MOTOR VEHICLE LAWS OF NORTH CAROLINA ANNOTATED

2020–2021 EDITION

Current through Session Laws 2020-97 of the 2020 Regular Session of the General Assembly, but does not reflect possible future codification directives relating to Session Laws 2020-95 through 2020-97 from the Revisor of Statutes pursuant to G.S. 164-10

Blue360° Media

**This publication is dedicated to the hard-working
law enforcement officers who risk their lives
every day to protect and serve the community.**

www.blue360media.com

To contact Blue360° Media, LLC, please call: **1-844-599-2887**

ISBN: 978-1-64130-924-0

Blue360° Media, LLC
2750 Rasmussen Rd., Suite 107
Park City, Utah 84098
1-844-599-2887
www.blue360media.com

(Pub. 30517)

PREFACE

We are pleased to offer to the law enforcement community the 2020–2021 edition of **Motor Vehicle Laws of North Carolina Annotated.** This compilation of selected laws is fully up to date with statutes, along with their annotations, current through Session Laws 2020-97 of the 2020 Regular Session of the General Assembly, but does not reflect possible future codification directives relating to Session Laws 2020-95 through 2020-97 from the Revisor of Statutes pursuant to G.S. 164-10. We continue to carry a listing of Sections Affected by 2020 Legislation. This edition also includes Highlights of Sections Affected by the 2020 North Carolina Legislative Session and North Carolina Police Procedure: Arrest, Search and Seizure, and Confession Law.

We are committed to providing law enforcement professionals with the most comprehensive, current, and useful publications possible. If you have comments and suggestions please call the Blue360° Media Publisher, 1-844-599-2887; email us at *support@blue 360media.com*; or visit our website at *www.blue360media.com*. Your valuable comments help keep this publication handy and more useful every year.

Visit the Blue360° Media home page at *www.blue360media.com* for an online bookstore, technical support, customer service, and other company information.

December 2020

IMPORTANT RESOURCES FOR NORTH CAROLINA LAW ENFORCEMENT OFFICERS

Pub. #	Featured Law Enforcement Titles
30517	Motor Vehicle Laws of North Carolina Annotated
30547	North Carolina Criminal and Traffic Law Manual

IMPORTANT RESOURCES FROM THE BLUE360° MEDIA OFFICER SERIES

Pub. #	Featured Law Enforcement Titles
80003	Active Threat: The First Responder Cooperative Response Plan *Bryon R. Betsinger, Battalion Chief (Ret.)*
80005	A First Responder's Guide to Providing Services to Special Needs Citizens *Bryon R. Betsinger, Battalion Chief (Ret.), Officer Brian Herritt (Ret.), C.P.P.*
74892	Criminal Procedure for Law and Justice Professionals *Larry E. Holtz*
33404	The Drug and Alcohol Impaired Driver *Jefferson L. Lankford, Judge, Arizona Court of Appeals (Ret.)*
29160	Criminal Evidence for Law and Justice Professionals *Larry E. Holtz*
37590	Officer's Search and Seizure Handbook *John A. Stephen*
75062	Effective Law Enforcement Report Writing *Larry E. Holtz*
37553	Officer's DUI Handbook *John B. Kwasnoski, John A. Stephen, Gerald N. Partridge*
29195	Drugs and the Law *Gary J. Miller*
32850	The Ideal Employee: Understanding Personality Tests *Dr. Donald J. Schroeder and Frank Lombardo*
37500	K9 Officer's Legal Handbook *Ken Wallentine*
27900	Tactical Spanish for Law Enforcement Officers *Jose Blanco*

To order, please visit: *www.blue360media.com*

Or call: 1-844-599-2887

TABLE OF CONTENTS

PART I

PART II
RELATED LAWS
SELECTED CONTENTS

YEARLY MOTOR VEHICLE REGISTRATION

	COMMERCIAL	PASSENGER	TOTAL
1921	13,743	136,815	150,558
1922	18,950	147,418	166,368
1923	21,324	190,408	211,732
1924	27,480	260,562	288,042
1925	28,903	312,223	341,126
1926	32,830	351,789	384,619
1927	42,246	391,724	434,400
1928	27,456	436,314	483,770
1929	56,535	447,055	503,590
1930	62,049	412,032	474,081
1931	62,693	379,755	442,448
1932	72,789	324,666	397,455
1933	81,279	327,816	409,095
1934	101,756	369,328	471,084
1935	113,446	398,610	512,076
1936	124,824	425,226	550,050
1937	133,358	453,302	586,660
1938	135,362	457,673	593,035
1939	145,383	486,918	632,301
1940	153,162	516,097	669,259
1941	168,252	568,856	737,108
1942	162,776	533,364	696,140
1943			669,625
1944	170,497	501,020	671,517
1945	183,906	502,530	686,436
1946	226,233	553,697	779,930
1947	267,924	615,574	883,498
1948	298,316	660,225	958,541
1949	309,864	720,455	1,030,319
1950	340,303	830,925	1,171,228
1951	358,451	889,373	1,247,824
1952	376,710	920,840	1,297,550

YEARLY MOTOR VEHICLE REGISTRATION

	COMMERCIAL	PASSENGER	TOTAL
1953	397,215	987.545	1,384,760
1954	409,343	1,028,480	1,437,823
1955	441,558	1,159,715	1,601,273
1956	463,462	1,208,478	1,671,940
1957	479,301	1,249,861	1,720,162
1958	475,128	1,233,196	1,708,324
1959	500,442	1,319,724	1,820,166
1960	521,292	1,386,696	1,907,988
1961	543,228	1,441,005	1,984,233
1962	570,676	1,486,212	2,056,888
1963	610,536	1,545,908	2,156,444
1964	644,431	1,613,575	2,258,006
1965	698,609	1,711,369	2,409,978
1966	752,611	1,834,506	2,587,117
1967	800,904	1,922,044	2,722,948
1968	877,399	2,021,021	2,898,420
1969	944,194	2,127,367	3,071,561
1970	1,008,775	2,209,517	3,218,292
1971	1,096,838	2,346,510	3,443,348
1972	1,101,886	2,511,591	3,613,477
1973	1,220,315	2,673,840	3,894,155
1974	1,245,438	2,763,448	4,008,886
1975	1,247,043	2,944,547	4,191,590
1976	1,471,774	3,090,526	4,562,300
1977	1,281,813	3,321,729	4,603,542
1978	1,367,648	3,447,221	4,814,869
1979	1,434,549	3,547,776	4,982,325
1980	1,465,283	3,629,531	5,094,814
1981	1,450,070	3,199,570	4,649,640
1982	1,573,878	3,360,060	4,933,938
1983	1,675,695	3,484,793	5,160,488
1984	1,763,586	3,619,426	5,383,012
1985	1,849,522	3,636,101	5,485,623
1986	1,856,512	3,754,473	5,610,985
1987	1,867,645	3,939,437	5,807,082
1988	1,823,456	3,768,813	5,592,269
1989	1,744,620	3,856,229	5,600,849
1990	1,758,307	3,893,419	5,651,726

	COMMERCIAL	PASSENGER	TOTAL
1991	1,754,395	3,921,933	5,676,328
1992	1,851,574	3,949,034	5,800,608
1993	1,854,825	4,128,043	5,982,868
1994	1,936,307	4,260,939	6,197,246
1995	1,979,473	4,312,831	6,292,304
1996	1,947,785	4,178,298	6,126,083
1997	1,802,152	4,453,352	6,255,504
1998	2,327,363	4,671,986	6,999,349
1999	2,370,861	4,698,583	7,069,444
2000	1,717,495	4,542,617	6,260,112
2001	1,738,585	4,675,262	6,413,847
2002	1,696,939	4,798,388	6,495,327
2003	1,709,073	4,862,646	6,571,719
2004	1,744,430	5,005,425	6,749,855
2005	1,816,492	5,300,362	7,116,854
2006	1,768,077	5,279,153	7,047,230
2007	1,802,804	5,410,609	7,213,413
2008	1,770,138	5,440,447	7,210,585
2009	1,709,279	5,341,609	7,050,888
2010	1,663,729	5,284,505	6,948,234
2011	1,732,256	5,570,138	7,302,394
2012	1,728,967	5,671,457	7,400,424
2013	1,729,658	5,739,187	7,468,845
2014	1,734,853	5,797,098	7,531,951
2015	1,774,658	5,975,223	7,749,881
2016	1,757,751	5,902,076	7,659,827
2017	1,793,140	6,004,198	7,797,338
2018	1,865,012	6,250,013	8,115,025
2019*	1,917,569	6,410,961	8,328,530

*Figures current through 10/31/2019.

TABLE OF SECTIONS AFFECTED BY 2020 LEGISLATION

Note: In addition to the sections listed below, users of this edition should be aware that additional section and case note annotations have also been appropriately incorporated throughout this publication. The sections with new and/or revised annotations do *not* appear in this listing.

CITATION	EFFECT	S.L.	BILL	BILL SECTION
20-4.01	Amended	40	H307	1
20-4.01	Amended	73	S739	1
20-4.01	Amended	51	H455	1(b)
20-24.1	Amended	77	S488	6.5(a)
20-37.7	Amended	17	H1169	9
20-52.1	Amended	51	H455	3(a)
20-72	Amended	51	H455	3(b)
20-79	Amended	51	H455	1(c)
20-79.02	Amended	51	H455	1(a)
20-79.1	Amended	77	S488	2, 4(a)
20-85	Amended	74	H308	7(c)
20-87	Amended	40	H307	2
20-121.1	Amended	40	H307	3
20-146.2	Amended	73	S739	4
20-150	Amended	18	S315	2(a)
Chapter 20, Art. 3, Part 11D	Added	73	S739	2
20-175.15	Added	73	S739	2
20-175.16	Added	73	S739	2
20-175.17	Added	73	S739	2
20-175.17	Added	73	S739	3(a)
20-175.18	Added	73	S739	2
20-183.2	Amended	73	S739	5
20-280.5	Amended	3	S704	4.36(a)
20-286	Amended	73	S739	6
20-288	Amended	77	S488	5(a)
20-295	Amended	77	S295	6(a)

CITATION	EFFECT	S.L.	BILL	BILL SECTION
20-305.7	Amended	51	H455	2
105-449.37	Amended	58	H1080	2.9
105-449.47	Amended	58	H1080	2.10(a)
105-499.49	Amended	58	H1080	2.10(b)

EXTENSION OF CREDENTIALS ISSUED BY THE DIVISION OF MOTOR VEHICLES (DMV)

A new act extends for five months the validity of any "credential" issued by DMV that expires on or after March 1, 2020 and before August 1, 2020. The act contains a list of 27 credentials, including driver's licenses, commercial driver's licenses, and vehicle registrations, and provides that the extension applies notwithstanding renewal, duration, or expiration provisions in various Ch. 20 statutes or any other provision of law. The act requires DMV to notify individuals affected by an extension, including information on new expiration dates and how the extension affects subsequent renewal and expiration dates. The act provides that a person may not be convicted or found responsible for any offense resulting from the failure to renew a credential issued by DMV if the person shows that the offense occurred during the period of the extension; however, if a credential expires after the extension, the expiration is treated as occurring on the date prescribed by law without regard to the extension. [Session Law 2020-3, SB704, §4.7]

PERSONAL DELIVERY DEVICES

- The general assembly authorized the use of personal delivery devices. A personal delivery device is defined as "An electrically powered device intended for transporting cargo that is equipped with automated driving technology that enables device operation with or without the remote support and supervision of a human and that does not exceed (i) a weight of 500 pounds, excluding cargo, (ii) a length of 40 inches, and (iii) a width of 30 inches."
- A business will be permitted to operate a personal delivery device in a pedestrian area (a sidewalk, crosswalk, school crossing zone, or safety zone) or on a street or highway, subject to certain conditions.
- The personal delivery device must be monitored by an operator who is able to remotely control the device.
- The personal delivery device may not exceed 10 miles per hour in a pedestrian area.
- The personal delivery device may be operated on a street or highway only if necessary to cross the street or highway or if a sidewalk is not accessible. Even then, the personal delivery device may not be operated on a street or highway

with a speed limit greater than 35 miles per hour. In those circumstances, the personal delivery device must be operated on the shoulder or extreme right of the roadway in the direction of traffic and must yield the right-of-way to vehicles. The personal delivery device may not be operated at a speed of more than 20 miles per hour on a street or highway.

- The personal delivery device must obey traffic and pedestrian control devices and signals, must yield the right of way to pedestrians, and may not "unreasonably interfere with any vehicle or pedestrian."
- A personal delivery device may not transport hazardous materials that require placarding under federal regulations.
- A personal delivery device must be marked with the name and contact information of the owner and a unique identification number. It must have a braking system that enables the device to come to a controlled stop. And, when operated at night, a personal delivery device must have lights on the front and rear that are visible and recognizable under normal atmospheric conditions from at least 500 feet.
- Violation of the rules for operation and equipment requirements for personal delivery devices, which are codified in new G.S. 20-175.8, is an infraction.
- A business that operates a personal delivery device must maintain an insurance policy that includes general liability coverage of at least $100,000 per claim for damages arising from the operation of a personal delivery device.
- Beginning December 1, 2020, a local government with jurisdiction over public streets, sidewalks and other ways of public passage may, to assure the safety of people using such streets and sidewalks, regulate the time and place for operation of personal delivery devices. A local government may not, however, prohibit the operation of personal delivery devices in its jurisdiction.
- Local government's authority to regulate such devices expands on December 1, 2022. On or after that date, a local government may ban operation of personal delivery devices within its jurisdiction. [Session Law 2020-73, SB739]

SELF-PROPELLED FARM EQUIPMENT

- Beginning on December 1, 2020, drivers are prohibited from overtaking and passing self-propelled farm equipment proceeding in the same direction when the farm equipment is making a left turn or signaling that it intends to make a left turn. [Session Law 2020-18, SB315, §2.(a)]

NORTH CAROLINA POLICE PROCEDURE

Arrest, Search and Seizure, and Confession Law

Note: *This is a general overview of the classical and current United States and North Carolina court decisions related to the Laws of Arrest, Search and Seizure, and Confession Law. As an overview, it should be used for a basic analysis of the general principles but not as a comprehensive presentation of the entire body of law. It is not to be used as a substitute for the opinion or advice of the appropriate legal counsel from the reader's department. To the extent possible, the information is current. However, very recent statutory and case law developments may not be covered.*

---

1. CONSTITUTIONAL CRIMINAL PROCEDURE

1.1. Constitutional Analysis

The Bill of Rights in the federal Constitution, and corresponding provisions in each state's constitution, provide citizens with certain fundamental safeguards from intrusive governmental conduct. Particularly relevant to situations involving law enforcement officials are the Fourth, Fifth, Sixth and, to a lesser extent, the First and Fourteenth Amendments.

The Fourth Amendment to the federal Constitution safeguards the "right of the people to be secure in their persons, houses, papers, and effects, against unreasonable searches and seizures[.]" Additionally, the Amendment commands that "no Warrants shall issue, but upon probable cause, supported by Oath or affirmation, and particularly describing the place to be searched, and the persons or things to be seized." The "ultimate touchstone of the Fourth Amendment is 'reasonableness.'"[1]

Similarly, Article I, § 20 of the North Carolina Constitution provides: "General warrants, whereby any officer or other person may be commanded to search suspected places without evidence of the act committed, or to seize any person or persons not named, whose offense is not particularly described and supported by evidence, are dangerous to liberty and shall not be granted." While this language "differs markedly from the language of the Fourth Amendment to the Constitution of the United States[,]" it "nevertheless ... prohibits unreasonable searches and seizures."[2]

1.1.1. New Federalism

When confronted with an unreasonable search and seizure, a state court is free, and indeed encouraged, to rely on its own constitution to provide greater protection to the privacy interests of its citizens than that afforded under parallel provisions of the federal Constitution. As a well-established principle of our federalist system, state constitutions may be the source of "individual liberties more expansive than those conferred by the federal Constitution."[3] This means that a state court is free as a matter of its own law to impose greater restrictions on police activity than those the United States Supreme Court holds to be necessary under federal constitutional standards. Indeed, the North Carolina Supreme Court has acknowledged, "[W]e have the authority to construe our own constitution differently from the construction by the United States Supreme Court of the Federal Constitution, as long as our citizens are thereby accorded no lesser rights than they are guaranteed by the parallel federal provision."[4]

The federal Constitution represents the baseline or "floor" of protection and, of course, a state may not drop below the federal floor;[5] it may, however, rely on its own state constitution to heighten that floor of protection. State law enforcement officers are cautioned, therefore, that their state may establish, as a matter of its own law, a ceiling of protection for its citizens which may have the effect of placing additional restrictions upon, or requiring the exercise of additional precautions by, its officers.[6]

1.1.2. Interpreting the North Carolina Constitution

In interpreting the North Carolina Constitution, courts are not bound by the United States Supreme Court's interpretation of the United States Constitution, even where the language is identical.[7] On this point,

---

[1] *Brigham City v. Stuart*, 547 U.S. 398, 403, 126 S. Ct. 1943 (2006).

[2] *State v. Arrington*, 311 N.C. 633, 643, 319 S.E.2d 254 (1984).

[3] *Pruneyard Shopping Center v. Robins,* 447 U.S. 74, 81, 100 S. Ct. 2035, 2040 (1980).

[4] *State v. Carter*, 322 N.C. 709, 713, 370 S.E.2d 553 (1988).

[5] Note also that in *Timbs v. Indiana*, 586 U.S. ___, 139 S.Ct. 682, 686-87 (2019), the United States Supreme Court held that the states cannot impose excessive fees, fines and forfeitures as criminal penalties. The Court's decision underscores that the Eighth Amendment's prohibition against "excessive fines" applies to states and localities as well as the federal government. Said the Court: "The Excessive Fines Clause is therefore incorporated by the Due Process Clause of the Fourteenth Amendment." *Id.*, 139 S.Ct. at 687.

[6] *See generally* Linde, *E. Pluribus — Constitutional Theory and State Courts,* 18 Ga. L. Rev. 165 (1984); Brennen, *State Constitutions and the Protection of Individual Rights,* 90 Harv. L. Rev. 489 (1977); Note, *The New Federalism, Toward a Principled Interpretation of the State Constitution,* 29 Stan. L. Rev. 297 (1977); Feldman & Abney, *The Double Security of Federalism: Protecting Individual Liberty Under the Arizona Constitution,* 20 Ariz. St. L.J. 115 (1988).

[7] *State v. Carter,* 322 N.C. 709, 370 S.E.2d 553 (1988).

the North Carolina Supreme Court has been clear. "In construing provisions of the Constitution of North Carolina, this Court is not bound by opinions of the Supreme Court of the United States construing even identical provisions in the Constitution of the United States."[8] However, "[i]n construing a provision of the state Constitution, [the North Carolina Supreme Court] find[s] highly persuasive the meaning given and the approach used by the United States Supreme Court in construing a similar provision of the federal Constitution."[9] Thus, although "Article I, Section 20 of the North Carolina Constitution contains different language [than the Fourth Amendment], it provides the same protection against unreasonable searches and seizures."[10] The North Carolina Supreme Court has been even more specific in this regard stating, "[B]ecause the text of Article I, Section 20 does not 'call[ ] for broader protection than that of the Fourth Amendment,' the probable cause analysis under the federal and state constitutions is identical."[11]

1.1.3. Rights of Crime Victims

Article I, § 37 of the North Carolina Constitution provides certain rights to victims of crime as follows:

Enumerated rights. When the crime or act of delinquency is one against or involving the person of the victim or is equivalent to a felony property crime, the victim is entitled to the following rights:

(a) The right upon request to reasonable, accurate, and timely notice of court proceedings of the accused.
    (1) The right upon request to be present at court proceedings of the accused.
(b) The right to be reasonably heard at any court proceeding involving the plea, conviction, adjudication, sentencing, or release of the accused.
(c) The right to receive restitution in a reasonably timely manner, when ordered by the court.
(d) The right to be given information about the crime or act of delinquency, how the criminal justice system works, the rights of victims, and the availability of services for victims.
(e) The right upon request to receive information about the conviction, adjudication, or final disposition and sentence of the accused.
(f) The right upon request to receive notification of escape, release, proposed parole or pardon of the accused, or notice of a reprieve or commutation of the accused's sentence.
(g) The right to present the victim's views and concerns to the Governor or agency considering any action that could result in the release of the accused, prior to such action becoming effective.
(h) The right to reasonably confer with the prosecution.

Additionally, the Crime Victims' Rights Act can be found at Chapter 15A, Article 46 of the North Carolina General Statutes. N.C.Gen.Stat. § 15A-831 provides for the responsibilities of law enforcement with regard to victims' rights.

§ 15A-831. Responsibilities of law enforcement agency
(a) As soon as practicable but within 72 hours after identifying a victim covered by this Article, the investigating law enforcement agency shall provide the victim with at least the following information in writing, on a form created by the Conference of District Attorneys:
    (1) The availability of medical services, if needed.
    (2) The availability of crime victims' compensation funds under Chapter 15B of the General Statutes and the address and telephone number of the agency responsible for dispensing the funds.

---

[8] *State v. Arrington,* 311 N.C. 633, 642, 319 S.E.2d 254 (1984) (citing *White v. Pate,* 308 N.C. 759, 304 S.E. 2d 199 (1983); *Bulova Watch Co. v. Brand Distributors Inc.,* 285 N.C. 467, 206 S.E. 2d 141 (1974)).
[9] *State v. Huff,* 325 N.C. 1, 33, 381 S.E.2d 635, 653 (1989) (citation omitted), *sentence vacated on other grounds,* 497 U.S. 1021, 110 S. Ct. 3266, 111 L. Ed. 2d 777 (1990).
[10] *State v. Elder,* 368 N.C. 70, 73, 773 S.E.2d 51 (2015).
[11] *State v. Allman,* 369 N.C. 292, 293, 794 S.E.2d 301 (2016) (quoting *State v. Miller,* 367 N.C. 702, 706, 766 S.E.2d 289, 292 (2014)).

(3) The address and telephone number of the district attorney's office that will be responsible for prosecuting the victim's case.

(4) The name and telephone number of an investigating law enforcement agency employee whom the victim may contact if the victim has not been notified of an arrest in the victim's case within six months after the crime was reported to the law enforcement agency.

(5) Information about an accused's opportunity for pretrial release.

(6) The name and telephone number of an investigating law enforcement agency employee whom the victim may contact to find out whether the accused has been released from custody.

(7) The informational sheet described in G.S. 50B-3(c1), if there was a personal relationship, as defined in G.S. 50B-1(b), with the accused.

(8) A list of each right enumerated under G.S. 15A-830.5(b).

(9) Information about any other rights afforded to victims by law.

(b) Within 72 hours after the arrest of a person believed to have committed a crime covered by this Article, the arresting law enforcement agency shall inform the investigating law enforcement agency of the arrest. Following receipt of this information, the investigating law enforcement agency shall notify the victim of the arrest within an additional 72 hours.

(c) Within 72 hours after receiving notification from the arresting law enforcement agency that the accused has been arrested, the investigating law enforcement agency shall also forward to the district attorney's office that will be responsible for prosecuting the case the defendant's name and the victim's name, address, and telephone number or other contact information, unless the victim refuses to disclose any or all of the information, in which case, the investigating law enforcement agency shall so inform the district attorney's office.

(d) Upon receiving the information in subsection (a) of this section, the victim shall, on a form created by the Conference of District Attorneys and provided by the investigating law enforcement agency, indicate whether the victim wishes to receive any further notices from the investigating law enforcement agency on the status of the accused during the pretrial process. If the victim elects to receive further notices during the pretrial process, the victim shall return the form to the investigating law enforcement agency within 10 business days of receipt of the form. The victim shall be responsible for notifying the investigating law enforcement agency of any changes in the victim's name, address, and telephone number.

(e) Upon receiving a form from the victim pursuant to subsection (d) of this section, the investigating law enforcement agency shall promptly share the form with the district attorney's office to facilitate compliance with the victim's preferences on notification.

1.2. The Fifth Amendment

The Fifth Amendment provides, in part, that no person shall be compelled to be a witness against oneself in a criminal case. The Supreme Court has also found that an integral part of an accused's right to be free from compelled incrimination is a judicially created right to have counsel present and a right to refuse to answer questions during a custodial interrogation, even though the Constitution does not specifically provide such a safeguard.

Similarly, Article 1, § 23 of the North Carolina Constitution provides: "In all criminal prosecutions, every person charged with crime has the right to be informed of the accusation and to confront the accusers and witnesses with other testimony, and to have counsel for defense, and not be compelled to give self-incriminating evidence, or to pay costs, jail fees, or necessary witness fees of the defense, unless found guilty."

The Fifth and Fourteenth Amendments of the federal Constitution, and Article I, § 19 of the North Carolina Constitution each contain a clause protecting a citizen from being punished without a proper legal proceeding. As we saw with Article I, § 20 of the North Carolina Constitution and the Fourth Amendment, here too the language is different. While the federal Constitution contains a "Due Process" clause, the North Carolina Constitution contains a "Law of the Land" clause and states in part:

No person shall be taken, imprisoned, or disseized of his freehold, liberties, or privileges, or outlawed, or exiled, or in any manner deprived of his life, liberty, or property, but by the law of the land.

The Supreme Court of North Carolina has determined that "[t]he term 'law of the land' as used in Article I, Section 19, of the Constitution of North Carolina, is synonymous with 'due process of law' as used in the Fourteenth Amendment to the Federal Constitution."[12] Due process means that no person shall be deprived of life, liberty or property without the due process of law. In the context of the rights of a criminal suspect, this provision has been construed as offering protection against certain fundamentally unfair governmental conduct, particularly the use of suggestive, prejudicial or discriminatory identification procedures.[13]

1.3. The Sixth Amendment

The Sixth Amendment provides that a defendant in a criminal case—and a suspect in a criminal investigation when the investigation has reached a critical stage—shall enjoy the right to counsel to aid in his defense. Article 1, § 23 of the North Carolina Constitution provides a similar right.

The Sixth Amendment is applicable to all state court proceedings by virtue of the Due Process Clause of the Fourteenth Amendment.[14] The right to counsel provided by the Sixth Amendment attaches when adversarial judicial proceedings are commenced against a defendant and remains throughout all critical stages of the proceedings.[15] The right attaches to initial proceedings, including formal charges, preliminary hearings, indictments, bills of information and arraignments.[16]

1.4. The Exclusionary Rule

1.4.1. General aspects

Although the Fourth Amendment does not specifically prohibit the use of evidence seized in violation of its terms, the Supreme Court has created a tool designed ultimately to safeguard Fourth Amendment rights. The tool is called the Exclusionary Rule and, since 1961, it has been disallowing the use of evidence obtained in violation of the Fourth Amendment in state as well as federal prosecutions.[17] Rather than a personal constitutional right belonging to the victim of an illegal search or seizure, the exclusionary rule operates as a judicially created remedy which protects Fourth Amendment rights generally by deterring wrongful police conduct.[18] "Deterrence," then, is the linchpin of the exclusionary rule.[19]

Simply stated, the exclusionary rule is a judicially-created device which is employed by the courts to prohibit the use of evidence at a criminal trial when that evidence has been seized by law enforcement officials in violation of the Constitution.

In North Carolina, courts have consistently held that exclusion of evidence is the required remedy for a violation of Article I, § 20 of the North Carolina Constitution. In *State v. Carter*,[20] the Supreme Court of North Carolina discussed the value of the exclusionary rule and declared, "We conclude that the exclusionary rule has been a potent force for achieving its intended deterrent purpose. Warrants today are more carefully prepared and scrutinized before issuance. Likewise, the exclusionary rule is responsible for the systematic, in-depth training

---

[12] *Rhyne v. K-Mart Corp.*, 358 N.C. 160, 180, 594 S.E.2d 1, 15 (2004) (quoting *In re Moore*, 289 N.C. 95, 98, 221 S.E.2d 307, 309 (1976)).

[13] *See Simmons v. United States,* 390 U.S. 377, 384, 88 S. Ct. 967, 971 (1968).

[14] This was made clear in *Gideon v. Wainright*, 372 U.S. 335, 344, 83 S. Ct. 792, 796 (1963).

[15] *See Kirby v. Illinois*, 406 U.S. 682, 689, 92 S. Ct. 1877 (1972).

[16] *See Kirby v. Illinois*, 406 U.S. 682, 689, 92 S. Ct. 1877 (1972).

[17] *See Mapp v. Ohio*, 367 U.S. 643, 81 S. Ct. 1684 (1961) ("all evidence obtained by searches and seizures in violation of the Constitution is, by that same authority, inadmissible in a state court").

[18] *United States v. Leon*, 468 U.S. 897, 104 S. Ct. 3405 (1984).

[19] *See United States v. Janis,* 428 U.S. 433, 96 S. Ct. 3021 (1976) (The "prime purpose" of the exclusionary rule, if not the sole one, is "to deter future unlawful police conduct."). As further explained in *United States v. Calandra,* 414 U.S. 338, 347-48, 94 S. Ct. 613, 619-20 (1974), "[t]he purpose of the exclusionary rule is not to redress the injury to the privacy of the search victim....Instead, the rule's prime purpose is to deter future unlawful police conduct and thereby effectuate the guarantee of the Fourth Amendment against unreasonable searches and seizures." The rule "is calculated to prevent, not to repair. Its purpose is to deter — to compel respect for the constitutional guaranty in the only effectively available way — by removing the incentive to disregard it." *Elkins v. United States,* 364 U.S. 206, 217, 80 S. Ct. 1437, 1444 (1960).

[20] *State v. Carter*, 322 N.C. 709, 370 S.E.2d 553 (1988).

of police forces in the law of search and seizure."[21] Moreover, the exclusionary rule has been codified in North Carolina at N.C.Gen.Stat. § 15A-974(a) which provides that evidence must be suppressed if:

(1) Its exclusion is required by the Constitution of the United States or the Constitution of the State of North Carolina; or

(2) It is obtained as a result of a substantial violation of the provisions of this Chapter. In determining whether a violation is substantial, the court must consider all the circumstances, including:

    a. The importance of the particular interest violated;
    b. The extent of the deviation from lawful conduct;
    c. The extent to which the violation was willful;
    d. The extent to which exclusion will tend to deter future violations of this Chapter.

The federal exclusionary rule does not generally apply to actions taken under a statute that is subsequently ruled to be invalid.[22] The rule also does not apply to private searches.[23]

Other than deterrence, the exclusionary rule advances the imperative of judicial integrity and removes the profit motive from unconstitutional actions. As Justice Clark, writing for the Supreme Court in *Mapp v. Ohio*,[24] declared:

There are those who say, as did Justice (then Judge) Cardozo, that under our constitutional exclusionary doctrine "the criminal is to go free because the constable has blundered." … In some cases this will undoubtedly be the result. But, … "there is another consideration—the imperative of judicial integrity." … The criminal goes free, if he must, but it is the law that sets him free. Nothing can destroy a government more quickly than its failure to observe its own laws, or worse, its disregard of the charter of its own existence.[25]

The remedy of exclusion applies generally to criminal prosecutions, prohibiting the use of evidence obtained in violation of federal or state constitutional rights.[26] The exclusionary rule has never been interpreted, however, to prohibit the use of illegally seized evidence in all proceedings or against all persons. As with any remedial device, the application of the rule has been restricted to those areas where its remedial objectives are thought to be best served.[27] If application of the exclusionary rule in a particular situation "does not result in appreciable deterrence," its use may be "unwarranted."[28]

The Fourth Amendment's exclusionary rule encompasses both the "primary evidence obtained as a direct result of an illegal search or seizure," and evidence later discovered and found to be derivative of an illegality.[29] This derivative, or secondary evidence, including an officer's testimony based on knowledge garnered as

---

[21] *State v. Carter*, 322 N.C. 709, 721, 370 S.E.2d 553 (1988).

[22] *See, e.g., Illinois v. Krull*, 480 U.S. 340, 107 S. Ct. 1160 (1987) (suppression is not required "when an officer's reliance on the constitutionality of a statute is objectively reasonable, but the statute is subsequently declared unconstitutional."). *See also Michigan v. DeFillippo*, 443 U.S. 31, 99 S. Ct. 2627 (1979) (An arrest "made in good-faith reliance on an ordinance, which at the time had not been declared unconstitutional, is valid regardless of a subsequent judicial determination of its unconstitutionality").

[23] *See United States v. Calandra*, 414 U.S. 338, 94 S. Ct. 613 (1974) (Exclusionary rule is "wholly inapplicable 'to a search or seizure, even an unreasonable one, effected by a private individual not acting as an agent of the Government or with the participation or knowledge of any governmental official.'") (citation omitted). *See also Burdeau v. McDowell*, 256 U.S. 465, 41 S. Ct. 574 (1921).

[24] *Mapp v. Ohio*, 367 U.S. 643, 81 S. Ct. 1684 (1961).

[25] *Mapp v. Ohio*, 367 U.S. 643, 659, 81 S. Ct. 1684, 1693-1694 (1961) (quoting *People v. Defore*, 242 N.Y. 13, 150 N.E. 585, 587 (1926)).

[26] *James v. Illinois*, 493 U.S. 307, 311, 110 S. Ct. 648, 651 (1990).

[27] *See United States v. Calandra*, 414 U.S. 338, 348, 94 S. Ct. 613, 620 (1974).

[28] *Compare United States v. Janis*, 428 U.S. 433, 459-60, 96 S. Ct. 3021, 3034 (1976) (illegally seized evidence may be used in a federal civil tax proceeding); *United States v. Calandra*, 414 U.S. 338, 348, 94 S. Ct. 613, 621-22 (1974) (illegally seized evidence may be used in grand jury proceedings); *United States v. Havens*, 446 U.S. 620, 627, 100 S. Ct. 1912, 1916-17 (1980) (illegally seized evidence may be used to impeach a defendant who takes the stand and testifies) *with I.N.S. v. Lopez-Mendoza*, 468 U.S. 1032, 104 S. Ct. 3479 (1984) (exclusionary rule not applicable to a civil deportation proceeding).

[29] *See Segura v. United States*, 468 U.S. 796, 804, 104 S. Ct. 3380 (1984).

a result of the illegal conduct, is often referred to as the *"fruit of the poisonous tree."*[30] To invoke the protection of the "poisonous tree" principle, the defendant must first demonstrate there was a primary illegality (*i.e.*, an unconstitutional search or arrest, or a coerced confession), and secondly, a nexus, or connection, between the illegality and the derivative evidence. The nexus between the illegal act and the subject evidence must be so strong that police can be said to have obtained the evidence only by an exploitation of their illegal actions. If another event or outside factor weakens the connection between the illegality and the evidence, a principle referred to as attenuation, so that the evidence can no longer be said to be a by-product of the unlawful conduct, then suppression would not be appropriate. The attenuating factor removes the stigma of the illegal law enforcement action, so that denying the admission of the seized evidence does not serve the deterrent purposes of the exclusionary rule.

Thus, the exclusionary rule is not monolithic. Even when there is a Fourth Amendment violation, the rule of exclusion will not apply when the costs of exclusion outweigh its deterrent benefits. As indicated above, when the link between the unconstitutional conduct and the discovery of the evidence is too attenuated to justify suppression the rule will not be applied.[31] In this regard, the United States Supreme Court has held that, pursuant to the "attenuation doctrine," evidence will be "admissible when the connection between unconstitutional police conduct and the evidence is remote or has been interrupted by some intervening circumstance, so that 'the interest protected by the constitutional guarantee that has been violated would not be served by suppression of the evidence obtained.'"[32]

There are three factors for a court to consider when determining whether unlawful conduct has been adequately attenuated. Those factors are: "(1) the elapsed time between the misconduct and the acquisition of the evidence, (2) the occurrence of intervening circumstances, and (3) the flagrancy and purpose of the improper law enforcement action."[33]

1.4.1.1. An unlawful stop and the subsequent discovery of an arrest warrant

In *Utah v. Strieff*,[34] during an unlawful investigative detention of defendant Edward Strieff, the investigating officer learned that Strieff had an outstanding arrest warrant for a traffic violation. The officer arrested Strieff pursuant to that warrant and a search incident to arrest uncovered a baggie of methamphetamine and drug paraphernalia. At court, the prosecution conceded that the officer lacked reasonable suspicion for the stop but argued that the evidence should not be suppressed because the existence of a valid arrest warrant attenuated the connection between the unlawful stop and the discovery of the contraband. *The United States Supreme Court agreed*, holding that the attenuation doctrine applies when an officer makes an unconstitutional investigatory stop; learns during that stop that the suspect is subject to a valid arrest warrant; and proceeds to arrest the suspect and seize incriminating evidence during a search incident to that arrest.[35] In this regard, the "valid arrest warrant was a sufficient intervening event to break the causal chain between the unlawful stop and the discovery of drug-related evidence on Strieff's person."[36]

Another exception involving the causal relationship between the unconstitutional act and the discovery of evidence is the "independent source" doctrine. This "allows trial courts to admit evidence obtained in an unlawful search if officers independently acquired it from a separate, independent source."[37] Similarly, the "inevitable discovery" rule "allows for the admission of evidence that would have been discovered even without the unconstitutional source."[38] And then there's the exclusionary rule's good-faith exception.

---

[30] *Wong Sun v. United States,* 371 U.S. 471, 83 S. Ct. 407 (1963) (emphasis added).

[31] *See Utah v. Strieff,* 579 U.S. ___, 136 S. Ct. 2056, 2059 (2016).

[32] *See Utah v. Strieff,* 579 U.S. ___, 136 S. Ct. 2056, 2059 (2016) (quoting *Hudson v. Michigan,* 547 U.S. 586, 593, 126 S. Ct. 2159, 2164 (2016)).

[33] *See Brown v. Illinois,* 422 U.S. 590, 603-04, 95 S. Ct. 2254, 2261-62 (1975); *see also Utah v. Strieff,* 579 U.S. ___, 136 S. Ct. 2056, 2061-62 (2016).

[34] *Utah v. Strieff,* 579 U.S. ___, 136 S. Ct. 2056 (2016).

[35] *Utah v. Strieff,* 579 U.S. ___, 136 S. Ct. 2056, 2059 (2016).

[36] *Utah v. Strieff,* 579 U.S. ___, 136 S. Ct. 2056, 2061 (2016).

[37] *See Utah v. Strieff,* 579 U.S. ___, 136 S. Ct. 2056, 2059 (2016).

[38] *See Utah v. Strieff,* 579 U.S. ___, 136 S. Ct. 2056, 2059 (2016).

1.4.2. The good-faith exception

In *United States v. Leon*,[39] the U.S. Supreme Court held that evidence should not be excluded from the prosecution's case if it was obtained by officers acting in reasonable reliance upon a search warrant, even if the warrant was ultimately found to be invalid. According to the Court, the primary benefit of the exclusionary rule is that it deters official misconduct by removing incentives to engage in unreasonable searches and seizures. The Court noted, however, that "the marginal or nonexistent benefits produced by suppressing evidence obtained in objectively reasonable reliance on a subsequently invalidated search warrant cannot justify the substantial costs of exclusion."[40] No deterrence of police misconduct occurs when the police reasonably rely on a warrant later found to be deficient.

The good-faith exception has been codified in North Carolina at N.C. Gen. Stat. § 15A-974(a) which provides in part, "Evidence shall not be suppressed under this subdivision if the person committing the violation of the provision or provisions under this Chapter acted under the objectively reasonable, good faith belief that the actions were lawful."

The United States Supreme Court has also held that suppression is inappropriate where an officer conducts a search or arrest in reasonable, good-faith reliance on a warrant issued by a neutral and detached magistrate, and that warrant is later found to be invalid due to a defect in form or because of a "technical error on the part of the issuing judge."[41] Similarly, the exclusionary rule will not apply to evidence seized pursuant to a warrant executed in good faith, where the warrant is subsequently deemed defective because of clerical errors.[42]

In *Arizona v. Evans*, a motorist was pulled over for a routine traffic stop. The officer's in-dash computer indicated the motorist had an outstanding warrant for his arrest. He was placed under arrest, and a search of his car revealed a bag of marijuana. The officer did not know that the warrant under which he arrested the motorist had been quashed, and a clerk forgot to make the appropriate entry. The motorist sought to have the evidence suppressed as the fruit of an unlawful arrest. The Supreme Court denied suppression, holding that the exclusionary rule does not require suppression of evidence seized in violation of the Fourth Amendment by an officer who acted in reasonable reliance upon a police record indicating the existence of an outstanding arrest warrant—a record that is later determined to be erroneous due to a clerical error of a court employee.[43] Similarly, the Court has held that when a police mistake is the result of isolated negligence, rather than systemic error or reckless disregard of constitutional requirements, suppression of evidence is not required.[44]

In *Davis v. United States*,[45] the federal Supreme Court expanded the good-faith exception to the exclusionary rule to include good-faith reliance upon binding appellate precedent that specifically authorized a particular practice but was subsequently overruled.

The United States Supreme Court also recognizes a good-faith exception to the exclusionary rule for actions taken under a statute that is subsequently ruled to be invalid.[46]

The Supreme Court has additionally recognized a reasonable mistake of law as a good-faith exception to the exclusionary rule. In *Heien v. North Carolina*,[47] the Court held that, under the Fourth Amendment, an officer's reasonable suspicion for a motor vehicle stop can rest on a reasonable mistake of law. According

---

[39] *United States v. Leon*, 468 U.S. 897, 104 S. Ct. 3405 (1984).

[40] *United States v. Leon*, 468 U.S. 897, 922, 104 S. Ct. 3405 (1984).

[41] *Massachusetts v. Sheppard,* 468 U.S. 981, 104 S. Ct. 3424, 3426 (1984).

[42] *Arizona v. Evans,* 514 U.S. 1, 115 S. Ct. 1185 (1995).

[43] *Arizona v. Evans,* 514 U.S. 1, 3, 14, 115 S. Ct. 1185, 1187, 1193 (1995).

[44] *Herring v. United States*, 555 U.S. 135, 129 S.Ct. 695 (2009). The mistake here was an arrest on a warrant that had been recalled five months earlier. The failure to update the computer database was deemed to be a "negligent omission."

[45] *Davis v. United States*, 564 U.S. 229, 240, 131 S. Ct. 2419, 2429 (2011).

[46] *See, e.g., Illinois v. Krull*, 480 U.S. 340, 107 S. Ct. 1160 (1987) (suppression is not required "when an officer's reliance on the constitutionality of a statute is objectively reasonable, but the statute is subsequently declared unconstitutional."); *Michigan v. DeFillippo*, 443 U.S. 31, 99 S. Ct. 2627 (1979) (An arrest "made in good-faith reliance on an ordinance, which at the time had not been declared unconstitutional, is valid regardless of a subsequent judicial determination of its unconstitutionality.").

[47] *Heien v. North Carolina,* 574 U.S. 54, 135 S. Ct. 530 (2014).

to the Court, the Fourth Amendment is not violated when a police officer pulls over a vehicle based on an "objectively reasonable, although mistaken, belief" that the traffic laws prohibited the conduct which was the basis for the stop. The defendant in *Heien* was a passenger in a car that was stopped by the police because the car had only one working brake light. Cocaine was recovered from the defendant during the stop. Upon appeal, the defendant contended that driving with only one brake light was not a violation and thus there was no basis for the traffic stop. Since the statute was an "ambiguous one," the Court determined that the officer's mistake was reasonable.[48]

1.4.3. The "Independent Source" Doctrine

"The Fourth Amendment does not require the suppression of evidence initially discovered during a police officer's illegal entry of private premises, if that evidence is also discovered during a later search pursuant to a valid warrant that is wholly independent of the initial illegal entry."[49] In this regard, the "independent source" doctrine "permits the introduction of evidence initially discovered during, or as a consequence of, an unlawful search, but later obtained independently from lawful activities untainted by the initial illegality."[50] The circumstances that justify the second lawful search must have no connection to the initial, unlawful conduct. In other words, the facts supporting the second search must arise wholly apart from those that purportedly justified the initial search (*e.g.*, a judicial finding of probable cause, and a warrant issued based on that finding, where the facts in the supporting affidavit derive completely from a source independent of facts garnered during an initial, illegal search).

In *Murray v. United States*,[51] officers conducting a narcotics investigation had probable cause to believe a large quantity of drugs was being stored in a warehouse. Before securing a warrant, they illegally entered the warehouse and confirmed their beliefs, finding several bales of marijuana. The officers subsequently applied for and obtained a search warrant but made no mention of their entry to the issuing judge, basing their application only on facts they had accumulated prior to the unlawful entry. The Supreme Court held that if the earlier information in the affidavit in fact supported the probable cause determination, so that the later seizure of the marijuana was not a result of the illegal entry, but rather the result of a warrant executed pursuant to the independent probable cause finding, the evidence should not be suppressed.

The North Carolina courts have recognized the Independent Source Doctrine. For example, in *State v. Phifer*,[52] the court upheld the admission of evidence despite an illegal search when "the officers, through lawful means, had independently obtained probable cause to suspect that the [area searched] contained contraband."[53]

1.4.4. The "Inevitable Discovery" Doctrine

The "inevitable discovery" doctrine is similar to the independent source doctrine; it enables courts to look to the facts and circumstances surrounding the discovery of the tainted evidence and asks whether the police would have discovered the evidence despite the illegality. "If the prosecution can establish by a preponderance of the evidence that the information ultimately or inevitably would have been discovered by lawful means, then the deterrence rationale has so little basis that the evidence should be received."[54] Generally, courts will find evidence would have been inevitably discovered if the evidence would have been discovered, in the same condition, through an independent line of investigation, and where the independent investigation was already in progress at the time of the illegal search. Thus, "[t]he inevitable discovery doctrine, with its distinct requirements, is in reality an extrapolation from the independent source doctrine:

---

[48] *Heien v. North Carolina*, 574 U.S. 54, 135 S. Ct. 530, 539 (2014).

[49] *Murray v. United States*, 487 U.S. 533, 108 S. Ct. 2529, 2536 (1987).

[50] *Murray v. United States*, 487 U.S. 533, 108 S. Ct. 2529, 2536 (1987).

[51] *Murray v. United States,* 487 U.S. 533, 108, S. Ct. 2529 (1988).

[52] *State v. Phifer*, 297 N.C. 216, 254 S.E.2d 586 (1979).

[53] *State v. Phifer*, 297 N.C. 216, 224-26, 254 S.E.2d 586 (1979).

[54] *Nix v. Williams*, 467 U.S. 431, 104 S. Ct. 2501, 2511 (1984).

Since the tainted evidence would be admissible if in fact discovered through an independent source, it should be admissible if it inevitably would have been discovered."[55]

In *Nix*,[56] two officers illegally obtained from a suspect the location of the body of a child he had murdered. The defendant argued that testimony concerning the location and condition of the body should be suppressed as a result of this illegality. The Supreme Court disagreed, holding that if the prosecution could demonstrate that the child's body would have been discovered without the benefit of the defendant's statements, suppression was not appropriate. In this case, there was an extremely good chance that the state could demonstrate the body's location would have been inevitably discovered, as there was a 200-member search party combing the area, which in fact was scheduled to search the area where the body was found.

Similarly, in *State v. Pope*,[57] evidence of a murder weapon found after the defendant's Fifth Amendment rights were violated was nevertheless properly admitted. The defendant had hidden the weapon in a truck, where it was recovered by police, but the owner's testimony that before selling the truck he had searched it and would have found the gun if it still had been there was proof enough of the inevitability of the discovery.

2. INVESTIGATIVE DETENTIONS

2.1. Levels of encounters

When reviewing the legality of police interactions with citizens, courts initially assess the nature and extent of the contact. To aid in this analysis, interactions, or encounters, are divided into three conceptual categories. First, there are encounters of a consensual nature. These are sometimes called "mere inquiries" or "mere field inquiries," which include a common law right to inquire—a right to ask a question enjoyed by all citizens, whether they work in law enforcement or not.

Occupying the next tier of encounters are interactions of a more intrusive character. These encounters are commonly called detentions, investigatory stops or *Terry* stops. An investigative detention ("*Terry* stop") is a "seizure" for purposes of the Fourth Amendment.[58] Such a "*Terry* stop" is reasonable when a law enforcement officer possesses specific and articulable facts which generate a "reasonable suspicion of criminal activity."[59] A "reasonable articulable suspicion" entails something more than an inchoate or unparticularized suspicion or "hunch," but less than the level of suspicion required for probable cause.[60] Since it is a less stringent standard than the probable cause standard, it certainly requires a quantum of proof that is less than preponderance of the evidence.

The final level of encounter is a formal arrest. To justify this action, law enforcement officials must possess a higher degree of suspicion, *i.e.,* "probable cause" to believe that a crime is being, or has been, perpetrated and that a specific person committed that crime.

This initial categorization of encounters is essential to a determination of the rights of the individual. If the encounter is consensual, the federal Constitution is not implicated because no seizure of a person, within the meaning of the Fourth Amendment, has taken place. However, if the encounter rises to the level of a detention or a full-scale arrest, then that person has been seized, and law enforcement conduct will be judged according to the standards of the Fourth Amendment. The person seized can then avail himself of Fourth Amendment protections.

2.2. Consensual encounters; the "mere inquiry"

There are some police-citizen encounters that do not require any level of constitutional justification because the interaction does not involve a "significant interference" with an individual's life, liberty or property. Law enforcement "officers do not violate the Fourth Amendment by merely approaching an individual

---

[55] *Murray v. United States*, 487 U.S. 533, 539, 108 S. Ct. 2529, 2534 (1988).
[56] *Nix v. Williams,* 467 *U.S.* 431, 104 S. Ct. 2501, 2511 (1984).
[57] *State v. Pope*, 333 N.C. 106, 423 S.E.2d 740 (1992).
[58] *See Terry v. Ohio,* 392 U.S. 1, 20-21, 88 S. Ct. 1868 (1968).
[59] *Terry v. Ohio,* 392 U.S. 1, 20-21, 88 S. Ct. 1868 (1968).
[60] *See United States v Sokolow*, 490 U.S. 1, 109 S. Ct. 1581 (1989).

on the street or in another public place, by asking him if he is willing to answer some questions, by putting questions to him if the person is willing to listen, or by offering in evidence in a criminal prosecution his voluntary answers to such questions."[61] Thus, when an officer approaches an individual in a public place and seeks voluntary cooperation though noncoercive questioning, there is no restraint on that person's liberty, and the person is not seized.

"Nor would the fact that the officer identifies himself as a police officer, without more, convert the encounter into a seizure requiring some level of objective justification."[62] "Even when law enforcement officers have no basis for suspecting a particular individual, they may pose questions, ask for identification, and request consent to search luggage provided they do not induce cooperation by coercive means[.] If a reasonable person would feel free to terminate the encounter, then he or she has not been seized."[63] These consensual encounters, called *"mere inquiries"* or *"field inquiries,"* require no constitutional justification because the interaction does not register on the constitutional scale; the encounter is not a "seizure" within the meaning of the Fourth Amendment.

Naturally, the person approached "need not answer any question put to him; indeed, he may decline to listen to the questions at all and may go on his way[.] He may not be detained even momentarily without reasonable, objective grounds for doing so; and his refusal to listen or answer does not, without more, furnish those grounds. [Thus,] if there is no detention—no seizure within the meaning of the Fourth Amendment—then no constitutional rights have been infringed."[64]

In *Terry v. Ohio*, the United States Supreme Court held that a seizure occurs "when the officer, by means of physical force or show of authority, has in some way restrained the liberty" of the individual.[65] Thereafter, in *INS v. Delgado*,[66] the Court refined this standard to mean that a seizure has occurred only "if, in view of all the circumstances surrounding the incident, a reasonable person would have believed that he was not free to leave." The Court further refined this standard in *Michigan v. Chesternut*,[67] by focusing not on whether a reasonable person would feel free to leave but on whether the officer's conduct would "have communicated to a reasonable person that he was not at liberty to ignore the police presence and go about his business." In *Chesternut*, the Court held that the defendant was not seized when an officer accelerated his patrol car and began to drive alongside him. The officer did not activate his siren or flashers, did not command the defendant to halt, did not display a weapon, and did not drive aggressively so as to block the defendant's path.

In 1991, the United States Supreme Court once again redefined the concept of "seizure" in *California v. Hodari D.*[68] The Court held that, even when an officer has manifested a "show of authority," a seizure within the meaning of the Fourth Amendment further "requires either physical force [or], where that is absent, submission to the assertion of authority."[69] Thus, under federal law, a seizure does not occur until either the suspect complies with an officer's "show of authority" or there is an application of physical force (however slight) to the suspect by the officer.

The determination of whether a police-citizen encounter has elevated to one requiring a constitutional justification is measured from a "reasonable person's" perspective. A police officer's belief that the citizen was "free to leave" is not probative. Rather, the correct inquiry is whether the citizen, under all of the attendant circumstances, *reasonably believed* he could walk away without answering any of the officer's questions. Therefore, officers who wish to maintain a police-citizen encounter as a mere inquiry should: (1) pose their

---

[61] *Florida v. Royer,* 460 U.S. 491, 497, 103 S. Ct. 1319, 1324 (1983); *see also Utah v. Strieff,* 579 U.S. ___, 136 S. Ct. 2056, 2063 (2016) ("[A] 'seizure does not occur simply because a police officer approaches an individual and asks a few questions.'") (quoting *Florida v. Bostick,* 501 U.S. 429, 434, 111 S. Ct. 2382 (1991)).

[62] *Florida v. Royer,* 460 U.S. 491, 497, 103 S. Ct. 1319, 1324 (1983).

[63] *United States v. Drayton,* 536 U.S. 194, 122 S. Ct. 2105, 2110 (2002).

[64] *Royer* at 498, 103 S. Ct. at 1324. *See also Illinois v. Wardlow,* 528 U.S. 119, 125, 120 S. Ct. 673, 676 (2000) (Since a "mere field inquiry" may be conducted without reasonable suspicion, the individual approached "has a right to ignore the police and go about his business.").

[65] *Terry v. Ohio,* 392 U.S. 1, 19, n.16, 88 S. Ct. 1868 (1968).

[66] *INS v. Delgado,* 466 U.S. 210, 215 104 S. Ct. 1758 (1984).

[67] *Michigan v. Chesternut,* 486 U.S. 567, 569 108 S. Ct. 1975 (1988).

[68] *California v. Hodari D.,* 499 U.S. 621, 111 S. Ct. 1547 (1991).

[69] *California v. Hodari D.,* 499 U.S. 621, 626, 111 S. Ct. 1547 (1991).

questions in a conversational manner; (2) avoid making demands or issuing orders; and (3) ensure that the questions they ask are not overbearing or harassing in nature.

"On the other hand, an encounter becomes a seizure if the officer engages in conduct a reasonable person would view as threatening or offensive[.] This would include such tactics as pursuing a person who has attempted to terminate the contact by departing, continuing to interrogate a person who has clearly expressed a desire not to cooperate, renewing an encounter with a person who earlier responded fully to police inquiries, calling to such a person to halt, holding a person's identification papers or other property, conducting a consensual search of the person in an 'authoritative manner,' bringing a drug-sniffing dog toward the person or his property, intercepting a phone call for the suspect, blocking the path of the suspect, physically grabbing and moving the suspect, drawing a weapon, calling for backup, and encircling the suspect by many officers[.]"[70]

2.2.1. Working the buses

Often an officer will approach a person in a public place (*i.e.*, airport, bus station, train, plane or bus, etc.). The officer needs no reasonable suspicion to ask questions, or ask for a person's identification, as long as a reasonable person would understand that he could refuse to cooperate. Thus, in *Florida v. Bostick*,[71] the United States Supreme Court held that a Fourth Amendment "seizure" does *not* occur when the police board a public bus during a scheduled stopover, approach a passenger at random, ask a few questions, ask to see the passenger's identification, and then request consent to search his bags—"so long as the officers do not convey a message that compliance with their request is required."[72] "[I]n order to determine whether a particular encounter constitutes a seizure, a court [will] consider all the circumstances surrounding the encounter to determine whether the police conduct would have communicated to a reasonable person that the person was not free to decline the officers' requests or otherwise terminate the encounter. That rule applies to encounters that take place on a city street, [on a train,] or in an airport lobby, and it applies equally to encounters on a bus."[73]

Similarly, in *United States v. Drayton*,[74] the Court held that the defendant was not seized when officers boarded a Greyhound bus during a scheduled stop in Tallahassee and began questioning the passengers, even when an officer asked consent to search the defendant's bag. Although the officers displayed their badges, they did not brandish weapons or make intimidating moves. They gave the passengers no reason to believe that they were required to answer the officers' questions and they left the aisle free so that passengers could exit the bus. Only one officer did the questioning and he spoke in a polite, quiet (not authoritative) voice: "Nothing he said would suggest to a reasonable person that he or she was barred from leaving the bus or otherwise terminating the encounter."

However, consider *Bond v. United States*,[75] wherein the Supreme Court held that, even if lawfully on a public bus during a scheduled stopover, an officer's physical manipulation of a bus passenger's carry-on luggage constitutes an unreasonable search and seizure under the Fourth Amendment.[76]

2.3. Investigative detentions; "stop and frisk"

Once it is determined that a police-citizen encounter has constitutional implications, that is, it has advanced beyond the point of a "mere inquiry," courts will examine, by reference to the totality of the circumstances, whether the official action was constitutionally justified. The circumstances will be viewed from the

---

[70] *See* 4 Wayne R. LaFave, *Search and Seizure, A Treatise on the Fourth Amendment* § 9.4(a), at pp. 601-06 (6th ed. 2020) (citing cases); *see also United States v. Lowe*, 791 F.3d 424 (3d Cir. 2015) (when "three marked police cars nearly simultaneously arrived on the scene and [f]our uniformed police officers" approached a defendant and his companion, "commanding them to show their hands," a seizure occurred.).

[71] *Florida v. Bostick*, 501 U.S. 429, 111 S. Ct. 2382 (1991).

[72] *Florida v. Bostick*, 501 U.S. 429, 111 S. Ct. 2388 (1991).

[73] *Florida v. Bostick*, 501 U.S. 429, 111 S. Ct. 2388, 2389 (1991).

[74] *United States v. Drayton*, 536 U.S. 194, 122 S. Ct. 2105 (2002).

[75] *Bond v. United States*, 529 U.S. 334, 120 S. Ct. 1462 (2000).

[76] *Bond v. United States*, 529 U.S. 334, 120 S. Ct. 1462, 1465 (2000).

vantage point of a prudent and reasonable law enforcement officer on the scene at the time of the encounter, who possesses a reasonable degree of training, experience and skill.

The next conceptual category in the hierarchy of encounters involves interactions that courts refer to as investigatory stops, temporary detentions, or *Terry* stops. In *Terry v. Ohio*,[77] the United States Supreme Court instructed:

> Where a police officer observes unusual conduct which leads him reasonably to conclude in light of his experience that criminal activity may be afoot and that the persons with whom he is dealing may be armed and presently dangerous, where in the course of investigating this behavior he identifies himself as a police [officer] and makes reasonable inquiries, and where nothing in the initial stages of the encounter serves to dispel his reasonable fear for his own or others' safety, he is entitled for the protection of himself and others in the area to conduct a carefully limited search of the outer clothing of such persons in an attempt to discover weapons which might be used to assault him.[78]

2.3.1. Reasonable articulable suspicion for a stop

The police-citizen encounter authorized by *Terry v. Ohio* has several distinct components. The first component concerns the level of "reasonable suspicion" that must exist before an "investigatory stop" may be conducted. This standard involves a level of belief which is something less than the probable cause standard needed to support an arrest. To justify such an intrusion, a law enforcement officer "must be able to point to specific and articulable facts which, taken together with rational inferences from those facts," collectively provide "'a particularized and objective basis' for suspecting the person stopped of criminal activity."[79] "Reasonable suspicion" as a "common sense, nontechnical conception[,]" deals with "'the factual and practical considerations of everyday life on which reasonable and prudent [persons], not legal technicians, act.'"[80]

The question whether an officer had a reasonable suspicion to support a particular investigative detention will be addressed by the courts by reference to an "objective" standard: Would the facts available to the officer at the moment of the stop or frisk warrant an officer "of reasonable caution in the belief that the action taken was appropriate?"[81] To determine if the standard has been met in a particular case, a court will give due weight, not to an officer's "unparticularized" suspicions or hunches, but to the "specific reasonable inferences" which the officer is entitled to draw from the facts in light of her experience.[82] Thus, more is required than mere generalizations and subjective impressions. The officer must be able to articulate specific facts gleaned from the "totality of the circumstances"—the whole picture—from which she reasonably inferred that the person confronted was involved in criminal activity. Reasonable suspicion will be evaluated in the context of the totality of the circumstances as viewed through the eyes of a reasonable, trained officer in the same or similar circumstances, combining objective facts with such an officer's subjective interpretation of those facts.

In *United States v. Arvizu*,[83] the U.S. Supreme Court further explained that the "totality of the circumstances" approach for determining whether a detaining officer has a "particularized and objective basis" for suspecting legal wrongdoing "allows officers to draw on their own experience and specialized training to make inferences from and deductions about the cumulative information available to them that 'might well

---

[77] *Terry v. Ohio*, 392 *U.S.* 1, 26, 88 S. Ct. 1868, 1882 (1968).

[78] *Terry v. Ohio*, 392 *U.S.* 1, 30-31, 88 S. Ct. 1868, 1884-85 (1968).

[79] *Terry v. Ohio*, 392 *U.S.* 1, 21, 88 S. Ct. 1868, 1880 (1968); *Ornelas v. United States*, 517 U.S. 690, 116 S. Ct. 1657, 1661 (1996) (quoting *United States v. Cortez*, 449 U.S. 411, 417-18, 101 S. Ct. 690, 694-95 (1981)); *see also United States v. Arvizu*, 534 U.S. 266, 122 S. Ct. 744 (2002) ("the Fourth Amendment is satisfied if the officer's action is supported by reasonable suspicion to believe that criminal activity 'may be afoot'").

[80] *Ornelas v. United States*, 517 U.S. 690, 695, 115 S. Ct. 1657, 1661 (1996) (quoting *Illinois v. Gates*, 462 U.S. 213, 231, 103 S. Ct. 2317 (1983)).

[81] *Terry v. Ohio*, 392 *U.S.* 1, 22, 88 S. Ct. 1868, 1880 (1968).

[82] *Terry v. Ohio*, 392 *U.S.* 1, 27, 88 S. Ct. 1868, 1883 (1968); *see also Ornelas v. United States*, 517 U.S. 690, 116 S. Ct. 1657, 1663 (1996) (due deference should be given to the inferences drawn by an officer who necessarily "views the facts through the lens of his police experience and expertise").

[83] *United States v. Arvizu*, 534 U.S. 266, 122 S. Ct. 744 (2002).

elude an untrained person.'"[84] In this analysis, the officer is not required to rule out "the possibility of inno-cent conduct."[85] Many times, facts and circumstances susceptible to innocent explanation when considered in isolation will, when viewed together, as a whole, suffice to form a reasonable and articulable suspicion of criminal activity. Moreover, a police officer's deductions are particularly entitled to deference because, in analyzing the totality of the circumstances, law enforcement officers are permitted, if not required, to con-sider "the modes or patterns of operation of certain kinds of lawbreakers. From these data, a trained officer draws inferences and makes deductions—inferences and deductions that might well elude an untrained person."[86]

State v. Wilson[87] is an excellent example. There, a SWAT team was securing a house that was located in an area where there had been numerous reports of gun violence. The police were openly maintaining a perime-ter around the premises to protect the SWAT team from outside interference. The defendant walked onto the premises and past Officer Christian who was standing near the street. Officer Ayers, who was standing closer to the house, overheard the defendant mention that he wanted to get his moped. Officer Ayers approached the defendant and noticed a heavy object in his pocket. Believing that the object might be a firearm, Officer Ayers asked the defendant if he was carrying any weapons. The defendant said he was not, and Officer Ayers then instructed him to turn around so that Officer Ayers could frisk him. Officer Ayers then observed the grip of a handgun protruding from the defendant's pocket. Officer Ayers seized the weapon and detained the defendant who was ultimately charged with possession of a firearm by a felon.

The North Carolina Supreme Court noted that, on review of the defendant's motion to suppress, the "Court of Appeals erred by focusing solely on one finding of fact instead of the totality of the circumstances, as *Terry* requires. The Court of Appeals correctly stated that 'unusual behavior does not necessarily equal behavior leading a reasonable officer to believe criminal activity was afoot.' This reasoning, though, does not take into account the *particular* unusual behavior at issue here and the totality of the circumstances sur-rounding it."[88] The court described the totality of the circumstances and held:

> These circumstances include police officers having responded to shootings at and near the house in the past, Officer Ayers' observation that defendant was likely armed, and defendant's apparent lie about possessing a weapon. Combining these circumstances with defendant's unusual choice to cross a police perimeter to purportedly retrieve his moped during an active SWAT team sweep, there were more than enough facts to establish a reasonable suspicion that criminal activity may have been afoot. The warrantless detention and search of defendant therefore did not violate the Fourth Amendment.[89]

In *State v. Fletcher*,[90] the police received information from two sources that the person they were looking for was a tall Black male with dark pants and a white shirt. Officers saw a person fitting the description moments later within two blocks of the location of the sources. The North Carolina Supreme Court held "that the proximity in time and location and the accuracy of the physical description of the race, gender, and clothing of the suspect gave the officers reasonable suspicion to make an investigative stop of the defendant."[91]

By contrast, in *State v. Ellis*,[92] Trooper Stevens did not have the requisite reasonable suspicion to stop the defendant. There, while assisting a motorist at the side of the road, Trooper Stevens observed a passing car from which the defendant was "gesturing with his middle finger."[93] Trooper Stevens pursued the vehicle for

---

[84] *United States v. Arvizu*, 534 U.S. 266, 122 S. Ct. 744, 750-51 (2002) (citation omitted).

[85] *United States v. Arvizu*, 534 U.S. 266, 122 S. Ct. 744, 753 (2002).

[86] *United States v. Cortez*, 449 U.S. 411, 418, 101 S Ct. 690, 695 (1981).

[87] *State v. Wilson*, 821 S.E.2d 811 (N.C. 2018).

[88] *State v. Wilson*, 821 S.E.2d 811, 817 (N.C. 2018) (citing *State v. Johnson*, 370 N.C. 32, 803 S.E.2d 137 (2017)).

[89] *State v. Wilson*, 821 S.E.2d 811, 817 (N.C. 2018) (citing *Terry v. Ohio*, 392 *U.S.* 1, 22, 88 S. Ct. 1868, 1880 (1968)).

[90] *State v. Fletcher*, 348 N.C. 292, 500 S.E.2d 668 (1998).

[91] *State v. Fletcher*, 348 N.C. 292, 302-03, 500 S.E.2d 668 (1998). See also *State v. Baker*, 247 N.C. App. 246, 785 S.E.2d 782 (2016) (finding reasonable suspicion to make stop where two witnesses described car and proximity in time and location to location of crime).

[92] *State v. Ellis*, 374 N.C. 340, 841 S.E.2d 247 (2020).

[93] *State v. Ellis*, 374 N.C. 340, 344, 841 S.E.2d 247 (2020).

approximately half a mile, did not observe any traffic violations, and then pulled the vehicle over on suspicion of disorderly conduct. The North Carolina Supreme Court found the facts insufficient to give rise to a reasonable suspicion of disorderly conduct. Said the court:

> Based on the facts in the record, we are unable to infer that, by gesturing with his middle finger, defendant was intending to or was likely to provoke a violent reaction from another driver that would cause a breach of the peace.[94]

2.3.1.1. The scope of an investigative detention

A determination that an officer possessed reasonable suspicion, justifying a detention, is only the first step in determining the legality of a stop. A reviewing court will ask initially if the officer's action was justified at its inception, and secondly whether it was reasonably related in scope to the circumstances which justified the interference in the first place. An examination of the scope of the stop addresses the following: (i) the length of the detention, and (ii) the methods employed during the stop. The duration and methods employed during the stop must be tailored to serve the purpose of confirming or dispelling the officer's suspicions. If those concerns are confirmed, and an officer's observations during the detention create probable cause, an arrest may be made. If the suspicions are dispelled, then the suspect should be let go. The detention must be sufficiently limited in temporal duration to satisfy the conditions of an investigative seizure. The nature of the questioning and level of force employed during the detention must be similarly limited. Even though an initial stop may be justified, if the detention exceeds the scope authorized by its justification, *i.e.*, "reasonable suspicion of criminal activity," it will be deemed an illegal stop, and any incriminating evidence found thereafter will not be admissible in court.

In *United States v. Sharpe*,[95] the Supreme Court would not hold that an investigative detention, based on reasonable suspicion, which lasts 20 minutes or longer, is a violation of the Fourth Amendment's prohibition on unlawful seizures. "Obviously, if an investigative stop continues indefinitely, at some point it can no longer be justified as an investigative stop." However, the Court refused to place a rigid time limitation on *Terry*-type investigatory stops. "While it is clear that the brevity of the invasion of the individual's Fourth Amendment interests is an important factor in determining whether the seizure is so minimally intrusive as to be justifiable on reasonable suspicion," courts will also consider the law enforcement purposes to be served by the stop as well as the time reasonably needed to effectuate those purposes.[96]

Therefore, when a court determines whether a detention is too long in duration to be justified as an investigative stop, it will examine whether the police "diligently pursued a means of investigation that was likely to confirm or dispel their suspicions quickly, during which time it was necessary to detain the defendant." The court will make this assessment by considering whether the police acted swiftly in developing the situation. The question will not be whether some other alternative was available, but "whether the police acted unreasonably in failing to recognize or to pursue it."[97] As the court stated in *United States v. McCarthy*[98]: "There is no talismanic time beyond which any stop justified on the basis of *Terry* becomes an unreasonable seizure under the Fourth Amendment." Rather, in determining whether an investigative stop is too long, "common sense and ordinary human experience must govern over rigid criteria."

2.3.1.2. Stop and identify

The United States Supreme Court has addressed the issue of whether the police can insist on identification. In *Hiibel v. Sixth Judicial Dist. Court of Nevada, Humboldt Co.*,[99] the United States Supreme Court, in upholding Nevada's "stop and identify" law, declared that the *Terry* line of cases "permit a State to require a suspect

---

[94] *State v. Ellis*, 374 N.C. 340, 344, 841 S.E.2d 247 (2020).

[95] *United States v. Sharpe,* 470 U.S. 675, 105 S. Ct. 1568 (1985).

[96] *See also State v. Thorpe*, 232 N.C. App. 468, 754 S.E.2d 213 (2014); *State v. McClendon*, 350 N.C. 630, 517 S.E.2d 128 (1999); *State v. Fletcher*, 348 N.C. 292, 500 S.E.2d 668 (1998).

[97] *United States v. Sharpe,* 470 U.S. 675, 105 S. Ct. 1568, 1576 (1985).

[98] *United States v. McCarthy*, 77 F.3d 522, 530 (1st Cir. 1996).

[99] *Hiibel v. Sixth Judicial Dist. Court of Nev.*, 542 U.S. 177, 185, 124 S. Ct. 2451 (2004).

to disclose his name in the course of a Terry stop." The officer may not, however, "stop a citizen and demand identification without any specific basis for believing he is involved in criminal activity."[100] The officer must have a reasonable suspicion to support the investigative stop.

In *Hiibel*, the defendant was arrested for obstruction because he refused to provide his identity to the police during a valid *Terry* stop. Hiibel argued that Nevada's "stop and identify" statute, which requires a person detained by the police to disclose his identity, violated the Fourth Amendment. The Court disagreed, noting that "[o]btaining a suspect's name in the course of a *Terry* stop serves important government interests" because "[k]nowledge of identity may inform an officer that a suspect is wanted for another offense, or has a record of violence or mental disorder."[101]

In North Carolina "[r]efusing to identify oneself to a police officer during a *valid* stop may constitute a violation of N.C.G.S. § 14-223"[102] which provides:

> If any person shall willfully and unlawfully resist, delay or obstruct a public officer in discharging or attempting to discharge a duty of his office, he shall be guilty of a Class 2 misdemeanor.

2.3.1.3. The "least intrusive means" test

In *Florida v. Royer*,[103] the U.S. Supreme Court instructed that a reasonable investigative detention is one that is "temporary," lasting "no longer than is necessary to effectuate the purpose of the stop." The Court then went on to state that "the investigative methods employed should be the least intrusive means reasonably available to verify or dispel the officer's suspicion in a short period of time."[104] The "least intrusive means" language is "directed at the length of the investigative stop, not at whether the police had a less intrusive means to verify their suspicions before stopping *Royer*. The reasonableness of the officer's decision to stop a suspect does not turn on the availability of less intrusive investigatory techniques. Such a rule," noted the Court, "would unduly hamper the police's ability to make swift, on-the-spot decisions."[105]

Naturally, if the detention lasts too long, or if the officers' conduct is too intrusive, the stop may transform into an arrest. As explained by the court in *United States v. Ruiz*:[106]

> A *Terry* stop based on reasonable suspicion can ripen into a *de facto* arrest that must be based on probable cause if it continues too long or becomes unreasonably intrusive.... The investigation following a *Terry* stop must be reasonably related in scope and duration to the circumstances that justified the stop in the first instance so that it is a minimal intrusion on the individual's Fourth Amendment interests.

With respect to the duration of the stop, there is no rigid time limit placed on *Terry* stops; and a defendant's actions can contribute to a permissible extension of the stop. For example, in *United States v. Vega*,[107] the court held that a 62-minute delay was reasonable given that the defendant initially consented to a search of his garage, but then changed his mind. Assuming reasonable suspicion exists (as it did in *Ruiz*), "a reasonable delay attributable to arranging for a canine unit to conduct a sniff may permissibly extend the duration of a stop."[108] The officers in *Ruiz* detained the defendant "for less than 20 minutes prior to obtaining his consent to search the car, which," the court held, was "a reasonable duration, given that there is nothing in the record to suggest that the officers acted less than diligently."[109]

---

[100] *United States v. Henderson*, 463 F.3d 27, 45 (1st Cir. 2006).

[101] *Hiibel v. Sixth Judicial Dist. Court of Nev.*, 542 U.S. 177, 186, 124 S. Ct. 2451 (2004).

[102] *State v. Ellis*, 374 N.C. 340, 343, 841 S.E.2d 247 (2020). *See also State v. Friend*, 237 N.C. App. 490, 493, 768 S.E.2d 146 (2014) (holding that the failure to provide information about one's identity during a lawful stop can constitute resistance, delay, or obstruction within the meaning of N.C.G.S. § 14-223).

[103] *Florida v. Royer*, 460 U.S. 491, 500, 103 S. Ct. 1319, 1325 (1983).

[104] *Florida v. Royer*, 460 U.S. 491, 500, 103 S. Ct. 1319, 1325 (1983).

[105] *United States v. Sokolow*, 490 U.S. 1, 11, 109 S. Ct. 1581, 1587 (1989).

[106] *United States v. Ruiz*, 785 F.3d 1134, 1143 (7th Cir. 2015) (citations and internal quotes omitted).

[107] *United States v. Vega*, 72 F.3d 507, 515 (7th Cir. 1995).

[108] *United States v. Ruiz*, 785 F.3d 1134, 1144 (7th Cir. 2015).

[109] *United States v. Ruiz*, 785 F.3d 1134, 1144 (7th Cir. 2015).

2.3.1.4. Transporting suspects

In *Dunaway v. New York*,[110] the Supreme Court held that officers are not permitted to transport a suspect to police headquarters for questioning without his consent and without probable cause for an arrest. According to the Court, whenever a law enforcement officer removes a suspect from where he is found and transports that suspect to police headquarters for questioning without his consent and without probable cause (for his arrest), the detention is, in all important respects, indistinguishable from a traditional arrest and is unlawful. Merely because a suspect is not told he is under arrest, is not "booked," and would not have an arrest record if the interrogation proves fruitless, does not make such a detention analogous to the type authorized by *Terry v. Ohio*. Rather, such a "detention for custodial interrogation—regardless of its label—intrudes so severely on interests protected by the Fourth Amendment" that the familiar requirement of probable cause is thereby triggered.

In *Kaupp v. Texas*,[111] the Supreme Court reaffirmed that, in the absence of probable cause for an arrest, it is unlawful for law enforcement officials to transport a suspect, against his will, to the station for questioning.

This principle was underscored in *Lincoln v. Barnes*,[112] where members of the police SWAT team fatally shot John Lincoln at his mother's residence. The shooting took place in front of John's 18-year-old daughter, Erin. After the shooting, Erin was removed from the home, placed in handcuffs, and put in the backseat of a police vehicle. Although she did not fight, struggle, or resist, she did ask the officer why she was being taken into custody. According to the officers, they were holding Erin because they needed to get a statement from her. After being held in the back of the patrol car for about two hours, Erin was transported to the police station where she was interrogated for five hours, and was "forced to write out a statement. After the officers obtained her statement, Erin was permitted to leave."[113]

In this appeal, Erin asserted that the police violated her Fourth Amendment right to be free from unreasonable seizure by taking her into custody without a warrant, probable cause, or justifiable reason and interrogating her against her will for five hours, during which she was forced to write out a statement. She argued that her detention constituted a *de facto* arrest. *The Fifth Circuit Court of Appeals agreed.*

Here, there was no dispute that the officers involved in the incident did not have a reasonable suspicion that Erin was involved with any criminal wrongdoing or that there was probable cause to believe she had committed or was committing a crime. The rationale for her detention rested solely on her status as a witness to her father's shooting.

As emphasized in *Dunaway v. New York*, "detention for custodial interrogation—regardless of its label—intrudes so severely on interests protected by the Fourth Amendment as necessarily to trigger the traditional safeguards against illegal arrest."[114] This principle had been made clear in *Davis v. Mississippi*—namely, "that an investigatory detention that, for all intents and purposes, is indistinguishable from custodial interrogation, requires no less probable cause than a traditional arrest."[115]

"Accordingly, police violate the Fourth Amendment when, absent probable cause or the individual's consent, they seize and transport a person to the police station and subject her to prolonged interrogation."[116]

In *Hayes v. Florida*,[117] however, the Supreme Court indicated that, with prior judicial authorization (such as an investigative detention order), the police may be authorized to transport a suspect to the police station for fingerprinting, even in the absence of probable cause or consent. Here, the Court noted that there have been a number of cases that have suggested that "the Fourth Amendment would permit seizures for the purpose of fingerprinting, if there is reasonable suspicion that the suspect has committed a criminal act, if there is a reasonable basis for believing that fingerprinting will establish or negate the suspect's connection with that crime, and if the procedure is carried out with dispatch."

---

[110] *Dunaway v. New York,* 442 U.S. 200, 99 S. Ct. 2248 (1979).

[111] *Kaupp v. Texas*, 538 U.S. 626, 123 S. Ct. 1843 (2003).

[112] *Lincoln v. Barnes*, 855 F.3d 297 (5th Cir. 2017).

[113] *Lincoln v. Barnes*, 855 F.3d 297, 300 (5th Cir. 2017).

[114] *Lincoln v. Barnes*, 855 F.3d 297, 302 (5th Cir. 2017) (citation and internal quotes omitted).

[115] *Davis v. Mississippi*, 394 U.S. 721, 726-27, 89 S. Ct. 1394 (1969). *See also Hayes v. Florida*, 470 U.S. 811, 815, 105 S. Ct. 1643 (1985) ("None of our later cases have undercut the holding in Davis that transportation to and investigative detention at the station house without probable cause or judicial authorization together violate the Fourth Amendment.").

[116] *Lincoln v. Barnes*, 855 F.3d 297, 302 (5th Cir. 2017).

[117] *Hayes v. Florida*, 470 U.S. 811, 105 S. Ct. 1643 (1985).

2.3.1.5. Handcuffing suspects

While the use of handcuffs to restrain the person being detained is an indication that the detention is an arrest rather than a *Terry* stop, courts have held that a law enforcement officer's act of handcuffing a suspect during the course of a *Terry* stop will not *automatically* transform the investigative detention into an arrest. As observed by the court in *United States v. Glenna*,[118] "'neither handcuffing nor other restraints will *automatically* convert a *Terry* stop into a *de facto* arrest requiring probable cause.'"[119] If, in a rare case, common sense and ordinary human experience reasonably convince an officer that an investigative stop could be effectuated safely only in this manner, a court should uphold the officer's chosen method to investigate. Naturally, the "use of handcuffs substantially heightens the intrusiveness of a temporary detention."[120]

When the prosecution "seeks to prove that an investigatory detention involving the use of handcuffs did not exceed the limits of a *Terry* stop, it must be able to point to some specific fact or circumstance that could have supported a reasonable belief that the use of such restraints was necessary to carry out the legitimate purposes of the stop without exposing law enforcement officers, the public, or the suspect himself to an undue risk of harm."[121]

A number of other courts have held that the placing of a person in handcuffs may fall within the permissible scope of a temporary investigative detention under *Terry v. Ohio*. For example, in *United States v. Kapperman*,[122] the Eleventh Circuit noted that "neither handcuffing nor other restraints will *automatically* convert a *Terry* stop into a *de facto* arrest requiring probable cause. Just as probable cause to arrest will not justify using excessive force to detain a suspect[,] the use of a particular method to restrain a person's freedom of movement does not necessarily make police action tantamount to an arrest. The inquiry in either context is reasonableness."[123] Likewise, the Court of Appeals of North Carolina has stated, "When dealing with aggressive, noncooperative individuals, handcuffs and placing the suspect in the officer's car are acceptable methods of effecting an investigatory stop."[124]

2.3.1.6. Reasonable suspicion and executive orders

In North Carolina, the governor has the power to impose an executive order or a declaration during a state of emergency.[125] Municipalities and counties are similarly empowered.[126] For example, in March of 2019, via Executive Order No. 121, Governor Cooper ordered people to stay at home in an attempt to curb the rise of COVID-19 infections. Pursuant to N.C.Gen.Stat. § 14-288.20A, it is a crime to violate any such executive

---

[118] *United States v. Glenna*, 878 F.2d 967 (7th Cir. 1989).

[119] *United States v. Glenna*, 878 F.2d 967, 972 (7th Cir. 1989) (quoting *United States v. Kapperman*, 764, F.2d 786, 790 n.4 (11th Cir. 1985)).

[120] *United States v. Glenna*, 878 F.2d 967, 972 (7th Cir. 1989).

[121] *United States v. Acosta-Colon*, 157 F.3d 9, 18-19 (1st Cir. 1998).

[122] *United States v. Kapperman*, 764 F.2d 786 (11th Cir. 1985).

[123] *United States v. Kapperman*, 764 F.2d 786, 790 n.4 (11th Cir. 1985); *see also United States v. Tilmon*, 19 F.3d 1221, 1228 (7th Cir. 1994) ("handcuffing—once highly problematic—is becoming quite acceptable in the context of a *Terry* stop"); *United States v. Miller*, 974 F.2d 953, 957 (8th Cir. 1992) (handcuffing of *Terry* detainee permitted where the police were badly outnumbered); *Halvorsen v. Baird*, 146 F.3d 680, 683, 685 (9th Cir. 1998) (holding that handcuffing a person and moving him three blocks for questioning did not automatically turn a detention into an arrest when such actions were justified by reasons of officer safety and security); *United States v. Perdue*, 8 F.3d 1455, 1463 (10th Cir. 1993) (noting "recent trend allowing police to use handcuffs or place suspects on the ground during a *Terry* stop," and that "nine courts of appeal, including the Tenth Circuit, have determined that such intrusive precautionary measures do not necessarily turn a lawful *Terry* stop into an arrest"); *United States v. Purry*, 545 F.2d 217, 220 (U.S. App. D.C. 1976) (handcuffing of a defendant was reasonable, as a corollary of the lawful *Terry* stop, in order to maintain status quo while the officer sought more information); *United States v. Crittendon*, 883 F.2d 326, 329 (4th Cir. 1989) (upholding the use of handcuffs in the context of a *Terry* stop where it was reasonably necessary to protect the officer's safety); *United States v. Taylor*, 716 F.2d 701, 709 (9th Cir. 1983) ("use of handcuffs, if reasonably necessary, while substantially aggravating the intrusiveness of an investigatory stop, [does] not necessarily convert a *Terry* stop into an arrest necessitating probable cause").

[124] *State v. Thorpe*, 232 N.C. App. 468, 479, 754 S.E.2d 213 (2014).

[125] N.C.Gen.Stat. § 166A-19.30.

[126] N.C.Gen.Stat. § 166A-19.31.

order or declaration. However, such an order does not authorize suspicionless stops. There is no blanket exception to the Fourth Amendment's reasonableness requirement or the reasonable suspicion standard for criminal violations of executive orders or declarations. A stop to investigate a violation must be supported by reasonable suspicion.

2.3.2. Reasonable suspicion for a protective "frisk"

Another component of the *Terry* rule involves an inquiry separate from whether the initial stop and detention was permissible. This component questions whether there was sufficient cause for an officer to conduct a protective pat-down search or "frisk" of the person being detained. It permits an officer to protect himself and others by conducting a limited search of the person's outer clothing for weapons "where he has reason to believe that he is dealing with an armed and dangerous individual, regardless of whether he has probable cause to arrest the individual for a crime. The officer need not be absolutely certain that the individual is armed. The issue is whether a reasonably prudent [officer] in the circumstances would be warranted in the belief that his safety or that of others was in danger."[127] The scope of a pat-down search is limited to that which is reasonably designed to discover guns, knives, clubs, or other hidden instruments that could be used to assault an officer.[128] In this regard, courts will determine whether a reasonably prudent officer in the circumstances would be warranted in the belief that [the officer's] safety or that of others was in danger. The officer must be able to articulate specific facts, which together with rational inferences from those facts, reasonably warrant the intrusion. The determination whether a pat-down search is justified is made by examining the totality of the circumstances with which the police officer is confronted. Factors to weigh in deciding whether a pat-down search ("frisk") is justified include: any furtive gestures or movements made in response to the officers' presence; the location of the encounter; the time of day; whether the suspect ignored requests to stop; and whether the suspect's clothing could conceal a weapon.

You will remember that in *State v. Wilson*,[129] after the defendant breached the security perimeter that the police were maintaining during the SWAT team's sweep of a residence, Officer Ayers stopped and frisked him. The court held that "[b]ased on his training, experience, and observations, it was reasonable for Officer Ayers to suspect that defendant was armed."[130] In *State v. McGirt*[131] it was lawful for an officer to frisk a person who had been removed from a vehicle when the officer knew that the defendant was a convicted felon who was under investigation for cocaine trafficking and that cocaine dealers normally carry weapons.

In *Arizona v. Johnson*,[132] the U.S. Supreme Court addressed the authority of a police officer to conduct a frisk of a passenger in a motor vehicle which was temporarily seized for a traffic infraction. According to the Court, "in a traffic-stop setting, the first *Terry* condition—a lawful investigatory stop—is met whenever it is lawful for police to detain an automobile and its occupants pending inquiry into a vehicular violation. The police need not have, in addition, cause to believe any occupant of the vehicle is involved in criminal activity. To justify a pat-down of the driver or a passenger during a traffic stop, however, just as in the case of a pedestrian reasonably suspected of criminal activity, the police must harbor reasonable suspicion that the person subjected to the frisk is armed and dangerous."[133]

Significantly, there are no "routine" or "automatic" frisks; the reasonable suspicion must be that the person may be "armed and dangerous," not "drunk or impaired." Clearly, *Terry v. Ohio* does not permit police officers to engage in a practice of routinely frisking individuals, without concern for whether a particular person poses a danger.

---

[127] *Terry v. Ohio*, 392 U.S. 1, 27, 88 S. Ct. 1868, 1883 (1968).
[128] *Adams v. Williams*, 407 U.S. 143, 146, 92 S. Ct. 1921 (1972).
[129] *State v. Wilson*, 821 S.E.2d 811 (N.C. 2018).
[130] *State v. Wilson*, 821 S.E.2d 811, 817 (N.C. 2018).
[131] *State v. McGirt*, 122 N.C. App. 237, 468 S.E.2d 833 (1996), *aff'd per curiam*, 345 N.C. 624, 481 S.E.2d 288, *cert. denied*, U.S., 118 S. Ct. 180, 139 L. Ed. 2d 121 (1997).
[132] *Arizona v. Johnson*, 555 U.S. 323, 129 S. Ct. 781 (2009).
[133] *Arizona v. Johnson*, 555 U.S. 323, 129 S. Ct. 781, 784 (2009). *See also State v. Bouknight*, 252 N.C. App. 265, 797 S.E.2d 340 (2017) (totality of circumstances supported frisk of vehicle where a defendant was in a high crime area, his behavior was evasive, he seemed nervous and routine background check revealed prior arrests).

2.3.2.1. Anonymous tip—"Man with a Gun" call

In *Florida v. J.L.*,[134] the U.S. Supreme Court cautioned that an anonymous tip that a person is carrying a gun, *without more*, will not be sufficient to justify a police officer's stop and frisk of that person.

In *J.L.*, an anonymous tipster called the Miami-Dade Police and reported that "a young black male standing at a particular bus stop and wearing a plaid shirt was carrying a gun." Two officers responded to the tip and arrived at the bus stop about six minutes after receiving the dispatch. At the bus stop, the officers noticed three Black males "just hanging out." One of the three, defendant J.L., was wearing a plaid shirt. "Apart from the tip, the officers had no reason to suspect any of the three of illegal conduct." One officer "approached J.L., told him to put his hands up on the bus stop, frisked him, and seized a gun from J.L.'s pocket." A second officer frisked the other two individuals but found nothing.

The pivotal issue was whether the Court should adopt a "gun exception" to the general rule, originated in *Terry v. Ohio*, which prohibits stops and frisks on the basis of "bare-boned anonymous tips." Refusing to do so, the Court instructed that to justify a stop based solely on an anonymous tip, police must take steps to establish the reliability of the tip. If the anonymous tip is found to be so lacking in reliability that the constitutional standard of a "reasonable articulable suspicion" of criminal activity has not been satisfied, the stop and frisk will not be justified, even if it alleges "the illegal possession of a firearm." Said the Court:

> An accurate description of a subject's readily observable location and appearance is of course reliable in this limited sense: It will help the police correctly identify the person whom the tipster means to accuse. Such a tip, however, does not show that the tipster has knowledge of concealed criminal activity. *The reasonable suspicion here at issue requires that a tip be reliable in its assertion of illegality, not just in its tendency to identify a determinate person.*[135]

With regard to the issue whether an anonymous tip supports a reasonable suspicion to stop a suspect, North Carolina case law tracks federal precedent. The North Carolina Supreme Court has asserted that "an anonymous tip can form the basis of reasonable suspicion as long as there is sufficient indicia of reliability either from the tip alone or after police corroboration."[136] However, in *State v. Hughes*,[137] the tip was not enough to create a reasonable suspicion. There, "Detectives Bryan and McAvoy had a physical description of a dark skinned Jamaican whose name and clothing description could not be recalled, who was going to North Topsail Beach, who 'sometimes' came to Jacksonville on weekends before dark, who 'sometimes' took a taxi, and who 'sometimes' carried an overnight bag. The only other information the officers had was that defendant might be arriving on the 5:30 p.m. bus."[138] Moreover, "the only items of the informant's statement actually confirmed by the officers before the stop were that they saw a man meeting the suspect's description come from around a bus that had arrived in Jacksonville at approximately 3:50 p.m., that he was carrying an overnight bag, and that he left the station by taxi."[139] The court explained, "Without more, these details are insufficient corroboration because they could apply to many individuals. Furthermore, the officers did not see defendant get off the bus, and the bus arrived an hour and a half earlier than the tipster had predicted."[140]

2.3.3. The scope of the protective frisk

Yet another component of the *Terry* process concerns the permissible scope of the protective pat-down search or "frisk." Once a sufficient basis has been established for the investigatory detention and the limited pat-down search, the final inquiry is whether the search was narrowly restricted to the purpose such an intrusion is supposed to serve. Because the "sole justification" of the limited pat-down "is the protection of the police officer and others nearby," it must be "confined in scope to an intrusion reasonably designed to

---

[134] *Florida v. J.L.*, 529 U.S. 266, 120 S. Ct. 1375 (2000).
[135] *Florida v. J.L.*, 529 U.S. 266, 272, 120 S. Ct. 1375, 1379 (2000) (emphasis added).
[136] *State v. Hughes*, 353 N.C. 200, 208, 539 S.E.2d 625 (2000).
[137] *State v. Hughes*, 353 N.C. 200, 539 S.E.2d 625 (2000).
[138] *State v. Hughes*, 353 N.C. 200, 208-09, 539 S.E.2d 625 (2000).
[139] *State v. Hughes*, 353 N.C. 200, 209, 539 S.E.2d 625 (2000).
[140] *State v. Hughes*, 353 N.C. 200, 209, 539 S.E.2d 625 (2000).

discover guns, knives, clubs, or other hidden instruments for the assault of the police officer."[141] As the U.S. Supreme Court explained in *Adams v. Williams*[142]: "The purpose of this limited search is not to discover evidence of crime, but to allow the officer to pursue his investigation without fear of violence." In *Adams*, the Court upheld a protective frisk based on an informant's tip that a described suspect seated in a specific area at 2:15 a.m. was carrying narcotics and had a gun at his waist.

Accordingly, investigative stops or detentions may only be conducted when an officer has an objective reasonable suspicion that criminal activity may be afoot. The protective frisk of a suspect's outer clothing may be conducted only when the officer is in possession of additional specific and articulable facts from which he can reasonably infer that the individual he is confronting is armed and presently dangerous. Moreover, the frisk must be strictly limited in scope; designed solely to uncover hidden weapons. The facts must be objectively realistic and not be grounded in speculation, subjective feelings or intuition. To allow anything less "would invite intrusions upon constitutionally guaranteed rights based on nothing more substantial than inarticulate hunches," a result which courts will not allow.[143]

2.3.4. Plain touch

During the course of a pat-down, if a weapon is found, the officer may seize the item, and retain it, if its possession is unlawful. If the officer determines that the suspect is not armed, the purpose of the frisk is satisfied and the probing can proceed no further. However, if in the frisking process an object is detected, in a pocket or under clothing, that is clearly not a weapon, but rather, and just as obviously, contraband, the item may be seized under the "plain touch" or "plain feel" doctrine.[144] The rule here is that officers conducting a *Terry* frisk are entitled to seize any item whose contour, shape or mass make its identity immediately apparent as contraband. The officer must be able to immediately identify the item as contraband, without resort to further manipulation of the item.

Minnesota v. Dickerson set out the three requirements for "plain touch."[145] First, the officer must be lawfully *in the touching area*; that is, the officer must not violate the Fourth Amendment by arriving at the place from which the evidence could be tactilely perceived. Second, the officer must have some independent constitutional justification for placing his hands on the property or person in question. This requirement—though not unrelated to the mandate that the officer be lawfully in the perceiving area—should receive separate scrutiny which probes the independent and distinct constitutional justification for the touching of the person or evidentiary item. In this regard, the second prong of the plain touch formulation requires the officer's hands to be lawfully *on the touching area*. Finally, upon touching the area in question, the officer must, through the process of tactile recognition, garner probable cause to believe the object which she is touching constitutes evidence of crime, contraband, or is otherwise subject to official seizure. Additionally, the development of probable cause should be reasonably contemporaneous with the initial touching to avoid the danger of an inoffensive touching graduating into a governmental massage which, "by virtue of its intolerable intensity and scope," may violate the Fourth Amendment. In this respect, the recognition of the item as contraband must be *immediately apparent*.[146]

In *State v. Rich*,[147] as a detective was lawfully patting down the defendant, he felt "items consistent with controlled substances." The detective had five and a half years of law enforcement experience, had worked "a hundred or more" drug cases, and was familiar with cocaine, marijuana, and how those substances are typically packaged. Moreover, the detective believed the defendant was wanted by the Sampson County Special Investigations Division, which investigates all drug activity in the county. Based on the totality of the

---

[141] *Terry v. Ohio*, 392 U.S. 1, 29, 88 S. Ct. 1868, 1884 (1968).

[142] *Adams v. Williams*, 407 *U.S.* 143, 146, 92 S. Ct. 1921, 1923 (1972).

[143] *Terry v. Ohio*, 392 U.S. 1, 22, 88 S. Ct. 1868, 1880 (1968).

[144] *See Minnesota v. Dickerson*, 508 U.S. 366, 113 S. Ct. 2130 (1993). For a comprehensive discussion of the "plain touch" corollary, *see* Holtz, *The "Plain Touch" Corollary: A Natural and Foreseeable Consequence of the Plain View Doctrine*, 95 Dickinson L. Rev. 521 (1991). *See also* Larry E. Holtz, *Criminal Procedure for Law and Justice Professionals* (Blue360° Media).

[145] *Minnesota v. Dickerson*, 508 U.S. 366, 113 S. Ct. 2130 (1993).

[146] *Minnesota v. Dickerson*, 508 U.S. 366, 375, 113 S. Ct. 2130, 2137 (1993).

[147] *State v. Rich*, 248 N.C. App. 455, 790 S.E.2d 752 (2016).

circumstances the detective had probable cause to withdraw the object based on its plain feel through the fabric of the defendant's coat.[148]

2.3.5. Various factors to consider

As the previous discussion indicates, the police may briefly detain and question a person upon a reasonable suspicion, short of probable cause for arrest, that the person is involved in criminal activity. What is, or is not, reasonable suspicion depends on balancing, weighing and examining a variety of factors, taking into account the particular factual setting with which an officer is confronted. Some factors commonly cited by courts when determining the existence or absence of reasonable suspicion are as follows:

2.3.5.1. A suspect's prior criminal record

A law enforcement officer's knowledge of a suspect's criminal history, especially where that history involves weapons offenses, is a relevant factor in judging the reasonableness of a *Terry* frisk. Although an officer's knowledge of a suspect's criminal record *alone* is not sufficient to justify the initial stop of a suspect or to justify a frisk of a suspect once stopped, an officer's knowledge of a suspect's prior criminal activity in combination with other factors may lead to a reasonable suspicion that the suspect is presently armed and dangerous. Indeed, *Terry* itself acknowledges that police officers must be permitted to use their knowledge and experience in deciding whether to frisk a suspect. In many instances, a reasonable inference may be drawn that a suspect is armed and dangerous from the fact that he is known to have been armed and dangerous on previous occasions.[149]

Accordingly, given the volatile times in which we live, courts certainly cannot require police officers to ignore the fact that a suspect whom they are confronting has a history of criminal behavior, particularly weapons offenses. While a suspect's criminal history alone will not justify a *Terry* frisk, that history, coupled with other facts, may be sufficient.

2.3.5.2. An officer's training and experience

Officers are entitled to rely on their own knowledge, training and experience in forming reasonable suspicion, and even probable cause. State and federal courts have "long recognized the police officer's investigatory insight in evaluating probable cause."[150] The courts are consistently deferential to police officer training and experience. Otherwise, there would be little merit in securing able, trained officers to guard citizens and the public peace if their actions were to be measured by what might be probable cause to an untrained civilian.

In *United States v. Foster*,[151] an officer was patrolling an apartment complex where he had made 85 PCP-related arrests. He saw the defendant emerge from a still-running vehicle and walk toward a dumpster; the officer knew that PCP traffickers often hid their drugs in this dumpster area. The officer approached the defendant in the hope of initiating a consensual encounter; as soon as he stood face-to-face with him, he could smell PCP coming from the defendant's person. The officer asked the defendant his name and what he was doing in the area. The defendant was nervous during this brief conversation and attempted to return to his vehicle after about one minute. Based on his observations, the officer had reasonable suspicion to detain the defendant by handcuffing him and further questioning him. Because PCP users have a tendency to become violent, the officer had reasonable suspicion to frisk the defendant as well.

In *United States v. Orrego-Fernandez*,[152] a state trooper was driving along the highway when he noticed the defendant's pick-up truck, which appeared to have been altered. The truck frame was noticeably lower in the

---

[148] *State v. Rich*, 248 N.C. App. 455, *6, 790 S.E.2d 752 (2016). *See also State v. Richmond*, 215 N.C. App. 475, 715 S.E.2d 581 (2011).

[149] *See, e.g., Ybarra v. Illinois*, 444 U.S. 85, 93, 100 S. Ct. 338, 343 (1979) (implying that knowledge of a person's criminal history would be a factor supporting a legitimate frisk).

[150] Anna Lvovsky, *The Judicial Presumption of Police Expertise*, 130 Harv. L. Rev. 1995, 2026-27 (2017) (citing cases).

[151] *United States v. Foster*, 376 F.3d 577 (6th Cir. 2004).

[152] *United States v. Orrego-Fernandez*, 78 F.3d 1497 (10th Cir. 1996).

back than the front, so low that the leaf springs on the rear axle were only five inches above the pavement. The wheel well was solid black, with no metal slats visible, indicating that the bed was sitting directly on the frame. In addition, the trooper noticed that the gas tank was hanging two to three inches below the frame. The trooper had trained on a similar truck with a lowered gas tank; that truck had been equipped with a hidden compartment. The defendant's truck had a fresh, glossy coat of paint, which would have concealed any dents removed after altering the truck. Because this truck had several alterations consistent, in the trooper's experience, with a hidden compartment, he had reasonable suspicion for a stop.

In *State v. Sutton*,[153] Officer Sojack personally observed the defendant engage in what he believed, based on his training and experience, to be an illegal drug transaction. That observation, combined with information received from a pharmacist regarding the defendant's purchase of OxyContin, provided reasonable suspicion that criminal activity was afoot. Similarly, in *State v. Carmon*,[154] an officer's observation, at nighttime, of the defendant receiving a package and his belief, based on experience, that he had seen a drug transaction was sufficient to raise a reasonable suspicion.[155]

2.3.5.3. Knowledge of a recent crime in the area

An officer's awareness that a crime was recently committed in the vicinity is a pertinent consideration. For example, in *State v. Fletcher*,[156] Officer Justice responded to the scene of a vehicle break-in. At the scene the officer received information from the victim as well as a witness describing a man who was acting suspiciously nearby. Officer Justice informed Officer Harmon "to be on the lookout for a tall black male wearing a white t-shirt and black pants who was seen on foot at a certain location and moving in a certain direction. Officer Harmon saw a person fitting the description just moments later and within two blocks of the location specified."[157] The North Carolina Supreme Court held "that the proximity in time and location and the accuracy of the physical description of the race, gender, and clothing of the suspect gave the officers reasonable suspicion to make an investigative stop of defendant."[158]

2.3.5.4. High-crime/high drug-trafficking areas

A suspect's presence in a high-crime area, or an area known for drug trafficking, standing alone, is not a basis for reasonable suspicion. But a suspect's presence in such an area is an articulable fact. Coupled with other more solid observations, such presence can create reasonable suspicion that the suspect is engaged in the unlawful activity for which the neighborhood is known.[159]

In *State v. Fleming*,[160] an officer stopped and searched the defendant and another man because they were unfamiliar to him, the area was known to the officer to be a "'high drug area,'" it was midnight, and the two men walked away from the officer upon seeing him forty feet away.[161] The court held that "a generalized

---

[153] *State v. Sutton*, 167 N.C. App. 242, 605 S.E.2d 483 (2004).

[154] *State v. Carmon*, 156 N.C. App. 235, 576 S.E.2d 730 *aff'd per curiam*, 357 N.C. 500, 586 S.E.2d 90 (2003).

[155] See also *State v. Watson*, 119 N.C. App. 395, 398, 458 S.E.2d 519, 522 (1995) ("[A]n officer's experience and training can create reasonable suspicion. Defendant's actions must be viewed through the officer's eyes." (citation omitted)).

[156] *State v. Fletcher*, 348 N.C. 292, 500 S.E.2d 668 (1998).

[157] *State v. Fletcher*, 348 N.C. 292, 302, 500 S.E.2d 668 (1998).

[158] *State v. Fletcher*, 348 N.C. 292, 302-03, 500 S.E.2d 668 (1998). *See also State v. Rinck*, 303 N.C. 551, 558-60, 280 S.E.2d 912, 919-20 (1981) (reasonable basis for directing the defendants to stop existed where, while there was no witness to the homicide, two men were seen acting suspiciously at victim's house late at night and, within about 30 minutes of the homicide, were seen walking along the road within 200 feet of victim's house); *State v. Buie*, 297 N.C. 159, 162, 254 S.E.2d 26, 28 (reasonable grounds to stop a defendant where woman reported intruder in motel room at 4:10 a.m. and gave description to police of a Black male wearing dark clothing, approximately 5' 11" tall and weighing about 190 pounds, and where 20 minutes after the report and five to 10 minutes after a radio transmission of the description, an officer saw the defendant near the scene of the crime, wet, as if he had been running or perspiring heavily, and wearing a gold-colored leisure suit), *cert. denied*, 444 U.S. 971, 62 L. Ed. 2d 386, 100 S. Ct. 464 (1979).

[159] *See e.g., See Illinois v. Wardlow*, 528 U.S. 119, 123-24, 120 S. Ct. 673 (2000) ("flight combined with the fact that it occurred in a high crime area supported a finding of reasonable suspicion").

[160] *State v. Fleming*, 106 N.C. App. 165, 415 S.E.2d 782 (1992).

[161] *State v. Fleming*, 106 N.C. App. 165, 168, 415 S.E.2d 782 (1992).

suspicion that the defendant was engaged in criminal activity, based upon the time, place, and the officer's knowledge that defendant was unfamiliar to the area" was not a reasonable suspicion that could support the seizure of a defendant.[162]

Similarly, in *State v. Hayes*,[163] "[d]efendant and his companion were in an area where drug-related arrests had been made in the past; the men were walking back and forth on the sidewalk of a residential neighborhood on a Sunday afternoon; the officer did not believe either man lived in the neighborhood; and the officer observed in the car defendant and his companion had recently exited a gun under the seat not of defendant, but of his companion."[164] The court held that these facts did not support a reasonable suspicion that crime was afoot.

However, in *State v. Butler*,[165] the North Carolina Supreme Court did uphold a *Terry* stop in a known drug area. There:

[Officer] Hedges and his partner saw defendant, an unfamiliar figure, standing with a group of people on a Tampa street corner known as a "drug hole," an area frequented by drug dealers and users. Hedges had had the area under daily surveillance for several months. In the past six months, Hedges had made four to six arrests at the corner and knew that other arrests had occurred there. As Hedges and his partner approached the group, defendant and the officers made eye contact, at which point defendant immediately turned and walked away.

Their suspicions raised, the officers followed defendant and asked him for identification. Defendant handed Hedges a Florida driver's license. Before Hedges accepted the identification, he frisked defendant's person. Hedges testified that he conducted the frisk in order to discover any weapons and for his own protection during the face-to-face encounter with a person he suspected of drug activity.[166]

In holding that Officer Hedges had sufficient suspicion to make the stop, the court described the totality of the circumstances:

Those circumstances are: 1) defendant was seen in the midst of a group of people congregated together on a corner known as a "drug hole"; 2) Hedges had had the corner under daily surveillance for several months; 3) Hedges knew this corner to be a center of drug activity because he had made four to six drug-related arrests there in the past six months; 4) Hedges was aware of other arrests there as well; 5) defendant was a stranger to the officers; 6) upon making eye contact with the uniformed officers, defendant immediately moved away, behavior that is evidence of flight; and 7) it was Hedges' experience that people involved in drug traffic are often armed.[167]

The court concluded, "While no one of these circumstances alone necessarily satisfies Fourth Amendment requirements, we hold that, when considered in their totality, Officer Hedges had sufficient suspicion to make a lawful stop."[168]

Hand-to-hand transactions. In *State v. Mello*,[169] the officer observed the defendant not simply in a general high crime area, but on a specific corner known for drug activity that was the scene of recent, multiple drug-related arrests. Moreover, the fact that two pedestrians fled in the immediate aftermath of an interaction with the defendant that could be reasonably construed as a hand-to-hand drug transaction would clearly have raised a reasonable suspicion in the mind of a competent and experienced law enforcement officer that

---

162 *State v. Fleming*, 106 N.C. App. 165, 171, 415 S.E.2d 782 (1992).

163 *State v. Hayes*, 188 N.C. App. 313, 655 S.E.2d 726 (2008).

164 *State v. Hayes*, 188 N.C. App. 313, 315, 655 S.E.2d 726 (2008).

165 *State v. Butler*, 331 N.C. 227, 415 S.E.2d 719 (1992).

166 *State v. Butler*, 331 N.C. 227, 231-32, 415 S.E.2d 719 (1992).

167 *State v. Butler*, 331 N.C. 227, 233, 415 S.E.2d 719 (1992).

168 *State v. Butler*, 331 N.C. 227, 233, 415 S.E.2d 719 (1992).

169 *State v. Mello*, 200 N.C. App. 437, 684 S.E.2d 483 (2009) *aff'd*, 364 N.C. 421, 700 S.E.2d 224 (2010).

further investigation was warranted.[170] The investigatory detention was allowed and the evidence seized as a result of the stop was properly admitted at the defendant's trial.

2.3.5.5. Time period

The time of day or night in which the individual is observed is relevant, and a late hour may be a factor contributing to a reasonable suspicion. For example, in *Adams v. Williams*,[171] while properly investigating the activity of a person who was reported to be carrying narcotics and a concealed weapon and who was sitting alone in a car in a high-crime area at 2:15 a.m., the officer was held to have had ample reason to fear for his safety. However, merely being out in public at a late hour, without more, will not justify a stop.

2.3.5.6. Wanted flyers

In *United States v. Hensley*,[172] the United States Supreme Court held that "where police have been unable to locate a person suspected of involvement in a past crime, the ability to briefly stop that person, ask questions, or check identification in the absence of probable cause promotes the strong government interest in solving crimes and bringing offenders to justice." Thus, the law enforcement interests promoted by allowing one department to conduct investigative detentions based upon another department's bulletins or "Wanted Flyers" are considerable, while the intrusions on a person's Fourth and Fourteenth Amendment rights are minimal.

This was the first time the federal Supreme Court specifically addressed the issue of whether the police may stop and detain a person on information from a wanted flyer from another jurisdiction when the investigation is of a past or completed crime. Hensley was wanted for questioning in reference to an armed robbery. The Court held that the justification for the stop did not evaporate merely because the armed robbery had been completed. Therefore, when police have a reasonable suspicion, grounded in specific and articulable facts, that a person they encounter was involved, or wanted, in connection with a completed crime, then a *Terry*-type stop may be made to investigate that suspicion.

As explained in *Whiteley v. Warden*,[173] where the arresting officer relied on a radio bulletin advising officers that a warrant had been issued for the defendant's arrest:

Certainly, police officers called upon to aid other officers in executing arrest warrants are entitled to assume that the officers requesting aid offered the magistrate the information requisite to support an independent judicial assessment of probable cause. Where, however, the contrary turns out to be true, an otherwise illegal arrest cannot be insulated from challenge by the decision of the instigating officer to rely on fellow officers to make the arrest.[174]

2.3.5.7. Evasive conduct, furtive gestures, etc.

Evasive conduct and furtive gestures, along with concealing or attempting to conceal one's identity, are criteria an officer may weigh in assessing if his suspicion is reasonable. However, each individual observation, without more, will not create a reasonable suspicion of criminal activity. As to the furtive gesture, the law is clear that a furtive gesture alone is not a sufficient basis for probable cause. A furtive gesture in conjunction with other facts certainly could generate a reasonable suspicion, as well as probable cause.

---

[170] *See also State v. Clyburn,* 120 N.C. App. 377, 380-81, 462 S.E.2d 538, 540-41 (1995) (holding that an officer's reasonable belief that he had witnessed a hand-to-hand drug transaction helped provide a "reasonable suspicion to make an investigatory stop of defendant's vehicle").

[171] *Adams v. Williams,* 407 U.S. 143, 147-48, 92 S. Ct. 1921, 1924 (1972).

[172] *United States v. Hensley,* 469 U.S. 221, 105 S. Ct. 675 (1985).

[173] *Whiteley v. Warden,* 401 U.S. 560, 91 S. Ct. 1031 (1971).

[174] *Whiteley v. Warden,* 401 *U.S.* 560, 568, 91 S. Ct. 1031 (1971). *See also Hensley,* 469 U.S. 221, 231, 105 S. Ct. 675 (1985) ("*Whiteley* supports the proposition that when evidence is uncovered during a search incident to an arrest in reliance merely on a flyer or bulletin, its admissibility turns on whether the officers who *issued* the flyer possessed probable cause to make the arrest.") (emphasis in original).

2.3.5.8. Flight

A suspect's flight, when confronted with police presence, may give the officer reasonable suspicion to pursue and detain the suspect.[175] Note, however, that not all conduct that merely avoids contact with a law enforcement officer is considered flight from the officer.

In *Illinois v. Wardlow*,[176] the U.S. Supreme Court held that the sudden, unprovoked flight of a person in a high drug-trafficking area, upon sighting a police vehicle, creates a reasonable suspicion of criminal activity to support a temporary investigative detention (*Terry* stop) of the person. In this case, two uniformed officers were in the last car of a four-car police caravan that converged on an area of Chicago known for heavy narcotics trafficking, in order to investigate drug transactions. The officers observed the defendant, who was standing next to a building holding an opaque bag, look at the police caravan, then run in the opposite direction. Given the character of the area and the defendant's headlong flight ("the consummate act of evasion"), the officers had reasonable suspicion to stop him.[177] The Court in *Wardlow* would not, however, adopt a bright-line rule authorizing the temporary detention of *anyone* who flees at the mere sight of a police officer. Rather, reasonable suspicion to support such a detention must be determined by looking to the totality of the circumstances—the whole picture.

In *State v. Neal*,[178] Officer Herron ordered the defendant to drop his weapon and put his hands in the air. The defendant did not comply with Officer Herron's orders and instead fled the scene. Furthermore, during his flight, the defendant ran into the vehicle of the officers coming as backup for Officer Herron, and continued to flee by jumping a fence into the backyard of a nearby house. The totality of the circumstances, including the defendant's flight, gave rise to a reasonable, articulable suspicion for his stop. "Because the officers had a reasonable suspicion that Defendant was involved in criminal behavior, his detention was justified."[179]

In *State v. Griffin*,[180] upon approaching a checkpoint, the defendant "stopped in the middle of the road, even though he was not at an intersection, and appeared to attempt a three-point turn by beginning to turn left and continuing onto the shoulder." Noting that "'flight—wherever it occurs—is the consummate act of evasion: [i]t is not necessarily indicative of wrongdoing, but it is certainly suggestive of such,'"[181] the court found that there was reasonable suspicion that the defendant was violating the law. Accordingly, the stop was constitutional.

In *State v. Augustin*,[182] the facts that the defendant was out at an unusual hour in deteriorating weather, the defendant's companion lied about his name, they both gave vague answers about where they were coming from and the defendant's companion ran away as he was being searched all contributed to the officer's reasonable suspicion.[183]

2.3.5.9. Tips provided by informants

Information provided by someone outside the circles of law enforcement may provide sufficient justification for a stop if it carries with it sufficient indicia of reliability. Factors that bolster the reliability of information may include: the reliability and reputation of the person providing the tip; corroboration of the details contained in the tip by independent police work; and the extent to which any information provided by the informant has proved to be accurate or useful in the past. Anonymous tips, however, must be corroborated by other observations and supported by indicia of reliability, in order to generate a reasonable suspicion.

---

[175] *See State v. Neal*, 250 N.C. App. 824, 794 S.E.2d 562 (2016); *State v. Butler*, 331 N.C. 227, 415 S.E.2d 719 (1992).

[176] *Illinois v. Wardlow*, 528 U.S. 119, 120 S. Ct. 673 (2000).

[177] *Illinois v. Wardlow*, 528 U.S. 119, 124, 120 S. Ct. 673, 676 (2000).

[178] *State v. Neal*, 250 N.C. App. 824, 794 S.E.2d 562 (2016).

[179] *State v. Neal*, 250 N.C. App. 824, *9, 794 S.E.2d 562 (2016).

[180] *State v. Griffin*, 366 N.C. 473, 749 S.E.2d 444 (2013).

[181] *State v. Griffin*, 366 N.C. 473, 476, 749 S.E.2d 444 (2013) (quoting *Illinois v. Wardlow*, 528 U.S. 119, 124, 120 S. Ct. 673, 676 (2000)).

[182] *State v. Augustin*, 824 S.E.2d 854 (N.C. Ct. App. 2019).

[183] *See also State v. Mello*, 200 N.C. App. 437, 446-47, 684 S.E.2d 483, 490 (2009), *aff'd per curiam*, 364 N.C. 421, 421, 700 S.E.2d 224, 225 (2010) (holding that erratic behavior and flight exhibited *by the defendant's companions* could be used in the reasonable suspicion calculus).

For example, in *Alabama v. White*,[184] Montgomery police received an anonymous tip stating that the defendant, carrying a brown briefcase filled with cocaine, would leave a specific unit of an apartment building and travel in her brown Plymouth station wagon, which had a broken taillight, to a specific motel. Police watched the apartment complex and saw a brown Plymouth wagon with a broken taillight. They then watched the defendant, empty-handed, exit the specified apartment, get into the car and drive directly toward the motel. Even though not every detail in the tip turned out to be totally correct, the partial corroboration by police alone provided reasonable suspicion for a stop. Here, the United States Supreme Court found it

important that "the anonymous [tip] contained a range of details relating not just to easily obtained facts and conditions existing at the time of the tip, but to future actions of third parties ordinarily not easily predicted." The fact that the officers found a car precisely matching the caller's description in front of the 235 building is an example of the former. *Anyone could have "predicted" that fact because it was a condition presumably existing at the time of the call. What was important was the caller's ability to predict [White's] future behavior, because it demonstrated inside information—a special familiarity with [White's] affairs....*Because only a small number of people are generally privy to an individual's itinerary, it is reasonable for police to believe that a person with access to such information is likely to also have access to reliable information about that individual's illegal activities.[185]

In *State v. McRae*,[186] "Lieutenant Supervisor Charlie Revels of the Robeson County Sheriff's Department received a tip from a confidential source that an older black male named Richard McRae would that day be driving a green Grand Am with over 60 grams of cocaine within the city limits of Pembroke, North Carolina. The source had previously provided reliable information leading to several felony arrests. Lieutenant Revels sent out a dispatch advising all officers to be on the lookout for a black male driving a green Grand Am within the Pembroke city limits."[187] That evening, Officer Clark observed a green Grand Am driven by a Black male. While Officer Clark was following the Grand Am, the driver made a turn into a gas station without signaling. When the driver exited the car at the pumps, Officer Clark told him to have a seat in the patrol car. The Court of Appeals of North Carolina held that the tip combined with the defendant's failure to use a turn signal, provided reasonable suspicion justifying the stop.[188] Said the court:

Here, the reliable, confidential informant gave...specific information... He identified defendant by name—a name that Lieutenant Revels recognized as someone associated with the drug trade. The informant also described the specific car—a green Grand Am—rather than providing a general type of car, and he advised Lieutenant Revels that defendant would be driving the car within the city limits of Pembroke with 60 grams of cocaine in his possession. We hold that this tip from a proven, confidential informant was sufficient to provide reasonable suspicion to stop defendant.[189]

The tip in *State v. Carver*[190] was insufficient to justify a warrantless traffic stop. There, an anonymous tipster "indicated a car was in a ditch, someone was present who may be intoxicated, and a truck was preparing to

---

[184] *Alabama v. White*, 496 U.S. 325, 110 S. Ct. 2412 (1990).

[185] *Alabama v. White*, 496 U.S. 325, 332, 110 S. Ct. 2412, 2417 (1990) (quoting *Illinois v. Gates*, 462 U.S. 213, 245 (1983)) (emphasis added).

[186] *State v. McRae*, 203 N.C. App. 319, 691 S.E.2d 56 (2010).

[187] *State v. McRae*, 203 N.C. App. 319, 320, 691 S.E.2d 56 (2010).

[188] See also; *State v. Morton*, 363 N.C. 737, 738, 686 S.E.2d 510, 510, adopting *per curiam,* 198 N.C. App. 206, 217, 679 S.E.2d 437, 445 (2009) (Hunter, J., dissenting) (holding that "the detectives in this case had reasonable suspicion to believe defendant could be armed based solely on the confidential informant's tip that defendant was involved in a recent drive-by shooting and was wearing gang colors"); *State v. Downing*, 169 N.C. App. 790, 794-95, 613 S.E.2d 35, 38 (2005) (concluding that reasonable suspicion to stop a defendant's vehicle existed when previously-proven confidential informant told police the defendant would be transporting cocaine that day, the defendant was driving vehicle that matched description given by informant, tag numbers on vehicle were registered to the defendant, the defendant was driving on suspected route, and the defendant crossed into county at approximate time informant had indicated).

[189] *State v. McRae*, 203 N.C. App. 319, 325, 691 S.E.2d 56 (2010).

[190] *State v. Carver*, 828 S.E.2d 195 (N.C. Ct. App. 2019), *aff'd per curiam,* 377 N.C. 453, 837 S.E.2d 872 (Feb. 28, 2020).

pull the vehicle out of the ditch. There was no description of the car, the truck, or any individuals who may have been involved."[191] Deputy Franks responded to the scene and found a car that looked as if it had been in an accident. He also noticed a truck driving along the highway below the speed limit. After stopping the truck, the defendant, who was a passenger in the truck, was arrested for drunk driving. Said the court:

> When Deputy Franks passed the Cadillac and came up behind the truck, he saw no equipment to indicate the truck had pulled, or had been able to pull, a car out of a ditch. There were no chains or other apparatuses visible to the deputy. Deputy Franks could not see how many people were in the truck prior to the stop. He testified the truck was not operating in violation of the law. He believed it was a suspicious vehicle merely because of the fact it was on the highway.[192]

> Under the totality of the circumstances, Deputy Franks lacked reasonable suspicion to conduct a warrantless traffic stop of Mr. Griekspoor's truck. Nothing in the anonymous tip would have indicated *this* truck was the one that had pulled the car out of the ditch. The truck was merely driving along a public highway and not committing any driving infractions. Deputy Franks' stop of Mr. Griekspoor was nothing more than a warrantless search and seizure based upon a mere suspicion or a hunch.[193]

Citizen informants. Courts have found citizen informants credible because historically a citizen informant would have been a victim or a witness to criminal activity. Greater credibility has traditionally been accorded such persons who have been witnesses to criminal activity and who act with the intent to aid the police in law enforcement efforts rather than for any personal gain or payment for the information.[194]

2.3.5.10. Drug courier profiles

A drug courier profile is a collection of objective factors which may be innocent in and of themselves, but in conjunction with each other or other facts, lead officers to believe that the suspect is engaging in drug trafficking. In general, most courts consider those factors actually exhibited by a suspect to determine if they collectively demonstrate reasonable suspicion, without accepting any set or combination of factors as demonstrating reasonable suspicion *per se*. Although it has not addressed the specific question whether drug courier profiles alone can provide a basis for reasonable suspicion, the United States Supreme Court has approved the use of profile characteristics as permissible factors to be considered in the totality of circumstances analysis of reasonable suspicion.[195]

Thus, the "drug courier profile" is merely a shorthand way of referring to a group of characteristics that may indicate that a person is a drug courier. One word of caution: While conformity with just a few aspects of the profile may not sufficiently support a reasonable and articulable suspicion that criminal activity may be afoot in order to warrant a *Terry* stop of a suspect,[196] as explained by Justice Rehnquist, a police officer is nonetheless entitled to assess the totality of the circumstances surrounding the subject of her attention in light of that officer's experience and training, which, of course, may include "instruction on a 'drug courier profile.'"[197]

Often, undercover officers will survey airport or bus terminals for individuals matching a certain profile. Factors utilized in compiling this profile may include: a journey that originated in a source city for narcotics, or a short round trip, with a brief stay in such a city; the suspect carrying a hard-sided suitcase; the suspect

---

[191] *State v. Carver*, 828 S.E.2d 195, 200 (N.C. Ct. App. 2019), *aff'd per curiam*, 377 N.C. 453, 837 S.E.2d 872 (Feb. 28, 2020).

[192] *State v. Carver*, 828 S.E.2d 195, 199 (N.C. Ct. App. 2019), *aff'd per curiam*, 377 N.C. 453, 837 S.E.2d 872 (Feb. 28, 2020).

[193] *State v. Carver*, 828 S.E.2d 195, 200 (N.C. Ct. App. 2019), *aff'd per curiam*, 377 N.C. 453, 837 S.E.2d 872 (Feb. 28, 2020) (citing *State v. Kincaid*, 147 N.C. App. 94, 97, 555 S.E.2d 294 (2001)) (emphasis in original.)

[194] *State v. Watkins*, 337 N.C. 437, 446 S.E.2d 67 (1994) (facts considered as a whole, including report of a suspicious vehicle, created reasonable suspicion to detain a defendant for a brief investigatory stop).

[195] *See Florida v. Royer*, 460 U.S. 491, 494 n.2, 103 S. Ct. 1319, 1322 n.2 (1983) ("The 'drug courier profile' is an abstract of characteristics found to be typical of persons transporting illegal drugs."); *United States v. Sokolow*, 490 U.S. 1, 10, 109 S. Ct. 1581, 1587 (1989).

[196] *See Reid v. Georgia*, 448 U.S. 438, 100 S. Ct. 2752 (1980).

[197] *Florida v. Royer*, 460 U.S. 491, 525 n.6, 103 S. Ct. 1319, 1339 n.6 (1983) (Rehnquist J., dissenting).

appearing nervous when questioned; tickets that were paid for in cash; the suspect providing inconsistent or wavering answers to inquiries; furtive movements (*e.g.*, glancing over one's shoulder, not making eye contact, etc.).[198]

However, as the Court instructed in *Royer*, the "drug courier profile," while not an end in itself, is an effective means or investigative tool utilized by trained law enforcement officers as a systematic method of recognizing characteristics repeatedly found among those who traffic in illicit drugs. In his dissenting opinion, Justice Rehnquist described the profile as "the collective or distilled experience of narcotics officers concerning characteristics repeatedly seen in drug smugglers."[199]

Thus, in *Reid v. Georgia*,[200] the Court held that a DEA agent had no reasonable suspicion to detain a defendant where (1) the defendant had arrived from a source city for cocaine; (2) he arrived in the early morning; (3) he and his companion appeared to be trying to conceal that they were traveling together; and (4) they had no luggage other than their shoulder bags. The Court determined that the defendant's early morning arrival from a source city for drugs, carrying only a shoulder bag, "describe[s] a very large category of presumably innocent travelers, who would be subject to virtually random seizures were the Court to conclude that as little foundation as there was in this case could justify a seizure."[201]

In *Royer*, "the detectives' attention was attracted by the following facts which were considered to be within the profile: Royer was carrying American Tourister luggage, which appeared to be heavy; he was young, apparently between 25-35; he was casually dressed; he appeared pale and nervous, looking around at other people; he paid for his ticket in cash with a large number of bills; and rather than completing the airline identification tag to be attached to checked baggage, which had space for a name, address, and telephone number, he wrote only a name and the destination."[202] Upholding Royer's initial investigatory detention, the Court reasoned that when the officers learned that Royer was traveling under an assumed name, that fact, coupled with the facts already known by the officers which constituted a "drug courier profile"— "paying cash for a one-way ticket, the mode of checking the two bags, and Royer's appearance and conduct in general—were adequate grounds for suspecting Royer of carrying drugs and for temporarily detaining him and his luggage while they attempted to verify or dispel their suspicions."[203]

In a typical scenario, a suspect matching the profile is approached by officers and asked a few questions. Often, a threshold issue in such cases is the nature of the questioning. If the encounter is consensual, then no Fourth Amendment concerns arise. If, however, the officers' suspicions are aroused and a more aggressive investigatory posture is assumed, the encounter may escalate into a *Terry* type detention, and the scope of the encounter must conform to constitutional guidelines. The method employed by investigating officers should be of the least intrusive means reasonably necessary to verify or dispel the officer's suspicion in a short period of time. Although the initial stop may be justified, it may become so protracted, exceeding a time limit that the officer would reasonably need to confirm or dispel her suspicions about possible trafficking activity, that it becomes unreasonable. To pass constitutional muster, a detention not only must be justified at its inception, but also must be reasonably related in scope to the circumstances that justified it in the first instance.

If, and when, such an encounter progresses into a full-blown detention, another frequently adjudicated question involves the seizure of a suspect's luggage, purse, handbag or other personal item. The general rule is that officers may temporarily detain the property if they have reasonable suspicion that the item contains contraband. The seizure must be brief and related in duration to dispelling any suspicion about what the luggage contains.[204] Frequently, the luggage is subjected to a sniff-test (by a dog trained to recognize, by smell, the presence of narcotics or other drugs), or officers try to obtain consent to search the luggage. In such cases, a distinction must be drawn between detaining and actually opening and searching a container. Although police may temporarily detain a container based upon reasonable suspicion, they generally may not open it without a warrant, or some recognized exception to the warrant requirement.

---

[198] *See e.g., United States v. Sokolow*, 490 U.S. 1, 109 S. Ct. 1581 (1989).

[199] *Florida v. Royer*, 460 U.S. 491, 525 n.6, 103 S. Ct. 1319, 1339 n.6 (1983) (Rehnquist, J., dissenting).

[200] *Reid v. Georgia*, 448 U.S. 438, 100 S. Ct. 2752 (1980).

[201] *Reid v. Georgia*, 448 U.S. 438, 441, 100 S. Ct. 2752, 2754 (1980).

[202] *Florida v. Royer*, 460 U.S. 491, 494 n.2, 103 S. Ct. 1319, 1322 n.2 (1983).

[203] *Florida v. Royer*, 460 U.S. 491, 502, 103 S. Ct. 1319, 1326 (1983).

[204] *United States v. Place*, 462 U.S. 696, 103 S. Ct. 2637 (1983).

2.3.6. Mere inquiries, investigative stops and *Miranda*

In consensual encounters and in investigatory stops, the police are not required to administer the *Miranda* warning.[205] Inherent in the concept of a *Terry* stop is the right of the police to temporarily detain an individual to confirm or dispel their suspicions. Therefore, it is erroneous to focus solely on whether the defendant was free to leave. Rather, the proper inquiry is whether the individual was "in custody." Indeed, *Miranda* itself instructed that "[g]eneral on-the-scene questioning as to facts surrounding a crime or other general questioning of citizens in the fact-finding process is not affected by our holding."[206] Rather, the safeguards outlined in *Miranda* become applicable as soon as the suspect's freedom of action is curtailed to a degree associated with a formal arrest.

Once an arrest is made, however, or there is a detention equivalent to arrest, the person must be advised of her *Miranda* rights if the officer plans on questioning the person while she is in custody.[207]

2.3.7. Investigative detentions of vehicles; the "motor vehicle or traffic stop"

2.3.7.1. General aspects

In *Terry v. Ohio*,[208] the U.S. Supreme Court authorized a temporary investigative detention of a person when a law enforcement officer possesses a reasonable suspicion, based on "specific and articulable facts which, taken together with rational inferences from those facts, reasonably warrant" the belief that criminal activity may be afoot. Thereafter, in *Delaware v. Prouse*,[209] the Court extended the rationale of *Terry* to circumstances involving the temporary detention of motor vehicles. The officer in *Prouse* stopped the defendant's vehicle merely to check his driver's license and registration. The officer had observed neither traffic, equipment violations nor any other suspicious activity associated with the vehicle. In applying the exclusionary rule to the seizure of marijuana observed in plain view on the vehicle's floor, the Court held:

> [E]xcept in those situations in which there is at least articulable suspicion that a motorist is unlicensed or that an automobile is not registered, or that either the vehicle or an occupant is otherwise subject to seizure for violation of the law, stopping an automobile and detaining the driver in order to check his driver's license and the registration of the automobile are unreasonable under the Fourth Amendment.[210]

Thus, in Fourth Amendment terms, "a traffic stop entails a seizure of the driver 'even though the purpose of the stop is limited and the resulting detention quite brief.'"[211] The stop also entails a seizure of every passenger in the vehicle, along with the driver.[212] In *Brendlin v. California*, the United States Supreme Court observed that during a routine traffic stop, all passengers are subject to some scrutiny.[213]

Accordingly, the "[t]emporary detention of individuals during the stop of an automobile by the police, even if only for a brief period and for a limited purpose, constitutes a 'seizure' of 'persons' within the meaning of the [Fourth Amendment]."[214]

---

[205] *Berkemer v. McCarty,* 468 U.S. 420, 437-442, 104 S. Ct. 3138, 3149-50 (1984).

[206] *Miranda v. Arizona,* 384 U.S. 436, 477, 86 S. Ct. 1602, 1629 (1966); *see also id.* at 477-478, 86 S. Ct. at 1629-1630, where the Court pointed out that it "is an act of responsible citizenship for individuals to give whatever information they may have to aid in law enforcement. In such situations the compelling atmosphere inherent in the process of in-custody interrogation is not necessarily present."

[207] This topic is further explored in Section 8.3.2.

[208] *Terry v. Ohio,* 392 U.S. 1, 88 S. Ct. 1868, 1880 (1968).

[209] *Delaware v. Prouse,* 440 U.S. 648, 99 S. Ct. 1391 (1979).

[210] *Delaware v. Prouse,* 440 U.S. 648, 663, 99 S. Ct. 1391, 1401 (1979); *see also United States v. Shabazz,* 993 F.2d 431, 434 (5th Cir. 1993) ("It is clear that, as in the case of pedestrians, searches and seizures of motorists who are merely *suspected* of criminal activity are to be analyzed under the framework established in *Terry v. Ohio*[.]") (emphasis in original).

[211] *Brendlin v. California,* 551 U.S. 249, 127 S. Ct. 2400, 2406 (2007) (internal citations omitted).

[212] *Brendlin v. California,* 551 U.S. 249, 127 S. Ct. 2400, 2406 (2007).

[213] *Brendlin v. California,* 551 U.S. 249, 257, 127 S. Ct. 2400 (2007).

[214] *Whren v. United States,* 517 U.S. 806, 809-10, 116 S. Ct. 1769 (1996).

The propriety of conducting motor vehicle stops on the basis of a reasonable and articulable suspicion that an occupant is or has been engaged in criminal activity, including a motor vehicle violation, has been consistently upheld.[215] In upholding the lawfulness of investigative detentions of vehicles on the basis of a reasonable suspicion, courts have recognized that the physical characteristics of a motor vehicle and its use result in a lessened expectation of privacy therein:

> One has a lesser expectation of privacy in a motor vehicle because its function is transportation and it seldom serves as one's residence or as the repository of personal effects. A car has little capacity for escaping public scrutiny. It travels public thoroughfares where both its occupants and its contents are in plain view.[216] .

Moreover, motor vehicles are "justifiably the subject of pervasive regulation by the State. Every operator of a motor vehicle must expect that the State, in enforcing its regulations, will intrude to some extent upon that operator's privacy[.]"[217] In this respect, the Supreme Court has observed:

> Automobiles, unlike homes, are subject to pervasive and continuing governmental regulation and controls, including periodic inspection and licensing requirements. As an everyday occurrence, police stop and examine vehicles when license plates or inspection stickers have expired, or if other violations, such as exhaust fumes or excessive noise, are noted, or if headlights or other safety equipment are not in proper working order.[218]

It is clear, therefore, that "[a]lthough stopping a car and detaining its occupants constitute a seizure within the meaning of the Fourth Amendment, the governmental interest in investigating an officer's reasonable suspicion, based on specific and articulable facts, may outweigh the Fourth Amendment interest of the driver and passengers in remaining secure from the intrusion."[219]

Nonetheless, "[a]n individual operating or traveling in an automobile does not lose all reasonable expectation of privacy simply because the automobile and its use are subject to government regulation."[220]

> Automobile travel is a basic, pervasive, and often necessary mode of transportation to and from one's home, workplace, and leisure activities. Many people spend more hours each day traveling in cars than walking on the streets. Undoubtedly, many find a greater sense of security and privacy in traveling in an automobile than they do in exposing themselves by pedestrian or other modes of travel. Were the individual subject to unfettered governmental intrusion every time he entered an automobile, the security guaranteed by the Fourth Amendment would be seriously circumscribed. As *Terry v. Ohio*,[221] recognized, people are not [stripped] of all Fourth Amendment protection when they step from their

---

[215] *See e.g., Ornelas v. United States*, 517 U.S. 690, 116 S. Ct. 1657, 1660 (1996) ("An investigatory stop is permissible under the Fourth Amendment if supported by reasonable suspicion[.]"); *Alabama v. White*, 496 U.S. 325, 110 S. Ct. 2412 (1990) (motor vehicle stop on the basis of reasonable suspicion that the driver was in possession of cocaine upheld); *United States v. Cortez*, 449 U.S. 411, 101 S. Ct. 690 (1981) (totality of the circumstances "must yield a particularized suspicion" that the vehicle or its occupant was engaged in wrongdoing); *United States v. Brignoni-Ponce*, 422 U.S. 873, 95 S. Ct. 2574 (1975) (motor vehicle stop upheld where officers were "aware of specific and articulable facts, together with rational inferences from those facts, that reasonably warrant suspicion" that the vehicle contains undocumented immigrants); *New York v. Class*, 475 U.S. 106, 106 S. Ct. 960 (1986) (upholding stop of a defendant for driving above speed limit in a car with a cracked windshield in violation of traffic laws); *Pennsylvania v. Mimms*, 434 U.S. 106, 98 S. Ct. 330 (1977) (upholding motor vehicle stop where police officers observed expired license plate). *See also United States v. Hensley*, 469 U.S. 221, 226, 105 S. Ct. 675, 679 (1985) ("law enforcement agents may briefly stop a moving automobile to investigate a reasonable suspicion that its occupants are involved in criminal activity").

[216] *Cardwell v. Lewis*, 417 U.S. 583, 590, 94 S. Ct. 2464, 2469 (1974).

[217] *New York v. Class*, 475 U.S. 106, 113, 106 S. Ct. 960, 965 (1986).

[218] *South Dakota v. Opperman*, 428 U.S. 364, 368, 96 S. Ct. 3092, 3096 (1976); *see also Cady v. Dombrowski*, 413 U.S. 433, 441-42, 93 S. Ct. 2523, 2528 (1973); *California v. Carney*, 471 U.S. 386, 392, 105 S. Ct. 2066, 2069-70 (1985).

[219] *United States v. Hensley*, 469 U.S. 221, 226, 105 S. Ct. 675, 679 (1985).

[220] *Delaware v. Prouse*, 440 U.S. 648, 662, 99 S. Ct. 1391, 1400 (1979).

[221] *Terry v. Ohio*, 392 U.S. 1, 88 S. Ct. 1868, 1880 (1968).

homes onto the public sidewalks. Nor are they [stripped] of those interests when they step from the sidewalks into their automobiles.[222]

2.3.7.2. A tip of dangerous or erratic driving

In *Navarette v. California*,[223] in Mendocino County, California, a driver called 911 to report that a silver Ford F-150 pickup truck with a specified license plate had just run her off the road, at mile marker 88 on southbound Highway 1. Roughly 18 minutes after the call, a California Highway Patrol officer spotted the same truck at mile marker 69, 19 miles south of the reported incident. The U.S. Supreme Court ruled that, assuming the 911 call was anonymous, the officer nevertheless had reasonable suspicion to stop the truck. By reporting that she had been run off the road by a specific vehicle, the caller necessarily claimed eyewitness knowledge of the alleged dangerous driving—a driver's claim that another vehicle ran her off the road implies that the informant knows the other car was driven dangerously. That basis of knowledge lent significant support to the tip's reliability. In addition, the officer saw the truck in a location suggesting that the caller must have reported the incident soon after she was run off the road. The Court noted: "That sort of contemporaneous report has long been treated as especially reliable." In addition, 911 calls are recorded, which provides victims with an opportunity to identify the false tipster's voice and subject him to prosecution; a 911 caller's cell phone number can also be easily identified, further discouraging its use in giving false tips. Thus, the caller's use of the 911 system was another factor suggesting reliability. Finally, the Court noted that running another vehicle off the road "suggests lane positioning problems, decreased vigilance, impaired judgment, or some combination of those recognized drunk driving cues." Thus, there was reason to believe the driver of the truck might be intoxicated and therefore committing a crime. Under the totality of these circumstances, an investigatory stop was justified.

2.3.7.3. Observed violations

Driving in an erratic manner in and of itself justifies a stop. Officers do not violate the Fourth Amendment by stopping and questioning someone who just committed a traffic violation in the officer's presence. Moreover, routine traffic infractions, even minor ones, can provide the requisite reasonable suspicion to stop a vehicle.[224]

For example, stops have been upheld for:

- driving too quickly given the road conditions[225]
- inoperable tag light and limited expired license plate[226]
- speeding[227]
- following too closely[228]
- failure to use a turn signal[229]
- weaving briefly over the white line marking the edge of the road[230]

The North Carolina Supreme Court has held that "the reasonable suspicion standard applies to traffic stops 'whether the traffic violation was readily observed or merely suspected.'"[231] For example, in *State v. Johnson*,[232] Officer Gardin thought that the defendant was driving at an unsafe speed given the weather and

---

[222] *Delaware v. Prouse*, 440 U.S. 648, 662-63, 99 S. Ct. 1391, 1400-01 (1979).

[223] *Navarette v. California*, 572 U.S. 393, 134 S. Ct. 1683 (2014).

[224] *United States v. Palomino*, 100 F.3d 446 (6th Cir. 1996).

[225] *State v. Johnson*, 370 N.C. 32, 803 S.E.2d 137 (2017).

[226] *State v. Bouknight*, 252 N.C. App. 265, 797 S.E.2d 340 (2017).

[227] *State v. McClendon*, 350 N.C. 630, 517 S.E.2d 128 (1999).

[228] *State v. McClendon*, 350 N.C. 630, 517 S.E.2d 128 (1999).

[229] *State v. McRae*, 203 N.C. App. 319, 691 S.E.2d 56 (2010).

[230] *State v. Bullock*, 370 N.C. 256, 805 S.E.2d 671 (2017).

[231] *State v. Johnson*, 370 N.C. 32, 36, 803 S.E.2d 137 (2017) (quoting *State v. Styles*, 362 N.C. 412, 415, 665 S.E.2d 438 (2008)).

[232] *State v. Johnson*, 370 N.C. 32, 803 S.E.2d 137 (2017).

the conditions of the road in violation of N.C.G.S. § 220-141(a) which states, "[n]o person shall drive a vehicle on a highway or in a public vehicular area at a speed greater than is reasonable and prudent under the conditions then existing." The court explained, "in order to have reasonable suspicion to conduct a traffic stop based on a violation that an officer allegedly observed, the officer does not need to observe an actual traffic violation....To meet the reasonable suspicion standard, it is enough for the officer to *reasonably believe* that a driver has violated the law."[233] Accordingly, Officer Gardin's reasonable belief that the defendant violated N.C.G.S. § 220-141(a) was enough to justify the subsequent traffic stop.

2.3.7.3.1. The "owner is the driver" assumption

May a law enforcement officer, consistent with the Fourth Amendment, initiate an investigative traffic stop after running a vehicle's license plate and learning that the registered owner has a revoked driver's license? According to the Court in *Kansas v. Glover,*[234] the answer is *yes.*

In *Glover,* while on patrol in Douglas County, Kansas, Sheriff's Deputy Mark Mehrer ran a registration check on a Chevy pickup truck. This revealed that the truck was registered to Charles Glover, Jr., and that his license was revoked. The deputy did not observe any traffic violations but initiated a traffic stop based on his assumption that the driver was the registered owner. The driver (Glover) turned out to be the registered owner and the officer issued him a citation.

Finding the stop lawful, the Court held that, so long as there are no facts negating the "inference that the owner is the driver of the vehicle, the stop is reasonable."[235] In this case, before initiating the traffic stop, Deputy Mehrer observed an individual operating a pickup truck with a specific Kansas license plate. He also knew that the registered owner of the truck had a revoked license and that the model of the truck matched the observed vehicle. "From these three facts, Deputy Mehrer drew the commonsense inference that Glover was likely the driver of the vehicle, which provided more than reasonable suspicion to initiate the stop."[236]

"The fact that the registered owner of a vehicle is not always the driver of the vehicle does not negate the reasonableness of Deputy Mehrer's inference." Such is the case with all reasonable inferences, for "[t]o be reasonable is not to be perfect." Glover's revoked license does not render the inference unreasonable either. "Empirical studies demonstrate what common experience readily reveals: Drivers with revoked licenses frequently continue to drive and therefore to pose safety risks to other motorists and pedestrians."[237]

The Court cautioned, however, that the presence of additional facts might dispel reasonable suspicion. "For example, if an officer knows that the registered owner of the vehicle is in his mid-sixties but observes that the driver is in her mid-twenties, then the totality of the circumstances would not raise a suspicion that the particular individual being stopped is engaged in wrongdoing."[238]

2.3.7.4. Permissible activities at, and length of, a traffic stop

During a traffic stop, an officer may take certain actions and make various inquiries that are deemed to be within the scope of investigation related to the stop.[239] This assists the officer in addressing the violation and making a determination whether to issue a citation or warning or make an arrest. In this regard, the officer:

- May request the motorist's driver's license, registration and proof of insurance.
- May run a computer check.
- May ask the driver out of the vehicle.
- May ask a passenger out of the vehicle.

---

[233] *State v. Johnson*, 370 N.C. 32, 37-38, 803 S.E.2d 137 (2017).

[234] *Kansas v. Glover*, 589 U.S. ___, 140 S.Ct. 1183 (2020).

[235] *Kansas v. Glover*, 589 U.S. ___, 140 S.Ct. 1183, 1186 (2020).

[236] *Kansas v. Glover*, 589 U.S. ___, 140 S.Ct. 1183, 1188 (2020).

[237] *Kansas v. Glover*, 589 U.S. ___, 140 S.Ct. 1183, 1188 (2020).

[238] *Kansas v. Glover*, 589 U.S. ___, 140 S.Ct. 1183, 1191 (2020).

[239] *See, e.g., Pennsylvania v. Mimms*, 434 U.S. 106, 111, 98 S. Ct. 330 (1977) (an officer may, as a matter of course, order the driver to either step out of or remain inside the vehicle); *Maryland v. Wilson*, 519 U.S. 408, 414-15, 117 S. Ct. 882, 886 (1997) (the *Mimms* rule extends to passengers).

- May advise the motorist of the reason for the stop.
- May ask questions reasonably related to the reason for the stop.
- May ask questions about the purpose and itinerary of the motorist's trip, such as his point of origin, destination and travel plans.
- May ask reasonable questions in order to obtain additional information about the violation.
- May ask questions regarding the circumstances leading to the violation of the law.
- May ask unrelated questions so long as the questions do not measurably prolong the stop.
- Need not give *Miranda* warnings *unless* the driver is placed "in custody."

As the United States Supreme Court instructed in *Arizona v. Johnson*,[240] "[a]n officer's inquiries into matters unrelated to the justification for the traffic stop ... do not convert the encounter into something other than a lawful seizure, so long as those inquiries do not measurably extend the duration of the stop."

In *Rodriguez v. United States*,[241] the Court further instructed that "[b]eyond determining whether to issue a traffic ticket, an officer's mission includes ordinary inquiries incident to [the traffic] stop." Typically, "such inquiries involve checking the driver's license, determining whether there are outstanding warrants against the driver, and inspecting the automobile's registration and proof of insurance[.] These checks serve the same objective as enforcement of the traffic code: ensuring that vehicles on the road are operated safely and responsibly."[242]

Once the traffic stop is completed, however, officers may not continue to detain a car for the purpose of asking unrelated questions without a reasonable suspicion of criminal behavior. Generally, the permissible duration of a traffic stop depends on the reason the police officer pulls the car over. The duration and execution of a traffic stop is necessarily limited by the initial purpose of the stop. This rule grows out of the United States Supreme Court's explanation of a broader Fourth Amendment principle: "An investigatory detention must be temporary and last no longer than is necessary to effectuate the purpose of the stop."[243] In this regard, any investigation of the vehicle or its occupants beyond that required to complete the purpose of the traffic stop constitutes a separate seizure that must be supported by independent facts sufficient to justify the additional intrusion.

As stated in *Rodriguez v. United States*,[244] "a police stop exceeding the time needed to handle the matter for which the stop was made violates the Constitution's shield against unreasonable seizures. A seizure justified only by a police-observed traffic violation, therefore, 'become[s] unlawful if it is prolonged beyond the time reasonably required to complete th[e] mission' of issuing a ticket for the violation."[245] In *Rodriguez*,[246] the U.S. Supreme Court held that the Fourth Amendment does not permit a dog sniff conducted after completion of a traffic stop.[247]

In *Illinois v. Caballes*,[248] the investigative activity at issue did not impact the duration of the stop *at all*, as the police dog sniff was conducted by the K-9 officer *at the same time* the traffic officer was writing out a warning for the violation. The U.S. Supreme Court cautioned, however, that a "motor vehicle stop that is justified solely by the interest in issuing a warning or a ticket to the driver can become an unlawful seizure if it is prolonged beyond the time reasonably required to complete that mission."[249] Thus, the use of a

---

[240] *Arizona v. Johnson*, 555 U.S. 323, 333, 129 S. Ct. 781, 788 (2009).

[241] *Rodriguez v. United States*, 575 U.S. 348, 135 S. Ct. 1609, 1615 (2015).

[242] *See also Arizona v. Johnson*, 555 U.S. 323, 333, 129 S. Ct. 781, 788 (2009) ("An officer's inquiries into matters unrelated to the justification for the traffic stop ... do not convert the encounter into something other than a lawful seizure, so long as those inquiries do not measurably extend the duration of the stop."); *State v. Bullock*, 370 N.C. 256, 257-58, 805 S.E.2d 671, 673 (2017), *cert. denied*, 139 S. Ct. 1275, 203 L. Ed. 2d 280 (2019); *State v. Downey*, 251 N.C. App. 829, 796 S.E.2d 517 (2017), aff'd, 370 N.C. 507, 809 S.E.2d 566 (2018).

[243] *Florida v. Royer*, 460 U.S. 491, 500, 103 S. Ct. 1319, 1325 (1983).

[244] *Rodriguez v. United States*, 575 U.S. 348, 135 S. Ct. 1609 (2015).

[245] *Rodriguez v. United States*, 575 U.S. 348, 135 S. Ct. 1609, 1612 (2015) (quoting *Illinois v. Caballes*, 543 U.S. 405, 407, 125 S. Ct. 834, 837 (2005)).

[246] *Rodriguez v. United States*, 575 U.S. 348, 135 S. Ct. 1609 (2015).

[247] As stated in *Rodriguez*, the question is not "whether the dog sniff occurs before or after the officer issues a ticket," but "whether conducting the sniff prolongs—*i.e.*, adds time to—the stop[.]"

[248] *Illinois v. Caballes*, 543 U.S. 405, 125 S. Ct. 834 (2005).

[249] *Illinois v. Caballes*, 543 U.S. 405, 125 S. Ct. 834, 837 (2005).

drug-detection dog during an "unreasonably prolonged traffic stop" may "lead to the suppression of evidence if the dog sniff is conducted while the motorist is being unlawfully detained."[250]

Once an officer has determined that the driver has a valid license and the citation or ticket has been issued, the driver must be allowed to proceed on her way, without being subjected to further delay by police for additional questioning, unless the driver consents to such questioning or the officer discovers evidence establishing a reasonable suspicion of criminal activity unrelated to the initial traffic violation. For example, in *State v. Downey*,[251] Deputy Clifton had reasonable suspicion to extend the traffic stop based on six factors taken together— the defendant's nervous behavior, his use of a particular type of air freshener favored by drug traffickers, his prepaid cellphone, his use of a car registered to someone else, his suspicious responses to the officer's questioning, and his prior drug conviction.

In *State v. Bullock*,[252] after stopping the defendant for several traffic violations, Officer McDonough ordered the defendant to exit the vehicle, frisked him and placed him in the patrol car while he ran three database checks. While the checks were running, Officer McDonough talked with the defendant. "With these checks running in the background, Officer McDonough was free to talk with defendant at least up until the moment that all three database checks had been completed."[253] Once the database checks were complete, this conversation in conjunction with Officer McDonough's observations from earlier in the traffic stop created a reasonable suspicion sufficient to permit Officer McDonough to prolong the stop until he could have a dog sniff performed. Said the North Carolina Supreme Court:

> The Supreme Court indicated in *Rodriguez* that reasonable suspicion, if found, would have justified the prolonged seizure that led to the discovery of Rodriguez's methamphetamine. Officer McDonough prolonged the traffic stop of defendant's rental car only after the officer had formed reasonable suspicion that defendant was a drug courier, which allowed for the dog sniff that ultimately led to the discovery of heroin in the bag that was pulled from the rental car. Because this extension of the stop's duration was properly justified by reasonable suspicion, it poses no constitutional problem under *Rodriguez*.[254]

In sharp contrast to *Bullock* is *State v. Reed*,[255] a case which provided the North Carolina Supreme Court an opportunity to further define the parameters of a traffic stop. In *Reed*, Trooper Lamm initiated a traffic stop when he observed the car driven by the defendant speeding. Upon discovering that the car was rented to Ms. Peart who was the defendant's passenger, that the defendant was an authorized driver under the rental agreement, that the defendant had a New York driver's license and that the car was not stolen, Trooper Lamm requested that the defendant take a seat in the law enforcement vehicle. In the police cruiser, Trooper Lamm began to pose questions regarding the defendant's travel plans, his living arrangements with Peart, and who owned the dog that was in the car. Trooper Lamm additionally contacted the rental company and confirmed that the vehicle was properly in the possession of Peart. At this point, Trooper Lamm handed the defendant's paperwork and a warning ticket to him. Thereafter, and with the defendant still in the police cruiser, Trooper Lamm said to the defendant, "this ends the traffic stop and I'm going to ask you a few more questions if it is okay with you."[256] Trooper Lamm went on to ask the defendant if there was anything illegal in the vehicle and for permission to search it to which the defendant responded, "you could break the car down."[257] The defendant directed Trooper Lamm to Peart on the matter of searching the vehicle as she was the individual who had rented it. Ultimately another trooper arrived on the scene and positioned himself next to the passenger door of Trooper Lamm's police cruiser while the defendant sat inside and Trooper Lamm spoke with Peart.

---

[250] *Illinois v. Caballes*, 543 U.S. 405, 125 S. Ct. 834, 837 (2005); *see also Arizona v. Johnson*, 555 U.S. 323, 330, 129 S. Ct. 781 (2009) ("The seizure remains lawful only so long as [unrelated] inquiries do not measurably extend the duration of the stop.").

[251] *State v. Downey*, 251 N.C. App. 829, 796 S.E.2d 517 (2017), aff'd, 370 N.C. 507, 809 S.E.2d 566 (2018).

[252] *State v. Bullock*, 370 N.C. 256, 805 S.E.2d 671 (2017).

[253] *State v. Bullock*, 370 N.C. 256, 263, 805 S.E.2d 671 (2017).

[254] *State v. Bullock*, 370 N.C. 256, 264, 805 S.E.2d 671 (2017) (citing *Rodriguez v. United States*, 575 U.S. ___, 135 S. Ct. 1609 (2015)).

[255] *State v. Reed*, 2020 N.C. LEXIS 103 (Feb. 28, 2020).

[256] *State v. Reed*, 2020 N.C. LEXIS 103, *7 (Feb. 28, 2020).

[257] *State v. Reed*, 2020 N.C. LEXIS 103, *8 (Feb. 28, 2020).

In finding that Trooper Lamm "disregarded the basic tenets of the Fourth Amendment by prolonging the traffic stop at issue without defendant's voluntary consent or a reasonable, articulable suspicion of criminal activity,"[258] the North Carolina Supreme Court drew a distinction between these facts and those of *Bullock*. While the officer in *Bullock* conducted his conversation with the defendant simultaneously to running three database checks, Trooper Lamm specifically told the defendant that the traffic stop was concluded before asking him further questions. "This interaction, which was initiated by the law enforcement officer with defendant, occurred after the traffic stop was categorically recognized by the trooper to have concluded and before reasonable suspicion existed."[259] Thus, "the continued pursuit of involvement with defendant by Trooper Lamm wrongly prolonged the traffic stop, and [ ] defendant was unconstitutionally detained beyond the announced end of the traffic stop because reasonable suspicion did not exist to justify defendant's further detainment."[260]

When the reason for the stop evaporates upon approach of the motorist. In *United States v. McSwain*,[261] a police officer saw a vehicle with no front or rear license plate, but a temporary registration sticker in the rear window. The officer was unable to read the sticker, so he stopped the vehicle to verify the validity of the sticker. As he approached the vehicle, the officer observed that the sticker was valid, but he spoke to the driver and requested identification from the driver and a passenger. The driver did not have a license, but he provided other identification. The officer conducted a computer search and learned that the driver had a suspended license and a prior record of drug and gun violations. The officer returned to the vehicle, questioned the driver about his travel plans, and asked for consent to search. The subsequent search of the vehicle's trunk revealed drugs and a gun. On appeal from the defendant's unsuccessful motion to suppress, the court of appeals reversed, holding that the initially valid stop evolved into an unreasonable detention because once the officer saw that the sticker was valid, the purpose of the stop was satisfied and further detention to question the driver about his itinerary and to request his license and registration "exceeded the scope of the stop's underlying justification."[262] Because the officer's reasonable suspicion regarding the validity of the sticker was "completely dispelled *prior* to the time" he questioned the driver and requested his license, he lacked reasonable suspicion to prolong the detention.[263]

The reasoning of *McSwain* was initially adopted by the Illinois Supreme Court in *People v. Cummings*.[264] In *Cummings,* an officer checked a vehicle's registration and saw that its owner, a woman, had an outstanding warrant for her arrest. When he pulled the van over, he saw that the driver was a man. He still asked for license and insurance as "standard operating procedure" after pulling over a car, which led to a citation of the driver for driving with a suspended driver's license. In the first round of proceedings, the state Supreme Court determined that while the officer initially had a reasonable suspicion that the driver was subject to seizure, that suspicion disappeared when he saw that the driver was a man. The court stated that requesting the defendant's license impermissibly prolonged the stop because it was not related to the reason for the stop, and it violated the Fourth Amendment.[265]

On further appeal, the United States Supreme Court vacated the *Cummings* Court's decision, remanding the case to the Illinois Supreme Court to reconsider its opinion in light of *Rodriguez v. United States*.[266]

Upon remand, the Court, in *People v. Cummings*,[267] determined that the "sole question" was whether, in light of *Rodriguez*, the officer's request for a driver's license after concluding the defendant was not the woman wanted on the warrant, "impermissibly prolonged the stop, violating the fourth amendment."[268] The Court ruled:

[258] *State v. Reed*, 2020 N.C. LEXIS 103, *2 (Feb. 28, 2020).

[259] *State v. Reed*, 2020 N.C. LEXIS 103, *28 (Feb. 28, 2020).

[260] *State v. Reed*, 2020 N.C. LEXIS 103, *28 (Feb. 28, 2020).

[261] *United States v. McSwain*, 29 F.3d 558 (10th Cir. 1994).

[262] *United States v. McSwain,* 29 F.3d 558, 561 (10th Cir. 1994).

[263] *United States v. McSwain*, 29 F.3d 558, 561-62 (10th Cir. 1994) (emphasis in original).

[264] *People v. Cummings*, 2014 IL 115769, 6 N.E.3d 725 (2014).

[265] *People v. Cummings*, 2014 IL 115769, 6 N.E.3d 725, 731, 734 (2014).

[266] *Rodriguez v. United States*, 575 U.S. 348, 135 S. Ct. 1609 (2015); *see also Illinois v. Cummings*, 135 S. Ct. 1892 (2015).

[267] *People v. Cummings*, 2016 IL 115769, 46 *N.E.3d* 248 (2016).

[268] *People v. Cummings*, 2016 IL 115769, 46 *N.E.3d* 248, 250 (2016).

A traffic stop is analogous to a *Terry* stop, and its permissible duration is determined by the seizure's mission. The seizure's mission consists of the purpose of the stop—in *Rodriguez*, traffic enforcement—and "related safety concerns." Those related safety concerns include "ordinary inquiries incident to [the traffic] stop," and typically "involve checking the driver's license, determining whether there are outstanding warrants against the driver, and inspecting the automobile's registration and proof of insurance." Those checks serve also to enforce the traffic code....

Ordinary inquiries incident to the stop do not prolong the stop beyond its original mission, because those inquiries are a part of that mission....Nothing in *Rodriguez* suggests that license requests might be withdrawn from the list of ordinary inquiries for a nontraffic enforcement stop....

Thus, where a traffic stop is lawfully initiated, the interest in officer safety entitles the officer to know the identity of a driver with whom he is interacting. If the permissible inquiries include warrant and criminal history checks, as the *Rodriguez* Court found, they necessarily include less invasive driver's license requests.[269]

Accordingly, the Court held that "Officer Bland's stop of defendant was lawfully initiated. Though his reasonable suspicion the driver was subject to arrest vanished upon seeing defendant, Bland could still make the ordinary inquiries incident to a stop. The interest in officer safety permits a driver's license request of a driver lawfully stopped. Such ordinary inquiries are part of the stop's mission and do not prolong the stop, for fourth amendment purposes."[270] This ruling, determined the Court, is consistent with the decision in *Rodriguez v. United States,* which "makes clear that a driver's license request of a lawfully stopped driver is permissible irrespective of whether that request directly relates to the purpose for the stop."[271]

2.3.7.4.1. The VIN of a motor vehicle

The vehicle identification number (VIN), located inside the passenger compartment of a vehicle but visible from outside, does not receive Fourth Amendment protection; police may run a computer search on the number without probable cause or even reasonable suspicion.[272] In *New York v. Class,* two New York City police officers observed the defendant, Class, driving above the speed limit in an automobile with a cracked windshield. When the officers stopped his vehicle, the defendant exited and approached one of the officers. The other officer approached the defendant's vehicle to inspect the Vehicle Identification Number (VIN). The officer first checked the left door jamb in which pre-1969 automobiles had the VIN located. When the VIN was not found there, the officer reached into the interior of the vehicle to move some papers obscuring the area of the dashboard where the VIN is located in all post-1969 automobiles. "In doing so, [the officer] saw the handle of a gun protruding about one inch from underneath the driver's seat."[273] The officer immediately seized the gun and arrested the defendant.

Finding the officer's actions proper, the U.S. Supreme Court held that, in light of the "pervasive governmental regulation of the automobile and the efforts by the Federal Government to ensure that the VIN is placed in plain view," there is "no reasonable expectation of privacy in the VIN," and the viewing of the formerly obscured VIN was "not a violation of the Fourth Amendment."[274] According to the Court, "it is unreasonable to have an expectation of privacy in an object required by law to be located in a place ordinarily in plain view from the exterior of the automobile."[275] Analogous to the exterior of the automobile, the VIN "is thrust

---

[269] *People v. Cummings,* 2016 IL 115769, 46 N.E.3d 248, 251-252 (2016).

[270] *People v. Cummings,* 2016 IL 115769, 46 N.E.3d 248, 252-253 (2016).

[271] *People v. Cummings,* 2016 IL 115769, 46 N.E.3d 248, 253 (2016). *See also United States v. Holt,* 264 F.3d 1215, 1221-22 (10th Cir. 2001), *abrogated on other grounds by United States v. Stewart,* 473 F.3d 1265, 1269 (10th Cir. 2007), cited with approval in *Rodriguez* and *Cummings,* which approved criminal record and warrant checks, "even though the purpose of the stop had nothing to do with such prior criminal history."

[272] *See New York v. Class,* 475 U.S. 106, 106 S. Ct. 960, 966 (1986).

[273] *New York v. Class,* 475 U.S. 106, 106 S. Ct. 960, 963 (1986).

[274] *New York v. Class,* 475 U.S. 106, 106 S. Ct. 960, 966 (1986).

[275] *New York v. Class,* 475 U.S. 106, 106 S. Ct. 960, 966 (1986).

into the public eye, and thus to examine it [from the outside of the auto] does not constitute a search [within the meaning of the Fourth Amendment]."[276]

Here, it made no difference that the papers in the defendant's automobile obscured the VIN from the sight of the officer. Persons may not create a reasonable expectation of privacy where none would otherwise exist.

Similarly, reasonable suspicion is not required to run a computer check on a randomly selected license plate.

2.3.7.5. Roadblocks and checkpoints

In *Brower v. County of Inyo*,[277] the United States Supreme Court held that a Fourth Amendment "seizure" occurs when, during a motor vehicle pursuit of a fleeing suspect, police officials (1) place an unilluminated 18-wheel tractor-trailer across both lanes of a two-lane highway, (2) "effectively conceal" the truck behind a curve in the road in order to (3) block the path of the fleeing suspect, while at the same time, (4) positioning a police car with its headlights on, between the suspect's oncoming vehicle and the truck, so that the suspect would be "blinded" on his approach, and (5) this official conduct results in the suspect's death when he crashes into the police roadblock. According to the Court, a "seizure" occurs "when there is a governmental termination" of an individual's "freedom of movement *through means intentionally applied*."[278] "[A] roadblock is not just a significant show of authority to induce a voluntary stop, but is designed to produce a stop by physical impact if voluntary compliance does not occur."[279]

In *Michigan Dept. of State Police v. Sitz*,[280] the Supreme Court held that, when properly conducted, a state's use of highway sobriety checkpoints does not violate the Constitution. According to the Court, "the balance of the State's interest in preventing drunken driving, the extent to which [this state's] system can reasonably be said to advance that interest, and the degree of intrusion upon individual motorists who are briefly stopped, weighs in favor of [this state's] highway sobriety checkpoint program."[281]

In *Sitz*, Michigan implemented a program where checkpoints would be set up at predetermined sites along state roads. All drivers passing through would be stopped and checked for obvious signs of intoxication. If such indications were detected, the motorist would be taken out of the flow of traffic and an officer would check her license and registration. If warranted, the officer would conduct field sobriety tests. All other motorists would continue unimpeded after the initial screening. The check lasted 75 minutes, during which 126 vehicles passed through. The average delay was 25 seconds. Three motorists were detained on suspicion of intoxication, and two were arrested. Finding that the checkpoint passed constitutional muster, the Court noted:

(i) The State had a substantial interest in eliminating drunken driving, noting that "no one can seriously dispute the magnitude of the drunken driving problem [or the] State's interest in eradicating it."

(ii) This checkpoint advanced the State's interest in curbing the drunk driving problem, noting that the use of a permissible checkpoint is but one of many reasonable alternatives to remedying the problem, and "the choice among such reasonable alternatives remains with the governmental officials who have a unique understanding" of the problem and the resources available to combat it.

(iii) The intrusion, both objective and subjective, was slight, pointing out the brevity (25 seconds) of the average encounter. The Court also noted that any subjective intrusion, such as making a motorist fearful or annoyed, was diminished by the fact that motorists could plainly see all vehicles were being stopped.

In upholding the lawfulness of sobriety checkpoints, courts around the nation have identified several critical features that Driving While Intoxicated (DWI) Sobriety Checkpoints should have. These include:

---

[276] *New York v. Class*, 475 U.S. 106, 106 S. Ct. 960, 966 (1986).

[277] *Brower v. County of Inyo*, 489 U.S. 593, 109 S. Ct. 1378 (1989).

[278] *Brower v. County of Inyo*, 489 U.S. 593, 109 S. Ct. 1378, 1381 (1989) (emphasis in original).

[279] *Brower v. County of Inyo*, 489 U.S. 593, 109 S. Ct. 1378, 1382-83 (1989).

[280] *Michigan Dept. of State Police v. Sitz*, 496 U.S. 444, 110 S. Ct. 2481 (1990).

[281] Not all states permit DUI checkpoints. The following 12 states have held that DUI checkpoints are unlawful: Alaska, Idaho, Iowa, Michigan, Minnesota, Montana, Oregon, Rhode Island, Texas, Washington, Wisconsin and Wyoming. Although Missouri law allows checkpoints, the state prohibits the public funding of checkpoint programs.

GUIDELINES GOVERNING ROADSIDE CHECKPOINTS

DWI Roadblocks; Safety Checkpoints; Etc.

1. There must be a *legitimate State interest*—for the checkpoint, for example drunk driving, safety checkpoints, etc.

2. When establishing the checkpoint, there must be participation of command or high-ranking supervisory authority in the formulation of an administrative plan for the checkpoint consisting of a uniform set of written, standardized guidelines setting forth proper procedures to reduce officer discretion, and for checkpoint officers to follow when approaching vehicles, observing motorists, requesting drivers' licenses, checking for other violations, and sidetracking those drivers found to have violations. (Ideally, roadblock decisions should be made by the chief of police or other high-ranking supervisor officials).

a. The Guidelines should set forth explicit, neutral and predetermined limitations on the conduct of officers participating in the checkpoint. Discretion should be minimized by directing checkpoint officers to stop cars at predetermined intervals, *e.g.*, every vehicle, or every 3rd, 4th, or 10th, and vehicles having observable violations.

b. *Site selection.* The Guidelines must include the selection of the time, place and duration of the checkpoint, which should be based on identifiable statistical data showing the need for the checkpoint at the respective time and place. Consideration should be given to (1) areas known for high incidents of accidents, drunk driving or other traffic violations, (2) traffic volume, and (3) motorist and pedestrian safety. For example, a checkpoint established during the late evening hours on a weekend may be reasonable to detect drunk drivers, while continuing the roadblock through Monday morning during rush hour might not be reasonable.

c. The Guidelines must set forth the required number of checkpoint officers that will be needed to ensure that delays are held to a minimum. If an executive-level officer did not participate in the plan's formulation, it should not be implemented until that officer has reviewed and approved it.

3. The safety of the motoring public and the field officer must be given proper attention. To avoid frightening the travelling public, adequate on-the-scene warnings must be given (*for example, a large, obvious sign indicating that the motorist is about to be stopped, the nature of the checkpoint, and that all motorists must pass through; flashing lights; marked police vehicles; flares; and other reflectorized equipment*). In addition, advance general publicity of the checkpoint may be provided to deter drunk drivers from getting in cars in the first place.

4. The checkpoints must be sufficiently staffed by uniformed officers to ensure safety and prevent undue inconvenience to motorists and unreasonable interference with normal traffic flow. A predetermined, safe and convenient "pull over" or parking area should be established and used for vehicles or motorists having violations.

5. Officers participating in the checkpoint should be provided with specified, neutral and courteous procedures to follow when stopping motorists; and the officers chosen for the process should have sufficient experience to quickly identify intoxicated motorists (motorists should be detained only briefly); and carefully planned and predetermined procedures must be in place for operations that will involve the moving of a checkpoint from one location to another.

6. Upon completion of the checkpoint operation, the participating officers should submit, through the appropriate chain of command, full reports in writing of the conduct and results of the checkpoint to the administrative officer(s) who initiated or planned the operation.

7. Advance publicity of the intention of the police to establish DUI roadblocks, without designating specific locations at which they will be conducted, also serves to minimize any apprehension motorists may otherwise experience upon encountering one (although the lack of advance publicity is not sufficient to invalidate a roadblock).

Roadside checkpoints may not be performed where the program's primary purpose is to "detect evidence of ordinary criminal wrongdoing."[282] In order to conduct a motor vehicle stop for the purpose of discovering or interdicting illegal drugs, police officers must first possess a reasonable articulable suspicion that the motorist or other vehicle occupant is engaged in unlawful activity.

Also, under the Fourth Amendment, brief "information-seeking" highway checkpoints are not unconstitutional *per se*. In *Illinois v. Lidster*,[283] the police checkpoint involved a brief stop of motorists to ask for information about a recent hit-and-run accident that resulted in a death. The stop's objective was to ask for public assistance in finding the perpetrator of this "specific and known crime." The checkpoint was "appropriately tailored" to this goal; its interference with the liberty of motorists was minimal; and all vehicles were stopped in a systematic and non-discriminatory manner. As such, it was constitutional.

An attempt to avoid a checkpoint. Evading a marked DWI checkpoint is a specific and articulable fact that is sufficient to predicate reasonable suspicion for an investigatory stop. However, an officer's conclusion that a driver is attempting to avoid a checkpoint may be unreasonable in light of the circumstances of the stop—the time of day, the proximity of the turn to the checkpoint, or whether the driver's actions were typical considering the layout of the area and the normal flow of traffic. In *State v. Foreman*,[284] the North Carolina Supreme Court held that it was constitutionally permissible for an officer to stop a vehicle which had made a legal turn away from a posted driving while impaired checkpoint. There the officer observed a "quick left turn" away from the checkpoint at the precise point where the driver of the vehicle would have first become aware of its presence. The court explained, "Although a legal turn, by itself, is *not* sufficient to establish a reasonable, articulable suspicion, a legal turn in conjunction with other circumstances, such as the time, place and manner in which it is made, *may* constitute a reasonable, articulable suspicion which could justify an investigatory stop."[285]

2.3.7.6. Removing drivers or passengers from the motor vehicle

During a lawful traffic stop, the police may, as a matter of course, order the driver out of the vehicle pending completion of the stop.[286] This was made clear in *Pennsylvania v. Mimms*,[287] where the United States Supreme Court observed: "Rather than conversing while standing exposed to moving traffic, the officer may prefer to ask the driver of the vehicle to step out of the car and off onto the shoulder of the road where the inquiry may be pursued with greater safety to both."[288]

In *Maryland v. Wilson*,[289] the Court further held that rule of *Pennsylvania v. Mimms*—that a police officer may, as a matter of course, order the driver of a lawfully stopped car to exit his vehicle—extends to passengers.

2.3.7.7. A "*Terry*" frisk" of the vehicle's passenger compartment

The United States Supreme Court has noted that "roadside encounters between police and suspects are especially hazardous, and danger may arise from the possible presence of weapons in the area surrounding a suspect."[290] Thus, "the search of the passenger compartment of an automobile, limited to those areas in which a weapon may be placed or hidden, is permissible if the police officer possesses a reasonable belief based on 'specific and articulable facts which, taken together with the rational inferences from those facts, reasonably warrant' the officer in believing that the suspect is dangerous and the suspect may gain immediate control of

---

[282] *City of Indianapolis v. Edmond,* 531 U.S. 32, 121 S. Ct. 447, 454 (2000).

[283] *Illinois v. Lidster*, 540 U.S. 419, 124 S. Ct. 885 (2004).

[284] *State v. Foreman*, 351 N.C. 627, 527 S.E.2d 921 (2000).

[285] *State v. Foreman*, 351 N.C. 627, 631, 527 S.E.2d 921 (2000) (emphasis in original). *See also State v. Griffin*, 366 N.C. 473, 749 S.E.2d 444 (2013).

[286] *State v. Bullock*, 370 N.C. 256, 805 S.E.2d 671 (2017).

[287] *Pennsylvania v. Mimms*, 434 U.S. 106, 111, 98 S. Ct. 330 (1977) (an officer may, as a matter of course, order the driver to either step out of or remain inside the vehicle).

[288] *Pennsylvania v. Mimms*, 434 U.S. 106, 111, 98 S. Ct. 330, 333 (1977).

[289] *Maryland v. Wilson*, 519 U.S. 408, 414-415, 117 S. Ct. 882, 886 (1997).

[290] *Michigan v. Long*, 463 U.S. 1032, 1049, 103 S. Ct. 3469, 3481 (1983).

weapons."[291] The search must be limited in scope to the area that the suspect can reach easily, sometimes called the "zone within the wingspan" or "grabbable area." Officers must also limit the scope of the search solely to weapons, not evidence. A search can be valid even if the suspect has already been removed from the vehicle.

In *State v. Parker*[292], the Court of Appeals of North Carolina explained:

> When the law enforcement officer conducting a traffic stop reasonably believes that an occupant of the car is dangerous and may gain immediate control of a weapon, the officer may conduct a protective search of areas inside the passenger compartment of the vehicle where a weapon may be located. This brief search is known as a "vehicle frisk," and its purpose is to ensure officer safety. The scope of a valid "vehicle frisk" does not extend to searching for evidence.[293]

Thus, in *State v. Reddick*,[294] Officer Carson was justified in performing a *Terry* frisk on the defendant's vehicle after he observed the defendant doing a "security tap" on the center console. "Officer Carson also testified to his years of training and experience as a police officer and the connection between drug crimes and weapons as part of the basis for why he was concerned about a weapon being present in this case, in addition to defendant's 'aggressive' behavior. Under the totality of the circumstances, it was reasonable for Officer Carson to believe his and Officer Thompson's safety may have been in danger to justify his search of the console."[295]

In *State v. Bouknight*,[296] the defendant was stopped by two police officers for driving with an inoperable tag light and a "limited expired" license plate. After the defendant exhibited "nervous and evasive" behavior, both he and his vehicle were *Terry* frisked. Police discovered cocaine and a firearm inside the vehicle. The defendant was charged with several drug crimes, weapon crimes, and habitual felon status. He moved to suppress the evidence obtained from the vehicle. The appellate court denied the motion, noting that the defendant's prior arrests and his behavior provided the officers with a reasonable suspicion that he was hiding something.

Naturally, an officer may pat-down a driver or passenger during a traffic stop if there is a reasonable suspicion that they may be armed and dangerous.[297]

2.3.7.8. Pretextual stops

A "pretextual stop" may be defined as a traffic stop that occurs when an officer has probable cause or reasonable suspicion to believe that a motorist has violated a traffic law, but which the officer would not have made absent a desire, not supported by probable cause or reasonable suspicion, to investigate some other more serious offense.[298] For example, such a stop can arise when an officer observes a vehicle driving 26 miles per hour in a 25 m.p.h. zone, has some subjective reason to suspect that the vehicle is involved in the drug trade, and uses this minor violation of the traffic laws to investigate his hunch further.

Under the Fourth Amendment and federal case law, a stop is justified following any traffic violation, no matter how minor, even if the officer's true purpose is to investigate criminal activity completely unrelated to driving. Thus, in *Whren v. United States*,[299] the United States Supreme Court determined that when a motor vehicle stop is supported by probable cause or reasonable suspicion that the motorist committed a traffic violation, the stop is not invalid simply because the officer's underlying motivation was to investigate criminal activity unrelated to the traffic violation. Said the Court: "Ulterior motives do not invalidate police conduct that is justified on the basis of probable cause to believe a violation of the law has occurred."[300] The

---

[291] *Michigan v. Long*, 463 U.S. 1032, 1049, 103 S. Ct. 3469, 3481 (1983).

[292] *State v. Parker*, 183 N.C. App. 1, 644 S.E.2d 235, 241 (2007).

[293] *State v. Parker*, 183 N.C. App. 1, 8-9, 644 S.E.2d 235, 241 (2007) (citations and quotation marks omitted).

[294] *State v. Reddick*, 253 N.C. App. 841, 799 S.E.2d 908 (2017).

[295] *State v. Reddick*, 253 N.C. App. 841, *20-21, 799 S.E.2d 908 (2017).

[296] *State v. Bouknight*, 252 N.C. App. 265, 797 S.E.2d 340 (2017).

[297] *Arizona v. Johnson*, 555 U.S. 323, 129 S. Ct. 781, 784 (2009).

[298] *See, e.g., Whren v. United States,* 517 U.S. 806, 116 S. Ct. 1769 (1996); *Scott v. United States*, 436 U.S. 128, 138, 98 S. Ct. 1717 (1978).

[299] *Whren v. United States,* 517 U.S. 806, 116 S. Ct. 1769 (1996).

[300] *See also Arkansas v. Sullivan*, 532 U.S. 769, 121 S. Ct. 1876 (2001) (rejecting a defendant's argument that his arrest was merely a "pretext and sham to search" him and, therefore, violated the Fourth Amendment).

Court in *Whren* did pause to note that a motor vehicle stop motivated by an intent to single out members of a suspect class, such as race, would be obviously impermissible.

Thus, if there is an objectively valid reason for the stop, even one involving a minor traffic infraction, subjective intentions are irrelevant.[301]

Note also that an arrest is valid even if the criminal offense for which probable cause actually exists is not "closely related to the offense stated by the arresting officer at the time of arrest."[302] In other words, the officer's "subjective reason for making the arrest need not be the criminal offense as to which the known facts provide probable cause."[303] As the Supreme Court has consistently held:

> The fact that the officer does not have the state of mind which is hypothecated by the reasons which provide the legal justification for the officer's action does not invalidate the action taken as long as the circumstances, viewed objectively, justify that action.[304]

In *State v. McClendon*,[305] the North Carolina Supreme Court adopted the *Whren* holding and stated, "Therefore, for situations arising under our state Constitution, we hold that an objective standard, rather than a subjective standard, must be applied to determine the reasonableness of police action related to probable cause."[306] Accordingly, after *Whren*, "the inquiry is no longer what a reasonable officer *would* do but what a reasonable officer *could* do."[307]

2.3.8. Investigative detentions of property

Persons and vehicles are not the only potential subjects of a temporary investigative detention. Officers may temporarily seize and detain items of personal property when they possess a reasonable suspicion that the property is connected with criminal activity. The detention must last no longer than reasonably necessary for the purpose of determining if the item is in fact linked to a criminal endeavor. If a brief investigation reveals that it is not, then the property should be returned to the owner. The Fourth Amendment protects property as well as privacy.[308] Therefore, similar to the seizure of an individual, "seizures of property are subject to Fourth Amendment scrutiny."[309] This is true even when no search within the meaning of the Amendment has taken place.

For example, in *Soldal*, deputy sheriffs assisted the owners of a mobile home park in evicting the Soldal family. As the deputies stood and watched, the park owners wrenched the sewer and water connections off the side of the Soldal trailer, disconnected the telephone, tore the trailer's canopy and skirting, pulled it free from its moorings and towed it away. Finding the Fourth Amendment clearly applicable, the United States Supreme Court held:

> As a result of the state action in this case, the Soldals' domicile was not only seized, it literally was carried away, giving a new meaning to the term "mobile home." We fail to see how being unceremoniously dispossessed of one's home in the manner alleged to have occurred here can be viewed as anything but a seizure invoking the protection of the Fourth Amendment.... The Amendment protects the

---

[301] *See, e.g., United States v. Hill*, 195 F.3d 258 (6th Cir. 1999) (the stop of a defendant's rented U-Haul truck valid after the officer paced the defendant's speed at 62 m.p.h. in a 55 m.p.h. zone, even though he initially began following the defendant because, in his experience, rental trucks are often used to carry contraband).

[302] *Devenpeck v. Alford,* 543 U.S. 146, 153, 125 S. Ct. 588, 594 (2004).

[303] *Devenpeck v. Alford,* 543 U.S. 146, 153, 125 S. Ct. 588, 594 (2004).

[304] *Whren v. United States,* 517 U.S. 806, 813, 116 S. Ct. 1769 (quoting *Scott v. United States*, 436 U.S. 128, 138, 98 S. Ct. 1717 (1978)). In this regard, "evenhanded law enforcement is best achieved by the application of objective standards of conduct, rather than standards that depend upon the subjective state of mind of the officer." *Horton v. California*, 496 U.S. 128, 138, 110 S. Ct. 2301 (1990).

[305] *State v. McClendon*, 350 N.C. 630, 517 S.E.2d 128 (1999).

[306] *State v. McClendon*, 350 N.C. 630, 636, 517 S.E.2d 128 (1999).

[307] *State v. McClendon*, 350 N.C. 630, 635, 517 S.E.2d 128 (1999) (emphasis in original).

[308] *Soldal v. Cook Co.*, 506 U.S. 56, 113 S. Ct. 538 (1992).

[309] *Soldal v. Cook Co.*, 506 U.S. 56, 113 S. Ct. 538 (1992).

people from unreasonable searches and seizures of "their persons, houses, papers, and effects." ... [A]nd our cases unmistakably hold that the Amendment protects property as well as privacy.... We thus are unconvinced that ... the Fourth Amendment protects against unreasonable seizures of property only where privacy or liberty is also implicated.[310]

Property is detained most often when the police wish to detain luggage or a package to search it for drugs. In *United States v. Place*,[311] the U.S. Supreme Court held that the Fourth Amendment permits law enforcement officials to temporarily detain an individual's luggage for exposure to a trained narcotics detection dog on the basis of a reasonable suspicion that the luggage contains narcotics. Thus, "the limitations applicable to investigative detentions of the person should define the permissible scope of an investigative detention of the person's luggage on less than probable cause."[312]

The Court in *Place* went on to hold, however, that the 90-minute detention of the defendant's personal luggage for the purpose of arranging its exposure to a narcotics detection dog violated the Fourth Amendment because the investigating officers, although having ample time to do so, failed to diligently pursue a means of investigation which would have greatly minimized the length of the detention. Although the Court would not "adopt any outside limitation for a permissible *Terry* stop," it has never approved a seizure of the person for the prolonged 90-minute period involved in this case.

2.3.8.1. A trained "sniff" by a "canine cannabis connoisseur"[313]

During the course of its opinion in *Place*,[314] the Supreme Court had occasion to address the constitutionality of employing a narcotics-detection dog for the purpose of determining whether a particular item of property contains a controlled substance. Writing for the Court, Justice O'Connor instructed:

We have affirmed that a person possesses a privacy interest in the contents of personal luggage that is protected by the Fourth Amendment[.] A "canine sniff" by a well-trained narcotics detection dog, however, does not require opening the luggage. It does not expose non-contraband items that otherwise would remain hidden from public view, as does, for example, an officer's rummaging through the contents of the luggage. Thus, the manner in which information is obtained through this investigative technique is much less intrusive than a typical search. Moreover, the sniff discloses only the presence or absence of narcotics, a contraband item. Thus, despite the fact that the sniff tells the authorities something about the contents of the luggage, the information obtained is limited. This limited disclosure also ensures that the owner of the property is not subject to the embarrassment and inconvenience entailed in less discriminate and more intrusive investigative methods.

In these respects, the canine sniff is *sui generis* [*i.e.*, unique, in its own class]. We are aware of no other investigative procedure that is so limited both in the manner in which the information is obtained and in the content of the information revealed by the procedure. *Therefore, we conclude that the particular course of investigation that the agents intended to pursue here—exposure of [defendant's] luggage, which was located in a public place, to a trained canine—did not constitute a "search" within the meaning of the Fourth Amendment.*[315]

In *United States v. Jacobsen*,[316] the Court gave *Place* a broad interpretation and concluded that a police investigatory tool is not a "search" if it merely discloses the presence or absence of contraband. According to the *Jacobsen* Court, similar to the *Place* canine sniff, the likelihood that chemical tests (which merely disclose

---

[310] *Soldal v. Cook Co.*, 506 U.S. 56, 113 S. Ct. 538, 543-45 (1992).

[311] *United States v. Place*, 462 U.S. 696, 103 S. Ct. 2637 (1983).

[312] *United States v. Place*, 462 U.S. 696, 103 S. Ct. 2637, 2645 (1983).

[313] *United States v. Bronstein*, 521 F.2d 459, 460 (2d Cir. 1975).

[314] *United States v. Place*, 462 U.S. 696, 103 S. Ct. 2637 (1983).

[315] *United States v. Place*, 462 U.S. 696, 103 S. Ct. 2637, 2644-45 (1983) (emphasis added).

[316] *United States v. Jacobsen*, 466 U.S. 109, 104 S. Ct. 1652 (1984).

whether or not a certain substance is an illicit drug), "will actually compromise any legitimate interest in privacy seems much too remote to characterize the testing as a search subject to the Fourth Amendment."[317]

Finally, in *Smith v. Ohio*,[318] the Supreme Court emphasized that reasonable suspicion permits a brief detention of property, but not a search of it. "Although the Fourth Amendment may permit the detention for a brief period of property on the basis of only 'reasonable, articulable suspicion' that it contains contraband or evidence of criminal activity," it prohibits—"except in certain well-defined circumstances—the search of that property unless accomplished pursuant to a judicial warrant issued upon probable cause.... That guarantee protects alike the 'traveler who carries a toothbrush and a few articles of clothing in a paper bag' and 'the sophisticated executive with the locked attaché case.'"[319]

3. THE LAW OF ARREST

3.1. General aspects

An "arrest" may be defined as a substantial physical interference with the liberty of a person, resulting in his apprehension and detention. It is generally effected for the purpose of preventing a person from committing a criminal offense, or calling upon a person to answer or account for an alleged completed crime.

An arrest may be effected "actually" or "constructively." An *actual* arrest occurs when a duly empowered law enforcement officer intentionally employs physical force (*e.g.*, a physical touching of the person), and delivers a formal communication of a present intention to arrest (*e.g.*, "You are under arrest!"). A *constructive* arrest occurs without an intentional use of physical force and without a formal statement indicating an intention to take the person into custody. Moreover, in constructive arrest situations, the power or authority of the arresting officer, along with his intention to effect the arrest, is implied by all the circumstances surrounding the encounter. In either case, to determine whether an arrest has occurred, a court will examine whether physical force has been applied—which may be accomplished by a mere touching of the suspect—*or*, where that is absent, whether there has been a "*submission* to the assertion of authority."[320]

An arrest signifies the initial step toward a prospective prosecution and, as a governmental intrusion upon the "person," must be effectuated according to the dictates of the Fourth Amendment. Although the word "arrest" does not appear in the language of the Amendment, courts have consistently equated "arrest" with "seizure." In this respect, the United States Supreme Court has declared that "it is the command of the Fourth Amendment that no warrants either for searches or arrests shall issue *except upon probable cause*[.]"[321]

Accordingly, "the Fourth Amendment speaks equally to both searches and seizures, and ... an arrest, the taking hold of one's person, is quintessentially a seizure."[322]

3.2. The objective standard

To determine whether an arrest has taken place, a court will apply an objective standard, focusing on the reasonable impression conveyed to the person subjected to the apprehension and detention. In this respect, the relative inquiry is whether, in view of all the circumstances surrounding the police-citizen encounter, "a reasonable person would have believed that he was not free to leave" at the conclusion of the officer's inquiry.[323] Thus, a law enforcement officer's subjective view that a suspect was not free to leave—so long

---

[317] *United States v. Jacobsen*, 466 U.S. 109, 122-24, 104 S. Ct. 1652, 1661-62 (1984).

[318] *Smith v. Ohio*, 494 U.S. 541, 110 S. Ct. 1288 (1990).

[319] *Smith v. Ohio*, 494 U.S. 541, 110 S. Ct. 1288, 1289 (1990) (quoting *United States v. Ross*, 456 U.S. 798, 822, 102 S. Ct. 2157, 2171 (1982)).

[320] *California v. Hodari D.*, 499 U.S. 621, 626, 111 S. Ct. 1547, 1551 (1991) (emphasis in original).

[321] *Henry v. United States*, 361 U.S. 98, 100, 80 S. Ct. 168, 170 (1959) (emphasis added).

[322] *United States v. Watson*, 423 U.S. 411, 428, 96 S. Ct. 820, 830 (1976); *see also District of Columbia v. Wesby*, 583 U.S. ___, 138 S. Ct. 577, 585 (2018) ("Because arrests are 'seizures' of 'persons,' they must be reasonable."). Excerpts from the comprehensive discussion of the laws of arrest, search and seizure in Larry E. Holtz, *Criminal Procedure for Law and Justice Professionals* (Blue360° Media).

[323] *United States v. Mendenhall*, 446 U.S. 544, 554, 100 S. Ct. 1870, 1877 (1980).

as that view has not been conveyed to the person confronted—will not transform an objectively casual, voluntary encounter, or even a temporary investigative detention, into a full-blown arrest. Significantly, the United States Supreme Court, almost without exception, has evaluated alleged violations of the law of arrest (as well as the law of search and seizure) by undertaking "an objective assessment of an officer's actions in light of the facts and circumstances then known to him."[324] So long as the facts and circumstances, viewed objectively, justify an officer's course of action, such action will not be invalidated merely because the officer does not have the state of mind which technically parallels the constitutional rules which provide the legal justification for that course of action.[325]

The objective standard uniformly applied by the courts utilizes a "reasonable person" test to determine whether a particular police-citizen encounter requires a certain level of constitutional justification. The determination proceeds by reference to the "totality of the circumstances," *i.e.*, the whole picture.[326] Although the federal Supreme Court in *Michigan v. Chesternut* recognized that the reasonable person test may be "imprecise," for "what constitutes a restraint on liberty prompting a person to conclude that he is not free to 'leave' will vary, not only with the particular police conduct at issue, but also with the setting in which the conduct occurs[,]" it nonetheless concluded:

> The test's objective standard—looking to the reasonable man's interpretation of the conduct in question— allows police to determine in advance whether the conduct contemplated will implicate the Fourth Amendment....This "reasonable person" standard also ensures that the scope of the Fourth Amendment protection does not vary with the state of mind of the particular individual being approached.[327]

3.3. Factors to consider

To determine whether a police-citizen encounter has elevated into a Fourth Amendment arrest, courts will consider such factors as

- whether the encounter was consensual;
- the basis for the encounter (whether the officers had reasonable grounds to believe a criminal offense had occurred and the grounds for that belief);
- the duration of the encounter;
- the investigative methods used to confirm or dispel suspicions;
- an officer's statement that the individual is the subject of an investigation;
- an officer's statement that the individual is or is not free to leave;
- whether the officer(s) blocked the individual's path or impeded his progress;
- whether weapons were displayed, enforcement canines employed, or the use of force in any other way threatened;
- the number of law enforcement officers present and their demeanor;
- the location of the encounter (public or private);
- the extent to which the officer(s) restrained the individual;
- whether the individual was transported to another location against his will (how far and why);
- whether the individual was free to choose between terminating or continuing the encounter with the officer(s);
- whether the individual was transported to the police station in a patrol car or arranged his own transportation; and
- whether the individual was placed in a closed-off interview room or in an open, common area.[328]

---

[324] *Scott v. United States*, 436 U.S. 128, 137, 98 S. Ct. 1717, 1723 (1978).

[325] *Scott v. United States*, 436 U.S. 128, 138, 98 S. Ct. 1717, 1723 (1978); *see also Devenpeck v. Alford*, 543 U.S. 146, 125 S. Ct. 588, 593 (2004); *United States v. Robinson*, 414 U.S. 218, 236, 94 S. Ct. 467, 477 (1973).

[326] *Michigan v. Chesternut*, 486 U.S. 567, 108 S. Ct. 1975, 1979 (1989); *INS v. Delgado*, 466 U.S. 210, 215, 104 S. Ct. 1758, 1762 (1984).

[327] *Michigan v. Chesternut*, 486 U.S. 567, 108 S. Ct. 1975, 1979-80 (1989).

[328] *See United States v. Mendenhall*, 446 U.S. 544, 554-55, 100 S. Ct. 1870, 1877-78 (1980); *Florida v. Royer*, 460 U.S. 491, 499-503, 103 S. Ct. 1319, 1324-27 (1983); *United States v. Novak*, 870 F.2d 1345, 1351-52 (7th Cir. 1989); *United States v.*

3.4. The probable cause requirement

While the law, both on the state and federal levels, certainly prefers that an arrest be effected pursuant to a warrant, it is well settled that a law enforcement officer may effect a warrantless arrest when she has probable cause to believe that a crime has been or is being committed and that the person to be arrested has committed or is committing it.[329] Moreover, when an officer must decide whether a warrantless arrest in a given set of circumstances is justified, he is not limited to consideration only of evidence admissible in a courtroom. Rather, the officer may consider all the facts and circumstances surrounding the prospective arrest, even that information coming from (preferably reliable) hearsay sources, when making the probable cause determination. Thus, "[t]he validity of the arrest does not depend on whether the suspect actually committed a crime[, and] the mere fact that the suspect is later acquitted of the offense for which he is arrested is irrelevant to the validity of the arrest."[330]

The constitutional justification for an arrest, whether on the federal or state level, and whether effected with or without a warrant, is "probable cause."[331] An arrest based on probable cause serves several important interests that serve to justify the seizure. An arrest

- ensures that the suspect appears in court to answer charges;
- prevents the suspect from continuing his offense;
- safeguards evidence; and
- enables officers to conduct a more thorough in-custody investigation.[332]

Probable cause is an elusive term which seems to carry varied meanings depending upon who is making the analysis. Virtually all courts and commentators tend to agree that it is generally more than "reasonable suspicion" but less than actual proof. In this respect, the United States Supreme Court has made it "clear that the kinds and degree of proof and the procedural requirements necessary for a conviction are not prerequisites to a valid arrest."[333] The question, of course, then becomes *how much* more than suspicion and *how much* less than proof?

Probable cause does not mean that the arrestee actually committed the suspected crime, or that the officer possesses enough proof to convict the suspect at a trial, or even that the arrestee will go to trial for the alleged offense. It does mean that at the time of the arrest, a prudent, objective person in the position of the officer, taking into account her experience, knowledge and observations, would reasonably believe that a crime has been or is being committed. It is interesting to note at this juncture that the police are not required to effect an arrest the moment they believe probable cause has materialized. In this regard, the United States Supreme Court has observed:

There is no constitutional right to be arrested. The police are not required to guess at their peril the precise moment at which they have probable cause to arrest a suspect, risking a violation of the Fourth Amendment if they act too soon, and a violation of the Sixth Amendment if they wait too long. Law enforcement officers are under no constitutional duty to call a halt to a criminal investigation the moment they have the minimum evidence to establish probable cause, a quantum of evidence which may fall far short of the amount necessary to support a criminal conviction.[334]

Analysis of legal proof standards suggests that probable cause must find its place somewhere above reasonable suspicion but below a preponderant level of proof.[335] It is established by building upon reasonable

---

Hammock, 860 F.2d 390, 393 (11th Cir. 1988). Excerpts from the comprehensive discussion of the laws of arrest, search and seizure in Larry E. Holtz, *Criminal Procedure for Law and Justice Professionals* (Blue360° Media).

[329] Larry E. Holtz, *Criminal Procedure for Law and Justice Professionals*, §1.1 (Blue360° Media).

[330] *Michigan v. DeFillippo*, 443 U.S. 31, 36, 99 S. Ct. 2627, 2631 (1979).

[331] *See e.g., Michigan v. Summers*, 452 U.S. 692, 700, 101 S. Ct. 2587, 2593 (1981) (It is a "general rule that every arrest, and every seizure having the essential attributes of a formal arrest, is unreasonable unless it is supported by probable cause.").

[332] *See Virginia v. Moore*, 553 U.S. 164, 128 S. Ct. 1598, 1605 (2008); *see also id.* at 1605 ("[T]he police do not violate the fourth amendment when they make an arrest that is supported by probable cause but is prohibited by state law.").

[333] *Michigan v. DeFillippo*, 443 U.S. 31, 36, 99 S. Ct. 2627, 2631 (1979).

[334] *Hoffa v. United States*, 385 U.S. 293, 310, 87 S. Ct. 408, 417 (1966).

[335] *See e.g., Gerstein v. Pugh*, 420 U.S. 103, 121, 95 S. Ct. 854, 867 (1975) (probable cause "does not require the fine resolution of conflicting evidence that a reasonable-doubt or even a preponderance standard demands").

suspicion those additional facts necessary to indicate an objectively reasonable probability that an offense has been committed and the person in question is, in fact, a criminal participant. The officer builds his probable cause by a *step-by-step ascent* from his reasonable suspicion. Depending upon the nature of the activity and the particular investigation, this ascent may take days, weeks, or months; then again, it might literally occur in seconds.[336]

Naturally, before reaching the threshold, or *landing*, of "reasonable suspicion," there must be some sort of *stimulus* which evokes the attention of the officer. In this respect, an assortment of stimuli may be acquired through the officer's contact with persons, places, vehicles or property, including any information received in such regard. The stimuli then mix with the officer's experience, training and education, and law enforcement intuition to build a reasonable basis for the activity which will follow. The officer now begins his ascent toward the "reasonable suspicion" threshold, or *landing*.

As the officer follows up or investigates each aspect of the "seasoned" stimuli, he either begins to corroborate and strengthen it, or he dispels it from his agenda. If the investigation proves fruitful, the officer now begins to enter the realm of "reasonable suspicion." He then must be able to collect all the steps of the ascent and articulate them in specific and objectively reasonable language. Once this is accomplished, the officer is safely on the *landing* of "reasonable suspicion."

The officer builds his "probable cause" by a *step-by-step ascent* from his reasonable suspicion. Its threshold is reached when the "specific and articulable facts," aided by the rational inferences drawn therefrom, not only support a reasonable basis for suspicion,[337] but magnify that suspicion to such an extent that a reasonable person, objectively viewing all the facts, would be convinced that an offense did, in fact, occur, and the person in question is, in fact, a criminal participant.

Significantly, the degree or quantum of belief required before a court may conclude that probable cause exists is virtually the same for purposes of an arrest or a search. A court should not apply two standards when assessing the sufficiency of probable cause, that is, there should not be a dual determination of probable cause—one related to the probability level necessary for a search and seizure, and one related to a different probability level necessary for an arrest. Rather, the focus of the court's attention should always be on the quantum or sufficiency of those objective facts and circumstances surrounding the particular police procedure at the relevant time in order to determine whether the police possessed the requisite *degree* of belief prior to engaging in the challenged procedure.[338]

Naturally, the application of the same degree or quantum of belief—the probable cause standard—will take on a different analysis when the probabilities must be assessed against the facts and circumstances justifying an arrest as opposed to the facts and circumstances justifying a search and seizure. In this respect, *probable cause to arrest* may be found to exist when the facts and circumstances within the officer's knowledge are sufficient to permit a prudent person, or one of reasonable caution, to conclude that there is a fair probability that a criminal offense is being or has been committed, and the suspect is or has been a criminal participant. *Probable cause to search* may be found to exist when the facts and circumstances within the officer's knowledge are sufficient to permit a prudent person, or one of reasonable caution, to conclude that there is a fair probability that particularly described property which is subject to official seizure may be presently found in a particular place.

Finally, it is important for the officer to realize that her probable cause determinations, many times made in the haste and hustle of dangerous investigations, will not be judged by after-the-fact, desk-side analyses made by legal scholars using strict standards and exacting calculations. Rather, probable cause will be assessed by everyday commonsensical probabilities upon which ordinary, reasonable people act.[339]

---

[336] *See also Florida v. Harris,* 568 U.S. 237, 133 S. Ct. 1050, 1055 (2013) (probable cause is the kind of "fair probability" on which "reasonable and prudent" people act).

[337] *Terry v. Ohio,* 392 U.S. 1, 88 S. Ct. 1868 (1968).

[338] *See e.g., California v. Acevedo,* 500 U.S. 565, 111 S. Ct. 1982, 1989 (1991) ("the same probable cause to believe that a container holds drugs will allow the police to arrest the person transporting the container [in the passenger compartment of an automobile] and search it"); *Ybarra v. Illinois,* 444 U.S. 85, 105, 100 S. Ct. 338, 350 (1979) (Rehnquist, J., dissenting) ("Given probable cause to believe that a person possesses illegal drugs, the police need no warrant to conduct a full body search. They need only arrest that person and conduct the search incident to that arrest.").

[339] Excerpts from the comprehensive discussion of the laws of arrest, search and seizure in Larry E. Holtz, *Criminal Procedure for Law and Justice Professionals* (Blue360° Media).

Retaliatory arrest claims. In *Nieves v. Bartlett*,[340] the United States Supreme Court made it clear that the existence of probable cause to arrest will defeat a claim that the police retaliated against a person for his protected First Amendment speech.

Russell Bartlett was arrested by police officers Luis Nieves and Bryce Weight for disorderly conduct and resisting arrest on the last night of "Arctic Man," a week-long raucous winter sports festival held in a remote part of Alaska. According to Sergeant Nieves, at about 1:30 a.m., he was speaking with a group of partygoers when a seemingly intoxicated Bartlett started shouting at them not to talk to the police. When Nieves approached him, Bartlett began yelling at the officer to leave. Rather than escalate the situation, Nieves left. Minutes later, Bartlett saw Trooper Weight asking a minor whether he and his underage friends had been drinking. According to Weight, Bartlett approached in an aggressive manner, stood between Weight and the teenager, and yelled with slurred speech that Weight should not speak with the minor. Weight indicated that Bartlett then stepped very close to him in a combative way, so Weight pushed him back. Sergeant Nieves saw the confrontation and rushed over, arriving right after Weight pushed Bartlett. Nieves immediately initiated an arrest, and when Bartlett was slow to comply with his orders, the officers forced him to the ground. After he was handcuffed, Bartlett claims that Nieves said "bet you wish you would have talked to me now."

Bartlett sued under 42 *U. S. C.* §1983, claiming that the officers violated his First Amendment rights by arresting him in retaliation for his speech—*i.e.*, his initial refusal to speak with Nieves and his intervention in Weight's discussion with the minor.[341] The Supreme Court held that the existence of probable cause to arrest Bartlett precluded his First Amendment retaliatory arrest claim as a matter of law.[342] In rejecting Bartlett's contention that the issue is simply whether the officer "intended to punish the plaintiff for the plaintiff's protected speech," the Court said:

> Police officers conduct approximately 29,000 arrests every day—a dangerous task that requires making quick decisions in "circumstances that are tense, uncertain, and rapidly evolving." ... To ensure that officers may go about their work without undue apprehension of being sued, we generally review their conduct under objective standards of reasonableness.... Thus, when reviewing an arrest, we ask "whether the circumstances, viewed objectively, justify [the challenged] action," and if so, conclude "that action was reasonable whatever the subjective intent motivating the relevant officials." ... A particular officer's state of mind is simply "irrelevant," and it provides "no basis for invalidating an arrest."[343]

3.5. Involuntary transportation to the police station

In *Dunaway v. New York*,[344] the Supreme Court held that officers are not permitted to transport a suspect to police headquarters for questioning without his consent and without probable cause for an arrest. According

---

[340] *Nieves v. Bartlett*, 587 U.S. ___, 139 S.Ct. 1715 (2019).

[341] "[A]s a general matter the First Amendment prohibits government officials from subjecting an individual to retaliatory actions" for engaging in protected speech. *Hartman v. Moore*, 547 U. S. 250, 256, 126 S. Ct. 1695 (2006). If an official takes adverse action against someone based on that forbidden motive, and "non-retaliatory grounds are in fact insufficient to provoke the adverse consequences," the injured person may generally seek relief by bringing a First Amendment claim. *See also Crawford-El v. Britton*, 523 U. S. 574, 593, 118 S. Ct. 1584 (1998); *Mt. Healthy City Bd. of Ed. v. Doyle*, 429 U. S. 274, 283-284, 97 S. Ct. 568 (1977).

[342] While the existence of probable cause will generally defeat a retaliatory arrest claim, officers may not exercise their discretion not to arrest for the purpose of "exploit[ing] the arrest power as a means of suppressing speech." *Nieves v. Bartlett*, 587 U.S. ___, 139 S.Ct. 1715 (2019). "For example, at many intersections, jaywalking is endemic but rarely results in arrest. If an individual who has been vocally complaining about police conduct is arrested for jaywalking at such an intersection, it would seem insufficiently protective of First Amendment rights to dismiss the individual's retaliatory arrest claim on the ground that there was undoubted probable cause for the arrest." *Id.*

[343] *Nieves v. Bartlett*, 587 U.S. ___, 139 S.Ct. 1715 (2019) (quoting *Graham v. Connor*, 490 U. S. 386, 397, 109 S. Ct. 1865 (1989); *Atwater v. Lago Vista*, 532 U. S. 318, 351 & n.22, 121 S. Ct. 1536 (2001); *Harlow v. Fitzgerald*, 457 U. S. 800, 814-819, 102 S. Ct. 2727 (1982); *Devenpeck v. Alford*, 543 U. S. 146, 153, 155, 125 S. Ct. 588, 160 L. Ed. 2d 537 (2004)).

[344] *Dunaway v. New York,* 442 U.S. 200, 99 S. Ct. 2248 (1979).

to the Court, whenever a law enforcement officer removes a suspect from where he is found and transports that suspect to police headquarters for questioning without his consent and without probable cause (for his arrest), the detention is, in all important respects, indistinguishable from a traditional arrest and is unlawful. Merely because a suspect is not told he is under arrest, is not "booked," and would not have an arrest record if the interrogation proves fruitless, does not make such a detention analogous to the type authorized by *Terry v. Ohio*. Rather, such a "detention for custodial interrogation—regardless of its label—intrudes so severely on interests protected by the Fourth Amendment" that the familiar requirement of probable cause is thereby triggered. This principle had been made clear in *Davis v. Mississippi*—namely, "that an investigatory detention that, for all intents and purposes, is indistinguishable from custodial interrogation, requires no less probable cause than a traditional arrest."[345]

The Court, in *Kaupp v. Texas*,[346] reaffirmed that, in the absence of probable cause for an arrest, it is unlawful for law enforcement officials to transport a suspect, against his will, to the station for questioning. According to the Court, the "involuntary transport to a police station for questioning is sufficiently like arrest to invoke the traditional rule that arrests may constitutionally be made only on probable cause."

In *Hayes v. Florida*,[347] however, the Supreme Court indicated that, with prior judicial authorization (such as an investigative detention order), the police may be authorized to transport a suspect to the police station for fingerprinting, even in the absence of probable cause or consent. Here, the Court noted that there have been a number of cases that have suggested that "the Fourth Amendment would permit seizures for the purpose of fingerprinting, if there is reasonable suspicion that the suspect has committed a criminal act, if there is a reasonable basis for believing that fingerprinting will establish or negate the suspect's connection with that crime, and if the procedure is carried out with dispatch."

3.6. An officer's training, experience and expertise

An officer's specialized training, experience and expertise provide the officer with a unique ability to make judgments and assessments as to whether the law is or is not being violated. Unlike a layman, most law enforcement officials receive initial and continuing training for the job. Through years of experience, they also develop a specialized expertise in recognizing criminality in all its forms. In addition, "a good patrol officer considers it his business to develop so complete familiarity with his 'beat' that he is alerted by anything suspicious or unusual."[348]

As a general matter, courts will take into account an officer's training, experience and expertise in determining whether probable cause exists. In this regard, what constitutes probable cause for an arrest or a search and seizure must be determined from the standpoint of the officer, with his skills and knowledge, rather than from the standpoint of an average citizen under similar circumstances. Thus, probable cause is to be viewed from the vantage point of a prudent, reasonable, cautious police officer guided by his experience and training.[349]

---

[345] *Davis v. Mississippi*, 394 U.S. 721, 726-27, 89 S. Ct. 1394 (1969). *See also Hayes v. Florida*, 470 U.S. 811, 815, 105 S. Ct. 1643 (1985) ("None of our later cases have undercut the holding in Davis that transportation to and investigative detention at the station house without probable cause or judicial authorization together violate the Fourth Amendment."). For an extended discussion of this topic, *see* §2.3.1.4.

[346] *Kaupp v. Texas*, 538 U.S. 626, 123 S. Ct. 1843 (2003).

[347] *Hayes v. Florida*, 470 U.S. 811, 105 S. Ct. 1643 (1985).

[348] *Model Code of Pre-Arraignment Procedure* 297 (1975).

[349] *See United States v. Ortiz*, 422 U.S. 891, 95 S. Ct. 2585 (1975) ("officers are entitled to draw reasonable inferences from these facts in light of their knowledge of the area and their prior experience"); *Johnson v. United States*, 333 U.S. 10, 68 S. Ct. 367 (1948) (probable cause may be based on a distinctive odor where the officer is "qualified to know the odor"); *United States v. Smith*, 789 F.3d 923 (8th Cir. 2015) (probable cause established from officer's smell of marijuana in car, where officer "testified that he had been trained in the detection of controlled substances, including the odor of both raw and burned marijuana"); *United States v. Clarke*, 564 F.3d 949 (8th Cir. 2009) (probable cause established where officer "smelled an odor which, based on his training and extensive experience, he recognized as consistent with methamphetamine manufacturing"); *see also United States v. Peters*, 743 F.3d 1113 (7th Cir. 2014) (probable cause established where officer with 15 years of "significant training and experience in traffic enforcement" judged the distance between the vehicles "to be too short for cars moving so quickly").

3.7. The "fellow officer" / "collective knowledge" rule

Police are also entitled to rely on facts garnered by those with whom they work. When more than one officer is working on a particular case, a reviewing court will take into account all of the information known to all of the officers on the case (not just the information known to the one who made the arrest) to determine if there was probable cause to arrest. Thus, in *Karr v. Smith*,[350] the court held that, under the "fellow officer" rule, "probable cause is to be determined by the courts on the basis of the collective information of the police involved in the arrest, rather than exclusively on the extent of the knowledge of the particular officer who may actually make the arrest." Rather than focusing exclusively on the extent of the knowledge of the particular officer who may actually have made the arrest, courts will determine the existence of probable cause "on the basis of the collective information" known to the police—all the officers involved in the arrest. This is known as the *fellow officer rule*. Under this rule, "the collective information" of all the law enforcement officers "involved in an arrest can form the basis for probable cause, even though that information is not within the knowledge of the arresting officer."[351]

In *State v. Zuniga*,[352] the North Carolina Supreme Court stated, "It is well established that one law enforcement officer may rely upon bulletins from other officers as the basis for an arrest, but only so long as the originating officer himself had probable cause."[353] There, a suspect in a murder investigation fled on a bus headed to Arkansas. Aware that the bus would make a scheduled stop in Knoxville, Tennessee, the North Carolina police requested that the Knoxville police hold the defendant for investigative purposes. "Knoxville police, after conferring by telephone with the North Carolina authorities, met the bus in which defendant was believed to be riding. Defendant, the only Mexican male aboard the bus, was detained ... [and] taken to the Knoxville Police Department where he was placed in custody awaiting the arrival of North Carolina law enforcement authorities."[354] The defendant argued that at the time he was taken into custody, there was no probable cause to believe that the defendant had committed the crime for which he was later charged. However, because the North Carolina authorities had probable cause to believe that the defendant had committed a murder, the warrantless arrest in Knoxville was lawful.[355]

3.8. Other factors to consider

3.8.1. High crime areas

In addition to an officer's training and experience, the known reputation of an area for crime is also a relevant factor in determining whether probable cause or reasonable suspicion exists.[356]

3.8.2. Identification of suspect

An officer must be sure that the description of a suspect is sufficiently detailed before she can effectuate an arrest. If the description is too vague or general, the officer should refrain from making the mistake of arresting the suspect prematurely. Instead she should ask the suspect certain questions or keep the suspect

---

[350] *Karr v. Smith*, 774 F.2d 1029, 1031 (10th Cir. 1985).

[351] *See also Whiteley v. Warden*, 401 U.S. 560, 568, 91 S. Ct. 1031, 1037 (1971) ("Certainly, police officers called upon to aid other officers in executing arrest warrants are entitled to assume that the officers requesting aid offered the magistrate the information requisite to support an independent judicial assessment of probable cause."); *United States v. Rocha*, 916 F.2d 219, 238 (5th Cir. 1990) (the arresting officer "need not have personal knowledge of all the facts constituting probable cause but can rely upon the collective knowledge of the police when there is a communication among them").

[352] *State v. Zuniga*, 312 N.C. 251, 322 S.E.2d 140 (1984).

[353] *State v. Zuniga*, 312 N.C. 251, 260, 322 S.E.2d 140 (1984).

[354] *State v. Zuniga*, 312 N.C. 251, 253, 322 S.E.2d 140 (1984).

[355] *See also State v. Tilley*, 44 N.C. App. 313, 317, 260 S.E.2d 794 (1979) ("[P]robable cause for an arrest can be imputed from one officer to others acting at his request. The officers receiving the request are entitled to assume that the officer requesting aid had probable cause to believe that a crime had been committed.").

[356] *See Illinois v. Wardlow*, 528 U.S. 119, 125, 120 S. Ct. 673, 676 (2000) ("[T]he fact that the stop occurred in a 'high crime area' [is] among the relevant contextual considerations in a *Terry* analysis.").

under surveillance. Obviously, if those procedures are not practical, the officer should use common sense and take reasonable steps to keep the suspect under observation.

The victim is the best source of identification of a suspect. The courts will assume that the victim is reliable and obviously knows what he is talking about. Unless a police officer has reason not to believe a victim (*i.e.*, if he exhibits emotional or mental problems), the officer can rely on the victim for sufficient identification and probable cause to make an arrest, without having to verify the information.[357]

In *Ahlers v. Schebil*,[358] plaintiff had been arrested for solicitation and was being kept in the Washtenaw County Jail. Her allegation that the defendant, a corrections officer, had sexually assaulted her the night before, standing alone, established probable cause for the defendant's arrest, especially when bolstered by Sheriff's Department records that confirmed that there was a window of time when the assault could have occurred.

Occasionally a victim will tell a police officer that she is not absolutely certain of an identification or that a person only looks like the perpetrator of the crime. This information is usually insufficient to provide an officer with probable cause. However, probable cause will exist if the victim picks out a suspect's photograph.[359]

A police officer can also rely on a citizen who is not the victim of a crime to provide information which will constitute probable cause to make an arrest. While the courts have also found this type of citizen to be trustworthy, an officer must still verify that the citizen knows what she is talking about. This is known as the citizen's "basis of knowledge."

3.8.3. Informants

When a police officer relies upon a confidential informant for information, there are certain points that the officer must keep in mind. Before the courts will find probable cause based on the informant's information, the officer must be sure that the tip is reliable. Two important considerations in making this determination are the informant's "veracity" and "basis of knowledge."

In order to establish an informant's "veracity," an officer should determine the following: (i) whether the informant came forward in the past with accurate information (including the number of times, the nature of the prior cases, how often the information was true and correct, and how often the information has led to a successful arrest, prosecution or conviction); (ii) whether the informant made any criminal admissions (called declarations against her penal interest); (iii) whether the informant has a proper motive; (iv) whether the informant has a close relationship to key criminal targets; (v) whether the officer can confirm details of the informant's story; and (vi) whether the informant is an ordinary citizen who provides information solely to help solve a crime or prevent a future crime.[360]

In order to establish an informant's "basis of knowledge," the officer should consider the following: (i) whether the informant provided detailed information and a factual account *i.e.*, no rumors or innuendo; (ii) whether the informant spoke from personal knowledge; (iii) whether the information is provided with a relevant time frame; (iv) whether the informant was able to provide predictive information; and (v) whether the officer observed conduct directly corroborating the informant's report.[361]

If, under the totality of the circumstances—including the informant's "veracity" and "basis of knowledge"—the reliability of the tip can be established by the officer, probable cause for an arrest will exist. If an officer cannot fully establish an informant's "veracity," "reliability" or "basis of knowledge," a deficiency in either may be made up by independent police corroboration and an application of the totality of the circumstances. This approach was adopted by the United States Supreme Court in *Illinois v. Gates*.[362] Stating that probable cause is a fluid concept that is not readily or usefully reduced to a neat set of legal rules, the Court said:

---

[357] *See Ahlers v. Schebil,* 188 F.3d 365, 370 (6th Cir. 1999) ("[S]ince eyewitness' statements are based on firsthand observations, they are generally entitled to a presumption of reliability and veracity.").

[358] *Ahlers v. Schebil,* 188 F.3d 365 (6th Cir. 1999).

[359] *Ahlers v. Schebil,* 188 F.3d 365, 370 (6th Cir. 1999).

[360] *See* Larry E. Holtz, *Criminal Procedure for Law and Justice Professionals,* §3.2(a) (Blue360° Media).

[361] *See* Larry E. Holtz, *Criminal Procedure for Law and Justice Professionals,* §3.2(a) (Blue360° Media).

[362] *Illinois v. Gates,* 462 U.S. 213, 232, 238, 103 S. Ct. 2317 (1983).

We agree ... that an informant's "veracity," "reliability," and "basis of knowledge" are all highly relevant in determining the value of [the informant's] report. We do not agree, however, that these elements should be understood as entirely separate and independent requirements to be rigidly exacted in every case.... Rather, ... they should be understood simply as closely intertwined issues that may usefully illuminate the common-sense, practical question whether there is "probable cause" to believe that contraband or evidence is located in a particular place.[363]

Under the "totality of the circumstances" approach, the facts are to be viewed collectively, not in isolation. Many times, when the facts are viewed separately and in isolation, they may be prone to innocent explanation. But "this kind of divide-and-conquer approach is improper."[364] Instead, we must look at "the whole picture." When the North Carolina Supreme Court looked at the whole picture in *State v. Bone*,[365] it found probable cause to arrest. There, Detective Saul had been investigating the murder of an 88-year-old woman in her apartment for several months when he received an anonymous tip from an informant identifying the defendant as the murderer. The tipster provided the defendant's name, details about the crime, the name of the town the defendant resided in and his place of work. Detective Saul verified most of the information before approaching the defendant. Thereafter, he asked the defendant to accompany him to the police station where an interrogation ensued. After the interrogation, Detective Saul formally placed the defendant under arrest. In considering whether Detective Saul had probable cause to arrest the defendant, the court said:

The record establishes that Detective Saul had probable cause to arrest defendant ... In making an arrest, an officer "may rely upon information received through an informant, rather than upon his direct observations, so long as the informant's statement is reasonably corroborated by other matters within the officer's knowledge." This rule applies to anonymous informants as well as informants who have supplied reliable information in the past. Detective Saul was able to corroborate almost all of the information in the anonymous tip, including defendant's name, age, race, marital status, criminal status, and area of employment, as well as the street on which the victim lived. Detective Saul also knew that the murderer had entered through a window in the victim's house and that the victim was found with blood on her face; the anonymous tipster reported that the murderer had climbed in an open window and had hit the victim so hard she bled from her ears. These indicia of reliability gave credibility to the anonymous tipster.[366]

3.8.4. Flight, nervousness or evasive maneuvers

Flight, nervousness or evasive maneuvers when confronted with police presence, although not sufficient to create probable cause when standing alone, may create probable cause for arrest if coupled with a suspicion centering on the suspect.

For example, in *Illinois v. Wardlow*,[367] the defendant fled upon seeing police officers patrolling an area known for heavy narcotics trafficking. Two officers caught the defendant on the street, stopped him, and conducted a pat-down search for weapons. Upon discovering a .38 caliber handgun, the defendant was arrested. Finding the stop proper, the Court noted that an officer may, consistent with the Fourth Amendment, conduct a brief, investigatory stop when the officer has a reasonable, articulable suspicion that criminal activity is afoot.[368] Here, the fact that the stop occurred in a "high crime area" is among the relevant contextual considerations in a *Terry* analysis. However, in *Wardlow*, it was not merely the defendant's presence "in an area of heavy narcotics trafficking that aroused the officers' suspicion but his unprovoked flight upon noticing the

---

[363] *Illinois v. Gates*, 462 U.S. 213, 232, 230, 103 S. Ct. 2317 (1983). The law related to informants is further explored at Section 4.1.7.

[364] *District of Columbia v. Wesby*, 583 U.S. ___, 138 S. Ct. 577, 589 (2018).

[365] *State v. Bone*, 354 N.C. 1, 10-11, 550 S.E.2d 482 (2001).

[366] *State v. Bone*, 354 N.C. 1, 10-11, 550 S.E.2d 482 (2001)(quoting *Jones v. United States*, 362 U.S. 257, 269, 4 L. Ed. 2d 697, 707, 80 S. Ct. 725 (1960), *overruled on other grounds by United States v. Salvucci*, 448 U.S. 83, 65 L. Ed. 2d 619, 100 S. Ct. 2547 (1980); citing *Illinois v. Gates*, 462 U.S. 213, 244, 76 L. Ed. 2d 527, 552, 103 S. Ct. 2317 (1983)). *See also State v. Leach*, 166 N.C. App. 711, 603 S.E.2d 831 (2004).

[367] *Illinois v. Wardlow*, 528 U.S. 119, 120 S. Ct. 673 (2000).

[368] *Illinois v. Wardlow*, 528 U.S. 119, 120 S. Ct. 673, 675 (2000).

police."[369] And in developing a reasonable articulable suspicion, "nervous, evasive behavior" may be considered as a "pertinent factor." Said the Court:

> Headlong flight—wherever it occurs—is the consummate act of evasion: it is not necessarily indicative of wrongdoing, but it is certainly suggestive of such. In reviewing the propriety of an officer's conduct, courts do not have available empirical studies dealing with inferences drawn from suspicious behavior, and we cannot reasonably demand scientific certainty from judges or law enforcement officers where none exists.[370]

In *State v. Neal*,[371] Officer Herron ordered the defendant to drop his weapon and put his hands in the air. The defendant did not comply with Officer Herron's orders and instead fled the scene. Furthermore, during his flight, the defendant ran into the vehicle of the officers coming as backup for Officer Herron, and continued to flee by jumping a fence into the backyard of a nearby house. Noting that "[e]vasive conduct by the defendant is among the circumstances that may give rise to reasonable suspicion when coupled with other facts,"[372] the court held that the totality of the circumstances, including the defendant's flight, gave rise to a reasonable, articulable suspicion for his stop and subsequent arrest.

3.9. Arrest with a warrant

An arrest warrant has the purpose of interposing a probable cause determination by a neutral and detached magistrate or judge between the law enforcement officer and the person to be arrested. Placing this "check-point between the Government and the citizen implicitly acknowledges that an 'officer engaged in the often competitive enterprise of ferreting out crime' may lack sufficient objectivity to weigh correctly the strength of the evidence supporting the contemplated action against the individual's interests in protecting his own liberty and … privacy[.]"[373]

Pursuant to N.C.Gen.Stat. § 15A-401(a)(1), an officer may arrest a person when the officer has a warrant. When an arrest warrant issues, it demonstrates that a detached and neutral magistrate or judge has determined that probable cause exists to believe that the subject of the warrant has committed an offense. As such, the warrant necessarily serves to protect individuals from unreasonable searches and seizures. Once armed with an arrest warrant, a police officer has the right to execute the warrant by the arrest of the accused not only in a public place but also at his home.[374]

3.9.1. Contents of the arrest warrant

An arrest warrant must contain "a statement of the crime of which the person to be arrested is accused, and an order directing that the person so accused be arrested and held to answer to the charges made against him. It is based upon a showing of probable cause supported by oath or affirmation."[375] An arrest warrant may be served at "any time and at any place within the officer's territorial jurisdiction."[376]

3.9.1.1. Media ride-alongs

In executing an arrest warrant, the United States Supreme Court has held that a "media ride-along," where a reporter and photographer accompanied police while an arrest warrant was served in a suspect's home, violated the Constitution.[377]

---

[369] *Illinois v. Wardlow*, 528 U.S. 119, 120 S. Ct. 673, 675 (2000).

[370] *Illinois v. Wardlow*, 528 U.S. 119, 120 S. Ct. 673, 676 (2000).

[371] *State v. Neal*, 250 N.C. App. 824, 794 S.E.2d 562 (2016).

[372] *State v. Neal*, 250 N.C. App. 824, *8, 794 S.E.2d 562 (2016).

[373] *Steagald v. United States*, 451 U.S. 204, 212, 101 S. Ct. 1642, 1648 (1981) (quoting *Johnson v. United States*, 333 U.S. 10, 14, 68 S. Ct. 367, 369 (1948)).

[374] *Payton v. New York*, 455 U.S. 573, 100 S. Ct. 1371 (1980).

[375] N.C.Gen.Stat. § 15A-304.

[376] N.C.Gen.Stat. § 15A-401.

[377] *See Wilson v. Layne*, 526 U.S. 603, 119 S. Ct. 1692 (1999).

In *Wilson v. Layne*, as officers executed an arrest warrant in a private home, invited members of the media accompanied them. The officers were looking for a fugitive, Dominic Wilson, who had violated his probation on previous charges of robbery, theft, and assault. The computer report contained certain "caution indicators" that Wilson was "likely to be armed, to resist arrest, and to assaul[t] police."[378] Three arrest warrants issued for Wilson, one for each of the probation violations. Each warrant was addressed to "any duly authorized peace officer," and commanded the officer to arrest the subject and bring him "immediately" before the court. The warrants contained no reference to the presence or assistance of the media.

Holding that such a "media ride-along" violated the Fourth Amendment, the Court's analysis began with the famous *Semayne's Case* of 1603, where the English Court observed that "the house of every one is to him as his castle and fortress, as well for his defence against injury and violence, as for his repose."[379] This "centuries-old principle of the respect for the privacy of the home," is embodied in the Fourth Amendment.[380]

Although the officers in this case were entitled to enter the Wilson home in order to execute the arrest warrant for Dominic Wilson, they were not entitled to bring a newspaper reporter and a photographer with them. Clearly, the presence of reporters inside the home "was not related to the objectives of the authorized intrusion.…[T]he reporters did not engage in the execution of the warrant, and did not assist the police in their task."[381] Rather, the "Washington Post reporters in the Wilsons' home were working on a story for their own purposes. They were not present for the purpose of protecting the officers, much less the Wilsons."[382] Accordingly, the "media ride-along," employed in this case violated the Fourth Amendment.

3.9.2. Delay in making an arrest

A criminal suspect has no constitutional right to be arrested. There is no requirement that once law enforcement possesses probable cause to arrest, they do so immediately. Although the Sixth Amendment guarantees a defendant the right to a speedy trial, it does not guarantee the right to a speedy arrest.[383] However, a gap between the commission of the offense (or the time law enforcement becomes aware of it), and the arrest may be so protracted that it violates the Due Process Clause of the Fourteenth Amendment.

To prevail on such a claim, a defendant must show that (i) the delay caused actual and substantial prejudice to the defendant; and (ii) the delay was the product of deliberate action or inaction by law enforcement in order to gain a tactical advantage. To demonstrate prejudice, the defendant must show that real and tangible harm was done to her defense. The mere passage of time, and its effects, is not sufficient. The fact that "memories will dim, witnesses become inaccessible, and evidence will be lost" during the gap is inadequate to demonstrate that the defendant cannot receive a fair trial and insufficient to show a Due Process violation.[384]

3.9.3. Protective sweeps

In *Maryland v. Buie*,[385] the Supreme Court held that, during the course of an in-home arrest, law enforcement officers may conduct a "protective sweep" of the premises so long as the officers possess specific and articulable facts which, taken together with the rational inferences from those facts, give rise to a reasonable suspicion "that the area to be swept harbors an individual posing a danger to those on the arrest scene." In addition, "as an incident to the arrest, the officers [may], as a precautionary matter and *without probable cause or reasonable suspicion*, look in closets and other spaces immediately adjoining the place of arrest from which an attack could be launched."[386] Such a protective sweep, however, is aimed only at protecting the arresting

---

[378] *Wilson v. Layne*, 526 U.S. 603, 119 S. Ct. 1692, 1695 (1999).

[379] *Semayne's Case*, 77 Eng.Rep. 194, 195 (K.B. 1603).

[380] *Wilson v. Layne*, 526 U.S. 603, 119 S. Ct. 1692, 1697 (1999).

[381] *Wilson v. Layne*, 526 U.S. 603, 119 S. Ct. 1692, 1698 (1999).

[382] *Wilson v. Layne*, 526 U.S. 603, 119 S. Ct. 1692, 1698 (1999).

[383] *See Hoffa v. United States*, 385 U.S. 293, 310, 87 S. Ct. 408, 417 (1966).

[384] *United States v. Marion*, 404 U.S. 307, 92 S. Ct. 455 (1971) (without an arrest, the period of three years that lapsed between the end of defendants' crime and their indictment did not implicate the Sixth Amendment speedy trial provision).

[385] *Maryland v. Buie*, 494 U.S. 325, 110 S. Ct. 1093, 1098-99 (1990).

[386] *Maryland v. Buie*, 494 U.S. 325, 110 S. Ct. 1093, 1098-99 (1990) (emphasis added).

officers; it is *not* a full search of the premises, but only a brief "cursory inspection of those spaces where a person may be found."[387]

In *State v. Dial*,[388] the Court of Appeals of North Carolina upheld a protective sweep where deputies were attempting to serve an order for arrest. There, the defendant did not open the door until after 10 to 15 minutes of Deputy Burger knocking and announcing his presence, although Deputy Burger did hear shuffling on the other side of the door. Suddenly, the defendant stepped out with his hands raised. The court found the following factors provided a proper basis for the protective sweep: "[D]efendant's unusually long response time and resistance, the known potential threat of weapons inside the residence, shuffling noises that could have indicated more than one person inside the residence, defendant's alarming exit from the residence, and defendant's own actions that led him to be arrested in the open doorway."[389] The court noted that the deputies who performed the sweep did so quickly and that "they only looked in places where a person might be hiding."[390] Thus, the sweep was justified and the motion to suppress the evidence found in plain view during the sweep was properly denied.

In *State v. Wallace*,[391] the officers did not have reasonable and articulate suspicion to justify a protective sweep. In that case, officers were at a residence to gain information. The defendant answered the door immediately and offered no resistance. While the officers questioned the defendant, the door to the residence was closed behind them. "Defendants Jolly and Troy Wallace at all times talked to the officers in a calm manner and up until the time the officers heard footsteps in the residence, the interview with defendants Jolly and Wallace had been non-threatening. Although the officers did hear footsteps in the residence, the officers admitted in their testimony at trial that they were not afraid nor did they feel they were in a dangerous situation."[392] Under these circumstances, the protective sweep was not justified.

3.10. Arrest without a warrant

While the law certainly prefers that an arrest be made pursuant to a warrant, a law enforcement officer is nonetheless permitted to effect a *warrantless* arrest when she has probable cause to believe that a crime has been or is being committed and that the person to be arrested is a criminal participant. In this context, the term "crime" many times referred to as "felony," encompasses those offenses which carry a penalty of imprisonment for a year or more.

N.C.Gen.Stat. § 15A-401(b) provides for arrests without a warrant as follows:

Arrest by Officer Without a Warrant.—
(1) Offense in Presence of Officer.—An officer may arrest without a warrant any person who the officer has probable cause to believe has committed a criminal offense, or has violated a pretrial release order entered under G.S. 15A-534 or G.S. 15A-534.1(a)(2), in the officer's presence.
(2) Offense Out of Presence of Officer.— An officer may arrest without a warrant any person who the officer has probable cause to believe:
  a. Has committed a felony; or
  b. Has committed a misdemeanor, and:
    1. Will not be apprehended unless immediately arrested, or
    2. May cause physical injury to himself or others, or damage to property unless immediately arrested; or
  c. Has committed a misdemeanor under G.S. 14-72.1, 14-134.3, 20-138.1, or 20-138.2; or
  d. Has committed a misdemeanor under G.S. 14-33(a), 14-33(c)(1), 14-33(c)(2), or 14-34 when the offense was committed by a person with whom the alleged victim has a personal relationship as defined in G.S. 50B-1; or

---

[387] *Maryland v. Buie*, 494 U.S. 325, 110 S. Ct. 1093, 1099 (1990) (emphasis added).
[388] *State v. Dial*, 228 N.C. App. 83, 744 S.E.2d 144 (2013).
[389] *State v. Dial*, 228 N.C. App. 83, 89, 744 S.E.2d 144 (2013).
[390] *State v. Dial*, 228 N.C. App. 83, 89, 744 S.E.2d 144 (2013).
[391] *State v. Wallace*, 111 N.C. App. 581, 433 S.E.2d 238 (1993).
[392] *State v. Wallace*, 111 N.C. App. 581, 588, 433 S.E.2d 238 (1993).

e. Has committed a misdemeanor under G.S. 50B-4.1(a); or

f. Has violated a pretrial release order entered under G.S. 15A-534 or G.S. 15A-534.1(a)(2).

(3) Repealed by Session Laws 1991, c. 150.

(4) A law enforcement officer may detain an individual arrested for violation of an order limiting freedom of movement or access issued pursuant to G.S. 130A-475 or G.S. 130A-145 in the area designated by the State Health Director or local health director pursuant to such order. The person may be detained in such area until the initial appearance before a judicial official pursuant to G.S. 15A-511 and G.S. 15A-534.5.

When an officer must decide whether a warrantless arrest in a given set of circumstances is justified, she is not confined to consideration only of evidence admissible in a courtroom. Rather, the officer may consider all the facts and circumstances surrounding the prospective arrest, even that information coming from (preferably reliable) hearsay sources, when making the probable cause determination.

Once probable cause exists for the arrest of an individual, the arrest may take place without a warrant when it is effected in a public place. The Fourth Amendment permits such warrantless (felony) arrests even though the law enforcement officer had sufficient time to obtain a warrant.[393]

In *United States v. Watson*,[394] the Supreme Court refused to place a requirement of more than probable cause in a warrantless arrest situation. According to the Court, to require more than probable cause—*e.g.*, probable cause and exigent circumstances—would "encumber criminal prosecutions with endless litigation with respect to the existence of exigent circumstances, whether it was practicable to get a warrant, whether the suspect was about to flee, and the like."[395] Accordingly, the two critical components for warrantless criminal arrests remain: (1) probable cause, and (2) an offense punishable by imprisonment for a year or more.

Respecting lower level offenses, *i.e.*, offenses punishable by imprisonment for less than one year, most jurisdictions require that the offense occur *in the presence* of the law enforcement officer. *"Presence,"* in this respect, means that the arresting officer has gained knowledge of the offense directly, and this may be accomplished by the use of any of his senses.[396]

Most commonly, the "in presence" requirement is satisfied by an officer directly viewing or seeing the offense occur, even if the officer uses a telescope or binoculars. The "in presence" requirement may also be satisfied if the officer witnesses the offense through her sense of hearing, smell or touch. In this regard, it is not enough that an officer uses his senses *to learn that an offense has been committed*. The offense must be committed at the time the officer is on the scene. For example, an officer would not be authorized to make an in-presence arrest for a minor assault merely because he has been told by the victim that the perpetrator, who is still present at the scene, struck her prior to the arrival of the officer. This is so even if the victim's story is largely corroborated by the officer's observation of signs of injury on the victim's body. It has also been held that a minor theft offense did not occur in the officer's presence in a case where the officer viewed a grocery store's videotape of the offender engaging in the alleged shoplifting offense.[397]

There are, however, certain statutory exceptions to this rule.[398] An officer may make a warrantless arrest for an assault or battery when the suspect has a child in common with the victim, resides or has resided in the same household as the victim, has or has had a dating relationship with the victim, or is a spouse or former spouse of the victim, regardless of whether or not the offense occurs in the officer's presence.[399]

---

[393] *United States v. Watson*, 423 U.S. 411, 96 S. Ct. 820 (1976) (upholding a warrantless arrest, based upon probable cause, effected by a postal inspector at a public restaurant).

[394] *United States v. Watson*, 423 U.S. 411, 96 S. Ct. 820 (1976).

[395] *United States v. Watson*, 423 U.S. 411, 423-24, 96 S. Ct. 820, 828 (1976).

[396] *See Atwater v. City of Lago Vista*, 532 U.S. 318, 354, 121 S. Ct. 1536, 1557 (2001) ("If an officer has probable cause to believe that an individual has committed even a very minor criminal offense in his presence, he may, without violating the Fourth Amendment, arrest the offender.").

[397] *See Forgie-Buccioni v. Hannaford Bros., Inc.*, 413 F.3d 175, 180 (1st Cir. 2005) (a videotape alone does not provide a sufficient basis to satisfy the "in presence" requirement for warrantless arrests).

[398] *See* N.C.Gen.Stat. § 15A-401(b)(2)(c), (d), (e).

[399] *See* N.C.Gen.Stat. § 15A-401(b)(2)(d).

Naturally, if an officer actually observes someone committing an offense, then there is probable cause to make an arrest. Where the officer does not witness the actual acts that constitute the offense, circumstantial evidence may nonetheless provide probable cause to believe the crime has been committed.

In *Maryland v. Pringle*,[400] a car with three male occupants was stopped for speeding in the early morning hours. When the driver retrieved his license from the glove compartment, an officer noticed a large amount of cash. Because he found this suspicious, the officer asked for and received consent to search the car. Police found $763 in the glove compartment and five glassine bags of cocaine between the backseat armrest and the backseat. All three men denied ownership of the drug. Because the cocaine was accessible to all the men, it was reasonable to infer all three had knowledge of it and exercised domain and control over it. Police therefore had probable cause to arrest all three occupants, including the defendant, the front-seat passenger.

Note: *Private Persons.* A private person may "assist law-enforcement officers in effecting arrests and preventing escapes from custody when requested to do so by the officer. When so requested, a private person has the same authority to effect an arrest or prevent escape from custody as the officer making the request."[401] Otherwise, "[n]o private person may arrest another person."[402] However, pursuant to N.C.Gen.Stat. § 15A-404(b):

> A private person may detain another person when he has probable cause to believe that the person detained has committed in his presence:
> **(1)** A felony,
> **(2)** A breach of the peace,
> **(3)** A crime involving physical injury to another person, or
> **(4)** A crime involving theft or destruction of property.

The "detention must be in a reasonable manner considering the offense involved and the circumstances of the detention."[403] In addition:

> The detention may be no longer than the time required for the earliest of the following:
> **(1)** The determination that no offense has been committed.
> **(2)** Surrender of the person detained to a law-enforcement officer.[404]

Finally, "[a] private person who detains another must immediately notify a law-enforcement officer and must, unless he releases the person earlier...surrender the person detained to the law-enforcement officer."[405]

3.11. Entry of a dwelling to effect an arrest

In a landmark decision, the United States Supreme Court, in *Payton v. New* York,[406] held that, absent exigent circumstances, a law enforcement officer may not make a warrantless, nonconsensual entry into a suspect's home to arrest him, even though probable cause exists to believe the suspect is, in fact, the perpetrator of a felony. "[T]he Fourth Amendment has drawn a firm line at the entrance to the house. Absent exigent circumstances, that threshold may not reasonably be crossed without a warrant."[407]

According to the court, "physical entry of the home is the chief evil against which the wording of the Fourth Amendment is directed."[408] In the context of warrantless home entries, it should be emphasized that

---

[400] *Maryland v. Pringle*, 540 U.S. 366, 124 S. Ct. 795 (2003).
[401] N.C.Gen.Stat. § 15A-405(a).
[402] N.C.Gen.Stat. § 15A-404(a).
[403] N.C.Gen.Stat. § 15A-404(c).
[404] N.C.Gen.Stat. § 15A-404(d).
[405] N.C.Gen.Stat. § 15A-404(e).
[406] *Payton v. New York*, 445 U.S. 573, 100 S. Ct. 1371, 1374-75 (1980).
[407] *Payton v. New York*, 445 U.S. 573, 100 S. Ct. 1371, 1374-75 (1980).
[408] *United States v. United States Dist. Court*, 407 U.S. 297, 313, 92 S. Ct. 2125, 2134 (1972).

the doctrine of "exigent circumstances" will permit such an intrusion only where there is also probable cause to enter the home.

The federal Supreme Court has also accorded Fourth Amendment protection to hotel rooms. Similar to the home, absent exigent circumstances or consent, police officers need to meet the requirements of the Fourth Amendment before searching or seizing things or persons from hotel or motel rooms.[409]

3.11.1. The requirement of exigent circumstances in addition to probable cause

In *Kirk v. Louisiana*,[410] police officers conducted a surveillance of the defendant's home, based on an anonymous tip that drug sales were occurring there. After witnessing what appeared to be several drug purchases and allowing the buyers to leave the area, the officers stopped one of the buyers on the street outside the defendant's apartment. Immediately thereafter, the officers knocked on the door of the apartment, entered, and placed the defendant under arrest. A search incident to the arrest uncovered a vial of cocaine found in the defendant's underwear. In addition, while in the apartment, the officers observed other contraband in "plain view." Finding the entry, arrest and search invalid under the rule set forth in *Payton*, the United States Supreme Court said:

> Here, the police had neither an arrest warrant for [defendant], nor a search warrant for [his] apartment, when they entered his home, arrested him, and searched him. The officers testified at the suppression hearing that the reason for their actions was a fear that evidence would be destroyed, but the Louisiana Court of Appeal did not determine that such exigent circumstances were present....As *Payton* makes plain, police officers need either a warrant or probable cause plus exigent circumstances in order to make a lawful entry into a home.[411]

3.11.2. Exigent circumstances further explored

Generally, exigent circumstances are explained as those surrounding a fast moving, often tense, series of events which call for quick and decisive law enforcement action. These are factors that allow law enforcement agents to conduct a warrantless arrest, based on probable cause, when there exists an urgent need for official action and time to secure a warrant is not available. Factors considered in determining if exigent circumstances are present include: (i) whether the crime under investigation was recently committed; (ii) whether the offense was violent in nature; (iii) whether there was a reasonable belief the suspect was armed; (iv) the level of certainty that the suspect committed the offense; (v) the level of certainty that the suspect is in the building; (vi) whether the circumstances indicate that the suspect is a flight risk; (vii) the time of day; and (viii) the level of force officers need to obtain entry to the premises.[412]

The police generally must be unable to obtain a warrant in the time necessary to meet and defuse the situation, or at the very least, contacting a magistrate must be extremely impractical (*e.g.*, late hour, remote location). In such situations, the requirement of a warrant may be excused. The presence of these extreme circumstances mandates the compelling need for quick activity and makes warrantless in-home arrests reasonable within the meaning of the Fourth Amendment. If such circumstances were not present, a warrant would be required. Often cited examples of the risks created when officers hesitate in making a warrantless in-home arrest and instead seek to obtain a warrant before acting include the following: (i) the risk of injury or death to officers or bystanders; (ii) the potential destruction or concealment of valuable evidence; or (iii) the possibility that the suspect may flee and elude capture.

---

[409] *See e.g., Stoner v. California,* 376 U.S. 483, 487-88, 84 S. Ct. 889 (1964) (hotel clerk had no authority to permit a search of a defendant's room); *United States v. Jeffers,* 342 U.S. 48 51-52, 72 S. Ct. 93 (1951) (search of a hotel room not exclusively used by a defendant invalid absent exigent circumstances or consent); *McDonald v. United States,* 335 U.S. 451, 454, 69 S. Ct. 191 (1948) (no compelling reason to justify the search of a hotel room); *Johnson v. United States,* 333 U.S. 10, 14-15, 68 S. Ct. 367 (1948) (search of a hotel room without a warrant constitutionally invalid).

[410] *Kirk v. Louisiana,* 536 U.S. 635, 122 S. Ct. 2458 (2002).

[411] *Kirk v. Louisiana,* 536 U.S. 635, 122 S. Ct. 2458, 2459 (2002).

[412] *See, e.g., Dorman v. United States,* 435 F.2d 385 (D.C. Cir. 1970).

3.11.2.1. Community caretaking and emergency aid

Police officers may also enter a premise without a warrant to protect individuals in distress, to assist victims of crimes that have just occurred, or to investigate suspicious signs of impending danger. For an extended discussion of the "community caretaking" function of the police and the "emergency aid" exception to the warrant requirement, refer to §4.2.2.4 and §4.2.2.5.

Entering a home to stop a fight. In *Brigham City v. Stuart*,[413] four officers responded to a loud party at a residence at around 3:00 a.m. When they arrived, they heard sounds of an altercation occurring inside—"thumping and crashing" as well as people yelling "stop, stop" and "get off me." The officers looked in the front window but saw nothing; because the sounds seemed to be coming from the back of the house, they proceeded down the driveway to investigate further. From the end of the driveway, they could see two juveniles drinking beer in the back yard. When they entered the back yard, they saw an altercation taking place in the kitchen through a screen door and windows. "[F]our adults were attempting, with some difficulty, to restrain a juvenile." The juvenile, fists clenched, eventually "broke free, swung a fist and struck one of the adults in the face."[414] That adult then spit blood into the sink. The other three adults continued to restrain the juvenile, pressing him against a refrigerator with such force that it slid across the floor. The officers called out but were ignored. They then entered the residence and broke up the fight. The adults were arrested for contributing to the delinquency of a minor (because of the juveniles outside with beer), disorderly conduct and intoxication. The U.S. Supreme Court upheld this warrantless entry under the Fourth Amendment. According to the Court, the officers were confronted with ongoing violence. They had an objectively reasonable belief that "both the injured adult might need help and that the violence in the kitchen was just beginning." The Court noted that police are not required to wait until someone is unconscious (or semi-conscious) before entering: "The role of a peace officer includes preventing violence and restoring order, not simply rendering first aid to casualties; an officer is not like a boxing (or hockey) referee, poised to stop a bout only if it becomes too one-sided."[415]

3.11.2.2. Hot pursuit

Hot pursuit can be thought of as a specific application of the general "exigent circumstances" exception. In *Warden v. Hayden*,[416] the U.S. Supreme Court held that if police were in hot pursuit of a fleeing suspect, they were entitled to make a warrantless entry to effectuate the arrest if they had probable cause to believe the suspect committed a felony, and they believed he entered a specific dwelling. For example, if a drug dealer runs into a house when police approach her after a controlled buy and after they identify themselves, the officers may follow her into the house to make their arrest.[417] In *Welsh v. Wisconsin*,[418] however, the United States Supreme Court held this exception was not always applicable in situations where the suspect commits a misdemeanor, traffic offense, or other non-jailable or minor infraction.[419] In *Stanton v. Sims,* the U.S. Supreme Court pointed out that *Welsh* did not hold that a warrantless entry to arrest a misdemeanant is never justified, "but only that such entry should be rare."[420]

To justify a warrantless in-home arrest based on this exception, the prosecution must generally demonstrate that: (i) the pursuit was undertaken immediately after the crime (*i.e.*, it was "hot"); and (ii) there was a continuity of pursuit from the crime to the place of arrest.

Note also that a suspect may not, however, defeat an arrest which has been set in motion in a public place (*e.g.*, outside the doorway of the suspect's home), by retreating into the home.[421]

---

[413] *Brigham City v. Stuart*, 547 U.S. 398, 126 S. Ct. 1943 (2006).
[414] *Brigham City v. Stuart*, 547 U.S. 398, 126 S. Ct. 1943, 1946 (2006).
[415] *Brigham City v. Stuart*, 547 U.S. 398, 126 S. Ct. 1943, 1949 (2006).
[416] *Warden v. Hayden,* 387 U.S. 294, 87 S. Ct. 1642 (1967).
[417] *See Smith v. Stoneburner,* 716 F.3d 926 (6th Cir. 2013).
[418] *Welsh v. Wisconsin*, 466 U.S. 740, 104 S. Ct. 2091 (1984).
[419] *But see Stanton v. Sims*, 571 U.S. 3, 134 S. Ct. 3 (2013) (recognizing that courts are divided on the legality of warrantless hot-pursuit home entries for minor offenses).
[420] *Stanton v. Sims*, 571 U.S. 3, 134 S. Ct. 3, 6 (2013).
[421] *United States v. Santana*, 427 U.S. 38, 96 S. Ct. 2406 (1976).

3.11.3. Consent

Naturally, an entry to a home for an arrest will be lawful when based on a valid consent. Valid consent to enter may be given by the owner, or one entitled to possession of the premises, or one with common control or joint access to the premises for most purposes. Valid consent is that which is given voluntarily (*i.e.*, in the absence of overbearing conduct on the part of the law enforcement officials seeking permission), knowingly and intelligently. Consent may be either actually given or implied from conduct or acts. The validity, or voluntariness, of consent is determined by examining all of the facts and circumstances surrounding the encounter.

Under the "consent once removed" doctrine, if: (i) an undercover officer or informant enters a residence at the express invitation of someone with authority to consent; (ii) probable cause to arrest is established; and (iii) the officer or informant immediately summons help, then other officers may enter the residence to make an arrest.[422]

3.11.4. *Payton* violations and the limits of the exclusionary rule

Exactly how far will the exclusionary rule reach when a court determines that officers have violated the rule in *Payton* by effecting a warrantless nonconsensual entry into a suspect's home in order to make a routine felony arrest? In *New York v. Harris*,[423] the Supreme Court held that only that evidence which is obtained inside the home is the proper subject of suppression. So long as police have the requisite probable cause for the suspect's arrest (for a crime), any physical evidence or statements validly obtained after the arrest and outside the home will not be suppressed when neither is "the fruit of the fact that the arrest was made in the house rather than someplace else."[424] In this respect, the Court reasoned: "Even though we decline to suppress statements made *outside* the home following a *Payton* violation, the principal incentive to obey *Payton* still obtains: the police know that a warrantless entry will lead to the suppression of any evidence found or statements taken *inside* the home." Further, the Court observed:

> Nothing in the reasoning of [the *Payton*] case suggests that an arrest in a home without a warrant but with probable cause somehow renders unlawful continued custody of the suspect once he is removed from the house. There could be no valid claim here that Harris is immune from prosecution because his person was the fruit of an illegal arrest.... Nor is there any claim that the warrantless arrest required the police to release Harris or that Harris could not be immediately rearrested if momentarily released. Because the officers had probable cause to arrest Harris for a crime, Harris was not unlawfully in custody when he was removed to the station house, given *Miranda* warnings and allowed to talk.[425]

3.11.4.1. Minor offenses

In *Welsh v. Wisconsin*,[426] the Supreme Court held that the Fourth Amendment prohibits the warrantless entry into a suspect's home to effect his arrest when the underlying offense is a "nonjailable traffic offense," and the circumstances do not amount to an exigency. Hot-pursuit entries may receive different treatment by the courts.[427]

3.12. Entry of the home of a third party

Absent consent or exigent circumstances, law enforcement officers may not lawfully "search for the subject of an arrest warrant in the home of a third party without first obtaining a search warrant." This was made clear by the United States Supreme Court in *Steagald v. United States*.[428]

---

[422] *See United States v. Pollard*, 215 F.3d 643 (6th Cir. 2000).

[423] *New York v. Harris*, 495 U.S. 14, 110 S. Ct. 1640 (1990).

[424] *New York v. Harris*, 495 U.S. 14, 110 S. Ct. 1640, 1644 (1990).

[425] *New York v. Harris*, 495 U.S. 14, 110 S. Ct. 1640, 1643 (1990).

[426] *Welsh v. Wisconsin*, 466 U.S. 740, 104 S. Ct. 2091, 2093 (1984).

[427] *See e.g., Stanton v. Sims*, 571 U.S. 3, 134 S. Ct. 3 (2013).

[428] *Steagald v. United States*, 451 U.S. 204, 101 S. Ct. 1642 (1981).

3.13. The "knock and announce" rule

When executing an arrest warrant, law enforcement officers should knock on the door of a residence or business, announce their purpose and authority, and give the occupants a reasonable opportunity to answer before forcing their way inside.[429]

Under the rule, in order to enter a private home to make an arrest or to carry out a search, a police officer must expressly announce the purpose of his coming.[430] Along with a statement of the purpose of his coming, the officer must make a request for admittance before entering the house. These requirements have the two-fold purpose of protecting the privacy of residents by preventing police entry of the home without reasonable warning; and it reduces the possibility of danger to officer and citizen alike which might result from misunderstanding and misinterpretation of the purpose of the entry.

Compliance with the "knock and announce" rule is also mandated by North Carolina law and has been codified at N.C.Gen.Stat. § 15A-401(e) which provides in part:

A law-enforcement officer may enter private premises or a vehicle to effect an arrest when … [t]he officer has given, or made reasonable effort to give, notice of his authority and purpose to an occupant thereof, unless there is reasonable cause to believe that the giving of such notice would present a clear danger to human life.

Strict compliance with the rule may be excused in cases where exigent circumstances are present, or if events indicated that compliance with the "knock and announce" statute would be a useless gesture. Exigent circumstances exist where there is a good faith belief by the officer that evidence will be destroyed, an arrest will be frustrated or that lives will be endangered by delay. This rule applies even if a door is found open.[431] As held in *Richards v. Wisconsin*,[432] "[a] no-knock entry is justified when the police have a reasonable suspicion that knocking and announcing their presence, under the particular circumstances, would be dangerous or futile, or that it would inhibit the effective investigation of the crime, for example, allowing the destruction of evidence." This standard, held the Court, "as opposed to a probable cause requirement, strikes the appropriate balance between the legitimate law enforcement concerns at issue in the execution of search warrants and the individual privacy interests affected by no-knock entries[.] This showing is not high, but the police should be required to make it whenever the reasonableness of a no-knock entry is challenged."[433]

Pursuant to a federal Supreme Court ruling, a knock-and-announce violation does not trigger the exclusionary rule, particularly when the discovery of the evidence was independent of the officers' failure to comply with the statutory knock-and-announce requirement.[434]

In *State v. Narcisse*,[435] the court found sufficient compliance with the requirements that entrance be demanded and denied before a police officer can forcibly enter a dwelling for the purpose of making an arrest, "where the officer knocked, identified himself twice, heard a lot of scrambling and running noises coming from within the dwelling, and received no reply before he forcibly opened the door."[436]

3.14. Use of force to effect an arrest

The general rule is that reasonable force may be used to place a suspect under arrest. The permissible quantum of force employed varies from situation to situation. The analysis applied by courts to determine

---

[429] *See Ker v. California*, 374 U.S. 23, 83 S. Ct. 1623 (1963).

[430] *Miller v. United States*, 357 U.S. 301, 78 S. Ct. 1190 (1958).

[431] *Richards v. Wisconsin*, 520 U.S. 385, 117 S. Ct. 1416, 1421-22 (1997).

[432] *Richards v. Wisconsin*, 520 U.S. 385, 117 S. Ct. 1416 (1997).

[433] *Richards v. Wisconsin*, 520 U.S. 385, 117 S. Ct. 1416, 1421-22 (1997).

[434] *See Hudson v. Michigan*, 547 U.S. 586, 599, 126 S. Ct. 2159 (2006) ("[T]he social costs of applying the exclusionary rule to knock-and-announce violations are considerable; the incentive to such violations is minimal to begin with, and … the massive remedy of suppressing evidence of guilt is unjustified.").

[435] State v. Narcisse, 90 N.C. App. 414, 368 S.E.2d 654, cert. denied, 323 N.C. 368, 373 S.E.2d 553 (1988).

[436] State v. Narcisse, 90 N.C. App. 414, 422, 368 S.E.2d 654, cert. denied, 323 N.C. 368, 373 S.E.2d 553 (1988).

the reasonableness of an officer's actions, focuses on the police conduct, viewed objectively, in light of the circumstances confronting the officers at the time, without regard to their subjective intent or motivation.

All claims that "law enforcement officers have used excessive force—deadly or not—in the course of an arrest, investigatory stop, or other 'seizure' of a free citizen should be analyzed under the Fourth Amendment and its 'reasonableness' standard, rather than under a 'substantive due process' approach."[437] In this context, a "seizure" "triggering the Fourth Amendment's protections occurs only when government actors have, by means of physical force or show of authority," in some way "restrained the liberty of a citizen."

The proper application of force in the context of an arrest or investigatory stop requires "careful attention to the facts and circumstances of each particular case, including *the severity of the crime at issue, whether the suspect poses an immediate threat to the safety of the officers or others, and whether he is actively resisting arrest or attempting to evade arrest by flight.*"[438]

The ultimate inquiry is whether a reasonable officer, confronted with the same circumstances, would have reacted in the same way. Once a use of force is deemed reasonable under *Graham v. Connor,* it may not be found unreasonable by reference to some separate, earlier constitutional violation.[439]

Officers cannot use force—including pepper spray—on a detainee who has been subdued, has not been told he is under arrest, or has not been resisting arrest. Even when a suspect verbally and physically resists arrest, the use of pepper spray may constitute excessive force—for example if the crime was minor and the arrestee does not pose an immediate threat to officers. Finally, even when the use of pepper spray is justified, using a large amount (for example, enough to make a suspect pass out) or using the spray at a very close distance may constitute excessive force.[440]

In some situations, the use of deadly force is reasonable within the meaning of the Fourth Amendment. Deadly force does not mean force that necessarily results in the death of the suspect, but rather a level of force that is reasonably likely to cause death or serious bodily injury resulting in death. In *Tennessee v. Garner,*[441] the United States Supreme Court described the circumstances under which the use of deadly force may be reasonable for purposes of the Fourth Amendment. The Court said: "Where the officer has probable cause to believe that the suspect poses a threat of serious physical harm, either to the officer or to others, it is not constitutionally unreasonable to prevent escape by using deadly force." Thus, if the suspect threatens the officer with a weapon or there is probable cause to believe that he has committed a crime involving the "infliction or threatened infliction of serious physical harm," the use of deadly force is permissible. If the officer does not have probable cause to believe the above, reasonable, non-deadly force must be used to effect the arrest.

N.C.Gen.Stat. § 15A-401(d) and (e) provide:

(d) Use of Force in Arrest.—

  (1) Subject to the provisions of subdivision (2), a law-enforcement officer is justified in using force upon another person when and to the extent that he reasonably believes it necessary:

  a. To prevent the escape from custody or to effect an arrest of a person who he reasonably believes has committed a criminal offense, unless he knows that the arrest is unauthorized; or

  b. To defend himself or a third person from what he reasonably believes to be the use or imminent use of physical force while effecting or attempting to effect an arrest or while preventing or attempting to prevent an escape.

  (2) A law-enforcement officer is justified in using deadly physical force upon another person for a purpose specified in subdivision (1) of this subsection only when it is or appears to be reasonably necessary thereby:

  a. To defend himself or a third person from what he reasonably believes to be the use or imminent use of deadly physical force;

  b. To effect an arrest or to prevent the escape from custody of a person who he reasonably believes is attempting to escape by means of a deadly weapon, or who by his conduct or any

---

[437] *Graham v. Connor,* 490 U.S. 386, 109 S. Ct. 1865, 1871 (1989).

[438] *Graham v. Connor,* 490 U.S. 386, 109 S. Ct. 1865, 1871-72 (1989) (emphasis added).

[439] *See County of Los Angeles v. Mendez,* 581 U.S. ___, 137 S. Ct. 1539 (2017).

[440] *Grawey v. Drury,* 567 F.3d 302 (6th Cir. 2009).

[441] *Tennessee v. Garner,* 471 U.S. 1, 105 S. Ct. 1694 (1985).

other means indicates that he presents an imminent threat of death or serious physical injury to others unless apprehended without delay; or

c. To prevent the escape of a person from custody imposed upon him as a result of conviction for a felony.

Nothing in this subdivision constitutes justification for willful, malicious or criminally negligent conduct by any person which injures or endangers any person or property, nor shall it be construed to excuse or justify the use of unreasonable or excessive force.

(e) Entry on Private Premises or Vehicle; Use of Force.—

(1) A law-enforcement officer may enter private premises or a vehicle to effect an arrest when:

a. The officer has in his possession a warrant or order or a copy of the warrant or order for the arrest of a person, provided that an officer may utilize a copy of a warrant or order only if the original warrant or order is in the possession of a member of a law enforcement agency located in the county where the officer is employed and the officer verifies with the agency that the warrant is current and valid; or the officer is authorized to arrest a person without a warrant or order having been issued,

b. The officer has reasonable cause to believe the person to be arrested is present, and

c. The officer has given, or made reasonable effort to give, notice of his authority and purpose to an occupant thereof, unless there is reasonable cause to believe that the giving of such notice would present a clear danger to human life.

(2) The law-enforcement officer may use force to enter the premises or vehicle if he reasonably believes that admittance is being denied or unreasonably delayed, or if he is authorized under subsection (e)(1)c to enter without giving notice of his authority and purpose.

3.15. Procedures after arrest

Whenever a law enforcement officer arrests a person, the officer:

(1) Must inform the person arrested of the charge against him or the cause for his arrest.

(2) Must, with respect to any person arrested without a warrant and, for purpose of setting bail, with respect to any person arrested upon a warrant or order for arrest, take the person arrested before a judicial official without unnecessary delay.

(3) May, prior to taking the person before a judicial official, take the person arrested to some other place if the person so requests.

(4) May, prior to taking the person before a judicial official, take the person arrested to some other place if such action is reasonably necessary for the purpose of having that person identified.

(5) Must without unnecessary delay advise the person arrested of his right to communicate with counsel and friends and must allow him reasonable time and reasonable opportunity to do so.

(6) Must make available to the State on a timely basis all materials and information acquired in the course of all felony investigations. This responsibility is a continuing affirmative duty.[442]

No right to delay an arrest for prayer. In *Sause v. Bauer*,[443] the Supreme Court held that once an officer places a suspect under arrest and orders the suspect to enter a police vehicle for transportation to jail, the suspect has no right to delay that trip by insisting on first engaging in prayer—"conduct that, at another time, would be protected by the First Amendment." According to the Court, there is "no doubt that the First Amendment protects the right to pray. Prayer unquestionably constitutes the 'exercise' of religion. At the same time, there are clearly circumstances in which a police officer may lawfully prevent a person from praying at a particular time and place. For example, if an officer places a suspect under arrest and orders the suspect to enter a police vehicle for transportation to jail, the suspect does not have a right to delay that trip by insisting on first

---

[442] N.C.Gen.Stat. § 15A-501.
[443] *Sause v. Bauer*, 138 S. Ct. 2561 (2018).

engaging in conduct that, at another time, would be protected by the First Amendment."[444] However, "[w]hen an officer's order to stop praying is alleged to have occurred during the course of investigative conduct that implicates Fourth Amendment rights, the First and Fourth Amendment issues may be inextricable."[445]

When an individual is the subject of a warrantless arrest, he is entitled to a prompt judicial determination of probable cause. Note that if the person had been arrested pursuant to a warrant, a judge has already made a probable cause determination as a prerequisite to issuing the warrant.

A prompt judicial determination of probable cause has been held to mean that a judicial hearing must be held as soon as is reasonably feasible, and that should be *within 48 hours of the arrest*.[446]

A hearing provided within 48 hours may violate the promptness requirement if the arrested individual can prove that the probable cause determination was delayed in an unreasonable manner. Examples of unreasonable delays are ones for the purpose of gathering additional evidence against the defendant, or ones motivated by ill will toward the defendant. The judicial probable cause determination may be combined with other proceedings, like an arraignment. If the state fails to provide a determination within this 48-hour window, the burden of proof shifts to the government to demonstrate the existence of an emergency or other extraordinary circumstance justifying the delay. In evaluating whether a delay in a particular case is unreasonable, courts will allow a substantial degree of flexibility.

The government cannot justify the failure to provide a determination within 48 hours on the basis of an intervening weekend (*e.g.*, a person arrested on Thursday not given a hearing until Monday).

3.15.1. Authority to obtain fingerprints and photographs

Once a person is lawfully arrested and brought to police headquarters to be detained in custody, the person must be accurately identified. In this regard, "criminal identification is said to have two main purposes: (1) The identification of the accused as the person who committed the crime for which he is being held; and (2) the identification of the accused as the same person who has been previously charged with, or convicted of, other offenses against criminal law."[447] Thus, courts have determined that the process of fingerprinting and photographing arrestees is "a natural part of 'the administrative steps incident to arrest.'"[448] In fact, by the "middle of the 20th century, it was considered 'elementary that a person in lawful custody may be required to submit to photographing and fingerprinting as part of routine identification process.'"[449]

When the arrest is for a serious offense, taking and analyzing a cheek swab of the arrestee's DNA is, like fingerprinting and photographing, a legitimate police booking procedure that is reasonable under the Fourth Amendment.[450]

North Carolina has codified the procedure for taking photographs and fingerprints at N.C.Gen.Stat. § 15A-502 which provides:

§ 15A-502. Photographs and fingerprints
(a) A person charged with the commission of a felony or a misdemeanor may be photographed and his fingerprints may be taken for law-enforcement records only when he has been:
(1) Arrested or committed to a detention facility, or
(2) Committed to imprisonment upon conviction of a crime, or
(3) Convicted of a felony.

---

[444] *Sause v. Bauer,* 138 S. Ct. 2561 (2018).

[445] The Freedom of Religion clause set forth in the First Amendment clearly applies to the States through the Due Process Clause of the Fourteenth Amendment. *See Cantwell v. Connecticut,* 310 U.S. 296, 303-304, 60 S. Ct. 900, 903 (1940) (As is true with Congress, state legislatures shall make no law respecting an establishment of religion or prohibiting the free exercise thereof).

[446] *County of Riverside v. McLaughlin,* 500 U.S. 44, 111 S. Ct. 1661 (1991).

[447] *Maryland v. King,* 569 U.S. 435, 133 S. Ct. 1958, 1975 (2013) (internal quotes and citation omitted).

[448] *County of Riverside v. McLaughlin,* 500 U.S. 44, 58, 111 S. Ct. 1661 (1991); *Maryland v. King,* 569 U.S. 435, 133 S. Ct. 1958, 1976 (2013).

[449] *Maryland v. King,* 569 U.S. 435, 459, 133 S. Ct. 1958, 1976 (2013) (quoting *Smith v. United States,* 324 F.2d 879, 882 (D.C. Cir. 1963)).

[450] *Maryland v. King,* 569 U.S. 435, 133 S. Ct. 1958, 1980 (2013).

(a1) It shall be the duty of the arresting law-enforcement agency to cause a person charged with the commission of a felony to be fingerprinted and to forward those fingerprints to the State Bureau of Investigation.

(a2) It shall be the duty of the arresting law enforcement agency to cause a person charged with the commission of any of the following misdemeanors to be fingerprinted and to forward those fingerprints to the State Bureau of Investigation:

(1) G.S. 14-134.3 (Domestic criminal trespass), G.S. 15A-1382.1 (Offense that involved domestic violence), or G.S. 50B 4.1 (Violation of a valid protective order).

(2) G.S. 20-138.1 (Impaired driving), G.S. 20-138.2 (Impaired driving in commercial vehicle), G.S. 20-138.2A (Operating a commercial vehicle after consuming alcohol), and G.S. 20-138.2B (Operating various school, child care, EMS, firefighting, or law enforcement vehicles after consuming alcohol).

(3) G.S. 90-95(a)(3) (Possession of a controlled substance).

(a3) It shall be the duty of the arresting law enforcement agency to cause a person charged with a crime to provide to the magistrate as much of the following information as possible for the person arrested:

(1) Name including first, last, middle, maiden, and nickname or alias.

(2) Address including street, city, and state.

(3) Drivers license number and state of issuance.

(4) Date of birth.

(5) Sex.

(6) Race.

(7) Social Security number.

(8) Relationship to the alleged victim and whether it is a "personal relationship" as defined by G.S. 50B-1(b).

(a4) It shall be the duty of the arresting law enforcement agency to cause a person who has been charged with a misdemeanor offense of assault, stalking, or communicating a threat and held under G.S. 15A 534.1 to be fingerprinted and to forward those fingerprints to the State Bureau of Investigation.

(a5) It shall be the duty of the magistrate to enter into the court information system all information provided by the arresting law enforcement agency on the person arrested.

(a6) If the person cannot be identified by a valid form of identification, it shall be the duty of the arresting law-enforcement agency to cause a person charged with the commission of:

(1) Any offense involving impaired driving, as defined in G.S. 20-4.01(24a), or

(2) Driving while license revoked if the revocation is for an Impaired Driving License Revocation as defined in G.S. 20-28.2 to be fingerprinted and photographed.

(b) This section does not authorize the taking of photographs or fingerprints when the offense charged is a Class 2 or 3 misdemeanor under Chapter 20 of the General Statutes, "Motor Vehicles." Notwithstanding the prohibition in this subsection, a photograph may be taken of a person who operates a motor vehicle on a street or highway if:

(1) The person is cited by a law enforcement officer for a motor vehicle moving violation, and

(2) The person does not produce a valid drivers license upon the request of a law enforcement officer, and

(3) The law enforcement officer has a reasonable suspicion concerning the true identity of the person.

As used in this subsection, the phrase "motor vehicle moving violation" does not include the offenses listed in the third paragraph of G.S. 20-16(c)for which no points are assessed, nor does it include equipment violations specified in Part 9 of Article 3 of Chapter 20 of the General Statutes.

(b1) Any photograph authorized by subsection (b) of this section and taken by a law enforcement officer or agency:

(1) Shall only be taken of the operator of the motor vehicle, and only from the neck up.

(2) Shall be taken at either the location where the citation is issued, or at the jail if an arrest is made.

(3) Shall be retained by the law enforcement officer or agency until the final disposition of the case.

(4) Shall not be used for any purpose other than to confirm the identity of the alleged offender.

(5) Shall be destroyed by the law enforcement officer or agency upon a final disposition of the charge.

(c) This section does not authorize the taking of photographs or fingerprints of a juvenile alleged to be delinquent except under Article 21 of Chapter 7B of the General Statutes.

(d) This section does not prevent the taking of photographs, moving pictures, video or sound recordings, fingerprints, or the like to show a condition of intoxication or for other evidentiary use.

(e) Fingerprints or photographs taken pursuant to subsection (a), (a1), or (a2) of this section may be forwarded to the State Bureau of Investigation, the Federal Bureau of Investigation, or other law-enforcement agencies.

(f) If a person is charged with an offense for which fingerprints are required pursuant to this section but the person is not arrested for that offense, the court before which the charge is pending shall order the defendant to submit to fingerprinting by the Sheriff or other appropriate law enforcement agency at the earliest practical opportunity. If the person fails to appear for fingerprinting as ordered by the court, the sheriff shall so inform the court, and the court may initiate proceedings for criminal contempt against the person pursuant to G.S. 5A-15, including issue of an order for arrest pursuant to G.S. 5A-16, if necessary. The defendant shall continue to be subject to the court's order to provide fingerprints until submitted.

4. SEARCH & SEIZURE

4.1. The Warrant Requirement

4.1.1. Preliminary

The Fourth Amendment to the Constitution safeguards the "right of the people to be secure in their persons, houses, papers, and effects, against unreasonable searches and seizures[.]" Additionally, the Amendment commands that "no Warrants shall issue, but upon probable cause, supported by Oath or affirmation, and particularly describing the place to be searched, and the persons or things to be seized."

Generally, the United States Supreme Court has viewed a search and seizure as "*per se* unreasonable within the meaning of the Fourth Amendment unless it is accomplished pursuant to a judicial warrant issued upon probable cause and particularly describing the [places to be searched and] the items to be seized."[451] As a fundamental principle of constitutional criminal procedure, search warrants are strongly favored under both the federal Constitution and all state constitutions. The judicial preference which underscores the written warrant requirement is predicated upon the proposition that the necessity, validity and reasonableness of a prospective search or seizure can best be determined by a "neutral and detached magistrate" instead of a law enforcement officer. As the Supreme Court has stated, the warrant procedure serves primarily "to advise the citizen that the intrusion is authorized by law and [is] limited in its permissible scope[,] and to interpose a neutral magistrate between the citizen and the law enforcement officer 'engaged in the often competitive enterprise of ferreting out crime.'"[452]

The warrant procedure is not a mere formality. As the Court put it in *McDonald v. United States*:[453]

The presence of a search warrant serves a high function. Absent some grave emergency, the Fourth Amendment has interposed a magistrate between the citizen and the police. This was done not to shield criminals nor to make the home a safe haven for illegal activities. It was done so that an objective mind might weigh the need to invade that privacy in order to enforce the law. The right of privacy was deemed too precious to entrust to the discretion of those whose job is the detection of crime and the arrest of criminals....And so the Constitution requires a magistrate to pass on the desires of the

---

[451] *United States v. Place*, 462 U.S. 696, 701, 103 S. Ct. 2637, 2641 (1983).

[452] *National Treasury Employees Union v. Von Raab*, 489 U.S. 656, 109 S. Ct. 1384, 1391 (1989) (quoting *Johnson v. United States*, 333 U.S. 10, 14, 68 S. Ct. 367, 369 (1948)).

[453] *McDonald v. United States*, 335 U.S. 451, 455-56, 69 Ct. 191 (1978).

police before they violate the privacy of the home. We cannot be true to that constitutional requirement and excuse the absence of a search warrant without a showing by those who seek exemption from the constitutional mandate that the exigencies of the situation made that course imperative.

The driving force behind the Fourth Amendment, along with the history of its application, demonstrates that the Amendment's purpose and design is the protection of the "people" against arbitrary action by their own government. "People," for purposes of the Fourth Amendment means "people of the United States,"[454] referring to "a class of persons who are part of a national community or who have otherwise developed sufficient connections with this country to be considered part of that community."[455] Thus, it has been held that the Fourth Amendment has no application to an unlawful search and seizure conducted by federal agents outside the United States of premises owned by a foreign national, even though that foreign national (a Mexican citizen) is physically (and involuntarily) present in the United States for purposes of criminal prosecution.[456] Significantly, foreign nationals receive constitutional protection only "when they have come within the territory of the United States and developed substantial connections with this country."[457] Consequently, "once an alien lawfully enters and resides in this country he becomes invested with the rights guaranteed by the Constitution to all people within our borders."[458]

Similarly, Article I, § 20 of the North Carolina Constitution provides: "General warrants, whereby any officer or other person may be commanded to search suspected places without evidence of the act committed, or to seize any person or persons not named, whose offense is not particularly described and supported by evidence, are dangerous to liberty and shall not be granted." While this language "differs markedly from the language of the Fourth Amendment to the Constitution of the United States[,]" it "nevertheless ... prohibits unreasonable searches and seizures."[459] As with the Fourth Amendment, a search will be unreasonable unless it is made pursuant to a valid search warrant or justified by a recognized exception.

When an officer has obtained a warrant, upon review, an appellate court will accord "great deference" to the magistrate's finding of probable cause.[460] The federal Supreme Court's preference for a written warrant requires the reviewing court to ask only whether a reasonably cautious person could have concluded that there was a "substantial basis" for the finding of probable cause. If so, the warrant was properly issued.[461] Thus, search warrants and the underlying affidavits will be "read in a common-sense and realistic manner."

4.1.2. The search warrant affidavit

Generally, it is the law enforcement officer's responsibility to present the facts and circumstances comprising her probable cause to the appropriate issuing authority (judge, justice of the peace or magistrate) by way of application. This document is the search warrant "affidavit" and the officer who swears to the facts and circumstances contained in the affidavit is referred to as the "affiant." The warrant and the affidavit or testimony on which it is based must be legally sufficient, *i.e.*, they must contain sufficient facts demonstrating probable cause to believe that evidence will be found at the house, building, or other location or place where the person, property, or thing to be searched for and seized is situated.

Pursuant to North Carolina law, an application for a search warrant "must be supported by one or more affidavits particularly setting forth the facts and circumstances establishing probable cause to believe that the items [subject to seizure] are in the place[ ] ... to be searched."[462] A supporting affidavit is sufficient when

---

[454] *United States v. Verdugo-Urquidez*, 494 U.S. 259, 110 S. Ct. 1056, 1061 (1990).

[455] *United States v. Verdugo-Urquidez*, 494 U.S. 259, 110 S. Ct. 1056, 1061 (1990).

[456] *United States v. Verdugo-Urquidez*, 494 U.S. 259, 110 S. Ct. 1056, 1064 (1990).

[457] *United States v. Verdugo-Urquidez*, 494 U.S. 259, 110 S. Ct. 1056, 1064 (1990).

[458] *United States v. Verdugo-Urquidez*, 494 U.S. 259, 110 S. Ct. 1056, 1064 (1990) (citations omitted).

[459] *State v. Arrington*, 311 N.C. 633, 643, 319 S.E.2d 254 (1984).

[460] *Illinois v. Gates*, 462 U.S. 213, 103 S. Ct. 2317 (1983); *see also United States v. Leon*, 468 U.S. 897, 914, 104 S. Ct. 3405, 3416 (1984).

[461] *See Illinois v. Gates*, 462 U.S. 213, 103 S. Ct. 2317 (1983); *see also United States v. Ventresca*, 380 U.S. 102, 85 S. Ct. 741 (1965); *Brinegar v. United States*, 338 U.S. 160, 69 S. Ct. 1302 (1949).

[462] N.C.Gen.Stat. § 15A-244(3).

it gives the magistrate "reasonable cause to believe that the search will reveal the presence of the [items] sought on the premises described in the [warrant] application," and that those items "will aid in the apprehension or conviction of the offender."[463] New Hampshire case law makes clear that "when an officer seeks a warrant to search a residence, the facts set out in the supporting affidavit must show some connection or nexus linking the residence to illegal activity. Such a connection need not be direct, but it cannot be purely conclusory."[464]

For example, in *State v. Bailey*,[465] the affidavit did not contain any evidence that drugs were actually being sold at the residence. However, "the affiant was simply required to demonstrate *some* nexus between the apartment on East Chatham Street and criminal activity."[466]

Thus, the following key information included in the affidavit was sufficient to give rise to probable cause:

(1) Detective Rose personally observed an encounter between Taylor, White, and Tommasone in a secluded parking lot that he believed—based on his training and experience—likely involved the sale of drugs; (2) Detective Rose knew White and Tommasone had a history of dealing drugs; (3) when Taylor was pulled over shortly after leaving the parking lot, she confirmed that she had just purchased heroin from White; (4) an officer observed White and Tommasone travel from the scene of the drug deal to the residence on East Chatham Street, exit the vehicle, and go inside the apartment; and (5) Detective Rose knew that this address was, in fact, where White and Tommasone lived.[467]

4.1.3. Issuance of the warrant

Search warrants may be issued pursuant to N.C.Gen.Stat. § 15A-243 as follows:

§ 15A-243. Who may issue a search warrant
(a) A search warrant valid throughout the State may be issued by:
    (1) A Justice of the Supreme Court.
    (2) A judge of the Court of Appeals.
    (3) A judge of the superior court.
  (b) Other search warrants may be issued by:
    (1) A judge of the district court as provided in G.S. 7A-291.
    (2) A clerk as provided in G.S. 7A-180 and 7A-181.
    (3) A magistrate as provided in G.S. 7A-273.

An item is subject to seizure pursuant to a search warrant if there is probable cause to believe that it:

(1) Is stolen or embezzled; or
(2) Is contraband or otherwise unlawfully possessed; or
(3) Has been used or is possessed for the purpose of being used to commit or conceal the commission of a crime; or
(4) Constitutes evidence of an offense or the identity of a person participating in an offense.[468]

---

[463] *State v. Bright*, 301 N.C. 243, 249, 271 S.E.2d 368, 372 (1980).
[464] *State v. Bailey*, 374 N.C. 332, 335, 841 S.E.2d 277 (2020). *See State v. Arrington*, 311 N.C. 633, 641-42, 319 S.E.2d 254 (1984) (warrant supported by probable cause where affidavit described two tips leading to a "strong inference" that defendant growing and selling marijuana in mobile home); *State v. Allman*, 369 N.C. 292, 794 S.E.2d 301 (2016) (finding that it was reasonable for the magistrate to infer, based on the facts contained in the affidavit, that evidence of drug dealing would be found at the residence); *State v. Campbell*, 282 N.C. 125, 191 S.E.2d 752 (1972) (no probable cause where affidavit was purely conclusory).
[465] *State v. Bailey*, 374 N.C. 332, 841 S.E.2d 277 (2020).
[466] *State v. Bailey*, 374 N.C. 332, 338, 841 S.E.2d 277 (2020).
[467] *State v. Bailey*, 374 N.C. 332, 338, 841 S.E.2d 277 (2020).
[468] N.C.Gen.Stat. § 15A-242.

4.1.4. The particularity requirement

Under both the United States and North Carolina Constitutions, a warrant must "particularly describe" the place to be searched and the person and things to be seized. As stated in Article I, § 20 of the North Carolina Constitution "General warrants, whereby any officer or other person may be commanded to search suspected places without evidence of the act committed, or to seize any person or persons not named, whose offense is not particularly described and supported by evidence, are dangerous to liberty and shall not be granted." In addition, N.C.Gen.Stat. § 15A-246 requires a search warrant to contain both "[a] designation sufficient to establish with reasonable certainty the premises, vehicles, or persons to be searched;" and "[a] description or a designation of the items constituting the object of the search and authorized to be seized."

The "particularity" requirement was designed to prevent "the issue of warrants on loose, vague or doubtful bases of fact."[469] "The manifest purpose" of the requirement "was to prevent *general searches*."[470] Even before our Government came into existence, such general searches had been "deemed obnoxious to fundamental principles of liberty[, and are presently] denounced in the constitutions or statutes of every State in the Union."[471] As the Supreme Court explained in *Coolidge v. New Hampshire*,[472] the problem posed by the general warrant "is not that of intrusion *per se*, but of a general exploratory rummaging in a person's belongings." The problem is addressed by the Fourth Amendment's "particularity" requirement.[473] "By limiting the authorization to search to the specific areas and things for which there is probable cause to search, the requirement ensures that the search will be carefully tailored to its justifications and will not take on the character of the wide-ranging exploratory searches the Framers [of our Constitution] intended to prohibit."[474]

Accordingly, the specific "requirement that warrants shall particularly describe the *things to be seized* makes general searches under them impossible and prevents the seizure of one thing under a warrant describing another. As to what is to be taken, nothing is left to the discretion of the officer executing the warrant."[475] The companion requirement, that warrants shall particularly describe the *place to be searched*, is satisfied where "the description is such that the officer with a search warrant can with reasonable effort ascertain and identify the place intended."[476]

A valid warrant authorizes the executing officer to look for a particular item in any place it could logically be found. For example, illegal narcotics may be reasonably expected to be found in a dresser drawer; a stolen Harley Davidson motorcycle, on the other hand, would not.

There are two prongs of the particularity requirement: (i) a particularly described place, and (ii) particularly described items.

4.1.4.1. The places to be searched

The test for whether a sufficient description of the premises to be searched is given in a search warrant has been stated as follows: "It is enough if the description is such that the officer with a search warrant can, with reasonable effort, ascertain and identify the place intended."[477]

Generally, a description containing the address as it would appear on a mailing envelope, along with the name of the resident, and a cursory listing of the physical appearance of the building itself, is sufficient for single unit

---

[469] *Go-Bart Importing Co. v. United States*, 282 U.S. 344, 357, 51 S. Ct. 153, 158 (1931).

[470] *Maryland v. Garrison*, 480 U.S. 79, 107 S. Ct. 1013, 1017 (1987) (emphasis added).

[471] *Go-Bart Importing Co. v. United States*, 282 U.S. 344, 357, 51 S. Ct. 153, 158 (1931).

[472] *Coolidge v. New Hampshire*, 403 U.S. 443, 467, 91 S. Ct. 2022, 2038 (1971).

[473] *Coolidge v. New Hampshire*, 403 U.S. 443, 467, 91 S. Ct. 2022, 2038 (1971).

[474] *Maryland v. Garrison*, 480 U.S. 79, 107 S. Ct. 1013, 1017 (1987).

[475] *Marron v. United States*, 275 U.S. 192, 196, 48 S. Ct. 74, 76 (1927) (emphasis added). *See also State v. Foye*, 14 N.C. App. 200, 188 S.E.2d 67 (1972).

[476] *Steele v. United States*, 267 U.S. 498, 503, 45 S. Ct. 414, 416 (1925).

[477] *Steele v. United States*, 267 U.S. 498, 503, 45 S. Ct. 414, 416 (1925) (upholding the search of 609 West 46th Street under a warrant describing the premises as 611 West 46th Street, where the building was a large warehouse having both numbers and being only partly partitioned).

dwellings. Thus, in *State v. Moore*,[478] the search warrants description of the type and color of the residence in which the defendant resided, with a map to the residence attached, which listed the defendant's first name only, and stated that an informant had observed the defendant at the residence searched, but stated an incorrect address for the premises, was adequate. The court explained, "A search warrant must contain a designation sufficient to establish with reasonable certainty the premises, vehicles, or persons to be searched, and a description or a designation of the items constituting the object of the search and authorized to be seized."[479] Notably, "the address described in the search warrant may differ from the address of the residence actually searched."[480] Accordingly, "[S]tanding alone, an incorrect address on a search warrant will not invalidate the warrant where other designations are sufficient to establish with reasonable certainty the premises, vehicles, or persons to be searched, and a description or a designation of the items constituting the object of the search and authorized to be seized."[481]

A problem arises, however, when the place to be searched is in a multi-unit structure, like an apartment in a complex or an office in a professional building. The general rule is that the description must describe the specific sub-unit to be searched, not the whole building, unless the multi-unit character of the building is not apparent and the searching officers had no knowledge of it. If the description merely lists the address of a building which itself contains many residences or offices, and the law enforcement agents executing the warrant have no means to determine which of the individual units is to be searched, the warrant may be invalid.

Property that is within the curtilage of any dwelling house must also be described with specificity in a search warrant in order to justify a search of such property pursuant to that search warrant.

4.1.4.2. The things to be seized

The search warrant must also describe the items authorized to be seized, so that officers can reasonably identify the things intended, thus preventing a general exploratory rummaging in a person's belongings. The degree of particularity with which the items must be described will fluctuate, depending on the circumstances and individual attributes of the subject items.[482]

Note, however, that when executing a warrant, officers may seize contraband or other evidence not listed in the warrant, in plain view, if the requirements of that doctrine are met.[483]

4.1.4.2.1. Contraband goods

Generally, a lesser standard or degree of particularity is required in a search warrant for contraband goods such as illicit drugs, automatic weapons, explosives and the like.[484]

However, in *Groh v. Ramirez*,[485] the United States Supreme Court found a search warrant was plainly invalid when it provided no description of the type of evidence sought. The fact that the *application* for the warrant adequately described the "things to be seized" did not save it, because there were no words in the warrant incorporating other documents by reference and the application did not accompany the warrant (it had been sealed). Even though the search was conducted with restraint and only items listed in the application were seized, the search was deemed to be unlawful.

4.1.5. Judicial requirements

From the foregoing discussion, it is clear that the rules require issuance of a warrant by a magistrate or judge who must, after receiving an "oath or affirmation" from the warrant applicant, make an independent,

---

[478] *State v. Moore*, 152 N.C. App. 156, 566 S.E.2d 713 (2002).

[479] *State v. Moore*, 152 N.C. App. 156, 159, 566 S.E.2d 713 (2002).

[480] *State v. Moore*, 152 N.C. App. 156, 160, 566 S.E.2d 713 (2002).

[481] *State v. Hunter*, 208 N.C. App. 506, 509, 703 S.E.2d 776 (2010). *See also State v. Friday*, 808 S.E.2d 622 (N.C. Ct. App. 2018).

[482] *See State v. Foye*, 14 N.C. App. 200, 188 S.E.2d 67 (1972).

[483] For a further discussion of this area of law, refer to the *Plain View Doctrine*, § 5.3.

[484] *United States v. Rome*, 809 F.2d 665, 670 (10th Cir. 1987); *see also United States v. Caves*, 890 F.2d 87, 93 (8th Cir. 1989) (the degree of specificity required in a search warrant varies; less specificity is required when the object of the search constitutes controlled substances); *United States v. Grimaldi*, 606 F.2d 332 (1st Cir. 1979) (finding the phrase, "other paraphernalia used in the manufacture of counterfeit federal reserve notes" to be a sufficient description of items of contraband in a search warrant).

[485] *Groh v. Ramirez*, 540 U.S. 551, 124 S. Ct. 1284 (2004).

"neutral and detached" determination whether probable cause exists to believe that (1) particularly described property, (2) which is subject to official seizure, (3) may be presently found, (4) at a particular place.

4.1.5.1. The neutral and detached magistrate

A search warrant must be issued by a neutral and detached magistrate. "Neutral and detached" means that the warrant must be issued by a removed, impartial judge. Neutrality and detachment require "severance and disengagement" from the activities of law enforcement.[486] This requirement is premised on the notion "that a warrant authorized by a neutral and detached judicial officer is a more reliable safeguard against improper searches than the hurried judgment of a law enforcement officer[.]"[487] As stated by Justice Jackson in *Johnson v. United States*:[488] "The point of the Fourth Amendment, which often is not grasped by zealous officers, is not that it denies law enforcement the support of the usual inferences which reasonable men draw from evidence. Its protection consists in requiring that those inferences be drawn by a neutral and detached magistrate instead of being judged by the officer engaged in the often competitive enterprise of ferreting out crime."

In *Lo-Ji Sales Inc. v. New York*, the warrant was invalid when the magistrate who issued it went along on the raid he had authorized, and determined only when he saw certain materials what was obscene, and therefore what was to be seized. Similarly, in *Coolidge v. New Hampshire*,[489] where a warrant was issued by the state attorney general, who was also actively involved in the investigation, and later prosecuted the case at trial, the initial probable cause determination was patently improper, for it was not made by an impartial and remote observer. To ensure the requisite neutrality, the issuing judge must not play a role in the investigation or the search itself.

4.1.5.2. Oath or affirmation

The North Carolina and United States Constitutions require that search warrants must be supported by "Oath or affirmation." In addition, N.C.Gen.Stat. § 15A-244 requires that "[e]ach application for a search warrant must be made in writing upon oath or affirmation." In *State v. McCord*,[490] the application for a search warrant submitted to the judge by a detective in the murder investigation, which eventually implicated the defendant, met the requirements of this section; although the application itself did not state on its face that it was sworn, the trial court found that the detective was sworn and signed the attached sworn affidavit in the judge's presence.[491]

4.1.6. The probable cause requirement

After the application and affidavit for a search warrant is submitted to the magistrate, a review is conducted to determine whether probable cause exists sufficient to warrant a reasonable person to believe that seizable property would be found in a particular place or on a particular person. The probable cause standard for issuance of a search warrant is essentially the same as that for arrest, the difference being that police must have probable cause to believe that a crime has been committed, and that there is a substantial basis for inferring a fair probability that they will find certain evidence or contraband in a particular place.[492] When making a probable cause determination, the issuing magistrate is entitled to consider all the circumstances surrounding an alleged crime, *i.e.*, "the totality of the circumstances."

---

[486] *Shadwick v. City of Tampa,* 407 U.S. 345, 350, 92 S. Ct. 2119, 32 L. Ed. 2d 783 (1972).

[487] *Lo-Ji Sales Inc. v. New York*, 442 U.S. 319, 99 S.Ct. 2319 (1979).

[488] *Johnson v. United States*, 333 U.S. 10, 13-14, 68 S. Ct. 367, 369 (1948).

[489] *Coolidge v. New Hampshire,* 403 U.S. 443, 91 S. Ct. 2022, 2029 (1971).

[490] *State v. McCord*, 140 N.C. App. 634, 538 S.E.2d 633 (2000), *review denied*, 353 N.C. 392 (2001).

[491] *State v. McCord*, 140 N.C. App. 634, 538 S.E.2d 633 (2000), *review denied*, 353 N.C. 392 (2001).

[492] *See State v. Riddick*, 291 N.C. 399, 230 S.E.2d 506 (1976), *motion for reconsideration denied*, 293 N.C. 261, 247 S.E.2d 234 (1977); *State v. Dailey*, 33 N.C. App. 600, 235 S.E.2d 917, *appeal dismissed*, 293 N.C. 362, 237 S.E.2d 849 (1977); *State v. Eutsler*, 41 N.C. App. 182, 254 S.E.2d 250, *cert. denied*, 297 N.C. 614, 257 S.E.2d 438 (1979); *State v. Jones*, 299 N.C. 298, 261 S.E.2d 860 (1980); State v. Sheetz, 46 N.C. App. 641, 265 S.E.2d 914 (1980); *State v. Rook*, 304 N.C. 201, 283 S.E.2d 732 (1981), *cert. denied*, 455 U.S. 1038, 102 S. Ct. 1741, 72 L. Ed. 2d 155 (1982); *State v. McKinnon*, 306 N.C. 288, 293 S.E.2d 118 (1982).

Pursuant to N.C.Gen.Stat. § 15A-245:

(a) Before acting on the application, the issuing official may examine on oath the applicant or any other person who may possess pertinent information, but information other than that contained in the affidavit may not be considered by the issuing official in determining whether probable cause exists for the issuance of the warrant unless the information is either recorded or contemporaneously summarized in the record or on the face of the warrant by the issuing official. The information must be shown by one or more of the following:

(1) Affidavit; or

(2) Oral testimony under oath or affirmation before the issuing official; or

(3) Oral testimony under oath or affirmation presented by a sworn law enforcement officer to the issuing official by means of an audio and video transmission in which both parties can see and hear each other. Prior to the use of audio and video transmission pursuant to this subdivision, the procedures and type of equipment for audio and video transmission shall be submitted to the Administrative Office of the Courts by the senior regular resident superior court judge and the chief district court judge for a judicial district or set of districts and approved by the Administrative Office of the Courts.

(b) If the issuing official finds that the application meets the requirements of this Article and finds there is probable cause to believe that the search will discover items specified in the application which are subject to seizure under G.S. 15A-242, he must issue a search warrant in accordance with the requirements of this Article. The issuing official must retain a copy of the warrant and warrant application and must promptly file them with the clerk. If he does not so find, the official must deny the application.

With regard to the probable cause standard for the issuance of a search warrant, the North Carolina Supreme Court has said:

This standard for determining probable cause is flexible, permitting the magistrate to draw "reasonable inferences" from the evidence in the affidavit supporting the application for the warrant ... That evidence is viewed from the perspective of a police officer with the affiant's training and experience, and the commonsense judgments reached by officers in light of that training and specialized experience. Probable cause requires not certainty, but only "*a probability or substantial chance* of criminal activity." The magistrate's determination of probable cause is given "great deference" and "after-the-fact scrutiny should not take the form of a *de novo* review.""[493]

A criminal defendant may challenge the validity of a warrant, or the sufficiency of an affidavit, on constitutional grounds, or may allege the warrant does not fulfill the requirements of the warrant statute. A constitutional challenge would, for example, involve assertions that the facts as alleged do not establish "probable cause," or that the warrant did not "particularly" describe the place to be searched or things to be seized, as required by the Fourth Amendment. A statutory challenge would involve allegations that the procedures required by the statute were not followed by the authorities.

If the defendant shows that a search warrant contains false statements or material omissions made by the affiant either knowingly or with reckless disregard for the truth, then the remaining information in the affidavit must independently establish probable cause, or else the warrant will be invalid. In this respect, the United States Supreme Court in *Franks v. Delaware*[494] set forth the procedure as follows:

[W]here the defendant makes a substantial preliminary showing that a false statement knowingly and intentionally, or with reckless disregard for the truth, was included by the affiant in the warrant affidavit, and if the allegedly false statement is necessary to the finding of probable cause, the Fourth Amendment requires that a hearing be held at the defendant's request. In the event that at that hearing the allegation of perjury or reckless disregard is established by the defendant by a preponderance

---

[493] *State v. McKinney*, 368 N.C. 161, 164-64, 775 S.E.2d 821 (2015) (citations omitted) (emphasis in original).

[494] *Franks v. Delaware*, 438 U.S. 154, 98 S. Ct. 2674 (1978).

of the evidence, and, with the affidavit's false material set to one side, the affidavit's remaining content is insufficient to establish probable cause, the search warrant must be voided and the fruits of the search excluded to the same extent as if probable cause was lacking on the face of the affidavit.[495]

There is, however, "a presumption of validity with respect to the affidavit supporting the search warrant. To mandate an evidentiary hearing, the challenger's attack must be more than conclusory and must be supported by more than a mere desire to cross-examine. There must be allegations of deliberate falsehood or of reckless disregard for the truth, and those allegations must be accompanied by an offer of proof. They should point out specifically the portion of the warrant affidavit that is claimed to be false; and they should be accompanied by a statement of supporting reasons. Affidavits or sworn or otherwise reliable statements of witnesses should be furnished, or their absence satisfactorily explained. Allegations of negligence or innocent mistake are insufficient. *The deliberate falsity or reckless disregard whose impeachment is permitted today is only that of the affiant, not of any nongovernmental informant.*"[496]

4.1.6.1. The "totality of the circumstances" test

In order to determine whether probable cause exists, the magistrate or judge will utilize the "totality of the circumstances" test, which was first announced by the United States Supreme Court in *Illinois v. Gates.*[497] In *Gates*, the Court redefined over 15 years of law governing the issuance of search warrants based upon information received from police informants. The Court abandoned the rigid "two-pronged test" originally established in *Aguilar v. Texas* and *Spinelli v. United States*, and determined that in its place, the "totality of the circumstances" analysis should be used to test the sufficiency of probable cause.[498]

In so doing, the Court said: "We are convinced that this flexible, easily applied standard will better achieve the accommodation of public and private interests that the Fourth Amendment requires." According to the Court in *Gates,* the "task of the issuing magistrate is simply to make a practical, common-sense decision whether, given *all the circumstances* set forth in the affidavit before him, there is a fair probability that contraband or evidence of a crime will be found in a particular place."[499]

The *Gates* Court went on to say that it considered the "totality of the circumstances" approach to be a more "practical, non-technical" concept. Thus, the "assessment of probabilities" that flows from the evidence presented in support of the warrant must be seen and weighed not in terms of library analysis by scholars, but as understood by those versed in the field of law enforcement. Under the "totality of the circumstances" approach, the facts are to be viewed collectively, not in isolation. Many times, when the facts are viewed separately and in isolation, they may be prone to innocent explanation. But "this kind of divide-and-conquer approach is improper."[500] Instead, we must look at "the whole picture." According to the North Carolina Supreme Court, "[A]s long as the pieces fit together well and yield a fair probability that a police officer executing the warrant will find contraband or evidence of a crime at the place to be searched, a magistrate has probable cause to issue a warrant."[501] The North Carolina Supreme Court has adopted the *Gates* totality of the circumstances test.[502]

In *State v. Allman,*[503] the magistrate had a substantial basis to find that probable cause existed to issue the search warrant. There, "[d]efendant lived with Sean Whitehead and Jeremy Black, who were half-brothers, at 4844 Acres Drive in Wilmington, North Carolina. The police stopped a car that Black was driving. Whitehead

---

[495] *Franks v. Delaware*, 438 U.S. 154, 155-56, 98 S. Ct. 2674, 2676 (1978).

[496] *Franks v. Delaware*, 438 U.S. 154, 171, 98 S. Ct. 2674, 2684 (1978) (emphasis added).

[497] *Illinois v. Gates*, 462 U.S. 213, 103 S. Ct. 2317 (1983).

[498] *Illinois v. Gates*, 462 U.S. 213, 232, 103 S. Ct. 2317 (1983) (citing *Aguilar v. Texas*, 378 U.S. 108, 84 S. Ct. 1509 (1964); and *Spinelli v. United States*, 393 U.S. 410, 89 S. Ct. 584 (1969)).

[499] *Illinois v. Gates*, 462 U.S. 213, 103 S. Ct. 2317 (1983) (emphasis added); *see also Massachusetts v. Upton*, 466 U.S. 727, 104 S. Ct. 2805, 2088 (1984) (The "totality of the circumstances" analysis, *i.e.*, examining the "whole picture," is "more in keeping with the practical, common-sense decision demanded of the magistrate.").

[500] *District of Columbia v. Wesby*, 583 U.S. ___, 138 S. Ct. 577, 589 (2018).

[501] *State v. Allman*, 369 N.C. 292, 294, 794 S.E.2d 301 (2016).

[502] *State v. Arrington*, 311 N.C. 633, 643, 319 S.E.2d 254 (1984).

[503] *State v. Allman*, 369 N.C. 292, 794 S.E.2d 301 (2016).

was a passenger. Inside the car, the police found 8.1 ounces of marijuana and over $1600 in cash. This stop ultimately led to the issuance of a warrant to search defendant's home. Based on evidence found there, defendant was charged with six offenses pertaining to the manufacture, possession, and sale or delivery of illegal drugs."[504]

During the vehicle stop, Whitehead maintained that he and Black lived at 30 Twin Oaks Drive in Castle Hayne, North Carolina. However, when Detective Bacon went to that address, he discovered that neither man lived there. Instead he found their mother at the residence and she provided the actual address of her sons. Detective Bacon's affidavit in support of the warrant contained extensive allegations including, a description of the traffic stop, the criminal histories of Whitehead and Black, a statement from Whitehead's and Black's mother as to where the men actually lived, observations corroborating the statement from Whitehead's and Black's mother, discovery of a vehicle registered to Black outside the residence, and a recitation of Detective Bacon's extensive training in law enforcement and extensive experience with drug investigations and trials. The court acknowledged that, "nothing in Detective Bacon's affidavit directly linked defendant's home with evidence of drug dealing,"[505] but also noted that the two men had lied about their home address and explained that "a suspected drug dealer's lie about his address, in combination with other evidence of drug dealing, can give rise to probable cause to search his home."[506] Accordingly, "it was reasonable for the magistrate to infer that there could be evidence of drug dealing at 4844 Acres Drive."[507]

On the other hand, there was no basis for the magistrate to find reasonable cause to issue the search warrant in *State v. Lewis*.[508] In that case, the affidavit did not connect the defendant to the residence beyond the fact that he was arrested there and a vehicle matching the description of the one involved in the robbery was observed in the vicinity of the residence at that time. The North Carolina Supreme Court was especially critical of what was *not* included in the affidavit. Said the court:

> [Detective Tart's] affidavit failed to set forth any of the circumstances surrounding defendant's arrest at 7085 Laurinburg Road and offered no explanation as to why law enforcement officers had gone to that address in the first place. Notably, the affidavit did not include the fact that the address had been provided by Johnston County law enforcement officers. It also failed to include any details of Deputy Kavanaugh's conversation with defendant's stepfather—who had confirmed that defendant lived in the home—and contained no mention of the fact that a Kia Optima was parked in front of the residence at the time of defendant's arrest.[509]

The court concluded that "the information contained in the affidavit failed to establish the existence of probable cause to search the residence at 7085 Laurinburg Road. The affidavit simply did not connect defendant with the residence that the officers wished to search in any meaningful way beyond the mere fact that he was arrested there and that a dark blue Nissan Titan was observed in the vicinity of the house at that time. Defendant could have been present at 7085 Laurinburg Road at the time of his arrest for any number of reasons. Absent additional information linking him to the residence or connecting the house with criminal activity, no basis existed for the magistrate to infer that evidence of the robberies would likely be found inside the home."[510]

Three specific aspects of the subject, regarding the nature and quality of the information itself, or the specific source from which it came, pose special problems for courts when ascertaining the existence of probable cause: (i) the facts relied upon may be too old or no longer accurate (staleness); (ii) the use of third party informants, rather than direct observation or personal knowledge; and (iii) the facts relied upon establish that a crime may take place, and evidence of that crime may be found in a certain place in the future, but not at present (anticipatory warrants).

---

[504] *State v. Allman*, 369 N.C. 292, 292-93, 794 S.E.2d 301 (2016).
[505] *State v. Allman*, 369 N.C. 292, 297, 794 S.E.2d 301 (2016).
[506] *State v. Allman*, 369 N.C. 292, 297, 794 S.E.2d 301 (2016).
[507] *State v. Allman*, 369 N.C. 292, 296-97, 794 S.E.2d 301 (2016).
[508] *State v. Lewis*, 831 S.E.2d 37 (N.C. 2019).
[509] *State v. Lewis*, 831 S.E.2d 37, 45 (N.C. 2019).
[510] *State v. Lewis*, 831 S.E.2d 37, 45-46 (N.C. 2019).

4.1.6.2. Staleness of probable cause

The age of the information supporting a warrant application is a factor in determining probable cause. If too old, the information is stale, and probable cause may no longer exist. It is critical that probable cause to search exists *at the time a warrant is issued*. Probable cause to search is concerned with whether certain identifiable objects are probably to be found *at the present time* in a certain identifiable place. It cannot be assumed that evidence of a crime will remain indefinitely in a given place. Thus, staleness is a factor to weigh in determining if there is probable cause to search."[511]

Age alone, however, does not determine staleness. Determining whether probable cause exists is not merely an exercise in counting the days or even months between the facts relied on and the issuance of the warrant. Rather, courts will also examine the nature of the crime and the type of evidence. The circumstances will vary depending upon such factors as whether the crime is a single instance or an ongoing pattern of protracted violations, whether the inherent nature of a scheme suggests that it is probably continuing, and the nature of the property sought, that is, whether it is likely to be promptly disposed of or retained by the person committing the offense. [512]

There are, therefore, a number of factors that a court may consider when determining whether the information supporting the issuance of a warrant has grown stale. These factors include: (1) the nature and quality of the seized evidence (whether perishable and easily transferable or of enduring utility to its holder); (2) the ease with which the evidence may be disposed of; (3) the character of the place to be searched (whether one of incidental use for mere convenience or a secure base of operations); (4) the lapse of time between the information and the warrant; (5) the character of the criminal (whether isolated and fleeting or entrenched); and (6) the character of the crime (whether chance encounter or an entrenched, continuing illegal scheme).

In *State v. Rayfield*,[513] the defendant was indicted for multiple counts of sexual acts with K.C., a minor. The acts had taken place over a period of years from the time that K.C. was eight years old until she was 11. Among other things, the affidavit in support of a search warrant of the defendant's home asserted that he had shown K.C. pornographic videos and images in his home. The images were of the defendant having sexual intercourse with an unknown female, who K.C. believed was under 10 years old. The affidavit noted that the defendant was a registered sex offender and requested a search warrant for his home and the magazines, videos, computers, cell phones, and thumb drives located therein. The defendant argued that the three-and-one-half-year gap between the K.C.'s viewing of the pornography in his house and the time the affidavit was issued rendered those allegations stale.

The North Carolina Supreme Court disagreed and explained "'[W]here the affidavit properly recites facts indicating activity of a protracted and continuous nature, a course of conduct, the passage of time becomes less significant. The continuity of the offense may be the most important factor in determining whether the probable cause is valid or stale.'"[514] Moreover, "when items to be searched are not inherently incriminating and have enduring utility for the person to be searched, a reasonably prudent magistrate could conclude that the items can be found in the area to be searched. Here, the items sought by the search warrant—magazines, videos, computers, cell phones, hard drives, gaming systems, MP3 players, a camera, a video recorder, thumb drives, and other pictures or documents—were not incriminating in and of themselves and were of enduring

---

[511] *See Sgro v. United States*, 287 U.S. 206, 210-12, 53 S. Ct. 138, 140-41 (1932) ("it is manifest that the proof must be of facts so closely related to the time of the issue of the warrant as to justify a finding of probable cause at that time").

[512] *See, e.g., United States v. Foster*, 711 F.2d 871, 878 (9th Cir. 1983) ("The passage of time is not necessarily a controlling factor in determining the existence of probable cause. The court should also evaluate the nature of the criminal activity and the kind of property for which authorization to search is sought."); *Andresen v. State*, 24 Md. App. 128, 331 A.2d 78 (1975) *aff'd sub nom. Andresen v. Maryland*, 427 U.S. 463, 96 S. Ct. 2737 (1976) (considering the character of the crime, the criminal, the thing to be seized, and the place to be searched). The staleness inquiry is another component of the overall inquiry, which requires that the factual information provided in the affidavit establishes a fair probability that the evidence sought will be found at the location sought to be searched. *See United States v. Spikes*, 158 F.3d 913, 923-24 (6th Cir. 1998).

[513] *State v. Rayfield*, 231 N.C. App. 632, 752 S.E.2d 745 (2014).

[514] *State v. Rayfield*, 231 N.C. App. 632, 640, 752 S.E.2d 745 (2014) (quoting *State v. McCoy*, 100 N.C. App. 574, 577, 397 S.E.2d 355 (1990)).

utility to Defendant."[515] Accordingly, "the information contained in the search warrant was not stale and the magistrate had sufficient evidence to support a determination of probable cause."[516]

4.1.6.3. The "four corners" test

In analyzing whether probable cause exists to issue a search warrant, a reviewing court will use the "four corners test." This test requires that sufficient facts must appear on the face of the affidavit so that the reviewing court may judge whether the factual basis in the document alone provides probable cause.

The "four corners" test appears frequently in case law to support the principle that reviewing courts should consider only that information contained in the underlying affidavit in their probable cause review. In this regard, sufficient facts must appear on the face of the affidavit so that a magistrate's personal knowledge notwithstanding, a reviewing court can verify the existence of probable cause.[517]

4.1.7. Sources of information / informants

Law enforcement officers do not often rely on their own direct observations to provide the underlying facts supporting a warrant. In so many cases, a third-party will provide documentation of a crime's commission, and detail where evidence or contraband can be found. In this regard, one of the most valuable assets in the law-enforcement battle against crime is the police informant. In fact, over the course of time, the proper utilization of information imparted by informants has led the courts to "consistently accept the use of informants in the discovery of evidence of a crime as a legitimate investigatory procedure consistent with the Constitution."[518]

Generally, informants are classified into three distinct types: criminal informants, citizen informants, and anonymous tips. The "type" of informant becomes important when a determination must be made as to whether the information imparted provides a sufficient constitutional justification for a particular police action. Moreover, knowledge of the type of informant the police are dealing with becomes critical when a determination must be made as to how much independent police investigation must be employed to verify or corroborate the information reported. Thus, courts will consider the following factors in determining whether the hearsay information provided by an informant generates probable cause: (1) the reliability of the informant; (2) the details contained in the informant's tip; and (3) the degree to which the tip is corroborated by independent police surveillance and information. One factor alone should not control the judge's decision. For example, if an informant's tip is sufficiently corroborated by independent police work, then the tip may form the basis for probable cause even if little is known about the informant's reliability.

4.1.7.1. Criminal informants

In the totality-of-the-circumstances analysis, the reliability of a criminal informant's hearsay information, along with the informant's credibility, remains a relevant inquiry. In fact, the hallmark of the competent criminal investigator is the ability to clearly and thoroughly document in an affidavit not only the credibility of his confidential informant but the reliability of the information relayed and the informant's basis of knowledge.

---

[515] *State v. Rayfield*, 231 N.C. App. 632, 641, 752 S.E.2d 745 (2014) (citing *State v. Jones*, 299 N.C. 298, 261 S.E.2d 860 (1980)).

[516] *State v. Rayfield*, 231 N.C. App. 632, 641-41, 752 S.E.2d 745 (2014). *See also State v. Jones*, 299 N.C. 298, 261 S.E.2d 860 (1980) (upholding a search warrant when five months had elapsed between the time the witness saw the defendant's hatchet and gloves and the witness spoke to police because, *inter alia*, the items were not incriminating in and of themselves and had utility to the defendant); *State v. Pickard*, 178 N.C. App. 330, 336, 631 S.E.2d 203, 208 (2006) (holding that the affidavit provided the magistrate with a substantial basis for concluding that probable cause existed to issue a search warrant when the items sought—computers, computer equipment and accessories, cassette videos or DVDs, video cameras, digital cameras, film cameras, and accessories—were not particularly incriminating and were of enduring utility to the defendant).

[517] *See Illinois v. Gates*, 462, U.S. 213, 238, 103 S. Ct. 2317, 2332 (1983) ("The task of the issuing magistrate is simply to make a practical, common-sense decision whether, given all the circumstances set forth in the affidavit before him, including the 'veracity' and 'basis of knowledge' of persons supplying hearsay information, there is a fair probability that contraband or evidence of a crime will be found in a particular place.").

[518] *Arizona v. Fulminante*, 499 U.S. 279, 111 S. Ct. 1246, 1262-63 (1991) (Rehnquist, C.J., dissenting in part).

These items are "closely intertwined issues" which make up the "commonsense, practical question whether there is 'probable cause' to believe that contraband or evidence is located in a particular place."[519]

Perhaps the most common way reliability is established is by documenting the past use of the particular informant and the number of times the information imparted by that informant proved not only to be true and correct but also led to the arrest and successful prosecution of the subject of the information. A mere bare bones statement in an affidavit that an informant is reliable and has proved to be reliable in the past is not enough. Officers should strive to include: (1) how often the informant has been used; (2) the nature or character of the investigations in which the informant has previously supplied information (*e.g.*, narcotics, burglary, stolen property, arson, etc.); (3) how many times the information proved to be true and correct; (4) whether the information led to the arrest of the subject of the information; and (5) whether the subsequent prosecution led to conviction. Naturally, if any of the aforementioned indicators of reliability is absent or unknown, the affidavit would merely be silent in that regard.[520]

Reliability may also be adequately established if, during the course of supplying information, the informant supplies his own name to the police and includes a "statement against his penal interest."[521] For example, consider the case where the informant admits to buying narcotics on several occasions from a named individual. In such a case—where the informant admits to criminal conduct during the course of supplying information to the police—"[c]ommon sense in the important daily affairs of life would induce a prudent and disinterested observer to credit these statements. People do not lightly admit a crime and place critical evidence in the hands of the police in the form of their own admissions."[522] As the D.C. Circuit Court pointed out in *United States v. Clark*,[523] "officers could reasonably believe that precisely because [the informant] was actively engaged in drug trafficking, he would know—and thus be able to identify—the source of his trading goods; furthermore, because he was seeking leniency at the hands of the law, [the informant] would have little reason to prove himself an unreliable informant."

Reliability may be further enhanced if the informant provides the police with such information with the hope of changing his criminal ways. Indeed, we are in a time when cocaine addiction is on the verge of epidemic proportion, and the public is extensively aware of the devastation created by it. Consequently, when a cocaine user voluntarily turns in his supplier to the police in the hope of shaking his reliance on the drug, and in doing so admits to his own criminal conduct, *such evidence sharply increases the degree of reliability* needed for the issuance of a search warrant.

The informant's basis of knowledge may be established by documenting, in as much detail as possible, the informant's personal observations. This establishes how (and when) the informant came by her information, and demonstrates what precisely the informant personally saw, heard, smelled, tasted or touched. Persuasive in this regard would be details of the physical appearance of the target residence, exactly where in the residence the subject keeps or conceals the evidence or contraband, what the evidence or contraband looked like, how it was packaged, the name and detailed physical description of the subject and others who may also live at or occasion the target premises, and so on.[524] This type and degree of detail not only fortifies the reliability of the information supplied but constitutes a material consideration in the totality-of-the-circumstances analysis. Indeed, even if the informant's statements and the events the informant describes "diverge in minor ways, the magistrate may reasonably choose to credit the statements and disregard petty inconsistencies."[525]

The final ingredient in the totality-of-the-circumstances approach calls for the independent corroboration of as many of the facts relayed by the informant as possible. If time permits, all the information relayed

---

[519] *Illinois v. Gates*, 462 U.S. 213, 103 S. Ct. 2317, 2328 (1983).

[520] Excerpts from the comprehensive discussion of the laws of arrest, search and seizure in Larry E. Holtz, *Criminal Procedure for Law and Justice Professionals* (Blue360° Media); *see also United States v. Winarske*, 715 F.3d 1063 (8th Cir. 2013) (informant deemed reliable because of his "track record of providing accurate information on local criminal activity" where "his tips were accurate enough to lead police to solve about a dozen open burglary cases").

[521] *United States v. Harris* 403 U.S. 573, 583, 91 S. Ct. 2075, 2081-82 (1971).

[522] *United States v. Harris* 403 U.S. 573, 583, 91 S. Ct. 2075, 2082 (1971).

[523] *United States v. Clark*, 24 F.3d 299, 303 (D.C. Cir. 1994).

[524] *See, e.g., United States v. Hill*, 91 F.3d 1064, 1069 (8th Cir. 1996) (confidential informant's report was based on *direct observations* of the subject, entitling "'his tip to greater weight than might otherwise be the case'") (quoting *Illinois v. Gates*, 462 U.S. 213, 234, 103 S. Ct. 2317, 2330 (1983)).

[525] *See United States v. Schaefer*, 87 F.2d 562, 567 (1st Cir. 1996); *United States v. Zayas-Diaz*, 95 F.3d 105, 112 (1st Cir. 1996).

should be confirmed by independent investigation. In this respect, a deficiency in any of the foregoing elements may be counterbalanced by the officer's independent investigation—the touchstone of the totality-of-the-circumstances approach.[526]

In *State v. Arrington*,[527] the affidavit in support of a search warrant to search the defendant's mobile home and truck detailed the tips of two confidential informants. The "information supplied by the first informant establishe[d], against the informant's penal interest, that he had purchased marijuana from the defendant."[528] The second informant advised that there had been a steady flow of traffic to the defendant's residence for the last 24 hours and also during the last two months, thus creating "a strong inference that the illegal activity was continuing and had occurred within the last twenty-four hours."[529] The North Carolina Supreme Court concluded, "A common sense reading of the information supplied by both informants provides a substantial basis for the *probability* that the defendant had sold marijuana, had grown it in his own home, and was continuing to sell it from his home to a steady flow of drug users within the last twenty-four hours. No more is required under the Fourth Amendment."[530]

4.1.7.2. Citizen informants

In marked contrast to the criminal informant, an ordinary citizen presumably has no ties or connections with the criminal world. In this respect, courts will impart an assumption grounded in common experience that such a person, regarded as a law-abiding and cooperative member of the general public, is motivated by factors that are consistent with law enforcement goals. Consequently, an individual of this kind may be regarded as trustworthy and the information imparted by her to a law enforcement officer concerning a criminal episode would not especially entail further exploration or verification of the citizen's personal credibility or reliability before suitable action may be taken.

Clearly, a different rationale exists for establishing the reliability of named "citizen-informers" as opposed to the traditional idea of unnamed police contacts or informers who usually themselves are criminals. Information supplied to officers by the traditional police informer is not given in the spirit of a concerned citizen, but often is given in exchange for some concession, payment, or simply out of revenge against the subject. The nature of these persons and the information which they supply convey a certain impression of unreliability, and it is proper to demand that some evidence of their credibility and reliability be shown. As previously noted, one practical way of making such a showing is to point to accurate information which they have supplied in the past.

However, an ordinary citizen who reports a crime which has been committed in his presence, or that a crime is being or will be committed, stands on much different ground than a police informer. He is a witness to criminal activity who acts with an intent to aid the police in law enforcement because of his concern for society or for his own safety. He does not expect any gain or concession in exchange for his information. An informer of this type usually would not have more than one opportunity to supply information to the police.

Credibility and reliability in this respect may be further enhanced if the particular citizen is "more than the ordinary citizen," for example, fire fighters, first aid or ambulance squad members, security personnel and the like. These individuals, while not sworn law enforcement officers, are more involved and presumably more public spirited than the average citizen, and in and of themselves may be considered credible sources of information.

Finally, the information imparted by a citizen-informer who is herself a victim or complainant, should be taken at face value.[531] Particularly when an informant is named, her reliability may be presumed, and the affidavit need only establish that his observations arise from personal knowledge.

---

[526] Excerpts from the comprehensive discussion of the laws of arrest, search and seizure in Larry E. Holtz, *Criminal Procedure for Law and Justice Professionals* (Blue360° Media).

[527] *State v. Arrington*, 311 N.C. 633, 319 S.E.2d 254 (1984).

[528] *State v. Arrington*, 311 N.C. 633, 641, 319 S.E.2d 254 (1984).

[529] *State v. Arrington*, 311 N.C. 633, 641-41, 319 S.E.2d 254 (1984).

[530] *State v. Arrington*, 311 N.C. 633, 642, 319 S.E.2d 254 (1984). *See also State v. Beam*, 325 N.C. 217, 381 S.E.2d 327 (1989).

[531] *See, e.g., Easton v. City of Boulder*, 776 F.2d 1441, 1449 (10th Cir. 1985) ("[T]he skepticism and careful scrutiny usually found in cases involving informants, sometimes anonymous, from the criminal milieu, is appropriately relaxed if the

4.1.7.3. Fellow officers

During the course of various types of investigations, police must rely on facts and information imparted by fellow officers. As a general rule, courts will consider information stemming from the observations and discoveries of fellow officers inherently trustworthy, and consequently, further exploration or verification of a fellow officer's personal credibility or reliability is not required. In this respect, the Supreme Court has determined that "[o]bservations of fellow officers of the Government engaged in a common investigation are plainly a reliable basis for a warrant applied for by one of their number."[532]

4.1.7.4. Anonymous tips

Of all the types of information acted upon by law enforcement, the anonymous tip requires the most independent verification.[533] By its very nature, the anonymous tip carries with it none of the traditional indicators of reliability which may attach to information imparted by citizen informants or even criminal informants. Thus, to develop the reliability of information imparted by the anonymous tip, officers must engage in two critical procedures: (1) comprehensive detail development; and (2) independent verification.[534]

First, the individual who takes the call or receives the information must elicit as much detail as possible from the informer. Comprehensive detail development is crucial; it demonstrates the anonymous informant's "basis of knowledge," and provides substance and meaning to the second procedure in the development of reliability. Naturally, the call-taker should not initially attempt to ascertain the caller's identity. It is all too often that the question, "What is your name?", is followed by the sound of a dial tone. Rather, the call-taker should try to ascertain as much detail as possible as to what exactly the caller has observed (or is presently observing), the physical description of the subject of the caller's observations, how far away the subject was (or is presently) from the caller, whether the caller is presently watching the subject and if not, how long ago the observations were made, the exact location of the subject, whether there were or presently are any other people or vehicles in the area, and whether the caller would stay on the line while officers are dispatched. Once the call-taker has elicited as much detail as possible from the caller, the call-taker may then consider asking more "dangerous" questions, such as, "Are you a resident of the neighborhood?" "Do you live next to where these things are taking place?" "Where do you live?" "What is your name?"

The second step requires independent investigation directed at confirming or verifying each of the facts related in the anonymous tip. It is this independent corroboration which provides a foundation for a reviewing court to conclude that a substantial basis exists for crediting the hearsay information imparted by the anonymous tip. Significantly, as the officer proceeds to corroborate each of the details of the tip, it becomes increasingly evident that "'[b]ecause [the] informant is right about some things, he is more probably right about other facts[.]'"[535] Once an officer has personally verified every possible facet of the information contained in the tip, reasonable grounds may then exist to believe that the remaining unverified bit of information—that a criminal offense is occurring, or has occurred—is likewise true.[536] As the United States Supreme Court has stated, "such tips, particularly when supplemented by independent police investigation, frequently contribute to the solution of otherwise 'perfect crimes.'"[537]

---

informant is an identified victim."); *see also Sharrar v. Felsing*, 128 F.3d 810, 818 (3d Cir. 1997) ("When a police officer has received a reliable identification by a victim of his or her attacker, the police have probable cause to arrest.").

[532] *United States v. Ventresca*, 380 U.S. 102, 111, 85 S. Ct. 741, 747 (1965); *see also United States v. Griffin*, 827 F.2d 1108, 1112 (7th Cir. 1987) (the "affiant's fellow agents" may "'plainly [] be regarded as a reliable source by the magistrate'") (quoting *United States v. Pritchard*, 745 F.2d 1112, 1120 (7th Cir. 1984)). *Accord United States v. Cooper*, 949 F.2d 737, 745 (5th Cir. 1991) (if the combined knowledge of police from two different jurisdictions was such that they collectively had probable cause to believe criminal evidence was located in a robbery suspect's car, officers from either jurisdiction could lawfully have conducted a warrantless search).

[533] *See State v. Lowe*, 369 N.C. 360, 794 S.E.2d 282 (2016); *State v. Benters*, 367 N.C. 660, 766 S.E.2d 593 (2014).

[534] Larry E. Holtz, *Criminal Procedure for Law and Justice Professionals*, §2.3(a) (Blue360° Media).

[535] *Illinois v. Gates*, 462 U.S. 213, 234, 103 S. Ct. 2317, 2335 (1983) (quoting *Spinelli v. United States*, 393 U.S. 410, 427, 89 S. Ct. 584, 594 (1969) (White, J., concurring)).

[536] *Draper v. United States*, 358 U.S. 307, 79 S. Ct. 329 (1959).

[537] *Illinois v. Gates*, 462 U.S. 213, 234, 103 S. Ct. 2317, 2332 (1983). Excerpts from the comprehensive discussion of the laws of arrest, search and seizure in Larry E. Holtz, *Criminal Procedure for Law and Justice Professionals* (Blue360° Media).

4.1.8. Warrant execution; serving the warrant

4.1.8.1. Service

Pursuant to N.C.Gen.Stat. § 15A-252:

Before undertaking any search or seizure pursuant to the warrant, the officer must read the warrant and give a copy of the warrant application and affidavit to the person to be searched, or the person in apparent control of the premises or vehicle to be searched. If no one in apparent and responsible control is occupying the premises or vehicle, the officer must leave a copy of the warrant affixed to the premises or vehicle.

4.1.8.2. Entry and the "knock and announce" rule

Prior to entering a dwelling to execute a search warrant, police must knock and announce their presence, authority and purpose, and demand entry. This common law "knock and announce" principle "forms a part of the reasonableness inquiry under the Fourth Amendment."[538] The rule requires "notice in the form of an express announcement by the officers of their [authority and] purpose for demanding admission."[539] Compliance with the rule "is also a safeguard for the police themselves who might be mistaken for prowlers and be shot down by a fearful householder."[540] The roots of the "knock and announce" rule can be traced back through the English common law at least as far as the 1603 opinion in *Semayne's* case.[541]

The rule is codified in North Carolina law, which provides: "The officer executing a search warrant must, before entering the premises, give appropriate notice of his identity and purpose to the person to be searched, or the person in apparent control of the premises to be searched. If it is unclear whether anyone is present at the premises to be searched, he must give the notice in a manner likely to be heard by anyone who is present."[542] This statute is commonly referred to as the "knock and announce" law.

Accordingly, the "knock and announce" rule has three underlying purposes: (1) to reduce the risk of violence that inheres in an unannounced, forced entry; (2) to protect privacy by reducing the risk of entering the wrong premises; and (3) to prevent unnecessary physical damage to the property.

Officers are required to adhere to the "knock and announce" rule even if the entry could be made without the use of force, *i.e.*, by merely opening a closed but unlocked door,[543] or by the use of a passkey.[544] As the Supreme Court stated in *Sabbath*: "An unannounced intrusion into a dwelling … is no less an unannounced intrusion whether officers break down a door, force open a chain lock on a partially open door, open a locked door by use of a passkey, or, as here, open a closed but unlocked door."[545]

There is no constitutional mandate that an officer must knock and announce before entering a dwelling in every instance. Over the course of time, courts have recognized several exceptions to the "knock and announce" rule. Exceptions recognized to date include a reasonable suspicion that knocking and announcing would:

(1) present a threat of physical violence, *e.g.*, where the officers' peril would be increased if knocking preceded entry;

(2) be futile or a "useless gesture" (for example, where a prisoner escapes from the police and retreats to his dwelling, knocking and announcing would be considered a "useless gesture" or a "senseless ceremony" prior to entering the premises to regain custody of the escaping offender; *or* when no one is home at the target premises, knocking and announcing would be futile or a "useless gesture" when there is no one present to hear the police knocking);

---

[538] *Wilson v. Arkansas*, 514 U.S. 927, 115 S. Ct. 1914 (1995).

[539] *Miller v. United States*, 357 U.S. 301, 309, 78 S. Ct. 1190, 1196 (1958).

[540] *Miller v. United States*, 357 U.S. 301, 313 n.12, 78 S. Ct. 1190, 1198 n.12 (1958).

[541] *Semayne's* case, 5 Coke 91, 77 *Eng.Rep.* 194 (K.B. 1603).

[542] N.C.Gen.Stat. § 15A-249.

[543] *Sabbath v. United States*, 391 U.S. 585, 88 S. Ct. 1755 (1968).

[544] *Munoz v. United States*, 325 F.2d 23 (9th Cir. 1963).

[545] *Sabbath v. United States*, 391 U.S. 585, 590, 88 S. Ct. 1755, 1798 (1968).

(3) cause the arrest to be frustrated, when entry of a premises is necessary to execute an "arrest" warrant or effect a warrantless arrest with exigent circumstances; or
(4) result in the loss or destruction of evidence, and immediate action is required to preserve the evidence.[546]

Thus, in *State v. Sumpter*,[547] there was no suppression when Detective Gaines, in executing search warrant for drugs, simultaneously announced his presence and entered residence. The court found it significant that "no occupant in the present case objected to the officers' entry through the unlocked door."[548] More importantly, "Detective Davis testified that, based on his training and experience, persons who use and sell crack cocaine usually carry weapons and that firearms and ammunition are often found during searches for drugs pursuant to search warrants. Detective Davis observed a number of persons enter through the door without knocking or receiving an invitation from an occupant to enter. The door was unlocked at the time the officers entered."[549] Moreover, "drugs such as crack cocaine, the object of the search, may be destroyed within a matter of seconds by flushing them down the toilet."[550] While Detective Gaines violated the "literal" provisions of N.C.Gen.Stat. § 15A-249, the violation was not "substantial" and did not require that the evidence be suppressed.[551]

In *Richards v. Wisconsin*,[552] however, the United States Supreme Court refused to adopt a blanket exception for felony drug investigations, rejecting the Wisconsin rule that

police officers are never required to knock and announce their presence when executing a search warrant in a felony drug investigation." Rather, in order "to justify a no-knock entry, *the police must have a reasonable suspicion that knocking and announcing their presence, under the particular circumstances, would be dangerous or futile, or that it would inhibit the effective investigation of the crime by, for example, allowing the destruction of evidence.* This standard—as opposed to a probable cause requirement—strikes the appropriate balance between the legitimate law enforcement concerns at issue in the execution of search warrants and the individual privacy interests affected by no-knock entries....This showing is not high, but the police should be required to make it whenever the reasonableness of a no-knock entry is challenged.[553]

Naturally, if at the time of search warrant procurement, the affiant possesses a reasonable suspicion that one or more of the foregoing factors are present, a judge would be "acting within the Constitution to authorize a 'no knock' entry."[554]

4.1.8.2.1. The time between the announcement and the entry

Officers may not knock and announce their presence, authority, and purpose and *immediately* enter the target premises. Although there is no set time for every case, to pass constitutional muster, the time lapse between the police announcement and any forced entry must be reasonable under the circumstances, but not necessarily extensive in length.[555]

In *United States v. Banks*,[556] the U.S. Supreme Court held that, under the "totality of the circumstances" presented, a 15- to 20-second wait between an officer's knock and announcement of authority and the forcible entry satisfied the Fourth Amendment. In *Banks*, based on information that Banks was selling cocaine at his

---

[546] *See Wilson v. Arkansas*, 514 U.S. 927, 115 S. Ct. 1914, 1919 (1995); *United States v. Banks*, 540 U.S. 31, 124 S. Ct. 521, 525 (2003).
[547] *State v. Sumpter*, 150 N.C. App. 431, 563 S.E.2d 60 (2002).
[548] *State v. Sumpter*, 150 N.C. App. 431, 434, 563 S.E.2d 60 (2002).
[549] *State v. Sumpter*, 150 N.C. App. 431, 433, 563 S.E.2d 60 (2002).
[550] *State v. Sumpter*, 150 N.C. App. 431, 434, 563 S.E.2d 60 (2002).
[551] *State v. Sumpter*, 150 N.C. App. 431, 434, 563 S.E.2d 60 (2002).
[552] *Richards v. Wisconsin*, 520 U.S. 385, 117 S. Ct. 1416 (1997).
[553] *Richards v. Wisconsin*, 520 U.S. 385, 117 S. Ct. 1416, 1421-22 (1997) (emphasis added).
[554] *United States v. Banks*, 540 U.S. 31, 124 S. Ct. 521, 525 (2003).
[555] See *State v. Gaines*, 33 N.C. App. 66, 234 S.E.2d 42 (1977) (Holding the amount of time required to be given between notice and entry must depend on the particular circumstances).
[556] *United States v. Banks*, 540 U.S. 31, 124 S. Ct. 521 (2003).

home, police officers and FBI agents obtained a warrant to search his two-bedroom apartment. "As soon as they arrived there, about 2 o'clock on a Wednesday afternoon, officers posted in front called out 'police search warrant' and rapped hard enough on the door to be heard by officers at the back door. There was no indication whether anyone was home, and after waiting for 15 to 20 seconds with no answer, the officers broke open the front door with a battering ram."[557] Banks was in the shower at the time. The search uncovered weapons, crack cocaine, and other evidence of drug dealing.

As a general rule, held the Court, the police must wait "a reasonable time under all the circumstances." Here, the 15- to 20-second wait was reasonable.

Although officers should make every effort to comply with the "knock and announce" requirement, under the Fourth Amendment, a violation of the rule will not necessarily lead to the suppression of evidence. In this regard, the federal Supreme Court, in *Hudson v. Michigan*,[558] determined that "the social costs of applying the exclusionary rule to knock-and-announce violations are considerable; the incentive to such violations is minimal to begin with, and the extant deterrences against them are substantial[.] Resort to the massive remedy of suppressing evidence of guilt is unjustified."[559] The Court did note, however, that officers who violate the rule still face the threat of possible civil remedies (such as a lawsuit under 42 U.S.C. § 1983) or internal discipline by their employer.

4.1.9. Inventory and return

The inventory and return of seized items are governed by N.C.Gen.Stat. § 15A-254 which provides:

Upon seizing items pursuant to a search warrant, an officer must write and sign a receipt itemizing the items taken and containing the name of the court by which the warrant was issued. If the items were taken from a person, the receipt must be given to the person. If items are taken from a place or vehicle, the receipt must be given to the owner, or person in apparent control of the premises or vehicle if the person is present; or if he is not, the officer must leave the receipt in the premises or vehicle from which the items were taken.

4.1.9.1. Police need not inform owner of the procedures for property return

When law enforcement officers seize property under the authority of a search warrant, "due process requires them to take reasonable steps to give notice that the property has been taken so that the owner can pursue available remedies for its return."[560] Moreover, when the owner of the property is not present at the time of the search, such individualized notice that law enforcement officials have taken property is necessary "because the property owner would have no other reasonable means of ascertaining who was responsible for his loss."[561] There is no requirement, however, that officers inform the property owner of the procedures for seeking return of the seized property. As emphasized by the U.S. Supreme Court in *Perkins*, the Due Process Clause does not require law enforcement officials "to give detailed and specific instructions or advice to owners who seek return of property lawfully seized but no longer needed for police investigation or criminal prosecution."[562] Once the property owner is informed that his property has been seized, she can turn to published statutes, court rules, or case law to learn about the remedial procedures available for property return.[563]

4.1.10. Anticipatory warrants

An "anticipatory" search warrant is a warrant that is signed and issued by a judge based on an affidavit demonstrating probable cause to believe that, within a reasonable time in the future (but not at the time

---

[557] *United States v. Banks*, 540 U.S. 31, 124 S. Ct. 521, 523 (2003).

[558] *Hudson v. Michigan*, 547 U.S. 586, 126 S. Ct. 2159 (2006).

[559] *Hudson v. Michigan*, 547 U.S. 586, 126 S. Ct. 2159, 2168, 2170 (2006).

[560] *City of West Covina v. Perkins*, 525 U.S. 234, 119 S. Ct. 678, 681 (1999).

[561] *City of West Covina v. Perkins*, 525 U.S. 234, 119 S. Ct. 678, 681 (1999).

[562] *City of West Covina v. Perkins*, 525 U.S. 234, 119 S. Ct. 678, 679 (1999).

[563] *City of West Covina v. Perkins*, 525 U.S. 234, 119 S. Ct. 678, 681-82 (1999).

the affidavit is presented), contraband or criminal evidence will arrive at a particular place. When applying for an anticipatory warrant, the affiant-officer is, in essence, asserting that probable cause does not exist presently, but will exist following the occurrence of some "triggering event." The affidavit must demonstrate a fair probability that evidence of a crime or contraband will be found at the place to be searched if the triggering condition occurs, and probable cause to believe that the triggering condition will occur. When properly drafted and used, anticipatory warrants have been held to be constitutional and a valuable law enforcement tool.[564]

Such warrants are typically used when law enforcement officials have arranged or will be monitoring a controlled delivery of contraband. The anticipatory search warrant and the affidavit in support thereof must demonstrate several things not normally found in the traditional search warrant. First, the affidavit must set forth facts demonstrating a *strong probability* that the sought-after evidence will be at the target premises when the warrant is executed. A judge must be able to conclude from the affidavit that there is a strong probability that the continuation of the process already initiated by the shipment of contraband will in the natural course of events result in the consummation of the crime at the time and place anticipated.

In *United States v. Grubbs*,[565] the defendant purchased a videotape of child pornography from a website operated by an undercover postal inspector. Authorities arranged a controlled delivery of the videotape, then obtained a search warrant for the defendant's home; the affidavit in support of the warrant specifically provided that the warrant was not to be executed "unless and until the parcel has been delivered by a person(s) and has been physically taken into the residence." After the defendant's wife signed for the videotape, the warrant was lawfully executed. The affidavit in this case clearly established that contraband would be present in the defendant's home once the videotape was delivered—child pornography is obviously illegal. In addition, there was probable cause to believe this condition would be satisfied; although it was possible the defendant might have refused delivery, he was unlikely to do so after having ordered the videotape. Therefore, this was a valid anticipatory warrant.

In *State v. Smith*,[566] the Court of Appeals of North Carolina recognized that an anticipatory search warrant "must minimize the officer's discretion in deciding whether or not the 'triggering event' has occurred to 'almost ministerial proportions.' This means the events which trigger probable cause must be specified in the warrant to a point 'similar to a search party's discretion in locating the place to be searched.'"[567] Because the affidavit in *Smith* was written in the present or past tense and did not express contingency or anticipation of a future event, the search pursuant to the warrant was not allowed.

The warrant clearly identified the triggering events in *State v. Carrillo*,[568] where the police obtained an anticipatory warrant to search the defendant's apartment. There, the United States Customs Service intercepted a package mailed from an address in Mexico and addressed to the defendant at his residence in Pitt County. U.S. Customs Inspector Richard Rice determined that the package contained a large amount of cocaine concealed inside three ceramic turtles.[569] The police secured an anticipatory warrant to search the defendant's apartment after the package was delivered to him.

An officer, disguised as a delivery man, delivered the package to the defendant, who accepted delivery, signed for the package and carried it into his apartment. Thereafter, the police executed the anticipatory warrant. Inside the defendant's apartment, the police found the package as well as broken pieces of glass turtles containing trace amounts of cocaine. With regard to the triggering events identified in the warrant, the court observed with favor, "Here, the language used in the supporting affidavit not only identifies the triggering events as occurring in the future, but also states the future condition upon which the warrant will *not* be executed."[570] Accordingly, the search was upheld.

---

[564] *United States v. Grubbs,* 547 U.S. 90, 126 S. Ct. 1494, 1499 (2006); *see also State v. Carrillo,* 164 N.C. App. 204, 595 S.E.2d 219 (2004).

[565] *United States v. Grubbs,* 547 U.S. 90, 126 S. Ct. 1494 (2006).

[566] *State v. Smith,* 124 N.C. App. 565, 478 S.E.2d 237 (1996).

[567] *State v. Smith,* 124 N.C. App. 565, 572, 478 S.E.2d 237 (1996) (quoting *United States v. Ricciardelli,* 998 F.2d 8 (1st Cir. 1993)).

[568] *State v. Carrillo,* 164 N.C. App. 204, 595 S.E.2d 219 (2004).

[569] *State v. Carrillo,* 164 N.C. App. 204, 205, 595 S.E.2d 219 (2004).

[570] *State v. Carrillo,* 164 N.C. App. 204, 208, 595 S.E.2d 219 (2004) (emphasis in original).

4.1.11. Scope of the search

As a general rule, the "scope" of a lawful search is "defined by the object of the search and the places in which there is probable cause to believe that it may be found."[571] Whenever a search is made pursuant to the authority of a valid search warrant, it may naturally extend to the entire area covered by the warrant's description. Therefore, if the residence to be searched is identified by street number, the search is not limited to the dwelling house, but may also extend to the garage and other structures deemed to be within the curtilage and the yard within the curtilage.

When a law enforcement officer executes a warrant authorizing the search of only a portion of a particular structure, only that portion may be searched. Thus, if the warrant specifically authorized a search of the third floor of a building, the officer may not lawfully search any other floor. And when the probable cause delineated in the warrant describes stolen property believed to be in the garage, that information would not support a search for that item in an upstairs bedroom.[572]

Individual rooms, places or objects within the described premises do not require any additional showing of probable cause when their access requires an additional act of entry. As the United States Supreme Court explained in *Ross*:

A lawful search of fixed premises generally extends to the entire area in which the object of the search may be found and is not limited by the possibility that separate acts of entry or opening may be required to complete the search. Thus, a warrant that authorizes an officer to search a home for illegal weapons also provides authority to open closets, chests, drawers, and containers in which the weapon might be found. A warrant to open a footlocker to search for marijuana would also authorize the opening of packages found inside. A warrant to search a vehicle would support a search of every part of the vehicle that might contain the object of the search.[573]

Accordingly, when law enforcement officers are engaged in a legitimate search pursuant to a warrant whose "purpose and limits have been precisely defined, nice distinctions between glove compartments, upholstered seats, trunks, and wrapped packages, in the case of a vehicle, must give way to the interest in the prompt and efficient completion of the task at hand."[574]

A critical distinction, however, must be drawn between the premises to be searched and vehicles at the premises. In this respect, a warrant to search a building does not include authority to search vehicles at the premises, and, the authority to search a vehicle does not include authority to enter private premises to effect a search of a vehicle within those premises.

4.1.11.1. The authority to detain occupants

The United States Supreme Court has also held that, "for Fourth Amendment purposes," a "warrant to search for contraband founded on probable cause implicitly carries with it the limited authority to detain the occupants of the premises while a proper search is conducted."[575] Officers may detain anyone found in the residence, regardless of whether or not the occupant is a suspect named in the warrant, and may use reasonable force in detaining the occupants.[576] This rule is codified in North Carolina at N.C.Gen.Stat. § 15A-256 which provides:

---

[571] *United States v. Ross*, 456 U.S. 798, 824, 102 S. Ct. 2157, 2172 (1982).

[572] *United States v. Ross*, 456 U.S. 798, 824, 102 S. Ct. 2157, 2172 (1982).

[573] *United States v. Ross*, 456 U.S. 798, 821, 102 S. Ct. 2157, 2170-71 (1982).

[574] *United States v. Ross*, 456 U.S. 798, 820-821, 102 S. Ct. 2157, 2171 (1982).

[575] *Michigan v. Summers*, 452 U.S. 692, 705, 101 S. Ct. 2587, 2595 (1981).

[576] *Muehler v. Mena*, 544 U.S. 93, 125 S. Ct. 1465 (2005) (police justified in handcuffing woman for two to three hours while executing search warrant for weapons at the residence of a suspected gang member); *cf. Illinois v. McArthur*, 531 U.S. 326, 121 S. Ct. 946 (2001) (Police could detain a defendant on the front porch outside his home for two hours while they obtained a search warrant when they had probable cause to believe that marijuana was hidden inside the home, and that the defendant would destroy this contraband if allowed to enter unescorted; noting with favor that detention lasted only long enough for police, acting with diligence, to obtain a warrant).

An officer executing a warrant directing a search of premises not generally open to the public or of a vehicle other than a common carrier may detain any person present for such time as is reasonably necessary to execute the warrant. If the search of such premises or vehicle and of any persons designated as objects of the search in the warrant fails to produce the items named in the warrant, the officer may then search any person present at the time of the officer's entry to the extent reasonably necessary to find property particularly described in the warrant which may be concealed upon the person, but no property of a different type from that particularly described in the warrant may be seized or may be the basis for prosecution of any person so searched. For the purpose of this section, all controlled substances are the same type of property.

In *Michigan v. Summers*, the U.S. Supreme Court observed that there are three important law enforcement interests that, taken together, justify the detention of an occupant who is on the premises during the execution of a search warrant: (1) officer safety; (2) facilitating the orderly completion of the search; and (3) preventing flight.[577]

A person may not, however, be detained incident to the execution of a search warrant unless the person is within the *immediate vicinity* of the premises to be searched—in other words, that area in which an occupant poses a real threat to the safe and efficient execution of the warrant. Courts can consider a number of factors to determine whether an occupant was detained within the immediate vicinity of the premises to be searched, including the lawful limits of the premises, whether the occupant was within the line of sight of his dwelling, and the ease of reentry from the occupant's location.[578] In *Bailey*, the defendant's detention was unlawful when he left the house to be searched and had driven about a mile from the home before the officers stopped and searched him.

The authority to detain those present but not named in the warrant does not include the authority to search those persons, absent an independent justification for the search. Thus, in *Ybarra v. Illinois*,[579] the Court held that a valid warrant to search for narcotics at a particular tavern did not also provide the officers with the authority to automatically search or frisk any person who happens to be on the premises during the execution of that warrant. According to the Court, a person's mere presence at the target premises, standing in close proximity "to others independently suspected of criminal activity does not, without more, give rise to probable cause to search that person.... This requirement cannot be undercut or avoided by simply pointing to the fact that coincidentally there exists probable cause to search or seize another or to search the premises where the person may happen to be."[580] Additionally, the "'narrow scope' of the *Terry* [rule] does not permit a frisk for weapons on less than reasonable belief or suspicion directed at the person to be frisked, even though that person happens to be on the premises where an authorized narcotics search is taking place."[581]

In *State v. Wilson*,[582] both the detention and the search were allowed where police officers had reason to believe that criminal activity may have been afoot. Having discussed this case with regard to a *Terry* stop, a brief review of the facts here will suffice. In *Wilson*, the defendant had arrived on the scene while the Winston-Salem Police Department was in the process of actively securing a home in order to execute a search warrant. The defendant penetrated the perimeter securing the scene, walked past an officer, and announced that he was going to retrieve his moped. After disobeying the officer's command to stop, the defendant proceeded down the driveway toward the home, at which point officers detained and frisked him. Officers recovered a firearm, and the defendant was charged with possession of a firearm by a felon.[583]

In determining whether the defendant had been lawfully seized, the North Carolina Supreme Court recognized "three parts of the *Summers* rule: 'a warrant to search for contraband founded on probable cause implicitly carries with it the limited authority to detain [(1)]' the occupants,' (2) who are 'within the immediate vicinity of the premises to be searched,' and (3) who are present 'during the execution of a search warrant'. These three parts roughly correspond to the 'who,' 'where,' and 'when' of a lawful suspicionless

577 *Michigan v. Summers*, 452 U.S. 692, 101 S. Ct. 2587 (1981).
578 *Bailey v. United States*, 568 U.S. 186, 133 S. Ct. 1031 (2013).
579 *Ybarra v. Illinois*, 444 U.S. 85, 100 S. Ct. 338 (1979).
580 *Ybarra v. Illinois*, 444 U.S. 85, 100 S. Ct. 338, 342 (1979).
581 *Ybarra v. Illinois*, 444 U.S. 85, 100 S. Ct. 338, 342 (1979).
582 *State v. Wilson*, 371 N.C. 920, 821 S.E.2d 811 (N.C. 2018).
583 *State v. Wilson*, 371 N.C. 920, 922, 821 S.E.2d 811 (N.C. 2018).

seizure incident to the execution of a search warrant."[584] Determining that the second and third prongs were "straightforward," the court focused its inquiry on whether the defendant was an "occupant" of the premises during the execution of the search warrant.[585] The court ultimately concluded that a person is an "occupant" for purposes of the rule ""if he poses a real threat to the safe and efficient execution of a search warrant."[586] Accordingly, while the defendant was not inside the premises during the execution of the search warrant, he "posed a real threat to the safe and efficient execution of the search warrant [and] ...would have *occupied* the area being searched if he had not been restrained."[587] Moreover, the subsequent frisk of the defendant was a permissible *Terry* frisk given the reasonable suspicion that criminal activity was afoot.[588]

In direct contrast with *Wilson* is *State v. Thompson*.[589] There, the "[d]efendant was cleaning his vehicle in the street when officers arrived to execute the search warrant. The officers approached Defendant to question him. Defendant remained inside his vehicle and told the officers that he did not live in the apartment, but that his girlfriend did. At no point did Defendant attempt to approach the apartment. Nor did he exhibit nervousness or agitation, disobey or protest the officers' directives, appear to be armed, or undertake to interfere with the search."[590] Accordingly, he was not an "occupant" pursuant to the *Summers* rule and his seizure was unjustified.

4.1.11.2. Media ride-alongs

In *Wilson v. Layne*,[591] and *Hanlon v. Berger*,[592] the United States Supreme Court held that "it is a violation of the Fourth Amendment for police to bring members of the media or other third parties into a home during the execution of a warrant when the presence of the third parties in the home was not in aid of the execution of the warrant."

4.2. Exceptions to the warrant requirement (warrantless searches)

As an established principle of contemporary criminal procedure, searches and seizures conducted without a written warrant are "*per se* unreasonable within the meaning of the Fourth Amendment,"[593] unless they fall within one of the recognized exceptions to the Fourth Amendment's written warrant requirement.[594] There is a strong judicial preference for the acquisition of a search warrant by a law enforcement officer prior to intruding into an individual's realm of privacy, and this requirement is not to be dispensed with lightly. The rule demonstrates the desirability of placing a judge's probable cause determination, and assessment of whether the circumstances are exigent (where applicable), between the law enforcement officer and the victim of the search or seizure, to provide the necessary security against unreasonable intrusions into an individual's right to privacy.

As observed in *United States v. Ventresca*,[595] "an evaluation of the constitutionality of a search warrant should begin with the rule that the informed and deliberate determinations of magistrates empowered to issue warrants ...are to be preferred over the hurried action of officers who may happen to make arrests. This preference for a written warrant indicates that in a doubtful or marginal case, a search may be sustainable where without one it would fall."

---

[584] *State v. Wilson*, 371 N.C. 920, 821 S.E.2d 811, 815 (N.C. 2018)(quoting *Michigan v. Summers*, 452 U.S. 692, 705, 101 S. Ct. 2587 (1981); *Bailey v. United States*, 568 U.S. 186, 201, 133 S. Ct. 1031 (2013) and citing *Muehler v. Mena*, 544 U.S. 93, 125 S. Ct. 1465 (2005)).

[585] *State v. Wilson*, 371 N.C. 920, 924-25, 821 S.E.2d 81 (N.C. 2018).

[586] *State v. Wilson*, 371 N.C. 920, 925, 821 S.E.2d 811 (N.C. 2018).

[587] *State v. Wilson*, 371 N.C. 920, 925, 821 S.E.2d 811 (N.C. 2018) (emphasis in original).

[588] *State v. Wilson*, 371 N.C. 920, 821 S.E.2d 811, 817 (N.C. 2018).

[589] *State v. Thompson*, 2019 N.C. App. LEXIS 703 (Ct. App. Aug. 20, 2019).

[590] *State v. Thompson*, 2019 N.C. App. LEXIS 703, *13-14 (Ct. App. Aug. 20, 2019).

[591] *Wilson v. Layne*, 526 U.S. 603, 119 S. Ct. 1692, 1699 (1999).

[592] *Hanlon v. Berger*, 526 U.S. 808, 119 S. Ct. 1706 (1999).

[593] *United States v. Place*, 462 U.S. 696, 701, 103 S. Ct. 2637, 2641 (1983).

[594] *See, e.g., Thompson v. Louisiana*, 469 U.S. 17, 105 S. Ct. 409, 411 (1984); *Mincey v. Arizona*, 437 U.S. 385, 98 S. Ct. 2408, 2412 (1978); *United States v. Edwards*, 415 U.S. 800, 802, 94 S. Ct. 1234, 1236 (1974).

[595] *United States v. Ventresca*, 380 U.S. 102, 105-06, 85 S. Ct. 741 (1965) (citations and internal quotes omitted).

Once a search or seizure is conducted without a warrant, the burden is upon the Government, as the party seeking to validate the warrantless search, to bring it clearly within one of the recognized exceptions created by the United States Supreme Court.[596] Thus, the Constitution does not, however, prohibit all warrantless searches or seizures; the Constitution only forbids "unreasonable searches and seizures."[597]

Over the course of time, the United States Supreme Court has carved out of the Fourth Amendment several carefully tailored exceptions to its warrant requirement. Those formally recognized include:

(1) Search incident to a lawful arrest
(2) Exigent circumstances
(3) Consent
(4) Automobile exception
(5) Impound/inventory
(6) Open fields
(7) Plain view
(8) Abandonment
(9) Administrative and Regulatory searches
(10) Non-governmental (private) searches

The following materials discuss each of the judicially recognized exceptions to the written warrant requirement and explore the impact each has on law enforcement.

4.2.1. Search incident to a lawful arrest

Generally, the courts address this exception in two broad areas: a search of a person incident to arrest and a search of a vehicle incident to arrest.

4.2.1.1. The person of the arrestee and the area within his immediate control

When a law enforcement officer effects a lawful custodial arrest based on probable cause, she is permitted to conduct a contemporaneous search of the person of the arrestee. Such a search safeguards the arresting officer and others nearby from harm while ensuring that the arrestee will not discard or destroy evidence.

Before a search incident to an arrest may be deemed valid, however, the arrest itself must be lawful. An officer may not justify an arrest by the search and at the same time justify the search by the arrest.[598] In this respect, if an officer makes an unlawful arrest, any evidence seized during the search incident to that arrest will be inadmissible in court. Thus, the propriety of the incident search depends upon the validity of the arrest.

An incident search of an individual's person may not, therefore, be undertaken for the purpose of gathering evidential justification for that individual's arrest. Even if the desired evidence is found on the individual's person, an arrest thereafter will not be valid in the absence of probable cause for the arrest based on information separate and distinct from that which the search of the person disclosed. As the Supreme Court stated in *Sibron v. New York*: "It is axiomatic that an incident search may not precede an arrest and serve as part of its justification."[599]

It has been held, however, that so long as probable cause for an arrest exists prior to the undertaking of any search of the prospective arrestee's person, it does not matter whether the search immediately precedes

---

[596] *See, e.g., Riley v. California*, 573 U.S. 373, 134 S. Ct. 2473, 2482 (2014) ("In the absence of a warrant, a search is reasonable only if it falls within a specific exception to the warrant requirement."); *see also Kentucky v. King*, 563 U.S. 452, 131 S. Ct. 1849, 1856-57 (2011).

[597] *Terry v. Ohio*, 392 U.S. 1, 9, 88 S. Ct. 1868, 1873 (1968); *Elkins v. United States*, 364 U.S. 206, 222, 80 S. Ct. 1437, 1446 (1960).

[598] *Johnson v. United States*, 333 U.S. 10, 16-17, 68 S. Ct. 367, 370 (1948).

[599] *Sibron v. New York*, 392 U.S. 40, 63, 88 S. Ct. 1889, 1902 (1968); *see also Smith v. Ohio*, 494 U.S. 541, 110 S. Ct. 1288, 1290 (1990) (The exception for searches incident to arrest "does not permit the police to search any citizen without a warrant or probable cause so long as an arrest immediately follows.").

or follows the formal arrest.[600] As the United States Supreme Court explained in *Rawlings v. Kentucky*,[601] "where the formal arrest followed quickly on the heels of the challenged search of [an individual's] person, we do not believe it particularly important that the search preceded the arrest rather than vice versa," so long as what the search disclosed was "not necessary to support probable cause to arrest." In these circumstances, if the arrest is lawful—apart from the search or what the search disclosed—and if the arrest and the search occurred as continuous steps in a single, integrated transaction, then the evidence disclosed by the search should not be lost merely because, in the precise sequence of events, the search preceded the arrest. It has been held, however, that a search will be unconstitutional, even if the officer had probable cause to arrest at the time, if an actual arrest is not made subsequent to the search.[602]

There is no requirement that the probable cause justifying the lawful custodial arrest, and therefore a search incident to that arrest, be "for the charge eventually prosecuted."[603] "Probable cause need only exist as to any offense that *could be charged* under the circumstances."[604] This means that an officer with probable cause to believe a person has committed *any offense justifying a full custodial arrest* has the authority to conduct a search incident to that arrest.

Once an individual has been lawfully arrested, not only may the police conduct a full search of the individual's person but they may also conduct a search of the area within that person's immediate control. This rule was pronounced by the United States Supreme Court in the landmark case of *Chimel v. California*,[605] where it was held that a valid custodial arrest creates the circumstance which justifies the contemporaneous warrantless search of the person arrested and of the immediately surrounding area. According to the Court, such contemporaneous searches incident to arrest have long been considered valid because of the law enforcement need "to remove any weapons that [the arrestee] might seek to use in order to resist arrest or effect his escape" and the need to prevent the destruction or concealment of evidence.[606] The Court said: "A gun on a table or in a drawer in front of one who is arrested can be as dangerous to the arresting officer as one concealed in the clothing of the person arrested."[607]

The reasons underlying such search need not, however, be litigated in every case.[608]

4.2.1.1.1. Strip searches

Naturally, a "full search of the person" does not include a strip search. A "strip search" requires a person to remove her clothing to expose underclothing, breasts, buttocks, or genitalia. It is no doubt a severe intrusion into one's privacy. Nonetheless, strip searches are not per se illegal or unconstitutional.

In *State v. Battle*,[609] the defendant was subjected to a roadside strip search. The Court of Appeals of North Carolina asserted, "A valid search incident to arrest, however, will not normally permit a law enforcement officer to conduct a roadside strip search."[610] Accordingly, the court held, "For a search to comply with the requirements of Fourth Amendment jurisprudence, there must be sufficient supporting facts and exigent circumstances *prior* to initiating a strip search to justify this heightened intrusion into a suspect's right to privacy."[611] Holding that the strip search violated the defendant's Fourth Amendment right against unreasonable searches and seizures the court said:

---

[600] *State v. Bone*, 354 N.C. 1, 550 S.E.2d 482 (2001).

[601] *Rawlings v. Kentucky*, 448 U.S. 98, 111, 100 S. Ct. 2556, 2564-65 (1980).

[602] *See Bennett v. City of Eastpointe*, 410 F.3d 810 (6th Cir. 2005).

[603] *United States v. Bizier*, 111 F.3d 214, 218 (1st Cir. 1997).

[604] *Barna v. City of Perth Amboy*, 42 F.3d 809, 819 (3d Cir. 1994) (emphasis added).

[605] *Chimel v. California*, 395 U.S. 752, 89 S. Ct. 2034 (1969).

[606] *Chimel v. California*, 395 U.S. 752, 763, 89 S. Ct. 2034, 2040 (1969).

[607] *Chimel v. California*, 395 U.S. 752, 763, 89 S. Ct. 2034, 2040 (1969). *See also State v. Harris*, 279 N.C. 307, 182 S.E.2d 364 (1971); *State v. Hardy*, 299 N.C. 445, 263 S.E.2d 711 (1980); *State v. Bone*, 354 N.C. 1, 550 S.E.2d 482 (2001); *State v. Goode*, 350 N.C. 247, 512 S.E.2d 414 (1999).

[608] *See New York v. Belton*, 453 U.S. 454, 460-61, 101 S. Ct. 2860, 2864 (1981); *United States v. Robinson*, 414 U.S. 218, 235, 94 S. Ct. 467, 476 (1973); *see also Agnello v. United States*, 269 U.S. 20, 30, 46 S. Ct. 4, 5 (1925).

[609] *State v. Battle*, 202 N.C. App. 376, 688 S.E.2d 805 (2010).

[610] *State v. Battle*, 202 N.C. App. 376, 387-88, 688 S.E.2d 805 (2010).

[611] *State v. Battle*, 202 N.C. App. 376, 392, 688 S.E.2d 805 (2010) (emphasis in original).

The search in the case before us was conducted in daylight, on a street with both pedestrians and vehicles in the immediate vicinity. No evidence was presented at the hearing, and thus no findings of fact were made, that the detectives had any evidence other than the confidential informant's tip that Defendant had ever been involved in any drug activity whatsoever. There was no evidence presented that Detective Curl knew Defendant to have any prior history of purchasing drugs or drug use, much less drug sales. Detective Curl testified that there was not any specific information concerning who in the vehicle might have the drugs. Though the confidential informant's tip was confirmed in many aspects before the strip search, no drugs were found in the Oldsmobile or on Murfree, the main focus of the detectives. Most importantly, the confidential informant provided no information that Defendant would have drugs on her person, much less hidden in her underwear.[612]

In *State v. Fowler*,[613] the Court of Appeals of North Carolina found both probable cause and exigent circumstances sufficient to uphold two strip searches of the defendant. Officer Bignall had received information from a reliable confidential informant indicating that the defendant would be carrying three grams of cocaine. Prior to the strip search, a search of the defendant's vehicle and the defendant did not produce the cocaine. Regarding exigent circumstances, Officer Bignall "knew defendant had prior experience with intake procedures at the jail and that he could reasonably expect that defendant would attempt to rid himself of any evidence in order to prevent his going to jail."[614] Moreover, the strip searches "were conducted in a discreet manner and in a discreet location, away from the roadside, and were limited in scope to finding drugs on defendant's person."[615] Accordingly, "the strip searches of defendant's person conducted incident to his arrest ... were reasonable and did not violate his constitutional privacy interests.'"[616]

A strip search shall be performed by a person of the same sex as the person being searched and shall be performed in a place that prevents the search from being observed by a person not conducting or necessary to assist with the search.

4.2.1.1.2. Fingerprints, photographs and DNA

As part of the authority to conduct a search incident to arrest, once a person is brought to police headquarters to be detained in custody, the person must be accurately identified. In this regard, "criminal identification is said to have two main purposes: '(1) The identification of the accused as the person who committed the crime for which he is being held; and (2) the identification of the accused as the same person who has been previously charged with, or convicted of, other offenses against criminal law.'"[617] Thus, courts have determined that the process of fingerprinting and photographing arrestees is "a natural part of the administrative steps incident to arrest."[618] In fact, by the "middle of the 20th century, it was considered 'elementary that a person in lawful custody may be required to submit to photographing and fingerprinting as part of routine identification processes.'"[619] In North Carolina this practice has been codified at N.C.Gen.Stat. § 15A-502 which provides in part:

(a) A person charged with the commission of a felony or a misdemeanor may be photographed and his fingerprints may be taken for law-enforcement records only when he has been:
   (1) Arrested or committed to a detention facility, or
   (2) Committed to imprisonment upon conviction of a crime, or
   (3) Convicted of a felony.

---

[612] *State v. Battle*, 202 N.C. App. 376, 401-02, 688 S.E.2d 805 (2010). *But see State v. Smith*, 342 N.C. 407, 464 S.E.2d 45 (1995) (holding scope of roadside search not unreasonable).
[613] *State v. Fowler*, 220 N.C. App. 263, 725 S.E.2d 624 (2012).
[614] *State v. Fowler*, 220 N.C. App. 263, 271-71, 725 S.E.2d 624 (2012).
[615] *State v. Fowler*, 220 N.C. App. 263, 274, 725 S.E.2d 624 (2012).
[616] *State v. Fowler*, 220 N.C. App. 263, 274, 725 S.E.2d 624 (2012).
[617] *Maryland v. King*, 569 U.S. 435, 458, 133 S. Ct. 1958, 1975 (2013) (internal citation omitted).
[618] *County of Riverside v. McLaughlin*, 500 U.S. 44, 58, 111 S. Ct. 1661 (1991); *Maryland v. King*, 569 U.S. 435, 133 S. Ct. 1958, 1976 (2013).
[619] *Maryland v. King*, 569 U.S. 435, 459, 133 S. Ct. 1958, 1976 (2013) (quoting *Smith v. United States*, 324 F.2d 879, 882 (CADC 1963)).

(a1) It shall be the duty of the arresting law-enforcement agency to cause a person charged with the commission of a felony to be fingerprinted and to forward those fingerprints to the State Bureau of Investigation.

(a2) It shall be the duty of the arresting law enforcement agency to cause a person charged with the commission of any of the following misdemeanors to be fingerprinted and to forward those fingerprints to the State Bureau of Investigation:

(1) G.S. 14-134.3 (Domestic criminal trespass), G.S. 15A-1382.1 (Offense that involved domestic violence), or G.S. 50B 4.1 (Violation of a valid protective order).

(2) G.S. 20-138.1 (Impaired driving), G.S. 20-138.2 (Impaired driving in commercial vehicle), G.S. 20-138.2A (Operating a commercial vehicle after consuming alcohol), and G.S. 20-138.2B (Operating various school, child care, EMS, firefighting, or law enforcement vehicles after consuming alcohol).

(3) G.S. 90-95(a)(3) (Possession of a controlled substance).

(a3) It shall be the duty of the arresting law enforcement agency to cause a person charged with a crime to provide to the magistrate as much of the following information as possible for the person arrested:

(1) Name including first, last, middle, maiden, and nickname or alias.

(2) Address including street, city, and state.

(3) Drivers license number and state of issuance.

(4) Date of birth.

(5) Sex.

(6) Race.

(7) Social Security number.

(8) Relationship to the alleged victim and whether it is a "personal relationship" as defined by G.S. 50B-1(b).

(a4) It shall be the duty of the arresting law enforcement agency to cause a person who has been charged with a misdemeanor offense of assault, stalking, or communicating a threat and held under G.S. 15A 534.1 to be fingerprinted and to forward those fingerprints to the State Bureau of Investigation....

(a6) If the person cannot be identified by a valid form of identification, it shall be the duty of the arresting law-enforcement agency to cause a person charged with the commission of:

(1) Any offense involving impaired driving, as defined in G.S. 20-4.01(24a), or

(2) Driving while license revoked if the revocation is for an Impaired Driving License Revocation as defined in G.S. 20-28.2 to be fingerprinted and photographed.

(b) This section does not authorize the taking of photographs or fingerprints when the offense charged is a Class 2 or 3 misdemeanor under Chapter 20 of the General Statutes, "Motor Vehicles." Notwithstanding the prohibition in this subsection, a photograph may be taken of a person who operates a motor vehicle on a street or highway if:

(1) The person is cited by a law enforcement officer for a motor vehicle moving violation, and

(2) The person does not produce a valid drivers license upon the request of a law enforcement officer, and

(3) The law enforcement officer has a reasonable suspicion concerning the true identity of the person.

As used in this subsection, the phrase "motor vehicle moving violation" does not include the offenses listed in the third paragraph of G.S. 20-16(c)for which no points are assessed, nor does it include equipment violations specified in Part 9 of Article 3 of Chapter 20 of the General Statutes.

(b1) Any photograph authorized by subsection (b) of this section and taken by a law enforcement officer or agency:

(1) Shall only be taken of the operator of the motor vehicle, and only from the neck up.

(2) Shall be taken at either the location where the citation is issued, or at the jail if an arrest is made.

(3) Shall be retained by the law enforcement officer or agency until the final disposition of the case.

(4) Shall not be used for any purpose other than to confirm the identity of the alleged offender.

(5) Shall be destroyed by the law enforcement officer or agency upon a final disposition of the charge.

(c) This section does not authorize the taking of photographs or fingerprints of a juvenile alleged to be delinquent except under Article 21 of Chapter 7B of the General Statutes.

The United States Supreme Court has also held that the DNA identification of an arrestee "is a reasonable search that can be considered part of a routine booking procedure. When officers make an arrest supported by probable cause to hold for a serious offense and they bring the suspect to the station to be detained in custody, taking and analyzing a cheek swab of the arrestee's DNA is, like fingerprinting and photographing, a legitimate police booking procedure that is reasonable under the Fourth Amendment."[620] In North Carolina, N.C.Gen.Stat. § 15A-266.3A requires that a DNA sample be obtained from any person arrested for the following:

(1) G.S. 14-16.6(b), Assault with a deadly weapon on executive, legislative, or court officer; and G.S. 14-16.6(c), Assault inflicting serious bodily injury on executive, legislative, or court officer.
(1a) G.S. 14-17, First and Second Degree Murder.
(2) G.S. 14-18, Manslaughter.
(2a) Any felony offense in Article 6A, Unborn Victims.
(3) Any offense in Article 7B, Rape and Other Sex Offenses.
(4) G.S. 14-28, Malicious castration; G.S. 14-29, Castration or other maiming without malice afore-thought; G.S. 14-30, Malicious maiming; G.S. 14-30.1, Malicious throwing of corrosive acid or alkali; G.S. 14-31, Maliciously assaulting in a secret manner; G.S. 14-32, Felonious assault with deadly weapon with intent to kill or inflicting serious injury; G.S. 14-32.1(e), Aggravated assault or assault and battery on an individual with a disability; G.S. 14-32.2(a) when punishable pursuant to G.S. 14-32.2(b)(1), Patient abuse and neglect, intentional conduct proximately causes death; G.S. 14-32.3(a), Domestic abuse of disabled or elder adults resulting in injury; G.S. 14-32.4, Assault inflicting serious bodily injury or injury by strangulation; G.S. 14-33.2, Habitual misdemeanor assault; G.S. 14-34.1, Discharging certain barreled weapons or a firearm into occupied property; G.S. 14-34.2, Assault with a firearm or other deadly weapon upon governmental officers or employees, company police officers, or campus police officers; G.S. 14-34.4, Adulterated or misbranded food, drugs, etc.; intent to cause serious injury or death; intent to extort; G.S. 14-34.5, Assault with a firearm on a law enforcement, probation, or parole officer or on a person employed at a State or local detention facility; G.S. 14-34.6, Assault or affray on a firefighter, an emergency medical technician, medical responder, emergency department nurse, or emergency department physician; G.S. 14-34.7, Assault inflicting serious injury on a law enforcement, probation, or parole officer or on a person employed at a State or local detention facility; G.S. 14-34.9, Discharging a firearm from within an enclosure; and G.S. 14-34.10, Discharge firearm within enclosure to incite fear.
(5) Any offense in Article 10, Kidnapping and Abduction, or Article 10A, Human Trafficking.
(5a) Any offense in Article 13, Malicious Injury or Damage by Use of Explosive or Incendiary Device or Material.
(6) G.S. 14-51, First and second degree burglary; G.S. 14-53, Breaking out of dwelling house burglary; G.S. 14-54(a1), Breaking or entering buildings with intent to terrorize or injure; G.S. 14-54.1, Breaking or entering a place of religious worship; and G.S. 14-57, Burglary with explosives.
(7) Any offense in Article 15, Arson.
(8) G.S. 14-87, Armed robbery; Common law robbery punishable pursuant to G.S. 14-87.1; and G.S. 14-88, Train robbery.
(8a) G.S. 14-163.1(a1), Assaulting a law enforcement agency animal, an assistance animal, or a search and rescue animal willfully killing the animal.
(9) Any offense which would require the person to register under the provisions of Article 27A of Chapter 14 of the General Statutes, Sex Offender and Public Protection Registration Programs.
(10) G.S. 14-196.3, Cyberstalking.
(10a) G.S. 14-202, Secretly peeping into room occupied by another person.
(10b) G.S. 14-258.2, Possession of dangerous weapon in prison resulting in bodily injury or escape; G.S. 14-258.3, Taking of hostage, etc., by prisoner; and G.S. 14-258.4, Malicious conduct by prisoner.

---

[620] *Maryland v. King*, 569 U.S. 435, 133 S. Ct. 1958, 1980 (2013).

(11) G.S. 14-277.3A, Stalking.

(12) G.S. 14-288.9, Assault on emergency personnel with a dangerous weapon or substance.

(13) G.S. 14-288.21, Unlawful manufacture, assembly, possession, storage, transportation, sale, purchase, delivery, or acquisition of a nuclear, biological, or chemical weapon of mass destruction; exceptions; and G.S. 14-288.22, Unlawful use of a nuclear, biological, or chemical weapon of mass destruction.

(14) G.S. 14-318.4(a), Child abuse inflicting serious injury and G.S. 14-318.4(a3), Child abuse inflicting serious bodily injury.

(15) G.S. 14-360(a1), Cruelty to animals; maliciously kill by intentional deprivation of necessary sustenance; and G.S. 14-360(b), Cruelty to animals; maliciously torture, mutilate, maim, cruelly beat, disfigure, poison, or kill.

(16) G.S. 14-401.22(e), Attempt to conceal evidence of non-natural death by dismembering or destroying remains.

Additionally, this section also applies to arrests for attempting, solicitation of another to commit, conspiracy to commit, and aiding and abetting another to commit any of the above crimes.[621]

4.2.1.1.3. The search must be substantially contemporaneous with the arrest

In *Vale v. Louisiana*,[622] the federal Supreme Court re-emphasized that "[a] search may be incident to an arrest 'only if it is substantially contemporaneous with the arrest and is confined to the *immediate* vicinity of the arrest.'"[623] Donald Vale was arrested on the steps leading to his home. Incident to the arrest, a search was conducted inside Vale's home, and a quantity of narcotics was found in the rear bedroom. Finding the search unlawful, the Court stated: "If a search of a house is to be upheld as incident to an arrest, that arrest must take place *inside the house*,... not somewhere outside—whether two blocks away,... twenty feet away,... or on the sidewalk near the front steps."[624] Naturally, even if the arrest does take place inside the house, the search incident to the arrest must be confined to the area within the arrestee's "immediate control."[625]

While a proper search incident to an arrest should be conducted contemporaneously with the arrest, *i.e.*, immediately preceding or succeeding the actual physical act of arrest, it has been held that a search of articles in the possession of the defendant at the time of arrest may not only be conducted at the time of the arrest, but may instead be conducted later, and at a different location, if a reasonable explanation for the delay is put forth.[626] Thus, searches and seizures that could be made on the spot at the time of arrest may legally be conducted later when the accused arrives at the place of detention.[627]

4.2.1.1.3.1. *Items carried by the arrestee*

In *United States v. Fleming*,[628] the Seventh Circuit upheld the seizure and search of two closed paper bags which were in the possession of the individuals arrested. The search of defendant Fleming's bag occurred immediately upon his arrest. The search of defendant Rolenc's bag occurred approximately five minutes after his arrest, when additional backup officers arrived on the scene. Fleming's bag contained $10,000 in cash and Rolenc's bag contained a quantity of cocaine. In the appeal which followed their conviction, the defendants argued that the searches of the bags, after the bags had been recovered from them and were securely in police custody, were illegal in the absence of a warrant, consent, or exigent

---

[621] N.C.Gen.Stat. § 15A-266.3A(g).

[622] *Vale v. Louisiana*, 399 U.S. 30, 90 S. Ct. 1969 (1970).

[623] *Vale v. Louisiana*, 399 U.S. 30, 90 S. Ct. 1969, 1971 (1970) (citations omitted; emphasis added).

[624] *Vale v. Louisiana*, 399 U.S. 30, 90 S. Ct. 1969, 1971 (1970) (citations omitted; emphasis added).

[625] *Chimel v. California*, 395 U.S. 752, 89 S. Ct. 2034 (1969).

[626] *See United States v. Edwards*, 415 U.S. 800 (1974) (delay of 10 hours between arrest and station house search permissible).

[627] *See State v. Wilkerson*, 363 N.C. 382, 683 S.E.2d 174 (2009).

[628] *United States v. Fleming*, 677 F.2d 602 (7th Cir. 1982).

circumstances. The court, however, refused "to impose on police a requirement that the search be abso-lutely contemporaneous with the arrest, no matter what the peril to themselves or to bystanders."[629] In this respect, the court stated: "It is surely possible for a *Chimel* search to be undertaken too long after the arrest and too far from the arrestee's person. That is the lesson of *Chadwick*. But we do not consider that the presence of more officers than suspects invalidated the immediate search of Fleming's bag. Nor do we think that a five-minute delay between seizing Rolenc's bag and opening it, occasioned by [the officer's] handcuffing Rolenc and moving with him to the street, defeated [the officer's] right to search under *Chimel* principles."[630] Significantly, at the point when the police first seized the bags, "the bags were within Flem-ing's and Rolenc's grabbing area."[631]

4.2.1.1.4. Minor offenses

When a law enforcement officer has effected a full custodial arrest of a motorist for driving with a revoked license, that officer may thereafter conduct a full search of the person of that motorist as a contemporane-ous incident of that lawful arrest. In *United States v. Robinson*,[632] the Court held that the general authority to search incident to a lawful custodial arrest should not be qualified or limited on "an assumption that persons arrested for the offense of driving while their licenses have been revoked are less likely to possess danger-ous weapons than are those arrested for other crimes." The Court wrote, "*A custodial arrest of a suspect based on probable cause is a reasonable intrusion under the Fourth Amendment; that intrusion being lawful, a search incident to the arrest requires no additional justification. It is the fact of the lawful arrest which establishes the authority to search*[.]"[633] Accordingly, "in the case of a lawful custodial arrest a full search of the person is not only an exception to the warrant requirement of the Fourth Amendment, but is also a 'reasonable' search under that Amendment."[634]

4.2.1.1.5. Search incident to citation rejected

In *Knowles v. Iowa*,[635] the Supreme Court rejected the contention that the "search incident to arrest" excep-tion to the written warrant requirement includes searches "incident to citation." According to the Court, "[o]nce Knowles was stopped for speeding and issued a citation, all the evidence necessary to prosecute that offense had been obtained. No further evidence of excessive speed was going to be found either on the person of the offender or in the passenger compartment of the car."[636] On this basis, the Court also expressly rejected the Iowa Supreme Court's reasoning that, "so long as the arresting officer had probable cause to make a custodial arrest, there need not in fact have been a custodial arrest."[637]

4.2.1.1.6. Blood and breath alcohol

In *Birchfield v. North Dakota*,[638] the United States Supreme Court addressed the issue whether motorists lawfully arrested for drunk driving may be convicted of a crime or otherwise penalized for refusing to sub-mit to blood-alcohol testing. According to the Court, the answer was yes for breath, but no for blood. In this regard, incident to a lawful drunk-driving arrest, "the Fourth Amendment allows warrantless breath tests, but as a general rule does not allow warrantless blood draws[.]"[639]

---

[629] *United States v. Fleming*, 677 F.2d 602, 607 (7th Cir. 1982).
[630] *United States v. Fleming*, 677 F.2d 602, 607-08 (7th Cir. 1982).
[631] *United States v. Fleming*, 677 F.2d 602, 607 (7th Cir. 1982).
[632] *United States v. Robinson*, 414 U.S. 218, 94 S. Ct. 467 (1973).
[633] *United States v. Robinson*, 414 U.S. 218, 94 S. Ct. 467 (1973) (emphasis added).
[634] *United States v. Robinson*, 414 U.S. 218, 235, 94 S. Ct. 467, 477 (1973).
[635] *Knowles v. Iowa*, 525 U.S. 113, 119 S. Ct. 484 (1998).
[636] *Knowles v. Iowa*, 525 U.S. 113, 119 S. Ct. 484, 487 (1998).
[637] *Knowles v. Iowa*, 525 U.S. 113, 119 S. Ct. 484, 487 (1998).
[638] *Birchfield v. North Dakota*, 579 U.S. ___, 136 S. Ct. 2160 (2016).
[639] *Birchfield v. North Dakota*, 579 U.S. ___, 136 S. Ct. 2160, 2185 n.8 (2016).

After the United States Supreme Court decided *Birchfield*, and based on the reasoning therein, the North Carolina Supreme Court held that "blood draws may only be performed after either obtaining a warrant, obtaining valid consent from the defendant, or under exigent circumstances with probable cause."[640]

4.2.1.1.7. Cell phones

In *Riley v. California*,[641] the U.S. Supreme Court addressed searches of data contained in modern-day cell phones. Finding that a warrant is generally required for such searches, the Court held that the digital data on a suspect's cell phone—including texts, e-mails, photos and call logs—may not be searched incident to arrest. However, officers may examine the physical aspects of a phone to ensure that it will not be used as a weapon—for example, to determine whether there is a razor blade hidden between the phone and its case.

4.2.1.1.7.1. Cell phone location data

In *Carpenter v. United States*,[642] the Court held that a Fourth Amendment search occurs when law enforcement officials access historical cell phone records that provide a comprehensive chronicle of the user's past movements. The case involved the Government's acquisition of wireless carrier cell-site records revealing the location of Carpenter's cell phone whenever it made or received calls. In all, the Government was able to obtain cell-site location information (CSLI) documenting 12,898 location points that cataloged Carpenter's movements over 127 days—an average of 101 data points per day.

The question before the Court was how to apply the Fourth Amendment to the personal location information maintained by a third party (Carpenter's wireless carriers Sprint and MetroPCS) and law enforcement's "ability to chronicle a person's past movements through the record of his cell phone signals." Much like GPS tracking of a vehicle addressed in *United States v. Jones*,[643] CSLI is detailed, encyclopedic, and effortlessly compiled. In fact, "when the Government tracks the location of a cell phone it achieves near perfect surveillance, as if it had attached an ankle monitor to the phone's user." Accordingly, the Court concluded:

> Given the unique nature of cellphone location records, the fact that the information is held by a third party does not by itself overcome the user's claim to Fourth Amendment protection. Whether the Government employs its own surveillance technology as in *Jones* or leverages the technology of a wireless carrier, we hold that an individual maintains a legitimate expectation of privacy in the record of his physical movements as captured through CSLI. The location information obtained from Carpenter's wireless carriers was the product of a search[, and] ... the Government must generally obtain a warrant supported by probable cause before acquiring such records.[644]

The Government, in *Carpenter*, acquired the cell-site records pursuant to a court order issued under the Stored Communications Act, which required the Government to show "reasonable grounds" for believing that the records were "relevant and material to an ongoing investigation."[645] That showing, according to the Court, falls well short of the probable cause required for a warrant. "Under the standard in the Stored Communications Act[,] law enforcement need only show that the cell-site evidence might be pertinent to an ongoing investigation—a 'gigantic' departure from the probable cause rule ... Consequently, an order issued under Section 2703(d) of the Act is not a permissible mechanism for accessing historical cell-site records. Before compelling a wireless carrier to turn over a subscriber's CSLI, the Government's obligation is a familiar one—get a warrant."[646]

---

[640] *State v. Romano*, 369 N.C. 678, 692, 800 S.E.2d 644 (2017).

[641] *Riley v. California*, 573 U.S. 373, 134 S. Ct. 2473 (2014).

[642] *Carpenter v. United States,* 585 U.S. ___, 138 S. Ct. 2206 (2018).

[643] *United States v. Jones*, 565 U.S. 400, 132 S. Ct. 945 (2012).

[644] *Carpenter v. United States*, 585 U.S. ___, 138 S. Ct. 2206, 2217 (2018). In deciding this case, the Court rejected the contention that Carpenter lacked a reasonable expectation of privacy in the location information collected by the FBI because he had shared that information with his wireless carriers.

[645] 18 U.S.C. § 2703(d).

[646] *Carpenter v. United States*, 585 U.S. ___, 138 S. Ct. 2206, 2221 (2018).

Noting that *Carpenter* "only established the government must obtain a warrant before it can access a phone company's *historical* CSLI" the Court of Appeals of North Carolina has "decline[d] to extend the holding in *Carpenter* to real-time or prospective CSLI."[647]

Emergency circumstances. Even though the Government will generally need a warrant to access cell-site location information, "case-specific exceptions may support a warrantless search of an individual's cell-site records under certain circumstances. 'One well-recognized exception applies when the exigencies of the situation make the needs of law enforcement so compelling that [a] warrantless search is objectively reasonable under the Fourth Amendment.'... Such exigencies include the need to pursue a fleeing suspect, protect individuals who are threatened with imminent harm, or prevent the imminent destruction of evidence."[648]

"As a result, if law enforcement is confronted with an urgent situation, such fact-specific threats will likely justify the warrantless collection of CSLI. Lower courts, for instance, have approved warrantless searches related to bomb threats, active shootings, and child abductions[, and the *Carpenter* case] does not call into doubt warrantless access to CSLI in such circumstances."[649]

4.2.1.2. Motor vehicle searches incident to arrest

In *Chimel v. California*,[650] the U.S. Supreme Court held that, as a permissible incident of a lawful custodial arrest, the police may not only conduct a warrantless search of the person of the arrestee, but also of the area within the arrestee's immediate control, meaning the area within his reach.

> [I]t is entirely reasonable for the arresting officer to search for and seize any evidence on the arrestee's person in order to prevent its concealment or destruction. *And the area into which an arrestee might reach in order to grab a weapon or evidentiary items must, of course, be governed by a like rule.* A gun on a table or in a drawer in front of one who is arrested can be as dangerous to the arresting officer as one concealed in the clothing of the person arrested. There is ample justification, therefore, for a search of the arrestee's person *and the area "within his immediate control"—construing that phrase to mean the area from within which he might gain possession of a weapon or destructible evidence.*[651]

Although the *Chimel* principle may be stated simply enough—that a search incident to arrest may not go beyond the area within the immediate control of the arrestee—many courts have struggled with determining the precise area that would be within the immediate control of the arrestee, particularly when that area arguably includes the interior of an automobile and the arrestee is its recent occupant.

In *New York v. Belton*,[652] the U.S. Supreme Court established a bright-line rule for "the proper scope of a search of the interior of an automobile incident to a lawful custodial arrest of its occupants" after the arrestees are no longer in it. The *Belton* "bright line" rule provided: When an officer has made "a lawful custodial arrest of the occupant of an automobile," the officer "may, as a contemporaneous incident of that arrest, search the passenger compartment of that automobile" including "any containers found within the passenger compartment."[653]

In *Thornton v. United States*,[654] the U.S. Supreme Court determined that the rule of *Belton* was not limited to situations where the officer made contact with the occupant while the occupant was inside the vehicle. According to the Court, "*Belton* governs even when an officer does not make contact until the person arrested has left the vehicle."[655] Similar to Belton, Thornton was arrested for the possession of marijuana and cocaine.

Justice Scalia's concurrence in *Thornton* emphasized that:

---

647 *State v. Thomas*, 2019 N.C. App. LEXIS 846, *11, (Ct. App. Oct. 15, 2019).
648 *Carpenter v. United States*, 585 U.S. __, 138 S. Ct. 2206, 2222-23 (2018) (citations and internal quotes omitted).
649 *Carpenter v. United States*, 585 U.S. __, 138 S. Ct. 2206, 2223 (2018).
650 *Chimel v. California*, 395 U.S. 752, 89 S. Ct. 2034 (1969).
651 *Chimel v. California*, 395 U.S. 752, 763, 89 S. Ct. 2034, 2040 (1969) (emphasis added).
652 *New York v. Belton*, 453 U.S. 454, 101 S. Ct. 2860, 863 (1981).
653 *New York v. Belton*, 453 U.S. 454, 101 S. Ct. 2860, 863 (1981).
654 *Thornton v. United States*, 541 U.S. 615, 124 S. Ct. 2127 (2004).
655 *Thornton v. United States*, 541 U.S. 615, 124 S. Ct. 2127 (2004).

[C]onducting a *Chimel* search is not the Government's right; it is an exception—justified by necessity—to a rule that would otherwise render the search unlawful. If "sensible police procedures" require that suspects be handcuffed and put in squad cars, then police should handcuff suspects, put them in squad cars, and not conduct the search. Indeed, if an officer leaves a suspect unrestrained nearby just to manufacture authority to search, one could argue that the search is unreasonable precisely because the dangerous conditions justifying it existed only by virtue of the officer's failure to follow sensible procedures....

If *Belton* searches are justifiable, it is not because the arrestee might grab a weapon or evidentiary item from his car, but simply because the car might contain evidence relevant to the crime for which he was arrested....

I would therefore limit *Belton* searches to cases where it is reasonable to believe evidence relevant to the crime of arrest might be found in the vehicle. In this case, as in *Belton*, [defendant] was lawfully arrested for a drug offense. It was reasonable for Officer Nichols to believe that further contraband or similar evidence relevant to the crime for which he had been arrested might be found in the vehicle from which he had just alighted and which was still within his vicinity at the time of arrest. I would affirm the decision below on that ground.[656]

Thereafter, in *Arizona v. Gant*,[657] the United States Supreme Court abandoned the *Belton* rule and held that the police "may search a vehicle incident to a recent occupant's arrest only if the arrestee is within reaching distance of the passenger compartment at the time of the search or it is reasonable to believe the vehicle contains evidence of the offense of arrest. When these justifications are absent, a search of an arrestee's vehicle will be unreasonable unless police obtain a warrant or show that another exception to the warrant requirement applies."[658]

The two components of Arizona v. Gant are outlined below.

1) *The "possibility of access" component.* The police may search a vehicle incident to a recent occupant's arrest "when the arrestee is unsecured and within reaching distance of the passenger compartment at the time of the search."[659] A critical aspect of this "possibility of access" component is that it is to be applied "at the time of the search," not at some earlier time. This is significant because, as pointed out by the dissent, "in the great majority of cases, an officer making an arrest is able to handcuff the arrestee and remove him to a secure place before conducting a search incident to the arrest."[660] "Because officers have many means of ensuring the safe arrest of vehicle occupants, it will be the rare case in which an officer is unable to fully effectuate an arrest so that a real possibility of access to the arrestee's vehicle remains."[661] Nonetheless, so long as the arrestee is *unsecured* and "within reaching distance of the passenger compartment" "a search incident to arrest is reasonable under the Fourth Amendment."[662]

2) *The "likelihood of discovering offense-related evidence" component.* Recall that *Chimel v. California* limited searches incident to arrest to "the arrestee's person and the area 'within his immediate control'—construing that phrase to mean the area from within which he might gain possession of a weapon or destructible evidence." Although it does not follow from *Chimel*, the *Gant* Court also held that "circumstances unique to the vehicle context" justify a search incident to a lawful arrest when it is "reasonable to believe the vehicle contains evidence of the offense of arrest."[663] This

---

656 *Thornton v. United States*, 541 U.S. 615, 124 S. Ct. 2127, 2133-38 (2004).
657 *Arizona v. Gant*, 556 U.S. 332, 129 S. Ct. 1710 (2009).
658 *Arizona v. Gant*, 556 U.S. 332, 129 S. Ct. 1710, 1723 (2009).
659 *Arizona v. Gant*, 556 U.S. 332, 129 S. Ct. 1710, 1719 (2009).
660 *Arizona v. Gant*, 556 U.S. 332, 129 S. Ct. 1710, 1730 (2009) (Alito, J., dissenting).
661 *Arizona v. Gant*, 556 U.S. 332, 129 S. Ct. 1710, 1719 n.4 (2009).
662 *Arizona v. Gant*, 556 U.S. 332, 129 S. Ct. 1710, 1719 n.4 (2009).
663 *Arizona v. Gant*, 556 U.S. 332, 129 S. Ct. 1710, 1719 (2009) (citing *Thornton v. United States*, 541 U.S. 615, 124 S. Ct. 2127, 2137 (2004) (Scalia, J., concurring)).

component appears to contain a new and additional power for officers conducting searches of vehicles incident to arrest—a power having nothing to do with the *Chimel* rationale. Nonetheless, officers are cautioned that "[i]n many cases, as when a recent occupant is arrested for a traffic violation, there will be no reasonable basis to believe the vehicle contains relevant evidence."[664] What remains to be seen is whether this component of *Gant* requires a simple purpose or nature-of-the-offense analysis, or whether there needs to be an inquiry into the "likelihood," "probability" or "possibility" that the vehicle contains relevant evidence.

In *United States v. McCraney*,[665] the defendant was stopped for failure to dim his high-beams upon the approach of an oncoming car, then arrested for driving while suspended. An officer then searched the defendant's car, finding a gun under the driver's seat. At the time of the search, the defendant and his passenger were standing two to three feet behind the car's rear bumper. Although neither had been handcuffed yet, they were surrounded by three officers. Thus, they were no longer within "reaching distance" of the passenger compartment. Because police could not reasonably expect to find evidence of the defendant's suspension in the car, neither component of *Gant* was applicable, and the court determined that the search was unconstitutional, and that the gun should be suppressed.

In *State v. Mbacke*,[666] the North Carolina Supreme Court upheld a search of the defendant's car pursuant to the second *Gant* component. There, the defendant was properly arrested and secured in the back seat of a patrol car when the officers returned to the defendant's vehicle and searched it. In attempting to define the "reason to believe" standard set out in *Gant*, the North Carolina Supreme Court held that "when investigators have a reasonable and articulable basis to believe that evidence of the offense of arrest might be found in a suspect's vehicle after the occupants have been removed and secured, the investigators are permitted to conduct a search of that vehicle."[667]

4.2.2. Exigent circumstances

The situations that often fall under the exigent circumstances exception to the warrant requirement can be grouped into three general categories. An exigency exists if: (i) there is a reasonable probability that evidence—either contraband, instrumentalities used in the crime, or the fruits of the crime—is being or will be destroyed or concealed; (ii) it is likely a suspect will flee; or (iii) there is a real danger to people. The rationale advanced for permitting warrantless searches under such circumstances is that extreme situations dictate that police act quickly, where there is no time to secure a warrant. The warrant requirement may be dispensed with when officers take actions that are necessary responses to an emergency situation. Courts permit warrantless searches where officers have probable cause and a qualifying emergent set of circumstances.[668]

For example, in *State v. Johnson*,[669] the Court of Appeals of North Carolina found "exigent circumstances" justifying a warrantless search. In *Johnson*, a police officer received a tip from a confidential reliable informant that the defendant was standing on the street in front of some apartments and offering cocaine for sale. The officer immediately proceeded to the apartments located about 20 minutes away from the police station. The officer did not obtain a search warrant. Upon arriving at the apartments and locating the defendant, the officer conducted an "emergency search" and discovered three bags of heroin. The court concluded that the distance of the defendant from the police station and the "known mobility of the drug 'pusher,' justified the officer in proceeding directly to the defendant without first proceeding to a magistrate's office to obtain a search warrant which would have caused substantial delay in arriving at the scene and the probable absence of the purported drug violator."[670]

---

[664] *Arizona v. Gant*, 556 U.S. 332, 343, 129 S. Ct. 1710, 1719 (2009) (citing *Atwater v. Lago Vista*, 532 U.S. 318, 324, 121 S. Ct. 1536, 1541 (2001)).

[665] *United States v. McCraney*, 674 F.3d 614 (6th Cir. 2012).

[666] *State v. Mbacke*, 365 N.C. 403, 721 S.E.2d 218 (2012).

[667] *State v. Mbacke*, 365 N.C. 403, 409-10, 721 S.E.2d 218 (2012).

[668] *State v. Allison*, 298 N.C. 135, 257 S.E.2d 417 (1979).

[669] *State v. Johnson*, 29 N.C. App. 698, 225 S.E.2d 650 (1976).

[670] *State v. Johnson*, 29 N.C. App. 698, 701, 225 S.E.2d 650 (1976).

In determining whether exigent circumstances exist to justify a warrantless seizure, courts will examine a number of factors to determine whether the police actions were reasonable. First and foremost, the police must have probable cause to believe that the premises contain contraband or evidence of a crime. In addition to probable cause, the police must demonstrate the existence of an actual emergency and articulate specific and objective facts which reveal a necessity for immediate action. In determining whether an exigency exists, court will examine such factors as: (1) the degree of urgency involved and amount of time necessary to obtain a warrant; (2) the reasonable belief that contraband is about to be removed or destroyed; (3) the possibility of danger to the police officers guarding the site of the contraband; (4) information indicating the possessors of contraband are aware that the police are on their trail; and (5) the ready destructibility of the contraband and the police knowledge that traffickers of the suspected contraband characteristically attempt to dispose of the destructible contraband and escape.[671]

In *Dorman v. United States*,[672] the court set forth several additional factors (often cited by numerous courts around the nation) as helpful in assessing whether exigent circumstances are present in cases involving serious crimes and a reasonable probability of imminent danger to life, serious damage to property, destruction of evidence, or the likelihood of flight. These factors include whether: (1) the crime under investigation was recently committed; (2) there was any deliberate or unjustified delay by the police during which time a warrant could have been obtained; (3) a grave offense was involved, particularly a crime of violence; (4) there was reasonable belief that the suspect was armed; (5) the police officers were acting on a clear showing of probable cause; (6) there was a likelihood that the suspect would escape if she was not swiftly apprehended; (7) there was strong reason to believe that the suspect was on the premises; and (8) the police entry was made peaceably, albeit nonconsensually.[673]

4.2.2.1. Destruction or removal of evidence

4.2.2.1.1. Crime scenes

Preliminarily, it is important to note that there is no "crime scene" exception to the written warrant requirement. This was made clear in *Mincey v. Arizona*,[674] where the United States Supreme Court held that the exigent circumstances surrounding the investigation of a serious crime does not permit the creation of a "crime scene exception" to the written warrant requirement. According to the Court, the seriousness of the offense under investigation does not itself create "exigent circumstances of the kind that under the Fourth Amendment justify a warrantless search." Therefore, "the warrantless search of Mincey's apartment was not constitutionally permissible simply because a homicide had recently occurred there."[675]

Similarly, the United States Supreme Court in *Thompson v. Louisiana*,[676] held that the Fourth Amendment will not tolerate a "murder scene exception" to the written warrant requirement.[677]

4.2.2.1.1.1. Protective, victim/suspect fan-out searches

In one portion of the United States Supreme Court's opinion in *Mincey v. Arizona*, the Court recognized "the right of the police to respond to emergency situations [and to make] warrantless entries and searches when they reasonably believe that a *person* within is in need of immediate aid."[678] Additionally, "when the police come upon a scene of a homicide they may make a prompt warrantless search of the area to see if other victims or if a killer is still on the premises."[679] In this respect, "*[t]he need to protect or preserve life or*

---

671 *United States v. Rubin*, 474 F.2d 262, 268 (3d Cir. 1973). *See also State v. Wallace*, 111 N.C. App. 581, 433 S.E.2d 238 (1993).
672 *Dorman v. United States*, 435 F.2d 385 (D.C. App. 1970).
673 *Dorman v. United States*, 435 F.2d 385, 392-93 (D.C. App. 1970).
674 *Mincey v. Arizona*, 437 U.S. 385, 98 S. Ct. 2408 (1978).
675 *Mincey v. Arizona*, 437 U.S. 385, 98 S. Ct. 2408, 2415 (1978).
676 *Thompson v. Louisiana*, 469 U.S. 17, 105 S. Ct. 409 (1984).
677 *See also Flippo v. West Virginia*, 528 U.S. 11, 120 S. Ct. 7 (1999).
678 *Mincey v. Arizona*, 437 U.S. 385, 392, 98 S. Ct. 2408, 2413 (1978) (emphasis added).
679 *Mincey v. Arizona*, 437 U.S. 385, 392, 98 S. Ct. 2408, 2413 (1978).

avoid serious injury is justification for what would be otherwise illegal absent an exigency or emergency."[680] Naturally, during the course of this protective, victim/suspect fan-out search, "police may seize any evidence that is in plain view[.]"[681]

In *State v. Woods*,[682] the Court of Appeals of North Carolina considered whether under the exigent circumstances exception to the warrant requirement of the Fourth Amendment law enforcement officers may enter a home without a warrant for the purpose of investigating a probable burglary. The court found that the officers' warrantless entry into the defendant's home, upon finding the back door ajar, a recently broken window and the security alarm sounding, did not violate the Fourth Amendment. However, once inside, the officers' search of a chest of drawers, chair and cabinet "did not comport with the defined exceptions to the warrant requirement."[683]

4.2.2.1.2. Evidence about to be destroyed

Where police have an objectively reasonable belief that evidence is being or about to be destroyed, a warrantless entry may be permitted under this exception. In order to invoke this exception, the state must demonstrate that the seized evidence is of an "evanescent" nature (*i.e.*, an easily destructible item, like narcotics, which can be easily burned, secreted or flushed). For example, in *State v. Corbitt*,[684] a warrantless search was allowed where "Officer Geddings knocked on the front door of Corbitt's residence; Officer Geddings smelled marijuana; Officer Geddings saw several "shadow figures" run to another room on the side of the house and return two seconds later; and nobody in the house came to the door until after a minute."[685] However, the same was not true in *State v. Nowell*.[686] There, law enforcement officers participated in a controlled delivery of approximately 50 pounds of marijuana to Nowell's residence. They entered when they became worried that the defendant was about to "roll a joint." Said the court: "Based on the totality of the circumstances, evidence the parties were going to destroy the amount of marijuana required for one "joint" from the approximately fifty pounds of marijuana present in the residence is not an exigent circumstance."[687]

4.2.2.1.3. Narcotics and other dangerous drugs

The fact that the grounds for arrest involve narcotics, standing alone, does not create an exigent circumstance. In this regard, the U.S. Supreme Court in *Vale v. Louisiana*,[688] held that a narcotics arrest, which takes place on the steps outside the arrestee's home, does not provide its own "exigent circumstance" so as to justify a warrantless entry or search of the home.

4.2.2.1.4. Pending the arrival of a search warrant

It has been held, however, that when the police have probable cause to believe a person has hidden contraband or criminal evidence within his home, the officers may prevent that person from entering his home while officers obtain a search warrant. Thus, in *Illinois v. McArthur*,[689] the U.S. Supreme Court observed: "[T]he police officers in this case had probable cause to believe that a home contained contraband, which was evidence of a crime. They reasonably believed that the home's resident, if left free of any restraint, would destroy that evidence." It was reasonable, therefore, for the officers to restrict the resident from entering the home pending the acquisition of a search warrant. The period of restraint—two hours— was "no longer than reasonably necessary for the police, acting with diligence, to obtain the warrant." In

---

[680] *Mincey v. Arizona*, 437 U.S. 385, 392, 98 S. Ct. 2408, 2413 (1978) (emphasis added).
[681] *Mincey v. Arizona*, 437 U.S. 385, 392, 98 S. Ct. 2408, 2413 (1978).
[682] *State v. Woods*, 136 N.C. App. 386, 524 S.E.2d 363 (2000).
[683] *State v. Woods*, 136 N.C. App. 386, 393, 524 S.E.2d 363 (2000).
[684] *State v. Corbitt*, 217 N.C. App. 400, 720 S.E.2d 29 (2011).
[685] *State v. Corbitt*, 217 N.C. App. 400, *5-6, 720 S.E.2d 29 (2011).
[686] *State v. Nowell*, 144 N.C. App. 636, 550 S.E.2d 807 (2001).
[687] *State v. Nowell*, 144 N.C. App. 636, 643, 550 S.E.2d 807 (2001).
[688] *Vale v. Louisiana*, 399 U.S. 30, 90 S. Ct. 1969, 1972 (1970).
[689] *Illinois v. McArthur*, 531 U.S. 326, 121 S. Ct. 946 (2001).

McArthur, the Court also held that, pending the arrival of a search warrant, if a person detained outside of his home asks to enter the home, officers may enter with him to ensure that evidence is not destroyed. The need to "preserve evidence" of this "jailable" drug offense "was sufficiently urgent or pressing to justify" the restriction that entry would be permitted only in the company of an officer. "In this case, the police had good reason to fear that, unless restrained, McArthur would destroy the drugs before they could return with a warrant. The reasonable restraint imposed by the police merely prevented McArthur from entering his home 'unaccompanied.'"[690] In this respect, the Court said, "the reasonableness of the greater restriction (preventing reentry) implies the reasonableness of the lesser (permitting reentry conditioned on observation)."[691]

The Court of Appeals of North Carolina encountered facts similar to those in *McArthur* when deciding *State v. Murray.*[692] There, police had probable cause to believe that the defendant was maintaining a methamphetamine lab in his residence. Upon their arrival, they encountered the defendant standing in the driveway, they detected the odor of methamphetamine production and observed items associated with its production. After the defendant refused to consent to a search of his residence, the officers informed him that they were securing the residence and seeking a search warrant. They additionally warned the defendant not to reenter the residence. However, the defendant disregarded this warning and reentered the home, grabbing a jar of brown liquid on his way in and proceeding to the back of the residence. Thereafter, the police arrested him. A subsequent search pursuant to a warrant uncovered chemicals used in the production of methamphetamine. Said the court:

> Considering the informant's tip, the defendant's behavior in the officers' presence, the odor emanating from defendant's residence, and the incriminating evidence observed in plain view, the totality of the circumstances provides probable cause to believe that a search of the residence would reveal a meth lab.

> As in *McArthur,* the officers had good reason to fear evidence would be destroyed if defendant reentered the residence. Because the officers had probable cause to believe that meth was being produced in the residence, and since they had specifically asked the defendant whether meth was being produced in the residence, the officers had good reason to fear that defendant would destroy evidence of meth production if he had been allowed to reenter the residence unaccompanied.[693]

The court was additionally persuaded by the "officers' efforts to minimize the nature of the intrusion into defendant's privacy, while diligently seeking and obtaining a valid search warrant within approximately a four-hour period. This was no longer than necessary for the officers to obtain a warrant."[694] Accordingly, the warrantless seizure of the defendant's residence was upheld.

4.2.2.1.4.1. *When the knock and announce prompts the sound of evidence destruction*

In *Kentucky v. King,*[695] the Supreme Court determined that a warrantless home entry will be justified by "exigent circumstances" in a situation where the police, by knocking on the door of a residence and announcing their presence, cause the occupants to attempt to destroy evidence. Here, even though this exigency may have been "police created," the officers' actions prior to their entry into the apartment were "entirely lawful."[696] "[T]he exigent circumstances rule applies when the police do not gain entry to premises by means of an actual or threatened violation of the Fourth Amendment."[697]

The United States Supreme Court remanded the case to the Kentucky Supreme Court for a determination as to whether an exigency was in fact present. The state court concluded that "the Commonwealth

---

[690] *Illinois v. McArthur,* 531 U.S. 326, 332, 121 S. Ct. 946, 950 (2001).
[691] *Illinois v. McArthur,* 531 U.S. 326, 335, 121 S. Ct. 946, 952 (2001).
[692] *State v. Murray,* 2009 N.C. App. LEXIS 1222 (Ct. App. Aug. 4, 2009).
[693] *State v. Murray,* 2009 N.C. App. LEXIS 1222, *8 (Ct. App. Aug. 4, 2009).
[694] *State v. Murray,* 2009 N.C. App. LEXIS 1222, *10 (Ct. App. Aug. 4, 2009).
[695] *Kentucky v. King,* 563 U.S. 452, 131 S. Ct. 1849 (2011).
[696] *Kentucky v. King,* 563 U.S. 452, 131 S. Ct. 1849, 1854 (2011).
[697] *Kentucky v. King,* 563 U.S. 452, 131 S. Ct. 1849, 1862 (2011).

failed to meet its burden of demonstrating exigent circumstances justifying a warrantless entry." During the suppression hearing, the officer repeatedly referred to the "possible" destruction of evidence. He stated that he heard people moving inside the apartment. He never articulated the specific sounds he heard which led him to believe that evidence was about to be destroyed. "In fact, the sounds as described at the suppression hearing were indistinguishable from ordinary household sounds, and were consistent with the natural and reasonable result of a knock on the door. Nothing in the record suggests that the sounds officers heard were anything more than the occupants preparing to answer the door."[698] Consequently, the court, concluded that exigent circumstances did not exist when police made a warrantless entry of the apartment.

4.2.2.1.5. Blood alcohol

The natural dissipation of alcohol in the blood does not automatically justify a warrantless blood test of a drunk-driving suspect.[699] In those drunk-driving investigations where police officers can reasonably obtain a warrant before a blood sample can be drawn without significantly undermining the efficacy of the search, the Fourth Amendment mandates that they do so. Exceptions to this requirement must be decided on a case to case basis, based on facts showing that securing a warrant would have been impractical.[700]

For example, in *Mitchell v. Wisconsin*,[701] a plurality of the U.S. Supreme Court held that a warrant is not required for a blood test when an officer has probable cause to believe a motorist has been driving while under the influence of alcohol, but the motorist is unconscious and cannot be given a breath test. In such cases, held the Court, "the exigent circumstances rule almost always permits a blood test without a warrant. When a breath test is impossible, enforcement of the drunk-driving laws depends upon the administration of a blood test. And when a police officer encounters an unconscious driver, it is very likely that the driver would be taken to an emergency room and that his blood would be drawn for diagnostic purposes even if the police were not seeking BAC information. In addition, police officers most frequently come upon unconscious drivers when they report to the scene of an accident, and under those circumstances, the officers' many responsibilities—such as attending to other injured drivers or passengers and preventing further accidents—may be incompatible with the procedures that would be required to obtain a warrant. Thus, *when a driver is unconscious, the general rule is that a warrant is not needed.*"[702]

However, the North Carolina Supreme Court has been clear that this rule applies only if the motorist is unconscious. In *State v. Romano*,[703] the North Carolina Supreme Court considered the constitutionality of N.C.Gen.Stat.§ 20-16.2(b) as applied to the defendant in that case. Pursuant to N.C.Gen.Stat. § 20-16.2(b), "If a law enforcement officer has reasonable grounds to believe that a person has committed an implied-consent offense, and the person is unconscious or otherwise in a condition that makes the person incapable of refusal, the law enforcement officer may direct the taking of a blood sample or may direct the administration of any other chemical analysis that may be effectively performed." In *Romano*, the defendant was belligerent and combative throughout his encounters with law enforcement and medical personnel. He was medicated at the hospital in an attempt to calm him down. Meanwhile, Sergeant Fowler told the treating nurse that she would need a blood draw for law enforcement purposes. The defendant was not advised of his chemical analysis rights before being medicated. The treating nurse drew blood for medical purposes but drew more than was necessary and offered the excess to Sergeant Fowler. Before accepting it, Sergeant Fowler attempted to gain consent from the defendant but was unable to wake him.

The court noted that it would not have taken long for Sergeant Fowler to obtain a warrant as magistrates were available nearby. Moreover, there were multiple law enforcement personnel on the scene making it

---

[698] *King v. Commonwealth*, 386 S.W.3d 119, 122 (Ky. 2012).
[699] *See Missouri v. McNeely*, 569 U.S. 141, 165, 133 S. Ct. 1552, 1568 (2013).
[700] *Missouri v. McNeely*, 569 U.S. 141, 151, 133 S. Ct. 1552, 1560 (2013).
[701] *Mitchell v. Wisconsin*, 588 U.S. ___, 139 S. Ct. 2525 (2019).
[702] *Mitchell v. Wisconsin*, 588 U.S. ___, 139 S. Ct. 2525 (2019) (emphasis added).
[703] *State v. Romano*, 369 N.C. 678, 800 S.E.2d 644 (2017).

possible for one to leave the hospital and obtain a warrant. Considering the reasoning of *Birchfield*, the court concluded that "blood draws may only be performed after either obtaining a warrant, obtaining valid consent from the defendant, or under exigent circumstances with probable cause."[704] Accordingly, "N.C.Gen.Stat. § 20-16.2(b) was unconstitutionally applied to defendant."[705]

4.2.2.2. Safety of the officer or others

If the officer believes that the suspect is armed or that the suspect presents a real and immediate danger to the officers or other people, a warrantless entry may be permitted.

For example, in *Brigham City, Utah v. Stuart*,[706] the U.S. Supreme Court held that the police "may enter a home without a warrant to render emergency assistance to an injured occupant or to protect an occupant from imminent danger." The facts of the case unfolded in late July, at about 3 a.m., when "four police officers responded to a call regarding a loud party at a residence. Upon arriving at the house, they heard shouting from inside, and proceeded down the driveway to investigate. There, they observed two juveniles drinking beer in the backyard. They entered the backyard and saw—through a screen door and windows—an altercation taking place in the kitchen of the home."[707] At the time, "four adults were attempting, with some difficulty, to restrain a juvenile. The juvenile eventually broke free, swung a fist and struck one of the adults in the face." The victim of the blow was then observed spitting blood into a nearby sink. "The other adults continued to try to restrain the juvenile, pressing him up against a refrigerator with such force that the refrigerator began moving across the floor. At this point, an officer opened the screen door and announced the officers' presence. Amid the tumult, nobody noticed. The officer entered the kitchen and again cried out, and as the occupants slowly became aware that the police were on the scene, the altercation ceased."[708] The officers subsequently arrested the adults, charging them with various offenses.

Finding the officers' actions proper, the Court said: "Here, the officers were confronted with *ongoing* violence occurring *within* the home.... We think the officers' entry here was plainly reasonable under the circumstances." It was clear to the Court that "the officers had an objectively reasonable basis for believing both that the injured adult might need help and that the violence in the kitchen was just beginning. Nothing in the Fourth Amendment required them to wait until another blow rendered someone 'unconscious' or 'semi-conscious' or worse before entering. The role of a peace officer includes preventing violence and restoring order, not simply rendering first aid to casualties; an officer is not like a boxing (or hockey) referee, poised to stop a bout only if it becomes too one-sided."[709]

In *Michigan v. Fisher*,[710] several officers responded to a complaint of a disturbance—a man was reportedly "going crazy" at a residence. Upon arrival, the officers found a household in considerable chaos: a pickup truck in the driveway with its front smashed, damaged fenceposts along the side of the property, and three broken house windows, the glass still on the ground outside. The officers also noticed blood on the hood of the pickup and on clothes inside of it, as well as on one of the doors to the house. Through a window, the officers could see the defendant inside, screaming and throwing things. The back door was locked, and a couch had been placed to block the front door. The officers knocked, but the defendant would not answer. They saw the defendant had a cut on his hand and asked if he needed medical help, but the defendant ignored these questions and demanded, with accompanying profanity, that they get a search warrant. One of the officers then pushed his way inside. The Court ruled that this warrantless entry was justified under the "Emergency Aid" doctrine because of the defendant's violent behavior. Although the officers had not seen the defendant hit anyone, they did see him throwing things, and it was objectively reasonable to believe that these projectiles might have a human target (perhaps a spouse or a child), or that the defendant would hurt himself in the course of his rage.

---

[704] *State v. Romano*, 369 N.C. 678, *9, 800 S.E.2d 644 (2017).
[705] *State v. Romano*, 369 N.C. 678, *9, 800 S.E.2d 644 (2017).
[706] *Brigham City, Utah v. Stuart*, 547 U.S. 398, 126 S. Ct. 1943 (2006).
[707] *Brigham City, Utah v. Stuart*, 547 U.S. 398, 126 S. Ct. 1943, 1946 (2006).
[708] *Brigham City, Utah v. Stuart*, 547 U.S. 398, 126 S. Ct. 1943, 1946 (2006).
[709] *Brigham City, Utah v. Stuart*, 547 U.S. 398, 126 S. Ct. 1943, 1949 (2006).
[710] *Michigan v. Fisher*, 558 U.S. 45, 130 S. Ct. 546 (2009).

4.2.2.2.1. When there is an imminent threat of violence

In *Ryburn v. Huff*,[711] two Burbank, California, officers responded to a call at a high school. The principal informed them that a student, Vincent Huff, was rumored to have written a letter threatening to "shoot up" the school and asked them to investigate. In interviewing Vincent's classmates, the officers learned he was a frequent target of bullying who had been absent from school for two days. The officers found this to be a cause for concern, as they had received training on targeted school violence and were aware that these characteristics are common among perpetrators of school shootings. The officers decided to continue their investigation by interviewing Vincent. At his house, the officers knocked on the door and announced several times they were with the Burbank Police Department. No one answered the door or otherwise responded to the knocks. One of the officers then called the home telephone. The officers could hear the phone ringing inside the house, but no one picked up. They next tried calling the cell phone of Vincent's mother, Mrs. Huff. When Mrs. Huff answered the phone, she indicated that both she and Vincent were inside the house; however, when the officers indicated they were outside and asked to speak with her, she hung up. One or two minutes later, Mrs. Huff and Vincent walked out of the house and stood on the front steps. The officers advised Vincent that they were there to discuss the threats. Vincent, apparently aware of the rumor that was circulating at his school, responded, "I can't believe you're here for that." An officer asked Mrs. Huff if they could continue the discussion inside the house, but she refused; in the officer's experience, it was "extremely unusual" for a parent to decline an officer's request to interview a juvenile inside. He also found it odd that Mrs. Huff never asked the officers the reason for their visit. The officer then asked if there were any guns in the house. Mrs. Huff responded by immediately turning around and running into the house. The officers followed her in. There, after a brief argument with Vincent's father, the interview continued for five to 10 minutes. The officers concluded the rumor about Vincent was false and left. The Huffs brought an action claiming the police violated their rights by entering their home without a warrant. The Supreme Court disagreed, finding that Mrs. Huff's odd behavior, combined with the information the officers gathered at the school, could have led reasonable officers to believe "that there could be weapons inside the house, and that family members or the officers themselves were in danger."

4.2.2.2.1.1. Burglary in progress

When a law enforcement officer has probable cause to believe that a burglary or other crime is in progress, or has just occurred, and that someone within the premises might be in need of assistance, sufficient exigent circumstances arise to justify an immediate warrantless entry of the premises.[712]

4.2.2.3. Hot/fresh pursuit

This doctrine may be analyzed as a specific application of the exigent circumstance doctrine discussed above. A warrantless entry of a private dwelling will be allowed when police are in hot pursuit of a suspect who they have probable cause to believe committed a felony. The pursuing officers must also have probable cause to believe the suspect entered a specific dwelling. After following the suspect into a dwelling, the police may seize contraband, weapons, instrumentalities or fruits of crime that are in plain view.[713]

In *United States v. Johnson*,[714] the police watched as the defendant sat on his great-grandmother's front porch while other people on the porch made their way out into the street to engage in apparent drug transactions with passing cars; the defendant seemed to be in charge of the operation. Eventually, a Geo Tracker

---

[711] *Ryburn v. Huff*, 565 U.S. 469, 132 S. Ct. 987 (2012).

[712] *See Murdock v. Stout*, 54 F.3d 1437, 1442 (9th Cir. 1995); *see also United States v. Brown*, 449 F.3d 741, 748 (6th Cir. 2006) ("This and other circuits have held that an officer may lawfully enter a residence without a warrant under the exigent circumstances exception when the officer reasonably believes a burglary is in progress."); *see also Reardon v. Wroan*, 811 F.2d 1025, 1029-30 (7th Cir. 1987).

[713] *See, e.g., Warden v. Hayden*, 387 U.S. 294, 299 (1967) (while police are engaged in hot pursuit of a suspect and weapons, any other evidence of criminal behavior may be seized and admitted if it was discovered in a place where the suspect or weapons might be located).

[714] *United States v. Johnson*, 488 F.3d 690 (6th Cir. 2007).

drove up in front of the house, and the defendant walked down to meet it; when the Tracker drove off, the defendant had a white baggie and a scale in his hands. Two officers, wearing tactical vests with patches reading "POLICE" moved in to attempt to stop the Tracker, but could not. Upon seeing the officers, the defendant ran up the stairs and into the house. According to the Sixth Circuit, the officers made a valid hot pursuit entry when they followed him inside, even though they did not have a warrant.

In *State v. Guevara*,[715] the defendant "suddenly with[drew] into his home and slam[med] the door, created the appearance that he was fleeing or trying to escape."[716] Moreover, there was a young child nearby. As such, exigent circumstances permitted the police officer's warrantless entry.

4.2.2.4. Emergency aid

There are many situations in which the police are required to enter premises without a warrant and without probable cause to believe a crime has occurred. Police officers perform various tasks in addition to conducting criminal investigations and identifying and apprehending criminal suspects. Beyond the "crime fighting" function, the police are also expected to: (1) "reduce the opportunities for the commission of some crimes through preventative patrol and other measures"; (2) "aid individuals who are in danger of physical harm"; (3) "assist those who cannot care for themselves"; (4) "resolve conflict"; (5) "create and maintain a feeling of security in the community"; and (6) "provide other services on an emergency basis."[717]

As observed by the former Chief Justice (then Judge) Burger in *Wayne v. United States*,[718] in such situations there must be a "balancing of interests and needs." In this regard, "[w]hen policemen, firemen or other public officers are confronted with evidence which would lead a prudent and reasonable official to see a need to act to protect life or property, they are authorized to act on that information, even if ultimately found erroneous."[719]

Thus, when an emergency arises—for example, a medical emergency—the police should not be required to hold a belief that the imminent death of a person is probable, or that there is a near certainty as to the presence of a person at risk in a premises. Rather, the test should be whether the police have "a prudent and reasonably based belief" that, at the premises, there is a potential medical or other emergency of unknown dimension. As stated in *Wayne*:

> [A] warrant is not required to break down a door to enter a burning home to rescue occupants or extinguish a fire, to prevent a shooting or to bring emergency aid to an injured person. The need to protect or preserve life or avoid serious injury is justification for what would be otherwise illegal absent an exigency or emergency. Fires or dead bodies are reported to the police by cranks where no fires or bodies are to be found.... But the business of policemen and firemen is *to act*, not to speculate or meditate on whether the report is correct. People could well die in emergencies if police tried to act with the calm deliberation associated with the judicial process. Even the apparently dead often are saved by swift police response.[720]

What gives rise to the genuine exigency is the police need to protect or preserve life or prevent serious injury.

The "emergency aid" doctrine has been treated by most courts as a recognized exception to the written warrant requirement.[721] A close examination of it, however, reveals that it is nothing more than a "species of exigent circumstances."[722] The "emergency aid" doctrine stems from a common sense understanding that *exi-*

---

[715] *State v. Guevara*, 349 N.C. 243, 506 S.E.2d 711 (1998).

[716] *State v. Guevara*, 349 N.C. 243, 250, 506 S.E.2d 711 (1998).

[717] *ABA Standards for Criminal Justice* § 1-1.1 (2d ed. 1980).

[718] *Wayne v. United States*, 318 F.2d 205, 212 (D.C. Cir. 1963).

[719] *Wayne v. United States*, 318 F.2d 205, 212 (D.C. Cir. 1963).

[720] *Wayne v. United States*, 318 F.2d 205, 212 (D.C. Cir. 1963) (emphasis in original).

[721] *See* 3 Wayne R. LaFave, *Search and Seizure, A Treatise on the Fourth Amendment* § 6.6(a) (6th ed. 2020) (and the cases listed therein).

[722] *But see Sutterfield v. City of Milwaukee*, 751 F.3d 542 (7th Cir. 2014), where the court identified a distinction between the emergency aid doctrine and exigent circumstances. "Exigency," observed the court, "is defined by a time-urgent need to act that makes resort to the warrant process impractical." *Id.*at 559. But here, where the police were responding to a

gent circumstances may require public safety officials, such as the police, firefighters, or paramedics, to enter a dwelling without a warrant for the purpose of protecting or preserving life, or preventing serious injury. The primary rationale for the doctrine is that the Fourth Amendment does not require that public safety officials stand by in the face of an imminent danger and delay potential lifesaving measures while critical and precious time is expended obtaining a warrant.

In *State v. Scott*,[723] the North Carolina Supreme Court held that a warrantless search of the crawl space under the defendant's home was not unreasonable where the officer was summoned to the scene to investigate a missing person report, his knocks on the door went unanswered, he observed large green flies indicative of a decaying corpse, and smelled what he believed to be rotting flesh. Said the court:

> We further conclude that the subsequent search of the residence pursuant to the search warrant was reasonable and that the statements of defendant were not taken as a result of any illegal search.... Once the officer had found the body of Ms. Funderburke under the house—suggested by the presence of flies and the smell of decaying flesh—he was confronted with a potential emergency. He had reason to believe that an injured person might be in the house or that the perpetrator was in the house and would be dangerous if the perpetrator's presence was unknown.[724]

In *State v. Cline*,[725] an officer who was looking for a parent of a small child found naked and alone at the side of the road entered a nearby home through a door that was ajar and found the defendant asleep and a bathtub with plants later determined to be marijuana. The court concluded that although the officer did not hear any sounds from within the residence or observe any blood or other signs suggesting criminal activity, a reasonable officer in his position could have believed that a party was in need of immediate assistance inside the home, such that entering without obtaining a warrant was justified.

To justify a warrantless entry or search under the "emergency aid" doctrine, the following elements must be satisfied:

(1) The officer must have an objectively reasonable basis to believe that an emergency requires that he provide immediate assistance to protect or preserve life or property, or to prevent serious injury;

(2) The search must not be primarily motivated by intent to arrest and seize evidence;[726] and

(3) There must be some basis, approximating probable cause, to believe that there is a reasonable nexus or connection between the emergency and the area or places to be searched.

Once the police respond and enter a premises pursuant to this exigency, they have the right to restore or maintain the status quo during the emergency to control the dangerous or dynamic situation. This right enables the officer to take a number of intrusive actions ranging from a command to halt to a seizure of an individual. During the investigation of an emergency situation, the police may search for weapons to protect themselves and others and may look for injured or missing persons.

---

psychiatrist's 911 call about a suicidal patient, "it is not at all clear to us, nor would it have been to the police, that the mere passage of time without apparent incident was sufficient to alleviate any concern that Sutterfield might yet harm herself." *Id.* at 562. Moreover, "in emergency aid cases, where the police are acting to protect someone from imminent harm, there frequently is no suspicion of wrongdoing at the moment that the police take action." *Id.* at 564.

[723] *State v. Scott*, 343 N.C. 313, 471 S.E.2d 605 (1996).

[724] *State v. Scott*, 343 N.C. 313, 329, 471 S.E.2d 605 (1996).

[725] *State v. Cline*, 205 N.C. App. 676, 696 S.E.2d 554 (2010).

[726] The United States Supreme Court, in *Brigham City v. Stuart*, 547 U.S. 398, 404, 126 S.Ct. 1943, 1948 (2006), has eliminated this prong of the emergency aid exception. According to the U.S. Supreme Court, "[a]n action is 'reasonable' under the Fourth Amendment, regardless of the individual officer's state of mind, 'as long as the circumstances, viewed objectively, justify [the] action.'" *Id.* (quoting *Scott v. United States*, 436 U.S. 128, 138, 98 S. Ct. 1717 (1978). In this regard, the officer's "subjective motivation is irrelevant." *See Bond v. United States*, 529 U.S. 334, 338, n. 2, 120 S. Ct. 1462 (2000) ("The parties properly agree that the subjective intent of the law enforcement officer is irrelevant in determining whether that officer's actions violate the Fourth Amendment[;] the issue is not his state of mind, but the objective effect of his actions.").

In upholding warrantless entries based on the "emergency aid" doctrine, many courts have observed that the officers would have been derelict in their duty had they not acted. In the final analysis, the prosecution is not required to prove that an actual emergency existed at the time of the officers' warrantless entry. Rather, the government need only show that the facts and circumstances surrounding the entry and search were such that the officers reasonably believed there existed an emergency that made obtaining a search warrant impracticable.

Thus, the key factor in such cases is the officer's objectively reasonable belief that, given the totality of the circumstances, a person is in need of assistance. For example, warrantless entries have been upheld where immediate police action was necessary to:

- rescue people from a burning building;
- seek an occupant reliably reported to be missing;
- seek a person known to be suffering from a gunshot or knife wound;
- seek a person who was so badly beaten that he is probably dead;
- seek a person who had been repeatedly struck with a pipe until he stopped moving;
- check on an odor of rotting flesh;
- check on the well-being of unattended children;
- ensure that a weapon within the premises does not remain accessible to children there;
- assist a person reported to be ill or injured;
- seek possible victims of violence in premises recently burglarized;
- seek possible victims in premises where shots have been fired;
- investigate where disarray and blood stains indicate a recent affray has occurred;
- discover the location of explosives;
- retrieve an object which had obstructed the breathing passage of a child, where the child's doctor needed to examine the object to provide proper medical treatment;
- locate a high school student who, a short time earlier, swallowed an undetermined amount of cocaine and ran home;
- attempt to discover what substance might have been eaten by several children who were critically ill;
- respond to a credible threat of suicide;[727]
- ensure the prompt involuntary commitment of a person who is apparently mentally ill and dangerous;
- respond to a fight within a premises;
- check out an occupant's hysterical telephone call to the police;
- determine the well-being of the occupants of a residence where screams were recently heard by neighbors who were unable to get anyone to answer the phone at the residence;
- seek persons possibly affected by detected noxious fumes in the home; and
- enter a hotel room based on a hotel guest's report of an armed robbery and the reasonable belief that a victim or gunman was still in the room.[728]

Once inside the premises, an officer's conduct "must be carefully limited to achieving the objective which justified the entry—the officer may do no more than is reasonably necessary to ascertain whether someone is

---

[727] See, e.g., Sutterfield v. City of Milwaukee, 751 F.3d 542 (7th Cir. 2014); Rice v. ReliaStar Life Ins. Co., 770 F.3d 1122 (5th Cir. 2014) (no Fourth Amendment violation where officers entered house in attempt to prevent suicide); United States v. Timmann, 741 F.3d 1170, 1180 (11th Cir. 2013) (discussing Roberts v. Spielman, 643 F.3d 899, 902 (11th Cir. 2011) (warrantless entry justified on sister-in-law's report of possible suicide based on prior attempts, bipolar disorder, presence of vehicle, televisions on, and no answer at door)); United States v. Uscanga-Ramirez, 475 F.3d 1024 (8th Cir. 2007) (warrantless entry into locked bedroom justified by potential for suicide where wife told officers husband was not suicidal but was armed with gun and distraught over end of marriage); Seibert v. State, 923 So.2d 460, 467-68 (Fla. 2006) (officers' forced entry justified by roommate report of suicidal threat with large kitchen knife nearby).

[728] See 3 Wayne R. LaFave, Search and Seizure, A Treatise on the Fourth Amendment § 6.6(a) (6th ed. 2020), at 633-48, and the cases listed therein. See also Brigham City, Utah v. Stuart, 547 U.S. 398, 126 S. Ct. 1943 (2006); Michigan v. Fisher, 558 U.S. 45, 130 S. Ct. 546 (2009).

in need of assistance and to provide that assistance."[729] If the officer determines that her assistance is, in fact, not needed, the officer must immediately depart the premises, rather than exploring further. If, however, the officer's "emergency aid" entry results in the "plain view" discovery of evidence of a crime or contraband, that evidence may be admissible under "plain view" principles.

4.2.2.4.1. Firefighters

Clearly, firefighters may make a warrantless entry into a burning building and seize any evidence of arson in plain view. As Justice Stewart explained:

> A burning building clearly presents an exigency of sufficient proportions to render a warrantless entry "reasonable." Indeed, it would defy reason to suppose that fire[fighters] must secure a warrant or consent before entering a burning structure to put out the blaze.[730]

They may also remain for a reasonable time after the blaze is extinguished to investigate its cause. However, additional entries to investigate further must be made pursuant to the search warrant requirement.[731]

There are two types of warrants available to the investigating fire official, and the "object of the search determines the type of warrant required."[732] If the fire official's prime objective is to determine the cause and origin of a recent fire, an "administrative warrant" must be obtained. "Probable cause to issue an administrative warrant exists if reasonable legislative, administrative, or judicially prescribed standards for conducting an inspection are satisfied with respect to a particular dwelling."[733] This procedural requirement is accomplished by the official personally appearing before a judge, who will examine the official's affidavit and/or take her sworn testimony. At this meeting, the official must show that (1) a "fire of undetermined origin has occurred on the premises," (2) the "scope of the proposed search is reasonable[,]" (3) the "search will not intrude unnecessarily on the fire victim's privacy," and (4) the "search will be executed at a reasonable and convenient time."[734]

If, however, the fire official's prime objective is to gather evidence of criminal activity, *e.g.*, arson, a "criminal search warrant" must be secured. This is accomplished only upon a showing (before a judge) of probable cause to believe that relevant evidence will be found in the place to be searched.

Naturally, if, during the course of a valid administrative search, evidence of arson is discovered, the official may lawfully seize that evidence under the "plain view" doctrine. "This evidence may then be used to establish probable cause to obtain a criminal search warrant."[735]

4.2.2.5. Community caretaking

Care should be taken to distinguish the "emergency aid" doctrine from the "community caretaking" function of the police, which is very often used in the motor vehicle stop context. In this regard, it is now well recognized that, in addition to investigating crimes, the police also engage in "community caretaking" functions, which are "totally divorced from the detection, investigation, or acquisition of evidence relating to the violation of a criminal statute."[736] *Cady v. Dombrowski* was the first United States Supreme Court case to recognize a community caretaking exception. It involved the search of an automobile operated by Chester Dombrowski, a Chicago police officer, who had been involved in an accident while visiting Wisconsin. During the accident investigation, local police became concerned that Dombrowski's service revolver was in the vehicle. At the

---

[729] 3 Wayne R. LaFave, *Search and Seizure, A Treatise on the Fourth Amendment* § 6.6(a) (6th ed. 2020), at 649-52.

[730] *Michigan v. Tyler,* 436 U.S. 499, 509, 98 S. Ct. 1942, 1950 (1978).

[731] *See Michigan v. Tyler,* 436 U.S. 499, 509, 98 S. Ct. 1942, 1950 (1978); *see also Steigler v. Anderson,* 496 F.2d 793, 795-96 (3d Cir. 1974).

[732] *Michigan v. Clifford,* 464 U.S. 287, 294, 104 S. Ct. 641, 647 (1984).

[733] *Michigan v. Clifford,* 464 U.S. 287, 294 n.5, 104 S. Ct. 641, 647 n.5 (1984); *see also Camara v. Municipal Court,* 387 U.S. 523, 538, 87 S. Ct. 1727, 1735-36 (1967).

[734] *Michigan v. Clifford,* 464 U.S. 287, 294, 104 S. Ct. 641, 647 (1984).

[735] *Michigan v. Clifford,* 464 U.S. 287, 294, 104 S. Ct. 641, 647 (1984).

[736] *Cady v. Dombrowski,* 413 U.S. 433, 441, 93 S. Ct. 2523, 2528 (1973).

time, Dombrowski appeared intoxicated to the officers, and offered conflicting versions of the accident. When no gun was found on Dombrowski's person, an officer checked the front seat and the glove compartment of the wrecked car, but to no avail. The officers' effort to find the weapon was motivated by the obligation of the police "to protect the public from the possibility that a revolver would fall into untrained or perhaps malicious hands."[737] Although no weapon was found in the vehicle, the Wisconsin officers did discover, in the trunk, various items that linked Dombrowski to a murder.

The Court held that the police search for the gun was lawful under the officers' "community caretaking" function.

> Because of the extensive regulation of motor vehicles and traffic, and also because of the frequency with which a vehicle can become disabled or involved in an accident on public highways, the extent of police-citizen contact involving automobiles will be substantially greater than police-citizen contact in a home or office.... Local police officers ... frequently investigate vehicle accidents in which there is no claim of criminal liability and engage in what, for want of a better term, may be described as *community caretaking functions, totally divorced from the detection, investigation, or acquisition of evidence relating to the violation of a criminal statute.*[738]

In *Cady*, the Court clearly distinguished automobile searches from searches of a home, pointing out that a search of a vehicle may be reasonable "although the result might be the opposite in a search of a home."[739] That distinction led to the Third Circuit declaring that the "community caretaking" doctrine simply "cannot be used to justify warrantless searches of a home."[740]

So, according to the United States Supreme Court, the defining characteristic of community caretaking functions is that they are totally unrelated to the criminal investigation duties of the police. In *State v. Smathers*,[741] the Court of Appeals of North Carolina adopted the community caretaking doctrine as a valid exception to the warrant requirement when it said, "Thus, we now formally recognize the community caretaking exception as a means of establishing the reasonableness of a search or seizure under the Fourth Amendment."[742] In so doing, the court adopted a three-pronged test that it believed "provides a flexible framework within which officers can safely perform their duties in the public's interest while still protecting individuals from unreasonable government intrusions."[743] The court explained:

> [u]nder [the] test, ... the State has the burden of proving that: (1) a search or seizure within the meaning of the Fourth Amendment has occurred; (2) if so, that under the totality of the circumstances an objectively reasonable basis for a community caretaking function is shown; and (3) if so, that the public need or interest outweighs the intrusion upon the privacy of the individual.[744]

The court has since noted that "in cases where the community caretaking doctrine has been held to justify a warrantless search, the facts unquestionably suggest a public safety issue."[745] Applying the test, the *Smathers* court held that an officer's stop of the defendant after he observed the defendant's vehicle strike an animal that ran into the road fit into the exception and was reasonable under the Fourth Amendment.[746]

---

[737] *Cady v. Dombrowski*, 413 U.S. 433, 443, 93 S. Ct. 2523, 2528 (1973).

[738] *Cady v. Dombrowski*, 413 U.S. 433, 442, 93 S. Ct. 2523 (1973) (emphasis added).

[739] *Cady v. Dombrowski*, 413 U.S. 433, 440, 93 S. Ct. 2523 (1973) (emphasis added).

[740] *See Ray v. Township of Warren*, 626 F.3d 170, 177 (3d Cir. 2010). *Compare State v. Bogan*, 200 N.J. 61, 975 A.2d 377 (2009) (upholding the warrantless entry of an apartment under the community caretaking function of the police). *See* Larry E. Holtz, *Criminal Procedure for Law and Justice Professionals* (Blue360° Media), for a further discussion of this issue.

[741] *State v. Smathers*, 232 N.C. App. 120, 753 S.E.2d 380 (2014).

[742] *State v. Smathers*, 232 N.C. App. 120, 126, 753 S.E.2d 380 (2014).

[743] *State v. Smathers*, 232 N.C. App. 120, 128, 753 S.E.2d 380 (2014).

[744] *State v. Smathers*, 232 N.C. App. 120, 128-29, 753 S.E.2d 380 (2014).

[745] *State v. Brown*, 827 S.E.2d 534, 538 (N.C. Ct. App. 2019).

[746] *State v. Smathers*, 232 N.C. App. 120, 131, 753 S.E.2d 380 (2014).

4.2.2.5.1. Protective custody

Should an officer observe an individual conducting himself in a manner that causes the officer to reasonably believe that the individual is a person requiring treatment for mental illness, the officer may take the individual into protective custody and transport the individual to a medical center or other community mental health crises intervention center for services.

A person requires treatment if, as a result of mental illness: (i) the person can reasonably be expected within the near future to intentionally or unintentionally seriously physically injure himself or another person, and (ii) who has engaged in acts or made significant threats that are substantially supportive of this expectation; or (iii) the person is unable to understand his need for treatment and as a result can be expected to cause significant physical harm to himself or another person.

4.2.3. Consent searches

4.2.3.1. General aspects

As a recognized exception to the written warrant requirement, consensual searches continue to provide the law enforcement community with access to those areas in which an officer, desirous of searching, has less than the requisite probable cause to conduct a constitutional search or to secure a warrant. When a search is conducted pursuant to a valid consent, it may be conducted without a warrant and without probable cause.[747]

As observed by the United States Supreme Court:

"Consent searches are part of the standard investigatory techniques of law enforcement agencies" and are "a constitutionally permissible and wholly legitimate aspect of effective police activity." It would be unreasonable—indeed, absurd—to require police officers to obtain a warrant when the sole owner or occupant of a house or apartment voluntarily consents to a search. The owner of a home has a right to allow others to enter and examine the premises, and there is no reason why the owner should not be permitted to extend this same privilege to police officers if that is the owner's choice. Where the owner believes that he or she is under suspicion, the owner may want the police to search the premises so that their suspicions are dispelled. This may be particularly important where the owner has a strong interest in the apprehension of the perpetrator of a crime and believes that the suspicions of the police are deflecting the course of their investigation. An owner may want the police to search even where they lack probable cause, and if a warrant were always required, this could not be done. And even where the police could establish probable cause, requiring a warrant despite the owner's consent would needlessly inconvenience everyone involved—not only the officers and the magistrate but also the occupant of the premises, who would generally either be compelled or would feel a need to stay until the search was completed.[748]

When a person consents to a search of his property, he relinquishes his constitutional right to be free from unreasonable searches and seizures. Therefore, in order to be valid, the consent must be "voluntarily" given.[749] To be voluntary, the consent must be unequivocal and specific. In this respect, mere acquiescence cannot substitute for free consent. The consent must also be freely and intelligently given, uncontaminated by any duress or coercion, actual or implied. In all cases, "the question whether a consent to a search was in fact 'voluntary' or was the product of duress or coercion, express or implied, is a question of fact to be determined from the totality of the circumstances."[750] Moreover, the prosecution has the burden of proof to show by a preponderance of the evidence that the consent to search was freely and voluntarily given.[751]

---

[747] *United States v. Matlock,* 415 U.S. 164, 165, 94 S. Ct. 988, 990 (1974); *Schneckloth v. Bustamonte,* 412 U.S. 218, 222, 93 S. Ct. 2041, 2045 (1973); *see also* N.C.Gen.Stat. § 15A-221.

[748] *Fernandez v. California,* 571 U.S. 292, 134 S. Ct. 1126, 1132 (2014) (quoting *Schneckloth v. Bustamonte,* 412 U.S. 218, 228, 231-32, 93 S. Ct. 2041, 2045 (1973)).

[749] *Bumper v. North Carolina,* 391 U.S. 543, 548, 88 S. Ct. 1788 (1968).

[750] *Schneckloth v. Bustamonte,* 412 U.S. 218, 227, 93 S. Ct. 2041, 2047-48 (1973).

[751] *Schneckloth v. Bustamonte,* 412 U.S. 218, 227, 93 S. Ct. 2041, 2047-48 (1973).

North Carolina has codified the search pursuant to consent exception to the warrant requirement at N.C.Gen.Stat. § 15A-221 which provides:

(a) Authority to Search and Seize Pursuant to Consent.— Subject to the limitations in the other provisions of this Article, a law-enforcement officer may conduct a search and make seizures, without a search warrant or other authorization, if consent to the search is given.

(b) Definition of "Consent".— As used in this Article, "consent" means a statement to the officer, made voluntarily and in accordance with the requirements of G.S. 15A-222, giving the officer permission to make a search.

Pursuant to N.C.Gen.Stat. § 15A-222, consent must be given:

(1) By the person to be searched;

(2) By the registered owner of a vehicle to be searched or by the person in apparent control of its operation and contents at the time the consent is given;

(3) By a person who by ownership or otherwise is reasonably apparently entitled to give or withhold consent to a search of premises.

4.2.3.2. The right to refuse

There is no requirement that officers tell an individual she has a right to refuse permission to search. "The law today is that knowledge of the right to refuse is but one factor in the totality of the circumstances to be examined in construing the reasonability of a search."[752] This aspect of the law of consent was underscored in *United States v. Drayton*, where the Court "rejected in specific terms the suggestion that police officers must always inform citizens of their right to refuse when seeking permission to conduct a warrantless consent search."[753] While knowledge of the right to refuse consent is one factor to be taken into account, there is no *per se* rule calling for a presumption of invalidity if a citizen consented without explicit notification that she was free to refuse to cooperate.[754]

4.2.3.3. Determining whether the consent was voluntary or coerced

There are several factors that a court will examine to determine whether a consent was voluntarily given or coerced. Factors which may suggest that consent was coerced include: (1) the presence of abusive, overbearing, or dictatorial police procedures; (2) police use of psychological ploys, or subtle psychological pressure or language, or a tone of voice which indicates that compliance with the request might be compelled; (3) statements or acts on the part of the police which convey to the consenting party that he is not free to refuse the search or to walk away from the officer; (4) that consent was obtained despite the consenting party's denial of guilt; (5) that consent was obtained only after the consenting party had refused initial requests for consent to search; (6) that consent was given after the police blocked or otherwise impaired the consenting party's progress, or in some other way physically restrained the individual, for example, by the use of handcuffs, by surrounding the individual with uniformed officers, by physically maneuvering the individual in a particular direction, by coercing the individual to move from a public area to a private area or office, or by the intimidating use of enforcement canines; (7) that consent was obtained only after the investigating officer retained possession of the consenting party's identification or plane, train or bus ticket; (8) that consent was obtained only after an officer informed the consenting party that if he were innocent, he would cooperate with the police; and (9) that the consent was given by a person already in custody or placed

---

[752] *Schneckloth v. Bustamonte*, 412 U.S. 218, 227, 93 S. Ct. 2041, 2047-48 (1973); *see also United States v. Drayton*, 536 U.S. 194, 206, 122 S. Ct. 2105, 2113 (2002) (Officers do not have a constitutional duty to inform a suspect of his "right to refuse when seeking permission to conduct a warrantless consent search.")

[753] *United States v. Drayton*, 536 U.S. 194, 206, 122 S. Ct. 2105, 2113 (2002); *see also Ohio v. Robinette*, 519 U.S. 33, 39-40, 117 S. Ct. 417 (1996).

[754] *United States v. Drayton*, 536 U.S. 194, 207, 122 S. Ct. 2105, 2113 (2002).

under arrest, and (i) the arrest occurred late at night, (ii) the arrest was made with a display of weaponry, (iii) the arrest was made by a forcible entry or by use of force against the person, (iv) the arrestee was placed in handcuffs or otherwise kept under close restraint after his arrest, (v) the police used the custody to make repeated requests for consent, and (vi) that the custody was used as leverage, in the sense that the arrestee was told he would be released if he gave consent.

Among the factors suggesting that the consent was voluntarily given are: (1) that the consenting party was not under arrest or in custody at the time the consent was given; (2) that (if in custody) the consenting party's custodial status was voluntary; (3) that consent was given where the consenting party had reason to believe that the police would find no contraband; (4) that the consenting party was aware of his constitutional right to refuse consent; (5) that the consenting party was informed by the police prior to the request for consent of what exactly they were looking for; (6) that the consenting party signed a "consent-to-search" form prior to the search; (7) that the consenting party admitted his guilt before giving consent; (8) that the consenting party affirmatively assisted the police in conducting the search; (9) that the consenting party used his own key to provide the police with access to the area to be searched; (10) that the consenting party demonstrated a cooperative posture throughout the encounter; (11) that the consenting party was not in any way restrained by the police; (12) that the consenting party knew the officers conducting the search; (13) that the consenting party was educated or intelligent; and (14) that the consenting party was no stranger to the criminal justice system.[755]

Note that if, in an attempt to gain consent to search a residence, officers mislead a person by saying or implying they have a warrant and will search anyway, when in reality they do not, any permission given is invalid.[756] However, the threat to obtain a warrant, while bearing on the voluntariness of consent, is not treated the same. Stating that a warrant can and will be obtained, if police in fact have the requisite grounds, will not automatically vitiate an ensuing consent.[757]

4.2.3.4. Express or implied consent

A consent sufficient to avoid the necessity of a warrant may be express or implied from the circumstances surrounding the police-citizen encounter. In fact, an *implied* consent has been held to be as effective as any express consent to search. A consent may be "implied" when it is found to exist merely because of the person's particular responses to police inquiry or the person's conduct in engaging in a certain activity.[758] Thus, an implied voluntary consent may be found where the defendant has initiated police contact and has adopted a cooperative posture in the mistaken belief that he could thereby divert or prevent police suspicion of him.

4.2.3.5. Common authority

A valid consent may also be obtained from one other than the accused, *i.e.*, from a third party, so long as the consenting third party has the authority to bind the accused. In these circumstances, the inquiry whether a third-party consent is constitutionally valid focuses on whether the consenting third party possesses *common authority* over or other sufficient relationship to the premises or effects sought to be

---

[755] *United States v. Mendenhall*, 446 U.S. 544, 555-57, 100 S. Ct. 1870, 1877-78 (1980); *United States v. Watson*, 423 U.S. 411, 424, 96 S. Ct. 820, 828 (1976); *United States v. Carter*, 854 F.2d 1102, 1106 (8th Cir. 1988); *United States v. Galberth*, 846 F.2d 983 (5th Cir. 1988); *United States v. Morrow*, 731 F.2d 233, 236 (4th Cir. 1984); *United States v. Ruigomez*, 702 F.2d 61, 65 (5th Cir. 1983); *United States v. Robinson*, 690 F.2d 869, 875 (11th Cir. 1982); *United States v. Setzer*, 654 F.2d 354, 357-58 (5th Cir. Unit B 1981), *cert. denied*, 459 U.S. 1041, 103 S. Ct. 457 (1982). *See also State v. Brown*, 306 N.C. 151, 293 S.E.2d 569 (1982); *State v. Steen*, 352 N.C. 227, 536 S.E.2d 1 (2000).

[756] *Bumper v. North Carolina*, 391 U.S. 543, 549, 88 S.Ct. 1788, 1792 (1968).

[757] *United States v. Salvo*, 133 F.3d 943 (6th Cir. 1998).

[758] *See, e.g., United States v. Price*, 599 F.2d 494 (2d Cir. 1979) (valid search where a defendant told police he did not care if they searched bag because it was not his and he had picked it up by mistake); *cf. North Carolina v. Butler*, 441 U.S. 369, 375-76, 99 S. Ct. 1755, 1758-59 (1979) (an express waiver is not invariably necessary to support a finding that the defendant waived his rights).

inspected.[759] The concept of third-party consent rests not upon the law of property, however, but upon the "mutual use of the property by persons generally having joint access or control for most purposes, so that it is reasonable to recognize that any of the cohabitants has the right to permit the inspection in his own right and that others have assumed the risk that one of their number might permit the common area to be searched."[760] Naturally, the prosecution must also demonstrate that the third-party consent was given freely and voluntarily.

In *State v. McDowell*,[761] the defendant lived in an apartment with his girlfriend, Karen Curtis, "a twenty-two-year-old woman who is mentally retarded, dropped out of high school in the twelfth grade but can write her own name and can read to some extent."[762] The police searched the home she shared with the defendant pursuant to her consent. The North Carolina Supreme Court found that Curtis possessed common authority with the defendant over the searched premises. The court noted that Curtis "continues to have legal custody of her child and has never been declared legally incompetent."[763] Finding "sufficient evidence in the record that she understood the nature and consequences of her action in signing the form and that she voluntarily consented,"[764] the court upheld the search under the rule of common authority.

In *State v. Mitchell*,[765] Officers Saine and Francisco arrived at the defendant's home in response to a 911 call reporting a domestic violence incident in addition to alleging that the defendant had recently been involved in an armed robbery. Upon arriving at the home, the officers separated the defendant and his girlfriend, Ms. Fink, who were both home at the time. The defendant remained outside while Ms. Fink spoke with Officer Francisco inside the residence. Alone with Officer Francisco, Ms. Fink confirmed the domestic violence incident and also corroborated the allegation regarding the armed robbery. Ms. Fink then led Officer Francisco upstairs to show him potentially incriminating evidence which she had found in the home. Thereafter, the officers obtained a search warrant and conducted a search of the home.

The defendant argued that the search was improper as he had not provided consent. The court noted that, although the defendant was reluctant to remain outside, he never objected to the officers' entry into his home. Thus, the officers were justified in entering the home. Moreover, they did not search the home before obtaining the warrant. Rather, "Ms. Fink simply showed the officers items she had discovered prior to their arrival at the home."[766]

Even where the party granting permission does not in fact have legally sufficient control over the premises, the consent may nonetheless be valid under the Fourth Amendment if the officer reasonably believes that the party had common control.[767] This is the rule for "apparent authority."

4.2.3.6. Co-occupants

When one co-occupant of a residence consents to a search, but another co-occupant is also physically present and expressly objects to the search, then any subsequent search and seizure is unreasonable and invalid as to the objecting party.[768] In *Randolph*, the defendant's wife called police regarding a domestic disturbance. When officers arrived, the defendant was not home, but his wife alleged that he had a cocaine habit, and that he had drug paraphernalia in the house. While officers were speaking with the defendant's wife, the defendant returned home. He denied he had a drug habit, but also refused to consent to a search of the residence. Undeterred, the officer who asked the defendant for consent then turned to the defendant's wife and asked her; she readily agreed to let him search, leading the officer to a bedroom, where the officer saw a section of a drinking straw covered with a powdery residue. Because the defendant had been present at the start of the search and objected to it, the contraband the officer observed could not be used against

---

[759] *Matlock v. United States*, 415 U.S. 164, 169-172, 94 S. Ct. 988, 993 (1974).
[760] *Matlock v. United States*, 415 U.S. 164, 169-172, 94 S. Ct. 988, 993 (1974).
[761] *State v. McDowell*, 329 N.C. 363, 407 S.E.2d 200 (1991).
[762] *State v. McDowell*, 329 N.C. 363, 376, 407 S.E.2d 200 (1991).
[763] *State v. McDowell*, 329 N.C. 363, 376, 407 S.E.2d 200 (1991).
[764] *State v. McDowell*, 329 N.C. 363, 377, 407 S.E.2d 200 (1991).
[765] *State v. Mitchell*, 822 S.E.2d 51 (N.C. Ct. App. 2018).
[766] *State v. Mitchell*, 822 S.E.2d 51, 55 (N.C. Ct. App. 2018).
[767] *Illinois v. Rodriguez*, 497 U.S. 177, 110 S. Ct. 2793 (1990).
[768] *Georgia v. Randolph*, 547 U.S. 103, 120, 126 S. Ct. 1515, 1527 (2006).

him. The rule in *Randolph* does not apply, however, if the objecting occupant is not physically present at the residence—this is true even if police are the reason for the occupant's absence (*i.e.*, if the occupant was lawfully detained or arrested prior to the request for consent to search being made).[769]

Although a police officer may not remove someone from the premises for the purpose of preventing an objection, the officer is not required to locate an absent person to obtain the person's consent.[770]

4.2.3.7. Consent provided by a minor

In *State v. Weathers*,[771] the North Carolina Supreme Court held that a minor possessed the authority to give law enforcement officers consent to search. There, Tammy Thomas, the defendant's stepdaughter, who lived with him frequently, consented to the search. The court held, "Tammy Thomas was a resident of the premises and, therefore, had the authority to consent to a search of the house and bedroom which she shared with defendant."[772] When examining whether such a consent is valid, courts will examine the person's age, intelligence, maturity, and education level.

4.2.3.8. Traffic stops

Following a valid traffic stop, there is no requirement that an officer tell an individual that he is free to leave before asking for permission to search his vehicle.[773] It has been held, however, that a driver's right to refuse consent falls within constitutional protections against unreasonable searches. The exercise of that right cannot be penalized by making the refusal part of the foundation for a search.

4.2.3.9. Scope of the consent

The search must be limited to those areas to which the defendant actually or implicitly gives permission to search.[774] The scope of the search is generally determined with reference to that which the officer is seeking, *i.e.*, to areas or containers where the stated subject of the search could be located. For example, in *Florida v. Jimeno*,[775] the U.S. Supreme Court approved the search of a paper bag, found on the floor of a car, for narcotics, after the defendant had given consent to a general search of his car. The Court concluded that, based on these facts, it was reasonable for the searching officer to believe the scope of the consent given permitted him to open the bag. The defendant knew the purpose of the search was to look for drugs, and it was objectively reasonable to assume drugs could be found there.

Consent to search may be limited in scope, and consent may be revoked. Any evidence obtained up to the time wherein the suspect revoked his consent is admissible. Once the suspect revokes his consent to search, however, the police must stop the search, unless some other basis justifies a continuation. If the police, for example, find illegal drugs during a consent search, they may arrest the suspect. They may then conduct a search incident to arrest, even if the suspect withdraws his consent to search after the discovery of illegal drugs. Because the illegal drugs were discovered before the withdrawal of the consent, they would be admissible. The continued search after the withdrawal of consent would be permitted because it would be based on a search incident to arrest rather than consent.

In *State v. Pearson*,[776] after being stopped on an interstate highway, the defendant signed a waiver giving consent to a search of his car. Thereafter, the police frisked the defendant and found small bags of cocaine and marijuana hidden in his crotch area. The North Carolina Supreme Court held, "The consent signed by the

---

[769] *See Fernandez v. California*, 571 U.S. 292, 134 S. Ct. 1126 (2014); *State v. Mitchell*, 822 S.E.2d 51 (N.C. Ct. App. 2018); *State v. McDowell*, 329 N.C. 363, 407 S.E.2d 200 (1991).

[770] *Georgia v. Randolph*, 547 U.S. 103, 121-122, 126 S. Ct. 1515, 1527 (2006).

[771] *State v. Weathers*, 339 N.C. 441, 451 S.E.2d 266 (1994).

[772] *State v. Weathers*, 339 N.C. 441, 452-53, 451 S.E.2d 266 (1994).

[773] *Ohio v. Robinette*, 519 U.S. 33, 117 S. Ct. 417 (1996).

[774] N.C. Gen. Stat. § 15A-223.

[775] *Florida v. Jimeno*, 500 U.S. 248, 111 S. Ct. 1801 (1991).

[776] *State v. Pearson*, 348 N.C. 272, 498 S.E.2d 599 (1998).

defendant applied only to the vehicle. We cannot broaden the consent to include the defendant's person."[777] Similarly in *State v. Stone*,[778] "the defendant, acting as a 'reasonable person,' would not have understood that his general consent to a search permitted the officer to pull his pants away and look into his genital area with a flashlight."[779]

4.2.4. Automobile exception

4.2.4.1. General aspects

One of the "specifically established and well-delineated exceptions" to the warrant requirement is the "automobile exception," created by the United States Supreme Court in *Carroll v. United States*.[780] In that case, the United States Supreme Court established the exception as a result of an automobile's mobility, which makes it impractical to obtain a warrant.[781]

Under the Fourth Amendment, and the so-called "automobile exception," if police have probable cause to believe a readily mobile automobile contains contraband or evidence of a crime, they may lawfully conduct a warrantless search of the entire automobile, and any containers therein that may reasonably be expected to conceal the object of their search.[782] This rule applies equally to all compartments, containers and packages found within the vehicle "in which the object of the search may be found."[783]

Under the Fourth Amendment, separate exigent circumstances are not required.[784] Even if the officers have time to obtain a warrant before searching, they are not required to do so.

In *State v. Isleib*,[785] the North Carolina Supreme Court declared, "We hold that no exigent circumstances other than the motor vehicle itself are required in order to justify a warrantless search of a motor vehicle if there is probable cause to believe that it contains the instrumentality of a crime or evidence pertaining to a crime and the vehicle is in a public place."[786] Later, the Court of Appeals of North Carolina explained the automobile exception as follows:

A search of a vehicle on a public roadway or public vehicular area is properly conducted without a warrant as long as probable cause exists for the search. "Probable cause exists where 'the facts and circumstances within their [the officers'] knowledge and of which they had reasonable trustworthy information [are] sufficient in themselves to warrant a man of reasonable caution in the belief that' an offense has been or is being committed." In utilizing an informant's tip, probable cause is determined using a 'totality-of-the circumstances' analysis which 'permits a balanced assessment of the relative weights of all the various indicia of reliability (and unreliability) attending an informant's tip.'[787]

---

[777] *State v. Pearson*, 348 N.C. 272, 277, 498 S.E.2d 599 (1998).
[778] *State v. Stone*, 362 N.C. 50, 653 S.E.2d 414 (2007).
[779] *State v. Stone*, 362 N.C. 50, 56, 653 S.E.2d 414 (2007).
[780] *Carroll v. United States*, 267 U.S. 132, 153-54, 45 S. Ct. 280, 285 (1925).
[781] *Carroll v. United States*, 267 U.S. 132, 153, 45 S. Ct. 280, 285 (1925) (acknowledging the difference in practicality of obtaining a warrant for stationary objects like a store or dwelling and obtaining a warrant for objects like a ship or automobile, given the fact that "[a] vehicle can be quickly moved out of the locality or jurisdiction in which the warrant must be sought").
[782] *See United States v. Ross*, 456 U.S. 798, 820-21, 102 S. Ct. 2157, 2172-73 (1982) (The scope of a warrantless search of a lawfully stopped vehicle based on probable cause "is no narrower—and no broader—than the scope of a search" that could be authorized by a search warrant.).
[783] *United States v. Ross*, 456 U.S. 798, 820-21, 102 S. Ct. 2157, 2160, 2172, 2173 (1982); *see also California v. Carney*, 471 U.S. 386, 105 S. Ct. 2066 (1985) (automobile exception justified based on lower expectation of privacy in a vehicle); *Carroll v. United States*, 267 U.S. 132, 153-54, 45 S. Ct. 280 (1925) (warrantless automobile search supported by probable cause of a crime is lawful due to the mobility inherent in an automobile).
[784] *See Pennsylvania v. Labron*, 518 U.S. 938, 116 S. Ct. 2485 (1996). *See also Maryland v. Dyson*, 527 U.S. 465 (1999).
[785] *State v. Isleib*, 319 N.C. 634, 356 S.E.2d 573 (1987).
[786] *State v. Isleib*, 319 N.C. 634, 638, 356 S.E.2d 573 (1987).
[787] *State v. Earhart*, 134 N.C. App. 130, 133, 516 S.E.2d 883 (1999) (citing *State v. Isleib*, 319 N.C. 634, 356 S.E.2d 573 (1987); quoting *State v. Zuniga*, 312 N.C. 251, 261, 322 S.E.2d 140, 146 (1984)). *See also State v. Holmes*, 142 N.C. App. 614, 544 S.E.2d 18 (2001).

Thus, when Officer John observed smoke emanating from the defendant's vehicle and observed marijuana residue on the defendant's lap in *State v. Brown*,[788] the officer had probable cause to believe that the defendant's vehicle contained evidence of marijuana. Such independent probable cause was sufficient to enable Officer John to conduct a warrantless search of the defendant's vehicle for the purpose of determining the existence of controlled substances even without the consent of the defendant.

4.2.4.2. Closed packages in an automobile

In *California v. Acevedo*,[789] the U.S. Supreme Court held that the police are not required to obtain a warrant to open a closed package located in a motor vehicle when their probable cause relates to the package and not the entire vehicle. The Court wrote, "The line between probable cause to search a vehicle and probable cause to search a package in that vehicle is not always clear." The better rule is that "the police may search an automobile and the containers within it where they have probable cause to believe contraband or evidence is contained." As the Court of Appeals of North Carolina has stated, "If a law enforcement officer has probable cause to believe that the vehicle contains evidence of a crime, the officer may conduct an immediate warrantless evidentiary search of the vehicle, including closed containers found therein."[790]

4.2.4.3. Passengers' belongings

When police have probable cause to believe an automobile contains contraband or evidence of a crime, they may search the entire car, including the contents of a *passenger's* personal belongings that may be capable of holding the object of the search.[791] According to the Supreme Court in *Wyoming v. Houghton,* effective law enforcement "would be appreciably impaired without the ability to search a passenger's personal belongings when there is reason to believe contraband or evidence of criminal wrongdoing is hidden in the car. As in all car-search cases, the 'ready mobility' of an automobile creates the risk that the evidence or contraband will be permanently lost while a warrant is obtained."[792] Thus, "police officers with probable cause to search a car may inspect passengers' belongings found in the car that are capable of concealing the object of the search." Moreover, such property may be searched, "whether or not its owner is present as a passenger or otherwise, because it may contain the contraband that the officer has reason to believe is in the car."[793]

4.2.4.4. Delayed searches

In *United States v. Johns*,[794] the U.S. Supreme Court held that a law enforcement officer may conduct a warrantless search of packages several days after those packages were removed from a lawfully stopped vehicle when the officer had probable cause to believe the packages contained contraband. When police have probable cause to believe a lawfully stopped vehicle contains contraband, they are entitled to conduct a warrantless "search of every part of the vehicle and its contents that may conceal the object of the search." The warrantless search of packages taken from that vehicle will not be deemed unreasonable merely because it occurs several days after the packages were unloaded from the vehicle. According to the Court, where officers are entitled to seize a package "and continue to have probable cause to believe that it contains contraband,...delay in the execution of the warrantless search is [not] necessarily unreasonable."[795]

---

[788] *State v. Brown*, 228 N.C. App. 282, 748 S.E.2d 774 (2013).

[789] *California v. Acevedo*, 500 U.S. 565, 111 S. Ct. 1982 (1991).

[790] *State v. Parker*, 183 N.C. App. 1, 10, 644 S.E.2d 235, 242 (2007) (quoting *California v. Acevedo*, 500 U.S. 565, 111 S. Ct. 1982, 114 L. Ed. 2d 619 (1991)).

[791] *Wyoming v. Houghton*, 526 U.S. 295, 119 S. Ct. 1297 (1999).

[792] *Wyoming v. Houghton*, 526 U.S. 295, 119 S. Ct. 1297, 1302 (1999).

[793] *Wyoming v. Houghton*, 526 U.S. 295, 119 S. Ct. 1297, 1304 (1999).

[794] *United States v. Johns*, 469 U.S. 478, 105 S. Ct. 881 (1985).

[795] *United States v. Johns*, 469 U.S. 478, 105 S. Ct. 881, 886-87 (1985); *see also Florida v. White,* 526 U.S. 559 (1999) (noting that if there is probable cause to believe that a vehicle itself is contraband, it may be seized from a public place without a warrant); *Texas v. White*, 423 U.S. 67, 68, 96 S. Ct. 304, 305 (1975) (As long as probable cause exists for a warrantless search of a vehicle on the scene, the search may also be conducted later after the vehicle has been moved to the station house);

4.2.4.5. K-9 searches

The Fourth Amendment does not require that police have a reasonable, articulable suspicion of criminal activity before allowing a well-trained narcotics detection dog to sniff the exterior of a vehicle during a lawful traffic stop, as long as this does not prolong the duration of the stop.[796] Officers may not, however, extend an otherwise completed traffic stop in order to conduct a dog sniff, absent reasonable suspicion that there is contraband in the vehicle.[797]

A reliable drug dog's alert on the exterior of a vehicle may be sufficient, in and of itself, to establish probable cause for a warrantless search of the interior. Note also that a positive alert followed by a negative alert does not necessarily eliminate an officer's probable cause.

In this regard, a narcotics detection dog's failed alert is not *per se* dispositive of probable cause, but merely one factor to be considered, and, more specifically, that the subsequent failed alert did not necessarily negate an earlier positive alert.

4.2.4.6. Odor of contraband

When a qualified person smells an odor sufficiently distinctive to identify contraband, the odor alone may provide probable cause to believe that contraband is present.[798]

Thus, when an officer detects an odor of a controlled substance coming from a vehicle, an officer has probable cause to conduct a search of the vehicle if testimony has been elicited that the officer has training and experience in the detection of the controlled substance.[799]

4.2.4.7. Motor homes

Does a fully mobile motor home, which is located in a public parking lot, fall within the "automobile exception" to the Fourth Amendment warrant requirement? In *California v. Carney*,[800] the United States Supreme Court said *yes*. The warrantless search of a fully mobile motor home, based upon probable cause, is proper under the "automobile exception" to the Fourth Amendment warrant requirement.[801]

The automobile exception will not apply, however, if the motor home is situated in such "a way or place that objectively indicates that it is being used as a residence."[802] Each of the following factors should be considered in determining whether the vehicle is being used as a residence and, therefore, whether a warrant must be obtained before its search: (1) the vehicle's location; (2) whether the vehicle is readily mobile or, instead, elevated on blocks or connected to utilities; (3) whether the vehicle is licensed; and (4) whether the vehicle has convenient access to a public road.[803]

4.2.4.8. GPS tracking

In *United States v. Jones*,[804] FBI agents installed a GPS tracking device on the undercarriage of the defendant's Jeep while it was parked in a public parking lot. Over the next 28 days, the agents used the device to

---

see also *Chambers v. Maroney*, 399 U.S. 42, 52, 90 S. Ct. 1975, 1981 (1970) ("The probable-cause factor" that developed on the scene "still obtained at the station house[.]").

[796] *Illinois v. Caballes*, 543 U.S. 405, 125 S. Ct. 834 (2005).

[797] *Rodriguez v. United States*, 575 U.S. 348, 135 S. Ct. 1609 (2015).

[798] *Taylor v. United States*, 286 U.S. 1, 52 S. Ct. 466 (1932); *Johnson v. United States*, 333 U.S. 10, 15, 68 S. Ct. 367 (1948).

[799] *See State v. Bethea*, 821 S.E.2d 316 (N.C. Ct. App. 2018) (odor of marijuana coming from the defendant's vehicle, which did not dissipate when the defendant was removed from the vehicle gave rise to probable cause to search the vehicle); *State v. Downing*, 169 N.C. App. 790, 796, 613 S.E.2d 35, 39 (2005) ("Plain smell of drugs by an officer is evidence to conclude there is probable cause for a search." (citation omitted)); *State v. Greenwood*, 301 N.C. 705, 273 S.E.2d 438 (1981) (the smell of marijuana gave the arresting officer probable cause to search the automobile for the contraband drug).

[800] *California v. Carney*, 471 U.S. 386, 105 S. Ct. 2066 (1985).

[801] *California v. Carney*, 471 U.S. 386, 105 S. Ct. 2066, 2070 (1985).

[802] *California v. Carney*, 471 U.S. 386, 105 S. Ct. 2066, 2071 n.3 (1985).

[803] *California v. Carney*, 471 U.S. 386, 105 S. Ct. 2066, 2071 n.3 (1985).

[804] *United States v. Jones*, 565 U.S. 400, 132 S. Ct. 945 (2012).

track the vehicle's movements (and once had to replace the device's battery when the Jeep was parked in a different public lot). By means of signals from multiple satellites, the device established the vehicle's location within 50 to 100 feet and communicated that location by cellular phone to an FBI computer. It relayed more than 2,000 pages of data over the four-week period. The U.S. Supreme Court found that installation of a GPS device, and the subsequent use of that device to monitor the vehicle's movements, constitutes a "search" within the meaning of the Fourth Amendment. The agents did more than conduct a visual inspection of the Jeep; by attaching the device to it, they encroached on a protected area. Because they did not first obtain a warrant, the Court held that the search was unlawful.

4.2.4.9. Driveway searches

In *Collins v. Virginia*,[805] the United States Supreme Court held that the automobile exception does not permit a law enforcement officer, uninvited and without a warrant, to enter the curtilage of a home in order to search a vehicle parked at the top of the home's driveway. According to the Court, "[t]he automobile exception does not afford the necessary lawful right of access to search a vehicle parked within a home or its curtilage because it does not justify an intrusion on a person's separate and substantial Fourth Amendment interest in his home and curtilage."[806]

4.2.5. Impound and inventory searches

4.2.5.1. General aspects

It is well recognized that police may conduct an inventory of the contents of lawfully impounded vehicles as a routine, administrative community caretaking function, in order to protect the vehicle and the property in it, to safeguard the police and others from potential danger, and to insure against claims of lost, stolen, or vandalized property.[807]

In *South Dakota v. Opperman*,[808] the defendant's illegally parked car was towed to the city impound lot where an officer of the Vermillion Police Department observed several articles of personal property within the vehicle. As the officer proceeded to inventory the contents of the car, he discovered a plastic bag containing marijuana in the unlocked glove compartment.

Finding the initial impoundment lawful, the United States Supreme Court determined that the automobile impoundment was sanctioned by the "community caretaking functions" incumbent upon law enforcement officials in situations wherein the public safety and efficient movement of vehicular traffic are in jeopardy.[809] Respecting the inventory, the Court ruled that such intrusions into automobiles legally "impounded or otherwise in lawful police custody" have been widely sustained as reasonable under the Fourth Amendment "where the process is aimed at securing or protecting the car and its contents."[810]

As a result, the Court declared that the officer in *Opperman* was

indisputably engaged in a caretaking search of a lawfully impounded automobile.... The inventory was conducted only after the car had been impounded for multiple parking violations. The owner, having left his car illegally parked for an extended period, and thus subject to impoundment, was not present

---

[805] *Collins v. Virginia*, 584 U.S. ___, 138 S. Ct. 1663 (2018).

[806] The United States Supreme Court remanded the case for a state court determination of whether the officer's warrantless intrusion may have been reasonable on a different basis. Upon remand, the Virginia Supreme Court held that the evidence discovered during the warrantless search was admissible under the good-faith exception to the exclusionary rule. Said the Court: "The exclusionary rule does not apply under the facts of this case because, at the time of the search, a reasonably well-trained police officer would not have known that the automobile exception did not permit him to search a motorcycle located a few feet across the curtilage boundary of a private driveway." *Collins v. Commonwealth*, 297 Va. 207, 227, 824 S.E.2d 485, 496 (2019).

[807] *South Dakota v. Opperman*, 428 U.S. 364, 369, 96 S. Ct. 3092, 3097 (1976).

[808] *South Dakota v. Opperman*, 428 U.S. 364, 96 S. Ct. 3092 (1976).

[809] *South Dakota v. Opperman*, 428 U.S. 364, 368, 96 S. Ct. 3092, 3096 (1976); *see also Cady v. Dombrowski*, 413 U.S. 433, 441, 93 S. Ct. 2523, 2528 (1973).

[810] *South Dakota v. Opperman*, 428 U.S. 364, 373, 96 S. Ct. 3092, 3099 (1976).

to make other arrangements for the safekeeping of his belongings. The inventory itself was prompted by the presence in plain view of a number of valuables inside the car.... [T]here is no suggestion whatever that this standard procedure, essentially like that followed throughout the country, was a pretext concealing an investigatory police motive. [Accordingly,] in following standard police procedures, prevailing throughout the country and approved by the overwhelming majority of courts, the conduct of [this officer] was not "unreasonable" under the Fourth Amendment.[811]

4.2.5.2. Pre-existing standardized procedures

In *Colorado v. Bertine*,[812] the Court held that law enforcement officers may, consistent with the Fourth Amendment, open closed containers while conducting a routine inventory search of an impounded vehicle. So long as the police department has "reasonable police regulations relating to inventory procedures" in place, such impound and inventory procedures, administered in good faith, "satisfy the Fourth Amendment."[813]

In *Florida v. Wells*,[814] the Court re-emphasized the importance of "standardized criteria" in the area of impounded motor vehicle inventory searches, and delivered a strong message to law enforcement agencies that a pre-existing *department policy* or written *general order* covering the subject of impounded motor vehicle inventories is required before the procedure will receive judicial approval.[815] In the absence of a standardized policy covering the subject of impounded vehicle inventory searches, and the opening of closed containers encountered during such procedures, a vehicle search will not be "sufficiently regulated to satisfy the Fourth Amendment."[816]

4.2.5.3. Booking procedures

In *Illinois v. Lafayette*,[817] the U.S. Supreme Court held that, in accordance with the routine booking process, it is reasonable under the Fourth Amendment "for police to search the personal effects of a person under lawful arrest as part of the administrative procedure at a police station house incident to booking and jailing the suspect."[818] According to the Court, "[a]t the station house, it is entirely proper for police to remove and list or inventory property found on the person or in the possession of an arrested person who is to be jailed."[819] Such a standardized procedure not only deters false claims, but also guards against theft or careless handling of property taken from the arrestee. Moreover, the Court observed that: "Arrested persons have also been known to injure themselves— or others—with belts, knives, drugs, or other items on their person while being detained. Dangerous instrumentalities—such as razor blades, bombs, or weapons—can be concealed in innocent-looking articles taken from the arrestee's possession."[820] Additionally, this procedure assists "the police in ascertaining or verifying the arrestee's identity."[821] These considerations therefore suggest that "a stationhouse search of every item carried on or by a person who has lawfully been taken into custody by the police will amply serve the important and legitimate governmental interests involved."[822]

In *Lafayette,* police arrested the defendant and transported him to precinct headquarters. At the time he was carrying a shoulder bag. The bag was opened, emptied, and found to contain contraband. The defendant argued that the search exceeded the scope of a permissible booking search. The Court disagreed, reasoning

---

[811] *South Dakota v. Opperman*, 428 U.S. 364, 375-76, 96 S. Ct. 3092, 3100 (1976).
[812] *Colorado v. Bertine*, 479 U.S. 367, 107 S. Ct. 738 (1987).
[813] *Colorado v. Bertine*, 479 U.S. 367, 107 S. Ct. 738, 742 (1987).
[814] *Florida v. Wells*, 495 U.S. 1, 110 S. Ct. 1632 (1990).
[815] *Florida v. Wells*, 495 U.S. 1, 110 S. Ct. 1632, 1635 (1990).
[816] *Florida v. Wells*, 495 U.S. 1, 110 S. Ct. 1632, 1635 (1990).
[817] *Illinois v. Lafayette*, 462 U.S. 640, 103 S. Ct. 2605 (1983).
[818] *Illinois v. Lafayette*, 462 U.S. 640, 103 S. Ct. 2605, 2608, 2611 (1983).
[819] *Illinois v. Lafayette*, 462 U.S. 640, 103 S. Ct. 2605, 2609 (1983).
[820] *Illinois v. Lafayette*, 462 U.S. 640, 103 S. Ct. 2605, 2609 (1983).
[821] *Illinois v. Lafayette*, 462 U.S. 640, 103 S. Ct. 2605, 2610 (1983).
[822] *Illinois v. Lafayette*, 462 U.S. 640, 103 S. Ct. 2605, 2610 (1983).

that the search served the important government interests of protecting the property of the arrestee, as well as protecting the police department from false claims. A routine booking and search is a reasonable way to promote these interests and thus is valid under the Fourth Amendment.[823]

5. PRIVACY EXPECTATIONS

5.1. Preliminary

At the federal level, in order to determine whether a particular area or object warrants Fourth Amendment protection, courts will engage in a two-part inquiry. The first part of the inquiry questions whether an individual has exhibited "an actual (or subjective) expectation of privacy" in the area or item in question.[824] Next, it must be determined whether the expectation is "one that society is prepared to recognize as 'reasonable.'"[825] Taken as a whole, the *Katz v. United States* "twofold requirement" stands for the proposition that "wherever an individual may harbor a reasonable 'expectation of privacy,' ... he is entitled to be free from unreasonable governmental intrusion."[826] On the other hand, one cannot have a reasonable expectation of privacy in what is knowingly exposed to public view.[827]

"The touchstone of Fourth Amendment analysis is whether a person has a 'constitutionally protected reasonable expectation of privacy.'"[828] In this respect, police conduct will implicate the Fourth Amendment only if it intrudes into an area (or significantly interferes with the possession of an item) in which an individual has "manifested a subjective expectation of privacy ... that society accepts as objectively reasonable."[829]

In certain cases, however, the constitutional protection may extend directly to a person's property, even though privacy or liberty interests may not be immediately implicated. For example, in *Soldal v. Cook County, Ill.*,[830] deputy sheriffs assisted the owners of a mobile home park in evicting the Soldal family. As the deputies stood and watched, the park owners wrenched the sewer and water connections off the side of the Soldal trailer, disconnected the telephone, tore the trailer's canopy and skirting, pulled it free from its moorings and towed it away. Finding the Fourth Amendment clearly applicable, the U.S. Supreme Court held:

> As a result of the state action in this case, the Soldals' domicile was not only seized, it literally was carried away, giving a new meaning to the term "mobile home." We fail to see how being unceremoniously dispossessed of one's home in the manner alleged to have occurred here can be viewed as anything but a seizure invoking the protection of the Fourth Amendment.... The Amendment protects the people from unreasonable searches and seizures of "their persons, houses, papers, and effects." ... [A]nd our cases unmistakably hold that the Amendment protects property as well as privacy.... We thus are unconvinced that ... the Fourth Amendment protects against unreasonable seizures of property only where privacy or liberty is also implicated.[831]

5.1.1. Listening devices

In *Katz v. United States*,[832] the Court determined that the police will violate the Fourth Amendment by electronically listening to and recording a person's words spoken into a telephone receiver in a public telephone booth without prior judicial authorization. In this regard, the Court determined that "the Fourth Amendment

---

[823] *See also State v. Butler*, 331 N.C. 227, 415 S.E.2d 719 (1992).

[824] *Katz v. United States*, 389 U.S. 347, 361, 88 S. Ct. 507, 516 (1967) (Harlan, J., concurring).

[825] *Katz v. United States*, 389 U.S. 347, 361, 88 S. Ct. 507, 516 (1967) (Harlan, J., concurring).

[826] *Terry v. Ohio*, 392 U.S. 1, 9, 88 S. Ct. 1868, 1873 (1968).

[827] *See Katz v. United States*, 389 U.S. 347, 88 S. Ct. 507 (1967). *See also State v. Perry*, 243 N.C. App. 156, 776 S.E.2d 528 (2015).

[828] *California v. Ciraolo*, 476 U.S. 207, 211, 106 S. Ct. 1809, 1811 (1986) (quoting *Katz v. United States*, 389 U.S. 347, 361, 88 S. Ct. 507, 516 (1967) (Harlan, J., concurring)).

[829] *California v. Greenwood*, 486 U.S. 35, 39, 108 S. Ct. 1625, 1628 (1988).

[830] *Soldal v. Cook County, Ill.*, 506 U.S. 56, 113 S. Ct. 538 (1992).

[831] *Soldal v. Cook County, Ill.*, 506 U.S. 56, 113 S. Ct. 538, 543-45 (1992).

[832] *Katz v. United States*, 389 U.S. 347, 88 S. Ct. 507 (1967).

governs not only the seizure of tangible items, but extends as well to the recording of oral statements over-heard without any 'technical [physical intrusion].'"[833] Thus, the FBI agents' conduct "in electronically listening to and recording the [defendant's] words violated the privacy upon which he justifiably relied while using the telephone booth and thus constituted a 'search and seizure' within the meaning of the Fourth Amendment. The fact that the electronic device employed to achieve that end did not happen to penetrate the wall of the booth can have no constitutional significance."[834]

5.1.2. Presence of the media during warrant execution

In *Wilson v. Layne*,[835] the Supreme Court held that "it is a violation of the Fourth Amendment for police to bring members of the media or other third parties into a home during the execution of [an arrest] warrant when the presence of the third parties in the home was not in aid of the execution of the warrant."[836]

5.1.3. Thermal imaging devices

In *Kyllo v. United States*,[837] the U.S. Supreme Court held that using a thermal imaging device to detect relative amounts of heat within the home, constitutes a Fourth Amendment "search." According to the Court where law enforcement officers use "a device that is not in general public use, to explore details of the home that would previously have been unknowable without physical intrusion, the surveillance is a 'search' and is presumptively unreasonable without a warrant."[838]

5.1.4. Use of a flashlight

A person's subjective expectation of privacy as to that which is located in an area of common access or view will be deemed unreasonable, and consequently, unworthy of Fourth Amendment protection. Therefore, visual observation of evidence located in such an unprotected area does not constitute a search within the meaning of the Fourth Amendment. Moreover, it has been held that no "search" takes place when police use artificial means, such as a flashlight, to illuminate a darkened area.[839] As explained in *Marshall v. United States*,[840]

When the circumstances of a particular case are such that the police officer's observations would not have constituted a search had it occurred in daylight, then the fact that the officer used a flashlight to pierce the nighttime darkness does not transform his observation into a search. Regardless of the time of day or night, the plain view rule must be upheld where the viewer is rightfully positioned....The plain view rule does not go into hibernation at sunset.[841]

---

[833] *Katz v. United States*, 389 U.S. 347, 88 S. Ct. 507, 512 (1967).

[834] *Katz v. United States*, 389 U.S. 347, 88 S. Ct. 507, 512 (1967).

[835] *Wilson v. Layne*, 526 U.S. 603, 119 S. Ct. 1692 (1999).

[836] *Wilson v. Layne*, 526 U.S. 603, 119 S. Ct. 1692, 1699 (1999); *see also Hanlon v. Berger*, 526 U.S. 808, 119 S. Ct. 1706 (1999) (reaching the same result in a situation involving the execution of a search warrant and the invited presence of a crew of photographers and reporters from the Cable News Network, Inc.).

[837] *Kyllo v. United States*, 533 U.S. 27, 121 S. Ct. 2038 (2001).

[838] *Kyllo v. United States*, 533 U.S. 27, 121 S. Ct. 2038, 2046 (2001).

[839] *See, e.g.*, *United States v. Dunn*, 480 U.S. 294, 107 S. Ct. 1134, 1141 (1987) ("officers' use of the beam of a flashlight, directed through the essentially open front of [defendant's] barn, did not transform their observations into an unreasonable search within the meaning of the Fourth Amendment"); *Texas v. Brown*, 460 U.S. 730, 739-40, 103 S. Ct. 1535, 1542 (1983) (officer's "action in shining his flashlight to illuminate the interior of [defendant's] car trenched upon no right secured to the latter by the Fourth Amendment"); *United States v. Lee*, 274 U.S. 559, 563, 47 S. Ct. 746, 748 (1927) ("[The] use of a search light is comparable to the use of a marine glass or a field glass. It is not prohibited by the Constitution."); *United States v. Rickus*, 737 F.2d 360, 366 n.3 (3d Cir. 1984) (The "use of a flashlight to aid the officer's vision did not transform the observations justified under the 'plain view doctrine' into an illegal search.").

[840] *Marshall v. United States*, 422 F.2d 185 (5th Cir. 1970).

[841] *Marshall v. United States*, 422 F.2d 185, 189 (5th Cir. 1970).

In *State v. Harris*,[842] Officers Canfield and Dula were lawfully at the defendant's residence investigating a dog biting incident. The officers knocked on the front door and the defendant answered. "While Officers Canfield and Dula stood at the door of the house waiting for other officers, they were able to see into the interior of the house and they observed a woman turning the lights off in the house. In an effort to see the woman's action, both officers shined their flashlights into the interior of the house. When the house was illuminated, both officers believed they saw a rifle in a corner that was within four to five feet of the woman."[843] Thereafter, the officers obtained a warrant and a search of the house produced a handgun, magazines and ammunition. The defendant was indicted for possession of a firearm by a felon.

The Court of Appeals of North Carolina explained, "In order to determine whether the use of the flashlight was a search within the meaning of the Fourth Amendment, we must first consider whether Defendant had a subjective expectation of privacy and if so, whether that expectation was reasonable."[844] The court held that the defendant did not have a subjective expectation of privacy in an area that was "'exposed to the public from an unprotected vantage point'"[845] and that the officers were not required to "'shield their eyes from that which was exposed to public view.'"[846] Accordingly there was no search and no Fourth Amendment violation.[847]

5.1.5. Drug field test not a search

In *United States v. Jacobsen*,[848] the U.S. Supreme Court held that a chemical field test "that merely discloses whether or not a particular substance is cocaine does not compromise any legitimate interest in privacy."[849] Here the Court explained that a field test discloses "only one fact previously unknown to [an officer]—whether or not a suspicious [substance is an illegal drug]."[850] "It is probably safe," stated the Court, "to assume that virtually all of the tests conducted under the circumstances [of this case] would result in a positive finding; in such cases, no legitimate interest has been compromised. But even if the results are negative—merely disclosing that the substance is something other than [a particular illegal drug]—such a result reveals nothing of special interest."[851] As in the case of the "sniff test" conducted by a trained narcotics detection dog, the likelihood that a chemical field test of suspected narcotics will actually compromise any legitimate interest in privacy "seems too remote to characterize the testing as a search subject to the Fourth Amendment."[852]

5.1.6. Use of a drug-sniffing dog on a homeowner's porch

In *Florida v. Jardines*,[853] the Court held that an officer's "use of a trained drug-sniffing dog to investigate the home and its immediate surroundings is a 'search' within the meaning of the Fourth Amendment."[854] Since the canine search in this case was performed without a warrant or probable cause, it was an illegal search. It therefore rendered invalid the warrant that issued based upon the information gathered in that search, and inadmissible the evidence so obtained.

---

[842] *State v. Harris*, 216 N.C. App. 586, 718 S.E.2d 424 (2011).

[843] *State v. Harris*, 216 N.C. App. 586, *2, 718 S.E.2d 424 (2011).

[844] *State v. Harris*, 216 N.C. App. 586, *7-8, 718 S.E.2d 424 (2011).

[845] *State v. Harris*, 216 N.C. App. 586, *9, 718 S.E.2d 424 (2011) (quoting *State v. Tarantino*, 322 N.C. 386, 390, 368 S.E.2d 588 (1988)).

[846] *State v. Harris*, 216 N.C. App. 586, *9, 718 S.E.2d 424 (2011) (quoting *State v. Tarantino*, 322 N.C. 386, 391, 368 S.E.2d 588 (1988)).

[847] cf. *State v. Tarantino*, 322 N.C. 386, 391, 368 S.E.2d 588 (1988) (holding a defendant had reasonable expectation of privacy where detective used a flashlight to look through cracks in the building after climbing to the second floor porch, door was padlocked and windows were boarded up).

[848] *United States v. Jacobsen*, 466 U.S. 109, 104 S. Ct. 1652 (1984).

[849] *United States v. Jacobsen*, 466 U.S. 109, 104 S. Ct. 1652, 1662 (1984).

[850] *United States v. Jacobsen*, 466 U.S. 109, 104 S. Ct. 1652, 1661 (1984).

[851] *United States v. Jacobsen*, 466 U.S. 109, 104 S. Ct. 1652, 1662 (1984).

[852] *United States v. Jacobsen*, 466 U.S. 109, 104 S. Ct. 1652, 1662 (1984).

[853] *Florida v. Jardines*, 569 U.S. 1, 133 S. Ct. 1409 (2013).

[854] *Florida v. Jardines*, 569 U.S. 1, 11-12, 133 S. Ct. 1409, 1417-18 (2013).

Rather than using a pure "expectation of privacy" analysis under *Katz v. United States*, the Court reasoned: "[W]e need not decide whether the officers' investigation of Jardines' home violated his expectation of privacy under *Katz*. One virtue of the Fourth Amendment's property-rights baseline is that it keeps easy cases easy. That the officers learned what they learned only by physically intruding on Jardines' property to gather evidence is enough to establish that a search occurred."[855] Here, the *Jardines* Court required not only a trespass, but also some attempted information-gathering, to find that a search had occurred. The *Jardines* information-gathering was the use of a drug-sniffing dog—conduct that the Supreme Court has held is not a search when the police have not trespassed. Thereafter, the North Carolina Supreme Court warned, "[T]he Court's recent decision in [*Jardines*] places police on a much shorter leash when employing dog sniffs in and around the home."[856]

5.1.7. The VIN of an automobile

In *New York v. Class*,[857] the federal Supreme Court held that there is "no reasonable expectation of privacy in the VIN" of an automobile. As a result, the police may run a computer search on the number without probable cause or even reasonable suspicion. Similarly, reasonable suspicion is not required to run a computer check on a randomly selected license plate.

5.1.8. Reasonable expectations of privacy and a person's physical appearance

5.1.8.1. Facial characteristics

In *United States v. Dionisio*,[858] the U.S. Supreme Court announced that no person has a reasonable expectation of privacy in his "facial characteristics" for one cannot reasonably expect that his face will be a mystery to the world. Thus, in *State v. McDowell*,[859] the defendant's Fourth Amendment rights were not violated when a parole officer took his photo. The North Carolina Supreme Court explained, "[A]n individual's personal traits, such as his facial appearance or the tone and manner of his voice, are not within the purview of the fourth amendment's protection against unreasonable searches and seizures. One does not have a reasonable expectation of privacy in those features which serve to distinguish one individual from another and which are exposed to the view of others as a matter of course."[860]

5.1.8.2. Fingerprints

Similarly, no person can have a reasonable expectation of privacy in her fingerprints.[861]

5.1.8.3. The physical characteristics of a person's voice

In *United States v. Dionisio*,[862] the U.S. Supreme Court held that "[t]he physical characteristics of a person's voice, its tone and manner, as opposed to the content of a specific conversation, are constantly exposed to the public," so that "[n]o person can have a reasonable expectation of privacy that others will not know the sound

---

[855] *Florida v. Jardines*, 569 U.S. 1, 11-12, 133 S. Ct. 1409, 1417-18 (2013); *see also Kyllo v. United States*, 533 U.S. 27, 121 S. Ct. 2038 (2001) (surveillance is a search when the government uses a physical intrusion to explore details of the home, including its curtilage; "the antiquity of the tools that they bring along is irrelevant").

[856] *State v. Miller*, 367 N.C. 702, 708, 766 S.E.2d 289 (2014).

[857] *New York v. Class*, 475 U.S. 106, 106 S. Ct. 960 (1986).

[858] *United States v. Dionisio*, 410 U.S. 1, 14, 93 S. Ct. 764, 771 (1973).

[859] *State v. McDowell*, 301 N.C. 279, 271 S.E.2d 286 (1980).

[860] *State v. McDowell*, 301 N.C. 279, 289, 271 S.E.2d 286 (1980).

[861] *See Cupp v. Murphy*, 412 U.S. 291, 295, 93 S. Ct. 2000, 2003 (1973) (no reasonable expectation of privacy attaches to one's fingerprints, which are mere "physical characteristics" that are "constantly exposed to the public"). *See also State v. McDowell*, 301 N.C. 279, 271 S.E.2d 286 (1980); *State v. Sharpe*, 284 N.C. 157, 200 S.E.2d 44 (1973) (holding seizure of hair samples did not violate the Fourth Amendment).

[862] *United States v. Dionisio*, 410 U.S. 1, 93 S. Ct. 764 (1973).

of his voice[.]"[863] "Like a man's facial characteristics, or handwriting, his voice is repeatedly produced for others to hear."[864]

5.1.8.4. Handwriting

In United *States v. Mara*, a companion case to *United States v. Dionisio*, the United States Supreme Court reached the same result as to a person's handwriting.[865]

5.1.8.5. Soles of a person's shoes

The visual inspection of the soles of a detainee's shoes has been held not to constitute a "search" within the meaning of the Fourth Amendment.[866]

5.1.9. Arrest records

In *Paul P. v. Verniero*,[867] in upholding sex offender registration and community notification laws, the Third Circuit determined "that arrest records and related information are not protected by a right to privacy."

5.1.10. The passenger area of a commercial bus

In *United States v. Ramos*,[868] the defendant hid a clear plastic bag containing drug paraphernalia between the seats of a commercial bus when, during a scheduled stop, the bus was boarded by police officers. One of the officers recovered the bag, placed the defendant under arrest and discovered another plastic bag on the defendant's person, this one containing cocaine base.

In the appeal following the denial of his motion to suppress, the defendant argued that when he hid "the bag containing empty vials in the crevice between the seats, he clearly possessed a reasonable expectation of privacy in that bag[,]" just as he would were he instead traveling with "a valise or a suitcase."[869] Additionally, the defendant argued that the crevice between the seats should be treated as "the constitutional equivalent of an opaque container," with the seats constituting "an area in which an occupant may reasonably expect fourth amendment protection."[870] The court disagreed.

Preliminarily, the court noted that the plastic bag the defendant hid between the seats was transparent. Therefore, "he could have no expectation of privacy in the bag itself," for the Fourth Amendment "provides protection to the owner of only a 'container that conceals its contents from plain view.'"[871]

In addition, the court determined that the area in which the defendant secreted the plastic bag is not one in which he could reasonably expect any degree of privacy. According to the court, "[a] passenger on a commercial bus certainly has no property interest in the crevice between the seats or for that matter in the rack above the seats, the area beneath the seats, or anywhere else that personal effects may be stowed. Nor are we aware of any socially recognized expectation of privacy in the interior of a bus."[872]

---

[863] *United States v. Dionisio*, 410 U.S. 1, 14, 93 S. Ct. 764, 771 (1973).

[864] *United States v. Dionisio*, 410 U.S. 1, 14, 93 S. Ct. 764, 771 (1973).

[865] *See United States v. Mara*, 410 U.S. 19, 93 S. Ct. 774 (1973) ("Handwriting, like speech, is repeatedly shown to the public, and there is no more expectation of privacy in the physical characteristics of a person's script than there is in the tone of his voice."); *see also United States v. Euge*, 444 U.S. 707, 100 S. Ct. 874 (1980) ("compulsion of handwriting exemplars is neither a search nor a seizure subject to Fourth Amendment protections").

[866] *See also State v. Bone*, 354 N.C. 1, 550 S.E.2d 482 (2001).

[867] *Paul P. v. Verniero*, 170 F.3d 396 (3d Cir. 1999).

[868] *United States v. Ramos*, 960 F.2d 1065 (D.C. Cir. 1992).

[869] *United States v. Ramos*, 960 F.2d 1065, 1067 (D.C. Cir. 1992).

[870] *United States v. Ramos*, 960 F.2d 1065, 1067 (D.C. Cir. 1992).

[871] *United States v. Ramos*, 960 F.2d 1065, 1067 (D.C. Cir. 1992) (citations omitted).

[872] *United States v. Ramos*, 960 F.2d 1065, 1067-68 (D.C. Cir. 1992).

5.1.11. Rental cars

In *Byrd v. United States*,[873] the United States Supreme Court held that a driver of a rental car has a reasonable expectation of privacy in the car, even when she is the sole occupant of the vehicle and is not listed as an authorized driver on the rental agreement. According to the Court, permitting an unauthorized driver to take the wheel of a rental car may be a violation of the rental agreement, but that has nothing to do with the driver's reasonable expectation of privacy in the rental car.

The facts of the case unfolded in mid-September, when the state police pulled over a car driven by defendant Terrence Byrd, the only person in the car. During the stop, "the troopers learned that the car was rented and that Byrd was not listed on the Budget rental-car agreement as an authorized driver. For this reason, the troopers told Byrd they did not need his consent to search the car, including its trunk where he had stored personal effects. A search of the trunk uncovered body armor and 49 bricks of heroin."[874] Byrd moved to suppress the evidence as the fruit of an unlawful search. The trial court denied the motion, reasoning that, because Byrd was not listed on the rental agreement, he lacked a reasonable expectation of privacy in the car. *The United States Supreme Court disagreed*, holding that, "as a general rule, someone in otherwise lawful possession and control of a rental car has a reasonable expectation of privacy in it even if the rental agreement does not list him or her as an authorized driver."[875]

Naturally, the person must be in lawful possession of the vehicle.

> A burglar plying his trade in a summer cabin during the off season, for example, may have a thoroughly justified subjective expectation of privacy, but it is not one which the law recognizes as "legitimate." Likewise, a person present in a stolen automobile at the time of the search may not object to the lawfulness of the search of the automobile. No matter the degree of possession and control, the car thief would not have a reasonable expectation of privacy in a stolen car.[876]

5.1.12. Parking lots

There is no legitimate expectation of privacy in an open parking lot, visible to the public.[877] In *State v. Williford*,[878] the police seized a cigarette butt from a shared parking lot directly in front of the defendant's four-unit apartment building. The lot was uncovered, it included five to seven parking spaces used by the four units, and the spaces were not assigned to particular units. Although the area between the road and the parking lot was heavily wooded, there was no gate restricting access to the lot and there were no signs which suggested either that access to the parking lot was restricted or that the lot was private. The Court of Appeals of North Carolina concluded that the "parking lot was not a location where defendant possessed 'a reasonable and legitimate expectation of privacy that society is prepared to accept.'"[879]

> *The following doctrines concern areas, and objects within those areas, or classes of property, with respect to which courts have consistently held individuals do not have a reasonable expectation of privacy. Because*

---

[873] *Byrd v. United States*, 548 U.S. ___, 138 S. Ct. 1518 (2018).

[874] *Byrd v. United States*, 548 U.S. ___, 138 S. Ct. 1518, 1523 (2018).

[875] *Byrd v. United States*, 548 U.S. ___, 138 S. Ct. 1518, 1524 (2018).

[876] *Byrd v. United States*, 548 U.S. ___, 138 S. Ct. 1518, 1529 (2018).

[877] *See United States v. Ludwig*, 10 F.3d 1523 (10th Cir. 1993) (a defendant could claim no reasonable expectation of privacy in a motel parking lot that was open, unfenced, and visible from the public roads bordering it); *United States v. Dunkel*, 900 F.2d 105, 107 (7th Cir. 1990) (a defendant had no legitimate expectation of privacy in the parking lot of a private office; lot was open to invitees of eight tenants and was not fenced), *vacated on other grounds*, 498 U.S. 1043, 111 S. Ct. 747 (1991); *United States v. Reed*, 733 F.2d 492, 501 (8th Cir. 1984) (officer's initial entry into business lot was not a search where lot was bound on three sides by public streets and visible from streets on two sides, and its fenced gate was completely open to a public street); *United States v. Edmonds*, 611 F.2d 1386, 1388 (5th Cir. 1980) (no legitimate expectation of privacy found in a business loading dock and parking lot).

[878] *State v. Williford*, 239 N.C. App. 123, 767 S.E.2d 139 (2015).

[879] *State v. Williford*, 239 N.C. App. 123, 128, 767 S.E.2d 139 (2015) (internal citation omitted).

there is no privacy expectation, no search within the meaning of the Constitution may be deemed to have taken place. Technically, the Fourth Amendment is not implicated.

5.2. Open fields

The "open fields" doctrine, originally set forth in *Hester v. United States*,[880] authorizes law enforcement officers to enter and search an "open" field without a warrant. In *Hester*, Justice Holmes explained that the special and unique safeguards provided by the Fourth Amendment to the people in their "persons, houses, papers, and effects," is not extended to open fields. Open fields are not "houses," nor may they be considered "effects."

In *Oliver v. United States,* the United States Supreme Court held that the defendant's act of fencing in a secluded field and placing locked gates and "No Trespassing" signs on the property did not create a constitutionally protected area where one never existed. As a result, the police did not need a search warrant or probable cause to search the "open field."[881]

It is important to recognize that the phrase "open field" is a term of art that applies to any unoccupied or undeveloped area outside of the curtilage. Areas may fall within this legal definition that are neither "open" nor a "field" as those terms are used in common speech.[882] As explained in *Oliver*, "open fields do not provide the setting for those intimate activities that the [Fourth] Amendment is intended to shelter from government interference or surveillance."[883] Not only is there no societal interest in protecting the privacy of crop cultivation or field irrigation, "as a practical matter, these lands usually are accessible to the public and the police in ways that a home, an office, or commercial structure would not be."[884] A typical example would be the common viewing of such fields by airplane or helicopter. The final analysis always boils down to the question of whether a person has a "constitutionally protected reasonable expectation of privacy" in the particular area in question.[885]

5.2.1. The "curtilage"

The home, of course, since the inception of this nation, has been one of these areas which commands the sanctity and privacy recognized by our society. Privacy has also been extended to the "curtilage"—the "land immediately surrounding and associated with the home."[886] This land, termed the "curtilage," of the home, is treated as a part of the home; it is not only separate, but distinguished from neighboring open fields.

Generally, the "curtilage" is the enclosed space of the grounds and buildings immediately surrounding a dwelling house. It is an area to which extends the intimate activity associated with the sanctity of a person's home and the privacies of life, and therefore has been considered part of the home itself for Fourth Amendment purposes.

In *United States v. Dunn*,[887] the Supreme Court held that the area near the defendant's barn, located approximately 50 yards from a fence surrounding a ranch house, was not within the curtilage of the house for Fourth Amendment purposes. Citing *Oliver v. United States*, the Court in *Dunn* reiterated that "the Fourth Amendment protects the curtilage of a house and that the extent of the curtilage is determined by factors that bear upon whether an individual reasonably may expect that the area in question should be treated as the home itself."[888] The "central component" of the curtilage inquiry is "whether the area harbors the 'intimate

---

[880] *Hester v. United States*, 265 U.S. 57, 44 S. Ct. 445 (1924).

[881] *Oliver v. United States*, 466 U.S. 170, 104 S. Ct. 1735 (1984).

[882] *See, e.g., United States v. Hatfield*, 333 F.3d 1189 (10th Cir. 2003).

[883] *Oliver v. United States*, 466 U.S. 170, 179, 104 S. Ct. 1735, 1741 (1984).

[884] *Oliver v. United States*, 466 U.S. 170, 179, 104 S. Ct. 1735, 1741 (1984).

[885] *See Katz v. United States*, 389 U.S. 347, 88 S. Ct. 507 (1967) (The Fourth Amendment will only protect those expectations that society is prepared to recognize as "reasonable.").

[886] *See Oliver v. United States*, 466 U.S. 170, 180, 104 S. Ct. 1735, 1742 (1984); *State v. Piland*, 822 S.E.2d 876 (N.C. Ct. App. 2018); *State v. Grice*, 367 N.C. 753, 767 S.E.2d 312 (2015); *State v. Ellis*, 829 S.E.2d 912 (N.C. Ct. App. 2019).

[887] *United States v. Dunn*, 480 U.S. 294, 107 S. Ct. 1134 (1987).

[888] *United States v. Dunn*, 480 U.S. 294, 107 S. Ct. 1134, 1139 (1987).

activity associated with the sanctity of a man's home and the privacies of life.'"[889] Thus, "curtilage questions should be resolved with particular reference to four factors:

(1) the proximity of the area claimed to be curtilage to the home;
(2) whether the area is included within an enclosure surrounding the home;
(3) the nature of the uses to which the area is put; and
(4) the steps taken by the resident to protect the area from observation by people passing by."[890]

While not a finely-tuned mechanical formula, these factors nonetheless are "useful analytical tools" which may be used to determine "whether the area in question is so intimately tied to the home itself that it should be placed under the home's 'umbrella' of Fourth Amendment protection."[891]

Be aware that police do not violate the curtilage merely by walking up to the front door and knocking, just as any other member of the public might do. In *Florida v. Jardines*,[892] however, the Court held that an officer's "use of a trained drug-sniffing dog to investigate the home and its immediate surroundings is a 'search' within the meaning of the Fourth Amendment."[893] Since the canine search in this case was performed without a warrant or probable cause, it was an illegal search. It therefore rendered invalid the warrant that issued based upon the information gathered in that search, and inadmissible the evidence so obtained.

Rather than using a pure "expectation of privacy" analysis under *Katz v. United States*,[894] the Court reasoned: "[W]e need not decide whether the officers' investigation of Jardines' home violated his expectation of privacy under *Katz*. One virtue of the Fourth Amendment's property-rights baseline is that it keeps easy cases easy. That the officers learned what they learned only by physically intruding on Jardines' property to gather evidence is enough to establish that a search occurred."[895]

5.2.1.1. A home's driveway

In *Collins v. Virginia*,[896] the United States Supreme Court held that the automobile exception does not permit a law enforcement officer, uninvited and without a warrant, to enter the curtilage of a home in order to search a vehicle parked at the top of the home's driveway.

In *Collins,* during the investigation of two traffic incidents involving violations committed by an operator of an orange and black motorcycle with an extended frame, Officer David Rhodes learned that the motorcycle likely was stolen and in the possession of defendant Ryan Collins. While investigating, Officer Rhodes discovered photographs on Collins' Facebook page of an orange and black motorcycle parked at the top of a driveway of a house. The officer tracked down the address of the house, drove there, and parked on the street. "It was later established that Collins' girlfriend lived in the house and that Collins stayed there a few nights per week."

"From his parked position on the street, Officer Rhodes saw what appeared to be a motorcycle with an extended frame covered with a white tarp, parked at the same angle and in the same location on the driveway as in the Facebook photograph." The officer took a photograph of the covered motorcycle from the sidewalk, and then walked onto the residential property and up to the top of the driveway to where the motorcycle was parked. "Officer Rhodes pulled off the tarp, revealing a motorcycle that looked like the one from the speeding incident. He then ran a search of the license plate and vehicle identification numbers, which confirmed that the motorcycle was stolen. After gathering this information, Officer Rhodes took a photograph of the

---

889 *United States v. Dunn*, 480 U.S. 294, 107 S. Ct. 1134, 1139 (1987) (citations omitted).
890 *United States v. Dunn*, 480 U.S. 294, 107 S. Ct. 1134, 1139 (1987).
891 *United States v. Dunn*, 480 U.S. 294, 107 S. Ct. 1134, 1139 (1987).
892 *Florida v. Jardines*, 569 U.S. 1, 133 S. Ct. 1409 (2013).
893 *Florida v. Jardines*, 569 U.S. 1, 133 S. Ct. 1409, 1417-18 (2013).
894 *Katz v. United States*, 389 U.S. 347, 361, 88 S. Ct. 507, 516 (1967).
895 *Katz v. United States*, 389 U.S. 347, 361, 88 S. Ct. 507, 516 (1967); *see also Kyllo v. United States*, 533 U.S. 27, 121 S. Ct. 2038 (2001) (surveillance is a search when the government uses a physical intrusion to explore details of the home, including its curtilage; "the antiquity of the tools that they bring along is irrelevant").
896 *Collins v. Virginia*, 584 U.S. ___, 138 S. Ct. 1663 (2018).

uncovered motorcycle, put the tarp back on, left the property, and returned to his car to wait for Collins." When Collins returned home and admitted that the motorcycle was his, the officer arrested him.

In this case, the Court initially decided that the part of the driveway where Collins' motorcycle was parked and subsequently searched was "curtilage." Just like "the front porch, side garden, or area outside the front window, the driveway enclosure where Officer Rhodes searched the motorcycle constitutes an area adjacent to the home and to which the activity of home life extends, and so is properly considered curtilage."

"In physically intruding on the curtilage of Collins' home to search the motorcycle, Officer Rhodes not only invaded Collins' Fourth Amendment interest in the item searched, *i.e.*, the motorcycle, but also invaded Collins' Fourth Amendment interest in the curtilage of his home." And the automobile exception, held the Court, cannot be used to justify the invasion of the curtilage.

"Just as an officer must have a lawful right of access to any contraband he discovers in plain view in order to seize it without a warrant, and just as an officer must have a lawful right of access in order to arrest a person in his home, so too, an officer must have a lawful right of access to a vehicle in order to search it pursuant to the automobile exception. The automobile exception does not afford the necessary lawful right of access to search a vehicle parked within a home or its curtilage because it does not justify an intrusion on a person's separate and substantial Fourth Amendment interest in his home and curtilage."[897]

5.2.2. The "knock and talk"

In general, the "knock and talk" procedure is a law enforcement tactic in which the police, who possess some information that they believe warrants further investigation, but that is insufficient to constitute probable cause for a search warrant, approach the person suspected of engaging in illegal activity at the person's residence (even knock on the front door), identify themselves as police officers, and request consent to search for the suspected illegality or illicit items.

Thus, absent signs or other indications to the contrary, police may enter the curtilage of a home to the extent that they can just walk up to the front door, the same way any other visitor might, with the intent to gain the occupant's consent to a search or to otherwise acquire information from the occupant. Clearly, a "knock and talk" procedure, when performed within its scope, is not a search at all. The proper scope of a knock and talk is determined by the "implied license" that is granted to solicitors, hawkers, and peddlers of all kinds. In this regard, an officer not armed with a warrant may approach a home and knock, precisely because that is "no more than any private citizen might do."[898] As explained in *Kentucky v. King*,[899]

> When law enforcement officers who are not armed with a warrant knock on a door, they do no more than any private citizen might do. And whether the person who knocks on the door and requests the opportunity to speak is a police officer or a private citizen, the occupant has no obligation to open the door or to speak.... When the police knock on a door but the occupants choose not to respond or to speak, "the investigation will have reached a conspicuously low point," and the occupants "will have

---

[897] The United States Supreme Court remanded the case for a state court determination of whether the officer's warrantless intrusion may have been reasonable on a different basis. Upon remand, the Virginia Supreme Court held that the evidence discovered during the warrantless search was admissible under the good-faith exception to the exclusionary rule. Said the Court: "The exclusionary rule does not apply under the facts of this case because, at the time of the search, a reasonably well-trained police officer would not have known that the automobile exception did not permit him to search a motorcycle located a few feet across the curtilage boundary of a private driveway." *Collins v. Commonwealth*, 297 Va. 207, 227, 824 S.E.2d 485, 496 (2019).

[898] *Florida v. Jardines*, 569 U.S. 1, 6, 8, 133 S. Ct. 1409, 1415 (2013); *see also Carroll v. Carman*, 574 U.S. 13, 135 S. Ct. 348, 351 (2014) (open to the suggestion that an unsuccessful attempt at a "knock and talk" visit at the front door does not automatically prohibit officers from trying the back door or other parts of the property that are open to visitors); *United States v. Titemore*, 335 F. Supp. 2d 502, 505-06 (D. Vt. 2004) ("[T]he law does not require an officer to determine which door most closely approximates the Platonic form of 'main entrance' and then, after successfully completing this metaphysical inquiry, approach only that door. An officer making a 'knock and talk' visit may approach any part of the building where uninvited visitors could be expected."), *aff'd*, 437 F.3d 251 (2d Cir. 2006).

[899] *Kentucky v. King*, 563 U.S. 452, 131 S. Ct. 1849 (2011).

the kind of warning that even the most elaborate security system cannot provide."...And even if an occupant chooses to open the door and speak with the officers, the occupant need not allow the officers to enter the premises and may refuse to answer any questions at any time.[900]

Naturally, the implied license to approach a house and knock "has certain spatial and temporal limits. A visitor must stick to the path that is typically used to approach a front door, such as a paved walkway. A visitor cannot traipse through the garden, meander into the backyard, or take other circuitous detours that veer from the pathway that a visitor would customarily use....Nor, as a general matter, may a visitor come to the front door in the middle of the night without an express invitation."[901]

The North Carolina Supreme Court has "recognized the right of police officers to conduct knock and talk investigations, so long as they do not rise to the level of Fourth Amendment searches."[902] Thus, in *State v. Smith*,[903] the detectives did not violate the Fourth Amendment in entering the defendant's property by way of his driveway to ask questions about the previous day's shooting because it was not established that the defendant consistently displayed a "No Trespassing" sign on his property or that he took consistent steps to physically prevent visitors from entering. However, "law enforcement may not use a knock and talk as a pretext to search the home's curtilage."[904]

5.3. Plain view

5.3.1. General aspects

The "plain view" doctrine, as originally set forth in *Coolidge v. New Hampshire*,[905] and later modified by *Texas v. Brown*,[906] authorizes law enforcement officers to seize evidence of a crime, contraband, or other items subject to official seizure without first obtaining a search warrant. So long as an officer has a prior constitutional justification for an intrusion into an individual's realm of privacy, and in the course thereof discovers a piece of incriminating evidence, a warrantless seizure of that evidence is authorized.

Although the "plain view" doctrine is often characterized as one of the exceptions to the written warrant requirement, the Supreme Court has indicated that "[i]f an article is already in plain view, neither its observation nor its seizure would involve any invasion of privacy."[907] Thus, it may be said that the plain view doctrine simply "provides the grounds for seizure of an item when an officer's access to an object has some prior justification under the Fourth Amendment."[908] In this respect, rather than being viewed as an independent exception to the warrant requirement, the doctrine merely "serves 'to supplement the prior justification—whether it be a warrant for another object, hot pursuit, search incident to lawful arrest, or some other legitimate reason for being present'" in the viewing area.[909] The constitutional requirements that follow, therefore, must attach, not to the government's *observation* of an item lawfully discovered in plain view, but to its *seizure* of that item. In these circumstances, it is the seizure by the government of a

---

[900] *Kentucky v. King*, 563 U.S. 452, 469-70, 131 S. Ct. 1849, 1862 (2011); *see also Florida v. Jardines*, 569 U.S. 1, 21, 133 S. Ct. 1409, 1423 (2013) ("Even when the objective of a 'knock and talk' is to obtain evidence that will lead to the homeowner's arrest and prosecution, the license to approach still applies. In other words, gathering evidence—even damning evidence—is a lawful activity that falls within the scope of the license to approach. And when officers walk up to the front door of a house, they are permitted to see, hear, and smell whatever can be detected from a lawful vantage point.") (Alito, J., dissenting, joined by Roberts, C.J., Kennedy, J, and Breyer, J).

[901] *Florida v. Jardines*, 569 U.S. 1, 19-20, 133 S. Ct. 1409, 1422 (2013) (Alito, J., dissenting, joined by Roberts, C.J., Kennedy, J, and Breyer, J).

[902] *State v. Marrero*, 248 N.C. App. 787, 790, 789 S.E.2d 560, 564 (2016).

[903] *State v. Smith*, 246 N.C. App. 170, 783 S.E.2d 504 (2016).

[904] *State v. Huddy*, 253 N.C. App. 148, 152, 799 S.E.2d 650 (2017) (citation omitted).

[905] *Coolidge v. New Hampshire*, 403 U.S. 443, 91 S. Ct. 2022 (1971).

[906] *Texas v. Brown*, 460 U.S. 730, 103 S. Ct. 1535 (1983).

[907] *Horton v. California*, 496 U.S. 128, 110 S. Ct. 2301, 2306 (1990).

[908] *Texas v. Brown*, 460 U.S. 730, 738 103 S. Ct. 1535, 1541 (1983).

[909] *Horton v. California*, 496 U.S. 128, 110 S. Ct. 2301, 2307 (1990) (quoting *Coolidge v. New Hampshire*, 403 U.S. 443, 466, 91 S. Ct. 2022, 2038 (1971)).

citizen's property which clearly invades the owner's possessory interest, and as a result, the dispossession must be constitutionally justified.[910]

Historically, the Supreme Court required three conditions to be satisfied before the "plain view" doctrine could be invoked. First, the law enforcement officer must have been lawfully in the viewing area. This required the initial intrusion to be constitutionally reasonable, *i.e.*, officers may not violate the Constitution in arriving at the place from which the evidence could be plainly viewed. Second, an officer's discovery of the incriminating evidence must have been inadvertent. The officer could not have known in advance where the items were located nor intend to seize them beforehand. This requirement traditionally guarded against the transformation of an initially valid (and therefore limited) search into a "general" one. Finally, the incriminating character of the evidence must have been "immediately apparent," and since 1987, this has meant that the officer must have "probable cause" to associate the item with criminal activity.[911] Naturally, even with all the requirements met, the officer must still "'have a lawful right of access to the object itself.'"[912]

In *Horton v. California*,[913] the Supreme Court eliminated the "inadvertence" requirement, reasoning that "evenhanded law enforcement is best achieved by the application of objective standards of conduct, rather than standards that depend upon the subjective state of mind of the officer."[914] Thus, even though an officer may be interested in an item of evidence and fully expects to find it in the course of a search, that subjective fact "should not invalidate its seizure if the search is confined in area and duration by the terms of a warrant or a valid exception to the warrant requirement."[915]

Accordingly, under the "plain view" doctrine, a warrantless seizure of an object is lawful if the following requirements are met:

(1) The officer must be lawfully in the viewing area; that is, an officer may not violate the Constitution in arriving at the place from which the evidence could be plainly viewed;

(2) The item's incriminating character is immediately apparent (here, the officer must have probable cause to believe the evidence is somehow associated with criminal activity); and

(3) The officer must have a lawful right of access to the evidence.

If these requirements are satisfied, the evidence may then be immediately seized without a search warrant. This seizure is constitutional, for it "involves no invasion of privacy and is presumptively reasonable[.]"[916]

In *State v. Grice*,[917] the police responded to a tip that the defendant was growing marijuana at his home and conducted a knock and talk investigation. Detective's Guseman and Allen drove into the driveway and parked behind the defendant's car. Detective Guseman knocked at the door while Detective Allen remained in the driveway. From the driveway, Detective Allen spotted marijuana growing in buckets about 15 yards away. Both officers approached the buckets and seized the plants before they obtained a search warrant. Applying the *Horton* elements, the North Carolina Supreme Court reasoned that the detectives were lawfully in the viewing area to perform a knock and talk. Secondly, "based on their training and experience, [the officers] instantly recognized the plants as marijuana."[918] With regard to the third *Horton* element, the court held that

---

[910] *Horton v. California*, 496 U.S. 128, 110 S. Ct. 2301, 2306 (1990); *see also United States v. Jacobsen*, 466 U.S. 109, 113, 104 S. Ct. 1652, 1656 (1984); *United States v. Jackson*, 131 F.3d 1105, 1108 (4th Cir. 1997) ("The 'plain view' doctrine provides an exception to the warrant requirement for the *seizure* of property, but it does not provide an exception for a search.") (emphasis in original).

[911] *Arizona v. Hicks*, 480 U.S. 321, 327, 107 S. Ct. 1149, 1153 (1987).

[912] *Collins v. Virginia*, 584 U.S. ___, 138 S.Ct. 1663, 1672 (2018) (quoting *Horton*).

[913] *Horton v. California*, 496 U.S. 128, 110 S. Ct. 2301 (1990).

[914] *Horton v. California*, 496 U.S. 128, 110 S. Ct. 2301, 2309 (1990).

[915] *Horton v. California*, 496 U.S. 128, 110 S. Ct. 2301, 2309 (1990).

[916] *Horton v. California*, 496 U.S. 128, 110 S. Ct. 2301, 2310 (1990); *Texas v. Brown*, 460 U.S. 730, 741-42, 103 S. Ct. 1535, 1543 (1983); *see also Payton v. New York*, 445 U.S. 573, 587, 100 S. Ct. 1371, 1380 (1980); *Collins v. Virginia*, 584 U.S. ___, 138 S.Ct. 1663, 1672 (2018).

[917] *State v. Grice*, 367 N.C. 753, 767 S.E.2d 312 (2015). *See also State v. Harvey*, 281 N.C. 1, 187 S.E.2d 706 (1972).

[918] *State v. Grice*, 367 N.C. 753, 757, 767 S.E.2d 312 (2015).

"[t]he presence of the clearly identifiable contraband justified walking further into the curtilage."[919] The court explained:

> The officers were at the home in daylight; the contraband nature of the plants was readily apparent; the officers took only the plants, leaving behind the buckets and caretaking implements surrounding them; and the officers left immediately after seizing the plants. The officers did not cross or open any fence or barrier, nor did they use the sighting of the plants as an excuse to conduct a general search of the rest of the property. In other words, they did not travel outside the category of property covered by the initial invitation to enter the curtilage. Under these circumstances, the warrantless seizure of clearly identifiable contraband left in plain view of defendant's driveway was not unreasonable and the motion to suppress was properly denied.[920]

When a police dog "nuzzles" an item into plain view. In *State v. Miller*,[921] Officer Hill, Officer Fox and his police dog, Jack, responded to a possible break-in at the defendant's house. Because the front door of the home was locked and a window at the back of the home had been broken, police were concerned that an intruder was inside. While Office Fox and Officer Hill were preparing to search the home, the defendant's mother arrived with a key to the house and consented to a search of the residence. Officer Fox deployed Jack inside the house and, during the search, the dog alerted to a closet which the officers opened. In the closet were two large trash bags. "[A]s soon as they opened the closet door, Jack 'immediately' stuck his nose inside one of the trash bags and nuzzled the bag open"[922] revealing marijuana. The officers finished their protective sweep of the house, found no intruders, obtained a search warrant and seized the drugs. According to the court, the main question was:

> Whether a police dog's instinctive action, unguided and undirected by the police, that brings evidence not otherwise in plain view into plain view is a search within the meaning of the Fourth Amendment. Nipping at the heels of near uniformity in the federal circuit courts that have addressed the issue in strictly "search" terms, we hold that such action is not a search.[923]

5.3.2. Use of a flashlight

No "search" takes place when police use artificial means, such as a flashlight, to illuminate a darkened area.[924] Accordingly, the use of a flashlight to view an object does not make a plain-view observation unlawful.[925]

5.3.3. Aerial observations

Courts have found that it is unreasonable to have a privacy expectation in the aerial view of one's property. This is due to the fact that any private citizen may obtain such a view. Since there is no protected privacy interest in the view, police may conduct aerial searches without a warrant.[926] In *California v. Ciraolo*,[927] the U.S. Supreme Court held that the Fourth Amendment was not violated by the warrantless, naked-eye aerial observation, at an altitude of 1,000 feet, of marijuana plants growing in a person's fenced-in backyard, within

---

[919] *State v. Grice*, 367 N.C. 753, 758, 767 S.E.2d 312 (2015).

[920] *State v. Grice*, 367 N.C. 753, 762, 767 S.E.2d 312 (2015).

[921] *State v. Miller*, 367 N.C. 702, 766 S.E.2d 289 (2014).

[922] *State v. Miller*, 367 N.C. 702, 704, 766 S.E.2d 289 (2014).

[923] *State v. Miller*, 367 N.C. 702, 712, 766 S.E.2d 289 (2014).

[924] *See, e.g., United States v. Dunn*, 480 U.S. 294, 107 S. Ct. 1134, 1141 (1987) (The officers' flashlight beam, directed through the essentially open front of a defendant's barn, "did not transform their observations into an unreasonable search within the meaning of the Fourth Amendment.").

[925] *United States v. Reed*, 114 F.3d 644 (6th Cir. 1998). *See also State v. Harris*, 216 N.C. App. 586, 718 S.E.2d 424 (2011).

[926] *Dow Chemical Co. v. United States*, 476 U.S. 227, 234-35, 106 S. Ct. 1819, 1824 (1986).

[927] *California v. Ciraolo*, 476 U.S. 207, 106 S. Ct. 1809 (1986).

the curtilage of his home. The Court wrote: "In an age where private and commercial flight in the public airways is routine, it is unreasonable for [a person] to expect that his marijuana plants [growing in his fenced-in backyard curtilage] were constitutionally protected from being observed with the naked eye from an altitude of 1,000 feet."[928]

In *Florida v. Riley*,[929] the U.S. Supreme Court similarly determined that the surveillance of the interior of a partially covered greenhouse in a residential backyard from the vantage point of a helicopter located 400 feet above the greenhouse did not constitute a "search" for which a warrant is required under the Fourth Amendment.

5.4. Abandonment

5.4.1. General aspects

The relevance of abandoned property in the realm of constitutional criminal procedure lies in the notion that the safeguards of the Fourth Amendment simply do not extend to it. When a person abandons property, he is said to bring his right of privacy therein to an end and may not later complain about its subsequent seizure and use in evidence against him.

The keynote to the concept of abandonment is the actor's intention to relinquish all claim to the property—either personal or real—with the concomitant intention of not reclaiming or resuming ownership, possession, or control over it. Once this situation exists, it may then be said that the actor's relinquishment took place under circumstances which demonstrate that he retained no reasonable expectation of privacy in the property so discarded. For example, in *Abel v. United States*,[930] an FBI agent undertook a warrantless search of the defendant's hotel room immediately after the defendant had paid his bill and vacated the room. During the search, the entire contents of the room's wastepaper basket were seized and found to contain evidence which was subsequently used against the defendant in his espionage prosecution. Finding the search and seizure entirely lawful, the Supreme Court explained:

> [A]t the time of the search, [defendant] had vacated the room. The hotel then had the exclusive right to its possession, and the hotel management freely gave its consent that the search be made. Nor was it unlawful to seize the entire contents of the wastepaper basket, even though some of its contents had no connection with crime.... *[Defendant] had abandoned these articles*. He had thrown them away. [So there] can be nothing unlawful in the Government's appropriation of such abandoned property.[931]

As a result, for criminal procedure purposes, the relevant inquiry is whether the actor, by dispossessing himself of his property, has so relinquished his reasonable expectation of privacy in that property that a subsequent government inspection and appropriation of that property cannot be said to constitute a "search and seizure" within the meaning of the Fourth Amendment. As the federal Supreme Court noted, there can be "no seizure in the sense of the law" when law enforcement officers examine "the contents of [personal property] after it ha[s] been abandoned."[932]

When an individual abandons an item of personal property, such as by dropping evidence while fleeing from police, he relinquishes a reasonable expectation of privacy in the discarded item. A showing of actual intent to abandon is not necessary. It is only necessary to show that the individual asserting a privacy interest in the property in question had relinquished sufficient control over the property so that he no longer had any reasonable expectation of privacy in the object or item.

For example, we already discussed that the parking lot from which police seized a cigarette butt in *State v. Williford*,[933] was not a place where the defendant possessed "a reasonable and legitimate expectation of

---

[928] *California v. Ciraolo*, 476 U.S. 207, 106 S. Ct. 1809, 1813 (1986).

[929] *Florida v. Riley*, 488 U.S. 445, 109 S. Ct. 693 (1989).

[930] *Abel v. United States*, 362 U.S. 217, 80 S. Ct. 683 (1960).

[931] *Abel v. United States*, 362 U.S. 217, 241, 80 S. Ct. 683 (1960) (emphasis added).

[932] *Hester v. United States*, 265 U.S. 57, 58, 44 S. Ct. 445 (1924).

[933] *State v. Williford*, 239 N.C. App. 123, 767 S.E.2d 139 (2015) (internal quotations and citation omitted).

privacy that society is prepared to accept."[934] Additionally, the court explained that "it is well established that '[w]here the presence of the police is lawful and the discard occurs in a public place where the defendant cannot reasonably have any continued expectancy of privacy in the discarded property, the property will be deemed abandoned for purposes of search and seizure.'"[935] Similarly, in *State v. Cromartie*,[936] the defendant abandoned any reasonable expectation of privacy in an aspirin box when he threw it during a search of his person. However, "when one discards property as the product of some illegal police activity, he will not be held to have voluntarily abandoned the property or to have necessarily lost his reasonable expectation of privacy with respect to it."[937]

5.4.1.1. Throwing or discarding property

In *Smith v. Ohio*,[938] the Supreme Court disallowed a search of property that had been placed on the hood of the defendant's car. There, plainclothes police officers observed the defendant carrying a grocery bag in what one of them described as a "gingerly" manner. When the officers identified themselves as police officers and approached the defendant, he threw the bag onto the hood of his car. The officer asked the defendant what the bag contained but the defendant did not answer, whereupon the officer opened the bag and found drug paraphernalia inside. In holding that the search was not justified, the court accepted the Ohio Supreme courts conclusion that "a citizen who attempts to protect his private property from inspection, after throwing it on a car to respond to a police officer's inquiry, clearly has not abandoned that property."[939]

Note also that where officers do not have a justification for their initial actions (*e.g.*, detaining without reasonable suspicion), and the item is discarded in response to this unlawful activity, the evidence may be suppressed as the fruit of illegal law enforcement activity. In this instance, courts say that the unlawful police action forced the abandonment.

5.4.2. Abandoned structures

Police do not need a search warrant before entering structures that, by all objective manifestations, appear abandoned. A court will weigh the totality of the circumstances in determining whether police could reasonably believe a structure has been abandoned, including: (i) its outward appearance; (ii) its overall condition; (iii) the state of the vegetation on the premises; (iv) whether barriers have been erected and securely fastened in all openings; (v) indications that the home is not being serviced with gas or electricity; (vi) a lack of appliances or furniture typically found in a dwelling home; (vii) the length of time it takes for temporary barriers to be replaced with functional doors and windows; (viii) the history surrounding the premises and its prior use; and (ix) any complaints of illicit activity occurring in the structure.

5.4.3. Curbside garbage

The Supreme Court, in *California v. Greenwood*,[940] held that the Fourth Amendment does not prohibit the warrantless seizure and search of garbage left for collection outside the curtilage of a home. According to the U.S. Supreme Court, when garbage is left for collection outside the curtilage of one's home, it is sufficiently exposed to the public so that any search or seizure thereof falls outside the parameters of the Fourth Amendment.[941] Thus, a person will have no reasonable expectation of privacy in items deposited in a public

---

[934] *State v. Williford*, 239 N.C. App. 123, 128, 767 S.E.2d 139 (2015) (internal citation omitted).

[935] *State v. Williford*, 239 N.C. App. 123, 129, 767 S.E.2d 139 (2015) (quoting *State v. Cromartie*, 55 N.C. App. 221, 224, 284 S.E.2d 728, 730 (1981)).

[936] *State v. Cromartie*, 55 N.C. App. 221, 284 S.E.2d 728 (1981).

[937] *State v. Cromartie*, 55 N.C. App. 221, 225, 284 S.E.2d 728 (1981) (citing *State v. Cooke*, 54 N.C. App. 33, 282 S.E.2d 800 (1981)).

[938] *Smith v. Ohio*, 494 U.S. 541, 110 S. Ct. 1288, 1290 (1990).

[939] *Smith v. Ohio*, 494 U.S. 541, 543-544, 110 S. Ct. 1288, 1290 (1990).

[940] *California v. Greenwood*, 486 U.S. 35, 108 S. Ct. 1625 (1988).

[941] *California v. Greenwood*, 486 U.S. 35, 108 S. Ct. 1625, 1628 (1988).

area, conveyed to a third-party for collection, and "readily accessible to animals, children, scavengers, snoops, and other members of the public."[942]

5.4.4. Denying ownership

If a defendant disclaims ownership of property or any possessory interest, police may use such a denial as sufficient proof of either an intent to abandon the property or a lack of ownership of the property.

A number of circuits have similarly held that an abandonment occurs where, in response to police questioning, a suspect denies ownership of the property in question.[943] Accordingly, discarding something while fleeing, tossing something in the trash, or denying ownership are all ways that a person may be found to have abandoned property so as to relinquish a reasonable expectation of privacy in it.

5.4.4.1. Silence in response to a police inquiry about ownership

An abandonment of property would not be found solely from a person's silence or failure to respond to a police officer's questions regarding ownership of an item. As one commentator reasoned, "To equate a passive failure to claim potentially incriminating evidence with an affirmative abandonment of property would be to twist both logic and experience in a most uncomfortable knot."[944]

6. ADMINISTRATIVE AND REGULATORY SEARCHES

6.1. Administrative searches

Searches and seizures may be undertaken by a state and its agents wholly apart from those pursued by law enforcement agencies. Whether the search or seizure is reasonable under the Fourth Amendment depends on an analysis of the totality of the circumstances and the nature of the search or seizure itself. In most typical cases involving law enforcement practice and procedure, there is a constitutional preference for a judicial determination of probable cause and the issuance of a written warrant. Yet, there are recognized exceptions to the warrant requirement, and in the area of regulatory and administrative searches, the courts will apply two types of analyses: "balancing of interests" and "special needs."

6.1.1. The "balancing of interests" analysis

In some circumstances, courts will apply a general Fourth Amendment "balancing test," examining the totality of the circumstances to assess, on the one side, the degree to which a search or seizure intrudes upon a person's reasonable expectation of privacy, and, on the other side, the degree to which it is needed for the promotion of legitimate governmental interests.[945]

For example, in *Michigan Dept. of State Police v. Sitz*,[946] the Supreme Court utilized a "balancing of interests" analysis in upholding the constitutionality of highway sobriety checkpoints. According to the Court, this test

---

[942] *California v. Greenwood,* 486 U.S. 35, 108 S. Ct. 1625, 1629 (1988).

[943] *See United States v. Carrasquillo,* 877 F.2d 73 (D.C. Cir. 1989) (abandonment found where train passenger denied ownership of garment bag under his feet and no other person claimed it); *United States v. McBean,* 861 F.2d 1570 (11th Cir. 1988) (a defendant abandoned any reasonable expectation of privacy in the contents of luggage in the trunk of his car when he told police that it was not his luggage and that he knew nothing of its contents); *United States v. Roman,* 849 F.2d 920 (5th Cir. 1988) (abandonment found where a defendant checked his suitcases at an airport and then told agents that he had not checked any luggage and had no baggage other than his carry-on bag). *See also United States v. Clark,* 891 F.2d 501 (4th Cir. 1989); *United States v. Moskowitz,* 883 F.2d 1142 (2d Cir. 1989); *United States v. Nordling,* 804 F.2d 1466 (9th Cir. 1986); *United States v. Lucci,* 758 F.2d 153 (6th Cir. 1985), *cert. denied,* 474 U.S. 843, 106 S. Ct. 129 (1985).

[944] *State v. Joyner,* 66 Haw. 543, 669 P.2d 152 (1983). *But see United States v. Adams,* 583 F.2d 457 (6th Cir. 2009) (police, in a hotel room by consent, asked to whom jacket on the floor belonged, and no one, including the defendant, claimed ownership; the defendant had thus abandoned any privacy interest in the jacket).

[945] *Brown v. Texas,* 443 U.S. 47, 99 S. Ct. 2637 (1979); *Samson v. California,* 547 U.S. 843, 126 S. Ct. 2193, 2197 (2006).

[946] *Michigan Dept. of State Police v. Sitz,* 496 U.S. 444, 110 S. Ct. 2481 (1990).

involved balancing the state's substantial interest in preventing harm caused by drunk drivers, the degree to which sobriety checkpoints advance that public interest, and the minimal level of intrusion upon individual motorists who are briefly stopped.[947]

Similarly, the Supreme Court, in *Illinois v. Lidster*,[948] upheld the brief stop of motorists at a roadside checkpoint, where police sought information about a recent hit-and-run fatal accident. Utilizing the *Brown v. Texas* "balancing of interests" approach, the Court looked to the gravity of the public concerns served by such a seizure, the degree to which the seizure advanced the public interest, and the severity of the interference with individual liberty.

6.1.2. The "special needs" analysis

There are some areas of law enforcement and criminal procedure, where "special needs," beyond the normal need for law enforcement, authorize government action without the standard constitutional justifications which typically apply. In this regard, the Supreme Court has utilized a "special needs" analysis to carve out an exception to the familiar probable cause and judicial warrant requirements normally associated with the Fourth Amendment.

The first use of the "special needs" analysis may be found in Justice Blackmun's concurrence in *New Jersey v. T.L.O.*,[949] where it was determined that a school official's search of a student's belongings based on individualized suspicion was reasonable. In this regard, Justice Blackmun explained that probable cause and a warrant were not required where "special needs, beyond the normal need for law enforcement, make the warrant and probable-cause requirements impracticable."[950]

While the "balancing of interests" approach is an easier test for the prosecution to satisfy, the "special needs" approach involves a more stringent analysis. In this regard, if a "special need" does exist, courts may then make an exception to the probable cause and warrant requirements only after balancing the nature and quality of the intrusion on the individual's constitutional rights against "the importance of the governmental interests alleged to justify the intrusion."[951]

In *State v. Grady*,[952] the North Carolina Supreme Court considered the constitutionality of mandatory lifetime satellite-based monitoring (SBM) on certain offenders. Specifically, the court considered individuals who are not on probation, parole, or post-release supervision but are subject to SBM pursuant to N.C.Gen. Stat. § 14-208.40A by virtue of being a recidivist. The court held that the intrusion of mandatory lifetime SBM on legitimate Fourth Amendment interests of those individuals outweighed the promotion of legitimate governmental interests. The court reasoned that such individuals do not have a greatly diminished privacy interest and the SBM program constituted a substantial intrusion into those privacy interests without any showing by the State that the program furthered its interest in solving crimes, preventing sex crimes, or protecting the public.

6.1.2.1. School searches

In *New Jersey v. T.L.O.*, the Supreme Court held that the Fourth Amendment's prohibition on unreasonable searches and seizures applies to searches conducted by public school officials. "In carrying out searches and other disciplinary functions pursuant to [publicly mandated educational and disciplinary] policies, [public] school officials act as representatives of the State, not merely as surrogates for the parents, and they cannot claim the parents' immunity from the strictures of the Fourth Amendment."[953] The Court balanced the student's legitimate expectation of privacy and personal security against such public school needs as

---

[947] *See also United States v. Martinez-Fuerte*, 428 U.S. 543, 96 S. Ct. 3074 (1976) (applying the "balancing of interests" approach to approve highway checkpoints for detecting undocumented immigrants).

[948] *Illinois v. Lidster*, 540 U.S. 419, 427-28, 124 S. Ct. 885, 890-91 (2004).

[949] *New Jersey v. T.L.O.*, 469 U.S. 325, 351, 105 S. Ct. 733, 747-48 (1985) (Blackmun, J., concurring).

[950] *New Jersey v. T.L.O.*, 469 U.S. 325, 351, 105 S. Ct. 733, 748 (1985) (Blackmun, J., concurring).

[951] *See United States v. Place*, 462 U.S. 696, 703, 103 S. Ct. 2637, 2642 (1983).

[952] *State v. Grady*, 831 S.E.2d 542 (N.C. 2019).

[953] *New Jersey v. T.L.O.*, 469 U.S. 325, 105 S. Ct. 733, 741 (1985).

maintaining discipline and order in the classrooms and on school grounds, and preservation of the educational environment.

In striking that balance, the Court ruled: First, public school officials are not subject to the warrant requirement.[954] Requiring a warrant would "unduly interfere with the maintenance of the swift and informal disciplinary procedures needed in schools."[955] Second, the level of suspicion applicable to public school officials has been reduced from probable cause to a standard which turns "simply on the reasonableness, under all of the circumstances, of the search."[956] Reasonableness will be assessed by a two-fold inquiry: "first, one must consider whether the action was justified at its inception[;] second, one must determine whether the search as actually conducted was reasonably related in scope to the circumstances which justified the interference in the first place."[957]

6.1.2.1.1. An unreasonable strip search

In *Safford Unified School District #1 v. Redding*,[958] the U.S. Supreme Court applied the rationale of *New Jersey v. T.L.O.* to hold that school officials violated a 13-year-old student's Fourth Amendment rights when the school nurse and an administrative assistant searched the student's bra and underpants acting on reasonable suspicion that she had brought forbidden prescription and over-the-counter drugs to school. According to the Court, because there were no reasons to suspect the drugs presented a danger or were concealed in her underwear, "the search did violate the Constitution[.]"[959]

6.1.2.2. Government employers

In *O'Connor v. Ortega*,[960] the Supreme Court held that the "special needs" of government workplaces permit government employers and supervisors to conduct warrantless, work-related searches of employees' desks, file cabinets and offices without a warrant or probable cause. Moreover, the same principles applicable to a government employer's search of an employee's office, desk, or file cabinet applies when the employer examines text messages sent and received on a device the employer owned and issued to employees.[961]

6.1.2.3. Probation and parole

Similarly, in *Griffin v. Wisconsin*,[962] the Court held that "a State's operation of a probation system, like its operation of a school, government office or prison, or its supervision of a regulated industry, likewise presents 'special needs' beyond normal law enforcement that may justify departures from the usual warrant and probable-cause requirements." According to the Court, "supervision" in the probation system is the "special need" of the state "permitting a degree of impingement upon privacy that would not be constitutional if applied to the public at large."[963]

---

[954] *New Jersey v. T.L.O.*, 469 U.S. 325, 105 S. Ct. 733, 743 (1985).

[955] *New Jersey v. T.L.O.*, 469 U.S. 325, 105 S. Ct. 733, 743 (1985).

[956] *New Jersey v. T.L.O.*, 469 U.S. 325, 105 S. Ct. 733, 744-45 (1985).

[957] *New Jersey v. T.L.O.*, 469 U.S. 325, 105 S. Ct. 733, 744 (1985) (citations omitted); *see also Board of Educ. of Indep. Sch. Dist. No. 92 v. Earls,* 536 U.S. 822, 829-30, 122 S. Ct. 2559, 2564 (2002) (applying "special needs" principles to validate school's drug testing of all students participating in competitive extracurricular activities); *Vernonia Sch. Dist. 47J v. Acton,* 515 U.S. 646, 653, 115 S. Ct. 2386, 2391 (1995) (applying a "special needs" analysis to sustain drug-testing programs for student athletes).

[958] *Safford Unified School District #1 v. Redding,* 557 U.S. 364, 129 S. Ct. 2633 (2009).

[959] *Safford Unified School District #1 v. Redding,* 557 U.S. 364, 129 S. Ct. 2633, 2637 (2009).

[960] *O'Connor v. Ortega,* 480 U.S. 709, 107 S. Ct. 1492 (1987).

[961] *See City of Ontario v. Quon,* 560 U.S. 746, 130 S. Ct. 2619 (2010).

[962] *Griffin v. Wisconsin,* 483 U.S. 868, 873-74, 107 S. Ct. 3164, 3168 (1987).

[963] *Griffin v. Wisconsin,* 483 U.S. 868, 875, 107 S. Ct. 3164, 3169 (1987); *see also United States v. Knights,* 534 U.S. 112, 122 S. Ct. 587 (2001) (The warrantless search of a probationer's home, supported by a reasonable suspicion and authorized by his probation, was reasonable under the Fourth Amendment); *Pennsylvania Bd. of Probation v. Scott,* 524 U.S. 357, 118 S. Ct. 2014 (1988) (The exclusionary rule, which generally prohibits the use at criminal trials of evidence obtained in violation of the Fourth Amendment, does not apply in parole revocation hearings).

6.1.2.4. Drug testing

In upholding mandatory, suspicionless drug testing of United States Customs Service employees seeking promotion to drug-interdiction positions, the U.S. Supreme Court, in *National Treasury Employees Union v. Von Raab*,[964] instructed:

[W]here a Fourth Amendment intrusion serves special governmental needs, beyond the normal need for law enforcement, it is necessary to balance the individual's privacy expectations against the Government's interests to determine whether it is impractical to require a warrant or some level of individualized suspicion in the particular context.[965]

In *Chandler v. Miller*,[966] however, the Supreme Court struck down a Georgia statutory provision requiring that candidates for specified state political offices pass a urinalysis drug test within 30 days prior to qualifying for election. The Court reasoned that Georgia had failed to show a special need important enough to override the individual privacy interests of the candidates. The Court found that the "certification requirement is not well designed to identify candidates who violate anti-drug laws" and that the statute failed to show any concrete danger posed by a state official possibly using drugs.[967]

6.1.2.4.1. Hotel/motel registries

In *City of Los Angeles v. Patel*,[968] the Supreme Court struck down a city of Los Angeles law that required hotel/motel operators to make their registries available to the police on demand. The purpose of the record-keeping requirement was "to deter criminal conduct, on the theory that criminals will be unwilling to carry on illicit activities in motel rooms if they must provide identifying information at check-in. Because this deterrent effect will only be accomplished if motels actually do require guests to provide the required information, the ordinance also authorize[d] police to conduct random spot checks of motels' guest registers to ensure that they are properly maintained."[969] According to the Court, the provision of the "Los Angeles Municipal Code that requires hotel operators to make their registries available to the police on demand"—is "facially unconstitutional because it penalizes them for declining to turn over their records without affording them any opportunity for precompliance review."[970]

6.2. Regulatory searches

As a general principle, the Fourth Amendment's prohibition against unreasonable searches and seizures is applicable to commercial businesses as well as private dwellings.[971] While an owner or operator of a commercial establishment may have a lesser expectation of privacy in the establishment's premises than that enjoyed by a homeowner in his dwelling place, the owner or operator nonetheless maintains a legitimate expectation of privacy in the commercial establishment.[972] This expectation of privacy exists with respect to

---

[964] *National Treasury Employees Union v. Von Raab*, 489 U.S. 656, 109 S. Ct. 1384 (1989).

[965] *National Treasury Employees Union v. Von Raab*, 489 U.S. 656, 665, 109 S. Ct. 1384, 1390 (1989).

[966] *Chandler v. Miller*, 520 U.S. 305, 117 S.Ct. 1295 (1997).

[967] *See also Ferguson v. City of Charleston*, 532 U.S. 67 (2001) (Court struck down a policy which required state hospital employees to perform drug tests on urine samples taken from pregnant women, without the informed consent of the women, then to report positive results to police, who arrested the women if they refused to enter a drug treatment program. The Court found that the "central and indispensable" purpose of this policy was to generate evidence for law enforcement purposes, not to provide medical treatment, and noted that police were actively involved in the development of this policy as well as its day-to-day administration).

[968] *City of Los Angeles v. Patel*, 576 U.S. 409, 135 S. Ct. 2443 (2015).

[969] *City of Los Angeles v. Patel*, 576 U.S. 409, 428, 135 S. Ct. 2443, 2457 (2015) (SCALIA, J. dissenting).

[970] *City of Los Angeles v. Patel*, 576 U.S. 409, 412, 135 S. Ct. 2443, 2447 (2015).

[971] *New York v. Burger*, 482 U.S. 691, 107 S. Ct. 2636 (1987); *See v. City of Seattle*, 387 U.S. 541, 543, 546, 87 S. Ct. 1737, 1739, 1741 (1967).

[972] *Donovan v. Dewey*, 452 U.S. 594, 101 S. Ct. 2534 (1981).

administrative inspections designed to enforce regulatory schemes as well as to traditional searches conducted by police for the gathering of evidence of a crime.[973]

Normally, prior to conducting a regulatory search, officers are required to obtain an administrative search warrant. In "closely regulated industries," however, "an exception to the warrant requirement has been carved out for searches of premises pursuant to an administrative inspection scheme."[974] As the Third Circuit stated in *Lovgren v. Byrne*,[975]

> [O]ne who is engaged in an industry, that is pervasively regulated by the government or that has been historically subject to such close supervision, is ordinarily held to be on notice that periodic inspections will occur and, accordingly, has [a significantly reduced] expectation of privacy in the areas where he knows those inspections will occur.[976]

Thus, it has been held that in certain circumstances, government investigators conducting searches or inspections of "closely regulated" businesses need not adhere to the usual warrant or probable-cause requirements as long as their searches meet reasonable legislative or administrative standards.[977]

In order to be constitutionally valid, a warrantless, administrative inspection of a closely regulated commercial establishment must satisfy three requirements:

1) There must be a substantial government interest in the regulatory scheme under which the warrantless, administrative inspection is conducted;
2) The warrantless, administrative inspection must be necessary to further the regulatory scheme; and
3) The warrantless inspection, by reason of the certainty of its terms and regularity of its application, must provide a constitutionally sufficient substitute for a search warrant. In this respect, similar to a search warrant, the regulatory scheme under which the inspection is conducted must advise the property owner that: (a) the administrative inspection is being conducted under legal authority; (b) by reason of that authority, the scope of the inspection is clearly defined; and (c) the discretion of the inspecting officer is appropriately limited.[978]

When each of the three requirements is satisfied, the warrantless, administrative inspection is constitutionally reasonable and the discovery of evidence of crimes in the course of an otherwise proper administrative inspection should not render the search illegal or the administrative scheme suspect.[979]

6.3. Fire Scenes

6.3.1. Preliminary considerations

An individual's reasonable expectation of privacy and his Fourth Amendment protections are not diminished simply because the official conducting the search at the fire scene "wears the uniform of a firefighter rather than a policeman, or because his purpose is to ascertain the cause of a fire rather than to look for

---

[973] *See New York v. Burger*, 482 U.S. 691, 699, 107 S. Ct. 2636, 2642 (1987); *see also Marshall v. Barlow's Inc.*, 436 U.S. 307, 312-13, 98 S. Ct. 1816, 1820 (1978).

[974] *Shoemaker v. Handel*, 795 F.2d 1136, 1142 (3d Cir. 1986).

[975] *Lovgren v. Byrne*, 787 F.2d 857 (3d Cir. 1986).

[976] *Lovgren v. Byrne*, 787 F.2d 857, 865 (3d Cir. 1986).

[977] *See, e.g., New York v. Burger*, 482 U.S. 691, 702-03, 107 S. Ct. 2636, 2643 (1987) (warrantless inspections of automobile junkyard businesses come within exception for closely regulated industries); *Donovan v. Dewey*, 452 U.S. 594, 605, 101 S. Ct. 2534, 2541 (1981) (warrantless inspections under the Federal Mine Safety and Health Act); *United States v. Biswell*, 406 U.S. 311, 316-17, 92 S. Ct. 1593, 1596-97 (1972) (warrantless inspection of pawnshops licensed to sell guns); *Colonnade Catering Corp. v. United States*, 397 U.S. 72, 76-77, 90 S. Ct. 774, 777 (1970) (liquor industry); *Shoemaker v. Handel*, 795 F.2d 1136, 1142(3d Cir. 1986) (horse racing).

[978] *New York v. Burger*, 482 U.S. 691, 702, 713, 107 S. Ct. 2636, 2644, 2649 (1987).

[979] *See New York v. Burger*, 482 U.S. 691, 716, 107 S. Ct. 2636, 2651 (1987). *See also State v. Sapatch*, 108 N.C. App. 321, 423 S.E.2d 510 (1992).

evidence of a crime, or because the fire might have been started deliberately."[980] Firefighters, like police officers, are public officials, and as such, are subject to the constraints of the federal and state constitutions.[981]

A hot fire scene, *i.e., a burning building*, "clearly presents an exigency of sufficient proportions to render a warrantless entry 'reasonable.' Indeed, it would defy reason to suppose that firemen must secure a warrant or consent before entering a burning structure to put out the blaze."[982] If a firefighter—once inside the building and during the course of fighting the blaze—discovers evidence of arson that is in "plain view," he may lawfully seize that evidence. Accordingly, "an entry to fight a fire requires no warrant," and, once inside the building, if evidence of arson is discovered, it is seizable and "admissible at trial[.]"[983] If, however, investigating fire officials during this time period "find probable cause to believe that arson has occurred and require further access to gather evidence for a possible prosecution, they [must] obtain a warrant ... upon a traditional showing of probable cause applicable to searches for evidence of crime."[984] Fire officials do not, however, need a "warrant to remain in a building *for a reasonable amount of time* to investigate the cause of a blaze after it has been extinguished."[985]

6.3.2. The warrant requirement and fire scene entries

Whenever a fire official wishes to re-enter a "cold" fire scene in the absence of consent, exigent (emergency) circumstances, or complete devastation or destruction, a warrant is required. A "cold" fire scene may be defined as an area containing property which has been freshly fire-damaged, existing at a time when the fire has been completely extinguished and all fire and police officials have departed. Any entries during this "cold" period will be considered by the courts as being *beyond* the "reasonable time to investigate the cause of a blaze after it has been extinguished," in the absence of consent, exigent circumstances, or total devastation.[986] Cold-scene entries and searches require a warrant.

There are two types of warrants available to the investigating fire official, and the "object of the search determines the type of warrant required."[987]

6.3.2.1. To determine cause and origin

If the fire official's prime objective is to determine the *cause* and *origin* of a recent fire, an "administrative warrant" must be obtained. "Probable cause to issue an administrative warrant exists if reasonable legislative, administrative, or judicially prescribed standards for conducting an inspection are satisfied with respect to a particular dwelling."[988] This procedural requirement is accomplished by the official personally appearing before a judge, who will examine the official's affidavit and/or take his sworn testimony. At this meeting, the official must show that: (1) a "fire of undetermined origin has occurred on the premises"; (2) the "scope of the proposed search is reasonable"; (3) the "search will not intrude unnecessarily on the fire victim's privacy"; and (4) the "search will be executed at a reasonable and convenient time."[989]

Before a judge will authorize the issuance of an administrative warrant to conduct an investigation into the cause of a fire, she will want to know: (1) the "number of prior entries"; (2) the "scope of the search"; (3) the "time of day when it is proposed to be made"; (4) the "lapse of time since the fire"; (5) the "continued use of the building"; and (6) the "owner's efforts to secure it against intruders[.]"[990]

---

[980] *Michigan v. Tyler*, 436 U.S. 499, 506, 98 S. Ct. 1942, 1948 (1978).

[981] *Michigan v. Tyler*, 436 U.S. 499, 506, 98 S. Ct. 1942, 1948 (1978).

[982] *Michigan v. Tyler*, 436 U.S. 499, 509, 98 S. Ct. 1942, 1950 (1978).

[983] *Michigan v. Tyler*, 436 U.S. 499, 512, 98 S. Ct. 1942, 1951 (1978).

[984] *Michigan v. Tyler*, 436 U.S. 499, 511, 98 S. Ct. 1942, 1951 (1978).

[985] *Michigan v. Tyler*, 436 U.S. 499, 511, 98 S. Ct. 1942, 1951 (1978) (emphasis added).

[986] *Michigan v. Tyler*, 436 U.S. 499, 510, 98 S. Ct. 1942, 1950 (1978).

[987] *Michigan v. Clifford,* 464 U.S. 287, 294, 104 S. Ct. 641, 647 (1984).

[988] *Michigan v. Clifford,* 464 U.S. 287, 294 n.5, 104 S. Ct. 641, 647 n.5 (1984); *see also Camara v. Municipal Court,* 387 U.S. 523, 538, 87 S. Ct. 1727, 1735-36 (1967).

[989] *Michigan v. Clifford,* 464 U.S. 287, 294,104 S. Ct. 641, 647 (1984). Note that "convenience" here refers to that time convenient to the fire victim, not the fire official.

[990] *Michigan v. Tyler,* 436 U.S. 499, 98 S. Ct. 1942, 1949 (1978).

6.3.2.2. To search for evidence of arson

If, however, the fire official's prime objective is to gather evidence of criminal activity, *e.g.*, arson, a "criminal search warrant" must be secured. This is accomplished only upon a showing (before a judge) of "probable cause to believe that relevant evidence will be found in the place to be searched."[991] Probable cause will be found to exist "where the facts and circumstances within a person's knowledge and of which he has reasonably trustworthy information are sufficient in themselves to warrant a man of reasonable caution and prudence in the belief that an offense has been or is being committed."[992]

Naturally, if, during the course of a valid administrative search, evidence of arson is discovered, the official may lawfully seize that evidence under the "plain view" doctrine. "This evidence may then be used to establish probable cause to obtain a criminal search warrant."[993] The *Clifford* Court warns, however, that "[f]ire officials may not…rely on this evidence to increase the scope of their administrative search without first making a successful showing of probable cause to an independent judicial officer."[994] Additionally, the keynote to an administrative warrant is the "specific limitation" in the scope of the official inspection. Therefore, "[a]n administrative search into the cause of a recent fire does not give fire officials license to roam freely through the fire victim's private residence."[995]

Because there is no bright line separating the firefighter's investigation into the cause of a fire from an investigatory search for evidence of arson, questions naturally arise as to when the administrative search becomes "excessive in scope," and whether the scope of such a search should necessarily expand or constrict in relation to the nature of the particular structure involved.

6.4. Border Searches

From before the adoption of the Fourth Amendment, to today, border searches "have been considered to be 'reasonable' by the single fact that the person or item in question had entered into our country from outside. There has never been any additional requirement that the reasonableness of a border search depended on the existence of probable cause. This longstanding recognition that searches at our borders without probable cause and without a warrant are nonetheless 'reasonable' has a history as old as the Fourth Amendment itself."[996]

In *United States v. Oriakhi*,[997] the Fourth Circuit held that the border search exception "extends to all routine searches at the nation's borders, irrespective of whether persons or effects are entering or exiting from the country."[998] Regarding such exit searches, every other federal circuit addressing this issue has held that the exception applies regardless of whether the person or items are entering or leaving the United States.[999]

The statutory authority of customs officers to conduct searches at the borders is derived from several sources. For example, federal law provides that "all persons coming into the United States from foreign countries shall be liable to detention and search by authorized officers and agents of the Government under [Treasury Department] regulations."[1000] One such regulation provides that "all persons, baggage, and merchandise arriving in the Customs territory of the United States from places outside thereof are liable to inspection and search by a customs officer."[1001] In addition, federal law provides that such officers "may stop, search and

---

[991] *Michigan v. Tyler*, 436 U.S. 499, 98 S. Ct. 1942, 1949 (1978).
[992] *Draper v. United States*, 358 U.S. 307, 313, 79 S. Ct. 329, 333 (1959).
[993] *Michigan v. Clifford*, 464 U.S. 287, 294, 104 S. Ct. 641, 647 (1984).
[994] *Michigan v. Clifford*, 464 U.S. 287, 294, 104 S. Ct. 641, 647 (1984).
[995] *Michigan v. Clifford*, 464 U.S. 287, 298, 104 S. Ct. 641, 649 (1984).
[996] *United States v. Ramsey*, 431 U.S. 606, 619, 97 S. Ct. 1972, 1980 (1977).
[997] *United States v. Oriakhi*, 57 F.3d 1290 (4th Cir. 1995).
[998] *United States v. Oriakhi*, 57 F.3d 1290, 1297 (4th Cir. 1995).
[999] *See, e.g., United States v. Ezeiruaku*, 936 F.2d 136, 143 (3d Cir. 1991); *United States v. Hernandez-Salazar*, 813 F.2d 1126, 1137 (11th Cir. 1987); *United States v. Des Jardins*, 747 F.2d 499, 504 (9th Cir. 1984); *United States v. Udofot*, 711 F.2d 831, 839-40 (8th Cir. 1983); *United States v. Ajlouny*, 629 F.2d 830, 834 (2d Cir. 1980); *see also Julian v. United States*, 463 U.S. 1308, 103 S. Ct. 3522 (1983) (Rehnquist, Circuit Justice) (a chambers opinion applying the border search exception articulated in *Ramsey* to a person and his effects as he attempted to *depart* the country on a flight destined for Peru).
[1000] 19 U.S.C. § 1582.
[1001] 19 C.F.R. § 162.6.

examine, any vehicle, beast or person, on which or whom he or they shall suspect there is merchandise which is subject to duty, or shall have been introduced into the United States in any manner contrary to law[.]"[1002]

Case law interpretation of these enactments provides that "routine searches" of the persons and effects of entrants are "not subject to any requirement of reasonable suspicion, probable cause or warrant."[1003] With respect to such "routine searches," there need not be any suspicion of illegality directed to the particular person or thing to be searched.

Not all border searches are exempt from the Fourth Amendment requirement of reasonableness. Rather, the exemption relates to only those border searches that are considered "*routine*." The main question is what constitutes a routine border search as opposed to one that is not routine.

The cases point to the following parameters constituting a "routine" border search requiring no particularized suspicion:

a) An initial stop and detention of an individual for questioning is permissible;
b) Searches of a traveler's luggage and personal effects, including the contents of a purse, wallet or pockets are deemed routine;
c) A request to remove outer garments, such as a coat, jacket, shoes or boots for the purpose of a search is likewise considered routine; and
d) A pat-down, commonly referred to as a frisk, is within the permissible limits of a routine border search.

Naturally, if a search is deemed to be non-routine, reasonable suspicion is required. In the context of a border search, customs officers may consider such factors as excessive nervousness, unusual conduct, loose fitting or bulky clothing, an itinerary showing brief stops in known drug source countries, lack of employment, inadequate or unusual luggage, and evasive or contradictory answers. While these factors are not exhaustive, they provide useful guideposts in analyzing the numerous factual variations customs officials may encounter.

In *United States v. Flores-Montano*,[1004] the United States Supreme Court addressed the question whether the removal or dismantling of a motorist's fuel tank was a "routine" border search for which no suspicion whatsoever is required. In this case, at the international border in southern California, customs officials seized 37 kilograms—a little more than 81 pounds—of marijuana from defendant Manuel Flores-Montano's gas tank. Chief Justice Rehnquist, speaking for a unanimous Court, held that the routine border search in question did not require reasonable suspicion. According to the Court,

> The Government's interest in preventing the entry of unwanted persons and effects is at its zenith at the international border. Time and again, we have stated that "searches made at the border, pursuant to the longstanding right of the sovereign to protect itself by stopping and examining persons and property crossing into this country, are reasonable simply by virtue of the fact that they occur at the border."…That interest in protecting the borders is illustrated in this case by the evidence that smugglers frequently attempt to penetrate our borders with contraband secreted in their automobiles' fuel tank. Over the past 5½ fiscal years, there have been 18,788 vehicle drug seizures at the southern California ports of entry. Of those 18,788, gas tank drug seizures have accounted for 4,619 of the vehicle drug seizures, or approximately 25%.[1005]

The Court rejected the defendant's contention that he had "a privacy interest in his fuel tank, and that the suspicionless disassembly of his tank [was] an invasion of his privacy."[1006] According to the Court, "the expectation of privacy is less at the border than it is in the interior.…We have long recognized that automobiles seeking entry into this country may be searched.…It is difficult to imagine how the search of a gas tank,

---

[1002] 19 U.S.C. § 482.
[1003] *United States v. Montoya de Hernandez*, 473 U.S. 531, 537, 105 S. Ct. 3304, 3309 (1985).
[1004] *United States v. Flores-Montano*, 541 U.S. 149, 124 S. Ct. 1582 (2004).
[1005] *United States v. Flores-Montano*, 541 U.S. 149, 124 S. Ct. 1582, 1585-86 (2004) (citations omitted).
[1006] *United States v. Flores-Montano*, 541 U.S. 149, 124 S. Ct. 1582, 1586 (2004).

which should be solely a repository for fuel, could be more of an invasion of privacy than the search of the automobile's passenger compartment."[1007]

Accordingly, the Court held that "the Government's authority to conduct suspicionless inspections at the border includes the authority to remove, disassemble, and reassemble a vehicle's fuel tank. While it may be true that some searches of property are so destructive as to require a different result, this was not one of them."[1008]

7. PRIVATE SEARCHES

7.1. General aspects

The Fourth Amendment to the federal Constitution begins by commanding that the "right of the people to be secure in their persons, houses, papers, and effects, against unreasonable searches and seizures, shall not be violated...." A *search* compromises an individual's interest in privacy and takes place "when an expectation of privacy that society is prepared to recognize as reasonable is infringed."[1009] A *seizure* "deprives the individual of dominion over his or her ... property,"[1010] and constitutes a "meaningful interference" with the owner's possessory interests in that property.[1011]

These principles do not, however, apply to private action. In fact, over the course of time, they have been consistently interpreted as prohibiting only unreasonable *government* action; they are "wholly inapplicable 'to a search or seizure, even an unreasonable one, effected by a private individual not acting as an agent of the Government or with the participation or knowledge of any governmental official.'"[1012] Therefore, evidence obtained by private citizens in pursuit of personal goals will not implicate the commands of the Fourth Amendment, and may thereafter be turned over to the government, so long as no government official played a part in the search or in the acquisition of the evidence. In this respect, the United States Supreme Court has explained:

> Although the Fourth Amendment does not apply to a search or seizure, even an arbitrary one, effected by a private party on his own initiative, the Amendment protects against such intrusions if the private party acted as an instrument or agent of the government.[1013]

"Whether a private party should be deemed an agent or instrument of the Government for [constitutional] purposes necessarily turns on the degree of the Government's participation in the private party's activities[,] a question that can only be resolved 'in light of all the circumstances.'"[1014]

7.2. The target of the exclusionary rule

Accordingly, the target of the exclusionary rule is "official," not "private," misconduct.[1015] For purposes of the discussion which follows, the pivotal factor will be whether the private individual, in light of all the circumstances, must be regarded as having acted as an "instrument" or "agent" of the police.

[1007] *United States v. Flores-Montano*, 541 U.S. 149, 124 S. Ct. 1582, 1586 (2004).

[1008] *United States v. Flores-Montano*, 541 U.S. 149, 124 S. Ct. 1582, 1587 (2004).

[1009] *United States v. Jacobsen*, 466 U.S. 109, 113, 104 S. Ct. 1652, 1656 (1984); *see also Horton v. California*, 496 U.S. 128, 110 S. Ct. 2301, 2306 (1990).

[1010] *Horton v. California*, 496 U.S. 128, 110 S. Ct. 2301, 2306 (1990).

[1011] *Maryland v. Macon*, 472 U.S. 463, 469, 105 S. Ct. 2778, 2782 (1985); *United States v. Jacobsen*, 466 U.S. 109, 113, 104 S. Ct. 1652, 1656 (1984).

[1012] *United States v. Jacobsen*, 466 U.S. 109, 113-14, 104 S. Ct. 1652, 1656 (1984) (quoting *Walter v. United States*, 447 U.S. 649, 662, 100 S. Ct. 2395, 2404 (1980)); *see also Burdeau v. McDowell*, 256 U.S. 465, 41 S. Ct. 574 (1921).

[1013] *Skinner v. Railway Labor Executives Ass'n.*, 489 U.S. 602, 614, 109 S. Ct. 1402, 1411 (1989).

[1014] *Skinner v. Railway Labor Executives Ass'n.*, 489 U.S. 602, 614, 109 S. Ct. 1402, 1411 (1989) (quoting *Coolidge v. New Hampshire*, 403 U.S. 443, 91 S. Ct. 2022, 2026 (1971)); *see also Hoagburg v. Harrah's Marina Hotel Casino*, 585 F. Supp. 1167, 1171, 1174 (D.N.J. 1984).

[1015] *United State v. King*, 55 F.3d 1193 (6th Cir. 1995).

A person will act as a "police agent" if:

(a) The police instigate, encourage, or foster the search;
(b) There is joint participation between private citizens and police officers;
(c) The police have significantly involved themselves in the search; or
(d) The police have pre-knowledge of the private individual's expressed intent to conduct a search or seizure and acquiesce in its effectuation.

If an unlawful private search or seizure is performed with any of the aforementioned relationships existing between the police and the private person(s) effecting the search or seizure, the Fourth Amendment's Exclusionary Rule will bar the admissibility of any evidence obtained. On the other hand, if it is found that the police had no significant connection with the private search or seizure, or any knowledge of it until after the fact, the evidence delivered to them may be admitted.[1016]

In *United States v. Jacobsen*,[1017] the Supreme Court ruled that the following set of circumstances *did not* give rise to a "governmental" search within the meaning of the Fourth Amendment to the Constitution:

Federal Express employees opened a damaged cardboard box and, pursuant to written company policy regarding insurance claims, examined the contents. Within the box they found five to six pieces of crumbled newspaper covering a tube about 10 inches long. The tube was made of silver duct tape. The employees then cut into the tube and found a series of four ziplock plastic bags, the outermost enclosing the other three, and the innermost containing about six ounces of a suspicious-looking white powder.

The employees then notified the DEA. Before the DEA agent arrived, the Federal Express employees put everything back into the cardboard box. When the DEA agent arrived, he opened the box, opened the duct tape tube, opened the plastic baggies, and conducted a field test of the white powder. The powder tested positive for cocaine. The DEA agent seized the cocaine.

According to the Court, the owner of the package "could have no privacy interest in the contents of the package, since it remained unsealed and since the Federal Express employees had just examined the package and had, on their own accord, invited the federal agent to their offices for the express purpose of viewing its contents."[1018] As a result, the DEA agent's inspection "of what a private party had freely made available for his inspection did not violate the Fourth Amendment."[1019]

This case is a prime example of the typical "third-party intervention" case. Because the initial violation of Jacobsen's privacy was the result of private action, the Court determined that the Fourth Amendment was not violated when the DEA agents re-examined the package.

Where the police expand the scope of the initial private search, however, the third-party intervention exception may no longer apply to the fruits of the expanded search. Thus, in *Walter v. United States*,[1020] where a shipping company erroneously delivered 12 cartons to "L'Eggs Products, Inc." instead of to "Leggs, Inc." When the L'Eggs Products employees opened the cartons, they discovered film canisters inside, with labels that indicated that they contained scenes of sexual activity. The employees did not screen the films or otherwise view their content. They did, however, call the FBI, whose agents picked up the cartons and viewed the films utilizing a projector.

The Supreme Court held that the FBI agents' viewing of the films was a warrantless search which violated the Fourth Amendment. According to the Court, the FBI's viewing of the films was a separate search that had

---

[1016] *See Coolidge v. New Hampshire*, 403 U.S. 443, 487-88, 91 S. Ct. 2022, 2048-49 (1971). *But see Flagg Bros. v. Brooks*, 436 U.S. 149, 98 S. Ct. 1729 (1978) (where the Court intimated that where state involvement in private action constitutes *no more* than mere acquiescence or tacit approval, the private action is not automatically transformed into state action).

[1017] *United States v. Jacobsen*, 466 U.S. 109, 104 S. Ct. 1652 (1984).

[1018] *United States v. Jacobsen*, 466 U.S. 109, 104 S. Ct. 1652, 1659-60 (1984).

[1019] *United States v. Jacobsen*, 466 U.S. 109, 104 S. Ct. 1652, 1660 (1984).

[1020] *Walter v. United States*, 447 U.S. 649, 100 S. Ct. 2395 (1980).

expanded the scope of the private search. "The projection of the films was a significant expansion of the search that had been conducted previously by a private party and therefore must be characterized as a separate search. That separate search was not supported by any exigency, or by a warrant even though one could have been obtained.... Since the additional search conducted by the FBI—the screening of the films—was not supported by any justification, it violated that Amendment."[1021]

The same was true in *State v. Terrell*,[1022] where the defendant's girlfriend, Ms. Jones, found a thumb drive belonging to him while searching his briefcase. Ms. Jones plugged the thumb drive into a shared computer and discovered that it contained what she termed, "inappropriate images of women and ... children"[1023] including one of her granddaughter. Ms. Jones brought the thumb drive to the police station and handed it over to Detective Bailey, explaining to him what she had discovered. Thereafter, Detective Bailey personally viewed the contents of the thumb drive and observed what he believed to be child pornography.

The North Carolina Supreme Court reasoned that a thumb drive potentially contains vast information in various folders and subfolders. "Accordingly, the extent to which an individual's expectation of privacy in the contents of an electronic storage device is frustrated depends upon the extent of the private search and the nature of the device and its contents."[1024] The court concluded, "It is clear that Ms. Jones's limited search did not frustrate defendant's legitimate expectation of privacy in the *entire* contents of his thumb drive and that Detective Bailey's follow-up search to locate the image of Sandy was not permissible under *Jacobsen* because he did not possess 'a virtual certainty that nothing else of significance was in the [thumb drive] and that a manual inspection of the [thumb drive] and its contents would not tell him anything more than he already had been told' by Jones."[1025]

8. CONFESSION LAW

8.1. Introduction

8.1.1. The Fifth Amendment

The Fifth Amendment to the Federal Constitution commands that *no person "shall be compelled in any criminal case to be a witness against himself."*[1026]

This provision represents the constitutional right which has come to be recognized as the "privilege against self-incrimination." It has been made applicable to the states through the Fourteenth Amendment by the United States Supreme Court's decision in *Malloy v. Hogan*.[1027] In *Malloy*, the Supreme Court ruled that the privilege against self-incrimination is a "fundamental right," and, as such, is binding upon the states in the same manner the Fifth Amendment safeguards persons from the federal government. The Court employed the Fourteenth Amendment's Due Process Clause as the vehicle through which the privilege was made binding upon the states. In pertinent part, the Due Process Clause provides that no state shall "deprive any person of life, liberty, or property, without *due process of law....*"[1028]

The privilege to be free from self-incrimination has been described as the "essential mainstay of our adversary system," and "the constitutional foundation underlying the privilege is the respect a government—state or federal—must accord to the dignity and integrity of its citizens."[1029]

[1021] *Walter v. United States*, 447 U.S. 649, 657-59, 100 S. Ct. 2395, 2402-03 (1980).

[1022] *State v. Terrell*, 2019 N.C. LEXIS 784 (Aug. 16, 2019).

[1023] *State v. Terrell*, 2019 N.C. LEXIS 784, *2, (Aug. 16, 2019).

[1024] *State v. Terrell*, 2019 N.C. LEXIS 784, *25, (Aug. 16, 2019).

[1025] *State v. Terrell*, 2019 N.C. LEXIS 784, *27, (Aug. 16, 2019) (emphasis in original) (quoting *United States v. Jacobsen*, 466 U.S. 109, 119, 104 S. Ct. 1652 (1984)). *See also State v. Mitchell*, 822 S.E.2d 51 (N.C. Ct. App. 2018); *State v. Kornegay*, 313 N.C. 1, 326 S.E.2d 881 (1985).

[1026] U.S. Const. amend. V (emphasis added).

[1027] *Malloy v. Hogan*, 378 U.S. 1, 84 S. Ct. 1489 (1964).

[1028] U.S. Const. amend. XIV § 1 (emphasis added).

[1029] *Miranda v. Arizona*, 384 U.S. 436, 460, 86 S. Ct. 1602, 1620 (1966).

The Supreme Court in *Miranda* perceived an intimate connection between the constitutional privilege against self-incrimination and "police custodial questioning" which takes place in a "police dominated atmosphere."[1030]

8.1.2. The *Miranda* Requirements

Miranda dealt with "the admissibility of statements obtained from an individual who is subjected to custodial police interrogation and the necessity for procedures which assure that the individual is accorded his privilege under the Fifth Amendment to the Constitution not to be compelled to incriminate himself."[1031]

Chief Justice Warren, speaking for the U.S. Supreme Court, concluded that "the privilege is fulfilled only when the person is guaranteed the right 'to remain silent unless he chooses to speak in the unfettered exercise of his own free will.'"[1032]

"Coercive" custodial interrogation is the "evil" which the Court addressed in *Miranda*. "Custodial interrogation" is defined as "questioning initiated by law enforcement officers after a person has been taken into custody or otherwise deprived of his freedom of action in any significant way."[1033] This concept of custodial interrogation is what the Court had in mind when it previously "spoke of an investigation which had focused on an accused."[1034]

The necessary procedural safeguards emanating from *Miranda* are as follows:

Prior to any questioning, the person must be warned that he has the right to remain silent, that any statement he does make [can and will] be used [against him in a court of law], and that he has a right to the presence of an attorney, . . . and that if he cannot afford an attorney one will be appointed for him prior to any questioning if he so desires.[1035]

Good practice dictates that the individual also be clearly informed that he may ask for counsel at any time during custodial questioning, and, in addition, that the questioning will cease at any time the person desires counsel. In addition, the warning given must convey that the suspect has the right to have an attorney present not only at the outset of interrogation, but at all times. In this regard, the Supreme Court, in *Florida v. Powell*,[1036] emphasized that, as a matter of law, an individual held for questioning "must be clearly informed that he has the right to consult with a lawyer *and to have the lawyer with him during interrogation.*" These rights apply regardless of the nature or severity of the offense.[1037]

Accordingly, prior to custodial interrogation, the person must be informed of the following:

- You have the right to remain silent.
- Anything you say can and will be used against you in a court of law.
- You have the right to consult with an attorney and have an attorney present during questioning.
- If you cannot afford an attorney, one can be provided to you before questioning at no cost.
- You may ask for an attorney at any time during questioning, and questioning will stop if at any time you ask for an attorney.

Thereafter, if the individual

indicates in any manner and at any stage of the process that he wishes to consult with an attorney before speaking there can be no questioning. Likewise, if the individual is alone and *indicates in any*

[1030] *Miranda v. Arizona*, 384 U.S. 436, 458, 86 S. Ct. 1602, 1619 (1966).

[1031] *Miranda v. Arizona*, 384 U.S. 436, 439, 86 S. Ct. 1602, 1609 (1966).

[1032] *Miranda v. Arizona*, 384 U.S. 436, 460, 86 S. Ct. 1602, 1620 (1966) (quoting *Malloy v. Hogan*, 378 U.S. 1, 8, 84 S. Ct. 1489, 1493 (1964)).

[1033] *Miranda v. Arizona*, 384 U.S. 436, 444, 86 S. Ct. 1602, 1612 (1966).

[1034] *Miranda v. Arizona*, 384 U.S. 436, 444 n.4, 86 S. Ct. 1602, 1612 n.4 (1966) (referring to *Escobedo v. Illinois*, 378 U.S. 478, 84 S. Ct. 1758 (1964)).

[1035] *Miranda v. Arizona*, 384 U.S. 436, 444, 479, 86 S. Ct. 1602, 1612, 1630 (1966).

[1036] *Florida v. Powell*, 559 U.S. 50, 130 S. Ct. 1195, 1203 (2010).

[1037] *See Berkemer v. McCarty*, 468 U.S. 420, 104 S.Ct. 3138 (1984).

manner that he does not wish to be interrogated, the police may not question him. The mere fact that he might have answered some questions on his own does not deprive him of the right to refrain from answering any further inquiries until he has consulted with an attorney and thereafter consents to be questioned.[1038]

Thus, as a general matter, the prosecution must demonstrate that the *Miranda* warnings were administered to the accused prior to any custodial interrogation. At the time of questioning, the accused may, of course, waive her *Miranda* rights, provided the waiver is made *voluntarily, knowingly, and intelligently.*[1039] Failure to establish adherence to *Miranda's* procedural safeguards—the administration of the warnings and receipt of an appropriate waiver—renders any and all statements obtained from an accused in any ensuing custodial interrogation inadmissible at trial, at least in the prosecution's case-in-chief.[1040]

"The *Miranda* Court did of course caution that the Constitution requires no 'particular solution for the inherent compulsions of the interrogation process,' and left it open to a State to meet its burden by adopting 'other procedures…at least as effective in apprising accused persons' of their rights[.] The Court indeed acknowledged that, in barring introduction of a statement obtained without the required warnings, *Miranda* might exclude a confession that [] would not [be] condemn[ed] as 'involuntary in traditional terms,'…and for this reason [the Court has] sometimes called the *Miranda* safeguards 'prophylactic' in nature."[1041]

In *Dickerson v. United States,*[1042] the Court, for the first time since *Miranda v. Arizona* was decided, had occasion to determine whether it should overrule *Miranda* and replace it with a test of "voluntariness" as the touchstone of a confession's admissibility, with the now-familiar warnings being just one factor in the analysis.

The *Dickerson* case addressed whether a federal statute,[1043] enacted two years after *Miranda* was decided, was an unconstitutional attempt by Congress to legislatively overrule *Miranda*. To nullify *Miranda*, the federal statute set forth a rule providing that the admissibility of an accused's confession or admission should turn only on whether or not it was voluntarily made. In a 7-to-2 opinion, the *Dickerson* Court declared:

> *Miranda*, being a constitutional decision of this Court, may not be in effect overruled by an Act of Congress, and we decline to overrule *Miranda* ourselves. We therefore hold that *Miranda* and its progeny in this Court govern the admissibility of statements made during custodial interrogation in both state and federal courts.[1044]

The *Dickerson* Court reemphasized that *Miranda* "laid down 'concrete constitutional guidelines for law enforcement agencies and courts to follow.'"[1045] Those guidelines mandate the administration of four warnings which have now "come to be known colloquially as '*Miranda* rights.'"[1046] The *Miranda* warnings, held the *Dickerson* Court, are constitutional in dimension; the warnings have "become embedded in routine police practice to the point where the warnings have become part of our national culture."[1047]

8.1.3. The *Miranda* Formula

From the foregoing discussion, it is clear that prior to any custodial interrogation, law enforcement officers are required to administer the *Miranda* warnings to the person about to be questioned. The formula should be as easy

---

[1038] *Miranda v. Arizona*, 384 U.S. 436, 444-45, 86 S. Ct. 1602, 1612 (1966) (emphasis added).

[1039] *Miranda v. Arizona*, 384 U.S. 436, 444-45, 86 S. Ct. 1602, 1612 (1966).

[1040] *See Michigan v. Tucker*, 417 U.S. 433, 444, 94 S. Ct. 2357, 2364 (1974) (recognizing that *Miranda's* "procedural safeguards were not themselves rights protected by the Constitution but were instead measures to insure that the right against compulsory self-incrimination was protected").

[1041] *Withrow v. Williams*, 507 U.S. 680, 113 S. Ct. 1745, 1752 (1993) (quoting *Miranda v. Arizona*, 384 U.S. 436, 457, 467, 86 S. Ct. 1602, 1618, 1624 (1966)).

[1042] *Dickerson v. United States*, 530 U.S. 428, 120 S. Ct. 2326 (2000).

[1043] 18 U.S.C. § 3501.

[1044] *Dickerson v. United States*, 530 U.S. 428, 120 S. Ct. 2326, 2329-30 (2000).

[1045] *Dickerson v. United States*, 530 U.S. 428, 120 S. Ct. 2326, 2331 (2000) (citation omitted).

[1046] *Dickerson v. United States*, 530 U.S. 428, 120 S. Ct. 2326, 2331 (2000) (citation omitted).

[1047] *Dickerson v. United States*, 530 U.S. 428, 120 S. Ct. 2326, 2335-36 (2000).

as 1 + 1 = 2; that is, "custody" + "interrogation" = the requirement that *Miranda* warnings be given.[1048] As the materials in this section will demonstrate, however, the formula is easier to recite than to apply. For law enforcement, the desired, ultimate result is the acquisition of a valid confession, fully admissible at trial. In order for that to occur, officers are at all times required to scrupulously honor each of the rights contained within the *Miranda* warnings.

Assuming that a criminal suspect is "in custody" and that law enforcement officials have administered the appropriate warnings, there are several courses that the interview may take. The first, and perhaps most straightforward, course that an interview session may take is:

1) a custodial suspect;
2) is given *Miranda* warnings;
3) thereafter voluntarily, knowingly and intelligently waives his rights; and
4) gives a full confession.

Second, a custodial suspect may blurt out a confession before the authorities have an opportunity to administer the *Miranda* warnings.

A third direction in which an interview session may head is illustrated by the following:

1) a custodial suspect;
2) is given *Miranda* warnings; and
3) thereafter indicates that she does not want to talk—the suspect invokes her right to remain silent.

Fourth, an interview session may proceed as follows:

1) a custodial suspect;
2) is given *Miranda* warnings; and
3) thereafter indicates that he wants a lawyer—the suspect invokes his right to counsel.

Fifth, the suspect may change her mind; in this instance:

1) a custodial suspect;
2) is given *Miranda* warnings;
3) indicates that she wants;
   a. to remain silent; or
   b. a lawyer; but
4) sometime thereafter changes her mind and indicates a desire to communicate with the authorities, to open up a dialogue about the investigation.

Sixth, outside influences may interrupt or affect an interview, for example, where

1) a custodial suspect;
2) is given *Miranda* warnings; and
3) voluntarily, knowingly and intelligently waives his rights, but at some time during the process;
4) an attorney, family member or close friend of the suspect;
   a. notifies the authorities of his pending or actual arrival at the station house; and / or
   b. advises the authorities not to question the suspect.

The following sections explore each of the above-described paths down which an interview or questioning session may travel.[1049] There are, however, several preliminary issues that need to be addressed. For

---

[1048] *State v. Johnson*, 371 N.C. 870, 821 S.E.2d 822 (2018); *State v. Hammonds*, 370 N.C. 158, 804 S.E.2d 438 (2017).
[1049] Excerpts from the comprehensive discussion of the laws of arrest, search and seizure in Larry E. Holtz, *Criminal Procedure for Law and Justice Professionals* (Blue360° Media).

example, "What constitutes custody?" "What constitutes interrogation?" and, "Is a validly obtained confession, by itself, sufficient to support a criminal conviction?"

8.2. Interviews and Confessions

Lawfully obtained admissions and confessions continue to play an integral role in the law enforcement scheme and are extremely persuasive at trial. The ability of law enforcement to obtain a valid, uncoerced confession has been described as "not an evil but an unmitigated good."[1050] As the Supreme Court observed in *McNeil v. Wisconsin*, "[a]dmissions of guilt resulting from valid *Miranda* waivers 'are more than merely "desirable"; they are essential to society's compelling interest in finding, convicting, and punishing those who violate the law.'"[1051] The introduction of an admission or a confession at trial "is like no other evidence. Indeed, 'the defendant's own confession is probably the most probative and damaging evidence that can be admitted against him.... The admissions of a defendant come from the actor himself, the most knowledgeable and unimpeachable source of information about his past conduct. Certainly, confessions have profound impact on the jury[.]'"[1052]

8.2.1. Preliminary issues

8.2.1.1. Uncorroborated confessions and the "*corpus delicti*" rule

As a general rule, "an accused may not be convicted on his own uncorroborated confession."[1053] This rule has been previously recognized by the U.S. Supreme Court in *Warszower v. United States*[1054] and *Isaacs v. United States*,[1055] and has been "consistently applied in the lower federal courts and in the overwhelming majority of state courts[.]"[1056] "Its purpose is to prevent 'errors in convictions based upon untrue confessions alone,' [and] its foundation lies in a long history of judicial experience with confessions and in the realization that sound law enforcement requires police investigations which extend beyond the words of the accused."[1057]

"The corroboration rule, at its inception, served an extremely limited function. In order to convict of serious crimes of violence, then capital offenses, independent proof was required that someone had indeed inflicted the violence, the so-called *corpus delicti*. Once the existence of the crime was established, however, the guilt of the accused could be based on his own otherwise uncorroborated confession."[1058]

While the rule requiring corroboration is well settled, the question is what is the quantum of proof independent of the confession that the prosecution must introduce before the confession may be considered evidential? "There has been considerable debate concerning the quantum of corroboration necessary to substantiate the existence of the crime charged. It is agreed that the corroborative evidence does not have to prove the offense beyond a reasonable doubt, or even by a preponderance, as long as there is substantial independent evidence that the offense has been committed, and the evidence as a whole proves beyond a reasonable doubt that defendant is guilty."[1059] The debate has centered largely about two questions: "(1) whether corroboration is necessary for all elements of the offense established by admissions alone," and "(2) whether it is sufficient if the corroboration merely fortifies the truth of the confession, without independently establishing the crime charged[.]"[1060] The Supreme Court has answered both questions in the affirmative. "All

---

[1050] *McNeil v. Wisconsin*, 501 U.S. 171, 111 S. Ct. 2204, 2210 (1991).

[1051] *McNeil v. Wisconsin*, 501 U.S. 171, 111 S. Ct. 2204, 2210 (1991) (citation omitted).

[1052] *Arizona v. Fulminante*, 499 U.S. 279, 296, 111 S. Ct. 1246, 1257 (1991) (quoting *Bruton v. United States*, 391 U.S. 123, 139-40, 88 S. Ct. 1620, 1630 (1968) (White, J., dissenting)).

[1053] *Smith v. United States*, 348 U.S. 147, 75 S. Ct. 194, 152 (1954).

[1054] *Warszower v. United States*, 312 U.S. 342, 61 S. Ct. 603 (1941).

[1055] *Isaacs v. United States*, 159 U.S. 487, 16 S. Ct. 51 (1895).

[1056] *Smith v. United States*, 348 U.S. 147, 75 S. Ct. 194, 152-53 (1954).

[1057] *Smith v. United States*, 348 U.S. 147, 75 S. Ct. 194, 153 (1954).

[1058] *Smith v. United States*, 348 U.S. 147, 75 S. Ct. 194, 153-54 (1954).

[1059] *Smith v. United States*, 348 U.S. 147, 75 S. Ct. 194, 155-56 (1954).

[1060] *Smith v. United States*, 348 U.S. 147, 75 S. Ct. 194, 156 (1954).

elements of the offense must be established by independent evidence or corroborated admissions, but one available mode of corroboration is for the independent evidence to bolster the confession itself and thereby prove the offense 'through' the statements of the accused."[1061]

In *State v. Parker*,[1062] acknowledging the shortcomings of the traditional *corpus delicti* rule, the North Carolina Supreme Court adopted its own rule for non-capital cases and "expanded the type of corroboration which may be sufficient to establish the trustworthiness of the confession."[1063] The court declared:

> We adopt a rule in non-capital cases that when the State relies upon the defendant's confession to obtain a conviction, it is no longer necessary that there be independent proof tending to establish the *corpus delicti* of the crime charged if the accused's confession is supported by substantial independent evidence tending to establish its trustworthiness, including facts that tend to show the defendant had the opportunity to commit the crime.[1064]

In adopting the *Parker* rule, the court emphasized:

> [W]hen independent proof of loss or injury is lacking, there must be *strong* corroboration of *essential* facts and circumstances embraced in the defendant's confession. Corroboration of insignificant facts or those unrelated to the commission of the crime will not suffice. We emphasize this point because although we have relaxed our corroboration rule somewhat, we remain advertent to the reason for its existence, that is, to protect against convictions for crimes that have not in fact occurred.[1065]

For example, in *State v. Cox*,[1066] the defendant was a passenger in a car that attempted to avoid a DWI checkpoint by pulling into a residential driveway. When the driver fled on foot, the defendant was one of three remaining passengers in the car. The officers found a firearm within 10 to 12 feet of the open car door that the defendant later admitted belonged to him. The court reasoned, "Even though the night was cool and the grass was wet with condensation, the firearm was dry and warm, indicating that it came from inside the car. Near the firearm officers found marijuana packaged in a manner consistent with packaging for sale. The officers also found a firearm at the feet of one of the other passengers. These are not 'insignificant facts' or facts 'unrelated to the commission of the crime.' Rather, these facts strongly corroborate 'essential facts and circumstances embraced in [ ] defendant's confession.' They link defendant temporally and spatially to the firearm. Thus, the circumstances preceding defendant's confession—circumstances that were observed by law enforcement officers—establish the trustworthiness of the confession."[1067]

Once the *corpus delicti* of the crime is established, the accused's confession is admissible.

8.2.1.2. Electronic recordings of custodial interrogations

The United States Supreme Court has yet to extend the Due Process Clause of the United States Constitution to require that electronic recordings be made of custodial interrogations.[1068] However, in North Carolina,

---

[1061] *Smith v. United States*, 348 U.S. 147, 75 S. Ct. 194, 156 (1954).

[1062] *State v. Parker*, 315 N.C. 222, 337 S.E.2d 487 (1985).

[1063] *State v. Trexler*, 316 N.C. 528, 532, 342 S.E.2d 878 (1986).

[1064] *State v. Parker*, 315 N.C. 222, 236, 337 S.E.2d 487 (1985).

[1065] *State v. Parker*, 315 N.C. 222, 236, 337 S.E.2d 487 (1985) (emphasis in original).

[1066] *State v. Cox*, 367 N.C. 147, 749 S.E.2d 271 (2013).

[1067] *State v. Cox*, 367 N.C. 147, 153, 749 S.E.2d 271 (2013) (quoting *State v. Parker*, 315 N.C. 222, 236, 337 S.E.2d 487 (1985)). *See also State v. Trexler*, 316 N.C. 528, 342 S.E.2d 878 (1986).

[1068] *See generally California v. Trombetta*, 467 U.S. 479, 104 S. Ct. 2528 (1984). To date, however, twenty-seven states and the District of Columbia now require or encourage, in one form or another, custodial interrogations to be recorded. *See Stephan v. State*, 711 P.2d 1156, 1159 (Alaska 1985); *Ark. R. Crim. P.* 4.7 (Arkansas); *Cal. Penal Code* § 859.5 (2017) (California); *Colo. Rev. Stat.* § 16-3-601 (2016) (Colorado); *Conn. Gen. Stat.* § 54-1o(b) (2014) (Connecticut); *D.C. Code* §§ 5-116.01-116.03 (2005) (District of Columbia); 705 *Ill. Comp. Stat.* 405/5-401.5 and 725 *Ill. Comp. Stat.* 5/103-2.1 (2017) (Illinois); *Ind. R. Evid.* 617 (Indiana); *Kan. Stat. Ann.* § 22-4620 (2017) (Kansas); *Me. Stat. tit.* 25, § 2803-B (2015) (Maine); *Md. Code Ann., Crim. Proc.* §§ 2-402 and 2-403 (2008) (Maryland); *Commonwealth v. DiGiambattista*, 442 Mass. 423, 813 N.E.2d 516, 533-34 (Mass.

N.C.Gen.Stat. § 15A-211 provides that certain interrogations must be recorded in their entirety. Such interrogations include any Class A, B1, or B2 felony, and any Class C felony of rape, sex offense, or assault with a deadly weapon with intent to kill inflicting serious injury when the interrogation is conducted at a place of detention.[1069] In addition, any custodial interrogation of a juvenile must be recorded in its entirety regardless of where it is conducted.[1070] A place of detention includes a jail, police or sheriff's station, correctional or detention facility, holding facility for prisoners, or other facility where persons are held in custody in connection with criminal charges.[1071] Pursuant to N.C.Gen.Stat. § 15A-211(g), the following do not have to be recorded:

(1) A statement made by the accused in open court during trial, before a grand jury, or at a preliminary hearing.

(2) A spontaneous statement that is not made in response to a question.

(3) A statement made during arrest processing in response to a routine question.

(4) A statement made during a custodial interrogation that is conducted in another state by law enforcement officers of that state.

(5) A statement obtained by a federal law enforcement officer.

(6) A statement given at a time when the interrogators are unaware that the person is suspected of an offense to which this Article applies.

(7) A statement used only for impeachment purposes and not as substantive evidence.

8.2.1.3. Volunteered statements

Not all admissions or confessions obtained in the absence of *Miranda* warnings are inadmissible. The formula set forth in the preceding section—*custody* + *interrogation* = the requirement that *Miranda* warnings be given—teaches that law enforcement officials may, without the administration of *Miranda* warnings, question a criminal suspect who is not in custody. Moreover, officers may utilize any admission or confession volunteered by an in-custody criminal suspect when no interrogation (express or implied) has taken place. In this respect, the Court in *Miranda* emphasized that "[a]ny statement given freely and voluntarily without any compelling influences is, of course, admissible in evidence."[1072] Law enforcement officials are by no means required to stop people from speaking when they step forward to confess to a crime. Volunteered statements of any kind are not barred by the Fifth Amendment and their admissibility has not been affected by the Court's ruling in *Miranda*.[1073]

8.2.2. What constitutes custody?

8.2.2.1. General aspects

In *Miranda v. Arizona*, the U.S. Supreme Court held that pre-interrogation warnings are required in the context of custodial interrogations, given "the compulsion inherent in custodial surroundings."[1074] The Court defined "custodial interrogation" as "questioning initiated by law enforcement officers after a person has been taken into custody or otherwise deprived of his freedom of action in any significant way."[1075]

2004); *Mich. Comp. Laws* §§ 763.7-11 (2013) (Michigan); *State v. Scales*, 518 N.W.2d 587, 592 (Minn. 1994); *Mo. Rev. Stat.* § 590.700 (2017) (Missouri); *Mont. Code Ann.* §§ 46-4-406-411 (2009) (Montana); *Neb. Rev. Stat.* §§ 29-4501-4508 (2008) (Nebraska); Nev. Rev. Stat. Ann. § 171.1239 (2019) (Nevada); *NJ. Court Rules* 3:17 (New Jersey); *N.M. Stat. Ann.* § 29-1-16 (2006) (New Mexico); *N.Y. Crim. Proc. Law* § 60.45 (2018) (New York); *N.C. Gen. Stat.* Ann. § 15A-211 (2011) (North Carolina); *Or. Rev. Stat. Ann.* § 133.400 (2018) (Oregon); *Tex. Crim. Proc. Code Ann.* art. 2.32 and *art.* 38.22, § 3 (2017) (Texas); *Utah R. Evid.* 616 (Utah); *Vt. Stat. Ann. tit.* 13, § 5585 (2015) (Vermont); *Va. Code Ann.* § 19.2-390.04 (2020) (Virginia); Wis. Stat. Ann. § 968.073 (2019) (Wisconsin).

[1069] N.C.Gen.Stat. § 15A-211(b).

[1070] N.C.Gen.Stat. § 15A-211(b).

[1071] N.C.Gen.Stat. § 15A-211(c)(3).

[1072] *Miranda v. Arizona*, 384 U.S. 436, 478, 86 S. Ct. 1602, 1630 (1966).

[1073] *Rhode Island v. Innis*, 446 U.S. 291, 300-01, 100 S. Ct. 1682 (1980).

[1074] *Miranda v. Arizona*, 384 U.S. 436, 458, 86 S. Ct. 1602, 1619 (1966).

[1075] *Miranda v. Arizona*, 384 U.S. 436, 444, 86 S. Ct. 1602, 1612 (1966); *see also Stansbury v. California*, 511 U.S. 318 (1994).

Whether or not a suspect is in custody for purposes of *Miranda* is an objective determination, based on all of the components of the setting.[1076] It is determined on the basis of "how a reasonable person in the suspect's situation would perceive his circumstances."[1077] The "initial determination of custody depends on the objective circumstances of the interrogation, not on the subjective views harbored by either the interrogating officers or the person being questioned."[1078] In this regard, a "noncustodial setting," will not be transformed into a "custodial" one, even where the police investigation has focused on a particular suspect as a primary target.[1079]

In *Thompson v. Keohane*,[1080] the U.S. Supreme Court provided the following description of the *Miranda* custody test:

> Two discrete inquiries are essential to the determination: first, what were the circumstances surrounding the interrogation; and second, given those circumstances, would a reasonable person have felt he or she was not at liberty to terminate the interrogation and leave. Once the scene is set and the players' lines and actions are reconstructed, the court must apply an objective test to resolve the ultimate inquiry: was there a formal arrest or restraint on freedom of movement of the degree associated with a formal arrest.[1081]

Thus, in determining whether an interrogation is custodial requires an examination of all the circumstances surrounding the questioning. Among the factors courts will consider are: (1) the purpose of the questioning; (2) location, length, mood and mode of the questioning, and whether it was hostile or coercive; (3) the number of police officers present; (4) the presence or absence of family and friends of the individual; (5) any indicia of formal arrest or other signs of restraint, such as the show of weapons or force, physical restraint, booking or fingerprinting; (6) whether the suspect was informed that she was free to leave; (7) the manner by which the individual arrived at the place of questioning; (8) the age, intelligence, and mental makeup of the accused; (9) the intentions of the officers; and (10) the extent of knowledge of the officers and the focus of the investigation.[1082]

No single factor is determinative. Courts will examine and weigh these factors and then make an objective determination as to what a reasonable person would perceive if he were in the defendant's position.

In *State v. Hammonds*,[1083] the defendant was confined in a hospital due to a civil commitment order. While he was hospitalized under that order, two detectives questioned him about a recent armed robbery for "about an hour and a half" without informing him of his *Miranda* rights. The defendant made incriminating statements after being told the following:

> So let's think about Monday night again and what took place Monday evening, okay. All right. And then after we talk about this, we're going to get up and walk out and you can have your supper and you can watch some Christmas shows on TV and rest, okay. And we're going to go back to work and we're going to leave you alone.[1084]

[1076] *See State v. Hammonds*, 370 N.C. 158, 804 S.E.2d 438 (2017).

[1077] *Yarborough v. Alvarado*, 541 U.S. 652, 662, 124 S. Ct. 2140, 2148 (2004); *State v. Hammonds*, 370 N.C. 158, 804 S.E.2d 438 (2017).

[1078] *Stansbury v. California*, 511 U.S. 318, 323, 114 S. Ct. 1526, 1529 (1994).

[1079] *See Beckwith v. United States*, 425 U.S. 341, 347-47, 96 S. Ct. 1612, 1616 (1976); *see also Minnesota v. Murphy*, 465 U.S. 420, 431, 104 S. Ct. 1136, 1144 (1984) ("The mere fact that an investigation has focused on a suspect does not trigger the need for *Miranda* warnings in noncustodial settings."); *Stansbury v. California*, 511 U.S. 318, 323, 114 S. Ct. 1526, 1528-29 (1994) ("a police officer's subjective view that an individual under questioning is a suspect, if undisclosed, does not bear upon the question whether the individual is in custody for purposes of *Miranda*.").

[1080] *Thompson v. Keohane*, 516 U.S. 99, 116 S. Ct. 457 (1995).

[1081] *Thompson v. Keohane*, 516 U.S. 99, 112, 116 S. Ct. 457, 465 (1995).

[1082] *See also United States v. Booth*, 669 F.2d 1231 (9th Cir. 1981), where the Ninth Circuit further explained that in order to determine whether a person is "in custody" or has been significantly deprived of his freedom of action so as to trigger the requirement that *Miranda* warnings be given, courts will analyze "the totality of circumstances," specifically examining such pertinent factors as: (1) the duration of the detention; (2) the nature and degree of the pressure applied to detain the individual; (3) the physical surroundings of the questioning; and (4) the language used by the officer.

[1083] *State v. Hammonds*, 370 N.C. 158, 804 S.E.2d 438 (2017).

[1084] *State v. Hammonds*, 370 N.C. 158, 166, 804 S.E.2d 438 (2017).

After considering the totality of the circumstances, the North Carolina Supreme Court concluded that "these statements, made to a suspect whose freedom is already severely restricted because of an involuntary commitment, would lead a reasonable person in this position to believe he was not 'at liberty to terminate the interrogation' without first answering his interrogators' questions about his suspected criminal activity."[1085] Therefore, the defendant was in custody for purposes of *Miranda* and the failure of police to advise him of his rights under *Miranda* rendered his incriminating statements inadmissible. Accordingly, the defendant's conviction was vacated.[1086]

8.2.2.2. A motor vehicle stop is not *Miranda* custody

"Custody," for purposes of *Miranda*, "is a term of art that specifies circumstances that are thought generally to present a serious danger of coercion. In determining whether a person is in custody in this sense, the initial step is to ascertain whether, in light of 'the objective circumstances of the interrogation,' ... a 'reasonable person [would] have felt he or she was not at liberty to terminate the interrogation and leave.'"[1087]

"Determining whether an individual's freedom of movement was curtailed, however, is simply the first step in the analysis, not the last. Not all restraints on freedom of movement amount to custody for purposes of *Miranda*."[1088] In addition, there is the question of "whether the relevant environment presents the same inherently coercive pressures as the type of station house questioning at issue in *Miranda*."[1089]

Thus, in *Berkemer v. McCarty*,[1090] the Court held that the roadside questioning of a motorist who was pulled over in a routine traffic stop did not constitute custodial interrogation. In *Berkemer,* the Court did acknowledge that "a traffic stop significantly curtails the 'freedom of action' of the driver and the passengers," and that it is generally "a crime either to ignore a policeman's signal to stop one's car or, once having stopped, to drive away without permission." Indeed, "few motorists," noted the Court, "would feel free either to disobey a directive to pull over or to leave the scene of a traffic stop without being told they might do so."[1091] Nonetheless, the Court "held that a person detained as a result of a traffic stop is not in *Miranda* custody because such detention does not 'sufficiently impair [the detained person's] free exercise of his privilege against self-incrimination to require that he be warned of his constitutional rights.'"[1092]

Accordingly, "the temporary and relatively nonthreatening detention involved in a traffic stop or *Terry* stop ... does not constitute *Miranda* custody."[1093]

8.2.2.3. Stationhouse questioning

In *Oregon v. Mathiason*,[1094] the U.S. Supreme Court held that *Miranda* warnings *are not* required when law enforcement officers question a suspect who is not under arrest nor "in custody" when such questioning takes place within the confines of the police station house. According to the Court, "police officers are not required to administer *Miranda* warnings to everyone whom they question. Nor is the requirement of warnings to be imposed simply because the questioning takes place in the station house, or because the questioned person

---

[1085] *State v. Hammonds*, 370 N.C. 158, 166, 804 S.E.2d 438 (2017) (quoting *J.D.B. v. North Carolina*, 564 U.S. 261, 270, 131 S. Ct. 2394 (2011)).

[1086] *See also State v. Waring*, 364 N.C. 443, 701 S.E.2d 615 (2010); *State v. Garcia*, 358 N.C. 382, 597 S.E.2d 724 (2004); *State v. Buchanan*, 355 N.C. 264, 559 S.E.2d 785 (2002) (finding custody where interrogators accompanied the defendant to the bathroom, with an officer staying with him at all times).

[1087] *Howes v. Fields*, 565 U.S. 499, 132 S. Ct. 1181, 1189 (2012) (citations omitted).

[1088] *Howes v. Fields*, 565 U.S. 499, 132 S. Ct. 1181, 1189 (2012).

[1089] *Howes v. Fields*, 565 U.S. 499, 132 S. Ct. 1181, 1189 (2012).

[1090] *Berkemer v. McCarty*, 468 U.S. 420, 104 S. Ct. 3138 (1984).

[1091] *Berkemer v. McCarty*, 468 U.S. 420, 436, 104 S. Ct. 3138, 3149 (1984).

[1092] *Howes v. Fields*, 565 U.S. 499, 132 S. Ct. 1181, 1190 (2012) (quoting *Berkemer v. McCarty,* 468 U.S. 420, 437, 104 S. Ct. 3138, 3151 (1984)).

[1093] *Maryland v. Shatzer*, 559 U.S. 98, 130 S. Ct. 1213, 1224 (2010); *see also Pennsylvania v. Bruder*, 488 U.S. 9, 109 S. Ct. 205, 206 (1988) (persons temporarily detained during an ordinary motor vehicle stop are not in custody for purposes of *Miranda*). *See also State v. Brooks*, 337 N.C. 132, 446 S.E.2d 579 (1994).

[1094] *Oregon v. Mathiason*, 429 U.S. 492, 97 S. Ct. 711 (1977).

is one whom the police suspect. *Miranda* warnings are required only where there has been such a restriction on a person's freedom as to render him 'in custody.'"[1095]

In *California v. Beheler*,[1096] the U.S. Supreme Court similarly held that "*Miranda* warnings are not required simply because the questioning takes place in the station house, or because the questioned person is one whom the police suspect." Rather, the police "are required to give *Miranda* warnings only where there has been such a restriction on a person's freedom as to render him *in custody.*"

In *State v. Garcia*,[1097] the defendant was transported to the police station at his own request. "[D]efendant's conversation was polite, lighthearted, and casual while en route to the police station. Upon arrival, he was free to move about unescorted to get a drink of water from the fountain. Thereafter, defendant was asked to wait in an unlocked interview room. A plain-clothed, unarmed officer conducted defendant's interview. At no time did either party raise his voice. Defendant was not threatened in any way, and no promises were made to him. He was not handcuffed at any time preceding, during, or immediately following the interview."[1098] The North Carolina Supreme Court held that the defendant was not in custody for purposes of *Miranda*.

8.2.2.4. Hospital settings

Generally, there is no *per se* rule for hospitals in a *Miranda* custody inquiry. Each case must be decided on its own facts. The majority approach, however, as stated in *State v. Pontbriand*, is that "the restraint on freedom of movement incumbent in hospitalization does not, on its own, constitute custody for *Miranda* purposes."[1099] Thus, in *Pontbriand*, the Court considered the defendant's "illness and medical confinement only to the extent that, as part of the totality of the circumstances surrounding the interview, they would impact a reasonable person's belief that he or she was actually in police custody, unable to leave or refuse to answer police questioning."[1100]

In *State v. Sweatt*,[1101] the statements the defendant made in a hospital treatment room were properly admitted at trial. There, the defendant had been injured in a high-speed automobile crash. The North Carolina Supreme Court noted that there were no police guards placed at the defendant's door to confine him to the hospital. Because there were "no overt actions of the officers themselves which show actual custody,"[1102] *Miranda* warnings were not required.

8.2.2.5. When the suspect is a juvenile, age should be taken into account

In *J.D.B. v. North Carolina*,[1103] the U.S. Supreme Court held that the *Miranda* custody analysis includes consideration of a juvenile suspect's age. "[S]o long as the child's age was known to the officer at the time of police questioning, or would have been objectively apparent to a reasonable officer, its inclusion in the custody analysis is consistent with the objective nature of that test. This is not to say that a child's age will be a determinative, or even a significant, factor in every case."[1104] "Just as police officers are competent to account for other objective circumstances that are a matter of degree such as the length of questioning or

---

[1095] *Oregon v. Mathiason*, 429 U.S. 492, 97 S. Ct. 711, 714 (1977).

[1096] *California v. Beheler*, 463 U.S. 1121, 103 S. Ct. 3517 (1983).

[1097] *State v. Garcia*, 358 N.C. 382, 597 S.E.2d 724 (2004).

[1098] *State v. Garcia*, 358 N.C. 382, 397, 597 S.E.2d 724 (2004).

[1099] *State v. Pontbriand*, 2005 VT 20 ¶14, 178 Vt. 120, 126, 878 A2d 227, 231 ("[C]ustody is not established merely because a suspect is unable to leave the hospital due to his or her medical condition.") (citing *United States v. Robertson*, 19 F.3d 1318, 1321 (10th Cir. 1994) (hospitalized suspect not in custody where officers did not restrict his freedom of movement through physical restraint or display of authority); *United States v. Martin*, 781 F.2d 671, 673 (9th Cir. 1985) (hospitalized suspect not in custody where police were not responsible for hospitalization and did not unnecessarily extend it); *Commonwealth v. Ellis*, 379 Pa. Super. 337, 549 A.2d 1323, 1333 (Pa. Super. Ct. 1988) (holding that appellant was not in custody for Miranda purposes where police officer questioned him while he awaited treatment in hospital emergency room).

[1100] *State v. Pontbriand*, 2005 VT 20 ¶14, 178 Vt. 120, 126, 878 A2d 227, 232.

[1101] *State v. Sweatt*, 333 N.C. 407, 427 S.E.2d 112 (1993).

[1102] *State v. Sweatt*, 333 N.C. 407, 418, 427 S.E.2d 112 (1993).

[1103] *J.D.B. v. North Carolina*, 564 U.S. 261, 131 S. Ct. 2394 (2011).

[1104] *J.D.B. v. North Carolina*, 564 U.S. 261, 131 S. Ct. 2394, 2406 (2011) (citing, for example, teenagers nearing age 18).

the number of officers present, so too are they competent to evaluate the effect of relative age....In short, officers and judges need no imaginative powers, knowledge of developmental psychology, training in cognitive science, or expertise in social and cultural anthropology to account for a child's age. They simply need the common sense to know that a 7-year-old is not a 13-year-old and neither is an adult."[1105]

8.2.2.6. Prison custody is not *Miranda* custody

In *Howes v. Fields*,[1106] the Supreme Court rejected the idea that a prison inmate is *always* "in custody" within the meaning of *Miranda* whenever he is taken aside and questioned about events that occurred outside the prison walls.

The prisoner, Randall Fields, while serving a sentence in Michigan, "was escorted by a corrections officer to a conference room where two sheriff's deputies questioned him about allegations that, before he came to prison, he had engaged in sexual conduct with a 12-year-old boy."[1107] Fields was questioned for over five hours. "At the beginning of the interview, Fields was told that he was free to leave and return to his cell"; that he "could leave whenever he wanted." He was not handcuffed and the door to the conference room was sometimes open and sometimes shut. Fields eventually confessed to engaging in sex acts with the boy.

Ruling that Fields was not in *Miranda* custody, the Court emphasized that the questioning of a prisoner is *not always* custodial "when the prisoner is removed from the general prison population and questioned about events that occurred outside the prison."[1108] On the contrary, the Court has repeatedly declined to adopt any such categorical rule. For example, in *Maryland v. Shatzer*,[1109] the U.S. Supreme Court determined that an inmate's return to the general prison population after an actual custodial interrogation constituted a break in "*Miranda* custody." Clearly, if "a break in custody can occur while a prisoner is serving an uninterrupted term of imprisonment, it must follow that imprisonment alone is not enough to create a custodial situation within the meaning of *Miranda*."[1110]

Accordingly, when a prisoner is questioned, "the determination of custody should focus on all of the features of the interrogation. These include the language that is used in summoning the prisoner to the interview and the manner in which the interrogation is conducted." In this case, Fields was "not taken into custody for purposes of *Miranda*."

8.2.3. What constitutes interrogation?

8.2.3.1. General aspects

One of the many recurring problems in this area is the question of what particular type of police conduct constitutes "interrogation." *Miranda* suggested that "interrogation" referred only to actual "questioning initiated by law enforcement officers."[1111] But what of the concern about the coerciveness of the "interrogation environment"? There are times that the creative and inventive officer may overpower the will of the individual questioned *without asking any questions whatsoever*. It is this type of "psychological ploy" which necessarily undermines the privilege against compulsory self-incrimination, and such ploys may thereby be treated as the "functional equivalent" of interrogation.

Interestingly, to determine whether an interrogation has taken place, the first question to ask is not, "What did the officer say or do?" That question comes second. The first question is: "At what stage of the criminal proceedings is the officer-defendant interaction occurring?" The answer to this question is critical for it may change the definition of the term "interrogation." Indeed, under the law of some states, it may even determine whether a criminal defendant may be questioned at all.

[1105] *J.D.B. v. North Carolina*, 564 U.S. 261, 131 S. Ct. 2394, 2407 (2011).

[1106] *Howes v. Fields*, 565 U.S. 499, 132 S. Ct. 1181 (2012).

[1107] *Howes v. Fields*, 565 U.S. 499, 132 S. Ct. 1181, 1185 (2012).

[1108] *Howes v. Fields*, 565 U.S. 499, 132 S. Ct. 1181, 1187 (2012).

[1109] *Maryland v. Shatzer*, 559 U.S. 98, 130 S. Ct. 1213 (2010).

[1110] *Howes v. Fields*, 565 U.S. 499, 132 S. Ct. 1181, 1190 (2012).

[1111] *Miranda v. Arizona*, 384 U.S. 436, 444, 86 S. Ct. 1602, 1612 (1966).

In determining the stage of the criminal proceedings in which the officer-defendant interaction is occurring, there are two time periods with which to be concerned. The first covers those events occurring *prior* to the initiation of formal criminal charges. The second time period begins at the initiation of formal charges and continues at least through trial. Once formal criminal charges have been initiated, any confrontational law-enforcement procedure involving the defendant (for example, an in-person lineup or an interrogation) is generally called a "critical stage" in the prosecution. The term "critical stage" is used because, at the moment formal criminal charges are initiated, the defendant's Sixth Amendment right to counsel attaches.

Thus, any law enforcement procedures involving a particular defendant that occur prior to the initiation of formal charges take place in what the courts call the "Fifth-Amendment setting." Procedures occurring after formal charges take place in the "Sixth-Amendment setting."

For purposes of defining the term "interrogation" in a Fifth-Amendment setting, the focus will be upon the perceptions of the suspect, rather than on the intent or design of the police. The critical question will be whether the police used any words or actions that they *knew or should have known* were "reasonably likely to elicit an incriminating response from the suspect."[1112] In the Sixth-Amendment setting, the focus is upon the intent or design of the police, and the critical question will be whether officers *deliberately elicited* incriminating information from a defendant in the absence of counsel after a formal charge against the defendant had been filed.[1113]

8.2.3.2. The Fifth-Amendment setting

In *Miranda*, the Court defined "custodial interrogation" as "*questioning* initiated by law enforcement officers after a person has been taken into custody or otherwise deprived of his freedom of action in any significant way." Here, the concern was that the "interrogation environment" created by the interplay of interrogation and custody would "subjugate the individual to the will of his examiner" and thereby undermine the privilege against compulsory self-incrimination.

In *Rhode Island v. Innis*,[1114] the Supreme Court addressed the police use of a psychological ploy to prompt an admission from a suspect after his arrest but before any formal charges had been filed (a time period known as the "Fifth-Amendment" setting). Since there was no direct questioning of the suspect, the Court examined whether the suspect's incriminating response, in this Fifth-Amendment setting, was or was not the product of "any words or actions on the part of the police (other than those normally attendant to arrest and custody) that the *police should know are (or should have known were) reasonably likely to elicit an incriminating response from the suspect.*"[1115] "Incriminating response" refers to "any response—whether inculpatory or exculpatory—that the prosecution may seek to introduce at trial." The *reasonably-likely-to-elicit standard* thus "focuses primarily upon the perceptions of the suspect, rather than the intent of the police." This focus reflects the fact that the *Miranda* safeguards were designed to vest a suspect in custody with an added measure of protection against coercive police practices, without regard to objective proof of the underlying intent of the police. A practice that the police should know is reasonably likely to evoke an incriminating response from a suspect thus amounts to interrogation.

In *Innis*, the police were investigating the murder of a taxicab driver. He had died from what appeared to be a shotgun blast to the back of his head. The day after the driver's body was found, the police received a call from another taxicab driver reporting that he had just been robbed by a "man wielding a sawed-off shotgun." After the driver identified the defendant from a photo line-up, the police began searching for him.

Within a few hours, the defendant was spotted, arrested, and advised of his *Miranda* rights. The defendant stated that he understood his rights and wanted to speak to an attorney. The officers then placed the defendant in a "caged wagon," a four-door police car with a wire screen mesh between the front and rear seats, and drove him to headquarters. During the ride to the police station, the following conversation took place among the officers:

[1112] *Rhode Island v. Innis*, 446 U.S. 291, 301, 100 S. Ct. 1682, 1689-90 (1980).

[1113] *Massiah v. United States*, 377 U.S. 201, 206, 84 S. Ct. 1199, 1203 (1964).

[1114] *Rhode Island v. Innis*, 446 U.S. 291, 100 S. Ct. 1682 (1980).

[1115] *Rhode Island v. Innis*, 446 U.S. 291, 100 S. Ct. 1682, 1689-90 (1980) (emphasis added).

I frequent this area while on patrol and there's a lot of handicapped children running around in this area, and God forbid one of them might find a weapon with shells and they might hurt themselves ... it would be too bad if the little girl would pick up the gun, maybe kill herself.

Defendant then interrupted the conversation and requested that the officers turn the patrol car around so he could show them where the gun was located. Defendant stated that he understood his rights, but he "wanted to get the gun out of the way because of the kids in the area in the school." The defendant then directed the police to a nearby field and pointed out the hidden shotgun.

According to the Court, because the defendant's incriminating response was not the product of words or actions of the police that they *should have known were reasonably likely to elicit an incriminating response*, their actions did not constitute "interrogation" within the meaning of *Miranda*.[1116]

In *State v. Hensley*,[1117] Detective Enoch's attempts to manipulate the defendant into making an incriminating statement amounted to an interrogation. There, Detective Enoch had cultivated a positive relationship with the defendant, who he was investigating with respect to allegations of a sexual offense. Detective Enoch was scheduled to meet with the defendant when he discovered that the defendant was in the intensive care unit at the hospital after an attempted overdose. The next day, Detective Enoch went to the hospital to serve arrest warrants on the defendant and to take him into custody. "When defendant was ready to be released from the hospital, Detective Enoch took defendant into custody. Detective Enoch testified that defendant seemed 'a little weak' and 'a little medicated,' enough so that Detective Enoch had to help defendant into his patrol car. Detective Enoch did not advise defendant of his *Miranda* rights when he took him into custody. Detective Enoch transported defendant to the Sheriff's Department. While waiting for defendant to be released from the hospital and on the way to the Sheriff's Department, Detective Enoch and defendant had '[a] lot of casual conversation.'"[1118] On the way to the police station, Detective Enoch told the defendant that their conversation would not be "on the record," but then moved the conversation toward the investigation. Detective Enoch then let the defendant know that Enoch was "in trouble" with his wife for coming to work on a Saturday and asked the defendant if he would agree to speak with him the next day. In response, the defendant made the following statement: "'Mike I do not want you to think that I am a bad person, but I do not find anything sexual about children, but I was drinking very heavily and smoking pot and I guess the combination of the two will make a guy do something he normally would not do[.]'"[1119]

The Court of Appeals of North Carolina held that "Detective Enoch 'should have known' his conduct was likely to elicit an incriminating response from defendant."[1120] Especially because "Detective Enoch knew that defendant was peculiarly susceptible to an appeal to defendant's relationship with Detective Enoch from his previous interviews and dealings with defendant."[1121] "However, more importantly, Detective Enoch knew that defendant was still under the effects of the attempted overdose on prescription medication and alcohol and would therefore be peculiarly susceptible to persuasion."[1122] Accordingly, the defendant was subjected to an interrogation by Detective Enoch and entitled to *Miranda* warnings.[1123]

8.2.3.2.1. Providing information about the crime

In general, an officer's statements that provide a defendant with information about the charges against him, about inculpatory evidence located by the police, or about statements made by witnesses or codefendants, which allow a defendant to make an informed and intelligent reassessment of his decision whether to speak to the police, do not constitute interrogation.

[1116] *Rhode Island v. Innis*, 446 U.S. 291, 100 S. Ct. 1682, 1691 (1980). *See also State v. Golphin,* 352 N.C. 364, 406, 533 S.E.2d 168, 199 (2000).

[1117] *State v. Hensley*, 201 N.C. App. 607, 687 S.E.2d 309 (2010).

[1118] *State v. Hensley*, 201 N.C. App. 607, 611, 687 S.E.2d 309 (2010).

[1119] *State v. Hensley*, 201 N.C. App. 607, 611, 687 S.E.2d 309 (2010).

[1120] *State v. Hensley*, 201 N.C. App. 607, 616, 687 S.E.2d 309 (2010).

[1121] *State v. Hensley*, 201 N.C. App. 607, 616-17, 687 S.E.2d 309 (2010).

[1122] *State v. Hensley*, 201 N.C. App. 607, 617, 687 S.E.2d 309 (2010).

[1123] *See also State v. McQueen,* 324 N.C. 118, 127, 377 S.E.2d 38, 44 (1989); *State v. Vick*, 341 N.C. 569, 461 S.E.2d 655 (1995); *State v. Forney*, 310 N.C. 126, 310 S.E.2d 20 (1984).

8.2.3.2.2. Consent searches

As a general rule, a police officer's request for consent to search a particular area is not "interrogation" within the meaning of *Miranda*, and an individual's subsequent response granting or denying consent is not "testimonial" for purposes of the Fifth Amendment privilege against self-incrimination.[1124]

8.2.3.3. The Sixth-Amendment setting

In this setting, the courts apply a stricter approach to define "interrogation." The question is whether the police "deliberately elicited" incriminating statements.

8.2.3.3.1. The "Christian Burial" case

In *Brewer v. Williams*,[1125] the famous "Christian Burial" case, the Supreme Court held that, in this "Sixth-Amendment setting," defendant Williams was "interrogated" in violation of his Sixth Amendment right to counsel.

The facts unfolded on the afternoon of December 24, when 10-year-old Pamela Powers went with her family to the YMCA in Des Moines, Iowa, to watch a wrestling tournament in which her brother was participating. When she failed to return from a trip to the washroom, an unsuccessful search for her began.

Robert Williams, who had recently escaped from a mental hospital, was a resident of the YMCA. Soon after the girl's disappearance, Williams was seen leaving the YMCA carrying some clothing and a large bundle wrapped in a blanket. He placed the large bundle in his car and drove off. His abandoned car was found the following day in Davenport, Iowa, roughly 160 miles east of Des Moines. A warrant was then issued in Des Moines for his arrest on a charge of abduction.

On the morning of December 26, acting on the advice of an attorney, Williams turned himself in to the Davenport police, where he was booked on the charge specified in the arrest warrant. After advising Williams of his *Miranda* rights, the Davenport police telephoned representatives of the Des Moines Police Department and advised them that Williams had surrendered. At the time, Williams' attorney was still at Des Moines police headquarters. The attorney spoke with Williams on the telephone and, in the presence of a police detective named Leaming, the attorney advised Williams that Des Moines police officers would be driving to Davenport to pick him up, that the officers would not interrogate him or mistreat him, and that Williams was not to talk to the officers about Pamela Powers until after consulting with him upon his return to Des Moines. Detective Leaming and a fellow officer would be driving to Davenport to pick up Williams. Prior to the trip, Williams was arraigned before a judge in Davenport on the outstanding arrest warrant. (This started the Sixth-Amendment setting.).

Detective Leaming and his fellow officer arrived in Davenport at about noon to pick up Williams and return him to Des Moines. The two detectives, along with Williams, then set out on the 160-mile drive. Leaming knew that Williams was a former mental patient and knew also that he was deeply religious. Not long after leaving Davenport and reaching the interstate highway, Detective Leaming addressed Williams as "Reverend," and said:

> I want to give you something to think about while we're traveling down the road....Number one, I want you to observe the weather conditions, it's raining, it's sleeting, it's freezing, driving is very treacherous, visibility is poor, it's going to be dark early this evening. They are predicting several inches of snow for tonight, and I feel that you yourself are the only person that knows where this little girl's body is, that you yourself have only been there once, and if you get a snow on top of it, you yourself may be unable to find it. And, since we will be going right past the area on the way into Des Moines, I feel that we could stop and locate the body, that the parents of this little girl should be entitled to a

---

[1124] *United States v. Glenna*, 878 F.2d 967, 971 (7th Cir. 1989); *see also United States v. LeGrone*, 43 F.3d 332 (7th Cir. 1994) ("[B]ecause requesting consent to search is not likely to elicit an incriminating statement, such questioning is not interrogation, and thus *Miranda* warnings are not required."); *Cody v. Solem*, 755 F.2d 1323, 1330 (8th Cir. 1985) ("Simply put, a consent to search is not an incriminating statement."); *Smith v. Wainwright*, 581 F.2d 1149, 1152 (5th Cir. 1978) ("A consent to search is not a self-incriminating statement."); *United States v. Lemon*, 550 F.2d 467, 472 (9th Cir. 1977) ("A consent to search is not the type of incriminating statement toward which the fifth amendment is directed. It is not in itself 'evidence of a testimonial or communicative nature.'").

[1125] *Brewer v. Williams*, 430 U.S. 387, 97 S. Ct. 1232 (1977).

Christian burial for the little girl who was snatched away from them on Christmas Eve and murdered. And I feel we should stop and locate it on the way in, rather than waiting until morning and trying to come back out after a snow storm and possibly not being able to find it at all.[1126]

As they continued towards Des Moines, just as they approached Mitchellville, Williams said that he would show the officers where the body was. He then directed the police to the body of Pamela Powers.

Holding that Williams was "interrogated," the Court said: The police detective "deliberately and design-edly set out to elicit information from Williams just as surely as—and perhaps more effectively than—if he had formally interrogated him." The detective's "Christian burial speech" was "tantamount to interrogation." Because the detective did not obtain from Williams a waiver of his right to counsel prior to that "interroga-tion," neither Williams' incriminating statements themselves nor any testimony describing his having led the police to the victim's body can constitutionally be admitted into evidence.[1127]

Once adversary judicial proceedings have been initiated against the defendant and the right to counsel has attached, it is at this point in the proceedings that "the government has committed itself to prosecute," and "the adverse positions of the government and the defendant have solidified."[1128]

8.2.3.3.2. After indictment

In *Patterson v. Illinois*,[1129] the Supreme Court held that the police are not barred from initiating communication, exchanges, or conversations with a defendant whose Sixth Amendment right to counsel has arisen with his indict-ment. Such a defendant should not be equated with a preindictment suspect who, while being questioned, asserts his Fifth Amendment right to counsel which would bar further questioning of such suspect unless he initiates the meeting. The mere fact that a defendant's Sixth Amendment right to counsel "came into existence with his indict-ment, *i.e.*, that he had such a right at the time of his questioning, does not distinguish him from the preindictment interrogatee whose right to counsel is in existence and available for his exercise while he is questioned." Like the preindictment setting, the request for an attorney in the post-indictment setting would also prohibit the police from any further questioning unless the accused himself initiates further communication. Here, the Court also held that the *Miranda* warnings were adequate, in a Sixth Amendment, post-indictment setting, to sufficiently apprise an accused of the nature of his Sixth Amendment rights and the consequences of abandoning them.

In *Michigan v. Harvey*,[1130] the Court observed

Although a defendant may sometimes later regret his decision to speak with police, the Sixth Amend-ment does not disable a criminal defendant from exercising his free will. To hold that a defendant is inherently incapable of relinquishing his right to counsel once it is invoked would be "to imprison a man in his privileges and call it the Constitution."[1131]

8.2.3.3.3. When the right to counsel attaches

The Sixth Amendment provides that, "[i]n all *prosecutions,* the accused shall enjoy the right [to] have the Assistance of Counsel for his defence."[1132] As the Supreme Court has explained, the Sixth Amendment right

---

[1126] *Brewer v. Williams,* 430 U.S. 387, 392-93, 97 S. Ct. 1232 (1977).

[1127] *See also Fellers v. United States,* 540 U.S. 519, 524, 124 S. Ct. 1019, 1022 (2004) (reaffirming application of the "deliberate-elicitation standard" for Sixth Amendment cases) (citing *United States v. Henry,* 447 U.S. 264, 270, 100 S. Ct. 2183 (1980)) ("The question here is whether under the facts of this case a Government agent 'deliberately elicited' incriminating state-ments"). The *Fellers* Court also "expressly distinguished this standard from the Fifth Amendment custodial-interrogation standard." *See id.,* 124 S. Ct. at 1023 (citing *Rhode Island v. Innis,* 446 U.S. 291, 100 S. Ct. 1682 (1980)).

[1128] *See Brewer v. Williams,* 430 U.S. 387, 97 S. Ct. 1232 (1977); *Maine v. Moulton,* 474 U.S. 159, 175, 106 S. Ct. 477 (1985).

[1129] *Patterson v. Illinois,* 487 U.S. 285, 108 S. Ct. 2389 (1988).

[1130] *Michigan v. Harvey,* 494 U.S. 344, 110 S. Ct. 1176 (1990).

[1131] *Michigan v. Harvey,* 494 U.S. 344, 110 S. Ct. 1176, 1182 (1990) (quoting *Adams v. United States ex rel. McCann,* 317 U.S. 269, 280, 63 S. Ct. 236, 242 (1942)).

[1132] U.S. Const. amend. VI (emphasis added). Note that the, spelling of "defence" is from the original document. "Defence" = British English; "defense" = American English.

to counsel "is limited by its terms," and therefore, "it does not attach until a prosecution is commenced."[1133] Commencement of prosecution, for purposes of the attachment of the right to counsel, has been tied to "the initiation of adversary judicial criminal proceedings—whether by way of formal charge, preliminary hearing, indictment, information, or arraignment."[1134] These pretrial proceedings are often considered to be "critical" stages because "the results might well settle the accused's fate and reduce the trial itself to a mere formality."[1135] Thus, at the earliest, "[a] defendant's right to rely on counsel as a 'medium' between the defendant and the State attaches upon the initiation of formal charges."[1136]

In *Rothgery v. Gillespie County, Texas*,[1137] the Court clarified that a defendant's right to counsel, guaranteed by the Sixth Amendment, attaches "at the first appearance before a judicial officer at which a defendant is told of the formal accusation against him and restrictions are imposed on his liberty."[1138] Moreover, the attachment of the right does not require that a public prosecutor be aware of that initial proceeding or involved in its conduct.[1139]

Once the right has attached for a given charge, the suspect cannot be questioned about that charge without counsel present. This rule applies not only to law enforcement officers, but also any government agents who "deliberately elicit" incriminating statements (*e.g.* jailhouse informants). A suspect can, however, be questioned regarding other offenses for which the Sixth Amendment right has not yet attached without violating that provision.[1140]

In *State v. Taylor*,[1141] the North Carolina Supreme Court considered whether the issuance of an arrest warrant for first-degree murder alone is sufficient to trigger the Sixth Amendment right to counsel. There, the defendant was arrested and detained in Florida pending extradition to North Carolina on first-degree murder and robbery charges. The court concluded that the defendant's right to counsel did not attach at the issuance of the arrest warrant as "'the right to counsel exists to protect the accused during trial-type confrontations with the prosecutor'"[1142] and "[a]n arrest warrant for first-degree murder is not a sufficient charging document upon which a defendant can be tried."[1143]

8.3. *Miranda*

8.3.1. Administration; when to advise

In *Duckworth v. Eagan*,[1144] the Supreme Court observed that in *Miranda v. Arizona*,[1145] "the court established certain procedural safeguards that require police to advise criminal suspects of their rights under the Fifth and Fourteenth Amendments before commencing custodial interrogation. In now familiar words, the Court reminded that

[A suspect] must be warned prior to any questioning [1] that he has the right to remain silent, [2] that anything he says can be used against him in a court of law, [3] that he has the right to the presence

---

[1133] *Rothgery v. Gillespie County, Texas,* 554 U.S. 191, 198, 128 S. Ct. 2578 (2008) (quoting *McNeil v. Wisconsin*, 501 U.S. 171, 175, 111 S. Ct. 2204 (1991)).

[1134] *Rothgery v. Gillespie County, Texas,* 554 U.S. 191, 198, 128 S. Ct. 2578 (2008); *see also Kirby v. Illinois,* 406 U.S. 682, 689, 92 S. Ct. 1877, 1882 (1972).

[1135] *United States v. Wade,* 388 U.S. 218, 224, 87 S. Ct. 1926 (1967); *see also Powell v. Alabama,* 287 U.S. 45, 57, 53 S. Ct. 55 (1932) (stating that the right to counsel "during perhaps the most critical period of the proceedings"—that is, from the time of a criminal defendant's arraignment until the beginning of his trial—is as important "as the trial itself.").

[1136] *Michigan v. Harvey,* 494 U.S. 344, 353, 110 S. Ct. 1176, 1181 (1990).

[1137] *Rothgery v. Gillespie County, Texas,* 554 U.S. 191, 128 S. Ct. 2578 (2008).

[1138] *Rothgery v. Gillespie County, Texas,* 554 U.S. 191, 128 S. Ct. 2578, 2581 (2008).

[1139] *Rothgery v. Gillespie County, Texas,* 554 U.S. 191, 128 S. Ct. 2578 (2008).

[1140] *McNeil v. Wisconsin*, 501 U.S. 171, 111 S.Ct. 2204 (1991). Suspects can even be questioned regarding an offense which is "factually related" to the offense for which this right has been invoked, as long as the offenses are not the same for Double Jeopardy purposes. *Texas v. Cobb*, 532 U.S. 162, 173-74, 121 S. Ct. 1335, 1343 (2001).

[1141] *State v. Taylor*, 354 N.C. 28, 550 S.E.2d 141 (2001).

[1142] *State v. Taylor*, 354 N.C. 28, 36, 550 S.E.2d 141 (2001).

[1143] *State v. Taylor*, 354 N.C. 28, 36, 550 S.E.2d 141 (2001).

[1144] *Duckworth v. Eagan*, 492 U.S. 195, 109 S. Ct. 2875 (1989).

[1145] *Miranda v. Arizona*, 384 U.S. 436, 86 S. Ct. 1602 (1966).

of an attorney, and [4] that if he cannot afford an attorney one will be appointed for him prior to any questioning if he so desires."[1146]

While there is no requirement that a suspect be given the *Miranda* warnings verbatim,[1147] the "crucial test is whether the words in the context used, considering the age, background and intelligence of the individual being interrogated, impart a clear, understandable warning of all of his rights."[1148] "The inquiry is simply whether the warnings reasonably convey to a suspect his rights as required by *Miranda*."[1149]

In *Florida v. Powell*,[1150] the U.S. Supreme Court emphasized that, as a matter of law, an individual held for questioning "must be clearly informed that he has the right to consult with a lawyer *and to have the lawyer with him during interrogation*."[1151]

Miranda's third warning—the only one at issue here—has been held in subsequent cases to require, "as an absolute prerequisite to interrogation, that an individual held for questioning [] be clearly informed that he has the right to consult with a lawyer and *to have the lawyer with him during interrogation*."[1152]

8.3.1.1. When the administration of the *Miranda* warnings has become stale

Clearly, once *Miranda* warnings are given, they are "not to be accorded unlimited efficacy or perpetuity."[1153] But at the same time, a suspect need not be advised of his constitutional rights more than once unless the time of warning and the time of subsequent interrogation are too remote in time from one another. The cases do not require that the warnings be repeated after an interruption in the questioning.[1154]

The United States Supreme Court has confirmed this approach in *Wyrick v. Fields*,[1155] where the defendant was arrested on a rape charge and requested a polygraph examination. Prior to the polygraph examination, the defendant had waived his rights to have his attorney present and to remain silent. At the conclusion of the test, the examiner informed the defendant that the test revealed that the defendant had been deceitful. The examiner asked if the defendant wished to explain the results. The defendant then admitted to having sexual contact with the victim, but claimed it was consensual. The defendant sought to suppress these statements. The Supreme Court, in examining the "totality of the circumstances," noted that there was nothing to suggest that the completion of the test and the defendant's being asked to explain the results were significant enough occurrences to cause the defendant to immediately forget his rights under *Miranda* or render his statements involuntary. The Court held that the initial warning and waiver would still be valid, "unless the circumstances changed so seriously that [the suspect's] answers no longer were voluntary, or unless [the suspect] no longer was making a 'knowing and intelligent relinquishment or abandonment' of his rights."[1156]

Since the *Miranda* staleness issue involves an examination of the "totality of the circumstances," the amount of time that elapsed between the warning and subsequent interrogation is not the sole dispositive factor in determining whether there has been a violation of *Miranda*. A close examination of the issue reveals a lack of consistency across different jurisdictions. For example, some courts have required a re-advisement

---

[1146] *Duckworth v. Eagan*, 492 U.S. 195, 109 S. Ct. 2875, 2879 (1989) (quoting *Miranda v. Arizona*, 384 U.S. 436, 479, 86 S. Ct. 1602, 1630 (1966)).

[1147] *See California v. Prysock*, 453 U.S. 355, 359-60, 101 S. Ct. 2806 (1981) (stating that *Miranda* does not require a "talismanic incantation" of the warnings, but rather only the fully effective equivalent of such warnings).

[1148] *See Coyote v. United States*, 380 F.2d 305, 308 (10th Cir. 1967).

[1149] *Duckworth v. Eagan*, 492 U.S. 195, 203, 109 S. Ct. 2875, 2880 (1989) (internal quotes omitted).

[1150] *Florida v. Powell*, 559 U.S. 50, 130 S. Ct. 1195 (2010).

[1151] *Florida v. Powell*, 559 U.S. 50, 130 S. Ct. 1195, 1203 (2010) (emphasis added).

[1152] *Florida v. Powell*, 559 U.S. 50, 130 S. Ct. 1195, 1203 (2010) (emphasis added).

[1153] *United States v. Hopkins*, 433 F.2d 1041, 1045 (5th Cir. 1970).

[1154] *See, e.g., United States v. Edwards*, 581 F.3d 604, 606 (7th Cir. 2009); *United States v. Ferrer-Montoya*, 483 F.3d 565, 569 (8th Cir. 2007); *United States v. Rodriguez-Preciado*, 399 F.3d 1118, 1128-29 (9th Cir. 2005).

[1155] *Wyrick v. Fields*, 459 U.S. 42, 103 S. Ct. 394 (1982).

[1156] *Wyrick v. Fields*, 459 U.S. 42, 47, 103 S. Ct. 394, 396 (1982) (quoting *Edwards v. Arizona*, 451 U.S. 477, 483, 101 S.Ct. 1880, 1884 (1981)).

of *Miranda* rights after four hours,[1157] 18 hours,[1158] two days,[1159] and three days.[1160] While at the same time, other courts have held that a re-advisement was *not necessary* after several hours,[1161] three hours,[1162] five hours,[1163] nine hours,[1164] 12 hours,[1165] 15 hours,[1166] 17 hours,[1167] two days,[1168] three days,[1169] and all the way up to a week or more if law enforcement asks if the suspect remembers his rights.[1170]

The analysis is dependent upon the facts of a particular situation. For example, the following factors may be useful in determining whether the *Miranda* warnings have gone stale:

(1) the length of time between the giving of the first warnings and the subsequent interrogation[;] (2) whether the warnings and the subsequent interrogation were given in the same or different places[;] (3) whether the warnings were given and the subsequent interrogation conducted by the same or different officers[;] (4) the extent to which the subsequent statement differed from any previous statements[; and] (5) the apparent intellectual and emotional state of the suspect.[1171]

8.3.1.2. When a suspect becomes the "focus" or "target" of an investigation

In *Stansbury v. California*,[1172] the Supreme Court held that a person's right to receive *Miranda* warnings is *not* triggered when she becomes a suspect in, or the focus of, an officer's investigation. According to the Court, a law enforcement officer's obligation to administer *Miranda* warnings attaches *only* where there has been such a restriction on a person's freedom as to render her "in custody." A person's *Miranda* rights are not triggered by virtue of the fact that he has become the focus of an officer's suspicions. Case law "makes clear, in no uncertain terms, that any inquiry into whether the interrogating officers have focused their suspicions upon the individual being questioned (assuming those suspicions remain undisclosed) is not relevant for purposes of *Miranda*."[1173]

8.3.1.3. On the scene questioning

Miranda warnings are not required before general, on-the-scene questions intended to investigate the facts surrounding an apparent crime.[1174] "In determining whether specific questions constitute custodial interrogation or general on-the-scene questioning, [North Carolina courts have] found the following factors

---

[1157] *People v. Sanchez*, 88 Misc. 2d 929, 391 N.Y.S.2d 513 (1977).

[1158] *United States v. Jones*, 147 F. Supp. 2d 752 (E.D. Mich. 2001).

[1159] *Franklin v. State*, 6 Md. App. 572, 252 A.2d 487 (1969).

[1160] *People v. Quirk*, 129 Cal. App. 3d 618, 181 Cal. Rptr. 301 (1982).

[1161] *United States v. Diaz*, 814 F.2d 454, 460 and n. 6 (7th Cir. 1987) (Here, the warnings were given at the hotel where Diaz was arrested, and his inculpatory statements came during the subsequent booking).

[1162] *Jarrell v. Balkcom*, 735 F.2d 1242, 1253-54 (11th Cir. 1984).

[1163] *Stumes* v. Solem, 752 F.2d 317, 320 (8th Cir. 1985).

[1164] *United States ex rel. Henne v. Fike*, 563 F.2d 809, 813-14 (7th Cir. 1977).

[1165] *Commonwealth v. Wideman*, 460 Pa. 699, 334 A.2d 594, 598-99 (Pa. 1975).

[1166] *People v. Dela Pena*, 72 F.3d 767, 769-70 (9th Cir. 1995).

[1167] *State v. Myers*, 345 A.2d 500 (Me. 1975).

[1168] *Babcock v. State*, 473 S.W.2d 941 (Tex. Crim. App. 1971).

[1169] *Maguire v. United States*, 396 F.2d 327 (9th Cir. 1968); *Johnson v. State*, 56 Ala. App. 583, 324 So. 2d 298 (1975).

[1170] *Martin v. Wainwright*, 770 F.2d 918 (11th Cir. 1985), *modified on denial of rehearing*, 781 F.2d 185 (11th Cir. 1986); *Biddy v. Diamond*, 516 F.2d 118 (5th Cir. 1975).

[1171] *State v. Miah S.*, 290 Neb. 607, 618, 861 N.W.2d 406, 415 (2015) (quoting *State v. McZorn*, 288 N.C. 417, 43 4, 219 S.E.2d 201, 212 (1975)), *judgment vacated in part*, 428 U.S. 904, 96 S. Ct. 3210 (1976); *see also State v. DeWeese*, 213 W. Va. 339, 582 S.E.2d 786 (2003).

[1172] *Stansbury v. California*, 511 U.S. 318, 114 S. Ct. 1526 (1994).

[1173] *See also Beckwith v. United States*, 425 U.S. 341, 347-047, 96 S. Ct. 1612, 1616 (1976) (A "noncustodial setting," will not be transformed into a "custodial" one, even where the police investigation has focused on a particular suspect as a primary target); *Minnesota v. Murphy*, 465 U.S. 420, 431, 104 S. Ct. 1136, 1144 (1984) ("The mere fact that an investigation has focused on a suspect does not trigger the need for *Miranda* warnings in noncustodial settings.").

[1174] *See Miranda v. Arizona*, 384 U.S. 436, 477, 86 S. Ct. 1602, 1629 (1966).

to be relevant: (1) the nature of the interrogator, (2) the time and place of the interrogation, (3) the degree to which suspicion had been focused on the defendant, (4) the nature of the interrogation and (5) the extent to which defendant was restrained or free to leave. While none of the factors standing alone is determinative, each factor is relevant."[1175]

8.3.2. *Miranda* and motor vehicle offenses

There is no requirement that a law enforcement officer administer *Miranda* warnings during the course of a traffic stop where the officer temporarily detains a motorist in order to ask a few brief questions and issue a traffic citation. As held in *Berkemer v. McCarty*,[1176] an ordinary traffic stop, by its very nature "is presumptively temporary and brief," lasting "only a few minutes."[1177] It generally involves no more than a check of credentials and issuance of citations for violations observed. Therefore, "persons temporarily detained pursuant to such stops are not 'in custody' for the purposes of *Miranda*."[1178]

Recall that officers need only administer the *Miranda* warnings prior to "custodial" interrogation. In *McCarty*, the defendant was not "in custody" until "he was formally placed under arrest and instructed to get into the police car." Here, the Court noted that a traffic stop significantly curtails the "freedom of action" of the driver and the passengers, if any, of the detained vehicle. Moreover, under the Fourth Amendment, the stopping of a motor vehicle and the detaining of its occupants is a "seizure" which requires a constitutional justification. But, this temporary stop, like the *Terry* stop, does not constitute "custody" for purposes of *Miranda*.

As in the case of the typical *Terry* stop, which is not subject to the dictates of *Miranda*, the similarly noncoercive aspect of ordinary traffic stops prompted the Court to hold that "persons temporarily detained pursuant to such stops are not 'in custody' for the purposes of *Miranda*."[1179]

It also has been held that when a drunk-driving suspect slurs his speech and exhibits a lack of muscular coordination in response to custodial police questioning, those responses are not "testimonial" in nature such that, if elicited in the absence of *Miranda* warnings, they will be deemed inadmissible.[1180] In this regard, a DUI defendant's responses to custodial police questioning "are not rendered inadmissible by *Miranda* merely because the slurred nature of his speech was incriminating. The physical inability to articulate words in a clear manner due to 'the lack of muscular coordination of his tongue and mouth'... is not itself a testimonial component of [an intoxicated motorist's] responses to [an officer's] questions."[1181]

The "sixth birthday" question. During Muniz's traffic stop, he was asked, "Do you know what the date was of your sixth birthday?" The Court held that Muniz's answer constituted a "testimonial response," and "was incriminating, not just because of his delivery, but also because of his answer's *content*." One could infer from an intoxicated motorist's answer (that he did not *know* the proper date) that his mental state was confused.

Here, "the incriminating inference of impaired mental faculties stemmed, not just from the fact that Muniz slurred his response, but also from a testimonial aspect of that response."[1182] Accordingly, because "Muniz's response to the sixth birthday question was testimonial, the response should have been suppressed."[1183]

8.3.2.1. The routine "booking question" exception to *Miranda*

In *Muniz*, the Supreme Court also held that an in-custody accused's responses to routine booking questions, such as, "What is your name? Address? Height? Weight? Eye color? Date of birth? and Current age?" need not be suppressed when asked without prior administration of *Miranda* warnings. While such questions may involve "custodial interrogation," within the meaning of *Miranda*, the responses to such questions in

---

[1175] *State v. Crudup*, 157 N.C. App. 657, 660-61, 580 S.E.2d 21 (2003) (citing *State v. Clay*, 39 N.C. App. 150, 155, 249 S.E.2d 843, 846-47 (1978), *rev'd on other grounds by* 297 N.C. 555, 256 S.E.2d 176 (1979)).
[1176] *Berkemer v. McCarty*, 468 U.S. 420, 104 S. Ct. 3138 (1984).
[1177] *Berkemer v. McCarty*, 468 U.S. 420, 104 S. Ct. 3138, 3149 (1984).
[1178] *Berkemer v. McCarty*, 468 U.S. 420, 104 S. Ct. 3138, 3151 (1984).
[1179] *See also Pennsylvania v. Bruder*, 488 U.S. 9, 109 S. Ct. 205 (1988).
[1180] *Pennsylvania v. Muniz*, 496 U.S. 582, 110 S. Ct. 2638 (1990).
[1181] *Pennsylvania v. Muniz*, 496 U.S. 582, 110 S. Ct. 2638, 2644-45 (1990).
[1182] *Pennsylvania v. Muniz*, 496 U.S. 582, 110 S. Ct. 2638, 2649 (1990).
[1183] *Pennsylvania v. Muniz*, 496 U.S. 582, 110 S. Ct. 2638 (1990).

the absence of *Miranda* "are nonetheless admissible because the questions fall within [the] 'routine booking question' exception which exempts from *Miranda's* coverage questions to secure the 'biographical data necessary to complete booking or pretrial services.'"[1184] These types of questions are asked for "record-keeping purposes only," and therefore "appear reasonably related to the police's administrative concerns."[1185]

8.3.2.2. Physical sobriety tests

Once a suspected drunk driver is in custody, the police request that he perform physical sobriety tests or submit to a breathalyzer examination does not constitute "interrogation" within the meaning of *Miranda*. In this regard, the *Muniz* Court noted that when an officer's dialogue with a drunk-driving suspect concerning physical sobriety tests consists primarily of carefully scripted instructions as to how the tests are to be performed, the request and the instructions are "not likely to be perceived as calling for any verbal response and therefore [are] not 'words or actions' constituting custodial interrogation."[1186] Similarly, "*Miranda* does not require suppression of [volunteered statements] made when [a suspected intoxicated motorist is] asked to submit to a breathalyzer examination." Requesting a suspected drunk driver to perform several balance tests, or take a breathalyzer test does not constitute interrogation within the meaning of *Miranda*.[1187]

8.3.3. The public safety exception

In *New York v. Quarles*,[1188] the Supreme Court held that the need for answers to questions in situations which pose a significant threat to the public safety justify a law enforcement officer's delay in advising an arrestee of his *Miranda* rights. In this case, the Court created a "*public safety exception*" to the requirement that *Miranda* warnings be administered before a suspect's answers may be admitted into evidence, and the availability of this exception does not depend upon the subjective motivation of the individual police officers involved.

In *Quarles*, officers were stopped while on patrol by a female who advised the officers that she was just raped. The female gave a particularized description of the suspect and further stated that he ran into a supermarket located nearby and was carrying a gun. The officers located the suspect in the supermarket and proceeded to stop and frisk him. The frisk revealed a concealed shoulder holster, which was empty. At this point, the officers placed the suspect under arrest, handcuffed him, and then asked him one question: "Where is the gun?" The arrestee motioned to the gun's location and the officers immediately recovered a loaded .38 caliber revolver from an empty carton. At this point the officers read the arrestee his rights as required by *Miranda*.

The Court determined that the circumstances in this case presented overriding considerations of public safety to justify the officers' failure to administer *Miranda* warnings before they asked a question devoted to locating the abandoned gun. "Public safety must be paramount to adherence to the literal language of the prophylactic rules enunciated in *Miranda*." Here, the police were presented with the immediate necessity of ascertaining the location of a gun which they had every reason to believe the suspect had just removed from his holster and discarded in the supermarket. So long as the gun was concealed somewhere in the supermarket, with its whereabouts unknown, it posed many significant dangers to the public safety. Administration of *Miranda* in such circumstances might deter a suspect from responding and have a result of creating a significant danger to the public—that of a concealed loaded gun in a public area.

[1184] *Pennsylvania v. Muniz*, 496 U.S. 582, 110 S. Ct. 2638, 2650 (1990).

[1185] *Pennsylvania v. Muniz*, 496 U.S. 582, 110 S. Ct. 2638, 2650 (1990). *See also State v. Ladd*, 308 N.C. 272, 302 S.E.2d 164 (1983) (Holding interrogation does not encompass routine informational questions posited to a defendant during the booking process); *State v. Banks*, 322 N.C. 753, 760, 370 S.E.2d 398 (1988)("[T]he *Miranda* requirements are inapplicable to routine questions asked during the booking process unless such questions are designed to elicit incriminating information from a suspect."). But see *State v. Diaz*, 831 S.E.2d 532 (N.C. 2019) (holding a defendant's statement of his date of birth on his affidavit was testimonial because he was charged with abduction of a child and statutory rape, which required proof that the victim was at least four years younger than the defendant and that the defendant was more than four but less than six years older than the defendant).

[1186] *Pennsylvania v. Muniz*, 496 U.S. 582, 603, 110 S. Ct. 2638, 2651 (1990).

[1187] *Pennsylvania v. Muniz*, 496 U.S. 582, 604, 110 S. Ct. 2638, 2652 (1990).

[1188] *New York v. Quarles*, 467 U.S. 649, 104 S. Ct. 2626 (1984).

The facts in *State v. Simmons*[1189] are very similar to those in *Quarles*. In Simmons, officers had reason to believe that the defendant had pursued a victim while brandishing a firearm on a major, public road. After apprehending the defendant, the officers discovered that he was unarmed. The Court of Appeals of North Carolina held that it was reasonable for the officers to conclude that the defendant had discarded the firearm outside. Because the area was heavily trafficked, "asking Defendant where he had hidden the gun was reasonably necessary in order 'to secure … [police] safety or the safety of the public.'"[1190]

In *State v. al-Bayyinah*,[1191] Officer Myers was alone and unarmed when he finally caught up with the defendant in the woods. Because the defendant had been involved in a stabbing, Officer Myers knew that the defendant might have a knife in his possession. Thus, he asked the defendant where the knife was. "Under the circumstances this question was necessary to secure Officer Myers' own safety, a purpose that falls within the public safety exception to *Miranda*."[1192] Accordingly, the question was excepted from the *Miranda* rule.[1193]

8.3.4. The impeachment exception

The "impeachment exception" to *Miranda*'s exclusionary rule provides the prosecution with a means to rebut a defendant's false or fabricated testimony, or attack the credibility of a defendant who offers testimony that contradicts a previously given, albeit inadmissible, statement. In *Walder v. United States*,[1194] the U.S. Supreme Court carved out an exception to the exclusionary rule for purposes of impeaching a defendant's credibility at trial. The Court explained: "It is one thing to say that the Government cannot make an affirmative use of evidence unlawfully obtained. It is quite another to say that the defendant can turn the illegal method by which evidence in the Government's possession was obtained to his own advantage, and provide himself with a shield against contradiction of his untruths."[1195]

8.3.5. Physical fruits of an unwarned statement

In *United States v. Patane*,[1196] the Supreme Court declined to extend the fruit of the poisonous tree doctrine to exclude physical evidence obtained through voluntary but unwarned confessions. There, the officer attempted to read the defendant his rights, and the defendant interrupted and informed the officer that he was aware of his rights. The officer proceeded to act on information he received prior to the interaction and asked the defendant, a convicted felon, if he had a firearm in his residence. After the defendant hesitated in responding, the officer persisted, and, ultimately, the defendant informed the officer of the location of a pistol in his home, and the officer seized the firearm. Prior to trial, the defendant filed a motion to suppress the pistol, arguing in part that the officer unlawfully obtained the firearm as the fruit of an unwarned statement.

The U.S. Supreme Court held that the admission of the physical fruits of a voluntary statement into evidence will not implicate the Self-Incrimination Clause, finding "no justification for extending the *Miranda* rule to [that] context."[1197] The Court reasoned that "the *Miranda* rule is a prophylactic employed to protect against violations of the Self-Incrimination Clause."[1198] Moreover, the Supreme Court explained that "the core protection afforded by the Self-Incrimination Clause is a prohibition on compelling a criminal defendant to testify against himself at trial[,]" and "[t]he Clause cannot be violated by the introduction of nontestimonial

---

[1189] *State v. Simmons*, 253 N.C. App. 841, 799 S.E.2d 909 (2017).

[1190] *State v. Simmons*, 253 N.C. App. 841, *4, 799 S.E.2d 909 (2017) (quoting *State v. Brooks*, 337 N.C. 132, 144, 446 S.E.2d 579 (1994)).

[1191] *State v. al-Bayyinah*, 359 N.C. 741, 616 S.E.2d 500 (2005).

[1192] *State v. al-Bayyinah*, 359 N.C. 741, 750, 616 S.E.2d 500 (2005).

[1193] *See also State v. Crudup*, 157 N.C. App. 657, 580 S.E.2d 21 (2003); *State v. Brooks*, 337 N.C. 132, 446 S.E.2d 579 (1994).

[1194] *Walder v. United States*, 347 U.S. 62, 74 S. Ct. 354 (1954).

[1195] *Walder v. United States*, 347 U.S. 62, 65, 74 S. Ct. 354, 356 (1954); *see also Harris v. New York*, 401 U.S. 222, 91 S. Ct. 643 (1971) ("The shield provided by *Miranda* cannot be perverted into a license to use perjury by way of a defense, free from the risk of confrontation with prior inconsistent utterances."); *Oregon v. Hass*, 420 U.S. 714, 723, 95 S. Ct. 1215, 1223 (1975).

[1196] *United States v. Patane*, 542 U.S. 630, 124 S. Ct. 2620 (2004).

[1197] *United States v. Patane*, 542 U.S. 630, 636-37, 124 S. Ct. 2620 (2004).

[1198] *United States v. Patane*, 542 U.S. 630, 636, 124 S. Ct. 2620 (2004).

evidence obtained as a result of voluntary statements."[1199] Finally, the Court drew an important distinction between unreasonable searches that violate the Fourth Amendment and failure to properly "Mirandize" a suspect, and concluded that the exclusion of unwarned statements at trial is a sufficient remedy for *Miranda* violations.[1200]

8.4. Events surrounding the interrogation process

8.4.1. Invocation of rights

8.4.1.1. The right to remain silent

The Supreme Court in *Miranda v. Arizona* was very clear in its command that once a suspect invokes her right to remain silent, "all questioning must cease." An individual who seeks to invoke his right to remain silent must do so unambiguously.[1201] *Miranda* did not discuss, however, whether, and under what circumstances, law enforcement authorities may resume questioning the suspect. In *Michigan v. Mosley*,[1202] the U.S. Supreme Court revisited this issue and noted that a strict, literal reading of the phrase "all questioning must cease" would lead to "absurd and unintended results."[1203] According to the Court, "a blanket prohibition against the taking of voluntary statements or a permanent immunity from further interrogation, regardless of the circumstances, would transform the *Miranda* safeguards into wholly irrational obstacles to legitimate police investigative activity, and deprive suspects of an opportunity to make informed and intelligent assessments of their interests."[1204]

Accordingly, the *Mosley* Court concluded that *Miranda* did not impose an absolute ban on the resumption of questioning following an invocation of the right to remain silent by a person in custody. The Court held that "the admissibility of statements obtained after the person in custody has decided to remain silent depends under *Miranda* on whether his 'right to cut off questioning' was 'scrupulously honored.'"[1205] Mosley's expression of his desire to remain silent was deemed "scrupulously honored" based on the facts that: (1) Mosley had been advised of his *Miranda* rights before both interrogations; (2) the officer conducting the first interrogation immediately ceased all questioning when Mosley expressed his desire to remain silent; (3) the second interrogation occurred after a significant time lapse; (4) the second interrogation was conducted in another location; (5) by another officer; and (6) it related to a different offense.

8.4.1.1.1. Booking questions

May an accused be deemed to have invoked his Fifth Amendment privilege simply by remaining silent during pedigree questioning? In *United States v. Montana*,[1206] the Second Circuit said yes. Generally, after receiving the *Miranda* warnings, an accused's silence in the face of repeated questioning "has been held sufficient to invoke the Fifth Amendment privilege,... or at least sufficient to create an ambiguity requiring the authorities either to cease interrogation or to limit themselves to clarifying questions[.]"[1207] In *Montana*, the Second Circuit could see "no basis for distinguishing silence in the face of pedigree questions from silence in the face of more substantive interrogation."[1208] "If a suspect refuses to answer even non-incriminating

---

[1199] *United States v. Patane*, 542 U.S. 630, 637, 124 S. Ct. 2620 (2004).

[1200] *United States v. Patane*, 542 U.S. 630, 641-42, 124 S. Ct. 2620 (2004).

[1201] *Berghuis v. Thompkins*, 560 U.S. 370, 381-82, 130 S. Ct. 2250 (2010). In *Berghuis*, the United States Supreme Court determined that a defendant's prolonged silence in response to police questioning did not constitute an unambiguous invocation of the right to remain silent. The Court noted that the defendant never said that "he wanted to remain silent" or that "he did not want to talk with the police" and held that if he had "made either of these simple, unambiguous statements, he would have invoked his 'right to cut off questioning.'" *Id.* at 382 (citing *Michigan v. Mosley*, 423 U.S. 96, 103, 96 S. Ct. 321 (1975)).

[1202] *Michigan v. Mosley*, 423 U.S. 96, 96 S. Ct. 321 (1975).

[1203] *Michigan v. Mosley*, 423 U.S. 96, 102, 96 S. Ct. 321, 325 (1975).

[1204] *Michigan v. Mosley*, 423 U.S. 96, 102, 96 S. Ct. 321, 325 (1975).

[1205] *Michigan v. Mosley*, 423 U.S. 96, 102-03, 96 S. Ct. 321, 326 (1975).

[1206] *United States v. Montana*, 958 F.2d 516 (2d Cir. 1992).

[1207] *United States v. Montana*, 958 F.2d 516, 518 (2d Cir. 1992) (citations omitted).

[1208] *United States v. Montana*, 958 F.2d 516, 518 (2d Cir. 1992) (citations omitted).

pedigree questions," reasoned the court, "the interrogating officer cannot reasonably conclude that he will immediately thereafter consent to answer incriminating ones."[1209] The court held, therefore, that an in-custody accused invokes his right to remain silent by declining to answer pedigree questions.[1210]

8.4.1.1.2. A suspect's silence and impeachment

A suspect's silence after being arrested and read the *Miranda* warnings cannot be used at trial to impeach the suspect.[1211] *Doyle's* rule does not apply—*i.e.*, a defendant's silence may be used to impeach his exculpatory testimony—if the silence occurred either (1) before arrest or (2) after arrest and before *Miranda* warnings were given.[1212] This is because, under the United States Constitution, use of a defendant's silence only deprives a defendant of due process when the government has given the defendant a reason to believe both that he has a right to remain silent and that his invocation of that right will not be used against him, which typically only occurs post-arrest and post-*Miranda*.

8.4.1.2. The right to counsel

When an in-custody suspect requests counsel, all questioning must stop. This was made clear by the Supreme Court in *Edwards v. Arizona*.[1213] *Edwards* held that once a suspect invokes the right to counsel, "a valid waiver of that right cannot be established by showing only that he responded to further *police initiated* custodial interrogation even if he has been advised of his rights."[1214]

Although the Fifth Amendment privilege against self-incrimination does not expressly provide for the right to counsel, courts construe that right as implicitly existing in the Fifth-Amendment setting as a "preventative measure" that protects an accused from self-incrimination. The correlative right to counsel found in the *Miranda* warnings is said to be necessary "to make the process of police interrogation conform to the dictates of the [Fifth Amendment] privilege."[1215]

The assertion of a suspect's right to an attorney while being questioned in police custody is "an invocation of his Fifth Amendment rights, requiring that all interrogation must cease."[1216] If the accused indicates in any manner that he may desire a lawyer, the police may not ask him any further questions or reinitiate questioning "until counsel has been made available to him, *unless the accused himself initiates further communication, exchanges or conversations with the police*."[1217] In these circumstances, courts will question first whether the accused invoked his right to counsel. If so, the inquiry next addresses whether the accused or the police initiated further communications or exchanges about the investigation.

If it is determined that the police initiated further questioning after a previous assertion of the right to counsel, any statements made by the accused will be inadmissible at trial unless, at the time of the second or subsequent questioning, the accused had been given an opportunity "to confer with [an] attorney and to have him present during" the second or subsequent questioning session.[1218] If, however, it is determined that the accused himself initiated further communication, exchanges or conversations about the investigation, the inquiry would then be whether, after providing the accused with a fresh set of *Miranda* warnings, the police

---

[1209] *United States v. Montana*, 958 F.2d 516, 518 (2d Cir. 1992) (citations omitted).

[1210] *United States v. Montana*, 958 F.2d 516, 517 (2d Cir. 1992).

[1211] *Doyle v. Ohio*, 426 U.S. 610, 619, 96 S.Ct. 2240, 2245 (1976) ("After an arrested person is formally advised by an officer of the law that he has a right to remain silent, the unfairness occurs when the prosecution, in the presence of the jury, is allowed to undertake impeachment on the basis of what may be the exercise of that right.").

[1212] *See Fletcher v. Weir*, 455 U.S. 603, 605-07, 102 S. Ct. 1309 (1982); *Jenkins v. Anderson*, 447 U.S. 231, 239-40, 100 S. Ct. 2124 (1980).

[1213] *Edwards v. Arizona*, 451 U.S. 477, 101 S. Ct. 1880 (1981).

[1214] *Edwards v. Arizona*, 451 U.S. 477, 484-85, 101 S. Ct. 1880, 1884-85 (1981).

[1215] *Miranda v. Arizona*, 384 U.S. 436, 466, 86 S. Ct. 1602, 1623 (1966).

[1216] *Edwards v. Arizona*, 451 U.S. 477, 485, 101 S. Ct. 1880, 1885 (1981).

[1217] *Edwards v. Arizona*, 451 U.S. 477, 485, 101 S. Ct. 1880, 1885 (1981) (emphasis added).

[1218] *Edwards v. Arizona*, 451 U.S. 477, 485, 101 S. Ct. 1880, 1885 (1981); *see also Minnick v. Mississippi*, 498 U.S. 146, 111 S. Ct. 486, 491 (1990) ("when counsel is requested, interrogation must cease, and officials may not reinitiate interrogation without counsel present, whether or not the accused has consulted with his attorney").

received "a valid waiver of the right to counsel and the right to silence[,]" that is, whether the accused voluntarily, knowingly and intelligently waived his rights based on "the totality of the circumstances, including the necessary fact that the accused, not the police, reopened the dialogue with the authorities."[1219]

In *Minnick v. Mississippi*,[1220] the Supreme Court held that once an accused requests counsel during custodial interrogation and is then given the opportunity to consult with an attorney, the police may not thereafter initiate further questioning without the attorney present. According to the Court, "when counsel is requested, interrogation must cease, and officials may not reinitiate interrogation without counsel present, whether or not the accused has consulted with his attorney."[1221] Clearly, "the Fifth Amendment protection of *Edwards* is not terminated or suspended by consultation with counsel." The requirement dictates that counsel be *present* during the interrogation.

In *Smith v. Illinois*,[1222] the Court pointed out that, on occasion, an accused's asserted request for counsel may be ambiguous or equivocal. But in this case, no one has pointed to anything Smith previously had said that might have cast doubt on the meaning of his statement, "I'd like to do that," upon learning that he had the right to his counsel's presence. Nor is there anything in that statement itself which would suggest anything inherently ambiguous or equivocal. "Where nothing about the request for counsel or the circumstances leading up to the request would render it ambiguous, all questioning must cease."

However, in *Davis v. United States*,[1223] the Court held that a defendant's "remark to the NIS agents—'Maybe I should talk to a lawyer'—was not a request for counsel." Consequently, the NIS agents "were not required to stop questioning [defendant], though it was entirely proper for them to clarify whether [defendant] in fact wanted a lawyer."[1224] The Court wrote, "after a knowing and voluntary waiver of the *Miranda* rights, law enforcement officers may continue questioning until and unless the suspect *clearly requests* an attorney."[1225]

8.4.1.2.1. A request for counsel during non-custodial questioning

In *McNeil v. Wisconsin*,[1226] the Supreme Court noted: "We have in fact never held that a person can invoke his *Miranda* rights anticipatorily, in a context other than 'custodial interrogation[.]' ... If the *Miranda* right to counsel can be invoked at a preliminary hearing, it could be argued, there is no logical reason why it could not be invoked by a letter prior to arrest, or indeed even prior to identification as a suspect. Most rights must be asserted when the government seeks to take the action they protect against. The fact that we have allowed the *Miranda* right to counsel, once asserted, to be effective with respect to future custodial interrogation *does not necessarily mean that we will allow it to be asserted initially outside the context of custodial interrogation, with similar effect.*"[1227]

[1219] *Edwards v. Arizona*, 451 U.S. 477, 486 n.9, 101 S. Ct. 1880, 1885 n.9 (1981).

[1220] *Minnick v. Mississippi*, 498 U.S. 146, 111 S. Ct. 486 (1990).

[1221] *Minnick v. Mississippi*, 498 U.S. 146, 111 S. Ct. 486, 491 (1990).

[1222] *Smith v. Illinois*, 469 U.S. 91, 105 S. Ct. 490 (1984).

[1223] *Davis v. United States*, 512 U.S. 452, 114 S. Ct. 2350 (1994).

[1224] *Davis v. United States*, 512 U.S. 452, 114 S. Ct. 2350, 2357 (1994).

[1225] *See also Ledbetter v. Edwards*, 35 F.3d 1062 (6th Cir. 1994) (a defendant's statement "It would be nice [to have an attorney]" too ambiguous to require cessation of questioning); *State v. Knight*, 369 N.C. 640, 799 S.E.2d 603 (2017); *State v. Simpson*, 314 N.C. 359, 334 S.E.2d 53 (1985).

[1226] *McNeil v. Wisconsin*, 501 U.S. 171, 111 S. Ct. 2204 (1991).

[1227] *McNeil v. Wisconsin*, 501 U.S. 171, 111 S. Ct. 2204, 2211 n.3 (1991) (emphasis added). Relying on *McNeil v. Wisconsin*, an overwhelming number of federal courts have also held that a defendant cannot invoke his *Miranda* rights outside the context of custodial interrogation. *See, e.g., United States v. Bautista*, 145 F.3d 1140, 1151 (10th Cir. 1998) ("we do not suggest that a person can invoke his *Miranda* rights anticipatorily in any situation, *i.e.*, in a context other than custodial interrogation"; *United States v. Grimes*, 142 F.3d 1342, 1348 (11th Cir. 1998) ("*Miranda* rights may be invoked only during custodial interrogation or when interrogation is imminent"); *United States v. LaGrone*, 43 F.3d 332 (7th Cir. 1994); *United States v. Thompson*, 35 F.3d 100, 104 (2d Cir. 1994) (a defendant's filing of the notice of appearance "did not occur in the context of custodial interrogation"); *Alston v. Redman*, 34 F.3d 1237, 1246 (3d Cir. 1994) (The *Miranda* right to counsel may not be invoked outside the context of custodial interrogation, in anticipation of a future interrogation; "to be effective, a request for *Miranda* counsel must be made within the context of custodial interrogation and no sooner."); *United States v. Wright*, 962 F.2d 953, 956 (9th Cir. 1992) ("to extend *Miranda-Edwards* protection as [the defendant] urges would, on the other hand, make it virtually impossible for any defendant charged with one crime ever to be questioned about unrelated

8.4.1.2.2. Conditional requests

May a law enforcement officer continue questioning a suspect after the suspect states that he would not give a written statement unless his attorney was present but has "no problem" talking about the incident? In *Connecticut v. Barrett*,[1228] the U.S. Supreme Court said *yes*. In this case, it was "undisputed that Barrett desired the presence of counsel before making a written statement. Had the police obtained such a statement without meeting the waiver standards of *Edwards*, it would clearly be inadmissible. Barrett's limited requests for counsel, however, were accompanied by affirmative announcements of his willingness to speak with the authorities. The fact that officials took the opportunity provided by Barrett to obtain an oral confession is quite consistent with the Fifth Amendment. *Miranda* gives the defendant a right to choose between speech and silence, and Barrett chose to speak."[1229] Accordingly, Barrett's oral confession was found to be admissible.

8.4.1.2.3. When the accused initiates further conversation

After an accused has been advised of his *Miranda* rights and requests counsel, does his subsequent question of "Well, what is going to happen to me now?" constitute a sufficient *initiation* of further conversation so as to satisfy the rule set forth in *Edwards v. Arizona*? In *Oregon v. Bradshaw*,[1230] the Court said, *yes*. Recall that in *Edwards,* the Court held that "after the right to counsel had been asserted by an accused, further interrogation should not take place 'unless the accused himself *initiates* further communication, exchanges, or conversations with the police.'" The rule was "designed to safeguard an accused in police custody from being badgered by police officers" into confessing. Once the *Edwards* rule is satisfied—that is, it is shown that the accused initiated further conversation with the law enforcement authorities—there is a second inquiry that will be made by the courts. The courts will then require the police and the prosecution to demonstrate that the accused thereafter voluntarily, knowingly and intelligently waived his right to counsel and right to remain silent.

8.4.1.2.4. Offenses unrelated to the subject of the initial interrogation

Once a suspect has requested the assistance of counsel during custodial interrogation, may the police subject that suspect to further questioning about an offense that is wholly unrelated to the subject of their initial interrogation? In *Arizona v. Roberson*,[1231] the Supreme Court said *no*. Once a suspect has requested an attorney during custodial interrogation, the police are prohibited from subjecting that suspect to further questioning—regardless of whether that questioning concerns the offense at issue or a wholly unrelated offense—"unless the [suspect] himself initiates further communication, exchanges, or conversations with the police."[1232]

8.4.1.2.5. The *Shatzer* 14-day rule

In *Maryland v. Shatzer*,[1233] the U.S. Supreme Court held that once the suspect has been released from *Miranda* custody for *14 days,* the police may reapproach the suspect and ask whether he is now willing to answer questions. According to the Court, a 14-day period "provides plenty of time for the suspect to get reacclimated to his normal life, to consult with friends and counsel, and to shake off any residual coercive effects of his prior custody."[1234]

---

criminal activity if, the first time in court on the first offense charged, he asked for counsel to be present at future interviews. This would not serve the prophylactic purposes of *Miranda*"); *United States v. Cooper*, 85 F. Supp. 2d 1, 23 (D.D.C. 2000) ("a request for counsel under *Miranda* must be made within the custodial context").

[1228] *Connecticut v. Barrett*, 479 U.S. 523, 107 S. Ct. 828 (1987).

[1229] *Connecticut v. Barrett*, 479 U.S. 523, 107 S. Ct. 828 (1987).

[1230] *Oregon v. Bradshaw,* 462 U.S. 1039, 103 S. Ct. 2830 (1983).

[1231] *Arizona v. Roberson*, 486 U.S. 675, 108 S. Ct. 2093 (1988).

[1232] *Arizona v. Roberson*, 486 U.S. 675, 108 S. Ct. 2093, 2096 (1988).

[1233] *Maryland v. Shatzer*, 559 U.S. 98, 130 S. Ct. 1213 (2010).

[1234] *Maryland v. Shatzer*, 559 U.S. 98, 130 S. Ct. 1213, 1223 (2010).

Recall that in *Edwards v. Arizona*, the Court created a *presumption* that once a suspect invokes the *Miranda* right to counsel, any waiver of that right in response to a subsequent police attempt at custodial interrogation is *involuntary*. The *Edwards* presumption is designed to preserve "the integrity of an accused's choice to communicate with police only through counsel," by preventing police from badgering him into waiving his previously asserted *Miranda* rights.

In the typical case, the suspect is arrested and is held in uninterrupted pretrial custody while the crime is being actively investigated. While *Edwards* did not address whether this rule survives a break in custody, lower courts have uniformly held that a break in custody ends the *Edwards* presumption. Here, in *Shatzer*, Justice Scalia, speaking for the Court, announced: "[L]aw enforcement officers need to know, with certainty and beforehand, when renewed interrogation is lawful. And while it is certainly unusual for this Court to set forth precise time limits governing police action, it is not unheard-of." Accordingly, 14 days is an appropriate period of time to avoid the consequence of the *Edwards* presumption. "That provides plenty of time for the suspect to get reacclimated to his normal life, to consult with friends and counsel, and to shake off any residual coercive effects of his prior custody."

As with the Fifth Amendment, once the accused has invoked his Sixth Amendment right to counsel after adversary proceedings have been commenced, this assertion must be scrupulously honored by law enforcement officers.

In *Montejo v. Louisiana*,[1235] the Supreme Court determined that if the police initiate interrogation after a defendant's assertion, at an arraignment or similar proceeding, of his right to counsel, any subsequent waiver of the defendant's right to counsel for that police-initiated interrogation will still be *valid*. In this case, the Court took the significant step of overruling *Michigan v. Jackson*,[1236] which had previously held that, "if police initiate interrogation after a defendant's assertion, at an arraignment or similar proceeding, of his right to counsel, any waiver of the defendant's right to counsel for that police-initiated interrogation [was] *invalid*."[1237] According to the Court, there is no reason "to assume that a defendant like Montejo, who has done *nothing at all* to express his intentions with respect to his Sixth Amendment rights, would not be perfectly amenable to speaking with the police without having counsel present. And no reason exists to prohibit the police from inquiring." The rule of *Jackson* was designed "to prevent police from badgering defendants into changing their minds about their rights, but a defendant who never asked for counsel has not yet made up his mind in the first instance."

8.4.2. Waiver of rights

8.4.2.1. General aspects

To be valid, a criminal defendant's waiver of his rights must be made voluntarily, knowingly, and intelligently, and the government bears the burden of proof. Under the federal Constitution, the prosecution must prove waiver by a "preponderance of the evidence."[1238] When a court assesses the voluntariness of a waiver of rights, it considers the characteristics of the suspect and the totality of the circumstances surrounding the interrogation. Relevant factors will include, but not be limited to:

- The method and context in which the suspect's constitutional rights were read.
- The background, experience and conduct of the suspect, including the suspect's age, education and intelligence.
- The suspect's previous encounters with law enforcement.
- How and by what method the suspect was advised of his constitutional rights.
- The length of the detention.
- The nature of the questioning and whether it was repeated or prolonged.
- Whether physical or mental punishment, coerciveness, or mental exhaustion was involved.
- Whether the suspect was deprived of food, sleep or medical attention.

[1235] *Montejo v. Louisiana*, 556 U.S. 778, 129 S. Ct. 2079 (2009).
[1236] *Michigan v. Jackson*, 475 U.S. 625, 106 S. Ct. 1404 (1986).
[1237] *Michigan v. Jackson*, 475 U.S. 625, 636, 106 S. Ct. 1404, 1411 (1986).
[1238] *Colorado v. Connelly*, 479 U.S. 157, 107 S. Ct. 515, 523 (1986).

- Whether the suspect was injured, intoxicated or drugged, or in ill health.
- Whether law enforcement officials made an express promise of leniency or sentence.[1239]

North Carolina courts will consider:

- The circumstances under which the interrogation was conducted, for example the location, the presence or absence of restraints, and the suspect's opportunity to communicate with family or an attorney.
- The treatment of the suspect, for example the duration of the session or consecutive sessions, availability of food and drink, opportunity to take breaks or use restroom facilities, and the use of actual physical violence or psychologically strenuous interrogation tactics.
- The appearance and demeanor of the officers, for example whether they were uniformed, whether weapons were displayed, and whether they used raised voices or made shows of violence.
- The statements made by the officers, including threats or promises or attempts to coerce a confession through trickery or deception.
- The characteristics of the defendant himself, including his age, mental condition, familiarity with the criminal justice system, and demeanor during questioning.[1240]

8.4.2.1.1. Voluntariness—a two-step analysis

As a general proposition, the admissibility of a confession depends upon whether it was voluntarily made. "The ultimate issue is whether the confession was the product of an essentially free and unconstrained choice by its maker. 'If it is, if he has willed to confess, it may be used against him. If it is not, if his will has been overborne and his capacity for self-determination critically impaired, the use of his confession offends due process.'"[1241] Unlike the use of physical coercion, however, use of psychologically-oriented methods during questioning are not inherently coercive. The critical inquiry in such cases is whether the person's decision to confess results from a free and self-directed choice rather than from an overbearing of the suspect's will.[1242] A court's inquiry into waiver has two distinct dimensions: (1) the relinquishment of the right must have been voluntary in the sense that it was the product of free and deliberate choice rather than intimidation, coercion or deception; and (2) the waiver must have been made with a full awareness of both the nature of the right being abandoned and the consequences of the decision to abandon it.

8.4.2.1.2. A free and unconstrained choice; inducements to confess

Police are not permitted to employ unreasonable or improper inducements which impair a suspect's decision whether to give a statement or seek legal counsel. The rule applies to those situations where the police prompt an admission or confession by suggesting a benefit if the suspect forgoes her rights. This reasoning was first announced in *Bram v. United States*,[1243] where the United States Supreme Court declared: "[A] confession, in order to be admissible, must be free and voluntary: that is, [it] must not be extracted by any sort of threats of violence, nor obtained by any direct or implied promises, however slight, nor by exertion of any

---

[1239] *See Colorado v. Connelly*, 479 U.S. 157, 107 S. Ct. 515, 522 (1986); *see also Schneckloth v. Bustamonte*, 412 U.S. 218, 226, 93 S. Ct. 2041, 2047-48 (1973).

[1240] *State v. Johnson*, 371 N.C. 870, 821 S.E.2d 822 (2018). *See also State v. Hardy*, 339 N.C. 207, 451 S.E.2d 600 (1994); *State v. Kemmerlin*, 356 N.C. 446, 458, 573 S.E.2d 870, 881 (2002); *State v. Hyde*, 352 N.C. 37, 45, 530 S.E.2d 281, 288 (2000).

[1241] *Arizona v. Fulminante*, 499 U.S. 279, 111 S. Ct. 1246, 1261 (1991) (quoting *Culombe v. Connecticut*, 367 U.S. 568, 602, 81 S. Ct. 1860, 1879 (1961)); *see also Blackburn v. Alabama*, 361 U.S. 199, 206, 80 S. Ct. 274, 279 (1960) ("coercion can be mental as well as physical, and ... the blood of the accused is not the only hallmark of an unconstitutional inquisition"). *See also State v. Hardy*, 339 N.C. 207, 451 S.E.2d 600 (1994).

[1242] *See Arizona v. Fulminante*, 499 U.S. 279, 111 S. Ct. 1246, 1252-53 (1991) (confession held involuntary where a defendant, an alleged child murderer in danger of physical violence from other inmates, was motivated to confess when a fellow inmate (a government agent) promised to protect him in exchange for the confession); *Payne v. Arkansas*, 356 U.S. 560, 561, 78 S. Ct. 844, 846 (1958) (confession held to be coerced because the interrogating officer had promised that if the accused confessed, the officer would protect him from an angry mob outside the jailhouse door).

[1243] *Bram v. United States*, 168 U.S. 532, 542-43, 18 S. Ct. 183, 187 (1897).

improper influence[.]" Involuntariness may also be shown by an express promise of leniency, such as the police telling the defendant that, in return for his cooperation, his punishment would be less severe. Clearly, "threats of physical violence" will "render involuntary a confession obtained thereafter."[1244]

Thus, in *State v. Johnson*,[1245] the court considered the following before concluding that the defendant was not induced to confess.

> [The] defendant came to the police department headquarters on his own without police escort, was not shackled or handcuffed, and retained possession of his personal cell phone while inside the interview room. Defendant was placed in an interview room with two plainclothes police officers on the second floor of a secure law enforcement facility. At one point, his cell phone rang and it appears from the record that officers would have allowed him to answer had he chosen to do so. Officers made no threats of physical violence but did interrogate defendant rigorously and raised their voices. Defendant was told, contradictorily and repeatedly, that officers both could not promise him anything and that the district attorney would "work with him" and would "go easier on him" if he cooperated and gave them truthful information.... Defendant was in his mid-thirties, had obtained his GED, and was articulate, intelligent, literate, and knowledgeable about the criminal justice system and its processes.[1246]

The court concluded that the defendant's statements to officers were voluntarily made.[1247]

8.4.2.1.2.1. A knowing and intelligent choice

The question of whether a waiver of rights was the product of force, threat, duress, improper influence, or any other type of coercive police activity is only half the equation. The second step in the inquiry questions whether the waiver was given "knowingly and intelligently." Among other things, this requires that the administration of the *Miranda* warnings be more than a mere perfunctory exercise. This second aspect requires that the defendant comprehend the plain meaning of his basic *Miranda* rights. Here, the prosecution will be asked to show that any such waiver was not only knowing and voluntary, but that the suspect understood the right that she was waiving.

Knowledge of all the subjects of questioning. In *Colorado v. Spring*,[1248] the United States Supreme Court held that "a suspect's awareness of all the possible subjects of questioning in advance of interrogation is not relevant to determining whether the suspect voluntarily, knowingly, and intelligently waived his Fifth Amendment privilege." Spring had been arrested for firearms violations. Prior to his arrest, law enforcement agents received information that Spring killed a man in Colorado. Spring signed a written form stating that he understood and waived his *Miranda* rights but was not advised as to the topics of the interrogation. After being questioned about the firearms violations, law enforcement agents inquired whether Spring had shot anyone. Spring admitted, "I shot another guy once." Agents then asked Spring if he shot a man in Colorado, which he denied. In a subsequent interrogation and while still under arrest for the firearms violations, Spring was again given the *Miranda* warnings, signed a written waiver, and admitted that he killed a man in Colorado. On appeal, Spring argued that he did not waive his *Miranda* rights during the first interview because "he was not informed that he would be questioned about the Colorado murder."

Finding the *Miranda* waiver valid, the Court observed that a waiver of Fifth Amendment rights depends upon: (1) whether the decision was a deliberate choice or the product of intimidation, coercion, or deception;

[1244] *See, e.g., Lynum v. Illinois*, 372 U.S. 528, 537, 83 S. Ct. 917 (1963) (a defendant's confession involuntary when police told her that her state financial aid would be cut off and her six children taken from her unless she "cooperated" with them); *State v. Johnson*, 371 N.C. 870, 821 S.E.2d 822 (2018).

[1245] *State v. Johnson*, 371 N.C. 870, 821 S.E.2d 822 (2018).

[1246] *State v. Johnson*, 371 N.C. 870, 879-81, 821 S.E.2d 822 (2018).

[1247] *State v. Johnson*, 371 N.C. 870, 882, 821 S.E.2d 822 (2018). *See also State v. Booker*, 306 N.C. 302, 310, 293 S.E.2d 78, 83 (1982) (five and one-half hour interview held not coercive); *State v. Hardy*, 339 N.C. 207, 451 S.E.2d 600 (1994) (finding statements that when viewed in isolation could be interpreted to contain implicit promises or threats but did not necessarily mandate a conclusion of coercion when viewed in context).

[1248] *Colorado v. Spring*, 479 U.S. 564, 577, 107 S. Ct. 851 (1987).

and (2) made with full awareness of the nature of the right being abandoned and the consequences of the decision to abandon it. According to the Court, "[t]he Constitution does not require that a criminal suspect know and understand every possible consequence of a waiver of the Fifth Amendment privilege." Nor will mere silence by law enforcement officials as to the subject matter of an interrogation constitute "trickery" sufficient to invalidate a suspect's waiver of *Miranda* rights, and we expressly decline so to hold today."

Implied waivers. Although the State need not show that a waiver of *Miranda* rights was express," the giving of an uncoerced statement following the provision of *Miranda* warnings, may be sufficient to demonstrate a valid waiver."[1249] Thus, an "implicit waiver" of the right to remain silent may be "sufficient to admit a suspect's statement into evidence."[1250] To establish "an implied waiver of the right to remain silent," the State must show "that a *Miranda* warning was given and that it was understood by the accused."[1251] "As a general proposition, the law can presume that an individual who, with a full understanding of his or her rights, acts in a manner inconsistent with their exercise has made a deliberate choice to relinquish the protection those rights afford."[1252]

8.4.2.1.3. Juveniles

A knowing and intelligent waiver of *Miranda* also means that the suspect had the ability to understand the very words used in the warnings. It need not mean the ability to understand far-reaching legal and strategic effects of waiving one's rights, or to appreciate how widely or deeply an interrogation may probe, or to withstand the influence of stress or fancy; but to waive rights intelligently and knowingly, one must at least understand basically what those rights encompass and minimally what their waiver will entail.[1253]

North Carolina has codified the procedures with regard to the interrogation of a juvenile. Pursuant to N.C.Gen.Stat. § 7B-2101:

(a) Any juvenile in custody must be advised prior to questioning:
  (1) That the juvenile has a right to remain silent;
  (2) That any statement the juvenile does make can be and may be used against the juvenile;
  (3) That the juvenile has a right to have a parent, guardian, or custodian present during questioning; and
  (4) That the juvenile has a right to consult with an attorney and that one will be appointed for the juvenile if the juvenile is not represented and wants representation.
(b) When the juvenile is less than 16 years of age, no in-custody admission or confession resulting from interrogation may be admitted into evidence unless the confession or admission was made in the presence of the juvenile's parent, guardian, custodian, or attorney. If an attorney is not present, the parent, guardian, or custodian as well as the juvenile must be advised of the juvenile's rights as set out in subsection (a) of this section; however, a parent, guardian, or custodian may not waive any right on behalf of the juvenile.
(c) If the juvenile indicates in any manner and at any stage of questioning pursuant to this section that the juvenile does not wish to be questioned further, the officer shall cease questioning.
(d) Before admitting into evidence any statement resulting from custodial interrogation, the court shall find that the juvenile knowingly, willingly, and understandingly waived the juvenile's rights.

The North Carolina Supreme Court has explained, "The relevant statutory language is clearly intended to codify the rights afforded to a juvenile subjected to custodial interrogation pursuant to *Miranda* in addition

---

[1249] *See Berghuis v. Thompkins*, 560 U.S. 370, 384, 130 S. Ct. 2250 (2010).

[1250] *Berghuis v. Thompkins*, 560 U.S. 370, 384, 130 S. Ct. 2250 (2010) (citing *North Carolina v. Butler*, 441 U.S. 369, 376, 99 S. Ct. 1755 (1979)).

[1251] *Berghuis v. Thompkins*, 560 U.S. 370, 384, 130 S. Ct. 2250 (2010).

[1252] *Berghuis v. Thompkins*, 560 U.S. 370, 385, 130 S. Ct. 2250 (2010).

[1253] *See* Larry E. Holtz, *Miranda in a Juvenile Setting: A Child's Right to Silence*, 78 J. Crim. L. & Criminology 534, 536-37, 546-56 (1987) (citing evidence that most youths lack proper comprehension of rights under police interrogation; providing a simplified version of *Miranda* warnings—a "Youth Rights Form."). *Compare Reno v. Flores,* 507 U.S. 292, 113 S. Ct. 1439, 1451 (1993) ("juveniles are capable"—at least 16- and 17-year-olds—"of 'knowingly and intelligently' waiving their right against self-incrimination") (citing *Fare v. Michael C.*, 442 U.S. 707, 724-27, 99 S. Ct. 2560, 2571-73 (1979), and *United States v. Saucedo-Velasquez,* 843 F.2d 832, 835 (5th Cir. 1988) (applying Fare to a juvenile foreign national)).

to affording a juvenile the State statutory right to have a parent, guardian, or custodian present during the interrogation process."[1254]

8.4.2.1.4. Intoxicated suspects

Suspects who are in pain, intoxicated or on drugs may not be able to give a knowing, intelligent and voluntary waiver. In such cases, the prosecution has the burden of showing by a preponderance of the evidence that the waiver was voluntary, knowing and intelligent.[1255]

8.4.2.1.5. Lying to a suspect

Lying to a suspect will not, by itself, render a confession involuntary. In *Frazier v. Cupp*,[1256] the United States Supreme Court held that the defendant's confession was admissible notwithstanding the fact that the police falsely told him that another person had confessed. The Court noted that the defendant was a mature person of normal intelligence and that the questioning session lasted only slightly over an hour.[1257]

In *Frazier,* the police falsely told a defendant that his codefendant had already confessed. The court concluded that "the fact that the police misrepresented the statements [the codefendant] had made is, while relevant, insufficient in our view to make this otherwise voluntary confession inadmissible."[1258]

In *Holland v. McGinnis,*[1259] the court stated that "of the numerous varieties of police trickery," a "lie that relates to a suspect's connection to the crime is the least likely to render a confession involuntary." The court went on to say the following:

> Such misrepresentations, of course, may cause a suspect to confess, but causation alone does not constitute coercion; if it did, all confessions following interrogations would be involuntary because "it can almost always be said that the interrogation caused the confession." ... Thus, the issue is not causation, but the degree of improper coercion, and in this instance the degree was slight. Inflating evidence of Holland's guilt interfered little, if at all, with his "free and deliberate choice" of whether to confess, ... for it did not lead him to consider anything beyond his own beliefs regarding his actual guilt or innocence, his moral sense of right and wrong, and his judgment regarding the likelihood that the police had garnered enough valid evidence linking him to the crime. In other words, the deception did not interject the type of extrinsic considerations that would overcome Holland's will by distorting an otherwise rational choice of whether to confess or remain silent.[1260]

8.4.2.1.6. An initial failure to warn

Does an initial failure of a law enforcement officer to administer *Miranda* warnings "taint" subsequent admissions made after a suspect has been fully advised of, and has waived, his constitutional rights? In *Oregon v. Elstad,*[1261] the Supreme Court said *no.* A suspect "who has once responded to unwarned yet uncoercive

---

[1254] *State v. Saldierna,* 371 N.C. 407, 421-22, 817 S.E.2d 174 (2018). *See also State v. Fincher,* 309 N.C. 1, 19, 305 S.E.2d 685, 697 (1983); *State v. Spence,* 36 N.C. App. 627, 244 S.E.2d 442 (1978).

[1255] *Colorado v. Connelly,* 479 U.S. 157 (1986). *See also State v. McKoy,* 323 N.C. 1, 22, 372 S.E.2d 12, 23 (1988), *sentence vacated on other grounds,* 494 U.S. 433, 110 S. Ct. 1227, 108 L. Ed. 2d 369 (1990); *State v. Parton,* 303 N.C. 55, 277 S.E.2d 410 (1981) (finding no error in trial court's denial of the defendant's motion to suppress his confession to murder given after receiving *Miranda* warnings when the trial court found the statements to be voluntary, even though the arresting officer believed the defendant to be intoxicated but the defendant was not staggering and was coherent); *State v. Wilkerson,* 363 N.C. 382, 431, 683 S.E.2d 174 (2009) ("An inculpatory statement is admissible unless the defendant is so intoxicated that he is unconscious of the meaning of his words.").

[1256] *Frazier v. Cupp,* 394 U.S. 731, 89 S. Ct. 1420 (1969).

[1257] *Frazier v. Cupp,* 394 U.S. 731, 739, 89 S. Ct. 1420, 1425 (1969).

[1258] *Frazier v. Cupp,* 394 U.S. 731, 739, 89 S. Ct. 1420, 1425 (1969).

[1259] *Holland v. McGinnis,* 963 F.2d 1044, 1051 (7th Cir. 1992).

[1260] *Holland v. McGinnis,* 963 F.2d 1044, 1051 (7th Cir. 1992).

[1261] *Oregon v. Elstad,* 470 U.S. 298, 105 S. Ct. 1285 (1985).

questioning is not thereby disabled from waiving his rights and confessing after he has been given the requisite *Miranda* warnings."[1262] Said the Court:

> [A]bsent deliberately coercive or improper tactics in obtaining the initial statement, the mere fact that a suspect has made an unwarned admission does not warrant a presumption of compulsion. A subsequent administration of *Miranda* warnings to a suspect who has given a voluntary but unwarned statement ordinarily should suffice to remove the conditions that precluded admission of the earlier statement. In such circumstances, the finder of fact may reasonably conclude that the suspect made a rational and intelligent choice whether to waive or invoke his rights.[1263]

8.4.2.1.7. Deliberate "end runs" around *Miranda*

In *Missouri v. Seibert*,[1264] the Court addressed the technique of interrogating in successive, unwarned and warned phases. At the trial court level, one of the officers testified that the strategy of withholding *Miranda* warnings until after interrogating and drawing out a confession was promoted not only by his own department, but by a national police training organization. The object of "question first" / "warn later" is to render *Miranda* warnings ineffective by waiting for a particularly opportune time to give them, after the suspect has already confessed. Finding such a practice *improper*, the Court said:

> By any objective measure, ... it is likely that if the interrogators employ the technique of withholding warnings until after interrogation succeeds in eliciting a confession, the warnings will be ineffective in preparing the suspect for successive interrogation, close in time and similar in content. After all, the reason that question-first is catching on is as obvious as its manifest purpose, which is to get a confession the suspect would not make if he understood his rights at the outset; the sensible underlying assumption is that with one confession in hand before the warnings, the interrogator can count on getting its duplicate, with trifling additional trouble.

> Upon hearing warnings only in the aftermath of interrogation and just after making a confession, a suspect would hardly think he had a genuine right to remain silent, let alone persist in so believing once the police began to lead him over the same ground again. A more likely reaction on a suspect's part would be perplexity about the reason for discussing rights at that point, bewilderment being an unpromising frame of mind for knowledgeable decision. What is worse, telling a suspect that "anything you say can and will be used against you," without expressly excepting the statement just given, could lead to an entirely reasonable inference that what he has just said will be used, with subsequent silence being of no avail. Thus, when *Miranda* warnings are inserted in the midst of coordinated and continuing interrogation, they are likely to mislead and deprive a defendant of knowledge essential to his ability to understand the nature of his rights and the consequences of abandoning them.[1265]

The Court also rejected the prosecution's argument that a confession repeated at the end of an interrogation sequence envisioned in a question-first strategy is admissible on the authority of *Oregon v. Elstad*.[1266] In *Elstad*, the failure to preliminarily provide the *Miranda* warnings was, at most, an "oversight." The *Elstad* questioning session had "none of the earmarks of coercion."[1267] Thus, it is fair to read *Elstad* as treating the officer's failure to first administer the warnings as "a good-faith *Miranda* mistake, not only open to correction by careful warnings before systematic questioning in that particular case, but posing no threat to warn-first practice generally."[1268]

[1262] *Oregon v. Elstad*, 470 U.S. 298, 105 S. Ct. 1285, 1298 (1985).

[1263] *Oregon v. Elstad*, 470 U.S. 298, 314, 105 S. Ct. 1285 (1985).

[1264] *Missouri v. Seibert*, 542 U.S. 600, 124 S. Ct. 2601 (2004).

[1265] *Missouri v. Seibert*, 542 U.S. 600, 124 S. Ct. 2601, 2610-11 (2004).

[1266] *Oregon v. Elstad*, 470 U.S. 298, 105 S. Ct. 1285 (1985).

[1267] *Missouri v. Seibert*, 542 U.S. 600, 124 S. Ct. 2601, 2611 (2004).

[1268] *Missouri v. Seibert*, 542 U.S. 600, 124 S. Ct. 2601, 2612 (2004).

Here, in *Seibert*, the facts "reveal a police strategy adapted to undermine the *Miranda* warnings. The unwarned interrogation was conducted in the station house, and the questioning was systematic, exhaustive, and managed with psychological skill. When the police were finished there was little, if anything, of incriminating potential left unsaid."[1269]

Accordingly, "[b]ecause the question-first tactic effectively threatens to thwart *Miranda*'s purpose of reducing the risk that a coerced confession would be admitted, and because the facts here do not reasonably support a conclusion that the warnings given could have served their purpose," the Court held that Seibert's post-warning statements were inadmissible.[1270]

Missouri v. Seibert was a plurality opinion. Although a plurality of the justices would consider all two-stage interrogations eligible for a *Seibert* inquiry, Justice Kennedy's opinion narrowed the *Seibert* exception to those cases involving the deliberate use of the two-step procedure to weaken *Miranda*'s protections. In this regard, both the plurality and Justice Kennedy agree that where law enforcement officers deliberately employ a two-step interrogation to obtain a confession and where separations of time and circumstance and additional curative warnings are absent or fail to apprise a reasonable person in the suspect's shoes of his rights, the trial court should suppress the confession. This narrow test—that excludes confessions made after a deliberate, objectively ineffective mid-stream warning—represents most states' application of the *Seibert* holding.[1271]

Thus, when making a suppression determination, a trial court should conduct an initial inquiry into whether the prosecution has established that the police did not deliberately use a two-step interrogation procedure to obtain a confession. If the court determines that the use of the procedure was deliberate, then the court should determine whether curative measures (*e.g.*, an additional warning or a substantial break in time and circumstances between the pre- and post-warning statements) were employed, such that the suspect would understand the import and effect of the warning at the time of the later statement. If not, then the statements should be inadmissible. If, however, the trial court determines that the prosecution established that the police did not deliberately use a two-step technique to undermine *Miranda*, then it should apply the voluntariness test enunciated in *Elstad*.

North Carolina courts will perform a slightly different inquiry. In North Carolina, "[w]hen a defendant asserts that his or her *Miranda* rights have been violated as a result of successive rounds of custodial interrogation, some portion of which was unwarned, the question for the court is whether the warnings effectively apprised him of his rights and whether he made a voluntary, knowing, and intelligent waiver of his right to remain silent."[1272]

8.4.2.2. Illegal detention

The United States Supreme Court has held that a confession made by an accused during a period of illegal detention is inadmissible.[1273] The rule is based, in part, on the notion that an unlawful or "unwarranted detention" may lead "to tempting utilization of intensive interrogation, easily gliding into the evils of 'the third degree.'"[1274] The mandate of what is now known as "the *McNabb-Mallory* rule," was handed down by the Court in the context of its supervisory authority over the federal courts, and for the purpose of adequately enforcing "the congressional requirement of prompt arraignment."[1275] It is not, therefore, constitutionally compelled.[1276]

[1269] *Missouri v. Seibert*, 542 U.S. 600, 124 S. Ct. 2601, 2612 (2004).

[1270] *Missouri v. Seibert*, 542 U.S. 600, 124 S. Ct. 2601, 2613 (2004).

[1271] *See, e.g., Verigan v. People*, 2018 CO 53, ¶ 34, 420 P.3d 247, 254 (concluding that "*Seibert* does create a precedential rule, namely, the rule set forth in Justice Kennedy's concurring opinion").

[1272] *State v. Johnson*, 371 N.C. 870, 876, 821 S.E.2d 822 (2018).

[1273] *Mallory v. United States*, 354 U.S. 449, 455, 77 S. Ct. 1356, 1360 (1957); *McNabb v. United States*, 318 U.S. 332, 344-45, 63 S. Ct. 608, 615 (1943).

[1274] *Mallory v. United States*, 354 U.S. 449, 453, 77 S. Ct. 1356, 1358 (1957).

[1275] *Mallory v. United States*, 354 U.S. 449, 463, 77 S. Ct. 1356, 1359 (1957).

[1276] *See also Taylor v. Alabama*, 457 U.S. 687, 102 S. Ct. 2664, 2667 (1982) (A confession "obtained through custodial interrogation after an illegal arrest should be excluded unless intervening events break the causal connection between the illegal arrest and confession so that the confession is sufficiently an act of free will" to remove the initial illegality).

8.4.2.3. Outside influences

Often in the interrogation process, factors outside or extrinsic to the actual questioning session may work to undermine the integrity of the process or the voluntariness of the defendant's responses. How an officer deals with such outside influences will, in many cases, determine the admissibility of any statements the defendant may make.

In *Moran v. Burbine*,[1277] the Supreme Court held that law enforcement officers were permitted to continue to question a person who was in custody and who has properly waived his *Miranda* rights without telling him that a lawyer (who was contacted by his sister) has been trying to reach him. In this regard, the conduct of the police in failing to advise a suspect in custody that a lawyer (who was contacted by the suspect's sister) has been trying to reach him has no bearing on the validity of the waiver of his *Miranda* rights. "Events occurring outside of the presence of the suspect and entirely unknown to him surely can have no bearing on the capacity to comprehend and knowingly relinquish a constitutional right."

Thus, when the investigators continued to question the defendant after his attorney arrived at the sheriff's office in *State v. Phillips*,[1278] there was no constitutional violation. "The interrogation began before attorney Cunningham arrived at the sheriff's office. Defendant never stated that he wanted the questioning to stop or that he wanted to speak with an attorney. Accordingly, the investigators did not violate defendant's state and federal constitutional rights to counsel by continuing to question him after attorney Cunningham's arrival at the sheriff's office and request to see defendant."[1279]

A suspect's internal compulsion to confess. In *Colorado v. Connelly*,[1280] the accused, who suffered from "command hallucinations" incident to chronic schizophrenia, heard the "voice of God" telling him to confess. The United States Supreme Court held that his confession was not "coerced" within the meaning of the Fifth Amendment because it was not the product of police overreaching. Observing that the Fifth Amendment simply does not address itself to "moral and psychological pressures to confess emanating from sources other than official coercion," the Court held that "coercive police activity is a necessary predicate" to the finding that a confession is not "voluntary" within the meaning of the Fifth Amendment and the Due Process Clause of the Fourteenth Amendment."[1281]

9. FOREIGN NATIONALS

9.1. Notification of Rights

The Vienna Convention on Consular Relations (VCCR) is a binding multi-lateral treaty to which about 170 nations, including the United States, are parties. It was drafted in 1963 with the purpose, evident in its preamble, of contributing "to 'the development of friendly relations among nations, irrespective of their differing constitutional and social systems.'"[1282] The VCCR addresses the functions of a consular post established by the nation sending the consul (the sending State) in the nation receiving the consul (the receiving State).

Under Article 36(1)(b) (ratified by the United States in 1969), when a foreign national (including an undocumented immigrant or foreign national with a "green card") is arrested or detained on criminal or immigration charges, she must be informed *without delay* of the right to have the consular officials of her home country notified and the right to communicate with those consular officials. This notice should be given in addition to, not instead of, the *Miranda* warnings.

Most law enforcement agencies have adopted policies and procedures consistent with the standards set forth in the *Standards for Law Enforcement Agencies*, from the Commission on Accreditation for Law Enforcement Agencies, including those for consular notification and access. "Without delay" is generally interpreted

---

[1277] *Moran v. Burbine*, 475 U.S. 412, 106 S. Ct. 1135 (1986).
[1278] *State v. Phillips*, 365 N.C. 103, 711 S.E.2d 122 (2011).
[1279] *State v. Phillips*, 365 N.C. 103, 112, 711 S.E.2d 122 (2011).
[1280] *Colorado v. Connelly*, 479 U.S. 157, 107 S. Ct. 515 (1986).
[1281] *Colorado v. Connelly*, 479 U.S. 157, 170, 107 S. Ct. 515, 522 (1986).
[1282] *See Sanchez-Llamas v. Oregon*, 548 U.S. 331, 337, 126 S. Ct. 2669, 2674 (2006) (quoting VCCR, 21 *U.S.T.* 77, 79 (1963)).

to mean that a detained foreign national must be advised of his Article 36 rights as soon as law enforcement realizes the person is a foreign national, or is probably a foreign national.

Brief, routine detentions, such as for a traffic violation or accident investigation, do not trigger this requirement. However, if the foreign national is required to accompany a law enforcement officer to a place of detention or is detained for a number of hours or overnight, the consular notification requirement will apply.

In addition, when a foreign national from one of the following countries is arrested or detained, the nearest consular officials *must* be notified without delay, *regardless* of the person's wishes.

These countries include the following:

Albania	Mauritius
Algeria	Moldova
Anguilla	Mongolia
Antigua and Barbuda	Montserrat
Armenia	Nigeria
Azerbaijan	Philippines
Bahamas	Poland (nonpermanent residents only)
Barbados	Romania
Belarus	Russia
Belize	St. Kitts and Nevis
Bermuda	St. Lucia
British Virgin Islands	St. Vincent and the Grenadines
Brunei	Seychelles
Bulgaria	Sierra Leone
Cayman Islands	Singapore
China (including Macao and Hong Kong)	Slovakia
Costa Rica	Tajikistan
Cyprus	Tanzania
Czech Republic	Tonga
Dominica	Trinidad and Tobago
Fiji	Tunisia
Gambia	Turkmenistan
Georgia	Turks and Caicos Islands
Ghana	Tuvalu
Grenada	Ukraine
Guyana	United Kingdom (Residents' passports may
Hungary	bear the name "United Kingdom," or the
Jamaica	name of the specific territory, such as
Kazakhstan	Anguilla, Bermuda, British Virgin Islands,
Kiribati	Cayman Islands, Montserrat, or the Turks
Kuwait	and Caicos Islands)
Kyrgyzstan	Uzbekistan
Malaysia	Zambia
Malta	Zimbabwe

For all other countries, law enforcement must inform the foreign national that they may have their consular officer notified of the arrest or detention and may communicate with them. The foreign national can accept or decline the offer to notify. In all cases, consular notification should be made within 24-72 hours after the initial arrest. Law enforcement should document the response and the notification in the event that there are any questions later.

Note: Under no circumstances should any information indicating that a foreign national may have applied for asylum in the United States or elsewhere be disclosed to that person's government. The following statement is suggested by the U.S. Department of State when consular notification is at the foreign national's option:

As a non-U.S. citizen who is being arrested or detained, you are entitled to have us notify your country's consular representatives here in the United States. A consular official from your country may be able to help you obtain legal counsel and may contact your family and visit you in detention, among other things. If you want us to notify your country's consular officials, you can request this notification now or at any time in the future. After your consular officials are notified, they may call or visit you. Do you want us to notify your country's consular officials?

The following statement is suggested when consular notification is mandatory:

Because of your nationality, we are required to notify your country's consular representatives here in the United States that you have been arrested or detained. After your consular officials are notified, they may call or visit you. You are not required to accept their assistance, but they may be able to help you obtain legal counsel and may contact your family and visit you in detention, among other things. We will be notifying your country's consular officials as soon as possible.

Telephone and fax numbers of the foreign embassies and consulates in the United States and translations of the above statements into selected languages are available at the U.S. Department of State website, http://travel.state.gov.

Although law enforcement officers should make every effort to comply with these requirements, failure to do so is not necessarily a constitutional violation and should not result in the suppression of evidence.[1283]

Regarding individual rights, the Supreme Court has expressly declined to decide whether Article 36 of the Vienna Convention creates individual rights that are enforceable in domestic courts.[1284]

9.2. Waiver of Rights

In a case involving a suspect who is a citizen of another country, a court will still examine the totality of the circumstances surrounding any waiver of Fifth Amendment rights, the same as in a case involving a citizen of the United States. However, the court will pay special attention to such factors as: whether the defendant signed a written waiver; whether the advice of rights was in the defendant's native language; whether the defendant appeared to understand those rights; whether the defendant had the assistance of a translator; whether the defendant's rights were explained painstakingly; and whether the defendant had any experience with the American criminal justice system.[1285]

9.3. Diplomatic Immunity

As a principle of international law, "diplomatic immunity" provides that certain foreign government officials are not subject to the jurisdiction of local courts and other authorities for both their official and, to a large extent, their personal activities.

[1283] *Sanchez-Llamas v. Oregon*, 548 U.S. 331, 126 S. Ct. 2669 (2006); *United States v. Emuegbunam*, 268 F.3d 377 (6th Cir. 2001). *See also United States v. Page*, 232 F.3d 536, 540 (6th Cir. 2000) ("[W]e join our colleagues in the First, Ninth, and Eleventh Circuits in concluding that although some judicial remedies may exist, there is no right in a criminal prosecution to have evidence excluded or an indictment dismissed due to a violation of Article 36.") (citing *United States v. Li*, 206 F.3d 56, 60 (1st Cir. 2000); *United States v. Lombera-Camorlinga*, 206 F.3d 882 (9th Cir. 2000); and *United States v. Cordoba-Mosquera*, 212 F.3d 1194 (11th Cir. 2000)).

[1284] *See Medellin v. Texas*, 552 U.S. 491, 506 n.4, 128 S. Ct. 1346 (2008) (We "assume, without deciding, that Article 36 grants foreign nationals an individually enforceable right to request that their consular officers be notified of their detention, and an accompanying right to be informed by authorities of the availability of consular notification."). *But see Sanchez-Llamas v. Oregon*, 548 U.S. 331, 346, 126 S. Ct. 2669, 2680 (2006) (noting that the Vienna Convention does not explicitly provide for a judicial remedy, and declining to impose one on state courts); *State v. Herrera*, 195 N.C. App. 181, 194, 672 S.E.2d 71 (2009) ("[W]ithout deciding whether Article 36 of the Vienna Convention provides a defendant with an individual right, we hold that the trial court did not err by denying defendant's motion to suppress ... written statements solely due to the State's failure to inform him of his right to contact the Honduran Consulate.").

[1285] *United States v. Amano*, 229 F.3d 801 (9th Cir. 2000).

International law requires that law enforcement authorities of the United States extend certain privileges and immunities to members of foreign diplomatic missions and consular posts. The failure of law enforcement officials to fully respect the privileges and immunities of foreign diplomatic and consular personnel may complicate diplomatic relations between the United States and other foreign nations. It also may lead to harsher treatment of U.S. personnel abroad since the principle of reciprocity is integral to diplomatic and consular relations.

Diplomatic immunity does not exempt diplomatic officers from the obligation of conforming with national and local laws and regulations. Diplomatic immunity is not intended to serve as a license for such persons to flout the law and purposely avoid liability for their actions. The purpose of these privileges and immunities is not to benefit individuals but to ensure the efficient and effective performance of their official missions. This is a crucial point for law-enforcement officers to understand in their dealings with foreign diplomatic and consular personnel. While police officers are obliged under international customary and treaty law to recognize the immunity of the envoy, they must not ignore or condone the commission of crimes. The proper performance of police procedures in such cases is often essential in order for the United States to formulate appropriate measures through diplomatic channels to deal with such offenders.[1286]

It is important that the law enforcement authorities of the United States always treat foreign diplomatic and consular personnel with respect and with due regard for the privileges and immunities to which they are entitled under international law. Any shortcomings have the potential of casting into doubt the commitment of the United States to carry out its international obligations or of negatively influencing larger foreign policy interests. Appropriate caution on the part of law enforcement authorities should never escalate into a total "hands off" attitude in connection with criminal law enforcement actions involving diplomats. Foreign diplomats who violate traffic laws should be cited. Allegations of serious crimes should be fully investigated, promptly reported to the Department of State, and procedurally developed to the maximum permissible extent. Local law enforcement authorities should never be inhibited in their efforts to protect the public welfare in extreme situations. The U.S. Department of State should be advised promptly of any serious difficulties arising in connection with diplomatic or consular personnel. It has provided offices to assist police authorities in verifying individuals who may enjoy inviolability or immunity. Police departments should feel free to contact the Department of State for general advice in any matter bearing on diplomatic or consular personnel.

For a comprehensive law enforcement guide on Diplomatic and Consular Immunity, refer to https://www.state.gov/documents/organization/150546.pdf

---

[1286] Excerpts from *Diplomatic and Consular Immunity: Guidance for Law Enforcement and Judicial Authorities.* (United States Department of State, Office of Foreign Missions).

MOTOR VEHICLE LAWS OF NORTH CAROLINA ANNOTATED

TABLE OF CONTENTS

TABLE OF CONTENTS

Table of Contents

TABLE OF CONTENTS

Table of Contents

CHAPTER 20.
MOTOR VEHICLES

ARTICLE 1.
DIVISION OF MOTOR VEHICLES

§ 20-1. Division of Motor Vehicles established

The Division of Motor Vehicles of the Department of Transportation is established. This Chapter sets out the powers and duties of the Division.

History.
1941, c. 36, s. 1; 1949, c. 1167; 1973, c. 476, s. 193; 1975, c. 716, s. 5; c. 863; 1987, c. 827, s. 2; c. 847, s. 1; 1995 (Reg. Sess., 1996), c. 756, s. 1

LOCAL MODIFICATION. --Dare: 1995, c. 196, s. 1;(As to Chapter 20) city of Charlotte: 2001-88; (As to Chapter 20) city of Salisbury: 2003-130.

EDITOR'S NOTE. --

As to the inapplicability of the contested case provisions of Chapter 150B to the Department of Transportation, except as provided in G.S. 136-29, see G.S. 150B-1(e).

Session Laws 2012-85, s. 12, provides: "When the Division of Motor Vehicles has completed the implementation of the Division's Next Generation Secure Driver License System, the Commissioner of Motor Vehicles shall certify to the Revisor of Statutes that the Division of Motor Vehicles has completed the implementation. When making the certification, the Commissioner of Motor Vehicles shall reference S.L. 2011-35, S.L. 2011-228, and the session law number of this act." On August 21, 2019, the Commissioner of Motor Vehicles certified to the Revisor of Statutes that the Next Generation Secure Driver License System was fully implemented in January 2016.

Session Laws 2013-360, s. 34.28, provides: "The Department of Transportation and the Department of Public Safety shall not transfer any personnel or functions of the License & Theft Bureau of the Department of Transportation's Division of Motor Vehicles or enter into any agreement regarding transfer of personnel or functions of the License & Theft Bureau until passage of an act of the General Assembly authorizing the transfer."

Session Laws 2013-360, s. 1.1, provides: "This act shall be known as the 'Current Operations and Capital Improvements Appropriations Act of 2013.'"

Session Laws 2013-360, s. 38.2, provides: "Except for statutory changes or other provisions that clearly indicate an intention to have effects beyond the 2013-2015 fiscal biennium, the textual provisions of this act apply only to funds appropriated for, and activities occurring during, the 2013-2015 fiscal biennium."

Session Laws 2013-360, s. 38.5, is a severability clause.

Session Laws 2019-231, s. 4.14(a) -(c), provides: "(a) Expand Performance Dashboard. -- The Department of Transportation shall expand its performance dashboard available on the Department's home page of the Department's Web site to track the following information about the Division of Motor Vehicles:

"(1) The number of conventional hybrid vehicle new registrations issued per month and year-to-date.

"(2) The number of conventional hybrid vehicle registrations renewed per month and year-to-date.

"(3) The total number of conventional hybrid vehicles currently registered.

"(4) The number of plug-in hybrid vehicle new registrations issued per month and year-to-date.

"(5) The number of plug-in hybrid vehicle registrations renewed per month and year-to-date.

"(6) The total number of plug-in hybrid vehicles currently registered.

"(7) The number of plug-in electric vehicle new registrations issued per month and year-to-date.

"(8) The number of plug-in electric vehicle registrations renewed per month and year-to-date.

"(9) The total number of plug-in electric vehicles currently registered.

"(b) Definitions. -- For purposes of this section: (i) a 'conventional hybrid vehicle' means a vehicle that uses both a motor fuel engine and an electric motor that cannot be plugged in and recharged, (ii) a 'plug-in hybrid vehicle' means a vehicle that uses both a motor fuel engine and an electric motor with a battery that may be recharged by plugging into an outlet or charging station, and (iii) a 'plug-in electric vehicle' means a vehicle that exclusively uses an on-board battery that may be recharged by plugging into an outlet or charging station.

"(c) Implementation Date. -- The expansion of the Department's performance dashboard required under subsection (a) of this section shall be completed by January 1, 2020."

Session Laws 2019-231, s. 5.3, provides: "Except for statutory changes or other provisions that clearly indicate an intention to have effects beyond the 2019-2021 fiscal biennium, the textual provisions of this act apply only to funds appropriated for, and activities occurring during, the 2019-2021 fiscal biennium."

Session Laws 2019-231, s. 5.5, is a severability clause.

CITED in State v. Wyrick, 35 N.C. App. 352, 241 S.E.2d 355 (1978); Lee v. Gore, 206 N.C. App. 374, 698 S.E.2d 179 (2010), aff'd, 717 S.E.2d 356, 2011 N.C. LEXIS 660 (2011).

LEGAL PERIODICALS. --

For note on the conflict between the North Carolina Motor Vehicle Act and the UCC, see 65 N.C.L. Rev. 1156 (1987).

For legislative survey on motor vehicle law, see 22 Campbell L. Rev. 253 (2000).

§ 20-2. Commissioner of Motor Vehicles; rules

(a) **Commissioner and Assistants.** -- The Division of Motor Vehicles shall be administered by the Commissioner of Motor Vehicles, who shall be appointed by and serve at the pleasure of the Secretary of the Department of Transportation. The Commissioner shall be paid an annual salary to be fixed by the Governor and allowed traveling expenses as allowed by law.

In any action, proceeding, or matter of any kind, to which the Commissioner of Motor Vehicles is a party or in which he may have an interest, all pleadings, legal notices, proof of claim, warrants for collection, certificates of tax liability, executions, and other legal documents, may be signed and verified on behalf of the Commissioner of Motor Vehicles by the Assistant Commissioner of Motor Vehicles or by any director or assistant director of any section of the Division of Motor Vehicles or by any other agent or employee of the Division so authorized by the Commissioner of Motor Vehicles.

(b) **Rules.** -- The Commissioner may adopt rules to implement this Chapter. Chapter 150B of the General Statutes governs the adoption of rules by the Commissioner.

History.
1941, c. 36, s. 2; 1945, c. 527; 1955, c. 472; 1975, c. 716, s. 5; 1983, c. 717, s. 5; 1983 (Reg. Sess., 1984), c. 1034, s. 164; 1991, c. 477, s. 4;2012-142, s. 25.1 (b)

EDITOR'S NOTE. --
Session Laws 2012-142, s. 25.1(f), made the amendments to this section by Session Laws 2012-142, s. 25.1(b), applicable to persons appointed to the positions of Commissioner of Motor Vehicles, "State Personnel Director" [now the Director of the Office of State Human Resources], Director of the North Carolina Museum of Art, and State Chief Information Officer on or after January 1, 2013.

EFFECT OF AMENDMENTS. --
Session Laws 2012-142, s. 25.1(b), effective July 1, 2012, substituted "Governor and allowed traveling" for "General Assembly in the Current Operations Appropriations Act and allowed his traveling" in the last sentence of the first paragraph of subsection (a). For applicability, see Editor's note.
CITED in Thompson Cadillac-Oldsmobile, Inc. v. Silk Hope Auto, Inc., 87 N.C. App. 467, 361 S.E.2d 418 (1987); Murray v. Justice, 96 N.C. App. 169, 385 S.E.2d 195 (1989).

§ 20-3. Organization of Division

The Commissioner, subject to the approval of the Secretary of the Department of Transportation, shall organize and administer the Division in such manner as he may deem necessary to conduct the work of the Division.

History.
1941, c. 36, s. 3; 1975, c. 716, s. 5

§ 20-3.1. Purchase of additional airplanes

The Division of Motor Vehicles shall not purchase additional airplanes without the express authorization of the General Assembly.

History.
1963, c. 911, s. 1 1/2; 1971, c. 198; 1975, c. 716, s. 5

N.C. Gen. Stat. § 20-4

Repealed by Session Laws 2002-190, s. 4, effective January 1, 2003.

EDITOR'S NOTE. --
Session Laws 2002-190, s. 1, provides: "All statutory authority, powers, duties, and functions, including rulemaking, budgeting, purchasing, records, personnel, personnel positions, salaries, property, and unexpended balances of appropriations, allocations, reserves, support costs, and other funds allocated to the Department of Transportation, Division of Motor Vehicles Enforcement Section, for the regulation and enforcement of commercial motor vehicles, oversize and overweight vehicles, motor carrier safety, and mobile and manufactured housing are transferred to and vested in the Department of Crime Control and Public Safety. This transfer has all the elements of a Type I transfer as defined in G.S. 143A-6.

"The Department of Crime Control and Public Safety shall be considered a continuation of the transferred portion of the Department of Transportation, Division of Motor Vehicles Enforcement Section, for the purpose of succession to all rights, powers, duties, and obligations of the Enforcement Section and of those rights, powers, duties, and obligations exercised by the Department of Transportation, Division of Motor Vehicles on behalf of the Enforcement Section. Where the Department of Transportation, the Division of Motor Vehicles, or the Enforcement Section, or any combination thereof are referred to by law, contract, or other document, that reference shall apply to the Department of Crime Control and Public Safety.

"All equipment, supplies, personnel, or other properties rented or controlled by the Department of Transportation, Division of Motor Vehicles Enforcement Section for the regulation and enforcement of commercial motor vehicles, oversize and overweight vehicles, motor carrier safety, and mobile and manufactured housing shall be administered by the Department of Crime Control and Public Safety."

Session Laws 2002-190, s. 17, provides: "The Governor shall resolve any dispute between the Department of Transportation and the Department of Crime Control and Public Safety concerning the implementation of this act [Session Laws 2002-190]."

This section has more than one version with varying effective dates. To view a complete list of the versions of this section see Table of Contents.

§ 20-4.01. Definitions

Unless the context requires otherwise, the following definitions apply throughout this Chapter to the defined words and phrases and their cognates:

(1) **Airbag.** -- A motor vehicle inflatable occupant restraint system device that is part of a supplemental restraint system.

(1a) **Alcohol.** -- Any substance containing any form of alcohol, including ethanol, methanol, propanol, and isopropanol.

(1b) **Alcohol Concentration.** -- The concentration of alcohol in a person, expressed either as:

a. Grams of alcohol per 100 milliliters of blood; or

b. Grams of alcohol per 210 liters of breath.

The results of a defendant's alcohol concentration determined by a chemical analysis of the defendant's breath or blood shall be reported to the hundredths. Any result between hundredths shall be reported to the next lower hundredth.

(1c) **All-Terrain Vehicle or ATV.** -- A motorized vehicle 50 inches or less in width that is designed to travel on three or more low-pressure tires and manufactured for off-highway use. The terms "all-terrain vehicle" or "ATV" do not include a golf cart or a utility vehicle, as defined in this section, or a riding lawn mower.

(1d) **Business District.** -- The territory prescribed as such by ordinance of the Board of Transportation.

(2) **Canceled.** -- As applied to drivers' licenses and permits, a declaration that a license or permit which was issued through error or fraud, or to which G.S. 20-15(a) applies, is void and terminated.

(2a) **Class A Motor Vehicle.** -- A combination of motor vehicles that meets either of the following descriptions:

a. Has a combined GVWR of at least 26,001 pounds and includes as part of the combination a towed unit that has a GVWR of at least 10,001 pounds.

b. Has a combined GVWR of less than 26,001 pounds and includes as part of the combination a towed unit that has a GVWR of at least 10,001 pounds.

(2b) **Class B Motor Vehicle.** -- Any of the following:

a. A single motor vehicle that has a GVWR of at least 26,001 pounds.

b. A combination of motor vehicles that includes as part of the combination a towing unit that has a GVWR of at least 26,001 pounds and a towed unit that has a GVWR of less than 10,001 pounds.

(2c) **Class C Motor Vehicle.** -- Any of the following:

a. A single motor vehicle not included in Class B.

b. A combination of motor vehicles not included in Class A or Class B.

(3) Repealed by Session Laws 1979, c. 667, s. 1.

(3a) **Chemical Analysis.** -- A test or tests of the breath, blood, or other bodily fluid or substance of a person to determine the person's alcohol concentration or presence of an impairing substance, performed in accordance with G.S. 20-139.1, including duplicate or sequential analyses.

(3b) **Chemical Analyst.** -- A person granted a permit by the Department of Health and Human Services under G.S. 20-139.1 to perform chemical analyses.

(3c) **Commercial Drivers License (CDL).** -- A license issued by a state to an individual who resides in the state that authorizes the individual to drive a class of commercial motor vehicle. A "nonresident commercial drivers license (NRCDL)" is issued by a state to an individual who resides in a foreign jurisdiction.

(3d) **Commercial Motor Vehicle.** -- Any of the following motor vehicles that are designed or used to transport passengers or property:

a. A Class A motor vehicle that has a combined GVWR of at least 26,001 pounds and includes as part of the combination a towed unit that has a GVWR of at least 10,001 pounds.

b. A Class B motor vehicle.

c. A Class C motor vehicle that meets either of the following descriptions:

1. Is designed to transport 16 or more passengers, including the driver.

2. Is transporting hazardous materials and is required to be placarded in accordance with 49 C.F.R. Part 172, Subpart F.

d. Repealed by Session Laws 1999, c. 330, s. 9, effective December 1, 1999.

(4) **Commissioner.** -- The Commissioner of Motor Vehicles.

(4a) **Conviction.** -- A conviction for an offense committed in North Carolina or another state:

a. In-State. When referring to an offense committed in North Carolina, the term means any of the following:

1. A final conviction of a criminal offense, including a no contest plea.

2. A determination that a person is responsible for an infraction, including a no contest plea.

3. An unvacated forfeiture of cash in the full amount of a bond required by Article 26 of Chapter 15A of the General Statutes.

4. A third or subsequent prayer for judgment continued within any five-year period.

5. Any prayer for judgment continued if the offender holds a commercial drivers license or if the offense occurs in a commercial motor vehicle.

b. Out-of-State. When referring to an offense committed outside North Carolina, the term means any of the following:

1. An unvacated adjudication of guilt.

2. A determination that a person has violated or failed to comply with the law in a court of original jurisdiction or an authorized administrative tribunal.

3. An unvacated forfeiture of bail or collateral deposited to secure the person's appearance in court.

4. A violation of a condition of release without bail, regardless of whether or not the penalty is rebated, suspended, or probated.

5. A final conviction of a criminal offense, including a no contest plea.

6. Any prayer for judgment continued, including any payment of a fine or court costs, if the offender holds a commercial drivers license or if the offense occurs in a commercial motor vehicle.

(4b) **Counterfeit supplemental restraint system component.** -- A replacement supplemental restraint system component, including an airbag, that displays a mark identical to, or substantially similar to, the genuine mark of a motor vehicle manufacturer or a supplier of parts to the manufacturer of a motor vehicle, without authorization from the manufacturer or supplier.

(4c) **Crash.** -- Any event that results in injury or property damage attributable directly to the motion of a motor vehicle or its load. The terms collision, accident, and crash and their cognates are synonymous.

(5) **Dealer.** -- Every person engaged in the business of buying, selling, distributing, or exchanging motor vehicles, trailers, or semitrailers in this State, and having an established place of business in this State.

The terms "motor vehicle dealer," "new motor vehicle dealer," and "used motor vehicle dealer" as used in Article 12 of this Chapter have the meaning set forth in G.S. 20-286.

(5a) **Dedicated natural gas vehicle.** -- A four-wheeled motor vehicle that meets each of the following requirements:

a. Is made by a manufacturer primarily for use on public streets, roads, and highways and meets National Highway Traffic Safety Administration standards included in 49 C.F.R. § 571.

b. Has not been modified from original manufacturer specifications with regard to power train or any manner of powering the vehicle.

c. Is powered solely by natural gas.

d. Is rated at not more than 8,500 pounds unloaded gross vehicle weight.

e. Has a maximum speed capability of at least 65 miles per hour.

(5b) **Disqualification.** -- A withdrawal of the privilege to drive a commercial motor vehicle.

(6) **Division.** -- The Division of Motor Vehicles acting directly or through its duly authorized officers and agents.

(7) **Driver.** -- The operator of a vehicle, as defined in subdivision (25). The terms "driver" and "operator" and their cognates are synonymous.

(7a) **Electric Assisted Bicycle.** -- A bicycle with two or three wheels that is equipped with a seat or saddle for use by the rider, fully operable pedals for human propulsion, and an electric motor of no more than 750 watts, whose maximum speed on a level surface when powered solely by such a motor is no greater than 20 miles per hour.

(7b) **Electric Personal Assistive Mobility Device.** -- A self-balancing nontandem two-wheeled device, designed to transport one person, with a propulsion system that limits the maximum speed of the device to 15 miles per hour or less.

(7c) **Employer.** -- Any person who owns or leases a commercial motor vehicle or assigns a person to drive a commercial motor vehicle and would be subject to the alcohol and controlled substance testing provisions of 49 C.F.R. § 382 and also includes any consortium or third-party administrator administering the alcohol and controlled substance testing program on behalf of owner-operators subject to the provisions of 49 C.F.R. § 382.

(8) **Essential Parts.** -- All integral and body parts of a vehicle of any type required

to be registered hereunder, the removal, alteration, or substitution of which would tend to conceal the identity of the vehicle or substantially alter its appearance, model, type, or mode of operation.

(9) **Established Place of Business.** -- Except as provided in G.S. 20-286, the place actually occupied by a dealer or manufacturer at which a permanent business of bargaining, trading, and selling motor vehicles is or will be carried on and at which the books, records, and files necessary and incident to the conduct of the business of automobile dealers or manufacturers shall be kept and maintained.

(10) **Explosives.** -- Any chemical compound or mechanical mixture that is commonly used or intended for the purpose of producing an explosion and which contains any oxidizing and combustive units or other ingredients in such proportions, quantities, or packing that an ignition by fire, by friction, by concussion, by percussion, or by detonator of any part of the compound or mixture may cause such a sudden generation of highly heated gases that the resultant gaseous pressures are capable of producing destructible effects on contiguous objects or of destroying life or limb.

(11) **Farm Tractor.** -- Every motor vehicle designed and used primarily as a farm implement for drawing plows, mowing machines, and other implements of husbandry.

(11a) **For-Hire Motor Carrier.** -- A person who transports passengers or property by motor vehicle for compensation.

(12) **Foreign Vehicle.** -- Every vehicle of a type required to be registered hereunder brought into this State from another state, territory, or country, other than in the ordinary course of business, by or through a manufacturer or dealer and not registered in this State.

(12a) **Fuel cell electric vehicle.** -- A four-wheeled motor vehicle that does not have the ability to be propelled by a gasoline engine and that meets each of the following requirements:

a. Is made by a manufacturer primarily for use on public streets, roads, and highways and meets National Highway Traffic Safety Administration standards included in 49 C.F.R. § 571.

b. Has not been modified from original manufacturer specifications with regard to power train or any manner of powering the vehicle.

c. Uses hydrogen and a fuel cell to produce electricity on board to power an electric motor to propel the vehicle.

d. Is rated at not more than 8,500 pounds unloaded gross vehicle weight.

e. Has a maximum speed capability of at least 65 miles per hour.

(12b) **Golf Cart.** -- A vehicle designed and manufactured for operation on a golf course for sporting or recreational purposes and that is not capable of exceeding speeds of 20 miles per hour.

(12c) **Gross Combination Weight Rating (GCWR).** -- Defined in 49 C.F.R. § 390.5.

(12d) **Gross Combined Weight (GCW).** -- The total weight of a combination (articulated) motor vehicle, including passengers, fuel, cargo, and attachments.

(12e) **Gross Vehicle Weight (GVW).** -- The total weight of a vehicle, including passengers, fuel, cargo, and attachments.

(12f) **Gross Vehicle Weight Rating (GVWR).** -- The value specified by the manufacturer as the maximum loaded weight a vehicle is capable of safely hauling. The GVWR of a combination vehicle is the GVWR of the power unit plus the GVWR of the towed unit or units. When a vehicle is determined by an enforcement officer to be structurally altered in any way from the manufacturer's original design in an attempt to increase the hauling capacity of the vehicle, the GVWR of that vehicle shall be deemed to be the greater of the license weight or the total weight of the vehicle or combination of vehicles for the purpose of enforcing this Chapter. For the purpose of classification of commercial drivers license and skills testing, the manufacturer's GVWR shall be used.

(12g) **Hazardous Materials.** -- Any material that has been designated as hazardous under 49 U.S.C. § 5103 and is required to be placarded under Subpart F of Part 172 of Title 49 of the Code of Federal Regulations, or any quantity of a material listed as a select agent or toxin under Part 73 of Title 42 of the Code of Federal Regulations.

(12h) **High-Mobility Multipurpose Wheeled Vehicle (HMMWV).** -- A four-wheel drive vehicle produced for military or government use and commonly referred to as a "HMMWV" or "Humvee".

(13) **Highway.** -- The entire width between property or right-of-way lines of every way or place of whatever nature, when any part thereof is open to the use of the public as a matter of right for the purposes of vehicular traffic. The terms "highway" and "street" and their cognates are synonymous.

(14) **House Trailer.** -- Any trailer or semitrailer designed and equipped to provide living or sleeping facilities and drawn by a motor vehicle. This term shall not include a manufactured home as defined in subdivision (18a) of this section.

Chapter 20

(14a) **Impairing Substance.** -- Alcohol, controlled substance under Chapter 90 of the General Statutes, any other drug or psychoactive substance capable of impairing a person's physical or mental faculties, or any combination of these substances.

(15) **Implement of Husbandry.** -- Every vehicle which is designed for agricultural purposes and used exclusively in the conduct of agricultural operations.

(15a) **Inoperable Vehicle.** -- A motor vehicle that is substantially disassembled and for this reason is mechanically unfit or unsafe to be operated or moved upon a public street, highway, or public vehicular area.

(16) **Intersection.** -- The area embraced within the prolongation of the lateral curblines or, if none, then the lateral edge of roadway lines of two or more highways which join one another at any angle whether or not one such highway crosses the other.

Where a highway includes two roadways 30 feet or more apart, then every crossing of each roadway of such divided highway by an intersecting highway shall be regarded as a separate intersection. In the event that such intersecting highway also includes two roadways 30 feet or more apart, then every crossing of two roadways of such highways shall be regarded as a separate intersection.

(17) **License.** -- Any driver's license or any other license or permit to operate a motor vehicle issued under or granted by the laws of this State including:

a. Any temporary license or learner's permit;

b. The privilege of any person to drive a motor vehicle whether or not such person holds a valid license; and

c. Any nonresident's operating privilege.

(18) **Local Authorities.** -- Every county, municipality, or other territorial district with a local board or body having authority to adopt local police regulations under the Constitution and laws of this State.

(18a) **Manufactured Home.** -- Defined in G.S. 143-143.9(6).

(19) **Manufacturer.** -- Every person, resident, or nonresident of this State, who manufactures or assembles motor vehicles.

(20) **Manufacturer's Certificate.** -- A certification on a form approved by the Division, signed by the manufacturer, indicating the name of the person or dealer to whom the therein-described vehicle is transferred, the date of transfer and that such vehicle is the first transfer of such vehicle in ordinary trade and commerce. The description of the vehicle shall include the make, model, year, type of body, identification number or numbers, and such other information as the Division may require.

(21) **Metal Tire.** -- Every tire the surface of which in contact with the highway is wholly or partly of metal or other hard, nonresilient material.

(21a) Repealed by Session Laws 2016-90, s. 13(a), effective December 1, 2016, and applicable to offenses committed on or after that date.

(21b) **Motor Carrier.** -- A for-hire motor carrier or a private motor carrier.

(22) **Motorcycle.** -- A type of passenger vehicle as defined in G.S. 20-4.01(27).

(23) **Motor Vehicle.** -- Every vehicle which is self-propelled and every vehicle designed to run upon the highways which is pulled by a self-propelled vehicle. Except as specifically provided otherwise, this term shall not include mopeds or electric assisted bicycles.

(23a) **Nonfunctional airbag.** -- A replacement airbag that meets any of the following criteria:

a. The airbag was previously deployed or damaged.

b. The airbag has an electric fault that is detected by the vehicle's airbag diagnostic systems when the installation procedure is completed and the vehicle is returned to the customer who requested the work to be performed or when ownership is intended to be transferred.

c. The airbag includes a part or object, including a supplemental restraint system component that is installed in a motor vehicle to mislead the owner or operator of the motor vehicle into believing that a functional airbag has been installed.

d. The airbag is subject to the prohibitions of 49 U.S.C. § 30120(j).

(24) **Nonresident.** -- Any person whose legal residence is in some state, territory, or jurisdiction other than North Carolina or in a foreign country.

(24a) **Offense Involving Impaired Driving.** -- Any of the following offenses:

a. Impaired driving under G.S. 20-138.1.

b. Any offense set forth under G.S. 20-141.4 when conviction is based upon impaired driving or a substantially similar offense under previous law.

c. First or second degree murder under G.S. 14-17 or involuntary manslaughter under G.S. 14-18 when conviction is based upon impaired driving or a substantially similar offense under previous law.

d. An offense committed in another jurisdiction which prohibits substantially similar conduct prohibited by the offenses in this subsection.

e. A repealed or superseded offense substantially similar to impaired driving, including offenses under former G.S. 20-138 or G.S. 20-139.

f. Impaired driving in a commercial motor vehicle under G.S. 20-138.2, except that convictions of impaired driving under G.S. 20-138.1 and G.S. 20-138.2 arising out of the same transaction shall be considered a single conviction of an offense involving impaired driving for any purpose under this Chapter.

g. Habitual impaired driving under G.S. 20-138.5.

A conviction under former G.S. 20-140(c) is not an offense involving impaired driving.

(24b) **On-track equipment.** -- Any railcar, rolling stock, equipment, vehicle, or other device that is operated on stationary rails.

(25) **Operator.** -- A person in actual physical control of a vehicle which is in motion or which has the engine running. The terms "operator" and "driver" and their cognates are synonymous.

(25a) **Out of Service Order.** -- A declaration that a driver, a commercial motor vehicle, or a motor carrier operation is out-of-service.

(26) **Owner.** -- A person holding the legal title to a vehicle, or in the event a vehicle is the subject of a chattel mortgage or an agreement for the conditional sale or lease thereof or other like agreement, with the right of purchase upon performance of the conditions stated in the agreement, and with the immediate right of possession vested in the mortgagor, conditional vendee or lessee, said mortgagor, conditional vendee or lessee shall be deemed the owner for the purpose of this Chapter. For the purposes of this Chapter, the lessee of a vehicle owned by the government of the United States shall be considered the owner of said vehicle.

(27) **Passenger Vehicles.** --

a. **Ambulances.** -- Vehicles equipped for transporting wounded, injured, or sick persons.

b. **Autocycle.** -- A three-wheeled motorcycle that has a steering wheel, pedals, seat safety belts for each occupant, antilock brakes, completely or partially enclosed seating that does not require the operator to straddle or sit astride, and is otherwise manufactured to comply with federal safety requirements for motorcycles.

c. **Child care vehicles.** -- Vehicles under the direction and control of a child care facility, as defined in G.S. 110-86(3), and driven by an owner, employee, or agent of the child care facility for the primary purpose of transporting children to and from the child care facility, or to and from a place for participation in an event or activity in connection with the child care facility.

d. **Common carriers of passengers.** -- Vehicles operated under a certificate of authority issued by the Utilities Commission for operation on the highways of this State between fixed termini or over a regular route for the transportation of persons for compensation.

e. **Excursion passenger vehicles.** -- Vehicles transporting persons on sight-seeing or travel tours.

f. **For-hire passenger vehicles.** -- Vehicles transporting persons for compensation. This classification shall not include the following:

1. Vehicles operated as ambulances.

2. Vehicles operated by the owner where the costs of operation are shared by the passengers.

3. Vehicles operated pursuant to a ridesharing arrangement as defined in G.S. 136-44.21.

4. Vehicles transporting students for the public school system under contract with the State Board of Education.

5. Vehicles leased to the United States of America or any of its agencies on a nonprofit basis.

6. Vehicles used for human service.

7. Vehicles used for volunteer transportation.

8. Vehicles operated in a TNC service, excluding vehicles operated in connection with a brokering transportation network company, regulated under Article 10A of Chapter 20 of the General Statutes.

g. **Low-speed vehicle.** -- A four-wheeled electric vehicle whose top speed is greater than 20 miles per hour but less than 25 miles per hour.

g1. **Mini-truck.** -- A motor vehicle designed, used, or maintained primarily for the transportation of property and having four wheels, an engine displacement of 660cc or less, an overall length of 130 inches or less, an overall height of 78 inches or less, and an overall width of 60 inches or less.

g2. **Modified utility vehicle.** -- A motor vehicle that (i) is manufactured for off-road use with equipment required by G.S. 20-121.1(2), except a vehicle identification number, and (ii) has four wheels, an engine displacement greater than 2,400 cubic centimeters, an overall length of 142 inches or greater, an overall width of 58 inches or greater, an overall height of 70 inches or greater, a maximum speed capability of 40 miles per hour or greater, and does not require an operator or passenger to straddle a seat. "Modified utility vehicle" does not include an all-terrain vehicle, golf cart, or utility vehicle, as defined in this section, or a riding lawn mower.

h. **Motorcycles.** -- Vehicles having a saddle for the use of the rider and designed to travel on not more than three wheels in contact with the ground, including autocycles, motor scooters, and motor-driven bicycles, but excluding tractors and utility vehicles equipped with an additional form of device designed to transport property, three-wheeled vehicles while being used by law-enforcement agencies, electric assisted bicycles, and mopeds as defined in sub-subdivision d1. of this subdivision.

i. **Motor-driven bicycle.** -- A vehicle with two or three wheels, a steering handle, one or two saddle seats, pedals, and a motor that cannot propel the vehicle at a speed greater than 20 miles per hour on a level surface. This term shall not include an electric assisted bicycle as defined in subdivision (7a) of this section.

j. **Moped.** -- A vehicle, other than a motor-driven bicycle or electric assisted bicycle, that has two or three wheels, no external shifting device, a motor that does not exceed 50 cubic centimeters piston displacement and cannot propel the vehicle at a speed greater than 30 miles per hour on a level surface. The motor may be powered by electricity, alternative fuel, motor fuel, or a combination of each.

k. **Motor home or house car.** -- A vehicular unit, designed to provide temporary living quarters, built into as an integral part, or permanently attached to, a self-propelled motor vehicle chassis or van. The vehicle must provide at least four of the following

facilities: cooking, refrigeration or ice-box, self-contained toilet, heating or air conditioning, a portable water supply system including a faucet and sink, separate 110-125 volt electrical power supply, or an LP gas supply.

l. **Private passenger vehicles.** -- All other passenger vehicles not included in the above definitions.

m. **School activity bus.** -- A vehicle, generally painted a different color from a school bus, whose primary purpose is to transport school students and others to or from a place for participation in an event other than regular classroom work. The term includes a public, private, or parochial vehicle that meets this description.

n. **School bus.** -- A vehicle whose primary purpose is to transport school students over an established route to and from school for the regularly scheduled school day, that is equipped with alternately flashing red lights on the front and rear and a mechanical stop signal, that is painted primarily yellow below the roofline, and that bears the plainly visible words "School Bus" on the front and rear. The term includes a public, private, or parochial vehicle that meets this description.

o. **U-drive-it passenger vehicles.** -- Passenger vehicles included in the definition of U-drive-it vehicles set forth in this section.

(28) **Person.** -- Every individual, firm, partnership, association, corporation, governmental agency, or combination thereof of whatsoever form or character.

(28a) **Personal delivery device.** -- An electrically powered device intended for transporting cargo that is equipped with automated driving technology that enables device operation with or without the remote support and supervision of a human and that does not exceed (i) a weight of 500 pounds, excluding cargo, (ii) a length of 40 inches, and (iii) a width of 30 inches.

(28b) **Plug-in electric vehicle.** -- A four-wheeled motor vehicle that does not have the ability to be propelled by a gasoline engine and that meets each of the following requirements:

a. Is made by a manufacturer primarily for use on public streets, roads, and highways and meets National Highway Traffic Safety Administration standards included in 49 C.F.R. § 571.

b. Has not been modified from original manufacturer specifications with regard to power train or any manner of powering the vehicle.

c. Is rated at not more than 8,500 pounds unloaded gross vehicle weight.

d. Has a maximum speed capability of at least 65 miles per hour.

e. Draws electricity from a battery that has all of the following characteristics:

1. A capacity of not less than four kilowatt hours.

2. Capable of being recharged from an external source of electricity.

(29) **Pneumatic Tire.** -- Every tire in which compressed air is designed to support the load.

(29a) **Private Motor Carrier.** -- A person who transports passengers or property by motor vehicle in interstate commerce and is not a for-hire motor carrier.

(30) **Private Road or Driveway.** -- Every road or driveway not open to the use of the public as a matter of right for the purpose of vehicular traffic.

(31) **Property-Hauling Vehicles.** --

a. Vehicles used for the transportation of property.

b., c. Repealed by Session Laws 1995 (Regular Session, 1996), c. 756, s. 4.

d. **Semitrailers.** -- Vehicles without motive power designed for carrying property or persons and for being drawn by a motor vehicle, and so constructed that part of their weight or their load rests upon or is carried by the pulling vehicle.

e. **Trailers.** -- Vehicles without motive power designed for carrying property or persons wholly on their own structure and to be drawn by a motor vehicle, including "pole trailers" or a pair of wheels used primarily to balance a load rather than for purposes of transportation.

f. Repealed by Session Laws 1995 (Regular Session, 1996), c. 756, s. 4.

(31a) **Provisional Licensee.** -- A person under the age of 18 years.

(32) **Public Vehicular Area.** -- Any area within the State of North Carolina that meets one or more of the following requirements:

a. The area is used by the public for vehicular traffic at any time, including by way of illustration and not limitation any drive, driveway, road, roadway, street, alley, or parking lot upon the grounds and premises of any of the following:

1. Any public or private hospital, college, university, school, orphanage, church, or any of the institutions, parks or other facilities maintained and supported by the State of North Carolina or any of its subdivisions.

2. Any service station, drive-in theater, supermarket, store, restaurant, or office building, or any other business, residential, or municipal establishment providing parking space whether the business or establishment is open or closed.

3. Any property owned by the United States and subject to the jurisdiction of the State of North Carolina. (The inclusion of property owned by the United States in this definition shall not limit assimilation of North Carolina law when applicable under the provisions of Title 18, United States Code, section 13).

b. The area is a beach area used by the public for vehicular traffic.

c. The area is a road used by vehicular traffic within or leading to a gated or non-gated subdivision or community, whether or not the subdivision or community roads have been offered for dedication to the public.

d. The area is a portion of private property used by vehicular traffic and designated by the private property owner as a public vehicular area in accordance with G.S. 20-219.4.

(32a) **Ramp Meter.** -- A traffic control device that consists of a circular red and circular green display placed at a point along an interchange entrance ramp.

(32b) **Recreational Vehicle.** -- A vehicular type unit primarily designed as temporary living quarters for recreational, camping, or travel use that either has its own motive power or is mounted on, or towed by, another vehicle. The basic entities are camping trailer, fifth-wheel travel trailer, motor home, travel trailer, and truck camper. This term shall not include a manufactured home as defined in G.S. 143-143.9(6). The basic entities are defined as follows:

a. **Camping trailer.** -- A vehicular portable unit mounted on wheels and constructed with collapsible partial side walls that fold for towing by another vehicle and unfold at the campsite to provide temporary living quarters for recreational, camping, or travel use.

b. **Fifth-wheel trailer.** -- A vehicular unit mounted on wheels designed to provide temporary living quarters for recreational, camping, or travel use, of a size and weight that does not require a special highway movement permit and designed to be towed by a motorized vehicle that contains a towing mechanism that is mounted above or forward of the tow vehicle's rear axle.

c. **Motor home.** -- As defined in G.S. 20-4.01(27)k.

d. **Travel trailer.** -- A vehicular unit mounted on wheels, designed to provide temporary living quarters for recreational, camping, or travel use, and of a size or weight that does not require a special highway movement permit when towed by a motorized vehicle.

e. **Truck camper.** -- A portable unit that is constructed to provide temporary living quarters for recreational, camping, or travel use, consisting of a roof, floor, and sides and is designed to be loaded onto and unloaded from the bed of a pickup truck.

(32c) **Regular Drivers License.** -- A license to drive a commercial motor vehicle that is exempt from the commercial drivers license requirements or a noncommercial motor vehicle.

(33) a. Flood Vehicle. -- A motor vehicle that has been submerged or partially submerged in water to the extent that damage to the body, engine, transmission, or differential has occurred.

b. Non-U.S.A. Vehicle. -- A motor vehicle manufactured outside of the United States and not intended by the manufacturer for sale in the United States.

c. **Reconstructed Vehicle.** -- A motor vehicle of a type required to be registered hereunder that has been materially altered from original construction due to removal, addition or substitution of new or used essential parts; and includes glider kits and custom assembled vehicles.

d. **Salvage Motor Vehicle.** -- Any motor vehicle damaged by collision or other occurrence to the extent that the cost of repairs to the vehicle and rendering the vehicle safe for use on the public streets and highways would exceed seventy-five percent (75%) of its fair retail market value, whether or not the motor vehicle has been declared a total loss by an insurer. Repairs shall include the cost of parts and labor. Fair market retail values shall be as found in the NADA Pricing Guide Book or other publications approved by the Commissioner.

e. **Salvage Rebuilt Vehicle.** -- A salvage vehicle that has been rebuilt for title and registration.

f. **Junk Vehicle.** -- A motor vehicle which is incapable of operation or use upon the highways and has no resale value except as a source of parts or scrap, and shall not be titled or registered.

(33a) **Relevant Time after the Driving.** -- Any time after the driving in which the driver still has in his body alcohol consumed before or during the driving.

(33b) **Reportable Crash.** -- A crash involving a motor vehicle that results in one or more of the following:

a. Death or injury of a human being.

b. Total property damage of one thousand dollars ($ 1,000) or more, or property damage of any amount to a vehicle seized pursuant to G. S. 20-28.3.

(33c) **Reserve components of the Armed Forces of the United States.** -- The organizations listed in Title 10 United States Code, section 10101, which specifically includes the Army and Air National Guard.

(34) **Resident.** -- Any person who resides within this State for other than a temporary or transitory purpose for more than six months shall be presumed to be a resident of this State; but absence from the State for more than six months shall raise no presumption that the person is not a resident of this State.

(35) **Residential District.** -- The territory prescribed as such by ordinance of the Department of Transportation.

(36) **Revocation or Suspension.** -- Termination of a licensee's or permittee's privilege to drive or termination of the registration of a vehicle for a period of time stated in an order of revocation or suspension. The terms "revocation" or "suspension" or a combination of both terms shall be used synonymously.

(37) **Road Tractors.** -- Vehicles designed and used for drawing other vehicles upon the highway and not so constructed as to carry any part of the load, either independently or as a part of the weight of the vehicle so drawn.

(38) **Roadway.** -- That portion of a highway improved, designed, or ordinarily used for vehicular travel, exclusive of the shoulder. In the event a highway includes two or more separate roadways the term "roadway" as used herein shall refer to any such roadway separately but not to all such roadways collectively.

(39) **Safety Zone.** -- Traffic island or other space officially set aside within a highway for the exclusive use of pedestrians and which is so plainly marked or indicated by proper signs as to be plainly visible at all times while set apart as a safety zone.

Chapter 20

(40) **Security Agreement.** -- Written agreement which reserves or creates a security interest.

(41) **Security Interest.** -- An interest in a vehicle reserved or created by agreement and which secures payments or performance of an obligation. The term includes but is not limited to the interest of a chattel mortgagee, the interest of a vendor under a conditional sales contract, the interest of a trustee under a chattel deed of trust, and the interest of a lessor under a lease intended as security. A security interest is "perfected" when it is valid against third parties generally.

(41a) **Serious Traffic Violation.** -- A conviction of one of the following offenses when operating a commercial or other motor vehicle:

a. Excessive speeding, involving a single charge of any speed 15 miles per hour or more above the posted speed limit.

b. Careless and reckless driving.

c. A violation of any State or local law relating to motor vehicle traffic control, other than a parking violation, arising in connection with a fatal accident.

d. Improper or erratic lane changes.

e. Following the vehicle ahead too closely.

f. Driving a commercial motor vehicle without obtaining a commercial drivers license.

g. Driving a commercial motor vehicle without a commercial drivers license in the driver's possession.

h. Driving a commercial motor vehicle without the proper class of commercial drivers license or endorsements for the specific vehicle group being operated or for the passenger or type of cargo being transported.

i. Unlawful use of a mobile telephone under G.S. 20-137.4A or Part 390 or Part 392 of Title 49 of the Code of Federal Regulations while operating a commercial motor vehicle.

(42) **Solid Tire.** -- Every tire of rubber or other resilient material which does not depend upon compressed air for the support of the load.

(43) **Specially Constructed Vehicles.** -- Motor vehicles required to be registered under this Chapter and that fit within one of the following categories:

a. **Replica vehicle.** -- A vehicle, excluding motorcycles, that when assembled replicates an earlier year, make, and model vehicle.

b. **Street rod vehicle.** -- A vehicle, excluding motorcycles, manufactured prior to 1949 that has been materially altered or has a body constructed from nonoriginal materials.

c. **Custom-built vehicle.** -- A vehicle, including motorcycles, reconstructed or assembled by a nonmanufacturer from new or used parts that has an exterior that does not replicate or resemble any other manufactured vehicle. This category also includes any motorcycle that was originally sold unassembled and manufactured from a kit or that has been materially altered or that has a body constructed from nonoriginal materials.

(44) **Special Mobile Equipment.** -- Defined in G.S. 105-164.3.

(44a) **Specialty Vehicles.** -- Vehicles of a type required to be registered under this Chapter that are modified from their original construction for an educational, emergency services, or public safety use.

(45) **State.** -- A state, territory, or possession of the United States, District of Columbia, Commonwealth of Puerto Rico, a province of Canada, or the Sovereign Nation of the Eastern Band of the Cherokee Indians with tribal lands, as defined in 18 U.S.C. § 1151, located within the boundaries of the State of North Carolina. For provisions in this Chapter that apply to commercial drivers licenses, "state" means a state of the United States and the District of Columbia.

(46) **Street.** -- A highway, as defined in subdivision (13). The terms "highway" and "street" and their cognates are synonymous.

(46a) **Supplemental restraint system.** -- A passive inflatable motor vehicle occupant crash protection system designed for use in conjunction with a seat belt assembly as defined in 49 C.F.R. § 571.209, and includes one or more airbags and all components required to ensure that an airbag works as designed by the vehicle manufacturer, including both of the following:

a. The airbag operates as designed in the event of a crash.

b. The airbag is designed in accordance with federal motor vehicle safety standards for the specific make, model, and year of the motor vehicle in which it is or will be installed.

(47) **Suspension.** -- Termination of a licensee's or permittee's privilege to drive or termination of the registration of a vehicle for a period of time stated in an order of revocation or suspension. The terms "revocation" or "suspension" or a combination of both terms shall be used synonymously.

(48) **Truck Tractors.** -- Vehicles designed and used primarily for drawing

Chapter 20

other vehicles and not so constructed as to carry any load independent of the vehicle so drawn.

(48a) *(Effective until December 31, 2024)* U-drive-it vehicles. -- The following vehicles that are either rented to a person, to be operated by that person, or loaned by a franchised motor vehicle dealer, with or without charge, to a customer of that dealer who is having a vehicle serviced or repaired by the dealer:

    a. A private passenger vehicle other than the following:

       1. A private passenger vehicle of nine-passenger capacity or less that is rented for a term of one year or more.

       2. A private passenger vehicle that is rented to public school authorities for driver-training instruction.

    b. A property-hauling vehicle under 7,000 pounds that does not haul products for hire and that is rented for a term of less than one year.

    c. Motorcycles.

(48a) *(Effective December 31, 2024)* U-drive-it vehicles. -- The following vehicles that are rented to a person, to be operated by that person:

    a. A private passenger vehicle other than the following:

       1. A private passenger vehicle of nine-passenger capacity or less that is rented for a term of one year or more.

       2. A private passenger vehicle that is rented to public school authorities for driver-training instruction.

    b. A property-hauling vehicle under 7,000 pounds that does not haul products for hire and that is rented for a term of less than one year.

    c. Motorcycles.

(48b) **Under the Influence of an Impairing Substance.** -- The state of a person having his physical or mental faculties, or both, appreciably impaired by an impairing substance.

(48c) **Utility Vehicle.** -- A motor vehicle that is (i) designed for off-road use and (ii) used for general maintenance, security, agricultural, or horticultural purposes. "Utility vehicle" does not include an all-terrain vehicle or golf cart, as defined in this section, or a riding lawn mower.

(49) **Vehicle.** -- Every device in, upon, or by which any person or property is or may be transported or drawn upon a highway, excepting devices moved by human power or used exclusively upon fixed rails or tracks; provided, that for the purposes of this Chapter bicycles and electric assisted bicycles shall be deemed vehicles and every rider of a bicycle or an electric assisted bicycle upon a highway shall be subject to the provisions of this Chapter applicable to the driver of a vehicle except those which by their nature can have no application. This term shall not include a device which is designed for and intended to be used as a means of transportation for a person with a mobility impairment, or who uses the device for mobility enhancement, is suitable for use both inside and outside a building, including on sidewalks, and is limited by design to 15 miles per hour when the device is being operated by a person with a mobility impairment, or who uses the device for mobility enhancement. This term shall not include (i) an electric personal assistive mobility device as defined in subdivision (7b) of this section or (ii) a personal delivery device as defined by this section. Unless the context requires otherwise, and except as provided under G.S. 20-109.2, 47-20.6, or 47-20.7, a manufactured home shall be deemed a vehicle.

(50) **Wreckers.** -- Vehicles with permanently attached cranes used to move other vehicles; provided, that said wreckers shall be equipped with adequate brakes for units being towed.

History.
1973, c. 1330, s. 1; 1975, cc. 94, 208; c. 716, s. 5; c. 743; c. 859, s. 1; 1977, c. 313; c. 464, s. 34; 1979, c. 39; c. 423, s. 1; c. 574, ss. 1-4; c. 667, s. 1; c. 680; 1981, c. 606, s. 3; c. 792, s. 2; 1983, c. 435, s. 8; 1983 (Reg. Sess., 1984), c. 1101, ss. 1-3; 1985, c. 509, s. 6; 1987, c. 607, s. 2; c. 658, s. 1; 1987 (Reg. Sess., 1988), c. 1069; c. 1105, s. 1; c. 1112, ss. 1-3; 1989, c. 455, ss. 1, 2; c. 727, s. 219(1); c. 771, ss. 1, 18; 1991, c. 449, s. 2;c. 726, ss. 1 -4; 1991 (Reg. Sess., 1992), c. 1015, s. 1; 1993 (Reg. Sess., 1994), c. 761, s. 22; 1995, c. 191, s. 1;1995 (Reg. Sess., 1996), c. 756, ss. 2-4; 1997-379, s. 5.1;1997-443, s. 11A.8;1997-456, s. 27;1998-149, s. 1;1998-182, ss. 1, 1.1, 26; 1998-217, s. 62(e);1999-330, s. 9;1999-337, s. 28(c) -(e); 1999-406, s. 14;1999-452, ss. 1 -5; 2000-155, s. 9;2000-173, s. 10(c);2001-212, s. 2;2001-341, ss. 1, 2; 2001-356, ss. 1, 2; 2001-441, s. 1;2001-487, ss. 50(a), 51; 2002-72, s. 19(b);2002-98, ss. 1 -3; 2003-397, s. 1;2005-282, s. 1;2005-349, ss. 1 -3; 2006-253, s. 8;2007-56, s. 4;2007-382, ss. 2, 3; 2007-455, s. 1;2007-493, s. 1;2008-156, s. 1;2009-274, s. 1;2009-405, ss. 1, 4; 2009-416, ss. 1, 2; 2010-129, s. 1;2011-95, s. 1;2011-206, s. 1;2013-410, s. 47.5;2014-58, s. 10(a), (c), (d); 2014-115, s. 28.3;2015-125, s. 1;2015-163, s. 1;2015-232, s. 1.1(a);2015-237, s. 2;2016-59, s. 1;2016-90, ss. 12.5(a), 13(a); 2016-94, s. 35.20(a);2017-69, s. 2.1(a);2017-102, s. 5.2(a), (b); 2018-27, s. 4.5(b);2018-42, s. 3(b);2019-34, s. 1;2019-36, s. 1;2019-155, s. 1;2019-227, s. 1(a), (b); 2020-40, s. 1;2020-51, s. 1(b);2020-73, s. 1

SUBDIVISION (48A) SET OUT TWICE. --The first version of subdivision (48a) set out above is effective until December 31, 2024. The second version of subdivision (48a) set out above is effective December 31, 2024.

EDITOR'S NOTE. --

Subdivisions (0.1), (0.2) and (1) were redesignated as subdivisions (1a), (1b) and (1c) and the subunits of subdivision (33) were renumbered pursuant to Session Laws 1997-456, s. 27 which authorized the Revisor of Statutes to renumber or reletter sections and parts of sections having a number or letter designation that is incompatible with the General Assembly's computer database.

Subdivisions (48a) and (48b) were designated as such under the direction of the Revisor of Statutes.

Sections 20-138, 20-139, and 20-140(c), referred to in this section, were repealed by Session Laws 1983, c. 435, s. 23.

Session Laws 1999-406, s. 18, states that this act does not obligate the General Assembly to appropriate additional funds, and that this act shall be implemented with funds available or appropriated to the Department of Transportation and the Administrative Office of the Courts.

Subdivisions (5a), defining "Dedicated natural gas vehicle" and (12a), defining "Fuel cell electric vehicle" were originally enacted by Session Laws 2011-206, s. 1, as subdivisions (28b) and (28c), respectively. At the direction of the Revisor of Statutes, they were redesignated to maintain alphabetical order, and former subdivisions (5a) and (12)(a) through (12)(f) were redesignated accordingly.

Session Laws 2014-58, s. 14, made subdivision (32a), as added by Session Laws 2014-58, s. 10(a), and the renumbering of former subdivisions (32a) and (32b) as subdivisions (32b) and (32c) by Session Laws 2014-58, s. 10(c) and (d), applicable to offenses committed on or after December 1, 2014.

Session Laws 2015-125, s. 10, made the substitution of "Except as specifically provided otherwise, this term" for "This" in the second sentence of subdivision (23) of this section by Session Laws 2015-125, s. 1, applicable to offenses committed on or after July 1, 2016. Session Laws 2015-163, s. 1, which added subdivision (27)a, renumbered former subdivision (27)a as subdivision (27)a1, and inserted "autocycles" in subdivision (27)d, was effective October 1, 2015.

Session Laws 2015-163, s. 14, provides, in part: "Prosecutions for offenses committed before the effective date of this act are not abated or affected by this act, and the statutes that would be applicable but for this act remain applicable to those prosecutions." Session Laws 2015-163, s. 1, which added subdivision (27)a., renumbered former subdivision (27)a. as subdivision (27)a1., and inserted "autocycles" in subdivision (27)d., was effective October 1, 2015.

Session Laws 2015-232, s. 1.1(b), as amended by Session Laws 2018-27, s. 4.5(b) and 2018-42, s. 3(b), and by Session Laws 2020-51, s. 1(b), made the amendments to subdivision (48a) by Session Laws 2015-232, s. 1.1(a), effective August 25, 2015, and expire December 31, 2024.

Session Laws 2016-90, s. 13(j), made the amendments to this section by Session Laws 2016-90, s. 13(a), applicable to offenses committed on or after December 1, 2016.

Session Laws 2016-94, s. 35.20(h), made the amendment to subdivision (2) of this section by Session Laws 2016-94, s. 35.20(a), applicable to drivers licenses issued or renewed on or after July 1, 2016, and hearings requested on or after July 1, 2016.

The bracketed words "[The basic entities are defined as followswere added at the end of the first paragraph of subdivision (32b) at the direction of the Revisor of Statutes. The omission was subsequently corrected in amendment by Session Laws 2017-102, s. 5.2(a).

Session Laws 2016-94, s. 1.2, provides: "This act shall be known as the 'Current Operations and Capital Improvements Appropriations Act of 2016.'"

Session Laws 2016-94, s. 39.4, provides: "Except for statutory changes or other provisions that clearly indicate an intention to have effects beyond the 2016-2017 fiscal year, the textual provisions of this act apply only to funds appropriated for, and activities occurring during, the 2016-2017 fiscal year."

Session Laws 2016-94, s. 39.7, is a severability clause.

Session Laws 2017-102, s. 5.2(b) provides: "The Revisor of Statutes is authorized to reletter the definitions in G.S. 20-4.01(27) and G.S. 20-4.01(32b) to place them in alphabetical order. The Revisor of Statutes may conform any citations that change as a result of the relettering." Pursuant to that authority, subsubdivisions (27)a. through h. and (32b)a. through e. were reordered to maintain alphabetical order. The reference in subdivision (32b)c. was conformed.

Session Laws 2018-27, s. 5, is a severability clause.

Session Laws 2019-36, s. 6, made subdivision (24b), as added by Session Laws 2019-36, s. 1, effective December 1, 2019, and applicable to offenses committed on or after that date.

Session Laws 2019-155, s. 4, makes the amendments to this section by Session Laws 2019-155, s. 1, effective October 1, 2019, and applicable to offenses committed on or after that date.

Session Laws 2020-73, s. 7, made the enactment of subdivision (28a), the renumbering of former subdivision (28a) as subdivision (28b), and the amendment of subdivision (49) by Session Laws 2020-73, s. 1, effective December 1, 2020, and applicable to offenses committed on or after that date.

EFFECT OF AMENDMENTS. --

Session Laws 2003-397, s. 1, effective January 1, 2005, added subdivisions (41a)f. through h.

Session Laws 2006-253, s. 8, effective December 1, 2006, and applicable to offenses committed on or after December 1, 2006, rewrote subdivisions (32) and (45).

Session Laws 2007-56, s. 4, effective May 23, 2007, and applicable to drivers licenses issued or renewed on or after that date, substituted "fraud, or to which G.S. 20-15(a)(3) applies," for "fraud" in subdivision (2).

Session Laws 2007-382, s. 2, in the first sentence of subdivision (27)d4, inserted "plainly visible" before "words" and deleted "in letters at least 8 inches in height" following "front and rear" at the end of the sentence. For effective date and applicability, see Editor's note.

Session Laws 2007-382, s. 3, in the first sentence of subdivision (27)d4, inserted "that is painted primarily yellow below the roofline." For effective date and applicability, see Editor's note.

Session Laws 2007-455, s. 1, effective December 1, 2007, inserted "gated or non-gated" and inserted "or community" twice in subdivision (32)c.

Session Laws 2007-493, s. 1, effective August 30, 2007, substituted "Any offense set forth" for "Death by vehicle" in subdivision (24a)b. For applicability provisions, see Editor's note.

Session Laws 2008-156, s. 1, effective August 3, 2008, rewrote subdivision (12c); and added the last sentence in subdivision (45).

Session Laws 2009-274, s. 1, effective July 10, 2009, and applicable to all licenses expiring on or after that date, added subdivision (33c).

Session Laws 2009-405, ss. 1 and 4, effective October 1, 2009, added subdivision (15a) and rewrote subdivision (43).

Session Laws 2009-416, ss. 1, 2, effective March 31, 2010 and applicable to offenses committed on or after that date, added subdivision (4a)b 6 and added the language following "commercial motor vehicle" in subsection (7b).

Session Laws 2010-129, s. 1, effective July 21, 2010, added subdivisions (12c) through (12e); and redesignated former subdivision (12c) as subdivision (12f), therein twice deleting "(1 October 2007 Edition)" following "Code of Federal Regulations."

Session Laws 2011-95, s. 1, effective May 26, 2011, added subdivision (28a).

Session Laws 2011-206, s. 1, effective June 23, 2011, added subdivisions (28b) and (28c).

Session Laws 2013-410, s. 47.5, effective August 23, 2013, rewrote subdivisions (1c) and (48c), which formerly read "All-Terrain Vehicle or ATV. -- A motorized off-highway vehicle designed to travel on three or four low-pressure tires, having a seat designed to be straddled by the operator and handlebars for steering control" and "Utility Vehicle. -- Vehicle designed and manufactured for general maintenance, security, recreational, and landscaping purposes, but does not include vehicles designed and used primarily for the transportation of persons or property on a street or highway" respectively.

Session Laws 2014-58, s. 10(a), (c), and (d), effective December 1, 2014, inserted subdivision (32a), and redesignated former subdivisions (32a) and (32b) as present subdivisions (32b) and (32c). See Editor's note for applicability.

Session Laws 2014-115, s. 28.3, effective August 11, 2014, added subdivision (41a)i.

Session Laws 2015-125, s. 1, effective July 1, 2016, substituted "Except as specifically provided otherwise, this term" for "This" in the second sentence of subdivision (23). For applicability, see editor's note.

Session Laws 2015-163, s. 1, effective October 1, 2015, added subdivision (27)a; renumbered former subdivision (27)a as subdivision (27)a1; and inserted "autocycles" in subdivision (27)d. For applicability, see editor's note.

Session Laws 2015-232, s. 1.1(a), as amended by Session Laws 2018-27, s. 4.5(b), Session Laws 2018-42, s. 3(b), and Session Laws 2020-51, s. 1(b), inserted "or loaned by a franchised motor vehicle dealer, with or without charge, to a customer of that dealer who is having a vehicle serviced or repaired by the dealer" at the end of the first paragraph of subdivision (48a). For effective date and expiration, see editor's note.

Session Laws 2015-237, s. 2, effective October 1, 2015, in subdivision (27)b, added the subdivision (27) b.1 through 7 designations, added subdivision (27)b.8, and made minor stylistic changes.

Session Laws 2016-59, s. 1, effective July 1, 2017, added the second sentence in subdivision (14); added subdivision (18a); added the third sentence in subdivision (32b); and added the last sentence in subdivision (49).

Session Laws 2016-90, s. 12.5(a), effective July 11, 2016, in subdivision (27)a., substituted "antilock brakes, completely or partially enclosed seating" for "antilock brakes, air bag protection, completely enclosed seating."

Session Laws 2016-90, s. 13(a), effective December 1, 2016, added subdivision (7a) and renumbered former subdivisions (7a) and (7b) as subdivisions (7b) and (7c) accordingly; deleted former subdivision (21a) pertaining to mopeds; in subdivision (23), substituted "mopeds or electric assisted bicycles" for "mopeds as defined in G.S. 20-4.01(27)d1; added subdivision (27) c2.; in subdivision (27)d., substituted "agencies, electric assisted bicycles" for "agencies," "sub-subdivision d1" for "subdivision d1," and "subdivision" for "subsection"; rewrote subdivision (27)d1, and, in subdivision (49), substituted "bicycles and electric assisted bicycles shall be deemed vehicles and every rider of a bicycle or an electric assisted bicycle" for "bicycles shall be deemed vehicles and every rider of a bicycle" in the first sentence proviso, and substituted "subdivision (7b) of this section" for "G.S. 20-4.01(7a)" at the end of the last sentence. See editor's note for applicability.

Session Laws 2016-94, s. 35.20(a), effective July 1, 2016, substituted "G.S. 20-15(a)" for "G.S. 20-15(a)(3)" near the end of subdivision (2). See editor's note for applicability.

Session Laws 2017-69, s. 2.1(a), effective June 28, 2017, added subdivision (12h).

Session Laws 2017-102, s. 5.2(a), effective July 12, 2017, added "The basic entities are defined as follows" at the end of the introductory paragraph in subdivision (32b).

Session Laws 2019-34, s. 1, effective June 21, 2019, added subsection (27)g1.

Session Laws 2019-36, s. 1, added subdivision (24b). For effective date and applicability, see editor's note.

Session Laws 2019-155, s. 1, effective October 1, 2019, added subdivisions (1), (4b), (23a) and (46a);

and designated former subdivision (4b) as (4c). For effective date and applicability, see editor's note.

Session Laws 2019-34, s. 1(a) and (b), effective September 27, 2019, inserted 'does not have the ability to be propelled by a gasoline engine and that" in the introductory paragraph of subdivisions (12a) and (28a).

Session Laws 2020-40, s. 1, effective October 1, 2020, added sub-subdivision (27)g2.

Session Laws 2020-73, s. 1, added subdivision (28a); renumbered former subdivision (28a) as subdivision (28b); and, in subdivision (49), added clause (ii) and made related stylistic changes. For effective date and applicability, see editor's note.

I. IN GENERAL.

CONSTITUTIONALITY. --For case reaffirming the constitutionality of G.S. 20-138.1(a)(2) and subdivision (33a) of this section, see State v. Denning, 316 N.C. 523, 342 S.E.2d 855 (1986).

IN CONSTRUING A HOMEOWNERS ASSOCIATION'S DECLARATION OF COVENANTS, CONDITIONS AND RESTRICTIONS (CC&RS), PROPERTY OWNERS' RELIANCE ON G.S. 20-4.01(32A) AND (27) D2, AND G.S. 20-354.2 (defining travel trailer, camping trailer, motor vehicle, and motor home or house car) was misplaced; the statutes were enacted between six and sixteen years after the association's CC&Rs (referring to campers and all similar property) were drafted and recorded. The statutory provisions were not material to the issue of the drafters' intent in 1985 when the CC&Rs were drafted and recorded. Schwartz v. Banbury Woods Homeowners Ass'n, 196 N.C. App. 584, 675 S.E.2d 382 (2009), review denied, 363 N.C. 856, 694 S.E.2d 391, 2010 N.C. LEXIS 230 (2010).

BUSINESS DISTRICT. --As to what constituted a business district within the meaning of subdivision (1) of former G.S. 20-38, see Mitchell v. Melts, 220 N.C. 793, 18 S.E.2d 406 (1942); Hinson v. Dawson, 241 N.C. 714, 86 S.E.2d 585 (1955); Black v. Penland, 255 N.C. 691, 122 S.E.2d 504 (1961).

DRIVER. --Although distinctions may have been made between driving and operating in prior case law and prior statutes regulating motor vehicles, such a distinction is not supportable under G.S. 20-138.1. Since "driver" is defined in this section simply as an "operator" of a vehicle, the legislature intended the two words to be synonymous. State v. Coker, 312 N.C. 432, 323 S.E.2d 343 (1984).

Although a distinction may have been made between driving and operating in prior case law and statutes regulating vehicles, no such distinction is supportable under this section since a "driver" is defined as an "operator." It is clear that the legislature intended the two words to be synonymous. State v. Dellinger, 73 N.C. App. 685, 327 S.E.2d 609 (1985).

IMPAIRING SUBSTANCE. --State of North Carolina presented sufficient evidence to prove the elements of driving while under the influence of an impairing substance as defendant collided with the rear end of another vehicle in a restaurant drive-thru, officers noted signs of impairment, defendant admitted to having earlier consumed alprazolam, an officer testified that defendant indicated impairment in a HGN test, and another officer who performed a drug recognition evaluation testified that defendant was impaired by a central nervous system depressant. State v. Fincher, 259 N.C. App. 159, 814 S.E.2d 606 (2018).

OPERATOR includes a person in the driver's seat of a motor vehicle when the engine is running. State v. Carter, 15 N.C. App. 391, 190 S.E.2d 241 (1972).

In a prosecution for driving under the influence and driving while license was revoked, evidence that defendant was seated behind the wheel of a car which had the motor running was sufficient to prove that defendant was the operator of the car under subdivision (25). State v. Turner, 29 N.C. App. 163, 223 S.E.2d 530 (1976).

Although distinctions may have been made between driving and operating in prior case law and prior statutes regulating motor vehicles, such a distinction is not supportable under G.S. 20-138.1. Since "driver" is defined in this section simply as an "operator" of a vehicle, the legislature intended the two words to be synonymous. State v. Coker, 312 N.C. 432, 323 S.E.2d 343 (1984).

A horseback rider is an "operator" who is in "control of a vehicle which is in motion" where the horse is ridden upon a street, highway or public vehicular area. State v. Dellinger, 73 N.C. App. 685, 327 S.E.2d 609 (1985).

Evidence held sufficient for a reasonable jury to infer that defendant, who was found asleep in driver's seat in car which had run off the road and into a fence, was under the influence of an impairing substance when he drove the vehicle. State v. Mack, 81 N.C. App. 578, 345 S.E.2d 223 (1986).

OWNER. --This section defines "owner" and former G.S. 20-279.1 defined "owner" in essentially the same way. Nationwide Mut. Ins. Co. v. Hayes, 276 N.C. 620, 174 S.E.2d 511 (1970).

A defendant who advanced money for the purchase of a used car as security took a title-retaining contract on the vehicle and permitted its delivery to the purchasers, one of whom was operating it when an accident occurred, could not be liable to the persons injured, since a conditional vendee, lessee, or mortgagor of a motor vehicle is deemed to be the owner, and liability on the part of the defendant could arise only by application of the doctrine of respondeat superior. Such facts do not show the necessary relationship. High Point Sav. & Trust Co. v. King, 253 N.C. 571, 117 S.E.2d 421 (1960).

Where the owner of trucks leased them to another corporation under an agreement requiring lessor to carry insurance and maintain the vehicles and giving lessee control over the operation of the trucks with right to use same exclusively for the transportation and delivery of lessee's goods, the lessor was not a contract carrier within the meaning of the statutes as they stood in 1949, since the lessor merely leased its vehicles and was not a carrier of any kind, and lessee was solely a private carrier, and therefore lessor was not liable for additional assessment at the "for-hire" rates under the statute. Equipment Fin. Corp. v. Scheidt, 249 N.C. 334, 106 S.E.2d 555 (1959).

Where the vendee paid the entire purchase price, had exclusive possession and use of the vehicle, obtained the insurance coverage for it, and paid the premium therefor, this sufficed to give him a clear equitable interest in the vehicle, and that equitable interest sufficed, under the particular facts and circumstances, to make him the "owner" of the vehicle within the coverage intent of the policy, interpreted in light of the purpose and intent of Article 9A, the Motor Vehicle Safety and Financial Responsibility Act of 1953. Ohio Cas. Ins. Co. v. Anderson, 59 N.C. App. 621, 298 S.E.2d 56 (1982).

Except under special circumstances not present in this case, the statute limits the definition of the word "owner" to the person holding legal title. Jenkins v. Aetna Cas. & Sur. Co., 324 N.C. 394, 378 S.E.2d 773 (1989).

Where evidence established that buyer paid four hundred dollars ($400.00) cash as the total price for a car and took immediate possession of the vehicle, but never received the certificate of title, buyer was not the "owner" of the car as that term is defined in G.S. 20-4.01(26); therefore, provision in insurance policy excluding coverage for liability arising from the use of a vehicle "owned" by buyer did not apply. Jenkins v. Aetna Cas. & Sur. Co., 324 N.C. 394, 378 S.E.2d 773 (1989).

Although a vehicle's owner gave the vehicle to her son, she never transferred title, and thus at the time of a later accident the owner remained the legal owner of the vehicle; a trial court erred in holding that the owner's insurance policy terminated when the son's policy was issued on the same car because the automatic termination clause in the owner's policy's only applied if the owner obtained other insurance, and since the owner's policy and the son's policy were procured by different persons, the owner's policy did not automatically terminate. Progressive Am. Ins. Co. v. State Farm Mut. Auto. Ins. Co., 184 N.C. App. 688, 647 S.E.2d 111 (2007).

Under G.S. 25-2-509(3), a buyer bore the risk of loss of a mobile home that was destroyed by fire for G.S. 20-4.01(26) purposes as: (1) Nationwide Mutual Insurance Co. v. Hayes, 174 S.E.2d 511 (N.C. 1970), did not apply to the breach of contract case; (2) the risk of loss passed to the buyer on the buyer's receipt of the mobile home; and (3) when the sales agreement was executed, the buyer accepted the mobile home and the seller made tender of delivery due to an as is, where is clause in the agreement. Singletary v. P & A Invs., Inc., 212 N.C. App. 469, 712 S.E.2d 681 (2011).

In a case in which defendant was convicted of felony conversion, the trial court erred by denying defendant's motion to dismiss as the State did not produce sufficient evidence that the alleged victim owned the vehicle because the alleged victim never received title to the vehicle; without title to the vehicle, the alleged victim did not meet the definition of owner; a lien encumbered the vehicle that the alleged victim could not remove; and ownership was essential to establishing the elements of felony conversion. State v. Falana, 254 N.C. App. 329, 802 S.E.2d 582 (2017).

FOR PURPOSES OF TORT LAW AND LIABILITY INSURANCE COVERAGE, NO OWNERSHIP PASSES to the purchaser of a motor vehicle which requires registration until: (1) The owner executes, in the presence of a person authorized to administer oaths, an assignment and warranty of title on the reverse of the certificate of title, including the name and address of the transferee; (2) there is an actual or constructive delivery of the motor vehicle; and (3) the duly assigned certificate of title is delivered to the transferee (or lienholder in secured transactions). Jenkins v. Aetna Cas. & Sur. Co., 324 N.C. 394, 378 S.E.2d 773 (1989).

Since actual title had not passed, an insurer had to provide coverage to its insured while driving a non-owned vehicle, even though the insured was in the process of buying the vehicle, as North Carolina required actual title to pass for ownership under G.S. 20-4.01(26); the insurer was responsible to a passenger who was injured in a collision with a non-owned vehicle being driven by the insured. Hernandez v. Nationwide Mut. Ins. Co., 171 N.C. App. 510, 615 S.E.2d 425 (2005), cert. denied, 360 N.C. 63, 621 S.E.2d 624 (2005).

DEFINITION OF "OWNER" APPLIES TO ARTICLE 9A. --The definition of "owner" in subdivision (26) of this section applies throughout this Chapter, and thus to Article 9A, the Motor Vehicle Safety and Financial Responsibility Act of 1953, unless the context otherwise requires. It thus must be read into every liability insurance policy within the purview of Article 9A, unless the context otherwise requires. Ohio Cas. Ins. Co. v. Anderson, 59 N.C. App. 621, 298 S.E.2d 56 (1982).

DELETION OF "OWNER" FROM G.S. 20-279.1 WAS MERELY TO AVOID REPETITION. --Prior to 1973 the definition of "owner" appeared in G.S. 20-279.1(9) (repealed in 1973), which was applicable solely to Article 9A, the Motor Vehicle Safety and Financial Responsibility Act of 1953. The General Assembly placed this definition in this section. The apparent purpose was to eliminate unnecessary repetition of this definition in separate articles of this Chapter, not to make the definition inapplicable to Article 9A. Ohio Cas. Ins. Co. v. Anderson, 59 N.C. App. 621, 298 S.E.2d 56 (1982).

ONE WHO DOES NOT HOLD LEGAL TITLE TO A VEHICLE CANNOT OBTAIN OWNER'S LIABILITY INSURANCE THEREON. Nationwide Mut. Ins. Co. v. Edwards, 67 N.C. App. 1, 312 S.E.2d 656 (1984).

PUBLIC VEHICULAR AREA. --Evidence held to permit a finding that at the time in question portion of park grounds legally in use as a parking lot was a "public vehicular area" within the meaning and intent of that phrase as used in subdivision (32), so as to permit a conviction under G.S. 20-138.1(a) for impaired driving thereon. State v. Carawan, 80 N.C. App. 151, 341 S.E.2d 96, cert. denied, 317 N.C. 337, 346 S.E.2d 141 (1986).

Evidence held sufficient to permit a finding that handicapped or wheelchair ramp in motel parking lot in front of motel door upon which most of defendant's

Chapter 20

car had been stopped was part of a "public vehicular area" within the meaning and intent of that phrase as used in subdivision (32). State v. Mabe, 85 N.C. App. 500, 355 S.E.2d 186 (1987).

Area where an accident between plaintiff and defendant's truck occurred was a public vehicular area and not a roadway. The accident occurred in the traffic lane of a parking lot generally open to and used by the public for vehicular traffic upon the premises of a business establishment which provided parking space for its customers. Although the lot was held open for use by the public, there was no evidence that the general public had a legally enforceable right to use the lot. Corns v. Hall, 112 N.C. App. 232, 435 S.E.2d 88 (1993).

Street in mobile home park, owned by one individual who had divided the property into lots for lease, that was not marked as private, and was available for use by residents, their guests and other visitors, was a public vehicular area within the meaning of subsection (32). State v. Turner, 117 N.C. App. 457, 451 S.E.2d 19 (1994).

Where the evidence established that a private club was licensed by the State to serve alcohol to guests of members as well as to members themselves, the club's parking lot could be used as a thoroughfare by members of the general public, there were no signs posted in the club's parking lot prohibiting the public from parking there and no signs posted stating that the parking lot was private property, nor was there any security or membership cards allowing members exclusive access to the parking lot, the evidence was sufficient to support a peremptory instruction that the club's parking lot was a "public vehicular area" as a matter of law. State v. Snyder, 343 N.C. 61, 468 S.E.2d 221 (1996).

A sign prohibiting loitering in a parking lot did not change the nature of the property; thus, a car wash was still a business providing parking for its customers, and as such, the premises was a "public vehicular area" under this section. State v. Robinette, 124 N.C. App. 212, 476 S.E.2d 387 (1996).

Defendant's possession of an open container of alcohol in his car in a gas station parking lot was not illegal since a parking lot of a service station was a public vehicular area and the open container law only prohibited open containers on highways and highway right-of-ways. State v. Coleman, 228 N.C. App. 76, 743 S.E.2d 62 (2013).

Officer's belief that possession of an open container of alcohol in a car in a public vehicular area was illegal could not support a Terry stop since the belief was unreasonable given that the open container law was neither novel nor complex and clearly prohibited the possession of an open container only on highways and highway right-of-ways, and the distinction between a highway and a public vehicular area was familiar to law enforcement officers. State v. Coleman, 228 N.C. App. 76, 743 S.E.2d 62 (2013).

Trial court erred in denying defendant's motion to dismiss the charge of habitual impaired driving because there was no evidence concerning the ownership of the vacant lot where defendant operated a moped or that the lot had been designated as a public vehicular area by the owner; in order to show an area meets the definition of public vehicular area there must be some evidence demonstrating the property is similar in nature to those examples provided by the General Assembly in the statute. State v. Ricks, 237 N.C. App. 359, 764 S.E.2d 692 (2014).

Definition of a public vehicular area contemplates areas generally open to and used by the public for vehicular traffic as a matter of right or areas used for vehicular traffic that are associated with places generally open to and used by the public, such as driveways and parking lots to institutions and businesses open to the public. State v. Ricks, 237 N.C. App. 359, 764 S.E.2d 692 (2014).

Even assuming there was sufficient evidence to allow the jury to decide whether a vacant lot was a public vehicular area, the trial court erred in abbreviating the definition of public vehicular area in the instructions and by preventing defendant from arguing his position in accordance with the statute; the entire definition of public vehicular area is significant to a determination of whether an area meets the definition, and the examples are not separable from the statute State v. Ricks, 237 N.C. App. 359, 764 S.E.2d 692 (2014).

"REPORTABLE CRASH." --Defendant was properly convicted of giving false information for a motor vehicle crash report in violation of G.S. 20-279.31(b) because, inter alia, an accident in which defendant was involved was a "reportable crash," under the provisions of G.S. 20-4.01(33b). State v. Hernandez, 188 N.C. App. 193, 655 S.E.2d 426 (2008).

RESIDENTIAL DISTRICT. --For cases construing earlier statutory definitions of "residential district," see Reid v. City Coach Co., 215 N.C. 469, 2 S.E.2d 578, 123 A.L.R. 140 (1939); Mitchell v. Melts, 220 N.C. 793, 18 S.E.2d 406 (1942); Goddard v. Williams, 251 N.C. 128, 110 S.E.2d 820 (1959), overruled in part, Young v. Woodall, 343 N.C. 459, 471 S.E.2d 357 (1996).

REVOCATION. --The contention that a revocation remains in effect not only throughout the period stated in the order of revocation but also until the person whose license was revoked applies for a restoration of his license and pays the restoration fee required is contrary to the definition of "revocation" in this section. Ennis v. Garrett, 279 N.C. 612, 184 S.E.2d 246 (1971).

Where petitioner, who was driving without his license, was stopped and charged with driving while impaired, and then appeared before a magistrate who revoked his driver's license for 10 days, petitioner's license had been validly revoked when he was stopped the next day; thus, he was properly charged with committing a moving violation during a period of revocation by operating a motor vehicle. Eibergen v. Killens, 124 N.C. App. 534, 477 S.E.2d 684 (1996).

When a person's driver's license is suspended or revoked, it is the surrendering of the privilege to drive, not the license card itself, that is of significance. Eibergen v. Killens, 124 N.C. App. 534, 477 S.E.2d 684 (1996).

As the terms "revoked" and "suspended" with respect to defendant's driver's license were used interchangeably in statutes pursuant to G.S. 20-4.01(47), defendant's claim that there was a fatal variance between the indictment, which indicated that defendant's license was revoked, and the proof offered at trial that defendant's license was suspended, lacked merit. State v. Lloyd, 187 N.C. App. 174, 652 S.E.2d 299 (2007), cert. denied, 363 N.C. 586, 683 S.E.2d 214 (2009).

"STREET." --Trial court did not err in denying defendant's motion to suppress evidence a police officer seized from his vehicle pursuant to a traffic stop because the trial court's findings supported its conclusion that the officer had reasonable suspicion that defendant had violated G.S. 20-129 by failing to have taillights in proper working order; considering the totality of the circumstances, the officer reasonably believed that a street in an apartment complex was a public road for purposes of G.S. 20-129(a)(4) and that under the weather conditions at the time of the stop, defendant was required to have his taillights on while his windshield wipers were in use, and the officer's reasonable, albeit assumed to be mistaken, belief did not render the stop unconstitutional. State v. Hopper, -- N.C. App. --, 692 S.E.2d 166 (Apr. 20, 2010).

EXPUNCTION. --Inasmuch as felonious speeding to elude arrest is not an offense involving impaired driving per G.S. 20-4.01(24a), the trial court made an error of law in determining that defendant was ineligible for expunction of the offense of fleeing to elude arrest. State v. Neira, -- N.C. App. --, 840 S.E.2d 890 (2020).

PROOF OF IMPAIRED DRIVING. --In a case in which defendant passed a tow truck on the shoulder and struck and killed the victim, the trial court erred in denying his motions to dismiss the driving while impaired charge because the trooper formed his opinion of impairment entirely through passive observation of defendant, and he did not request defendant to perform any of the several field tests officers often use to gauge a motorist's impairment; he did not ask defendant if or when he had ingested any impairing substances; and trooper's observations occurred about five hours after the collision occurred. State v. Nazzal, -- N.C. App. --, 840 S.E.2d 881 (2020).

APPLIED in State v. Springs, 26 N.C. App. 757, 217 S.E.2d 200 (1975); State v. Lesley, 29 N.C. App. 169, 223 S.E.2d 532 (1976); Williams v. Wachovia Bank & Trust Co., 292 N.C. 416, 233 S.E.2d 589 (1977); Smith v. Powell, 32 N.C. App. 563, 232 S.E.2d 863 (1977); State v. Bowen, 67 N.C. App. 512, 313 S.E.2d 196 (1984); Indiana Lumbermens Mut. Ins. Co. v. Unigard Indem. Co., 76 N.C. App. 88, 331 S.E.2d 741 (1985); Roseboro Ford, Inc. v. Bass, 77 N.C. App. 363, 335 S.E.2d 214 (1985); Continental Tel. Co. v. Gunter, 99 N.C. App. 741, 394 S.E.2d 228 (1990); Hoover v. State Farm Mut. Ins. Co., 156 N.C. App. 418, 576 S.E.2d 396 (2003); Pa. Nat'l Mut. Ins. Co. v. Strickland, 178 N.C. App. 547, 631 S.E.2d 845 (2006), review denied, 361 N.C. 221, 642 S.E.2d 445 (2007); Batts v. Lumbermen's Mut. Cas. Ins. Co., 192 N.C. App. 533, 665 S.E.2d 578 (2008); State v. Narron, 193 N.C. App. 76, 666 S.E.2d 860 (2008), review denied, 363 N.C. 135,

674 S.E.2d 140 (2009), cert. denied, 558 U.S. 818, 130 S. Ct. 71, 175 L. Ed. 2d 26 (2009); State v. Hopper, 205 N.C. App. 175, 695 S.E.2d 801 (2010).

CITED in McLeod v. Nationwide Mut. Ins. Co., 115 N.C. App. 283, 444 S.E.2d 487, cert. denied, 337 N.C. 694, 448 S.E.2d 528 (1994); State v. Priddy, 115 N.C. App. 547, 445 S.E.2d 610, cert. denied, 337 N.C. 805, 449 S.E.2d 751 (1994); State v. Bradley, 32 N.C. App. 666, 233 S.E.2d 603 (1977); Harper v. Peters, 42 N.C. App. 62, 255 S.E.2d 791 (1979); Lupo v. Powell, 44 N.C. App. 35, 259 S.E.2d 777 (1979); Oroweat Employees Credit Union v. Stroupe, 48 N.C. App. 338, 269 S.E.2d 211 (1980); State v. Ray, 54 N.C. App. 473, 283 S.E.2d 823 (1981); State v. Bost, 55 N.C. App. 612, 286 S.E.2d 632 (1982); Perry v. Aycock, 68 N.C. App. 705, 315 S.E. 791 (1984); State v. Rose, 312 N.C. 441, 323 S.E.2d 339 (1984); State v. Coker, 312 N.C. 432, 323 S.E.2d 343 (1984); State v. Shuping, 312 N.C. 421, 323 S.E.2d 350 (1984); Carter v. Holland (In re Carraway), 65 Bankr. 51 (Bankr. E.D.N.C. 1986); Lawing v. Lawing, 81 N.C. App. 159, 344 S.E.2d 100 (1986); Brooks v. Pembroke City Jail, 722 F. Supp. 1294 (E.D.N.C. 1989); North Carolina Farm Bureau Mut. Ins. Co. v. Warren, 326 N.C. 444, 390 S.E.2d 138 (1990); Alberti v. Manufactured Homes, Inc., 329 N.C. 727, 407 S.E.2d 819 (1991); State Auto. Mut. Ins. Co. v. Hoyle, 106 N.C. App. 199, 415 S.E.2d 764 (1992); State v. Stafford, 114 N.C. App. 101, 440 S.E.2d 846 (1994); State v. Crawford, 125 N.C. App. 279, 480 S.E.2d 422 (1997); Wooten v. Town of Topsail Beach, 127 N.C. App. 739, 493 S.E.2d 285 (1997), cert. denied, 348 N.C. 78, 505 S.E.2d 888 (1998); Butler v. Green Tree Fin. Servicing Corp. (In re Wester), 229 Bankr. 348 (Bankr. E.D.N.C. 1998); State v. Clapp, 135 N.C. App. 52, 519 S.E.2d 90 (1999); Halter v. J.C. Penney Life Ins. Co., 1999 U.S. Dist. LEXIS 21386 (M.D.N.C. Nov. 30, 1999); Cooke v. Faulkner, 137 N.C. App. 755, 529 S.E.2d 512 (2000); State v. Smith, 139 N.C. App. 209, 533 S.E.2d 518 (2000); Clontz v. St. Mark's Evangelical Lutheran Church, 157 N.C. App. 325, 578 S.E.2d 654, cert. denied, 357 N.C. 249, 582 S.E.2d 29 (2003); Erwin v. Tweed, 159 N.C. App. 579, 583 S.E.2d 717 (2003), cert. denied, 358 N.C. 234, 593 S.E.2d 780 (2004), aff'd, 359 N.C. 64, 602 S.E.2d 359 (2004); State v. Winslow, 169 N.C. App. 137, 609 S.E.2d 463 (2005), review denied, in part, 359 N.C. 642, 617 S.E.2d 660 (2005); State v. Jones, 186 N.C. App. 405, 651 S.E.2d 589 (2007), aff'd, 362 N.C. 341, 661 S.E.2d 733 (2008); Great American Ins. Co. v. Freeman, 192 N.C. App. 497, 665 S.E.2d 536 (2008); Bissette v. Auto-Owners Ins. Co., 208 N.C. App. 321, 703 S.E.2d 168 (2010); State v. Leyshon, 211 N.C. App. 511, 710 S.E.2d 282 (2011); State v. Braswell, 222 N.C. App. 176, 729 S.E.2d 697 (2012); State v. McKenzie, 225 N.C. App. 208, 736 S.E.2d 591 (2013), rev'd 367 N.C. 112, 750 S.E.2d 521, 2013 N.C. LEXIS 1019 (2013), rev'd 748 S.E.2d 145, 2013 N.C. LEXIS 1019 (2013); Walters v. Cooper, 226 N.C. App. 166, 739 S.E.2d 185 (2013), aff'd 367 N.C. 117, 748 S.E.2d 144, 2013 N.C. LEXIS 1021 (2013); Irving v. Charlotte-Mecklenburg Bd. of Educ., 230 N.C. App. 265, 750 S.E.2d 1 (2013), rev'd, 368 N.C. 609, 781 S.E.2d 282, 2016 N.C. LEXIS 30 (2016); State v. Smathers, 232

N.C. App. 120, 753 S.E.2d 380 (2014), review denied, 755 S.E.2d 616, 2014 N.C. LEXIS 193 (2014)..

II. TYPES OF VEHICLES.

VEHICLES -- LEGISLATIVE INTENT. --The North Carolina legislature intended the provisions of the traffic laws of North Carolina applicable to the drivers of "vehicles" to apply to horseback riders irrespective of whether a horse is a vehicle. State v. Dellinger, 73 N.C. App. 685, 327 S.E.2d 609 (1985).

"COMMERCIAL MOTOR VEHICLE". --The defendant's contention that he did not violate this section because he was not driving a "commercial motor vehicle" was without merit; the tractor-trailer was a commercial vehicle within the statutory definition although the defendant was driving it for his own private use and although he had detached the trailer portion of the tractor-trailer. State v. Jones, 140 N.C. App. 691, 538 S.E.2d 228 (2000).

FARM TRACTOR. --Farm tractors are not to be considered motor vehicles within the provisions of the Uniform Driver's License Act or the Motor Vehicle Safety and Financial Responsibility Act. Brown v. Fidelity & Cas. Co., 241 N.C. 666, 86 S.E.2d 433 (1955) (decided under repealed G.S. 20-226).

The Motor Vehicles Act expressly defines a "farm tractor" as a "motor vehicle." Therefore, an instruction imparting to a farm tractor and trailer on a highway special hazard status per se and rendering a motorist who collides with a farm tractor and trailer on a highway negligent per se, regardless of the circumstances or the conduct of the tractor-trailer operator constituted prejudicial error. Davis v. Gamble, 55 N.C. App. 617, 286 S.E.2d 629 (1982).

Construing the definitions of "farm tractor" and "vehicle" together in pari materia, it is apparent that the General Assembly intended that while farm tractors are motor implements of husbandry, they were vehicles within the meaning of former G.S. 20-138 when operated upon a highway by one under the influence of intoxicating liquor or narcotic drugs. State v. Green, 251 N.C. 141, 110 S.E.2d 805 (1959).

TRUCKS. --Trucks, even if used for private purposes, are not private passenger type autos. Harleysville Mut. Ins. Co. v. Packer, 60 F.3d 1116 (4th Cir. 1995).

MOTORCYCLE. --The definition of the term "motorcycle" in former G.S. 20-38 did not describe the "mailster," a class of motor vehicle generally known as a "motor scooter." LeCroy v. Nationwide Mut. Ins. Co., 251 N.C. 19, 110 S.E.2d 463 (1959).

The statutory definition of the term "motorcycle" has no application in an action based on an insurance contract's interpretation of the word "automobile." LeCroy v. Nationwide Mut. Ins. Co., 251 N.C. 19, 110 S.E.2d 463 (1959).

Statutory definition cited in Anderson v. Life & Cas. Ins. Co., 197 N.C. 72, 147 S.E. 693 (1929), holding that the expression "motor-driven car" in an insurance policy excluded a motorcycle.

ELECTRIC SCOOTER FELL WITHIN STATUTORY DEFINITION OF VEHICLE. --Defendant's electric scooter, which was not self-balancing, with its two wheels in tandem, and which did not fall within the two statutory exceptions from a vehicle under G.S. 20-138.1(e) with regard to horses, bicycles, and lawnmowers or G.S. 20-4.01(49) as to transportation for a person with a mobility impairment, fell within the legislature's definition of vehicle in G.S. 20-4.01(49) and, because the evidence at trial showed that his breath alcohol concentration following arrest was 0.13, there was sufficient evidence to uphold defendant's conviction for impaired driving under G.S. 20-138.1. State v. Crow, 175 N.C. App. 119, 623 S.E.2d 68 (2005).

LOW-BOY TRAILER AND MACK TRUCK WERE NOT PRIVATE PASSENGER MOTOR VEHICLES as they did not have a pickup body and were not delivery sedans nor panel trucks. Nationwide Mut. Ins. Co. v. Mabe, 342 N.C. 482, 467 S.E.2d 34 (1996).

A MOBILE HOME IS A MOTOR VEHICLE and is subject to the mandatory provisions of the statutes relating to the registration of motor vehicles in this State. King Homes, Inc. v. Bryson, 273 N.C. 84, 159 S.E.2d 329 (1968).

It is clear under North Carolina law that a mobile home is a "motor vehicle" for purposes of the statutes dealing with registration and ownership of motor vehicles. In re Meade, 174 Bankr. 49 (Bankr. M.D.N.C. 1994).

MOBILE HOME IS A MOTOR VEHICLE FOR PURPOSES OF PERFECTING SECURITY INTEREST. --Plaintiff's argument that owner no longer intended to operate her mobile home upon the highway did not nullify defendant's properly perfected security interest in the mobile home. Peoples Sav. & Loan Assoc. v. Citicorp Acceptance Co., 103 N.C. App. 762, 407 S.E.2d 251, cert. denied, 330 N.C. 197, 412 S.E.2d 59 (1991).

MODULAR HOME. --Although the title to a modular home is initially acquired through a bill of sale, once installed title must pass by way of a real property deed unlike a mobile home or trailer which passes by transfer of a certificate of origin and motor vehicle title. Briggs v. Rankin, 127 N.C. App. 477, 491 S.E.2d 234 (1997), aff'd, 348 N.C. 686, 500 S.E.2d 663 (1998).

BICYCLE AS VEHICLE. --A bicycle is a vehicle and its rider is a driver within the meaning of the motor vehicle law. Low v. Futrell, 271 N.C. 550, 157 S.E.2d 92 (1967); Sadler v. Purser, 12 N.C. App. 206, 182 S.E.2d 850 (1971); Townsend v. Frye, 30 N.C. App. 634, 228 S.E.2d 56, cert. denied, 291 N.C. 178, 229 S.E.2d 689 (1976).

The operation of a bicycle upon a public highway is governed by the rules governing motor vehicles insofar as the nature of the vehicle permits. Webb v. Felton, 266 N.C. 707, 147 S.E.2d 219 (1966).

A bicycle is a vehicle, and the rider of a bicycle upon the highway is subject to the applicable provisions of the statutes relating to motor vehicles. Van Dyke v. Atlantic Greyhound Corp., 218 N.C. 283, 10 S.E.2d 727 (1940).

A bicycle is a vehicle, and is subject to the provisions of Article 3 of this Chapter, except those which by their nature can have no application. Tarrant v. Pepsi-Cola Bottling Co., 221 N.C. 390, 20 S.E.2d 565

(1942); Oxendine v. Lowry, 260 N.C. 709, 133 S.E.2d 687 (1963).

In interpreting an underinsured motorist excess provision, a bicycle involved in an accident with a car was considered to be a vehicle pursuant to G.S. 20-4.01(49), since it was operated upon a highway. Sitzman v. Gov't Emples. Ins. Co., 182 N.C. App. 259, 641 S.E.2d 838 (2007).

HANDCART. --A handcart, being moved solely by human power, is excluded from the category of vehicles defined in subdivision (38) of former G.S. 20-38 (now subdivision (49) of this section). Lewis v. Watson, 229 N.C. 20, 47 S.E.2d 484 (1948).

When neither named insured owned a rental car, as defined in G.S. 20-4.04(26), which was being driven by a family member when it was involved in a motor vehicle accident, a trial court erred in granting summary judgment to plaintiff insurer in its declaratory action against defendant insurer because it was impossible to determine which insurer's policy provided primary coverage due to the identical wording in the "excess" clauses of their respective policies; thus, the "excess" clauses were mutually repugnant and neither clause was given effect. Integon Nat'l Ins. Co. v. Phillips, 212 N.C. App. 623, 712 S.E.2d 381 (2011).

SCHOOL ACTIVITY BUS. --North Carolina Industrial Commission did not have jurisdiction over a driver's action to recover for the alleged negligence of a local board of education employee in the operation of an activity bus because the waiver of governmental immunity provided in the Tort Claims Act did not apply; the school activity bus did not meet the requirement of the statute that the Commission had jurisdiction over a public school bus or school transportation service vehicle. Irving v. Charlotte-Mecklenburg Bd. of Educ., 368 N.C. 609, 781 S.E.2d 282 (2016).

III. HIGHWAYS.

CONSTRUCTION OF SUBDIVISION (13). --The definition of "highway" in subdivision (13) is to be construed so as to give its terms their plain and ordinary meaning. Smith v. Powell, 293 N.C. 342, 238 S.E.2d 137 (1977).

The legislature has provided that, unless the context requires otherwise, the word "highway" is to be given the same connotation in all of the provisions of Chapter 20, whether they be penal, remedial or otherwise. Thus, the well known principles of statutory construction that a penal statute is to be strictly construed and a statute designed to promote safety is to be liberally construed have no application. Smith v. Powell, 293 N.C. 342, 238 S.E.2d 137 (1977).

"HIGHWAY" DISTINGUISHED FROM ROADWAY. --The definitions of "highway" and "roadway," considered together, show that the legislature in defining "highway" intended to make it clear that the entire "width" between the right-of-way lines is included in a "highway" as distinguished from a "roadway." Smith v. Powell, 293 N.C. 342, 238 S.E.2d 137 (1977).

DEFINITION OF "HIGHWAY" IS CONCERNED WITH WIDTH, NOT DEPTH. --While it is true that a "highway" or a "street" is not limited to its surface so far as the right of the State to use, maintain and protect it from damage and private use are concerned, and in this sense, it includes not only the entire thickness of the pavement and the prepared base upon which it rests but also so much of the depth as may not unfairly be used as streets are used for the laying therein of drainage systems and conduits for sewer, water and other services, nevertheless, the primary concern of the legislature in defining "highway" as used in Chapter 20 was with the "width," not the depth. "Width" means "the lineal extent of a thing from side to side." Smith v. Powell, 293 N.C. 342, 238 S.E.2d 137 (1977).

PORTION OF SIDEWALK AS HIGHWAY. --The portion of a sidewalk between a street and a filling station, open to the use of the public as a matter of right for the purposes of vehicular traffic, was a "highway" within the meaning of former G.S. 20-138, prohibiting drunken driving. State v. Perry, 230 N.C. 361, 53 S.E.2d 288 (1949).

AREA BENEATH HIGHWAY BRIDGE NOT "HIGHWAY". --A petitioner who drove a motor vehicle only within the limits of the area beneath a highway bridge did not drive on a "highway" as that term is used in G.S. 20-16.2. Smith v. Powell, 293 N.C. 342, 238 S.E.2d 137 (1977).

EMERGENCY STRIP ADJACENT TO INTERSTATE HIGHWAYS falls within the literal language of the definition of "highway" as contained in this section. State v. Kelley, 65 N.C. App. 159, 308 S.E.2d 720 (1983).

INTERSECTION. --With reference to the right-of-way as between two vehicles approaching and entering an intersection, the law of this State makes no distinction between a "T" intersection and one at which the two highways cross each other completely. Dawson v. Jennette, 278 N.C. 438, 180 S.E.2d 121 (1971).

Where one public highway joins another, but does not cross it, the point where they join is an intersection of public highways. Goss v. Williams, 196 N.C. 213, 145 S.E. 169 (1928).

When the failure to explain the law so the jury could apply it to the facts is specifically called to the court's attention by a juror's request for information, it should tell the jury how to find the intersection of the streets as fixed by statute, and how, when the motorist reaches the intersection, he is required to drive in making a left turn. Pearsall v. Duke Power Co., 258 N.C. 639, 129 S.E.2d 217 (1963).

IV. INVOLVING ALCOHOL.

ALCOHOL CONCENTRATION. --Police officer who had been issued a permit to perform chemical analysis under the authority of G.S. 20-139.1(b) by the Department of Human Resources was permitted by subdivision (0.2) of this section (now subdivision (1b)) to express alcohol concentration in terms of 210 liters of breath, as well as 100 milliliters of blood. State v. Midgett, 78 N.C. App. 387, 337 S.E.2d 117 (1985).

"CHEMICAL ANALYST" for purposes of G.S. 20-139.1 includes a person who was validly licensed by the Department of Human Resources to perform chemical analyses immediately prior to the enactment of the Safe Roads Act. To hold otherwise would mean that an individual licensed to perform chemical analyses under one statute would automatically lose his license when the testing procedures are merely recodified in another statute. Obviously the legislature did not intend that result. State v. Dellinger, 73 N.C. App. 685, 327 S.E.2d 609 (1985).

DRIVING WHILE IMPAIRED. --Sufficient evidence supported a conviction of driving while impaired, G.S. 20-138.1, because a trooper testified that the reading on the Intoxilyzer 5000 rounded down, that he administered the Intoxilyzer test two times, and that each administration showed defendant's BAC to be .08. State v. Arrington, 215 N.C. App. 161, 714 S.E.2d 777 (2011), decided under former G.S. 143B-262.4.

Defendant's impaired driving charge was not dismissed because, (1) under the corpus delicti rule, defendant's admission was corroborated with a wrecked vehicle, a shoe matching defendant's shoe in the vehicle's driver's side footwell, the absence of others in the area, defendant's consistent injury, and the lack of another explanation for the wreck, and (2) defendant's blood alcohol level was above the statutory limit. State v. Hines, 259 N.C. App. 358, 816 S.E.2d 182 (2018).

Context of finding the existence of a grossly aggravating factor based upon a prior driving while impaired conviction in superior court requires an interpretation that a "prior conviction" not be limited to only those not pending on direct appeal in the appellate courts; because there is no language limiting that definition to a "final" conviction or only those not challenged on appeal, the courts have no authority to interpret the statute as imposing such a limitation. State v. Cole, 262 N.C. App. 466, 822 S.E.2d 456 (2018).

Evidence was sufficient to support defendant's conviction of driving while impaired because the officer found defendant in the driver's seat of a stationary vehicle with the engine running, the officer testified that defendant was apparently sleeping, there was a strong odor of alcohol on the defendant's breath, the defendant's speech was slurred, officers saw an alcohol bottle between the defendant's legs, defendant admitted that the defendant had consumed alcohol, defendant's blood test results indicated that the blood contained alcohol, THC, THCA, amphetamine, and methamphetamine, and defendant refused to submit to an intoxilyzer test. State v. Hoque, -- N.C. App. --, 837 S.E.2d 464 (2020).

OFFENSE INVOLVING IMPAIRED DRIVING -- SIMILAR OFFENSE IN ANOTHER JURISDICTION. --Although the definitions of "impairment" under North Carolina and New York laws are not identical and the statutes do not "mirror" one another, they are "substantially equivalent"; consequently, the trial court did not err in determining that defendant's prior conviction under New York law was a grossly aggravating factor in sentencing him under North Carolina law. State v. Parisi, 135 N.C. App. 222, 519 S.E.2d 531 (1999).

UNDER INFLUENCE OF IMPAIRING SUBSTANCE. --The offense of impaired driving is proven by evidence that defendant drove a vehicle on any highway in this State while his physical or mental faculties, or both, were "appreciably impaired by an impairing substance." State v. George, 77 N.C. App. 580, 335 S.E.2d 768 (1985).

Where the tortfeasor rear-ended the injured party's vehicle, the trial court erred in granting the tortfeasor's motion for summary judgment on the injured party's punitive damages claim, because the tortfeasor failed to show that he was not under the influence of an impairing substance under G.S. 20-4.01(14a), where he admitted to drinking two beers and taking three prescription drugs before the accident; the tortfeasor offered no evidence that the prescription drugs, mixed with alcohol, were not an impairing substance. Byrd v. Adams, 152 N.C. App. 460, 568 S.E.2d 640 (2002), cert. denied, 356 N.C. 433, 568 S.E.2d 640 (2002).

Admissible trial evidence established beyond a reasonable doubt that defendant was driving a vehicle while under the influence of alcohol in violation of G.S. 20-138.1; evidence showing that defendant was under the influence of alcohol included, inter alia: (1) weaving; (2) erratic braking; (3) driving 70 MPH in a 50 MPH zone; (4) the strong odor of alcohol on defendant's person; (5) defendant's unsteady balance; and (6) his statement that he had consumed alcohol. United States v. Van Hazel, 468 F. Supp. 2d 792 (E.D.N.C. 2006).

Lab report of defendant's blood sample indicated that three of the drugs found in defendant's blood were listed in N.C. Gen. Stat. ch. 90 as Schedule II controlled substances, and therefore were impairing substances under G.S. 20-4.01(14a). State v. Braswell, 222 N.C. App. 176, 729 S.E.2d 697 (2012).

CROSS REFERENCES. --
As to designation of an area of private property as a public vehicular area, see G.S. 20-219.4.

LEGAL PERIODICALS. --
For note discussing the definition of "driving" under the North Carolina Safe Roads Act, in light of State v. Fields, 77 N.C. App. 404, 335 S.E.2d 69 (1985), see 64 N.C.L. Rev. 127 (1986).

OPINIONS OF THE ATTORNEY GENERAL
TRAILERS DESIGNED TO RUN UPON THE HIGHWAYS and pulled by a self-propelled vehicle are motor vehicles for the purposes of this Chapter. See opinion of the Attorney General to Clyde R. Cook, Jr., Asst. Comm'r of Motor Vehicles, 60 N.C.A.G. 90 (1992).

"PUBLIC VEHICULAR AREA" includes streets leading into privately owned trailer parks which rent, lease and sell individual lots. See opinion of Attorney General to Mr. Henry A. Harkey, Assistant District Attorney, 45 N.C.A.G. 284 (1976).

THE PARKING LOT OF THE RESTAURANT is within the definition of "public vehicular area" under subdivision (32) of this section when the restaurant is closed. See opinion of Attorney General to Mr. James C. Yeatts, III, Assistant District Attorney, 17-B Judicial District, 52 N.C.A.G. 6 (1982).

SECTION 20-217, A SAFETY STATUTE DESIGNED TO PREVENT THE PASSING OF A SCHOOL BUS displaying its mechanical stop signal while receiving or discharging passengers, has no application to a

Chapter 20

"public vehicular area." See opinion of Attorney General to Mr. Alan Leonard, District Attorney, Twenty-Ninth Judicial District, -- N.C.A.G. -- (Mar. 9, 1987).

VEHICLE WHICH IS CONSTRUCTIVE TOTAL LOSS NOW DEFINED AS SALVAGE VEHICLE UNDER THIS SECTION. See opinion of Attorney General to Mr. James E. Rhodes, Director, Vehicle Registration Section, Division of Motor Vehicles, North Carolina Department of Transportation, -- N.C.A.G. -- (May 20, 1988).

AS TO TREATMENT BY INSURER OF WRECKED VEHICLE AS CONSTRUCTIVE TOTAL LOSS, thereby declaring it a total loss, so as to harmonize subdivision (33)(d) and G.S. 20-109.1(a)(1). See opinion of Attorney General to Mr. James E. Rhodes, Director, Vehicle Registration Section, Division of Motor Vehicles, North Carolina Department of Transportation, -- N.C.A.G. -- (May 20, 1988).

NEW DEFINITION OF SALVAGE MOTOR VEHICLE ENACTED BY SESSION LAWS 1987, C. 607 IN SUBDIVISION (33)(D) AND G.S. 20-109.1 MUST BE READ IN PARI MATERIA. See opinion of Attorney General to Mr. James E. Rhodes, Director, Vehicle Registration Section, Division of Motor Vehicles, North Carolina Department of Transportation, -- N.C.A.G. -- (May 20, 1988).

PRIVATE CARRIERS OPERATED BY DRIVERS EMPLOYED IN LOGGING OPERATIONS ARE ENTITLED TO THE EXEMPTION FOR "FARM" VEHICLES UNDER G.S. 20-37.16(E)(3) IF agricultural or forest products being transported were raised and grown by farmer/forester and he does not engage in business of buying products for resale. Then he and his employees could transport such forest products within 150 miles of farm in vehicles not used in common or contract motor carrier operations without obtaining a commercial driver's license. Conversely, if forest products were not raised and grown by forester, or he engages in buying forest products for resale, transporting of those products by him or his employees would not be exempt from commercial driver's license requirements for, as to those forest products, forester was not a farmer. See opinion of Attorney General to Rep. Beverly M. Purdue, 3rd District: Craven, Lenoir, Pamlico Counties, 60 N.C.A.G. 30 (1990).

This section has more than one version with varying effective dates. To view a complete list of the versions of this section see Table of Contents.

§ 20-4.02. Quadrennial adjustment of certain fees and rates

(a) **Adjustment for Inflation.** -- Beginning July 1, 2020, and every four years thereafter, the Division shall adjust the fees and rates imposed pursuant to the statutes listed in this subsection for inflation in accordance with the Consumer Price Index computed by the Bureau of Labor Statistics. The adjustment for per transaction rates in subdivision (8a) of this subsection shall be rounded to the nearest cent and all other adjustments under this subsection shall be rounded to the nearest twenty-five cents (25 cent(s)):

(1) G.S. 20-7.
(2) G.S. 20-11.
(3) G.S. 20-14.
(4) G.S. 20-16.
(5) G.S. 20-26.
(6) G.S. 20-37.15.
(7) G.S. 20-37.16.
(8) G.S. 20-42(b).
(8a) G.S. 20-63(h), with respect to the per transaction rates set in that subsection.
(9) G.S. 20-85(a)(1) through (10).
(10) G.S. 20-85.1.
(11) G.S. 20-87, except for the additional fee set forth in G.S. 20-87(6) for private motorcycles.
(12) G.S. 20-88.
(13) G.S. 20-289.
(14) G.S. 20-385.
(15) G.S. 44A-4(b)(1).

(b) **Computation.** -- In determining the rate of inflation to use when making an adjustment pursuant to subsection (a) of this section, the Division shall base the rate on the percent change in the annual Consumer Price Index over the preceding four-year period.

(c) **Rules.** -- The provisions of Chapter 150B of the General Statutes shall not apply to the inflation adjustment required by this section.

(d) **Consultation and Publication.** -- At least 90 days prior to making an adjustment pursuant to subsection (a) of this section, and notwithstanding any provision of G.S. 12-3.1 to the contrary, the Division shall (i) consult with the Joint Legislative Commission on Governmental Operations, (ii) provide a report to the chairs of the Senate Appropriations Committee on Department of Transportation and the House of Representatives Appropriations Committee on Transportation, and (iii) publish notice of the fees that will be in effect in the offices of the Division and on the Division's Web site.

(e) **Effective Date.** -- Any adjustment to fees or rates under this section applicable to a motor vehicle sold or leased by a motor vehicle dealer, as defined in G.S. 20-286(11), is only applicable to a motor vehicle sale or lease made on or after the effective date of the fee or rate adjustment regardless of the date of submission of a title and registration application for the motor vehicle to the Division. No adjustment to fees or rates under this section applies to a motor vehicle sale or lease made prior to the effective date of the fee or rate adjustment.

History.
2015-241, s. 29.30(s); 2016-120, s. 1; 2018-42, s. 8.
  EDITOR'S NOTE. --
Session Laws 2015-241, s. 29.30(u), made this section effective July 1, 2020.

Session Laws 2015-241, s. 1.1, provides: "This act shall be known as 'The Current Operations and Capital Improvements Appropriations Act of 2015.'"

Session Laws 2015-241, s. 33.4, provides: "Except for statutory changes or other provisions that clearly indicate an intention to have effects beyond the 2015-2017 fiscal biennium, the textual provisions of this act apply only to funds appropriated for, and activities occurring during, the 2015-2017 fiscal biennium."

Session Laws 2015-241, s. 33.6, is a severability clause.

EFFECT OF AMENDMENTS. --
Session Laws 2016-120, s. 1, effective July 28, 2016, substituted "fees and rates" for "fees" in the section heading; rewrote subsection (a); substituted "making an adjustment" for "adjusting the fees" in subsection (b); substituted "the inflation adjustment" for "the adjustment of fees" in subsection (c); and substituted "making an adjustment" for "adjusting the fees" in subsection (d).

Session Laws 2018-42, s. 8, effective June 22, 2018, added subsection (e).

§ 20-4.03. Administrative hearing fees

(a) **Authorization.** -- The Division is authorized to charge a fee to any person who requests an administrative hearing before the Division in accordance with this Chapter.

(b) **Requirements for Requesting a Hearing.** -- Any request for an administrative hearing before the Division must be in writing and accompanied by the total applicable administrative hearing fee charged by the Division. An administrative hearing shall not be granted by the Division unless the administrative hearing request complies with the requirements of this subsection. Notwithstanding any provision of this Chapter to the contrary, any pending revocation, suspension, civil penalty assessment, or other adverse action shall not be stayed upon receipt of an administrative hearing request unless the request complies with the requirements of this subsection.

(c) **Report.** -- Beginning October 1, 2018, and quarterly thereafter, the Division shall submit a report to the Fiscal Research Division of the General Assembly detailing all of the following for each month of the applicable quarter and for each type of administrative hearing:

(1) The total number of administrative hearings.

(2) The total amount of revenue collected.

(3) The total number of fee waivers granted.

(4) The counties where the administrative hearings were held.

(5) The average amount of time required to conduct an administrative hearing, with the time required of hearing officers and the time required of administrative personnel listed separately.

History.
2017-57, s. 34.32(b);2017-197, s. 7.3(a);2018-5, s. 34.23(d)

EDITOR'S NOTE. --
Session Laws 2014-100, s. 34.9(a), as amended by Session Laws 2017-57, s. 34.32(a), provides: "The Department of Transportation, Division of Motor Vehicles, shall develop a schedule of fees to recover the costs incurred by the Hearings Unit of the Division of Motor Vehicles for the performance of administrative hearings required by law or under rules adopted under G.S. 20-2(b). The proceeds of the fees developed in accordance with this section shall be deposited in a fund established for the Hearings Unit. Except as otherwise provided by an act of the General Assembly, the Hearings Unit shall be funded solely from the proceeds collected from the fees developed in accordance with this section. The plan and proposed schedule shall address, at a minimum, the following:

"(1) Current hearing process and recommended modifications to achieve cost efficiencies, including proposed revisions to existing laws or rules.

"(2) Historical and projected funding requirements for each category of hearing performed by the Division.

"(3) Schedule of fees and projected receipts.

"(4) Proposed processes and rules for the collection of fees and the refunding of fees for hearings initiated by the Division in which the original decision of the Division is reversed.

"(5) Implementation milestones."

Session Laws 2017-57, s. 34.32(c), provides: "The Division of Motor Vehicles may adopt temporary rules to implement the provisions of Section 34.9 of S.L. 2014-100, as amended by Section 29.30A of S.L. 2015-241 and subsection (a) of this section. Temporary rules adopted in accordance with this section shall remain in effect until permanent rules that replace the temporary rules become effective."

Session Laws 2017-57, s. 34.32(d), made this section effective January 1, 2018, and applicable to administrative hearings requested on or after that date.

Session Laws 2017-57, s. 1.1, provides: "This act shall be known as the 'Current Operations Appropriations Act of 2017.'"

Session Laws 2017-57, s. 39.6, is a severability clause.

Session Laws 2018-5, s. 34.23(a) -(c), (e), provides: "(a) Revised Budget. -- The Office of State Budget and Management, in consultation with the Division of Motor Vehicles, shall adjust the Hearing Unit's certified budget for the 2018-2019 fiscal year to correctly align total requirements and receipts to reflect the requirement set forth in Section 34.9 of S.L. 2014-100, as amended by Section 29.30A of S.L. 2015-241 and Section 34.32 of S.L. 2017-57, that all functions supporting the Hearing Unit's operating budget under Fund Code 1304 be fully receipt-supported from the fee proceeds collected by the Hearings Unit.

"(b) Position Elimination. -- The Division of Motor Vehicles may eliminate vacant and filled positions to achieve the requirement set forth in subsection (a) of this section. If filled positions are eliminated under this subsection, the Division of Motor Vehicles shall eliminate the positions in accordance with G.S. 126-7.1. All positions identified by the Division of Motor Vehicles for elimination under this subsection shall be eliminated by no later than October 1, 2018.

"(c) Position Elimination Report. -- By October 15, 2018, the Division of Motor Vehicles shall submit a report to the Joint Legislative Transportation Oversight Committee detailing the elimination of any positions under subsection (b) of this section.

"(e) Requirement for Submission of First Hearings Report. -- Notwithstanding any provision of G.S. 20-4.03(c), as enacted by subsection (d) of this section, to the contrary, the report required under G.S. 20-4.03(c) for October 1, 2018, shall include all of the information required under G.S. 20-4.03(c) for the period from January 1, 2018, through October 1, 2018."

Session Laws 2018-5, s. 1.1, provides: "This act shall be known as the 'Current Operations Appropriations Act of 2018.'"

Session Laws 2018-5, s. 39.4, provides: "Except for statutory changes or other provisions that clearly indicate an intention to have effects beyond the 2018-2019 fiscal year, the textual provisions of this act apply only to funds appropriated for, and activities occurring during, the 2018-2019 fiscal year."

Session Laws 2018-5, s. 39.7, is a severability clause.

EFFECT OF AMENDMENTS. --

Session Laws 2017-197, s. 7.3(a), effective January 1, 2018, in subsection (a) substituted "any person who requests" for "individuals who request."

Session Laws 2018-5, s. 34.23(d), effective July 1, 2018, added subsection (c).

ARTICLE 1A.
RECIPROCITY AGREEMENTS AS TO REGISTRATION AND LICENSING

§ 20-4.1. Declaration of policy

It is the policy of this State to promote and encourage the fullest possible use of its highway system by authorizing the making and execution of motor vehicle reciprocal registration agreements, arrangements and declarations with other states, provinces, territories and countries with respect to vehicles registered in this and such other states, provinces, territories and countries thus contributing to the economic and social development and growth of this State.

History.
1961, c. 642, s. 1

§ 20-4.2. Definitions

As used in this Article:

(1) "Commercial vehicle" means any vehicle which is operated in furtherance of any commercial enterprise.

(2) "Commissioner" means the Commissioner of Motor Vehicles of North Carolina.

(3) "Division" means the Division of Motor Vehicles of North Carolina.

(4) "Jurisdiction" means and includes a state, district, territory or possession of the United States, a foreign country and a state or province of a foreign country.

(5) "Properly registered," as applied to place of registration, means:

a. The jurisdiction where the person registering the vehicle has his legal residence, or

b. In the case of a commercial vehicle, including a leased vehicle, the jurisdiction in which it is registered if the commercial enterprise in which such vehicle is used has a place of business therein, and, if the vehicle is most frequently dispatched, garaged, serviced, maintained, operated or otherwise controlled in or from such place of business, and, the vehicle has been assigned to such place of business, or

c. In the case of a commercial vehicle, including leased vehicles, the jurisdiction where, because of an agreement or arrangement between two or more jurisdictions, or pursuant to a declaration, the vehicle has been registered as required by said jurisdiction.

d. In case of doubt or dispute as to the proper place of registration of a vehicle, the Division shall make the final determination, but in making such determination, may confer with departments of the other jurisdictions affected.

History.
1961, c. 642, s. 1; 1975, c. 716, s. 5; 1979, c. 470, s. 2
APPLIED in Cox v. Miller, 26 N.C. App. 749, 217 S.E.2d 198 (1975).

§ 20-4.3. Commissioner may make reciprocity agreements, arrangements or declarations

The Commissioner of Motor Vehicles shall have the authority to execute or make agreements, arrangements or declarations to carry out the provisions of this Article.

History.
1961, c. 642, s. 1

§ 20-4.4. Authority for reciprocity agreements; provisions; reciprocity standards

(a) The Commissioner may enter into an agreement or arrangement for interstate or intrastate operations with the duly authorized representatives of another jurisdiction, granting to vehicles or to owners of vehicles which are properly registered or licensed in such jurisdiction and for which evidence of compliance is supplied, benefits, privileges and exemptions from the payment, wholly or partially, of any taxes, fees, or other charges imposed upon such vehicles or owners with respect to the operation or ownership of such vehicles under the laws of this State. Such an agreement or arrangement shall provide that vehicles properly registered or licensed in this State when operated upon highways of such other jurisdiction shall receive exemptions, benefits and privileges of a similar kind or to a similar degree as are extended to vehicles properly registered or licensed in such jurisdiction when operated in this State. Each such agreement or arrangement shall, in the judgment of the Commissioner, be in the best interest of this State and the citizens thereof and shall be fair and equitable to this State and the citizens thereof, and all of the same shall be determined on the basis and recognition of the benefits which accrue to the economy of this State from the uninterrupted flow of commerce.

(b) When the Commissioner enters into a reciprocal registration agreement or arrangement with another jurisdiction which has a motor vehicle tax, license or fee which is not subject to waiver by a reciprocity agreement, the Commissioner is empowered and authorized to provide as a condition of the agreement or arrangement that owners of vehicles licensed in such other jurisdiction shall pay some equalizing tax or fee to the Division. The failure of any owner or operator of a vehicle to pay the taxes or fees provided in the agreement or arrangement shall prohibit them from receiving any benefits therefrom and they shall be required to register their vehicles and pay taxes as if there was no agreement or arrangement.

History.
1961, c. 642, s. 1; 1971, c. 588; 1975, c. 716, s. 5

§ 20-4.5. Base-state registration reciprocity

An agreement or arrangement entered into, or a declaration issued under the authority of this Article may contain provisions authorizing the registration or licensing in another jurisdiction of vehicles located in or operated from a base in such other jurisdiction which vehicles otherwise would be required to be registered or licensed in some other state; and in such event the exemptions, benefits and privileges extended by such agreement, arrangement or declaration shall apply to such vehicles, when properly licensed or registered in such base jurisdiction.

History.
1961, c. 642, s. 1

N.C. Gen. Stat. § 20-4.6

Repealed by Session Laws 1997-122, s. 1.

§ 20-4.7. Extension of reciprocal privileges to lessees authorized

An agreement or arrangement entered into, or a declaration issued under the authority of this Article, may contain provisions under which a leased vehicle properly registered by the lessor thereof may be entitled, subject to terms and conditions stated therein, to the exemptions, benefits and privileges extended by such agreement, arrangement or declaration.

History.
1961, c. 642, s. 1

§ 20-4.8. Automatic reciprocity, when

On and after July 1, 1961, if no agreement, arrangement or declaration is in effect with respect to another jurisdiction as authorized by this Article, any vehicle properly registered or licensed in such other jurisdiction and for which evidence of compliance supplied shall receive, when operated in this State, the same exemptions, benefits and privileges granted by such other jurisdiction to vehicles properly registered in this State. Reciprocity extended under this section shall apply to commercial vehicles only when engaged exclusively in interstate operations.

History.
1961, c. 642, s. 1

§ 20-4.9. Suspension of reciprocity benefits

Agreements, arrangements or declarations made under the authority of this Article may include provisions authorizing the Division to suspend or cancel the exemptions, benefits or privileges granted thereunder to a vehicle which is in violation of any of the conditions or terms of such agreements, arrangements or declarations or is in violation of the laws of this State relating to motor vehicles or rules and regulations lawfully promulgated thereunder.

History.
1961, c. 642, s. 1; 1975, c. 716, s. 5

§ 20-4.10. Agreements to be written, filed and available for distribution

All agreements, arrangements or declarations or amendments thereto shall be in writing

Chapter 20

and shall be filed in the office of the Commissioner. Copies thereof shall be made available by the Commissioner upon request and upon payment of a fee therefor in an amount necessary to defray the costs of reproduction thereof.

History.
1961, c. 642, s. 1

§ 20-4.11. Reciprocity agreements in effect at time of Article

All reciprocity registration agreements, arrangements and declarations relating to vehicles in force and effect July 1, 1961, shall continue in force and effect until specifically amended or revoked as provided by law or by such agreements or arrangements.

History.
1961, c. 642, s. 1

§ 20-4.12. Article part of and supplemental to motor vehicle registration law

This Article shall be, and construed as, a part of and supplemental to the motor vehicle registration law of this State.

History.
1961, c. 642, s. 1

§§ 20-4.13 through 20-4.17

Reserved for future codification purposes.

ARTICLE 1B.
RECIPROCAL PROVISIONS AS TO ARREST OF NONRESIDENTS

§ 20-4.18. Definitions

Unless the context otherwise requires, the following words and phrases, for the purpose of this Article, shall have the following meanings:

(1) **Citation.** -- Any citation, summons, ticket, or other document issued by a law-enforcement officer for the violation of a traffic law, ordinance, rule or regulation.

(2) **Collateral or Bond.** -- Any cash or other security deposited to secure an appearance following a citation by a law-enforcement officer.

(3) Repealed by Session Laws 1979, c. 667, s. 2.

(4) **Nonresident.** -- A person who holds a license issued by a reciprocating state.

(5) **Personal Recognizance.** -- An agreement by a nonresident to comply with

the terms of the citation issued to the nonresident.

(6) **Reciprocating State.** -- Any state or other jurisdiction which extends by its laws to residents of North Carolina substantially the rights and privileges provided by this Article.

(7) **State.** -- The State of North Carolina.

History.
1973, c. 736; 1979, c. 667, s. 2; 1981, c. 508; 1999-452, s. 6

§ 20-4.19. Issuance of citation to nonresident; officer to report noncompliance

(a) Notwithstanding other provisions of this Chapter, a law-enforcement officer observing a violation of this Chapter or other traffic regulation by a nonresident shall issue a citation as appropriate and shall not, subject to the provisions of subsection (b) of this section, require such nonresident to post collateral or bond to secure appearance for trial, but shall accept such nonresident's personal recognizance; provided, however, that the nonresident shall have the right upon request to post collateral or bond in a manner provided by law and in such case the provisions of this Article shall not apply.

(b) A nonresident may be required to post collateral or bond to secure appearance for trial if the offense is one which would result in the suspension or revocation of a person's license under the laws of this State.

(c) Upon the failure of the nonresident to comply with the citation, the clerk of court shall report the noncompliance to the Division. The report of noncompliance shall clearly identify the nonresident; describe the violation, specifying the section of the statute, code, or ordinance violated; indicate the location and date of offense; and identify the vehicle involved.

History.
1973, c. 736; 1975, c. 716, s. 5; 1991, c. 682, s. 1;1999-452, s. 7

§ 20-4.20. Division to transmit report to reciprocating state; suspension of license for noncompliance with citation issued by reciprocating state

(a) Upon receipt of a report of noncompliance, the Division shall transmit a certified copy of such report to the official in charge of the issuance of licenses in the reciprocating state in which the nonresident resides or by which he is licensed.

(b) When the licensing authority of a reciprocating state reports that a person holding a North Carolina license has failed to comply with a citation issued in such state, the Commissioner shall forthwith suspend such person's license. The order of suspension shall indicate the reason for the order, and shall notify the person that his license shall remain suspended until he has furnished evidence satisfactory to the Commissioner that he has complied with the terms of the citation which was the basis for the suspension order by appearing before the tribunal to which he was cited and complying with any order entered by said tribunal.

(c) A copy of any suspension order issued hereunder may be furnished to the licensing authority of the reciprocating state.

(d) The Commissioner shall maintain a current listing of reciprocating states hereunder. Such lists shall from time to time be disseminated among the appropriate departments, divisions, bureaus, and agencies of this State; the principal law-enforcement officers of the several counties, cities, and towns of this State; and the licensing authorities in reciprocating states.

(e) The Commissioner shall have the authority to execute or make agreements, arrangements, or declarations to carry out the provisions of this Article.

History.
1973, c. 736; 1975, c. 716, s. 5; 1979, c. 104

   G.

S. 20-25 CREATES NO RIGHT TO APPEAL A SUSPENSION UNDER G.S. 20/Y-4.20(B). The General Assembly simply has not yet provided for appeals from suspension under G.S. 20-4.20(b). Palmer v. Wilkins, 73 N.C. App. 171, 325 S.E.2d 697 (1985). CITED in Cooke v. Faulkner, 137 N.C. App. 755, 529 S.E.2d 512 (2000).

ARTICLE 1C.
DRIVERS LICENSE COMPACT

§ 20-4.21. Title of Article

This Article is the Drivers License Compact and may be cited by that name.

History.
1993, c. 533, s. 1

§ 20-4.22. Commissioner may make reciprocity agreements, arrangements, or declarations

The Commissioner may execute or make agreements, arrangements, or declarations to implement this Article.

History.
1993, c. 533, s. 1

§ 20-4.23. Legislative findings and policy

(a) **Findings. --** The General Assembly and the states that are members of the Drivers License Compact find that:

(1) The safety of their streets and highways is materially affected by the degree of compliance with state laws and local ordinances relating to the operation of motor vehicles.

(2) The violation of a law or an ordinance relating to the operation of a motor vehicle is evidence that the violator engages in conduct that is likely to endanger the safety of persons and property.

(3) The continuance in force of a license to drive is predicated upon compliance with laws and ordinances relating to the operation of motor vehicles in whichever jurisdiction the vehicle is operated.

(b) **Policy. --** It is the policy of the General Assembly and of each of the states that is a member of the Drivers License Compact to:

(1) Promote compliance with the laws, ordinances, and administrative rules and regulations of a member state relating to the operation of motor vehicles.

(2) Make the reciprocal recognition of licenses to drive and the eligibility for a license to drive more just and equitable by making consideration of overall compliance with motor vehicle laws, ordinances, and administrative rules and regulations a condition precedent to the continuance or issuance of any license that authorizes the holder of the license to operate a motor vehicle in a member state.

History.
1993, c. 533, s. 1
CITED in Ward v. Carmona, 368 N.C. 35, 770 S.E.2d 70 (2015).

§ 20-4.24. Reports of convictions; effect of reports

(a) **Reports. --** A state that is a member of the Drivers License Compact shall report to another member state of the compact a conviction for any of the following:

(1) Manslaughter or negligent homicide resulting from the operation of a motor vehicle.

(2) Driving a motor vehicle while impaired.

(3) A felony in the commission of which a motor vehicle was used.

(4) Failure to stop and render aid in the event of a motor vehicle accident resulting in the death or personal injury of another.

If the laws of a member state do not describe the listed violations in precisely the words used in this subsection, the member state shall construe the descriptions to apply to offenses of the member state that are substantially similar to the ones described.

A state that is a member of the Drivers License Compact shall report to another member state of the compact a conviction for any other offense or any other information concerning convictions that the member states agree to report.

(b) **Effect.** -- A state that is a member of the Drivers License Compact shall treat a report of a conviction received from another member state of the compact as a report of the conduct that resulted in the conviction. For a conviction required to be reported under subsection (a), a member state shall give the same effect to the report as if the conviction had occurred in that state. For a conviction that is not required to be reported under subsection (a), a member state shall give the effect to the report that is required by the laws of that state. G.S. 20-23 governs the effect in this State of convictions that are not required to be reported under subsection (a).

History.
1993, c. 533, s. 1

§ 20-4.25. Review of license status in other states upon application for license in member state

Upon application for a license to drive, the licensing authority of a state that is a member of the Drivers License Compact must determine if the applicant has ever held, or currently holds, a license to drive issued by another member state. The licensing authority of the member state where the application is made may not issue the applicant a license to drive if:

(1) The applicant has held a license, but it has been revoked for a violation and the revocation period has not ended. If the revocation period is for more than one year and it has been at least one year since the license was revoked, the licensing authority may allow the applicant to apply for a new license if the laws of the licensing authority's state permit the application.

(2) The applicant currently holds a license to drive issued by another member state and does not surrender that license.

History.
1993, c. 533, s. 1

§ 20-4.26. Effect on other laws or agreements

Except as expressly required by the provisions of this Article, this Article does not affect the right of a member state to the Drivers License Compact to apply any of its other laws relating to licenses to drive to any person or circumstance, nor does it invalidate or prevent any driver license agreement or other cooperative arrangement between a member state and a state that is not a member.

History.
1993, c. 533, s. 1

§ 20-4.27. Effect on other State driver license laws

To the extent that this Article conflicts with general driver licensing provisions in this Chapter, this Article prevails. Where this Article is silent, the general driver licensing provisions apply.

History.
1993, c. 533, s. 1

§ 20-4.28. Administration and exchange of information

The head of the licensing authority of each member state is the administrator of the Drivers License Compact for that state. The administrators, acting jointly, have the power to formulate all necessary procedures for the exchange of information under this compact. The administrator of each member state shall furnish to the administrator of each other member state any information or documents reasonably necessary to facilitate the administration of this compact.

History.
1993, c. 533, s. 1

§ 20-4.29. Withdrawal from Drivers License Compact

A member state may withdraw from the Drivers License Compact. A withdrawal may not become effective until at least six months after the heads of all other member states have received notice of the withdrawal. Withdrawal does not affect the validity or applicability by the licensing authorities of states remaining members of the compact of a report of a conviction occurring prior to the withdrawal.

History.
1993, c. 533, s. 1

§ 20-4.30. Construction and severability

This Article shall be liberally construed to effectuate its purposes. The provisions of this Article are severable; if any part of this Article is declared to be invalid by a court, the invalidity does not affect other parts of this Article that can be given effect without the invalid provision. If the Drivers License Compact is declared invalid by a court in a member state, the compact remains in full force and effect in the remaining member states and in full force and effect for all severable matters in that member state.

History.
1993, c. 533, s. 1

ARTICLE 2.
UNIFORM DRIVER'S LICENSE ACT

§ 20-5. Title of Article

This Article may be cited as the Uniform Driver's License Act.

History.
1935, c. 52, s. 31
LEGISLATIVE PURPOSE. --This Article was designed under the police power in furtherance of the safety of the users of the State's highways. Harrell v. Scheidt, 243 N.C. 735, 92 S.E.2d 182 (1956).
AND AUTHORITY. --The General Assembly has full authority to prescribe the conditions upon which licenses to operate automobiles are issued, and to designate the agency through which, and the conditions upon which licenses, when issued shall be suspended or revoked. Honeycutt v. Scheidt, 254 N.C. 607, 119 S.E.2d 777 (1961).
DIVISION GIVEN EXCLUSIVE POWER TO ISSUE, SUSPEND AND REVOKE LICENSES. --This Article vests exclusively in the State Department (now Division) of Motor Vehicles the issuance, suspension and revocation of licenses to operate motor vehicles. Honeycutt v. Scheidt, 254 N.C. 607, 119 S.E.2d 777 (1961); Gibson v. Scheidt, 259 N.C. 339, 130 S.E.2d 679 (1963).

OPINIONS OF THE ATTORNEY GENERAL
AUTHORITY TO REQUIRE DOCUMENTED PROOF FOR NAME CHANGES. --The Division of Motor Vehicles does not have authority to establish a policy to require documented proof from the Register of Deeds or official court documents for name changes on driver's licenses and identification cards as the only method of establishing a name change. See opinion of Attorney General to Mr. William S. Hiatt, Commissioner of Motor Vehicles, 58 N.C.A.G. 4 (1988).

N.C. Gen. Stat. § 20-6

Repealed by Session Laws 1973, c. 1330, s. 39.

§ 20-7. Issuance and renewal of drivers licenses

(a) **License Required.** -- To drive a motor vehicle on a highway, a person must be licensed by the Division under this Article or Article 2C of this Chapter to drive the vehicle and must carry the license while driving the vehicle. The Division issues regular drivers licenses under this Article and issues commercial drivers licenses under Article 2C.

A license authorizes the holder of the license to drive any vehicle included in the class of the license and any vehicle included in a lesser class of license, except a vehicle for which an endorsement is required. To drive a vehicle for which an endorsement is required, a person must obtain both a license and an endorsement for the vehicle. A regular drivers license is considered a lesser class of license than its commercial counterpart.

The classes of regular drivers licenses and the motor vehicles that can be driven with each class of license are:

(1) **Class A.** -- A Class A license authorizes the holder to drive any of the following:

a. A Class A motor vehicle that is exempt under G.S. 20-37.16 from the commercial drivers license requirements.

b. A Class A motor vehicle that has a combined GVWR of less than 26,001 pounds and includes as part of the combination a towed unit that has a GVWR of at least 10,001 pounds.

(2) **Class B.** -- A Class B license authorizes the holder to drive any Class B motor vehicle that is exempt under G.S. 20-37.16 from the commercial drivers license requirements.

(3) **Class C.** -- A Class C license authorizes the holder to drive any of the following:

a. A Class C motor vehicle that is not a commercial motor vehicle.

b. When operated by a volunteer member of a fire department, a rescue squad, or an emergency medical service (EMS) in the performance of duty, a Class A or Class B fire-fighting, rescue, or EMS motor vehicle or a combination of these vehicles.

c. A combination of noncommercial motor vehicles that have a GVWR of more than 10,000 pounds but less than 26,001 pounds. This sub-subdivision does not apply to a Class C license holder less than 18 years of age.

The Commissioner may assign a unique motor vehicle to a class that is different from the class in which it would otherwise belong.

A person holding a commercial drivers license issued by another jurisdiction must apply for a transfer and obtain a North Carolina issued commercial drivers license within 30 days of becoming a resident. Any other new resident of North Carolina who has a drivers license issued by another jurisdiction must obtain a license from the Division within 60 days after becoming a resident.

(a1) **Motorcycles and Mopeds.** -- To drive a motorcycle, a person shall have one of the following:

(1) A full provisional license with a motorcycle learner's permit.

(2) A regular drivers license with a motorcycle learner's permit.

(3) A full provisional license with a motorcycle endorsement.

(4) A regular drivers license with a motorcycle endorsement.

Subsection (a2) of this section sets forth the requirements for a motorcycle learner's permit. To obtain a motorcycle endorsement, a person shall pay the fee set in subsection (i) of this section. In addition, to obtain an endorsement, a person age 18 or older shall demonstrate competence to drive a motorcycle by passing a knowledge test concerning motorcycles, and by passing a road test or providing proof of successful completion of one of the following:

(1) The North Carolina Motorcycle Safety Education Program Basic Rider Course or Experienced Rider Course.

(2) Any course approved by the Commissioner consistent with the instruction provided through the Motorcycle Safety Instruction Program established under G.S. 115D-72.

A person less than 18 years of age shall demonstrate competence to drive a motorcycle by passing a knowledge test concerning motorcycles and providing proof of successful completion of one of the following:

(1) Repealed by Session Laws 2012-85, s. 1, effective July 1, 2012.

(2) The North Carolina Motorcycle Safety Education Program Basic Rider Course or Experienced Rider Course.

(3) Any course approved by the Commissioner consistent with the instruction provided through the Motorcycle Safety Instruction Program established under G.S. 115D-72.

A person less than 18 years of age with a motorcycle endorsement may not drive a motorcycle with a passenger.

Neither a drivers license nor a motorcycle endorsement is required to drive a moped.

(a2) **Motorcycle Learner's Permit.** -- The following persons are eligible for a motorcycle learner's permit:

(1) A person who is at least 16 years old but less than 18 years old and has a full provisional license issued by the Division.

(2) A person who is at least 18 years old and has a license issued by the Division.

To obtain a motorcycle learner's permit, an applicant shall pass a vision test, a road sign test, and a knowledge test specified by the Division. An applicant who is less than 18 years old shall successfully complete the North Carolina Motorcycle Safety Education Program Basic Rider Course or any course approved by the Commissioner consistent with the instruction provided through the Motorcycle Safety Instruction Program established under G.S. 115D-72. A motorcycle learner's permit expires twelve months after it is issued and may be renewed for one additional six-month period. The holder of a motorcycle learner's permit may not drive a motorcycle with a passenger. The fee for a motorcycle learner's permit is the amount set in G.S. 20-7(*l*) for a learner's permit.

(a3) **Autocycles.** -- For purposes of this section, the term "motorcycle" shall not include autocycles. To drive an autocycle, a person shall have a regular drivers license.

(b) Repealed by Session Laws 1993, c. 368, s. 1, c. 533, s. 12.

(b1) **Application.** -- To obtain an identification card, learners permit, or drivers license from the Division, a person shall complete an application form provided by the Division, present at least two forms of identification approved by the Commissioner, be a resident of this State, and, except for an identification card, demonstrate his or her physical and mental ability to drive safely a motor vehicle included in the class of license for which the person has applied. At least one of the forms of identification shall indicate the applicant's residence address. The Division may copy the identification presented or hold it for a brief period of time to verify its authenticity. To obtain an endorsement, a person shall demonstrate his or her physical and mental ability to drive safely the type of motor vehicle for which the endorsement is required.

The application form shall request all of the following information, and it shall contain the disclosures concerning the request for an applicant's social security number required by section 7 of the federal Privacy Act of 1974, Pub. L. No. 93-579:

(1) The applicant's full name.

(2) The applicant's mailing address and residence address.

(3) A physical description of the applicant, including the applicant's sex, height, eye color, and hair color.

(4) The applicant's date of birth.

(5) The applicant's valid social security number.

(6) The applicant's signature.

The Division shall not issue an identification card, learners permit, or drivers license to an applicant who fails to provide the applicant's valid social security number.

(b2) **Disclosure of Social Security Number.** -- The social security number of an applicant is not a public record. The Division may not disclose an applicant's social security number except as allowed under federal law. A violation of the disclosure restrictions is punishable as provided in 42 U.S.C. § 408, and amendments to that law.

In accordance with 42 U.S.C. 405 and 42 U.S.C. 666, and amendments thereto, the Division may disclose a social security number obtained under subsection (b1) of this section only as follows:

(1) For the purpose of administering the drivers license laws.

(2) To the Department of Health and Human Services, Child Support Enforcement Program for the purpose of establishing paternity or child support or enforcing a child support order.

(3) To the Department of Revenue for the purpose of verifying taxpayer identity.

(4) To the Office of Indigent Defense Services of the Judicial Department for the purpose of verifying the identity of a represented client and enforcing a court order to pay for the legal services rendered.

(5) To each county jury commission for the purpose of verifying the identity of deceased persons whose names should be removed from jury lists.

(6) To the State Chief Information Officer for the purposes of G.S. 143B-1385.

(7) To the Department of Commerce, Division of Employment Security, for the purpose of verifying employer and claimant identity.

(8) To the Judicial Department for the purpose of administering the criminal and motor vehicle laws.

(b3) The Division shall adopt rules implementing the provisions of subsection (b1) of this section with respect to proof of residency in this State. Those rules shall ensure that applicants submit verified or verifiable residency and address information that can be reasonably considered to be valid and that is provided on any of the following:

(1) A document issued by an agency of the United States or by the government of another nation.

(2) A document issued by another state.

(3) A document issued by the State of North Carolina, or a political subdivision of this State. This includes an agency or instrumentality of this State.

(4) A preprinted bank or other corporate statement.

(5) A preprinted business letterhead.

(6) Any other document deemed reliable by the Division.

(b4) Examples of documents that are reasonably reliable indicators of residency include, but are not limited to, any of the following:

(1) A pay stub with the payee's address.

(2) A utility bill showing the address of the applicant-payor.

(3) A contract for an apartment, house, modular unit, or manufactured home with a North Carolina address signed by the applicant.

(4) A receipt for personal property taxes paid.

(5) A receipt for real property taxes paid to a North Carolina locality.

(6) A current automobile insurance policy issued to the applicant and showing the applicant's address.

(7) A monthly or quarterly financial statement from a North Carolina regulated financial institution.

(8), (9) Repealed by Session Laws 2015-294, s. 12, effective October 1, 2015, and applicable to contracts entered into on or after that date.

(b5) The Division rules adopted pursuant to subsection (b3) of this section shall also provide that if an applicant cannot produce any documentation specified in subsection (b3) or (b4) of this section, the applicant, or in the case of a minor applicant a parent or legal guardian of the applicant, may complete an affidavit, on a form provided by the Division and sworn to before an official of the Division, indicating the applicant's current residence address. The affidavit shall contain the provisions of G.S. 20-15(a) and G.S. 20-17(a)(5) and shall indicate the civil and criminal penalties for completing a false affidavit.

(c) **Tests.** -- To demonstrate physical and mental ability, a person must pass an examination. The examination may include road tests, vision tests, oral tests, and, in the case of literate applicants, written tests, as the Division may require. The tests must ensure that an applicant recognizes the handicapped international symbol of access, as defined in G.S. 20-37.5. The Division may not require a person who applies to renew a license that has not expired to take a written test or a road test unless one or more of the following applies:

(1) The person has been convicted of a traffic violation since the person's license was last issued.

(2) The applicant suffers from a mental or physical condition that impairs the person's ability to drive a motor vehicle.

The Division shall require sign and symbol testing upon initial issuance of a license. The Division shall require vision

Chapter 20

testing as a part of required in-person, in-office renewals of a license.

The Division may not require a person who is at least 60 years old to parallel park a motor vehicle as part of a road test. A person shall not use an autocycle to complete a road test under this subsection.

(c1) **Insurance.** -- The Division may not issue a drivers license to a person until the person has furnished proof of financial responsibility. Proof of financial responsibility shall be in one of the following forms:

(1) A written certificate or electronically-transmitted facsimile thereof from any insurance carrier duly authorized to do business in this State certifying that there is in effect a nonfleet private passenger motor vehicle liability policy for the benefit of the person required to furnish proof of financial responsibility. The certificate or facsimile shall state the effective date and expiration date of the nonfleet private passenger motor vehicle liability policy and shall state the date that the certificate or facsimile is issued. The certificate or facsimile shall remain effective proof of financial responsibility for a period of 30 consecutive days following the date the certificate or facsimile is issued but shall not in and of itself constitute a binder or policy of insurance.

(2) A binder for or policy of nonfleet private passenger motor vehicle liability insurance under which the applicant is insured, provided that the binder or policy states the effective date and expiration date of the nonfleet private passenger motor vehicle liability policy.

The preceding provisions of this subsection do not apply to applicants who do not own currently registered motor vehicles and who do not operate nonfleet private passenger motor vehicles that are owned by other persons and that are not insured under commercial motor vehicle liability insurance policies. In such cases, the applicant shall sign a written certificate to that effect. Such certificate shall be furnished by the Division and may be incorporated into the license application form. Any material misrepresentation made by such person on such certificate shall be grounds for suspension of that person's license for a period of 90 days.

For the purpose of this subsection, the term "nonfleet private passenger motor vehicle" has the definition ascribed to it in Article 40 of General Statute Chapter 58.

The Commissioner may require that certificates required by this subsection be on a form approved by the Commissioner.

The requirement of furnishing proof of financial responsibility does not apply to a person who applies for a renewal of his or her drivers license.

Nothing in this subsection precludes any person from showing proof of financial responsibility in any other manner authorized by Articles 9A and 13 of this Chapter.

(d) Repealed by Session Laws 1993, c. 368, s. 1.

(e) **Restrictions.** -- The Division may impose any restriction it finds advisable on a drivers license. It is unlawful for the holder of a restricted license to operate a motor vehicle without complying with the restriction and is the equivalent of operating a motor vehicle without a license. If any applicant shall suffer from any physical or mental disability or disease that affects his or her operation of a motor vehicle, the Division may require to be filed with it a certificate of the applicant's condition signed by a medical authority of the applicant's community designated by the Division. The Division may, in its discretion, require the certificate to be completed and submitted after a license or renewal has been issued based on the applicant's performance during a road test administered by the Division. Upon submission, the certificate shall be reviewed in accordance with the procedure set forth in G.S. 20-9(g)(3). This certificate shall in all cases be treated as confidential and subject to release under G.S. 20-9(g)(4)h. Nothing in this subsection shall be construed to prevent the Division from refusing to issue a license, either restricted or unrestricted, to any person deemed to be incapable of safely operating a motor vehicle based on information observed or received by the Division, including observations during a road test and medical information submitted about the applicant. An applicant may seek review pursuant to G.S. 20-9(g)(4) of a licensing decision made on the basis of a physical or mental disability or disease. This subsection does not prohibit deaf persons from operating motor vehicles who in every other way meet the requirements of this section.

(f) **Duration and Renewal of Licenses.** -- Drivers licenses shall be issued and renewed pursuant to the provisions of this subsection:

(1) **Duration of license for persons under age 18.** -- A full provisional license issued to a person under the age of 18 expires 60 days following the person's twenty-first birthday.

(2) **Duration of original license for persons at least 18 years of age or older.** -- A drivers license issued to a person at least 18 years old but less than 66 years old expires on the birthday of the licensee in the eighth year after issuance. A drivers license issued to a person at least 66 years old expires on the birthday of the licensee in the fifth year after issuance. A commercial drivers license expires on the

Chapter 20

birthday of the licensee in the fifth year after issuance. A commercial drivers license that has a vehicles carrying passengers (P) and school bus (S) endorsement issued pursuant to G.S. 20-37.16 expires on the birthday of the licensee in the third year after issuance, if the licensee is certified to drive a school bus in North Carolina.

(2a) **Duration of renewed licenses. --** A renewed drivers license that was issued by the Division to a person at least 18 years old but less than 66 years old expires eight years after the expiration date of the license that is renewed. A renewed drivers license that was issued by the Division to a person at least 66 years old expires five years after the expiration date of the license that is renewed. A renewed commercial drivers license expires five years after the expiration date of the license that is renewed.

(3) **Duration of license for certain other drivers. --** The durations listed in subdivisions (1), (2) and (2a) of this subsection are valid unless the Division determines that a license of shorter duration should be issued when the applicant holds valid documentation issued by, or under the authority of, the United States government that demonstrates the applicant's legal presence of limited duration in the United States. In no event shall a license of limited duration expire later than the expiration of the authorization for the applicant's legal presence in the United States.

(3a) **When to renew. --** A person may apply to the Division to renew a license during the 180-day period before the license expires. The Division may not accept an application for renewal made before the 180-day period begins.

(3b) Renewal for certain members of the Armed Forces of the United States and reserve components of the Armed Forces of the United States.

a. The Division may renew a drivers license, without limitation on the period of time before the license expires, if the person applying for renewal is a member of the Armed Forces of the United States or of a reserve component of the Armed Forces of the United States and provides orders that place the member on active duty and duty station outside this State.

b. A person who is a member of a reserve component of the Armed Forces of the United States whose license bears an expiration date that occurred while the person was on active duty outside this State shall be considered to have a valid license until 60 days after the date of release from active duty

upon showing proof of the release date, unless the license was rescinded, revoked, or otherwise invalidated under some other provision of law. Notwithstanding the provisions of this subsubdivision, no license shall be considered valid more than 18 months after the date of expiration.

(4) **Renewal by mail. --** The Division may renew by mail a drivers license issued by the Division to a person who meets any of the following descriptions:

a. Is a member of the Armed Forces of the United States or a reserve component of the Armed Forces of the United States serving on active duty and is stationed outside this State.

b. Is a resident of this State and has been residing outside the State for at least 30 continuous days.

When renewing a license by mail, the Division may waive the examination that would otherwise be required for the renewal and may impose any conditions it finds advisable. A license renewed by mail is a temporary license that expires 60 days after the person to whom it is issued returns to this State.

(5) **License to be sent by mail. --** The Division shall issue to the applicant a temporary driving certificate valid for 60 days, unless the applicant is applying for renewal by mail under subdivision (4) of this subsection. The temporary driving certificate shall be valid for driving purposes and shall not be valid for identification purposes, except when conducting business with the Division and not otherwise prohibited by federal law. The Division shall produce the applicant's drivers license at a central location and send it to the applicant by first-class mail at the residence address provided by the applicant, unless the applicant is ineligible for mail delivery by the United States Postal Service at the applicant's residence. If the United States Postal Service documents that it does not deliver to the residential address provided by the applicant, and the Division has verified the applicant's residential address by other means, the Division may mail the drivers license to the post office box provided by the applicant. Applicants whose only mailing address prior to July 1, 2008, was a post office box in this State may continue to receive their license at that post office box, provided the applicant's residential address has been verified by the Division.

(6) **Remote renewal or conversion. --** Subject to the following requirements and limitations, the Division may offer remote renewal of a drivers license or remote

conversion of a full provisional license issued by the Division:

a. **Requirements.** -- To be eligible for remote renewal or conversion under this subdivision, a person must meet all of the following requirements:

1. The license holder possesses either (i) a valid Class C drivers license or (ii) a valid full provisional license and is at least 18 years old at the time of the remote conversion.

2. The license holder's current license includes no restrictions other than a restriction for corrective lenses.

3. The license holder attests, in a manner designated by the Division, that (i) the license holder is a resident of the State and currently resides at the address on the license to be renewed or converted, (ii) the license holder's name as it appears on the license to be renewed or converted has not changed, and (iii) all other information required by the Division for an in-person renewal under this Article has been provided completely and truthfully. If the license holder does not currently reside at the address on the license to be renewed or converted, the license holder may comply with the address requirement of this sub-sub-subdivision by providing the address at which the license holder resides at the time of the remote renewal or conversion request.

4. For a remote renewal, the most recent renewal was an in-person renewal and not a remote renewal under this subdivision.

5. The license holder is otherwise eligible for renewal or conversion under this subsection.

b. **Waiver of requirements.** -- When renewing or converting a drivers license pursuant to this subdivision, the Division may waive the examination and photograph that would otherwise be required for the renewal or conversion.

c. **Duration of remote renewal or conversion.** -- A drivers license issued to a person by remote renewal or conversion under this subdivision expires according to the following schedule:

1. For a person at least 18 years old but less than 66 years old, on the birthday of the licensee in the eighth year after issuance.

2. For a person at least 66 years old, on the birthday of the licensee in the fifth year after issuance.

d. **Rules.** -- The Division shall adopt rules to implement this subdivision.

e. **Federal law.** -- Nothing in this subdivision shall be construed to supersede any more restrictive provisions for renewal or conversion of drivers licenses prescribed by federal law or regulation.

f. **Definition.** -- For purposes of this subdivision, "remote renewal or conversion" means renewal of a drivers license or conversion of a full provisional license by mail, telephone, electronic device, or other secure means approved by the Commissioner.

(g) Repealed by Session Laws 1979, c. 667, s. 6.

(h) Repealed by Session Laws 1979, c. 113, s. 1.

(i) **Fees.** -- The fee for a regular drivers license is the amount set in the following table multiplied by the number of years in the period for which the license is issued:

Class of Regular License	Fee For Each Year
Class A	$ 5.00
Class B	$ 5.00
Class C	$ 5.00

The fee for a motorcycle endorsement is two dollars and thirty cents ($ 2.30) for each year of the period for which the endorsement is issued. The appropriate fee shall be paid before a person receives a regular drivers license or an endorsement.

(i1) **Restoration Fee.** -- Any person whose drivers license has been revoked pursuant to the provisions of this Chapter, other than G.S. 20-17(a)(2) shall pay a restoration fee of sixty five dollars ($ 65.00). A person whose drivers license has been revoked under G.S. 20-17(a)(2) shall pay a restoration fee of one hundred thirty dollars ($ 130.00). The fee shall be paid to the Division prior to the issuance to such person of a new drivers license or the restoration of the drivers license. The restoration fee shall be paid to the Division in addition to any and all fees which may be provided by law. This restoration fee shall not be required from any licensee whose license was revoked or voluntarily surrendered for medical or health reasons whether or not a medical evaluation was conducted pursuant to this Chapter. The sixty five dollar ($ 65.00) fee, and the first one hundred five dollars ($ 105.00) of the one hundred thirty dollar ($ 130.00) fee, shall be deposited in the Highway Fund. Twenty five dollars ($ 25.00) of the one hundred thirty dollar ($ 130.00) fee shall be used to fund a statewide chemical alcohol testing program administered by the Forensic Tests for Alcohol Branch of the Chronic Disease and Injury Section of the Department of Health and Human Services. Notwithstanding any other provision of law, a restoration fee assessed pursuant to this subsection may be waived by the Division when (i) the restoration fee remains unpaid for more than 10 years from the date of assessment and (ii) the person responsible for payment of the restoration fee has been issued a drivers license by the Division after the effective date of the revocation for which the restoration fee is owed. The Office of State Budget and Management shall annually report to the General Assembly the amount of fees deposited in the General Fund and transferred to the Forensic Tests for Alcohol Branch of the Chronic Disease and Injury Section of the Department of Health and Human Services under this subsection.

(j) **Highway Fund.** -- The fees collected under this section and G.S. 20-14 shall be placed in the Highway Fund.

(j1) [Maintenance of Organ Donor Registry Internet Site.] The Division of Motor Vehicles shall retain a portion of five cents ($ 0.05) collected for the issuance of each drivers license and duplicate license to offset the actual cost of developing and maintaining the online Organ Donor Internet site established pursuant to G.S. 20-43.2. The remainder of the five cents ($ 0.05) shall be credited to the License to Give Trust Fund established under G.S. 20-7.4 and shall be used for the purposes authorized under G.S. 20-7.4 and G.S. 20-7.5.

(k) Repealed by Session Laws 1991, c. 726, s. 5.

(*l*) **Learner's Permit.** -- A person who is at least 18 years old may obtain a learner's permit. A learner's permit authorizes the permit holder to drive a specified type or class of motor vehicle while in possession of the permit. A learner's permit is valid for a period of 18 months after it is issued. The fee for a learner's permit is twenty dollars ($ 20.00). A learner's permit may be renewed, or a second learner's permit may be issued, for an additional period of 18 months. The permit holder must, while operating a motor vehicle over the highways, be accompanied by a person who is licensed to operate the motor vehicle being driven and is seated beside the permit holder.

(*l* -1) Repealed by Session Laws 1991, c. 726, s. 5.

(m) **Instruction Permit.** -- The Division upon receiving proper application may in its discretion issue a restricted instruction permit effective for a school year or a lesser period to any of the following applicants:

(1) An applicant who is less than 18 years old and is enrolled in a drivers education program that is approved by the State Superintendent of Public Instruction and is offered at a public high school, a nonpublic secondary school, or a licensed drivers training school.

(2) A restricted instruction permit authorizes the holder of the permit to drive a specified type or class of motor vehicle when in possession of the permit, subject to any restrictions imposed by the Division. The restrictions the Division may impose on a permit include restrictions to designated areas and highways and restrictions prohibiting operation except when an approved instructor is occupying a seat beside the permittee. A restricted instruction permit is not required to have a distinguishing number or a picture of the person to whom the permit is issued.

(n) **Format.** -- A drivers license issued by the Division must be tamperproof and must contain all of the following information:

(1) An identification of this State as the issuer of the license.

(2) The license holder's full name.

(3) The license holder's residence address.

(4) A color photograph of the license holder applied to material that is measured by the industry standard of security and durability and is resistant to tampering and reproduction.

(5) A physical description of the license holder, including sex, height, eye color, and hair color.

(6) The license holder's date of birth.

(7) An identifying number for the license holder assigned by the Division. The identifying number may not be the license holder's social security number.

(8) Each class of motor vehicle the license holder is authorized to drive and any endorsements or restrictions that apply.

(9) The license holder's signature.

(10) The date the license was issued and the date the license expires.

The Commissioner shall ensure that applicants 21 years old or older are issued drivers licenses and special identification cards that are printed in a horizontal format. The Commissioner shall ensure that applicants under the age of 21 are issued drivers licenses and special identification cards that are printed in a vertical format, that distinguishes them from the horizontal format, for ease of identification of individuals under age 21 by members of industries that regulate controlled products that are sale restricted by age and law enforcement officers enforcing these laws.

At the request of an applicant for a drivers license, a license issued to the applicant must contain the applicant's race, which shall be designated with the letters "AI" for an applicant who is American Indian.

(o) Repealed by Session Laws 1991, c. 726, s. 5.

(p) The Division must give the clerk of superior court in each county at least 50 copies of the driver license handbook free of charge. The clerk must give a copy to a person who requests it.

(q) **Active Duty Military Designation.** -- The Division shall develop a military designation for drivers licenses that may, upon request, be granted to North Carolina residents on active duty and to their spouses and dependent children. A drivers license with a military designation on it may be renewed by mail no more than two times during the license holder's lifetime. A license renewed by mail under this subsection is a permanent license and does not expire when the license holder returns to the State. A drivers license with a military designation on it issued to a person on active duty may be renewed up to one year prior to its expiration upon presentation of military or Department of Defense credentials.

(q1) **Veteran Military Designation.** -- The Division shall develop a military designation for drivers licenses and identification cards that may, upon request, be granted to North Carolina residents who are honorably discharged from military service in the Armed Forces of the United States. An applicant requesting this designation must produce a Form DD-214 showing the applicant has been honorably discharged from the Armed Forces of the United States.

(q2) **Deaf or Hard of Hearing Designation.** -- The Division shall develop, in consultation with the Department of Public Safety, the State Highway Patrol, the Division of Services for the Deaf and Hard of Hearing, and pursuant to this subsection, a drivers license designation that may, upon request, be granted to a person who is deaf or hard of hearing. The Division shall comply with the following requirements applicable to the designation:

(1) At the request of a person who is deaf or hard of hearing, the Division shall place a unique symbol on the front of the person's license. The unique symbol placed on the license shall not include any further descriptor. The Division shall record the designation in the electronic record associated with the person's drivers license.

(2) At the request of a person who is deaf or hard of hearing, the Division shall enter the drivers license symbol and a descriptor into the electronic record of any motor vehicle registered in the same name of the deaf or hard of hearing person.

(3) For the purposes of this subsection, a person shall be considered to be deaf or hard of hearing if they provide verification or documentation substantiating their hearing loss that is recommended by the Division of Services for the Deaf and Hard of Hearing as acceptable. The Division of Motor Vehicles shall consult with the Division of Services for the Deaf and the Hard of Hearing to identify acceptable forms of verification that do not result in undue burden to the person requesting the designation of hearing loss. Acceptable documentation shall include any of the following:

a. Documentation of certification or examination by a medical, health, or audiology professional showing evidence of hearing loss.

b. Affidavit executed by the person, their parent, or guardian attesting to the person's hearing loss.

c. Documentation deemed by the Division of Motor Vehicles to qualify as satisfactory proof of the person's hearing loss.

(4) Nothing in this subsection shall be construed as authorizing the issuance of a drivers license to a person ineligible under G.S. 20-9.

(5) Nothing in this subsection shall be construed as prohibiting the issuance of a drivers license to a person otherwise eligible under the law.

(6) Any individual who chooses to register or not to register shall not be deemed to have waived any protections under the law.

(7) Information collected under this subsection shall only be available to law enforcement and only for the purpose of ensuring mutually safe interactions between law enforcement and persons who are deaf or hard of hearing. It shall not be accessed or used for any other purpose.

(8) The right to make the decision for inclusion or removal of the designation from the database is entirely voluntary and shall only be made by the person who holds the drivers license associated with the designation.

(9) The Division, in conjunction with the Department of Health and Human Services, shall develop a process for removal of the designation authorized by this subsection that is available online, by mail, or in person.

(r) **Waiver of Vision Test.** -- The following license holders shall be exempt from any required eye exam when renewing a drivers license by mail under either subsection (f) of this section or subsection (q) of this section if, at the time of renewal, the license holder is serving in a combat zone or a qualified hazardous duty zone:

(1) A member of the Armed Forces of the United States.

(2) A member of a reserve component of the Armed Forces of the United States.

(s) Notwithstanding the requirements of subsection (b1) of this section that an applicant present a valid social security number, the Division shall issue a drivers license of limited duration, under subsection (f) of this section, to an applicant present in the United States who holds valid documentation issued by, or under the authority of, the United States government that demonstrates the applicant's legal presence of limited duration in the United States if the applicant presents that valid documentation and meets all other requirements for a license of limited duration. Notwithstanding the requirements of subsection (n) of this section addressing background colors and borders, a drivers license of limited duration issued under this section shall bear a distinguishing mark or other designation on the face of the license clearly denoting the limited duration of the license.

(t) Use of Bioptic Telescopic Lenses. --

(1) An applicant using bioptic telescopic lenses shall be eligible for a regular Class C drivers license under this section if the applicant meets all of the following:

a. Demonstrates a visual acuity of at least 20/200 in one or both eyes and a field of 70 degrees horizontal vision with or without corrective carrier lenses, or if the person has vision in one eye only, the person demonstrates a field of at least 40 degrees temporal and 30 degrees nasal horizontal vision.

b. Demonstrates a visual acuity of at least 20/70 in one or both eyes with the bioptic telescopic lenses and without the use of field expanders.

c. Provides a report of examination by an ophthalmologist or optometrist, on a form prescribed by the Division, for the Division to determine if all field of vision requirements are met or additional testing is needed.

d. Successfully passes a road test administered by the Division. This requirement is waived if the applicant is a new resident of North Carolina who has a valid drivers license issued by another jurisdiction that requires a road test.

e. Meets all other criteria for licensure.

(2) In addition to the requirements listed in subdivision (1) of this subsection, the Division shall require an applicant using bioptic telescopic lenses to successfully complete a behind-the-wheel training and assessment program prescribed by the Division. This requirement is waived if the applicant has successfully completed a behind-the-wheel training and assessment program as a condition of licensure in another jurisdiction.

(3) Applicants using bioptic telescopic lenses shall be eligible for a limited learner's permit or provisional drivers license issued pursuant to G.S. 20-11, provided the requirements of this subsection are met and any other required testing or documentation is completed and submitted with the application.

(4) Applicants issued a regular Class C drivers license, limited learner's permit, or provisional drivers license shall be subject to the following restrictions on the license issued:

a. The license or permit holder shall not be eligible for any endorsements.

b. The license or permit shall permit the operation of motor vehicles only during the period beginning one-half hour after sunrise and ending one-half hour before sunset.

(5) Applicants issued a regular Class C drivers license may drive motor vehicles between the period beginning one-half hour before sunset and ending one-half hour after sunrise if the applicant meets the following requirements:

a. Demonstrates a visual acuity of at least 20/40 in one or both eyes with the bioptic telescopic lenses and without the use of field expanders.

b. Provides a report of examination by an ophthalmologist or optometrist in accordance with sub-subdivision c. of subdivision (1) of this subsection that does not recommend restricting the applicant to driving a motor vehicle only during the period beginning one-half hour after sunrise and ending one-half hour before sunset.

History.

1935, c. 52, s. 2; 1943, c. 649, s. 1; c. 787, s. 1; 1947, c. 1067, s. 10; 1949, c. 583, ss. 9, 10; c. 826, ss. 1, 2; 1951, c. 542, ss. 1, 2; c. 1196, ss. 1-3; 1953, cc. 839, 1284, 1311; 1955, c. 1187, ss. 2-6; 1957, c. 1225; 1963, cc. 754, 1007, 1022; 1965, c. 410, s. 5; 1967, c. 509; 1969, c. 183; c. 783, s. 1; c. 865; 1971, c. 158; 1973, cc. 73, 705; c. 1057, ss. 1, 3; 1975, c. 162, s. 1; c. 295; c. 296, ss. 1, 2; c. 684; c. 716, s. 5; c. 841; c. 875, s. 4; c. 879, s. 46; 1977, c. 6; c. 340, s. 3; c. 354, s. 1; c. 865, ss. 1, 3; 1979, c. 37, s. 1; c. 113; c. 178, s. 2; c. 667, ss. 3-11, 41; c. 678, ss. 1-3; c. 801, ss. 5, 6; 1981, c. 42; c. 690, ss. 8-10; c. 792, s. 3; 1981 (Reg. Sess., 1982), c. 1257, s. 1; 1983, c. 443, s. 1; 1985, c. 141, s. 4; c. 682, ss. 1, 2; 1987, c. 869, ss. 10, 11; 1989, c. 436, ss. 1, 2; c. 771, s. 5; c. 786, s. 4; 1991, c. 478, s. 1;c. 689, s. 325;c. 726, s. 5;1991 (Reg. Sess., 1992), c. 1007, s. 27;

c. 1030, s. 10; 1993, c. 368, s. 1;c. 533, ss. 2, 3, 12; 1993 (Reg. Sess., 1994), c. 595, ss. 1, 2; c. 750, s. 1; c. 761, s. 1.1; 1995 (Reg. Sess., 1996), c. 675, s. 1; 1997-16, ss. 5, 8, 9; 1997-122, ss. 2, 3; 1997-377, s. 1;1997-433, s. 4;1997-443, ss. 11A.122, 32.20; 1997-456, s. 32, 33; 1998-17, s. 1;1998-149, s. 2;2000-120, ss. 14, 15; 2000-140, s. 93.1(a);2001-424, ss. 12.2(b), 27.10A(a)-(d); 2001-513, s. 32(a);2003-152, ss. 1, 2; 2003-284, s. 36.1;2004-189, s. 5(a), (c); 2004-203, s. 2;2005-276, s. 44.1(a), (q); 2005-349, s. 4;2006-257, ss. 1, 2; 2006-264, s. 35.2;2007-56, ss. 1 -3; 2007-249, s. 1;2007-350, s. 1;2007-512, s. 5;2008-202, ss. 2, 3; 2008-217, s. 1;2008-221, s. 1;2009-274, ss. 2, 3; 2009-451, s. 9.5(a);2009-492, ss. 1, 2; 2010-130, s. 1;2010-131, ss. 1, 2; 2010-132, s. 1;2011-35, ss. 1, 2; 2011-183, ss. 21, 127(a); 2011-326, s. 28;2011-381, s. 2;2012-78, s. 1;2012-85, ss. 1, 2; 2012-142, s. 9.16;2012-145, s. 2.2;2013-195, s. 2;2013-231, s. 1;2013-360, s. 7.10(a);2014-58, s. 5;2014-100, s. 34.8(a);2014-115, s. 56.8(c);2015-163, s. 2;2015-238, s. 2.1;2015-241, ss. 7A.4(b), 29.30(a), 29.30(a1), 29.36; 2015-294, s. 12;2016-75, s. 1;2016-90, ss. 6(a), 8(a), 9(a); 2017-191, s. 1;2018-74, s. 10(a);2018-145, s. 14;2019-199, s. 7(a);2019-227, s. 3(a), (b)

EDITOR'S NOTE. --

Session Laws 1985, c. 141, s. 6 provided that the amendment thereby would become effective September 1, 1986. Section 6 further provided that if the Congress of the United States repeals the mandate established by the Surface Transportation Assistance Act of 1982 relating to National Uniform Drinking Age of 21 as found in Section 6 of Public Law 98-363, or a court of competent jurisdiction declares the provision to be unconstitutional or otherwise invalid, then ss. 1, 2, 2.1, 4, and 5 of the act shall expire upon the certification of the Secretary of State that the federal mandate has been repealed or has been invalidated, and the statutes amended by ss. 1, 2, 2.1, 4, and 5 shall revert to the form they would have without the amendments made by these sections.

Session Laws 1987 (Reg. Sess., 1988), c. 1112 would have amended subsections (a) and (i) of this section effective June 1, 1989, through June 30, 1989, so as to make changes regarding the requirements for and entitlements of certain licenses, with certain exceptions for persons holding a Class C license issued before June 1, 1989. Session Laws 1989, c. 771, s. 18, effective June 1, 1989, repealed Session Laws 1987 (Reg. Sess., 1988), c. 1112; therefore, the provisions of c. 1112 never went into effect.

Session Laws 1993, c. 368, which amended this section, in s. 5 provides: "A drivers license or a special identification card issued by the Division of Motor Vehicles before January 1, 1995, and renewed by the Division after that date is considered the first drivers license or special identification card issued by the Division for purposes of determining when the license or card expires."

Session Laws 1997-16, s. 10 provides that the act does not appropriate funds to the Division to implement the act nor does it obligate the General Assembly to appropriate funds to implement this act.

Session Laws 2001-424, ss. 27.10A(b) to (d) enacted new subsections which the act numbered (b2), (b3), and (b4). As the section already contained a subsection (b2), at the direction of the Reviser of Statutes these subsections have been renumbered (b3), (b4), and (b5).

Session Laws 2004-189, s. 5(c), as amended by Session Laws 2005-276, s. 44.1(q), was codified as G.S. 20-7(j1) at the direction of the Revisor of Statutes.

Session Laws 2005-276, s. 1.2, provides: "This act shall be known as the 'Current Operations and Capital Improvements Appropriations Act of 2005.'"

Session Laws 2005-276, s. 46.3, provides: "Except for statutory changes or other provisions that clearly indicate an intention to have effects beyond the 2005-2007 fiscal biennium, the textual provisions of this act apply only to funds appropriated for, and activities occurring during, the 2005-2007 fiscal biennium."

Session Laws 2005-276, s. 46.5, is a severability clause.

Session Laws 2011-35, s. 3, as amended by Session Laws 2012-85, s. 2, which added "Active Duty" to the subsection (q) heading, and added subsection (q1), provides:

"SECTION 3. This act becomes effective on the later of the following dates and applies to drivers licenses issued on or after that date:

"(1) January 1, 2013.

"(2) The first day of a month that is 30 days after the Commissioner of Motor Vehicles certifies to the Revisor of Statutes that the Division of Motor Vehicles has completed the implementation of the Division's Next Generation Secure Driver License System." On August 21, 2019, the Commissioner of Motor Vehicles certified to the Revisor of Statutes that the Next Generation Secure Driver License System was fully implemented in January 2016.

Session Laws 2012-85, s. 12, provides: "When the Division of Motor Vehicles has completed the implementation of the Division's Next Generation Secure Driver License System, the Commissioner of Motor Vehicles shall certify to the Revisor of Statutes that the Division of Motor Vehicles has completed the implementation. When making the certification, the Commissioner of Motor Vehicles shall reference S.L. 2011-35, S.L. 2011-228, and the session law number of this act." On August 21, 2019, the Commissioner of Motor Vehicles certified to the Revisor of Statutes that the Next Generation Secure Driver License System was fully implemented in January 2016.

Session Laws 2014-100, s. 34.8(b), made subdivision (f)(6), as added by Session Laws 2014-100, s. 34.8(a), effective August 7, 2014, and applicable to drivers licenses renewed on or after the Division of Motor Vehicles adopts rules under G.S. 20-7(f)(6)d.

Session Laws 2015-163, s. 2, which added subsection (a3) and added the last sentence of the second paragraph in subsection (c), was effective October 1, 2015.

Session Laws 2015-163, s. 14, provides, in part: "Prosecutions for offenses committed before the effective date of this act are not abated or affected by this act, and the statutes that would be applicable but for this act remain applicable to those prosecutions."

Session Laws 2015-241, s. 29.30(u), made the amendments to subsections (i), (i1), and (l) of this section by Session Laws 2015-241, s. 29.30(a1), applicable to issuances, renewals, restorations, and requests on or after January 1, 2016.

Session Laws 2015-241, s. 1.1, provides: "This act shall be known as 'The Current Operations and Capital Improvements Appropriations Act of 2015.'"

Session Laws 2015-241, s. 33.6, is a severability clause.

Session Laws 2015-294, s. 17, made the repeal of subdivisions (b4)(8) and (9) of this section by Session Laws 2015-294, s. 12, applicable to contracts entered into on or after October 1, 2015.

Session Laws 2016-75, s. 2, made the amendment to subsection (n) by Session Laws 2016-75, s. 1, applicable to drivers licenses issued or renewed on or after October 1, 2016.

Session Laws 2016-90, s. 6(f), made the deletion of the former first sentence of subdivision (m)(2), which pertained to applicants for certification as a school bus driver, by Session Laws 2016-90, s. 6(a), applicable to offenses committed on or after January 1, 2017.

Session Laws 2016-90, s. 8(b), provides: "This section becomes effective January 1, 2017. The extended period of validity applies to temporary driving certificates issued on or after that date."

Session Laws 2016-94, s. 35.20(h), made the amendment to subsection (e) of this section by Session Laws 2016-94, s. 35.20(b), applicable to drivers licenses issued or renewed on or after July 1, 2016 and hearings requested on or after July 1, 2016.

Session Laws 2016-94, s. 1.2, provides: "This act shall be known as the 'Current Operations and Capital Improvements Appropriations Act of 2016.'"

Session Laws 2016-94, s. 39.4, provides: "Except for statutory changes or other provisions that clearly indicate an intention to have effects beyond the 2016-2017 fiscal year, the textual provisions of this act apply only to funds appropriated for, and activities occurring during, the 2016-2017 fiscal year."

Session Laws 2016-94, s. 39.7, is a severability clause.

Session Laws 2017-41, s. 6.1(a), (b), provides: "(a) The General Assembly recognizes that not having a drivers license is a barrier to education, employment, health care, and other community-based activities for older youth in foster care, as defined in G.S. 131D-10.2(9), working toward independence. One of the biggest barriers to accessing a drivers license for such youth is the ability to obtain insurance. Therefore, to assist in this effort, the Department of Health and Human Services, Division of Social Services, shall establish a two-year pilot program that shall reimburse, on a first-come, first-served basis, youth and caregivers' costs associated with drivers license education, drivers license fees, insurance costs, and any other costs associated with obtaining a drivers license. The Division shall take appropriate steps to ensure proper advertising of the pilot program.

"(b) The Division of Social Services shall report on the pilot project to the Joint Legislative Oversight Committee on Health and Human Services by March 1, 2018."

Session Laws 2020-3, s. 4.7(a) -(h), as amended by Session Laws 2020-97, ss. 3.15(a), 3.16(a), provides: "(a) Definition. -- For purposes of this section, 'credential' means any of the following issued by the Division of Motor Vehicles:

"(1) Drivers license.

"(2) Learner's permit.

"(3) Limited learner's permit.

"(4) Limited provisional license.

"(5) Full provisional license.

"(6) Commercial drivers license.

"(7) Commercial learner's permit.

"(8) Temporary driving certificate.

"(9) Special identification card.

"(10) Handicapped placard.

"(11) Vehicle registration.

"(12) Temporary vehicle registration.

"(13) Dealer license plate.

"(14) Transporter plate.

"(15) Loaner/Dealer 'LD' plate.

"(16) Vehicle inspection authorization.

"(17) Inspection station license.

"(18) Inspection mechanic license.

"(19) Transportation network company permit.

"(20) Motor vehicle dealer license.

"(21) Sales representative license.

"(22) Manufacturer license.

"(23) Distributor license.

"(24) Wholesaler license.

"(25) Driver training school license.

"(26) Driver training school instructor license.

"(27) Professional housemoving license.

"(b) Extend Validity of Credentials. -- Notwithstanding renewal, duration, or expiration provisions of G.S. 20-7, 20-11, 20-37.6, 20-37.7, 20-37.13, 20-50, 20-66, 20-79, 20-79.02, 20-79.2, 20-183.4B, 20-183.4D, 20-280.3, 20-288, 20-324, and 20-359, or any other provision of law to the contrary, the Division of Motor Vehicles shall extend for a period of five months the validity of any credential that expires on or after March 1, 2020, and before August 1, 2020. The Division shall extend for a period of five months the validity of any credential listed in subdivisions (6), (7), (9), (10), and (18) of subsection (a) of this section that expires on or after March 1, 2020, and before the date 30 days after the date the Governor (i) rescinds Executive Order No. 116 or (ii) issues another executive order lifting restrictions on Division of Motor Vehicles functions. Notwithstanding G.S. 20-37.13(h) and G.S. 20-37.13A(a), the Division of Motor Vehicles is authorized to waive the requirement that commercial drivers license and commercial learner's permit holders have a medical examination and certification, as required by federal law, consistent with any waiver of medical qualifications standards issued by the Federal Motor Carrier Safety Administration. A credential extended under this section shall expire five months from the date it otherwise expires as prescribed by law prior to this section. However, the subsequent expiration of a credential extended under this section shall occur on the date prescribed by law prior to this section without regard to the extension. The Division shall notify individuals affected by an extension granted under this section, including information on new expiration dates and how the extension affects subsequent renewal and expiration dates.

"(b1) Extension of Intrastate Medical Waivers. -- Notwithstanding the limitation on duration of waivers in G.S. 20-37.13A(b), the Division of Motor Vehicles may extend for up to five months the validity of a medical waiver issued by the Division under G.S. 20-37.13A if the waiver expires on or after March 1, 2020, and before the date 30 days after the date the Governor (i) rescinds Executive Order No. 116 or (ii) issues another executive order lifting restrictions on Division of Motor Vehicles functions, and the Division's Medical Review Unit determines the extension is appropriate.

"(c) Driving Eligibility Certificates. -- Notwithstanding G.S. 20-11(n)(3), a driving eligibility certificate dated on or after February 9, 2020, and before March 10, 2020, remains valid and may be accepted by the Division of Motor Vehicles to meet the requirements for a license or permit issued under G.S. 20-11 until 30 days after the date the Governor rescinds Executive Order No. 116 or the date the Division reopens all drivers license offices, whichever is earlier.

"(d) Waive Penalties. -- Notwithstanding any provision of law to the contrary, the Division shall waive any fines, fees, or penalties associated with failing to renew a credential during the period of time the credential is valid by extension under subsection (b) of this section.

"(e) Motor Vehicle Taxes. -- Notwithstanding any provision of law to the contrary, due dates for motor vehicle taxes that are tied to registration expiration under Article 22A of Chapter 105 of the General Statutes shall be extended to correspond with extended expiration dates under subsection (b) of this section.

"(f) Validity by Extension a Defense. -- A person may not be convicted or found responsible for any offense resulting from failure to renew a credential issued by the Division if, when tried for that offense, the person shows that the offense occurred during the period of time the credential is valid by extension under subsection (b) of this section.

"(g) Report. -- Within 30 days of the extensions made under subsection (b) of this section, the Division shall submit a report to the Joint Legislative Transportation Oversight Committee and the Fiscal Research Division detailing implementation of this section.

"(h) Effective Date. -- This section is effective retroactively to March 1, 2020, and applies to expirations occurring on or after that date."

Session Laws 2020-3, s. 5, is a severability clause.

Session Laws 2020-97, s. 4.5, is a severability clause.

EFFECT OF AMENDMENTS. --

Session Laws 2004-189, s. 5.(a), effective November 1, 2004, in subsection (i), under the heading "Fee For Each Year," substituted "4.30" for "4.25" twice, and substituted "3.05" for "3.00."

Session Laws 2004-203, s. 2, effective August 17, 2004, in subsection (b1), substituted "an identification card, learners permit, or drivers" for "a drivers," inserted "except for an identification card" preceding "demonstrate his or her," and made a related punctuation change.

Session Laws 2005-276, s. 44.1(a), effective October 1, 2005, in subsection (i), in the first paragraph, substituted "$4.00" for "$4.30" and "3.05" in the list of fees; in subsection (i1), substituted "fifty-dollars ($50.00)" for "twenty-five dollars ($25.00)" twice, substituted "seventy-five dollars ($75.00)" for "fifty dollars ($50.00)" and substituted "fifty-dollar ($50.00) fee, and the first fifty dollars ($50.00) of the seventy-five-dollar ($75.00) fee" for "twenty-five dollar ($25.00) fee, and the first twenty-five dollars ($25.00) of the fifty-dollar ($50.00) fee" and "the seventy-five-dollar ($75.00) fee" for "the fifty-dollar ($50.00) fee"; and in subsection (*l*) substituted "fifteen dollars ($15.00)" for "ten dollars ($10.00)."

Session Laws 2005-349, s. 4, effective September 30, 2005, in the next-to-last paragraph of subsection (a), added the first sentence and substituted "Any other" for "A" at the beginning of the second sentence.

Session Laws 2006-257, s. 1, effective January 1, 2007, rewrote subsection (f); and s. 2 added subdivision (f)(5) effective July 1, 2008.

Session Laws 2006-264, s. 35.2, effective August 27, 2006, in subsection (b1), deleted the former second to last paragraph relating to applicants who do not have social security numbers, and in the last paragraph, deleted "either" following "to provide" and "or the applicant's valid Taxpayer Identification Number" from the end; rewrote subsection (f); and added subsection (s).

Session Laws 2007-56, s. 1, effective retroactively to January 1, 2007, and applicable to drivers licenses issued or renewed on or after that date, rewrote subdivisions (f)(1), (2) and (3), and added subdivisions (f)(2a) and (f)(3a).

Session Laws 2007-249, s. 1, effective July 20, 2007, added subdivision (b2)(4).

Session Laws 2007-512, s. 5, effective October 1, 2007, added subdivision (b2)(5).

Session Laws 2008-202, ss. 2 and 3, effective August 8, 2008, in subdivision (f)(5), added the language beginning "unless the applicant is ineligible for mail delivery" to the end of the subdivision; in subdivision (n)(4), inserted "or a properly applied laser engraved picture on polycarbonate material"; in the second full paragraph in subsection (n), deleted the former first sentence, which read: "The Commissioner may waive the requirement of a color photograph on a license if the license holder proves to the satisfaction of the Commissioner that taking the photograph would violate the license holder's religious convictions"; and made minor grammatical changes.

Session Laws 2008-221, s. 1, effective September 1, 2008, added subdivisions (a)(3)c.

Session Laws 2009-451, s. 9.5(a), effective July 1, 2009, in subsection (i1), in the first paragraph, substituted "G.S. 20-17(a)(2)" for "G.S. 20-17(2)" in the first sentence, substituted "G.S. 20-17(a)(2) shall pay a restoration fee of seventy-five dollars ($75.00)" for "G.S. 20-17(2) shall pay a restoration fee of seventy-five dollars ($75.00) until the end of the fiscal year in which the cumulative total amount of fees deposited under this subsection in the General Fund exceeds ten million dollars ($10,000,000), and shall pay a restoration fee of fifty dollars ($50.00) thereafter" in the second sentence, and deleted "shall certify to the Department of Transportation and the General Assembly when the cumulative total amount of fees deposited in the General Fund under this subsection exceeds ten million dollars ($10,000,000), and" preceding "shall annually report" in the last sentence; in the second paragraph, inserted "from" near the beginning, "the sum of five hundred thirty-seven thousand four hundred fifty-five dollars ($537,455)" near the middle, and substituted "operating expenses of the Bowles Center for Alcohol Studies at the University of North Carolina at Chapel Hill" for "the Center for Alcohol Studies Endowment at The University of North Carolina at Chapel Hill, but not to exceed this cumulative total of ten million dollars ($10,000,000)" at the end.

Session Laws 2010-130, s. 1, effective September 1, 2010, in the first paragraph in subsection (i1), in the second sentence, substituted "one hundred dollars ($100.00)" for "seventy-five dollars ($75.00)," in the sixth sentence, substituted "one-hundred-dollar ($100.00) fee" for "seventy-five-dollar ($75.00) fee," deleted the former seventh sentence, which read: "The remaining twenty-five dollars ($25.00) of the seventy-five-dollar ($75.00) fee shall be deposited in the General Fund of the State," added the seventh and eighth sentences, and in the last sentence, inserted "and transferred to the Forensic Tests for Alcohol Branch of the Chronic Disease and Injury Section of the Department of Health and Human Services."

Session Laws 2010-131, ss. 1 and 2, effective January 1, 2011, and applicable to any drivers license issued on or after that date, in subdivisions (f)(2) and (f)(2a), twice substituted "66 years old" for "54 years old."

Session Laws 2010-132, s. 1, effective December 1, 2010, and applicable to offenses committed on or after that date, in subdivision (f)(2), added the third sentence, and in the last sentence, substituted "expires on the birthday of the licensee three years after the date of issuance" for "shall expire on the birth date of the licensee three years after the date of issuance"; and added the last sentence in subdivision (f)(2a).

Session Laws 2011-35, ss. 1 and 2, as amended by Session Laws 2011-326, s. 28, added "Active Duty" to the subsection (q) heading; and added subsection (q1). See editor's note for effective date and applicability.

Session Laws 2011-183, ss. 21 and 127(a), effective June 20, 2011, in subdivision (f)(3b), inserted the first three occurrences of "of the United States"; and in subdivision (f)(4)a., inserted the first occurrence of "of the United States."; and in subsection (q1), twice substituted "Armed Forces of the United States" for "United States Armed Forces."

Session Laws 2012-78, s. 1, effective January 1, 2013, added the second sentence in subsection (s). For applicability, see Editor's note.

Session Laws 2012-85, s. 1, effective July 1, 2012, rewrote subsection (a1); and in the last paragraph, substituted "knowledge test" for "written test" in the first sentence, and substituted the language beginning "complete the North CarolinaMotorcycle Safety" for "complete the Motorcycle Safety Foundation Basic Rider Course or the North CarolinaMotorcycle Safety Education Program Basic Rider Course" in the second sentence.

Session Laws 2012-142, s. 9.16, as added by Session Laws 2012-145, s. 2.2, effective July 1, 2012, in the second paragraph of subsection (i1), substituted "Effective with the 2011-2012 fiscal year" for "It is the intent of the General Assembly to annually appropriate" at the beginning, and inserted "shall be transferred annually" in the middle.

Session Laws 2013-195, s. 2, effective July 1, 2013, added "and 60 days for a commercial drivers license" in the first sentence of subdivision (f)(5).

Session Laws 2013-231, s. 1, effective July 3, 2013, added subsection (t).

Session Laws 2013-360, s. 7.10(a), effective July 26, 2013, added subdivision (b2)(6).

Session Laws 2014-58, s. 5, effective July 7, 2014, rewrote subdivision (n)(4), which read "A color photograph, or a properly applied laser engraved picture on polycarbonate material, of the license holder, taken by the Division."

Session Laws 2014-100, s. 34.8(a), added subdivision (f)(6). For effective date and applicability, see Editor's note.

Session Laws 2014-115, s. 56.8(c), effective August 11, 2014, substituted "Chief Information Officer" for "Controller" in subdivision (b2)(6).

Session Laws 2015-163, s. 2, effective October 1, 2015, added subsection (a3); and added the last sentence of the second paragraph in subsection (c). For applicability, see editor's note.

Session Laws 2015-238, s. 2.1, effective September 10, 2015, added subdivision (b2)(7).

Session Laws 2015-241, s. 7A.4(b), effective September 18, 2015, rewrote subdivision (b2)(6), which formerly read: "To the Office of the State Chief Information Officer for the purposes of G.S. 143B-426.38A."

Session Laws 2015-241, s. 29.30(a), effective October 1, 2015, in subsection (i1), substituted "and the first seventy-five dollars ($75.00) of the one-hundred-dollar ($100.00) fee" for "and the first fifty dollars ($50.00) of the one-hundred-dollar ($100.00) fee" in the sixth sentence, deleted the former seventh sentence, which read: "The remainder of the one-hundred-dollar ($100.00) fee shall be deposited in the General Fund," and deleted the former last paragraph, relating to operating expenses of the Bowles Center for Alcohol Studies.

Session Laws 2015-241, s. 29.30(a1), effective January 1, 2016, in subsection (i), substituted "$5.00" for "$4.00" throughout the second column of the table, and substituted "two dollars and thirty cents ($2.30)" for "one dollar and seventy-five cents ($1.75)"; in subsection (i1), substituted "sixty-five dollars ($65.00)" for "fifty dollars ($50.00)" and "one-hundred-thirty-dollar ($130.00)" for "one-hundred-dollar ($100.00)" throughout, and substituted "one hundred five dollars ($105.00)" for "seventy-five dollars ($75.00)" in the sixth sentence; and substituted "twenty dollars ($20.00)" for "fifteen dollars ($15.00)" in subsection (l). For applicability, see editor's note.

Session Laws 2015-241, s. 29.36, effective July 1, 2015, in subdivision (f)(6), inserted "Subject to the following requirements and limitations," and rewrote the former last sentence of the introductory paragraph to be a new subdivision (f)(6)f.

Session Laws 2015-294, s. 12, effective October 1, 2015, deleted former subdivisions (b4)(8) and (b4)(9), pertaining to matricula consular or similar documents. For applicability, see editor's note.

Session Laws 2016-75, s. 1, effective October 1, 2016, substituted "race, which shall be designated with the letters 'AI' for an applicant who is American Indian" for "race" near the end of subsection (n). See editor's note for applicability.

Session Laws 2016-90, s. 6(a), effective January 1, 2017, in subdivision (m)(2), deleted the former first sentence, which read: "An applicant for certification under G.S. 20-218 as a school bus driver" from the beginning of the subdivision. See editor's note for applicability.

Session Laws 2016-90, s. 8(a), in subdivision (f)(5), substituted "60 days" for "20 days, and 60 days for a commercial drivers license" near the middle of the first sentence, and substituted "purposes and shall not be valid for identification purposes, except when conducting business with the Division and not otherwise prohibited by federal law" for "purposes only and shall not be valid for identification purposes" at the end of the second sentence. See editor's note for effective date and applicability.

Session Laws 2016-90, s. 9(a), effective October 1, 2016, added the second paragraph in subsection (c).

Session Laws 2016-94, s. 35.20(b), effective July 1, 2016, rewrote subsection (e). See editor's note for applicability.

Session Laws 2017-191, s. 1, effective January 1, 2018, added subsection (q2).

Session Laws 2018-74, s. 10(a), effective July 1, 2018, substituted "confidential and subject to release under G.S. 20-9(g)(4)h" for "confidential" in subsection (e).

Session Laws 2018-145, s. 14, effective December 27, 2018, added subdivision (b2)(8).

Session Laws 2019-199, s. 7(a), effective October 1, 2019, inserted the next-to-last sentence in subsection (i1).

Session Laws 2019-227, s. 3(a), (b), effective September 27, 2019, in subdivision (f)(6), inserted "or conversion" following "renewal" and "or converted" following "renewed" throughout, inserted "or remote conversion of a full provisional license" in the introductory paragraph, added clause (ii) in sub-sub-subdivision a.1., added the last sentence in sub-sub-subdivision

a.3., inserted "For a remote renewal" in sub-sub-subdivision a.4., inserted "or conversion of a full provisional license" in sub-subdivision f.; and made stylistic changes.

THIS SECTION AND G.S. 20-35, BEING IN PARI MATERIA, MUST BE CONSTRUED TOGETHER, and, if possible, they must be reconciled and harmonized. State v. Tolley, 271 N.C. 459, 156 S.E.2d 858 (1967).

PENALTY. --Any person convicted of operating a motor vehicle over any highway in this State without having first been licensed as such operator, in violation of subsection (a) of this section, is guilty of a misdemeanor; and, under former G.S. 20-35(b), was subject to punishment by imprisonment for a term of not more than six months. The superior court, even if it had jurisdiction in other respects, had no authority to pronounce judgment imposing a prison sentence of two years for this criminal offense. State v. Wall, 271 N.C. 675, 157 S.E.2d 363 (1967).

A VIOLATION OF THIS SECTION IS NOT STATUTORILY A LESSER INCLUDED offense of G.S. 20-28. State v. Cannon, 38 N.C. App. 322, 248 S.E.2d 65 (1978).

The defendant could not be prosecuted for driving while his license was permanently revoked in violation of G.S. 20-28 because of the prohibition against double jeopardy, where the defendant had previously pled guilty to driving without a license in violation of this section based upon the same event. While a violation of this section is not statutorily a lesser included offense of a violation of G.S. 20-28, under the "additional facts test" of double jeopardy when applied to the defendant's offenses, the two offenses were the same both in fact and in law since the evidence that the defendant was driving an automobile while his license had been permanently revoked would sustain a conviction for driving without a license. State v. Cannon, 38 N.C. App. 322, 248 S.E.2d 65 (1978).

SUBSECTION (I1) OF THIS SECTION DOES NOT EXPRESSLY EXTEND THE PERIOD OF A SUSPENSION, CANCELLATION OR REVOCATION; it merely provides for the payment of a fee for an administrative act by the Department (now Division). Ennis v. Garrett, 279 N.C. 612, 184 S.E.2d 246 (1971).

The contention that a revocation remains in effect not only throughout the period stated in the order of revocation but also until the person whose license was revoked applies for a restoration of his license and pays the restoration fee required by subsection (i1) of this section is contrary to the definition of "revocation" in former G.S. 20-6 [now in G.S. 20-4.01(36)]. Ennis v. Garrett, 279 N.C. 612, 184 S.E.2d 246 (1971).

DRIVING WITHOUT A LICENSE IS NEGLIGENT PER SE. --Under this section it is negligence per se for one to drive a motor vehicle without a license, but such negligence must be the proximate cause of injury in order to be actionable. Hoke v. Atlantic Greyhound Corp., 226 N.C. 692, 40 S.E.2d 345 (1946).

Trial court did not err in admitting testimony that decedent did not have motorcycle endorsement at time of accident. Violation of this section is negligence per se. Ward v. McDonald, 100 N.C. App. 359, 396 S.E.2d 337 (1990).

PROBABLE CAUSE FOR ARREST. --Where trooper could have placed defendant under arrest for not carrying his driver's license, but merely choose to ask defendant to step back to the patrol car so that he could check defendant's license information and so that he could further investigate defendant's intoxication based upon defendant's unsteady movements and smell of alcohol and after defendant failed field sobriety tests he was placed under arrest and advised of his rights, the seizure was constitutionally permissible and there was sufficient probable cause for arrest. State v. Johnston, 115 N.C. App. 711, 446 S.E.2d 135 (1994).

SUFFICIENT EVIDENCE SUPPORTED CONVICTION. --Denial of defendant juvenile's operating a vehicle without a license under G.S. 20-7(a) charge was supported by sufficient evidence since: (1) defendant admitted at the accident scene that he drove the vehicle that collided with a utility pole; (2) the motor vehicle the officer discovered upon arrival at the accident scene was still warm, which tended to show that the car had recently been driven; (3) the only persons in the vicinity of the accident scene when the officer arrived were defendant and his friends; (4) the wrecked vehicle was registered to defendant's mother; and (5) there was ample additional evidence showing the trustworthiness of defendant's admission for purposes of the corpus delicti doctrine. In re A.N.C., 225 N.C. App. 315, 750 S.E.2d 835 (2013), review denied 367 N.C. 269, 752 S.E.2d 151, 2013 N.C. LEXIS 1386 (2013).

APPLIED in State v. Green, 266 N.C. 785, 147 S.E.2d 377 (1966); State v. White, 18 N.C. App. 31, 195 S.E.2d 576 (1973); In re Frye, 32 N.C. App. 384, 232 S.E.2d 301 (1977); Hinson v. Jarvis, 190 N.C. App. 607, 660 S.E.2d 604 (2008), review dismissed, as moot, 363 N.C. 126, 675 S.E.2d 365 (2009), review denied, 363 N.C. 126, 675 S.E.2d 366 (2009).

CITED in State v. Payne, 213 N.C. 719, 197 S.E. 573 (1938); Brown v. Fidelity & Cas. Co., 241 N.C. 666, 86 S.E.2d 433 (1955); Beaver v. Scheidt, 251 N.C. 671, 111 S.E.2d 881 (1960); Parks v. Washington, 255 N.C. 478, 122 S.E.2d 70 (1961); State v. White, 3 N.C. App. 31, 164 S.E.2d 36 (1968); State v. Newborn, 11 N.C. App. 292, 181 S.E.2d 214 (1971); State v. Baxley, 15 N.C. App. 544, 190 S.E.2d 401 (1972); Williams v. Wachovia Bank & Trust Co., 292 N.C. 416, 233 S.E.2d 589 (1977); United States v. Dixon, 729 F. Supp. 1113 (W.D.N.C. 1990); State v. Green, 103 N.C. App. 38, 404 S.E.2d 363 (1991); State v. Hudson, 103 N.C. App. 708, 407 S.E.2d 583 (1991); Craig v. Faulkner, 151 N.C. App. 581, 565 S.E.2d 733 (2002); State v. McKinney, 153 N.C. App. 369, 570 S.E.2d 238 (2002); State v. Hernandez, 188 N.C. App. 193, 655 S.E.2d 426 (2008); State v. Veazey, 191 N.C. App. 181, 662 S.E.2d 683 (2008).

CROSS REFERENCES. --
As to jurisdiction of prosecution under this section, see note to G.S. 7A-272. As to expiration of H and X endorsements, see G.S. 20-37.16. As to criminal record checks of applicants and of current employees who are involved in the manufacture or production of drivers licenses and identification cards, see G.S. 114-19.24.

LEGAL PERIODICALS. --
For comment on the 1953 amendments, see 31 N.C.L. Rev. 412 (1953).
For survey of 1978 constitutional law, see 57 N.C.L. Rev. 958 (1979).
For 1997 Legislative Survey, see 20 Campbell L. Rev. 491.
For article, "Local Enforcement of Federal Immigration Law: Should North Carolina Communities Implement 287(g) Authority," see 86 N.C.L. Rev. 1710 (2008).

OPINIONS OF THE ATTORNEY GENERAL
DRIVING WITHOUT LICENSE AS LESSER INCLUDED OFFENSE OF DRIVING WHILE LICENSE SUSPENDED OR REVOKED. --See opinion of Attorney General to Mr. Charles B. Winberry, Chief District Prosecutor, Seventh Judicial District, 40 N.C.A.G. 427 (1970).

This section has more than one version with varying effective dates. To view a complete list of the versions of this section see Table of Contents.

N.C. Gen. Stat. § 20-7.01

Repealed by Session Laws 1979, c. 667, s. 43.

This section has more than one version with varying effective dates. To view a complete list of the versions of this section see Table of Contents.

§ 20-7.1. Notice of change of address or name

(a) **Address.** -- A person whose address changes from the address stated on a drivers license must notify the Division of the change within 60 days after the change occurs. If the person's address changed because the person moved, the person must obtain a duplicate license within that time limit stating the new address. A person who does not move but whose address changes due to governmental action may not be charged with violating this subsection. A person who has provided an e-mail or electronic address to the Division pursuant to G.S. 20-48(a) shall notify the Division of any change or discontinuance of that e-mail or electronic address within 30 days after the change or discontinuance.

(b) **Name.** -- A person whose name changes from the name stated on a drivers license must notify the Division of the change within 60 days after the change occurs and obtain a duplicate drivers license stating the new name.

(c) **Fee.** -- G.S. 20-14 sets the fee for a duplicate license.

History.
1975, c. 223, s. 1; 1979, c. 970; 1983, c. 521, s. 1; 1997-122, s. 4; 2016-90, s. 10(a)

EFFECT OF AMENDMENTS. --

Session Laws 2016-90, s. 10(a), effective October 1, 2016, added the last sentence in subsection (a).

CITED in State v. Atwood, 290 N.C. 266, 225 S.E.2d 543 (1976).

OPINIONS OF THE ATTORNEY GENERAL

LICENSE MUST SHOW CURRENT ADDRESS. -- See opinion of Attorney General to Mr. Edward Powell, Commissioner of Motor Vehicles, 45 N.C.A.G. 194 (1976).

N.C. Gen. Stat. § 20-7.2

Repealed by Session Laws 1987, c. 581, s. 2.

§ 20-7.3. Availability of organ, eye, and tissue donor cards at motor vehicle offices

The Division shall make organ, eye, and tissue donor cards available to interested individuals in each office authorized to issue drivers licenses or special identification cards. The Division shall obtain donor cards from qualified organ, eye, or tissue procurement organizations or tissue banks, as defined in G.S. 130A-412.4(31). The Division shall offer organ donation information and a donor card to each applicant for a drivers license. The organ donation information shall include the following:

(1) A statement informing the individual that federally designated organ procurement organizations and eye banks have read-only access to the Department-operated Organ Donor Registry Internet site (hereafter "Donor Registry") listing those individuals who have stated to the Division of Motor Vehicles the individual's intent to be an organ donor and have an organ donation symbol on the individual's drivers license or special identification card.

(2) The type of information that will be made available on the Donor Registry.

History.

2001-481, s. 3;2004-189, s. 3;2007-538, s. 7

EDITOR'S NOTE. --

Session Laws 2004-189, s. 5(c), as amended by Session Laws 2005-276, s. 44.1(q), provides: "The Division of Motor Vehicles shall retain a portion of five cents ($0.05) collected for the issuance of each drivers license and duplicate license to offset the actual cost of developing and maintaining the online Organ Donor Internet site established pursuant to Section 1 of this act. The remainder of the five cents ($0.05) shall be credited to the License to Give Trust Fund established under G.S. 20-7.4 and shall be used for the purposes authorized under G.S. 20-7.4 and G.S. 20-7.5."

Session Laws 2007-538, s. 11, provides: "The North Carolina Department of Transportation, Division of Motor Vehicles, in cooperation with the License to Give Trust Fund Commission, shall use available grant-in-aid funds from the State and federal governments and other sources to enhance online access such that donors and prospective donors may update, amend, or revoke information on the donor's or prospective donor's drivers license or donor card."

EFFECT OF AMENDMENTS. --

Session Laws 2004-189, s. 3, effective January 1, 2005, inserted "organ donation information and" preceding "a donor card" in the third sentence; and added the last sentence and subdivisions (1) and (2).

Session Laws 2007-538, s. 7, effective October 1, 2007, in the second sentence of the introductory paragraph, substituted "G.S. 130A-412.4(31)" for "G.S. 130A-403"; in subdivision (1), substituted "Organ Donor Registry Internet site (hereafter 'Donor Registry')" for "Organ Donor Internet site"; and in subdivision (2), substituted "Donor Registry." for "Organ Donor Internet site."

§ 20-7.4. License to Give Trust Fund established

(a) There is established the License to Give Trust Fund. Revenue in the Fund includes amounts credited by the Division as required by law, and other funds. Any surplus in the Fund shall not revert but shall be used for the purposes stated in this section. The Fund shall be kept on deposit with the State Treasurer, as in the case of other State Funds, and may be invested by the State Treasurer in any lawful securities for investment of State funds. The License to Give Trust Fund is subject to oversight by the State Auditor pursuant to Article 5A of Chapter 147 of the General Statutes.

(b) The purposes for which funds may be expended by the License to Give Trust Fund Commission from the License to Give Trust Fund are as follows:

(1) As grants-in-aid for initiatives that educate about and promote organ and tissue donation and health care decision making at life's end.

(2) Expenses of the License to Give Trust Fund Commission as authorized in G.S. 20-7.5.

History.

2004-189, s. 4(a);2015-241, s. 27.8(a);2015-276, s. 6.5

EDITOR'S NOTE. --

Session Laws 2004-189, s. 5(c), as amended by Session Laws 2005-276, s. 44.1(q), provides: "The Division of Motor Vehicles shall retain a portion of five cents ($0.05) collected for the issuance of each drivers license and duplicate license to offset the actual cost of developing and maintaining the online Organ Donor Internet site established pursuant to Section 1 of this act. The remainder of the five cents ($0.05) shall be credited to the License to Give Trust Fund established under G.S. 20-7.4 and shall be used for the purposes authorized under G.S. 20-7.4 and G.S. 20-7.5."

Session Laws 2015-276, s. 6.5, repealed Session Laws 2015-241, s. 27.8, which amended this section. Session Laws 2015-276, s. 7, made the repeal effective October 20, 2015, applicable to offenses committed on or after that date, and provides, in part, that "Prosecutions for offenses committed before the effective date of this act are not abated or affected by this act, and the statutes that would be applicable but for this act remain applicable to those prosecutions."

Session Laws 2015-276, s. 7, provides: "Sections 1 and 2 of this act become effective December 1, 2015, and apply to offenses committed on or after that date. The remainder of this act is effective when this act becomes law [October 20, 2015] and applies to offenses committed on or after that date. Prosecutions for offenses committed before the effective date of this act are not abated or affected by this act, and the statutes that would be applicable but for this act remain applicable to those prosecutions."

EFFECT OF AMENDMENTS. --

Session Laws 2015-241, s. 27.8(a), effective September 18, 2015, and applicable to grants awarded on or after that date, amended subdivision (b)(1) by inserting "matching" and adding the second and third sentences, which read: "A grant-in-aid provided pursuant to this subdivision shall be matched on the basis of one dollar ($1.00) in grant funds for every one dollar ($1.00) in nongrant funds. Matching funds shall not include other State funds. The Commission shall not provide a grant under this subdivision until the grantee provides evidence satisfactory to the Commission that the grantee has sufficient nongrant funds to match." Session Laws 2015-241, s. 27.8(a), was subsequently repealed by Session Laws 2015-276, s. 6.5, effective October 20, 2015. For applicability, see editor's note.

§ 20-7.5. License to Give Trust Fund Commission established

(a) There is established the License to Give Trust Fund Commission. The Commission shall be located in the Department of Administration for budgetary and administrative purposes only. The Commission may allocate funds from the License to Give Trust Fund for the purposes authorized in G.S. 20-7.4. The Commission shall have 15 members, appointed as follows:

(1) Four members by the General Assembly, upon the recommendation of the President Pro Tempore of the Senate:

a. One representative of Carolina Donor Services.

b. One representative of LifeShare of The Carolinas.

c. Two members who have demonstrated an interest in organ and tissue donation and education.

(2) Four members by the General Assembly, upon the recommendation of the Speaker of the House of Representatives:

a. One representative of The North Carolina Eye Bank, Inc.

b. One representative of The Carolinas Center for Hospice and End-of-Life Care.

c. Two members who have demonstrated an interest in promoting advance care planning education.

(3) Seven members by the Governor:

a. Three members representing organ, tissue, and eye recipients, families of recipients, or families of donors. Of these three, one each from the mountain, heartland, and coastal regions of the State.

b. One member who is a transplant physician licensed to practice medicine in this State.

c. One member who has demonstrated an interest in organ and tissue donation and education.

d. One member who has demonstrated an interest in promoting advance care planning education.

e. A representative of the North Carolina Department of Transportation.

(b) The Commission shall elect from its membership a chair and a vice-chair for two-year terms. The Secretary of Administration shall provide meeting facilities for the Commission as required by the Chair.

(c) The members of the Commission shall receive per diem and necessary travel and subsistence expenses in accordance with G.S. 138-5 and G.S. 138-6, as applicable. Per diem, subsistence, and travel expenses of the members shall be paid from the License to Give Trust Fund.

(d) The members of the Commission shall comply with G.S. 14-234 prohibiting conflicts of interest. In addition to the restrictions imposed under G.S. 14-234, a member shall not vote on, participate in the deliberations of, or otherwise attempt through his or her official capacity to influence the vote on allocations of moneys from the License to Give Trust Fund to a nonprofit entity of which the member is an officer, director, or employee, or to a governmental entity of which the member is an employee or a member of the governing board. A violation of this subsection is a Class 1 misdemeanor.

History.

2004-189, s. 4(b)

EDITOR'S NOTE. --

Session Laws 2004-189, s. 5(c), as amended by Session Laws 2005-276, s. 44.1(q), provides: "The Division of Motor Vehicles shall retain a portion of five cents ($0.05) collected for the issuance of each drivers license and duplicate license to offset the actual cost of developing and maintaining the online Organ Donor Internet site established pursuant to Section 1 of this act. The remainder of the five cents ($0.05) shall be credited to the License to Give Trust Fund established under G.S. 20-7.4 and shall be used for the purposes authorized under G.S. 20-7.4 and G.S. 20-7.5."

§ 20-7.6. Powers and duties of the License to Give Trust Fund Commission

The License to Give Trust Fund Commission has the following powers and duties:

(1) Establish general policies and guidelines for awarding grants-in-aid to nonprofit entities to conduct education and awareness activities on organ and tissue donation and advance care planning.

(2) Accept gifts or grants from other sources to further the purposes of the License to Give Trust Fund. Such gifts or grants shall be transmitted to the State Treasurer for credit to the Fund.

(3) Hire staff or contract for other expertise for the administration of the Fund. Expenses related to staffing shall be paid from the License to Give Trust Fund.

History.
2004-189, s. 4(b);2015-241, s. 27.8(b);2015-276, s. 6.5
EDITOR'S NOTE. --
Session Laws 2004-189, s. 5(c), as amended by Session Laws 2005-276, s. 44.1(q), provides: "The Division of Motor Vehicles shall retain a portion of five cents ($0.05) collected for the issuance of each drivers license and duplicate license to offset the actual cost of developing and maintaining the online Organ Donor Internet site established pursuant to Section 1 of this act. The remainder of the five cents ($0.05) shall be credited to the License to Give Trust Fund established under G.S. 20-7.4 and shall be used for the purposes authorized under G.S. 20-7.4 and G.S. 20-7.5."

Session Laws 2015-276, s. 6.5, repealed Session Laws 2015-241, s. 27.8, which amended this section. Session Laws 2015-276, s. 7, made the repeal effective October 20, 2015, applicable to offenses committed on or after that date, and provides, in part, that "Prosecutions for offenses committed before the effective date of this act are not abated or affected by this act, and the statutes that would be applicable but for this act remain applicable to those prosecutions."
EFFECT OF AMENDMENTS. --
Session Laws 2015-241, s. 27.8(b), effective September 18, 2015, and applicable to grants awarded on or after that date, amended subdivision (1) by adding "In accordance with G.S. 20-7.4(b)" at the beginning and inserting "matching" between "awarding" and "grants-in-aid." Session Laws 2015-241, s. 27.8(b), was subsequently repealed by Session Laws 2015-276, s. 6.5, effective October 20, 2015.

§ 20-8. Persons exempt from license

The following are exempt from license hereunder:

(1) Any person while operating a motor vehicle the property of and in the service of the Armed Forces of the United States. This shall not be construed to exempt any operators of the United States Civilian Conservation Corps motor vehicles;

(2) Any person while driving or operating any road machine, farm tractor, or implement of husbandry temporarily operated or moved on a highway;

(3) A nonresident who is at least 16 years of age who has in his immediate possession a valid driver's license issued to him in his home state or country if the nonresident is operating a motor vehicle in this State in accordance with the license restrictions and vehicle classifications that would be applicable to him under the laws and regulations of his home state or country if he were driving in his home state or country. This exemption specifically applies to nonresident military spouses, regardless of their employment status, who are temporarily residing in North Carolina due to the active duty military orders of a spouse.

(4) to (6) Repealed by Session Laws 1979, c. 667, s. 13.

(7) Any person who is at least 16 years of age and while operating a moped.

History.
1935, c. 52, s. 3; 1963, c. 1175; 1973, c. 1017; 1975, c. 859, s. 2; 1979, c. 574, s. 7; c. 667, s. 13; 1983, c. 436; 2009-274, s. 4
EFFECT OF AMENDMENTS. --
Session Laws 2009-274, s. 4, effective July 10, 2009, and applicable to all licenses expiring on or after that date, substituted "Armed Forces" for "armed forces" in subdivision (1).
CITED in Brown v. Fidelity & Cas. Co., 241 N.C. 666, 86 S.E.2d 433 (1955); State v. Leyshon, 211 N.C. App. 511, 710 S.E.2d 282 (2011).
LEGAL PERIODICALS. --
For survey of 1978 constitutional law, see 57 N.C.L. Rev. 958 (1979).
OPINIONS OF THE ATTORNEY GENERAL
EXEMPTION FOR ONE DRIVING FARM TRACTOR APPLIES ONLY TO ONE ACTUALLY ENGAGED IN FARMING OPERATIONS. --See opinion of Attorney General to LTC Charles B. Pierce, N.C. State Highway Patrol, 41 N.C.A.G. 832 (1972).

§ 20-9. What persons shall not be licensed

(a) To obtain a regular drivers license, a person must have reached the minimum age set in the following table for the class of license sought:

Class of Regular License	Minimum Age
Class A	18
Class B	18
Class C	16

G.S. 20-37.13 sets the age qualifications for a commercial drivers license.

(b) The Division shall not issue a drivers license to any person whose license has been suspended or revoked during the period for which the license was suspended or revoked.

(b1) The Division shall not issue a drivers license to any person whose permit or license has been suspended or revoked under G.S. 20-13.2(c1) during the suspension or revocation period, unless the Division has restored the person's permit or license under G.S. 20-13.2(c1).

(c) The Division shall not issue a drivers license to any person who is an habitual drunkard or is an habitual user of narcotic drugs or barbiturates, whether or not the use is in accordance with the prescription of a physician.

(d) Repealed by Session Laws 2012-194, s. 8, effective July 17, 2012.

(e) The Division shall not issue a drivers license to any person when in the opinion of the Division the person is unable to exercise reasonable and ordinary control over a motor vehicle while operating the vehicle upon the highways, nor shall a license be issued to any person who is unable to understand highway warnings or direction signs.

(f) The Division shall not issue a drivers license to any person whose license or driving privilege is in a state of cancellation, suspension, or revocation in any jurisdiction, if the acts or things upon which the cancellation, suspension, or revocation in the other jurisdiction was based would constitute lawful grounds for cancellation, suspension, or revocation in this State had those acts or things been done or committed in this State. However, any such cancellation shall not prohibit issuance for a period in excess of 18 months.

(g) The Division may issue a restricted or unrestricted drivers license under the following conditions to an otherwise eligible applicant suffering from a physical or mental disability or disease that affects his or her ability to exercise reasonable and ordinary control of a motor vehicle:

(1) The applicant submits to the Division a certificate in the form prescribed in subdivision (2) of this subsection. The Division may request the certificate at the applicant's initial application, at any time following the issuance of the license, or at the initial application and any time following the issuance of the license. Until a license issued under this subdivision expires, is cancelled, or is revoked, the license continues in force as long as the licensee presents to the Division a certificate in the form prescribed in subdivision (2) of this subsection at the intervals determined by the Division to be in the best interests of public safety.

(2) The Division may request a signed certificate from a health care provider duly licensed to practice medicine in the United States that the applicant or licensee has submitted to a physical examination by the health care provider. The certificate shall be devised by the Commissioner with the advice of qualified experts in the field of diagnosing and treating physical and mental disabilities and diseases as the Commissioner may select to assist him or her and shall be designed to elicit the maximum medical information necessary to aid in determining whether or not it would be a hazard to public safety to permit the applicant or licensee to operate a motor vehicle, including, if such is the fact, the examining provider's statement that the applicant or licensee is under medication and treatment and that the applicant's or licensee's physical or mental disability or disease is controlled. The certificate shall contain a waiver of privilege and the recommendation of the examining provider to the Commissioner as to whether a license should be issued to the applicant or licensee and whether the applicant or licensee can safely operate a motor vehicle.

(3) The Commissioner is not bound by the recommendation of the examining health care provider but shall give fair consideration to the recommendation in exercising his or her discretion in making licensing decisions, the criterion being whether or not, upon all the evidence, it appears that it is safe to permit the applicant or licensee to operate a motor vehicle. The burden of proof of this fact is upon the applicant or licensee. In deciding whether to issue, restrict, cancel, or deny a license, the Commissioner may be guided by the opinion of experts in the field of diagnosing and treating the specific physical or mental disability or disease suffered by an applicant or licensee and the experts may be compensated for their services on an equitable basis. The Commissioner may also take into consideration any other factors which bear on the issue of public safety.

(4) Whenever a license is restricted, cancelled, or denied by the Commissioner on the basis of a physical or mental disability or disease, the action may be reviewed by a reviewing board upon written request of the applicant or licensee filed with the Division within 10 days after receipt of notice given in accordance with G.S. 20-48 of the action taken. The reviewing board shall consist of the Commissioner or the Commissioner's authorized representative and at least two medical professionals selected by the Commissioner and duly licensed to practice medicine by the appropriate licensing authority in the State. The medical

professionals selected by the Commissioner may be compensated for their services on an equitable basis, including reimbursement for ordinary and necessary travel expenses. The Commissioner or the Commissioner's authorized representative, plus any two medical professionals selected by the Commissioner, shall constitute a quorum. The procedure for hearings authorized by this section shall be as follows:

a. Applicants shall be afforded an opportunity for hearing, after reasonable notice of not less than 10 days, before the review board established by this subdivision. The notice shall be in writing and shall be delivered to the applicant in person or sent by certified mail, with return receipt requested. The notice shall state the time, place, and subject of the hearing. If a hearing is requested under this subdivision to contest a restriction placed on a license under subdivision (3) of this subsection, the restriction shall be stayed unless the Division determines there is an imminent threat to public safety if continued unrestricted driving is permitted. No stay shall be granted if a hearing is requested under this subdivision to contest a denial or cancellation of a license under subdivision (3) of this subsection. Nothing in this sub-subdivision authorizes the stay of a restriction placed on a license pursuant to another provision of law.

b. The review board may compel the attendance of witnesses and the production of such books, records, and papers as it desires at a hearing authorized by this section. Upon request of an applicant or licensee, a subpoena to compel the attendance of any witness or a subpoena duces tecum to compel the production of any books, records, or papers shall be issued by the board. Subpoenas shall be directed to the sheriff of the county where the witness resides or is found and shall be served and returned in the same manner as a subpoena in a criminal case. Fees of the sheriff and witnesses shall be the same as that allowed in the district court in cases before that court and shall be paid in the same manner as other expenses of the Division of Motor Vehicles are paid. In any case of disobedience or neglect of any subpoena served on any person, or the refusal of any witness to testify to any matters regarding which the witness may be lawfully interrogated, the district court or superior court where the

disobedience, neglect, or refusal occurs, or any judge thereof, on application by the board, shall compel obedience or punish as for contempt.

c. A hearing may be continued upon motion of the applicant or licensee for good cause shown with approval of the board or upon order of the board.

d. The board shall pass upon the admissibility of evidence at a hearing but the applicant or licensee affected may at the time object to the board's ruling, and, if evidence offered by an applicant or licensee is rejected, the party may proffer the evidence, and the proffer shall be made a part of the record. The board shall not be bound by common law or statutory rules of evidence which prevail in courts of law or equity and may admit and give probative value to evidence which possesses probative value commonly accepted by reasonably prudent persons in the conduct of their affairs. It may exclude incompetent, immaterial, irrelevant, and unduly repetitious evidence. Uncontested facts may be stipulated by agreement between an applicant or licensee and the board, and evidence relating to stipulated facts may be excluded. All evidence, including records and documents in the possession of the Division of Motor Vehicles or the board, of which the board desires to avail itself shall be made a part of the record. Documentary evidence may be received in the form of copies or excerpts, or by incorporation by reference. The board shall prepare an official record, which shall include testimony and exhibits. A record of the testimony and other evidence submitted shall be taken, but it shall not be necessary to transcribe shorthand notes or electronic recordings unless requested for purposes of court review.

e. Every decision and order adverse to an applicant or licensee shall be in writing or stated in the record and shall be accompanied by findings of fact and conclusions of law. The findings of fact shall consist of a concise statement of the board's conclusions on each contested issue of fact. The applicant or licensee shall be notified of the board's decision in person or by registered mail with return receipt requested. A copy of the board's decision with accompanying findings and conclusions shall be delivered or mailed upon request to the applicant's or licensee's attorney of record or to the applicant or licensee, if he or she has no attorney.

f. Actions of the reviewing board are subject to judicial review as provided under Chapter 150B of the General Statutes.

g. Repealed by Session Laws 1977, c. 840.

h. All records and evidence collected and compiled by the Division and the reviewing board shall not be considered public records within the meaning of Chapter 132 of the General Statutes and may be made available to the public only upon an order of a court of competent jurisdiction. An applicant or licensee may obtain, without a court order, a copy of records and evidence collected and compiled under this subdivision about the applicant or licensee by submitting a written request to the Division, signing any release forms required by the Division, and remitting the required fee set by the Division. All information furnished by, about, or on behalf of an applicant or licensee under this section shall be without prejudice and shall be for the use of the Division, the reviewing board, or the court in administering this section and shall not be used in any manner as evidence, or for any other purposes in any trial, civil or criminal. The prohibition on release and use under this sub-subdivision applies without regard to who authored or produced the information collected, compiled, and used by the Division under this subdivision.

(h) The Division shall not issue a drivers license to an applicant who currently holds a license to drive issued by another state unless the applicant surrenders the license.

(i) The Division shall not issue a drivers license to an applicant who has resided in this State for less than 12 months until the Division has searched the National Sex Offender Public Registry to determine if the person is currently registered as a sex offender in another state. The following applies in this subsection:

(1) If the Division finds that the person is currently registered as a sex offender in another state, the Division shall not issue a drivers license to the person until the person submits proof of registration pursuant to Article 27A of Chapter 14 of the General Statutes issued by the sheriff of the county where the person resides.

(2) If the person does not appear on the National Sex Offender Public Registry, the Division shall issue a drivers license but shall require the person to sign an affidavit acknowledging that the person has been notified that if the person is a sex offender, then the person is required to register

pursuant to Article 27A of Chapter 14 of the General Statutes.

(3) If the Division is unable to access all states' information contained in the National Sex Offender Public Registry, but the person is otherwise qualified to obtain a drivers license, then the Division shall issue the drivers license but shall first require the person to sign an affidavit stating that: (i) the person does not appear on the National Sex Offender Public Registry and (ii) acknowledging that the person has been notified that if the person is a sex offender, then the person is required to register pursuant to Article 27A of Chapter 14 of the General Statutes. The Division shall search the National Sex Offender Public Registry for the person within a reasonable time after access to the Registry is restored. If the person does appear in the National Sex Offender Public Registry, the person is in violation of G.S. 20-30, and the Division shall immediately revoke the drivers license and shall promptly notify the sheriff of the county where the person resides of the offense.

(4) Any person denied a license or whose license has been revoked by the Division pursuant to this subsection has a right to file a petition within 30 days thereafter for a hearing in the matter in the superior court of the county where the person resides, or to petition the resident judge of the district or judge holding the court of that district, or special or emergency judge holding a court in the district, and the court or judge is hereby vested with jurisdiction. The court or judge shall set the matter for hearing upon 30 days' written notice to the Division. At the hearing, the court or judge shall take testimony and examine the facts of the case and shall determine whether the petitioner is entitled to a license under this subsection and whether the petitioner is in violation of G.S. 20-30.

History.
1935, c. 52, s. 4; 1951, c. 542, s. 3; 1953, c. 773; 1955, c. 118, s. 7; 1967, cc. 961, 966; 1971, c. 152; c. 528, s. 11; 1973, cc. 135, 441; c. 476, s. 128; c. 1331, s. 3; 1975, c. 716, s. 5; 1979, c. 667, ss. 14, 41; 1983, c. 545; 1987, c. 827, s. 1; 1989, c. 771, s. 7;1991, c. 726, s. 6;1993, c. 368, s. 2;c. 533, s. 4;1999-243, s. 4;1999-452, s. 8;2003-14, s. 1;2006-247, s. 19(c);2007-182, s. 2;2012-194, s. 8;2016-94, s. 35.20(c);2018-74, s. 10(b);2018-142, s. 3(a)

EDITOR'S NOTE. --
Session Laws 1989, c. 168, ss. 3 and 4, effective May 30, 1989, would have amended subdivisions (c)(9) and (c)(10) of this section; however, these subdivisions do not exist in this section. The amendment apparently should have been to G.S. 20-118. Session

Laws 2018-142, s. 5, effective December 14, 2018, repealed Session Laws 1989, c. 168, s. 4.

Session Laws 1993, c. 368, which amended this section, in s. 5 provides: "A drivers license or a special identification card issued by the Division of Motor Vehicles before January 1, 1995, and renewed by the Division after that date is considered the first drivers license or special identification card issued by the Division for purposes of determining when the license or card expires."

Session Laws 2016-94, s. 35.20(h), made the amendments to this section by Session Laws 2016-94, s. 35.20(d), applicable to drivers licenses issued or renewed on or after July 1, 2016 and hearings requested on or after July 1, 2016.

Session Laws 2016-94, s. 1.2, provides: "This act shall be known as the 'Current Operations and Capital Improvements Appropriations Act of 2016.'"

Session Laws 2016-94, s. 39.4, provides: "Except for statutory changes or other provisions that clearly indicate an intention to have effects beyond the 2016-2017 fiscal year, the textual provisions of this act apply only to funds appropriated for, and activities occurring during, the 2016-2017 fiscal year."

Session Laws 2016-94, s. 39.7, is a severability clause.

EFFECT OF AMENDMENTS. --

Session Laws 2006-247, s. 19(c), effective December 1, 2006, and applicable to all applications for a drivers license, learner's permit, instruction permit, or special identification card submitted on or after that date, added subsection (i).

Session Laws 2007-182, s. 2, effective July 5, 2007, substituted "Commission for Public Health" for "Commission for Health Services" seven times in subdivision (g)(4).

Session Laws 2012-194, s. 8, effective July 17, 2012, repealed subsection (d), which read: "No driver's license shall be issued to any applicant who has been previously adjudged insane or an idiot, imbecile, or feebleminded, and who has not at the time of such application been restored to competency by judicial decree or released from a hospital for the insane or feebleminded upon a certificate of the superintendent that such person is competent, nor then unless the Division is satisfied that such person is competent to operate a motor vehicle with safety to persons and property."

Session Laws 2016-94, s. 35.20(c), effective July 1, 2016, rewrote subsections (e) and (g). See editor's note for applicability.

Session Laws 2018-74, s. 10(b), effective July 1, 2018, in sub-subdivision (g)(4)h, inserted "except as authorized in this sub-subdivision" in the third sentence and added the last sentence.

Session Laws 2018-142, s. 3(a), effective December 14, 2018, rewrote the section.

STATUTES GOVERNING DRIVING PRIVILEGES CIVIL IN NATURE. --Administration of statutes governing the issuance, revocation, suspension and cancellation of driving privileges is civil, rather than penal, in nature. Smith v. Wilkins, 75 N.C. App. 483, 331 S.E.2d 159 (1985).

WHERE THE LAW DIRECTS SUSPENSION, REVOCATION, OR NONISSUANCE OF A DRIVER'S LICENSE, THE GROUNDS ARE CONVICTIONS FOR MOVING VIOLATIONS, or other statutory violations relating to highway safety, or situations where an individual's capacity to operate a motor vehicle safely are manifestly questionable. Evans v. Roberson, 69 N.C. App. 644, 317 S.E.2d 715 (1984), rev'd on other grounds and modified, 314 N.C. 315, 333 S.E.2d 228 (1985).

ALCOHOLISM. --Findings and conclusions by the Driver License Medical Review Board were sufficient to support its order that petitioner not be granted driving privileges where the board found that petitioner had an alcohol problem; the board gave fair consideration to the recommendation of petitioner's physician that he be granted driving privileges, but the recommendation did not have to be expressly rejected by the board. McCormick v. Peters, 48 N.C. App. 365, 269 S.E.2d 168 (1980).

EPILEPSY. --Prior to 1967, subsection (d) of this section prohibited the licensing of anyone who had been diagnosed as having grand mal epilepsy. In 1967 this section was amended to delete the words "grand mal epileptic." Ormond v. Garrett, 8 N.C. App. 662, 175 S.E.2d 371 (1970).

The Division of Motor Vehicles was without authority to deny or withhold petitioner's license to operate a motor vehicle upon the highways of the State where the record showed that once or twice a year petitioner, who suffered from epilepsy, had an epileptic seizure and that with one exception when petitioner blacked out while driving and ran off the road, all the seizures had occurred in his sleep, and all the other evidence tended to show that his seizures were controlled and that he had exercised reasonable and ordinary control over his vehicle while operating it upon the highways. Chesnutt v. Peters, 300 N.C. 359, 266 S.E.2d 623 (1980).

Where the record on appeal contained no evidence that petitioner suffered from an "uncontrolled seizure disorder," although it did show that petitioner had suffered seizures from time to time, the whole record did not support the finding required by this section that petitioner be suffering from a mental or physical disability that prevents him from exercising reasonable and ordinary control in the operation of a motor vehicle on the highways. Chesnutt v. Peters, 44 N.C. App. 484, 261 S.E.2d 223, aff'd, 300 N.C. 359, 266 S.E.2d 623 (1980).

OUT-OF-STATE SUSPENSION AS BASIS FOR REVOCATION. --Under this section the Department (now Division) of Motor Vehicles must apply the period of revocation of the other state, since the person was a resident of the other state and was subject to and controlled by the laws of that state at the time the offense was committed. Parks v. Howland, 4 N.C. App. 197, 166 S.E.2d 701 (1969).

PURPOSE OF SUBSECTION (F). --Subsection (f) is clearly designed to promote public safety on the highways and to protect motorists on North Carolina's highways from the hazards created by a person who has demonstrated disregard for the rules of safety while operating a motor vehicle. The enactment of laws to assure public safety on the state's highways is a valid exercise of the police power by the legislature. Smith v. Wilkins, 75 N.C. App. 483, 331 S.E.2d 159 (1985).

SUBSECTION (F) IMPOSES NO DURATIONAL RESIDENCY REQUIREMENT to obtain a North Carolina driver's license, but requires only that the individual's license not be in a revoked status in another jurisdiction, and, consequently, does not violate the right to travel under the federal constitution. Smith v. Wilkins, 75 N.C. App. 483, 331 S.E.2d 159 (1985).

PERSONS WHOSE LICENSES ARE REVOKED ELSEWHERE AND THEN MOVE TO STATE. --All people who, as the result of traffic convictions, have their licenses revoked in other jurisdictions and then move to North Carolina are treated similarly under subsection (f), which is all that is required by the equal protection clause of the U.S. Const., Amend. XIV. Smith v. Wilkins, 75 N.C. App. 483, 331 S.E.2d 159 (1985).

A PETITIONER SEEKING JUDICIAL REVIEW OF A DECISION OF THE NORTH CAROLINA DRIVER LICENSE MEDICAL REVIEW BOARD must file such petition in the Superior Court of Wake County pursuant to G.S. 150B-45 and may not obtain a hearing under G.S. 20-25 in the superior court of the county in which he resides. Cox v. Miller, 26 N.C. App. 749, 217 S.E.2d 198 (1975).

APPLIED in In re Frye, 32 N.C. App. 384, 232 S.E.2d 301 (1977).

CITED in Hoke v. Atlantic Greyhound Corp., 226 N.C. 692, 40 S.E.2d 345 (1946); Nationwide Mut. Ins. Co. v. Chantos, 293 N.C. 431, 238 S.E.2d 597 (1977); Craig v. Faulkner, 151 N.C. App. 581, 565 S.E.2d 733 (2002).

LEGAL PERIODICALS. --

For note on reporting patients for review of driver's license, see 48 N.C.L. Rev. 1003 (1970).

For note discussing the extension of the family purpose doctrine to motorcycles and private property, see 14 Wake Forest L. Rev. 699 (1978).

OPINIONS OF THE ATTORNEY GENERAL

RELEASE OF DEPARTMENT OF MOTOR VEHICLE RECORDS. --The Department of Motor Vehicles is required by the Drivers Privacy Protection Act, 18 U.S.C. § 2721 et seq., to redact "personal information" and "highly restricted personal information" from documents, such as accident reports, provided to the public. Otherwise, the requirements of the Public Records Act, G.S. 132-1 et seq., should be complied with by DMV and local law enforcement agencies. Motor vehicle registration information provided by DMV to local taxing authorities should also be provided upon request in accordance with the Public Records Act. See opinion of Attorney General to Mr. George Tatum, Commissioner, North Carolina Division of Motor Vehicles, 2005 N.C.A.G. 1 (02/09/05).

§ 20-9.1. Physicians, psychologists, and other medical providers providing medical information on drivers with physical or mental disabilities or diseases

(a) Notwithstanding G.S. 8-53 for physicians and G.S. 8-53.3 for psychologists, or any other law relating to confidentiality of communications between physicians, psychologists, or other medical providers and their patients, a physician, psychologist, or other medical provider duly licensed in the State of North Carolina may disclose after consultation with the patient to the Commissioner information about a patient who has a physical or mental disability or disease that the physician, psychologist, or other medical provider believes may affect the patient's ability to safely operate a motor vehicle. This information shall be limited to the patient's name, address, date of birth, and diagnosis.

(b) The information provided to the Commissioner pursuant to subsection (a) of this section shall be confidential and shall be used only for the purpose of determining the qualifications of the patient to operate a motor vehicle.

(c) A physician, psychologist, or other medical provider disclosing or not disclosing information pursuant to this section, or conducting an evaluation and making a recommendation to the Division regarding a person's ability to safely operate a motor vehicle, is immune from any civil or criminal liability that might otherwise be incurred or imposed based on the action taken provided that the physician, psychologist, or other medical provider was acting in good faith and without malice. In any proceeding involving liability, good faith and lack of malice are presumed.

History.

1997-464, s. 1;2016-94, s. 35.20(d)

EDITOR'S NOTE. --

Session Laws 2016-94, s. 35.20(h), made the amendments to this section by Session Laws 2016-94, s. 35.20(d), applicable to drivers licenses issued or renewed on or after July 1, 2016 and hearings requested on or after July 1, 2016.

Session Laws 2016-94, s. 1.2, provides: "This act shall be known as the 'Current Operations and Capital Improvements Appropriations Act of 2016.'"

Session Laws 2016-94, s. 39.4, provides: "Except for statutory changes or other provisions that clearly indicate an intention to have effects beyond the 2016-2017 fiscal year, the textual provisions of this act apply only to funds appropriated for, and activities occurring during, the 2016-2017 fiscal year."

Session Laws 2016-94, s. 39.7, is a severability clause.

EFFECT OF AMENDMENTS. --

Session Laws 2016-94, s. 35.20(d), effective July 1, 2016, rewrote the section heading; and rewrote subsections (a) and (c). See editor's note for applicability.

§ 20-9.2. Selective service system registration requirements

(a) Any male United States citizen or immigrant who is at least 18 years of age but less than 26 years of age shall be registered in compliance with the requirements of the Military Selective Service Act, 50 U.S.C. § 453 (1948), when applying for the issuance, renewal, or duplication of a drivers license, commercial drivers license, or identification card.

(b) The Division shall forward in an electronic format the necessary personal information of the applicants identified in subsection (a) of this section required for registration to the Selective Service System. An application for the issuance, renewal, or duplication of a drivers license, commercial drivers license, or identification card constitutes an affirmation that the applicant has already registered with the Selective Service System or that he authorizes the Division to forward the necessary information to the Selective Service System for registration. The Division shall notify the applicant that his application for the issuance, renewal, or duplication of a drivers license, commercial drivers license, or identification card serves as his consent to be registered with the Selective Service System pursuant to this section.

(c) This section does not apply to special identification cards issued pursuant to G.S. 20-37.7(d)(5) or (6).

History.
2002-162, s. 1;2014-111, s. 14
  EFFECT OF AMENDMENTS. --
  Session Laws 2014-111, s. 14, effective August 6, 2014, added subsection (c).

§ 20-9.3. Notification of requirements for sex offender registration

The Division shall provide notice to each person who applies for the issuance of a drivers license, learner's permit, or instruction permit to operate a motor vehicle, and to each person who applies for an identification card, that if the person is a sex offender, then the person is required to register pursuant to Article 27A of Chapter 14 of the General Statutes.

History.
2006-247, s. 19(b)
  EDITOR'S NOTE. --
  Session Laws 2006-247, s. 19(e), made this section effective December 1, 2006, and applicable to all applications for a drivers license, learner's permit, instruction permit, or special identification card submitted on or after that date.

§ 20-10. Age limits for drivers of public passenger-carrying vehicles

It shall be unlawful for any person, whether licensed under this Article or not, who is under the age of 18 years to drive a motor vehicle while in use as a public passenger-carrying

vehicle. For purposes of this section, an ambulance when operated for the purpose of transporting persons who are sick, injured, or otherwise incapacitated shall not be treated as a public passenger-carrying vehicle.

No person 14 years of age or under, whether licensed under this Article or not, shall operate any road machine, farm tractor or motor driven implement of husbandry on any highway within this State. Provided any person may operate a road machine, farm tractor, or motor driven implement of husbandry upon a highway adjacent to or running in front of the land upon which such person lives when said person is actually engaged in farming operations.

History.
1935, c. 52, s. 5; 1951, c. 764; 1967, c. 343, s. 4; 1971, c. 1231, s. 1
LOCAL MODIFICATION. --Cumberland: 1965, c. 1152, s. 3.
CITED in State v. Hopper, 205 N.C. App. 175, 695 S.E.2d 801 (2010).

§ 20-10.1. Mopeds

It shall be unlawful for any person who is under the age of 16 years to operate a moped as defined in G.S. 20-4.01(27)j. upon any highway or public vehicular area of this State.

History.
1979, c. 574, s. 8; 2002-72, s. 6;2016-90, s. 13(b);2017-102, s. 5.2(b)
  EDITOR'S NOTE. --
  Session Laws 2016-90, s. 13(j), made the amendment to this section by Session Laws 2016-90, s. 13(b), applicable to offenses committed on or after December 1, 2016.
  Session Laws 2017-102, s. 5.2(b) provides: "The Revisor of Statutes is authorized to reletter the definitions in G.S. 20-4.01(27) and G.S. 20-4.01(32b) to place them in alphabetical order. The Revisor of Statutes may conform any citations that change as a result of the relettering." Pursuant to that authority, the reference to G.S. 20-4.01(27)d1. in this section was changed to G.S. 20-4.01(27)j.
  EFFECT OF AMENDMENTS. --
  Session Laws 2016-90, s. 13(b), effective December 1, 2016, substituted "G.S. 20-4.01(27)d1" for "G.S. 105-164.3." See editor's note for applicability.

§ 20-11. Issuance of limited learner's permit and provisional drivers license to person who is less than 18 years old

(a) **Process.** -- Safe driving requires instruction in driving and experience. To ensure that a person who is less than 18 years old has both instruction and experience before obtaining a drivers license, driving privileges are granted first on a limited basis and are then expanded in accordance with the following process:

(1) **Level 1.** -- Driving with a limited learner's permit.

(2) **Level 2.** -- Driving with a limited provisional license.

(3) **Level 3.** -- Driving with a full provisional license.

A permit or license issued under this section must indicate the level of driving privileges granted by the permit or license.

(b) **Level 1.** -- A person who is at least 15 years old but less than 18 years old may obtain a limited learner's permit if the person meets all of the following requirements:

(1) Passes a course of driver education prescribed in G.S. 115C-215 or a course of driver instruction at a licensed commercial driver training school.

(2) Passes a written test administered by the Division.

(3) Has a driving eligibility certificate or a high school diploma or its equivalent.

(c) **Level 1 Restrictions.** -- A limited learner's permit authorizes the permit holder to drive a specified type or class of motor vehicle only under the following conditions:

(1) The permit holder must be in possession of the permit.

(2) A supervising driver must be seated beside the permit holder in the front seat of the vehicle when it is in motion. No person other than the supervising driver can be in the front seat.

(3) For the first six months after issuance, the permit holder may drive only between the hours of 5:00 a.m. and 9:00 p.m.

(4) After the first six months after issuance, the permit holder may drive at any time.

(5) Every person occupying the vehicle being driven by the permit holder must have a safety belt properly fastened about his or her body, or be restrained by a child passenger restraint system as provided in G.S. 20-137.1(a), when the vehicle is in motion.

(6) The permit holder shall not use a mobile telephone or other additional technology associated with a mobile telephone while operating the motor vehicle on a public street or highway or public vehicular area.

(d) **Level 2.** -- A person who is at least 16 years old but less than 18 years old may obtain a limited provisional license if the person meets all of the following requirements:

(1) Has held a limited learner's permit issued by the Division for at least 12 months.

(2) Has not been convicted of a motor vehicle moving violation or seat belt infraction or a violation of G.S. 20-137.3 during the preceding six months.

(3) Passes a road test administered by the Division.

(4) Has a driving eligibility certificate or a high school diploma or its equivalent.

(5) Has completed a driving log, on a form approved by the Division, detailing a minimum of 60 hours as the operator of a motor vehicle of a class for which the driver has been issued a limited learner's permit. The log must show at least 10 hours of the required driving occurred during nighttime hours. No more than 10 hours of driving per week may be counted toward the 60-hour requirement. The driving log must be signed by the supervising driver and submitted to the Division at the time the applicant seeks to obtain a limited provisional license. If the Division has cause to believe that a driving log has been falsified, the limited learner's permit holder shall be required to complete a new driving log with the same requirements and shall not be eligible to obtain a limited provisional license for six months.

(e) **Level 2 Restrictions.** -- A limited provisional license authorizes the license holder to drive a specified type or class of motor vehicle only under the following conditions:

(1) The license holder shall be in possession of the license.

(2) The license holder may drive without supervision in any of the following circumstances:

a. From 5:00 a.m. to 9:00 p.m.

b. When driving directly to or from work.

c. When driving directly to or from an activity of a volunteer fire department, volunteer rescue squad, or volunteer emergency medical service, if the driver is a member of the organization.

(3) The license holder may drive with supervision at any time. When the license holder is driving with supervision, the supervising driver shall be seated beside the license holder in the front seat of the vehicle when it is in motion. The supervising driver need not be the only other occupant of the front seat, but shall be the person seated next to the license holder.

(4) When the license holder is driving the vehicle and is not accompanied by the supervising driver, there may be no more than one passenger under 21 years of age in the vehicle. This limit does not apply to passengers who are members of the license holder's immediate family or whose primary residence is the same household as the license holder. However, if a family member or member of the same household as the license holder who is younger than

21 years of age is a passenger in the vehicle, no other passengers under 21 years of age, who are not members of the license holder's immediate family or members of the license holder's household, may be in the vehicle.

(5) Every person occupying the vehicle being driven by the license holder shall have a safety belt properly fastened about his or her body, or be restrained by a child passenger restraint system as provided in G.S. 20-137.1(a), when the vehicle is in motion.

(6) The license holder shall not use a mobile telephone or other additional technology associated with a mobile telephone while operating the vehicle on a public street or highway or public vehicular area.

(f) **Level 3.** -- A person who is at least 16 years old but less than 18 years old may obtain a full provisional license if the person meets all of the following requirements:

(1) Has held a limited provisional license issued by the Division for at least six months.

(2) Has not been convicted of a motor vehicle moving violation or seat belt infraction or a violation of G.S. 20-137.3 during the preceding six months.

(3) Has a driving eligibility certificate or a high school diploma or its equivalent.

(4) Has completed a driving log, on a form approved by the Division, detailing a minimum of 12 hours as the operator of a motor vehicle of a class for which the driver is licensed. The log must show at least six hours of the required driving occurred during nighttime hours. The driving log must be signed by the supervising driver for any hours driven outside the provisions of subdivision (e)(2) of this section and submitted to the Division at the time the applicant seeks to obtain a full provisional license. If the Division has cause to believe that a driving log has been falsified, the limited provisional licensee shall be required to complete a new driving log with the same requirements and shall not be eligible to obtain a full provisional license for six months.

A person who meets these requirements may obtain a full provisional license by mail.

(g) **Level 3 Restrictions.** -- The restrictions on Level 1 and Level 2 drivers concerning time of driving, supervision, and passenger limitations do not apply to a full provisional license. However, the prohibition against operating a motor vehicle while using a mobile telephone under G.S. 20-137.3(b) shall apply to a full provisional license.

(h) **Exception for Persons 16 to 18 Who Have an Unrestricted Out-of-State License.** -- A person who is at least 16 years old but less than 18 years old, who was a resident of another state and has an unrestricted drivers license issued by that state, and who becomes a resident of this State may obtain one of the following upon the submission of a driving eligibility certificate or a high school diploma or its equivalent:

(1) A temporary permit, if the person has not completed a drivers education program that meets the requirements of the Superintendent of Public Instruction but is currently enrolled in a drivers education program that meets these requirements. A temporary permit is valid for the period specified in the permit and authorizes the holder of the permit to drive a specified type or class of motor vehicle when in possession of the permit, subject to any restrictions imposed by the Division concerning time of driving, supervision, and passenger limitations. The period must end within 10 days after the expected completion date of the drivers education program in which the applicant is enrolled.

(2) A full provisional license, if the person has completed a drivers education program that meets the requirements of the Superintendent of Public Instruction, has held the license issued by the other state for at least 12 months, and has not been convicted during the preceding six months of a motor vehicle moving violation, a seat belt infraction, or an offense committed in another jurisdiction that would be a motor vehicle moving violation or seat belt infraction if committed in this State.

(2a) A full provisional license, if the person has completed a drivers education program that meets the requirements of the Superintendent of Public Instruction, has held both a learner's permit and a restricted license from another state for at least six months each, the Commissioner finds that the requirements for the learner's permit and restricted license are comparable to the requirements for a learner's permit and restricted license in this State, and the person has not been convicted during the preceding six months of a motor vehicle moving violation, a seat belt infraction, or an offense committed in another jurisdiction that would be a moving violation or a seat belt infraction if committed in this State.

(3) A limited provisional license, if the person has completed a drivers education program that meets the requirements of the Superintendent of Public Instruction but either did not hold the license issued by the other state for at least 12 months or was convicted during the preceding six

months of a motor vehicle moving violation, a seat belt infraction, or an offense committed in another jurisdiction that would be a motor vehicle moving violation or seat belt infraction if committed in this State.

(h1) **Exception for Persons 16 to 18 Who Have an Out-of-State Restricted License.** -- A person who is at least 16 years old but less than 18 years old, who was a resident of another state and has a restricted drivers license issued by that state, and who becomes a resident of this State may obtain one of the following:

(1) A limited provisional license, if the person has completed a drivers education program that meets the requirements of the Superintendent of Public Instruction, held the restricted license issued by the other state for at least 12 months, and whose parent or guardian certifies that the person has not been convicted during the preceding six months of a motor vehicle moving violation, a seat belt infraction, or an offense committed in another jurisdiction that would be a motor vehicle moving violation or seat belt infraction if committed in this State.

(2) A limited learners permit, if the person has completed a drivers education program that meets the requirements of the Superintendent of Public Instruction but either did not hold the restricted license issued by the other state for at least 12 months or was convicted during the preceding six months of a motor vehicle moving violation, a seat belt infraction, or an offense committed in another jurisdiction that would be a motor vehicle moving violation or seat belt infraction if committed in this State. A person who qualifies for a limited learners permit under this subdivision and whose parent or guardian certifies that the person has not been convicted of a moving violation in the preceding six months shall be deemed to have held a limited learners permit in this State for each month the person held a restricted license in another state.

(h2) **Exception for Persons Age 15 Who Have an Out-of-State Unrestricted or Restricted License.** -- A person who is age 15, who was a resident of another state, has an unrestricted or restricted drivers license issued by that state, and who becomes a resident of this State may obtain a limited learners permit if the person has completed a drivers education program that meets the requirements of the Superintendent of Public Instruction. A person who qualifies for a limited learners permit under this subsection and whose parent or guardian certifies that the person has not been convicted of a moving violation in the preceding six months shall be deemed to have held a limited

learners permit in this State for each month the person held an unrestricted or restricted license in another state.

(h3) **Exception for Persons Less Than Age 18 Who Have a Federally Issued Unrestricted or Restricted License.** -- A person who is less than age 18, who has an unrestricted or restricted drivers license issued by the federal government, and who becomes a resident of this State may obtain a limited provisional license or a provisional license if the person has completed a drivers education program substantially equivalent to the drivers education program that meets the requirements of the Superintendent of Public Instruction. A person who qualifies for a limited provisional license or a provisional license under this subsection and whose parent or guardian certifies that the person has not been convicted of a moving violation in the preceding six months shall be deemed to have held a limited provisional license or a provisional license in this State for each month the person held an unrestricted or restricted license issued by the federal government.

(i) **Application.** -- An application for a permit or license authorized by this section must be signed by both the applicant and another person. That person must be:

(1) The applicant's parent or guardian;

(2) A person approved by the applicant's parent or guardian; or

(3) A person approved by the Division.

(4) With respect to minors in the legal custody of the county department of social services, any of the following:

a. A guardian ad litem or attorney advocate appointed to advocate for the minor under G.S. 7B-601.

b. The director of the county department of social services or the director's designee.

c. If no person listed in subsubdivision a. or b. of this subdivision is available, the court with continuing jurisdiction over the minor's placement under G.S. 7B-1000(b).

(j) **Duration and Fee.** -- A limited learner's permit expires on the eighteenth birthday of the permit holder. A limited provisional license expires on the eighteenth birthday of the license holder. A limited learner's permit or limited provisional license issued under this section that expires on a weekend or State holiday shall remain valid through the fifth regular State business day following the date of expiration. A full provisional license expires on the date set under G.S. 20-7(f). The fee for a limited learner's permit or a limited provisional license is twenty dollars ($ 20.00). The fee for a full provisional license is the amount set under G.S. 20-7(i).

(k) **Supervising Driver.** -- A supervising driver shall be a parent, grandparent, or guardian of the permit holder or license holder or a responsible person approved by the parent or guardian or the Division. A supervising driver shall be a licensed driver who has been licensed for at least five years. At least one supervising driver shall sign the application for a permit or license.

(*l*) **Violations.** -- It is unlawful for the holder of a limited learner's permit, a temporary permit, or a limited provisional license to drive a motor vehicle in violation of the restrictions that apply to the permit or license. Failure to comply with a restriction concerning the time of driving or the presence of a supervising driver in the vehicle constitutes operating a motor vehicle without a license. Failure to comply with the restriction regarding the use of a mobile telephone while operating a motor vehicle is an infraction punishable by a fine of twenty-five dollars ($ 25.00). Failure to comply with any other restriction, including seating and passenger limitations, is an infraction punishable by a monetary penalty as provided in G.S. 20-176. Failure to comply with the provisions of subsections (e) and (g) of this section shall not constitute negligence per se or contributory negligence by the driver or passenger in any action for the recovery of damages arising out of the operation, ownership or maintenance of a motor vehicle. Any evidence of failure to comply with the provisions of subdivisions (1), (2), (3), (4), and (5) of subsection (e) of this section shall not be admissible in any criminal or civil trial, action, or proceeding except in an action based on a violation of this section. No drivers license points or insurance surcharge shall be assessed for failure to comply with seating and occupancy limitations in subsection (e) of this section. No drivers license points or insurance surcharge shall be assessed for failure to comply with subsection (e) or (g) of this section regarding the use of a mobile telephone while operating a motor vehicle.

(m) **Insurance Status.** -- The holder of a limited learner's permit is not considered a licensed driver for the purpose of determining the inexperienced operator premium surcharge under automobile insurance policies.

(n) **Driving Eligibility Certificate.** -- A person who desires to obtain a permit or license issued under this section must have a high school diploma or its equivalent or must have a driving eligibility certificate. A driving eligibility certificate must meet the following conditions:

(1) The person who is required to sign the certificate under subdivision (4) of this subsection must show that he or she has determined that one of the following requirements is met:

a. The person is currently enrolled in school and is making progress toward obtaining a high school diploma or its equivalent.

b. A substantial hardship would be placed on the person or the person's family if the person does not receive a certificate.

c. The person cannot make progress toward obtaining a high school diploma or its equivalent.

(1a) The person who is required to sign the certificate under subdivision (4) of this subsection also must show that one of the following requirements is met:

a. The person who seeks a permit or license issued under this section is not subject to subsection (n1) of this section.

b. The person who seeks a permit or license issued under this section is subject to subsection (n1) of this section and is eligible for the certificate under that subsection.

(2) It must be on a form approved by the Division.

(3) It must be dated within 30 days of the date the person applies for a permit or license issuable under this section.

(4) It must be signed by the applicable person named below:

a. The principal, or the principal's designee, of the public school in which the person is enrolled.

b. The administrator, or the administrator's designee, of the nonpublic school in which the person is enrolled.

c. The person who provides the academic instruction in the home school in which the person is enrolled.

c1. The person who provides the academic instruction in the home in accordance with an educational program found by a court, prior to July 1, 1998, to comply with the compulsory attendance law.

d. The designee of the board of directors of the charter school in which the person is enrolled.

e. The president, or the president's designee, of the community college in which the person is enrolled.

Notwithstanding any other law, the decision concerning whether a driving eligibility certificate was properly issued or improperly denied shall be appealed only as provided under the rules adopted in accordance with G.S. 115C-12(28), 115D-5(a3), or 115C-566, whichever is applicable, and may not be appealed under this Chapter.

(n1) Lose Control; Lose License.

(1) The following definitions apply in this subsection:

a. **Applicable State entity.** -- The State Board of Education for public schools and charter schools, the State Board of Community Colleges for community colleges, or the Secretary of Administration for nonpublic schools and home schools.

b. **Certificate.** -- A driving eligibility certificate that meets the conditions of subsection (n) of this section.

c. **Disciplinary action.** -- An expulsion, a suspension for more than 10 consecutive days, or an assignment to an alternative educational setting for more than 10 consecutive days.

d. **Enumerated student conduct.** -- One of the following behaviors that results in disciplinary action:

1. The possession or sale of an alcoholic beverage or an illegal controlled substance on school property.

2. The bringing, possession, or use on school property of a weapon or firearm that resulted in disciplinary action under G.S. 115C-390.10 or that could have resulted in that disciplinary action if the conduct had occurred in a public school.

3. The physical assault on a teacher or other school personnel on school property.

e. **School.** -- A public school, charter school, community college, nonpublic school, or home school.

f. **School administrator.** -- The person who is required to sign certificates under subdivision (4) of subsection (n) of this section.

g. **School property.** -- The physical premises of the school, school buses or other vehicles under the school's control or contract and that are used to transport students, and school-sponsored curricular or extracurricular activities that occur on or off the physical premises of the school.

h. **Student.** -- A person who desires to obtain a permit or license issued under this section.

(2) Any student who was subject to disciplinary action for enumerated student conduct that occurred either after the first day of July before the school year in which the student enrolled in the eighth grade or after the student's fourteenth birthday, whichever event occurred first, is subject to this subsection.

(3) A student who is subject to this subsection is eligible for a certificate when the school administrator determines that the student has exhausted all administrative appeals connected to the disciplinary action and that one of the following conditions is met:

a. The enumerated student conduct occurred before the student reached the age of 15, and the student is now at least 16 years old.

b. The enumerated student conduct occurred after the student reached the age of 15, and it is at least one year after the date the student exhausted all administrative appeals connected to the disciplinary action.

c. The student needs the certificate in order to drive to and from school, a drug or alcohol treatment counseling program, as appropriate, or a mental health treatment program, and no other transportation is available.

(4) A student whose permit or license is denied or revoked due to ineligibility for a certificate under this subsection may otherwise be eligible for a certificate if, after six months from the date of the ineligibility, the school administrator determines that one of the following conditions is met:

a. The student has returned to school or has been placed in an alternative educational setting, and has displayed exemplary student behavior, as defined by the applicable State entity.

b. The disciplinary action was for the possession or sale of an alcoholic beverage or an illegal controlled substance on school property, and the student subsequently attended and successfully completed, as defined by the applicable State entity, a drug or alcohol treatment counseling program, as appropriate.

History.

1935, c. 52, s. 6; 1953, c. 355; 1955, c. 1187, s. 8; 1963, c. 968, ss. 2, 2A; 1965, c. 410, s. 3; c. 1171; 1967, c. 694; 1969, c. 37; 1973, c. 191, ss. 1, 2; c. 664, ss. 1, 2; 1975, c. 79; c. 716, s. 5; 1979, c. 101; c. 667, ss. 15, 16, 41; 1981 (Reg. Sess., 1982), c. 1257, s. 2; 1989 (Reg. Sess., 1990), c. 1021, s. 11; 1991, c. 689, s. 326;1993, c. 539, s. 319;1994, Ex. Sess., c. 24, s. 14(c);1997-16, s. 1;1997-443, s. 32.20;1997-507, s. 1;1998-149, ss. 2.1, 2.2, 2.3, 2.4, 2.5; 1998-212, s. 9.21(c);1999-243, ss. 1, 2; 1999-276, s. 1;1999-387, s. 4;1999-452, s. 9;2001-194, s. 1;2001-487, s. 51.5(a);2002-73, ss. 1, 2; 2002-159, s. 30;2005-276, s. 44.1(b);2006-177, ss. 2 -7; 2011-145, s. 28.37(d);2011-282, s. 15;2011-381, s. 3;2011-385, ss. 1 -3; 2011-412, s. 3.2;2015-135, s. 4.2;2015-241, s. 29.30(b)

EDITOR'S NOTE. --

Session Laws 1997-16, s. 10 provides that this act does not appropriate funds to the Division to implement this act nor does it obligate the General Assembly to appropriate funds to implement this act.

Session Laws 2011-145, s. 1.1, provides: "This act shall be known as the 'Current Operations and Capital Improvements Appropriations Act of 2011.'"

Session Laws 2011-145, s. 32.5 is a severability clause.

Session Laws 2015-241, s. 29.30(u), made the amendments to subsection (j) of this section by Session Laws 2015-241, s. 29.30(b), applicable to issuances, renewals, restorations, and requests on or after January 1, 2016.

Session Laws 2015-241, s. 1.1, provides: "This act shall be known as 'The Current Operations and Capital Improvements Appropriations Act of 2015.'"

Session Laws 2015-241, s. 33.6, is a severability clause.

Session Laws 2016-23, s. 6(a) -(c), provides: "(a) Notwithstanding State Board of Education policy, GCS-R-004, or any other provision of law, if a student enrolled in a North Carolina public school or charter school under subsection (a) of Section 5 of this act [S.L. 2016-23, s. 5(a) pertains to the impact on public school student enrollment as a result of certification of the boundary between North Carolina and South Carolina] obtains a beginner's permit in South Carolina, the student shall be eligible to participate in behind-the-wheel instruction as part of a driver education course offered by the local school administrative unit in which the student is enrolled.

"(b) Notwithstanding G.S. 20-11(b)(1), a student who (i) as a result of the boundary certification becomes a legal resident of North Carolina on the date of the certification and (ii) is enrolled in a South Carolina school district in which his or her residence was located prior to certification or in the South Carolina statewide public charter school district may meet the requirement in G.S. 20-11(b)(1) for obtaining a limited learner's permit if the student passes a course of driver education offered by the South Carolina high school in which the student is enrolled.

"(c) The Department of Transportation, Division of Motor Vehicles, in collaboration with the State Board of Education, shall develop a procedure for any North Carolina resident who is a student enrolled in a South Carolina school pursuant to the conditions described in subsection (b) of this section to satisfy the driver eligibility certificate requirements of G.S. 20-11 to obtain and continue to hold a limited or full provisional license under this section."

Session Laws 2016-23, s. 12(a), is a severability clause.

Session Laws 2020-3, s. 4.7(a) -(h), as amended by Session Laws 2020-97, ss. 3.15(a), 3.16(a), provides: "(a) Definition. -- For purposes of this section, 'credential' means any of the following issued by the Division of Motor Vehicles:

"(1) Drivers license.
"(2) Learner's permit.
"(3) Limited learner's permit.
"(4) Limited provisional license.
"(5) Full provisional license.
"(6) Commercial drivers license.
"(7) Commercial learner's permit.
"(8) Temporary driving certificate.
"(9) Special identification card.
"(10) Handicapped placard.
"(11) Vehicle registration.
"(12) Temporary vehicle registration.
"(13) Dealer license plate.
"(14) Transporter plate.
"(15) Loaner/Dealer 'LD' plate.
"(16) Vehicle inspection authorization.
"(17) Inspection station license.
"(18) Inspection mechanic license.
"(19) Transportation network company permit.
"(20) Motor vehicle dealer license.
"(21) Sales representative license.
"(22) Manufacturer license.
"(23) Distributor license.
"(24) Wholesaler license.
"(25) Driver training school license.
"(26) Driver training school instructor license.
"(27) Professional housemoving license.

"(b) Extend Validity of Credentials. -- Notwithstanding renewal, duration, or expiration provisions of G.S. 20-7, 20-11, 20-37.6, 20-37.7, 20-37.13, 20-50, 20-66, 20-79, 20-79.02, 20-79.2, 20-183.4B, 20-183.4D, 20-280.3, 20-288, 20-324, and 20-359, or any other provision of law to the contrary, the Division of Motor Vehicles shall extend for a period of five months the validity of any credential that expires on or after March 1, 2020, and before August 1, 2020. The Division shall extend for a period of five months the validity of any credential listed in subdivisions (6), (7), (9), (10), and (18) of subsection (a) of this section that expires on or after March 1, 2020, and before the date 30 days after the date the Governor (i) rescinds Executive Order No. 116 or (ii) issues another executive order lifting restrictions on Division of Motor Vehicles functions. Notwithstanding G.S. 20-37.13(h) and G.S. 20-37.13A(a), the Division of Motor Vehicles is authorized to waive the requirement that commercial drivers license and commercial learner's permit holders have a medical examination and certification, as required by federal law, consistent with any waiver of medical qualifications standards issued by the Federal Motor Carrier Safety Administration. A credential extended under this section shall expire five months from the date it otherwise expires as prescribed by law prior to this section. However, the subsequent expiration of a credential extended under this section shall occur on the date prescribed by law prior to this section without regard to the extension. The Division shall notify individuals affected by an extension granted under this section, including information on new expiration dates and how the extension affects subsequent renewal and expiration dates.

"(b1) Extension of Intrastate Medical Waivers. -- Notwithstanding the limitation on duration of waivers in G.S. 20-37.13A(b), the Division of Motor Vehicles may extend for up to five months the validity of a medical waiver issued by the Division under G.S. 20-37.13A if the waiver expires on or after March 1, 2020, and before the date 30 days after the date the Governor (i) rescinds Executive Order No. 116 or (ii) issues another executive order lifting restrictions on Division of Motor Vehicles functions, and the Division's Medical Review Unit determines the extension is appropriate.

"(c) Driving Eligibility Certificates. -- Notwithstanding G.S. 20-11(n)(3), a driving eligibility certificate dated on or after February 9, 2020, and before March 10, 2020, remains valid and may be accepted by the Division of Motor Vehicles to meet the requirements for a license or permit issued under G.S. 20-11 until 30 days after the date the Governor rescinds Executive Order No. 116 or the date the Division reopens all drivers license offices, whichever is earlier.

"(d) Waive Penalties. -- Notwithstanding any provision of law to the contrary, the Division shall waive any fines, fees, or penalties associated with failing to renew a credential during the period of time the credential is valid by extension under subsection (b) of this section.

"(e) Motor Vehicle Taxes. -- Notwithstanding any provision of law to the contrary, due dates for motor vehicle taxes that are tied to registration expiration under Article 22A of Chapter 105 of the General Statutes shall be extended to correspond with extended expiration dates under subsection (b) of this section.

"(f) Validity by Extension a Defense. -- A person may not be convicted or found responsible for any offense resulting from failure to renew a credential issued by the Division if, when tried for that offense, the person shows that the offense occurred during the period of time the credential is valid by extension under subsection (b) of this section.

"(g) Report. -- Within 30 days of the extensions made under subsection (b) of this section, the Division shall submit a report to the Joint Legislative Transportation Oversight Committee and the Fiscal Research Division detailing implementation of this section.

"(h) Effective Date. -- This section is effective retroactively to March 1, 2020, and applies to expirations occurring on or after that date."

Session Laws 2020-3, s. 5, is a severability clause.

Session Laws 2020-30, s. 1(a) -(c), provides: "(a) Notwithstanding G.S. 20-11(d)(3), the Division of Motor Vehicles shall waive the requirement that an applicant pass a road test in order to obtain a Level 2 limited provisional license if the applicant meets all other requirements to obtain the license.

"(b) In addition to all other requirements for a Level 3 full provisional license set out in G.S. 20-11, a Level 2 limited provisional license holder who receives a waiver under subsection (a) of this section must pass a road test administered by the Division in order to obtain a Level 3 full provisional license.

"(c) This section is effective when it becomes law [June 19, 2020] and applies to applications for provisional licenses submitted on or after that date. Subsection (a) of this section expires on the date the Division resumes administering road tests for Level 2 limited provisional license applicants."

Session Laws 2020-97, s. 4.5, is a severability clause.

EFFECT OF AMENDMENTS. --
Session Laws 2005-276, s. 44.1(b), effective October 1, 2005, substituted "fifteen dollars ($15.00)" for "ten dollars ($10.00)" in subsection (j).

Session Laws 2006-177, ss. 2 -7, effective December 1, 2006, and applicable to offenses committed on or after that date, added subdivisions (c)(6) and (e)(6); inserted "or a violation of G.S. 20-137.3" in the middle of subdivisions (d)(2) and (f)(2); added the last sentence in subsection (g); and, in subsection (l), added the third sentence, substituted "subsections (e) and (g)" for "subsection (e)" in the fifth sentence, inserted "of subdivisions (1), (2), (3), (4), and (5)" in the middle of the sixth sentence, and added the last sentence.

Session Laws 2011-145, s. 28.37(d), effective July 1, 2011, updated the section reference in subdivision (b)(1).

Session Laws 2011-282, s. 15, effective June 23, 2011, and applicable beginning with the 2011-2012 school year, substituted "G.S. 115C-390.10" for "G.S. 115C-391(d1)" in subdivision (n1)(1)d.2.

Session Laws 2011-385, ss. 1 through 3, as amended by Session Laws 2011-412, s. 3.2, in sub-subdivisions (e)(2)b. and (e)(2)c., inserted "directly"; and added subdivisions (d)(5) and (f)(4). For effective date and applicability, see editor's note.

Session Laws 2015-135, s. 4.2, effective October 1, 2015, added subdivision (i)(4).

Session Laws 2015-241, s. 29.30(b), effective January 1, 2016, substituted "twenty dollars ($20.00)" for "fifteen dollars ($15.00)" in the next-to-last sentence of subsection (j). For applicability, see editor's note.

CONFLICTING PRESUMPTIONS. --While this section created a presumption that plaintiff, mother of the driver, occupying the front passenger seat, had the right to control and direct the operation of the vehicle by her son, who was operating under a learner's permit, but the facts of the case also implicated a conflicting presumption, namely the rule of law that her husband as owner of the vehicle and a passenger therein the vehicle had the right to control and direct its operation unless he relinquished that right, based on plaintiff's and her husband's equal rights to control son's operation of the vehicle, person who actually exercised the right to control son's driving would bear responsibility therefor. McFetters v. McFetters, 98 N.C. App. 187, 390 S.E.2d 348, cert. denied, 327 N.C. 140, 394 S.E.2d 177 (1990).

PRESUMPTION OF CONTROL. --This section creates a presumption that the statutorily approved person occupying the front passenger seat has the right to control and direct the operation of the vehicle. Stanfield v. Tilghman ex rel. Stanfield, 117 N.C. App. 292, 450 S.E.2d 751 (1994), rev'd on other grounds, 342 N.C. 389, 464 S.E.2d 294 (1995).

While front seat passenger who was a licensed driver was presumed to have "the right to control" the vehicle, this presumption does not translate into an irrebuttable presumption "of control" so as to impute negligence or establish contributory negligence, as a matter of law, without regard for exigent circumstances or general negligence principles. Stanfield v. Tilghman, 342 N.C. 389, 464 S.E.2d 294 (1995).

Sanctions imposed under G.S. 1A-1-11 were not an abuse of discretion because the trial court found that there was absolutely no basis in the law for any negligence claim against a backseat passenger where it was not alleged that the passenger had any legal right or duty to control the operation of the motor vehicle driven by an underaged driver who was unlicensed under G.S. 20-11; further, there were insufficient allegations to establish a legal basis for liability for any vicarious liability, and plaintiffs' counsel had signed and certified the complaint as having merit. Harris v. DaimlerChrysler Corp., 180 N.C. App. 551, 638 S.E.2d 260 (2006).

STATUTORILY APPROVED PERSON MAY RECOVER DAMAGES. --The negligence of a driver, operating an automobile under a valid learner's permit pursuant to subsection (b), is not imputed to the statutorily approved person who occupies the seat next to the permittee and who has the right to control and direct the permittee's operation of the car. Therefore, the statutorily approved person is not precluded from recovering damages for personal injuries sustained as a result of the permittee's sudden negligence. Stanfield v. Tilghman, 342 N.C. 389, 464 S.E.2d 294 (1995).

IF THE PERMITTEE'S NEGLIGENT OPERATION OF A VEHICLE WAS IMPUTED, IN ALL INSTANCES AS A MATTER OF LAW TO THE SUPERVISING ADULT, such adults, including driver education instructors, would be less inclined to serve as supervisors over a permittee's practice driving, thus militating against our public policy and practice regarding drivers' education. Stanfield v. Tilghman, 342 N.C. 389, 464 S.E.2d 294 (1995).

CITED in Monk v. Cowan Transp., Inc., 121 N.C. App. 588, 468 S.E.2d 407 (1996).

LEGAL PERIODICALS. --

For 1997 legislative survey, see 20 Campbell L. Rev. 491.

OPINIONS OF THE ATTORNEY GENERAL

"LOSE CONTROL, LOSE YOUR LICENSE" LEGISLATION. --The application of G.S. 20-11(n1)(1)d.2. does not require a one-year loss of the driver's license or learner's permit for a home school student who used a weapon or firearm in a lawful manner under the supervision of his or her parent/guardian on the property of the parent/guardian. See opinion of Attorney General to R. Glen Peterson, General Counsel, N.C. Department of Administration, 2000 N.C. AG LEXIS 11 (6/5/2000).

N.C. Gen. Stat. § 20-11.1

Repealed by Session Laws 1965, c. 410, s. 4.

N.C. Gen. Stat. § 20-12

Repealed by Session Laws 1997-16, s. 6.

§ 20-12.1. Impaired supervision or instruction

(a) It is unlawful for a person to serve as a supervising driver under G.S. 20-7(*l*) or G.S.

20-11 or as an approved instructor under G.S. 20-7(m) in any of the following circumstances:

(1) While under the influence of an impairing substance.

(2) After having consumed sufficient alcohol to have, at any relevant time after the driving, an alcohol concentration of 0.08 or more.

(b) An offense under this section is an implied-consent offense under G.S. 20-16.2.

History.

1977, c. 116, ss. 1, 2; 1981, c. 412, s. 4; c. 747, s. 66; 1983, c. 435, s. 9; 1993, c. 285, s. 2;1997-16, s. 7;1997-443, s. 32.20

EDITOR'S NOTE. --

Session Laws 1997-16, s. 10 provides that this act does not appropriate funds to the Division to implement this act nor does it obligate the General Assembly to appropriate funds to implement this act.

§ 20-13. Suspension of license of provisional licensee

(a) The Division may suspend, with or without a preliminary hearing, the operator's license of a provisional licensee upon receipt of notice of the licensee's conviction of a motor vehicle moving violation, in accordance with subsection (b), if the offense was committed while the person was still a provisional licensee. As used in this section, the phrase "motor vehicle moving violation" does not include the offenses listed in the third paragraph of G.S. 20-16(c) for which no points are assessed, nor does it include equipment violations specified in Part 9 of Article 3 of this Chapter. However, if the Division revokes without a preliminary hearing and the person whose license is being revoked requests a hearing before the effective date of the revocation, the licensee retains his license unless it is revoked under some other provision of the law, until the hearing is held, the person withdraws his request, or he fails to appear at a scheduled hearing.

(b) The Division may suspend the license of a provisional licensee as follows:

(1) For the first motor vehicle moving violation, the Division may not suspend the license of the provisional licensee.

(2) For conviction of a second motor vehicle moving violation committed within 12 months of the date the first offense was committed, the Division may suspend the licensee's license for up to 30 days.

(3) For conviction of a third motor vehicle moving violation committed within 12 months of the date the first offense was committed, the Division may suspend the licensee's license for up to 90 days.

(4) For conviction of a fourth motor vehicle moving violation committed within 12 months of the date the first offense was

committed, the Division may suspend the licensee's license for up to six months.

The Division may, in lieu of suspension and with the written consent of the licensee, place the licensee on probation for a period of not more than 12 months on such terms and conditions as the Division sees fit to impose.

If the Division suspends the provisional licensee's license for at least 90 days without a preliminary hearing, the parent, guardian or other person standing in loco parentis of the provisional licensee may request a hearing to determine if the provisional licensee's license should be restored on a probationary status. The Division may wait until one-half the period of suspension has expired to hold the hearing. The Division may place the licensee on probation for up to 12 months on such terms and conditions as the Division sees fit to impose, if the licensee consents in writing to the terms and conditions of probation.

(c) In the event of conviction of two or more motor vehicle moving offenses committed on a single occasion, a licensee shall be charged, for purposes of this section, with only one moving offense, except as otherwise provided.

(d) The suspension provided for in this section is in addition to any other remedies which the Division may have against a licensee under other provisions of law; however, when the license of any person is suspended under this section and at the same time is also suspended under other provisions of law, the suspensions run concurrently.

(e) Repealed by Session Laws 1987, c. 869, s. 14, effective January 1, 1988.

History.
1963, c. 968, s. 1; 1965, c. 897; 1967, c. 295, s. 1; 1971, c. 120, ss. 1, 2; 1973, c. 439; 1975, c. 716, s. 5; 1979, c. 555, s. 1; 1983, c. 538, ss. 1, 2; 1983 (Reg. Sess., 1984), c. 1101, s. 3; 1987, c. 744, ss. 3, 4; c. 869, s. 14

WHERE THE LAW DIRECTS SUSPENSION, REVOCATION, OR NONISSUANCE OF A DRIVER'S LICENSE, the grounds are convictions for moving violations, or other statutory violations relating to highway safety, or situations where an individual's capacity to operate a motor vehicle safely are manifestly questionable. Evans v. Roberson, 69 N.C. App. 644, 317 S.E.2d 715 (1984), rev'd on other grounds and modified, 314 N.C. 315, 333 S.E.2d 228 (1985).

OPINIONS OF THE ATTORNEY GENERAL
OPERATION OF VEHICLE WITH IMPROPER TAILLIGHTS IS A MOVING VIOLATION. --See opinion of Attorney General to Mr. Henry M. Whitesides, Fourteenth Solicitorial District, 41 N.C.A.G. 211 (1971).

N.C. Gen. Stat. § 20-13.1

Repealed by Session Laws 1979, c. 555, s. 2.

§ 20-13.2. Grounds for revoking provisional license

(a) The Division must revoke the license of a person convicted of violating the provisions of G.S. 20-138.3 upon receipt of a record of the licensee's conviction.

(b) If a person is convicted of an offense involving impaired driving and the offense occurs while he is less than 21 years old, his license must be revoked under this section in addition to any other revocation required or authorized by law.

(c) If a person willfully refuses to submit to a chemical analysis pursuant to G.S. 20-16.2 while he is less than 21 years old, his license must be revoked under this section, in addition to any other revocation required or authorized by law. A revocation order entered under authority of this subsection becomes effective at the same time as a revocation order issued under G.S. 20-16.2 for the same willful refusal.

(c1) Upon receipt of notification from the proper school authority that a person no longer meets the requirements for a driving eligibility certificate under G.S. 20-11(n), the Division must expeditiously notify the person that his or her permit or license is revoked effective on the tenth calendar day after the mailing of the revocation notice. The Division must revoke the permit or license of that person on the tenth calendar day after the mailing of the revocation notice. Notwithstanding subsection (d) of this section, the length of revocation must last for the following periods:

(1) If the revocation is because of ineligibility for a driving eligibility certificate under G.S. 20-11(n)(1), then the revocation shall last until the person's eighteenth birthday.

(2) If the revocation is because of ineligibility for a driving eligibility certificate under G.S. 20-11(n1), then the revocation shall be for a period of one year.

For a person whose permit or license was revoked due to ineligibility for a driving eligibility certificate under G.S. 20-11(n)(1), the Division must restore a person's permit or license before the person's eighteenth birthday, if the person submits to the Division one of the following:

(1) A high school diploma or its equivalent.

(2) A driving eligibility certificate as required under G.S. 20-11(n).

If the Division restores a permit or license that was revoked due to ineligibility for a driving eligibility certificate under G.S. 20-11(n)(1), any record of revocation or suspension shall be expunged by the Division from the person's driving record. The Division shall

Chapter 20

not expunge a suspension or revocation record if a person has had a prior expunction from the person's driving record for any reason.

For a person whose permit or license was revoked due to ineligibility for a driving eligibility certificate under G.S. 20-11(n1), the Division shall restore a person's permit or license before the end of the revocation period, if the person submits to the Division a driving eligibility certificate as required under G.S. 20-11(n).

Notwithstanding any other law, the decision concerning whether a driving eligibility certificate was properly issued or improperly denied shall be appealed only as provided under the rules adopted in accordance with G.S. 115C-12(28), 115D-5(a3), or 115C-566, whichever is applicable, and may not be appealed under this Chapter.

(c2) The Division must revoke the permit or license of a person under the age of 18 upon receiving a record of the person's conviction for malicious use of an explosive or incendiary device to damage property (G.S. 14-49(b) and (b1)); conspiracy to injure or damage by use of an explosive or incendiary device (G.S. 14-50); making a false report concerning a destructive device in a public building (G.S. 14-69.1(c)); perpetrating a hoax concerning a destructive device in a public building (G.S. 14-69.2(c)); possessing or carrying a dynamite cartridge, bomb, grenade, mine, or powerful explosive on educational property (G.S. 14-269.2(b1)); or causing, encouraging, or aiding a minor to possess or carry a dynamite cartridge, bomb, grenade, mine, or powerful explosive on educational property (G.S. 14-269.2(c1)).

(d) The length of revocation under this section shall be one year. Revocations under this section run concurrently with any other revocations.

(e) Before the Division restores a driver's license that has been suspended or revoked under any provision of this Article, other than G.S. 20-24.1, the person seeking to have his driver's license restored shall submit to the Division proof that he has notified his insurance agent or company of his seeking the restoration and that he is financially responsible. Proof of financial responsibility shall be in one of the following forms:

(1) A written certificate or electronically-transmitted facsimile thereof from any insurance carrier duly authorized to do business in this State certifying that there is in effect a nonfleet private passenger motor vehicle liability policy for the benefit of the person required to furnish proof of financial responsibility. The certificate or facsimile

shall state the effective date and expiration date of the nonfleet private passenger motor vehicle liability policy and shall state the date that the certificate or facsimile is issued. The certificate or facsimile shall remain effective proof of financial responsibility for a period of 30 consecutive days following the date the certificate or facsimile is issued but shall not in and of itself constitute a binder or policy of insurance or

(2) A binder for or policy of nonfleet private passenger motor vehicle liability insurance under which the applicant is insured, provided that the binder or policy states the effective date and expiration date of the nonfleet private passenger motor vehicle liability policy.

The preceding provisions of this subsection do not apply to applicants who do not own currently registered motor vehicles and who do not operate nonfleet private passenger motor vehicles that are owned by other persons and that are not insured under commercial motor vehicle liability insurance policies. In such cases, the applicant shall sign a written certificate to that effect. Such certificate shall be furnished by the Division and may be incorporated into the restoration application form. Any material misrepresentation made by such person on such certificate shall be grounds for suspension of that person's license for a period of 90 days.

For the purposes of this subsection, the term "nonfleet private passenger motor vehicle" has the definition ascribed to it in Article 40 of General Statute Chapter 58.

The Commissioner may require that certificates required by this subsection be on a form approved by the Commissioner. The financial responsibility required by this subsection shall be kept in effect for not less than three years after the date that the license is restored. Failure to maintain financial responsibility as required by this subsection shall be grounds for suspending the restored driver's license for a period of thirty (30) days. Nothing in this subsection precludes any person from showing proof of financial responsibility in any other manner authorized by Articles 9A and 13 of this Chapter.

History.
1983, c. 435, s. 33; 1987, c. 869, s. 12; 1989, c. 436, s. 3;1993, c. 285, s. 8;1995, c. 506, ss. 3, 4, 5; 1997-507, s. 2;1999-243, s. 3;1999-257, s. 4;2013-133, s. 1

EFFECT OF AMENDMENTS. --
Session Laws 2013-133, s. 1, effective December 1, 2013, added the last two sentences in the second paragraph of subsection (c1). For applicability, see Editor's note.

LEGAL PERIODICALS. --

For survey on new penalties for criminal behavior in schools, see 22 Campbell L. Rev. 253 (2000).

OPINIONS OF THE ATTORNEY GENERAL

REGARDING THE APPLICATION OF THIS SECTION TO THREE SEPARATE GROUPS OF DRIVERS BASED UPON WHEN DRIVING PRIVILEGES WERE RECEIVED, see opinion of Attorney General to Michael E. Ward, State Superintendent of Public Instruction, N.C.General Assembly, 1999 N.C.A.G. 11 (10/14/99).

§ 20-13.3. Immediate civil license revocation for provisional licensees charged with certain offenses

(a) **Definitions.** -- As used in this section, the following words and phrases have the following meanings:

(1) **Clerk.** -- As defined in G.S. 15A-101(2).

(2) **Criminal moving violation.** -- A violation of Part 9 or 10 of Article 3 of this Chapter which is punishable as a misdemeanor or a felony offense. This term does not include the offenses listed in the third paragraph of G.S. 20-16(c) for which no points are assessed, nor does it include equipment violations specified in Part 9 of Article 3 of this Chapter.

(3) **Judicial official.** -- As defined in G.S. 15A-101(5).

(4) **Provisional licensee.** -- A person under the age of 18 who has a limited learner's permit, a limited provisional license, or a full provisional license issued pursuant to G.S. 20-11.

(5) **Revocation report.** -- A sworn statement by a law enforcement officer containing facts indicating that the conditions of subsection (b) of this section have been met.

(b) **Revocations for Provisional Licensees Charged With Criminal Moving Violation.** -- A provisional licensee's permit or license is subject to revocation under this section if a law enforcement officer has reasonable grounds to believe that the provisional licensee has committed a criminal moving violation, the provisional licensee is charged with that offense, and the provisional licensee is not subject to a civil revocation pursuant to G.S. 20-16.5.

(c) **Duty of Law Enforcement Officers to Notify Provisional Licensee and Report to Judicial Officials.** -- If a provisional licensee's permit or license is subject to revocation under this section, the law enforcement officer must execute a revocation report. It is the specific duty of the law enforcement officer to make sure that the report is expeditiously filed with a judicial official as required by this section. If no initial appearance is required on the underlying criminal moving violation at the time of the issuance of the charge, the law enforcement officer must verbally notify the provisional licensee that the provisional licensee's permit or license is subject to revocation pursuant to this section and must provide the provisional licensee with a written form containing notice of the process for revocation and hearing under this section.

(c1) **Which Judicial Official Must Receive Report.** -- The judicial official with whom the revocation report must be filed is:

(1) The judicial official conducting the initial appearance on the underlying criminal moving violation.

(2) The clerk of superior court in the county in which the underlying criminal charge has been brought if no initial appearance is required.

(d) **Procedure If Report Filed With Judicial Official When Provisional Licensee Is Present.** -- If an initial appearance is required, the law enforcement officer must file the revocation report with the judicial official conducting the initial appearance on the underlying criminal moving violation. If a properly executed revocation report concerning a provisional licensee is filed with a judicial official when the person is present before that official, the judicial official shall, after completing any other proceedings involving the provisional licensee, determine whether there is probable cause to believe that the conditions of subsection (b) of this section have been met. If the judicial official determines there is such probable cause, the judicial official shall enter an order revoking the provisional licensee's permit or license. In addition to setting it out in the order, the judicial official shall personally inform the provisional licensee of the right to a hearing as specified in subsection (d2) of this section and that the provisional licensee's permit or license remains revoked pending the hearing. The period of revocation is for 30 days and begins at the time the revocation order is issued and continues for 30 additional calendar days. The judicial official shall give the provisional licensee a copy of the revocation order, which shall include the beginning date of the revocation and shall clearly state the final day of the revocation period and the date on which the provisional licensee's permit or license will again become valid. The provisional licensee shall not be required to surrender the provisional licensee's permit or license; however, the provisional licensee shall not be authorized to drive at any time or for any purpose during the period of revocation.

(d1) **Procedure If Report Filed With Clerk of Court When Provisional Licensee Not Present.** -- When a clerk receives a properly executed report under subdivision (2) of subsection (c1) of this section and the provisional licensee named in the revocation report is not present before the clerk, the clerk shall determine whether there is probable cause to believe that the conditions of subsection (b) of this section have been met. If the clerk determines there is such probable cause, the clerk shall mail to the provisional licensee a revocation order by first-class mail. The order shall inform the provisional licensee that the period of revocation is for 30 days, that the revocation becomes effective on the fourth day after the order is deposited in the United States mail and continues for 30 additional calendar days, of the right to a hearing as specified in subsection (d2) of this section, and that the revocation remains in effect pending the hearing. The provisional licensee shall not be required to surrender the provisional licensee's permit or license; however, the provisional licensee shall not be authorized to drive at any time or for any purpose during the period of revocation.

(d2) **Hearing Before Magistrate or Judge If Provisional Licensee Contests Validity of Revocation.** -- A provisional licensee whose permit or license is revoked under this section may request in writing a hearing to contest the validity of the revocation. The request may be made at the time of the person's initial appearance, or within 10 days of the effective date of the revocation to the clerk or a magistrate designated by the clerk, and may specifically request that the hearing be conducted by a district court judge. The Administrative Office of the Courts must develop a hearing request form for any provisional licensee requesting a hearing. Unless a district court judge is requested, the hearing must be conducted within the county by a magistrate assigned by the chief district court judge to conduct such hearings. If the provisional licensee requests that a district court judge hold the hearing, the hearing must be conducted within the district court district as defined in G.S. 7A-133 by a district court judge assigned to conduct such hearings. The revocation remains in effect pending the hearing, but the hearing must be held within three working days following the request if the hearing is before a magistrate or within ten working days if the hearing is before a district court judge. The request for the hearing must specify the grounds upon which the validity of the revocation is challenged, and the hearing must be limited to the grounds specified in the request. A witness may submit his evidence by affidavit unless he is subpoenaed to appear. Any person who appears and testifies is subject to questioning by the judicial official conducting the hearing, and the judicial official may adjourn the hearing to seek additional evidence if the judicial official is not satisfied with the accuracy or completeness of evidence. The provisional licensee contesting the validity of the revocation may, but is not required to, testify in his own behalf. Unless contested by the person requesting the hearing, the judicial official may accept as true any matter stated in the revocation report. If any relevant condition under subsection (b) of this section is contested, the judicial official must find by the greater weight of the evidence that the condition was met in order to sustain the revocation. At the conclusion of the hearing, the judicial official must enter an order sustaining or rescinding the revocation. The judicial official's findings are without prejudice to the provisional licensee contesting the revocation and to any other potential party as to any other proceedings, civil or criminal, that may involve facts bearing upon the conditions in subsection (b) of this section considered by the judicial official. The decision of the judicial official is final and may not be appealed in the General Court of Justice. If the hearing is not held and completed within three working days of the written request for a hearing before a magistrate or within ten working days of the written request for a hearing before a district court judge, the judicial official must enter an order rescinding the revocation, unless the provisional licensee contesting the revocation contributed to the delay in completing the hearing. If the provisional licensee requesting the hearing fails to appear at the hearing or any rescheduling thereof after having been properly notified, the provisional licensee forfeits the right to a hearing.

(e) **Report to Division.** -- The clerk shall notify the Division of the issuance of a revocation order pursuant to this section within two business days of the issuance of the revocation order. The notification shall identify the person whose provisional license has been revoked and specify the beginning and end date of the revocation period.

(f) **Effect of Revocations.** -- A revocation under this section revokes a provisional licensee's privilege to drive in North Carolina. Revocations under this section are independent of and run concurrently with any other revocations, except for a revocation pursuant to G.S. 20-16.5. Any civil revocation issued pursuant to G.S. 20-16.5 for the same underlying conduct as a revocation under this section shall have the effect of terminating a revocation pursuant to this section. No court imposing a period of revocation following conviction for an offense involving impaired driving may give credit for any period of revocation imposed under this section. A person whose license is revoked pursuant to this section is not eligible to receive a limited driving privilege.

(g) **Designation of Proceedings.** -- Proceedings under this section are civil actions and must be identified by the caption "In the Matter of   " and filed as directed by the Administrative Office of the Courts.

(h) No drivers license points or insurance surcharge shall be assessed for a revocation pursuant to this section. Possession of a drivers license revoked pursuant to this section shall not be a violation of G.S. 20-30.

(i) The Administrative Office of the Courts shall adopt forms to implement this section.

History.
2011-385, s. 4;2011-412, s. 3.2;2012-168, s. 3

EFFECT OF AMENDMENTS. --

Session Laws 2012-168, s. 3, effective October 1, 2012, added subsections (c1), (d1), (d2) and (i); in subsection (c), inserted "Notify Provisional Licensee and" in the subsection heading, deleted "and must take the provisional licensee before a judicial official for an initial appearance" at the end of the first sentence, and added the last sentence; in subsection (d), rewrote the subsection heading, added "If an initial appearance is required" at the beginning of the first sentence, and added the fourth sentence; and added the last sentence in subsection (h). For applicability, see Editor's note.

§ 20-14. Duplicate licenses

A person may obtain a duplicate of a license issued by the Division by paying a fee of thirteen dollars ($ 13.00) and giving the Division satisfactory proof that any of the following has occurred:

(1) The person's license has been lost or destroyed.

(2) It is necessary to change the name or address on the license.

(3) Because of age, the person is entitled to a license with a different color photographic background or a different color border.

(4) The Division revoked the person's license, the revocation period has expired, and the period for which the license was issued has not expired.

History.
1935, c. 52, s. 9; 1943, c. 649, s. 2; 1969, c. 783, s. 2; 1975, c. 716, s. 5; 1979, c. 667, s. 41; 1981, c. 690, s. 11; 1983, c. 443, s. 3; 1991, c. 682, s. 2;c. 689, s. 327;1991 (Reg. Sess., 1992), c. 1007, s. 28; 1995 (Reg. Sess., 1996), c. 675, s. 2; 2004-189, s. 5(b);2005-276, s. 44.1(c);2015-241, s. 29.30(c)

EDITOR'S NOTE. --

Session Laws 2004-189, s. 5(c), as amended by Session Laws 2005-276, s. 44.1(q), provides: "The Division of Motor Vehicles shall retain a portion of five cents ($0.05) collected for the issuance of each drivers license and duplicate license to offset the actual cost of developing and maintaining the online Organ Donor Internet site established pursuant to Section 1 of this act. The remainder of the five cents ($0.05) shall be credited to the License to Give Trust Fund established under G.S. 20-7.4 and shall be used for the purposes authorized under G.S. 20-7.4 and G.S. 20-7.5."

Session Laws 2015-241, s. 29.30(u), made the amendment to this section by Session Laws 2015-241,

s. 29.30(c), applicable to issuances, renewals, restorations, and requests on or after January 1, 2016.

Session Laws 2015-241, s. 1.1, provides: "This act shall be known as 'The Current Operations and Capital Improvements Appropriations Act of 2015.'"

Session Laws 2015-241, s. 33.6, is a severability clause.

Session Laws 2018-134, 3rd Ex. Sess., s. 1.1, provides: "This act shall be known as 'The Hurricane Florence Emergency Response Act.'" Session Laws 2018-134, 3rd Ex. Sess., s. 5.5(a)-(c), provides: "(a) Notwithstanding G.S. 20-14, 20-37.7, 20-85, and 20-88.03, the Governor may waive any fees assessed by the Division of Motor Vehicles under those sections for the following:

"(1) A duplicate drivers license, duplicate commercial drivers license, or duplicate special identification card.

"(2) A special identification card issued to a person for the first time.

"(3) An application for a duplicate or corrected certificate of title.

"(4) A replacement registration plate.

"(5) An application for a duplicate registration card.

"(6) Late payment of a motor vehicle registration renewal fee.

"(b) The waiver authorized under subsection (a) of this section only applies to residents of counties impacted by Hurricane Florence, as determined by the Governor. A resident is allowed a refund of any fee assessed and collected by the Division of Motor Vehicles and waived pursuant to this section. The Division shall post notice of the availability of a refund on its Web site.

"(c) This section is effective when it becomes law and applies to fees assessed or collected on or after September 13, 2018. This section expires December 31, 2018."

EFFECT OF AMENDMENTS. --

Session Laws 2004-189, s. 5(b), effective November 1, 2004, substituted "ten dollars and five cents ($10.05)" for "ten dollars ($10.00)."

Session Laws 2005-276, s. 44.1(c), effective October 1, 2005, substituted "ten dollars ($10.00)" for "ten dollars and five cents ($10.05)" in the introductory paragraph.

Session Laws 2015-241, s. 29.30(c), effective January 1, 2016, substituted "thirteen dollars ($13.00)" for "ten dollars ($10.00)"in the introductory language. For applicability, see editor's note.

CITED in State v. Teasley, 9 N.C. App. 477, 176 S.E.2d 838 (1970).

§ 20-15. Authority of Division to cancel license or endorsement

(a) The Division shall have authority to cancel any driver's license upon determining any of the following:

(1) The licensee was not entitled to the issuance of the license under this Chapter.

(2) The licensee failed to give the required or correct information on the license application or committed fraud in making the application.

(3) The licensee is no longer authorized under federal law to be legally present in the United States.

(4) The licensee suffers from a physical or mental disability or disease that affects his or her ability to safely operate a motor vehicle, as determined by the applicable State or federal law, rule, or regulation.

(5) The licensee has failed to submit the certificate required under G.S. 20-7(e) and G.S. 20-9(g).

(b) Upon such cancellation, the licensee must surrender the license so cancelled to the Division.

(c) Any person whose license is canceled under this section for failure to give the required or correct information, or for committing fraud, in an application for a commercial drivers license shall be prohibited from reapplying for a commercial drivers license for a period of 60 days from the date of cancellation.

(d) The Division shall have authority to revoke an H endorsement of a commercial drivers license holder if the person with the endorsement is determined by the federal Transportation Security Administration to constitute a security threat, as specified in 49 C.F.R. § 1572.5(d)(4).

History.
1935, c. 52, s. 10; 1943, c. 649, s. 3; 1975, c. 716, s. 5; 1979, c. 667, s. 41; 2005-349, s. 5;2007-56, s. 5;2016-94, s. 35.20(e)

EDITOR'S NOTE. --
Session Laws 2016-94, s. 35.20(h) made subdivisions (a)(4) and (5), as added by Session Laws 2016-94, s. 35.20(e), applicable to drivers licenses issued or renewed on or after July 1, 2016 and hearings requested on or after July 1, 2016.

Session Laws 2016-94, s. 1.2, provides: "This act shall be known as the 'Current Operations and Capital Improvements Appropriations Act of 2016.'"

Session Laws 2016-94, s. 39.4, provides: "Except for statutory changes or other provisions that clearly indicate an intention to have effects beyond the 2016-2017 fiscal year, the textual provisions of this act apply only to funds appropriated for, and activities occurring during, the 2016-2017 fiscal year."

Session Laws 2016-94, s. 39.7, is a severability clause.

EFFECT OF AMENDMENTS. --
Session Laws 2005-349, s. 5, effective September 30, 2005, added "or endorsement" to the section heading and added subsections (c) and (d).

Session Laws 2007-56, s. 5, effective May 23, 2007, and applicable to drivers licenses issued or renewed on or after that date, rewrote subsection (a).

Session Laws 2016-94, s. 35.20(e), effective July 1, 2016, added subdivisions (a)(4) and (a)(5). ee editor's note for applicability.

CITED in Parks v. Howland, 4 N.C. App. 197, 166 S.E.2d 701 (1969).

§ 20-15.1. Revocations when licensing privileges forfeited

The Division shall revoke the license of a person whose licensing privileges have been forfeited under G.S. 15A-1331.1, 50-13.12, and 110-142.2. If a revocation period set by this Chapter is longer than the revocation period resulting from the forfeiture of licensing privileges, the revocation period in this Chapter applies.

History.
1994, Ex. Sess., c. 20, s. 2;1995, c. 538, s. 2(a);2012-194, s. 45(b)

EFFECT OF AMENDMENTS. --
Session Laws 2012-194, s. 45(b), effective July 17, 2012, substituted "G.S. 15A-1331.1" for "G.S. 15A-1331A".

§ 20-16. Authority of Division to suspend license

(a) The Division shall have authority to suspend the license of any operator with or without a preliminary hearing upon a showing by its records or other satisfactory evidence that the licensee:

(1) through (4) Repealed by Session Laws 1979, c. 36;

(5) Has, under the provisions of subsection (c) of this section, within a three-year period, accumulated 12 or more points, or eight or more points in the three-year period immediately following the reinstatement of a license which has been suspended or revoked because of a conviction for one or more traffic offenses;

(6) Has made or permitted an unlawful or fraudulent use of such license or a learner's permit, or has displayed or represented as his own, a license or learner's permit not issued to him;

(7) Has committed an offense in another state, which if committed in this State would be grounds for suspension or revocation;

(8) Has been convicted of illegal transportation of alcoholic beverages;

(8a) Has been convicted of impaired instruction under G.S. 20-12.1;

(8b) Has violated on a military installation a regulation of that installation prohibiting conduct substantially similar to conduct that constitutes impaired driving under G.S. 20-138.1 and, as a result of that violation, has had his privilege to drive on that installation revoked or suspended after an administrative hearing authorized by the commanding officer of the installation and that commanding officer has general court martial jurisdiction;

(9) Has, within a period of 12 months, been convicted of (i) two or more charges of speeding in excess of 55 and not more than 80 miles per hour, (ii) one or more charges of reckless driving and one or more charges of speeding in excess of 55 and not more than 80 miles per hour, or (iii) one or more charges of aggressive driving and one or more charges of speeding in excess of 55 and not more than 80 miles per hour;

(10) Has been convicted of operating a motor vehicle at a speed in excess of 75 miles per hour on a public road or highway where the maximum speed is less than 70 miles per hour;

(10a) Has been convicted of operating a motor vehicle at a speed in excess of 80 miles per hour on a public highway where the maximum speed is 70 miles per hour; or

(11) Has been sentenced by a court of record and all or a part of the sentence has been suspended and a condition of suspension of the sentence is that the operator not operate a motor vehicle for a period of time.

However, if the Division revokes without a preliminary hearing and the person whose license is being revoked requests a hearing before the effective date of the revocation, the licensee retains his license unless it is revoked under some other provision of the law, until the hearing is held, the person withdraws his request, or he fails to appear at a scheduled hearing.

(b) Pending an appeal from a conviction of any violation of the motor vehicle laws of this State, no driver's license shall be suspended by the Division of Motor Vehicles because of such conviction or because of evidence of the commission of the offense for which the conviction has been had.

(c) The Division shall maintain a record of convictions of every person licensed or required to be licensed under the provisions of this Article as an operator and shall enter therein records of all convictions of such persons for any violation of the motor vehicle laws of this State and shall assign to the record of such person, as of the date of commission of the offense, a number of points for every such conviction in accordance with the following schedule of convictions and points, except that points shall not be assessed for convictions resulting in suspensions or revocations under other provisions of laws: Further, any points heretofore charged for violation of the motor vehicle inspection laws shall not be considered by the Division of Motor Vehicles as a basis for suspension or revocation of driver's license:

Schedule of Point Values

Passing stopped school bus 5
Aggressive driving.......................................5
Reckless driving...4
Hit and run, property damage only.............. 4
Following too close.......................................4
Driving on wrong side of road 4
Illegal passing...4
Failure to yield right-of-way to pedestrian pursuant to G.S. 20-158(b)(2)b......................4
Failure to yield right-of-way to bicycle, motor scooter, or motorcycle..........................4
Running through stop sign 3
Speeding in excess of 55 miles per hour.......3
Failing to yield right-of-way.........................3
Running through red light............................3
No driver's license or license expired more than one year 3
Failure to stop for siren...............................3
Driving through safety zone 3
No liability insurance...................................3
Failure to report accident where such report is required..3
Speeding in a school zone in excess of the posted school zone speed limit.....................3
Failure to properly restrain a child in a restraint or seat belt..2
All other moving violations........................... 2
Littering pursuant to G.S. 14-399 when the littering involves the use of a motor vehicle 1

Schedule of Point Values for
Violations While Operating a
Commercial Motor Vehicle

Passing stopped school bus 8
Rail-highway crossing violation.................... 6
Careless and reckless driving in violation of G.S. 20-140(f...6
Speeding in violation of G.S. 20-141(j3).........6
Aggressive driving.......................................6
Reckless driving...5
Hit and run, property damage only..............5
Following too close.......................................5
Driving on wrong side of road......................5
Illegal passing...5
Failure to yield right-of-way to pedestrian pursuant to G.S. 20-158(b)(2)b.....................5
Failure to yield right-of-way to bicycle, motor scooter, or motorcycle..........................5
Running through stop sign 4
Speeding in excess of 55 miles per hour.......4
Failing to yield right-of-way.........................4
Running through red light............................4
No driver's license or license expired more than one year 4
Failure to stop for siren...............................4
Driving through safety zone 4
No liability insurance...................................4
Failure to report accident where such report is required...4

Speeding in a school zone in excess of the posted school zone speed limit 4
Possessing alcoholic beverages in the passenger area of a commercial motor vehicle 4
All other moving violations 3
Littering pursuant to G.S. 14-399 when the littering involves the use of a motor vehicle 1

The above provisions of this subsection shall only apply to violations and convictions which take place within the State of North Carolina. The Schedule of Point Values for Violations While Operating a Commercial Motor Vehicle shall not apply to any commercial motor vehicle known as an "aerial lift truck" having a hydraulic arm and bucket station, and to any commercial motor vehicle known as a "line truck" having a hydraulic lift for cable, if the vehicle is owned, operated by or under contract to a public utility, electric or telephone membership corporation or municipality and used in connection with installation, restoration or maintenance of utility services.

No points shall be assessed for conviction of the following offenses:

Overloads
Over length
Over width
Over height
Illegal parking
Carrying concealed weapon
Improper plates
Improper registration
Improper muffler
Improper display of license plates or dealers' tags
Unlawful display of emblems and insignia
Failure to display current inspection certificate.

In case of the conviction of a licensee of two or more traffic offenses committed on a single occasion, such licensee shall be assessed points for one offense only and if the offenses involved have a different point value, such licensee shall be assessed for the offense having the greater point value.

Upon the restoration of the license or driving privilege of such person whose license or driving privilege has been suspended or revoked because of conviction for a traffic offense, any points that might previously have been accumulated in the driver's record shall be cancelled.

Whenever any licensee accumulates as many as seven points or accumulates as many as four points during a three-year period immediately following reinstatement of his license after a period of suspension or revocation, the Division may request the licensee to attend a conference regarding such licensee's driving record. The Division may also afford any licensee who has accumulated as many as seven points or any licensee who has accumulated as many as four points within a three-year period immediately

following reinstatement of his license after a period of suspension or revocation an opportunity to attend a driver improvement clinic operated by the Division and, upon the successful completion of the course taken at the clinic, three points shall be deducted from the licensee's conviction record; provided, that only one deduction of points shall be made on behalf of any licensee within any five-year period.

When a license is suspended under the point system provided for herein, the first such suspension shall be for not more than 60 days; the second such suspension shall not exceed six months and any subsequent suspension shall not exceed one year.

Whenever the driver's license of any person is subject to suspension under this subsection and at the same time also subject to suspension or revocation under other provisions of laws, such suspensions or revocations shall run concurrently.

In the discretion of the Division, a period of probation not to exceed one year may be substituted for suspension or for any unexpired period of suspension under subsections (a)(1) through (a)(10a) of this section. Any violation of probation during the probation period shall result in a suspension for the unexpired remainder of the suspension period. Any accumulation of three or more points under this subsection during a period of probation shall constitute a violation of the condition of probation.

(d) Upon suspending the license of any person as authorized in this section, the Division shall immediately notify the licensee in writing and upon his request shall afford him an opportunity for a hearing, not to exceed 60 days after receipt of the request, unless a preliminary hearing was held before his license was suspended. Upon such hearing the duly authorized agents of the Division may administer oaths and may issue subpoenas for the attendance of witnesses and the production of relevant books and papers and may require a reexamination of the licensee. Upon such hearing the Division shall either rescind its order of suspension, or good cause appearing therefor, may extend the suspension of such license. Provided further upon such hearing, preliminary or otherwise, involving subsections (a)(1) through (a) (10a) of this section, the Division may for good cause appearing in its discretion substitute a period of probation not to exceed one year for the suspension or for any unexpired period of suspension. Probation shall mean any written agreement between the suspended driver and a duly authorized representative of the Division and such period of probation shall not exceed one year, and any violation of the probation agreement during the probation period shall result in a suspension for the unexpired remainder of the suspension period. The authorized agents of the Division shall have the same powers in connection with a preliminary hearing prior to suspension as this subsection provided in connection with hearings held after suspension. These agents shall also have the authority to take possession of a surrendered license on behalf of the Division if the suspension is upheld and the licensee requests that the suspension begin immediately.

(e) The Division may conduct driver improvement clinics for the benefit of those who have been convicted of one or more violations of this Chapter. Each driver attending a driver improvement clinic shall pay a fee of sixty-five dollars ($ 65.00).

(e1) Notwithstanding any other provision of this Chapter, if the Division suspends the license of an operator pursuant to subdivisions (a)(9), (a)(10), or (a)(10a) of this section, upon the first suspension only, a district court judge may allow the licensee a limited driving privilege or license for a period not to exceed 12 months, provided he has not been convicted of any other motor vehicle moving violation within the previous 12 months. The limited driving privilege shall be issued in the same manner and under the terms and conditions prescribed in G.S. 20-16.1(b)(1), (2), (3), (4), and (5).

(e2) If the Division revokes a person's drivers license pursuant to G.S. 20-17(a)(16), a judge may allow the licensee a limited driving privilege for a period not to exceed the period of revocation. The limited driving privilege shall be issued in the same manner and under the terms and conditions prescribed in G.S. 20-16.1(b)(1), (2), (3), (4), (5), and (g).

History.

1935, c. 52, s. 11; 1947, c. 893, ss. 1, 2; c. 1067, s. 13; 1949, c. 373, ss. 1, 2; c. 1032, s. 2; 1953, c. 450; 1955, c. 1152, s. 15; c. 1187, ss. 9-12; 1957, c. 499, s. 1; 1959, c. 1242, ss. 1-2; 1961, c. 460, ss. 1, 2(a); 1963, c. 1115; 1965, c. 130; 1967, c. 16; 1971, c. 234, ss. 1, 2; c. 793, ss. 1, 2; c. 1198, ss. 1, 2; 1973, c. 17, ss. 1, 2; 1975, c. 716, s. 5; 1977, c. 902, s. 1; 1979, c. 36; c. 667, ss. 18, 41; 1981, c. 412, s. 4; c. 747, ss. 33, 66; 1981 (Reg. Sess., 1982), c. 1256; 1983, c. 435, s. 10; c. 538, ss. 3-5; c. 798; 1983 (Reg. Sess., 1984), c. 1101, s. 4; 1987, c. 744, ss. 1, 2; 1987 (Reg. Sess., 1988), c. 1037, s. 75; 1989, c. 784, s. 9;1991, c. 682, s. 3;1999-330, s. 7;1999-452, s. 10;2000-109, s. 7(d);2000-117, s. 2;2000-155, s. 10;2001-352, s. 2;2004-172, s. 3;2004-193, ss. 2, 3; 2005-276, s. 44.1(d);2015-241, s. 29.30(d)

EDITOR'S NOTE. --

A reference to subdivisions (a)(1) through (a)(10a) of this section appears in the last paragraph of subsection (c) and in subsection (d). Subdivisions (a)(1) through (a)(4) were repealed by Session Laws 1979, c. 36.

Session Laws 2015-241, s. 29.30(u), made the amendment to subsection (e) of this section by Session Laws 2015-241, s. 29.30(d), applicable to issuances, renewals, restorations, and requests on or after January 1, 2016.

Session Laws 2015-241, s. 1.1, provides: "This act shall be known as 'The Current Operations and Capital Improvements Appropriations Act of 2015.'"

Session Laws 2015-241, s. 33.6, is a severability clause.

EFFECT OF AMENDMENTS. --

Session Laws 2004-172, s. 3, effective December 1, 2004, in subsection (c), inserted "Failure to yield right-of-way to pedestrian pursuant to G.S. 20-158(b)(2)b . . . 4" and "Failure to yield right-of-way to bicycle, motor scooter, or motorcycle.. 4" preceding "Running through stop sign.. 3" under "Schedule of Point Values," inserted "Failure to yield right-of-way to pedestrian pursuant to G.S. 20-158(b)(2)b . . . 5" and "Failure to yield right-of-way to bicycle, motor scooter, or motorcycle.. 5" preceding "Running through stop sign" under "Schedule of Point Values for Violations While Operating a Commercial Motor Vehicle."

Session Laws 2004-193, ss. 2 and 3, effective December 1, 2004, in subdivision (a)(9), inserted "(i)" preceding "two or more," substituted "hour, (ii)" for "hour, or of," and added ",or (iii) one or more charges of aggressive driving and one or more charges of speeding in excess of 55 and not more than 80 miles per hour" at the end of the sentence; in subsection (c), inserted "Aggressive driving.. 5" in the "Schedule of Point Values," and inserted "Aggressive driving.. 6" in the "Schedule of Point Values for Violations While Operating a Commercial Motor Vehicle."

Session Laws 2005-276, s. 44.1(d), effective October 1, 2005, substituted "fifty dollars ($50.00)" for "twenty-five dollars ($25.00)" in subsection (e).

Session Laws 2015-241, s. 29.30(d), effective January 1, 2016, substituted "sixty-five dollars ($65.00)" for "fifty dollars ($50.00)" in subsection (e). For applicability, see editor's note.

I. IN GENERAL.

OPERATION OF MOTOR VEHICLE ON HIGHWAY IS A PERSONAL PRIVILEGE. --A license to operate motor vehicles on the public highways of North Carolina is a personal privilege and property right which may not be denied a citizen of this State who is qualified therefor under its statutes. In re Donnelly, 260 N.C. 375, 132 S.E.2d 904 (1963).

ALBEIT A CONDITIONAL ONE. --The right of a citizen to travel upon the public highways is a common right, but the exercise of that right may be regulated or controlled in the interest of public safety under the police power of the State. The operation of a motor vehicle on such highways is not a natural right. It is a conditional privilege, which may be suspended or revoked under the police power. Honeycutt v. Scheidt, 254 N.C. 607, 119 S.E.2d 777 (1961).

LICENSEE MAY NOT BE DEPRIVED OF SUCH PRIVILEGE EXCEPT AS PROVIDED BY STATUTES. --A license to operate a motor vehicle may be suspended or revoked only in accordance with statutory provisions as they are written and construed in this jurisdiction. In re Donnelly, 260 N.C. 375, 132 S.E.2d 904 (1963).

A license to operate a motor vehicle is a privilege in the nature of a right of which the licensee may not be

Chapter 20

deprived save in the manner and upon the conditions prescribed by statute. Gibson v. Scheidt, 259 N.C. 339, 130 S.E.2d 679 (1963).

POWER TO ISSUE, SUSPEND OR REVOKE A DRIVER'S LICENSE IS VESTED EXCLUSIVELY IN THE DIVISION of Motor Vehicles, subject to review by the superior court and, upon appeal, by the appellate division. Smith v. Walsh, 34 N.C. App. 287, 238 S.E.2d 157 (1977).

Power to suspend or revoke a driver's license is exclusively in the Department (now Division) of Motor Vehicles, subject to review by the superior court. State v. Warren, 230 N.C. 299, 52 S.E.2d 879 (1949).

NO DISCRETIONARY POWER IS CONFERRED ON SUPERIOR COURT. --Under subdivision (a)(10) of this section and G.S. 20-19(b), the discretionary authority to suspend petitioner's license for a period not exceeding 12 months was vested exclusively in the Division of Motor Vehicles. No discretionary power was conferred upon a superior court. Smith v. Walsh, 34 N.C. App. 287, 238 S.E.2d 157 (1977).

Where the facts as found by the trial court were in exact conformity with the suspension provisions of subdivision (a)(5), the Department (now Division) had complete authority by law to suspend petitioner's license, and the superior court judge had no authority to substitute his discretion for that of the Department (now Division). In re Grubbs, 25 N.C. App. 232, 212 S.E.2d 414 (1975).

When a person is convicted of a criminal offense, the court has no authority to pronounce judgment suspending or revoking his operator's license or prohibiting him from operating a motor vehicle during a specified period. State v. Cole, 241 N.C. 576, 86 S.E.2d 203 (1955).

JUDICIAL REVIEW OF SUSPENSIONS AND REVOCATIONS. --Discretionary suspension and revocations of licenses by the Department (now Division) of Motor Vehicles are reviewable under G.S. 20-25, but mandatory revocations under G.S. 20-17 are not so reviewable. In re Wright, 228 N.C. 584, 46 S.E.2d 696 (1948). See State v. Cooper, 224 N.C. 100, 29 S.E.2d 18 (1944); Winesett v. Scheidt, 239 N.C. 190, 79 S.E.2d 501 (1954); Fox v. Scheidt, 241 N.C. 31, 84 S.E.2d 259 (1954); State v. Cole, 86 S.E.2d 203 (1955); Harrell v. Scheidt, 243 N.C. 735, 92 S.E.2d 182 (1956).

PROVISIONS OF SUBSECTION (D) AND OTHER STATUTES SATISFY REQUIREMENTS OF DUE PROCESS. --The provisions of G.S. 20-48, together with the provisions of subsection (d) of this section, relating to the right of review, and the provisions of G.S. 20-25, relating to the right of appeal, satisfy the requirements of procedural due process. State v. Teasley, 9 N.C. App. 477, 176 S.E.2d 838, appeal dismissed, 277 N.C. 459, 177 S.E.2d 900 (1970); State v. Atwood, 27 N.C. App. 445, 219 S.E.2d 521 (1975), rev'd on other grounds, 290 N.C. 266, 225 S.E.2d 543 (1976).

FORMER SUBDIVISION (A)(5) UNCONSTITUTIONAL. --Before its amendment in 1959, subdivision (a)(5) of this section provided for suspension of the license of a driver who was "an habitual violator of the traffic laws." This provision was held to be an unconstitutional grant of legislative power to the Department (now Division) of Motor Vehicles, since it did not contain any fixed standard or guide to which the Department (now Division) must conform but on the contrary left it to the sole discretion of the Commissioner of the Department (now Division) to determine when a driver was an habitual violator of the traffic laws. Harvel v. Scheidt, 249 N.C. 699, 107 S.E.2d 549 (1959), holding also that a point system set up and used by the Department (now Division) did not furnish an adequate standard or guide.

WHERE THE LAW DIRECTS SUSPENSION, REVOCATION, OR NONISSUANCE OF A DRIVER'S LICENSE, THE GROUNDS ARE CONVICTIONS FOR MOVING VIOLATIONS, or other statutory violations relating to highway safety, or situations where an individual's capacity to operate a motor vehicle safely are manifestly questionable. Evans v. Roberson, 69 N.C. App. 644, 317 S.E.2d 715 (1984), rev'd on other grounds and modified, 314 N.C. 315, 333 S.E.2d 228 (1985).

APPLIED in Whedbee v. Powell, 41 N.C. App. 250, 254 S.E.2d 645 (1979); Baggett v. Peters, 49 N.C. App. 435, 271 S.E.2d 581 (1980); Belk v. Peters, 63 N.C. App. 196, 303 S.E.2d 641 (1983).

CITED in State ex rel. Commissioner of Ins. v. North Carolina Auto. Rate Admin. Office, 293 N.C. 365, 239 S.E.2d 48 (1977); In re Nowell, 293 N.C. 235, 237 S.E.2d 246 (1977); Heritage Village Church & Missionary Fellowship, Inc. v. State, 40 N.C. App. 429, 253 S.E.2d 473 (1979); State v. Robinson, 40 N.C. App. 514, 253 S.E.2d 311 (1979); Noyes v. Peters, 40 N.C. App. 763, 253 S.E.2d 584 (1979); State v. MaGee, 75 N.C. App. 357, 330 S.E.2d 825 (1985); Davis v. Hiatt, 92 N.C. App. 748, 376 S.E.2d 44 (1989); State v. Nobles, 107 N.C. App. 627, 422 S.E.2d 78 (1992); 333 N.C. 787, 429 S.E.2d 716 (1993); Shavitz v. City of High Point, 270 F. Supp. 2d 702 (M.D.N.C. 2003); State v. Scott, 167 N.C. App. 783, 607 S.E.2d 10 (2005); Shavitz v. City of High Point, 177 N.C. App. 465, 630 S.E.2d 4 (2006), review denied, appeal dismissed, 361 N.C. 430, 648 S.E.2d 845 (2007).

II. SPECIFIC OFFENSES.

ENUMERATED OFFENSES ARE "MOVING VIOLATIONS". --The legislature considered the enumerated offenses in this section, including "no operator's (now 'driver's') license," to be moving violations. Underwood v. Howland, 274 N.C. 473, 164 S.E.2d 2 (1968).

REVOCATION OR SUSPENSION NOT MANDATORY FOR RECKLESS DRIVING. --The offense of reckless driving in violation of G.S. 20-140 is not an offense for which, upon conviction, the revocation or suspension of an operator's license is mandatory. In re Bratton, 263 N.C. 70, 138 S.E.2d 809 (1964).

SUBDIVISION (A)(9) OF THIS SECTION DID NOT REPEAL BY IMPLICATION G.S. 20-17(6). --Section 20-17(6) authorizing the mandatory revocation of a driver's license upon two convictions of reckless driving within a 12-month period was not repealed by implication by the subsequent enactment of subdivision (a)(9) of this section authorizing the

Chapter 20

discretionary suspension of a driver's license upon one or more convictions of reckless driving and one or more convictions of speeding in excess of 44 (now 55) mph and not more than 75 (now 80) mph, within a 12-month period. Person v. Garrett, 280 N.C. 163, 184 S.E.2d 873 (1971).

EFFECT OF POINT SYSTEM ON SUBDIVISION (A)(9). --The provisions of the 1959 amendment, establishing the point system, did not purport to repeal, modify or change in any manner the provisions of subdivision (a)(9) of this section. Honeycutt v. Scheidt, 254 N.C. 607, 119 S.E.2d 777 (1961).

Hence, in canceling the points accumulated over the period stipulated in subsection (c) of this section, upon which a suspension may be ordered, such cancellation does not cancel or change the number of convictions upon which a license may be suspended under the provisions of subdivision (a)(9). Honeycutt v. Scheidt, 254 N.C. 607, 119 S.E.2d 777 (1961).

The Department (now Division) of Motor Vehicles properly suspends a motor vehicle operator's license upon proof that the licensee had been convicted of speeding 60 miles per hour in a 50-mile-per-hour zone on two separate occasions within a 12-month period, even though one of the occasions had theretofore been used as the basis for a prior suspension of the license. Honeycutt v. Scheidt, 254 N.C. 607, 119 S.E.2d 777 (1961).

CONVICTION OF DRUNKEN DRIVING IN ANOTHER STATE. --Upon a receipt of notification from the highway department of another state that a resident of this State had there been convicted of drunken driving, the Department (now Division) of Motor Vehicles has the right to suspend the driving license of such person. In re Wright, 228 N.C. 301, 45 S.E.2d 370 (1947).

FAILURE TO APPEAR FOR TRIAL FOR DRIVING UNDER THE INFLUENCE IN ANOTHER STATE. --Motorist who received citation for driving under the influence in South Carolina and then forfeited bond by not appearing in court had his driver's license properly revoked even though no warrant was issued. Sykes v. Hiatt, 98 N.C. App. 688, 391 S.E.2d 834 (1990).

REVOCATION OF LICENSE IN ANOTHER STATE. --North Carolina Department of Transportation Division of Motor Vehicles may suspend the license of a driver whose license was suspended in another state, even though it was later reinstated in that state. Olive v. Faulkner, 148 N.C. App. 187, 557 S.E.2d 642 (2001).

III. JUDICIAL PROCEEDINGS.

CONVICTION MUST BE FOLLOWED BY APPEALABLE JUDGMENT. --In view of the provision in G.S. 20-24(c) to the effect that a "conviction," when used in this Article, shall mean a final conviction, it would seem that before a license may be revoked pursuant to the provisions of this section, there must be a conviction of two or more offenses enumerated in subdivision (a)(9) of this section, followed by a judgment from which an appeal might have been or may be taken. Barbour v. Scheidt, 246 N.C. 169, 97 S.E.2d 855 (1957).

CONVICTION IS NOT FINAL WHERE PRAYER FOR JUDGMENT IS CONTINUED ON PAYMENT OF COSTS. --Where, in prosecutions for speeding, prayer for judgment is continued upon payment of the costs, there are no final convictions within the purview of G.S. 20-24(c), and defendant's license to drive may not be revoked pursuant to this section. Barbour v. Scheidt, 246 N.C. 169, 97 S.E.2d 855 (1957).

JUDGMENT IN EXCESS OF JURISDICTION OF COURT. --A judgment of the superior court requiring a defendant to surrender his license to drive a motor vehicle and prohibiting him from operating such vehicles for a specified period is in excess of the jurisdiction of such court and is void. State v. Cooper, 224 N.C. 100, 29 S.E.2d 18 (1944).

A provision in a judgment in a prosecution for violation of a statutory provision regulating the operation of motor vehicles, that defendant's license be surrendered and that defendant not operate a motor vehicle on the public highways for a stipulated period, is void and will be stricken on appeal. State v. Warren, 230 N.C. 299, 52 S.E.2d 879 (1949).

COURT MAY MAKE SURRENDER OF LICENSE A CONDITION TO SUSPENSION OF SENTENCE. --While the Department (now Division) of Motor Vehicles is given the exclusive authority to suspend or revoke a driver's license, a court, either upon a plea of guilty or nolo contendere, may make the surrender of defendant's driver's license a condition upon which prison sentence or other penalty is suspended. Winesett v. Scheidt, 239 N.C. 190, 79 S.E.2d 501 (1954).

IV. ADMINISTRATIVE PROCEEDINGS.

SUSPENSION OF LICENSE A CIVIL PROCEEDING. --A proceeding to suspend an operator's license under this section is civil and not criminal in its nature. Honeycutt v. Scheidt, 254 N.C. 607, 119 S.E.2d 777 (1961).

SECTION CONSTRUED WITH G.S. 20-23. --This section and G.S. 20-23 are parts of the same statute relating to the same subject matter and must be construed in pari materia. In re Wright, 228 N.C. 584, 46 S.E.2d 696 (1948).

This section is the real source of authority. Section 20-23 prescribes a rule of evidence and adds the power of revocation, when this section is the basis of action. In re Wright, 228 N.C. 584, 46 S.E.2d 696 (1948).

EXTRATERRITORIAL JURISDICTION NOT CONFERRED. --The words "other satisfactory evidence" in this section refer to the form of notice of conviction in another state, and confer no extraterritorial jurisdiction of the offense itself. In re Donnelly, 260 N.C. 375, 132 S.E.2d 904 (1963).

This section and G.S. 20-23 do not contemplate a suspension or revocation of license by reason of a conviction in North Carolina of an alleged offense committed beyond its borders. In re Donnelly, 260 N.C. 375, 132 S.E.2d 904 (1963).

BUT EVIDENCE RELATIVE TO OFFENSES OUTSIDE STATE MAY BE CONSIDERED. --It is proper for the Department's (now Division's) hearing agent to hear and consider evidence bearing on guilt and innocence, among other things, relative to

Chapter 20

offenses outside the State, as assist him in reaching a decision in the exercise of discretionary authority. In re Donnelly, 260 N.C. 375, 132 S.E.2d 904 (1963).

EFFECT OF CONVICTION OR PLEA OF NOLO CONTENDERE TO OFFENSE REQUIRING MANDATORY REVOCATION. --Where the Department (now Division) of Motor Vehicles suspends or revokes a driver's license under the provisions of this section, the Department (now Division) must notify the licensee, and upon request afford him a hearing which is de novo, with right of appeal as prescribed by this section, and where the Department (now Division) elects to proceed under this section, it may not contend that the licensee has no right of appeal because of a conviction of or a plea of nolo contendere to an offense requiring mandatory revocation of license. Winesett v. Scheidt, 239 N.C. 190, 79 S.E.2d 501 (1954).

DIVISION NOT REQUIRED TO HAVE VALID WARRANT OR VALID JUDGMENT IN FILES. --This section authorizes the Department (now Division) to suspend the license of any driver with or without preliminary hearing upon a showing by its records that the licensee has committed an enumerated offense. It does not require the Department (now Division) to have in its files a "valid warrant" nor a "valid judgment" before it is authorized to take action. Tilley v. Garrett, 8 N.C. App. 556, 174 S.E.2d 617 (1970).

"SATISFACTORY EVIDENCE". --This section uses the phrase "satisfactory evidence." Satisfactory evidence is such as a reasonable mind might accept as adequate to support a conclusion. It is equivalent to sufficient evidence, which is defined to be such evidence as in amount is adequate to justify the court or jury in adopting the conclusion in support of which it was adduced. Winesett v. Scheidt, 239 N.C. 190, 79 S.E.2d 501 (1954).

ADMISSIBILITY OF DIVISION RECORDS. --The records of the Department (now Division) of Motor Vehicles, properly authenticated, are competent for the purpose of establishing the status of a person's operator's license and driving privilege. State v. Rhodes, 10 N.C. App. 154, 177 S.E.2d 754 (1970).

A defendant is entitled to have the contents of the official record of the status of his driver's license limited, if he so requests, to the formal parts thereof, including the certification and seal, plus the fact that under official action of the Department (now Division) of Motor Vehicles the defendant's license was in a state of revocation or suspension on the date he is charged with committing the offense under G.S. 20-28. State v. Rhodes, 10 N.C. App. 154, 177 S.E.2d 754 (1970).

BURDEN OF PROOF. --In the administrative hearing under subsection (d) of this section the burden of proof is upon the Department (now Division) to show "good cause" for extending the suspension of petitioner's license. Joyner v. Garrett, 279 N.C. 226, 182 S.E.2d 553 (1971).

Upon the hearing held under subsection (d) of this section the burden is upon the Department (now Division) to show that petitioner has willfully refused to take the test. Joyner v. Garrett, 279 N.C. 226, 182 S.E.2d 553 (1971).

RIGHT OF LICENSEE TO BE CONFRONTED BY AND CROSS-EXAMINE ADVERSE WITNESS. --At the administrative hearing, under subsection (d) of this section, the licensee has the right to be confronted by any witness whose testimony is used against him and to cross-examine the witness if he so desires. However, this is a right which the licensee waives if he does not assert it in apt time. Joyner v. Garrett, 279 N.C. 226, 182 S.E.2d 553 (1971).

WHEN LICENSEE ENTITLED TO REVIEW. --A licensee is entitled to a review whenever the suspension, cancellation, or revocation of a license is made in the discretion of the Department (now Division) of Motor Vehicles, whether under this section, or G.S. 20-23, or any other provision of the statute. Carmichael v. Scheidt, 249 N.C. 472, 106 S.E.2d 685 (1959).

REMEDY FOR IMPROPER DEPRIVATION OF LICENSE. --If a person has been improperly deprived of his license by the Department (now Division) of Motor Vehicles due to mistake in law or fact, his remedy is to apply for a hearing as provided by subsection (d) of this section, or by petitioning the superior court pursuant to G.S. 20-25. At a hearing under either of these statutory provisions, he would be permitted to show that the suspension was erroneous. One cannot contemptuously ignore the quasi-judicial determinations made by the Department (now Division) of Motor Vehicles. Beaver v. Scheidt, 251 N.C. 671, 111 S.E.2d 881 (1960).

CROSS REFERENCES. --
As to period of suspension or revocation, see G.S. 20-19 and note to G.S. 20-17.

LEGAL PERIODICALS. --
For brief discussion of the 1949 amendments, see 27 N.C.L. Rev. 371, 372 (1949).

For article on administrative hearing for suspension of driver's license, see 30 N.C.L. Rev. 27 (1951).

For note as to effect of plea of nolo contendere, see 32 N.C.L. Rev. 549 (1954).

For a survey of 1996 developments in constitutional law, see 75 N.C.L. Rev. 2315 (1997).

OPINIONS OF THE ATTORNEY GENERAL
OPERATION OF VEHICLE WITH IMPROPER TAILLIGHTS CARRIES TWO POINTS AS A MOVING VIOLATION. --See opinion of Attorney General to Mr. Henry M. Whitesides, Fourteenth Solicitorial District, 41 N.C.A.G. 211 (1971).

§ 20-16.01. Double penalties for offenses committed while operating a commercial motor vehicle

Any person who commits an offense for which points may be assessed pursuant to the Schedule of Point Values for Violations While Operating a Commercial Motor Vehicle as provided in G.S. 20-16(c) may be assessed double the amount of any fine or penalty authorized by statute.

History.
1999-330, s. 8

EDITOR'S NOTE. --

The number of this section was assigned by the Revisor of Statutes, the number in Session Laws 1999-330, s. 10 having been 20-16A.

§ 20-16.1. Mandatory suspension of driver's license upon conviction of excessive speeding; limited driving permits for first offenders

(a) Notwithstanding any other provisions of this Article, the Division shall suspend for a period of 30 days the license of any driver without preliminary hearing on receiving a record of the driver's conviction of either (i) exceeding by more than 15 miles per hour the speed limit, either within or outside the corporate limits of a municipality, if the person was also driving at a speed in excess of 55 miles per hour at the time of the offense, or (ii) driving at a speed in excess of 80 miles per hour at the time of the offense.

(b) (1) Upon a first conviction only of violating subsection (a), the trial judge may when feasible allow a limited driving privilege or license to the person convicted for proper purposes reasonably connected with the health, education and welfare of the person convicted and his family. For purposes of determining whether conviction is a first conviction, no prior offense occurring more than seven years before the date of the current offense shall be considered. The judge may impose upon such limited driving privilege any restrictions as in his discretion are deemed advisable including, but not limited to, conditions of days, hours, types of vehicles, routes, geographical boundaries and specific purposes for which limited driving privilege is allowed. Any such limited driving privilege allowed and restrictions imposed thereon shall be specifically recorded in a written judgment which shall be as near as practical to that hereinafter set forth and shall be signed by the trial judge and shall be affixed with the seal of the court and shall be made a part of the records of the said court. A copy of said judgment shall be transmitted to the Division of Motor Vehicles along with any driver's license in the possession of the person convicted and a notice of the conviction. Such permit issued hereunder shall be valid for 30 days from the date of issuance by trial court. Such permit shall constitute a valid license to operate motor vehicles of the class or type that would be allowed by the person's license if it were not currently revoked upon the streets and highways of this or any other state in accordance with the restrictions noted thereon and shall be subject to all provisions of law relating to driver's license, not by their nature, rendered inapplicable.

(2) The judgment issued by the trial judge as herein permitted shall as near as practical be in form and content as follows:

This cause coming on to be heard and being heard before the Honorable , Judge presiding, and it appearing to the court that the defendant, has been convicted of the offense of excessive speeding in violation of G.S. 20-16.1(a), and it further appearing to the court that the defendant should be issued a restrictive driving license and is entitled to the issuance of a restrictive driving privilege under and by the authority of G.S. 20-16.1(b);

Now, therefore, it is ordered, adjudged and decreed that the defendant be allowed to operate a motor vehicle under the following conditions and under no other circumstances.

Name:_____
Race:_____Sex:_____
Height:_____Weight:_____
Color of Hair:_____Color of Eyes:_____
Birth Date:_____
Driver's License Number:_____
Signature of Licensee:_____
Conditions of Restriction:_____
Type of Vehicle:_____
Geographic Restrictions:_____
Hours of Restriction:_____
Other Restrictions:_____

This limited license shall be effective from_____to_____subject to further orders as the court in its discretion may deem necessary and proper.

This the_____day of_____,_____

_____
(Judge Presiding)

(3) Upon conviction of such offense outside the jurisdiction of this State the person so convicted may apply to a district court judge of the district or set of districts as defined in G.S. 7A-41.1(a) in which he resides for limited driving privileges hereinbefore defined. Upon such application the judge shall have the authority to issue such limited driving privileges in the same manner as if he were the trial judge.

(4) Any violation of the restrictive driving privileges as set forth in the judgment of the trial judge allowing such privileges shall constitute the offense of driving while license has been suspended as set forth in G.S. 20-28. Whenever a person is charged with operating a motor vehicle in violation of the restrictions, the limited driving privilege shall be suspended pending the final disposition of the charge.

(5) This section is supplemental and in addition to existing law and shall not be construed so as to repeal any existing provision contained in the General Statutes of North Carolina.

(c) Upon conviction of a similar second or subsequent offense which offense occurs within one year of the first or prior offense, the license of such operator shall be suspended for 60 days, provided such first or prior offense occurs subsequent to July 1, 1953.

(d) Notwithstanding any other provisions of this Article, the Division shall suspend for a period of 60 days the license of any driver without preliminary hearing on receiving a record of such driver's conviction of having violated the laws against speeding described in subsection (a) and of having violated the laws against reckless driving on the same occasion as the speeding offense occurred.

(e) The provisions of this section shall not prevent the suspension or revocation of a license for a longer period of time where the same may be authorized by other provisions of law.

(f) Repealed by Session Laws 1987, c. 869, s. 14.

(g) Any judge granting limited driving privileges under this section shall, prior to granting such privileges, be furnished proof and be satisfied that the person being granted such privileges is financially responsible. Proof of financial responsibility shall be in one of the following forms:

    (1) A written certificate or electronically-transmitted facsimile thereof from any insurance carrier duly authorized to do business in this State certifying that there is in effect a nonfleet private passenger motor vehicle liability policy for the benefit of the person required to furnish proof of financial responsibility. The certificate or facsimile shall state the effective date and expiration date of the nonfleet private passenger motor vehicle liability policy and shall state the date that the certificate or facsimile is issued. The certificate or facsimile shall remain effective proof of financial responsibility for a period of 30 consecutive days following the date the certificate or facsimile is issued but shall not in and of itself constitute a binder or policy of insurance or

    (2) A binder for or policy of nonfleet private passenger motor vehicle liability insurance under which the applicant is insured, provided that the binder or policy states the effective date and expiration date of the nonfleet private passenger motor vehicle liability policy.

The preceding provisions of this subsection do not apply to applicants who do not own currently registered motor vehicles and who do not operate nonfleet private passenger motor vehicles that are owned by other persons and that are not insured under commercial motor vehicle liability insurance policies. In such cases, the applicant shall sign a written certificate to that effect. Such certificate shall be furnished by

the Division. Any material misrepresentation made by such person on such certificate shall be grounds for suspension of that person's license for a period of 90 days.

For the purpose of this subsection "nonfleet private passenger motor vehicle" has the definition ascribed to it in Article 40 of General Statute Chapter 58.

The Commissioner may require that certificates required by this subsection be on a form approved by the Commissioner. Such granting of limited driving privileges shall be conditioned upon the maintenance of such financial responsibility during the period of the limited driving privilege. Nothing in this subsection precludes any person from showing proof of financial responsibility in any other manner authorized by Articles 9A and 13 of this Chapter.

History.
1953, c. 1223; 1955, c. 1187, s. 15; 1959, c. 1264, s. 4; 1965, c. 133; 1975, c. 716, s. 5; c. 763; 1979, c. 667, ss. 19, 41; 1983, c. 77; 1987, c. 869, ss. 13, 14; 1989, c. 436, s. 4;770, s. 57; 1995 (Reg. Sess., 1996), c. 652, s. 2; 1999-456, s. 59;2004-199, s. 13(a)

EFFECT OF AMENDMENTS. --
Session Laws 2004-199, s. 13(a), effective August 17, 2004, substituted "a district court judge" for "the resident judge of the superior court" in the first sentence of subsection (b)(3).

THE OPERATION OF A MOTOR VEHICLE ON A PUBLIC HIGHWAY IS NOT A NATURAL RIGHT. It is a conditional privilege which the State in the interest of public safety acting under its police power may regulate or control, and the State may suspend or revoke the driver's license. Shue v. Scheidt, 252 N.C. 561, 114 S.E.2d 237 (1960).

THIS SECTION WAS ENACTED TO PROMOTE HIGHWAY SAFETY by providing for the mandatory suspension of a driver's license upon conviction of excessive speeding and reckless driving. Shue v. Scheidt, 252 N.C. 561, 114 S.E.2d 237 (1960).

AND NOT TO PUNISH LICENSEE. --The suspension or revocation of a driver's license is no part of the punishment for the violation or violations of traffic laws. The purpose of the suspension or revocation of a driver's license is to protect the public and not to punish the licensee. Shue v. Scheidt, 252 N.C. 561, 114 S.E.2d 237 (1960).

IT APPLIES TO VIOLATION OF G.S. 20-141(D). -- This section applies where a driver is convicted of driving his passenger automobile at a speed of 75 miles per hour on a public highway in a 45-mile-per-hour speed zone established under subsection (d) of G.S. 20-141. Shue v. Scheidt, 252 N.C. 561, 114 S.E.2d 237 (1960).

WHERE THE LAW DIRECTS SUSPENSION, REVOCATION, OR NONISSUANCE OF A DRIVER'S LICENSE, THE GROUNDS ARE CONVICTIONS FOR MOVING VIOLATIONS, or other statutory violations relating to highway safety, or situations where an individual's capacity to operate a motor vehicle safely are manifestly questionable. Evans v. Roberson, 69 N.C. App. 644, 317 S.E.2d 715 (1984), rev'd on other grounds and modified, 314 N.C. 315, 333 S.E.2d 228 (1985).

NOLO CONTENDERE HAS SAME EFFECT AS CONVICTION. --As a basis for suspension or revocation of an operator's license, a plea of nolo contendere has the same effect as a conviction or plea of guilty of such offense. Gibson v. Scheidt, 259 N.C. 339, 130 S.E.2d 679 (1963).

CITED in Underwood v. Howland, 274 N.C. 473, 164 S.E.2d 2 (1968); Rice v. Peters, 48 N.C. App. 697, 269 S.E.2d 740 (1980).

CROSS REFERENCES. --
As to mandatory revocation of license for refusal to submit to chemical test to determine alcoholic content of blood, see G.S. 20-16.2.

OPINIONS OF THE ATTORNEY GENERAL
LIMITED DRIVING PRIVILEGE MAY NOT BE EXTENDED TO COVER DISCRETIONARY REVOCATION BY DIVISION. --Subsection (b) applies to offenses of speeding 71 mph through 75 mph, speeds in excess of 75 mph, and speeds in excess of 80 mph. When a limited permit is issued pursuant to subsection (b) of this section by the court upon conviction or a plea of guilty to a speeding charge requiring a mandatory 30-day revocation and such speed is such as to give rise to a discretionary revocation by the Division of Motor Vehicles for a greater period, the limited driving privilege issued by the court may not be extended to cover the revocation by the Division of Motor Vehicles. See Opinion of Attorney General to Mr. E. Burt Aycock, Jr., Assistant District Attorney, 45 N.C.A.G. 112 (1975).

§ 20-16.2. Implied consent to chemical analysis; mandatory revocation of license in event of refusal; right of driver to request analysis

(a) **Basis for Officer to Require Chemical Analysis; Notification of Rights. --** Any person who drives a vehicle on a highway or public vehicular area thereby gives consent to a chemical analysis if charged with an implied-consent offense. Any law enforcement officer who has reasonable grounds to believe that the person charged has committed the implied-consent offense may obtain a chemical analysis of the person.

Before any type of chemical analysis is administered the person charged shall be taken before a chemical analyst authorized to administer a test of a person's breath or a law enforcement officer who is authorized to administer chemical analysis of the breath, who shall inform the person orally and also give the person a notice in writing that:

(1) You have been charged with an implied-consent offense. Under the implied-consent law, you can refuse any test, but

your drivers license will be revoked for one year and could be revoked for a longer period of time under certain circumstances, and an officer can compel you to be tested under other laws.

(2) Repealed by Session Laws 2006-253, s. 15, effective December 1, 2006, and applicable to offenses committed on or after that date.

(3) The test results, or the fact of your refusal, will be admissible in evidence at trial.

(4) Your driving privilege will be revoked immediately for at least 30 days if you refuse any test or the test result is 0.08 or more, 0.04 or more if you were driving a commercial vehicle, or 0.01 or more if you are under the age of 21.

(5) After you are released, you may seek your own test in addition to this test.

(6) You may call an attorney for advice and select a witness to view the testing procedures remaining after the witness arrives, but the testing may not be delayed for these purposes longer than 30 minutes from the time you are notified of these rights. You must take the test at the end of 30 minutes even if you have not contacted an attorney or your witness has not arrived.

(a1) **Meaning of Terms. --** Under this section, an "implied-consent offense" is an offense involving impaired driving, a violation of G.S. 20-141.4(a2), or an alcohol-related offense made subject to the procedures of this section. A person is "charged" with an offense if the person is arrested for it or if criminal process for the offense has been issued.

(b) **Unconscious Person May Be Tested.** -- If a law enforcement officer has reasonable grounds to believe that a person has committed an implied-consent offense, and the person is unconscious or otherwise in a condition that makes the person incapable of refusal, the law enforcement officer may direct the taking of a blood sample or may direct the administration of any other chemical analysis that may be effectively performed. In this instance the notification of rights set out in subsection (a) and the request required by subsection (c) are not necessary.

(c) **Request to Submit to Chemical Analysis. --** A law enforcement officer or chemical analyst shall designate the type of test or tests to be given and may request the person charged to submit to the type of chemical analysis designated. If the person charged willfully refuses to submit to that chemical analysis, none may be given under the provisions of this section, but the refusal does not preclude testing under other applicable procedures of law.

(c1) **Procedure for Reporting Results and Refusal to Division.** -- Whenever a person refuses to submit to a chemical analysis, a person has an alcohol concentration of 0.15 or more, or a person's drivers license has an alcohol concentration restriction and the results of the chemical analysis establish a violation of the restriction, the law enforcement officer and the chemical analyst shall without unnecessary delay go before an official authorized to administer oaths and execute an affidavit(s) stating that:

(1) The person was charged with an implied-consent offense or had an alcohol concentration restriction on the drivers license;

(2) A law enforcement officer had reasonable grounds to believe that the person had committed an implied-consent offense or violated the alcohol concentration restriction on the drivers license;

(3) Whether the implied-consent offense charged involved death or critical injury to another person, if the person willfully refused to submit to chemical analysis;

(4) The person was notified of the rights in subsection (a); and

(5) The results of any tests given or that the person willfully refused to submit to a chemical analysis.

If the person's drivers license has an alcohol concentration restriction, pursuant to G.S. 20-19(c3), and an officer has reasonable grounds to believe the person has violated a provision of that restriction other than violation of the alcohol concentration level, the officer and chemical analyst shall complete the applicable sections of the affidavit and indicate the restriction which was violated. The officer shall immediately mail the affidavit(s) to the Division. If the officer is also the chemical analyst who has notified the person of the rights under subsection (a), the officer may perform alone the duties of this subsection.

(d) **Consequences of Refusal; Right to Hearing before Division; Issues.** -- Upon receipt of a properly executed affidavit required by subsection (c1), the Division shall expeditiously notify the person charged that the person's license to drive is revoked for 12 months, effective on the tenth calendar day after the mailing of the revocation order unless, before the effective date of the order, the person requests in writing a hearing before the Division. Except for the time referred to in G.S. 20-16.5, if the person shows to the satisfaction of the Division that his or her license was surrendered to the court, and remained in the court's possession, then the Division shall credit the amount of time for which the license was in the possession of the court against the 12-month revocation period

required by this subsection. If the person properly requests a hearing, the person retains his or her license, unless it is revoked under some other provision of law, until the hearing is held, the person withdraws the request, or the person fails to appear at a scheduled hearing. The hearing officer may subpoena any witnesses or documents that the hearing officer deems necessary. The person may request the hearing officer to subpoena the charging officer, the chemical analyst, or both to appear at the hearing if the person makes the request in writing at least three days before the hearing. The person may subpoena any other witness whom the person deems necessary, and the provisions of G.S. 1A-1, Rule 45, apply to the issuance and service of all subpoenas issued under the authority of this section. The hearing officer is authorized to administer oaths to witnesses appearing at the hearing. The hearing shall be conducted in the county where the charge was brought, and shall be limited to consideration of whether:

(1) The person was charged with an implied-consent offense or the driver had an alcohol concentration restriction on the drivers license pursuant to G.S. 20-19;

(2) A law enforcement officer had reasonable grounds to believe that the person had committed an implied-consent offense or violated the alcohol concentration restriction on the drivers license;

(3) The implied-consent offense charged involved death or critical injury to another person, if this allegation is in the affidavit;

(4) The person was notified of the person's rights as required by subsection (a); and

(5) The person willfully refused to submit to a chemical analysis.

If the Division finds that the conditions specified in this subsection are met, it shall order the revocation sustained. If the Division finds that any of the conditions (1), (2), (4), or (5) is not met, it shall rescind the revocation. If it finds that condition (3) is alleged in the affidavit but is not met, it shall order the revocation sustained if that is the only condition that is not met; in this instance subsection (d1) does not apply to that revocation. If the revocation is sustained, the person shall surrender his or her license immediately upon notification by the Division.

(d1) **Consequences of Refusal in Case Involving Death or Critical Injury.** -- If the refusal occurred in a case involving death or critical injury to another person, no limited driving privilege may be issued. The 12-month revocation begins only after all other periods of revocation have terminated unless the person's license is revoked under G.S. 20-28, 20-28.1, 20-19(d), or 20-19(e). If the revocation is based on those sections, the revocation under this subsection begins at the time and in the manner specified in subsection (d) for revocations under this section. However, the person's eligibility for a hearing to determine if the revocation under those sections should be rescinded is postponed for one year from the date on which the person would otherwise have been eligible for the hearing. If the person's driver's license is again revoked while the 12-month revocation under this subsection is in effect, that revocation, whether imposed by a court or by the Division, may only take effect after the period of revocation under this subsection has terminated.

(e) **Right to Hearing in Superior Court.** -- If the revocation for a willful refusal is sustained after the hearing, the person whose license has been revoked has the right to file a petition in the superior court district or set of districts defined in G.S. 7A-41.1, where the charges were made, within 30 days thereafter for a hearing on the record. The superior court review shall be limited to whether there is sufficient evidence in the record to support the Commissioner's findings of fact and whether the conclusions of law are supported by the findings of fact and whether the Commissioner committed an error of law in revoking the license.

(e1) **Limited Driving Privilege after Six Months in Certain Instances.** -- A person whose driver's license has been revoked under this section may apply for and a judge authorized to do so by this subsection may issue a limited driving privilege if:

(1) At the time of the refusal the person held either a valid drivers license or a license that had been expired for less than one year;

(2) At the time of the refusal, the person had not within the preceding seven years been convicted of an offense involving impaired driving;

(3) At the time of the refusal, the person had not in the preceding seven years willfully refused to submit to a chemical analysis under this section;

(4) The implied consent offense charged did not involve death or critical injury to another person;

(5) The underlying charge for which the defendant was requested to submit to a chemical analysis has been finally disposed of:

    a. Other than by conviction; or

    b. By a conviction of impaired driving under G.S. 20-138.1, at a punishment level authorizing issuance of a limited driving privilege under G.S. 20-179.3(b), and the defendant has complied with at least one of the mandatory conditions of probation listed

for the punishment level under which the defendant was sentenced;

(6) Subsequent to the refusal the person has had no unresolved pending charges for or additional convictions of an offense involving impaired driving;

(7) The person's license has been revoked for at least six months for the refusal; and

(8) The person has obtained a substance abuse assessment from a mental health facility and successfully completed any recommended training or treatment program.

Except as modified in this subsection, the provisions of G.S. 20-179.3 relating to the procedure for application and conduct of the hearing and the restrictions required or authorized to be included in the limited driving privilege apply to applications under this subsection. If the case was finally disposed of in the district court, the hearing shall be conducted in the district court district as defined in G.S. 7A-133 in which the refusal occurred by a district court judge. If the case was finally disposed of in the superior court, the hearing shall be conducted in the superior court district or set of districts as defined in G.S. 7A-41.1 in which the refusal occurred by a superior court judge. A limited driving privilege issued under this section authorizes a person to drive if the person's license is revoked solely under this section or solely under this section and G.S. 20-17(2). If the person's license is revoked for any other reason, the limited driving privilege is invalid.

(f) **Notice to Other States as to Nonresidents.** -- When it has been finally determined under the procedures of this section that a nonresident's privilege to drive a motor vehicle in this State has been revoked, the Division shall give information in writing of the action taken to the motor vehicle administrator of the state of the person's residence and of any state in which the person has a license.

(g) Repealed by Session Laws 1973, c. 914.

(h) Repealed by Session Laws 1979, c. 423, s. 2.

(i) **Right to Chemical Analysis before Arrest or Charge.** -- A person stopped or questioned by a law enforcement officer who is investigating whether the person may have committed an implied consent offense may request the administration of a chemical analysis before any arrest or other charge is made for the offense. Upon this request, the officer shall afford the person the opportunity to have a chemical analysis of his or her breath, if available, in accordance with the procedures required by G.S. 20-139.1(b). The request constitutes the person's consent to be transported by the law enforcement officer to the place where the chemical analysis is to be administered. Before the chemical analysis is made, the person shall confirm the request in writing and shall be notified:

(1) That the test results will be admissible in evidence and may be used against you in any implied consent offense that may arise;

(2) Your driving privilege will be revoked immediately for at least 30 days if the test result is 0.08 or more, 0.04 or more if you were driving a commercial vehicle, or 0.01 or more if you are under the age of 21.

(3) That if you fail to comply fully with the test procedures, the officer may charge you with any offense for which the officer has probable cause, and if you are charged with an implied consent offense, your refusal to submit to the testing required as a result of that charge would result in revocation of your driving privilege. The results of the chemical analysis are admissible in evidence in any proceeding in which they are relevant.

History.

1963, c. 966, s. 1; 1965, c. 1165; 1969, c. 1074, s. 1; 1971, c. 619, ss. 3-6; 1973, c. 206, ss. 1, 2; cc. 824, 914; 1975, c. 716, s. 5; 1977, c. 812; 1979, c. 423, s. 2; 1979, 2nd Sess., c. 1160; 1981, c. 412, s. 4; c. 747, s. 66; 1983, c. 87; c. 435, s. 11; 1983 (Reg. Sess., 1984), c. 1101, ss. 5-8; 1987, c. 797, s. 3; 1987 (Reg. Sess., 1988), c. 1037, ss. 76, 77; c. 1112; 1989, c. 771, ss. 13, 14, 18; 1991, c. 689, s. 233.1(c);1993, c. 285, ss. 3, 4; 1995, c. 163, s. 1;1997-379, ss. 3.1₁-3.3; 1998-182, s. 28;1999-406, ss. 1, 10; 2000-155, s. 5;2006-253, s. 15;2007-493, ss. 25, 27; 2011-119, s. 1

EDITOR'S NOTE. --

Session Laws 1999-406, s. 18, states that this act does not obligate the General Assembly to appropriate additional funds, and that this act shall be implemented with funds available or appropriated to the Department of Transportation and the Administrative Office of the Courts.

EFFECT OF AMENDMENTS. --

Session Laws 2006-253, s. 15, effective December 1, 2006, and applicable to offenses committed on or after that date, rewrote the section.

Session Laws 2007-493, s. 25, effective August 30, 2007, inserted "district or set of districts defined in G.S. 7A-41.1, where the charges were made, within 30 days thereafter" in the first sentence of subsection (e).

Session Laws 2007-493, s. 27, effective December 1, 2007, and applicable to offenses committed on or after that date, substituted "concentration of 0.15" for "concentration of 0.16" in the introductory paragraph of subsection (c1).

Session Laws 2011-119, s. 1, effective December 1, 2011, and applicable to offenses committed on or after that date, inserted "a violation of G.S. 20-141.4(a2)" in subsection (a1).

I. IN GENERAL.

EDITOR'S NOTE. --Many of the cases annotated below were decided under this section as it read prior

to the 1993 amendment which reduced the blood alcohol content for driving while impaired and related offenses from 0.10 to 0.08.

BECAUSE THIS SECTION IMPOSES A PENALTY, IT MUST BE STRICTLY CONSTRUED. Price v. North Carolina Dep't of Motor Vehicles, 36 N.C. App. 698, 245 S.E.2d 518, appeal dismissed, 295 N.C. 551, 248 S.E.2d 728 (1978), overruled on other grounds, Seders v. Powell, 298 N.C. 453, 259 S.E.2d 518 (1979).

CONSTRUCTION WITH G.S. 20-138.1 --A civil superior court determination, on appeal from an administrative hearing, pursuant to this section, regarding an allegation of willful refusal, estops the relitigation of that same issue in a defendant's criminal prosecution for DWI. The district attorney and the Attorney General both represent the interests of the people of North Carolina, regardless of whether it be the district attorney in a criminal trial court or the Attorney General in a civil or criminal appeal. State v. Summers, 351 N.C. 620, 528 S.E.2d 17 (2000).

THOUGH THIS SECTION MUST BE READ IN CONJUNCTION WITH G.S. 20-139.1 to determine the procedures governing the administering of chemical analyses, this section, and that statute alone, sets forth the procedures governing notification of rights pursuant to a chemical analysis. Nicholson v. Killens, 116 N.C. App. 473, 448 S.E.2d 542 (1994).

EVIDENCE IN LICENSE REVOCATION HEARING NOT SUBJECT TO EXCLUSIONARY RULE. --Whether or not law enforcement officers had reasonable and articulable suspicion to stop a driver, the evidence that resulted from the stop was not subject to the exclusionary rule; evidence in a license revocation hearing is not subject to the exclusionary rule. Hartman v. Robertson, 208 N.C. App. 692, 703 S.E.2d 811 (2010).

CONSENT DEEMED GIVEN. --Anyone who operates a motor vehicle upon the highways of the State is deemed to have given consent to a breathalyzer test. State v. Allen, 14 N.C. App. 485, 188 S.E.2d 568 (1972).

PURPOSE OF PROCEDURES. --The administrative procedures provided for in this section are designed to promote breathalyzer tests as a valuable tool for law-enforcement officers in their enforcing the laws against driving under the influence while also protecting the rights of the State's citizens. Rice v. Peters, 48 N.C. App. 697, 269 S.E.2d 740 (1980).

THE PURPOSE OF ADMINISTERING THE BREATHALYZER TEST IS TO PRODUCE AN ACCURATE RESULT. Bell v. Powell, 41 N.C. App. 131, 254 S.E.2d 191 (1979).

THE PURPOSE OF THE STATUTE IS FULFILLED WHEN THE ARRESTEE IS GIVEN THE OPTION TO SUBMIT OR REFUSE to submit to a breathalyzer test and his decision is made after having been advised of his rights in a manner provided by the statute. Rice v. Peters, 48 N.C. App. 697, 269 S.E.2d 740 (1980).

OPTION TO REFUSE IS NOT CONSTITUTIONALLY MANDATED. --This section only "coerces" a breathalyzer test in the limited instances in which the law-enforcement officer has reasonable grounds

Chapter 20

to believe that the driver has violated the law. In such situations the State could constitutionally require that the driver submit to an examination without any option to refuse. Montgomery v. North Carolina DMV, 455 F. Supp. 338 (W.D.N.C. 1978), aff'd, 599 F.2d 1048 (4th Cir. 1979).

The State is not constitutionally required to give an accused an option to refuse the breathalyzer test. Etheridge v. Peters, 45 N.C. App. 358, 263 S.E.2d 308, aff'd, 301 N.C. 76, 269 S.E.2d 133 (1980).

EFFECT OF REFUSAL. --Persons being requested to submit to chemical analysis do not have to be informed that a refusal can result in the denial of their right to seek a limited driving privilege as a part of the notification requirement of this section. Nowell v. Killens, 119 N.C. App. 567, 459 S.E.2d 37 (1995).

NOR IS IT IMPERMISSIBLE FOR STATE TO ALLOW OPTION. --It is not impermissible nor a violation of equal protection of the laws for the State to allow drivers an option of refusing a breathalyzer examination that could be constitutionally required in exchange for risking license suspension of six months if the proper procedures are followed and the officer has probable cause to believe that the accused has driven a motor vehicle while under the influence of intoxicating liquor (now has committed an implied-consent offense). Montgomery v. North Carolina DMV, 455 F. Supp. 338 (W.D.N.C. 1978), aff'd, 599 F.2d 1048 (4th Cir. 1979).

THE STATUTORY DISTINCTION UNDER THIS SECTION IS BASED ON WHETHER A MOTORIST REFUSES TO SUBMIT TO A BREATH TEST. Since the motorist may not be subjected to such a test unless, pursuant to subsection (d) of this section, the law-enforcement officer has reasonable grounds to believe the person had been driving or operating a motor vehicle upon a highway or public vehicular area while under the influence of intoxicating liquor (now had committed an implied-consent offense), the State could have required that the motorist submit to the test without any refusal option and without any infringement of the constitutional rights against self-incrimination or against unreasonable searches and seizures. Montgomery v. North Carolina DMV, 455 F. Supp. 338 (W.D.N.C. 1978), aff'd, 599 F.2d 1048 (4th Cir. 1979).

UNCONSCIOUS DRIVER. --Requiring the arrest of an unconscious driver would serve no sensible purpose; in such a case, the formal requirements of subsection (a) of this section are not meant to apply. State v. Hollingsworth, 77 N.C. App. 36, 334 S.E.2d 463 (1985).

In a prosecution for involuntary manslaughter and driving under the influence, the performance of a blood alcohol test on blood seized from an unconscious defendant pursuant to subsection (b) of this section did not violate the defendant's rights under U.S. Const., Amend. IV and N.C. Const., Art. 1, § 20, relating to search and seizure, because of (1) the existence of probable cause to arrest; (2) the limited nature of the intrusion upon the person; and (3) the destructibility of the evidence. State v. Hollingsworth, 77 N.C. App. 36, 334 S.E.2d 463 (1985).

Where defendant was already sedated and unconscious when a police officer arrived at a hospital to obtain a blood sample for chemical analysis such that officer did not advise defendant of his right to refuse the test, the trial court properly concluded that defendant was rendered unconscious by the doctors based solely on a medical decision to treat him, that the officer had nothing to do with this decision, and that defendant's statutory rights were not violated in that the officer who conducted the chemical analysis complied with the requirements of this section and G.S. 20-139.1. State v. Garcia-Lorenzo, 110 N.C. App. 319, 430 S.E.2d 290 (1993).

Trial court properly granted defendant's motion to suppress blood draw evidence a police officer collected from a nurse because the record did not affirmatively show that the officer had reasonable grounds to believe defendant, who was unconscious during the blood draw, committed the implied consent offense of driving while intoxicated; the record did not affirmatively show that defendant was intoxicated while he drove, but it raised a question as to whether defendant became very intoxicated. State v. Romano, 247 N.C. App. 212, 785 S.E.2d 168 (2016), modified and aff'd, 800 S.E.2d 644, 2017 N.C. LEXIS 398 (N.C. 2017).

Based on the United States Supreme Court's Fourth Amendment precedent regarding consent, the blood draw from defendant could not be justified under subsection (b) as a per se categorical exception to the warrant requirement; the implied-consent statute, as well as a person's decision to drive on public roads, are factors to consider when analyzing whether a suspect has consented to a blood draw, but the statute alone does not create a per se exception to the warrant requirement. State v. Romano, 369 N.C. 678, 800 S.E.2d 644 (2017).

Treating subsection (b) as an irrevocable rule of implied consent does not comport with the consent exception to the warrant requirement because such treatment does not require an analysis of the voluntariness of consent based on the totality of the circumstances. State v. Romano, 369 N.C. 678, 800 S.E.2d 644 (2017).

Trial court correctly suppressed defendant's blood sample because subsection (b) was unconstitutional as applied to defendant since it permitted a warrantless search that violated the Fourth Amendment; blood draws could only be performed after obtaining a warrant, valid consent from the defendant, or under exigent circumstances with probable cause, but the officer who took possession of defendant's blood did not get a warrant, and there were no exigent circumstances. State v. Romano, 369 N.C. 678, 800 S.E.2d 644 (2017).

NOTICE. --Police officer's placement of written rights form with defendant's emergency room chart was tantamount to "giving" defendant notice in writing; in light of the treatment defendant was receiving for his injuries, there was effectively no other means by which the notice could have been given to him. State v. Lovett, 119 N.C. App. 689, 460 S.E.2d 177 (1995).

REASONABLE GROUNDS SYNONYMOUS WITH PROBABLE CAUSE. --In determining whether a charging officer had reasonable grounds to believe a petitioner committed an implied consent offense within the meaning of this section, the term reasonable grounds should be viewed as synonymous with probable cause. Moore v. Hodges, 116 N.C. App. 727, 449 S.E.2d 218 (1994).

THIS SECTION DOES NOT LIMIT THE INTRODUCTION OF OTHER COMPETENT EVIDENCE as to a defendant's alcohol concentration, including other chemical tests. This statute allows other competent evidence of a defendant's blood alcohol level in addition to that obtained from chemical analysis pursuant to this section and G.S. 20-139.1. State v. Drdak, 330 N.C. 587, 411 S.E.2d 604 (1992).

RELATION TO DWI CHARGE. --The decision by Division of Motor Vehicles (DMV) to rescind the revocation of defendant's driver's license was independent of, and inconsequential to, defendant's criminal trial for driving while impaired (DWI). State v. O'Rourke, 114 N.C. App. 435, 442 S.E.2d 137 (1994).

REASONABLE GROUNDS DRIVER COMMITTED IMPLIED-CONSENT OFFENSE. --Superior court did not err in affirming the decision of the North CarolinaDMV to revoke a driver's license under G.S. 20-16.2 because the superior court's findings of fact supported the conclusion of law that a law enforcement officer had reasonable grounds to believe that the driver had committed an implied-consent offense; competent evidence supported the findings that the driver stopped past an intersection midway into it then turned right onto a road and that the officer followed the driver and estimated his speed was 65 in a 45 mph zone at the time of the initial stop. Hartman v. Robertson, 208 N.C. App. 692, 703 S.E.2d 811 (2010).

DEFENDANT'S SUBJECTIVE UNDERSTANDING NOT KEY. --Admissibility of the results of a chemical analysis test are not conditioned on a defendant's subjective understanding of the information disclosed to him pursuant to the requirements of the statute, and as long as the rights are disclosed to a defendant, the requirements of the statute are satisfied and it is immaterial whether the defendant comprehends them; in this case, the officer complied with the statute when he read defendant his rights in English and provided him written form copies of those rights, and thus the trial court did not err in denying defendant's motion to suppress. State v. Kap Mung, 251 N.C. App. 311, 795 S.E.2d 284 (2016).

COLLATERAL ESTOPPEL -- PRIVITY OF PARTIES. --The state is collaterally estopped from litigating issues in a criminal DWI case when those exact issues have been relitigated in a civil license revocation hearing with the Attorney General representing the DMV in superior court; defendant was found to have not refused to take the breathalyzer test in the earlier proceeding, so that the results of the single breath analysis were inadmissible, and privity of parties existed, as both the Attorney General and the District Attorney represent the same party, which is the people of the State of North Carolina. State v. Summers,

132 N.C. App. 636, 513 S.E.2d 575 (1999), aff'd, 351 N.C. 620, 528 S.E.2d 17 (2000).

Revocation of driving privileges was not barred by collateral estoppel. The dismissal of a driver's criminal case due to a violation of his right to have a witness present during the chemical test did not reach the issue of whether his refusal to take the test was willful under G.S. 20-16.2(d). Powers v. Tatum, 196 N.C. App. 639, 676 S.E.2d 89 (2009), review denied, stay denied, 363 N.C. 583, 681 S.E.2d 784 (2009).

PROPRIETY OF AN INITIAL STOP OF IS NOT WITHIN THE STATUTORILY-PRESCRIBED PURVIEW OF A LICENSE REVOCATION HEARING because reasonable and articulable suspicion for an initial stop is not an issue to be reviewed pursuant to G.S. 20-16.2; according to G.S. 20-16.2, the only inquiry with respect to the law enforcement officer is the requirement that he or she have reasonable grounds to believe that the person had committed an implied-consent offense. Hartman v. Robertson, 208 N.C. App. 692, 703 S.E.2d 811 (2010).

THE QUANTUM OF PROOF NECESSARY TO ESTABLISH PROBABLE CAUSE TO ARREST in criminal driving while impaired cases and civil license revocation proceedings, notwithstanding the different burdens on the remaining elements, is virtually identical. Brower v. Killens, 122 N.C. App. 685, 472 S.E.2d 33 (1996), discretionary review improvidently allowed, 345 N.C. 625, 481 S.E.2d 86 (1997).

NO RIGHT TO HAVE WITNESS PRESENT. --Procedures for obtaining the blood sample did not have to comply with the requirements of this section because defendant refused a breath test of his blood alcohol level, and defendant did not have a right to have a witness present. State v. Shepley, 237 N.C. App. 174, 764 S.E.2d 658 (2014).

MODIFICATION OF RIGHTS FORM. --Arresting officer's modification of the rights form related to a material requirement under G.S. 20-16.2(c1) -- namely, whether petitioner submitted to breathalyzer testing. The officer's failure to modify the rights form in front of a magistrate or official authorized to administer oaths stripped the DMV of jurisdiction to revoke petitioner's driver's license. Wolski v. N.C. DMV, 252 N.C. App. 422, 798 S.E.2d 152 (2017), review denied, 803 S.E.2d 389, 2017 N.C. LEXIS 592 (N.C. 2017).

APPLIED in Durland v. Peters, 42 N.C. App. 25, 255 S.E.2d 650 (1979); Harper v. Peters, 42 N.C. App. 62, 255 S.E.2d 791 (1979); State v. McLawhorn, 43 N.C. App. 695, 260 S.E.2d 138 (1979); Rawls v. Peters, 45 N.C. App. 461, 263 S.E.2d 330 (1980); Byrd v. Wilkins, 69 N.C. App. 516, 317 S.E.2d 108 (1984); State ex rel. Edmisten v. Tucker, 312 N.C. 326, 323 S.E.2d 294 (1984); State v. Gunter, 111 N.C. App. 621, 433 S.E.2d 191 (1993); State v. McGill, 114 N.C. App. 479, 442 S.E.2d 166 (1994); Gibson v. Faulkner, 132 N.C. App. 728, 515 S.E.2d 452 (1999), decided prior to the 2000 amendment; State v. Streckfuss, 171 N.C. App. 81, 614 S.E.2d 323 (2005); Lee v. Gore, 206 N.C. App. 374, 698 S.E.2d 179 (2010), aff'd, 717 S.E.2d 356, 2011 N.C. LEXIS 660 (2011).

CITED in Church v. Powell, 40 N.C. App. 254, 252 S.E.2d 229 (1979); State v. Harper, 82 N.C. App. 398,

346 S.E.2d 223 (1986); State v. Knoll, 84 N.C. App. 228, 352 S.E.2d 463 (1987); State v. Bumgarner, 97 N.C. App. 567, 389 S.E.2d 425 (1990); State v. Jones, 106 N.C. App. 214, 415 S.E.2d 774 (1992); State v. Nobles, 107 N.C. App. 627, 422 S.E.2d 78 (1992); Melton v. Hodges, 114 N.C. App. 795, 443 S.E.2d 83 (1994); Nowell v. Killens, 119 N.C. App. 567, 459 S.E.2d 37 (1995); State v. Pyatt, 125 N.C. App. 147, 479 S.E.2d 218 (1997); Ferguson v. Killens, 129 N.C. App. 131, 497 S.E.2d 722 (1998); State v. Bartlett, 130 N.C. App. 79, 502 S.E.2d 53 (1998); State v. Summers, 351 N.C. 620, 528 S.E.2d 17 (2000); State v. Jacobs, 162 N.C. App. 251, 590 S.E.2d 437 (2004); Steinkrause v. Tatum, 201 N.C. App. 289, 689 S.E.2d 379 (2009), review denied, 363 N.C. 859, N.C. LEXIS 198 (2010); State v. Townsend, 236 N.C. App. 456, 762 S.E.2d 898 (2014); State v. Sisk, 238 N.C. App. 553, 766 S.E.2d 694 (2014), cert. denied 780 S.E.2d 566, 2015 N.C. LEXIS 1242 (2015).State v. Perry, 254 N.C. App. 202, 802 S.E.2d 566, review denied, 807 S.E.2d 568, 2017 N.C. LEXIS 970 (2017).

II. ADMINISTRATION OF TEST.

ADMINISTRATION OF BREATHALYZER TEST IS NOT DEPENDENT UPON THE LEGALITY OF THE ARREST, but hinges solely upon the law-enforcement officer having reasonable grounds to believe the person to have been driving or operating a motor vehicle on a highway or public vehicular area while under the influence of intoxicating liquor (now committed an implied-consent offense). State v. Eubanks, 283 N.C. 556, 196 S.E.2d 706 (1973); State v. Stewardson, 32 N.C. App. 344, 232 S.E.2d 308 (1977); In re Gardner, 39 N.C. App. 567, 251 S.E.2d 723 (1979).

Subsection (a) of this section provides that administration of the breathalyzer test hinges solely upon the law-enforcement officer having reasonable grounds to believe the person to have been operating a motor vehicle on the highway while under the influence of intoxicating liquor (now committed an implied-consent offense), and not upon the illegality of the arrest for that offense. In re Pinyatello, 36 N.C. App. 542, 245 S.E.2d 185 (1978).

OFFICERS AUTHORIZED TO REQUEST TEST. --Subsection (c) of this section does not provide that the "arresting officer" (now charging officer) is the sole person authorized to request that the petitioner submit to the test. The phrase "arresting officer" (now charging officer) merely distinguishes between the two law-enforcement officers present at the administration of the test and makes it clear that the breathalyzer operator who gives the warning set out in subsection (a) of this section is not the officer authorized to request that the petitioner take the test. Oldham v. Miller, 38 N.C. App. 178, 247 S.E.2d 767 (1978).

Considering the 1973 amendments to subsections (a) and (c) of this section together it is clear that the modification in subsection (c) that changed the phrase "law-enforcement officer" to "arresting officer" (now charging officer) was designed to distinguish between the law-enforcement officer with reasonable grounds to believe that the suspect was driving under

the influence of alcohol (now committed an implied-consent offense) and the law-enforcement officer who is to administer the test and give the warning. Oldham v. Miller, 38 N.C. App. 178, 247 S.E.2d 767 (1978).

State was required, pursuant to G.S. 20-16.2 and 20-139.1, to re-advise the defendant of the defendant's implied consent rights before requesting the defendant take a blood test; the state's failure to adhere to these statutory requirements required suppression of the results of the blood test. State v. Williams, 234 N.C. App. 445, 759 S.E.2d 350 (2014).

NOTICE OF RIGHTS --Where defendant was convicted of driving while impaired, the trial court did not err in denying defendant's motion to suppress intoxilyzer test results, as the police officer's placing of a copy of defendant's rights in front of defendant was sufficient to comply with G.S. 20-16.2(a), even though the officer did not physically hand the copy to defendant. State v. Thompson, 154 N.C. App. 194, 571 S.E.2d 673 (2002).

NOTICE OF RIGHTS NEED NOT PRECEDE REQUEST TO SUBMIT TO TEST. --Subsection (c) of this section does not require that the accused be requested to submit to a breathalyzer test after being informed of his statutory rights. Rice v. Peters, 48 N.C. App. 697, 269 S.E.2d 740 (1980).

ONE REQUEST BY OFFICER SUFFICIENT. --Petitioner's contention that he did not willfully refuse to submit to a chemical analysis at the request of the charging officer since the officer did not request any additional chemical analysis after the first test was completed was without merit, as the statutes require the charging officer to request a chemical analysis based on sequential breath samples, not a sequence of requests for separate chemical analyses, and thus officer's original request that petitioner submit to a chemical analysis was sufficient to comply with the requirements of subsection (c) of this section. Tolbert v. Hiatt, 95 N.C. App. 380, 382 S.E.2d 453 (1989).

ACCUSED NEED NOT BE WARNED THAT RESULTS MAY BE USED AGAINST HIM. --An accused subjected to a blood or breath test need not be warned that the results may be used against him. State v. Sykes, 20 N.C. App. 467, 201 S.E.2d 544, aff'd, 285 N.C. 202, 203 S.E.2d 849 (1974).

As breathalyzer results are not testimonial evidence, Miranda warnings are not required prior to administering a breathalyzer. State v. White, 84 N.C. App. 111, 351 S.E.2d 828, cert. denied, 319 N.C. 227, 353 S.E.2d 404 (1987).

BUT BEFORE THE TEST IS ADMINISTERED, AN ACCUSED MUST BE PERMITTED TO CALL AN ATTORNEY AND TO SELECT A WITNESS to observe testing procedures. State v. Sykes, 20 N.C. App. 467, 201 S.E.2d 544, aff'd, 285 N.C. 202, 203 S.E.2d 849 (1974).

RIGHT TO BLOOD TEST. --The trial court acted within its discretion in rejecting the defendant's allegation that he had requested and been denied a blood test, where the defendant was given an opportunity to use the telephone to make certain calls to his girlfriend and attorney and could have called, but did not call, a medical expert or hospital for the purposes of conducting a blood test. State v. Tappe, 139 N.C. App. 33, 533 S.E.2d 262 (2000).

RIGHT TO HAVE A WITNESS TO BREATHA-LYZER TEST. --To deny a defendant access to a witness to observe his breathalyzer test when the State's sole evidence of the offense of driving while impaired is the personal observations of the authorities would constitute a flagrant violation of defendant's constitutional right to obtain witnesses under N.C. Const., Art. 1, § 23 as a matter of law and would require that the charges be dismissed. State v. Ferguson, 90 N.C. App. 513, 369 S.E.2d 378, cert. denied, 323 N.C. 367, 373 S.E.2d 551 (1988).

Where officer refused defendant's unequivocal request that his wife be permitted to observe his taking of breathalyzer test, the trial court erred in admitting the results of the breathalyzer test at trial; fact that defendant later did take the breathalyzer, after he was first refused permission to have his wife witness the test, could not be construed to be a waiver of his right to have a witness. State v. Myers, 118 N.C. App. 452, 455 S.E.2d 492 (1995).

Although a witness who arrived to observe intoxilyzer testing failed to specifically tell the front desk why she was at the police station, defendant's G.S. 20-16.2(a) right to have the witness present during the test was violated as the arresting officer knew the witness was en route, the witness timely arrived at the police station, and the witness made a reasonable effort to make her presence known. State v. Hatley, 190 N.C. App. 639, 661 S.E.2d 43 (2008).

Defendant's suppression motion was improperly denied where: (1) after being arrested, defendant chose to have a witness present under G.S. 20-16.2(a); (2) in the presence of the arresting officer, defendant made contact with his selected witness by telephone and asked her to come and witness the administration of the Intoxilyzer test; (3) less than 20 minutes later, his witness arrived at the public safety center; and (4) despite multiple attempts to obtain access to defendant, the witness was not present when the Intoxilyzer test was administered, because she was still being told to wait in the lobby. State v. Buckheit, 223 N.C. App. 269, 735 S.E.2d 345 (2012).

NO RIGHT TO HAVE WITNESS PRESENT. --Because defendant's blood draw was performed pursuant to a valid search warrant, defendant did not have a constitutional right to have a witness present for the blood draw, and the trial court properly denied defendant's motion to suppress the blood evidence and dismiss the impaired driving charge. State v. Chavez, 237 N.C. App. 475, 767 S.E.2d 581 (2014).

FAILURE TO INDICATE DESIRE TO HAVE WITNESS AS WAIVER. --Petitioner, having failed to indicate at the time he refused to take breathalyzer examination test that he desired to have a witness present, waived his statutory right to delay the test until after his witness arrived, even if the witness arrived within the 30-minute period. McDaniel v. DMV,

96 N.C. App. 495, 386 S.E.2d 73, cert. denied, 326 N.C. 364, 389 S.E.2d 815 (1990).

THE EFFECT OF SUBSECTION (A) of this section is to require a defendant to exercise his rights in a timely manner. State v. Lloyd, 33 N.C. App. 370, 235 S.E.2d 281 (1977).

SUBSECTION (A) COMPLIED WITH. --Having placed the information required by subsection (a) in writing before the defendant, the operator was not required to make defendant read it. The operator complied fully with the statute when he orally advised defendant and placed the required information in writing before defendant with the opportunity on defendant's part to read the same. State v. Carpenter, 34 N.C. App. 742, 239 S.E.2d 596 (1977), cert. denied, 294 N.C. 183, 241 S.E.2d 518 (1978).

Where defendant was informed of his rights, signed a form containing those rights and submitted to the chemical analysis, defendant was adequately notified of his rights as required by subsection (a). State v. Watson, 122 N.C. App. 596, 472 S.E.2d 28 (1996).

RIGHT TO COUNSEL --When a defendant was arrested for driving while impaired, his right to consult with counsel as specified in G.S. 20-16.2(a)(6) controlled over the right stated in G.S. 15A-105(5) because anyone who accepted the privilege of driving on North Carolina's highways consented to the use of a breathalyzer test and had no constitutional right to consult a lawyer to void that consent; thus, so defendant had no right to consult counsel other than that provided for in G.S. 20-16.2(a)(6). State v. Rasmussen, 158 N.C. App. 544, 582 S.E.2d 44 (2003), cert. denied, 357 N.C. 581, 589 S.E.2d 362 (2003).

When defendant was arrested for driving while impaired, his right to consult with counsel as specified in G.S. 20-16.2(a)(6) was not violated because he did not unambiguously identify the person who was present as his witness to the breathalyzer test as his attorney and did not affirmatively ask to speak to her before the test was administered. State v. Rasmussen, 158 N.C. App. 544, 582 S.E.2d 44 (2003), cert. denied, 357 N.C. 581, 589 S.E.2d 362 (2003).

Officer was not required to wait for the full 30 minutes under G.S. 20-16.2(a)(6) before administering a breathalyzer test as a driver gave no clear indication that the driver wanted to call an attorney; the officer had reasonable grounds to believe that the driver had committed an implied consent offense based on the combination of the driver's evasion of a checkpoint, the odor of alcohol surrounding the driver, and a brief conversation with the driver. White v. Tippett, 187 N.C. App. 285, 652 S.E.2d 728 (2007).

TIME LIMIT ON RIGHT TO CALL ATTORNEY AND SELECT WITNESS. --The 30-minute time limit referred to by subdivision (a)(6) of this section applies both to the purpose of calling an attorney and to the purpose of selecting a witness to view the testing procedure. Seders v. Powell, 298 N.C. 453, 259 S.E.2d 544 (1979).

The fact that as a matter of grace the legislature has given defendant the right to refuse to submit to chemical analysis, and suffer the consequences for refusing, does not convert this step in the investigation into a critical stage in the prosecution entitling defendant to more than the 30 minutes provided in the statute to secure a lawyer. Otherwise, defendant would be able to delay the analysis until its results would be of doubtful value. State v. Howren, 312 N.C. 454, 323 S.E.2d 335 (1984).

The 30-minute grace period is available only when a petitioner intends to exercise his rights to call an attorney or have a witness present under the statute. Rock v. Hiatt, 103 N.C. App. 578, 406 S.E.2d 638 (1991).

THE 30-MINUTE PERIOD FROM THE ADVISING OF RIGHTS IS A MATTER OF LEGISLATIVE GRACE. In re Vallender, 81 N.C. App. 291, 344 S.E.2d 62 (1986).

THE BREATHALYZER TEST WILL BE DELAYED A MAXIMUM OF 30 MINUTES from the time defendant is notified of his rights. State v. Lloyd, 33 N.C. App. 370, 235 S.E.2d 281 (1977).

THE PURPOSE OF THE 30-MINUTE DELAY is to allow the defendant, who exercises his rights, a reasonable but limited amount of time to procure the presence of a lawyer, doctor, nurse or witness. State v. Lloyd, 33 N.C. App. 370, 235 S.E.2d 281 (1977).

The 1973 amendment of this section which inserted "for this purpose" in the place of "for these purposes" in subdivision (a)(6) did so at the same time that it enumerated three other rights accruing to a driver faced with the prospect of a breathalyzer test. The limiting words were inserted to apply to the single generic right enumerated in subdivision (a)(6) of this section, the right to have advice and support during the testing process, as opposed to the other rights enumerated in the proceeding subdivisions of this section. Seders v. Powell, 298 N.C. 453, 259 S.E.2d 544 (1979).

TIME LIMIT IS CONSTITUTIONALLY SOUND. --Allowing the driver 30 minutes time to decide whether to submit to the test, while providing that he is deemed to have refused at the expiration of the 30 minutes, is a constitutionally sound principle. Etheridge v. Peters, 45 N.C. App. 358, 263 S.E.2d 308, aff'd, 301 N.C. 76, 269 S.E.2d 133 (1980).

NO CONSTITUTIONAL RIGHT TO CONFER WITH COUNSEL. --A person enjoys no constitutional right to confer with counsel before deciding whether to submit to the breathalyzer test. Etheridge v. Peters, 45 N.C. App. 358, 263 S.E.2d 308, aff'd, 301 N.C. 76, 269 S.E.2d 133 (1980).

The operator of a motor vehicle has no constitutional right to confer with counsel prior to a decision to submit to the breathalyzer test. Seders v. Powell, 298 N.C. 453, 259 S.E.2d 544 (1979).

SECTION 15A-501(5) NOT APPLICABLE TO BREATHALYZER TESTS. --Section 15A-501(5) which gives a criminal defendant a right to consult with counsel within a reasonable time after arrest, does not apply to breathalyzer tests. It would be incongruous to hold that subdivision (a)(6) of this section requires an accused to select a witness to view for him the testing procedure within 30 minutes but

allows a greater period for the purpose of calling an attorney since, in virtually every situation, it would be easier for an accused to contact an attorney by telephone within 30 minutes than to contact anyone else and have them travel to the breathalyzer room to observe the test within that same time period. Seders v. Powell, 298 N.C. 453, 259 S.E.2d 544 (1979).

The legislature did not intend for the "reasonable time" contemplated by G.S. 15A-501(5), a part of the Criminal Procedure Act, to apply to the specialized situation contemplated by this section, a civil matter involving the administrative removal of driving privileges as a result of refusing to submit to a breathalyzer test. When two statutes apparently overlap, it is well established that the statute special and particular shall control over the statute general in nature, even if the general statute is more recent, unless it clearly appears that the legislature intended the general statute to control. Seders v. Powell, 298 N.C. 453, 259 S.E.2d 544 (1979).

TEST ADMINISTERED WHETHER OR NOT REQUESTED PERSONS HAVE ARRIVED. --Even if the defendant does exercise his rights within 30 minutes of notification, the test can and will be administered after the lapse of 30 minutes regardless of whether the requested persons have arrived. State v. Lloyd, 33 N.C. App. 370, 235 S.E.2d 281 (1977).

PRESENCE OF COUNSEL DURING ENTIRE PROCESS NOT REQUIRED. --An accused has no absolute right to demand that an attorney view the entire process involved in administering the test, including the preliminary steps necessary to ready the machine itself. State v. Martin, 46 N.C. App. 514, 265 S.E.2d 456, cert. denied, 301 N.C. 102, 273 S.E.2d 307 (1980).

THE POLICE ARE NOT REQUIRED TO DELAY TESTING UNLESS THE DEFENDANT EXERCISES HIS RIGHTS. State v. Lloyd, 33 N.C. App. 370, 235 S.E.2d 281 (1977).

WHEN DELAY OF LESS THAN 30 MINUTES PERMISSIBLE. --This section provides for a delay not in excess of 30 minutes for defendant to exercise his rights, and a delay of less than 30 minutes is permissible where the record is barren of any evidence to support a contention, if made, that a lawyer or witness would have arrived to witness the proceeding had the operator delayed the test to the maximum time of 30 minutes. State v. Buckner, 34 N.C. App. 447, 238 S.E.2d 635 (1977).

Subdivision (a)(6) of this section constitutes a maximum of 30 minutes delay for the defendant to obtain a lawyer or witness. It does not require that the administering officer wait 30 minutes before giving the test when the defendant has waived the right to have a lawyer or witness present or when it becomes obvious that defendant does not intend to exercise this right. State v. Buckner, 34 N.C. App. 447, 238 S.E.2d 635 (1977).

There was no error in the testing procedures or in the admission of the test results where there was a period of 25 minutes after notification to the defendant of his rights during which the defendant made no effort to exercise rights, and where, at the time the test was administered, the defendant made no effort to exercise his rights. State v. Lloyd, 33 N.C. App. 370, 235 S.E.2d 281 (1977).

TEST NOT REQUIRED TO BE ADMINISTERED WITHIN 30 MINUTES. --This section does not require that the breathalyzer test be administered within 30 minutes of the time a person's rights are read to him. Pappas v. North Carolina Dep't of Motor Vehicles, 42 N.C. App. 497, 256 S.E.2d 829 (1979).

REQUEST MADE BY OFFICER TO TECHNICIAN. --That portion of this section which provides that the test or tests shall be administered upon request of a law-enforcement officer having reasonable grounds to believe the person to have been driving a motor vehicle upon the public highways of this State while under the influence of intoxicating liquor (now committed an implied-consent offense), refers to the request being made by the officer to the technician who will give the test, rather than being directed to the suspect. State v. Randolph, 273 N.C. 120, 159 S.E.2d 324 (1968), decided under this section as it stood before the 1969 amendment.

PERSON TESTED MUST FOLLOW DIRECTIONS OF BREATHALYZER OPERATOR. --The full import of subsection (c) of this section requires an operator of a motor vehicle, who has been charged with the offense of driving under the influence of intoxicating liquor, to take a breathalyzer test, which means the person to be tested must follow the instructions of the breathalyzer operator. A failure to follow such instruction provides an adequate basis for the trial court to conclude that petitioner willfully refused to take a chemical test of breath in violation of law. Bell v. Powell, 41 N.C. App. 131, 254 S.E.2d 191 (1979).

REFUSAL TO REMOVE OBJECT FROM MOUTH. --Where breathalyzer operator noticed a piece of paper in the corner of petitioner's mouth and ordered him to remove it, and where petitioner refused, petitioner's refusal to obey the breathalyzer operator's instructions was a refusal to take the breathalyzer test under subsection (c) of this section, since a reasonable method for determining that the subject has not "eaten" in 15 minutes is to prohibit him from placing foreign objects in his mouth. Tolbert v. Hiatt, 95 N.C. App. 380, 382 S.E.2d 453 (1989).

RIGHT TO BE READVISED NOT TRIGGERED. --Superior court properly refused to suppress intoxilyzer results because the re-advisement requirement was never triggered; the officer's request that defendant provide another sample for the same chemical analysis of the breath on a second intoxilyzer machine was not one for a subsequent chemical analysis. State v. Cole, 262 N.C. App. 466, 822 S.E.2d 456 (2018).

DEFENDANT'S RIGHTS NOT DENIED BY OFFICER'S STATEMENTS. --Where defendant was fully and completely advised of his rights before a breathalyzer test was administered to him, the officer's error in stating that defendant could have a physician, registered nurse or a qualified technician or qualified person of his own choosing to administer the test under the direction of a law officer instead of

stating that defendant could have a qualified person of his own choosing to administer a test or tests in addition to any administered at the direction of the law-enforcement officer did not deny defendant his rights. State v. Green, 27 N.C. App. 491, 219 S.E.2d 529 (1975).

TRIAL COURT'S REVOCATION WAS BASED ON ADEQUATE FINDINGS OF FACT, as the court's finding that petitioner willfully refused without just cause or excuse to submit to a chemical analysis upon the request of the charging officer was the finding of an ultimate fact, indicating that the court rejected all opposing inferences raised by petitioner's evidence that the refusal was not willful or was excused, and as such, the court's finding permitted adequate appellate review of the ultimate fact at issue. Tolbert v. Hiatt, 95 N.C. App. 380, 382 S.E.2d 453 (1989).

TRIAL COURT ERRED IN ENJOINING COMMISSIONER OF MOTOR VEHICLES FROM REVOKING PETITIONER'S LICENSE on the grounds that proper procedures were not followed in administering the breathalyzer test; the validity of testing procedures is not relevant where a motorist has refused to take the test. In re Rogers, 94 N.C. App. 505, 380 S.E.2d 599 (1989).

III. REVOCATION OF LICENSE FOR REFUSAL TO TAKE TEST.

PURPOSE. --The administrative punishment of license revocation is designed to promote breathalyzer examinations which provide the State law-enforcement officers with more accurate evidence of possible driving under the influence violations. Montgomery v. North Carolina DMV, 455 F. Supp. 338 (W.D.N.C. 1978), aff'd, 599 F.2d 1048 (4th Cir. 1979).

RULE OF EVIDENCE DID NOT APPLY. --Reports of a police officer and sergeant and the affidavit of the officer were properly admitted in a license revocation proceeding as under this rule, the North Carolina Rules of Evidence did not apply to North Carolina Division of Motor Vehicle (DMV) proceedings pursuant to G.S. 20-16.2; the Rules of Evidence do not apply to DMV hearings held pursuant to G.S. 20-16.2. Johnson v. Robertson, 227 N.C. App. 281, 742 S.E.2d 603 (2013).

REVOCATION OF A DRIVER'S LICENSE DOES NOT DEPRIVE THE LICENSEE OF ANY FUNDAMENTAL CONSTITUTIONAL RIGHT. Montgomery v. North Carolina DMV, 455 F. Supp. 338 (W.D.N.C. 1978), aff'd, 599 F.2d 1048 (4th Cir. 1979).

The evidence sought from a breathalyzer examination is directly related to the State's need to enforce the laws governing the operation of motor vehicles on the State's roads. The administrative penalty is appropriately designed to deny a right directly related to the laws whose enforcement may be hindered by refusal to take a breathalyzer examination. Montgomery v. North Carolina DMV, 455 F. Supp. 338 (W.D.N.C. 1978), aff'd, 599 F.2d 1048 (4th Cir. 1979).

FINDING THAT DRIVER'S REFUSAL TO TAKE INTOXILYZER TEST WAS UNRELATED TO RIGHT TO HAVE WITNESS PRESENT. --Trial court properly determined that a driver refused to take an

Intoxilyzer test for reasons unrelated to a violation of his right to have a witness present under G.S. 20-16.2. By concluding that the driver's refusal was willful, the trial court resolved any issue of whether the refusal was related to the State's violation of the driver's right to have a witness present during chemical analysis. Powers v. Tatum, 196 N.C. App. 639, 676 S.E.2d 89 (2009), review denied, stay denied, 363 N.C. 583, 681 S.E.2d 784 (2009).

A HEARING UNDER SUBSECTION (D) OF THIS SECTION SATISFIES THE CONSTITUTIONAL DUE PROCESS REQUIREMENT. Montgomery v. North Carolina DMV, 455 F. Supp. 338 (W.D.N.C. 1978), aff'd, 599 F.2d 1048 (4th Cir. 1979).

Subsection (d) of this section provides an adequate opportunity for a hearing prior to revocation of a license for failure to submit to a breathalyzer examination. Montgomery v. North Carolina DMV, 455 F. Supp. 338 (W.D.N.C. 1978), aff'd, 599 F.2d 1048 (4th Cir. 1979).

PROPERTY RIGHTS NOT DENIED. --Where plaintiff refused to submit to a breathalyzer examination and later received notice that his driver's license would be suspended, the plaintiff was not deprived of any property right without procedural due process. Although a notice of revocation was issued prior to a hearing the plaintiff was provided a right to a hearing, before revocation was effectuated. In fact the plaintiff requested and received an administrative hearing a trial de novo in superior court, and consideration of his appeals of the superior court's decision by both the North Carolina Court of Appeals and the North Carolina Supreme Court prior to actual revocation. Montgomery v. North Carolina DMV, 455 F. Supp. 338 (W.D.N.C. 1978), aff'd, 599 F.2d 1048 (4th Cir. 1979).

SUSPENSIONS FOR REFUSAL TO TAKE TEST AND FOR IMPAIRED DRIVING DISTINGUISHED. --The suspension of a license for refusal to submit to a chemical test at the time of an arrest for drunken (now impaired) driving and a suspension which results from a plea of guilty or a conviction of that charge are separate and distinct revocations. Joyner v. Garrett, 279 N.C. 226, 182 S.E.2d 553 (1971); Vuncannon v. Garrett, 17 N.C. App. 440, 194 S.E.2d 364 (1973); Creech v. Alexander, 32 N.C. App. 139, 231 S.E.2d 36, cert. denied, 293 N.C. 589, 239 S.E.2d 263 (1977).

The suspension of a license which results from a plea of guilty or a conviction for drunken (now impaired) driving in no way exempts the licensee from the mandatory effects of the 60-day suspension of his license if he willfully refused to take a chemical test. Joyner v. Garrett, 279 N.C. 226, 182 S.E.2d 553 (1971); Creech v. Alexander, 32 N.C. App. 139, 231 S.E.2d 36, cert. denied, 293 N.C. 589, 239 S.E.2d 263 (1977).

The Department (now Division) of Motor Vehicles had authority to suspend for 60 days the limited driving privilege granted a defendant convicted of drunken (now impaired) driving for defendant's willful refusal to take a breathalyzer test at the time of his arrest. Vuncannon v. Garrett, 17 N.C. App. 440, 194 S.E.2d 364 (1973).

WHERE THE LAW DIRECTS SUSPENSION, RE-VOCATION, OR NONISSUANCE OF A DRIVER'S LICENSE, SOME OF the grounds are convictions for moving violations, or other statutory violations relating to highway safety, or situations where an individual's capacity to operate a motor vehicle safely are manifestly questionable. Evans v. Roberson, 69 N.C. App. 644, 317 S.E.2d 715 (1984), rev'd on other grounds and modified, 314 N.C. 315, 333 S.E.2d 228 (1985).

LEGALITY OF ARREST. --Subsection (d) of this section makes no reference to any question concerning the legality of the arrest as coming within the scope of the inquiry. In re Gardner, 39 N.C. App. 567, 251 S.E.2d 723 (1979).

The petitioner's driving privilege was properly revoked because of his unwillingness to take the breathalyzer test, whether or not his warrantless arrest was legal under G.S. 15A-401, where the arrest was constitutionally valid by virtue of the fact that the arresting officer had ample information to provide him with probable cause to arrest the petitioner for operating a motor vehicle upon a public highway while under the influence of intoxicants (now committing an implied-consent offense). In re Gardner, 39 N.C. App. 567, 251 S.E.2d 723 (1979).

THIS SECTION DOES NOT REQUIRE THAT A SUSPECTED DRUNK DRIVER SUBMIT TO A CHEMICAL TEST. It does, however, provide that a suspect who "willfully refuses" a request to submit to the test will have his driving privileges automatically revoked for a period of six months. The standard of "willful refusal" in this context is clear. Once apprised of one's rights and having received a request to submit, a driver is allowed 30 minutes in which to make a decision. A "willful refusal" occurs whenever a driver (1) is aware that he has a choice to take or to refuse to take the test; (2) is aware of the time limit within which he must take the test; (3) voluntarily elects not to take the test; and (4) knowingly permits the prescribed 30 minute time limit to expire before he elects to take the test. Mathis v. North Carolina DMV, 71 N.C. App. 413, 322 S.E.2d 436 (1984).

BURDEN OF PROOF. --Under this section, the respondent Commissioner of Motor Vehicles had the burden of proof to show that petitioner willfully refused to submit to a chemical analysis. Rock v. Hiatt, 103 N.C. App. 578, 406 S.E.2d 638 (1991).

THE WORD "REFUSE" AS USED IN THIS SECTION means the declination of a request or demand, or the omission to comply with some requirement of law, as the result of a positive intention to disobey. Joyner v. Garrett, 279 N.C. 226, 182 S.E.2d 553 (1971).

A DEFENDANT'S REFUSAL TO SUBMIT TO AN INTOXILYZER TEST can give rise to proceedings to revoke his driver's license only if it is a willful refusal. State v. Summers, 132 N.C. App. 636, 513 S.E.2d 575 (1999), aff'd, 351 N.C. 620, 528 S.E.2d 17 (2000).

DRIVER'S WILLFUL REFUSAL TO SUBMIT TO A CHEMICAL ANALYSIS COULD BE USED TO REVOKE HIS DRIVER'S LICENSE even though the arrest was not in compliance with G.S. 15A-401 (b)(2).

Quick v. North Carolina DMV, 125 N.C. App. 123, 479 S.E.2d 226 (1997).

A WILLFUL REFUSAL TO SUBMIT TO A CHEMICAL TEST WITHIN THE MEANING OF THIS SECTION OCCURS WHERE a motorist: (1) is aware that he has a choice to take or to refuse to take the test; (2) is aware of the time limit within which he must take the test; (3) voluntarily elects not to take the test; and (4) knowingly permits the prescribed 30 minute time limit to expire before he elects to take the test. Etheridge v. Peters, 301 N.C. 76, 269 S.E.2d 133 (1980).

ONE MAY REFUSE THE TEST UNDER THIS SECTION BY INACTION AS WELL AS BY WORDS. Refusal, in this context, is the declination of a request or demand, or the omission to comply with some requirement of law, as the result of a positive intention to disobey. A finding that a driver did refuse to take the test is equivalent to a finding that the driver willfully refused to take the test. Mathis v. North Carolina DMV, 71 N.C. App. 413, 322 S.E.2d 436 (1984).

DELAY AFTER BEING INFORMED OF RIGHTS HELD REFUSAL TO SUBMIT TO TEST. --Where the breathalyzer operator once fully informed petitioner of his rights with regard to the breath test, there was no obligation upon him to remind petitioner of the effect of his refusal to submit to the test, and petitioner's delay in taking the breathalyzer test, was at his own peril even though he stated that he was awaiting his attorney. Therefore, the trial court could properly find, that defendant had refused to submit to the breathalyzer test. Creech v. Alexander, 32 N.C. App. 139, 231 S.E.2d 36, cert. denied, 293 N.C. 589, 239 S.E.2d 263 (1977); Seders v. Powell, 39 N.C. App. 491, 250 S.E.2d 690, aff'd, 298 N.C. 453, 259 S.E.2d 544 (1979).

Where plaintiff was requested to take the test pursuant to this section and acknowledged an understanding of his rights, and where plaintiff was told of the 30 minute time limit and was repeatedly asked if he would take the test before it expired, plaintiff's initial 20-minute silence in response to those requests does not toll the 30 minute period. Otherwise, any suspect could evade the possible repercussions of testing by simply refusing to cooperate. Mathis v. North Carolina DMV, 71 N.C. App. 413, 322 S.E.2d 436 (1984).

The trial court did not err in finding that petitioner willfully refused to submit to a breath test by concluding that the 30 minute waiting period began to run at 1:39 a.m., when he was advised of his rights, instead of 1:54 a.m., when the formal request was made. In re Vallender, 81 N.C. App. 291, 344 S.E.2d 62 (1986).

DELAY OF MORE THAN 30 MINUTES WHILE AWAITING ATTORNEY. --Where petitioner's right to "call an attorney" was satisfied, petitioner had no right to delay the test in excess of 30 minutes while awaiting the arrival of his attorney. His declination to submit to the test was, therefore, a willful refusal under this section. Price v. North Carolina Dep't of Motor Vehicles, 36 N.C. App. 698, 245 S.E.2d 518, appeal dismissed, 295 N.C. 551, 248 S.E.2d 728 (1978), overruled on other grounds, Seders v. Powell, 298 N.C. 453, 259 S.E.2d 544 (1979); Etheridge v. Peters, 45 N.C. App. 358, 263 S.E.2d 308, aff'd, 301 N.C. 76, 269 S.E.2d 133 (1980).

Plaintiff had no right to delay the test in excess of 30 minutes while waiting for his attorney to return his call. His declination to take the breathalyzer test was thus a willful refusal under this section. Seders v. Powell, 39 N.C. App. 491, 250 S.E.2d 690, aff'd, 298 N.C. 453, 259 S.E.2d 544 (1979).

REFUSAL TO PROVIDE MORE THAN TWO SAMPLES. --Where petitioner provided two breath samples resulting in readings of .28 and .31 and then refused to provide any more samples, her conduct amounted to a willful refusal under subsection (c) of this section within the meaning of G.S. 20-139.1(b3). Watson v. Hiatt, 78 N.C. App. 609, 337 S.E.2d 871 (1985).

FAILURE TO FOLLOW INSTRUCTIONS AS WILLFUL REFUSAL. --Evidence showed that petitioner failed to follow the instructions of the breathalyzer operator where he repeatedly put his fingers in his mouth and failed to blow long enough into the machine to get a sufficient sample; failure to follow the instructions of the breathalyzer operator is an adequate basis for the trial court to conclude that petitioner willfully refused to submit to a chemical analysis. Tedder v. Hodges, 119 N.C. App. 169, 457 S.E.2d 881 (1995).

RIGHT TO FULL DE NOVO REVIEW. --Any person whose driver's license has been suspended under subsection (d) of this section has the right to a full de novo review by a superior court judge. This means the court must hear the matter on its merits from beginning to end as if no trial or hearing had been held by the Department (now Division) and without any presumption in favor of its decision. Joyner v. Garrett, 279 N.C. 226, 182 S.E.2d 553 (1971).

CORRECT STANDARD OF REVIEW WAS APPLIED. --Superior court applied the correct standard of review of a license revocation proceeding under this section where it stated that it did not conduct a de novo review of the facts and instead reviewed the record to determine whether there was sufficient evidence in the record to support the Commissioner of the North Carolina Division of Motor Vehicle's findings of fact. Johnson v. Robertson, 227 N.C. App. 281, 742 S.E.2d 603 (2013).

DUTY OF COURT TO DETERMINE "WILLFUL REFUSAL." --"Willful refusal" to take a breathalyzer test is a necessary requirement under this section and the trial court has the duty of judicially determining this question. Sermons v. Peters, 51 N.C. App. 147, 275 S.E.2d 218, cert. denied, 302 N.C. 630, 280 S.E.2d 441 (1981).

FAILURE OF COURT TO RESOLVE EVIDENCE OF WILLFUL REFUSAL. --Where evidence on whether petitioner knowingly permitted the prescribed 30-minute time period to expire before he took the test was conflicting, and the trial court made no attempt to resolve it in its order, trial court erred in determining that petitioner had "willfully refused" to submit to a chemical analysis under this section, and the case would be remanded to the trial court for additional findings based upon the evidence. Rock v. Hiatt, 103 N.C. App. 578, 406 S.E.2d 638 (1991).

Chapter 20

FAILURE OF COURT TO FIND FACTS. --Notwithstanding the failure of the trial court to find facts with regard to whether the plaintiff was arrested on reasonable grounds within the meaning of subsection (d) of this section, there was no need to remand for a further finding of facts or to award the plaintiff a new trial, since the facts leading up to the arrest were essentially uncontradicted, and only the conclusion to be drawn from them was disputed. Poag v. Powell, 39 N.C. App. 363, 250 S.E.2d 93, cert. denied, 296 N.C. 736, 254 S.E.2d 178 (1979).

OFFICER'S SWORN REPORT IS NOT PRIMA FACIE EVIDENCE OF REFUSAL TO SUBMIT TO TEST. --This section does not make the law-enforcement officer's sworn report prima facie evidence that the arrested person willfully refused to submit to the breathalyzer test. Therefore, if he objects to its introduction, the report cannot be used as evidence against him. Joyner v. Garrett, 279 N.C. 226, 182 S.E.2d 553 (1971).

BUT IS SUFFICIENT IN ABSENCE OF TIMELY OBJECTION. --In the absence of a timely objection as to its introduction, the officer's sworn report was sufficient evidence to sustain the Department's (now Division's) suspension of petitioner's license. Joyner v. Garrett, 279 N.C. 226, 182 S.E.2d 553 (1971).

Trooper's failure to comply with subsection (a) in the face of petitioner's refusal to submit resulted in the rescission of the revocation of petitioner's license. Nicholson v. Killens, 116 N.C. App. 473, 448 S.E.2d 542 (1994).

WILLFULNESS FOUND. --Although the evidence before a superior court was conflicting, the findings of fact 24 and 30 complied with G.S. 1A-1, N.C. R. Civ. P. 52(a) and were the ultimate findings of fact required to support a conclusion that a driver's refusal to submit to chemical analysis was willful as defined in G.S. 20-16.2. The officers asserted that the driver was marked as a refusal after refusing the test because he was innocent, and he testified that he refused the test because his right to have a witness present was violated; however, the driver conceded through finding of fact 30 that he did not know whether or not his witness was present, and therefore did not know that his rights had been violated. Powers v. Tatum, 196 N.C. App. 639, 676 S.E.2d 89 (2009), review denied, stay denied, 363 N.C. 583, 681 S.E.2d 784 (2009).

WILLFUL REFUSAL NOT SHOWN. --Superior court did not err by reversing the administrative decision of the Division of Motor Vehicles hearing officer revoking petitioner's driver's license because the evidence did not show that petitioner willfully refused to submit to a chemical analysis, as it was undisputed that when petitioner blew a second time, the breath test machine registered "mouth alcohol" as the result of the sample.

COMPLIANCE. --After being informed and kept apprised of his rights, a driver was given the option to take or refuse an Intoxilyzer test, and the purpose of G.S. 20-16.2 was thus fulfilled. The driver was informed of his statutory rights, given the opportunity to exercise those rights, kept informed of the thirty-minute time period as it elapsed, made aware of the choice he had to take or refuse the test, and provided multiple opportunities to submit to the test; the driver was not marked as a refusal until four minutes past the elapsed time limit. Powers v. Tatum, 196 N.C. App. 639, 676 S.E.2d 89 (2009), review denied, stay denied, 363 N.C. 583, 681 S.E.2d 784 (2009).

PROPERLY EXECUTED AFFIDAVIT REQUIREMENT --Construing G.S. 20-16.2 strictly, as courts are compelled to do, the plain language of the statute requires that the Division of Motor Vehicles of the Department of Transportation receive a properly executed affidavit that includes all the requirements set forth in G.S. 20-16.2(c1) before the Division is vested with the authority to revoke a driver's license pursuant to G.S. 20-16.2. Lee v. Gore, 202 N.C. App. 133, 688 S.E.2d 734 (2010).

Construing the plain language of G.S. 20-16.2, the form DHHS 3908 could not be construed as part of the affidavit. Lee v. Gore, 202 N.C. App. 133, 688 S.E.2d 734 (2010).

There was no evidence that the officer swore before the magistrate in any manner that the driver had willfully refused to submit to the chemical analysis, and the form DHHS 3908 could not serve as a substitute for a properly executed affidavit; therefore, because the Division of Motor Vehicles of the Department of Transportation never received a properly executed affidavit required by G.S. 20-16.2(c1), the Division had no authority to revoke the driver's license pursuant to G.S. 20-16.2, or any other statute. Absent the authority to revoke the driver's license, there was also no authority pursuant to G.S. 20-16.2 for the Division to conduct a review hearing, or for appellate review in the superior court, and therefore, the rulings of hearing officer and the superior court affirming the revocation of the driver's license were void. Lee v. Gore, 202 N.C. App. 133, 688 S.E.2d 734 (2010).

Trial court erred in reversing a suspension of a licensee's driving privileges by the Division of Motor Vehicles, as a police trooper's affidavit complied with G.S. 20-16.2(c1), despite a clerical error in his affidavit as to the time when the refusal occurred; time of refusal was not a requirement in the affidavit, and the trial court was bound by the hearing officer's finding on the time issue. Hoots v. Robertson, 214 N.C. App. 181, 715 S.E.2d 199 (2011).

Because G.S. 20-16.2(d) required that the DMV receive a properly executed affidavit from law enforcement swearing to a willful refusal to submit to chemical analysis before revoking driving privileges, and the officer failed to check the form indicating that petitioner's refusal was willful, the DMV lacked the authority to revoke petitioner's driving privileges. Lee v. Gore, 365 N.C. 227, 717 S.E.2d 356 (2011).

REASONABLE GROUNDS TO BELIEVE DRIVER WAS IMPAIRED. --Evidence was sufficient to support the Division of Motor Vehicles' (DMV) determination that the officer had reasonable grounds to believe that the driver was driving while impaired, and therefore the superior court erred by reversing the DMV's decision revoking the driver's license for refusing to

Chapter 20

submit to chemical analysis under G.S. 20-16.2, where the arresting officer observed the driver with glassy, bloodshot eyes and slightly slurred speech, the driver used enough mouthwash to create a strong odor detectable by the officer from outside the car, and he lied to the officer about using the mouthwash. Farrell v. Thomas, 247 N.C. App. 64, 784 S.E.2d 657 (2016).

COURT OF APPEALS IMPROPERLY RE-WEIGHED EVIDENCE AND MADE CREDIBILITY DETERMINATIONS. --Court of appeals erred in determining that the North Carolina Division of Motor Vehicles improperly concluded that a driver willfully refused to submit to a chemical analysis because it engaged in the prohibited exercises of reweighing evidence and making witness credibility determinations; the driver was instructed repeatedly about the process of submitting to a valid chemical analysis, and despite those warnings, he remained noncompliant. Brackett v. Thomas, 371 N.C. 121, 814 S.E.2d 86 (2018).

IV. EVIDENCE IN PROSECUTION FOR DRUNKEN DRIVING.

CHEMICAL ANALYSES OF BLOOD OR BREATH ARE NOT WITHIN THE PROTECTION OF U.S. CONST., AMEND. V AND XIV, or N.C. Const., Art. I, § 23, as such chemical analyses are not evidence which is "testimonial" or "communicative" in nature. State v. White, 84 N.C. App. 111, 351 S.E.2d 828, cert. denied, 319 N.C. 227, 353 S.E.2d 404 (1987).

RESULTS OF TEST ARE NOT EVIDENCE WITHIN PRIVILEGE AGAINST SELF-INCRIMINATION. -- The taking of a breath sample from an accused for the purpose of test is not evidence of a testimonial or communicative nature within the privilege against self-incrimination, and for that reason the requirements of Miranda are inapplicable to a breathalyzer test administered pursuant to the statutes. State v. Sykes, 285 N.C. 202, 203 S.E.2d 849 (1974).

EXCLUSIONARY RULE INAPPLICABLE. --It was error to reverse the revocation of a driver's license due to the exclusion, in criminal proceedings, of evidence derived from an officer's stop of the driver's vehicle without reasonable suspicion, because (1) the exclusionary rule did not apply in license revocation proceedings, so the relevant question was whether the officer had reasonable grounds to believe the driver had been driving while impaired, and (2) ample evidence showed such grounds, as the driver smelled of alcohol, had bloodshot eyes, admitted drinking, swayed noticeably on exiting the vehicle, and failed a sobriety test. Combs v. Robertson, 239 N.C. App. 135, 767 S.E.2d 925 (2015).

ADMISSIBILITY OF RESULTS WHEN TEST NOT PROPERLY PERFORMED. --Testimony concerning the results of blood tests may be admitted into evidence even though the tests were not performed in accordance with this section and G.S. 20-139.1 under the "other competent evidence" exception contained in G.S. 20-139.1. State v. Byers, 105 N.C. App. 377, 413 S.E.2d 586 (1992).

CONSIDERATION OF ALCOSENSOR RESULTS. --It is permissible to consider the results of alcosensor test in determining whether trooper had reasonable

grounds to believe petitioner had committed an implied consent offense. Moore v. Hodges, 116 N.C. App. 727, 449 S.E.2d 218 (1994).

THE STATE IS NOT LIMITED TO EVIDENCE OF BLOOD ALCOHOL CONCENTRATION WHICH WAS PROCURED IN ACCORDANCE WITH THE PROCEDURES OF THIS STATUTE; testing pursuant to a search warrant is a type of "other competent evidence" referred to in G.S. 20-139.1. State v. Davis, 142 N.C. App. 81, 542 S.E.2d 236 (2001), cert. denied, 353 N.C. 386, 547 S.E.2d 818 (2001).

FAILURE TO ADVISE DEFENDANT OF RIGHTS AND TO OBTAIN CONSENT TO BLOOD TEST. --Trial court properly granted defendant's motion to suppress blood draw evidence a police officer collected from a nurse who was treating defendant because the officer did not advise defendant of his rights and did not obtain his written or oral consent to the blood test; the State's post hoc actions did not overcome the presumption that the warrantless search was unreasonable, and it offended the Fourth Amendment and the State Constitution. State v. Romano, 247 N.C. App. 212, 785 S.E.2d 168 (2016), modified and aff'd, 800 S.E.2d 644, 2017 N.C. LEXIS 398 (N.C. 2017).

EFFECT OF FAILURE TO ADVISE DEFENDANT OF RIGHT TO REFUSE TEST. --Under this section, failure to advise a defendant of his right to refuse the breathalyzer test does not render the results of the test inadmissible in court. State v. Allen, 14 N.C. App. 485, 188 S.E.2d 568 (1972).

Failure by officers to advise defendant of his right to refuse to take a breathalyzer test does not render the result of the test inadmissible in evidence, defendant having impliedly consented to the test by virtue of driving an automobile on the public highways of the State, and the test having been administered after arrest and without the use of force or violence. State v. McCabe, 1 N.C. App. 237, 161 S.E.2d 42 (1968).

Where the defendant by his voluntary and overt actions makes it clear that he will not voluntarily submit to the breathalyzer test, it is not necessary for the State to present evidence that the defendant was advised of his right to refuse to take the breathalyzer test before evidence of that refusal may be used against him at a trial for driving under the influence, as is allowed pursuant to G.S. 20-139.1. State v. Simmons, 51 N.C. App. 440, 276 S.E.2d 765 (1981).

FAILURE TO ADVISE DEFENDANT OF RIGHT TO ATTORNEY AND WITNESS. --Where the State offered no evidence upon the question of whether defendant had been notified of his right to call an attorney and to select a witness to view breathalyzer testing procedures in accordance with subsection (a) of this section, results of the test were inadmissible, and admission of the results over defendant's objection constituted prejudicial error. State v. Shadding, 17 N.C. App. 279, 194 S.E.2d 55, cert. denied, 283 N.C. 108, 194 S.E.2d 636 (1973).

REFUSAL OF TEST ADMISSIBLE. --The failure to warn the defendant that the officer could seek alternate methods of testing did not render defendant's refusal inadmissible. State v. Davis, 142 N.C. App. 81,

542 S.E.2d 236 (2001), cert. denied, 353 N.C. 386, 547 S.E.2d 818 (2001).

FAILURE TO ADVISE DEFENDANT OF RIGHT TO ADDITIONAL TEST. --The failure of the State to establish that defendant was accorded the statutory right to have another test, in addition to the others which he was properly accorded, renders the results of the breathalyzer test inadmissible in evidence. State v. Fuller, 24 N.C. App. 38, 209 S.E.2d 805 (1974).

Where the defendant is not advised of his rights under subsection (a), including, under subdivision (a)(5), the right to have another alcohol concentration test performed by a qualified person of his own choosing, the State's test is inadmissible in evidence. State v. Gilbert, 85 N.C. App. 594, 355 S.E.2d 261 (1987).

RESULTS OF THE BREATHALYZER TEST WERE ADMISSIBLE even though defendant's initial "commitment" to take the test was obtained before he was advised of his statutory rights embodied in subsection (a) of this section. State v. Sykes, 285 N.C. 202, 203 S.E.2d 849 (1974).

REFUSAL OF TEST MAY NOT BE USED AS ASSUMPTION OF GUILT. --This section does not say that if a person refuses to submit to the test, it will be used as an assumption of guilt in court. State v. Mobley, 273 N.C. 471, 160 S.E.2d 334 (1968), decided prior to the 1969 amendment.

TESTIMONY OF CHARGING OFFICER. --It is settled law that the arresting (now charging) officer may testify as to a refusal to take the breathalyzer test at a trial for driving under the influence. State v. Simmons, 51 N.C. App. 440, 276 S.E.2d 765 (1981).

DEFENDANT'S INCRIMINATING STATEMENTS DEEMED HARMLESS ERROR. --Admission of evidence that after defendant blew into breathalyzer and was shown the reading, he made statements indicating his disbelief at the result, thus allegedly creating an inference that he had registered a reading in excess of the legal limit on the first test, was harmless in light of other evidence of defendant's guilt, including his refusal to take a second test. State v. Wike, 85 N.C. App. 516, 355 S.E.2d 221 (1987).

OTHER OFFICER NOT REQUIRED TO ADVISE DEFENDANT. --Subsection (a) does not require an officer, other than the charging officer, to advise defendants of their statutory rights in order for the State to admit into evidence, at the criminal prosecution for driving while impaired, the results of, or refusal to submit to, chemical analysis. State v. Abdereazeq, 122 N.C. App. 727, 471 S.E.2d 445 (1996).

ADEQUATE ADVICE GIVEN. --Evidence, including state trooper's testimony and defendant's telephone call subsequent to refusal to sign written form, supported trial court's finding that defendant had been adequately advised of his chemical test rights as required by this section. Gibson v. Faulkner, 132 N.C. App. 728, 515 S.E.2d 452 (1999), decided prior to the 2000 amendment.

REASONABLE GROUNDS SHOWN. --The evidence surrounding petitioner's accident, including the reason for its occurrence, taken with the odor of alcohol about petitioner, her mumbled speech, her admission that she had been drinking liquor earlier, and the results of the alcosensor test were clearly sufficient to give trooper reasonable grounds to believe that petitioner had been driving while impaired. Moore v. Hodges, 116 N.C. App. 727, 449 S.E.2d 218 (1994).

CROSS REFERENCES. --
For definition of "public vehicular area," see G.S. 20-4.01, subdivision (32). As to the availability of test records, see G.S. 20-27.

LEGAL PERIODICALS. --
For comment on chemical tests and implied consent, see 42 N.C.L. Rev. 841 (1964).

For article on tests for intoxication, see 45 N.C.L. Rev. 34 (1966).

For survey of 1978 law on criminal procedure, see 57 N.C.L. Rev. 1007 (1979).

For survey of 1979 law on criminal procedure, see 58 N.C.L. Rev. 1404 (1980).

For note discussing North Carolina's validation of the warrantless seizure of blood from an unconscious suspect, in light of State v. Hollingsworth, 77 N.C. App. 36, 334 S.E.2d 463 (1985), see 21 Wake Forest L. Rev. 1071 (1986).

For note, "North Carolina and Pretrial Civil Revocation of an Impaired Driver's License and the Double Jeopardy Clause," see 18 Campbell L. Rev. 391 (1996).

For a survey of 1996 developments in constitutional law, see 75 N.C.L. Rev. 2315 (1997).

OPINIONS OF THE ATTORNEY GENERAL

DEPARTMENT (NOW DIVISION) OF MOTOR VEHICLES MAY REVOKE LIMITED DRIVING PRIVILEGE GRANTED BY A COURT. --See opinion of Attorney General to Mr. Joe W. Garrett, Commissioner, N.C. Department of Motor Vehicles, 40 N.C.A.G. 414 (1970).

REVOCATION FOR REFUSAL TO SUBMIT TO TEST IS CONTINGENT UPON FIRST HAVING BEEN CHARGED FOR IMPAIRED DRIVING. --See opinion of Attorney General to Lt. M. S. Niven, 43 N.C.A.G. 81 (1973).

PERSON AUTHORIZED TO ADMINISTER A CHEMICAL TEST is a breathalyzer operator who holds a permit issued by the Commission for Health Services (now Department of Human Resources) pursuant to G.S. 20-139.1(b). See Opinion of Attorney General to Dr. Arthur J. McBay, Office, Chief Medical Examiner, 42 N.C.A.G. 326 (1973).

ADVISING ACCUSED OF RIGHTS. --See opinion of Attorney General to Robert Powell, 41 N.C.A.G. 326 (1971).

RUNNING OF 30 MINUTES PRIOR TO TESTING DEFENDANT. --See opinion of Attorney General to LTC Charles B. Pierce, N.C. State Highway Patrol, 41 N.C.A.G. 242 (1971).

SUSPECT NOT ENTITLED TO DRIVE OWN CAR TO TEST SITE. --A person who requests a pre-arrest chemical test pursuant to G.S. 20-16.2(i) does not have to be permitted to drive his own vehicle to the test site. See Opinion of Attorney General to Chief P.L. McIver, Garner Police Department, Garner, N.C., 47 N.C.A.G. 89 (1977).

SERVICE OF PICK-UP NOTICE. --If a subject upon whom a law-enforcement officer is serving a notice to pick up a driver's license revoked under G.S. 20-16.2(c) states that he has requested a hearing pursuant to G.S. 20-16.2(d), the officer should not serve the pick-up notice until he has verification from the Department of Motor Vehicles that no valid request for hearing has been made. See opinion of Attorney General to Major John Laws, N.C. State Highway Patrol, 40 N.C.A.G. 403 (1969).

§ 20-16.3. Alcohol screening tests required of certain drivers; approval of test devices and manner of use by Department of Health and Human Services; use of test results or refusal

(a) **When Alcohol Screening Test May Be Required; Not an Arrest.** -- A law-enforcement officer may require the driver of a vehicle to submit to an alcohol screening test within a relevant time after the driving if the officer has:

(1) Reasonable grounds to believe that the driver has consumed alcohol and has:

a. Committed a moving traffic violation; or

b. Been involved in an accident or collision; or

(2) An articulable and reasonable suspicion that the driver has committed an implied-consent offense under G.S. 20-16.2, and the driver has been lawfully stopped for a driver's license check or otherwise lawfully stopped or lawfully encountered by the officer in the course of the performance of the officer's duties.

Requiring a driver to submit to an alcohol screening test in accordance with this section does not in itself constitute an arrest.

(b) **Approval of Screening Devices and Manner of Use.** -- The Department of Health and Human Services is directed to examine and approve devices suitable for use by law-enforcement officers in making on-the-scene tests of drivers for alcohol concentration. For each alcohol screening device or class of devices approved, the Department must adopt regulations governing the manner of use of the device. For any alcohol screening device that tests the breath of a driver, the Department is directed to specify in its regulations the shortest feasible minimum waiting period that does not produce an unacceptably high number of false positive test results.

(c) **Tests Must Be Made with Approved Devices and in Approved Manner.** -- No screening test for alcohol concentration is a valid one under this section unless the device used is one approved by the Department and the screening test is conducted in accordance with the applicable regulations of the Department as to the manner of its use.

(d) **Use of Screening Test Results or Refusal by Officer.** -- The fact that a driver showed a positive or negative result on an alcohol screening test, but not the actual alcohol concentration result, or a driver's refusal to submit may be used by a law-enforcement officer, is admissible in a court, or may also be used by an administrative agency in determining if there are reasonable grounds for believing:

(1) That the driver has committed an implied-consent offense under G.S. 20-16.2; and

(2) That the driver had consumed alcohol and that the driver had in his or her body previously consumed alcohol, but not to prove a particular alcohol concentration. Negative results on the alcohol screening test may be used in factually appropriate cases by the officer, a court, or an administrative agency in determining whether a person's alleged impairment is caused by an impairing substance other than alcohol.

History.
1973, c. 312, s. 1; c. 476, s. 128; 1981, c. 412, s. 4; c. 747, s. 66; 1983, c. 435, s. 12; 2006-253, s. 7

EFFECT OF AMENDMENTS. --
Session Laws 2006-253, s. 7, effective December 1, 2006, and applicable to offenses committed on or after that date, rewrote the section and section heading.

CONSIDERATION OF ALCOSENSOR RESULTS. --It is permissible to consider the results of alcosensor test in determining whether trooper had reasonable grounds to believe petitioner had committed an implied consent offense. Moore v. Hodges, 116 N.C. App. 727, 449 S.E.2d 218 (1994).

Statutory language that allowed an officer to consider the numerical reading of the Alco-sensor test was supplanted by the current version of the statute, which prohibits the actual alcohol concentration result from being used in determining if there are reasonable grounds for believing that the driver has committed an implied-consent offense; in light of the absence of any numerical reading in the record, the state's argument would allow law enforcement to evade review when arresting individuals for impaired driving after conducting alcohol screening tests, and the argument was without merit. State v. Overocker, 236 N.C. App. 423, 762 S.E.2d 921 (2014).

ADMISSION INTO EVIDENCE. --Results of defendant's alcohol screening test were not admissible as substantive evidence of alcohol use in a prosecution for driving while his license was revoked, and could be admitted only as evidence in support of probable cause for the arrest or to show impairment by a substance other than alcohol. State v. Bartlett, 130 N.C. App. 79, 502 S.E.2d 53 (1998).

Alco-sensor test results were not admissible in the event of a rehearing on defendant's contempt charge under G.S. 5A-11 because the results were used to show that defendant was impaired and that alcohol was the cause of the impairment, and thus the results were inadmissible under G.S. 20-16.3(d). State v. Ford, 164 N.C. App. 566, 596 S.E.2d 846 (2004).

ADMISSION OF ACTUAL NUMBERS. --Although the admission of the actual numerical results of defendant's alco-sensor test during the pre-trial hearing was error, defendant was not entitled to a new trial because the actual numerical results were never admitted into evidence at trial before the jury. State v. Townsend, 236 N.C. App. 456, 762 S.E.2d 898 (2014).

In a driving while impaired case, because the trooper only testified to the positive test results from the portable breath tests, without revealing the actual alcohol concentration, his testimony was not erroneously admitted. State v. Wiles, -- N.C. App. --, 841 S.E.2d 321 (2020).

SOBRIETY CHECKPOINT. --Order suppressing evidence obtained by roadway checkpoint was error because no evidence suggested that the stated proper purpose of checkpoint (sobriety) was a mask for another, unconstitutional purpose, and as such the trial court was in error in holding that the lack of such evidence required it to exclude the evidence obtained by the stop; from the available evidence, it was clear that the actual purpose of the checkpoint was the same as its stated purpose: to check for sobriety. State v. Burroughs, 185 N.C. App. 496, 648 S.E.2d 561 (2007).

CITED in State v. Hunter, 299 N.C. 29, 261 S.E.2d 189 (1980); Powers v. Powers, 130 N.C. App. 37, 502 S.E.2d 398 (1998); State v. Mitchell, 154 N.C. App. 186, 571 S.E.2d 640 (2002).

§ 20-16.3A. Checking stations and roadblocks

(a) A law-enforcement agency may conduct checking stations to determine compliance with the provisions of this Chapter. If the agency is conducting a checking station for the purposes of determining compliance with this Chapter, it must:

 (1) Repealed by Session Laws 2006-253, s. 4, effective December 1, 2006, and applicable to offenses committed on or after that date.

 (2) Designate in advance the pattern both for stopping vehicles and for requesting drivers that are stopped to produce drivers license, registration, or insurance information.

 (2a) Operate under a written policy that provides guidelines for the pattern, which need not be in writing. The policy may be either the agency's own policy, or if the agency does not have a written policy, it may be the policy of another law enforcement agency, and may include contingency provisions for altering either pattern if actual traffic conditions are different from those anticipated, but no individual officer may be given discretion as to which vehicle

is stopped or, of the vehicles stopped, which driver is requested to produce drivers license, registration, or insurance information. If officers of a law enforcement agency are operating under another agency's policy, it must be stated in writing.

 (3) Advise the public that an authorized checking station is being operated by having, at a minimum, one law enforcement vehicle with its blue light in operation during the conducting of the checking station.

(a1) A pattern designated by a law enforcement agency pursuant to subsection (a) of this section shall not be based on a particular vehicle type, except that the pattern may designate any type of commercial motor vehicle as defined in G.S. 20-4.01(3d). The provisions of this subsection shall apply to this Chapter only and are not to be construed to restrict any other type of checkpoint or roadblock which is lawful and meets the requirements of subsection (c) of this section.

(b) An officer who determines there is a reasonable suspicion that an occupant has violated a provision of this Chapter, or any other provision of law, may detain the driver to further investigate in accordance with law. The operator of any vehicle stopped at a checking station established under this subsection may be requested to submit to an alcohol screening test under G.S. 20-16.3 if during the course of the stop the officer determines the driver had previously consumed alcohol or has an open container of alcoholic beverage in the vehicle. The officer so requesting shall consider the results of any alcohol screening test or the driver's refusal in determining if there is reasonable suspicion to investigate further.

(c) Law enforcement agencies may conduct any type of checking station or roadblock as long as it is established and operated in accordance with the provisions of the United States Constitution and the Constitution of North Carolina.

(d) The placement of checkpoints should be random or statistically indicated, and agencies shall avoid placing checkpoints repeatedly in the same location or proximity. This subsection shall not be grounds for a motion to suppress or a defense to any offense arising out of the operation of a checking station.

History.
1983, c. 435, s. 22; 2006-253, s. 4;2011-216, s. 1
 EFFECT OF AMENDMENTS. --
Session Laws 2006-253, s. 4, effective December 1, 2006, and applicable to offenses committed on or after that date, rewrote the section and section heading.
Session Laws 2011-216, s. 1, added subsection (a1).
For effective date and applicability, see Editor's note.
LEGISLATIVE INTENT. --Language of G.S. 20-16.3A made clear that the legislature did not

intend for it to cover all license checks. State v. Tarlton, 146 N.C. App. 417, 553 S.E.2d 50 (2001).

WRITTEN POLICY REQUIRED. --Trial court did not err by granting defendant's motion to suppress because the sheriff's department had no written policy providing guidelines for motor vehicle law checking stations as statutorily mandated and the General Assembly specifically included language in the statute that it shall not be a basis for a motion to suppress, meanwhile excluding the same language in another subsection. State v. White, 232 N.C. App. 296, 753 S.E.2d 698 (2014).

CHECKING STATION IN ACCORD WITH GUIDELINES. --Where the findings showed that checking station was conducted in accordance with required guidelines, motion to suppress was not proper. State v. Barnes, 123 N.C. App. 144, 472 S.E.2d 784 (1996).

Sobriety checkpoint complied with G.S. 20-16.3A because it provided for preliminary screening of every driver and allowed further investigation only if the officer had a reasonable articulable suspicion that the driver was impaired. State v. Colbert, 146 N.C. App. 506, 553 S.E.2d 221 (2001).

No error occurred from suppressing checkpoint evidence because the well-marked checkpoint was administered under a written plan to check all drivers, under N.C. Gen. Stat. § 20-16.3A, at a predetermined location where a large number of intoxicated driving offenses occurred, with predetermined start and end times. State v. Townsend, 236 N.C. App. 456, 762 S.E.2d 898 (2014).

CHECKPOINT FOR LAWFUL PURPOSE. --An attempt to increase police presence in an affected area while conducting a checkpoint for a recognized lawful purpose was not akin to operating a checkpoint for the general detection of crime. State v. McDonald, 239 N.C. App. 559, 768 S.E.2d 913 (2015).

REASONABLENESS OF CHECKPOINT. --Trial court erred in failing to adequately determine the reasonableness of the checkpoint, as it made no findings concerning the gravity of the public concerns served by the checkpoint, no findings as to whether the checkpoint was appropriately tailored to meets its primary purposes, and no findings addressing whether the location of the checkpoint or the manner it was conducted were subject to supervision. State v. McDonald, 239 N.C. App. 559, 768 S.E.2d 913 (2015).

PERMISSIBILITY OF MONITORING CHECKPOINT AVOIDANCE --It is reasonable and permissible for an officer to monitor a checkpoint's entrance for vehicles whose drivers may be attempting to avoid the checkpoint. An officer, in conjunction with the totality of the circumstances or the checkpoint plan, may, also, pursue and stop a vehicle which has turned away from a checkpoint within its perimeters for reasonable inquiry to determine why the vehicle turned away. North Carolina's interest in combating intoxicated drivers outweighs the minimal intrusion that an investigatory stop may impose upon a motorist under these circumstances. State v. Foreman, 351 N.C. 627, 527 S.E.2d 921 (2000).

POLICE OFFICERS WERE NOT REQUIRED TO FOLLOW THE REQUIREMENTS OF THIS SECTION where the stop which resulted in defendant/drunk driver's arrest did not arise pursuant to an impaired driving check but arose as the result of a false report of breaking and entering. State v. Covington, 138 N.C. App. 688, 532 S.E.2d 221 (2000).

CITED in State v. Bowden, 177 N.C. App. 718, 630 S.E.2d 208 (2006); State v. Collins, 219 N.C. App. 374, 724 S.E.2d 82 (2012); State v. White, 232 N.C. App. 296, 753 S.E.2d 698 (2014); State v. Townsend, 236 N.C. App. 456, 762 S.E.2d 898 (2014).

LEGAL PERIODICALS. --
For comment, "DWI Roadblocks: Are They Constitutional in North Carolina?," see 21 Wake Forest L. Rev. 779 (1986).

For note, "Blurred Lines: State v. Griffin and the Resulting Uncertainty in North Carolina Courts Regarding the Constitutional Analysis of Traffic Checkpoints," see 36 N.C. Cent. L. Rev. 130 (2013).

N.C. Gen. Stat. § 20-16.4

Repealed by Session Laws 1989, c. 691, s. 4.

§ 20-16.5. Immediate civil license revocation for certain persons charged with implied-consent offenses

(a) **Definitions. --** As used in this section the following words and phrases have the following meanings:

(1) **Law Enforcement Officer. --** As described in G.S. 20-16.2(a1).

(2) **Clerk. --** As defined in G.S. 15A-101(2).

(3) **Judicial Official. --** As defined in G.S. 15A-101(5).

(4) **Revocation Report. --** A sworn statement by a law enforcement officer and a chemical analyst containing facts indicating that the conditions of subsection (b) have been met, and whether the person has a pending offense for which the person's license had been or is revoked under this section. When one chemical analyst analyzes a person's blood and another chemical analyst informs a person of his rights and responsibilities under G.S. 20-16.2, the report must include the statements of both analysts.

(5) **Surrender of a Driver's License.** -- The act of turning over to a court or a law-enforcement officer the person's most recent, valid driver's license or learner's permit issued by the Division or by a similar agency in another jurisdiction, or a limited driving privilege issued by a North Carolina court. A person who is validly licensed but who is unable to locate his license card may file an affidavit with the clerk setting out facts that indicate that he is unable to locate his license card and that he is validly licensed; the filing of the

affidavit constitutes a surrender of the person's license.

(b) **Revocations for Persons Who Refuse Chemical Analyses or Who Are Charged With Certain Implied-Consent Offenses.** -- A person's driver's license is subject to revocation under this section if:

(1) A law enforcement officer has reasonable grounds to believe that the person has committed an offense subject to the implied-consent provisions of G.S. 20-16.2;

(2) The person is charged with that offense as provided in G.S. 20-16.2(a);

(3) The law enforcement officer and the chemical analyst comply with the procedures of G.S. 20-16.2 and G.S. 20-139.1 in requiring the person's submission to or procuring a chemical analysis; and

(4) The person:

a. Willfully refuses to submit to the chemical analysis;

b. Has an alcohol concentration of 0.08 or more within a relevant time after the driving;

c. Has an alcohol concentration of 0.04 or more at any relevant time after the driving of a commercial motor vehicle; or

d. Has any alcohol concentration at any relevant time after the driving and the person is under 21 years of age.

(b1) **Precharge Test Results as Basis for Revocation.** -- Notwithstanding the provisions of subsection (b), a person's driver's license is subject to revocation under this section if:

(1) The person requests a precharge chemical analysis pursuant to G.S. 20-16.2(i); and

(2) The person has:

a. An alcohol concentration of 0.08 or more at any relevant time after driving;

b. An alcohol concentration of 0.04 or more at any relevant time after driving a commercial motor vehicle; or

c. Any alcohol concentration at any relevant time after driving and the person is under 21 years of age; and

(3) The person is charged with an implied-consent offense.

(c) **Duty of Law Enforcement Officers and Chemical Analysts to Report to Judicial Officials.** -- If a person's driver's license is subject to revocation under this section, the law enforcement officer and the chemical analyst must execute a revocation report. If the person has refused to submit to a chemical analysis, a copy of the affidavit to be submitted to the Division under G.S. 20-16.2(c) may be substituted for the revocation report if it contains the information required by this section. It is the specific duty of the law enforcement officer to make

sure that the report is expeditiously filed with a judicial official as required by this section.

(d) **Which Judicial Official Must Receive Report.** -- The judicial official with whom the revocation report must be filed is:

(1) The judicial official conducting the initial appearance on the underlying criminal charge if:

a. No revocation report has previously been filed; and

b. At the time of the initial appearance the results of the chemical analysis, if administered, or the reports indicating a refusal, are available.

(2) A judicial official conducting any other proceeding relating to the underlying criminal charge at which the person is present, if no report has previously been filed.

(3) The clerk of superior court in the county in which the underlying criminal charge has been brought if subdivisions (1) and (2) are not applicable at the time the law enforcement officer must file the report.

(e) **Procedure if Report Filed with Judicial Official When Person Is Present.** -- If a properly executed revocation report concerning a person is filed with a judicial official when the person is present before that official, the judicial official shall, after completing any other proceedings involving the person, determine whether there is probable cause to believe that each of the conditions of subsection (b) has been met. If he determines that there is such probable cause, he shall enter an order revoking the person's driver's license for the period required in this subsection. The judicial official shall order the person to surrender his license and if necessary may order a law-enforcement officer to seize the license. The judicial official shall give the person a copy of the revocation order. In addition to setting it out in the order the judicial official shall personally inform the person of his right to a hearing as specified in subsection (g), and that his license remains revoked pending the hearing. The revocation under this subsection begins at the time the revocation order is issued and continues until the person's license has been surrendered for the period specified in this subsection, and the person has paid the applicable costs. The period of revocation is 30 days, if there are no pending offenses for which the person's license had been or is revoked under this section. If at the time of the current offense, the person has one or more pending offenses for which his license had been or is revoked under this section, the revocation shall remain in effect until a final judgment, including all appeals, has been entered for the current offense and for all pending offenses. In no event, may the period of revocation under this subsection be less than 30 days. If within five working days of the effective date of the order, the person does not surrender his license or demonstrate that he is not currently licensed, the clerk shall immediately issue a pick-up order. The pick-up order shall be issued to a member of a local law-enforcement agency if the law enforcement officer was employed by the agency at the time of the charge and the person resides in or is present in the agency's territorial jurisdiction. In all other cases, the pick-up order shall be issued to an officer or inspector of the Division. A pick-up order issued pursuant to this section is to be served in accordance with G.S. 20-29 as if the order had been issued by the Division.

(f) **Procedure if Report Filed with Clerk of Court When Person Not Present.** -- When a clerk receives a properly executed report under subdivision (d)(3) and the person named in the revocation report is not present before the clerk, the clerk shall determine whether there is probable cause to believe that each of the conditions of subsection (b) has been met. For purposes of this subsection, a properly executed report under subdivision (d)(3) may include a sworn statement by the law enforcement officer along with an affidavit received directly by the Clerk from the chemical analyst. If he determines that there is such probable cause, he shall mail to the person a revocation order by first-class mail. The order shall direct that the person on or before the effective date of the order either surrender his license to the clerk or appear before the clerk and demonstrate that he is not currently licensed, and the order shall inform the person of the time and effective date of the revocation and of its duration, of his right to a hearing as specified in subsection (g), and that the revocation remains in effect pending the hearing. Revocation orders mailed under this subsection become effective on the fourth day after the order is deposited in the United States mail. If within five working days of the effective date of the order, the person does not surrender his license to the clerk or appear before the clerk to demonstrate that he is not currently licensed, the clerk shall immediately issue a pick-up order. The pick-up order shall be issued and served in the same manner as specified in subsection (e) for pick-up orders issued pursuant to that subsection. A revocation under this subsection begins at the date specified in the order and continues until the person's license has been revoked for the period specified in this subsection and the person has paid the applicable costs. If the person has no pending offenses for which his license had been or is revoked under this section, the period of revocation under this subsection is:

    (1) Thirty days from the time the person surrenders his license to the court, if the surrender occurs within five working days of the effective date of the order; or

    (2) Thirty days after the person appears before the clerk and demonstrates that he is not currently licensed to drive, if the appearance occurs within five working days of the effective date of the revocation order; or

    (3) Forty-five days from the time:

        a. The person's drivers license is picked up by a law-enforcement officer following service of a pick-up order; or

        b. The person demonstrates to a law-enforcement officer who has a pick-up order for his license that he is not currently licensed; or

        c. The person's drivers license is surrendered to the court if the surrender occurs more than five working days after the effective date of the revocation order; or

        d. The person appears before the clerk to demonstrate that he is not currently licensed, if he appears more than five working days after the effective date of the revocation order.

If at the time of the current offense, the person has one or more pending offenses for which his license had been or is revoked under this section, the revocation shall remain in effect until a final judgment, including all appeals, has been entered for the current offense and for all pending offenses. In no event may the period of revocation for the current offense be less than the applicable period of revocation in subdivision (1), (2), or (3) of this subsection. When a pick-up order is issued, it shall inform the person of his right to a hearing as specified in subsection (g), and that the revocation remains in effect pending the hearing. An officer serving a pick-up order under this subsection shall return the order to the court indicating the date it was served or that he was unable to serve the order. If the license was surrendered, the officer serving the order shall deposit it with the clerk within three days of the surrender.

(g) **Hearing before Magistrate or Judge if Person Contests Validity of Revocation.** -- A person whose license is revoked under this section may request in writing a hearing to contest the validity of the revocation. The request may be made at the time of the person's initial appearance, or within 10 days of the effective date of the revocation to the clerk or a magistrate designated by the clerk, and may specifically request that the hearing be conducted by a district court judge. The Administrative Office of the Courts must develop a hearing request form for any person requesting a hearing. Unless a district court judge is requested, the hearing must be conducted within the county by a magistrate assigned by the chief district court judge to conduct such hearings. If the person requests that a district court judge hold the hearing, the hearing must be conducted within the district court district as defined in G.S. 7A-133 by a district court judge assigned to conduct such hearings. The revocation remains in effect pending the hearing, but the hearing must be held within three working days following the request if the hearing is before a magistrate or within five working days if the hearing is before a district court judge. The request for the hearing must specify the grounds upon which the validity of the revocation is challenged and the hearing must be limited to the grounds specified in the request. A witness may submit his evidence by affidavit unless he is subpoenaed to appear. Any person who appears and testifies is subject to questioning by the judicial official conducting the hearing, and the judicial official may adjourn the hearing to seek additional evidence if he is not satisfied with the accuracy or completeness of evidence. The person contesting the validity of the revocation may, but is not required to, testify in his own behalf. Unless contested by the person requesting the hearing, the judicial official may accept as true any matter stated in the revocation report. If any relevant condition under subsection (b) is contested, the judicial official must find by the greater weight of the evidence that the condition was met in order to sustain the revocation. At the conclusion of the hearing the judicial official must enter an order sustaining or rescinding the revocation. The judicial official's findings are without prejudice to the person contesting the revocation and to any other potential party as to any other proceedings, civil or criminal, that may involve facts bearing upon the conditions in subsection (b) considered by the judicial official. The decision of the judicial official is final and may not be appealed in the General Court of Justice. If the hearing is not held and completed within three working days of the written request for a hearing before a magistrate or within five working days of the written request for a hearing before a district court judge, the judicial official must enter an order rescinding the revocation, unless the person contesting the revocation contributed to the delay in completing the hearing. If the person requesting the hearing fails to appear at the hearing or any rescheduling thereof after having been properly notified, he forfeits his right to a hearing.

(h) **Return of License.** -- After the applicable period of revocation under this section, or if the magistrate or judge orders the revocation rescinded, the person whose license was revoked may apply to the clerk for return of his surrendered license. Unless the clerk finds that the person is not eligible to use the surrendered license, he must return it if:

(1) The applicable period of revocation has passed and the person has tendered payment for the costs under subsection (j); or

(2) The magistrate or judge has ordered the revocation rescinded.

If the license has expired, he may return it to the person with a caution that it is no longer valid. Otherwise, if the person is not eligible to use the license and the license was issued by the Division or in another state, the clerk must mail it to the Division. If the person has surrendered his copy of a limited driving privilege and he is no longer eligible to use it, the clerk must make a record that he has withheld the limited driving privilege and forward that record to the clerk in the county in which the limited driving privilege was issued for filing in the case file. If the person's license is revoked under this section and under another section of this Chapter, the clerk must surrender the license to the Division if the revocation under this section can terminate before the other revocation; in such cases, the costs required by subsection (j) must still be paid before the revocation under this section is terminated.

(i) **Effect of Revocations.** -- A revocation under this section revokes a person's privilege to drive in North Carolina whatever the source of his authorization to drive. Revocations under this section are independent of and run concurrently with any other revocations. No court imposing a period of revocation following conviction of an offense involving impaired driving may give credit for any period of revocation imposed under this section. A person whose license is revoked pursuant to this section is not eligible to receive a limited driving privilege except as specifically authorized by G.S. 20-16.5(p).

(j) **Costs.** -- Unless the magistrate or judge orders the revocation rescinded, a person whose license is revoked under this section must pay a fee of one hundred dollars ($ 100.00) as costs for the action before the person's license may be returned under subsection (h) of this section. Fifty percent (50%) of the costs collected under this section shall be credited to the General Fund. Twenty-five percent (25%) of the costs collected under this section shall be used to fund a statewide chemical alcohol testing program administered by the Injury Control Section of the Department of Health and Human Services. The remaining twenty-five percent (25%) of the costs collected under this section shall be remitted to the county for the sole purpose of reimbursing the county for jail expenses incurred due to enforcement of the impaired driving laws.

(k) **Report to Division.** -- Except as provided below, the clerk shall mail a report to the Division:

(1) If the license is revoked indefinitely, within 10 working days of the revocation of the license; and

(2) In all cases, within 10 working days of the return of a license under this section or of the termination of a revocation of the driving privilege of a person not currently licensed.

The report shall identify the person whose license has been revoked, specify the date on which his license was revoked, and indicate whether the license has been returned. The report must also provide, if applicable, whether the license is revoked indefinitely. No report need be made to the Division, however, if there was a surrender of the driver's license issued by the Division, a 30-day minimum revocation was imposed, and the license was properly returned to the person under subsection (h) within five working days after the 30-day period had elapsed.

(*l*) **Restoration Fee for Unlicensed Persons.** -- If a person whose license is revoked under this section has no valid license, he must pay the restoration fee required by G.S. 20-7 before he may apply for a license from the Division.

(m) **Modification of Revocation Order.** -- Any judicial official presiding over a proceeding under this section may issue a modified order if he determines that an inappropriate order has been issued.

(n) **Exception for Revoked Licenses.** -- Notwithstanding any other provision of this section, if the judicial official required to issue a revocation order under this section determines that the person whose license is subject to revocation under subsection (b):

(1) Has a currently revoked driver's license;

(2) Has no limited driving privilege; and

(3) Will not become eligible for restoration of his license or for a limited driving privilege during the period of revocation required by this section,

the judicial official need not issue a revocation order under this section. In this event the judicial official must file in the records of the civil proceeding a copy of any documentary evidence and set out in writing all other evidence on which he relies in making his determination.

(o) **Designation of Proceedings.** -- Proceedings under this section are civil actions, and must be identified by the caption "In the Matter of " and filed as directed by the Administrative Office of the Courts.

(p) **Limited Driving Privilege.** -- A person whose drivers license has been revoked for a specified period of 30 or 45 days under this section may apply for a limited driving privilege if:

(1) At the time of the alleged offense the person held either a valid drivers license

or a license that had been expired for less than one year;

(2) Does not have an unresolved pending charge involving impaired driving except the charge for which the license is currently revoked under this section or additional convictions of an offense involving impaired driving since being charged for the violation for which the license is currently revoked under this section;

(3) The person's license has been revoked for at least 10 days if the revocation is for 30 days or 30 days if the revocation is for 45 days; and

(4) The person has obtained a substance abuse assessment from a mental health facility and registers for and agrees to participate in any recommended training or treatment program.

A person whose license has been indefinitely revoked under this section may, after completion of 30 days under subsection (e) or the applicable period of time under subdivision (1), (2), or (3) of subsection (f), apply for a limited driving privilege. In the case of an indefinite revocation, a judge of the division in which the current offense is pending may issue the limited driving privilege only if the privilege is necessary to overcome undue hardship and the person meets the eligibility requirements of G.S. 20-179.3, except that the requirements in G.S. 20-179.3(b)(1)c. and G.S. 20-179.3(e) shall not apply. Except as modified in this subsection, the provisions of G.S. 20-179.3 relating to the procedure for application and conduct of the hearing and the restrictions required or authorized to be included in the limited driving privilege apply to applications under this subsection. Any district court judge authorized to hold court in the judicial district is authorized to issue such a limited driving privilege. A limited driving privilege issued under this section authorizes a person to drive if the person's license is revoked solely under this section. If the person's license is revoked for any other reason, the limited driving privilege is invalid.

History.
1983, c. 435, s. 14; 1983 (Reg. Sess., 1984), c. 1101, ss. 11-17; 1985, c. 690, ss. 1, 2; 1987 (Reg. Sess., 1988), c. 1037, s. 80, c. 1112; 1989, c. 771, ss. 15, 16, 18; 1991, c. 689, s. 233.1(a);1993, c. 285, ss. 5, 6; 1997-379, ss. 3.4 -3.8; 1997-443, s. 11A.9;1997-486, ss. 2 -6; 1998-182, ss. 29, 30; 1999-406, s. 13;2000-140, s. 103A;2000-155, s. 15;2001-487, ss. 6, 7; 2003-104, s. 1;2007-323, s. 30.10(e);2007-493, s. 17

EDITOR'S NOTE. --
Session Laws 1999-237, s. 11.62(a) provides that the Administrative Office of the Courts shall transfer

all funds collected under G.S. 20-16.5(j) that are designated for the chemical alcohol testing program to the Department of Health and Human Services on a monthly basis.

Session Laws 1999-237, s. 11.62(b) provides that any funds collected under G.S. 20-16.5(j) that are designated for the chemical alcohol testing program of the Department of Health and Human Services and are not needed for that program shall be transferred annually to the Governor's Highway Safety program for grants to local law enforcement agencies for training and enforcement of the laws on driving while impaired. Transferred funds shall be spent within 13 months of receipt of the funds and amounts received by the Governor's Highway Safety Program shall not revert until the June 30 following the 13-month period.

For an earlier provision on funds collected under subsection (j), see Session Laws 1995-324, s. 26.5.

Session Laws 1999-406, s. 18, states that the act does not obligate the General Assembly to appropriate additional funds, and that the act shall be implemented with funds available or appropriated to the Department of Transportation and the Administrative Office of the Courts.

EFFECT OF AMENDMENTS. --

Session Laws 2007-323, s. 30.10(e), effective August 1, 2007, and applicable to all costs assessed or collected on or after that date, rewrote subsection (j).

Session Laws 2007-493, s. 17, effective August 30, 2007, substituted "law enforcement officer" for "charging officer" throughout the section. For applicability provision, see Editor's note.

EDITOR'S NOTE. --Many of the cases decided below were decided under this section as it read prior to the 1993 amendment which reduced the blood alcohol content for driving while impaired and related offenses from 0.10 to 0.08.

CONSTITUTIONALITY. --The summary 10-day revocation required by this section does not violate the equal protection rights guaranteed by the State and federal Constitutions. Henry v. Edmisten, 315 N.C. 474, 340 S.E.2d 720 (1986).

The Safe Roads Act's prehearing suspension provisions do not deprive persons whose licenses have been suspended for a 10-day period following their failure of a breath analysis test of property without due process of law. Henry v. Edmisten, 315 N.C. 474, 340 S.E.2d 720 (1986).

Because the summary 10-day license revocation under this section upon a person's failure to pass a breath analysis test is a remedial measure reasonably related to the State's interest in highway safety, the law of the land is satisfied by judicial review of the State's action to determine if there is probable cause to believe the conditions justifying revocation exist. The Safe Roads Act provides for such review, as under subsection (e) of this section, before revocation can take place, a detached and impartial judicial officer must scrutinize every condition of revocation to determine if each condition probably has been met. Henry v. Edmisten, 315 N.C. 474, 340 S.E.2d 720 (1986).

The ten-day driver's license revocation under this section did not constitute punishment as such, and therefore, defendant's subsequent criminal conviction for DWI did not violate the Double Jeopardy Clause. State v. Oliver, 343 N.C. 202, 470 S.E.2d 16 (1996).

Revocation of one's driver's license under this section and subsequent convictions of DWI under G.S. 20-138.1 do not violate the prohibition against double jeopardy. State v. Rogers, 124 N.C. App. 364, 477 S.E.2d 221 (1996).

IMPACT OF DOUBLE JEOPARDY CLAUSE. -- The plaintiff failed to prove that North Carolina's prior imposition of a thirty-day period of administrative license revocation under G.S. 20-16.5 constituted a criminal punishment within the meaning of the Double Jeopardy Clause of the Fifth Amendment, U.S. Const. Amend. V, and barred plaintiff's prosecution for the offense of driving while impaired in violation of G.S. 20-138.1. Brewer v. Kimel, 256 F.3d 222 (4th Cir. 2001).

Because a 30-day license revocation is a civil sanction rather than a criminal penalty, the Double Jeopardy Clause does not bar a defendant's subsequent criminal prosecution for driving while impaired by alcohol. State v. Evans, 145 N.C. App. 324, 550 S.E.2d 853 (2001).

Revocation of defendant's driver's license did not constitute jeopardy for double jeopardy purposes because it was not a punishment. State v. Streckfuss, 171 N.C. App. 81, 614 S.E.2d 323 (2005).

THIS SECTION DOES NOT REQUIRE A FINDING OF SCIENTER. Brewer v. Kimel, 256 F.3d 222 (4th Cir. 2001).

THE SUMMARY 10-DAY REVOCATION PROCEDURE OF THIS SECTION IS NOT A PUNISHMENT, but a highway safety measure. Henry v. Edmisten, 315 N.C. 474, 340 S.E.2d 720 (1986).

DURATION OF 10-DAY REVOCATION. --Under subsection (e) of this section, the summary 10-day revocation continues until the person has paid the applicable costs and at least 10 days have elapsed from the date the revocation order is issued. Henry v. Edmisten, 315 N.C. 474, 340 S.E.2d 720 (1986), rejecting the contention that revocation continues until 10 days from the date the revocation order is issued and the date the person has paid the applicable costs, whichever occurs last.

THE THIRTY-DAY ADMINISTRATIVE LICENSE REVOCATION PROVISION RATIONALLY SERVES LEGITIMATE REMEDIAL GOALS and is not excessive in relation to these goals. Brewer v. Kimel, 256 F.3d 222 (4th Cir. 2001).

REVOCATION PROPER. --Where petitioner, who was driving without his license, was stopped and charged with driving while impaired, and then appeared before a magistrate who revoked his driver's license for 10 days, petitioner's license had been validly revoked when he was stopped the next day; thus, he was properly charged with committing a moving violation during a period of revocation by operating a motor vehicle. Eibergen v. Killens, 124 N.C. App. 534, 477 S.E.2d 684 (1996).

Chapter 20

STANDING TO CHALLENGE SECTION. --The mere fact that plaintiff suffered the adverse effects of this section in October, 1983, did not give him standing to challenge the statute in federal court after his license had been returned to him. Crow v. North Carolina, 642 F. Supp. 953 (W.D.N.C. 1986).

APPELLATE REVIEW DECLINED DUE TO FAILURE TO CONTEST REVOCATION APPROPRIATELY. --Appellate court declined to address defendant's argument that the revocation report was not properly executed and was not "expeditiously filed" with the court because defendant failed to contest the validity of the revocation through the means prescribed in G.S. 20-16.5. State v. Hinchman, 192 N.C. App. 657, 666 S.E.2d 199 (2008).

APPLIED in State ex rel. Edmisten v. Tucker, 312 N.C. 326, 323 S.E.2d 294 (1984); State v. Howren, 312 N.C. 454, 323 S.E.2d 335 (1984); Harris v. Testar, Inc., 243 N.C. App. 33, 777 S.E.2d 776 (2015).

CITED in State v. Simmons, 205 N.C. App. 509, 698 S.E.2d 95 (2010); State v. McKenzie, 225 N.C. App. 208, 736 S.E.2d 591 (2013), rev'd 367 N.C. 112, 750 S.E.2d 521, 2013 N.C. LEXIS 1019 (2013), rev'd 748 S.E.2d 145, 2013 N.C. LEXIS 1019 (2013).

LEGAL PERIODICALS. --
For note, "North Carolina and Pretrial Civil Revocation of an Impaired Driver's License and the Double Jeopardy Clause," see 18 Campbell L. Rev. 391 (1996).

For a survey of 1996 developments in constitutional law, see 75 N.C.L. Rev. 2315 (1997).

For 1997 legislative survey, see 20 Campbell L. Rev. 417.

OPINIONS OF THE ATTORNEY GENERAL
EXPUNCTION OF CRIMINAL RECORDS. --Section 15A-146, which prescribes procedures for expunction of criminal records, does not apply to records of civil drivers license revocations maintained by the Division of Motor Vehicles and, therefore, does not require the Division of Motor Vehicles to expunge records of a 30-day drivers license revocation under G.S. 20-16.5 based on the same operation of a vehicle that gave rise to a criminal charge against the driver which is subsequently dismissed. See opinion of Attorney General to Mr. Mike Bryant, Director, Driver License Section, N.C. Division of Motor Vehicles, 2001 N.C. AG LEXIS 22 (6/13/2001).

§ 20-17. Mandatory revocation of license by Division

(a) The Division shall forthwith revoke the license of any driver upon receiving a record of the driver's conviction for any of the following offenses:

    (1) Manslaughter (or negligent homicide) resulting from the operation of a motor vehicle.

    (2) Either of the following impaired driving offenses:

        a. Impaired driving under G.S. 20-138.1.

        b. Impaired driving under G.S. 20-138.2, if the driver's alcohol concentration level was.06 or higher. For the purposes of this subsubdivision, the driver's alcohol concentration level result, obtained by chemical analysis, shall be conclusive and is not subject to modification by any party, with or without approval by the court.

    (3) Any felony in the commission of which a motor vehicle is used.

    (4) Failure to stop and render aid in violation of G.S. 20-166(a) or (b).

    (5) Perjury or the making of a false affidavit or statement under oath to the Division under this Article or under any other law relating to the ownership of motor vehicles.

    (6) Conviction, within a period of 12 months, of (i) two charges of reckless driving, (ii) two charges of aggressive driving, or (iii) one or more charges of reckless driving and one or more charges of aggressive driving.

    (7) Conviction upon one charge of aggressive driving or reckless driving while engaged in the illegal transportation of intoxicants for the purpose of sale.

    (8) Conviction of using a false or fictitious name or giving a false or fictitious address in any application for a drivers license, or learner's permit, or any renewal or duplicate thereof, or knowingly making a false statement or knowingly concealing a material fact or otherwise committing a fraud in any such application or procuring or knowingly permitting or allowing another to commit any of the foregoing acts.

    (9) Any offense set forth under G.S. 20-141.4.

    (10) Repealed by Session Laws 1997-443, s. 19.26(b).

    (11) Conviction of assault with a motor vehicle.

    (12) A second or subsequent conviction of transporting an open container of alcoholic beverage under G.S. 20-138.7.

    (13) A second or subsequent conviction, as defined in G.S. 20-138.2A(d), of driving a commercial motor vehicle after consuming alcohol under G.S. 20-138.2A.

    (14) A conviction of driving a school bus, school activity bus, or child care vehicle after consuming alcohol under G.S. 20-138.2B.

    (15) A conviction of malicious use of an explosive or incendiary device to damage property (G.S. 14-49(b) and (b1)); making a false report concerning a destructive device in a public building (G.S. 14-69.1(c)); perpetrating a hoax concerning a destructive device in a public building (G.S. 14-69.2(c)); possessing or carrying a dynamite

cartridge, bomb, grenade, mine, or powerful explosive on educational property (G.S. 14-269.2(b1)); or causing, encouraging, or aiding a minor to possess or carry a dynamite cartridge, bomb, grenade, mine, or powerful explosive on educational property (G.S. 14-269.2(c1)).

(16) A second or subsequent conviction of larceny of motor fuel under G.S. 14-72.5. A conviction for violating G.S. 14-72.5 is a second or subsequent conviction if at the time of the current offense the person has a previous conviction under G.S. 14-72.5 that occurred in the seven years immediately preceding the date of the current offense.

(b) On the basis of information provided by the child support enforcement agency or the clerk of court, the Division shall:

(1) Ensure that no license or right to operate a motor vehicle under this Chapter is renewed or issued to an obligor who is delinquent in making child support payments when a court of record has issued a revocation order pursuant to G.S. 110-142.2 or G.S. 50-13.12. The obligor shall not be entitled to any other hearing before the Division as a result of the revocation of his license pursuant to G.S. 110-142.2 or G.S. 50-13.12; or

(2) Revoke the drivers license of any person who has willfully failed to complete court-ordered community service and a court has issued a revocation order. This revocation shall continue until the Division receives certification from the clerk of court that the person has completed the court-ordered community service. No person whose drivers license is revoked pursuant to this subdivision shall be entitled to any other hearing before the Division as a result of this revocation.

History.
1935, c. 52, s. 12; 1947, c. 1067, s. 14; 1967, c. 1098, s. 2; 1971, c. 619, s. 7; 1973, c. 18, s. 1; c. 1081, s. 3; c. 1330, s. 2; 1975, c. 716, s. 5; c. 831; 1979, c. 667, ss. 20, 41; 1981, c. 412, s. 4; c. 747, s. 66; 1983, c. 435, s. 15; 1989, c. 771, s. 11;1991, c. 726, s. 7;1993 (Reg. Sess., 1994), c. 761, s. 1; 1995, c. 506, s. 7;c. 538, s. 2(b);1997-234, s. 3;1997-443, s. 19.26(b);1998-182, s. 18;1999-257, s. 4.1;2001-352, s. 3;2001-487, s. 52;2004-193, ss. 4, 5; 2006-253, s. 22.2;2007-493, s. 2

EDITOR'S NOTE. --
The subsection (b) designation was assigned by the Revisor of Statutes, the designation in Session Laws 1995, c. 538, s. 2(b) having been subdivision (12); the subsection (a) designation was added as well.

EFFECT OF AMENDMENTS. --
Session Laws 2004-193, ss. 4 and 5, effective December 1, 2004, rewrote subdivision (a)(6); and inserted "aggressive driving or" preceding "reckless" in subdivision (a)(7).

Session Laws 2006-253, s. 22.2, effective December 1, 2006, and applicable to offenses committed on or after that date, rewrote subdivision (a)(2)b.

Session Laws 2007-493, s. 2, effective August 30, 2007, substituted "Any offense set forth under G.S. 20-141.4." for "Death by vehicle as defined in G.S. 20-141.4." in subdivision (a)(9).

EDITOR'S NOTE. --Many of the cases below were decided prior to the 1993 (Reg. Sess., 1994) amendment which lowered the alcohol concentration from 0.10 to 0.08.

I. IN GENERAL.

WHERE THE LAW DIRECTS SUSPENSION, REVOCATION, OR NONISSUANCE OF A DRIVER'S LICENSE, the grounds are convictions for moving violations, or other statutory violations relating to highway safety, or situations where an individual's capacity to operate a motor vehicle safely are manifestly questionable. Evans v. Roberson, 69 N.C. App. 644, 317 S.E.2d 715 (1984), rev'd on other grounds and modified, 314 N.C. 315, 333 S.E.2d 228 (1985).

REVOCATION OF LICENSE NOT PART OF COURT'S PUNISHMENT. --The revocation of a license to operate a motor vehicle is not a part of, nor within the limits of, punishment to be fixed by the court wherein the offender is tried. When the conviction has become final, the revocation of the license by the Department (now Division) of Motor Vehicles is a measure flowing from the police power of the State designed to protect users of the State's highways. Harrell v. Scheidt, 243 N.C. 735, 92 S.E.2d 182 (1956).

MINISTERIAL DUTY. --Mandatory revocation of an operator's license under this section is the performance of a ministerial duty. Fox v. Scheidt, 241 N.C. 31, 84 S.E.2d 259 (1954).

The record of a conviction which has become final suffices to invoke the ministerial duty of performing the mandatory requirement of the statute by the Department (now Division) of Motor Vehicles. Harrell v. Scheidt, 243 N.C. 735, 92 S.E.2d 182 (1956).

The revocation of a license by the Division of Motor Vehicles is nothing more than the performance of a ministerial duty by that administrative agency, and is in no sense a "judgment" that can preclude the superior court from acting on a petition filed in that court pursuant to the habitual offenders provisions of the General Statutes. In re Woods, 33 N.C. App. 86, 234 S.E.2d 45 (1977).

NO ACTION OR ORDER OF THE COURT IS REQUIRED to put the revocation of the license into effect. Harrell v. Scheidt, 243 N.C. 735, 92 S.E.2d 182 (1956); Barbour v. Scheidt, 246 N.C. 169, 97 S.E.2d 855 (1957).

"FORTHWITH" DOES NOT MEAN THE ABSOLUTE EXCLUSION OF ANY INTERVAL of time, but means only that no unreasonable length of time shall intervene before performance. State v. Ball, 255 N.C. 351, 121 S.E.2d 604 (1961).

This section does not require the Commissioner (now Division) to act instantaneously. State v. Ball, 255 N.C. 351, 121 S.E.2d 604 (1961).

The word "forthwith" in this section does not require instantaneous action but only action within a reasonable length of time. Simpson v. Garrett, 15 N.C. App. 449, 190 S.E.2d 251 (1972); State v. Ward, 31 N.C. App. 104, 228 S.E.2d 490 (1976).

AND ACTION BY DIVISION WITHIN 11 DAYS OF NOTICE REASONABLY COMPLIED WITH SECTION. --Where the Department (now Division) of Motor Vehicles acted within 11 days after it received notice of plaintiff's second conviction for reckless driving, this was reasonable compliance with this section. Simpson v. Garrett, 15 N.C. App. 449, 190 S.E.2d 251 (1972).

INJUNCTION NOT AVAILABLE TO PLAINTIFF WHO COULD HAVE PREVENTED DELAY IN START OF REVOCATION PERIOD. --Where the elapse of approximately 15 months between plaintiff's last conviction for reckless driving and the order of revocation was not caused by defendant, Commissioner of Motor Vehicles or his Department (now Division), but the delay apparently resulted from the failure of the clerk of the court where plaintiff was last convicted to act promptly in forwarding a record of the conviction to the Department (now Division) of Motor Vehicles, and plaintiff could have prevented any delay in the start of the revocation period by surrendering his license to the clerk and obtaining a receipt therefor at the time of his second conviction, plaintiff was not entitled to injunctive relief. Simpson v. Garrett, 15 N.C. App. 449, 190 S.E.2d 251 (1972).

APPLIES ONLY TO CONVICTION IN NORTH CAROLINA COURT. --The mandatory provision of this section applies only to a conviction in a North Carolina court. Carmichael v. Scheidt, 249 N.C. 472, 106 S.E.2d 685 (1959).

THIS SECTION DOES NOT SPECIFICALLY REQUIRE NOTICE, and revocation under this statute is not reviewable in court. State v. Teasley, 9 N.C. App. 477, 176 S.E.2d 838, appeal dismissed, 277 N.C. 459, 177 S.E.2d 900 (1970).

The surrendering of his license, and the forwarding of it to the Department (now Division) by the court, gives the licensee sufficient notice that his operator's license has been revoked. State v. Teasley, 9 N.C. App. 477, 176 S.E.2d 838, appeal dismissed, 277 N.C. 459, 177 S.E.2d 900 (1970).

NOTICE AND RECORD SHOWING REVOCATION UNDER SECTION. --An official notice and record of "revocation of license" for the specified reason of "conviction of involuntary manslaughter" mailed to a driver by the Department (now Division) of Motor Vehicles was held to show that the license was revoked under this section rather than suspended under G.S. 20-16, and did not support a finding by the trial court that the license was suspended under the latter statute. Mintz v. Scheidt, 241 N.C. 268, 84 S.E.2d 882 (1954).

DIVISION NOT ESTOPPED TO ASSERT THAT IT ACTED UNDER SECTION. --Where the Department (now Division) of Motor Vehicles revokes a driver's license under the mandatory provisions of this section, the Department (now Division) will not be stopped

from asserting that it was acting under the provisions of this section by reason of a letter subsequently written to the licensee granting him a hearing under G.S. 20-16(c) [now subsection (d)], since in such instance a hearing is authorized by law. Mintz v. Scheidt, 241 N.C. 268, 84 S.E.2d 882 (1954).

FAILURE TO NOTIFY DMV OF CHANGE OF ADDRESS. --Where there was no court record indicating defendant's plea, nor the court's allocution to her, with respect to her guilty plea to a charge of failing to notify the Department of Motor Vehicles of a change of address pursuant to G.S. 20-17, such was more than a technical non-compliance with the reporting requirements of G.S. 15A-1022 and G.S. 15A-1026, but instead was sufficient to establish prejudice requiring that the conviction thereunder be vacated and the matter remanded. State v. Glover, 156 N.C. App. 139, 575 S.E.2d 835 (2003).

PLEA OF NOLO CONTENDERE. --This section mandatorily required the Department (now Division) of Motor Vehicles to revoke the petitioner's license upon receipt of the record from the superior court of his plea of nolo contendere, which in that case for the purposes of that case was equivalent to a conviction on the charge of driving a motor vehicle while under the influence of intoxicating liquor upon the public highways (now impaired driving). Fox v. Scheidt, 241 N.C. 31, 84 S.E.2d 259 (1954).

As a basis for suspension or revocation of an operator's license, a plea of nolo contendere has the same effect as a conviction or plea of guilty of such offense. Gibson v. Scheidt, 259 N.C. 339, 130 S.E.2d 679 (1963).

A plea of nolo contendere to a charge of manslaughter resulting from the operation of an automobile supports the revocation of the driver's license under the mandatory provisions of this section. Mintz v. Scheidt, 241 N.C. 268, 84 S.E.2d 882 (1954).

NO CONTEST PLEA MAY BE USED AS PRIOR CONVICTION. --The judgment entered on a plea of no contest to a previous charge of driving with a blood alcohol content of .10 percent or more may be used as a prior conviction by the DMV for purposes of revoking a driver's license. Davis v. Hiatt, 326 N.C. 462, 390 S.E.2d 338 (1990).

CERTIORARI TO REVIEW MANDATORY SUSPENSION. --Petitioner whose driving privilege was mandatorily suspended under subdivision (2) of this section (now subdivision (a)(2)) and G.S. 20-19(e) did not have the right to appeal under G.S. 20-25 or under the Administrative Procedure Act, Chapter 150B. However, the Superior Court could review the actions of the Commissioner by issuing a writ of certiorari. Davis v. Hiatt, 326 N.C. 462, 390 S.E.2d 338 (1990).

Where petitioner, seeking conditional restoration of his driving privileges, pled sufficient facts to show he did not have right to appeal from final decision of DMV, he could then have petitioned for writ of certiorari to have case reviewed by superior court. Thus, superior court had jurisdiction to review case. Penuel v. Hiatt, 100 N.C. App. 268, 396 S.E.2d 85 (1990).

REVIEW OF REVOCATION. --Mandatory revocations under this section are not reviewable under

G.S. 20-25. In re Wright, 228 N.C. 584, 46 S.E.2d 696 (1948); Winesett v. Scheidt, 239 N.C. 190, 79 S.E.2d 501 (1954); Fox v. Scheidt, 241 N.C. 31, 84 S.E.2d 259 (1954); Harrell v. Scheidt, 243 N.C. 735, 92 S.E.2d 182 (1956).

There is no right of judicial review when the revocation is mandatory pursuant to the provisions of this section. In re Austin, 5 N.C. App. 575, 169 S.E.2d 20 (1969); Rhyne v. Garrett, 18 N.C. App. 565, 197 S.E.2d 235 (1973).

The mandatory provision of this section is not subject to judicial review. Carmichael v. Scheidt, 249 N.C. 472, 106 S.E.2d 685 (1959).

REVIEW OF REFUSAL TO REINSTATE LICENSE. --Once the right to drive has been mandatorily revoked and a petitioner unsuccessfully seeks to have the license reinstated by the DMV, no superior court review of the denial is mandated unless the denial was arbitrary or illegal, because reinstatement is not a legal right but is an act of grace. Alpiser v. Eagle Pontiac-GMC-Isuzu, Inc., 97 N.C. App. 610, 389 S.E.2d 293 (1990).

COURT ORDER REQUIRING CONDITIONAL RESTORATION HELD ERROR. --Where petitioner offered no support for his allegation that the DMV's denial of a conditional restoration of his license, which had been mandatorily revoked under this section, was an arbitrary and capricious act and was in disregard of the law set forth in G.S. 20-19, it was error for the superior court to enter an order requiring the DMV to conditionally restore petitioner's driving privileges. Penuel v. Hiatt, 97 N.C. App. 616, 389 S.E.2d 289 (1990).

APPLIED in Whedbee v. Powell, 41 N.C. App. 250, 254 S.E.2d 645 (1979); State v. Finger, 72 N.C. App. 569, 324 S.E.2d 894 (1985); State v. Curtis, 73 N.C. App. 248, 326 S.E.2d 90 (1985); State v. Bowes, 159 N.C. App. 18, 583 S.E.2d 294 (2003), cert. denied, 358 N.C. 156, 592 S.E.2d 698 (2004).

CITED in Henry v. Edmisten, 315 N.C. 474, 340 S.E.2d 720 (1986); Cole v. Faulkner, 155 N.C. App. 592, 573 S.E.2d 614 (2002).

II. IMPAIRED DRIVING.

REVOCATION OF A DRIVER'S LICENSE IS MANDATORY whenever it is made to appear that the licensee has been found guilty of driving a motor vehicle while under the influence of intoxicating liquor or a narcotic drug (now impaired driving). Parks v. Howland, 4 N.C. App. 197, 166 S.E.2d 701 (1969); In re Austin, 5 N.C. App. 575, 169 S.E.2d 20 (1969).

Under G.S. 20-17(a)(2), defendant's driver's license was subject to mandatory revocation for one year because she was convicted under G.S. 20-138.1 for driving with an alcohol concentration of 0.16. State v. Benbow, 169 N.C. App. 613, 610 S.E.2d 297 (2005).

PERIOD OF REVOCATION. --Where there is mandatory revocation under subdivision (2) of this section (now subdivision (a)(2)), the period of revocation shall be as provided in G.S. 20-19. Carmichael v. Scheidt, 249 N.C. 472, 106 S.E.2d 685 (1959); In re Austin, 5 N.C. App. 575, 169 S.E.2d 20 (1969).

EVIDENCE that defendant had been convicted of operating an automobile while under the influence of intoxicants (now impaired driving) was competent on the question as to whether a driver's license issued to defendant had been legally revoked. State v. Stewart, 224 N.C. 528, 31 S.E.2d 534 (1944).

FAILURE TO APPEAR FOR TRIAL FOR DRIVING UNDER THE INFLUENCE IN ANOTHER STATE. --Motorist who received citation for driving under the influence in South Carolina and then forfeited bond by not appearing in court had his driver's license properly revoked even though no warrant was issued. Sykes v. Hiatt, 98 N.C. App. 688, 391 S.E.2d 834 (1990).

III. RECKLESS DRIVING.

PROVISIONS MANDATORY. -- The provisions of G.S. 20-17(6) (now subdivision (a)(6)) are mandatory. Snyder v. Scheidt, 246 N.C. 81, 97 S.E.2d 461 (1957).

The provisions of subdivision (6) of this section (now subdivision (a)(6)) and G.S. 20-19(f) are mandatory and not discretionary. Simpson v. Garrett, 15 N.C. App. 449, 190 S.E.2d 251 (1972).

SECTION 20-16(A)(9) DID NOT REPEAL SUBDIVISION (6) NOW SUBDIVISION (A)(6)) OF THIS SECTION BY IMPLICATION. --Subdivision (6) (now subdivision (a)(6)) of this section authorizing the mandatory revocation of a driver's license upon two convictions of reckless driving within a 12-month period was not repealed by implication by the subsequent enactment of G.S. 20-16(a)(9) authorizing the discretionary suspension of a driver's license upon one or more convictions of reckless driving and one or more convictions of speeding in excess of 44 (now 55) mph and not more than 75 (now 80) mph within a 12-month period. Person v. Garrett, 280 N.C. 163, 184 S.E.2d 873 (1971).

THE WORD "CONVICTION," as used in subdivision (6) (now subdivision (a)(6)), refers to a final conviction by a court of competent jurisdiction. Snyder v. Scheidt, 246 N.C. 81, 97 S.E.2d 461 (1957).

DATE OF OFFENSE, NOT DATE OF CONVICTION, CONTROLS. --Subdivision (6) (now subdivision (a)(6)) of this section directs the revocation of a driver's license for one year upon his conviction of two charges of reckless driving committed within a period of 12 months, and if both offenses were committed within a 12-month period, it is immaterial that the conviction of the second offense was entered more than 12 months after the first. The date of the offense, not the date of the conviction, is the determinative factor. Snyder v. Scheidt, 246 N.C. 81, 97 S.E.2d 461 (1957).

NOTICE OF SECOND CONVICTION MUST PRECEDE REVOCATION. --The Department (now Division) of Motor Vehicles was not authorized under this section to revoke plaintiff's license before it received notice of his second conviction for reckless driving. Simpson v. Garrett, 15 N.C. App. 449, 190 S.E.2d 251 (1972).

REVOCATION NOT MANDATORY FOR RECKLESS DRIVING. --The offense of reckless driving in violation of G.S. 20-140 is not an offense for which, upon conviction, the revocation or suspension of an operator's license is mandatory. In re Bratton, 263 N.C. 70, 138 S.E.2d 809 (1964).

CROSS REFERENCES. --

As to power to suspend or revoke license generally, see G.S. 20-16 and note. As to period of suspension or revocation, see G.S. 20-19.

LEGAL PERIODICALS. --

For 1997 legislative survey, see 20 Campbell L. Rev. 417.

For survey on new penalties for criminal behavior in schools, see 22 Campbell L. Rev. 253 (2000).

§ 20-17.1. Revocation of license of mental incompetents, alcoholics and habitual users of narcotic drugs

(a) The Commissioner, upon receipt of notice that any person has been legally adjudicated incompetent or has been involuntarily committed to an institution for the treatment of alcoholism or drug addiction, shall forthwith make inquiry into the facts for the purpose of determining whether such person is competent to operate a motor vehicle. If a person has been adjudicated incompetent under Chapter 35A of the General Statutes, in making an inquiry into the facts, the Commissioner shall consider the clerk of court's recommendation regarding whether the incompetent person should be allowed to retain his or her driving privilege. Unless the Commissioner is satisfied that such person is competent to operate a motor vehicle with safety to persons and property, he shall revoke such person's driving privilege. Provided that if such person requests, in writing, a hearing, he shall retain his license until after the hearing, and if the revocation is sustained after such hearing, the person whose driving privilege has been revoked under the provisions of this section, shall have the right to a review by the review board as provided in G.S. 20-9(g)(4) upon written request filed with the Division.

(b) If any person shall be adjudicated as incompetent or is involuntarily committed for the treatment of alcoholism or drug addiction, the clerk of the court in which any such adjudication is made shall forthwith send a certified copy of abstract thereof to the Commissioner.

(c) Repealed by Session Laws 1973, c. 475, s. 3 1/2.

(d) It is the intent of this section that the provisions herein shall be carried out by the Commissioner of Motor Vehicles for the safety of the motoring public. The Commissioner shall have authority to make such agreements as are necessary with the persons in charge of every institution of any nature for the care and treatment of alcoholics or habitual users of narcotic drugs, to effectively carry out the duty hereby imposed and the person in charge of the institutions described above shall cooperate with and assist the Commissioner of Motor Vehicles.

(e) Notwithstanding the provisions of G.S. 8-53, 8-53.2, and Article 3 of Chapter 122C of the General Statutes, the person or persons in charge of any institution as set out in subsection (a) hereinabove shall furnish such information as may be required for the effective enforcement of this section. Information furnished to the Division of Motor Vehicles as provided herein shall be confidential and the Commissioner of Motor Vehicles shall be subject to the same penalties and is granted the same protection as is the department, institution or individual furnishing such information. No criminal or civil action may be brought against any person or agency who shall provide or submit to the Commissioner of Motor Vehicles or his authorized agents the information as required herein.

(f) Revocations under this section may be reviewed as provided in G.S. 20-9(g)(4).

History.

1947, c. 1006, s. 9; 1953, c. 1300, s. 36; 1955, c. 1187, s. 16; 1969, c. 186, s. 1; c. 1125; 1971, c. 208, ss. 1, 1 1/2; c. 401, s. 1; c. 767; 1973, c. 475, s. 3 1/2; c. 1362; 1975, c. 716, s. 5; 1983, c. 768, s. 3; 1987, c. 720, s. 1; 2008-182, s. 1

EFFECT OF AMENDMENTS. --

Session Laws 2008-182, s. 1, effective October 1, 2008, and applicable to persons adjudicated incompetent under Chapter 35A of the General Statutes on or after that date, added the second sentence of subsection (a).

CONSTITUTIONALITY. --This section is neither vague nor overbroad. Jones v. Penny, 387 F. Supp. 383 (M.D.N.C. 1974).

A legitimate State interest may be rationally advanced by the classification drawn in this section, thus it does not deny equal protection of the laws to those involuntarily committed. Jones v. Penny, 387 F. Supp. 383 (M.D.N.C. 1974).

To decide that those whose institutionalization was legally coerced present, as a class, significantly greater highway safety problems and thus require renewed scrutiny as to driving skills is, whatever its wisdom or efficacy or validity in a particular case, not irrational under the equal protection clause. Jones v. Penny, 387 F. Supp. 383 (M.D.N.C. 1974).

That North Carolina has not chosen in this section to include "all alcoholics and drug addicts" is not irrational. Jones v. Penny, 387 F. Supp. 383 (M.D.N.C. 1974).

This section fairly informs those it affects of the standard against which their conduct will be measured, and thus there is no constitutional infirmity presented. Jones v. Penny, 387 F. Supp. 383 (M.D.N.C. 1974).

THE PHRASE "IS SATISFIED" IN SUBSECTION (A). --This section imparts an objective standard, and the phrase "is satisfied" refers to the conclusion the Commissioner reaches after his inquiry into the facts for the purpose of determining whether such person is competent to operate a motor vehicle with safety to persons and property. Jones v. Penny, 387 F. Supp. 383 (M.D.N.C. 1974).

Chapter 20

THERE IS NO SUBSTANTIVE CONSTITUTIONAL RIGHT TO DRIVE AN AUTOMOBILE. Jones v. Penny, 387 F. Supp. 383 (M.D.N.C. 1974).

BUT ONCE LICENSES ARE ISSUED, THEIR CONTINUED POSSESSION MAY BECOME ESSENTIAL in the pursuit of a livelihood, and suspension of issued licenses thus involves State action that adjudicates important interests of the licensees; in such cases the licenses are not to be taken away without that procedural due process required by U.S. Const., Amend. XIV. Jones v. Penny, 387 F. Supp. 383 (M.D.N.C. 1974).

PERSONS INVOLUNTARILY COMMITTED ARE ENTITLED TO NOTICE AND HEARING before the Department (now Division) of Motor Vehicles prior to any revocation of their driving privileges. Jones v. Penny, 387 F. Supp. 383 (M.D.N.C. 1974).

THE TYPE OF "FACTS" TO BE LOOKED INTO AND THE SCOPE OF THE "INQUIRY" are tied to the obvious purpose of this section: to determine driving competency. By themselves they set no standard against which the plaintiff's privilege is judged. Jones v. Penny, 387 F. Supp. 383 (M.D.N.C. 1974).

WHERE THE LAW DIRECTS SUSPENSION, REVOCATION, OR NONISSUANCE OF A DRIVER'S LICENSE, the grounds are convictions for moving violations, or other statutory violations relating to highway safety, or situations where an individual's capacity to operate a motor vehicle safely are manifestly questionable. Evans v. Roberson, 69 N.C. App. 644, 317 S.E.2d 715 (1984), rev'd on other grounds and modified, 314 N.C. 315, 333 S.E.2d 228 (1985).

PERIOD OF REVOCATION. --The one-year period in G.S. 20-19(f) applies to this section. Jones v. Penny, 387 F. Supp. 383 (M.D.N.C. 1974).

LEGAL PERIODICALS. --

For note on reporting patients for review of driver's license, see 48 N.C.L. Rev. 1003 (1970).

§ 20-17.1A. Restoration of license for person adjudicated to be restored to competency

If otherwise eligible under G.S. 20-7 and any other applicable provision of law, the Division shall restore the drivers license of a person adjudicated to be restored to competency under G.S. 35A-1130 upon receiving notice from the clerk of court in which the adjudication is made. Nothing in this section shall be construed as requiring the Division to restore the drivers license of a person if (i) the person's drivers license was revoked because of a conviction or other act requiring revocation and (ii) the person has not met the requirements set forth in this Article for restoration of the person's drivers license.

History.
2015-165, s. 1
EDITOR'S NOTE. --
Session Laws 2015-165, s. 3 made this section effective October 1, 2015.

N.C. Gen. Stat. § 20-17.2

Repealed by Session Laws 2006-253, s. 25, effective December 1, 2006, and applicable to offenses committed on or after that date.

§ 20-17.3. Revocation for underage purchasers of alcohol

The Division shall revoke for one year the driver's license of any person who has been convicted of violating any of the following:

(1) G.S. 18B-302(c), (e), or (f).

(2) G.S. 18B-302(b), if the violation occurred while the person was purchasing or attempting to purchase an alcoholic beverage.

(3) G.S. 18B-302(a1).

If the person's license is currently suspended or revoked, then the revocation under this section shall begin at the termination of that revocation. A person whose license is revoked under this section for a violation of G.S. 18B-302(a1) or G.S. 18B-302(c) shall be eligible for a limited driving privilege under G.S. 20-179.3.

History.
1983, c. 435, s. 36; 2007-537, s. 3
EFFECT OF AMENDMENTS. --
Session Laws 2007-537, s. 3, effective December 1, 2007, and applicable to offenses committed on or after that date, in subdivision (1), substituted "G.S. 18B-302(c), (e), or (f)" for "G.S.18B-302(c)(1), (e), or (f)"; added subdivision (3); added the last sentence of the section; and made minor stylistic and punctuation changes.

§ 20-17.4. Disqualification to drive a commercial motor vehicle

(a) **One Year. --** Any of the following disqualifies a person from driving a commercial motor vehicle for one year if committed by a person holding a commercial drivers license, or, when applicable, committed while operating a commercial motor vehicle by a person who does not hold a commercial drivers license:

(1) A first conviction of G.S. 20-138.1, driving while impaired, for a holder of a commercial drivers license that occurred while the person was driving a motor vehicle that is not a commercial motor vehicle.

(2) A first conviction of G.S. 20-138.2, driving a commercial motor vehicle while impaired.

(3) A first conviction of G.S. 20-166, hit and run.

(4) A first conviction of a felony in the commission of which a commercial motor vehicle was used or the first conviction of a felony in which any motor vehicle is used by a holder of a commercial drivers license.

(5) Refusal to submit to a chemical test when charged with an implied-consent offense, as defined in G.S. 20-16.2.

(6) A second or subsequent conviction, as defined in G.S. 20-138.2A(d), of driving a commercial motor vehicle after consuming alcohol under G.S. 20-138.2A.

(7) A civil license revocation under G.S. 20-16.5, or a substantially similar revocation obtained in another jurisdiction, arising out of a charge that occurred while the person was either operating a commercial motor vehicle or while the person was holding a commercial drivers license.

(8) A first conviction of vehicular homicide under G.S. 20-141.4 or vehicular manslaughter under G.S. 14-18 occurring while the person was operating a commercial motor vehicle.

(9) Driving a commercial motor vehicle during a period when the person's commercial drivers license is revoked, suspended, cancelled, or the driver is otherwise disqualified from operating a commercial motor vehicle.

(a1) **Ten-Day Disqualification.** -- A person who is convicted for a first offense of driving a commercial motor vehicle after consuming alcohol under G.S. 20-138.2A is disqualified from driving a commercial motor vehicle for 10 days.

(b) **Modified Life.** -- A person who has been disqualified from driving a commercial motor vehicle for a conviction or refusal described in subsection (a) who, as the result of a separate incident, is subsequently convicted of an offense or commits an act requiring disqualification under subsection (a) is disqualified for life. The Division may adopt guidelines, including conditions, under which a disqualification for life under this subsection may be reduced to 10 years.

(b1) **Life Without Reduction.** -- A person is disqualified from driving a commercial motor vehicle for life, without the possibility of reinstatement after 10 years, if that person is convicted of a third or subsequent violation of G.S. 20-138.2, a fourth or subsequent violation of G.S. 20-138.2A, or if the person refuses to submit to a chemical test a third time when charged with an implied-consent offense, as defined in G.S. 20-16.2, that occurred while the person was driving a commercial motor vehicle.

(c) **Life.** -- A person is disqualified from driving a commercial motor vehicle for life if that person either uses a commercial motor vehicle in the commission of any felony involving the manufacture, distribution, or dispensing of a controlled substance, or possession with intent to manufacture, distribute, or dispense a controlled substance or is the holder of a commercial drivers license at the time of the commission of any such felony.

(c1) **Life.** -- A person shall be disqualified from driving a commercial motor vehicle for life, without the possibility of reinstatement, if that person has had a commercial drivers license reinstated in the past and is convicted of another major disqualifying offense as defined in 49 C.F.R. § 383.51(b).

(d) **Less Than a Year.** -- A person is disqualified from driving a commercial motor vehicle for 60 days if that person is convicted of two serious traffic violations, or 120 days if convicted of three or more serious traffic violations, arising from separate incidents occurring within a three-year period, committed in a commercial motor vehicle or while holding a commercial drivers license. This disqualification shall be in addition to, and shall be served at the end of, any other prior disqualification. For purposes of this subsection, a "serious violation" includes violations of G.S. 20-140(f) and G.S. 20-141(j3).

(e) **Three Years.** -- A person is disqualified from driving a commercial motor vehicle for three years if that person is convicted of an offense or commits an act requiring disqualification under subsection (a) and the offense or act occurred while the person was transporting a hazardous material that required the motor vehicle driven to be placarded.

(f) **Revocation Period.** -- A person is disqualified from driving a commercial motor vehicle for the period during which the person's regular or commercial drivers license is revoked, suspended, or cancelled.

(g) **Violation of Out-of-Service Order.** -- Any person holding a commercial learner's permit or commercial drivers license or required to have a commercial learner's permit or commercial drivers license convicted for violating an out-of-service order, except as described in subsection (h) of this section, shall be disqualified as follows:

(1) A person is disqualified from driving a commercial vehicle for a period of no less than 180 days and no more than one year if convicted of a first violation of an out-of-service order while operating a commercial motor vehicle.

(2) A person is disqualified for a period of no less than two years and no more than five years if convicted of a second violation of an out-of-service order while operating a commercial motor vehicle during any 10-year period, arising from separate incidents.

(3) A person is disqualified for a period of no less than three years and no more than five years if convicted of a third or subsequent violation of an out-of-service order while operating a commercial motor vehicle during any 10-year period, arising from separate incidents.

(h) **Violation of Out-of-Service Order; Special Rule for Hazardous Materials**

and Passenger Offenses. -- Any person holding a commercial learner's permit or commercial drivers license or required to have a commercial learner's permit or commercial drivers license convicted for violating an out-of-service order while transporting hazardous materials, as defined in 49 C.F.R. § 383.5, or while operating a commercial vehicle designed or used to transport 16 or more passengers, including the driver, shall be disqualified as follows:

(1) A person is disqualified for a period of no less than 180 days and no more than two years if convicted of a first violation of an out-of-service order while operating a commercial motor vehicle.

(2) A person is disqualified for a period of no less than three years and no more than five years if convicted of a second or subsequent violation of an out-of-service order while operating a commercial motor vehicle during any 10-year period, arising from separate incidents.

(3) A person is disqualified for a period of no less than three years and no more than five years if convicted of a third or subsequent violation of an out-of-service order while operating a commercial motor vehicle during any 10-year period arising from separate incidents.

(i) **Disqualification for Out-of-State Violations.** -- The Division shall withdraw the privilege to operate a commercial vehicle of any resident of this State or person transferring to this State upon receiving notice of the person's conviction or Administrative Per Se Notice in another state for an offense that, if committed in this State, would be grounds for disqualification, even if the offense occurred in another jurisdiction prior to being licensed in this State where no action had been taken at that time in the other jurisdiction. The period of disqualification shall be the same as if the offense occurred in this State.

(j) **Disqualification of Persons Without Commercial Drivers Licenses.** -- Any person convicted of an offense that requires disqualification under this section, but who does not hold a commercial drivers license, shall be disqualified from operating a commercial vehicle in the same manner as if the person held a valid commercial drivers license.

(k) **Disqualification for Railroad Grade Crossing Offenses.** -- Any person convicted of a violation of G.S. 20-142.1 through G.S. 20-142.5, when the driver is operating a commercial motor vehicle, shall be disqualified from driving a commercial motor vehicle as follows:

(1) A person is disqualified for a period of 60 days if convicted of a first violation of a railroad grade crossing offense listed in this subsection.

(2) A person is disqualified for a period of 120 days if convicted during any three-year period of a second violation of any combination of railroad grade crossing offenses listed in this subsection.

(3) A person is disqualified for a period of one year if convicted during any three-year period of a third or subsequent violation of any combination of railroad grade crossing offenses listed in this subsection.

(*l*) **Disqualification for Testing Positive in a Drug or Alcohol Test.** -- Upon receipt of notice of a positive drug or alcohol test, or of refusal to participate in a drug or alcohol test, pursuant to G.S. 20-37.19(c), the Division must disqualify a CDL holder from operating a commercial motor vehicle for a minimum of 30 days and until receipt of proof of successful completion of assessment and treatment by a substance abuse professional in accordance with 49 C.F.R. § 382.503.

(m) **Disqualifications of Drivers Who Are Determined to Constitute an Imminent Hazard.** -- The Division shall withdraw the privilege to operate a commercial motor vehicle for any resident of this State for a period of 30 days in accordance with 49 C.F.R. § 383.52.

(n) **Disqualification for Conviction of Criminal Offense That Requires Registration Under the Sex Offender and Public Protection Registration Programs.** -- Effective December 1, 2009, except as otherwise provided by this subsection, a person convicted of a violation that requires registration under Article 27A of Chapter 14 of the General Statutes is disqualified from driving a commercial motor vehicle that requires a commercial drivers license with a P or S endorsement for the period of time during which the person is required to maintain registration under Article 27A of Chapter 14 of the General Statutes. If a person who is registered pursuant to Article 27A of Chapter 14 of the General Statutes on December 1, 2009, also has a valid commercial drivers license with a P or S endorsement that was issued on or before December 1, 2009, then the person is not disqualified under this subsection until that license expires, provided the person does not commit a subsequent offense that requires registration under Article 27A of Chapter 14 of the General Statutes.

(o) **Disqualification for Passing Stopped School Bus.** -- Any person whose drivers license is revoked under G.S. 20-217 is disqualified from driving a commercial motor vehicle for the period of time in which the person's drivers license remains revoked under G.S. 20-217.

History.
1989, c. 771, s. 3;1991, c. 726, s. 8;1993, c. 533, s. 5;1998-149, s. 3;1998-182, s. 19;2000-109, s. 7(e);2002-72, s. 7;2003-397, s. 2;2005-156, s. 2;2005-349, s.

Chapter 20

6;2007-492, s. 1;2008-175, s. 1;2009-416, s. 3;2009-491, s. 2;2013-293, s. 3;2016-90, s. 6(c), (d)

EDITOR'S NOTE. --

Session Laws 1987 (Reg. Sess., 1988), c. 1112, s. 12 also enacted a G.S. 20-17.4, to be effective June 1, 1989, through June 30, 1989, and to provide for mandatory revocation of a Class A or Class B license for drivers convicted of impaired driving in a commercial vehicle. Session Laws 1989, c. 771, s. 18, effective June 1, 1989, repealed Session Laws 1987 (Reg. Sess., 1988), c. 1112; therefore, G.S. 20-17.4, as enacted by c. 1112, never went into effect.

Session Laws 2016-90, s. 6(f), made the rewriting of subsections (g) and (h) by Session Laws 2016-90, s. 6(c) and (d), applicable to offenses committed on or after January 1, 2017.

EFFECT OF AMENDMENTS. --

Session Laws 2005-156, s. 2, effective December 1, 2005, added subsection (*l*).

Session Laws 2005-349, s. 6, effective September 30, 2005, rewrote subsection (a); added the present second sentence of subsection (d); added "suspended, or cancelled" at the end of subsection (f); in subsection (i), in the first sentence, inserted "or person transferring to this State," "or Administrative Per Se Notice," and "even if the offense occurred in another jurisdiction prior to being licensed in this State where no action had been taken at that time in the other jurisdiction"; and added subsection (m).

Session Laws 2007-492, s. 1, effective August 30, 2007, in subsection (*l*), substituted "Based on" for "for Testing Positive in a" in the subsection heading, inserted "or of refusal to participate in a drug or alcohol test," and substituted "Division must disqualify a CDL holder" for "Division shall disqualify a driver."

Session Laws 2008-175, s. 1, effective December 1, 2008, and applicable to offenses committed on or after that date, in subdivision (a)(7), substituted "either operating a commercial motor vehicle or while the person was holding a commercial drivers license" for "operating a commercial motor vehicle"; in subsection (c), inserted "either" and added "or is the holder of a commercial drivers license at the time of the commission of any such felony"; in subsection (d), substituted "arising from separate incidents occurring within a three-year period, committed in a commercial motor vehicle or while holding a commercial drivers license" for "committed in a commercial motor vehicle arising from separate incidents occurring within a three-year period"; and, in subsection (*l*), substituted "for Testing Positive in a" for "Based on" and inserted "for a minimum of 30 days and."

Session Laws 2009-416, s. 3, effective March 31, 2010, and applicable to offenses committed on or after that date, added subsection (c1).

Session Laws 2013-293, s. 3, effective December 1, 2013, added subsection (o). For applicability, see Editor's note.

Session Laws 2016-90, s. 6(c), (d), effective January 1, 2017, rewrote subsections (g) and (h). See editor's note for applicability.

DOUBLE JEOPARDY VIOLATION. --Prosecuting defendant for driving while impaired subjected him to double jeopardy because his prior one-year commercial driver's license disqualification under G.S. 20-17.4(a)(7) due to his breath test results was so punitive that it constituted a prior criminal punishment. State v. McKenzie, 225 N.C. App. 208, 736 S.E.2d 591 (2013), rev'd 367 N.C. 112, 750 S.E.2d 521, 2013 N.C. LEXIS 1019 (2013), rev'd 748 S.E.2d 145, 2013 N.C. LEXIS 1019 (2013).

G.

S. 20-17.4 is so punitive that it becomes a criminal punishment; therefore, prosecution for driving while impaired subsequent to license disqualification under G.S. 20-17.4 constitutes impermissible double jeopardy. State v. McKenzie, 225 N.C. App. 208, 736 S.E.2d 591 (2013), rev'd 367 N.C. 112, 750 S.E.2d 521, 2013 N.C. LEXIS 1019 (2013), rev'd 748 S.E.2d 145, 2013 N.C. LEXIS 1019 (2013).

§ 20-17.5. Effect of disqualification

(a) **When No Accompanying Revocation.** -- A person who is disqualified as the result of a conviction that requires disqualification but not revocation may keep any regular Class C drivers license the person had at the time of the offense resulting in disqualification. If the person had a Class A or Class B regular drivers license or a commercial drivers license when the offense occurred, all of the following apply:

(1) The person must give the license to the court that convicts the person or, if the person is not present when convicted, to the Division.

(2) The person may apply for a regular Class C drivers license.

(b) **When Revocation and Disqualification.** -- When a person is disqualified as the result of a conviction that requires both disqualification and revocation, all of the following apply:

(1) The person must give any drivers license the person has to the court that convicts the person or, if the person is not present when convicted, to the Division.

(2) The person may obtain limited driving privileges to drive a noncommercial motor vehicle during the revocation period to the extent the law would allow limited driving privileges if the person had been driving a noncommercial motor vehicle when the offense occurred. The same procedure, eligibility requirements, and mandatory conditions apply to limited driving privileges authorized by this subdivision that would apply if the person had been driving a noncommercial motor vehicle when the offense occurred.

(3) If the disqualification period is longer than the revocation period, the person may apply for a regular Class C drivers license at the end of the revocation period.

(c) **Refusal to Take Chemical Test.** -- When a person is disqualified for refusing to take a chemical test, all of the following apply:

(1) The person must give any license the person has to a court, a law enforcement officer, or the Division, in accordance with G.S. 20-16.2 and G.S. 20-16.5.

(2) The person may obtain limited driving privileges to drive a noncommercial motor vehicle during the period the person's license is revoked for the refusal that disqualified the person to the extent the law would allow limited driving privileges if the person had been driving a noncommercial motor vehicle at the time of the refusal. The same procedure, eligibility requirements, and mandatory conditions apply to limited driving privileges authorized by this subdivision that would apply if the person had been driving a noncommercial motor vehicle at the time of the refusal.

(3) If the disqualification period is longer than the revocation period, the person may apply for a regular Class C drivers license at the end of the revocation period.

(d) **Obtaining Class C Regular License.** -- A person who is authorized by this section to apply for a regular Class C drivers license and who meets all of the following criteria may obtain a regular Class C drivers license without taking a test:

(1) The person must have had a Class A or Class B regular drivers license or a commercial drivers license when the person was disqualified.

(2) The person's license must have been issued by the Division.

(3) The person's license must not have expired by the date the person applies for a regular Class C drivers license.

Upon application and payment of the fee set in G.S. 20-14 for a duplicate license, the Division shall issue a person who meets these criteria a regular Class C drivers license. The license shall include the same endorsements and restrictions as the former Class A regular, Class B regular, or commercial drivers license, to the extent they apply to a regular Class C drivers license. A regular Class C drivers license issued to a person who meets these criteria expires the same day as the license it replaces.

G.S. 20-7 governs the issuance of a regular Class C drivers license to a person who is authorized by this section to apply for a regular Class C drivers license but who does not meet the listed criteria. In accordance with that statute, the Division may require the person to take a test and the person must pay the license fee.

(e) **Restoration Fee.** -- A person who is disqualified must pay the restoration fee set in G.S. 20-7(i1) the first time any of the following events occurs as a result of the same disqualification:

(1) The Division reinstates a Class A regular drivers license, a Class B regular drivers license, or a commercial drivers license the person had at the time of the disqualification by issuing the person a duplicate license.

(2) The Division issues a Class A regular drivers license, a Class B regular drivers license, or a commercial drivers license to the person.

(3) If the person's license was revoked because of the conviction or act requiring disqualification, the Division issues a regular Class C drivers license to the person.

The restoration fee does not apply the second time any of these events occurs as a result of the same disqualification.

History.
1991, c. 726, s. 9

§ 20-17.6. Restoration of a license after a conviction of driving while impaired or driving while less than 21 years old after consuming alcohol or drugs

(a) **Scope.** -- This section applies to a person whose license was revoked as a result of a conviction of any of the following offenses:

(1) G.S. 20-138.1, driving while impaired (DWI).

(2) G.S. 20-138.2, commercial DWI.

(3) G.S. 20-138.3, driving while less than 21 years old after consuming alcohol or drugs.

(4) G.S. 20-138.2A, driving a commercial motor vehicle with an alcohol concentration of greater than 0.00 and less than 0.04, if the person's drivers license was revoked under G.S. 20-17(a)(13).

(5) G.S. 20-138.2B, driving a school bus, a school activity bus, or a child care vehicle with an alcohol concentration of greater than 0.00, if the person's drivers license was revoked under G.S. 20-17(a)(14).

(b) **Requirement for Restoring License.** -- The Division must receive a certificate of completion for a person who is subject to this section before the Division can restore that person's license. The revocation period for a person who is subject to this section is extended until the Division receives the certificate of completion.

(c) **Certificate of Completion.** -- To obtain a certificate of completion, a person must have a substance abuse assessment and, depending on the results of the assessment, must complete either an alcohol and drug education traffic (ADET) school or a substance abuse treatment program. The substance abuse assessment must be conducted by one of the entities authorized by the Department of Health and Human Services to conduct assessments. G.S. 122C-142.1 describes the procedure for obtaining a certificate of completion.

(d) **Notice of Requirement.** -- When a court reports to the Division a conviction of a person who is subject to this section, the Division must send the person written notice of the requirements of this section and of the consequences of failing to comply with these requirements. The notification must include a statement that the person may contact the local area mental health, developmental disabilities, and substance abuse program for a list of agencies and entities in the person's area that are authorized to make a substance abuse assessment and provide the education or treatment needed to obtain a certificate of completion.

(e) **Effect on Limited Driving Privileges.** -- A person who is subject to this section is not eligible for limited driving privileges if the revocation period for the offense that caused the person to become subject to this section has ended and the person's license remains revoked only because the Division has not obtained a certificate of completion for that person. The issuance of limited driving privileges during the revocation period for the offense that caused the person to become subject to this section is governed by the statutes that apply to that offense.

History.
1995, c. 496, ss. 1, 11, 12; 1997-443, s. 11A.118(a);1998-182, s. 20

EDITOR'S NOTE. --
Session Laws 1995, c. 496, ss. 11 and 12, which substituted "less than 21 years old" for "a provisional licensee" in the catchline and in subdivision (a)(3), were to become effective only if House Bill 353 of the 1995 General Assembly was enacted. House Bill 353 was ratified as Session Laws 1995, c. 506, on July 28, 1995.

INDEFINITE REVOCATION. --Although the trial court should have submitted the aggravating factor in G.S. 20-179(c)(2), providing that at the time of the offense, defendant was driving while defendant's license was revoked, as defined by G.S. 20-28, and the revocation was an impaired driving revocation under G.S. 20-28.2(a), the error was harmless beyond a reasonable doubt. Defendant's driving record, admitted by the State, showed that defendant's driver's license was indefinitely revoked due to an impaired driving conviction and that the license had not been reinstated, which meant that evidence of the aggravating factor was overwhelming and uncontroverted such that a sentence beyond the statutory maximum could be imposed. State v. Coffey, 189 N.C. App. 382, 658 S.E.2d 73 (2008).

§ 20-17.7. Commercial motor vehicle out-of-service fines authorized

The Secretary of Public Safety may adopt rules implementing fines for violation of out-of-service criteria as defined in 49 C.F.R. § 390.5. These fines may not exceed the schedule of fines adopted by the Commercial Motor Vehicle Safety Alliance that is in effect on the date of the violations.

History.
1999-330, s. 1;2002-159, s. 31.5(b);2002-190, s. 3;2011-145, s. 19.1(g)

EDITOR'S NOTE. --
Session Laws 2002-190, s. 17, provides: "The Governor shall resolve any dispute between the Department of Transportation and the Department of Crime Control and Public Safety concerning the implementation of this act [Session Laws 2002-190]."

Session Laws 2017-108, s. 17.1(a) -(d), provides: "(a) Rule. -- Until the effective date of the revised permanent rule that the State Highway Patrol is required to adopt pursuant to subsection (c) of this section, the State Highway Patrol shall implement 14B NCAC 07C.0101 (Safety of Operation and Equipment), as provided in subsection (b) of this section.

"(b) Implementation. -- Notwithstanding 14B NCAC 07C.0101, the State Highway Patrol shall exempt covered farm vehicles engaged in intrastate commerce from the requirements of 49 C.F.R. § 390.21.

"(c) Additional Rule-Making Authority. -- The State Highway Patrol shall adopt rules to amend 14B NCAC 07C.0101, consistent with subsection (b) of this section.

"(d) Effective Date. -- Subsection (b) of this section expires on the date that rules adopted pursuant to subsection (c) of this section become effective. The remainder of this section is effective when it becomes law."

EFFECT OF AMENDMENTS. --
Session Laws 2011-145, s. 19.1(g), effective January 1, 2012, substituted "Public Safety" for "Crime Control and Public Safety."

§ 20-17.8. Restoration of a license after certain driving while impaired convictions; ignition interlock

(a) **Scope.** -- This section applies to a person whose license was revoked as a result of a conviction of driving while impaired, G.S. 20-138.1, and:

    (1) The person had an alcohol concentration of 0.15 or more;

    (2) The person has been convicted of another offense involving impaired driving, which offense occurred within seven years immediately preceding the date of the offense for which the person's license has been revoked; or

    (3) The person was sentenced pursuant to G.S. 20-179(f3).

For purposes of subdivision (1) of this subsection, the results of a chemical analysis, as shown by an affidavit or affidavits executed pursuant to G.S. 20-16.2(c1), shall be used by the Division to determine that person's alcohol concentration.

(a1) **Additional Scope.** -- This section applies to a person whose license was revoked as a result of a conviction of habitual impaired driving, G.S. 20-138.5.

(b) **Ignition Interlock Required.** -- Except as provided in subsection (*l*) of this section, when the Division restores the license of a person who is subject to this section, in addition to any other restriction or condition, it shall require the person to agree to and shall indicate on the person's drivers license the following restrictions for the period designated in subsection (c):

(1) A restriction that the person may operate only a vehicle that is equipped with a functioning ignition interlock system of a type approved by the Commissioner. The Commissioner shall not unreasonably withhold approval of an ignition interlock system and shall consult with the Division of Purchase and Contract in the Department of Administration to ensure that potential vendors are not discriminated against.

(2) A requirement that the person personally activate the ignition interlock system before driving the motor vehicle.

(3) An alcohol concentration restriction as follows:

a. If the ignition interlock system is required pursuant only to subdivision (a)(1) of this section, a requirement that the person not drive with an alcohol concentration of 0.04 or greater;

b. If the ignition interlock system is required pursuant to subdivision (a)(2) or (a)(3) of this section, or subsection (a1) of this section, a requirement that the person not drive with an alcohol concentration of greater than 0.00; or

c. If the ignition interlock system is required pursuant to subdivision (a)(1) of this section, and the person has also been convicted, based on the same set of circumstances, of: (i) driving while impaired in a commercial vehicle, G.S. 20-138.2, (ii) driving while less than 21 years old after consuming alcohol or drugs, G.S. 20-138.3, (iii) a violation of G.S. 20-141.4, or (iv) manslaughter or negligent homicide resulting from the operation of a motor vehicle when the offense involved impaired driving, a requirement that the person not drive with an alcohol concentration of greater than 0.00.

(c) **Length of Requirement.** -- The requirements of subsection (b) shall remain in effect for:

(1) One year from the date of restoration if the original revocation period was one year;

(2) Three years from the date of restoration if the original revocation period was four years; or

(3) Seven years from the date of restoration if the original revocation was a permanent revocation.

(c1) **Vehicles Subject to Requirement.** -- A person subject to this section shall have all registered vehicles owned by that person equipped with a functioning ignition interlock system of a type approved by the Commissioner. The Commissioner shall not issue a license to a person subject to this section until presented with proof of the installation of an ignition interlock system in all registered vehicles owned by the person. In order to avoid an undue financial hardship, a person subject to this section may seek a waiver from the Division for any vehicle registered to that person that is relied upon by another member of that person's family for transportation and that the vehicle is not in the possession of the person subject to this section. The Division shall determine such waiver on a case-by-case basis following an assessment of financial hardship to the person subject to this restriction. The Commissioner shall cancel the drivers license of any person subject to this section for registration of a motor vehicle owned by the person without an installed ignition interlock system or removal of the ignition interlock system from a motor vehicle owned by the person, other than when changing ignition interlock providers or upon sale of the vehicle.

(d) **Effect of Limited Driving Privileges.** -- If the person was eligible for and received a limited driving privilege under G.S. 20-179.3, with the ignition interlock requirement contained in G.S. 20-179.3(g5), the period of time for which that limited driving privilege was held shall be applied towards the requirements of subsection (c).

(e) **Notice of Requirement.** -- When a court reports to the Division a conviction of a person who is subject to this section, the Division must send the person written notice of the requirements of this section and of the consequences of failing to comply with these requirements. The notification must include a statement that the person may contact the Division for information on obtaining and having installed an ignition interlock system of a type approved by the Commissioner.

(f) **Effect of Violation of Restriction.** -- A person subject to this section who violates any of the restrictions of this section commits the offense of driving while license revoked for impaired driving under G.S. 20-28(a1) and is subject to punishment and license revocation as provided in that section. If a law enforcement officer has reasonable grounds to believe that a person subject to this section has consumed alcohol while driving or has driven while he has remaining in his body any alcohol previously consumed, the suspected offense of driving while license is revoked is an alcohol-related offense subject to the implied-consent provisions of G.S. 20-16.2. If a person subject to this section is charged with driving while license revoked by violating a condition of subsection (b) of this section, and a judicial official determines that there is probable cause for the charge, the person's license is suspended pending the resolution of the case, and the judicial official must require the person to surrender the license. The judicial official must also notify the person that he is not entitled to drive until his case is resolved. An alcohol concentration report from the ignition interlock system shall not be admissible as evidence of driving while license revoked, nor shall it be admissible in an administrative revocation proceeding as provided in subsection (g) of this section, unless the person operated a vehicle when the ignition interlock system indicated an alcohol concentration in violation of the restriction placed upon the person by subdivision (b)(3) of this section.

(g) **Effect of Violation of Restriction When Driving While License Revoked Not Charged.** -- A person subject to this section who violates any of the restrictions of this section, but is not charged or convicted of driving while license revoked pursuant to G.S. 20-28(a), shall have the person's license revoked by the Division for a period of one year.

(h) **Beginning of Revocation Period.** -- If the original period of revocation was imposed pursuant to G.S. 20-19(d) or (e), any remaining period of the original revocation, prior to its reduction, shall be reinstated and the revocation required by subsection (f) or (g) of this section begins after all other periods of revocation have terminated.

(i) **Notification of Revocation.** -- If the person's license has not already been surrendered to the court, the Division must expeditiously notify the person that the person's license to drive is revoked pursuant to subsection (f) or (g) of this section effective on the tenth calendar day after the mailing of the revocation order.

(j) **Right to Hearing Before Division; Issues.** -- If the person's license is revoked pursuant to subsection (g) of this section, before the effective date of the order issued under subsection (i) of this section, the person may request in writing a hearing before the Division. Except for the time referred to in G.S. 20-16.5, if the person shows to the satisfaction of the Division that the person's license was surrendered to

the court and remained in the court's possession, then the Division shall credit the amount of time for which the license was in the possession of the court against the revocation period required by subsection (g) of this section. If the person properly requests a hearing, the person retains the person's license, unless it is revoked under some other provision of law, until the hearing is held, the person withdraws the request, or the person fails to appear at a scheduled hearing. The hearing officer may subpoena any witnesses or documents that the hearing officer deems necessary. The person may request the hearing officer to subpoena the charging officer, the chemical analyst, or both to appear at the hearing if the person makes the request in writing at least three days before the hearing. The person may subpoena any other witness whom the person deems necessary, and the provisions of G.S. 1A-1, Rule 45, apply to the issuance and service of all subpoenas issued under the authority of this section. The hearing officer is authorized to administer oaths to witnesses appearing at the hearing. The hearing must be conducted in the county where the charge was brought, except when the evidence of the violation is an alcohol concentration report from an ignition interlock system, the hearing may be conducted in the county where the person resides. The hearing must be limited to consideration of whether:

(1) The drivers license of the person had an ignition interlock requirement; and

(2) The person:

a. Was driving a vehicle that was not equipped with a functioning ignition interlock system; or

b. Did not personally activate the ignition interlock system before driving the vehicle; or

c. Drove the vehicle in violation of an applicable alcohol concentration restriction prescribed by subdivision (b) (3) of this section.

If the Division finds that the conditions specified in this subsection are met, it must order the revocation sustained. If the Division finds that the condition of subdivision (1) is not met, or that none of the conditions of subdivision (2) are met, it must rescind the revocation. If the revocation is sustained, the person must surrender the person's license immediately upon notification by the Division. If the revocation is sustained, the person may appeal the decision of the Division pursuant to G.S. 20-25.

(k) **Restoration After Violation.** -- When the Division restores the license of a person whose license was revoked pursuant to subsection (f) or (g) of this section and the revocation occurred prior to completion of time period required by subsection (c) of this section, in addition to any other restriction or condition, it shall require the person to comply with the conditions of subsection (b) of this section until the person has complied with those conditions for the cumulative period of time as set forth in subsection (c) of this section. The period of time for which the person successfully complied with subsection (b) of this section prior to revocation pursuant to subsection (f) or (g) of this section shall be applied towards the requirements of subsection (c) of this section.

(*l*) **Medical Exception to Requirement. --** A person subject to this section solely for the reason set forth in subdivision (a)(1) of this section and who has a medically diagnosed physical condition that makes the person incapable of personally activating an ignition interlock system may request an exception to the requirements of this section from the Division. The Division shall not issue an exception to this section unless the person has submitted to a physical examination by two or more physicians or surgeons duly licensed to practice medicine in this State or in any other state of the United States and unless such examining physicians or surgeons have completed and signed a certificate in the form prescribed by the Division. Such certificate shall be devised by the Commissioner with the advice of those qualified experts in the field of diagnosing and treating physical disorders that the Commissioner may select and shall be designed to elicit the maximum medical information necessary to aid in determining whether or not the person is capable of personally activating an ignition interlock system. The certificate shall contain a waiver of privilege and the recommendation of the examining physician to the Commissioner as to whether the person is capable of personally activating an ignition interlock system.

The Commissioner is not bound by the recommendations of the examining physicians but shall give fair consideration to such recommendations in acting upon the request for medical exception, the criterion being whether or not, upon all the evidence, it appears that the person is in fact incapable of personally activating an ignition interlock system. The burden of proof of such fact is upon the person seeking the exception.

Whenever an exception is denied by the Commissioner, such denial may be reviewed by a reviewing board upon written request of the person seeking the exception filed with the Division within 10 days after receipt of such denial. The composition, procedures, and review of the reviewing board shall be as provided in G.S. 20-9(g)(4). This subsection shall not apply to persons subject to an ignition interlock requirement

under this section for the reasons set forth in subdivision (a)(2) or (a)(3) of this section.

History.
1999-406, s. 3;2000-155, ss. 1 -3; 2001-487, s. 8;2006-253, ss. 22.3, 22.4; 2007-493, ss. 5, 10, 28; 2009-369, ss. 5, 6; 2011-191, s. 3;2013-348, s. 1;2014-108, s. 1(a);2014-115, s. 61.5;2015-186, s. 4;2015-264, s. 86;2017-176, s. 2(b)

EDITOR'S NOTE. --
The number of this section was assigned by the Revisor of Statutes, the number in Session Laws 1999-406, s. 3 having been 20-17.7.

Session Laws 1999-406, s. 18, states that the act does not obligate the General Assembly to appropriate additional funds, and that the act shall be implemented with funds available or appropriated to the Department of Transportation and the Administrative Office of the Courts.

Session Laws 2009-369, s. 7, as amended by Session Laws 2014-115, s. 61.5, and as amended by Session Laws 2017-176, s. 2(b), provides: "This act becomes effective December 1, 2009, and applies to applications for reinstatement that occur on or after that date." Session Laws 2017-176, s. 2(b) repealed the expiration date for amendments by Session Laws 2009-369, ss. 5 and 6, retroactively effective December 1, 2016.

Session Laws 2014-108, s. 1(b) made amendments to subsection (j) of this section by Session Laws 2014-108, s. 1(a), effective October 1, 2014, and applicable to hearings requested on or after that date.

Session Laws 2015-186, s. 1, provides: "This act shall be known as the 'North Carolina Drivers License Restoration Act.'"

Session Laws 2015-186, s. 7, as amended by Session Laws 2015-264, s. 86, provides: "This act becomes effective December 1, 2015, and applies to offenses committed on or after that date. Prosecutions for offenses committed before the effective date of this act are not abated or affected by this act, and the statutes that would be applicable but for this act remain applicable to those prosecutions." Session Laws 2015-186, s. 4, inserted "for impaired driving" and substituted "G.S. 20-28(a1)" for "G.S. 20-28(a)" in the first sentence of subsection (f).

EFFECT OF AMENDMENTS. --
Session Laws 2006-253, ss. 22.3 and 22.4, inserted "Except as provided in subsection (*l*) of this section" at the beginning of subsection (b), and added subsection (*l*). For effective date and applicability, see Editor's note.

Session Laws 2007-493, s. 10, effective August 30, 2007, substituted "(iii) a violation of G.S. 20-141.4" for "(iii) felony death by vehicle, G.S. 20-141.4(a1)" in subdivision (b)(3)c.

Session Laws 2007-493, s. 28, effective December 1, 2007, and applicable to offenses committed on or after that date, in subsection (a), substituted "concentration of 0.15" for "concentration of 0.16" in subdivision (a)(1), and added the last paragraph of the subsection.

Session Laws 2009-369, ss. 5 and 6, effective December 1, 2009, and applicable to applications for reinstatement that occur on or after that date, added subsection (a1), and in subdivision (b)(3)b., inserted "or subsection (a1)" near the middle.

Session Laws 2011-191, s. 3, effective December 1, 2011, and applicable to offenses committed on or after that date, added subdivision (a)(3) and made a related grammatical change; and in subdivision (b)(3)b., inserted "or (a)(3) of this section."

Session Laws 2013-348, s. 1, effective October 1, 2013, in subsection (c1), added the second, fourth, and fifth sentences, and substituted "In order to avoid an undue..to that person that is" for "unless the Division determines that one or more specific registered vehicles owned by that person are" in the third sentence; deleted the last two sentences in subsection (f), which read "If a person subject to this section is charged with driving while license revoked by violating the requirements of subsection (c1) of this section, and no other violation of this section is alleged, the court may make a determination at the hearing of the case that the vehicle, on which the ignition interlock system was not installed, was relied upon by another member of that person's family for transportation and that the vehicle was not in the possession of the person subject to this section, and therefore the vehicle was not required to be equipped with a functioning ignition interlock system. If the court determines that the vehicle was not required to be equipped with a functioning ignition interlock system and the person subject to this section has committed no other violation of this section, the court shall find the person not guilty of driving while license revoked."; and, in subsection (l), inserted "solely for the reason set forth in subdivision (a)(1) of this section and" in the first sentence, and added the last sentence. For applicability, see Editor's note.

Session Laws 2014-108, s. 1(a), rewrote the former last sentence of the introductory paragraph of subsection (j) as the last two sentences, and added the exception therein. See Editor's note for effective date and applicability.

Session Laws 2015-186, s. 4, effective December 1, 2015, inserted "for impaired driving" and substituted "G.S. 20-28(a1)" for "G.S. 20-28(a)" in the first sentence of subsection (f). For effective date and applicability, see Editor's note.

NO EXCEPTIONS TO IGNITION INTERLOCK DEVICE. --G.S. 20-17.8 does not provide any exceptions to the mandatory ignition interlock device. State v. Benbow, 169 N.C. App. 613, 610 S.E.2d 297 (2005).

REVIEW PROCESS. --There is no review process under G.S. 20-17.8 which would allow a defendant to present her arguments to the Division of Motor Vehicles (DMV); G.S. 20-17.8(j) governs appeals of a DMV decision in cases where a person has violated the requirements of G.S. 20-17.8, but it does not govern instances where a person seeks an exemption from the requirement. State v. Benbow, 169 N.C. App. 613, 610 S.E.2d 297 (2005).

NO RIGHT TO APPEAL MANDATORY REVOCATION. --There is no right to appeal to a court where the cancellation of the license is mandatory, and the

provisions of G.S. 20-17.8 are mandatory; thus, the district court could not review, under G.S. 20-25, a decision by the Division of Motor Vehicles that decided not to reinstate, without a requisite ignition interlock device, the license of a driver whose license had been suspended for violating G.S. 20-17.8. State v. Benbow, 169 N.C. App. 613, 610 S.E.2d 297 (2005).

§ 20-17.8A. Tampering with ignition interlock systems

Any person who tampers with, circumvents, or attempts to circumvent an ignition interlock device required to be installed on a motor vehicle pursuant to judicial order, statute, or as may be otherwise required as a condition for an individual to operate a motor vehicle, for the purpose of avoiding or altering testing on the ignition interlock device in the operation or attempted operation of a vehicle, or altering the testing results received or results in the process of being received on the ignition interlock device, is guilty of a Class 1 misdemeanor. Each act of tampering, circumvention, or attempted circumvention under this statute shall constitute a separate violation.

History.
2011-381, s. 1

EDITOR'S NOTE. --
Session Laws 2011-381, s. 6, made this section effective December 1, 2011, and applicable to offenses committed on or after that date. Session Laws 2011-381, s. 6, further provides: "Prosecutions for offenses committed before the effective date of this act [December 1, 2011] are not abated or affected by this act, and the statutes that would be applicable but for this act remain applicable to those prosecutions."

§ 20-17.9. Revocation of commercial drivers license with a P or S endorsement upon conviction of certain offenses

The Division shall revoke the commercial drivers license with a P or S endorsement of any person convicted of any offense on or after December 1, 2009, that requires registration under Article 27A of Chapter 14 of the General Statutes. The person may apply for the issuance of a new commercial drivers license pursuant to this Chapter, but, pursuant to G.S. 20-17.4, shall remain disqualified from obtaining a commercial drivers license with a P or S endorsement for the period of time during which the person is required to maintain registration.

History.
2009-491, s. 3

EDITOR'S NOTE. --
Session Laws 2009-491, s. 7, provides: "This act becomes effective December 1, 2009. This act applies to persons whose initial registration under Article 27A

of Chapter 14 of the General Statutes occurs on or after December 1, 2009, and to persons who are registered under Article 27A of Chapter 14 of the General Statutes prior to December 1, 2009, and continue to be registered on or after December 1, 2009. The criminal penalties enacted by this act apply to offenses occurring on or after December 1, 2009."

§ 20-18. Conviction of offenses described in § 20-181 not ground for suspension or revocation

Conviction of offenses described in G.S. 20-181 shall not be cause for the suspension or revocation of driver's license under the terms of this Article.

History.

1939, c. 351, s. 2; 1955, c. 913, s. 1; 1979, c. 667, s. 41 CITED in State v. McDaniels, 219 N.C. 763, 14 S.E.2d 793 (1941).

§ 20-19. Period of suspension or revocation; conditions of restoration

(a) When a license is suspended under subdivision (8) or (9) of G.S. 20-16(a), the period of suspension shall be in the discretion of the Division and for such time as it deems best for public safety but shall not exceed six months.

(b) When a license is suspended under subdivision (10) of G.S. 20-16(a), the period of suspension shall be in the discretion of the Division and for such time as it deems best for public safety but shall not exceed a period of 12 months.

(c) When a license is suspended under any other provision of this Article which does not specifically provide a period of suspension, the period of suspension shall be not more than one year.

(c1) When a license is revoked under subdivision (2) of G.S. 20-17, and the period of revocation is not determined by subsection (d) or (e) of this section, the period of revocation is one year.

(c2) When a license is suspended under G.S. 20-17(a)(14), the period of revocation for a first conviction shall be for 10 days. For a second or subsequent conviction as defined in G.S. 20-138.2B(d), the period of revocation shall be one year.

(c3) **Restriction; Revocations. --** When the Division restores a person's drivers license which was revoked pursuant to G.S. 20-13.2(a), G.S. 20-23 when the offense involved impaired driving, G.S. 20-23.2, subdivision (2) of G.S. 20-17(a), subdivision (1) or (9) of G.S. 20-17(a) when the offense involved impaired driving, G.S. 20-138.5(d), or this subsection, in addition to any other restriction or condition, it shall place the applicable restriction on the person's drivers license as follows:

(1) For the first restoration of a drivers license for a person convicted of driving while impaired, G.S. 20-138.1, or a drivers license revoked pursuant to G.S. 20-23 or G.S. 20-23.2 when the offense for which the person's license was revoked prohibits substantially similar conduct which if committed in this State would result in a conviction of driving while impaired under G.S. 20-138.1, that the person not operate a vehicle with an alcohol concentration of 0.04 or more at any relevant time after the driving;

(2) For the second or subsequent restoration of a drivers license for a person convicted of driving while impaired, G.S. 20-138.1, or a drivers license revoked pursuant to G.S. 20-23 or G.S. 20-23.2 when the offense for which the person's license was revoked prohibits substantially similar conduct which if committed in this State would result in a conviction of driving while impaired under G.S. 20-138.1, that the person not operate a vehicle with an alcohol concentration greater than 0.00 at any relevant time after the driving;

(3) For any restoration of a drivers license for a person convicted of driving while impaired in a commercial motor vehicle, G.S. 20-138.2, habitual impaired driving, G.S. 20-138.5, driving while less than 21 years old after consuming alcohol or drugs, G.S. 20-138.3, felony death by vehicle, G.S. 20-141.4(a1), manslaughter or negligent homicide resulting from the operation of a motor vehicle when the offense involved impaired driving, or a revocation under this subsection, that the person not operate a vehicle with an alcohol concentration of greater than 0.00 at any relevant time after the driving;

(4) For any restoration of a drivers license revoked pursuant to G.S. 20-23 or G.S. 20-23.2 when the offense for which the person's license was revoked prohibits substantially similar conduct which if committed in this State would result in a conviction of driving while impaired in a commercial motor vehicle, G.S. 20-138.2, driving while less than 21 years old after consuming alcohol or drugs, G.S. 20-138.3, a violation of G.S. 20-141.4, or manslaughter or negligent homicide resulting from the operation of a motor vehicle when the offense involved impaired driving, that the person not operate vehicle with an alcohol concentration of greater than 0.00 at any relevant time after the driving.

In addition, the person seeking restoration of a license must agree to submit to a chemical analysis in accordance with G.S. 20-16.2 at the request of a law enforcement officer who has reasonable grounds to believe the person is operating a motor vehicle on a highway or public vehicular area in violation of the restriction specified in this subsection. The person must also agree that, when requested by a law enforcement officer, the person will agree to be transported by the law enforcement officer to the place where chemical analysis is to be administered.

The restrictions placed on a license under this subsection shall be in effect (i) seven years from the date of restoration if the person's license was permanently revoked, (ii) until the person's twenty-first birthday if the revocation was for a conviction under G.S. 20-138.3, and (iii) three years in all other cases.

A law enforcement officer who has reasonable grounds to believe that a person has violated a restriction placed on the person's drivers license shall complete an affidavit pursuant to G.S. 20-16.2(c1). On the basis of information reported pursuant to G.S. 20-16.2, the Division shall revoke the drivers license of any person who violates a condition of reinstatement imposed under this subsection. An alcohol concentration report from an ignition interlock system shall not be used as the basis for revocation under this subsection. A violation of a restriction imposed under this subsection or the willful refusal to submit to a chemical analysis shall result in a one-year revocation. If the period of revocation was imposed pursuant to subsection (d) or (e), or G.S. 20-138.5(d), any remaining period of the original revocation, prior to its reduction, shall be reinstated and the one-year revocation begins after all other periods of revocation have terminated.

(c4) **Applicable Procedures.** -- When a person has violated a condition of restoration by refusing a chemical analysis, the notice and hearing procedures of G.S. 20-16.2 apply. When a person has submitted to a chemical analysis and the results show a violation of the alcohol concentration restriction, the notification and hearing procedures of this section apply.

(c5) **Right to Hearing Before Division; Issues.** -- Upon receipt of a properly executed affidavit required by G.S. 20-16.2(c1), the Division must expeditiously notify the person charged that the person's license to drive is revoked for the period of time specified in this section, effective on the tenth calendar day after the mailing of the revocation order unless, before the effective date of the order, the person requests in writing a hearing before the Division. Except for the time referred to in G.S. 20-16.5, if the person shows to the satisfaction of the Division that the person's license was surrendered to

the court and remained in the court's possession, then the Division shall credit the amount of time for which the license was in the possession of the court against the revocation period required by this section. If the person properly requests a hearing, the person retains the person's license, unless it is revoked under some other provision of law, until the hearing is held, the person withdraws the request, or the person fails to appear at a scheduled hearing. The hearing officer may subpoena any witnesses or documents that the hearing officer deems necessary. The person may request the hearing officer to subpoena the charging officer, the chemical analyst, or both to appear at the hearing if the person makes the request in writing at least three days before the hearing. The person may subpoena any other witness whom the person deems necessary, and the provisions of G.S. 1A-1, Rule 45, apply to the issuance and service of all subpoenas issued under the authority of this section. The hearing officer is authorized to administer oaths to witnesses appearing at the hearing. The hearing must be conducted in the county where the charge was brought, and must be limited to consideration of whether:

(1) The charging officer had reasonable grounds to believe that the person had violated the alcohol concentration restriction;

(2) The person was notified of the person's rights as required by G.S. 20-16.2(a);

(3) The drivers license of the person had an alcohol concentration restriction; and

(4) The person submitted to a chemical analysis upon the request of the charging officer, and the analysis revealed an alcohol concentration in excess of the restriction on the person's drivers license.

If the Division finds that the conditions specified in this subsection are met, it must order the revocation sustained. If the Division finds that any of the conditions (1), (2), (3), or (4) is not met, it must rescind the revocation. If the revocation is sustained, the person must surrender the person's license immediately upon notification by the Division.

(c6) **Appeal to Court.** -- There is no right to appeal the decision of the Division. However, if the person properly requested a hearing before the Division under subsection (c5) and the Division held such a hearing, the person may within 30 days of the date the Division's decision is mailed to the person, petition the superior court of the county in which the hearing took place for discretionary review on the record of the revocation. The superior court may stay the imposition of the revocation only if the court finds that the person is likely to succeed on the merits of the case and will suffer irreparable harm if such a stay is not granted. The stay shall not exceed 30 days. The reviewing court shall review the record only and shall be limited to determining if the Division hearing officer followed proper procedures and if the hearing officer made sufficient findings of fact to support the revocation. There shall be no further appeal.

(d) When a person's license is revoked under (i) G.S. 20-17(a)(2) and the person has another offense involving impaired driving for which he has been convicted, which offense occurred within three years immediately preceding the date of the offense for which his license is being revoked, or (ii) G.S. 20-17(a)(9) due to a violation of G.S. 20-141.4(a3), the period of revocation is four years, and this period may be reduced only as provided in this section. The Division may conditionally restore the person's license after it has been revoked for at least two years under this subsection if he provides the Division with satisfactory proof that:

(1) He has not in the period of revocation been convicted in North Carolina or any other state or federal jurisdiction of a motor vehicle offense, an alcoholic beverage control law offense, a drug law offense, or any other criminal offense involving the possession or consumption of alcohol or drugs; and

(2) He is not currently an excessive user of alcohol, drugs, or prescription drugs, or unlawfully using any controlled substance. The person may voluntarily submit themselves to continuous alcohol monitoring for the purpose of proving abstinence from alcohol consumption during a period of revocation immediately prior to the restoration consideration.

a. Monitoring periods of 120 days or longer shall be accepted by the Division as evidence of abstinence if the Division receives sufficient documentation that reflects that the person abstained from alcohol use during the monitoring period.

b. The continuous alcohol monitoring system shall be a system approved under G.S. 15A-1343.3.

c. The Division may establish guidelines for the acceptance of evidence of abstinence under this subdivision.

If the Division restores the person's license, it may place reasonable conditions or restrictions on the person for the duration of the original revocation period.

(e) When a person's license is revoked under (i) G.S. 20-17(a)(2) and the person has two or more previous offenses involving impaired driving for which the person has been convicted, and the most recent offense occurred within the five years immediately preceding the date of the offense for which the person's license is being revoked, (ii) G.S. 20-17(a)(2) and the person was

sentenced pursuant to G.S. 20-179(f3) for the offense resulting in the revocation, or (iii) G.S. 20-17(a)(9) due to a violation of G.S. 20-141.4(a4), the revocation is permanent.

(e1) Notwithstanding subsection (e) of this section, the Division may conditionally restore the license of a person to whom subsection (e) applies after it has been revoked for at least three years under subsection (e) if the person provides the Division with satisfactory proof of all of the following:

(1) In the three years immediately preceding the person's application for a restored license, the person has not been convicted in North Carolina or in any other state or federal court of a motor vehicle offense, an alcohol beverage control law offense, a drug law offense, or any criminal offense involving the consumption of alcohol or drugs.

(2) The person is not currently an excessive user of alcohol, drugs, or prescription drugs, or unlawfully using any controlled substance. The person may voluntarily submit themselves to continuous alcohol monitoring for the purpose of proving abstinence from alcohol consumption during a period of revocation immediately prior to the restoration consideration.

a. Monitoring periods of 120 days or longer shall be accepted by the Division as evidence of abstinence if the Division receives sufficient documentation that reflects that the person abstained from alcohol use during the monitoring period.

b. The continuous alcohol monitoring system shall be a system approved under G.S. 15A-1343.3.

c. The Division may establish guidelines for the acceptance of evidence of abstinence under this subdivision.

(e2) Notwithstanding subsection (e) of this section, the Division may conditionally restore the license of a person to whom subsection (e) applies after it has been revoked for at least 24 months under G.S. 20-17(a)(2) if the person provides the Division with satisfactory proof of all of the following:

(1) The person has not consumed any alcohol for the 12 months preceding the restoration while being monitored by a continuous alcohol monitoring device of a type approved by the Division of Adult Correction and Juvenile Justice of the Department of Public Safety.

(2) The person has not in the period of revocation been convicted in North Carolina or any other state or federal jurisdiction of a motor vehicle offense, an alcoholic beverage control law offense, a drug law offense, or any other criminal offense involving the

possession or consumption of alcohol or drugs.

(3) The person is not currently an excessive user of drugs or prescription drugs.

(4) The person is not unlawfully using any controlled substance.

(e3) If the Division restores a person's license under subsection (e1), (e2), or (e4) of this section, it may place reasonable conditions or restrictions on the person for any period up to five years from the date of restoration.

(e4) When a person's license is revoked under G.S. 20-138.5(d), the Division may conditionally restore the license of that person after it has been revoked for at least 10 years after the completion of any sentence imposed by the court, if the person provides the Division with satisfactory proof of all of the following:

(1) In the 10 years immediately preceding the person's application for a restored license, the person has not been convicted in North Carolina or in any other state or federal court of a motor vehicle offense, an alcohol beverage control law offense, a drug law offense, or any other criminal offense.

(2) The person is not currently a user of alcohol, unlawfully using any controlled substance, or an excessive user of prescription drugs.

(f) When a license is revoked under any other provision of this Article which does not specifically provide a period of revocation, the period of revocation shall be one year.

(g) When a license is suspended under subdivision (11) of G.S. 20-16(a), the period of suspension shall be for a period of time not in excess of the period of nonoperation imposed by the court as a condition of the suspended sentence; further, in such case, it shall not be necessary to comply with the Motor Vehicle Safety and Financial Responsibility Act in order to have such license returned at the expiration of the suspension period.

(g1) When a license is revoked under subdivision (12) of G.S. 20-17, the period of revocation is six months for conviction of a second offense and one year for conviction of a third or subsequent offense.

(g2) When a license is revoked under G.S. 20-17(a)(16), the period of revocation is 90 days for a second conviction and six months for a third or subsequent conviction. The term "second or subsequent conviction" shall have the same meaning as found in G.S. 20-17(a)(16).

(h) Repealed by Session Laws 1983, c. 435, s. 17.

(i) *(For applicability, see Editor's note)* When a person's license is revoked under G.S. 20-17(a)(1) or G.S. 20-17(a)(9), and the offense is one involving impaired driving and a fatality, the revocation is permanent. The Division may, however, conditionally restore the person's license after it has been revoked for at least five years under this subsection if he provides the Division with satisfactory proof that:

(1) In the five years immediately preceding the person's application for a restored license, he has not been convicted in North Carolina or in any other state or federal court of a motor vehicle offense, an alcohol beverage control law offense, a drug law offense, or any criminal offense involving the consumption of alcohol or drugs; and

(2) He is not currently an excessive user of alcohol or drugs.

If the Division restores the person's license, it may place reasonable conditions or restrictions on the person for any period up to seven years from the date of restoration.

(j) The Division is authorized to issue amended revocation orders issued under subsections (d) and (e), if necessary because convictions do not respectively occur in the same order as offenses for which the license may be revoked under those subsections.

(k) Before the Division restores a driver's license that has been suspended or revoked under G.S. 20-138.5(d), or under any provision of this Article, other than G.S. 20-24.1, the person seeking to have his driver's license restored shall submit to the Division proof that he has notified his insurance agent or company of his seeking the restoration and that he is financially responsible. Proof of financial responsibility shall be in one of the following forms:

(1) A written certificate or electronically-transmitted facsimile thereof from any insurance carrier duly authorized to do business in this State certifying that there is in effect a nonfleet private passenger motor vehicle liability policy for the benefit of the person required to furnish proof of financial responsibility. The certificate or facsimile shall state the effective date and expiration date of the nonfleet private passenger motor vehicle liability policy and shall state the date that the certificate or facsimile is issued. The certificate or facsimile shall remain effective proof of financial responsibility for a period of 30 consecutive days following the date the certificate or facsimile is issued but shall not in and of itself constitute a binder or policy of insurance or

(2) A binder for or policy of nonfleet private passenger motor vehicle liability insurance under which the applicant is insured, provided that the binder or policy states the effective date and expiration date of the nonfleet private passenger motor vehicle liability policy.

The preceding provisions of this subsection do not apply to applicants who do not own currently registered motor vehicles and who do not operate nonfleet private passenger motor vehicles that are owned by other persons and that are not insured under commercial motor vehicle liability insurance policies. In such cases, the applicant shall sign a written certificate to that effect. Such certificate shall be furnished by the Division and may be incorporated into the restoration application form. Any material misrepresentation made by such person on such certificate shall be grounds for suspension of that person's license for a period of 90 days.

For the purposes of this subsection, the term "nonfleet private passenger motor vehicle" has the definition ascribed to it in Article 40 of General Statute Chapter 58.

The Commissioner may require that certificates required by this subsection be on a form approved by the Commissioner. The financial responsibility required by this subsection shall be kept in effect for not less than three years after the date that the license is restored. Failure to maintain financial responsibility as required by this subsection shall be grounds for suspending the restored driver's license for a period of thirty (30) days. Nothing in this subsection precludes any person from showing proof of financial responsibility in any other manner authorized by Articles 9A and 13 of this Chapter.

History.
1935, c. 52, s. 13; 1947, c. 1067, s. 15; 1951, c. 1202, ss. 2-4; 1953, c. 1138; 1955, c. 1187, ss. 13, 17, 18; 1957, c. 499, s. 2; c. 515, s. 1; 1959, c. 1264, s. 11A; 1969, c. 242; 1971, c. 619, ss. 8-10; 1973, c. 1445, ss. 1-4; 1975, c. 716, s. 5; 1979, c. 903, ss. 4-6; 1981, c. 412, s. 4; c. 747, ss. 34, 66; 1983, c. 435, s. 17; 1983 (Reg. Sess., 1984), c. 1101, s. 18; 1987, c. 869, s. 12; 1987 (Reg. Sess., 1988), c. 1112; 1989, c. 436, s. 5; c. 771, s. 18; 1995, c. 506, s. 8; 1998-182, s. 21; 1999-406, s. 2; 1999-452, ss. 11, 12; 2000-140, ss. 3, 4; 2000-155, s. 6; 2001-352, s. 4; 2007-165, s. 1(a), (b); 2007-493, ss. 11 -14; 2008-187, s. 9; 2009-99, s. 1; 2009-369, ss. 1 -4; 2009-500, ss. 1, 2; 2011-145, s. 19.1(h); 2011-191, s. 2; 2014-115, s. 61.5; 2017-176, s. 2(b); 2017-186, s. 2 (jjjj)

EDITOR'S NOTE. --
Session Laws 1999-406, s. 18, states that the act does not obligate the General Assembly to appropriate additional funds, and that the act shall be implemented with funds available or appropriated to the Department of Transportation and the Administrative Office of the Courts.

Session Laws 2007-493, s. 33, as amended by Session Laws 2009-99, s. 1, provides: "Sections 26, 27, 28, 29, 30, and 31 of this act become effective December 1, 2007, and apply to offenses committed on or after that date. Section 14 of this act applies to persons whose waiting period for a hearing on conditional restoration commences on or after the effective date of this act. The remainder of this act is effective when it

becomes law. Prosecutions for offenses committed before the effective date of this act are not abated or affected by this act, and the statutes that would be applicable but for this act remain applicable to those prosecutions."

Subsection (e), as originally amended by Session Laws 2007-165, s. 1(b), had two subdivisions designated (e)(1) and two subdivisions designated (e)(2). Session Laws 2008-187 corrected the subsection (e) designation scheme.

The amendment by Session Laws 2007-493, s. 14, rewrote subsection (i), and was effective August 30, 2007, and applicable to persons whose waiting period for a hearing on conditional restoration commences on or after that date, pursuant to Session Laws 2007-493, s. 33, as amended by Session Laws 2009-99, s. 1.

Subsection (e), as originally amended by Session Laws 2007-165, s. 1(b), had two subdivisions designated (e)(1) and two subdivisions designated (e)(2). Session Laws 2008-187 corrected the subsection (e) designation scheme.

Session Laws 2009-369, s. 7, as amended by Session Laws 2014-115, s. 61.5, and as amended by Session Laws 2017-176, s. 2(b), provides: "This act becomes effective December 1, 2009, and applies to applications for reinstatement that occur on or after that date." Session Laws 2017-176, s. 2(b) repealed the expiration date for amendments by Session Laws 2009-369, ss. 1 -4, retroactively effective December 1, 2016.

EFFECT OF AMENDMENTS. --
Session Laws 2008-187, s. 9, effective August 7, 2008, rewrote subsection (e) as present subsections (e), (e1), (e2), and (e3).

Session Laws 2009-369, ss. 1 through 4, as amended by Session Laws 2014-115, s. 61.5, effective December 1, 2009, and applicable to applications for reinstatement that occur on or after that date, in subsection (c3), in the introductory language, inserted "G.S. 20-138.5(d)"; in subdivision (c3)(3), inserted "habitual impaired driving, G.S. 20-138.5"; in the last paragraph of subsection (c3), inserted "or G.S. 20-138.5(d)"; in subsection (e3) substituted "(e1), (e2), or (e4)" for "(e1) or (e2)"; added subsection (e4); and in subsection (k), inserted "G.S. 20-138.5(d), or under" in the introductory language.

Session Laws 2009-500, ss. 1 and 2, effective for hearings or proceedings occurring on or after December 1, 2009, added the second sentence in subdivisions (d)(2) and (e1)(2); and added subdivisions (d)(2) a.-(d)(2)c and (e1)(2)a.-(e1)(2)c.

Session Laws 2011-145, s. 19.1(h), effective January 1, 2012, substituted "Division of Adult Correction of the Department of Public Safety" for "Department of Correction" in subdivision (e2)(1).

Session Laws 2011-191, s. 2, effective December 1, 2011, and applicable to offenses committed on or after that date, in subsection (e), inserted (ii), redesignated former (ii) as (iii), and made a related change.

Session Laws 2017-186, s. 2 (jjjj), effective December 1, 2017, inserted "and Juvenile Justice" in subdivision (e2)(1).

THE POWER TO ISSUE, SUSPEND OR REVOKE A DRIVER'S LICENSE IS VESTED EXCLUSIVELY

Chapter 20

IN THE DIVISION of Motor Vehicles, subject to review by the superior court and, upon appeal, by the appellate division. Smith v. Walsh, 34 N.C. App. 287, 238 S.E.2d 157 (1977).

Under G.S. 20-16(a)(10) and subsection (b) of this section, the discretionary authority to suspend petitioner's license for a period not exceeding 12 months was vested exclusively in the Division of Motor Vehicles. No discretionary power was conferred upon a superior court. Smith v. Walsh, 34 N.C. App. 287, 238 S.E.2d 157 (1977).

SUBSECTION (E) OF THIS SECTION IS NOT OVERBROAD IN VIOLATION OF THE CONSTITUTION since no conduct within the purview of the phrase "violation of liquor laws of North Carolina," including the commission of the crime of public drunkenness, is a constitutionally protected activity. In re Harris, 37 N.C. App. 590, 246 S.E.2d 532 (1978).

SUBSECTION (E) IS NOT UNCONSTITUTIONALLY VAGUE. --The phrase "liquor laws" in subsection (e) of this section, is not a term so vague that men of common intelligence must necessarily guess at its meaning and differ as to its application. In re Harris, 37 N.C. App. 590, 246 S.E.2d 532 (1978).

IN ENACTING SUBSECTION (E) OF THIS SECTION, THE LEGISLATURE WAS DEMANDING COMPLETE COMPLIANCE WITH ALL LAWS GOVERNING THE USE OF DRUGS, ALCOHOL, AND MOTOR VEHICLES. In re Harris, 37 N.C. App. 590, 246 S.E.2d 532 (1978).

THE PURPOSE OF THIS SECTION is to provide a uniform standard period for the withholding of the privilege to operate a motor vehicle following certain offenses. Wagoner v. Hiatt, 111 N.C. App. 448, 432 S.E.2d 417 (1993).

VIOLATION OF "ALCOHOLIC BEVERAGES LAWS". --The legislature fully intended to include the crime of public drunkenness in the phrase "violation of liquor (now 'alcoholic beverages') laws of North Carolina" in subsection (e) of this section. In re Harris, 37 N.C. App. 590, 246 S.E.2d 532 (1978).

OUT-OF-STATE CONVICTION TO BE COUNTED AS CONVICTION FOR PURPOSE OF SUBSECTION (E). --An out-of-state conviction of operating a motor vehicle upon the public highway while under the influence of intoxicating liquor or an impairing drug (now impaired driving) is to be counted as a conviction for the purpose of the operation of the mandatory provision of subsection (e). In re Oates, 18 N.C. App. 320, 196 S.E.2d 596 (1973).

NO CONTEST PLEA MAY BE USED AS PRIOR CONVICTION. --The judgment entered on a plea of no contest to a previous charge of driving with a blood alcohol content of .10 percent or more may be used as a prior conviction by the DMV for purposes of revoking a driver's license. Davis v. Hiatt, 326 N.C. 462, 390 S.E.2d 338 (1990).

CERTIORARI TO REVIEW MANDATORY SUSPENSION. --Petitioner whose driving privilege was mandatorily suspended under G.S. 20-17(2) and G.S. 20-19(e) did not have the right to appeal under G.S. 20-25 or under the Administrative Procedure Act,

Chapter 150B. However, the superior court could review the actions of the Commissioner by issuing a writ of certiorari. Davis v. Hiatt, 326 N.C. 462, 390 S.E.2d 338 (1990).

Where petitioner, seeking conditional restoration of his driving privileges, pled sufficient facts to show he did not have right to appeal from final decision of DMV, he could then have petitioned for writ of certiorari to have case reviewed by superior court. Thus, superior court had jurisdiction to review case. Penuel v. Hiatt, 100 N.C. App. 268, 396 S.E.2d 85 (1990).

REVIEW OF PERMANENT REVOCATION UNDER SUBSECTION (E). --Where the Department (now Division) of Motor Vehicles permanently revoked plaintiff's driver's license for a third offense of driving while under the influence, the departmental action was mandatory, and the superior court was without authority to revoke or make any order with reference thereto. Rhyne v. Garrett, 18 N.C. App. 565, 197 S.E.2d 235 (1973).

Trial court correctly reviewed the North Carolina Division of Motor Vehicles' cancellation of a driver's conditionally restored driving privileges under a petition for writ of certiorari rather than de novo review because although there was no right to appeal a cancellation or revocation under G.S. 20-25, the driver could seek certiorari pursuant to G.S. 20-19(e). Cole v. Faulkner, 155 N.C. App. 592, 573 S.E.2d 614 (2002).

REVIEW OF REFUSAL TO REINSTATE LICENSE. --Once the right to drive has been mandatorily revoked and a petitioner unsuccessfully seeks to have the license reinstated by the DMV, no superior court review of the denial is mandated unless the denial was arbitrary or illegal, because reinstatement is not a legal right but is an act of grace. Alpiser v. Eagle Pontiac-GMC-Isuzu, Inc., 97 N.C. App. 610, 389 S.E.2d 293 (1990).

THE PROVISIONS OF SUBSECTION (F) OF THIS SECTION ARE MANDATORY. Snyder v. Scheidt, 246 N.C. 81, 97 S.E.2d 461 (1957).

The provisions of G.S. 20-17(6) and subsection (f) of this section are mandatory and not discretionary. Simpson v. Garrett, 15 N.C. App. 449, 190 S.E.2d 251 (1972).

SUBSECTION (F)'S ONE-YEAR PERIOD APPLIES TO G.S. 20-17.1. Jones v. Penny, 387 F. Supp. 383 (M.D.N.C. 1974).

SUBSECTIONS (D) AND (J) of this section must be read together, giving consideration both to the legislative intent of ensuring standard penalties for the same offenses and to the policy of preventing circumvention of this section. Wagoner v. Hiatt, 111 N.C. App. 448, 432 S.E.2d 417 (1993).

DIVISION REQUIRED TO REVOKE LICENSE FOR STATUTORY PERIOD. --Upon receiving a record of an operator's or chauffeur's conviction upon two charges of reckless driving committed within a period of 12 months, the Department (now Division) of Motor Vehicles is required to forthwith revoke the license of such persons for the statutory period. Simpson v. Garrett, 15 N.C. App. 449, 190 S.E.2d 251 (1972).

Where there is mandatory revocation under subdivision (2) of G.S. 20-17, the period of revocation shall be as provided in this section. Carmichael v. Scheidt, 249 N.C. 472, 106 S.E.2d 685 (1959); In re Austin, 5 N.C. App. 575, 169 S.E.2d 20 (1969).

EFFECTIVE DATE OF REVOCATION. --A revocation based on a second offense for driving while under the influence of intoxicating liquor or a narcotic drug (now impaired driving) must be for a period of three (now four) years, and the effective date of the revocation for such period should not begin prior to the date of the second conviction. Likewise, when a license is permanently revoked, the effective date of such revocation should not be earlier than the date of the conviction for the third offense. Carmichael v. Scheidt, 249 N.C. 472, 106 S.E.2d 685 (1959).

PERIOD OF SUSPENSION RUNS FROM DATE OF ORDER BY DIVISION. --When within five days from receipt of notice of conviction the Department (now Division) ordered the revocation of an operator's license for one year, the revocation was in effect until the same date in the following year, and did not expire one year from the date of conviction or the date of receipt of notice by the Department (now Division). State v. Ball, 255 N.C. 351, 121 S.E.2d 604 (1961).

INJUNCTION NOT AVAILABLE TO PLAINTIFF WHO COULD HAVE PREVENTED DELAY IN START OF REVOCATION PERIOD. --Where the elapse of approximately 15 months between plaintiff's last conviction for reckless driving and the order of revocation was not caused by defendant, Commissioner of Motor Vehicles or his Department (now Division), but the delay apparently resulted from the failure of the clerk of the court where plaintiff was last convicted to act promptly in forwarding a record of the conviction to the Department (now Division) of Motor Vehicles, and plaintiff could have prevented any delay in the start of the revocation period by surrendering his license to the clerk and obtaining a receipt therefor at the time of his second conviction, plaintiff was not entitled to injunctive relief. Simpson v. Garrett, 15 N.C. App. 449, 190 S.E.2d 251 (1972).

REINSTATEMENT OR THE RECEIPT OF A NEW LICENSE DURING THE REVOCATION PERIOD IS NOT A LEGAL RIGHT of the defendant, but an act of grace which the General Assembly permits, but does not require, the Department (now Division) to apply. The authority to exercise or apply this act of grace is granted to the Department (now Division), not to the courts. In re Austin, 5 N.C. App. 575, 169 S.E.2d 20 (1969).

COURT ORDER REQUIRING CONDITIONAL RESTORATION HELD ERROR. --Where petitioner offered no support for his allegation that the DMV's denial of a conditional restoration of his license, which had been mandatorily revoked under G.S. 20-17, was an arbitrary and capricious act and was in disregard of the law set forth in this section, it was error for the Superior Court to enter an order requiring the DMV to conditionally restore petitioner's driving privileges. Penuel v. Hiatt, 97 N.C. App. 616, 389 S.E.2d 289, aff'd on petition to rehear, 100 N.C. App. 268, 396 S.E.2d 85 (1990).

WARRANT NEED NOT CHARGE SECOND OFFENSE IN ORDER TO SUPPORT REVOCATION UNDER SUBSECTION (D). --Where defendant's driver's license had previously been suspended for a period of one year for conviction of driving while under the influence of intoxicating liquor, and defendant pleaded guilty to another such offense upon warrant not charging a second offense, the Department (now Division) of Motor Vehicles, upon receipt of the report of the later conviction, must revoke defendant's license for the period provided by subsection (d) of this section. Harrell v. Scheidt, 243 N.C. 735, 92 S.E.2d 182 (1956).

RIGHT TO INHERIT FROM LIFE INSURANCE POLICIES. --While paternity had to be established for an illegitimate child to inherit from a father who died intestate, North Carolina had no statute requiring that paternity be established for an illegitimate child to benefit from a life insurance policy, and the policy at issue in defendant claimant's case did not exclude illegitimate children unless paternity had been judicially established. Fort Dearborn Life Ins. Co. v. Turner, 521 F. Supp. 2d 499 (E.D.N.C. Oct. 3, 2007).

APPLIED in Fox v. Scheidt, 241 N.C. 31, 84 S.E.2d 259 (1954); State v. Moore, 247 N.C. 368, 101 S.E.2d 26 (1957); Honeycutt v. Scheidt, 254 N.C. 607, 119 S.E.2d 777 (1961); Gibson v. Scheidt, 259 N.C. 339, 130 S.E.2d 679 (1963); In re Woods, 33 N.C. App. 86, 234 S.E.2d 45 (1977); State v. Finger, 72 N.C. App. 569, 324 S.E.2d 894 (1985); State v. Curtis, 73 N.C. App. 248, 326 S.E.2d 90 (1985); Smith v. Wilkins, 75 N.C. App. 483, 331 S.E.2d 159 (1985).

CITED in State v. Letterlough, 6 N.C. App. 36, 169 S.E.2d 269 (1969); State v. Teasley, 9 N.C. App. 477, 176 S.E.2d 838 (1970); Ennis v. Garrett, 279 N.C. 612, 184 S.E.2d 246 (1971); Cooke v. Faulkner, 137 N.C. App. 755, 529 S.E.2d 512 (2000); State v. Benbow, 169 N.C. App. 613, 610 S.E.2d 297 (2005); State v. Coffey, 189 N.C. App. 382, 658 S.E.2d 73 (2008); Powers v. Tatum, 196 N.C. App. 639, 676 S.E.2d 89 (2009), review denied, stay denied, 363 N.C. 583, 681 S.E.2d 784 (2009).

CROSS REFERENCES. --
As to Division of Adult Correction and Juvenile Justice of the Department of Public Safety establishing regulations for continuous alcohol monitoring systems, see G.S. 15A-1343.3.

LEGAL PERIODICALS. --
For survey of 1978 constitutional law, see 57 N.C.L. Rev. 958 (1979).

N.C. Gen. Stat. § 20-20

Repealed by Session Laws 1981, c. 938, s. 5.
CROSS REFERENCES. --
For present provisions concerning the surrender of an operator's license which has been revoked or suspended, see G.S. 20-45(b).

§ 20-20.1. Limited driving privilege for certain revocations

(a) **Definitions. --** The following definitions apply in this section:

Chapter 20

(1) **Limited driving privilege.** -- A judgment issued by a court authorizing a person with a revoked drivers license to drive under specified terms and conditions.

(2) **Nonstandard working hours.** -- Anytime other than 6:00 A.M. until 8:00 P.M. on Monday through Friday.

(3) **Standard working hours.** -- Anytime from 6:00 A.M. until 8:00 P.M. on Monday through Friday.

(4) **Underlying offense.** -- The offense for which a person's drivers license was revoked when the person was charged under G.S. 20-28(a), driving with a revoked license, or under G.S. 20-28.1, committing a motor vehicle moving offense while driving with a revoked license.

(b) **Eligibility.** -- A person is eligible to apply for a limited driving privilege under this section if all of the following conditions apply:

(1) The person's license is currently revoked under G.S. 20-28(a) or G.S. 20-28.1.

(2) The person has complied with the revocation for the period required in subsection (c) of this section immediately preceding the date the person files a petition for a limited driving privilege under this section.

(3) The person's underlying offense is not an offense involving impaired driving and, if the person's license is revoked under G.S. 20-28.1 for committing a motor vehicle moving offense while driving with a revoked license, the moving offense is not an offense involving impaired driving.

(4) The revocation period for the underlying offense has expired.

(5) The revocation under G.S. 20-28(a) or G.S. 20-28.1 is the only revocation in effect.

(6) The person is not eligible to receive a limited driving privilege under any other law.

(7) The person has not held a limited driving privilege issued under this section at anytime during the three years prior to the date the person files the current petition.

(8) The person has no pending charges for any motor vehicle offense in this or in any other state and has no unpaid motor vehicle fines or penalties in this or in any other state.

(9) The person's drivers license issued by another state has not been revoked by that state.

(10) G.S. 20-9(e) or G.S. 20-9(f) does not prohibit the Division from issuing the person a license.

(c) **Compliance Period.** -- The following table sets out the period during which a person must comply with a revocation under G.S. 20-28(a) or G.S. 20-28.1 to be eligible for a limited driving privilege under this section:

Revocation Period	Compliance Period
1 Year	90 Days
2 Years	1 Year
Permanent	2 Years

(d) **Petition.** -- A person may apply for a limited driving privilege under this section by filing a petition. A petition filed under this section is separate from the action that resulted in the initial revocation and is a civil action. A petition must be filed in district court in the county of the person's residence as reflected by the Division's records or, if the Division's records are inaccurate, in the county of the person's actual residence. A person must attach to a petition a copy of the person's motor vehicle record. A petition must include a sworn statement that the person filing the petition is eligible for a limited driving privilege under this section.

A court, for good cause shown, may issue a limited driving privilege to an eligible person in accordance with this section. The costs required under G.S. 7A-305(a) and G.S. 20-20.2 apply to a petition filed under this section. The clerk of court for the court that issues a limited driving privilege under this section must send a copy of the limited driving privilege to the Division.

(e) **Scope of Privilege.** -- A limited driving privilege restricts the person to essential driving related to one or more of the purposes listed in this subsection. Any driving that is not related to the purposes authorized in this subsection is unlawful even though done at times and upon routes that may be authorized by the privilege. Except as otherwise provided, all driving must be for a purpose and done within the restrictions specified in the privilege.

The permissible purposes for a limited driving privilege are:

(1) Travel to and from the person's place of employment and in the course of employment.

(2) Travel necessary for maintenance of the person's household.

(3) Travel to provide emergency medical care for the person or for an immediate family member of the person who resides in the same household with the person. Driving related to emergency medical care is authorized at anytime and without restriction as to routes.

(f) **Employment Driving in Standard Working Hours.** -- The court may authorize driving for employment-related purposes during standard working hours without specifying times and routes for the driving. If the person is required to drive for essential employment-related purposes only during standard working hours, the limited driving privilege must prohibit driving during nonstandard working hours unless the driving is for emergency medical care or for authorized household maintenance. The limited driving privilege must state the name and address of the person's employer and may, in the discretion of the court, include other information and restrictions applicable to employment-related driving.

(g) **Employment Driving in Nonstandard Working Hours.** -- If a person is required to drive during nonstandard working hours for an essential employment-related purpose and the person provides documentation of that fact to the court, the court may authorize the person to drive for that purpose during those hours. If the person is self-employed, the documentation must be attached to or made a part of the limited driving privilege. If the person is employed by another, the limited driving privilege must state the name and address of the person's employer and may, in the discretion of the court, include other information and restrictions applicable to employment-related driving. If the court determines that it is necessary for the person to drive during nonstandard working hours for an employment-related purpose, the court may authorize the person to drive subject to these limitations:

(1) If the person is required to drive to and from a specific place of employment at regular times, the limited driving privilege must specify the general times and routes by which the person may drive to and from work and must restrict driving to those times and routes.

(2) If the person is required to drive to and from work at a specific place but is unable to specify the times during which the driving will occur, the limited driving privilege must specify the general routes by which the person may drive to and from work and must restrict driving to those general routes.

(3) If the person is required to drive to and from work at regular times but is unable to specify the places at which work is to be performed, the limited driving privilege must specify the general times and geographic boundaries within which the person may drive and must restrict driving to those times and boundaries.

(4) If the person can specify neither the times nor places in which the person will be driving to and from work, the limited driving privilege must specify the geographic boundaries within which the person may drive and must restrict driving to those boundaries.

(h) **Household Maintenance.** -- A limited driving privilege may allow driving for maintenance of the household only during standard working hours. The court, at its discretion, may impose additional restrictions on driving for the maintenance of the household.

(i) **Restrictions.** -- A limited driving privilege that is not authorized by this section or that does not contain the restrictions required by law is invalid. A limited driving privilege issued under this section is subject to the following conditions:

(1) **Financial responsibility.** -- A person applying for a limited driving privilege under this section must provide the court proof of financial responsibility acceptable under G.S. 20-16.1(g) and must maintain the financial responsibility during the period of the limited driving privilege.

(2) **Alcohol restrictions.** -- A person who received a limited driving privilege under this section may not consume alcohol while driving or drive at anytime while the person has remaining in the person's body any alcohol or controlled substance previously consumed, unless the controlled substance was lawfully obtained and taken in therapeutically appropriate amounts.

(3) **Others.** -- The court may impose any other reasonable restrictions or conditions necessary to achieve the purposes of this section.

(j) **Term and Reinstatement.** -- The term of a limited driving privilege issued under this section is the shorter of one year or the length of time remaining in the revocation period imposed under G.S. 20-28(a) or G.S. 20-28.1. When the term of the limited driving privilege expires, the Division must reinstate the person's license if the person meets all of the conditions listed in this subsection. The Division may impose restrictions or conditions on the new license in accordance with G.S. 20-7(e). The conditions are:

(1) Payment of the restoration fee as required under G.S. 20-7(i1).

(2) Providing proof of financial responsibility as required under G.S. 20-7(c1).

(3) Providing the proof required for reinstatement of a license under G.S. 20-28(c1).

(k) **Modification.** -- A court may modify or revoke a person's limited driving privilege issued under this section upon a showing that the circumstances have changed sufficiently to justify modification or revocation. If the judge who issued the privilege is not presiding in the court in which the privilege was issued, a presiding judge in that court may modify or revoke the privilege. The judge must indicate in the order of modification or revocation the reasons for the order or make specific findings indicating the reason for the order and enter those findings in the record of the case. When a court issues an order of modification or revocation, the clerk of court must send a copy of the order to the Division.

(*l*) **Effect of Violation.** -- A violation of a limited driving privilege issued under this section constitutes the offense of driving while license revoked under G.S. 20-28. When a person is charged with operating a motor vehicle in violation of the limited driving privilege, the limited driving privilege is suspended pending the final disposition of the charge.

History.
2007-293, s. 1;2007-323, s. 30.11(d);2007-345, s. 9.1(c);2008-118, s. 2.9(b)
EDITOR'S NOTE. --
Session Laws 2007-293, s. 3, made this section effective December 1, 2007, and applicable to revocations that occur before, on, or after December 1, 2007.
EFFECT OF AMENDMENTS. --
Session Laws 2008-118, s. 2.9(b), effective July 1, 2008, substituted "and G.S. 20-20.2" for "and (a3)" in the second paragraph of subsection (d).

§ 20-20.2. Processing fee for limited driving privilege

Upon the issuance of a limited driving privilege by a court under this Chapter, the applicant or petitioner must pay, in addition to any other costs associated with obtaining the privilege, a processing fee of one hundred dollars ($ 100.00). The applicant or petitioner shall pay this fee to the clerk of superior court in the county in which the limited driving privilege is issued. The fee must be remitted to the State Treasurer and used for support of the General Court of Justice. The failure to pay this fee shall render the privilege invalid.

History.
2007-323, s. 30.11(b);2007-345, s. 9.1(b)
EDITOR'S NOTE. --
Session Laws 2007-323, s. 30.11(e), made this section effective August 1, 2007, and applicable to costs assessed or collected on or after August 1, 2007.
EFFECT OF AMENDMENTS. --
Session Laws 2007-345, s. 9.1(b), effective August 1, 2007, and applicable to costs assessed on or after that date, substituted "a processing fee of one hundred dollars ($100.00)" for "the processing fee imposed under G.S. 7A-305(a3)" at the end of the first sentence, and added the third sentence.

§ 20-21. No operation under foreign license during suspension or revocation in this State

Any resident or nonresident whose driver's license or right or privilege to operate a motor vehicle in this State has been suspended or revoked as provided in this Article shall not operate a motor vehicle in this State under a license, permit or registration issued by another jurisdiction or otherwise during such suspension, or after such revocation until a new license is obtained when and as permitted under this Article.

History.
1935, c. 52, s. 15; 1979, c. 667, s. 41

§ 20-22. Suspending privileges of nonresidents and reporting convictions

(a) The privilege of driving a motor vehicle on the highways of this State given to a nonresident hereunder shall be subject to suspension or revocation by the Division in like manner and for like cause as a driver's license issued hereunder may be suspended or revoked.

(b) The Division is further authorized, upon receiving a record of the conviction in this State of a nonresident driver of a motor vehicle of any offense under the motor vehicle laws of this State, to forward a certified copy of such record to the motor vehicle administrator in the state wherein the person so convicted is a resident.

History.
1935, c. 52, s. 16; 1975, c. 716, s. 5; 1979, c. 667, s. 41
REVOCATION OF OUT-OF-STATE LICENSE. --Revocation of defendant's South Dakota driver's license for failure to submit to a chemical analysis was permissible. State v. Streckfuss, 171 N.C. App. 81, 614 S.E.2d 323 (2005).
CITED in Morrisey v. Crabtree, 143 F. Supp. 105 (M.D.N.C. 1956); Lee v. Gore, 206 N.C. App. 374, 698 S.E.2d 179 (2010), aff'd, 717 S.E.2d 356, 2011 N.C. LEXIS 660 (2011).
OPINIONS OF THE ATTORNEY GENERAL
NONRESIDENT CONVICTED IN NORTH CAROLINA COURT. --Upon conviction of a nonresident of driving while under the influence in a North Carolina court, his privilege to drive in North Carolina will be revoked. The court may allow a nonresident a limited privilege to operate a motor vehicle in North Carolina. The court should not require nonresidents to surrender driver's licenses issued by states other than North Carolina. See opinion of Attorney General to Honorable John S. Gardner, District Court Judge, Sixteenth Judicial District, 40 N.C.A.G. 420 (1969).

§ 20-23. Revoking resident's license upon conviction in another state

The Division may revoke the license of any resident of this State upon receiving notice of the person's conviction in another state of an offense set forth in G.S. 20-26(a).

History.
1935, c. 52, s. 17; 1971, c. 486, s. 2; 1975, c. 716, s. 5; 1979, c. 667, s. 22; 1993, c. 533, s. 6
SECTION CONSTRUED WITH G.S. 20-16 AND G.S. 20-25. --This section, G.S. 20-16 and G.S. 20-25 must be construed in pari materia. In re Wright, 228 N.C. 584, 46 S.E.2d 696 (1948).
SECTION IS NOT MANDATORY. --The Department (now Division) of Motor Vehicles, under provisions of this section, is merely authorized, not directed,

to suspend or revoke the license of any resident of this State upon receiving notice of the conviction of such person in another state of any offense therein which, if committed in this State, would be grounds for the suspension or revocation of the license. Carmichael v. Scheidt, 249 N.C. 472, 106 S.E.2d 685 (1959).

DISCRETION OF DIVISION. --Under the provisions of this section, it is discretionary with the Department (now Division) to suspend or revoke an operator's license upon receiving notice of his conviction in another state of an offense which, if committed in this State, would be grounds for suspension or revocation. State v. Teasley, 9 N.C. App. 477, 176 S.E.2d 838, appeal dismissed, 277 N.C. 459, 177 S.E.2d 900 (1970).

NOTICE MAY BE FROM ANY SOURCE. --This section does not limit the notice of conviction in another state upon which the Department (now Division) may act to notice from a judicial tribunal or other official agency. Under the wording of the statute, from whatever source the notice may come, the Department (now Division) may act. In re Wright, 228 N.C. 584, 46 S.E.2d 696 (1948).

LICENSEE MAY SHOW INVALIDITY OF OUT-OF-STATE CONVICTION. --Where an order of the Department (now Division) of Motor Vehicles permanently revoking the license of a driver upon a third conviction for operating a motor vehicle while under the influence of intoxicating liquor (now impaired driving) was based in part upon notice of the licensee's conviction of that offense in another state, the licensee had the right to show, if he could, that the proceedings in such other state were irregular, invalid and insufficient to support the reported conviction, and he was entitled to a hearing de novo in the superior court upon his petition for review. The sustaining of a demurrer to such petition was error, petitioner being entitled to an adjudication of the validity of the out-of-state conviction in order to determine whether the revocation should be permanent or for the period of time prescribed by subsection (d) of G.S. 20-19. Carmichael v. Scheidt, 249 N.C. 472, 106 S.E.2d 685 (1959).

CONVICTION OF DRUNKEN DRIVING. --Upon a receipt of notification from the highway department of another state that a resident of this State had there been convicted of drunken (now impaired) driving, the Department (now Division) of Motor Vehicles had the right to suspend the driving license of such person. In re Wright, 228 N.C. 301, 45 S.E.2d 370 (1947).

FAILURE TO APPEAR AT TRIAL FOR DRIVING UNDER THE INFLUENCE IN ANOTHER STATE. --Motorist who received citation for driving under the influence in South Carolina and then forfeited bond by not appearing in court had his driver's license properly revoked even though no warrant was issued. Sykes v. Hiatt, 98 N.C. App. 688, 391 S.E.2d 834 (1990).

CROSS REFERENCES. --
As to Division's authority to suspend license, see G.S. 20-16.

LEGAL PERIODICALS. --
For note on choice of law rules in North Carolina, see 48 N.C.L. Rev. 243 (1970).

§ 20-23.1. Suspending or revoking operating privilege of person not holding license

In any case where the Division would be authorized to suspend or revoke the license of a person but such person does not hold a license, the Division is authorized to suspend or revoke the operating privilege of such a person in like manner as it could suspend or revoke his license if such person held a driver's license, and the provisions of this Chapter governing suspensions, revocations, issuance of a license, and driving after license suspended or revoked, shall apply in the discretion of the Division in the same manner as if the license has been suspended or revoked.

History.
1955, c. 1187, s. 19; 1969, c. 186, s. 2; 1975, c. 716, s. 5; 1979, c. 667, s. 41

DRIVING DURING PERIOD OF SUSPENSION CONSTITUTES VIOLATION OF G.S. 20-28. --Under the provisions of this section and G.S. 20-28(a), when a person who does not hold a driver's license has his operating privilege revoked or suspended in the manner and under the conditions prescribed by statute, and while such operating privilege is thus suspended or revoked he drives a motor vehicle upon the highways of this State, he violates G.S. 20-28(a). State v. Newborn, 11 N.C. App. 292, 181 S.E.2d 214 (1971).

§ 20-23.2. Suspension of license for conviction of offense involving impaired driving in federal court

Upon receipt of notice of conviction in any court of the federal government of an offense involving impaired driving, the Division is authorized to revoke the driving privilege of the person convicted in the same manner as if the conviction had occurred in a court of this State.

History.
1969, c. 988; 1971, c. 619, s. 11; 1975, c. 716, s. 5; 1979, c. 903, s. 12; 1981, c. 412, s. 4; c. 747, s. 66; 1983, c. 435, s. 18

WHERE THE LAW DIRECTS SUSPENSION, REVOCATION, OR NONISSUANCE OF A DRIVER'S LICENSE, the grounds are convictions for moving violations, or other statutory violations relating to highway safety, or situations where an individual's capacity to operate a motor vehicle safely are manifestly questionable. Evans v. Roberson, 69 N.C. App. 644, 317 S.E.2d 715 (1984), rev'd on other grounds and modified, 314 N.C. 315, 333 S.E.2d 228 (1985).

§ 20-24. When court or child support enforcement agency to forward license to Division and report convictions, child support delinquencies, and prayers for judgment continued

(a) **License.** -- A court that convicts a person of an offense that requires revocation of the person's drivers license or revokes a person's drivers license pursuant to G.S. 50-13.12 shall require the person to give the court any regular or commercial drivers license issued to that person. A court that convicts a person of an offense that requires disqualification of the person but would not require revocation of a regular drivers license issued to that person shall require the person to give the court any Class A or Class B regular drivers license and any commercial drivers license issued to that person.

The clerk of court in a non-IV-D case, and the child support enforcement agency in a IV-D case, shall accept a drivers license required to be given to the court under this subsection. A clerk of court or the child support enforcement agency who receives a drivers license shall give the person whose license is received a copy of a dated receipt for the license. The receipt must be on a form approved by the Commissioner. A revocation or disqualification for which a license is received under this subsection is effective as of the date on the receipt for the license.

The clerk of court or the child support enforcement agency shall notify the Division of a license received under this subsection either by forwarding to the Division the license, a record of the conviction for which the license was received, a copy of the court order revoking the license for failure to pay child support for which the license was received, and the original dated receipt for the license or by electronically sending to the Division the information on the license, the record of conviction or court order revoking the license for failure to pay child support, and the receipt given for the license. The clerk of court or the child support enforcement agency must forward the required items unless the Commissioner has given the clerk of court or the child support enforcement agency approval to notify the Division electronically. If the clerk of court or the child support enforcement agency notifies the Division electronically, the clerk of court or the child support enforcement agency must destroy a license received after sending to the Division the required information. The clerk of court or the child support enforcement agency shall notify the Division within 30 days after entry of the conviction or court order revoking the license for failure to pay child support for which the license was received.

(b) **Convictions, Court Orders of Drivers License Revocations, and PJCs.** -- The clerk of court shall send the Division a record of any of the following:

(1) A conviction of a violation of a law regulating the operation of a vehicle.

(2) A conviction for which the convicted person is placed on probation and a condition of probation is that the person not drive a motor vehicle for a period of time, stating the period of time for which the condition applies.

(3) A conviction of a felony in the commission of which a motor vehicle is used, when the judgment includes a finding that a motor vehicle was used in the commission of the felony.

(4) A conviction that requires revocation of the drivers license of the person convicted and is not otherwise reported under subdivision (1).

(4a) A court order revoking drivers license pursuant to G.S. 50-13.12.

(5) An order entering prayer for judgment continued in a case involving an alleged violation of a law regulating the operation of a vehicle.

The child support enforcement agency shall send the Division a record of any court order revoking drivers license pursuant to G.S. 110-142.2(a)(1).

With the approval of the Commissioner, the clerk of court or the child support enforcement agency may forward a record of conviction, court order revoking drivers license, or prayer for judgment continued to the Division by electronic data processing means.

(b1) In any case in which the Division, for any reason, does not receive a record of a conviction or a prayer for judgment continued until more than one year after the date it is entered, the Division may, in its discretion, substitute a period of probation for all or any part of a revocation or disqualification required because of the conviction or prayer for judgment continued.

(c) Repealed by Session Laws 1991, c. 726, s. 10.

(d) **Scope.** -- This Article governs drivers license revocation and disqualification. A drivers license may not be revoked and a person may not be disqualified except in accordance with this Article.

(e) **Special Information.** -- A judgment for a conviction for an offense for which special information is required under this subsection shall, when appropriate, include a finding of the special information. The convictions for which special information is required and the specific information required is as follows:

(1) **Homicide.** -- If a conviction of homicide involves impaired driving, the judgment must indicate that fact.

(2) G.S. 20-138.1, Driving While Impaired. -- If a conviction under G.S. 20-138.1 involves a commercial motor vehicle, the judgment must indicate that fact. If a conviction under G.S. 20-138.1 involves a commercial motor vehicle that was transporting a hazardous substance required to

be placarded, the judgment must indicate that fact.

(3) G.S. 20-138.2, Driving Commercial Motor Vehicle While Impaired. -- If the commercial motor vehicle involved in an offense under G.S. 20-138.2 was transporting a hazardous material required to be placarded, a judgment for that offense must indicate that fact.

(4) G.S. 20-166, Hit and Run. -- If a conviction under G.S. 20-166 involves a commercial motor vehicle, the judgment must indicate that fact. If a conviction under G.S. 20-166 involves a commercial motor vehicle that was transporting a hazardous substance required to be placarded, the judgment must indicate that fact.

(5) **Felony Using Commercial Motor Vehicle.** -- If a conviction of a felony in which a commercial motor vehicle was used involves the manufacture, distribution, or dispensing of a controlled substance, or possession with intent to manufacture, distribute, or dispense a controlled substance, the judgment must indicate that fact. If a commercial motor vehicle used in a felony was transporting a hazardous substance required to be placarded, the judgment for that felony must indicate that fact.

History.

1935, c. 52, s. 18; 1949, c. 373, ss. 3, 4; 1955, c. 1187, s. 14; 1959, c. 47; 1965, c. 38; 1973, c. 19; 1975, cc. 46, 445; c. 716, s. 5; c. 871, s. 1; 1979, c. 667, s. 41; 1981, c. 416; c. 839; 1983, c. 294, s. 5; c. 435, s. 19; 1985, c. 764, s. 18; 1985 (Reg. Sess., 1986), c. 852, s. 17; 1987, c. 581, s. 1; c. 658, s. 2; 1989, c. 771, s. 10;1991, c. 726, s. 10;1993, c. 533, s. 7;1995, c. 538, s. 2(c)

LOCAL MODIFICATION. --Hertford as to subsection (b): 1953, c. 1059; Washington, as to subsection (b): 1953, c. 765.

JURISDICTION TO REVOKE LICENSE. --A municipal court is without authority to revoke a driver's license, the power to suspend or revoke drivers' licenses being vested exclusively in the Department of Revenue, subject to the right of review by the superior court, as provided in G.S. 20-25. State v. McDaniels, 219 N.C. 763, 14 S.E.2d 793 (1941).

MEANING OF FORFEITURE OF BAIL OR COLLATERAL. --"Bail" as here used means security for a defendant's appearance in court to answer a criminal charge there pending. Ordinarily it is evidenced by a bond or recognizance which becomes a record of the court. The forfeiture thereof is a judicial act. In re Wright, 228 N.C. 584, 46 S.E.2d 696 (1948).

The mere deposit of security with an arresting officer or magistrate pending issuance and service of warrant, which deposit is retained without the semblance of judicial or legal forfeiture, is not a forfeiture of "bail" within the meaning of subsection (c) of this section. In re Wright, 228 N.C. 584, 46 S.E.2d 696

(1948); In re Donnelly, 260 N.C. 375, 132 S.E.2d 904 (1963).

Where no warrant is served, no legal action is pending in court; and when no legal action is pending, there can be no valid judgment of forfeiture of bail. In re Donnelly, 260 N.C. 375, 132 S.E.2d 904 (1963).

BOND FORFEITURE HELD TO BE EQUIVALENT TO A CONVICTION of driving while under the influence of an intoxicant. Rhyne v. Garrett, 18 N.C. App. 565, 197 S.E.2d 235 (1973).

PLEA OF NOLO CONTENDERE. --Where the petitioner entered a plea of nolo contendere to the charge of a second offense of operating an automobile upon the public highways of the State while under the influence of intoxicating liquor (now impaired driving), which plea was accepted by the court, for the purposes of that case in that court, such plea was equivalent to a plea of guilty, or conviction by a jury, and subsection (a) of this section required that court to enter a notation of such conviction upon the license of petitioner to operate an automobile in North Carolina, and to compel the surrender to it of such license then held by petitioner, and thereupon to forward the license, together with a record of the conviction, to the Department (now Division) of Motor Vehicles. Fox v. Scheidt, 241 N.C. 31, 84 S.E.2d 259 (1954).

"FINAL CONVICTION." --Where defendant pleaded guilty to driving without a license, and judge's order granted a prayer for judgment continued on condition that plaintiff not violate any motor vehicle laws and that plaintiff make a $75.00 contribution to the school board, the condition "that he make a $75.00 contribution to the school board" constituted an invalid condition as it is not restitution and it is not a fine. Thus it is not punishment that would render the judgment a final conviction and require or allow Division of Motor Vehicle to revoke plaintiff's license. Florence v. Hiatt, 101 N.C. App. 539, 400 S.E.2d 118 (1991).

WHEN CONVICTION FINAL. --The conviction alone, without the imposition of a judgment from which an appeal might be taken, is not a final conviction within the terms of subsection (c). Barbour v. Scheidt, 246 N.C. 169, 97 S.E.2d 855 (1957).

A conviction in a criminal case is not final within the meaning of subsection (c) of this section where no judgment is imposed on the verdict, but merely an order is entered continuing prayer for judgment upon payment of costs. Barbour v. Scheidt, 246 N.C. 169, 97 S.E.2d 855 (1957).

TRIAL COURT IS REQUIRED TO FORWARD RECORD OF CONVICTION. --This section requires that the trial courts shall forward to the Department (now Division) a record of the conviction of any person. Tilley v. Garrett, 8 N.C. App. 556, 174 S.E.2d 617 (1970).

BUT COURT IS NOT REQUIRED TO FORWARD WARRANT AND JUDGMENT. --This section does not require that the warrant and judgment, or certified copies thereof, shall be forwarded by the trial court. Tilley v. Garrett, 8 N.C. App. 556, 174 S.E.2d 617 (1970).

Chapter 20

FORWARDING OF LICENSE AS NOTICE OF REVOCATION. --The surrendering of his license and forwarding of it to the Department (now Division) by the court gives the licensee sufficient notice that his operator's license has been revoked. State v. Teasley, 9 N.C. App. 477, 277 N.C. 459, 176 S.E.2d 838, 176 S.E.2d 838, appeal dismissed, 277 N.C. 459, 177 S.E.2d 900 (1970).

THIS SECTION DESIGNATES CLERKS OF COURT AND ASSISTANT AND DEPUTY CLERKS OF COURT AS AGENTS OF THE DEPARTMENT (NOW DIVISION) OF MOTOR VEHICLES for receipt of driver's licenses in cases where revocation is required. Simpson v. Garrett, 15 N.C. App. 449, 190 S.E.2d 251 (1972).

INJUNCTION NOT AVAILABLE TO PLAINTIFF WHO COULD HAVE PREVENTED DELAY IN START OF REVOCATION PERIOD. --Where the elapse of approximately 15 months between plaintiff's last conviction for reckless driving and the order of revocation was not caused by defendant Commissioner of Motor Vehicles or his Department (now Division), but the delay apparently resulted from the failure of the clerk of the court where plaintiff was last convicted to act promptly in forwarding a record of the conviction to the Department (now Division) of Motor Vehicles, and plaintiff could have prevented any delay in the start of the revocation period by surrendering his license to the clerk and obtaining a receipt therefor at the time of his second conviction, plaintiff was not entitled to injunctive relief. Simpson v. Garrett, 15 N.C. App. 449, 190 S.E.2d 251 (1972).

FAILURE TO APPEAR AT TRIAL FOR DRIVING UNDER THE INFLUENCE IN ANOTHER STATE. --Motorist who received citation for driving under the influence in South Carolina and then forfeited bond by not appearing in court had his driver's license properly revoked even though no warrant was issued. Sykes v. Hiatt, 98 N.C. App. 688, 391 S.E.2d 834 (1990).

CONDITION IN ORDER HELD UNENFORCEABLE. --Where defendant pleaded guilty to driving without license, the condition in judge's order that plaintiff make a contribution to the school board was unenforceable surplusage. It was not restitution because the school board was not an aggrieved party. It was not a fine because it was directed to an entity other than the county for use by the public schools. Florence v. Hiatt, 101 N.C. App. 539, 400 S.E.2d 118 (1991).

APPLIED in State v. Ball, 255 N.C. 351, 121 S.E.2d 604 (1961); In re Sparks, 25 N.C. App. 65, 212 S.E.2d 220 (1975); State v. Finger, 72 N.C. App. 569, 324 S.E.2d 894 (1985).

CITED in Winesett v. Scheidt, 239 N.C. 190, 79 S.E.2d 501 (1954); Harrell v. Scheidt, 243 N.C. 735, 92 S.E.2d 182 (1956); Walters v. Cooper, 226 N.C. App. 166, 739 S.E.2d 185 (2013), aff'd 367 N.C. 117, 748 S.E.2d 144, 2013 N.C. LEXIS 1021 (2013).

CROSS REFERENCES. --
For present provisions regarding definitions for "conviction", which were formerly found in subsection (c) of this section, see G.S. 20-4.01(4a).

OPINIONS OF THE ATTORNEY GENERAL
SURRENDER OF OUT-OF-STATE LICENSE NOT REQUIRED. --Upon conviction of a nonresident for a traffic violation for which revocation or suspension of driving privilege is mandatory, the court should not require such nonresident to surrender a driver's license issued him by his state. See opinion of Attorney General to Honorable John S. Gardner, District Court Judge, Sixteenth Judicial District, 40 N.C.A.G. 420 (1969).

§ 20-24.1. Revocation for failure to appear or pay fine, penalty or costs for motor vehicle offenses

(a) The Division must revoke the driver's license of a person upon receipt of notice from a court that the person was charged with a motor vehicle offense and he:

(1) failed to appear, after being notified to do so, when the case was called for a trial or hearing; or

(2) failed to pay a fine, penalty, or court costs ordered by the court.

Revocation orders entered under the authority of this section are effective on the sixtieth day after the order is mailed or personally delivered to the person.

(b) A license revoked under this section remains revoked until the person whose license has been revoked:

(1) disposes of the charge in the trial division in which he failed to appear when the case was last called for trial or hearing; or

(2) demonstrates to the court that he is not the person charged with the offense; or

(3) pays the penalty, fine, or costs ordered by the court; or

(4) demonstrates to the court that his failure to pay the penalty, fine, or costs was not willful and that he is making a good faith effort to pay or that the penalty, fine, or costs should be remitted.

Upon receipt of notice from the court that the person has satisfied the conditions of this subsection applicable to his case, the Division must restore the person's license as provided in subsection (c). In addition, if the person whose license is revoked is not a resident of this State, the Division may notify the driver licensing agency in the person's state of residence that the person's license to drive in this State has been revoked.

(b1) A defendant must be afforded an opportunity for a trial or a hearing within a reasonable time of the defendant's appearance. Upon motion of a defendant, the court must order that a hearing or a trial be heard within a reasonable time.

(c) If the person satisfies the conditions of subsection (b) that are applicable to his case before the effective date of the revocation order, the revocation order and any entries on his driving record relating to it shall be deleted and the person does not have to pay the restoration fee set by G.S. 20-7(i1). For all other revocation orders issued pursuant to this section, G.S. 50-13.12 or G.S. 110-142.2, the person must pay the restoration fee and satisfy any other applicable requirements of this Article before the person may be relicensed.

(d) To facilitate the prompt return of licenses and to prevent unjustified charges of driving while license revoked, the clerk of court, upon request, must give the person a copy of the notice it sends to the Division to indicate that the person has complied with the conditions of subsection (b) applicable to his case. If the person complies with the condition before the effective date of the revocation, the notice must indicate that the person is eligible to drive if he is otherwise validly licensed.

(e) As used in this section and in G.S. 20-24.2, the word offense includes crimes and infractions created by this Chapter.

(f) If a license is revoked under subdivision (2) of subsection (a) of this section, and for no other reason, the person subject to the order may apply to the court for a limited driving privilege valid for up to one year or until any fine, penalty, or court costs ordered by the court are paid. The court may grant the limited driving privilege in the same manner and under the terms and conditions prescribed in G.S. 20-16.1. A person is eligible to apply for a limited driving privilege under this subsection only if the person has not had a limited driving privilege granted under this subsection within the three years prior to application.

History.
1985, c. 764, s. 19; 1985 (Reg. Sess., 1986), c. 852, ss. 4-6, 9, 17; 1987, c. 581, s. 4; 1991, c. 682, s. 4;1993, c. 313, s. 1;1995, c. 538, s. 2(d);2020-77, s. 6.5(a)
EDITOR'S NOTE. --
Session Laws 2020-77, s. 6.5(b), made subsection (f) of this section, as added by Session Laws 2020-77, s. 6.5(a), effective December 1, 2020, and applicable to applications for limited driving privileges filed on or after that date.
EFFECT OF AMENDMENTS. --
Session Laws 2020-77, s. 6.5(a), added subsection (f). For effective date and applicability, see editor's note.
CITED in White v. Williams, 111 N.C. App. 879, 433 S.E.2d 808 (1993).

§ 20-24.2. Court to report failure to appear or pay fine, penalty or costs

(a) The court must report to the Division the name of any person charged with a motor vehicle offense under this Chapter who:

(1) Fails to appear to answer the charge as scheduled, unless within 20 days after the scheduled appearance, he either appears in court to answer the charge or disposes of the charge pursuant to G.S. 7A-146; or

(2) Fails to pay a fine, penalty, or costs within 40 days of the date specified in the court's judgment.

(b) The reporting requirement of this section and the revocation mandated by G.S. 20-24.1 do not apply to offenses in which an order of forfeiture of a cash bond is entered and reported to the Division pursuant to G.S. 20-24. If an order is sent to the Division by the clerk through clerical mistake or other inadvertence, the clerk's office that sent the report of noncompliance must withdraw the report and send notice to the Division which shall correct its records accordingly.

History.
1985, c. 764, s. 3; 1985 (Reg. Sess., 1986), c. 852, ss. 3, 17; 1987, c. 581, s. 3; 1991, c. 682, s. 5;2015-247, s. 1(b)
EDITOR'S NOTE. --
This section was formerly G.S. 15A-1117, as enacted by Session Laws 1985, c. 764, s. 3. It was rewritten and recodified as this section by Session Laws 1985 (Reg. Sess., 1986), c. 852, s. 3, effective September 1, 1986.
Session Laws 2015-247, which, in s. 1(b), amended subdivision (a)(2) by substituting "40 days" for "20 days," in s. 1(c) provides: "This section becomes effective December 1, 2015, except that a failure to pay after 20 days occurring before the effective date of this act is not abated or affected by this act and the statutes that would be applicable but for this act remain applicable to that failure to pay."
EFFECT OF AMENDMENTS. --
Session Laws 2015-247, s. 1(b), effective December 1, 2015, substituted "40 days" for "20 days" in subdivision (a)(2). For applicability, see editor's note.
CITED in White v. Williams, 111 N.C. App. 879, 433 S.E.2d 808 (1993).

§ 20-25. Right of appeal to court

Any person denied a license or whose license has been canceled, suspended or revoked by the Division, except where such cancellation is mandatory under the provisions of this Article, shall have a right to file a petition within 30 days thereafter for a hearing in the matter in the superior court of the county wherein such person shall reside, or to the resident judge of the district or judge holding the court of that district, or special or emergency judge holding a court in such district in which the violation was committed, and such court or judge is hereby vested with jurisdiction and it shall be its or his duty to set the matter for hearing upon 30 days' written notice to the Division, and thereupon to take testimony and examine into the facts of the case, and to determine whether the petitioner is entitled to a license or is subject to

Chapter 20

suspension, cancellation or revocation of license under the provisions of this Article. Provided, a judge of the district court shall have limited jurisdiction under this section to sign and enter a temporary restraining order only.

History.
1935, c. 52, s. 19; 1975, c. 716, s. 5; 1987, c. 659, s. 1

POWER TO SUSPEND OR REVOKE LICENSES VESTED EXCLUSIVELY IN DEPARTMENT (NOW DIVISION) OF MOTOR VEHICLES. --By Session Laws 1941, c. 36 (G.S. 20-1, 20-2, 20-3 and 20-4), the power to suspend or revoke drivers' licenses after July 1, 1941, vested exclusively in the newly created Department (now Division) of Motor Vehicles, subject to the same right of review by the superior court as existed prior to that date. State v. Cooper, 224 N.C. 100, 29 S.E.2d 18 (1944).

SECTION CONSTRUED WITH G.S. 20-23. --This section and G.S. 20-23 must be construed in pari materia. In re Wright, 228 N.C. 584, 46 S.E.2d 696 (1948).

A LICENSE TO OPERATE A MOTOR VEHICLE IS A PRIVILEGE IN THE NATURE OF A RIGHT of which the licensee may not be deprived save in the manner and upon the conditions prescribed by statute. These, under express provisions of this section, include full de novo review by a superior court judge, at the election of the licensee, in all cases except where the suspension or revocation is mandatory. Underwood v. Howland, 274 N.C. 473, 164 S.E.2d 2 (1968).

PROVISIONS SATISFY REQUIREMENTS OF DUE PROCESS. --The provisions of G.S. 20-48, together with the provisions of G.S. 20-16(d), relating to the right of review, and the provisions of this section, relating to the right of appeal, satisfy the requirements of procedural due process. State v. Teasley, 9 N.C. App. 477, 176 S.E.2d 838, appeal dismissed, 277 N.C. 459, 177 S.E.2d 900 (1970); State v. Atwood, 27 N.C. App. 445, 219 S.E.2d 521 (1975), rev'd on other grounds, 290 N.C. 266, 225 S.E.2d 543 (1976).

THIS SECTION CREATES NO RIGHT TO APPEAL A SUSPENSION UNDER G.S. 20/Y-4.20(B). The General Assembly simply has not yet provided for appeals from suspension under G.S. 20-4.20(b). Palmer v. Wilkins, 73 N.C. App. 171, 325 S.E.2d 697 (1985).

A PETITIONER SEEKING JUDICIAL REVIEW OF A DECISION OF THE NORTH CAROLINA DRIVER LICENSE MEDICAL REVIEW BOARD must file such petition in the superior court of Wake County pursuant to former G.S. 150A-45 and may not obtain a hearing under the present section in the superior court of the county in which he resides. Cox v. Miller, 26 N.C. App. 749, 217 S.E.2d 198 (1975).

CERTIORARI TO REVIEW MANDATORY SUSPENSION. --Petitioner whose driving privilege was mandatorily suspended under G.S. 20-17(2) and G.S. 20-19(e) did not have the right to appeal under this section or under the Administrative Procedure Act, Chapter 150B. However, the superior court could review the actions of the Commissioner by issuing a writ of certiorari. Davis v. Hiatt, 326 N.C. 462, 390 S.E.2d 338 (1990).

Where petitioner, seeking conditional restoration of his driving privileges, pled sufficient facts to show he did not have right to appeal from final decision of DMV, he could then have petitioned for writ of certiorari to have case reviewed by superior court. Thus, superior court had jurisdiction to review case. Penuel v. Hiatt, 100 N.C. App. 268, 396 S.E.2d 85 (1990).

DISCRETIONARY SUSPENSIONS AND REVOCATIONS OF DRIVING LICENSES BY THE DEPARTMENT (NOW DIVISION) OF MOTOR VEHICLES ARE REVIEWABLE under this section. State v. Cooper, 224 N.C. 100, 29 S.E.2d 18 (1944); In re Wright, 228 N.C. 584, 46 S.E.2d 696 (1948).

Trial court correctly reviewed the North Carolina Division of Motor Vehicles' cancellation of a driver's conditionally restored driving privileges under a petition for writ of certiorari rather than de novo review because although there was no right to appeal a cancellation or revocation under G.S. 20-25, the driver could seek certiorari pursuant to G.S. 20-19(e). Cole v. Faulkner, 155 N.C. App. 592, 573 S.E.2d 614 (2002).

Discretionary revocations and suspensions may be reviewed by the court under this section, while mandatory revocations and suspensions may not. Underwood v. Howland, 274 N.C. 473, 164 S.E.2d 2 (1968); Taylor v. Garrett, 7 N.C. App. 473, 173 S.E.2d 31 (1970).

Discretionary revocation of a driver's license is reviewable under the provisions of this section but mandatory revocations are not. In re Austin, 5 N.C. App. 575, 169 S.E.2d 20 (1969).

BY TRIAL DE NOVO. --All suspensions, cancellations and revocations of driving licenses made in the discretion of the Department (now Division) of Motor Vehicles, whether under G.S. 20-16, 20-23 or any other provision of this Chapter, are reviewable by trial de novo. In re Wright, 228 N.C. 584, 46 S.E.2d 696 (1948).

The hearing in the superior court is de novo, and the court is not bound by the findings of fact or the conclusions of law made by the Department (now Division). In re Wright, 228 N.C. 301, 45 S.E.2d 370 (1947); Fox v. Scheidt, 241 N.C. 31, 84 S.E.2d 259 (1954).

Upon the filing of a petition for review, it is the duty of the judge, after notice to the Department (now Division), "to take testimony and examine into the facts of the case, and to determine whether the petitioner is entitled to a license or is subject to suspension, cancellation, or revocation of license under the provisions of this Article." This is more than a review as upon a writ of certiorari. It is a rehearing de novo, and the judge is not bound by the findings of fact or the conclusions of law made by the Department (now Division). Else why "take testimony," "examine into the facts," and "determine" the question at issue? Parks v. Howland, 4 N.C. App. 197, 166 S.E.2d 701 (1969).

Any person whose driver's license has been suspended under G.S. 20-16.2(d) has the right to a full de novo review by a superior court judge. This means the court must hear the matter on its merits from beginning to end as if no trial or hearing had been held by the Department (now Division) and without any presumption in favor of its decision. Joyner v. Garrett, 279 N.C. 226, 182 S.E.2d 553 (1971).

G.

S. 20-25 CREATES NO RIGHT TO APPEAL A REVOCATION UNDER G.S. 20-138.5, since G.S. 20-138.5 appears in Article 3 rather than Article 2. Following a conviction for habitual impaired driving, under that section, permanent revocation is mandatory and the trial court lacks the authority to provide relief. Cooke v. Faulkner, 137 N.C. App. 755, 529 S.E.2d 512 (2000).

BUT MANDATORY REVOCATIONS UNDER G.S. 20-17 ARE NOT REVIEWABLE. And no right accrues to a licensee who petitions for a review of the order of the Department (now Division) when it acts under the terms of G.S. 20-17, for then its action is mandatory. In re Wright, 228 N.C. 584, 46 S.E.2d 696 (1948); Winesett v. Scheidt, 239 N.C. 190, 79 S.E.2d 501 (1954); Fox v. Scheidt, 241 N.C. 31, 84 S.E.2d 259 (1954); Mintz v. Scheidt, 241 N.C. 268, 84 S.E.2d 882 (1954).

There is no right of judicial review when the revocation is mandatory pursuant to the provisions of G.S. 20-17. In re Austin, 5 N.C. App. 575, 169 S.E.2d 20 (1969); Rhyne v. Garrett, 18 N.C. App. 565, 197 S.E.2d 235 (1973).

There is no right to appeal to a court where the cancellation of the license is mandatory, and the provisions of G.S. 20-17.8 are mandatory; thus, the district court could not review, under G.S. 20-25, a decision by the Division of Motor Vehicles that decided not to reinstate, without a requisite ignition interlock device, the license of a driver whose license had been suspended for violating G.S. 20-17.8. State v. Benbow, 169 N.C. App. 613, 610 S.E.2d 297 (2005).

MANDATORY REVOCATION WAS NOT REVIEWABLE UNDER G.S. 150B-43. --Where revocation issued by Division of Motor Vehicles (DMV) was mandatory, superior court did not have jurisdiction to review order of revocation pursuant to G.S. 150B-43 as licenses issued under Chapter 20 are expressly excluded under G.S. 150B-2. Davis v. Hiatt, 326 N.C. 462, 390 S.E.2d 338 (1990).

THE JURISDICTION VESTED BY THIS SECTION IS NOT A DELEGATION OF LEGISLATIVE AND ADMINISTRATIVE AUTHORITY. The review is judicial and is governed by the standards and guides which are applicable to other judicial proceedings. In re Wright, 228 N.C. 584, 46 S.E.2d 696 (1948).

SUCH JURISDICTION IS NOT THE LIMITED, INHERENT POWER OF COURTS TO REVIEW THE DISCRETIONARY ACTS OF AN ADMINISTRATIVE OFFICER. The power is conferred by statute, and the statute must be looked to in order to ascertain the nature and extent of the review contemplated by the legislature. In re Wright, 228 N.C. 301, 45 S.E.2d 370 (1947).

THE SECTION IMPOSES ADDITIONAL JURISDICTION. --The court has inherent authority to review the discretionary action of an administrative agency whenever such action affects personal or property rights, upon a prima facie showing, by petition for a writ of certiorari, that such agency has acted arbitrarily, capriciously, or in disregard of law. This section dispenses with the necessity of an application

for writ of certiorari, provides for direct approach to the courts and enlarges the scope of the hearing. That the legislature had full authority to impose this additional jurisdiction upon the courts is beyond question. In re Wright, 228 N.C. 584, 46 S.E.2d 696 (1948).

BUT NO DISCRETIONARY POWER IS CONFERRED UPON THE COURT in reviewing the suspension or revocation of driving licenses, and the court may determine only if, upon the facts, petitioner's license is subject to suspension or revocation under the provisions of the statute. In re Wright, 228 N.C. 584, 46 S.E.2d 696 (1948).

On appeal and hearing de novo in the superior court, that court is not vested with discretionary authority. It makes judicial review of the facts, and if it finds that the license of petitioner is in fact and in law subject to suspension or revocation, the order of the Department (now Division) must be affirmed; otherwise not. In re Donnelly, 260 N.C. 375, 132 S.E.2d 904 (1963); Smith v. Walsh, 34 N.C. App. 287, 238 S.E.2d 157 (1977).

No discretionary power is conferred upon the court in matters pertaining to the revocation of licenses. If, under the facts found by the judge, the statute requires the suspension or revocation of petitioner's license, the order of the Department (now Division) entered in conformity with the facts found must be affirmed. Joyner v. Garrett, 279 N.C. 226, 182 S.E.2d 553 (1971).

FAILURE OF THE SECTION TO PROVIDE STANDARDS FOR THE GUIDANCE OF THE COURTS DOES NOT INVALIDATE IT or negate the jurisdiction. In re Wright, 228 N.C. 584, 46 S.E.2d 696 (1948).

REMEDY FOR IMPROPER DEPRIVATION OF LICENSE. --If an individual has been improperly deprived of his license by the Department (now Division) of Motor Vehicles due to a mistake of law or fact, his remedy is to apply for a hearing as provided by G.S. 20-16(d), or by application to the superior court as permitted by this section. At a hearing held pursuant to either of these sections, he would be permitted to show that the suspension was erroneous. He could not ignore the quasi-judicial determination made by the Department (now Division). Beaver v. Scheidt, 251 N.C. 671, 111 S.E.2d 881 (1960).

HEARING BY DIVISION IS PREREQUISITE TO COURT REVIEW. --Section 20-16(d) provides for a rehearing by the Department (now Division) of Motor Vehicles upon application of a licensee whose license has been suspended, and this procedure should be followed and should be made to appear in the petition before review by the superior court. In re Wright, 228 N.C. 301, 45 S.E.2d 370 (1947).

ERRORS IN ADMINISTRATIVE PROCEEDINGS ARE RENDERED HARMLESS BY HEARING DE NOVO. --If any errors were committed in the administrative proceedings, they are rendered harmless by the hearing de novo on appeal. Joyner v. Garrett, 279 N.C. 226, 182 S.E.2d 553 (1971).

HEARING MUST BE SUFFICIENTLY FORMAL TO PERMIT APPELLATE REVIEW. --Although a hearing conducted pursuant to this section may be as informal as the particular judge permits, nevertheless there should be sufficient formality in compiling a record of the proceeding so as to permit an appellate review. Tilley v. Garrett, 8 N.C. App. 556, 174 S.E.2d 617 (1970).

BURDEN OF PROOF. --Since the hearing on appeal in the superior court is de novo, if the Department (now Division) has the burden of proof at the first hearing held under G.S. 20-16(d), obviously it also has the burden at the de novo hearing in the superior court. Joyner v. Garrett, 279 N.C. 226, 182 S.E.2d 553 (1971).

PLAINTIFF MAY NOT COMPLAIN THAT DIVISION HAS NO VALID WARRANT AND VALID JUDGMENT IN RECORDS. --If the plaintiff has been improperly deprived of his license by the Department (now Division) due to a mistake of law or fact, he is entitled to show that the suspension was erroneous; however, he has no ground to complain that the Department (now Division) does not have as a part of its records a "valid warrant" and a "valid judgment." Plaintiff has available to him the records of the court in which he is alleged to have been convicted by which he may show whether the conviction was valid. Tilley v. Garrett, 8 N.C. App. 556, 174 S.E.2d 617 (1970).

CANCELLATION OF SUSPENSION. --Petitioner was arrested in South Carolina, charged with operating a motor vehicle while under the influence of intoxicants. He gave bond for appearance, but no warrant was served on him and no trial had, and his bond was forfeited. His license was suspended by the Department (now Division) of Motor Vehicles upon information of the highway department of South Carolina that he had been found guilty of driving while intoxicated. Upon review the superior court found, in addition, that the suspension was based upon misinformation and further that petitioner in fact was not guilty. It was held that the findings supported the court's order directing the respondent to cancel the suspension and to restore license to petitioner. In re Wright, 228 N.C. 301, 45 S.E.2d 370 (1947).

DENIAL OF LICENSE ON PETITION FOR REINSTATEMENT. --If a petitioner is unlawfully and illegally denied a license upon a hearing on a petition for reinstatement of his license, the judge of the superior court, upon proper allegations in a petition and proper notice to the respondent as provided in this section, is authorized to take testimony, examine the facts of the case, and determine whether the petitioner was illegally and unlawfully denied a license under the provisions of the Uniform Driver's License Act. In re Austin, 5 N.C. App. 575, 169 S.E.2d 20 (1969).

REVIEW OF REVOCATION BASED ON CONVICTION OF OFFENSE IN ANOTHER STATE. --The fact that the Department (now Division) of Motor Vehicles, in the exercise of its discretion, accepted the certification of a conviction in another state at its face value did not foreclose the petitioner's right to review as provided in this section. In other words, the General Assembly has never made it mandatory on the Department (now Division) to suspend or revoke the license of a resident of this State based on the conviction of such person in another state of any offense

therein which, if committed in this State, would make the revocation mandatory. Carmichael v. Scheidt, 249 N.C. 472, 106 S.E.2d 685 (1959).

On appeal from a suspension of a resident's license under G.S. 20-23, it is the conviction in another state that is under review in the superior court. In re Donnelly, 260 N.C. 375, 132 S.E.2d 904 (1963).

The superior court of North Carolina may not determine the guilt of a license holder, with respect to offenses alleged to have been committed in another state, as the sole predicate for suspension or revocation of his license. In re Donnelly, 260 N.C. 375, 132 S.E.2d 904 (1963).

APPLIED in Noyes v. Peters, 40 N.C. App. 763, 253 S.E.2d 584 (1979).

CITED in In re Harris, 37 N.C. App. 590, 246 S.E.2d 532 (1978); Seders v. Powell, 298 N.C. 453, 259 S.E.2d 544 (1979); Gaither v. Peters, 63 N.C. App. 559, 305 S.E.2d 763 (1983); Mathis v. North Carolina DMV, 71 N.C. App. 413, 322 S.E.2d 436 (1984); Smith v. Wilkins, 75 N.C. App. 483, 331 S.E.2d 159 (1985); In re Vallender, 81 N.C. App. 291, 344 S.E.2d 62 (1986); In re Rogers, 94 N.C. App. 505, 380 S.E.2d 599 (1989); Richardson v. Hiatt, 95 N.C. App. 196, 381 S.E.2d 866 (1989); Ferguson v. Killens, 129 N.C. App. 131, 497 S.E.2d 722 (1998); State v. Leyshon, 211 N.C. App. 511, 710 S.E.2d 282 (2011).

§ 20-26. Records; copies furnished; charge

(a) The Division shall keep a record of all applications for a drivers license, all tests given an applicant for a drivers license, all applications for a drivers license that are denied, all drivers licenses issued, renewed, cancelled, or revoked, all disqualifications, all convictions affecting a drivers license, and all prayers for judgment continued that may lead to a license revocation. When the Division cancels or revokes a commercial drivers license or disqualifies a person, the Division shall update its records to reflect that action within 10 days after the cancellation, revocation, or disqualification becomes effective. When a person who is not a resident of this State is convicted of an offense or commits an act requiring revocation of the person's commercial drivers license or disqualification of the person, the Division shall notify the licensing authority of the person's state of residence.

The Division shall keep records of convictions occurring outside North Carolina for the offenses of exceeding a stated speed limit of 55 miles per hour or more by more than 15 miles per hour, driving while license suspended or revoked, careless and reckless driving, engaging in prearranged speed competition, engaging willfully in speed competition, hit-and-run driving resulting in damage to property, unlawfully passing a stopped school bus, illegal transportation of alcoholic beverages, and the offenses included in G.S. 20-17. The Division shall also keep records of convictions occurring outside

North Carolina for any serious traffic violation that involves a commercial motor vehicle and is not otherwise required to be kept under this subsection.

(b) The Division shall furnish certified copies of license records required to be kept by subsection (a) of this section to State, county, municipal and court officials of this State for official use only, without charge. A certified copy of a driver's records kept pursuant to subsection (a) may be sent by the Police Information Network. In addition to the uses authorized by G.S. 8-35.1, a copy certified under the authority of this section is admissible as prima facie evidence of the status of the person's license. The Attorney General and the Commissioner of Motor Vehicles are authorized to promulgate such rules and regulations as may be necessary to implement the provision of this subsection.

(b1) The registered or declared weight set forth on the vehicle registration card or a certified copy of the Division record sent by the Department of Public Safety or otherwise is admissible in any judicial or administrative proceeding and shall be prima facie evidence of the registered or declared weight.

(c) The Division shall furnish copies of license records required to be kept by subsection (a) of this section in accordance with G.S. 20-43.1 to other persons for uses other than official upon prepayment of the following fees:

    (1) Limited extract copy of license record, for period up to three years .... $ 10.00

    (2) Complete extract copy of license record 10.00

    (3) Certified true copy of complete license record .... 14.00.

    All fees received by the Division under this subsection shall be credited to the Highway Fund.

(d) The charge for records provided pursuant to this section shall not be subject to the provisions of Chapter 132 of the General Statutes.

(e) In the event of a mistake on the part of any person in ordering license records under subsection (c) of this section, the Commissioner may refund or credit to that person up to sixty-five percent (65%) of the amount paid for the license records.

(f) On and after July 1, 1988, the Division shall expeditiously furnish to insurance agents, insurance companies, and to insurance support organizations as defined in G.S. 58-39-15(12), for the purpose of rating nonfleet private passenger motor vehicle insurance policies, through electronic data processing means or otherwise, copies of or information pertaining to license records that are required to be kept pursuant to subsection (a) of this section.

History.

1935, c. 52, s. 20; 1961, c. 307; 1969, c. 783, s. 3; 1971, c. 486, s. 1; 1975, c. 716, s. 5; 1979, c. 667, s. 23; c. 903, ss. 9, 10; 1981, c. 145, s. 1; c. 412, s. 4; c. 690, s. 13; c. 747, s. 66; 1983, c. 435, s. 20; c. 761, s. 149; 1987, c. 869, s. 16; 1987 (Reg. Sess., 1988), c. 1112, ss. 14, 17; 1989, c. 771, ss. 9, 17, 18; 1991, c. 689, s. 330;c. 726, s. 11;1997-443, s. 32.25(b);2005-276, s. 44.1(e);2014-100, s. 17.1(q);2015-241, s. 29.30(e)

EDITOR'S NOTE. --

Session Laws 2015-241, s. 29.30(u), made the amendment to subsection (c) of this section by Session Laws 2015-241, s. 29.30(e), applicable to issuances, renewals, restorations, and requests on or after January 1, 2016.

Session Laws 2015-241, s. 1.1, provides: "This act shall be known as 'The Current Operations and Capital Improvements Appropriations Act of 2015.'"

Session Laws 2015-241, s. 33.6, is a severability clause.

EFFECT OF AMENDMENTS. --

Session Laws 2014-100, s. 17.1(q), effective July 1, 2014, substituted "Department of Public Safety" for "Division of Criminal Information" in subsection (b1).

Session Laws 2015-241, s. 29.30(e), effective January 1, 2016, substituted "$10.00" for "$8.00" in subdivision (c)(1), substituted "$10.00" for "$8.00" in subdivision (c)(2); and substituted "$14.00" for "$11.00" in subdivision (c)(3). For applicability, see editor's note.

DUTY TO MAINTAIN. --To convict defendant of driving while his license was revoked, the State had to prove he had knowledge of the revocation, and the State moved to admit defendant's driving record; while hearsay, the portions of the documents certifying their accuracy and attesting that the suspension orders were sent to defendant constituted substantive evidence of his commission of the offense, and as the driving records were created in compliance with the motor vehicle department's obligations to maintain such records and provide notice to motorists, the records were not testimonial. State v. Clark, 242 N.C. App. 141, 775 S.E.2d 28 (2015).

FAILURE TO APPEAR AT TRIAL FOR DRIVING UNDER THE INFLUENCE IN ANOTHER STATE. --Motorist who received citation for driving under the influence in South Carolina and then forfeited bond by not appearing in court had his driver's license properly revoked even though no warrant was issued. Sykes v. Hiatt, 98 N.C. App. 688, 391 S.E.2d 834 (1990).

OPINIONS OF THE ATTORNEY GENERAL

ACCIDENTS ARE NOT REQUIRED TO BE SHOWN ON RECORDS. --See opinion of Attorney General to Mr. Fred Colquitt, Director, Driver's License Section, Department of Motor Vehicles, 45 N.C.A.G. 218 (1976).

DIVISION MAY NOT FURNISH LISTINGS FOR COMMERCIAL PURPOSES. --The Division of Motor Vehicles is not required or permitted under the statutes to sell or furnish selective listings (i.e., by age, sex, etc.) in bulk or on computer tapes from the driver's license files for commercial purposes. Opinion

Chapter 20

of Attorney General to Mr. Zeb Hocutt, Jr., Director, Driver License Section, Division of Motor Vehicles, 47 N.C.A.G. 59 (1977).

§ 20-27. Availability of records

(a) All records of the Division pertaining to application and to drivers' licenses, except the confidential medical report referred to in G.S. 20-7, of the current or previous five years shall be open to public inspection in accordance with G.S. 20-43.1, at any reasonable time during office hours and copies shall be provided pursuant to the provisions of G.S. 20-26.

(b) All records of the Division pertaining to chemical tests as provided in G.S. 20-16.2 shall be available to the courts as provided in G.S. 20-26(b).

History.
1935, c. 52, s. 21; 1975, c. 716, s. 5; 1979, c. 667, s. 24; c. 903, s. 11; 1981, c. 145, s. 2; 1997-443, s. 32.25(c)

§ 20-27.1. Unlawful for sex offender to drive commercial passenger vehicle or school bus without appropriate commercial license or while disqualified

A person who drives a commercial passenger vehicle or a school bus and who does not have a valid commercial drivers license with a P or S endorsement because the person was convicted of a violation that requires registration under Article 27A of Chapter 14 of the General Statutes is guilty of a Class F felony.

History.
2009-491, s. 4
EDITOR'S NOTE. --
Session Laws 2009-491, s. 7, provides: "This act becomes effective December 1, 2009. This act applies to persons whose initial registration under Article 27A of Chapter 14 of the General Statutes occurs on or after December 1, 2009, and to persons who are registered under Article 27A of Chapter 14 of the General Statutes prior to December 1, 2009, and continue to be registered on or after December 1, 2009. The criminal penalties enacted by this act apply to offenses occurring on or after December 1, 2009."

§ 20-28. Unlawful to drive while license revoked, after notification, or while disqualified

(a) **Driving While License Revoked.** -- Except as provided in subsections (a1) or (a2) of this section, any person whose drivers license has been revoked who drives any motor vehicle upon the highways of the State while the license is revoked is guilty of a Class 3 misdemeanor.

(a1) **Driving While License Revoked for Impaired Driving.** -- Any person whose drivers license has been revoked for an impaired driving revocation as defined in G.S. 20-28.2(a) and who drives any motor vehicle upon the highways of the State is guilty of a Class 1 misdemeanor. Upon conviction, the person's license shall be revoked for an additional period of one year for the first offense, two years for the second offense, and permanently for a third or subsequent offense.

If the person's license was originally revoked for an impaired driving revocation, the court may order as a condition of probation that the offender abstain from alcohol consumption and verify compliance by use of a continuous alcohol monitoring system, of a type approved by the Division of Adult Correction and Juvenile Justice of the Department of Public Safety, for a minimum period of 90 days.

The restoree of a revoked drivers license who operates a motor vehicle upon the highways of the State without maintaining financial responsibility as provided by law shall be punished as for driving without a license.

(a2) **Driving Without Reclaiming License.** -- A person convicted under subsection (a) or (a1) of this section shall be punished as if the person had been convicted of driving without a license under G.S. 20-35 if the person demonstrates to the court that either of the following is true:

(1) At the time of the offense, the person's license was revoked solely under G.S. 20-16.5 and one of the following applies:

  a. The offense occurred more than 45 days after the effective date of a revocation order issued under G.S. 20-16.5(f) and the period of revocation was 45 days as provided under subdivision (3) of that subsection; or

  b. The offense occurred more than 30 days after the effective date of the revocation order issued under any other provision of G.S. 20-16.5.

(2) At the time of the offense the person had met the requirements of G.S. 50-13.12, or G.S. 110-142.2 and was eligible for reinstatement of the person's drivers license privilege as provided therein.

In addition, a person punished under this subsection shall be treated for drivers license and insurance rating purposes as if the person had been convicted of driving without a license under G.S. 20-35, and the conviction report sent to the Division must indicate that the person is to be so treated.

(a3) **Driving After Notification or Failure to Appear.** -- A person shall be guilty of a Class 1 misdemeanor if:

(1) The person operates a motor vehicle upon a highway while that person's license is revoked for an impaired drivers license revocation after the Division has sent

notification in accordance with G.S. 20-48; or

(2) The person fails to appear for two years from the date of the charge after being charged with an implied-consent offense.

Upon conviction, the person's drivers license shall be revoked for an additional period of one year for the first offense, two years for the second offense, and permanently for a third or subsequent offense. The restoree of a revoked drivers license who operates a motor vehicle upon the highways of the State without maintaining financial responsibility as provided by law shall be punished as for driving without a license.

(b) Repealed by Session Laws 1993 (Reg. Sess., 1994), c. 761, s. 3.

(c) **When Person May Apply for License.** -- A person whose license has been revoked may apply for a license as follows:

(1) If revoked under subsection (a1) of this section for one year, the person may apply for a license after 90 days.

(2) If punished under subsection (a2) of this section and the original revocation was pursuant to G.S. 20-16.5, in order to obtain reinstatement of a drivers license, the person must obtain a substance abuse assessment and show proof of financial responsibility to the Division. If the assessment recommends education or treatment, the person must complete the education or treatment within the time limits specified by the Division.

(3) If revoked under subsection (a3) of this section for one year, the person may apply for a license after one year.

(4) If revoked under this section for two years, the person may apply for a license after one year.

(5) If revoked under this section permanently, the person may apply for a license after three years.

(c1) Upon the filing of an application the Division may, with or without a hearing, issue a new license upon satisfactory proof that the former licensee has not been convicted of a moving violation under this Chapter or the laws of another state, a violation of any provision of the alcoholic beverage laws of this State or another state, or a violation of any provisions of the drug laws of this State or another state when any of these violations occurred during the revocation period. For purposes of this subsection, a violation of subsection (a) of this section shall not be considered a moving violation.

(c2) The Division may impose any restrictions or conditions on the new license that the Division considers appropriate for the balance of the revocation period. When the revocation period is permanent, the restrictions and conditions imposed by the Division may not exceed three years.

(c3) A person whose license is revoked for violation of subsection (a1) of this section where the person's license was originally revoked for an impaired driving revocation, or a person whose license is revoked for a violation of subsection (a3) of this section, may only have the license conditionally restored by the Division pursuant to the provisions of subsection (c4) of this section.

(c4) For a conditional restoration under subsection (c3) of this section, the Division shall require at a minimum that the driver obtain a substance abuse assessment prior to issuance of a license and show proof of financial responsibility. If the substance abuse assessment recommends education or treatment, the person must complete the education or treatment within the time limits specified. If the assessment determines that the person abuses alcohol, the Division shall require the person to install and use an ignition interlock system on any vehicles that are to be driven by that person for the period of time that the conditional restoration is active.

(c5) For licenses conditionally restored pursuant to subsections (c3) and (c4) of this section, the Division shall cancel the license and impose the remaining revocation period if any of the following occur:

(1) The person violates any condition of the restoration.

(2) The person is convicted of any moving offense in this or another state.

(3) The person is convicted for a violation of the alcoholic beverage or controlled substance laws of this or any other state.

(d) **Driving While Disqualified.** -- A person who was convicted of a violation that disqualified the person and required the person's drivers license to be revoked who drives a motor vehicle during the revocation period is punishable as provided in subsection (a1) of this section. A person who has been disqualified who drives a commercial motor vehicle during the disqualification period is guilty of a Class 1 misdemeanor and is disqualified for an additional period as follows:

(1) For a first offense of driving while disqualified, a person is disqualified for a period equal to the period for which the person was disqualified when the offense occurred.

(2) For a second offense of driving while disqualified, a person is disqualified for a period equal to two times the period for which the person was disqualified when the offense occurred.

(3) For a third offense of driving while disqualified, a person is disqualified for life.

Chapter 20

The Division may reduce a disqualification for life under this subsection to 10 years in accordance with the guidelines adopted under G.S. 20-17.4(b). A person who drives a commercial motor vehicle while the person is disqualified and the person's drivers license is revoked is punishable for both driving while the person's license was revoked and driving while disqualified.

History.

1935, c. 52, s. 22; 1945, c. 635; 1947, c. 1067, s. 16; 1955, c. 1020, s. 1; c. 1152, s. 18; c. 1187, s. 20; 1957, c. 1046; 1959, c. 515; 1967, c. 447; 1973, c. 47, s. 2; cc. 71, 1132; 1975, c. 716, s. 5; 1979, c 377, ss. 1, 2; c. 667, s. 41; 1981, c. 412, s. 4; c. 747, s. 66; 1983, c. 51; 1983 (Reg. Sess., 1984), c. 1101, s. 18A; 1989, c. 771, s. 4;1991, c. 509, s. 2;c. 726, s. 12;1993, c. 539, ss. 320 -322; 1994, Ex. Sess., c. 24, s. 14(c);1993 (Reg. Sess., 1994), c. 761, ss. 2, 3; 1995, c. 538, s. 2(e), (f); 2002-159, s. 6;2006-253, s. 22.1;2007-493, ss. 4, 19; 2012-146, s. 8;2013-360, s. 18B.14(f);2015-186, s. 2;2015-264, ss. 38(a), 86; 2017-186, s. 2 (kkkk)

EDITOR'S NOTE. --

Session Laws 2012-146, s. 11, made the amendment to this section by Session Laws 2012-146, s. 8, effective December 1, 2012, and applicable to offenses committed or any custody and visitation orders issued on or after that date.

Session Laws 2015-186, s. 1, provides: "This act shall be known as the 'North Carolina Drivers License Restoration Act.'"

Session Laws 2015-186, which, in s. 2, rewrote the section, in s. 7, as amended by Session Laws 2015-264, s. 86, provides: "This act becomes effective December 1, 2015, and applies to offenses committed on or after that date. Prosecutions for offenses committed before the effective date of this act are not abated or affected by this act, and the statutes that would be applicable but for this act remain applicable to those prosecutions."

Session Laws 2015-264, which, in s. 38(a), rewrote subsection (a2), in s. 38(c), provides: "This section becomes effective December 1, 2015, and applies to convictions on or after that date. Prosecutions for offenses committed before the effective date of this section are not abated or affected by this section, and the statutes that would be applicable but for this section remain applicable to those prosecutions."

EFFECT OF AMENDMENTS. --

Session Laws 2006-253, s. 22.1, effective December 1, 2006, and applicable to offenses committed on or after that date, rewrote the section catchline; added subsection (a2); rewrote subsection (c); redesignated former subsection (c) as present subsections (c1) and (c2); and added subsections (c3) through (c5).

Session Laws 2007-493, ss. 4 and 19, effective August 30, 2007, in subdivision (a2)(1), substituted "person operates a motor vehicle" for "person drives"; and in subsection (c4), substituted "that the conditional restoration is active" for "set forth in G.S. 20-17.8(c)"

at the end of the last sentence. For applicability provision, see Editor's note.

Session Laws 2012-146, s. 8, effective December 1, 2012, added the present second paragraph in subsection (a). For applicability, see Editor's note.

Session Laws 2013-360, s. 18B.14(f), effective December 1, 2013, inserted "Class 3 misdemeanor unless the person's license was originally revoked for an impaired driving revocation, in which case the person is guilty of a" in the first sentence in subsection (a). For applicability, see Editor's note.

Session Laws 2015-186, s. 2, effective December 1, 2015, rewrote the section. For applicability, see editor's note.

Session Laws 2015-264, s. 38(a), effective December 1, 2015, rewrote subsection (a2). For effective date and applicability, see editor's note.

Session Laws 2017-186, s. 2 (kkkk), effective December 1, 2017, inserted "and Juvenile Justice" in the second paragraph of subsection (a1).

I. IN GENERAL.

THE RIGHT TO OPERATE A MOTOR VEHICLE UPON THE PUBLIC HIGHWAYS IS NOT AN UNRESTRICTED RIGHT but a privilege which can be exercised only in accordance with the legislative restrictions fixed thereon. State v. Tharrington, 1 N.C. App. 608, 162 S.E.2d 140 (1968).

IN THIS SECTION THE GENERAL ASSEMBLY ANTICIPATED THERE WOULD BE HARDSHIP CASES where the violation of subsection (a) would be technical rather than wilful. Gibson v. Scheidt, 259 N.C. 339, 130 S.E.2d 679 (1963).

WHERE THE PETITIONER WAS CONVICTED OF VIOLATING THIS SECTION THE REVOCATION OF HIS LICENSE WAS MANDATORY, and the exercise of limited discretion by the division under subsection (a) of this section does not change the mandatory character of the revocation. Noyes v. Peters, 40 N.C. App. 763, 253 S.E.2d 584 (1979).

SUSPENSION OR REVOCATION OF LICENSE UNDER SUBSECTION (A) NOT PROPER WITHOUT CONVICTION. --Where plaintiff has never been convicted of or tried for the offense defined in subsection (a) of this section, unless and until he is so tried and convicted, subsection (a) vests no authority in the Department (now Division) in respect of the suspension or revocation of his operator's license. Gibson v. Scheidt, 259 N.C. 339, 130 S.E.2d 679 (1963).

OPERATION MUST HAVE OCCURRED DURING SUSPENSION OR REVOCATION. --To constitute a violation of subsection (a) of this section, the operation of a motor vehicle must occur "while such license is suspended or revoked," that is, during the period of suspension or revocation. State v. Sossamon, 259 N.C. 374, 130 S.E.2d 638 (1963).

Subsection (a) of this section deals solely and directly with the offense of driving while one's operator's license is suspended or revoked and contains provisions bearing directly upon periods of suspension and revocation upon conviction. In re Bratton, 263 N.C. 70, 138 S.E.2d 809 (1964).

Chapter 20

One violates this section if he operates a motor vehicle on a public highway while his operator's license is in a state of suspension. State v. Blacknell, 270 N.C. 103, 153 S.E.2d 789 (1967).

To constitute a violation of subsection (a) of this section there must be: (1) operation of a motor vehicle by a person; (2) on a public highway; (3) while his operator's license is suspended or revoked. State v. Cook, 272 N.C. 728, 158 S.E.2d 820 (1968); State v. Hughes, 6 N.C. App. 287, 170 S.E.2d 78 (1969); State v. Springs, 26 N.C. App. 757, 217 S.E.2d 200 (1975).

In order to convict a person of a violation of subsection (a) of this section, such person must have: (1) operated a motor vehicle; (2) on a public highway; and (3) while his operator's license or operating privilege was lawfully suspended or revoked. State v. Newborn, 11 N.C. App. 292, 181 S.E.2d 214 (1971).

In order to constitute a violation of this section, defendant must be found guilty of driving "while" his license is revoked, and a verdict specifically finding defendant guilty of driving "after" his license was revoked is therefore defective. State v. McDonald, 21 N.C. App. 136, 203 S.E.2d 397 (1974).

To convict for a violation of subsection (a) of this section, the State must prove: (1) the operation of a motor vehicle, (2) on a public highway, (3) while one's operator's license is suspended or revoked. State v. Chester, 30 N.C. App. 224, 226 S.E.2d 524 (1976).

A conviction under subsection (a) of this section requires that the State prove beyond a reasonable doubt (1) the operation of a motor vehicle by a person, (2) on a public highway, (3) while his operator's license is suspended or revoked. State v. Atwood, 290 N.C. 266, 225 S.E.2d 543 (1976).

OFFENSE MUST HAVE OCCURRED UPON PUBLIC HIGHWAY. --The trial judge's failure to require the jury to find beyond a reasonable doubt that the offense occurred upon a public highway was prejudicial error. State v. Harris, 10 N.C. App. 553, 180 S.E.2d 29 (1971); State v. Springs, 26 N.C. App. 757, 217 S.E.2d 200 (1975).

WHAT TERM "HIGHWAY" ENCOMPASSES. --The term "highway" encompasses "highway of the State" or "public highway for purposes of framing a valid arrest warrant." State v. Bigelow, 19 N.C. App. 570, 199 S.E.2d 494 (1973).

INTENT IMMATERIAL. --The operation of a motor vehicle upon the highways of the State by a person whose driver's license has been revoked is unlawful, regardless of intent, since the specific performance of the act forbidden constitutes the offense itself. State v. Correll, 232 N.C. 696, 62 S.E.2d 82 (1950).

A person has no right to drive his car upon the highways of North Carolina after his license has been revoked and it makes no difference what the person's intentions are in so doing. State v. Tharrington, 1 N.C. App. 608, 162 S.E.2d 140 (1968); State v. Hurley, 18 N.C. App. 285, 196 S.E.2d 542 (1973).

There is nothing in subsection (a) of this section which would imply that knowledge or intent is a part of the crime of operating a motor vehicle after one's license has been suspended. State v. Teasley, 9 N.C.

App. 477, 176 S.E.2d 838, appeal dismissed, 277 N.C. 459, 177 S.E.2d 900 (1970); State v. Hurley, 18 N.C. App. 285, 196 S.E.2d 542 (1973).

ACTUAL OR CONSTRUCTIVE KNOWLEDGE REQUIRED FOR CONVICTION. --The legislature intended that there be actual or constructive knowledge of the suspension or revocation in order for there to be a conviction under this section. State v. Atwood, 290 N.C. 266, 225 S.E.2d 543 (1976).

While a specific intent is not an element of the offense of operating a motor vehicle on a public highway while one's license is suspended or revoked, the burden is on the State to prove that defendant had knowledge at the time charged that his operator's license was suspended or revoked. State v. Chester, 30 N.C. App. 224, 226 S.E.2d 524 (1976).

The surrendering of defendant's license to the trial court, and the forwarding of it to the DMV, gave defendant sufficient notice that his driver's license had been revoked. State v. Finger, 72 N.C. App. 569, 324 S.E.2d 894, cert. denied, 313 N.C. 606, 332 S.E.2d 80 (1985).

Trial court erred in denying defendant's motion to dismiss the charge against him of driving while license revoked, as the State did not present sufficient evidence that defendant knew his license was revoked, in part because the State was unable to show that defendant had been notified of the alleged revocation. State v. Cruz, 173 N.C. App. 689, 620 S.E.2d 251 (2005).

EXCLUSION OF EVIDENCE OF OPERABILITY UPHELD. --Where defendant admitted that he was sitting behind the wheel of an automobile while the motor was running, that he put the car into drive three times and that the car moved forward on each occasion, failure to allow defendant to introduce evidence that the vehicle he was alleged to have been operating was not operable was not prejudicial and did not entitle him to a new trial for the offenses of habitual impaired driving and driving during revocation, as defendant demonstrated in the presence of a police officer that the car in which he was seated was a device in which a person might be transported for purposes of G.S. 20-4.01(49). State v. Clapp, 135 N.C. App. 52, 519 S.E.2d 90 (1999).

STATE'S BURDEN OF PROOF. --To sustain a charge against a defendant for driving while his license was revoked, the State had to prove that he (1) operated a motor vehicle, (2) on a public highway, (3) while his operator's license was suspended or revoked, (4) with knowledge of the suspension or revocation. State v. Woody, 102 N.C. App. 576, 402 S.E.2d 848 (1991).

REQUIREMENTS OF NECESSITY DEFENSE NOT MET. --Regardless of whether the defense of necessity should be recognized in North Carolina, the evidence in defendant's case clearly did not meet the requirements of this defense. State v. Gainey, 84 N.C. App. 107, 351 S.E.2d 819 (1987).

SUFFICIENT EVIDENCE. --Sufficient evidence supported defendant's conviction for driving while defendant's license was revoked because defendant stipulated (1) defendant's license was revoked for driving while impaired, and (2) defendant had three prior such convictions within ten years of the revocation. State v. Hines, 259 N.C. App. 358, 816 S.E.2d 182 (2018).

SUFFICIENT EVIDENCE DEFENDANT WAS "DRIVING." --While there was no eyewitness establishing that defendant was the driver of the car involved in an accident, evidence that the vehicle involved in an accident was registered to defendant, that defendant was found walking on a road near the scene of the accident, and that defendant had injuries consistent with person who was driving in a car accident was sufficient to survive a motion to dismiss. State v. Foye, 220 N.C. App. 37, 725 S.E.2d 73 (2012).

OFFENSE BY PERSON NOT HOLDING LICENSE. --Under the provisions of G.S. 20-23.1 and subsection (a) of this section, when a person who does not hold a driver's license has his operating privilege revoked or suspended in the manner and under the conditions prescribed by statute, and while such operating privilege is thus suspended or revoked he drives a motor vehicle upon the highways of this State, he violates subsection (a). State v. Newborn, 11 N.C. App. 292, 181 S.E.2d 214 (1971).

SPECIAL ARRAIGNMENT NOT REQUIRED ON CHARGE OF DRIVING WHILE LICENSE PERMANENTLY REVOKED. --A special arraignment need not be held in order for defendant to be convicted of driving while license permanently revoked. Section 15A-928 applies solely to those charges in which the defendant's prior conviction raises an offense of lower grade to one of higher grade. State v. Wells, 59 N.C. App. 682, 298 S.E.2d 73 (1982).

MAXIMUM TERM OF 18 MONTHS AND MINIMUM TERM OF 12 MONTHS DOES NOT EXCEED STATUTORY MAXIMUM for the crime of driving while license permanently revoked. Since only the minimum punishment of not less than one year is specified in subsection (b) of this section, this statute must be read together with G.S. 14-3, applicable to motor vehicle misdemeanors contained in sections other than Article 3 of this Chapter, to find the maximum term of imprisonment. State v. Wells, 59 N.C. App. 682, 298 S.E.2d 73 (1982).

APPLIED in State v. Meadows, 234 N.C. 657, 68 S.E.2d 406 (1951); Beaver v. Scheidt, 251 N.C. 671, 111 S.E.2d 881 (1960); State v. Sossamon, 259 N.C. 378, 130 S.E.2d 640 (1963); State v. Blackwelder, 263 N.C. 96, 138 S.E.2d 787 (1964); State v. Letterlough, 6 N.C. App. 36, 169 S.E.2d 269 (1969); State v. Rowland, 13 N.C. App. 253, 185 S.E.2d 296 (1971); State v. Guffey, 283 N.C. 94, 194 S.E.2d 827 (1973); State v. Toler, 18 N.C. App. 149, 196 S.E.2d 295 (1973); State v. Phillips, 25 N.C. App. 313, 212 S.E.2d 906 (1975); State v. Burbank, 59 N.C. App. 543, 297 S.E.2d 602 (1982); State v. Beasley, 66 N.C. App. 288, 311 S.E.2d 347 (1984); State v. Finger, 72 N.C. App. 569, 324 S.E.2d 894 (1985); State v. Cooney, 72 N.C. App. 649, 325 S.E.2d 15 (1985); State v. Carrington, 74 N.C. App. 40, 327 S.E.2d 594 (1985); State v. Cornelius, 104 N.C.

App. 583, 410 S.E.2d 504 (1991); State v. Bartlett, 130 N.C. App. 79, 502 S.E.2d 53 (1998).

CITED in State v. Jordan, 155 N.C. App. 146, 574 S.E.2d 166 (2002); State v. Bowden, 177 N.C. App. 718, 630 S.E.2d 208 (2006); Hinson v. Jarvis, 190 N.C. App. 607, 660 S.E.2d 604 (2008), review dismissed, as moot, 363 N.C. 126, 675 S.E.2d 365 (2009), review denied, 363 N.C. 126, 675 S.E.2d 366 (2009); State v. Hopper, 205 N.C. App. 175, 695 S.E.2d 801 (2010); State v. Davis, 208 N.C. App. 26, 702 S.E.2d 507 (2010); State v. Dewalt, 209 N.C. App. 187, 703 S.E.2d 872 (2011); State v. Leyshon, 211 N.C. App. 511, 710 S.E.2d 282 (2011); State v. Fox, 216 N.C. App. 153, 716 S.E.2d 261 (2011); State v. White, 232 N.C. App. 296, 753 S.E.2d 698 (2014); State v. Sitosky, 238 N.C. App. 558, 767 S.E.2d 623 (2014); State v. Adams, 250 N.C. App. 664, 794 S.E.2d 357 (2016), review denied, 797 S.E.2d 15, 2017 N.C. LEXIS 181 (2017), cert. dismissed, 369 N.C. 562, 799 S.E.2d 48, 2017 N.C. LEXIS 336 (N.C. 2017).

II. PROCEDURE.

A VIOLATION OF G.S. 20-7 IS NOT STATUTORILY A LESSER INCLUDED OFFENSE OF THIS SECTION. State v. Cannon, 38 N.C. App. 322, 248 S.E.2d 65 (1978).

DOUBLE JEOPARDY BARS PROSECUTION UNDER THIS SECTION WHERE DEFENDANT ALREADY PLED GUILTY TO G.S. 20-7. --The defendant could not be prosecuted for driving while his license was permanently revoked in violation of this section because of the prohibition against double jeopardy, where the defendant had previously pled guilty to driving without a license in violation of G.S. 20-7 is not statutorily a lesser included offense of a violation of this section, under the "additional facts test" of double jeopardy when applied to the defendant's offenses, the two offenses were the same both in fact and in law since the evidence that the defendant was driving an automobile while his license had been permanently revoked would sustain a conviction for driving without a license. State v. Cannon, 38 N.C. App. 322, 248 S.E.2d 65 (1978).

A WARRANT IS FATALLY DEFECTIVE WHICH DOES NOT ALLEGE IN WORDS OR IN SUBSTANCE AN ESSENTIAL ELEMENT of the offense defined in subsection (a) of this section. State v. Sossamon, 259 N.C. 374, 130 S.E.2d 638 (1963).

WARRANT NEED NOT SPECIFICALLY REFER TO SECTION. --A warrant charging that the named defendant did unlawfully and willfully operate a motor vehicle on public streets or highways while his license was suspended sufficiently charges defendant's violation of this section without specific reference to the statute. State v. Blacknell, 270 N.C. 103, 153 S.E.2d 789 (1967).

WARRANT NEED NOT ALLEGE THAT DEFENDANT WAS DRIVING ON "PUBLIC" HIGHWAY. --A warrant for driving while driver's license was suspended is not fatally defective in failing to allege that defendant was driving upon a "public" street or highway, since this section uses the phrase "highways of the State." State v. Martin, 13 N.C. App. 613, 186

S.E.2d 647, cert. denied and appeal dismissed, 281 N.C. 156, 188 S.E.2d 364 (1972).

INDICTMENT HELD SUFFICIENT. --Indictments for driving while license revoked and speeding to elude arrest were not made defective by their failure to list all elements of the crime of driving with license revoked, because they gave defendant sufficient notice of the nature and cause of the charges against him. State v. Scott, 167 N.C. App. 783, 607 S.E.2d 10 (2005).

ADMISSIBILITY OF DIVISION RECORDS. --The records of the Department (now Division), properly authenticated, are competent for the purpose of establishing the status of a person's operator's license and driving privilege. State v. Teasley, 9 N.C. App. 477, 176 S.E.2d 838, appeal dismissed, 277 N.C. 459, 177 S.E.2d 900 (1970); State v. Rhodes, 10 N.C. App. 154, 177 S.E.2d 754 (1970).

In a prosecution of a defendant for driving while his license was suspended, a properly certified copy of the driver's license record of defendant on file with the Department (now Division) of Motor Vehicles is admissible as evidence that the defendant's license was in a state of revocation for a period covering the date of the offense for which he was charged. State v. Herald, 10 N.C. App. 263, 178 S.E.2d 120 (1970).

Certification by an employee of the Department (now Division) of Motor Vehicles that the original of an order of security requirement or suspension of driving privilege was mailed to defendant on a specified date at his address shown on the records of the Department (now Division) of Motor Vehicles is sufficient to render admissible a copy of the document in a prosecution of a defendant for driving while his license was suspended. State v. Herald, 10 N.C. App. 263, 178 S.E.2d 120 (1970).

A defendant is entitled to have the contents of the official record of the status of his driver's license limited, if he so requests, to the formal parts thereof, including the certification and seal, plus the fact that under official action of the Department (now Division) of Motor Vehicles the defendant's license was in a state of revocation or suspension on the date he is charged with committing the offense under this section. State v. Rhodes, 10 N.C. App. 154, 177 S.E.2d 754 (1970).

Where a defendant failed to request that the contents of his certified driving record be limited to the portions thereof relating to the status of his license on the day he was charged with driving while his license was revoked, he could not complain on appeal that the record indicated that he had been involved in a number of accidents. State v. Herald, 10 N.C. App. 263, 178 S.E.2d 120 (1970).

ADMISSION INTO EVIDENCE OF DEFENDANT'S PRIOR CONVICTIONS for driving while impaired and for hit-and-run did not unfairly prejudice defendant in prosecution for driving while his license was revoked, where defendant admitted driving van while his license was revoked. State v. Gainey, 84 N.C. App. 107, 351 S.E.2d 819 (1987).

Admission of evidence concerning defendant's convictions for failure to follow a truck route and improper turning was improper under G.S. 8C-1, Rule 609, but the error was not prejudicial to the defendant in prosecution for driving while his license was revoked, where defendant admitted driving van while his license was revoked. State v. Gainey, 84 N.C. App. 107, 351 S.E.2d 819 (1987).

COLLATERAL ATTACK ON ORDER OF REVOCATION NOT PERMITTED. --Defendant could not, when on trial for the criminal offense of driving while his license was revoked, collaterally attack the record of revocation which did not on its face disclose invalidity. State v. Ball, 255 N.C. 351, 121 S.E.2d 604 (1961).

BURDEN OF PROOF AND PRESUMPTION OF KNOWLEDGE. --The State satisfies the burden of proving that defendant had knowledge at the time charged that his operator's license was suspended or revoked when, nothing else appearing, it has offered evidence of compliance with the notice requirements of G.S. 20-48 because of the presumption that he received notice and had such knowledge. State v. Chester, 30 N.C. App. 224, 226 S.E.2d 524 (1976).

Since defendant chose not to present any evidence at trial, the State met its burden of producing substantial evidence on each element of driving while license revoked in G.S. 20-28(a) by offering evidence that the Department of Motor Vehicles had sent defendant 18 notices of the revocation of defendant's license in compliance with G.S. 20-48(a). State v. Coltrane, 188 N.C. App. 498, 656 S.E.2d 322 (2008), review denied, 362 N.C. 476, 666 S.E.2d 760 (2008).

MAILING OF NOTICE UNDER G.S. 20-48 RAISES PRIMA FACIE PRESUMPTION OF KNOWLEDGE. --For purposes of a conviction for driving while license is suspended or revoked, mailing of the notice under G.S. 20-48 raises only a prima facie presumption that defendant received the notice and thereby acquired knowledge of the suspension or revocation. State v. Atwood, 290 N.C. 266, 225 S.E.2d 543 (1976).

THE FAILURE OF THE TRIAL COURT TO CHARGE ON KNOWLEDGE OF REVOCATION pursuant to this section in support of an aggravated sentence under G.S. 20-141.5 was not erroneous where the State's evidence tended to show that it complied with the provisions for giving notice of revocation or suspension of a driver's license found in G.S. 20-48 and the defendant neither contested that evidence nor offered contrary evidence. State v. Funchess, 141 N.C. App. 302, 540 S.E.2d 435 (2000).

WHEN INSTRUCTIONS AS TO KNOWLEDGE REQUIRED. --In a prosecution for violation of subsection (a) of this section where the evidence for the State discloses that the Division complied with the notice requirements of G.S. 20-48: (1) Where there is no evidence that defendant did not receive the notice mailed by the division, it is not necessary for the trial court to charge on guilty knowledge; (2) Where there is some evidence of failure of defendant to receive the notice or some other evidence sufficient to raise the issue, then the trial court must, in order to comply with

G.S. 1-180 (now repealed) and apply the law to the evidence, instruct the jury that guilty knowledge by the defendant is necessary to convict; and (3) Where all the evidence indicates that defendant had no notice or knowledge of the suspension or revocation of license, a nonsuit should be granted. State v. Chester, 30 N.C. App. 224, 226 S.E.2d 524 (1976); State v. Hayes, 31 N.C. App. 121, 228 S.E.2d 460 (1976).

Trial court erred in convicting defendant of driving a motor vehicle while his license was revoked because, while the State provided evidence that notice of defendant's driver's license revocation had been mailed in accordance with the statutory requirements, defendant testified that he did not receive the notice from the Department of Motor Vehicles and suggested that, since he shared his name and address with his father, he never received actual notice of his license's revocation, the trial court failed to instruct the jury that it could find defendant guilty only if he had knowledge of his license's revocation, and there was a reasonable possibility that the jury, properly instructed, would have acquitted him. State v. Green, 258 N.C. App. 87, 811 S.E.2d 666 (2018).

FAILURE TO PROVE THAT DEFENDANT HAD NOTICE OF REVOCATION. --Where the State offered no evidence that defendant had been notified that his license was revoked and defendant's plea of not guilty required the State to prove beyond a reasonable doubt every element of the offense charged, defendant's conviction for that charge was reversed. State v. Richardson, 96 N.C. App. 270, 385 S.E.2d 194 (1989).

EVIDENCE SUFFICIENT TO PROVE DEFENDANT WAS OPERATOR. --In a prosecution for driving under the influence and driving while license was revoked, evidence that defendant was seated behind the wheel of a car which had the motor running was sufficient to prove that defendant was the operator of the car under G.S. 20-4.01(25). State v. Turner, 29 N.C. App. 163, 223 S.E.2d 530 (1976).

HARMLESS ERROR. --Although the trial court should have submitted the aggravating factor in G.S. 20-179(c)(2), providing that at the time of the offense, defendant was driving while defendant's license was revoked, as defined by G.S. 20-28, and the revocation was an impaired driving revocation under G.S. 20-28.2(a), the error was harmless beyond a reasonable doubt. Defendant's driving record, admitted by the State, showed that defendant's driver's license was indefinitely revoked due to an impaired driving conviction and that the license had not been reinstated, which meant that evidence of the aggravating factor was overwhelming and uncontroverted such that a sentence beyond the statutory maximum could be imposed. State v. Coffey, 189 N.C. App. 382, 658 S.E.2d 73 (2008).

Defendant failed to demonstrate prejudicial error regarding a jury instruction for driving while license revoked, although the trial court erroneously instructed the jury that the State had proved defendant's knowledge of the suspension, because it immediately correctly instructed that the State had the burden of providing defendant had received notice of the suspension. State v. Armstrong, 203 N.C. App. 399, 691 S.E.2d 433 (2010).

LEGAL PERIODICALS. --
For survey of 1976 case law on criminal law, see 55 N.C.L. Rev. 976 (1977).

OPINIONS OF THE ATTORNEY GENERAL
MINIMUM PUNISHMENT MANDATORY. --The minimum punishment of imprisonment for one year under subsection (b) of this section is mandatory and may not be suspended. See opinion of Attorney General to Honorable Samuel L. Osborne, District Court Judge, Twenty-Third Judicial District, 50 N.C.A.G. 88 (1981).

§ 20-28.1. Conviction of moving offense committed while driving during period of suspension or revocation of license

(a) Upon receipt of notice of conviction of any person of a motor vehicle moving offense, such offense having been committed while such person's driving privilege was in a state of suspension or revocation, the Division shall revoke such person's driving privilege for an additional period of time as set forth in subsection (b) hereof. For purposes of this section a violation of G.S. 20-7(a), 20-24.1, or 20-28(a) or (a2) shall not be considered a "motor vehicle moving offense" unless the offense occurred in a commercial motor vehicle or the person held a commercial drivers license at the time of the offense.

(b) When a driving privilege is subject to revocation under this section, the additional period of revocation shall be as follows:

(1) A first such revocation shall be for one year;

(2) A second such revocation shall be for two years; and

(3) A third or subsequent such revocation shall be permanent.

(c) A person whose license has been revoked under this section for one year may apply for a license after 90 days. A person whose license has been revoked under this section for two years may apply for a license after 12 months. A person whose license has been revoked under this section permanently may apply for a license after three years. Upon the filing of an application, the Division may, with or without a hearing, issue a new license upon satisfactory proof that the former licensee has not been convicted of a moving violation under this Chapter or the laws of another state, or a violation of any provision of the alcoholic beverage laws of this State or another state, or a violation of any provision of the drug laws of this State or another state when any of these violations occurred during the revocation period. The Division may impose any restrictions or conditions on the new license that the Division considers appropriate for the balance of the revocation period. When the revocation period is permanent, the restrictions and conditions imposed by the Division may not exceed three years.

(d) Repealed by Session Laws 1979, c. 378, s. 2.

History.

1965, c. 286; 1969, c. 348; 1971, c. 163; 1973, c. 47, s. 2; 1975, c. 716, s. 5; 1979, c. 378, ss. 1, 2; 1981, c. 412, s. 4; c. 747, s. 66; 1991, c. 509, s. 1;c. 682, s. 6;c. 726, s. 22.1;2015-186, s. 3;2015-264, s. 86

EDITOR'S NOTE. --

Session Laws 2015-186, s. 1, provides: "This act shall be known as the 'North Carolina Drivers License Restoration Act.'"

Session Laws 2015-186, which, in s. 3, deleted "except a conviction punishable under G.S. 20-28(a1)" following "motor vehicle moving offense" in the first sentence and added the last sentence of subsection (a), in s. 7, as amended by Session Laws 2015-264, s. 86, provides: "This act becomes effective December 1, 2015, and applies to offenses committed on or after that date. Prosecutions for offenses committed before the effective date of this act are not abated or affected by this act, and the statutes that would be applicable but for this act remain applicable to those prosecutions."

EFFECT OF AMENDMENTS. --

Session Laws 2015-186, s. 3, effective December 1, 2015, deleted "except a conviction punishable under G.S. 20-28(a1)" following "motor vehicle moving offense" in the first sentence and added the last sentence of subsection (a). For effective date and applicability, see Editor's note.

IT IS CLEAR THAT A VIOLATION OF ANY PROVISION OF THE MOTOR VEHICLE LAWS is a basis for denying reinstatement. The statute's application is not limited to motor vehicle laws involving moving violations or those involving highway safety. Evans v. Roberson, 314 N.C. 315, 333 S.E.2d 228 (1985).

APPLICATION OF SECTION. --This section does not apply to a conviction of a "motor vehicle moving offense" during the interim between the termination of an original order of revocation and the payment of the fee required by G.S. 20-7(i1). Ennis v. Garrett, 279 N.C. 612, 184 S.E.2d 246 (1971).

ODOMETER ALTERATION PROHIBITED BY G.S. 20-343 IS A VIOLATION OF THE MOTOR VEHICLE LAWS OF NORTH CAROLINA as that term is used in subsection (c) of this section. Evans v. Roberson, 314 N.C. 315, 333 S.E.2d 228 (1985).

EFFECT OF TERMINATION OF REVOCATION PERIOD. --When the period of revocation stated in the original order of revocation terminates, the license is no longer "in a state of suspension or revocation" within the meaning of this section. Ennis v. Garrett, 279 N.C. 612, 184 S.E.2d 246 (1971).

When the period of revocation stated in the original order of revocation terminates, the former holder of the license may not immediately resume driving. Before he may do so the fee required by G.S. 20-7(i1) must be paid. Ennis v. Garrett, 279 N.C. 612, 184 S.E.2d 246 (1971).

When the period of revocation stated in the original order of revocation terminates, the former holder of the license is simply a person without a valid operator's or chauffeur's license; if, before payment of the fee required by G.S. 20-7(i1), he operates a motor vehicle upon a highway of this State, he is subject to the penalties provided for one who operates a motor vehicle without a valid operator's or chauffeur's license. Ennis v. Garrett, 279 N.C. 612, 184 S.E.2d 246 (1971).

SUSPENSION DUE TO INSURANCE AGENT'S FAILURE TO GIVE NOTICE OF INSURANCE. --Where, by error, a licensee's insurance agent failed to furnish the Commissioner notice of the existence of liability insurance on her car and received notification of suspension of her license for lack of liability insurance but she continued to drive, relying on her agent to correct his error, subsequent moving violations during the period of the suspension make revocation for an additional period mandatory under this section even though the suspension would not have been entered if the Commissioner had been properly advised of the existence of liability insurance. Carson v. Godwin, 269 N.C. 744, 153 S.E.2d 473 (1967).

REVOCATION OF DRIVING PRIVILEGE. --When a person's driver's license is suspended or revoked, it is the surrendering of the privilege to drive, not the license card itself, that is of significance. Eibergen v. Killens, 124 N.C. App. 534, 477 S.E.2d 684 (1996).

Where petitioner, who was driving without his license, was stopped and charged with driving while impaired, and then appeared before a magistrate who revoked his driver's license for 10 days, petitioner's license had been validly revoked when he was stopped the next day; thus, he was properly charged with committing a moving violation during a period of revocation by operating a motor vehicle. Eibergen v. Killens, 124 N.C. App. 534, 477 S.E.2d 684 (1996).

FORMER PROVISIONS CONSTRUED. --See Underwood v. Howland, 274 N.C. 473, 164 S.E.2d 2 (1968).

APPLIED in Taylor v. Garrett, 7 N.C. App. 473, 173 S.E.2d 31 (1970).

CITED in Walters v. Cooper, 226 N.C. App. 166, 739 S.E.2d 185 (2013), aff'd 367 N.C. 117, 748 S.E.2d 144, 2013 N.C. LEXIS 1021 (2013).

§ 20-28.2. Forfeiture of motor vehicle for impaired driving after impaired driving license revocation; forfeiture for felony speeding to elude arrest

(a) **Meaning of "Impaired Driving License Revocation". --** The revocation of a person's drivers license is an impaired driving license revocation if the revocation is pursuant to:

    (1) G.S. 20-13.2, 20-16(a)(8b), 20-16.2, 20-16.5, 20-17(a)(2), 20-17(a)(12), or 20-138.5; or

    (2) G.S. 20-16(a)(7), 20-17(a)(1), 20-17(a)(3), 20-17(a)(9), or 20-17(a)(11), if the offense involves impaired driving; or

    (3) The laws of another state and the offense for which the person's license is revoked prohibits substantially similar conduct which if committed in this State would result in a revocation listed in subdivisions (1) or (2).

Chapter 20

(a1) **Definitions.** -- As used in this section and in G.S. 20-28.3, 20-28.4, 20-28.5, 20-28.7, 20-28.8, 20-28.9, 20-54.1, and 20-141.5, the following terms mean:

(1) **Fair Market Value.** -- The value of the seized motor vehicle, as determined in accordance with the schedule of values adopted by the Commissioner pursuant to G.S. 105-187.3.

(1a) **Impaired Driving Acknowledgment.** -- A written document acknowledging that:

a. The motor vehicle was operated by a person charged with an offense involving impaired driving, and:

1. That person's drivers license was revoked as a result of a prior impaired drivers license revocation; or

2. That person did not have a valid drivers license, and did not have liability insurance.

b. If the motor vehicle is again operated by this particular person, and the person is charged with an offense involving impaired driving, then the vehicle is subject to impoundment and forfeiture if (i) the offense occurs while that person's drivers license is revoked, or (ii) the offense occurs while the person has no valid drivers license, and has no liability insurance.

c. A lack of knowledge or consent to the operation will not be a defense in the future, unless the motor vehicle owner has taken all reasonable precautions to prevent the use of the motor vehicle by this particular person and immediately reports, upon discovery, any unauthorized use to the appropriate law enforcement agency.

(2) **Innocent Owner.** -- A motor vehicle owner:

a. Who, if the offense resulting in seizure was an impaired driving offense, did not know and had no reason to know that (i) the defendant's drivers license was revoked, or (ii) that the defendant did not have a valid drivers license, and that the defendant had no liability insurance; or

b. Who, if the offense resulting in seizure was an impaired driving offense, knew that (i) the defendant's drivers license was revoked, or (ii) that the defendant had no valid drivers license, and that the defendant had no liability insurance, but the defendant drove the vehicle without the person's expressed or implied permission, and the owner files a police report for unauthorized use of the motor vehicle and agrees to

prosecute the unauthorized operator of the motor vehicle, or who, if the offense resulting in seizure was a felony speeding to elude arrest offense, did not give the defendant express or implied permission to drive the vehicle, and the owner files a police report for unauthorized use of the motor vehicle and agrees to prosecute the unauthorized operator of the motor vehicle; or

c. Whose vehicle was reported stolen; or

d. Repealed by Session Laws 1999-406, s. 17.

e. Who is (i) a rental car company as defined in G.S. 66-201(a) and the vehicle was driven by a person who is not listed as an authorized driver on the rental agreement as defined in G.S. 66-201; or (ii) a rental car company as defined in G.S. 66-201(a) and the vehicle was driven by a person who is listed as an authorized driver on the rental agreement as defined in G.S. 66-201 and if the offense resulting in seizure was an impaired driving offense, the rental car company has no actual knowledge of the revocation of the renter's drivers' license at the time the rental agreement is entered, or if the offense resulting in seizure was a felony speeding to elude arrest offense, the rental agreement expressly prohibits use of the vehicle while committing a felony; or

f. Who is in the business of leasing motor vehicles, who holds legal title to the motor vehicle as a lessor at the time of seizure and, if the offense resulting in seizure was an impaired driving offense, who has no actual knowledge of the revocation of the lessee's drivers license at the time the lease is entered.

(2a) **Insurance Company.** -- Any insurance company that has coverage on or is otherwise liable for repairs or damages to the motor vehicle at the time of the seizure.

(2b) **Insurance Proceeds.** -- Proceeds paid under an insurance policy for damage to a seized motor vehicle less any payments actually paid to valid lienholders and for towing and storage costs incurred for the motor vehicle after the time the motor vehicle became subject to seizure.

(3) **Lienholder.** -- A person who holds a perfected security interest in a motor vehicle at the time of seizure.

(3a) **Motor Vehicle Owner.** -- A person in whose name a registration card or certificate of title for a motor vehicle is issued at the time of seizure.

(4) **Order of Forfeiture. --** An order by the court which terminates the rights and ownership interest of a motor vehicle owner in a motor vehicle and any insurance proceeds or proceeds of sale in accordance with G.S. 20-28.2.

(5) Repealed by Session Laws 1998-182, s. 2.

(6) **Registered Owner. --** A person in whose name a registration card for a motor vehicle is issued at the time of seizure.

(7) Repealed by Session Laws 1998-182, s. 2.

(8) **Speeding to Elude Arrest Acknowledgment. --** A written document acknowledging that:

    a. The motor vehicle was operated by a person charged with felony speeding to elude arrest pursuant to G.S. 20-141.5(b) or (b1).

    b. If the motor vehicle is again operated by this particular person and the person is charged with felony speeding to elude arrest pursuant to G.S. 20-141.5(b) or (b1), then the vehicle is subject to impoundment and forfeiture.

    c. A lack of knowledge or consent to the operation will not be a defense in the future unless the motor vehicle owner has taken all reasonable precautions to prevent the use of the motor vehicle by this particular person and immediately reports upon discovery any unauthorized use to the appropriate law enforcement agency.

(9) **State Surplus Property Agency. --** The Department of Administration.

(b) **When Motor Vehicle Becomes Property Subject to Order of Forfeiture; Impaired Driving and Prior Revocation. --** A judge may determine whether the vehicle driven by an impaired driver at the time of the offense becomes subject to an order of forfeiture. The determination may be made at any of the following times:

(1) A sentencing hearing for the underlying offense involving impaired driving.

(2) A separate hearing after conviction of the defendant.

(3) A forfeiture hearing held at least 60 days after the defendant failed to appear at the scheduled trial for the underlying offense, and the defendant's order of arrest for failing to appear has not been set aside.

The vehicle shall become subject to an order of forfeiture if the greater weight of the evidence shows that the defendant is guilty of an offense involving impaired driving, and that the defendant's license was revoked pursuant to an impaired driving license revocation as defined in subsection (a) of this section.

(b1) **When a Motor Vehicle Becomes Property Subject to Order of Forfeiture; No License and No Insurance. --** A judge may determine whether the vehicle driven by an impaired driver at the time of the offense becomes subject to an order of forfeiture. The determination may be made at any of the following times:

(1) A sentencing hearing for the underlying offense involving impaired driving.

(2) A separate hearing after conviction of the defendant.

(3) A forfeiture hearing held at least 60 days after the defendant failed to appear at the scheduled trial for the underlying offense, and the defendant's order of arrest for failing to appear has not been set aside.

The vehicle shall become subject to an order of forfeiture if the greater weight of the evidence shows that the defendant is guilty of an offense involving impaired driving, and: (i) the defendant was driving without a valid drivers license, and (ii) the defendant was not covered by an automobile liability policy.

(b2) **When a Motor Vehicle Becomes Property Subject to Order of Forfeiture; Felony Speeding to Elude Arrest. --** A judge may determine whether the vehicle driven at the time of the offense becomes subject to an order of forfeiture. The determination may be made at any of the following times:

(1) A sentencing hearing for the underlying felony speeding to elude arrest offense.

(2) A separate hearing after conviction of the defendant.

(3) A forfeiture hearing held at least 60 days after the defendant failed to appear at the scheduled trial for the underlying offense, and the defendant's order of arrest for failing to appear has not been set aside.

The vehicle shall become subject to an order of forfeiture if the greater weight of the evidence shows that the defendant is guilty of felony speeding to elude arrest pursuant to G.S. 20-141.5(b) or (b1).

(c) **Duty of Prosecutor to Notify Possible Innocent Parties. --** In any case in which a prosecutor determines that a motor vehicle driven by a defendant may be subject to forfeiture under this section and the motor vehicle has not been permanently released to a nondefendant vehicle owner pursuant to G.S. 20-28.3(e1), a defendant owner pursuant to G.S. 20-28.3(e2), or a lienholder, pursuant to G.S. 20-28.3(e3), the prosecutor shall notify the defendant, each motor vehicle owner, and each lienholder that the motor vehicle may be subject to forfeiture and that the defendant, motor vehicle owner, or the lienholder may intervene to protect that person's interest. The notice may be served by any means reasonably likely to provide actual notice, and shall be served at least 10 days before the hearing at which an order of forfeiture may be entered.

(c1) **Motor Vehicles Involved in Accidents.** -- If a motor vehicle subject to forfeiture was damaged while the defendant operator was committing the underlying offense resulting in seizure, or was damaged incident to the seizure of the motor vehicle, the Division shall determine the name of any insurance companies that are the insurers of record with the Division for the motor vehicle at the time of the seizure or that may otherwise be liable for repair to the motor vehicle. In any case where a seized motor vehicle was involved in an accident, the Division shall notify the insurance companies that the claim for insurance proceeds for damage to the seized motor vehicle shall be paid to the clerk of superior court of the county where the motor vehicle driver was charged to be held and disbursed pursuant to further orders of the court. Any insurance company that receives written or other actual notice of seizure pursuant to this section shall not be relieved of any legal obligation under any contract of insurance unless the claim for property damage to the seized motor vehicle minus the policy owner's deductible is paid directly to the clerk of court. The insurance company paying insurance proceeds to the clerk of court pursuant to this section shall be immune from suit by the motor vehicle owner for any damages alleged to have occurred as a result of the motor vehicle seizure. The proceeds shall be held by the clerk. The clerk shall disburse the insurance proceeds pursuant to further orders of the court.

(d) **Forfeiture Hearing.** -- Unless a motor vehicle that has been seized pursuant to G.S. 20-28.3 has been permanently released to an innocent owner pursuant to G.S. 20-28.3(e1), a defendant owner pursuant to G.S. 20-28.3(e2), or to a lienholder pursuant to G.S. 20-28.3(e3), the court shall conduct a hearing on the forfeiture of the motor vehicle. The hearing may be held at the sentencing hearing on the underlying offense resulting in seizure, at a separate hearing after conviction of the defendant, or at a separate forfeiture hearing held not less than 60 days after the defendant failed to appear at the scheduled trial for the underlying offense and the defendant's order of arrest for failing to appear has not been set aside. If at the forfeiture hearing, the judge determines that the motor vehicle is subject to forfeiture pursuant to this section and proper notice of the hearing has been given, the judge shall order the motor vehicle forfeited. If at the sentencing hearing or at a forfeiture hearing, the judge determines that the motor vehicle is subject to forfeiture pursuant to this section and proper notice of the hearing has been given, the judge shall order the motor vehicle forfeited unless another

motor vehicle owner establishes, by the greater weight of the evidence, that such motor vehicle owner is an innocent owner as defined in this section, in which case the trial judge shall order the motor vehicle released to the innocent owner pursuant to the provisions of subsection (e) of this section. In any case where the motor vehicle is ordered forfeited, the judge shall:

(1) a. Authorize the sale of the motor vehicle at public sale or allow the county board of education to retain the motor vehicle for its own use pursuant to G.S. 20-28.5; or

b. Order the motor vehicle released to a lienholder pursuant to the provisions of subsection (f) of this section; and

(2) a. Order any proceeds of sale or insurance proceeds held by the clerk of court to be disbursed to the county board of education; and

b. Order any outstanding insurance claims be assigned to the county board of education in the event the motor vehicle has been damaged in an accident incident to the seizure of the motor vehicle.

If the judge determines that the motor vehicle is subject to forfeiture pursuant to this section, but that notice as required by subsection (c) has not been given, the judge shall continue the forfeiture proceeding until adequate notice has been given. In no circumstance shall the sentencing of the defendant be delayed as a result of the failure of the prosecutor to give adequate notice.

(e) **Release of Vehicle to Innocent Motor Vehicle Owner.** -- At a forfeiture hearing, if a nondefendant motor vehicle owner establishes by the greater weight of the evidence that: (i) the motor vehicle was being driven by a person who was not the only motor vehicle owner or had no ownership interest in the motor vehicle at the time of the underlying offense and (ii) the petitioner is an "innocent owner", as defined by this section, a judge shall order the motor vehicle released to that owner, conditioned upon payment of all towing and storage charges incurred as a result of the seizure and impoundment of the motor vehicle.

Release to an innocent owner shall only be ordered upon satisfactory proof of:

(1) The identity of the person as a motor vehicle owner;

(2) The existence of financial responsibility to the extent required by Article 13 of this Chapter or by the laws of the state in which the vehicle is registered; and

(3) Repealed by Session Laws 1998-182, s. 2, effective December 1, 1998.

(4) The execution of:

a. An impaired driving acknowledgment as defined in subdivision (a1)(1a) of this section if the seizure was for an offense involving impaired driving; or

b. A speeding to elude arrest acknowledgment as defined in subdivision (a1)(8) of this section if the seizure was for violation of G.S. 20-141.5(b) or (b1).

If the nondefendant owner is a lessor, the release shall also be conditioned upon the lessor agreeing not to sell, give, or otherwise transfer possession of the forfeited motor vehicle to the defendant or any person acting on the defendant's behalf. A lessor who refuses to sell, give, or transfer possession of a seized motor vehicle to the defendant or any person acting on the behalf of the defendant shall not be liable for damages arising out of the refusal.

No motor vehicle subject to forfeiture under this section shall be released to a nondefendant motor vehicle owner if the records of the Division indicate the motor vehicle owner had previously signed an impaired driving acknowledgment or a speeding to elude arrest acknowledgment, as required by this section, and the same person was operating the motor vehicle at the time of the current seizure unless the innocent owner shows by the greater weight of the evidence that the motor vehicle owner has taken all reasonable precautions to prevent the use of the motor vehicle by this particular person and immediately reports, upon discovery, any unauthorized use to the appropriate law enforcement agency. A determination by the court at the forfeiture hearing held pursuant to subsection (d) of this section that the petitioner is not an innocent owner is a final judgment and is immediately appealable to the Court of Appeals.

(f) **Release to Lienholder.** -- At a forfeiture hearing, the trial judge shall order a forfeited motor vehicle released to the lienholder upon payment of all towing and storage charges incurred as a result of the seizure of the motor vehicle if the judge determines, by the greater weight of the evidence, that:

(1) The lienholder's interest has been perfected and appears on the title to the forfeited vehicle;

(2) The lienholder agrees not to sell, give, or otherwise transfer possession of the forfeited motor vehicle to the defendant or to the motor vehicle owner who owned the motor vehicle immediately prior to forfeiture, or any person acting on the defendant's or motor vehicle owner's behalf;

(3) The forfeited motor vehicle had not previously been released to the lienholder;

(4) The owner is in default under the terms of the security instrument evidencing the interest of the lienholder and as a consequence of the default the lienholder is entitled to possession of the motor vehicle; and

(5) The lienholder agrees to sell the motor vehicle in accordance with the terms of its agreement and pursuant to the provisions of Part 6 of Article 9 of Chapter 25 of the General Statutes. Upon the sale of the motor vehicle, the lienholder will pay to the clerk of court of the county in which the vehicle was forfeited all proceeds from the sale, less the amount of the lien in favor of the lienholder, and any towing and storage costs paid by the lienholder.

A lienholder who refuses to sell, give, or transfer possession of a forfeited motor vehicle to the defendant, the vehicle owner who owned the motor vehicle immediately prior to forfeiture, or any person acting on the behalf of the defendant or motor vehicle owner shall not be liable for damages arising out of such refusal. The defendant, the motor vehicle owner who owned the motor vehicle immediately prior to forfeiture, and any person acting on the defendant's or motor vehicle owner's behalf are prohibited from purchasing the motor vehicle at any sale conducted by the lienholder.

(g) Repealed by Session Laws 1998-182, s. 2, effective December 1, 1998.

(h) Any order issued pursuant to this section authorizing the release of a seized vehicle shall require the payment of all towing and storage charges incurred as a result of the seizure and impoundment of the motor vehicle. This requirement shall not be waived.

History.
1983, c. 435, s. 21; 1983 (Reg. Sess., 1984), c. 1101, s. 19; 1989 (Reg. Sess., 1990), c. 1024, s. 6; 1997-379, s. 1.1;1997-456, s. 30;1998-182, s. 2;1999-406, ss. 11, 12, 17; 2000-169, s. 28;2001-362, s. 7;2006-253, s. 31;2007-493, ss. 7, 8, 21; 2013-243, s. 1;2013-410, s. 18(a);2015-241, s. 27.3(a)

EDITOR'S NOTE. --
Session Laws 1999-406, s. 18, states that the act does not obligate the General Assembly to appropriate additional funds, and that the act shall be implemented with funds available or appropriated to the Department of Transportation and the Administrative Office of the Courts.

Subdivisions (a1)(1), (1a) and (1b) as amended by Session Laws 2013-243, s. 1, were renumbered as subdivisions (a1)(1a), (8), and (1), respectively, at the direction of the Revisor of Statutes.

EFFECT OF AMENDMENTS. --
Session Laws 2006-253, s. 31, effective December 1, 2006, and applicable to offenses committed on or after

that date, rewrote subdivisions (a1)(1) and (2), and subsections (b) and (b1).

Session Laws 2007-493, ss. 7, 8 and 21, effective August 30, 2007, in subdivision (a)(1), deleted "20-17.2," preceding "or 20-138.5"; in subdivisions (b)(1) and (b1) (1), inserted "sentencing"; and in the last sentence of subsections (b) and (b1), substituted "defendant is guilty of an offense involving impaired" for "underlying offense involved impaired." For applicability provisions, see Editor's note.

Session Laws 2013-243, s. 1, effective December 1, 2013, added "forfeiture for felony speeding to elude arrest" in the section heading; rewrote subsections (a1) and (e); added subsection (b2); substituted "offense resulting in seizure" for "offense involving impaired driving" in subsections (c1) and (d). For applicability, see Editor's note.

Session Laws 2013-410, s. 18(a), effective December 1, 2013, in sub-subdivision (a1)(2)e., substituted "a rental car company as defined in G.S. 66-201(a) and the vehicle was driven by a person who is listed as" for "is," and inserted "on the rental agreement as defined in G.S. 66-201" and made minor stylistic changes.

Session Laws 2015-241, s. 27.3(a), effective July 1, 2015, added subdivision (a1)(9).

HARMLESS ERROR. --Although the trial court should have submitted the aggravating factor in G.S. 20-179(c)(2), providing that at the time of the offense, defendant was driving while defendant's license was revoked, as defined by G.S. 20-28, and the revocation was an impaired driving revocation under G.S. 20-28.2(a), the error was harmless beyond a reasonable doubt. Defendant's driving record, admitted by the State, showed that defendant's driver's license was indefinitely revoked due to an impaired driving conviction and that the license had not been reinstated, which meant that evidence of the aggravating factor was overwhelming and uncontroverted such that a sentence beyond the statutory maximum could be imposed. State v. Coffey, 189 N.C. App. 382, 658 S.E.2d 73 (2008).

CITED in Old Salem Foreign Car Serv., Inc. v. Webb, 159 N.C. App. 93, 582 S.E.2d 673 (2003).

LEGAL PERIODICALS. --

For 1997 legislative survey, see 20 Campbell L. Rev. 417.

§ 20-28.3. Seizure, impoundment, forfeiture of motor vehicles for offenses involving impaired driving while license revoked or without license and insurance, and for felony speeding to elude arrest

(a) **Motor Vehicles Subject to Seizure for Impaired Driving Offenses.** -- A motor vehicle that is driven by a person who is charged with an offense involving impaired driving is subject to seizure if:

(1) At the time of the violation, the drivers license of the person driving the motor vehicle was revoked as a result of a prior

impaired driving license revocation as defined in G.S. 20-28.2(a); or

(2) At the time of the violation:

a. The person was driving without a valid drivers license, and

b. The driver was not covered by an automobile liability policy.

For the purposes of this subsection, a person who has a complete defense, pursuant to G.S. 20-35, to a charge of driving without a drivers license, shall be considered to have had a valid drivers license at the time of the violation.

(a1) **Motor Vehicles Subject to Seizure for Felony Speeding to Elude Arrest.** -- A motor vehicle is subject to seizure if it is driven by a person who is charged with the offense of felony speeding to elude arrest pursuant to G.S. 20-141.5(b) or (b1).

(b) **Duty of Officer.** -- If the charging officer has probable cause to believe that a motor vehicle driven by the defendant may be subject to forfeiture under this section, the officer shall seize the motor vehicle and have it impounded. If the officer determines prior to seizure that the motor vehicle had been reported stolen, the officer shall not seize the motor vehicle pursuant to this section. If the officer determines prior to seizure that the motor vehicle was a rental vehicle driven by a person not listed as an authorized driver on the rental contract, the officer shall not seize the motor vehicle pursuant to this section, but shall make a reasonable effort to notify the owner of the rental vehicle that the vehicle was stopped and that the driver of the vehicle was not listed as an authorized driver on the rental contract. Probable cause may be based on the officer's personal knowledge, reliable information conveyed by another officer, records of the Division, or other reliable sources. The seizing officer shall notify the Division as soon as practical but no later than 24 hours after seizure of the motor vehicle of the seizure in accordance with procedures established by the Division.

(b1) **Written Notification of Impoundment.** -- Within 48 hours of receipt within regular business hours of the notice of seizure, the Division shall issue written notification of impoundment to any lienholder of record and to any motor vehicle owner who was not operating the motor vehicle at the time of the offense. A notice of seizure received outside regular business hours shall be considered to have been received at the start of the next business day. The notification of impoundment shall be sent by first-class mail to the most recent address contained in the Division's records. If the motor vehicle is registered in another state, notice shall be sent to the address shown on the records of the state where the motor vehicle is registered. This written notification shall provide notice that the motor vehicle has been seized, state the reason for the seizure and the procedure for requesting release of the motor vehicle. Additionally, if the motor vehicle was damaged while the operator was committing an offense resulting in seizure or incident to the seizure, the Division shall issue written notification of the seizure to the owner's insurance company of record and to any other insurance companies that may be insuring other motor vehicles involved in the accident. The Division shall prohibit title to a seized motor vehicle from being transferred by a motor vehicle owner unless authorized by court order.

(b2) **Additional Notification to Lienholders.** -- In addition to providing written notification pursuant to subsection (b1) of this section, within eight hours of receipt within regular business hours of the notice of seizure, the Division shall notify by facsimile any lienholder of record that has provided the Division with a designated facsimile number for notification of impoundment. The facsimile notification of impoundment shall state that the vehicle has been seized, state the reason for the seizure, and notify the lienholder of the additional written notification that will be provided pursuant to subsection (b1) of this section. The Division shall establish procedures to allow a lienholder to provide one designated facsimile number for notification of impoundment for any vehicle for which the lienholder is a lienholder of record and shall maintain a centralized database of the provided facsimile numbers. The lienholder must provide a facsimile number at which the Division may give notification of impoundment at anytime.

(c) **Review by Magistrate.** -- Upon determining that there is probable cause for seizing a motor vehicle, the seizing officer shall present to a magistrate within the county where the driver was charged an affidavit of impoundment setting forth the basis upon which the motor vehicle has been or will be seized for forfeiture. The magistrate shall review the affidavit of impoundment and if the magistrate determines the requirements of this section have been met, shall order the motor vehicle held. The magistrate may request additional information and may hear from the defendant if the defendant is present. If the magistrate determines the requirements of this section have not been met, the magistrate shall order the motor vehicle released to a motor vehicle owner upon payment of towing and storage fees. If the motor vehicle has not yet been seized, and the magistrate determines that seizure is appropriate, the magistrate shall issue an order of seizure of the motor vehicle. The magistrate shall provide a copy of the order of seizure to the clerk of court. The clerk shall provide copies of the order of seizure to the district attorney and the attorney for the county board of education.

(c1) **Effecting an Order of Seizure.** -- An order of seizure shall be valid anywhere in the State. Any officer with territorial jurisdiction and who has subject matter jurisdiction for violations of this Chapter may use such force as may be reasonable to seize the motor vehicle and to enter upon the property of the defendant to accomplish the seizure. An officer who has probable cause to believe the motor vehicle is concealed or stored on private property of a person other than the defendant may obtain a search warrant to enter upon that property for the purpose of seizing the motor vehicle.

(d) **Custody of Motor Vehicle.** -- Unless the motor vehicle is towed pursuant to a statewide or regional contract, or a contract with the county board of education, the seized motor vehicle shall be towed by a commercial towing company designated by the law enforcement agency that seized the motor vehicle. Seized motor vehicles not towed pursuant to a statewide or regional contract or a contract with a county board of education shall be retrieved from the commercial towing company within a reasonable time, not to exceed 10 business days, by the county board of education or their agent who must pay towing and storage fees to the commercial towing company when the motor vehicle is retrieved. If either a statewide or regional contractor, or the county board of education, chooses to contract for local towing services, all towing companies on the towing list for each law enforcement agency with jurisdiction within the county shall be given written notice and an opportunity to submit proposals prior to a contract for local towing services being awarded. The seized motor vehicle is under the constructive possession of the county board of education for the county in which the operator of the vehicle is charged at the time the vehicle is delivered to a location designated by the county board of education or delivered to its agent pending release or sale, or in the event a statewide or regional contract is in place, under the constructive possession of the State Surplus Property Agency on behalf of the State at the time the vehicle is delivered to a location designated by the State Surplus Property Agency or delivered to its agent pending release or sale. Absent a statewide or regional contract that provides otherwise, each county board of education may elect to have seized motor vehicles stored on property owned or leased by the county board of education and charge a reasonable fee for storage, not to exceed ten dollars ($ 10.00) per calendar day. In the alternative, the county board of education may contract with a commercial towing and storage facility or other private entity for the towing, storage, and disposal of seized motor vehicles, and a storage fee of not more than ten dollars ($ 10.00) per calendar day may be charged. Except for gross negligence or intentional misconduct, neither the State Surplus Property Agency, the county board of education, nor any of their employees, shall be liable to the owner or lienholder for damage to or loss of the motor vehicle or its contents, or to the owner of personal property in a seized vehicle, during the time the motor vehicle is being towed or stored pursuant to this subsection.

(e) **Release of Motor Vehicle Pending Trial.** -- A motor vehicle owner, other than the driver at the time of the underlying offense resulting in the seizure, may apply to the clerk of superior court in the county where the charges are pending for pretrial release of the motor vehicle.

The clerk shall release the motor vehicle to a nondefendant motor vehicle owner conditioned upon payment of all towing and storage charges incurred as a result of seizure and impoundment of the motor vehicle under the following conditions:

(1) The motor vehicle has been seized for not less than 24 hours;

(2) Repealed by Session Laws 1998-182, s. 3, effective December 1, 1998.

(3) A bond in an amount equal to the fair market value of the motor vehicle as defined by G.S. 20-28.2 has been executed and is secured by a cash deposit in the full amount of the bond, by a recordable deed of trust to real property in the full amount of the bond, by a bail bond under G.S. 58-71-1(2), or by at least one solvent surety, payable to the county school fund and conditioned on return of the motor vehicle, in substantially the same condition as it was at the time of seizure and without any new or additional liens or encumbrances, on the day of any hearing scheduled and noticed by the district attorney under G.S. 20-28.2(c), unless the motor vehicle has been permanently released;

(4) Execution of either:

a. An impaired driving acknowledgment as described in G.S. 20-28.2(a1) (1a) if the seizure was for an offense involving impaired driving; or

b. A speeding to elude arrest acknowledgment as defined in G.S. 20-28.2(a1)(8) if the seizure was for violation of G.S. 20-141.5(b) or (b1).

(5) A check of the records of the Division indicates that the requesting motor vehicle owner has not previously executed an acknowledgment naming the operator of the seized motor vehicle; and

(6) A bond posted to secure the release of this motor vehicle under this subsection has not been previously ordered forfeited under G.S. 20-28.5.

In the event a nondefendant motor vehicle owner who obtains temporary possession of a seized motor vehicle pursuant to this subsection does not return the motor vehicle on the day of the forfeiture hearing as noticed by the district attorney under G.S. 20-28.2(c) or otherwise violates a condition of pretrial release of the seized motor vehicle as set forth in this subsection, the bond posted shall be ordered forfeited and an order of seizure shall be issued by the court. Additionally, a nondefendant motor vehicle owner or lienholder who willfully violates any condition of pretrial release may be held in civil or criminal contempt.

(e1) **Pretrial Release of Motor Vehicle to Innocent Owner.** -- A nondefendant motor vehicle owner may file a petition with the clerk of court seeking a pretrial determination that the petitioner is an innocent owner. The clerk shall consider the petition and make a determination as soon as may be feasible. At any proceeding conducted pursuant to this subsection, the clerk is not required to determine the issue of forfeiture, only the issue of whether the petitioner is an innocent owner. If the clerk determines that the petitioner is an innocent owner, the clerk shall release the motor vehicle to the petitioner subject to the same conditions as if the petitioner were an innocent owner under G.S. 20-28.2(e). The clerk shall send a copy of the order authorizing or denying release of the vehicle to the district attorney and the attorney for the county board of education. An order issued under this subsection finding that the petitioner failed to establish that the petitioner is an innocent owner may be reconsidered by the court as part of the forfeiture hearing conducted pursuant to G.S. 20-28.2(d).

(e2) **Pretrial Release of Motor Vehicle to Defendant Owner.** --

(1) If the seizure was for an offense involving impaired driving, a defendant motor vehicle owner may file a petition with the clerk of court seeking a pretrial determination that the defendant's license was not revoked pursuant to an impaired driving license revocation as defined in G.S. 20-28.2(a). The clerk shall schedule a hearing before a judge of the division in which the underlying criminal charge is pending for a hearing to be held within 10 business days or as soon thereafter as may be feasible. Notice of the hearing shall be given to the defendant, the district attorney, and the attorney for the county board of education. The clerk shall forward a copy of the petition to the district attorney for the district attorney's review. If, based on available information, the district attorney determines that the defendant's motor vehicle is not subject to forfeiture, the district attorney may note the State's consent to the release

of the motor vehicle on the petition and return the petition to the clerk of court who shall enter an order releasing the motor vehicle to the defendant upon payment of all towing and storage charges incurred as a result of the seizure and impoundment of the motor vehicle, subject to the satisfactory proof of the identity of the defendant as a motor vehicle owner and the existence of financial responsibility to the extent required by Article 13 of this Chapter, and no hearing shall be held. The clerk shall send a copy of the order of release to the attorney for the county board of education. At any pretrial hearing conducted pursuant to this subdivision, the court is not required to determine the issue of the underlying offense of impaired driving only the existence of a prior drivers license revocation as an impaired driving license revocation. Accordingly, the State shall not be required to prove the underlying offense of impaired driving. An order issued under this subdivision finding that the defendant failed to establish that the defendant's license was not revoked pursuant to an impaired driving license revocation as defined in G.S. 20-28.2(a) may be reconsidered by the court as part of the forfeiture hearing conducted pursuant to G.S. 20-28.2(d).

(2) If the seizure was for a felony speeding to elude arrest offense, a defendant motor vehicle owner may apply to the clerk of superior court in the county where the charges are pending for pretrial release of the motor vehicle. The clerk shall release the motor vehicle to the defendant motor vehicle owner conditioned upon payment of all towing and storage charges incurred as a result of seizure and impoundment of the motor vehicle under the following conditions:

a. The motor vehicle has been seized for not less than 24 hours;

b. A bond in an amount equal to the fair market value of the motor vehicle as defined by G.S. 20-28.2 has been executed and is secured by a cash deposit in the full amount of the bond, by a recordable deed of trust to real property in the full amount of the bond, by a bail bond under G.S. 58-71-1(2), or by at least one solvent surety, payable to the county school fund and conditioned on return of the motor vehicle, in substantially the same condition as it was at the time of seizure and without any new or additional liens or encumbrances, on the day of any hearing scheduled and noticed by the district attorney under G.S. 20-28.2(c), unless the motor vehicle has been permanently released;

c. A bond posted to secure the release of this motor vehicle under this subdivision has not been previously ordered forfeited under G.S. 20-28.5.

In the event a defendant motor vehicle owner who obtains temporary possession of a seized motor vehicle pursuant to this subdivision does not return the motor vehicle on the day of the forfeiture hearing as noticed by the district attorney under G.S. 20-28.2(c) or otherwise violates a condition of pretrial release of the seized motor vehicle as set forth in this subdivision, the bond posted shall be ordered forfeited, and an order of seizure shall be issued by the court. Additionally, a defendant motor vehicle owner who willfully violates any condition of pretrial release may be held in civil or criminal contempt.

(e3) **Pretrial Release of Motor Vehicle to Lienholder. --**

(1) A lienholder may file a petition with the clerk of court requesting the court to order pretrial release of a seized motor vehicle. The lienholder shall serve a copy of the petition on all interested parties which shall include the registered owner, the titled owner, the district attorney, and the county board of education attorney. Upon 10 days' prior notice of the date, time, and location of the hearing sent by the lienholder to all interested parties, a judge, after a hearing, shall order a seized motor vehicle released to the lienholder conditioned upon payment of all towing and storage costs incurred as a result of the seizure and impoundment of the motor vehicle if the judge determines, by the greater weight of the evidence, that:

a. Default on the obligation secured by the motor vehicle has occurred;

b. As a consequence of default, the lienholder is entitled to possession of the motor vehicle;

c. The lienholder agrees to sell the motor vehicle in accordance with the terms of its agreement and pursuant to the provisions of Part 6 of Article 9 of Chapter 25 of the General Statutes. Upon sale of the motor vehicle, the lienholder will pay to the clerk of court of the county in which the driver was charged all proceeds from the sale, less the amount of the lien in favor of the lienholder, and any towing and storage costs paid by the lienholder;

d. The lienholder agrees not to sell, give, or otherwise transfer possession of the seized motor vehicle while the motor vehicle is subject to forfeiture, or the forfeited motor vehicle after the forfeiture hearing, to the defendant or the motor vehicle owner; and

e. The seized motor vehicle while the motor vehicle is subject to forfeiture, or the forfeited motor vehicle after the forfeiture hearing, had not previously been released to the lienholder as a result of a prior seizure involving the same defendant or motor vehicle owner.

(2) The clerk of superior court may order a seized vehicle released to the lienholder conditioned upon payment of all towing and storage costs incurred as a result of the seizure and impoundment of the motor vehicle at any time when all interested parties have, in writing, waived any rights that they may have to notice and a hearing, and the lienholder has agreed to the provision of subdivision (1)d. above. A lienholder who refuses to sell, give, or transfer possession of a seized motor vehicle while the motor vehicle is subject to forfeiture, or a forfeited motor vehicle after the forfeiture hearing, to:

a. The defendant;

b. The motor vehicle owner who owned the motor vehicle immediately prior to seizure pending the forfeiture hearing, or to forfeiture after the forfeiture hearing; or

c. Any person acting on the behalf of the defendant or the motor vehicle owner,

shall not be liable for damages arising out of such refusal. However, any subsequent violation of the conditions of release by the lienholder shall be punishable by civil or criminal contempt.

(f), (g) Repealed by Session Laws 1998-182, s. 3, effective December 1, 1998.

(h) **Insurance Proceeds. --** In the event a motor vehicle is damaged incident to the conduct of the defendant which gave rise to the defendant's arrest and seizure of the motor vehicle pursuant to this section, the county board of education, or its authorized designee, is authorized to negotiate the county board of education's interest with the insurance company and to compromise and accept settlement of any claim for damages. Property insurance proceeds accruing to the defendant, or other owner of the seized motor vehicle, shall be paid by the responsible insurance company directly to the clerk of superior court in the county where the motor vehicle driver was charged. If the motor vehicle is declared a total loss by the insurance company liable for the damages to the motor vehicle, the clerk of superior court, upon application of the county board of education, shall enter an order that the motor vehicle be released

to the insurance company upon payment into the court of all insurance proceeds for damage to the motor vehicle after payment of towing and storage costs and all valid liens. The clerk of superior court shall provide the Division with a certified copy of the order entered pursuant to this subsection, and the Division shall transfer title to the insurance company or to such other person or entity as may be designated by the insurance company. Insurance proceeds paid to the clerk of court pursuant to this subsection shall be subject to forfeiture pursuant to G.S. 20-28.5 and shall be disbursed pursuant to further orders of the court. An affected motor vehicle owner or lienholder who objects to any agreed upon settlement under this subsection may file an independent claim with the insurance company for any additional monies believed owed. Notwithstanding any other provisions in this Chapter, nothing in this section or G.S. 20-28.2 shall require an insurance company to make payments in excess of those required pursuant to its policy of insurance on the seized motor vehicle.

(i) **Expedited Sale of Seized Motor Vehicles in Certain Cases. --** In order to avoid additional liability for towing and storage costs pending resolution of the criminal proceedings of the defendant, the State Surplus Property Agency or county board of education may, after expiration of 90 days from the date of seizure, sell any motor vehicle having a fair market value of one thousand five hundred dollars ($ 1,500) or less. The county board of education may also sell a motor vehicle, regardless of the fair market value, any time the outstanding towing and storage costs exceed eighty-five percent (85%) of the fair market value of the vehicle, or with the consent of all the motor vehicle owners. Any sale conducted pursuant to this subsection shall be conducted in accordance with the provisions of G.S. 20-28.5(a) or G.S. 20-28.5(a1), as applicable, and the proceeds of the sale, after the payment of outstanding towing and storage costs or reimbursement of towing and storage costs paid by a person other than the defendant, shall be deposited with the clerk of superior court. If an order of forfeiture is entered by the court, the court shall order the proceeds held by the clerk to be disbursed as provided in G.S. 20-28.5(b). If the court determines that the motor vehicle is not subject to forfeiture, the court shall order the proceeds held by the clerk to be disbursed first to pay the sale, towing, and storage costs, second to pay outstanding liens on the motor vehicle, and the balance to be paid to the motor vehicle owners.

(j) **Retrieval of Certain Personal Property. --** At reasonable times, the entity charged with storing the motor vehicle may permit owners of personal property not affixed to the motor vehicle to retrieve those items from the motor vehicle, provided satisfactory proof of ownership of the motor vehicle or the items of personal property is presented to the storing entity.

(k) **County Board of Education Right to Appear and Participate in Proceedings.** -- The attorney for the county board of education shall be given notice of all proceedings regarding offenses related to a motor vehicle subject to forfeiture under this section. However, the notice requirement under this subsection does not apply to proceedings conducted under G.S. 20-28.3(e1). The attorney for the county board of education shall also have the right to appear and to be heard on all issues relating to the seizure, possession, release, forfeiture, sale, and other matters related to the seized vehicle under this section. With the prior consent of the county board of education, the district attorney may delegate to the attorney for the county board of education any or all of the duties of the district attorney under this section. Clerks of superior court, law enforcement agencies, and all other agencies with information relevant to the seizure, impoundment, release, or forfeiture of motor vehicles are authorized and directed to provide county boards of education with access to that information and to do so by electronic means when existing technology makes this type of transmission possible.

(*l*) **Payment of Fees Upon Conviction.** -- If the driver of a motor vehicle seized pursuant to this section is convicted of the underlying offense resulting in the seizure of a motor vehicle pursuant to this section, the defendant shall be ordered to pay as restitution to the county board of education, the motor vehicle owner, or the lienholder the cost paid or owing for the towing, storage, and sale of the motor vehicle to the extent the costs were not covered by the proceeds from the forfeiture and sale of the motor vehicle. If the underlying offense resulting in the seizure is felony speeding to elude arrest pursuant to G.S. 20-141.5(b) or (b1) and the defendant's conviction is for misdemeanor speeding to elude arrest pursuant to G.S. 20-141.5(a), whether or not the reduced charge is by plea agreement, the defendant shall be ordered to pay as restitution to the county board of education, the motor vehicle owner, or the lienholder the cost paid or owing for the towing and storage of the motor vehicle. In addition, a civil judgment for the costs under this section in favor of the party to whom the restitution is owed shall be docketed by the clerk of superior court. If the defendant is sentenced to an active term of imprisonment, the civil judgment shall become effective and be docketed when the defendant's conviction becomes final. If the defendant is placed on probation, the civil judgment in the amount found by a judge during the probation revocation or termination hearing to be due shall become effective and be docketed by the clerk when the defendant's probation is revoked or terminated.

(m) **Trial Priority.** -- District court trials of offenses involving forfeitures of motor vehicles pursuant to G.S. 20-28.2 shall be scheduled on the arresting officer's next court date or within 30 days of the offense, whichever comes first.

Once scheduled, the case shall not be continued unless all of the following conditions are met:

(1) A written motion for continuance is filed with notice given to the opposing party prior to the motion being heard.

(2) The judge makes a finding of a "compelling reason" for the continuance.

(3) The motion and finding are attached to the court case record.

Upon a determination of guilt, the issue of vehicle forfeiture shall be heard by the judge immediately, or as soon thereafter as feasible, and the judge shall issue the appropriate orders pursuant to G.S. 20-28.2(d).

Should a defendant appeal the conviction to superior court, any party who has not previously been heard on a petition for pretrial release under subsection (e1) or (e3) of this section or any party whose motor vehicle has not been the subject of a forfeiture hearing held pursuant to G.S. 20-28.2(d) may be heard on a petition for pretrial release pursuant to subsection (e1) or (e3) of this section. The provisions of subsection (e) of this section shall also apply to seized motor vehicles pending trial in superior court. Where a motor vehicle was released pursuant to subsection (e) of this section pending trial in district court, the release of the motor vehicle continues, and the terms and conditions of the original bond remain the same as those required for the initial release of the motor vehicle under subsection (e) of this section, pending the resolution of the underlying offense involving impaired driving in superior court.

(n) Any order issued pursuant to this section authorizing the release of a seized vehicle shall require the payment of all towing and storage charges incurred as a result of the seizure and impoundment of the motor vehicle. This requirement shall not be waived.

History.
1997-379, s. 1.2;1997-456, s. 31;1998-182, s. 3;1998-217, s. 62(a)-(c); 2000-169, s. 29;2001-362, ss. 1, 2, 3, 4, 5, 6; 2001-487, s. 9;2006-253, s. 32;2013-243, s. 2;2015-241, s. 27.3(b)

EDITOR'S NOTE. --

The subdivisions in subsection (e3) have been redesignated at the direction of the Revisor of Statutes.

Session Laws 2009-461, ss. 1 and 2, provide: "SECTION 1. Notwithstanding the authority of the

Secretary of Crime Control and Public Safety to adopt rules for the maintenance and operation of a Highway Patrol rotation wrecker system, the amendments to 14A NCAC 09H.0321(10), which became effective on July 18, 2008, are void and unenforceable to the extent such amendments:

"(1) Limit submission of initial applications and re-applications for inclusion in the Highway Patrol rotation wrecker list to an annual open enrollment period.

"(2) Limit vehicle storage fees to the maximum allowed by G.S. 20-28.3.

"(3) Require that towing and recovery fees be within fifteen percent (15%) of the median price charged within the applicable Highway Patrol Troop.

"Notwithstanding the limitations set out in this section, the Highway Patrol may require that wrecker services, when responding to rotation wrecker calls, charge reasonable fees for services rendered and that any fee charged for rotation services not exceed the wrecker service's charges for nonrotation service calls that provide the same service, labor, and conditions.

"SECTION 2.

The Secretary of Crime Control and Public Safety shall adopt amendments to 14A NCAC 09H.0321(10) to conform to the requirements of this act."

EFFECT OF AMENDMENTS. --

Session Laws 2006-253, s. 32, effective December 1, 2006, and applicable to offenses committed on or after that date, added "or without license and insurance" to the end of the section catchline and rewrote subsection (a).

Session Laws 2013-243, s. 2, effective December 1, 2013, added "and for felony speeding to elude arrest" in the section heading; substituted "the Division" for "the executive agency designated under subsection (b1) of this section" and "Division" for "executive agency" throughout; inserted "for Impaired Driving Offenses" in the subsection heading of subsection (a); rewrote the first and sixth sentences in subsection (b1); rewrote subdivision(e)(4); in subsection (e2), inserted the subdivision designation and "If the seizure was for an offense involving impaired driving" in subdivision (1) and added subdivision (2); in subsection (k), deleted "involving impaired driving" preceding "related to a motor vehicle" and added "under this section" at the end of the first sentence; in subsection (l), rewrote the first sentence and added the second sentence; and in subsection (m), deleted "impaired driving" following "District court trials of" in the first sentence; and made stylistic changes throughout. For applicability, see Editor's note.

Session Laws 2015-241, s. 27.3(b), effective July 1, 2015, in subsection (d), substituted "not to exceed 10 business days" for "not to exceed 10 days" in the second sentence, substituted "State Surplus Property Agency" for "Department of Public Instruction" twice in the fourth sentence, substituted "ten dollars ($10.00) per calendar day" for "ten dollars ($10.00) per day" in the fifth and sixth sentences, and in the seventh sentence inserted "neither the State Surplus Property Agency" and substituted "nor any of their

employees, shall be liable" for "or any of its employees, shall not be liable"; and in subsection (i), inserted "State Surplus Property Agency or" in the first sentence, and inserted "or G.S. 20-28.5(a1), as applicable" in the third sentence.

DWI SEIZURE STATUTES WERE DEEMED CONSTITUTIONAL in spite of a "law of the land" challenge, indicating that these statutes have a legitimate objective -- keeping impaired drivers and their cars off of the roads -- and that the means chosen to further the goals -- seizing the cars, even when they belong to people other than the drivers -- is directly related to said objective. State v. Chisholm, 135 N.C. App. 578, 521 S.E.2d 487 (1999).

CITED in Old Salem Foreign Car Serv., Inc. v. Webb, 159 N.C. App. 93, 582 S.E.2d 673 (2003); Bowles Auto., Inc. v. N.C. DMV, 203 N.C. App. 19, 690 S.E.2d 728 (2010), review denied, 364 N.C. 324, 700 S.E.2d 746, 2010 N.C. LEXIS 590 (2010).

OPINIONS OF THE ATTORNEY GENERAL

DUTY OF LOCAL BOARD OF EDUCATION. --Whenever a vehicle is towed by a company that is not under statewide or regional contract, the local board of education must retrieve the vehicle and pay the towing and storage charges within 10 days; the fact that the local board of education or the Department of Public Instruction has entered into a statewide or regional contract with another towing company is immaterial. See opinion of Attorney General to David E. Inabinett, Brinkley Walser, P.L.L.C., 2000 N.C. AG LEXIS 2 (1/14/2000).

§ 20-28.4. Release of impounded motor vehicles by judge

(a) **Release Upon Conclusion of Trial. --** If the driver of a motor vehicle seized pursuant to G.S. 20-28.3:

(1) Is subsequently not convicted of the underlying offense resulting in seizure due to dismissal or a finding of not guilty; or

(2) The judge at a forfeiture hearing conducted pursuant to G.S. 20-28.2(d) finds that the criteria for forfeiture have not otherwise been met; and

(3) The vehicle has not previously been released to a lienholder pursuant to G.S. 20-28.3(e3),

the seized motor vehicle or insurance proceeds held by the clerk of court pursuant to G.S. 20-28.2(c1) or G.S. 20-28.3(h) shall be released to the motor vehicle owner conditioned upon payment of towing and storage costs. The court shall not waive the payment of towing and storage costs. The court shall include in its order notice to the owner of the seized motor vehicle still being held, that within 30 days of the date of the court's order, the owner must make payment of the outstanding towing and storage costs for the motor vehicle and retrieve the motor vehicle, or give notice

Chapter 20

to Division of Motor Vehicles requesting a judicial hearing on the validity of any mechanics' lien on the motor vehicle for towing and storage costs.

(b) Notwithstanding G.S. 44A-2(d), if the owner of the seized motor vehicle does not obtain release of the vehicle within 30 days from the date of the court's order, the possessor of the seized motor vehicle has a mechanics' lien on the seized motor vehicle for the full amount of the towing and storage charges incurred since the motor vehicle was seized and may dispose of the seized motor vehicle pursuant to Article 1 of Chapter 44A of the General Statutes. Notice of the right to a judicial hearing on the validity of the mechanics' lien given to the owner of the motor vehicle in open court in accordance with subsection (a) of this section or delivery to the owner of the vehicle of a copy of the court's order entered in accordance with subsection (a) of this section shall satisfy the notice requirement of G.S. 44A-4(b).

History.
1997-379, s. 1.3;1998-182, s. 4;2001-362, s. 8;2004-128, s. 4;2013-243, s. 3

EFFECT OF AMENDMENTS. --
Session Laws 2004-128, s. 4, effective October 1, 2004, added subsection designations; added the last sentence in subsection (a); and added the last sentence in subsection (b).

Session Laws 2013-243, s. 3, effective December 1, 2013, substituted "the underlying offense resulting in seizure" for "an offense involving impaired driving" in subdivision (a)(1); and substituted "finds that the criteria for forfeiture have not otherwise been met" for "fails to find that the drivers license was revoked as a result of a prior impaired driving license revocation as defined in G.S. 20-28.2" in subdivision (a)(2). For applicability, see Editor's note.

CITED in Bowles Auto., Inc. v. N.C. DMV, 203 N.C. App. 19, 690 S.E.2d 728 (2010), review denied, 364 N.C. 324, 700 S.E.2d 746, 2010 N.C. LEXIS 590 (2010).

§ 20-28.5. Forfeiture of impounded motor vehicle or funds

(a) **Sale of Vehicle in Possession of County Board of Education.** -- A motor vehicle in the possession or constructive possession of a county board of education ordered forfeited and sold or a seized motor vehicle authorized to be sold pursuant to G.S. 20-28.3(i), shall be sold at a public sale conducted in accordance with the provisions of Article 12 of Chapter 160A of the General Statutes, applicable to sales authorized pursuant to G.S. 160A-266(a)(2), (3), or (4), subject to the notice requirements of this subsection, and shall be conducted by the county board of education or a person acting on its behalf. Notice of sale, including the date, time, location, and manner of sale, shall be given by

first-class mail to all motor vehicle owners of the vehicle to be sold at the address shown by the records of the Division. Written notice of sale shall also be given to all lienholders on file with the Division. Notice of sale shall be given to the Division in accordance with the procedures established by the Division. Notices required to be given under this subsection shall be mailed at least 10 days prior to the date of sale. A lienholder shall be permitted to purchase the motor vehicle at any such sale by bidding in the amount of its lien, if that should be the highest bid, without being required to tender any additional funds, other than the towing and storage fees. The county board of education, or its agent, shall not sell, give, or otherwise transfer possession of the forfeited motor vehicle to the defendant, the motor vehicle owner who owned the motor vehicle immediately prior to forfeiture, or any person acting on the defendant's or motor vehicle owner's behalf.

(a1) **Sale of Vehicle in Possession of the State Surplus Property Agency.** -- A motor vehicle in the possession or constructive possession of the State Surplus Property Agency ordered forfeited and sold or a seized motor vehicle authorized to be sold pursuant to G.S. 20-28.3(i) shall be sold at a public sale conducted in accordance with the provisions of Article 3A of Chapter 143 of the General Statutes, subject to the notice requirements of this subsection, and shall be conducted by the State Surplus Property Agency or a person acting on its behalf. Notice of sale, including the date, time, location, and manner of sale, shall be given by first-class mail to all motor vehicle owners of the vehicle to be sold at the address shown by the records of the Division. Written notice of sale shall also be given to all lienholders on file with the Division. Notice of sale shall be given to the Division in accordance with the procedures established by the State Surplus Property Agency. Notices required to be given under this subsection shall be mailed at least 10 days prior to the date of sale. A lienholder shall be permitted to purchase the motor vehicle at any such sale by bidding in the amount of its lien, if that should be the highest bid, without being required to tender any additional funds, other than the towing and storage fees. The State Surplus Property Agency, or its agent, shall not sell, give, or otherwise transfer possession of the forfeited motor vehicle to the defendant, the motor vehicle owner who owned the motor vehicle immediately prior to forfeiture, or any person acting on the defendant's or motor vehicle owner's behalf.

(b) **Proceeds of Sale.** -- Proceeds of any sale conducted under this section, G.S. 20-28.2(f)(5), or G.S. 20-28.3(e3)(3), shall first be applied to all costs incurred by the State Surplus Property Agency or county board of education and then to satisfy towing and storage costs. The balance of the proceeds of sale, if any, shall be used to satisfy any other existing liens of record that were properly recorded prior to the date of initial seizure of the vehicle. Any remaining balance shall be paid to the county school fund in the county in which the motor vehicle was ordered forfeited. If there is more than one school board in the county, then the net proceeds of sale, after reimbursement to the county board of education of reasonable administrative costs incurred in connection with the forfeiture and sale of the motor vehicle, shall be distributed in the same manner as fines and other forfeitures. The sale of a motor vehicle pursuant to this section shall be deemed to extinguish all existing liens on the motor vehicle and the motor vehicle shall be transferred free and clear of any liens.

(c) **Retention of Motor Vehicle.** -- A board of education may, at its option, retain any forfeited motor vehicle for its use upon payment of towing and storage costs. If the motor vehicle is retained, any valid lien of record at the time of the initial seizure of the motor vehicle shall be satisfied by the county board of education relieving the motor vehicle owner of all liability for the obligation secured by the motor vehicle. If there is more than one school board in the county, and the motor vehicle is retained by a board of education, then the fair market value of the motor vehicle, less the costs for towing, storage, reasonable administrative costs, and liens paid, shall be used to determine and pay the share due each of the school boards in the same manner as fines and other forfeitures.

(d) Repealed by Session Laws 1998-182, s. 5, effective December 1, 1998.

(e) **Order of Forfeiture; Appeals.** -- An order of forfeiture is stayed pending appeal of a conviction for an offense that is the basis for the order. When the conviction of an offense that is the basis for an order of forfeiture is appealed from district court, the issue of forfeiture shall be heard in superior court de novo. Appeal from a final order of forfeiture shall be to the Court of Appeals.

History.
1997-379, s. 1.4;1998-182, s. 5;1998-217, s. 62(d);1999-456, s. 11;2015-241, s. 27.3(c)

EFFECT OF AMENDMENTS. --

Session Laws 2015-241, s. 27.3(c), effective July 1, 2015, in subsection (a), substituted "Sale of Vehicle in Possession of County Board of Education" for "Sale" in the subsection heading, and inserted "in the possession or constructive possession of a county board of education" near the beginning of the first sentence; added subsection (a1); and substituted "all costs incurred by the State Surplus Property Agency or county board of education" for "the cost of sale" in subsection (b).

CITED in Old Salem Foreign Car Serv., Inc. v. Webb, 159 N.C. App. 93, 582 S.E.2d 673 (2003).

N.C. Gen. Stat. § 20-28.6

Repealed by Session Laws 1998-182, s. 6, effective December 1, 1998, and applicable to offenses committed, contracts entered, and motor vehicles seized on or after that date.

§ 20-28.7. Responsibility of Division of Motor Vehicles

The Division shall establish procedures by rule to provide for the orderly seizure, forfeiture, sale, and transfer of motor vehicles pursuant to the provisions of G.S. 20-28.2, 20-28.3, 20-28.4, and 20-28.5.

History.
1997-379, s. 1.6;1998-182, s. 7

§ 20-28.8. Reports to the Division

In any case in which a vehicle has been seized pursuant to G.S. 20-28.3, in addition to any other information that must be reported pursuant to this Chapter, the clerk of superior court shall report to the Division by electronic means the execution of an impaired driving acknowledgment as defined in G.S. 20-28.2(a1)(1a), a speeding to elude arrest acknowledgment as defined in G.S. 20-28.2(a1)(8), the entry of an order of forfeiture as defined in G.S. 20-28.2(a1)(4), and the entry of an order of release as defined in G.S. 20-28.3 and G.S. 20-28.4. Each report shall include any of the following information that has not previously been reported to the Division in the case: the name, address, and drivers license number of the defendant; the name, address, and drivers license number of the nondefendant motor vehicle owner, if known; and the make, model, year, vehicle identification number, state of registration, and vehicle registration plate number of the seized vehicle, if known.

History.
1998-182, s. 8;2013-243, s. 4

EFFECT OF AMENDMENTS. --

Session Laws 2013-243, s. 4, effective December 1, 2013, inserted "impaired driving" and "a speeding to elude arrest acknowledgment as defined in G.S. 20-28.2(a1)(8)" in the first sentence. For applicability, see Editor's note.

§ 20-28.9. Authority for the State Surplus Property Agency to administer a statewide or regional towing, storage, and sales program for vehicles forfeited

(a) The State Surplus Property Agency is authorized to enter into a contract for a statewide service or contracts for regional services to tow, store, process, maintain, and sell motor vehicles seized pursuant to G.S. 20-28.3. All motor vehicles seized under G.S. 20-28.3 shall be subject to contracts entered into pursuant to this section. Contracts shall be let by the State Surplus Property Agency in accordance with the provisions of Article 3 of Chapter 143 of the General Statutes. All contracts shall ensure the safety of the motor vehicles while held and any funds arising from the sale of any seized motor vehicle. The contract shall require the contractor to maintain and make available to the agency a computerized up-to-date inventory of all motor vehicles held under the contract, together with an accounting of all accrued charges, the status of the vehicle, and the county school fund to which the proceeds of sale are to be paid. The contract shall provide that the contractor shall pay the towing and storage charges owed on a seized vehicle to a commercial towing company at the time the seized vehicle is obtained from the commercial towing company, with the contractor being reimbursed this expense when the vehicle is released or sold. The State Surplus Property Agency shall not enter into any contract under this section under which the State will be obligated to pay a deficiency arising from the sale of any forfeited motor vehicle.

(b) The State Surplus Property Agency, through its contractor or contractors designated in accordance with subsection (a) of this section, may charge a reasonable fee for storage not to exceed ten dollars ($ 10.00) per calendar day for the storage of seized vehicles pursuant to G.S. 20-28.3.

(c) Repealed by Session Laws 2015-241, s. 27.3(d), effective July 1, 2015.

History.
1998-182, s. 8;2014-115, s. 2.2;2015-241, s. 27.3(d);2015-264, s. 38.3(a)

EFFECT OF AMENDMENTS. --
Session Laws 2014-115, s. 2.2, effective August 11, 2014, deleted "driving while impaired" preceding "vehicles" in the section heading.

Session Laws 2015-241, s. 27.3(d), effective July 1, 2015, twice substituted "State Surplus Property Agency" for "Department of Public Instruction" and twice substituted "State Surplus Property Agency" for "Department"; in subsection (a) added the fourth sentence; and deleted former subsection (c), relating to the collection of administrative fees.

Session Laws 2015-264, s. 38.3(a), effective July 1, 2015, deleted the former fourth sentence of subsection (a), which read "Nothing in this section shall be construed to prohibit the State Surplus Property Agency from entering into contracts pursuant to this section for some regions of the State while performing the work of towing, storing, processing, maintaining, and selling motor vehicles seized pursuant to G.S. 20-28.3 itself in other regions of the State."

§ 20-29. Surrender of license

Any person operating or in charge of a motor vehicle, when requested by an officer in uniform, or, in the event of accident in which the vehicle which he is operating or in charge of shall be involved, when requested by any other person, who shall refuse to write his name for the purpose of identification or to give his name and address and the name and address of the owner of such vehicle, or who shall give a false name or address, or who shall refuse, on demand of such officer or such other person, to produce his license and exhibit same to such officer or such other person for the purpose of examination, or who shall refuse to surrender his license on demand of the Division, or fail to produce same when requested by a court of this State, shall be guilty of a Class 2 misdemeanor. Pickup notices for drivers' licenses or revocation or suspension of license notices and orders or demands issued by the Division for the surrender of such licenses may be served and executed by patrolmen or other peace officers or may be served in accordance with G.S. 20-48. Patrolmen and peace officers, while serving and executing such notices, orders and demands, shall have all the power and authority possessed by peace officers when serving the executing warrants charging violations of the criminal laws of the State.

History.
1935, c. 52, s. 23; 1949, c. 583, s. 7; 1975, c. 716, s. 5; 1979, c. 667, s. 25; 1981, c. 938, s. 1; 1993, c. 539, s. 323;1994, Ex. Sess., c. 24, s. 14(c)

STOP OF DEFENDANT IN PRIVATE DRIVEWAY IS "SEIZURE" WITHIN U.S. CONST., AMEND. XIV. --Where a patrolman, while not engaged in any patrol of the highway for purposes of observing traffic or making random license checks, spontaneously decided to stop petitioner, not while petitioner was "on a public highway" nor while petitioner was operating a vehicle, but instead while petitioner was in a private driveway, although petitioner would have had a meritorious defense to any prosecution based on failure to display his license, he was not entitled to invoke self-help against what was, at the time, an arguable lawful arrest, and petitioner's conviction for assaulting the highway patrolman can survive despite the finding that the officer's initial stop and demand were illegal as an unreasonable search and seizure under U.S. Const., Amend. XIV. Keziah v. Bostic, 452 F. Supp. 912 (W.D.N.C. 1978).

SUFFICIENCY OF WARRANT. --A warrant under this section was fatally defective where it failed to aver that defendant refused to exhibit his license upon request while operating or in charge of a motor vehicle. The warrant should also have named the officer who demanded the right to inspect the license. State v. Danziger, 245 N.C. 406, 95 S.E.2d 862 (1957).

REFUSAL TO DISPLAY LICENSE. --Refusal of defendant, who hit another car with his vehicle in dentist's offstreet parking area, to display his license when requested clearly violated this section. State v. Adams, 88 N.C. App. 139, 362 S.E.2d 789 (1987).

APPLIED in State v. Clark, 21 N.C. App. 35, 203 S.E.2d 103 (1974); State v. Keziah, 24 N.C. App. 298, 210 S.E.2d 436 (1974); State v. Cornelius, 104 N.C. App. 583, 410 S.E.2d 504 (1991).

CITED in State v. Greenwood, 47 N.C. App. 731, 268 S.E.2d 835 (1980); State v. Hudson, 103 N.C. App. 708, 407 S.E.2d 583 (1991); State v. Johnston, 115 N.C. App. 711, 446 S.E.2d 135 (1994); State v. Phillips, 152 N.C. App. 679, 568 S.E.2d 300 (2002), appeal dismissed, 356 N.C. 442, 573 S.E.2d 162 (2002).

§ 20-29.1. Commissioner may require reexamination; issuance of limited or restricted licenses

The Commissioner of Motor Vehicles, having good and sufficient cause to believe that a licensed operator is incompetent or otherwise not qualified to be licensed, may, upon written notice of at least five days to such licensee, require him to submit to a reexamination to determine his competency to operate a motor vehicle. Upon the conclusion of such examination, the Commissioner shall take such action as may be appropriate, and may suspend or revoke the license of such person or permit him to retain such license, or may issue a license subject to restrictions or upon failure of such reexamination may cancel the license of such person until he passes a reexamination. Refusal or neglect of the licensee to submit to such reexamination shall be grounds for the cancellation of the license of the person failing to be reexamined, and the license so canceled shall remain canceled until such person satisfactorily complies with the reexamination requirements of the Commissioner. The Commissioner may, in his discretion and upon the written application of any person qualified to receive a driver's license, issue to such person a driver's license restricting or limiting the licensee to the operation of a single prescribed motor vehicle or to the operation of a particular class or type of motor vehicle. Such a limitation or restriction shall be noted on the face of the license, and it shall be unlawful for the holder of such limited or restricted license to operate any motor vehicle or class of motor vehicle not specified by such restricted or limited license, and the operation by such licensee of motor vehicles not specified by such license shall be deemed the equivalent of operating a motor vehicle without any driver's license. Any such restricted or limited licensee may at any time surrender such restricted or limited license and apply for and receive an unrestricted driver's license upon meeting the requirements therefor.

History.
1943, c. 787, s. 2; 1949, c. 1121; 1971, c. 546; 1979, c. 667, ss. 26, 41

NOTICE OF SUSPENSION REQUIRED. --A requirement for notice is made by G.S. 20-16(d) in all cases in which a license is suspended under the authority of that section. Even though a similar requirement for notice does not appear in this section, a reading of this Chapter, in which both sections appear, makes it clear that the legislature intended that notice be given to the licensee when the Commissioner suspends a license under this section as well as when suspension is made under the authority of G.S. 20-16. State v. Hughes, 6 N.C. App. 287, 170 S.E.2d 78 (1969). In any case in which a license is suspended under the authority of this section, the Commissioner of Motor Vehicles is required to notify the licensee of such suspension. That such notice is required is made more apparent when it is realized that even a failure to pass a reexamination conducted under this section does not necessarily result in suspension of the license. State v. Hughes, 6 N.C. App. 287, 170 S.E.2d 78 (1969).

§ 20-30. Violations of license, learner's permit, or special identification card provisions

It shall be unlawful for any person to commit any of the following acts:

(1) To display or cause to be displayed or to have in possession a driver's license, learner's permit, or special identification card, knowing the same to be fictitious or to have been canceled, revoked, suspended or altered.

(2) To counterfeit, sell, lend to, or knowingly permit the use of, by one not entitled thereto, a driver's license, learner's permit, or special identification card.

(3) To display or to represent as one's own a drivers license, learner's permit, or special identification card not issued to the person so displaying same.

(4) To fail or refuse to surrender to the Division upon demand any driver's license, learner's permit, or special identification card that has been suspended, canceled or revoked as provided by law.

(5) To use a false or fictitious name or give a false or fictitious address in any application for a driver's license, learner's permit, or special identification card, or any renewal or duplicate thereof, or knowingly to make a false statement or knowingly conceal a material fact or otherwise commit a fraud in any such application, or for any person to procure, or knowingly permit or allow another to commit any of the foregoing acts. Any license, learner's permit, or special identification card procured as aforesaid shall be void from the issuance thereof, and any moneys paid therefor shall be forfeited to the State. Any person violating the provisions of this subdivision shall be guilty of a Class 1 misdemeanor.

(6) To make a color photocopy or otherwise make a color reproduction of a drivers license, learner's permit, or special identification card which has been color-photocopied or otherwise reproduced in color, unless such color photocopy or other color reproduction was authorized by the Commissioner or is made to comply with G.S. 163-230.2. It shall be lawful to make a black and white photocopy of a drivers license, learner's permit, or special identification card or otherwise make a black and white reproduction of a drivers license, learner's permit, or special identification card.

(7) To sell or offer for sale any reproduction or facsimile or simulation of a driver's license, learner's permit, or special identification card. The provisions of this subdivision shall not apply to agents or employees of the Division while acting in the course and scope of their employment. Any person, firm or corporation violating the provisions of this subsection shall be guilty of a Class I felony.

(8) To possess more than one commercial drivers license or to possess a commercial drivers license and a regular drivers license. Any commercial drivers license other than the one most recently issued is subject to immediate seizure by any law enforcement officer or judicial official. Any regular drivers license possessed at the same time as a commercial drivers license is subject to immediate seizure by any law enforcement officer or judicial official.

(9) To present, display, or use a drivers license, learner's permit, or special identification card that contains a false or fictitious name in the commission or attempted commission of a felony. Any person violating the provisions of this subdivision shall be guilty of a Class I felony.

History.
1935, c. 52, s. 24; 1951, c. 542, s. 4; 1967, c. 1098, s. 1; 1973, c. 18, s. 2; 1975, c. 716, s. 5; 1979, c. 415; c. 667, ss. 27, 41; 1979, 2nd Sess., c. 1316, s. 22; 1989, c. 771, s. 8;1991, c. 726, s. 13;1991 (Reg. Sess., 1992), c. 1007, s. 29; 1993, c. 539, s. 1247;1994, Ex. Sess., c. 24, s. 14(c);1999-299, s. 1;2001-461, s. 1.1;2001-487, s. 50(b);2011-381, s. 4;2019-239, s. 1.3(c)

EDITOR'S NOTE. --
Session Laws 2019-239, s. 1.3(d), provides: "On or before May 1, 2020, the State Board of Elections shall report to the Joint Legislative Elections Oversight Committee and the General Assembly as to its plans to implement Sections 1.2 and 1.3 of this act and any recommendations for statutory changes necessary to implement these provisions."

Session Laws 2019-239, s. 1.6, provides: "Rule Making. -- The State Board of Elections shall adopt

emergency rules for the implementation of this Part in accordance with G.S. 150B-21.1A. This section does not require any rule making if not otherwise required by law."

Session Laws 2019-239, s. 7, made the amendment to subdivision (6) of this section by Session Laws 2019-239, s. 1.3(c), effective January 1, 2020, and applicable to elections conducted on or after that date.

Session Laws 2019-239, s. 5.14, is a severability clause.

EFFECT OF AMENDMENTS. --
Session Laws 2011-381, s. 4, added "or special identification card" throughout subdivisions (1) through (5), (7), and (9), and in the section heading; and made related changes. For effective date and applicability, see Editor's note.

Session Laws 2019-239, s. 1.3(c), inserted "or is made to comply with G.S. 163-230.2" at the end of the first sentence of subdivision (6). For effective date and applicability, see editor's note.

THE OFFENSE DESCRIBED IN G.S. 20-30(5) IS NOT A LESSER INCLUDED OFFENSE OF G.S. 20-31 dealing with perjury. State v. Finger, 72 N.C. App. 569, 324 S.E.2d 894, cert. denied, 313 N.C. 606, 332 S.E.2d 80 (1985).

APPLIED in State v. Hayes, 31 N.C. App. 121, 228 S.E.2d 460 (1976).

§ 20-31. Making false affidavits perjury

Any person who shall make any false affidavit, or shall knowingly swear or affirm falsely, to any matter or thing required by the terms of this Article to be sworn to or affirmed shall be guilty of a Class I felony.

History.
1935, c. 52, s. 25; 1993, c. 539, s. 1249;1994, Ex. Sess., c. 24, s. 14(c)

THE OFFENSE DESCRIBED IN G.S. 20-30(5) IS NOT A LESSER INCLUDED OFFENSE OF this section. State v. Finger, 72 N.C. App. 569, 324 S.E.2d 894, cert. denied, 313 N.C. 606, 332 S.E.2d 80 (1985).

§ 20-32. Unlawful to permit unlicensed minor to drive motor vehicle

It shall be unlawful for any person to cause or knowingly permit any minor under the age of 18 years to drive a motor vehicle upon a highway as an operator, unless such minor shall have first obtained a license to so drive a motor vehicle under the provisions of this Article.

History.
1935, c. 52, s. 26; 1973, c. 684

EDITOR'S NOTE. --The cases treated below were decided under a corresponding provision of an earlier law.

VIOLATION OF AGE LIMIT AS NEGLIGENCE. --Where a person within the age prohibited by the statute runs an automobile upon and injures a pedestrian, the violation of the statute is negligence per se, and a charge by the court that it is a circumstance from which the jury could infer negligence is reversible error. Taylor v. Stewart, 172 N.C. 203, 90 S.E. 134 (1916).

LIABILITY FOR INJURIES. --While it is negligence per se for one within the prohibited age to run an automobile, it is necessary that such negligence proximately cause the injury for damages to be recovered on that account, with the burden of proof on the plaintiff to show it by the preponderance of the evidence. Taylor v. Stewart, 172 N.C. 203, 90 S.E. 134 (1916).

PERMITTING OPERATION OF CAR BY PERSON UNDER LEGAL AGE IS NEGLIGENCE PER SE. --Under this section it is negligence per se for the owner of a car or one having it under his control to permit a person under legal age to operate it, but such negligence must be proximate cause of injury in order to be actionable. Hoke v. Atlantic Greyhound Corp., 226 N.C. 692, 40 S.E.2d 345 (1946).

LIABILITY OF OWNER FOR TORTS OF DRIVER. --See Cates v. Hall, 171 N.C. 360, 88 S.E. 524 (1916); Williams v. May, 173 N.C. 78, 91 S.E. 604 (1917); Wilson v. Polk, 175 N.C. 490, 95 S.E. 849 (1918). For a complete treatment, see 2 N.C.L. Rev. 181 (1924).

LIABILITY OF FATHER WHERE DRIVER IS MINOR SON. --While ordinarily a father is not held responsible in damages for the negligent acts of his minor son done without his knowledge and consent, such may be inferred, as where the father constantly permitted his 13-year-old son to run his automobile. Taylor v. Stewart, 172 N.C. 203, 90 S.E. 134 (1916). See Clark v. Sweaney, 176 N.C. 529, 97 S.E. 474 (1918). See also 2 N.C.L. Rev. 181 (1924).

QUESTION FOR JURY. --It was for the jury to determine whether a competent and careful chauffeur of more mature years could have avoided the injury under the circumstances, or whether the accident was due to the fact that a lad within the prohibited age was running the vehicle at the time. Taylor v. Stewart, 172 N.C. 203, 90 S.E. 134 (1916).

INSTRUCTION. --An instruction to the effect that it would be negligence per se for defendant to permit his child under the legal driving age to operate his automobile but that defendant could not be held liable unless the jury found from the preponderance of the evidence that such negligence was the proximate or one of the proximate causes of the injury, was held sufficient to cover this aspect of the case. Hoke v. Atlantic Greyhound Corp., 227 N.C. 412, 42 S.E.2d 593 (1947).

N.C. Gen. Stat. § 20-33

Repealed by Session Laws 1979, c. 667, s. 28.

§ 20-34. Unlawful to permit violations of this Article

No person shall authorize or knowingly permit a motor vehicle owned by him or under his control to be driven by any person who has no legal right to do so or in violation of any of the provisions of this Article.

History.
1935, c. 52, s. 28

UNDER THIS SECTION, THERE IS NO DISTINCTION IN MEANING BETWEEN THE WORDS "AUTHORIZE" AND "PERMIT"; either action would constitute a violation of this section. Thompson v. Three Guys Furn. Co., 122 N.C. App. 340, 469 S.E.2d 583 (1996).

NO DUTY TO INQUIRE FURTHER INTO DRIVING CREDENTIALS. --Grant of summary judgment in favor of the rental company in the administratrix's wrongful death and survival action was appropriate under G.S. 20-34 where the driver presented the rental company with an unexpired New Jersey driver's license and the rental company had no duty to inquire further into the driver's driving credentials. Cowan v. Jack, 922 So. 2d 559 (Dec. 21, 2005).

§ 20-34.1. Violations for wrongful issuance of a drivers license or a special identification card

(a) An employee of the Division or of an agent of the Division who does any of the following commits a Class I felony:

(1) Charges or accepts any money or other thing of value, except the required fee, for the issuance of a drivers license or a special identification card.

(2) Knowing it is false, accepts false proof of identification submitted for a drivers license or a special identification card.

(3) Knowing it is false, enters false information concerning a drivers license or a special identification card in the records of the Division.

(b) **Defenses Precluded.** -- The fact that the Division does not issue a license or a special identification card after an employee or an agent of the Division charges or accepts money or another thing of value for its issuance is not a defense to a criminal action under this section. It is not a defense to a criminal action under this section to show that the person who received or was intended to receive the license or special identification card was eligible for it.

(c) **Dismissal.** -- An employee of the Division who violates this section shall be dismissed from employment and may not hold any public office or public employment in this State for five years after the violation. If a person who violates this section is an employee of the agent of the Division, the Division shall cancel the contract of the agent unless the agent dismisses that person. A person dismissed by an agent because of a violation of this section may not hold any public office or public employment in this State for five years after the violation.

History.

1951, c. 211; 1975, c. 716, s. 5; 1979, c. 667, s. 41; 1993, c. 533, s. 8;c. 539, s. 1250;1994, Ex. Sess., c. 14, s. 30;c. 24, s. 14(c)

§ 20-35. Penalties for violating Article; defense to driving without a license

(a) **Penalty.** -- Except as otherwise provided in subsection (a1) or (a2) of this section, a violation of this Article is a Class 2 misdemeanor unless a statute in the Article sets a different punishment for the violation. If a statute in this Article sets a different punishment for a violation of the Article, the different punishment applies.

(a1) The following offenses are Class 3 misdemeanors:

(1) Failure to obtain a license before driving a motor vehicle, in violation of G.S. 20-7(a).

(2) Failure to comply with license restrictions, in violation of G.S. 20-7(e).

(3) Permitting a motor vehicle owned by the person to be operated by an unlicensed person, in violation of G.S. 20-34.

(a2) A person who does any of the following is responsible for an infraction:

(1) Fails to carry a valid license while driving a motor vehicle, in violation of G.S. 20-7(a).

(2) Operates a motor vehicle with an expired license, in violation of G.S. 20-7(f).

(3) Fails to notify the Division of an address change for a drivers license within 60 days after the change occurs, in violation of G.S. 20-7.1.

(b) Repealed by Session Laws 1993 (Reg. Sess., 1994), c. 761, s. 4.

(c) **Defenses.** -- A person may not be found responsible for failing to carry a regular drivers license if, when tried for that offense, the person produces in court a regular drivers license issued to the person that was valid when the person was charged with the offense. A person may not be found responsible for driving a motor vehicle with an expired drivers license if, when tried for that offense, the person shows all the following:

(1) That, at the time of the offense, the person had an expired license.

(2) The person renewed the expired license within 30 days after it expired and now has a drivers license.

(3) The person could not have been charged with driving without a license if the person had the renewed license when charged with the offense.

History.

1935, c. 52, s. 29; 1991, c. 726, s. 14;1993, c. 539, s. 324;1994, Ex. Sess., c. 24, s. 14(c);1993 (Reg. Sess., 1994), c. 761, s. 4; 2013-360, s. 18B.14(g);2013-385, s. 4

EFFECT OF AMENDMENTS. --

Session Laws 2013-360, s. 18B.14(g), effective December 1, 2013, added "Except as otherwise provided in subsection (a1) of this section" in subsection (a); and added subsection (a1). For applicability, see Editor's note.

Session Laws 2013-385, s. 4, effective December 1, 2013, added "or (a2)" in subsection (a); deleted former subdivisions (a1)(2), (a1)(4), and (a1)(5); redesignated former subdivisions (a1)(3) and (a1)(6) as present subdivisions (a1)(2) and (a1)(3); added subsection (a2); and, in subsection (c), substituted "found responsible for" for "convicted of" twice and "with an expired" for "without a regular." For applicability, see Editor's note.

THIS SECTION AND G.S. 20-7, BEING IN PARI MATERIA, MUST BE CONSTRUED TOGETHER, and, if possible, they must be reconciled and harmonized. State v. Tolley, 271 N.C. 459, 156 S.E.2d 858 (1967).

PROBABLE CAUSE. --Corporal had probable cause to justify defendant's arrest because as when the corporal approached defendant's vehicle he noticed an open beer can, when defendant rolled down his window the corporal detected an odor of alcohol, and when he asked for defendant's license and registration, defendant responded that he did not have a license. Therefore, the corporal could have arrested defendant for either driving with an open container or driving without a valid operator's license. State v. Jackson, 262 N.C. App. 329, 821 S.E.2d 656 (2018).

STIPULATION TO PRIOR MISDEMEANOR. --Trial court did not err by sentencing defendant as a Level II offender based on his stipulation that he was previously convicted of a Class 2 misdemeanor because defendant, as the person most familiar with the facts surrounding his offense, stipulated that his "no operator's license" conviction was a Class 2 misdemeanor, as such he stipulated that the facts underlying his conviction justified that classification, and the trial court was under no duty to pursue further inquiry. State v. Salter, 264 N.C. App. 724, 826 S.E.2d 803 (2019).

EXCESSIVE PENALTY. --Any person convicted of operating a motor vehicle over any highway in this State without having first been licensed as such operator, in violation of G.S. 20-7(a), was guilty of a misdemeanor, and, under former G.S. 20-7(o) and former subsection (b) of this section, was subject to punishment by imprisonment for a term of not more than six months. The superior court, even if it had jurisdiction in other respects, had no authority to pronounce judgment imposing a prison sentence of two years for this criminal offense. State v. Wall, 271 N.C. 675, 157 S.E.2d 363 (1967).

CITED in Hoke v. Atlantic Greyhound Corp., 226 N.C. 692, 40 S.E.2d 345 (1946); State v. Johnston, 115 N.C. App. 711, 446 S.E.2d 135 (1994); Hinson v. Jarvis, 190 N.C. App. 607, 660 S.E.2d 604 (2008), review dismissed, as moot, 363 N.C. 126, 675 S.E.2d 365 (2009), review denied, 363 N.C. 126, 675 S.E.2d 366 (2009).

CROSS REFERENCES. --

As to jurisdiction of prosecution under this section, see notes to G.S. 7A-271 and 7A-272.

§ 20-36. Ten-year-old convictions not considered

Except for offenses occurring in a commercial motor vehicle, offenses by the holder of a commercial drivers license involving a noncommercial motor vehicle, or a second failure to submit to a chemical test when charged with an implied-consent offense, as defined in G.S. 20-16.2, that occurred while the person was driving a commercial motor vehicle, no conviction of any other violation of the motor vehicle laws shall be considered by the Division in determining whether any person's driving privilege shall be suspended or revoked or in determining the appropriate period of suspension or revocation after 10 years has elapsed from the date of that conviction.

History.

1971, c. 15; 1975, c. 716, s. 5; 1998-182, s. 22;2005-349, s. 7;2009-416, s. 4

EFFECT OF AMENDMENTS. --

Session Laws 2005-349, s. 7, effective September 30, 2005, substituted "Except for offenses occurring in a commercial motor vehicle" for "Except for a second or subsequent conviction for violating G.S. 20-138.2, a third or subsequent violation of G.S. 20-138.2A."

Session Laws 2009-416, s. 4, effective March 31, 2010, and applicable to offenses committed on or after that date, inserted "offenses by the holder of a commercial drivers license involving a noncommercial motor vehicle."

OPINIONS OF THE ATTORNEY GENERAL

TEN-YEAR LIMITATION APPLICABLE TO DIVISION OF MOTOR VEHICLE ACTION ONLY. --See opinion of Attorney General to Honorable Robert A. Collier, Jr., 41 N.C.A.G. 322 (1971).

§ 20-37. Limitations on issuance of licenses

There shall be no driver's license issued within this State other than that provided for in this Article, nor shall there be any other examination required: Provided, however, that cities and towns shall have the power to license, regulate and control drivers and operators of taxicabs within the city or town limits and to regulate and control operators of taxicabs operating between the city or town to points, not incorporated, within a radius of five miles of said city or town.

History.

1935, c. 52, s. 34; 1943, c. 639, s. 2; 1979, c. 667, s. 41

AUTHORITY TO LICENSE AND REGULATE TAXICABS. --In adopting this section the General Assembly delegated the authority to license taxicabs and regulate their use on public streets to the several municipalities. Suddreth v. City of Charlotte, 223 N.C. 630, 27 S.E.2d 650 (1943).

In the exercise of this delegated power, it is the duty of the municipal authorities in their sound discretion, to determine what ordinances or regulations are reasonably necessary for the protection of the public or the better government of the town; and when in the exercise of such discretion an ordinance is adopted, it is presumed to be valid; and, the courts will not declare it invalid unless it is clearly shown to be so. State v. Stallings, 230 N.C. 252, 52 S.E.2d 901 (1949).

Under such delegated power a city may require, as a condition incident to the privilege of operating a taxicab on its streets, that the driver of such taxicab or other insignia while operating a taxicab, to show that he is a duly licensed taxicab driver. State v. Stallings, 230 N.C. 252, 52 S.E.2d 901 (1949).

CITED in Victory Cab Co. v. City of Charlotte, 234 N.C. 572, 68 S.E.2d 433 (1951); Morrisey v. Crabtree, 143 F. Supp. 105 (M.D.N.C. 1956).

LEGAL PERIODICALS. --

For comment on the 1943 amendment to this section, see 21 N.C.L. Rev. 358 (1943).

§ 20-37.01. Drivers License Technology Fund

The Drivers License Technology Fund is established in the Department of Transportation as a nonreverting, interest-bearing special revenue account. The revenue in the Fund at the end of a fiscal year does not revert, and earnings on the Fund shall be credited to the Fund annually. All money collected by the Commissioner pursuant to G.S. 20-37.02 shall be remitted to the State Treasurer and held in the Fund. Money held in the Fund shall be used to supplement funds otherwise available to the Division for information technology and office automation needs. The Commissioner shall report by February 1 and August 1 of each year to the Joint Legislative Commission on Governmental Operations, the chairs of the Senate and House of Representatives Appropriation Committees, and the chairs of the Senate and House of Representatives Appropriations Subcommittees on Transportation on all money collected and deposited in the Fund and on the proposed expenditure of funds collected during the preceding six months.

History.

2001-461, s. 4;2001-487, s. 42(c)

EDITOR'S NOTE. --

Session Laws 2001-461, s. 6, made this section effective November 14, 2001.

Session Laws 2001-461, s. 6, also provides: "The electronic system to be established pursuant to Section 4 of this act [which enacted G.S. 20-37.01 and 20-37.02] shall not be operated by the Commissioner until such time as the Drivers License Technology Fund contains sufficient funds to meet the purposes of Section 4 of this act and only for so long as adequate funds are available to operate the electronic system."

§ 20-37.02. Verification of drivers license information

(a) The Commissioner shall establish and operate an electronic system that can be used to verify drivers licenses and identification cards issued by the Division and the dates of birth on these documents in order to facilitate access to drivers license information by retailers and persons holding ABC permits to prevent the utilization of fictitious identification for the purpose of underage purchases of certain age-restricted products or to commit certain crimes.

(b) The electronic system established and operated by the Commissioner pursuant to subsection (a) of this section shall allow a retailer, as defined in G.S. 105-164.3(195), a person who holds an ABC permit, as defined in G.S. 18B-101(2), or an agent of the retailer or a person holding an ABC permit, to verify the validity of a drivers license or identification card issued by the Division and the date of birth of the person issued the drivers license or identification card. The Commissioner shall make drivers license and identification card information available in a read-only format, and the information to be made available shall not exceed the information contained on the face of the drivers license. The Division shall not keep a record of the inquiry. The retailer or a person holding an ABC permit may retain such information as is necessary to provide evidence that the person's drivers license or identification card was validated or that the person's age was verified. A retailer or permittee shall agree to comply with the requirements of this section prior to using the system.

(c) Except for purposes allowed in this section, a person using the electronic system established in accordance with subsection (a) of this section shall not collect or retain any information obtained through the use of the electronic system, nor transfer or make accessible to a third party any information obtained through an inquiry permitted under this section. A violation of the provisions of this subsection shall be punished as a Class 2 misdemeanor.

(d) A retailer or permittee using the electronic system established pursuant to this section shall be responsible for the costs of the equipment and communication lines approved by the Division needed by the retailer or permittee to access the system.

(e) The establishment and operation of an electronic system pursuant to this section may be funded through grants received from the State, the federal government, a private entity, or any other funding source made available to the Drivers License Technology Fund. All funds obtained through grants to the Fund shall be remitted to the State Treasurer to be held in the Drivers License Technology Fund established in G.S. 20-37.01.

History.
2001-461, s. 4
EDITOR'S NOTE. --
Session Laws 2001-461, s. 6, made this section effective November 14, 2001.
Session Laws 2001-461, s. 6, also provides: "The electronic system to be established pursuant to Section 4 of this act [which enacted G.S. 20-37.01 and 20-37.02] shall not be operated by the Commissioner until such time as the Drivers License Technology Fund contains sufficient funds to meet the purposes of Section 4 of this act and only for so long as adequate funds are available to operate the electronic system."
Session Laws 2019-169, s. 3.1(c), provides: "The Revisor of Statutes is authorized to renumber the subdivisions of G.S. 105-164.3 to ensure that the subdivisions are listed in alphabetical order and in a manner that reduces the current use of alphanumeric designations, to make conforming changes, and to reserve sufficient space to accommodate future additions to the statutory section." At the direction of the Revisor of Statutes, a reference was conformed in subsection (b).

ARTICLE 2A.
AFFLICTED, DISABLED OR HANDICAPPED PERSONS

N.C. Gen. Stat. § 20-37.1

Repealed by Session Laws 1989, c. 157, s. 1.

§§ 20-37.2 through 20-37.4

Repealed by Session Laws 1991, c. 411, s. 5.

§ 20-37.5. Definitions

Unless the context requires otherwise, the following definitions apply throughout this Article to the defined words and phrases and their cognates:

(1) "Distinguishing license plate" means a license plate that displays the International Symbol of Access using the same color, size of plate, and size of letters or numbers as a regular plate.

(1a) *(Effective March 1, 2020)* Guardian. -- Any of the following:

a. **Custodian.** -- As defined in G.S. 7B-101(8).

b. **General guardian.** -- As defined in G.S. 35A-1202(7).

c. **Guardian of the person.** -- As defined in G.S. 35A-1202(10).

(2) "Handicapped" shall mean a person with a mobility impairment who, as determined by a licensed physician:

a. Cannot walk 200 feet without stopping to rest;

b. Cannot walk without the use of, or assistance from, a brace, cane, crutch, another person, prosthetic device, wheelchair, or other assistive device;

c. Is restricted by lung disease to such an extent that the person's forced (respiratory) expiratory volume of one second, when measured by spirometry, is less than one liter, or the arterial oxygen tension is less than 60 mm/hg on room air at rest;

d. Uses portable oxygen;

e. Has a cardiac condition to the extent that the person's functional limitations are classified in severity as Class III or Class IV according to standards set by the American Heart Association;

f. Is severely limited in their ability to walk due to an arthritic, neurological, or orthopedic condition; or

g. Is totally blind or whose vision with glasses is so defective as to prevent the performance of ordinary activity for which eyesight is essential, as certified by a licensed ophthalmologist, optometrist, or the Division of Services for the Blind.

(3) "International Symbol of Access" means the symbol adopted by Rehabilitation International in 1969 at its Eleventh World Congress on Rehabilitation of the Disabled.

(4) "Removable windshield placard" means a two-sided, hooked placard which includes on each side:

a. The International Symbol of Access, which is at least three inches in height, centered on the placard, and is white on a blue shield;

b. An identification number;

c. An expiration date that is visible from at least 20 feet and the month and year of expiration; and

d. The seal or other identification of the issuing authority.

History.
1967, c. 296, s. 5; 1977, c. 340, s. 1; 1991, c. 411, s. 1;2009-493, s. 1;2019-213, s. 1(a)

EFFECT OF AMENDMENTS. --
Session Laws 2009-493, s. 1, effective January 1, 2010, and applicable to placards that are issued or renewed on or after that date, inserted "that is visible from at least 20 feet and the month and year of expiration " in subdivision (4)c.

Session Laws 2019-213, s. 1(a), effective March 1, 2020, added subdivision (1a).
CITED in Brown v. North Carolina DMV, 987 F. Supp. 451 (E.D.N.C. 1997), aff'd, 166 F.3d 698 (4th Cir. 1999).

§ 20-37.6. Parking privileges for handicapped drivers and passengers

(a) **General Parking.** -- Any vehicle that is driven by or is transporting a person who is handicapped and that displays a distinguishing license plate, a removable windshield placard, or a temporary removable windshield placard may be parked for unlimited periods in parking zones restricted as to the length of time parking is permitted. This provision has no application to those zones or during times in which the stopping, parking, or standing of all vehicles is prohibited or which are reserved for special types of vehicles. Any qualifying vehicle may park in spaces designated as restricted to vehicles driven by or transporting the handicapped.

(b) **Distinguishing License Plates.** -- If the registered owner of a vehicle is handicapped or the registered owner certifies that the registered owner is the guardian or parent of a handicapped person, the registered owner may apply for and display a distinguishing license plate. This license plate shall be issued for the normal fee applicable to standard license plates. Any vehicle owner who qualifies for a distinguishing license plate shall be notified by the Division at the time the plate is issued that the applicant is also eligible to receive one removable windshield placard and, upon request, shall be issued a placard at that time. A vehicle with a distinguishing license plate may be lawfully used when a handicapped person is not a driver or passenger so long as the vehicle is not using handicapped privileges including parking in a space designated with a sign pursuant to subsection (d) of this section.

(c) **Distinguishing Placards.** -- A handicapped person may apply for the issuance of a removable windshield placard or a temporary removable windshield placard. Upon request, one additional placard may be issued to applicants who do not have a distinguishing license plate. Any organization which, as determined and certified by the State Vocational Rehabilitation Agency, regularly transports handicapped persons may also apply. These organizations may receive one removable windshield placard for each transporting vehicle. When the removable windshield or temporary removable windshield placard is properly displayed, all parking rights and privileges extended to vehicles displaying a distinguishing license plate issued pursuant to subsection (b) shall apply. The removable windshield placard or the temporary removable windshield placard shall be displayed so that it may be viewed from the front and rear of the vehicle by hanging it from the front windshield rearview mirror of a vehicle using a parking space allowed for handicapped persons. When there is no inside rearview mirror, or when the placard cannot reasonably be hung from the rearview mirror by the handicapped person, the placard shall be displayed on the driver's side of the dashboard. A removable windshield placard placed on a motorized wheelchair or similar vehicle shall be displayed in a clearly visible location. The Division shall establish procedures for the issuance of the placards and may charge a fee sufficient to pay the actual cost of issuance, but in no event less than five dollars ($ 5.00) per placard. The Division shall issue a placard registration card with each placard issued to a handicapped person. The registration card shall bear the name of the person to whom the placard is issued, the person's address, the placard number, and an expiration date. The registration card shall be in the vehicle in which the placard is being used, and the person to whom the placard is issued shall be the operator or a passenger in the vehicle in which the placard is displayed.

(c1) **Application and Renewal; Medical Certification.** -- The initial application for a distinguishing license plate, removable windshield placard, or temporary removable windshield placard shall be accompanied by a certification of a licensed physician, a licensed ophthalmologist, a licensed optometrist, a licensed physician assistant, a licensed nurse practitioner, or the Division of Services for the Blind that the applicant or person in the applicant's custody or care is handicapped or by a disability determination by the United States Department of Veterans Affairs that the applicant or person in the applicant's custody or care is handicapped. For an initial application for a temporary removable windshield placard only, the certification that the applicant is handicapped may be made by a licensed certified nurse midwife. The application for a temporary removable windshield placard shall contain additional certification to include the period of time the certifying authority determines the applicant will have the disability. Distinguishing license plates shall be renewed annually, but subsequent applications shall not require a medical certification that the applicant is handicapped, except that a registered owner that certified pursuant to subsection (b) of this section that the registered owner is the guardian or parent of a handicapped person must recertify every five years. Removable windshield placards shall be renewed every five years, and, except for a person certified as totally and permanently disabled at the time of the initial application or a prior renewal under this subsection, the renewal shall require a medical recertification that the person is handicapped;

provided that a medical certification shall not be required to renew any placard that expires after the person to whom it is issued is 80 years of age. Temporary removable windshield placards shall expire no later than six months after issuance.

(c2) **Existing Placards; Expiration; Exchange for New Placards.**-- All existing placards shall expire on January 1, 1992. No person shall be convicted of parking in violation of this Article by reason of an expired placard if the defendant produces in court, at the time of trial on the illegal parking charge, an expired placard and a renewed placard issued within 30 days of the expiration date of the expired placard and which would have been a defense to the charge had it been issued prior to the time of the alleged offense. Existing placards issued on or after July 1, 1989, may be exchanged without charge for the new placards.

(c3) It shall be unlawful to sell a distinguishing license plate, a removable windshield placard, or a temporary removable windshield placard issued pursuant to this section. A violation of this subsection shall be a Class 2 misdemeanor and may be punished pursuant to G.S. 20-176(c) and (c1).

(d) **Designation of Parking Spaces.** -- Designation of parking spaces for handicapped persons on streets and public vehicular areas shall comply with G.S. 136-30. A sign designating a parking space for handicapped persons shall state the maximum penalty for parking in the space in violation of the law. For purposes of this section, a parking space designated for handicapped persons includes clearly marked access aisles, and all provisions, restrictions, and penalties applicable to parking in spaces designated for handicapped persons also apply to clearly marked access aisles.

(d1) Repealed by Session Laws 1991, c. 530, s. 4.

(e) **Enforcement of Handicapped Parking Privileges.** -- It shall be unlawful:

(1) To park or leave standing any vehicle in a space designated with a sign pursuant to subsection (d) of this section for handicapped persons when the vehicle does not display the distinguishing license plate, removable windshield placard, temporary removable windshield placard as provided in this section, a disabled veteran registration plate issued under G.S. 20-79.4, or a partially disabled veteran registration plate issued under G.S. 20-79.4;

(2) For any person not qualifying for the rights and privileges extended to handicapped persons under this section to exercise or attempt to exercise such rights or privileges by the unauthorized use of a distinguishing license plate, removable windshield placard, or temporary removable

windshield placard issued pursuant to the provisions of this section;

(3) To park or leave standing any vehicle so as to obstruct a curb ramp or curb cut for handicapped persons as provided for by the North Carolina Building Code or as designated in G.S. 136-44.14;

(4) For those responsible for designating parking spaces for the handicapped to erect or otherwise use signs not conforming to G.S. 20-37.6(d) for this purpose.

This section is enforceable in all public vehicular areas.

(f) **Penalties for Violation.** --

(1) A violation of G.S. 20-37.6(e)(1), (2) or (3) is an infraction which carries a penalty of at least one hundred dollars ($ 100.00) but not more than two hundred fifty dollars ($ 250.00) and whenever evidence shall be presented in any court of the fact that any automobile, truck, or other vehicle was found to be parked in a properly designated handicapped parking space in violation of the provisions of this section, it shall be prima facie evidence in any court in the State of North Carolina that the vehicle was parked and left in the space by the person, firm, or corporation in whose name the vehicle is registered and licensed according to the records of the Division. No evidence tendered or presented under this authorization shall be admissible or competent in any respect in any court or tribunal except in cases concerned solely with a violation of this section.

(2) A violation of G.S. 20-37.6(e)(4) is an infraction which carries a penalty of at least one hundred dollars ($ 100.00) but not more than two hundred fifty dollars ($ 250.00) and whenever evidence shall be presented in any court of the fact that a nonconforming sign is being used it shall be prima facie evidence in any court in the State of North Carolina that the person, firm, or corporation with ownership of the property where the nonconforming sign is located is responsible for violation of this section. Building inspectors and others responsible for North Carolina State Building Code violations specified in G.S. 143-138(h) where such signs are required by the Handicapped Section of the North Carolina State Building Code, may cause a citation to be issued for this violation and may also initiate any appropriate action or proceeding to correct such violation.

(3) A law-enforcement officer, including a company police officer commissioned by the Attorney General under Chapter 74E of the General Statutes, or a campus police officer commissioned by the Attorney General under Chapter 74G of the General Statutes,

may cause a vehicle parked in violation of this section to be towed. The officer is a legal possessor as provided in G.S. 20-161(d) (2). The officer shall not be held to answer in any civil or criminal action to any owner, lienholder or other person legally entitled to the possession of any motor vehicle removed from a space pursuant to this section, except where the motor vehicle is willfully, maliciously, or negligently damaged in the removal from the space to a place of storage.

(4) Notwithstanding any other provision of the General Statutes, the provisions of this section relative to handicapped parking shall be enforced by State, county, city and other municipal authorities in their respective jurisdictions whether on public or private property in the same manner as is used to enforce other parking laws and ordinances by said agencies.

History.
1971, c. 374, s. 1; 1973, cc. 126, 1384; 1977, c. 340, s. 2; 1979, c. 632; 1981, c. 682, s. 7; 1983, c. 326, ss. 1, 2; 1985, c. 249; c. 586; c. 764, s. 24; 1985 (Reg. Sess., 1986), c. 852, s. 17; 1987, c. 843; 1989, c. 760, s. 3;1989 (Reg. Sess., 1990), c. 1052, ss. 1-3.1; 1991, c. 411, s. 2;c. 530, s. 4;c. 672, s. 5;c. 726, s. 23;c. 761, s. 5;1991 (Reg. Sess., 1992), c. 1007, s. 30; c. 1043, s. 4; 1993, c. 373, s. 1;1994, Ex. Sess., c. 14, s. 31;1999-265, s. 1;2005-231, s. 11;2009-493, s. 2;2015-22, s. 1;2015-29, s. 1;2016-25, ss. 1, 2; 2017-111, s. 1;2018-77, s. 4;2019-199, s. 8;2019-213, s. 1(b)

LOCAL MODIFICATION. --City of Charlotte: 2001-88; city of Jacksonville: 1987 (Reg. Sess., 1988), c. 997.

EDITOR'S NOTE. --
Session Laws 2015-16, s. 1 provides: "The Division of Motor Vehicles shall study ways to decrease the misuse of windshield placards issued to handicapped persons. Included within this study shall be the cost, feasibility, and advisability of (i) requiring the inclusion of more personally identifying information on the windshield placard, including a picture of the handicapped person who was issued the placard, (ii) linking the windshield placard to the handicapped person's drivers license or special identification card, and (iii) linking the windshield placard to the license plate issued to the handicapped person or the owner of the vehicle in which the handicapped person is or will be transported. The Division shall report its findings and recommendations, including any legislative proposals, to the Joint Legislative Transportation Oversight Committee on or before January 15, 2016."

Session Laws 2015-22, s. 2, made the substitution of "shall be notified by the Division at the time the plate is issued that the applicant is also eligible to receive one removable windshield placard and, upon request, shall be issued a placard at that time" for "may also receive one removable windshield placard" in the last sentence of subsection (b) of this section by Session Laws 2015-22, s. 1, applicable to applications for a distinguishing license plate received on or after July 1, 2015.

Session Laws 2015-29, s. 2, provides: "The Division of Motor Vehicles shall develop or update the appropriate forms and procedures necessary to implement this act."

Session Laws 2020-3, s. 4.7(a) -(h), as amended by Session Laws 2020-97, ss. 3.15(a), 3.16(a), provides: "(a) Definition. -- For purposes of this section, 'credential' means any of the following issued by the Division of Motor Vehicles:

"(1) Drivers license.
"(2) Learner's permit.
"(3) Limited learner's permit.
"(4) Limited provisional license.
"(5) Full provisional license.
"(6) Commercial drivers license.
"(7) Commercial learner's permit.
"(8) Temporary driving certificate.
"(9) Special identification card.
"(10) Handicapped placard.
"(11) Vehicle registration.
"(12) Temporary vehicle registration.
"(13) Dealer license plate.
"(14) Transporter plate.
"(15) Loaner/Dealer 'LD' plate.
"(16) Vehicle inspection authorization.
"(17) Inspection station license.
"(18) Inspection mechanic license.
"(19) Transportation network company permit.
"(20) Motor vehicle dealer license.
"(21) Sales representative license.
"(22) Manufacturer license.
"(23) Distributor license.
"(24) Wholesaler license.
"(25) Driver training school license.
"(26) Driver training school instructor license.
"(27) Professional housemoving license.

"(b) Extend Validity of Credentials. -- Notwithstanding renewal, duration, or expiration provisions of G.S. 20-7, 20-11, 20-37.6, 20-37.7, 20-37.13, 20-50, 20-66, 20-79, 20-79.02, 20-79.2, 20-183.4B, 20-183.4D, 20-280.3, 20-288, 20-324, and 20-359, or any other provision of law to the contrary, the Division of Motor Vehicles shall extend for a period of five months the validity of any credential that expires on or after March 1, 2020, and before August 1, 2020. The Division shall extend for a period of five months the validity of any credential listed in subdivisions (6), (7), (9), (10), and (18) of subsection (a) of this section that expires on or after March 1, 2020, and before the date 30 days after the date the Governor (i) rescinds Executive Order No. 116 or (ii) issues another executive order lifting restrictions on Division of Motor Vehicles functions. Notwithstanding G.S. 20-37.13(h) and G.S. 20-37.13A(a), the Division of Motor Vehicles is authorized to waive the requirement that commercial drivers license and commercial learner's permit holders have a medical examination and certification, as required by federal law, consistent with any waiver of medical qualifications standards issued by the Federal Motor Carrier Safety Administration. A

credential extended under this section shall expire five months from the date it otherwise expires as prescribed by law prior to this section. However, the subsequent expiration of a credential extended under this section shall occur on the date prescribed by law prior to this section without regard to the extension. The Division shall notify individuals affected by an extension granted under this section, including information on new expiration dates and how the extension affects subsequent renewal and expiration dates.

"(b1) Extension of Intrastate Medical Waivers. -- Notwithstanding the limitation on duration of waivers in G.S. 20-37.13A(b), the Division of Motor Vehicles may extend for up to five months the validity of a medical waiver issued by the Division under G.S. 20-37.13A if the waiver expires on or after March 1, 2020, and before the date 30 days after the date the Governor (i) rescinds Executive Order No. 116 or (ii) issues another executive order lifting restrictions on Division of Motor Vehicles functions, and the Division's Medical Review Unit determines the extension is appropriate.

"(c) Driving Eligibility Certificates. -- Notwithstanding G.S. 20-11(n)(3), a driving eligibility certificate dated on or after February 9, 2020, and before March 10, 2020, remains valid and may be accepted by the Division of Motor Vehicles to meet the requirements for a license or permit issued under G.S. 20-11 until 30 days after the date the Governor rescinds Executive Order No. 116 or the date the Division reopens all drivers license offices, whichever is earlier.

"(d) Waive Penalties. -- Notwithstanding any provision of law to the contrary, the Division shall waive any fines, fees, or penalties associated with failing to renew a credential during the period of time the credential is valid by extension under subsection (b) of this section.

"(e) Motor Vehicle Taxes. -- Notwithstanding any provision of law to the contrary, due dates for motor vehicle taxes that are tied to registration expiration under Article 22A of Chapter 105 of the General Statutes shall be extended to correspond with extended expiration dates under subsection (b) of this section.

"(f) Validity by Extension a Defense. -- A person may not be convicted or found responsible for any offense resulting from failure to renew a credential issued by the Division if, when tried for that offense, the person shows that the offense occurred during the period of time the credential is valid by extension under subsection (b) of this section.

"(g) Report. -- Within 30 days of the extensions made under subsection (b) of this section, the Division shall submit a report to the Joint Legislative Transportation Oversight Committee and the Fiscal Research Division detailing implementation of this section.

"(h) Effective Date. -- This section is effective retroactively to March 1, 2020, and applies to expirations occurring on or after that date."
Session Laws 2020-3, s. 5, is a severability clause.
Session Laws 2020-97, s. 4.5, is a severability clause.

EFFECT OF AMENDMENTS. --

Session Laws, 2005-231, s. 11, effective July 28, 2005, inserted "of the General Statutes, or a campus police officer commissioned by the Attorney General under Chapter 74G of the General Statutes" in the first sentence of subdivision (f)(3).

Session Laws 2009-493, s. 2, effective January 1, 2010, and applicable to placards that are issued or renewed on or after that date, added the last three sentences in subsection (c).

Session Laws 2015-22, s. 1, effective July 1, 2015, substituted "shall be notified by the Division at the time the plate is issued that the applicant is also eligible to receive one removable windshield placard and, upon request, shall be issued a placard at that time" for "may also receive one removable windshield placard" in the last sentence in subsection (b). For applicability, see editor's note.

Session Laws 2015-29, s. 1, effective July 1, 2016, inserted "except for a person certified as totally and permanently disabled at the time of the initial application or a prior renewal under this subsection" in the fourth sentence of subsection (c1).

Session Laws 2016-25, ss. 1 and 2, effective June 22, 2016, substituted "of a licensed physician, a licensed ophthalmologist, a licensed optometrist, or the Division of Services for the Blind that the applicant is handicapped or by a disability determination by the United States Department of Veterans Affairs" for "of a licensed physician, ophthalmologist, or optometrist or of the Division of Services for the Blind" in the first sentence of subsection (c1); and substituted "under G.S. 20-79.4, or a partially disabled veteran registration plate issued under G.S. 20-79.4" for "under G.S. 20-79.4" at the end of subsection (e)(1).

Session Laws 2017-111, s. 1, effective July 12, 2017, in subsection (c1), substituted "Medical Certification" for Physician's Certification" in the subsection heading; inserted "a licensed physician assistant, a licensed nurse practitioner" in the first sentence; and added the second sentence.

Session Laws 2018-77, s. 4, effective June 25, 2018, inserted "provided that a medical certification shall not be required to renew any placard that expires after the person to whom it is issued is 80 years of age" in the next to last sentence of subsection (c1).

Session Laws 2019-199, s. 8, effective August 21, 2019, added the last sentence to subsection (d).

Session Laws 2019-213, s. 1(b), effective March 1, 2020, in subsection (b), deleted "Handicapped Car Owners" at the beginning, rewrote the first sentence, and added the last sentence; in subsection (c), deleted "Handicapped Drivers and Passengers" at the beginning; in subsection (c1), inserted "or a person in the applicant's custody or care" twice and inserted "except that a registered owner that certified pursuant to subsection (b) of this section that the registered owner is the guardian or parent of a handicapped person must recertify every five years."

PLACARD FEE. --Where plaintiffs charged that the fee for a handicapped placard violated their rights under the Americans With Disabilities Act and filed

an action for declaratory judgment, the action was barred by the 11th Amendment to the Federal Constitution.Brown v. North Carolina DMV, 987 F. Supp. 451 (E.D.N.C. 1997), aff'd, 166 F.3d 698 (4th Cir. 1999). CITED in Brown v. North Carolina DMV, 166 F.3d 698 (4th Cir. 1999).

§ 20-37.6A. Parking privileges for out-of-state handicapped drivers and passengers

Any vehicle displaying an out-of-State handicapped license plate, placard, or other evidence of handicap issued by the appropriate authority of the appropriate jurisdiction may park in any space reserved for the handicapped pursuant to G.S. 20-37.6.

History.

1981, c. 48; 1991, c. 411, s. 3;1991 (Reg. Sess., 1992), c. 1007, s. 31

ARTICLE 2B.
SPECIAL IDENTIFICATION CARDS FOR NONOPERATORS

§ 20-37.7. Special identification card

(a) **Eligibility.** -- A person who is a resident of this State is eligible for a special identification card.

(b) **Application.** -- To obtain a special identification card from the Division, a person must complete the application form used to obtain a drivers license.

(b1) **Search National Sex Offender Public Registry.** -- The Division shall not issue a special identification card to an applicant who has resided in this State for less than 12 months until the Division has searched the National Sex Offender Public Registry to determine if the person is currently registered as a sex offender in another state. The following applies in this subsection:

(1) If the Division finds that the person is currently registered as a sex offender in another state, the Division shall not issue a special identification card to the person until the person submits proof of registration pursuant to Article 27A of Chapter 14 of the General Statutes issued by the sheriff of the county where the person resides.

(2) If the person does not appear on the National Sex Offender Public Registry, the Division shall issue a special identification card but shall require the person to sign an affidavit acknowledging that the person has been notified that if the person is a sex offender, then the person is required to register pursuant to Article 27A of Chapter 14 of the General Statutes.

(3) If the Division is unable to access all states' information contained in the National Sex Offender Public Registry, but the person is otherwise qualified to obtain a special identification card, then the Division shall issue the card but shall first require the person to sign an affidavit stating that: (i) the person does not appear on the National Sex Offender Public Registry and (ii) acknowledging that the person has been notified that if the person is a sex offender, then the person is required to register pursuant to Article 27A of Chapter 14 of the General Statutes. The Division shall search the National Sex Offender Public Registry for the person within a reasonable time after access to the Registry is restored. If the person does appear in the National Sex Offender Public Registry, the person is in violation of G.S. 20-37.8, and the Division shall promptly notify the sheriff of the county where the person resides of the offense.

(4) Any person denied a special identification card by the Division pursuant to this subsection has a right to file a petition within 30 days thereafter for a hearing in the matter in the superior court of the county where the person resides, or to petition the resident judge of the district or judge holding the court of that district, or special or emergency judge holding a court in the district, and the court or judge is hereby vested with jurisdiction. The court or judge shall set the matter for hearing upon 30 days' written notice to the Division. At the hearing, the court or judge shall take testimony and examine the facts of the case and shall determine whether the petitioner is entitled to a special identification card under this subsection and whether the petitioner is in violation of G.S. 20-37.8.

(c) **Format.** -- A special identification card shall include a color photograph of the special identification card holder and shall be similar in size, shape, and design to a drivers license, but shall clearly state that it does not entitle the person to whom it is issued to operate a motor vehicle. A special identification card issued to an applicant must have the same background color that a drivers license issued to the applicant would have.

(d) **Expiration and Fee.** -- A special identification card issued to a person for the first time under this section expires when a drivers license issued on the same day to that person would expire. A special identification card renewed under this section expires when a drivers license renewed by the card holder on the same day would expire. The Division shall offer renewal of a special identification card in person and online on the Division's Web site.

The fee for a special identification card is the same as the fee set in G.S. 20-14 for a duplicate license. The fee does not apply to a special identification card issued to a resident of this State as follows:

(1) The applicant is legally blind.

(2) The applicant is at least 17 years old.

(3) The applicant has been issued a drivers license but the drivers license is cancelled under G.S. 20-15, in accordance with G.S. 20-9(e) and (g), as a result of a physical or mental disability or disease.

(4) The applicant is homeless. To obtain a special identification card without paying a fee, a homeless person must present a letter to the Division from the director of a facility that provides care or shelter to homeless persons verifying that the person is homeless.

(5), (6) Repealed by Session Laws 2018-144, s. 1.3(a), effective December 19, 2018.

(7) The applicant has a developmental disability. To obtain a special identification card without paying a fee pursuant to this subdivision, an applicant must present a letter from his or her primary care provider certifying that the applicant has a developmental disability. For purposes of this subdivision, the term "developmental disability" has the same meaning as in G.S. 122C-3.

(d1) For a person who has a physician's letter certifying that a severe disability causes the person to be homebound, the Division shall adopt rules allowing for application for or renewal of a special photo identification card under this section by means other than a personal appearance.

(d2) Notwithstanding subsection (b) of this section, for a person whose valid drivers license, permit, or endorsement, is required to be seized or surrendered due to cancellation, disqualification, suspension, or revocation under applicable State law, the Division shall issue a special identification card to that person without application, if eligible to receive a special identification card, upon receipt by the Division of the seized or surrendered document. The Division shall issue and mail, via first-class mail to that person's address on file, a special identification card pursuant to this subsection at no charge.

(e) **Offense.** -- Any fraud or misrepresentation in the application for or use of a special identification card issued under this section is a Class 2 misdemeanor.

(f) **Records.** -- The Division shall maintain a record of all recipients of a special identification card.

(g) **No State Liability.** -- The fact of issuance of a special identification card pursuant to this section shall not place upon the State of North Carolina or any agency thereof any liability for the misuse thereof and the acceptance thereof as valid identification is a matter left entirely to the discretion of any person to whom such card is presented.

(h) **Advertising.** -- The Division may utilize the various communications media throughout the State to inform North Carolina residents of the provisions of this section.

History.
1973, c. 438, s. 1; 1975, c. 716, s. 5; 1979, c. 469, c. 667, s. 30; 1981, c. 673, ss. 1, 2; c. 690, s. 12; 1981 (Reg. Sess., 1982), c. 1257, s. 3; 1983, c. 443, s. 2; 1983 (Reg. Sess., 1984), c. 1062, s. 7; 1985, c. 141, s. 5; 1991, c. 689, s. 328;1993, c. 368, s. 3;c. 490, ss. 1, 2; c. 539, s. 325; c. 553, s. 77; 1994, Ex. Sess., c. 24, s. 14(c);1993 (Reg. Sess., 1994), c. 750, s. 2; 2006-247, s. 19(d);2009-493, s. 3;2013-233, ss. 1, 2; 2013-381, s. 3.1;2016-80, s. 1;2017-6, s. 3;2018-142, s. 3(b);2018-144, s. 1.3(a);2020-17, s. 9

RECODIFICATION; TECHNICAL AND CONFORMING CHANGES. --Session Laws 2017-6, s. 3, provides, in part: "The Revisor of Statutes shall recodify Chapter 138A of the General Statutes, Chapter 120C of the General Statutes, as well as Chapter 163 of the General Statutes, as amended by this act, into a new Chapter 163A of the General Statutes to be entitled 'Elections and Ethics Enforcement Act,' as enacted by Section 4 of this act. The Revisor may also recodify into the new Chapter 163A of the General Statutes other existing statutory laws relating to elections and ethics enforcement that are located elsewhere in the General Statutes as the Revisor deems appropriate." The Revisor was further authorized to make additional technical and conforming changes to catchlines, internal citations, and other references throughout the General Statutes to effectuate this recodification. Pursuant to this authority, the Revisor of Statutes substituted "163A-1145" for "163-166.13" and "163A-1389(13)" for "163-275(13)" in subdivisions (d)(5) and (6); and substituted "163A-883" for "163-82.19" in subdivision (d)(6).

Subdivisions (d)(5) and (6) were repealed by Session Laws 2018-144, s. 1.3(a), effective December 19, 2018.

EDITOR'S NOTE. --
Session Laws 1985, c. 141, s. 6 provides that the amendment thereby is effective September 1, 1986. Section 6 further provides that if the Congress of the United States repeals the mandate established by the Surface Transportation Assistance Act of 1982 relating to National Uniform Drinking Age of 21 as found in Section 6 of Public Law 98-363, or a court of competent jurisdiction declares the provision to be unconstitutional or otherwise invalid, then ss. 1, 2, 2.1, 4 and 5 of the act shall expire upon the certification of the Secretary of State that the federal mandate has been repealed or has been invalidated, and the statutes amended by ss. 1, 2, 2.1, 4 and 5 shall revert to the form they would have without the amendments made by these sections.

Session Laws 2013-233, s. 1, was codified as subsection (d1) of this section at the direction of the Revisor of Statutes.

Session Laws 2013-381, s. 6.2(6), provides: "At any primary and election between May 1, 2014, and January 1, 2016, any registered voter may present that voter's photo identification to the elections officials at the voting place but may not be required to do so. At each primary and election between May 1, 2014, and January 1, 2016, each voter presenting in person shall be notified that photo identification will be needed to vote beginning in 2016 and be asked if that voter has one of the forms of photo identification appropriate for voting. If that voter indicates he or she does not have one or more of the types of photo identification appropriate for voting, that voter shall be asked to sign an acknowledgment of the photo identification requirement and be given a list of types of photo identification appropriate for voting and information on how to obtain those types of photo identification. The list of names of those voters who signed an acknowledgment is a public record."

Session Laws 2013-381, s. 60.1, is a severability clause.

Session Laws 2016-80, s. 2, made subdivision (d)(7), as added by Session Laws 2016-80, s. 1, applicable to special identification cards issued on or after October 1, 2016.

Session Laws 2018-134, 3rd Ex. Sess., s. 1.1, provides: "This act shall be known as 'The Hurricane Florence Emergency Response Act.'" Session Laws 2018-134, 3rd Ex. Sess., s. 5.5(a)-(c), provides: "(a) Notwithstanding G.S. 20-14, 20-37.7, 20-85, and 20-88.03, the Governor may waive any fees assessed by the Division of Motor Vehicles under those sections for the following:

"(1) A duplicate drivers license, duplicate commercial drivers license, or duplicate special identification card.

"(2) A special identification card issued to a person for the first time.

"(3) An application for a duplicate or corrected certificate of title.

"(4) A replacement registration plate.

"(5) An application for a duplicate registration card.

"(6) Late payment of a motor vehicle registration renewal fee.

"(b) The waiver authorized under subsection (a) of this section only applies to residents of counties impacted by Hurricane Florence, as determined by the Governor. A resident is allowed a refund of any fee assessed and collected by the Division of Motor Vehicles and waived pursuant to this section. The Division shall post notice of the availability of a refund on its Web site.

"(c) This section is effective when it becomes law and applies to fees assessed or collected on or after September 13, 2018. This section expires December 31, 2018."

Session Laws 2018-144, s. 1.3(b), provides: "The issuance of special identification cards without application for any person whose valid drivers license, permit, or endorsement is received by the Division upon seizure or surrender, as required by G.S. 20-37.7(d2), as enacted by this act, shall begin no later than May 1, 2019."

Session Laws 2019-4 provides in its preamble: "Whereas, in November 2018, the voters of North Carolina approved a constitutional amendment requiring every voter offering to vote in person to present photographic identification before voting; and

"Whereas, the approved constitutional amendment became effective upon certification of the November 6, 2018, election results; and

"Whereas, the General Assembly of North Carolina enacted S.L. 2018-144 in December 2018, setting forth the general laws governing the requirements of photographic identification for voting in person and the exceptions thereto, and setting forth a time line of implementation for the 2019 elections and thereafter; and

Whereas, S.L. 2018-144 also contained reforms to the process of absentee voting by mail and those reforms require rule making and other implementation efforts from the State Board of Elections; and

"Whereas, in February 2019, the need for a special congressional election to fill a vacancy in the United States House of Representatives has arisen due to unforeseen circumstances, and the Governor has determined a schedule for such special election; and

"Whereas, in March 2019, the State Board of Elections issued an order to conduct a new election in a separate United States House of Representatives district and has determined a schedule for such new election; and

"Whereas, the schedule of the two additional elections generates concerns about the ability of the county boards of election and the State Board of Elections to ensure uniformity in the requirement to present photographic identification before voting in person; and

"Whereas, the absentee voting by mail reforms in S.L. 2018-144 require rule making and other administrative procedures on the part of the State Board of Elections which will not be completed prior to the two additional 2019 congressional elections; and

"Whereas, the State Board of Elections needs legislative clarity regarding absentee voting by mail in order to conduct the two additional 2019 congressional elections in an orderly fashion; Now, therefore,"

Session Laws 2019-4, s. 1(a), provides: "S.L. 2018 144 shall not apply to any election held in 2019 for which the filing period opens prior to the date set forth in Section 1.5(a)(8) of S.L. 2018 144."

Session Laws 2019-4, s. 1(b), provides: "Notwithstanding Section 1(a) of this act, all implementation and educational efforts set forth in S.L. 2018-144 during 2019 by the State and counties shall continue."

Session Laws 2020-3, s. 4.7(a) -(h), as amended by Session Laws 2020-97, ss. 3.15(a), 3.16(a), provides: "(a) Definition. -- For purposes of this section, 'credential' means any of the following issued by the Division of Motor Vehicles:

"(1) Drivers license.

"(2) Learner's permit.

"(3) Limited learner's permit.

"(4) Limited provisional license.

"(5) Full provisional license.

"(6) Commercial drivers license.

"(7) Commercial learner's permit.

"(8) Temporary driving certificate.

"(9) Special identification card.

"(10) Handicapped placard.

"(11) Vehicle registration.

"(12) Temporary vehicle registration.

"(13) Dealer license plate.

"(14) Transporter plate.

"(15) Loaner/Dealer 'LD' plate.

"(16) Vehicle inspection authorization.

"(17) Inspection station license.

"(18) Inspection mechanic license.

"(19) Transportation network company permit.

"(20) Motor vehicle dealer license.

"(21) Sales representative license.

"(22) Manufacturer license.

"(23) Distributor license.

"(24) Wholesaler license.

"(25) Driver training school license.

"(26) Driver training school instructor license.

"(27) Professional housemoving license.

"(b) Extend Validity of Credentials. -- Notwithstanding renewal, duration, or expiration provisions of G.S. 20-7, 20-11, 20-37.6, 20-37.7, 20-37.13, 20-50, 20-66, 20-79, 20-79.02, 20-79.2, 20-183.4B, 20-183.4D, 20-280.3, 20-288, 20-324, and 20-359, or any other provision of law to the contrary, the Division of Motor Vehicles shall extend for a period of five months the validity of any credential that expires on or after March 1, 2020, and before August 1, 2020. The Division shall extend for a period of five months the validity of any credential listed in subdivisions (6), (7), (9), (10), and (18) of subsection (a) of this section that expires on or after March 1, 2020, and before the date 30 days after the date the Governor (i) rescinds Executive Order No. 116 or (ii) issues another executive order lifting restrictions on Division of Motor Vehicles functions. Notwithstanding G.S. 20-37.13(h) and G.S. 20-37.13A(a), the Division of Motor Vehicles is authorized to waive the requirement that commercial drivers license and commercial learner's permit holders have a medical examination and certification, as required by federal law, consistent with any waiver of medical qualifications standards issued by the Federal Motor Carrier Safety Administration. A credential extended under this section shall expire five months from the date it otherwise expires as prescribed by law prior to this section. However, the subsequent expiration of a credential extended under this section shall occur on the date prescribed by law prior to this section without regard to the extension. The Division shall notify individuals affected by an extension granted under this section, including information on new expiration dates and how the extension affects subsequent renewal and expiration dates.

"(b1) Extension of Intrastate Medical Waivers. -- Notwithstanding the limitation on duration of waivers in G.S. 20-37.13A(b), the Division of Motor Vehicles may extend for up to five months the validity of a medical waiver issued by the Division under G.S. 20-37.13A if the waiver expires on or after March 1, 2020, and before the date 30 days after the date the

Governor (i) rescinds Executive Order No. 116 or (ii) issues another executive order lifting restrictions on Division of Motor Vehicles functions, and the Division's Medical Review Unit determines the extension is appropriate.

"(c) Driving Eligibility Certificates. -- Notwithstanding G.S. 20-11(n)(3), a driving eligibility certificate dated on or after February 9, 2020, and before March 10, 2020, remains valid and may be accepted by the Division of Motor Vehicles to meet the requirements for a license or permit issued under G.S. 20-11 until 30 days after the date the Governor rescinds Executive Order No. 116 or the date the Division reopens all drivers license offices, whichever is earlier.

"(d) Waive Penalties. -- Notwithstanding any provision of law to the contrary, the Division shall waive any fines, fees, or penalties associated with failing to renew a credential during the period of time the credential is valid by extension under subsection (b) of this section.

"(e) Motor Vehicle Taxes. -- Notwithstanding any provision of law to the contrary, due dates for motor vehicle taxes that are tied to registration expiration under Article 22A of Chapter 105 of the General Statutes shall be extended to correspond with extended expiration dates under subsection (b) of this section.

"(f) Validity by Extension a Defense. -- A person may not be convicted or found responsible for any offense resulting from failure to renew a credential issued by the Division if, when tried for that offense, the person shows that the offense occurred during the period of time the credential is valid by extension under subsection (b) of this section.

"(g) Report. -- Within 30 days of the extensions made under subsection (b) of this section, the Division shall submit a report to the Joint Legislative Transportation Oversight Committee and the Fiscal Research Division detailing implementation of this section.

"(h) Effective Date. -- This section is effective retroactively to March 1, 2020, and applies to expirations occurring on or after that date."

Session Laws 2020-3, s. 5, is a severability clause.

Session Laws 2020-97, s. 4.5, is a severability clause.

EFFECT OF AMENDMENTS. --

Session Laws 2006-247, s. 19(d), effective December 1, 2006, and applicable to all applications for a drivers license, learner's permit, instruction permit, or special identificaton card submitted on or after that date, added subsection (b1).

Session Laws 2009-493, s. 3, effective August 26, 2009, added "or who has been issued a drivers license but the drivers license is cancelled under G.S. 20-15, in accordance with G.S. 20-9(e) and (g), as a result of a physical or mental disability or disease" at the end of the second sentence in the second paragraph of subsection (d).

Session Laws 2013-233, ss. 1 and 2, effective July 1, 2014, added "including a color photograph of the special identification card holder and" in subsection (c); and added subsection (d1).

Session Laws 2013-381, s. 3.1, effective January 1, 2014, in subsection (d) inserted "as follows" at the end of the second paragraph and inserted the subdivision

(d)(1) through (4) designations; in subdivision (d)(1), substituted "The applicant" for "who"; in subdivision (d)(2), inserted "The applicant"; in subdivision (d)(3), inserted the first sentence; and added subdivisions (d) (5) and (d)(6).

Session Laws 2016-80, s. 1, effective October 1, 2016, added subdivision (d)(7). See editor's note for applicability.

Session Laws 2018-142, s. 3(b), effective December 14, 2018, in subsection (b1), added "The following applies in this subsection:" at the end; rewrote subdivision (b1)(4); in subsection (c), inserted "shall" preceding "be similar in size"; and in subdivision (d) (3), deleted "or who" following "applicant."

Session Laws 2018-144, s. 1.3(a), effective December 19, 2018, in subdivision (d)(2), substituted "17 years old" for "70 years old" following "at least"; deleted subdivisions (d)(5) and (d)(6); and added subsection (d2).

Session Laws 2020-17, s. 9, effective June 12, 2020, added the last sentence in the first paragraph of subsection (d).

LIABILITY OF STATE FOR NEGLIGENT ISSUANCE. --Where plaintiff suffered personal injury proximately caused by a Division of Motor Vehicles employee who in the course of his employment issued a special identification card in plaintiff's name to another person, this section did not prohibit an action against the State for misuse of a special identification card issued by the State; the legislature by the enactment of this section did not contemplate that the State would escape liability if a special identification card was negligently issued. Talbot v. North Carolina Dep't of Transp., 95 N.C. App. 446, 382 S.E.2d 447 (1989).

CITED in State v. Fair, 77 N.C. App. 681, 335 S.E.2d 783 (1985); N.C. State Conf. of the NAACP v. McCrory, 997 F. Supp. 2d 322 (M.D.N.C. Aug. 8, 2014).

§ 20-37.8. Fraudulent use prohibited

(a) It shall be unlawful for any person to use a false or fictitious name or give a false or fictitious address in any application for a special identification card or knowingly to make a false statement or knowingly conceal a material fact or otherwise commit a fraud in any such application or to obtain or possess more than one such card for a fraudulent purpose or knowingly to permit or allow another to commit any of the foregoing acts.

(b) It shall be unlawful for any person to present, display, or use a special identification card which contains a false or fictitious name in the commission or attempted commission of a felony.

(c) A violation of subsection (a) of this section shall constitute a Class 2 misdemeanor. A violation of subsection (b) of this section shall constitute a Class I felony.

History.

1979, c. 603, s. 1; 1993, c. 539, s. 326;1994, Ex. Sess., c. 24, s. 14(c);1999-299, s. 2

§ 20-37.9. Notice of change of address or name

(a) **Address.** -- A person whose address changes from the address stated on a special identification card must notify the Division of the change within 60 days after the change occurs. If the person's address changed because the person moved, the person must obtain a new special identification card within that time limit stating the new address. A person who does not move but whose address changes due to governmental action may not be charged with violating this subsection.

(b) **Name.** -- A person whose name changes from the name stated on a special identification card must notify the Division of the change within 60 days after the change occurs and obtain a new special identification card stating the new name.

(c) **Fee.** -- G.S. 20-37.7 sets the fee for a special identification card.

History.
1981, c. 521, s. 2; 1991, c. 689, s. 329;1997-122, s. 6

ARTICLE 2C.
COMMERCIAL DRIVER LICENSE

§ 20-37.10. Title of Article

This Article may be cited as the Commercial Driver License Act.

History.
1989, c. 771, s. 2

§ 20-37.11. Purpose

The purpose of this Article is to implement the federal Commercial Motor Vehicle Safety Act of 1986, 49 U.S.C. Chapter 36, and reduce or prevent commercial motor vehicle accidents, fatalities, and injuries by:

(1) Permitting commercial drivers to hold one license;

(2) Disqualifying commercial drivers who have committed certain serious traffic violations, or other specified offenses; and

(3) Strengthening commercial driver licensing and testing standards.

To the extent that this Article conflicts with general driver licensing provisions, this Article prevails. Where this Article is silent, the general driver licensing provisions apply.

History.
1989, c. 771, s. 2

§ 20-37.12. Commercial drivers license required

(a) On or after April 1, 1992, no person shall operate a commercial motor vehicle on the highways of this State unless he has first been issued and is in immediate possession of a commercial drivers license with applicable endorsements valid for the vehicle he is driving; provided, a person may operate a commercial motor vehicle after being issued and while in possession of a commercial driver learner's permit and while accompanied by the holder of a commercial drivers license valid for the vehicle being driven.

(b) The out-of-service criteria as referred to in 49 C.F.R. Subchapter B apply to a person who drives a commercial motor vehicle. No person shall drive a commercial motor vehicle on the highways of this State in violation of an out-of-service order.

(c) Repealed by Session Laws 1991, c. 726, s. 15.

(d) Any person who is not a resident of this State, who has been issued a commercial drivers license by his state of residence, or who holds any license recognized by the federal government that grants the privilege of driving a commercial motor vehicle, who has that license in his immediate possession, whose privilege to drive any motor vehicle is not suspended, revoked, or cancelled, and who has not been disqualified from driving a commercial motor vehicle shall be permitted without further examination or licensure by the Division to drive a commercial motor vehicle in this State.

(e) G.S. 20-7 sets the time period in which a new resident of North Carolina must obtain a license from the Division. The Commissioner may establish by rule the conditions under which the test requirements for a commercial drivers license may be waived for a new resident who is licensed in another state.

(f) A person shall not be convicted of failing to carry a commercial drivers license if, by the date the person is required to appear in court for the violation, the person produces to the court a commercial drivers license issued to the person that was valid on the date of the offense.

History.
1989, c. 771, s. 2;1991, c. 726, s. 15;1997-122, s. 5;1998-149, s. 4;2003-397, s. 3;2009-416, s. 5

EFFECT OF AMENDMENTS. --
Session Laws 2009-416, s. 5, effective March 31, 2010, and applicable to offenses committed on or after that date, inserted "or who holds any license recognized by the federal government that grants the privilege of driving a commercial motor vehicle" in subsection (d).

§ 20-37.13. Commercial drivers license qualification standards

(a) No person shall be issued a commercial drivers license unless the person meets all of the following requirements:

(1) Is a resident of this State.

(2) Is 21 years of age.

(3) Has passed a knowledge test and a skills test for driving a commercial motor vehicle that comply with minimum federal standards established by federal regulation enumerated in 49 C.F.R., Part 383, Subparts F, G, and H.

(4) Has satisfied all other requirements of the Commercial Motor Vehicle Safety Act in addition to other requirements of this Chapter or federal regulation.

(5) Has held a commercial learner's permit for a minimum of 14 days.

For the purpose of skills testing and determining commercial drivers license classification, only the manufacturer's GVWR shall be used.

The tests shall be prescribed and conducted by the Division. Provided, a person who is at least 18 years of age may be issued a commercial drivers license if the person is exempt from, or not subject to, the age requirements of the federal Motor Carrier Safety Regulations contained in 49 C.F.R., Part 391, as adopted by the Division.

(b) The Division may permit a person, including an agency of this or another state, an employer, a private driver training facility, or an agency of local government, to administer the skills test specified by this section, provided:

(1) The test is the same as that administered by the Division; and

(2) The third party has entered into an agreement with the Division which complies with the requirements of 49 C.F.R. § 383.75. The Division may charge a fee to applicants for third-party testing authority in order to investigate the applicants' qualifications and to monitor their program as required by federal law.

(b1) The Division shall allow a third party to administer a skills test for driving a commercial motor vehicle pursuant to subsection (b) of this section any day of the week.

(c) Prior to October 1, 1992, the Division may waive the skills test for applicants licensed at the time they apply for a commercial drivers license if:

(1) For an application submitted by April 1, 1992, the applicant has not, and certifies that he or she has not, at any time during the two years immediately preceding the date of application done any of the following and for an application submitted after April 1, 1992, the applicant has not, and certifies that he or she has not, at any time during the two years preceding April 1, 1992:

a. Had more than one drivers license, except during the 10-day period beginning on the date he or she is issued a drivers license, or unless, prior to December 31, 1989, he or she was required to have more than one license by a State law enacted prior to June 1, 1986;

b. Had any drivers license or driving privilege suspended, revoked, or cancelled;

c. Had any convictions involving any kind of motor vehicle for the offenses listed in G.S. 20-17 or had any convictions for the offenses listed in G.S. 20-17.4;

d. Been convicted of a violation of State or local laws relating to motor vehicle traffic control, other than a parking violation, which violation arose in connection with any reportable traffic accident; or

e. Refused to take a chemical test when charged with an implied consent offense, as defined in G.S. 20-16.2; and

(2) The applicant certifies, and provides satisfactory evidence, that he or she is regularly employed in a job requiring the operation of a commercial motor vehicle, and he or she either:

a. Has previously taken and successfully completed a skills test that was administered by a state with a classified licensing and testing system and the test was behind the wheel in a vehicle representative of the class and, if applicable, the type of commercial motor vehicle for which the applicant seeks to be licensed; or

b. Has operated for the relevant two-year period under subpart (1)a. of this subsection, a vehicle representative of the class and, if applicable, the type of commercial motor vehicle for which the applicant seeks to be licensed.

(c1) The Division may waive the skills test for any qualified military applicant at the time the applicant applies for a commercial drivers license if the applicant is currently licensed at the time of application and meets all of the following:

(1) The applicant has passed all required written knowledge exams.

(2) The applicant has not, and certifies that the applicant has not, at any time during the two years immediately preceding the date of application done any of the following:

a. Had any drivers license or driving privilege suspended, revoked, or cancelled.

b. Had any convictions involving any kind of motor vehicle for the offenses listed in G.S. 20-17 or had any convictions for the offenses listed in G.S. 20-17.4.

    c. Been convicted of a violation of military, State, or local laws relating to motor vehicle traffic control, other than a parking violation, which violation arose in connection with any reportable traffic accident.

    d. Refused to take a chemical test when charged with an implied consent offense, as defined in G.S. 20-16.2.

    e. Had more than one drivers license, except for a drivers license issued by the military.

    (3) The applicant certifies, and provides satisfactory evidence on the date of application, that the applicant is a retired, discharged, or current member of an active or reserve component of the Armed Forces of the United States and is regularly employed or was regularly employed within the one-year period immediately preceding the date of application in a military position requiring the operation of a commercial motor vehicle, and the applicant meets either of the following requirements:

    a. Repealed by Session Laws 2013-201, s. 1, effective June 26, 2013.

    b. Has operated for the two-year period immediately preceding the date of application a vehicle representative of the class and, if applicable, the type of commercial motor vehicle for which the applicant seeks to be licensed, and has taken and successfully completed a skills test administered by the military.

    c. For an applicant who is a retired or discharged member of an active or reserve component of the Armed Forces of the United States, the applicant (i) has operated for the two-year period immediately preceding the date of retirement or discharge a vehicle representative of the class and, if applicable, the type of commercial motor vehicle for which the applicant seeks to be licensed, and has taken and successfully completed a skills test administered by the military, (ii) has retired or received either an honorable or general discharge, and (iii) has retired or been discharged from the Armed Forces within the one-year period immediately preceding the date of application.

    (c2) The one-year period referenced in subdivision (3) of subsection (c1) of this section applies unless a different period is provided by federal law. An applicant may provide his or her Form DD 214, "Certificate of Release or Discharge from Active Duty," and his or her drivers license issued by the military, to satisfy the certification required by subdivision (3) of subsection (c1) of this section. An applicant who is retired or discharged must provide a drivers license issued by the military that was valid at the time of his or her retirement or discharge when using the process in this subsection to satisfy the certification required by subdivision (3) of subsection (c1) of this section.

    (c3) The Division may waive the knowledge and skills test for a qualified military applicant who has been issued a military license that authorizes the holder to operate a motor vehicle representative of the class and endorsements for which the applicant seeks to be licensed. The applicant must certify and provide satisfactory evidence on the date of application that the applicant meets all of the following requirements:

    (1) The applicant is a current or former member of an active or reserve component of the Armed Forces of the United States and was issued a military license that authorized the applicant to operate a vehicle that is representative of the class and type of commercial motor vehicle for which the applicant seeks to be licensed and whose military occupational specialty or rating are eligible for waiver, as allowed by the Federal Motor Carrier Safety Administration.

    (2) The applicant is or was, within the year prior to the date of application, regularly employed in a military position requiring operation of a motor vehicle representative of the class of commercial motor vehicle for which the applicant seeks to be licensed.

    (3) The applicant meets the qualifications listed in subdivision (2) of subsection (c1) of this section.

    (d) A commercial drivers license or learner's permit shall not be issued to a person while the person is subject to a disqualification from driving a commercial motor vehicle, or while the person's drivers license is suspended, revoked, or cancelled in any state; nor shall a commercial drivers license be issued unless the person who has applied for the license first surrenders all other drivers licenses issued by the Division or by another state. If a person surrenders a drivers license issued by another state, the Division must return the license to the issuing state for cancellation.

    (e) A commercial learner's permit may be issued to an individual who holds a regular Class C drivers license and has passed the knowledge test for the class and type of commercial motor vehicle the individual will be driving. The permit is valid for a period not to exceed 180 days. The fee for a commercial driver learner's permit is the same as the fee set by G.S. 20-7 for a regular learner's permit.

    (f) Notwithstanding subsection (e) of this section, a commercial driver learner's permit with

Chapter 20

a P or S endorsement shall not be issued to any person who is required to register under Article 27A of Chapter 14 of the General Statutes.

(g) The issuance of a commercial driver learner's permit is a precondition to the initial issuance of a commercial drivers license. The issuance of a commercial driver learner's permit is also a precondition to the upgrade of a commercial drivers license if the upgrade requires a skills test.

(h) The Division shall promptly notify any driver who fails to meet the medical certification requirements in accordance with 49 C.F.R. § 383.71. The Division shall give the driver 60 days to provide the required documentation. If the driver fails to provide the required commercial drivers license medical certification documentation within the period allowed, the Division shall automatically downgrade a commercial drivers license to a class C regular drivers license.

History.

1989, c. 771, s. 2;1991, c. 726, s. 16;1991 (Reg. Sess., 1992), c. 916, s. 1; 2005-349, s. 8;2009-274, s. 4;2009-491, s. 5;2009-494, s. 1;2011-183, s. 22;2013-195, s. 1;2013-201, s. 1;2014-115, s. 28.5(a), (b); 2015-115, s. 1;2016-90, s. 6(b);2018-74, s. 9(a)

EDITOR'S NOTE. --

Session Laws 2009-491, s. 7, provides in part: "This act [which aded subsection (f)] applies to persons whose initial registration under Article 27A of Chapter 14 of the General Statutes occurs on or after December 1, 2009, and to persons who are registered under Article 27A of Chapter 14 of the General Statutes prior to December 1, 2009, and continue to be registered on or after December 1, 2009. The criminal penalties enacted by this act apply to offenses occurring on or after December 1, 2009."

Session Laws 2016-90, s. 6(f), made the amendment to subsection (e) by Session Laws 2016-90, s. 6(b), applicable to offenses committed on or after January 1, 2017.

Session Laws 2020-3, s. 4.7(a) -(h), as amended by Session Laws 2020-97, ss. 3.15(a), 3.16(a), provides: "(a) Definition. -- For purposes of this section, 'credential' means any of the following issued by the Division of Motor Vehicles:

"(1) Drivers license.

"(2) Learner's permit.

"(3) Limited learner's permit.

"(4) Limited provisional license.

"(5) Full provisional license.

"(6) Commercial drivers license.

"(7) Commercial learner's permit.

"(8) Temporary driving certificate.

"(9) Special identification card.

"(10) Handicapped placard.

"(11) Vehicle registration.

"(12) Temporary vehicle registration.

"(13) Dealer license plate.

"(14) Transporter plate.

"(15) Loaner/Dealer 'LD' plate.

"(16) Vehicle inspection authorization.

"(17) Inspection station license.

"(18) Inspection mechanic license.

"(19) Transportation network company permit.

"(20) Motor vehicle dealer license.

"(21) Sales representative license.

"(22) Manufacturer license.

"(23) Distributor license.

"(24) Wholesaler license.

"(25) Driver training school license.

"(26) Driver training school instructor license.

"(27) Professional housemoving license.

"(b) Extend Validity of Credentials. -- Notwithstanding renewal, duration, or expiration provisions of G.S. 20-7, 20-11, 20-37.6, 20-37.7, 20-37.13, 20-50, 20-66, 20-79, 20-79.02, 20-79.2, 20-183.4B, 20-183.4D, 20-280.3, 20-288, 20-324, and 20-359, or any other provision of law to the contrary, the Division of Motor Vehicles shall extend for a period of five months the validity of any credential that expires on or after March 1, 2020, and before August 1, 2020. The Division shall extend for a period of five months the validity of any credential listed in subdivisions (6), (7), (9), (10), and (18) of subsection (a) of this section that expires on or after March 1, 2020, and before the date 30 days after the date the Governor (i) rescinds Executive Order No. 116 or (ii) issues another executive order lifting restrictions on Division of Motor Vehicles functions. Notwithstanding G.S. 20-37.13(h) and G.S. 20-37.13A(a), the Division of Motor Vehicles is authorized to waive the requirement that commercial drivers license and commercial learner's permit holders have a medical examination and certification, as required by federal law, consistent with any waiver of medical qualifications standards issued by the Federal Motor Carrier Safety Administration. A credential extended under this section shall expire five months from the date it otherwise expires as prescribed by law prior to this section. However, the subsequent expiration of a credential extended under this section shall occur on the date prescribed by law prior to this section without regard to the extension. The Division shall notify individuals affected by an extension granted under this section, including information on new expiration dates and how the extension affects subsequent renewal and expiration dates.

"(b1) Extension of Intrastate Medical Waivers. -- Notwithstanding the limitation on duration of waivers in G.S. 20-37.13A(b), the Division of Motor Vehicles may extend for up to five months the validity of a medical waiver issued by the Division under G.S. 20-37.13A if the waiver expires on or after March 1, 2020, and before the date 30 days after the date the Governor (i) rescinds Executive Order No. 116 or (ii) issues another executive order lifting restrictions on Division of Motor Vehicles functions, and the Division's Medical Review Unit determines the extension is appropriate.

"(c) Driving Eligibility Certificates. -- Notwithstanding G.S. 20-11(n)(3), a driving eligibility certificate dated on or after February 9, 2020, and before March 10, 2020, remains valid and may be accepted by the Division of Motor Vehicles to meet the requirements for a license or permit issued under G.S. 20-11 until 30 days after the date the Governor rescinds Executive Order No. 116 or the date the Division reopens all drivers license offices, whichever is earlier.

"(d) Waive Penalties. -- Notwithstanding any provision of law to the contrary, the Division shall waive any fines, fees, or penalties associated with failing to renew a credential during the period of time the credential is valid by extension under subsection (b) of this section.

"(e) Motor Vehicle Taxes. -- Notwithstanding any provision of law to the contrary, due dates for motor vehicle taxes that are tied to registration expiration under Article 22A of Chapter 105 of the General Statutes shall be extended to correspond with extended expiration dates under subsection (b) of this section.

"(f) Validity by Extension a Defense. -- A person may not be convicted or found responsible for any offense resulting from failure to renew a credential issued by the Division if, when tried for that offense, the person shows that the offense occurred during the period of time the credential is valid by extension under subsection (b) of this section.

"(g) Report. -- Within 30 days of the extensions made under subsection (b) of this section, the Division shall submit a report to the Joint Legislative Transportation Oversight Committee and the Fiscal Research Division detailing implementation of this section".

"(h) Effective Date. -- This section is effective retroactively to March 1, 2020, and applies to expirations occurring on or after that date."

Session Laws 2020-3, s. 5, is a severability clause.

Session Laws 2020-97, s. 4.5, is a severability clause.

EFFECT OF AMENDMENTS. --

Session Laws 2005-349, s. 8, effective September 30, 2005, in subsection (a), substituted "Subparts F, G and H" for "Subparts G and H" at the end of subdivision (a)(3), and added the next-to-last paragraph of the subsection.

Session Laws 2009-274, s. 4, effective July 10, 2009, and applicable to all licenses expiring on or after that date, substituted "Armed Forces" for "armed forces" in subdivision (c1)(3).

Session Laws 2009-494, s. 1, effective January 1, 2010, and applicable to any commercial drivers license issued on or after that date, added subsection (c1).

Session Laws 2011-183, s. 22, effective June 20, 2011, in subsections (a) and (d), made minor stylistic changes; throughout subsection (c), inserted "or she" following "he"; and in subdivision (c1)(3), substituted "component of the Armed Forces of the United States" for "component of a branch of the United States Armed Forces."

Session Laws 2013-195, s. 1, effective July 1, 2013, added subsection (b1).

Session Laws 2013-201, s. 1, effective June 26, 2013, in subsection (c1), substituted "any qualified military applicant" for "applicants" and "the applicant applies" for "they apply," and inserted "is currently licensed at the time of application and"; added sub-subdivision (c1)(2)e.; in subdivision (c1)(3), inserted "retired, discharged, or current" and "or was regularly employed within the 90-day period immediately preceding the date of application," and substituted "military position" for "job" and "meets either of the following requirements" for "either"; deleted sub-subdivision (c1)(3)a.; added sub-subdivision (c1)(3)c.; and made minor punctuation and stylistic changes in sub-subdivisions (c1)(2)a. through (c1)(2)c.

Session Laws 2014-115, s. 28.5(a), effective August 11, 2014, in subsection (a), added "meets all of the following requirements" to the introductory paragraph; added subdivision (a)(5); added subsections (g) and (h); and made minor, stylistic changes.

Session Laws 2015-115, s. 1, effective June 24, 2015, substituted "one-year" for "90-day" in subdivisions (c1)(3) and (c1)(3)(c); and added subsection (c2).

Session Laws 2016-90, s. 6(b), effective January 1, 2017, in subsection (e), deleted "driver" following "A commercial" near the beginning of the first sentence, substituted "180 days" for "six months and may be renewed or reissued only once within a two year period" at the end of the second sentence, and deleted the former fourth sentence, which read: "G.S. 20-7(m) governs the issuance of a restricted instruction permit for a prospective school bus driver" from the end of the subsection. See editor's note for applicability.

Session Laws 2018-74, s. 9(a), effective October 1, 2018, added subsection (c3).

CITED in State v. Hernandez, 188 N.C. App. 193, 655 S.E.2d 426 (2008).

§ 20-37.13A. Medical qualifications standards; waiver for intrastate drivers

(a) Medical Qualifications Standards Applicable to Commercial Drivers. — All commercial drivers license holders and applicants for commercial drivers licenses must meet the medical qualifications standards set forth in 49 C.F.R. § 391.41. As allowed under G.S. 20-9(g)(4)h., the Division may release information it deems necessary to any other State or federal government agency for purposes of determining an individual's ability to safely operate a commercial motor vehicle or to obtain a commercial drivers license.

(b) Intrastate Medical Waiver. — Any person unable to meet the standards in 49 C.F.R. § 391.41, as adopted by the Division, may apply for a medical waiver that, if approved, will authorize intrastate operation of a commercial motor vehicle. Applications for the medical waiver must be submitted to the Division in

Chapter 20

writing. Waivers may be granted for no more than two years.

(c) Intrastate Operation Subject to Waiver. — Any person granted an intrastate commercial drivers license medical waiver is permitted to maintain a commercial drivers license and operate a commercial motor vehicle in intrastate commerce subject to the following conditions:

(1) The commercial drivers license must display a restriction to signify it is only valid for intrastate operation.

(2) The holder of the license must submit to medical recertification at intervals set by the Division.

(3) The holder of the license must timely submit all documentation required by the Division.

(4) Failure to meet any condition within the time period allowed will result in an automatic downgrade of the license holder's commercial drivers license to a Class C regular drivers license.

History.

2016-90, s. 6(e); 2018-74, s. 10(c).

EDITOR'S NOTE. --

Session Laws 2016-90, s. 6(f), made this section effective January 1, 2017, and applicable to offenses committed on or after that date.

Session Laws 2020-3, s. 4.7(a) -(h), as amended by Session Laws 2020-97, ss. 3.15(a), 3.16(a), provides:

"(a) Definition. -- For purposes of this section, 'credential' means any of the following issued by the Division of Motor Vehicles:

"(1) Drivers license.

"(2) Learner's permit.

"(3) Limited learner's permit.

"(4) Limited provisional license.

"(5) Full provisional license.

"(6) Commercial drivers license.

"(7) Commercial learner's permit.

"(8) Temporary driving certificate.

"(9) Special identification card.

"(10) Handicapped placard.

"(11) Vehicle registration.

"(12) Temporary vehicle registration.

"(13) Dealer license plate.

"(14) Transporter plate.

"(15) Loaner/Dealer 'LD' plate.

"(16) Vehicle inspection authorization.

"(17) Inspection station license.

"(18) Inspection mechanic license.

"(19) Transportation network company permit.

"(20) Motor vehicle dealer license.

"(21) Sales representative license.

"(22) Manufacturer license.

"(23) Distributor license.

"(24) Wholesaler license.

"(25) Driver training school license.

"(26) Driver training school instructor license.

"(27) Professional housemoving license.

"(b) Extend Validity of Credentials. -- Notwithstanding renewal, duration, or expiration provisions of G.S. 20-7, 20-11, 20-37.6, 20-37.7, 20-37.13, 20-50, 20-66, 20-79, 20-79.02, 20-79.2, 20-183.4B, 20-183.4D, 20-280.3, 20-288, 20-324, and 20-359, or any other provision of law to the contrary, the Division of Motor Vehicles shall extend for a period of five months the validity of any credential that expires on or after March 1, 2020, and before August 1, 2020. The Division shall extend for a period of five months the validity of any credential listed in subdivisions (6), (7), (9), (10), and (18) of subsection (a) of this section that expires on or after March 1, 2020, and before the date 30 days after the date the Governor (i) rescinds Executive Order No. 116 or (ii) issues another executive order lifting restrictions on Division of Motor Vehicles functions. Notwithstanding G.S. 20-37.13(h) and G.S. 20-37.13A(a), the Division of Motor Vehicles is authorized to waive the requirement that commercial drivers license and commercial learner's permit holders have a medical examination and certification, as required by federal law, consistent with any waiver of medical qualifications standards issued by the Federal Motor Carrier Safety Administration. A credential extended under this section shall expire five months from the date it otherwise expires as prescribed by law prior to this section. However, the subsequent expiration of a credential extended under this section shall occur on the date prescribed by law prior to this section without regard to the extension. The Division shall notify individuals affected by an extension granted under this section, including information on new expiration dates and how the extension affects subsequent renewal and expiration dates.

"(b1) Extension of Intrastate Medical Waivers. -- Notwithstanding the limitation on duration of waivers in G.S. 20-37.13A(b), the Division of Motor Vehicles may extend for up to five months the validity of a medical waiver issued by the Division under G.S. 20-37.13A if the waiver expires on or after March 1, 2020, and before the date 30 days after the date the Governor (i) rescinds Executive Order No. 116 or (ii) issues another executive order lifting restrictions on Division of Motor Vehicles functions, and the Division's Medical Review Unit determines the extension is appropriate.

"(c) Driving Eligibility Certificates. -- Notwithstanding G.S. 20-11(n)(3), a driving eligibility certificate dated on or after February 9, 2020, and before March 10, 2020, remains valid and may be accepted by the Division of Motor Vehicles to meet the requirements for a license or permit issued under G.S. 20-11 until 30 days after the date the Governor rescinds Executive Order No. 116 or the date the Division reopens all drivers license offices, whichever is earlier.

"(d) Waive Penalties. -- Notwithstanding any provision of law to the contrary, the Division shall waive any fines, fees, or penalties associated with failing to renew a credential during the period of time the credential is valid by extension under subsection (b) of this section.

"(e) Motor Vehicle Taxes. -- Notwithstanding any provision of law to the contrary, due dates for motor vehicle taxes that are tied to registration expiration under Article 22A of Chapter 105 of the General Statutes shall be extended to correspond with extended expiration dates under subsection (b) of this section.

"(f) Validity by Extension a Defense. -- A person may not be convicted or found responsible for any offense resulting from failure to renew a credential issued by the Division if, when tried for that offense, the person shows that the offense occurred during the period of time the credential is valid by extension under subsection (b) of this section.

"(g) Report. -- Within 30 days of the extensions made under subsection (b) of this section, the Division shall submit a report to the Joint Legislative Transportation Oversight Committee and the Fiscal Research Division detailing implementation of this section.

"(h) Effective Date. -- This section is effective retroactively to March 1, 2020, and applies to expirations occurring on or after that date."

Session Laws 2020-3, s. 5, is a severability clause.

Session Laws 2020-97, s. 4.5, is a severability clause.

EFFECT OF AMENDMENTS. --

Session Laws 2018-74, s. 10(c), effective July 1, 2018, added the last sentence of subsection (a).

§ 20-37.14. Nonresident commercial driver license

The Division may issue a nonresident commercial driver license (NRCDL) to a resident of a foreign jurisdiction if the United States Secretary of Transportation has determined that the commercial motor vehicle testing and licensing standards in the foreign jurisdiction do not meet the testing standards established in 49 C.F.R., Part 383. The word "Nonresident" must appear on the face of the NRCDL. An applicant must surrender any NRCDL issued by another state. Prior to issuing a NRCDL, the Division shall establish the practical capability of revoking, suspending, or cancelling the NRCDL and disqualifying that person with the same conditions applicable to the commercial driver license issued to a resident of this State.

History.
1989, c. 771, s. 2

§ 20-37.14A. Prohibit issuance or renewal of certain categories of commercial drivers licenses to sex offenders

(a) Effective December 1, 2009, the Division shall not issue or renew a commercial drivers license with a P or S endorsement to any person who is required to register under Article 27A of Chapter 14 of the General Statutes.

(b) The Division shall not issue a commercial drivers license with a P or S endorsement to an applicant until the Division has searched both the statewide registry and the National Sex Offender Public Registry to determine if the person is currently registered as a sex offender in North Carolina or another state.

(1) If the Division finds that the person is currently registered as a sex offender in either North Carolina or another state, the Division, in compliance with subsection (a) of this section, shall not issue a commercial drivers license with a P or S endorsement to the person.

(2) If the Division is unable to access either the statewide registry or all of the states' information contained in the National Sex Offender Public Registry, but the person is otherwise qualified to obtain a commercial drivers license with a P or S endorsement, then the Division shall issue the commercial drivers license with the P or S endorsement but shall first require the person to sign an affidavit stating that the person does not appear on either the statewide registry or the National Sex Offender Public Registry. The Division shall search the statewide registry and the National Sex Offender Public Registry for the person within a reasonable time after access to the statewide registry or the National Sex Offender Public Registry is restored. If the person does appear in either registry, the person is in violation of this section, and the Division shall immediately cancel the commercial drivers license and shall promptly notify the sheriff of the county where the person resides of the offense.

(3) Any person denied a commercial license with a P or S endorsement or who is disqualified from driving a commercial motor vehicle that requires a commercial drivers license with a P or S endorsement by the Division pursuant to this subsection shall have a right to file a petition within 30 days thereafter for a hearing in the matter, in the superior court of the county where the person resides, or to the resident judge of the district or judge holding the court of that district, or special or emergency judge holding a court in such district. The court or judge is vested with jurisdiction to hear the petition, and it shall be the duty of the judge or court to set the matter for hearing upon 30 days' written notice to the Division, and thereupon to take testimony and examine into the facts of the case and

to determine whether the petitioner is entitled to a commercial drivers license with a P or S endorsement under the provisions of this subsection.

(c) Any person who makes a false affidavit, or who knowingly swears or affirms falsely, to any matter or thing required by the terms of this section to be affirmed to or sworn is guilty of a Class I felony.

History.
2009-491, s. 6

EDITOR'S NOTE. --
Session Laws 2009-491, s. 7, provides: "This act becomes effective December 1, 2009. This act applies to persons whose initial registration under Article 27A of Chapter 14 of the General Statutes occurs on or after December 1, 2009, and to persons who are registered under Article 27A of Chapter 14 of the General Statutes prior to December 1, 2009, and continue to be registered on or after December 1, 2009. The criminal penalties enacted by this act apply to offenses occurring on or after December 1, 2009."

§ 20-37.15. Application for commercial drivers license

(a) An application for a commercial drivers license must include the information required by G.S. 20-7 for a regular drivers license and a consent to release driving record information.

(a1) The application must be accompanied by a nonrefundable application fee of forty dollars ($ 40.00). This fee does not apply in any of the following circumstances:

(1) When an individual surrenders a commercial driver learner's permit issued by the Division when submitting the application.

(2) When the application is to renew a commercial drivers license issued by the Division.

This fee shall entitle the applicant to three attempts to pass the written knowledge test without payment of a new fee. No application fee shall be charged to an applicant eligible for a waiver under G.S. 20-37.13(c).

(b) When the holder of a commercial drivers license changes his name or residence address, an application for a duplicate shall be made as provided in G.S. 20-7.1 and a fee paid as provided in G.S. 20-14.

History.
1989, c. 771, s. 2;1991, c. 726, s. 17;1993 (Reg. Sess., 1994), c. 750, s. 3; 2005-276, s. 44.1(f);2015-241, s. 29.30(f)

EDITOR'S NOTE. --
Session Laws 2015-241, s. 29.30(u), made the amendment to subsection (a1) of this section by Session Laws 2015-241, s. 29.30(f), applicable to

issuances, renewals, restorations, and requests on or after January 1, 2016.

EFFECT OF AMENDMENTS. --
Session Laws 2005-276, s. 44.1(f), effective October 1, 2005, and applicable to fees collected on or after that date, substituted "thirty dollars ($30.00)" for "twenty dollars ($20.00)" in the introductory paragraph of subsection (a1).

Session Laws 2015-241, s. 29.30(f), effective January 1, 2016, substituted "forty dollars ($40.00)" for "thirty dollars ($30.00)" in first sentence of the introductory language of subsection (a1). For applicability, see editor's note.

§ 20-37.16. Content of license; classifications and endorsements; fees

(a) A commercial drivers license must be marked "Commercial Drivers License" or "CDL" and must contain the information required by G.S. 20-7 for a regular drivers license.

(b) The classes of commercial drivers licenses are:

(1) Class A CDL -- A Class A commercial drivers license authorizes the holder to drive any Class A motor vehicle.

(2) Class B CDL -- A Class B commercial drivers license authorizes the holder to drive any Class B motor vehicle.

(3) Class C CDL -- A Class C commercial drivers license authorizes the holder to drive any Class C motor vehicle.

(c) **Endorsements. --** The endorsements required to drive certain motor vehicles are as follows:

Endorsement	Vehicles That Can Be Driven
H	Vehicles, regardless of size or class, except tank vehicles, when transporting hazardous materials that require the vehicle to be placarded
M	Motorcycles
N	Tank vehicles not carrying hazardous materials
P	Vehicles carrying passengers
S	School bus
T	Double trailers
X	Tank vehicles carrying hazardous materials.

To qualify for any of the above endorsements, an applicant shall pass a knowledge test. To obtain an H or an X endorsement, an applicant must take a test. This requirement applies when a person first obtains an H or an X endorsement and each time a person renews an H or an X endorsement. An applicant who has an H or an X endorsement issued by another state who applies for an H or an X endorsement must take a test unless the person has passed a test that covers the information set out in 49 C.F.R. § 383.121 within the preceding two years. For purposes of this subsection, the term "motorcycle" shall not include autocycles. Autocycles shall be subject to the requirements under this section for motor vehicles.

(c1) Expired.

(c2) **Expiration of H and X Endorsements.** -- Hazardous materials endorsements shall be renewed every five years or less so that individuals subject to a Transportation Security Administration security screening required pursuant to 49 C.F.R. § 383.141 may receive the screening and be authorized to renew the endorsements of H or X to transport hazardous materials. Notwithstanding G.S. 20-7(f), a commercial drivers license that contains an H or X endorsement as defined in subsection (c) of this section shall expire on the date of expiration of the licensee's security threat assessment conducted by the Transportation Security Administration of the United States Department of Homeland Security. When the commercial drivers license also contains an S endorsement and the licensee is certified to drive a school bus in this State, the commercial drivers license shall expire as provided in G.S. 20-7(f). The H and X endorsements on a commercial drivers license shall expire when the commercial drivers license expires.

(d) The fee for a Class A, B, or C commercial drivers license is twenty dollars ($ 20.00) for each year of the period for which the license is issued. The fee for each endorsement is four dollars ($ 4.00) for each year of the period for which the endorsement is issued. The fees required under this section do not apply to employees of the Driver License Section of the Division who are designated by the Commissioner.

(e) The requirements for a commercial drivers license do not apply to vehicles used for personal use such as recreational vehicles. A commercial drivers license is also waived for the following classes of vehicles as permitted by regulation of the United States Department of Transportation:

(1) Vehicles owned or operated by the Department of Defense, including the National Guard, while they are driven by active duty military personnel, or members of the National Guard when on active duty, in the pursuit of military purposes.

(2) Any vehicle when used as firefighting or emergency equipment for the purpose of preserving life or property or to execute governmental functions, including, but not limited to, necessary maintenance, training, or required operation for official business of the department.

(3) A farm vehicle that meets all of the following criteria:

    a. Is controlled and operated by the farmer or the farmer's employee and used exclusively for farm use.

    b. Is used to transport either agricultural products, farm machinery, or farm supplies, both to or from a farm.

    c. Is not used in the operations of a for-hire motor carrier.

    d. Is used within 150 miles of the farmer's farm.

    A farm vehicle includes a forestry vehicle that meets the listed criteria when applied to the forestry operation.

(f) For the purposes of this section, the term "school bus" has the same meaning as in 49 C.F.R. § 383.5.

History.
1989, c. 771, s. 2;1991, c. 726, s. 18;1993, c. 368, s. 4;1993 (Reg. Sess., 1994), c. 750, ss. 4, 6; 1995 (Reg. Sess., 1996), c. 695, s. 1; c. 756, s. 5; 1998-149, s. 5;2003-397, ss. 4, 5; 2005-276, s. 44.1(g);2005-349, s. 9;2011-228, s. 1;2012-85, s. 3;2015-163, s. 3;2015-241, s. 29.30(g);2018-74, s. 15

EDITOR'S NOTE. --
Session Laws 1993, c. 368, which amended this section, in s. 5 provides: "A drivers license or a special identification card issued by the Division of Motor Vehicles before January 1, 1995, and renewed by the Division after that date is considered the first drivers license or special identification card issued by the Division for purposes of determining when the license or card expires."

Session Laws 2003-397, s. 7, provides, in part, that s. 5, which added subsection (c1), expires September 30, 2005.

Session Laws 2011-228, s. 2, as amended by Session Laws 2012-85, s. 3, provides: "This act becomes effective on the later of the following dates and applies to endorsements issued for commercial drivers licenses issued on or after that date:

"(1) January 1, 2013.

"(2) The first day of a month that is 30 days after the Commissioner of Motor Vehicles certifies to the Revisor of Statutes that the Division of Motor Vehicles has completed the implementation of the Division's Next Generation Secure Driver License System." On August 21, 2019, the Commissioner of Motor Vehicles certified to the Revisor of Statutes that the Next Generation Secure Driver License System was fully implemented in January 2016.

Session Laws 2012-85, s. 12, provides: "When the Division of Motor Vehicles has completed the implementation of the Division's Next Generation Secure Driver License System, the Commissioner of Motor Vehicles shall certify to the Revisor of Statutes that the Division of Motor Vehicles has completed the implementation. When making the certification, the Commissioner of Motor Vehicles shall reference S.L. 2011-35, S.L. 2011-228, and the session law number of this act." On August 21, 2019, the Commissioner of Motor Vehicles certified to the Revisor of Statutes that the Next Generation Secure Driver License System was fully implemented in January 2016.

Chapter 20

Session Laws 2015-241, s. 29.30(u), made the amendment to subsection (d) of this section by Session Laws 2015-241, s. 29.30(g), applicable to issuances, renewals, restorations, and requests on or after January 1, 2016.

Session Laws 2015-241, s. 1.1, provides: "This act shall be known as 'The Current Operations and Capital Improvements Appropriations Act of 2015.'"

Session Laws 2015-241, s. 33.6, is a severability clause.

EFFECT OF AMENDMENTS. --

Session Laws 2003-397, ss. 4 and 5, effective October 1, 2003, in the table in subsection (c), inserted "S" under the "Endorsement" column and inserted "School bus" under the "Vehicles That Can Be Driven column"; inserted subsection (c1); in the last sentence of subsection (d), deleted "a person whose license is restricted to driving a school bus or school activity bus or to" following "do not apply to"; and added subsection (f). See Editor's note for expiration of s. 5 of Laws 2003-397.

Session Laws 2005-276, s. 44.1(g), effective October 1, 2005, and applicable to fees collected on or after that date, substituted "fifteen dollars ($15.00)" for "ten dollars ($10.00)" and "three dollars ($3.00)" for "one dollar and twenty-five cents ($1.25)" in subsection (d).

Session Laws 2005-349, s. 9, effective September 30, 2005, and applicable to offenses committed on or after that date, added the first sentence of the paragraph following the table in subsection (c).

Session Laws 2011-228, s. 1, added subsection (c2). For effective date, see Editor's note.

Session Laws 2015-163, s. 3, effective October 1, 2015, added the last two sentences of the second paragraph in subsection (c).

Session Laws 2015-241, s. 29.30(g), effective January 1, 2016, in subsection (d), substituted "twenty dollars ($20.00)" for "fifteen dollars ($15.00)" in first sentence and substituted "four dollars ($4.00)" for "three dollars ($3.00)" in the second sentence. For applicability, see editor's note.

Session Laws 2018-74, s. 15, effective July 1, 2018, inserted "including, but not limited\ to, necessary maintenance, training, or required operation for official business of the department" in subdivision (c)(2).

OPINIONS OF THE ATTORNEY GENERAL

PRIVATE CARRIERS OPERATED BY DRIVERS EMPLOYED IN LOGGING OPERATIONS ARE ENTITLED TO THE EXEMPTION FOR "FARM" VEHICLES UNDER G.S. 20-37.16(E)(3) IF agricultural or forest products being transported were raised and grown by farmer/forester and he does not engage in business of buying products for resale. Then he and his employees could transport such forest products within 150 miles of farm in vehicles not used in common or contract motor carrier operations without obtaining commercial driver's license. Conversely, if forest products were not raised and grown by forester, or he engages in buying of forest products for resale, transporting of those products by him or his employees would not be exempt from commercial driver's

license requirements for, as to those forest products, forester was not a farmer. See opinion of Attorney General to Rep. Beverly M. Purdue, 3rd District: Craven, Lenoir, Pamlico Counties, 60 N.C.A.G. 30 (1990).

§ 20-37.17. Record check and notification of license issuance

Before issuing a commercial driver license, the Division shall obtain driving record information from the Commercial Driver License Information System (CDLIS), the National Driver Register, and from each state in which the person has been licensed.

Within 10 days after issuing a commercial driver license, the Division shall notify CDLIS of the issuance of the commercial driver license, providing all information necessary to ensure identification of the person.

History.
1989, c. 771, s. 2

§ 20-37.18. Notification required by driver

(a) Any driver holding a commercial driver license issued by this State who is convicted of violating any State law or local ordinance relating to motor vehicle traffic control in any other state, other than parking violations, shall notify the Division in the manner specified by the Division within 30 days of the date of the conviction.

(b) Any driver holding a commercial driver license issued by this State who is convicted of violating any State law or local ordinance relating to motor vehicle traffic control in this or any other state, other than parking violations, shall notify his employer in writing of the conviction within 30 days of the date of conviction.

(c) Any driver whose commercial driver license is suspended, revoked, or cancelled by any state, or who loses the privilege to drive a commercial motor vehicle in any state for any period, including being disqualified from driving a commercial motor vehicle, or who is subject to an out-of-service order, shall notify his employer of that fact before the end of the business day following the day the driver received notice of that fact.

(d) Any person who applies to be a commercial motor vehicle driver shall provide the employer, at the time of the application, with the following information for the 10 years preceding the date of application:

(1) A list of the names and addresses of the applicant's previous employers for which the applicant was a driver of a commercial motor vehicle;

(2) The dates between which the applicant drove for each employer; and

(3) The reason for leaving that employer.

The applicant shall certify that all information furnished is true and complete. Any employer may require an applicant to provide additional information.

History.
1989, c. 771, s. 2

§ 20-37.19. Employer responsibilities

(a) Each employer shall require the applicant to provide the information specified in G.S. 20-37.18(c).

(b) No employer shall knowingly allow, permit, or authorize a driver to drive a commercial motor vehicle during any period:

(1) In which the driver has had his commercial driver license suspended, revoked, or cancelled by any state, is currently disqualified from driving a commercial vehicle, or is subject to an out-of-service order in any state; or

(2) In which the driver has more than one driver license; [or]

(3) In which the driver, the commercial motor vehicle being operated, or the motor carrier operation, is subject to an out-of-service order.

(c) The employer of any employee or applicant who tests positive or of any employee who refuses to participate in a drug or alcohol test required under 49 C.F.R. Part 382 and 49 C.F.R. Part 655 must notify the Division in writing within five business days following the employer's receipt of confirmation of a positive drug or alcohol test or of the employee's refusal to participate in the test. The notification must include the driver's name, address, drivers license number, social security number, and results of the drug or alcohol test or documentation from the employer of the refusal by the employee to take the test.

History.
1989, c. 771, s. 2;2005-156, s. 1;2007-492, s. 2;2009-416, s. 6
EFFECT OF AMENDMENTS. --
Session Laws 2005-156, s. 1, effective December 1, 2005, added subsection (c).
Session Laws 2007-492, s. 2, effective August 30, 2007, rewrote subsection (c).
Session Laws 2009-416, s. 6, effective March 31, 2010 and applicable to offenses committed on or after that date, added subdivision (b)(3).

§ 20-37.20. Notification of traffic convictions

(a) **Out-of-state Resident. --** Within 10 days after receiving a report of the conviction of any nonresident holder of a commercial driver license for any violation of State law or local ordinance relating to motor vehicle traffic control, other than parking violations, committed in a commercial vehicle, the Division shall notify the driver licensing authority in the licensing state of the conviction.

(b) **Foreign Diplomat. --** The Division must notify the United States Department of State within 15 days after it receives one or more of the following reports for a holder of a drivers license issued by the United States Department of State:

(1) A report of a conviction for a violation of State law or local ordinance relating to motor vehicle traffic control, other than parking violations.

(2) A report of a civil revocation order.

History.
1989, c. 771, s. 2;2001-498, s. 7;2002-159, s. 31;2006-209, s. 7
EFFECT OF AMENDMENTS. --
Session Laws 2001-498, s. 7, inserted the subsection designation and catchline for subsection (a), and added subsection (b). For effective date of this amendment, see editor's note.

§ 20-37.20A. Driving record notation for testing positive in a drug or alcohol test

Upon receipt of notice pursuant to G.S. 20-37.19(c) of positive result in an alcohol or drug test of a person holding a commercial drivers license, and subject to any appeal of the disqualification pursuant to G.S. 20-37.20B, the Division shall place a notation on the driving record of the driver. A notation of a disqualification pursuant to G.S. 20-17.4(l) shall be retained on the record of a person for a period of three years following the end of any disqualification of that person.

History.
2005-156, s. 3;2008-175, s. 2
EFFECT OF AMENDMENTS. --
Session Laws 2008-175, s. 2, effective December 1, 2008, and applicable to offenses committed on or after that date, substituted "three years" for "two years" in the last sentence.

§ 20-37.20B. Appeal of disqualification for testing positive in a drug or alcohol test

Following receipt of notice pursuant to G.S. 20-37.19(c) of a positive test in an alcohol or drug test, the Division shall notify the driver of the pending disqualification of the driver to operate a commercial vehicle and the driver's right to a hearing if requested within 20 days of the date of the notice. If the Division receives no request for a hearing, the disqualification shall become effective at the end of the 20-day period. If the driver requests a hearing, the disqualification shall be stayed pending outcome of the hearing. The hearing shall take place at the offices of the Division of Motor Vehicles in Raleigh. The hearing shall be limited to issues of testing procedure and protocol. A copy of a positive test result accompanied by certification by the testing officer of the accuracy of the laboratory protocols that resulted in the test result shall be prima facie evidence of a confirmed positive test result. The decision of the Division hearing officer may be appealed in accordance with the procedure of G.S. 20-19(c6).

History.
2005-156, s. 4

§ 20-37.21. Penalties

(a) Any person who drives a commercial motor vehicle in violation of G.S. 20-37.12 shall be guilty of a Class 3 misdemeanor and, upon conviction, shall be fined not less than two hundred fifty dollars ($ 250.00) for a first offense and not less than five hundred dollars ($ 500.00) for a second or subsequent offense. In addition, the person shall be subject to a civil penalty pursuant to the provisions of 49 C.F.R. § 383.53(b).

(b) Any person who violates G.S. 20-37.18 shall have committed an infraction and, upon being found responsible, shall pay a penalty of not less than one hundred dollars ($ 100.00) nor more than five hundred dollars ($ 500.00).

(c) Any employer who violates G.S. 20-37.19 shall have committed an infraction and, upon being found responsible, shall pay a penalty of not less than five hundred dollars ($ 500.00) nor more than one thousand dollars ($ 1,000). In addition, upon conviction, the employer shall be subject to a civil penalty of not less than two thousand seven hundred fifty dollars ($ 2,750) nor more than eleven thousand dollars ($ 11,000).

(d) An employer who knowingly allows, requires, permits, or otherwise authorizes an employee to violate any railroad grade requirements contained in G.S. 20-142.1 through G.S. 20-142.5 shall pay a civil penalty of not more than ten thousand dollars ($ 10,000).

History.
1989, c. 771, s. 2;1993, c. 539, s. 327;1994, Ex. Sess., c. 24, s. 14(c);2005-349, s. 10;2009-416, s. 7
EFFECT OF AMENDMENTS. --
Session Laws 2005-349, s. 10, effective September 30, 2005, and applicable to offenses committed on or after that date, added the last sentences of subsections (a) and (c), and added subsection (d).
Session Laws 2009-416, s. 7, effective March 31, 2010, and applicable to offenses committed on or after that date, in subsection (a), deleted "upon conviction" following "In addition" and substituted "pursuant to the provisions of 49 C.F.R. § 383.53(b)" for "of not

less than one thousand one hundred dollars ($1,100) for the first offense and not more than two thousand seven hundred fifty dollars ($2,750) for a second or subsequent offense."

§ 20-37.22. Rule making authority

The Division may adopt any rules necessary to carry out the provisions of this Article.

History.
1989, c. 771, s. 2
CITED in Hensley v. Nat'l Freight Transp., Inc., 193 N.C. App. 561, 668 S.E.2d 349 (2008), aff'd, 363 N.C. 255, 675 S.E.2d 333 (2009).

§ 20-37.23. Authority to enter agreements

The Commissioner shall have the authority to execute or make agreements, arrangements, or declarations to carry out the provisions of this Article.

History.
1989, c. 771, s. 2

N.C. Gen. Stat. § 20-38

Repealed by Session Laws 1973, c. 1330, s. 39.
EDITOR'S NOTE. --
G.S. 20-38 was enacted as Part 1 of Article 3. It was transferred as a result of the enactment of Article 2C.

ARTICLE 2D.
IMPLIED-CONSENT OFFENSE PROCEDURES

§ 20-38.1. Applicability

The procedures set forth in this Article shall be followed for the investigation and processing of an implied-consent offense as defined in G.S. 20-16.2. The trial procedures shall apply to any implied-consent offense litigated in the District Court Division.

History.
2006-253, s. 5
EDITOR'S NOTE. --
Session Laws 2006-253, s. 33, made this Article effective December 1, 2006, and applicable to offenses committed on or after that date.

§ 20-38.2. Investigation

A law enforcement officer who is investigating an implied-consent offense or a vehicle crash that occurred in the officer's territorial jurisdiction is authorized to investigate and seek evidence of the driver's impairment anywhere in-state or out-of-state, and to make arrests at any place within the State.

History.
2006-253, s. 5

§ 20-38.3. Police processing duties

Upon the arrest of a person, with or without a warrant, but not necessarily in the order listed, a law enforcement officer:

(1) Shall inform the person arrested of the charges or a cause for the arrest.

(2) May take the person arrested to any place within the State for one or more chemical analyses at the request of any law enforcement officer and for any evaluation by a law enforcement officer, medical professional, or other person to determine the extent or cause of the person's impairment.

(3) May take the person arrested to some other place within the State for the purpose of having the person identified, to complete a crash report, or for any other lawful purpose.

(4) May take photographs and fingerprints in accordance with G.S. 15A-502.

(5) Shall take the person arrested before a judicial official for an initial appearance after completion of all investigatory procedures, crash reports, chemical analyses, and other procedures provided for in this section.

History.
2006-253, s. 5

§ 20-38.4. Initial appearance

(a) **Appearance Before a Magistrate. --** Except as modified in this Article, a magistrate shall follow the procedures set forth in Article 24 of Chapter 15A of the General Statutes.

(1) A magistrate may hold an initial appearance at any place within the county and shall, to the extent practicable, be available at locations other than the courthouse when it will expedite the initial appearance.

(2) In determining whether there is probable cause to believe a person is impaired, the magistrate may review all alcohol screening tests, chemical analyses, receive testimony from any law enforcement officer concerning impairment and the circumstances of the arrest, and observe the person arrested.

(3) If there is a finding of probable cause, the magistrate shall consider whether the person is impaired to the extent that the provisions of G.S. 15A-534.2 should be imposed.

(4) The magistrate shall also:

a. Inform the person in writing of the established procedure to have others appear at the jail to observe his condition or to administer an additional chemical analysis if the person is unable to make bond; and

b. Require the person who is unable to make bond to list all persons he wishes to contact and telephone numbers on a form that sets forth the procedure for contacting the persons listed. A copy of this form shall be filed with the case file.

(b) The Administrative Office of the Courts shall adopt forms to implement this Article.

History.
2006-253, s. 5
IRREPARABLE PREJUDICE NOT DEMONSTRATED. --Although the magistrate had not complied with G.S. 20-38.4, defendant could not demonstrate irreparable prejudice where she was able to, and in fact did, make several phone calls from jail to family and friends. State v. Ledbetter, 261 N.C. App. 71, 819 S.E.2d 591 (2018), review dismissed, 372 N.C. 716, 830 S.E.2d 820, 2019 N.C. LEXIS 695 (2019).
CITED in State v. Ledbetter, 243 N.C. App. 746, 779 S.E.2d 164 (2015).

§ 20-38.5. Facilities

(a) The Chief District Court Judge, the Department of Health and Human Services, the district attorney, and the sheriff shall:

(1) Establish a written procedure for attorneys and witnesses to have access to the chemical analysis room.

(2) Approve the location of written notice of implied-consent rights in the chemical analysis room in accordance with G.S. 20-16.2.

(3) Approve a procedure for access to a person arrested for an implied-consent offense by family and friends or a qualified person contacted by the arrested person to obtain blood or urine when the arrested person is held in custody and unable to obtain pretrial release from jail.

(b) Signs shall be posted explaining to the public the procedure for obtaining access to the room where the chemical analysis of the breath is administered and to any person arrested for an implied-consent offense. The initial signs shall be provided by the Department of Transportation, without costs. The signs shall thereafter be maintained by the county for all county buildings and the county courthouse.

(c) If the instrument for performing a chemical analysis of the breath is located in a State or municipal building, then the head of the highway patrol for the county, the chief of police for the city or that person's designee shall be substituted for the sheriff when determining signs and access to the chemical analysis room. The signs shall be maintained by the owner of the building. When a breath testing instrument is in a motor vehicle or at a temporary location, the Department of Health and Human Services shall alone perform the functions listed in subdivisions (a)(1) and (a)(2) of this section.

History.
2006-253, s. 5

§ 20-38.6. Motions and district court procedure

(a) The defendant may move to suppress evidence or dismiss charges only prior to trial, except the defendant may move to dismiss the charges for insufficient evidence at the close of the State's evidence and at the close of all of the evidence without prior notice. If, during the course of the trial, the defendant discovers facts not previously known, a motion to suppress or dismiss may be made during the trial.

(b) Upon a motion to suppress or dismiss the charges, other than at the close of the State's evidence or at the close of all the evidence, the State shall be granted reasonable time to procure witnesses or evidence and to conduct research required to defend against the motion.

(c) The judge shall summarily grant the motion to suppress evidence if the State stipulates that the evidence sought to be suppressed will not be offered in evidence in any criminal action or proceeding against the defendant.

(d) The judge may summarily deny the motion to suppress evidence if the defendant failed to make the motion pretrial when all material facts were known to the defendant.

(e) If the motion is not determined summarily, the judge shall make the determination after a hearing and finding of facts. Testimony at the hearing shall be under oath.

(f) The judge shall set forth in writing the findings of fact and conclusions of law and preliminarily indicate whether the motion should be granted or denied. If the judge preliminarily indicates the motion should be granted, the judge shall not enter a final judgment on the motion until after the State has appealed to superior court or has indicated it does not intend to appeal.

History.
2006-253, s. 5

CONSTITUTIONALITY. --State's right to appeal a district court's preliminary determination indicating that it would grant a defendant's pretrial motion to suppress or dismiss made in accordance with G.S. 20-38.6(a) does not deprive defendants charged with implied-consent offenses of their guaranteed freedom from former jeopardy because at the time a defendant's pretrial motions to suppress or dismiss are made, heard, and decided by the district court, the defendant has not yet been put to trial before the trier of fact, and, so, jeopardy has not yet attached to the proceedings, and the General Assembly intended the pretrial motions to suppress evidence or dismiss charges made in accordance with G.S. 20-38.6(a) to address only procedural matters including, but not limited to, delays in the processing of a defendant, limitations imposed on a defendant's access to witnesses, and challenges to the results of a breathalyzer; by enacting G.S. 20-38.6(a), (f) and G.S. 20-38.7(a), the General Assembly has granted the State a right of appeal to superior court only from a district court's preliminary determination indicating that it would grant a defendant's pretrial motion to suppress evidence or dismiss charges on an implied-consent offense which (1) is made and decided in district court at a time before jeopardy has attached to the proceedings, i.e., before the district court sits as the trier of fact to adjudicate the defendant's guilt, and (2) is entirely unrelated to the sufficiency of evidence as to any element of the offense or to defendant's guilt or innocence. State v. Fowler, 197 N.C. App. 1, 676 S.E.2d 523 (2009), review denied, 364 N.C. 129, 696 S.E.2d 695 (2010).

Pretrial motion requirement of G.S. 20-38.6(a) does not infringe on the fundamental right to a fair trial of defendants charged with implied-consent offenses appearing in district court because although, unlike other defendants appearing in district court, G.S. 20-38.6(a) generally requires defendants charged with implied-consent offenses to make motions to suppress evidence or dismiss charges prior to trial, the express language of G.S. 20-38.6(a) also protects defendants against any disadvantage they could suffer as a result of the absence of a statutory right to discovery in district court, since any unfair surprise that might arise from the discovery of facts not previously known to a defendant is tempered by allowing defendants to make motions to suppress or dismiss during the course of the trial on the basis of newly discovered facts. State v. Fowler, 197 N.C. App. 1, 676 S.E.2d 523 (2009), review denied, 364 N.C. 129, 696 S.E.2d 695 (2010).

State's appeal from a district court's preliminary determination indicating that it would grant a defendant's pretrial motion made in accordance with G.S. 20-38.6(a) on an implied-consent offense charge does not infringe on a defendant's fundamental right to a speedy trial because the General Assembly's decision to refrain from establishing a time by which the State must give notice of appeal from a district court's preliminary determination indicating that it would grant a defendant's pretrial motion made in accordance with § 20-38.6(a) will require an examination of the circumstances of each particular case in which a defendant alleges that the State acted in violation of his or her fundamental right to a speedy trial by subjecting that defendant to undue delay. State v. Fowler, 197 N.C. App. 1, 676 S.E.2d 523 (2009), review denied, 364 N.C. 129, 696 S.E.2d 695 (2010).

G.

S. 20-38.6(a), (f) and G.S. 20-38.7(a) do not violate substantive due process because they are not unreasonable, arbitrary or capricious, and are substantially related to the valid object sought to be obtained; the Legislature determined that the pretrial procedures codified in G.S. 20-38.6(a), (f) and G.S. 20-38.7(a) would serve as a means to improve the safety of the motoring public of North Carolina. State v. Fowler, 197 N.C. App. 1, 676 S.E.2d 523 (2009), review denied, 364 N.C. 129, 696 S.E.2d 695 (2010).

G.

S. 20-38.6(a), (f) and G.S. 20-38.7(a) do not violate the Equal Protection Clause of the United States Constitution or of the North Carolina Constitution because the Legislature's objective to improve the safety of the motoring public of North Carolina is a legitimate objective and the procedures established by G.S. 20-38.6(a), (f), and G.S. 20-38.7(a) are rationally related to that objective; no classification between different groups has been created, but all defendants charged with an implied-consent offense appearing in district court will be subject to the same procedural requirements established by G.S. 20-38.6(a), (f) and G.S. 20-38.7(a), State v. Fowler, 197 N.C. App. 1, 676 S.E.2d 523 (2009), review denied, 364 N.C. 129, 696 S.E.2d 695 (2010).

In an implied-consent case in which a superior court held that G.S. 20-38.6(f) and G.S. 20-38.7(a) were unconstitutional under the separation of powers, on the face of the relevant State constitutional provisions alone, N.C. Const., Art. IV, §§ 1, 13(2), and 12(3), (4), and (6), the General Assembly acted within its constitutional authority by enacting the challenged statutes that prescribed the jurisdiction of the district and superior courts, and provide a system of appeal from district to superior court. State v. Mangino, 200 N.C. App. 430, 683 S.E.2d 779 (2009), dismissed, 364 N.C. 621, 705 S.E.2d 378, 2010 N.C. LEXIS 1072 (2010).

JURISDICTION. --Trial court could not determine that it did not have jurisdiction to hear the appeal of the district court's granting of defendant's motion to suppress evidence. After considering an appeal pursuant to G.S. 20-38.7(a), the trial court was required to enter an order remanding the matter to the district court with instructions to grant or deny defendant's NG.S. 20-38.6 motion to suppress, especially since (1) G.S. 20-38.7(a) did not have a 10-day time limit for appeal; and (2) the State's notice of appeal otherwise met the G.S. 15A-1432(b) requirements for appealing a matter from the district court to the trial court. State v. Palmer, 197 N.C. App. 201, 676 S.E.2d 559 (2009), review denied, 363 N.C. 810, -- S.E.2d --, 2010 N.C. LEXIS 47 (2010).

G.

S. 20-38.6(a), (f) and G.S. 20-38.7(a) do not violate the separation of powers doctrine of the North Carolina Constitution because there is no usurpation of the judicial power of the State by the Legislature in the enactment of these statutory provisions. State v. Fowler, 197 N.C. App. 1, 676 S.E.2d 523 (2009), review denied, 364 N.C. 129, 696 S.E.2d 695 (2010).

MOTION TO DISMISS. --Superior court erred when it concluded that it appeared the district court's conclusions of law granting defendant's motion to dismiss under G.S. 20-38.6(a) were based upon the findings of fact that were cited in the district court's order because there was no indication in the record that the State had the opportunity to present all of its evidence prior to the district court's preliminary determination indicating that it would dismiss the charge against defendant. State v. Fowler, 197 N.C. App. 1, 676 S.E.2d 523 (2009), review denied, 364 N.C. 129, 696 S.E.2d 695 (2010).

PROCEDURES OF G.S. 20-38.6(A), (F) AND G.S. 20-38.7(A) DO NOT APPLY TO THE APPELLATE DIVISION because by enacting these provisions, the General Assembly created rules which affect the procedure and practice of the superior and district court divisions only, as it is constitutionally permitted to do pursuant to N.C. Const., Art. IV, § 13, cl. 2; because the General Assembly is constitutionally authorized to create rules of procedure and practice for the superior and district courts, to prescribe the jurisdiction and powers of the district courts, and to circumscribe the jurisdiction of the superior courts, a constitutional amendment is not required for the General Assembly to promulgate a rule of procedure and practice pertaining exclusively to the superior and district courts. State v. Fowler, 197 N.C. App. 1, 676 S.E.2d 523 (2009), review denied, 364 N.C. 129, 696 S.E.2d 695 (2010).

RIGHT TO APPEAL. --State had no statutory right of appeal because the superior court order specifically stated that the basis for the hearing was the State's appeal of the district court's pretrial indication granting defendant's motion to suppress; however, the court of appeals exercised its discretion to grant the State's petition for writ of certiorari pursuant to N.C. R. App. P. 21(a)(1) because the State contended that the superior court exceeded its jurisdiction. State v. Osterhoudt, 222 N.C. App. 620, 731 S.E.2d 454 (2012).

Because the district court did not enter an order "finally denying" defendant's motion to suppress, the court of appeals was unable to review the issues presented in his appeal from his no contest plea; if the ruling is not a final order for purposes of the State's appeal, it is likewise not a final order for purposes of defendant's appeal. State v. Hutton, 244 N.C. App. 128, 780 S.E.2d 202 (2015).

CITED in State v. Morgan, 189 N.C. App. 716, 660 S.E.2d 545 (2008), review denied, stay denied, 362 N.C. 686, 671 S.E.2d 329 (2008), review dismissed, as moot, 362 N.C. 686, 671 S.E.2d 329 (2008); State v. Wilson, 225 N.C. App. 246, 736 S.E.2d 614 (2013); State v. Loftis, 250 N.C. App. 449, 792 S.E.2d 886 (2016).

§ 20-38.7. Appeal to superior court

(a) The State may appeal to superior court any district court preliminary determination granting a motion to suppress or dismiss. If there is a dispute about the findings of fact, the superior court shall not be bound by the findings of the district court but shall determine the matter de novo. Any further appeal shall be governed by Article 90 of Chapter 15A of the General Statutes.

(b) The defendant may not appeal a denial of a pretrial motion to suppress or to dismiss but may appeal upon conviction as provided by law.

(c) Notwithstanding the provisions of G.S. 15A-1431, for any implied-consent offense that is first tried in district court and that is appealed to superior court by the defendant for a trial de novo as a result of a conviction, when an appeal is withdrawn or a case is remanded back to district court, the sentence imposed by the district court is vacated and the district court shall hold a new sentencing hearing and shall consider any new convictions unless one of the following conditions is met:

(1) If the appeal is withdrawn pursuant to G.S. 15A-1431(c), the prosecutor has certified to the clerk, in writing, that the prosecutor has no new sentencing factors to offer the court.

(2) If the appeal is withdrawn and remanded pursuant to G.S. 15A-1431(g), the prosecutor has certified to the clerk, in writing, that the prosecutor has no new sentencing factors to offer the court.

(3) If the appeal is withdrawn and remanded pursuant to G.S. 15A-1431(h), the prosecutor has certified to the clerk, in writing, that the prosecutor consents to the withdrawal and remand and has no new sentencing factors to offer the court.

(d) Following a new sentencing hearing in district court pursuant to subsection (c) of this section, a defendant has a right of appeal to the superior court only if:

(1) The sentence is based upon additional facts considered by the district court that were not considered in the previously vacated sentence, and

(2) The defendant would be entitled to a jury determination of those facts pursuant to G.S. 20-179.

A defendant who has a right of appeal under this subsection, gives notice of appeal, and subsequently withdraws the appeal shall have the sentence imposed by the district court reinstated by the district court as a final judgment that is not subject to further appeal.

History.

2006-253, s. 5;2007-493, s. 9;2008-187, s. 10;2015-150, s. 5;2015-264, s. 39(a)

EDITOR'S NOTE. --

Session Laws 2015-150, s. 6, made the rewriting of subsection (c) of this section by Session Laws 2015-150, s. 5, applicable to appeals filed on or after December 1, 2015.

Session Laws 2015-264, s. 91.7 contains a severability clause.

EFFECT OF AMENDMENTS. --

Session Laws 2007-493, s. 9, effective August 30, 2007, deleted "and, if the defendant has any pending charges of offenses involving impaired driving, shall delay sentencing in the remanded case until all cases are resolved" at the end of subsection (c); and added subsection (d).

Session Laws 2008-187, s. 10, effective August 7, 2008, substituted "sentence" for "judgment" at the end of subdivision (d)(1).

Session Laws 2015-150, s. 5, effective December 1, 2015, rewrote subsection (c) and added subdivisions (c)(1) through (c)(3). For applicability, see editor's note.

Session Laws 2015-264, s. 39(a), effective December 1, 2015, substituted "G.S. 15A-1431(h)" for "G.S. 15A-1341(h)" in subdivision (c)(3).

CONSTITUTIONALITY. --G.S. 20-38.6(a), (f) and G.S. 20-38.7(a) do not violate substantive due process because they are not unreasonable, arbitrary or capricious, and are substantially related to the valid object sought to be obtained; the Legislature determined that the pretrial procedures codified in G.S. 20-38.6(a), (f) and G.S. 20-38.7(a) would serve as a means to improve the safety of the motoring public of North Carolina. State v. Fowler, 197 N.C. App. 1, 676 S.E.2d 523 (2009), review denied, 364 N.C. 129, 696 S.E.2d 695 (2010).

State's right to appeal a district court's preliminary determination indicating that it would grant a defendant's pretrial motion to suppress or dismiss made in accordance with G.S. 20-38.6(a) does not deprive defendants charged with implied-consent offenses of their guaranteed freedom from former jeopardy because at the time a defendant's pretrial motions to suppress or dismiss are made, heard, and decided by the district court, the defendant has not yet been put to trial before the trier of fact, and, so, jeopardy has not yet attached to the proceedings, and the General Assembly intended the pretrial motions to suppress evidence or dismiss charges made in accordance with G.S. 20-38.6(a) to address only procedural matters including, but not limited to, delays in the processing of a defendant, limitations imposed on a defendant's access to witnesses, and challenges to the results of a breathalyzer; by enacting G.S. 20-38.6(a), (f) and G.S. 20-38.7(a), the General Assembly has granted the State a right of appeal to superior court only from a district court's preliminary determination indicating that it would grant a defendant's pretrial motion to suppress evidence or dismiss charges on an implied-consent offense which (1) is made and decided in district court at a time before jeopardy has attached to the proceedings, i.e., before the district court sits as the trier of fact to adjudicate the defendant's guilt, and (2) is entirely unrelated to the sufficiency of evidence as to any element of the offense or to defendant's guilt or innocence. State v. Fowler, 197 N.C. App. 1, 676 S.E.2d 523 (2009), review denied, 364 N.C. 129, 696 S.E.2d 695 (2010).

G.

S. 20-38.6(a), (f) and G.S. 20-38.7(a) do not violate the Equal Protection Clause of the United States

Constitution or of the North Carolina Constitution because the Legislature's objective to improve the safety of the motoring public of North Carolina is a legitimate objective and the procedures established by G.S. 20-38.6(a), (f), and G.S. 20-38.7(a) are rationally related to that objective; no classification between different groups has been created, but all defendants charged with an implied-consent offense appearing in district court will be subject to the same procedural requirements established by G.S. 20-38.6(a), (f) and G.S. 20-38.7(a), State v. Fowler, 197 N.C. App. 1, 676 S.E.2d 523 (2009), review denied, 364 N.C. 129, 696 S.E.2d 695 (2010).

In an implied-consent case in which a superior court held that G.S. 20-38.6(f) and G.S. 20-38.7(a) were unconstitutional under the separation of powers, on the face of the relevant State constitutional provisions alone, N.C. Const., Art. IV, §§ 1, 13(2), and 12(3), (4), and (6), the General Assembly acted within its constitutional authority by enacting the challenged statutes that prescribed the jurisdiction of the district and superior courts, and provide a system of appeal from district to superior court. State v. Mangino, 200 N.C. App. 430, 683 S.E.2d 779 (2009), dismissed, 364 N.C. 621, 705 S.E.2d 378, 2010 N.C. LEXIS 1072 (2010).

PROCEDURES OF G.S. 20-38.6(A), (F) AND G.S. 20-38.7(A) DO NOT APPLY TO THE APPELLATE DIVISION because by enacting these provisions, the General Assembly created rules which affect the procedure and practice of the superior and district court divisions only, as it is constitutionally permitted to do pursuant to N.C. Const,. Art. IV, § 13, cl. 2; because the General Assembly is constitutionally authorized to create rules of procedure and practice for the superior and district courts, to prescribe the jurisdiction and powers of the district courts, and to circumscribe the jurisdiction of the superior courts, a constitutional amendment is not required for the General Assembly to promulgate a rule of procedure and practice pertaining exclusively to the superior and district courts. State v. Fowler, 197 N.C. App. 1, 676 S.E.2d 523 (2009), review denied, 364 N.C. 129, 696 S.E.2d 695 (2010).

JURISDICTION. --Trial court could not determine that it did not have jurisdiction to hear the appeal of the district court's granting of defendant's motion to suppress evidence. After considering an appeal pursuant to G.S. 20-38.7(a), the trial court was required to enter an order remanding the matter to the district court with instructions to grant or deny defendant's G.S. 20-38.6 motion to suppress, especially since (1) G.S. 20-38.7(a) did not have a 10-day time limit for appeal; and (2) the State's notice of appeal otherwise met the G.S. 15A-1432(b) requirements for appealing a matter from the district court to the trial court. State v. Palmer, 197 N.C. App. 201, 676 S.E.2d 559 (2009), review denied, 363 N.C. 810, -- S.E.2d --, 2010 N.C. LEXIS 47 (2010).

G.

S. 20-38.6(a), (f) and G.S. 20-38.7(a) do not violate the separation of powers doctrine of the North Carolina Constitution because there is no usurpation of the judicial power of the State by the Legislature in the enactment of these statutory provisions. State v.

Fowler, 197 N.C. App. 1, 676 S.E.2d 523 (2009), review denied, 364 N.C. 129, 696 S.E.2d 695 (2010).

RIGHT TO APPEAL. --Because a superior court must remand a matter heard pursuant to G.S. 20-38.7(a) to a district court for a final entry of judgment on a defendant's pretrial motion, the State will not be able to appeal to the appellate division pursuant to G.S. 15A-979(c) if the superior court determines that a defendant's pretrial motion to suppress should be granted. State v. Fowler, 197 N.C. App. 1, 676 S.E.2d 523 (2009), review denied, 364 N.C. 129, 696 S.E.2d 695 (2010).

State had no statutory right of appeal because the superior court order specifically stated that the basis for the hearing was the State's appeal of the district court's pretrial indication granting defendant's motion to suppress; however, the court of appeals exercised its discretion to grant the State's petition for writ of certiorari pursuant to N.C. R. App. P. 21(a)(1) because the State contended that the superior court exceeded its jurisdiction. State v. Osterhoudt, 222 N.C. App. 620, 731 S.E.2d 454 (2012).

Because the district court did not enter an order "finally denying" defendant's motion to suppress, the court of appeals was unable to review the issues presented in his appeal from his no contest plea; if the ruling is not a final order for purposes of the State's appeal, it is likewise not a final order for purposes of defendant's appeal. State v. Hutton, 244 N.C. App. 128, 780 S.E.2d 202 (2015).

CITED in State v. Bryan, 230 N.C. App. 324, 749 S.E.2d 900 (2013), review denied and cert. denied 755 S.E.2d 615, 2014 N.C. LEXIS 208 (2014); State v. Miller, 368 N.C. 729, 783 S.E.2d 194 (2016); State v. Loftis, 250 N.C. App. 449, 792 S.E.2d 886 (2016).

ARTICLE 3.
MOTOR VEHICLE ACT OF 1937

PART 1.
GENERAL PROVISIONS

N.C. Gen. Stat. § 20-38.100

Reserved for future codification purposes.

PART 2.
AUTHORITY AND DUTIES OF COMMISSIONER AND DIVISION

§ 20-39. Administering and enforcing laws; rules and regulations; agents, etc.; seal; fees

(a) The Commissioner is hereby vested with the power and is charged with the duty of administering and enforcing the provisions of this

Article and of all laws regulating the operation of vehicles or the use of the highways, the enforcement or administration of which is now or hereafter vested in the Division.

(b) The Commissioner is hereby authorized to adopt and enforce such rules and regulations as may be necessary to carry out the provisions of this Article and any other laws the enforcement and administration of which are vested in the Division.

(c) The Commissioner is authorized to designate and appoint such agents, field deputies, and clerks as may be necessary to carry out the provisions of this Article.

(d) The Commissioner shall adopt an official seal for the use of the Division.

(e) The Commissioner is authorized to cooperate with and provide assistance to the Environmental Management Commission, or appropriate local government officials, and to develop, adopt, and ensure enforcement of necessary rules and regulations, regarding programs of motor vehicle emissions inspection/maintenance required for areas in which ambient air pollutant concentrations exceed National Ambient Air Quality Standards. The Commissioner is further authorized to allow offices of the Division that provide vehicle titling and registration services and commission contractors of the Division under G.S. 20-63 to serve, upon agreement with the Wildlife Resources Commission, as vessel agents under G.S. 75A-5.2.

(f) The Commissioner is authorized to charge and collect the following fees for the verification of equipment to be used on motor vehicles or to be sold in North Carolina, when that approval is required pursuant to this Chapter:

    (1) When a federal standard has been established, the fee shall be equal to the cost of verifying compliance with the applicable federal standard; or

    (2) When no federal standard has been established, the fee shall be equal to the cost of verifying compliance with the applicable State standard. Any motor vehicle manufacturer or distributor who is required to certify his products under the National Traffic and Motor Vehicle Safety Act of 1966, as from time to time amended, may satisfy the provisions of this section by submitting an annual written certification to the Commissioner attesting to the compliance of his vehicles with applicable federal requirements. Failure to comply with the certification requirement or failure to meet the federal standards will subject the manufacturer or distributor to the fee requirements of this subsection.

(g), (h) Repealed by Session Laws 2001-424, s. 6.14(e), effective September 26, 2001.

    (i) Notwithstanding the requirements of G.S. 20-7.1 and G.S. 20-67(a), the Commissioner may correct the address records of drivers license and registration plate holders as shown in the files of the Division to that shown on notices and renewal cards returned to the Division with new addresses provided by the United States Postal Service.

History.

1937, c. 407, s. 4; 1975, c. 716, s. 5; 1979, 2nd Sess., c. 1180, s. 1; 1983, c. 223; c. 629, s. 2; c. 768, ss. 25.1, 25.2; 1985, c. 767, ss. 1, 2; 1987, c. 552; 1991, c. 53, s. 1;c. 654, s. 1;1993, c. 539, s. 328;1994, Ex. Sess., c. 24, s. 14(c);1995, c. 507, s. 6.2(b);1996, 2nd Ex. Sess., c. 18, s. 23(a);1997-256, s. 8;1997-347, s. 4;1997-401, s. 4;1997-418, s. 3;1997-443, s. 20.10(a), (b); 2001-424, ss. 6.14(e), 6.14(f); 2015-241, s. 29.38

EDITOR'S NOTE. --

Session Laws 1993 (Reg. Sess., 1994), c. 769, s. 2, provides: "This act shall be known as 'The Current Operations and Capital Improvements Appropriations Act of 1994.'"

Session Laws 1993 (Reg. Sess., 1994), c. 769, s. 20, provides: "The Division of Motor Vehicles shall report quarterly, beginning in January 1995, to the Joint Legislative Transportation Oversight Committee and the Fiscal Research Division, on the Emission Inspection Program's compliance with regulations the Environmental Protection Agency adopted for the inspection and maintenance activities required in the Clean Air Amendments of 1990. The report shall include the receipts and expenditures from the Emissions Program Account."

EFFECT OF AMENDMENTS. --

Session Laws 2015-241, s. 29.38, effective July 1, 2015, added the last sentence in subsection (e).

COMMISSIONER IMMUNE FROM LIABILITY FOR MERE NEGLIGENCE IN PERFORMANCE OF HIS DUTIES. --There can be little doubt that the Commissioner exercises some portion of the sovereign power of the State, and as such, is a public officer, and is immune from liability for mere negligence in the performance of his duties. Thompson Cadillac-Oldsmobile, Inc. v. Silk Hope Auto., Inc., 87 N.C. App. 467, 361 S.E.2d 418 (1987).

IMMUNITY OF INSPECTOR FOR NEGLIGENCE. --Inspector employed by the enforcement section of the DMV was a public official, immune from liability for negligent acts. Murray v. Justice, 96 N.C. App. 169, 385 S.E.2d 195, cert. denied, 326 N.C. 364, 389 S.E.2d 115 (1990).

CROSS REFERENCES. --

As to Commissioner and organization of Division, see G.S. 20-2 and 20-3. For definitions applicable throughout this Chapter, see G.S. 20-4.01. For requirements regarding marking and issuance of license plates for publicly owned vehicles, see G.S. 20-39.1.

§ 20-39.1. Publicly owned vehicles to be marked; private license plates on publicly owned vehicles

(a) Except as otherwise provided in this section, the executive head of every department of State government and every county, institution, or agency of the State shall mark every motor vehicle owned by the State, county, institution, or agency with a statement that the vehicle belongs to the State, county, institution, or agency. The requirements of this subsection are complied with if:

(1) The vehicle has imprinted on the license plate, above the license number, the words "State Owned" and the vehicle has affixed to the front the words "State Owned";

(2) In the case of a county, the vehicle has painted or affixed on its side a circle not less than eight inches in diameter showing a replica of the seal of the county; or

(3) In the case of vehicles assigned to members of the Council of State, the vehicle has imprinted on the license plate the license number assigned to the appropriate member of the Council of State pursuant to G.S. 20-79.5(a); a member of the Council of State shall not be assessed any registration fee if the member elects to have a State-owned motor vehicle assigned to the member designated by the official plate number.

(b) A motor vehicle used by any State or county officer or official for transporting, apprehending, or arresting persons charged with violations of the laws of the United States or the laws of this State is not required to be marked as provided in subsection (a) of this section. The Commissioner may lawfully provide private license plates to local, State, or federal departments or agencies for use on publicly owned or leased vehicles used for those purposes. Private license plates issued under this subsection shall be issued on an annual basis and the records of issuance shall be maintained in accordance with the provisions of G.S. 20-56.

(c) A motor vehicle used by a county for transporting day or residential facility clients of area mental health, developmental disabilities, and substance abuse authorities established under Article 4 of Chapter 122C of the General Statutes is not required to be marked as provided in subsection (a) of this section. The Commissioner may lawfully provide private license plates to counties for use on publicly owned or leased vehicles used for that purpose. Private license plates issued under this subsection shall be issued on an annual basis and the records of issuance shall be maintained in accordance with the provisions of G.S. 20-56.

(c1) A motor vehicle used by the Department of Agriculture and Consumer Services exclusively for Meat and Poultry compliance officers to conduct inspections is not required to be marked as provided in subsection (a) of this section. The Commissioner may lawfully provide private license plates to the Department of Agriculture and Consumer Services for use on publicly owned or leased vehicles used for this purpose. Private license plates issued under this subsection shall be issued on an annual basis and the records of issuance shall be maintained in accordance with the provisions of G.S. 20-56.

(d) For purposes of this section, the term "private license plate" refers to a license plate that would normally be issued to a private party and therefore lacks any markings indicating that it has been assigned to a publicly owned vehicle. "Confidential" license plates are a specialized form of private license plate for which a confidential registration has been authorized under subsection (e) of this section. "Fictitious" license plates are a specialized form of private license plate for which a fictitious registration has been issued under subsection (f) or (g) of this section.

(e) Upon approval and request of the Director of the State Bureau of Investigation, the Commissioner shall issue confidential license plates to local, State, or federal law enforcement agencies, the Department of Public Safety, agents of the Internal Revenue Service, and agents of the Department of Defense in accordance with the provisions of this subsection. Applicants in these categories shall provide satisfactory evidence to the Director of the State Bureau of Investigation of the following:

(1) The confidential license plate requested is to be used on a publicly owned or leased vehicle that is primarily used for transporting, apprehending, or arresting persons charged with violations of the laws of the United States or the State of North Carolina;

(2) The use of a confidential license plate is necessary to protect the personal safety of an officer or for placement on a vehicle used primarily for surveillance or undercover operations; and

(3) The application contains an original signature of the head of the requesting agency or department or, in the case of a federal agency, the signature of the senior ranking officer for that agency in this State.

Confidential license plates issued under this subsection shall be issued on an annual basis and the Division shall maintain a separate registration file for vehicles bearing confidential license plates. That file shall be confidential for the use of the Division and is not a public record within the meaning of Chapter 132 of the General Statutes. Upon the annual renewal of the registration of a vehicle for which a confidential status has been established under this section, the registration shall lose its confidential status unless the agency or department supplies the Director of the

State Bureau of Investigation with information demonstrating that an officer's personal safety remains at risk or that the vehicle is still primarily used for surveillance or undercover operations at the time of renewal.

(f) The Commissioner may to the extent necessary provide law enforcement officers of the Division on special undercover assignments with motor vehicle operator's licenses and motor vehicle license plates under assumed names, using false or fictitious addresses. The Commissioner shall be responsible for the request for issuance and use of such licenses and license plates, and may direct the immediate return of any license or license plate issued pursuant to this subsection.

(g) The Commissioner may, upon the request of the Director of the State Bureau of Investigation and to the extent necessary, lawfully provide local, State, and federal law enforcement officers on special undercover assignments and to agents of the Department of Defense with motor vehicle drivers licenses and motor vehicle license plates under assumed names, using false or fictitious addresses. Fictitious license plates shall only be used on publicly owned or leased vehicles. A request for fictitious licenses and license plates by a local, State or federal law enforcement agency or department or by the Department of Defense shall be made in writing to the Director of the State Bureau of Investigation and shall contain an original signature of the head of the requesting agency or department or, in the case of a federal agency, the signature of the senior ranking officer for that agency in this State.

Prior to the issuance of any fictitious license or license plate, the Director of the State Bureau of Investigation shall make a specific written finding that the request is justified and necessary. The Director shall maintain a record of all such licenses, license plates, assumed names, false or fictitious addresses, and law enforcement officers using the licenses or license plates. That record shall be confidential and is not a public record within the meaning of Chapter 132 of the General Statutes. The Director shall request the immediate return of any license or registration that is no longer necessary.

Licenses and license plates provided under this subsection shall expire six months after initial issuance unless the Director of the State Bureau of Investigation has approved an extension in writing. The head of the local, State, or federal law enforcement agency or the Department of Defense shall be responsible for the use of the licenses and license plates and shall return them immediately to the Director for cancellation upon either (i) their expiration, (ii) request of the Director of the State

Bureau of Investigation, or (iii) request of the Commissioner. Failure to return a license or license plate issued pursuant to this subsection shall be punished as a Class 2 misdemeanor. At no time shall the number of valid licenses issued under this subsection exceed two hundred nor shall the number of valid license plates issued under this subsection exceed one hundred twenty-five unless the Director determines that exceptional circumstances justify exceeding those amounts. However, fictitious licenses and license plates issued to special agents of the State Bureau of Investigation, State alcohol law enforcement agents, and the Department of Defense shall not be counted against the limitation on the total number of fictitious licenses and plates established by this subsection and shall be renewable annually.

(h) No private, confidential, or fictitious license plates issued under this section shall be used on privately owned vehicles under any circumstances.

(i) The Commissioner shall administer the issuance of private plates for publicly owned vehicles under the provisions of this section to ensure strict compliance with those provisions. The Division shall report to the Joint Legislative Commission on Governmental Operations by January 1 and July 1 of each year on the total number of private plates issued to each agency, and the total number of fictitious licenses and plates issued by the Division.

History.
2001-424, s. 6.14(a);2001-424, s. 6.14(b);2001-487, ss. 53, 54; 2003-152, ss. 3, 4; 2003- 284, ss. 6.5(a), (b); 2004-124, s. 6.5(a), (b); 2005-276, s. 6.18(a);2011-145, s. 19.1(g);2017-108, s. 10

EDITOR'S NOTE. --
Session Laws 2017-108, s. 21, is a severability clause.

EFFECT OF AMENDMENTS. --
Session Laws 2011-145, s. 19.1(g), effective January 1, 2012, substituted "Public Safety" for "Crime Control and Public Safety" in subsection (e).

Session Laws 2017-108, s. 10, effective July 12, 2017, added subsection (c1).

§ 20-40. Offices of Division

The Commissioner shall maintain an office in Wake County, North Carolina, or a surrounding county, and in such places in the State as the Commissioner deems necessary to properly carry out the provisions of this Article.

History.
1937, c. 407, s. 5; 2018-5, s. 34.24(c)

EDITOR'S NOTE. --
Session Laws 2018-5, s. 34.24(a) and (b), as amended by Session Laws 2020-3, s. 4.8(a), provides: "(a) All Division of Motor Vehicles employees and

contractors working at the Division of Motor Vehicles building located on New Bern Avenue in the City of Raleigh shall begin vacating the property by October 1, 2020.

"(b) By no later than August 1, 2018, the Department of Administration shall issue a Request for Proposal (RFP) seeking leased office space or spaces for the Division of Motor Vehicles employees and contractors currently working at the Division building located on New Bern Avenue in the City of Raleigh. The geographic scope of the RFP shall include Wake County and surrounding counties."

Session Laws 2018-5, s. 1.1, provides: "This act shall be known as the 'Current Operations Appropriations Act of 2018.'"

Session Laws 2018-5, s. 39.4, provides: "Except for statutory changes or other provisions that clearly indicate an intention to have effects beyond the 2018-2019 fiscal year, the textual provisions of this act apply only to funds appropriated for, and activities occurring during, the 2018-2019 fiscal year."

Session Laws 2018-5, s. 39.7, is a severability clause.

Session Laws 2020-3, s. 5, is a severability clause.

EFFECT OF AMENDMENTS. --
Session Laws 2018-5, s. 34.24(c), effective July 1, 2018, substituted "Wake County, North Carolina, or a surrounding county" for "Raleigh, North Carolina" and substituted "the Commissioner deems" for "he shall deem."

§ 20-41. Commissioner to provide forms required

The Commissioner shall provide suitable forms for applications, certificates of title and registration cards, registration number plates and all other forms requisite for the purpose of this Article, and shall prepay all transportation charges thereon.

History.
1937, c. 407, s. 6

§ 20-42. Authority to administer oaths and certify copies of records

(a) Officers and employees of the Division designated by the Commissioner are, for the purpose of administering the motor vehicle laws, authorized to administer oaths and acknowledge signatures, and shall charge for the acknowledgment of signatures a fee according to the following schedule:

(1) One signature $ 2.00
(2) Two signatures 3.00
(3) Three or more signatures 4.00

Funds received under the provisions of this subsection shall be used to defray a part of the costs of distribution of license plates, registration certificates and certificates of title issued by the Division.

(b) The Commissioner and officers of the Division designated by the Commissioner may prepare under the seal of the Division and deliver upon request a certified copy of any document of the Division for a fee. The fee for a document, other than an accident report under G.S. 20-166.1, is thirteen dollars ($ 13.00). The fee for an accident report is five dollars ($ 5.00). A certified copy shall be admissible in any proceeding in any court in like manner as the original thereof, without further certification. The certification fee does not apply to a document furnished for official use to a judicial official or to an official of the federal government, a state government, or a local government.

History.
1937, c. 407, s. 7; 1955, c. 480; 1961, c. 861, s. 1; 1967, c. 691, s. 41; c. 1172; 1971, c. 749; 1975, c. 716, s. 5; 1977, c. 785; 1979, c. 801, s. 7; 1981, c. 690, ss. 22, 23; 1991, c. 689, s. 331;1995, c. 191, s. 8;2005-276, s. 44.1(h);2015-241, s. 29.30(h)

EDITOR'S NOTE. --
Session Laws 2015-241, s. 29.30(u), made the amendment to subsection (b) of this section by Session Laws 2015-241, s. 29.30(h), applicable to issuances, renewals, restorations, and requests on or after January 1, 2016.

Session Laws 2015-241, s. 1.1, provides: "This act shall be known as 'The Current Operations and Capital Improvements Appropriations Act of 2015.'"

Session Laws 2015-241, s. 33.6, is a severability clause.

EFFECT OF AMENDMENTS. --
Session Laws 2005-276, s. 44.1(h), effective October 1, 2005, and applicable to fees collected on or after that date, substituted "ten dollars ($10.00)" for "five dollars ($5.00)" and "five dollars ($5.00)" for "four dollars ($4.00)" in subsection (b).

Session Laws 2015-241, s. 29.30(h), effective January 1, 2016, substituted "thirteen dollars ($13.00)" for "ten dollars ($10.00)" in second sentence of subsection (b). For applicability, see editor's note.

DIVISION'S RECORDS ARE COMPETENT TO ESTABLISH STATUS OF LICENSE AND DRIVING PRIVILEGE. --The records of the Department (now Division), properly authenticated, are competent for the purpose of establishing the status of a person's operator's license and driving privilege. State v. Teasley, 9 N.C. App. 477, 176 S.E.2d 838, appeal dismissed, 277 N.C. 459, 177 S.E.2d 900 (1970); State v. Rhodes, 10 N.C. App. 154, 177 S.E.2d 754 (1970).

AS WELL AS ACTIONS PREVIOUSLY TAKEN BY DIVISION. --Records of the Department (now Division) are competent to prove, among other things, the status of an individual's license and actions previously taken by the Department (now Division). State v. Mabry, 18 N.C. App. 492, 197 S.E.2d 44 (1973).

BUT NOT TO PROVE CONTENTS OF COURT RECORDS. --Records of the Department (now Division) of Motor Vehicles are not competent to prove the contents of the records of a court of law. State v. Mabry, 18 N.C. App. 492, 197 S.E.2d 44 (1973).

ADMISSIBILITY OF CERTIFIED COPIES OF RECORDS. --The effect of subsection (b) is to provide merely that properly certified copies of the Department's (now Division's) records are admissible in like manner as the original thereof. State v. Mabry, 18 N.C. App. 492, 197 S.E.2d 44 (1973).

THERE IS NO ERROR IN ALLOWING A PROPERLY CERTIFIED COPY OF A RECORD OF THE DIVISION TO BE READ INTO EVIDENCE by the district attorney, as opposed to having the document passed among the jurors. State v. Miller, 288 N.C. 582, 220 S.E.2d 326 (1975).

DEFENDANT WAS ENTITLED TO HAVE THE CONTENTS OF THE OFFICIAL RECORD OF THE STATUS OF HIS DRIVER'S LICENSE LIMITED, if he so requested, to the formal parts thereof, including the certification and seal, plus the fact that under official action of the Department (now Division) of Motor Vehicles the defendant's license was in a state of revocation or suspension on the date he was charged with committing an offense under G.S. 20-28. State v. Rhodes, 10 N.C. App. 154, 177 S.E.2d 754 (1970).

NO RESTRICTION ON GENERAL RULE AS TO STAMPED, PRINTED OR TYPEWRITTEN SIGNATURES. --This section does not impose upon the general rule that a stamped, printed or typewritten signature is a good signature the restriction that the signature be made under the hand of the person making it. State v. Watts, 289 N.C. 445, 222 S.E.2d 389 (1976).

APPLIED in State v. Moore, 247 N.C. 368, 101 S.E.2d 26 (1957); State v. Blacknell, 270 N.C. 103, 153 S.E.2d 789 (1967); State v. Hughes, 6 N.C. App. 287, 170 S.E.2d 78 (1969).

CITED in State v. Corl, 250 N.C. 252, 108 S.E.2d 608 (1959); State v. Knight, 261 N.C. 17, 134 S.E.2d 101 (1964); State v. Letterlough, 6 N.C. App. 36, 169 S.E.2d 269 (1969); State v. Parker, 20 N.C. App. 146, 201 S.E.2d 35 (1973); State v. Carlisle, 20 N.C. App. 358, 201 S.E.2d 704 (1973); State v. Salter, 29 N.C. App. 372, 224 S.E.2d 247 (1976).

CROSS REFERENCES. --

As to copy of record kept by Commissioner, etc., certified by Commissioner, as evidence, see G.S. 8-37.

§ 20-43. Records of Division

(a) All records of the Division, other than those declared by law to be confidential for the use of the Division, shall be open to public inspection during office hours in accordance with G.S. 20-43.1. A signature recorded in any format by the Division for a drivers license or a special identification card is confidential and shall not be released except for law enforcement purposes or to the State Chief Information Officer for purposes of G.S. 143B-1385 or the State Board of Elections in connection with its official duties under Chapter 163 of the General Statutes. A photographic image recorded in any

format by the Division for a drivers license or a special identification card is confidential and shall not be released except for law enforcement purposes or to the State Chief Information Officer for the purposes of G.S. 143B-1385 or the State Board of Elections in connection with its official duties under Chapter 163 of the General Statutes.

(b) The Commissioner, upon receipt of notification from another state or foreign country that a certificate of title issued by the Division has been surrendered by the owner in conformity with the laws of such other state or foreign country, may cancel and destroy such record of certificate of title.

History.

1937, c. 407, s. 8; 1947, c. 219, s. 1; 1971, c. 1070, s. 1; 1975, c. 716, s. 5; 1995, c. 195, s. 1;1997-443, s. 32.25(d);2013-360, s. 7.10(b);2014-115, s. 56.8(d);2015-241, s. 7A.4(c);2016-94, s. 24.1;2017-6, s. 3;2018-146, ss. 3.1(a), (b), 6.1.

RE-RECODIFICATION; TECHNICAL AND CONFORMING CHANGES. --Session Laws 2017-6, s. 3, provides, in part: "The Revisor of Statutes shall recodify Chapter 138A of the General Statutes, Chapter 120C of the General Statutes, as well as Chapter 163 of the General Statutes, as amended by this act, into a new Chapter 163A of the General Statutes to be entitled 'Elections and Ethics Enforcement Act,' as enacted by Section 4 of this act. The Revisor may also recodify into the new Chapter 163A of the General Statutes other existing statutory laws relating to elections and ethics enforcement that are located elsewhere in the General Statutes as the Revisor deems appropriate." The Revisor was further authorized to make additional technical and conforming changes to catchlines, internal citations, and other references throughout the General Statutes to effectuate this recodification. Pursuant to this authority, the Revisor of Statutes substituted "Bipartisan State Board of Elections and Ethics Enforcement" for "State Board of Elections" and "Subchapter III of Chapter 163A" for "Chapter 163" in subsection (a).

Session Laws 2018-146, ss. 3.1(a), (b), and 6.1, repealed Session Laws 2017-6, s. 3, and authorized the Revisor of Statutes to re-recodify Chapter 163A into Chapters 163, 138A, and 120C and to revert the changes made by the Revisor pursuant to Session Laws 2017-6, s. 3. Pursuant to this authority, the Revisor of Statutes reverted the changes to references in subsection (a).

EFFECT OF AMENDMENTS. --

Session Laws 2013-360, s. 7.10(b), effective July 26, 2013, in subsection (a), deleted "photographic image or" preceding "signature recorded" in the second sentence and added the last sentence.

Session Laws 2014-115, s. 56.8(d), effective August 11, 2014, substituted "Chief Information Officer" for "Controller" in the last sentence of subsection (a).

Session Laws 2015-241, s. 7A.4(c), effective July 1, 2015, near the end of subsection (a), deleted "Office of the" preceding "State Chief Information" and substituted "G.S. 143B-1385" for "G.S. 143B-426.38A."

Session Laws 2016-94, s. 24.1, effective July 1, 2016, in subsection (a), added "or to the State Chief Information Officer for purposes of G.S. 143B-1385 or the State Board of Elections in connection with its official duties under Chapter 163 of the General Statutes" at the end of the first sentence, and added "G.S. 143B-1385 or the State Board of Elections in connection with its official duties under Chapter 163 of the General Statutes" at the end of the last sentence. CITED in Hodgson v. Hyatt Realty & Inv. Co., 353 F. Supp. 1363 (M.D.N.C. 1973).

§ 20-43.1. Disclosure of personal information in motor vehicle records

(a) The Division shall disclose personal information contained in motor vehicle records in accordance with the federal Driver's Privacy Protection Act of 1994, as amended, 18 U.S.C. §§ 2721, et seq.

(b) As authorized in 18 U.S.C. § 2721, the Division shall not disclose personal information for the purposes specified in 18 U.S.C. § 2721(b) (11).

(c) The Division shall not disclose personal information for the purposes specified in 18 U.S.C. § 2721(b)(12) unless the Division receives prior written permission from the person about whom the information is requested.

(d) As authorized in 18 U.S.C. § 2721, the Division may disclose personal information to federally designated organ procurement organizations and eye banks operating in this State for the purpose of identifying individuals who have indicated an intent to be an organ donor. Personal information authorized under this subsection is limited to the individual's first, middle, and last name, date of birth, address, sex, county of residence, and drivers license number. Employees of the Division who provide access to or disclosure of information in good-faith compliance with this subsection are not liable in damages for access to or disclosure of the information.

(e) As authorized in 18 U.S.C. § 2721, the Division may also provide copies of partial crash report data collected pursuant to G.S. 20-166.1, partial driver license data kept pursuant to G.S. 20-26(a), and partial vehicle registration application data collected pursuant to G.S. 20-52 in bulk form to persons, private companies, or other entities, for uses other than official, upon payment of a fee of three cents (3 cent(s)) per individual record. The Division shall not furnish such data except upon execution by the recipient of a written agreement to comply with the Driver's Privacy Protection Act of 1994, as amended, 18 U.S.C. §§ 2721, et seq. The information released to persons, private companies, or other entities, for uses other than official,

pursuant to this subsection, shall not be a public record pursuant to Chapter 132 of the General Statutes.

(f) E-mail addresses or other electronic addresses provided to the Division are personal information for purposes of this section and shall only be disclosed in accordance with this section.

History.
1997-443, s. 32.25(a);1999-237, s. 27.9(b);2004-189, s. 2;2011-145, s. 31.29;2016-90, s. 10(b)

EDITOR'S NOTE. --
Session Laws 1998-23, s. 17.1, as amended by Session Laws 1998-212, s. 27.18(a), had provided that notwithstanding any other provision of law, the Division of Motor Vehicles shall not disclose personal information in its records for purposes specified in 18 U.S.C. § 2721(b)(12) prior to January 1, 2000; and further provides that this section shall not expire until January 1, 2000. Session Laws 1999-237, s. 27.9(a), repealed Session Laws 1998-23, s. 17.1, as amended.

Session Laws 2004-189, s. 5(c), as amended by Session Laws 2005-276, s. 44.1(q), provides: "The Division of Motor Vehicles shall retain a portion of five cents ($0.05) collected for the issuance of each drivers license and duplicate license to offset the actual cost of developing and maintaining the online Organ Donor Internet site established pursuant to Section 1 of this act. The remainder of the five cents ($0.05) shall be credited to the License to Give Trust Fund established under G.S. 20-7.4 and shall be used for the purposes authorized under G.S. 20-7.4 and G.S. 20-7.5."

Session Laws 2011-145, s. 1.1, provides: "This act shall be known as the 'Current Operations and Capital Improvements Appropriations Act of 2011.'"

Session Laws 2011-145, s. 32.5 is a severability clause.

EFFECT OF AMENDMENTS. --
Session Laws 2004-189, s. 2, effective January 1, 2005, added subsection (d).

Session Laws 2011-145, s. 31.29, effective July 1, 2011, added subsection (e).

Session Laws 2016-90, s. 10(b), effective October 1, 2016, added subsection (f).

OPINIONS OF THE ATTORNEY GENERAL
MOTOR VEHICLE ACCIDENT REPORTS are public records, but should be released only after the Division of Motor Vehicles has redacted personal identifying information in accordance with the federal Drivers Privacy Protection Act. See opinion of Attorney General to Mr. George Tatum, Commissioner, North Carolina Division of Motor Vehicles, 2005 N.C. AG LEXIS 1 (2/9/05).

RELEASE OF DEPARTMENT OF MOTOR VEHICLE RECORDS. --The Department of Motor Vehicles is required by the Drivers Privacy Protection Act, 18 U.S.C. § 2721, et seq., to redact "personal information" and "highly restricted personal information" from documents, such as accident reports, provided to the public. Otherwise, the requirements of the Public Records Act, G.S. 132-1 et seq., should be complied with by DMV and local law enforcement agencies. Motor vehicle registration information provided by DMV to local taxing authorities should also be provided upon request in accordance with the Public Records Act. See opinion of Attorney General to Mr. George Tatum, Commissioner, North Carolina Division of Motor Vehicles, 2005 N.C.A.G. 1 (02/09/05).

§ 20-43.2. Internet access to organ donation records by organ procurement organizations

(a) The Department of Transportation, Division of Motor Vehicles, shall establish and maintain a statewide, online Organ Donor Registry Internet site (hereafter "Donor Registry"). The purpose of the Donor Registry is to enable federally designated organ procurement organizations and eye banks to have access 24 hours per day, seven days per week to obtain relevant information on the Donor Registry to determine, at or near death of the donor or a prospective donor, whether the donor or prospective donor has made, amended, or revoked an anatomical gift through a symbol on the donor's or prospective donor's drivers license, special identification card, or other manner. The data available on the Donor Registry shall be limited to the individual's first, middle, and last name, date of birth, address, sex, county of residence, and drivers license number. The Division of Motor Vehicles shall ensure that only federally designated organ procurement organizations and eye banks operating in this State have access to the Donor Registry in read-only format. The Division of Motor Vehicles shall enable federally designated organ procurement organizations and eye banks operating in this State to have online access in read-only format to the Donor Registry through a unique identifier and password issued to the organ procurement organization or eye bank by the Division of Motor Vehicles. Employees of the Division who provide access to or disclosure of information in good-faith compliance with this section are not liable in damages for access to or disclosure of the information.

(b) When accessing and using information obtained from the Donor Registry, federally designated organ procurement organizations and eye banks shall comply with the requirements of Part 3A of Article 16 of Chapter 130A of the General Statutes.

(c) Personally identifiable information on a donor registry about a donor or prospective donor may not be used or disclosed without the express consent of the donor, prospective donor, or person that made the anatomical gift for any purpose other than to determine, at or near death of the donor or prospective donor, whether the donor or prospective donor has made, amended, or revoked an anatomical gift.

(d) This section does not prohibit any person from creating or maintaining a donor registry that is not established by or under contract with the State. Any such registry must comply with subsections (b) and (c) of this section.

History.
2004-189, s. 1;2007-538, s. 2
    EDITOR'S NOTE. --
    Session Laws 2004-189, s. 1, has been codified as this section at the direction of the Revisor of Statutes.
    Session Laws 2004-189, s. 5(c), as amended by Session Laws 2005-276, s. 44.1(q), provides: "The Division of Motor Vehicles shall retain a portion of five cents ($0.05) collected for the issuance of each drivers license and duplicate license to offset the actual cost of developing and maintaining the online Organ Donor Internet site established pursuant to Section 1 of this act. The remainder of the five cents ($0.05) shall be credited to the License to Give Trust Fund established under G.S. 20-7.4 and shall be used for the purposes authorized under G.S. 20-7.4 and G.S. 20-7.5."
    EFFECT OF AMENDMENTS. --
    Session Laws 2007-538, s. 2, effective October 1, 2007, rewrote this section.

§ 20-43.3. Authorization for the collection of data to enforce the Federal Motor Carrier Safety Administration's Performance and Registration Information Systems Management (PRISM) program

The Division is authorized to collect and maintain necessary motor carrier or commercial motor vehicle data in a manner that complies with the information system established by the United States Secretary of Transportation under 49 U.S.C. § 31106.

History.
2019-196, s. 1
    EDITOR'S NOTE. --
    Session Laws 2019-196, s. 5, made this section, as added by Session Laws 2019-196, s. 1, effective November 12, 2019.

§ 20-43.4. Current list of licensed drivers to be provided to jury commissions

(a) The Commissioner of Motor Vehicles shall provide to each county jury commission an alphabetical list of all persons that the Commissioner has determined are residents of the county, who will be 18 years of age or older as of the first day of January of the following year, and licensed to drive a motor vehicle as of July 1 of each odd-numbered year, provided that if an annual master jury list is being prepared under G.S. 9-2(a), the list to be provided to the county jury commission shall be updated and provided annually.

(b) The list shall include those persons whose license to drive has been suspended, and those former licensees whose license has been canceled, except that the list shall not include the name of any formerly licensed driver whose license is expired and has not been renewed for eight years or more. The list shall contain the address and zip code of each driver, plus the driver's date of birth, sex, social security number, and drivers license number, and may be in either printed or computerized form, as requested by each county. Before providing the list to the county jury commission, the Commissioner shall have computer-matched the list with the voter registration list of the State Board of Elections to eliminate duplicates. The Commissioner shall also remove from the list the names of those residents of the county who are (i) issued a drivers license of limited duration under G.S. 20-7(s), (ii) issued a drivers license of regular duration under G.S. 20-7(f) and who hold a valid permanent resident card issued by the United States, or (iii) who are recently deceased, which names shall be supplied to the Commissioner by the State Registrar under G.S. 130A-121(b). The Commissioner shall include in the list provided to the county jury commission names of registered voters who do not have drivers licenses, and shall indicate the licensed or formerly licensed drivers who are also registered voters, the licensed or formerly licensed drivers who are not registered voters, and the registered voters who are not licensed or formerly licensed drivers.

(c) The list so provided shall be used solely for jury selection and election records purposes and no other. Information provided by the Commissioner to county jury commissions and the State Board of Elections under this section shall remain confidential, shall continue to be subject to the disclosure restriction provisions of G.S. 20-43.1, and shall not be a public record for purposes of Chapter 132 of the General Statutes.

History.
1981, c. 720, s. 2; 1983, c. 197, ss. 1, 1.1; c. 754; c. 768, s. 25.3; 2003-226, s. 7(c);2007-512, s. 3;2012-180, s. 11.5;2017-6, s. 3;2018-146, ss. 3.1(a), (b), 6.1

RE-RECODIFICATION; TECHNICAL AND CONFORMING CHANGES. --Session Laws 2017-6, s. 3, provides, in part: "The Revisor of Statutes shall recodify Chapter 138A of the General Statutes, Chapter 120C of the General Statutes, as well as Chapter 163 of the General Statutes, as amended by this act, into a new Chapter 163A of the General Statutes to be entitled 'Elections and Ethics Enforcement Act,' as enacted by Section 4 of this act. The Revisor may also recodify into the new Chapter 163A of the General Statutes other existing statutory laws relating to elections and ethics enforcement that are located elsewhere in the General Statutes as the Revisor deems appropriate." The Revisor was further authorized to

make additional technical and conforming changes to catchlines, internal citations, and other references throughout the General Statutes to effectuate this recodification. Pursuant to this authority, the Revisor of Statutes substituted "Bipartisan State Board of Elections and Ethics Enforcement" for "State Board of Elections" in subsections (b) and (c).

Session Laws 2018-146, ss. 3.1(a), (b), and 6.1, repealed Session Laws 2017-6, s. 3, and authorized the Revisor of Statutes to re-recodify Chapter 163A into Chapters 163, 138A, and 120C and to revert the changes made by the Revisor pursuant to Session Laws 2017-6, s. 3. Pursuant to this authority, the Revisor of Statutes reverted the changes to references in subsections (b) and (c).

EDITOR'S NOTE. --
Session Laws 2003-226, s. 1, provides: "The purpose of this act is to ensure that the State of North Carolina has a system for all North Carolina elections that complies with the requirements for federal elections set forth in the federal Help America Vote Act of 2002, Public Law 107-252, 116 Stat. 1666 (2002), codified at 42 U.S.C. §§ 15481-15485.

"The General Assembly finds that the education and training of election officials as required by G.S. 163-82.34 has met and continues to meet the mandate for the education and training of precinct officials and other election officials in section 254(a)(3) of the Help America Vote Act of 2002. The General Assembly further finds that the establishment, development, and continued operation of the statewide list maintenance program for voter registration set forth in G.S. 163-82.14 has met and continues to meet the mandates of section 303(a)(2) of the Help America Vote Act of 2002.

"In certain other areas of the election statutes and other laws, the General Assembly finds that the statutes must be amended to comply with the Help America Vote Act."

EFFECT OF AMENDMENTS. --
Session Laws 2003-226, s. 7.(c), effective January 1, 2004, and applicable with respect to all primaries and elections held on or after that date, in the first sentence, substituted "the Commissioner" for "he," deleted "as of July 1, 1983, and" following "to drive a motor vehicle," and substituted "odd-numbered year" for "biennium thereafter"; in the third sentence, substituted "the driver's" for "his" and inserted "and drivers license number"; inserted the fourth and fifth sentences; in the sixth sentence, inserted "and election records"; and added the last sentence.

Session Laws 2007-512, s. 3, effective October 1, 2007, inserted "updated and" near the end of the first sentence; added the exception at the end of the second sentence; inserted "social security number," in the third sentence; and added the fifth sentence.

Session Laws 2012-180, s. 11.5, effective July 12, 2012, designated the existing provisions as subsections (a), (b) and (c); in subsection (a), added "master" preceding "jury list"; and in fourth sentence of subsection (b), added "(i) issued a drivers license of limited duration under G.S. 20-7(s), (ii) issued a drivers license of regular duration under G.S. 20-7(f) and who hold a valid permanent resident card issued by the United States, or (iii) who are", and added "names" preceding "shall be."

§ 20-44. Authority to grant or refuse applications

The Division shall examine and determine the genuineness, regularity and legality of every application for registration of a vehicle and for a certificate of title therefor, and of any other application lawfully made in the Division, and may in all cases make investigation as may be deemed necessary or require additional information, and shall reject any such application if not satisfied of the genuineness, regularity, or legality thereof or the truth of any statement contained therein, or for any other reason, when authorized by law.

History.
1937, c. 407, s. 9; 1975, c. 716, s. 5

§ 20-45. Seizure of documents and plates

(a) The Division is authorized to take possession of any certificate of title, registration card, permit, license, or registration plate issued by it upon expiration, revocation, cancellation, or suspension thereof, or which is fictitious, or which has been unlawfully or erroneously issued, or which has been unlawfully used.

(b) The Division may give notice to the owner, licensee or lessee of its authority to take possession of any certificate of title, registration card, permit, license, or registration plate issued by it and require that person to surrender it to the Commissioner or the Commissioner's officers or agents. Any person who fails to surrender the certificate of title, registration card, permit, license, or registration plate or any duplicate thereof, upon personal service of notice or within 10 days after receipt of notice by mail as provided in G.S. 20-48, shall be guilty of a Class 2 misdemeanor.

(c) Any sworn law enforcement officer with jurisdiction, including a member of the State Highway Patrol, is authorized to seize the certificate of title, registration card, permit, license, or registration plate, if the officer has electronic or other notification from the Division that the item has been revoked or cancelled, or otherwise has probable cause to believe that the item has been revoked or cancelled under any law or statute, including G.S. 20-311. If a criminal proceeding relating to a certificate of title, registration card, permit, or license is pending, the law enforcement officer in possession of that item shall retain the item pending the entry of a final judgment by a court with jurisdiction. If there is no criminal proceeding pending, the law enforcement officer shall deliver the item to the Division.

(d) Any law enforcement officer who seizes a registration plate pursuant to this section shall report the seizure to the Division within 48 hours of the seizure and shall return the registration plate, but not a fictitious registration plate, to the Division within 10 business days of the seizure.

History.
1937, c. 407, s. 10; 1975, c. 716, s. 5; 1981, c. 938, s. 2; 1993, c. 539, s. 329;1994, Ex. Sess., c. 24, s. 14(c);2005-357, s. 1;2006-105, ss. 2.1, 2.2; 2006-264, s. 98.1;2017-102, s. 6

EFFECT OF AMENDMENTS. --
Session Laws 2005-357, s. 1, effective December 1, 2005, rewrote subsection (b) and added subsections (c) and (d).

Session Laws 2006-105, ss. 2.1 and 2.2, effective July 13, 2006, substituted "a certificate of title, registration card, permit, or license" for "the item" in the second sentence of subsection (c); and substituted "seizure and shall return the registration plate, but not a fictitious registration plate, to the Division within 10 business days of the seizure" for "seizure" in subsection (d).

Session Laws 2006-264, s. 98.1, effective August 27, 2006, substituted "jurisdiction, including a member of the State Highway Patrol" for "jurisdiction" in the first sentence of subsection (c).

Session Laws 2017-102, s. 6, effective July 12, 2017, deleted "hereby" following "The Division is" in subsection (a); substituted "the Commisioner's officers or agents" for "his officers or agents" in subsection (b); and substituted "G.S. 20-311" for "G.S. 20-309(e)" in subsection (c).

N.C. Gen. Stat. § 20-46

Repealed by Session Laws 1979, c. 99.

§ 20-47. Division may summon witnesses and take testimony

(a) The Commissioner and officers of the Division designated by him shall have authority to summon witnesses to give testimony under oath or to give written deposition upon any matter under the jurisdiction of the Division. Such summons may require the production of relevant books, papers, or records.

(b) Every such summons shall be served at least five days before the return date, either by personal service made by any person over 18 years of age or by registered mail, but return acknowledgment is required to prove such latter service. Failure to obey such a summons so served shall constitute a Class 2 misdemeanor. The fees for the attendance and travel of witnesses shall be the same as for witnesses before the superior court.

(c) The superior court shall have jurisdiction, upon application by the Commissioner, to enforce all lawful orders of the Commissioner under this section.

History.
1937, c. 407, s. 12; 1975, c. 716, s. 5; 1993, c. 539, s. 330;1994, Ex. Sess., c. 24, s. 14(c)
CROSS REFERENCES. --
As to fees of witnesses generally, see G.S. 7A-314. As to penalties for persons convicted of misdemeanors for violations of this Article, see G.S. 20-176.

§ 20-48. Giving of notice

(a) Whenever the Division is authorized or required to give any notice under this Chapter or other law regulating the operation of vehicles, unless a different method of giving such notice is otherwise expressly prescribed, such notice shall be given either by personal delivery thereof to the person to be so notified or by deposit in the United States mail of such notice in an envelope with postage prepaid, addressed to such person at his address as shown by the records of the Division. The giving of notice by mail is complete upon the expiration of four days after such deposit of such notice. In lieu of providing notice by personal delivery or United States mail, the Division may give notice under this Chapter by e-mail or other electronic means if the person to be notified has consented to receiving notices via electronic means and has provided the Division an e-mail address or other like electronic address for receiving the notices. Proof of the giving of notice in any such manner pursuant to this section may be made by a notation in the records of the Division that the notice was sent to a particular address, physical or electronic, and the purpose of the notice. A certified copy of the Division's records may be sent by the Police Information Network, facsimile, or other electronic means. A copy of the Division's records sent under the authority of this section is admissible as evidence in any court or administrative agency and is sufficient evidence to discharge the burden of the person presenting the record that notice was sent to the person named in the record, at the physical or electronic address indicated in the record, and for the purpose indicated in the record. There is no requirement that the actual notice or letter be produced.

(a1) A person may consent to receive any notice under this Chapter by electronic delivery by completing a written or electronic authorization for this method of delivery. The authorization must advise the person that all of the following apply to consent to electronic delivery of a notice:

　(1) Consent is effective until it is revoked in accordance with the procedure set by the Division.

　(2) At the option of the Division, electronic delivery may be the only method of delivery.

　(3) A notice sent by electronic delivery to an e-mail or electronic address is considered to have been received even if the person to whom it is sent does not receive it.

(a2) A person who consents to electronic notification pursuant to this section shall notify the Division of any change or discontinuance of any e-mail or electronic address provided to the Division in accordance with the provisions of this section and G.S. 20-7.1(a). Upon the failure of a person to notify the Division of any change or discontinuance of an electronic notification pursuant to this section, any notices sent to the original or discontinued electronic address shall be deemed to have been received by the person and a copy of the Division's records sent under the authority of this section is sufficient evidence that notice was sent to the person named in the record, at the physical or electronic address indicated in the record, and for the purpose indicated in the record.

(b) Notwithstanding any other provision of this Chapter at any time notice is now required by registered mail with return receipt requested, certified mail with return receipt requested may be used in lieu thereof and shall constitute valid notice to the same extent and degree as notice by registered mail with return receipt requested.

(c) The Commissioner shall appoint such agents of the Division as may be needed to serve revocation notices required by this Chapter. The fee for service of a revocation notice by personal delivery shall be fifty dollars ($ 50.00).

History.
1937, c. 407, s. 13; 1955, c. 1187, s. 21; 1971, c. 1231, s. 1; 1975, c. 326, s. 3; c. 716, s. 5; 1983, c. 761, s. 148; 1985, c. 479, s. 171; 2006-253, s. 21;2016-90, s. 10(c)
EFFECT OF AMENDMENTS. --
Session Laws 2006-253, s. 21, effective December 1, 2006, and applicable to offenses committed on or after that date, rewrote subsection (a).

Session Laws 2016-90, s. 10(c), effective October 1, 2016, in subsection (a), added the third sentence, in the fourth sentence, substituted "any such manner pursuant to this section" for "either such manner" near the beginning, and inserted "physical or electronic" near the end, and, in the next-to-last sentence, inserted "physical or electronic"; added subsections (a1) and (a2); and, in subsection (c), substituted "revocation notice by personal delivery" for "notice" near the middle of the last sentence.

DUE PROCESS REQUIREMENTS SATISFIED. -- The provisions of this section, together with the provisions of G.S. 20-16(d), relating to the right of review, and the provisions of G.S. 20-25, relating to the right of appeal, satisfy the requirements of procedural due process. State v. Teasley, 9 N.C. App. 477, 176 S.E.2d

838, appeal dismissed, 277 N.C. 459, 177 S.E.2d 900 (1970).

This section affords the defendant procedural due process with respect to the manner of giving him notice of the revocation or suspension of his driving privileges. State v. Hayes, 31 N.C. App. 121, 228 S.E.2d 460 (1976).

SECTION REASONABLY CALCULATED TO GIVE NOTICE OF PROPOSED AND ACTUAL SUSPENSION. --This section, providing for the manner in which notice is to be given, is reasonably calculated to assure that notice will reach the intended party and afford him the opportunity of resisting or avoiding the proposed suspension, as well as to give him notification of the actual suspension of his operator's license and driving privilege. State v. Teasley, 9 N.C. App. 477, 176 S.E.2d 838, appeal dismissed, 277 N.C. 459, 177 S.E.2d 900 (1970).

COMPLIANCE WITH SECTION AS CONSTRUCTIVE NOTICE OF SUSPENSION. --Compliance by the Department (now Division) with the procedure set forth in this section as to notice of suspension of an operator's license and driving privilege constitutes constructive notice to the defendant that his license has been suspended. State v. Teasley, 9 N.C. App. 477, 176 S.E.2d 838, appeal dismissed, 277 N.C. 459, 177 S.E.2d 900 (1970).

PRIMA FACIE PRESUMPTION OF RECEIPT FROM MAILING OF NOTICE. --For purposes of a conviction for driving while one's license is suspended or revoked, mailing of the notice under this section raises only a prima facie presumption that defendant received the notice and thereby acquired knowledge of the suspension or revocation, and defendant is not by this section denied the right to rebut the presumption. State v. Atwood, 290 N.C. 266, 225 S.E.2d 543 (1976); State v. Sellers, 58 N.C. App. 43, 293 S.E.2d 226, cert. denied and appeal dismissed, 306 N.C. 749, 295 S.E.2d 485 (1982).

For purposes of a conviction for driving while license is suspended or revoked, mailing of the notice under this section raises only a prima facie presumption that defendant received the notice and thereby acquired knowledge of the suspension or revocation. Thus, defendant is not by this statute denied the right to rebut this presumption. State v. Curtis, 73 N.C. App. 248, 326 S.E.2d 90 (1985).

THE STATE SATISFIES THE BURDEN OF PROVING THAT DEFENDANT HAD KNOWLEDGE at the time charged that his operator's license was suspended or revoked when, nothing else appearing, it has offered evidence of compliance with the notice requirements of this section because of the presumption that he received notice and had such knowledge. State v. Chester, 30 N.C. App. 224, 226 S.E.2d 524 (1976); State v. Sellers, 58 N.C. App. 43, 293 S.E.2d 226, cert. denied and appeal dismissed, 306 N.C. 749, 295 S.E.2d 485 (1982); State v. Curtis, 73 N.C. App. 248, 326 S.E.2d 90 (1985).

WHEN THERE IS SOME EVIDENCE TO REBUT THE PRESUMPTION OF RECEIPT OF NOTICE AND KNOWLEDGE, THE ISSUE OF GUILTY

KNOWLEDGE IS RAISED and must be determined by the jury under appropriate instruction from the trial court. State v. Sellers, 58 N.C. App. 43, 293 S.E.2d 226, cert. denied and appeal dismissed, 306 N.C. 749, 295 S.E.2d 485 (1982).

THE FAILURE OF THE TRIAL COURT TO CHARGE ON KNOWLEDGE OF REVOCATION pursuant to G.S. 20-28 in support of an aggravated sentence under G.S. 20-141.5 was not erroneous where the State's evidence tended to show that it complied with the provisions for giving notice of revocation or suspension of a driver's license found in this section and the defendant neither contested that evidence nor offered contrary evidence. State v. Funchess, 141 N.C. App. 302, 540 S.E.2d 435 (2000).

KNOWLEDGE OF REVOCATION. --Trial court erred in denying defendant's motion to dismiss the charge against him of driving while license revoked, as the State did not present sufficient evidence that defendant knew his license was revoked, in part because the State was unable to show that defendant had been notified of the alleged revocation. State v. Cruz, 173 N.C. App. 689, 620 S.E.2d 251 (2005).

Since defendant chose not to present any evidence at trial, the State met its burden of producing substantial evidence on each element of driving while license revoked in G.S. 20-28(a) by offering evidence that the Department of Motor Vehicles had sent defendant 18 notices of the revocation of defendant's license in compliance with G.S. 20-48(a). State v. Coltrane, 188 N.C. App. 498, 656 S.E.2d 322 (2008), review denied, 362 N.C. 476, 666 S.E.2d 760 (2008).

To convict defendant of driving while his license was revoked, the State had to prove he had knowledge of the revocation, and the State moved to admit defendant's driving record; while hearsay, the portions of the documents certifying their accuracy and attesting that the suspension orders were sent to defendant constituted substantive evidence of his commission of the offense, and as the driving records were created in compliance with the motor vehicle department's obligations to maintain such records and provide notice to motorists, the records were not testimonial. State v. Clark, 242 N.C. App. 141, 775 S.E.2d 28 (2015).

Trial court erred in convicting defendant of driving a motor vehicle while his license was revoked because, while the State provided evidence that notice of defendant's driver's license revocation had been mailed in accordance with the statutory requirements, defendant testified that he did not receive the notice from the Department of Motor Vehicles and suggested that, since he shared his name and address with his father, he never received actual notice of his license's revocation, the trial court failed to instruct the jury that it could find defendant guilty only if he had knowledge of his license's revocation, and there was a reasonable possibility that the jury, properly instructed, would have acquitted him. State v. Green, 258 N.C. App. 87, 811 S.E.2d 666 (2018).

DEFENDANT'S ADDRESS IS RELEVANT TO THE CHARGE OF DRIVING WHILE HIS LICENSE WAS PERMANENTLY REVOKED, since the State has the burden of proving that defendant had knowledge of the revocation prior to the date of his arrest in order to sustain a conviction. State v. Sellers, 58 N.C. App. 43, 293 S.E.2d 226, cert. denied and appeal dismissed, 306 N.C. 749, 295 S.E.2d 485 (1982).

FULL SIGNATURE AND NOTARIZATION NOT REQUIRED ON CERTIFICATE OF NOTICE. --There is nothing in this section which requires that the certificate to prove that the notice of revocation was mailed in accordance with the statute contain the full signature of the employee making the certificate or that such certificate be notarized. State v. Johnson, 25 N.C. App. 630, 214 S.E.2d 278, cert. denied, 288 N.C. 247, 217 S.E.2d 671 (1975).

Initialed certificate lacking notary's authentication meets all the requirements of this section and provides prima facie evidence of the genuineness of such certificate, the truth of the statements made in such certificate, and the official character of the person who purportedly initialed and executed it. State v. Johnson, 25 N.C. App. 630, 214 S.E.2d 278, cert. denied, 288 N.C. 247, 217 S.E.2d 671 (1975).

ADMISSIBILITY OF COPY OF DIVISION ORDER ON CERTIFICATION OF MAILING OF ORIGINAL. --Certification by an employee of the Department (now Division) of Motor Vehicles that the original of an order of security requirement or suspension of driving privilege was mailed to defendant on a specified date at his address shown on the records of the Department (now Division) was sufficient to render admissible a copy of the document in a prosecution of defendant for driving while his license was suspended. State v. Herald, 10 N.C. App. 263, 178 S.E.2d 120 (1970).

APPLIED in State v. Hughes, 6 N.C. App. 287, 170 S.E.2d 78 (1969); State v. Phillips, 25 N.C. App. 313, 212 S.E.2d 906 (1975); State v. Finger, 72 N.C. App. 569, 324 S.E.2d 894 (1985).

CITED in Ellis v. White, 156 N.C. App. 16, 575 S.E.2d 809 (2003).

§ 20-49. Police authority of Division

The Commissioner and such officers and inspectors of the Division as he shall designate and all members of the Highway Patrol and law enforcement officers of the Department of Public Safety shall have the power:

(1) Of peace officers for the purpose of enforcing the provisions of this Article and of any other law regulating the operation of vehicles or the use of the highways.

(2) To make arrests upon view and without warrant for any violation committed in their presence of any of the provisions of this Article or other laws regulating the operation of vehicles or the use of the highways.

(3) At all time to direct all traffic in conformance with law, and in the event of a fire or other emergency or to expedite traffic or to insure safety, to direct traffic as conditions may require, notwithstanding the provisions of law.

(4) When on duty, upon reasonable belief that any vehicle is being operated in violation of any provision of this Article or of any other law regulating the operation of vehicles to require the driver thereof to stop and exhibit his driver's license and the registration card issued for the vehicle, and submit to an inspection of such vehicle, the registration plates and registration card thereon or to an inspection and test of the equipment of such vehicle.

(5) To inspect any vehicle of a type required to be registered hereunder in any public garage or repair shop or in any place where such vehicles are held for sale or wrecking, for the purpose of locating stolen vehicles and investigating the title and registration thereof.

(6) To serve all warrants relating to the enforcement of the laws regulating the operation of vehicles or the use of the highways.

(7) To investigate traffic accidents and secure testimony of witnesses or of persons involved.

(8) To investigate reported thefts of motor vehicles, trailers and semitrailers and make arrest for thefts thereof.

(9) For the purpose of determining compliance with the provisions of this Chapter, to inspect all files and records of the persons hereinafter designated and required to be kept under the provisions of this Chapter or of the registrations of the Division:

    a. Persons dealing in or selling and buying new, used or junked motor vehicles and motor vehicle parts; and

    b. Persons operating garages or other places where motor vehicles are repaired, dismantled, or stored.

History.
1937, c. 407, s. 14; 1955, c. 554, s. 1; 1975, c. 716, s. 5; 1979, c. 93; 2002-159, s. 31.5(b);2002-190, s. 5;2011-145, s. 19.1(g)

EDITOR'S NOTE. --
Session Laws 2002-190, s. 1, provides: "All statutory authority, powers, duties, and functions, including rulemaking, budgeting, purchasing, records, personnel, personnel positions, salaries, property, and unexpended balances of appropriations, allocations, reserves, support costs, and other funds allocated to the Department of Transportation, Division of Motor Vehicles Enforcement Section, for the regulation and enforcement of commercial motor vehicles, oversize and overweight vehicles, motor carrier safety, and mobile and manufactured housing are transferred to and vested in the Department of Crime Control and Public Safety. This transfer has all the elements of a Type I transfer as defined in G.S. 143A-6.

Chapter 20

"The Department of Crime Control and Public Safety shall be considered a continuation of the transferred portion of the Department of Transportation, Division of Motor Vehicles Enforcement Section, for the purpose of succession to all rights, powers, duties, and obligations of the Enforcement Section and of those rights, powers, duties, and obligations exercised by the Department of Transportation, Division of Motor Vehicles on behalf of the Enforcement Section. Where the Department of Transportation, the Division of Motor Vehicles, or the Enforcement Section, or any combination thereof are referred to by law, contract, or other document, that reference shall apply to the Department of Crime Control and Public Safety.

"All equipment, supplies, personnel, or other properties rented or controlled by the Department of Transportation, Division of Motor Vehicles Enforcement Section for the regulation and enforcement of commercial motor vehicles, oversize and overweight vehicles, motor carrier safety, and mobile and manufactured housing shall be administered by the Department of Crime Control and Public Safety."

Session Laws 2002-190, s. 17, provides: "The Governor shall resolve any dispute between the Department of Transportation and the Department of Crime Control and Public Safety concerning the implementation of this act [Session Laws 2002-190]."

EFFECT OF AMENDMENTS. --

Session Laws 2011-145, s. 19.1(g), effective January 1, 2012, substituted "Public Safety" for "Crime Control and Public Safety" in the introductory paragraph.

SUBDIVISIONS (2) AND (4) OF THIS SECTION ARE NOT IRRECONCILABLE WITH G.S. 20-183. State v. Allen, 15 N.C. App. 670, 190 S.E.2d 714 (1972), rev'd on other grounds, 282 N.C. 503, 194 S.E.2d 9 (1973).

DUTIES OF AN INSPECTOR FOR THE DIVISION OF MOTOR VEHICLES PROVIDE FOR THE EXERCISE OF SOME PORTION OF THE SOVEREIGN POWER OF THE STATE, and as such said inspector is considered a public officer immune from liability for mere negligence in the performance of his duties. Thompson Cadillac-Oldsmobile, Inc. v. Silk Hope Auto., Inc., 87 N.C. App. 467, 361 S.E.2d 418 (1987).

INSPECTION OF A CAR'S IDENTIFICATION NUMBER differs from a search of a vehicle and seizure of its contents in one important aspect. The occupants of the car cannot harbor an expectation of privacy concerning the identification of the vehicle. State v. Baker, 65 N.C. App. 430, 310 S.E.2d 101 (1983), cert. denied, 312 N.C. 85, 321 S.E.2d 900 (1984).

A police officer should be freer to inspect the identification number without a warrant than he is to search a car for purely private property. State v. Baker, 65 N.C. App. 430, 310 S.E.2d 101 (1983), cert. denied, 312 N.C. 85, 321 S.E.2d 900 (1984).

The State requires manufacturers to identify vehicles by affixing identification numbers which are also recorded in registries where the police and any interested person may inspect them. Since identification numbers are, at the least, quasi-public information, a search of that part of the car displaying the number is but a minimal invasion of a person's privacy. State v. Baker, 65 N.C. App. 430, 310 S.E.2d 101 (1983), cert. denied, 312 N.C. 85, 321 S.E.2d 900 (1984).

APPLIED in State v. Clark, 21 N.C. App. 35, 203 S.E.2d 103 (1974).

CITED in State v. Francum, 39 N.C. App. 429, 250 S.E.2d 705 (1979).

§ 20-49.1. Supplemental police authority of Division officers

(a) In addition to the law enforcement authority granted in G.S. 20-49 or elsewhere, the Commissioner and the officers and inspectors of the Division whom the Commissioner designates have the authority to enforce criminal laws under any of the following circumstances:

(1) When they have probable cause to believe that a person has committed a criminal act in their presence and at the time of the violation they are engaged in the enforcement of laws otherwise within their jurisdiction.

(2) When they are asked to provide temporary assistance by the head of a State or local law enforcement agency or his designee and the request is within the scope of the agency's subject matter jurisdiction.

While acting pursuant to this subsection, the Division officers shall have the same powers vested in law enforcement officers by statute or common law. When acting pursuant to subdivision (2) of this subsection, the Division officers shall not be considered an officer, employee, or agent of the State or local law enforcement agency or designee asking for temporary assistance. Nothing in this section shall be construed to expand the Division officers' authority to initiate or conduct an independent investigation into violations of criminal laws outside the scope of their subject matter or territorial jurisdiction.

(b) In addition to the law enforcement authority granted in G.S. 20-49 or elsewhere, the Commissioner and the officers and inspectors of the Division whom the Commissioner designates have the authority to investigate drivers license fraud and identity thefts related to drivers license fraud and to make arrests for these offenses.

History.
2004-148, s. 1

§ 20-49.2. Supplemental authority of State Highway Patrol Motor Carrier Enforcement officers

In addition to law enforcement authority granted in G.S. 20-49 or elsewhere, all sworn

Motor Carrier Enforcement officers of the State Highway Patrol shall have the authority to enforce criminal laws under the following circumstances:

(1) When they have probable cause to believe that a person has committed a criminal act in their presence and at the time of the violation they are engaged in the enforcement of laws otherwise within their jurisdiction.

(2) When they are asked to provide temporary assistance by the head of a State or local law enforcement agency or his designee and the request is within the scope of the agency's subject matter jurisdiction.

While acting pursuant to this section, they shall have the same powers invested in law enforcement officers by statute or common law. When acting pursuant to subdivision (2) of this section, they shall not be considered an officer, employee, or agent for the State or local law enforcement agency or designee asking for temporary assistance. Nothing in this statute shall be construed to expand their authority to initiate or conduct an independent investigation into violations of criminal laws outside the scope of their subject matter or territorial jurisdiction.

History.
2004-148, s. 2
EDITOR'S NOTE. --
As enacted, this section contained a subsection (c), but no subsection (a) or (b). This section has been set out in the form above at the direction of the Revisor of Statutes.

§ 20-49.3. Bureau of License and Theft; custody of seized vehicles

(a) **Vehicles Seized by the Division of Motor Vehicles.** -- Notwithstanding any other provision of law, the Division of Motor Vehicles, Bureau of License and Theft, may retain any vehicle seized by the Division of Motor Vehicles, Bureau of License and Theft, in the course of any investigation authorized by the provisions of G.S. 20-49 or G.S. 20-49.1 and forfeited to the Division by a court of competent jurisdiction.

(b) **Vehicles Seized by the United States Government.** -- Notwithstanding any other provision of law, the Division may accept custody and ownership of any vehicle seized by the United States Government, forfeited by a court of competent jurisdiction, and turned over to the Division.

(c) **Use of Vehicles.** -- All vehicles forfeited to, or accepted by, the Division pursuant to this section shall be used by the Bureau of License and Theft to conduct undercover operations and inspection station compliance checks throughout the State.

(d) **Disposition of Seized Vehicles.** -- Upon determination by the Commissioner of Motor Vehicles that a vehicle transferred pursuant to the provisions of this section is of no further use to the agency for use in official investigations, the vehicle shall be sold as surplus property in the same manner as other vehicles owned by the law enforcement agency and the proceeds from the sale after deducting the cost of sale shall be paid to the treasurer or proper officer authorized to receive fines and forfeitures to be used for the school fund of the county in the county in which the vehicle was seized, provided, that any vehicle transferred to any law enforcement agency under the provisions of this Article that has been modified to increase speed shall be used in the performance of official duties only and not for resale, transfer, or disposition other than as junk. The Division shall also reimburse the appropriate county school fund for any diminution in value of any vehicle seized under subsection (a) of this section during its period of use by the Division. Any vehicle seized outside of this State shall be sold as surplus property in the same manner as other vehicles owned by the law enforcement agency and the proceeds from the sale after deducting the cost of sale shall be paid to the treasurer and placed in the Civil Fines and Forfeitures Fund established pursuant to G.S. 115C-457.1.

History.
2009-495, s. 1

PART 3.
REGISTRATION AND CERTIFICATES OF TITLES OF MOTOR VEHICLES

§ 20-50. Owner to secure registration and certificate of title; temporary registration markers

(a) A vehicle intended to be operated upon any highway of this State must be registered with the Division in accordance with G.S. 20-52, and the owner of the vehicle must comply with G.S. 20-52 before operating the vehicle. A vehicle that is leased to an individual who is a resident of this State is a vehicle intended to be operated upon a highway of this State.

The Commissioner of Motor Vehicles or the Commissioner's duly authorized agent is empowered to grant a special one-way trip permit to move a vehicle without license upon good cause being shown. When the owner of a vehicle leases the vehicle to a carrier of passengers or property and the vehicle is actually used by the carrier in the operation of its business, the license plates may be obtained by the

Chapter 20

lessee, upon written consent of the owner, after the certificate of title has been obtained by the owner. When the owner of a vehicle leases the vehicle to a farmer and the vehicle is actually used by the farmer in the operation of a farm, the license plates may be obtained by the farmer at the applicable farmer rate, upon written consent of the owner, after the certificate of title has been obtained by the owner. The lessee shall make application on an appropriate form furnished by the Division and file such evidence of the lease as the Division may require.

(b) The Division may issue a temporary license plate for a vehicle. A temporary license plate is valid for the period set by the Division. The period may not be less than 10 days nor more than 60 days.

A person may obtain a temporary license plate for a vehicle by filing an application with the Division and paying the required fee. An application must be filed on a form provided by the Division.

The fee for a temporary license plate that is valid for 10 days is ten dollars ($ 10.00). The fee for a temporary license plate that is valid for more than 10 days is the amount that would be required with an application for a license plate for the vehicle. If a person obtains for a vehicle a temporary license plate that is valid for more than 10 days and files an application for a license plate for that vehicle before the temporary license plate expires, the person is not required to pay the fee that would otherwise be required for the license plate.

A temporary license plate is subject to the following limitations and conditions:

(1) It may be issued only upon proper proof that the applicant has met the applicable financial responsibility requirements.

(2) It expires on midnight of the day set for expiration.

(3) It may be used only on the vehicle for which issued and may not be transferred, loaned, or assigned to another.

(4) If it is lost or stolen, the person who applied for it must notify the Division.

(5) It may not be issued by a dealer.

(6) The provisions of G.S. 20-63, 20-71, 20-110 and 20-111 that apply to license plates apply to temporary license plates insofar as possible.

History.
1937, c. 407, s. 15; 1943, c. 648; 1945, c. 956, s. 3; 1947, c. 219, s. 2; 1953, c. 831, s. 3; 1957, c. 246, s. 2; 1961, c. 360, s. 1; 1963, c. 552, s. 1; 1973, c. 919; 1975, c. 462; c. 716, s. 5; c. 767, s. 1; 1995, c. 394, s. 1;1999-438, s. 26;2005-276, s. 44.1(i);2015-241, s. 29.35(b)

LOCAL MODIFICATION. --Moore: 1995, c. 13, s. 3, as amended by 2002-82, s. 2, as amended by 2005-11, s. 2;city of Conover: 2003-124, s. 1, as amended by 2004-58, s. 1, 2007-204, s. 1, 2007-259, s. 1, 2009-459, s. 5, 2011-171, s. 1, and 2013-172, s. 1;Lowell: 2003-124, s. 1, as amended by 2004-58, s. 1, 2007-204, s. 1, 2007-259, s. 1, 2009-459, s. 5, 2011-171, s. 1, and 2013-172, s. 1;town of Beech Mountain: 2003-124, s. 1, as amended by 2007-204, s. 1, 2007-259, s. 1, 2009-459, s. 6;town of Caswell Beach: 2006-149, s. 1.1;town of Cramerton: 2003-124, s. 1, as amended by 2004-58, 2007-204, s. 1, 2007-259, 2009-459, 2011-171, s. 1, and 2013-172, s. 1;town of North Topsail Beach: 2003-124, s. 1, as amended by 2004-59, s. 1, 2007-204, s. 1, 2007-259, s. 1, 2009-459, s. 5, 2011-171, s. 1, and 2013-172, s. 1;town of Seven Devils: 2003-124, s. 1, as amended by 2004-58, s. 1, 2007-204, s. 1, 2007-259, s. 1, 2009-459, s. 5, 2011-171, s. 1, and 2013-172, s. 1.

EDITOR'S NOTE. --
Session Laws 2015-241, s. 29.35(d), made the amendment to subsection (b) of this section by Session Laws 2015-241, s. 29.35(b), applicable to sales made on or after January 1, 2016.

Session Laws 2015-241, s. 1.1, provides: "This act shall be known as 'The Current Operations and Capital Improvements Appropriations Act of 2015.'"

Session Laws 2015-241, s. 33.6, is a severability clause.

Session Laws 2016-23, s. 9(a), (b), provides: "(a) Definition. -- For purposes of this section, 'impacted person' shall mean any person who is the owner of a motor vehicle titled and registered in South Carolina and who has now been determined to be a resident of North Carolina as a result of a boundary certification agreed to by the states of North Carolina and South Carolina.

"(b) The Division of Motor Vehicles of the Department of Transportation shall require title, registration, and the payment of highway use tax from impacted persons in the same manner as it currently uses for persons moving to North Carolina from another state."

Session Laws 2016-23, s. 12(a), is a severability clause.

Session Laws 2020-3, s. 4.7(a) -(h), as amended by Session Laws 2020-97, ss. 3.15(a), 3.16(a), provides: "(a) Definition. -- For purposes of this section, 'credential' means any of the following issued by the Division of Motor Vehicles:

"(1) Drivers license.

"(2) Learner's permit.

"(3) Limited learner's permit.

"(4) Limited provisional license.

"(5) Full provisional license.

"(6) Commercial drivers license.

"(7) Commercial learner's permit.

"(8) Temporary driving certificate.

"(9) Special identification card.

"(10) Handicapped placard.

"(11) Vehicle registration.

"(12) Temporary vehicle registration.

"(13) Dealer license plate.

"(14) Transporter plate.

"(15) Loaner/Dealer 'LD' plate.

"(16) Vehicle inspection authorization.

"(17) Inspection station license.

Chapter 20

"(18) Inspection mechanic license.

"(19) Transportation network company permit.

"(20) Motor vehicle dealer license.

"(21) Sales representative license.

"(22) Manufacturer license.

"(23) Distributor license.

"(24) Wholesaler license.

"(25) Driver training school license.

"(26) Driver training school instructor license.

"(27) Professional housemoving license.

"(b) Extend Validity of Credentials. -- Notwithstanding renewal, duration, or expiration provisions of G.S. 20-7, 20-11, 20-37.6, 20-37.7, 20-37.13, 20-50, 20-66, 20-79, 20-79.02, 20-79.2, 20-183.4B, 20-183.4D, 20-280.3, 20-288, 20-324, and 20-359, or any other provision of law to the contrary, the Division of Motor Vehicles shall extend for a period of five months the validity of any credential that expires on or after March 1, 2020, and before August 1, 2020. The Division shall extend for a period of five months the validity of any credential listed in subdivisions (6), (7), (9), (10), and (18) of subsection (a) of this section that expires on or after March 1, 2020, and before the date 30 days after the date the Governor (i) rescinds Executive Order No. 116 or (ii) issues another executive order lifting restrictions on Division of Motor Vehicles functions. Notwithstanding G.S. 20-37.13(h) and G.S. 20-37.13A(a), the Division of Motor Vehicles is authorized to waive the requirement that commercial drivers license and commercial learner's permit holders have a medical examination and certification, as required by federal law, consistent with any waiver of medical qualifications standards issued by the Federal Motor Carrier Safety Administration. A credential extended under this section shall expire five months from the date it otherwise expires as prescribed by law prior to this section. However, the subsequent expiration of a credential extended under this section shall occur on the date prescribed by law prior to this section without regard to the extension. The Division shall notify individuals affected by an extension granted under this section, including information on new expiration dates and how the extension affects subsequent renewal and expiration dates.

"(b1) Extension of Intrastate Medical Waivers. -- Notwithstanding the limitation on duration of waivers in G.S. 20-37.13A(b), the Division of Motor Vehicles may extend for up to five months the validity of a medical waiver issued by the Division under G.S. 20-37.13A if the waiver expires on or after March 1, 2020, and before the date 30 days after the date the Governor (i) rescinds Executive Order No. 116 or (ii) issues another executive order lifting restrictions on Division of Motor Vehicles functions, and the Division's Medical Review Unit determines the extension is appropriate.

"(c) Driving Eligibility Certificates. -- Notwithstanding G.S. 20-11(n)(3), a driving eligibility certificate dated on or after February 9, 2020, and before March 10, 2020, remains valid and may be accepted by the Division of Motor Vehicles to meet the requirements for a license or permit issued under G.S. 20-11

until 30 days after the date the Governor rescinds Executive Order No. 116 or the date the Division reopens all drivers license offices, whichever is earlier.

"(d) Waive Penalties. -- Notwithstanding any provision of law to the contrary, the Division shall waive any fines, fees, or penalties associated with failing to renew a credential during the period of time the credential is valid by extension under subsection (b) of this section.

"(e) Motor Vehicle Taxes. -- Notwithstanding any provision of law to the contrary, due dates for motor vehicle taxes that are tied to registration expiration under Article 22A of Chapter 105 of the General Statutes shall be extended to correspond with extended expiration dates under subsection (b) of this section.

"(f) Validity by Extension a Defense. -- A person may not be convicted or found responsible for any offense resulting from failure to renew a credential issued by the Division if, when tried for that offense, the person shows that the offense occurred during the period of time the credential is valid by extension under subsection (b) of this section.

"(g) Report. -- Within 30 days of the extensions made under subsection (b) of this section, the Division shall submit a report to the Joint Legislative Transportation Oversight Committee and the Fiscal Research Division detailing implementation of this section.

"(h) Effective Date. -- This section is effective retroactively to March 1, 2020, and applies to expirations occurring on or after that date."

Session Laws 2020-3, s. 5, is a severability clause.

Session Laws 2020-97, s. 4.5, is a severability clause.

EFFECT OF AMENDMENTS. --

Session Laws 2005-276, s. 44.1(i), effective October 1, 2005, and applicable to fees collected on or after that date, substituted "five dollars ($5.00)" for "three dollars ($3.00)" in the third paragraph of subsection (b).

Session Laws 2015-241, s. 29.35(b), effective January 1, 2016, substituted "ten dollars ($10.00" for "five dollars ($5.00)" in the first sentence of the third paragraph in subsection (b). For applicability, see editor's note.

A "CERTIFICATE OF NUMBER" REQUIRED BY § 75A-5 IS NOT A "CERTIFICATE OF TITLE" to be compared with that required by this section for vehicles intended to be operated on the highways. Lane v. Honeycutt, 14 N.C. App. 436, 188 S.E.2d 604, cert. denied, 281 N.C. 622, 190 S.E.2d 466 (1972).

AS TO THE APPLICABILITY OF THE MANDATORY PROVISIONS OF MOTOR VEHICLES TO MOBILE HOMES, see King Homes, Inc. v. Bryson, 273 N.C. 84, 159 S.E.2d 329 (1968).

REGISTRATION AND CERTIFICATE OF TITLE NOT REQUIRED. --Where purchaser of real property did not need to transport permanently attached mobile home along the highways and had no intention of doing so, purchaser was not required to register the mobile home nor to obtain a certificate of title; the mobile home was permanently affixed to the land when the property was deeded to the debtors and all parties intended the transaction to be one involving the sale of real property. In re Meade, 174 Bankr. 49 (Bankr. M.D.N.C. 1994).

REASONABLE SUSPICION VEHICLE DID NOT HAVE PROPER REGISTRATION TAG. --Officer possessed reasonable suspicion to believe that defendant was operating defendant's vehicle without a proper registration tag because the tag displayed was just a piece of paper with a date written on it, rather than the piece of cardboard that car dealers normally hand out when a vehicle is purchased. State v. Smith, 192 N.C. App. 690, 666 S.E.2d 191 (2008), cert. denied 130 S. Ct. 3325, 2010 U.S. LEXIS 4297, 176 L. Ed. 2d 1221 (U.S. 2010).

FOR COMPARISON OF MORTGAGE REGISTRATION STATUTE WITH PRIOR SIMILAR STATUTE, see Carolina Disct. Corp. v. Landis Motor Co., 190 N.C. 157, 129 S.E. 414 (1925).

MODULAR HOMES. --Although the title to a modular home is initially acquired through a bill of sale, once installed title must pass by way of a real property deed unlike a mobile home or trailer which passes by transfer of a certificate of origin and motor vehicle title. Briggs v. Rankin, 127 N.C. App. 477, 491 S.E.2d 234 (1997), aff'd, 348 N.C. 686, 500 S.E.2d 663 (1998).

APPLIED in Hawkins v. M & J Fin. Corp., 238 N.C. 174, 77 S.E.2d 669 (1953).

CITED in Southern Auto Fin. Co. v. Pittman, 253 N.C. 550, 117 S.E.2d 423 (1960); Community Credit Co. v. Norwood, 257 N.C. 87, 125 S.E.2d 369 (1962); Pilot Freight Carriers, Inc. v. Scheidt, 263 N.C. 737, 140 S.E.2d 383 (1965); State v. White, 3 N.C. App. 31, 164 S.E.2d 36 (1968); Nationwide Mut. Ins. Co. v. Hayes, 276 N.C. 620, 174 S.E.2d 511 (1970); United States v. Powers, 439 F.2d 373 (4th Cir. 1971); Ferguson v. Morgan, 282 N.C. 83, 191 S.E.2d 817 (1972); Williams v. Wachovia Bank & Trust Co., 292 N.C. 416, 233 S.E.2d 589 (1977); BarclaysAmerican/Credit Co. v. Riddle, 57 N.C. App. 662, 292 S.E.2d 177 (1982); Peoples Sav. & Loan Assoc. v. Citicorp Acceptance Co., 103 N.C. App. 762, 407 S.E.2d 251 (1991); State v. Hudson, 103 N.C. App. 708, 407 S.E.2d 583 (1991); Butler v. Green Tree Fin. Servicing Corp. (In re Wester), 229 Bankr. 348 (Bankr. E.D.N.C. 1998).

LEGAL PERIODICALS. --

For note discussing the extension of the family purpose doctrine to motorcycles and private property, see 14 Wake Forest L. Rev. 699 (1978).

OPINIONS OF THE ATTORNEY GENERAL

THIS SECTION REQUIRES THE OWNER OF A MOTOR VEHICLE TO REGISTER THE VEHICLE AND OBTAIN A CERTIFICATE OF TITLE from the Department (now Division) of Motor Vehicles. See opinion of Attorney General to Mr. Eric L. Gooch, Director, Sales and Use Tax Division, North Carolina Department of Revenue, 40 N.C.A.G. 446 (1969).

N.C. Gen. Stat. § 20-50.1

Repealed by Session Laws 1979, c. 574, s. 5.

CROSS REFERENCES. --

For present provisions covering the subject matter of the repealed section, see G.S. 20-51, subdivision (9).

N.C. Gen. Stat. § 20-50.2

Repealed by Session Laws 1991, c. 624, s. 4.

N.C. Gen. Stat. § 20-50.3

Repealed by Session Laws 2005-294, s. 10, effective July 1, 2013, and applicable to combined tax and registration notices issued on or after that date. See Editor's note.

History.

1991, c. 624, s. 5;1991 (Reg. Sess., 1992), c. 961, s. 11; 2005-294, s. 10;2006-259, s. 31.5;2007-527, s. 22(b);2008-134, s. 65;2011-330, s. 42(a);2012-79, s. 3.6;2013-414, s. 70(d);repealed by 2005-294, s. 10, effective July 1, 2013

EDITOR'S NOTE. --

Former G.S. 20-50.3 pertained to division to furnish county assessors registration lists.

Session Laws 2005-294, s. 13, as amended by Session Laws 2006-259, s. 31.5, as amended by 2007-527, s. 22(b), as amended by Session Laws 2008-134, s. 65, as amended by Session Laws 2011-330, s. 42(a), as amended by Session Laws 2012-79, s. 3.6, and as amended by Session Laws 2013-414, s. 70(d), provides: "Sections 4 and 8 of this act become effective January 1, 2006. Sections 1, 2, 3, 5, 6, 7, 10, and 11 of this act become effective July 1, 2013, and apply to combined tax and registration notices issued on or after that date. Counties may continue to collect property taxes on motor vehicles for taxable years beginning on or before September 1, 2013, under the provisions of Article 22A of Chapter 105 of the General Statutes as those statutes are in effect on June 30, 2013. Sections 12 and 13 of this act are effective when they become law. Nothing in this act shall require the General Assembly to appropriate funds to implement it for the biennium ending June 30, 2007."

§ 20-50.4. Division to refuse to register vehicles on which county and municipal taxes and fees are not paid and when there is a failure to meet court-ordered child support obligations

(a) **Property Taxes Paid with Registration.** -- The Division shall refuse to register a vehicle on which county and municipal taxes and fees have not been paid.

(b) **Delinquent Child Support Obligations.** -- Upon receiving a report from a child support enforcement agency that sanctions pursuant to G.S. 110-142.2(a)(3) have been imposed, the Division shall refuse to register a vehicle for the owner named in the report until the Division receives certification pursuant to G.S. 110-142.2 that the payments are no longer considered delinquent.

History.

1991, c. 624, s. 5;1995, c. 538, s. 2(g);1995 (Reg. Sess., 1996), c. 741, ss. 1, 2; 2005-294, s. 11;2006-259, s. 31.5;2007-527, s. 22(b);2008-134, s. 65;2011-330, s. 42(a);2012-79, s. 3.6;2013-414, s. 70(d)

EDITOR'S NOTE. --

Session Laws 2005-294, s. 13, as amended by Session Laws 2006-259, s. 31.5, as amended by 2007-527, s. 22(b), as amended by Session Laws 2008-134, s. 65, as amended by Session Laws 2011-330, s. 42(a), and as amended by Session Laws 2012-79, s. 3.6, and as amended by Session Laws 2013-414, s. 70(d), provides: "Sections 4 and 8 of this act become effective January 1, 2006. Sections 1, 2, 3, 5, 6, 7, 10, and 11 of this act become effective July 1, 2013, and apply to combined tax and registration notices issued on or after that date. Counties may continue to collect property taxes on motor vehicles for taxable years beginning on or before September 1, 2013, under the provisions of Article 22A of Chapter 105 of the General Statutes as those statutes are in effect on June 30, 2013. Sections 12 and 13 of this act are effective when they become law. Nothing in this act shall require the General Assembly to appropriate funds to implement it for the biennium ending June 30, 2007."

The amendment by Session Laws 2012-79, s. 3.6, of Session Laws 2005-294, s. 13, as amended by Session Laws 2006-259, s. 31.5, as amended by Session Laws 2007-527, s. 22(b), as amended by Session Laws 2008-134, s. 65, and as amended by Session Laws 2011-330, s. 42(a), was retroactively effective to July 1, 2011.

EFFECT OF AMENDMENTS. --

Session Laws 2005-294, s. 11, in the section heading, substituted "county and municipal taxes and fees are not paid" for "taxes are delinquent" and rewrote subsection (a). For effective date, see Editor's note.

§ 20-51. Exempt from registration

The following shall be exempt from the requirement of registration and certificate of title:

(1) Any such vehicle driven or moved upon a highway in conformance with the provisions of this Article relating to manufacturers, dealers, or nonresidents.

(2) Any such vehicle which is driven or moved upon a highway only for the purpose of crossing such highway from one property to another.

(3) Any implement of husbandry, farm tractor, road construction or maintenance machinery or other vehicle which is not self-propelled that was designed for use in work off the highway and which is operated on the highway for the purpose of going to and from such nonhighway projects.

(4) Any vehicle owned and operated by the government of the United States.

(5) Farm tractors equipped with rubber tires and trailers or semitrailers when attached thereto and when used by a farmer, his tenant, agent, or employee in transporting his own farm implements, farm supplies, or farm products from place to place on the same farm, from one farm to another, from farm to market, or from market to farm. This exemption shall extend also to any tractor, implement of husbandry, and trailer or semitrailer while on any trip within a radius of 10 miles from the point of loading, provided that the vehicle does not exceed a speed of 35 miles per hour. This section shall not be construed as granting any exemption to farm tractors, implements of husbandry, and trailers or semitrailers which are operated on a for-hire basis, whether money or some other thing of value is paid or given for the use of such tractors, implements of husbandry, and trailers or semitrailers.

(6) Any trailer or semitrailer attached to and drawn by a properly licensed motor vehicle when used by a farmer, his tenant, agent, or employee in transporting unginned cotton, peanuts, soybeans, corn, hay, tobacco, silage, cucumbers, potatoes, all vegetables, fruits, greenhouse and nursery plants and flowers, Christmas trees, livestock, live poultry, animal waste, pesticides, seeds, fertilizers or chemicals purchased or owned by the farmer or tenant for personal use in implementing husbandry, irrigation pipes, loaders, or equipment owned by the farmer or tenant from place to place on the same farm, from one farm to another, from farm to gin, from farm to dryer, or from farm to market, and when not operated on a for-hire basis. The term "transporting" as used herein shall include the actual hauling of said products and all unloaded travel in connection therewith.

(7) Those small farm trailers known generally as tobacco-handling trailers, tobacco trucks or tobacco trailers when used by a farmer, his tenant, agent or employee, when transporting or otherwise handling tobacco in connection with the pulling, tying or curing thereof.

(8) Any vehicle which is driven or moved upon a highway only for the purpose of crossing or traveling upon such highway from one side to the other provided the owner or lessee of the vehicle owns the fee or a leasehold in all the land along both sides of the highway at the place or crossing.

(9) Repealed by Session Laws 2014-114, s. 2, effective July 1, 2015, and applicable to offenses committed on or after that date.

(10) Devices which are designed for towing private passenger motor vehicles or vehicles not exceeding 5,000 pounds gross weight. These devices are known generally as "tow dollies." A tow dolly is a two-wheeled device without motive power designed for towing disabled motor vehicles

Chapter 20

and is drawn by a motor vehicle in the same manner as a trailer.

(11) Devices generally called converter gear or dollies consisting of a tongue attached to either a single or tandem axle upon which is mounted a fifth wheel and which is used to convert a semitrailer to a full trailer for the purpose of being drawn behind a truck tractor and semitrailer.

(12) Motorized wheelchairs or similar vehicles not exceeding 1,000 pounds gross weight when used for pedestrian purposes by a handicapped person with a mobility impairment as defined in G.S. 20-37.5.

(13) Any vehicle registered in another state and operated temporarily within this State by a public utility, a governmental or cooperative provider of utility services, or a contractor for one of these entities for the purpose of restoring utility services in an emergency outage.

(14) Electric personal assistive mobility devices as defined in G.S. 20-4.01(7b).

(15) Any vehicle that meets all of the following:

a. Is designed for use in work off the highway.

b. Is used for agricultural quarantine programs under the supervision of the Department of Agriculture and Consumer Services.

c. Is driven or moved on the highway for the purpose of going to and from nonhighway projects.

d. Is identified in a manner approved by the Division of Motor Vehicles.

e. Is operated by a person who possesses an identification card issued by the Department of Agriculture and Consumer Services.

(16) A vehicle that meets all of the following conditions is exempt from the requirement of registration and certificate of title. The provisions of G.S. 105-449.117 continue to apply to the vehicle and to the person in whose name the vehicle would be registered.

a. Is an agricultural spreader vehicle. An "agricultural spreader vehicle" is a vehicle that is designed for off-highway use on a farm to spread feed, fertilizer, seed, lime, or other agricultural products.

b. Is driven on the highway only for the purpose of going from the location of its supply source for fertilizer or other products to and from a farm.

c. Does not exceed a speed of 45 miles per hour.

d. Does not drive outside a radius of 50 miles from the location of its supply source for fertilizer and other products.

e. Is driven by a person who has a license appropriate for the class of the vehicle.

f. Is insured under a motor vehicle liability policy in the amount required under G.S. 20-309.

g. Displays a valid federal safety inspection decal if the vehicle has a gross vehicle weight rating of at least 10,001 pounds.

(17) A header trailer when transported to or from a dealer, or after a sale or repairs, to the farm or another dealership.

History.
1937, c. 407, s. 16; 1943, c. 500; 1949, c. 429; 1951, c. 705, s. 2; 1953, c. 826, ss. 2, 3; c. 1316, s. 1; 1961, cc. 334, 817; 1963, c. 145; 1965, c. 1146; 1971, c. 107; 1973, cc. 478, 757, 964; 1979, c. 574, s. 6; 1981 (Reg. Sess., 1982), c. 1286; 1983, cc. 288, 732; 1987, c. 608; 1989, c. 157, s. 2;1991, c. 411, s. 4;1995, c. 50, s. 4;1999-281, s. 2;2002-98, s. 4;2002-150, s. 1;2006-135, s. 2;2007-194, s. 1;2007-527, s. 41;2012-78, ss. 2, 3; 2014-114, s. 2;2015-263, s. 7;2016-90, s. 13(i)

EDITOR'S NOTE. --
The number of subdivision (15) was designated as such by the Revisor of Statutes, the number in Session Laws 2002-150, s. 1, having been (14).

Session Laws 2012-78, s. 18, provides: "Prosecutions for offenses committed before the effective date of the section of this act that modifies the offense [June 26, 2012] are not abated or affected by this act, and the statutes that would be applicable but for this act remain applicable to those prosecutions."

Session Laws 2014-114, s. 5, made the repeal of subdivision (9) of this section by Session Laws 2014-114, s. 2, effective July 1, 2015, and applicable to offenses committed on or after that date.

Session Laws 2015-263, s. 38(a) contains a severability clause.

Session Laws 2016-90, s. 13(j), made the amendment to subdivision (14) of this section by Session Laws 2016-90, s. 13(i), applicable to offenses committed on or after December 1, 2016.

EFFECT OF AMENDMENTS. --
Session Laws 2006-135, s. 2, effective July 19, 2006, substituted "potatoes, all vegetables, fruits, greenhouse and nursery plants and flowers, Christmas trees," for "potatoes," in subdivision (6).

Session Laws 2007-194, s. 1, effective July 1, 2007, added subdivision (16).

Session Laws 2007-527, s. 41, effective August 31, 2007, added the language following "all of the following" at the end of the introductory paragraph of subdivision (16).

Session Laws 2012-78, ss. 2 and 3, effective June 26, 2012, in the first sentence in subdivision (6), added "livestock, live poultry, animal waste, pesticides, seeds,"; and added subdivision (17).

Session Laws 2014-114, s. 2, repealed subdivision (9), which read "Mopeds as defined in G.S. 20-4.01(27)d1." See Editor's note for effective date and applicability.

Session Laws 2015-263, s. 7, effective September 30, 2015, inserted "feed" and deleted "on a field" at the end of the second sentence of subdivision (16)a; and substituted "45 miles per hour" for "35 miles per hour" in subdivision (16)c.

Session Laws 2016-90, s. 13(i), effective December 1, 2016, in subdivision (14), substituted "G.S. 20-4.01(7b)" for "G.S. 20-4.01(7a)." See editor's note for applicability.

FARM TRACTORS ARE NOT TO BE CONSIDERED MOTOR VEHICLES within the statute relating to registration and certificates of titles of motor vehicles. Brown v. Fidelity & Cas. Co., 241 N.C. 666, 86 S.E.2d 433 (1955).

CITED in Hawkins v. M & J Fin. Corp., 238 N.C. 174, 77 S.E.2d 669 (1953); Butler v. Green Tree Fin. Servicing Corp. (In re Wester), 229 Bankr. 348 (Bankr. E.D.N.C. 1998); Bowles Auto., Inc. v. N.C. DMV, 203 N.C. App. 19, 690 S.E.2d 728 (2010), review denied, 364 N.C. 324, 700 S.E.2d 746, 2010 N.C. LEXIS 590 (2010).

CROSS REFERENCES. --
As to manufacturers and dealers, see G.S. 20-79. As to nonresidents, see G.S. 20-83.

§ 20-52. Application for registration and certificate of title

(a) An owner of a vehicle subject to registration must apply to the Division for a certificate of title, a registration plate, and a registration card for the vehicle. To apply, an owner must complete an application provided by the Division. The application shall contain a preprinted option that co-owners may use to title the vehicle as a joint tenancy with right of survivorship. The co-owners' designation of a joint tenancy with right of survivorship on the application shall be valid notwithstanding whether this designation appears on the assignment of title. The application must request all of the following information and may request other information the Division considers necessary:

(1) The owner's name.

(1a) If the owner is an individual, the following information:

a. The owner's mailing address and residence address.

b. One of the following at the option of the applicant:

1. The owner's North Carolina drivers license number or North Carolina special identification card number.

2. The owner's home state drivers license number or home state special identification card number and valid active duty military identification card number or military dependent identification card number if the owner is a person or the spouse or dependent child of a person on active duty in the Armed Forces of the United States who is stationed in this State or deployed outside this State from a home base in this State. The owner's inability to provide a photocopy or reproduction of a military or military dependent identification card pursuant to any prohibition of the United States government or any agency thereof against the making of such photocopy or reproduction shall not operate to prevent the owner from making an application for registration and certificate of title pursuant to this subdivision.

3. The owner's home state drivers license number or home state special identification card number and proof of enrollment in a school in this State if the owner is a permanent resident of another state but is currently enrolled in a school in this State.

4. The owner's home state drivers license number or home state special identification card number if the owner provides a signed affidavit certifying that the owner intends to principally garage the vehicle in this State and provides the address where the vehicle is or will be principally garaged. For purposes of this section, "principally garage" means the vehicle is garaged for six or more months of the year on property in this State which is owned, leased, or otherwise lawfully occupied by the owner of the vehicle.

5. The owner's home state drivers license number or home state special identification card number, provided that the application is made pursuant to a court authorized sale or a sale authorized by G.S. 44A-4 for the purpose of issuing a title to be registered in another state or country.

6. The co-owner's home state drivers license number or home state special identification card number if at least one co-owner provides a North Carolina drivers license number or North Carolina special identification number.

7. The owner's home state drivers license number or special identification card number if the application is for a motor home or house car, as defined in G.S. 20-4.01(27) k., or for a house trailer, as defined in G.S. 20-4.01(14).

(1b) If the owner is a firm, partnership, a corporation, or another entity, the address of the entity.

(2) A description of the vehicle, including the following:

    a. The make, model, type of body, and vehicle identification number of the vehicle.

    b. Whether the vehicle is new or used and, if a new vehicle, the date the manufacturer or dealer sold the vehicle to the owner and the date the manufacturer or dealer delivered the vehicle to the owner.

(3) A statement of the owner's title and of all liens upon the vehicle, including the names and addresses of all lienholders in the order of their priority, and the date and nature of each lien.

(4) -- (6) Repealed by Session Laws 2017-69, s. 2(a), effective July 1, 2017.

(7) A statement that the owner has proof of financial responsibility, as required by Article 9A or Article 13 of this Chapter.

(a1) An owner who would otherwise be capable of attaining a drivers license or special identification card from this State or any other state, except for a medical or physical condition that can be documented to, and verified by, the Division, shall be issued a registration plate and certificate of title if the owner provides a signed affidavit certifying that the owner intends to principally garage the vehicle in this State and provides the address where the vehicle is or will be principally garaged.

(b) When such application refers to a new vehicle purchased from a manufacturer or dealer, such application shall be accompanied with a manufacturer's certificate of origin that is properly assigned to the applicant. If the new vehicle is acquired from a dealer or person located in another jurisdiction other than a manufacturer, the application shall be accompanied with such evidence of ownership as is required by the laws of that jurisdiction duly assigned by the disposer to the purchaser, or, if no such evidence of ownership be required by the laws of such other jurisdiction, a notarized bill of sale from the disposer.

(c) Unless otherwise prohibited by federal law, an application for a certificate of title, salvage certificate of title, a registration plate, a registration card, and any other document required by the Division to be submitted with the application and requiring a signature may be submitted to the Division with an electronic signature in accordance with Article 40 of Chapter 66 of the General Statutes. The required notarization of any electronic signature on any application or document submitted to the Division pursuant to this subsection may be performed electronically in accordance with Article 2 of Chapter 10B of the General Statutes. The Division will not certify or approve a specific electronic process or vendor. Any entity offering an electronic signature process assumes all responsibility and liability for the accuracy of the signature. The Division shall be held harmless from any liability to a claim arising from applications submitted with an inaccurate electronic signature pursuant to this subsection.

History.
1937, c. 407, s. 17; 1961, c. 835, ss. 2, 3; 1975, c. 716, s. 5; 1991, c. 183, s. 2;1993 (Reg. Sess., 1994), c. 750, s. 5; 2007-164, s. 4;2007-209, ss. 1, 2; 2007-443, s. 6;2007-481, ss. 4 -7; 2008-124, s. 4.1;2009-274, s. 4;2015-270, s. 1;2016-90, s. 10.5(a);2017-69, s. 2(a), (b); 2017-102, s. 5.2(b);2019-153, s. 1

EDITOR'S NOTE. --
Session Laws 2017-102, s. 5.2(b) provides: "The Revisor of Statutes is authorized to reletter the definitions in G.S. 20-4.01(27) and G.S. 20-4.01(32b) to place them in alphabetical order. The Revisor of Statutes may conform any citations that change as a result of the relettering." Pursuant to that authority, the reference to G.S. 20-4.01(27)d2. in sub-sub-subdivision (a)(1a)b.7. was changed to G.S. 20-4.01(27)k.

EFFECT OF AMENDMENTS. --
Session Laws 2008-124, s. 4.1, effective July 28, 2008, substituted "G.S. 58-37-1(4a)" for "G.S. 58-37-1" in subdivision (a)(4).

Session Laws 2009-274, s. 4, effective July 10, 2009, and applicable to all licenses expiring on or after that date, substituted "Armed Forces" for "armed forces" in the first sentence of subdivision (a)(1a)b.2.

Session Laws 2015-270, s. 1, effective August 1, 2016, added subsection (c).

Session Laws 2016-90, s. 10.5(a), effective January 1, 2017, added the third and fourth sentences in the introductory language of subsection (a).

Session Laws 2017-69, s. 2(a), (b), effective July 1, 2017, deleted subdivisions (a)(4) through (a)(6), and added subdivision (a)(7).

Session Laws 2019-153, s. 1, effective October 1, 2019, inserted "salvage certificate of title" in the first sentence and added the last three sentences of subsection (c).

A MOBILE HOME IS A MOTOR VEHICLE, and is subject to the mandatory provisions of the statutes relating to the registration of motor vehicles in this State. King Homes, Inc. v. Bryson, 273 N.C. 84, 159 S.E.2d 329 (1968).

DUTY OF CARE OF LIENHOLDER. --Trial court did not err in dismissing counterclaim based on defendants' contention that because lienholder controlled the processes of perfecting its security interest and obtaining the certificate of title, it owed the debtor-purchaser a duty of care with regard to completing these matters, as defendants did not establish the existence of a duty of care owed to them by plaintiff on the basis of statute. NCNB Nat'l Bank v. Gutridge, 94 N.C. App. 344, 380 S.E.2d 408, cert. denied, 325 N.C. 432, 384 S.E.2d 539 (1989).

APPLIED in State v. Baker, 65 N.C. App. 430, 310 S.E.2d 101 (1983).

CITED in Community Credit Co. v. Norwood, 257 N.C. 87, 125 S.E.2d 369 (1962); Ferguson v. Morgan, 282 N.C. 83, 191 S.E.2d 817 (1972); Peoples Sav. & Loan Assoc. v. Citicorp Acceptance Co., 103 N.C. App. 762, 407 S.E.2d 251 (1991); Singletary v. P & A Invs., Inc., 212 N.C. App. 469, 712 S.E.2d 681 (2011).

§ 20-52.1. Manufacturer's certificate of transfer of new motor vehicle

(a) Any manufacturer transferring a new motor vehicle to another shall, at the time of the transfer, supply the transferee with a manufacturer's certificate of origin assigned to the transferee.

(b) Any dealer transferring a new vehicle to another dealer shall, at the time of transfer, give such transferee the proper manufacturer's certificate assigned to the transferee.

(c) Upon sale of a new vehicle by a dealer to a consumer-purchaser, the dealer shall execute in the presence of a person authorized to administer oaths an assignment of the manufacturer's certificate of origin for the vehicle, including in such assignment the name and address of the transferee and no title to a new motor vehicle acquired by a dealer under the provisions of subsections (a) and (b) of this section shall pass or vest until such assignment is executed and the motor vehicle delivered to the transferee.

Any dealer transferring title to, or an interest in, a new vehicle shall deliver the manufacturer's certificate of origin duly assigned in accordance with the foregoing provision to the transferee at the time of delivering the vehicle, except that where a security interest is obtained in the motor vehicle from the transferee in payment of the purchase price or otherwise, the transferor shall deliver the manufacturer's certificate of origin to the lienholder and the lienholder shall forthwith forward the manufacturer's certificate of origin together with the transferee's application for certificate of title and necessary fees to the Division. Any person who delivers or accepts a manufacturer's certificate of origin assigned in blank shall be guilty of a Class 2 misdemeanor, unless done in accordance with subsection (d) of this section.

(d) When a manufacturer's statement of origin or an existing certificate of title on a motor vehicle is unavailable, a motor vehicle dealer licensed under Article 12 of this Chapter may also transfer title to a vehicle to another by certifying in writing in a sworn statement to the Division signed by the dealer principal, general manager, general sales manager, controller, owner, or other manager of the dealership that, to the best of the signatory's knowledge and information as of the date of sworn certification, all prior perfected liens on the vehicle that are known or reasonably ascertainable by the signatory have been paid and that the motor vehicle dealer, despite having used reasonable diligence, is unable to obtain the vehicle's statement of origin or certificate of title. For purposes of this subsection, a dealer may certify that the dealer is unable to obtain the vehicle's statement of origin or certificate of title because the statement of origin or certificate of title was either (i) not delivered to the dealer or (ii) lost or misplaced. The Division is authorized to require any information it deems necessary for the transfer of the vehicle and shall develop a form for this purpose. The knowing and intentional filing of a false sworn certification with the Division pursuant to this subsection shall constitute a Class H felony. A dealer principal, owner, or manager who is not a signatory of the sworn certification under this subsection may only be charged for a criminal violation for filing a false certification under this subsection by another dealership employee if the dealer principal, owner, or manager had actual knowledge of the falsity of the sworn certification at the time the sworn certification was submitted to the Division. The dealer shall hold harmless and indemnify the consumer-purchaser from any damages arising from the use of the procedure authorized by this subsection. No person shall have a cause of action against the Division or Division contractors arising from the transfer of a vehicle by a sworn certification pursuant to this section.

History.

1961, c. 835, s. 4; 1967, c. 863; 1975, c. 716, s. 5; 1993, c. 539, s. 331;1994, Ex. Sess., c. 24, s. 14(c);2000-182, s. 1;2018-42, s. 2(a);2018-145, s. 4;2019-181, s. 5(a);2020-51, s. 3(a)

EDITOR'S NOTE. --

Session Laws 2018-42, s. 2(f), provides: "The Division of Motor Vehicles, in consultation with the North Carolina Automobile Dealers Association, Inc., shall study the following:

"(1) The impacts of this section on Division processes and procedures, along with recommended statutory changes to further improve the lawful transfer of motor vehicles.

"(2) Methods to ensure consumer protection in the motor vehicle transfer process.

"(3) Potential changes to the Division's electronic lien and title program or other processes that could assist with reducing the delay in the release of a satisfied security interest in a motor vehicle.

"(4) Any other issues the Division deems appropriate.

"The Division shall report its findings, including any legislative recommendations, to the Joint Legislative Transportation Oversight Committee by December 31, 2020."

EFFECT OF AMENDMENTS. --

Session Laws 2018-42, s. 2(a), as amended by Session Laws 2018-145, s. 4, effective March 1, 2019, rewrote subsection (d), which read: "When a manufacturer's statement of origin or an existing certificate of title on a motor vehicle is unavailable, a motor vehicle dealer licensed under Article 12 of this Chapter may also transfer title to another by certifying in writing in a sworn statement to the Division that all prior perfected liens on the vehicle have been paid and that the motor vehicle dealer, despite having used reasonable diligence, is unable to obtain the vehicle's statement of origin or certificate of title. The Division is authorized to develop a form for this purpose. The filing of a false sworn certification with the Division pursuant to this subsection shall constitute a Class H felony. The dealer shall hold harmless the consumer-purchaser from any damages arising from the use of the procedure authorized by this subsection."

Session Laws 2019-181, s. 5(a), effective July 26, 2019, substituted "owner, or other manager" for "or owner" in the first sentence of subsection (d).

Session Laws 2020-51, s. 3(a), effective June 30, 2020, deleted "currently titled in this State" following "to a vehicle" in the first sentence of subsection (d).

A MOBILE HOME IS A MOTOR VEHICLE, and is subject to the mandatory provisions of the statutes relating to the registration of motor vehicles in this State. King Homes, Inc. v. Bryson, 273 N.C. 84, 159 S.E.2d 329 (1968).

THIS SECTION IS ONE SEGMENT OF AN ENTIRE STATUTORY SCHEME OF POLICE REGULATIONS designed and intended to provide a simple expeditious mode of tracing titles to motor vehicles so as to (1) facilitate the enforcement of the highway safety statutes, (2) minimize the hazards of theft, and (3) provide safeguards against fraud, imposition, and sharp practices in connection with the sale and transfer of motor vehicles. American Clipper Corp. v. Howerton, 311 N.C. 151, 316 S.E.2d 186 (1984).

THIS SECTION WAS DESIGNED FOR THE PROTECTION OF THE PUBLIC GENERALLY, to regulate the transfer of new motor vehicles from manufacturers to dealers and, ultimately, to consumers. American Clipper Corp. v. Howerton, 311 N.C. 151, 316 S.E.2d 186 (1984).

THIS SECTION WAS NOT DESIGNED TO PROVIDE A METHOD FOR MANUFACTURERS TO PROTECT THEMSELVES AGAINST THEIR DEALERS' DEFAULTS by withholding manufacturer's statements of origin on vehicles transferred to dealers for ultimate sale to consumers. American Clipper Corp. v. Howerton, 311 N.C. 151, 316 S.E.2d 186 (1984).

SUBSECTION (A) OF THIS SECTION IS NOT PERMISSIVE. American Clipper Corp. v. Howerton, 311 N.C. 151, 316 S.E.2d 186 (1984).

DUTY OF CARE OF LIENHOLDER. --Trial court did not err in dismissing counterclaim based on defendants' contention that because lienholder controlled the processes of perfecting its security interest and obtaining the certificate of title, it owed the debtor-purchaser a duty of care with regard to completing these matters, as defendants did not establish the existence of a duty of care owed to them by plaintiff on the basis of statute. NCNB Nat'l Bank v. Gutridge, 94 N.C. App. 344, 380 S.E.2d 408, cert. denied, 325 N.C. 432, 384 S.E.2d 539 (1989).

CITED in Bank of Alamance v. Isley, 74 N.C. App. 489, 328 S.E.2d 867 (1985).

LEGAL PERIODICALS. --

For 1984 survey, "The Application of the North Carolina Motor Vehicle Act and the Uniform Commercial Code to the Sale of Motor Vehicles by Consignment," see 63 N.C.L. Rev. 1105 (1985).

For note on the conflict between the North Carolina Motor Vehicle Act and the UCC, see 65 N.C.L. Rev. 1156 (1987).

§ 20-53. Application for specially constructed, reconstructed, or foreign vehicle

(a) In the event the vehicle to be registered is a specially constructed, reconstructed, or foreign vehicle, such fact shall be stated in the application, and with reference to every foreign vehicle which has been registered outside of this State, the owner shall surrender to the Division all registration cards, certificates of title or notarized copies of original titles on vehicles 35 model years old and older, or other evidence of such foreign registration as may be in his possession or under his control, except as provided in subsection (b) hereof. After initial review, the Division shall return to the owner any original titles presented on vehicles 35 model years old and older appropriately marked indicating that the title has been previously submitted.

(b) Where, in the course of interstate operation of a vehicle registered in another state, it is desirable to retain registration of said vehicle in such other state, such applicant need not surrender, but shall submit for inspection said evidence of such foreign registration, and the Division in its discretion, and upon a proper showing, shall register said vehicle in this State but shall not issue a certificate of title for such vehicle.

(c), (d) Repealed by Session Laws 1965, c. 734, s. 2.

(e) No title shall be issued to an initial applicant for (i) out-of-state vehicles that are 1980 model year or older or (ii) a specially constructed vehicle prior to the completion of a vehicle verification conducted by the License and Theft Bureau of the Division of Motor Vehicles. These verifications shall be conducted as soon as practical. For an out-of-state vehicle that is 1980 model year or older, this inspection shall consist of verifying the public vehicle identification number to ensure that it matches the vehicle and ownership documents. No covert vehicle identification numbers are to be examined on an out-of-state vehicle 1980 model year or older unless the inspector develops probable cause to believe that the ownership documents or public vehicle identification number presented does not match the vehicle being examined. However, upon such application and the submission of any required documentation, the Division shall be authorized to register the vehicle pending the completion of the verification of the vehicle. The registration shall be valid for one year but shall not be renewed unless and until the vehicle examination has been completed.

If an inspection and verification is not conducted by the License and Theft Bureau of the Division of Motor Vehicles within 15 days after receiving a request for such and the inspector has no probable cause to believe that the ownership documents or public vehicle identification number presented does not match the vehicle being examined, the vehicle shall be deemed to have satisfied all inspection and verification requirements and title shall issue to the owner within 15 days thereafter. If an inspection and verification is timely performed and the vehicle passes the inspection and verification, title shall issue to the owner within 15 days of the date of the inspection.

(f) If a vehicle owner desires a vehicle title classification change, he or she may, upon proper application, be eligible for a reclassification.

History.
1937, c. 407, s. 18; 1949, c. 675; 1953, c. 853; 1957, c. 1355; 1965, c. 734, s. 2; 1975, c. 716, s. 5; 2009-405, s. 5;2013-349, s. 1;2016-90, s. 11(a)

EFFECT OF AMENDMENTS. --
Session Laws 2009-405, s. 5, effective August 5, 2009, in subsection (a), inserted "or notarized copies of original titles on vehicles 35 model years old and older," made a related change and added the last sentence; and added subsections (e) and (f).

Session Laws 2013-349, s. 1, effective July 23, 2013, added the second paragraph in subsection (e).

Session Laws 2016-90, s. 11(a), effective January 1, 2017, in the first paragraph of subsection (e), substituted "1980 model year or older" for "35 years old or older" throughout.

LEGAL PERIODICALS. --
For comment on former subsection (c) of this section, see 27 N.C.L. Rev. 471 (1949).

§ 20-53.1. Specially constructed vehicle certificate of title and registration

(a) Specially constructed vehicles shall be titled in the following manner:

(1) Replica vehicles shall be titled as the year, make, and model of the vehicle intended to be replicated. A label of "Replica" shall be applied to the title and registration card. All replica vehicle titles shall be labeled "Specially Constructed Vehicle."

(2) The model year of a street rod vehicle shall continue to be recognized as the manufacturer's assigned model year. The manufacturer's name shall continue to be used as the make with a label of "Street Rod" applied to the title and registration card. All street rod vehicle titles shall be labeled "Specially Constructed Vehicle."

(3) Custom-built vehicles shall be titled and registered showing the make as "Custom-built," and the year the vehicle was built shall be the vehicle model year. All custom-built vehicle titles shall be labeled "Specially Constructed Vehicle."

(b) Inoperable vehicles may be titled, but no registration may be issued until such time as the License and Theft Bureau inspects the vehicle to ensure it is substantially assembled. Once a vehicle has been verified as substantially assembled pursuant to an inspection by the License and Theft Bureau, the Commissioner shall title the vehicle by classifying it in the proper category and collecting all highway use taxes applicable to the value of the car at the time the vehicle is retitled to a proper classification, as described in this section.

(c) Motor vehicle certificates of title and registration cards issued pursuant to this section shall be labeled in accordance with this section. As used in this section, "labeled" means that the title and registration card shall contain a designation that discloses if the vehicle is classified as any of the following:

(1) Specially constructed vehicle.

(2) Inoperable vehicle.

History.
2009-405, s. 2

N.C. Gen. Stat. § 20-53.2

Reserved for future codification purposes.

§ 20-53.3. Appeal of specially constructed vehicle classification determination to Vehicle Classification Review Committee

(a) Any person aggrieved by the Division's determination of the appropriate vehicle classification for a specially constructed vehicle may request review of that determination by the Vehicle Classification Review Committee. This review shall be initiated by completing a Vehicle Classification Review Request and returning the request to the Division. The Vehicle Classification Review Request shall be made on a form provided by the Division. The decision of the Review Committee may be appealed to the Commissioner of Motor Vehicles.

(b) The Vehicle Classification Review Committee shall consist of five members as follows:

(1) Two members shall be personnel of the License and Theft Bureau of the

Division of Motor Vehicles appointed by the Commissioner.

(2) One member shall be a member of the public with expertise in antique or specially constructed vehicles appointed by the Commissioner from a list of nominees provided by the Antique Automobile Club of America.

(3) One member shall be a member of the public with expertise in antique or specially constructed vehicles appointed by the Commissioner from a list of nominees provided by the Specialty Equipment Market Association.

(4) One member shall be a member of the public with expertise in antique or specially constructed vehicles appointed by the Commissioner from a list of nominees provided by the National Corvette Restorers Society.

(c) Members of the Vehicle Classification Review Committee shall serve staggered two-year terms. Initial appointments shall be made on or before October 1, 2009. The initial appointment of one of the members from the License and Theft Bureau and the member nominated by the Antique Automobile Club of America shall be for one year. The initial appointments of the remaining members shall be for two years. At the expiration of these initial terms, appointments shall be for two years. A member of the Committee may be removed at any time by unanimous vote of the remaining four members. Vacancies shall be filled in the manner set out in subsection (b) of this section.

History.
2009-405, s. 6

§ 20-53.4. Registration of mopeds; certificate of title

(a) **Registration.** -- Mopeds shall be registered with the Division. The owner of the moped shall pay the same base fee and be issued the same type of registration card and plate issued for a motorcycle. In order to be registered with the Division and operated upon a highway or public vehicular area, a moped must meet the following requirements:

(1) The moped has a manufacturer's certificate of origin.

(2) The moped was designed and manufactured for use on highways or public vehicular areas.

(b) **Certificate of Title.** -- Notwithstanding G.S. 20-52 and G.S. 20-57, the owner of a moped is not required to apply for, and the Division is not required to issue, a certificate of title.

History.
2014-114, s. 1; 2015-125, s. 9

EDITOR'S NOTE. --
Session Laws 2014-114, s. 5, made this section effective July 1, 2015, and applicable to offenses committed on or after that date.

Session Laws 2014-114, s. 4, provides: "The Joint Legislative Transportation Oversight Committee shall study whether additional statutory changes are needed to ensure the safe operation of mopeds. The report shall include data on (i) the number of mopeds involved in traffic accidents, (ii) the number and types of injuries resulting from traffic accidents involving mopeds, and (iii) the causes for the traffic accidents involving mopeds. The Committee shall also study whether insurance should be required to operate a moped on a public street or highway. The Committee shall report its findings, together with any recommended legislation, to the 2015 Regular Session of the General Assembly upon its convening."

EFFECT OF AMENDMENTS. --
Session Laws 2015-125, s. 9, effective July 1, 2015, added "certificate of title" in the section heading; inserted "(a) Registration." in subsection (a); and added subsection (b).

§ 20-53.5. Titling and registration of HMMWV

(a) **Registration and Certificate of Title.** -- The Division shall register and issue a certificate of title for an HMMWV if all of the following conditions are met:

(1) The applicant for the title and registration of the HMMWV has provided to the Division a sworn affidavit from a manufacturer, motor vehicle dealer, or seller of the HMMWV certifying that the vehicle complies with all applicable federal motor vehicle safety standards for vehicles designed for highway use.

(2) The vehicle has a vehicle identification number that matches the vehicle ownership documents. If the vehicle does not have a vehicle identification number, the Division shall assign one to the vehicle prior to registration. The existence of a valid vehicle identification number for the vehicle shall be verified by the License and Theft Bureau of the Division prior to its registration and titling.

(b) **Applicability of This Chapter.** -- All provisions of this Chapter shall apply to an HMMWV, including the provisions of Article 3A and Article 9A of this Chapter, to the same extent they would apply to any other registered motor vehicle.

(c) **Fees.** -- The vehicle registration fees applicable to property-hauling vehicles shall apply to the registration of an HMMWV.

(d) **No Liability for Operations.** -- Neither the State nor its commission contract agents shall be liable for any injury or damages resulting from the operation of an HMMWV registered or titled pursuant to this section.

History.
2017-69, s. 2.1(b)
EDITOR'S NOTE. --
Session Laws 2017-69, s. 3, made this section effective June 28, 2017.

§ 20-54. Authority for refusing registration or certificate of title

The Division shall refuse registration or issuance of a certificate of title or any transfer of registration upon any of the following grounds:

(1) The application contains a false or fraudulent statement, the applicant has failed to furnish required information or reasonable additional information requested by the Division, or the applicant is not entitled to the issuance of a certificate of title or registration of the vehicle under this Article.

(2) The vehicle is mechanically unfit or unsafe to be operated or moved upon the highways.

(3) The Division has reasonable ground to believe that the vehicle is a stolen or embezzled vehicle, or that the granting of registration or the issuance of a certificate of title would constitute a fraud against the rightful owner or another person who has a valid lien against the vehicle.

(4) The registration of the vehicle stands suspended or revoked for any reason as provided in the motor vehicle laws of this State, except in such cases to abide by the ignition interlock installation requirements of G.S. 20-17.8.

(5) The required fee has not been paid, including any additional registration fees or taxes due pursuant to G.S. 20-91(c).

(6) The vehicle is not in compliance with the inspection requirements of Part 2 of Article 3A of this Chapter or a civil penalty assessed as a result of the failure of the vehicle to comply with that Part has not been paid.

(7) The Division has been notified that the motor vehicle has been seized by a law enforcement officer and is subject to forfeiture pursuant to G.S. 20-28.2, et seq., or any other statute. However, the Division shall not prevent the renewal of existing registration prior to an order of forfeiture.

(8) The vehicle is a golf cart or utility vehicle.

(9) The applicant motor carrier is subject to an order issued by the Federal Motor Carrier Safety Administration or the Division. The Division shall deny registration of a vehicle of a motor carrier if the applicant fails to disclose material information required, or if the applicant has made a materially false statement on the application, or if the applicant has applied as a subterfuge for the real party in interest who has been issued a federal out-of-service order, or if the applicant's business is operated, managed, or otherwise controlled by or affiliated with a person who is ineligible for registration, including the applicant entity, a relative, family member, corporate officer, or shareholder. The Division shall deny registration for a vehicle that has been assigned for safety to a commercial motor carrier who has been prohibited from operating by the Federal Motor Carrier Safety Administration or a carrier whose business is operated, managed, or otherwise controlled by or affiliated with a person who is ineligible for registration, including the owner, a relative, family member, corporate officer, or shareholder.

(10) The North Carolina Turnpike Authority has notified the Division that the owner of the vehicle has not paid the amount of tolls, fees, and civil penalties the owner owes the Authority for use of a Turnpike project.

(11) The Division has been notified (i) pursuant to G.S. 20-217(g2) that the owner of the vehicle has failed to pay any fine imposed pursuant to G.S. 20-217 or (ii) pursuant to G.S. 153A-246(b)(14) that the owner of the vehicle has failed to pay a civil penalty due under G.S. 153A-246.

(12) The owner of the vehicle has failed to pay any penalty or fee imposed pursuant to G.S. 20-311.

(13) The Division has been notified by the State Highway Patrol that the owner of the vehicle has failed to pay any civil penalty and fees imposed by the State Highway Patrol for a violation of Part 9 of Article 3 of this Chapter.

History.
1937, c. 407, s. 19; 1975, c. 716, s. 5; 1993 (Reg. Sess., 1994), c. 754, s. 7; 1998-182, s. 9;2001-356, s. 3;2002-152, s. 1;2007-164, s. 5;2008-225, s. 7;2009-319, s. 1;2013-293, s. 4;2015-241, s. 29.31(b);2016-87, s. 4;2017-188, s. 3;2019-196, s. 2

LOCAL MODIFICATION. --Moore: 1995, c. 13, s. 3, as amended by 2002-82, s. 2, as amended by 2005-11, s. 2;city of Conover: 2003-124, s. 1, as amended by 2004-58, s. 1, 2007-204, s. 1, 2007-259, s. 1, 2009-459, s. 5, 2011-171, s. 1, and 2013-172, s. 1;city of Lowell: 2003-124, s. 1, as amended by 2004-58, s. 1, 2007-204, s. 1, 2007-259, s. 1, 2009-459, s. 5, 2011-171, s. 1, and 2013-172, s. 1;town of Beech Mountain: 2003-124, s. 1, as amended by 2007-204, s. 1, 2007-259, s. 1, 2009-459, s. 5, 2011-171, s. 1, and 2013-172, s. 1;town of Caswell Beach: 2006-149, s. 1.1;town of Cramerton: 2003-124, s. 1, as amended by 2004-58, 2007-204, s. 1, 2007-259, 2009-459, 2011-171, s. 1, and 2013-172,

s. 1;town of North Topsail Beach: 2003-124, s. 1, as amended by 2004-59, s. 1, 2007-204, s. 1, 2007-259, s. 1, 2009-459, s. 5, 2011-171, s. 1, and 2013-172, s. 1;town of Seven Devils: 2003-124, s. 1, as amended by 2004-58, s. 1, 2007-204, s. 1, 2007-259, s. 1, 2009-459, s. 5, 2011-171, s. 1, and 2013-172, s. 1.

EDITOR'S NOTE. --

Session Laws 2015-241, s. 29.31(c), made subivision (12), as added by Session Laws 2015-241, s. 29.31(b), applicable to lapses in financial responsibility occurring on or after January 1, 2016.

Session Laws 2015-241, s. 1.1, provides: "This act shall be known as 'The Current Operations and Capital Improvements Appropriations Act of 2015.'"

Session Laws 2015-241, s. 33.6, is a severability clause.

Session Laws 2016-87, s. 8, made subdivision (13), as added by Session Laws 2016-87, s. 4, applicable to violations committed on or after October 1, 2016.

Session Laws 2017-188, s. 7, reads in part: "Section 3 of this act [which added clause (ii) of subdivision (11) of this section] is effective one year after it becomes law and shall apply to the registration of any motor vehicle whose owner's failure to pay a civil penalty due under G.S. 153A-246 is reported by a county to the Division of Motor Vehicles on or after the effective date of this act." The act became law July 25, 2017.

EFFECT OF AMENDMENTS. --

Session Laws 2007-164, s. 5, effective July 1, 2007, added the language following "laws of this State" in subdivision (4); added the language following "not been paid" in subdivision (5); and made minor punctuation changes.

Session Laws 2008-225, s. 7, effective January 1, 2011, added subdivision (10).

Session Laws 2009-319, s. 1, effective July 17, 2009, deleted "emissions" preceding "inspection" in subdivision (6).

Session Laws 2013-293, s. 4, effective December 1, 2013, added subdivision (11). For applicability, see Editor's note.

Session Laws 2015-241, s. 29.31(b), effective January 1, 2016, added subdivision (12). For applicability, see editor's note.

Session Laws 2016-87, s. 4, effective October 1, 2016, added subdivision (13). See editor's note for applicability.

Session Laws 2017-188, s. 3, effective July 25, 2018, inserted the clause (i) designation and added (ii) in subdivision (11). For applicability, see editor's note.

Session Laws 2019-196, s. 2, effective November 12, 2019, rewrote subdivision (9), which formerly read: "The applicant motor carrier is subject to an order issued by the Federal Motor Carrier Safety Administration or the Division to cease all operations based on a finding that the continued operations of the motor carrier pose an 'imminent hazard' as defined in 49 C.F.R. § 386.72(b)(1)."

CROSS REFERENCES. --

As to fees, see G.S. 20-85.

§ 20-54.1. Forfeiture of right of registration

(a) Upon receipt of notice of conviction of a violation of an offense involving impaired driving while the person's license is revoked as a result of a prior impaired driving license revocation as defined in G.S. 20-28.2, the Division shall revoke the registration of all motor vehicles registered in the convicted person's name and shall not register a motor vehicle in the convicted person's name until the convicted person's license is restored, except in such cases to abide by the ignition interlock installation requirements of G.S. 20-17.8. Upon receipt of notice of revocation of registration from the Division, the convicted person shall surrender the registration on all motor vehicles registered in the convicted person's name to the Division within 10 days of the date of the notice.

(a1) Upon receipt of notice of conviction of a felony speeding to elude arrest offense under G.S. 20-141.5(b) or (b1), the Division shall revoke the registration of all motor vehicles registered in the convicted person's name and shall not register a motor vehicle in the convicted person's name until the convicted person's license is restored. Upon receipt of notice of revocation of registration from the Division, the convicted person shall surrender the registration on all motor vehicles registered in the convicted person's name to the Division within 10 days of the date of the notice.

(b) Upon receipt of a notice of conviction under subsection (a) or (a1) of this section, the Division shall revoke the registration of the motor vehicle seized, and the owner shall not be allowed to register the motor vehicle seized until the convicted operator's drivers license has been restored. The Division shall not revoke the registration of the owner of the seized motor vehicle if the owner is determined to be an innocent owner. The Division shall revoke the owner's registration only after the owner is given an opportunity for a hearing to demonstrate that the owner is an innocent owner as defined in G.S. 20-28.2. Upon receipt of notice of revocation of registration from the Division, the owner shall surrender the registration on the motor vehicle seized to the Division within 10 days of the date of the notice.

History.

1998-182, s. 10;2007-164, s. 6;2013-243, s. 5

EFFECT OF AMENDMENTS. --

Session Laws 2007-164, s. 6, effective July 1, 2007, added the exception at the end of the first sentence of subsection (a).

Session Laws 2013-243, s. 5, effective December 1, 2013, added subsection (a1); and inserted "or (a1)" in subsection (b). For applicability, see Editor's note.

Chapter 20

§ 20-55. Examination of registration records and index of seized, stolen, and recovered vehicles

The Division, upon receiving application for any transfer of registration or for original registration of a vehicle, other than a new vehicle sold by a North Carolina dealer, shall first check the engine and serial numbers shown in the application with its record of registered motor vehicles, and against the index of seized, stolen and recovered motor vehicles required to be maintained by this Article.

History.
1937, c. 407, s. 20; 1971, c. 1070, s. 2; 1975, c. 716, s. 5; 1998-182, s. 11

§ 20-56. Registration indexes

(a) The Division shall file each application received, and when satisfied as to the genuineness and regularity thereof, and that the applicant is entitled to register such vehicle and to the issuance of a certificate of title, shall register the vehicle therein described and keep a record thereof as follows:

(1) Under a distinctive registration number assigned to the vehicle;

(2) Alphabetically, under the name of the owner;

(3) Under the motor number or any other identifying number of the vehicle; and

(4) In the discretion of the Division, in any other manner it may deem advisable.

(b) Repealed by Session Laws 2001, c. 424, s. 6.14(g), effective September 26, 2001.

History.
1937, c. 407, s. 20 1/2; 1949, c. 583, s. 5; 1971, c. 1070, s. 3; 1975, c. 716, s. 5; 1991, c. 53, s. 2;2001-424, s. 6.14(g) CITED in Hawkins v. M & J Fin. Corp., 238 N.C. 174, 77 S.E.2d 669 (1953).

CROSS REFERENCES. --
For requirements regarding marking and issuance of license plates for publicly owned vehicles, see G.S. 20-39.1.

§ 20-57. Division to issue certificate of title and registration card

(a) The Division upon registering a vehicle shall issue a registration card and a certificate of title as separate documents.

(b) The registration card shall be delivered to the owner and shall contain upon the face thereof the name and address of the owner, the registration number assigned to the vehicle, and a description of the vehicle as determined by the Commissioner, provided that if there are more than two owners the Division may show only two owners on the registration card and indicate that additional owners exist by placing after the names listed "et al." An owner may obtain a copy of a registration card issued in the owner's name by applying to the Division for a copy and paying the fee set in G.S. 20-85.

(c) Every such registration card shall at all times be carried in the vehicle to which it refers or in the vehicle to which transfer is being effected, as provided by G.S. 20-64 at the time of its operation, and such registration card shall be displayed upon demand of any peace officer or any officer of the Division: Provided, however, any person charged with failing to so carry such registration card shall not be convicted if he produces in court a registration card theretofore issued to him and valid at the time of his arrest: Provided further, that in case of a transfer of a license plate from one vehicle to another under the provisions of G.S. 20-72, evidence of application for transfer shall be carried in the vehicle in lieu of the registration card.

(d) The certificate of title shall contain upon the face thereof the identical information required upon the face of the registration card except the abbreviation "et al." if such appears and in addition thereto the name of all owners, the date of issuance and all liens or encumbrances disclosed in the application for title. All such liens or encumbrances shall be shown in the order of their priority, according to the information contained in such application.

(e) The certificate of title shall contain upon the reverse side an assignment of title or interest and warranty by registered owner or registered dealer. The purchaser's application for North Carolina certificate of title shall be made on a form prescribed by the Commissioner and shall include a space for notation of liens and encumbrances on the vehicle at the time of transfer.

(f) Certificates of title upon which liens or encumbrances are shown shall be delivered or mailed by the Division to the holder of the first lien or encumbrance.

(g) Certificates of title shall bear thereon the seal of the Division.

(h) Certificates of title need not be renewed annually, but shall remain valid until canceled by the Division for cause or upon a transfer of any interest shown therein.

History.
1937, c. 407, s. 21; 1943, c. 715; 1961, c. 360, s. 2; c. 835, s. 5; 1963, c. 552, s. 2; 1973, c. 72; c. 764, ss. 1-3; c. 1118; 1975, c. 716, s. 5; 1979, c. 139; 1981, c. 690, s. 20; 1983, c. 252; 1991, c. 193, s. 7;2016-90, s. 12(a);2019-227, s. 2

EDITOR'S NOTE. --
Session Laws 2016-90, s. 12(c), made the deletion of the former first sentence of subsection (c) of this section, which required an owner's signature upon a registration card upon receipt, by Session Laws 2016-90, s. 12(a), applicable to registration cards issued on or after December 1, 2016.

EFFECT OF AMENDMENTS. --

Session Laws 2016-90, s. 12(a), effective December 1, 2016, in subsection (c), deleted the former first sentence, which read: "Every owner upon receipt of a registration card, shall write his signature thereon with pen and ink in the space provided" from the beginning of the subsection. See editor's note for applicability.

Session Laws 2019-227, s. 2, effective September 27, 2019, deleted "space for the owner's signature" preceding "the registration number assigned" in subsection (b).

APPLICATION. --While G.S. 20-57 is intended to govern a situation in which there is only one owner at issue, the party registering the vehicle, G.S. 20-72(b) is intended to govern a situation in which an ownership interest is being transferred between two parties. Batts v. Lumbermen's Mut. Cas. Ins. Co., 192 N.C. App. 533, 665 S.E.2d 578 (2008).

PERFECTED SECURITY INTEREST. --Debtors' objection to the creditor's claim was denied because the debtor's "consolidation loan" was effectively a refinancing transaction as it was an advance under an existing credit facility rather than an entirely new loan, and therefore, rescission notices under 15 U.S.C.S. § 1635(a) and 12 C.F.R. § 226.23(a)(1) were not required by law or by contract, and as a result, and because of the re-pledge of a mobile home, the creditor maintained its security interest in the mobile home, the truck, and the car, and its interest remained perfected because the certificates of title were continuously valid pursuant to G.S. 25-9-311(a)(2) and 20-57; the creditor had a secured claim in the amount of $24,248, secured by the mobile home, the truck, and the car, and an unsecured claim for the balance. In re Holland, 2011 Bankr. LEXIS 1853 (Bankr. E.D.N.C. May 19, 2011).

APPLIED in Oroweat Employees Credit Union v. Stroupe, 48 N.C. App. 338, 269 S.E.2d 211 (1980).

CITED in Hawkins v. M & J Fin. Corp., 238 N.C. 174, 77 S.E.2d 669 (1953); Community Credit Co. v. Norwood, 257 N.C. 87, 125 S.E.2d 369 (1962); State v. Green, 103 N.C. App. 38, 404 S.E.2d 363 (1991); Peoples Sav. & Loan Assoc. v. Citicorp Acceptance Co., 103 N.C. App. 762, 407 S.E.2d 251 (1991); State v. Hudson, 103 N.C. App. 708, 407 S.E.2d 583 (1991); State v. Veazey, 191 N.C. App. 181, 662 S.E.2d 683 (2008).

CROSS REFERENCES. --

As to authority for consumer finance licensee under Article 15 of Chapter 53 to collect from borrower recording fees required pursuant to G.S. 20-58 et seq., see G.S. 53-177.

LEGAL PERIODICALS. --

For survey of 1980 commercial law, see 59 N.C.L. Rev. 1079 (1981).

§ 20-58. Perfection by indication of security interest on certificate of title

(a) Except as provided in G.S. 20-58.8, a security interest in a vehicle of a type for which a certificate of title is required shall be perfected only as hereinafter provided:

(1) If the vehicle is not registered in this State, the application for notation of a security interest shall be the application for certificate of title provided for in G.S. 20-52.

(2) If the vehicle is registered in this State, the application for notation of a security interest shall be in the form prescribed by the Division, signed by the debtor, and contain the date of application of each security interest, and name and address of the secured party from whom information concerning the security interest may be obtained. The application must be accompanied by the existing certificate of title unless in the possession of a prior secured party or in the event the manufacturer's statement of origin or existing certificate of title (i) was not delivered to the dealer or (ii) was lost or misplaced on the date the dealer sells or transfers the motor vehicle. If there is an existing certificate of title issued by this or any other jurisdiction in the possession of a prior secured party, the application for notation of the security interest shall in addition contain the name and address of such prior secured party. An application for notation of a security interest may be signed by the secured party instead of the debtor when the application is accompanied by documentary evidence of the applicant's security interest in that motor vehicle signed by the debtor and by affidavit of the applicant stating the reason the debtor did not sign the application. In the event the certificate cannot be obtained for recordation of the security interest, when title remains in the name of the debtor, the Division shall cancel the certificate and issue a new certificate of title listing all the respective security interests.

(3) If the application for notation of security interest is made in order to continue the perfection of a security interest perfected in another jurisdiction, it may be signed by the secured party instead of the debtor. Such application shall be accompanied by documentary evidence of a perfected security interest. No such application shall be valid unless an application for a certificate of title has been made in North Carolina. The security interest perfected herein shall be subject to the provisions set forth in G.S. 20-58.5.

(b) If a manufacturer's statement of origin or an existing certificate of title on a motor vehicle was (i) not delivered to the dealer or (ii) was lost or misplaced on or prior to the date the dealer sells or transfers the motor vehicle, a first lienholder or his designee may file a notarized copy of an instrument creating and evidencing a security interest in the motor vehicle with the Division of Motor Vehicles. A filing pursuant

Chapter 20

to this subsection shall constitute constructive notice to all persons of the security interest in the motor vehicle described in the filing. The constructive notice shall be effective on the date of the security agreement if the filing is made within 20 days after the date of the security agreement. The constructive notice shall date from the date of the filing with the Division if it is made more than 20 days after the date of the security agreement. The notation of a security interest created under this subsection shall automatically expire 60 days after the date of the creation of the security interest, or upon perfection of the security interest as provided in subsection (a) of this section, whichever occurs first. A security interest notation made under this subsection and then later perfected under subsection (a) of this section shall be presumed to have been perfected on the date of the earlier filing. The Division may charge a fee not to exceed ten dollars ($ 10.00) for each notation of security interest filed pursuant to this subsection. The fee shall be credited to the Highway Fund. It shall constitute a Class H felony for a person to knowingly and intentionally file a false notice with the Division pursuant to this subsection. A dealer principal, owner, or manager of a motor vehicle dealership who is not a signatory of the notice required under this subsection may only be charged for a criminal violation for filing a false notice with the Division under this subsection by another dealership employee if the dealer principal, owner, or manager had actual knowledge of the falsity of the filing at the time the filing was submitted to the Division.

(c) An application for the notation of a security interest pursuant to subsection (a) of this section on a certificate of title for a manufactured home shall state the maturity date of the secured obligation. The Division shall include the stated maturity date for the certificate of title, including the notation of the maturity date on the certificate of title, in its public records and in any reports regarding the certificate of title provided to third parties. For the purposes of this subsection, the maturity date of the security interest is defined in G.S. 45-36.24.

History.
1937, c. 407, s. 22; 1955, c. 554, s. 2; 1961, c. 835, s. 6; 1969, c. 838, s. 1; 1975, c. 716, s. 5; 1979, c. 145, ss. 1, 2; c. 199; 2000-182, s. 2;2016-59, s. 2;2018-42, s. 2(b);2018-145, s. 4

EDITOR'S NOTE. --
Session Laws 2018-42, s. 2(f), provides: "The Division of Motor Vehicles, in consultation with the North Carolina Automobile Dealers Association, Inc., shall study the following:

"(1) The impacts of this section on Division processes and procedures, along with recommended statutory changes to further improve the lawful transfer of motor vehicles.

"(2) Methods to ensure consumer protection in the motor vehicle transfer process.

"(3) Potential changes to the Division's electronic lien and title program or other processes that could assist with reducing the delay in the release of a satisfied security interest in a motor vehicle.

"(4) Any other issues the Division deems appropriate.

"The Division shall report its findings, including any legislative recommendations, to the Joint Legislative Transportation Oversight Committee by December 31, 2020."

Session Laws 2020-77, s. 3(a) -(e), provides: "(a) Electronic Signatures for Applications for Notations of Security Interest Signed by Debtor. -- Notwithstanding any other provision of law to the contrary, an application for a notation of a security interest submitted to the Division of Motor Vehicles pursuant to G.S. 20-58(a)(2) signed by a debtor may be signed by electronic signature by the debtor without notarization provided the application is submitted by a licensed or regulated lender in this State having a lienholder identification number issued by the Division.

"(b) Certain Documentary Evidence Not Required for Applications Without Debtor Signature. -- Notwithstanding any other provision of law to the contrary, an application for a notation of a security interest submitted to the Division of Motor Vehicles pursuant to G.S. 20-58(a)(2) signed by the secured party instead of the debtor does not require documentary evidence of the applicant's security interest in that motor vehicle signed by the debtor provided the application is submitted by a licensed or regulated lender in this State having a lienholder identification number issued by the Division.

"(c) Manufactured Home Applicability. -- This section does not apply to applications for a notation of a security interest for manufactured homes.

"(d) Division Liability. -- Neither the Division nor its commission contractors shall be liable for any cause of action arising from a notation of security interest fraudulently or erroneously placed on a certificate of title for applications submitted to the Division pursuant to this section. Any entity offering an electronic signature process for applications submitted pursuant to this section assumes all responsibility and liability for the accuracy of the signature. The Division and its commission contractors shall be held harmless from any liability to a claim arising from applications submitted with an inaccurate electronic signature pursuant to this section.

"(e) This section is effective when it becomes law and applies to applications for notation of security interests submitted to the Division of Motor Vehicles on or after that date and before December 1, 2020."

EFFECT OF AMENDMENTS. --
Session Laws 2016-59, s. 2, effective July 1, 2017, added subsection (c).

Session Laws 2018-42, s. 2(b), as amended by Session Laws 2018-145, s. 4, effective March 1, 2019, in subsection (a), added "or in the event the manufacturer's statement of origin or existing certificate of title (i) was not delivered to the dealer or (ii) was lost or misplaced on the date the dealer sells or transfers the motor vehicle" at the end of the second sentence; and in subsection (b), substituted "If" for "When" at the beginning and "was (i) not delivered to the dealer or (ii) was lost or misplaced on or prior to the date the dealer sells or transfers the motor vehicle" for "is unavailable," and deleted "who holds a valid license as a motor vehicle dealer issued by the Commissioner under Article 12 of this Chapter" following "a first lienholder" in the first sentence, substituted "on the date of the security agreement" for "from the date of the filing" in the third sentence, deleted the former last sentence, which read: "A false filing with the Division pursuant to this subsection shall constitute a Class H felony", and added the last two sentences.

EDITOR'S NOTE. --Some of the cases cited below were decided under this section prior to the 1969 revision of G.S. 20-58 through 20-58.8.

LEGISLATIVE INTENT REGARDING SECURITY INTEREST IN MOBILE HOME. --The legislature intended that this section provide the exclusive method for a first mortgagee to perfect a security interest in a mobile home. Peoples Sav. & Loan Assoc. v. Citicorp Acceptance Co., 103 N.C. App. 762, 407 S.E.2d 251, cert. denied, 330 N.C. 197, 412 S.E.2d 59 (1991).

PURPOSE. --The manifest purpose of this and the following sections is to provide notice by recording the security interest on the certificate of title. Ferguson v. Morgan, 14 N.C. App. 520, 188 S.E.2d 672, rev'd on other grounds, 282 N.C. 83, 191 S.E.2d 817 (1972).

SCOPE. --With reference to vehicles subject to registration with the Division of Motor Vehicles, the provisions of G.S. 20-58 et seq. are the exclusive statutory authority governing the perfecting of security interests in motor vehicles. In re Holder, 94 Bankr. 395 (Bankr. M.D.N.C. 1988), aff'd, 892 F.2d 29 (1989).

SALE CONTEMPLATING REGULAR USE SUBJECTS VEHICLE TO STATUTE. --Once a sale of an automobile has occurred contemplating regular use, whether it be a sale of a complete or limited interest, the vehicle is then subject to North Carolina's certificate of title statute, G.S. 20-58 et seq. Bank of Alamance v. Isley, 74 N.C. App. 489, 328 S.E.2d 867 (1985).

PROVISIONS OF THE UNIFORM COMMERCIAL CODE AS TO THE PLACE FOR FILING FINANCING STATEMENTS HAVE NO APPLICATION TO VEHICLES SUBJECT TO REGISTRATION with the Department (now Division) of Motor Vehicles. Ferguson v. Morgan, 282 N.C. 83, 191 S.E.2d 817 (1972).

RECORDATION ON CERTIFICATE OF TITLE REQUIRED. --Security interests in vehicles requiring registration and certificates of title may be perfected only if recorded on the certificate of title. In re Meade, 174 Bankr. 49 (Bankr. M.D.N.C. 1994).

RECORDATION OF LIEN IN COUNTY OF RESIDENCE UNNECESSARY. --It is no longer necessary to record the mortgage or other lien on vehicles required to be registered under the State motor vehicle laws in the county where the debtor resides. Ferguson v. Morgan, 282 N.C. 83, 191 S.E.2d 817 (1972).

The certificate of title issued by the Department (now Division) now fixes the priority of liens. It is no longer

necessary to record the mortgage or other lien in the county where the debtor resides. Community Credit Co. v. Norwood, 257 N.C. 87, 125 S.E.2d 369 (1962).

PLEDGE NOT PROHIBITED. --No language of the 1961 act amending this section expressly prohibited the creation of a pledge. Wachovia Bank & Trust Co. v. Wayne Fin. Co., 262 N.C. 711, 138 S.E.2d 481 (1964).

THE LEGISLATURE DID NOT INTEND TO PREVENT A MORTGAGEE WITH ACTUAL POSSESSION FROM ACQUIRING A LIEN HAVING PRIORITY over liens not then perfected. Wachovia Bank & Trust Co. v. Wayne Fin. Co., 262 N.C. 711, 138 S.E.2d 481 (1964).

DUTY OF CARE OF LIENHOLDER. --Trial court did not err in dismissing counterclaim based on defendants' contention that because lienholder controlled the processes of perfecting its security interest and obtaining the certificate of title, it owed the debtor-purchaser a duty of care with regard to completing these matters, as defendants did not establish the existence of a duty of care owed to them by plaintiff on the basis of statute. NCNB Nat'l Bank v. Gutridge, 94 N.C. App. 344, 380 S.E.2d 408, cert. denied, 325 N.C. 432, 384 S.E.2d 539 (1989).

PERFECTION OF FEDERAL TAX LIEN ON MOTOR VEHICLE. --While the normal method for recording a lien on a motor vehicle is to record it on the certificate of title, G.S. 20-58.8(b)(2) makes that method of perfecting a lien expressly inapplicable to federal tax liens. In re Williams, 109 Bankr. 179 (Bankr. W.D.N.C. 1989).

A federal tax lien attaches to all real and personal property of the debtors pursuant to federal law, and is perfected by the filing of a notice of tax lien. Where that was accomplished in accordance with federal regulation and G.S. 44-68.1(b)(2) (see now G.S. 44-68.10 et seq.), the IRS lien attached to and was secured by debtors' automobiles, regardless of the fact that no lien was noted on the automobiles' titles. In re Williams, 109 Bankr. 179 (Bankr. W.D.N.C. 1989).

FAILURE TO PROPERLY EFFECT SECURITY INTEREST. --Debtor was the owner of the automobile at issue and the creditor did not retain an ownership interest, only a security interest in the vehicle, when the debtor and the creditor entered into a promissory note and security agreement whereby the debtor agreed to purchase the automobile; however, because the creditor failed to properly perfect the security interest in the vehicle under G.S. 20-58, the trustee's interest was superior pursuant to 11 U.S.C. § 544. Ivey v. Wilson (In re Payne), 2006 Bankr. LEXIS 4199 (Bankr. M.D.N.C. Dec. 6, 2006).

POSSESSION INSUFFICIENT TO PERFECT SECURITY INTEREST IN VEHICLE. --Only way to perfect a security interest in a vehicle in North Carolina is by a notation on the certificate of title, not mere possession. In re In re Mills Int'l, Inc., 2015 Bankr. LEXIS 958 (Bankr. E.D.N.C. Mar. 27, 2015).

Where judgment creditor seized two of debtor's vehicles, thereby creating liens pre-petition, because liens were never perfected under North Carolina law, debtor retained interest in vehicles as of petition date, vehicles were property of estate, and vehicles were therefore subject to turnover. In re Hutton, 2017 Bankr. LEXIS 2419 (Bankr. E.D.N.C. Aug. 25, 2017).

WHEN A LEVY HAS BEEN MADE ON AN AUTOMOBILE PURSUANT TO AN EXECUTION, it is the duty of the officer to report the levy to the Department (now Division) in a form prescribed by it. The levy so reported is subordinate to all liens therefore noted on the certificate. Community Credit Co. v. Norwood, 257 N.C. 87, 125 S.E.2d 369 (1962).

AS TO PLAINTIFF'S ESTOPPEL FROM ASSERTING LIEN ON VEHICLES WHERE IT DID NOTHING TO PERFECT ITS SECURITY INTEREST, see Wayne Fin. Corp. v. Shivar, 8 N.C. App. 489, 174 S.E.2d 876 (1970).

LATE-PERFECTED SECURITY INTEREST IS NOT RETROACTIVELY VALID AGAINST AN INNOCENT THIRD PARTY who acquired an automobile for value. Bank of Alamance v. Isley, 74 N.C. App. 489, 328 S.E.2d 867 (1985).

A SECURITY INTEREST IN A MOBILE HOME is subject to the same perfection requirements as an automobile. Carter v. Holland (In re Carraway), 65 Bankr. 51 (Bankr. E.D.N.C. 1986).

Plaintiff's argument that owner no longer intended to operate her mobile home upon the highway did not nullify defendant's properly perfected security interest in the mobile home. Peoples Sav. & Loan Assoc. v. Citicorp Acceptance Co., 103 N.C. App. 762, 407 S.E.2d 251, cert. denied, 330 N.C. 197, 412 S.E.2d 59 (1991).

Debtor's Chapter 13 bankruptcy plan could not be confirmed under 11 U.S.C.S. § 1325 because it valued secured claim mortgage company held on debtor's mobile home at $13,080, when evidence that was offered under 11 U.S.C.S. § 506 showed that home had replacement value of $20,714; company had valid lien on home and its accessions under G.S. 20-58 and G.S. 25-9-311 because home was personal property and company notated its lien on home's certificate of title, and court was not bound by testimony debtor's expert and company's expert offered to support their conclusions that home was worth, respectively, $17,200 and $31,900. In re Edwards, 2017 Bankr. LEXIS 4430 (Bankr. E.D.N.C. Dec. 29, 2017).

CITED in Nationwide Mut. Ins. Co. v. Hayes, 276 N.C. 620, 174 S.E.2d 511 (1970); Moser v. Employers Com. Union Ins. Co. of Am., 25 N.C. App. 309, 212 S.E.2d 664 (1975); Paccar Fin. Corp. v. Harnett Transf., Inc., 51 N.C. App. 1, 275 S.E.2d 243 (1981); Barclaysamerican/Credit Co. v. Riddle, 57 N.C. App. 662, 292 S.E.2d 177 (1982); In re Millerburg, 61 Bankr. 125 (Bankr. E.D.N.C. 1986); Butler v. Green Tree Fin. Servicing Corp. (In re Wester), 229 Bankr. 348 (Bankr. E.D.N.C. 1998).

LEGAL PERIODICALS. --

For case law survey as to credit transactions, see 44 N.C.L. Rev. 956 (1966).

OPINIONS OF THE ATTORNEY GENERAL

PERFECTION OF SECURITY INTEREST. --A security interest in a motor vehicle is not valid against third parties unless perfected by application for notation upon the certificate of title for the vehicle as provided in this and the following sections. See opinion of Attorney General to Mr. Eric L. Gooch, Director, Sales and Use Tax Division, North Carolina Department of Revenue, 40 N.C.A.G. 446 (1969).

§ 20-58.1. Duty of the Division upon receipt of application for notation of security interest

(a) Upon receipt of an application for notation of security interest, the required fee and accompanying documents required by G.S. 20-58, the Division, if it finds the application and accompanying documents in order, shall either endorse upon the certificate of title or issue a new certificate of title containing, the name and address of each secured party, and the date of perfection of each security interest as determined by the Division. The Division shall deliver or mail the certificate to the first secured party named in it and shall also notify the new secured party that his security interest has been noted upon the certificate of title.

(b) If the certificate of title is in the possession of some prior secured party, the Division, when satisfied that the application is in order, shall procure the certificate of title from the secured party in whose possession it is being held, for the sole purpose of noting the new security interest. Upon request of the Division, a secured party in possession of a certificate of title shall forthwith deliver or mail the certificate of title to the Division. Such delivery of the certificate does not affect the rights of any secured party under his security agreement.

History.

1961, c. 835, s. 6; 1969, c. 838, s. 1; 1975, c. 716, s. 5; 1979, c. 145, s. 3

DATE OF PERFECTION OF LIEN. --Section 20-58.2 provides expressly that the security interest evidenced by a security agreement is perfected as of the date of delivery of the application to the Department (now Division) and payment of the required fee. Ferguson v. Morgan, 282 N.C. 83, 191 S.E.2d 817 (1972).

Where both owner and creditor did all they were required to do and could do to perfect lien, under G.S. 20-58.2, which relates solely and specifically to the date of perfection of the lien, the security interest was perfected as of the date of delivery of the application to the Department (now Division). Ferguson v. Morgan, 282 N.C. 83, 191 S.E.2d 817 (1972).

LATE-PERFECTED SECURITY INTEREST IS NOT RETROACTIVELY VALID AGAINST AN INNOCENT THIRD PARTY who acquired an automobile for value. Bank of Alamance v. Isley, 74 N.C. App. 489, 328 S.E.2d 867 (1985).

CITED in Wayne Fin. Corp. v. Shivar, 8 N.C. App. 489, 174 S.E.2d 876 (1970); Ferguson v. Morgan, 282 N.C. 83, 191 S.E.2d 817 (1972).

Chapter 20

LEGAL PERIODICALS. --

For 1984 survey, "The Application of the North Carolina Motor Vehicle Act and the Uniform Commercial Code to the Sale of Motor Vehicles by Consignment," see 63 N.C.L. Rev. 1105 (1985).

§ 20-58.2. Date of perfection

If the application for notation of security interest with the required fee is delivered to the Division within 20 days after the date of the security agreement, the security interest is perfected as of the date of the execution of the security agreement. Otherwise, the security interest is perfected as of the date of delivery of the application to the Division.

History.

1961, c. 835, s. 6; 1969, c. 838, s. 1; 1975, c. 716, s. 5; 1991, c. 414, s. 1

DATE OF PERFECTION OF SECURITY INTEREST. --This section provides expressly that the security interest evidenced by a security agreement is perfected as of the date of delivery of the application to the Department (now Division) and payment of the required fee. Ferguson v. Morgan, 282 N.C. 83, 191 S.E.2d 817 (1972).

Where both owner and creditor did all they were required to do and could do to perfect lien, under this section, which relates solely and specifically to the date of perfection of the lien, the security interest was perfected as of the date of delivery of the application to the Department (now Division). Ferguson v. Morgan, 282 N.C. 83, 191 S.E.2d 817 (1972).

Under this section, perfection of the security interest in a motor vehicle occurs when the application and proper fee are delivered to the Division of Motor Vehicles. Bank of Alamance v. Isley, 74 N.C. App. 489, 328 S.E.2d 867 (1985).

Perfection by notation on an automobile's certificate of title occurs when the application and proper fee are delivered to the DMV. In re Millerburg, 61 Bankr. 125 (Bankr. E.D.N.C. 1986).

Creditor's security interest in a bankruptcy debtor's vehicle was void since the creditor attempted to record the interest electronically prior to the debtor's bankruptcy petition date but the filing was blocked and was not accepted by the appropriate State agency until after the petition date, and thus the interest was perfected in violation of the automatic bankruptcy stay. Saslow v. Porsche Fin. Servs. (In re Ware), 2003 Bankr. LEXIS 2444 (Bankr. M.D.N.C. Dec. 15, 2003).

LATE-PERFECTED SECURITY INTEREST IS NOT RETROACTIVELY VALID AGAINST AN INNOCENT THIRD PARTY who acquired an automobile for value. Bank of Alamance v. Isley, 74 N.C. App. 489, 328 S.E.2d 867 (1985).

RELATION BACK OF LIEN. --The lien, if the agreement to pay is filed with the Department (now Division) within 10 (now 20) days from its date, relates back to the day the lien was created. Wachovia Bank & Trust Co. v. Wayne Fin. Co., 262 N.C. 711, 138

S.E.2d 481 (1964), decided under § 20-58 as it stood before the 1969 revision of §§ 20-58 through 20-58.8.

In order for the date of perfection to relate back to the purchase date or date of creation of the security interest, proper application must be made to the Division of Motor Vehicles on or within 10 (now 20) days from the date of purchase. In re Holder, 94 Bankr. 395 (Bankr. M.D.N.C. 1988), aff'd, 892 F.2d 29 (1989).

CITED in Carter v. Holland (In re Carraway), 65 Bankr. 51 (Bankr. E.D.N.C. 1986); Wachovia Bank & Trust Co. v. Holder, 94 Bankr. 394 (M.D.N.C. 1988); Wachovia Bank & Trust Co. v. Bringle, 892 F.2d 29 (4th Cir. 1989); Peoples Sav. & Loan Assoc. v. Citicorp Acceptance Co., 103 N.C. App. 762, 407 S.E.2d 251 (1991).

§ 20-58.3. Notation of assignment of security interest on certificate of title

An assignee of a security interest may have the certificate of title endorsed or issued with the assignee named as the secured party, upon delivering to the Division on a form prescribed by the Division, with the required fee, an assignment by the secured party named in the certificate together with the certificate of title. The assignment must contain the address of the assignee from which information concerning the security interest may be obtained. If the certificate of title is in the possession of some other secured party the procedure prescribed by G.S. 20-58.1(b) shall be followed.

History.

1961, c. 835, s. 6; 1969, c. 838, s. 1; 1975, c. 716, s. 5

LEGAL PERIODICALS. --

For note on commercial reasonableness and the public sale in North Carolina, see 17 Wake Forest L. Rev. 153 (1981).

§ 20-58.3A. Automatic expiration of security interest in manufactured home; renewal of security interests in manufactured homes

(a) For the purposes of this section, the term "secured party" means the secured party named on a certificate of title for a manufactured home and those parties that succeed to the rights of the secured party as a secured creditor by assignment or otherwise. The term "borrower" means the homeowner or the debtor on the obligation secured by the security interest noted on the certificate of title for a manufactured home.

(b) With the exception of a security interest in a manufactured home perfected pursuant to G.S. 20-58(c), unless satisfied pursuant to G.S. 20-58.4 or G.S. 20-109.2, the perfection of a security interest in a manufactured home that is perfected by a notation on the certificate of title shall automatically expire 30 years after the date of the issuance of the original certificate of

Chapter 20

title containing the notation of the security interest, unless a different maturity date is stated on the title.

(c) Unless satisfied pursuant to G.S. 20-58.4 or G.S. 20-109.2, the perfection of a security interest in a manufactured home perfected by a notation on the certificate of title pursuant to G.S. 20-58(c) shall automatically expire as follows:

(1) If the perfection of the security interest has not been renewed as provided in this section, on the earlier of (i) 90 days after the maturity date stated on the application for the security interest or (ii) 15 years plus 180 days after the date of issuance of the original certificate of title containing the notation of the security interest.

(2) If the perfection of the security interest has been renewed as provided in this section, on the earlier of (i) 10 years after the date of the renewal of the perfection of the security interest, (ii) 90 days after the original maturity date of the security interest, if the original maturity date has not been extended, or (iii) 90 days after any extended maturity date stated on the application of renewal.

(d) Prior to the date that perfection of a secured party's security interest in a manufactured home automatically expires pursuant to subsection (b) or (c) of this section, the secured party may deliver to the Division an application for renewal of the perfection of the secured party's security interest. The application for the renewal of the perfection of the secured party's security interest shall be in a form prescribed by the Division. Nothing in this section shall be construed to extend the maturity date of the secured obligation unless an agreement in writing has been executed by the borrower extending the original maturity date. The application for renewal of the perfection of the secured party's security interest shall contain all of the following:

(1) The secured party's signature.

(2) The existing certificate of title, unless it is in the possession of a prior secured party.

(3) An affirmative statement of any agreement executed by the borrower to extend the maturity date.

(4) If the application is submitted by the assignee or successor in interest of the secured party listed on the certificate of title, documentary evidence that the applicant is the assignee or successor in interest of the secured party listed on the certificate of title.

(5) The name and address of the party from whom information concerning the security interest may be obtained.

(6) Any other information requested by the Division.

(e) Upon receipt of the application for renewal of the perfection of the secured party's security interest, the Division shall do one of the following:

(1) If the existing certificate of title is included with the application for renewal, the Division shall issue a new certificate of title bearing the original or extended maturity date of the security interest.

(2) If the existing certificate of title is in the possession of a prior secured party, the Division, if satisfied as to the genuineness and regularity of the application for renewal, may request the certificate of title from the party in possession for the purpose of notating the original or extended maturity date of the security interest. Once the notations have been made, the Division shall return the certificate of title to the possession of the secured party.

(3) If the existing certificate of title is not obtained upon request, the Division shall cancel the existing certificate of title and issue a new certificate of title. The new certificate of title shall list all known security interests and shall bear notation that shows the original or extended maturity date of the security interest.

(f) An application for the renewal of a secured party's security interest pursuant to this section shall be effective to renew the perfection of the security interest as of the date the application is delivered to the Division. Each renewed security interest shall retain its original date of perfection and the perfection shall thereafter expire on the earlier to occur of (i) 10 years after the date of renewal of the perfection of the security interest, (ii) 90 days after the original maturity date of the security interest, if the original maturity date has not been extended, or (iii) 90 days after any extended maturity date stated on the application of renewal. Perfection of a security interest in a manufactured home may be renewed more than once pursuant to this section.

(g) The Division shall not be subject to a claim under Article 31 of Chapter 143 of the General Statutes related to the renewal of the perfection of a security interest or the failure to acknowledge or give effect to an expired perfection of a security interest on a certificate of title for a manufactured home pursuant to this section if the claim is based on reliance by the Division on any application for renewal submitted to the Division by a third party pursuant to this section or based on the automatic expiration of a perfection of a security interest pursuant to this section.

History.
2016-59, s. 3;2018-74, s. 16.3(b)

EDITOR'S NOTE. --

Session Laws 2016-59, s. 10, made this section effective July 1, 2017.

EFFECT OF AMENDMENTS. --

Session Laws 2018-74, s. 16.3(b), effective October 1, 2018, inserted "or the failure to acknowledge or give effect to an expired perfection of a security interest" and "or based on the automatic expiration of a perfection of a security interest pursuant to this section" in subsection (g).

§ 20-58.4. Release of security interest

(a) Upon the satisfaction or other discharge of a security interest in a vehicle for which the certificate of title is in the possession of the secured party, the secured party shall, within the earlier of 10 days after demand or 30 days from the date of satisfaction, execute a release of his security interest, in the space provided therefor on the certificate or as the Division prescribes, and mail or deliver the certificate and release to the next secured party named therein, or if none, to the owner or other person authorized to receive the certificate for the owner.

(a1) Upon the satisfaction or other discharge of a security interest in a vehicle for which the certificate of title data is notated by a lien through electronic means pursuant to G.S. 20-58.4A, the secured party shall, within seven business days from the date of satisfaction, send electronic notice of the release of the security interest to the Division through the electronic lien release system established pursuant to G.S. 20-58.4A. The electronic notice of the release of the security interest sent to the Division by the secured party shall direct that a physical certificate of title be mailed or delivered to the address noted by the secured party providing notice of the satisfaction or other discharge of the security interest. Upon receipt by the Division of an electronic notice of the release of the security interest, the Division shall mail or deliver a certificate of title to the address noted by the secured party within three business days.

(b) Upon the satisfaction or other discharge of a security interest in a vehicle for which the certificate of title is in the possession of a prior secured party, the secured party whose security interest is satisfied shall within 10 days execute a release of his security interest in such form as the Division prescribes and mail or deliver the same to the owner or other person authorized to receive the same for the owner.

(c) An owner, upon securing the release of any security interest in a vehicle shown upon the certificate of title issued therefor, may exhibit the documents evidencing such release, signed by the person or persons making such release, and the certificate of title to the Division which shall, when satisfied as to the genuineness and regularity of the release, issue to the owner either a new certificate of title in proper form or an endorsement or rider attached thereto showing the release of the security interest.

(d) If an owner exhibits documents evidencing the release of a security interest as provided in subsection (c) of this section but is unable to furnish the certificate of title to the Division because it is in possession of a prior secured party, the Division, when satisfied as to the genuineness and regularity of the release, shall procure the certificate of title from the person in possession thereof for the sole purpose of noting thereon the release of the subsequent security interest, following which the Division shall return the certificate of title to the person from whom it was obtained and notify the owner that the release has been noted on the certificate of title.

(e) If it is impossible for the owner to secure from the secured party the release contemplated by this section, the owner may exhibit to the Division such evidence as may be available showing satisfaction or other discharge of the debt secured, together with a sworn affidavit by the owner that the debt has been satisfied.

(e1) If the vehicle is a manufactured home, the owner may proceed in accordance with subsection (e) of this section or may, in the alternative, provide the Division with a sworn affidavit by the owner that the debt has been satisfied and that either:

(1) After diligent inquiry, the owner has been unable to determine the identity or the current location of the secured creditor or its successor in interest; or

(2) The secured creditor has not responded within 30 days to a written request from the owner to release the secured creditor's security interest.

For purposes of this subsection, the term "owner" shall mean any of the following: (i) the owner of the manufactured home; (ii) the owner of real property on which the manufactured home is affixed; or (iii) a title insurance company as insurer of an insured owner of real property on which the manufactured home is affixed.

(e2) The Division may treat either of the methods employed by the owner pursuant to subsection (e) or subsection (e1) of this section as a proper release for purposes of this section when satisfied as to the genuineness, truth and sufficiency thereof. Prior to cancellation of a security interest under the provisions of this subsection, at least 15 days' notice of the pendency thereof shall be given to the secured party at his last known address by the Division by registered letter. The Division shall not cancel a security interest pursuant to this subsection if, within 15 days after the Division gives notice, the secured party responds to the Division indicating that the security interest remains in effect.

(f) The Division shall not be subject to a claim under Article 31 of Chapter 143 of the General Statutes related to the release of the perfection of a security interest on a certificate of title for a manufactured home pursuant to this section if the claim is based on reliance by the Division on any release, affidavit, notation of the certificate of title, or documents evidencing the release or satisfaction of a security interest submitted to the Division by a third party pursuant to this section.

History.
1961, c. 835, s. 6; 1969, c. 838, s. 1; 1975, c. 716, s. 5; 2011-318, s. 1;2015-270, s. 2;2016-59, s. 4;2018-74, s. 16.3(a)
EFFECT OF AMENDMENTS. --
Session Laws 2015-270, s. 2, effective December 1, 2015, added subsection (a1).
Session Laws 2016-59, s. 4, effective July 1, 2017, rewrote former subsection (e) as present subsections (e) and (e2); and added subsections (e1) and (f).
Session Laws 2018-74, s. 16.3(a), effective October 1, 2018, added the last paragraph in subsection (e1).
FAILURE TO COMPLY. --Notwithstanding the full payment and discharge of the claim, the creditor failed for months and months to comply with G.S. 20-58.4, which required a secured creditor to release its lien on the title to a motor vehicle or a mobile home within 30 days of the full payment or within 10 days after receipt of written demand from the debtors or the attorney for the debtors following a final payment. A violation of this lien-release statute could also constitute a violation of the North Carolina Retail Installment Sales Act and furthermore an Unfair and Deceptive Trade Practice in Violation N.C. Gen. Stat. ch. 75; these statutes applied to bankruptcy debtors. The creditor was subject to statutory damages, legal fees, and expenses for its failure to comply with the North Carolina lien release statute. In re Sipe, 2001 Bankr. LEXIS 2199 (Bankr. W.D.N.C. July 18, 2001).

§ 20-58.4A. Electronic lien system

(a) **Implementation.** -- No later than January 1, 2015, the Division shall implement a statewide electronic lien system to process the notification, release, and maintenance of security interests and certificate of title data where a lien is notated, through electronic means instead of paper documents otherwise required by this Chapter. The Division may contract with a qualified vendor or vendors to develop and implement this statewide electronic lien system, or the Division may develop and make available to qualified service providers a well-defined set of information services that will enable secure access to the data and internal application components necessary to facilitate the creation of an electronic lien system.

(b) **Minimum Standards for a Vendor Implemented System.** -- When contracting with a qualified vendor or vendors to implement the system required in subsection (a) of this section, the Division shall set the following minimum standards:

(1) The Division shall issue a competitive request for proposal to assess the qualifications of any vendor or vendors responsible for the establishment and ongoing support of the statewide electronic lien system. The Division may also reserve the right to receive input regarding specifications for the electronic lien system from parties that do not respond to a request for proposal to establish and operate an electronic lien system.

(2) Any contract entered into with a vendor or vendors shall include no costs or charges payable by the Division to the vendor or vendors. The vendor or vendors shall reimburse the Division for documented reasonable implementation costs directly associated with the establishment and ongoing support of the statewide electronic lien system.

(3) Upon implementation of the electronic lien system pursuant to subsection (a) of this section, the qualified vendor or vendors may charge participating lienholders or their agents a per-transaction fee for each lien notification. The per-transaction lien notification fee shall be consistent with market pricing in an amount not to exceed three dollars and fifty cents ($ 3.50) for costs associated with the development and ongoing administration of the electronic lien system. The qualified vendor or vendors shall not charge lienholders or their agents any additional fee for lien releases, assignments, or transfers. To recover their costs, participating lienholders or their agents may charge the borrower of a motor vehicle loan or the lessee of an automotive lease an amount equal to the transaction fee per lien notification plus a fee in an amount not to exceed three dollars ($ 3.00) for each electronic transaction where a lien is notated.

(4) A qualified vendor or vendors may also serve as a service provider to lienholders, if all of the following conditions are met:

a. The contract with the vendor must include provisions specifically prohibiting the vendor from using information concerning vehicle titles for marketing or business solicitation purposes.

b. The contract with the vendor must include an acknowledgment by the vendor that it is required to enter into agreements to exchange electronic lien data with any service providers who offer electronic lien and title services in the State and who have been approved by the Division for participation in the system and with service providers who are not qualified vendors.

c. The Division must periodically monitor fees charged by a qualified vendor also serving as a service provider to lienholders and providing services as a qualified vendor to other service providers to ensure the vendor is not engaged in predatory pricing.

(c) **Minimum Standards for Division-Developed System.** -- If the Division chooses to develop an interface to enable service provider access to data to facilitate the creation of an electronic lien system, then the Division shall do so for a cost not to exceed two hundred fifty thousand dollars ($ 250,000) and set the following minimum standards:

(1) The Division shall establish qualifications for third-party service providers offering electronic lien services and establish a qualification process that will vet applications developed by service providers for compliance with defined security and architecture standards as follows:

a. Qualifications shall be posted within 60 days of the effective date of this section.

b. Interested service providers shall respond by providing qualifications within 30 days of posting.

c. The Division shall notify service providers of their approval.

d. Within 30 days of approval, each qualified service provider shall remit payment in an amount equal to the development costs as a fraction of the number of qualified service providers participating in the electronic lien services.

e. If there is a service provider who later wishes to participate but did not apply or pay the initial development costs, then that provider may apply to participate if the provider meets all qualifications and pays the same amount in development costs as other participating service providers.

(2) Each qualified service provider shall remit to the Division an annual fee not to exceed three thousand dollars ($ 3,000) on a date prescribed by the Division to be used for the operation and maintenance of the electronic lien system.

(3) Any contract entered into with a service provider shall include no costs or charges payable by the Division to the service provider.

(4) Upon implementation of the electronic lien system pursuant to subsection (a) of this section, the service provider may charge participating lienholders or their agents a per-transaction fee consistent with market pricing.

(5) The contract with the service provider must include provisions specifically prohibiting the service provider from using information concerning vehicle titles for marketing or business solicitation purposes.

(d) Qualified vendors and service providers shall have experience in directly providing electronic solutions to State motor vehicle departments or agencies.

(e) Notwithstanding any requirement in this Chapter that a lien on a motor vehicle shall be noted on the face of the certificate of title, if there are one or more liens or encumbrances on the motor vehicle or mobile home, the Division may electronically transmit the lien to the first lienholder and notify the first lienholder of any additional liens. Subsequent lien satisfactions may be electronically transmitted to the Division and shall include the name and address of the person satisfying the lien.

(f) When electronic transmission of liens and lien satisfactions is used, a certificate of title need not be issued until the last lien is satisfied and a clear certificate of title is issued to the owner of the vehicle.

(g) When a vehicle is subject to an electronic lien, the certificate of title for the vehicle shall be considered to be physically held by the lienholder for purposes of compliance with State or federal odometer disclosure requirements.

(h) A duly certified copy of the Division's electronic record of the lien shall be admissible in any civil, criminal, or administrative proceeding in this State as evidence of the existence of the lien.

(i) **Mandatory Participation.** -- All individuals and lienholders who conduct at least five transactions annually shall utilize the electronic lien system implemented in subsection (a) of this section to record information concerning the perfection and release of a security interest in a vehicle.

(j) **Effect of Electronic Notice or Release.** -- An electronic notice or release of a security interest made through the electronic system implemented pursuant to subsection (a) of this section shall have the same force and effect as a notice or release on a paper document provided under G.S. 20-58 through G.S. 20-58.8.

(k) Nothing in this section shall preclude the Division from collecting a title fee for the preparation and issuance of a title.

(l) The Division may convert an existing paper title to an electronic lien upon request of a primary lienholder. The Division or a party contracting with the Division under this section is authorized to collect a fee not to exceed three dollars ($ 3.00) for each conversion.

History.
2013-341, s. 1;2014-100, s. 34.7(a);2014-115, s. 29(a), (b); 2015-264, s. 40;2018-42, s. 1

EFFECT OF AMENDMENTS. --

Session Laws 2014-100, s. 34.7(a), effective January 1, 2015, added subsection (*l*).

Session Laws 2014-115, s. 29(a), (b), effective August 11, 2014, substituted "January 1, 2015" for "July 1, 2014" in the first sentence of subsection (a) and substituted "January 1, 2016" for "July 1, 2015" in subsection (i).

Session Laws 2015-264, s. 40, effective October 1, 2015, substituted "July 1, 2016" for "January 1, 2016" in subsection (i).

Session Laws 2018-42, s. 1, effective June 22, 2018, substituted "All individuals and lienholders who conduct at least five transactions annually shall" for "Beginning July 1, 2016, all individuals and lienholders who are normally engaged in the business or practice of financing motor vehicles, and who conduct at least five transactions annually, shall" in subsection (i).

CERTIFICATION REQUIRED. --Electronic Lien and Titling Report (ELT Report) proffered by creditor was not admissible and thus, was not prima facie evidence of creditor's claim, because it was hearsay and creditor made no effort to qualify the ELT Report under an exception such as the business or public records exception, and it was apparent that such effort would not have succeeded even if made given that the exceptions themselves required a showing that the evidence was reliable. Further, North Carolina's statutory scheme itself required that ELT Reports be "certified" in order to constitute admissible evidence, and creditor's ELT Report did not meet that standard. In re Ramos, 2020 Bankr. LEXIS 1465 (Bankr. E.D.N.C. June 3, 2020).

§ 20-58.5. Duration of security interest in favor of corporations which dissolve or become inactive

Any security interest recorded in favor of a corporation which, since the recording of such security interest, has dissolved or become inactive for any reason, and which remains of record as a security interest of such corporation for a period of more than three years from the date of such dissolution or becoming inactive, shall become null and void and of no further force and effect.

History.
1961, c. 835, s. 6; 1969, c. 838, s. 1; 1979, c. 145, s. 4

CROSS REFERENCES. --

As to perfection of security interest, see G.S. 20-58.

§ 20-58.6. Duty of secured party to disclose information

A secured party named in a certificate of title shall, upon written request of the Division, the owner or another secured party named on the certificate, disclose information when called upon by such person, within 10 days after his lien shall have been paid and satisfied, and any person convicted under this section shall be fined not more than fifty dollars ($ 50.00) or imprisoned not more than 30 days.

History.
1937, c. 407, s. 23; 1975, c. 716, s. 5

§ 20-58.7. Cancellation of certificate

The cancellation of a certificate of title shall not, in and of itself, affect the validity of a security interest noted on it.

History.
1961, c. 835, s. 6; 1969, c. 838, s. 1

CITED in Peoples Sav. & Loan Assoc. v. Citicorp Acceptance Co., 103 N.C. App. 762, 407 S.E.2d 251 (1991).

§ 20-58.8. Applicability of §§ 20-58 to 20-58.8; use of term "lien"

(a) Repealed by Session Laws 2000, c. 169, s. 30, effective July 1, 2001.

(b) The provisions of G.S. 20-58 through 20-58.8 inclusive shall not apply to or affect:

(1) A lien given by statute or rule of law for storage of a motor vehicle or to a supplier of services or materials for a vehicle;

(2) A lien arising by virtue of a statute in favor of the United States, this State or any political subdivision of this State; or

(3) A security interest in a vehicle created by a manufacturer or by a dealer in new or used vehicles who holds the vehicle in his inventory.

(c) When the term "lien" is used in other sections of this Chapter, or has been used prior to October 1, 1969, with reference to transactions governed by G.S. 20-58 through 20-58.8, to describe contractual agreements creating security interests in personal property, the term "lien" shall be construed to refer to a "security interest" as the term is used in G.S. 20-58 through 20-58.8 and the Uniform Commercial Code.

History.
1961, c. 835, s. 6; 1969, c. 838, s. 1; 2000-169, s. 30

EDITOR'S NOTE. --

The Uniform Commercial Code, referred to in this section, is codified as Chapter 25, G.S. 25-1-101 et seq.

CAR HELD IN INVENTORY BY A USED CAR BUSINESS fell within the provisions of subdivision (b)(3) of this section and G.S. 25-9-302(3)(b). North Carolina Nat'l Bank v. Robinson, 78 N.C. App. 1, 336 S.E.2d 666 (1985).

PERFECTION OF FEDERAL TAX LIEN ON MOTOR VEHICLE. --While the normal method for recording a lien on a motor vehicle is to record it on the certificate of title, subdivision (b)(2) makes that method of perfecting a lien expressly inapplicable to federal tax liens. In re Williams, 109 Bankr. 179 (Bankr. W.D.N.C. 1989).

A federal tax lien attaches to all real and personal property of the debtors pursuant to federal law, and is perfected by the filing of a notice of tax lien. Where that was accomplished in this case in accordance with federal regulation and former G.S. 44-68.1(b)(2), the IRS lien attached to and was secured by debtors' automobiles, regardless of the fact that no lien was noted on the automobiles' titles. In re Williams, 109 Bankr. 179 (Bankr. W.D.N.C. 1989).

APPLIED in American Clipper Corp. v. Howerton, 311 N.C. 151, 316 S.E.2d 186 (1984).

N.C. Gen. Stat. § 20-58.9

Repealed by Session Laws 1969, c. 838, s. 3.

§ 20-58.10. Effective date of §§ 20-58 to 20-58.9

The provisions of G.S. 20-58 through 20-58.9 inclusive shall be effective and relate to the perfecting and giving notice of security interests entered into on and after January 1, 1962.

History.
1961, c. 835, s. 6

APPLIED in Community Credit Co. v. Norwood, 257 N.C. 87, 125 S.E.2d 369 (1962); Ferguson v. Morgan, 282 N.C. 83, 191 S.E.2d 817 (1972).

CITED in Peoples Sav. & Loan Assoc. v. Citicorp Acceptance Co., 103 N.C. App. 762, 407 S.E.2d 251 (1991).

§ 20-59. Unlawful for lienor who holds certificate of title not to surrender same when lien satisfied

It shall be unlawful and constitute a Class 3 misdemeanor for a lienor who holds a certificate of title as provided in this Article to refuse or fail to surrender such certificate of title to the person legally entitled thereto, when called upon by such person, within 10 days after his lien shall have been paid and satisfied.

History.
1937, c. 407, s. 23; 1993, c. 539, s. 332;1994, Ex. Sess., c. 24, s. 14(c)

§ 20-60. Owner after transfer not liable for negligent operation

The owner of a motor vehicle who has made a bona fide sale or transfer of his title or interest, and who has delivered possession of such vehicle and the certificate of title thereto properly endorsed to the purchaser or transferee, shall not be liable for any damages thereafter resulting from negligent operation of such vehicle by another.

History.
1937, c. 407, s. 24

§ 20-61. Owner dismantling or wrecking vehicle to return evidence of registration

Except as permitted under G.S. 20-62.1, any owner dismantling or wrecking any vehicle shall forward to the Division the certificate of title, registration card and other proof of ownership, and the registration plates last issued for such vehicle, unless such plates are to be transferred to another vehicle of the same owner. In that event, the plates shall be retained and preserved by the owner for transfer to such other vehicle. No person, firm or corporation shall dismantle or wreck any motor vehicle without first complying with the requirements of this section. The Commissioner upon receipt of certificate of title and notice from the owner thereof that a vehicle has been junked or dismantled may cancel and destroy such record of certificate of title.

History.
1937, c. 407, s. 25; 1947, c. 219, s. 3; 1961, c. 360, s. 3; 1975, c. 716, s. 5; 2007-505, s. 2

EFFECT OF AMENDMENTS. --
Session Laws 2007-505, s. 2, effective December 1, 2007, and applicable to offenses committed and motor vehicles purchased on or after that date, inserted "Except as permitted under G.S. 20-62.1" at the beginning of the paragraph.

N.C. Gen. Stat. § 20-62

Repealed by Session Laws 1993, c. 533, s. 9.

§ 20-62.1. Purchase of vehicles for purposes of scrap or parts only

(a) **Records for Scrap or Parts. --** A secondary metals recycler, as defined in G.S. 66-420(8), and a salvage yard, as defined in G.S. 20-137.7(6), purchasing motor vehicles solely for the purposes of dismantling or wrecking such motor vehicles for the recovery of scrap metal or for the sale of parts only, shall comply with the provisions of G.S. 20-61 and subsection (a1) of this section, provided, however, that a secondary metals recycler or salvage yard may purchase a motor vehicle without a certificate of title, if the motor vehicle is 10 model years old or older and the secondary metals recycler or salvage yard comply with the following requirements:

(1) Maintain a record on a form, or in a format, as approved by the Division of Motor Vehicles (DMV) of all purchase transactions of motor vehicles. The following

information shall be maintained for trans-actions of motor vehicles:

a. The name, address, and contact information of the secondary metals recycler or salvage yard.

b. The name, initials, or other identi-fication of the individual entering the information.

c. The date of the transaction.

d. A description of the motor vehicle, including the year, make, and model to the extent practicable.

e. The vehicle identification number (VIN) of the vehicle.

f. The amount of consideration given for the motor vehicle.

g. A written statement signed by the seller or the seller's agent certifying that (i) the seller or the seller's agent has the lawful right to sell and dispose of the motor vehicle, (ii) the motor ve-hicle is at least 10 model years old, and (iii) the motor vehicle is not subject to any security interest or lien.

g1. A written statement that the mo-tor vehicle will be scrapped or crushed for disposal or dismantled for parts only.

h. The name, address, and drivers li-cense number of the person from whom the motor vehicle is being purchased.

i. A photocopy or electronic scan of a valid drivers license or identification card issued by the DMV of the seller of the motor vehicle, or seller's agent, to the secondary metals recycler or salvage yard, or in lieu thereof, any other identification card containing a photograph of the seller as issued by any state or federal agency of the United States: provided, that if the buyer has a copy of the seller's photo identification on file, the buyer may reference the identification that is on file, without making a separate photo-copy for each transaction. If seller has no identification as described in this sub-subdivision, the secondary metals recycler or salvage yard shall not com-plete the transaction.

(1a) Verify with the DMV whether or not the motor vehicle has been reported stolen. The DMV shall develop a method to allow a person subject to this section to verify, at the time of the transaction, through the use of the Internet, that the vehicle has not been reported stolen, and that also allows for the DMV's response to be printed and retained by the person making the request. One of the following shall apply following the DMV response:

a. If the Division of Motor Vehicles confirms that the motor vehicle has been reported stolen, the secondary metals recycler or salvage yard shall not complete the transaction and shall notify the DMV of the current location of the vehicle and the identifying in-formation of the person attempting to transfer the vehicle.

b. If the Division of Motor Vehicles confirms that the motor vehicle has not been stolen, the secondary metals recy-cler or salvage yard may proceed with the transaction and shall not be held criminally or civilly liable if the motor vehicle later turns out to be a stolen vehicle, unless the secondary metals recycler had knowledge that the motor vehicle was a stolen vehicle.

c. If the Division of Motor Vehicles has not received information from a federal, State, or local department or independent source that a vehicle has been stolen and reports pursuant to this section that a vehicle is not stolen, any person damaged does not have a cause of action against the Division.

(2) Maintain the information required under subdivision (1) of this subsection, and the record confirming that the vehicle was not stolen, required under subdivision (1a) of this subsection, for not less than two years from the date of the purchase of the motor vehicle.

(a1) **Reporting Requirement.** -- Within 72 hours of each day's close of business, a second-ary metals recycler or salvage yard purchasing a motor vehicle under this section shall submit to the National Motor Vehicle Title Informa-tion System (NMVTIS) such information con-tained in subdivision (1) of subsection (a) of this section, along with any other information or statement pertaining to the intended disposi-tion of the motor vehicle, as may be required. The information shall be in a format that will satisfy the requirement for reporting informa-tion in accordance with rules adopted by the United States Department of Justice in 28 C.F.R. § 25.56. A secondary metals recycler or salvage yard may comply with this subsection by reporting the information required by this subsection to a third-party consolidator as long as the third-party consolidator reports the in-formation to the NMVTIS in compliance with the provisions of this subsection.

(b) **Inspection of Motor Vehicles and Records.** -- At any time it appears a second-ary metals recycler, salvage yard, or any other person involved in secondary metals opera-tions is open for business, a law enforcement officer shall have the right to inspect the fol-lowing:

(1) Any and all motor vehicles in the pos-session of the secondary metals recycler,

Chapter 20

the salvage yard, or any other person involved in secondary metals operations.

    (2) Any records required to be maintained under subsection (a) of this section.

    (b1) **Availability of Information.** -- The information obtained by the Division of Motor Vehicles pursuant to this section shall be made available to law enforcement agencies only. The information submitted pursuant to this section is confidential and shall not be considered a public record as that term is defined in G.S. 132-1.

    (c) **Violations.** -- Any person who knowingly and willfully violates any of the provisions of this section, or any person who falsifies the statement required under subsection (a)(1)g. of this section, shall be guilty of a Class I felony and shall pay a minimum fine of one thousand dollars ($ 1,000). The court may order a defendant seller under this subsection to make restitution to the secondary metals recycler or salvage yard or lien holder for any damage or loss caused by the defendant seller arising out of an offense committed by the defendant seller.

    (d) **Confiscation of Vehicle or Tools Used in Illegal Sale.** -- Any motor vehicle used to transport another motor vehicle illegally sold under this section may be seized by law enforcement and is subject to forfeiture by the court, provided, however, that no vehicle used by any person in the transaction of a sale of regulated metals is subject to forfeiture unless it appears that the owner or other person in charge of the motor vehicle is a consenting party or privy to the commission of a crime, and a forfeiture of the vehicle encumbered by a bona fide security interest is subject to the interest of the secured party who had no knowledge of or consented to the act.

Whenever property is forfeited under this subsection by order of the court, the law enforcement agency having custody of the property shall sell any forfeited property which is not required to be destroyed by law and which is not harmful to the public, provided that the proceeds are remitted to the Civil Fines and Forfeitures Fund established pursuant to G.S. 115C-457.1.

    (e) **Exemptions.** -- As used in this section, the term "motor vehicle" shall not include motor vehicles which have been mechanically flattened, crushed, baled, or logged and sold for purposes of scrap metal only.

    (f) **Preemption.** -- No local government shall enact any local law or ordinance with regards to the regulation of the sale of motor vehicles to secondary metals recyclers or salvage yards.

History.

2007-505, s. 1;2012-46, s. 30;2013-323, s. 2;2013-410, s. 28(a)

EDITOR'S NOTE. --

Session Laws 2007-505, s. 4, makes this section effective December 1, 2007, and applicable to offenses committed and motor vehicles purchased on or after that date.

The reference in subsection (a) to "G.S. 66-415(8)" was changed to "G.S. 66-420(8)" at the direction of the Revisor of Statutes to conform to the renumbering of that section by the Revisor.

EFFECT OF AMENDMENTS. --

Session Laws 2012-46, s. 30, substituted "G.S. 66-415(8)" for "G.S. 66-11(a)(3)" in the introductory paragraph of subsection (a). For effective date, applicability, and change of the internal reference from "G.S. 66-415(8)" to "G.S. 66-420(8)," see Editor's notes.

Session Laws 2013-323, s. 2, effective for reports and transactions occurring on or after December 1, 2013, added subdivision (a)(1)g1., subdivision (a)(1a), and subsections (a1) and (b1); in subsection (a), substituted "shall comply with the provisions of G.S. 20-61 and subsection (a1) of this section" for "must comply with the provision of G.S. 20-61"; inserted "on a form, or in a format, as approved by the Division of Motor Vehicles (DMV)" in subdivision (a)(1); substituted "name, address, and contact information" for "name and address" in subdivision (a)(1)a.; inserted "year" preceding "make" in sub-subdivision (a)(1)d.; in subdivision (a)(1)g., inserted the clause "(i)" designation and added clauses (ii) and (iii); in subdivision (a)(1)h., substituted "name, address, and drivers license number" for "name and address" and "DMV" for "Division of Motor Vehicles"; in subdivision (a)(2), inserted "and the record confirming that the vehicle was not stolen, required under subdivision (1a) of this subsection"; in subsection (c), substituted "Class I felony and shall pay a minimum fine of one thousand dollars ($1,000)" for "Class 1 misdemeanor for a first offense. A second or subsequent violation of this section is a Class I felony" and added "or lien holder"; and made stylistic changes. For applicability, see Editor's note.

Session Laws 2013-410, s. 28(a), effective August 23, 2013, added subdivision (a)(1a)c.

§ 20-63. Registration plates furnished by Division; requirements; replacement of regular plates with First in Flight plates, First in Freedom plates, or National/State Mottos plates; surrender and reissuance; displaying; preservation and cleaning; alteration or concealment of numbers; commission contracts for issuance

    (a) The Division upon registering a vehicle shall issue to the owner one registration plate for a motorcycle, trailer or semitrailer and for every other motor vehicle. Registration plates issued by the Division under this Article shall be and remain the property of the State, and it shall be lawful for the Commissioner or his duly authorized agents to summarily take possession of any plate or plates which he has reason to believe is being illegally used, and to keep in his possession such plate or plates pending investigation and legal disposition of the same. Whenever the Commissioner finds that any registration plate issued for any vehicle pursuant to the provisions of this Article has become illegible or is in such a condition that the numbers thereon may not be readily distinguished, he may require that such registration plate, and its companion when there are two registration plates, be surrendered to the Division. When said registration plate or plates are so surrendered to the Division, a new registration plate or plates shall be issued in lieu thereof without charge. The owner of any vehicle who receives notice to surrender illegible plate or plates on which the numbers are not readily distinguishable and who willfully refuses to surrender said plates to the Division shall be guilty of a Class 2 misdemeanor.

(b) Every license plate must display the registration number assigned to the vehicle for which it is issued, the name of the State of North Carolina, which may be abbreviated, and the year number for which it is issued or the date of expiration. A plate issued for a commercial vehicle, as defined in G.S. 20-4.2(1), and weighing 26,001 pounds or more, must bear the word "commercial," unless the plate is a special registration plate authorized in G.S. 20-79.4 or the commercial vehicle is a trailer or is licensed for 6,000 pounds or less. The plate issued for vehicles licensed for 7,000 pounds through 26,000 pounds must bear the word "weighted," unless the plate is a special registration plate authorized in G.S. 20-79.4.

A registration plate issued by the Division for a private passenger vehicle or for a private hauler vehicle licensed for 6,000 pounds or less shall be, at the option of the owner, either (i) a "First in Flight" plate, (ii) a "First in Freedom" plate, or (iii) a "National/State Mottos" plate. A "First in Flight" plate shall have the words "First in Flight" printed at the top of the plate above all other letters and numerals. The background of the "First in Flight" plate shall depict the Wright Brothers biplane flying over Kitty Hawk Beach, with the plane flying slightly upward and to the right. A "First in Freedom" plate shall have the words "First in Freedom" printed at the top of the plate above all other letters and numerals. The background of the "First in Freedom" plate may include an image chosen by the Division that is representative of the Mecklenburg Declaration of 1775 or the Halifax Resolves of 1776. A "National/State Mottos" plate shall have in words the motto of the United States "In God We Trust" printed at the top of the plate above all other letters and numerals and have in words the State motto "To Be Rather Than To Seem". The background of the "National/State Mottos" plate shall include an image chosen by the Division that is representative of the American Flag.

(b1) The following special registration plates do not have to be a "First in Flight" plate, "First in Freedom" plate, or "National/State Mottos" plate as provided in subsection (b) of this section. The design of the plates that are not "First in Flight" plates, "First in Freedom" plates, or "National/State Mottos" plate must be developed in accordance with G.S. 20-79.4(a3). For special plates authorized in G.S. 20-79.7 on or after July 1, 2013, the Division may not issue the plate on a background under this subsection unless it receives the required number of applications set forth in G.S. 20-79.3A(a).

(1) AIDS Awareness -- Expired July 1, 2016.

(2) Alpha Phi Alpha.

(3) **ARTS NC.**

(4) Back Country Horsemen of North Carolina -- Expired July 1, 2016.

(5) Battle of Kings Mountain.

(6) Big Rock Blue Marlin Tournament.

(7) Blue Ridge Parkway Foundation.

(8) Buddy Pelletier Surfing Foundation.

(9) Carolina Panthers.

(10) Carolina Raptor Center -- Expired July 1, 2016.

(11) Carolinas Credit Union Foundation -- Expired July 1, 2016.

(12) Choose Life.

(13) Coastal Land Trust.

(14) Colorectal Cancer Awareness.

(15) Core Sound Waterfowl Museum and Heritage Center.

(16) Donate Life.

(17) Ducks Unlimited.

(18) Farmland Preservation -- Expired July 1, 2016.

(19) First in Forestry.

(20) Fox Hunting -- Expired July 1, 2016.

(21) Friends of the Appalachian Trail.

(22) Friends of the Great Smoky Mountains National Park.

(23) Guilford Battleground Company.

(24) Home Care and Hospice.

(25) Hospice Care -- Expired July 1, 2016.

(26) In God We Trust.

(27) Kappa Alpha Psi Fraternity.

(28) Keeping The Lights On.

(29) Lung Cancer Research -- Expired July 1, 2016.

(30) Mountains-to-Sea Trail, Inc.

(31) National Wild Turkey Federation.

(32) Native Brook Trout.

(33) NC Civil War -- Expired July 1, 2016.

(34) NC Coastal Federation.

(35) NC Horse Council.

(36) NC Mining -- Expired July 1, 2016.

(37) NC State Parks.

(38) NC Surveyors.

(39) NC Tennis Foundation.

(40) NC Trout Unlimited.

(41) North Carolina Aquarium Society.

(42) North Carolina Green Industry Council -- Expired July 1, 2016.

(43) North Carolina Sheriffs' Association.

(44) North Carolina State Flag -- Expired July 1, 2016.

(45) North Carolina Wildlife Habitat Foundation.

(46) North Carolina Zoological Society.

(47) Order of the Long Leaf Pine.

(48) Pisgah Conservancy.

(49) POW/MIA Bring Them Home.

(50) Red Drum -- Expired July 1, 2016.

(51) Rocky Mountain Elk Foundation.

(52) Save the Honey Bee (SB).

(53) S.T.A.R. -- Expired July 1, 2016.

(54) Stock Car Racing Theme.

(55) Support Our Troops.

(56) Travel and Tourism -- Expired July 1, 2016.

(57) United States Service Academy.

(58) US Equine Rescue League -- Expired July 1, 2016.

(c) Such registration plate and the required numerals thereon, except the year number for which issued, shall be of sufficient size to be plainly readable from a distance of 100 feet during daylight.

(d) Registration plates issued for a motor vehicle other than a motorcycle, trailer, or semi-trailer shall be attached thereto, one in the front and the other in the rear: Provided, that when only one registration plate is issued for a motor vehicle other than a truck-tractor, said registration plate shall be attached to the rear of the motor vehicle. The registration plate issued for a truck-tractor shall be attached to the front thereof. Provided further, that when only one registration plate is issued for a motor vehicle and this motor vehicle is transporting a substance that may adhere to the plate so as to cover or discolor the plate or if the motor vehicle has a mechanical loading device that may damage the plate, the registration plate may be attached to the front of the motor vehicle.

Any motor vehicle of the age of 35 years or more from the date of manufacture may bear the license plates of the year of manufacture instead of the current registration plates, if the current registration plates are maintained within the vehicle and produced upon the request of any person.

The Division shall provide registered owners of motorcycles and property hauling motorcycle trailers attached to the rear of motorcycles with suitably reduced size registration plates, approximately four by seven inches in size, that are issued on a multiyear basis in accordance with G.S. 20-88(c), or on an annual basis as otherwise provided in this Chapter.

(e) **Preservation and Cleaning of Registration Plates.** -- It shall be the duty of each and every registered owner of a motor vehicle to keep the registration plates assigned to such motor vehicle reasonably clean and free from dust and dirt, and such registered owner, or any person in his employ, or who operates such motor vehicle by his authority, shall, upon the request of any proper officer, immediately clean such registration plates so that the numbers thereon may be readily distinguished, and any person who shall neglect or refuse to so clean a registration plate, after having been requested to do so, shall be guilty of a Class 3 misdemeanor.

(f) **Operating with False Numbers.** -- Any person who shall willfully operate a motor vehicle with a registration plate which has been repainted or altered or forged shall be guilty of a Class 2 misdemeanor.

(g) **Alteration, Disguise, or Concealment of Numbers.** -- Any operator of a motor vehicle who shall willfully mutilate, bend, twist, cover or cause to be covered or partially covered by any bumper, light, spare tire, tire rack, strap, or other device, or who shall paint, enamel, emboss, stamp, print, perforate, or alter or add to or cut off any part or portion of a registration plate or the figures or letters thereon, or who shall place or deposit or cause to be placed or deposited any oil, grease, or other substance upon such registration plates for the purpose of making dust adhere thereto, or who shall deface, disfigure, change, or attempt to change any letter or figure thereon, or who shall display a number plate in other than a horizontal upright position, shall be guilty of a Class 2 misdemeanor. Any operator of a motor vehicle who shall willfully cover or cause to be covered any part or portion of a registration plate or the figures or letters thereon by any device designed or intended to prevent or interfere with the taking of a clear photograph of a registration plate by a traffic control or toll collection system using cameras commits an infraction and shall be penalized under G.S. 14-3.1. Any operator of a motor vehicle who shall otherwise intentionally cover any number or registration renewal sticker on a registration plate with any material that makes the number or registration renewal sticker illegible commits an infraction and shall be penalized under G.S. 14-3.1. Any operator of a motor vehicle who covers any registration plate with any frame or transparent, clear, or color-tinted cover that makes a number or letter included in the vehicle's registration, the State name on the plate, or a number or month on the registration renewal sticker on the plate illegible commits an infraction and shall be penalized under G.S. 14-3.1.

(h) **Commission Contracts for Issuance of Plates and Certificates.** -- All registration plates, registration certificates, and certificates of title issued by the Division, outside of those issued from the office of the Division located in Wake, Cumberland, or Mecklenburg Counties and those issued and handled through the United States mail, shall be issued insofar as practicable and possible through commission contracts entered into by the Division for the issuance of the plates and certificates in localities throughout North Carolina, including military installations within this State, with persons, firms, corporations or governmental subdivisions of the State of North Carolina. The Division shall make a reasonable effort in every locality, except as noted above, to enter into a commission contract for the issuance of the plates and certificates and a record of these efforts shall be maintained in the Division. In the event the Division is unsuccessful in making commission contracts, it shall issue the plates and certificates through the regular employees of the Division. Whenever registration plates, registration certificates, and certificates of title are issued by the Division through commission contract arrangements, the Division shall provide proper supervision of the distribution. Nothing contained in this subsection allows or permits the operation of fewer outlets in any county in this State than are now being operated.

The terms of a commission contract entered under this subsection shall specify the duration of the contract and either include or incorporate by reference standards by which the Division may supervise and evaluate the performance of the commission contractor. The duration of an initial commission contract may not exceed eight years and the duration of a renewal commission contract may not exceed two years. The Division may award monetary performance bonuses, not to exceed an aggregate total of ninety thousand dollars ($ 90,000) annually, to commission contractors based on their performance.

The amount of compensation payable to a commission contractor is determined on a per transaction basis. The collection of the highway use tax and the removal of an inspection stop are each considered a separate transaction for which one dollar and fifty-six cents ($ 1.56) compensation shall be paid. The issuance of a limited registration "T" sticker and the collection of property tax are each considered a separate transaction for which compensation at the rate of one dollar and thirty cents ($ 1.30) and one dollar and eight cents ($ 1.08) respectively, shall be paid by counties and municipalities as a cost of the combined motor vehicle registration renewal and property tax collection system. The performance at the same time of one or more of the transactions below is considered a single transaction for which one dollar and seventy-five cents ($ 1.75) compensation shall be paid:

(1) Issuance of a registration plate, a registration card, a registration sticker, or a certificate of title.

(2) Issuance of a handicapped placard or handicapped identification card.

(3) Acceptance of an application for a personalized registration plate.

(4) Acceptance of a surrendered registration plate, registration card, or registration renewal sticker, or acceptance of an affidavit stating why a person cannot surrender a registration plate, registration card, or registration renewal sticker.

(5) Cancellation of a title because the vehicle has been junked.

(6) Acceptance of an application for, or issuance of, a refund for a fee or a tax, other than the highway use tax.

(7) Receipt of the civil penalty imposed by G.S. 20-311 for a lapse in financial responsibility or receipt of the restoration fee imposed by that statute.

(8) Acceptance of a notice of failure to maintain financial responsibility for a motor vehicle.

(8a) Collection of civil penalties imposed for violations of G.S. 20-183.8A.

(8b), (9) Repealed by Session Laws 2013-372, s. 2(a), effective July 1, 2013.

(10) Acceptance of a temporary lien filing.

(11) Conversion of an existing paper title to an electronic lien upon request of a primary lienholder.

(h1) Commission contracts entered into by the Division under this subsection shall also provide for the payment of an additional one dollar ($ 1.00) of compensation to commission contract agents for any transaction assessed a fee under subdivision (a)(1), (a)(2), (a)(3), (a)(7), (a)(8), or (a)(9) of G.S. 20-85.

(h2) Upon the closing of the only contract license plate agency in a county, the Division shall as soon as practicable designate a temporary location for the issuance of all registration plates, registration certificates, and certificates of title issued by the Division for that county. The designation shall be posted at the former agency location for not less than 30 days and shall include the street address and telephone number of the temporary location. A former contract agent shall allow the posting of this required notice at the former location for a period of not less than 30 days. A failure to comply with the posting requirements of this section by a former contract agent shall be a Class 3 misdemeanor.

(i) **Electronic Applications and Collections.** -- The Division shall accept electronic applications for the issuance of registration plates, registration certificates, salvage certificates of title, and certificates of title, and is authorized to electronically collect fees from online motor vehicle registration vendors under contract with the Division.

(j) The Division shall contract with at least two online motor vehicle registration vendors which may enter into contracts with motor vehicle dealers to complete and file Division required documents for the issuance of a certificate of title, registration plate, or registration card or a duplicate certificate of title, registration plate, or registration card for a motor vehicle, upon purchase or sale of a vehicle. Vendors under contract with the Division pursuant to this subsection may also enter into contracts with used motor vehicle dealers whose primary business is the sale of salvage vehicles on behalf of insurers to complete and file documents required by the Division for the issuance of a salvage certificate of title.

(k) Commission contract agents are authorized to enter into contracts with online motor vehicle registration vendors which are under contract with the Division to complete and file Division required documents for the issuance of a certificate of title, registration plate, or registration card or a duplicate certificate of title, registration plate, or registration card for a motor vehicle.

History.
1937, c. 407, s. 27; 1943, c. 726; 1951, c. 102, ss. 1-3; 1955, c. 119, s. 1; 1961, c. 360, s. 4; c. 861, s. 2; 1963, c. 552, s. 6; c. 1071; 1965, c. 1088; 1969, c. 1140; 1971, c. 945; 1973, c. 629; 1975, c. 716, s. 5; 1979, c. 470, s. 1; c. 604, s. 1; c. 917, s. 4; 1981, c. 750; c. 859, s. 76; 1983, c. 253, ss. 1-3; 1985, c. 257; 1991 (Reg. Sess., 1992), c. 1007, s. 32; 1993, c. 539, ss. 333 -336; 1994, Ex. Sess., c. 24, s. 14(c);1997-36, s. 1;1997-443, s. 32.7(a);1997-461, s. 1;1998-160, s. 3;1998-212, ss. 15.4(a), 27.6(a); 1999-452, ss. 13, 14; 2000-182, s. 3;2001-424, s. 27.21;2001-487, s. 50(c);2002-159, s. 31.1;2003-424, s. 1;2004-77, s. 1;2004-79, s. 1;2004-131, s. 1;2004-185, s. 1;2005-216, s. 1;2006-209, s. 1;2006-213, s. 4;2007-243, s. 1;2007-400, s. 1;2007-483, s. 1;2007-488, ss. 2 -5; 2008-225, s. 8;2009-445, s. 24(b1);2009-456, s. 1;2010-96, s. 40(a);2010-132, ss. 2, 3; 2011-382, s. 4;2011-392, ss. 1, 1.1; 2012-79, s. 1.12(a);2013-87, s. 1;2013-372, s. 2(a);2013-376, s. 9(a), (b), (d); 2014-3, s. 13.2;2014-96, s. 2;2014-100, ss. 8.11(e), 34.7(b), 34.28(a); 2015-241, ss. 29.32(a), 29.40(a); 2015-264, s. 40.6(a);2015-286, s. 3.5(a);2016-120, s. 2;2017-107, s. 1;2017-114, s. 1;2018-5, s. 34.27(a);2018-74, ss. 12(a), 16.10; 2018-77, s. 2(a);2019-153, s. 2;2019-213, s. 2(a);2019-231, s. 4.18(a)
INACTIVE SPECIAL INTEREST PLATES. --Pursuant to G.S. 20-79.8(a), several special plates authorized by G.S. 20-79.4 prior to October 1, 2014, expired as a matter of law on July 1, 2016, because the number of applications required for their production was not received by the Division of Motor Vehicles. At the direction of the Revisor of Statutes, pursuant to G.S. 20-79.8(c), those special plates not meeting this requirement have been set out as expired effective July 1, 2016.

EDITOR'S NOTE. --
Subdivisions (b)(21) through (b)(24), as enacted by Session Laws 2007-483, s. 1, have been redesignated as subdivisions (b)(22) through (b)(25), at the direction of the Revisor of Statutes.

Session Laws 2011-382, s. 1, provides: "The Joint Legislative Program Evaluation Oversight Committee shall include in the 2011-2012 Work Plan for the Program Evaluation Division of the General Assembly a study to evaluate the Division of Motor Vehicles' Commission Contract for the Issuance of Plates and Certificates program, authorized in G.S. 20-63(h), to determine the cost-effectiveness and savings that can be effected by changing or maintaining the current operating procedures and to develop any plans or practices that, if implemented, would result in increased operating efficiency of the Division of Motor Vehicles' Commission Contract program."

Session Laws 2011-382, s. 2, provides: "The Program Evaluation Division shall submit its findings and recommendations for Section 1 of this act to the Joint Legislative Program Evaluation Oversight Committee, the Joint Legislative Transportation Oversight Committee, and the Fiscal Research Division at a date to be determined by the Joint Legislative Program Evaluation Oversight Committee."

Session Laws 2011-382, s. 3, provides: "The Commissioner of Motor Vehicles shall not cancel or amend any commission contracts for any reason other than malfeasance, misfeasance, or nonfeasance of the commission contractor until the study required by this act is complete and final recommendations have been acted upon by the Joint Legislative Program Evaluation Oversight Committee."

Session Laws 2011-392, s. 1.1, effective July 1, 2016, repealed subsection (b1). Session Laws 2013-376, s. 9(b), effective July 29, 2013, repealed Session Laws 2011-392, s. 1.1. Session Laws 2013-376, s. 9(d), amended the effective date provision in Session Laws 2011-392, s. 12, to remove the reference to Session Laws 2011-392, s. 1.1.

Session Laws 2011-392, s. 9, provides: "Notwithstanding Section 8 of this act, any special registration plate authorized in G.S. 20-79.7, prior to July 1, 2011, shall expire, as a matter of law, on July 1, 2013, if the number of applications required for the production of the special registration plate has not been received by the Division of Motor Vehicles on or before that date. Upon notification of expiration of the authorization for any special plate by the Division pursuant to this section, the Revisor of Statutes shall verify that the authorization for each special registration plate listed has expired and shall notate such expiration in the applicable statutes. If an authorization for a special registration plate listed in G.S. 20-79.4 expires, the Revisor of Statutes shall revise the subdivision referring to the special registration plate to leave the name of the special plate authorized and the date the special registration plate's authorization expired. If an authorization for a special registration plate listed in G.S. 20-79.4 expires, the Revisor of Statutes shall also make corresponding changes to reflect the expiration of the special registration plate's authorization, if applicable, in G.S. 20-63(b), 20-79.7, and 20-81.12."

Session Laws 2011-392, s. 11, provides: "The Department of Crime Control and Public Safety [now Department of Public Safety] and the Department of

Transportation shall study whether, for purposes of effective law enforcement, full-color special license plates should continue to be authorized or be phased out, with all special license plates being on the First in Flight background. The study shall also include an estimate of the replacement costs and recommendations for funding those costs. The Departments shall report their findings and make recommendations to the Joint Legislative Transportation Oversight Committee on or before the convening of the 2012 Regular Session of the 2011 General Assembly. The Joint Legislative Transportation Oversight Committee shall make any legislative recommendations based on the study to the 2012 Regular Session of the 2011 General Assembly."

Session Laws 2013-372, s. 2(c), as amended by Session Laws 2014-3, s. 13.1, provides: "Notwithstanding G.S. 20-63(h), as amended by subsection (a) of this section, the transaction rate of one dollar and six cents ($1.06) applies to the collection of property tax by commission contractors for vehicles whose registration renewals expire on or between September 30, 2013, and June 30, 2014."

Session Laws 2013-372, s. 3, provides: "Implementation by the Division of Motor Vehicles of the Department of Transportation of an integrated computer system that combines vehicle registration with the collection of property tax includes training commission contractors under G.S. 20-63(h) on the use of that integrated computer system. The cost of the system training required of the commission contractors on or after April 1, 2013, and before July 1, 2013, is a cost of the combined motor vehicle registration renewal and property tax collection system and is payable from the Combined Motor Vehicle and Registration Account, established under G.S. 105-330.10."

Session Laws 2014-3, s. 13.1(b), provides: "The Division of Motor Vehicles must compensate license plate agents the additional fee for the collection of property taxes as provided in this section. For the period between March 1, 2014, and the date the Division of Motor Vehicles is able to implement the additional fee, the Division must calculate the difference in the fee for agents contracting with the Division authorized by this section and the fee authorized in S.L. 2013-372. The Division must calculate the difference by September 1, 2014. The difference in the fee must be paid to the agents by reducing future remittances of tax payments to counties and municipalities under the Tax and Tag Together Program in equal amounts over a three month period."

Session Laws 2014-3, s. 13.5, made the amendment to this section by Session Laws 2014-3, s. 13.2, applicable to collections of property tax on or after July 1, 2014.

Session Laws 2014-96, s. 1(a), provides: "Any special registration plate authorized under G.S. 20-79.4 that expired as a matter of law on July 1, 2013, pursuant to G.S. 20-79.8, is reenacted. The corresponding provisions for fees under G.S. 20-79.7(a1) and (b) and any other corresponding requirements for the plates under G.S. 20-81.12 are also reenacted. A special registration plate reenacted under this section is subject to the requirements of G.S. 20-63(b1) if the plate is

authorized to be on a background other than a "First in Flight" background."

Session Laws 2014-96, s. 1(b), provides: "This section is effective when it becomes law. A special registration plate reenacted by this section shall expire, as a matter of law, on October 1, 2014, if the required number of applications for the special registration plate has not been received by the Division of Motor Vehicles by that date. The notification procedure and the responsibilities of the Revisor of Statutes for a special registration plate that expires pursuant to this subsection shall be in accordance with G.S. 20-79.8 except that the notification date shall be no later than October 15, 2015. The Division shall not accept applications for nor advertise any special registration plate that has expired pursuant to this subsection."

Subdivisions (b1)(44) through (47) as added by Session Laws 2014-96, s. 2, were renumbered as (b1)(45) through (48) at the direction of the Revisor of Statutes.

Session Laws 2014-100, s. 34.28(d), made the amendment to this section by Session Laws 2014-100, s. 34.28(a), effective July 1, 2015, and applicable to registration plates issued on or after that date.

Session Laws 2015-241, s. 29.32(b), provides: "All commission contracts entered into by the Division of Motor Vehicles under G.S. 20-63(h) after the effective date of this subsection shall specify the duration of the contract and include or incorporate by reference the standards required under subsection (a) of this section. No later than July 1, 2018, all other commission contracts entered into by the Division of Motor Vehicles shall specify the duration of the contract and include or incorporate by reference the standards required under subsection (a) of this section."

Session Laws 2015-241, s. 29.32(c), made the compensation rates set forth in subsection (h) of this section, as amended by Session Laws 2015-241, s. 29.32(a), effective July 1, 2015, and applicable to transactions on or after that date.

Session Laws 2015-241, s. 29.40(s), provides: "Subsections (r) and (s) of this section are effective when this act becomes law. The remainder of this section is effective 90 days after this act becomes law."

Session Laws 2015-241, s. 1.1, provides: "This act shall be known as 'The Current Operations and Capital Improvements Appropriations Act of 2015.'"

Session Laws 2015-241, s. 33.4, provides: "Except for statutory changes or other provisions that clearly indicate an intention to have effects beyond the 2015-2017 fiscal biennium, the textual provisions of this act apply only to funds appropriated for, and activities occurring during, the 2015-2017 fiscal biennium."

Session Laws 2015-241, s. 33.6, is a severability clause.

Session Laws 2015-264, s. 40.6(c), provides: "Nothing in G.S. 20-63(b1) or G.S. 20-79.3A(a) shall be construed as requiring an additional 200 applications for the Division of Motor Vehicles to issue a full-color background 'Kappa Alpha Psi Fraternity' special registration plate in accordance with G.S. 20-63(b1), as amended by subsection (a) of this section."

Session Laws 2015-264, s. 40.6(d) provides: "This section becomes effective 90 days after S.L. 2015-241 becomes law." Session Laws 2015-241 became law September 18, 2015.

Session Laws 2015-264, s. 91.7, is a severability clause.

Session Laws 2016-120, s. 3, provides: "The Division of Motor Vehicles of the Department of Transportation is directed to study the following and to report its findings and recommendations to the Joint Legislative Transportation Oversight Committee by December 1, 2017:

"(1) The number of State vehicle inspection stops that were overridden in the two most recent fiscal years due to the failure of data to be transmitted timely from an inspection station to the State Titling and Registration System (STARS) or due to other reasons.

"(2) Any changes, in the process or in the law, required to reduce or eliminate the need for commission contractors to override, through a cumbersome data entry process, an incorrect State inspection stop.

"(3) The number of vehicles registered in the State in the two most recent fiscal years that were subject to inspection under federal law.

"(4) The process by which data is entered in STARS to reflect that a vehicle has met the federal inspection requirement and whether this process can be made simpler."

Subdivisions (b1)(54) through (56), as added by Session Laws 2017-114, s. 1, were renumbered as subdivisions (b1)(55) through (57) at the direction of the Revisor of Statutes.

Session Laws 2018-5, s. 1.1, provides: "This act shall be known as the 'Current Operations Appropriations Act of 2018.'"

Session Laws 2018-5, s. 39.7, is a severability clause.

Session Laws 2018-74, s. 12(a), and 2018-77, s. 2(a) are identical, effective February 1, 2019, and reenacted subdivision (b1)(47) as it existed immediately before its repeal.

Session Laws 2019-213, s. 2(e), provides: "The Revisor of Statutes is authorized to alphabetize, number, and renumber the special registration plates listed in G.S. 20-63(b1), 20-79.4(b), and 20-81.12 to ensure that all the special registration plates are listed in alphabetical order and numbered accordingly." Pursuant to this authority, the subdivisions in subsection (b1) have been renumbered.

Session Laws 2019-227, s. 7, provides: "The Joint Legislative Transportation Oversight Committee shall study the feasibility of making digital license plates available to the public as an alternative to traditional physical registration plates currently issued by the Division of Motor Vehicles. The Committee shall report its findings, together with any recommended legislation, to the 2020 Regular Session of the 2019 General Assembly."

Session Laws 2019-231, s. 4.18(b), made the amendment to subsection (h) of this section by Session Laws 2019-231, s. 4.18(a), effective October 18, 2019, and applicable to transactions on or after that date.

Session Laws 2019-231, s. 5.3, provides: "Except for statutory changes or other provisions that clearly

indicate an intention to have effects beyond the 2019-2021 fiscal biennium, the textual provisions of this act apply only to funds appropriated for, and activities occurring during, the 2019-2021 fiscal biennium." Session Laws 2019-231, s. 5.5, is a severability clause.

EFFECT OF AMENDMENTS. --

Session Laws 2004-77, s. 1, effective October 1, 2004, and applicable to fees assessed on or after that date inserted subsection (h1).

Session Laws 2004-79, s. 1, effective October 1, 2004, and applicable to acts committed on or after that date, inserted the second and fourth sentences of subsection (g).

Session Laws 2004-131, s. 1, effective July 29, 2004, added subdivision (b)(6).

Session Laws 2004-185, s. 1, effective October 1, 2004, added the subdivision designated herein as subdivision (b)(7).

Session Laws 2005-216, s. 1, effective July 20, 2005, added subdivisions (b)(8) through (b)(14).

Session Laws 2006-209, s. 1, effective August 8, 2006, added subdivisions (b)(15) through (b)(20).

Session Laws 2006-213, s. 4, effective July 1, 2008, and applicable to lapses occurring on or after that date, substituted "G.S. 20-311" for "G.S. 20-309" in subdivision (h)(7).

Session Laws 2007-243, s. 1, effective July 20, 2007, added subsection (h2).

Session Laws 2007-400, s. 1, effective August 21, 2007, added subdivision (b)(21).

Session Laws 2007-483, s. 1, effective August 30, 2007, added subdivisions (b)(22) through (b)(25).

Session Laws 2007-488, ss. 2 through 5, effective August 30, 2007, in subsection (h), inserted "Charlotte and" in the first sentence; in subsection (i), substituted "shall accept" for "is authorized to accept" and "is authorized to electronically collect fees from online motor vehicle registration vendors under contract with the Division" for "to electronically collect fees and penalties"; and added subsections (j) and (k).

Session Laws 2008-225, s. 8, effective December 1, 2008, inserted "or toll collection" following "traffic control" twice in subsection (g).

Session Laws 2009-445, s. 24(b1), effective August 7, 2009, inserted "issued without collection of property taxes or fees under G.S. 105-330.5" in subdivision (h)(1).

Session Laws 2009-456, s. 1, effective December 1, 2009, and applicable to offenses committed on or after that date, in subsection (g), inserted the next-to-last sentence and in the last sentence, substituted "do not prevent" for "are not designed or intended to prevent." See Editor's note for applicability.

Session Laws 2010-96, s. 40(a), effective December 1, 2010, and applicable to offenses committed on or after that date, in the last sentence in subsection (g), substituted "transparent, clear" for "transparent clear" and "number or letter included in the vehicles registration" for "number or letter on the plate."

Session Laws 2010-132, ss. 2 and 3, effective December 1, 2010, and applicable to offenses committed on or after that date, in the first paragraph in subsection (b), in the first sentence, substituted "Every license plate must display" for "Every license plate shall have displayed upon it," and in the last sentence, added "unless the plate is a special registration plate authorized in G.S. 20-79.4"; and in subsection (g), in the second and third sentences, substituted "shall be penalized" for "shall be fined," added the last sentence, and deleted the former last two sentences, which read: "Any operator of a motor vehicle who covers the State name, year sticker, or month sticker on a registration plate with a license plate frame commits an infraction and shall be fined under G.S. 14-3.1. Nothing in this subsection shall prohibit the use of transparent covers that do not prevent or interfere with the taking of a clear photograph of a registration plate by a traffic control or toll collection system using cameras."

Session Laws 2011-382, s. 4, effective June 27, 2011, in the first sentence of subsection (h), substituted "Charlotte, Fort Bragg and Raleigh offices" for "Charlotte and Raleigh offices" and inserted "including military installations within this State."

Session Laws 2011-392, s. 1, effective June 30, 2011, in the last paragraph of subsection (b), deleted "Except as otherwise provided in this subsection" from the beginning; and added the subsection (b1) designation, and therein, in the first paragraph, added "as provided in subsection (b) of this section" in the first sentence, and added the last sentence.

Session Laws 2012-79, s. 1.12(a), effective June 26, 2012, added subdivision (b1)(43).

Session Laws 2013-87, s. 1, effective July 1, 2013, substituted "office of the Division located in Wake, Cumberland, or Mecklenburg Counties" for "Charlotte, Fort Bragg and Raleigh offices of the Division" in the first sentence of subsection (h).

Session Laws 2013-372, s. 2(a), effective July 1, 2013, in the second paragraph of subsection (h), substituted "is" for "shall be" following "use tax" in the second sentence, added the third sentence, and in the fourth sentence, substituted "transactions below is" for "remaining transactions listed in this subsection shall be" and deleted the former third paragraph, which read: "A transaction is any of the following activities:"; in subdivision (h)(1), deleted "issued without collection of property taxes or fees under G.S. 105-330.5" following "card" and "renewal" preceding "sticker"; and deleted subdivisions (h)(8b) and (h)(9), pertaining to sale of inspection stickers to inspection stations and collection of the highway use tax.

Session Laws 2013-376, s. 9(a), effective July 29, 2013, rewrote the second and third sentences of subsection (b1), which formerly read "The design of the plates that are not 'First in Flight' plates must be approved by the Division and the State Highway Patrol for clarity and ease of identification. When the Division registers a vehicle or renews the registration of a vehicle on or after July 1, 2015, the Division must send the owner a replacement special license plate in a standardized format in accordance with subsection (b) of this section and G.S. 20-79.4(a3)."

Session Laws 2014-3, s. 13.2, effective July 1, 2014, in subsection (h), substituted "one dollar and six cents ($1.06)" for "seventy one cents ($0.71)" in the third sentence of the second paragraph, and made a minor stylistic change. See Editor's note for applicability.

Session Laws 2014-96, s. 2, effective August 1, 2014, added subdivisions (b1)(44) through (b1)(47).

Session Laws 2014-100, s. 8.11(e), effective July 1, 2014, added subdivision (b1)(44).

Session Laws 2014-3, s. 13.2, effective July 1, 2014, in subsection (h), substituted "one dollar and six cents ($1.06)" for "seventy one cents ($0.71)" in the third sentence of the second paragraph, and made a minor stylistic change. See Editor's note for applicability.

Session Laws 2014-96, s. 2, effective August 1, 2014, added subdivisions (b1)(45) through (b1)(48).

Session Laws 2014-100, s. 8.11(e), effective July 1, 2014, added subdivision (b1)(44).

Session Laws 2014-100, s. 34.7(b), effective January 1, 2015, added subdivision (h)(11).

Session Laws 2014-100, s. 34.28(a), inserted "or First in Freedom plates" or similar language in the section heading and subsection (b1); and rewrote the second paragraph in subsection (b) to add the "First in Freedom" plates and the last two sentences. See Editor's note for effective date and applicability.

Session Laws 2015-241, s. 29.32(a), effective July 1, 2015, in subsection (h), inserted the second paragraph, and in the last paragraph, rewrote the first sentence, and the dollar amounts throughout. For applicability, see editor's note.

Session Laws 2015-241, s. 29.40(a), effective December 17, 2015, added subdivisions (b1)(49) through (b1)(52). For effective date, see editor's note.

Session Laws 2015-264, s. 40.6(a), effective December 17, 2015, added subdivision (b1)(53). For effective date, see editor's note.

Session Laws 2015-286, s. 3.5(a), effective January 1, 2016, rewrote the third paragraph of subsection (d), which read "The Division shall provide registered owners of motorcycles and motorcycle trailers with suitably reduced size registration plates."

Session Laws 2016-120, s. 2, effective October 1, 2016, substituted "and the removal of an inspection stop are each" for "is" in the second sentence of the third paragraph of subsection (h).

Session Laws 2017-107, s. 1, effective July 1, 2017, added subdivision (b1)(54).

Session Laws 2017-114, s. 1, effective July 18, 2017, in subsection (b1), substituted "the required number of applications set forth in G.S. 20-79.3A(a)" for "at least 200 applications for the plate in addition to the applications required under G.S. 20-79.4 or G.S. 20-81.12"; and added subdivisions (b1)(55) through (57).

Session Laws 2018-5, s. 34.27(a), effective July 1, 2018, in the heading, inserted "or National/State Mottos plates" and made related changes; in the second paragraph of subsection (b), in the first sentence, inserted "or (iii) a 'National/State Mottos' plate" and made related changes and added the last sentence; and, in subsection (b1), inserted "or 'National/State Mottos' plate" twice and made related changes.

Session Laws 2018-74, s. 16.10, effective July 1, 2018, rewrote the former last sentence of subsection (b), which read "A 'National/State Mottos' plate shall (i) be a white plate, (ii) have above all other letters and numerals the motto of the United States 'In God We Trust' printed in gold lettering over a background containing the American flag, (iii) have the letters and numerals of the plate number in dark blue lettering, (iv) have below the plate number 'North Carolina' printed in light blue bold Arial Black capitalized font, and (v) have at the bottom of the plate the State motto 'To Be Rather Than To Seem' printed in dark blue lettering matching the North Carolina flag and italicized" and added the last sentence.

Session Laws 2018-74, s. 12(a), and 2018-77, s. 2(a), are identical, both effective February 1, 2019, and both reenacted subdivision (b1)(47) as that subdivision existed immediately before its repeal.

Session Laws 2019-153, s. 2, effective October 1, 2019, inserted "salvage certificates of title" in subsection (i); and added the last sentence in subsection (j).

Session Laws 2019-213, s. 2(a), effective March 1, 2020, added subdivisions (b1)(28) and (b1)(49).

Session Laws 2019-231, s. 4.18(a), in the third paragraph of subsection (h), substituted "one dollar and fifty-six cents ($1.56)" for "one dollar and thirty cents ($1.30)" in the second sentence and substituted "one dollar and seventy-five cents ($1.75)" for "one dollar and forty-six cents ($1.46)" in the fourth sentence. For effective date and applicability, see editor's note.

LICENSE PLATES ARE A RECEIPT FOR THE PRIVILEGE OF USING NORTH CAROLINA HIGHWAYS; thus any aid they give to commerce relates only to intrastate movements. Hodgson v. Hyatt Realty & Inv. Co., 353 F. Supp. 1363 (M.D.N.C. 1973).

THE LEGISLATURE DID NOT INTEND TO AID OR FACILITATE THE FUNCTIONING OF AN INTERSTATE FACILITY, in this case the State highways. Hodgson v. Hyatt Realty & Inv. Co., 353 F. Supp. 1363 (M.D.N.C. 1973).

THE TAX COLLECTION FROM LICENSE SALES UNDER SUBSECTION (H) IS ESSENTIALLY A LOCAL ACTIVITY which Congress did not intend to include under the Fair Labor Standards Act. Hodgson v. Hyatt Realty & Inv. Co., 353 F. Supp. 1363 (M.D.N.C. 1973).

AND THOSE COMMISSIONED TO SELL LICENSE PLATES ARE NOT DEALING IN INTERSTATE COMMERCE, but perform a general tax-collecting effort. Hodgson v. Hyatt Realty & Inv. Co., 353 F. Supp. 1363 (M.D.N.C. 1973).

PURPOSE OF SUBSECTION (H). --Subsection (h) of this section was intended to further the public convenience by setting up local license plate distribution points throughout the State, as well as to eliminate the necessity of employing temporary Department (now Division) personnel for a 45-day period between January 1 and February 15 of each year when the vast bulk of the license plates are issued. Hodgson v. Hyatt Realty & Inv. Co., 353 F. Supp. 1363 (M.D.N.C. 1973).

A NORTH CAROLINA LICENSE PLATE REMAINS THE PROPERTY OF THE STATE AND CAN BE SUMMARILY SEIZED under certain conditions under subsection (a). Hodgson v. Hyatt Realty & Inv. Co., 353 F. Supp. 1363 (M.D.N.C. 1973).

AIDING AND ABETTING UNLAWFUL USE OF PLATE. --Guilt attaches to anyone who knowingly aids and abets the unlawful use of a license plate. Woodruff v. Holbrook, 255 N.C. 740, 122 S.E.2d 709 (1961).

THE MAXIMUM PUNISHMENT FOR A VIOLATION OF THIS SECTION or G.S. 20-111 would be that prescribed by G.S. 20-176(b), namely, a fine of not more than $100.00 or imprisonment in the county or municipal jail for not more than 60 days, or both such fine and imprisonment. State v. Tolley, 271 N.C. 459, 156 S.E.2d 858 (1967).

CITED in State v. Hudson, 103 N.C. App. 708, 407 S.E.2d 583 (1991); State v. Veazey, 191 N.C. App. 181, 662 S.E.2d 683 (2008).

§ 20-63.01. Bonds required for commission contractors

(a) A guaranty bond is required for each commission contractor that is not a governmental subdivision of this State that is granted a contract to issue license plates or conduct business pursuant to G.S. 20-63. Provided, however, a commission contractor that is unable to secure a bond may, with the consent of the Division, provide an alternative to a guaranty bond, as provided in subsection (c) of this section.

The Division may revoke, with cause, a contract with a commission contractor that fails to maintain a bond or an alternative to a bond, pursuant to this section.

(b) (1) When application is made for a contract or contract renewal, the applicant shall file a guaranty bond with the clerk of the superior court and/or the register of deeds of the county in which the commission contractor will be located. The bond shall be in favor of the Division. The bond shall be executed by the applicant as principal and by a bonding company authorized to do business in this State. The bond shall be conditioned to provide indemnification to the Division for a loss of revenue for any reason, including bankruptcy, employee embezzlement or theft, foreclosure, or ceasing to operate.

(2) The bond shall be in an amount determined by the Division to be adequate to provide indemnification to the Division under the terms of the bond. The bond amount shall be at least one hundred thousand dollars ($ 100,000).

(3) The bond shall remain in force and effect until cancelled by the guarantor. The guarantor may cancel the bond upon 30 days' notice to the Division. Cancellation of the bond shall not affect any liability incurred or accrued prior to the termination of the notice period.

(4) The Division may be able to negotiate bonds for contractors who qualify for bonds as a group under favorable rates

or circumstances. If so, the Division may require those contractors who can qualify for the group bond to obtain their bond as part of a group of contractors. The Division may deduct the premiums for any bonds it may be able to negotiate at group rates from the commissioned contractors' compensation.

(c) An applicant that is unable to secure a bond may seek a waiver of the guaranty bond from the Division and approval of one of the guaranty bond alternatives set forth in this subsection. With the approval of the Division, an applicant may file with the clerk of the superior court and/or the register of deeds of the county in which the commission contractor will be located, in lieu of a bond:

(1) An assignment of a savings account in an amount equal to the bond required (i) that is in a form acceptable to the Division; (ii) that is executed by the applicant; (iii) that is executed by a federally insured depository institution or a trust institution authorized to do business in this State; and (iv) for which access to the account in favor of the State of North Carolina is subject to the same conditions as for a bond in subsection (b) of this section.

(2) A certificate of deposit (i) that is executed by a federally insured depository institution or a trust institution authorized to do business in this State; (ii) that is either payable to the State of North Carolina, unrestrictively endorsed to the Division of Motor Vehicles; in the case of a negotiable certificate of deposit, is unrestrictively endorsed to the Division of Motor Vehicles; or in the case of a nonnegotiable certificate of deposit, is assigned to the Division of Motor Vehicles in a form satisfactory to the Division; and (iii) for which access to the certificate of deposit in favor of the State of North Carolina is subject to the same conditions as for a bond in subsection (b) of this section.

History.
2007-488, s. 1;2017-25, s. 1(b)
EDITOR'S NOTE. --
Session Laws 2007-488, s. 1, enacted this section as G.S. 20-63A. It has been renumbered as this section at the direction of the Revisor of Statutes.
EFFECT OF AMENDMENTS. --
Session Laws 2017-25, s. 1(b), effective June 2, 2017, and substituted "federally insured depository institution or a trust institution authorized to do business in this State" for "state or federal savings and loan association, state bank, or national bank that is doing business in North Carolina and whose accounts are insured by a federal depositors corporation" or similar language in subdivisions (c)(1) and (c)(2); and made minor stylistic changes.

§ 20-63.02. Advisory committee of commission contractors

(a) **Committee and Duties.** -- An advisory committee is established and is designated the License Plate Agent (LPA) Advisory Committee. The Division and the LPA Advisory Committee are directed to work together to ensure excellent and efficient customer service with respect to vehicle titling and registration services provided through commission contracts awarded under G.S. 20-63. As part of this effort, the Division and the Committee must periodically review all forms and instructions used in the vehicle titling and registration process to ensure that they are readily understandable and not duplicative. The Committee must meet at least quarterly.

(b) **Membership and Terms.** -- The LPA Advisory Committee consists of persons who are on the staff of the Division of Motor Vehicles and six persons appointed by the North Carolina Association of Motor Vehicle Registration Contractors. The Commissioner determines the number of Division staff persons to appoint to the Committee and designates the chair of the Committee. Members of the Committee appointed by the Commissioner serve ex officio. Members of the Committee appointed by the Association serve two-year terms beginning on July 1 of an odd-numbered year. A member who serves for a specific term continues to serve after the expiration of the member's term until a successor is appointed.

(c) **Expenses.** -- Members of the LPA Advisory Committee are allowed the per diem, subsistence, and travel allowances established under G.S. 138-5 for service on State boards and commissions.

History.
2013-372, s. 1(a)

§ 20-63.1. Division may cause plates to be reflectorized

(a) Registration Plate Standards. -- The Division of Motor Vehicles is hereby authorized to cause vehicle license plates for 1968 and future years to be completely treated with reflectorized materials designed to increase visibility and legibility of license plates at night. The Division of Motor Vehicles shall develop standards for reflectivity that use the most current technology available while maintaining a competitive bid process.

(b) Registration Plate Mandatory Replacement. -- All registration plates shall be replaced every seven years.

History.
1967, c. 8; 1975, c. 716, s. 5; 2019-227, s. 5(a)

Chapter 20

§ 20-64. Transfer of registration plates to another vehicle

(a) Except as otherwise provided in this Article, registration plates shall be retained by the owner thereof upon disposition of the vehicle to which assigned, and may be assigned to another vehicle, belonging to such owner and of a like vehicle category within the meaning of G.S. 20-87 and 20-88, upon proper application to the Division and payment of a transfer fee and such additional fees as may be due because the vehicle to which the plates are to be assigned requires a greater registration fee than that vehicle to which the license plates were last assigned. In cases where the plate is assigned to another vehicle belonging to such owner, and is not of a like vehicle category within the meaning of G.S. 20-87 and 20-88, the owner shall surrender the plate to the Division and receive therefor a plate of the proper category, and the unexpired portion of the fee originally paid by the owner for the plate so surrendered shall be a credit toward the fee charged for the new plate of the proper category. Provided, that the owner shall not be entitled to a cash refund when the registration fee for the vehicle to which the plates are to be assigned is less than the registration fee for that vehicle to which the license plates were last assigned. An owner assigning or transferring plates to another vehicle as provided herein shall be subject to the same assessments and penalties for use of the plates on another vehicle or for improper use of the plates, as he could have been for the use of the plates on the vehicle to which last assigned. Provided, however, that upon compliance with the requirements of this section, the registration plates of vehicles owned by and registered in the name of a corporation may be transferred and assigned to a like vehicle category within the meaning of G.S. 20-87 and 20-88, upon the showing that the vehicle to which the transfer and assignment is to be made is owned by a corporation which is a wholly owned subsidiary of the corporation applying for such transfer and assignment.

(b) Upon a change of the name of a corporation or a change of the name under which a proprietorship or partnership is doing business, the corporation, partnership or proprietorship shall forthwith apply for correction of the certificate of title of all vehicles owned by such corporation, partnership or proprietorship so as to correctly reflect the name of the corporation or the name under which the proprietorship or partnership is doing business, and pay the fees required by law.

(c) Upon a change in the composition of a partnership, ownership of vehicles belonging to such partnership shall not be deemed to have changed so long as one partner of the predecessor partnership remains a partner in the reconstituted partnership, but the reconstituted partnership shall forthwith apply for correction of the certificate of title of all vehicles owned by such partnership so as to correctly reflect the composition of the partnership and the name under which it is doing business, if any, and pay the fees required by law.

(d) When a proprietorship or partnership is incorporated, the corporation shall retain license plates assigned to vehicles belonging to it and may use the same, provided the corporation applies for and obtains transfers of the certificates of title of all vehicles and pays the fees required by law.

(e) Upon death of the owner of a registered vehicle, such registration shall continue in force as a valid registration until the end of the year for which the license is issued unless ownership of the vehicle passes or is transferred to any person other than the surviving spouse before the end of the year.

(f) The owner or transferor of a registered vehicle who surrenders the registration plate to the division may secure a refund for the unexpired portion of such plate prorated on a monthly basis, beginning the first day of the month following surrender of the plate to the division, provided the annual fee of such surrendered plate is sixty dollars ($ 60.00) or more. This refund may not exceed one half of the annual license fee. No refund shall be made unless the owner or transferor furnishes proof of financial responsibility on the registered vehicle effective until the date of the surrender of the plate. Proof of financial responsibility shall be furnished in a manner prescribed by the Commissioner.

(g) The Commissioner of Motor Vehicles shall have the power to make such rules and regulations as he may deem necessary for the administration of transfers of license plates and vehicles under this Article.

History.

1937, c. 407, s. 28; 1945, c. 576, s. 1; 1947, c. 914, s. 1; 1951, c. 188; c. 819, s. 1; 1961, c. 360, s. 5; 1963, cc. 1067, 1190; 1967, c. 995; 1973, c. 1134; 1975, c. 716, s. 5; 1981, c. 227; 2004-167, s. 1;2004-199, s. 59;2007-491, s. 5

EDITOR'S NOTE. --

Session Laws 2007-491, s. 47, provides in part: "The procedures for review of disputed tax matters enacted by this act apply to assessments of tax that are not final as of the effective date of this act and to claims for refund pending on or filed on or after the effective date of this act. This act does not affect matters for which a petition for review was filed with the Tax Review Board under G.S. 105-241.2 [repealed] before the effective date of this act. The repeal of G.S. 105-122(c) and G.S. 105-130.4(t) and Sections 11 and 12 apply to requests for alternative apportionment formulas filed on or after the effective date of this act. A petition filed with the Tax Review Board for an apportionment formula before the effective date of this act is considered a request under G.S. 105-122(c1) or G.S. 105-130.4(t1), as appropriate."

EFFECT OF AMENDMENTS. --
Session Laws 2004-167, s. 1, as amended by Session Laws 2004-199, s. 59, effective January 1, 2006, deleted the former fourth sentence of subsection (a) which read: "Provided, however, registration plates may not be transferred under this section after December 31 of the year for which issued."

Session Laws 2007-491, s. 5, effective January 1, 2008, deleted the former last sentence of subsection (f), which read: "Any unauthorized refund may be recovered in the manner set forth in G.S. 20-99."

CITED in Nationwide Mut. Ins. Co. v. Hayes, 276 N.C. 620, 174 S.E.2d 511 (1970).

N.C. Gen. Stat. § 20-64.1

Repealed by Session Laws 1995 (Regular Session, 1996), c. 756, s. 6.

EDITOR'S NOTE. --
Section 62-278 in Chapter 62 as rewritten is in substance a reenactment of this former section.

N.C. Gen. Stat. § 20-64.2

Repealed by Session Laws 2010-132, s. 4, effective December 1, 2010.

History.
1957, c. 402; 1975, c. 716, s. 5

EDITOR'S NOTE. --
This section is repealed by Session Laws 2010-132, s. 4, effective December 1, 2010, and applicable to offenses committed on or after that date.

N.C. Gen. Stat. § 20-65

Repealed by Session Laws 1979, 2nd Session, c. 1280, s. 1.

§ 20-66. Renewal of vehicle registration

(a) **Annual Renewal. --** The registration of a vehicle must be renewed annually. In accordance with G.S. 105-330.5(b), upon receiving written consent from the owner of the vehicle, the Division may send any required notice of renewal electronically to an e-mail address provided by the owner of the vehicle. To renew the registration of a vehicle, the owner of the vehicle must file an application with the Division and pay the required registration fee. The Division may receive and grant an application for renewal of registration at any time before the registration expires.

(b) **Method of Renewal. --** When the Division renews the registration of a vehicle, it must issue a new registration card for the vehicle and either a new registration plate or a registration renewal sticker. The Division may renew a registration plate for any type of vehicle by means of a renewal sticker.

(b1) Repealed by Session Laws 1993, c. 467, s. 2.

(c) **Renewal Stickers. --** A single registration renewal sticker issued by the Division must be displayed on the registration plate that it renews in the place prescribed by the Commissioner and must indicate the period for which it is valid. Except where physical differences between a registration renewal sticker and a registration plate render a provision of this Chapter inapplicable, the provisions of this Chapter relating to registration plates apply to registration renewal stickers.

(d), (e) Repealed by Session Laws 1993 (Reg. Sess., 1994), c. 761, § 5.

(f) Repealed by Session Laws 1993, c. 467, s. 2.

(g) **When Renewal Sticker Expires. --** The registration of a vehicle that is renewed by means of a registration renewal sticker expires at midnight on the last day of the month designated on the sticker. It is lawful, however, to operate the vehicle on a highway until midnight on the fifteenth day of the month following the month in which the sticker expired.

The Division may vary the expiration dates of registration renewal stickers issued for a type of vehicle so that an approximately equal number expires at the end of each month, quarter, or other period consisting of one or more months. When the Division implements registration renewal for a type of vehicle by means of a renewal sticker, it may issue a registration renewal sticker that expires at the end of any monthly interval.

(g1) **Expiration of Registration by Other Means. --** The registration of a vehicle renewed by means of a new registration plate expires at midnight on the last day of the year in which the registration plate was issued. It is lawful, however, to operate the vehicle on a highway through midnight February 15 of the following year.

(h) Repealed by Session Laws 2004-167, s. 3, as amended by Session Laws 2004-199, s. 59, effective January 1, 2006.

(i) **Property Tax Consolidation. --** When the Division receives an application under subsection (a) for the renewal of registration before the current registration expires, the Division shall grant the application if it is made for the purpose of consolidating the property taxes payable by the applicant on classified motor vehicles, as defined in G.S. 105-330. The registration fee for a motor vehicle whose registration cycle is changed under this subsection shall be reduced by a prorated amount. The prorated amount is one-twelfth of the registration fee in effect when the motor vehicle's registration was last renewed multiplied by the number of full months remaining in the motor vehicle's current registration cycle, rounded to the nearest multiple of twenty-five cents (25 cent(s)).

(j) **Inspection Prior to Renewal of Registration.** -- The Division shall not renew the registration of a vehicle unless it has a current safety or emissions inspection.

(k) Repealed by Session Laws 2008-190, s. 1, effective October 1, 2008.

History.

1937, c. 407, s. 30; 1955, c. 554, s. 3; 1973, c. 1389, s. 1; 1975, c. 716, s. 5; 1977, c. 337; 1979, 2nd Sess., c. 1280, ss. 2, 3; 1981 (Reg. Sess., 1982), c. 1258, s. 1; 1985 (Reg. Sess., 1986), c. 982, s. 24; 1991, c. 624, ss. 6, 7; c. 672, s. 7; c. 726, s. 23; 1993, c. 467, s. 2;1993 (Reg. Sess., 1994), c. 761, s. 5; 2004-167, ss. 2, 3; 2004-199, s. 59;2007-503, s. 1;2008-190, s. 1;2014-108, s. 2(a);2015-108, s. 2;2016-90, s. 7(a);2017-96, s. 1

EDITOR'S NOTE. --

Session Laws 2007-503 [s. 1 of which added subsections (j) and (k)], effective October 1, 2008, is applicable to offenses committed on or after that date.

Session Laws 2016-90, s. 7(b), made subsection (g1), as added by Session Laws 2016-90, s. 7(a), applicable to registration renewals on or after October 1, 2016.

Session Laws 2020-3, s. 4.7(a) -(h), as amended by Session Laws 2020-97, ss. 3.15(a), 3.16(a), provides: "(a) Definition. -- For purposes of this section, 'credential' means any of the following issued by the Division of Motor Vehicles:

"(1) Drivers license.

"(2) Learner's permit.

"(3) Limited learner's permit.

"(4) Limited provisional license.

"(5) Full provisional license.

"(6) Commercial drivers license.

"(7) Commercial learner's permit.

"(8) Temporary driving certificate.

"(9) Special identification card.

"(10) Handicapped placard.

"(11) Vehicle registration.

"(12) Temporary vehicle registration.

"(13) Dealer license plate.

"(14) Transporter plate.

"(15) Loaner/Dealer 'LD' plate.

"(16) Vehicle inspection authorization.

"(17) Inspection station license.

"(18) Inspection mechanic license.

"(19) Transportation network company permit.

"(20) Motor vehicle dealer license.

"(21) Sales representative license.

"(22) Manufacturer license.

"(23) Distributor license.

"(24) Wholesaler license.

"(25) Driver training school license.

"(26) Driver training school instructor license.

"(27) Professional housemoving license.

"(b) Extend Validity of Credentials. -- Notwithstanding renewal, duration, or expiration provisions

of G.S. 20-7, 20-11, 20-37.6, 20-37.7, 20-37.13, 20-50, 20-66, 20-79, 20-79.02, 20-79.2, 20-183.4B, 20-183.4D, 20-280.3, 20-288, 20-324, and 20-359, or any other provision of law to the contrary, the Division of Motor Vehicles shall extend for a period of five months the validity of any credential that expires on or after March 1, 2020, and before August 1, 2020. The Division shall extend for a period of five months the validity of any credential listed in subdivisions (6), (7), (9), (10), and (18) of subsection (a) of this section that expires on or after March 1, 2020, and before the date 30 days after the date the Governor (i) rescinds Executive Order No. 116 or (ii) issues another executive order lifting restrictions on Division of Motor Vehicles functions. Notwithstanding G.S. 20-37.13(h) and G.S. 20-37.13A(a), the Division of Motor Vehicles is authorized to waive the requirement that commercial drivers license and commercial learner's permit holders have a medical examination and certification, as required by federal law, consistent with any waiver of medical qualifications standards issued by the Federal Motor Carrier Safety Administration. A credential extended under this section shall expire five months from the date it otherwise expires as prescribed by law prior to this section. However, the subsequent expiration of a credential extended under this section shall occur on the date prescribed by law prior to this section without regard to the extension. The Division shall notify individuals affected by an extension granted under this section, including information on new expiration dates and how the extension affects subsequent renewal and expiration dates.

"(b1) Extension of Intrastate Medical Waivers. -- Notwithstanding the limitation on duration of waivers in G.S. 20-37.13A(b), the Division of Motor Vehicles may extend for up to five months the validity of a medical waiver issued by the Division under G.S. 20-37.13A if the waiver expires on or after March 1, 2020, and before the date 30 days after the date the Governor (i) rescinds Executive Order No. 116 or (ii) issues another executive order lifting restrictions on Division of Motor Vehicles functions, and the Division's Medical Review Unit determines the extension is appropriate.

"(c) Driving Eligibility Certificates. -- Notwithstanding G.S. 20-11(n)(3), a driving eligibility certificate dated on or after February 9, 2020, and before March 10, 2020, remains valid and may be accepted by the Division of Motor Vehicles to meet the requirements for a license or permit issued under G.S. 20-11 until 30 days after the date the Governor rescinds Executive Order No. 116 or the date the Division reopens all drivers license offices, whichever is earlier.

"(d) Waive Penalties. -- Notwithstanding any provision of law to the contrary, the Division shall waive any fines, fees, or penalties associated with failing to renew a credential during the period of time the credential is valid by extension under subsection (b) of this section.

"(e) Motor Vehicle Taxes. -- Notwithstanding any provision of law to the contrary, due dates for motor vehicle taxes that are tied to registration expiration under Article 22A of Chapter 105 of the General Statutes shall be extended to correspond with extended expiration dates under subsection (b) of this section.

"(f) Validity by Extension a Defense. -- A person may not be convicted or found responsible for any offense resulting from failure to renew a credential issued by the Division if, when tried for that offense, the person shows that the offense occurred during the period of time the credential is valid by extension under subsection (b) of this section.

"(g) Report. -- Within 30 days of the extensions made under subsection (b) of this section, the Division shall submit a report to the Joint Legislative Transportation Oversight Committee and the Fiscal Research Division detailing implementation of this section.

"(h) Effective Date. -- This section is effective retroactively to March 1, 2020, and applies to expirations occurring on or after that date."
Session Laws 2020-3, s. 5, is a severability clause.
Session Laws 2020-97, s. 4.5, is a severability clause.
EFFECT OF AMENDMENTS. --
Session Laws 2004-167, ss. 2 and 3, as amended by Session Laws 2004-199, s. 59, effective January 1, 2006, deleted part of the second sentence and deleted the last sentence of the first paragraph of subsection (g) which read: "if the vehicle is not registered under the International Registration Plan. If the vehicle is registered under the International Registration Plan, it is not lawful to operate the vehicle on a highway after the sticker expires"; and repealed subsection (h).

Session Laws 2014-108, s. 2(a), effective January 1, 2015, in the first sentence of subsection (c), inserted "single" and substituted "is valid" for "and the registration plate on which it is displayed are valid."

Session Laws 2015-108, s. 2, effective January 1, 2016, added the second sentence of subsection (a).

Session Laws 2016-90, s. 7(a), effective October 1, 2016, added subsection (g1). See editor's note for applicability.

Session Laws 2017-96, s. 1, effective July 12, 2017, rewrote subsection (g1) which formerly read: "Expiration of Registration by Other Means. -- The registration of a vehicle renewed by means of a new registration plate expires at midnight on February 15 of each year."

N.C. Gen. Stat. § 20-66.1

Repealed by Session Laws 1973, c. 1389, s. 2.
CROSS REFERENCES. --
For present provisions on renewal of vehicle registrations, see G.S. 20-66.

§ 20-67. Notice of change of address or name

(a) **Address.** -- A person whose address changes from the address stated on a certificate of title or registration card must notify the Division of the change within 60 days after the change occurs. The person may obtain a duplicate certificate of title or registration card stating the new address but is not required to do so. A person who does not move but whose address changes due to governmental action may not be charged with violating this subsection.

(b) **Name.** -- A person whose name changes from the name stated on a certificate of title or registration card must notify the Division of the change within 60 days after the change occurs. The person may obtain a duplicate certificate of title or registration card but is not required to do so.

(c) **Fee.** -- G.S. 20-85 sets the fee for a duplicate certificate of title or registration card.

History.
1937, c. 407, s. 31; 1955, c. 554, s. 4; 1975, c. 716, s. 5; 1979, c. 106; 1997-122, s. 7
CITED in State v. Teasley, 9 N.C. App. 477, 176 S.E.2d 838 (1970).

§ 20-68. Replacement of lost or damaged certificates, cards and plates

(a) In the event any registration card or registration plate is lost, mutilated, or becomes illegible, the owner or legal representative of the owner of the vehicle for which the same was issued, as shown by the records of the Division, shall immediately make application for and may obtain a duplicate or a substitute or a new registration under a new registration number, as determined to be most advisable by the Division, upon the applicant's furnishing under oath information satisfactory to the Division and payment of required fee.

(b) If a certificate of title is lost, stolen, mutilated, destroyed or becomes illegible, the first lienholder or, if none, the owner or legal representative of the owner named in the certificate, as shown by the records of the Division, shall promptly make application for and may obtain a duplicate upon furnishing information satisfactory to the Division. It shall be mailed to the first lienholder named in it or, if none, to the owner. The Division shall not issue a new certificate of title upon application made on a duplicate until 15 days after receipt of the application. A person recovering an original certificate of title for which a duplicate has been issued shall promptly surrender the original certificate to the Division.

History.
1937, c. 407, s. 32; 1961, c. 360, s. 7; c. 835, s. 7; 1975, c. 716, s. 5
CROSS REFERENCES. --
As to fees for duplicate certificate, see G.S. 20-85.

§ 20-69. Division authorized to assign new engine number

The owner of a motor vehicle upon which the engine number or serial number has become illegible or has been removed or obliterated shall immediately make application to the Division for a new engine or serial number for such motor vehicle. The Division, when satisfied that the applicant is the lawful owner of the vehicle referred to in such application is hereby authorized to assign a new engine or serial number thereto, and shall require that such number, together with the name of this State, or a symbol indicating this State, be stamped upon the engine, or in the event such number is a serial number, then upon such portion of the motor vehicle as shall be designated by the Division.

History.
1937, c. 407, s. 33; 1975, c. 716, s. 5

§ 20-70. Division to be notified when another engine is installed or body changed

(a) Whenever a motor vehicle registered hereunder is altered by the installation of another engine in place of an engine, the number of which is shown in the registration records, or the installation of another body in place of a body, the owner of such motor vehicle shall immediately give notice to the Division in writing on a form prepared by it, which shall state the number of the former engine and the number of the newly installed engine, the registration number of the motor vehicle, the name of the owner and any other information which the Division may require. Whenever another engine has been substituted as provided in this section, and the notice given as required hereunder, the Division shall insert the number of the newly installed engine upon the registration card and certificate of title issued for such motor vehicle.

(b) Whenever a new engine or serial number has been assigned to and stamped upon a motor vehicle as provided in G.S. 20-69, or whenever a new engine has been installed or body changed as provided in this section, the Division shall require the owner to surrender to the Division the registration card and certificate of title previously issued for said vehicle. The Division shall also require the owner to make application for a duplicate registration card and a duplicate certificate of title showing the new motor or serial number thereon or new style of body, and upon receipt of such application and fee, as for any other duplicate title, the Division shall issue to said owner a duplicate registration and a duplicate certificate of title showing thereon the new number in place of the original number or the new style of body.

(c) The notification and registration requirements contained in subsections (a) and (b) of this section regarding an engine change shall be required only if the motor vehicle into which

a new engine is installed uses an engine number as the sole means to identify the vehicle.

History.
1937, c. 407, s. 34; 1943, c. 726; 1975, c. 716, s. 5; 2009-405, s. 3

EFFECT OF AMENDMENTS. --
Session Laws 2009-405, s. 3, effective August 5, 2009, added subsection (c).

CROSS REFERENCES. --
As to fee for duplicate registration card and certificate of title, see G.S. 20-85.

§ 20-71. Altering or forging certificate of title, registration card or application, a felony; reproducing or possessing blank certificate of title

(a) Any person who, with fraudulent intent, shall alter any certificate of title, registration card issued by the Division, or any application for a certificate of title or registration card, or forge or counterfeit any certificate of title or registration card purported to have been issued by the Division under the provisions of this Article, or who, with fraudulent intent, shall alter, falsify or forge any assignment thereof, or who shall hold or use any such certificate, registration card, or application, or assignment, knowing the same to have been altered, forged or falsified, shall be guilty of a felony and upon conviction thereof shall be punished in the discretion of the court.

(b) It shall be unlawful for any person with fraudulent intent to reproduce or possess a blank North Carolina certificate of title or facsimile thereof. Any person, firm or corporation violating the provisions of this section shall be guilty of a Class I felony.

History.
1937, c. 407, s. 35; 1959, c. 1264, s. 2; 1971, c. 99; 1975, c. 716, s. 5; 1979, c. 499; 1993, c. 539, s. 1251;1994, Ex. Sess., c. 24, s. 14(c)
APPLIED in Smart Fin. Co. v. Dick, 256 N.C. 669, 124 S.E.2d 862 (1962).

§ 20-71.1. Registration evidence of ownership; ownership evidence of defendant's responsibility for conduct of operation

(a) In all actions to recover damages for injury to the person or to property or for the death of a person, arising out of an accident or collision involving a motor vehicle, proof of ownership of such motor vehicle at the time of such accident or collision shall be prima facie evidence that said motor vehicle was being operated and used with the authority, consent, and knowledge of the owner in the very transaction out of which said injury or cause of action arose.

(b) Proof of the registration of a motor vehicle in the name of any person, firm, or corporation, shall for the purpose of any such action, be prima facie evidence of ownership and that such motor vehicle was then being operated by and under the control of a person for whose conduct the owner was legally responsible, for the owner's benefit, and within the course and scope of his employment.

History.

1951, c. 494; 1961, c. 975

BY ENACTING THIS SECTION THE LEGISLATURE CHANGED THE PRIOR COMMON LAW. Broadway v. Webb, 462 F. Supp. 429 (W.D.N.C. 1977).

LEGISLATIVE INTENT. --By enacting this section the legislature showed a clear intent to provide victims of automobile accidents with the opportunity to recover from the owner as well as the driver of a car involved in an accident. Broadway v. Webb, 462 F. Supp. 429 (W.D.N.C. 1977).

This statute shows a clear legislative intent to provide victims of highway collisions with the opportunity to recover from the owner as well as the driver of the vehicle involved in the accident. It enables the plaintiff relying on an agency theory to submit a prima facie case to the jury. DeArmon v. B. Mears Corp., 67 N.C. App. 640, 314 S.E.2d 124 (1984), rev'd in part, 312 N.C. 749, 325 S.E.2d 223 (1985).

North Carolina has an obligation to protect persons using North Carolina roads built and maintained to a large degree with North Carolina taxpayers' funds, whether they are citizens of this State or out-of-state citizens. DeArmon v. B. Mears Corp., 67 N.C. App. 640, 314 S.E.2d 124 (1984), rev'd in part, 312 N.C. 749, 325 S.E.2d 223 (1985).

PURPOSE OF SECTION. --The evident purpose of this section was to require that proof of ownership of an offending motor vehicle should be regarded as prima facie evidence that it was being operated at the time of the accident by authority of the owner, doubtless having in view the decision in Carter v. Thurston Motor Lines, 227 N.C. 193, 41 S.E.2d 586 (1947), overruled on other grounds in Knight v. Associated Transp., Inc., 255 N.C. 122 S.E.2d 64 (1961), and to provide that, in the absence of proof of ownership, proof of motor vehicle registration in the name of a person would be prima facie evidence that the motor vehicle was being operated by one for whose conduct such person was legally responsible. Travis v. Duckworth, 237 N.C. 471, 75 S.E.2d 309 (1953).

The purpose of this section is to establish a ready means of proving agency in any case where it is charged that the negligence of a nonowner operator causes damage to the property or injury to the person of another or for the death of a person arising out of an accident or collision involving a motor vehicle. It does not have, and was not intended to have, any other force or effect. State v. Cotten, 2 N.C. App. 305, 163 S.E.2d 100 (1968).

The purpose of this section is to establish a ready means of proving agency in any case where it is charged that the negligence of a nonowner operator causes damage to the property or injury to the person of another. It does not and was not intended to have any other force or effect. Phillips v. Utica Mut. Ins. Co., 4 N.C. App. 655, 167 S.E.2d 542 (1969).

The plain and obvious purpose of this section is to enable plaintiff to submit a prima facie case of agency to the jury which it can decide to accept or reject. Scallon v. Hooper, 49 N.C. App. 113, 270 S.E.2d 496 (1980), cert. denied, 301 N.C. 722, 276 S.E.2d 284 (1981).

The sole purpose of subsection (b) is to facilitate proof of ownership and agency where a vehicle is operated by one other than the owner. The statute makes out a prima facie case which, nothing else appearing, permits but does not compel a finding for plaintiff on the issue of agency. DeArmon v. B. Mears Corp., 312 N.C. 749, 325 S.E.2d 223 (1985).

THE TWO SUBSECTIONS OF THIS SECTION ARE IDENTICAL IN THEIR OBJECTIVE. While the language used in subsection (a) is not as apt as that used in subsection (b), the intent and meaning of the two are the same. Hartley v. Smith, 239 N.C. 170, 79 S.E.2d 767 (1954); State v. Cotten, 2 N.C. App. 305, 163 S.E.2d 100 (1968).

The legislature used the language "was being operated and used with the authority, consent, and knowledge of the owner" in subsection (a) of this section to connote "under the direction and control of the owner," and when one acts under the direction and control of another, he is an agent or employee. It did not intend to give greater force and effect to mere proof of registration than to the admission or actual proof of ownership. In short, proof of registration is prima facie proof of ownership under subsection (b), which in turn is prima facie proof of agency under subsection (a). Hartley v. Smith, 239 N.C. 170, 79 S.E.2d 767 (1954).

SUBSECTION (B) SHIFTS THE BURDEN OF GOING FORWARD WITH EVIDENCE to those persons better able to establish the facts than are plaintiffs. DeArmon v. B. Mears Corp., 312 N.C. 749, 325 S.E.2d 223 (1985).

SCOPE OF SECTION. --This section applies in all actions to recover damages for injury to the person or to property, or for the death of a person, arising out of an accident or a collision involving a motor vehicle, and the rule of evidence established thereby applies whenever a factual determination as to alleged agency is to be made, whether by the court to resolve a question of fact or by a jury to resolve an issue of fact. Howard v. Sasso, 253 N.C. 185, 116 S.E.2d 341 (1960).

Actions of the emergency vehicle driver were attributed to her employer, the county, pursuant to G.S. 20-71.1. Earp v. Peters, 2008 U.S. Dist. LEXIS 77393 (W.D.N.C. July 2, 2008).

THIS SECTION WAS PLAINLY MEANT TO APPLY IN A CIVIL CASE. State v. Cotten, 2 N.C. App. 305, 163 S.E.2d 100 (1968).

THIS SECTION CREATES A PRESUMPTION OF OWNERSHIP ONLY IN THOSE SPECIFIC INSTANCES ENUMERATED. State v. Cotten, 2 N.C. App. 305, 163 S.E.2d 100 (1968).

Chapter 20

SECTION CREATES NO PRESUMPTION THAT OWNER WAS DRIVER. --This section does not provide that proof of ownership of an automobile, or proof of the registration of an automobile in the name of any person, shall be prima facie evidence that the owner of the automobile, or the person in whose name it was registered, was the driver of the automobile at the time of a wreck. Parker v. Wilson, 247 N.C. 47, 100 S.E.2d 258 (1957); Johnson v. Fox, 254 N.C. 454, 119 S.E.2d 185 (1961).

THIS SECTION MAKES NO REFERENCE TO ANY AUTHORITY OF THE DRIVER TO AFFECT THE OWNER'S LIABILITY to other persons otherwise than by the driver's conduct in the operation and control of the vehicle. Branch v. Dempsey, 265 N.C. 733, 145 S.E.2d 395 (1965).

SECTION APPLIES ONLY WHERE PLAINTIFF RELIES ON DOCTRINE OF RESPONDEAT SUPERIOR. --This section was designed and intended to apply, and does apply, only in those cases where the plaintiff seeks to hold an owner liable for the negligence of a nonowner operator under the doctrine of respondeat superior. Roberts v. Hill, 240 N.C. 373, 82 S.E.2d 373 (1954); Jones v. Farm Bureau Mut. Auto. Ins. Co., 159 F. Supp. 404 (E.D.N.C. 1958); Howard v. Sasso, 253 N.C. 185, 116 S.E.2d 341 (1960); State v. Cotten, 2 N.C. App. 305, 163 S.E.2d 100 (1968).

This section applies when plaintiff, upon sufficient allegations, seeks to hold the owner liable for the negligence of a nonowner operator under the doctrine of respondeat superior. Dupree v. Batts, 276 N.C. 68, 170 S.E.2d 918 (1969); Phillips v. Utica Mut. Ins. Co., 4 N.C. App. 655, 167 S.E.2d 542 (1969); Allen v. Schiller, 6 N.C. App. 392, 169 S.E.2d 924 (1969).

Since the owner of a vehicle may be held liable for the negligence of an nonowner/operator under the doctrine of respondeat superior, proof of ownership is sufficient to take the case to the jury on the question of the legal responsibility of the defendant for the operation of the vehicle. DeArmon v. B. Mears Corp., 67 N.C. App. 640, 314 S.E.2d 124 (1984), rev'd in part, 312 N.C. 749, 325 S.E.2d 223 (1985).

SECTION DOES NOT APPLY WHERE PLAINTIFF ATTEMPTS TO PROVE THE OWNER'S LIABILITY UNDER THE "FAMILY PURPOSE DOCTRINE." Fox v. Albea, 250 N.C. 445, 109 S.E.2d 197 (1959).

NOR TO AN ACTION BETWEEN INSURERS SEEKING DECLARATION OF RIGHTS AND OBLIGATIONS. --An action which is not an action to recover damages for injury to the person or to the property or for the death of a person arising out of an accident or collision involving a motor vehicle, but is an action brought by an insurer against another insurer to have the court declare the rights and obligations of the insurers under their policies of insurance, is not the type of case to which this section was intended to apply. Aetna Cas. & Sur. Co. v. Lumbermen's Mut. Cas. Co., 11 N.C. App. 490, 181 S.E.2d 727 (1971).

THIS SECTION DOES NOT MAKE THE MERCHANT WHO SUPPLIES PARTS OR THE MECHANIC WHO PERFORMS WORK AND SUPPLIES PARTS RESPONSIBLE for the operation of a repaired or rebuilt motor vehicle. Rick v. Murphy, 251 N.C. 162, 110 S.E.2d 815 (1959), holding garage operator who supplied body from wrecked car he owned to be used with parts from customer's wrecked car to make a motor vehicle for the customer was not owner of such motor vehicle.

THIS SECTION APPLIES TO AN ACCIDENT OCCURRING PRIOR TO ITS EFFECTIVE DATE, UNLESS AN ACTION WAS PENDING at the time of its effective date. Spencer v. McDowell Motor Co., 236 N.C. 239, 72 S.E.2d 598 (1952).

THIS SECTION MERELY CREATES A RULE OF EVIDENCE. Duckworth v. Metcalf, 268 N.C. 340, 150 S.E.2d 485 (1966).

This section creates a rule of evidence, and has no other or further force or effect. Mitchell v. White, 256 N.C. 437, 124 S.E.2d 137 (1962).

This section was designed to create a rule of evidence. Its purpose is to establish a ready means of proving agency in any case where it is charged that the negligence of a nonowner operator causes damage to the property or injury to the person of another. It does not have, and was not intended to have, any other or further force or effect. Hartley v. Smith, 239 N.C. 170, 79 S.E.2d 767 (1954). See also, Roberts v. Hill, 240 N.C. 373, 82 S.E.2d 373 (1954); Osborne v. Gilreath, 241 N.C. 685, 86 S.E.2d 462 (1955); Elliott v. Killian, 242 N.C. 471, 87 S.E.2d 903 (1955); Fox v. Albea, 250 N.C. 445, 109 S.E.2d 197 (1959); Lynn v. Clark, 252 N.C. 289, 113 S.E.2d 427 (1960); Howard v. Sasso, 253 N.C. 185, 116 S.E.2d 341 (1960); Taylor v. Parks, 254 N.C. 266, 118 S.E.2d 779 (1961); Chappell v. Dean, 258 N.C. 412, 128 S.E.2d 830 (1963).

This section was designed and intended to, and does, establish a rule of evidence which facilitates proof of ownership and agency in automobile collision cases where one of the vehicles is operated by a person other than the owner. It was not enacted and designed to render proof unnecessary, nor does proof of registration or ownership make out a prima facie case for the jury on the issue of negligence. Neither is it sufficient to send the case to the jury, or support a finding favorable to plaintiff under the negligence issue, or to support a finding against a defendant on the issue of negligence. Branch v. Dempsey, 265 N.C. 733, 145 S.E.2d 395 (1965).

The presumption of this section relates to the rule of evidence and procedure rather than to substantive rights. Randall Ins., Inc. v. O'Neill, 258 N.C. 169, 128 S.E.2d 239 (1962).

This section is simply a rule of evidence to shift the burden of going forward with the proof to those persons better able to establish the true facts than are plaintiffs. Manning v. State Farm Mut. Auto. Ins. Co., 243 F. Supp. 619 (W.D.N.C. 1965).

The prima facie showing of agency under subsection (b) is a rule of evidence and not one of substantive law. DeArmon v. B. Mears Corp., 312 N.C. 749, 325 S.E.2d 223 (1985).

G.

S. 20-71.1 was a rule of evidence, not a rule of law, and, contrary to a passenger's assertion, an estate's admission that the decedent owned the motor vehicle involved in a traffic accident did not suffice to establish a prima facie case of liability against the estate under the legal doctrine of respondeat superior; the dismissal of the passenger's claim against the estate based on the decedent's ownership of the auto was proper because the claim against the driver was a claim against an agent, and, since the driver was named as a party, proper service was required. Because the summons as to the driver was allowed to lapse and the statute of limitations had since run, the driver had no liability to impute to the estate, and neither the driver nor the estate could have been determined judicially to have been negligent. Atkinson v. Lesmeister, 186 N.C. App. 442, 651 S.E.2d 294 (2007).

SECTION DOES NOT CHANGE BASIC RULE AS TO LIABILITY. --This section did not change the basic rule as to liability. It did establish a new rule of evidence, changing radically the requirements as to what the injured plaintiff must show in evidence in order to have his case passed on by the jury. Jyachosky v. Wensil, 240 N.C. 217, 81 S.E.2d 644 (1954).

OR CHANGE PREREQUISITES TO LIABILITY UNDER DOCTRINE OF RESPONDEAT SUPERIOR. --This section did not change the elements prerequisite to liability under the doctrine of respondeat superior. To establish liability under this doctrine, the injured plaintiff must allege and prove that the operator was the agent of the owner, and that this relationship existed at the time and in respect of the very transaction out of which the injury arose. Whiteside v. McCarson, 250 N.C. 673, 110 S.E.2d 295 (1959); Belmany v. Overton, 270 N.C. 400, 154 S.E.2d 538 (1967).

It is elementary that a principal or employer is not liable for injury due to a negligent act or omission of his agent or employee when such agent or employee had departed from the course of his employment and embarked upon a mission or frolic of his own. Duckworth v. Metcalf, 268 N.C. 340, 150 S.E.2d 485 (1966).

NOR DOES THIS SECTION ABROGATE THE WELL-SETTLED RULE OF LAW THAT MERE OWNERSHIP OF AN AUTOMOBILE DOES NOT IMPOSE LIABILITY upon the owner for injury to another by the negligent operation of the vehicle on the part of a driver who was not, at the time of the injury, the employee or agent of the owner or who was not, at such time, acting in the course of his employment or agency. Duckworth v. Metcalf, 268 N.C. 340, 150 S.E.2d 485 (1966).

Proof that one owns a motor vehicle which is operated in a negligent manner, causing injury to another, is not sufficient to impose liability on the owner. The injured party, if he is to recover from the owner, must allege and prove facts (1) calling for an application of the doctrine of respondeat superior, or (2) negligence of the owner himself in (a) providing the driver with a vehicle known to be dangerous because of its defective condition, or (b) permitting a known incompetent

driver to use the vehicle on the highway. Beasley v. Williams, 260 N.C. 561, 133 S.E.2d 227 (1963).

OR COMPEL A VERDICT AGAINST OWNER. --Proof of ownership of the automobile by one not the driver makes out a prima facie case of agency of the driver for the owner at the time of the driver's negligent act or omission, but it does not compel a verdict against the owner upon the principle of respondeat superior. Duckworth v. Metcalf, 268 N.C. 340, 150 S.E.2d 485 (1966).

THE RULE OF EVIDENCE ESTABLISHED BY THIS SECTION APPLIES WHENEVER A FACTUAL DETERMINATION AS TO ALLEGED AGENCY IS TO BE MADE, whether by the court to resolve a question of fact or by a jury to resolve an issue of fact. Howard v. Sasso, 253 N.C. 185, 116 S.E.2d 341 (1960).

THE RELATIONSHIP OF LESSOR AND LESSEE IS NOT THAT OF PRINCIPAL AND AGENT. DeArmon v. B. Mears Corp., 312 N.C. 749, 325 S.E.2d 223 (1985).

PROOF OF OWNERSHIP IS PRIMA FACIE PROOF OF AGENCY. Branch v. Dempsey, 265 N.C. 733, 145 S.E.2d 395 (1965).

Upon a showing of ownership, the artificial force of the prima facie rule under this section seems to permit a finding of agency. Torres v. Smith, 269 N.C. 546, 153 S.E.2d 129 (1967).

Evidence of ownership and registration of a motor vehicle involved in a collision must, by force of this statute, be regarded as prima facie evidence that at the time and place of the injury caused by it the motor vehicle was being operated with the authority, consent and knowledge and under the control of a person for whose conduct the defendant was legally responsible. Allen v. Schiller, 6 N.C. App. 392, 169 S.E.2d 924 (1969).

Where the owner of equipment leased both the equipment and operator to another under circumstances wherein the owner retained control over the manner in which the equipment was to be operated, the operator may have been the agent of the owner-lessor. DeArmon v. B. Mears Corp., 312 N.C. 749, 325 S.E.2d 223 (1985).

Where an owner of a truck leased both the truck and driver to another, the operator of the truck was not thereafter the agent of the owner if by the terms of the lease itself or other circumstances the owner relinquished all right to control the truck's operation. DeArmon v. B. Mears Corp., 312 N.C. 749, 325 S.E.2d 223 (1985).

Given that plaintiffs alleged that defendants owned the tractor that defendant driver was driving at the time of a wreck and the evidence indicated that they were the tractor's owners, plaintiffs were entitled to rely upon the statutory presumption of control under G.S. 20-71.1(b), and therefore established a prima facie case of a principal-agent relationship between the defendants as the tractor's owners and defendant the driver of the tractor. Shinn v. Greeness, 218 F.R.D. 478 (M.D.N.C. 2003).

AND IS SUFFICIENT TO TAKE CASE TO JURY. --Proof of ownership of the motor vehicle involved in the injury complained of, by force of this section, must

Chapter 20

be regarded as sufficient to carry the case to the jury on the question of the legal responsibility of the defendant for the operation of the vehicle. Travis v. Duckworth, 237 N.C. 471, 75 S.E.2d 309 (1953); Kellogg v. Thomas, 244 N.C. 722, 94 S.E.2d 903 (1956); Scott v. Lee, 245 N.C. 68, 95 S.E.2d 89 (1956); Johnson v. Wayne Thompson, Inc., 250 N.C. 665, 110 S.E.2d 306 (1959).

Where there is sufficient evidence of negligence of the operator of a motor vehicle to be submitted to the jury on that issue, evidence that the vehicle was registered in the name of another defendant takes the issue of such other defendant's liability to the jury. Ennis v. Dupree, 258 N.C. 141, 128 S.E.2d 231 (1962).

This section is construed to mean that proof of ownership alone carries the case to the jury on the issue of agency. Humphries v. Going, 59 F.R.D. 583 (E.D.N.C. 1973).

AN ADMISSION OF THE OWNERSHIP OF ONE OF THE VEHICLES INVOLVED IN A COLLISION IS SUFFICIENT TO MAKE OUT A PRIMA FACIE CASE OF AGENCY sufficient to support, but not to compel, a verdict against the owner under the doctrine of respondeat superior for damages proximately caused by the negligence of the driver. Hartley v. Smith, 239 N.C. 170, 79 S.E.2d 767 (1954); Elliott v. Killian, 242 N.C. 471, 87 S.E.2d 903 (1955); Davis v. Lawrence, 242 N.C. 496, 87 S.E.2d 915 (1955); Hatcher v. Clayton, 242 N.C. 450, 88 S.E.2d 104 (1955); Caughron v. Walker, 243 N.C. 153, 90 S.E.2d 305 (1955); Brown v. Nesbitt, 271 N.C. 532, 157 S.E.2d 85 (1967); Scallon v. Hooper, 49 N.C. App. 113, 270 S.E.2d 496 (1980), cert. denied, 301 N.C. 722, 276 S.E.2d 284 (1981); Norman v. Royal Crown Bottling Co., 49 N.C. App. 661, 272 S.E.2d 355 (1980).

Admission of ownership of the vehicle involved in the collision requires the submission to the jury of the question of liability under the doctrine of respondeat superior. Wilcox v. Glover Motors, Inc., 269 N.C. 473, 153 S.E.2d 76 (1967).

ADMISSION BY DEFENDANT TRUCK OWNER that his truck was being operated by codefendant was sufficient, as against such owner, to permit a finding that codefendant was driving the truck and, therefore, to bring into operation this section, making such fact prima facie proof that codefendant was the agent of the truck owner and was driving the truck in the course of his employment as such agent. Branch v. Dempsey, 265 N.C. 733, 145 S.E.2d 395 (1965).

AND TO ENTITLE PLAINTIFF TO INSTRUCTION ON SECTION. --Plaintiff in a wrongful death action was entitled to an instruction, even absent a special request by plaintiff, on this section, where it was stipulated that one defendant who was not the driver was the registered owner of the vehicle at the time of the accident, and an instruction on the statute was required even though plaintiff presented no positive evidence that defendant driver was defendant owner's agent. Scallon v. Hooper, 49 N.C. App. 113, 270 S.E.2d 496 (1980), cert. denied, 301 N.C. 722, 276 S.E.2d 284 (1981).

PLAINTIFF WAS ENTITLED TO HAVE HIS CASE SUBMITTED TO THE JURY WHERE

DEFENDANT ADMITTED OWNERSHIP of the automobile and conceded that it was registered in his name. White v. Vananda, 13 N.C. App. 19, 185 S.E.2d 247 (1971).

PROOF OF LEGAL TITLE TO AN AUTOMOBILE MAKES AT LEAST A PRIMA FACIE SHOWING OF OWNERSHIP in the one in whose name the title is registered. Guilford Nat'l Bank v. Southern Ry., 319 F.2d 825 (4th Cir. 1963), cert. denied, 375 U.S. 985, 84 S. Ct. 518, 11 L. Ed. 2d 473 (1964).

Under this section all that is now required for submission of the issue to the jury is that the injured party show ownership of the motor vehicle, which may be done prima facie by proof that the motor vehicle was registered in the name of the person sought to be charged. Jyachosky v. Wensil, 240 N.C. 217, 81 S.E.2d 644 (1954).

Proof of registration of a motorcycle in the name of driver's father was prima facie evidence of ownership by him and agency in the driver under this section. Such prima facie evidence of ownership in the father was sufficient to carry the case to the jury against him, notwithstanding that further evidence was sufficient, if true, to rebut the prima facie evidence that the father owned the motorcycle and that the minor was driving it as his agent. Bowen v. Gardner, 275 N.C. 363, 168 S.E.2d 47 (1969).

BUT PRIMA FACIE CASE OF AGENCY DOES NOT COMPEL A VERDICT AGAINST DEFENDANT. --This section makes out a prima facie case of agency which will support, but does not compel, a verdict against defendant upon the principle of respondeat superior. Chappell v. Dean, 258 N.C. 412, 128 S.E.2d 830 (1963).

While this section makes admitted ownership of a truck prima facie evidence that the operator was acting as the owner's agent or employee within the scope of his employment, sufficient to carry the case to the jury, it does not compel the finding by the jury that the driver was negligent or that he was the agent or employee of the owner and at the time acting within the scope of his employment. Brothers v. Jernigan, 244 N.C. 441, 94 S.E.2d 316 (1956).

Where a trial judge is presented only with a prima facie showing of agency mandated by subsection (b) on the one hand, and defendant's evidence establishing the absence of agency on the other, the only issue becomes whether the judge believes defendant's evidence. If the judge does, then plaintiff's prima facie showing disappears and the judge must conclude that no agency relationship exists. If he does not believe defendant's evidence, then he may conclude for plaintiff on the agency issue. Either conclusion must be based on proper findings. DeArmon v. B. Mears Corp., 312 N.C. 749, 325 S.E.2d 223 (1985).

The prima facie showing of agency under this section only permits, and does not compel, a finding for the plaintiff on the issue of agency. Thompson v. Three Guys Furn. Co., 122 N.C. App. 340, 469 S.E.2d 583 (1996).

The prima facie showing of agency under G.S. 20-71.1(b) is a rule of evidence and not one of substantive law. The statute makes out a prima facie case which, nothing else appearing, permits but does not compel a finding for plaintiff on the issue of agency. Shinn v. Greeness, 218 F.R.D. 478 (M.D.N.C. 2003).

AS PLAINTIFF HAS BURDEN OF PROVING AGENCY. --Proof of registration or admission of ownership furnishes, by virtue of the statute, prima facie evidence that the driver was agent of the owner in the operation, and is sufficient to support, but not compel, a verdict on the agency issue. It takes the issue to the jury. Even so, plaintiff must allege, and has the burden of proving, agency. Mitchell v. White, 256 N.C. 437, 124 S.E.2d 137 (1962).

The burden of proof continues to rest upon the plaintiff to prove an agency relationship between the driver and the owner at the time of the driver's negligence which caused the injury. Duckworth v. Metcalf, 268 N.C. 340, 150 S.E.2d 485 (1966).

This section creates no presumption of law, and it does not shift the burden of the issue from plaintiff to defendant. Chappell v. Dean, 258 N.C. 412, 128 S.E.2d 830 (1963).

This section does not relieve plaintiff of the duty to allege and the burden of proving agency. Chappell v. Dean, 258 N.C. 412, 128 S.E.2d 830 (1963).

Trial court incorrectly denied defendants' motions under G.S. 1A-1, Rule 50(a); this section merely provides prima facie evidence of motor vehicle ownership, but does not remove plaintiff's burden of proof as to agency which, in this case, he failed to carry as to the first defendant and which issue the court removed in error from the jury as to the second defendant. Winston v. Brodie, 134 N.C. App. 260, 517 S.E.2d 203 (1999).

AND ALLEGING ULTIMATE FACTS. --The provisions of this section are a rule of evidence and do not relieve a plaintiff of alleging the ultimate facts on which to base a cause of actionable negligence. Parker v. Underwood, 239 N.C. 308, 79 S.E.2d 765 (1954).

BOTH NEGLIGENCE AND AGENCY MUST BE ALLEGED AND PROVED BY PLAINTIFF. --This section was not enacted and designed to render proof unnecessary, nor does proof of registration or ownership make out a prima facie case for the jury on the issue of negligence. Neither is it sufficient to send the case to the jury, or to support a finding favorable to plaintiff under the negligence issue, or to support a finding against a defendant on the issue of negligence. It does not constitute evidence of negligence. It is instead directed solely to the question of agency of a nonowner operator of a motor vehicle involved in an accident. It is still necessary for the party aggrieved to allege both negligence and agency in his pleading and to prove both at the trial. Hartley v. Smith, 239 N.C. 170, 79 S.E.2d 767 (1954).

It is still necessary for the party aggrieved to allege both negligence and agency in his pleading and to prove both at the trial. Branch v. Dempsey, 265 N.C. 733, 145 S.E.2d 395 (1965); Belmany v. Overton, 270 N.C. 400, 154 S.E.2d 538 (1967).

This section establishes a rule of evidence, but does not relieve a plaintiff from alleging and proving negligence and agency. Osborne v. Gilreath, 241 N.C. 685, 86 S.E.2d 462 (1955).

This section presupposes a cause of action based on allegations of agency and of actionable negligence, and therefore, if the complaint fails to allege agency or actionable negligence, it is demurrable and is insufficient to support a verdict for damages against the owner of the vehicle. Lynn v. Clark, 252 N.C. 289, 113 S.E.2d 427 (1960).

While proof of registration is prima facie evidence of ownership and that the agent was acting for the owner's benefit and in the scope of his employment, there must be an allegation of agency to make evidence of agency admissible against the principal. Dupree v. Batts, 276 N.C. 68, 170 S.E.2d 918 (1969).

Defendant's admission and stipulation that the automobile involved in the accident was registered in her name was evidence sufficient to support, but not compel, a finding for plaintiffs that defendant was legally responsible for the acts and omissions of the codefendant in the operation and parking of the automobile; but before plaintiffs could recover, they had to prove by evidence competent against the owner defendant that the codefendant was negligent and that her negligence was the proximate cause of plaintiffs' damages. Tuttle v. Beck, 7 N.C. App. 337, 172 S.E.2d 90 (1970).

AS ABSENT EVIDENCE THAT DEFENDANT IS THE OWNER OF THE VEHICLE, PLAINTIFF IS NOT ENTITLED TO THE BENEFIT OF THIS SECTION. Freeman v. Biggers Bros., 260 N.C. 300, 132 S.E.2d 626 (1963).

Where plaintiff offered no evidence to support her allegation that defendant was the registered owner of an automobile operated by his son, she could not benefit by the presumption of agency created by this section. Griffin v. Pancoast, 257 N.C. 52, 125 S.E.2d 310 (1962).

THE ULTIMATE ISSUE IS FOR JURY DETERMINATION, notwithstanding that the only positive evidence tends to show explicitly and clearly that the operator, whether driving with or without the owner's consent, was on a purely personal mission at the time of the collision. Whiteside v. McCarson, 250 N.C. 673, 110 S.E.2d 295 (1959).

By reason of this section, the agency issue is for determination by the jury. Moore v. Crocker, 264 N.C. 233, 141 S.E.2d 307 (1965); Allen v. Schiller, 6 N.C. App. 392, 169 S.E.2d 924 (1969).

LICENSE PLATES AS PRIMA FACIE EVIDENCE OF OWNERSHIP. --A prima facie case of ownership was made out by virtue of this section when license plates issued to driver were on the vehicle, even though the car described on the registration did not have the same body style as the vehicle actually being driven. Rick v. Murphy, 251 N.C. 162, 110 S.E.2d 815 (1959).

NAME ON VEHICLE AS PRIMA FACIE EVIDENCE OF OWNERSHIP. --Where common carrier of freight operated tractor-trailer units on public highway bearing the insignia or name of such carrier, and one of their motor vehicles was involved in a collision or inflicts injury upon another, evidence that the name or insignia of the defendant was painted or inscribed on the motor vehicle which inflicted the injury constituted prima facie evidence that the defendant was the owner of such vehicle and that the driver thereof was operating it for and on behalf of defendant. Freeman v. Biggers Bros., 260 N.C. 300, 132 S.E.2d 626 (1963).

REBUTTAL OF PRESUMPTION OF AGENCY BY PLAINTIFF'S OWN EVIDENCE. --Where defendant admitted that, at the time of the accident, he was the owner of one of the vehicles involved in the collision, but plaintiff elicited testimony from her own witnesses of declarations made by defendant to the effect that, at the time in question, the driver had taken defendant's automobile without defendant's authorization, knowledge or consent, and was not at the time defendant's agent or employee or acting in the course and scope of any employment by defendant, plaintiff's own evidence rebutted the presumption created by this section, and such evidence not being contradicted by any other evidence of either plaintiff or defendant, nonsuit on the issue of agency was proper. Taylor v. Parks, 254 N.C. 266, 118 S.E.2d 779 (1961).

NO PRESUMPTION OR INFERENCE OF AGENCY BEFORE OR AFTER OPERATION OF VEHICLE. --This section creates no presumption and gives rise to no inference as to the existence of any agency relation before the operation of the vehicle begins or after it stops. Branch v. Dempsey, 265 N.C. 733, 145 S.E.2d 395 (1965).

In the absence of evidence of agency, apart from the mere act of driving a motor vehicle registered in the name of another, the agency must be deemed to have terminated when the driver has brought the vehicle to a final stop and has left it. Branch v. Dempsey, 265 N.C. 733, 145 S.E.2d 395 (1965).

WHENEVER THE FACTS WITH RESPECT TO AGENCY ARE ESTABLISHED, WITHOUT CONTRADICTION, IT IS THE DUTY OF THE COURT TO DISREGARD THIS SECTION, even to the point of setting aside a verdict which this section permits. Manning v. State Farm Mut. Auto. Ins. Co., 243 F. Supp. 619 (W.D.N.C. 1965).

PEREMPTORY INSTRUCTION IN DEFENDANT'S FAVOR WHERE DRIVER WAS ON A PURELY PERSONAL MISSION. --Where ownership of the vehicle involved was sufficient to take the case to the jury under this section, the trial court's directed verdict in favor of defendant owner was harmless error where the evidence clearly established that the driver of the vehicle was on a purely personal mission at the time of the accident, thereby entitling defendant, without request, to a peremptory instruction on the issue of the owner's liability. Gwaltney v. Keaton, 29 N.C. App. 91, 223 S.E.2d 506 (1976).

Where plaintiff relied solely on this section to take the issue of agency to the jury, and defendant's evidence tended to show that the driver was on a purely personal mission at the time of the accident, defendant, without request therefor, was entitled to a peremptory instruction, related directly to the particular facts shown by defendant's positive evidence, to answer the issue of agency in the negative. A general instruction to so answer the issue if the jury believed the facts to be as defendant's evidence tended to show, without relating the instruction directly to defendant's evidence in the particular case, was insufficient. Belmany v. Overton, 270 N.C. 400, 154 S.E.2d 538 (1967).

In any case in which a plaintiff, as against the registered owner of a motor vehicle, relied solely upon this section to prove the agency of a nonowner operator, and in which all of the positive evidence in the case was to the effect that the operator was on a mission of his own and not on any business for the registered owner, it was the duty of the trial judge, even if there was evidence that the registered owner gave the operator permission to use the vehicle, to instruct the jury that, if they believed the evidence and found the facts to be as the evidence tended to show, that is, that the operator was on a mission of his own, they would answer the agency issue in the negative. And it was prejudicial error for the court, in such circumstances, to fail to so instruct the jury, even if there was no special request therefor. Chappel v. Dean, 258 N.C. 412, 128 S.E.2d 830 (1963).

Where plaintiff relies solely on the provisions of this section on the issue of respondeat superior and introduces no evidence, but defendant introduces evidence tending to show that the driver was on a purely personal mission of his own at the time of the accident, there is no evidence upon which the court may instruct the jury in plaintiff's favor on the issue, and the court's explanation of the rule of evidence prescribed by the statute is sufficient; but as to the defendant's evidence, the court is required, even in the absence of a request for special instructions, to give an explicit instruction applying defendant's evidence to the issue and charging that if the jury should find the facts to be as defendant's evidence tends to show, the issue should be answered in the negative. Whiteside v. McCarson, 250 N.C. 673, 110 S.E.2d 295 (1959).

Where evidence disclosed that an employee was driving vehicle registered in the name of his employer, and there was also evidence that the employee was driving on the occasion in question on a purely personal mission without the knowledge or consent of the employer, the court properly submitted the issue of the employer's liability to the jury under instructions that if the jury should find that the employee was engaged in a purely personal mission without the knowledge or consent of the employer the jury should answer the issue in the negative. Skinner v. Jernigan, 250 N.C. 657, 110 S.E.2d 301 (1959).

Defendant was entitled to a peremptory instruction when plaintiff relied solely on this section and defendant offered uncontradicted evidence on the issue of agency tending to show that the driver was on a purely personal mission or errand at the time of the collision; but there is no authority that a peremptory instruction may be given in favor of a defendant who offers no evidence whatsoever on the critical issue. Scallon v. Hooper, 49 N.C. App. 113, 270 S.E.2d 496 (1980), cert. denied, 301 N.C. 722, 276 S.E.2d 284 (1981).

Where plaintiff relied solely upon subsection (b), presenting no other evidence of agency, and defendant

Chapter 20

presented positive, contradicting evidence which, if believed, established the nonexistence of an agency relationship between owner and operator, defendant was entitled to a peremptory instruction on the agency, issue, or in a nonjury hearing, to a conclusion, based on proper findings, that no agency relationship existed. The statutory presumption is not weighed against defendant's evidence by the trier of facts. DeArmon v. B. Mears Corp., 312 N.C. 749, 325 S.E.2d 223 (1985).

INSTRUCTION WHERE EVIDENCE SHOWS THAT DRIVER WAS CO-OWNER WITH REGISTERED OWNER. --Evidence that a vehicle operated by a woman was registered in the name of her husband was prima facie evidence that she was driving as his agent, but even so, parol evidence was competent to show that the husband and wife were in fact co-owners, and when there was such evidence, it was error for the court to peremptorily instruct the jury to answer the issue of agency in the affirmative. Rushing v. Polk, 258 N.C. 256, 128 S.E.2d 675 (1962).

A MODEL INSTRUCTION IS AVAILABLE AS A GUIDE FOR EXPLAINING THIS SECTION to the jury. Scallon v. Hooper, 49 N.C. App. 113, 270 S.E.2d 496 (1980), cert. denied, 301 N.C. 722, 276 S.E.2d 284 (1981).

THE INSTRUCTION MUST RELATE DIRECTLY TO PARTICULAR FACTS shown by defendant's positive evidence. Scallon v. Hooper, 49 N.C. App. 113, 270 S.E.2d 496 (1980), cert. denied, 301 N.C. 722, 276 S.E.2d 284 (1981).

RIGHT TO HAVE OWNER JOINED FOR CONTRIBUTION. --Where, in an action by a passenger against the drivers involved in a collision, plaintiff made out a prima facie case of negligence on the part of the driver of the car, proof or admissions that additional defendant was the registered owner of the car established prima facie that the driver was such owner's agent and was acting in the course and scope of the employment, and entitled the defendants to have the owner of the car joined for contribution. McPherson v. Haire, 262 N.C. 71, 136 S.E.2d 224 (1964).

SERVICE ON NONRESIDENT OWNER OF VEHICLE. --Under this section, ownership of a vehicle involved in an accident is sufficient proof of agency to support service of process on the nonresident owner whose agent is alleged to have negligently injured plaintiff by operation of the vehicle on North Carolina highways. Todd v. Thomas, 202 F. Supp. 45 (E.D.N.C. 1962). See also Davis v. St. Paul-Mercury Indem. Co., 294 F.2d 641 (4th Cir. 1961).

COMPULSORY NONSUIT HELD ERROR. --Where a judgment of compulsory nonsuit of plaintiff's action against a defendant who was the driver of the automobile involved in the action was improvidently entered, the trial court also erred in entering a judgment of compulsory nonsuit against another defendant, for the reason that the automobile was registered in the latter's name, and therefore plaintiff was entitled to go to the jury against him by virtue of the provisions of this section. Hamilton v. McCash, 257 N.C. 611, 127 S.E.2d 214 (1962).

IMPUTATION TO HUSBAND OF WIFE'S NEGLIGENCE HELD IMPROPER. --Where title to an automobile stood in wife's name, imputation to her husband of her alleged negligence in driving the vehicle while her husband was riding as a passenger in the automobile could not be predicated upon evidence showing that the husband made deferred payments on the purchase price of the car, paid the expenses incident to maintaining the car, and treated the car for tax purposes as a depreciable asset of his business enterprise. Guilford Nat'l Bank v. Southern Ry., 319 F.2d 825 (4th Cir. 1963), cert. denied, 375 U.S. 985, 84 S. Ct. 518, 11 L. Ed. 2d 473 (1964).

OWNER-OCCUPANT OF CAR ORDINARILY HAS THE RIGHT TO DIRECT ITS OPERATION by the driver. Randall v. Rogers, 262 N.C. 544, 138 S.E.2d 248 (1964).

HENCE, HE IS RESPONSIBLE FOR DRIVER'S NEGLIGENCE IRRESPECTIVE OF AGENCY, as such, and the provisions of this section. Randall v. Rogers, 262 N.C. 544, 138 S.E.2d 248 (1964).

APPLIED in Hensley v. Harris, 242 N.C. 599, 89 S.E.2d 155 (1955); Knight v. Associated Transp., Inc., 255 N.C. 462, 122 S.E.2d 64 (1961); Tharpe v. Newman, 257 N.C. 71, 125 S.E.2d 315 (1962); Hawley v. Indemnity Ins. Co. of N. Am., 257 N.C. 381, 126 S.E.2d 161 (1962); Salter v. Lovick, 257 N.C. 619, 127 S.E.2d 273 (1962); Smith v. Simpson, 260 N.C. 601, 133 S.E.2d 474 (1963); Yates v. Chappell, 263 N.C. 461, 139 S.E.2d 728 (1965); Passmore v. Smith, 266 N.C. 717, 147 S.E.2d 238 (1966); Jackson v. Baldwin, 268 N.C. 149, 150 S.E.2d 37 (1966); Morris v. Bigham, 6 N.C. App. 490, 170 S.E.2d 534 (1969); Nolan v. Boulware, 21 N.C. App. 347, 204 S.E.2d 701 (1974); Jones v. Allred, 52 N.C. App. 38, 278 S.E.2d 521 (1981); Hargett v. Reed, 95 N.C. App. 292, 382 S.E.2d 791 (1989); Brewer v. Spivey, 108 N.C. App. 174, 423 S.E.2d 95 (1992).

CITED in State v. Scoggin, 236 N.C. 19, 72 S.E.2d 54 (1952); Chatfield v. Farm Bureau Mut. Auto. Ins. Co., 208 F.2d 250 (4th Cir. 1953); Northwest Cas. Co. v. Kirkman, 119 F. Supp. 828 (M.D.N.C. 1954); Ransdell v. Young, 243 N.C. 75, 89 S.E.2d 773 (1955); Williamson v. Varner, 252 N.C. 446, 114 S.E.2d 92 (1960); Tart v. Register, 257 N.C. 161, 125 S.E.2d 754 (1962); Parlier v. Barnes, 260 N.C. 341, 132 S.E.2d 684 (1963); Perkins v. Cook, 272 N.C. 477, 158 S.E.2d 584 (1968); United Roasters, Inc. v. Colgate-Palmolive Co., 485 F. Supp. 1049 (E.D.N.C. 1980); Duffer v. Royal Dodge, Inc., 51 N.C. App. 129, 275 S.E.2d 206 (1981); Cranford v. Helms, 53 N.C. App. 337, 280 S.E.2d 756 (1981); Mercer v. Crocker, 73 N.C. App. 634, 327 S.E.2d 31 (1985); Lawing v. Lawing, 81 N.C. App. 159, 344 S.E.2d 100 (1986); State v. Williams, 90 N.C. App. 120, 367 S.E.2d 345 (1988); Tittle v. Case, 101 N.C. App. 346, 399 S.E.2d 373 (1991).

LEGAL PERIODICALS. --

For case note discussing cases arising under this section, see 41 N.C.L. Rev. 124 (1962).

For note on permissive user under the omnibus clause, see 41 N.C.L. Rev. 232 (1963).

For note discussing the extension of the family purpose doctrine to motorcycles and private property, see 14 Wake Forest L. Rev. 699 (1978).

Chapter 20

PART 3A.
SALVAGE TITLES

§ 20-71.2. Declaration of purpose

The titling of salvage motor vehicles constitutes a problem in North Carolina because members of the public are sometimes misled into believing a motor vehicle has not been damaged by collision, fire, flood, accident, or other cause or that the vehicle has not been altered, rebuilt, or modified to such an extent that it impairs or changes the original components of the motor vehicle. It is therefore in the public interest that the Commissioner of Motor Vehicles issue rules to give public notice of the titling of such vehicles and to carry out the provisions of this Part of the motor vehicle laws of North Carolina.

History.

1987, c. 607, s. 1

CITED in Wilson v. Sutton, 124 N.C. App. 170, 476 S.E.2d 467 (1996).

OPINIONS OF THE ATTORNEY GENERAL

MAIN OBJECTIVE OF SECTION TO PRESERVE INFORMATION OF PRIOR HISTORY OF DAMAGED VEHICLES. --In this section the General Assembly clearly indicated that its main objective in enacting Session Laws 1987, c. 607, was to preserve information regarding the prior history of damaged vehicles for the benefit of subsequent buyers. Any reading of the statute contrary to that purpose would be inappropriate. See opinion of Attorney General to Mr. James E. Rhodes, Director, Vehicle Registration Section, Division of Motor Vehicles, North Carolina Department of Transportation, 58 N.C.A.G. 38 (May 20, 1988).

§ 20-71.3. Salvage and other vehicles -- titles and registration cards to be branded

(a) Motor vehicle certificates of title and registration cards issued pursuant to G.S. 20-57 shall be branded in accordance with this section.

As used in this section, "branded" means that the title and registration card shall contain a designation that discloses if the vehicle is classified as any of the following:

(1) Salvage Motor Vehicle.

(2) Salvage Rebuilt Vehicle.

(3) Reconstructed Vehicle.

(4) Flood Vehicle.

(5) Non-U.S.A. Vehicle.

(6) Any other classification authorized by law.

(a1) Any motor vehicle that is declared a total loss by an insurance company licensed and approved to conduct business in North Carolina, in addition to the designations noted in subsection (a) of this section, shall:

(1) Have the title and registration card marked "TOTAL LOSS CLAIM".

(2) Have a tamperproof permanent marker inserted into the doorjamb of that vehicle by the Division, at the time of the final inspection of the reconstructed vehicle, that states "TOTAL LOSS CLAIM VEHICLE". Should that vehicle be later reconstructed, repaired, or rebuilt, a permanent tamperproof marker shall be inserted in the doorjamb of the reconstructed, repaired, or rebuilt vehicle.

(b) Any motor vehicle up to and including six model years old damaged by collision or other occurrence, that is to be retitled in this State, shall be subject to preliminary and final inspections by the Enforcement Section of the Division. For purposes of this section, the term "six model years" shall be calculated by counting the model year of the vehicle's manufacture as the first model year and the current calendar year as the final model year.

These inspections serve as antitheft measures and do not certify the safety or roadworthiness of a vehicle.

(c) The Division shall not retitle a vehicle described in subsection (b) of this section that has not undergone the preliminary and final inspections required by that subsection.

(d) Any motor vehicle up to and including six model years old that has been inspected pursuant to subsection (b) of this section may be retitled with an unbranded title based upon a title application by the rebuilder with a supporting affidavit disclosing all of the following:

(1) The parts used or replaced.

(2) The major components replaced.

(3) The hours of labor and the hourly labor rate.

(4) The total cost of repair.

(5) The existence, if applicable, of the doorjamb "TOTAL LOSS CLAIM VEHICLE" marker.

The unbranded title shall be issued only if the cost of repairs, including parts and labor, does not exceed seventy-five percent (75%) of its fair market retail value.

(e) Any motor vehicle more than six model years old damaged by collision or other occurrence that is to be retitled by the State may be retitled, without inspection, with an unbranded title based upon a title application by the rebuilder with a supporting affidavit disclosing all of the following:

(1) The parts used or replaced.

(2) The major components replaced.

(3) The hours of labor and the hourly labor rate.

(4) The total cost of repair.

(5) The existence, if applicable, of the doorjamb "TOTAL LOSS CLAIM VEHICLE" marker.

(6) The cost to replace the air bag restraint system.

The unbranded title shall be issued only if the cost of repairs, including parts and labor and excluding the cost to replace the air bag restraint system, does not exceed seventy-five percent (75%) of its fair market retail value.

(f) The Division shall maintain the affidavits required by this section and make them available for review and copying by persons researching the salvage and repair history of the vehicle.

(g) Any motor vehicle that has been branded in another state shall be branded with the nearest applicable brand specified in this section, except that no junk vehicle or vehicle that has been branded junk in another state shall be titled or registered.

(h) A branded title for a salvage motor vehicle damaged by collision or other occurrence shall be issued as follows:

(1) For motor vehicles up to and including six model years old, a branded title shall be issued if the cost of repairs, including parts and labor, exceeds seventy-five percent (75%) of its fair market value at the time of the collision or other occurrence.

(2) For motor vehicles more than six model years old, a branded title shall be issued if the cost of repairs, including parts and labor and excluding the cost to replace the air bag restraint system, exceeds seventy-five percent (75%) of its fair market value at the time of the collision or other occurrence.

(i) Once the Division has issued a branded title for a motor vehicle all subsequent titles for that motor vehicle shall continue to reflect the branding.

(j) The Division shall prepare necessary forms and doorjamb marker specifications and may adopt rules required to carry out the provisions of this Part.

History.
1987, c. 607, s. 1; 1987 (Reg. Sess., 1988), c. 1105, s. 2; 1989, c. 455, ss. 2, 3; 1989 (Reg. Sess., 1990), c. 916, s. 1; 1997-443, s. 32.26;1998-212, s. 27.8(a);2003-258, s. 1

EDITOR'S NOTE. --
Session Laws 2001-492, s. 5, effective December 4, 2001, provides: "The Division of Motor Vehicles shall issue or reissue an unbranded title for vehicles titled in this State between July 20, 2001, and November 1, 2001, pursuant to G.S. 20-71.3 if the vehicle was a motor vehicle damaged by collision or other occurrence and if the cost of repairs, including parts, did not exceed seventy-five percent (75%) of its fair market value. Transfers of vehicles issued or reissued unbranded titles pursuant to this section [s. 5 of Session Laws 2001-492] shall be subject to the disclosure requirements of G.S. 20-71.4." Initially s. 6 of Session

Laws 2001-492, had provided a November 1, 2001, sunset for s. 5. However, Session Laws 2001-487, s. 123.5 deleted the sunset provision.

LEGAL PERIODICALS. --
See Legislative Survey, 21 Campbell L. Rev. 323 (1999).

OPINIONS OF THE ATTORNEY GENERAL
"SATISFACTORY EVIDENCE" IN ORDER FOR THE DIVISION TO ISSUE AN UNBRANDED TITLE, if the vehicle also met the 75% standard of this section, would be evidence satisfactory to the division that the vehicle which was the subject of the application would meet requirements of the titling state for an unbranded title if repaired in that state. This could be a copy of the titling state's statutory or regulatory process if clear, and otherwise, a statement from an authorized official within the titling agency confirming the vehicle meets the criteria of their state for an unbranded title. See opinion of Attorney General to Ms. Carol Nemitz, Director, Vehicle Registration Section, Division of Motor Vehicles, 59 N.C.A.G. 48 (1989).

SECTION REQUIRES APPLICANT TO PROVIDE "SATISFACTORY EVIDENCE". --This section requires that the applicant for a North Carolina title provide the "satisfactory evidence" of the vehicle's eligibility for an unbranded title in the state where currently titled. See opinion of Attorney General to Ms. Carol Nemitz, Director, Vehicle Registration Section, Division of Motor Vehicles, 59 N.C.A.G. 48 (1989).

SATISFACTORY EVIDENCE WOULD HAVE TO BE VEHICLE SPECIFIC. --The "satisfactory evidence" for issuance of an unbranded title would have to be vehicle specific. See opinion of Attorney General to Ms. Carol Nemitz, Director, Vehicle Registration Section, Division of Motor Vehicles, 59 N.C.A.G. 48 (1989).

IF THE TITLING STATE HAS NO PROCEDURE FOR REMOVING A BRAND on a salvage vehicle title, North Carolina has no means by which an unbranded title can be issued here. See opinion of Attorney General to Ms. Carol Nemitz, Director, Vehicle Registration Section, Division of Motor Vehicles, 59 N.C.A.G. 48 (1989).

THE DATE OF APPLICATION FOR A TITLE DETERMINES WHICH LAW TO APPLY for purposes of processing salvage title vehicles. See opinion of Attorney General to Ms. Carol Nemitz, Director, Vehicle Registration Section, Division of Motor Vehicles, 59 N.C.A.G. 48 (1989).

RECORDS OF DISCLOSURE FORMS. --The Division of Motor Vehicles may prepare forms to carry out the provisions of this section, but there is no requirement that it keep records of the disclosure forms it may create. However, while there is no statutory provision requiring the division to disclose a prior title history showing that a vehicle was once damaged, there is no prohibition against this practice as a public service if the division should voluntarily undertake to do it. See opinion of Attorney General to Ms. Carol Nemitz, Director, Vehicle Registration Section, Division of Motor Vehicles, 59 N.C.A.G. 48 (1989).

VEHICLE DECLARED TOTAL LOSS BY INSURER DOES NOT HAVE TO MEET 75% TEST

TO BE SALVAGE VEHICLE. The tests are independent. See opinion of Attorney General to Mr. James E. Rhodes, Director, Vehicle Registration Section, Division of Motor Vehicles, North Carolina Department of Transportation, 58 N.C.A.G. 38 (May 20, 1988).

THIS SECTION PROVIDES NO BASIS FOR DMV TO RELAX 75% OF REPAIR COST FACTOR IN DETERMINING IF VEHICLE IS SALVAGE UNDER SUBDIVISION (D) OF G.S. 20-4-01(33). The standard is mandated by statute. See opinion of Attorney General to Mr. James E. Rhodes, Director, Vehicle Registration Section, Division of Motor Vehicles, North Carolina Department of Transportation, 58 N.C.A.G. 38 (May 20, 1988).

NO PROCEDURE WHICH ALLOWS DMV TO AVOID BRANDING TITLE OF MOTOR VEHICLE, BRANDED IN ANOTHER STATE, with the nearest applicable brand specified in the new North Carolina statute. The requirement in this section is mandatory and does not authorize reevaluation of the branding decision that was made in another state. See opinion of Attorney General to Mr. James E. Rhodes, Director, Vehicle Registration Section, Division of Motor Vehicles, North Carolina Department of Transportation, 58 N.C.A.G. 38 (May 20, 1988).

§ 20-71.4. Failure to disclose damage to a vehicle shall be a misdemeanor

(a) It shall be unlawful for any transferor of a motor vehicle to do any of the following:

(1) Transfer a motor vehicle up to and including five model years old when the transferor has knowledge that the vehicle has been involved in a collision or other occurrence to the extent that the cost of repairing that vehicle, excluding the cost to replace the air bag restraint system, exceeds twenty-five percent (25%) of its fair market retail value at the time of the collision or other occurrence, without disclosing that fact in writing to the transferee prior to the transfer of the vehicle.

(2) Transfer a motor vehicle when the transferor has knowledge that the vehicle is, or was, a flood vehicle, a reconstructed vehicle, or a salvage motor vehicle, without disclosing that fact in writing to the transferee prior to the transfer of the vehicle.

(3) Transfer a motor vehicle when the transferor has knowledge that a counterfeit supplemental restraint system, or a nonfunctional airbag, or no airbag has been installed in the vehicle. For purposes of this subdivision, in the event the owners of a franchised motor vehicle dealer, as defined in G.S. 20-286(8b), have no actual knowledge that a counterfeit supplemental restraint system component or nonfunctional air bag has been installed in a vehicle, knowledge by any other person shall not be imputed to the franchised motor vehicle dealer or its owners, and the franchised motor vehicle dealer or its owners shall not be deemed to have committed an unlawful act under this subdivision.

(a1) For purposes of this section, the term "five model years" shall be calculated by counting the model year of the vehicle's manufacture as the first model year and the current calendar year as the final model year. Failure to disclose any of the information required under subsection (a) of this section that is within the knowledge of the transferor will also result in civil liability under G.S. 20-348. The Commissioner may prepare forms to carry out the provisions of this section.

(b) It shall be unlawful for any person to remove the title or supporting documents to any motor vehicle from the State of North Carolina with the intent to conceal damage (or damage which has been repaired) occurring as a result of a collision or other occurrence.

(c) It shall be unlawful for any person to remove, tamper with, alter, or conceal the "TOTAL LOSS CLAIM VEHICLE" tamperproof permanent marker that is affixed to the doorjamb of any total loss claim vehicle. It shall be unlawful for any person to reconstruct a total loss claim vehicle and not include or affix a "TOTAL LOSS CLAIM VEHICLE" tamperproof permanent marker to the doorjamb of the rebuilt vehicle. Violation of this subsection shall constitute a Class I felony, punishable by a fine of not less than five thousand dollars ($ 5,000) for each offense.

(d) Violation of subsections (a) and (b) of this section shall constitute a Class 2 misdemeanor.

(e) The provisions of this section shall not apply to a State agency that assists the United States Department of Defense with purchasing, transferring, or titling a vehicle to another State agency, a unit of local government, a volunteer fire department, or a volunteer rescue squad.

History.
1987, c. 607, s. 1; 1987 (Reg. Sess., 1988), c. 1105, s. 3; 1989, c. 455, s. 4;1989 (Reg. Sess., 1990), c. 916, s. 2; 1993, c. 539, s. 337;1994, Ex. Sess., c. 24, s. 14(c);1998-212, s. 27.8(b);2003-258, s. 2;2009-550, s. 2(a);2019-155, s. 2

EDITOR'S NOTE. --
Session Laws 2001-492, s. 5, effective December 4, 2001, provides: "The Division of Motor Vehicles shall issue or reissue an unbranded title for vehicles titled in this State between July 20, 2001, and November 1, 2001, pursuant to G.S. 20-71.3 if the vehicle was a motor vehicle damaged by collision or other occurrence and if the cost of repairs, including parts, did not exceed seventy-five percent (75%) of its fair market value. Transfers of vehicles issued or reissued unbranded titles pursuant to this section [s. 5 of Session Laws 2001-492] shall be subject to the disclosure

requirements of G.S. 20-71.4." Initially s. 6 of Session Laws 2001-492, had provided a November 1, 2001, sunset for s. 5. However, Session Laws 2001-487, s. 123.5 deleted the sunset provision.

Session Laws 2019-155, s. 4, makes subdivision (a) (3) as added by Session Laws 2019-155, s. 2, effective October 1, 2019, and applicable to offenses committed on or after that date.

EFFECT OF AMENDMENTS. --

Session Laws 2009-550, s. 2(a), effective August 28, 2009, added subsection (e).

Session Laws 2019-155, s. 2, effective October 1, 2019, added subdivision (a)(3). For effective date and applicability, see editor's note.

FRAUDULENT INTENT MUST BE PLEADED FOR CIVIL LIABILITY --In order to properly plead a cause of action under this section and G.S. 20-348(a), a plaintiff must allege fraudulent intent in addition to a violation of the provisions of this section. Bowman v. Alan Vester Ford Lincoln Mercury, 151 N.C. App. 603, 566 S.E.2d 818 (2002).

DAMAGE TO VEHICLE OBVIOUS. --Where defendant ignored statements made by the previous owner, signs of damage to the truck, and owner failed to provide a damage disclosure statement to plaintiff, defendant was either grossly negligent or recklessly disregarded indications made by the previous owner, and knew or reasonably should have known of damage to the vehicle which exceeded twenty-five percent (25%) of the vehicle's fair market value. Payne v. Parks Chevrolet, Inc., 119 N.C. App. 383, 458 S.E.2d 716 (1995).

DEFENDANTS VIOLATED THIS SECTION AND G.S. 75-1.1 WHEN THEY DID NOT GIVE PLAINTIFFS A WRITTEN DAMAGE DISCLOSURE statement that van had been involved in a collision to the extent that the cost of the van's repairs exceeded twenty-five percent of its fair market retail value. Wilson v. Sutton, 124 N.C. App. 170, 476 S.E.2d 467 (1996).

DEFENDANTS COMMITTED UNFAIR AND DECEPTIVE TRADE PRACTICES where car sold by defendants was severely structurally damaged, was not safe to operate, and plaintiff was misled by defendants into believing otherwise. Huff v. Autos Unlimited, Inc., 124 N.C. App. 410, 477 S.E.2d 86 (1996), cert. denied, 346 N.C. 279, 486 S.E.2d 546 (1997).

SECTION NOT APPLICABLE. --Vehicle purchasers' negligence claim against the previous owners' lender was properly dismissed where the transferee was the seller, who had purchased the vehicle at auction; thus, any duty owed under G.S. 20-71.4 was to the seller. Sain v. Adams Auto Grp., Inc., 244 N.C. App. 657, 781 S.E.2d 655 (2015).

CITED in Blankenship v. Town & Country Ford, Inc., 155 N.C. App. 161, 574 S.E.2d 132 (2002), cert. denied, appeal dismissed, 357 N.C. 61, 579 S.E.2d 384 (2003).

OPINIONS OF THE ATTORNEY GENERAL

SUBSECTION (A) REQUIREMENT FALLS ON PERSON WHO KNOWS ABOUT DAMAGE. --The requirement in subsection (a) of this section that a written disclosure of damage that exceeds 25% of the vehicle's fair market value be given to the buyer prior to transfer falls upon any person who knows or reasonably should know about the damage. See opinion of Attorney General to Ms. Carol Nemitz, Director, Vehicle Registration Section, Division of Motor Vehicles, 59 N.C.A.G. 48 (1989).

RECORDS OF DISCLOSURE FORMS. --The Division of Motor Vehicles may prepare forms to carry out subsection (a) of this section, but there is no requirement that it keep records of the disclosure forms it may create. However, while there is no statutory provision requiring the division to disclose a prior title history showing that a vehicle was once damaged, there is no prohibition against this practice as a public service if the division should voluntarily undertake to do it. See opinion of Attorney General to Ms. Carol Nemitz, Director, Vehicle Registration Section, Division of Motor Vehicles, 59 N.C.A.G. 48 (1989).

PART 4.
TRANSFER OF TITLE OR INTEREST

§ 20-72. Transfer by owner

(a) Whenever the owner of a registered vehicle transfers or assigns his title or interests thereto, he shall remove the license plates. The registration card and plates shall be forwarded to the Division unless the plates are to be transferred to another vehicle as provided in G.S. 20-64. If they are to be transferred to and used with another vehicle, then the endorsed registration card and the plates shall be retained and preserved by the owner. If such registration plates are to be transferred to and used with another vehicle, then the owner shall make application to the Division for assignment of the registration plates to such other vehicle under the provisions of G.S. 20-64. Such application shall be made within 20 days after the date on which such plates are last used on the vehicle to which theretofore assigned.

(b) In order to assign or transfer title or interest in any motor vehicle registered under the provisions of this Article, the owner shall execute in the presence of a person authorized to administer oaths an assignment and warranty of title on the reverse of the certificate of title in form approved by the Division, including in such assignment the name and address of the transferee; and no title to any motor vehicle shall pass or vest until such assignment is executed and the motor vehicle delivered to the transferee. The provisions of this section shall not apply to any foreclosure or repossession under a chattel mortgage or conditional sales contract or any judicial sale. The provisions of this subsection shall not apply to (i) any transfer to an insurer pursuant to G.S. 20-109.1(b)(2) or (ii) any transfer to a used motor vehicle dealer pursuant to G.S. 20-109.1(e1). The provisions of this subsection requiring that an assignment and warranty of title be executed in the presence of a person authorized to administer oaths shall not apply to any transfer of title to or from an insurer pursuant to G.S. 20-109.1.

When a manufacturer's statement of origin or an existing certificate of title on a motor vehicle is unavailable, a motor vehicle dealer licensed under Article 12 of this Chapter may also transfer title to a vehicle to another by certifying in writing in a sworn statement to the Division that is signed by the dealer principal, general manager, general sales manager, controller, owner, or other manager of the dealership that, to the best of the signatory's knowledge and information as of the date of the sworn certification, all prior perfected liens on the vehicle that are known or reasonably ascertainable by the signatory have been paid and that the motor vehicle dealer, despite having used reasonable diligence, was unable to obtain the vehicle's statement of origin or certificate of title. For purposes of this subsection, a dealer may certify that the dealer is unable to obtain the vehicle's statement of origin or certificate of title if the statement of origin or certificate of title has either (i) not been delivered to the dealer or (ii) has been lost or misplaced. The Division is authorized to request any information it deems necessary to transfer the vehicle and shall develop a form for this purpose. The knowing and intentional filing of a false sworn certification with the Division pursuant to this subsection shall constitute a Class H felony. A dealer principal, owner, or manager of a motor vehicle dealership who is not a signatory of the sworn certification required under this subsection may only be charged for a criminal violation for filing a false certification under this subsection by another dealership employee if the dealer principal, owner, or manager had actual knowledge of the falsity of the sworn certification at the time the sworn certification was submitted to the Division.

Any person transferring title or interest in a motor vehicle shall deliver the certificate of title duly assigned in accordance with the foregoing provision to the transferee at the time of delivering the vehicle, except when a certificate of title is unavailable as provided in this subsection or in G.S. 20-72.1, and except that where a security interest is obtained in the motor vehicle from the transferee in payment of the purchase price or otherwise, the transferor shall deliver the certificate of title to the lienholder and the lienholder shall forward the certificate of title together with the transferee's application for new title and necessary fees to the Division within 20 days. If the title to a vehicle is unavailable and the dealer transfers the vehicle on a sworn certification pursuant to this section or G.S. 20-52.1, and the title is subsequently

received or found by the dealer, the dealer shall retain a copy for its records and submit the title to the Division. Any person who delivers or accepts a certificate of title assigned in blank shall be guilty of a Class 2 misdemeanor. No person shall have a cause of action against the Division or Division contractors arising from the transfer of a vehicle by a sworn certification pursuant to this section.

The title to a salvage vehicle shall be forwarded to the Division as provided in G.S. 20-109.1, except with respect to the title of any salvage vehicle transferred pursuant to G.S. 20-109.1(b)(2) or G.S. 20-109.1(e1).

(c) When the Division finds that any person other than the registered owner of a vehicle has in his possession a certificate of title to the vehicle on which there appears an endorsement of an assignment of title but there does not appear in the assignment any designation to show the name and address of the assignee or transferee, the Division shall be authorized and empowered to seize and hold said certificate of title until the assignor whose name appears in the assignment appears before the Division to complete the execution of the assignment or until evidence satisfactory to the Division is presented to the Division to show the name and address of the transferee.

History.
1937, c. 407, s. 36; 1947, c. 219, ss. 4, 5; 1955, c. 554, ss. 5, 6; 1961, c. 360, s. 8; c. 835, s. 8; 1963, c. 552, ss. 3, 4; 1971, c. 678; 1973, c. 1095, s. 2; 1975, c. 716, s. 5; 1993, c. 539, s. 338;1994, Ex. Sess., c. 24, s. 14(c);2000-182, s. 4;2013-400, s. 2;2018-42, s. 2(c);2018-145, s. 4;2019-153, s. 3;2019-181, s. 5(b);2020-51, s. 3(b)

EDITOR'S NOTE. --
Session Laws 2018-42, s. 2(f), provides: "The Division of Motor Vehicles, in consultation with the North Carolina Automobile Dealers Association, Inc., shall study the following:

"(1) The impacts of this section on Division processes and procedures, along with recommended statutory changes to further improve the lawful transfer of motor vehicles.

"(2) Methods to ensure consumer protection in the motor vehicle transfer process.

"(3) Potential changes to the Division's electronic lien and title program or other processes that could assist with reducing the delay in the release of a satisfied security interest in a motor vehicle.

"(4) Any other issues the Division deems appropriate.

"The Division shall report its findings, including any legislative recommendations, to the Joint Legislative Transportation Oversight Committee by December 31, 2020."

EFFECT OF AMENDMENTS. --
Session Laws 2013-400, s. 2, effective October 1, 2013, in subsection (b), added the last sentence in the first paragraph, and added "except with respect to the

title of any salvage vehicle transferred pursuant to
G.S. 20-109.1(b)(2) or G.S. 20-109.1(e1)" at the end of
the last paragraph.

Session Laws 2018-42, s. 2(c), as amended by Session Laws 2018-145, s. 4, effective March 1, 2019, in
subsection (b), rewrote the second paragraph, and in
the third paragraph, added "when a certificate of title
is unavailable as provided in this subsection or in G.S.
20-72.1, and except" in the first sentence, and added
the second and last sentences.

Session Laws 2019-153, s. 3, effective October 1,
2019, added the fourth sentence in subsection (b).

Session Laws 2019-181, s. 5(b), effective July 26,
2019, substituted "owner, or other manager" for "or
owner" preceding "of the dealership" in the first sentence of the second paragraph in subsection (b).

Session Laws 2020-51, s. 3(b), effective June 30,
2020, deleted "currently titled in this State" following
"to a vehicle" in the first sentence of the second paragraph of subsection (b).

REQUIREMENTS MANDATORY. --By explicit
terms of this section and by interpretation of the Supreme Court, there are definite and mandatory requirements governing transfer of legal title and ownership to a motor vehicle. Nationwide Mut. Ins. Co. v.
Hayes, 276 N.C. 620, 174 S.E.2d 511 (1970).

The requirements of this section are not within
the discretion of automobile buyers and sellers; the
requirements are mandatory. Thompson Cadillac-Oldsmobile, Inc. v. Silk Hope Auto., Inc., 87 N.C. App.
467, 361 S.E.2d 418 (1987).

STRICT COMPLIANCE REQUIRED. --Strict compliance with the requirements of assignment and
warranty of title and a statement of all liens and
encumbrances is necessary in every sale of motor vehicles. Seymour v. W.S. Boyd Sales Co., 257 N.C. 603,
127 S.E.2d 265 (1962), decided under this section as it
stood before the 1963 amendment.

APPLICATION TO BANKRUPTCY EXEMPTIONS. --Chapter 7 female debtor was not entitled
to exemptions under G.S. 1C-1601(a)(3) and G.S. 1C-1601(a)(2) for a vehicle that was titled solely in the
name of the male co-debtor; G.S. 20-72 equated a
transfer of title with the transfer of ownership, and
thus she had no legal interest the in vehicle and the
Trustee had superior lien rights under 11 U.S.C.S.
§ 544(a)(1). In re Thams, 2011 Bankr. LEXIS 939
(Bankr. W.D.N.C. Mar. 10, 2011).

Female debtor was entitled to claim automobile
and wildcard exemptions pursuant to G.S. 1C-1601(a)
(3) and (a)(2), where, although title to a vehicle was
solely in the male debtor's name, the presumption of
ownership was rebutted by testimony showing that
the vehicle was purchased with funds from an equity
line belonging to both debtors, that the certificate of
title was issued to the male debtor for logistical purposes only, and that the female debtor primarily drove
that vehicle, while the other vehicle was purchased
primarily for the male debtor. Further, both debtors
explicitly claimed an equitable interest in the vehicle
on Schedule B. In re Jourdan, 2013 Bankr. LEXIS 863
(Bankr. E.D.N.C. Mar. 8, 2013).

THE LEGISLATURE DID NOT INTEND TO REPEAL THE MOTOR VEHICLES ACT BY THE GENERAL REPEALER OF THE UNIFORM COMMERCIAL CODE. Nationwide Mut. Ins. Co. v. Hayes, 276
N.C. 620, 174 S.E.2d 511 (1970).

UNIFORM COMMERCIAL CODE DOES NOT
OVERRIDE THE EARLIER MOTOR VEHICLE
STATUTES relating to the transfer of ownership of
a motor vehicle for the purpose of tort law and liability insurance coverage. Nationwide Mut. Ins. Co. v.
Hayes, 276 N.C. 620, 174 S.E.2d 511 (1970).

SUBSECTION (B) PREVAILS OVER U.C.C.
--Subsection (b) of this section contains specific, definite and comprehensive terms concerning the transfer
of ownership of a motor vehicle, while the Uniform
Commercial Code does not refer to transfer of ownership of motor vehicles, but only refers to the passing
of title to property generally described as "goods." Although the word "automobile" comes within the general term of "goods," automobiles are a special class of
goods which have long been heavily regulated by public regulatory acts. Subsection (b) is a special statute
and the Uniform Commercial Code is a general statute. Thus, the special statute, even though earlier in
point of time, must prevail. Nationwide Mut. Ins. Co. v.
Hayes, 276 N.C. 620, 174 S.E.2d 511 (1970).

"TITLE" AS USED IN SUBSECTION (B) SYNONYMOUS WITH "OWNERSHIP." --The words "title"
and "ownership" are words that may be used interchangeably, and the legislature in enacting the 1963
amendment to subsection (b) of this section used the
word "title" as a synonym for the word "ownership."
Nationwide Mut. Ins. Co. v. Hayes, 276 N.C. 620, 174
S.E.2d 511 (1970).

In enacting the 1963 amendment to subsection (b)
of this section, providing that title to a motor vehicle
cannot be transferred from one owner to another until the certificate of title has been duly executed and
the vehicle delivered to the transferee, the legislature
used the word "title" as a synonym for the word "ownership." Nationwide Mut. Ins. Co. v. Fireman's Fund
Ins. Co., 279 N.C. 240, 182 S.E.2d 571 (1971).

NO MATERIAL CONFLICT WILL ARISE BETWEEN THE FINANCIAL RESPONSIBILITY ACT
OF 1953 (G.S. 20-279.1 ET SEQ.) AND SUBSECTION (B) of this section, as amended by the legislature in 1963, by holding subsection (b) of this section
to be controlling as to ownership of a motor vehicle
for purposes of tort liability and insurance coverage.
Rather, such an interpretation would strengthen and
complement the purposes of the Financial Responsibility Act of 1953. Nationwide Mut. Ins. Co. v. Hayes,
276 N.C. 620, 174 S.E.2d 511 (1970).

GOVERNS WHERE OWNERSHIP TRANSFERRED BETWEEN TWO PARTIES. --While G.S.
20-57 is intended to govern a situation in which there
is only one owner at issue, the party registering the
vehicle, G.S. 20-72(b) is intended to govern a situation in which an ownership interest is being transferred between two parties. The first party being the
original owner of the vehicle; the second party being
the future owner of the vehicle. Batts v. Lumbermen's

Mut. Cas. Ins. Co., 192 N.C. App. 533, 665 S.E.2d 578 (2008).

WHEN TITLE TO MOTOR VEHICLE PASSES GENERALLY. --No title passes to the purchaser of a motor vehicle until the certificate of title has been assigned by the vendor and delivered to the vendee or his agent, and application has been made for a new certificate of title. International Serv. Ins. Co. v. Iowa Nat'l Mut. Ins. Co., 276 N.C. 243, 172 S.E.2d 55 (1970); Younts v. State Farm Mut. Auto. Ins. Co., 281 N.C. 582, 189 S.E.2d 137 (1972).

When a dealer transfers a vehicle registered under this Chapter, it must execute a reassignment and warranty of title on the reverse of the certificate of title, and title to such vehicle shall not pass or vest until such reassignment is executed and the motor vehicle is delivered to the transferee. The dealer must also deliver the duly assigned certificate of title to the transferee or lienholder at the time the vehicle is delivered. North Carolina Nat'l Bank v. Robinson, 78 N.C. App. 1, 336 S.E.2d 666 (1985).

TRANSFER OF TITLE AS WARRANTY OF TITLE. --Defendant, by admitting that it transferred title to plaintiff, admitted that it also warranted title to the automobiles sold. Thompson Cadillac-Oldsmobile, Inc. v. Silk Hope Auto., Inc., 87 N.C. App. 467, 361 S.E.2d 418 (1987).

PASSAGE OF TITLE FOR PURPOSES OF TORT LAW AND INSURANCE COVERAGE. --After July 1, 1963, the effective date of the 1963 amendment to this section, for purposes of tort law and liability insurance coverage, no ownership passes to the purchaser of a motor vehicle which requires registration under the Motor Vehicle Act of 1937 until (1) the owner executes, in the presence of a person authorized to administer oaths, an assignment and warranty of title on the reverse of the certificate of title, including the name and address of the transferee, (2) there is an actual or constructive delivery of the motor vehicle, and (3) the duly assigned certificate of title is delivered to the transferee. In the event a security interest is obtained in the motor vehicle from the transferee, the requirement of delivery of the duly assigned certificate of title is met by delivering it to the lienholder. Nationwide Mut. Ins. Co. v. Hayes, 276 N.C. 620, 174 S.E.2d 511 (1970); Roseboro Ford, Inc. v. Bass, 77 N.C. App. 363, 335 S.E.2d 214 (1985); Jenkins v. Aetna Cas. & Sur. Co., 324 N.C. 394, 378 S.E.2d 773 (1989).

"[F]or purposes of tort law and liability insurance coverage, no ownership passes to the purchaser of a motor vehicle which requires registration" until transfer of legal title is effected as provided in this section. The general rule then, as between vendor and vendee, is that the vendee does not acquire "valid owner's liability insurance until legal title has been transferred or assigned" to the vendee by the vendor. Jenkins v. Aetna Cas. & Sur. Co., 91 N.C. App. 388, 371 S.E.2d 761 (1988), rev'd on other grounds, 324 N.C. 394, 378 S.E.2d 773 (1989).

Insureds' newly acquired vehicle was not covered on the date of an accident under the auto insurance policy issued to the insureds by the insurer because the insureds did not timely notify the insurer of the acquisition of the vehicle under the terms of their insurance policy and the issuance of a registration card by the North Carolina Department of Motor Vehicles, under G.S. 20-72(b), was not a necessary requirement for the ownership interest in the vehicle to vest in the insureds. Batts v. Lumbermen's Mut. Cas. Ins. Co., 192 N.C. App. 533, 665 S.E.2d 578 (2008).

FAILURE TO TAKE RECEIPT OF TITLE. --Where evidence established that buyer paid four hundred dollars ($400.00) cash as the total price for a car and took immediate possession of the vehicle, but never received the certificate of title, buyer was not the "owner" of the Camaro as that term is defined in G.S. 20-4.01(26); therefore, provision in policy excluding coverage for liability arising from the use of a vehicle "owned" by buyer did not apply. Jenkins v. Aetna Cas. & Sur. Co., 324 N.C. 394, 378 S.E.2d 773 (1989).

A vehicle dealer who sold a vehicle to a private consumer, who paid with a dishonored check, effectively placed the car into the stream of commerce to the extent that a second car dealer, who purchased the car from the buyer, could be construed as a good-faith purchaser of the car in spite of the fact that the first dealer never provided the consumer with a certificate of title. Sale Chevrolet, Buick, BMW, Inc. v. Peterbilt of Florence, Inc., 133 N.C. App. 177, 514 S.E.2d 747 (1999).

THE 1961 AMENDMENTS TO SUBSECTION (B) AND G.S. 20-75 CHANGED THE LAW with respect to transfer of ownership of motor vehicles. International Serv. Ins. Co. v. Iowa Nat'l Mut. Ins. Co., 276 N.C. 243, 172 S.E.2d 55 (1970).

AS TO PASSAGE OF TITLE TO MOTOR VEHICLES PRIOR TO JULY 1, 1961, see International Serv. Ins. Co. v. Iowa Nat'l Mut. Ins. Co., 276 N.C. 243, 172 S.E.2d 55 (1970); Nationwide Mut. Ins. Co. v. Hayes, 276 N.C. 620, 174 S.E.2d 511 (1970).

AS TO DEFERRAL OF VESTING OF TITLE UNDER SUBSECTION (B) AS AMENDED IN 1961 AND BEFORE ITS AMENDMENT IN 1963 until the purchaser had the old certificate endorsed to him and made application for a new certificate, see Community Credit Co. v. Norwood, 257 N.C. 87, 125 S.E.2d 369 (1962). See also, Home Indem. Co. v. West Trade Motors, Inc., 258 N.C. 647, 129 S.E.2d 248 (1963).

DUTY OF PURCHASER TO SECURE OLD CERTIFICATE OF TITLE AND APPLY FOR NEW ONE. --This section and G.S. 20-75 make it the duty of the purchaser to secure from his vendor the old certificate of title duly endorsed or assigned and to apply for a new certificate. They do not relate to the duty of the Department (now Division) to issue a new certificate. Community Credit Co. v. Norwood, 257 N.C. 87, 125 S.E.2d 369 (1962).

There is no longer a requirement under the Motor Vehicle Act that a purchaser apply for a new certificate of title before title may pass or vest. North Carolina Nat'l Bank v. Robinson, 78 N.C. App. 1, 336 S.E.2d 666 (1985).

FOR PURPOSES OF LIABILITY INSURANCE COVERAGE, ownership of a motor vehicle which requires registration under the Motor Vehicle Act of 1937 does not pass until transfer of legal title is effected as provided in subsection (b). Indiana Lumbermens Mut. Ins. Co. v. Unigard Indem. Co., 76 N.C. App. 88, 331 S.E.2d 741 (1985), cert. denied, 314 N.C. 666, 335 S.E.2d 494 (1985).

CONTROLLING EFFECT OF UCC OVER SECURITY INTERESTS AND PRIORITIES. --Notwithstanding the title transfer provisions of the Motor Vehicle Act, an automobile purchaser may be a "buyer in the ordinary course of business" as that term is used in G.S. 25-2-403 and G.S. 25-9-307, even though the certificate of title has not yet been reassigned. Moreover, it was the legislature's intent to have the UCC control issues of security interests and priorities. North Carolina Nat'l Bank v. Robinson, 78 N.C. App. 1, 336 S.E.2d 666 (1985).

The UCC should control over the Motor Vehicle Act when automobiles are used as collateral and are held in inventory for sale. North Carolina Nat'l Bank v. Robinson, 78 N.C. App. 1, 336 S.E.2d 666 (1985).

BUYERS WHO GAVE VALUE FOR A USED CAR DISPLAYED ON A DEALER'S LOT and received a 20-day temporary marker in June, 1983, which car was covered by a dealer inventory security agreement in effect since April 1, 1970, and on which the credit company retained the title certificate, which was in the name of the dealer, had a superior right to possession of the car when the credit company's agent came to repossess it on June 19, 1983, as it was no longer part of the dealer's inventory; and buyers were entitled to possession of the car in their action for wrongful conversion. North Carolina Nat'l Bank v. Robinson, 78 N.C. App. 1, 336 S.E.2d 666 (1985).

WARRANTY OF TITLE AND STATEMENT OF LIENS AND ENCUMBRANCES REQUIRED UNDER FORMER LAW. --Prior to the 1963 amendment to this section, subsection (b) made it the duty of the vendor of a registered vehicle to endorse his certificate of title to the transferee with a statement of all liens or encumbrances, to be verified by the oath of the owner. Home Indem. Co. v. West Trade Motors, Inc., 258 N.C. 647, 129 S.E.2d 248 (1963).

The seller of a motor vehicle was required to endorse, and deliver to or for the buyer, an assignment and warranty of title and a statement of all liens and encumbrances, even where a conditional sale was involved. Seymour v. W.S. Boyd Sales Co., 257 N.C. 603, 127 S.E.2d 265 (1962), decided under this section as it stood before the 1963 amendment.

NO LIEN CREATED BY CHATTEL MORTGAGE PRIOR TO ACQUISITION OF TITLE. --Where the purchaser of a motor vehicle executed a chattel mortgage which was registered prior to the acknowledgment of assignment of the certificate of title by the seller and the forwarding of an application for a new certificate to the Department (now Division) of Motor Vehicles, the chattel mortgage did not create a lien on the vehicle, since the purchaser, at the time it was executed, did not have title, and the instrument could operate only as a contract to execute a chattel mortgage upon the acquisition of title. National Bank v.

Greensboro Motor Co., 264 N.C. 568, 142 S.E.2d 166 (1965). As to perfecting security interest, see G.S. 20-58 et seq.

WHEN A SALE IS MADE TO A DEALER, it is not necessary to transmit the certificate of title to the Department (now Division) of Motor Vehicles until the dealer resells. Home Indem. Co. v. West Trade Motors, Inc., 258 N.C. 647, 129 S.E.2d 248 (1963).

VEHICLE NOT A "NON-OWNED AUTO" AS TO EITHER POLICY. --Trial court erred in holding that an owner's insurance policy terminated when the son's policy was issued on the same car because the automatic termination clause in the owner's policy's only applied if the owner obtained other insurance, and the owner's policy and the son's policy were procured by different persons; the vehicle was not a "non-owned auto" as to either policy because it was furnished for the regular use of the son, and because each policies' "share of the loss" was limited to the proportion that the limit of liability bore to the total of all applicable limits, and because both policies had the same limit, the policies were required to share pro rata in the damages to the vehicle. Progressive Am. Ins. Co. v. State Farm Mut. Auto. Ins. Co., 184 N.C. App. 688, 647 S.E.2d 111 (2007).

Risk of loss provisions in the Uniform Commercial Code were not overridden in a breach of contract case by the North Carolina Motor Vehicle Act, specifically G.S. 20-72, as set forth in Nationwide Mutual Insurance Co. v. Hayes, 174 S.E.2d 511 (N.C. 1970), as the requirements of Hayes that the case involved a tort or liability insurance issue were not met. Singletary v. P & A Invs., Inc., 212 N.C. App. 469, 712 S.E.2d 681 (2011).

APPLIED in Hawkins v. M & J Fin. Corp., 238 N.C. 174, 77 S.E.2d 669 (1953) (as to subsection (b)); Gaddy v. State Farm Mut. Auto. Ins. Co., 32 N.C. App. 714, 233 S.E.2d 613 (1977).

CITED in North Carolina Farm Bureau Mut. Ins. Co. v. Ayazi, 106 N.C. App. 475, 417 S.E.2d 81 (1992); Manning v. State Farm Mut. Auto. Ins. Co., 243 F. Supp. 619 (W.D.N.C. 1965); Younts v. State Farm Mut. Auto. Ins. Co., 13 N.C. App. 426, 185 S.E.2d 730 (1972); Moser v. Employers Com. Union Ins. Co. of Am., 25 N.C. App. 309, 212 S.E.2d 664 (1975); Ohio Cas. Ins. Co. v. Anderson, 59 N.C. App. 621, 298 S.E.2d 56 (1982); American Clipper Corp. v. Howerton, 311 N.C. 151, 316 S.E.2d 186 (1984); Hargett v. Reed, 95 N.C. App. 292, 382 S.E.2d 791 (1989); State v. Morris, 103 N.C. App. 246, 405 S.E.2d 351 (1991); Hughes v. Young, 115 N.C. App. 325, 444 S.E.2d 248 (1994); Lynn v. West, 134 F.3d 582 (4th Cir. 1998), cert. denied, 525 U.S. 813, 119 S. Ct. 47, 142 L. Ed. 2d 36 (1998) (But see Milligan v. State, 135 N.C. App. 781, 522 S.E.2d 330 (1999)); Hernandez v. Nationwide Mut. Ins. Co., 171 N.C. App. 510, 615 S.E.2d 425 (2005), cert. denied, 360 N.C. 63, 621 S.E.2d 624 (2005); Bissette v. Auto-Owners Ins. Co., 208 N.C. App. 321, 703 S.E.2d 168 (2010).

CROSS REFERENCES. --
As to fees, see G.S. 20-85.
LEGAL PERIODICALS. --
For note as to the requirements of this section through G.S. 20-78, see 32 N.C.L. Rev. 545 (1954).

Chapter 20

For case law survey on time of acquisition of title to motor vehicles, see 41 N.C.L. Rev. 444 (1963).

For note on the conflict between the North Carolina Motor Vehicle Act and the UCC, see 65 N.C.L. Rev. 1156 (1987).

§ 20-72.1. Transfer by owner when a certificate of title is unavailable; consumer remedies

(a) Notwithstanding any other provision in this Article, when a manufacturer's statement of origin or an existing certificate of title on a motor vehicle is unavailable, a motor vehicle dealer licensed under Article 12 of this Chapter shall deliver the manufacturer's statement of origin or certificate of title to the Division within 20 days of receipt of the title, but no later than 60 days following the later of the date of the sale or transfer of the vehicle or the date of the creation of a security interest in the vehicle pursuant to G.S. 20-58(b). The dealer may offer the vehicle for sale provided that the purchaser is given written notice prior to sale that the dealer is not in possession of the manufacturer's statement of origin or certificate of title and that the purchaser may be entitled to liquidated damages pursuant to subsection (b) of this section if the dealer fails to deliver the manufacturer's statement of origin or certificate of title to the Division in accordance with this subsection. For purposes of this subsection, a vehicle's manufacturer's statement of origin or existing certificate of title shall be considered unavailable under either of the following circumstances:

    (1) The manufacturer's statement of origin or certificate of title has not been actually delivered to the dealer on or prior to the date the dealer sold or transferred the vehicle.

    (2) The manufacturer's statement of origin or certificate of title was lost or misplaced on or prior to the date the dealer sold or transferred the vehicle.

(b) In any case where a dealer fails to deliver the manufacturer's statement of origin or certificate of title to the Division within the 60-day time period allowed in subsection (a) of this section, the vehicle purchaser may elect to receive liquidated damages from the dealer in the amount of five percent (5%) of the vehicle purchase price, not to exceed one thousand dollars ($ 1,000), provided that the dealer receives written demand for liquidated damages from the purchaser within 10 days after the expiration of the 60-day period provided in subsection (a) of this section. The liquidated damages provided in this subsection shall be payable by the dealer within 30 days after the receipt of the purchaser's written demand. Nothing in this section shall be construed to limit any other civil remedies or consumer protections available to the vehicle purchaser. Nothing in this section shall be construed to prohibit a motor vehicle dealer who pays liquidated damages or other valuable consideration to a vehicle purchaser or lessee from obtaining a release from the purchaser or lessee for any other damages or liability arising out of or related to the sale or lease of the vehicle.

(c) Notwithstanding any other provision in this Article, a motor vehicle dealer licensed under Article 12 of this Chapter may sell or transfer a motor vehicle when a manufacturer's statement of origin or an existing certificate of title on the motor vehicle is unavailable and the motor vehicle is sold or transferred to a current lessee of the motor vehicle regardless of whether the payment of any residual amount or payoff amount for the vehicle has been made to the lessor who holds legal title to the motor vehicle at the time of the sale or transfer. The vehicle purchaser notice requirement in subsection (a) of this section, liquidated damages requirements in subsections (a) and (b) of this section, and sworn certification requirements of G.S. 20-52.1(d) and G.S. 20-72(b) shall not be applicable when a motor vehicle is sold or transferred to the current lessee of the motor vehicle.

History.
2018-42, s. 2(d); 2018-145, s. 4; 2019-181, s. 5(c)

EDITOR'S NOTE. --

Session Laws 2018-42, s. 2(h), as amended by Session Laws 2018-145, s. 4, made this section effective March 1, 2019.

Session Laws 2018-42, s. 2(f), provides: "The Division of Motor Vehicles, in consultation with the North Carolina Automobile Dealers Association, Inc., shall study the following:

"(1) The impacts of this section on Division processes and procedures, along with recommended statutory changes to further improve the lawful transfer of motor vehicles.

"(2) Methods to ensure consumer protection in the motor vehicle transfer process.

"(3) Potential changes to the Division's electronic lien and title program or other processes that could assist with reducing the delay in the release of a satisfied security interest in a motor vehicle.

"(4) Any other issues the Division deems appropriate.

"The Division shall report its findings, including any legislative recommendations, to the Joint Legislative Transportation Oversight Committee by December 31, 2020."

EFFECT OF AMENDMENTS. --

Session Laws 2019-181, s. 5(c), effective July 26, 2019, deleted the second and third sentences of subdivision (a)(2), which read "If the motor vehicle being sold or transferred is a used motor vehicle, the dealer is required to make application to the Division for a duplicate title within five working days of the date of the sale or transfer of the vehicle. If the vehicle being sold or transferred is a new motor vehicle, the dealer is required to request a new or duplicate manufacturer's statement of origin from the applicable manufacturer or distributor within five working days of the date of the sale or transfer of the vehicle"; added the last sentence of subsection (b); and added subsection (c).

§ 20-73. New owner must get new certificate of title

(a) **Time Limit.** -- A person to whom a vehicle is transferred, whether by purchase or otherwise, must apply to the Division for a new certificate of title. An application for a certificate of title must be submitted within 28 days after the vehicle is transferred. A person who must follow the procedure in G.S. 20-76 to get a certificate of title and who applies for a title within the required 20-day time limit or who transfers title to a vehicle pursuant to a sworn certificate pursuant to G.S. 20-52.1(d) is considered to have complied with this section even when the Division issues a certificate of title to the person after the time limit has elapsed.

A person may apply directly for a certificate of title or may allow another person, such as the person from whom the vehicle is transferred or a person who has a lien on the vehicle, to apply for a certificate of title on that person's behalf. A person to whom a vehicle is transferred is responsible for getting a certificate of title within the time limit regardless of whether the person allowed another to apply for a certificate of title on the person's behalf.

(b) **Exceptions.** -- This section does not apply to any of the following:

(1) A dealer or an insurance company to whom a vehicle is transferred when the transfer meets the requirements of G.S. 20-75.

(2) A State agency that assists the United States Department of Defense with purchasing, transferring, or titling a vehicle to another State agency, a unit of local government, a volunteer fire department, or a volunteer rescue squad.

(c) **Penalties.** -- A person to whom a vehicle is transferred who fails to apply for a certificate of title within the required time is subject to a civil penalty of twenty dollars ($ 20.00) and is guilty of a Class 2 misdemeanor. A person who undertakes to apply for a certificate of title on behalf of another person and who fails to apply for a title within the required time is subject to a civil penalty of twenty dollars ($ 20.00). When a person to whom a vehicle is transferred fails to obtain a title within the required time because a person who undertook to apply for the certificate of title did not do so within the required time, the Division may impose a civil penalty only on the person who undertook to apply for the title. Civil penalties collected under this subsection shall be credited to the Highway Fund.

History.
1937, c. 407, s. 37; 1939, c. 275; 1947, c. 219, s. 6; 1961, c. 360, s. 9; 1975, c. 716, s. 5; 1991, c. 689, s. 332;1993, c. 539, s. 339;1994, Ex. Sess., c. 24, s. 14(c);2005-276, s. 44.1(j);2009-81, s. 1;2009-550, s. 2(b);2015-241, s. 29.30(i);2018-42, s. 2(g);2018-145, s. 4

EDITOR'S NOTE. --
Session Laws 2015-241, s. 29.30(u), made the amendment to subsection (c) of this section by Session Laws 2015-241, s. 29.30(i), applicable to issuances, renewals, restorations, and requests on or after January 1, 2016.

Session Laws 2015-241, s. 1.1, provides: "This act shall be known as 'The Current Operations and Capital Improvements Appropriations Act of 2015.'"

Session Laws 2015-241, s. 33.6, is a severability clause.

Session Laws 2018-42, s. 2(f), provides: "The Division of Motor Vehicles, in consultation with the North Carolina Automobile Dealers Association, Inc., shall study the following:

"(1) The impacts of this section on Division processes and procedures, along with recommended statutory changes to further improve the lawful transfer of motor vehicles.

"(2) Methods to ensure consumer protection in the motor vehicle transfer process.

"(3) Potential changes to the Division's electronic lien and title program or other processes that could assist with reducing the delay in the release of a satisfied security interest in a motor vehicle.

"(4) Any other issues the Division deems appropriate.

"The Division shall report its findings, including any legislative recommendations, to the Joint Legislative Transportation Oversight Committee by December 31, 2020."

EFFECT OF AMENDMENTS. --
Session Laws 2005-276, s. 44.1(j), effective October 1, 2005, and applicable to fees collected on or after that date, substituted "fifteen dollars ($15.00)" for "ten dollars ($10.00)" twice in subsection (c).

Session Laws 2009-81, s. 1, effective June 11, 2009, in subsection (a), in the first paragraph, added the last sentence, and rewrote subsection (b).

Session Laws 2009-550, s. 2(b), effective August 28, 2009, in subdivision (b)(2), substituted "with purchasing, transferring, or titling" for "in purchasing or transferring" and inserted "another State agency."

Session Laws 2015-241, s. 29.30(i), effective January 1, 2016, substituted "twenty dollars ($20.00)" for "fifteen dollars ($15.00)" twice in subsection (c). For applicability, see editor's note.

Session Laws 2018-42, s. 2(g), as amended by Session Laws 2018-145, s. 4, effective March 1, 2019, inserted "or who transfers title to a vehicle pursuant to a sworn certificate to G.S. 20-52.1(d)" in the second sentence of subsection (a).

BURDEN IS ON VENDEE TO APPLY FOR NEW CERTIFICATE OF TITLE. --The burden is imposed on the vendee, or as this section describes him, the transferee, to present the certificate and make application for a new certificate of title within 20 days, and a willful failure to do so is expressly declared to be a misdemeanor. When the certificate of title is delivered to a lienholder, it is nonetheless the duty of the purchaser to see that the certificate is forwarded to the Department (now Division) of Motor Vehicles. Home Indem. Co. v. West Trade Motors, Inc., 258 N.C. 647, 129 S.E.2d 248 (1963).

VENDOR SHOULD NOT BE PENALIZED FOR VENDEE'S FAILURE. --There is nothing in the 1961 amendments to this Part which suggests that dealer, a vendor, should be penalized and held liable because of the failure of a purchaser to perform his statutory duty. Home Indem. Co. v. West Trade Motors, Inc., 258 N.C. 647, 129 S.E.2d 248 (1963).

There is nothing in the statute which suggests dealer, a vendor, should be penalized and held liable because of the failure of a purchaser to perform his statutory duty. International Serv. Ins. Co. v. Iowa Nat'l Mut. Ins. Co., 5 N.C. App. 236, 168 S.E.2d 66 (1969), modified on other grounds and aff'd, 276 N.C. 243, 172 S.E.2d 55 (1970).

APPLICATION MUST BE IN PROPER FORM. -- The statute necessarily implies that the application for a new certificate should be in proper form. Community Credit Co. v. Norwood, 257 N.C. 87, 125 S.E.2d 369 (1962).

CITED in International Serv. Ins. Co. v. Iowa Nat'l Mut. Ins. Co., 276 N.C. 243, 172 S.E.2d 55 (1970).

§ 20-74. Penalty for making false statement about transfer of vehicle

A dealer or another person who, in an application required by this Division, knowingly makes a false statement about the date a vehicle was sold or acquired shall be guilty of a Class 3 misdemeanor.

History.
1937, c. 407, s. 38; 1939, c. 275; 1961, c. 360, s. 10; 1975, c. 716, s. 5; 1979, c. 801, s. 8; 1981, c. 690, s. 21; 1991, c. 689, s. 333;1993, c. 539, s. 340;1994, Ex. Sess., c. 24, s. 14(c)

COMPLIANCE WITH REGISTRATION STATUTES MANDATORY. --It is manifest both from the express language of the registration statutes and from this companion penal enforcement provision that compliance with the registration statutes is mandatory and calls for substantial observance. Hawkins v. M & J Fin. Corp., 238 N.C. 174, 77 S.E.2d 669 (1953).

CITED in Community Credit Co. v. Norwood, 257 N.C. 87, 125 S.E.2d 369 (1962); International Serv. Ins. Co. v. Iowa Nat'l Mut. Ins. Co., 276 N.C. 243, 172 S.E.2d 55 (1970); Nationwide Mut. Ins. Co. v. Hayes, 7 N.C. App. 294, 172 S.E.2d 269 (1970); State v. Morris, 103 N.C. App. 246, 405 S.E.2d 351 (1991).

CROSS REFERENCES. --
As to duty of new owner to secure new certificate of title, see G.S. 20-73.

§ 20-75. When transferee is a charitable organization, dealer, or insurance company

A transferee of a vehicle registered under this Article is not required to register the vehicle or forward the certificate of title to the Division as provided in G.S. 20-73 when the transferee is any of the following:

(1) A dealer who is licensed under Article 12 of this Chapter and who holds the vehicle for resale.

(2) An insurance company taking the vehicle for sale or disposal for salvage purposes where the title is taken or requested as a part of a bona fide claim settlement transaction and only for the purpose of resale.

(3) A charitable organization operating under section 501(c)(3) of the Internal Revenue Code (26 U.S.C. § 501(c)(3)) and the vehicle was donated to the charitable organization solely for purposes of resale by the charitable organization.

To assign or transfer title or interest in the vehicle, the charitable organization or dealer shall execute, in the presence of a person authorized to administer oaths, a reassignment and warranty of title on the reverse of the certificate of title in the form approved by the Division, which shall include the name and address of the transferee. To assign or transfer title or interest in the vehicle, the insurance company shall execute a reassignment and warranty of title on the reverse of the certificate of title in the form approved by the Division, which shall include the name and address of the transferee. The title to the vehicle shall not pass or vest until the reassignment is executed and the motor vehicle delivered to the transferee.

The dealer transferring title or interest in a motor vehicle shall deliver the certificate of title duly assigned in accordance with the foregoing provision to the transferee at the time of delivering the vehicle, except:

(1) Where a security interest in the motor vehicle is obtained from the transferee in payment of the purchase price or otherwise, the dealer shall deliver the certificate of title to the lienholder and the lienholder shall forward the certificate of title together with the transferee's application for new certificate of title and necessary fees to the Division within 20 days; or

(2) Where the transferee has the option of cancelling the transfer of the vehicle within 10 days of delivery of the vehicle, the dealer shall deliver the certificate of title to the

transferee at the end of that period. Delivery need not be made if the contract for sale has been rescinded in writing by all parties to the contract.

Any person who delivers or accepts a certificate of title assigned in blank shall be guilty of a Class 2 misdemeanor.

The title to a salvage vehicle shall be forwarded to the Division as provided in G.S. 20-109.1, except with respect to the title of any salvage vehicle transferred pursuant to G.S. 20-109.1(b)(2) or G.S. 20-109.1(e1).

History.
1937, c. 407, s. 39; 1961, c. 835, s. 9; 1963, c. 552, s. 5; 1967, c. 760; 1973, c. 1095, s. 3; 1975, c. 716, s. 5; 1993, c. 440, s. 12;c. 539, s. 341;1994, Ex. Sess., c. 24, s. 14(c);1997-327, s. 2.1;2013-400, s. 3;2018-43, s. 2;2019-153, s. 4

EFFECT OF AMENDMENTS. --
Session Laws 2013-400, s. 3, effective October 1, 2013, inserted "or requested" in subdivision (2) of the first paragraph; and added "except with respect to the title of any salvage vehicle transferred pursuant to G.S. 20-109.1(b)(2) or G.S. 20-109.1(e1)" at the end of the section.

Session Laws 2018-43, s. 2, effective June 22, 2018, inserted "a charitable organization" and made related changes in the section heading and the second paragraph; and reorganized the first paragraph by transferring language from the end of the paragraph to the introductory language and adding subdivision (3).

Session Laws 2019-153, s. 4, effective October 1, 2019, substituted "organization or dealer" for "organization, dealer, or insurance company" in the first sentence and added the second sentence in the second full paragraph.

THE 1961 AMENDMENTS TO THIS SECTION AND G.S. 20-72(B) CHANGED THE LAW with respect to transfer of ownership of motor vehicles. International Serv. Ins. Co. v. Iowa Nat'l Mut. Ins. Co., 276 N.C. 243, 172 S.E.2d 55 (1970).

WHEN A DEALER TRANSFERS A VEHICLE REGISTERED UNDER THIS CHAPTER, it must execute a reassignment and warranty of title on the reverse of the certificate of title, and title to such vehicle shall not pass or vest until such reassignment is executed and the motor vehicle delivered to the transferee. The dealer must also deliver the duly assigned certificate of title to the transferee or lienholder at the time the vehicle is delivered. North Carolina Nat'l Bank v. Robinson, 78 N.C. App. 1, 336 S.E.2d 666 (1985).

APPLICATION FOR NEW CERTIFICATE OF TITLE. --There is no longer a requirement under the Motor Vehicle Act that a purchaser apply for a new certificate of title before title may pass or vest. North Carolina Nat'l Bank v. Robinson, 78 N.C. App. 1, 336 S.E.2d 666 (1985).

CONTROLLING EFFECT OF UCC OVER SECURITY INTERESTS AND PRIORITIES. --Notwithstanding the title transfer provisions of the Motor Vehicle Act, an automobile purchaser may be

a "buyer in the ordinary course of business" as that term is used in G.S. 25-2-403 and G.S. 25-9-307, even though the certificate of title has not yet been reassigned. Moreover, it was the legislature's intent to have the UCC control issues of security interests and priorities. North Carolina Nat'l Bank v. Robinson, 78 N.C. App. 1, 336 S.E.2d 666 (1985).

The UCC should control over the Motor Vehicle Act when automobiles are used as collateral and are held in inventory for sale. North Carolina Nat'l Bank v. Robinson, 78 N.C. App. 1, 336 S.E.2d 666 (1985).

CUSTOM OF USED CAR DEALERS TO ACCEPT A BLANK ENDORSEMENT OF THE TITLE by the owner and to transfer title directly to a purchaser upon an anonymous notarization was violative of the letter and spirit of the motor vehicle registration statutes and could not be asserted as a ground for equitable estoppel. Hawkins v. M & J Fin. Corp., 238 N.C. 174, 77 S.E.2d 669 (1953).

BUYERS WHO GAVE VALUE FOR A USED CAR DISPLAYED ON DEALER'S LOT and received a 20-day temporary marker in June, 1983, which car was covered by a dealer inventory security agreement in effect since April 1, 1970, and on which the credit company retained the title certificate, which was in the name of the dealer, had superior right to possession of the car when the credit company's agent came to repossess it on June 19, 1983, as it was no longer part of the dealer's inventory; and buyers were entitled to possession of the car in their action for wrongful conversion. North Carolina Nat'l Bank v. Robinson, 78 N.C. App. 1, 336 S.E.2d 666 (1985).

CITED in Rushing v. Polk, 258 N.C. 256, 128 S.E.2d 675 (1962); Nationwide Mut. Ins. Co. v. Hayes, 276 N.C. 620, 174 S.E.2d 511 (1970); Singletary v. P & A Invs., Inc., 212 N.C. App. 469, 712 S.E.2d 681 (2011).

§ 20-75.1. Conditional delivery of motor vehicles

Notwithstanding G.S. 20-52.1, 20-72, and 20-75, nothing contained in those sections prohibits a dealer from entering into a contract with any purchaser for the sale of a vehicle and delivering the vehicle to the purchaser under terms by which the dealer's obligation to execute the manufacturer's certificate of origin or the certificate of title is conditioned on the purchaser obtaining financing for the purchase of the vehicle. Liability, collision, and comprehensive insurance on a vehicle sold and delivered conditioned on the purchaser obtaining financing for the purchaser of the vehicle shall be covered by the dealer's insurance policy until such financing is finally approved and execution of the manufacturer's certificate of origin or execution of the certificate of title. Upon final approval and execution of the manufacturer's certificate of origin or the certificate of title, and upon the purchaser having liability insurance on another vehicle, the delivered vehicle shall be covered by the purchaser's insurance policy beginning at the time of final financial approval and execution of the manufacturer's certificate of origin or the certificate of title. The dealer shall notify the insurance agency servicing the purchaser's insurance policy or the purchaser's insurer of the purchase on the day of, or if the insurance agency or insurer is not open for business, on the next business day following approval of the purchaser's financing and execution of the manufacturer's certificate of origin or the certificate of title. This subsection is in addition to any other provisions of law or insurance policies and does not repeal or supersede those provisions.

History.

1993, c. 328, s. 1

STANDING. --Parties allegedly injured in an automobile accident had no standing in a declaratory judgment action in which insurers sought a declaration as to coverage obligations because (1) the alleged injured parties were not named insureds in any policy potentially providing coverage to an estate the parties sued, and (2) the alleged injured parties could not assert standing under G.S. 20-75.1, as that statute did not address the rights of third-party victims, so the statute did not directly and adversely impact the alleged injured parties. Smith v. USAA Cas. Ins. Co., 261 N.C. App. 40, 819 S.E.2d 610 (2018).

CITED in Hester v. Hubert Vester Ford, Inc., 239 N.C. App. 22, 767 S.E.2d 129 (2015).

§ 20-76. Title lost or unlawfully detained; bond as condition to issuance of new certificate

(a) Whenever the applicant for the registration of a vehicle or a new certificate of title thereto is unable to present a certificate of title thereto by reason of the same being lost or unlawfully detained by one in possession, or the same is otherwise not available, the Division is hereby authorized to receive such application and to examine into the circumstances of the case, and may require the filing of affidavits or other information; and when the Division is satisfied that the applicant is entitled thereto and that G.S. 20-72 has been complied with, it is hereby authorized to register such vehicle and issue a new registration card, registration plate or plates and certificates of title to the person entitled thereto, upon payment of proper fees.

(b) Whenever the applicant for a new certificate of title is unable to satisfy the Division that he is entitled thereto as provided in subsection (a) of this section, the applicant may nevertheless obtain issuance of a new certificate of title by filing a bond with the Division as a condition to the issuance thereof. The bond shall be in the form prescribed by the Division and shall be executed by the applicant. It shall be accompanied by the deposit of cash with the Division,

be executed as surety by a person, firm or corporation authorized to conduct a surety business in this State or be in the nature of a real estate bond as described in G.S. 20-279.24(a). The bond shall be in an amount equal to one and one-half times the value of the vehicle as determined by the Division and conditioned to indemnify any prior owner or lienholder, any subsequent purchaser of the vehicle or person acquiring any security interest therein, and their respective successors in interest, against any expense, loss or damage, reason of the issuance of the certificate of title to the vehicle or on account of any defect in or undisclosed security interest in the right, title and interest of the applicant in and to the vehicle. Any person damaged by issuance of the certificate of title shall have a right of action to recover on the bond for any breach of its conditions, but the aggregate liability of the surety to all persons shall not exceed the amount of the bond. The bond, and any deposit accompanying it, shall be returned at the end of three years or prior thereto if the vehicle is no longer registered in this State and the currently valid certificate of title is surrendered to the Division, unless the Division has been notified of the pendency of an action to recover on the bond.

(c) Whenever an applicant for the registration of a moped is unable to present a manufacturer's certificate of origin for the moped, the applicant must submit an affidavit stating why the applicant does not have the manufacturer's certificate of origin and attesting that the applicant is entitled to registration. Upon receipt of the application and accompanying affidavit, the Division shall issue the applicant a registration card and plate. The Division may not require the applicant to post a bond as required under subsection (b) of this section. A person damaged by issuance of the registration card does not have a right of action against the Division.

History.

1937, c. 407, s. 40; 1947, c. 219, s. 7; 1961, c. 360, s. 11; c. 835, s. 10; 1975, c. 716, s. 5; 2014-114, s. 3

EDITOR'S NOTE. --

Session Laws 2014-114, s. 5, made subsection (c) of this section as added by Session Laws 2014-114, s. 3, effective July 1, 2015, and applicable to offenses committed on or after that date.

EFFECT OF AMENDMENTS. --

Session Laws 2014-114, s. 3, added subsection (c). See Editor's note for effective date and applicability.

CROSS REFERENCES. --

For fee schedule, see G.S. 20-85.

§ 20-77. Transfer by operation of law; sale under mechanic's or storage lien; unclaimed vehicles

(a) Whenever the title or interest of an owner in or to a vehicle shall pass to another by operation of law, as upon order in bankruptcy, execution sale, repossession upon default in performing the terms of a lease or executory sales contract, or otherwise than by voluntary transfer, the transferee shall secure a new certificate of title upon proper application, payment of the fees provided by law, and presentation of the last certificate of title, if available and such instruments or documents of authority or certified copies thereof as may be sufficient or required by law to evidence or effect a transfer of interest in or to chattels in such cases.

(b) In the event of transfer as upon inheritance or devise, the Division shall, upon a receipt of a certified copy of a will, letters of administration and/or a certificate from the clerk of the superior court showing that the motor vehicle registered in the name of the decedent owner has been assigned to the owner's surviving spouse as part of the spousal year's allowance, transfer both title and license as otherwise provided for transfers. If a decedent dies intestate and no administrator has qualified or the clerk of superior court has not issued a certificate of assignment as part of the spousal year's allowance, or if a decedent dies testate with a small estate and leaving a purported will, which, in the opinion of the clerk of superior court, does not justify the expense of probate and administration and probate and administration is not demanded by any interested party entitled by law to demand same, and provided that the purported will is filed in the public records of the office of the clerk of the superior court, the Division may upon affidavit executed by all heirs effect such transfer. The affidavit shall state the name of the decedent, date of death, that the decedent died intestate or testate and no administration is pending or expected, that all debts have been paid or that the proceeds from the transfer will be used for that purpose, the names, ages and relationship of all heirs and devisees (if there be a purported will), and the name and address of the transferee of the title. A surviving spouse may execute the affidavit and transfer the interest of the decedent's minor or incompetent children where such minor or incompetent does not have a guardian. A transfer under this subsection shall not affect the validity nor be in prejudice of any creditor's lien.

(c) **Mechanic's or Storage Lien.** -- In any case where a vehicle is sold under a mechanic's or storage lien, or abandoned property, the Division shall be given a 20-day notice as provided in G.S. 20-114.

(d) An operator of a place of business for garaging, repairing, parking or storing vehicles for the public in which a vehicle remains unclaimed for 10 days, or the landowners upon whose property a motor vehicle has been abandoned for more than 30 days, shall, within five days after the expiration of that period, report the vehicle as unclaimed to the Division. Failure to make the report shall constitute a Class 3 misdemeanor. Persons who are required to make this report and who fail to do so within the time period specified may collect other charges due but may not collect storage charges for the period of time between when they were required to make this report and when they actually did send the report to the Division by certified mail.

Any vehicle which remains unclaimed after report is made to the Division may be sold by the operator or landowner in accordance with the provisions relating to the enforcement of liens and the application of proceeds of sale of Article 1 of Chapter 44A. The Division shall make all forms required by the Division to effectuate a sale under this subsection available on the Division's Web site, and the Division shall allow for the electronic submission of these forms. Any form required by the Division to effectuate a sale under this subsection that requires a signature may be submitted with an electronic signature in accordance with Article 40 of Chapter 66 of the General Statutes.

(e) Any person, who shall sell a vehicle to satisfy a mechanic's or storage lien or any person who shall sell a vehicle as upon order in bankruptcy, execution sale, repossession upon default in performing the terms of a lease or executory sales contract, or otherwise by operation of law, shall remove any license plates attached thereto and return them to the Division.

History.
1937, c. 407, s. 41; 1943, c. 726; 1945, cc. 289, 714; 1955, c. 296, s. 1; 1959, c. 1264, s. 3; 1961, c. 360, ss. 12, 13; 1967, c. 562, s. 8; 1971, cc. 230, 512, 876; 1973, c. 1386, ss. 1, 2; c. 1446, s. 21; 1975, c. 438, s. 2; c. 716, s. 5; 1993, c. 539, s. 342;1994, Ex. Sess., c. 24, s. 14(c);1995 (Reg. Sess., 1996), c. 635, s. 1; 2003-336, s. 1;2011-284, s. 14;2017-57, s. 34.41(a)

EFFECT OF AMENDMENTS. --
Session Laws 2011-284, s. 14, effective June 24, 2011, in subsection (b), in the first sentence, substituted "inheritance or devise" for "inheritance, devise or bequest" and "assigned to the owner's surviving spouse as part of the spousal year's allowance" for "assigned to his widow as part of her year's support," and in the second sentence, substituted "spousal" for "widow's."

Session Laws 2017-57, s. 34.41(a), effective October 1, 2017, added the last two sentences in subsection (d) and made plural stylistic changes.
CITED in Younts v. State Farm Mut. Auto. Ins. Co., 281 N.C. 582, 189 S.E.2d 137 (1972).

CROSS REFERENCES. --
For fee schedule, see G.S. 20-85.

LEGAL PERIODICALS. --
For article concerning liens on personal property not governed by the Uniform Commercial Code, see 44 N.C.L. Rev. 322 (1966).

§ 20-78. When Division to transfer registration and issue new certificate; recordation

(a) The Division, upon receipt of a properly endorsed certificate of title, application for transfer thereof and payment of all proper fees, shall issue a new certificate of title as upon an original registration. The Division, upon receipt of an application for transfer of registration plates, together with payment of all proper fees, shall issue a new registration card transferring and assigning the registration plates and numbers thereon as upon an original assignment of registration plates. The Division, upon receipt of an application for transfer thereof and payment of all proper fees, but without receipt of a properly endorsed certificate of title, shall issue a salvage certificate of title pursuant to G.S. 20-109.1(b)(2) or G.S. 20-109.1(e1).

(b) The Division shall maintain a record of certificates of title issued by the Division for a period of 20 years. After 20 years, the Division shall maintain a record of the last two owners.

The Commissioner is hereby authorized and empowered to provide for the photographic or photostatic recording of certificate of title records in such manner as he may deem expedient. The photographic or photostatic copies herein authorized shall be sufficient as evidence in tracing of titles of the motor vehicles designated therein, and shall also be admitted in evidence in all actions and proceedings to the same extent that the originals would have been admitted.

History.
1937, c. 407, s. 42; 1943, c. 726; 1947, c. 219, s. 8; 1961, c. 360, s. 14; 1971, c. 1070, s. 4; 1975, c. 716, s. 5; 1999-452, s. 15;2013-400, s. 4

EFFECT OF AMENDMENTS. --
Session Laws 2013-400, s. 4, effective October 1, 2013, added the last sentence in subsection (a).
APPLIED in Hawkins v. M & J Fin. Corp., 238 N.C. 174, 77 S.E.2d 669 (1953).
CITED in Morrisey v. Crabtree, 143 F. Supp. 105 (M.D.N.C. 1956); Sutton v. Sutton, 35 N.C. App. 670, 242 S.E.2d 644 (1978).

CROSS REFERENCES. --
For fee schedule, see G.S. 20-85.

§ 20-78.1. Terminal rental adjustment clauses; vehicle leases that are not sales or security interests

Notwithstanding any other provision of law, a lease transaction does not create a sale or security interest in a motor vehicle or trailer merely because the lease contains a terminal rental adjustment clause that provides that the rental price is permitted or required to be adjusted up or down by reference to the amount of money realized upon the sale or other disposition of the motor vehicle or trailer.

History.
2011-223, s. 1

PART 5.
ISSUANCE OF SPECIAL PLATES

§ 20-79. Dealer license plates

(a) **How to Get a Dealer Plate. --** The Division may issue a person licensed under Article 12 of this Chapter the appropriate classification of dealer license plate. A person eligible for a dealer license plate may obtain one by filing an application with the Division and paying the required fee. An application must be filed on a form provided by the Division. The required fee is the amount set by G.S. 20-87(7).

(b) **Number of Plates. --** A dealer who was licensed under Article 12 of this Chapter for the previous 12-month period ending December 31 may obtain the number of dealer license plates allowed by the following table; the number allowed is based on the number of motor vehicles the dealer sold during the relevant 12-month period and the average number of qualifying sales representatives the dealer employed during that same 12-month period:

Vehicles Sold In Relevant 12-Month Period	Maximum Number of Plates
Fewer than 12	3
At least 12 but less than 25	6
At least 25 but less than 37	7
At least 37 but less than 49	8
49 or more	At least 8, but no more than 5 times the average number of qualifying sales representatives employed by the dealer during the relevant 12-month period.

A dealer who was not licensed under Article 12 of this Chapter for part or all of the previous 12-month period ending December 31 may obtain the number of dealer license plates that equals four times the number of qualifying sales representatives employed by the dealer on the date the dealer files the application. A "qualifying sales representative" is a sales representative who works for the dealer at least 25 hours a week on a regular basis and is compensated by the dealer for this work.

A dealer who sold fewer than 49 motor vehicles the previous 12-month period ending December 31 but has sold at least that number since January 1 may apply for additional dealer license plates at any time. The maximum number of dealer license plates the dealer may obtain is the number the dealer could have obtained if the dealer had sold at least 49 motor vehicles in the previous 12-month period ending December 31.

A dealer who applies for a dealer license plate must certify to the Division the number of motor vehicles the dealer sold in the relevant period. Making a material misstatement in an application for a dealer license plate is grounds for the denial, suspension, or revocation of a dealer's license under G.S. 20-294.

A dealer engaged in the alteration and sale of specialty vehicles may apply for up to two dealer plates in addition to the number of dealer plates that the dealer would otherwise be entitled to under this section.

This subsection does not apply to manufacturers licensed under Article 12 of this Chapter.

(c) **Form and Duration.** -- A dealer license plate is subject to G.S. 20-63, except for the requirement that the plate display the registration number of a motor vehicle and the requirement that the plate be a "First in Flight" plate, a "First in Freedom" plate, or a "National/State Mottos" plate. A dealer license plate must have a distinguishing symbol identifying the plate as a dealer license plate. The symbol may vary depending upon the classification of dealer license plate issued. The Division must provide suitably reduced sized license plates for motorcycle dealers and manufacturers.

A dealer license plate is issued for a period of one year. The Division shall vary the expiration dates of dealer registration renewals so that an approximately equal number expires at the end of each month, quarter, or other period consisting of one or more months. A dealer license plate may be transferred from one vehicle to another. When the Division issues a dealer plate, it may issue a registration that expires at the end of any monthly interval. When one of the following occurs, a dealer must surrender to the Division all dealer license plates issued to the dealer:

(1) The dealer surrenders the license issued to the dealer under Article 12 of this Chapter.

(2) The Division suspends or revokes the license issued to the dealer under Article 12 of this Chapter.

(3) The Division rescinds the dealer license plates because of a violation of the restrictions on the use of a dealer license plate.

To obtain a dealer license plate after it has been surrendered, the dealer must file a new application for a dealer license plate and pay the required fee for the plate.

(d) **(Effective until December 31, 2024) Restrictions on Use.** -- A dealer license plate may be displayed only on a motor vehicle that meets all of the following requirements:

(1) Is part of the inventory of the dealer.

(2) Is not consigned to the dealer.

(3) Is covered by liability insurance that meets the requirements of Article 9A of this Chapter.

(4) Is not used by the dealer in another business in which the dealer is engaged.

(5) Is driven on a highway by a person who meets one of the following descriptions:

a. Has a demonstration permit to test-drive the motor vehicle and carries the demonstration permit while driving the motor vehicle.

b. Is an officer or sales representative of the dealer and is driving the vehicle for a business purpose of the dealer.

c. Is an employee of the dealer and is driving the vehicle in the course of employment.

d. Is an employee of the dealer or of a contractor of the dealer and is driving the vehicle within a 20-mile radius of a place where the vehicle is being repaired or otherwise prepared for sale.

e. Is an employee of the dealer or of a contractor of the dealer and is transporting the vehicle to or from a vehicle auction or to the dealer's established salesroom.

f. Is an officer, sales representative, or other employee of an independent or franchised motor vehicle dealer or is an immediate family member of an officer, sales representative, or other employee of an independent or franchised motor vehicle dealer.

(6) A copy of the registration card for the dealer plate issued to the dealer is carried by the person operating the motor vehicle or, if the person is operating the motor vehicle in this State, the registration card is maintained on file at the dealer's address listed on the registration card, and the registration card must be able to be produced within 24 hours upon request of any law enforcement officer.

A dealer may issue a demonstration permit for a motor vehicle to a person licensed to drive that type of motor vehicle. A demonstration permit authorizes each person named in the permit to drive the motor vehicle described in the permit for up to 96 hours after the time the permit is issued. A dealer may, for good cause, renew

Chapter 20

a demonstration permit for one additional 96-hour period. A franchised motor vehicle dealer is not prohibited from using a demonstration permit pursuant to this subsection by reason of the dealer's receipt of incentive or warranty compensation or other reimbursement or consideration from a manufacturer, factory branch, distributor, distributor branch or from a third-party warranty, maintenance, or service contract company relating to the use of the vehicle as a demonstrator or service loaner.

A dealer may not lend, rent, lease, or otherwise place a dealer license plate at the disposal of a person except as authorized by this subsection.

(d) **(Effective December 31, 2024) Restrictions on Use. --** A dealer license plate may be displayed only on a motor vehicle that meets all of the following requirements:

(1) Is part of the inventory of the dealer.

(2) Is not consigned to the dealer.

(3) Is covered by liability insurance that meets the requirements of Article 9A of this Chapter.

(4) Is not used by the dealer in another business in which the dealer is engaged.

(5) Is driven on a highway by a person who meets one of the following descriptions:

    a. Has a demonstration permit to test-drive the motor vehicle and carries the demonstration permit while driving the motor vehicle.

    b. Is an officer or sales representative of the dealer and is driving the vehicle for a business purpose of the dealer.

    c. Is an employee of the dealer and is driving the vehicle in the course of employment.

    d. Is an employee of the dealer or of a contractor of the dealer and is driving the vehicle within a 20-mile radius of a place where the vehicle is being repaired or otherwise prepared for sale.

    e. Is an employee of the dealer or of a contractor of the dealer and is transporting the vehicle to or from a vehicle auction or to the dealer's established salesroom.

    f. Is an officer, sales representative, or other employee of an independent or franchised motor vehicle dealer or is an immediate family member of an officer, sales representative, or other employee of an independent or franchised motor vehicle dealer.

(6) A copy of the registration card for the dealer plate issued to the dealer is carried by the person operating the motor vehicle or, if the person is operating the motor vehicle in this State, the registration card is maintained on file at the dealer's address listed on the registration card, and the registration card must be able to be produced within 24 hours upon request of any law enforcement officer.

A dealer may issue a demonstration permit for a motor vehicle to a person licensed to drive that type of motor vehicle. A demonstration permit authorizes each person named in the permit to drive the motor vehicle described in the permit for up to 96 hours after the time the permit is issued. A dealer may, for good cause, renew a demonstration permit for one additional 96-hour period.

A dealer may not lend, rent, lease, or otherwise place a dealer license plate at the disposal of a person except as authorized by this subsection.

(e) **Sanctions. --** The following sanctions apply when a motor vehicle displaying a dealer license plate is driven in violation of the restrictions on the use of the plate:

(1) The individual driving the motor vehicle is responsible for an infraction and is subject to a penalty of one hundred dollars ($ 100.00).

(2) The dealer to whom the plate is issued is subject to a civil penalty imposed by the Division of two hundred fifty dollars ($ 250.00).

(3) The Division may rescind all dealer license plates issued to the dealer whose plate was displayed on the motor vehicle.

A penalty imposed under subdivision (1) of this subsection is payable to the county where the infraction occurred, as required by G.S. 14-3.1. A civil penalty imposed under subdivision (2) of this subsection shall be credited to the Highway Fund as nontax revenue.

(f) **Transfer of Dealer Registration. --** No change in the name of a firm, partnership or corporation, nor the taking in of a new partner, nor the withdrawal of one or more of the firm, shall be considered a new business; but if any one or more of the partners remain in the firm, or if there is change in ownership of less than a majority of the stock, if a corporation, the business shall be regarded as continuing and the dealers' plates originally issued may continue to be used.

(g) **Penalties. --** The clear proceeds of all civil penalties, civil forfeitures, and civil fines that are collected by the Department of Transportation pursuant to this section shall be remitted to the Civil Penalty and Forfeiture Fund in accordance with G.S. 115C-457.2.

(h) **Definition. --** For purposes of this section, the term "dealer" means a person who is licensed under Article 12 of this Chapter.

History.

1937, c. 407, s. 43; 1947, c. 220, s. 2; 1949, c. 583, s. 3; 1951, c. 985, s. 2; 1959, c. 1264, s. 3.5; 1961, c. 360, s. 15; 1975, c. 716, s. 5; 1979, c. 239; c. 612, s. 1; 1985, c. 764, s. 21; 1985 (Reg. Sess., 1986), c. 852, s. 17; 1989, c. 770, s. 74.1(a);1993, c. 321, s. 169.4;c. 440, s. 2;c. 539, s. 343;1993 (Reg. Sess., 1994), c. 697, ss. 1, 2; c. 761, s. 6; 1994, Ex. Sess., c. 24, s. 14(c);1997-335, s. 1;2001-212, s. 1;2004-167, s. 4;2004-199, s. 59;2005-276, s. 6.37(q);2007-291, s. 1;2007-481, s. 1;2010-132, s. 5;2011-318, s. 2;2014-100, s. 34.28(b);2015-232, s. 1.4(a);2015-264, s. 42(b);2016-90, s. 13.5;2018-5, s. 34.27(b);2018-27, s. 4.5(c);2018-42, s. 3(c);2020-51, s. 1(c)

SUBSECTION (D) SET OUT TWICE. --The first version of subsection (d) set out above is effective until December 31, 2024. The second version of subsection (d) set out above is effective December 31, 2024.

EDITOR'S NOTE. --

Session Laws 2014-100, s. 34.28(d), made the amendment to subsection (c) of this section by Session Laws 2014-100, s. 34.28(b), effective July 1, 2015, and applicable to registration plates issued on or after that date.

Session Laws 2015-232, s. 1.4(b), as amended by Session Laws 2018-27, s. 4.5(c), Session Laws 2018-42, s. 3(c), and Session Laws 2020-51, s. 1(c), made the last sentence of the next-to-last paragraph of subsection (d), as added by Session Laws 2015-232, s. 1.4(a), effective August 25, 2015, and expires December 31, 2024.

Session Laws 2018-5, s. 1.1, provides: "This act shall be known as the 'Current Operations Appropriations Act of 2018.'"

Session Laws 2018-5, s. 39.7, is a severability clause.

Session Laws 2018-27, s. 5, is a severability clause.

Session Laws 2020-3, s. 4.7(a) -(h), as amended by Session Laws 2020-97, ss. 3.15(a), 3.16(a), provides: "(a) Definition. -- For purposes of this section, 'credential' means any of the following issued by the Division of Motor Vehicles:

"(1) Drivers license.

"(2) Learner's permit.

"(3) Limited learner's permit.

"(4) Limited provisional license.

"(5) Full provisional license.

"(6) Commercial drivers license.

"(7) Commercial learner's permit.

"(8) Temporary driving certificate.

"(9) Special identification card.

"(10) Handicapped placard.

"(11) Vehicle registration.

"(12) Temporary vehicle registration.

"(13) Dealer license plate.

"(14) Transporter plate.

"(15) Loaner/Dealer 'LD' plate.

"(16) Vehicle inspection authorization.

"(17) Inspection station license.

"(18) Inspection mechanic license.

"(19) Transportation network company permit.

"(20) Motor vehicle dealer license.

"(21) Sales representative license.

"(22) Manufacturer license.

"(23) Distributor license.

"(24) Wholesaler license.

"(25) Driver training school license.

"(26) Driver training school instructor license.

"(27) Professional housemoving license.

"(b) Extend Validity of Credentials. -- Notwithstanding renewal, duration, or expiration provisions of G.S. 20-7, 20-11, 20-37.6, 20-37.7, 20-37.13, 20-50, 20-66, 20-79, 20-79.02, 20-79.2, 20-183.4B, 20-183.4D, 20-280.3, 20-288, 20-324, and 20-359, or any other provision of law to the contrary, the Division of Motor Vehicles shall extend for a period of five months the validity of any credential that expires on or after March 1, 2020, and before August 1, 2020. The Division shall extend for a period of five months the validity of any credential listed in subdivisions (6), (7), (9), (10), and (18) of subsection (a) of this section that expires on or after March 1, 2020, and before the date 30 days after the date the Governor (i) rescinds Executive Order No. 116 or (ii) issues another executive order lifting restrictions on Division of Motor Vehicles functions. Notwithstanding G.S. 20-37.13(h) and G.S. 20-37.13A(a), the Division of Motor Vehicles is authorized to waive the requirement that commercial drivers license and commercial learner's permit holders have a medical examination and certification, as required by federal law, consistent with any waiver of medical qualifications standards issued by the Federal Motor Carrier Safety Administration. A credential extended under this section shall expire five months from the date it otherwise expires as prescribed by law prior to this section. However, the subsequent expiration of a credential extended under this section shall occur on the date prescribed by law prior to this section without regard to the extension. The Division shall notify individuals affected by an extension granted under this section, including information on new expiration dates and how the extension affects subsequent renewal and expiration dates.

"(b1) Extension of Intrastate Medical Waivers. -- Notwithstanding the limitation on duration of waivers in G.S. 20-37.13A(b), the Division of Motor Vehicles may extend for up to five months the validity of a medical waiver issued by the Division under G.S. 20-37.13A if the waiver expires on or after March 1, 2020, and before the date 30 days after the date the Governor (i) rescinds Executive Order No. 116 or (ii) issues another executive order lifting restrictions on Division of Motor Vehicles functions, and the Division's Medical Review Unit determines the extension is appropriate.

"(c) Driving Eligibility Certificates. -- Notwithstanding G.S. 20-11(n)(3), a driving eligibility certificate dated on or after February 9, 2020, and before March 10, 2020, remains valid and may be accepted by the Division of Motor Vehicles to meet the requirements for a license or permit issued under G.S. 20-11 until 30 days after the date the Governor rescinds Executive Order No. 116 or the date the Division reopens all drivers license offices, whichever is earlier.

"(d) Waive Penalties. -- Notwithstanding any provision of law to the contrary, the Division shall waive any fines, fees, or penalties associated with failing to renew a credential during the period of time the credential is valid by extension under subsection (b) of this section.

"(e) Motor Vehicle Taxes. -- Notwithstanding any provision of law to the contrary, due dates for motor vehicle taxes that are tied to registration expiration under Article 22A of Chapter 105 of the General Statutes shall be extended to correspond with extended expiration dates under subsection (b) of this section.

"(f) Validity by Extension a Defense. -- A person may not be convicted or found responsible for any offense resulting from failure to renew a credential issued by the Division if, when tried for that offense, the person shows that the offense occurred during the period of time the credential is valid by extension under subsection (b) of this section.

"(g) Report. -- Within 30 days of the extensions made under subsection (b) of this section, the Division shall submit a report to the Joint Legislative Transportation Oversight Committee and the Fiscal Research Division detailing implementation of this section.

"(h) Effective Date. -- This section is effective retroactively to March 1, 2020, and applies to expirations occurring on or after that date."

Session Laws 2020-3, s. 5, is a severability clause.

Session Laws 2020-97, s. 4.5, is a severability clause.

EFFECT OF AMENDMENTS. --

Session Laws 2010-132, s. 5, effective December 1, 2010, and applicable to offenses committed on or after that date, in the first paragraph in subsection (b), increased the maximum number of plates by 2 in the first four entries, and in the last entry, substituted "At least 8, but no more than 5 times the average number" for "At least 6, but no more than 4 times the average number"; added subdivisions (d)(5)d. and (d)(5)e.; in subdivision (e)(1), substituted "one hundred dollars ($100.00)" for "fifty dollars ($50.00)"; and in subdivision (e)(2), substituted "two hundred fifty dollars ($250.00)" for "two hundred dollars ($200.00)."

Session Laws 2014-100, s. 34.28(b), inserted "or a 'First in Freedom' plate" at the end of the first sentence in subsection (c). See Editor's note for effective date and applicability.

Session Laws 2015-232, s. 1.4(a), as amended by Session Laws 2018-27, s. 4.5(c), Session Laws 2018-42, s. 3(c), and Session Laws 2020-51, s. 1(c), added the last sentence of the next-to-last paragraph of subsection (d). For effective date and expiration, see editor's note.

Session Laws 2015-264, s. 42(b), effective October 1, 2015, removed former designations (i) and (ii) and inserted "from" preceding "a third-party warranty" in the last sentence of the next-to-last paragraph of subsection (d).

Session Laws 2016-90, s. 13.5, effective July 11, 2016, in subdivision (d)(5)f., substituted "an independent or franchised" for "a franchised."

Session Laws 2018-5, s. 34.27(b), effective July 1, 2018, substituted ""First in Flight' plate, a 'First in Freedom' plate, or a 'National/State Mottos' plate" for ""First in Flight' plate or a 'First in Freedom' plate" in the first paragraph of subsection (c).

§ 20-79.01. Special sports event temporary license plates

(a) **Application.** -- A dealer who is licensed under Article 12 of this Chapter and who agrees to loan to another for use at a special sports event a vehicle that could display a dealer license plate if driven by an officer or employee of the dealer may obtain a temporary special sports event license plate for that vehicle by filing an application with the Division and paying the required fee. A "special sports event" is a sports event that is held no more than once a year and is open to the public. An application must be filed on a form provided by the Division and contain the information required by the Division. The fee for a temporary special sports event license plate is five dollars ($ 5.00).

(b) **Form and Duration.** -- A temporary special sports event license plate must state on the plate the date it was issued, the date it expires, and the make, model, and serial number of the vehicle for which it is issued. A temporary special sports event license plate may be issued for no more than 45 days. The dealer to whom the plate is issued must destroy the plate on or before the date it expires.

(c) **Restrictions on Use.** -- A temporary special sports event license plate may be displayed only on the vehicle for which it is issued. A vehicle displaying a temporary special sports event license plate may be driven by anyone who is licensed to drive the type of vehicle for which the plate is issued and may be driven for any purpose.

History.
1993, c. 440, s. 13

§ 20-79.02. Loaner/Dealer "LD" license plate for franchised dealer loaner vehicles

(a) **Application; Fee.** -- A franchised motor vehicle dealer, as defined in G.S. 20-286(8b) and licensed in accordance with Article 12 of this Chapter, who agrees to loan, with or without charge, a new motor vehicle owned by the dealer to a customer of the dealer who is having his or her vehicle serviced by the dealer, may obtain a Loaner/Dealer "LD" license plate for the vehicle by filing an application with the Division and paying the required fee. Receipt by a franchised motor vehicle dealer of compensation or other consideration from a manufacturer, distributor, manufacturer branch, distributor branch, third-party warranty, maintenance or service contract company, or other third-party source related to a vehicle, including, but not limited to, incentive compensation or reimbursement for maintenance, repairs, or other work performed on the vehicle, does not prevent the franchised motor vehicle dealer from receiving an LD license plate for the vehicle. An application must be filed on a form provided by the Division and contain the information required by the Division. The annual fee for an LD license plate is two hundred dollars ($ 200.00) per 12 calendar months.

(b) **Number of Plates. --** There is no limit on the number of LD license plates that a franchised motor vehicle dealer may be issued, provided that the applicable annual fee for each plate is paid.

(c) **Form and Duration. --** An LD license plate is subject to G.S. 20-63, except for the requirement that the plate display the registration number of a motor vehicle and the requirement that the plate be a "First in Flight" plate, "First in Freedom" plate, or a "National/State Mottos" plate. An LD license plate must have a distinguishing symbol identifying the plate as an LD license plate. Subject to the limitations in this section, an LD license plate may continue in existence perpetually and may be transferred to other vehicles in the dealer's loaner fleet when the vehicle on which the LD license plate is displayed has been sold or leased to a third party or otherwise removed from the dealer's loaner fleet.

(d) **Restrictions on Use. --** The following restrictions apply with regard to the use and display of an LD license plate:

(1) An LD license plate may be displayed only on a motor vehicle that meets all of the following requirements:

a. Is part of the inventory of a franchised motor vehicle dealer.

b. Is not consigned to the franchised motor vehicle dealer or affiliate.

c. Is covered by liability insurance that meets the requirements of Article 9A of this Chapter; provided, however, that nothing herein prevents or prohibits a franchised motor vehicle dealer from contractually shifting the risk of loss and insurance requirements contained in Article 9A of this Chapter to an individual or entity to which a vehicle is loaned.

d. Is not used by the franchised motor vehicle dealer in another business in which the dealer is engaged.

e. Is driven on a highway by a customer of the franchised motor vehicle dealer who is having a vehicle serviced or repaired by the dealer.

(2) The person operating the motor vehicle must carry a copy of the assignment by the franchised motor vehicle dealer and a copy of the registration card for the LD license plate issued to the franchised motor vehicle dealer, or, if the person is operating the motor vehicle in this State, the registration card must be maintained on file at the franchised motor vehicle dealer's address listed on the registration card, and the registration card must be able to be produced within 24 hours upon request of a law enforcement officer.

(3) A vehicle displaying an LD license plate may be driven only by a person who is licensed to drive the type of motor vehicle for which the plate is issued.

(4) An LD license plate may be displayed only on the motor vehicle for which it has been assigned by the franchised motor vehicle dealer.

(5) The franchised motor vehicle dealer to whom an LD license plate is issued is responsible for completing and maintaining documentation prescribed by the Division relating to the assignment of each motor vehicle on which an LD license plate is displayed to a customer of the franchised dealer.

(e) **Penalties. --** A driver of a motor vehicle or a franchised motor vehicle dealer who violates a restriction on the use or display of an LD license plate as set out in subsection (d) of this section is subject to the penalties listed in this subsection. The clear proceeds of all civil penalties, civil forfeitures, and civil fines that are collected pursuant to this section shall be remitted to the Civil Penalty and Forfeiture Fund in accordance with G.S. 115C-457.2. The penalties are as follows:

(1) The driver of the motor vehicle who violates a restriction on the use or display of an LD license plate is responsible for an infraction and is subject to a penalty of one hundred dollars ($ 100.00).

(2) A franchised motor vehicle dealer to whom the plate is issued who violates a restriction on the use or display of an LD license plate is subject to an infraction and is subject to a penalty of two hundred fifty dollars ($ 250.00). The Division may rescind all LD license plates issued to the franchised motor vehicle dealer for knowing repeated violations of subsection (d) of this section.

(f) **Transfer of Dealer Registration. --** A change in the name of a firm, partnership, or corporation is not considered a new business, and the franchised motor vehicle dealer's LD license plates may continue to be used.

(g) **Applicability. --** Prior to January 1, 2025, a new motor vehicle dealer may, but is not required to, display an LD license plate on a service loaner vehicle. Beginning on or after January 1, 2025, a new motor vehicle dealer shall display an LD license plate on any new motor vehicle placed into service as a loaner vehicle if either of the following circumstances exists:

 (1) The new motor vehicle dealer is receiving incentive or warranty compensation from a manufacturer, factory branch, distributor, or distributor branch for the use of the vehicle as a service loaner.

 (2) The new motor vehicle dealer is receiving a fee or other compensation from the dealer's customers for the use of the vehicle as a service loaner.

History.

2015-232, s. 1.3(a);2018-5, s. 34.27(c);2018-27, s. 4.5(a);2018-42, s. 3(a);2020-51, s. 1(a)

EDITOR'S NOTE. --

Session Laws 2015-232, s. 1.3(b), made this section effective July 1, 2016.

Session Laws 2018-5, s. 1.1, provides: "This act shall be known as the 'Current Operations Appropriations Act of 2018.'"

Session Laws 2018-5, s. 39.7, is a severability clause.

Session Laws 2018-27, s. 5, is a severability clause.

Session Laws 2020-3, s. 4.7(a) -(h), as amended by Session Laws 2020-97, ss. 3.15(a), 3.16(a), provides: "(a) Definition. -- For purposes of this section, 'credential' means any of the following issued by the Division of Motor Vehicles:

"(1) Drivers license.

"(2) Learner's permit.

"(3) Limited learner's permit.

"(4) Limited provisional license.

"(5) Full provisional license.

"(6) Commercial drivers license.

"(7) Commercial learner's permit.

"(8) Temporary driving certificate.

"(9) Special identification card.

"(10) Handicapped placard.

"(11) Vehicle registration.

"(12) Temporary vehicle registration.

"(13) Dealer license plate.

"(14) Transporter plate.

"(15) Loaner/Dealer 'LD' plate.

"(16) Vehicle inspection authorization.

"(17) Inspection station license.

"(18) Inspection mechanic license.

"(19) Transportation network company permit.

"(20) Motor vehicle dealer license.

"(21) Sales representative license.

"(22) Manufacturer license.

"(23) Distributor license.

"(24) Wholesaler license.

"(25) Driver training school license.

"(26) Driver training school instructor license.

"(27) Professional housemoving license.

"(b) Extend Validity of Credentials. -- Notwithstanding renewal, duration, or expiration provisions of G.S. 20-7, 20-11, 20-37.6, 20-37.7, 20-37.13, 20-50, 20-66, 20-79, 20-79.02, 20-79.2, 20-183.4B, 20-183.4D, 20-280.3, 20-288, 20-324, and 20-359, or any other

provision of law to the contrary, the Division of Motor Vehicles shall extend for a period of five months the validity of any credential that expires on or after March 1, 2020, and before August 1, 2020. The Division shall extend for a period of five months the validity of any credential listed in subdivisions (6), (7), (9), (10), and (18) of subsection (a) of this section that expires on or after March 1, 2020, and before the date 30 days after the date the Governor (i) rescinds Executive Order No. 116 or (ii) issues another executive order lifting restrictions on Division of Motor Vehicles functions. Notwithstanding G.S. 20-37.13(h) and G.S. 20-37.13A(a), the Division of Motor Vehicles is authorized to waive the requirement that commercial drivers license and commercial learner's permit holders have a medical examination and certification, as required by federal law, consistent with any waiver of medical qualifications standards issued by the Federal Motor Carrier Safety Administration. A credential extended under this section shall expire five months from the date it otherwise expires as prescribed by law prior to this section. However, the subsequent expiration of a credential extended under this section shall occur on the date prescribed by law prior to this section without regard to the extension. The Division shall notify individuals affected by an extension granted under this section, including information on new expiration dates and how the extension affects subsequent renewal and expiration dates.

"(b1) Extension of Intrastate Medical Waivers. -- Notwithstanding the limitation on duration of waivers in G.S. 20-37.13A(b), the Division of Motor Vehicles may extend for up to five months the validity of a medical waiver issued by the Division under G.S. 20-37.13A if the waiver expires on or after March 1, 2020, and before the date 30 days after the date the Governor (i) rescinds Executive Order No. 116 or (ii) issues another executive order lifting restrictions on Division of Motor Vehicles functions, and the Division's Medical Review Unit determines the extension is appropriate.

"(c) Driving Eligibility Certificates. -- Notwithstanding G.S. 20-11(n)(3), a driving eligibility certificate dated on or after February 9, 2020, and before March 10, 2020, remains valid and may be accepted by the Division of Motor Vehicles to meet the requirements for a license or permit issued under G.S. 20-11 until 30 days after the date the Governor rescinds Executive Order No. 116 or the date the Division reopens all drivers license offices, whichever is earlier.

"(d) Waive Penalties. -- Notwithstanding any provision of law to the contrary, the Division shall waive any fines, fees, or penalties associated with failing to renew a credential during the period of time the credential is valid by extension under subsection (b) of this section.

"(e) Motor Vehicle Taxes. -- Notwithstanding any provision of law to the contrary, due dates for motor vehicle taxes that are tied to registration expiration under Article 22A of Chapter 105 of the General Statutes shall be extended to correspond with extended expiration dates under subsection (b) of this section.

"(f) Validity by Extension a Defense. -- A person may not be convicted or found responsible for any offense resulting from failure to renew a credential issued by the Division if, when tried for that offense, the person shows that the offense occurred during the period of time the credential is valid by extension under subsection (b) of this section.

"(g) Report. -- Within 30 days of the extensions made under subsection (b) of this section, the Division shall submit a report to the Joint Legislative Transportation Oversight Committee and the Fiscal Research Division detailing implementation of this section.

"(h) Effective Date. -- This section is effective retroactively to March 1, 2020, and applies to expirations occurring on or after that date."

Session Laws 2020-3, s. 5, is a severability clause.

Session Laws 2020-97, s. 4.5, is a severability clause.

EFFECT OF AMENDMENTS. --

Session Laws 2018-5, s. 34.27(c), effective July 1, 2018, substituted ""First in Flight' plate, 'First in Freedom' plate, or a 'National/State Mottos' plate" for ""First in Flight' or 'First in Freedom' plate" in the first sentence of subsection (c).

Session Laws 2018-27, s. 4.5(a), and Session Laws 2018-42, s. 3(a), are identical, both effective June 22, 2018, and both substituted "January 1, 2021" for "January 1, 2019" twice in the introductory paragraph of subsection (g).

Session Laws 2020-51, s. 1(a), effective June 30, 2020, substituted "2025" for "2021" twice in the introductory language of subsection (g).

§ 20-79.1. Use of temporary registration plates or markers by purchasers of motor vehicles in lieu of dealers' plates

(a) The Division may, subject to the limitations and conditions hereinafter set forth, deliver temporary registration plates or markers designed by said Division to a dealer duly registered under the provisions of this Article who applies for at least 25 such plates or markers and who encloses with the application a fee of one dollar ($ 1.00) for each plate or marker for which application is made. The application shall be made upon a form prescribed and furnished by the Division. The Division shall provide methods for physical and electronic application submission and payment. Any electronic application submitted to the Division under this subsection may include a method for electronic signature by the dealer. Dealers, subject to the limitations and conditions hereinafter set forth, may issue temporary registration plates or markers to owners of vehicles, provided that owners comply with the pertinent provisions of this section.

(b) Every dealer who has made application for temporary registration plates or markers shall maintain in permanent form a record of all temporary registration plates or markers delivered to him, and shall also maintain in permanent form a record of all temporary registration plates or markers issued by him, and in addition thereto, shall maintain in permanent form a record of any other information pertaining to the receipt or the issuance of temporary registration plates or markers that the Division may require. Each record shall be kept for a period of at least one year from the date of entry of such record. Every dealer shall allow full and free access to such records during regular business hours, to duly authorized representatives of the Division and to peace officers.

(c) Every dealer who issues temporary registration plates or markers shall also issue a temporary registration certificate upon a form furnished by the Division and deliver it with the registration plate or marker to the owner.

(d) A dealer shall:

(1) Not issue, assign, transfer, or deliver temporary registration plates or markers to anyone other than a bona fide purchaser or owner of a vehicle which he has sold.

(2) Not issue a temporary registration plate or marker without first obtaining from the purchaser or owner a written application for titling and registration of the vehicle and the applicable fees.

(3) Within 20 days of the issuance of a temporary registration plate or marker, mail or deliver the application and fees to the Division or deliver the application and fees to a local license agency for processing. Delivery need not be made if the contract for sale has been rescinded by all parties to the contract.

(4) Not deliver a temporary registration plate to anyone purchasing a vehicle that has an unexpired registration plate that is to be transferred to the purchaser.

(5) Not lend to anyone, or use on any vehicle that he may own, any temporary registration plates or markers.

A dealer may issue temporary markers, without obtaining the written application for titling and registration or collecting the applicable fees, to nonresidents for the purpose of removing the vehicle from the State.

(e) Every dealer who issues temporary plates or markers shall write clearly and indelibly on the face of the temporary registration plate or marker:

(1) The dates of issuance and expiration;

(2) The make, motor number, and serial numbers of the vehicle; and

(3) Any other information that the Division may require.

It shall be unlawful for any person to issue a temporary registration plate or marker containing any misstatement of fact or to knowingly write any false information on the face of the plate or marker.

(f) If the Division finds that the provisions of this section or the directions of the Division are not being complied with by the dealer, the Division may suspend, after a hearing, the right of a dealer to issue temporary registration plates or markers. Nothing in this section shall be deemed to require a dealer to collect or receive property taxes from any person.

(g) Every person to whom temporary registration plates or markers have been issued shall permanently destroy such temporary registration plates or markers immediately upon receiving the limited registration plates or the annual registration plates from the Division: Provided, that if the limited registration plates or the annual registration plates are not received within 30 days of the issuance of the temporary registration plates or markers, the owner shall, notwithstanding, immediately upon the expiration of such 30-day period, permanently destroy the temporary registration plates or markers.

(h) Temporary registration plates or markers shall expire and become void upon the receipt of the limited registration plates or the annual registration plates from the Division, or upon the rescission of a contract to purchase a motor vehicle, or upon the expiration of 30 days from the date of issuance, depending upon whichever event shall first occur. No refund or credit or fees paid by dealers to the Division for temporary registration plates or markers shall be allowed, except in the event that the Division discontinues the issuance of temporary registration plates or markers or unless the dealer discontinues business. In this event the unissued registration plates or markers with the unissued registration certificates shall be returned to the Division and the dealer may petition for a refund. Upon the expiration of the 30 days from the date of issuance, a second 30-day temporary registration plate or marker may be issued by the dealer upon showing the vehicle has been sold or leased, and that the dealer, having used reasonable diligence, is unable to obtain the vehicle's statement of origin or certificate of title so that the lien may be perfected. For purposes of this subsection, a dealer shall be considered unable to obtain the vehicle's statement of origin or certificate of title if the statement of origin or certificate of title either (i) has not been delivered to the dealer or (ii) was lost or misplaced.

(i) A temporary registration plate or marker may be used on the vehicle for which issued only and may not be transferred, loaned, or assigned to another. In the event a temporary registration plate or marker or temporary registration certificate is lost or stolen, the owner shall permanently destroy the remaining plate or marker or certificate and no operation of the vehicle for which the lost or stolen registration certificate, registration plate or marker has been issued shall be made on the highways until the regular license plate is received and attached thereto.

(j) The Commissioner of Motor Vehicles shall have the power to make such rules and regulations, not inconsistent herewith, as he shall deem necessary for the purpose of carrying out the provisions of this section.

(k) The provisions of G.S. 20-63, 20-71, 20-110 and 20-111 shall apply in like manner to temporary registration plates or markers as is applicable to nontemporary plates.

(l) The Division is authorized to enter into agreements to utilize commission contractors under contract with the Division under G.S. 20-63(h) to distribute temporary registration plates to dealers as provided in this section. The Division must provide compensation to commission contractors for distributing temporary registration plates at the transaction rate established for issuing registration documents in G.S. 20-63(h)(1). The Division must provide commission contractors with any forms, equipment, and supplies necessary for distributing temporary registration plates and provide appropriate guidance and supervision of the distribution. If the Division enters into agreements with commission contractors under this subsection, the Division shall make every effort to enter into agreements with commission contractors across all geographic regions of the State in order to make temporary registration plates accessible to all dealers.

History.
1957, c. 246, s. 1; 1963, c. 552, s. 8; 1975, c. 716, s. 5; 1985, c. 95; c. 263; 1997-327, ss. 1, 2; 2000-182, s. 5;2007-471, s. 1;2009-445, s. 25(a);2010-95, s. 22(d);2013-414, s. 70(c);2018-42, ss. 2(e), 4; 2018-145, s. 4;2019-181, s. 5(d);2020-77, ss. 2, 4(a)

EDITOR'S NOTE. --
Session Laws 2018-42, s. 2(f), provides: "The Division of Motor Vehicles, in consultation with the North Carolina Automobile Dealers Association, Inc., shall study the following:

"(1) The impacts of this section on Division processes and procedures, along with recommended statutory changes to further improve the lawful transfer of motor vehicles.

"(2) Methods to ensure consumer protection in the motor vehicle transfer process.

"(3) Potential changes to the Division's electronic lien and title program or other processes that could assist with reducing the delay in the release of a satisfied security interest in a motor vehicle.

"(4) Any other issues the Division deems appropriate.

"The Division shall report its findings, including any legislative recommendations, to the Joint Legislative Transportation Oversight Committee by December 31, 2020."

Session Laws 2020-77, s. 4(b), made the amendment of subsection (a) of this section by Session

Laws 2020-77, s. 4(a), effective October 1, 2020, and applicable to dealer applications for temporary registration plates or markers submitted on or after that date.

EFFECT OF AMENDMENTS. --

Session Laws 2007-471, s. 1, in subsection (f), substituted "the Division may" for "he may" and added the second sentence; inserted "limited registration plates or the" twice in subsection (g) and once in subsection (h). See Editor's Note for contingent effective date.

Session Laws 2018-42, s. 2(e), as amended by Session Laws 2018-145, s. 4, effective March 1, 2019, added the last sentence in subsection (h).

Session Laws 2018-42, s. 4, effective June 22, 2018, substituted "20 days of the issuance of a temporary registration plate or marker" for "10 working days" and "rescinded by all" for "rescinded in writing by all" in subdivision (d)(3).

Session Laws 2019-181, s. 5(d), effective July 26, 2019, substituted "sold or leased" for "sold, a temporary lien has been filed as provided in G.S. 20-58" in the fourth sentence of subsection (h).

Session Laws 2020-77, s. 2, effective July 1, 2020, added subsection (l).

Session Laws 2020-77, s. 4(a), in subsection (a), added the third and fourth sentences and made minor stylistic changes. For effective date and applicability, see editor's note.

REASONABLE SUSPICION TEMPORARY TAG WAS IMPROPER. --Officer possessed reasonable suspicion to believe that defendant was operating defendant's vehicle without a proper registration tag because the tag displayed was just a piece of paper with a date written on it, rather than the piece of cardboard that car dealers normally hand out, which contains the dates of issuance and expiration, the make, the motor number, and the serial numbers of the vehicle. State v. Smith, 192 N.C. App. 690, 666 S.E.2d 191 (2008), cert. denied 130 S. Ct. 3325, 2010 U.S. LEXIS 4297, 176 L. Ed. 2d 1221 (U.S. 2010).

APPLIED in State v. Gray, 55 N.C. App. 568, 286 S.E.2d 357 (1982); State v. Burke, 212 N.C. App. 654, 712 S.E.2d 704 (2011), aff'd 720 S.E.2d 388, 2012 N.C. LEXIS 23 (N.C. 2012).

CITED in Home Indem. Co. v. West Trade Motors, Inc., 258 N.C. 647, 129 S.E.2d 248 (1963); State v. Hudson, 103 N.C. App. 708, 407 S.E.2d 583 (1991).

§ 20-79.1A. Limited registration plates

(a) **Eligibility.** -- A limited registration plate is issuable to any of the following:

(1) A person who applies, either directly or through a dealer licensed under Article 12 of this Chapter, for a title to a motor vehicle and a registration plate for the vehicle and who submits payment for the applicable title and registration fees but does not submit payment for any municipal corporation property taxes on the vehicle. A person who submits payment for municipal corporation property taxes receives an annual registration plate.

(2) A person who applies for a plate for a vehicle that was previously registered with the Division but whose registration has not been current for at least a year because the plate for the vehicle was surrendered or the vehicle's registration expired over a year ago.

(b) **Form and Authorization.** -- A limited registration plate must be clearly and visibly designated as "temporary." The plate expires on the last day of the second month following the date of application of the limited registration plate. The plate may be used only on the vehicle for which it is issued and may not be transferred, loaned, or assigned to another. If the plate is lost or stolen, the vehicle for which the plate was issued may not be operated on a highway until a replacement limited registration plate or a regular license plate is received and attached to the vehicle.

(c) **Registration Certificate.** -- The Division is not required to issue a registration certificate for a limited registration plate. A combined tax and registration notice issued under G.S. 105-330.5 serves as the registration certificate for the plate.

History.

2007-471, s. 2;2009-445, ss. 24(b), 25(a); 2010-95, ss. 22(c), (d); 2013-414, s. 70(b), (c); 2014-3, s. 14.24

EFFECT OF AMENDMENTS. --

Session Laws 2009-445, s. 24(b), rewrote this section. See Editor's Note for applicability and effective date provisions.

Session Laws 2014-3, s. 14.24, effective May 29, 2014, added the subsection and subdivision designations; added the subsection headings; inserted present subdivision (a)(2); and made related changes.

§ 20-79.2. Transporter plates

(a) **Who Can Get a Plate.** -- The Division may issue a transporter plate authorizing the limited operation of a motor vehicle in the circumstances listed in this subsection. A person who receives a transporter plate must have proof of financial responsibility that meets the requirements of Article 9A of this Chapter. The person to whom a transporter plate may be issued and the circumstances in which the vehicle bearing the plate may be operated are as follows:

(1) To a business or a dealer to facilitate the manufacture, construction, rebuilding, or delivery of new or used truck cabs or bodies between manufacturer, dealer, seller, or purchaser.

(2) To a financial institution that has a recorded lien on a motor vehicle to repossess the motor vehicle.

(3) To a dealer or repair facility to pick up and deliver a motor vehicle that is to be repaired, is to undergo a safety or emissions inspection, or is to otherwise be prepared for sale by a dealer, to road-test the vehicle, if it is repaired or inspected within a 20-mile radius of the place where it is repaired or inspected, and to deliver the vehicle to the dealer. A repair facility may not receive more than two transporter plates for this purpose.

(4) To a business that has at least 10 registered vehicles to move a motor vehicle that is owned by the business and is a replaced vehicle offered for sale.

(5) To a dealer or a business that contracts with a dealer and has a business privilege license to take a motor vehicle either to or from a motor vehicle auction where the vehicle will be or was offered for sale. The title to the vehicle, a bill of sale, or written authorization from the dealer or auction must be inside the vehicle when the vehicle is operated with a transporter plate.

(6) To a business or dealer to road-test a repaired truck whose GVWR is at least 15,000 pounds when the test is performed within a 10-mile radius of the place where the truck was repaired and the truck is owned by a person who has a fleet of at least five trucks whose GVWRs are at least 15,000 pounds and who maintains the place where the truck was repaired.

(7) To a business or dealer to move a mobile office, a mobile classroom, or a mobile or manufactured home, or to transport a newly manufactured travel trailer, fifth-wheel trailer, or camping trailer between a manufacturer and a dealer. Any transporter plate used under this subdivision may not be used on the power unit.

(8) To a business to drive a motor vehicle that is registered in this State and is at least 35 years old to and from a parade or another public event and to drive the motor vehicle in that event. A person who owns one of these motor vehicles is considered to be in the business of collecting those vehicles.

(9) To a dealer to drive a motor vehicle that is part of the inventory of a dealer to and from a motor vehicle trade show or exhibition or to, during, and from a parade in which the motor vehicle is used.

(10) To drive special mobile equipment in any of the following circumstances:

　　a. From the manufacturer of the equipment to a facility of a dealer.

　　b. From one facility of a dealer to another facility of a dealer.

　　c. From a dealer to the person who buys the equipment from the dealer.

(b) **How to Get a Plate.** -- A business or a dealer may obtain a transporter plate by filing an application with the Division and paying the required fee. An application must be on a form provided by the Division and contain the information required by the Division. The fee for a transporter plate is one-half the fee set in G.S. 20-87(5) for a passenger motor vehicle of not more than 15 passengers.

(b1) **Number of Plates.** -- The total number of Dealer-Transporter or dealer plates issued to a dealer may not exceed the total number of plates that can be issued to the dealer under G.S. 20-79(b). Transporter plates issued to a dealer shall bear the words "Dealer-Transporter." This subsection does not apply to a person who is not a dealer.

(b2) **Sanctions.** -- The following sanctions apply when a motor vehicle displaying a "Dealer-Transporter" or "Transporter" license plate is driven in violation of the restrictions on the use of the plate or of the requirement to have proof of financial responsibility:

(1) The individual driving the motor vehicle is responsible for an infraction and is subject to a penalty of one hundred dollars ($ 100.00).

(2) The dealer or business to whom the plate is issued is subject to a civil penalty imposed by the Division of two hundred fifty dollars ($ 250.00) per occurrence.

(3) The Division may rescind all dealer license plates, dealer transporter plates, or transporter plates issued to the dealer or business whose plate was displayed on the motor vehicle.

(4) A person who sells, rents, leases, or otherwise provides a transporter plate to another person in exchange for the money or any other thing of value is guilty of a Class I felony. A conviction for a violation of this subdivision is considered a felony involving moral turpitude for purposes of G.S. 20-294.

A penalty imposed under subdivision (1) of this subsection is payable to the county where the infraction occurred, as required by G.S. 14-3.1. A civil penalty imposed under subdivision (2) of this subsection shall be credited to the Highway Fund as nontax revenue. A law enforcement officer having probable cause to believe that a transporter plate is being used in violation of this section may seize the plate.

(c) **Form, Duration, and Transfer.** -- A transporter plate is subject to G.S. 20-63, except for the requirement that the plate display the registration number of a motor vehicle and the requirement that the plate be a "First in Flight" plate, a "First in Freedom" plate, or a "National/State Mottos" plate. A transporter plate shall have a distinguishing symbol identifying the plate as a transporter plate. The symbol may vary depending upon the classification of transporter plate issued. A transporter plate is issued for a period of one year. The Division shall vary the expiration dates of transporter registration renewals so that an approximately equal number expires at the end of each month, quarter, or other period consisting of one or more months. When the Division issues a transporter plate, it may issue a registration that expires at the end of any monthly interval. During the year for which it is issued, a business or dealer may transfer a transporter plate from one vehicle to another as long as the vehicle is driven only for a purpose authorized by subsection (a) of this section. The Division must rescind a transporter plate that is displayed on a motor vehicle driven for a purpose that is not authorized by subsection (a) of this section.

(d) **County.** -- A county may obtain one transporter plate, without paying a fee, by filing an application with the Division on a form to be provided by the Division. A transporter plate issued pursuant to this subsection may only be used to transport motor vehicles as part of a program established by the county to receive donated motor vehicles and make them available to low-income individuals.

If a motor vehicle is operated on the highways of this State using a transporter plate authorized by this section, all of the following requirements shall be met:

(1) The driver of the vehicle shall have in his or her possession the certificate of title for the motor vehicle, which has been properly reassigned by the previous owner to the county or the affected donor program.

(2) The vehicle shall be covered by liability insurance that meets the requirements of Article 9A of this Chapter.

The form and duration of the transporter plate shall be as provided in subsection (c) of this section.

(e) Any vehicle being operated on the highways of this State using a transporter plate shall have proof of financial responsibility that meets the requirement of Article 9A of this Chapter.

History.
1961, c. 360, s. 21; 1969, c. 600, s. 1; 1975, c. 222; 1979, c. 473, ss. 1, 2; c. 627, ss. 1-3; 1981, c. 727, ss. 1, 2; 1983, c. 426; 1987, c. 520; 1993, c. 440, s. 4;1995, c. 50, s. 1;1997-335, s. 2;2001-147, s. 1;2010-132, s. 6;2014-100, s. 34.28(c);2018-5, s. 34.27(d)

EDITOR'S NOTE. --
Session Laws 2014-100, s. 34.28(d), made the amendment to subsection (c) of this section by Session Laws 2014-100, s. 34.28(c), effective July 1, 2015, and applicable to registration plates issued on or after that date.

Session Laws 2018-5, s. 1.1, provides: "This act shall be known as the 'Current Operations Appropriations Act of 2018.'"

Session Laws 2018-5, s. 39.7, is a severability clause.

Session Laws 2020-3, s. 4.7(a) -(h), as amended by Session Laws 2020-97, ss. 3.15(a), 3.16(a), provides: "(a) Definition. -- For purposes of this section, 'credential' means any of the following issued by the Division of Motor Vehicles:

"(1) Drivers license.

"(2) Learner's permit.

"(3) Limited learner's permit.

"(4) Limited provisional license.

"(5) Full provisional license.

"(6) Commercial drivers license.

"(7) Commercial learner's permit.

"(8) Temporary driving certificate.

"(9) Special identification card.

"(10) Handicapped placard.

"(11) Vehicle registration.

"(12) Temporary vehicle registration.

"(13) Dealer license plate.

"(14) Transporter plate.

"(15) Loaner/Dealer 'LD' plate.

"(16) Vehicle inspection authorization.

"(17) Inspection station license.

"(18) Inspection mechanic license.

"(19) Transportation network company permit.

"(20) Motor vehicle dealer license.

"(21) Sales representative license.

"(22) Manufacturer license.

"(23) Distributor license.

"(24) Wholesaler license.

"(25) Driver training school license.

"(26) Driver training school instructor license.

"(27) Professional housemoving license.

"(b) Extend Validity of Credentials. -- Notwithstanding renewal, duration, or expiration provisions of G.S. 20-7, 20-11, 20-37.6, 20-37.7, 20-37.13, 20-50, 20-66, 20-79, 20-79.02, 20-79.2, 20-183.4B, 20-183.4D, 20-280.3, 20-288, 20-324, and 20-359, or any other provision of law to the contrary, the Division of Motor Vehicles shall extend for a period of five months the validity of any credential that expires on or after March 1, 2020, and before August 1, 2020. The Division shall extend for a period of five months the validity of any credential listed in subdivisions (6), (7), (9), (10), and (18) of subsection (a) of this section that expires on or after March 1, 2020, and before the date 30 days after the date the Governor (i) rescinds Executive Order No. 116 or (ii) issues another executive order lifting restrictions on Division of Motor Vehicles functions. Notwithstanding G.S. 20-37.13(h) and G.S. 20-37.13A(a), the Division of Motor Vehicles is authorized to waive the requirement that commercial drivers license and commercial learner's permit holders have a medical examination and certification, as required by federal law, consistent with any waiver of medical qualifications standards issued by the Federal Motor Carrier Safety Administration. A credential extended under this section shall expire five months from the date it otherwise expires as prescribed by law prior to this section. However, the subsequent expiration of a credential extended under this section shall occur on the date prescribed by law prior to this section without regard to the extension. The Division shall notify individuals affected by an extension granted under this section, including information on new expiration dates and how the extension affects subsequent renewal and expiration dates.

"(b1) Extension of Intrastate Medical Waivers. -- Notwithstanding the limitation on duration of waivers in G.S. 20-37.13A(b), the Division of Motor Vehicles may extend for up to five months the validity of a medical waiver issued by the Division under G.S. 20-37.13A if the waiver expires on or after March 1, 2020, and before August 1, 2020, and the Division's Medical Review Unit determines the extension is appropriate.

"(c) Extension of Intrastate Medical Waivers. -- Notwithstanding the limitation on duration of waivers in G.S. 20-37.13A(b), the Division of Motor Vehicles may extend for up to five months the validity of a medical waiver issued by the Division under G.S. 20-37.13A if the waiver expires on or after March 1, 2020, and before the date 30 days after the date the Governor (i) rescinds Executive Order No. 116 or (ii) issues another executive order lifting restrictions on Division of Motor Vehicles functions, and the Division's Medical Review Unit determines the extension is appropriate.

"(d) Waive Penalties. -- Notwithstanding any provision of law to the contrary, the Division shall waive any fines, fees, or penalties associated with failing to renew a credential during the period of time the credential is valid by extension under subsection (b) of this section.

"(e) Motor Vehicle Taxes. -- Notwithstanding any provision of law to the contrary, due dates for motor vehicle taxes that are tied to registration expiration under Article 22A of Chapter 105 of the General Statutes shall be extended to correspond with extended expiration dates under subsection (b) of this section.

"(f) Validity by Extension a Defense. -- A person may not be convicted or found responsible for any offense resulting from failure to renew a credential issued by the Division if, when tried for that offense, the person shows that the offense occurred during the period of time the credential is valid by extension under subsection (b) of this section.

"(g) Report. -- Within 30 days of the extensions made under subsection (b) of this section, the Division shall submit a report to the Joint Legislative Transportation Oversight Committee and the Fiscal Research Division detailing implementation of this section.

"(h) Effective Date. -- This section is effective retroactively to March 1, 2020, and applies to expirations occurring on or after that date."

Session Laws 2020-3, s. 5, is a severability clause.

Session Laws 2020-97, s. 4.5, is a severability clause.

EFFECT OF AMENDMENTS. --

Session Laws 2014-100, s. 34.28(b), inserted "or a 'First in Freedom' plate" at the end of the first sentence in subsection (c). See Editor's note for effective date and applicability.

Session Laws 2018-5, s. 34.27(d), effective July 1, 2018, inserted "or a 'National/State Mottos' plate" in subsection (c) and made related changes.

N.C. Gen. Stat. § 20-79.3

Repealed by Session Laws 1993, c. 440, s. 5.

§ 20-79.3A. Requirements to establish a special registration plate

(a) **Minimum Number of Paid Applications.** -- An applicant under this section is a person, organization, or other legal entity seeking authorization to establish a special registration plate for a motor vehicle or a motorcycle. An applicant must obtain the minimum number of paid applications from potential purchasers before submitting a Special Registration Plate Development Application to the Division. A "paid application" means an application completed by a potential purchaser and submitted to the applicant requesting purchase of the special registration plate being proposed by the applicant plus payment of the proposed additional fee amount. The minimum number of paid applications is as follows:

(1) 300 for a special registration plate on a standard background described in G.S. 20-63(b).

(2) 500 for a special registration plate on a background authorized under G.S. 20-63(b1).

(b) **Application.** -- An applicant must submit all of the items listed in this subsection to the Division by February 15 in order for a bill authorizing the special registration plate to be considered for approval during the legislative session being held that year. The Division shall consider an application received after February 15 for approval in the legislative session that begins in the year following the submission date. The application items must include:

(1) A completed Special Registration Plate Development Application.

(2) A fee equal to number of paid applications received by the applicant, which shall be no less than the minimum number of paid applications required under subsection (a) of this section, multiplied by the proposed additional fee amount stated on the Special Registration Plate Development Application submitted by the applicant.

(c) **Report to General Assembly.** -- On or before March 15 of each year, the Division shall submit to the Chairs of the House and Senate Transportation Committees, the Chairs of the House and Senate Finance Committees, and the Legislative Analysis Division of the General

Assembly a report that identifies each applicant that has applied for a special registration plate to be authorized in the legislative session being held that year and indicates whether the applicant met the requirements of this section. If an applicant meets the requirements of this section, then a bill may be considered during the legislative session being held that year to authorize a special registration plate for the applicant that submitted the application.

(d) **Legislative Approval.** -- If a special registration plate requested under this section is approved by law, the applicant must submit all of the following items to the Division no later than 60 days after the act approving the plate becomes law. If the applicant fails to timely submit the items required under this subsection, the authorization for the special registration plate shall expire in accordance with G.S. 20-79.8(a1). The items to be submitted are:

(1) The final artwork for the plate. The Division must review the artwork to ensure it complies with the standardized format established by G.S. 20-79.4(a3).

(2) A list of purchasers who submitted to the applicant a paid application for the special registration plate and any additional fees submitted by potential purchasers to the applicant after submission of the Special Registration Plate Development Application.

(e) **Legislative Disapproval.** -- If the special registration plate is not authorized in the legislative session in which the authorization was sought, the Division shall refund to the applicant the fee submitted under subdivision (2) of subsection (b) of this section.

(f) **Issuance.** -- Within 180 days after receipt of the requester's design and the minimum number of paid applications, the Division shall issue the special registration plate.

History.
2014-96, s. 3(a);2018-142, s. 4(a)
EDITOR'S NOTE. --
Session Laws 2014-96, s. 3(b) provides: "This section becomes effective October 1, 2014, and applies to requests for the establishment of new special registration plates on or after that date or to requests for the reenactment of special registration plates for which the authorization expired on or after that date."

Session Laws 2014-96, s. 3(c), provides: "Notwithstanding the deadlines established in G.S. 20-79.3A(b) and (c), as enacted by this act, the Division shall accept through April 1, 2015, Special Registration Plate Development Applications and shall report the list of qualified applicants to the General Assembly in accordance with G.S. 20-79.3A(c) by May 1, 2015, for a bill to be considered during the 2015 Regular Session of the 2015 General Assembly authorizing a special registration plate requested by an applicant."

Session Laws 2014-96, s. 4(a), provides: "The Division of Motor Vehicles shall develop an application form for use by an applicant to be completed by potential purchasers of a proposed special registration plate. The form must include an explanation of the application process, the fees that must be submitted to the applicant with the application, and the refund process. Specifically, the form must state that the applicant, and not the Division of Motor Vehicles, is responsible for collecting the fees and for refunding the fees to potential purchasers if the request for a special registration plate is not approved by the General Assembly. The form must also include space for the applicant to provide identifying information of the person or organization seeking the special registration plate and point of contact information."

Session Laws 2014-96, s. 4(b), provides: "This section is effective when it becomes law [August 1, 2014]. The Division of Motor Vehicles must, by October 1, 2014, develop the form required by this section and make it available on the Division's Web site along with an explanation of the special registration plate application process established under this act."

Session Laws 2014-96, s. 5(a), provides: "The Division of Motor Vehicles shall develop a Special Registration Plate Development Application Form for use by an applicant seeking to establish or to reauthorize a special registration plate. The form shall require the following information:

"(1) The applicant's identifying information, including point of contact information.

"(2) A description of the proposed plate, including a draft copy of the proposed plate design in substantially final form that conforms to the specifications set by the Division.

"(3) The proposed fee for the plate, which must be a minimum of ten dollars ($10.00) that is remitted to the Special Registration Plate Account. If an applicant is proposing a fee in excess of the amount remitted to the Special Registration Plate Account, the applicant must state the additional fee amount and describe the proposed use of the additional fee proceeds.

"(4) The name of at least one current member of the General Assembly who would sponsor legislation to authorize the special registration plate.

"(5) A statement that must be signed by the applicant indicating that the applicant has obtained the minimum number of paid applications and will submit the list of purchasers and the final artwork to the Division within 60 days of legislation authorizing the requested special registration plate becoming law."

Session Laws 2014-96, s. 5(b), provides: "This section is effective when it becomes law [August 1, 2014]. The Division of Motor Vehicles must, by February 1, 2015, develop the form required by this section and make it available on the Division's Web site. The Division must, by February 1, 2015, make the necessary programming changes to be able to accept Special Registration Plate Development Applications in accordance with this act."

Session Laws 2014-96, s. 7, provides: "The Revenue Laws Study Committee is directed as follows as it relates to registration plates:

"(1) To identify whether the process for requests to establish or reauthorize special registration plates under this act requires any modifications and to examine the costs incurred by the Division of Motor Vehicles to administer special registration plates.

"(2) To study whether certain governmental entities should have different eligibility or renewal requirements for permanent registration plates; to study whether nongovernmental entities should be eligible for permanent plates and, if so, what the criteria should be; and to examine the costs incurred by the Division of Motor Vehicles to administer permanent registration plates.

"The Committee shall report its findings, together with any recommended legislation, to the 2015 Regular Session of the 2015 General Assembly upon its convening."

Session Laws 2015-264, s. 40.6(c), provides: "Nothing in G.S. 20-63(b1) or G.S. 20-79.3A(a) shall be construed as requiring an additional 200 applications for the Division of Motor Vehicles to issue a full-color background 'Kappa Alpha Psi Fraternity' special registration plate in accordance with G.S. 20-63(b1), as amended by subsection (a) of this section."

Session Laws 2019-213, s. 2(f), provides: "The POW/MIA Bring Them Home plate authorized by this section is not subject to the requirements to establish a new special registration plate in G.S. 20-79.3A and the expiration of special registration plate authorization in G.S. 20-79.8."

EFFECT OF AMENDMENTS. --
Session Laws 2018-142, s. 4(a), effective December 15, 2018, in subsection (c), substituted "Legislative Analysis" for "Research" preceding "Division of the General Assembly"; and in subsection (d), inserted "than" preceding "60 days after."

LEGAL PERIODICALS. --
For note, "Specialty License Plates: The Product of Government Speech, Private Speech, or Both?," see 7 Charlotte L. Rev. 255 (2016).

§ 20-79.4. Special registration plates

(a) **General.** -- Upon application and payment of the required registration fees, a person may obtain from the Division a special registration plate for a motor vehicle registered in that person's name if the person qualifies for the registration plate. A holder of a special registration plate who becomes ineligible for the plate, for whatever reason, must return the special plate within 30 days. A special registration plate may not be issued for a vehicle registered under the International Registration Plan. A special registration plate may be issued for a commercial vehicle that is not registered under the International Registration Plan. A special registration plate may not be developed using a name or logo for which a trademark has been issued unless the holder of the trademark licenses, without charge, the State to use the name or logo on the special registration plate.

(a1) **Qualifying for a Special Plate.** -- In order to qualify for a special plate, an applicant shall meet all of the qualifications set out in this section. The Division of Motor Vehicles shall verify the qualifications of an individual to whom any special plate is issued to ensure only qualified applicants receive the requested special plates.

(a2) **Special Plates Based Upon Military Service.** -- The Department of Military and Veterans Affairs shall be responsible for verifying and maintaining all verification documentation for all special plates that are based upon military service. The Department shall not issue a special plate that is based on military service unless the application is accompanied by a motor vehicle registration (MVR) verification form signed by the Secretary of Military and Veterans Affairs, or the Secretary's designee, showing that the Department of Military and Veterans Affairs has verified the applicant's credentials and qualifications to hold the special plate applied for.

(1) Unless a qualifying condition exists requiring annual verification, no additional verification shall be required to renew a special registration plate either in person or through an online service.

(2) If the Department of Military and Veterans Affairs determines a special registration plate has been issued due to an error on the part of the Division of Motor Vehicles, the plate shall be recalled and canceled.

(3) If the Department of Military and Veterans Affairs determines a special registration plate has been issued to an applicant who falsified documents or has fraudulently applied for the special registration plate, the Division of Motor Vehicles shall revoke the special plate and take appropriate enforcement action.

(a3) The Division shall develop, in consultation with the State Highway Patrol and the Division of Adult Correction and Juvenile Justice, a standardized format for special license plates. The format shall allow for the name of the State and the license plate number to be reflective and to contrast with the background so it may be easily read by the human eye and by cameras installed along roadways as part of tolling and speed enforcement. A designated segment of the plate shall be set aside for unique design representing various groups and interests. Nothing in this subsection shall be construed to require the recall of existing special license plates.

(b) **Types.** -- The Division shall issue the following types of special registration plates:

(1) **82nd Airborne Division Association Member.** -- Issuable to a member of the 82nd Airborne Division Association, Inc. The plate shall bear the insignia of the 82nd Airborne Division Association, Inc. The Division may not issue the plate

authorized by this subdivision unless it receives at least 300 applications for the plate.

(2) **Administrative Officer of the Courts.** -- Issuable to the Director of the Administrative Office of the Courts. The plate shall bear the phrase "J-20".

(3) **AIDS Awareness.** -- Expired July 1, 2016.

(4) **Air Medal Recipient.** -- Issuable to the recipient of the Air Medal. The plate shall bear the emblem of the Air Medal and the words "Air Medal".

(5) **Alpha Kappa Alpha Sorority.** -- Issuable to the registered owner of a motor vehicle. The plate shall bear the sorority's symbol and name. The Division may not issue the plate authorized by this subdivision unless it receives at least 300 applications for the plate.

(6) **Alpha Phi Alpha Fraternity.** -- Issuable to a member or supporter of the Alpha Phi Alpha Fraternity in accordance with G.S. 20-81.12. The plate shall bear the fraternity's symbol and name.

(7) **ALS Research.** -- Issuable to a registered owner of a motor vehicle in accordance with G.S. 20-81.12. The plate shall bear a picture of a baseball and the phrase "Cure ALS."

(8) **Alternative Fuel Vehicles.** -- Expired July 1, 2016.

(9) **Amateur Radio Operator.** -- Issuable to an amateur radio operator who holds an unexpired and unrevoked amateur radio license issued by the Federal Communications Commission and who asserts to the Division that a portable transceiver is carried in the vehicle. The plate shall bear the phrase "Amateur Radio". The plate shall bear the operator's official amateur radio call letters, or call letters with numerical or letter suffixes so that an owner of more than one vehicle may have the call letters on each.

(10) **American Legion.** -- Issuable to a member of the American Legion. The plate shall bear the words "American Legion" and the emblem of the American Legion. The Division may not issue the plate authorized by this subdivision unless it receives at least 300 applications for the plate.

(11) **American Red Cross.** -- Expired July 1, 2016.

(12) **Animal Lovers.** -- Issuable to the registered owner of a motor vehicle in accordance with G.S. 20-81.12. The plate may bear a picture of a dog and cat and the phrase "I Care."

(13) **ARC of North Carolina.** -- Expired July 1, 2016.

(14) **Armed Forces Expeditionary Medal Recipient.** -- Expired July 1, 2016.

(15) **Arthritis Foundation.** -- Expired July 1, 2016.

(16) **ARTS NC.** -- Issuable to the registered owner of a motor vehicle in accordance with G.S. 20-81.12. The plate shall bear the phrase "The Creative State" with a logo designed by ARTS North Carolina, Inc.

(17) **Audubon North Carolina.** -- Expired July 1, 2016.

(18) **Autism Society of North Carolina.** -- Issuable to the registered owner of a motor vehicle in accordance with G.S. 20-81.12. The plate shall bear the phrase "Autism Society of North Carolina", and the logo of the Autism Society.

(19) **Aviation Maintenance Technician.** -- Expired July 1, 2016.

(20) **Back Country Horsemen of North Carolina.** -- Expired July 1, 2016.

(21) **Battle of Kings Mountain.** -- Issuable to the registered owner of a motor vehicle in accordance with G.S. 20-81.12. The plate shall bear the phrase "Battle of Kings Mountain" with a representation of Kings Mountain on it. The plate authorized by this subdivision is not subject to the provisions of G.S. 20-79.3A or G.S. 20-79.8.

(22) **Be Active NC.** -- Expired July 1, 2016.

(23) **Big Rock Blue Marlin Tournament.** -- Issuable to the registered owner of a motor vehicle in accordance with G.S. 20-81.12. The plate shall bear the words "Big Rock Blue Marlin Tournament" and include a representation of a blue marlin.

(24) **Blue Knights.** -- Expired July 1, 2016.

(25) **Boy Scouts of America.** -- Expired July 1, 2016.

(26) **Brain Injury Awareness.** -- Expired July 1, 2016.

(27) **Breast Cancer Awareness.** -- Issuable to the registered owner of a motor vehicle. The plate shall bear the phrase "Early Detection Saves Lives" and a representation of a pink ribbon. The Division must receive 300 or more applications for the plate before it may be developed.

(28) **Breast Cancer Earlier Detection.** -- Expired July 1, 2016.

(29) **Brenner Children's Hospital.** -- Expired July 1, 2016.

(30) **Bronze Star Recipient.** -- Issuable to a recipient of the Bronze Star. The plate shall bear the emblem of the Bronze Star and the words "Bronze Star".

(31) **Bronze Star Valor Recipient.** -- Issuable to a recipient of the Bronze Star Medal for valor in combat. The plate shall

bear the emblem of the Bronze Star with a "Combat V" emblem and the words "Bronze Star." To be eligible for this plate, the applicant must provide documentation that the medal was issued for valor in combat.

(32) **Buddy Pelletier Surfing Foundation.** -- Issuable to the registered owner of a motor vehicle in accordance with G.S. 20-81.12. The plate shall bear the words "Buddy Pelletier Surfing Foundation" and bear the logo of the Foundation.

(33) **Buffalo Soldiers.** -- Expired July 1, 2016.

(34) **Carolina Panthers.** -- Issuable to the registered owner of a motor vehicle in accordance with G.S. 20-81.12. The plate shall bear the phrase "Keep Pounding", the logo of the Carolina Panthers, and the letters "CP". The Division shall not develop a plate under this subdivision without a license to use copyrighted or registered words, symbols, trademarks, or designs associated with the plate. The Division shall not pay a royalty for the license to use the copyrighted or registered words, symbols, trademarks, or designs associated with the plate. The plate authorized by this subdivision is not subject to the provisions of G.S. 20-79.3A or G.S. 20-79.8.

(35) **Carolina Raptor Center.** -- Expired July 1, 2016.

(36) **Carolina Regional Volleyball Association.** -- Expired July 1, 2016.

(37) **Carolina's Aviation Museum.** -- Expired July 1, 2016.

(38) **Carolinas Credit Union Foundation.** -- Expired July 1, 2016.

(39) **Carolinas Golf Association.** -- Issuable to the registered owner of a motor vehicle in accordance with G.S. 20-81.12. The plate shall bear the phrase "Carolinas Golf Association" and an emblem of the Carolinas Golf Association.

(40) **Celebrate Adoption.** -- Expired July 1, 2016.

(41) **Charlotte Checkers.** -- Expired July 1, 2016.

(42) **Childhood Cancer Awareness.** -- Expired July 1, 2016.

(43) **Choose Life.** -- Issuable to a registered owner of a motor vehicle in accordance with G.S. 20-81.12. The plate shall bear the phrase "Choose Life."

(44) **Civic Club.** -- Issuable to a member of a nationally recognized civic organization whose member clubs in the State are exempt from State corporate income tax under G.S. 105-130.11(a)(5). Examples of these clubs include Jaycees, Kiwanis, Optimist, Rotary, Ruritan, and Shrine. The plate shall bear a word or phrase identifying the civic club and the emblem of the civic club. A person may obtain from the Division a special registration plate under this subdivision for the registered owner of a motor vehicle or a motorcycle. The registration fees and the restrictions on the issuance of a specialized registration plate for a motorcycle are the same as for any motor vehicle. The Division may not issue a civic club plate authorized by this subdivision unless it receives at least 300 applications for that civic club plate.

(45) **Civil Air Patrol Member.** -- Issuable to an active member of the North Carolina Wing of the Civil Air Patrol. The plate shall bear the phrase "Civil Air Patrol". A plate issued to an officer member shall begin with the number "201" and the number shall reflect the seniority of the member; a plate issued to an enlisted member, a senior member, or a cadet member shall begin with the number "501".

(46) **Class D Citizen's Radio Station Operator.** -- Issuable to a Class D citizen's radio station operator. For an operator who has been issued Class D citizen's radio station call letters by the Federal Communications Commission, the plate shall bear the operator's official Class D citizen's radio station call letters. For an operator who has not been issued Class D citizen's radio station call letters by the Federal Communications Commission, the plate shall bear the phrase "Citizen's Band Radio".

(47) **Clerk of Superior Court.** -- Expired July 1, 2016.

(48) **Coast Guard Auxiliary Member.** -- Issuable to an active member of the United States Coast Guard Auxiliary. The plate shall bear the phrase "Coast Guard Auxiliary".

(49) **Coastal Conservation Association.** -- Expired July 1, 2016.

(50) **Coastal Land Trust.** -- Issuable to the registered owner of a motor vehicle in accordance with G.S. 20-81.12. The plate shall bear the phrase "Coastal Land Trust" with a logo designed by the North Carolina Coastal Land Trust.

(51) **Cold War Veteran.** -- Expired July 1, 2016.

(52) **Collegiate Insignia Plate.** -- Issuable to the registered owner of a motor vehicle in accordance with G.S. 20-81.12. The plate may bear a phrase or an insignia representing a public or private college or university.

(53) **Colorectal Cancer Awareness.** -- Issuable to the registered owner of a motor vehicle in accordance with G.S. 20-81.12. The plate shall bear (i) the phrase "It Takes a Warrior to Battle Cancer!" across the top of the plate, (ii) a symbol on

the left side of the plate of a blue ribbon with two wings that are colored blue, grey, and black, (iii) the phrase "Blue Ribbon Warrior" above the symbol, (iv) the phrase "Colorectal Cancer Awareness" below the symbol, and (v) the letters "CC" on the right side of the plate. The plate authorized under this subdivision is not subject to G.S. 20-79.3A(c) or the deadline set forth in G.S. 20-79.3A(b).

(54) **Combat Infantry Badge Recipient.** -- Expired July 1, 2016.

(55) **Combat Veteran.** -- Expired July 1, 2016.

(56) **Commercial Fishing.** -- Expired July 1, 2016.

(57) **Concerned Bikers Association/ABATE of North Carolina.** -- Expired July 1, 2016.

(58) **Corvette Club.** -- Expired July 1, 2016.

(59) **County Commissioner.** -- Issuable to a county commissioner of a county in this State. The plate shall bear the words "County Commissioner" followed first by a number representing the commissioner's county and then by a letter or number that distinguishes plates issued to county commissioners of the same county. The number of a county shall be the order of the county in an alphabetical list of counties that assigns number one to the first county in the list and a letter or number to distinguish different cars owned by the county commissioners in that county. The plate authorized by this subdivision is not subject to the provisions of G.S. 20-79.3A or G.S. 20-79.8.

(60) **Crystal Coast.** -- Expired July 1, 2016.

(61) **Daniel Stowe Botanical Garden.** -- Expired July 1, 2016.

(62) **Daughters of the American Revolution.** -- Expired July 1, 2016.

(63) **Delta Sigma Theta Sorority.** -- Issuable to the registered owner of a motor vehicle. The plate shall bear the sorority's name and symbol. The Division must receive 300 or more applications for the plate before it may be developed.

(64) **Disabled Veteran.** -- Issuable to a veteran of the Armed Forces of the United States who suffered a 100% service-connected disability. A person may obtain from the Division a special registration plate under this subdivision for the registered owner of a motor vehicle or a motorcycle.

(65) **Distinguished Flying Cross.** -- Issuable to a recipient of the Distinguished Flying Cross. The plate shall bear the emblem of the Distinguished Flying Cross and the words "Distinguished Flying Cross".

(66) **District Attorney.** -- Issuable to a North Carolina or United States District Attorney. The plate issuable to a North Carolina district attorney shall bear the letters "DA" followed by a number that represents the prosecutorial district the district attorney serves. The plate for a United States attorney shall bear the phrase "U.S. Attorney" followed by a number that represents the district the attorney serves, with 1 being the Eastern District, 2 being the Middle District, and 3 being the Western District.

(67) **Donate Life.** -- Issuable to the registered owner of a motor vehicle in accordance with G.S. 20-81.12. The plate shall bear the phrase "Donate Life" with a logo designed by Donate Life North Carolina.

(68) **Don't Tread on Me.** -- Expired July 1, 2016.

(69) **Ducks Unlimited.** -- Issuable to the registered owner of a motor vehicle in accordance with G.S. 20-81.12. The plate shall bear the logo of Ducks Unlimited, Inc., and shall bear the words: "Ducks Unlimited".

(70) **E-911 Telecommunicator.** -- Expired July 1, 2016.

(71) **Eagle Scout.** -- Issuable to a young man who has been certified as an Eagle Scout by the Boy Scouts of America, or to his parents or guardians. The plate shall bear the insignia of the Boy Scouts of America and shall bear the words "Eagle Scout". The Division may not issue the plate authorized by this subdivision unless it receives at least 300 applications for the plate.

(72) **Eastern Band of Cherokee Indians.** -- Issuable to a member of the Eastern Band of Cherokee Indians who presents to the Division a tribal identification card. The plate may bear a phrase or emblem representing the Eastern Band of Cherokee Indians. The plate authorized by this subdivision is not subject to the provisions of G.S. 20-79.3A.

(73) **El Pueblo.** -- Expired July 1, 2016.

(74) **Emergency Medical Technician.** -- Expired July 1, 2016.

(75) **Farmland Preservation.** -- Expired July 1, 2016.

(76) **Fire Department or Rescue Squad Member.** -- Issuable to an active regular member or volunteer member of a fire department, rescue squad, or both a fire department and rescue squad. The plate shall bear the words "Firefighter", "Rescue Squad", or "Firefighter-Rescue Squad".

(77) **First in Forestry.** -- Issuable to the registered owner of a motor vehicle. The plate shall bear the words "First in Forestry". The Division may not issue the plate authorized by this subdivision unless it receives at least 300 applications for the plate.

Chapter 20

(78) **First in Turf.** -- Expired July 1, 2016.

(79) **First Tee.** -- Expired July 1, 2016.

(80) **Flag of the United States of America.** -- Expired July 1, 2016.

(81) **Fox Hunting.** -- Expired July 1, 2016.

(82) **Fraternal Order of Police.** -- The plate authorized by this subdivision shall bear a representation of the Fraternal Order of Police emblem containing the letters "FOP". The Division must receive 300 applications for the plate before it may be developed. The plate is issuable to one of the following:

    a. A person who presents proof of active membership in the State Lodge, Fraternal Order of Police for the year in which the license plate is sought.

    b. The surviving spouse of a person who was a member of the State Lodge, Fraternal Order of Police, so long as the surviving spouse continues to renew the plate and does not remarry.

(83) **Future Farmers of America.** -- Expired July 1, 2016.

(84) **Girl Scout Gold Award recipient.** -- Expired July 1, 2016.

(85) **Girl Scouts.** -- Expired July 1, 2016.

(86) **Gold Star Lapel Button.** -- Issuable to the recipient of the Gold Star lapel button. The plate shall bear the emblem of the Gold Star lapel button and the words "Gold Star".

(87) **Goodness Grows.** -- Expired July 1, 2016.

(88) **Greensboro Symphony Guild.** -- Expired July 1, 2016.

(89) **Greyhound Friends of North Carolina.** -- Expired July 1, 2016.

(90) **Guilford Battleground Company.** -- Issuable to the registered owner of a motor vehicle in accordance with G.S. 20-81.12. The plate shall bear the phrase "Revolutionary" used by the Guilford Battleground Company and an image that depicts General Nathaniel Greene.

(91) **Harley Owners' Group.** -- Issuable to the registered owner of a motor vehicle in accordance with G.S. 20-81.12. The plate shall be designed in consultation with and approved by the Harley-Davidson Motor Company, Inc., and shall bear the words and trademark of the "Harley Owners' Group".

(92) **High Point Furniture Market 100th Anniversary.** -- Expired July 1, 2016.

(93) **High School Insignia Plate.** -- Issuable to the registered owner of a motor vehicle in accordance with G.S. 20-81.12. The plate may bear a phrase or an insignia representing a public high school in North Carolina.

(94) **Historic Vehicle Owner.** -- Issuable for a motor vehicle that is at least 30 years old measured from the date of manufacture. The plate for an historic vehicle shall bear the word "Antique" unless the vehicle is a model year 1943 or older. The plate for a vehicle that is a model year 1943 or older shall bear the word "Antique" or the words "Horseless Carriage", at the option of the vehicle owner.

(95) **Historical Attraction Plate.** -- Issuable to the registered owner of a motor vehicle in accordance with G.S. 20-81.12. The plate may bear a phrase or an insignia representing a publicly owned or nonprofit historical attraction located in North Carolina.

(96) **Hollerin'.** -- Expired July 1, 2016.

(97) **Home Care and Hospice.** -- Issuable to the registered owner of a motor vehicle in accordance with G.S. 20-81.12. The plate shall bear the phrase "Home Care and Hospice" and the letters "HH" on the right side of the plate.

(98) **Home of American Golf.** -- Expired July 1, 2016.

(99) **HOMES4NC Plate.** -- Issuable to the registered owner of a motor vehicle in accordance with G.S. 20-81.12. The plate shall bear "HOMES4NC", the logo of the North Carolina Association of Realtors Housing Opportunity Foundation, and shall be developed in conjunction with that organization. The Division may not issue the plate authorized by this subdivision unless it receives at least 300 applications for the plate.

(100) **Honorary Plate.** -- Issuable to a member of the Honorary Consular Corps, who has been certified by the U. S. State Department, the plate shall bear the words "Honorary Consular Corps" and a distinguishing number based on the order of issuance.

(101) **Hospice Care.** -- Expired July 1, 2016.

(102) **I.B.P.O.E.W.** -- Expired July 1, 2016.

(103) **I Support Teachers.** -- Expired July 1, 2016.

(104) **In God We Trust.** -- Issuable to the registered owner of a motor vehicle in accordance with G.S. 20-81.12. The plate shall bear the phrase "In God We Trust."

(105) **International Association of Fire Fighters.** -- The plate authorized by this subdivision shall bear the logo of the International Association of Fire Fighters. The Division may not issue the plate unless it receives at least 300 applications for the plate. The plate is issuable to one of the following in accordance with G.S. 20-81.12:

a. A person who presents proof of active membership in the International Association of Fire Fighters for the year in which the license plate is sought.

b. The surviving spouse of a person who was a member of the International Association of Fire Fighters, so long as the surviving spouse continues to renew the plate and does not remarry.

(106) **Jaycees.** -- Expired July 1, 2016.

(107) **Judge or Justice.** -- Issuable to a sitting or retired judge or justice in accordance with G.S. 20-79.6.

(108) **Juvenile Diabetes Research Foundation.** -- Issuable to the registered owner of a motor vehicle in accordance with G.S. 20-81.12. The plate shall bear the phrase "Juvenile Diabetes Research" and the "sneaker" logo of the nonprofit group Juvenile Diabetes Research Foundation International, Inc.

(109) **Kappa Alpha Order.** -- Expired July 1, 2016.

(110) **Kappa Alpha Psi Fraternity.** -- Issuable to the registered owner of a motor vehicle who is a member of the Kappa Alpha Psi Fraternity. The plate shall bear the fraternity's symbol and name. The Division may not issue the plate authorized by this subdivision unless it receives at least 300 applications for the plate.

(111) **Keeping The Lights On.** -- Issuable to a registered owner of a motor vehicle in accordance with G.S. 20-81.12. The plate shall have a background of mountains to the coast and bear a picture of a line worker on a utility pole on the left and the phrase "Keeping The Lights On" at the top of the registration plate.

(112) **Kick Cancer for Kids.** -- Issuable to the registered owner of a motor vehicle in accordance with G.S. 20-81.12. The plate shall bear the words "Kick Cancer for Kids" and a representation of a gold ribbon with children's handprints surrounding the ribbon.

(113) **Kids First.** -- Issuable to the registered owner of a motor vehicle in accordance with G.S. 20-81.12. The plate may bear the phrase "Kids First" and a logo of children's hands.

(114) **Legion of Merit.** -- Issuable to a recipient of the Legion of Merit award. The plate shall bear the emblem and name of the Legion of Merit decoration.

(115) **Legion of Valor.** -- Issuable to a recipient of one of the following military decorations: the Congressional Medal of Honor, the Distinguished Service Cross, the Navy Cross, the Air Force Cross, or the Coast Guard Cross. The plate shall bear the emblem and name of the recipient's decoration.

(116) **Legislator.** -- Issuable to a member of the North Carolina General Assembly. The plate shall bear "The Great Seal of the State of North Carolina" and, as appropriate, the word "Senate" or "House" followed by the Senator's or Representative's assigned seat number.

(117) **Leukemia & Lymphoma Society.** -- Expired July 1, 2016.

(118) **Lifetime Sportsman.** -- Expired July 1, 2016.

(119) **Litter Prevention.** -- Issuable to the registered owner of a motor vehicle in accordance with G.S. 20-81.12. The plate may bear a phrase and picture appropriate to the subject of litter prevention in North Carolina.

(120) **Lung Cancer Research.** -- Expired July 1, 2016.

(121) **Maggie Valley Trout Festival.** -- Expired July 1, 2016.

(122) **Magistrate.** -- Issuable to a current or retired North Carolina magistrate. A plate issued to a current magistrate shall bear the letters "MJ" followed by a number indicating the district court district the magistrate serves, then by a hyphen, and then by a number indicating the seniority of the magistrate. The Division shall use the number "9" to designate District Court Districts 9 and 9B. A plate issued to a retired magistrate shall bear the phrase "Magistrate, Retired", the letters "MJX" followed by a hyphen and the number that indicates the district court district the magistrate served, followed by a letter based on the order of issuance of the plates.

(123) **March of Dimes.** -- Expired July 1, 2016.

(124) **Marine Corps League.** -- Issuable to a member of the Marine Corps League. The plate shall bear the words "Marine Corps League" or the letters "MCL" and the emblem of the Marine Corps League. The Division may not issue the plate authorized by this subdivision unless it receives at least 150 applications for the plate.

(125) **Marshal.** -- Issuable to a United States Marshal. The plate shall bear the phrase "U.S. Marshal" followed by a number that represents the district the Marshal serves, with 1 being the Eastern District, 2 being the Middle District, and 3 being the Western District.

(126) **Mayor.** -- Expired July 1, 2016.

(127) **Military Reservist.** -- Issuable to a member of a reserve component of the Armed Forces of the United States. The plate shall bear the name and insignia of the appropriate reserve component. Plates

shall be numbered sequentially for members of a component with the numbers 1 through 5000 reserved for officers, without regard to rank.

(128) **Military Retiree.** -- Issuable to an individual who has retired from the Armed Forces of the United States. The plate shall bear the word "Retired" and the name and insignia of the branch of service from which the individual retired.

(129) **Military Veteran.** -- Issuable to an individual who served honorably in the Armed Forces of the United States. The plate shall bear the words "U.S. Military Veteran" and the name and insignia of the branch of service in which the individual served. The plate authorized by this subdivision is not subject to the provisions of G.S. 20-79.3A or G.S. 20-79.8.

(130) **Military Wartime Veteran.** -- Issuable to either a member or veteran of the Armed Forces of the United States who served during a period of war who received a campaign or expeditionary ribbon or medal for their service. If the person is a veteran of the Armed Forces of the United States, then the veteran must be separated from the Armed Forces of the United States under honorable conditions. The plate shall bear a word or phrase identifying the period of war and a replica of the campaign badge or medal awarded for that war. The Division may not issue the plate authorized by this subdivision unless it receives a total of 300 applications for all periods of war, combined, to be represented on this plate. A "period of war" is any of the following:

　　a. World War I, meaning the period beginning April 16, 1917, and ending November 11, 1918.

　　b. World War II, meaning the period beginning December 7, 1941, and ending December 31, 1946.

　　c. The Korean Conflict, meaning the period beginning June 27, 1950, and ending January 31, 1955.

　　d. The Vietnam Era, meaning the period beginning August 5, 1964, and ending May 7, 1975.

　　e. Desert Storm, meaning the period beginning August 2, 1990, and ending April 11, 1991.

　　f. Operation Enduring Freedom, meaning the period beginning October 24, 2001, and ending at a date to be determined.

　　g. Operation Iraqi Freedom, meaning the period beginning March 19, 2003, and ending at a date to be determined.

　　h. Any other campaign, expedition, or engagement for which the United States Department of Defense authorizes a campaign badge or medal.

(131) **Mission Foundation.** -- Expired July 1, 2016.

(132) **Morehead Planetarium.** -- Expired July 1, 2016.

(133) **Morgan Horse Club.** -- Expired July 1, 2016.

(134) **Mothers Against Drunk Driving.** -- Expired July 1, 2016.

(135) **Mountains-to-Sea Trail.** -- Issuable to the registered owner of a motor vehicle in accordance with G.S. 20-81.12. The plate shall bear the phrase "Mountains-to-Sea Trail" with a background designed by the Friends of the Mountains-to-Sea Trail, Inc.

(136) **Municipal Council.** -- Expired July 1, 2016.

(137) **Municipality Plate.** -- Expired July 1, 2016.

(138) **National Defense Service Medal.** -- Expired July 1, 2016.

(139) **National Guard Member.** -- Issuable to an active or a retired member of the North Carolina National Guard. The plate shall bear the phrase "National Guard". A plate issued to an active member shall bear a number that reflects the seniority of the member; a plate issued to a commissioned officer shall begin with the number "1"; a plate issued to a noncommissioned officer with a rank of E7, E8, or E9 shall begin with the number "1601"; a plate issued to an enlisted member with a rank of E6 or below shall begin with the number "3001". The plate issued to a retired or separated member shall indicate the member's retired status.

(140) **National Kidney Foundation.** -- Expired July 1, 2016.

(141) **National Law Enforcement Officers Memorial.** -- Expired July 1, 2016.

(142) **National Multiple Sclerosis Society.** -- Issuable to the registered owner of a motor vehicle in accordance with G.S. 20-81.12. The plate shall have the logo of the National Multiple Sclerosis Society and the telephone number "1-800-FIGHT MS" on the plate.

(143) **National Rifle Association.** -- Issuable to the registered owner of a motor vehicle. The plate shall bear a phrase or insignia representing the National Rifle Association of America. The Division must receive 300 or more applications for the plate before it may be developed.

(144) **National Wild Turkey Federation.** -- Issuable to the registered owner of a motor vehicle. The plate shall bear the design of a strutting wild turkey and dogwood blossoms and the words "Working For The

Chapter 20

Wild Turkey." The Division must receive 300 or more applications for the plate before it may be developed.

(145) **Native American.** -- Issuable to the registered owner of a motor vehicle in accordance with G.S. 20-81.12. The plate may bear a phrase or an insignia representing Native Americans. The Division must receive 300 or more applications for the plate before it may be developed.

(146) **Native Brook Trout.** -- Issuable to the registered owner of a motor vehicle in accordance with G.S. 20-81.12. The plate shall bear the phrase "Native Brook Trout" with a picture of a brook trout native to North Carolina in the background.

(147) **NC Agribusiness.** -- Expired July 1, 2016.

(148) **NCAMC/NCACC Clerk.** -- Expired July 1, 2016.

(149) **NC Beekeepers.** -- Expired July 1, 2016.

(150) **NC Children's Promise.** -- Expired July 1, 2016.

(151) **NC Civil War.** -- Expired July 1, 2016.

(152) **NC Coastal Federation.** -- Issuable to the registered owner of a motor vehicle in accordance with G.S. 20-81.12. The plate shall bear a phrase used by the North Carolina Coastal Federation and an image that depicts the coastal area of the State.

(153) **NC FIRST Robotics.** -- Expired July 1, 2016.

(154) **NC Fisheries Association.** -- Expired July 1, 2016.

(155) **NC Horse Council.** -- Issuable to the registered owner of a motor vehicle in accordance with G.S. 20-81.12. The plate shall bear the phrase "NC Horse Council" and a logo designed by the North Carolina Horse Council, Inc.

(156) **NC Mining.** -- Expired July 1, 2016.

(157) **NCSC.** -- Expired July 1, 2016.

(158) **NC Surveyors.** -- Issuable to the registered owner of a motor vehicle in accordance with G.S. 20-81.12. The plate shall bear the phrase "Following In Their Footsteps", a picture representing a surveyor, and the letters "PS" on the right side of the plate.

(159) **NC Tennis Foundation.** -- Issuable to the registered owner of a motor vehicle in accordance with G.S. 20-81.12. The plate shall bear the phrase "Play Tennis" and the image of an implement of the tennis sport.

(160) **NC Trout Unlimited.** -- Issuable to the registered owner of a motor vehicle in accordance with G.S. 20-81.12. The plate shall bear the phrase "Back the Brookie" and an image that depicts a North Carolina brook trout.

(161) **NC Veterinary Medical Association.** -- Expired July 1, 2016.

(162) **NC Victim Assistance Network.** -- Expired July 1, 2016.

(163) **NC Wildlife Federation.** -- Expired July 1, 2016.

(164) **NC Youth Soccer Association.** -- Expired July 1, 2016.

(165) **North Carolina 4-H Development Fund.** -- Expired July 1, 2016.

(166) **North Carolina Bluegrass Association.** -- Expired July 1, 2016.

(167) **North Carolina Cattlemen's Association.** -- Expired July 1, 2016.

(168) **North Carolina Emergency Management Association.** -- Expired July 1, 2016.

(169) **North Carolina Green Industry Council.** -- Expired July 1, 2016.

(170) **North Carolina Libraries.** -- Expired July 1, 2016.

(171) **North Carolina Master Gardener.** -- Issuable to the registered owner of a motor vehicle in accordance with G.S. 20-81.12. The plate shall bear the letters "MG" with a logo representing the North Carolina Master Gardeners.

(172) **North Carolina Paddle Festival.** -- Expired July 1, 2016.

(173) **North Carolina Sheriffs' Association.** -- Issuable to the registered owner of a motor vehicle in accordance with G.S. 20-81.12. The plate may bear a phrase and logo selected by the North Carolina Sheriffs' Association, Inc.

(174) **North Carolina State Flag.** -- Expired July 1, 2016.

(175) **North Carolina Wildlife Habitat Foundation.** -- Issuable to the owner of a motor vehicle in accordance with G.S. 20-81.12. The plate shall bear the logo of the North Carolina Wildlife Habitat Foundation on the left side. The numbers or other writing on the plate shall be black and the border shall be black. The plate shall be developed by the Division in consultation with and approved by the North Carolina Wildlife Habitat Foundation. The Division may not issue the plate authorized by this subdivision unless it receives at least 300 applications for the plate.

(176) **Nurses.** -- Issuable to the registered owner of a motor vehicle in accordance with G.S. 20-81.12. The plate shall bear the phrase "First in Nursing" and a representation relating to nursing.

(177) **Olympic Games.** -- Issuable to the registered owner of a motor vehicle in accordance with G.S. 20-81.12. The plate may

bear a phrase or insignia representing the Olympic Games.

(178) **Omega Psi Phi Fraternity.** -- Issuable to the registered owner of a motor vehicle in accordance with G.S. 20-81.12. The plate shall bear the fraternity's symbol and name.

(179) **Operation Coming Home.** -- Expired July 1, 2016.

(180) **Order of the Eastern Star Prince Hall Affiliated.** -- Issuable to an active member of the Order of the Eastern Star Prince Hall Affiliated in accordance with G.S. 20-81.12. The plate shall bear the Order of the Eastern Star Prince Hall Affiliated logo.

(181) **Order of the Long Leaf Pine.** -- Issuable to a person who has received the award of membership in the Order of the Long Leaf Pine from the Governor. The plate shall bear the phrase "Order of the Long Leaf Pine."

(182) **Outer Banks Preservation Association.** -- Expired July 1, 2016.

(183) **Pamlico-Tar River Foundation.** -- Expired July 1, 2016.

(184) **Pancreatic Cancer Awareness.** -- Expired July 1, 2016.

(185) **Paramedics.** -- Expired July 1, 2016.

(186) **Partially Disabled Veteran.** -- Issuable to a veteran of the Armed Forces of the United States who suffered a service connected disability of less than 100%. A person may obtain from the Division a special registration plate under this subdivision for the registered owner of a motor vehicle or a motorcycle.

(187) **Pearl Harbor Survivor.** -- Issuable to a veteran of the Armed Forces of the United States who was present at and survived the attack on Pearl Harbor on December 7, 1941. The plate will bear the phrase "Pearl Harbor Survivor" and the insignia of the Pearl Harbor Survivors' Association.

(188) P.E.O. Sisterhood. -- Expired July 1, 2016.

(189) **Personalized.** -- Issuable to the registered owner of a motor vehicle. The plate will bear the letters or letters and numbers requested by the owner. The Division may refuse to issue a plate with a letter combination that is offensive to good taste and decency. The Division may not issue a plate that duplicates another plate.

(190) **Piedmont Airlines.** -- This plate is issuable to the registered owner of a motor vehicle in accordance with G.S. 20-81.12. The plate authorized by this subdivision shall bear the phrase "PA" and the Piedmont Speed Bird logo.

(191) **Pisgah Conservancy.** -- Issuable to the registered owner of a motor vehicle in accordance with G.S. 20-81.12. The plate shall bear (i) the phrase "The Pisgah Conservancy", (ii) a representation of Looking Glass Rock and rhododendron flowers, and (iii) a background of a blue sky.

(192) **POW/MIA.** -- Expired July 1, 2016.

(193) **POW/MIA Bring Them Home.** -- The plate shall have the phrase "POW/MIA Bring Them Home" with artwork submitted by Rolling Thunder, Inc., Chapter #1 North Carolina and reviewed by the Division to ensure compliance with G.S. 20-79.4(a3). A person may obtain from the Division a special registration plate under this subdivision for the registered owner of a motor vehicle or a motorcycle. The division may not issue a plate authorized under this subdivision until it receives at least 350 applications for the plate. Applications for motor vehicle special registration plates and motorcycle special registration plates received by the Division each count towards the minimum number of applications necessary to issue a plate under this subdivision.

(194) **Prince Hall Mason.** -- This plate is issuable to the registered owner of a motor vehicle in accordance with G.S. 20-81.12. The plate shall bear the phrase "Prince Hall Mason" and a picture of the Masonic symbol.

(195) **Prisoner of War.** -- Issuable to the following:

a. A member or veteran member of the Armed Forces of the United States who has been captured and held prisoner by forces hostile to the United States while serving in the Armed Forces of the United States.

b. The surviving spouse of a person who had a prisoner of war plate at the time of death so long as the surviving spouse continues to renew the plate and does not remarry.

(196) **Professional Engineer.** -- Expired July 1, 2016.

(197) **Professional Sports Fan.** -- Issuable to the registered owner of a motor vehicle. The plate shall bear the logo of a professional sports team located in North Carolina. The Division shall receive 300 or more applications for a professional sports fan plate before a plate may be issued.

(198) **Prostate Cancer Awareness.** -- Expired July 1, 2016.

(199) **Purple Heart Recipient.** -- Issuable to a recipient of the Purple Heart award. The plate shall bear the phrase "Purple Heart Veteran, Combat Wounded." A person may obtain from the Division a

special registration plate under this subdivision for the registered owner of a motor vehicle or a motorcycle. A motorcycle plate issued under this subdivision shall bear a depiction of the Purple Heart Medal and the phrase "Purple Heart Veteran, Combat Wounded."

(200) **Red Drum.** -- Expired July 1, 2016.

(201) **Red Hat Society.** -- Expired July 1, 2016.

(202) **Register of Deeds.** -- Issuable to a register of deeds of a county of this State. The plate shall bear the words "Register of Deeds" and the letter "R" followed by a number representing the county of the register of deeds. The number of a county shall be the order of the county in an alphabetical list of counties that assigns number one to the first county in the list. A plate issued to a retired register of deeds shall bear the phrase "Register of Deeds, Retired," followed by a number that indicates the county where the register of deeds served and a designation indicating the retired status of the register of deeds. For purposes of this subdivision, a "retired register of deeds" is a person (i) with at least 10 years of service as a register of deeds of a county of this State and (ii) who no longer holds that office for any reason other than removal under G.S. 161-27.

(203) **Relay for Life.** -- Expired July 1, 2016.

(204) **Retired Law Enforcement Officers.** -- The plate authorized by this subdivision shall bear the phrase "Retired Law Enforcement Officer" and a representation of a law enforcement badge. The Division must receive 300 or more applications for the plate before it may be developed. The plate is issuable to one of the following:

a. A retired law enforcement officer presenting to the Division, along with the application for the plate, a copy of the officer's retired identification card or letter of retirement.

b. The surviving spouse of a person who had a retired law enforcement officer plate at the time of death so long as the surviving spouse continues to renew the plate and does not remarry.

(205) **Retired Legislator.** -- Issuable to a retired member of the North Carolina General Assembly in accordance with G.S. 20-81.12. A person who has served in the North Carolina General Assembly is a retired member for purposes of this subdivision. The plate shall bear "The Great Seal of the State of North Carolina" and, as appropriate, the phrase "Retired Senate Member" or "Retired House Member" followed by a number representing the retired

member's district with the letters "RM". If more than one retired member is from the same district, then the number shall be followed by a letter from A through Z. The plates shall be issued in the order applications are received.

(206) **Retired State Highway Patrol.** -- The plate authorized by this subdivision shall bear the phrase "SHP, Retired." The Division may not issue the plate authorized by this subdivision unless it receives at least 300 applications for the plate. The plate is issuable to one of the following:

a. An individual who has retired from the North Carolina State Highway Patrol, presenting to the Division, along with the application for the plate, a copy of the retiree's retired identification card or letter of retirement.

b. The surviving spouse of a person who had retired from the State Highway Patrol who, along with the application for the plate, presents a copy of the deceased retiree's identification card or letter of retirement and certifies in writing that the retiree is deceased and that the applicant is not remarried.

(207) **RiverLink.** -- Expired July 1, 2016.

(208) **Rocky Mountain Elk Foundation.** -- Issuable to the registered owner of a motor vehicle in accordance with G.S. 20-81.12. The plate shall bear the phrase "Rocky Mountain Elk Foundation" and a logo approved by the Rocky Mountain Elk Foundation, Inc.

(209) **Ronald McDonald House.** -- Issuable to the registered owner of a motor vehicle in accordance with G.S. 20-81.12. The plate shall bear the phrase "House and Hands" with the words "Ronald McDonald House Charities" below the emblem and the letters "RH".

(210) **Save the Honey Bee (HB).** -- Issuable to the registered owner of a motor vehicle in accordance with G.S. 20-81.12. The plate shall bear the phrase "Save the Honey Bee", a picture representing a honey bee, and the letters "HB" on the right side of the plate.

(211) **Save the Honey Bee (SB).** -- Issuable to the registered owner of a motor vehicle in accordance with G.S. 20-81.12. The plate shall bear the phrase "Save the Honey Bee", a picture representing a honey bee on a blue flower inside of a hexagon, a honeycomb background, and the letters "SB" on the right side of the plate.

(212) **Save the Sea Turtles.** -- Issuable to the registered owner of a motor vehicle in accordance with G.S. 20-81.12. The plate may bear the phrase "Save the Sea Turtles" and a representation related to sea turtles.

Chapter 20

(213) **Scenic Rivers.** -- Expired July 1, 2016.

(214) **School Board.** -- Expired July 1, 2016.

(215) **School Technology.** -- Expired July 1, 2016.

(216) **SCUBA.** -- Issuable to the registered owner of a motor vehicle in accordance with G.S. 20-81.12. The plate shall bear the phrase "SCUBA" and a logo of the Diver Down Flag.

(217) **Shag Dancing.** -- Issuable to the registered owner of a motor vehicle in accordance with G.S. 20-81.12. The plate may bear the phrase "I'd Rather Be Shaggin'" and a picture representing shag dancing.

(218) **Share the Road.** -- Issuable to the registered owner of a motor vehicle in accordance with G.S. 20-81.12. The plate shall bear a representation of a bicycle and the phrase "Share the Road".

(219) **Sheriff.** -- Issuable to a current sheriff or to a retired sheriff who served as sheriff for at least 10 years before retiring. A plate issued to a current sheriff shall bear the word "Sheriff" and the letter "S" followed by a number that indicates the county the sheriff serves. A plate issued to a retired sheriff shall bear the phrase "Sheriff, Retired", the letter "S" followed by a number that indicates the county the sheriff served, and the letter "X" indicating the sheriff's retired status.

(220) **Sigma Gamma Rho Sorority.** -- Expired July 1, 2016.

(221) **Silver Star Recipient.** -- Issuable to a recipient of the Silver Star. The plate shall bear the emblem of the Silver Star and the words "Silver Star".

(222) **Silver Star Recipient/Disabled Veteran.** -- Issuable to a recipient of the Silver Star who is also a veteran of the Armed Forces of the United States who suffered a one hundred percent (100%) service-connected disability. The plate shall bear the emblem of the Silver Star laid over the universal symbol for the handicapped and the words "Silver Star." For the purposes of a fee for this plate, it shall be treated as a one hundred percent (100%) Disabled Veteran plate.

(223) **Sneads Ferry Shrimp Festival.** -- Expired July 1, 2016.

(224) **Soil and Water Conservation.** -- Expired July 1, 2016.

(225) **Special Forces Association.** -- Expired July 1, 2016.

(226) **Special Olympics.** -- Expired July 1, 2016.

(227) **Sport Fishing.** -- Expired July 1, 2016.

(228) **Square Dance Clubs.** -- Issuable to a member of a recognized square dance organization exempt from corporate income tax under G.S. 105-130.11(a)(5). The plate shall bear a word or phrase identifying the club and the emblem of the club. The Division shall not issue a dance club plate authorized by this subdivision unless it receives at least 300 applications for that dance club plate.

(229) **S.T.A.R.** -- Expired July 1, 2016.

(230) **State Attraction.** -- Issuable to the registered owner of a motor vehicle in accordance with G.S. 20-81.12. The plate may bear a phrase or an insignia representing a publicly owned or nonprofit State or federal attraction located in North Carolina.

(231) **State Government Official.** -- Issuable to elected and appointed members of State government in accordance with G.S. 20-79.5.

(232) **Stock Car Racing Theme.** -- Issuable to the registered owner of a motor vehicle pursuant to G.S. 20-81.12. This is a series of plates bearing an emblem, seal, other symbol or design displaying themes of professional stock car auto racing, or professional stock car auto racing drivers. The Division shall not develop any plate in the series without a license to use copyrighted or registered words, symbols, trademarks, or designs associated with the plate. The plate shall be designed in consultation with and approved by the person authorized to provide the State with the license to use the words, symbols, trademarks, or designs associated with the plate. The Division shall not pay a royalty for the license to use the copyrighted or registered words, symbols, trademarks, or designs associated with the plate.

(233) **Street Rod Owner.** -- Expired July 1, 2016.

(234) **Support NC Education.** -- Expired July 1, 2016.

(235) **Support Our Troops.** -- Issuable to the registered owner of a motor vehicle in accordance with G.S. 20-81.12. The plate shall bear a picture of a soldier and a child and shall bear the words: "Support Our Troops".

(236) **Support Soccer.** -- Issuable to the registered owner of a motor vehicle in accordance with G.S. 20-81.12. The plate shall bear the phrase "Support Soccer" and a logo designed by the North Carolina Soccer Hall of Fame, Inc.

(237) **Surveyor Plate.** -- Issuable to the registered owner of a motor vehicle in accordance with G.S. 20-81.12. The plate shall bear the words "Following In Their Footsteps" and shall bear a picture of a transit.

(238) **Sustainable Fisheries.** -- Expired July 1, 2016.

(239) **Sweet Potato.** -- Expired July 1, 2016.

(240) **Tarheel Classic Thunderbird Club.** -- Expired July 1, 2016.

(241) **Toastmasters Club.** -- Expired July 1, 2016.

(242) **Tobacco Heritage.** -- Issuable to the registered owner of a motor vehicle. The plate shall bear a picture of a tobacco leaf and plow. The Division may not issue the plate authorized by this subdivision unless it receives at least 300 applications for the plate.

(243) **Topsail Island Shoreline Protection.** -- Expired July 1, 2016.

(244) **Town of Oak Island.** -- Expired July 1, 2016.

(245) **Transportation Personnel.** -- Issuable to various members of the Divisions of the Department of Transportation. The plate shall bear the letters "DOT" followed by a number from 1 to 85, as designated by the Governor.

(246) **Travel and Tourism.** -- Expired July 1, 2016.

(247) **Turtle Rescue Team.** -- Expired July 1, 2016.

(248) **United States Service Academy.** -- Issuable to a graduate of one of the service academies, upon furnishing to the Division proof of graduation. The plate shall bear the name of the specific service academy with an emblem that designates the specific service academy being represented. The Division, with the cooperation of each service academy, shall develop a special plate for each of the service academies. The Division must receive a combined total of 600 or more applications for all the plates authorized by this subdivision before a specific service academy plate may be developed. The plates authorized by this subdivision are not subject to the provisions of G.S. 20-79.3A or G.S. 20-79.8.

(249) **University Health Systems of Eastern Carolina.** -- Expired July 1, 2016.

(250) **US Equine Rescue League.** -- Expired July 1, 2016.

(251) U.S. Navy Submarine Veteran. -- Issuable to a veteran of the United States Navy Submarine Service. The plate shall bear the phrase "United States Navy Submarine Veteran" and shall bear a representation of the Submarine Service Qualification insignia overlaid upon a representation of the State of North Carolina. The Division may not issue the plate authorized by this subdivision unless it receives at least 150 applications for the plate.

(252) U.S. Representative. -- Issuable to a United States Representative for North Carolina. The plate shall bear the phrase "U.S. House" and shall be issued on the basis of Congressional district numbers.

(253) U.S. Senator. -- Issuable to a United States Senator for North Carolina. The plates shall bear the phrase "U.S. Senate" and shall be issued on the basis of seniority represented by the numbers 1 and 2.

(254) **USA Triathlon.** -- Expired July 1, 2016.

(255) **USO of NC.** -- Expired July 1, 2016.

(256) **The V Foundation for Cancer Research.** -- Issuable to the registered owner of a motor vehicle in accordance with G.S. 20-81.12. The plate shall bear a phrase and insignia representing The V Foundation for Cancer Research.

(257) **Veterans of Foreign Wars.** -- Issuable to a member or a supporter of the Veterans of Foreign Wars. The plate shall bear the words "Veterans of Foreign Wars" or "VFW" and the emblem of the VFW. The Division may not issue the plate authorized by this subdivision unless it receives at least 300 applications for the plate.

(258) **Victory Junction Gang Camp.** -- Expired July 1, 2016.

(259) **Vietnam Veterans of America.** -- Expired July 1, 2016.

(260) **Volunteers in Law Enforcement.** -- Expired July 1, 2016.

(261) **Watermelon.** -- Issuable to the registered owner of a motor vehicle. The plate shall bear a picture representing a slice of watermelon. The Division may not issue the plate authorized by this subdivision unless it receives at least 300 applications for the plate.

(262) **Wildlife Resources.** -- Issuable to the registered owner of a motor vehicle in accordance with G.S. 20-81.12. The plate shall bear a picture representing a native wildlife species occurring in North Carolina.

(263) **Wrightsville Beach.** -- Issuable to a registered owner of a motor vehicle in accordance with G.S. 20-81.12. The plate shall bear the Town of Wrightsville Beach logo followed by the four assigned or personalized characters ending with the suffix WB.

(264) **YMCA.** -- Expired July 1, 2016.

(265) **Zeta Phi Beta Sorority.** -- Issuable to the registered owner of a motor vehicle in accordance with G.S. 20-81.12. The plate shall bear the sorority's name and symbol.

(c) Repealed by Session Laws 1991 (Regular Session, 1992), c. 1042, s. 1.

History.
1991, c. 672, s. 2;c. 726, s. 23;1991 (Reg. Sess., 1992), c. 1042, s. 1; 1993, c. 543, s. 2;1995, c. 326, ss. 1 -3;

c. 433, ss. 1, 4.1; 1997-156, s. 1;1997-158, s. 1;1997-339, s. 1;1997-427, s. 1;1997-461, ss. 2 -4; 1997-477, s. 1;1997-484, ss. 1 -3; 1998-155, s. 1;1998-160, ss. 1, 2; 1998-163, ss. 3 -5; 1999-220, s. 3.1;1999-277, s. 1;1999-314, s. 1;1999-403, s. 1;1999-450, s. 1;1999-452, s. 16;2000-159, ss. 1, 2; 2001-40, s. 1;2001-483, s. 1;2001-498, ss. 1(a), 1(b), 2; 2002-134, ss. 1 -4; 2002-159, s. 68;2003-10, s. 1;2003-11, s. 1;2003-68, s. 1;2003-424, s. 2;2004-131, s. 2;2004-182, s. 1;2004-185, s. 2;2004-200, s. 1;2005-216, ss. 2, 3; 2006-209, ss. 2, 7; 2007-400, s. 2;2007-470, s. 1;2007-483, ss. 2, 8(d); 2007-522, s. 1;2009-121, s. 1;2009-274, s. 4;2009-376, s. 1;2010-39, s. 1;2011-145, ss. 2;19.1(h); 2011-183, s. 23;2011-392, ss. 2, 3; 2012-194, ss. 45.7, 57; 2013-376, ss. 1, 2, 9(e); 2013-414, s. 57(a);2014-100, s. 8.11(b);2015-241, ss. 24.1(m), 14.30(s), 29.40(b), (f), (g), (i), (j), (*l*)-(o), (q); 2015-264, s. 40.6(b);2015-268, s. 7.3(a);2017-100, s. 1;2017-107, ss. 2, 5; 2017-114, ss. 2, 5; 2017-186, s. 2 (*llll*); 2018-7, ss. 1(a), 1(c); 2018-74, ss. 11(a), 11(d), 11(e), 12(b), 14(a); 2018-77, ss. 1(a), 2(b), 3.5(a), (d); 2019-213, s. 2(b);2019-231, s. 4.15(a)

INACTIVE SPECIAL INTEREST PLATES. --Pursuant to G.S. 20-79.8 (a), several special plates authorized by G.S. 20-79.4 prior to October 1, 2014, expired as a matter of law on July 1, 2016, because the number of applications required for their production was not received by the Division of Motor Vehicles. At the direction of the Revisor of Statutes, pursuant to G.S. 20-79.8(c), those special plates not meeting this requirement have been set out as expired effective July 1, 2016.

EDITOR'S NOTE. --
Session Laws 2006-209, s. 8, as amended by Session Laws 2011-330, s. 46, provides: "As applied to G.S. 20-79.4, the authority in G.S. 164-10 for the Legislative Services Office to reletter or renumber section subdivisions includes the authority to renumber all the subdivisions in G.S. 20-79.4(b) in sequential and alphabetical order and to eliminate mixed number-letter subdivision designations."

Subdivisions in subsection (b) of this section have been renumbered periodically, pursuant to Session Laws 2006-209, s. 8, which authorized the Revisor of Statutes to renumber subdivisions in subsection (b) in sequential and alphabetical order and to eliminate mixed number-letter subdivision designations. Subsection (b) was again renumbered in 2009.

Session Laws 2000-159 s. 9(c), directs the Department of Transportation, the Department of Environment and Natural Resources, and the Department of Public Instruction to cooperatively develop the phrase and picture to be used on the litter prevention registration plate authorized under G.S. 20-79.4(b)(22a).

Session Laws 2001-498, s. 8, provided that the amendment by Session Laws 2001-498, s. 1(b), which added subdivisions (b)(16c) and (b)(36b) [now subdivisions (53) and (106)], relating to the Harley Owners' Group and the Rocky Mountain Elk Foundation, would expire on June 30, 2006. However, Session Laws 2006-209, s. 7, amended Session Laws 2001-498, s. 8, to delete the sunset provision, so special plates

for Harley Owners' Group and Rocky Mountain Elk Foundation will not expire.

Session Laws 2009-456, s. 2, provides: "The Joint Legislative Transportation Oversight Committee, in consultation with the Revenue Laws Study Committee, must study the authorization of special registration plates under Part 5 of Article 3 of Chapter 20 of the General Statutes and the issuance of special registration plates with a design that is not a 'First in Flight' design. As part of its study, the Division of Motor Vehicles must report to the Committee the special registration plates that have been authorized but for which the Division has not received the minimum 300 applications. It is the intent of the General Assembly to repeal the authorization for a special plate that has not received at least 300 applications within two years of its authorization."

Session Laws 2011-392, s. 9, provides: "Notwithstanding Section 8 of this act, any special registration plate authorized in G.S. 20-79.7, prior to July 1, 2011, shall expire, as a matter of law, on July 1, 2013, if the number of applications required for the production of the special registration plate has not been received by the Division of Motor Vehicles on or before that date. Upon notification of expiration of the authorization for any special plate by the Division pursuant to this section, the Revisor of Statutes shall verify that the authorization for each special registration plate listed has expired and shall notate such expiration in the applicable statutes. If an authorization for a special registration plate listed in G.S. 20-79.4 expires, the Revisor of Statutes shall revise the subdivision referring to the special registration plate to leave the name of the special plate authorized and the date the special registration plate's authorization expired. If an authorization for a special registration plate listed in G.S. 20-79.4 expires, the Revisor of Statutes shall also make corresponding changes to reflect the expiration of the special registration plate's authorization, if applicable, in G.S. 20-63(b), 20-79.7, and 20-81.12."

Session Laws 2011-392, s. 10, provides: "The Revisor of Statutes is authorized to alphabetize, number, and renumber the special registration plates listed in G.S. 20-79.4 to ensure that all the special registration plates are listed in alphabetical order and numbered accordingly." The special registration plates listed in G.S. 20-79.4 have been renumbered at the direction of the Revisor of Statutes, pursuant to this provision.

Session Laws 2013-376, s. 2, effective July 29, 2013, provides: "G.S. 20-79.4(b)(52) and G.S. 20-79.4(b)(119) [now (b)(122)] are reenacted."

Session Laws 2014-96, s. 1(a), provides: "Any special registration plate authorized under G.S. 20-79.4 that expired as a matter of law on July 1, 2013, pursuant to G.S. 20-79.8, is reenacted. The corresponding provisions for fees under G.S. 20-79.7(a1) and (b) and any other corresponding requirements for the plates under G.S. 20-81.12 are also reenacted. A special registration plate reenacted under this section is subject to the requirements of G.S. 20-63(b1) if the plate is authorized to be on a background other than a 'First in Flight' background."

Session Laws 2014-96, s. 1(b), provides: "This section is effective when it becomes law [August 1, 2014]. A special registration plate reenacted by this section shall expire, as a matter of law, on October 1, 2014, if the required number of applications for the special registration plate has not been received by the Division of Motor Vehicles by that date. The notification procedure and the responsibilities of the Revisor of Statutes for a special registration plate that expires pursuant to this subsection shall be in accordance with G.S. 20-79.8 except that the notification date shall be no later than October 15, 2015. The Division shall not accept applications for nor advertise any special registration plate that has expired pursuant to this subsection."

Session Laws 2014-96, s. 7, provides: "The Revenue Laws Study Committee is directed as follows as it relates to registration plates:

"(1) To identify whether the process for requests to establish or reauthorize special registration plates under this act requires any modifications and to examine the costs incurred by the Division of Motor Vehicles to administer special registration plates.

"(2) To study whether certain governmental entities should have different eligibility or renewal requirements for permanent registration plates; to study whether nongovernmental entities should be eligible for permanent plates and, if so, what the criteria should be; and to examine the costs incurred by the Division of Motor Vehicles to administer permanent registration plates.

"The Committee shall report its findings, together with any recommended legislation, to the 2015 Regular Session of the 2015 General Assembly upon its convening."

Session Laws 2014-100, s. 8.11(f), provides: "The Revisor of Statutes is authorized to alphabetize, number, and renumber the special registration plates listed in G.S. 20-79.4(b) to ensure that all the special registration plates are listed in alphabetical order and numbered accordingly."

Session Laws 2014-100, s. 1.1, provides: "This act shall be known as 'The Current Operations and Capital Improvements Appropriations Act of 2014.'"

Session Laws 2014-100, s. 38.4, provides: "Except for statutory changes or other provisions that clearly indicate an intention to have effects beyond the 2014-2015 fiscal year, the textual provisions of this act apply only to funds appropriated for, and activities occurring during, the 2014-2015 fiscal year."

Session Laws 2014-100, s. 38.7, is a severability clause.

Session Laws 2015-241, s. 29.40(e), provides: "The Division of Motor Vehicles shall not issue, and shall not produce, any more special registration plates developed for the Carolina Panthers under the authority in G.S. 20-79.4(b)(185)."

Session Laws 2015-241, s. 29.40(f), provides: "G.S. 20-79.4(b)(122) and G.S. 20-79.4(b)(234), as they existed on September 30, 2014, are reenacted."

Session Laws 2015-241, s. 29.40(j), provides: "G.S. 20-79.4(b)(171), as it existed on June 30, 2015, is

reenacted. The corresponding provisions for fees under G.S. 20-79.7(a1) and (b) and any other corresponding requirements for the plates under G.S. 20-81.12 are also reenacted."

Session Laws 2015-241, s. 29.40 (*l*), provides: "G.S. 20-79.4(b)(56), as it existed on September 30, 2014, is reenacted."

Session Laws 2015-241, s. 29.40(n), provides: "G.S. 20-79.4(b)(21), G.S. 20-81.12(b76), and the corresponding provisions for fees under G.S. 20-79.7(a) and (b), as they existed on September 30, 2014, are reenacted."

Session Laws 2015-241, s. 29.40(q), provides: "The Revisor of Statutes is authorized to alphabetize, number, and renumber the special registration plates listed in G.S. 20-79.4(b) to ensure that all the special registration plates are listed in alphabetical order and numbered accordingly."

Session Laws 2015-241, s. 29.40(s), provides: "Subsections (r) and (s) of this section are effective when this act becomes law. The remainder of this section is effective 90 days after this act becomes law." [September 18, 2015]

Session Laws 2015-241, s. 1.1, provides: "This act shall be known as 'The Current Operations and Capital Improvements Appropriations Act of 2015.'"

Session Laws 2015-241, s. 33.4, provides: "Except for statutory changes or other provisions that clearly indicate an intention to have effects beyond the 2015-2017 fiscal biennium, the textual provisions of this act apply only to funds appropriated for, and activities occurring during, the 2015-2017 fiscal biennium."

Session Laws 2015-241, s. 33.6, is a severability clause.

Session Laws 2015-264, s. 40.6(d) provides: "This section becomes effective 90 days after S.L. 2015-241 becomes law." Session Laws 2015-241 became law September 18, 2015.

Session Laws 2015-268, s. 7.3(a), made the amendment of this section by Session Laws 2015-241, s. 24.1(m), effective July 1, 2015.

Session Laws 2017-100, s. 1, provides: "G.S. 20-79.4(b)(255) [now (b)(260)], as it existed immediately before its repeal under Section 1(b) of S.L. 2014-96, is reenacted"

Session Laws 2017-107, s. 5, provides: "The Revisor of Statutes is authorized to alphabetize, number, and renumber the special registration plates listed in G.S. 20-79.4(b) to ensure that all the special registration plates are listed in alphabetical order and numbered accordingly."

Session Laws 2017-114, s. 5, provides: "The Revisor of Statutes is authorized to alphabetize, number, and renumber the special registration plates listed in G.S. 20-79.4(b) to ensure that all the special registration plates are listed in alphabetical order and numbered accordingly."

Session Laws 2018-7, s. 1(c) and Session Laws 2018-74, s. 11(d), provide: "The Revisor of Statutes is authorized to alphabetize, number, and renumber the special registration plates listed in G.S. 20-79.4(b) to ensure that all the special registration plates are listed in alphabetical order and numbered accordingly."

Chapter 20

Session Laws 2018-77, s. 3.5, effective February 1, 2019, was repealed by Acts 2018-74, s. 11(e), effective February 1, 2019. Session Laws 2018-77, s. 3.5(a), (d) would have added (b)(179) [Order of the Eastern Star Prince Hall Affiliated] (identical to the subdivision as added by Session Laws 2018-74, s. 11(a)) and authorized renumbering of subdivisions in subsection (b).

Session Laws 2019-213, s. 2(e), provides: "The Revisor of Statutes is authorized to alphabetize, number, and renumber the special registration plates listed in G.S. 20-63(b1), 20-79.4(b), and 20-81.12 to ensure that all the special registration plates are listed in alphabetical order and numbered accordingly."

Pursuant to this authority, the subdivisions in subsection (b) have been renumbered. Former subdivision (b)(7), ALS Research, had expired July 1, 2016, and Session Laws 2019-213, s. 2(b) added a new subdivision (b)(7), ALS Research.

Session Laws 2019-231, s. 4.15(b), provides that the substitution of "30 years old" for "35 years old" in subdivision (b)(94) of this section by Session Laws 2019-231, s. 4.15(a), is effective October 18, 2019, and applicable to applications for Historic Vehicle Owner registration plates made on or after that date.

Session Laws 2019-231, s. 5.3, provides: "Except for statutory changes or other provisions that clearly indicate an intention to have effects beyond the 2019-2021 fiscal biennium, the textual provisions of this act apply only to funds appropriated for, and activities occurring during, the 2019-2021 fiscal biennium."

Session Laws 2019-231, s. 5.5, is a severability clause.

EFFECT OF AMENDMENTS. --
Session Laws 2004-131, s. 2, effective July 29, 2004, redesignated former subdivision (b)(19a) as (b)(19b), and inserted new subdivision (b)(19a).

Session Laws 2004-182, s. 1, effective August 10, 2004, redesignated former subdivision (b)(28) as present subdivision (b)(27i) and inserted new subdivision (b)(28).

Session Laws 2004-185, s. 2, effective October 1, 2004, inserted subdivision (b)(44c).

Session Laws 2004-200, s. 1, effective August 17, 2004, in subsection (b), inserted subdivisions (10a), (11e), (14a),(16f), (18a), (28e), and (41a), and rewrote subdivision (36a).

Session Laws 2005-216, ss. 2 and 3, effective July 20, 2005, in subsection (a), added the second and last sentences and deleted the former last sentence which read: "A holder of a special registration plate who becomes ineligible for the plate, for whatever reason, must return the special plate within 30 days."; added subdivisions (b)(1b), (b)(1d), (b)(3b), (b)(3d), (b)(3 l), (b)(8d), (b)(8g), (b)(10e), (b)(16c), (b)(24a), (b)(27 l), (b)(28c), (b)(28p), (b)(28w), (b)(38c), (b)(38d), (b)(38f), (b)(45h) and (b)(50a); redesignated former (b)(3b) as present (b)(3c), former (b)(3c) as present (b)(3e), former (b)(3e) as present (b)(3f), former (b)(16c) as present (b)(16d), and deleted the last sentence which read: "The Division shall not develop this plate unless the Harley-Davidson Motor Company, Inc., licenses, without charge, the State to use the words and trademark of the Harley

Owners' Group on the plate.", former (b)(28a) as present (b)(28f), former (b)(28b) as present (b)(28i), former (b)(28d) as present (b)(28m), former (b)(28e) as present (b)(28r), former (b)(28g) as present (b)(28y); in subdivision (b)(27b), added f. and g. and redesignated former f. as present h.; in subdivision (b)(28), deleted the former third sentence which read: "The Division shall not use the name and logo of the National Rifle Association of America on the plate unless the National Rifle Association of America licenses, without charge, the State to use the name and logo on the plate."; in subdivision (b)(34) deleted the last sentence which read: "The Division shall not develop a professional sports fan plate unless the professional sports team licenses, without charge, the State to use the official team logo on the plate."; and in subdivision (b)(35d) deleted the second sentence which read: "The Division shall not use the name and logo of The Red Hat Society, Inc., on the plate unless The Red Hat Society, Inc., licenses, without charge, the State to use the name and logo on the plate."

Session Laws 2006-209, s. 2, effective August 8, 2006, in subdivision (b)(3h) [now (b)(15)], added "in accordance with G.S. 20-81.12" at the end of the first sentence, and deleted the third sentence, which read: "The Division must receive 300 or more applications for the plate before it may be developed."; added subdivisions (b)(3n), (b)(14e), (b)(15c), (b)(16b), (b)(16f), (b)(20f), (b)(22c), (b)(22k), (b)(28k), (b)(22g), (b)(45a), and (b)(46c) [now (b)(19), (b)(43), (b)(46), (b)(51), (b)(54), (b)(63), (b)(67), (b)(68), (b)(84), (b)(124), (b)(131)]; rewrote subdivision (b)(19b) [now (b)(60)]; and added sub-subdivision (b)(36a)c [now (b)(104)d.].

Session Laws 2007-400, s. 2, effective August 21, 2007, added subdivisions (b)(13a) and (b)(68a).

Session Laws 2007-470, s. 1, effective August 29, 2007, added subdivision (40a).

Session Laws 2007-483, s. 2, effective August 30, 2007, added subdivisions (b)(2a), (b)(6a) (now (b)(5a)), (b)(14a), (b)(15a), (b)(58a), (b)(58b) (now (b)(56a)), (b)(61a), (b)(78a), (b)(85a), (b)(100a); and deleted the former last sentence in subdivision (b)(54), which read: "The Division may not issue the plate authorized by this subdivision unless it receives at least 300 applications for the plate".

Session Laws 2007-483, s. 8(d), effective October 1, 2007, in subdivision (b)(15), deleted "in accordance with G.S. 20-81.12" at the end of the first sentence and added the last sentence.

Session Laws 2007-522, s. 1, effective August 31, 2007, added subdivision (b)(16a) (now (b)(15b)).

Session Laws 2009-121, s. 1, effective June 19, 2009, added subsections (a1) and (a2).

Session Laws 2009-274, s. 4, effective July 10, 2009, and applicable to all licenses expiring on or after that date, substituted "Armed Forces" for "armed forces" in subdivisions (b)(36), (b)(43), (b)(85), (b)(86), (b)(108), (b)(109), and (b)(113)a.

Session Laws 2009-376, s. 1, effective July 31, 2009, rewrote subdivision (b)(120).

Session Laws 2010-39, s. 1, effective July 1, 2010, in the introductory paragraph in subdivision (b)(88), in the first sentence, added "who received a campaign or expeditionary ribbon or medal for their service" and rewrote the fourth sentence, which formerly read: "Except for World War II and Korean Conflict plates, the Division may not issue a plate authorized by this subdivision unless it receives at least 300 applications for that plate."

Session Laws 2011-183, s. 23, effective June 20, 2011, throughout subdivisions (b)(33), (b)(87), and (b)(88), substituted "Armed Forces" for "armed services"; in subdivision (b)(33), inserted the last occurrence of "of the United States"; in subdivision (b)(36), twice inserted "of the United States"; in subdivision (b)(88), inserted the last two occurrences of "of the United States"; and in subdivision (b)(113)a., added "of the United States" at the end. [Subdivisions (b)(33), (b)(36), (b)(87), (b)(88), and (b)(113) have been renumbered as (b)(49), (b)(52), (b)(119), (b)(120), and (b)(167), respectively.]

Session Laws 2011-145, s. 19.1(h), effective January 1, 2011, substituted "Division of Adult Correction" for "Department of Correction" in subsection (a3).

Session Laws 2011-392, ss. 2, 3, effective June 30, 2011, rewrote the section.

Session Laws 2012-194, s. 45.7, effective July 17, 2012, deleted "and the letters 'PH'" following "Wounded'" in the first sentence of subdivision (b)(170).

Session Laws 2012-194, s. 57, effective July 17, 2012, substituted "phrases 'Proud Supporter,' 'American Red Cross,' and the official American Red Cross logo." for "phrase 'American Red Cross Saving Lives' and a red cross" in subdivision (b)(11).

Session Laws 2013-376, s. 1, effective July 29, 2013, in subsection (b), alphabetically added the following subdivisions: "Charlotte Checkers," "First Tee," "Flag of the United States of America," "I.B.P.O.E.W.," "Mission Foundation," "Morehead Planetarium," "Municipality Plate," "National Law Enforcement Officers Memorial," "Native Brook Trout," "NC FIRST Robotics," "NCSC," "North Carolina Bluegrass Association," "North Carolina Cattlemen's Association," "Operation Coming Home," "Order of the Long Leaf Pine," "Pancreatic Cancer Awareness," "Professional Engineer," "Red Drum," "RiverLink," "Sneads Ferry Shrimp Festival," "Turtle Rescue Team," "Volunteers in Law Enforcement," and "YMCA"; substituted "Valor" for "Combat" in subdivision (b)(29); in the subdivision entitled "Legion of Valor," added "or the Coast Guard Cross" and made a minor stylistic change; substituted subdivision heading "NCAMC/NCACC Clerk" for "City/County Clerk" and substituted "municipal" for "city or town" or similar language throughout, and "NCAMC" for "City" and "NCACC" for "County"; deleted the former subdivision entitled "Phi Beta Sigma Fraternity"; added the last sentence in the subdivision entitled "Register of Deeds"; added the second and fifth sentences in the subdivision entitled "Retired Legislator"; and in the subdivision entitled "Vietnam Veterans of America," added the third and fourth sentences and "either type of" in the fifth sentence. For applicability, see Editor's note.

Session Laws 2013-376, s. 2, effective July 29, 2013, reenacted subdivisions (b)(52) and (b)(119).

Session Laws 2013-376, s. 9(e), effective July 29, 2013, in subsection (a3), inserted "name of the State and the" and "reflective and to contrast with the background so it may be."

Session Laws 2013-414, s. 57(a), effective August 23, 2013, inserted an undesignated subdivision under subsection (b), entitled "North Carolina Paddle Festival."

Session Laws 2014-100, s. 8.11(b), effective July 1, 2014, in subsection (b), inserted subdivision (98a).

Session Laws 2015-241, s. 14.30(s), effective July 1, 2015, substituted "Department of Natural and Cultural Resources" for "Department of Cultural Resources" in subdivision (b)(144).

Session Laws 2015-241, s. 24.1(m), effective July 1, 2015, in subsection (a2), substituted "Department of Military and Veterans Affairs" for "Division of Veterans Affairs" and "Secretary of Military and Veterans Affairs" for "Director of the Division of Veterans Affairs." For effective date, see editor's note.

Session Laws 2015-241, s. 29.40(b), (g), (i), (m), and (o), effective December 17, 2015, in subsection (b), added special registration plate types "Carolina Panthers," "NC Surveyors," "North Carolina Sheriffs' Association," "Save the Honey Bee (HB)," and "Save the Honey Bee (SB)"; rewrote the last sentence in subdivisions (b)(21), (b)(57), and (b)(123); in subdivision (b)(193), inserted "of a county of this State" in the first sentence and added the last sentence; in subdivision (b)(239), substituted "(600)" for "(300)" in the next-to-last sentence and added the last sentence. For effective date, see editor's note.

Session Laws 2015-264, s. 40.6(b), effective October 1, 2015, inserted "who is a member of the Kappa Alpha Psi Fraternity" following "owner of a motor vehicle" in the first sentence of subdivision (b)(106).

Session Laws 2017-100, s. 1, effective July 12, 2017, reenacted subdivision (b)(260) ["Zeta Phi Beta"].

Session Laws 2017-107, s. 2, effective July 1, 2017, in subsection (b), added special license plate entitled "Pisgah Conservancy."

Session Laws 2017-114, s. 2, effective July 18, 2017, in subsection (b), added special license plates entitled "Big Rock Blue Marlin Tournament," "Colorectal Cancer Awareness" and "Kick Cancer for Kids."

Session Laws 2017-186, s. 2 (*llll*), effective December 1, 2017, inserted "and Juvenile Justice" in the first sentence of subsection (a3).

Session Laws 2018-7, s. 1(a), effective June 13, 2018, added subdivision (b)(72) [Eastern Band of Cherokee Indians].

Session Laws 2018-74, s. 11(a), effective February 1, 2019, added subdivision (b)(179) [Order of the Eastern Star Prince Hall Affiliated].

Session Laws 2018-74, s. 12(b), and Session Laws 2018-77, s. 2(b), are identical, both effective February 1, 2019, and both reenacted subdivision (b)(6) [Alpha Phi Alpha Fraternity] as it existed immediately before its repeal.

Session Laws 2018-74, s. 14(a), effective July 1, 2018, inserted "in accordance with G.S. 20-81.12" in subdivision (b)(104) [now (b)(105) International Association of Fire Fighters].

Session Laws 2018-77, s. 1(a), effective June 25, 2018, in subsection (b), added the last sentence in subdivisions (b)(64) [Disabled Veteran] and (b)(183) [now (b)(185) Partially Disabled Veteran].

Session Laws 2018-77, s. 1(a), effective June 25, 2018, in subsection (a), inserted "and except for the special registration plate listed in subdivision (2) of this subsection" in the first sentence and added the second sentence.

Session Laws 2019-213, s. 2(b), effective March 1, 2020, added subdivisions (b)(7), (b)(111), (b)(193) and (b)(263). For renumbering of subdivisions, see editor's note.

Session Laws 2019-231, s. 4.15(a), substituted "30 years old" for "35 years old" in subdivision (b)(94). For effective date and applicability, see editor's note.

THE SONS OF CONFEDERATE VETERANS MET THE REQUIREMENTS of this section for issuance of special registration license plates, where the organization was similar to organizations listed in this section; it was "nationally recognized," engaged in charitable and benevolent community activities, and was listed in the comprehensive encyclopedia of associations. North Carolina Div. of Sons of Confederate Veterans v. Faulkner, 131 N.C. App. 775, 509 S.E.2d 207 (1998).

ISSUANCE OF PLATE PRELIMINARILY ENJOINED. --State officials were preliminarily enjoined from issuing "Choose Life" license plates because plaintiffs, automobile owners who wanted to purchase a license plate expressing support for abortion rights, showed a likelihood of success on their claim that the State, by authorizing the "Choose Life" plate without offering an abortion rights alternative, engaged in impermissible viewpoint discrimination in violation of the First Amendment. ACLU of N.C. v. Conti, 835 F. Supp. 2d 51 (E.D.N.C. Dec. 8, 2011).

§ 20-79.5. Special registration plates for elected and appointed State government officials

(a) **Plates.** -- The State government officials listed in this section are eligible for a special registration plate under G.S. 20-79.4. The plate shall bear the number designated in the following table for the position held by the official.

Position	Number on Plate
Governor	1
Lieutenant Governor	2
Speaker of the House of Representatives	3
President Pro Tempore of the Senate	4
Secretary of State	5
State Auditor	6
State Treasurer	7
Superintendent of Public Instruction	8
Attorney General	9
Commissioner of Agriculture	10
Commissioner of Labor	11
Commissioner of Insurance	12
Speaker Pro Tempore of the House	13
Legislative Services Officer	14
Secretary of Administration	15
Secretary of Environmental Quality	16
Secretary of Revenue	17
Secretary of Health and Human Services	18
Secretary of Commerce	19
Secretary of Public Safety	20
Secretary of Natural and Cultural Resources	21
Secretary of Military and Veterans Affairs	22
Governor's Staff	23-29
State Budget Officer	30
Director of the Office of State Human Resources	31
Chair of the State Board of Education	32
President of the U.N.C. System	33
President of the Community Colleges System	34
State Board Member, Commission Member, or State Employee Not Named in List	35-43
Alcoholic Beverage Control Commission	44-46
Assistant Commissioners of Agriculture	47-48
Deputy Secretary of State	49
Deputy State Treasurer	50
Assistant State Treasurer	51
Deputy Commissioner for the Department of Labor	52
Chief Deputy for the Department of Insurance	53
Assistant Commissioner of Insurance	54
Deputies and Assistant to the Attorney General	55-65
Board of Economic Development Nonlegislative Member	66-88
State Ports Authority Nonlegislative Member	89-96
Utilities Commission Member	97-103
State Board Member, Commission Member, or State Employee Not Named in List	104
Post-Release Supervision and Parole Commission Member	105-107
State Board Member, Commission Member, or State Employee Not Named in List	108-200

(b) **Designation.** -- When the table in subsection (a) designates a range of numbers for certain officials, the number given an official in that group shall be assigned. The Governor shall assign a number for members of the Governor's staff, nonlegislative members of the Board of Economic Development, nonlegislative members of the State Ports Authority, members of State boards and commissions, and for State employees. The Attorney General shall assign a number for the Attorney General's deputies and assistants.

The first number assigned to the Alcoholic Beverage Control Commission is reserved for the Chair of that Commission. The remaining numbers shall be assigned to the Alcoholic Beverage Control Commission members on the basis of seniority. The first number assigned to the Utilities Commission is reserved for the Chair of that Commission. The remaining numbers shall be assigned to the Utilities Commission members on the basis of seniority. The first number assigned to the Post-Release Supervision and Parole Commission is reserved for the Chair of that Commission. The remaining numbers shall be assigned to the Post-Release Supervision and Parole Commission members on the basis of seniority.

History.
1991, c. 672, s. 2;c. 726, s. 23;1991 (Reg. Sess., 1992), c. 959, s. 1; 1996, 2nd Ex. Sess., c. 18, s. 8(a);1997-443, ss. 11A.118(a), 11A.119(a); 2000-137, s. 4.(e); 2006-203, s. 14;2007-483, s. 3(a);2011-145, s. 19.1(g), (i), (m); 2012-83, s. 4;2013-382, s. 9.1(c);2015-241, ss. 24.1(n), 14.30(t), (v); 2015-268, s. 7.3(a)

EDITOR'S NOTE. --
Session Laws 2013-382, s. 9.1(b), provides: "The following entities and positions created by Chapter 126 of the General Statutes are hereby renamed by this act:

"(1) The State Personnel Commission is renamed the 'North Carolina Human Resources Commission.'

"(2) The Office of State Personnel is renamed the 'North Carolina Office of State Human Resources.'

"(3) The State Personnel Director is renamed the 'Director of the North Carolina Office of State Human Resources.'"

Session Laws 2013-382, s. 9.1(c), provides: "Modification of References. -- The Revisor of Statutes shall delete any references in the General Statutes to the State Personnel Act, State Personnel Commission, the State Personnel Director, and the Office of State Personnel (or any derivatives thereof) and substitute references to the North Carolina Human Resources Act, the State Human Resources Commission, the Director of the Office of State Human Resources, and the Office of Human Resources (or the appropriate derivative thereof) to effectuate the renaming set forth in this section wherever conforming changes are necessary."

Session Laws 2013-382, s. 9.2, provides: "No action or proceeding pending on the effective date of this section, brought by or against the State Personnel Commission, the Director of the Office of State Personnel, or the Office of State Personnel, shall be affected by any provision of this section, but the same may be prosecuted or defended in the new name of the Commission, Director, and Office. In these actions and proceedings, the renamed Commission, Director, or Office shall be substituted as a party upon proper application to the courts or other public bodies." This Act became effective August 21, 2013.

Session Laws 2013-382, s. 9.3, provides: "Any business or other matter undertaken or commanded by the former State Personnel Commission, State Personnel Director, or Office of State Personnel regarding any State program, office, or contract or pertaining to or connected with their respective functions, powers, obligations, and duties that are pending on the date this act becomes effective may be conducted and completed by the Commission, Director, or Office in the same manner and under the same terms and conditions and with the same effect as if conducted and completed by the formerly named commission, director, or office." This Act became effective August 21, 2013.

Session Laws 2015-268, s. 7.3(a), made the amendment of this section by Session Laws 2015-241, s. 24.1(n), effective July 1, 2015.

EFFECT OF AMENDMENTS. --
Session Laws 2006-203, s. 14, effective July 1, 2007, deleted "Advisory Budget Commission Nonlegislative Member 32-41" from the list of government officials eligible for a special registration plate in subsection (a); and deleted "nonlegislative members of the Advisory Budget Commission" following "Governor's staff" in the first sentence of subsection (b).

Session Laws 2007-483, s. 3(a), effective January 1, 2008, in the table in subsection (a), inserted "President of the Community Colleges System" and "State Board Member, Commission Member, or State Employee Not Named in the List" the first and second times it appears in the "Position" column, and in the "Number on Plate" column, inserted "34," "35-43," and "104," and substituted "32" for "42," "33" for "43," "97-103" for "97-104," "105-107" for "105-109," and "108-200" for "110-200."

Session Laws 2011-145, s. 19.1(g), (i), and (m), effective January 1, 2012, in subsection (a), substituted the first occurrence of "Secretary of Public Safety" for "Secretary of Correction" (number 20), the second occurrence for "Secretary of Crime Control and Public Safety" (number 22), and the third occurrence for "Secretary of Juvenile Justice and Delinquency Prevention" (number 23).

Session Laws 2012-83, s. 4, effective June 26, 2012, in the table in subsection (a), deleted "Secretary of Public Safety 22" and "Secretary of Public Safety 23"; and in the "Number on Plate" column substituted "22-29" for "24-29".

Session Laws 2013-382, s. 9.1(c), effective August 21, 2013, in the table in subsection (a), substituted "Director of the Office of State Human Resources" for "State Personnel Director."

Session Laws 2015-241, s. 24.1(n), effective July 1, 2015, in the table in subsection (a), inserted the row that includes "Secretary of Military and Veterans Affairs" and "22" and substituted "23-29" for "22-29" in the second column for row beginning with "Governor's Staff."

Session Laws 2015-241, s. 14.30(t), effective July 1, 2015, in subsection (a), substituted "Secretary of Natural and Cultural Resources" for "Secretary of Cultural Resources" and "Secretary of Environmental Quality" for "Secretary of Environment and Natural Resources" in the table.

§ 20-79.6. Special registration plates for members of the judiciary

(a) **Supreme Court.** -- A special plate issued to a Justice of the North Carolina Supreme Court shall bear the words "Supreme Court" and the Great Seal of North Carolina and a number from 1 through 7. The Chief Justice of the Supreme Court of North Carolina shall be issued the plate bearing the number 1 and the remaining plates shall be issued to the Associate Justices on the basis of seniority.

Special plates issued to retired members of the Supreme Court shall bear a number indicating the member's position of seniority at the time of retirement followed by the letter "X" to indicate the member's retired status.

(a1) **Court of Appeals.** -- A special plate issued to a Judge of the North Carolina Court of Appeals shall bear the words "Court of Appeals" and the Great Seal of North Carolina and a number beginning with the number 1. The Chief Judge of the North Carolina Court of Appeals shall be issued a plate with the number 1 and the remaining plates shall be issued to the Associate Judges with the numbers assigned on the basis of seniority.

Special plates issued to retired members of the Court of Appeals shall bear a number indicating the member's position of seniority at the time of retirement followed by the letter "X" to indicate the member's retired status.

(b) **Superior Court.** -- A special plate issued to a resident superior court judge shall bear the letter "J" followed by a number indicative of the judicial district the judge serves. The number issued to the senior resident superior court judge shall be the numerical designation of the judge's judicial district, as defined in G.S. 7A-41.1(a)(1). If a district has more than one regular resident superior court judge, a special plate for a resident superior court judge of that district shall bear the number issued to the senior resident superior court judge followed by a hyphen and a letter of the alphabet beginning with the letter "A" to indicate the judge's seniority.

For any grouping of districts having the same numerical designation, other than districts where there are two or more resident superior court judges, the number issued to the senior resident superior court judge shall be the number the districts in the set have in common. A special plate issued to the other regular resident superior court judges of the set of districts shall bear the number issued to the senior resident superior court judge followed by a hyphen and a letter of the alphabet beginning with the letter "A" to indicate the judge's seniority among all of the regular resident superior court judges of the set of districts. The letter assigned to a resident superior court judge will not necessarily correspond with the letter designation of the district the judge serves.

Where there are two or more regular resident superior court judges for the district or set of districts, the registration plate with the letter "A" shall be issued to the judge who, from among all the regular resident superior court judges of the district or set of districts, has the most continuous service as a regular resident superior court judge; provided if two or more judges are of equal service, the oldest of those judges shall receive the next letter registration plate. Thereafter, registration plates shall be issued based on seniority within the district or set of districts.

A special judge, emergency judge, or retired judge of the superior court shall be issued a special plate bearing the letter "J" followed by a number designated by the Administrative Office of the Courts with the approval of the Chief Justice of the Supreme Court of North Carolina. The plate for a retired judge shall have the letter "X" after the designated number to indicate the judge's retired status.

(c) **District Court.** -- A special plate issued to a North Carolina district court judge shall bear the letter "J" followed by a number. For the chief judge of the district court district, the number shall be equal to the sum of the numerical designation of the district court district the chief judge serves, plus 100. The number for all other judges of the district courts serving within the same district court district shall be the same number as appears on the special plate issued to the chief district judge followed by a letter of the alphabet beginning with the letter "A" to indicate the judge's seniority. A retired district court judge shall be issued a similar plate except that the numerical designation shall be followed by the letter "X" to indicate the judge's retired status.

(d) **United States.** -- A special plate issued to a Justice of the United States Supreme Court, a Judge of the United States Circuit Court of Appeals, or a District Judge of the United States District Court residing in North Carolina shall bear the words "U.S. J" followed by a number beginning with "1". The number shall reflect the judge's seniority based on continuous service as a United States Judge as designated by the Secretary of State. A judge who has retired or taken senior status shall be issued a similar plate except that the number shall be based on the date of the judge's retirement or assumption of senior status and shall follow the numerical designation of active justices and judges.

History.
1991, c. 672, s. 2;c. 726, s. 23;1999-403, s. 5;1999-456, s. 67.1

§ 20-79.7. Fees for special registration plates and distribution of the fees

(a) **Free of Charge.** -- Upon request, and except for the special registration plate listed in subdivision (2) of this subsection, the Division shall annually provide and issue free of charge a single special registration plate listed in this subsection to a person qualified to receive the plate in accordance with G.S. 20-79.4(a2). For the special registration plate listed in subdivision (2) of this subsection, and upon request, the Division shall annually provide and issue free of charge a single registration plate for both a motor vehicle and a motorcycle to a person qualified to receive each plate in accordance with G.S. 20-79.4(a2). This subsection does not apply to a special registration plate issued for a vehicle that has a registered weight greater than 6,000 pounds. The regular motor vehicle registration fees in G.S. 20-88 apply if the registered weight of the vehicle is greater than 6,000 pounds:

(1) A Legion of Valor registration plate to a recipient of the Legion of Valor award.

(2) A 100% Disabled Veteran registration plate to a 100% disabled veteran.

(3) An Ex-Prisoner of War registration plate to an ex-prisoner of war.

(4) A Bronze Star Valor registration plate to a recipient of the Bronze Star Medal for valor in combat award.

(5) A Silver Star registration plate to a recipient of the Silver Star award.

(a1) **(Effective until March 1, 2020) Fees.** -- All other special registration plates are subject to the regular motor vehicle registration fee in G.S. 20-87 or G.S. 20-88 plus an additional fee in the following amount:

Special Plate	Additional Fee Amount
Alpha Phi Alpha Fraternity	$ 30.00
American Red Cross	Expired July 1, 2016
Animal Lovers	$ 30.00
Arthritis Foundation	Expired July 1, 2016
ARTS NC	$ 30.00
Back Country Horsemen of NC	Expired July 1, 2016
Big Rock Blue Marlin Tournament	$ 30.00
Boy Scouts of America	Expired July 1, 2016
Brenner Children's Hospital	Expired July 1, 2016
Carolina Panthers	$ 30.00
Carolina Raptor Center	Expired July 1, 2016
Carolinas Credit Union Foundation	Expired July 1, 2016
Carolinas Golf Association	$ 30.00
Coastal Conservation Association	Expired July 1, 2016
Coastal Land Trust	$ 30.00
Colorectal Cancer Awareness	$ 30.00
Crystal Coast	Expired July 1, 2016
Daniel Stowe Botanical Garden	Expired July 1, 2016
El Pueblo	Expired July 1, 2016
Farmland Preservation	Expired July 1, 2016
First in Forestry	$ 30.00
First Tee	Expired July 1, 2016
Girl Scouts	Expired July 1, 2016
Greensboro Symphony Guild	Expired July 1, 2016
Historical Attraction	$ 30.00
Home Care and Hospice	$ 30.00
Home of American Golf	Expired July 1, 2016
HOMES4NC	$ 30.00
Hospice Care	Expired July 1, 2016
In God We Trust	$ 30.00
Kick Cancer for Kids	$ 30.00
Maggie Valley Trout Festival	Expired July 1, 2016
Morehead Planetarium	Expired July 1, 2016
Morgan Horse Club	Expired July 1, 2016
Mountains-to-Sea Trail	$ 30.00
Municipality Plate	Expired July 1, 2016
NC Civil War	Expired July 1, 2016
NC Coastal Federation	$ 30.00
NC FIRST Robotics	Expired July 1, 2016
NCSC	Expired July 1, 2016

NC Veterinary Medical Association	Expired July 1, 2016
National Kidney Foundation	Expired July 1, 2016
National Law Enforcement Officers Memorial	Expired July 1, 2016
Native Brook Trout	$ 30.00
North Carolina 4-H Development Fund	Expired July 1, 2016
North Carolina Bluegrass Association	Expired July 1, 2016
North Carolina Cattlemen's Association	Expired July 1, 2016
North Carolina Emergency Management Association	Expired July 1, 2016
North Carolina Green Industry Council	Expired July 1, 2016
North Carolina Libraries	Expired July 1, 2016
North Carolina Paddle Festival	Expired July 1, 2016
North Carolina Sheriffs' Association	$ 30.00
Operation Coming Home	Expired July 1, 2016
Outer Banks Preservation Association	Expired July 1, 2016
Pamlico-Tar River Foundation	Expired July 1, 2016
Pancreatic Cancer Awareness	Expired July 1, 2016
P.E.O. Sisterhood	Expired July 1, 2016
Personalized	$ 30.00
Pisgah Conservancy	$ 30.00
Red Drum	Expired July 1, 2016
Retired Legislator	$ 30.00
RiverLink	Expired July 1, 2016
Ronald McDonald House	$ 30.00
Share the Road	$ 30.00
S.T.A.R.	Expired July 1, 2016
State Attraction	$ 30.00
Stock Car Racing Theme	$ 30.00
Support NC Education	Expired July 1, 2016
Support Our Troops	$ 30.00
Sustainable Fisheries	Expired July 1, 2016
Toastmasters Club	Expired July 1, 2016
Topsail Island Shoreline Protection	Expired July 1, 2016
Travel and Tourism	Expired July 1, 2016
Turtle Rescue Team	Expired July 1, 2016
United States Service Academy	$ 30.00
Wildlife Resources	$ 30.00
Volunteers in Law Enforcement	Expired July 1, 2016
YMCA	Expired July 1, 2016
AIDS Awareness	Expired July 1, 2016
Buffalo Soldiers	Expired July 1, 2016
Charlotte Checkers	Expired July 1, 2016
Choose Life	$ 25.00
Collegiate Insignia	$ 25.00
First in Turf	Expired July 1, 2016
Goodness Grows	Expired July 1, 2016
High School Insignia	$ 25.00
I.B.P.O.E.W.	Expired July 1, 2016
Kids First	$ 25.00
National Multiple Sclerosis Society	$ 25.00
National Wild Turkey Federation	$ 25.00
NC Agribusiness	Expired July 1, 2016
NC Children's Promise	Expired July 1, 2016
NC Surveyors	$ 25.00
Nurses	$ 25.00
Olympic Games	$ 25.00
Professional Engineer	Expired July 1, 2016
Rocky Mountain Elk Foundation	$ 25.00
Special Olympics	Expired July 1, 2016
Support Soccer	$ 25.00
Surveyor Plate	$ 25.00
The V Foundation for Cancer Research Division	$ 25.00
University Health Systems of Eastern Carolina	Expired July 1, 2016

ALS Association, Jim "Catfish " Hunter Chapter	Expired July 1, 2016
ARC of North Carolina	Expired July 1, 2016
Audubon North Carolina	Expired July 1, 2016
Autism Society of North Carolina	$ 20.00
Battle of Kings Mountain	$ 20.00
Be Active NC	Expired July 1, 2016
Brain Injury Awareness	Expired July 1, 2016
Breast Cancer Earlier Detection	Expired July 1, 2016
Buddy Pelletier Surfing Foundation	$ 20.00
Concerned Bikers Association/ABATE of North Carolina	Expired July 1, 2016
Daughters of the American Revolution	Expired July 1, 2016
Donate Life	$ 20.00
Ducks Unlimited	$ 20.00
Fraternal Order of Police	$ 20.00
Greyhound Friends of North Carolina	Expired July 1, 2016
Guilford Battleground Company	$ 20.00
Harley Owners' Group	$ 20.00
International Association of Fire Fighters	$ 20.00
I Support Teachers	Expired July 1, 2016
Jaycees	Expired July 1, 2016
Juvenile Diabetes Research Foundation	$ 20.00
Kappa Alpha Order	Expired July 1, 2016
Litter Prevention	$ 20.00
March of Dimes	Expired July 1, 2016
Mission Foundation	Expired July 1, 2016
Native American	$ 20.00
NC Fisheries Association	Expired July 1, 2016
NC Horse Council	$ 20.00
NC Mining	Expired July 1, 2016
NC Tennis Foundation	$ 20.00
NC Trout Unlimited	$ 20.00
NC Victim Assistance	Expired July 1, 2016
NC Wildlife Federation	Expired July 1, 2016
NC Wildlife Habitat Foundation	$ 20.00
NC Youth Soccer Association	Expired July 1, 2016
North Carolina Master Gardener	$ 20.00
Omega Psi Phi Fraternity	$ 20.00
Order of the Eastern Star Prince Hall Affiliated	$ 20.00
Order of the Long Leaf Pine	$ 20.00
Piedmont Airlines	$ 20.00
Prince Hall Mason	$ 20.00
Save the Sea Turtles	$ 20.00
Scenic Rivers	Expired July 1, 2016
School Technology	Expired July 1, 2016
SCUBA	$ 20.00
Soil and Water Conservation	Expired July 1, 2016
Special Forces Association	Expired July 1, 2016
US Equine Rescue League	Expired July 1, 2016
USO of NC	Expired July 1, 2016
Zeta Phi Beta Sorority	$ 20.00
Carolina Regional Volleyball Association	Expired July 1, 2016
Carolina's Aviation Museum	Expired July 1, 2016
Leukemia & Lymphoma Society	Expired July 1, 2016
Lung Cancer Research	Expired July 1, 2016
NC Beekeepers	Expired July 1, 2016
Save the Honey Bee (HB)	$ 15.00
Save the Honey Bee (SB)	$ 15.00
Shag Dancing	$ 15.00
Active Member of the National Guard	None
Bronze Star Combat Recipient	None
Bronze Star Recipient	None
Combat Veteran	Expired July 1, 2016

100% Disabled Veteran	None
Eastern Band of Cherokee Indians	None
Ex-Prisoner of War	None
Gold Star Lapel Button	None
Legion of Merit	None
Legion of Valor	None
Military Veteran	None
Military Wartime Veteran	None
Partially Disabled Veteran	None
Pearl Harbor Survivor	None
Purple Heart Recipient	None
Silver Star Recipient	None
All Other Special Plates	$ 10.00.

(a1) **(Effective March 1, 2020) Fees.** -- All other special registration plates are subject to the regular motor vehicle registration fee in G.S. 20-87 or G.S. 20-88 plus an additional fee in the following amount:

Special Plate	Additional Fee Amount
Alpha Phi Alpha Fraternity	$ 30.00
ALS Research	$ 30.00
American Red Cross	Expired July 1, 2016
Animal Lovers	$ 30.00
Arthritis Foundation	Expired July 1, 2016
ARTS NC	$ 30.00
Back Country Horsemen of NC	Expired July 1, 2016
Big Rock Blue Marlin Tournament	$ 30.00
Boy Scouts of America	Expired July 1, 2016
Brenner Children's Hospital	Expired July 1, 2016
Carolina Panthers	$ 30.00
Carolina Raptor Center	Expired July 1, 2016
Carolinas Credit Union Foundation	Expired July 1, 2016
Carolinas Golf Association	$ 30.00
Coastal Conservation Association	Expired July 1, 2016
Coastal Land Trust	$ 30.00
Colorectal Cancer Awareness	$ 30.00
Crystal Coast	Expired July 1, 2016
Daniel Stowe Botanical Garden	Expired July 1, 2016
El Pueblo	Expired July 1, 2016
Farmland Preservation	Expired July 1, 2016
First in Forestry	$ 30.00
First Tee	Expired July 1, 2016
Girl Scouts	Expired July 1, 2016
Greensboro Symphony Guild	Expired July 1, 2016
Historical Attraction	$ 30.00
Home Care and Hospice	$ 30.00
Home of American Golf	Expired July 1, 2016
HOMES4NC	$ 30.00
Hospice Care	Expired July 1, 2016
In God We Trust	$ 30.00
Keeping the Lights On	$ 30.00
Kick Cancer for Kids	$ 30.00
Maggie Valley Trout Festival	Expired July 1, 2016
Morehead Planetarium	Expired July 1, 2016
Morgan Horse Club	Expired July 1, 2016
Mountains-to-Sea Trail	$ 30.00
Municipality Plate	Expired July 1, 2016
NC Civil War	Expired July 1, 2016
NC Coastal Federation	$ 30.00
NC FIRST Robotics	Expired July 1, 2016
NCSC	Expired July 1, 2016
NC Veterinary Medical Association	Expired July 1, 2016

Chapter 20

National Kidney Foundation	Expired July 1, 2016
National Law Enforcement Officers Memorial	Expired July 1, 2016
Native Brook Trout	$ 30.00
North Carolina 4-H Development Fund	Expired July 1, 2016
North Carolina Bluegrass Association	Expired July 1, 2016
North Carolina Cattlemen's Association	Expired July 1, 2016
North Carolina Emergency Management Association	Expired July 1, 2016
North Carolina Green Industry Council	Expired July 1, 2016
North Carolina Libraries	Expired July 1, 2016
North Carolina Paddle Festival	Expired July 1, 2016
North Carolina Sheriffs' Association	$ 30.00
Operation Coming Home	Expired July 1, 2016
Outer Banks Preservation Association	Expired July 1, 2016
Pamlico-Tar River Foundation	Expired July 1, 2016
Pancreatic Cancer Awareness	Expired July 1, 2016
P.E.O. Sisterhood	Expired July 1, 2016
Personalized	$ 30.00
Pisgah Conservancy	$ 30.00
Red Drum	Expired July 1, 2016
Retired Legislator	$ 30.00
RiverLink	Expired July 1, 2016
Ronald McDonald House	$ 30.00
Share the Road	$ 30.00
S.T.A.R.	Expired July 1, 2016
State Attraction	$ 30.00
Stock Car Racing Theme	$ 30.00
Support NC Education	Expired July 1, 2016
Support Our Troops	$ 30.00
Sustainable Fisheries	Expired July 1, 2016
Toastmasters Club	Expired July 1, 2016
Topsail Island Shoreline Protection	Expired July 1, 2016
Travel and Tourism	Expired July 1, 2016
Turtle Rescue Team	Expired July 1, 2016
United States Service Academy	$ 30.00
Wildlife Resources	$ 30.00
Volunteers in Law Enforcement	Expired July 1, 2016
YMCA	Expired July 1, 2016
AIDS Awareness	Expired July 1, 2016
Buffalo Soldiers	Expired July 1, 2016
Charlotte Checkers	Expired July 1, 2016
Choose Life	$ 25.00
Collegiate Insignia	$ 25.00
First in Turf	Expired July 1, 2016
Goodness Grows	Expired July 1, 2016
High School Insignia	$ 25.00
I.B.P.O.E.W.	Expired July 1, 2016
Kids First	$ 25.00
National Multiple Sclerosis Society	$ 25.00
National Wild Turkey Federation	$ 25.00
NC Agribusiness	Expired July 1, 2016
NC Children's Promise	Expired July 1, 2016
NC Surveyors	$ 25.00
Nurses	$ 25.00
Olympic Games	$ 25.00
Professional Engineer	Expired July 1, 2016
Rocky Mountain Elk Foundation	$ 25.00
Special Olympics	Expired July 1, 2016
Support Soccer	$ 25.00
Surveyor Plate	$ 25.00
The V Foundation for Cancer Research Division	$ 25.00
University Health Systems of Eastern Carolina	Expired July 1, 2016
ALS Association, Jim "Catfish " Hunter Chapter	Expired July 1, 2016

Chapter 20

ARC of North Carolina	Expired July 1, 2016
Audubon North Carolina	Expired July 1, 2016
Autism Society of North Carolina	$ 20.00
Battle of Kings Mountain	$ 20.00
Be Active NC	Expired July 1, 2016
Brain Injury Awareness	Expired July 1, 2016
Breast Cancer Earlier Detection	Expired July 1, 2016
Buddy Pelletier Surfing Foundation	$ 20.00
Concerned Bikers Association/ABATE of North Carolina	Expired July 1, 2016
Daughters of the American Revolution	Expired July 1, 2016
Donate Life	$ 20.00
Ducks Unlimited	$ 20.00
Fraternal Order of Police	$ 20.00
Greyhound Friends of North Carolina	Expired July 1, 2016
Guilford Battleground Company	$ 20.00
Harley Owners' Group	$ 20.00
International Association of Fire Fighters	$ 20.00
I Support Teachers	Expired July 1, 2016
Jaycees	Expired July 1, 2016
Juvenile Diabetes Research Foundation	$ 20.00
Kappa Alpha Order	Expired July 1, 2016
Litter Prevention	$ 20.00
March of Dimes	Expired July 1, 2016
Mission Foundation	Expired July 1, 2016
Native American	$ 20.00
NC Fisheries Association	Expired July 1, 2016
NC Horse Council	$ 20.00
NC Mining	Expired July 1, 2016
NC Tennis Foundation	$ 20.00
NC Trout Unlimited	$ 20.00
NC Victim Assistance	Expired July 1, 2016
NC Wildlife Federation	Expired July 1, 2016
NC Wildlife Habitat Foundation	$ 20.00
NC Youth Soccer Association	Expired July 1, 2016
North Carolina Master Gardener	$ 20.00
Omega Psi Phi Fraternity	$ 20.00
Order of the Eastern Star Prince Hall Affiliated	$ 20.00
Order of the Long Leaf Pine	$ 20.00
Piedmont Airlines	$ 20.00
POW/MIA Bring Them Home	$ 20.00
Prince Hall Mason	$ 20.00
Save the Sea Turtles	$ 20.00
Scenic Rivers	Expired July 1, 2016
School Technology	Expired July 1, 2016
SCUBA	$ 20.00
Soil and Water Conservation	Expired July 1, 2016
Special Forces Association	Expired July 1, 2016
US Equine Rescue League	Expired July 1, 2016
USO of NC	Expired July 1, 2016
Wrightsville Beach	$ 20.00
Zeta Phi Beta Sorority	$ 20.00
Carolina Regional Volleyball Association	Expired July 1, 2016
Carolina's Aviation Museum	Expired July 1, 2016
Leukemia & Lymphoma Society	Expired July 1, 2016
Lung Cancer Research	Expired July 1, 2016
NC Beekeepers	Expired July 1, 2016
Save the Honey Bee (HB)	$ 15.00
Save the Honey Bee (SB)	$ 15.00
Shag Dancing	$ 15.00
Active Member of the National Guard	None
Bronze Star Combat Recipient	None

Bronze Star Recipient	None
Combat Veteran	Expired July 1, 2016
100% Disabled Veteran	None
Eastern Band of Cherokee Indians	None
Ex-Prisoner of War	None
Gold Star Lapel Button	None
Legion of Merit	None
Legion of Valor	None
Military Veteran	None
Military Wartime Veteran	None
Partially Disabled Veteran	None
Pearl Harbor Survivor	None
Purple Heart Recipient	None
Silver Star Recipient	None
All Other Special Plates	$ 10.00.

(b) **(Effective until March 1, 2020) Distribution of Fees.** -- The Special Registration Plate Account and the Collegiate and Cultural Attraction Plate Account are established within the Highway Fund. The Division must credit the additional fee imposed for the special registration plates listed in subsection (a) of this section among the Special Registration Plate Account (SRPA), the Collegiate and Cultural Attraction Plate Account (CCAPA), the Clean Water Management Trust Fund (CWMTF), which is established under G.S. 143B-135.234, and the Parks and Recreation Trust Fund, which is established under G.S. 143B-135.56 as follows:

Special Plate	SRPA	CCAPA	NHTF	PRTF
AIDS Awareness -- Expired July 1, 2016				
Alpha Phi Alpha Fraternity	$ 10	$ 20	0	0
ALS Association, Jim "Catfish" Hunter Chapter -- Expired July 1, 2016				
American Red Cross -- Expired July 1, 2016				
Animal Lovers	$ 10	$ 20	0	0
ARC of North Carolina -- Expired July 1, 2016				
Arthritis Foundation -- Expired July 1, 2016				
ARTS NC	$ 10	$ 20	0	0
Audubon North Carolina -- Expired July 1, 2016				
Autism Society of North Carolina	$ 10	$ 10	0	0
Back Country Horsemen of NC -- Expired July 1, 2016				
Battle of Kings Mountain	$ 10	$ 10	0	0
Be Active NC -- Expired July 1, 2016				
Big Rock Blue Marlin Tournament	$ 10	$ 20	0	0
Boy Scouts of America -- Expired July 1, 2016				
Brain Injury Awareness -- Expired July 1, 2016				
Breast Cancer Earlier Detection -- Expired July 1, 2016				
Brenner Children's Hospital -- Expired July 1, 2016				
Buddy Pelletier Surfing Foundation	$ 10	$ 10	0	0
Buffalo Soldiers -- Expired July 1, 2016				
Carolina Panthers	$ 10	$ 20	0	0
Carolina Raptor Center -- Expired July 1, 2016				
Carolina Regional Volleyball Association -- Expired July 1, 2016				
Carolina's Aviation Museum -- Expired July 1, 2016				
Carolinas Credit Union Foundation -- Expired July 1, 2016				
Carolinas Golf Association	$ 10	$ 20	0	0
Charlotte Checkers -- Expired July 1, 2016				
Choose Life	$ 10	$ 15	0	0
Coastal Conservation Association -- Expired July 1, 2016				
Coastal Land Trust	$ 10	$ 20	0	0
Colorectal Cancer Awareness	$ 10	$ 20	0	0
Concerned Bikers Association / ABATE of North Carolina -- Expired July 1, 2016				
Crystal Coast -- Expired July 1, 2016				

Chapter 20

Daniel Stowe Botanical Gardens --
Expired July 1, 2016
Daughters of the American Revolution -- Expired July 1, 2016

	SRPA	CCAPA	NHTF	PRTF
Donate Life	$ 10	$ 10	0	0
Ducks Unlimited	$ 10	$ 10	0	0

El Pueblo -- Expired July 1, 2016
Farmland Preservation -- Expired July 1, 2016

First in Forestry	$ 10	$ 10	$ 10	0

First in Turf -- Expired July 1, 2016
First Tee -- Expired July 1, 2016

Fraternal Order of Police	$ 10	$ 10	0	0

Girl Scouts -- Expired July 1, 2016
Goodness Grows -- Expired July 1, 2016
Greensboro Symphony Guild -- Expired July 1, 2016
Greyhound Friends of North Carolina -- Expired July 1, 2016

Guilford Battleground Company	$ 10	$ 10	0	0
Harley Owners' Group	$ 10	$ 10	0	0
High School Insignia	$ 10	$ 15	0	0
Historical Attraction	$ 10	$ 20	0	0
Home Care and Hospice	$ 10	$ 20	0	0

Home of American Golf -- Expired July 1, 2016

HOMES4NC	$ 10	$ 20	0	0

Hospice Care -- Expired July 1, 2016
I.B.P.O.E.W. -- Expired July 1, 2016

Special Plate	SRPA	CCAPA	NHTF	PRTF
In God We Trust	$ 10	$ 20	0	0
In-State Collegiate Insignia	$ 10	$ 15	0	0
International Association of Fire Fighters	$ 10	$ 10	0	0

I Support Teachers -- Expired July 1,
2016 Jaycees -- Expired July 1, 2016

Juvenile Diabetes Research Foundation	$ 10	$ 10	0	0

Kappa Alpha Order -- Expired July 1, 2016

Kick Cancer for Kids	$ 10	$ 20	0	0
Kids First	$ 10	$ 15	0	0

Leukemia & Lymphoma Society -- Expired July 1, 2016

Litter Prevention	$ 10	$ 10	0	0

Lung Cancer Research -- Expired July 1, 2016
Maggie Valley Trout Festival -- Expired July 1, 2016
March of Dimes -- Expired July 1, 2016
Mission Foundation -- Expired July 1,
2016 Morgan Horse Club -- Expired July 1,
2016 Morehead Planetarium -- Expired July 1, 2016

Mountains-to-Sea Trail	$ 10	$ 20	0	0

Municipality Plate -- Expired July 1,
2016 National Kidney Foundation -- Expired July 1, 2016
National Law Enforcement Officers
Memorial -- Expired July 1, 2016

National Multiple Sclerosis Society	$ 10	$ 15	0	0
National Wild Turkey Federation	$ 10	$ 15	0	0
Native American	$ 10	$ 10	0	0

NC Agribusiness -- Expired July 1, 2016
NC Beekeepers -- Expired July 1, 2016
NC Children's Promise -- Expired July 1, 2016
NC Civil War -- Expired July 1, 2016

NC Coastal Federation	$ 10	$ 20	0	0

NC 4-H Development Fund -- Expired July 1, 2016
NC FIRST Robotics -- Expired July 1, 2016
NC Fisheries Association -- Expired July 1, 2016

NC Horse Council	$ 10	$ 10	0	0

NC Mining -- Expired July 1, 2016
NCSC -- Expired July 1, 2016

NC Surveyors	$ 10	$ 15	0	0

NC Tennis Foundation	$ 10	$ 10	0	0
NC Trout Unlimited	$ 10	$ 10	0	0
NC Veterinary Medical Association -- Expired July 1, 2016				
NC Victim Assistance -- Expired July 1, 2016				
NC Wildlife Federation -- Expired July 1, 2016				
NC Wildlife Habitat Foundation	$ 10	$ 10	0	0
NC Youth Soccer Association -- Expired July 1, 2016				
North Carolina Bluegrass Association -- Expired July 1, 2016				
North Carolina Cattlemen's Association -- Expired July 1, 2016				
North Carolina Emergency Management Association -- Expired July 1, 2016				
North Carolina Green Industry Council -- Expired July 1, 2016				
North Carolina Libraries -- Expired July 1, 2016				
North Carolina Master Gardener	$ 10	$ 10	0	0
North Carolina Paddle Festival -- Expired July 1, 2016				
North Carolina Sheriffs' Association	$ 10	$ 20	0	0
Nurses	$ 10	$ 15	0	0
Olympic Games	$ 10	$ 15	0	0
Omega Psi Phi Fraternity	*$ 10*	*$ 10*	*0*	*0*
Operation Coming Home -- Expired July 1, 2016				
Order of the Eastern Star Prince Hall Affiliated	*$ 10*	*$ 10*	*0*	*0*
Order of the Long Leaf Pine	*$ 10*	*$ 10*	*0*	*0*
Out-of-state Collegiate Insignia	*$ 10*	*0*	*$ 15*	*0*
Special Plate	*SRPA*	*CCAPA*	*NHTF*	*PRTF*
Outer Banks Preservation Association -- Expired July 1, 2016				
Pamlico-Tar River Foundation -- Expired July 1, 2016				
Pancreatic Cancer Awareness -- Expired July 1, 2016				
P.E.O. Sisterhood -- Expired July 1, 2016				
Personalized	*$ 10*	*0*	*$ 15*	*$ 5*
Piedmont Airlines	*$ 10*	*$ 10*	*0*	*0*
Pisgah Conservancy	*$ 10*	*$ 20*	*0*	*0*
Prince Hall Mason	*$ 10*	*$ 10*	*0*	*0*
Professional Engineer -- Expired July 1, 2016				
Retired Legislator	*$ 10*	*$ 20*	*0*	*0*
RiverLink -- Expired July 1, 2016				
Rocky Mountain Elk Foundation	*$ 10*	*$ 15*	*0*	*0*
Ronald McDonald House	$ 10	$ 20	0	0
Save the Honey Bee (HB)	$ 10	$ 5	0	0
Save the Honey Bee (SB)	$ 10	$ 5	0	0
Save the Sea Turtles	$ 10	$ 10	0	0
Scenic Rivers -- Expired July 1, 2016				
School Technology -- Expired July 1, 2016 SCUBA	$ 10	$ 10	0	0
Shag Dancing	$ 10	$ 5	0	0
Share the Road	$ 10	$ 20	0	0
Sneads Ferry Shrimp Festival -- Expired July 1, 2016				
Soil and Water Conservation -- Expired July 1, 2016				
Special Forces Association -- Expired July 1, 2016				
Special Olympics -- Expired July 1, 2016 S.T.A.R. -- Expired July 1, 2016				
State Attraction	$ 10	$ 20	0	0
Stock Car Racing Theme	$ 10	$ 20	0	0
Support NC Education -- Expired July 1, 2016				
Support Our Troops	$ 10	$ 20	0	0
Support Soccer	$ 10	$ 15	0	0
Surveyor Plate	$ 10	$ 15	0	0
Sustainable Fisheries -- Expired July 1, 2016				
The V Foundation for Cancer Research	$ 10	$ 15	0	0
Toastmasters Club -- Expired July 1, 2016				
Topsail Island Shoreline Protection -- Expired July 1, 2016				
Travel and Tourism -- Expired July 1, 2016				

Turtle Rescue Team -- Expired July 1, 2016
University Health Systems of Eastern Carolina --
　　Expired July 1, 2016

United States Service Academy	$ 10	$ 20	0	0

US Equine Rescue League -- Expired July 1, 2016
USO of NC -- Expired July 1, 2016
Volunteers in Law Enforcement -- Expired July 1, 2016

Wildlife Resources	$ 10	$ 20	0	0

YMCA -- Expired July 1, 2016

Zeta Phi Beta Sorority	$ 10	$ 10	0	0
All other Special Plates	$ 10	0	0	0.

(b) **(Effective March 1, 2020) Distribution of Fees. --** The Special Registration Plate Account and the Collegiate and Cultural Attraction Plate Account are established within the Highway Fund. The Division must credit the additional fee imposed for the special registration plates listed in subsection (a1) of this section among the Special Registration Plate Account (SRPA), the Collegiate and Cultural Attraction Plate Account (CCAPA), the Clean Water Management Trust Fund (CWMTF), which is established under G.S. 143B-135.234, and the Parks and Recreation Trust Fund, which is established under G.S. 143B-135.56, as follows:

Special Plate	SRPA	CCAPA	NHTF	PRTF
AIDS Awareness -- Expired July 1, 2016				
Alpha Phi Alpha Fraternity	$ 10	$ 20	0	0
ALS Association, Jim "Catfish " Hunter Chapter -- Expired July 1, 2016				
ALS Research	$ 10	$ 20	0	0
American Red Cross -- Expired July 1, 2016				
Animal Lovers	$ 10	$ 20	0	0
ARC of North Carolina -- Expired July 1, 2016				
Arthritis Foundation -- Expired July 1, 2016				
ARTS NC	$ 10	$ 20	0	0
Audubon North Carolina -- Expired July 1, 2016				
Autism Society of North Carolina	$ 10	$ 10	0	0
Back Country Horsemen of NC -- Expired July 1, 2016				
Battle of Kings Mountain	$ 10	$ 10	0	0
Be Active NC -- Expired July 1, 2016				
Big Rock Blue Marlin Tournament	$ 10	$ 20	0	0
Boy Scouts of America -- Expired July 1, 2016				
Brain Injury Awareness -- Expired July 1, 2016				
Breast Cancer Earlier Detection -- Expired July 1, 2016				
Brenner Children's Hospital -- Expired July 1, 2016				
Buddy Pelletier Surfing Foundation	$ 10	$ 10	0	0
Buffalo Soldiers -- Expired July 1, 2016				
Carolina Panthers	$ 10	$ 20	0	0
Carolina Raptor Center -- Expired July 1, 2016				
Carolina Regional Volleyball Association -- Expired July 1, 2016				
Carolina's Aviation Museum -- Expired July 1, 2016				
Carolinas Credit Union Foundation -- Expired July 1, 2016				
Carolinas Golf Association	$ 10	$ 20	0	0
Charlotte Checkers -- Expired July 1,2016				
Choose Life	$ 10	$ 15	0	0
Coastal Conservation Association -- Expired July 1, 2016				
Coastal Land Trust	$ 10	$ 20	0	0
Colorectal Cancer Awareness	$ 10	$ 20	0	0
Concerned Bikers Association/ABATE of North Carolina -- Expired July 1, 2016				
Crystal Coast -- Expired July 1, 2016				
Daniel Stowe Botanical Gardens -- Expired July 1, 2016				
Daughters of the American Revolution -- Expired July 1, 2016				
Donate Life	$ 10	$ 10	0	0

	SRPA	CCAPA	NHTF	PRTF
Ducks Unlimited	$ 10	$ 10	0	0
El Pueblo -- Expired July 1, 2016				
Farmland Preservation -- Expired July 1, 2016				
First in Forestry	$ 10	$ 10	$ 10	0
First in Turf -- Expired July 1, 2016				
First Tee -- Expired July 1, 2016				
Fraternal Order of Police	$ 10	$ 10	0	0
Girl Scouts -- Expired July 1, 2016				
Goodness Grows -- Expired July 1, 2016				
Greensboro Symphony Guild -- Expired July 1, 2016				
Greyhound Friends of North Carolina -- Expired July 1, 2016				
Guilford Battleground Company	$ 10	$ 10	0	0
Harley Owners' Group	$ 10	$ 10	0	0
High School Insignia	$ 10	$ 15	0	0
Historical Attraction	$ 10	$ 20	0	0
Home Care and Hospice	$ 10	$ 20	0	0
Home of American Golf -- Expired July 1, 2016				
HOMES4NC	$ 10	$ 20	0	0
Hospice Care -- Expired July 1, 2016				
I.B.P.O.E.W. -- Expired July 1, 2016				

Special Plate	SRPA	CCAPA	NHTF	PRTF
In God We Trust	$ 10	$ 20	0	0
In-State Collegiate Insignia	$ 10	$ 15	0	0
International Association of Fire Fighters	$ 10	$ 10	0	0
I Support Teachers -- Expired July 1, 2016				
Jaycees -- Expired July 1, 2016				
Juvenile Diabetes Research Foundation	$ 10	$ 10	0	0
Kappa Alpha Order -- Expired July 1, 2016				
Keeping The Lights On	$ 10	$ 20	0	0
Kick Cancer for Kids	$ 10	$ 20	0	0
Kids First	$ 10	$ 15	0	0
Leukemia & Lymphoma Society -- Expired July 1, 2016				
Litter Prevention	$ 10	$ 10	0	0
Lung Cancer Research -- Expired July 1, 2016				
Maggie Valley Trout Festival -- Expired July 1, 2016				
March of Dimes -- Expired July 1, 2016				
Mission Foundation -- Expired July 1,				
2016 Morgan Horse Club -- Expired July 1,				
2016 Morehead Planetarium -- Expired July 1, 2016				
Mountains-to-Sea Trail	$ 10	$ 20	0	0
Municipality Plate -- Expired July 1, 2016				
National Kidney Foundation -- Expired July 1, 2016				
National Law Enforcement Officers Memorial -- Expired July 1, 2016				
National Multiple Sclerosis Society	$ 10	$ 15	0	0
National Wild Turkey Federation	$ 10	$ 15	0	0
Native American	$ 10	$ 10	0	0
NC Agribusiness -- Expired July 1, 2016				
NC Beekeepers -- Expired July 1, 2016				
NC Children's Promise -- Expired July 1, 2016				
NC Civil War -- Expired July 1, 2016				
NC Coastal Federation	$ 10	$ 20	0	0
NC 4-H Development Fund -- Expired July 1, 2016				
NC FIRST Robotics -- Expired July 1, 2016				
NC Fisheries Association -- Expired July 1, 2016				
NC Horse Council	$ 10	$ 10	0	0
NC Mining -- Expired July 1, 2016				
NCSC -- Expired July 1, 2016				
NC Surveyors	$ 10	$ 15	0	0
NC Tennis Foundation	$ 10	$ 10	0	0
NC Trout Unlimited	$ 10	$ 10	0	0
NC Veterinary Medical Association -- Expired July 1, 2016				

Chapter 20

NC Victim Assistance -- Expired July 1, 2016
NC Wildlife Federation -- Expired July 1, 2016

	SRPA	CCAPA	NHTF	PRTF
NC Wildlife Habitat Foundation	$ 10	$ 10	0	0

NC Youth Soccer Association -- Expired July 1, 2016
North Carolina Bluegrass Association -- Expired July 1, 2016
North Carolina Cattlemen's Association -- Expired July 1, 2016
North Carolina Emergency Management Association --
    Expired July 1, 2016
North Carolina Green Industry Council -- Expired
    July 1, 2016
North Carolina Libraries -- Expired July 1, 2016

	SRPA	CCAPA	NHTF	PRTF
North Carolina Master Gardener	$ 10	$ 10	0	0

North Carolina Paddle Festival -- Expired July 1, 2016

	SRPA	CCAPA	NHTF	PRTF
North Carolina Sheriffs' Association	$ 10	$ 20	0	0
Nurses	$ 10	$ 15	0	0
Olympic Games	$ 10	$ 15	0	0
Omega Psi Phi Fraternity	*$ 10*	*$ 10*	*0*	*0*

Operation Coming Home -- Expired July 1, 2016

	SRPA	CCAPA	NHTF	PRTF
Order of the Eastern Star Prince Hall Affiliated	*$ 10*	*$ 10*	*0*	*0*
Order of the Long Leaf Pine	*$ 10*	*$ 10*	*0*	*0*
Special Plate	*SRPA*	*CCAPA*	*NHTF*	*PRTF*
Out-of-state Collegiate Insignia	*$ 10*	*0*	*$ 15*	*0*

Outer Banks Preservation Association   -- Expired July 1, 2016
Pamlico-Tar River Foundation -- Expired July 1, 2016
Pancreatic Cancer Awareness -- Expired July 1, 2016
P.E.O. Sisterhood -- Expired July 1, 2016

	SRPA	CCAPA	NHTF	PRTF
Personalized	*$ 10*	*0*	*$ 15*	*$ 5*
Piedmont Airlines	*$ 10*	*$ 10*	*0*	*0*
Pisgah Conservancy	*$ 10*	*$ 20*	*0*	*0*
POW/MIA Bring Them Home	*$ 10*	*$ 10*	*0*	*0*
Prince Hall Mason	*$ 10*	*$ 10*	*0*	*0*

Professional Engineer -- Expired July 1, 2016

	SRPA	CCAPA	NHTF	PRTF
Retired Legislator	*$ 10*	*$ 20*	*0*	*0*

RiverLink -- Expired July 1, 2016

	SRPA	CCAPA	NHTF	PRTF
Rocky Mountain Elk Foundation	*$ 10*	*$ 15*	*0*	*0*
Ronald McDonald House	$ 10	$ 20	0	0
Save the Honey Bee (HB)	$ 10	$ 5	0	0
Save the Honey Bee (SB)	$ 10	$ 5	0	0
Save the Sea Turtles	$ 10	$ 10	0	0

Scenic Rivers -- Expired July 1, 2016
School Technology -- Expired July 1,

	SRPA	CCAPA	NHTF	PRTF
2016 SCUBA	$ 10	$ 10	0	0
Shag Dancing	$ 10	$ 5	0	0
Share the Road	$ 10	$ 20	0	0

Sneads Ferry Shrimp Festival -- Expired July 1, 2016
Soil and Water Conservation -- Expired July 1, 2016
Special Forces Association -- Expired July 1, 2016
Special Olympics -- Expired July 1, 2016
S.T.A.R. -- Expired July 1, 2016

	SRPA	CCAPA	NHTF	PRTF
State Attraction	$ 10	$ 20	0	0
Stock Car Racing Theme	$ 10	$ 20	0	0

Support NC Education -- Expired July 1, 2016

	SRPA	CCAPA	NHTF	PRTF
Support Our Troops	$ 10	$ 20	0	0
Support Soccer	$ 10	$ 15	0	0
Surveyor Plate	$ 10	$ 15	0	0

Sustainable Fisheries -- Expired July 1, 2016

	SRPA	CCAPA	NHTF	PRTF
The V Foundation for Cancer Research	$ 10	$ 15	0	0

Toastmasters Club -- Expired July 1, 2016
Topsail Island Shoreline Protection -- Expired July 1, 2016
Travel and Tourism -- Expired July 1, 2016
Turtle Rescue Team -- Expired July 1, 2016

University Health Systems of Eastern
  Carolina -- Expired July 1, 2016

United States Service Academy	$ 10	$ 20	0	0

US Equine Rescue League -- Expired July 1, 2016
USO of NC -- Expired July 1, 2016
Volunteers in Law Enforcement -- Expired July 1, 2016

Wildlife Resources	$ 10	$ 20	0	0
Wrightsville Beach	$ 10	$ 10	0	0

YMCA -- Expired July 1, 2016

Zeta Phi Beta Sorority	$ 10	$ 10	0	0
All other Special Plates	$ 10	0	0	0.

(c) **Use of Funds in Special Registration Plate Account. --**

(1) The Division shall deduct the costs of special registration plates, including the costs of issuing, handling, and advertising the availability of the special plates, from the Special Registration Plate Account.

(2) From the funds remaining in the Special Registration Plate Account after the deductions in accordance with subdivision (1) of this subsection, there is annually appropriated from the Special Registration Plate Account the sum of one million three hundred thousand dollars ($ 1,300,000) to provide operating assistance for the Visitor Centers:

a. on U.S. Highway 17 in Camden County, ninety-two thousand eight hundred fifty-seven dollars ($ 92,857);

b. on U.S. Highway 17 in Brunswick County, ninety-two thousand eight hundred fifty-seven dollars ($ 92,857);

c. on U.S. Highway 441 in Macon County, ninety-two thousand eight hundred fifty-seven dollars ($ 92,857);

d. in Watauga County, ninety-two thousand eight hundred fifty-seven dollars ($ 92,857);

e. on U.S. Highway 29 in Caswell County, ninety-two thousand eight hundred fifty-seven dollars ($ 92,857);

f. on U.S. Highway 70 in Carteret County, ninety-two thousand eight hundred fifty-seven dollars ($ 92,857);

g. on U.S. Highway 64 in Tyrrell County, ninety-two thousand eight hundred fifty-seven dollars ($ 92,857);

h. at the intersection of U.S. Highway 701 and N.C. 904 in Columbus County, ninety-two thousand eight hundred fifty-seven dollars ($ 92,857);

i. on U.S. Highway 221 in McDowell County, ninety-two thousand eight hundred fifty-seven dollars ($ 92,857);

j. on Staton Road in Transylvania County, ninety-two thousand eight hundred fifty-seven dollars ($ 92,857);

k. in the Town of Fair Bluff, Columbus County, near the intersection of U.S. Highway 76 and N.C. 904, ninety-two thousand eight hundred fifty-seven dollars ($ 92,857);

l. on U.S. Highway 421 in Wilkes County, ninety-two thousand eight hundred fifty-seven dollars ($ 92,857); and

m. at the intersection of Interstate 73 and Interstate 74 in Randolph County, ninety-two thousand eight hundred fifty-eight dollars ($ 92,858) each, for two centers.

(3) The Division shall transfer fifty percent (50%) of the remaining revenue in the Special Registration Plate Account quarterly, and funds are hereby appropriated to the Department of Transportation to be used solely for the purpose of beautification of highways. These funds shall be administered by the Department of Transportation for beautification purposes not inconsistent with good landscaping and engineering principles. The Division shall transfer the remaining revenue in the Special Registration Plate Account quarterly to the Highway Fund to be used for the Roadside Vegetation Management Program.

History.
1967, c. 413; 1971, c. 42; 1973, c. 507, s. 5; c. 1262, s. 86; 1975, c. 716, s. 5; 1977, c. 464, s. 3; c. 771, s. 4; 1979, c. 126, ss. 1, 2; 1981 (Reg. Sess., 1982), c. 1258, s. 6; 1983, c. 848; 1985, c. 766; 1987, c. 252; c. 738, s. 140; c. 830, ss. 113(a), 116(a)-(c); 1989, c. 751, s. 7(1);c. 774, s. 1;1989 (Reg. Sess., 1990), c. 814, s. 31; 1991, c. 672, s. 3;c. 726, s. 23;1991 (Reg. Sess., 1992), c. 959, s. 2; c. 1042, s. 2; c. 1044, ss. 33, 34; 1993, c. 321, s. 169.3(a);c. 543, s. 3;1995, c. 163, s. 2;c. 324, s. 18.7(a);c. 433, ss. 2, 3; c. 507, s. 18.17(a); 1996, 2nd Ex. Sess., c. 18, s. 19.11(e);1997-443, s. 11A.118(a);1997-477, ss. 2, 3; 1997-484, ss. 4, 5; 1998-163, s. 1;1999-277, ss. 2, 3; 1999-403, ss. 2, 3; 1999-450, ss. 2, 3; 2000-159, ss. 3, 4; 2001-414, s. 32;2001-498, ss. 3(a), 3(b), 4(a), 4(b); 2002-134, ss. 5, 6; 2003-11, ss. 2, 3; 2003-68, ss. 2, 3; 2003-424, ss. 3, 4; 2004-124, s. 30.3A;2004-131, ss. 3, 4; 2004-185, ss. 3, 4; 2004-200, ss. 2, 3; 2005-216, ss. 4, 5; 2005-276, s. 28.16;2006-209, ss. 3, 4, 7; 2007-323, s. 27.20(b);2007-345, s. 10.1;2007-400, ss. 3, 4; 2007-483, ss. 4, 5, 8(a), (b); 2009-228, s. 1;2010-31, ss. 11.4(i), (j), 28.11; 2010-132, s. 7;2011-145, s. 28.30(b);2011-392, ss. 4, 5, 5.1; 2012-79, s. 1.12(b);2013-360, ss. 14.3(c), 34.22; 2013-376, ss. 3, 4, 9(c), (d); 2013-414, s. 57(b), (c); 2014-100, s. 8.11(d);2015-241, ss. 14.30(dd), 29.30B(a), 29.36A, 29.40(c), (h), (j), (n); 2017-100, s. 2;2017-107, s. 3;2017-114, s. 3;2018-7, s. 1(b);2018-74, ss. 11(b), (e),

Chapter 20

12(c)-(e), 13, 14(b); 2018-77, ss. 1(b), 2(c)-(e), 3.5(b); 2019-32, s. 1(c);2019-213, s. 2(c)

SUBSECTIONS (A1) AND (B) SET OUT TWICE. --The first version of subsections (a1) and (b) set out above is effective until March 1, 2020. The second version of subsections (a1) and (b) set out above is effective March 1, 2020.

INACTIVE SPECIAL INTEREST PLATES. --Pursuant to G.S. 20-79.8 (a), several special plates authorized by G.S. 20-79.4 prior to October 1, 2014, expired as a matter of law on July 1, 2016, because the number of applications required for their production was not received by the Division of Motor Vehicles. At the direction of the Revisor of Statutes, pursuant to G.S. 20-79.8(c), those special plates not meeting this requirement have been set out as expired effective July 1, 2016.

EDITOR'S NOTE. --

This is former G.S. 20-81.3, recodified as G.S. 20-79.7 by Session Laws 1991, c. 672, s. 3.

Session Laws 2014-96, s. 1(a), provides: "Any special registration plate authorized under G.S. 20-79.4 that expired as a matter of law on July 1, 2013, pursuant to G.S. 20-79.8, is reenacted. The corresponding provisions for fees under G.S. 20-79.7(a1) and (b) and any other corresponding requirements for the plates under G.S. 20-81.12 are also reenacted. A special registration plate reenacted under this section is subject to the requirements of G.S. 20-63(b1) if the plate is authorized to be on a background other than a 'First in Flight' background."

Session Laws 2014-96, s. 1(b), provides: "This section is effective when it becomes law [August 1, 2014]. A special registration plate reenacted by this section shall expire, as a matter of law, on October 1, 2014, if the required number of applications for the special registration plate has not been received by the Division of Motor Vehicles by that date. The notification procedure and the responsibilities of the Revisor of Statutes for a special registration plate that expires pursuant to this subsection shall be in accordance with G.S. 20-79.8 except that the notification date shall be no later than October 15, 2015. The Division shall not accept applications for nor advertise any special registration plate that has expired pursuant to this subsection."

Session Laws 2015-241, s. 29.40(h), provides: "The fee amount set for 'Military Veteran' special registration plates in G.S. 20-79.7(a1) is reenacted."

Session Laws 2015-241, s. 29.40(j), which reenacts provisions related to Order of the Long Leaf Pine, provides: "G.S. 20-79.4(b)(171), as it existed on June 30, 2015, is reenacted. The corresponding provisions for fees under G.S. 20-79.7(a1) and (b) and any other corresponding requirements for the plates under G.S. 20-81.12 are also reenacted."

Session Laws 2015-241, s. 29.40(n), which reenacts provisions related to Battle of Kings Mountain plates, provides: "G.S. 20-79.4(b)(21), G.S. 20-81.12(b76), and the corresponding provisions for fees under G.S. 20-79.7(a) and (b), as they existed on September 30, 2014, are reenacted."

Session Laws 2015-241, s. 29.40(s), provides: "Subsections (r) and (s) of this section are effective when this act becomes law [September 18, 2015]. The remainder of this section is effective 90 days after this act becomes law."

Session Laws 2015-241, s. 1.1, provides: "This act shall be known as 'The Current Operations and Capital Improvements Appropriations Act of 2015.'"

Session Laws 2015-241, s. 33.4, provides: "Except for statutory changes or other provisions that clearly indicate an intention to have effects beyond the 2015-2017 fiscal biennium, the textual provisions of this act apply only to funds appropriated for, and activities occurring during, the 2015-2017 fiscal biennium."

Session Laws 2015-241, s. 33.6, is a severability clause.

Session Laws 2017-100, s. 2, provides: "The fee amount and distribution set for 'Zeta Phi Beta' special registration plates in G.S. 20-79.7(a1) and (b) immediately before their repeal under Section 1(b) of S.L. 2014-96 are reenacted."

Session Laws 2018-77, s. 3.5, effective February 1, 2019, was repealed by Acts 2018-74, s. 11(e), effective February 1, 2019. Session Laws 2018-77, s. 3.5(b) would have added entries for Order of the Eastern Star Prince Hall Affiliated in subsections (a1) and (b) identical to the amendments by Session Laws 2018-74, s. 11(b).

Session Laws 2019-32, s. 7, provides: "This act becomes effective July 1, 2019. All rules, regulations, and decisions made by the predecessor boards and authorities reconstituted in this act shall remain in full force and effect until and unless duly modified by the successor entities."

EFFECT OF AMENDMENTS. --

Session Laws 2001-498, ss. 3(b) and 4(b), effective December 19, 2001, inserted entries for the following Special Plates in subsection (a) and in subsection (b) as amended by Session Laws 2001-414: Harley Owners' Group and Rocky Mountain Elk Foundation. For expiration of these amendments, see editor's note.

Session Laws 2003-424, ss. 3 and 4, effective January 1, 2004, in subsection (a), in the special plate and additional fee amount columns, inserted "Crystal Coast $30.00" at the beginning, inserted "Personalized $30.00" following "Historical Attraction $30.00," inserted "Buffalo Soldiers $25.00" following "State Attraction $30.00," inserted "Rocky Mountain Elk Foundation $25.00" following the first "(Effective until June 30, 2006)," inserted "Surveyor Plate $25.00" following "Special Olympics $25.00," inserted "Be Active NC $20.00" following "Audubon North Carolina $20.00," deleted "Rocky Mountain Elk Foundation $25.00" following "Omega Psi Phi Fraternity $20.00," inserted "Zeta Phi Beta Sorority $20.00" following "Wildlife Resources $20.00," and deleted "Personalized $20.00" following "Zeta Phi Beta Sorority $20.00"; and rewrote subsection (b).

Session Laws 2004-124, s. 30.3A, effective July 1, 2004, rewrote subdivision (c)(2).

Session Laws 2004-131, ss. 3 and 4, effective July 29, 2004, inserted entries for "In God We Trust" special plates in subsections (a) and (b).

Session Laws 2004-185, ss. 3 and 4, effective October 1, 2004, in subsection (a), inserted "Stock Car Racing Theme" following "State Attraction" under the "Special Plate" column, and inserted "$30.00" following "$30.00" under the "Additional Fee Amount" column; and in subsection (b), inserted "Stock Car Racing Theme" following "State Attraction" in the "Special Plate" column, inserted "$10" following "$10" in the "SRPA" column, inserted "$20" following "$20" in the "CCAPA" column, inserted "0" following "0" in the "NHTF" column, and inserted "0" following "0" in the "PRTF" column.

Session Laws 2004-200, ss. 2 and 3, effective August 17, 2004, in subsection (a), inserted special plate fees for "El Pueblo," "HOMES4NC," "North Carolina 4-H Development Fund," "High School Insignia," and "Daughters of the American Revolution," and changed the fee for the "First in Forestry" from "$20.00" to "$30.00"; and in subsection (b), provided for the distribution of fees collected from such special plates.

Session Laws 2005-216, ss. 4 and 5, effective July 20, 2005, added numerous entries for the special plate fees in subsections (a) and (b).

Session Laws 2005-276, s. 28.16, effective July 1, 2005, in subdivision (c)(2), in the introductory paragraph, substituted "one million dollars ($1,000,000)" for "nine hundred thousand dollars ($900,000)"; added sub-subdivision (c)(2)j. and made minor stylistic and punctuation changes.

Session Laws 2006-209, ss. 3, 4, effective August 8, 2006, added numerous entries for the special plate fees in subsections (a) and (b). See Editor's note.

Session Laws 2007-323, s. 27.20(b), as added by Session Laws 2007-345, s. 10.1, effective July 1, 2007, substituted "Special Registration Plate Account quarterly, and funds are hereby appropriated" for "Account quarterly" in subdivision (c)(3).

Session Laws 2007-400, ss. 3, 4, effective August 21, 2007, added the "Back Country Horsemen of NC" and "Maggie Valley Trout Festival" entries for the special plate fees in subsections (a) and (b).

Session Laws 2007-483, ss. 4 and 5, effective August 30, 2007, in subsection (a), inserted the following entries: "Home Care and Hospice," "Hospice Care," "National Kidney Foundation," "AIDS Awareness," "ALS Association, Jim 'Catfish' Hunter Chapter," "Brain Injury Awareness," "Breast Cancer Earlier Detection," "Juvenile Diabetes Research Foundation," "NC Tennis Foundation," "Gold Star Lapel Button," and substituted "$30.00" for "$25.00" in the fee entry for NC Coastal Federation; and in subsection (b), added the following entries: "AIDS Awareness," "ALS Association, Jim 'Catfish' Hunter Chapter," "Brain Injury Awareness," "Breast Cancer Earlier Detection," "Home Care and Hospice," "Hospice Care," "Juvenile Diabetes Research Foundation," "National Kidney Foundation," "NC Tennis Foundation," and substituted "$20" for "$15" in the CCAPA column for the NC Coastal Federation.

Session Laws 2007-483, s. 8(a) and (b), effective October 1, 2007, deleted the Breast Cancer Awareness entries which preceded the Breast Cancer Earlier Detection entries in subsections (a) and (b).

Session Laws 2009-228, s. 1, effective June 30, 2009, deleted "other than those designated as interstate" from the end of the first sentence in subdivision (c)(3)b.

Session Laws 2010-31, s. 11.4(i) and (j), effective October 1, 2010, in subsection (a), relocated the entry for "Animal Lovers" and increased the respective additional fee amount by ten dollars; and in subsection (b), inserted "of this section" in the first paragraph, and under the entry for "Animal Lovers" increased the CCAPA amount by ten dollars.

Session Laws 2010-31, s. 28.11, effective July 1, 2010, in subdivision (c)(2), substituted "one million two hundred thousand dollars ($1,200,000)" for "one million dollars ($1,000.000)" in the introductory paragraph and added subdivisions (c)(2)k. and (c)(2)l. and made a related punctuation change.

Session Laws 2010-132, s. 7, effective December 1, 2010, and applicable to offenses committed on or after that date, in the first paragraph in subsection (a), in the first sentence, substituted "a single Legion of Valor, 100% Disabled Veteran, and Ex-Prisoner of War registration plate" for "one registration plate," and added "each year," added the second sentence, and in the last sentence, deleted "including additional Legion of Valor, 100% Disabled Veteran, and Ex-Prisoner of War" following "special registration plates."

Session Laws 2011-145, s. 28.30(b), effective July 1, 2011, substituted "one million three hundred thousand dollars ($1,300,000)" for "one million two hundred thousand dollars ($1,200,000)" in the introductory paragraph of subdivision (c)(2); made minor stylistic changes in subdivisions (c)(2)k. and (c)(2)l.; and added subdivision (c)(2)m.

Session Laws 2011-392, ss. 4 and 5, effective June 30, 2011, rewrote subsections (a) and (b).

Session Laws 2012-79, s. 1.12(b), effective June 26, 2012, in subsection (a), raised the additional fees for "Morgan Horse Club" and "Sustainable Fisheries" special registration plates from $20.00 to $30.00.

Session Laws 2013-360, s. 14.3(c), effective August 1, 2013, in subsection (b), substituted "Clean Water Management Trust Fund (CWMTF)" for "Natural Heritage Trust Fund (NHTF)," "G.S. 113A-253" for "G.S. 113-77.7," and "CWMTF" for "NHTF" in the table heading.

Session Laws 2013-360, s. 34.22, effective July 1, 2013, substituted "ninety-two thousand eight hundred fifty-seven dollars ($92,857)" for "($100,000)" in subdivisions (c)(2)a. through (c)(2) l.; and substituted "ninety-two thousand eight hundred fifty-eight dollars ($92,858) each, for two centers" for "($100,000)" in subdivision (c)(2)m.

Session Laws 2013-376, ss. 3 and 4, effective July 29, 2013, rewrote former subsection (a) as subsections (a) and (a1), adding subdivisions (a)(3) and (4); added the following entries in the charts in subsections (a1) and (b): First Tee, Morehead Planetarium, Municipality

Plate, NC FIRST Robotics, NCSC, National Law Enforcement Officers Memorial, North Carolina Bluegrass Association, North Carolina Cattlemen's Association, Operation Coming Home, Pancreatic Cancer Awareness, RiverLink, Turtle Rescue Team, Volunteers in Law Enforcement, YMCA, Charlotte Checkers, I.B.P.O.E.W., Professional Engineer, Fraternal Order of Police, Mission Foundation, Order of the Long Leaf Pine, and deleted the entries for Phi Beta Sigma Fraternity in both charts; added the entries for Native Brook Trout, Red Drum, Bronze Star Combat recipient, Bronze Star Recipient, Combat Veteran, Legion of Merit, Military Veteran, Military Wartime Veteran, Partially Disabled Veteran, Pearl Harbor Survivor, and Silver Star Recipient in subsection (a1); and, in subsection (b), inserted an entry for Snead's Ferry Shrimp Festival.

Session Laws 2013-414, s. 57(b) and (c), effective August 23, 2013, added entries for North Carolina Paddle Festival in the charts in subsections (a1) and (b).

Session Laws 2014-100, s. 8.11(d), effective July 1, 2014, in the tables in subsections (a1) and (b), inserted the row concerning "I Support Teachers" and deleted the row concerning "Support Public Schools."

Session Laws 2015-241, ss. 14.30(dd) and 29.36A, effective July 1, 2015, substituted "143B-135.234" for "113A-253" and "143B-135.56" for "113-44.15" in subsection (b); and deleted "the Town of Bonne" preceding "Watauga County" in subdivision (c)(2)d.

Session Laws 2015-241, s. 29.30B(a), effective October 1, 2015, rewrote subdivision (c)(3).

Session Laws 2015-241, s. 29.40(c), effective December 17, 2015, in the table in subsections (a1) and (b), added entries for special plates "Carolina Panthers," "North Carolina Sheriffs' Association," "NC Surveyors," "Save the Honey Bee (HB)," and "Save the Honey Bee (SB)," and "United States Service Academy." For effective date, see editor's note.

Session Laws 2017-100, s. 2, effective July 12, 2017, reenacted the fee amount and distribution set for "Zeta Phi Beta" in subsections (a1) and (b).

Session Laws 2017-107, s. 3, effective July 1, 2017, in the tables in subsections (a1) and (b), inserted the rows concerning "Pisgah Conservancy."

Session Laws 2017-114, s. 3, effective July 18, 2017, in the tables in subsections (a1) and (b), inserted the rows concerning "Big Rock Blue Marlin Tournament," "Colorectal Cancer Awareness" and "Kick Cancer for Kids."

Session Laws 2018-7, s. 1(b), effective June 13, 2018, added the entry for "Eastern Band of Cherokee Indians" to the table in subsection (a1).

Session Laws 2018-74, s. 11(b), effective February 1, 2019, added the entry for "Order of the Eastern Star Prince Hall Affiliated" in subsections (a1), (b).

Session Laws 2018-74, s. 12(c) -(e), and Session Laws 2018-77, s. 2(c) -(e), effective February 1, 2019, are identical, and in subsection (a1), reenacted the special registration plates for Alpha Phi Alpha Fraternity, modified the amount to ($30), and reordered the table accordingly; and in subsection (b), reenacted

Alpha Phi Alpha Fraternity special registration plates, modified to $10 the SRPA and modified to $20 the CCAP.

Session Laws 2018-74, s. 13, 14(b), effective July 1, 2018, in subsection (a1), substituted "$30.00" for "$20.00" in the entry for "Wildlife Resources"; substituted "$20" for "$10" in the entry for "Wildlife Resources" in subsection (b); and added the entry for "International Association of Fire Fighters" in subsections (a1) and (b).

Session Laws 2018-77, s. 1(b), effective June 25, 2018, in subsection (a), inserted the exception in the first sentence, and added the second sentence.

Session Laws 2019-32, s. 1(c), effective July 1, 2019, in the second sentence of subsection (b), substituted "G.S. 143B 135.234" for "G.S. 113A 253" and "G.S. 143B 135.56" for "G.S. 113-44.15". For effective date and applicability, see editor's note.

Session Laws 2019-213, s. 2(c), effective March 1, 2020, in subsections (a1) and (b), inserted entries for ALS Research, Keeping The Lights On, POW IA Bring Them Home, and Wrightsville Beach; and in the introductory paragraph of subsection (b), substituted "subsection (a1)" for "subsection (a)."

CITED in Hodgson v. Hyatt Realty & Inv. Co., 353 F. Supp. 1363 (M.D.N.C. 1973).

§ 20-79.8. Expiration of special registration plate authorization

(a) **Expiration of Plates Authorized Prior to October 1, 2014.** -- A special registration plate authorized after July 1, 2011, and before October 1, 2014, pursuant to G.S. 20-79.4 shall expire, as a matter of law, on July 1 of the second calendar year following the year in which the special plate was authorized if the number of required applications for the authorized special plate has not been received by the Division. The Division shall not accept applications for nor advertise any special registration plate that has expired pursuant to this section.

(a1) **Expiration of Plates Authorized On or After October 1, 2014.** -- A special registration plate authorized on or after October 1, 2014, pursuant to G.S. 20-79.4, shall expire as a matter of law upon an applicant's failure to submit to the Division all of the items required under G.S. 20-79.3A(d) within 60 days of the act approving the special registration plate becoming law. The Division shall not accept applications for nor advertise any special registration plate that has expired pursuant to this section.

(b) **Notification.** -- The Division shall notify the Revisor of Statutes in writing, not later than August 1 of each year, which special registration plate authorizations have expired as a matter of law pursuant to subsection (a) of this section. The Division shall publish a copy of the written notification sent to the Revisor of Statutes pursuant to this subsection on a Web site maintained by the Division or the Department of Transportation.

(c) **Revisor of Statutes Responsibilities.** -- Upon notification of expiration of the authorization for any special registration plate by the Division pursuant to this section, the Revisor of Statutes shall verify that the authorization for each special registration plate listed has expired and shall notate the expiration in the applicable statutes. If an authorization for a special registration plate listed in G.S. 20-79.4 expires, the Revisor of Statutes shall revise the subdivision referring to the special registration plate to leave the name of the special registration plate authorized and the date the special registration plate's authorization expired. If an authorization for a special registration plate listed in G.S. 20-79.4 expires, the Revisor of Statutes shall also make corresponding changes to reflect the expiration of the special registration plate's authorization, if applicable, in G.S. 20-63(b), 20-79.7, and 20-81.12.

History.
2011-392, s. 8;2014-96, s. 6
EDITOR'S NOTE. --
Session Laws 2011-392, s. 9, provides: "Notwithstanding Section 8 of this act, any special registration plate authorized in G.S. 20-79.7, prior to July 1, 2011, shall expire, as a matter of law, on July 1, 2013, if the number of applications required for the production of the special registration plate has not been received by the Division of Motor Vehicles on or before that date. Upon notification of expiration of the authorization for any special plate by the Division pursuant to this section, the Revisor of Statutes shall verify that the authorization for each special registration plate listed has expired and shall notate such expiration in the applicable statutes. If an authorization for a special registration plate listed in G.S. 20-79.4 expires, the Revisor of Statutes shall revise the subdivision referring to the special registration plate to leave the name of the special plate authorized and the date the special registration plate's authorization expired. If an authorization for a special registration plate listed in G.S. 20-79.4 expires, the Revisor of Statutes shall also make corresponding changes to reflect the expiration of the special registration plate's authorization, if applicable, in G.S. 20-63(b), 20-79.7, and 20-81.12."

Session Laws 2011-392, s. 10, provides: "The Revisor of Statutes is authorized to alphabetize, number, and renumber the special registration plates listed in G.S. 20-79.4 to ensure that all the special registration plates are listed in alphabetical order and numbered accordingly."

Session Laws 2014-96, s. 1(a), provides: "Any special registration plate authorized under G.S. 20-79.4 that expired as a matter of law on July 1, 2013, pursuant to G.S. 20-79.8, is reenacted. The corresponding provisions for fees under G.S. 20-79.7(a1) and (b) and any other corresponding requirements for the plates under G.S. 20-81.12 are also reenacted. A

special registration plate reenacted under this section is subject to the requirements of G.S. 20-63(b1) if the plate is authorized to be on a background other than a 'First in Flight' background."

Session Laws 2014-96, s. 1(b), provides: "This section is effective when it becomes law [August 1, 2014]. A special registration plate reenacted by this section shall expire, as a matter of law, on October 1, 2014, if the required number of applications for the special registration plate has not been received by the Division of Motor Vehicles by that date. The notification procedure and the responsibilities of the Revisor of Statutes for a special registration plate that expires pursuant to this subsection shall be in accordance with G.S. 20-79.8 except that the notification date shall be no later than October 15, 2015. The Division shall not accept applications for nor advertise any special registration plate that has expired pursuant to this subsection."

Session Laws 2014-96, s. 7, provides: "The Revenue Laws Study Committee is directed as follows as it relates to registration plates:

"(1) To identify whether the process for requests to establish or reauthorize special registration plates under this act requires any modifications and to examine the costs incurred by the Division of Motor Vehicles to administer special registration plates.

"(2) To study whether certain governmental entities should have different eligibility or renewal requirements for permanent registration plates; to study whether nongovernmental entities should be eligible for permanent plates and, if so, what the criteria should be; and to examine the costs incurred by the Division of Motor Vehicles to administer permanent registration plates.

"The Committee shall report its findings, together with any recommended legislation, to the 2015 Regular Session of the 2015 General Assembly upon its convening."

Session Laws 2019-213, s. 2(f), provides: "The POW/MIA Bring Them Home plate authorized by this section is not subject to the requirements to establish a new special registration plate in G.S. 20-79.3A and the expiration of special registration plate authorization in G.S. 20-79.8."

EFFECT OF AMENDMENTS. --
Session Laws 2014-96, s. 6, effective August 1, 2014, in subsection (a), substituted "Expiration of Plates Authorized Prior to October 1, 2014" for "Expiration" in the subsection heading, and inserted "after July 1, 2011, and before October 1, 2014" in the first sentence; inserted subsection (a1); substituted "August 1" for "July 15" in the first sentence of subsection (b); and made a minor stylistic change.

§§ 20-80 through 20-81.2

Repealed by Session Laws 1991, c. 672, s. 1, as amended by Session Laws 1991, c. 726, s. 23.

N.C. Gen. Stat. § 20-81.3

Recodified as § 20-79.7 by Session Laws 1991, c. 672, s. 3, as amended by Session Laws 1991, c. 726, s. 23.

§§ 20-81.4 through 20-81.11

Repealed by Session Laws 1991, c. 672, s. 1, as amended by Session Laws 1991, c. 726, s. 23.

§ 20-81.12. Collegiate insignia plates and certain other special plates

(a) **AIDS Awareness.** -- Expired July 1, 2016.

(b) **Alpha Phi Alpha Fraternity.** -- The Division shall transfer quarterly the money in the Collegiate and Cultural Attraction Plate Account derived from the sale of the Alpha Phi Alpha Fraternity plates to the Education Consortium of North Carolina, Inc., for scholarships for the benefit of African-American males attending accredited North Carolina colleges and universities.

(b1) **ALS Research.** -- The Division shall transfer quarterly the money in the Collegiate and Cultural Attraction Plate Account derived from the sale of ALS Research plates to The ALS Association of North Carolina Chapter to support ALS research.

(b2) **American Red Cross.** -- Expired July 1, 2016.

(b3) **Animal Lovers Plates.** -- The Division must receive 300 or more applications before an animal lovers plate may be developed. The Division shall transfer quarterly the money in the Collegiate and Cultural Attraction Plate Account derived from the sale of the animal lovers plate to the Spay/Neuter Account established in G.S. 19A-62.

(b4) **ARC of North Carolina.** -- Expired July 1, 2016.

(b5) **Arthritis Foundation.** -- Expired July 1, 2016.

(b6) **ARTS NC.** -- The Division must receive 300 or more applications for the ARTS NC plate before the plate may be developed. The Division must transfer quarterly the money in the Collegiate and Cultural Attraction Plate Account derived from the sale of ARTSNC plates to ARTS North Carolina, Inc., to provide funding to promote the arts in North Carolina.

(b7) **Audubon North Carolina Plates.** -- Expired July 1, 2016.

(b8) **Autism Society of North Carolina.** -- The Division must receive 300 or more applications for an Autism Society of North Carolina plate before the plate may be developed. The Division must transfer quarterly the money in the Collegiate and Cultural Attraction Plate Account derived from the sale of Autism Society of North Carolina plates to the Autism Society of North Carolina, Inc., for support services to individuals with autism and their families.

(b9) **Back Country Horsemen of North Carolina.** -- Expired July 1, 2016.

(b10) **Battle of Kings Mountain.** -- The Division shall transfer quarterly the money in the Collegiate and Cultural Attraction Plate Account derived from the sale of "Battle of Kings Mountain" plates by transferring fifty percent (50%) to the Kings Mountain Tourism Development Authority and fifty percent (50%) to Kings Mountain Gateway Trails, Inc., to be used to develop tourism to the area and provide safe and adequate trails for visitors to the park.

(b11) **Battleship North Carolina.** -- The Division must receive 300 or more applications for the "Battleship North Carolina" plate before the plate may be developed. The Division must transfer quarterly the money in the Collegiate and Cultural Attraction Plate Account derived from the sale of "Battleship North Carolina" plates to the U.S.S. North Carolina Battleship Commission to provide funding for information and education about the role of the Battleship U.S.S. North Carolina in history and for administrative and operating costs of the U.S.S. North Carolina Battleship Commission.

(b12) **Be Active NC.** -- Expired July 1, 2016.

(b13) **Big Rock Blue Marlin Tournament.** -- The Division shall transfer quarterly the money in the Collegiate and Cultural Attraction Plate Account derived from the sale of Big Rock Blue Marlin Tournament plates to the Big Rock Blue Marlin Tournament to be used to fund charities in North Carolina.

(b14) **Boy Scouts of America.** -- Expired July 1, 2016.

(b15) **Brain Injury Awareness.** -- Expired July 1, 2016.

(b16) **Breast Cancer Earlier Detection.** -- Expired July 1, 2016.

(b17) **Brenner Children's Hospital.** -- Expired July 1, 2016.

(b18) **Buddy Pelletier Surfing Foundation.** -- The Division must receive 300 or more applications for the Buddy Pelletier Surfing Foundation plate before the plate may be developed. The Division shall transfer quarterly the money in the Collegiate and Cultural Attraction Plate Account derived from the sale of the Buddy Pelletier Surfing Foundation to the Foundation to fund the Foundation's scholastic and humanitarian aid programs.

(b19) **Buffalo Soldiers.** -- Expired July 1, 2016.

(b20) **Carolina Panthers.** -- The Division shall transfer quarterly one-half of the money in the Collegiate and Cultural Attraction Plate Account derived from the sale of Carolina Panthers plates to the Keep Pounding Fund of the

Carolinas Healthcare Foundation, Inc., to be used to support cancer research at the Carolinas Medical Center, and shall transfer quarterly one-half of the money in the Collegiate and Cultural Attraction Plate Account derived from the sale of the Carolina Panthers plates to the Carolina Panthers Charities Fund of the Foundation for the Carolinas to be used to create new athletic opportunities for children, support their educational needs, and promote healthy lifestyles for families.

(b21) **Carolina Raptor Center.** -- Expired July 1, 2016.

(b22) **Carolina Regional Volleyball Association.** -- Expired July 1, 2016.

(b23) **Carolina's Aviation Museum.** -- Expired July 1, 2016.

(b24) **Carolinas Credit Union Foundation.** -- Expired July 1, 2016.

(b25) **Carolinas Golf Association.** -- The Division must receive 300 or more applications for the "Carolinas Golf Association" plate before the plate may be developed. The Division shall transfer quarterly the money in the Collegiate and Cultural Attraction Plate Account derived from the sale of "Carolinas Golf Association" plates to the Carolinas Golf Association to be used to promote amateur golf in North Carolina.

(b26) **Charlotte Checkers.** -- Expired July 1, 2016.

(b27) **Choose Life.** -- The Division must receive 300 or more applications for a "Choose Life" plate before the plate may be developed. The Division shall transfer quarterly the money in the Collegiate and Cultural Attraction Plate Account derived from the sale of "Choose Life" plates to the Carolina Pregnancy Care Fellowship, which shall distribute the money annually to nongovernmental, not-for-profit agencies that provide pregnancy services that are limited to counseling and/or meeting the physical needs of pregnant women. Funds received pursuant to this section shall not be distributed to any agency, organization, business, or other entity that provides, promotes, counsels, or refers for abortion and shall not be distributed to any entity that charges women for services received.

(b28) **Coastal Conservation Association.** -- Expired July 1, 2016.

(b29) **Coastal Land Trust.** -- The Division must receive 300 or more applications for the "Coastal Land Trust" plate before the plate may be developed. The Division shall transfer quarterly the money in the Collegiate and Cultural Attraction Plate Account derived from the sale of the "Coastal Land Trust" plates to the North Carolina Coastal Land Trust to be used to acquire open space and natural areas, to ensure conservation education, to promote good land stewardship, to set aside lands for conservation, and for other administrative and operating costs.

(b30) **Collegiate Insignia Plates.** -- Except for a collegiate insignia plate for a public military college or university, the Division must receive 300 or more applications for a collegiate insignia license plate for a college or university before a collegiate license plate may be developed. For a collegiate insignia license plate for a public military college or university, the Division must receive 100 or more applications before a collegiate license plate may be developed. The color, design, and material for the plate must be approved by both the Division and the alumni or alumnae association of the appropriate college or university. The Division must transfer quarterly the money in the Collegiate and Cultural Attraction Plate Account derived from the sale of in-State collegiate insignia plates to the Board of Governors of The University of North Carolina for in-State, public colleges and universities and to the respective board of trustees for in-State, private colleges and universities in proportion to the number of collegiate plates sold representing that institution for use for academic enhancement.

(b31) **Colorectal Cancer Awareness.** -- The Division must receive 300 or more applications for a Colorectal Cancer Awareness plate before the plate may be developed. The Division shall transfer quarterly the money in the Collegiate and Cultural Attraction Plate Account derived from the sale of Colorectal Cancer Awareness plates to the Colon Cancer Coalition to be used to promote prevention and early detection of colorectal cancer and to provide support to persons affected.

(b32) **Concerned Bikers Association/ABATE of North Carolina.** -- Expired July 1, 2016.

(b33) **Crystal Coast.** -- Expired July 1, 2016.

(b34) **Daniel Stowe Botanical Garden.** -- Expired July 1, 2016.

(b35) **Daughters of the American Revolution.** -- Expired July 1, 2016.

(b36) **Donate Life.** -- The Division must receive 300 or more applications for the "Donate Life" plate before the plate may be developed. The Division must transfer quarterly the money in the Collegiate and Cultural Attraction Plate Account derived from the sale of "Donate Life" plates to Donate Life North Carolina to be divided equally among Donate Life North Carolina and each of the transplant centers in North Carolina to include Bowman Gray Medical Center, Carolinas Medical Center, Duke University, East Carolina University, and the University of North Carolina at Chapel Hill. The transplant centers shall use all of the proceeds received from this plate to provide funding for expenses incurred by needy families, recipients, and expenses related to organ donation.

Chapter 20

(b37) **Ducks Unlimited Plates.** -- The Division must receive 300 or more applications for a Ducks Unlimited plate and receive any necessary licenses from Ducks Unlimited, Inc., for use of their logo before the plate may be developed. The Division shall transfer quarterly the money in the Collegiate and Cultural Attraction Plate Account derived from the sale of Ducks Unlimited plates to the Wildlife Resources Commission to be used to support the conservation programs of Ducks Unlimited, Inc., in this State.

(b38) **El Pueblo.** -- Expired July 1, 2016.

(b39) **Farmland Preservation.** -- Expired July 1, 2016.

(b40) **First in Forestry.** -- The Division must receive 300 or more applications for the First in Forestry plate before the plate may be developed. The Division shall transfer quarterly one-half of the money in the Collegiate and Cultural Attraction Plate Account derived from the sale of the First in Forestry plates to the North Carolina Forest Service of the Department of Agriculture and Consumer Services for a State forests and forestry education program and shall transfer quarterly one-half of the money in the Collegiate and Cultural Attraction Plate Account derived from the sale of the First in Forestry plates to the Forest Education and Conservation Foundation for their programs.

(b41) **First in Turf.** -- Expired July 1, 2016.

(b42) **First Tee.** -- Expired July 1, 2016.

(b43) **Fraternal Order of Police.** -- The Division shall transfer quarterly the money in the Collegiate and Cultural Attraction Plate Account derived from the sale of Fraternal Order of Police plates to The North Carolina Fraternal Order of Police to support the State Lodge.

(b44) **Girl Scouts.** -- Expired July 1, 2016.

(b45) **Goodness Grows Plates.** -- Expired July 1, 2016.

(b46) **Greensboro Symphony Guild.** -- Expired July 1, 2016.

(b47) **Greyhound Friends of North Carolina.** -- Expired July 1, 2016.

(b48) **Guilford Battleground Company.** -- The Division must receive 300 or more applications for a Guilford Battleground Company plate before the plate may be developed. The Division shall transfer quarterly the money in the Collegiate and Cultural Attraction Plate Account derived from the sale of Guilford Battleground Company plates to the Guilford Battleground Company for its programs.

(b49) **Harley Owners' Group.** -- The Division must receive 300 or more applications for a Harley Owners' Group plate before the plate may be developed. The Division shall transfer quarterly the money in the Collegiate and Cultural Attraction Plate Account derived from the sale of Harley Owners' Group plates to the State Board of Community Colleges to support the motorcycle safety instruction program established pursuant to G.S. 115D-72.

(b50) **High School Insignia Plate.** -- The Division must receive 300 or more applications for a high school insignia plate for a public high school in North Carolina before a high school insignia plate may be issued for that school. The Division must transfer quarterly the money in the Collegiate and Cultural Attraction Plate Account derived from the sale of high school insignia plates to the Department of Public Instruction to be deposited into the State Aid to Local School Administrative Units account. The Division must also send the Department of Public Instruction information as to the number of plates sold representing a particular high school. The Department of Public Instruction must annually transfer the money in the State Aid to Local School Administrative Units account that is derived from the sale of the high school insignia plates to the high schools which have a high school insignia plate in proportion to the number of high school insignia plates sold representing that school. The high school must use the money for academic enhancement.

(b51) **Historical Attraction Plates.** -- The Division must receive 300 or more applications for an historical attraction plate representing a publicly owned or nonprofit historical attraction located in North Carolina and listed below before the plate may be developed. The Division must transfer quarterly the money in the Collegiate and Cultural Attraction Plate Account derived from the sale of historical attraction plates to the organizations named below in proportion to the number of historical attraction plates sold representing that organization:

(1) **Historical Attraction Within Historic District.** -- The revenue derived from the special plate shall be transferred quarterly to the appropriate Historic Preservation Commission, or entity designated as the Historic Preservation Commission, and used to maintain property in the historic district in which the attraction is located. As used in this subdivision, the term "historic district" means a district created under G.S. 160A-400.4.

(2) **Nonprofit Historical Attraction.** -- The revenue derived from the special plate shall be transferred quarterly to the nonprofit corporation that is responsible for maintaining the attraction for which the plate is issued and used to develop and operate the attraction.

(3) **State Historic Site.** -- The revenue derived from the special plate shall be transferred quarterly to the Department of Natural and Cultural Resources and used to develop and operate the site for which the plate is issued. As used in this

subdivision, the term "State historic site" has the same meaning as in G.S. 121-2(11).

(b52) **Home Care and Hospice.** -- The Division must receive 300 or more applications for the Home Care and Hospice plate before the plate may be developed. The Division must transfer quarterly the money in the Collegiate and Cultural Attraction Plate Account derived from the sale of Home Care and Hospice plates to The Association for Home and Hospice Care of North Carolina for its educational programs in support of home care and hospice care in North Carolina.

(b53) **Home of American Golf.** -- Expired July 1, 2016.

(b54) HOMES4NC. -- The Division must receive 300 or more applications for the HOMES4NC plate before the plate may be developed. The Division shall transfer quarterly the money in the Collegiate and Cultural Attraction Plate Account derived from the sale of the HOMES4NC plates to the NCAR Housing Opportunity Foundation to promote safe, decent, and affordable housing for all in North Carolina.

(b55) **Hospice Care.** -- Expired July 1, 2016.

(b56) I.B.P.O.E.W. -- Expired July 1, 2016.

(b57) **I Support Teachers Plates.** -- Expired July 1, 2016.

(b58) **In God We Trust.** -- The Division must receive 300 or more applications for the In God We Trust plate before the plate may be developed. The Division shall transfer quarterly the money in the Collegiate and Cultural Attraction Plate Account derived from the sale of the In God We Trust plates to the Department of Public Safety to be deposited into The N.C. National Guard Soldiers and Airmen Assistance Fund of The Minuteman Partnership to help provide assistance to the families of North Carolina National Guardsmen who have been activated and deployed in federal service.

(b59) **International Association of Fire Fighters.** -- The Division shall transfer quarterly the money in the Collegiate and Cultural Attraction Plate Account derived from the sale of "International Association of Fire Fighters" plates to the Professional Firefighters of North Carolina Charitable Fund.

(b60) **Jaycees.** -- Expired July 1, 2016.

(b61) **Juvenile Diabetes Research Foundation.** -- The Division must receive 300 or more applications for the Juvenile Diabetes Research Foundation plate before the plate may be developed. The Division must transfer quarterly the money in the Collegiate and Cultural Attraction Plate Account derived from the sale of Juvenile Diabetes Research Foundation plates to the Triangle Eastern North Carolina Chapter of the Juvenile Diabetes Research Foundation International, Inc., to provide funding for research to cure diabetes. The Foundation must distribute the amount it receives to all Juvenile

Diabetes Research Foundation, Inc., chapters located in the State in equal shares.

(b62) **Kappa Alpha Order.** -- Expired July 1, 2016.

(b63) **Keeping The Lights On.** -- The Division shall transfer quarterly the money in the Collegiate and Cultural Attraction Plate Account derived from the sale of Keeping The Lights On plates to the UNC Jaycee Burn Center.

(b64) **Kick Cancer for Kids.** -- The Division shall transfer quarterly the money in the Collegiate and Cultural Attraction Plate Account derived from the sale of Kick Cancer for Kids plates as follows:

(1) Fifty percent (50%) to The Children's Oncology Group Foundation to be used to provide support for the mission and goals of the Foundation.

(2) Fifty percent (50%) to Riley's Army, Inc., to be used to provide support to children with cancer and their families.

(b65) **Kids First Plates.** -- The Division must receive 300 or more applications for a Kids First plate before the plate may be developed. The Division shall transfer quarterly the money in the Collegiate and Cultural Attraction Plate Account derived from the sale of Kids First plates to the North CarolinaChildren's Trust Fund established in G.S. 7B-1302.

(b66) **Leukemia & Lymphoma Society.** -- Expired July 1, 2016.

(b67) **Litter Prevention Plates.** -- The Division must receive 300 or more applications for a Litter Prevention plate before the plate may be developed. The Division shall transfer quarterly the money in the Collegiate and Cultural Attraction Plate Account derived from the sale of the litter prevention plates to the Litter Prevention Account created pursuant to G.S. 136-125.1.

(b68) **Lung Cancer Research.** -- Expired July 1, 2016.

(b69) **Maggie Valley Trout Festival.** -- Expired July 1, 2016.

(b70) **March of Dimes Plates.** -- Expired July 1, 2016.

(b71) **Mission Foundation.** -- Expired July 1, 2016.

(b72) **Morehead Planetarium.** -- Expired July 1, 2016.

(b73) **Morgan Horse Club.** -- Expired July 1, 2016.

(b74) **Mountains-to-Sea Trail.** -- The Division must receive 300 or more applications for the "Mountains-to-Sea Trail" plate before the plate may be developed. The Division shall transfer quarterly the money in the Collegiate and Cultural Attraction Plate Account derived from the sale of "Mountains-to-Sea Trail" plates to the Friends of the Mountains-to-Sea Trail, Inc., to be used to fund trail projects and related administrative and operating expenses.

Chapter 20

(b75) **Municipality Plate.** -- Expired July 1, 2016.

(b76) **National Kidney Foundation.** -- Expired July 1, 2016.

(b77) **National Law Enforcement Officers Memorial.** -- Expired July 1, 2016.

(b78) **National Multiple Sclerosis Society.** -- The Division must receive 300 or more applications for the National Multiple Sclerosis Society plate before the plate may be developed. The Division shall transfer quarterly the money in the Collegiate and Cultural Attraction Plate Account derived from the sale of the National Multiple Sclerosis Society plates to the National Multiple Sclerosis Society for its public awareness programs.

(b79) **National Wild Turkey Federation.** -- The Division must receive 300 or more applications for the National Wild Turkey Federation plate before the plate may be developed. The Division shall transfer quarterly the money in the Collegiate and Cultural Attraction Plate Account derived from the sale of the National Wild Turkey Federation plates to the North Carolina State Chapter of the National Wild Turkey Federation for special projects to benefit the public.

(b80) **Native American.** -- The Division must receive 300 or more applications for the "Native American" plate before the plate may be developed. The Division shall transfer quarterly the money in the Collegiate and Cultural Attraction Plate Account derived from the sale of "Native American" plates to the Native American College Fund for scholarships to be awarded to Native American students from North Carolina.

(b81) **Native Brook Trout.** -- The Division must receive 300 or more applications for the Native Brook Trout plate before the plate may be developed. The Division must transfer quarterly the money in the Collegiate and Cultural Attraction Plate Account derived from the sale of Native Brook Trout plates to the North Carolina Wildlife Resources Commission to be used to fund public access to and habitat protection of brook trout waters.

(b82) **NC Agribusiness.** -- Expired July 1, 2016.

(b83) **NC Beekeepers.** -- Expired July 1, 2016.

(b84) **NC Children's Promise.** -- Expired July 1, 2016.

(b85) **NC Civil War.** -- Expired July 1, 2016.

(b86) **NC Coastal Federation.** -- The Division must receive 300 or more applications for a NC Coastal Federation plate before the plate may be developed. The Division shall transfer quarterly the money in the Collegiate and Cultural Attraction Plate Account derived from the sale of NC Coastal Federation plates to the North Carolina Coastal Federation, Inc.

(b87) **NC FIRST Robotics.** -- Expired July 1, 2016.

(b88) **NC Fisheries Association.** -- Expired July 1, 2016.

(b89) **NC Horse Council.** -- The Division must receive 300 or more applications for the "NC Horse Council" plate before the plate may be developed. The Division shall transfer quarterly the money in the Collegiate and Cultural Attraction Plate Account derived from the sale of "NC Horse Council" plates to the North Carolina Horse Council, Inc., to promote and enhance the equine industry in North Carolina.

(b90) **NC Mining.** -- Expired July 1, 2016.

(b91) **NCSC.** -- Expired July 1, 2016.

(b92) **NCSurveyors.** -- The applicable requirements of G.S. 20-79.3A shall be met before the NCSurveyors plate may be developed. The Division shall transfer quarterly the money in the Collegiate and Cultural Attraction Plate Account derived from the sale of NCSurveyors plates to the North Carolina Society of Surveyors Education Foundation, Inc., to be used to grant financial assistance to those persons genuinely interested in pursuing or continuing to pursue a formal education in the field of surveying.

(b93) **NC Tennis Foundation.** -- The Division must receive 300 or more applications for the NC Tennis Foundation plate before the plate may be developed. The Division must transfer quarterly the money in the Collegiate and Cultural Attraction Plate Account derived from the sale of NC Tennis Foundation plates to the North Carolina Tennis Foundation, Inc., to provide funding for development and growth of tennis as a sport in North Carolina.

(b94) **NC Trout Unlimited.** -- The Division must receive 300 or more applications for an NC Trout Unlimited plate before the plate may be developed. The Division shall transfer quarterly the money in the Collegiate and Cultural Attraction Plate Account derived from the sale of NC Trout Unlimited plates to North Carolina Trout Unlimited for its programs.

(b95) **NC Veterinary Medical Association.** -- Expired July 1, 2016.

(b96) **NC Victim Assistance Network.** -- Expired July 1, 2016.

(b97) **NC Wildlife Federation.** -- Expired July 1, 2016.

(b98) **NC Youth Soccer Association.** -- Expired July 1, 2016.

(b99) **North Carolina 4-H Development Fund.** -- Expired July 1, 2016.

(b100) **North Carolina Bluegrass Association.** -- Expired July 1, 2016.

(b101) **North Carolina Cattlemen's Association.** -- Expired July 1, 2016.

(b102) **North Carolina Emergency Management Association.** -- Expired July 1, 2016.

(b103) **North Carolina Green Industry Council.** -- Expired July 1, 2016.

(b104) **North Carolina Libraries.** -- Expired July 1, 2016.

(b105) **North Carolina Master Gardener.** -- The Division must receive 300 or more applications for the "North Carolina Master Gardener" plate before the plate may be developed. The Division shall transfer quarterly the money in the Collegiate and Cultural Attraction Plate Account derived from the sale of "North Carolina Master Gardener" plates to the Master Gardener's Endowment Fund maintained by the Agricultural Foundation of North Carolina State University to be used for educational programs by trained volunteers who work in partnership with their county Cooperative Extension offices to extend information in consumer horticulture.

(b106) **North Carolina Paddle Festival.** -- Expired July 1, 2016.

(b107) **North Carolina Sheriffs' Association.** -- The applicable requirements of G.S. 20-79.3A shall be met before the North Carolina Sheriffs' Association plate may be developed. The Division shall transfer quarterly the money in the Collegiate and Cultural Attraction Plate Account derived from the sale of North Carolina Sheriffs' Association plates to the North Carolina Sheriffs' Association, Inc., to support the operating expenses of the North Carolina Sheriffs' Association.

(b108) **North Carolina Wildlife Habitat Foundation.** -- The Division must receive 300 or more applications for the North Carolina Wildlife Habitat Foundation plate before the plate may be developed. The Division shall transfer quarterly the money in the Collegiate and Cultural Attraction Plate Account derived from the sale of the North Carolina Wildlife Habitat Foundation plates to the North Carolina Wildlife Habitat Foundation for its programs.

(b109) **Nurses.** -- The Division must receive 300 or more applications for a Nurses plate before the plate may be developed. The Division shall transfer quarterly the money in the Collegiate and Cultural Attraction Plate Account derived from the sale of Nurses plates to the NC Foundation for Nursing for nursing scholarships for citizens of North Carolina to be awarded annually.

(b110) **Olympic Games.** -- The Division may not issue an Olympic Games special plate unless it receives 300 or more applications for the plate and the U.S. Olympic Committee licenses, without charge, the State to develop a plate bearing the Olympic Games symbol and name. The Division must transfer quarterly the money in the Collegiate and Cultural Attraction Plate Account derived from the sale of Olympic Games plates to North Carolina Amateur Sports, which will allocate the funds as follows:

(1) Sixty-seven percent (67%) to the U.S. Olympic Committee to assist in training Olympic athletes.

(2) Thirty-three percent (33%) to North Carolina Amateur Sports to assist with administration of the State Games of North Carolina.

(3) Repealed by Session Laws 2013-376, s. 7, effective July 29, 2013.

(b111) **Omega Psi Phi Fraternity Plates.** -- The Division must receive 300 or more applications for an Omega Psi Phi Fraternity plate and receive any necessary licenses, without charge, from Omega Psi PhiFraternity, Incorporated, before the plate may be developed. The Division must transfer quarterly the money in the Collegiate and Cultural Attraction Plate Account derived from the sale of Omega Psi Phi Fraternity plates to the Carolina Uplift Foundation, Inc., for youth activity and scholarship programs.

(b112) **Operation Coming Home.** -- Expired July 1, 2016.

(b113) **Order of the Eastern Star Prince Hall Affiliated.** -- The Division shall transfer quarterly the money in the Collegiate and Cultural Attraction Plate Account derived from the sale of "Order of the Eastern Star Prince Hall Affiliated" plates to The Most Worshipful Prince Hall Grand Lodge of Free and Accepted Masons of North Carolina and Jurisdiction, Inc.

(b114) **Order of the Long Leaf Pine.** -- The Order of the Long Leaf Pine plate is not subject to the provisions of G.S. 20-79.3A or G.S. 20-79.8, including the minimum number of applications required under G.S. 20-63(b1). The Division shall transfer quarterly the money in the Collegiate and Cultural Attraction Plate Account derived from the sale of Order of the Long Leaf Pine plates to the General Fund.

(b115) **Outer Banks Preservation Association.** -- Expired July 1, 2016.

(b116) **Pamlico-Tar River Foundation.** -- Expired July 1, 2016.

(b117) **Pancreatic Cancer Awareness.** -- Expired July 1, 2016.

(b118) P.E.O. Sisterhood. -- Expired July 1, 2016.

(b119) **Phi Beta Sigma Fraternity.** -- The Division must receive 300 or more applications for the "Phi Beta Sigma Fraternity" plate before the plate may be developed. The Division shall transfer quarterly the money in the Collegiate and Cultural Attraction Plate Account derived from the sale of "Phi Beta Sigma Fraternity" plates to the Phi Beta SigmaFraternity, Inc., to provide funding for scholarships, education, and professional development, or similar programs. None of the proceeds from this special plate may be distributed to any board member as compensation or as an honorarium.

(b120) **Piedmont Airlines.** -- The Division must receive 300 or more applications for a

Chapter 20

"Piedmont Airlines" plate before the plate may be developed. The Division must transfer quarterly the money in the Collegiate and Cultural Attraction Plate Account derived from the sale of "Piedmont Airlines" plates to Piedmont Silver Eagles Charitable Funds, Inc., to be used for scholarships and family assistance for Piedmont Airlines employees and their families, including surviving spouses and dependents, suffering economic hardship.

(b121) **Pisgah Conservancy.** -- The applicable requirements of G.S. 20-79.3A shall be met before the Pisgah Conservancy plate may be developed. The Division shall transfer quarterly the money in the Collegiate and Cultural Attraction Plate Account derived from the sale of Pisgah Conservancy plates to The Pisgah Conservancy to be used to provide support for the mission and goals of the Conservancy.

(b122) **POW/MIA Bring Them Home.** -- The Division shall transfer quarterly the money in the Collegiate and Cultural Attraction Plate Account derived from the sale of POW/MIA Bring Them Home plates to Rolling Thunder, Inc., Chapter #1 North Carolina.

(b123) **Prince Hall Mason.** -- The Division must receive 300 or more applications for a Prince Hall Mason plate before the plate may be developed. The Division must transfer quarterly the money in the Collegiate and Cultural Attraction Plate Account derived from the sale of Prince Hall Mason plates to The Most Worshipful Prince Hall Grand Lodge of Free and Accepted Masons of North Carolina and Jurisdiction, Inc., to be used for scholarships, family assistance, and other charitable causes.

(b124) **Professional Engineer.** -- Expired July 1, 2016.

(b125) **Red Drum.** -- Expired July 1, 2016.

(b126) **Retired Legislator.** -- The Division shall transfer quarterly the money in the Collegiate and Cultural Attraction Plate Account derived from the sale of Retired Legislator plates to the State Capitol Foundation, Inc., to be used to provide support for the mission and goals of the foundation.

(b127) **RiverLink.** -- Expired July 1, 2016.

(b128) **Rocky Mountain Elk Foundation.** -- The Division must receive 300 or more applications for a Rocky Mountain Elk Foundation plate before the plate may be developed. The Division must transfer quarterly the money in the Collegiate and Cultural Attraction Account derived from the sale of Rocky Mountain Elk Foundation plates to Rocky Mountain Elk Foundation, Inc.

(b129) **Ronald McDonald House.** -- The Division must receive 300 or more applications for the "Ronald McDonald House" plate before the plate may be developed. The Division shall transfer quarterly the money in the Collegiate and Cultural Attraction Plate Account derived from the sale of "Ronald McDonald House" plates to Ronald McDonald House Charities of North Carolina, Inc., to be used for Ronald McDonald Houses located within North Carolina and related administrative and operating expenses.

(b130) **Save the Honey Bee (HB).** -- The applicable requirements of G.S. 20-79.3A shall be met before the Save the Honey Bee plate may be developed. The Division shall transfer quarterly the money in the Collegiate and Cultural Attraction Plate Account derived from the sale of Save the Honey Bee plates to the North Carolina State University Apiculture Program.

(b131) **Save the Honey Bee (SB).** -- The applicable requirements of G.S. 20-79.3A shall be met before the Save the Honey Bee plate may be developed. The Division shall transfer quarterly one-half of the money in the Collegiate and Cultural Attraction Plate Account derived from the sale of Save the Honey Bee plates to the Grandfather Mountain Stewardship Foundation to be used to support the Honey Bee Haven and honey bee educational programs and shall transfer one-half of the money in the Collegiate and Cultural Attraction Plate Account derived from the sale of Save the Honey Bee plates to the North Carolina State University Apiculture Program to be used to support work on honey bee biology and apicultural science.

(b132) **Save the Sea Turtles.** -- The Division must receive 300 or more applications for a Save the Sea Turtles plate before the plate may be developed. The Division must transfer quarterly the money in the Collegiate and Cultural Attraction Plate Account derived from the sale of Save the Sea Turtles plates to The Karen Beasley Sea Turtle Rescue and Rehabilitation Center.

(b133) **Scenic Rivers Plates.** -- Expired July 1, 2016.

(b134) **School Technology Plates.** -- Expired July 1, 2016.

(b135) **SCUBA.** -- The Division must receive 300 or more applications for the SCUBA plate before the plate may be developed. The Division shall transfer quarterly the money in the Collegiate and Cultural Plate Account derived for the sale of the SCUBA plates to the Division of Marine Fisheries for the purpose of developing the State's artificial reefs.

(b136) **Shag Dancing.** -- The Division must receive 300 or more applications for the Shag Dancing plate before the plate may be developed. The Division shall transfer quarterly the money in the Collegiate and Cultural Attraction Plate Account derived from the sale of Shag Dancing plates to the Hall of Fame Foundation.

(b137) **Share the Road.** -- The Division must receive 300 or more applications for the Share the Road plate before the plate may be developed. The Division shall transfer quarterly the money in the Collegiate and Cultural Attraction Plate Account derived from the sale of the Share the Road plates to the Department of Transportation, Division of Bicycle and Pedestrian Transportation, for its programs.

(b138) **Soil and Water Conservation Plates.** -- Expired July 1, 2016.

(b139) **Special Forces Association.** -- Expired July 1, 2016.

(b140) **Special Olympics Plates.** -- Expired July 1, 2016.

(b141) S.T.A.R. -- Expired July 1, 2016.

(b142) **State Attraction Plates.** -- The Division must receive 300 or more applications for a State attraction plate before the plate may be developed. The Division must transfer quarterly the money in the Collegiate and Cultural Attraction Plate Account derived from the sale of State attraction plates to the organizations named below in proportion to the number of State attraction plates sold representing that organization:

(1) **Aurora Fossil Museum.** -- The revenue derived from the special plate shall be transferred quarterly to the Aurora Fossil Museum Foundation, Inc., to be used for educational programs, for enhancing collections, and for operating expenses of the Aurora Fossil Museum.

(2) **Blue Ridge Parkway Foundation.** -- The revenue derived from the special plate shall be transferred quarterly to Blue Ridge Parkway Foundation for use in promoting and preserving the Blue Ridge Parkway as a scenic attraction in North Carolina. A person may obtain from the Division a special registration plate under this subdivision for the registered owner of a motor vehicle or a motorcycle. The registration fees and the restrictions on the issuance of a specialized registration plate for a motorcycle are the same as for any motor vehicle. The Division must receive a minimum of 300 applications to develop a special registration plate for a motorcycle.

(3) **Friends of the Appalachian Trail.** -- The revenue derived from the special plate shall be transferred quarterly to The Appalachian Trail Conference to be used for educational materials, preservation programs, trail maintenance, trailway and viewshed acquisitions, trailway and viewshed easement acquisitions, capital improvements for the portions of the Appalachian Trail and connecting trails that are located in North Carolina, and related administrative and operating expenses.

(4) **Friends of the Great Smoky Mountains National Park.** -- The revenue derived from the special plate shall be transferred quarterly to the Friends of the Great Smoky Mountains National Park, Inc., to be used for educational materials, preservation programs, capital improvements for the portion of the Great Smoky Mountains National Park that is located in North Carolina, and operating expenses of the Great Smoky Mountains National Park.

(5) **The North Carolina Aquariums.** -- The revenue derived from the special plate shall be transferred quarterly to the North Carolina Aquarium Society, Inc., for its programs in support of the North Carolina Aquariums.

(6) **The North Carolina Arboretum.** -- The revenue derived from the special plate shall be transferred quarterly to The North Carolina Arboretum Society and used to help the Society obtain grants for the North Carolina Arboretum and for capital improvements to the North Carolina Arboretum.

(7) **The North Carolina Maritime Museum.** -- The revenue derived from the special plate shall be transferred quarterly to Friends of the Museum, North Carolina Maritime Museum, Inc., to be used for educational programs and conservation programs and for operating expenses of the North Carolina Maritime Museum.

(8) **The North Carolina Museum of Natural Sciences.** -- The revenue derived from the special plate shall be transferred quarterly to the Friends of the North Carolina State Museum of Natural Sciences for its programs in support of the museum.

(9) **North Carolina State Parks.** -- The revenue derived from the special plate shall be transferred quarterly to Friends of State Parks, Inc., for its educational, conservation, and other programs in support of the operations of the State Parks System established in Part 32 of Article 7 [Article 2] of Chapter 143B of the General Statutes.

(10) **The North Carolina Transportation Museum.** -- The revenue derived from the special plate shall be transferred quarterly to the North Carolina Transportation Museum Foundation to be used for educational programs and conservation programs and for operating expenses of the North Carolina Transportation Museum.

(11) **The North Carolina Zoological Society.** -- The revenue derived from the special plate shall be transferred quarterly to The North Carolina Zoological Society, Incorporated, to be used for educational programs and conservation programs at the North Carolina Zoo at Asheboro and for operating expenses of the North Carolina Zoo at Asheboro.

(12) **"Old Baldy," Bald Head Island Lighthouse.** -- The revenue derived from

Chapter 20

515

the special plate shall be transferred quarterly to the Old Baldy Foundation, Inc., for its programs in support of the Bald Head Island Lighthouse.

(13) U.S.S. North Carolina Battleship Commission. -- The revenue derived from the special plate shall be transferred quarterly to the U.S.S. North Carolina Battleship Commission to be used for educational programs and preservation programs on the U.S.S. North Carolina (BB-55) and for operating expenses of the U.S.S. North Carolina Battleship Commission.

(b143) **Stock Car Racing Theme.** -- The Division may issue any plate in this series without a minimum number of applications if the person providing the State with the license to use the words, logos, trademarks, or designs associated with the plate produces the plate for the State without a minimum order quantity.

The cost of the Stock Car Racing Theme plate shall include all costs to produce blank plates for issuance by the Division. Notwithstanding G.S. 66-58(b), the Division or the Division of Adult Correction and Juvenile Justice of the Department of Public Safety may contract for the production of the blank plates in this series to be issued by the Division, provided the plates meet or exceed the State's specifications including durability and retroreflectivity, and provided the plates are manufactured using high-quality embossable aluminum. The cost of the blank plates to the State shall be substantially equivalent to the price paid to the Division of Adult Correction and Juvenile Justice of the Department of Public Safety for license tags, as provided in G.S. 66-58(b)(15).

The Division shall transfer quarterly the money in the Collegiate and Cultural Attraction Plate Account derived from the sale of Stock Car Racing Theme plates to the North Carolina Motorsports Foundation, Inc.; except that the Division shall transfer quarterly the money in the Collegiate and Cultural Attraction Plate Account derived from the sale of Charlotte Motor Speedway plates to Speedway Children's Charities.

(b144) **Support NC Education.** -- Expired July 1, 2016.

(b145) **Support Our Troops.** -- The Division must receive 300 or more applications for a Support Our Troops plate before the plate may be developed. The Division shall transfer quarterly the money in the Collegiate and Cultural Attraction Plate Account derived from the sale of Support Our Troops plates to NC Support Our Troops, Inc., to be used to provide support and assistance to the troops and their families.

(b146) **Support Soccer.** -- The Division must receive 300 or more applications for the "Support Soccer" plate before the plate may be developed. The Division shall transfer quarterly the money in the Collegiate and Cultural Attraction Plate Account derived from the sale of "Support Soccer" plates to the North Carolina Soccer Hall of Fame, Inc., to provide funding to promote the sport of soccer in North Carolina.

(b147) **Surveyor Plate.** -- The Division must receive 300 or more applications for a Surveyor plate before the plate may be developed. The Division shall transfer quarterly the money in the Collegiate and Cultural Attraction Plate Account derived from the sale of Surveyor plates to The North Carolina Society of Surveyors Education Foundation, Inc., for public educational programs.

(b148) **Sustainable Fisheries.** -- Expired July 1, 2016.

(b149) **Toastmasters Club.** -- Expired July 1, 2016.

(b150) **Topsail Island Shoreline Protection.** -- Expired July 1, 2016.

(b151) **Travel and Tourism.** -- Expired July 1, 2016.

(b152) **Turtle Rescue Team.** -- Expired July 1, 2016.

(b153) **United States Service Academy.** -- The Division must transfer quarterly the money in the Collegiate and Cultural Attraction Plate Account derived from the sale of United States Service Academy plates to the United Services Organization of North Carolina to support its mission to lead the way to enriching the lives of America's military in North Carolina.

(b154) **University Health Systems of Eastern Carolina.** -- Expired July 1, 2016.

(b155) **US Equine Rescue League.** -- Expired July 1, 2016.

(b156) **USO of NC.** -- Expired July 1, 2016.

(b157) **The V Foundation for Cancer Research.** -- The Division must receive 300 or more applications for a V Foundation plate before the plate may be developed. The Division shall transfer quarterly the money in the Collegiate and Cultural Attraction Plate Account derived from the sale of V Foundation plates to The V Foundation for Cancer Research to fund cancer research grants.

(b158) **Volunteers in Law Enforcement.** -- Expired July 1, 2016.

(b159) **Wildlife Resources Plates.** -- The Division must receive 300 or more applications for a wildlife resources plate with a picture representing a particular native wildlife species occurring in North Carolina before the plate may be developed. The Division must transfer quarterly the money in the Collegiate and Cultural Attraction Plate Account derived from the sale of wildlife resources plates to the Wildlife Conservation Account established by G.S. 143-247.2.

(b160) **Wrightsville Beach.** -- The Division shall transfer quarterly the money in the Collegiate and Cultural Attraction Plate Account derived from the sale of Wrightsville Beach plates to the Town of Wrightsville Beach to help fund the Town's continuing efforts to maintain and improve recreational opportunities for residents and visitors of Wrightsville Beach.

(b161) **YMCA.** -- Expired July 1, 2016.

(b162) **Zeta Phi Beta Sorority.** -- The Division must receive 300 or more applications for a Zeta Phi Beta Sorority plate before the plate may be developed. The Division shall transfer quarterly the money in the Collegiate and Cultural Attraction Plate Account derived from the sale of Zeta Phi Beta Sorority plates to the Zeta Phi Beta Sorority Education Foundation, through the Raleigh office, for the benefit of undergraduate scholarships in this State.

(c) **General.** -- An application for a special license plate named in this section may be made at any time during the year. If the application is made to replace an existing current valid plate, the special plate must be issued with the appropriate decals attached. No refund shall be made to the applicant for any unused portion remaining on the original plate. The request for a special license plate named in this section may be combined with a request that the plate be a personalized license plate.

(c1) In accordance with G.S. 143C-1-2, the transfers mandated in this section are appropriations made by law.

(d) through (g) Repealed by Session Laws 1991 (Regular Session, 1992), c. 1042, s. 3.

History.

1991, c. 758, s. 1;1991 (Reg. Sess., 1992), c. 1007, s. 33; c. 1042, s. 3; 1993, c. 543, s. 5;1995, c. 433, s. 4;1997-427, s. 2;1997-477, s. 4;1997-484, s. 6;1999-277, s. 4;1999-403, s. 4;1999-450, s. 4;2000-159, ss. 5, 6; 2000-163, s. 3;2001-498, ss. 6(a), 6(b); 2002-134, s. 7;2003-11, s. 4;2003-68, s. 4;2003-424, ss. 5, 6; 2004-131, s. 5;2004-185, s. 5;2004-200, s. 4;2005-216, ss. 6, 7; 2005-435, s. 40;2006-209, ss. 5, 6, 7; 2007-323, s. 27.20(a);2007-345, s. 10.1;2007-400, ss. 5, 6; 2007-483, ss. 6(a), 7, 8(c); 2010-31, s. 11.4(m);2010-95, s. 35;2011-145, ss. 19.1(g), (h), 13.25(*ll*); 2011-392, ss. 6, 7; 2013-155, s. 2;2013-360, s. 14.3B;2013-376, ss. 5 -8; 2013-414, s. 57(d);2014-100, s. 8.11(c);2015-241, ss. 14.30(dd1), 15.4(a), 29.40(d), (j), (k), (n), (p); 2017-100, s. 3;2017-107, s. 4;2017-114, s. 4;2017-186, ss. 2 (mmmm), 3(a); 2018-74, ss. 11(c), (e), 12(f), 14(c), 14.5; 2018-77, ss. 2(f), 3, 3.5(c); 2019-213, s. 2(d)

INACTIVE SPECIAL INTEREST PLATES. --Pursuant to G.S. 20-79.8(a), several special plates authorized by G.S. 20-79.4 prior to October 1, 2014, expired as a matter of law on July 1, 2016, because the number of applications required for their production was not received by the Division of Motor Vehicles. At the direction of the Revisor of Statutes, pursuant to G.S. 20-79.8(c), those special plates not meeting this requirement have been set out as expired effective July 1, 2016.

EDITOR'S NOTE. --

The bracketed reference in subdivision (b2)(9) was added at the direction of the Revisor of Statutes.

Session Laws, 2004-131, s. 5, Session Laws 2004-185, s. 5, and Session Laws 2004-200, s. 4, each amended this section by inserting a new subsection (b31). This section has been set out in the form above at the direction of the Revisor of Statutes.

The subsection designation for subsection (b11) was assigned by the Revisor of Statutes, the designation in Session Laws 1999-450, s. 4 having been (b10).

This section was amended by Session Laws 2000-163, s. 3 in the coded bill drafting format. It failed to incorporate the addition of subsection (b10) by Session Laws 1999-403, s. 4, and the subsequent renumbering of subsection (b10) as added by Session Laws 1999-450, s. 4, as subsection (b11). The section has been set out in the form above at the direction of the Revisor of Statutes.

Session Laws 2001-498, s. 8, provided that s. 6(b), which amended this section by adding subsections (b21) and (b22), would expire on June 30, 2006. However, Session Laws 2006-209, s. 7, amended Session Laws 2001-498, s. 8, to delete the sunset provision, so subsections (b21) and (b22) will not expire.

Subsections (b62) through (b70), as enacted by Session Laws 2007-483, s. 7, have been redesignated as subsections (b64) through (b72) at the direction of the Revisor of Statutes.

Pursuant to Session Laws 2011-145, s. 13.22A(dd), and at the direction of the Revisor of Statutes, the reference in subsection (b8) of this section to "G.S. 106-844" was substituted for the former reference to "G.S. 143B-297.1." G.S. 143B-294 through G.S. 143B-297.1 were recodified as G.S. 106-840 through G.S. 106-844, by Session Laws 2011-145, s. 13.22A(e), effective July 1, 2011.

Session Laws 2011-392, s. 9, provides: "Notwithstanding Section 8 of this act, any special registration plate authorized in G.S. 20-79.7, prior to July 1, 2011, shall expire, as a matter of law, on July 1, 2013, if the number of applications required for the production of the special registration plate has not been received by the Division of Motor Vehicles on or before that date. Upon notification of expiration of the authorization for any special plate by the Division pursuant to this section, the Revisor of Statutes shall verify that the authorization for each special registration plate listed has expired and shall notate such expiration in the applicable statutes. If an authorization for a special registration plate listed in G.S. 20-79.4 expires, the Revisor of Statutes shall revise the subdivision referring to the special registration plate to leave the name of the special plate authorized and the date the special registration plate's authorization expired. If an authorization for a special registration plate listed in G.S. 20-79.4 expires, the Revisor of Statutes shall also make corresponding changes to reflect the expiration of the special registration plate's authorization, if applicable, in G.S. 20-63(b), 20-79.7, and 20-81.12."

Subsections (b)(93) through (b109.1), added by Session Laws 2011-392, s. 7, were redesignated as (b92) through (b109) at the direction of the Revisor of Statutes.

Session Laws 2013-414, s. 57(e), provides: "The Revisor of Statutes is authorized to alphabetize, number, and renumber the special registration plates listed in G.S. 20-81.12(b2) to ensure that all the special registration plates are listed in alphabetical order and numbered accordingly." Pursuant to this authority, the subdivisions in subsection (b2) have been reordered to achieve alphabetical order.

Session Laws 2014-96, s. 1(a), provides: "Any special registration plate authorized under G.S. 20-79.4 that expired as a matter of law on July 1, 2013, pursuant to G.S. 20-79.8, is reenacted. The corresponding provisions for fees under G.S. 20-79.7(a1) and (b) and any other corresponding requirements for the plates under G.S. 20-81.12 are also reenacted. A special registration plate reenacted under this section is subject to the requirements of G.S. 20-63(b1) if the plate is authorized to be on a background other than a "First in Flight" background."

Session Laws 2014-96, s. 1(b), provides: "This section is effective when it becomes law [August 1, 2014]. A special registration plate reenacted by this section shall expire, as a matter of law, on October 1, 2014, if the required number of applications for the special registration plate has not been received by the Division of Motor Vehicles by that date. The notification procedure and the responsibilities of the Revisor of Statutes for a special registration plate that expires pursuant to this subsection shall be in accordance with G.S. 20-79.8 except that the notification date shall be no later than October 15, 2015. The Division shall not accept applications for nor advertise any special registration plate that has expired pursuant to this subsection."

Session Laws 2015-241, s. 29.40(j), which reenacted provisions related to Order of the Long Leaf Pine, provides: "G.S. 20-79.4(b)(171), as it existed on June 30, 2015, is reenacted. The corresponding provisions for fees under G.S. 20-79.7(a1) and (b) and any other corresponding requirements for the plates under G.S. 20-81.12 are also reenacted."

Session Laws 2015-241, s. 29.40(n), provides: "G.S. 20-79.4(b)(21), G.S. 20-81.12(b76), and the corresponding provisions for fees under G.S. 20-79.7(a) and (b), as they existed on September 30, 2014, are reenacted."

Session Laws 2015-241, s. 29.40(s), provides: "Subsections (r) and (s) of this section are effective when this act becomes law. The remainder of this section is effective 90 days after this act becomes law."

Session Laws 2015-241, s. 1.1, provides: "This act shall be known as 'The Current Operations and Capital Improvements Appropriations Act of 2015.'"

Session Laws 2015-241, s. 33.6, is a severability clause.

Session Laws 2017-100, s. 3, provides: "G.S. 20-81.12(b30), as it existed immediately before its repeal under Section 1(b) of S.L. 2014-96, is reenacted."

Subsections (b155) through (b157), as added by Session Laws 2017-114, s. 4, were renumbered as subsections (b156) through (b158) at the direction of the Revisor of Statutes.

Session Laws 2017-186, s. 3(a), provides: "The Revisor of Statutes shall change any additional references in the General Statutes to the 'Division of Adult Correction' to the 'Division of Adult Correction and Juvenile Justice.'" Pursuant to this authority, the first occurrence of "Division of Adult Correction" was changed to "Division of Adult Correction and Juvenile Justice."

Session Laws 2018-77, s. 3.5, effective February 1, 2019, was repealed by Acts 2018-74, s. 11(e), effective February 1, 2019. Session Laws 2018-77, s. 3.5(c) would have added (b159) for Order of the Eastern Star Prince Hall Affiliated identical to the amendment by Session Laws 2018-74, s. 11(c).

Session Laws 2019-213, s. 2(e), provides: "The Revisor of Statutes is authorized to alphabetize, number, and renumber the special registration plates listed in G.S. 20-63(b1), 20-79.4(b), and 20-81.12 to ensure that all the special registration plates are listed in alphabetical order and numbered accordingly." Pursuant to that authority, subsections (a), (b), and (b1) through (b160) were renumbered.

EFFECT OF AMENDMENTS. --

Session Laws 2003-424, ss. 5 and 6, effective January 1, 2004, in subsection (b2), renumbered former subdivision (1) as present (1a), renumbered former subdivision (1a) as present (1c), and renumbered former subdivision (1b) as present (1d), and inserted present subdivisions (1) and (1b); and added subsections (b26), (b27), (b28), (b29), and (b30).

Session Laws 2004-131, s. 5, effective July 29, 2004, inserted subsection (b31).

Session Laws 2004-185, s. 5, effective October 1, 2004, inserted the subsection designated herein as subsection (b38).

Session Laws 2004-200, s. 4, effective August 17, 2004, added the subsections designated herein as subsections (b32) through (b37).

Session Laws 2005-216, ss. 6 and 7, effective July 20, 2005, redesignated subdivisions (b2)(1a), (1b), (1c) and (1d) as subdivisions (b2)(1c), (1g), (1m) and (1p), respectively, and added subdivisions (b2)(1j), (1t); and added subsections (b39) through (b52).

Session Laws 2005-435, s. 40, effective September 27, 2005, substituted "G.S. 113A-253" for "G.S. 113-45.3" at the end of subsection (b7).

Session Laws 2006-209, ss. 5, 6, effective August 8, 2006, added subdivision (b2)(1i); and added subsections (b53) through (b61).

Session Laws 2007-323, s. 27.20(a), as added by Session Laws 2007-345, s. 10.1, effective July 1, 2007, added subsection (c1).

Session Laws 2007-400, ss. 5 and 6, effective August 21, 2007, in subdivision (b2)(1), added the last three sentences; and added subsections (b62) and (b63).

Session Laws 2007-483, s. 6(a), effective July 1, 2007, and applicable to fees transferred from the

Collegiate and Cultural Attraction Plate Account on or after that date, in subsection (b14), in the second sentence, substituted "must transfer" for "shall transfer" and substituted "the Carolina Uplift Foundation, Inc., for youth activity and scholarship programs" for "the United Negro College Fund, Inc., through the Winston-Salem Area Office for the benefit of UNCF colleges in this State".

Session Laws 2007-483, s. 7, effective August 30, 2007, added subsections (b62) through (b70) (now (b64) through (b72)).

Session Laws 2007-483, s. 8(c), effective October 1, 2007, repealed subsection (b53), which related to the Breast Cancer Awareness specialty license plate. See Editor's note.

Session Laws 2010-31, s. 11.4(m), effective October 1, 2010, substituted "G.S. 19A-62" for "G.S. 19A-60" in subsection (b11).

Session Laws 2010-95, s. 35, effective July 17, 2010, substituted "G.S. 19A-62" for "G.S. 19A-60" in subsection (b11).

Session Laws 2011-145, s. 19.1(g), (h), effective January 1, 2012, substituted "Public Safety" for "Crime Control and Public Safety" in subsection (b31); and substituted "Division of Adult Correction of the Department of Public Safety" for "Department of Correction" twice in subsection (b38).

Session Laws 2011-145, s. 13.25 (ll), effective July 1, 2011, inserted "of the Department of Agriculture and Consumer Services" in the second sentence of subsection (b35).

Session Laws 2011-392, ss. 6 and 7, effective June 30, 2011, added subdivisions (b2)(1), (b2)(6), and (b2)(12), and made related redesignations; and added subsections (b73) through (b125).

Session Laws 2013-155, s. 2, effective July 1, 2013, substituted "North Carolina Forest Service" for "Division of Forest Resources" in subsection (b35).

Session Laws 2013-360, s. 14.3B, effective July 1, 2013, rewrote subdivision (b2)(5), which formerly read "North Carolina State Parks. -- One-half of the revenue derived from the special plate shall be transferred quarterly to Natural Heritage Trust Fund established under G.S. 113-77.7, and the remaining revenue shall be transferred quarterly to the Parks and Recreation Trust Fund established under G.S. 113-44.15."

Session Laws 2013-376, ss. 5 -8, effective July 29, 2013, added subdivision (b2)(10) -- The North Carolina Transportation Museum; in subsection (b4), substituted "North Carolina Amateur Sports" for "the N.C. Health and Fitness Foundation, Inc."; in subdivision (b4)(1), substituted "Sixty-seven percent (67%)" for "Fifty percent (50%)" and made a minor stylistic change; substituted "Thirty-three percent (33%)" for "Twenty-five percent (25%)" in subdivision (b4)(2); and deleted subdivision (b4)(3), which allocated 25% of the funds to the Governor's Council on Physical Fitness; in subsection (b38), added the exception at the end of the last paragraph; and added subsections (b126) through (b147).

Session Laws 2013-414, s. 57(d), effective August 23, 2013, added subsection (b148).

Session Laws 2014-100, s. 8.11(c), effective July 1, 2014, in subsection (b12), twice substituted "I Support Teachers Plates" for "Support Public Schools Plates" and substituted "North Carolina Education Endowment Fund established pursuant to G.S. 115C-472.16" for "Fund for the Reduction of Class Size in Public Schools created pursuant to G.S. 115C-472.10" and made minor stylistic changes.

Session Laws 2015-241, ss. 14.30(dd1) and 15.4(a), effective July 1, 2015, substituted "Department of Natural and Cultural Resources" for "Department of Cultural Resources" in subdivision (b)(3) and subsection (b100); substituted "Part 32 of Article 7 of Chapter 143B" for "Article 2C of Chapter 113" in subdivision (b2)(9); substituted "G.S. 143B-135.234" for "G.S. 113A-253" in subsection (b7); and substituted "Department of Commerce" for "Division of Tourism, Film, and Sports Development" in subsection (b124).

Session Laws 2015-241, s. 29.40(d), (k), and (p), effective December 17, 2015, deleted the former first sentence in subsection (b76), which read: "The Division must receive 300 or more applications for the 'Battle of Kings Mountain' plate before the plate may be developed"; rewrote subsection (b140); added the subsection heading in subsection (b148); and added subsections (b149) through (b154). For effective date, see editor's note.

Session Laws 2017-100, s. 3, effective July 12, 2017, reenacted subsection (b30).

Session Laws 2017-107, s. 4, effective July 1, 2017, added subsection (b155).

Session Laws 2017-114, s. 4, effective July 18, 2017, added subsections (b156) through (b157).

Session Laws 2017-186, s. 2 (mmmm), effective December 1, 2017, inserted "and Juvenile Justice" in the last sentence of the second paragraph of subsection (b38).

Session Laws 2018-74, s. 11(c), effective February 1, 2019, added subsection (b159).

Session Laws 2018-74, s. 12(f), and Session Laws 2018-77, s. 2(f), effective February 1, 2019, are identical, and reenacted subsection (b39) and deleted the first sentence, which read "The Division must receive 300 or more applications for the Alpha Phi Alpha Fraternity plate before the plate may be developed" and substituted "Education Consortium of North Carolina, Inc." for "Association of North Carolina Alphamen (ANCA) Educational Foundation" and deleted "in ANCA" preceding "attending."

Session Laws 2018-74, ss. 14(c), 14.5, effective July 1, 2018, added subsection (b160); and inserted "including the minimum number of applications required under G.S. 20-63(b1)" in subsection (b140).

Session Laws 2018-77, s. 3, effective June 25, 2018, inserted the exception at the beginning of the first sentence and added the second sentence in subsection (a).

Session Laws 2019-213, s. 2(d), effective March 1, 2020, added subsections (b3), (b63), (b122), and (b160).

LEGAL PERIODICALS. --

For note, "Specialty License Plates: The Product of Government Speech, Private Speech, or Both?," see 7 Charlotte L. Rev. 255 (2016).

N.C. Gen. Stat. § 20-82

Repealed by Session Laws 1995, c. 163, s. 3.

PART 6.
VEHICLES OF NONRESIDENTS OF STATE; PERMANENT PLATES; HIGHWAY PATROL

§ 20-83. Registration by nonresidents

(a) When a resident carrier of this State interchanges a properly licensed trailer or semitrailer with another carrier who is a resident of another state, and adequate records are on file in his office to verify such interchanges, the North Carolina licensed carrier may use the trailer licensed in such other state the same as if it is his own during the time the nonresident carrier is using the North Carolina licensed trailer.

(b) Motor vehicles duly registered in a state or territory which are not allowed exemptions by the Commissioner, as provided for in the preceding paragraph, desiring to make occasional trips into or through the State of North Carolina, or operate in this State for a period not exceeding 30 days, may be permitted the same use and privileges of the highways of this State as provided for similar vehicles regularly licensed in this State, by procuring from the Commissioner trip licenses upon forms and under rules and regulations to be adopted by the Commissioner, good for use for a period of 30 days upon the payment of a fee in compensation for said privilege equivalent to one tenth of the annual fee which would be chargeable against said vehicle if regularly licensed in this State: Provided that only one such permit allowed by this section shall be issued for the use of the same vehicle within the same registration year. Provided, however, that nothing in this provision shall prevent the extension of the privileges of the use of the roads of this State to vehicles of other states under the reciprocity provisions provided by law: Provided further, that nothing herein contained shall prevent the owners of vehicles from other states from licensing such vehicles in the State of North Carolina under the same terms and the same fees as like vehicles are licensed by owners resident in this State.

(c) Every nonresident, including any foreign corporation carrying on business within this State and owning and operating in such business any motor vehicle, trailer or semitrailer within this State, shall be required to register each such vehicle and pay the same fees therefor as is required with reference to like vehicles owned by residents of this State.

History.

1937, c. 407, s. 47; 1941, cc. 99, 365; 1957, c. 681, s. 1; 1961, c. 642, s. 4; 1967, c. 1090

CITED in Butler v. Green Tree Fin. Servicing Corp. (In re Wester), 229 Bankr. 348 (Bankr. E.D.N.C. 1998).

LEGAL PERIODICALS. --

For comment on the 1941 amendments to this section, see 19 N.C.L. Rev. 514 (1941).

§ 20-84. Permanent registration plates; State Highway Patrol

(a) **General. --** The Division may issue a permanent registration plate for a motor vehicle owned by one of the entities authorized to have a permanent registration plate in this section. To obtain a permanent registration plate, an authorized representative of the entity must provide proof of ownership, provide proof of financial responsibility as required by G.S. 20-309, and pay a fee of six dollars ($ 6.00). A permanent plate issued under this section may be transferred as provided in G.S. 20-78 to a replacement vehicle of the same classification. A permanent registration plate issued under this section must be a distinctive color and bear the word "permanent". In addition, a permanent registration plate issued under subdivision (b) (1) of this section must have distinctive color and design that is readily distinguishable from all other permanent registration plates issued under this section. Every eligible entity that receives a permanent registration plate under this section shall ensure that the permanent registration plate is registered under a single name. That single name shall be the full legal name of the eligible entity.

(b) **Permanent Registration Plates. --** The Division may issue permanent plates for the following motor vehicles:

(1) A motor vehicle owned by the State or one of its agencies.

(2) A motor vehicle owned by a county, city or town.

(3) A motor vehicle owned by a board of education.

(3a) A motor vehicle that is owned and exclusively operated by a nonprofit corporation authorized under G.S. 115C-218.5 to operate a charter school and identified by a permanent decal or painted marking disclosing the name of the nonprofit corporation. The motor vehicle shall only be used for student transportation and official charter school related activities.

(4) Repealed by Session Laws 2012-159, s. 1, effective July 1, 2012.

(5) A motor vehicle owned by the civil air patrol.

(6) A motor vehicle owned by an incorporated emergency rescue squad.

(7) through (9) Repealed by Session Laws 2012-159, s. 1, effective July 1, 2012.

(10) A motor vehicle owned by a rural fire department, agency, or association.

(11) Repealed by Session Laws 2012-159, s. 1, effective July 1, 2012.

(12) A motor vehicle owned by a local chapter of the American National Red Cross and used for emergency or disaster work.

(13) through (16) Repealed by Session Laws 2012-159, s. 1, effective July 1, 2012.

(17) A motor vehicle owned by a community college. A community college vehicle purchased with State equipment funds shall be issued a permanent registration plate with the same distinctive color and design as a permanent registration plate issued under subdivision (1) of this subsection.

(18) A motor vehicle that is owned and operated by a sanitary district created under Part 2 of Article 2 of Chapter 130A of the General Statutes.

(19) Any motor vehicle owned by a federally recognized tribe.

(20) A motor vehicle owned by a public transportation service provider that is a designated recipient or direct recipient of Federal Transit Administration formula grant funds pursuant to 49 U.S.C. § 5311 or 49 U.S.C. § 5307.

(c) **State Highway Patrol.** -- In lieu of all other registration requirements, the Commissioner shall each year assign to the State Highway Patrol, upon payment of six dollars ($ 6.00) per registration plate, a sufficient number of regular registration plates of the same letter prefix and in numerical sequence beginning with number 100 to meet the requirements of the State Highway Patrol for use on Division vehicles assigned to the State Highway Patrol. The commander of the Patrol shall, when such plates are assigned, issue to each member of the State Highway Patrol a registration plate for use upon the Division vehicle assigned to the member pursuant to G.S. 20-190 and assign a registration plate to each Division service vehicle operated by the Patrol. An index of such assignments of registration plates shall be kept at each State Highway Patrol radio station and a copy of it shall be furnished to the registration division of the Division. Information as to the individual assignments of the registration plates shall be made available to the public upon request to the same extent and in the same manner as regular registration information. The commander, when necessary, may reassign registration plates provided that the reassignment shall appear upon the index required under this subsection within 20 days after the reassignment.

(d) **Revocation.** -- The Division may revoke all permanent registration plates issued to eligible entities for vehicles that are 90 days or more past due for a vehicle inspection, as required by G.S. 20-183.4C. This subsection does not limit or restrict the authority of the Division to revoke permanent registration plates pursuant to other applicable law.

History.
1937, c. 407, s. 48; 1939, c. 275; 1949, c. 583, s. 1; 1951, c. 388; 1953, c. 1264; 1955, cc. 368, 382; 1967, c. 284; 1969, c. 800; 1971, c. 460, s. 1; 1975, c. 548; c. 716, s. 5; 1977, c. 370, s. 1; 1979, c. 801, s. 9; 1981 (Reg. Sess., 1982), c. 1159; 1983, c. 593, ss. 1, 2; 1987 (Reg. Sess., 1988), c. 885; 1991 (Reg. Sess., 1992), c. 1030, s. 11; 1997-443, s. 11A.118(a);1999-220, s. 3;2000-159, s. 7;2012-159, s. 1;2014-101, s. 6.6(a);2014-108, s. 3(a);2015-241, s. 29.40(r);2016-94, s. 35.16

EDITOR'S NOTE. --
Session Laws 1971, c. 460, which amended this section, provided in s. 1.1, that the addition of the last paragraph to this section "shall not be construed as abrogating or modifying the provisions of G.S. 14-250."

Session Laws 2012-159, s. 3, provides: "Except for State entities issued permanent registration plates under G.S. 20-84(b)(1), the Division of Motor Vehicles shall cancel all permanent registration plates issued to non-State entities and reissue permanent registration plates with a new design to eligible non-State entities by January 15, 2013. The Division shall determine the new design of the permanent registration plates reissued to eligible non-State entities."

Session Laws 2014-101, s. 6.6(b), repeals subdivision (b)(3a) of this section, effective July 1, 2015.

Session Laws 2014-101, s. 8, made subdivision (b)(3a) of this section, as added by Session Laws 2014-101, s. 6.6(a), effective August 6, 2014, and applicable beginning with the 2014-2015 school year.

Session Laws 2015-241, s. 29.40(r), provides: "G.S. 20-84(b)(3a), as it existed on June 30, 2015, is reenacted."

Session Laws 2015-241, s. 1.1, provides: "This act shall be known as 'The Current Operations and Capital Improvements Appropriations Act of 2015.'"

Session Laws 2015-241, s. 33.6, is a severability clause.

Session Laws 2016-94, s. 1.2, provides: "This act shall be known as the 'Current Operations and Capital Improvements Appropriations Act of 2016.'"

Session Laws 2016-94, s. 39.7, is a severability clause.

Chapter 20

EFFECT OF AMENDMENTS. --

Session Laws 2012-159, s. 1, effective July 1, 2012, in subsection (a), substituted "entities" for "persons" in the first sentence, substituted "an authorized representative of the entity" for "a person" in the second sentence, and added the last sentence; repealed subdivisions (b)(4), (b)(7) through (b)(9), (b)(11), and (b)(13) through (b)(16); added subdivision (b)(17); and added subsection (d).

Session Laws 2014-101, s. 6.6(a), effective August 6, 2014, added subdivision (b)(3a). See Editor's note for applicability.

Session Laws 2014-108, s. 3(a), effective August 6, 2014, added subdivisions (b)(18) and (19).

Session Laws 2016-94, s. 35.16, effective July 1, 2016, added subdivision (b)(20).

CROSS REFERENCES. --

As to motor vehicles owned by local boards of education, see G.S. 115C-520.

OPINIONS OF THE ATTORNEY GENERAL

PERMANENT REGISTRATION OF MOTOR VEHICLE LEASED TO MUNICIPALITY IS IMPROPER. --See opinion of Attorney General to Mr. James H. Stamey, Department of Motor Vehicles, 41 N.C.A.G. 798 (1972).

N.C. Gen. Stat. § 20-84.1

Repealed by Session Laws 1999-220, s. 4, effective July 1, 1999.

PART 6A.
RENTAL VEHICLES

§ 20-84.2. Definition; reciprocity; Commissioner's powers

(a) The term rental vehicle when used herein shall mean and include any motor vehicle which is rented or leased to another by its owner for a period of not more than 30 days solely for the transportation of the lessee or the private hauling of the lessee's personal property.

(b) Rental vehicles owned or operated by any nonresident person engaged in the business of leasing such vehicles for use in intrastate or interstate commerce shall be extended full reciprocity and exempted from registration fees only in instances where:

    (1) Such person has validly licensed all rental vehicles owned by him in the state wherein the owner actually resides; provided, that such state affords equal recognition, either in fact or in law to such vehicles licensed in the State of North Carolina and operating similarly within the owner's state of residence; and further provided, that such person is not engaged in this State in the business of leasing rental vehicles; or where

    (2) Such person operates vehicles which are a part of a common fleet of vehicles which are easily identifiable as a part of such fleet and such person has validly licensed in the State of North Carolina a percentage of the total number of vehicles in each weight classification in such fleet which represents the percentage of total miles travelled in North Carolina by all vehicles in each weight classification of such fleet to total miles travelled in all jurisdictions in which such fleet is operated by all vehicles in each weight classification of such fleet.

(c) The Commissioner of Motor Vehicles requires such person to submit under oath such information as is deemed necessary for fairly administering this section. The Commissioner's determination, after hearing, as to the number of vehicles in each weight classification to be licensed in North Carolina shall be final.

Any person who licenses vehicles under subsection (b)(2) above shall keep and preserve for three years the mileage records on which the percentage of the total fleet is determined. Upon request these records shall be submitted or made available to the Commissioner of Motor Vehicles for audit or review, or the owner or operator shall pay reasonable costs of an audit by the duly appointed representative of the Commissioner at the place where the records are kept.

If the Commissioner determines that the person licensing vehicles under subsection (b)(2) above should have licensed more vehicles in North Carolina or that such person's records are insufficient for proper determination the Commissioner may deny that person the right or any further benefits under this subsection until the correct number of vehicles have been licensed, and all taxes determined by the Commissioner to be due have been paid.

(d) Upon payment by the owner of the prescribed fee, the Division shall issue registration certificates and plates for the percentage of vehicles determined by the Commissioner. Thereafter, all rental vehicles properly identified and licensed in any state, territory, province, country or the District of Columbia, and belonging to such owner, shall be permitted to operate in this State on an interstate or intrastate basis.

History.

1959, c. 1066; 1971, c. 808; 1973, c. 1446, s. 23; 1975, c. 716, s. 5

EDITOR'S NOTE. --

Part 6.1 was renumbered as Part 6A pursuant to Session Laws 1997-456, s. 27 which authorized the Revisor of Statutes to renumber or reletter sections and parts of section having a number or letter designation that is incompatible with the General Assembly's computer database.

PART 7.
TITLE AND REGISTRATION FEES

§ 20-85. Schedule of fees

(a) The following fees are imposed concerning a certificate of title, a registration card, or a registration plate for a motor vehicle. These fees are payable to the Division and are in addition to the tax imposed by Article 5A of Chapter 105 of the General Statutes:

(1) Each application for certificate
    of title.. $ 52.00
(2) Each application for duplicate
    or corrected certificate of title.............20.00
(3) Each application of repossessor
    for certificate of title............................20.00
(4) Each transfer of registration 20.00
(5) Each set of replacement
    registration plates...............................20.00
(6) Each application for duplicate
    registration card..................................20.00
(7) Each application for recording
    supplementary lien..............................20.00
(8) Each application for renewing
    a security interest on a certificate
    of title or removing a lien or security
    interest from a certificate of title.......20.00
(9) Each application for certificate of
    title for a motor vehicle transferred
    to a manufacturer, as defined in
    G.S. 20-286, or a motor vehicle retailer
    for the purpose of resale......................20.00
(10) Each application for a salvage
    certificate of title made by an insurer
    pursuant to G.S. 20-109.1 or by a
    used motor vehicle dealer pursuant
    to G.S. 20-109.1(e1) 20.00
(11) Each set of replacement Stock Car
    Racing Theme plates issued under
    G.S. 20-79.4...25.00.

(a1) *(Effective until June 30, 2031)* One dollar ($ 1.00) of the fee imposed for any transaction assessed a fee under subdivision (a)(1), (a)(2), (a)(3), (a)(7), (a)(8), or (a)(9) of this section shall be credited to the North Carolina Highway Fund. The Division shall use the fees derived from transactions with commission contract agents for the payment of compensation to commission contract agents. An additional twenty cents (20 cent(s)) of the fee imposed for any transaction assessed a fee under subdivision (a)(1) of this section shall be credited to the Mercury Pollution Prevention Fund in the Department of Environmental Quality.

(a1) *(Effective June 30, 2031)* One dollar ($ 1.00) of the fee imposed for any transaction assessed a fee under subdivision (a)(1), (a)(2), (a)(3), (a)(7), (a)(8), or (a)(9) of this section shall be credited to the North Carolina Highway Fund. The Division shall use the fees derived from transactions with commission contract agents for the payment of compensation to commission contract agents.

(a2) From the fees collected under subdivisions (a)(1) through (a)(9) of this section, the Department shall annually credit the sum of four hundred thousand dollars ($ 400,000) to the Reserve for Visitor Centers in the Highway Fund.

(b) Except as otherwise provided in subsections (a1) and (a2) of this section, the fees collected under subdivisions (a)(1) through (a)(9) of this section shall be credited to the North Carolina Highway Trust Fund. The fees collected under subdivision (a)(10) of this section shall be credited to the Highway Fund.

(c) The Division shall not collect a fee for a certificate of title for a motor vehicle entitled to a permanent registration plate under G.S. 20-84.

History.
1937, c. 407, s. 49; 1943, c. 648; 1947, c. 219, s. 9; 1955, c. 554, s. 4; 1961, c. 360, s. 19; c. 835, s. 11; 1975, c. 430; c. 716, s. 5; c. 727; c. 875, s. 4; c. 879, s. 46; 1979, c. 801, s. 11; 1981, c. 690, s. 19; 1989, c. 692, s. 2.1;c. 700, s. 1;c. 770, s. 74.11;1991, c. 193, s. 8;1993, c. 467, s. 5;1995, c. 50, s. 2;c. 390, s. 34;c. 509, s. 135.2(i), (j); 1999-220, s. 2;2004-77, s. 2;2004-185, s. 6;2005-276, s. 44.1(k);2005-384, s. 2;2006-255, s. 5;2006-264, s. 35.5;2007-142, s. 8;2011-145, ss. 28.30(a), 31.11; 2011-391, s. 54;2013-183, s. 2.1;2013-360, s. 34.16(b);2013-400, s. 5;2015-241, ss. 14.30(u), 29.30(j); 2016-59, s. 5;2016-94, ss. 14.1(a), 35.3(a); 2017-57, s. 34.37(a);2019-153, s. 5;2020-74, s. 7(c)
SUBSECTION (A1) SET OUT TWICE. --The first version of subsection (a1) set out above is effective until June 30, 2031. The second version of subsection (a1) set out above is effective June 30, 2031.

EDITOR'S NOTE. --
Session Laws 2003-383, s. 4, provides that the General Assembly reaffirms its intent that the proceeds of the issuance of any bonds pursuant to the Highway Bond Act of 1996, Session Laws 1995 (Reg. Sess., 1996), c. 590, s. 7, shall be used only for the purposes stated in that act, and for no other purpose.

Session Laws 2005-384, which in s. 2, amended subsections (a) and (a1), in s. 4, as amended by Session Laws 2006-255, s. 5, provides that the amendments become effective October 1, 2005, and expire July 1, 2026.

Session Laws 2005-384, s. 4, as amended by Session Laws 2006-255, s. 5, provided: "Sections 1, 3, and 4 of this act are effective when this act becomes law, except that G.S. 130A-310.53, 130A-310.54(c), and 130A-310.55 become effective 1 July 2007. Section 2 of this act becomes effective 1 October 2005. Each vehicle

Chapter 20

manufacturer that is subject to the requirements of this act shall provide the information required by G.S. 130A-310.52(b) [repealed], either individually or as a group of manufacturers, on or before 1 January 2007. This act expires on 1 July 2026."

Session Laws 2011-145, s. 28.30(a), contains an apparent error, in its directory language, referring to "G.S. 20-85.1(a1)", rather than G.S. 20-85(a1), as the statutory section amended. The amendment has been given effect at the direction of the Revisor of Statutes to reflect the apparent intention of the Legislature.

Session Laws 2013-183, s. 7.1(b), provided: "This act is effective only if the General Assembly appropriates funds in the Current Operations and Capital Improvements Appropriations Act of 2013 to implement this act." Session Laws 2013-360, s. 34.30, effective July 1, 2013, repealed Session Laws 2013-183, s. 7.1(b).

Session Laws 2013-360, s. 1.1, provides: "This act shall be known as the 'Current Operations and Capital Improvements Appropriations Act of 2013.'"

Session Laws 2013-360, s. 38.5, is a severability clause.

Session Laws 2015-241, s. 29.30(u), made the amendment to subsection (a) of this section by Session Laws 2015-241, s. 29.30(j), applicable to issuances, renewals, restorations, and requests on or after January 1, 2016.

Session Laws 2015-241, s. 1.1, provides: "This act shall be known as 'The Current Operations and Capital Improvements Appropriations Act of 2015.'"

Session Laws 2015-241, s. 33.6, is a severability clause.

Session Laws 2016-94, s. 14.1(a), amended Session Laws 2007-142, s. 9, to remove the December 31, 2017 expiration date for that act.

Session Laws 2016-94, s. 35.3(b), made the amendment to subsection (a1) of this section by Session Laws 2016-94, s. 35.3(a), applicable to fees paid on or after July 1, 2016.

Session Laws 2016-94, s. 1.2, provides: "This act shall be known as the 'Current Operations and Capital Improvements Appropriations Act of 2016.'"

Session Laws 2016-94, s. 39.4, provides: "Except for statutory changes or other provisions that clearly indicate an intention to have effects beyond the 2016-2017 fiscal year, the textual provisions of this act apply only to funds appropriated for, and activities occurring during, the 2016-2017 fiscal year."

Session Laws 2016-94, s. 39.7, is a severability clause. Session Laws 2016-124, 3rd Ex. Sess., s. 5.9(a)-(c), provides: "(a) Notwithstanding G.S. 20-14, 20-37.7, 20-85, and 20-88.03, the Governor may waive any fees assessed by the Division of Motor Vehicles under those sections for the following:

"(1) A duplicate drivers license, commercial drivers license, or special identification card.

"(2) A special identification card issued to a person for the first time.

"(3) An application for a duplicate or corrected certificate of title.

"(4) A replacement registration plate.

"(5) An application for a duplicate registration card.

"(6) Late payment of a motor vehicle registration renewal fee.

"(b) The waiver authorized under subsection (a) of this section applies only to residents of counties impacted by Hurricane Matthew, as determined by the Governor.

"(c) This section is effective when it becomes law and applies to fees assessed or collected on or after October 1, 2016. This section expires December 1, 2016."

Session Laws 2017-57, s. 34.37(b), as amended by Session Laws 2020-74, s. 7(c), made subsection (a1) of this section, as amended by Session Laws 2017-57, s. 34.37(a), effective July 1, 2017, and provides that it expires on June 30, 2031.

Session Laws 2017-57, s. 1.1, provides: "This act shall be known as the 'Current Operations Appropriations Act of 2017.'"

Session Laws 2017-57, s. 39.6, is a severability clause. Session Laws 2018-134, 3rd Ex. Sess., s. 1.1, provides: "This act shall be known as 'The Hurricane Florence Emergency Response Act.'" Session Laws 2018-134, 3rd Ex. Sess., s. 5.5(a)-(c), provides: "(a) Notwithstanding G.S. 20-14, 20-37.7, 20-85, and 20-88.03, the Governor may waive any fees assessed by the Division of Motor Vehicles under those sections for the following:

"(1) A duplicate drivers license, duplicate commercial drivers license, or duplicate special identification card.

"(2) A special identification card issued to a person for the first time.

"(3) An application for a duplicate or corrected certificate of title.

"(4) A replacement registration plate.

"(5) An application for a duplicate registration card.

"(6) Late payment of a motor vehicle registration renewal fee.

"(b) The waiver authorized under subsection (a) of this section only applies to residents of counties impacted by Hurricane Florence, as determined by the Governor. A resident is allowed a refund of any fee assessed and collected by the Division of Motor Vehicles and waived pursuant to this section. The Division shall post notice of the availability of a refund on its Web site.

"(c) This section is effective when it becomes law and applies to fees assessed or collected on or after September 13, 2018. This section expires December 31, 2018."

EFFECT OF AMENDMENTS. --

Session Laws 2016-94, s. 39.7, is a severability clause.

Session Laws 2004-185, s. 1, effective October 1, 2004, added subdivision (a)(11).

Session Laws 2005-276, s. 44.1(k), effective October 1, 2005, and applicable to fees collected on or after that date, rewrote the fees in subdivisions (a)(1) through (a)(10).

Session Laws 2005-384, s. 2, effective October 1, 2005, in subsection (a), substituted "$40.00" for "$39.00" in subdivision (a)(1) and substituted "$15.00" for "$14.00" in subdivisions (a)(2), (a)(3), and (a)(7) through (a)(9); in subsection (a1), substituted "One dollar $1.00.. section shall" for "An additional one dollar ($1.00) fee shall be imposed for any transaction assessed a fee under subdivision (a)(1), (a)(2), (a)(3), (a)(7), (a)(8), or (a)(9) of this section. The fees collected pursuant to this section shall" and added the last sentence. For expiration of amendments see the Editor's note.

Session Laws 2006-264, s. 35.5, effective August 27, 2006, substituted "Except as otherwise provided in subsection (a1) of this section, the" for "the" in subsection (b).

Session Laws 2011-145, ss. 28.30(a) and 31.11, as amended by Session Laws 2011-391, s. 54, effective July 1, 2011, added the last sentence in the introductory paragraph of subsection (a1) and added subdivisions (a1)(1) and (a1)(2); and in the next-to-last sentence of the introductory paragraph of subsection (a1), substituted "fifty cents (50 cent(s))" for "one dollar ($1.00)."

Session Laws 2013-183, s. 2.1, effective July 1, 2013, deleted the last sentence in subsections (a1) and (b); deleted subdivisions (a)(1) and (a)(2); added subsection (a2); and substituted "subsections (a1) and (a2)" for "subsection (a1)" in subsection (b).

Session Laws 2013-360, s. 34.16(b), effective July 1, 2013, deleted the former second sentence in subsection (a1), which read "The Division shall use the fees derived from transactions with the Division for technology improvements."

Session Laws 2013-400, s. 5, effective October 1, 2013, added "or by a used motor vehicle dealer pursuant to subdivision (b)(2) or subsection (e1) of G.S. 20-109.1" in subdivision (a)(10).

Session Laws 2015-241, s. 14.30(u), effective July 1, 2015, substituted "Department of Environmental Quality" for "Department of Environment and Natural Resources" in subsection (a1).

Session Laws 2007-142, s. 8, as amended by Session Laws 2016-94, s. 14.1(a), effective July 1, 2007, substituted "Mercury Switch Removal Account" for "Mercury Pollution Prevention Account" in subsection (a1).

Session Laws 2015-241, s. 29.30(j), effective January 1, 2016, substituted "$52.00" for "$40.00" in subdivision (a)(1), and substituted "20.00" for "15.00" in subdivisions (a)(2) through (a)(10). For applicability, see Editor's note.

Session Laws 2016-59, s. 5, effective July 1, 2017, in subdivision (a)(8), inserted "renewing a security interest on a certificate of title or" and "or security interest."

Session Laws 2016-94, s. 35.3(a), effective July 1, 2016, deleted the former last sentence in subsection (a1), which read: "An additional fifty cents (50 cent(s)) of the fee imposed for any transaction assessed a fee under subdivision (a)(1) of this section shall be credited to the Mercury Switch Removal Account in the Department of Environmental Quality." For applicability, see Editor's note.

Session Laws 2017-57, s. 34.37(a), added the last sentence in subsection (a1). For effective date and expiration date, see Editor's note.

Session Laws 2019-153, s. 5, effective October 1, 2019, rewrote subdivision (a)(10), which formerly read: "Each application for a salvage certificate of title made by an insurer or by a used motor vehicle dealer pursuant to subdivision (b)(2) or subsection (e1) of G.S. 20-109.1".

§ 20-85.1. Registration by mail; one-day title service; fees

(a) The owner of a vehicle registered in North Carolina may renew that vehicle registration by mail.

(b) The Commissioner and the employees of the Division designated by the Commissioner may prepare and deliver upon request a certificate of title, charging a fee of ninety-eight dollars ($ 98.00) for one-day title service, in lieu of the title fee required by G.S. 20-85(a). The fee for one-day title service must be paid by cash or by certified check. This fee shall be credited to the Highway Trust Fund.

(c) Repealed by Session Laws 2010-132, s. 8, effective December 1, 2010, and applicable to offenses committed on or after that date.

History.
1983, c. 50, s. 1; 1989, c. 692, s. 2.2;c. 700, s. 1;1991, c. 689, s. 324;2005-276, s. 44.1 (*l*); 2010-132, s. 8;2015-241, s. 29.30(k)

EDITOR'S NOTE. --
Session Laws 2003-383, s. 4, provides that the General Assembly reaffirms its intent that the proceeds of the issuance of any bonds pursuant to the Highway Bond Act of 1996, Session Laws 1995 (Reg. Sess. 1996), c. 590, s. 7, shall be used only for the purposes stated in that act, and for no other purpose.

Session Laws 2015-241, s. 29.30(u), made the amendment to subsection (b) of this section by Session Laws 2015-241, s. 29.30(k), applicable to issuances, renewals, restorations, and requests on or after January 1, 2016.

Session Laws 2015-241, s. 1.1, provides: "This act shall be known as 'The Current Operations and Capital Improvements Appropriations Act of 2015.'"

Session Laws 2015-241, s. 33.6, is a severability clause.

EFFECT OF AMENDMENTS. --
Session Laws 2005-276, s. 44.1(l), effective October 1, 2005, and applicable to fees collected on or after that date, substituted "seventy-five dollars ($75.00)" for "fifty dollars ($50.00)" in subsection (b).

Session Laws 2010-132, s. 8, effective December 1, 2010, and applicable to offenses committed on or after that date, deleted the last sentence in subsection (a), which read: "A postage and handling fee of one dollar ($1.00) per vehicle to be registered shall be charged for this service"; added the last sentence in subsection (b); and deleted subsection (c), which read: "The fee collected under subsection (a) shall be credited to the Highway Fund. The fee collected under subsection (b) shall be credited to the Highway Trust Fund."

Chapter 20

Session Laws 2015-241, s. 29.30(k), effective January 1, 2016, substituted "ninety-eight dollars ($98.00)" for "seventy-five dollars ($75.00)" in subsection (b). For applicability, see editor's note.

§ 20-86. Penalty for engaging in a "for-hire" business without proper license plates

Any person, firm or corporation engaged in the business of transporting persons or property for compensation, except as otherwise provided in this Article, shall, before engaging in such business, pay the license fees prescribed by this Article and secure the license plates provided for vehicles operated for hire. Any person, firm or corporation operating vehicles for hire without having paid the tax prescribed or using private plates on such vehicles shall be liable for an additional tax of twenty-five dollars ($ 25.00) for each vehicle in addition to the normal fees provided in this Article; provided, that when the vehicle subject to for-hire license has attached thereto a trailer or semitrailer, each unit in the combination, including the tractor, trailer and/or semitrailer, shall be subject to the additional tax as herein prescribed; provided, further that the additional tax herein provided shall not apply to trailers having a gross weight of 3,000 pounds or less.

History.
1937, c. 407, s. 50; 1965, c. 659

§ 20-86.1. International Registration Plan

(a) The registration fees required under this Article may be proportioned for vehicles which qualify and are licensed under the provisions of the International Registration Plan.

(b) Notwithstanding any other provisions of this Chapter, the Commissioner is hereby authorized to promulgate and enforce such rules and regulations as may be necessary to carry out the provisions of any agreement entered pursuant to the International Registration Plan.

History.
1975, c. 767, s. 2; 1981, c. 859, s. 77; c. 1127, s. 53

§ 20-87. Passenger vehicle registration fees

These fees shall be paid to the Division annually for the registration and licensing of passenger vehicles, according to the following classifications and schedules:

(1) **For-Hire Passenger Vehicles.** — The fee for a for-hire passenger vehicle with a capacity of 15 passengers or less is one hundred dollars ($ 100.00). The fee for a for-hire passenger vehicle with a capacity of more than 15 passengers is one dollar and eighty cents ($ 1.80) per hundred pounds of empty weight of the vehicle.

(2) **U-Drive-It Vehicles.** — U-drive-it vehicles shall pay the following tax:

Motorcycles:	1-passenger capacity	$ 23.00
	2-passenger capacity	30.00
	3-passenger capacity	34.00
Automobiles:	15 or fewer passengers	$ 66.00
Buses:	16 or more passengers	$ 2.60 per hundred pounds of empty weight
Trucks under 7,000 pounds that do not haul products for hire:	4,000 pounds	$ 54.00
	5,000 pounds	$ 66.00
	6,000 pounds	$ 80.00.

(3) Repealed by Session Laws 1981, c. 976, s. 3.

(4) **Limousine Vehicles.** — For-hire passenger vehicles on call or demand which do not solicit passengers indiscriminately for hire between points along streets or highways, shall be taxed at the same rate as for-hire passenger vehicles under *G.S. 20-87(1)* but shall be issued appropriate registration plates to distinguish such vehicles from taxicabs.

(5) **Private Passenger Vehicles.** — There shall be paid to the Division annually, as of the first day of January, for the registration and licensing of private passenger vehicles, fees according to the following classifications and schedules:

Private passenger vehicles of not more than fifteen passengers......................... $ 36.00

Private passenger vehicles over fifteen passengers.......................... 40.00

Provided, that a fee of only one dollar and thirty cents ($ 1.30) shall be charged for any vehicle given by the federal government to any veteran on account of any disability suffered during war so long as such vehicle is owned by the original donee or other veteran entitled to receive such gift under Title 38, section 252, United States Code Annotated.

(6) Private Motorcycles. — The base fee on private passenger motorcycles shall be twenty dollars ($ 20.00); except that when a motorcycle is equipped with an additional form of device designed to transport persons or property, the base fee shall be thirty dollars ($ 30.00). An additional fee of four dollars ($ 4.00) is imposed on each private motorcycle registered under this subdivision in addition to the base fee. The revenue from the additional fee, in addition to any other funds appropriated for this purpose, shall be used to fund the Motorcycle Safety Instruction Program created in G.S. 115D-72.

(7) Dealer License Plates. — The fee for a dealer license plate is the regular fee for each of the first five plates issued to the same dealer and is one-half the regular fee for each additional dealer license plate issued to the same dealer. The "regular fee" is the fee set in subdivision (5) of this section for a private passenger motor vehicle of not more than 15 passengers.

(8) Driveaway Companies. — Any person engaged in the business of driving new motor vehicles from the place of manufacture to the place of sale in this State for compensation shall pay a fee of one-half of the amount that would otherwise be payable under this section for each set of plates.

(9) House Trailers. — In lieu of other registration and license fees levied on house trailers under this section or G.S. 20-88, the registration and license fee on house trailers shall be fourteen dollars ($ 14.00) for the license year or any portion thereof.

(10) Special Mobile Equipment. — The fee for special mobile equipment for the license year or any part of the license year is two times the fee in subdivision (5) for a private passenger motor vehicle of not more than 15 passengers.

(11) Any vehicle fee determined under this section according to the weight of the vehicle shall be increased by the sum of four dollars ($ 4.00) to arrive at the total fee.

(12) Low-Speed Vehicles, Mini-Trucks, and Modified Utility Vehicles. — The fee for a low-speed vehicle, mini-truck, or modified utility vehicle is the same as the fee for private passenger vehicles of not more than 15 passengers. However, the fee for any low-speed vehicle, mini-truck, or modified utility vehicle that is offered for rent shall be the same as the fee for a U-drive-it automobile.

(13) Additional fee for certain electric vehicles. — At the time of an initial registration or registration renewal, the owner of a plug-in electric vehicle that is not a low-speed vehicle and that does not rely on a nonelectric source of power shall pay a fee in the amount of one hundred thirty dollars ($ 130.00) in addition to any other required registration fees.

History.
1937, c. 407, s. 51; 1939, c. 275; 1943, c. 648; 1945, c. 564, s. 1; c. 576, s. 2; 1947, c. 220, s. 3; c. 1019, ss. 1-3; 1949, c. 127; 1951, c. 819, ss. 1, 2; 1953, c. 478; c. 826, s. 4; 1955, c. 1313, s. 2; 1957, c. 1340, s. 3; 1961, c. 1172, s. 1a; 1965, c. 927; 1967, c. 1136; 1969, c. 600, ss. 3-11; 1971, c. 952; 1973, c. 107; 1975, c. 716, s. 5; 1981, c. 976, ss. 1-4; 1981 (Reg. Sess., 1982), c. 1255; 1983, c. 713, s. 61; c. 761, ss. 142, 143, 145; 1985, c. 454, s. 2; 1987, c. 333; 1989, c. 755, ss. 2, 4; c. 770, ss. 74.2, 74.3; 1989 (Reg. Sess., 1990), c. 830, s. 1; 1991 (Reg. Sess., 1992), c. 1015, s. 2; 1993, c. 320, s. 5; c. 440, s. 7; 1995 (Reg. Sess., 1996), c. 756, s. 7; 1999-438, s. 27; 1999-452, s. 17; 2001-356, s. 4; 2001-414, s. 31; 2002-72, s. 8; 2004-167, s. 5; 2004-199, s. 59; 2005-276, s. 44.1(m); 2013-360, s. 34.21(a); 2015-237, s. 3; 2015-241, s. 29.30 (1); 2019-34, s. 2; 2020-40, s. 2

EDITOR'S NOTE. —
Session Laws 2015-241, s. 29.30(u), made the amendment to this section by Session Laws 2015-241, s. 29.30 (l), applicable to issuances, renewals, restorations, and requests on or after January 1, 2016.

Session Laws 2015-241, s. 1.1, provides: "This act shall be known as 'The Current Operations and Capital Improvements Appropriations Act of 2015.'"

Session Laws 2015-241, s. 33.6, is a severability clause.

EFFECT OF AMENDMENTS. —
Session Laws 2004-167, s. 5, as amended by Session Laws 2004-199, s. 59, effective January 1, 2006, in the first paragraph, inserted "fees" following "These," deleted "as of the first day of January" following "annually," and deleted "fees" following "passenger vehicles."

Session Laws 2005-276, s. 44.1(m), effective October 1, 2005, and applicable to fees collected on or after that date, in subdivision (2), substituted "$51.00" for "$41.00" and "$2.00" for "$1.40"; in subdivision (5), substituted "$28.00" for "$20.00" and "31.00" for "23.00"; in subdivision (6), substituted "fifteen dollars ($15.00)" for "nine dollars ($9.00)" and "twenty-two dollars ($22.00)" for "sixteen dollars ($16.00)"; and in subdivision (9), substituted "eleven dollars ($11.00)" for "seven dollars ($7.00)."

Session Laws 2013-360, s. 34.21(a), effective January 1, 2014, added subdivision (13). For applicability, see Editor's note.

Session Laws *2015-237, s. 3*, effective October 1, 2015, rewrote subdivision (1).

Session Laws *2015-241, s. 29.30 (l)*, effective January 1, 2016, rewrote the dollar amounts throughout subdivisions (1), (2), (5), (6), (9), (11), and (13). For applicability, see editor's note.

Session Laws *2019-34, s. 2*, effective June 21, 2019, subdivision (12), inserted "and Mini-Trucks" in the catchline and "or mini-trucks" in the first sentence, added the second sentence; and made a stylistic change.

Session Laws *2020-40, s. 2*, effective October 1, 2020, in subdivision (12), substituted "Vehicles, Mini-Trucks, and Modified Utility Vehicles" for "Vehicles and Mini-Trucks" in the subdivision heading and substituted "vehicle, mini-truck, or modified utility vehicle" for "vehicle or mini-truck" in the first and second sentences.

Case Notes

FOR CASE CITING CORRESPONDING PROVISIONS OF FORMER LAW, see *Safe Bus v. Maxwell, 214 N.C. 12, 197 S.E. 567 (1938)*.

CITED in *Victory Cab Co. v. City of Charlotte, 234 N.C. 572, 68 S.E.2d 433 (1951); Airlines Transp. v. Tobin, 198 F.2d 249 (4th Cir. 1952); Pilot Freight Carriers, Inc. v. Scheidt, 263 N.C. 737, 140 S.E.2d 383 (1965)*.

§ 20-87.1. Interchange of passenger buses with nonresident common carriers of passengers

When a resident common carrier of passengers of this State interchanges a properly licensed bus with another common carrier of passengers who is a resident of another state, and adequate records are on file in its office to verify such interchanges, the North Carolina licensed common carrier of passengers may use the bus licensed in such other state the same as if it is its own during the time the nonresident carrier is using the North Carolina licensed bus.

History.

1971, c. 871, s. 1; 1975, c. 716, s. 5; 1981, c. 976, s. 5

§ 20-88. Property-hauling vehicles

(a) **Determination of Weight.** -- For the purpose of licensing, the weight of self-propelled property-carrying vehicles shall be the empty weight and heaviest load to be transported, as declared by the owner or operator; provided, that any determination of weight shall be made only in units of 1,000 pounds or major fraction thereof, weights of over 500 pounds counted as 1,000 and weights of 500 pounds or less disregarded. The declared gross weight of self-propelled property-carrying vehicles operated in conjunction with trailers or semitrailers shall include the empty weight of the vehicles to be operated in the combination and the heaviest load to be transported by such combination at any time during the registration period, except that the gross weight of a trailer or semitrailer is not required to be included when the operation is to be in conjunction with a self-propelled property-carrying vehicle which is licensed for 6,000 pounds or less gross weight and the gross weight of such combination does not exceed 9,000 pounds, except wreckers as defined under G.S. 20-4.01(50). Those property-hauling vehicles registered for 4,000 pounds shall be permitted a tolerance of 500 pounds above the weight permitted under the table of weights and rates appearing in subsection (b) of this section.

(b) The following fees are imposed on the annual registration of self-propelled property-hauling vehicles; the fees are based on the type of vehicle and its weight:

SCHEDULE OF WEIGHTS AND RATES

Rates Per Hundred Pound	Gross Weight
Farmer Rate	
Not over 4,000 pounds	$ 0.38
4,001 to 9,000 pounds inclusive	.52
9,001 to 13,000 pounds inclusive	.65
13,001 to 17,000 pounds inclusive	.88
Over 17,000 pounds	1.00

Rates Per Hundred Pound	Gross Weight
General Rate	
Not over 4,000 pounds	$ 0.77
4,001 to 9,000 pounds inclusive	1.05
9,001 to 13,000 pounds inclusive	1.30
13,001 to 17,000 pounds inclusive	1.77
Over 17,000 pounds	2.00

(1) The minimum fee for a vehicle licensed under this subsection is thirty dollars ($ 30.00) at the farmer rate and thirty-six dollars ($ 36.00) at the general rate.

(2) The term "farmer" as used in this subsection means any person engaged in the raising and growing of farm products on a farm in North Carolina not less than 10 acres in area, and who does not engage in the business of buying products for resale.

(3) License plates issued at the farmer rate shall be placed upon trucks and truck-tractors that are operated for the primary purpose of carrying or transporting the applicant's farm products, raised or produced on the applicant's farm, and farm supplies. The license plates shall not be used on a vehicle operated in hauling for hire.

(4) "Farm products" means any food crop, livestock, poultry, dairy products, flower bulbs, or other nursery products and other agricultural products designed to be used for food purposes, including in the term "farm products" also cotton, tobacco, logs, bark, pulpwood, tannic acid wood and other forest products grown, produced, or processed by the farmer.

(5) The Division shall issue necessary rules and regulations providing for the recall, transfer, exchange or cancellation of "farmer" plates, when vehicle bearing such plates shall be sold or transferred.

(5a) Notwithstanding any other provision of this Chapter, license plates issued pursuant to this subsection at the farmer rate may be purchased for any three-month period at one fourth of the annual fee.

(6) There shall be paid to the Division annually the following fees for "wreckers" as defined under G.S. 20-4.01(50): a wrecker fully equipped weighing 7,000 pounds or less, ninety-eight dollars ($ 98.00); wreckers weighing in excess of 7,000 pounds shall pay one hundred ninety-two dollars ($ 192.00). Fees to be prorated monthly. Provided, further, that nothing herein shall prohibit a licensed dealer from using a dealer's license plate to tow a vehicle for a customer.

(c) The fee for a semitrailer or trailer is twenty-five dollars ($ 25.00) for each year or part of a year. The fee is payable each year. Upon the application of the owner of a semitrailer or trailer, the Division may issue a multiyear plate and registration card for the semitrailer or trailer for a fee of ninety-eight dollars ($ 98.00). A multiyear plate and registration card for a semitrailer or trailer are valid until the owner transfers the semitrailer or trailer to another person or surrenders the plate and registration card to the Division. A multiyear plate may not be transferred to another vehicle.

The Division shall issue a multiyear semitrailer or trailer plate in a different color than an annual semitrailer or trailer plate and shall include the word "multiyear" on the plate. The Division may not issue a multiyear plate for a house trailer.

(d) Rates on trucks, trailers and semitrailers wholly or partially equipped with solid tires shall be double the above schedule.

(e) Repealed by Session Laws 1981, c. 976, s. 6.

(f) Repealed by Session Laws 1995, c. 163, s. 6.

(g) Repealed by Session Laws 1969, c. 600, s. 17.

(h) Repealed by Session Laws 1979, c. 419.

(i) Any vehicle fee determined under this section according to the weight of the vehicle shall be increased by the sum of four dollars ($ 4.00) to arrive at the total fee.

(j) No heavy vehicle subject to the use tax imposed by Section 4481 of the Internal Revenue Code of 1954 (26 U.S.C. 4481) may be registered or licensed pursuant to G.S. 20-88 without proof of payment of the use tax imposed by that law. The proof of payment shall be on a form prescribed by the United States Secretary of Treasury pursuant to the provisions of 23 U.S.C. 141(d).

(k) A person may not drive a vehicle on a highway if the vehicle's gross weight exceeds its declared gross weight. A vehicle driven in violation of this subsection is subject to the axle-group weight penalties set in G.S. 20-118(e). The penalties apply to the amount by which the vehicle's gross weight exceeds its declared weight.

(l) The Division shall issue permanent truck and truck-tractor plates to Class A and Class B Motor Vehicles and shall include the word "permanent" on the plate. The permanent registration plates issued pursuant to this section shall be subject to annual registration fees set in this section. The Division shall issue the necessary rules providing for the recall, transfer, exchange, or cancellation of permanent plates issued pursuant to this section.

(m) Any vehicle weighing greater than the gross weight limits found in G.S. 20-118(b)(3), as authorized by G.S. 20-118(c)(12), (c)(14), and (c)(15), must be registered for the maximum weight allowed for the vehicle configuration as listed in G.S. 20-118(b). A vehicle driven in violation of this subsection is subject to the axle group penalties set out in G.S. 20-118(e). The penalties apply to the amount by which the vehicle's maximum gross weight as listed in G.S. 20-118(b) exceeds its declared weight.

History.
1937, c. 407, s. 52; 1939, c. 275; 1941, cc. 36, 227; 1943, c. 648; 1945, c. 569, s. 1; c. 575, s. 1; c. 576, s. 3; c. 956, ss. 1, 2; 1949, cc. 355, 361; 1951, c. 583; c. 819, ss. 1, 2; 1953, c. 568; c. 694, s. 1; c. 1122; 1955, c. 554, s. 8; 1957, c. 681, s. 2; c. 1215; 1959, c. 571; 1961, c. 685; 1963, c. 501; c. 702, ss. 2, 3; 1967, c. 1095, ss. 1, 2; 1969, c. 600, ss. 12-17; c. 1056, s. 1; 1973, c. 154, ss. 1, 2; c. 291; 1975, c. 716, s. 5; 1977, c. 638; 1979, c. 419; c. 631; 1981, c. 67; c. 690, ss. 29, 30; c. 976, s. 6; 1983, c. 43; c. 190, s. 1; c. 761, s. 144; c. 768, s. 4; 1991 (Reg. Sess., 1992), c. 947, s. 1; 1993, c. 467, s. 4;c. 543, s. 1;1995, c. 109, s. 1;c. 163, s. 6;1995 (Reg. Sess., 1996), c. 756, s. 8; 1997-466, s. 1;2004-167, ss. 6, 7; 2004-199, s. 59;2005-276, s. 44.1(n);2008-221, s. 2;2012-78, s. 4;2013-92, s. 1;2015-241, s. 29.30(o)

EDITOR'S NOTE. --
Session Laws 2015-241, s. 29.30(u), made the amendment to subsections (b), (c), and (i) of this section by Session Laws 2015-241, s. 29.30(o), applicable to issuances, renewals, restorations, and requests on or after January 1, 2016.

Session Laws 2015-241, s. 1.1, provides: "This act shall be known as 'The Current Operations and Capital Improvements Appropriations Act of 2015.'"

Session Laws 2015-241, s. 33.6, is a severability clause.

EFFECT OF AMENDMENTS. --
Session Laws 2004-167, ss. 6 and 7, as amended by Session Laws 2004-199, s. 59, effective January 1, 2006, in subdivision (b)(6), deleted "as of the first of

January," following "annually" in the first sentence and substituted "monthly" for "quarterly" in the second to last sentence; and deleted "on or before January 1 of" following "fee is payable" in the second sentence of subsection (c).

Session Laws 2005-276, s. 44.1(n), effective October 1, 2005, and applicable to fees collected on or after that date, in subsection (b), in the Schedule of Rates, rewrote the farmer rates and the general rates; in subdivision (b)(1), substituted "twenty-four dollars ($24.00)" for "seventeen dollars and fifty cents ($17.50)" and "twenty-eight dollars ($28.00)" for "twenty-one dollars and fifty cents ($21.50)"; and in subsection (c), substituted "nineteen dollars ($19.00)" for "ten dollars ($10.00)."

Session Laws 2008-221, s. 2, effective September 1, 2008, rewrote subdivision (b)(3).

Session Laws 2012-78, s. 4, effective June 26, 2012, added subsection (m).

Session Laws 2013-92, s. 1, effective June 12, 2013, substituted "gross weight limits found in G.S. 20-118(b)(3)" for "limits found in G.S. 20-118(b)" in the first sentence of subsection (m).

Session Laws 2015-241, s. 29.30(o), effective January 1, 2016, rewrote the dollar amounts throughout subsections (b), (c), and (i). For applicability, see editor's note.

COMPUTATION OF TAX. --Until the legislature prescribes some other rule for measurement, the tax must be computed by ascertaining the miles actually traveled by outbound shipments from the place where the carrier takes possession of the shipment, the point of origin, to the State line; and for inbound shipments, the miles actually traveled from the State line to the place where the carrier surrenders possession of the shipment to the consignee, the point of destination. The miles the shipment actually moves in this State is the numerator. The total miles actually traveled by the shipment from the point of origin to the point of destination is the denominator. That fraction determines the portion of the revenue derived from each shipment which is subject to North Carolina's six percent tax. Pilot Freight Carriers, Inc. v. Scheidt, 263 N.C. 737, 140 S.E.2d 383 (1965).

CITED in Equipment Fin. Corp. v. Scheidt, 249 N.C. 334, 106 S.E.2d 555 (1959).

LEGAL PERIODICALS. --

For comment on the 1941 amendment, see 19 N.C.L. Rev. 514 (1941).

OPINIONS OF THE ATTORNEY GENERAL

UNDER SUBDIVISIONS (2), (3), (4) AND (5) OF SUBSECTION (B), LARGE LUMBER AND PAPER COMPANIES ENGAGED IN TREE FARMING are entitled to license their trucks used to transport logs from the forest to their mills and lumber, bark and wood chips from their mills to place of sale, provided the firm or corporation is, in fact, a tree farmer and does not buy timber or forestry products for resale or haul manufactured forestry products for hire. See opinion of Attorney General to Gonzalie Rivers, Director, License and Theft Division, Department of Motor Vehicles, 41 N.C.A.G. 273 (1971).

COMMON CARRIER FILING HEREUNDER MAY NOT REPORT ONLY LOADED MILES FOR PURPOSE OF DETERMINING GROSS RECEIPTS FOR TAX DUE. --See opinion of Attorney General to Mr. Victor J. Hines, Director, Common Carrier Tax Division, N.C. Department of Motor Vehicles, 43 N.C.A.G. 106 (1973).

METHOD OF REPORTING IN CERTAIN CIRCUMSTANCES MAY BE CHANGED AT OTHER THAN BEGINNING OF TAX YEAR. --See opinion of Attorney General to Mr. Victor J. Hines, Director, Common Carrier Tax Division, N.C. Department of Motor Vehicles, 43 N.C.A.G. 106 (1973).

§ 20-88.01. Revocation of registration for failure to register for or comply with road tax or pay civil penalty for buying or selling non-tax-paid fuel

(a) **Road Tax. --** The Secretary of Revenue may notify the Commissioner of those motor vehicles that are registered or are required to be registered under Article 36B of Chapter 105 and whose owners or lessees, as appropriate, are not in compliance with Article 36B, 36C, or 36D of Chapter 105. When notified, the Commissioner shall withhold or revoke the registration plate for the vehicle.

(b) **Non-tax-paid Fuel. --** The Secretary of Revenue may notify the Commissioner of those motor vehicles for which a civil penalty imposed under G.S. 105-449.118 has not been paid. When notified, the Commissioner shall withhold or revoke the registration plate of the vehicle.

History.

1983, c. 713, s. 54; 1989, c. 692, s. 6.1;c. 770, s. 74.5;1991, c. 613, s. 4;1995, c. 390, s. 11

§ 20-88.02. Registration of logging vehicles

Upon receipt of an application on a form prescribed by it, the Division shall register trucks and tractor trucks used exclusively in connection with logging operations, as provided in section 4483(e) of the Internal Revenue Code and 26 C.F.R. § 41.4483-6 for the collection of the federal heavy vehicle use tax. For the purposes of this section, "logging" shall mean the harvesting of timber and transportation from a forested site to places of sale.

Fees for the registration of vehicles under this section shall be the same as those ordinarily charged for the type of vehicle being registered.

History.

1985, c. 458, s. 1; 2010-132, s. 9

EFFECT OF AMENDMENTS. --

Session Laws 2010-132, s. 9, effective December 1, 2010, and applicable to offenses committed on or after that date, in the first paragraph, substituted "shall register trucks and tractor trucks" for "shall register trucks, tractor trucks, trailers, and semi-trailers" and "with logging operations, as provided in section 4483(e) of the Internal Revenue Code and 26 C.F.R. § 41.4483-6 for the collection of the federal heavy vehicle use tax" for "with logging operations in a separate category."

§ 20-88.03. Late fee; motor vehicle registration

(a) **Late Fee.** -- In addition to the applicable fees required under this Article for the registration of a motor vehicle and any interest assessed under G.S. 105-330.4, the Division shall charge a late fee according to the following schedule to a person who pays the applicable registration fee required under this Article after the registration expires:

(1) If the registration has been expired for less than one month, a late fee of fifteen dollars ($ 15.00).

(2) If the registration has been expired for one month or greater, but less than two months, a late fee of twenty dollars ($ 20.00).

(3) If the registration has been expired for two months or greater, a late fee of twenty-five dollars ($ 25.00).

(b) **Proceeds.** -- The clear proceeds of any late fee charged under this section shall be remitted to the Civil Penalty and Forfeiture Fund in accordance with G.S. 115C-457.2. The clear proceeds of the late fee charged under this section shall be used to provide a dedicated source of revenue for the drivers education program administered by the Department of Public Instruction in accordance with G.S. 115C-215.

(c) **Construction.** -- For purposes of this section, payment by mail of a registration fee required under this Article is considered to be made on the date shown on the postmark stamped by the United States Postal Service. If payment by mail is not postmarked or does not show the date of mailing, the payment is considered to be made on the date the Division receives the payment.

(d) **Grace Period Inapplicable.** -- The 15-day grace period provided in G.S. 20-66(g) shall not apply to any late fee assessed under this section.

(e) **Surrender of Registration Plate.** -- Nothing in this section shall be construed as requiring the Division to assess a late fee under this section if, on or prior to the date the registration expires, the owner surrenders to the Division the registration plate issued for the vehicle.

History.
2015-241, s. 29.30(m);2015-268, s. 8.2(a);2016-94, s. 35.13;2017-57, s. 5.4(d)

EDITOR'S NOTE. --
Session Laws 2015-241, s. 29.30(u), as amended by Session Laws 2016-94, s. 35.13, provides, in part: "Subsection (m) of this section [which enacted this section] becomes effective July 1, 2016, and applies to renewal motor vehicle registrations on or after that date." Session Laws 2016-94, s. 35.13 further amended Session Laws 2015-241, s. 29.30(u), by deleting "Subsection (m) of this section expires December 31, 2017." This section will not expire December 31, 2017.

Session Laws 2015-268, s. 8.2(b), made subdivisions (d) and (e) as added by Session Laws 2015-268, s. 8.2(a), effective July 1, 2016.

Session Laws 2015-241, s. 1.1, provides: "This act shall be known as 'The Current Operations and Capital Improvements Appropriations Act of 2015.'"

Session Laws 2015-241, s. 33.4, provides: "Except for statutory changes or other provisions that clearly indicate an intention to have effects beyond the 2015-2017 fiscal biennium, the textual provisions of this act apply only to funds appropriated for, and activities occurring during, the 2015-2017 fiscal biennium."

Session Laws 2015-241, s. 33.6, is a severability clause. Session Laws 2016-124, 3rd Ex. Sess., s. 5.9(a)-(c), provides: "(a) Notwithstanding G.S. 20-14, 20-37.7, 20-85, and 20-88.03, the Governor may waive any fees assessed by the Division of Motor Vehicles under those sections for the following:

"(1) A duplicate drivers license, commercial drivers license, or special identification card.

"(2) A special identification card issued to a person for the first time.

"(3) An application for a duplicate or corrected certificate of title.

"(4) A replacement registration plate.

"(5) An application for a duplicate registration card.

"(6) Late payment of a motor vehicle registration renewal fee.

"(b) The waiver authorized under subsection (a) of this section applies only to residents of counties impacted by Hurricane Matthew, as determined by the Governor.

"(c) This section is effective when it becomes law and applies to fees assessed or collected on or after October 1, 2016. This section expires December 1, 2016."

Session Laws 2017-57, s. 1.1, provides: "This act shall be known as the 'Current Operations Appropriations Act of 2017.'"

Session Laws 2017-57, s. 39.6, is a severability clause. Session Laws 2018-134, 3rd Ex. Sess., s. 1.1, provides: "This act shall be known as 'The Hurricane Florence Emergency Response Act.'" Session Laws 2018-134, 3rd Ex. Sess., s. 5.5(a)-(c), provides: "(a) Notwithstanding G.S. 20-14, 20-37.7, 20-85, and 20-88.03, the Governor may waive any fees assessed by the Division of Motor Vehicles under those sections for the following:

"(1) A duplicate drivers license, duplicate commercial drivers license, or duplicate special identification card.

"(2) A special identification card issued to a person for the first time.

"(3) An application for a duplicate or corrected certificate of title.

"(4) A replacement registration plate.

"(5) An application for a duplicate registration card.

"(6) Late payment of a motor vehicle registration renewal fee.

"(b) The waiver authorized under subsection (a) of this section only applies to residents of counties impacted by Hurricane Florence, as determined by the Governor. A resident is allowed a refund of any fee assessed and collected by the Division of Motor Vehicles and waived pursuant to this section. The Division shall post notice of the availability of a refund on its Web site.

"(c) This section is effective when it becomes law and applies to fees assessed or collected on or after September 13, 2018. This section expires December 31, 2018."

EFFECT OF AMENDMENTS. --

Session Laws 2015-268, s. 8.2(a), effective July 1, 2016, added subsections (d) and (e).

Session Laws 2017-57, s. 5.4(d), effective July 1, 2017, added the second sentence in subsection (b).

§ 20-88.1. Driver education

(a) through (b1) Repealed by Session Laws 2011-145, s. 28.37(c), effective July 1, 2011.

(c) Repealed by Session Laws 2014-100, s. 8.15(a), effective July 1, 2015.

(d) The Division shall prepare a driver license handbook that explains the traffic laws of the State and shall periodically revise the handbook to reflect changes in these laws. The Division, in consultation with the State Highway Patrol, the North Carolina Sheriff's Association, and the North Carolina Association of Chiefs of Police, shall include in the driver license handbook a description of law enforcement procedures during traffic stops and the actions that a motorist should take during a traffic stop, including appropriate interactions with law enforcement officers. At the request of the Department of Public Instruction, the Division shall provide free copies of the handbook to that Department for use in the program of driver education offered at public high schools.

History.

1957, c. 682, s. 1; 1965, c. 410, s. 1; 1975, c. 431; c. 716, s. 5; 1977, c. 340, s. 4; c. 1002; 1983, c. 761, s. 141; 1985 (Reg. Sess., 1986), c. 982, s. 25; 1991, c. 689, s. 32(a);1993 (Reg. Sess., 1994), c. 761, s. 7; 1997-16, s. 3;1997-443, s. 32.20;2011-145, s. 28.37(c);2014-100, s. 8.15(a);2017-95, s. 1

EDITOR'S NOTE. --

Session Laws 1997-16, s. 10 provides that this act does not appropriate funds to the Division to implement this act nor does it obligate the General Assembly to appropriate funds to implement this act.

Session Laws 2014-100, s. 8.15(b), provides: "It is the intent of the General Assembly that, beginning with the 2015-2016 fiscal year, the driver education program administered by the Department of Public Instruction in accordance with G.S. 115C-215 shall no longer be paid out of the Highway Fund based on an annual appropriation by the General Assembly. Local boards of education shall use funds available to them, including a fee for instruction charged to students pursuant to G.S. 115C-216(g), to offer noncredit driver education courses in high schools."

Session Laws 2014-100, s. 1.1, provides: "This act shall be known as 'The Current Operations and Capital Improvements Appropriations Act of 2014.'"

Session Laws 2014-100, s. 38.4, provides: "Except for statutory changes or other provisions that clearly indicate an intention to have effects beyond the 2014-2015 fiscal year, the textual provisions of this act apply only to funds appropriated for, and activities occurring during, the 2014-2015 fiscal year."

Session Laws 2014-100, s. 38.7, is a severability clause.

EFFECT OF AMENDMENTS. --

Session Laws 2011-145, s. 28.37(c), effective July 1, 2011, rewrote the section.

Session Laws 2014-100, s. 8.15(a), effective July 1, 2015, repealed subsection (c) which read "Expenses incurred by the State in carrying out the provisions of the driver education program administered by the Department of Public Instruction in accordance with G.S. 115C-215 shall be paid out of the Highway Fund based on an annual appropriation by the General Assembly."

Session Laws 2017-95, s. 1, effective January 1, 2018, added the second sentence in subsection (d).

CROSS REFERENCES. --

As to administration of driver education program by the Department of Public Instruction, see G.S. 115C-215. As to requirement that boards of education provide courses in operation of motor vehicles, see G.S. 115C-216.

N.C. Gen. Stat. § 20-89

Repealed by Session Laws 1981, c. 976, s. 7.

N.C. Gen. Stat. § 20-90

Repealed by Session Laws 1981, c. 976, s. 8.

§ 20-91. Audit of vehicle registrations under the International Registration Plan

(a) Repealed by Session Laws 1995 (Regular Session, 1996), c. 756, s. 9.

(b) The Department of Revenue may audit a person who registers or is required to register a vehicle under the International Registration Plan to determine if the person has paid the registration fees due under this Article. A person who registers a vehicle under the International Registration Plan must keep any records used to determine the information when registering the vehicle. The records must be kept for three years after the date of the registration to which the records apply. The Department of Revenue may examine these records during business hours. If the records are not located in North Carolina and an auditor must travel to the location of the records, the registrant shall reimburse North Carolina for per diem and travel expense incurred in the performance of the audit. If more than one registrant is audited on the same out-of-state trip, the per diem and travel expense may be prorated.

The Secretary of Revenue may enter into reciprocal audit agreements with other agencies of this State or agencies of another jurisdiction for the purpose of conducting joint audits of any registrant subject to audit under this section.

(c) If an audit is conducted and it becomes necessary to assess the registrant for deficiencies in registration fees or taxes due based on the audit, the assessment will be determined based on the schedule of rates prescribed for that registration year, adding thereto and as a part thereof an amount equal to five percent (5%) of the tax to be collected. If, during an audit, it is determined that:

(1) A registrant failed or refused to make acceptable records available for audit as provided by law; or

(2) A registrant misrepresented, falsified or concealed records, then all plates and cab cards shall be deemed to have been issued erroneously and are subject to cancellation. The Commissioner, based on information provided by the Department of Revenue audit, may assess the registrant for an additional percentage up to one hundred percent (100%) North Carolina registration fees at the rate prescribed for that registration year, adding thereto and as a part thereof an amount equal to five percent (5%) of the tax to be collected. The Commissioner may cancel all registration and reciprocal privileges.

As a result of an audit, no assessment shall be issued and no claim for refund shall be allowed which is in an amount of less than ten dollars ($ 10.00).

The results of any audit conducted under this section shall be provided to the Division. The notice of any assessments shall be sent by the Division to the registrant by registered or certified mail at the address of the registrant as it appears in the records of the Division of Motor Vehicles in Raleigh. The notice, when sent in accordance with the requirements indicated above, will be sufficient regardless of whether or not it was ever received.

The failure of any registrant to pay any additional registration fees or tax within 30 days after the billing date, shall constitute cause for revocation of registration license plates, cab cards and reciprocal privileges, or shall constitute cause for the denial of registration of a vehicle registered through the International Registration Plan or a vehicle no longer registered through the International Registration Plan.

(d) Repealed by Session Laws 1995 (Regular Session, 1996), c. 756, s. 9.

History.
1937, c. 407, s. 55; 1939, c. 275; 1941, c. 36; 1943, c. 726; 1945, c. 575, s. 3; 1947, c. 914, s. 2; 1951, c. 190, s. 1; c. 819, s. 1; 1955, c. 1313, s. 2; 1967, c. 1079, s. 2; 1975, c. 716, s. 5; c. 767, s. 3; 1981, c. 859, s. 78; c. 976, s. 9; c. 1127, s. 53; 1995 (Reg. Sess., 1996), c. 756, s. 9; 2005-435, s. 22;2007-164, s. 7;2007-484, s. 41.5

EFFECT OF AMENDMENTS. --
Session Laws 2005-435, s. 22, effective September 27, 2005, in subsection (b), substituted "Department of Revenue" for "Division" throughout and deleted "provided to the Division" following "determine the information" in the second sentence; substituted "Secretary of Revenue" for "Commissioner" in the second paragraph of subsection (b); inserted "based on information provided by the Department of Revenue audit" in the second sentence of subdivision (c)(2); in the third paragraph of subsection (c), added the first sentence, inserted "by the Division" in the second sentence and made a minor stylistic change.

Session Laws 2007-164, s. 7, as amended by Session Laws 2007-484, s. 41.5, effective July 1, 2008, added the language following "reciprocal privileges" at the end of the last paragraph of subsection (c).

§§ 20-91.1, 20-91.2

Repealed by Session Laws 2007-491, s. 2, effective January 1, 2008.

EDITOR'S NOTE. --
Session Laws 2007-491, s. 47, provides in part: "The procedures for review of disputed tax matters enacted by this act apply to assessments of tax that are not final as of the effective date of this act and to claims for refund pending on or filed on or after the effective date of this act. This act does not affect matters for which a petition for review was filed with the Tax Review Board under G.S.105-241.2 before the effective date of this act. The repeal of G.S.105-122(c) and G.S.105-130.4(t) and Sections 11 and 12 apply to requests for alternative apportionment formulas filed on or after the effective date of this act. A petition filed with the Tax Review Board for an apportionment formula before the effective date of this act is considered a request under G.S.105-122(c1) or G.S.105-130.4(t1), as appropriate."

N.C. Gen. Stat. § 20-92

Repealed by Session Laws 1995 (Regular Session, 1996), c. 756, s. 10.

N.C. Gen. Stat. § 20-93

Repealed by Session Laws 1981, c. 976, s. 10.

§ 20-94. Partial payments

In the purchase of licenses, where the gross amount of the license fee to any one owner amounts to more than four hundred dollars ($ 400.00), half of such payment may, if the Commissioner is satisfied of the financial responsibility of such owner, be deferred until six months from the month of renewal in any calendar year upon the execution to the Commissioner of a draft upon any bank or trust company upon forms to be provided by the Commissioner in an amount equivalent to one half of such fee, plus a carrying charge of three percent (3%) of the deferred portion of the license fee: Provided, that any person using any tag so purchased after the first day of six months from the month of renewal in any such year without having first provided for the payment of such draft, shall be guilty of a Class 2 misdemeanor. No further license plates shall be issued to any person executing such a draft after the due date of any such draft so long as such draft or any portion thereof remains unpaid. Any such draft being dishonored and not paid shall be subject to the penalties prescribed in G.S. 20-178 and shall be immediately turned over by the Commissioner to his duly authorized agents and/or the State Highway Patrol, to the end that this provision may be enforced. When the owner of the vehicles for which a draft has been given sells or transfers ownership to all vehicles covered by the draft, such draft shall become payable immediately, and such vehicles shall not be transferred by the Division until the draft has been paid. Any one owner whose gross license fee amounts to more than two hundred dollars ($ 200.00) but not more than four hundred dollars ($ 400.00) may also be permitted to sign a draft in accordance with the foregoing provisions of this section provided such owner makes application for the draft during the month of renewal.

History.
1937, c. 407, s. 58; 1943, c. 726; 1945, c. 49, ss. 1, 2; 1947, c. 219, s. 10; 1953, c. 192; 1967, c. 712; 1975, c. 716, s. 5; 1979, c. 801, s. 12; 1987 (Reg. Sess., 1988), c. 938; 1989, c. 661; 1993, c. 539, s. 344;1994, Ex. Sess., c. 24, s. 14(c)2004-167, s. 8;2004-199, s. 59
EFFECT OF AMENDMENTS. --
Session Laws 2004-167, s. 8, as amended by Session Laws 2004-199, s. 59, effective January 1, 2006, in the first sentence, substituted "six months from the month of renewal" for "June 1," and substituted "six months from the month of renewal" for "June," and in the last sentence, deleted "on or before February 1" following "for the draft," and substituted "month of renewal" for "license renewal period."

§ 20-95. Prorated fee for license plate issued for other than a year

(a) **Calendar-Year Plate.** -- The fee for a calendar-year license plate issued on or after April 1 of a year is a percentage of the annual fee determined in accordance with the following table:

Date Plate Issued	Percentage of Annual Fee
April 1 through June 30	75%
July 1 through September 30	50
October 1 through December 31	25.

(a1) **Plate With Renewal Sticker.** -- The fee for a license plate whose registration is renewed by means of a registration renewal sticker for a period of other than 12 months is a prorated amount of the annual fee. The prorated amount is one-twelfth of the annual fee multiplied by the number of full months in the period beginning the date the renewal sticker becomes effective until the date the renewal sticker expires, rounded to the nearest dollar.

(b) **Scope.** -- This section does not apply to license plates issued pursuant to G.S. 20-79.1, 20-79.2, 20-84, 20-84.1, 20-87(9) or (10), and 20-88(c).

History.
1937, c. 407, s. 59; 1947, c. 914, s. 3; 1979, c. 476; 1991, c. 672, s. 6;c. 726, s. 23;1993, c. 440, s. 6;1993 (Reg. Sess., 1994), c. 761, s. 8
EDITOR'S NOTE. --
Former section 20-84.1, referred to in subsection (b) above, has been repealed.

§ 20-96. Detaining property-hauling vehicles or vehicles regulated by the Motor Carrier Safety Regulation Unit until fines or penalties and taxes are collected

(a) **Authority to Detain Vehicles.** -- A law enforcement officer may seize and detain the following property-hauling vehicles operating on the highways of the State:

    (1) A property-hauling vehicle with an overload in violation of G.S. 20-88(k) and G.S. 20-118.

    (2) A property-hauling vehicle that does not have a proper registration plate as required under G.S. 20-118.3.

    (3) A property-hauling vehicle that is owned by a person liable for any overload penalties or assessments due and unpaid for more than 30 days.

    (4) A property-hauling vehicle that is owned by a person liable for any taxes or penalties under Article 36B of Chapter 105 of the General Statutes.

    (5) Any commercial vehicle operating under the authority of a motor carrier when the motor carrier has been assessed a fine

pursuant to G.S. 20-17.7 and that fine has not been paid.

(6) A property-hauling vehicle operating in violation of G.S. 20-119.

The officer may detain the vehicle until the delinquent fines or penalties and taxes are paid and, in the case of a vehicle that does not have the proper registration plate, until the proper registration plate is secured.

(b) **Storage; Liability.** -- When necessary, an officer who detains a vehicle under this section may have the vehicle stored. The motor carrier under whose authority the vehicle is being operated or the owner of a vehicle that is detained or stored under this section is responsible for the care of any property being hauled by the vehicle and for any storage charges. The State shall not be liable for damage to the vehicle or loss of the property being hauled.

(c) The authority of a law enforcement officer to seize a motor vehicle pursuant to subsection (a) of this section shall not be affected by the statutes of limitations set out in Chapter 1 of the North Carolina General Statutes.

History.

1937, c. 407, s. 60; 1943, c. 726; 1949, c. 583, s. 8; c. 1207, s. 41/2; c. 1253; 1951, c. 1013, ss. 1-3; 1953, c. 694, ss. 2, 3; 1955, c. 554, s. 9; 1957, c. 65, s. 11; 1959, c. 1264, s. 5; 1973, c. 507, s. 5; 1985, c. 116, ss. 1-3; 1993, c. 539, s. 345;1994, Ex. Sess., c. 24, s. 14(c);1995, c. 109, s. 2;1999-452, s. 18;2000-67, s. 25.11;2005-361, s. 1;2010-129, s. 2

EFFECT OF AMENDMENTS. --

Session Laws 2005-361, s. 1, effective October 1, 2005, added subdivision (a)(6).

Session Laws 2010-129, s. 2, effective July 21, 2010, added subsection (c).

THE PHRASE "ADDITIONAL TAX PROVIDED IN THIS SECTION WHEN THEIR VEHICLES ARE OPERATED IN EXCESS OF THE LICENSED WEIGHT or.. in excess of the maximum weight provided in G.S. 20-118" refers to the overloading charge set out in this section. Cedar Creek Enters., Inc. v. State Dep't of Motor Vehicles, 290 N.C. 450, 226 S.E.2d 336 (1976).

MONETARY CHARGE PRESCRIBED IN SECTION AS "TAX." --By using the word "tax" to include penalties, G.S. 20-91.2 [repealed] indicates that the monetary charge prescribed in this section is defined as a "tax" and is therefore subject to G.S. 20-91.1 [repealed]. Cedar Creek Enters., Inc. v. State Dep't of Motor Vehicles, 290 N.C. 450, 226 S.E.2d 336 (1976).

By labeling the required payment for overloading as an "additional tax," this section effectively defines the "penalties prescribed in G.S. 20-118" that must be paid upon a violation of this section as a "tax." Cedar Creek Enters., Inc. v. State Dep't of Motor Vehicles, 290 N.C. 450, 226 S.E.2d 336 (1976).

INVALID PENALTY. --Where the DMV assessed a penalty for operating a vehicle on the highways with a gross weight in excess of that allowed under the license obtained pursuant to this section, but not in excess of the maximum axle weight limits, and such penalty was not authorized by G.S. 20-118, such penalty violated N.C. Const., Art. IV, § 1 and 3, since there was no reasonable necessity for conferring absolute judicial discretion in the DMV. Young's Sheet Metal & Roofing, Inc. v. Wilkins, 77 N.C. App. 180, 334 S.E.2d 419 (1985), decided prior to the 1985 amendment to this section.

§ 20-97. Taxes credited to Highway Fund; municipal vehicle taxes

(a) **State Taxes to Highway Fund.** -- All taxes levied under this Article are compensatory taxes for the use and privileges of the public highways of this State. The taxes collected shall be credited to the State Highway Fund. Except as provided in this section, no county or municipality shall levy any license or privilege tax upon any motor vehicle licensed by the State.

(b) Repealed by Session Laws 2015-241, s. 29.27A(a), effective July 1, 2016.

(b1) **Municipal Vehicle Tax.** -- A city or town may levy an annual municipal vehicle tax upon any vehicle resident in the city or town. The aggregate annual municipal vehicle tax levied, including any annual municipal vehicle tax authorized by local legislation, may not exceed thirty dollars ($ 30.00) per vehicle. A city or town may use the net proceeds from the municipal vehicle tax as follows:

(1) **General purpose.** -- Not more than five dollars ($ 5.00) of the tax levied may be used for any lawful purpose.

(2) **Public transportation.** -- Not more than five dollars ($ 5.00) of the tax levied may be used for financing, constructing, operating, and maintaining local public transportation systems. This subdivision only applies to a city or town that operates a public transportation system as defined in G.S. 105-550.

(3) **Public streets.** -- The remainder of the tax levied may be used for maintaining, repairing, constructing, reconstructing, widening, or improving public streets in the city or town that do not form a part of the State highway system.

(c) Repealed by Session Laws 2015-241, s. 29.27A(a), effective July 1, 2016.

(d) **Municipal Taxi Tax.** -- Cities and towns may levy a tax of not more than fifteen dollars ($ 15.00) per year upon each vehicle operated in the city or town as a taxicab. The proceeds of the tax may be used for any lawful purpose.

(e) **No Additional Local Tax.** -- No county, city or town may impose a franchise tax, license tax, or other fee upon a motor carrier unless the tax is authorized by this section.

Chapter 20

History.

1937, c. 407, s. 61; 1941, c. 36; 1943, c. 639, ss. 3, 4; 1975, c. 716, s. 5; 1977, c. 433, s. 1; c. 880, s. 1; 1979, c. 173, s. 1; c. 216, s. 1; c. 217; c. 248, s. 1; c. 398; c. 400, s. 1; c. 458; c. 530, s. 1; c. 790; 1979, 2nd Sess., c. 1152; c. 1153, s. 1; c. 1155, s. 1; c. 1189; c. 1308, s. 1; 1981, cc. 74, 129, 210, 228, 310, 311, 312, 315, 368, 370, s. 10; c. 415, s. 10; cc. 857, 858, 991; 1981 (Reg. Sess., 1982), cc. 1202, 1250; 1983, cc. 9, 75; c. 106, s. 1; c. 188, ss. 1, 2; 1993, c. 321, s. 146, c. 479, s. 4;c. 456, s. 1;1997-417, s. 2;2009-166, s. 2(b);2015-241, s. 29.27A(a)

LOCAL MODIFICATION. --Alleghany: 1993, c. 456, s. 1.1, 1993 (Reg. Sess., 1994), c. 761, s. 9; Cabarrus: 2005-116, s. 1;Caswell: 1977, c. 420; 1987, c. 334; 1989, c. 527, s. 2;Pamlico: 1993 (Reg. Sess., 1994), c. 751, s. 4; city of Charlotte: 1985 (Reg. Sess., 1986), c. 1009; 1991, c. 209; 1993, c. 345, s. 1;city of Durham: 2003-329, s. 1, as amended by 2004-103, s. 1, and 2008-31, s. 1 (expires June 30, 2009; repealed by 2009-166, s. 1;see editor's notes for applicability and effective date); city of Greensboro: 1991, c. 31; city of Greenville: 1993, c. 200, s. 1;city of Henderson: 1987 (Reg. Sess., 1988), c. 1066; city of Kinston: 1991 (Reg. Sess., 1992), c. 838; city of Oxford: 2008-29, s. 1;city of Raleigh: 1991, c. 229, repealed by Session Laws 2007-333, s. 2(a) (repealed effective upon the date the City of Raleigh acts to levy an additional tax under the act and is effective for taxes imposed for taxable years beginning on or after July 1, 2007); 2007-333, 2(b), as amended by 2009-160, s. 1 (effective upon the date the City of Raleigh acts to levy an additional tax under the act and is effective for taxes imposed for taxable years beginning on or after July 1, 2007); city of Winston-Salem: 2005-278, ss. 2, 3; town of Ahoskie: 1989 (Reg. Sess., 1990), c. 893; town of Apex: 2007-108, s. 2 (as to subsection (b), effective for taxes imposed for taxable years beginning on or after July 1, 2007); town of Black Mountain: 2005-306, s. 2 (as to subsection (c)); town of Carrboro: 1991, c. 392, s. 3;1995, c. 339, s. 5.1;2005-306, s. 1 (as to subsection (b)); town of Cary: 1993, c. 325, s. 1;town of Chapel Hill: 2008-16, s. 2;town of Cornelius: 1985 (Reg. Sess., 1986), c. 109; town of Creedmoor: 1987, c. 610, as amended by 2008-29, s. 2;town of Davidson: 1985 (Reg. Sess., 1986), c. 1009; town of Garner: 2007-73, s. 2 (as to subsection (b), effective for taxes imposed for taxable years beginning on or after July 1, 2007); town of Hillsborough: 1991, (Reg. Sess., 1992), c. 822; town of Holly Springs: 2007-73, s. 2 (as to subsection (b), effective for taxes imposed for taxable years beginning on or after July 1, 2007); town of Huntersville: 1985 (Reg. Sess., 1986), c. 1009; town of Knightdale: 2007-73, s. 2 (as to subsection (b), effective for taxes imposed for taxable years beginning on or after July 1, 2007); town of Matthews: 1985 (Reg. Sess., 1986), c. 1009; 1991, c. 209; 1993, c. 345, s. 1;2007-109, ss. 1, 2 (as to subsections (a) and (b), effective for taxes imposed for taxable years beginning on or after July 1, 2007); town of Mint Hill: 1985 (Reg. Sess., 1986), c. 1009; town of Morrisville: 2007-108, s. 2 (as to subsection (b), effective for taxes imposed for taxable years beginning on or after July 1, 2007); town of Murfreesboro: 1987 (Reg. Sess., 1988), c. 953

(effective retroactively as of July 1, 1987); town of Pineville: 1985 (Reg. Sess., 1986), c. 1009; town of Rolesville: 2007-73, s. 2 (as to subsection (b), effective for taxes imposed for taxable years beginning on or after July 1, 2007).

EDITOR'S NOTE. --

Session Laws 2005-278, s. 4, provides that Chapter 56 of the 1993 Session Laws is repealed effective upon the date the City of Winston-Salem acts to levy an additional tax under this act.

Session Laws 2009-166, s. 1 repeals 2003-329, s. 1, 2004-103, s. 1, and 2008-31, which authorized the City of Durham to levy up to ten dollars ($10.00) per year for general purposes, and provides: "The repeal of these acts shall not affect the authority of the City of Durham to levy the General Municipal Vehicle Tax in G.S. 20-97(b) of five dollars ($5.00)."

Session Laws 2009-166, s. 4, provides: "Section 1 of this act is effective when the City of Durham levies a tax under Section 2 of this act. The remainder of this act is effective when it becomes law. This act does not affect the rights or liabilities of the State, a taxpayer, or another person arising under a statute amended or repealed by this act before the effective date of its amendment or repeal; nor does it affect the right to any refund or credit of a tax that accrued under the amended or repealed statute before the effective date of its amendment or repeal."

EFFECT OF AMENDMENTS. --

Session Laws 2015-241, s. 29.27A(a), effective July 1, 2016, deleted former subsection (b), relating to the general municipal vehicle tax; added subsection (b1); and deleted former subsection (c), relating to the municipal vehicle tax for public transportation.

FOR HISTORICAL BACKGROUND OF SUBSECTIONS (A) AND (B), see Victory Cab Co. v. City of Charlotte, 234 N.C. 572, 68 S.E.2d 433 (1951).

LEGISLATIVE POLICY TO LIMIT MUNICIPAL TAXING POWERS. --An examination of the legislative history of this section shows a fixed and unvarying legislative policy to curb the powers of municipalities in taxing motor vehicles of all kinds, including taxicabs. Victory Cab Co. v. City of Charlotte, 234 N.C. 572, 68 S.E.2d 433 (1951).

THIS SECTION EXPRESSLY PROHIBITS A MUNICIPALITY FROM LEVYING A LICENSE OR PRIVILEGE TAX in excess of $1.00 upon the use of any motor vehicle licensed by the State; it must be construed with and operates as an exception to and limitation upon the general power to levy license and privilege taxes upon businesses, trades and professions granted by charter and former G.S. 160-56. Cox v. Brown, 218 N.C. 350, 11 S.E.2d 152 (1940).

Municipalities are prohibited by this section from levying a license or privilege tax for use of its streets by motor trucks. C.D. Kenny Co. v. Town of Brevard, 217 N.C. 269, 7 S.E.2d 542 (1940).

MUNICIPAL ORDINANCE HELD VOID. --Provisions of a municipal ordinance imposing a license tax upon the operation of passenger vehicles for hire in addition to the $1.00 theretofore imposed by it upon motor vehicles generally, were void, and such additional municipal tax could not be sustained upon the theory that it was a tax upon the business of operating a motor vehicle for hire rather than ownership of the vehicle, since the word "business" and the word "use" as used in the statutes mean the same thing. Cox v. Brown, 218 N.C. 350, 11 S.E.2d 152 (1940).

THOSE COMMISSIONED TO SELL LICENSE PLATES ARE NOT DEALING IN INTERSTATE COMMERCE, but perform a general tax collecting effort. Hodgson v. Hyatt Realty & Inv. Co., 353 F. Supp. 1363 (M.D.N.C. 1973).

TAXES FINANCE CONSTRUCTION AND MAINTENANCE OF HIGHWAYS. --The construction and maintenance of the State's highways are financed, in part, by taxes based on the use of the highways by motor vehicles. Pilot Freight Carriers, Inc. v. Scheidt, 263 N.C. 737, 140 S.E.2d 383 (1965).

VILLAGE OF BALD HEAD ISLAND EXEMPT. --General assembly has explicitly authorized the Village of Bald Head Island, North Carolina, to exempt itself from G.S. ch. 20, Art. 2, which includes G.S. 20-97. Bald Head Island, Ltd. v. Village of Bald Head Island, 175 N.C. App. 543, 624 S.E.2d 406 (2006).

FOR CASES DECIDED UNDER CORRESPONDING PROVISIONS OF FORMER LAW, see State v. Fink, 179 N.C. 712, 103 S.E. 16 (1920); Southeastern Express Co. v. City of Charlotte, 186 N.C. 668, 120 S.E. 475 (1923); State v. Jones, 191 N.C. 371, 131 S.E. 734 (1926).

APPLIED in Cooke v. Futrell, 37 N.C. App. 441, 246 S.E.2d 65 (1978).

CROSS REFERENCES. --
As to authority of cities to impose motor vehicle license taxes, and to waive such taxes for certain persons, see G.S. 160A-213.

LEGAL PERIODICALS. --
For comment on the 1943 amendment, see 21 N.C.L. Rev. 358 (1943).

OPINIONS OF THE ATTORNEY GENERAL
WHEN VEHICLE IS "RESIDENT" IN MUNICIPALITY. --The considerations determinative of when a vehicle is "resident" in a municipality, as the term is used in subsection (a) of this section, are the residence of the owner, the "residence" of the vehicle, whether or not the owner is an individual person, the type of vehicle and its use. See opinion of Attorney General to Gillam & Gillam, 45 N.C.A.G. 185 (1975).

APPLICABILITY OF LICENSE TAX AND LICENSE PLATE DISPLAY REQUIREMENTS. --Under this section, the license tax and the requirement that license plates be displayed are applicable to vehicles which become "resident" in the town after January 1 of any year. See opinion of Attorney General to Gillam & Gillam, 45 N.C.A.G. 185 (1975).

LICENSE TAX LIABILITY WHERE VEHICLE BECOMES RESIDENT IN ANOTHER MUNICIPALITY IN SAME YEAR. --If a license plate is once issued for a motor vehicle during a particular year by a municipality, the owner is liable for another one dollar ($1.00) license tax during the same year if the vehicle becomes "resident" in another municipality. See opinion of Attorney General to Gillam & Gillam, 45 N.C.A.G. 185 (1975).

§§ 20-98, 20-99

Repealed by Session Laws 2007-491, s. 2, effective January 1, 2008.
EDITOR'S NOTE. --
Session Laws 2007-491, s. 47, provides in part: "The procedures for review of disputed tax matters enacted by this act apply to assessments of tax that are not final as of the effective date of this act and to claims for refund pending on or filed on or after the effective date of this act. This act does not affect matters for which a petition for review was filed with the Tax Review Board under G.S.105-241.2 before the effective date of this act. The repeal of G.S.105-122(c) and G.S.105-130.4(t) and Sections 11 and 12 apply to requests for alternative apportionment formulas filed on or after the effective date of this act. A petition filed with the Tax Review Board for an apportionment formula before the effective date of this act is considered a request under G.S.105-122(c1) or G.S.105-130.4(t1), as appropriate."
CROSS REFERENCES. --
For present provisions as to refund of overpayment, see now G.S. 105-163.16.

§ 20-100. Vehicles junked or destroyed by fire or collision

Upon satisfactory proof to the Commissioner that any motor vehicle, duly licensed, has been completely destroyed by fire or collision, or has been junked and completely dismantled so that the same can no longer be operated as a motor vehicle, the owner of such vehicle may be allowed on the purchase of a new license for another vehicle a credit equivalent to the unexpired proportion of the cost of the original license, dating from the first day of the next month after the date of such destruction.

History.
1937, c. 407, s. 64; 1939, c. 369, s. 1
CITED in State v. Ezell, 159 N.C. App. 103, 582 S.E.2d 679 (2003).

§ 20-101. Certain business vehicles to be marked

(a) A motor vehicle that is subject to 49 C.F.R. Part 390, the federal motor carrier safety regulations, shall be marked as required by that Part.

(b) A motor vehicle with a gross vehicle weight rating of more than 26,000 pounds that is used in intrastate commerce shall have (i) the name of the owner and (ii) the motor carrier's identification number preceded by the letters "USDOT" and followed by the letters "NC" printed on each side of the vehicle in letters not less than three inches in height. The provisions of this subsection shall not apply if any of the following are true:

(1) The motor vehicle is subject to 49 C.F.R. Part 390.

(2) The motor vehicle is of a type listed in 49 C.F.R. 390.3(f).

(3) The motor vehicle is licensed at the farmer rate under G.S. 20-88.

(c) A motor vehicle that is subject to regulation by the North Carolina Utilities Commission shall be marked as required by that Commission and as otherwise required by this section.

(d) A motor vehicle equipped to tow or transport another motor vehicle, hired for the purpose of towing or transporting another motor vehicle, shall have the name and address of the registered owner of the vehicle, and the name of the business or person being hired if different, printed on each side of the vehicle in letters not less than three inches in height. This subsection shall not apply to motor vehicles subject to 49 C.F.R. Part 390.

History.

1937, c. 407, s. 65; 1951, c. 819, s. 1; 1967, c. 1132; 1985, c. 132; 1995 (Reg. Sess., 1996), c. 756, s. 12; 2000-67, s. 25.8;2001-487, s. 50(d);2007-404, s. 1;2009-376, s. 3;2012-41, s. 1;2017-108, s. 15

EDITOR'S NOTE. --

Session Laws 2017-108, s. 21, is a severability clause.

EFFECT OF AMENDMENTS. --

Session Laws 2007-404, s. 1, effective December 1, 2007, added subsection (d) and designated the former first three paragraphs as subsections (a) through (c); and substituted "49 C.F.R. Part 390" for "those regulations" in subsection (b).

Session Laws 2009-376, s. 3, effective October 1, 2009, and applicable to civil penalties assessed and offenses committed on or after that date, rewrote subsection (b).

Session Laws 2012-41, s. 1, effective December 1, 2012, in subsection (b), substituted "26,000 pounds" for "10,000 pounds", inserted "(i)" in the middle of the first sentence, inserted "and (ii) the motor carrier's identification number preceded by the letters 'US-DOT' and followed by the letters 'NC'", substituted "than three inches in height. The provisions of this subsection shall not apply if any of the following are true" for "that three inches in height, unless either of the following applies"; rewrote subdivision (b)(2), which formerly read: "The motor vehicle is a farm vehicle as further described in G.S. 20-118(c)(4), (c) (5), or (c)(12)'"; and substituted "printed on each" for "printed on the" in the first sentence in subsection (d). For applicability, see Editor's note.

Session Laws 2017-108, s. 15, effective July 12, 2017, added subdivision (b)(3).

OPINIONS OF THE ATTORNEY GENERAL

AS TO INAPPLICABILITY TO TAXICAB WHICH SEATS NINE OR FEWER PASSENGERS AND IS NOT OPERATED ON A REGULAR ROUTE OR BETWEEN TERMINI, see opinion of Attorney General to Mr. W. Vance McCown, 41 N.C.A.G. 547 (1971).

§ 20-101.1. Conspicuous disclosure of dealer administrative fees.

(a) A motor vehicle dealer shall not charge an administrative, origination, documentary, procurement, or other similar administrative fee related to the sale or lease of a motor vehicle, whether or not that fee relates to costs or charges that the dealer is required to pay to third parties or is attributable to the dealer's internal overhead or profit, unless the dealer complies with all of the following requirements:

(1) The dealer shall post a conspicuous notice in the sales or finance area of the dealership measuring at least 24 inches on each side informing customers that a fee regulated by this section may or will be charged and the amount of the fee.

(2) The fact that the dealer charges a fee regulated by this section and the amount of the fee shall be disclosed whenever the dealer engages in the price advertising of vehicles.

(3) The amount of a fee regulated by this section shall be separately identified on the customer's buyer's order, purchase order, or bill of sale.

(b) Nothing contained in this section or elsewhere under the law of this State shall be deemed to prohibit a dealer from, in the dealer's discretion, deciding not to charge an administrative, origination, documentary, procurement, or other similar administrative fee or reducing the amount of the fee in certain cases, as the dealer may deem appropriate.

(c) Notwithstanding the terms of any contract, franchise, novation, or agreement, it shall be unlawful for any manufacturer, manufacturer branch, distributor, or distributor branch to prevent, attempt to prevent, prohibit, coerce, or attempt to coerce, any new motor vehicle dealer located in this State from charging any administrative, origination, documentary, procurement, or other similar administrative fee related to the sale or lease of a motor vehicle. It shall further be unlawful for any manufacturer, manufacturer branch, distributor, or distributor branch, notwithstanding the terms of any contract, franchise, novation, or agreement, to prevent or prohibit any new motor vehicle dealer in this State from participating in any program relating to the sale of motor vehicles or reduce the amount of compensation to be paid to any dealer in this State, based upon the dealer's willingness to refrain from charging or reduce the amount of any administrative, origination, documentary, procurement, or other similar administrative fee related to the sale or lease of a motor vehicle.

(d) This section does not apply to a dealer fee related to the online registration of a motor vehicle when the dealer fee is separately stated on

Chapter 20

the buyer's order, purchase order, retail installment sales agreement, lease, or bill of sale.

History.
2001-487, s. 123.5;2001-492, s. 1;2014-108, s. 4(a)
EDITOR'S NOTE. --
Session Laws 2001-492, s. 3, provides: "Nothing
contained in Section 1 or 2 above [ss. 1 or 2 of Session
Laws 2001-492, which enacted G.S. 20-101.1 and 20-
101.2] or elsewhere under the law of this State shall
be deemed as imposing any civil or criminal liability
on motor vehicle dealers located in this State for failure to disclose any of the information required to be
in Sections 1 and 2 above prior to the effective date
of this act."
Session Laws 2001-492, s. 6, as amended by Session
Laws 2001-487, s. 123.5, made this section effective
December 31, 2001.
EFFECT OF AMENDMENTS. --
Session Laws 2014-108, s. 4(a), effective October 1,
2014, added subsection (d).

§ 20-101.2. Conspicuous disclosure of dealer finance yield charges

(a) A motor vehicle dealer shall not charge a
fee or receive a commission or other compensation for providing, procuring, or arranging
financing for the retail purchase or lease of a
motor vehicle, unless the dealer complies with
both of the following requirements:

(1) The dealer shall post a conspicuous
notice in the sales or finance area of the
dealership measuring at least 24 inches
on each side informing customers that the
dealer may receive a fee, commission, or
other compensation for providing, procuring, or arranging financing for the retail
purchase or lease of a motor vehicle, for
which the customer may be responsible.

(2) The dealer shall disclose conspicuously on the purchase order or buyer's order, or on a separate form provided to the
purchaser at or prior to the closing on the
sale of the vehicle, that the dealer may receive a fee, commission, or other compensation for providing, procuring, or arranging
financing for the retail purchase or lease
of a motor vehicle, for which the customer
may be responsible.

(b) Nothing contained in this section or elsewhere under the law of this State shall be
deemed to require that a motor vehicle dealer
disclose to any actual or potential purchaser the
dealer's contractual arrangements with any finance company, bank, leasing company, or other
lender or financial institution, or the amount of
markup, profit, or compensation that the dealer
will receive in any particular transaction or series of transactions from the charging of such
fees.

History.
2001-487, s. 123.5;2001-492, s. 2
EDITOR'S NOTE. --
Session Laws 2001-492, s. 3, provides: "Nothing
contained in Section 1 or 2 above [ss. 1 or 2 of Session
Laws 2001-492, which enacted G.S. 20-101.1 and 20-
101.2] or elsewhere under the law of this State shall
be deemed as imposing any civil or criminal liability
on motor vehicle dealers located in this State for failure to disclose any of the information required to be
in Sections 1 and 2 above prior to the effective date
of this act."
Session Laws 2001-492, s. 6, as amended by Session
Laws 2001-487, s. 123.5, made this section effective
December 31, 2001.

§ 20-101.3. Conspicuous disclosure of dealer shop and other service-related fees

(a) **Requirement.** -- A motor vehicle dealer
shall not charge shop fees in conjunction with
service work performed by the dealer, or other
discretionary fees relating to environmental
or regulatory compliance, record retention, or
other costs incurred by the dealer in conjunction with service work performed by the dealer,
whether or not the fees are attributable to or
include the dealer's internal overhead or profit,
unless the dealer complies with both of the following requirements:

(1) The dealer shall post a conspicuous
notice in the service area of the dealership
measuring at least 24 inches on each side
informing customers that fees regulated by
this section may or will be charged and that
customers should inquire of dealership personnel if they would like to know the type
and amount or basis of the fees charged by
the dealer.

(2) The total amount of all fees regulated
by this section shall be disclosed on the customer's repair order or repair invoice. Nothing in this subdivision shall be construed
as requiring a dealer to list separately each
fee charged by the dealer.

(b) **Discretion.** -- Notwithstanding any provision of law to the contrary, a dealer is not required to charge a shop or other service-related
fee regulated under this section and may reduce
the amount of any or all fees charged.

(c) Notwithstanding any other section of this
Chapter, the fees covered by this section shall
not be considered a warranty expense and are
not subject to the compensation requirements
of G.S. 20-305.1.

History.
2017-148, s. 5
EDITOR'S NOTE. --
Session Laws 2017-148, s. 6, is a severability
clause.

Chapter 20

Session Laws 2017-148, s. 7, made this section effective January 1, 2018, and applicable to fees charged on or after that date.

PART 8.
ANTI-THEFT AND ENFORCEMENT PROVISIONS

§ 20-102. Report of stolen and recovered motor vehicles

Every sheriff, chief of police, or peace officer upon receiving reliable information that any vehicle registered hereunder has been stolen shall report such theft to the Division. Any said officer upon receiving information that any vehicle, which he has previously reported as stolen, has been recovered, shall report the fact of such recovery to the Division.

History.
1937, c. 407, s. 66; 1975, c. 716, s. 5; 2005-182, s. 4
EFFECT OF AMENDMENTS. --
Session Laws 2005-182, s. 4, effective December 1, 2005, and applicable to offenses committed on or after that date, deleted "immediately" preceding "report" in the first and second sentences.

§ 20-102.1. False report of theft or conversion a misdemeanor

A person who knowingly makes to a peace officer or to the Division a false report of the theft or conversion of a motor vehicle shall be guilty of a Class 2 misdemeanor.

History.
1963, c. 1083; 1975, c. 716, s. 5; 1993, c. 539, s. 346;1994, Ex. Sess., c. 24, s. 14(c)

§ 20-102.2. Report of failure to return hired motor vehicles

Every sheriff, chief of police, or peace officer, upon receiving a vehicle theft report, warrant, or other reliable information that any rental, for-hire, or leased vehicle registered pursuant to this Chapter has not been returned as set forth in G.S. 14-167, shall report the failure to the National Crime Information Center. Any officer upon receiving information concerning the recovery of a vehicle that the officer previously reported as not having been returned shall report the recovery to the National Crime Information Center. The officer shall also attempt to notify the reporting party of the location and condition of the recovered vehicle by telephone, if the telephone number of the reporting party is available or readily accessible.

History.
2005-182, s. 5
EDITOR'S NOTE. --
Session Laws 2005-182, s. 6, made this section effective December 1, 2005, and applicable to offenses committed on or after that date.

§ 20-103. Reports by owners of stolen and recovered vehicles

The owner, or person having a lien or encumbrance upon a registered vehicle which has been stolen or embezzled, may notify the Division of such theft or embezzlement, but in the event of an embezzlement may make such report only after having procured the issuance of a warrant for the arrest of the person charged with such embezzlement. Every owner or other person who has given any such notice must notify the Division of the recovery of such vehicle.

History.
1937, c. 407, s. 67; 1975, c. 716, s. 5

§ 20-104. Action by Division on report of stolen or embezzled vehicles

(a) The Division, upon receiving a report of a stolen or embezzled vehicle as hereinbefore provided, shall file and appropriately index the same and shall immediately suspend the registration of the vehicle so reported, and shall not transfer the registration of the same until such time as it is notified in writing that such vehicle has been recovered.

(b) The Division shall at least once each month compile and maintain at its headquarters office a list of all vehicles which have been stolen or embezzled or recovered as reported to it during the preceding month, and such lists shall be open to inspection by any peace officer or other persons interested in any such vehicle.

History.
1937, c. 407, s. 68; 1975, c. 716, s. 5

N.C. Gen. Stat. § 20-105

Repealed by Session Laws 1973, c. 1330, s. 39.
CROSS REFERENCES. --
For present provisions as to unauthorized use of a conveyance, see G.S. 14-72.2.

§ 20-106. Receiving or transferring stolen vehicles

Recodified as G.S. 14-71.2 by Session Laws 2019-186, s. 1(c), effective December 1, 2019, and applicable to offenses committed on or after that date.

History.

1937, c. 407, s. 70; 1979, c. 760, s. 5; 1979, 2nd Sess., c. 1316, s. 47; 1981, c. 63, s. 1; c. 179, s. 14; 1993, c. 539, s. 1252;1994, Ex. Sess., c. 24, s. 14(c).

CONSTITUTIONALITY. --This section is constitutional. State v. Lockamy, 31 N.C. App. 713, 230 S.E.2d 565 (1976).

The language "or has reason to believe has been stolen or unlawfully taken" does not create a matter of conjecture as to what is prohibited and is not unconstitutionally vague so as to deprive the defendant of due process of law. State v. Rook, 26 N.C. App. 33, 215 S.E.2d 159, appeal dismissed, 288 N.C. 250, 217 S.E.2d 674 (1975).

PURPOSE OF SECTION. --The purpose of this section is to discourage the possession of stolen vehicles by one who knows a vehicle is stolen or has reason to believe that it is stolen. State v. Rook, 26 N.C. App. 33, 215 S.E.2d 159, appeal dismissed, 288 N.C. 250, 217 S.E.2d 674 (1975); State v. Abrams, 29 N.C. App. 144, 223 S.E.2d 516 (1976); State v. Murchinson, 39 N.C. App. 163, 249 S.E.2d 871 (1978), overruled on other grounds in State v. Wesson, 45 N.C. App. 510, 263 S.E.2d 298 (1980).

ELEMENTS --Defendant charged with possession of stolen property under G.S. 14-71.1 or possession of a stolen vehicle under G.S. 20-106 could be convicted if the State produced sufficient evidence that defendant possessed stolen property (i.e. a vehicle), which he knew or had reason to believe had been stolen or taken. State v. Bailey, 157 N.C. App. 80, 577 S.E.2d 683 (2003).

PROVISION AS TO POLICE OFFICERS AN EXCEPTION AND NOT AN ELEMENT OF OFFENSE. --The provision exculpating police officers in the line of duty was apparently placed in the statute out of an abundance of legislative caution. Such a provision may have been thought necessary in light of the fact that the crime charged merely requires possession with knowledge that the vehicle is stolen, not criminal intent. The provision is an exception to the statute, not an element of the offense. State v. Murchinson, 39 N.C. App. 163, 249 S.E.2d 871 (1978), overruled on other grounds in State v. Wesson, 45 N.C. App. 510, 263 S.E.2d 298 (1980).

NO FELONIOUS INTENT REQUIRED. --Neither the construction of this section nor the purpose for which it was enacted compels a requirement that the doer of the act have a felonious intent. State v. Abrams, 29 N.C. App. 144, 223 S.E.2d 516 (1976).

This section requires only that the State prove defendant knew or had reason to believe that the vehicle in his possession was stolen. No felonious intent is required. State v. Murchinson, 39 N.C. App. 163, 249 S.E.2d 871 (1978), overruled on other grounds in State v. Wesson, 45 N.C. App. 510, 263 S.E.2d 298 (1980).

Because the purpose of this section is to discourage the possession of stolen vehicles the State need only prove that the defendant knew or had reason to believe that the vehicle in his possession was stolen. No felonious intent is required. State v. Baker, 65 N.C.

App. 430, 310 S.E.2d 101 (1983), cert. denied, 312 N.C. 85, 321 S.E.2d 900 (1984).

G.

S. 14-71 NOT LESSER INCLUDED OFFENSE. --The offenses under this section and G.S. 14-71 are separate offenses; the latter is not a lesser included offense under the former. State v. Carlin, 37 N.C. App. 228, 245 S.E.2d 586 (1978), overruled on other grounds, State v. Wesson, 45 N.C. App. 510, 263 S.E.2d 298 (1980).

SUFFICIENCY OF INDICTMENT. --Indictment was sufficient to give defendant notice of the basis of the habitual felon indictment because the indictment stated that defendant possessed a stolen vehicle, which conveyed exactly the same meaning as saying that a defendant was in possession of a stolen vehicle. Moreover, the indictment also referenced the case number, date, and county of the prior conviction, which was sufficient to allow a person of common understanding to comprehend which felony conviction was being referenced even if the language describing the offense had been unclear. State v. Griffin, 213 N.C. App. 625, 713 S.E.2d 185 (2011), dismissed 719 S.E.2d 623, 2011 N.C. LEXIS 1042 (N.C. 2011), cert. dismissed, 747 S.E.2d 559, 2013 N.C. LEXIS 873 (2013).

DOUBLE JEOPARDY --Defendant's conviction and sentencing for possession of a stolen vehicle, in violation of G.S. 20-106, and possession of stolen property, in violation of G.S. 14-71.1, for possession of the same vehicle, violated double jeopardy because the Legislature did not intend to punish a defendant twice for possession of the same property. State v. Bailey, 157 N.C. App. 80, 577 S.E.2d 683 (2003).

UNAUTHORIZED USE IS NOT A LESSER INCLUDED OFFENSE OF POSSESSION OF STOLEN VEHICLE. --Unauthorized use of a motor vehicle is not a lesser-included offense of possession of a stolen vehicle and State v. Oliver is overruled to the extent that it is inconsistent with this opinion; unauthorized use of a motor vehicle contains an essential element, taking or operating, that is not included in possession of a stolen vehicle, and thus the trial court did not err in denying defendant's request to instruct the jury on unauthorized use of a motor vehicle. State v. Robinson, 368 N.C. 402, 777 S.E.2d 755 (2015).

EVIDENCE HELD INSUFFICIENT TO SHOW KNOWLEDGE OR REASON TO KNOW. --Evidence that defendant was in possession of stolen vehicle approximately one month after it was stolen was not sufficient to raise an inference that defendant knew or had reason to believe that the automobile was stolen, where the evidence offered by the State demonstrated the intervening agency of others. State v. Leonard, 34 N.C. App. 131, 237 S.E.2d 347 (1977).

Evidence tending to show that public vehicle identification number plate on an automobile had been replaced was not sufficient to raise an inference that defendant knew or had reason to believe that the vehicle was stolen, where there was no evidence that the alteration was made by defendant or with his knowledge. State v. Leonard, 34 N.C. App. 131, 237 S.E.2d 347 (1977).

Decision of the North Carolina Criminal Justice Education and Training Standards Commission, which revoked and suspended a law enforcement officer's certification as a result of finding that he violated G.S. 20-106 by knowingly possessing a stolen vehicle, was reversed and remanded for the Commission to consider the elements of the offense of possession of a stolen vehicle because the Commission's order merely citing the statute was insufficient evidence to satisfy the elements of the statute. Powell v. N.C. Crim. Justice Educ. & Training Stds. Comm'n, 165 N.C. App. 848, 600 S.E.2d 56 (2004).

EFFECT OF DOCTRINE OF POSSESSION OF RECENTLY STOLEN GOODS. --The doctrine of possession of recently stolen goods is, under appropriate circumstances, applicable to justify denial of a motion for nonsuit in a case charging illegal possession of a stolen vehicle pursuant to this section. State v. Murchinson, 39 N.C. App. 163, 249 S.E.2d 871 (1978), overruled on other grounds in State v. Wesson, 45 N.C. App. 510, 263 S.E.2d 298 (1980).

EVIDENCE OF POSSESSION HELD SUFFICIENT. --Where defendant had control over vehicle, since he was driving it, the State's evidence in the case was sufficient to go to the jury on the element of possession. State v. Suitt, 94 N.C. App. 571, 380 S.E.2d 570 (1989).

Evidence was sufficient to show defendant knew or had reason to think the car he was driving was stolen as (1) he was driving the car several hours after it was stolen; (2) he said the vehicle belonged to a "friend" whose name he would not give; (3) the car's owner said he gave no one permission to drive it on the day in question; and (4) defendant had the owner's keys. State v. Bailey, 157 N.C. App. 80, 577 S.E.2d 683 (2003).

JURY INSTRUCTIONS. --In light of case law on which the court was bound, despite the discrepancy discovered, the trial court did not err in denying defendant's request for an instruction on unauthorized use of a motor vehicle as a lesser-included offense of possession of a stolen vehicle. State v. Robinson, 236 N.C. App. 446, 763 S.E.2d 178 (2014), modified 777 S.E.2d 755, 2015 N.C. LEXIS 1058 (2015).

Defendant failed to show plain error in the jury instructions for possession of a stolen motor vehicle, as the instruction "is in the car, such as driving" related to the theory of actual possession, and the possession element could be satisfied if the jury found that defendant was operating the vehicle; the jury could have inferred that defendant operated the vehicle and was not merely a passenger, and he failed to show that absent any purported error, a different verdict was probable. State v. Quinones, -- N.C. App. --, 811 S.E.2d 734 (2018).

APPLIED in State v. Craver, 70 N.C. App. 555, 320 S.E.2d 431 (1984).

CITED in State v. Marsh, 187 N.C. App. 235, 652 S.E.2d 744 (2007), review denied 2010 N.C. LEXIS 466 (2010), overruled in part by State v. Tanner, 2010 N.C. LEXIS 423 (2010).

CROSS REFERENCES. --
As to seizure and forfeiture of conveyances used in committing a crime under this section, see G.S. 14-86.1. As to penalty for a felony violation of this Article, see G.S. 20-177.

LEGAL PERIODICALS. --
For survey of 1976 case law on criminal law, see 55 N.C.L. Rev. 976 (1977).

§ 20-106.1. Fraud in connection with rental of motor vehicles

Any person with the intent to defraud the owner of any motor vehicle or a person in lawful possession thereof, who obtains possession of said vehicle by agreeing in writing to pay a rental for the use of said vehicle, and further agreeing in writing that the said vehicle shall be returned to a certain place, or at a certain time, and who willfully fails and refuses to return the same to the place and at the time specified, or who secretes, converts, sells or attempts to sell the same or any part thereof shall be guilty of a Class I felony.

History.
1961, c. 1067; 1993, c. 539, s. 1253;1994, Ex. Sess., c. 24, s. 14(c)

CITED in Nationwide Mut. Ins. Co. v. Land, 78 N.C. App. 342, 337 S.E.2d 180 (1985); Nationwide Mut. Ins. Co. v. Land, 318 N.C. 551, 350 S.E.2d 500 (1986).

§ 20-106.2. Sublease and loan assumption arranging regulated

(a) As used in this section:

(1) "Buyer" means a purchaser of a motor vehicle under the terms of a retail installment contract. "Buyer" shall include any co-buyer on the retail installment contract.

(2) "Lease" means an agreement between a lessor and lessee whereby the lessee obtains the possession and use of a motor vehicle for the period of time, for the purposes, and for the consideration set forth in the agreement whether or not the agreement includes an option to purchase the motor vehicle; provided, however, "lease" shall not include a residential rental agreement of a manufactured home which is subject to Chapter 42 of the General Statutes.

(3) "Lessor" means any person who in the regular course of business or as a part of regular business activity leases motor vehicles under motor vehicle lease agreements, purchases motor vehicle lease agreements, or any sales finance company that purchases motor vehicle lease agreements.

(4) "Lessee" means a person who obtains possession and use of a motor vehicle through a motor vehicle lease agreement.

"Lessee" shall include any co-lessee listed on the motor vehicle lease agreement.

(5) "Person" means an individual, partnership, corporation, association or any other group however organized.

(6) "Security interest" means an interest in personal property that secures performance of an obligation.

(7) "Secured party" means a lender, seller, or other person in whose favor there is a security interest, including a person to whom accounts or retail installment sales contracts have been sold.

(8) "Sublease" means an agreement whether written or oral:

a. To transfer to a third party possession of a motor vehicle which is and will, while in that third party's possession, remain the subject of a security interest which secures performance of a retail installment contract or consumer loan; or

b. To transfer or assign to a third party any of the buyer's rights, interests, or obligations under the retail installment contract or consumer loan; or

c. To transfer to a third party possession of a motor vehicle which is and will, while in the third party's possession, remain the subject of a motor vehicle lease agreement; or

d. To transfer or assign to a third party any of the lessee's or buyer's rights, interests, or obligations under the motor vehicle lease agreement.

(9) "Sublease arranger" means a person who engages in the business of inducing by any means buyers and lessees to enter into subleases as sublessors and inducing third parties to enter into subleases as sublessees, however such contracts may be called. "Sublease arranger" does not include the publisher, owner, agent or employee of a newspaper, periodical, radio station, television station, cable-television system or other advertising medium which disseminates any advertisement or promotion of any act governed by this section.

(10) "Third party" means a person other than the buyer or the lessee of the vehicle.

(11) "Transfer" means to transfer possession of a motor vehicle by means of a sale, loan assumption, lease, sublease, or lease assignment.

(b) A sublease arranger commits an offense if the sublease arranger arranges a sublease of a motor vehicle and:

(1) Does not first obtain written authorization for the sublease from the vehicle's secured party or lessor; or

(2) Accepts a fee without having first obtained written authorization for the sublease from the vehicle's secured party or lessor; or

(3) Does not disclose the location of the vehicle on the request of the vehicle's buyer, lessee, secured party, or lessor; or

(4) Does not provide to the third party new, accurate disclosures under the Consumer Credit Protection Act, 15 U.S.C. Section 1601, et seq.; or

(5) Does not provide oral and written notice to the buyer or lessee that he will not be released from liability; or

(6) Does not ensure that all rights under warranties and service contracts regarding the motor vehicle transfer to the third party, unless a pro rata rebate for any unexpired coverage is applied to reduce the third party's cost under the sublease; or

(7) Does not take reasonable steps to ensure that the third party is financially able to assume the payment obligations of the buyer or lessee according to the terms of the lease agreement, retail installment contract, or consumer loan.

(c) It is not a defense to prosecution under subsection (b) of this section that the motor vehicle's buyer or lessee, secured party or lessor has violated a contract creating a security interest or lease in the motor vehicle, nor may any sublease arranger shift to the lessee, buyer or third party the arranger's duty under subdivision (b)(1) or (b)(2) to obtain prior written authorization for formation of a sublease.

(d) An offense under subdivision (b)(1) or (b)(2) of this section is a Class I felony.

(e) All other offenses under subsection (b) of this section are Class 1 misdemeanors. Each failure to disclose the location of the vehicle under subdivision (b)(3) shall constitute a separate offense.

(f) Any buyer, lessee, sublessee, secured party or lessor injured or damaged by reason of any act in violation of this section, whether or not there is a conviction for the violation, may file a civil action to recover damages based on the violation with the following available remedies:

(1) Three times the amount of any actual damages or fifteen hundred dollars ($1500), whichever is greater;

(2) Equitable relief, including a temporary restraining order, a preliminary or permanent injunction, or restitution of money or property;

(3) Reasonable attorney fees and costs; and

(4) Any other relief which the court deems just.

The rights and remedies provided by this section are in addition to any other rights and remedies provided by law.

(g) This section and G.S. 14-114 and G.S. 14-115 are mutually exclusive and prosecution under those sections shall not preclude criminal prosecution or civil action under this section.

History.

1989 (Reg. Sess., 1990), c. 1011; 1993, c. 539, ss. 347, 1254; 1994, Ex. Sess., c. 24, s. 14(c)

§ 20-107. Injuring or tampering with vehicle

(a) Any person who either individually or in association with one or more other persons willfully injures or tampers with any vehicles or breaks or removes any part or parts of or from a vehicle without the consent of the owner is guilty of a Class 2 misdemeanor.

(b) Any person who with intent to steal, commit any malicious mischief, injury or other crime, climbs into or upon a vehicle, whether it is in motion or at rest, or with like intent attempts to manipulate any of the levers, starting mechanism, brakes, or other mechanism or device of a vehicle while the same is at rest and unattended or with like intent sets in motion any vehicle while the same is at rest and unattended, is guilty of a Class 2 misdemeanor.

History.

1937, c. 407, s. 71; 1965, c. 621, s. 1; 1993, c. 539, s. 348;1994, Ex. Sess., c. 24, s. 14(c)

SUBSECTION (A) NOT A LESSER INCLUDED OFFENSE OF G.S. 14-56. --A lesser included offense is one composed of some, but not all, of the elements of the greater crime, and which does not have any element not included in the greater offense; while most of the elements of subsection (a) of this section are present in G.S. 14-56, neither injuring or tampering with the vehicle itself nor breaking or removing a part of it (elements of this section) are part of the greater offense found in G.S. 14-56. State v. Carver, 96 N.C. App. 230, 385 S.E.2d 145 (1989).

NEITHER PART OF G.S. 20-107 IS A LESSER INCLUDED OFFENSE OF G.S. 14-56. --While most of the elements of G.S. 20-107(a) are present in G.S. 14-56, neither injuring or tampering with the vehicle itself, nor breaking or removing a part of the car are part of the offense in G.S. 14-56; thus, neither part of G.S. 20-107 is a lesser included offense of G.S. 14-56. State v. Jackson, 162 N.C. App. 695, 592 S.E.2d 575 (2004).

CITED in Kirschbaum v. McLaurin Parking Co., 188 N.C. App. 782, 656 S.E.2d 683 (2008).

§ 20-108. Vehicles or component parts of vehicles without manufacturer's numbers

(a) Any person who knowingly buys, receives, disposes of, sells, offers for sale, conceals, or has in his possession any motor vehicle, or engine or transmission or component part which has been stolen or removed from a motor vehicle and from which the manufacturer's serial or engine number or other distinguishing number or identification mark or number placed thereon under assignment from the Division has been removed, defaced, covered, altered, or destroyed for the purpose of concealing or misrepresenting the identity of said motor vehicle or engine or transmission or component part is guilty of a Class 2 misdemeanor.

(b) The Commissioner and such officers and inspectors of the Division of Motor Vehicles as he has designated may take and possess any motor vehicle or component part if its engine number, vehicle identification number, or manufacturer's serial number has been altered, changed, or obliterated or if such officer has probable cause to believe that the driver or person in charge of the motor vehicle or component part has violated subsection (a) above. Any officer who so takes possession of a motor vehicle or component part shall immediately notify the Division of Motor Vehicles and the rightful owner, if known. The notification shall contain a description of the motor vehicle or component part and any other facts that may assist in locating or establishing the rightful ownership thereof or in prosecuting any person for a violation of the provisions of this Article.

(c) Within 15 days after seizure of a motor vehicle or component part pursuant to this section, the Division shall send notice by certified mail to the person from whom the property was seized and to all claimants to the property whose interest or title is in the registration records in the Division of Motor Vehicles that the Division has taken custody of the motor vehicle or component part. The notice shall also contain the following information:

(1) The name and address of the person or persons from whom the motor vehicle or component part was seized;

(2) A statement that the motor vehicle or component part has been seized for investigation as provided in this section and that the motor vehicle or component part will be released to the rightful owner:

a. Upon a determination that the identification number has not been altered, changed, or obliterated; or

b. Upon presentation of satisfactory evidence of the ownership of the motor vehicle or component part if no other person claims an interest in it within 30 days of the date the notice is mailed. Otherwise, a hearing regarding the disposition of the motor vehicle or component part may take place in a court having jurisdiction.

(3) The name and address of the officer to whom evidence of ownership of the motor vehicle or component part may be presented; and

(4) A copy statement of the text contained in this section.

(d) Whenever a motor vehicle or component part comes into the custody of an officer, the Division of Motor Vehicles may commence a civil action in the District Court in the county in which the motor vehicle or component part was seized to determine whether the motor vehicle or component part should be destroyed, sold, converted to the use of the Division or otherwise disposed of by an order of the court. The Division shall give notice of the commencement of such an action to the person from whom the motor vehicle or component part was seized and all claimants to the property whose interest or title is in the registration records of the Division of Motor Vehicles. Notice shall be by certified mail sent within 10 days after the filing of the action. In addition, any possessor of a motor vehicle or component part described in this section may commence a civil action under the provisions of this section, to which the Division of Motor Vehicles may be made a party, to provide for the proper disposition of the motor vehicle or component part.

(e) Nothing in this section shall preclude the Division of Motor Vehicles from returning a seized motor vehicle or component part to the owner following presentation of satisfactory evidence of ownership, and, if determined necessary, requiring the owner to obtain an assignment of an identification number for the motor vehicle or component part from the Division of Motor Vehicles.

(f) No court order providing for disposition shall be issued unless the person from whom the motor vehicle or component was seized and all claimants to the property whose interest or title is in the registration records in the Division of Motor Vehicles are provided a postseizure hearing by the court having jurisdiction. Ten days' notice of the postseizure hearing shall be given by certified mail to the person from whom the motor vehicle was seized and all claimants to the property whose interest or title is in the registration records in the Division of Motor Vehicles. If such motor vehicle or component part has been held or identified as evidence in a pending civil or criminal action or proceeding, no final disposition of such motor vehicle or component part shall be ordered without prior notice to the parties in said proceeding.

(g) At a hearing held pursuant to any action filed by the Division to determine the disposition of any motor vehicle or component part seized pursuant to this section, the court shall consider the following:

(1) If the evidence reveals either that the motor vehicle or component part identification number has not been altered, changed or obliterated or that the identification

number has been altered, changed, or obliterated but satisfactory evidence of ownership has been presented, the motor vehicle or component part shall be returned to the person entitled to it. If ownership cannot be established, nothing in this section shall preclude the return of said motor vehicle or component part to a good faith purchaser following the presentation of satisfactory evidence of ownership thereof and, if necessary, upon the good faith purchaser's obtaining an assigned number from the Division of Motor Vehicles and posting a reasonable bond for a period of three years. The amount of the bond shall be set by the court.

(2) If the evidence reveals that the motor vehicle or component part identification number has been altered, changed, or obliterated and satisfactory evidence of ownership has not been presented, the motor vehicle or component part shall be destroyed, sold, converted to the use of the Division of Motor Vehicles or otherwise disposed of, as provided for by order of the court.

(h) At the hearing, the Division shall have the burden of establishing, by a preponderance of the evidence, that the motor vehicle or component part has been stolen or that its identification number has been altered, changed, or obliterated.

(i) At the hearing any claimant to the motor vehicle or component part shall have the burden of providing satisfactory evidence of ownership.

(j) An officer taking into custody a motor vehicle or component part under the provisions of this section is authorized to obtain necessary removal and storage services, but shall incur no personal liability for such services. The person or company so employed shall be entitled to reasonable compensation as a claimant under (e), and shall not be deemed an unlawful possessor under (a).

History.
1937, c. 407, s. 72; 1965, c. 621, s. 2; 1973, c. 1149, ss. 1, 2; 1975, c. 716, s. 5; 1983, c. 592; 1985, c. 764, s. 22; 1985 (Reg. Sess., 1986), c. 852, s. 17; 1993, c. 539, s. 349;1994, Ex. Sess., c. 24, s. 14(c)

NOTICE REQUIREMENT. --Buyer of a vehicle seized by the division of motor vehicles was entitled to notice and a hearing as outlined in G.S. 20-108; a trial court's summary judgment dismissing a claim brought by the buyer against the division was error where the record was devoid of evidence that the division gave the buyer notice complying with the requirements of G.S. 20-108(c). Citifinancial, Inc. v. Messer, 167 N.C. App. 742, 606 S.E.2d 453 (2005), cert. denied, 359 N.C. 410, 612 S.E.2d 317 (2005).

LIABILITY FOR STORAGE SERVICES. --North Carolina Division of Motor Vehicles was liable under

Chapter 20

G.S. 20-108(j) to an automotive company for a more than half-million dollar storage bill for stolen motorcycles and parts seized by the Division during an investigation of a theft ring where the Division ran up an eight-year tab at the automotive company's expense. Bowles Auto., Inc. v. N.C. DMV, 203 N.C. App. 19, 690 S.E.2d 728 (2010), review denied, 364 N.C. 324, 700 S.E.2d 746, 2010 N.C. LEXIS 590 (2010).

CROSS REFERENCES. --

For provision that G.S. 14-160.1, relating to the alteration, destruction or removal of permanent identification marks from personal property, shall not affect this section, see G.S. 14-160.1(d).

§ 20-109. Altering or changing engine or other numbers

(a) It shall be unlawful and constitute a felony for:

(1) Any person to willfully deface, destroy, remove, cover, or alter the manufacturer's serial number, transmission number, or engine number; or

(2) Any vehicle owner to knowingly permit the defacing, removal, destroying, covering, or alteration of the serial number, transmission number, or engine number; or

(3) Any person except a licensed vehicle manufacturer as authorized by law to place or stamp any serial number, transmission number, or engine number upon a vehicle, other than one assigned thereto by the Division; or

(4) Any vehicle owner to knowingly permit the placing or stamping of any serial number or motor number upon a motor vehicle, except such numbers as assigned thereto by the Division.

A violation of this subsection shall be punishable as a Class I felony.

(b) It shall be unlawful and constitute a felony for:

(1) Any person, with intent to conceal or misrepresent the true identity of the vehicle, to deface, destroy, remove, cover, alter, or use any serial or motor number assigned to a vehicle by the Division; or

(2) Any vehicle owner, with intent to conceal or misrepresent the true identity of the vehicle, to permit the defacing, destruction, removal, covering, alteration, or use of a serial or motor number assigned to a vehicle by the Division; or

(3) Any vehicle owner, with the intent to conceal or misrepresent the true identity of a vehicle, to permit the defacing, destruction, removal, covering, alteration, use, gift, or sale of any manufacturer's serial number, serial number plate, or any part or parts of a vehicle containing the serial number or portions of the serial number.

A violation of this subsection shall be punishable as a Class I felony.

History.

1937, c. 407, s. 73; 1943, c. 726; 1953, c. 216; 1965, c. 621, s. 3; 1967, c. 449; 1973, c. 1089; 1975, c. 716, s. 5; 1979, c. 760, s. 5; 1979, 2nd Sess., c. 1316, s. 47; 1981, c. 63, s. 1;;1987, c. 512; 1993, c. 539, s. 1255;1994, Ex. Sess., c. 24, s. 14(c)

ASSIGNMENT OF NUMBER BY DIVISION AS ESSENTIAL ELEMENT OF OFFENSE UNDER SUBDIVISION (B)(1). --The requirement that a serial or motor number alleged to have been altered be one assigned to a vehicle by the Division of Motor Vehicles of the Department of Transportation is an essential element of the offense condemned by subdivision (b)(1) of this section. Before the State is entitled to a conviction, it must prove the presence of this element beyond a reasonable doubt from the evidence. State v. Wyrick, 35 N.C. App. 352, 241 S.E.2d 355 (1978).

CROSS REFERENCES. --

For provision that G.S. 14-160.1, relating to the alteration, destruction or removal of permanent identification marks from personal property, shall not affect this section, see G.S. 14-160.1(d).

§ 20-109.1. Surrender of titles to salvage vehicles

(a) **Option to Keep Title. --** When a vehicle is damaged to the extent that it becomes a salvage vehicle and the owner submits a claim for the damages to an insurer, the insurer must determine whether the owner wants to keep the vehicle after payment of the claim. If the owner does not want to keep the vehicle after payment of the claim, the procedures in subsection (b) of this section apply. If the owner wants to keep the vehicle after payment of the claim, the procedures in subsection (c) of this section apply.

(b) **Transfer to Insurer. --**

(1) If a salvage vehicle owner does not want to keep the vehicle, the owner must assign the vehicle's certificate of title to the insurer when the insurer pays the claim. The insurer must send the assigned title to the Division within 10 days after receiving it from the vehicle owner. The Division must then send the insurer a form to use to transfer title to the vehicle from the insurer to a person who buys the vehicle from the insurer. If the insurer sells the vehicle, the insurer must complete the form and give it to the buyer. If the buyer rebuilds the vehicle, the buyer may apply for a new certificate of title to the vehicle.

(2) If a salvage vehicle owner fails to assign and deliver the vehicle's certificate of title to the insurer within 30 days of the payment of the claim in accordance with subdivision (b)(1) of this section, the insurer, without surrendering the certificate of title,

may, at any time thereafter, request that the Division send the insurer a form to use to transfer title to the vehicle from the insurer to a person who buys the vehicle from the insurer. The request shall be made on a form prescribed by the Division and shall be accompanied by proof of payment of the claim and proof of notice sent to the owner and any lienholder requesting the vehicle's certificate of title. If the records of the Division indicate there is an outstanding lien against the vehicle immediately before the payment of the claim and if the payment was made to a lienholder or to a lienholder and the owner jointly, the proof of payment shall include evidence that funds were paid to the first lienholder shown on the records of the Division. The notice must be sent by the insurer at least 30 days prior to requesting the Division send the insurer a form to use to transfer title and must be sent by certified mail or by another commercially available delivery service providing proof of delivery to the address on record with the Division. Upon the Division's receipt of such request, the vehicle's certificate of title is deemed to be assigned to the insurer. Notwithstanding any outstanding liens against the vehicle, the Division must send the insurer a form to use to transfer title to the vehicle from the insurer to a person who buys the vehicle from the insurer. The Division's issuance of the form extinguishes all existing liens on the motor vehicle. If the insurer sells the vehicle, the insurer must complete the form and give it to the buyer. In such a sale by the insurer, the motor vehicle shall be transferred free and clear of any liens. If the buyer rebuilds the vehicle, the buyer may apply for a new certificate of title to the vehicle.

(3) Notwithstanding any other provision of law, with respect to a vehicle described in this subsection, the following shall be exempt from the requirements of notarization, including exemption from the notarization of electronic signature requirements of G.S. 20-52(c):

a. The transfer of ownership on the certificate of title.

b. Any power of attorney required in connection with the transfer of ownership to the insurer.

c. Any required odometer disclosure statement.

d. The application for a salvage certificate of title.

e. The transfer of ownership on the salvage certificate of title issued.

f. Any statement pursuant to subdivision (2) of subsection (b) of this section.

g. Any statement on the salvage certificate of title issued.

(c) **Owner Keeps Vehicle.** -- If a salvage vehicle owner wants to keep the vehicle, the insurer must give the owner an owner-retained salvage form. The owner must complete the form and give it to the insurer when the insurer pays the claim. The owner's signature on the owner-retained salvage form must be notarized. The insurer must send the completed form to the Division within 10 days after receiving it from the vehicle owner. The Division must then note in its vehicle registration records that the vehicle listed on the form is a salvage vehicle.

(d) **Theft Claim on Salvage Vehicle.** -- An insurer that pays a theft loss claim on a vehicle and, upon recovery of the vehicle, determines that the vehicle has been damaged to the extent that it is a salvage vehicle must send the vehicle's certificate of title to the Division within 10 days after making the determination. The Division and the insurer must then follow the procedures set in subdivision (1) of subsection (b) of this section.

(e) **Out-of-State Vehicle.** -- A person who acquires a salvage vehicle that is registered in a state that does not require surrender of the vehicle's certificate of title must send the title to the Division within 10 days after the vehicle enters this State. The Division and the person must then follow the procedures set in subdivision (1) of subsection (b) of this section.

(e1) **Owner or Lienholder Abandons Vehicle.** -- If an insurer requests a used motor vehicle dealer, the primary business of which is the sale of salvage vehicles on behalf of insurers, to take possession of a salvage vehicle that is the subject of an insurance claim and subsequently the insurer does not take ownership of the vehicle, the insurer may direct the used motor vehicle dealer to release the vehicle to the owner or lienholder. The insurer shall provide the used motor vehicle dealer a release statement authorizing the used motor vehicle dealer to release the vehicle to the vehicle's owner or lienholder.

Upon receiving a release statement from an insurer, the used motor vehicle dealer shall send notice to the owner and any lienholder of the vehicle informing the owner or lienholder that the vehicle is available for pick up. The notice shall include an invoice for any outstanding charges owed to the used motor vehicle dealer. The notice shall inform the owner and any lienholder that the owner or lienholder has 30 days from the date of the notice, and upon payment of applicable charges owed to the used motor vehicle dealer, to pick up the vehicle from the used motor vehicle dealer. Notice under this subsection must be sent by certified mail or by another commercially available delivery service providing proof of delivery to the address on record with the Division.

Chapter 20

If the owner or any lienholder of the vehicle does not pick up the vehicle within 30 days after notice was sent to the owner and any lienholder in accordance with this subsection, the vehicle shall be considered abandoned, the vehicle's certificate of title is deemed to be assigned to the used motor vehicle dealer, and the used motor vehicle dealer, without surrendering the certificate of title, may request that the Division send the used motor vehicle dealer a form to use to transfer title to the vehicle from the used motor vehicle dealer to a person who buys the vehicle from the used motor vehicle dealer. The request shall be accompanied by a copy of the notice required by this subsection and proof of delivery of the notice required by this subsection sent to the owner and any lienholder. Notwithstanding any outstanding liens against the vehicle, the Division must send the used motor vehicle dealer a form to use to transfer title to the vehicle from the used motor vehicle dealer to a person who buys the vehicle from the used motor vehicle dealer. The Division's issuance of the form extinguishes all existing liens on the motor vehicle. If the used motor vehicle dealer sells the vehicle, the used motor vehicle dealer must complete the form and give it to the buyer. In such a sale by the used motor vehicle dealer, the motor vehicle shall be transferred free and clear of any liens. If the buyer rebuilds the vehicle, the buyer may apply for a new certificate of title.

(f) **Sanctions.** -- Violation of this section is a Class 1 misdemeanor. In addition to this criminal sanction, a person who violates this section is subject to a civil penalty of up to one hundred dollars ($ 100.00), to be imposed in the discretion of the Commissioner.

(g) **Fee.** -- G.S. 20-85 sets the fee for issuing a salvage certificate of title.

(h) **Claims.** -- The Division shall not be subject to a claim under Article 31 of Chapter 143 of the General Statutes related to the cancellation of a title pursuant to this section if the claim is based on reliance by the Division on any proof of payment or proof of notice submitted to the Division by a third party pursuant to subdivision (b)(2) or subsection (e1) of this section.

History.
1973, c. 1095, s. 1; 1975, c. 716, s. 5; c. 799; 1983, c. 713, s. 94; 1989, c. 455, s. 5;1993, c. 539, s. 350;1994, Ex. Sess., c. 24, s. 14(c);1995, c. 50, s. 3;c. 517, s. 33.1;2013-400, s. 1;2019-153, s. 6

EFFECT OF AMENDMENTS. --
Session Laws 2013-400, s. 1, effective October 1, 2013, inserted the subdivision (b)(1) designation and added subdivision (b)(2); inserted "subdivision (1) of" in subsections (d) and (e); and added subsections (e1) and (h).

Session Laws 2019-153, s. 6, effective October 1, 2019, added subdivision (b)(3).

INTENT OF SECTION. --The intent of this section is to see that insurance companies which obtain salvage vehicles as a result of paying a total loss claim, repair them, and then sell them, surrender their evidence of title to the State, so that the reissued certificate of title might reflect that the vehicle has been previously wrecked. Allen v. American Sec. Ins. Co., 53 N.C. App. 239, 280 S.E.2d 471 (1981).

SCOPE OF SECTION. --This section appears to be directed only toward insurance companies who obtain salvage vehicles as a result of paying a total loss claim, repair them, and then sell them. Allen v. American Sec. Ins. Co., 53 N.C. App. 239, 280 S.E.2d 471 (1981).

CONSTRUCTIVE AND ACTUAL TOTAL LOSS DISTINGUISHED. --A vehicle is considered a constructive total loss any time repair becomes economically impractical. Hence, under this definition, a constructive total loss is something quite different from an actual total loss, which is generally defined as occurring when the cost of repairs exceeds the fair market value of the vehicle prior to the collision. Allen v. American Sec. Ins. Co., 53 N.C. App. 239, 280 S.E.2d 471 (1981).

TOTAL LOSS REFERRED TO IN THIS SECTION MUST BE AN ACTUAL TOTAL LOSS, since only if the insurance company pays the full precollision value of a vehicle can the vehicle's owner be expected to give up his rights in the vehicle, including his right to the proceeds from salvage of the vehicle. Allen v. American Sec. Ins. Co., 53 N.C. App. 239, 280 S.E.2d 471 (1981).

SECTION INAPPLICABLE WHERE CONSTRUCTIVE TOTAL LOSS CLAIM PAID. --As it is unlikely that the legislature intended to force the owner of a wrecked vehicle to give up title and possession of his vehicle for less than its reasonable precollision value, this section applies only to the payment of an actual total loss claim, and is inapplicable where a substantially lower constructive total loss claim is paid. Allen v. American Sec. Ins. Co., 53 N.C. App. 239, 280 S.E.2d 471 (1981).

CITED in Wilson v. Sutton, 124 N.C. App. 170, 476 S.E.2d 467 (1996).

OPINIONS OF THE ATTORNEY GENERAL
"CONSTRUCTIVE TOTAL LOSS" VEHICLES AS WELL AS "ACTUAL TOTAL LOSS" VEHICLES ARE WITHIN THE DEFINITION OF SALVAGE MOTOR VEHICLE. See opinion of Attorney General to Mr. James E. Rhodes, Director, Vehicle Registration Section, Division of Motor Vehicles, North Carolina Department of Transportation, 58 N.C.A.G. 38 (May 20, 1988).

AS TO TREATMENT BY INSURER OF WRECKED VEHICLE AS A CONSTRUCTIVE TOTAL LOSS, so as to harmonize G.S. 20-4.01(33)(d) and subdivision (a)(1) of this section, see opinion of Attorney General to Mr. James E. Rhodes, Director, Vehicle Registration Section, Division of Motor Vehicles, North Carolina Department of Transportation, 58 N.C.A.G. 38 (May 20, 1988).

NEW DEFINITIONS OF SALVAGE MOTOR VEHICLE ENACTED BY SESSION LAWS 1987, C. 607

IN G.S. 20-4.01(33)(D) AND THIS SECTION MUST BE READ IN PARI MATERIA. See opinion of Attorney General to Mr. James E. Rhodes, Director, Vehicle Registration Section, Division of Motor Vehicles, North Carolina Department of Transportation, 58 N.C.A.G. 38 (May 20, 1988).

§ 20-109.2. Surrender of title to manufactured home

(a) **Surrender of Title. --** If a certificate of title has been issued for a manufactured home, the owner listed on the title has the title, and the manufactured home qualifies as real property as defined in G.S. 105-273(13), the owner listed on the title shall submit an affidavit to the Division that the manufactured home meets this definition and surrender the certificate of title to the Division.

(a1) **Surrender When Title Not Available. --** If a certificate of title has been issued for a manufactured home, no issued title is available, and the manufactured home qualifies as real property as defined in G.S. 105-273(13), the owner listed on the title shall be deemed to have surrendered the title to the Division if the owner of the real property on which the manufactured home is affixed (i) submits an affidavit to the Division that the manufactured home meets the definition of real property under G.S. 105-273(13) and in compliance with subsection (b) of this section and (ii) submits a tax record showing the manufactured home listed for ad valorem taxes as real property pursuant to Article 17 of Chapter 105 of the General Statutes in the name of the record owner of the real property on which the manufactured home is affixed.

(b) **Affidavit. --** The affidavit must be in a form approved by the Commissioner and shall include or provide for all of the following information:

(1) The manufacturer and, if applicable, the model name of the manufactured home affixed to real property upon which cancellation is sought.

(2) The vehicle identification number and serial number of the manufactured home affixed to real property upon which cancellation is sought.

(3) The legal description of the real property on which the manufactured home is affixed, stating that the owner of the manufactured home also owns the real property or that the owner of the manufactured home has entered into a lease with a primary term of at least 20 years for the real property on which the manufactured home is affixed with a copy of the lease or a memorandum thereof pursuant to G.S. 47-18 attached to the affidavit, if not previously recorded.

(4) A description of any security interests in the manufactured home affixed to real property upon which cancellation is sought.

(5) A section for the Division's notation or statement that either the procedure in subsection (a) of this section for surrendering the title has been surrendered and the title has been cancelled by the Division or the affiant submits this affidavit pursuant to subsection (a1) of this section to have the title deemed surrendered by the owner listed on the certificate of title.

(6) An affirmative statement that the affiant is (i) the record owner of the real property on which the manufactured home is affixed and the lease for the manufactured home does not include a provision allowing the owner listed on the certificate of title to dispose of the manufactured home prior to the end of the primary term of the lease or (ii) is the owner of the manufactured home and either owns the real property on which the manufactured home is affixed or has entered into a lease with a primary term of at least 20 years for the real property on which the manufactured home is affixed.

(7) The affiant affirms that he or she has sent notice of this cancellation by hand delivery or by first-class mail to the last known address of the owner listed on the certificate of title prior to filing this affidavit with the Division.

(c) **Cancellation. --** Upon compliance with the procedures in subsection (a) or (a1) of this section for surrender of title, the Division shall rescind and cancel the certificate of title. If a security interest has been recorded on the certificate of title and not released by the secured party, the Division may not cancel the title without written consent from all secured parties. After canceling the title, the Division shall return the original of the affidavit to the affiant, or to the secured party having the first recorded security interest, with the Division's notation or statement that the title has been surrendered and has been cancelled by the Division. The affiant or secured party shall file the affidavit returned by the Division with the office of the register of deeds of the county where the real property is located. The Division may charge five dollars ($ 5.00) for a cancellation of a title under this section.

(d) **Application for Title After Cancellation. --** If the owner of a manufactured home whose certificate of title has been cancelled under this section subsequently seeks to separate the manufactured home from the real property, the owner may apply for a new certificate of title. The owner must submit to the Division an affidavit containing the same information set out in subsection (b) of this section, verification that the manufactured home has been removed from the real property, verification of the identity of the current owner of the real property upon which the manufactured home was located, and written consent of any affected owners of recorded mortgages, deeds of trust, or security interests in the real property where the manufactured home was placed. The Commissioner may require evidence sufficient to demonstrate that all affected owners of security interests have been notified and consent. Upon receipt of this information, together with a title application and required fee, the Division shall issue a new title for the manufactured home in the name of the current owner of the real property upon which the manufactured home was located.

(e) **Sanctions.** -- Any person who violates this section is subject to a civil penalty of up to one hundred dollars (\$ 100.00), to be imposed in the discretion of the Commissioner.

(f) **No Right of Action.** -- A person damaged by the cancellation of a certificate of title pursuant to subsection (a1) of this section does not have a right of action against the Division.

History.
2001-506, s. 2;2003-400, s. 1;2013-79, s. 1;2016-59, s. 6

EDITOR'S NOTE. --
Session Laws 2016-59, s. 10, made the amendment to subsection (d) of this section by Session Laws 2016-59, s. 6, applicable to titles issued on or after August 1, 2016.

EFFECT OF AMENDMENTS. --
Session Laws 2013-79, s. 1, effective July 1, 2013, in subsection (a), inserted "certificate of", "the owner listed on the title has the title" and "listed on the title"; added subsections (a1) and (f) and subdivisions (b)(6) and (b)(7); inserted "affixed to real property upon which cancellation is sought" in subdivisions (b)(1), (b)(2), and (b)(4); substituted "affixed" for "placed" in subdivision (b)(3); rewrote subdivision (b)(5), which read "A section for the Division's notation or statement that the title has been surrendered and cancelled by the Division"; and in subsection (c), substituted "with the procedures in subsection (a) or (a1) of this section" for "by the owner with the procedure" in the first sentence, and substituted "affiant" for "owner" in the third and fourth sentences.

Session Laws 2016-59, s. 6, effective August 1, 2016, in subsection (d), inserted "verification of the identity of the current owner of the real property upon which the manufactured home was located" near the middle of the second sentence, and substituted "shall issue a new title for the manufactured home in the name of the current owner of the real property upon which the manufactured home was located" for "is authorized to issue a new title for the manufactured home" at the end of the last sentence. See editor's note for applicability.

§ 20-109.3. Disposition of vehicles abandoned by charitable organizations

(a) If a charitable organization operating under section 501(c)(3) of the Internal Revenue Code (26 U.S.C. § 501(c)(3)) requests a licensed used motor vehicle dealer, whose primary business is the sale of salvage vehicles on behalf of insurers or charitable organizations, to take possession of a donated vehicle that is currently titled in this State, and the vehicle title is not provided to the used motor vehicle dealer at the time of donation or within 10 days of the donation, then the following provisions apply:

(1) The used motor vehicle dealer receiving the vehicle on behalf of the charitable organization shall send notice to the last registered owner and any reasonably ascertainable lienholders of the vehicle informing the owner or lienholder that the vehicle has been donated to the named charitable organization. The notice shall set forth the current location of the vehicle, the name of the charitable organization to which the vehicle was donated, and the name of the vehicle donor. The notice shall inform the owner or lienholder that, if the owner or lienholder objects to the donation of the vehicle, the owner or lienholder has 30 days from the date of the notice to provide proof of ownership and reclaim the vehicle from the used motor vehicle dealer at no charge. Notice under this subdivision must be sent by certified mail or by another commercially available delivery service providing proof of delivery to the address on record with the Division.

(2) If the owner or any lienholder of the vehicle receives notice but fails to object to the donation and pick up the vehicle within 30 days, any claim to the vehicle by the owner or lienholder is considered abandoned, the certificate of title to the vehicle is deemed to be transferred to the charitable organization by the owner, and the lien is deemed to be extinguished. The charitable organization, or the used motor vehicle dealer acting on its behalf through a power of attorney, may then execute an application for duplicate title with transfer upon payment of any applicable fees. The application for duplicate title with transfer shall be accompanied by a copy of the written donation statement, a copy of the notice required by subdivision (1) of this subsection, and proof of delivery of the notice sent to the owner and any lienholder. If the application is being executed by the used motor vehicle dealer on behalf of the charitable organization, a copy of the power of attorney shall also be submitted with the application.

(3) Upon receipt of an application for duplicate title with transfer, any additional documentation required under subdivision (2) of this subsection and payment of required fees, the Division shall issue a title to the donated vehicle in the name of the charitable organization and mail the title,

free and clear of any liens, to the used motor vehicle dealer possessing the vehicle.

(4) If the notice required under subdivision (1) of this subsection is not received or is returned as undeliverable, the used motor vehicle dealer may file a special proceeding to obtain an order allowing the vehicle to be sold. In such a proceeding, the used motor vehicle dealer may include more than one vehicle.

(5) If the donated vehicle is not currently titled in this State, does not appear in the Division's records, or the owner and any lienholders are not otherwise reasonably ascertainable for any reason, the used motor vehicle dealer may institute a civil action in the county where the vehicle is being held for authorization to sell that vehicle as salvage on behalf of the charitable organization. In such a proceeding, the used motor vehicle dealer may include more than one vehicle. If the court enters an order authorizing the sale of the vehicle, upon proper application and payment of the appropriate taxes and fees, the Division shall issue a salvage branded title to the person who purchases the vehicle at a subsequent sale.

(b) No person shall have a cause of action against the Division or Division contractors arising from the issuance of a title pursuant to this section, and the Division and Division contractors shall not be held liable for any damages arising from the transfer or subsequent operation of any vehicle titled or sold pursuant to this section.

History.
2018-43, s. 1
EDITOR'S NOTE. --
Session Laws 2018-43, s. 6, made this section effective June 22, 2018.

§ 20-110. When registration shall be rescinded

(a) The Division shall rescind and cancel the registration of any vehicle which the Division shall determine is unsafe or unfit to be operated or is not equipped as required by law.

(b) The Division shall rescind and cancel the registration of any vehicle whenever the person to whom the registration card or registration number plates therefor have been issued shall make or permit to be made any unlawful use of the said card or plates or permit the use thereof by a person not entitled thereto.

(c) Repealed by Session Laws 1993, c. 440, s. 8.

(d) The Division shall rescind and cancel the certificate of title to any vehicle which has been erroneously issued or fraudulently obtained or is unlawfully detained by anyone not entitled to possession.

(e) and (f) Repealed by Session Laws 1993, c. 440, s. 8.

(g) The Division shall rescind and cancel the registration plates issued to a carrier of passengers or property which has been secured by such carrier as provided under G.S. 20-50 when the license is being used on a vehicle other than the one for which it was issued or which is being used by the lessor-owner after the lease with such lessee has been terminated.

(h) The Division may rescind and cancel the registration or certificate of title on any vehicle on the grounds that the application therefor contains any false or fraudulent statement or that the holder of the certificate was not entitled to the issuance of a certificate of title or registration.

(i) The Division may rescind and cancel the registration or certificate of title of any vehicle when the Division has reasonable grounds to believe that the vehicle is a stolen or embezzled vehicle, or that the granting of registration or the issuance of certificate of title constituted a fraud against the rightful owner or person having a valid lien upon such vehicle.

(j) The Division may rescind and cancel the registration or certificate of title of any vehicle on the grounds that the registration of the vehicle stands suspended or revoked under the motor vehicle laws of this State.

(k) The Division shall rescind and cancel a certificate of title when the Division finds that such certificate has been used in connection with the registration or sale of a vehicle other than the vehicle for which the certificate was issued.

(l) The Division may rescind and cancel the registration and certificate of title of a vehicle when presented with evidence, such as a sworn statement, that the vehicle has been transferred to a person who has failed to get a new certificate of title for the vehicle as required by G.S. 20-73. A person may submit evidence to the Division by mail.

(m) The Division shall rescind and cancel the registration of vehicles of a motor carrier that is the subject of an order issued by the Federal Motor Carrier Safety Administration or the Division.

(n) The Division shall rescind and cancel the registration of a vehicle of a motor carrier if the applicant fails to disclose material information required, or if the applicant has made a materially false statement on the application, or if the applicant has applied as a subterfuge for the real party in interest who has been issued a federal out-of-service order, or if the applicant's business is operated, managed, or otherwise controlled by or affiliated with a person who is ineligible for registration, including the applicant entity, a relative, family member, corporate officer, or shareholder. The Division shall rescind and cancel the registration for a vehicle that has been assigned for safety to a commercial motor carrier who has been prohibited from operating by the Federal Motor Carrier Safety Administration or a carrier whose business is operated, managed, or otherwise controlled by or affiliated with a person who is ineligible for registration, including the owner, a relative, family member, corporate officer, or shareholder.

History.
1937, c. 407, s. 74; 1945, c. 576, s. 5; 1947, c. 220, s. 4; 1951, c. 985, s. 1; 1953, c. 831, s. 4; 1955, c. 294, s. 1; c. 554, s. 11; 1975, c. 716, s. 5; 1981, c. 976, s. 11; 1991, c. 183, s. 1;1993, c. 440, s. 8;2002-152, s. 2;2019-196, s. 3

EDITOR'S NOTE. --
Session Laws 2002-152, s. 6, provides: "The Division shall adopt rules to implement the provisions of this act."

EFFECT OF AMENDMENTS. --
Session Laws 2019-196, s. 3, effective November 12, 2019, rewrote subsection (m), which formerly read: "The Division shall rescind and cancel the registration of vehicles of a motor carrier that is subject to an order issued by the Federal Motor Carrier Safety Administration or the Division to cease all operations based on a finding that the continued operations of the motor carrier pose an 'imminent hazard' as defined in 49 C.F.R. § 386.72(b)(1)"; and added subsection (n).

§ 20-111. Violation of registration provisions

It shall be unlawful for any person to commit any of the following acts:

(1) To drive a vehicle on a highway, or knowingly permit a vehicle owned by that person to be driven on a highway, when the vehicle is not registered with the Division in accordance with this Article or does not display a current registration plate. Violation of this subdivision is a Class 3 misdemeanor.

(2) To display or cause or permit to be displayed or to have in possession any registration card, certificate of title or registration number plate knowing the same to be fictitious or to have been canceled, revoked, suspended or altered, or to willfully display an expired license or registration plate on a vehicle knowing the same to be expired. Violation of this subdivision is a Class 3 misdemeanor.

(3) The giving, lending, or borrowing of a license plate for the purpose of using same on some motor vehicle other than that for which issued shall make the giver, lender, or borrower guilty of a Class 3 misdemeanor.

Where license plate is found being improperly used, such plate or plates shall be revoked or canceled, and new license plates must be purchased before further operation of the motor vehicle.

(4) To fail or refuse to surrender to the Division, upon demand, any title certificate, registration card or registration number plate which has been suspended, canceled or revoked as in this Article provided. Service of the demand shall be in accordance with G.S. 20-48.

(5) To use a false or fictitious name or address in any application for the registration of any vehicle or for a certificate of title or for any renewal or duplicate thereof, or knowingly to make a false statement or knowingly to conceal a material fact or otherwise commit a fraud in any such application. A violation of this subdivision shall constitute a Class 1 misdemeanor.

(6) To give, lend, sell or obtain a certificate of title for the purpose of such certificate being used for any purpose other than the registration, sale, or other use in connection with the vehicle for which the certificate was issued. Any person violating the provisions of this subdivision shall be guilty of a Class 2 misdemeanor.

History.
1937, c. 407, s. 75; 1943, c. 592, s. 2; 1945, c. 576, s. 6; c. 635; 1949, c. 360; 1955, c. 294, s. 2; 1961, c. 360, s. 20; 1975, c. 716, s. 5; 1981, c. 938, s. 3; 1993, c. 440, s. 9;c. 539, ss. 351 -353; 1994, Ex. Sess., c. 24, s. 14(c);2013-360, s. 18B.14(i)

EDITOR'S NOTE. --
Session Laws 1989, c. 168, ss. 3 and 4, effective May 30, 1989, would have amended subdivisions (c) (9) and (c)(10) of this section; however, these subdivisions do not exist in this section. The amendment apparently should have been to G.S. 20-118. Session Laws 2018-142, s. 5, effective December 14, 2018, repealed Session Laws 1989, c. 168, s. 4.

EFFECT OF AMENDMENTS. --
Session Laws 2013-360, s. 18B.14(i), effective December 1, 2013, added the last sentence in subdivisions (1) and (2). For applicability, see Editor's note.

CONSTITUTIONALITY. --G.S. 20-111(1) and G.S. 20-313 bear a real and substantial relationship to public safety, and, therefore, he General Assembly had ample authority, under its police power, to enact the sections of the statute and to make their violation a criminal offense because there are ample public safety justifications for the vehicle registration and financial responsibility requirements; if a defendant does not wish to follow these statutory requirements, he may exercise his right to travel in a variety of other ways, and if he wishes, he may walk, ride a bicycle or horse, or travel as a passenger in an automobile, bus, airplane or helicopter, but he cannot operate a motor vehicle on the public highways. State v. Sullivan, 201

N.C. App. 540, 687 S.E.2d 504 (2009), appeal denied, 364 N.C. 247, 699 S.E.2d 921 (2010), cert. denied, 562 U.S. 1138, 131 S. Ct. 937, 178 L. Ed. 2d 754, 2011 U.S. LEXIS 574 (U.S. 2011).

G.

S. 20-111 and G.S. 20-313 are not void for vagueness because the purpose of the statutes is very clear, and there is nothing in these statutes that forbids or requires doing an act in terms so vague that men of common intelligence must necessarily guess at its meaning and differ as to its application; defendant failed to demonstrate how the statutes failed to give him the type of fair notice that was necessary to enable him or anyone else operating a motor vehicle to conform their conduct to the law. State v. Sullivan, 201 N.C. App. 540, 687 S.E.2d 504 (2009), appeal denied, 364 N.C. 247, 699 S.E.2d 921 (2010), cert. denied, 562 U.S. 1138, 131 S. Ct. 937, 178 L. Ed. 2d 754, 2011 U.S. LEXIS 574 (U.S. 2011).

PROBABLE CAUSE FOR ARREST. --Civil claims against an inspector with the North Carolina Division of Motor Vehicles were properly dismissed upon summary judgment on the basis of sovereign and qualified immunity, where plaintiff's arrest was supported by probable cause; the inspector had firsthand knowledge that plaintiff's vehicle was not registered to plaintiff and that plaintiff was attempting to operate an unregistered vehicle on a highway while possessing a canceled/revoked registration card. Ellis v. White, 156 N.C. App. 16, 575 S.E.2d 809 (2003).

THE MAXIMUM PUNISHMENT FOR A VIOLATION OF THIS SECTION or G.S. 20-63 would be that prescribed by G.S. 20-176(b), namely, a fine of not more than $100.00 or imprisonment in the county or municipal jail for not more than 60 days, or both such fine and imprisonment. State v. Tolley, 271 N.C. 459, 156 S.E.2d 858 (1967).

MOTION TO DISMISS IMPROPERLY DENIED. --Trial court erred in denying defendant's motion to dismiss the charge of operating a vehicle while displaying an expired registration plate as no substantial evidence showed that defendant displayed an expired registration plate on a vehicle; and, in fact, the officer testified that he stopped defendant's car because there was no license plate on it. State v. Money, -- N.C. App. --, 843 S.E.2d 257 (2020).

APPLIED in State v. Green, 266 N.C. 785, 147 S.E.2d 377 (1966); State v. Gray, 55 N.C. App. 568, 286 S.E.2d 357 (1982); State v. Harrell, 96 N.C. App. 426, 386 S.E.2d 103 (1989).

CITED in State v. White, 3 N.C. App. 31, 164 S.E.2d 36 (1968); State v. Scott, 71 N.C. App. 570, 322 S.E.2d 613 (1984); State v. Green, 103 N.C. App. 38, 404 S.E.2d 363 (1991); State v. Washington, 193 N.C. App. 670, 668 S.E.2d 622 (2008).

§ 20-112. Making false affidavit perjury

Any person who shall knowingly make any false affidavit or shall knowingly swear or affirm falsely to any matter or thing required by the terms of this Article to be sworn or affirmed to shall be guilty of a Class I felony.

History.
1937, c. 407, s. 76; 1993, c. 539, s. 1256;1994, Ex. Sess., c. 24, s. 14(c)

CROSS REFERENCES. --
As to revocation of license in the event of conviction of perjury or the making of false affidavits, etc., see G.S. 20-17.

N.C. Gen. Stat. § 20-113

Repealed by Session Laws 1995 (Regular Session, 1996), c. 756, s. 13.

§ 20-114. Duty of officers; manner of enforcement

(a) For the purpose of enforcing the provisions of this Article, it is hereby made the duty of every police officer of any incorporated city or village, and every sheriff, deputy sheriff, and all other lawful officers of any county to arrest within the limits of their jurisdiction any person known personally to any such officer, or upon the sworn information of a creditable witness, to have violated any of the provisions of this Article, and to immediately bring such offender before any magistrate or officer having jurisdiction, and any such person so arrested shall have the right of immediate trial, and all other rights given to any person arrested for having committed a misdemeanor. Every officer herein named who shall neglect or refuse to carry out the duties imposed by this Chapter shall be liable on his official bond for such neglect or refusal as provided by law in like cases.

(b) It shall be the duty of all sheriffs, police officers, deputy sheriffs, deputy police officers, and all other officers within the State to cooperate with and render all assistance in their power to the officers herein provided for, and nothing in this Article shall be construed as relieving said sheriffs, police officers, deputy sheriffs, deputy police officers, and other officers of the duties imposed on them by this Chapter.

(c) It shall also be the duty of every law enforcement officer to make immediate report to the Commissioner of all motor vehicles reported to the officer as abandoned or that are seized by the officer for being used for illegal transportation of alcoholic beverages or other unlawful purposes, or seized and are subject to forfeiture pursuant to G.S. 20-28.2, et seq., or any other statute, and no motor vehicle shall be sold by any sheriff, police or peace officer, or by any person, firm or corporation claiming a mechanic's or storage lien, or under judicial proceedings, until notice on a form approved by the Commissioner shall have been given the Commissioner at least 20 days before the date of such sale.

History.

1937, c. 407, s. 78; 1943, c. 726; 1967, c. 862; 1971, c. 528, s. 13; 1981, c. 412, s. 4; c. 747, s. 66; 1998-182, s. 12

CITED in Shay v. Nixon, 45 N.C. App. 108, 262 S.E.2d 294 (1980).

§ 20-114.1. Willful failure to obey law-enforcement or traffic-control officer; firemen as traffic-control officers; appointment, etc., of traffic-control officers

(a) No person shall willfully fail or refuse to comply with any lawful order or direction of any law-enforcement officer or traffic-control officer invested by law with authority to direct, control or regulate traffic, which order or direction related to the control of traffic.

(b) In addition to other law enforcement or traffic control officers, uniformed regular and volunteer firemen and uniformed regular and volunteer members of a rescue squad may direct traffic and enforce traffic laws and ordinances at the scene of or in connection with fires, accidents, or other hazards in connection with their duties as firemen or rescue squad members. Except as herein provided, firemen and members of rescue squads shall not be considered law enforcement or traffic control officers.

(b1) Any member of a rural volunteer fire department or volunteer rescue squad who receives no compensation for services shall not be liable in civil damages for any acts or omissions relating to the direction of traffic or enforcement of traffic laws or ordinances at the scene of or in connection with a fire, accident, or other hazard unless such acts or omissions amount to gross negligence, wanton conduct, or intentional wrongdoing.

(c) The chief of police of a local or county police department or the sheriff of any county is authorized to appoint traffic-control officers, who shall have attained the age of 18 years and who are hereby authorized to direct, control, or regulate traffic within their respective jurisdictions at times and places specifically designated in writing by the police chief or the sheriff. A traffic-control officer, when exercising this authority, must be attired in a distinguishing uniform or jacket indicating that he is a traffic-control officer and must possess a valid authorization card issued by the police chief or sheriff who appointed him. Unless an earlier expiration date is specified, an authorization card shall expire two years from the date of its issuance. In order to be appointed as a traffic-control officer, a person shall have received at least three hours of training in directing, controlling, or regulating traffic under the supervision of a law-enforcement officer. A traffic-control officer shall be subject to the rules and regulations of the respective local or county police department or sheriff's office as well as the lawful command of any other law-enforcement officer. The appointing police chief or sheriff shall have the right to revoke the appointment of any traffic-control officer at any time with or without cause. The appointing police chief or sheriff shall not be held liable for any act or omission of a traffic-control officer. A traffic-control officer shall not be deemed to be an agent or employee of the respective local or county police department or of the sheriff's office, nor shall he be considered a law-enforcement officer except as provided herein. A traffic-control officer shall not have nor shall he exercise the power of arrest.

(d) No police chief or sheriff who is authorized to appoint traffic-control officers under subsection (c) of this section shall appoint any person to direct, control, or regulate traffic unless there is indemnity against liability of the traffic-control officer for wrongful death, bodily injury, or property damage that is proximately caused by the negligence of the traffic-control officer while acting within the scope of his duties as a traffic-control officer. Such indemnity shall provide a minimum of twenty-five thousand dollars ($ 25,000) for the death of or bodily injury to one person in any one accident, fifty thousand dollars ($ 50,000) for the death of or bodily injury to two or more persons in any one accident, and ten thousand dollars ($ 10,000) for injury to or destruction of property of others in any one accident.

History.

1961, c. 879; 1969, c. 59; 1983, c. 483, ss. 1-3; 1987, c. 146, ss. 1, 3

EDITOR'S NOTE. --

Session Laws 1985, c. 591, repealed Session Laws 1983, c. 483, s. 4, which had exempted certain counties and municipalities from the provisions of the 1983 Act.

HAND MOTIONS. --In an impaired driving case, the appellate court disagreed with defendant that he was compelled to stop pursuant to G.S. 20-114.1(a). A police officer's hand motion for defendant to stop his vehicle was not related to the control of traffic and there were no circumstances that would indicate to a reasonable person that the officer was acting as a traffic control officer. State v. Wilson, 250 N.C. App. 781, 793 S.E.2d 737 (2016), aff'd, 808 S.E.2d 266, 2017 N.C. LEXIS 1014 (N.C. 2017).

NO PROBABLE CAUSE FOR ARREST. --The defendant police officer who stated that the plaintiff bus driver was under arrest for violating G.S. 20-90(11) (now repealed) could later justify that arrest by reference to G.S. 20-114.1 because the offenses were sufficiently related; nevertheless, summary judgment was still not proper where he may have lacked probable cause to arrest her, even under this section; the facts tended to show that plaintiff was approached by an "angry," "out of control" man wearing shorts, a plain t-shirt, and boots who "flashed something" at her "quickly;" asserted he was both a truck driver and a police officer; boarded her bus; ordered her to move her bus; grabbed her arm, unfastened her seatbelt, and told her she was under arrest; then exited her bus without writing her a citation or formally taking her into custody; furthermore, at no point did plaintiff acknowledge his status as a police officer nor was she even looking in his direction when he attempted to show her his badge at the window of the bus. Glenn-Robinson v. Acker, 140 N.C. App. 606, 538 S.E.2d 601 (2000).

CITED in Bland v. City of Wilmington, 278 N.C. 657, 180 S.E.2d 813 (1971); Warren v. Parks, 31 N.C. App. 609, 230 S.E.2d 684 (1976).

N.C. Gen. Stat. § 20-114.3

Repealed by Session Laws 2007-433, s. 3(a), (b), effective October 1, 2007.

EDITOR'S NOTE. --

Session Laws 2007-4, s. 1, effective March 26, 2007, amended subsection (c) by inserting the towns of Atlantic Beach, Burgaw, Carolina Beach, Emerald Isle, Indian Beach, Kure Beach, Oakboro, North Topsail Beach, Pine Knoll Shores, and Topsail Beach, and the cities of Albemarle and Rockingham, and rearranging the town of Stanley to fall in alphabetical order. However, since Session Laws 2007-433, s. 3(a), (b), repealed this section effective October 1, 2007, the amendment by 2007-4, s. 1, has not been given effect.

As amended, Session Laws 2004-108, s. 2, applied to 10 or more jurisdictions and was codified as this section at the direction of the Revisor of Statutes.

CROSS REFERENCES. --

For present similar provisions concerning use of all-terrain vehicles on certain highways by law-enforcement officers, fire, rescue, and emergency services personnel, and employees of certain municipalities, see G.S. 20-171.23 and 20-171.24.

PART 9.
THE SIZE, WEIGHT, CONSTRUCTION AND EQUIPMENT OF VEHICLES

§ 20-115. Scope and effect of regulations in this Part

It shall be unlawful for any person to drive or move or for the owner to cause or knowingly permit to be driven or moved on any highway any vehicle or vehicles of a size or weight exceeding the limitations stated in this Part, or any vehicle or vehicles which are not so constructed or equipped as required in this Part, or the rules and regulations of the Department of Transportation adopted pursuant to this Part and the maximum size and weight of vehicles specified in this Part shall be lawful throughout this State, and local authorities shall have no power or authority to alter the limitations except as express authority may be granted in this Article.

History.

1937, c. 407, s. 79; 1973, c. 507, s. 5; 1977, c. 464, s. 34; 1985 (Reg. Sess., 1986), c. 852, s. 8; 2015-264, s. 8(a)

EFFECT OF AMENDMENTS. --

Session Laws 2015-264, s. 8(a), effective October 1, 2015, substituted "this Part" for "this title" in the section heading and two times near the middle of the sentence; substituted "to this Part" for "thereto" near the middle of the sentence; substituted "in this Part" for "herein" near the middle of the sentence; and made a minor stylistic change near the end of the sentence.

CIVIL ACTIONS BASED ON ALLEGED VIOLATION --Trial court properly dismissed an injured party's claim against a church and a landowner, alleging that the church and the landowner where negligent because they allowed children younger than 12 years old to ride on an open flatbed trailer during a church festival in violation of G.S. 20-135.2B, because the festival occurred on private property and G.S. 20-135.2B did not apply to activities that occurred on private property. Clontz v. St. Mark's Evangelical Lutheran Church, 157 N.C. App. 325, 578 S.E.2d 654, cert. denied, 357 N.C. 249, 582 S.E.2d 29 (2003).

APPLIED in Richmond Cnty. Bd. of Educ. v. Cowell, 243 N.C. App. 116, 776 S.E.2d 244 (2015).

LEGAL PERIODICALS. --

Legal Periodicals. - See Legislative Survey, 21 Campbell L. Rev. 323 (1999).

§ 20-115.1. Limitations on tandem trailers and semitrailers on certain North Carolina highways

(a) Motor vehicle combinations consisting of a truck tractor and two trailing units may be operated in North Carolina only on highways of the interstate system (except those exempted by the United States Secretary of Transportation pursuant to 49 USC 2311(i)) and on those sections of the federal-aid primary system designated by the United States Secretary of Transportation. No trailer or semitrailer operated in this combination shall exceed 28 feet in length; Provided, however, a 1982 or older year model trailer or semitrailer of up to 28 1/2 feet in length may operate in a combination permitted by this section for trailers or semitrailers which are 28 feet in length.

(b) Motor vehicle combinations consisting of a semitrailer of not more than 53 feet in length and a truck tractor may be operated on all primary highway routes of North Carolina provided the motor vehicle combination meets the requirements of this subsection. The Department may, at any time, prohibit motor vehicle combinations on portions of any route on the State highway system. If the Department prohibits a motor vehicle combination on any route, it shall submit a written report to the Joint Legislative Transportation Oversight Committee within six months of the prohibition clearly documenting through traffic engineering studies that the operation of a motor vehicle combination on that route cannot be safely accommodated and that the route does not have sufficient capacity to handle the vehicle combination. To operate on a primary highway route, a motor vehicle combination described in this subsection must meet all of the following requirements:

(1) The motor vehicle combination must comply with the weight requirements in G.S. 20-118.

(2) A semitrailer in excess of 48 feet in length must meet one or more of the following conditions:

(a) The distance between the kingpin of the trailer and the rearmost axle, or a point midway between the two rear axles, if the two rear axles are a tandem axle, does not exceed 41 feet.

(b) The semitrailer is used exclusively or primarily to transport vehicles in connection with motorsports competition events, and the distance between the kingpin of the trailer and the rearmost axle, or a point midway between the two rear axles, if the two rear axles are a tandem axle, does not exceed 46 feet.

(3) A semitrailer in excess of 48 feet must be equipped with a rear underride guard of substantial construction consisting of a continuous lateral beam extending to within four inches of the lateral extremities of the semitrailer and located not more than 30 inches from the surface as measured with the vehicle empty and on a level surface.

(c) Motor vehicles with a width not exceeding 102 inches may be operated on the interstate highways (except those exempted by the United States Secretary of Transportation pursuant to 49 USC 2316(e)) and other qualifying federal-aid highways designated by the United States Secretary of Transportation, with traffic lanes designed to be a width of 12 feet or more and any other qualifying federal-aid primary system highway designated by the United States Secretary of Transportation if the Secretary has determined that the designation is consistent with highway safety.

(d) Notwithstanding the provisions of subsections (a) and (b) of this section which limit the length of trailers which may be used in motor vehicle combinations in this State on highways of the interstate system (except those exempted by the United States Secretary of Transportation pursuant to 49 USC 2311(i)) and on those

sections of the federal-aid primary system designated by the United States Secretary of Transportation, there is no limitation of the length of the truck tractor which may be used in motor vehicle combinations on these highways and therefore, in compliance with Section 411(b) of the Surface Transportation Act of 1982, there is no overall length limitation for motor vehicle combinations regulated by this section.

(e) The length and width limitations in this section are subject to exceptions and exclusions for safety devices and specialized equipment as provided for in 49 USC 2311(d)(h) and Section 416 of the Surface Transportation Act of 1982 as amended (49 USC 2316).

(f) Motor vehicle combinations operating pursuant to this section shall have reasonable access between (i) highways on the interstate system (except those exempted by the United States Secretary of Transportation pursuant to 49 USC 2311(i) and 49 USC 2316(e)) and other qualifying federal-aid highways as designated by the United States Secretary of Transportation and (ii) terminals, facilities for food, fuel, repairs, and rest and points of loading and unloading by household goods carriers and by any truck tractor-semitrailer combination in which the semitrailer has a length not to exceed 28 1/2 feet and a width not to exceed 102 inches as provided in subsection (c) of this section and which generally operates as part of a vehicle combination described in subsection (a) of this section. The North Carolina Department of Transportation may, on streets and highways on the State highway system, and any municipality may, on streets and highways on the municipal street system, impose reasonable restrictions based on safety considerations on any truck tractor-semitrailer combination in which the semitrailer has a length not to exceed 28 1/2 feet and which generally operates as part of a vehicle combination described in subsection (a) of this section. "Reasonable access" to facilities for food, fuel, repairs and rest shall be deemed to be those facilities which are located within three road miles of the interstate or designated highway. The Department of Transportation is authorized to promulgate rules and regulations providing for "reasonable access." The Department may approve reasonable access routes for one particular type of STAA (Surface Transportation Assistance Act) dimensioned vehicle when significant, substantial differences in their operating characteristics exist.

(g) Under certain conditions, and after consultation with the Joint Legislative Commission on Governmental Operations, the North Carolina Department of Transportation may designate State highway system roads in addition to those highways designated by the United States Secretary of Transportation for use by the vehicle combinations authorized in this section. Such designations by the Department shall only be made under the following conditions:

(1) A determination of the public convenience and need for such designation;

(2) A traffic engineering study which clearly shows the road proposed to be designated can safely accommodate and has sufficient capacity to handle these vehicle combinations; and

(3) A public hearing is held or the opportunity for a public hearing is provided in each county through which the designated highway passes, after two weeks notice posted at the courthouse and published in a newspaper of general circulation in each county through which the designated State highway system road passes, and consideration is given to the comments received prior to the designation.

(4) The Department may designate routes for one particular type of STAA (Surface Transportation Assistance Act) dimensioned vehicle when significant, substantial differences in their operating characteristics exist.

The Department may not designate any portion of the State highway system that has been deleted or exempted by the United States Secretary of Transportation based on safety considerations. For the purpose of this section, any highway designated by the Department shall be deemed to be the same as a federal-aid primary highway designated by the United States Secretary of Transportation pursuant to 49 USC 2311 and 49 USC 2316, and the vehicle combinations authorized in this section shall be permitted to operate on such highway.

(h) Any owner of a semitrailer less than 50 feet in length in violation of subsections (a) or (b) is responsible for an infraction and is subject to a penalty of one hundred dollars ($ 100.00). Any owner of a semitrailer 50 feet or greater in length in violation of subsection (b) is responsible for an infraction and subject to a penalty of two hundred dollars ($ 200.00).

(i) Any driver of a vehicle with a semitrailer less than 50 feet in length violating subsections (a) or (b) of this section is guilty of a Class 3 misdemeanor punishable only by a fine of one hundred dollars ($ 100.00). Any driver of a vehicle with a semitrailer 50 feet or more in length violating subsection (b) of this section is guilty of a Class 3 misdemeanor punishable only by a fine of two hundred dollars ($ 200.00).

(j) Notwithstanding any other provision of this section, a manufacturer of trailer frames, with a permit issued pursuant to G.S. 20-119, is authorized to transport the trailer frame to another location within three miles of the first place of manufacture to the location of completion on any public street or highway if the width

of the trailer frame does not exceed 14 feet and oversize markings and safety flags are used during transport. Trailer frames transported pursuant to this subsection shall not exceed 7,000 pounds, and the vehicle towing the trailer frame shall have a towing capacity greater than 10,000 pounds and necessary towing equipment. The transport of trailer frames under this subsection shall only be done during daylight hours.

History.

1983, c. 898, s. 1; 1985, c. 423, ss. 1-7; 1989, c. 790, ss. 1, 3, 3.1; 1993, c. 533, s. 10;c. 539, s. 354;1994, Ex. Sess., c. 24, s. 14(c);1998-149, s. 6;2007-77, ss. 2, 3; 2008-160, s. 1;2008-221, ss. 3, 4

EFFECT OF AMENDMENTS. --

Session Laws 2007-77, ss. 2 and 3, effective June 14, 2007, added the last sentence in subsection (f) and added subdivision (g)(4).

Session Laws 2008-160, s. 1, effective August 3, 2008, added subsection (j).

Session Laws 2008-221, ss. 3 and 4, effective September 1, 2008, rewrote subsection (b); and deleted the first sentence in the concluding paragraph of subsection (g) regarding designating portions of highway within municipal corporate limits and made related changes.

CITED in King v. Town of Chapel Hill, 367 N.C. 400, 758 S.E.2d 364 (2014).

OPINIONS OF THE ATTORNEY GENERAL

USE OF SHORTCUT ROUTE BY TWIN TRAILERS. --The Department of Transportation may not by regulation designate or authorize the use of a shortcut route between routes on the National Twin Trailer Network, as an access route for use by twin trailers. See opinion of Attorney General to Mr. James E. Harrington, Secretary of Transportation, 58 N.C.A.G. 8 (Jan. 4, 1988).

Twin trailers are not authorized to use shortcuts between routes on the National Twin Trailer System routes on which a terminal is not located. See opinion of Attorney General to Mr. James E. Harrington, Secretary of Transportation, 58 N.C.A.G. 8 (Jan. 4, 1988).

§ 20-116. Size of vehicles and loads

(a) The total outside width of any vehicle or the load thereon shall not exceed 102 inches, except as otherwise provided in this section. When hogsheads of tobacco are being transported, a tolerance of six inches is allowed. When sheet or bale tobacco is being transported the load must not exceed a width of 114 inches at the top of the load and the bottom of the load at the truck bed must not exceed the width of 102 inches inclusive of allowance for load shifting or settling. Vehicles (other than passenger buses) that do not exceed the overall width of 102 inches and otherwise provided in this section may be operated in accordance with G.S. 20-115.1(c), (f), and (g).

(b) No passenger-type vehicle or recreational vehicle shall be operated on any highway with any load carried thereon extending beyond the line of the fenders on the left side of such vehicle nor extending more than six inches beyond the line of the fenders on the right side thereof.

(c) No vehicle, unladen or with load, shall exceed a height of 13 feet, six inches. Provided, however, that neither the State of North Carolina nor any agency or subdivision thereof, nor any person, firm or corporation, shall be required to raise, alter, construct or reconstruct any underpass, wire, pole, trestle, or other structure to permit the passage of any vehicle having a height, unladen or with load, in excess of 12 feet, six inches. Provided further, that the operator or owner of any vehicle having an overall height, whether unladen or with load, in excess of 12 feet, six inches, shall be liable for damage to any structure caused by such vehicle having a height in excess of 12 feet, six inches.

(d) **Maximum Length.** -- The following maximum lengths apply to vehicles. A truck-tractor and semitrailer shall be regarded as two vehicles for the purpose of determining lawful length and license taxes.

(1) Except as otherwise provided in this subsection, a single vehicle having two or more axles shall not exceed 40 feet in length overall of dimensions inclusive of front and rear bumpers.

(2) Trucks transporting unprocessed cotton from farm to gin, or unprocessed sage from farm to market shall not exceed 50 feet in length overall of dimensions inclusive of front and rear bumpers.

(3) Recreational vehicles shall not exceed 45 feet in length overall, excluding bumpers and mirrors.

(4) Vehicles owned or leased by State, local, or federal government, when used for official law enforcement or emergency management purposes, shall not exceed 45 feet in length overall, excluding bumpers and mirrors.

(e) Except as provided by G.S. 20-115.1, no combination of vehicles coupled together shall consist of more than two units and no such combination of vehicles shall exceed a total length of 60 feet inclusive of front and rear bumpers, subject to the following exceptions: Motor vehicle combinations of one semitrailer not more than 53 feet in length and a truck tractor (power unit) may exceed the 60-foot maximum length. Said maximum overall length limitation shall not apply to vehicles operated in the daytime when transporting poles, pipe, machinery or other objects of a structural nature which cannot readily be dismembered, nor to such vehicles transporting such objects operated at nighttime by a public utility when required for emergency repair of public service facilities or properties, provided the trailer length does not exceed 53 feet in length, but in respect to such night transportation every such vehicle and the load thereon shall be equipped with a sufficient number of clearance lamps on both sides and marker lamps upon the extreme ends of said projecting load to clearly mark the dimensions of such load: Provided that vehicles designed and used exclusively for the transportation of motor vehicles shall be permitted an overhang tolerance front or rear not to exceed five feet. Provided, that wreckers may tow a truck, combination tractor and trailer, trailer, or any other disabled vehicle or combination of vehicles to a place for repair, parking, or storage within 50 miles of the point where the vehicle was disabled and may tow a truck, tractor, or other replacement vehicle to the site of the disabled vehicle. Provided further, that the said limitation that no combination of vehicles coupled together shall consist of more than two units shall not apply to trailers not exceeding three in number drawn by a motor vehicle used by municipalities for the removal of domestic and commercial refuse and street rubbish, but such combination of vehicles shall not exceed a total length of 50 feet inclusive of front and rear bumpers. Provided further, that the said limitation that no combination of vehicles coupled together shall consist of more than two units shall not apply to a combination of vehicles coupled together by a saddle mount device used to transport motor vehicles in a driveway service when no more than three saddle mounts are used and provided further, that equipment used in said combination is approved by the safety regulations of the Federal Highway Administration and the safety rules of the Department of Public Safety.

(f) The load upon any vehicle operated alone, or the load upon the front vehicle of a combination of vehicles, shall not extend more than three feet beyond the foremost part of the vehicle. Under this subsection "load" shall include the boom on a self-propelled vehicle.

A utility pole carried by a self-propelled pole carrier may extend beyond the front overhang limit set in this subsection if the pole cannot be dismembered, the pole is less than 80 feet in length and does not extend more than 10 feet beyond the front bumper of the vehicle, and either of the following circumstances apply:

(1) It is daytime and the front of the extending load of poles is marked by a flag of the type required by G.S. 20-117 for certain rear overhangs.

(2) It is nighttime, operation of the vehicle is required to make emergency repairs to utility service, and the front of the extending load of poles is marked by a light of the type required by G.S. 20-117 for certain rear overhangs.

As used in this subsection, a "self-propelled pole carrier" is a vehicle designed to carry a pole on the side of the vehicle at a height of at least five feet when measured from the bottom of the brace used to carry the pole. A self-propelled pole carrier may not tow another vehicle when carrying a pole that extends beyond the front overhang limit set in this subsection.

(g) (1) No vehicle shall be driven or moved on any highway unless the vehicle is constructed and loaded to prevent any of its load from falling, blowing, dropping, sifting, leaking, or otherwise escaping therefrom, and the vehicle shall not contain any holes, cracks, or openings through which any of its load may escape. However, sand may be dropped for the purpose of securing traction, or water or other substance may be sprinkled, dumped, or spread on a roadway in cleaning or maintaining the roadway. For purposes of this subsection, the terms "load" and "leaking" do not include water accumulated from precipitation.

(2) A truck, trailer, or other vehicle licensed for more than 7,500 pounds gross vehicle weight that is loaded with rock, gravel, stone, or any other similar substance, other than sand, that could fall, blow, leak, sift, or drop shall not be driven or moved on any highway unless:

a. The height of the load against all four walls does not extend above a horizontal line six inches below their tops when loaded at the loading point; and

b. The load is securely covered by tarpaulin or some other suitable covering to prevent any of its load from falling, dropping, sifting, leaking, blowing, or otherwise escaping therefrom.

(3) A truck, trailer, or other vehicle licensed for 7,500 pounds or less gross vehicle weight and loaded with rock, gravel, stone, or any other similar substance that could fall, blow, leak, or sift, or licensed for any gross vehicle weight and loaded with sand, shall not be driven or moved on any highway unless:

a. The height of the load against all four walls does not extend above a horizontal line six inches below the top when loaded at the loading point;

b. The load is securely covered by tarpaulin or some other suitable covering; or

c. The vehicle is constructed to prevent any of its load from falling, dropping, sifting, leaking, blowing, or otherwise escaping therefrom.

(4) This section shall not be applicable to or in any manner restrict the transportation of seed cotton, poultry or livestock, or silage or other feed grain used in the feeding of poultry or livestock.

(h) Whenever there exist two highways of the State highway system of approximately the same distance between two or more points, the Department of Transportation may, when in the opinion of the Department of Transportation, based upon engineering and traffic investigation, safety will be promoted or the public interest will be served, designate one of the highways the "truck route" between those points, and to prohibit the use of the other highway by heavy trucks or other vehicles of a gross vehicle weight or axle load limit in excess of a designated maximum. In such instances the highways selected for heavy vehicle traffic shall be designated as "truck routes" by signs conspicuously posted, and the highways upon which heavy vehicle traffic is prohibited shall likewise be designated by signs conspicuously posted showing the maximum gross vehicle weight or axle load limits authorized for those highways. The operation of any vehicle whose gross vehicle weight or axle load exceeds the maximum limits shown on signs over the posted highway shall constitute a Class 2 misdemeanor: Provided, that nothing in this subsection shall prohibit a truck or other motor vehicle whose gross vehicle weight or axle load exceeds that prescribed for those highways from using them when its destination is located solely upon that highway, road or street: Provided, further, that nothing in this subsection shall prohibit passenger vehicles or other light vehicles from using any highways designated for heavy truck traffic.

(i) Repealed by Session Laws 1973, c. 1330, s. 39.

(j) Nothing in this section shall be construed to prevent the operation of self-propelled grain combines or other self-propelled farm equipment with or without implements, not exceeding 25 feet in width on any highway, unless the operation violates a provision of this subsection. Farm equipment includes a vehicle that is designed exclusively to transport compressed seed cotton from a farm to a gin and has a self-loading bed. Combines or equipment which exceed 10 feet in width may be operated only if they meet all of the conditions listed in this subsection. A violation of one or more of these conditions does not constitute negligence per se.

(1) The equipment may only be operated during daylight hours.

(2) The equipment must display a red flag on front and rear ends or a flashing warning light. The flags or lights shall be attached to the equipment as to be visible from both directions at all times while being operated on the public highway for not less than 300 feet.

(3) Equipment covered by this section, which by necessity must travel more than 10 miles or where by nature of the terrain or obstacles the flags or lights referred to in subdivision (2) of this subsection are not visible from both directions for 300 feet at any point along the proposed route, must be

preceded at a distance of 300 feet and followed at a distance of 300 feet by a flagman in a vehicle having mounted thereon an appropriate warning light or flag. No flagman in a vehicle shall be required pursuant to this subdivision if the equipment is being moved under its own power or on a trailer from any field to another field, or from the normal place of storage of the vehicle to any field, for no more than ten miles and if visible from both directions for 300 feet at any point along the proposed route.

(4) Every piece of equipment so operated shall operate to the right of the center line unless the combined width of the traveling lane and the accessible shoulder is less than the width of the equipment.

(5) Repealed by Session Laws 2008-221, s. 6, effective September 1, 2008.

(6) When the equipment is causing a delay in traffic, the operator of the equipment shall move the equipment off the paved portion of the highway at the nearest practical location until the vehicles following the equipment have passed.

(7) The equipment shall be operated in the designed transport position that minimizes equipment width. No removal of equipment or appurtenances is required under this subdivision.

(8) Equipment covered by this subsection shall not be operated on a highway or section of highway that is a fully controlled access highway or is a part of the National System of Interstate and Defense Highways without authorization from the North Carolina Department of Transportation. The Department shall develop an authorization process and approve routes under the following conditions:

    a. Persons shall submit an application to the Department requesting authorization to operate equipment covered by this subsection on a particular route that is part of a highway or section of highway that is a fully controlled access highway or is a part of the National System of Interstate and Defense Highways.

    b. The Department shall have a period of 30 days from receipt of a complete application to approve or reject the application. A complete application shall be deemed approved if the Department does not take action within 30 days of receipt by the Department; such a route may then be used by the original applicant.

    c. The Department shall approve an application upon a showing that the route is necessary to accomplish one or more of the following:

        1. Prevent farming operations from traveling more than five miles longer than the requested route during the normal course of business.

        2. Prevent excess traffic delays on local or secondary roads.

        3. Allow farm equipment access due to dimension restrictions on local or secondary roads.

    d. For applications that do not meet the requirements of sub-subdivision c. of this subdivision, the Department may also approve an application upon review of relevant safety factors.

    e. The Department may consult with the North Carolina State Highway Patrol, the North Carolina Department of Agriculture and Consumer Services, or other parties concerning an application.

    f. Any approved route may be subject to any of the following additional conditions:

        1. A requirement that the subject equipment be followed by a flag vehicle with flashing lights that shall be operated at all times on the route so as to be visible from a distance of at least 300 feet.

        2. Restrictions on maximum and minimum speeds of the equipment.

        3. Restrictions on the maximum dimensions of the equipment.

        4. Restrictions on the time of day that the equipment may be operated on the approved route.

    g. The Department shall publish all approved routes, including any conditions on the routes' use, and shall notify appropriate State and local law enforcement officers of any approved route.

    h. Once approved for use and published by the Department, a route may be used by any person who adheres to the route, including any conditions on the route's use imposed by the Department.

    i. The Department may revise published routes as road conditions on the routes change.

(k) Nothing in this section shall be construed to prevent the operation of passenger buses having an overall width of 102 inches, exclusive of safety equipment, upon the highways of this State which are 20 feet or wider and that are designated as the State primary system, or as municipal streets, when, and not until, the federal law and regulations thereunder permit the operation of passenger buses having a width of

102 inches or wider on the National System of Interstate and Defense Highways.

(*l*) Nothing in this section shall be construed to prevent the operation of passenger buses that are owned and operated by units of local government, operated as a single vehicle only and having an overall length of 45 feet or less, on public streets or highways. The Department of Transportation may prevent the operation of buses that are authorized under this subsection if the operation of such buses on a street or highway presents a hazard to passengers of the buses or to the motoring public.

(m) Notwithstanding subsection (a) of this section, a boat or boat trailer with an outside width of less than 120 inches may be towed without a permit. The towing of a boat or boat trailer 102 inches to 114 inches in width may take place on any day of the week, including weekends and holidays, and may take place at night. The towing of a boat or boat trailer 114 inches to 120 inches in width may take place on any day of the week, including weekends and holidays from sun up to sun down. A boat or boat trailer in excess of 102 inches but less than 120 inches must be equipped with a minimum of two operable amber lamps on the widest point of the boat and the boat trailer such that the dimensions of the boat and the boat trailer are clearly marked and visible.

(n) Vehicle combinations used in connection with motorsports competition events that include a cab or other motorized vehicle unit with living quarters, and an attached enclosed specialty trailer, the combination of which does not exceed 90 feet in length, may be operated on the highways of this State, provided that such operation takes place for one or more of the following purposes:

(1) Driving to or from a motorsports competition event.

(2) For trips conducted for the purpose of purchasing fuel or conducting repairs or other maintenance on the competition vehicle.

(3) For other activities related to motorsports purposes, including, but not limited to, performance testing of the competition vehicle.

The Department of Transportation may prohibit combinations authorized by this subsection from specific routes, pursuant to G.S. 20-115.1(b).

(o) Any vehicle carrying baled hay from place to place on the same farm, from one farm to another, from farm to market, or from market to farm that does not exceed 12 feet in width may be operated on the highways of this State. Vehicles carrying baled hay that exceed 10 feet in width may only be operated under the following conditions:

(1) The vehicle may only be operated during daylight hours.

(2) The vehicle shall display a red flag or a flashing warning light on both the rear and front ends. The flags or lights shall be attached to the equipment as to be visible from both directions at all times while being operated on the public highway for not less than 300 feet.

(p) Notwithstanding any provision of this section to the contrary, the following may operate on the highways of this State without an oversize permit for the purpose of Department snow removal and snow removal training operations:

(1) Truck supporting snow plows with blades not exceeding 12 feet in width. A truck operated pursuant to this subdivision shall have adequate illumination when the plow is in the up and the down positions; visible signal lights; and a plow that is angled so that the minimum width is exposed to oncoming traffic during periods of travel between assignments.

(2) Motor graders not exceeding 102 inches in width, measured from the outside edge of the tires. A motor grader operated pursuant to this subdivision shall have adequate illumination when the moldboard is in the up and down positions; visible signal lights; and a moldboard that is angled not to exceed 102 inches during periods of travel between assignments.

History.

1937, c. 246; c. 407, s. 80; 1943, c. 213, s. 1; 1945, c. 242, s. 1; 1947, c. 844; 1951, c. 495, s. 1; c. 733; 1953, cc. 682, 1107; 1955, c. 296, s. 2; c. 729; 1957, c. 65, s. 11; cc. 493, 1183, 1190; 1959, c. 559; 1963, c. 356, s. 1; c. 610, ss. 1, 2; c. 702, s. 4; c. 1027, s. 1; 1965, c. 471; 1967, c. 24, s. 4; c. 710; 1969, cc. 128, 880; 1971, cc. 128, 680, 688, 1079; 1973, c. 507, s. 5; c. 546; c. 1330, s. 39; 1975, c. 148, ss. 1-5; c. 716, s. 5; 1977, c. 464, s. 34; 1979, cc. 21, 218; 1981, c. 169, s. 1; 1983, c. 724, s. 2; 1985, c. 587; 1987, c. 272; 1989, c. 277, s. 1;c. 790, s. 2;1991, c. 112, s. 1;c. 449, ss. 1, 2.1; 1993, c. 539, s. 355;1994, Ex. Sess., c. 24, s. 14(c);1995 (Reg. Sess., 1996), c. 573, s. 1; c. 756, s. 14; 1998-149, s. 7;1999-438, s. 28;2000-185, s. 2;2001-341, ss. 3, 4; 2001-512, s. 2;2002-72, s. 19(c);2002-159, s. 31.5(b);2002-190, s. 2;2003-383, s. 8;2005-248, s. 2;2007-77, s. 1;2007-194, ss. 2, 3; 2007-484, s. 5;2007-499, s. 1;2008-221, ss. 5, 6; 2008-229, s. 1;2009-7, s. 1;2009-127, s. 1;2009-128, s. 1;2011-145, s. 19.1(g);2012-33, s. 1;2012-78, s. 5;2013-413, s. 59.2(f);2014-115, s. 17;2015-263, ss. 5, 6(a); 2015-264, s. 41;2015-286, s. 1.8(a)

LOCAL MODIFICATION. --Dare: 1985 (Reg. Sess., 1986), c. 964; city of Charlotte: 2014-71, ss. 2, 3 (as to subsection (*l*), permitting city of Charlotte to operate passenger buses of 45 feet or less throughout the state and 60 feet or less within Mecklenburg County and contiguous counties).

EDITOR'S NOTE. --

Session Laws 2001-512, s. 15, provides: "This act shall not be construed to obligate the General Assembly to appropriate any funds to implement the provisions of this act. Every agency to which this act applies shall implement the provisions of this act from funds otherwise appropriated or available to the agency."

Session Laws 2002-190, s. 17, provides: "The Governor shall resolve any dispute between the Department of Transportation and the Department of Crime Control and Public Safety concerning the implementation of this act [Session Laws 2002-190]."

Session Laws 2008-229 [s. 1 of which added subsection (m) to this section] was House Bill 2167, which was vetoed by the Governor on August 17, 2008. The General Assembly, in a special session on August 27, 2008, voted to override the Governor's veto. Session Laws 2008-229 became law notwithstanding the Governor's veto on August 27, 2008.

Session Laws 2015-263, s. 4(a) -(e), provides: "(a) 19A NCAC 02D.0607 (Permits-Weight, Dimensions and Limitations). -- Until the effective date of the revised permanent rule that the Department of Transportation is required to adopt pursuant to Section 4(d) of this act, the Department shall implement 19A NCAC 02D.0607 (Permits-Weight, Dimensions and Limitations) as provided in subsections (b) and (c) of this section.

"(b) Implementation. -- Notwithstanding subdivision (h)(1) of 19A NCAC 02D.0607 (Permits-Weight, Dimensions and Limitations), the Secretary of Transportation shall allow movement of a permitted oversize vehicle between sunrise and sunset Monday through Sunday. However, a 16-foot-wide mobile or modular home unit with a maximum three-inch gutter edge is restricted to travel from 9:00 A.M. to 2:30 P.M. Monday through Sunday. A 16-foot-wide unit is authorized to continue operation after 2:30 P.M., but not beyond sunset, when traveling on an approved route as determined by an engineering study and the unit is being exported out-of-state.

"(c) Implementation. -- Notwithstanding subdivision (h)(2) of 19A NCAC 02D.0607 (Permits-Weight, Dimensions and Limitations), the Secretary of Transportation shall only prohibit movement of a permitted oversize vehicle and vehicle combination after noon on the weekday preceding the three holidays of Independence Day, Thanksgiving Day, and Christmas Day until noon on the weekday following a holiday. If the observed holiday falls on the weekend, travel is restricted from noon on the preceding Friday until noon on the following Monday.

"(d) Additional Rule-Making Authority. -- The Department of Transportation shall adopt rules to amend 19A NCAC 02D.0607 (Permits-Weight, Dimensions and Limitations) consistent with subsections (b) and (c) of this section. Notwithstanding G.S. 150B-19(4), the rule adopted by the Department pursuant to this section shall be substantively identical to the provisions of subsections (b) and (c) of this section. Rules adopted pursuant to this section are not subject to Part 3 of Article 2A of Chapter 150B of the General Statutes. Rules adopted pursuant to this section shall

become effective as provided in G.S. 150B-21.3(b1) as though 10 or more written objections had been received as provided by G.S. 150B-21.3(b2).

"(e) Effective Date. -- Subsections (b) and (c) of this section expire on the date that rules adopted pursuant to subsection (d) of this act become effective."

Session Laws 2015-263, s. 38(a), is a severability clause.

Subsection (p) was originally enacted by Session Laws 2015-264, s. 41, as subsection (o). The subsection has been redesignated at the direction of the Revisor of Statutes.

EFFECT OF AMENDMENTS. --

Session Laws 2005-248, s. 2, effective August 4, 2005, rewrote the second sentence in subsection (e).

Session Laws 2007-77, s. 1, effective June 14, 2007, inserted "Motor vehicle combinations of one semi-trailer of not more than 48 feet in length and a truck tractor (power unit) may exceed the 60-foot maximum length" in the first sentence of subsection (e).

Session Laws 2007-194, ss. 2 and 3, effective July 1, 2007, substituted "50 feet" for "48 feet" in subdivision (d)(2); and, in subsection (j), in the introductory language, substituted a period for a colon in the first sentence, inserted the second sentence, substituted "All" for "Provided that all" at the beginning of the third sentence, and made minor stylistic and punctuation changes.

Session Laws 2007-484, s. 5, effective August 30, 2007, deleted the last sentence in subsection (c) which read: "The term 'automobile transport' as used in this subsection shall mean only vehicles engaged exclusively in transporting automobiles, trucks and other commercial vehicles."

Session Laws 2007-499, s. 1, effective August 30, 2007, added subsection (l).

Session Laws 2008-221, ss. 5 and 6, effective September 1, 2008, in subsection (e), substituted "53 feet" for "48 feet" in the second sentence; and rewrote subsection (j).

Session Laws 2009-7, s. 1, effective March 6, 2009, added subsection (n).

Session Laws 2009-127, s. 1, effective June 19, 2009, inserted "or unprocessed sage from farm to market" in subdivision (d)(2).

Session Laws 2011-145, s. 19.1(g), effective January 1, 2012, substituted "Public Safety" for "Crime Control and Public Safety" in subsection (e).

Session Laws 2012-33, s. 1, effective June 20, 2012, added subdivision (d)(4).

Session Laws 2012-78, s. 5, effective June 26, 2012, in the introductory paragraph of subsection (j), substituted "unless the operation violates a provision of this subsection" for "except a highway or section of highway that is a fully controlled access highway or is a part of the National System of Interstate and Defense Highways"; in subdivision (j)(2), substituted "rear ends or a flashing warning light" for "rear ends" in the first sentence, deleted the second sentence, which read: "The flags shall not be smaller than three feet wide and four feet long."; and substituted "flags or lights shall be" for "flags shall be attached to a stick, pole, staff, etc., not less than four feet long and they shall be" in the last sentence; in subdivision (j) (3), added "or lights" to the first sentence; and added subdivision (j)(8).

Session Laws 2013-413, s. 59.2(f), substituted "the terms 'load' and 'leaking' do" for "load does" in subdivision (g)(1). For effective date, see editors note.

Session Laws 2015-263, s. 5, effective September 30, 2015, added subsection (o).

Session Laws 2015-263, s. 6(a), effective September 30, 2015, rewrote subdivision (j)(4).

Session Laws 2015-264, s. 41, effective October 1, 2015, added subsection (p).

Session Laws 2015-286, s. 1.8(a), effective October 22, 2015, rewrote subdivision (g)(3).

VEHICLES TRANSPORTING POLES IN THE DAYTIME ARE EXEMPT FROM THE REQUIREMENTS OF SUBSECTION (E) of this section, and therefore during the daytime it is not negligence per se to transport without a special permit a 40-foot pole on a trailer. Ratliff v. Duke Power Co., 268 N.C. 605, 151 S.E.2d 641 (1966).

EVIDENCE HELD INSUFFICIENT TO SUSTAIN VIOLATION OF SUBSECTION (J). --Defendant's contention that plaintiff violated subsection (j) of this section, which constitutes negligence per se, was untenable where there was no evidence in the record that plaintiff's combine exceeded 10 feet in width so as to bring the case within the purview of subsection (j), plaintiff's evidence, taken in the light most favorable to him, showing that the combine was nine feet 11 inches in width while being moved upon the road and defendant's evidence tending only to show the width of the combine when in actual operation and not when being moved along the highway. Furr v. Overcash, 254 N.C. 611, 119 S.E.2d 465 (1961).

SECTION NOT CONCLUSIVE ON CONTRIBUTORY NEGLIGENCE OF PASSENGER. --This section, prohibiting the extension of any part of the load of a passenger vehicle beyond the line of the fenders on the left side of such vehicle, imposes a duty for the safety of other vehicles on the highway, and is not conclusive on the question of contributory negligence of a passenger riding on the running board, with none of his body extending beyond the line of the fenders, who is injured by the negligent operation of another vehicle. Roberson v. Carolina Taxi Serv., 214 N.C. 624, 200 S.E. 363 (1939).

DRIVER NOT CONTRIBUTORILY NEGLIGENT WHERE NO WARNING SIGNS. --North Carolina Department of Transportation was liable under the Tort Claims Act, G.S. 143-291 et seq., for failing to post adequate signage at a railroad crossing that was difficult to cross for low vehicles due to the grade of the road where the Department had a duty to put up signs to warn of the risk, pursuant to G.S. 136-18(5), and it instead chose to direct trucks on an alternate route after finding that signs often went unheeded; the failure to post such warnings was a breach of its duty and was the proximate cause of a truck driver's tractor-trailer getting stuck on the crossing and thereafter hit by a train, and there was no contributory negligence by the truck driver who bypassed the alternate route because there were no warning signs or weight limit signs posted pursuant to G.S. 20-116(h). Smith v. N.C. DOT, 156 N.C. App. 92, 576 S.E.2d 345 (2003).

AS TO HEIGHT OF VEHICLE, Dennis v. City of Albemarle, 242 N.C. 263, 87 S.E.2d 561, appeal dismissed, 243 N.C. 221, 90 S.E.2d 532 (1955).

APPLIED in Adams v. Mills, 312 N.C. 181, 322 S.E.2d 164 (1984).

CITED in Hobbs v. Drewer, 226 N.C. 146, 37 S.E.2d 121 (1946); Lyday v. Southern Ry., 253 N.C. 687, 117 S.E.2d 778 (1961); State Hwy. Comm'n v. Raleigh Farmers Mkt., Inc., 263 N.C. 622, 139 S.E.2d 904 (1965); Reynolds v. United States, 805 F. Supp. 336 (W.D.N.C. 1992).

OPINIONS OF THE ATTORNEY GENERAL

SUBSECTION (G) DOES NOT REQUIRE THE PEAK OF A LOAD ON A TRUCK, TRAILER OR OTHER VEHICLE TO BE SIX INCHES BELOW A HORIZONTAL LINE SIX INCHES BELOW THE TOP OF ALL FOUR SIDEWALLS. --See opinion of Attorney General to Colonel Edwin C. Guy, North Carolina State Highway Patrol, 41 N.C.A.G. 708 (1972).

PROVISO TO SUBSECTION (G) DOES NOT APPLY TO TRANSPORTATION OF EMPTY, UNLOADED POULTRY CONTAINERS. --See opinion of Attorney General to Mr. Broxie Nelson, Raleigh City Attorney, 43 N.C.A.G. 340 (1974).

SUBSECTION (G) APPLIES TO A BASICALLY UNLOADED TRUCK THAT IS DEPOSITING MATERIAL ON THE ROAD. --See opinion of Attorney General to Mr. Randy Jones, Department of Natural Resources & Community Development, Oct. 3, 1979.

TWIN TRAILERS ARE NOT AUTHORIZED TO USE SHORTCUTS between routes on the National Twin Trailer System routes on which a terminal is not located. See opinion of Attorney General to Mr. James E. Harrington, Secretary of Transportation, 58 N.C.A.G. 8 (Jan. 4, 1988).

§ 20-117. Flag or light at end of load

(a) **General Provisions.** -- Whenever the load on any vehicle shall extend more than four feet beyond the rear of the bed or body thereof, there shall be displayed at the end of such load, in such position as to be clearly visible at all times from the rear of such load, a red or orange flag not less than 18 inches both in length and width, except that from sunset to sunrise there shall be displayed at the end of any such load a red or amber light plainly visible under normal atmospheric conditions at least 200 feet from the rear of such vehicle. At no time shall a load extend more than 14 feet beyond the rear of the bed or body of the vehicle, with the exception of vehicles transporting forestry products or utility poles.

(b) **Commercial Motor Vehicles.** -- A commercial motor vehicle, or a motor vehicle with a GVWR of 10,001 pounds or more that is engaged in commerce, that is being used to tow a load or that has a load that protrudes from the rear or sides of the vehicle shall comply with the provisions of 49 C.F.R. Part 393.

Chapter 20

History.

1937, c. 407, s. 81; 1985, c. 455; 1997-178, s. 1;2005-361, s. 2;2009-376, s. 4

EFFECT OF AMENDMENTS. --

Session Laws 2005-361, s. 2, effective October 1, 2005, added the last sentence.

PURPOSE OF SECTION. --The obvious purpose of this section is to promote the safety of one following a loaded vehicle upon the highway. Ratliff v. Duke Power Co., 268 N.C. 605, 151 S.E.2d 641 (1966).

THE CLEAR MEANING OF THIS SECTION IS THAT DURING DAYLIGHT HOURS A RED FLAG SHALL BE DISPLAYED FROM THE END OF THE PROJECTING LOAD so that there shall be visible to a user of the highway following the vehicle at least 12 inches of the flag's length and 12 inches of the flag's width. Ratliff v. Duke Power Co., 268 N.C. 605, 151 S.E.2d 641 (1966).

THE REQUIREMENT OF THIS SECTION IS NOT MET BY DRAPING A RED FLAG OVER THE TOP OF THE LOAD so that only a fringe of it is visible to one following the vehicle upon the highway. Ratliff v. Duke Power Co., 268 N.C. 605, 151 S.E.2d 641 (1966).

VIOLATION OF SECTION AS NEGLIGENCE. --Violation of this section during the daylight hours, by failure to comply with its requirements applicable to such time, is negligence. Ratliff v. Duke Power Co., 268 N.C. 605, 151 S.E.2d 641 (1966).

Violation of this section by failure to display at night a light, such as is required hereby, is negligence. Ratliff v. Duke Power Co., 268 N.C. 605, 151 S.E.2d 641 (1966).

Failure of defendant to display a red light at the end of lumber which extended more than four feet beyond the rear of the bed or body of the truck, plainly visible under normal atmospheric conditions at least 200 feet from the rear of the truck, between one-half hour after sunset and one-half hour before sunrise, as required by this section, was negligence. Weavil v. Myers, 243 N.C. 386, 90 S.E.2d 733 (1956).

AS TO FORMER LAW, see Williams v. Frederickson Motor Express Lines, 198 N.C. 193, 151 S.E. 197 (1930).

APPLIED in Bumgardner v. Allison, 238 N.C. 621, 78 S.E.2d 752 (1953).

CITED in C. C. T. Equip. Co. v. Hertz Corp., 256 N.C. 277, 123 S.E.2d 802 (1962).

§ 20-117.1. Requirements for mirrors and fuel container

(a) **Rear-Vision Mirrors. --** Every bus, truck, and truck tractor with a GVWR of 10,001 pounds or more shall be equipped with two rear-vision mirrors, one at each side, firmly attached to the outside of the motor vehicle, and located as to reflect to the driver a view of the highway to the rear and along both sides of the vehicle. Only one outside mirror shall be required, on the driver's side, on trucks which are so constructed that the driver also has a view to the rear by means of an interior mirror. In driveaway-towaway operations, a driven vehicle shall have at least one mirror furnishing a clear view to the rear, and if the interior mirror does not provide the clear view, an additional mirror shall be attached to the left side of the driven vehicle to provide the clear view to the rear.

(b) **Fuel Container Not to Project. --** No part of any fuel tank or container or intake pipe shall project beyond the sides of the motor vehicle.

History.

1949, c. 1207, s. 1; 1951, c. 819, s. 1; 1955, c. 1157, ss. 1, 4; 1991, c. 113, s. 1;c. 761, s. 6

§ 20-118. Weight of vehicles and load

(a) For the purposes of this section, the following definitions apply:

(1), (2) Repealed by Session Laws 2018-142, s. 5(b), effective December 14, 2018.

(3) **Axle group. --** Any two or more consecutive axles on a vehicle or combination of vehicles.

(4) **Gross weight. --** The weight of any single axle, tandem axle, or axle group of a vehicle or combination of vehicles plus the weight of any load thereon.

(5) **Light-traffic roads. --** Any highway on the State Highway System, excepting routes designated I, U.S. or N.C., posted by the Department of Transportation to limit the axle weight below the statutory limits.

(6) **Single axle weight. --** The gross weight transmitted by all wheels whose centers may be included between two parallel transverse vertical planes 40 inches apart, extending across the full width of the vehicle.

(7) **Tandem axle weight. --** The gross weight transmitted to the road by two or more consecutive axles whose centers may be included between parallel vertical planes spaced more than 40 inches and not more than 96 inches apart, extending across the full width of the vehicle.

(b) The following weight limitations apply to vehicles operating on the highways of the State:

(1) The single-axle weight of a vehicle or combination of vehicles shall not exceed 20,000 pounds.

(2) The tandem-axle weight of a vehicle or combination of vehicles shall not exceed 38,000 pounds.

(3) The gross weight imposed upon the highway by any axle group of a vehicle or combination of vehicles shall not exceed the maximum weight given for the respective distance between the first and last axle of the group of axles measured longitudinally to the nearest foot as set forth in the following table:

Chapter 20

Distance Between Axles*	Maximum Weight in Pounds for any Group of Two or More Consecutive Axles					
	2 Axles	3 Axles	4 Axles	5 Axles	6 Axles	7 Axles
4	38000					
5	38000					
6	38000					
7	38000					
8 or less	38000	38000				
more than 8	38000	42000				
9	39000	42500				
10	40000	43500				
11		44000				
12		45000	50000			
13		45500	50500			
14		46500	51500			
15		47000	52000			
16		48000	52500	58000		
17		48500	53500	58500		
18		49500	54000	59000		
19		50000	54500	60000		
20		51000	55500	60500	66000	
21		51500	56000	61000	66500	
22		52500	56500	61500	67000	
23		53000	57500	62500	68000	
24		54000	58000	63000	68500	74000
25		54500	58500	63500	69000	74500
26		55500	59500	64000	69500	75000
27		56000	60000	65000	70000	75500
28		57000	60500	65500	71000	76500
29		57500	61500	66000	71500	77000
30		58500	62000	66500	72000	77500
31		59000	62500	67500	72500	78000
32		60000	63500	68000	73000	78500
33		64000	68500	74000	79000	
34		64500	69000	74500	80000	
35		65500	70000	75000		
36		66000**	70500	75500		
37		66500**	71000	76000		
38		67500**	72000	77000		
39		68000	72500	77500		
40		68500	73000	78000		
41		69500	73500	78500		
42		70000	74000	79000		
43		70500	75000	80000		
44		71500	75500			
45		72000	76000			
46		72500	76500			
47		73500	77500			
48		74000	78000			
49		74500	78500			
50		75500	79000			
51		76000	80000			
52		76500				
53		77500				
54		78000				
55		78500				
56		79500				
57		80000				

*Distance in Feet Between the Extremes of any Group of Two or More Consecutive Axles.
**See exception in subdivision (c)(1) of this section.

(4) The Department of Transportation may establish light-traffic roads and further restrict the axle weight limit on such light-traffic roads lower than the statutory limits. The Department of Transportation has the authority to designate any highway on the State Highway System, excluding routes designated by I, U.S. and N.C., as a light-traffic road when in the opinion of the Department of Transportation, the road is inadequate to carry and will be injuriously affected by vehicles using the road carrying the maximum axle weight. All such roads so designated shall be conspicuously posted as light-traffic roads and the maximum axle weight authorized shall be displayed on proper signs erected thereon.

(c) **Exceptions.** -- The following exceptions apply to subsections (b) and (e) of this section:

(1) Two consecutive sets of tandem axles may carry a gross weight of 34,000 pounds each without penalty provided the overall distance between the first and last axles of the consecutive sets of tandem axles is 36 feet or more.

(2) When a vehicle is operated in violation of subdivision (b)(1), (b)(2), or (b)(3) of this section, but the gross weight of the vehicle or combination of vehicles does not exceed that permitted by subdivision (b)(3) of this section, the owner of the vehicle shall be permitted to shift the load within the vehicle, without penalty, from one axle to another to comply with the weight limits in the following cases:

a. Where the single-axle load exceeds the statutory limits, but does not exceed 21,000 pounds.

b. Where the vehicle or combination of vehicles has tandem axles, but the tandem-axle weight does not exceed 40,000 pounds.

(3) When a vehicle is operated in violation of subdivision (b)(4) of this section, the owner of the vehicle shall be permitted, without penalty, to shift the load within the vehicle from one axle to another to comply with the weight limits where the single-axle weight does not exceed the posted limit by 2,500 pounds.

(4) A truck or other motor vehicle shall be exempt from the light-traffic road limitations provided for pursuant to subdivision (b)(4) of this section, when transporting supplies, material, or equipment necessary to carry out a farming operation engaged in the production of meats and agricultural crops and livestock or poultry by-products or a business engaged in the harvest or processing of seafood when the destination of the vehicle and load is located solely upon a light-traffic road.

(5) The light-traffic road limitations provided for pursuant to subdivision (b)(4) of this section do not apply to a vehicle while that vehicle is transporting only the following from its point of origin on a light-traffic road to either one of the two nearest highways that is not a light-traffic road. If that vehicle's point of origin is a non-light-traffic road and that road is blocked by light-traffic roads from all directions and is not contiguous with other non-light-traffic roads, then the road at point of origin is treated as a light-traffic road for purposes of this subdivision:

a. Processed or unprocessed seafood transported from boats or any other point of origin to a processing plant or a point of further distribution.

b. Meats, live poultry, or agricultural crop products transported from a farm to a processing plant or market.

c. Forest products originating and transported from a farm or from woodlands to market without interruption or delay for further packaging or processing after initiating transport.

d. Livestock or live poultry transported from their point of origin to a processing plant or market.

e. Livestock by-products or poultry by-products transported from their point of origin to a rendering plant.

f. Recyclable material transported from its point of origin to a scrap-processing facility for processing. As used in this subpart, the terms "recyclable material" and "processing" have the same meaning as in G.S. 130A-290(a).

g. Garbage collected by the vehicle from residences or garbage dumpsters if the vehicle is fully enclosed and is designed specifically for collecting, compacting, and hauling garbage from residences or from garbage dumpsters. As used in this subpart, the term "garbage" does not include hazardous waste as defined in G.S. 130A-290(a), spent nuclear fuel regulated under G.S. 20-167.1, low-level radioactive waste as defined in G.S. 104E-5, or radioactive material as defined in G.S. 104E-5.

h. Treated sludge collected from a wastewater treatment facility.

i. Apples when transported from the orchard to the first processing or packing point.

j. Trees grown as Christmas trees from the field, farm, stand, or grove, and other forest products, including chips and bark, to a processing point.

k. Water, fertilizer, pesticides, seeds, fuel, and animal waste transported to or from a farm by a farm vehicle as defined in G.S. 20-37.16(e)(3).

(6) A truck or other motor vehicle shall be exempt from the light-traffic road limitations provided by subdivision (b)(4) of this section when the motor vehicles are owned, operated by or under contract to a public utility, electric or telephone membership corporation or municipality and are used in connection with installation, restoration, or emergency maintenance of utility services.

(7) A wrecker may tow any disabled truck or other motor vehicle or combination of vehicles to a place for repairs, parking, or storage within 50 miles from the point that the vehicle was disabled and may tow a truck, tractor, or other replacement vehicle to the site of the disabled vehicle without being in violation of this section provided that the wrecker and towed vehicle or combination of vehicles otherwise meet all requirements of this section.

(8) A firefighting vehicle operated by any member of a municipal or rural fire department in the performance of the member's duties, regardless of whether members of that fire department are paid or voluntary, and any vehicle of a voluntary lifesaving organization, when operated by a member of that organization while answering an official call, shall be exempt from the light-traffic road limitations provided by subdivision (b)(4) of this section.

(9) Repealed by Session Laws 1993 (Reg. Sess., 1994), c. 761, s. 12.

(10) Fully enclosed motor vehicles designed specifically for collecting, compacting, and hauling garbage from residences or from garbage dumpsters shall, when operating for those purposes, be allowed a single axle weight not to exceed 23,500 pounds on the steering axle on vehicles equipped with a boom, or on the rear axle on vehicles loaded from the rear. This exemption does not apply to vehicles operating on interstate highways, vehicles transporting hazardous waste as defined in G.S. 130A-290(a)(8), spent nuclear fuel regulated under G.S. 20-167.1, low-level radioactive waste as defined in G.S. 104E-5(9a), or radioactive material as defined in G.S. 104E-5(14).

(11) A truck or other motor vehicle shall be exempt for light-traffic road limitations issued under subdivision (b)(4) of this section when transporting heating fuel for on-premises use at a destination located on the light-traffic road.

(12) Subsections (b) and (e) of this section do not apply to a vehicle or vehicle combination that meets all of the conditions set out below:

a. Is transporting any of the following items within 150 miles of the point of origination:

1. Agriculture, dairy, and crop products transported from a farm or holding facility to a processing plant, feed mill, or market.

2. Water, fertilizer, pesticides, seeds, fuel, or animal waste transported to or from a farm.

3. Meats, livestock, or live poultry transported from the farm where they were raised to a processing plant or market.

3a. Feed or feed ingredients that are used in the feeding of poultry or livestock and transported from a storage facility, holding facility, or mill to a farm.

4. Forest products originating and transported from a farm or woodlands to market with delay interruption or delay for further packaging or processing after initiating transport.

5. Wood residuals, including wood chips, sawdust, mulch, or tree bark from any site.

6. Raw logs to market.

7. Trees grown as Christmas trees from field, farm, stand, or grove to a processing point.

b. Repealed by Session Laws 1993 (Reg. Sess., 1994), c. 761, s. 13.

b1. Does not operate on an interstate highway or exceed any posted bridge weight limits during transportation or hauling of agricultural products.

c. Meets any of the following vehicle configurations:

1. Does not exceed a single-axle weight of 22,000 pounds, a tandem-axle weight of 42,000 pounds, or a gross weight of 90,000 pounds.

2. Consists of a five or more axle combination vehicle that does not exceed a single-axle weight of 26,000 pounds, a tandem-axle weight of 44,000 pounds and a gross weight of 90,000 pounds, with a length of at least 48 feet between the center of axle one and the center of the last axle of the vehicle and a minimum of 11 feet between the center of axle one and the center of axle two of the vehicle.

3. Consists of a two-axle vehicle that does not exceed a gross

weight of 37,000 pounds and a single-axle weight of no more than 27,000 pounds, with a length of at least 14 feet between the center of axle one and the center of axle two of the vehicle.

d. Repealed by Session Laws 2012-78, s. 6, effective June 26, 2012.

(13) Vehicles specifically designed for fire fighting that are owned by a municipal or rural fire department. This exception does not apply to vehicles operating on interstate highways.

(14) Subsections (b) and (e) of this section do not apply to a vehicle that meets all of the conditions below, but all other enforcement provisions of this Article remain applicable:

a. Is hauling aggregates from a distribution yard or a State-permitted production site located within a North Carolina county contiguous to the North Carolina State border to a destination in another state adjacent to that county as verified by a weight ticket in the driver's possession and available for inspection by enforcement personnel.

b. Does not operate on an interstate highway or exceed any posted bridge weight limits.

c. Does not exceed 69,850 pounds gross vehicle weight and 53,850 pounds per axle grouping for tri-axle vehicles. For purposes of this subsection, a tri-axle vehicle is a single power unit vehicle with a three consecutive axle group on which the respective distance between any two consecutive axles of the group, measured longitudinally center to center to the nearest foot, does not exceed eight feet. For purposes of this subsection, the tolerance provisions of subsection (h) of this section do not apply, and vehicles must be licensed in accordance with G.S. 20-88.

d. Repealed by Session Laws 2001-487, s. 10, effective December 16, 2001.

e. Repealed by Session Laws 2012-78, s. 6, effective June 26, 2012.

(15) Subsections (b) and (e) of this section do not apply to a vehicle or vehicle combination that meets all of the conditions below, but all other enforcement provisions of this Article remain applicable:

a. Is transporting bulk soil, bulk rock, sand, sand rock, or asphalt millings from a site that does not have a certified scale for weighing the vehicle.

b. Does not operate on an interstate highway, a posted light-traffic road, except as provided by subdivision (c)

(5) of this section, or exceed any posted bridge weight limits.

c. Does not exceed a maximum gross weight 4,000 pounds in excess of what is allowed in subsection (b) of this section.

d. Does not exceed a single-axle weight of more than 22,000 pounds and a tandem-axle weight of more than 42,000 pounds.

e. Repealed by Session Laws 2012-78, s. 6, effective June 26, 2012.

(16) Subsections (b) and (e) of this section do not apply to a vehicle or vehicle combination that meets all of the conditions below, but all other enforcement provisions of this Article remain applicable:

a. Is hauling unhardened ready-mixed concrete.

b. Does not operate on an interstate highway or a posted light-traffic road, or exceed any posted bridge weight limits.

c. Has a single steer axle weight of no more than 22,000 pounds and a tandem-axle weight of no more than 46,000 pounds.

d. Does not exceed a maximum gross weight of 66,000 pounds on a three-axle vehicle with a length of at least 21 feet between the center of axle one and the center of axle three of the vehicle.

e. Does not exceed a maximum gross weight of 72,600 pounds on a four-axle vehicle with a length of at least 36 feet between the center of axle one and the center of axle four. The four-axle vehicle shall have a maximum gross weight of 66,000 pounds on axles one, two, and three with a length of at least 21 feet between the center of axle one and the center of axle three.

For purposes of this subdivision, no additional weight allowances in this section apply for the gross weight, single-axle weight, and tandem-axle weight, and the tolerance allowed by subsection (h) of this section does not apply.

(17) Subsections (b) and (e) of this section do not apply to a truck owned, operated by, or under contract to a public utility, electric or telephone membership corporation, or municipality that meets all of the conditions listed below, but all other enforcement provisions of this Article remain applicable:

a. Is being used in connection with the installation, restoration, or maintenance of utility services within a North Carolina county located in whole or in part west of Interstate 77, and the terrain, road widths, and other naturally occurring conditions prevent the safe navigation and operation of a truck having more than a single axle or using a trailer.

b. Does not operate on an interstate highway.

c. Does not exceed a single-axle weight of more than 28,000 pounds.

d. Does not exceed a maximum gross weight in excess of 48,000 pounds.

(18) Subsections (b) and (e) of this section do not apply to a vehicle or vehicle combination that meets all of the conditions set out below:

a. Is transporting metal commodities or construction equipment.

b. Does not operate on an interstate highway, a posted light traffic road, or exceed any posted bridge weight limit.

c. Does not exceed a single-axle weight of 22,000 pounds, a tandem-axle weight of 42,000 pounds, or a gross weight of 90,000 pounds.

(19) Any additional weight allowance authorized by 23 U.S.C. § 127, and applicable to all interstate highways, also applies to all State roads, unless the road is a posted road or posted bridge, or unless specifically prohibited by State law or a Department ordinance applicable to a specific road.

(d) The Department of Transportation is authorized to abrogate certain exceptions. The exceptions provided for in subdivisions (c)(4) and (c)(5) of this section as applied to any light-traffic road may be abrogated by the Department of Transportation upon a determination of the Department of Transportation that undue damage to the light-traffic road is resulting from vehicles exempted by subdivisions (c)(4) and (c)(5) of this section. In those cases where the exemption to the light-traffic roads are abrogated by the Department of Transportation, the Department shall post the road to indicate no exemptions.

(e) **Penalties. --**

(1) Except as provided in subdivision (2) of this subsection, for each violation of the single-axle or tandem-axle weight limits set in subdivision (b)(1), (b)(2), or (b)(4) of this section or axle weights authorized by special permit according to G.S. 20-119(a), the Department of Public Safety shall assess a civil penalty against the owner or registrant of the vehicle in accordance with the following schedule: for the first 1,000 pounds or any part thereof, four cents (4 cent(s)) per pound; for the next 1,000 pounds or any part thereof, six cents (6 cent(s)) per pound; and for each additional pound, ten cents (10 cent(s)) per pound. These penalties apply separately to each weight limit violated. In all cases of violation of the weight limitation, the penalty

shall be computed and assessed on each pound of weight in excess of the maximum permitted.

(2) The penalty for a violation of the single-axle or tandem-axle weight limits by a vehicle that is transporting an item listed in subdivision (c)(5) of this section is one-half of the amount it would otherwise be under subdivision (1) of this subsection.

(3) If an axle-group weight of a vehicle exceeds the weight limit set in subdivision (b)(3) of this section plus any tolerance allowed in subsection (h) of this section or axle-group weights or gross weights authorized by special permit under G.S. 20-119(a), the Department of Public Safety shall assess a civil penalty against the owner or registrant of the motor vehicle. The penalty shall be assessed on the number of pounds by which the axle-group weight exceeds the limit set in subdivision (b)(3) of this section, or by a special permit issued pursuant to G.S. 20-119, as follows: for the first 2,000 pounds or any part thereof, two cents (2) per pound; for the next 3,000 pounds or any part thereof, four cents (4) per pound; for each pound in excess of 5,000 pounds, ten cents (10) per pound. Tolerance pounds in excess of the limit set in subdivision (b)(3) of this section are subject to the penalty if the vehicle exceeds the tolerance allowed in subsection (h) of this section. These penalties apply separately to each axle-group weight limit violated. Notwithstanding any provision to the contrary, a vehicle with a special permit that is subject to additional penalties under this subsection based on a violation of any of the permit restrictions set out in G.S. 20-119(d1) shall be assessed a civil penalty, not to exceed ten thousand dollars ($ 10,000), based on the number of pounds by which the axle-group weight exceeds the limit set in subdivision (b)(3) of this section.

(4) The penalty for a violation of an axle-group weight limit by a vehicle that is transporting an item listed in subdivision (c)(5) of this section is one-half of the amount it would otherwise be under subdivision (3) of this subsection.

(5) A violation of a weight limit in this section or of a permitted weight under G.S. 20-119 is not punishable under G.S. 20-176.

(6) The penalty for violating the gross weight or axle-group weight by a dump truck or dump trailer vehicle transporting bulk soil, bulk rock, sand, sand rock, or asphalt millings intrastate from a site that does not have a certified scale for weighing the vehicle is one-half of the amount it otherwise would be under subdivisions (1) and (3) of this subsection.

(7) The clear proceeds of all civil penalties, civil forfeitures, and civil fines that are collected by the Department of Transportation pursuant to this section shall be remitted to the Civil Penalty and Forfeiture Fund in accordance with G.S. 115C-457.2.

(f) Repealed by Session Laws 1993 (Reg. Sess., 1994), c. 761, s. 15.

(g) This section does not permit the gross weight of any vehicle or combination in excess of the safe load carrying capacity established by the Department of Transportation on any bridge pursuant to G.S. 136-72.

(h) **Tolerance.** -- A vehicle may exceed maximum and the inner axle-group weight limitations set forth in subdivision (b)(3) of this section by a tolerance of ten percent (10%). This exception does not authorize a vehicle to exceed either the single-axle or tandem-axle weight limitations set forth in subdivisions (b)(1) and (b)(2) of this section, or the maximum gross weight limit of 80,000 pounds. This exception does not apply to a vehicle exceeding posted bridge weight limitations as posted under G.S. 136-72 or to vehicles operating on interstate highways. The tolerance allowed under this subsection does not authorize the weight of a vehicle to exceed the weight for which that vehicle is licensed under G.S. 20-88. No tolerance on the single-axle weight or the tandem-axle weight provided for in subdivisions (b)(1) and (b)(2) of this section shall be granted administratively or otherwise. The Department of Transportation shall report back to the Transportation Oversight Committee and to the General Assembly on the effects of the tolerance granted under this section, any abuses of this tolerance, and any suggested revisions to this section by that Department on or before May 1, 1998.

(i) Repealed by Session Laws 1993 (Reg. Sess., 1994), c. 761, s. 16.

(j) Repealed by Session Laws 1987, c. 392.

(k) A vehicle which is equipped with a self-loading bed and which is designed and used exclusively to transport compressed seed cotton from the farm to a cotton gin, or sage to market, may operate on the highways of the State, except interstate highways, with a tandem-axle weight not exceeding 50,000 pounds. Such vehicles are exempt from light-traffic road limitations only from point of origin on the light-traffic road to the nearest State-maintained road which is not posted to prohibit the transportation of statutory load limits. This exemption does not apply to restricted, posted bridge structures.

(*l*) A vehicle or vehicle combination that hauls unhardened ready-mixed concrete may be weighed with weigh in motion scales, but the vehicle or vehicle combination must be weighed static, allowing the drum to come to a complete stop.

History.

1937, c. 407, s. 82; 1943, c. 213, s. 2; cc. 726, 784; 1945, c. 242, s. 2; c. 569, s. 2; c. 576, s. 7; 1947, c. 1079; 1949, c. 1207, s. 2; 1951, c. 495, s. 2; c. 942, s. 1; c. 1013, ss. 5, 6, 8; 1953, cc. 214, 1092; 1959, c. 872; c. 1264, s. 6; 1963, c. 159; c. 610, ss. 3-5; c. 702, s. 5; 1965, cc. 483, 1044; 1969, c. 537; 1973, c. 507, s. 5; c. 1449, ss. 1, 2; 1975, c. 325; c. 373, s. 2; c. 716, s. 5; c. 735; c. 736, ss. 1-3; 1977, c. 461; c. 464, s. 34; 1977, 2nd Sess., c. 1178; 1981, c. 690, ss. 27, 28; c. 726; c. 1127, s. 53.1; 1983, c. 407; c. 724, s. 1; 1983 (Reg. Sess., 1984), c. 1116, ss. 105-109; 1985, c. 54; c. 274; 1987, c. 392; c. 707, ss. 1-4; 1991, c. 202, s. 1;1991 (Reg. Sess., 1992), c. 905, s. 1; 1993, c. 426, ss. 1, 2; c. 470, s. 1; c. 533, s. 11; 1993 (Reg. Sess., 1994), c. 761, ss. 10-16; 1995, c. 109, s. 3;c. 163, s. 4;c. 332, ss. 1 -3;c. 509, s. 135.1(b); 1995 (Reg. Sess., 1996), c. 756, s. 29; 1997-354, s. 1;1997-373, s. 1;1997-466, s. 2;1998-149, ss. 8, 9, 9.1; 1998-177, s. 1;1999-452, s. 23;2000-57, s. 1;2001-487, ss. 10, 50(e); 2002-126, s. 26.16(a);2004-145, ss. 1, 2; 2005-248, s. 1;2005-276, s. 6.37(o);2005-361, s. 3;2006-135, s. 1;2006-264, s. 37;2008-221, ss. 7, 8, 9; 2009-127, s. 2;2009-376, ss. 6, 16(a), 16(b); 2009-531, s. 1;2010-129, s. 3;2010-132, s. 10;2011-71, s. 1;2011-145, s. 19.1(g);2011-200, s. 1;2012-78, ss. 6, 13; 2013-120, s. 1;2013-134, s. 1;2015-263, s. 9(a);2016-90, s. 2.1(a);2018-74, s. 16.5;2018-142, s. 5(b)

EDITOR'S NOTE. --

Session Laws 2012-78, s. 15, provides: "Notwithstanding 19A NCAC 02D.0607(e)(3), the Department of Transportation may permit sealed ship containers as nondivisible loads as allowed by Federal Highway Administration policy. All Department of Transportation permitting rules applied to other nondivisible loads shall also apply to sealed ship containers."

Session Laws 2012-78, s. 16, provides: "The Department of Transportation shall initiate the process to conform the North Carolina Administrative Code to this act by striking the words 'not to exceed 94,500 pounds' from the first sentence of 19A NCAC 02D.0607(e)(3)."

Session Laws 2012-78, s. 18, provides: "Prosecutions for offenses committed before the effective date of the section of this act that modifies the offense [June 26, 2012] are not abated or affected by this act, and the statutes that would be applicable but for this act remain applicable to those prosecutions."

Session Laws 2015-263, s. 4(a) -(e), provides: "(a) 19A NCAC 02D.0607 (Permits-Weight, Dimensions and Limitations). -- Until the effective date of the revised permanent rule that the Department of Transportation is required to adopt pursuant to Section 4(d) of this act, the Department shall implement 19A NCAC 02D.0607 (Permits-Weight, Dimensions and Limitations) as provided in subsections (b) and (c) of this section.

"(b) Implementation. -- Notwithstanding subdivision (h)(1) of 19A NCAC 02D.0607 (Permits-Weight, Dimensions and Limitations), the Secretary of Transportation shall allow movement of a permitted oversize vehicle between sunrise and sunset Monday through Sunday. However, a 16-foot-wide mobile or modular home unit with a maximum three-inch gutter edge is restricted to travel from 9:00 A.M. to 2:30 P.M. Monday through Sunday. A 16-foot-wide unit is authorized to continue operation after 2:30 P.M., but not beyond sunset, when traveling on an approved route as determined by an engineering study and the unit is being exported out-of-state.

"(c) Implementation. -- Notwithstanding subdivision (h)(2) of 19A NCAC 02D.0607 (Permits-Weight, Dimensions and Limitations), the Secretary of Transportation shall only prohibit movement of a permitted oversize vehicle and vehicle combination after noon on the weekday preceding the three holidays of Independence Day, Thanksgiving Day, and Christmas Day until noon on the weekday following a holiday. If the observed holiday falls on the weekend, travel is restricted from noon on the preceding Friday until noon on the following Monday.

"(d) Additional Rule-Making Authority. -- The Department of Transportation shall adopt rules to amend 19A NCAC 02D.0607 (Permits-Weight, Dimensions and Limitations) consistent with subsections (b) and (c) of this section. Notwithstanding G.S. 150B-19(4), the rule adopted by the Department pursuant to this section shall be substantively identical to the provisions of subsections (b) and (c) of this section. Rules adopted pursuant to this section are not subject to Part 3 of Article 2A of Chapter 150B of the General Statutes. Rules adopted pursuant to this section shall become effective as provided in G.S. 150B-21.3(b1) as though 10 or more written objections had been received as provided by G.S. 150B-21.3(b2).

"(e) Effective Date. -- Subsections (b) and (c) of this section expire on the date that rules adopted pursuant to subsection (d) of this act become effective."

Session Laws 2015-263, s. 38(a), is a severability clause.

Session Laws 1989, c. 168, ss. 3 and 4, effective May 30, 1989, would have amended subdivisions (c)(9) and (c)(10) of this section; however, these subdivisions do not exist in this section. The amendment apparently should have been to G.S. 20-118. Session Laws 2018-142, s. 5, effective December 14, 2018, repealed Session Laws 1989, c. 168, s. 4.

EFFECT OF AMENDMENTS. --
Session Laws 2004-145, ss. 1 and 2, effective July 29, 2004, added "or is transporting bulk soil, bulk rock, sand, sand rock, or asphalt millings from a site that does not have a certified scale for weighing the vehicle" at the end of subdivision (c)(15)a; and added subdivision (e)(6).

Session Laws 2005-248, s. 1, effective August 4, 2005, rewrote subdivision (c)(7).

Session Laws 2005-276, s. 6.37(o), effective July 1, 2005, added subdivision (e)(7).

Session Laws 2005-361, s. 3, effective October 1, 2005, in subsection (e), inserted "or axle weights authorized by special permit according to G.S. 20-119(a)" and substituted "Crime Control and Public Safety" for "Transportation" in the first sentence of subdivision (1), inserted "or axle-group weights or gross weights

authorized by special permit under G.S. 20-119(a)" and substituted "Crime Control and Public Safety" for "Transportation" in the first sentence of subdivision (3), and inserted "or of a permitted weight under G.S. 20-119" in subdivision (5).

Session Laws 2006-135, s. 1, effective July 19, 2006, substituted "bark from any site" for "bark" in subdivision (c)(15)a.

Session Laws 2006-264, s. 37, effective August 27, 2006, added "located" preceding "within a North Carolina county" in subdivision (c)(14)a.

Session Laws 2008-221, ss. 7 -9, effective September 1, 2008, rewrote subdivision (c)(12); in subdivision (c)(15)a, inserted "is hauling raw logs to first market"; in subdivision (c)(15)b, inserted "except as provided by subdivision (c)(5) of this section"; substituted "50,000" for "44,000" at the end of the first sentence of subsection (k); and made minor grammatical changes.

Session Laws 2009-127, s. 2, effective June 19, 2009, in subsection (k), in the first sentence, deleted "From September 1 through March 1 of each year" at the beginning, and inserted "or sage to market" near the middle.

Session Laws 2009-376, s. 6, effective July 31, 2009, in subdivision (e)(3), in the second sentence, inserted "of this section, or by a special permit issued pursuant to G.S. 20-119", and added the last sentence.

Session Laws 2010-129, s. 3, effective October 1, 2010, and applicable to offenses committed on or after that date, added subdivisions (c)(12)d., (c)(14)e., and (c)(15)e.

Session Laws 2010-132, s. 10, effective December 1, 2010, and applicable to offenses committed on or after that date, added the last sentence in the introductory paragraph in subdivision (c)(5); in subdivision (c)(5)d., inserted "a processing plant or"; and in subdivision (c)(15)a., added "or is hauling animal waste products from the animal waste storage site to a farm or field."

Session Laws 2011-71, s. 1, effective October 1, 2011, and applicable to offenses committed on or after that date, added subdivision (c)(16).

Session Laws 2011-145, s. 19.1(g), effective January 1, 2012, substituted "Public Safety" for "Crime Control and Public Safety" in subdivisions (e)(1) and (e)(3).

Session Laws 2012-78, ss. 6 and 13, effective June 26, 2012, rewrote subdivisions (c)(5)b., (c)(5)c. and (c)(5)d.; substituted "and other forest products, including chips and bark, to a processing point" for "to first processing point" in subdivision (c)(5)j.; added subdivision (c)(5)k.; rewrote the introductory language of subdivision (c)(12); rewrote subdivisions (c)(12)a. and (c)(12)c.; deleted subdivision (c)(12)d., which read: "Is registered pursuant to G.S. 20-88 for the maximum weight allowed for the vehicle configuration as listed in subsection (b) of this section."; deleted subdivision (c)(14)e., which read: "Is registered pursuant to G.S. 20-88 for the maximum weight allowed for the vehicle configuration as listed in subsection (b) of this section."; rewrote subdivision (c)(15)a.; deleted subdivision (c)(15)e., which read: "Is registered pursuant to G.S. 20-88 for the maximum weight allowed for the vehicle configuration as listed in subsection (b) of this section."; rewrote subdivision (c)(16)c.; added subdivisions (c)(16)d. and (c)(16)e.; and added the last paragraph in subdivision (c)(16).

Session Laws 2013-120, s. 1, effective July 1, 2013, added subdivision (c)(12)a.3a.

Session Laws 2013-134, s. 1, effective January 1, 2014, added subdivision (c)(17).

Session Laws 2015-263, s. 9(a), effective October 1, 2015, rewrote subdivision (c)(12)(a)(1); deleted "by a farm vehicle as defined in G.S. 20-37.16 (e)(3)" at the end of subdivision (c)(12)(a)(2); and substituted "feed or feed ingredients that are used in" for "feed that is used in" in subdivision (c)(12)(a)(3a).

Session Laws 2016-90, s. 2.1(a), effective October 1, 2016, added subdivisions (c)(18) and (c)(19).

Session Laws 2018-74, s. 16.5, effective July 1, 2018, added subsection (l).

Session Laws 2018-142, s. 5(b), effective December 15, 2018, rewrote the section.

THE PENALTIES PRESCRIBED IN THIS SECTION ARE DEEMED A "TAX" under G.S. 20-96 and qualify as "any tax" as used in G.S. 20-91.1 [repealed]. Cedar Creek Enters., Inc. v. State Dep't of Motor Vehicles, 290 N.C. 450, 226 S.E.2d 336 (1976).

PAYMENTS AUTHORIZED BY G.S. 20-118(E) ARE PUNITIVE IN NATURE and are therefore subject to N.C. Const. Art. IX, § 7. N.C. Sch. Bds. Ass'n v. Moore, 160 N.C. App. 253, 585 S.E.2d 418 (2003).

ASSESSMENT OF ADDITIONAL OVERWEIGHT PENALTY SUBSTANTIALLY JUSTIFIED. --Trial court did not err in awarding attorney's fees to a company under G.S. 6-19.1 because the decision of the Secretary of Crime Control and Public Safety to assess an additional overweight penalty against the company was substantially justified, and although the Secretary erroneously assessed a separate overweight penalty against the company, since the Secretary showed that its action was not without substantial justification, he was not liable for attorney's fees. Daily Express, Inc. v. Beatty, 202 N.C. App. 441, 688 S.E.2d 791 (2010).

INVALID PENALTY. --Where the DMV assessed a penalty for operating a vehicle on the highways with a gross weight in excess of that allowed under the license obtained pursuant to G.S. 20-96, but not in excess of the maximum axle weight limits, and such penalty was not authorized by this section, such penalty violated N.C. Const., Art. IV, §§ 1 and 3, since there was no reasonable necessity for conferring absolute judicial discretion in the DMV. Young's Sheet Metal & Roofing, Inc. v. Wilkins, 77 N.C. App. 180, 334 S.E.2d 419 (1985), decided prior to the 1985 amendment to § 20-96.

Although it was uncontroverted that a trucking company did not have the required number of escorts for a truck operating under a special permit, G.S. 20-119(d) and G.S. 20-118(e) did not authorize the North Carolina Department of Crime Control and Public Safety to issue an additional overweight penalty based on the difference between the actual weight of the truck (181,180 pounds) and the statutory weight listed in G.S. 20-118(b) (80,000 pounds), where the actual weight did not violate the weight limit set out in the special permit. Daily Express, Inc. v. N.C. Deparment of Crime Control & Pub. Safety, 195 N.C. App. 288, 671 S.E.2d 587 (2009).

OPINIONS OF THE ATTORNEY GENERAL

THE PENALTIES PROVIDED IN FORMER SUBDIVISIONS (C)(5) AND (C)(12) OF THIS SECTION ARE MANDATORY. --See opinion of Attorney General to Mr. J.F. Alexander, 44 N.C.A.G. 307 (1975).

A TRUCK EQUIPPED WITH A TOTAL OF FOUR AXLES operating with one of the axles (air bag) in a raised position and not carrying any load is subject to the penalties prescribed by law if the weight of the truck exceeds the permissible limit for three axles. See opinion of Attorney General to Mr. J.G. Wilson, Director, License, Theft & Weight Enforcement, Division of Motor Vehicles, 52 N.C.A.G. 126 (1983).

MILITARY VEHICLES BEING OPERATED PURSUANT TO MILITARY ORDERS are not subject to subsection (b) of this section. See opinion of Attorney General to Col. L. M. Brinkley, Division of National Guard, 53 N.C.A.G. 54 (1984).

§ 20-118.1. Officers may weigh vehicles and require overloads to be removed

A law enforcement officer may stop and weigh a vehicle to determine if the vehicle's weight is in compliance with the vehicle's declared gross weight and the weight limits set in this Part. The officer may require the driver of the vehicle to drive to a scale located within five miles of where the officer stopped the vehicle.

Any person operating a vehicle or a combination of vehicles having a GVWR of 10,001 pounds or more or any vehicle transporting hazardous materials that is required to be placarded under 49 C.F.R. § 171-180 must enter a permanent weigh station or temporary inspection or weigh site as directed by duly erected signs or an electronic transponder for the purpose of being electronically screened for compliance, or weighed, or inspected.

If the vehicle's weight exceeds the amount allowable, the officer may detain the vehicle until the overload has been removed. Any property removed from a vehicle because the vehicle was overloaded is the responsibility of the owner or operator of the vehicle. The State is not liable for damage to or loss of the removed property.

Failure to permit a vehicle to be weighed or to remove an overload is a misdemeanor of the Class set in G.S. 20-176. An officer must weigh a vehicle with a scale that has been approved by the Department of Agriculture and Consumer Services.

A privately owned noncommercial horse trailer constructed to transport four or fewer horses shall not be required to stop at any permanent weigh station in the State while transporting horses, unless the driver of the vehicle hauling the trailer is directed to stop by a law enforcement officer. A 'privately owned noncommercial horse trailer' means a trailer used solely for the occasional transportation of horses and not for compensation or in furtherance of a commercial enterprise.

History.
1927, c. 148, s. 37; 1949, c. 1207, s. 3; 1951, c. 1013, s. 4; 1979, c. 436, ss. 1, 2; 1981 (Reg. Sess., 1982), c. 1259, s. 2; 1993, c. 539, s. 356;1994, Ex. Sess., c. 24, s. 14(c);1995, c. 109, s. 4;1997-261, s. 109;2001-487, s. 50(f);2003-338, s. 1

§ 20-118.2. Authority to fix higher weight limitations at reduced speeds for certain vehicles

The Department of Transportation is hereby authorized and empowered to fix higher weight limitations at reduced speeds for vehicles used in transporting property when the point of origin or destination of the motor vehicles is located upon any light traffic highway, county road, farm-to-market road, or any other roads of the secondary system only and/or to the extent only that the motor vehicle is necessarily using said highway in transporting the property from the bona fide point of origin of the property being transported or to the bona fide point of destination of said property and such weights may be different from the weight of those vehicles otherwise using such roads.

History.
1951, c. 1013, s. 7A; 1957, c. 65, s. 11; 1973, c. 507, s. 5; 1977, c. 464, s. 34

§ 20-118.3. Vehicle or combination of vehicles operated without registration plate subject to civil penalty

Any vehicle or combination of vehicles being operated upon the highway of this State either by a resident or nonresident without having been issued therefor a registration plate by the appropriate jurisdiction shall be subject to a civil penalty equal to the North Carolina annual fee for the gross weight of the vehicle and in addition thereto the license fee applicable for the remainder of the current registration year, provided a nonresident shall pay the North Carolina license fee or furnish satisfactory proof of payment of required registration fee to its base jurisdiction. The civil penalties provided for in this section shall not be enforceable through criminal sanctions and the provisions of G.S. 20-176 shall not apply to this section.

History.
1981 Reg. Sess., 1982, c. 1259, s. 1

CITED in Young's Sheet Metal & Roofing, Inc. v. Wilkins, 77 N.C. App. 180, 334 S.E.2d 419 (1985).

§ 20-118.4. Firefighting equipment exempt from size and weight restrictions while transporting or moving heavy equipment for emergency response and preparedness and fire prevention; permits

(a) **Exemption From Weight and Size Restrictions.** -- Any overweight or oversize vehicle owned and operated by a State or local government or cooperating federal agency is exempt from the weight and size restrictions of this Chapter and implementing rules while it is actively engaged in (i) a response to a fire under the authority of a forest ranger pursuant to G.S. 106-899(a); (ii) a county request for forest protection assistance pursuant to G.S. 106-906; (iii) a request for assistance under a state of emergency declared pursuant to G.S. 166A-19.20 or G.S. 166A-19.22, and any other applicable statutes and provisions of common law; (iv) a request for assistance under a disaster declared pursuant to G.S. 166A-19.21; or (v) performance of other required duties for emergency preparedness and fire prevention, when the vehicle meets the following conditions:

(1) The vehicle weight does not exceed the manufacturer's GVWR or 90,000 pounds gross weight, whichever is less.

(2) The tri-axle grouping weight does not exceed 50,000 pounds, tandem axle weight does not exceed 42,000 pounds, and the single axle weight does not exceed 22,000 pounds.

(3) A vehicle/vehicle combination does not exceed 12 feet in width and a total overall vehicle combination length of 75 feet from bumper to bumper.

(b) **Marking, Lighting, and Bridge Requirements.** -- Vehicle/vehicle combinations subject to an exemption or permit under this section shall not be exempt from the requirement of a yellow banner on the front and rear measuring a total length of seven feet by 18 inches bearing the legend "Oversize Load" in 10 inch black letters 1.5 inches wide, and red or orange flags measuring 18 inches square to be displayed on all sides at the widest point of load. In addition, when operating between sunset and sunrise, flashing amber lights shall be displayed on each side of the load at the widest point. Vehicle/vehicle combinations subject to an exemption or permit under this section shall not exceed posted bridge limits without prior approval from the Department of Transportation.

(c) Definition of "Response." -- A response lasts from the time an overweight or oversize vehicle is requested until the vehicle is returned to its base location and restored to a state of readiness for another response.

Chapter 20

(c1) Definition of "Preparedness and Fire Prevention." -- Movement of equipment for the purpose of hazardous fuel reduction, training, equipment maintenance, pre-suppression fire line installation, fire prevention programs, and equipment staging. In order to qualify for the exception in subsection (a) of this section, equipment must remain configured during movement for one or more of these purposes.

(d) **Discretionary Annual or Single Trip Permit for Emergency Response by a Commercial Vehicle.** -- The Department of Transportation may, in its discretion, issue an annual or single trip special use permit waiving the weight and size restrictions of this Chapter and implementing rules for a commercial overweight or oversize vehicle actively engaged in a response to a fire or a request for assistance from a person authorized to direct emergency operations. The Department of Transportation may condition the permit with safety measures that do not unreasonably delay a response. The Department of Transportation may issue the single trip special use permit upon verbal communication, provided the requestor submits appropriate documentation and fees on the next business day.

(e) **No Liability for Issuance of Permit Under This Section.** -- The action of issuing a permit by the Department of Transportation under this section is a governmental function and does not subject the Department of Transportation to liability for injury to a person or damage to property as a result of the activity.

History.
2007-290, s. 1;2012-12, s. 2(g);2012-78, s. 7

EDITOR'S NOTE. --
Session Laws 2007-290, s. 3, made this section effective July 27, 2007.

Pursuant to the recodifications by Session Laws 2011-145, s. 13.25(p), and at the direction of the Revisor of Statutes, "G.S. 106-899(a)" has been substituted for "G.S. 113-55(a)" and "G.S. 106-906" has been substituted for "G.S. 113-59" in the first sentence of subsection (a).

Session Laws 2012-78, s. 18, provides: "Prosecutions for offenses committed before the effective date of the section of this act that modifies the offense [June 26, 2012] are not abated or affected by this act, and the statutes that would be applicable but for this act remain applicable to those prosecutions."

EFFECT OF AMENDMENTS. --
Session Laws 2012-12, s. 2(g), effective October 1, 2012, in subsection (a), substituted "G.S. 166A-19.20 or G.S. 166A-19.22" for "G.S. 14-288.12, 14-288.13, 14-288.14, 14-288.15" and "G.S. 166A-19.21" for "G.S 166A-6 or G.S. 166A-8."

Session Laws 2012-78, s. 7, effective June 26, 2012, in the section heading, substituted "for emergency response and preparedness and fire prevention" for

"in an emergency"; in the introductory paragraph of subsection (a), deleted "During Emergency Response" from the end of the subsection (a) heading; added "or (v) performance of other required duties for emergency preparedness and fire prevention" in the introductory paragraph of subsection (a); substituted "red or orange flags" for "red flags" in subsection (b); and added subsection (c1).

§ 20-119. Special permits for vehicles of excessive size or weight; fees

(a) The Department of Transportation may, in its discretion, upon application, for good cause being shown therefor, issue a special permit in writing authorizing the applicant to operate or move a vehicle of a size or weight exceeding a maximum specified in this Article upon any highway under the jurisdiction and for the maintenance of which the body granting the permit is responsible. However, the Department is not authorized to issue any permit to operate or move over the State highways twin trailers, commonly referred to as double bottom trailers. Every such permit shall be carried in the vehicle to which it refers and shall be open to inspection by any peace officer. The authorities in any incorporated city or town may grant permits in writing and for good cause shown, authorizing the applicant to move a vehicle over the streets of such city or town, the size or weight exceeding the maximum expressed in this Article. The Department of Transportation shall issue rules to implement this section.

(a1) Where permitted by the posted road and bridge limits, the Department may issue a single trip permit for a vehicle or vehicle combination responding to an emergency event that could result in severe damage, injury, or loss of life or property resulting from any natural or man-made emergency as determined by either the Secretary of Public Safety or the Secretary of Transportation or their designees. A permit issued under this subsection may allow for travel from a specific origin to destination and return 24 hours a day, seven days a week, including holidays. Permits issued under this subsection shall include a requirement for banners, flags, and other safety devices, as determined by the Department, and a requirement for a law enforcement escort or a vehicle being operated by a certified escort vehicle operator if traveling between sunset and sunrise. To obtain authorization to travel during restricted times, application shall be made with any required documentation to the proper officials as designated by the Department. If an emergency permit is issued under this subsection, the requestor shall contact the Department of Transportation's central permit office on the next business day to complete any further documentation and pay the applicable fees.

(b) Upon the issuance of a special permit for an oversize or overweight vehicle by the Department of Transportation in accordance with this section, the applicant shall pay to the Department for a single trip permit a fee of twelve dollars ($ 12.00) for each dimension over lawful dimensions, including height, length, width, and weight up to 132,000 pounds. For overweight vehicles, the applicant shall pay to the Department for a single trip permit in addition to the fee imposed by the previous sentence a fee of three dollars ($ 3.00) per 1,000 pounds over 132,000 pounds.

Upon the issuance of an annual permit for a single vehicle, the applicant shall pay a fee in accordance with the following schedule:

Commodity: Annual Fee:

Annual Permit to

Move House Trailers or Trailer Frames $ 200.00

Annual Permit to Move Other Commodities $ 100.00

In addition to the fees set out in this subsection, applications for permits that require an engineering study for pavement or structures or other special conditions or considerations shall be accompanied by a nonrefundable application fee of one hundred dollars ($ 100.00).

This subsection does not apply to farm equipment or machinery being used at the time for agricultural purposes, nor to the moving of a house as provided for by the license and permit requirements of Article 16 of this Chapter. Fees will not be assessed for permits for oversize and overweight vehicles issued to any agency of the United States Government or the State of North Carolina, its agencies, institutions, subdivisions, or municipalities if the vehicle is registered in the name of the agency.

(b1) Neither the Department nor the Board may require review or renewal of annual permits, with or without fee, more than once per calendar year.

(b2) The Department shall issue single trip permits for the transport and delivery of a manufactured or modular home with a maximum width of 16 feet and a gutter edge that does not exceed three inches from the manufacturer to an authorized dealership within this State, for delivery of a manufactured or modular home by a manufacturer and authorized dealer or their transporters to a location within this State, and for transport and delivery of a manufactured or modular home by a homeowner from one location to another within this State. The Department shall promulgate rules that set the days allowed for transport and delivery, times of day transport or delivery may occur, the display and use of banners and escort vehicles for public safety purposes, and any other reasonable rules as are necessary to promote public safety and commerce. For the purposes of this subsection,

manufactured home and modular home shall have the same meanings as those terms are defined in G.S. 105-164.3.

(b3) For a special permit issued under this section for the transport and delivery of cargo, containers, or other equipment, the Department may allow travel after sunset if the Department determines it will be safe and expedite traffic flow. The Department shall not include a term or condition prohibiting travel after sunset for any permitted shipments going to or from international ports. Nothing in this subsection precludes the Department from restricting movements it determines to be unsafe.

(c) Nothing in this section shall require the Department of Transportation to issue any permit for any load.

(d) For each violation of any of the terms or conditions of a special permit issued or where a permit is required but not obtained under this section the Department of Public Safety shall assess a civil penalty for each violation against the registered owner of the vehicle as follows:

(1) A fine of one thousand five hundred dollars ($ 1,500) for operating without the proper number of certified escorts as determined by the actual loaded weight or size of the vehicle combination.

(1a) A fine of five hundred dollars ($ 500.00) for any of the following: operating without the issuance of a permit, moving a load off the route specified in the permit, falsifying information to obtain a permit, or failing to comply with dimension restrictions of a permit.

(2) A fine of two hundred fifty dollars ($ 250.00) for moving loads beyond the distance allowances of an annual permit covering the movement of house trailers from the retailer's premises or for operating in violation of time of travel restrictions.

(3) A fine of one hundred dollars ($ 100.00) for any other violation of the permit conditions or requirements imposed by applicable regulations.

The Department of Transportation may refuse to issue additional permits or suspend existing permits if there are repeated violations of subdivision (1), (1a), or (2) of this subsection.

(d1) In addition to the penalties assessed under subsection (d) of this section, the Department of Public Safety shall assess a civil penalty, not to exceed ten thousand dollars ($ 10,000), in accordance with G.S. 20-118(e)(1) and (e)(3) against the registered owner of the vehicle for any of the following:

(1) Operating without the issuance of a required permit.

(2) Operating off permitted route of travel.

(3) Failing to comply with travel restrictions of the permit.

(4) Operating without the proper vehicle registration or license for the class of vehicle being operated.

A violation of this subsection constitutes operating a vehicle without a special permit.

(e) It is the intent of the General Assembly that the permit fees provided in G.S. 20-119 shall be adjusted periodically to assure that the revenue generated by the fees is equal to the cost to the Department of administering the Oversize/Overweight Permit Unit Program within the Division of Highways. At least every two years, the Department shall review and compare the revenue generated by the permit fees and the cost of administering the program, and shall report to the Joint Legislative Transportation Oversight Committee created in G.S.120-70.50 its recommendations for adjustments to the permit fees to bring the revenues and the costs into alignment.

(f) The Department of Transportation shall issue rules to establish an escort driver training and certification program for escort vehicles accompanying oversize/overweight loads. Any driver operating a vehicle escorting an oversize/overweight load shall meet any training requirements and obtain certification under the rules issued pursuant to this subsection. These rules may provide for reciprocity with other states having similar escort certification programs. Certification credentials for the driver of an escort vehicle shall be carried in the vehicle and be readily available for inspection by law enforcement personnel. The escort and training certification requirements of this subsection shall not apply to the transportation of agricultural machinery until October 1, 2004. The Department of Transportation shall develop and implement an in-house training program for agricultural machinery escorts by September 1, 2004.

(g) The Department of Transportation shall issue annual overwidth permits for the following:

(1) A vehicle carrying agricultural equipment or machinery from the dealer to the farm or from the farm to the dealer that does not exceed 14 feet in width. A permit issued under this subdivision is valid for unlimited movement without escorts on all State highways where the overwidth vehicle does not exceed posted bridge and load limits.

(2) A boat or boat trailer whose outside width equals or exceeds 120 inches. A permit issued under this subdivision must restrict a vehicle's towing of the boat or boat trailer to daylight hours only.

(h) No law enforcement officer shall issue a citation to a person for a violation of this section if the officer is able to determine by electronic means that the person has a permit valid at the time of the violation but does not have the permit in his or her possession. Any person issued a citation pursuant to this section who does not have the permit in his or her possession at the time of the issuance of the citation shall not be responsible for a violation, and the Department of Public Safety may not impose any fines under this section if the person submits evidence to the Department of the existence of a permit valid at the time of the violation within 30 days of the date of the violation.

(i) One, two, or three steel coils, transported on the same vehicle, shall be considered a nondivisible load for purposes of permit issuance pursuant to this section.

History.
1937, c. 407, s. 83; 1957, c. 65, s. 11; 1959, c. 1129; 1973, c. 507, s. 5; 1977, c. 464, s. 34; 1981, c. 690, ss. 31, 32; c. 736, ss. 1, 2; 1989, c. 54; 1991, c. 604, ss. 1, 2; c. 689, s. 334; 1993, c. 539, s. 357;1994, Ex. Sess., c. 24, s. 14(c);2000-109, ss. 7(a), 7(f), 7(g); 2001-424, s. 27.10;2003-383, s. 7;2004-124, s. 30.3E(a), (b); 2004-145, s. 3;2005-361, s. 4;2007-290, s. 2;2008-160, s. 2;2008-229, s. 2;2009-376, ss. 7, 8; 2011-145, s. 19.1(g);2011-358, s. 1;2016-90, s. 2.1(b);2017-97, s. 1

EDITOR'S NOTE. --
Session Laws 2000-109, s. 7(g), was codified as subsection (e) of this section at the direction of the Revisor of Statutes, effective July 13, 2000. Pursuant to Session Laws 2000-109, s. 10(g), the first report required by s. 7(g) is due December 1, 2002.

Session Laws 2008-229 [s. 2 of which amended (g), (g)(1) and (g)(2)] was House Bill 2167, which was vetoed by the Governor on August 17, 2008. The General Assembly, in a special session on August 27, 2008, voted to override the Governor's veto. Session Laws 2008-229 became law notwithstanding the Governor's veto on August 27, 2008.

Session Laws 2012-78, s. 15, provides: "Notwithstanding 19A NCAC 02D.0607(e)(3), the Department of Transportation may permit sealed ship containers as nondivisible loads as allowed by Federal Highway Administration policy. All Department of Transportation permitting rules applied to other nondivisible loads shall also apply to sealed ship containers."

Session Laws 2012-78, s. 16, provides: "The Department of Transportation shall initiate the process to conform the North Carolina Administrative Code to this act by striking the words "not to exceed 94,500 pounds" from the first sentence of 19A NCAC 02D.0607(e)(3)."

Session Laws 2015-263, s. 4(a) -(e), provides: "(a) 19A NCAC 02D.0607 (Permits-Weight, Dimensions and Limitations). -- Until the effective date of the revised permanent rule that the Department of Transportation is required to adopt pursuant to Section 4(d) of this act, the Department shall implement 19A NCAC 02D.0607 (Permits-Weight, Dimensions and Limitations) as provided in subsections (b) and (c) of this section.

"(b) Implementation. -- Notwithstanding subdivision (h)(1) of 19A NCAC 02D.0607 (Permits-Weight, Dimensions and Limitations), the Secretary of Transportation shall allow movement of a permitted oversize vehicle between sunrise and sunset Monday through Sunday. However, a 16-foot-wide mobile or modular home unit with a maximum three-inch gutter edge is restricted to travel from 9:00 A.M. to 2:30 P.M. Monday through Sunday. A 16-foot-wide unit is authorized to continue operation after 2:30 P.M., but not beyond sunset, when traveling on an approved route as determined by an engineering study and the unit is being exported out-of-state.

"(c) Implementation. -- Notwithstanding subdivision (h)(2) of 19A NCAC 02D.0607 (Permits-Weight, Dimensions and Limitations), the Secretary of Transportation shall only prohibit movement of a permitted oversize vehicle and vehicle combination after noon on the weekday preceding the three holidays of Independence Day, Thanksgiving Day, and Christmas Day until noon on the weekday following a holiday. If the observed holiday falls on the weekend, travel is restricted from noon on the preceding Friday until noon on the following Monday.

"(d) Additional Rule-Making Authority. -- The Department of Transportation shall adopt rules to amend 19A NCAC 02D.0607 (Permits-Weight, Dimensions and Limitations) consistent with subsections (b) and (c) of this section. Notwithstanding G.S. 150B-19(4), the rule adopted by the Department pursuant to this section shall be substantively identical to the provisions of subsections (b) and (c) of this section. Rules adopted pursuant to this section are not subject to Part 3 of Article 2A of Chapter 150B of the General Statutes. Rules adopted pursuant to this section shall become effective as provided in G.S. 150B-21.3(b1) as though 10 or more written objections had been received as provided by G.S. 150B-21.3(b2).

"(e) Effective Date. -- Subsections (b) and (c) of this section expire on the date that rules adopted pursuant to subsection (d) of this act become effective."

EFFECT OF AMENDMENTS. --

Session Laws 2004-124, ss. 30.3E(a) and (b), effective July 1, 2004, added subsection (g); and added the last sentence in subsection (f).

Session Laws 2004-145, s. 3, effective January 1, 2005, added the subsection designated herein as subsection (h).

Session Laws 2005-361, s. 4, effective October 1, 2005, substituted "excessive size or weight" for "excessive size, weight, or number of units" in the section heading; in subsection (a), substituted "its discretion" for "their discretion" and deleted "or number of units" following "size or weight" in the first sentence, and deleted "but no rule shall provide that the permits issued pursuant to this section may be invalidated by law enforcement personnel" at the end of the subsection; and in subsection (d), in the first paragraph, inserted "or where a permit is required but not obtained," substituted "Crime Control and Public Safety" for

"Transportation" and "a civil penalty for each violation" for "a separate civil penalty"; and in subdivision (d)(1), inserted "the issuance of" and substituted "the number of properly certified escort vehicles required" for "escort vehicle requirements"; and added the last two sentences of the concluding paragraph of subsection (d).

Session Laws 2007-290, s. 2, effective July 27, 2007, added subsection (a1).

Session Laws 2008-160, s. 2, effective August 3, 2008, inserted "or Trailer Frames" on the list of commodities in subsection (b).

Session Laws 2009-376, ss. 7 and 8, effective October 1, 2009, and applicable to civil penalties assessed and offenses committed on or after that date, in subsection (d), in the introductory language, substituted "shall assess" for "may assess"; added present subdivision (d)(1); redesignated former subdivision (d)(1) as subdivision (d)(1a), deleted "or failing to comply with the number of properly certified escort vehicles required" from the end, and made a related change; in the last paragraph, substituted "subdivision (1), (1a), or (2)" for "subdivision (1) or (2)" in the first sentence, and deleted the former last two sentences, which read: "In addition to the penalties provided by this subsection, a civil penalty in accordance with G.S. 20-118(e) (1) and (3) may be assessed if a vehicle is operating without the issuance of a required permit, operating off permitted route of travel, operating without the proper number of certified escorts as determined by the actual loaded weight of the vehicle combination, fails to comply with travel restrictions of the permit, or operating with improper license. Fees assessed for permit violations under this subsection shall not exceed a maximum of twenty-five thousand dollars ($25,000)."; and added subsection (d1).

Session Laws 2011-145, s. 19.1(g), effective January 1, 2012, in subsections (a1), (d), (d1), and (h), substituted "Public Safety" for "Crime Control and Public Safety."

Session Laws 2011-358, s. 1, effective October 1, 2011, added subsection (b2).

Session Laws 2016-90, s. 2.1(b), effective October 1, 2016, added subsection (i).

Session Laws 2017-97, s. 1, effective July 12, 2017, added subsection (b3).

THIS SECTION WAS ENACTED FOR THE PROTECTION OF THE TRAVELING PUBLIC. Lyday v. Southern Ry., 253 N.C. 687, 117 S.E.2d 778 (1961).

FAILURE TO OBTAIN PERMIT AS NEGLIGENCE PER SE. --The failure to obtain a permit to operate oversize or overweight vehicles in violation of this section is negligence per se. Byers v. Standard Concrete Prods. Co., 268 N.C. 518, 151 S.E.2d 38 (1966).

WHETHER VIOLATION OF THIS SECTION BY PLAINTIFF CONSTITUTES CONTRIBUTORY NEGLIGENCE DEPENDS on whether or not such violation is a proximate cause, or one of the proximate causes, of the damages suffered by plaintiff. Lyday v. Southern Ry., 253 N.C. 687, 117 S.E.2d 778 (1961).

VEHICLES TRANSPORTING POLES IN THE DAYTIME ARE EXEMPT FROM THE

Chapter 20

REQUIREMENTS OF § 20-116(E), and therefore during the daytime it is not negligence per se to transport without a special permit a 40-foot pole on a trailer. Ratliff v. Duke Power Co., 268 N.C. 605, 151 S.E.2d 641 (1966).

IMPOSITION OF A FINE. --Although it was uncontroverted that a trucking company did not have the required number of escorts for a truck operating under a special permit, G.S. 20-119(d) and G.S. 20-118(e) did not authorize the North Carolina Department of Crime Control and Public Safety to issue an additional overweight penalty based on the difference between the actual weight of the truck (181,180 pounds) and the statutory weight listed in G.S. 20-118(b) (80,000 pounds), where the actual weight did not violate the weight limit set out in the special permit. Daily Express, Inc. v. N.C. Deparment of Crime Control & Pub. Safety, 195 N.C. App. 288, 671 S.E.2d 587 (2009).

Trial court did not err in awarding attorney's fees to a company under G.S. 6-19.1 because the decision of the Secretary of Crime Control and Public Safety to assess an additional overweight penalty against the company was substantially justified, and although the Secretary erroneously assessed a separate overweight penalty against the company, since the Secretary showed that its action was not without substantial justification, he was not liable for attorney's fees. Daily Express, Inc. v. Beatty, 202 N.C. App. 441, 688 S.E.2d 791 (2010).

CITED in C & H Transp. Co. v. North Carolina DMV, 34 N.C. App. 616, 239 S.E.2d 309 (1977).

§ 20-119.1. Use of excess overweight and oversize fees

Funds generated by overweight and oversize permit fees in excess of the cost of administering the program, as determined pursuant to G.S. 20-119(e), shall be used for highway and bridge maintenance required as a result of damages caused from overweight or oversize loads.

History.
2005-276, s. 28.5

§ 20-120. Operation of flat trucks on State highways regulated; trucks hauling leaf tobacco in barrels or hogsheads

It shall be unlawful for any person, firm or corporation to operate, or have operated on any public highway in the State any open, flat truck loaded with logs, cotton bales, boxes or other load piled on said truck, without having the said load securely fastened on said truck.

It shall be unlawful for any firm, person or corporation to operate or permit to be operated on any highway of this State a truck or trucks on which leaf tobacco in barrels or hogsheads is carried unless each section or tier of such barrels or hogsheads are reasonably securely fastened to such truck or trucks by metal chains or wire cables, or manila or hemp ropes of not less than five-eighths inch in diameter, to hold said barrels or hogsheads in place under any ordinary traffic or road condition: Provided that the provisions of this paragraph shall not apply to any truck or trucks on which the hogsheads or barrels of tobacco are arranged in a single layer, tier, or plane, it being the intent of this paragraph to require the use of metal chains or wire cables only when barrels or hogsheads of tobacco are stacked or piled one upon the other on a truck or trucks. Nothing in this paragraph shall apply to trucks engaged in transporting hogsheads or barrels of tobacco between factories and storage houses of the same company unless such hogsheads or barrels are placed upon the truck in tiers. In the event the hogsheads or barrels of tobacco are placed upon the truck in tiers same shall be securely fastened to the said truck as hereinbefore provided in this paragraph.

Any person violating the provisions of this section shall be guilty of a Class 2 misdemeanor.

History.
1939, c. 114; 1947, c. 1094; 1953, c. 240; 1993, c. 539, s. 358;1994, Ex. Sess., c. 24, s. 14(c)

§ 20-121. When authorities may restrict right to use highways

The Department of Transportation or local authorities may prohibit the operation of vehicles upon or impose restrictions as to the weight thereof, for a total period not to exceed 90 days in any one calendar year, when operated upon any highway under the jurisdiction of and for the maintenance of which the body adopting the ordinance is responsible, whenever any said highway by reason of deterioration, rain, snow or other climatic conditions will be damaged unless the use of vehicles thereon is prohibited or the permissible weights thereof reduced. The local authority enacting any such ordinance shall erect, or cause to be erected and maintained, signs designating the provisions of the ordinance at each end of that portion of any highway to which the ordinance is applicable, and the ordinance shall not be effective until or unless such signs are erected and maintained.

History.
1937, c. 407, s. 84; 1957, c. 65, s. 11; 1973, c. 507, s. 5; 1977, c. 464, s. 34

CROSS REFERENCES. --
As to powers of municipal corporations with regard to streets, see § 160A-296 et seq.

Chapter 20

§ 20-121.1. Operation of a low-speed vehicle, mini-truck, or modified utility vehicle on certain roadways.

The operation of a low-speed vehicle, mini-truck, or modified utility vehicle is authorized with the following restrictions:

(1) A low-speed vehicle may be operated only on streets and highways where the posted speed limit is 35 miles per hour or less. A mini-truck or modified utility vehicle may be operated only on streets and highways where the posted speed limit is 55 miles per hour or less. This does not prohibit a low-speed vehicle, mini-truck, or modified utility vehicle from crossing a road or street at an intersection where the road or street being crossed has a posted speed limit of more than 35 miles per hour.

(2) A low-speed vehicle, mini-truck, or modified utility vehicle shall be equipped with headlamps, stop lamps, turn signal lamps, tail lamps, reflex reflectors, parking brakes, rearview mirrors, windshields, windshield wipers, speedometer, seat belts, and a vehicle identification number. Any such required equipment shall be maintained in proper working order. If a modified utility vehicle does not have a vehicle identification number, upon application by the owner, the Division shall assign a vehicle identification number to the modified utility vehicle prior to registration.

(3) A low-speed vehicle, mini-truck, or modified utility vehicle shall be registered and insured in accordance with G.S. 20-50 and G.S. 20-309.

(4) The Department of Transportation may prohibit the operation of low-speed vehicles, mini-trucks, or modified utility vehicles on any road or highway if it determines that the prohibition is necessary in the interest of safety.

(5) Low-speed vehicles must comply with the safety standards in 49 C.F.R. § 571.500.

(6) Regardless of age, a mini-truck shall not qualify as an antique vehicle or historic vehicle as described in G.S. 20-79.4(b).

History.
2001-356, s. 5;2019-34, s. 3;2020-40, s. 3

EFFECT OF AMENDMENTS. --
Session Laws 2019-34, s. 3, effective June 21, 2019, inserted "or mini-truck" following "vehicle" throughout the section; inserted the second sentence in subdivision (1); added the second sentence in subdivision (2); and added subdivision (6).

Session Laws 2020-40, s. 3, effective October 1, 2020, substituted "vehicle, mini-truck, or modified utility truck vehicle" for "vehicle or mini-truck" throughout the section; and added the third sentence in subdivision (2).

§ 20-122. Restrictions as to tire equipment

(a) No vehicle will be allowed to move on any public highway unless equipped with tires of rubber or other resilient material which depend upon compressed air, for support of a load, except by special permission of the Department of Transportation which may grant such special permits upon a showing of necessity. This subsection shall have no application to the movement of farm vehicles on highways.

(b) No tire on a vehicle moved on a highway shall have on its periphery any block, stud, flange, cleat or spike or any other protuberance of any material other than rubber which projects beyond the tread of the traction surface of the tire, except that it shall be permissible to use farm machinery with tires having protuberances which will not injure the highway and except, also, that it shall be permissible to use tire chains of reasonable proportions upon any vehicle when required for safety because of snow, ice or other conditions tending to cause a vehicle to slide or skid. It shall be permissible to use upon any vehicle for increased safety, regular and snow tires with studs which project beyond the tread of the traction surface of the tire not more than one sixteenth of an inch when compressed.

(c) The Department of Transportation or local authorities in their respective jurisdictions may, in their discretion, issue special permits authorizing the operation upon a highway of traction engines or tractors having movable tracks with transverse corrugation upon the periphery of such movable tracks or farm tractors or other farm machinery.

(d) It shall not be unlawful to drive farm tractors on dirt roads from farm to farm: Provided, in doing so they do not damage said dirt roads or interfere with traffic.

History.
1937, c. 407, s. 85; 1939, c. 266; 1957, c. 65, s. 11; 1965, c. 435; 1973, c. 507, s. 5; 1977, c. 464, s. 34; 1979, c. 515 CITED in State Hwy. Comm'n v. Raleigh Farmers Mkt., Inc., 263 N.C. 622, 139 S.E.2d 904 (1965).

§ 20-122.1. Motor vehicles to be equipped with safe tires

(a) Every motor vehicle subject to safety equipment inspection in this State and operated on the streets and highways of this State shall be equipped with tires which are safe for the operation of the motor vehicle and which do not expose the public to needless hazard. Tires shall be considered unsafe if cut so as to expose tire cord, cracked so as to expose tire cord, or worn so as to expose tire cord or there is a visible tread separation or chunking or the tire has less than two thirty-seconds inch tread depth at two or more locations around the circumference of the tire in two adjacent major tread grooves, or if the tread wear indicators are in contact with the roadway at two or more locations around the circumference of the tire in two adjacent major tread grooves: Provided, the two thirty-seconds tread depth requirements of this section shall not apply to dual wheel trailers. For the purpose of this section, the following definitions shall apply:

(1) "Chunking" -- separation of the tread from the carcass in particles which may range from very small size to several square inches in area.

(2) "Cord" -- strands forming a ply in a tire.

(3) "Tread" -- portion of tire which comes in contact with road.

(4) "Tread depth" -- the distance from the base of the tread design to the top of the tread.

(a1) Any motor vehicle that has a GVWR of at least 10,001 pounds or more and is operated on the streets or highways of this State shall be equipped with tires that are safe for the operation of the vehicle and do not expose the public to needless hazard. A tire is unsafe if any of the following applies:

(1) It is cut, cracked, or worn so as to expose tire cord.

(2) There is a visible tread separation or chunking.

(3) The steering axle tire has less than four thirty-seconds inch tread depth at any location around the circumference of the tire on any major tread groove.

(4) Any nonsteering axle tire has less than two thirty-seconds inch tread depth around the circumference of the tire in any major tread groove.

(5) The tread wear indicators are in contact with the roadway at any location around the circumference of the tire on any major tread groove.

(b) The driver of any vehicle who is charged with a violation of this section shall be allowed 15 calendar days within which to bring the tires of such vehicle in conformance with the requirements of this section. It shall be a defense to any such charge that the person arrested produce in court, or submit to the prosecuting attorney prior to trial, a certificate from an official safety inspection equipment station showing that within 15 calendar days after such arrest, the tires on such vehicle had been made to conform with the requirements of this section or that such vehicle had been sold, destroyed, or permanently removed from the highways. Violation of this section shall not constitute negligence per se.

History.
1969, c. 378, s. 1; c. 1256; 1985, c. 93, ss. 1, 2; 2009-376, s. 5

EDITOR'S NOTE. --
Session Laws 1985, c. 93, s. 3 provided that the act would not apply to the manner in which tread depth is measured on tires used on farm vehicles which would be registered for less than a full calendar year.

EFFECT OF AMENDMENTS. --
Session Laws 2009-376, s. 5, effective October 1, 2009, and applicable to civil penalties assessed and offenses committed on or after that date, in subsection (a), in the introductory language, deleted the former fourth sentence, which read: "Provided further that as to trucks owned by farmers and operated exclusively in the carrying and transportation of the owner's farm products which are approved for daylight use only and which are equipped with dual wheels, the tread depth requirements of this section shall not apply to more than one wheel in each set of dual wheels."; and added subsection (a1).

§ 20-123. Trailers and towed vehicles

(a) The limitations in G.S. 20-116 on combination vehicles do not prohibit the towing of farm trailers not exceeding three in number nor exceeding a total length of 50 feet during the period from one-half hour before sunrise until one-half hour after sunset when a red flag of at least 12 inches square is prominently displayed on the last vehicle. The towing of farm trailers and equipment allowed by this subsection does not apply to interstate or federal numbered highways.

(b) No trailer or semitrailer or other towed vehicle shall be operated over the highways of the State unless such trailer or semitrailer or other towed vehicle be firmly attached to the rear of the towing unit, and unless so equipped that it will not snake, but will travel in the path of the vehicle drawing such trailer or semitrailer or other towed vehicle, which equipment shall at all times be kept in good condition.

(c) In addition to the requirements of subsections (a) and (b) of this section, the towed vehicle shall be attached to the towing unit by means of safety chains or cables which shall be of sufficient strength to hold the gross weight of the towed vehicle in the event the primary towing device fails or becomes disconnected while being operated on the highways of this State if the primary towing attachment is a ball hitch. Trailers and semitrailers having locking pins or bolts in the towing attachment to prevent disconnection, and the locking pins or bolts are of sufficient strength and condition to hold the gross weight of the towed vehicle, need not be equipped with safety chains or cables unless their operation is subject to the requirements of the Federal Motor Carrier Safety Regulations. Semitrailers in combinations of vehicles that are equipped with fifth wheel assemblies that include locking devices need not be equipped with safety chains or cables.

History.

1937, c. 407, s. 86; 1955, c. 296, s. 3; 1963, c. 356, s. 2; c. 1027, s. 2; 1965, c. 966; 1971, c. 639; 1973, c. 507, s. 5; 1975, c. 716, s. 5; 1977, c. 464, s. 34; 1981 (Reg. Sess., 1982), c. 1195; 1993, c. 71, s. 1;1995 (Reg. Sess., 1996), c. 756, s. 15

ONE USING A VEHICLE TRAILER ON THE PUBLIC HIGHWAYS IS REQUIRED TO EXERCISE REASONABLE CARE, both as to the equipment of the trailer and as to the operation of the vehicle to which it is attached. Miller v. Lucas, 267 N.C. 1, 147 S.E.2d 537 (1966).

In the case of a trailer not controlled in its movements by any person thereon, the operator of the vehicle to which the trailer is attached must exercise reasonable care to see that it is properly attached and that the progress of the two vehicles does not cause danger or injury. Miller v. Lucas, 267 N.C. 1, 147 S.E.2d 537 (1966).

SAFETY CHAINS REQUIRED FOR USE OF BALL HITCH. --G.S. 20-123(c) required the use of safety chains or cables when a ball hitch was the primary towing attachment; accordingly, a jury instruction regarding locking pins was not a correct statement of the law as it was undisputed that the primary towing attachment used by defendant to tow a trailer with his truck was a ball hitch. State v. Hall, 173 N.C. App. 735, 620 S.E.2d 309 (2005).

VIOLATION OF SECTION AS NEGLIGENCE PER SE. --A violation of this section, intended and designed to prevent injury to persons or property on the highways, is negligence per se. Miller v. Lucas, 267 N.C. 1, 147 S.E.2d 537 (1966).

LIABILITY FOR INJURY CAUSED BY DEFECT IN TRAILER HITCH. --As to liability of the owner of a motor vehicle with a trailer attached for loss or injury inflicted by reason of a defect in the trailer fastening or hitch resulting in the trailer breaking loose, see Miller v. Lucas, 267 N.C. 1, 147 S.E.2d 537 (1966).

CITED in State v. Gainey, 84 N.C. App. 107, 351 S.E.2d 819 (1987).

LEGAL PERIODICALS. --

For note on State regulation of twin-trailer trucks, see 4 Campbell L. Rev. 127 (1981).

§ 20-123.1. Steering mechanism

The steering mechanism of every self-propelled motor vehicle operated on the highway shall be maintained in good working order, sufficient to enable the operator to control the vehicle's movements and to maneuver it safely.

History.

1957, c. 1038, s. 3

§ 20-123.2. Speedometer

(a) Every self-propelled motor vehicle when operated on the highway shall be equipped with a speedometer which shall be maintained in good working order.

(b) Any person violating this section shall have committed an infraction and may be ordered to pay a penalty of not more than twenty-five dollars ($ 25.00). No drivers license points, insurance points or premium surcharge shall be assessed on or imputed to any party on account of a violation of this section.

History.

1989 (Reg. Sess., 1990), c. 822, s. 2

CROSS REFERENCES. --

As to violation of G.S. 20-123.2 being a lesser included offense in any violation of the speed restrictions contained in G.S. 20-141, see G.S. 20-141(o).

§ 20-124. Brakes

(a) Every motor vehicle when operated upon a highway shall be equipped with brakes adequate to control the movement of and to stop such vehicle or vehicles, and such brakes shall be maintained in good working order and shall conform to regulations provided in this section.

(b) Repealed by Session Laws 1973, c. 1330, s. 39.

(c) Every motor vehicle when operated on a highway shall be equipped with brakes adequate to control the movement of and to stop and hold such vehicle, and shall have all originally equipped brakes in good working order, including two separate means of applying the brakes. If these two separate means of applying the brakes are connected in any way, they shall be so constructed that failure of any one part of the operating mechanism shall not leave the motor vehicle without brakes.

(d) Every motorcycle and every motor-driven cycle when operated upon a highway shall be equipped with at least one brake which may be operated by hand or foot. For purposes of this section, the term "motorcycle" shall not include autocycles. Autocycles shall be subject to the requirements under this section for motor vehicles.

(e) Motor trucks and tractor-trucks with semi-trailers attached shall be capable of stopping on a dry, hard, approximately level highway free from loose material at a speed of 20 miles per hour within the following distances: Thirty feet with both hand and service brake applied simultaneously and 50 feet when either is applied separately, except that vehicles maintained and operated permanently for the transportation of property and which were registered in this or any other state or district prior to August, 1929, shall be capable of stopping on a dry, hard, approximately level highway free from loose material at a speed of 20 miles per hour within a distance of 50 feet with both hand and service brake applied simultaneously, and within a distance of 75 feet when either applied separately.

(e1) Every motor truck and truck-tractor with semitrailer attached, shall be equipped with brakes acting on all wheels, except trucks and truck-tractors having three or more axles need not have brakes on the front wheels if manufactured prior to July 25, 1980. However, such trucks and truck-tractors must be capable of complying with the performance requirements of G.S. 20-124(e).

(f) Every semitrailer, or trailer, or separate vehicle, attached by a drawbar or coupling to a towing vehicle, and having a gross weight of two tons, and all house trailers of 1,000 pounds gross weight or more, shall be equipped with brakes controlled or operated by the driver of the towing vehicle, which shall conform to the specifications set forth in subsection (e) of this section and shall be of a type approved by the Commissioner.

It shall be unlawful for any person or corporation engaged in the business of selling house trailers at wholesale or retail to sell or offer for sale any house trailer which is not equipped with the brakes required by this subsection.

This subsection shall not apply to house trailers being used as dwellings, or to house trailers not intended to be used or towed on public highways and roads. This subsection shall not apply to house trailers with a manufacturer's certificate of origin dated prior to December 31, 1974.

(g) The provisions of this section shall not apply to a trailer when used by a farmer, a farmer's tenant, agent, or employee if the trailer is exempt from registration by the provisions of G.S. 20-51. This exemption does not apply to trailers that are equipped with brakes from the manufacturer and that are manufactured after October 1, 2009.

(h) From and after July 1, 1955, no person shall sell or offer for sale for use in motor vehicle brake systems in this State any hydraulic brake fluid of a type and brand other than those approved by the Commissioner of Motor Vehicles. From and after January 1, 1970, no person shall sell or offer for sale in motor vehicle brake systems any brake lining of a type or brand other than those approved by the Commissioner of Motor Vehicles. Violation of the provisions of this subsection shall constitute a Class 2 misdemeanor.

History.

1937, c. 407, s. 87; 1953, c. 1316, s. 2; 1955, c. 1275; 1959, c. 990; 1965, c. 1031; 1967, c. 1188; 1969, cc. 787, 866; 1973, c. 1203; c. 1330, s. 39; 1993, c. 539, s. 359;1994, Ex. Sess., c. 24, s. 14(c);2009-376, ss. 10, 11; 2015-163, s. 4

EDITOR'S NOTE. --

Session Laws 2015-163, s. 14, provides, in part: "Prosecutions for offenses committed before the effective date of this act are not abated or affected by this act, and the statutes that would be applicable but for this act remain applicable to those prosecutions."

EFFECT OF AMENDMENTS. --

Session Laws 2009-376, ss. 10 and 11, effective October 1, 2009, and applicable to civil penalties assessed and offenses committed on or after that date, in subsection (e1), in the first sentence, substituted "truck-tractor" for "tractor-truck" near the beginning, and "wheels if manufactured prior to July 25, 1980" for "wheels, except that when such vehicles are equipped with at least two steerable axles, the wheels of one steerable axle need not have brakes" at the end; and in subsection (g), in the first sentence, substituted "a trailer" for "any trailer or semitrailer", "a farmer's tenant" for "his tenant", and "if the trailer" for "under such circumstances that such trailer or semitrailer"; and added the second sentence.

Session Laws 2015-163, s. 4, effective October 1, 2015, added the last two sentences of subsection (d).

PURPOSE OF SECTION. --This section was enacted to promote safe operation of motor vehicles on the highways. Stephens v. Southern Oil Co., 259 N.C. 456, 131 S.E.2d 39 (1963).

The purpose of this section is to protect from injury all persons using the highway, both occupants of the vehicle in question and others. Wilcox v. Glover Motors, Inc., 269 N.C. 473, 153 S.E.2d 76 (1967).

THE LANGUAGE OF THIS SECTION IS MANDATORY. Stephens v. Southern Oil Co., 259 N.C. 456, 131 S.E.2d 39 (1963).

BUT SECTION MUST BE GIVEN REASONABLE INTERPRETATION. --Although the language of this section is mandatory, the statute must be given a reasonable interpretation to promote its intended purpose. Stephens v. Southern Oil Co., 259 N.C. 456, 131 S.E.2d 39 (1963); Wilcox v. Glover Motors, Inc., 269 N.C. 473, 153 S.E.2d 76 (1967); Stone v. Mitchell, 5 N.C. App. 373, 168 S.E.2d 668 (1969).

THE LEGISLATURE DID NOT INTEND TO MAKE OPERATORS OF MOTOR VEHICLES INSURERS of the adequacy of their brakes. The operator must act with care and diligence to see that his brakes meet the standard prescribed by this section; but if because of some latent defect, unknown to the operator and not reasonably discoverable upon proper inspection, he is not able to control the movement of his car, he is not negligent, and for that reason not liable for injuries directly resulting from such loss of control; such injuries result from an unavoidable accident. Stephens v. Southern Oil Co., 259 N.C. 456, 131 S.E.2d 39 (1963); Wilcox v. Glover Motors, Inc., 269 N.C. 473, 153 S.E.2d 76 (1967); Stone v. Mitchell, 5 N.C. App. 373, 168 S.E.2d 668 (1969).

THE DUTY IMPOSED BY THIS SECTION RESTS BOTH UPON THE OWNER AND UPON THE DRIVER of the vehicle, though knowledge of a defect, or negligence in failing to discover it, on the part of the one would not necessarily be imputed to the other. Wilcox v. Glover Motors, Inc., 269 N.C. 473, 153 S.E.2d 76 (1967).

VIOLATION OF THIS SECTION AND OTHER SAFETY STATUTES IS NEGLIGENCE PER SE, unless the statute expressly provides otherwise. McCall v. Dixie Cartage & Warehousing, Inc., 272 N.C. 190, 158 S.E.2d 72 (1967).

One who fails to comply with the provisions of this section is negligent. Stephens v. Southern Oil Co., 259 N.C. 456, 131 S.E.2d 39 (1963).

Where the plaintiff has shown the defendant's brakes to be defective, this is negligence per se. Anderson v. Robinson, 8 N.C. App. 224, 174 S.E.2d 45 (1970).

Willingness of plaintiff's employee-driver and partner-owner to operate tractor on a public highway with defective or malfunctioning brakes and knowledge thereof is negligence as a matter of law. Rose v. Herring Tractor & Truck Co., 47 N.C. App. 643, 267 S.E.2d 717 (1980).

BUT SUCH VIOLATION MUST BE PROXIMATE CAUSE OF INJURY TO BE ACTIONABLE. --Violation of this section is negligence per se, but such violation must be proximate cause of injury to become actionable. Tysinger v. Coble Dairy Prods., 225 N.C. 717, 36 S.E.2d 246 (1945); Arnett v. Yeago, 247 N.C. 356, 100 S.E.2d 855 (1957); Watts v. Watts, 252 N.C. 352, 113 S.E.2d 720 (1960); Bundy v. Belue, 253 N.C. 31, 116 S.E.2d 200 (1960); Tate v. Bryant, 16 N.C. App. 132, 191 S.E.2d 433 (1972).

If the negligence resulting from failure to comply with the provisions of this section proximately causes injury, liability results. Stephens v. Southern Oil Co., 259 N.C. 456, 131 S.E.2d 39 (1963).

QUESTION OF PROXIMATE CAUSE IS FOR JURY. --Whether a violation of the provisions of this section is a proximate cause of an injury is for the jury to determine. Stephens v. Southern Oil Co., 259 N.C. 456, 131 S.E.2d 39 (1963).

REASONABLE EXCUSE FOR FAILURE TO COMPLY WITH SECTION. --In recognition of the principle that this statute must be reasonably construed and applied, defendant could offer proof of legal excuse in avoidance of his failure to have observed the duty created by this section, i.e., proof that an occurrence wholly without his fault and which proper care on his part would not have avoided made compliance with the section impossible at the moment complained of. Anderson v. Robinson, 8 N.C. App. 224, 174 S.E.2d 45 (1970).

The defendant may excuse violation of this section by showing a sudden and unexpected brake failure not the result of his failure to reasonably inspect the vehicle. Tate v. Bryant, 16 N.C. App. 132, 191 S.E.2d 433 (1972).

AS TO LIABILITY OF BAILOR AUTOMOBILE DEALER when he permits a prospective purchaser to test drive a vehicle with defective brakes, see Wilcox v. Glover Motors, Inc., 269 N.C. 473, 153 S.E.2d 76 (1967).

INFERENCE FROM RUNAWAY AUTOMOBILE. --The fact that an automobile ran down the street for a considerable distance immediately after it was parked permitted the inference that plaintiff's intestate did not turn its front wheels to the curb of the street, as required by this section and G.S. 20-163. Watts v. Watts, 252 N.C. 352, 113 S.E.2d 720 (1960).

DOCTRINE OF RES IPSA LOQUITUR does not apply to a brake failure several hours and many miles after delivery of the car to the bailee. Wilcox v. Glover Motors, Inc., 269 N.C. 473, 153 S.E.2d 76 (1967).

BRAKE FAILURE IS NOT NECESSARILY NEGLIGENCE. --While this section requires motorists to maintain their brakes in good working order, and failure to do so is negligence per se, the mere fact that one's brakes failed was not enough to establish a breach of the duty of due care. Mann v. Knight, 83 N.C. App. 331, 350 S.E.2d 122 (1986).

MOTORIST NOT LIABLE FOR UNEXPECTED BRAKE FAILURE. --Where a brake failure is sudden and unexpected and could not have been discovered even with reasonable inspection, the motorist will not be held liable. Mann v. Knight, 83 N.C. App. 331, 350 S.E.2d 122 (1986).

BREACH OF DUTY IN DELIVERY OF AUTOMOBILE WITH DEFECTIVE BRAKES HELD A JURY QUESTION. --Whether defendant breached duty to plaintiff's intestates by delivering to them an automobile when he knew, or by the exercise of ordinary care should have known, that its brakes were defective and its operation was dangerous was a question for the jury. Austin v. Austin, 252 N.C. 283, 113 S.E.2d 553 (1960).

EVIDENCE HELD SUFFICIENT TO NEGATIVE PRIMA FACIE CASE OF NEGLIGENCE. --Corporate defendant's evidence to the effect that brakes on the vehicle in question had been overhauled and relined and had worked perfectly until some two days thereafter, when they suddenly failed, causing the accident in suit, and that after the collision it was ascertained that the flange on one of the wheels was broken, permitting brake fluid to escape, required the court to instruct the jury that if they accepted defendant's evidence it was sufficient to negative the prima facie case of negligence made out by plaintiff's evidence of the failure of the brakes on defendant's vehicle. Stephens v. Southern Oil Co., 259 N.C. 456, 131 S.E.2d 39 (1963).

INSTRUCTION HELD TO BE HARMLESS. --A charge as to proper brakes on motor vehicles, in compliance with this section, where the evidence showed no mention of brakes, was a harmless inadvertence. Hopkins v. Colonial Stores, Inc., 224 N.C. 137, 29 S.E.2d 455 (1944), overruled on other grounds, 246 N.C. 618, 99 S.E.2d 771 (1957).

APPLIED in Burlington Indus., Inc. v. State Hwy. Comm'n, 262 N.C. 620, 138 S.E.2d 281 (1964).

CITED in Newbern v. Leary, 215 N.C. 134, 1 S.E.2d 384 (1939); Crotts v. Overnite Transp. Co., 246 N.C. 420, 98 S.E.2d 502 (1957); Jones v. C. B. Atkins Co., 259 N.C. 655, 131 S.E.2d 371 (1963); Warren v. Jeffries, 263 N.C. 531, 139 S.E.2d 718 (1965); State Hwy. Comm'n v. Raleigh Farmers Mkt., Inc., 263 N.C. 622, 139 S.E.2d 904 (1965); Vann v. Hayes, 266 N.C. 713, 147 S.E.2d 186 (1966); Butler v. Peters, 52 N.C. App. 357, 278 S.E.2d 283 (1981); Peal ex rel. Peal v. Smith, 115 N.C. App. 225, 444 S.E.2d 673 (1994).

Chapter 20

OPINIONS OF THE ATTORNEY GENERAL
FOLD-OUT CAMPER TRAILERS ARE NOT HOUSE TRAILERS. --See opinion of Attorney General to The Honorable Donald R. Kincaid, Member of Senate, N.C.General Assembly, 45 N.C.A.G. 210 (1976).

§ 20-125. Horns and warning devices

(a) Every motor vehicle when operated upon a highway shall be equipped with a horn in good working order capable of emitting sound audible under normal conditions from a distance of not less than 200 feet, and it shall be unlawful, except as otherwise provided in this section, for any vehicle to be equipped with or for any person to use upon a vehicle any siren, compression or spark plug whistle or for any person at any time to use a horn otherwise than as a reasonable warning or to make any unnecessary or unreasonable loud or harsh sound by means of a horn or other warning device. All such horns and warning devices shall be maintained in good working order and shall conform to regulation not inconsistent with this section to be promulgated by the Commissioner.

(b) Every vehicle owned or operated by a police department or by the Department of Public Safety including the State Highway Patrol or by the Wildlife Resources Commission or the Division of Marine Fisheries of the Department of Environmental Quality, or by the Division of Parks and Recreation of the Department of Natural and Cultural Resources, or by the North Carolina Forest Service of the Department of Agriculture and Consumer Services, and used exclusively for law enforcement, firefighting, or other emergency response purposes, or by the Division of Emergency Management, or by a fire department, either municipal or rural, or by a fire patrol, whether such fire department or patrol be a paid organization or a voluntary association, vehicles used by an organ procurement organization or agency for the recovery and transportation of human tissues and organs for transplantation, and every ambulance or emergency medical service emergency support vehicle used for answering emergency calls, shall be equipped with special lights, bells, sirens, horns or exhaust whistles of a type approved by the Commissioner of Motor Vehicles.

The operators of all such vehicles so equipped are hereby authorized to use such equipment at all times while engaged in the performance of their duties and services, both within their respective corporate limits and beyond.

In addition to the use of special equipment authorized and required by this subsection, the chief and assistant chiefs of any police department or of any fire department, whether the same be municipal or rural, paid or voluntary, county fire marshals, assistant fire marshals, transplant coordinators, and emergency management coordinators, are hereby authorized to use such special equipment on privately owned vehicles operated by them while actually engaged in the performance of their official or semiofficial duties or services either within or beyond their respective corporate limits.

And vehicles driven by law enforcement officers of the North Carolina Division of Motor Vehicles shall be equipped with a bell, siren, or exhaust whistle of a type approved by the Commissioner, and all vehicles owned and operated by the State Bureau of Investigation for the use of its agents and officers in the performance of their official duties may be equipped with special lights, bells, sirens, horns or exhaust whistles of a type approved by the Commissioner of Motor Vehicles.

Every vehicle used or operated for law enforcement purposes by the sheriff or any salaried deputy sheriff or salaried rural policeman of any county, whether owned by the county or not, may be, but is not required to be, equipped with special lights, bells, sirens, horns or exhaust whistles of a type approved by the Commissioner of Motor Vehicles. Such special equipment shall not be operated or activated by any person except by a law enforcement officer while actively engaged in performing law enforcement duties.

In addition to the use of special equipment authorized and required by this subsection, the chief and assistant chiefs of each emergency rescue squad which is recognized or sponsored by any municipality or civil preparedness agency, are hereby authorized to use such special equipment on privately owned vehicles operated by them while actually engaged in their official or semiofficial duties or services either within or beyond the corporate limits of the municipality which recognizes or sponsors such organization.

(c) Repealed by Session Laws 1979, c. 653, s. 2.

History.
1937, c. 407, s. 88; 1951, cc. 392, 1161; 1955, c. 1224; 1959, c. 166, s. 1; c. 494; c. 1170, s. 1; c. 1209; 1965, c. 257; 1975, c. 588; c. 734, s. 15; 1977, c. 52, s. 1; c. 438, s. 1; 1979, c. 653, s. 2; 1981, c. 964, s. 19; 1983, c. 32, s. 2; c. 768, s. 5; 1987, c. 266; 1989, c. 537; 1989 (Reg. Sess., 1990), c. 1020, s. 1; 1993 (Reg. Sess., 1994), c. 719, s. 2; 2011-145, s. 19.1(g);2013-415, s. 1(a);2015-241, s. 14.30(ee)

LOCAL MODIFICATION. --Brunswick: 1959, c. 211; Edgecombe: 1955, c. 1024.

EFFECT OF AMENDMENTS. --

Session Laws 2011-145, s. 19.1(g), effective January 1, 2012, substituted "Public Safety" for "Crime Control and Public Safety" in subsection (b).

Session Laws 2013-415, s. 1(a), effective October 1, 2013, in subsection (b), substituted "or" for "and" following "Every vehicle owned" and inserted "or by the Division of Parks and Recreation of the Department of Environment and Natural Resources, or by the North

Carolina Forest Service of the Department of Agriculture and Consumer Services" and "firefighting, or other emergency response" in the first sentence.

Session Laws 2015-241, s. 14.30(ee), effective July 1, 2015, in the first paragraph of subsection (b), substituted "Marine Fisheries of the Department of Environmental Quality" for "Marine Fisheries" and substituted "Department of Natural and Cultural Resources" for "Department of Environment and Natural Resources."

DISTINCTION BETWEEN VEHICLES MAKING NORMAL USE OF HIGHWAY AND THOSE ENGAGED IN EMERGENCY USES. --The legislature, in prescribing practical warning devices for use on motor vehicles, drew a distinction between vehicles making normal use of the highway and those engaged in emergency uses. For normal use, a horn audible for 200 feet under normal conditions was deemed adequate, under subsection (a) of this section; but something different and manifestly with a more authoritative voice and greater volume was expected of vehicles on emergency errands under subsection (b). McEwen Funeral Serv., Inc. v. Charlotte City Coach Lines, 248 N.C. 146, 102 S.E.2d 816 (1958).

APPLIED in State v. Speights, 12 N.C. App. 32, 182 S.E.2d 204 (1971).

CITED in State v. Speights, 280 N.C. 137, 185 S.E.2d 152 (1971).

OPINIONS OF THE ATTORNEY GENERAL

BLUE LIGHT MAY BE USED FOR LAW-ENFORCEMENT VEHICLES. --See opinion of Attorney General to Chief W.W. Pleasants, Durham Chief of Police, 40 N.C.A.G. 391 (1970), issued prior to 1979 repeal of subsection (c), which related specifically to the use of blue lights.

§ 20-125.1. Directional signals

(a) It shall be unlawful for the owner of any motor vehicle of a changed model or series designation indicating that it was manufactured or assembled after July 1, 1953, to register such vehicle or cause it to be registered in this State, or to obtain, or cause to be obtained in this State registration plates therefor, unless such vehicle is equipped with a mechanical or electrical signal device by which the operator of the vehicle may indicate to the operator of another vehicle, approaching from either the front or rear and within a distance of 200 feet, his intention to turn from a direct line. Such signal device must be of a type approved by the Commissioner of Motor Vehicles.

(b) It shall be unlawful for any dealer to sell or deliver in this State any motor vehicle of a changed model or series designation indicating that it was manufactured or assembled after July 1, 1953, if he knows or has reasonable cause to believe that the purchaser of such vehicle intends to register it or cause it to be registered in this State or to resell it to any other person for registration in and use upon the highways of this State, unless such motor vehicle is equipped with a mechanical or electrical signal device by which the operator of the vehicle may indicate to the operator of another vehicle, approaching from either of the front or rear or within a distance of 200 feet, his intention to turn from a direct line. Such signal device must be of a type approved by the Commissioner of Motor Vehicles: Provided that in the case of any motor vehicle manufactured or assembled after July 1, 1953, the signal device with which such motor vehicle is equipped shall be presumed prima facie to have been approved by the Commissioner of Motor Vehicles. Irrespective of the date of manufacture of any motor vehicle a certificate from the Commissioner of Motor Vehicles to the effect that a particular type of signal device has been approved by his Division shall be admissible in evidence in all the courts of this State.

(c) Trailers satisfying the following conditions are not required to be equipped with a directional signal device:

(1) The trailer and load does not obscure the directional signals of the towing vehicle from the view of a driver approaching from the rear and within a distance of 200 feet;

(2) The gross weight of the trailer and load does not exceed 4,000 pounds.

(d) Nothing in this section shall apply to motorcycles. For purposes of this section, the term "motorcycle" shall not include autocycles. Autocycles shall be subject to the requirements under this section for motor vehicles.

History.
1953, c. 481; 1957, c. 488, s. 1; 1963, c. 524; 1969, c. 622; 1975, c. 716, s. 5; 2015-163, s. 5

EDITOR'S NOTE. --
Session Laws 2015-163, s. 14, provides, in part: "Prosecutions for offenses committed before the effective date of this act are not abated or affected by this act, and the statutes that would be applicable but for this act remain applicable to those prosecutions."

EFFECT OF AMENDMENTS. --
Session Laws 2015-163, s. 5, effective October 1, 2015, added the last two sentences of subsection (d).

CITED in Butler v. Peters, 52 N.C. App. 357, 278 S.E.2d 283 (1981).

OPINIONS OF THE ATTORNEY GENERAL

ALL FARM TRAILERS MUST BE EQUIPPED WITH A STOP LAMP ACTIVATED BY THE FOOT BRAKE of the towing unit when operated upon the highways of this State. Additional lights or reflectors required depend on the time of day of operation, the atmospheric and weather conditions, the gross weight of the trailer and whether or not the trailer and load obscure the directional signals or stop light of the towing vehicle. See opinion of the Attorney General to Clyde R. Cook, Jr., Asst. Comm'r of Motor Vehicles, 60 N.C.A.G. 90 (1992).

§ 20-126. Mirrors

(a) No person shall drive a motor vehicle on the streets or highways of this State unless equipped with an inside rearview mirror of a type approved by the Commissioner, which provides the driver with a clear, undistorted, and reasonably unobstructed view of the highway to the rear of such vehicle; provided, a vehicle so constructed or loaded as to make such inside rearview mirror ineffective may be operated if equipped with a mirror of a type to be approved by the Commissioner located so as to reflect to the driver a view of the highway to the rear of such vehicle. A violation of this subsection shall not constitute negligence per se in civil actions. Farm tractors, self-propelled implements of husbandry and construction equipment and all self-propelled vehicles not subject to registration under this Chapter are exempt from the provisions of this section. Provided that pickup trucks equipped with an outside rearview mirror approved by the Commissioner shall be exempt from the inside rearview mirror provision of this section. Any inside mirror installed in any motor vehicle by its manufacturer shall be deemed to comply with the provisions of this subsection.

(b) It shall be unlawful for any person to operate upon the highways of this State any vehicle manufactured, assembled or first sold on or after January 1, 1966 and registered in this State unless such vehicle is equipped with at least one outside mirror mounted on the driver's side of the vehicle. Mirrors herein required shall be of a type approved by the Commissioner.

(c) No person shall operate a motorcycle upon the streets or highways of this State unless such motorcycle is equipped with a rearview mirror so mounted as to provide the operator with a clear, undistorted and unobstructed view of at least 200 feet to the rear of the motorcycle. No motorcycle shall be registered in this State after January 1, 1968, unless such motorcycle is equipped with a rearview mirror as described in this section. Violation of the provisions of this subsection shall not be considered negligence per se or contributory negligence per se in any civil action.

History.

1937, c. 407, s. 89; 1965, c. 368; 1967, c. 282, s. 1; c. 674, s. 2; c. 1139; 2002-159, ss. 22(a), 22(b).

EDITOR'S NOTE. --

Session Laws 1967, c. 282, s. 12 provided that any inside mirror installed in any motor vehicle by its manufacturer shall be deemed to comply with subsection (a) of this section.

VIOLATION OF THIS SECTION AND OTHER SAFETY STATUTES IS NEGLIGENCE PER SE, unless the statute expressly provides otherwise. McCall v. Dixie Cartage & Warehousing, Inc., 272 N.C. 190, 158 S.E.2d 72 (1967).

VEHICLE REGISTRATION. --Trial court erred in denying defendant's motion to suppress evidence discovered during the stop of his vehicle because the stop was based on a police officer's mistake of law that was not objectively reasonable where the statutory phrase "registered in this State" was susceptible to only one meaning; that the vehicle must be registered in North Carolina; and a reasonable officer reading the statute would understand the requirement did not apply to vehicles that, like defendant's vehicle, were registered in another state. State v. Eldridge, 249 N.C. App. 493, 790 S.E.2d 740 (2016).

CITED in Bechtler v. Bracken, 218 N.C. 515, 11 S.E.2d 721 (1940); State v. Veazey, 191 N.C. App. 181, 662 S.E.2d 683 (2008).

§ 20-127. Windows and windshield wipers

(a) **Windshield Wipers.** -- A vehicle that is operated on a highway and has a windshield shall have a windshield wiper to clear rain or other substances from the windshield in front of the driver of the vehicle and the windshield wiper shall be in good working order. If a vehicle has more than one windshield wiper to clear substances from the windshield, all the windshield wipers shall be in good working order.

(b) **Window Tinting Restrictions.** -- A window of a vehicle that is operated on a highway or a public vehicular area shall comply with this subsection. The windshield of the vehicle may be tinted only along the top of the windshield and the tinting may not extend more than five inches below the top of the windshield or below the AS1 line of the windshield, whichever measurement is longer. Provided, however, an untinted clear film which does not obstruct vision but which reduces or eliminates ultraviolet radiation from entering a vehicle may be applied to the windshield. Any other window of the vehicle may be tinted in accordance with the following restrictions:

(1) The total light transmission of the tinted window shall be at least thirty-five percent (35%). A vehicle window that, by use of a light meter approved by the Commissioner, measures a total light transmission of more than thirty-two percent (32%) is conclusively presumed to meet this restriction.

(2) The light reflectance of the tinted window shall be twenty percent (20%) or less.

(3) Tinted film or another material used to tint the window shall be nonreflective and shall not be red, yellow, or amber.

(b1) Notwithstanding subsection (b) of this section, a window of a vehicle that is operated on a public street or highway and which is subject to the provisions of Part 393 of Title 49 of the Code of Federal Regulations shall comply with the provisions of that Part.

(c) **Tinting Exceptions.** -- The window tinting restrictions in subsection (b) of this section apply without exception to the windshield of a vehicle. The window tinting restrictions in subdivisions (b)(1) and (b)(2) of this section do not apply to any of the following vehicle windows:

(1) A window of an excursion passenger vehicle, as defined in G.S. 20-4.01(27).

(2), (3) Repealed by Session Laws 2012-78, s. 8, effective December 1, 2012. For applicability, see Editor's notes.

(4) A window of a motor home, as defined in G.S. 20-4.01(27)k.

(5) A window of an ambulance, as defined in G.S. 20-4.01(27)a.

(6) The rear window of a property-hauling vehicle, as defined in G.S. 20-4.01(31).

(7) A window of a limousine.

(8) A window of a law enforcement vehicle.

(9) A window of a multipurpose vehicle that is behind the driver of the vehicle. A multipurpose vehicle is a passenger vehicle that is designed to carry 10 or fewer passengers and either is constructed on a truck chassis or has special features designed for occasional off-road operation. A minivan and a pickup truck are multipurpose vehicles.

(10) A window of a vehicle that is registered in another state and meets the requirements of the state in which it is registered.

(11) A window of a vehicle for which the Division has issued a medical exception permit under subsection (f) of this section.

(d) **Violations.** -- A person who does any of the following commits a Class 3 misdemeanor:

(1) Applies tinting to the window of a vehicle that is subject to a safety inspection in this State and the resulting tinted window does not meet the window tinting restrictions set in this section.

(2) Drives on a highway or a public vehicular area a vehicle that has a window that does not meet the window tinting restrictions set in this section.

(e) **Defense.** -- It is a defense to a charge of driving a vehicle with an unlawfully tinted window that the tinting was removed within 15 days after the charge and the window now meets the window tinting restrictions. To assert this defense, the person charged shall produce in court, or submit to the prosecuting attorney before trial, a certificate from the Division of Motor Vehicles or the Highway Patrol showing that the window complies with the restrictions.

(f) **Medical Exception.** -- A person who suffers from a medical condition that causes the person to be photosensitive to visible light may obtain a medical exception permit. To obtain a permit, an applicant shall apply in writing to the Drivers Medical Evaluation Program and have his or her doctor complete the required medical evaluation form provided by the Division. The permit shall be valid for five years from the date of issue, unless a shorter time is directed by the Drivers Medical Evaluation Program. The renewal shall require a medical recertification that the person continues to suffer from a medical condition requiring tinting.

A person may receive no more than two medical exception permits that are valid at any one time. A permit issued under this subsection shall specify the vehicle to which it applies, the windows that may be tinted, and the permitted levels of tinting. The permit shall be carried in the vehicle to which it applies when the vehicle is driven on a highway.

The Division shall give a person who receives a medical exception permit a sticker to place on the lower left-hand corner of the rear window of the vehicle to which it applies. The sticker shall be designed to give prospective purchasers of the vehicle notice that the windows of the vehicle do not meet the requirements of G.S. 20-127(b), and shall be placed between the window and the tinting when the tinting is installed. The Division shall adopt rules regarding the specifications of the medical exception sticker. Failure to display the sticker is an infraction punishable by a two hundred dollar ($ 200.00) fine.

History.

1937, c. 407, s. 90; 1953, c. 1254; 1955, c. 1157, s. 2; 1959, c. 1264, s. 7; 1967, c. 1077; 1985, c. 789; 1985 (Reg. Sess., 1986), c. 997; 1987, c. 567; 1987 (Reg. Sess., 1988), c. 1082, ss. 7-8.1; 1989, c. 770, s. 66;1991 (Reg. Sess., 1992), c. 1007, s. 34; 1993, c. 539, s. 360;1994, Ex. Sess., c. 24, s. 14(c);1993 (Reg. Sess., 1994), c. 683, s. 1; c. 754, s. 4; 1995, c. 14, s. 1;c. 473, s. 1;2000-75, s. 1;2012-78, s. 8;2013-360, s. 18B.14(j);2015-163, s. 13;2017-102, s. 5.2(b)

EDITOR'S NOTE. --

The designations of subsections (d) and (e) were assigned by the Revisor of Statutes, as the amendment by Session Laws 1995, c. 473, s. 1, contained two subsection (c)'s.

Session Laws 2000-75, s. 2, provides:

"The Medical Review Branch of the Division of Motor Vehicles shall issue rules and create forms and permits necessary for this program. Until funds for this program are appropriated by the General Assembly, the Medical Review Branch shall manually issue all medical exception permits and shall manually maintain the records related specifically to these permits.

"The Division of Motor Vehicles shall add the medical exception described in Section 1 of this act [which amended G.S. 20-127] to the STARS program, to allow the computerized issuance of medical exception permits and to allow computerized maintenance of the records related specifically to these permits when it is modifying that computer program for some other purpose.

Chapter 20

"The Division of Motor Vehicles shall report to the Joint Legislative Transportation Oversight Committee six months after the first medical exception permit is issued on the number of permits issued and the projected additional costs, if any, of operating the program."

Session Laws 2015-163, s. 14, provides, in part: "Prosecutions for offenses committed before the effective date of this act are not abated or affected by this act, and the statutes that would be applicable but for this act remain applicable to those prosecutions."

Session Laws 2017-102, s. 5.2(b) provides: "The Revisor of Statutes is authorized to reletter the definitions in G.S. 20-4.01(27) and G.S. 20-4.01(32b) to place them in alphabetical order. The Revisor of Statutes may conform any citations that change as a result of the relettering." Pursuant to that authority, the reference to G.S. 20-4.01(27)d2. and f. in subdivisions (c)(4) and (5) were changed to G.S. 20-4.01(27)k. and a. respectively.

EFFECT OF AMENDMENTS. --

Session Laws 2012-78, s. 8, effective December 1, 2012, added subsection (b1); repealed subdivision (c)(2), which read: "A window of a for-hire passenger vehicle, as defined in G.S. 20-4.01(27)b."; and repealed subdivision (c)(3), which read: "A window of a common carrier of passengers, as defined in G.S. 20-4.01(27)c." For applicability, see Editor's note.

Session Laws 2013-360, s. 18B.14(j), effective December 1, 2013, substituted "Class 3 misdemeanor" for "misdemeanor of the class set in G.S. 20-176" in subsection (d). For applicability, see Editor's note.

Session Laws 2015-163, s. 13, effective October 1, 2015, substituted "G.S. 20-4.01(27)" for "G.S. 20-4.01(27)a" at the end of subdivision (c)(1).

TRAFFIC STOP FOR VIOLATION OF WINDSHIELD TINTING RESTRICTIONS. --The windshield-tinting restrictions are not subject to any exception for vehicles registered in other states, and it is immaterial whether a defendant's windows were tinted in compliance with Florida law; thus, a deputy had the right to stop a vehicle where he reasonably suspected that defendant violated this section. State v. Schiffer, 132 N.C. App. 22, 510 S.E.2d 165 (1999).

CITED in State v. Veazey, 191 N.C. App. 181, 662 S.E.2d 683 (2008); State v. Williams, 215 N.C. App. 1, 714 S.E.2d 835 (2011), aff'd, 366 N.C. 110, 726 S.E. 2d 161, 2012 N.C. LEXIS 410 (N.C. 2012).

OPINIONS OF THE ATTORNEY GENERAL

FEDERAL SAFETY LAWS PREEMPT STATE REGULATION. --A State statute or regulation allowing 35% light transmittance through windows in motor vehicles would be preempted by current federal safety laws and standards regulating the same subject matter. See opinion of Attorney General to Mr. William S. Hiatt, Commissioner of Motor Vehicles, -- N.C.A.G. -- (Dec. 18, 1987).

§ 20-128. Exhaust system and emissions control devices

(a) No person shall drive a motor vehicle on a highway unless such motor vehicle is equipped with a muffler, or other exhaust system of the type installed at the time of manufacture, in good working order and in constant operation to prevent excessive or unusual noise, annoying smoke and smoke screens.

(b) It shall be unlawful to use a "muffler cutout" on any motor vehicle upon a highway.

(c) No motor vehicle registered in this State that was manufactured after model year 1967 shall be operated in this State unless it is equipped with emissions control devices that were installed on the vehicle at the time the vehicle was manufactured and these devices are properly connected.

(d) The requirements of subsection (c) of this section shall not apply if the emissions control devices have been removed for the purpose of converting the motor vehicle to operate on natural or liquefied petroleum gas or other modifications have been made in order to reduce air pollution and these modifications are approved by the Department of Environmental Quality.

History.

1937, c. 407, s. 91; 1971, c. 455, s. 1; 1983, c. 132; 1989, c. 727, s. 9;1997-443, s. 11A.119(a);2000-134, s. 6;2015-241, s. 14.30(u)

EFFECT OF AMENDMENTS. --

Session Laws 2015-241, s. 14.30(u), effective July 1, 2015, substituted "Department of Environmental Quality" for "Department of Environment and Natural Resources" in subsection (d).

FOR CASE HOLDING A WARRANT SUFFICIENT TO CHARGE VIOLATION OF THIS SECTION, see State v. Daughtry, 236 N.C. 316, 72 S.E.2d 658 (1952).

CITED in State v. Woolard, 260 N.C. 133, 132 S.E.2d 364 (1963); Stanley v. Department of Conservation & Dev., 284 N.C. 15, 199 S.E.2d 641 (1973).

§ 20-128.1. Control of visible emissions

(a) It shall be a violation of this Article:

(1) For any gasoline-powered motor vehicle registered and operated in this State to emit visible air contaminants under any mode of operation for longer than five consecutive seconds.

(2) For any diesel-powered motor vehicle registered and operated in this State to emit for longer than five consecutive seconds under any mode of operation visible air contaminants which are equal to or darker than the shade or density designated as No. 1 on the Ringelmann Chart or are equal to or darker than a shade or density of twenty percent (20%) opacity.

(b) Any person charged with a violation of this section shall be allowed 30 days within which to make the necessary repairs or modification to bring the motor vehicle into conformity with the standards of this section and to have the motor vehicle inspected and approved by the agency issuing the notice of violation. Any person who, within 30 days of receipt of a notice of violation, and prior to inspection and approval by the agency issuing the notice, receives additional notice or notices of violation, may exhibit a certificate of inspection and approval from the agency issuing the first notice in lieu of inspection and approval by the agencies issuing the subsequent notices.

(c) The provisions of this section shall be enforceable by all persons designated in G.S. 20-49; by all law-enforcement officers of this State within their respective jurisdictions; by the personnel of local air pollution control agencies within their respective jurisdictions; and by personnel of State air pollution control agencies throughout the State.

(d) Any person who fails to comply with the provisions of this section shall be subject to the penalties provided in G.S. 20-176.

History.
1971, c. 1167, s. 10
CITED in Stanley v. Department of Conservation & Dev., 284 N.C. 15, 199 S.E.2d 641 (1973).

§ 20-128.2. Motor vehicle emission standards

(a) The rules and regulations promulgated pursuant to G.S. 143-215.107(a)(6) shall be implemented when the Environmental Management Commission certifies to the Commissioner of Motor Vehicles that the ambient air quality in an area will be improved by the implementation of a motor vehicle inspection/maintenance program within a specified county or group of counties, as necessary to effect attainment or preclude violations of the National Ambient Air Quality Standards for carbon monoxide or ozone; provided the Environmental Management Commission may prescribe different vehicle emission limits for different areas as may be necessary and appropriate to meet the stated purposes of this section.

(b) Repealed by Session Laws 1993 (Reg. Sess., 1994), c. 754, s. 5.

History.
1979, 2nd Sess., c. 1180, s. 2; 1989, c. 391, s. 1;1993 (Reg. Sess., 1994), c. 754, s. 5

§ 20-129. Required lighting equipment of vehicles

(a) **When Vehicles Must Be Equipped.** -- Every vehicle upon a highway within this State shall be equipped with lighted headlamps and rear lamps as required for different classes of vehicles, and subject to exemption with reference to lights on parked vehicles as declared in G.S. 20-134:

(1) During the period from sunset to sunrise,

(2) When there is not sufficient light to render clearly discernible any person on the highway at a distance of 400 feet ahead, or

(3) Repealed by Session Laws 1989 (Reg. Sess., 1990), c. 822, s. 1.

(4) At any other time when windshield wipers are in use as a result of smoke, fog, rain, sleet, or snow, or when inclement weather or environmental factors severely reduce the ability to clearly discern persons and vehicles on the street and highway at a distance of 500 feet ahead, provided, however, the provisions of this subdivision shall not apply to instances when windshield wipers are used intermittently in misting rain, sleet, or snow. Any person violating this subdivision during the period from October 1, 1990, through December 31, 1991, shall be given a warning of the violation only. Thereafter, any person violating this subdivision shall have committed an infraction and shall pay a fine of five dollars ($ 5.00) and shall not be assessed court costs. No drivers license points, insurance points or premium surcharge shall be assessed on account of violation of this subdivision and no negligence or liability shall be assessed on or imputed to any party on account of a violation of this subdivision. The Commissioner of Motor Vehicles and the Superintendent of Public Instruction shall incorporate into driver education programs and driver licensing programs instruction designed to encourage compliance with this subdivision as an important means of reducing accidents by making vehicles more discernible during periods of limited visibility.

(b) **Headlamps on Motor Vehicles.** -- Every self-propelled motor vehicle other than motorcycles, road machinery, and farm tractors shall be equipped with at least two headlamps, all in good operating condition with at least one on each side of the front of the motor vehicle. Headlamps shall comply with the requirements and limitations set forth in G.S. 20-131 or 20-132.

(c) **Headlamps on Motorcycles.** -- Every motorcycle shall be equipped with at least one and not more than two headlamps which shall comply with the requirements and limitations set forth in G.S. 20-131 or 20-132. The headlamps on a motorcycle shall be lighted at all times while the motorcycle is in operation on highways or public vehicular areas. For purposes of this section, the term "motorcycle" shall not include autocycles. Autocycles shall be subject to the requirements under this section for motor vehicles.

(d) **Rear Lamps.** -- Every motor vehicle, and every trailer or semitrailer attached to a motor vehicle and every vehicle which is being drawn at the end of a combination of vehicles, shall have all originally equipped rear lamps or the equivalent in good working order, which lamps shall exhibit a red light plainly visible under normal atmospheric conditions from a distance of 500 feet to the rear of such vehicle. One rear lamp or a separate lamp shall be so constructed and placed that the number plate carried on the rear of such vehicle shall under like conditions be illuminated by a white light as to be read from a distance of 50 feet to the rear of such vehicle. Every trailer or semitrailer shall carry at the rear, in addition to the originally equipped lamps, a red reflector of the type which has been approved by the Commissioner and which is so located as to height and is so maintained as to be visible for at least 500 feet when opposed by a motor vehicle displaying lawful undimmed lights at night on an unlighted highway.

Notwithstanding the provisions of the first paragraph of this subsection, it shall not be necessary for a trailer weighing less than 4,000 pounds, or a trailer described in G.S. 20-51(6) weighing less than 6,500 pounds, to carry or be equipped with a rear lamp, provided such vehicle is equipped with and carries at the rear two red reflectors of a diameter of not less than three inches, such reflectors to be approved by the Commissioner, and which are so designed and located as to height and are maintained so that each reflector is visible for at least 500 feet when approached by a motor vehicle displaying lawful undimmed headlights at night on an unlighted highway.

The rear lamps of a motorcycle shall be lighted at all times while the motorcycle is in operation on highways or public vehicular areas.

(e) **Lamps on Bicycles.** -- Every bicycle shall be equipped with a reflex mirror on the rear and both of the following when operated at night on any public street, public vehicular area, or public greenway:

(1) A lighted lamp on the front thereof, visible under normal atmospheric conditions from a distance of at least 300 feet in front of such bicycle.

(2) A lamp on the rear, exhibiting a red light visible under like conditions from a distance of at least 300 feet to the rear of such bicycle, or the operator must wear clothing or a vest that is bright and visible from a distance of at least 300 feet to the rear of the bicycle.

(f) **Lights on Other Vehicles.** -- All vehicles not heretofore in this section required to be equipped with specified lighted lamps shall carry on the left side one or more lighted lamps or lanterns projecting a white light, visible under normal atmospheric conditions from a distance of not less than 500 feet to the front of such vehicle and visible under like conditions from a distance of not less than 500 feet to the rear of such vehicle, or in lieu of said lights shall be equipped with reflectors of a type which is approved by the Commissioner. Farm tractors operated on a highway at night must be equipped with at least one white lamp visible at a distance of 500 feet from the front of the tractor and with at least one red lamp visible at a distance of 500 feet to the rear of the tractor. Two red reflectors each having a diameter of at least four inches may be used on the rear of the tractor in lieu of the red lamp.

(g) No person shall sell or operate on the highways of the State any motor vehicle manufactured after December 31, 1955, and on or before December 31, 1970, unless it shall be equipped with a stop lamp on the rear of the vehicle. No person shall sell or operate on the highways of the State any motor vehicle, manufactured after December 31, 1970, unless it shall be equipped with stop lamps, one on each side of the rear of the vehicle. No person shall sell or operate on the highways of the State any motorcycle or motor-driven cycle, manufactured after December 31, 1955, unless it shall be equipped with a stop lamp on the rear of the motorcycle or motor-driven cycle. The stop lamps shall emit, reflect, or display a red or amber light visible from a distance of not less than 100 feet to the rear in normal sunlight, and shall be actuated upon application of the service (foot) brake. The stop lamps may be incorporated into a unit with one or more other rear lamps.

(h) **Backup Lamps.** -- Every motor vehicle originally equipped with white backup lamps shall have those lamps in operating condition.

History.
1937, c. 407, s. 92; 1939, c. 275; 1947, c. 526; 1955, c. 1157, ss. 3-5, 8; 1957, c. 1038, s. 1; 1967, cc. 1076, 1213; 1969, c. 389; 1973, c. 531, ss. 1, 2; 1979, c. 175; 1981, c. 549, s. 1; 1985, c. 66; 1987, c. 611; 1989 (Reg. Sess., 1990), c. 822, s. 1; 1991, c. 18, s. 1;1999-281, s. 1;2015-31, s. 1;2015-163, s. 6;2015-241, s. 29.36B(a);2016-90, s. 5.1(a);2017-211, s. 12(a)

EDITOR'S NOTE. --
Session Laws 2015-31, s. 3, made the amendment to subsection (g) by Session Laws 2015-31, s. 1, applicable to offenses committed on or after October 1, 2015.

Session Laws 2015-163, s. 14, provides, in part: "Prosecutions for offenses committed before the effective date of this act are not abated or affected by this act, and the statutes that would be applicable but for this act remain applicable to those prosecutions."

Session Laws 2015-241, s. 29.36B(b), made the amendment to subsection (g) of this section by Session

Laws 2015-241, s. 29.36B(a), applicable to offenses committed on or after October 1, 2015.

Session Laws 2016-90, s. 5.1(b), made the rewriting of subsection (e) of this section by Session Laws 2016-90, s. 5.1(a), applicable to offenses committed on or after December 1, 2016.

Session Laws 2017-211, s. 12(b), provides: "The Department of Transportation and the Department of Environmental Quality shall jointly study whether the frequency of vehicle safety inspections and vehicle emissions inspections should be decreased. The Departments shall consider public safety, air quality, savings to vehicle owners, impacts on State revenues, and any other factors the Departments deem necessary. No later than March 1, 2018, the Departments shall jointly report their findings and recommendations to the Joint Legislative Transportation Oversight Committee."

Session Laws 2017-211, s. 12(c) made subsection (h), as added by Session Laws 2017-211, s. 12(a), effective March 1, 2018, and applicable to offenses committed on or after that date.

Session Laws 2017-211, s. 21(a), is a severability clause.

EFFECT OF AMENDMENTS. --

Session Laws 2015-31, s. 1, effective October 1, 2015, in subsection (g), rewrote the first sentence, inserted the present second sentence, and substituted "lamps shall emit, reflect, or display" for "lamp shall display" in the present third sentence, and substituted "lamps" for "lamp" in the last sentence. For applicability, see editor's note.

Session Laws 2015-163, s. 6, effective October 1, 2015, added the last two sentences of subsection (c).

Session Laws 2015-241, s. 29.36B(a), effective October 1, 2015, in subsection (g), added the present first sentence, and substituted "December 31, 1955" for "December 31, 1970" in the present third sentence. For applicability, see editor's note.

Session Laws 2016-90, s. 5.1(a), effective December 1, 2016, rewrote subsection (e). See editor's note for applicability.

Session Laws 2017-211, s. 12(a), added subsection (h). For effective date and applicability, see editor's note.

THIS A SAFETY STATUTE enacted for the protection of persons and property. Brown v. Boren Clay Prods. Co., 5 N.C. App. 418, 168 S.E.2d 452 (1969).

PURPOSE OF SECTION. --This section was enacted to minimize the hazards incident to the movement of motor vehicles upon the public roads during the nighttime. Thomas v. Thurston Motor Lines, 230 N.C. 122, 52 S.E.2d 377 (1949).

This section was enacted for the protection of persons and property and in the interest of public safety and the preservation of human life. State v. Norris, 242 N.C. 47, 86 S.E.2d 916 (1955).

This section was enacted in the interest of public safety. Scarborough v. Ingram, 256 N.C. 87, 122 S.E.2d 798 (1961); Oxendine v. Lowry, 260 N.C. 709, 133 S.E.2d 687 (1963); White v. Mote, 270 N.C. 544, 155 S.E.2d 75 (1967).

EFFECT OF G.S. 20-161. --Section 20-161 does not conflict with nor reduce the obligation imposed on the operator of a motor vehicle stopped or parked on the highway at night to light his vehicle as required by this section and G.S. 20-134. Melton v. Crotts, 257 N.C. 121, 125 S.E.2d 396 (1962).

APPLICATION. --Provisions of G.S. 20-129 apply to all highways or streets as defined by G.S. 20-4.01. State v. Hopper, 205 N.C. App. 175, 695 S.E.2d 801 (2010).

WHAT CONSTITUTES VIOLATION OF SECTION. --Driving a motor vehicle without lights during the period from a half hour after sunset to a half hour before sunrise violates this section and is punishable as prescribed by § 20-176(b). State v. Eason, 242 N.C. 59, 86 S.E.2d 774 (1955).

Operating a motor vehicle on a public highway at night without lights is a violation of this section. Williamson v. Varner, 252 N.C. 446, 114 S.E.2d 92 (1960).

Defendant's Fourth Amendment rights were violated when defendant's vehicle was stopped due to a malfunctioning brake light because (1) G.S. 20-129(g) only required defendant to have one working brake light, which defendant did, (2) that statute did not require the vehicle's originally equipped stop lamps to be in good working order, as did G.S. 20-129(d), and (3) the malfunctioning brake light did not violate the safety inspection requirements of G.S. 20-183.3 or the requirements of NG.S. 20-129.1. State v. Heien, 214 N.C. App. 515, 714 S.E.2d 827 (2011).

INABILITY OF POLICE TO READ LICENSE PLATE. --Where police officers pulled within 50 feet of defendant's vehicle and were unable to read defendant's license plate, the officers had reasonable suspicion to stop defendant's vehicle for a violation of G.S. 20-129(d). State v. Ford, 208 N.C. App. 699, 703 S.E.2d 768 (2010).

FAILURE TO USE TAILLIGHTS WHILE WINDSHIELD WIPERS IN USE. --Trial court did not err in denying defendant's motion to suppress evidence a police officer seized from his vehicle pursuant to a traffic stop because the trial court's findings supported its conclusion that the officer had reasonable suspicion that defendant had violated G.S. 20-129 by failing to have taillights in proper working order; considering the totality of the circumstances, the officer reasonably believed that a street in an apartment complex was a public road for purposes of G.S. 20-129(a)(4) and that under the weather conditions at the time of the stop, defendant was required to have his taillights on while his windshield wipers were in use, and the officer's reasonable, albeit assumed to be mistaken, belief did not render the stop unconstitutional. State v. Hopper, -- N.C. App. --, 692 S.E.2d 166 (Apr. 20, 2010).

PROOF THAT STREET FORMS PART OF HIGHWAY SYSTEM REQUIRED. --The provisions of this section are not applicable to defendants' truck parked or stopped on a street in the city when plaintiff has neither allegation nor proof to show that the street forms a part of the State highway system. Coleman v. Burris, 265 N.C. 404, 144 S.E.2d 241 (1965).

VIOLATION AS NEGLIGENCE. -- Williamson v. Varner, 252 N.C. 446, 114 S.E.2d 92 (1960); Correll v. Gaskins, 263 N.C. 212, 139 S.E.2d 202 (1964); Faison v. T & S Trucking Co., 266 N.C. 383, 146 S.E.2d 450 (1966); McNulty v. Chaney, 1 N.C. App. 610, 162 S.E.2d 90 (1968); Brown v. Boren Clay Prods. Co., 5 N.C. App. 418, 168 S.E.2d 452 (1969); Hardison v. Williams, 21 N.C. App. 670, 205 S.E.2d 551 (1974).

Violation of this section constitutes negligence as a matter of law. Scarborough v. Ingram, 256 N.C. 87, 122 S.E.2d 798 (1961); Oxendine v. Lowry, 260 N.C. 709, 133 S.E.2d 687 (1963); White v. Mote, 270 N.C. 544, 155 S.E.2d 75 (1967); Bigelow v. Johnson, 49 N.C. App. 40, 270 S.E.2d 503 (1980), rev'd on other grounds, 303 N.C. 126, 277 S.E.2d 347 (1981).

One who operates a vehicle at night without lights, or with improper lights, is negligent. Reeves v. Campbell, 264 N.C. 224, 141 S.E.2d 296 (1965).

Operation of a tractor-trailer on the highways at night without burning the rear and clearance lights required by this section is negligence per se. Thomas v. Thurston Motor Lines, 230 N.C. 122, 52 S.E.2d 377 (1949).

Riding a bicycle on the highway at night without a lamp of any kind on the front thereof is a violation of this section and is negligence per se. Oxendine v. Lowry, 260 N.C. 709, 133 S.E.2d 687 (1963). See also Miller v. Enzor, 17 N.C. App. 510, 195 S.E.2d 86, cert. denied, 283 N.C. 393, 196 S.E.2d 276 (1973).

The violation of a safety statute which results in injury or death will constitute culpable negligence if the violation is willful, wanton, or intentional. But where there is an unintentional or inadvertent violation of the statute, such violation standing alone does not constitute culpable negligence. The inadvertent or unintentional violation of the statute must be accompanied by recklessness of probable consequences of a dangerous nature, when tested by the rule of reasonable prevision, amounting altogether to a thoughtless disregard of consequences or of a heedless indifference to the safety of others. State v. Gooden, 65 N.C. App. 669, 309 S.E.2d 707 (1983), cert. denied, 311 N.C. 766, 321 S.E.2d 150 (1984).

VIOLATION AS MISDEMEANOR. --Violation of this section is a misdemeanor under G.S. 20-176. Williamson v. Varner, 252 N.C. 446, 114 S.E.2d 92 (1960).

VIOLATION AS BASIS FOR TRAFFIC STOP. --Though an officer mistakenly believed that the driver of vehicle with one defective brake light was violating former G.S. 20-129, which required only one functioning brake light, under the totality of the circumstances, the officer had a reasonable, articulable suspicion that G.S. 20-129 was being violated, and his mistake of law was objectively reasonable; therefore, the traffic stop did not violate defendant's rights under U.S. Const. amend. IV. State v. Heien, 366 N.C. 271, 737 S.E.2d 351 (2012).

Police officer's error of law in stopping a vehicle for a violation of G.S. 20-129(g) because one of its two brake lights was out was objectively reasonable, thereby justifying the stop, where the statute had not previously been construed by North Carolina's appellate courts, and under the language of the statute, it was reasonable to conclude that the use of the word "other" meant that the rear lamps discussed in G.S. 20-129(d) included brake lights. Heien v. North Carolina, 574 U.S. 54, 135 S. Ct. 530, 190 L. Ed. 2d 475 (2014).

Superior court properly refused to suppress the results of roadside sobriety tests and an intoxilyzer test because an officer had reasonable suspicion to justify prolonging the traffic stop to investigate defendant's potential impairment; the superior court's findings in conjunction with the findings on defendant's performance on the roadside sobriety tests supported a conclusion that the officer had probable cause to arrest defendant for driving while, which justified the intoxilyzer test. State v. Cole, 262 N.C. App. 466, 822 S.E.2d 456 (2018).

LIGHTS ON MOTOR VEHICLES SERVE TWO PURPOSES. --The lights required by this section serve two purposes: (1) To enable the operator of the automobile to see what is ahead of him; and (2) to inform others of the approach of the automobile. Reeves v. Campbell, 264 N.C. 224, 141 S.E.2d 296 (1965); Bigelow v. Johnson, 49 N.C. App. 40, 270 S.E.2d 503 (1980), 303 N.C. 126, 277 S.E.2d 347 (1981).

THE FUNCTION OF A FRONT LIGHT OR HEADLIGHT, defined by this section and G.S. 20-131, is to produce a driving light sufficient, under normal atmospheric conditions, to enable the operator to see a person 200 feet ahead. O'Berry v. Perry, 266 N.C. 77, 145 S.E.2d 321 (1965); Miller v. Wright, 272 N.C. 666, 158 S.E.2d 824 (1968).

THE ADEQUACY OF HEADLIGHTS upon a motor vehicle, in normal atmospheric conditions, is determined by this section and G.S. 20-131. Miller v. Wright, 272 N.C. 666, 158 S.E.2d 824 (1968).

MEANING OF "HEADLAMP" UNDER SUBSECTION (C). --The legislature intended that a "headlamp" within the contemplation of subsection (c) of this section and G.S. 20-131 should be one that was specifically designed and constructed for use as a headlamp, and a five-cell flashlight attached to a motorcycle falls short of the headlamp requirement. Bigelow v. Johnson, 303 N.C. 126, 277 S.E.2d 347 (1981).

Although subsection (c) of this section and G.S. 20-131(a) do not contain a specific definition of a "headlamp," the legislature's use of the term "headlamp" indicates that not just any light source possessing the requisite brightness will suffice. Bigelow v. Johnson, 303 N.C. 126, 277 S.E.2d 347 (1981).

THIS SECTION DOES NOT PROVIDE FOR HEADLAMP SUBSTITUTES, however powerful or reasonable. Bigelow v. Johnson, 49 N.C. App. 40, 270 S.E.2d 503 (1980), rev'd on other grounds, 303 N.C. 126, 277 S.E.2d 347 (1981).

OPPORTUNITY TO OBSERVE WHETHER HEADLAMPS WERE ON. --Testimony of the plaintiff that she stopped at an intersection, looked both ways, and did not see lights coming from either direction, was evidence from which the jury could conclude that defendant approached the intersection without lights, since the plaintiff had adequate opportunity to observe whether headlights were on. McLean v. Henderson, 45 N.C. App. 707, 264 S.E.2d 120 (1980).

PURPOSE OF FRONT LAMP ON BICYCLE. --Subsection (e) of this section, relating to front lamps on bicycles, is designed for the benefit of those approaching a bicycle from the front and for the protection of the bicyclist. Oxendine v. Lowry, 260 N.C. 709, 133 S.E.2d 687 (1963).

PURPOSE OF RED REFLECTOR ON BICYCLE. -- The red reflector required under subsection (e) of this section is designed to protect the bicyclist from vehicles approaching from the rear and to give notice to such vehicles of the presence of the bicycle ahead. Oxendine v. Lowry, 260 N.C. 709, 133 S.E.2d 687 (1963).

INTENSITY OF LIGHT UNDER SUBSECTION (E). --Subsection (e) of this section in no way requires a light of such intensity as to render objects visible along the highway in front of the bicycle. Oxendine v. Lowry, 260 N.C. 709, 133 S.E.2d 687 (1963).

BICYCLE BEING CARRIED BY PEDESTRIAN. --Where plaintiff's evidence was to the effect that at nighttime he was carrying a child's bicycle, too small for him to ride, across a street intersection to a repair shop, and that he was hit by a vehicle entering the intersection against the stoplight at a high rate of speed, refusal to give defendant's requested instruction that failure to have a light on the bicycle was a violation of this section was not error, since under the circumstances plaintiff was a pedestrian rather than a cyclist. Holmes v. Blue Bird Cab, Inc., 227 N.C. 581, 43 S.E.2d 71 (1947).

ABSENCE OF FRONT LAMP ON BICYCLE NOT PROXIMATE CAUSE OF REAR-END COLLISION. --Where plaintiff's evidence failed to show that his bicycle was equipped with a lighted lamp on the front thereof, but did show that he had a reflecting mirror on its rear, and that plaintiff's bicycle was hit from the rear by a car operated by defendant, and there was no evidence that if the bicycle had been equipped with a front lamp the lamp would have been visible to a person approaching in an automobile from the rear of the bicycle, the only legitimate inference was that the absence of a lighted lamp on the front of the bicycle was not a proximate or contributing proximate cause of the collision, and the court could properly charge the jury to this effect. Oxendine v. Lowry, 260 N.C. 709, 133 S.E.2d 687 (1963).

PARKING ON HIGHWAY WITHOUT LIGHTS 40 MINUTES BEFORE SUNRISE IS UNLAWFUL. Smith v. Nunn, 257 N.C. 108, 125 S.E.2d 351 (1962).

LIGHTS ON DISABLED VEHICLE. --A tractor-trailer standing on the paved portion of a highway at nighttime is required to have the rear and clearance lights burning as provided by this section, regardless of whether or not the vehicle is disabled within the meaning of G.S. 20-161(c). Thomas v. Thurston Motor Lines, 230 N.C. 122, 52 S.E.2d 377 (1949).

It is negligence to permit a disabled bus to stand on a highway at night without lights, blocking a lane of traffic, without giving warning to approaching vehicles. Dezern v. Asheboro City Bd. of Educ., 260 N.C. 535, 133 S.E.2d 204 (1963).

NEGLIGENCE IN DRIVING SCHOOL BUS WITHOUT CLEARANCE LIGHTS. --Instruction that defendant would be chargeable with negligence if he drove a school bus having a width in excess of 80 inches on the highway during the nighttime without displaying burning clearance lights thereon as required by this section, was correct, even though the duty to keep the lighting system on the vehicle in good working order may have rested on defendant's employer and not on defendant, as the latter was not empowered to set a positive statute at naught merely because his employer furnished him a vehicle with a defective lighting system. Hansley v. Tilton, 234 N.C. 3, 65 S.E.2d 300 (1951).

RIGHT OF MOTORIST TO ASSUME THAT OTHER VEHICLE WILL DISPLAY LIGHTS. --A motorist has the right to act upon the assumption that no other motorist will permit a motor vehicle either to move or to stand on the highway without displaying thereon the lights required by this section and G.S. 20-134, until he has notice to the contrary. Chaffin v. Brame, 233 N.C. 377, 64 S.E.2d 276 (1951); United States v. First-Citizens Bank & Trust Co., 208 F.2d 280 (4th Cir. 1953); Towe v. Stokes, 117 F. Supp. 880 (M.D.N.C.), aff'd, 214 F.2d 563 (4th Cir. 1954).

Until he saw, or by the exercise of due care should have seen, the approach of defendant's car, plaintiff was entitled to assume and to act upon the assumption that no motorist would be traveling without lights in violation of this section. White v. Lacey, 245 N.C. 364, 96 S.E.2d 1 (1957).

WHETHER OBSTRUCTION SHOULD HAVE BEEN SEEN IS JURY QUESTION. --Generally speaking, where the statutes, as this section, or the decisions of the courts, require red lights as a warning of danger on any object in the highway and such lights are not present, it is a question for the jury to determine whether the driver at night should have seen the obstruction, notwithstanding the absence of red lights. Morris v. Sells-Floto Circus, Inc., 65 F.2d 782 (4th Cir. 1933).

DEFENDANT WAS HELD ENTITLED TO AN INSTRUCTION, even in the absence of a request therefor, that if the jury found by the greater weight of the evidence that plaintiff stopped his car and permitted it to stand, without lights, on the paved portion of the road in defendant's right lane of travel, such conduct on the part of plaintiff would constitute negligence as a matter of law, and that if the jury found by the greater weight of the evidence that such negligence was a proximate cause of the collision and plaintiff's injuries, the jury was to answer the contributory negligence issue, "Yes." Correll v. Gaskins, 263 N.C. 212, 139 S.E.2d 202 (1964).

NEGLIGENCE IN NOT HAVING A LIGHT ON THE REAR OF A TRUCK WILL NOT PRECLUDE RECOVERY against one who drove his car into the truck, unless it contributed to the injury. Hughes v. Luther, 189 N.C. 841, 128 S.E. 145 (1925).

PLAINTIFF'S RECOVERY HELD BARRED BY CONTRIBUTORY NEGLIGENCE. --Where plaintiff's evidence tended to show that he was driving at night along a highway covered with smoke from fires along its side and that he collided with the rear of an oil truck which was headed in the same direction and which had been stopped on the highway without rear lights in violation of this section, it was held that, conceding negligence on the part of defendant, plaintiff's evidence disclosed contributory negligence barring recovery as a matter of law, either in driving at a speed in excess of that at which he could stop within the distance to which his lights would disclose the existence of obstructions, or, if he could have seen the oil truck in time to have avoided a collision, in failing to do so. Sibbitt v. R. & W. Transit Co., 220 N.C. 702, 18 S.E.2d 203 (1942).

EVIDENCE HELD SUFFICIENT FOR JURY. --Evidence tending to show that the headlights on defendant's car were defective, that he was driving at a speed of 60 to 65 miles an hour and that, in a sudden effort to avoid colliding with another automobile which had been backed into the highway and which was apparently not in motion at the time, defendant drove off the road, causing the car to overturn, and inflicting serious injury to plaintiff, a guest in the car, required submission of the case to the jury. Stewart v. Stewart, 221 N.C. 147, 19 S.E.2d 242 (1942).

Evidence that car in which plaintiff was riding as a guest struck defendant's trailer, which was standing across the highway in the car's lane of traffic, and that the trailer did not have burning the lights required by this section, was sufficient to overrule defendant's motion to nonsuit and motion for a directed verdict in its favor on the issue of negligence, since the question of proximate cause under the evidence is for the jury. Thomas v. Thurston Motor Lines, 230 N.C. 122, 52 S.E.2d 377 (1949).

FOR EVIDENCE SHOWING VIOLATION OF SECTION, see Powell v. Lloyd, 234 N.C. 481, 67 S.E.2d 664 (1951); White v. Mote, 270 N.C. 544, 155 S.E.2d 75 (1967).

APPLIED in McKinnon v. Howard Motor Lines, 228 N.C. 132, 44 S.E.2d 735 (1947); Pascal v. Burke Transit Co., 229 N.C. 435, 50 S.E.2d 534 (1948); Gantt v. Hobson, 240 N.C. 426, 82 S.E.2d 384 (1954) (as to subsection (d)); Punch v. Landis, 258 N.C. 114, 128 S.E.2d 224 (1962); Griffin v. Watkins, 269 N.C. 650, 153 S.E.2d 356 (1967); Williamson v. McNeill, 8 N.C. App. 625, 175 S.E.2d 294 (1970).

CITED in Newbern v. Leary, 215 N.C. 134, 1 S.E.2d 384 (1939); Pike v. Seymour, 222 N.C. 42, 21 S.E.2d 884 (1942); Morris v. Jenrette Transp. Co., 235 N.C. 568, 70 S.E.2d 845 (1952); Morgan v. Cook, 236 N.C. 477, 73 S.E.2d 296 (1952); Hollifield v. Everhart, 237 N.C. 313, 74 S.E.2d 706 (1953); Smith v. City of Kinston, 249 N.C. 160, 105 S.E.2d 648 (1958); Meece v. Dickson, 252 N.C. 300, 113 S.E.2d 578 (1960); Smith v. Goldsboro Iron & Metal Co., 257 N.C. 143, 125 S.E.2d 377 (1962); State Hwy. Comm'n v. Raleigh Farmers Mkt., Inc., 263 N.C. 622, 139 S.E.2d 904 (1965); C & H Transp. Co. v. North Carolina DMV, 34 N.C. App. 616, 239 S.E.2d 309 (1977); State v. Stewart, 40 N.C. App. 693, 253 S.E.2d 638 (1979); Butler v. Peters, 52 N.C. App. 357, 278 S.E.2d 283 (1981); Mobley v. Hill, 80 N.C. App. 79, 341 S.E.2d 46 (1986); State v. Veazey, 191 N.C. App. 181,

662 S.E.2d 683 (2008); State v. Heien, 226 N.C. App. 280, 741 S.E.2d 1, aff'd, 367 N.C. 163, 749 S.E.2d 278, 2013 N.C. LEXIS 1157 (2013); State v. Coleman, 228 N.C. App. 76, 743 S.E.2d 62 (2013); State v. Eldridge, 249 N.C. App. 493, 790 S.E.2d 740 (2016).

OPINIONS OF THE ATTORNEY GENERAL

ALL FARM TRAILERS MUST BE EQUIPPED WITH A STOP LAMP ACTIVATED BY THE FOOT BRAKE of the towing unit when operated upon the highways of this State. Additional lights or reflectors required depend on the time of day of operation, the atmospheric and weather conditions, the gross weight of the trailer and whether or not the trailer and load obscure the directional signals or stop light of the towing vehicle. See opinion of the Attorney General to Clyde R. Cook, Jr., Asst. Comm'r of Motor Vehicles, 60 N.C.A.G. 90 (1992).

§ 20-129.1. Additional lighting equipment required on certain vehicles

In addition to other equipment required by this Chapter, the following vehicles shall be equipped as follows:

(1) On every bus or truck, whatever its size, there shall be the following:

On the rear, two reflectors, one at each side, and two stop lamps, one at each side.

(2) On every bus or truck 80 inches or more in overall width, in addition to the requirements in subdivision (1):

On the front, two clearance lamps, one at each side.

On the rear, two clearance lamps, one at each side.

On each side, two side marker lamps, one at or near the front and one at or near the rear.

On each side, two reflectors, one at or near the front and one at or near the rear.

(3) On every truck tractor:

On the front, two clearance lamps, one at each side.

On the rear, two stop lamps, one at each side.

(4) On every trailer or semitrailer having a gross weight of 4,000 pounds or more:

On the front, two clearance lamps, one at each side.

On each side, two side marker lamps, one at or near the front and one at or near the rear.

On each side, two reflectors, one at or near the front and one at or near the rear.

On the rear, two clearance lamps, one at each side, also two reflectors, one at each side, and two stop lamps, one at each side.

(5) On every pole trailer having a gross weight of 4,000 pounds or more:

On each side, one side marker lamp and one clearance lamp which may be in combination, to show to the front, side and rear.

On the rear of the pole trailer or load, two reflectors, one at each side.

(6) On every trailer, semitrailer or pole trailer having a gross weight of less than 4,000 pounds:

On the rear, two reflectors, one on each side. If any trailer or semitrailer is so loaded or is of such dimensions as to obscure the stoplight on the towing vehicle, then such vehicle shall also be equipped with two stop lamps, one at each side.

(7) Front clearance lamps and those marker lamps and reflectors mounted on the front or on the side near the front of a vehicle shall display or reflect an amber color.

(8) Rear clearance lamps and those marker lamps and reflectors mounted on the rear or on the sides near the rear of a vehicle shall display or reflect a red color.

(9) Stop lamps (and/or brake reflectors) on the rear of a motor vehicle shall be constructed so that the light emitted, reflected, or displayed is red, except that a motor vehicle originally manufactured with amber stop lamps may emit, reflect, or display an amber light. The light illuminating the license plate shall be white. All other lights shall be white, amber, yellow, clear or red.

(10) On every trailer and semitrailer which is 30 feet or more in length and has a gross weight of 4,000 pounds or more, one combination marker lamp showing amber and mounted on the bottom side rail at or near the center of each side of the trailer.

History.
1955, c. 1157, s. 4; 1969, c. 387; 1983, c. 245; 1987, c. 363, s. 1; 2000-159, s. 10;2015-31, s. 2

EDITOR'S NOTE. --
Session Laws 2015-31, s. 3, made the amendment to this section by Session Laws 2015-31, s. 2, applicable to offenses committed on or after October 1, 2015.

EFFECT OF AMENDMENTS. --
Session Laws 2015-31, s. 2, effective October 1, 2015, substituted "two stop lamps, one at each side" for "one stoplight" throughout the section; and rewrote the first sentence of subdivision (9). For applicability, see editor's note.

THIS SECTION WAS ENACTED IN THE INTEREST OF PUBLIC SAFETY. Scarborough v. Ingram, 256 N.C. 87, 122 S.E.2d 798 (1961); Oxendine v. Lowry, 260 N.C. 709, 133 S.E.2d 687 (1963); White v. Mote, 270 N.C. 544, 155 S.E.2d 75 (1967).

VIOLATION OF THIS SECTION CONSTITUTES NEGLIGENCE AS A MATTER OF LAW. Scarborough v. Ingram, 256 N.C. 87, 122 S.E.2d 798 (1961); Oxendine v. Lowry, 260 N.C. 709, 133 S.E.2d 687 (1963); White v. Mote, 270 N.C. 544, 155 S.E.2d 75 (1967).

STATUTE DID NOT AUTHORIZE STOP OF DEFENDANT'S VEHICLE. --Defendant's Fourth Amendment rights were violated when defendant's vehicle was stopped due to a malfunctioning brake light because (1) G.S. 20-129(g) only required defendant to have one working brake light, which defendant did, (2) that statute did not require the vehicle's originally equipped stop lamps to be in good working order, as did G.S. 20-129(d), and (3) the malfunctioning brake light did not violate the safety inspection requirements of G.S. 20-183.3 or the requirements of G.S. 20-129.1. State v. Heien, 214 N.C. App. 515, 714 S.E.2d 827 (2011).

APPLIED in Smith v. Goldsboro Iron & Metal Co., 257 N.C. 143, 125 S.E.2d 377 (1962); State v. Heien, 366 N.C. 271, 737 S.E.2d 351 (2012).

CITED in Atkins v. Moye, 277 N.C. 174, 176 S.E.2d 729 (1970); Butler v. Peters, 52 N.C. App. 357, 278 S.E.2d 283 (1981); State v. Coleman, 228 N.C. App. 76, 743 S.E.2d 62 (2013).

§ 20-129.2. Lighting equipment for mobile homes

Notwithstanding the provisions of G.S. 20-129 and 20-129.1, the lighting equipment required to be provided and equipped on a house trailer, mobile home, modular home, or structural component thereof shall be as designated by the Commissioner of Motor Vehicles and from time to time promulgated by regulation of the Division.

History.
1975, c. 716, s. 5; c. 833, s. 1

§ 20-130. Additional permissible light on vehicle

(a) **Spot Lamps.** -- Any motor vehicle may be equipped with not to exceed two spot lamps, except that a motorcycle shall not be equipped with more than one spot lamp, and every lighted spot lamp shall be so aimed and used upon approaching another vehicle that no part of the beam will be directed to the left of the center of the highway nor more than 100 feet ahead of the vehicle. No spot lamps shall be used on the rear of any vehicle. For purposes of this section, the term "motorcycle" shall not include autocycles. Autocycles shall be subject to the requirements under this section for motor vehicles.

(b) **Auxiliary Driving Lamps.** -- Any motor vehicle may be equipped with not to exceed two auxiliary driving lamps mounted on the front, and every such auxiliary driving lamp or lamps shall meet the requirements and limitations set forth in G.S. 20-131, subsection (c).

(c) **Restrictions on Lamps.** -- Any device, other than headlamps, spot lamps, or auxiliary driving lamps, which projects a beam of light of an intensity greater than 25 candlepower, shall be so directed that no part of the beam will strike the level of the surface on which the vehicle stands at a distance of more than 50 feet from the vehicle.

(d) **Electronically Modulated Headlamps.** -- Nothing contained in this Chapter shall prohibit the use of electronically modulated headlamps on motorcycles, law-enforcement and fire department vehicles, county fire marshals and Emergency Management coordinators, public and private ambulances, and rescue squad emergency service vehicles, provided such headlamps and light modulator are of a type or kind which have been approved by the Commissioner of Motor Vehicles.

(e) **High Mounted Flashing Deceleration Lamps.** -- Public transit vehicles may be equipped with amber, high mounted, flashing deceleration lamps on the rear of the vehicle.

(f) **Light Bar Lighting Device.** -- Notwithstanding any provision of this section to the contrary, and excluding vehicles described in subsection (d) of this section, and excluding vehicles listed in G.S. 20-130.1(b), no person shall drive a motor vehicle on the highways of this State while using a light bar lighting device. This subsection does not apply to or otherwise restrict use of a light bar lighting device with strobing lights. For purposes of this subsection, the term "light bar lighting device" means a bar-shaped lighting device comprised of multiple lamps capable of projecting a beam of light at an intensity greater than that set forth in subsection (c) of this section.

History.

1937, c. 407, s. 93; 1977, c. 104; 1989, c. 770, s. 7;2004-82, s. 1;2015-163, s. 7;2017-112, s. 1

EDITOR'S NOTE. --

Session Laws 2015-163, s. 14, provides, in part: "Prosecutions for offenses committed before the effective date of this act are not abated or affected by this act, and the statutes that would be applicable but for this act remain applicable to those prosecutions."

Session Laws 2017-112, s. 2, made subsection (f), as added by Session Laws 2017-112, s. 1, effective October 1, 2017, and applicable to offenses committed on or after that date.

EFFECT OF AMENDMENTS. --

Session Laws 2004-82, s. 1, effective July 1, 2004, added subsection (e).

Session Laws 2015-163, s. 7, effective October 1, 2015, added the last two sentences of subsection (a).

Session Laws 2017-112, s. 1, added subsection (f). For effective date and applicability, see editor's note.

APPLIED in Bigelow v. Johnson, 49 N.C. App. 40, 270 S.E.2d 503 (1980).

§ 20-130.1. Use of red or blue lights on vehicles prohibited; exceptions

(a) It is unlawful for any person to install or activate or operate a red light in or on any vehicle in this State. As used in this subsection, unless the context requires otherwise, "red light" means an operable red light not sealed in the manufacturer's original package which: (i) is designed for use by an emergency vehicle or is similar in appearance to a red light designed for use by an emergency vehicle; and (ii) can be operated by use of the vehicle's battery, vehicle's electrical system, or a dry cell battery. As used in this subsection, the term "red light" shall also mean any red light installed on a vehicle after initial manufacture of the vehicle.

(b) The provisions of subsection (a) of this section do not apply to the following:

    (1) A police vehicle.

    (2) A highway patrol vehicle.

    (3) A vehicle owned by the Wildlife Resources Commission and operated exclusively for law enforcement, firefighting, or other emergency response purposes.

    (4) An ambulance.

    (5) A vehicle used by an organ procurement organization or agency for the recovery and transportation of blood, human tissues, or organs for transplantation.

    (6) A fire-fighting vehicle.

    (7) A school bus.

    (8) A vehicle operated by any member of a municipal or rural fire department in the performance of his duties, regardless of whether members of that fire department are paid or voluntary.

    (9) A vehicle of a voluntary lifesaving organization (including the private vehicles of the members of such an organization) that has been officially approved by the local police authorities and which is manned or operated by members of that organization while answering an official call.

    (10) A vehicle operated by medical doctors or anesthetists in emergencies.

    (11) A motor vehicle used in law enforcement by the sheriff, or any salaried rural policeman in any county, regardless of whether or not the county owns the vehicle.

    (11a) A vehicle operated by the State Fire Marshal or his representatives in the performance of their duties, whether or not the State owns the vehicle.

    (12) A vehicle operated by any county fire marshal, assistant fire marshal, or emergency management coordinator in the performance of his duties, regardless of whether or not the county owns the vehicle.

    (13) A light required by the Federal Highway Administration.

Chapter 20

(14) A vehicle operated by a transplant coordinator who is an employee of an organ procurement organization or agency when the transplant coordinator is responding to a call to recover or transport human tissues or organs for transplantation.

(15) A vehicle operated by an emergency medical service as an emergency support vehicle.

(16) A State emergency management vehicle.

(17) An Incident Management Assistance Patrol vehicle operated by the Department of Transportation, when using rear-facing red lights while stopped for the purpose of providing assistance or incident management.

(18) A vehicle operated by the Division of Marine Fisheries of the Department of Environmental Quality or the Division of Parks and Recreation of the Department of Natural and Cultural Resources that is used for law enforcement, firefighting, or other emergency response purpose.

(19) A vehicle operated by the North Carolina Forest Service of the Department of Agriculture and Consumer Services that is used for law enforcement, firefighting, or other emergency response purpose.

(20) A vehicle operated by official members or Teams of REACT International, Inc., that is used to provide additional manpower authorized by law enforcement, firefighting, or other emergency response entities.

(c) It is unlawful for any person to possess a blue light or to install, activate, or operate a blue light in or on any vehicle in this State, except for a publicly owned vehicle used for law enforcement purposes or any other vehicle when used by law enforcement officers in the performance of their official duties. As used in this subsection, unless the context requires otherwise, "blue light" means any blue light installed on a vehicle after initial manufacture of the vehicle; or an operable blue light which:

(1) Is not (i) being installed on, held in inventory for the purpose of being installed on, or held in inventory for the purpose of sale for installation on a vehicle on which it may be lawfully operated or (ii) installed on a vehicle which is used solely for the purpose of demonstrating the blue light for sale to law enforcement personnel;

(1a) Is designed for use by an emergency vehicle, or is similar in appearance to a blue light designed for use by an emergency vehicle; and

(2) Can be operated by use of the vehicle's battery, the vehicle's electrical system, or a dry cell battery.

(c1) The provisions of subsection (c) of this section do not apply to the possession and installation of an inoperable blue light on a vehicle that is inspected by and registered with the Department of Motor Vehicles as a specially constructed vehicle and that is used primarily for participation in shows, exhibitions, parades, or holiday/weekend activities, and not for general daily transportation. For purposes of this subsection, "inoperable blue light" means a blue-colored lamp housing or cover that does not contain a lamp or other mechanism having the ability to produce or emit illumination.

(d) Repealed by Session Laws 1999-249, s. 1.

(e) Violation of subsection (a) or (c) of this section is a Class 1 misdemeanor.

History.
1943, c. 726; 1947, c. 1032; 1953, c. 354; 1955, c. 528; 1957, c. 65, s. 11; 1959, c. 166, s. 2; c. 1170, s. 2; 1967, c. 651, s. 1; 1971, c. 1214; 1977, c. 52, s. 2; c. 438, s. 2; 1979, c. 653, s. 1; c. 887; 1983, c. 32, s. 1; c. 768, s. 6; 1985 (Reg. Sess., 1986), c. 1027, s. 50; 1989, c. 537, s. 2;1989 (Reg. Sess., 1990), c. 1020, s. 2; 1991, c. 263, s. 1;1993, c. 539, s. 361;1994, Ex. Sess., c. 24, s. 14(c);1993 (Reg. Sess., 1994), c. 719, s. 1; 1995, c. 168, s. 1;1995 (Reg. Sess., 1996), c. 756, s. 16; 1999-249, s. 1;2005-152, s. 1;2009-526, s. 1;2009-550, s. 3;2010-132, s. 11;2013-415, s. 1(b);2015-241, s. 14.30(ff);2015-276, s. 2
LOCAL MODIFICATION. --Macon: 1985, c. 231.

EDITOR'S NOTE. --
Session Laws 2015-276, s. 7, provides: "Sections 1 and 2 of this act become effective December 1, 2015, and apply to offenses committed on or after that date. The remainder of this act is effective when this act becomes law [October 20, 2015] and applies to offenses committed on or after that date. Prosecutions for offenses committed before the effective date of this act are not abated or affected by this act, and the statutes that would be applicable but for this act remain applicable to those prosecutions."

EFFECT OF AMENDMENTS. --
Session Laws 2009-526, s. 1, effective August 26, 2009, added subsection (c1).

Session Laws 2009-550, s. 3, effective August 28, 2009, also added subsection (c1).

Session Laws 2010-132, s. 11, effective December 1, 2010, and applicable to offenses committed on or after that date, added subdivision (b)(17) and made a related change.

Session Laws 2013-415, s. 1(b), effective October 1, 2013, substituted "law enforcement, firefighting, or other emergency response purposes" for "law-enforcement purposes" in subdivision (b)(3); added subdivisions (b)(18), (b)(19), and (b)(20); and made minor stylistic changes.

Session Laws 2015-241, s. 14.30(ff), effective July 1, 2015, in subdivision (b)(18), substituted "Fisheries of the Department of Environmental Quality" for "Fisheries" and substituted "Department of Natural and Cultural Resources" for "Department of Environment and Natural Resources."

Session Laws 2015-276, s. 2, effective December 1, 2015, deleted "forward facing" preceding "red light installed" in the last sentence of subsection (a); and deleted "forward facing" preceding "blue light installed" in the last sentence of the first undesignated paragraph of subsection (c). For applicability, see editor's note.

APPLICATION OF SECTION TO VEHICLES OPERATED AT TIME LIGHTS ARE REQUIRED. --While this section declares that it shall be unlawful to display red lights visible in front of a vehicle, it may be fairly assumed that the General Assembly intended the section to apply to vehicles operated at the time when lights are required, as provided in G.S. 20-129. Hollifield v. Everhart, 237 N.C. 313, 74 S.E.2d 706 (1953).

CITED in State v. Guarascio, 205 N.C. App. 548, 696 S.E.2d 704 (2010).

§ 20-130.2. Use of amber lights on certain vehicles; limited use

(a) All wreckers operated on the highways of the State shall be equipped with an amber-colored flashing light which shall be so mounted and located as to be clearly visible in all directions from a distance of 500 feet, which light shall be activated when at the scene of an accident or recovery operation and when towing a vehicle which has a total outside width exceeding 96 inches or which exceeds the width of the towing vehicle. It shall be lawful to equip any other vehicle with a similar warning light including, but not by way of limitation, maintenance or construction vehicles or equipment of the Department of Transportation engaged in performing maintenance or construction work on the roads, maintenance or construction vehicles of any person, firm or corporation, Radio Emergency Associated Citizens Team (REACT) vehicles, and any other vehicles required to contain a warning light.

(b) Except as otherwise permitted under this Article, it shall be unlawful for any vehicle to operate a flashing or strobing amber light while in motion on a street or highway unless one of the following conditions apply:

(1) A law enforcement vehicle when in route to an emergency or when engaged in the chase or apprehension of violators of the law or of persons charged with or suspected of any violation.

(2) A fire, rescue, first responder, or emergency response vehicle in route to an emergency situation, when traveling in response to a fire alarm or responding to any other incident warranting the use of emergency lights and siren.

(3) When any vehicle, or vehicle's load exceeds a width of 102 inches, including oversize loads in accordance with G.S. 20-116.

(4) When the use of flashing or strobing lights is required by the Department of Transportation.

(5) When the vehicle must travel 15 miles per hour or more below the posted speed limit for safety reasons or is otherwise impeding traffic which could cause a danger to the public, in performing the vehicle's intended service, including waste management vehicles, utility vehicles, school buses, farm equipment, mail delivery vehicles, or any vehicle being used in a work zone.

(6) During a state of emergency declared by the Governor.

History.
1967, c. 651, s. 2; 1973, c. 507, s. 5; 1977, c. 464, s. 34; 1979, c. 1; c. 765; 1981, c. 390; 1991, c. 44, s. 1;2019-157, s. 3

EDITOR'S NOTE. --
Session Laws 2019-157, s. 1, provides: "This act shall be known and may be cited as the 'Officer Jason Quick Act.'"

Session Laws 2019-157, s. 4, makes subsection (b) of this section as added by Session Laws 2019-157, s. 3, effective December 1, 2019, and applicable to offenses committed on or after that date.

EFFECT OF AMENDMENTS. --
Session Laws 2019-157, s. 3, effective December 1, 2019, substituted "vehicles; limited use" for "vehicles" in the section heading; designated the existing provisions as subsection (a); and added subsection (b). For effective date and applicability, see editor's note.

CITED in Leisure Prods., Inc. v. Clifton, 44 N.C. App. 233, 260 S.E.2d 803 (1979).

§ 20-130.3. Use of white or clear lights on rear of vehicles prohibited; exceptions

It shall be unlawful for any person to willfully drive a motor vehicle in forward motion upon the highways of this State displaying white or clear lights on the rear of said vehicle. The provisions of this section shall not apply to the white light required by G.S. 20-129(d) or so-called backup lights lighted only when said vehicle is in reverse gear or backing. Violation of this section does not constitute negligence per se in any civil action.

History.
1973, c. 1071

§ 20-131. Requirements as to headlamps and auxiliary driving lamps

(a) The headlamps of motor vehicles shall be so constructed, arranged, and adjusted that, except as provided in subsection (c) of this section, they will at all times mentioned in G.S. 20-129, and under normal atmospheric conditions and on a level road, produce a driving light sufficient to render clearly discernible a person 200 feet ahead, but any person operating a motor vehicle upon the highways, when meeting another vehicle, shall so control the lights of the vehicle operated by him by shifting, depressing, deflecting, tilting, or dimming the headlight beams in such manner as shall not project a glaring or dazzling light to persons within a distance of 500 feet in front of such headlamp. Every new motor vehicle, other than a motorcycle or motor-driven cycle, registered in this State after January 1, 1956, which has multiple-beam road-lighting equipment shall be equipped with a beam indicator, which shall be lighted whenever the uppermost distribution of light from the headlamps is in use, and shall not otherwise be lighted. Said indicator shall be so designed and located that when lighted it will be readily visible without glare to the driver of the vehicle so equipped. For purposes of this section, the term "motorcycle" shall not include autocycles. Autocycles shall be subject to the requirements under this section for motor vehicles.

(b) Headlamps shall be deemed to comply with the foregoing provisions prohibiting glaring and dazzling lights if none of the main bright portion of the headlamp beams rises above a horizontal plane passing through the lamp centers parallel to the level road upon which the loaded vehicle stands, and in no case higher than 42 inches, 75 feet ahead of the vehicle.

(c) Whenever a motor vehicle is being operated upon a highway, or portion thereof, which is sufficiently lighted to reveal a person on the highway at a distance of 200 feet ahead of the vehicle, it shall be permissible to dim the headlamps or to tilt the beams downward or to substitute therefor the light from an auxiliary driving lamp or pair of such lamps, subject to the restrictions as to tilted beams and auxiliary driving lamps set forth in this section.

(d) Whenever a motor vehicle meets another vehicle on any highway it shall be permissible to tilt the beams of the headlamps downward or to substitute therefor the light from an auxiliary driving lamp or pair of such lamps subject to the requirement that the tilted headlamps or auxiliary lamp or lamps shall give sufficient illumination under normal atmospheric conditions and on a level road to render clearly discernible a person 75 feet ahead, but shall not project a glaring or dazzling light to persons in front of the vehicle: Provided, that at all times required in G.S. 20-129 at least two lights shall be displayed on the front of and on opposite sides of every motor vehicle other than a motorcycle, road roller, road machinery, or farm tractor.

(e) No city or town shall enact an ordinance in conflict with this section.

History.
1937, c. 407, s. 94; 1939, c. 351, s. 1; 1955, c. 1157, ss. 6, 7; 2015-163, s. 8

EDITOR'S NOTE. --
Session Laws 2015-163, s. 14, provides, in part: "Prosecutions for offenses committed before the effective date of this act are not abated or affected by this act, and the statutes that would be applicable but for this act remain applicable to those prosecutions."

EFFECT OF AMENDMENTS. --
Session Laws 2015-163, s. 8, effective October 1, 2015, added the last two sentences of subsection (a).

REQUIREMENTS OF SUBSECTION (A) AND G.S. 20-129(E) DISTINGUISHED. --The requirement of subsection (e) of G.S. 20-129 is entirely different from the requirement for motor vehicles, when used at night, as set forth in subsection (a) of this section. Oxendine v. Lowry, 260 N.C. 709, 133 S.E.2d 687 (1963).

MEANING OF "HEADLAMP." --The legislature intended that a "headlamp" within the contemplation of G.S. 20-129(c) and this section should be one that was specifically designed and constructed for use as a headlamp, and a five-cell flashlight attached to a motorcycle falls short of the headlamp requirement. Bigelow v. Johnson, 303 N.C. 126, 277 S.E.2d 347 (1981). Although G.S. 20-129(c) and subsection (a) of this section do not contain a specific definition of a "headlamp," the legislature's use of the term "headlamp" indicates that not just any light source possessing the requisite brightness will suffice. Bigelow v. Johnson, 303 N.C. 126, 277 S.E.2d 347 (1981).

THE FUNCTION OF A FRONT LIGHT OR HEADLIGHT, defined by G.S. 20-129 and this section, is to produce a driving light sufficient, under normal atmospheric conditions, to enable the operator to see a person 200 feet ahead. O'Berry v. Perry, 266 N.C. 77, 145 S.E.2d 321 (1965); Miller v. Wright, 272 N.C. 666, 158 S.E.2d 824 (1968).

THE FUNCTION OF A PARKING LIGHT is to enable a vehicle parked or stopped upon the highway to be seen under similar conditions from a distance of 500 feet to the front of such vehicle. O'Berry v. Perry, 266 N.C. 77, 145 S.E.2d 321 (1965).

THE ADEQUACY OF HEADLIGHTS upon a motor vehicle, in normal atmospheric conditions, is determined by this section and G.S. 20-129. Miller v. Wright, 272 N.C. 666, 158 S.E.2d 824 (1968).

PERMISSIBILITY OF DIMMING LIGHTS FOR BETTER VISIBILITY. --The duty of a motorist to dim or deflect his headlights is not restricted by this section solely to instances in which he is meeting oncoming traffic, since this section refers to "normal atmospheric conditions"; therefore, it may be permissible for a motorist to deflect his headlights when driving in fog or other atmospheric conditions in which deflected headlights afford better visibility. Short v. Chapman, 261 N.C. 674, 136 S.E.2d 40 (1964).

PERSONS LYING OR SLEEPING ON HIGHWAY. --As the law does not require a motorist to anticipate that a person may be lying or sleeping on the travelled portion of the highway, this statute does not require that persons lying or sleeping on the highway be rendered clearly discernible as human beings by motor vehicle headlights. Sink v. Sumrell, 41 N.C. App. 242, 254 S.E.2d 665 (1979).

PLAINTIFFS' RECOVERY HELD BARRED BY CONTRIBUTORY NEGLIGENCE. --In an action for damages due to negligence of defendants, where the evidence showed that plaintiffs, on a joint enterprise, driving their car about 2:00 A. M., at 40 or 45 miles per hour, with lights dimmed so that they could not see ahead over 75 to 100 feet, never applied the brakes and failed to see defendants' truck until after the collision, crashing into the back of the truck with terrific force, plaintiffs were guilty of contributory negligence which was a proximate cause of the accident, thereby barring their recovery. Pike v. Seymour, 222 N.C. 42, 21 S.E.2d 884 (1942).

DUTY OF DRIVER IS NOT MERELY TO LOOK BUT TO KEEP LOOKOUT. --It is the duty of the driver of a motor vehicle not merely to look, but to keep a lookout, in the direction of travel, and he is held to the duty of seeing what he ought to have seen. When a motorist travels into a completely blinded area for two or three seconds, with the knowledge that his vision has failed him, such behavior will be contributory negligence as a matter of law. Williams v. Hall, 100 N.C. App. 655, 397 S.E.2d 767 (1990).

DIRECTED VERDICT ON ISSUE OF CONTRIBUTORY NEGLIGENCE WAS IMPROPER where plaintiff testified that he was not completely blinded by the oncoming headlights as he approached the tractor-trailer and he could see much more than the edge of the road; the plaintiff may have been keeping a proper lookout without realizing that he was partially blinded only as to the area beyond the tractor-trailers' headlights. In such a deceptive visual situation, the plaintiff may not have knowingly driven into the blinded area, for it would have appeared as though he could see into the distant darkness. From the evidence there was insufficient evidence to establish that plaintiff was contributorily negligent as a matter of law. Williams v. Hall, 100 N.C. App. 655, 397 S.E.2d 767 (1990).

JURY QUESTION. --Whether or not defendant knew or should have known that the position of his cab and lights could blind oncoming drivers was a question for the jury. Williams v. Hall, 100 N.C. App. 655, 397 S.E.2d 767 (1990).

APPLIED in Cronenberg v. United States, 123 F. Supp. 693 (E.D.N.C. 1954); Williamson v. McNeill, 8 N.C. App. 625, 175 S.E.2d 294 (1970).

CITED in Newbern v. Leary, 215 N.C. 134, 1 S.E.2d 384 (1939); Singletary v. Nixon, 239 N.C. 634, 80 S.E.2d 676 (1954); as to subsections (a) and (d), in Keener v. Beal, 246 N.C. 247, 98 S.E.2d 19 (1957); Smith v. City of Kinston, 249 N.C. 160, 105 S.E.2d 648 (1958); Meeks v. Atkeson, 7 N.C. App. 631, 173 S.E.2d 509 (1970); Schaefer v. Wickstead, 88 N.C. App. 468, 363 S.E.2d 653 (1988).

CROSS REFERENCES. --
As to failure to dim headlights not being cause for suspension or revocation of driver's license, see G.S. 20-18. As to penalties imposed for failure to dim headlights, see G.S. 20-181.

§ 20-132. Acetylene lights

Motor vehicles eligible for a Historic Vehicle Owner special registration plate under G.S. 20-79.4 may be equipped with two acetylene headlamps of approximately equal candlepower when equipped with clear plane-glass fronts, bright six-inch spherical mirrors, and standard acetylene five-eighths foot burners not more and not less and which do not project a glaring or dazzling light into the eyes of approaching drivers.

History.
1937, c. 407, s. 95; 1995, c. 379, s. 18.1

§ 20-133. Enforcement of provisions

(a) The Commissioner is authorized to designate, furnish instructions to and to supervise official stations for adjusting headlamps and auxiliary driving lamps to conform with the provisions of G.S. 20-129. When headlamps and auxiliary driving lamps have been adjusted in conformity with the instructions issued by the Commissioner, a certificate of adjustment shall be issued to the driver of the motor vehicle on forms issued in duplicate by the Commissioner and showing date of issue, registration number of the motor vehicle, owner's name, make of vehicle and official designation of the adjusting station.

(b) The driver of any motor vehicle equipped with approved headlamps, auxiliary driving lamps, rear lamps or signal lamps, who is arrested upon a charge that such lamps are improperly adjusted or are equipped with bulbs of a candlepower not approved for use therewith, shall be allowed 48 hours within which to bring such lamps into conformance with the requirements of this Article. It shall be a defense to any such charge that the person arrested produce in court or submit to the prosecuting attorney a certificate from an official adjusting station showing that within 48 hours after such arrest such lamps have been made to conform with the requirements of this Article.

History.
1937, c. 407, s. 96

§ 20-134. Lights on parked vehicles

(a) Whenever a vehicle is parked or stopped upon a highway, whether attended or unattended during the times mentioned in G.S. 20-129, there shall be displayed upon such vehicle one or more lamps projecting a white or amber light visible under normal atmospheric conditions from a distance of 500 feet to the front of such vehicle, and projecting a red light visible under like conditions from a distance of 500 feet to the rear, except that local authorities may provide by ordinance that no lights need be displayed upon any such vehicle when parked in accordance with local ordinances upon a highway where there is sufficient light to reveal any person within a distance of 200 feet upon such highway.

(b) A motor vehicle operated on a highway by a rural letter carrier or by a newspaper delivery person shall be equipped and operated with flashing amber lights at any time the vehicle is being used in the delivery of mail or newspapers, regardless of whether the vehicle is attended or unattended.

History.
1937, c. 407, s. 97; 1959, c. 1264, s. 9; 1995 (Reg. Sess., 1996), c. 715, s. 1

PURPOSE OF SECTION. --This section is designed to promote safe use of the public highways. Beasley v. Williams, 260 N.C. 561, 133 S.E.2d 227 (1963).

EFFECT OF G.S. 20-161. --G.S. 20-161 does not conflict with nor reduce the obligation imposed on the operator of a motor vehicle stopped or parked on the highway at night to light his vehicle as required by this section and G.S. 20-129. Melton v. Crotts, 257 N.C. 121, 125 S.E.2d 396 (1962).

THIS SECTION IS INAPPLICABLE TO A MOTOR VEHICLE PARKED IN A RESIDENTIAL DISTRICT IN A CITY OR TOWN on a street which constitutes no part of the highway system. Smith v. Goldsboro Iron & Metal Co., 257 N.C. 143, 125 S.E.2d 377 (1962).

The provisions of this section are not applicable to defendants' truck parked or stopped on a street in the city when plaintiff has neither allegation nor proof to show that the street forms a part of the State highway system. Coleman v. Burris, 265 N.C. 404, 144 S.E.2d 241 (1965).

THE FUNCTION OF A PARKING LIGHT is to enable a vehicle parked or stopped upon the highway to be seen under similar conditions from a distance of 500 feet to the front of such vehicle. O'Berry v. Perry, 266 N.C. 77, 145 S.E.2d 321 (1965).

RIGHT OF MOTORIST TO ASSUME THAT OTHER VEHICLE WILL DISPLAY LIGHTS. --A motorist has the right to act upon the assumption that no other motorist will permit a motor vehicle either to move or to stand on the highway without displaying thereon the lights required by this section and G.S. 20-129, until he has notice to the contrary. Chaffin v. Brame, 233 N.C. 377, 64 S.E.2d 276 (1951); United States v. First-Citizens Bank & Trust Co., 208 F.2d 280 (4th Cir. 1953); Towe v. Stokes, 117 F. Supp. 880 (M.D.N.C.), aff'd, 214 F.2d 563 (4th Cir. 1954).

A VIOLATION OF THIS SECTION IS NEGLIGENCE PER SE. Correll v. Gaskins, 263 N.C. 212, 139 S.E.2d 202 (1964); Faison v. T & S Trucking Co., 266 N.C. 383, 146 S.E.2d 450 (1966); Edwards v. Mayes, 385 F.2d 369 (4th Cir. 1967); King v. Allred, 60 N.C. App. 380, 299 S.E.2d 248, rev'd on other grounds, 309 N.C. 113, 305 S.E.2d 554 (1983).

Parking on a paved highway at night, without flares or other warning, is negligence. Allen v. Dr. Pepper Bottling Co., 223 N.C. 118, 25 S.E.2d 388 (1943).

BUT IT IS NOT NECESSARILY UNLAWFUL IN ALL CASES TO PARK A VEHICLE AT NIGHT ON THE PAVED PORTION OF A HIGHWAY WITHOUT LIGHTS THEREON, as an emergency may arise thereby making it impossible to move such vehicle immediately. Pike v. Seymour, 222 N.C. 42, 21 S.E.2d 884 (1942).

IT WAS NEGLIGENCE TO PERMIT A DISABLED BUS TO STAND ON A HIGHWAY AT NIGHT without lights, blocking a lane of traffic, without giving warning to approaching vehicles. Dezern v. Asheboro City Bd. of Educ., 260 N.C. 535, 133 S.E.2d 204 (1963).

LEAVING A DISABLED MARINE CORPS WRECKER STANDING ON THE HIGHWAY in the nighttime without the lights and warning signals required by this section and G.S. 20-161 constituted negligence. United States v. First-Citizens Bank & Trust Co., 208 F.2d 280 (4th Cir. 1953).

PROXIMATE CAUSE AS A JURY QUESTION. --It is for the jury to decide whether, upon the evidence, a violation of this statute was a proximate cause of decedent's injuries. Edwards v. Mayes, 385 F.2d 369 (4th Cir. 1967).

The parking of a truck on a public highway at night without lights in violation of the statute is negligence per se, and the question of proximate cause is for the determination of the jury. Barrier v. Thomas & Howard Co., 205 N.C. 425, 171 S.E. 626 (1933), decided under corresponding section of former law.

EVIDENCE HELD SUFFICIENT FOR SUBMISSION TO JURY. --Evidence that the driver of a car left the vehicle standing unattended without lights at nighttime, partially on the hard surface, and that plaintiff was unable to stop before striking the rear of the vehicle when he first saw it upon resuming his bright lights after dimming his lights in response to oncoming traffic, was sufficient to be submitted to the jury on the issue of negligence. Beasley v. Williams, 260 N.C. 561, 133 S.E.2d 227 (1963).

DEFENDANT WAS ENTITLED TO AN INSTRUCTION, even in the absence of a request therefor, that if the jury found by the greater weight of the evidence that plaintiff stopped his car and permitted it to stand, without lights, on the paved portion of the road in defendant's right lane of travel, such conduct on the part of the plaintiff would constitute negligence as a matter of law, and that if the jury find by the greater weight of the evidence that such negligence was a proximate cause of the collision and plaintiff's injuries, the jury should answer the contributory negligence issue, "Yes." Correll v. Gaskins, 263 N.C. 212, 139 S.E.2d 202 (1964).

APPLIED in Bumgardner v. Allison, 238 N.C. 621, 78 S.E.2d 752 (1953); Kinsey v. Town of Kenly, 263 N.C. 376, 139 S.E.2d 686 (1965); King v. Allred, 309 N.C. 113, 305 S.E.2d 554 (1983); State v. Gooden, 65 N.C. App. 669, 309 S.E.2d 707 (1983).

CITED in McKinnon v. Howard Motor Lines, 228 N.C. 132, 44 S.E.2d 735 (1947); Keener v. Beal, 246

Chapter 20

N.C. 247, 98 S.E.2d 19 (1957); Vann v. Hayes, 266 N.C. 713, 147 S.E.2d 186 (1966); Puryear v. Cooper, 2 N.C. App. 517, 163 S.E.2d 299 (1968); Brown v. Boren Clay Prods. Co., 5 N.C. App. 418, 168 S.E.2d 452 (1969); Atkins v. Moye, 277 N.C. 179, 176 S.E.2d 789 (1970); McNair v. Boyette, 282 N.C. 230, 192 S.E.2d 457 (1972); Williamson v. Basinger, 30 N.C. App. 50, 226 S.E.2d 213 (1976); Thomas v. Deloatch, 45 N.C. App. 322, 263 S.E.2d 615 (1980); State v. Heien, 214 N.C. App. 515, 714 S.E.2d 827 (2011).

§ 20-135. Safety glass

(a) It shall be unlawful to operate knowingly, on any public highway or street in this State, any motor vehicle which is registered in the State of North Carolina and which shall have been manufactured or assembled on or after January 1, 1936, unless such motor vehicle be equipped with safety glass wherever glass is used in doors, windows, windshields, wings or partitions; or for a dealer to sell a motor vehicle manufactured or assembled on or after January 1, 1936, for operation upon the said highways or streets unless it be so equipped. The provisions of this Article shall not apply to any motor vehicle if such motor vehicle shall have been registered previously in another state by the owner while the owner was a bona fide resident of said other state.

(b) The term "safety glass" as used in this Article shall be construed as meaning glass so treated or combined with other materials as to reduce, in comparison with ordinary sheet glass or plate glass, the likelihood of injury to persons by glass when the glass is cracked or broken.

(c) The Division of Motor Vehicles shall approve and maintain a list of the approved types of glass, conforming to the specifications and requirements for safety glass as set forth in this Article, and in accordance with standards recognized by the United States Bureau of Standards, and shall not issue a license for or relicense any motor vehicle subject to the provisions of this Article unless such motor vehicle be equipped as herein provided with such approved type of glass.

(d) Repealed by Session Laws 1985, c. 764, s. 26.

History.

1937, c. 407, s. 98; 1941, c. 36; 1975, c. 716, s. 5; 1985, c. 764, s. 26; 1985 (Reg. Sess., 1986), c. 852, s. 17

N.C. Gen. Stat. § 20-135.1

Repealed by Session Laws 1995 (Regular Session, 1996), c. 756, s. 30.

§ 20-135.2. Safety belts and anchorages

(a) Every new motor vehicle registered in this State and manufactured, assembled, or sold after January 1, 1964, shall, at the time of registration, be equipped with at least two sets of seat safety belts for the front seat of the motor vehicle. Such seat safety belts shall be of such construction, design, and strength to support a loop load strength of not less than 5,000 pounds for each belt, and must be of a type approved by the Commissioner.

This subsection shall not apply to passenger motor vehicles having a seating capacity in the front seat of less than two passengers.

(b) After July 1, 1962, no seat safety belt shall be sold for use in connection with the operation of a motor vehicle on any highway of this State unless it shall be constructed and installed as to have a loop strength through the complete attachment of not less than 5,000 pounds and the buckle or closing device shall be of such construction and design that after it has received the aforesaid loop belt load it can be released with one hand with a pull of less than 45 pounds.

(c) The provisions of this section shall apply only to passenger vehicles of nine-passenger capacity or less, except motorcycles.

(d) For purposes of this section, the term "motorcycle" shall not include autocycles. Every autocycle registered in this State shall be equipped with seat safety belts for the front seats of the autocycle. The seat safety belts shall meet the same construction, design, and strength requirements under this section for seat safety belts in motor vehicles.

History.

1961, c. 1076; 1963, c. 288; 2015-163, s. 9

EDITOR'S NOTE. --

Session Laws 2015-163, s. 14, provides, in part: "Prosecutions for offenses committed before the effective date of this act are not abated or affected by this act, and the statutes that would be applicable but for this act remain applicable to those prosecutions."

EFFECT OF AMENDMENTS. --

Session Laws 2015-163, s. 9, effective October 1, 2015, added subsection (d).

NO STATUTORY DUTY TO USE SEAT BELTS. --Seat belt enactments are not absolute safety measures, and no statutory duty to use the belts can be implied from them. Miller v. Miller, 273 N.C. 228, 160 S.E.2d 65 (1968).

FAILURE OF A GUEST PASSENGER TO USE AN AVAILABLE SEAT BELT DOES NOT CONSTITUTE CONTRIBUTORY NEGLIGENCE barring recovery by the passenger for personal injuries received in an automobile accident caused by defendant driver's negligence. Miller v. Miller, 273 N.C. 228, 160 S.E.2d 65 (1968).

NOR DOES IT INVOKE DOCTRINE OF AVOIDABLE CONSEQUENCES. --The doctrine of avoidable consequences is not invoked by the failure of plaintiff guest passenger to use an available seat belt, since the failure to fasten the seat belt occurs before

Chapter 20

defendant's negligence. Miller v. Miller, 273 N.C. 228, 160 S.E.2d 65 (1968).

TRAFFIC STOP. --Initiation of a traffic stop was justified by a deputy's observation that defendant was not wearing his seatbelt as a passenger of a moving vehicle in violation of G.S. 20-135.2A(a). Because the deputy's conduct of asking defendant, who was unable to provide any identification, to exit the vehicle and frisking him for weapons did not extend the traffic stop's duration in any way, an additional showing that the deputy had reasonable suspicion of another crime was unnecessary. State v. Jones, 264 N.C. App. 225, 825 S.E.2d 260 (2019).

APPLIED in Calloway v. Ford Motor Co., 281 N.C. 496, 189 S.E.2d 484 (1972).

§ 20-135.2A. (See Editor's note) Seat belt use mandatory

(a) Except as otherwise provided in G.S. 20-137.1, each occupant of a motor vehicle manufactured with seat belts shall have a seatbelt properly fastened about his or her body at all times when the vehicle is in forward motion on a street or highway in this State.

(b) Repealed by Session Laws 2006-140, s. 1, effective December 1, 2006.

(c) This section shall not apply to any of the following:

(1) A driver or occupant of a noncommercial motor vehicle with a medical or physical condition that prevents appropriate restraint by a safety belt or with a professionally certified mental phobia against the wearing of vehicle restraints.

(2) A motor vehicle operated by a rural letter carrier of the United States Postal Service while performing duties as a rural letter carrier and a motor vehicle operated by a newspaper delivery person while actually engaged in delivery of newspapers along the person's specified route.

(3) A driver or passenger frequently stopping and leaving the vehicle or delivering property from the vehicle if the speed of the vehicle between stops does not exceed 20 miles per hour.

(4) Any vehicle registered and licensed as a property-carrying vehicle in accordance with G.S. 20-88, while being used for agricultural purposes in intrastate commerce.

(5) A motor vehicle not required to be equipped with seat safety belts under federal law.

(6) Any occupant of a motor home, as defined in G.S. 20-4.01(27)k, other than the driver and front seat passengers.

(7) Any occupant, while in the custody of a law enforcement officer, being transported in the backseat of a law enforcement vehicle.

(8) A passenger of a residential garbage or recycling truck while the truck is operating during collection rounds.

(d) Evidence of failure to wear a seat belt shall not be admissible in any criminal or civil trial, action, or proceeding except in an action based on a violation of this section or as justification for the stop of a vehicle or detention of a vehicle operator and passengers.

(d1) Failure of a rear seat occupant of a vehicle to wear a seat belt shall not be justification for the stop of a vehicle.

(e) Any driver or front seat passenger who fails to wear a seat belt as required by this section shall have committed an infraction and shall pay a penalty of twenty-five dollars and fifty cents ($ 25.50) plus the following court costs: the General Court of Justice fee provided for in G.S. 7A-304(a)(4), the telephone facilities fee provided for in G.S. 7A-304(a)(2a), and the law enforcement training and certification fee provided for in G.S. 7A-304(a)(3b). Any rear seat occupant of a vehicle who fails to wear a seat belt as required by this section shall have committed an infraction and shall pay a penalty of ten dollars ($ 10.00) and no court costs. Court costs assessed under this section are for the support of the General Court of Justice and shall be remitted to the State Treasurer. Conviction of an infraction under this section has no other consequence.

(f) No drivers license points or insurance surcharge shall be assessed on account of violation of this section.

(g) The Commissioner of Motor Vehicles and the Department of Public Instruction shall incorporate in driver education programs and driver licensing programs instructions designed to encourage compliance with this section as an important means of reducing the severity of injury to the users of restraint devices and on the requirements and penalties specified in this law.

(h) Repealed by Session Laws 1999-183, s. 3, effective October 1, 1999.

History.
1985, c. 222, s. 1; 1987, c. 623; 1991, c. 448, s. 1; 1994, Ex. Sess., c. 5, s. 1; 1997-16, s. 2; 1997-443, s. 32.20; 1999-183, ss. 1 -3; 2002-126, s. 29A.3(a); 2005-276, s. 43.1(g); 2006-66, s. 21.11; 2006-140, s. 1; 2006-221, s. 21(a); 2007-289, s. 1; 2007-404, s. 2; 2009-376, s. 12; 2009-451, s. 15.20(j); 2017-102, s. 5.2(b)

EDITOR'S NOTE. —
Session Laws 1985, c. 222, s. 2 made this section effective October 1, 1985. Section 2 further provides that the act shall cease to be effective if, and upon such date as, a final determination by lawful authority is made that the North Carolina law on mandatory safety belt usage does not meet the minimum criteria established by the United States Department of Transportation for State mandatory safety belt usage

laws necessary to rescind the federal rule requiring automobile manufacturers to phase in automatic occupant restraints in automobiles.

Session Laws *1997-16, s. 10* provides that this act does not appropriate funds to the Division to implement this act nor does it obligate the General Assembly to appropriate funds to implement this act.

Session Laws *2006-221, s. 21(a)*, provided that if Senate Bill 774 of the 2005 Regular Session [2006-140] becomes law, Session Laws *2006-66, s. 21.11* is repealed. Therefore subsection 20-135.2A(c) is set out above as amended by Session Laws 2006-140.

Session Laws *2017-102, s. 5.2(b)* provides: "The Revisor of Statutes is authorized to reletter the definitions in *G.S. 20-4.01(27)* and *G.S. 20-4.01(32b)* to place them in alphabetical order. The Revisor of Statutes may conform any citations that change as a result of the relettering." Pursuant to that authority, the reference to *G.S. 20-4.01(27)*d2. in subdivision (c) (6) was changed to *G.S. 20-4.01(27)*k.

EFFECT OF AMENDMENTS. —

Session Laws *2002-126, s. 135.2A(e)*, effective October 1, 2002, rewrote subsection (e). See editor's note.

Session Laws *2005-276, s. 43.1(g)*, effective September 1, 2005, and applicable to all costs assessed or collected on or after that date, substituted "seventy-five dollars ($75.00)" for "fifty dollars ($50.00)" in subsection (e).

Session Laws *2006-140, s. 1*, effective December 1, 2006, substituted "Except as otherwise provided in G.S. 20-137.1, each occupant of a" for "Each front seat occupant who is 16 years of age or older and each driver of a passenger" in subsection (a); repealed subsection (b); inserted "of a non commercial motor vehicle" in subdivision (c)(1); substituted "purposes in intrastate commerce" for "or commercial purposes" in subdivision (c)(4); made minor punctuation changes in subdivision (c)(5); added subdivision (c)(6) and subsection (d1); in subsection (e), inserted "front seat" near the beginning of the first sentence and inserted the second sentence; deleted "the Division of" following "The Commissioner of" in subsection (g).

Session Laws *2007-289, s. 1*, effective July 27, 2007, in subsection (c), substituted a period for a semicolon at the end of subdivisions (c)(1) through (c)(5) and added subdivision (c)(7).

Session Laws *2007-404, s. 2*, effective December 1, 2007, added subdivision (c)(8).

Session Laws *2009-376, s. 12*, effective October 1, 2009, and applicable to civil penalties assessed and offenses committed on or after that date, in subdivision (c)(8), deleted "driver or" preceding "passenger" near the beginning, and deleted "and while traveling to and from garbage and recycling material loading and unloading locations" from the end.

LEGISLATIVE INTENT. —

It is not entirely clear that, by enacting this section, the North Carolina legislature created an evidentiary privilege as contemplated by *F.R. Evid., Rule 501. United States v. Cartledge, 928 F.2d 93 (4th Cir. 1991),* rev'd on other grounds, *928 F.2d 93 (4th Cir. 1991).*

CONSTITUTIONALITY. —

Defendant failed to show that this section was an unreasonable, arbitrary, or capricious restriction on the operator or passenger in a passenger vehicle; the statute clearly contributes in a reasonable manner to the safety of travel on the streets and highways of the State, and is, therefore, a proper exercise of the police power of the *State by the General Assembly. State v. Swain, 92 N.C. App. 240, 374 S.E.2d 173 (1988).*

COMMON LAW RULE REGARDING INADMISSIBILITY OF SEATBELT EVIDENCE. —

North Carolina has a strong common law rule, now codified by statute, that evidence that a plaintiff did not fasten his seatbelt is inadmissible in any civil action. *Barron v. Ford Motor Co. of Canada Ltd., 965 F.2d 195 (7th Cir.),* cert. denied, *506 U.S. 1001, 113 S. Ct. 605, 121 L. Ed. 2d 541 (1992).*

The clearest articulation of North Carolina's common law rule against seatbelt evidence holds not that such evidence is inadmissible on all issues, but only that it is inadmissible to establish the plaintiff's failure to exercise due care to minimize the consequences of an accident should one occur. *Barron v. Ford Motor Co. of Canada Ltd., 965 F.2d 195 (7th Cir.),* cert. denied, *506 U.S. 1001, 113 S. Ct. 605, 121 L. Ed. 2d 541 (1992).*

The common law rule is founded on the desire of the North Carolina courts not to penalize the failure to fasten one's seatbelt, because nonuse is so rampant in the State that the average person could not be thought careless for failing to fasten his seatbelt. *Barron v. Ford Motor Co. of Canada Ltd., 965 F.2d 195 (7th Cir.),* cert. denied, *506 U.S. 1001, 113 S. Ct. 605, 121 L. Ed. 2d 541 (1992).*

INFANTS. —

Evidence that an infant killed in a car accident was improperly sitting on the lap of, and within the seat belt of, the occupant of the front passenger's seat was not admissible in a personal injury and wrongful death action arising out of the accident. *Chaney v. Young, 122 N.C. App. 260, 468 S.E.2d 837 (1996).*

LITERAL INTERPRETATION OF SUBSECTION (D) MAY BE INCORRECT. —This section is a mandatory seatbelt law, and evidence of nonuse can of course be introduced in a proceeding to impose a penalty for violation of the law. But if the statute is read literally, that is the only type of proceeding in which such evidence can be introduced. The literal interpretation of North Carolina's rule, though, is almost certainly incorrect. *In State v. Brewer, 328 N.C. 515, 522, 402 S.E.2d 380, 385 (1991),* a prosecution of a woman for murdering her disabled daughter by abandoning her car with the daughter in it on a railroad crossing, the Supreme Court of North Carolina remarked, without criticism, the introduction of evidence that the daughter knew how to release her seatbelt; it never occurred to anyone that such evidence might be inadmissible. *Barron v. Ford Motor Co. of Canada Ltd., 965 F.2d 195 (7th Cir.),* cert. denied, *506 U.S. 1001, 113 S. Ct. 605, 121 L. Ed. 2d 541 (1992).*

THIS SECTION PRECLUDES THE INTRODUCTION OF ANY EVIDENCE REGARDING SEAT

BELT USE, regardless of any knowledge of a specific hazard. *Hagwood v. Odom, 88 N.C. App. 513, 364 S.E.2d 190 (1988).*

The evidence of the failure of the defendant to use her seat belt was not admissible in a DWI trial. *State v. Williams, 113 N.C. App. 686, 440 S.E.2d 324 (1994).*

In an action arising from an automobile accident, a statutory prohibition in Conn. *Gen. Stat. §§ 14-100a(c) (3)* and *14-222* regarding evidence of contributory negligence based on failure to use a seat belt also applied to the misuse of a seat belt based on case law in other jurisdictions interpreting similar provisions, such as *G.S. 20-135.2A(d)* and *G.S. 20-137.1(d)* and *Kan. Stat. Ann. §§ 60-258a* and 8-1344. Ferentzy v. Ferentzy, (Aug. 4, 2008).

THIS SECTION PRECLUDES ANY INSTRUCTION TO THE JURY WHICH WOULD ALLOW MITIGATION OF DAMAGES for failure to wear a seat belt. *Hagwood v. Odom, 88 N.C. App. 513, 364 S.E.2d 190 (1988).*

UNDER THE LAW THAT OBTAINED PRIOR TO THIS SECTION, a motorist was not contributorily negligent for failure to use his seat belt unless the motorist with prior knowledge of a specific hazard, one not generally associated with highway travel, had failed or refused to fasten his seat belt. *Hagwood v. Odom, 88 N.C. App. 513, 364 S.E.2d 190 (1988).*

Under the law that obtained prior to this section, the failure to fasten one's seat belt could not be held to be a breach of the duty to minimize damages, as the duty to minimize damages arises only after the negligent act of defendant, and a plaintiff's failure to fasten his seat belt necessarily occurs before defendant's allegedly negligent act. *Hagwood v. Odom, 88 N.C. App. 513, 364 S.E.2d 190 (1988).*

USE OF EVIDENCE OF VIOLATION IS LIMITED. —

Although failure to wear a seat belt is a traffic violation under this section, subsection (d) prohibits using evidence of the seat belt violation other than in proceedings to enforce the traffic violation. *United States v. Cartledge, 928 F.2d 93 (4th Cir. 1991).*

NON-USE OF SEAT BELTS PROBABLE CAUSE. —

Officer had probable cause to stop vehicle in which defendant was a passenger where officer observed that neither the driver or the defendant passenger were wearing seat belts. Likewise, the officer was allowed to ask defendant passenger to exit the vehicle. *State v. Hamilton, 125 N.C. App. 396, 481 S.E.2d 98 (1997),* appeal dismissed and cert. denied, *345 N.C. 757, 485 S.E.2d 302 (1997).*

Police officer had probable cause pursuant to *U.S. Const., amend. IV* and *N.C. Const., Art. I, § 20* to stop defendant's vehicle because the officer witnessed defendant remove his seat belt while driving, a violation of *G.S. 20-135.2A(a). State v. Hernandez, 170 N.C. App. 299, 612 S.E.2d 420 (2005).*

DRIVER'S VIOLATION OF *G.S. 20-135.2A* DID NOT PROVIDE PROBABLE CAUSE TO ARREST DRIVER FOR VIOLATING *G.S. 14-223.* —In a *42 U.S.C.S. § 1983* case in which a university police

officer moved for summary judgment, asserting that he was entitled to qualified immunity, because a driver's violation of *G.S. 20-135.2A* did not provide probable cause to arrest the driver for violating *G.S. 14-223,* the officer's conduct in arresting him violated the driver's Fourth Amendment right. However, as the officer made a bad guess in a gray area as to whether the driver's actions violated *G.S. 14-223,* the right was not clearly established as required by the second prong of the Saucier test. *Bostic v. Rodriguez, 667 F. Supp. 2d 591 (E.D.N.C. 2009).*

FOR CASE HOLDING TRAFFIC STOP NOT PRETEXTUAL where officer stopped defendant on premise that defendant was not wearing a seat belt, see *State v. Morocco, 99 N.C. App. 421, 393 S.E.2d 545 (1990).*

IN THE 1987 AMENDMENT TO SUBSECTION (D) not only did the General Assembly retain the exclusion of the seat belt defense in civil cases, but expanded the act so as to exclude evidence of the failure to have a fastened seat belt in place in other criminal proceedings. *State v. Williams, 113 N.C. App. 686, 440 S.E.2d 324 (1994).*

CITED in *State v. McClendon, 130 N.C. App. 368, 502 S.E.2d 902 (1998); State v. Brewington, 170 N.C. App. 264, 612 S.E.2d 648 (2005),* cert. denied, *360 N.C. 67, 621 S.E.2d 881 (2005); State v. Cox, 253 N.C. App. 306, 800 S.E.2d 692 (2017),* review denied, *803 S.E.2d 153, 2017 N.C. LEXIS 579 (N.C. 2017).*

LEGAL PERIODICALS. —

For note, "The Seat Belt Defense and North Carolina's New Mandatory Usage Law." See 64 N.C.L. Rev. 1127 (1986).

§ 20-135.2B. Transporting children under 16 years of age in open bed or open cargo area of a vehicle prohibited; exceptions

(a) The operator of a vehicle having an open bed or open cargo area shall ensure that no child under 16 years of age is transported in the bed or cargo area of that vehicle. An open bed or open cargo area is a bed or cargo area without permanent overhead restraining construction.

(b) Subsection (a) of this section does not apply in any of the following circumstances:

(1) An adult is present in the bed or cargo area of the vehicle and is supervising the child.

(2) The child is secured or restrained by a seat belt manufactured in compliance with Federal Motor Vehicle Safety Standard No. 208, installed to support a load strength of not less than 5,000 pounds for each belt, and of a type approved by the Commissioner.

(3) An emergency situation exists.

(4) The vehicle is being operated in a parade.

(5) The vehicle is being operated in an agricultural enterprise, including providing transportation to and from the principal place of the agricultural enterprise.

(6) Repealed by Session Laws 2008-216, s. 1, effective October 1, 2008.

(c) Any person violating this section shall have committed an infraction and shall pay a penalty of not more than twenty-five dollars ($ 25.00), even if more than one child less than 16 years of age is riding in the open bed or open cargo area of a vehicle. A person found responsible for a violation of this section may not be assessed court costs.

(d) No drivers license points or insurance surcharge shall be assessed on account of violation of this section. A violation of this section shall not constitute negligence per se.

History.
1993 (Reg. Sess., 1994), c. 672, s. 1; 1995, c. 163, s. 7;1999-183, s. 4;2008-216, s. 1

EFFECT OF AMENDMENTS. --
Session Laws 2008-216, s. 1, effective October 1, 2008, and applicable to offenses committed on or after that date, substituted "16" for "12" in the section heading; in subsection (a), substituted "ensure" for "insure" and substituted "16" for "12"; deleted "pursuant to a valid permit" following "parade" in subdivision (b)(4); added "including providing transportation to and from the principal place of the agricultural enterprise" in subdivision (b)(5); deleted subdivision (b)(6) which read: "The vehicle is being operated in a county that has no incorporated area with a population in excess of 3,500"; rewrote subsection (c); and added the second sentence in subsection (d).

CIVIL ACTIONS BASED ON ALLEGED VIOLATION --Trial court properly dismissed an injured party's claim against a church and a landowner, alleging that the church and the landowner where negligent because they allowed children younger than 12 years old to ride on an open flatbed trailer during a church festival in violation of G.S. 20-135.2B, because the festival occurred on private property and G.S. 20-135.2B did not apply to activities that occurred on private property. Clontz v. St. Mark's Evangelical Lutheran Church, 157 N.C. App. 325, 578 S.E.2d 654, cert. denied, 357 N.C. 249, 582 S.E.2d 29 (2003).

CITED in State v. Veazey, 191 N.C. App. 181, 662 S.E.2d 683 (2008).

§ 20-135.3. Seat belt anchorages for rear seats of motor vehicles

(a) Every new motor vehicle registered in this State and manufactured, assembled or sold after July 1, 1966, shall be equipped with sufficient anchorage units at the attachment points for attaching at least two sets of seat safety belts for the rear seat of the motor vehicle. Such anchorage units at the attachment points shall be of such construction, design, and strength to support a loop load strength of not less than 5,000 pounds for each belt.

(b) The provisions of this section shall apply to passenger vehicles of nine-passenger capacity or less, except motorcycles.

(c) For purposes of this section, the term "motorcycle" shall not include autocycles. Every autocycle registered in this State shall be equipped with sufficient anchorage units at the attachment points for attaching seat safety belts for the rear seats of the autocycle. The anchorage unit shall meet the same construction, design, and strength requirements under this section for anchorage units in motor vehicles.

History.
1965, c. 372; 2015-163, s. 10;2016-90, s. 12.5(c)

EDITOR'S NOTE. --
Session Laws 2015-163, s. 14, provides, in part: "Prosecutions for offenses committed before the effective date of this act are not abated or affected by this act, and the statutes that would be applicable but for this act remain applicable to those prosecutions."

EFFECT OF AMENDMENTS. --
Session Laws 2015-163, s. 10, effective October 1, 2015, designated existing language as subsections (a) and (b); added subsection (c); and made minor stylistic change in subsection (a).

Session Laws 2016-90, s. 12.5(c), effective July 11, 2016, near the end of the second sentence in subsection (c), substituted "seats" for "seat."

§ 20-135.4. Certain automobile safety standards

(a) **Definitions. --** For the purposes of this section, the term "private passenger automobile" shall mean a four-wheeled motor vehicle designed principally for carrying passengers, for use on public roads and highways, except a multipurpose passenger vehicle which is constructed either on a truck chassis or with special features for occasional off-road operation.

(b), (c) Repealed by Session Laws 1975, c. 856.

(d) The manufacturer's specified height of any passenger motor vehicle shall not be elevated or lowered, either in front or back, more than six inches by modification, alteration, or change of the physical structure of said vehicle without prior written approval of the Commissioner of Motor Vehicles.

On or after January 1, 1975, no self-propelled passenger vehicle that has been so altered, modified or changed shall be operated upon any highway or public vehicular area without the prior written approval of the Commissioner.

History.
1971, c. 485; 1973, cc. 58, 1082; 1975, c. 856

OPINIONS OF THE ATTORNEY GENERAL
AS TO APPLICABILITY TO SPECIFIC VEHICLE, AND NONPREEMPTION BY FEDERAL LEGISLATION, see opinion of Attorney General to Mr. Joe W.

Garrett, Commissioner of Motor Vehicles, 41 N.C.A.G. 677 (1971).

§ 20-136. Smoke screens

(a) It shall be unlawful for any person or persons to drive, operate, equip or be in the possession of any automobile or other motor vehicle containing, or in any manner provided with, a mechanical machine or device designed, used or capable of being used for the purpose of discharging, creating or causing, in any manner, to be discharged or emitted, either from itself or from the automobile or other motor vehicle to which attached, any unusual amount of smoke, gas or other substance not necessary to the actual propulsion, care and keep of said vehicle, and the possession by any person or persons of any such device, whether the same is attached to any such motor vehicle, or detached therefrom, shall be prima facie evidence of the guilt of such person or persons of a violation of this section.

(b) Any person or persons violating the provisions of this section shall be guilty of a Class I felony.

History.
1937, c. 407, s. 99; 1993, c. 539, s. 1257;1994, Ex. Sess., c. 24, s. 14(c)

§ 20-136.1. Location of television, computer, or video players, monitors, and screens

No person shall drive any motor vehicle upon a public street or highway or public vehicular area while viewing any television, computer, or video player which is located in the motor vehicle at any point forward of the back of the driver's seat, and which is visible to the driver while operating the motor vehicle. This section does not apply to the use of global positioning systems; turn-by-turn navigation displays or similar navigation devices; factory-installed or aftermarket global positioning systems or wireless communications devices used to transmit or receive data as part of a digital dispatch system; equipment that displays audio system information, functions, or controls, or weather, traffic, and safety information; vehicle safety or equipment information; or image displays that enhance the driver's view in any direction, inside or outside of the vehicle. The provisions of this section shall not apply to law enforcement or emergency personnel while in the performance of their official duties, or to the operator of a vehicle that is lawfully parked or stopped.

History.
1949, c. 583, s. 4; 2009-376, s. 13

EFFECT OF AMENDMENTS. --
Session Laws 2009-376, s. 13, effective October 1, 2009, and applicable to civil penalties assessed and offenses committed on or after that date, rewrote the section.

§ 20-136.2. Counterfeit supplemental restraint system components and nonfunctional airbags

(a) It shall be unlawful for any person, firm, or corporation to knowingly import, manufacture, sell, offer for sale, distribute, install or reinstall a counterfeit supplemental restraint system or nonfunctional airbag in any motor vehicle, or other component device that causes a motor vehicle to fail to meet federal motor vehicle safety standards as provided in 49 C.F.R. § 571.208. Any person, firm, or corporation violating this section shall be guilty of a Class 1 misdemeanor, and violation constitutes an unfair and deceptive trade practice under G.S. 75-1.1. If a violation of this section contributes to a person's physical injury or death, the person, firm, or corporation violating this section shall be guilty of a Class H felony. For purposes of this section, in the event that a franchised motor vehicle dealer, as defined in G.S. 20-286(8b) or its owners, have no actual knowledge that a counterfeit supplemental restraint system component, nonfunctional airbag, or other component device has been imported, manufactured, sold, offered for sale, installed, or reinstalled in lieu of a supplemental restraint system component at the franchised motor vehicle dealer's place of business or elsewhere, knowledge by any other person shall not be imputed to the franchised motor vehicle dealer or its owners, and the franchised motor vehicle dealer or its owners shall not be deemed to have committed an unlawful act under this section and shall not have any criminal liability under this section.

(b) Nothing in this section is intended to prohibit automotive dealers, repair professionals, recyclers, original equipment manufacturers, or contractors from disposing of counterfeit supplemental restraint system components or nonfunctional airbags in accordance with federal and State law.

History.
2003-258, s. 3;2019-155, s. 3
EDITOR'S NOTE. --
Session Laws 2019-155, s. 4, makes the amendments to this section by Session Laws 2019-155, s. 3, effective October 1, 2019, and applicable to offenses committed on or after that date.
EFFECT OF AMENDMENTS. --
Session Laws 2019-155, s. 3, effective October 1, 2019, rewrote this section. For effective date and applicability, see editor's note.

N.C. Gen. Stat. § 20-137

Repealed by Session Laws 1995, c. 379, s. 18.2.

§ 20-137.1. Child restraint systems required

(a) Every driver who is transporting one or more passengers of less than 16 years of age shall have all such passengers properly secured in a child passenger restraint system or seat belt which meets federal standards applicable at the time of its manufacture.

(a1) A child less than eight years of age and less than 80 pounds in weight shall be properly secured in a weight-appropriate child passenger restraint system. In vehicles equipped with an active passenger-side front air bag, if the vehicle has a rear seat, a child less than five years of age and less than 40 pounds in weight shall be properly secured in a rear seat, unless the child restraint system is designed for use with air bags. If no seating position equipped with a lap and shoulder belt to properly secure the weight-appropriate child passenger restraint system is available, a child less than eight years of age and between 40 and 80 pounds may be restrained by a properly fitted lap belt only.

(b) The provisions of this section shall not apply: (i) to ambulances or other emergency vehicles; (ii) if all seating positions equipped with child passenger restraint systems or seat belts are occupied; or (iii) to vehicles which are not required by federal law or regulation to be equipped with seat belts.

(c) Any driver found responsible for a violation of this section may be punished by a penalty not to exceed twenty-five dollars ($ 25.00), even when more than one child less than 16 years of age was not properly secured in a restraint system. No driver charged under this section for failure to have a child under eight years of age properly secured in a restraint system shall be convicted if he produces at the time of his trial proof satisfactory to the court that he has subsequently acquired an approved child passenger restraint system for a vehicle in which the child is normally transported.

(d) A violation of this section shall have all of the following consequences:

(1) Two drivers license points shall be assessed pursuant to G.S. 20-16.

(2) No insurance points shall be assessed.

(3) The violation shall not constitute negligence per se or contributory negligence per se.

(4) The violation shall not be evidence of negligence or contributory negligence.

History.

1981, c. 804, ss. 1, 4, 5; 1985, c. 218; 1993 (Reg. Sess., 1994), c. 748, s. 1; 1999-183, ss. 6, 7; 2000-117, s. 1;2004-191, ss. 1, 2; 2007-6, s. 1

EDITOR'S NOTE. --
Session Laws 1981, c. 804, s. 6, provided: "This act shall become effective on July 1, 1982, and shall expire on June 30, 1985." The section was subsequently rewritten by Session Laws 1985, c. 218, effective July 1, 1985, and hence did not expire.

EFFECT OF AMENDMENTS. --
Session Laws 2004-191, ss. 1 and 2, effective January 1, 2005, substituted "eight years" for "five years" in subsections (a1) and (c), in subsection (a1), substituted "80 pounds" for "40 pounds," and added the last sentence; and added "for a vehicle in which the child is normally transported" at the end of the last sentence of subsection (c).

Session Laws 2007-6, s. 1, effective June 1, 2007, and applicable to offenses committed on or after that date, in subsection (b), deleted "(ii) when the child's personal needs are being attended to" and redesignated items (iii) and (iv) as items (ii) and (iii), respectively.

REGULATIONS PROMULGATED BY THE STATE DIVISION OF MOTOR VEHICLES designed to insure that manufacturers comply with applicable standards for child passenger restraint systems by requiring verification of any equipment regulated by this section are preempted by the National Motor Vehicle Safety Act of 1966, 15 U.S.C.A. § 1381 et seq., as amended. Juvenile Prods. Mfrs. Ass'n v. Edmisten, 568 F. Supp. 714 (E.D.N.C. 1983).

EVIDENCE OF CONTRIBUTORY NEGLIGENCE. --In an action arising from an automobile accident, a statutory prohibition in Conn.Gen. Stat. §§ 14-100a(c)(3) and 14-222 regarding evidence of contributory negligence based on failure to use a seat belt also applied to the misuse of a seat belt based on case law in other jurisdictions interpreting similar provisions, such as G.S. 20-135.2A(d) and G.S. 20-137.1(d) and Kan. Stat. Ann. §§ 60-258a and 8-1344. Ferentzy v. Ferentzy, (Aug. 4, 2008).

FAILURE TO RESTRAIN CHILD HELD NOT ACTIONABLE NEGLIGENCE. --Mother's failure to fasten her child in a child restraint system as required by this section as it existed at the time of the accident did not constitute actionable negligence and was therefore not the proximate cause of death of child. Thus, mother could not be held jointly liable for damages awarded to the child's estate in wrongful death action against other driver. State Farm Mut. Auto. Ins. Co. v. Holland, 324 N.C. 466, 380 S.E.2d 100 (1989) (decided under prior law).

IMPROPER RESTRAINT. --Evidence that an infant killed in a car accident was improperly sitting on the lap of, and within the seat belt of, the occupant of the front passenger's seat was not admissible in a personal injury and wrongful death action arising out of the accident. Chaney v. Young, 122 N.C. App. 260, 468 S.E.2d 837 (1996).

CITED in State v. Cox, 253 N.C. App. 306, 800 S.E.2d 692 (2017), review denied, 803 S.E.2d 153, 2017 N.C. LEXIS 579 (N.C. 2017).

§ 20-137.2. Operation of vehicles resembling law-enforcement vehicles unlawful; punishment

(a) It is unlawful for any person other than a law-enforcement officer of the State or of any county, municipality, or other political subdivision thereof, with the intent to impersonate a law-enforcement officer, to operate any vehicle, which by its coloration, insignia, lettering, and blue or red light resembles a vehicle owned, possessed, or operated by any law-enforcement agency.

(b) Violation of subsection (a) of this section is a Class 1 misdemeanor.

History.
1979, c. 567, s. 1; 1993, c. 539, s. 362; 1994, Ex. Sess., c. 24, s. 14(c)

§ 20-137.3. Unlawful use of a mobile phone by persons under 18 years of age

(a) **Definitions.** -- The following definitions apply in this section:

(1) **Additional technology.** -- Any technology that provides access to digital media including, but not limited to, a camera, music, the Internet, or games. The term does not include electronic mail or text messaging.

(2) **Mobile telephone.** -- A device used by subscribers and other users of wireless telephone service to access the service. The term includes: (i) a device with which a user engages in a call using at least one hand, and (ii) a device that has an internal feature or function, or that is equipped with an attachment or addition, whether or not permanently part of the mobile telephone, by which a user engages in a call without the use of either hand, whether or not the use of either hand is necessary to activate, deactivate, or initiate a function of such telephone.

(3) **Wireless telephone service.** -- A service that is a two-way real-time voice telecommunications service that is interconnected to a public switched telephone network and is provided by a commercial mobile radio service, as such term is defined by 47 C.F.R. § 20.3.

(b) **Offense.** -- Except as otherwise provided in this section, no person under the age of 18 years shall operate a motor vehicle on a public street or highway or public vehicular area while using a mobile telephone or any additional technology associated with a mobile telephone while the vehicle is in motion. This prohibition shall not apply to the use of a mobile telephone or additional technology in a stationary vehicle.

(c) **Seizure.** -- The provisions of this section shall not be construed as authorizing the seizure or forfeiture of a mobile telephone, unless otherwise provided by law.

(d) **Exceptions.** -- The provisions of subsection (b) of this section shall not apply if the use of a mobile telephone is for the sole purpose of communicating with:

(1) Any of the following regarding an emergency situation: an emergency response operator; a hospital, physician's office, or health clinic; a public or privately owned ambulance company or service; a fire department; or a law enforcement agency.

(2) The motor vehicle operator's parent, legal guardian or spouse.

(e) **Penalty.** -- Any person violating this section shall have committed an infraction and shall pay a fine of twenty-five dollars (\$ 25.00). This offense is an offense for which a defendant may waive the right to a hearing or trial and admit responsibility for the infraction pursuant to G.S. 7A-148. No drivers license points, insurance surcharge, or court costs shall be assessed as a result of a violation of this section.

History.
2006-177, s. 1; 2009-135, s. 1
EFFECT OF AMENDMENTS. --
Session Laws 2009-135, s. 1, effective December 1, 2009, and applicable to offenses committed on or after that date, in subdivision (a)(1), substituted "including, but not limited to, a camera, music" for "such as a camera, electronic mail, music" in the first sentence, and added the second sentence.
CITED in King v. Town of Chapel Hill, 367 N.C. 400, 758 S.E.2d 364 (2014).

§ 20-137.4. Unlawful use of a mobile phone

(a) **Definitions.** -- For purposes of this section, the following terms shall mean:

(1) **Additional technology.** -- As defined in G.S. 20-137.3(a)(1).

(2) **Emergency situation.** -- Circumstances such as medical concerns, unsafe road conditions, matters of public safety, or mechanical problems that create a risk of harm for the operator or passengers of a school bus.

(3) **Mobile telephone.** -- As defined in G.S. 20-137.3(a)(2).

(4) **School bus.** -- As defined in G.S. 20-4.01(27)n. The term also includes any school activity bus as defined in G.S. 20-4.01(27)m. and any vehicle transporting public, private, or parochial school students for compensation.

(b) **Offense.** -- Except as otherwise provided in this section, no person shall operate a school bus on a public street or highway or public vehicular area while using a mobile telephone or any additional technology associated with a mobile telephone while the school bus is in motion. This prohibition shall not apply to the use of a mobile telephone or additional technology associated with a mobile telephone in a stationary school bus.

(c) **Seizure.** -- The provisions of this section shall not be construed as authorizing the seizure or forfeiture of a mobile telephone or additional technology, unless otherwise provided by law.

(d) **Exceptions.** -- The provisions of subsection (b) of this section shall not apply to the use of a mobile telephone or additional technology associated with a mobile telephone for the sole purpose of communicating in an emergency situation.

(e) **Local Ordinances.** -- No local government may pass any ordinance regulating the use of mobile telephones or additional technology associated with a mobile telephone by operators of school buses.

(f) **Penalty.** -- A violation of this section shall be a Class 2 misdemeanor and shall be punishable by a fine of not less than one hundred dollars ($ 100.00). No drivers license points or insurance surcharge shall be assessed as a result of a violation of this section. Failure to comply with the provisions of this section shall not constitute negligence per se or contributory negligence by the operator in any action for the recovery of damages arising out of the operation, ownership, or maintenance of a school bus.

History.
2007-261, s. 1;2017-102, s. 5.2(b)
EDITOR'S NOTE. --
Session Laws 2007-261, s. 2, made this section effective December 1, 2007, and applicable to offenses committed on or after that date.

Session Laws 2017-102, s. 5.2(b) provides: "The Revisor of Statutes is authorized to reletter the definitions in G.S. 20-4.01(27) and G.S. 20-4.01(32b) to place them in alphabetical order. The Revisor of Statutes may conform any citations that change as a result of the relettering." Pursuant to that authority, the references to G.S. 20-4.01(27)d4. and d3. in subdivision (a)(4) were changed to G.S. 20-4.01(27)n. and m., respectively.

CONSTRUCTION. --While not entirely dispositive, the broadly worded title of G.S. 20-137.4 -- "Unlawful use of a mobile phone" -- tends to indicate an expansive intent to regulate, thus precluding municipalities from doing so. King v. Town of Chapel Hill, 367 N.C. 400, 758 S.E.2d 364 (2014).

§ 20-137.4A. Unlawful use of mobile telephone for text messaging or electronic mail

(a) **Offense.** -- It shall be unlawful for any person to operate a vehicle on a public street or highway or public vehicular area while using a mobile telephone to:

(1) Manually enter multiple letters or text in the device as a means of communicating with another person; or

(2) Read any electronic mail or text message transmitted to the device or stored within the device, provided that this prohibition shall not apply to any name or number stored in the device nor to any caller identification information.

(a1) **Motor Carrier Offense.** -- It shall be unlawful for any person to operate a commercial motor vehicle subject to Part 390 or 392 of Title 49 of the Code of Federal Regulations on a public street or highway or public vehicular area while using a mobile telephone or other electronic device in violation of those Parts. Nothing in this subsection shall be construed to prohibit the use of hands-free technology.

(b) **Exceptions.** -- The provisions of this section shall not apply to:

(1) The operator of a vehicle that is lawfully parked or stopped.

(2) Any of the following while in the performance of their official duties: a law enforcement officer; a member of a fire department; or the operator of a public or private ambulance.

(3) The use of factory-installed or aftermarket global positioning systems (GPS) or wireless communications devices used to transmit or receive data as part of a digital dispatch system.

(4) The use of voice operated technology.

(c) **Penalty.** -- A violation of this section while operating a school bus, as defined in G.S. 20-137.4(a)(4), shall be a Class 2 misdemeanor and shall be punishable by a fine of not less than one hundred dollars ($ 100.00). Any other violation of this section shall be an infraction and shall be punishable by a fine of one hundred dollars ($ 100.00) and the costs of court.

No drivers license points or insurance surcharge shall be assessed as a result of a violation of this section. Failure to comply with the provisions of this section shall not constitute negligence per se or contributory negligence per se by the operator in any action for the recovery of damages arising out of the operation, ownership, or maintenance of a vehicle.

History.
2009-135, s. 2;2012-78, s. 9
EFFECT OF AMENDMENTS. --
Session Laws 2012-78, s. 9, effective December 1, 2012, added subsection (a1). For applicability, see Editor's notes.

CITED in King v. Town of Chapel Hill, 367 N.C. 400, 758 S.E.2d 364 (2014).

§ 20-137.5. Child passenger safety technician; limitation of liability

(a) The following definitions apply in this section:

(1) **Certified child passenger safety technician.** -- A certified child passenger safety technician is an individual who has successfully completed the U.S. Department of Transportation National Highway Traffic Safety Administration's (NHTSA) National Standardized Child Passenger Safety Certification Training Program and who maintains a current child passenger safety technician or technician instructor certification through the current certifying body for the National Child Passenger Safety Training Program as designated by the National Highway Traffic Safety Administration.

(2) **Sponsoring organization.** -- A sponsoring organization is a person or organization other than a manufacturer of or employee or agent of a manufacturer of child safety seats that:

a. Offers or arranges for the public a nonprofit child safety seat educational program, checkup event, or checking station program utilizing certified child passenger safety technicians; or

b. Owns property upon which a nonprofit child safety seat educational program, checkup event, or checking station program for the public occurs utilizing certified child passenger safety technicians.

(b) **Limitation of Liability.** -- Except as provided in subsection (c) of this section, a certified child passenger safety technician or sponsoring organization shall not be liable to any person as a result of any act or omission that occurs solely in the inspection, installation, or adjustment of a child safety seat or in providing education regarding the installation or adjustment of a child safety seat if:

(1) The service is provided without fee or charge other than reimbursement for expenses, and

(2) The child passenger safety technician or sponsoring organization acts in good faith and within the scope of training for which the technician is currently certified.

(c) **Exceptions.** -- The limitation on liability shall not apply under any of the following conditions:

(1) The act or omission of the certified child passenger safety technician or sponsoring organization constitutes willful or wanton misconduct or gross negligence.

(2) The inspection, installation, or adjustment of a child safety seat or education provided regarding the installation or adjustment of a child safety seat is in conjunction with the for-profit sale of a child safety seat.

History.
2008-178, s. 1

PART 9A.
ABANDONED AND DERELICT MOTOR VEHICLES

§ 20-137.6. Declaration of purpose

Abandoned and derelict motor vehicles constitute a hazard to the health and welfare of the people of the State in that such vehicles can harbor noxious diseases, furnish shelter and breeding places for vermin, and present physical dangers to the safety and well-being of children and other citizens. It is therefore in the public interest that the present accumulation of abandoned and derelict motor vehicles be eliminated and that the future abandonment of such vehicles be prevented.

History.
1973, c. 720, s. 1

EDITOR'S NOTE. --
Session Laws 1973, c. 720, s. 2, provided: "This act shall not repeal or modify G.S. 20-162.3 and shall become effective on Sept. 3, 1973." Section 20-162.3 was transferred to G.S. 20-219.3 by Session Laws 1973, c. 1330, s. 36.

§ 20-137.7. Definitions of words and phrases

The following words and phrases when used in this Part shall for the purpose of this Part have the meaning respectively prescribed to them in this Part, except in those instances where the context clearly indicates a different meaning:

(1) "Abandoned vehicle" means a motor vehicle that has remained illegally on private or public property for a period of more than 10 days without the consent of the owner or person in control of the property.

(2) "Demolisher" means any person, firm or corporation whose business is to convert a motor vehicle into processed scrap or scrap metal or otherwise to wreck, or dismantle, such a vehicle.

(3) "Department" means the North Carolina Department of Transportation.

(4) "Derelict vehicle" means a motor vehicle:

a. Whose certificate of registration has expired and the registered and legal owner no longer resides at the address listed on the last certificate of registration on record with the North Carolina Department of Transportation; or

Chapter 20

611

b. Whose major parts have been removed so as to render the vehicle inoperable and incapable of passing inspection as required under existing standards; or

c. Whose manufacturer's serial plates, vehicle identification numbers, license number plates and any other means of identification have been removed so as to nullify efforts to locate or identify the registered and legal owner; or

d. Whose registered and legal owner of record disclaims ownership or releases his rights thereto; or

e. Which is more than 12 years old and does not bear a current license as required by the Department.

(5) "Officer" means any law-enforcement officer of the State, of any county or of any municipality including county sanitation officers.

(6) "Salvage yard" means a business or a person who possesses five or more derelict vehicles, regularly engages in buying and selling used vehicle parts.

(7) "Secretary" means the Secretary of the North Carolina Department of Transportation.

(8) "Tag" means any type of notice affixed to an abandoned or derelict motor vehicle advising the owner or the person in possession that the same has been declared an abandoned or derelict vehicle and will be treated as such, which tag shall be of sufficient size as to be easily discernible and contain such information as the Secretary deems necessary to enforce this Part.

(9) "Vehicle" means every device in, upon, or by which any person or property is or may be transported or drawn upon a highway by mechanical means.

(10) "Vehicle recycling" means the process whereby discarded vehicles (abandoned, derelict or wrecked) are collected and then processed by shredding, bailing or shearing to produce processed scrap iron and steel which is then remelted by steel mills and foundries to make raw materials which are subsequently used to manufacture new metal-based products for the consumer.

History.
1973, c. 720, s. 1

§ 20-137.8. Secretary may adopt rules and regulations

The Secretary is hereby vested with the power and is charged with the duties of administering the provisions of this Part and is authorized to adopt such rules and regulations as may be necessary to carry out the provisions thereof.

History.
1973, c. 720, s. 1

§ 20-137.9. Removal from private property

Any abandoned or any derelict vehicle in this State shall be subject to be removed from public or private property provided not objected to by the owner of the private property after notice as hereinafter provided and disposed of in accordance with the provisions of this Part, provided, that all abandoned motor vehicles left on any right-of-way of any road or highway in this State may be removed in accordance with G.S. 20-161.

History.
1973, c. 720, s. 1

§ 20-137.10. Abandoned and derelict vehicles to be tagged; determination of value

(a) When any vehicle is derelict or abandoned in this State, the Secretary shall cause a tag to be placed on the vehicle which shall be notice to the owner, the person in possession of the vehicle, or any lienholder that the same is considered to have been derelict or abandoned and is subject to forfeiture to the State.

(b) Repealed by Session Laws 1975, c. 438, s. 3.

(c) The tag shall serve as the only notice that if the vehicle is not removed within five days from the date reflected on the tag, it will be removed to a designated place to be sold. After the vehicle is removed, the Secretary shall give notice in writing to the person in whose name the vehicle was last registered at the last address reflected in the Department's records and to any lienholder of record that the vehicle is being held, designating the place where the vehicle is being held and that if it is not redeemed within 10 days from the date of the notice by paying all costs of removal and storage the same shall be sold for recycling purposes. The proceeds of the sale shall be deposited in the highway fund established for the purpose of administering the provisions of this Part.

(d) If the value of the vehicle is determined to be more than one hundred dollars ($ 100.00), and if the identity of the last registered owner cannot be determined or if the registration contains no address for the owner, or if it is impossible to determine with reasonable certainty the identification and addresses of any lienholders, notice by one publication in a newspaper of general circulation in the area where the vehicle was located shall be sufficient to meet all requirements of notice pursuant to this Part. The notice of publication may contain multiple listings of vehicles. Five days after date of publication the advertised vehicles may be sold. The proceeds of such sale shall be deposited in the highway fund established for the purpose of administering the provisions of this Part.

(d1) If the value of the vehicle is determined to be less than one hundred dollars ($ 100.00), and if the identity of the last registered owner cannot be determined or if the registration contains no address for the owner, or if it is impossible to determine with reasonable certainty the identification and addresses of any lienholders, no notice in addition to that required by subsection (a) hereof shall be required prior to sale.

(e) All officers, as defined in this Part, are given the authority to appraise or determine the value of derelict or abandoned vehicles as defined in this Part.

History.
1973, c. 720, s. 1; 1975, c. 438, s. 3

§ 20-137.11. Title to vest in State

Title to all vehicles sold or disposed of in accordance with this Part shall vest in the State. All manufacturers' serial number plates and any other identification numbers for all vehicles sold to any person other than a demolisher shall at the time of the sale be turned in to the Department for destruction. Any demolisher purchasing or acquiring any vehicle hereunder shall, under oath, state to the Department that the vehicles purchased or acquired by it have been shredded or recycled.

The Secretary shall remove and destroy all departmental records relating to such vehicles in such method and manner as he may prescribe.

History.
1973, c. 720, s. 1

§ 20-137.12. Secretary may contract for disposal

The Secretary is hereby authorized to contract with any federal, other state, county or municipal authority or private enterprise for tagging, collection, storage, transportation or any other services necessary to prepare derelict or abandoned vehicles for recycling or other methods of disposal. Publicly owned properties, when available, shall be provided as temporary collecting areas for the vehicles defined herein. The Secretary shall have full authority to sell such derelict or abandoned vehicles. If the Secretary deems it more advisable and practical, in addition, he is authorized to contract with private enterprise for the purchase of such vehicles for recycling.

History.
1973, c. 720, s. 1

§ 20-137.13. No liability for removal

No agent or employee of any federal, State, county or municipal government, no person or occupant of the premises from which any derelict or abandoned vehicle shall be removed, nor any person or firm contracting for the removal of or disposition of any such vehicle shall be held criminally or civilly liable in any way arising out of or caused by carrying out or enforcing any provisions of this Part.

History.
1973, c. 720, s. 1

§ 20-137.14. Enclosed, antique, registered and certain other vehicles exempt

The provisions of this Part shall not apply to vehicles located on used car lots, in private garages, enclosed parking lots, or on any other parking area on private property which is not visible from any public street or highway, nor to motor vehicles classified as antiques and registered under the laws of the State of North Carolina, those not required by law to be registered, or those in possession of a salvage yard as defined in G.S. 20-137.7, unless that vehicle presents some safety or health hazard or constitutes a nuisance.

History.
1973, c. 720, s. 1

PART 10.
OPERATION OF VEHICLES AND RULES OF THE ROAD

N.C. Gen. Stat. § 20-138

Repealed by Session Laws 1983, c. 435, s. 23.

§ 20-138.1. Impaired driving

(a) **Offense.** -- A person commits the offense of impaired driving if he drives any vehicle upon any highway, any street, or any public vehicular area within this State:

(1) While under the influence of an impairing substance; or

(2) After having consumed sufficient alcohol that he has, at any relevant time after the driving, an alcohol concentration of 0.08 or more. The results of a chemical analysis shall be deemed sufficient evidence to prove a person's alcohol concentration; or

(3) With any amount of a Schedule I controlled substance, as listed in G.S. 90-89, or its metabolites in his blood or urine.

(a1) A person who has submitted to a chemical analysis of a blood sample, pursuant to G.S. 20-139.1(d), may use the result in rebuttal as evidence that the person did not have, at a relevant time after driving, an alcohol concentration of 0.08 or more.

(b) **Defense Precluded. --** The fact that a person charged with violating this section is or has been legally entitled to use alcohol or a drug is not a defense to a charge under this section.

(b1) **Defense Allowed. --** Nothing in this section shall preclude a person from asserting that a chemical analysis result is inadmissible pursuant to G.S. 20-139.1(b2).

(c) **Pleading. --** In any prosecution for impaired driving, the pleading is sufficient if it states the time and place of the alleged offense in the usual form and charges that the defendant drove a vehicle on a highway or public vehicular area while subject to an impairing substance.

(d) **Sentencing Hearing and Punishment.** -- Impaired driving as defined in this section is a misdemeanor. Upon conviction of a defendant of impaired driving, the presiding judge shall hold a sentencing hearing and impose punishment in accordance with G.S. 20-179.

(e) **Exception. --** Notwithstanding the definition of "vehicle" pursuant to G.S. 20-4.01(49), for purposes of this section the word "vehicle" does not include a horse.

History.
1983, c. 435, s. 24; 1989, c. 711, s. 2;1993, c. 285, s. 1;2006-253, s. 9

EFFECT OF AMENDMENTS. --
Session Laws 2006-253, s. 9, effective December 1, 2006, and applicable to offenses committed on or after that date, in subdivision (a)(2), added the last sentence; added subdivision (a)(3) and subsections (a1) and (b1); substituted "shall" for "must" in subsection (d); and deleted "bicycle, or lawnmower" at the end of subsection (e).

I. IN GENERAL.
EDITOR'S NOTE. --Some of the cases cited below were decided under former G.S. 20-138 and 20-139 or corresponding provisions of prior law and prior to the 1993 amendment which reduced the blood alcohol content for driving while impaired and related offenses from 0.10 to 0.08.

CONSTITUTIONALITY. --The prohibition against driving upon the public highways when the amount of alcohol in one's blood is 0.10 (now 0.08) percent or more by weight contributes in a real and substantial way to the safety of other travelers and is a constitutional exercise of police power by the General Assembly. State v. Basinger, 30 N.C. App. 45, 226 S.E.2d 216 (1976).

G.
S. 20-139.1(b3) does not create an impermissible classification and the Safe Roads Act (G.S. 20-138.1 et seq.) does not deny the equal protection of the laws. State v. Howren, 312 N.C. 454, 323 S.E.2d 335 (1984).

Subdivision (a)(2) of this section does not contravene constitutional due process. State v. Rose, 312 N.C. 441, 323 S.E.2d 339 (1984).

Subdivision (a)(2) is not unconstitutionally vague and uncertain, nor does it violate a driver's substantive due process rights. State v. Ferrell, 75 N.C. App. 156, 330 S.E.2d 225, cert. denied and appeal dismissed, 314 N.C. 333, 333 S.E.2d 492 (1985).

For case reaffirming the constitutionality of subdivision (a)(2) of this section and G.S. 20-4.01(33a), see State v. Denning, 316 N.C. 523, 342 S.E.2d 855 (1986).

Revocation of one's driver's license under G.S. 20-16.5 and subsequent convictions of DWI under this section do not violate the prohibition against double jeopardy. State v. Rogers, 124 N.C. App. 364, 477 S.E.2d 221 (1996).

Appellate court declined to find G.S. 20-138.1 unconstitutional, because the challenged provision, "shall be deemed sufficient evidence to prove," did not create an evidentiary or factual presumption, but simply stated the standard for prima facie evidence of a defendant's alcohol concentration State v. Narron, 193 N.C. App. 76, 666 S.E.2d 860 (2008), review denied, 363 N.C. 135, 674 S.E.2d 140 (2009), cert. denied, 558 U.S. 818, 130 S. Ct. 71, 175 L. Ed. 2d 26 (2009).

IMPACT OF DOUBLE JEOPARDY CLAUSE. --Because a 30-day license revocation is a civil sanction rather than a criminal penalty, the Double Jeopardy Clause does not bar a defendant's subsequent criminal prosecution for driving while impaired by alcohol. State v. Evans, 145 N.C. App. 324, 550 S.E.2d 853 (2001).

The plaintiff failed to prove that North Carolina's prior imposition of a thirty-day period of administrative license revocation under G.S. 20-16.5 constituted a criminal punishment within the meaning of the Double Jeopardy Clause of the Fifth Amendment, U.S. Const. Amend. V, and barred plaintiff's prosecution for the offense of driving while impaired in violation of G.S. 20-138.1. Brewer v. Kimel, 256 F.3d 222 (4th Cir. 2001).

PROSECUTORIAL MISCONDUCT. --Defendant's conviction for driving while impaired in violation of G.S. 20-138.1 could not stand where the prosecutor read during closing arguments from another case the prosecutor had tried, which was outside of the record and not pertinent to defendant's case, and where that reading prejudiced the result of the trial. State v. Simmons, 205 N.C. App. 509, 698 S.E.2d 95 (2010).

TRIAL COURT ERRED IN ACCEPTING INCONSISTENT VERDICT OF NOT GUILTY of driving while impaired, under G.S.20-138.1, yet guilty of felony serious injury by vehicle, under G.S. 20-141.4(a3), because the elements of the greater crime statutorily required conviction of the lesser crime. State v. Mumford, 201 N.C. App. 594, 688 S.E.2d 458 (2010).

INEFFECTIVE ASSISTANCE OF COUNSEL. --Defendant did not show counsel's assistance was ineffective for not arguing a warrantless blood draw's constitutionality because defendant showed no prejudice, as (1) defendant could be convicted based on an officer's opinion of appreciable impairment, and (2) evidence of impairment aside from the blood draw was overwhelming. State v. Perry, 254 N.C. App. 202, 802 S.E.2d 566, review denied, 807 S.E.2d 568, 2017 N.C. LEXIS 970 (2017).

JURISDICTION OF STATE CAPITAL OFFICER. --Trial court erred by concluding that the arresting State Capitol Police officer had no jurisdiction to arrest defendant for DWI. State v. Dickerson, 125 N.C. App. 592, 481 S.E.2d 344 (1997).

CONSTRUCTION WITH G.S. 20-16.2 --A civil superior court determination, on appeal from an administrative hearing, pursuant to G.S. 20-16.2(e), regarding an allegation of willful refusal, estops the relitigation of that same issue in a defendant's criminal prosecution for DWI. The district attorney and the Attorney General both represent the interests of the people of North Carolina, regardless of whether it be the district attorney in a criminal trial court or the Attorney General in a civil or criminal appeal. State v. Summers, 351 N.C. 620, 528 S.E.2d 17 (2000).

As a trial court erred in failing to suppress the intoxilyzer testing evidence obtained after defendant was arrested for driving while impaired because defendant's right under G.S. 20.16.2(a) to have a witness present during the testing had been violated, the trial court also erred in accepting defendant's plea of guilty to the driving while impaired charge. State v. Hatley, 190 N.C. App. 639, 661 S.E.2d 43 (2008).

THE LEGISLATURE MAY CONSTITUTIONALLY MAKE IT A CRIME FOR PERSONS TO HAVE AN ALCOHOL CONCENTRATION OF 0.10 (NOW 0.08) or more at any relevant time after driving on the highways and public vehicular areas of this State and that is all subdivision (a)(2) of this section does. State v. Howren, 312 N.C. 454, 323 S.E.2d 335 (1984).

A legislature may not declare an individual guilty or presumptively guilty of crime. Subdivision (a)(2) of this section does not run afoul of that prohibition. By stating that anyone who drives a vehicle upon a highway, street, or public vehicular area after having consumed such an amount of alcohol that he has a blood-alcohol concentration of 0.10 (now 0.08) or more at any relevant time after the driver has committed the offense of driving while impaired, the legislature has merely stated the elements of the offense, proof of which constitutes guilt. State v. Howren, 312 N.C. 454, 323 S.E.2d 335 (1984).

Courts in other jurisdictions in considering challenges to driving while impaired statutes have agreed that a 0.10 (now 0.08) blood-alcohol concentration is not an unconstitutionally vague standard simply because a drinking driver does not know precisely when he has reached that level. These courts have adopted the position that all persons are presumed to know the law and a defendant who drinks and then drives takes the risk that his blood-alcohol content will exceed the legal maximum. The N.C. Superior Court agrees with this rationale. State v. Rose, 312 N.C. 441, 323 S.E.2d 339 (1984).

PURPOSE. --Former G.S. 20-138 was designed for the protection of human life or limb. State v. Stewardson, 32 N.C. App. 344, 232 S.E.2d 308, cert. denied, 292 N.C. 643, 235 S.E.2d 64 (1977).

ASSIMILATION OF SECTION INTO FEDERAL LAW. --Under 18 U.S.C. § 13 this section, the driving while impaired statute of North Carolina, is assimilated into federal law, but an offender can only be convicted of a misdemeanor in the federal court and his punishment therein cannot exceed a fine of $1,000 and imprisonment for a term in excess of one year. Such a misdemeanor is within the jurisdiction of the federal magistrates, subject to the provisions of 18 U.S.C. § 3401. United States v. Kendrick, 636 F. Supp. 189 (E.D.N.C. 1986).

COLLATERAL ESTOPPEL BARRED STATE FROM INTRODUCING EVIDENCE. --The State is collaterally estopped from litigating issues in a criminal DWI case when those exact issues have been relitigated in a civil license revocation hearing with the Attorney General representing the DMV in superior court; defendant was found to have not refused to take the breathalyzer test in the earlier proceeding, so that the results of the single breath analysis were inadmissible, and privity of parties existed, as both the Attorney General and the District Attorney represent the same party, which is the people of the State of North Carolina. State v. Summers, 132 N.C. App. 636, 513 S.E.2d 575 (1999), aff'd, 351 N.C. 620, 528 S.E.2d 17 (2000).

"DRIVING" CONSTRUED. --It could be fairly and logically inferred from the circumstantial evidence offered by the State that defendant drove his vehicle on the highway and that he did so while he was under the influence of intoxicating liquor, where defendant was found asleep and intoxicated sitting in the driver's seat of his car, which was stopped in its proper lane at a stop sign, with the lights out and the engine running; no one else was in or near the car; and defendant stated to the officer that he had gone to Zebulon earlier that night and was on his way home. State v. Carter, 15 N.C. App. 391, 190 S.E.2d 241 (1972).

One "drives" within the meaning of this section if he is in actual physical control of a vehicle which is in motion or which has the engine running. State v. Fields, 77 N.C. App. 404, 335 S.E.2d 69 (1985).

The trial court did not err in finding that the defendant was "driving" a vehicle within the meaning of this section when he sat behind the steering wheel in the driver's seat of the car and started the car's engine in order to make the heater operable, but the car remained motionless on the street. State v. Fields, 77 N.C. App. 404, 335 S.E.2d 69 (1985).

Although distinctions may have been made between driving and operating in prior case law and prior statutes regulating motor vehicles, such a distinction is not supportable under this section. Since "driver" is defined in G.S. 20-4.01 simply as an "operator" of a vehicle, the legislature intended the two words to be synonymous. State v. Coker, 312 N.C. 432, 323 S.E.2d 343 (1984).

One "drives" within the meaning of this section if he is in actual physical control of a vehicle which is in motion or which has the engine running. State v. Fields, 77 N.C. App. 404, 335 S.E.2d 69 (1985); State v. Mabe, 85 N.C. App. 500, 355 S.E.2d 186 (1987).

The trial court did not err in finding that the defendant was "driving" a vehicle within the meaning of this section when he sat behind the steering wheel in the driver's seat of the car and started the car's engine in order to make the heater operable, but the car remained motionless on the street. State v. Fields, 77 N.C. App. 404, 335 S.E.2d 69 (1985).

SUFFICIENT EVIDENCE DEFENDANT WAS "DRIVING." --While there was no eyewitness establishing that defendant was the driver of the car involved in an accident, evidence that the vehicle involved in an accident was registered to defendant, that defendant was found walking on a road near the scene of the accident, and that defendant had injuries consistent with person who was driving in a car accident was sufficient to survive a motion to dismiss. State v. Foye, 220 N.C. App. 37, 725 S.E.2d 73 (2012).

"OPERATE" CONSTRUED. --It could be fairly and logically inferred from the circumstantial evidence offered by the State that defendant drove his vehicle on the highway and that he did so while he was under the influence of intoxicating liquor, where defendant was found asleep and intoxicated sitting in the driver's seat of his car, which was stopped in its proper lane at a stop sign, with the lights out and the engine running; no one else was in or near the car; and defendant stated to the officer that he had gone to Zebulon earlier that night and was on his way home. State v. Carter, 15 N.C. App. 391, 190 S.E.2d 241 (1972).

Although distinctions may have been made between driving and operating in prior case law and prior statutes regulating motor vehicles, such a distinction is not supportable under this section. Since "driver" is defined in G.S. 20-4.01 simply as an "operator" of a vehicle, the legislature intended the two words to be synonymous. State v. Coker, 312 N.C. 432, 323 S.E.2d 343 (1984).

MEANING OF "OPERATOR". --In a prosecution for driving under the influence and driving while license was revoked, evidence that defendant was seated behind the wheel of a car which had the motor running was sufficient to prove that defendant was the operator of the car under G.S. 20-4.01(25). State v. Turner, 29 N.C. App. 163, 223 S.E.2d 530 (1976).

SUFFICIENT EVIDENCE THAT DEFENDANT PHYSICALLY CONTROLLED VEHICLE. --Evidence that defendant was seated behind the steering wheel of a car stopped on the handicapped or wheelchair ramp in a hotel parking lot, which car had its motor running, and that when aroused, the defendant himself turned off the car's engine, was sufficient to support a finding that the defendant was in actual physical control of the vehicle. State v. Mabe, 85 N.C. App. 500, 355 S.E.2d 186 (1987).

Trial court committed error by vacating a jury's verdict convicting the defendant of driving while

impaired because a rational juror could infer from the physical evidence that the defendant drove the subject vehicle, including: (1) the presence of blood on the driver's side of the air bag; (2) blood on the defendant; (3) a lack of blood on the passenger side; (4) a burn on the other occupant's shoulder consistent with the passenger side safety belt; and (5) the fact that the driver's seat was pushed too far back for the other occupant to drive the vehicle while sitting in that seat, despite the other occupant's claim that she drove the vehicle. State v. Hernandez, 188 N.C. App. 193, 655 S.E.2d 426 (2008).

EXCLUSION OF EVIDENCE OF OPERABILITY UPHELD. --Where defendant admitted that he was sitting behind the wheel of an automobile while the motor was running, that he put the car into drive three times and that the car moved forward on each occasion, failure to allow defendant to introduce evidence that the vehicle he was alleged to have been operating was not operable was not prejudicial and did not entitle him to a new trial for the offenses of habitual impaired driving and driving during revocation, as defendant demonstrated in the presence of a police officer that the car in which he was seated was a device in which a person might be transported for purposes of G.S. 20-4.01(49). State v. Clapp, 135 N.C. App. 52, 519 S.E.2d 90 (1999).

A HORSE IS A VEHICLE for the purpose of charging a violation of this section. State v. Dellinger, 73 N.C. App. 685, 327 S.E.2d 609 (1985).

Where the evidence showed that defendant was riding a horse on a street while defendant had an alcohol concentration of 0.18, the evidence was sufficient from which a jury could find that defendant drove a vehicle upon a street while under the influence of an impairing substance. State v. Dellinger, 73 N.C. App. 685, 327 S.E.2d 609 (1985).

FOR CASE HOLDING THAT FARM TRACTORS WERE "VEHICLES" within the meaning of former G.S. 20-138 when operated upon a highway by one under the influence of intoxicating liquor, see State v. Green, 251 N.C. 141, 110 S.E.2d 805 (1959).

PORTION OF SIDEWALK AS "HIGHWAY". --The portion of a sidewalk between a street and a filling station, open to the use of the public as a matter of right for the purposes of vehicular traffic, is a "highway." State v. Perry, 230 N.C. 361, 53 S.E.2d 288 (1949).

PARK GROUNDS AS PUBLIC VEHICULAR AREA. --Evidence held to permit a finding that at the time in question portion of park grounds legally in use as a parking lot was a "public vehicular area" within the meaning and intent of that phrase as used in G.S. 20-4.01(32), so as to permit a conviction under subsection (a) of this section for impaired driving thereon. State v. Carawan, 80 N.C. App. 151, 341 S.E.2d 96, cert. denied, 317 N.C. 337, 346 S.E.2d 141 (1986).

NO EVIDENCE WHETHER VACANT LOT WAS PUBLIC VEHICULAR AREA. --Trial court erred in denying defendant's motion to dismiss the charge of habitual impaired driving because there was no evidence concerning the ownership of the vacant lot where defendant operated a moped or that the lot had been designated as a public vehicular area by the owner; in order to show an area meets the definition of public vehicular area there must be some evidence demonstrating the property is similar in nature to those examples provided by the General Assembly in the statute. State v. Ricks, 237 N.C. App. 359, 764 S.E.2d 692 (2014).

MEANING OF "IMPAIRED." --Under our former "driving under the influence" statutes the test was whether the accused had drunk a sufficient quantity of intoxicating beverage or taken a sufficient amount of narcotic drugs to cause him to lose the normal control of his bodily or mental faculties, or both, to such an extent that there was an appreciable impairment of either or both of these faculties. This section consolidated existing impairment offenses into a single offense with two different methods of proof, but it does not appear to have changed the basic definition of "impaired." State v. Harrington, 78 N.C. App. 39, 336 S.E.2d 852 (1985).

PROOF OF IMPAIRED DRIVING. --The offense of impaired driving is proven by evidence that defendant drove a vehicle on any highway in this State while his physical or mental faculties, or both, were "appreciably impaired by an impairing substance." State v. George, 77 N.C. App. 580, 335 S.E.2d 768 (1985).

Trial court did not err in denying defendant's motion to dismiss the charge against him of driving while impaired, as the trustworthiness of defendant's confessions was adequately corroborated by witnesses who observed defendant arrive at the scene of the fatal accident. State v. Cruz, 173 N.C. App. 689, 620 S.E.2d 251 (2005).

Evidence defendant pulled into a handicap spot, the officer noticed an odor of alcohol coming from defendant, defendant had red and glassy eyes, defendant admitted to consuming alcohol hours before, the officer noted five out of six indicators of impairment on the horizontal gaze nystagmus test, and the officer believed that defendant was impaired, despite evidence tending to show defendant was driving properly and was steady on his feet, was sufficient to survive defendant's motions to dismiss. State v. Lindsey, 249 N.C. App. 516, 791 S.E.2d 496 (2016), appeal dismissed, review denied, 794 S.E.2d 520, 2016 N.C. LEXIS 1146 (2016).

In a case in which defendant passed a tow truck on the shoulder and struck and killed the victim, the trial court erred in denying his motions to dismiss the driving while impaired charge because the trooper formed his opinion of impairment entirely through passive observation of defendant, and he did not request defendant to perform any of the several field tests officers often use to gauge a motorist's impairment; he did not ask defendant if or when he had ingested any impairing substances; and trooper's observations occurred about five hours after the collision occurred. State v. Nazzal, -- N.C. App. --, 840 S.E.2d 881 (2020).

THERE WAS SUFFICIENT EVIDENCE THAT DEFENDANT WAS APPRECIABLY IMPAIRED where State trooper observed defendant driving erratically, defendant had a pronounced alcohol odor about him, and defendant admitted he had been drinking significantly. State v. Phillips, 127 N.C. App. 391, 489 S.E.2d 890 (1997).

Admissible trial evidence established beyond a reasonable doubt that defendant was driving a vehicle while under the influence of alcohol in violation of G.S. 20-138.1; evidence showing that defendant was under the influence of alcohol included, inter alia: (1) weaving; (2) erratic braking; (3) driving 70 MPH in a 50 MPH zone; (4) the strong odor of alcohol on defendant's person; (5) defendant's unsteady balance; and (6) his statement that he had consumed alcohol. United States v. Van Hazel, 468 F. Supp. 2d 792 (E.D.N.C. 2006).

SUBSTANTIAL EVIDENCE EXISTED FOR EACH ESSENTIAL ELEMENT OF DWI. --The trial court erred in dismissal of defendant's conviction for habitual driving while impaired under G.S. 20-138.5 because the State presented evidence that: (1) defendant was traveling at a speed in excess of sixty miles per hour; (2) defendant's vehicle had no motor vehicle tags; (3) defendant did not immediately stop after the arresting officer activated his red and blue lights and did not do so until after the officer accelerated to keep up with the vehicle and activated his airhorn more than once; (4) defendant did not stop in the rightmost lane of the four-lane highway, but rather stopped at a 'T' intersection in such a manner that defendant's and the officer's cars blocked the intersection; (5) defendant left his vehicle and started toward the officer's vehicle before being ordered to return to his vehicle; (6) upon approaching defendant's vehicle, the officer smelled a strong odor of alcohol; (7) the officer observed an open container of beer in the passenger area of defendant's vehicle; (8) defendant's coat was wet from what appeared to the officer to be beer waste; (9) defendant's speech was slurred; (10) defendant refused to take the ALCO-SENSOR test; and (11) defendant refused the Intoxilyzer test. Substantial evidence existed for each essential element of DWI, and viewing the evidence in a light most favorable to the State, revealed a reasonable inference of defendant's guilt based on direct and circumstantial evidence presented by the State, which was sufficient to support the jury's verdict of guilty. State v. Scott, 356 N.C. 591; 573 S.E.2d 866; 2002 N.C. LEXIS 1263 (2002). State v. Scott, 356 N.C. 591, 573 S.E.2d 866 (2002).

STATUTORY DUTY IMPOSED. --Pursuant to this section, a person under the influence of an impairing substance commits the offense of impaired driving if he drives a car on any public road. Thus, the statutory law imposes a duty on all persons to avoid driving while under the influence of an impairing substance. King v. Allred, 76 N.C. App. 427, 333 S.E.2d 758, cert. denied, 315 N.C. 184, 337 S.E.2d 857 (1985).

VIOLATION AS CULPABLE NEGLIGENCE. --A willful violation of former G.S. 20-138 would constitute culpable negligence if that violation was the proximate cause of death. State v. Atkins, 58 N.C.

App. 146, 292 S.E.2d 744, cert. denied and appeal dismissed, 306 N.C. 744, 295 S.E.2d 480 (1982).

An intentional, willful or wanton violation of a statute or ordinance designed for the protection of human life or limb, which proximately results in injury or death, is culpable negligence. State v. Griffith, 24 N.C. App. 250, 210 S.E.2d 431 (1974), cert. denied, 286 N.C. 546, 212 S.E.2d 168 (1975).

This section is a statute designed for the protection of human life and limb, and as such, it is a matter of law that a violation of its provisions constitutes culpable negligence. State v. McGill, 314 N.C. 633, 336 S.E.2d 90 (1985).

It is negligence per se to operate a vehicle while impaired within the meaning of this section. Baker v. Mauldin, 82 N.C. App. 404, 346 S.E.2d 240 (1986).

There was sufficient evidence of intent to support defendant's assault with a deadly weapon inflicting serious injury conviction as: (1) there was evidence that defendant had consumed 9 to 12 beers in a two-hour timeframe; (2) defendant's blood alcohol content was well-above the threshold for driving while impaired; (3) defendant got into a truck, ran over a sign, and continued driving; (4) defendant eventually ran off the road and crashed into the victims' truck; and (5) a violation of G.S. 20-138.1 constituted culpable negligence as a matter of law. State v. Davis, 197 N.C. App. 738, 678 S.E.2d 385 (2009), aff'd in part and rev'd in part 2010 N.C. LEXIS 585 (2010).

DEATH CAUSED BY A VIOLATION MAY CONSTITUTE MANSLAUGHTER. State v. Griffith, 24 N.C. App. 250, 210 S.E.2d 431 (1974), cert. denied, 286 N.C. 546, 212 S.E.2d 168 (1975); State v. Stewardson, 32 N.C. App. 344, 232 S.E.2d 308, cert. denied, 292 N.C. 643, 235 S.E.2d 64 (1977).

One who drives his automobile, in violation of statute, runs into another car, and thereby proximately causes the death of one of the occupants, is guilty of manslaughter at least. State v. Stansell, 203 N.C. 69, 164 S.E. 580 (1932).

Evidence that defendant was driving on the public highways of the State while under the influence of intoxicating liquor in violation of statute, and was driving recklessly in violation of G.S. 20-140, proximately causing the death of a passenger in his car, was sufficient to be submitted to the jury in a prosecution for manslaughter. State v. Blankenship, 229 N.C. 589, 50 S.E.2d 724 (1948).

While it is clear that driving while impaired is culpable negligence, in order to convict an impaired driver of involuntary manslaughter based upon his impairment, the State must show that while driving impaired defendant violated some other rule of the road, and that this violation was the proximate cause of the accident. State v. McGill, 73 N.C. App. 206, 326 S.E.2d 345 (1985).

When a death is caused by one who was driving under the influence of alcohol, only two elements must exist for the successful prosecution of manslaughter: A willful violation of G.S. 20-138 (now this section) and the causal link between that violation and the death. If these elements are present, the State need not demonstrate that defendant violated any other rule of the road, nor that his conduct was in any other way wrongful. State v. McGill, 314 N.C. 633, 336 S.E.2d 90 (1985).

BUT VIOLATION OF LAW MUST HAVE CAUSED ACCIDENT AND DEATH. --Death caused by a violation of statute may be manslaughter, but a condition precedent to conviction is that the violation of the law in this respect must have caused the wreck and the death of deceased. State v. Dills, 204 N.C. 33, 167 S.E. 459 (1933).

Precedent to a conviction of manslaughter for violation of either former G.S. 20-138 or G.S. 20-140(b) or both is that the violation of either one or both must have caused the accident and death of decedent. State v. Griffith, 24 N.C. App. 250, 210 S.E.2d 431 (1974), cert. denied, 286 N.C. 546, 212 S.E.2d 168 (1975).

AND A CAUSAL CONNECTION MUST BE SHOWN. --Statutory violation, if conceded, is not sufficient to sustain a prosecution for involuntary manslaughter unless a causal relation is shown between the breach of the statute and the death. State v. Lowery, 223 N.C. 598, 27 S.E.2d 638 (1943).

THE OFFENSE OF FELONY DEATH BY VEHICLE requires the identical essential elements to those required for a conviction of involuntary manslaughter predicated on a violation of this section, to wit: a willful violation of this section, and a causal link between that violation and the death. State v. Williams, 90 N.C. App. 615, 369 S.E.2d 832, cert. denied, 323 N.C. 369, 373 S.E.2d 555 (1988).

FELONY DEATH BY VEHICLE IS NOT A LESSER INCLUDED OFFENSE of involuntary manslaughter while driving under the influence of alcohol. State v. Williams, 90 N.C. App. 615, 369 S.E.2d 832, cert. denied, 323 N.C. 369, 373 S.E.2d 555 (1988).

INTENTIONAL ACT OF IMPAIRED DRIVING REQUIRED FOR VIOLATION OF G.S. 20-141.4. -- The phrase "intentionally causes the death of another person" as used within G.S. 20-141.4 refers not to the presence of a specific intent to cause death, but rather to the fact that the act which resulted in death is intentionally committed and is an act of impaired driving under this section. State v. Williams, 90 N.C. App. 615, 369 S.E.2d 832, cert. denied, 323 N.C. 369, 373 S.E.2d 555 (1988).

Even if defendant's willful attempt to elude arrest in violation of G.S. 20-141.5 was a cause of the victim's injury, his driving under the influence in violation of G.S. 20-138.1 could also be a proximate cause of the injury under G.S. 20-141.4(a3) because defendant's violation of G.S. 20-138.1 did not have to be the only proximate cause of the victim's injury in order for defendant to be found criminally liable; a showing that defendant's action of driving while under the influence was one of the proximate causes was sufficient. State v. Leonard, 213 N.C. App. 526, 711 S.E.2d 867 (2011).

FOR CASE HOLDING VIOLATION OF FORMER G.S. 14-387 NOT PROXIMATE CAUSE OF FATAL ACCIDENT, see State v. Miller, 220 N.C. 660, 18 S.E.2d 143 (1942).

VIOLATION OF SECTION AS DEFENSE TO WRONGFUL DEATH CLAIM. --Contributory negligence of plaintiffs' decedent, who was operating his vehicle in an impaired condition in violation of this section, was a defense to a wrongful death claim under this section based on defendants' alleged negligence in selling alcohol to an intoxicated person. Clark v. Inn West, 89 N.C. App. 275, 365 S.E.2d 682 (1988).

Plaintiff's wrongful death claim against a provider of alcohol alleging wilful and wanton negligence for serving the visibly intoxicated decedent alcohol after being requested to refrain from serving him was barred by the decedent's own actions in driving his vehicle while highly intoxicated. Sorrells v. M.Y.B. Hospitality Ventures, 332 N.C. 645, 423 S.E.2d 72 (1992).

QUESTION OF CONTRIBUTORY NEGLIGENCE of plaintiff's decedent, who was killed in an accident while riding as a passenger in a car driven by defendant, where defendant admitted in his answer that he was driving while mentally and physically impaired in violation of this section, was for the jury. Baker v. Mauldin, 82 N.C. App. 404, 346 S.E.2d 240 (1986).

ADMISSIBILITY OF RESULTS OF BLOOD TEST. --In a prosecution for drunken driving it is competent for an expert witness to testify as to the results of a test as to the alcoholic content of the defendant's blood, based on a sample taken less than an hour after the alleged offense, with defendant's consent. State v. Willard, 241 N.C. 259, 84 S.E.2d 899 (1954); State v. Moore, 245 N.C. 158, 95 S.E.2d 548 (1956).

Assuming blood specimen is obtained at or near the pertinent time and is identified and traced until chemical analysis thereof is made, testimony of a qualified expert (1) as to the making and results of a chemical analysis of such blood specimen to determine the alcoholic content thereof, and (2) as to the effects of certain percentages of alcohol in the bloodstream, is competent. State v. Paschal, 253 N.C. 795, 117 S.E.2d 749 (1961).

A qualified expert may testify as to the effect of certain percentages of alcohol in the bloodstream of human beings, provided the blood sample analyzed was timely taken, properly traced, and identified. State v. Webb, 265 N.C. 546, 144 S.E.2d 619 (1965).

RESULT OF BREATHALYZER TEST IS COMPETENT EVIDENCE. --The result of a breathalyzer test, when the qualifications of the person making the test and the manner of making it meet the requirements of G.S. 20-139.1, is competent evidence. State v. Cooke, 270 N.C. 644, 155 S.E.2d 165 (1967).

EVIDENCE OF RESULTS OF BREATHALYZER TEST GIVES RISE TO INFERENCE that defendant was under the influence. State v. Jenkins, 21 N.C. App. 541, 204 S.E.2d 919 (1974).

THE RESULT OF A BREATHALYZER ANALYSIS IS CRUCIAL TO A CONVICTION. State v. Smith, 312 N.C. 361, 323 S.E.2d 316 (1984).

PROOF OF VIOLATION OF SECTION. --This section creates one offense which may be proved by either or both theories detailed in subdivisions (a)(1) and (a)(2). State v. Coker, 312 N.C. 432, 323 S.E.2d 343 (1984).

PROBABLE CAUSE FOR STOP AND SEARCH. --Despite lack of an observed and verifiable traffic code violation by suspect, his driving 20 miles per hour below the speed limit and weaving within his lane were actions sufficient to raise the suspicion of an impaired driver in a reasonable and experienced trooper's mind; fact that driver was not charged with a DUI offense after being stopped and questioned was not relevant to trooper's initial suspicions so as to invalidate stop and search of car. State v. Jones, 96 N.C. App. 389, 386 S.E.2d 217 (1989), appeal dismissed, 326 N.C. 366, 389 S.E.2d 809 (1990).

PROBABLE CAUSE FOR ARREST. --Where petitioner was involved in a one-vehicle accident in which his car went off the road into a ditch, the accident occurred on a clear day in the middle of the afternoon, and petitioner told the arresting officer that he had fallen asleep at the wheel, the evidence surrounding the accident and petitioner's reason for its occurrence, coupled with the strong odor of alcohol detected from him, gave the officer reasonable grounds to arrest petitioner for impaired driving. Richardson v. Hiatt, 95 N.C. App. 196, 381 S.E.2d 866, rehearing granted, 95 N.C. App. 780, 384 S.E.2d 62 (1989).

Evidence that the officer smelled an odor of alcohol coming from defendant and observed five of six indicators of impairment upon administering an horizontal gaze nystagmus test, and defendant admitted he had consumed three beers hours before the stop provided probable cause to arrest defendant for DWI. State v. Lindsey, 249 N.C. App. 516, 791 S.E.2d 496 (2016), appeal dismissed, review denied, 794 S.E.2d 520, 2016 N.C. LEXIS 1146 (2016).

Probable cause existed to justify a police officer's second arrest of defendant for impaired driving, when less than three hours after defendant was arrested for driving while impaired and a half hour after he was released from the county jail, the officer saw defendant in the driver's seat of defendant's car at a gas station with no one else in the car and the engine running. The officer knew defendant's blood alcohol concentration based on a breath analysis following the first arrest and observed signs of impairment. State v. Clapp, 259 N.C. App. 839, 817 S.E.2d 222 (2018).

Trial court's factual findings failed to support the conclusion that the officer lacked probable cause to arrest defendant for driving while impaired, as the facts showed that defendant had been driving and admitted having consumed three beers, his eyes were red and glassy, a moderate odor of alcohol emanated from his person, and he exhibited multiple indicia of impairment while performing various sobriety tests, and thus, the trial court's grant of defendant's motion to suppress was improper. State v. Parisi, 372 N.C. 639, 831 S.E.2d 236 (2019).

PROBABLE CAUSE FOR ARREST LACKING. --Trial court did not err by granting defendant's motion to suppress because neither officer saw defendant drive, park, or get out of the truck and, therefore, the arresting officer lacked the requisite probable cause to arrest defendant for driving while impaired. State v. Fields, -- N.C. App. --, 836 S.E.2d 886 (2019).

DEFENSE OF COERCION, COMPULSION, OR DURESS. --The trial court was correct in refusing to instruct the jury on the defense of coercion, compulsion, or duress, as there was no evidence that defendant faced threatening conduct of any kind at the time officer saw him driving while intoxicated; although evidence tended to show that defendant was justifiably in fear for his safety when he drove away from pedestrian pursuers, it did not tend to show that he was still justifiably fearful 30 minutes later after his pursuers had been left many miles behind. State v. Cooke, 94 N.C. App. 386, 380 S.E.2d 382, cert. denied, 325 N.C. 433, 384 S.E.2d 542 (1989).

FAILURE TO INFORM DEFENDANT OF RIGHTS. --Where the defendant is not advised of his rights under G.S. 20-16.2(a), including, under G.S. 20-16.2(a)(5), the right to have another alcohol concentration test performed by a qualified person of his own choosing, the State's test is inadmissible in evidence. State v. Gilbert, 85 N.C. App. 594, 355 S.E.2d 261 (1987).

Statutory violations by magistrate, who failed to inform defendant of his rights to pretrial release under either the general provisions of G.S. 15A-511 or the more specific provisions of G.S. 15A-534.2, did not justify dismissal of driving while impaired charges. State v. Gilbert, 85 N.C. App. 594, 355 S.E.2d 261 (1987).

VIOLATION AS GROUNDS FOR SEEKING PUNITIVE DAMAGES. --In an action arising out of an automobile accident, defendant's operation of a motor vehicle in violation of this section, and failure of four sobriety tests, evidenced a willful and wanton disregard for plaintiffs' rights sufficient to warrant the submission of the issue of punitive damages to the jury. Ivey v. Rose, 94 N.C. App. 773, 381 S.E.2d 476 (1989).

PUNITIVE DAMAGES MAY BE RECOVERED AGAINST IMPAIRED DRIVERS IN CERTAIN SITUATIONS WITHOUT REGARD TO THE DRIVERS' MOTIVES OR INTENT. Huff v. Chrismon, 68 N.C. App. 525, 315 S.E.2d 711, cert. denied, 311 N.C. 756, 321 S.E.2d 134 (1984).

IMPROPER CONVICTION AS VIOLATION OF CODE OF JUDICIAL CONDUCT. --Acts of respondent judge in convicting defendants of reckless driving when they were charged with driving while impaired were acts which respondent knew to be improper and ultra vires, or beyond the powers of his office; therefore respondent's actions constituted conduct in violation of Code Jud. Con., Canons 2A and 3A(1). In re Martin, 333 N.C. 242, 424 S.E.2d 118 (1993).

APPLIED in State ex rel. Edmisten v. Tucker, 312 N.C. 326, 323 S.E.2d 294 (1984); State v. Harrell, 96 N.C. App. 426, 386 S.E.2d 103 (1989); State v. Parisi, 135 N.C. App. 222, 519 S.E.2d 531 (1999); State v. Jones, 353 N.C. 159, 538 S.E.2d 917 (2000); State v. Davis, 142 N.C. App. 81, 542 S.E.2d 236 (2001), cert. denied, 353 N.C. 386, 547 S.E.2d 818 (2001); State v. McDonald, 151 N.C. App. 236, 565 S.E.2d 273 (2002); Efird v. Hubbard, 151 N.C. App. 577, 565 S.E.2d 713 (2002); Harris v. Testar, Inc., 243 N.C. App. 33, 777 S.E.2d 776 (2015).

CITED in State v. Priddy, 115 N.C. App. 547, 445 S.E.2d 610, cert. denied, 337 N.C. 805, 449 S.E.2d 751 (1994); Camalier v. Jeffries, 340 N.C. 699, 460 S.E.2d 133; State v. Hollingsworth, 77 N.C. App. 36, 334 S.E.2d 463 (1985); United States v. Canane, 622 F. Supp. 279 (W.D.N.C. 1985); State v. Haislip, 79 N.C. App. 656, 339 S.E.2d 832 (1986); Crow v. North Carolina, 642 F. Supp. 953 (W.D.N.C. 1986); State v. Hicks, 84 N.C. App. 237, 352 S.E.2d 275 (1987); State v. Warren, 84 N.C. App. 235, 352 S.E.2d 276 (1987); State v. Drayton, 321 N.C. 512, 364 S.E.2d 121 (1988); State v. Weaver, 91 N.C. App. 413, 371 S.E.2d 759 (1988); Davis v. Hiatt, 92 N.C. App. 748, 376 S.E.2d 44 (1989); Clark v. Inn W., 324 N.C. 415, 379 S.E.2d 23 (1989); State v. Bailey, 93 N.C. App. 721, 379 S.E.2d 266 (1989); State v. Golden, 96 N.C. App. 249, 385 S.E.2d 346 (1989); State v. Brunson, 96 N.C. App. 347, 385 S.E.2d 542 (1989); McDaniel v. DMV, 96 N.C. App. 495, 386 S.E.2d 73 (1989); State v. McDonald, 97 N.C. App. 322, 387 S.E.2d 666 (1990); Penuel v. Hiatt, 97 N.C. App. 616, 389 S.E.2d 289 (1990); State v. Bumgarner, 97 N.C. App. 567, 389 S.E.2d 425 (1990); State v. Garvick, 98 N.C. App. 556, 392 S.E.2d 115 (1990); State v. Brunson, 327 N.C. 244, 393 S.E.2d 860 (1990); State v. Gwyn, 103 N.C. App. 369, 406 S.E.2d 145 (1991); State v. Mooneyhan, 104 N.C. App. 477, 409 S.E.2d 700 (1991); State v. Ham, 105 N.C. App. 658, 414 S.E.2d 577 (1992); Berrier v. Thrift, 107 N.C. App. 356, 420 S.E.2d 206 (1992); State v. Moore, 107 N.C. App. 388, 420 S.E.2d 691 (1992); State v. Stafford, 114 N.C. App. 101, 440 S.E.2d 846 (1994); Camalier v. Jeffries, 113 N.C. App. 303, 438 S.E.2d 427 (1994); State v. McGill, 114 N.C. App. 479, 442 S.E.2d 166 (1994); Peal ex rel. Peal v. Smith, 115 N.C. App. 225, 444 S.E.2d 673 (1994); Nicholson v. Killens, 116 N.C. App. 473, 448 S.E.2d 542 (1994); State v. Turner, 117 N.C. App. 457, 451 S.E.2d 19 (1994); State v. Snyder, 343 N.C. 61, 468 S.E.2d 221 (1996); State v. Crawford, 125 N.C. App. 279, 480 S.E.2d 422 (1997); State v. Shoff, 128 N.C. App. 432, 496 S.E.2d 590 (1998), appeal dismissed, cert. denied, 348 N.C. 289, 501 S.E.2d 923 (1998); Estate of Mullis v. Monroe Oil Co., 349 N.C. 196, 505 S.E.2d 131 (1998); State v. Pearson, 131 N.C. App. 315, 507 S.E.2d 301 (1998); Baker v. Provident Life & Accident Ins. Co., 171 F.3d 939 (4th Cir. 1999); State v. Moore, 132 N.C. App. 802, 513 S.E.2d 346 (1999); State v. Covington, 138 N.C. App. 688, 532 S.E.2d 221 (2000); McCrary v. Byrd, 136 N.C. App. 487, 524 S.E.2d 817 (2000); In re Inquiry Concerning a Judge (Brown), 351 N.C. 601, 527 S.E.2d 651 (2000); Cooke v. Faulkner, 137 N.C. App. 755, 529 S.E.2d 512 (2000); State v. Smith, 139 N.C. App. 209, 533 S.E.2d 518 (2000); State v. Lobohe, 143 N.C. App. 555, 547 S.E.2d 107 (2001); Iodice v. United States, 289 F.3d 270 (4th Cir. 2002); Davis v. N.C. Dep't of Crime Control & Pub. Safety, 151 N.C. App. 513, 565 S.E.2d 716 (2002); State v. Jordan, 155 N.C. App. 146, 574 S.E.2d 166 (2002); State v. Hudgins, 167 N.C. App. 705, 606 S.E.2d 443 (2005); State v. Winslow, 169 N.C. App. 137, 609 S.E.2d 463 (2005), review denied, in part,

359 N.C. 642, 617 S.E.2d 660 (2005); State v. Hurt, 361 N.C. 325, 643 S.E.2d 915 (2007); State v. McLamb, 186 N.C. App. 124, 649 S.E.2d 902 (2007), review denied, stay denied, 362 N.C. 368, 663 S.E.2d 433 (2008); State v. Haislip, 186 N.C. App. 275, 651 S.E.2d 243 (2007); Harrell v. Bowen, 362 N.C. 142, 655 S.E.2d 350 (2008); State v. Barnard, 362 N.C. 244, 658 S.E.2d 643 (2008); State v. Hinchman, 192 N.C. App. 657, 666 S.E.2d 199 (2008); State v. Maready, 362 N.C. 614, 669 S.E.2d 564 (2008); State v. Shockley, 201 N.C. App. 431, 689 S.E.2d 455 (2009); State v. Maready, 205 N.C. App. 1, 695 S.E.2d 771 (2010); State v. Blackmon, 208 N.C. App. 397, 702 S.E.2d 833 (2010); State v. Dewalt, 209 N.C. App. 187, 703 S.E.2d 872 (2011); Kennedy v. Polumbo, 209 N.C. App. 394, 704 S.E.2d 916 (2011); State v. Green, 209 N.C. App. 669, 707 S.E.2d 715 (2011); State v. Ziglar, 209 N.C. App. 461, 705 S.E.2d 417 (2011), review denied 365 N.C. 200, 710 S.E.2d 30, 2011 N.C. LEXIS 438 (N.C. 2011); State v. Petty, 212 N.C. App. 368, 711 S.E.2d 509 (2011); State v. Knudsen, 229 N.C. App. 271, 747 S.E.2d 641 (2013), review denied 367 N.C. 258, 749 S.E.2d 865, 2013 N.C. LEXIS 1223 (2013); State v. Marino, 229 N.C. App. 130, 747 S.E.2d 633 (2013), review denied, 749 S.E.2d 889, 2013 N.C. LEXIS 1276 (2013); State v. Kostick, 233 N.C. App. 62, 755 S.E.2d 411 (2014), review denied, 758 S.E.2d 872, 2014 N.C. LEXIS 432 (2014); State v. White, 232 N.C. App. 296, 753 S.E.2d 698 (2014); State v. Townsend, 236 N.C. App. 456, 762 S.E.2d 898 (2014); State v. Shaw, 236 N.C. App. 453, 763 S.E.2d 161 (2014); Mohr v. Matthews, 237 N.C. App. 448, 768 S.E.2d 10 (2014); State v. Hoskins, 242 N.C. App. 168, 775 S.E.2d 15 (2015); State v. Bartlett, 368 N.C. 309, 776 S.E.2d 672 (2015); State v. Loftis, 250 N.C. App. 449, 792 S.E.2d 886 (2016); State v. Cox, 253 N.C. App. 306, 800 S.E.2d 692 (2017), review denied, 803 S.E.2d 153, 2017 N.C. LEXIS 579 (N.C. 2017).

II. DRIVING UNDER THE INFLUENCE.

MEANING OF "UNDER THE INFLUENCE". --A person is under the influence of intoxicating liquor when he has drunk a sufficient quantity of intoxicating beverages to cause him to lose the normal control of his bodily or mental faculties, or both, to such an extent that there is an appreciable impairment of either or both of these faculties. State v. Carroll, 226 N.C. 237, 37 S.E.2d 688 (1946); State v. Lee, 237 N.C. 263, 74 S.E.2d 654 (1953); State v. Turberville, 239 N.C. 25, 79 S.E.2d 359 (1953); State v. Nall, 239 N.C. 60, 79 S.E.2d 354 (1953); State v. Hairr, 244 N.C. 506, 94 S.E.2d 472 (1956); State v. Green, 251 N.C. 141, 110 S.E.2d 805 (1959); State v. Bledsoe, 6 N.C. App. 195, 169 S.E.2d 520 (1969); Atkins v. Moye, 277 N.C. 179, 176 S.E.2d 789 (1970); State v. Combs, 13 N.C. App. 195, 185 S.E.2d 8 (1971); State v. Jenkins, 21 N.C. App. 541, 204 S.E.2d 919 (1974).

A person is under the influence of an intoxicant whenever he has consumed sufficient alcohol to appreciably impair his mental or bodily faculties or both. State v. Bunn, 283 N.C. 444, 196 S.E.2d 777 (1973).

One is under the influence of an intoxicant when he has consumed some quantity of an intoxicating beverage, whether it be a small or a large amount, one drink or several drinks, one bottle or can of beer or more than one, so as to cause him to lose the normal control of his bodily faculties or his mental faculties, or both of those faculties, to such an extent that there is an appreciable impairment of either bodily or mental faculties. State v. Felts, 5 N.C. App. 499, 168 S.E.2d 483 (1969).

"UNDER THE INFLUENCE OF AN INTOXICANT" AND "DRUNK" ARE NOT NECESSARILY SYNONYMOUS. Davis v. Rigsby, 261 N.C. 684, 136 S.E.2d 33 (1964). But see the earlier decision of State v. Carroll, 226 N.C. 237, 37 S.E.2d 688 (1946).

"Drunk," within the meaning of former G.S. 14-335, was not synonymous with "under the influence of intoxicating liquor." State v. Painter, 261 N.C. 332, 134 S.E.2d 638 (1964).

ONE NEED NOT BE DRUNK TO BE GUILTY OF DRIVING UNDER THE INFLUENCE. --It is not necessary for one to be drunk to violate prohibition against operating a motor vehicle while under the influence of some intoxicant, but a person need only be under the influence. State v. Felts, 5 N.C. App. 499, 168 S.E.2d 483 (1969).

PRESENCE IN DEFENDANT'S BLOOD. --It was undisputed that defendant ingested Oxycodone and Tramadol on the day he was involved in a car accident and that they were still present in his blood after the crash. Reasonable jurors could -- and did -- find that defendant was appreciably impaired. State v. Shelton, 263 N.C. App. 681, 824 S.E.2d 136, review denied, 826 S.E.2d 705, 2019 N.C. LEXIS 421 (2019).

USE OF BLOOD ALCOHOL LEVEL AS PROOF. -- See State v. Lockamy, 65 N.C. App. 75, 308 S.E.2d 750 (1983), decided under former G.S. 20-138.

Evidence was sufficient to convict defendant under the appreciably impaired prong of the statute but the jury was only given two options on the verdict sheet; thus, it was not possible to tell whether the jury found defendant guilty based on defendant's blood alcohol concentration level or due to the appreciable impairment of defendant's faculties. State v. Roach, 145 N.C. App. 159, 548 S.E.2d 841 (2001).

THE STATUTORY BLOOD ALCOHOL CONCENTRATION (BAC) IS NOT A SINE QUA NON OF DRIVING UNDER THE INFLUENCE. The State may prove driving under the influence where the BAC is entirely unknown or less than 0.10 (now 0.08). State v. Harrington, 78 N.C. App. 39, 336 S.E.2d 852 (1985).

BREATHALYZER READING OF 0.06 DOES NOT CREATE PRESUMPTION THAT DEFENDANT NOT IMPAIRED. --Contention that because a blood alcohol concentration of 0.10 (now 0.08) or more is illegal per se under subdivision (a)(2) of this section, a breathalyzer reading of 0.06 must create a presumption that the defendant is not impaired is totally without merit and has no basis in statutory or case law. State v. Sigmon, 74 N.C. App. 479, 328 S.E.2d 843 (1985).

BUT A PERSON DRUNK BY THE USE OF INTOXICATING LIQUOR IS NECESSARILY UNDER THE INFLUENCE of intoxicating liquor. State v.

Stephens, 262 N.C. 45, 136 S.E.2d 209 (1964); Southern Nat'l Bank v. Lindsey, 264 N.C. 585, 142 S.E.2d 357 (1965).

THE CORRECT TEST is not whether the party had drunk or consumed a spoonful or a quart of intoxicating beverage, but whether a person is under the influence of an intoxicating liquor by reason of his having drunk a sufficient quantity of an intoxicating beverage to cause him to lose normal control of his bodily or mental faculties, or both, to such an extent that there is an appreciable impairment of either or both of these faculties. State v. Ellis, 261 N.C. 606, 135 S.E.2d 584 (1964).

Intoxicating beverages affect different persons in different ways. Thus the courts have uniformly required proof of facts which would tend to show intoxication, rather than the mere consumption of alcoholic beverages. Atkins v. Moye, 8 N.C. App. 126, 174 S.E.2d 34, aff'd, 277 N.C. 179, 176 S.E.2d 789 (1970).

AS TO THE ELEMENTS OF OFFENSE OF DRIVING UNDER THE INFLUENCE, see State v. Haddock, 254 N.C. 162, 118 S.E.2d 411 (1961); State v. Kellum, 273 N.C. 348, 160 S.E.2d 76 (1968); State v. Carter, 15 N.C. App. 391, 190 S.E.2d 241 (1972); State v. Griggs, 27 N.C. App. 159, 218 S.E.2d 200 (1975); State v. Basinger, 30 N.C. App. 45, 226 S.E.2d 216 (1976); State v. Ray, 54 N.C. App. 473, 283 S.E.2d 823 (1981).

PRIOR CONVICTIONS ARE NOT AN ELEMENT OF THE OFFENSE of driving while impaired, but are now merely one of several factors relating to punishment. State v. Denning, 316 N.C. 523, 342 S.E.2d 855 (1986).

Where there was evidence that defendant had a blood alcohol concentration (BAC) of.09 some two and one-half hours after accident, and no evidence of drinking between the time of the accident and the sample, and police officer smelled a moderate odor of alcohol on defendant's person at the accident scene, observed her slurred speech and glassy eyes, and gave his opinion that she had consumed some controlled substance to an appreciable degree that would have affected both her mental and physical faculties, the evidence was sufficient to go to the jury on the question of DUI, regardless of additional expert extrapolation evidence. State v. Catoe, 78 N.C. App. 167, 336 S.E.2d 691, supersedeas granted, 315 N.C. 186, 338 S.E.2d 107 (1985), cert. denied, 316 N.C. 380, 344 S.E.2d 1 (1986).

BUT CAN BE OFFERED TO IMPEACH DEFENDANT --Trial court properly denied defendant's motion to dismiss for insufficient evidence, as testimony by the deputy who arrested defendant provided substantial evidence of defendant's impairment; an intoxilyzer test and field sobriety tests were not required to establish a defendant's faculties as being appreciably impaired, and the trial court properly denied defendant's motion in limine to suppress and bar the use of his prior DWI convictions, as a DWI conviction was a class 1 misdemeanor admissible for impeachment purposes under G.S. 8C-1, N.C. R. Evid. 609(a). State v. Gregory, 154 N.C. App. 718, 572 S.E.2d 838 (2002).

THE OFFENSE OF DRIVING UNDER THE INFLUENCE REQUIRES AN APPRECIABLE IMPAIRMENT of one's normal control of his bodily or mental faculties, or both. State v. Combs, 13 N.C. App. 195, 185 S.E.2d 8 (1971).

SHOWING OF A SLIGHT EFFECT ON DEFENDANT'S FACULTIES IS INSUFFICIENT. --It is not sufficient for a conviction for driving under the influence for the State to show that defendant drove an automobile upon a highway within the State when he had drunk a sufficient quantity of intoxicating liquor to affect however slightly his mental and physical faculties. The State must show that he has drunk a sufficient quantity of intoxicating liquor to cause him to lose the normal control of his bodily or mental faculties, or both, to such an extent that there was an appreciable impairment of either or both of these faculties. State v. Hairr, 244 N.C. 506, 94 S.E.2d 472 (1956).

VIOLATIONS MUST BE SHOWN BEYOND A REASONABLE DOUBT. --Before the State is entitled to a conviction for driving under the influence, it must show beyond a reasonable doubt that the defendant was driving a motor vehicle on a public highway of the State while under the influence of intoxicating liquor. State v. Carroll, 226 N.C. 237, 37 S.E.2d 688 (1946); State v. Lee, 237 N.C. 263, 74 S.E.2d 654 (1953); State v. Nall, 239 N.C. 60, 79 S.E.2d 354 (1953); State v. Hairr, 244 N.C. 506, 94 S.E.2d 472 (1956).

BUT CIRCUMSTANTIAL EVIDENCE MAY SUFFICE. --Though the evidence on the part of the State as to a violation is circumstantial, it may be sufficient to be submitted to a jury. State v. Newton, 207 N.C. 323, 177 S.E. 184 (1934).

PRIMA FACIE SHOWING OF VIOLATION. --The fact that a motorist has been drinking, when considered in connection with faulty driving such as following an irregular course on the highway or other conduct indicating an impairment of physical or mental faculties, is sufficient, prima facie, to show a violation. State v. Hewitt, 263 N.C. 759, 140 S.E.2d 241 (1965); Atkins v. Moye, 277 N.C. 179, 176 S.E.2d 789 (1970); State v. Cartwright, 12 N.C. App. 4, 182 S.E.2d 203 (1971); State v. Flannery, 31 N.C. App. 617, 230 S.E.2d 603 (1976).

AIDERS AND ABETTORS GUILTY AS PRINCIPALS. --The unlawful operation of a vehicle upon a highway within this State while under the influence of intoxicating liquor is a misdemeanor, and all who participate therein, as aiders and abettors or otherwise, are guilty as principals. State v. Nall, 239 N.C. 60, 79 S.E.2d 354 (1953).

When an owner places his motor vehicle in the hands of an intoxicated driver, sits by his side, and permits him, without protest, to operate the vehicle on a public highway while in a state of intoxication, the owner is as guilty as the man at the wheel. State v. Gibbs, 227 N.C. 677, 44 S.E.2d 201 (1947).

EVIDENCE INSUFFICIENT TO IMPLICATE FRIENDS OF DRUNK DRIVER. --The record did not contain substantial evidence that one, two or all of three minors aided and abetted defendant minor in committing the offense of driving while impaired under this section; while the record contained evidence that the three consumed alcoholic beverages together on the evening of the accident, and though they observed the defendant minor consume some of, or as much as, a six-pack of beer in a "short period of time." and did not stop him from driving while impaired, these activities did not render them guilty as principals of his driving while impaired offense. Smith v. Winn-Dixie Charlotte, Inc., 142 N.C. App. 255, 542 S.E.2d 288 (2001), cert. denied, 353 N.C. 452, 548 S.E.2d 528 (2001).

DRIVING UNDER THE INFLUENCE IN VIOLATION OF STATUTE IS NEGLIGENCE PER SE. Edwards v. Mayes, 385 F.2d 369 (4th Cir. 1967); Arant v. Ransom, 4 N.C. App. 89, 165 S.E.2d 671 (1969).

It is negligence per se for one to operate an automobile while under the influence of an intoxicant. Davis v. Rigsby, 261 N.C. 684, 136 S.E.2d 33 (1964); Southern Nat'l Bank v. Lindsey, 264 N.C. 585, 142 S.E.2d 357 (1965); Wardrick v. Davis, 15 N.C. App. 261, 189 S.E.2d 746 (1972).

Defendant was guilty of negligence per se in operating his pickup truck while under the influence of intoxicating liquor in violation of statute. Watters v. Parrish, 252 N.C. 787, 115 S.E.2d 1 (1960).

It is unlawful for any person who is under the influence of intoxicating liquor to drive any vehicle upon the highways within this State, and a violation is negligence. Atkins v. Moye, 277 N.C. 179, 176 S.E.2d 789 (1970).

BUT CAUSAL RELATION MUST BE SHOWN TO CONSTITUTE ACTIONABLE OR CONTRIBUTORY NEGLIGENCE. --Unquestionably a motorist is guilty of negligence if he operates a motor vehicle on the highway while under the influence of intoxicating liquor. Such conduct, however, will not constitute either actionable negligence or contributory negligence unless, like any other negligence, it is causally related to the accident. Atkins v. Moye, 277 N.C. 179, 176 S.E.2d 789 (1970). See also, Edwards v. Mayes, 385 F.2d 369 (4th Cir. 1967).

Mere proof that a motorist involved in a collision was under the influence of an intoxicant at the time does not establish a causal relation between his condition and the collision. His condition must have caused him to violate a rule of the road and to operate his vehicle in a manner which was a proximate cause of the collision. Atkins v. Moye, 277 N.C. 179, 176 S.E.2d 789 (1970).

CONSTITUTIONAL AND STATUTORY RIGHTS OF ACCUSED. --One who is detained by police officers under a charge of driving while under the influence of an intoxicant has the same constitutional and statutory rights as any other accused. State v. Hill, 277 N.C. 547, 178 S.E.2d 462 (1971); State v. Lawson, 285 N.C. 320, 204 S.E.2d 843 (1974).

APPLICABILITY OF MIRANDA RULES. --After defendant was arrested and placed in patrol car, the rules of Miranda were applicable to him just as to any other person in custody on a criminal charge. State v. Lawson, 285 N.C. 320, 204 S.E.2d 843 (1974).

RIGHT OF ACCUSED TO COMMUNICATE WITH COUNSEL AND OTHERS. --The denial of a request for permission to contact counsel as soon as a person is charged with a crime involving the element of intoxication is a denial of a constitutional right, resulting in irreparable prejudice to his defense. State v. Hill, 277 N.C. 547, 178 S.E.2d 462 (1971).

When one is taken into police custody for an offense of which intoxication is an essential element, time is of the essence, as intoxication does not last. Thus, if one accused of driving while intoxicated is to have witnesses for his defense, he must have access to his counsel, friends, relatives, or some disinterested person within a relatively short time after his arrest. State v. Hill, 277 N.C. 547, 178 S.E.2d 462 (1971).

A defendant's guilt or innocence of the offense of driving under the influence depends upon whether he is intoxicated at the time of his arrest. His condition then is the crucial and decisive fact to be proven. Permission to communicate with counsel and friends is of no avail if those who come to the jail in response to a prisoner's call are not permitted to see for themselves whether he is intoxicated. In this situation, the right of a defendant to communicate with counsel and friends implies, at the very least, the right to have them see, observe and examine him, with reference to his alleged intoxication. State v. Hill, 277 N.C. 547, 178 S.E.2d 462 (1971).

Application of a per se prejudice rule as set forth in State v. Hill, 277 N.C. 547, 178 S.E.2d 462 (1971) is inappropriate in cases involving a violation of subdivision (a)(2) of this section, driving with an alcohol concentration of 0.10 (now 0.08) or more. State v. Knoll, 84 N.C. App. 228, 352 S.E.2d 463 (1987), rev'd on other grounds, 322 N.C. 535, 369 S.E.2d 558 (1988).

Under this section, as amended, denial of access is no longer inherently prejudicial to a defendant's ability to gather evidence in support of his innocence in every driving while impaired case, since an alcohol concentration of 0.10 (now 0.08) is sufficient. State v. Gilbert, 85 N.C. App. 594, 355 S.E.2d 261 (1987), distinguishing State v. Hill, 277 N.C. 547, 178 S.E.2d 462 (1971), which was decided when the statute provided that a 0.10 (now 0.08) alcohol concentration merely created an inference of intoxication.

ADMISSIBILITY OF HORIZONTAL GAZE NYSTAGMUS TEST. --The state's failure to lay a proper foundation for the admission of a horizontal gaze nystagmus test was reversible error, where the defendant was convicted for driving while impaired as the defendant met his burden of showing a reasonable possibility that a different outcome would have been reached had the test results not been erroneously admitted. State v. Helms, 348 N.C. 578, 504 S.E.2d 293 (1998).

In a case where defendant was convicted of driving while impaired, defendant was not entitled to a new trial because, although the officer was not tendered as an expert in Horizontal Gaze Nystagmus (HGN) interpretation, defendant was not prejudiced by the admission of the officer's testimony regarding the HGN test as there was overwhelming evidence of defendant's impairment even without that testimony because the officer observed defendant's slurred speech, glassy, red eyes, and strong odor of alcohol; there were two positive breath test results; defendant did not successfully complete two other sobriety tests; and the blood alcohol test results indicated legal impairment with a blood alcohol content of 0.10. State v. Killian, 250 N.C. App. 443, 792 S.E.2d 883 (2016), review denied, stay lifted, stay denied, 797 S.E.2d 11, 2017 N.C. LEXIS 187 (2017).

THE ADMINISTRATION OF A BREATH ANALYSIS IS NOT A CRITICAL STAGE OF THE PROSECUTION for driving while impaired entitling defendant to counsel. For this reason, it was not error for the trial court to refuse to dismiss the driving while impaired charge based on a violation of defendant's right under U.S. Const., Amend. VI, to counsel at a critical stage of the prosecution. State v. Dellinger, 73 N.C. App. 685, 327 S.E.2d 609 (1985).

THERE IS NO CONSTITUTIONAL RIGHT TO HAVE AN ATTORNEY PRESENT PRIOR TO SUBMITTING TO CHEMICAL ANALYSIS. State v. Howren, 312 N.C. 454, 323 S.E.2d 335 (1984).

ODOR OF ALCOHOL INSUFFICIENT TO SHOW THAT DRIVER IS UNDER INFLUENCE. --An odor of alcohol on the breath of the driver of an automobile is evidence that he has been drinking. However, an odor, standing alone, is not evidence that a driver is under the influence of an intoxicant, and the mere fact that one has had a drink will not support such a finding. Atkins v. Moye, 277 N.C. 179, 176 S.E.2d 789 (1970); State v. Cartwright, 12 N.C. App. 4, 182 S.E.2d 203 (1971).

ADMISSIBILITY OF OFFICER'S OPINION. --In a prosecution for drunken driving, the arresting officer may be asked his opinion as to whether at the time the arrest was made the defendant was under the influence. State v. Warren, 236 N.C. 358, 72 S.E.2d 763 (1952).

In a prosecution for driving under the influence, two highway patrolmen who investigated the accident in which defendant was involved just before his arrest were properly allowed to testify that in their opinion defendant was under the influence of intoxicating liquor. State v. Mills, 268 N.C. 142, 150 S.E.2d 13 (1966).

ADMISSIBILITY OF OPINION OF LAY WITNESS. --A lay witness is competent to testify whether or not in his opinion a person was under the influence of an intoxicant on a given occasion on which he observed him. State v. Willard, 241 N.C. 259, 84 S.E.2d 899 (1954).

EVIDENCE HELD INSUFFICIENT FOR CONVICTION. --Where officers who reached the scene of an accident some 30 minutes after it occurred testified that in their opinion defendant driver was intoxicated or under the influence of something, and one of them testified that he smelled something on defendant's breath, but both testified that they did not know whether defendant's condition was due to drink or to injuries sustained by him in the accident, such evidence raised no more than a suspicion or conjecture as to whether defendant was driving under the influence of liquor or narcotic drugs, and defendant's motion as of nonsuit should have been allowed. State v. Hough, 229 N.C. 532, 50 S.E.2d 496 (1948).

Testimony of two witnesses to the effect that from the detection of some "foreign" odor of an intoxicant from the mouth of a man whom they had not seen before, who had been knocked unconscious by a blow on the head, they were of opinion that he was under the influence of intoxicating liquor, standing alone, was insufficient to constitute substantial evidence that the man, while driving an automobile on the highway, had been under the influence of intoxicants to the extent held necessary in State v. Carroll, 226 N.C. 237, 37 S.E.2d 688 (1946), to constitute a violation. State v. Flinchem, 228 N.C. 149, 44 S.E.2d 724 (1947).

State of North Carolina presented insufficient evidence to establish that defendant was impaired when defendant was driving defendant's vehicle as the State failed to present evidence that defendant's admitted impairment from earlier consuming methamphetamine began before or during the time of a motor vehicle accident that occurred when defendant was operating defendant's vehicle. State v. Eldred, 259 N.C. App. 345, 815 S.E.2d 742 (2018).

EVIDENCE HELD SUFFICIENT FOR CONVICTION. --Evidence was sufficient to support defendant's DUI conviction under G.S. 20-138.1, where a witness testified that she observed the car from first sighting until the car stopped and the police arrived, the witness did not see anyone exit the car and the car did not move, an officer testified that the driver was in driver's seat when the officer arrived and the officer spoke to defendant, defendant signed an Intoxilyzer rights form, and the administrator of Intoxilyzer testified to giving defendant the test. State v. Clowers, 217 N.C. App. 520, 720 S.E.2d 430 (2011).

Substantial evidence of each element of the crime of driving while impaired was presented because a lab report of defendant's blood sample indicated that three of the drugs found in defendant's blood were listed in N.C. Gen. Stat. ch. 90 as Schedule II controlled substances, and therefore were impairing substances under G.S. 20-4.01(14a). Moreover, defendant did not sufficiently perform the standardized field sobriety tests which defendant was asked to perform. State v. Braswell, 222 N.C. App. 176, 729 S.E.2d 697 (2012).

Evidence was sufficient to support defendant's conviction of driving while impaired because the officer found defendant in the driver's seat of a stationary vehicle with the engine running, the officer testified that defendant was apparently sleeping, there was a strong odor of alcohol on the defendant's breath, the defendant's speech was slurred, officers saw an alcohol bottle between the defendant's legs, defendant admitted that the defendant had consumed alcohol, defendant's blood test results indicated that the blood contained alcohol, THC, THCA, amphetamine, and methamphetamine, and defendant refused to submit to an intoxilyzer test. State v. Hoque, -- N.C. App. --, 837 S.E.2d 464 (2020).

IN A PROSECUTION FOR INVOLUNTARY MAN-SLAUGHTER INCIDENT TO DRIVING UNDER THE INFLUENCE, defendant's admission of being "intoxicated" or having "consumed too much beer" at 2:30 a.m. to 3:00 a.m. was sufficient evidence from which the jury could have inferred that he was impaired between 1:05 a.m. and 1:52 a.m., the time of the fatal accident. State v. Brown, 87 N.C. App. 13, 359 S.E.2d 265 (1987).

NO DOUBLE JEOPARDY VIOLATION. --Defendant's conviction on a charge of habitual impaired driving did not violate defendant's rights to be free of double jeopardy; recidivist statutes, such as habitual impaired driving, survived constitutional challenges regarding double jeopardy because they increased the severity of the punishment for the crime being prosecuted; they did not punish a previous crime a second time. State v. Bradley, 181 N.C. App. 557, 640 S.E.2d 432 (2007).

EVIDENCE OF IMPAIRMENT HELD SUFFI-CIENT. --In addition to evidence showing that defendant had a blood alcohol content of 0.06, evidence that defendant was arrested by a police officer who testified that in her opinion, defendant was under the influence of alcohol based on observation of defendant, defendant's driving on the occasion in question, the odor of alcohol about her person and her inability to perform satisfactorily certain sobriety tests constituted substantial evidence, separate and apart from the breathalyzer result, that defendant's mental and physical faculties were appreciably impaired under subdivision (a)(1) of this section. State v. Sigmon, 74 N.C. App. 479, 328 S.E.2d 843 (1985).

Where trooper could have placed defendant under arrest for not carrying his driver's license, but merely choose to ask defendant to step back to the patrol car so that he could check defendant's license information and so that he could further investigate defendant's intoxication based upon defendant's unsteady movements and the smell of alcohol, and after defendant failed the field sobriety tests he was placed under arrest and advised of his rights, the seizure was constitutionally permissible and there was sufficient probable cause for arrest. State v. Johnston, 115 N.C. App. 711, 446 S.E.2d 135 (1994).

Police officer's testimony that the officer observed the defendant driving on a street that was twice the width of a normal street out in the county and that the officer formed an opinion that the defendant was appreciably impaired after conducting a field sobriety test was sufficient to support the defendant's conviction for driving while impaired. State v. Mark, 154 N.C. App. 341, 571 S.E.2d 867 (2002), aff'd, 357 N.C. 242, 580 S.E.2d 693 (2003).

Trial court did not err in allowing expert testimony that defendant's blood alcohol content at the time of the crash was 0.08 based on an average alcohol elimination rate of 0.0165 because the State was not required to establish that level to prove that defendant was driving while impaired, and the evidence was sufficient for a DWI conviction regardless of the expert's testimony; the evidence established (1) that a trooper smelled an odor of alcohol on defendant's person at the accident scene, (2) that defendant needed assistance with walking to the patrol car, (3) that defendant had difficulty writing defendant's statement on the appropriate lines, (4) that defendant had a "blank face," and (5) that defendant did not perform satisfactorily on field sobriety tests administered by the trooper. State v. Taylor, 165 N.C. App. 750, 600 S.E.2d 483 (2004).

Conviction for impaired driving was supported by sufficient evidence, including evidence that defendant's driving was erratic, that she accelerated to hit a police vehicle after a police chase, that defendant admitted she had consumed alcohol before driving, a fact confirmed by a breathalyzer result showing a 0.07 breath alcohol concentration, and that an open half-filled bottle of vodka was found in the passenger area of her vehicle. State v. Wood, 174 N.C. App. 790, 622 S.E.2d 120 (2005).

Substantial evidence supported the trial court's denial of defendant's request for dismissal of the charge of driving while impaired under G.S. 20-138.1(a). The evidence showed that: (1) defendant had been drinking at a party shortly before defendant's arrest; (2) defendant had been operating the motor vehicle in question on a road shortly before defendant's arrest; (3) defendant was operating the vehicle well above the speed limit on the road and drove on the shoulder of the road; (4) defendant's eyes were red and glassy; (5) defendant smelled of alcohol; and (6) defendant had trouble maintaining defendant's balance while walking. State v. Coffey, 189 N.C. App. 382, 658 S.E.2d 73 (2008).

Denial of defendant's motion to dismiss the driving while impaired charge was proper where the evidence showed faulty driving, erratic behavior, and blood tests showing that defendant had consumed cocaine and alcohol. State v. Norton, 213 N.C. App. 75, 712 S.E.2d 387 (2011).

Defendant's admission to taking prescription medication on the morning of the accident and the result of field sobriety tests were sufficient to support defendant's conviction for driving while impaired. State v. Braswell, 222 N.C. App. 176, 729 S.E.2d 697 (2012).

PRESCRIPTION DRUG AS IMPAIRING SUBSTANCE. --Expert testimony that Floricet, the drug defendant alleged he took prior to driving, was an impairing substance and that a healthcare professional should have warned defendant of its effects led to the conclusion that defendant knew or should have known that it could impair him, and was thus that he was on notice that, by driving after taking Floricet, he risked crossing over the line into the territory of proscribed conduct. State v. Highsmith, 173 N.C. App. 600, 619 S.E.2d 586 (2005).

EVIDENCE HELD SUFFICIENT TO GO TO JURY. --Evidence that defendant was intoxicated was held amply sufficient to be submitted to the jury even in the absence of expert testimony as to the alcoholic content of defendant's blood. State v. Willard, 241 N.C. 259, 84 S.E.2d 899 (1954).

Chapter 20

Evidence that defendant was highly intoxicated when sheriff caught up with him after a chase was sufficient to take charge of driving under the influence of intoxicants to the jury. State v. Garner, 244 N.C. 79, 92 S.E.2d 445 (1956).

The State's evidence was sufficient to be submitted to the jury on the issue of whether defendant was guilty of drunken driving where it tended to show that defendant was driving on the wrong side of the road, that he had a strong odor of alcohol about him, that he was unsteady on his feet and that he had half a fifth of whiskey in his truck. State v. Cartwright, 12 N.C. App. 4, 182 S.E.2d 203 (1971).

For additional cases holding evidence sufficient for submission to the jury, see State v. Blankenship, 229 N.C. 589, 50 S.E.2d 724 (1948). See State v. Sawyer, 230 N.C. 713, 55 S.E.2d 464 (1949); State v. Simpson, 233 N.C. 438, 64 S.E.2d 568 (1951); State v. Cole, 241 N.C. 576, 86 S.E.2d 203 (1955); State v. St. Clair, 246 N.C. 183, 97 S.E.2d 840, modified on other grounds, 247 N.C. 228, 100 S.E.2d 493 (1957); State v. Green, 251 N.C. 40, 110 S.E.2d 609 (1959); State v. Mills, 268 N.C. 142, 150 S.E.2d 13 (1966); State v. Flannery, 31 N.C. App. 617, 230 S.E.2d 603 (1976).

Evidence held sufficient for a reasonable jury to infer that defendant who was found asleep in driver's seat in car which had run off the road and into a fence was under the influence of an impairing substance when he drove the vehicle. State v. Mack, 81 N.C. App. 578, 345 S.E.2d 223 (1986).

Defendant's electric scooter, which was not self-balancing, with its two wheels in tandem, and which did not fall within the two statutory exceptions from a vehicle under G.S. 20-138.1(e) with regard to horses, bicycles, and lawnmowers or G.S. 20-4.01(49) as to transportation for a person with a mobility impairment, fell within the legislature's definition of vehicle in G.S. 20-4.01(49) and, because the evidence at trial showed that his breath alcohol concentration following arrest was 0.13, there was sufficient evidence to uphold defendant's conviction for impaired driving under G.S. 20- 138.1. State v. Crow, 175 N.C. App. 119, 623 S.E.2d 68 (2005).

Denial of motion to dismiss was proper as the evidence could have supported a reasonable juror's conclusion that defendant could be found guilty under either prong of the driving while impaired statute. State v. Teate, 180 N.C. App. 601, 638 S.E.2d 29 (2006).

State of North Carolina presented sufficient evidence to prove the elements of driving while under the influence of an impairing substance as defendant collided with the rear end of another vehicle in a restaurant drive-thru, officers noted signs of impairment, defendant admitted to having earlier consumed alprazolam, an officer testified that defendant indicated impairment in a HGN test, and another officer who performed a drug recognition evaluation testified that defendant was impaired by a central nervous system depressant. State v. Fincher, 259 N.C. App. 159, 814 S.E.2d 606 (2018).

EVIDENCE SUFFICIENT TO SUPPORT FINDING THAT DEFENDANT WAS DRIVER.

--Defendant's extrajudicial statement in conjunction with circumstantial evidence that no one other than defendant, who was sitting in the driver' seat, was in the vehicle when the officer arrived on the scene was sufficient to withstand a motion to dismiss the driving while impaired charge. State v. Reeves, 218 N.C. App. 570, 721 S.E.2d 317 (2012).

EVIDENCE OF DRIVING INSUFFICIENT. --Only evidence of defendant's operation of a motor vehicle was his admission, which should have been suppressed; although defendant was sitting in the driver's seat of the vehicle, the vehicle's engine was not running when the detective approached the vehicle, there was no evidence of when the vehicle had arrived at the hotel parking lot, and there was no evidence that the vehicle's lights were on or that the engine was warm. State v. Burris, -- N.C. App. --, 2017 N.C. App. LEXIS 175 (Mar. 21, 2017).

A PERSON MAY BE "UNDER THE INFLUENCE" OF INTOXICANTS AND YET BE CAPABLE OF A SPECIFIC INTENT TO KILL. State v. Medley, 295 N.C. 75, 243 S.E.2d 374 (1978).

Evidence was sufficient to go to jury where defendant was involved in an automobile accident, at the accident scene defendant's breath smelled of alcohol, his speech was slurred, his eyes were red, glassy, and watery, he was swaying, staggering, and generally so unsteady on his feet that he had to use police car to steady himself, and he passed out on the way to the police station and again while waiting to be tested at the police station. State v. Barber, 93 N.C. App. 42, 376 S.E.2d 497, cert. denied, 324 N.C. 578, 381 S.E.2d 775 (1989).

III. DRIVING WITH 0.10 (NOW 0.08) PERCENT OR MORE ALCOHOL IN BLOOD.

EDITOR'S NOTE. --Many of the cases cited in the annotations under "III." were decided under this section as it read prior to the 1993 amendment, which reduced the blood alcohol content for driving while impaired and related offenses from 0.10 to 0.08.

AS TO THE ELEMENTS OF THIS OFFENSE, see State v. Basinger, 30 N.C. App. 45, 226 S.E.2d 216 (1976); State v. Donald, 51 N.C. App. 238, 275 S.E.2d 531 (1981).

SOURCE OF ALCOHOL NEED NOT BE INTOXICATING BEVERAGE. --The primary purpose for which the General Assembly enacted prohibition against driving with specific concentration of alcohol in blood was to regulate conduct for the safety of the public using the State's highways, and it would be contrary to the legislative intent to read into it a requirement that the source of alcohol be an intoxicating beverage. A person whose blood contains 0.10 (now 0.08) percent or more by weight of alcohol, regardless of the source of the alcohol, and who drives upon the highways within the State, violates the prohibition. State v. Hill, 31 N.C. App. 733, 230 S.E.2d 579 (1976), cert. denied, 272 N.C. 267, 233 S.E.2d 394 (1977).

AND STATE NEED NOT PROVE DEFENDANT KNEW HE WAS DRINKING ALCOHOL. --In order to convict a person of driving with a blood alcohol

Chapter 20

content of 0.10 (now 0.08) percent or more, the State need not prove that defendant must have known or had reasonable grounds to believe that he was drinking alcohol. State v. Hill, 31 N.C. App. 733, 230 S.E.2d 579 (1976), cert. denied, 292 N.C. 267, 233 S.E.2d 394 (1977).

IT IS NEGLIGENCE PER SE for person with a blood alcohol concentration of 0.10 (now 0.08) or more to operate a motor vehicle. Hinkamp v. AMC, 735 F. Supp. 176 (E.D.N.C. 1989), aff'd, 900 F.2d 252 (4th Cir. 1990).

EXPRESSION OF CONCENTRATION IN GRAMS PER MILLILITERS OR IN LITERS NOT REQUIRED. --There is no requirement in this section or elsewhere in the Motor Vehicle Code that a person's alcohol concentration be expressed in terms of grams per milliliters of blood or liters of breath, nor have the courts interpreted this section as requiring such specificity; moreover, where both the chemical analyst who testified about the test results and the trial court defined the term "alcohol concentration" for the jury so that it was completely clear what was meant by the term, there was no error in the admission of the test results. State v. Jones, 76 N.C. App. 160, 332 S.E.2d 494 (1985).

RIGHT OF ACCUSED TO COMMUNICATE WITH COUNSEL AND OTHERS. --Application of a per se prejudice rule as set forth in State v. Hill, 277 N.C. 547, 178 S.E.2d 462 (1971) is inappropriate in cases involving a violation of subdivision (a)(2) of this section, driving with an alcohol concentration of 0.10 (now 0.08) or more. State v. Knoll, 84 N.C. App. 228, 352 S.E.2d 463 (1987), rev'd on other grounds, 322 N.C. 535, 369 S.E.2d 558 (1988).

DEFENDANT HAS BURDEN TO PROVE PREJUDICE. --In cases arising under G.S. 20-138.1(a)(2), prejudice will not be assumed to accompany a violation of defendant's statutory rights, but rather, defendant must make a showing that he was prejudiced in order to gain relief. State v. Knoll, 322 N.C. 535, 369 S.E.2d 558 (1988).

DEFENDANTS MADE A SUFFICIENT SHOWING OF A SUBSTANTIAL STATUTORY VIOLATION and of the prejudice arising therefrom to warrant relief where the evidence showed that magistrates failed to advise defendants of their rights under G.S. 15A-511(b), 15A-533(b) and 15A-534(c) and deprived defendants of their rights to secure their liberty for a significant time during a critical period. State v. Knoll, 322 N.C. 535, 369 S.E.2d 558 (1988).

PROOF OF PREJUDICE RESULTING FROM DENIAL OF ACCESS. --While a defendant charged with an offense under this section might be prejudiced by a denial of access or unwarranted detention, at the very least, such defendant must show that lost evidence or testimony would have been helpful to his defense, that the evidence would have been significant, and that the evidence or testimony was lost as a result of the statutory deprivations of which he complains. State v. Knoll, 84 N.C. App. 228, 352 S.E.2d 463 (1987), rev'd on other grounds, 322 N.C. 535, 369 S.E.2d 558 (1988).

PROOF. --Once it is determined that the chemical analysis of defendant's breath is valid, then a reading of 0.10 (now 0.08) constitutes reliable evidence and is sufficient to satisfy the State's burden of proof as to this element of the offense of driving while impaired. State v. Shuping, 312 N.C. 421, 323 S.E.2d 350 (1984).

Defendant was not entitled to dismissal for a lack of evidence defendant operated a motor vehicle because (1) defendant admitted defendant had been driving, (2) the vehicle was parked by a hotel's front door, rather than in a parking spot, (3) defendant exited the driver's seat, and (4) the vehicle was registered to defendant. State v. Burris, 253 N.C. App. 525, 799 S.E.2d 452 (2017), review denied, 803 S.E.2d 158, 2017 N.C. LEXIS 601 (N.C. 2017).

EVIDENCE CORROBORATING DEFENDANT'S ADMISSIONS. --Evidence aliunde admissions by defendant was sufficient to corroborate defendant's admission that he drove vehicle which was found wrecked on a public highway or vehicular area after he had consumed alcohol and, when considered with his admissions, was sufficient to support a reasonable inference that at the time he was driving the motor vehicle he had consumed a sufficient amount of alcohol to raise his blood alcohol level to 0.10% (now 0.08) or greater at a relevant time after driving. State v. Trexler, 316 N.C. 528, 342 S.E.2d 878 (1986).

EXTRAPOLATION EVIDENCE. --In prosecution in which the jury found defendant guilty of DUI and driving on the wrong side of the road, testimony of expert witness that the average person displays a certain rate of decline in blood alcohol concentration (BAC) in the hours after the last consumption of alcohol, and that based on that average rate of decline, defendant's BAC, which was .09 some two and one-half hours after the accident, would have been approximately 0.13 at the time of the accident, was not improper. State v. Catoe, 78 N.C. App. 167, 336 S.E.2d 691, supersedeas granted, 315 N.C. 186, 338 S.E.2d 107 (1985), cert. denied, 316 N.C. 380, 344 S.E.2d 1 (1986).

In a case where defendant was convicted of driving while impaired, the trial court abused its discretion by admitting the challenged expert testimony on retrograde extrapolation because the State's expert witness conceded that she had no factual information from which she could assume that defendant was in a post-absorptive state, and her testimony did not satisfy the Daubert "fit" test as the expert's otherwise reliable analysis was not properly tied to the facts of the case; however, the error was harmless as the evidence was sufficient to show that, even without the challenged expert testimony, there was no reasonable possibility that the jury would have reached a different result. State v. Babich, 252 N.C. App. 165, 797 S.E.2d 359 (2017).

WILLFUL VIOLATION. --Defendant's .181 blood alcohol concentration unquestionably demonstrated a willful violation of G.S. 20-138.1. State v. Purdie, 93 N.C. App. 269, 377 S.E.2d 789 (1989).

LESSER INCLUDED OFFENSE. --As to offense of driving with a blood alcohol content of 0.10 (now

0.08) percent or more being a lesser included offense of driving under the influence, see State v. Basinger, 30 N.C. App. 45, 226 S.E.2d 216 (1976).

CONVICTION OF THE LESSER OFFENSE CONSTITUTED AN ACQUITTAL IN THE DISTRICT COURT OF THE GREATER OFFENSE. State v. McKenzie, 292 N.C. 170, 232 S.E.2d 424 (1977).

MANDATORY REVOCATION OF LICENSE. --Under G.S. 20-17(a)(2), defendant's driver's license was subject to mandatory revocation for one year because she was convicted under G.S. 20-138.1 for driving with an alcohol concentration of 0.16. State v. Benbow, 169 N.C. App. 613, 610 S.E.2d 297 (2005).

SUFFICIENT EVIDENCE SUPPORTED A CONVICTION of driving while impaired, G.S. 20-138.1, because a trooper testified that the reading on the Intoxilyzer 5000 rounded down, that he administered the Intoxylizer test two times, and that each administration showed defendant's BAC to be.08. State v. Arrington, 215 N.C. App. 161, 714 S.E.2d 777 (2011), decided under former G.S. 143B-262.4.

IV. PROCEDURE.

ISSUANCE OF CITATION TOLLED STATUTE OF LIMITATIONS. --It was error to affirm a decision upholding an order granting defendant's motion to dismiss because a citation issued for driving while subject to an impairing substance tolled the statute of limitations, and the citation was a constitutionally and statutorily proper criminal pleading that conveyed jurisdiction to the district court to try defendant; because a citation could serve as the charging document for misdemeanors, the purpose of the statute of limitations was satisfied by its issuance. State v. Curtis, 371 N.C. 355, 817 S.E.2d 187 (2018).

WARRANT HELD SUFFICIENT. --A warrant charging defendant with driving under the influence and reckless driving, which were treated as separate counts, was sufficient since each count charged all the essential elements constituting the violation of law charged. State v. Fuller, 24 N.C. App. 38, 209 S.E.2d 805 (1974).

SUMMONS SUFFICIENT --Summons which indicated the charged as "operate a motor vehicle on a street highway while subject to an impairing substance" and the date of the offense was a sufficient allegation of time in the usual form. State v. Friend, 219 N.C. App. 338, 724 S.E.2d 85 (2012).

RIGHT TO HAVE BREATHALYZER TEST WITNESSED. --To deny defendant access to a witness to observe his breathalyzer test when the State's sole evidence of the offense of driving while impaired is the personal observations of the authorities would constitute a flagrant violation of defendant's constitutional right to obtain witnesses under N.C. Const., Art. I, § 23 as a matter of law and would require that the charges be dismissed. State v. Ferguson, 90 N.C. App. 513, 369 S.E.2d 378, cert. denied, 323 N.C. 367, 373 S.E.2d 551 (1988).

Defendant's G.S. 20.138.1 conviction was vacated as his suppression motion was improperly denied where: (1) after being arrested, defendant chose to have a witness present under G.S. 20-16.2(a); (2) in the presence of the arresting officer, defendant made contact with his selected witness by telephone and asked her to come and witness the administration of the Intoxilyzer test; (3) less than 20 minutes later, his witness arrived at the public safety center; and (4) despite multiple attempts to obtain access to defendant, the witness was not present when the Intoxilyzer test was administered, because she was still being told to wait in the lobby. State v. Buckheit, 223 N.C. App. 269, 735 S.E.2d 345 (2012).

Defendant's Knoll motion was properly denied because, inter alia, defendant could call counsel and friends to observe defendant and help defendant obtain an independent chemical analysis. State v. Townsend, 236 N.C. App. 456, 762 S.E.2d 898 (2014).

JURY IS RESPONSIBLE FOR FINDING FACTS which support the conclusion that the elements of the offense have been proven beyond a reasonable doubt by the State. Once the offense is so proved, the jury has no further responsibility; it does not find aggravating or mitigating circumstances, or the existence of grossly aggravating factors. The jury only determines guilt or innocence of driving while impaired. Field v. Sheriff of Wake County, 654 F. Supp. 1367 (E.D.N.C. 1986), rev'd on other grounds, 831 F.2d 530 (4th Cir. 1987).

BIFURCATED PROCEDURE CONSTITUTIONAL. --The bifurcated procedure that the legislature has established for impaired driving cases, with the jury determining whether this section has been violated and the judge determining the length of punishment required under G.S. 20-179, is constitutional. State v. Field, 75 N.C. App. 647, 331 S.E.2d 221, cert. denied and appeal dismissed, 315 N.C. 186, 337 S.E.2d 582 (1985).

EVIDENCE OF WANTON CONDUCT HELD SUFFICIENT TO GO TO JURY. --In a negligence action, the evidence of the defendant's wanton conduct was sufficient to go to the jury, where defendant admitted: awareness of her own substantial intoxication, indifference to her duty under this section to avoid operating a motor vehicle while impaired, and obliviousness to the duty under G.S. 20-158 to stop at the five stoplights between the cocktail lounge and the accident. It was for the jury to determine whether defendant's negligence evinced a wilful or reckless indifference to the rights of others, and then, whether her wilful or wanton conduct was the proximate cause of the accident. King v. Allred, 76 N.C. App. 427, 333 S.E.2d 758, cert. denied, 315 N.C. 184, 337 S.E.2d 857 (1985).

SIMILARITY BETWEEN NORTH AND SOUTH CAROLINAS' DRIVING WHILE IMPAIRED STATUTES NOTICED JUDICIALLY. --Trial court did not err in taking judicial notice of similarity between South Carolina impaired driving statutes and North Carolina statute. Sykes v. Hiatt, 98 N.C. App. 688, 391 S.E.2d 834 (1990).

DEFENDANT MUST SHOW SUBSTANTIAL STATUTORY VIOLATION AND RESULTING PREJUDICE FOR DISMISSAL UNDER SUBDIVISION (A)(2) OF THIS SECTION. --To warrant dismissal of charge under subdivision (a)(2), defendant must make sufficient showing of substantial statutory violation and of prejudice arising therefrom. State v. Eliason, 100 N.C. App. 313, 395 S.E.2d 702 (1990).

Trial court did not err in denying defendant's pretrial motion to dismiss the G.S. 20-138.1 charge of driving while impaired against defendant because even though (1) there was no evidence, pursuant to G.S. 15A-534.2, that defendant was required to be held because the impairment of defendant's physical or mental faculties presented a danger, if defendant were released, of physical injury to defendant or others or damage to property, and (2) there was no evidence, pursuant to G.S. 15A-534(b), that defendant would pose a danger of injury to any person if defendant were released under conditions other than a secured bond, defendant was not irreparably prejudiced in the preparation of defendant's defense by the denial of defendant's G.S. 15A-533 right to timely pretrial release; defendant was not denied access to friends and family, such that defendant lost the opportunity to gather evidence. State v. Labinski, 188 N.C. App. 120, 654 S.E.2d 740 (2008), review denied, stay denied, 362 N.C. 367, 661 S.E.2d 889 (2008).

EVIDENCE HELD ADMISSIBLE. --No plain error existed in a trial court admitting evidence of defendant's empty prescription pill bottle, testimony by an officer identifying the pills from the label, and testimony by a pharmacist about the interaction between the pills and alcohol, as the evidence was relevant to show that defendant, who had been drinking, was driving while impaired. State v. Edwards, 170 N.C. App. 381, 612 S.E.2d 394 (2005).

PREJUDICIAL ERROR IN ERRONEOUS ADMISSION OF EVIDENCE. --Defendant met his burden of showing prejudicial error in the erroneous admission of retrograde extrapolation testimony of the State's witness where the officer testified that he never observed defendant exhibit slurred speech, reckless driving, weaving, difficulty with motor skills, difficulty answering questions, or difficulty following directions, there was no other evidence of appreciable physical and mental impairment, and thus, the evidence played a pivotal role in the guilty verdict for driving while impaired. State v. Hayes, 256 N.C. App. 559, 808 S.E.2d 446 (2017).

DISMISSAL IMPROPER. --Dismissal of a misdemeanor driving while impaired (DWI) charge was error because, for the trial court to properly dismiss pursuant to G.S. 15A-954(a)(1), it had to find and that the DWI statute was unconstitutional as applied, but the trial court made no such conclusion; rather, the trial court's conclusion centered on G.S. 20-139.1(d1), which it found was violated when defendant's blood was drawn in violation of constitutional provisions. Given State's stipulation that blood evidence would not be offered in evidence, the trial court was required to summarily grant defendant's motion to suppress. State v. Wilson, 225 N.C. App. 246, 736 S.E.2d 614 (2013).

MOTION TO DISMISS PROPERLY DENIED. --Trial court properly declined to dismiss defendant's driving while impaired charge because the State presented substantial evidence that defendant was driving while impaired based on an alcohol concentration of .08 or more. State v. Marley, 227 N.C. App. 613, 742 S.E.2d 634 (2013).

G.

S. 20-17.4 IS SO PUNITIVE THAT IT BECOMES A CRIMINAL PUNISHMENT; therefore, prosecution for driving while impaired subsequent to license disqualification under G.S. 20-17.4 constitutes impermissible double jeopardy. State v. McKenzie, 225 N.C. App. 208, 736 S.E.2d 591 (2013), rev'd 367 N.C. 112, 750 S.E.2d 521, 2013 N.C. LEXIS 1019 (2013), rev'd 748 S.E.2d 145, 2013 N.C. LEXIS 1019 (2013).

DOUBLE JEOPARDY VIOLATION. --Prosecuting defendant for driving while impaired subjected him to double jeopardy because his prior one-year commercial driver's license disqualification under G.S. 20-17.4(a)(7) due to his breath test results was so punitive that it constituted a prior criminal punishment. State v. McKenzie, 225 N.C. App. 208, 736 S.E.2d 591 (2013), rev'd 367 N.C. 112, 750 S.E.2d 521, 2013 N.C. LEXIS 1019 (2013), rev'd 748 S.E.2d 145, 2013 N.C. LEXIS 1019 (2013).

V. INSTRUCTIONS.

EVIDENCE HELD SUFFICIENT TO SUPPORT INSTRUCTION. --Evidence tending to show that defendant was seen driving his truck some 30 minutes before a highway patrolman reached the scene of the accident, that defendant had then been arrested and was in the custody of a deputy sheriff, that defendant was in a highly intoxicated condition, and that no intoxicating liquor was found in or about the vehicle was held sufficient to support an instruction in regard to the law if defendant at the time of the accident was driving while under the influence of intoxicating liquor. State v. Lindsey, 264 N.C. 588, 142 S.E.2d 355 (1965).

FOR CASE HOLDING THAT THE ISSUE OF INTOXICATION WAS IMPROPERLY SUBMITTED TO THE JURY, see Atkins v. Moye, 8 N.C. App. 126, 174 S.E.2d 34, aff'd, 277 N.C. 179, 176 S.E.2d 789 (1970).

INSTRUCTION UPHELD. --In a prosecution for drunken driving under former G.S. 14-387, an instruction that defendant was under the influence of intoxicating liquor if he had drunk enough to make him act or think differently than he would have acted or thought if he had not drunk any, regardless of the amount he drank, was held without error. State v. Harris, 213 N.C. 648, 197 S.E. 142 (1938).

In a prosecution for driving under the influence, an instruction that defendant was under the influence of intoxicants if he had drunk a sufficient amount to make him think or act differently than he would have done, regardless of the amount, and that he was "under the influence" if his mind and muscles did not normally coordinate or if he was abnormal in any degree from intoxicants was held without error. State v. Biggerstaff, 226 N.C. 603, 39 S.E.2d 619 (1946). But see, State v. Edwards, 9 N.C. App. 602, 176 S.E.2d 874 (1970), and State v. Harris, 10 N.C. App. 553, 180 S.E.2d 29 (1971), wherein a similar instruction was held error.

In an instruction stating the degree of impairment of the faculties necessary to render one "under the influence" of intoxicating liquor, the use of the word "perceptibly" instead of the word "appreciably," without explanation of what it meant, was not error. While the language of the rule in State v. Carroll, 226 N.C. 237, 37 S.E.2d 688 (1946), is preferred, there is not in the word "perceptible" sufficient difference in meaning and common understanding for the rule to have been misunderstood by the jury. State v. Lee, 237 N.C. 263, 74 S.E.2d 654 (1953).

An instruction that "under the influence of intoxicating liquor" meant that defendant at the time and place in question had by reason of having drunk some intoxicating beverage lost the normal control of the powers or functions of his body or mind, or both, so that such loss could be estimated or recognized, properly expressed the intent of the statute. State v. Combs, 13 N.C. App. 195, 185 S.E.2d 8 (1971).

An instruction that a person is under the influence of some intoxicating beverage within the meaning of the statute when he has drunk a sufficient quantity of some intoxicating beverage to cause him to lose the normal control of his mental or bodily faculties, his mental or bodily capabilities, to such an extent that there is appreciable or noticeable impairment of either one or both of those faculties was without error. State v. Robinette, 13 N.C. App. 224, 185 S.E.2d 9 (1971), cert. denied, 280 N.C. 304, 186 S.E.2d 178 (1972).

Trial court did not err in instructing the jury that it could consider whether defendant refused to submit to a breath test in deciding defendant's guilt for driving while impaired, as the officer testified that he gave defendant two opportunities to provide sufficient breath samples and defendant failed to complete the test either time. The officer opined that defendant was not attempting to give a sufficient sample, noting that defendant appeared to be breathing normally and he had never observed a person who was able to breath normally be unable to provide a sufficient sample. State v. Macon, 227 N.C. App. 152, 741 S.E.2d 688 (2013), review denied 367 N.C. 238, 748 S.E.2d 545, 2013 N.C. LEXIS 1025 (2013).

DEFENDANT DID NOT SHOW THAT INSTRUCTION AFFECTED VERDICT. --Although defendant argued that the instructions constituted plain error because the trial court stated that the substances in a toxicology report were impairing substances which could have caused the jury to believe that defendant was in fact impaired when driving a vehicle, the record showed sufficient evidence that defendant was in fact impaired. Thus, defendant did not show that the verdict was affected by the instruction. State v. Braswell, 222 N.C. App. 176, 729 S.E.2d 697 (2012).

DISJUNCTIVE INSTRUCTIONS AND NONUNANIMOUS VERDICTS. --Permitting the jury to consider the DWI defendant's driving both at the time of the accident as well as when he later returned to the accident scene in his truck did not result in him being convicted on less than a unanimous verdict, since this section proscribes a single offense, not crimes in the disjunctive, and even if all jurors did not agree as to the time and extent of the defendant's drunkenness, they unanimously found him guilty of the single offense of impaired driving. State v. McCaslin, 132 N.C. App. 352, 511 S.E.2d 347 (1999).

JURY INSTRUCTION PROPER ON THE DEFINITION OF "PUBLIC VEHICULAR AREA" because members of the public using car wash premises deserved no less protection from impaired drivers in the parking lot than on public streets or highways. State v. Robinette, 124 N.C. App. 212, 476 S.E.2d 387 (1996).

JURY INSTRUCTION ON PUBLIC VEHICULAR AREA IMPROPER. --Even assuming there was sufficient evidence to allow the jury to decide whether a vacant lot was a public vehicular area, the trial court erred in abbreviating the definition of public vehicular area in the instructions and by preventing defendant from arguing his position in accordance with the statute; the entire definition of public vehicular area is significant to a determination of whether an area meets the definition, and the examples are not separable from the statute State v. Ricks, 237 N.C. App. 359, 764 S.E.2d 692 (2014).

INSTRUCTION HELD ERRONEOUS. --An instruction that a person is under the influence of intoxicating liquor when "he has drunk a sufficient quantity of alcoholic liquor or beverage to affect, however slightly, his mind and his muscles, his mental and his physical faculties" is erroneous. State v. Carroll, 226 N.C. 237, 37 S.E.2d 688 (1946).

Trial judge's instruction that "a person would be under the influence of intoxicants if he had drunk a sufficient amount to make him think or act differently than he would otherwise have done, regardless of the amount, and he would be under the influence if his mind and muscles did not normally coordinate, or if he was abnormal in any degree from intoxicants" was erroneous. State v. Harris, 10 N.C. App. 553, 180 S.E.2d 29 (1971). But see, State v. Biggerstaff, 226 N.C. 603, 39 S.E.2d 619 (1946), wherein a similar instruction was approved.

In a drunken driving prosecution, trial court's instruction that a person is under the influence of intoxicants if he has consumed a sufficient amount to make him think or act differently than he otherwise would have done, regardless of the amount that he consumed, and that one is under the influence if his mind and muscles do not normally coordinate or if he is abnormal in any degree, is reversible error. State v. Edwards, 9 N.C. App. 602, 176 S.E.2d 874 (1970). But see, State v. Biggerstaff, 226 N.C. 603, 39 S.E.2d 619 (1946), wherein a similar instruction was approved.

Judgment convicting defendant of driving while impaired would be vacated where magistrate judge instructed the jury that it could rely on either of two independent grounds in determining whether defendant drove his vehicle while under the influence, as the jury could not legally convict him on the second ground, i.e., that the defendant had a blood alcohol concentration of at least .10 percent, since the court had suppressed evidence of blood alcohol concentration. United States v. Harris, 27 F.3d 111 (4th Cir. 1994).

Defendant arrested for driving while impaired was entitled to an instruction on the defense of entrapment where a jury could find defendant was not predisposed to drive while impaired; the officer who first encountered defendant when defendant was sleeping in his truck knew defendant was impaired; although defendant was not doing anything illegal, the officer told defendant to "move along"; at 4:30 a.m. in rainy weather the officer knew driving was defendant's only realistic means of "moving along"; when defendant left, the officer was waiting in the dark with his lights off; and as soon as defendant drove away the officer arrested him for driving while impaired. State v. Redmon, 164 N.C. App. 658, 596 S.E.2d 854 (2004).

INADVERTENT USE BY THE TRIAL JUDGE OF THE WORD "QUALITIES" IN PLACE OF THE WORD "FACULTIES" at one point in the charge could not have in any way misled the jury to defendant's prejudice. State v. Bledsoe, 6 N.C. App. 195, 169 S.E.2d 520 (1969).

USE OF THE TERM "ANY BEVERAGE CONTAINING ALCOHOL" rather than the term "intoxicating beverage" in the court's charge defining the expression "under the influence of intoxicating liquor" in a prosecution for drunken driving was not prejudicial. State v. Nall, 239 N.C. 60, 79 S.E.2d 354 (1953).

INSTRUCTION ON BREATHALYZER TEST. --In a prosecution for driving while under the influence of intoxicating liquor, there is no requirement that the jury be instructed that they must find that the breathalyzer test was administered in accordance with the pertinent regulations. State v. Jenkins, 21 N.C. App. 541, 204 S.E.2d 919 (1974).

CHARGE AS TO GOOD CHARACTER OF DEFENDANT. --Where defendant was charged with operating a motor vehicle on the public highway while under the influence of intoxicating liquor, in the absence of a request it was not incumbent upon the trial judge to charge specifically as to the effect of evidence of the good character of the defendant. This was not an essential feature of the case. State v. Glatly, 230 N.C. 177, 52 S.E.2d 277 (1949).

INSTRUCTION NOT MANDATED. --It is not mandated that the offense of driving with a blood alcohol content of 0.10 (now 0.08) percent or more be instructed on every time the offense of driving under the influence is charged. State v. McLawhorn, 43 N.C. App. 695, 260 S.E.2d 138 (1979), cert. denied, 299 N.C. 123, 261 S.E.2d 925 (1980).

In a prosecution for driving under the influence of intoxicating liquor, second offense, and driving with a revoked license, fourth offense, where evidence was introduced which indicated that a breathalyzer test revealed 0.11 percent alcohol by blood weight in defendant, it was not error to fail to instruct the jury on the offense of operating a vehicle on a public highway when blood alcohol content is 0.10 (now 0.08) percent by weight, since, although the instruction could have been given, the omission of the instruction was to defendant's benefit, since to convict defendant of

driving under the influence, the State had to prove beyond a reasonable doubt that defendant was under the influence of alcoholic beverages, while for a conviction of driving with a blood alcohol content of 0.10 (now 0.08) percent or more the State only needed to prove that the amount of alcohol in defendant's blood was 0.10 (0.08) percent or more by weight. Thus, by not instructing on the latter motor vehicle violation, the trial judge benefited defendant and handicapped the State. State v. McLawhorn, 43 N.C. App. 695, 260 S.E.2d 138 (1979), cert. denied, 299 N.C. 123, 261 S.E.2d 925 (1980).

In a prosecution for driving while impaired, the court was not required to instruct the jury that the breathalyzer result should not be considered by them unless they found first that the test was performed in accord with regulations promulgated by the Commission of Health Services [now the Commission for Public Health]. State v. DeVane, 81 N.C. App. 524, 344 S.E.2d 362 (1986).

FAILURE TO INSTRUCT AS TO SUBDIVISION (A)(2) NOT ERROR WHERE BREATHALYZER READING WAS 0.06. --Evidence of a per se 0.10 (now 0.08) violation under subdivision (a)(2) of this section was not sufficient to submit to the jury where breathalyzer result indicated a blood alcohol content of 0.06, and accordingly, it was not error for the trial court to fail to instruct the jury concerning subdivision (a)(2) on its own motion. State v. Sigmon, 74 N.C. App. 479, 328 S.E.2d 843 (1985).

FOR CASE HOLDING INSTRUCTIONS PREJUDICIAL WHERE ONE OF TWO DEFENDANTS WAS STATED BY THE COURT TO BE THE DRIVER, see State v. Swaringen, 249 N.C. 38, 105 S.E.2d 99 (1958).

VI. SENTENCING.

FAIR SENTENCING ACT. --A conviction of driving while impaired under this section, irrespective of the level of punishment imposed, constitutes a prior conviction of an offense punishable by more than sixty days' imprisonment for purposes of sentencing under the Fair Sentencing Act. State v. Santon, 101 N.C. App. 710, 401 S.E.2d 117 (1991).

INCREASE IN PUNISHMENT BASED ON AGGRAVATING FACTOR DID NOT DEPRIVE RIGHT TO JURY. --A trial judge's increasing punishment under the Safe Roads Act of 1983 after a finding of a grossly aggravating factor, that the defendant had a prior conviction for a similar offense within seven years, did not in any way deprive the defendant of his right to jury trial. State v. Denning, 76 N.C. App. 156, 332 S.E.2d 203 (1985), modified and aff'd, 316 N.C. 523, 342 S.E.2d 855 (1986).

FAILURE TO SUBMIT AGGRAVATING FACTORS TO JURY. --Trial court erred in failing to submit aggravating factors to the jury before imposing an aggravated sentence on defendant for his conviction of driving while impaired; as defendant was entitled to a jury trial on the charge, any aggravating factor had to be submitted to the jury before an aggravated sentence could be imposed. State v. Speight, 359 N.C. 602, 614 S.E.2d 262 (2005), vacated, remanded, North

Chapter 20

631

Carolina v. Speight, 126 S. Ct. 2977 (U.S. 2006) (as to Blakely error being subject to harmless review).

SERIOUS INJURY TO ANOTHER IS SENTENCING FACTOR. --Whether the defendant seriously injured another person was not an element of the crime of driving while impaired; it was a sentencing factor that the General Assembly deemed to be important in punishing those convicted of driving while impaired. State v. Field, 75 N.C. App. 647, 331 S.E.2d 221, cert. denied and appeal dismissed, 315 N.C. 186, 337 S.E.2d 582 (1985).

The existence of serious injury is not an element of the crime of impaired driving but merely a sentencing factor. Thus, in a sentencing hearing conducted after defendant pled guilty to driving while impaired, the trial court did not violate the Constitution by finding that defendant had caused serious injury as a result of his impaired driving, one of the aggravating factors in G.S. 20-179. Field v. Sheriff of Wake County, 831 F.2d 530 (4th Cir. 1987).

TRIAL COURT'S DECISION TO GRANT CONTINUANCE AND CLARITY OF CHARGING INSTRUMENT NOT SENTENCING FACTORS. --Where defendant's assignments of error related to the trial court's decision to grant a continuance and the clarity of the charging instrument, the errors were not sentencing issues pursuant to G.S. 15A-1444(a2) and defendant did not have an appeal by right or by certiorari for the entry of a plea of "no contest" to habitual driving while impaired and habitual felon status. State v. Moore, 156 N.C. App. 693, 577 S.E.2d 354 (2003).

BLAKELY ERRORS WERE HARMLESS. --Blakely errors committed by the trial court in sentencing defendant for DUI were harmless as defendant knowingly created a great risk of death to more than one person by means of a weapon or device that would normally be hazardous to more than one person since: (1) defendant operated defendant's vehicle in a reckless manner by speeding, driving while intoxicated and with THC and morphine in defendant's blood, and weaving in and out of traffic; (2) a reasonable person would have known that a great risk of death had been created; (3) defendant's blood alcohol concentration was 0.10 two hours after the collision; (4) defendant acknowledged that the two involuntary manslaughter convictions showed that in the course of conduct as to each offense defendant killed another; and (5) since there were two involuntary manslaughter convictions, the evidence used to prove an element of one offense could be used to support an aggravating factor of a separate joined offense. State v. Speight, 186 N.C. App. 93, 650 S.E.2d 452 (2007).

THE TRIAL COURT DID NOT ERR OR VIOLATE DOUBLE JEOPARDY PRINCIPLES IN SENTENCING THE DEFENDANT FOR BOTH IMPAIRED DRIVING and second degree murder. Driving while impaired is not a lesser included offense of second degree murder. State v. McAllister, 138 N.C. App. 252, 530 S.E.2d 859 (2000).

Double jeopardy did not require a driving while intoxicated (DWI) conviction had to be vacated where defendant was also convicted of second-degree murder because the legislature intended to create two separate offenses, and punishment for second degree murder was controlled by structured sentencing, while punishment for DWI was exempted from the structured sentencing provisions. State v. Armstrong, 203 N.C. App. 399, 691 S.E.2d 433 (2010).

DOUBLE JEOPARDY PREVENTED SENTENCING FOR BOTH FELONY DEATH BY VEHICLE AND DWI. --Trial court erred in sentencing defendant for both felony death by vehicle under G.S. 20-141.4(a1) and DWI under G.S. 20-138.1, because DWI was an element of felony death by vehicle. State v. Davis, 198 N.C. App. 443, 680 S.E.2d 239 (2009).

PRIOR OUT-OF-STATE CONVICTION. --There was no merit to defendant's argument that the trial court erroneously assigned prior record points to his out-of-state driving while impaired (DWI) convictions because in North Carolina, DWI is a Class 1 misdemeanor and the Alabama convictions could have resulted in imprisonment for more than six months, and, therefore, those convictions were properly classified as misdemeanors. State v. Armstrong, 203 N.C. App. 399, 691 S.E.2d 433 (2010).

CROSS REFERENCES. --

For Parole Commission's authority to parole and terminate supervision of persons convicted under this section, see G.S. 15A-1372(d). As to compensation for injury caused by sales of alcoholic beverages to underage persons, see G.S. 18B-120 et seq. For definition of "alcohol concentration," see G.S. 20-4.01(1b). As to felony and misdemeanor death by vehicle, see G.S. 20-141.4.

LEGAL PERIODICALS. --

For comment, "Liability of Commercial Vendors, Employers, and Social Hosts for Torts of the Intoxicated," see 19 Wake Forest L. Rev. 1013 (1983).

For note discussing the definition of "driving" under the North Carolina Safe Roads Act, in light of State v. Fields, 77 N.C. App. 404, 335 S.E.2d 69 (1985), see 64 N.C.L. Rev. 1278 (1986).

For note, "Constitutional Law-Enhanced Sentencing Under North Carolina's DWI Statute: Making Due Process Disappear -- Field v. Sheriff of Wake County, N.C.," see 23 Wake Forest L. Rev. 517 (1988).

For note, "North Carolina and Pretrial Civil Revocation of an Impaired Driver's License and the Double Jeopardy Clause," see 18 Campbell L. Rev. 391 (1996).

For a survey of 1996 developments in constitutional law, see 75 N.C.L. Rev. 2315 (1997).

For 1997 legislative survey, see 20 Campbell L. Rev. 417.

For comment, "North Carolina's Unconstitutional Expansion of an Ancient Maxim: Using DWI Fatalities to Satisfy First Degree Felony Murder," see 22 Campbell L. Rev. 169 (1999).

For note, "Ramifications of the 1997 DWIelony Prior Record Level Amendment to the Structured Sentencing Act: State of North Carolina v. Tanya Watts Gentry," see 22 Campbell L. Rev. 211 (1999).

For article, "A Comparative Analysis of Traffic Accident Systems," see 53 Wake Forest L. Rev. 365 (2018).

For article, "When Cars Crash: The Automobile's Tort Law Legacy," see 53 Wake Forest L. Rev. 293 (2018).

OPINIONS OF THE ATTORNEY GENERAL

AS TO APPLICABILITY OF STATUTE TO PERSONS OPERATING BICYCLES WITH HELPER MOTORS, see opinion of Attorney General to Mr. Michael v. F. Royster, Assistant District Attorney, Twenty-Sixth Judicial District, 45 N.C.A.G. 286 (1976), issued under former G.S. 20-138, 20-139. 316 N.C. 523, 342 S.E.2d 855 (1986), modified and aff'd.

DRIVEWAYS OF AN APARTMENT COMPLEX ARE "PUBLIC VEHICULAR AREAS." See opinion of Attorney General to Mr. C.C. Tarleton, 42 N.C.A.G. 107 (1972), issued under former G.S. 20-138, 20-139.

§ 20-138.2. Impaired driving in commercial vehicle

(a) **Offense.** -- A person commits the offense of impaired driving in a commercial motor vehicle if he drives a commercial motor vehicle upon any highway, any street, or any public vehicular area within the State:

(1) While under the influence of an impairing substance; or

(2) After having consumed sufficient alcohol that he has, at any relevant time after the driving, an alcohol concentration of 0.04 or more. The results of a chemical analysis shall be deemed sufficient evidence to prove a person's alcohol concentration; or

(3) With any amount of a Schedule I controlled substance, as listed in G.S. 90-89, or its metabolites in his blood or urine.

(a1) A person who has submitted to a chemical analysis of a blood sample, pursuant to G.S. 20-139.1(d), may use the result in rebuttal as evidence that the person did not have, at a relevant time after driving, an alcohol concentration of 0.04 or more.

(a2) In order to prove the gross vehicle weight rating of a vehicle as defined in G.S. 20-4.01(12f), the opinion of a person who observed the vehicle as to the weight, the testimony of the gross vehicle weight rating affixed to the vehicle, the registered or declared weight shown on the Division's records pursuant to G.S. 20-26(b1), the gross vehicle weight rating as determined from the vehicle identification number, the listed gross weight publications from the manufacturer of the vehicle, or any other description or evidence shall be admissible.

(b) **Defense Precluded.** -- The fact that a person charged with violating this section is or has been legally entitled to use alcohol or a drug is not a defense to a charge under this section.

(b1) **Defense Allowed.** -- Nothing in this section shall preclude a person from asserting that a chemical analysis result is inadmissible pursuant to G.S. 20-139.1(b2).

(c) **Pleading.** -- To charge a violation of this section, the pleading is sufficient if it states the time and place of the alleged offense in the usual form and charges the defendant drove a commercial motor vehicle on a highway, street, or public vehicular area while subject to an impairing substance.

(d) **Implied Consent Offense.** -- An offense under this section is an implied consent offense subject to the provisions of G.S. 20-16.2.

(e) **Punishment.** -- The offense in this section is a misdemeanor and any defendant convicted under this section shall be sentenced under G.S. 20-179. This offense is not a lesser included offense of impaired driving under G.S. 20-138.1, and if a person is convicted under this section and of an offense involving impaired driving under G.S. 20-138.1 arising out of the same transaction, the aggregate punishment imposed by the Court may not exceed the maximum punishment applicable to the offense involving impaired driving under G.S. 20-138.1.

(f) Repealed by Session Laws 1991, c. 726, s. 19.

(g) **Chemical Analysis Provisions.** -- The provisions of G.S. 20-139.1 shall apply to the offense of impaired driving in a commercial motor vehicle.

History.

1989, c. 771, s. 12;1991, c. 726, s. 19;1993, c. 539, s. 363;1994, Ex. Sess., c. 24, s. 14(c);1998-182, s. 24;2006-253, s. 10;2010-129, s. 1

EDITOR'S NOTE. --

Session Laws 1987 (Reg. Sess., 1988), c. 1112, s. 15 also enacted a G.S. 20-138.2, to be effective June 1, 1989 through June 30, 1989, which was almost identical to the G.S. 20-138.2 enacted by Session Laws 1989, c. 771, s. 12, effective September 1, 1990. Session Laws 1989, c. 771, s. 18, effective June 1, 1989, repealed Session Laws 1987 (Reg. Sess., 1988), c. 1112; therefore, G.S. 20-138.2, as enacted by c. 1112, never went into effect.

In subsection (a2) above, "G.S. 20-4.01(12f)," was substituted for "G.S. 20-4.01(12e)," to conform to renumbering in G.S. 20-4.01, as amended by Session Laws 2010-129, s. 1.

EFFECT OF AMENDMENTS. --

Session Laws 2006-253, s. 10, effective December 1, 2006, and applicable to offenses committed on or after that date, added the last sentence in subdivision (a) (2), added subdivision (a)(3) and subsections (a1), (a2) and (b1).

LEGISLATIVE INTENT. --Our legislature has adopted a breath alcohol per se offense as an alternative method of committing a driving while impaired offense, as it is immaterial whether the defendant is in fact impaired or whether his blood alcohol content is in excess of that permitted in the statutes. State v. Cothran, 120 N.C. App. 633, 463 S.E.2d 423 (1995).

"COMMERCIAL MOTOR VEHICLE". --The defendant's contention that he did not violate this section because he was not driving a "commercial motor

Chapter 20

vehicle" was without merit; the tractor-trailer was a commercial vehicle within the statutory definition although the defendant was driving it for his own private use and although he had detached the trailer portion of the tractor-trailer. State v. Jones, 140 N.C. App. 691, 538 S.E.2d 228 (2000).

CITED in Harrell v. Bowen, 362 N.C. 142, 655 S.E.2d 350 (2008); State v. Mumford, 201 N.C. App. 594, 688 S.E.2d 458 (2010); State v. Blackmon, 208 N.C. App. 397, 702 S.E.2d 833 (2010); State v. Leonard, 213 N.C. App. 526, 711 S.E.2d 867 (2011).

§ 20-138.2A. Operating a commercial vehicle after consuming alcohol

(a) **Offense.** -- A person commits the offense of operating a commercial motor vehicle after consuming alcohol if the person drives a commercial motor vehicle, as defined in G.S. 20-4.01(3d)a. and b., upon any highway, any street, or any public vehicular area within the State while consuming alcohol or while alcohol remains in the person's body.

(b) **Implied-Consent Offense.** -- An offense under this section is an implied-consent offense subject to the provisions of G.S. 20-16.2. The provisions of G.S. 20-139.1 shall apply to an offense committed under this section.

(b1) **Odor Insufficient.** -- The odor of an alcoholic beverage on the breath of the driver is insufficient evidence by itself to prove beyond a reasonable doubt that alcohol was remaining in the driver's body in violation of this section unless the driver was offered an alcohol screening test or chemical analysis and refused to provide all required samples of breath or blood for analysis.

(b2) **Alcohol Screening Test.** -- Notwithstanding any other provision of law, an alcohol screening test may be administered to a driver suspected of violation of subsection (a) of this section, and the results of an alcohol screening test or the driver's refusal to submit may be used by a law enforcement officer, a court, or an administrative agency in determining if alcohol was present in the driver's body. No alcohol screening tests are valid under this section unless the device used is one approved by the Department of Health and Human Services, and the screening test is conducted in accordance with the applicable regulations of the Department as to its manner and use.

(c) **Punishment.** -- Except as otherwise provided in this subsection, a violation of the offense described in subsection (a) of this section is a Class 3 misdemeanor and, notwithstanding G.S. 15A-1340.23, is punishable by a penalty of one hundred dollars ($ 100.00). A second or subsequent violation of this section is a misdemeanor punishable under G.S. 20-179. This offense is a lesser included offense of impaired driving of a commercial vehicle under G.S. 20-138.2.

(d) **Second or Subsequent Conviction Defined.** -- A conviction for violating this offense is a second or subsequent conviction if at the time of the current offense the person has a previous conviction under this section, and the previous conviction occurred in the seven years immediately preceding the date of the current offense. This definition of second or subsequent conviction also applies to G.S. 20-17(a)(13) and G.S. 20-17.4(a)(6).

History.
1998-182, s. 23;1999-406, s. 15;2000-140, s. 5;2000-155, s. 16;2007-182, s. 2;2008-187, s. 36(a)

EDITOR'S NOTE. --
Session Laws 1999-406, s. 18, states that this act does not obligate the General Assembly to appropriate additional funds, and that this act shall be implemented with funds available or appropriated to the Department of Transportation and the Administrative Office of the Courts.

EFFECT OF AMENDMENTS. --
Session Laws 2007-182, s. 2, effective July 5, 2007, substituted "Commission for Public Health" for "Commission for Health Services" in subsection (b2).

Session Laws 2008-187, s. 36(a), effective August 7, 2008, in the last sentence of subsection (b2), substituted "Department of Health and Human Services" for "Commission for Public Health" and substituted "Department" for "Commission."

§ 20-138.2B. Operating a school bus, school activity bus, child care vehicle, ambulance, other EMS vehicle, firefighting vehicle, or law enforcement vehicle after consuming alcohol

(a) **Offense.** -- A person commits the offense of operating a school bus, school activity bus, child care vehicle, ambulance, other emergency medical services vehicle, firefighting vehicle, or law enforcement vehicle after consuming alcohol if the person drives a school bus, school activity bus, child care vehicle, ambulance, other emergency medical services vehicle, firefighting vehicle, or law enforcement vehicle upon any highway, any street, or any public vehicular area within the State while consuming alcohol or while alcohol remains in the person's body. This section does not apply to law enforcement officers acting in the course of, and within the scope of, their official duties.

(b) **Implied-Consent Offense.** -- An offense under this section is an implied-consent offense subject to the provisions of G.S. 20-16.2. The provisions of G.S. 20-139.1 shall apply to an offense committed under this section.

(b1) **Odor Insufficient.** -- The odor of an alcoholic beverage on the breath of the driver is insufficient evidence by itself to prove beyond a reasonable doubt that alcohol was remaining in the driver's body in violation of this section unless the driver was offered an alcohol screening test or chemical analysis and refused to provide all required samples of breath or blood for analysis.

(b2) **Alcohol Screening Test.** -- Notwithstanding any other provision of law, an alcohol screening test may be administered to a driver suspected of violation of subsection (a) of this section, and the results of an alcohol screening test or the driver's refusal to submit may be used by a law enforcement officer, a court, or an administrative agency in determining if alcohol was present in the driver's body. No alcohol screening tests are valid under this section unless the device used is one approved by the Department of Health and Human Services, and the screening test is conducted in accordance with the applicable regulations of the Department as to its manner and use.

(c) **Punishment.** -- Except as otherwise provided in this subsection, a violation of the offense described in subsection (a) of this section is a Class 3 misdemeanor and, notwithstanding G.S. 15A-1340.23, is punishable by a penalty of one hundred dollars ($ 100.00). A second or subsequent violation of this section is a misdemeanor punishable under G.S. 20-179. This offense is a lesser included offense of impaired driving of a commercial vehicle under G.S. 20-138.1.

(d) **Second or Subsequent Conviction Defined.** -- A conviction for violating this offense is a second or subsequent conviction if at the time of the current offense the person has a previous conviction under this section, and the previous conviction occurred in the seven years immediately preceding the date of the current offense. This definition of second or subsequent conviction also applies to G.S. 20-19(c2).

History.
1998-182, s. 27;1999-406, s. 16;2000-140, s. 6;2000-155, s. 17;2007-182, s. 2;2008-187, s. 36(b);2013-105, s. 1

EDITOR'S NOTE. --
Session Laws 1999-406, s. 18, states that this act does not obligate the General Assembly to appropriate additional funds, and that this act shall be implemented with funds available or appropriated to the Department of Transportation and the Administrative Office of the Courts.

Session Laws 2013-105, s. 2, made the amendments to this section by Session Laws 2013-105, s. 1, applicable to offenses committed on or after December 1, 2013.

EFFECT OF AMENDMENTS. --
Session Laws 2007-182, s. 2, effective July 5, 2007, substituted "Commission for Public Health" for "Commission for Health Services" in subsection (b2).

Session Laws 2008-187, s. 36(b), effective August 7, 2008, in subsection (b2), substituted "Department of Health and Human Services" for "Commission for Public Health" and substituted "Department" for "Commission."

Session Laws 2013-105, s. 1, effective December 1, 2013, in the section catchline, substituted "child care vehicle, ambulance, other EMS vehicle, firefighting vehicle, or law enforcement" for "or child care vehicle"; and in subsection (a), twice inserted "ambulance other emergency medical services vehicle, firefighting vehicle, or law enforcement vehicle" and added the last sentence. For applicability, see Editor's note.

§ 20-138.2C. Possession of alcoholic beverages while operating a commercial motor vehicle

A person commits the offense of operating a commercial motor vehicle while possessing alcoholic beverages if the person drives a commercial motor vehicle, as defined in G.S. 20-4.01(3d), upon any highway, any street, or any public vehicular area within the State while having an open or closed alcoholic beverage in the passenger area of the commercial motor vehicle. This section shall not apply to the driver of a commercial motor vehicle that is also an excursion passenger vehicle, a for-hire passenger vehicle, a common carrier of passengers, or a motor home, if the alcoholic beverage is in possession of a passenger or is in the passenger area of the vehicle.

History.
1999-330, s. 2

§ 20-138.3. Driving by person less than 21 years old after consuming alcohol or drugs

(a) **Offense.** -- It is unlawful for a person less than 21 years old to drive a motor vehicle on a highway or public vehicular area while consuming alcohol or at any time while he has remaining in his body any alcohol or controlled substance previously consumed, but a person less than 21 years old does not violate this section if he drives with a controlled substance in his body which was lawfully obtained and taken in therapeutically appropriate amounts.

(b) **Subject to Implied-Consent Law.** -- An offense under this section is an alcohol-related offense subject to the implied-consent provisions of G.S. 20-16.2.

(b1) **Odor Insufficient.** -- The odor of an alcoholic beverage on the breath of the driver is insufficient evidence by itself to prove beyond a reasonable doubt that alcohol was remaining in the driver's body in violation of this section unless the driver was offered an alcohol screening test or chemical analysis and refused to provide all required samples of breath or blood for analysis.

(b2) **Alcohol Screening Test.** -- Notwithstanding any other provision of law, an alcohol screening test may be administered to a driver suspected of violation of subsection (a) of this section, and the results of an alcohol screening test or the driver's refusal to submit may be used by a law enforcement officer, a court, or an administrative agency in determining if alcohol was present in the driver's body. No alcohol screening tests are valid under this section unless the device used is one approved by the Department of Health and Human Services, and the screening test is conducted in accordance with the applicable regulations of the Department as to its manner and use.

(c) **Punishment; Effect When Impaired Driving Offense Also Charged. --** The offense in this section is a Class 2 misdemeanor. It is not, in any circumstances, a lesser included offense of impaired driving under G.S. 20-138.1, but if a person is convicted under this section and of an offense involving impaired driving arising out of the same transaction, the aggregate punishment imposed by the court may not exceed the maximum applicable to the offense involving impaired driving, and any minimum punishment applicable shall be imposed.

(d) **Limited Driving Privilege. --** A person who is convicted of violating subsection (a) of this section and whose drivers license is revoked solely based on that conviction may apply for a limited driving privilege as provided in G.S. 20-179.3. This subsection shall apply only if the person meets both of the following requirements:

(1) Is 18, 19, or 20 years old on the date of the offense.

(2) Has not previously been convicted of a violation of this section.

The judge may issue the limited driving privilege only if the person meets the eligibility requirements of G.S. 20-179.3, other than the requirement in G.S. 20-179.3(b)(1) c. G.S. 20-179.3(e) shall not apply. All other terms, conditions, and restrictions provided for in G.S. 20-179.3 shall apply. G.S. 20-179.3, rather than this subsection, governs the issuance of a limited driving privilege to a person who is convicted of violating subsection (a) of this section and of driving while impaired as a result of the same transaction.

History.

1983, c. 435, s. 34; 1985 (Reg. Sess., 1986), c. 852, s. 11; 1993, c. 539, s. 364;1994, Ex. Sess., c. 24, s. 14(c);1995, c. 506, s. 6;1997-379, ss. 4, 5.2; 2000-140, s. 7;2000-155, s. 18;2006-253, s. 11

EDITOR'S NOTE. --

Session Laws 2006-253, s. 1, provides: "This act shall be known as 'The Motor Vehicle Driver Protection Act of 2006.'"

EFFECT OF AMENDMENTS. --

Session Laws 2006-253, s. 11, effective December 1, 2006, and applicable to offenses committed on or after

that date, in subsection (b2), substituted "Department of Health and Human Services" for "Commission for Health Services" and "Department" for "Commission."

CONSTRUCTION WITH OTHER LAW. --The defendant's prior alcohol-related conviction pursuant to this section was relevant, because the impaired defendant caused a death and was charged with second-degree murder, and was admissible for the purpose of establishing malice, even though the prior offense imposed strict liability based upon defendant's age without regard to the quantity consumed. State v. Gray, 137 N.C. App. 345, 528 S.E.2d 46 (2000).

APPLIED in Harris v. Testar, Inc., 243 N.C. App. 33, 777 S.E.2d 776 (2015).

CITED in Iodice v. United States, 289 F.3d 270 (4th Cir. 2002); State v. Hinchman, 192 N.C. App. 657, 666 S.E.2d 199 (2008).

§ 20-138.4. Requirement that prosecutor explain reduction or dismissal of charge in implied-consent case

(a) Any prosecutor shall enter detailed facts in the record of any case subject to the implied-consent law or involving driving while license revoked for impaired driving as defined in G.S. 20-28.2 explaining orally in open court and in writing the reasons for his action if he:

(1) Enters a voluntary dismissal; or

(2) Accepts a plea of guilty or no contest to a lesser included offense; or

(3) Substitutes another charge, by statement of charges or otherwise, if the substitute charge carries a lesser mandatory minimum punishment or is not a case subject to the implied-consent law; or

(4) Otherwise takes a discretionary action that effectively dismisses or reduces the original charge in a case subject to the implied-consent law.

General explanations such as "interests of justice" or "insufficient evidence" are not sufficiently detailed to meet the requirements of this section.

(b) The written explanation shall be signed by the prosecutor taking the action on a form approved by the Administrative Office of the Courts and shall contain, at a minimum:

(1) The alcohol concentration or the fact that the driver refused.

(2) A list of all prior convictions of implied-consent offenses or driving while license revoked.

(3) Whether the driver had a valid drivers license or privilege to drive in this State as indicated by the Division's records.

(4) A statement that a check of the database of the Administrative Office of the Courts revealed whether any other charges against the defendant were pending.

(5) The elements that the prosecutor believes in good faith can be proved, and a list

of those elements that the prosecutor cannot prove and why.

(6) The name and agency of the charging officer and whether the officer is available.

(7) Any reason why the charges are dismissed.

(c) *(See Editor's note on effective date)* A copy of the form required in subsection (b) of this section shall be sent to the head of the law enforcement agency that employed the charging officer, to the district attorney who employs the prosecutor, and filed in the court file. The Administrative Office of the Courts shall electronically record this data in its database and make it available upon request.

History.
1983, c. 435, s. 25; 1987 (Reg. Sess., 1988), c. 1112; 1989, c. 771, s. 18;2006-253, s. 19;2007-493, s. 16

EDITOR'S NOTE. --
Session Laws 2006-253, s. 33, provides in part: "Sections 20.1, 20.2, and the requirement that the Administrative Office of the Courts electronically record certain data contained in subsection (c) of G.S. 20-138.4, as amended by Section 19 of this act, become effective after the next rewrite of the superior court clerks system by the Administrative Office of the Courts." The rewrite of the superior court clerk's system has not happened.

EFFECT OF AMENDMENTS. --
Session Laws 2006-253, s. 19, effective December 1, 2006, rewrote the section. See Editor's note for applicability.

Session Laws 2007-493, s. 16, effective August 30, 2007, substituted "in implied-consent case" for "involving impaired driving" in section catchline; in subdivision (a)(3), substituted "a case subject to the implied-consent law" for "an offense involving impaired driving"; and, in subdivision (a)(4), substituted "a case subject to the implied-consent law" for "the case involving impaidred driving." For applicability provision, see Editor's note.

§ 20-138.5. Habitual impaired driving

(a) A person commits the offense of habitual impaired driving if he drives while impaired as defined in G.S. 20-138.1 and has been convicted of three or more offenses involving impaired driving as defined in G.S. 20-4.01(24a) within 10 years of the date of this offense.

(b) A person convicted of violating this section shall be punished as a Class F felon and shall be sentenced to a minimum active term of not less than 12 months of imprisonment, which shall not be suspended. Sentences imposed under this subsection shall run consecutively with and shall commence at the expiration of any sentence being served.

(c) An offense under this section is an implied consent offense subject to the provisions of G.S. 20-16.2. The provisions of G.S. 20-139.1 shall apply to an offense committed under this section.

(d) A person convicted under this section shall have his license permanently revoked.

(e) If a person is convicted under this section, the motor vehicle that was driven by the defendant at the time the defendant committed the offense of impaired driving becomes property subject to forfeiture in accordance with the procedure set out in G.S. 20-28.2. In applying the procedure set out in that statute, an owner or a holder of a security interest is considered an innocent party with respect to a motor vehicle subject to forfeiture under this subsection if any of the following applies:

(1) The owner or holder of the security interest did not know and had no reason to know that the defendant had been convicted within the previous seven years of three or more offenses involving impaired driving.

(2) The defendant drove the motor vehicle without the consent of the owner or the holder of the security interest.

History.
1989 (Reg. Sess., 1990), c. 1039, s. 7; 1993, c. 539, s. 1258;1994, Ex. Sess., c. 14, s. 32;c. 24, s. 14(c);1993 (Reg. Sess., 1994), c. 761, s. 34.1; c. 767, s. 32; 1997-379, s. 6;2006-253, ss. 12, 13

EFFECT OF AMENDMENTS. --
Session Laws 2006-253, ss. 12 and 13, effective December 1, 2006, and applicable to offenses committed on or after that date, substituted "10" for "seven" in subsection (a); and added the last sentence in subsection (c).

CONSTITUTIONALITY. --Statute was not unconstitutional on its face because it was a recidivist statute that punished the most recent offense more severely, not a statute regarding a substantive offense that would be subject to double jeopardy analysis. State v. Vardiman, 146 N.C. App. 381, 552 S.E.2d 697 (2001), appeal dismissed, 355 N.C. 222, 559 S.E.2d 794 (2002), cert. denied, 537 U.S. 833, 123 S. Ct. 142, 154 L. Ed. 2d 51 (2002).

Defendant's argument, that the habitual driving while impaired statute violated the separation of powers and was an unconstitutional delegation of legislative authority to the executive branch because the district attorney was allowed to exercise discretion in enforcing the law, was rejected because defendant had not argued, nor did any evidence reflect an improper motive by the prosecutor regarding the charges upon which defendant was indicted and tried. State v. Johnson, 186 N.C. App. 673, 651 S.E.2d 907 (2007).

STATUTE DID NOT VIOLATE DOUBLE JEOPARDY. --Effect of G.S. 20-138.5 was that a defendant was punished more severely for a recent crime based on having committed previous crimes, not that the defendant was punished for those previous crimes again; therefore the statute did not violate the United

States and North Carolina Constitutions' prohibitions against double jeopardy. State v. Vardiman, 146 N.C. App. 381, 552 S.E.2d 697 (2001), appeal dismissed, 355 N.C. 222, 559 S.E.2d 794 (2002), cert. denied, 537 U.S. 833, 123 S. Ct. 142, 154 L. Ed. 2d 51 (2002).

Defendant's conviction on a charge of habitual impaired driving did not violate defendant's rights to be free of double jeopardy; recidivist statutes, such as habitual impaired driving, survived constitutional challenges regarding double jeopardy because they increased the severity of the punishment for the crime being prosecuted; they did not punish a previous crime a second time. State v. Bradley, 181 N.C. App. 557, 640 S.E.2d 432 (2007).

SUPERIOR COURT JURISDICTION. --The offense of habitual impaired driving as defined in this section constitutes a separate substantive felony offense which is properly within the original exclusive jurisdiction of the superior court. State v. Priddy, 115 N.C. App. 547, 445 S.E.2d 610, cert. denied, 337 N.C. 805, 449 S.E.2d 751 (1994).

AMENDMENT OF INDICTMENT. --Defendant argued unsuccessfully, in a case in which he appealed his habitual impaired driving conviction in violation of G.S. 20-138.5, that the district court erred in permitting the State to amend the indictment to change the look-back period from seven to 10 years. At all times, the indictment alleged the essential elements of the crime set out in G.S. 20-138.5(a), and the State's mistake did not involve an essential element of the crime, such as the date of a prior conviction; the incorrect recitation in the indictment of a seven-year look-back period was not essential to the indictment, and amendment of the indictment did not fundamentally change the nature of the charge asserted against defendant. State v. White, 202 N.C. App. 524, 689 S.E.2d 595 (2010).

ARRAIGNMENT. --Trial court did not commit reversible error by failing to personally address and arraign defendant under this section regarding the prior DWI convictions serving as the basis of the habitual impaired driving charge and the prior impaired driving revocation serving as the basis of the driving while license revoked for an impaired driving revocation charge because there was no indication that defendant was confused about the charges or that defense counsel was acting contrary to defendant's wishes by refusing to stipulate to the prior convictions and the State presented overwhelming evidence of defendant's guilt through testimony of the arresting officer. State v. Silva, 251 N.C. App. 678, 796 S.E.2d 72 (2017).

G.

S. 20-25 CREATES NO RIGHT TO APPEAL A REVOCATION UNDER THIS SECTION since this section appears in Article 3 rather than Article 2. Following a conviction for habitual impaired driving, under this section, permanent revocation is mandatory and the trial court lacks the authority to provide relief. Cooke v. Faulkner, 137 N.C. App. 755, 529 S.E.2d 512 (2000).

A CONVICTION FOR HABITUAL IMPAIRED DRIVING may serve as the basis for enhancement to habitual felon status. State v. Baldwin, 117 N.C. App. 713, 453 S.E.2d 193 (1995).

DETERMINATION OF PRIOR RECORD LEVEL. --Trial court impermissibly assigned points to defendant's three prior DWI convictions where those same three DWI convictions were the basis for her habitual DWI charge. State v. Gentry, 135 N.C. App. 107, 519 S.E.2d 68 (1999).

Trial court did not err in calculating defendant's prior record by including his driving while impaired convictions even though those convictions were also elements of his habitual impaired driving convictions; prior convictions of driving while impaired were the elements of the offense of habitual impaired driving, but G.S. 20-138.5(a) did not impose punishment for these previous crimes, it imposed an enhanced punishment for the latest offense, and the trial court's calculation of defendant's prior record level did not represent a double-counting of convictions. State v. Hyden, 175 N.C. App. 576, 625 S.E.2d 125 (2006).

EVIDENCE OF PRIOR CONVICTIONS. --The State could use a certified computer printout from the Administrative Office of the Courts to establish a prior conviction during the defendant's prosecution for impaired driving. State v. Ellis, 130 N.C. App. 596, 504 S.E.2d 787 (1998).

Habitual offender charge was supported by a judgment, signed by the presiding judge on the uniform citation form and included in the record on appeal and two other charges which had been consolidated for judgment but which were two separate offenses under this section. State v. Allen, 164 N.C. App. 665, 596 S.E.2d 261 (2004).

Defendant's conviction of driving while intoxicated under G.S. 20-138.5 was affirmed; all of the requirements of the charge were met, as a disputed prior conviction occurred within the statutory seven year period, and the trial court properly allowed the State to amend the indictment to state the date of the conviction, as time was not of the essence pursuant to G.S. 15-155. State v. Winslow, 169 N.C. App. 137, 609 S.E.2d 463 (2005), review denied, in part, 359 N.C. 642, 617 S.E.2d 660 (2005).

PREJUDICIAL ERROR IN ERRONEOUS ADMISSION OF EVIDENCE. --Defendant met his burden of showing prejudicial error in the erroneous admission of retrograde extrapolation testimony of the State's witness where the officer testified that he never observed defendant exhibit slurred speech, reckless driving, weaving, difficulty with motor skills, difficulty answering questions, or difficulty following directions, there was no other evidence of appreciable physical and mental impairment, and thus, the evidence played a pivotal role in the guilty verdict for driving while impaired. State v. Hayes, 256 N.C. App. 559, 808 S.E.2d 446 (2017).

SUFFICIENT EVIDENCE. --Defendant's impaired driving charge was not dismissed because, (1) under the corpus delicti rule, defendant's admission was corroborated with a wrecked vehicle, a shoe matching defendant's shoe in the vehicle's driver's side footwell, the absence of others in the area, defendant's consistent injury, and the lack of another explanation for the wreck, and (2) defendant's blood alcohol level was above the statutory limit. State v. Hines, 259 N.C. App. 358, 816 S.E.2d 182 (2018).

ENHANCEMENT OF SENTENCE. --This section did not prohibit defendant's felony sentence from being enhanced on the grounds that he was an habitual felon when elements necessary to prove that he was an habitual felon were the same as those elements which were used to support the underlying felony. State v. Misenheimer, 123 N.C. App. 156, 472 S.E.2d 191 (1996).

CITED in State v. Stafford, 114 N.C. App. 101, 440 S.E.2d 846 (1994); State v. Jernigan, 118 N.C. App. 240, 455 S.E.2d 163 (1995); State v. Smith, 139 N.C. App. 209, 533 S.E.2d 518 (2000); State v. Lobohe, 143 N.C. App. 555, 547 S.E.2d 107 (2001); State v. Gregory, 154 N.C. App. 718, 572 S.E.2d 838 (2002); State v. Burch, 160 N.C. App. 394, 585 S.E.2d 461 (2003); State v. Jones, 358 N.C. 473, 598 S.E.2d 125 (2004); State v. Taylor, 165 N.C. App. 750, 600 S.E.2d 483 (2004); State v. Highsmith, 173 N.C. App. 600, 619 S.E.2d 586 (2005); State v. Bowden, 177 N.C. App. 718, 630 S.E.2d 208 (2006); Harrell v. Bowen, 362 N.C. 142, 655 S.E.2d 350 (2008); State v. Best, 214 N.C. App. 39, 713 S.E.2d 556 (2011), review denied, 718 S.E.2d 397, 2011 N.C. LEXIS 935 (2011).

LEGAL PERIODICALS. --

For survey of developments in North Carolina Law (1992), see 71 N.C.L. Rev. 1893 (1993).

For comment, "North Carolina's Unconstitutional Expansion of an Ancient Maxim: Using DWI Fatalities to Satisfy First Degree Felony Murder," see 22 Campbell L. Rev. 169 (1999).

For note, "Ramifications of the 1997 DWIelony Prior Record Level Amendment to the Structured Sentencing Act: State of North Carolina v. Tanya Watts Gentry," see 22 Campbell L. Rev. 211 (1999).

For article, "Once, Twice, Four Times a Felon: North Carolina's Unconstitutional Recidivist Statutes," see 24 Campbell L. Rev. 115 (2001).

For comment, "Lots of Squeeze, Little (or No) Juice: North Carolina's Habitual Misdemeanor Larceny Statute, a Law Where Results Do Not Justify Costs," see 97 N.C.L. Rev. 432 (2019).

N.C. Gen. Stat. § 20-138.6

Reserved for future codification purposes.

§ 20-138.7. Transporting an open container of alcoholic beverage.

(a) **Offense.** -- No person shall drive a motor vehicle on a highway or the right-of-way of a highway:

(1) While there is an alcoholic beverage in the passenger area in other than the unopened manufacturer's original container; and

. (2) While the driver is consuming alcohol or while alcohol remains in the driver's body.

(a1) **Offense.** -- No person shall possess an alcoholic beverage other than in the unopened manufacturer's original container, or consume an alcoholic beverage, in the passenger area of a motor vehicle while the motor vehicle is on a highway or the right-of-way of a highway. For purposes of this subsection, only the person who possesses or consumes an alcoholic beverage in violation of this subsection shall be charged with this offense.

(a2) **Exception.** -- It shall not be a violation of subsection (a1) of this section for a passenger to possess an alcoholic beverage other than in the unopened manufacturer's original container, or for a passenger to consume an alcoholic beverage, if the container is:

(1) In the passenger area of a motor vehicle that is designed, maintained, or used primarily for the transportation of persons for compensation;

(2) In the living quarters of a motor home or house car as defined in G.S. 20-4.01(27) k.; or

(3) In a house trailer as defined in G.S. 20-4.01(14).

(a3) **Meaning of Terms.** -- Under this section, the term "motor vehicle" means any vehicle driven or drawn by mechanical power and manufactured primarily for use on public highways and includes mopeds.

(b) **Subject to Implied-Consent Law.** -- An offense under this section is an alcohol-related offense subject to the implied-consent provisions of G.S. 20-16.2.

(c) **Odor Insufficient.** -- The odor of an alcoholic beverage on the breath of the driver is insufficient evidence to prove beyond a reasonable doubt that alcohol was remaining in the driver's body in violation of this section, unless the driver was offered an alcohol screening test or chemical analysis and refused to provide all required samples of breath or blood for analysis.

(d) **Alcohol Screening Test.** -- Notwithstanding any other provision of law, an alcohol screening test may be administered to a driver suspected of violating subsection (a) of this section, and the results of an alcohol screening test or the driver's refusal to submit may be used by a law enforcement officer, a court, or an administrative agency in determining if alcohol was present in the driver's body. No alcohol screening tests are valid under this section unless the device used is one approved by the Commission for Public Health, and the screening test is conducted in accordance with the applicable regulations of the Commission as to the manner of its use.

(e) **Punishment; Effect When Impaired Driving Offense Also Charged.** -- Violation of subsection (a) of this section shall be a Class 3 misdemeanor for the first offense and shall be a Class 2 misdemeanor for a second or subsequent offense. Violation of subsection (a) of this section is not a lesser included offense of impaired driving under G.S. 20-138.1, but if a person is convicted under subsection (a) of this section and of an offense involving impaired driving arising out of the same transaction, the punishment imposed by the court shall not exceed the maximum applicable to the offense involving impaired driving, and any minimum applicable punishment shall be imposed. Violation of subsection (a1) of this section by the driver of the motor vehicle is a lesser-included offense of subsection (a) of this section. A violation of subsection (a) shall be considered a moving violation for purposes of G.S. 20-16(c).

Violation of subsection (a1) of this section shall be an infraction and shall not be considered a moving violation for purposes of G.S. 20-16(c).

(f) **Definitions.** -- If the seal on a container of alcoholic beverages has been broken, it is opened within the meaning of this section. For purposes of this section, "passenger area of a motor vehicle" means the area designed to seat the driver and passengers and any area within the reach of a seated driver or passenger, including the glove compartment. The area of the trunk or the area behind the last upright back seat of a station wagon, hatchback, or similar vehicle shall not be considered part of the passenger area. The term "alcoholic beverage" is as defined in G.S. 18B-101(4).

(g) **Pleading.** -- In any prosecution for a violation of subsection (a) of this section, the pleading is sufficient if it states the time and place of the alleged offense in the usual form and charges that the defendant drove a motor vehicle on a highway or the right-of-way of a highway with an open container of alcoholic beverage after drinking.

In any prosecution for a violation of subsection (a1) of this section, the pleading is sufficient if it states the time and place of the alleged offense in the usual form and charges that (i) the defendant possessed an open container of alcoholic beverage in the passenger area of a motor vehicle while the motor vehicle was on a highway or the right-of-way of a highway, or (ii) the defendant consumed an alcoholic beverage in the passenger area of a motor vehicle while the motor vehicle was on a highway or the right-of-way of a highway.

(h) **Limited Driving Privilege.** -- A person who is convicted of violating subsection (a) of this section and whose drivers license is revoked solely based on that conviction may apply for a limited driving privilege as provided for in G.S. 20-179.3. The judge may issue the limited driving privilege only if the driver meets the eligibility requirements of G.S. 20-179.3, other than the requirement in G.S. 20-179.3(b)(1)c. G.S. 20-179.3(e) shall not apply. All other terms, conditions, and restrictions provided for in G.S.

20-179.3 shall apply. G.S. 20-179.3, rather than this subsection, governs the issuance of a limited driving privilege to a person who is convicted of violating subsection (a) of this section and of driving while impaired as a result of the same transaction.

History.
1995, c. 506, s. 9;2000-155, s. 4;2002-25, s. 1;2006-66, s. 21.7;2007-182, s. 2;2013-348, s. 4;2017-102, s. 5.2(b)

EDITOR'S NOTE. --
Session Laws 2017-102, s. 5.2(b) provides: "The Revisor of Statutes is authorized to reletter the definitions in G.S. 20-4.01(27) and G.S. 20-4.01(32b) to place them in alphabetical order. The Revisor of Statutes may conform any citations that change as a result of the relettering." Pursuant to that authority, the reference to G.S. 20-4.01(27)d2. in subdivision (a2)(2) was changed to G.S. 20-4.01(27)k.

EFFECT OF AMENDMENTS. --
Session Laws 2000-155, s. 4, as amended by Session Laws 2002-25, s. 1, and as amended by Session Laws 2006-66, s. 21.7, effective September 1, 2000, deleted "after consuming alcohol" following "beverage" in the catchline; substituted "the right-of-way of a highway" for "public vehicular area" in subsection (a); in subdivision (a)(1), inserted "in the passenger area," and deleted "in passenger area" following "container"; added subsections (a1) through (a3); in subsection (e), deleted "punished as" preceding "Class 3" and "Class 2," deleted the former second sentence stating, "A fine imposed for a second or subsequent offense may not exceed one thousand dollars ($1,000)," substituted "subsection (a) of this section" for "this section " three times, added the next- to-last sentence, substituted "subsection (a)" for "this section," and added the last paragraph; and in subsection (g), substituted "subsection (a) of this section" for "this section," substituted "the right-of-way of a highway" for "public vehicular area" and added the last paragraph.

Session Laws 2007-182, s. 2, effective July 5, 2007, substituted "Commission for Public Health" for "Commission for Health Services" in subsection (d).

Session Laws 2013-348, s. 4, effective October 1, 2013, rewrote subsection (a3), which formerly read "Meaning of Terms. -- Under this section, the term 'motor vehicle' means only those types of motor vehicles which North Carolina law requires to be registered, whether the motor vehicle is registered in North Carolina or another jurisdiction." For applicability, see Editor's note.

DISTRICT COURT JURISDICTION. --District court had jurisdiction to try defendant for operating a motor vehicle with an open container of alcohol while alcohol remained in defendant's system because the citation issued to defendant identified the crime and stated defendant had an open container of alcohol after drinking, (2) defendant filed no motion objecting to the sufficiency of the offense charged in the citation, and (3) any failure to allege facts supporting every element of the offense was not a jurisdictional defect, as the North Carolina Constitution required no grand jury to make a probable cause determination for misdemeanors tried in district court as a jurisdictional prerequisite. State v. Jones, 255 N.C. App. 364, 805 S.E.2d 701 (2017), aff'd, 371 N.C. 548, 819 S.E.2d 340, 2018 N.C. LEXIS 911 (2018).

POSSESSION IN PUBLIC VEHICULAR AREA NOT ILLEGAL. --Defendant's possession of an open container of alcohol in his car in a gas station parking lot was not illegal since a parking lot of a service station was a public vehicular area, and this section only prohibited open containers on highways and highway right-of-ways. State v. Coleman, 228 N.C. App. 76, 743 S.E.2d 62 (2013).

Officer's belief that possession of an open container of alcohol in a car in a public vehicular area was illegal could not support a Terry stop since the belief was unreasonable given that the open container law was neither novel nor complex and clearly prohibited the possession of an open container only on highways and highway right-of-ways, and the distinction between a highway and a public vehicular area was familiar to law enforcement officers. State v. Coleman, 228 N.C. App. 76, 743 S.E.2d 62 (2013).

PROBABLE CAUSE. --Officer's search of defendant's car was unreasonable because the probable cause on which the search was based was tainted since defendant's incriminatory statements that gave rise to probable cause to search the car were elicited in response to the officer's manifestly false assertion that the officer had probable cause to search the car based on the presence of defendant's hip flask and the officer's suggestion that, with or without defendant's consent, the officer would proceed with the search. United States v. Saafir, 754 F.3d 262 (4th Cir. 2014).

Corporal had probable cause to justify defendant's arrest because as when the corporal approached defendant's vehicle he noticed an open beer can, when defendant rolled down his window the corporal detected an odor of alcohol, and when he asked for defendant's license and registration, defendant responded that he did not have a license. Therefore, the corporal could have arrested defendant for either driving with an open container or driving without a valid operator's license. State v. Jackson, 262 N.C. App. 329, 821 S.E.2d 656 (2018).

SUFFICIENT EVIDENCE. --Evidence was sufficient to support defendant's conviction of possessing an open container because the evidence showed that the officers testified that the officers saw an opened bottle of vodka in between defendant's legs while the defendant was seated in the driver's seat of a running car, the officers testified that the bottle contained liquid which one officer poured out at the scene of the arrest, the officers detected a strong odor of alcohol on defendant's breath, and defendant admitted that the defendant had consumed alcohol. State v. Hoque, -- N.C. App. --, 837 S.E.2d 464 (2020).

CITED in State v. Simmons, 205 N.C. App. 509, 698 S.E.2d 95 (2010); Harris v. Testar, Inc., 243 N.C. App. 33, 777 S.E.2d 776 (2015).

N.C. Gen. Stat. § 20-139

Repealed by Session Laws 1983, c. 435, s. 23.

§ 20-139.1. Procedures governing chemical analyses; admissibility; evidentiary provisions; controlled-drinking programs

(a) **Chemical Analysis Admissible.** -- In any implied-consent offense under G.S. 20-16.2, a person's alcohol concentration or the presence of any other impairing substance in the person's body as shown by a chemical analysis is admissible in evidence. This section does not limit the introduction of other competent evidence as to a person's alcohol concentration or results of other tests showing the presence of an impairing substance, including other chemical tests.

(b) **Approval of Valid Test Methods; Licensing Chemical Analysts.** -- The results of a chemical analysis shall be deemed sufficient evidence to prove a person's alcohol concentration. A chemical analysis of the breath administered pursuant to the implied-consent law is admissible in any court or administrative hearing or proceeding if it meets both of the following requirements:

(1) It is performed in accordance with the rules of the Department of Health and Human Services.

(2) The person performing the analysis had, at the time of the analysis, a current permit issued by the Department of Health and Human Services authorizing the person to perform a test of the breath using the type of instrument employed.

For purposes of establishing compliance with subdivision (b)(1) of this section, the court or administrative agency shall take notice of the rules of the Department of Health and Human Services. For purposes of establishing compliance with subdivision (b)(2) of this section, the court or administrative agency shall take judicial notice of the list of permits issued to the person performing the analysis, the type of instrument on which the person is authorized to perform tests of the breath, and the date the permit was issued. The Department of Health and Human Services may ascertain the qualifications and competence of individuals to conduct particular chemical analyses and the methods for conducting chemical analyses. The Department may issue permits to conduct chemical analyses to individuals it finds qualified subject to periodic renewal, termination, and revocation of the permit in the Department's discretion.

(b1) **When Officer May Perform Chemical Analysis.** -- Any person possessing a current permit authorizing the person to perform chemical analysis may perform a chemical analysis.

(b2) **Breath Analysis Results Preventive Maintenance.** -- The Department of Health and Human Services shall perform preventive maintenance on breath-testing instruments used for chemical analysis. A court or administrative agency shall take judicial notice of the preventive maintenance records of the Department. Notwithstanding the provisions of subsection (b), the results of a chemical analysis of a person's breath performed in accordance with this section are not admissible in evidence if:

(1) The defendant objects to the introduction into evidence of the results of the chemical analysis of the defendant's breath; and

(2) The defendant demonstrates that, with respect to the instrument used to analyze the defendant's breath, preventive maintenance procedures required by the regulations of the Department of Health and Human Services had not been performed within the time limits prescribed by those regulations.

(b3) **Sequential Breath Tests Required.** -- The methods governing the administration of chemical analyses of the breath shall require the testing of at least duplicate sequential breath samples. The results of the chemical analysis of all breath samples are admissible if the test results from any two consecutively collected breath samples do not differ from each other by an alcohol concentration greater than 0.02. Only the lower of the two test results of the consecutively administered tests can be used to prove a particular alcohol concentration. A person's refusal to give the sequential breath samples necessary to constitute a valid chemical analysis is a refusal under G.S. 20-16.2(c).

A person's refusal to give the second or subsequent breath sample shall make the result of the first breath sample, or the result of the sample providing the lowest alcohol concentration if more than one breath sample is provided, admissible in any judicial or administrative hearing for any relevant purpose, including the establishment that a person had a particular alcohol concentration for conviction of an offense involving impaired driving.

(b4) Repealed by Session Laws 2006-253, s. 16, effective December 1, 2006, and applicable to offenses committed on or after that date.

(b5) **Subsequent Tests Allowed.** -- A person may be requested, pursuant to G.S. 20-16.2, to submit to a chemical analysis of the person's blood or other bodily fluid or substance in addition to or in lieu of a chemical analysis of the breath, in the discretion of a law enforcement officer; except that a person charged with a violation of G.S. 20-141.4 shall be requested, at any relevant time after the driving, to provide a blood sample in addition to or in lieu of a chemical analysis of the breath. However, if a breath

sample shows an alcohol concentration of .08 or more, then requesting a blood sample shall be in the discretion of a law enforcement officer. If a subsequent chemical analysis is requested pursuant to this subsection, the person shall again be advised of the implied consent rights in accordance with G.S. 20-16.2(a). A person's willful refusal to submit to a chemical analysis of the blood or other bodily fluid or substance is a willful refusal under G.S. 20-16.2. If a person willfully refuses to provide a blood sample under this subsection, and the person is charged with a violation of G.S. 20-141.4, then a law enforcement officer with probable cause to believe that the offense involved impaired driving or was an alcohol-related offense made subject to the procedures of G.S. 20-16.2 shall seek a warrant to obtain a blood sample. The failure to obtain a blood sample pursuant to this subsection shall not be grounds for the dismissal of a charge and is not an appealable issue.

(b6) The Department of Health and Human Services shall post on a Web page a list of all persons who have a permit authorizing them to perform chemical analyses, the types of analyses that they can perform, the instruments that each person is authorized to operate, the effective dates of the permits, and the records of preventive maintenance. A court or administrative agency shall take judicial notice of whether, at the time of the chemical analysis, the chemical analyst possessed a permit authorizing the chemical analyst to perform the chemical analysis administered and whether preventive maintenance had been performed on the breath-testing instrument in accordance with the Department's rules.

(c) **Blood and Urine for Chemical Analysis.** -- Notwithstanding any other provision of law, when a blood or urine test is specified as the type of chemical analysis by a law enforcement officer, a physician, registered nurse, emergency medical technician, or other qualified person shall withdraw the blood sample and obtain the urine sample, and no further authorization or approval is required. If the person withdrawing the blood or collecting the urine requests written confirmation of the law enforcement officer's request for the withdrawal of blood or collecting the urine, the officer shall furnish it before blood is withdrawn or urine collected. When blood is withdrawn or urine collected pursuant to a law enforcement officer's request, neither the person withdrawing the blood nor any hospital, laboratory, or other institution, person, firm, or corporation employing that person, or contracting for the service of withdrawing blood or collecting urine, may be held criminally or civilly liable by reason of withdrawing the blood or collecting the urine, except that there is no immunity from liability for negligent acts or omissions. A person requested to withdraw blood or collect urine pursuant to this subsection may refuse to do so only if it reasonably appears that the procedure cannot be performed without endangering the safety of the person collecting the sample or the safety of the person from whom the sample is being collected. If the officer requesting the blood or urine requests a written justification for the refusal, the medical provider who determined the sample could not be collected safely shall provide written justification at the time of the refusal.

(c1) **Admissibility.** -- The results of a chemical analysis of blood or urine reported by the North Carolina State Crime Laboratory, the Charlotte, North Carolina, Police Department Laboratory, or any other laboratory approved for chemical analysis by the Department of Health and Human Services (DHHS), are admissible as evidence in all administrative hearings, and in any court, without further authentication and without the testimony of the analyst. For the purposes of this section, a "laboratory approved for chemical analysis" by the DHHS includes, but is not limited to, any hospital laboratory approved by DHHS pursuant to the program resulting from the federal Clinical Laboratory Improvement Amendments of 1988 (CLIA).

The results shall be certified by the person who performed the analysis. The provisions of this subsection may be utilized in any administrative hearing, but can only be utilized in cases tried in the district and superior court divisions, or in an adjudicatory hearing in juvenile court, if:

(1) The State notifies the defendant no later than 15 business days after receiving the report and at least 15 business days before the proceeding at which the evidence would be used of its intention to introduce the report into evidence under this subsection and provides a copy of the report to the defendant, and

(2) The defendant fails to file a written objection with the court, with a copy to the State, at least five business days before the proceeding at which the report would be used that the defendant objects to the introduction of the report into evidence.

If the defendant's attorney of record, or the defendant if that person has no attorney, fails to file a written objection as provided in this subsection, then the objection shall be deemed waived and the report shall be admitted into evidence without the testimony of the analyst. Upon filing a timely objection, the admissibility of the report shall be determined and governed by the appropriate rules of evidence.

If the proceeding at which the report would be introduced into evidence under this subsection is continued, the notice provided by the State, the written objection

filed by the defendant, or the failure of the defendant to file a written objection shall remain effective at any subsequent calendaring of that proceeding.

The report containing the results of any blood or urine test may be transmitted electronically or via facsimile. A copy of the affidavit sent electronically or via facsimile shall be admissible in any court or administrative hearing without further authentication. A copy of the report shall be sent to the charging officer, the clerk of superior court in the county in which the criminal charges are pending, the Division of Motor Vehicles, and the Department of Health and Human Services.

Nothing in this subsection precludes the right of any party to call any witness or to introduce any evidence supporting or contradicting the evidence contained in the report.

(c2) Repealed by Session Laws 2013-194, s. 1, effective June 26, 2013.

(c3) **Procedure for Establishing Chain of Custody Without Calling Unnecessary Witnesses.** --

(1) For the purpose of establishing the chain of physical custody or control of blood or urine tested or analyzed to determine whether it contains alcohol, a controlled substance or its metabolite, or any impairing substance, a statement signed by each successive person in the chain of custody that the person delivered it to the other person indicated on or about the date stated is prima facie evidence that the person had custody and made the delivery as stated, without the necessity of a personal appearance in court by the person signing the statement.

(2) The statement shall contain a sufficient description of the material or its container so as to distinguish it as the particular item in question and shall state that the material was delivered in essentially the same condition as received. The statement may be placed on the same document as the report provided for in subsection (c1) or the affidavit provided for in subsection (e1) of this section, as applicable.

(3) The provisions of this subsection may be utilized in any administrative hearing, but can only be utilized in cases tried in the district and superior court divisions, or in an adjudicatory hearing in juvenile court, if:

a. The State notifies the defendant no later than 15 business days after receiving the statement and at least 15 business days before the proceeding at which the statement would be used of its intention to introduce the statement into evidence under this subsection and provides a copy of the statement to the defendant, and

b. The defendant fails to file a written notification with the court, with a copy to the State, at least five business days before the proceeding at which the statement would be used that the defendant objects to the introduction of the statement into evidence.

If the defendant's attorney of record, or the defendant if that person has no attorney, fails to file a written objection as provided in this subsection, then the objection shall be deemed waived and the statement shall be admitted into evidence without the necessity of a personal appearance by the person signing the statement. Upon filing a timely objection, the admissibility of the statement shall be determined and governed by the appropriate rules of evidence.

If the proceeding at which the statement would be introduced into evidence under this subsection is continued, the notice provided by the State, the written objection filed by the defendant, or the failure of the defendant to file a written objection shall remain effective at any subsequent calendaring of that proceeding.

(4) Nothing in this subsection precludes the right of any party to call any witness or to introduce any evidence supporting or contradicting the evidence contained in the statement.

(c4) Repealed by Session Laws 2013-194, s. 1, effective June 26, 2013.

(c5) The testimony of an analyst regarding the results of a chemical analysis of blood or urine admissible pursuant to subsection (c1) of this section, and reported by that analyst, shall be permitted by remote testimony, as defined in G.S. 15A-1225.3, in all administrative hearings, and in any court, if all of the following occur:

(1) The State has provided a copy of the report to the attorney of record for the defendant, or to the defendant if that person has no attorney, as required by subsections (c1) and (c3) of this section.

(2) The State notifies the attorney of record for the defendant or the defendant if that person has no attorney, at least 15 business days before the proceeding at which the evidence would be used of its intention to introduce the testimony regarding the chemical analysis into evidence using remote testimony.

(3) The defendant's attorney of record, or the defendant if that person has no attorney, fails to file a written objection with the court, with a copy to the State, at least

five business days before the proceeding at which the testimony will be presented that the defendant objects to the introduction of the remote testimony.

If the defendant's attorney of record, or the defendant if that person has no attorney, fails to file a written objection as provided in this subsection, then the objection shall be deemed waived and the analyst shall be allowed to testify by remote testimony.

The method used for remote testimony authorized by this subsection shall allow the trier of fact and all parties to observe the demeanor of the analyst as the analyst testifies in a similar manner as if the analyst were testifying in the location where the hearing or trial is being conducted. The court shall ensure that the defendant's attorney, or the defendant if that person has no attorney, has a full and fair opportunity for examination and cross-examination of the analyst.

Nothing in this section shall preclude the right of any party to call any witness. Nothing in this subsection shall obligate the Administrative Office of the Courts or the State Crime Laboratory to incur expenses related to remote testimony absent an appropriation of funds for that purpose.

(d) **Right to Additional Test.** -- Nothing in this section shall be construed to prohibit a person from obtaining or attempting to obtain an additional chemical analysis. If the person is not released from custody after the initial appearance, the agency having custody of the person shall make reasonable efforts in a timely manner to assist the person in obtaining access to a telephone to arrange for any additional test and allow access to the person in accordance with the agreed procedure in G.S. 20-38.5. The failure or inability of the person who submitted to a chemical analysis to obtain any additional test or to withdraw blood does not preclude the admission of evidence relating to the chemical analysis.

(d1) **Right to Require Additional Tests.** -- If a person refuses to submit to any test or tests pursuant to this section, any law enforcement officer with probable cause may, without a court order, compel the person to provide blood or urine samples for analysis if the officer reasonably believes that the delay necessary to obtain a court order, under the circumstances, would result in the dissipation of the percentage of alcohol in the person's blood or urine.

(d2) Notwithstanding any other provision of law, when a blood or urine sample is requested under subsection (d1) of this section by a law enforcement officer, a physician, registered nurse, emergency medical technician, or other qualified person shall withdraw the blood and obtain the urine sample, and no further authorization or approval is required. If the person withdrawing the blood or collecting the urine requests written confirmation of the charging officer's request for the withdrawal of blood or obtaining urine, the officer shall furnish it before blood is withdrawn or urine obtained. A person requested to withdraw blood or collect urine pursuant to this subsection may refuse to do so only if it reasonably appears that the procedure cannot be performed without endangering the safety of the person collecting the sample or the safety of the person from whom the sample is being collected. If the officer requesting the blood or urine requests a written justification for the refusal, the medical provider who determined the sample could not be collected safely shall provide written justification at the time of the refusal.

(d3) When blood is withdrawn or urine collected pursuant to a law enforcement officer's request, neither the person withdrawing the blood nor any hospital, laboratory, or other institution, person, firm, or corporation employing that person, or contracting for the service of withdrawing blood, may be held criminally or civilly liable by reason of withdrawing that blood, except that there is no immunity from liability for negligent acts or omissions. The results of the analysis of blood or urine under this subsection shall be admissible if performed by the State Crime Laboratory or any other hospital or qualified laboratory.

(e) **Recording Results of Chemical Analysis of Breath.** -- A person charged with an implied-consent offense who has not received, prior to a trial, a copy of the chemical analysis results the State intends to offer into evidence may request in writing a copy of the results. The failure to provide a copy prior to any trial shall be grounds for a continuance of the case but shall not be grounds to suppress the results of the chemical analysis or to dismiss the criminal charges.

(e1) **Use of Chemical Analyst's Affidavit in District Court.** -- An affidavit by a chemical analyst sworn to and properly executed before an official authorized to administer oaths shall be admissible in evidence without further authentication and without the testimony of the analyst in any hearing or trial in the District Court Division of the General Court of Justice with respect to the following matters:

(1) The alcohol concentration or concentrations or the presence or absence of an impairing substance of a person given a chemical analysis and who is involved in the hearing or trial.

(2) The time of the collection of the blood, breath, or other bodily fluid or substance sample or samples for the chemical analysis.

(3) The type of chemical analysis administered and the procedures followed.

(4) The type and status of any permit issued by the Department of Health and Human Services that the analyst held on the date the analyst performed the chemical analysis in question.

(5) If the chemical analysis is performed on a breath-testing instrument for which regulations adopted pursuant to subsection (b) require preventive maintenance, the date the most recent preventive maintenance procedures were performed on the breath-testing instrument used, as shown on the maintenance records for that instrument.

The Department of Health and Human Services shall develop a form for use by chemical analysts in making this affidavit.

(e2) Except as governed by subsection (c1) or (c3) of this section, the State can only use the provisions of subsection (e1) of this section if:

(1) The State notifies the defendant no later than 15 business days after receiving the affidavit and at least 15 business days before the proceeding at which the affidavit would be used of its intention to introduce the affidavit into evidence under this subsection and provides a copy of the affidavit to the defendant, and

(2) The defendant fails to file a written notification with the court, with a copy to the State, at least five business days before the proceeding at which the affidavit would be used that the defendant objects to the introduction of the affidavit into evidence.

The failure to file a timely objection as provided in this subsection shall be deemed a waiver of the right to object to the admissibility of the affidavit, and the affidavit shall be admitted into evidence without the testimony of the analyst. Upon filing a timely objection, the admissibility of the report shall be determined and governed by the appropriate rules of evidence. The case shall be continued until the analyst can be present. The criminal case shall not be dismissed due to the failure of the analyst to appear, unless the analyst willfully fails to appear after being ordered to appear by the court. If the proceeding at which the affidavit would be introduced into evidence under this subsection is continued, the notice provided by the State, the written objection filed by the defendant, or the failure of the defendant to file a written objection shall remain effective at any subsequent calendaring of that proceeding.

Nothing in subsection (e1) or subsection (e2) of this section precludes the right of any party to call any witness or to introduce any evidence supporting or contradicting the evidence contained in the affidavit.

(f) **Evidence of Refusal Admissible.** -- If any person charged with an implied-consent offense refuses to submit to a chemical analysis or to perform field sobriety tests at the request of an officer, evidence of that refusal is admissible in any criminal, civil, or administrative action against the person.

(g) **Controlled-Drinking Programs.** -- The Department of Health and Human Services may adopt rules concerning the ingestion of controlled amounts of alcohol by individuals submitting to chemical testing as a part of scientific, experimental, educational, or demonstration programs. These regulations shall prescribe procedures consistent with controlling federal law governing the acquisition, transportation, possession, storage, administration, and disposition of alcohol intended for use in the programs. Any person in charge of a controlled-drinking program who acquires alcohol under these regulations must keep records accounting for the disposition of all alcohol acquired, and the records must at all reasonable times be available for inspection upon the request of any federal, State, or local law-enforcement officer with jurisdiction over the laws relating to control of alcohol. A controlled-drinking program exclusively using lawfully purchased alcoholic beverages in places in which they may be lawfully possessed, however, need not comply with the record-keeping requirements of the regulations authorized by this subsection. All acts pursuant to the regulations reasonably done in furtherance of bona fide objectives of a controlled-drinking program authorized by the regulations are lawful notwithstanding the provisions of any other general or local statute, regulation, or ordinance controlling alcohol.

(h) **Disposition of Blood Evidence.** -- Notwithstanding any other provision of law, any blood or urine sample subject to chemical analysis for the presence of alcohol, a controlled substance or its metabolite, or any impairing substance pursuant to this section may be destroyed by the analyzing agency 12 months after the case is filed or after the case is concluded in the trial court and not under appeal, whichever is later, without further notice to the parties. However, if a Motion to Preserve the evidence has been filed by either party, the evidence shall remain in the custody of the analyzing agency or the agency that collected the sample until dispositive order of a court of competent jurisdiction is entered.

History.
1963, c. 966, s. 2; 1967, c. 123; 1969, c. 1074, s. 2; 1971, c. 619, ss. 12, 13; 1973, c. 476, s. 128; c. 1081, s. 2; c. 1331, s. 3; 1975, c. 405; 1979, 2nd Sess., c. 1089; 1981, c. 412, s. 4; c. 747, s. 66; 1983, c. 435, s. 26; 1983 (Reg. Sess., 1984), c. 1101, s. 20; 1989, c. 727, s. 219(2);1991, c. 689, s. 233.1(b);1993, c. 285, s. 7;1997-379, ss. 5.3 -5.5; 1997-443, s. 11A.10;1997-443, s. 11A.123;1997-456, s. 34(b);2000-155, s. 8;2003-95, s. 1;2003-104, s. 2;2006-253, s. 16;2007-115, ss. 5, 6; 2007-493, ss. 3, 18, 22, 23; 2009-473, ss. 3 -6; 2011-19, ss. 5, 8; 2011-119, s. 2;2011-307, s. 9;2012-168, s. 6;2013-171, ss. 1, 4-6; 2013-194, s. 1;2013-338, s. 1;2014-119, s. 8(b);2015-173, s. 3;2015-276, s. 1;2016-10, s. 1

EDITOR'S NOTE. --
Session Laws 2009-473, s. 8, provides in part: "Nothing in this act shall be construed to abrogate any judicial or administrative rulings or decisions prior to the effective date of this act that (i) allowed or disallowed the introduction of evidence or (ii) validated or invalidated procedures used for the introduction of evidence."

Session Laws 2011-19, s. 1, provides: "This act shall be known as 'The Forensic Sciences Act of 2011.'"

Session Laws 2011-19, s. 3, provides: "The State Bureau of Investigation (SBI) shall encourage and seek collaborative opportunities and grant funds for research programs, in association, whenever possible, with the university system or independent nationally recognized forensic institutions, on human observer bias and sources of human error in forensic examinations. Such programs might include studies to determine the effects of contextual bias in forensic practice (e.g., studies to determine whether and to what extent the results of forensic analysis are influenced by knowledge regarding the background of the suspect and the investigator's theory of the case). In addition, research on sources of human error should be closely linked with research conducted to quantify and characterize the amount of error. Based on the results of these studies, and in consultation with the North Carolina Forensic Sciences Advisory Board, the North Carolina State Crime Laboratory should develop standard operating procedures (that will lay the foundation for model protocols) to minimize, to the extent possible, potential bias and sources of human error in forensic science. These standard operating procedures should apply to all forensic analyses that may be used in litigation."

Session Laws 2011-19, s. 4, as amended by Session Laws 2011-307, s. 8, and as amended by Session Laws 2012-168, s. 6.1, provides: "Forensic Scientists I, II, and III, forensic science supervisors, and forensic scientist managers professionals at the State Crime Laboratory shall be required to obtain individual certification consistent with international and ISO standards within 18 months of the date the scientist becomes eligible to seek certification according to the standards of the certifying entity or by January 1, 2013, or as soon as practicable after that date unless no certification is available. All such forensic scientists shall have access to the certification process."

Session Laws 2011-19, s. 5, provides: "The Revisor of Statutes shall replace the name of the State Bureau of Investigation Laboratory, or any other name which is identified with the State Bureau of Investigation Laboratory, with the name 'North Carolina State Crime Laboratory' wherever first used in a statute or session law and with 'State Crime Laboratory' at each subsequent location in the statute or session law."

Session Laws 2011-19, which, in s. 8, rewrote subsection (c2), in s. 11, as amended by Session Laws 2011-307, s. 9, as amended by Session Laws 2012-168, s. 6, and as amended by Session Laws 2013-338, s. 1, provides: "Sections 1 through 5 and Sections 9 through 11 are effective when this act becomes law [March 31, 2011], and Section 6 becomes effective July 1, 2011. Sections 7 and 8 of this act are effective when they become law; however, until July 1, 2016, the provisions of those sections shall apply only to the North Carolina State Crime Laboratory, and on or after July 1, 2016, the provisions of Sections 7 and 8 shall apply to all laboratories conducting forensic or chemical analysis for admission in the courts of this State. Nothing in this act is intended to amend or modify either the statutory or common law applicable to discovery in criminal cases which was applicable prior to the effective date of this act. Prosecutions for offenses committed before the effective date of this act are not abated or affected by this act, and the statutes that would be applicable but for this act remain applicable to those prosecutions."

Session Laws 2013-171, s. 10, made the amendment to subsections (c1), (c3), and (e1) by Session Laws 2013-171, ss. 4, 5, and 6, applicable to proceedings held on or after December 1, 2013, and verification forms received by the SBI on or after December 1, 2013.

Session Laws 2014-119, s. 8(c), made subsection (c5), as added by Session Laws 2014-119, s. 8(b), effective September 1, 2014, and applicable to testimony admitted on or after that date.

Session Laws 2015-173, s. 6, made the amendment to this section by Session Laws 2015-173, s. 6, applicable to notices of intent to introduce a statement or report provided by the State on or after that date. Section 5 of this act applies to ex parte hearings conducted on or after July 31, 2015.

Session Laws 2015-276, s. 7, provides: "Sections 1 and 2 of this act become effective December 1, 2015, and apply to offenses committed on or after that date. The remainder of this act is effective when this act becomes law [October 20, 2015] and applies to offenses committed on or after that date. Prosecutions for offenses committed before the effective date of this act are not abated or affected by this act, and the statutes that would be applicable but for this act remain applicable to those prosecutions."

Session Laws 2016-10, s. 2, made the amendment to this section by Session Laws 2016-10, s. 1, applicable to trials commencing on or after October 1, 2016.

EFFECT OF AMENDMENTS. --
Session Laws 2006-253, s. 16, effective December 1, 2006, and applicable to offenses committed on or after that date, rewrote the section.

Session Laws 2007-115, ss. 5 and 6, effective June 27, 2007, in subsection (c), in the third sentence, substituted "withdrawing blood or collecting urine" for "withdrawing blood" and "the blood or collecting the urine" for "that blood," and added the last two

sentences; and in subsection (d2), added the last two sentences.

Session Laws 2007-493, ss. 3, 18, 22 and 23, effective August 30, 2007, in subsection (b6), deleted "and file with the clerk of superior court in each county" following "Web page" in the first sentence, and inserted "or administrative agency" in the last sentence; in subsection (c1), deleted "and reported on a form approved by the Attorney General" at the end of the second sentence; in subsection (c2), substituted "accredited" for "certified," and "Directors/Laboratory Accreditation Board (ASCLD/LAB)" for "Directors (ASCLD),"; and, in subsection (d), substituted "G.S. 20-38.5" for "G.S. 20-38.4" at the end of the first sentence. For applicability provision, see Editor's note.

Session Laws 2013-171, s. 1, effective June 19, 2013, added subsection (h).

Session Laws 2013-171, ss. 4 -6, effective December 1, 2013, in subsection (c1), substituted "shall" for "may" preceding "be admitted into evidence" in the fourth sentence, in subdivision (c3)(3), substituted "shall be admitted into evidence" for "may be admitted into evidence" in the second sentence; and substituted "shall be admissible in evidence" for "is admissible in evidence" in the first sentence in subsection (e1). For applicability, see Editor's note.

Session Laws 2013-194, s. 1, effective June 26, 2013, in subsection (c1), added "(DHHS)" in the first sentence, and added that second sentence; and deleted subsections (c2), which pertained to accreditation of a laboratory under the International Laboratory Accreditation Cooperation (ILAC) Mutual Recognition Arrangement For Testing, and (c4), which required that evidence, to be admissible, be requested by law enforcement and be performed by an accredited lab.

Session Laws 2014-119, s. 8(b), effective September 1, 2014, added subsection (c5). See Editor's note for applicability.

Session Laws 2015-173, s. 3, effective July 31, 2015, and applicable to notices of intent to introduce a statement or report provided by the State on or after that date, inserted "the objection shall be deemed waived and" in subsections (c1) and (c5), and subdivision (c3)(3)(b).

Session Laws 2015-276, s. 1, effective December 1, 2015, inserted "at any relevant time after the driving" preceding "to provide a blood sample" in the first sentence of subsection (b5). For applicability, see editor's note.

Session Laws 2016-10, s. 1, effective October 1, 2016, added "no later than 15 business days after receiving the report and" following "The State notifies the defendant" near the beginning of subdivision (c1)(1); added the fourth sentence in subdivision (c1)(2); substituted "in subsection (c1) or the affidavit provided for in subsection (e1) of this section, as applicable" for "in subsection (c1) of this section" near the end of subdivision (c3)(2); added "no later than 15 business days after receiving the statement and" preceding "at least 15 business days" in subdivision (c3)(3); in subdivision (c3)(3), substituted "statement" for "report" preceding "shall be determined" and added the last sentence; substituted "(c1) or (c3) of this section" for "(c1), (c2), or (c3) of this section" in subsection (e2); added "no later than 15 business days after receiving the statement and" preceding "at least 15 business days" in subdivision (e2)(1); in subdivision (e2)(2), rewrote the second sentence which formerly read "The failure to file a timely objection as provided in this subsection shall be deemed a waiver of the right to object to the admissibility of the affidavit" and added the last sentence. See editor's note for applicability.

I. IN GENERAL.

EDITOR'S NOTE. --Many of the cases cited below were decided prior to 1969 and subsequent amendments, and prior to the 1993 reduction of the blood alcohol content for driving while impaired and related offenses from 0.10 to 0.08, and prior to the 2000 amendment of this section, which deleted the word "willful" preceding "refusal" in subsection (b3).

CONSTITUTIONALITY. --See State v. Jones, 63 N.C. App. 411, 305 S.E.2d 221, cert. denied and appeal dismissed, 309 N.C. 323, 307 S.E.2d 171 (1983).

Subsection (b2) does not provide an unconstitutional shifting of the burden of proof to defendant. The possibility that the breathalyzer may not have been properly maintained is a affirmative defense to be established by defendant and the State may permissibly put the burden of establishing affirmative defenses on the defendant. State v. Dellinger, 73 N.C. App. 685, 327 S.E.2d 609 (1985).

The requirement of subdivision (b)(3) of this section that defendants charged with impaired driving be given two breathalyzer tests after January 1, 1985, does not create an impermissible classification denying defendant equal protection of the laws. State v. Dellinger, 73 N.C. App. 685, 327 S.E.2d 609 (1985).

All individuals arrested for driving while impaired who are tested under model 900 breathalyzer are given same initial test to determine blood alcohol content. Regulations merely treat same group of people in a different way depending on results of first test. This classification is not of the type that can be considered denial of equal protection. State v. Garvick, 98 N.C. App. 556, 392 S.E.2d 115 (1990).

This section does not violate the Law of the Land Clause of Art. I, § 19 of the North Carolina Constitution.State v. Jones, 106 N.C. App. 214, 415 S.E.2d 774 (1992).

In a case in which defendant challenged the constitutionality of G.S. 20-139.1 on the basis that the previous caselaw concerning the exigency of testing for blood alcohol content was outdated, he did not present any caselaw that called into question that the diminution of blood alcohol content constituted an exigent circumstance. State v. Fletcher, 202 N.C. App. 107, 688 S.E.2d 94 (2010).

BECAUSE TESTING PURSUANT TO A SEARCH WARRANT IS A TYPE OF "OTHER COMPETENT EVIDENCE" REFERRED TO IN THIS STATUTE, the State is not limited to evidence of blood alcohol concentration which was procured in accordance with the procedures of G.S. 20-16.2. State v. Davis, 142 N.C. App. 81, 542 S.E.2d 236 (2001), cert. denied, 353 N.C. 386, 547 S.E.2d 818 (2001).

WILLFUL REFUSAL NOT REQUIRED. --Defendant's argument that because "willful refusal" is required before a driver's license is revoked under G.S. 20-16.2, the requirement of a willful refusal should be read into this section was without merit. State v. Pyatt, 125 N.C. App. 147, 479 S.E.2d 218 (1997).

Subsection (f) does not require a willful refusal before evidence of a refusal is admissible and the court will not read in this additional requirement. State v. Pyatt, 125 N.C. App. 147, 479 S.E.2d 218 (1997).

STATE'S FAILURE TO TAKE AND TO PRESERVE AN ADDITIONAL BREATH SAMPLE FOR INDEPENDENT TESTING BY DEFENDANT or to produce the control and test ampules for defendant's breathalyzer examination did not violate State or federal due process. State v. Jones, 106 N.C. App. 214, 415 S.E.2d 774 (1992).

MEANING OF "READINGS" IN SUBDIVISION (B3)(3). --When read in pari materia with statute's remaining provisions, term "readings" was intended by legislature to mean test "results" recorded by chemical analyst in hundredths, rounded down as provided in the commission regulations. State v. Tew, 326 N.C. 732, 392 S.E.2d 603 (1990).

SUBSECTION (B3) DOES NOT CREATE AN IMPERMISSIBLE CLASSIFICATION and the Safe Roads Act (G.S. 20-138.1 et seq.) does not deny the equal protection of the laws. State v. Howren, 312 N.C. 454, 323 S.E.2d 335 (1984).

Subsection (e1) is constitutional under the provisions of U.S. Const., Amend. VI and N.C. Const., Art. I, § 19 and 23. State v. Smith, 312 N.C. 361, 323 S.E.2d 316 (1984).

Subsection (e1) of this section does not violate the accused's right to confrontation. State v. Smith, 312 N.C. 361, 323 S.E.2d 316 (1984).

THIS SECTION RELATES ONLY TO CRIMINAL ACTIONS ARISING OUT OF THE OPERATION OF A MOTOR VEHICLE and has no application to the effect of voluntary intoxication upon criminal responsibility for assault and homicide. State v. Bunn, 283 N.C. 444, 196 S.E.2d 777 (1973).

The chemical analysis (breathalyzer) test authorized by this section is, by its express terms, applicable only to criminal actions arising out of the operation of a motor vehicle and has no application to criminal responsibility for homicide. State v. Medley, 295 N.C. 75, 243 S.E.2d 374 (1978).

BREATHALYZER TEST RESULTS ARE NOT ADMISSIBLE IN A BREAKING AND ENTERING CASE. State v. Wade, 14 N.C. App. 414, 188 S.E.2d 714, cert. denied, 281 N.C. 627, 190 S.E.2d 470 (1972).

ADMISSION OF TEST RESULTS HELD ERROR WHERE DEFENDANT HAD NOT BEEN DRIVING VEHICLE. --Where defendant was not driving or operating a vehicle at the time of alleged assault on a police officer, the court erred in admitting testimony showing the result of a breathalyzer test. State v.

Powell, 18 N.C. App. 732, 198 S.E.2d 70, cert. denied, 283 N.C. 757, 198 S.E.2d 727 (1973).

AS TO THE PROSPECTIVE EFFECT OF THE SECOND 1973 AMENDMENT, see State v. Bunton, 27 N.C. App. 704, 220 S.E.2d 354 (1975).

ADMISSION OF EVIDENCE OF REFUSAL TO SUBMIT TO TEST DOES NOT VIOLATE RIGHT AGAINST SELF-INCRIMINATION. --Admission of evidence of defendant's refusal to submit to the tests under this section does not violate his constitutional right against self-incrimination. State v. Flannery, 31 N.C. App. 617, 230 S.E.2d 603 (1976).

MIRANDA REQUIREMENTS INAPPLICABLE TO BREATHALYZER TEST. --Since the taking of a breath sample from an accused for the purpose of the test is not evidence of a testimonial or communicative nature within the privilege against self-incrimination, the requirements of Miranda v. Arizona, 394 U.S. 436, 86 S. Ct. 1602, 16 L. Ed. 2d 694, 10 A.L.R.3d 974 (1966) are inapplicable to a breathalyzer test administered pursuant to this section. State v. Flannery, 31 N.C. App. 617, 230 S.E.2d 603 (1976).

The breathalyzer operator is not required to remind the subject of his Miranda rights, since the test does not constitute evidence of a testimonial nature. State v. Spencer, 46 N.C. App. 507, 265 S.E.2d 451 (1980).

As breathalyzer results are not testimonial evidence, Miranda warnings are not required prior to administering a breathalyzer. State v. White, 84 N.C. App. 111, 351 S.E.2d 828, cert. denied, 319 N.C. 227, 353 S.E.2d 404 (1987).

DEFENDANT'S ALLEGEDLY INCRIMINATING STATEMENTS HELD HARMLESS. --Admission of evidence that after defendant blew into breathalyzer and was shown the reading, he made statements indicating his disbelief at the result, thus allegedly creating an inference that he had registered a reading in excess of the legal limit on the first test, was harmless in light of other evidence of defendant's guilt, including his refusal to take a second test. State v. Wike, 85 N.C. App. 516, 355 S.E.2d 221 (1987).

"CHEMICAL ANALYST" FOR PURPOSES OF THIS SECTION INCLUDES a person who was validly licensed by the Department of Human Resources to perform chemical analyses immediately prior to the enactment of the Safe Roads Act. To hold otherwise would mean that an individual licensed to perform chemical analyses under one statute would automatically lose his license when the testing procedures are merely recodified in another statute. Obviously the legislature did not intend that result. State v. Dellinger, 73 N.C. App. 685, 327 S.E.2d 609 (1985).

ALTHOUGH SUBSECTION (E) REQUIRES THAT THE CHEMICAL ANALYST RECORD THE RESULTS OF THE TEST and the time of collection and give a copy to the person submitting to the test, the court found there to be compliance where the defendant was given the required information on the test card printed by the machine after the test was performed. State v. Watson, 122 N.C. App. 596, 472 S.E.2d 28 (1996).

THE USE OF A CHEMICAL ANALYST'S AFFIDAVIT, IN LIEU OF THE ANALYST'S LIVE APPEARANCE, by the State in a criminal trial in the district court division of the general court of justice as proof of the facts noted in the chemical analyst's affidavit, does not deny to the criminal defendant any right or privilege granted by the Constitution of the United States or the Constitution of North Carolina. State v. Smith, 312 N.C. 361, 323 S.E.2d 316 (1984).

The legislature, through subsection (e1) of this section, has enacted a constitutionally permissible procedure attuned to scientific and technological advancements which have insured reliability in chemical testing for blood-alcohol concentration. State v. Smith, 312 N.C. 361, 323 S.E.2d 316 (1984).

OFFICER'S TESTIMONY ON QUALIFIED PERSON SUFFICIENT. --Trooper's testimony that the person drawing defendant's blood worked at the blood laboratory at the hospital was sufficient to show that the person was a qualified person under G.S. 20-139.1(c). State v. Hinchman, 192 N.C. App. 657, 666 S.E.2d 199 (2008).

COLLATERAL ESTOPPEL. --For purposes of the privity requirement for a collateral estoppel defense, the Attorney General, when representing the Department of Motor Vehicles in a license revocation appeal, and the district attorney, when representing the State in a criminal DWI proceeding, represent the same interest, that of State citizens prohibiting individuals who use intoxicating substances from using their roads. State v. Summers, 132 N.C. App. 636, 513 S.E.2d 575 (1999), aff'd, 351 N.C. 620, 528 S.E.2d 17 (2000).

The State was collaterally estopped in a DWI prosecution from submitting evidence of the defendant's refusal to take an intoxilyzer test, where the issue of refusal was litigated and decided in the defendant's favor in a prior civil license revocation proceeding, and the State did not appeal. State v. Summers, 132 N.C. App. 636, 513 S.E.2d 575 (1999), aff'd, 351 N.C. 620, 528 S.E.2d 17 (2000).

SUBSECTION (E1) HAS EFFECTIVELY CREATED A STATUTORY EXCEPTION TO THE HEARSAY RULE. State v. Smith, 312 N.C. 361, 323 S.E.2d 316 (1984).

The statutory exception to the hearsay rule created by subsection (e1) of this section has as its basis the sound reasoning which gave rise to the business and public records exceptions to the hearsay rule. State v. Smith, 312 N.C. 361, 323 S.E.2d 316 (1984).

Subsection (e1) reflects a rationale which complies fully with historically recognized legitimate reasons for exceptions to the general rule against hearsay evidence. State v. Smith, 312 N.C. 361, 323 S.E.2d 316 (1984).

THE SCIENTIFIC AND TECHNOLOGICAL ADVANCEMENTS IN BREATH ANALYSIS FOR ALCOHOL CONCENTRATION have removed the necessity for a subjective determination of impairment, so appropriate for cross-examination, and have increasingly removed the operator as a material element in the objective determination of blood-alcohol concentration. Indeed, the legislature's recognition of the reliable and accurate innovation of blood-alcohol concentration testing is manifested in G.S. 20-138.1(a)(2) which now provides that a person who after having consumed sufficient alcohol that he has, at any relevant time after driving, an alcohol concentration of 0.10 (now 0.08) or more commits the offense of impaired driving. State v. Smith, 312 N.C. 361, 323 S.E.2d 316 (1984).

The science of breath analysis for alcohol concentration has become increasingly reliable, increasingly less dependent on human skill of operation, and increasingly accepted as a means for measuring blood-alcohol concentration. State v. Smith, 312 N.C. 361, 323 S.E.2d 316 (1984).

WHERE DEFENDANT BY HIS VOLUNTARY AND OVERT ACTIONS MAKES IT CLEAR THAT HE WILL NOT VOLUNTARILY SUBMIT TO BREATHALYZER TEST, it is not necessary for the State to present evidence that the defendant was advised of his right to refuse to take the breathalyzer test before evidence of that refusal may be used against him at a trial for driving under the influence, as is allowed pursuant to this section. State v. Simmons, 51 N.C. App. 440, 276 S.E.2d 765 (1981).

THIS SECTION CONTEMPLATES SITUATIONS IN WHICH MORE THAN TWO SAMPLES MAY BE REQUIRED to constitute a valid chemical analysis. Watson v. Hiatt, 78 N.C. App. 609, 337 S.E.2d 871 (1985).

REFUSAL TO GIVE MORE THAN TWO SAMPLES. --Where petitioner provided two breath samples resulting in readings of .28 and .31 and then refused to provide any more samples, her conduct amounted to a willful refusal under G.S. 20-16.2(c), within the meaning of subsection (b3) of this section. Watson v. Hiatt, 78 N.C. App. 609, 337 S.E.2d 871 (1985).

SUFFICIENT EVIDENCE EXISTED TO CONCLUDE THAT PETITIONER REFUSED TO GIVE SEQUENTIAL BREATH SAMPLES and that petitioner's conduct constituted a willful refusal under this section, and defendant's contention that the test was not performed according to applicable rules and regulations was irrelevant to the revocation proceedings. Gibson v. Faulkner, 132 N.C. App. 728, 515 S.E.2d 452 (1999), decided prior to the 2000 amendment.

REFUSAL TO REMOVE OBJECT FROM MOUTH. --Where breathalyzer operator noticed a piece of paper in the corner of petitioner's mouth and ordered him to remove it, and where petitioner refused, petitioner's refusal to obey the breathalyzer operator's instructions was a refusal to take the breathalyzer test under G.S. 20-16.2(c), since a reasonable method for determining that the subject has not "eaten" in 15 minutes is to prohibit him from placing foreign objects in his mouth. Tolbert v. Hiatt, 95 N.C. App. 380, 382 S.E.2d 453 (1989).

STANDARDS NOT MET. --Retrograde extrapolation from an officer's report of smelling alcohol on the breath of defendant more than 10 hours after an accident did not meet the rigorous standards applied to

chemical analyses of breath, blood, and urine under G.S. 20-139.1. State v. Davis, 208 N.C. App. 26, 702 S.E.2d 507 (2010).

CHAIN OF CUSTODY OF EVIDENCE. --If all the evidence can reasonably support a conclusion that the blood sample analyzed is the same as that taken from the defendant then it is admissible into evidence. The fact that the defendant can show potential weak spots in the chain of custody only relates to the weight to be given the evidence establishing the chain of custody. State v. Bailey, 76 N.C. App. 610, 334 S.E.2d 266 (1985), overruled on other grounds, State v. Drdak, 330 N.C. 587, 411 S.E.2d 604 (1992).

APPLIED in State v. Powell, 264 N.C. 73, 140 S.E.2d 705 (1965); State v. Randolph, 273 N.C. 120, 159 S.E.2d 324 (1968); State v. Mobley, 273 N.C. 471, 160 S.E.2d 334 (1968); State v. Sherrill, 15 N.C. App. 590, 190 S.E.2d 405 (1972); State v. Fuller, 24 N.C. App. 38, 209 S.E.2d 805 (1974); State v. Hurley, 28 N.C. App. 478, 221 S.E.2d 743 (1976); Byrd v. Wilkins, 69 N.C. App. 516, 317 S.E.2d 108 (1984); State v. Watts, 72 N.C. App. 661, 325 S.E.2d 505 (1985); State v. Garcia-Lorenzo, 110 N.C. App. 319, 430 S.E.2d 290 (1993); State v. Gunter, 111 N.C. App. 621, 433 S.E.2d 191 (1993); State v. Summers, 351 N.C. 620, 528 S.E.2d 17 (2000); State v. McDonald, 151 N.C. App. 236, 565 S.E.2d 273 (2002); State v. Narron, 193 N.C. App. 76, 666 S.E.2d 860 (2008), review denied, 363 N.C. 135, 674 S.E.2d 140 (2009), cert. denied, 558 U.S. 818, 130 S. Ct. 71, 175 L. Ed. 2d 26 (2009); State v. Meadows, 201 N.C. App. 707, 687 S.E.2d 305 (2010), review denied 2010 N.C. LEXIS 453 (2010); State v. Simmons, 205 N.C. App. 509, 698 S.E.2d 95 (2010).

CITED in State v. Brown, 13 N.C. App. 327, 185 S.E.2d 453 (1971); Gwaltney v. Keaton, 29 N.C. App. 91, 223 S.E.2d 506 (1976); State v. Hill, 31 N.C. App. 733, 230 S.E.2d 579 (1976); In re Arthur, 291 N.C. 640, 231 S.E.2d 614 (1977); State v. Lockamy, 65 N.C. App. 75, 308 S.E.2d 750 (1983); In re Redwine, 312 N.C. 482, 322 S.E.2d 769 (1984); State v. Knoll, 84 N.C. App. 228, 352 S.E.2d 463 (1987); In re Rogers, 94 N.C. App. 505, 380 S.E.2d 599 (1989); State v. Freund, 326 N.C. 795, 392 S.E.2d 608 (1990); Nicholson v. Killens, 116 N.C. App. 473, 448 S.E.2d 542 (1994); State v. Abdereazeq, 122 N.C. App. 727, 471 S.E.2d 445 (1996); Powers v. Powers, 130 N.C. App. 37, 502 S.E.2d 398 (1998); State v. Wilson, 225 N.C. App. 246, 736 S.E.2d 614 (2013); State v. Townsend, 236 N.C. App. 456, 762 S.E.2d 898 (2014); State v. McCrary, 237 N.C. App. 48, 764 S.E.2d 477 (2014), aff'd 780 S.E.2d 554, 2015 N.C. LEXIS 1262 (2015).

II. ADMINISTRATION AND USE OF BREATHALYZER TEST.

THE BREATHALYZER TEST IS A CHEMICAL TEST for the testing of a person's breath for the purpose of determining the alcoholic content of his blood. State v. Hill, 9 N.C. App. 279, 176 S.E.2d 41 (1970), rev'd on other grounds, 277 N.C. 547, 178 S.E.2d 462 (1971).

PROCEDURE FOR REQUESTING CHEMICAL TESTS NOT DIFFERENT FROM § 20-16.2. --The General Assembly did not intend to establish a different procedure for requesting chemical tests under this section than it provided in G.S. 20-16.2. State v. Flannery, 31 N.C. App. 617, 230 S.E.2d 603 (1976).

ONE REQUEST BY OFFICER SUFFICIENT. --Petitioner's contention that he did not willfully refuse to submit to a chemical analysis at the request of the charging officer since the officer did not request any additional chemical analysis after the first test was completed was without merit, as the statutes require the charging officer to request a chemical analysis based on sequential breath samples, not a sequence of requests for separate chemical analyses, and thus officer's original request that petitioner submit to a chemical analysis was sufficient to comply with the requirements of G.S. 20-16.2(c). Tolbert v. Hiatt, 95 N.C. App. 380, 382 S.E.2d 453 (1989).

TEST PURSUANT TO A WARRANT. --Where the officer obtained a blood sample from defendant pursuant to a warrant, after defendant refused to submit to a breath test of his blood alcohol level, the results were admissible. State v. Shepley, 237 N.C. App. 174, 764 S.E.2d 658 (2014).

THE RESULT OF A BREATHALYZER ANALYSIS IS CRUCIAL TO A CONVICTION. State v. Smith, 312 N.C. 361, 323 S.E.2d 316 (1984).

TEST MUST HAVE BEEN TIMELY MADE. --For the test to cast any light on a defendant's condition at the time of the alleged crime, the test must have been timely made. State v. Cooke, 270 N.C. 644, 155 S.E.2d 165 (1967).

POLICE OFFICER'S INSTRUCTIONS. --A police officer was not required to repeat all the steps in the breath alcohol test process, but only the step requiring the subject to blow into the instrument, before administering the third test to the defendant, which was required because the results of the first two tests differed by more than.02. State v. Moore, 132 N.C. App. 802, 513 S.E.2d 346 (1999).

IN THE INTEREST OF ACCURACY. --Since it is the degree of intoxication at the time of the occurrence in question which is relevant, the sooner after the event the breathalyzer test is made, the more accurate will be the estimate of blood alcohol concentration at the time of the act in issue. State v. Cooke, 270 N.C. 644, 155 S.E.2d 165 (1967).

TIME OF TEST GOES TO WEIGHT OF EVIDENCE. --The fact that three hours had passed from the time the defendant operated a vehicle until breathalyzer test was given went to the weight to be given the evidence, rather than its admissibility, and the breathalyzer evidence was properly admitted. State v. George, 77 N.C. App. 470, 336 S.E.2d 93 (1985), appeal dismissed and petition denied, 316 N.C. 197, 341 S.E.2d 581 (1986).

OBSERVATION PERIOD. --Given that the record showed that the officer observed defendant over the course of a period of 21 minutes, during which defendant did not ingest alcohol or other fluids, regurgitate, vomit, eat, or smoke, and during which the officer only lost direct sight of defendant for very brief intervals, the trial court did not err in determining that the officer failed to comply with the applicable observation period requirement prior the administration of a

breath test. State v. Roberts, 237 N.C. App. 551, 767 S.E.2d 543 (2014).

THIS SECTION REQUIRES TWO THINGS BEFORE A CHEMICAL ANALYSIS OF A PERSON'S BREATH OR BLOOD CAN BE CONSIDERED VALID. First, that such analysis shall be performed according to methods approved by the State Board of Health (now by the Commission for Public Health), and second, that such analysis be made by a person possessing a valid permit issued by the State Board of Health (now by the Department of Human Resources) for this purpose. State v. Powell, 279 N.C. 608, 184 S.E.2d 243 (1971); State v. Chavis, 15 N.C. App. 566, 190 S.E.2d 374 (1972); State v. Eubanks, 283 N.C. 556, 196 S.E.2d 706 (1973); State v. Franks, 87 N.C. App. 265, 360 S.E.2d 473 (1987).

The State must establish under subsection (b) of this section (1) that the person administering the test possessed "a valid permit issued by the Department of Human Resources for this purpose" and (2) that the test was "performed according to methods approved by the Commission for Health Services." State v. Martin, 46 N.C. App. 514, 265 S.E.2d 456, cert. denied, 301 N.C. 102 (1980); State v. George, 77 N.C. App. 470, 336 S.E.2d 93 (1985), appeal dismissed and petition denied, 316 N.C. 197, 341 S.E.2d 581 (1986).

It was necessary for a State trooper conducting a chemical analysis test against a drunk driver to hold a permit issued by the Department of Health and Human Services; proper foundation had to be established that the trooper had a permit in order for the test results to be admitted into evidence. State v. Roach, 145 N.C. App. 159, 548 S.E.2d 841 (2001).

EXPRESSION OF TEST RESULTS IN TERMS OF BREATH OR BLOOD. --Police officer who was issued a permit to perform chemical analysis under the authority of subsection (b) of this section by the Department of Human Resources was permitted by G.S. 20-4.01(0.2) (now G.S. 20-4.01(1b)) to express alcohol concentration in terms of 210 liters of breath, as well as 100 milliliters of blood. State v. Midgett, 78 N.C. App. 387, 337 S.E.2d 117 (1985).

REGULATIONS GOVERNING SECOND AND SUBSEQUENT SAMPLES. --Commission of Health Services [now the Commission for Public Health] operational procedure designating a specific time, namely, at the reappearance of the words "blow sample" on the machine for the collection of the second breath sample, met the requirements of this section that Commission regulations provide time requirements as to the collection of second and subsequent samples. State v. Lockwood, 78 N.C. App. 205, 336 S.E.2d 678 (1985).

HIGHER OF TWO ANALYSES MAY NOT BE INTRODUCED. --Subdivision (b3)(3) of this section restricts the State from seeking to introduce into evidence the higher of two chemical analyses as proof of a defendant's alcohol concentration. State v. Harper, 82 N.C. App. 398, 346 S.E.2d 223 (1986).

TESTIMONY AS TO IDENTICAL SEQUENTIAL TESTS NOT PREJUDICIAL. --While subdivision (b3)(3) of this section protects a defendant from a conviction based on the higher of two breathalyzer test results, it was not prejudicial for the court to allow testimony that two breathalyzer tests were administered to defendant, where both breathalyzer test results were 0.12, and where defendant did not object or move to strike prior testimony that a sequential breathalyzer test was administered to him. State v. Harper, 82 N.C. App. 398, 346 S.E.2d 223 (1986).

CONSECUTIVELY ADMINISTERED TESTS REQUIREMENT MET. --Where the time of the first reading was 11:15 a.m., and the time of the second reading was 11:26 a.m., and because these readings were taken from "consecutively administered tests" on adequate breath samples given within 11 minutes of one another and the readings were within .01 of one another, the requirement of sequential testing was complied with, despite the fact that between the time of these two readings defendant had given two insufficient breath samples. State v. White, 84 N.C. App. 111, 351 S.E.2d 828, cert. denied, 319 N.C. 227, 353 S.E.2d 404, appeal dismissed, 319 N.C. 409, 354 S.E.2d 887 (1987).

Trial court did not commit reversible error when it allowed admission into evidence of the lesser of defendant's sequential and consecutive Intoxilyzer results. The Intoxilyzer results were admissible based on consecutive testing, not based on defendant's refusal; thus defendant's conviction rested squarely on admissible evidence. State v. Shockley, 201 N.C. App. 431, 689 S.E.2d 455 (2009).

Defendant's breath test results were sequential because the fact that the test results were printed on separate tickets did not change their sequential character when they were taken within an eleven minute period and the only intervening event was the resetting of the breath test machine for the second test. State v. Cathcart, 227 N.C. App. 347, 742 S.E.2d 321 (2013).

TIMELINESS OF SEQUENTIAL BREATH TESTS UNDER SUBDIVISION (B3)(1) OF THIS SECTION. --Use of words "as soon as feasible" in duplicate sequential breath samples regulations, in substance meets time requirements of subdivision (b3)(1) of this section. State v. Garvick, 98 N.C. App. 556, 392 S.E.2d 115 (1990).

PURPOSE OF SEQUENTIAL TESTING IS TO INSURE ACCURACY OF READINGS. "Sequential tests are required to minimize the time between tests." Sequential testing is also designed to assure that factors outside control of both State and defendant do not affect result. Shutting down instrument, adding new ampul, and restarting from beginning would not accomplish either purpose. State v. Garvick, 98 N.C. App. 556, 392 S.E.2d 115 (1990).

SUBSECTION (B3) OF THIS SECTION DOES NOT REQUIRE TWO CHEMICAL ANALYSES but merely requires testing of at least duplicate sequential breath samples. State v. Garvick, 98 N.C. App. 556, 392 S.E.2d 115 (1990).

QUALIFICATIONS REQUIRED TO ADMINISTER BREATHALYZER TEST. --A person holding a valid permit issued by the State Board of Health (now

by the Department of Human Resources) is qualified to administer a breathalyzer test. When such permit is introduced in evidence, the permittee is competent to testify as to the results of the test. State v. King, 6 N.C. App. 702, 171 S.E.2d 33 (1969); State v. Powell, 10 N.C. App. 726, 179 S.E.2d 785, aff'd, 279 N.C. 608, 184 S.E.2d 243 (1971).

HOW MANDATE OF SUBSECTION (B) AS TO QUALIFICATIONS OF PERSON ADMINISTERING TEST CAN BE MET. --The mandate of subsection (b) of this section can be met in one of three ways: (1) by stipulation between the defendant and the State that the individual who administers the test holds a valid permit issued by the Department of Human Resources; or (2) by offering the permit of the individual who administers the test into evidence and in the event of conviction from which an appeal is taken, by bringing forward the exhibit as a part of the record on appeal; or (3) by presenting any other evidence which shows that the individual who administered the test holds a valid permit issued by the Department of Human Resources. State v. Mullis, 38 N.C. App. 40, 247 S.E.2d 265 (1978).

NOTIFICATION OF RIGHTS. --Though G.S. 20-16.2 must be read in conjunction with this section to determine the procedures governing the administering of chemical analyses, G.S. 20-16.2, and that statute alone, sets forth the procedures governing notification of rights pursuant to a chemical analysis. Nicholson v. Killens, 116 N.C. App. 473, 448 S.E.2d 542 (1994).

THE BURDEN OF PROVING COMPLIANCE WITH SUBSECTION (B) LIES WITH THE STATE and the failure to offer any proof is not sanctioned by the courts. State v. Gray, 28 N.C. App. 506, 221 S.E.2d 765 (1976).

IN ANY PROPER MANNER. --It is left open for the State to prove compliance with the requirements of this section in any proper and acceptable manner. State v. Powell, 10 N.C. App. 726, 179 S.E.2d 785, aff'd, 279 N.C. 608, 184 S.E.2d 243 (1971); State v. Chavis, 15 N.C. App. 566, 190 S.E.2d 374 (1972); State v. Warf, 16 N.C. App. 431, 192 S.E.2d 37 (1972); State v. Eubanks, 283 N.C. 556, 196 S.E.2d 706 (1973).

FAILURE TO SHOW COMPLIANCE WITH SUBSECTION (B) AS PREJUDICIAL ERROR. --Failure of the State to produce evidence of the test operator's compliance with subsection (b) of this section must be deemed prejudicial error. State v. Gray, 28 N.C. App. 506, 221 S.E.2d 765 (1976).

State's failure to lay the proper foundation for the admission of evidence of the results of a breathalyzer test entitles defendant to a new trial. State v. Gray, 28 N.C. App. 506, 221 S.E.2d 765 (1976).

Defendant was entitled to a new trial in a prosecution under former G.S. 20-138 where the trial court allowed into evidence the results of a breathalyzer test without a showing by the State that the test was administered according to methods approved by the State Board of Health (now by the Commission for Public Health) and that the test was administered by a person possessing a valid permit issued by the

Board of Health (now by the Department of Human Resources). State v. Warf, 16 N.C. App. 431, 192 S.E.2d 37 (1972).

NEITHER OPERATOR'S PERMIT NOR COPY OF APPROVED METHODS MUST BE INTRODUCED. --Although permissible, it is not required that either the permit or a certified copy of the methods approved by the State Board of Health (now by the Commission for Public Health) be introduced into evidence by the State before testimony of the results of the breathalyzer test can be given. State v. Powell, 10 N.C. App. 726, 179 S.E.2d 785, aff'd, 279 N.C. 608, 184 S.E.2d 243 (1971).

AND FAILURE TO INTRODUCE COPY OF RULES DOES NOT MAKE OFFICER'S TESTIMONY INCOMPETENT. --Failure to introduce in evidence a certified copy of the rules and regulations containing the approved methods of administering a breathalyzer test does not make an officer's testimony as to the results of a test incompetent. State v. Powell, 279 N.C. 608, 184 S.E.2d 243 (1971).

A WITNESS MAY TESTIFY THAT HE ADMINISTERED THE TEST IN ACCORDANCE WITH THE RULES AND REGULATIONS established, without introducing a copy of such rules and regulations in evidence. State v. Powell, 10 N.C. App. 726, 179 S.E.2d 785, aff'd, 279 N.C. 608, 184 S.E.2d 243 (1971).

WITNESS TESTIMONY AS TO THE CUSTOMARY PROCEDURES followed in administering tests using the Breathalyzer model 900 machine was sufficient, and properly admitted under G.S. 8C-1, Rule 406, to prove defendant's test was administered in accordance with "approved methods" required by this section, where copies of the actual test and the arresting officer's personal notes concerning the case had been discarded as customary after approximately five years. State v. Tappe, 139 N.C. App. 33, 533 S.E.2d 262 (2000).

STATEMENT BY STATE TROOPER WHO ADMINISTERED BREATHALYZER TEST TO DEFENDANT THAT HE HELD A PARTICULAR CERTIFICATE NUMBER from the Department of Human Resources stating that he was qualified as a breathalyzer operator provided the basis for a reasonable inference that he possessed a valid permit at the time he administered the test to defendant, although it was not established when the permit was issued. State v. Doggett, 41 N.C. App. 304, 254 S.E.2d 793 (1979).

WITNESS' POSSESSION OF PERMIT NOT SHOWN. --The testimony of a witness that he had been to school, studied and graduated from the "school for breathalyzer operators put on by the Community College in Raleigh" was not sufficient to satisfy the requirements of the statute that he possess a valid permit issued by the State Board of Health (now by the Department of Human Resources). State v. Caviness, 7 N.C. App. 541, 173 S.E.2d 12 (1970).

Testimony that a witness had "a license to administer the breathalyzer" was not sufficient to satisfy the requirement of this section that to be considered valid the analysis must be performed by an individual possessing a valid permit issued by the State Board of

Health (now by the Department of Human Resources) for this purpose. State v. Caviness, 7 N.C. App. 541, 173 S.E.2d 12 (1970).

THE STATE NEED NOT OFFER PROOF OF "PREVENTIVE MAINTENANCE PROCEDURES." State v. Martin, 46 N.C. App. 514, 265 S.E.2d 456, cert. denied, 301 N.C. 102 (1980).

WHEN RESULT OF BREATHALYZER TEST IS COMPETENT EVIDENCE. --The result of a breathalyzer test, when the qualifications of the person making the test and the manner of making it meet the requirements of this section, is competent evidence in a criminal prosecution under G.S. 20-138 (now G.S. 20-138.1). State v. Cooke, 270 N.C. 644, 155 S.E.2d 165 (1967); State v. Coley, 17 N.C. App. 443, 194 S.E.2d 372, cert. denied, 283 N.C. 258, 195 S.E.2d 690 (1973). See also, State v. Cummings, 267 N.C. 300, 148 S.E.2d 97 (1966).

VARIANCE IN TEST RESULTS. --Where first of two tests of defendant's breath showed an alcohol concentration between .22 and .23 grams of alcohol per 210 liters of breath, and second showed a concentration of .20 grams, evidence obtained from breathalyzer readings should not be suppressed where rounded-down readings are within .02 of each other. "Readings" was intended by the Legislature to mean the test "results" recorded by the chemical analyst in hundredths, rounded down as provided in the commission regulations. State v. Tew, 326 N.C. 732, 392 S.E.2d 603 (1990).

EVIDENCE WAS SUFFICIENT TO LAY FOUNDATION FOR INTRODUCTION OF "RESULT" OF BREATHALYZER ANALYSIS, the result being that defendant refused to submit to such analysis, where sheriff, who administered breathalyzer test to defendant, testified that he was licensed to operate breathalyzer by North Carolina Department of Health and Human Services, that breathalyzer instrument was in working order on the date in question, and that after giving defendant third opportunity to provide breath sample, officer concluded that defendant willfully refused to take breathalyzer. State v. Barber, 93 N.C. App. 42, 376 S.E.2d 497 (1989).

ASSUMING ARGUENDO THAT PROSECUTOR'S QUESTION REGARDING LOWER OF TWO BREATHALYZER TEST RESULTS WAS IMPROPER, the trial court promptly took appropriate corrective measures by sustaining defendant's objection as to the form of the question and instructing the jury to disregard it; such measures were sufficient to cure any possible prejudice resulting from the prosecutor's question. State v. McDonald, 97 N.C. App. 322, 387 S.E.2d 666 (1990).

RESULT OF BREATHALYZER HELD NOT COMPETENT EVIDENCE. --Where the only evidence was that the officer who administered the breathalyzer test to defendant had a "certificate" to operate the breathalyzer instrument and there was no evidence to show who issued such "certificate," it was error to admit the officer's testimony concerning the results of the test, entitling the defendant to a new trial. State v. Franks, 87 N.C. App. 265, 360 S.E.2d 473 (1987).

STATE IS NOT REQUIRED TO PRODUCE AN EXPERT WITNESS TO TESTIFY CONCERNING A BREATHALYZER TEST; admissibility of such testimony is governed by the rules set forth in State v. Powell, 279 N.C. 608, 184 S.E.2d 243 (1971); State v. Luckey, 54 N.C. App. 178, 282 S.E.2d 490 (1981).

BREATHALYZER TEST MAY CARRY STATE'S CASE TO JURY. --A breathalyzer test which is otherwise relevant and competent and which shows 0.10 (now 0.08) percent or more by weight of alcohol in defendant's blood will carry the State's case to the jury for its determination of whether defendant was under the influence of alcoholic beverages at the time charged. State v. Cooke, 270 N.C. 644, 155 S.E.2d 165 (1967).

BUT JURY IS STILL AT LIBERTY TO ACQUIT. --Despite the results of the breathalyzer test, the jury is still at liberty to acquit defendant if they find that his guilt is not proven beyond a reasonable doubt, and the court should explain this to the jury. State v. Cooke, 270 N.C. 644, 155 S.E.2d 165 (1967).

The jury is at liberty to acquit defendant if it should find that his guilt was not proven beyond a reasonable doubt. State v. Royall, 14 N.C. App. 214, 188 S.E.2d 50, cert. denied, 281 N.C. 515, 189 S.E.2d 35 (1972).

III. LIMITATION ON ROLE OF ARRESTING OFFICER.

ARRESTING OFFICER CANNOT ADMINISTER TEST. --An officer cannot administer the breathalyzer test if he was at the scene of the crime and participated in the arrest. State v. Spencer, 46 N.C. App. 507, 265 S.E.2d 451 (1980).

Chemical analysis test was not valid because it was performed by the arresting officer; admission of such evidence was error. State v. Roach, 145 N.C. App. 159, 548 S.E.2d 841 (2001).

REASON FOR LIMITATION AS TO WHO MAY ADMINISTER TEST. --The principle that underlies the limitation seems to be that, in the interest of fairness as well as the appearance of fairness, an officer whose judgment in selecting a defendant for arrest or in making the arrest may be at issue at trial should not administer the chemical test that will either confirm or refute the soundness of his earlier judgment in causing the arrest. State v. Jordan, 35 N.C. App. 652, 242 S.E.2d 192 (1978).

The purpose of the limitation is to assure that the test will be fairly and impartially made. State v. Stauffer, 266 N.C. 358, 145 S.E.2d 917 (1966); State v. Jordan, 35 N.C. App. 652, 242 S.E.2d 192 (1978).

OFFICER WHO WAS PRESENT AT THE SCENE OF THE ARREST FOR THE PURPOSE OF ASSISTING IF NECESSARY WAS AN "ARRESTING OFFICER" within the meaning of this section, even though a different officer actually placed his hand upon the defendant and informed him that he was under arrest. State v. Stauffer, 266 N.C. 358, 145 S.E.2d 917 (1966).

POLICEMAN HELD NOT AN "ARRESTING OFFICER". --Where defendant was already under arrest and was seated in the patrol car of the arresting officer when the officer who administered the test first arrived on the scene, which latter officer had not been called to the scene for any purpose of assisting in the arrest, but arrived at the scene merely because it happened to be on his direct route to the police station, and stopped there solely to assist in moving defendant's car out of the way of traffic, despite the fact that such officer testified on cross-examination by defendant's counsel that if trouble had developed with defendant he would have assisted the arresting officer with that too, these facts did not make him an arresting officer. State v. Dail, 25 N.C. App. 552, 214 S.E.2d 219, cert. denied, 288 N.C. 245, 217 S.E.2d 669 (1975).

OFFICER WHO PREVIOUSLY ARRESTED DEFENDANT ON SIMILAR CHARGE MAY ADMINISTER TEST. --Where an officer had nothing to do with defendant's second arrest, his arrest of defendant on a similar charge earlier in the morning did not bring him within the disqualification. State v. Jordan, 35 N.C. App. 652, 242 S.E.2d 192 (1978).

THIS SECTION IS NOT VIOLATED WHEN THE REQUEST COMES FROM THE ARRESTING OFFICER. State v. Flannery, 31 N.C. App. 617, 230 S.E.2d 603 (1976).

THE ARRESTING OFFICER IS QUALIFIED TO TESTIFY AS TO DEFENDANT'S REFUSAL TO SUBMIT TO TESTS. State v. Flannery, 31 N.C. App. 617, 230 S.E.2d 603 (1976); State v. Simmons, 51 N.C. App. 440, 276 S.E.2d 765 (1981).

IV. ASSISTING DEFENDANT IN SECURING ADDITIONAL TEST.

ALL THAT THIS SECTION REQUIRES OF THE ARRESTING OFFICER IS THAT HE ASSIST DEFENDANT IN CONTACTING DOCTOR; he is not required in addition to transport defendant to the doctor. State v. Bunton, 27 N.C. App. 704, 220 S.E.2d 354 (1975); State v. Bumgarner, 97 N.C. App. 567, 389 S.E.2d 425 (1990), disc. rev. denied and appeal dismissed, 326 N.C. 599, 393 S.E.2d 873 (1990).

Law enforcement officers may not hinder a driver from obtaining an independent sobriety test, but their constitutional duties in North Carolina go no further than allowing a defendant access to a telephone and allowing medical personnel access to a driver held in custody. State v. Bumgarner, 97 N.C. App. 567, 389 S.E.2d 425 (1990), disc. rev. denied and appeal dismissed, 326 N.C. 599, 393 S.E.2d 873 (1990).

REFUSAL OF ARRESTING OFFICER TO SIGN FORMS, AUTHORIZING THAT BLOOD SAMPLE BE SENT from hospital that did not perform certain type of analysis to hospital that did, was not a violation of defendant's rights under subsection (d) of this section so as to render prior breathalyzer results inadmissible, since the officer complied with the mandate of this section by taking defendant to a physician of his choice for the prior test and it was defendant's responsibility to obtain an analysis of the blood sample. State v. Sawyer, 26 N.C. App. 728, 217 S.E.2d 116, cert. denied, 288 N.C. 395, 218 S.E.2d 469 (1975).

NO WRONGFUL VIOLATION OF DEFENDANT'S RIGHTS FOUND. --The trial court acted within its discretion in rejecting the defendant's allegation that he had requested and been denied a blood test, where the defendant was given an opportunity to use the telephone to make certain calls to his girlfriend and attorney and could have called, but did not call, a medical expert or hospital for the purposes of conducting a blood test. State v. Tappe, 139 N.C. App. 33, 533 S.E.2d 262 (2000).

V. ADMINISTRATION AND USE OF BLOOD TEST.

THIS SECTION DOES NOT LIMIT THE INTRODUCTION OF OTHER COMPETENT EVIDENCE as to a defendant's alcohol concentration, including other chemical tests. This statute allows other competent evidence of a defendant's blood alcohol level in addition to that obtained from chemical analysis pursuant to this section and G.S. 20-16.2. State v. Drdak, 330 N.C. 587, 411 S.E.2d 604 (1992).

WITHDRAWAL OF BLOOD BY NURSE. --Where officers testified that a nurse was present to withdraw petitioner's blood, and one officer further testified that the nurse was "authorized to do that," and there was no evidence to the contrary, the State carried its burden of proof to show compliance with this section. Richardson v. Hiatt, 95 N.C. App. 196, 381 S.E.2d 866, rehearing granted, 95 N.C. App. 780, 384 S.E.2d 62 (1989).

State met the State's burden to demonstrate that the person who drew the blood was qualified because the trial court found that the officer indicated that at the hospital a nurse entered the emergency room to perform the blood draw, defendant indicated that a nurse entered the room, the officer observed the blood draw, the nurse signed on the rights form, the officer could not remember the nurse's name, the nurse asked defendant if the nurse could take the defendant's blood, and defendant told the nurse no. State v. Hoque, -- N.C. App. --, 837 S.E.2d 464 (2020).

FAILURE TO ADVISE. --State was required, pursuant to G.S. 20-16.2 and 20-139.1, to re-advise the defendant of the defendant's implied consent rights before requesting the defendant take a blood test; the state's failure to adhere to these statutory requirements required suppression of the results of the blood test. State v. Williams, 234 N.C. App. 445, 759 S.E.2d 350 (2014).

RIGHT TO BE READVISED NOT TRIGGERED. --Trial court did not err in admitting evidence of the results of defendant's blood test because the prospect of defendant submitting to a blood test originated with defendant, as opposed to originating with a state trooper, his statutory right to be readvised of his implied consent rights was not triggered State v. Sisk, 238 N.C. App. 553, 766 S.E.2d 694 (2014), cert. denied 780 S.E.2d 566, 2015 N.C. LEXIS 1242 (2015).

Superior court properly refused to suppress intoxilyzer results because the re-advisement requirement of the statute was never triggered; the officer's request that defendant provide another sample for the same chemical analysis of the breath on a second intoxilyzer machine was not one for a subsequent chemical analysis under the statute. State v. Cole, 262 N.C. App. 466, 822 S.E.2d 456 (2018).

TEST OBTAINED PURSUANT TO WARRANT. --Because defendant's blood draw was performed pursuant to a valid search warrant, defendant did not have a constitutional right to have a witness present for the blood draw, and the trial court properly denied defendant's motion to suppress the blood evidence and dismiss the impaired driving charge. State v. Chavez, 237 N.C. App. 475, 767 S.E.2d 581 (2014).

ADMISSIBILITY OF RESULTS WHEN TEST NOT PROPERLY PERFORMED. --Testimony concerning the results of blood tests may be admitted into evidence even though the tests were not performed in accordance with G.S. 20-16.2 and this section under the "other competent evidence" exception contained in this section. State v. Byers, 105 N.C. App. 377, 413 S.E.2d 586 (1992).

LAW ENFORCEMENT OFFICER'S BELIEF THAT DELAY CAUSED BY OBTAINING COURT ORDER WOULD RESULT IN DISSIPATION OF PERCENTAGE OF BLOOD ALCOHOL. --In a case in which defendant did not question whether he had refused to submit to a test or whether probable cause existed in order to compel a blood test, but he did contend that the police officer's belief that the delay caused by obtaining a court order would result in the dissipation of his percentage of blood alcohol was unreasonable and not grounded in fact or knowledge, competent evidence existed to suggest that the belief was reasonable. The officer opined that the entire process of driving to the magistrate's office, standing in line, filling out the required forms, returning to the hospital, and having defendant's blood drawn would have taken anywhere from two to three hours, and while other evidence existed that could have supported a contrary finding, the trial court's finding of fact as to the officer's reasonable belief was supported by competent evidence. State v. Fletcher, 202 N.C. App. 107, 688 S.E.2d 94 (2010).

CROSS REFERENCES. -- For provision regarding the offense of impaired driving, see G.S. 20-138.1. For the North Carolina State Crime Laboratory Ombudsman, see G.S. 114-16.2.

LEGAL PERIODICALS. -- For article on tests for intoxication, see 45 N.C.L. Rev. 34 (1966).

For survey of 1978 law on criminal procedure, see 57 N.C.L. Rev. 1007 (1979).

For note discussing North Carolina's Validation of the Warrantless Seizure of Blood from an Unconscious Suspect, in Light of State v. Hollingsworth, 77 N.C. App. 36, 334 S.E.2d 463 (1985), see 21 Wake Forest L. Rev. 1071 (1986).

For a survey of 1996 developments in constitutional law, see 75 N.C.L. Rev. 2315 (1997).

For 1997 legislative survey, see 20 Campbell L. Rev. 417.

For article, "Another 'Straightforward Application': The Impact of Melendez-Diaz on Forensic Testing and Expert Testimony in Controlled Substance Cases," see 33 Campbell L. Rev. 1 (2010).

Chapter 20

OPINIONS OF THE ATTORNEY GENERAL

EDITOR'S NOTE. --Many of the opinions of the Attorney General cited below were decided prior to the 1969 and subsequent amendments.

AS TO PERSONS QUALIFIED TO GIVE BLOOD TESTS, see opinion of Attorney General to Dr. Jacob Koomen, State Health Director, 40 N.C.A.G. 429 (1970).

AN ARRESTING OFFICER MAY NOT COLLECT A BREATH SAMPLE FOR SUBSEQUENT ANALYSIS BY QUALIFIED OPERATION OF A TESTING DEVICE. --See opinion of Attorney General to Mr. Jacob Koomen, M.D., M.P.H., State Health Director, 41 N.C.A.G. 792 (1972).

SUBSECTION (A) DOES NOT REQUIRE THAT DEFENDANT'S ALCOHOL CONCENTRATION BE EXPRESSED in "grams per 100 milliliters of blood" or "grams per 210 liters of breath" in order for the results to be admissible in evidence. See opinion of Attorney General to Mr. Joel H. Brewer, Assistant District Attorney, Ninth Judicial District, 54 N.C.A.G. 93 (1985).

THE WORDS "TEST OR TESTS" IN SUBSECTION (D) of this section are modified by the adjective "chemical" and refer only to chemical analyses of bodily substances to determine the alcohol content of the blood. See opinion of Attorney General to Mr. Howard D. Cole, Assistant Prosecutor, Eighteenth Judicial District, 40 N.C.A.G. 401 (1969).

THE WORD "CONTACTING" IN SUBSECTION (D) of this section appears to mean "establishing communication with." In most cases this will involve assisting the accused in establishing telephonic communication with the person selected. The law-enforcement officer must allow the person selected to perform the additional test to have access to the body of the accused, but he is not required to transport the accused to the hospital or the doctor. See opinion of Attorney General to Mr. Howard D. Cole, Assistant Prosecutor, Eighteenth Judicial District, 40 N.C.A.G. 401 (1969).

DEFENDANT HAS THE RIGHT AT ANY TIME TO REQUEST AN ADDITIONAL TEST by a qualified person of his own choosing. However, such test is "in addition to any administered at the direction of a law-enforcement officer," and "the person tested" by the law-enforcement officer cannot delay the officer's tests for that purpose. See opinion of Attorney General to Mr. Howard D. Cole, Assistant Prosecutor, Eighteenth Judicial District, 40 N.C.A.G. 401 (1969).

WARNINGS TO WHICH DEFENDANT IS ENTITLED. --Since September 1, 1969, by virtue of the new language added to G.S. 20-16.2(b) by Session Laws 1969, c. 1074, the officer must notify the accused that he is "permitted to call an attorney and to select a witness to view for him the testing procedures". Prior to the 1969 act, the law-enforcement officer was not required to give the defendant any warnings with respect to the chemical test or notify him of any rights regarding it. See opinion of Attorney General to Mr. Howard D. Cole, Assistant Prosecutor, Eighteenth Judicial District, 40 N.C.A.G. 401 (1969).

THE OFFICER NEED NOT GIVE A WARNING THAT DEFENDANT HAS NO RIGHT TO AN INDEPENDENT TEST ADMINISTERED BY A QUALIFIED PERSON OF HIS OWN CHOOSING UNLESS HE FIRST SUBMITS TO A CHEMICAL TEST given by the State. The only restriction upon administration of the officer's test is that the officer must permit the accused "to call an attorney and to select a witness to view for him the testing procedures," but "the testing procedures shall not be delayed for these purposes for a period of time over thirty (30) minutes from the time the accused person is notified of these rights." See opinion of Attorney General to Mr. Howard D. Cole, Assistant Prosecutor, Eighteenth Judicial District, 40 N.C.A.G. 401 (1969).

OFFICER NEED NOT ASSIST ONE WHO REFUSES TO SUBMIT TO TEST TO SECURE INDEPENDENT TESTING. --If defendant fails or refuses to submit to a chemical test given at the direction of a law-enforcement officer, yet asks for an independent test given by a qualified person, the officer need not assist defendant in contacting a qualified person to administer the test, as the officer is only required to assist "any person who has submitted to the chemical test under the provisions of G.S. 20-16.2." See opinion of Attorney General to Mr. Howard D. Cole, Assistant Prosecutor, Eighteenth Judicial District, 40 N.C.A.G. 401 (1969).

A BLOOD ALCOHOL LEVEL OF LESS THAN 0.10 (NOW 0.08) PERCENT IS NOT CONCLUSIVE ON A DRUNKEN DRIVING CHARGE. --See opinion of Attorney General to the Honorable George H. Martin, Magistrate, Clay County, 40 N.C.A.G. 430 (1970).

§ 20-140. Reckless driving

(a) Any person who drives any vehicle upon a highway or any public vehicular area carelessly and heedlessly in willful or wanton disregard of the rights or safety of others shall be guilty of reckless driving.

(b) Any person who drives any vehicle upon a highway or any public vehicular area without due caution and circumspection and at a speed or in a manner so as to endanger or be likely to endanger any person or property shall be guilty of reckless driving.

(c) Repealed by Session Laws 1983, c. 435, s. 23.

(d) Reckless driving as defined in subsections (a) and (b) is a Class 2 misdemeanor.

(e) Repealed by Session Laws 1983, c. 435, s. 23.

(f) A person is guilty of the Class 2 misdemeanor of reckless driving if the person drives a commercial motor vehicle carrying a load that is subject to the permit requirements of G.S. 20-119 upon a highway or any public vehicular area either:

 (1) Carelessly and heedlessly in willful or wanton disregard of the rights or safety of others; or

 (2) Without due caution and circumspection and at a speed or in a manner so as to endanger or be likely to endanger any person or property.

History.

1937, c. 407, s. 102; 1957, c. 1368, s. 1; 1959, c. 1264, s. 8; 1973, c. 1330, s. 3; 1979, c. 903, ss. 7, 8; 1981, c. 412, s. 4; c. 466, s. 7; c. 747, s. 66; 1983, c. 435, s. 23; 1985, c. 764, s. 28; 1985 (Reg. Sess., 1986), c. 852, s. 17; 1993, c. 539, s. 365;1994, Ex. Sess., c. 24, s. 14(c);2000-109, s. 7(b)

I. IN GENERAL.

EDITOR'S NOTE. --Many of the cases cited below were decided under corresponding provisions of former law.

THIS SECTION IS A SAFETY STATUTE. State v. Colson, 262 N.C. 506, 138 S.E.2d 121 (1964).

This section is a safety statute, designed for the protection of life, limb and property. State v. Weston, 273 N.C. 275, 159 S.E.2d 883 (1968).

PURPOSE OF SECTION. --This section was enacted for the protection of persons and property and in the interest of public safety and the preservation of human life. State v. Norris, 242 N.C. 47, 86 S.E.2d 916 (1955).

This section is designed to prevent injury to persons or property and to prohibit the careless and reckless driving of automobiles on the public highways. State v. Colson, 262 N.C. 506, 138 S.E.2d 121 (1964).

The reckless driving and speed statutes are designed for the protection of life, limb and property. State v. Ward, 258 N.C. 330, 128 S.E.2d 673 (1962).

THIS SECTION AND G.S. 20-141 CONSTITUTE THE HUB OF THE MOTOR TRAFFIC LAW around which all other provisions regulating the operation of automobiles revolve. Kolman v. Silbert, 219 N.C. 134, 12 S.E.2d 915 (1941).

A PERSON MAY VIOLATE THIS SECTION BY EITHER OF THE COURSES OF CONDUCT DEFINED IN SUBSECTIONS (A) AND (B), OR IN BOTH RESPECTS. State v. Dupree, 264 N.C. 463, 142 S.E.2d 5 (1965); Haynes v. Busby, 15 N.C. App. 106, 189 S.E.2d 653 (1972).

VIOLATIONS COMMITTED IN ONE CONTINUOUS OPERATION OF VEHICLE CONSTITUTE ONE OFFENSE. --If a defendant is guilty of the acts condemned either under subsection (a) or (b), or both, in one continuous operation of his vehicle, he is guilty of one offense of reckless driving and is not guilty of two separate offenses. State v. Lewis, 256 N.C. 430, 124 S.E.2d 115 (1962).

TRIAL ON WARRANTS ON APPEAL FROM MAYOR'S COURT HELD A NULLITY. --Where defendant was tried in a mayor's court on charges of operating a motor vehicle while under the influence of intoxicating liquor and reckless driving, and on appeal to the superior court, judgment was pronounced exceeding that permitted for the offense of reckless driving alone, it was held that the mayor's court was without jurisdiction of the charge of operating a motor vehicle while under the influence of intoxicating liquor, and even conceding that it had jurisdiction of the charge of reckless driving, the sentence exceeded that permitted for that offense, so that the trial of defendant in the superior court upon the warrants, without a bill of indictment first being found and returned, was

a nullity. State v. Johnson, 214 N.C. 319, 199 S.E. 96 (1938).

CONVICTION DOES NOT AUTHORIZE SUSPENSION OF LICENSE. --The offense of reckless driving in violation of this section is not an offense for which the Department (now Division) of Motor Vehicles is authorized by G.S. 20-16 to suspend an operator's license. In re Bratton, 263 N.C. 70, 138 S.E.2d 809 (1964).

NOR MANDATORY REVOCATION THEREOF. --The offense of reckless driving in violation of this section is not an offense for which, upon conviction, the revocation of an operator's license is mandatory under G.S. 20-17. In re Bratton, 263 N.C. 70, 138 S.E.2d 809 (1964).

AN ACQUITTAL OF RECKLESS DRIVING IN THE RECORDER'S COURT WILL NOT BAR A PROSECUTION FOR MANSLAUGHTER in the superior court arising out of the same occurrence, as the two offenses differ both in grade and kind and are not the same in law or in fact, the one is not a lesser degree of the other, and the recorder is without jurisdiction over the charge of manslaughter. State v. Midgett, 214 N.C. 107, 198 S.E. 613 (1938).

An acquittal of reckless driving in a court having jurisdiction to try defendant for that offense would not bar prosecution of defendant in the superior court for involuntary manslaughter arising out of the same occurrence. Reckless driving and speed competition are not lesser included offenses of the charge of involuntary manslaughter. State v. Sawyer, 11 N.C. App. 81, 180 S.E.2d 387 (1971).

DOUBLE JEOPARDY. --Defendant's convictions for speeding, reckless driving, and speeding to elude arrest, aggravated to a felony for speeding and reckless driving, violated double jeopardy because (1) speeding and reckless driving were elements of the third crime, since speeding and reckless driving increased the maximum penalty, and (2) the legislature intended to impose alternate, not separate, punishments, since all the statutes sought to deter the same conduct. State v. Mulder, 233 N.C. App. 82, 755 S.E.2d 98 (2014).

IMPROPER CONVICTION AS VIOLATION OF CODE OF JUDICIAL CONDUCT. --Acts of respondent judge in convicting defendants of reckless driving when they were charged with driving while impaired were acts which respondent knew to be improper and ultra vires, or beyond the powers of his office; therefore respondent's actions constituted conduct in violation of Code Jud. Con., Canons 2A and 3A(1). In re Martin, 333 N.C. 242, 424 S.E.2d 118 (1993).

REASONABLE SUSPICION FOR POLICE TO STOP. --Defendant's conduct in failing to stop at a road checkpoint, but instead, driving through it and nearly striking an officer, gave the officer reasonable suspicion that defendant had committed several crimes, including violations of G.S. 20-141.5(a) and G.S. 20-140(a); the officer's stop and arrest of defendant were valid. State v. Mitchell, 358 N.C. 63, 592 S.E.2d 543 (2004).

In a case in which defendant, who had been charged with violating 8 U.S.C.S. § 1326(a) and (b)(2), filed a motion to suppress all information law enforcement collected following his arrest that revealed his true identity, he unsuccessfully argued that his arrest was not lawful. The objective evidence supported a reasonable, articulable suspicion that he violated G.S. 20-140. United States v. Rosas-Herrera, 2011 U.S. Dist. LEXIS 116363 (M.D.N.C. Oct. 7, 2011), aff'd, 2012 U.S. App. LEXIS 25593 (4th Cir. N.C. 2012).

APPLIED in State v. Flinchem, 228 N.C. 149, 44 S.E.2d 724 (1947); State v. Williams, 237 N.C. 435, 75 S.E.2d 301 (1953); State v. McIntyre, 238 N.C. 305, 77 S.E.2d 698 (1953); State v. Turberville, 239 N.C. 25, 79 S.E.2d 359 (1953); State v. McRae, 240 N.C. 334, 82 S.E.2d 67 (1954); Redden v. Bynum, 256 N.C. 351, 123 S.E.2d 734 (1962); State v. Stroud, 256 N.C. 458, 124 S.E.2d 136 (1962); Benson v. Sawyer, 257 N.C. 765, 127 S.E.2d 549 (1962); Parker v. Bruce, 258 N.C. 341, 128 S.E.2d 561 (1962); Rundle v. Grubb Motor Lines, 300 F.2d 333 (4th Cir. 1962); Queen v. Jarrett, 258 N.C. 405, 128 S.E.2d 894 (1963); Scott v. Darden, 259 N.C. 167, 130 S.E.2d 42 (1963); State v. Wells, 259 N.C. 173, 130 S.E.2d 299 (1963); Williams v. Tucker, 259 N.C. 214, 130 S.E.2d 306 (1963); Russell v. Hamlett, 259 N.C. 273, 130 S.E.2d 395 (1963); Faulk v. Althouse Chem. Co., 259 N.C. 395, 130 S.E.2d 684 (1963); Jones v. C. B. Atkins Co., 259 N.C. 655, 131 S.E.2d 371 (1963); State v. Woolard, 260 N.C. 133, 132 S.E.2d 364 (1963); Scott v. Clark, 261 N.C. 102, 134 S.E.2d 181 (1964); Britt v. Mangum, 261 N.C. 250, 134 S.E.2d 235 (1964); Porter v. Pitt, 261 N.C. 482, 135 S.E.2d 42 (1964); Randall v. Rogers, 262 N.C. 544, 138 S.E.2d 248 (1964); Hall v. Little, 262 N.C. 618, 138 S.E.2d 282 (1964); Kight v. Seymour, 263 N.C. 790, 140 S.E.2d 410 (1965); Farmers Oil Co. v. Miller, 264 N.C. 101, 141 S.E.2d 41 (1965); Bongardt v. Frink, 265 N.C. 130, 143 S.E.2d 286 (1965); State v. Abernathy, 265 N.C. 724, 145 S.E.2d 2 (1965); Drumwright v. Wood, 266 N.C. 198, 146 S.E.2d 1 (1966); Wells v. Bissette, 266 N.C. 774, 147 S.E.2d 210 (1966); Atwood v. Holland, 267 N.C. 722, 148 S.E.2d 851 (1966); State v. Moses, 272 N.C. 509, 158 S.E.2d 617 (1968); Morris v. Brigham, 6 N.C. App. 490, 170 S.E.2d 534 (1969); State v. Grissom, 17 N.C. App. 374, 194 S.E.2d 227 (1973); State v. McLawhorn, 43 N.C. App. 695, 260 S.E.2d 138 (1979); State v. Wells, 59 N.C. App. 682, 298 S.E.2d 73 (1982).

CITED in Hancock v. Wilson, 211 N.C. 129, 189 S.E. 631 (1937); State v. Crews, 214 N.C. 705, 200 S.E. 378 (1939); Newbern v. Leary, 215 N.C. 134, 1 S.E.2d 384 (1939); Bechtler v. Bracken, 218 N.C. 515, 11 S.E.2d 721 (1940); Etheridge v. Etheridge, 222 N.C. 616, 24 S.E.2d 477 (1943); Hoke v. Atlantic Greyhound Corp., 226 N.C. 692, 40 S.E.2d 345 (1946); State v. Wooten, 228 N.C. 628, 46 S.E.2d 868 (1948); Singletary v. Nixon, 239 N.C. 634, 80 S.E.2d 676 (1954); State v. Bournais, 240 N.C. 311, 82 S.E.2d 115 (1954); Troxler v. Central Motor Lines, 240 N.C. 420, 82 S.E.2d 342 (1954); Hennis Freight Lines v. Burlington Mills Corp., 246 N.C. 143, 97 S.E.2d 850 (1957); Rick v. Murphy, 251 N.C. 162, 110 S.E.2d 815 (1959); Hunt v. Crawford, 253 N.C. 381, 117 S.E.2d 18 (1960); Fleming v. Drye, 253 N.C. 545, 117 S.E.2d 416 (1960); Pridgen v. Uzzell, 254 N.C. 292, 118 S.E.2d 755 (1961); Gathings

v. Sehorn, 255 N.C. 503, 121 S.E.2d 873 (1961); Pittman v. Swanson, 255 N.C. 681, 122 S.E.2d 814 (1961); Powell v. Clark, 255 N.C. 707, 122 S.E.2d 706 (1961); Mason v. Gillikin, 256 N.C. 527, 124 S.E.2d 537 (1962); Hall v. Poteat, 257 N.C. 458, 125 S.E.2d 924 (1962); Greene v. Meredith, 264 N.C. 178, 141 S.E.2d 287 (1965); Southern Nat'l Bank v. Lindsey, 264 N.C. 585, 142 S.E.2d 357 (1965); Webb v. Felton, 266 N.C. 707, 147 S.E.2d 219 (1966); Hout v. Harvell, 270 N.C. 274, 154 S.E.2d 41 (1967); Mabe v. Green, 270 N.C. 276, 154 S.E.2d 91 (1967); Reeves v. Hill, 272 N.C. 352, 158 S.E.2d 529 (1968); Toler v. Brink's, Inc., 1 N.C. App. 315, 161 S.E.2d 208 (1968); Rogers v. Rogers, 2 N.C. App. 668, 163 S.E.2d 645 (1968); State v. White, 3 N.C. App. 31, 164 S.E.2d 36 (1968); Basden v. Sutton, 7 N.C. App. 6, 171 S.E.2d 77 (1969); Wilder v. Edwards, 7 N.C. App. 513, 173 S.E.2d 72 (1970); Broadnax v. Deloatch, 8 N.C. App. 620, 174 S.E.2d 314 (1970); Huggins v. Kye, 10 N.C. App. 221, 178 S.E.2d 127 (1970); Brewer v. Harris, 279 N.C. 288, 182 S.E.2d 345 (1971); Southwire Co. v. Long Mfg. Co., 12 N.C. App. 335, 183 S.E.2d 253 (1971); McNair v. Boyette, 282 N.C. 230, 192 S.E.2d 457 (1972); State v. Pate, 29 N.C. App. 35, 222 S.E.2d 741 (1976); State v. McKenzie, 29 N.C. App. 524, 225 S.E.2d 151 (1976); State v. Burrus, 30 N.C. App. 250, 226 S.E.2d 677 (1976); State v. Hill, 31 N.C. App. 733, 230 S.E.2d 579 (1976); State v. McKenzie, 292 N.C. 170, 232 S.E.2d 424 (1977); State v. Snead, 35 N.C. App. 724, 242 S.E.2d 530 (1978); State v. Snead, 295 N.C. 615, 247 S.E.2d 893 (1978); State v. Davis, 37 N.C. App. 735, 247 S.E.2d 14 (1978); State v. Robinson, 40 N.C. App. 514, 253 S.E.2d 311 (1979); State v. Covington, 48 N.C. App. 209, 268 S.E.2d 231 (1980); State v. Donald, 51 N.C. App. 238, 275 S.E.2d 531 (1981); State v. Hefler, 60 N.C. App. 466, 299 S.E.2d 456 (1983); State v. Hefler, 310 N.C. 135, 310 S.E.2d 310 (1984); State v. McGill, 73 N.C. App. 206, 326 S.E.2d 345 (1985); State v. Harrington, 78 N.C. App. 39, 336 S.E.2d 852 (1985); State v. Graves, 83 N.C. App. 126, 349 S.E.2d 320 (1986); Body ex rel. Body v. Varner, 107 N.C. App. 219, 419 S.E.2d 208 (1992); Peal ex rel. Peal v. Smith, 115 N.C. App. 225, 444 S.E.2d 673 (1994); In re Inquiry Concerning a Judge (Brown), 351 N.C. 601, 527 S.E.2d 651 (2000); State v. Funchess, 141 N.C. App. 302, 540 S.E.2d 435 (2000); State v. Phillips, 152 N.C. App. 679, 568 S.E.2d 300 (2002), appeal dismissed, 356 N.C. 442, 573 S.E.2d 162 (2002); Shinn v. Greeness, 218 F.R.D. 478 (M.D.N.C. 2003); State v. Stokes, 174 N.C. App. 447, 621 S.E.2d 311 (2005); State v. Hinchman, 192 N.C. App. 657, 666 S.E.2d 199 (2008); State v. Dewalt, 209 N.C. App. 187, 703 S.E.2d 872 (2011); State v. Jackson, 212 N.C. App. 167, 710 S.E.2d 414 (2011); State v. Banks, 213 N.C. App. 599, 713 S.E.2d 754 (2011); State v. Hawk, 236 N.C. App. 177, 762 S.E.2d 883 (2014).

II. STANDARD OF CARE, NEGLIGENCE AND LIABILITY.

THIS SECTION PRESCRIBES A STANDARD OF CARE, and the standard fixed by the legislature is absolute. Aldridge v. Hasty, 240 N.C. 353, 82 S.E.2d 331 (1954); Kellogg v. Thomas, 244 N.C. 722, 94 S.E.2d 903 (1956); Lamm v. Gardner, 250 N.C. 540, 108 S.E.2d

847 (1959); Bondurant v. Mastin, 252 N.C. 190, 113 S.E.2d 292 (1960); Stockwell v. Brown, 254 N.C. 662, 119 S.E.2d 795 (1961); Boykin v. Bissette, 260 N.C. 295, 132 S.E.2d 616 (1963).

FUNDAMENTAL TO THE RIGHT TO OPERATE ANY MOTOR VEHICLE IS THE RULE OF THE PRUDENT MAN DECLARED IN THIS SECTION, that he shall operate with due care and circumspection so as not to endanger others by his reckless driving. McEwen Funeral Serv. v. Charlotte City Coach Lines, 248 N.C. 146, 102 S.E.2d 816 (1958).

DUTY OF MOTORIST GENERALLY. --Every operator of a motor vehicle is required to exercise reasonable care to avoid injury to persons or property of another, and a failure to so operate proximately resulting in injury to another gives rise to a cause of action. Scarlette v. Grindstaff, 258 N.C. 159, 128 S.E.2d 221 (1962); Miller v. Lucas, 267 N.C. 1, 147 S.E.2d 537 (1966).

A motorist must at all times operate his vehicle with due caution and circumspection, with due regard for the rights and safety of others, and at such speed and in such manner as will not endanger or be likely to endanger the lives or property of others. Morris v. Minix, 4 N.C. App. 634, 167 S.E.2d 494 (1969).

A motorist must operate his vehicle at a reasonable rate of speed, keep a lookout for persons on or near the highway, decrease his speed when any special hazard exists with respect to pedestrians, and, if circumstances warrant, he must give warning of his approach by sounding his horn. Morris v. Minix, 4 N.C. App. 634, 167 S.E.2d 494 (1969).

A motorist is under duty at all times to operate his vehicle at a reasonable rate of speed and maintain constant attention to the highway. Williams v. Henderson, 230 N.C. 707, 55 S.E.2d 462 (1949); Goodson v. Williams, 237 N.C. 291, 74 S.E.2d 762 (1953); Price v. Miller, 271 N.C. 690, 157 S.E.2d 347 (1967).

It is the duty of one proceeding along a public highway to maintain a proper lookout and to exercise due care to avoid colliding with vehicles entering the highway from private premises. Davis v. Imes, 13 N.C. App. 521, 186 S.E.2d 641 (1972).

THE DRIVER OF AN AUTOMOBILE IS REQUIRED AT ALL TIMES TO OPERATE HIS VEHICLE WITH DUE REGARD TO TRAFFIC AND CONDITIONS of the highway, and to keep his car under control and decrease his speed when special hazards exist by reason of weather or highway conditions or when necessary to avoid colliding with any other vehicle. This requirement, as expressed in this section and G.S. 20-141, constitutes the hub of the motor vehicle law around which other provisions regulating the operation of motor vehicles revolve. Cox v. Lee, 230 N.C. 155, 52 S.E.2d 355 (1949); Beasley v. Williams, 260 N.C. 561, 133 S.E.2d 227 (1963).

UNLAWFULNESS MAY DEPEND ON CIRCUMSTANCES. --Driving an automobile with tires which are known to be worn out and slick, on a highway which is wet and slippery, at a rate of speed not ordinarily unlawful, under this section may be unlawful

under all the circumstances shown by the evidence. Waller v. Hipp, 208 N.C. 117, 179 S.E. 428 (1935).

In light of the provisions of this section and G.S. 20-141, it is clear that whether or not a speed of 55 miles an hour is lawful depends upon the circumstances at the time. These sections provide that a motorist must at all times drive with due caution and circumspection and at a speed and in a manner so as not to endanger or be likely to endanger any person or property. At no time may a motorist lawfully drive at a speed greater than is reasonable and prudent under the conditions then existing. Primm v. King, 249 N.C. 228, 106 S.E.2d 223 (1958).

The principle that the mere fact of a collision with a vehicle ahead furnishes some evidence that the following motorist was negligent as to speed, was following too closely, or failed to keep a proper lookout is not absolute; the negligence, if any, depends upon the circumstances. Powell v. Cross, 263 N.C. 764, 140 S.E.2d 393 (1965).

CARE REQUIRED IN EMERGENCY. --While the operator of a public automobile is obligated to exercise a high degree of care, he is not charged with the necessity either of possessing superhuman powers of anticipation or of exercising such powers in a threatened emergency. Love v. Queen City Lines, 206 N.C. 575, 174 S.E. 514 (1934).

EFFECT OF USING PRUDENCE AFTER VIOLATION. --A reckless violation which put a driver in such position that he could not avoid an injury, though he attempted to do so after the danger became apparent, is not excused by the subsequent attempt. State v. Gray, 180 N.C. 697, 104 S.E. 647 (1920).

If the peril suddenly confronting the defendant was due to excessive speed or to his failure to maintain a proper lookout, the fact that care was exercised after the discovery of the peril would not excuse the negligent conduct which was the proximate cause of the injury and damage. Brunson v. Gainey, 245 N.C. 152, 95 S.E.2d 514 (1956).

The fact that defendant at length made an effort to avoid an accident does not avail him when it appears that his recklessness was responsible for his inability to control his vehicle. State v. Ward, 258 N.C. 330, 128 S.E.2d 673 (1962).

WHEN MOTORIST IS GUILTY OF RECKLESS DRIVING. --Under this section, a person is guilty of reckless driving (1) if he drives an automobile on a public highway in this State, carelessly and heedlessly, in a willful or wanton disregard of the rights or safety of others, or (2) if he drives an automobile on a public highway in this State without due caution and circumspection and at a speed or in a manner so as to endanger or be likely to endanger any person or property. State v. Folger, 211 N.C. 695, 191 S.E. 747 (1937). See also, State v. Norris, 242 N.C. 47, 86 S.E.2d 916 (1955).

Under this section a person is guilty of reckless driving if he drives an automobile on a public highway in this State without due caution and circumspection and at a speed or in a manner so as to endanger or be likely to endanger any person or property. State v.

Floyd, 15 N.C. App. 438, 190 S.E.2d 353, cert. denied, 281 N.C. 760, 191 S.E.2d 363 (1972).

Court refused to review G.S. 20-140, the careless and reckless statute, as to a trial court's ruling that 14 C.F.R. § 91.13 was too vague and ambiguous to constitute North Carolina's public policy in the context of the wrongful termination of an at-will employee. G.S. 20-140 was a reckless driving motor vehicle statute and the instant case involved safety relating to a flight engineer's schedule. McDonnell v. Tradewind Airlines, Inc., 194 N.C. App. 674, 670 S.E.2d 302 (2009), review denied, 363 N.C. 128, 675 S.E.2d 657 (2009).

MERE FAILURE TO KEEP A REASONABLE LOOKOUT DOES NOT CONSTITUTE RECKLESS DRIVING. To this must be added dangerous speed or perilous operation. Dunlap v. Lee, 257 N.C. 447, 126 S.E.2d 62 (1962); State v. Dupree, 264 N.C. 463, 142 S.E.2d 5 (1965); Ingle v. Roy Stone Transf. Corp., 271 N.C. 276, 156 S.E.2d 265 (1967); Haynes v. Busby, 15 N.C. App. 106, 189 S.E.2d 653 (1972).

WHILE THE FACT OF A REAR-END COLLISION OFFERS SOME EVIDENCE OF NEGLIGENCE, IT IS NOT SUFFICIENT to present the question of defendant's violation of this section when the fact of accident is combined only with the failure to keep a proper lookout, and not with excessive speed or following too closely. Nance v. Williams, 2 N.C. App. 345, 163 S.E.2d 47 (1968).

ENTERING INTERSECTION CLOSELY IN FRONT OF PLAINLY VISIBLE AUTOMOBILE. --The act of a driver in entering an intersection so closely in front of an automobile which is plainly visible to him, approaching along an intersecting four-lane highway, that the driver of the car does not have sufficient time in the exercise of reasonable care to avoid a collision, constitutes a violation of subsections (a) and (b) of this section, and is negligence per se. Snell v. Caudle Sand & Rock Co., 267 N.C. 613, 148 S.E.2d 608 (1966).

DRIVING ON WRONG SIDE OF ROAD. --The mere fact that defendant's automobile was on the left of the center line in the direction in which it was traveling when the collision occurred, without any evidence that it was being operated at a dangerous speed or in a perilous manner, except being on the wrong side of the road some 40 feet before the collision, does not show on defendant's part an intentional or willful violation of subsection (b) of this section; nor does it show an unintentional violation of subsection (a) accompanied by such recklessness or carelessness of probable consequences of a dangerous nature, when tested by the rule of reasonable prevision, amounting to a thoughtless disregard of consequences, or a heedless indifference to the safety of others, as imports criminal responsibility; and, hence, does not make out a case of reckless driving sufficient to carry the case to the jury. State v. Dupree, 264 N.C. 463, 142 S.E.2d 5 (1965).

SKIDDING. --The mere skidding of a motor vehicle is not evidence of, and does not imply, negligence. But skidding may form the basis of a recovery where it and the resulting damage is caused from some fault of the operator amounting to negligence on his part. Webb v. Clark, 264 N.C. 474, 141 S.E.2d 880 (1965).

When the condition of a road is such that skidding may be reasonably anticipated, the driver of a vehicle must exercise care commensurate with the danger to keep the vehicle under control so as to avoid injury to occupants of the vehicle and others on or off the highway. Webb v. Clark, 264 N.C. 474, 141 S.E.2d 880 (1965).

VIOLATION OF TRAFFIC REGULATION. --The simple violation of a traffic regulation which does not involve actual danger to life, limb or property, while importing civil liability if damage or injury ensue, would not perforce constitute the criminal offense of reckless driving. State v. Cope, 204 N.C. 28, 167 S.E. 456 (1933); State v. Floyd, 15 N.C. App. 438, 190 S.E.2d 353, cert. denied, 281 N.C. 760, 191 S.E.2d 363 (1972).

Neither the intentional nor the unintentional violation of a traffic law without more constitutes reckless driving. Ingle v. Roy Stone Transf. Corp., 271 N.C. 276, 156 S.E.2d 265 (1967); Haynes v. Busby, 15 N.C. App. 106, 189 S.E.2d 653 (1972).

WHAT IS ADMITTED BY PLEADING GUILTY TO RECKLESS DRIVING. --By pleading guilty to reckless driving, defendant admits he was operating a car in a criminally negligent and unreasonable manner and in doing so exposed those traveling on the road, as well as those situated adjacent to it, to unnecessary danger. Wyatt v. Gilmore, 57 N.C. App. 57, 290 S.E.2d 790 (1982).

A VIOLATION OF THIS SECTION IS NEGLIGENCE PER SE. Stegall v. Sledge, 247 N.C. 718, 102 S.E.2d 115 (1958); Carswell v. Lackey, 253 N.C. 387, 117 S.E.2d 51 (1960); Robbins v. Harrington, 255 N.C. 416, 121 S.E.2d 584 (1961); Dunlap v. Lee, 257 N.C. 447, 126 S.E.2d 62 (1962); Boykin v. Bissette, 260 N.C. 295, 132 S.E.2d 616 (1963); Southern Nat'l Bank v. Lindsey, 264 N.C. 585, 142 S.E.2d 357 (1965); Ingle v. Roy Stone Transf. Corp., 271 N.C. 276, 156 S.E.2d 265 (1967).

Reckless driving is made up of continuing acts, or a series of acts, which, in themselves, constitute negligence. Ingle v. Roy Stone Transf. Corp., 271 N.C. 276, 156 S.E.2d 265 (1967).

BUT QUESTION OF PROXIMATE CAUSE IS ORDINARILY FOR JURY. --The violation of this and succeeding sections enacted for the safety of those driving upon the highway is negligence per se, and when such violation is admitted or established, the question of proximate cause is ordinarily for the jury. Godfrey v. Queen City Coach Co., 201 N.C. 264, 159 S.E. 412 (1931); King v. Pope, 202 N.C. 554, 163 S.E. 447 (1932).

The better rule under this and the following section is that except where the evidence is so conclusive that there could be, in the minds of reasonable men, no doubt as to the plaintiff's negligence contributing to the injury, the question should be left to the jury. Morris v. Sells-Floto Circus, Inc., 65 F.2d 782 (4th Cir. 1933).

Chapter 20

FINDINGS BY JURY SUPPORTING CONCLUSION OF VIOLATION OF SECTION. --Findings by the jury that certain acts imported a thoughtless disregard for the consequences or a heedless indifference to the safety and rights of others would support a conclusion that the minor plaintiff operated her car in violation of this section. That would constitute negligence per se and, if a proximate cause of the collision, would constitute actionable negligence. Ford v. Jones, 6 N.C. App. 722, 171 S.E.2d 103 (1969).

FACTUAL QUESTION FOR JURY. --Whether defendant was correct in believing movement could be made in safety under the circumstances was a factual question for the jury. Williams v. Hall, 100 N.C. App. 655, 397 S.E.2d 767 (1990).

THE LANGUAGE OF THIS SECTION DEFINES CULPABLE NEGLIGENCE. State v. Roberson, 240 N.C. 745, 83 S.E.2d 798 (1954); State v. Dupree, 264 N.C. 463, 142 S.E.2d 5 (1965); Southern Nat'l Bank v. Lindsey, 264 N.C. 585, 142 S.E.2d 357 (1965).

The language in each subsection of the reckless driving statute defines culpable negligence. Ingle v. Roy Stone Transf. Corp., 271 N.C. 276, 156 S.E.2d 265 (1967); Ford v. Jones, 6 N.C. App. 722, 171 S.E.2d 103 (1969); Haynes v. Busby, 15 N.C. App. 106, 189 S.E.2d 653 (1972).

An intentional, willful, or wanton violation of a statute or ordinance, designed for the protection of human life or limb, which proximately results in injury or death, is culpable negligence. State v. Griffith, 24 N.C. App. 250, 210 S.E.2d 431 (1974), cert. denied, 286 N.C. 546, 212 S.E.2d 168 (1975).

WHAT IS CULPABLE NEGLIGENCE. --Culpable negligence is such recklessness or carelessness, proximately resulting in injury or death, as imports a thoughtless disregard of consequences or a heedless indifference to the safety and rights of others. The intentional, willful or wanton violation of a safety statute or ordinance which proximately results in injury is culpable negligence; an unintentional violation, unaccompanied by recklessness or probable consequences of a dangerous nature, when tested by the rule of reasonable prevision, is not. Ingle v. Roy Stone Transf. Corp., 271 N.C. 276, 156 S.E.2d 265 (1967); Ford v. Jones, 6 N.C. App. 722, 171 S.E.2d 103 (1969); Haynes v. Busby, 15 N.C. App. 106, 189 S.E.2d 653 (1972).

The violation of a safety statute which results in injury or death will constitute culpable negligence if the violation is willful, wanton, or intentional. But, where there is an unintentional or inadvertent violation of the statute, such violation standing alone does not constitute culpable negligence. The inadvertent or unintentional violation of the statute must be accompanied by recklessness of probable consequences of a dangerous nature, when tested by the rule of reasonable prevision, amounting altogether to a thoughtless disregard of consequences or of a heedless indifference to the safety of others. State v. Weston, 273 N.C. 275, 159 S.E.2d 883 (1968).

CULPABLE NEGLIGENCE AND ACTIONABLE NEGLIGENCE DISTINGUISHED. --Culpable negligence in the law of crimes is something more than actionable negligence in the law of torts. State v. Roberson, 240 N.C. 745, 83 S.E.2d 798 (1954).

Where there is an unintentional or inadvertent violation of this section, such violation, standing alone, does not constitute culpable negligence in the law of crimes as distinguished from actionable negligence in the law of torts. The inadvertent or unintentional violation of the statute must be accompanied by recklessness of probable consequences of a dangerous nature, when tested by the rule of reasonable prevision, amounting altogether to a thoughtless disregard of consequences or of a heedless indifference to the safety of others. State v. Sealy, 253 N.C. 802, 117 S.E.2d 793 (1961).

EVIDENCE HELD SUFFICIENT TO SHOW ACTIONABLE NEGLIGENCE. --Evidence of greatly excessive speed in violation of the speed restrictions of G.S. 20-141, and of reckless driving in violation of this section, were sufficient to make out a case of actionable negligence. Bell v. Maxwell, 246 N.C. 257, 98 S.E.2d 33 (1957).

All the evidence tended to show that plaintiff's decedent was killed by the actionable negligence of the driver of the automobile in which he was a passenger in driving it at an excessive speed in violation of former subdivision (4) of G.S. 20-141(b), and in a reckless manner in violation of this section. Bridges v. Graham, 246 N.C. 371, 98 S.E.2d 492 (1957).

IF PLAINTIFF'S EVIDENCE DOES NOT ESTABLISH CIVIL NEGLIGENCE, A FORTIORI, IT WILL NOT PROVE RECKLESS DRIVING, which is criminal negligence. Ford v. Jones, 6 N.C. App. 722, 171 S.E.2d 103 (1969).

VIOLATION OF THIS SECTION GIVES RISE TO BOTH CIVIL AND CRIMINAL LIABILITY. Ingle v. Roy Stone Transf. Corp., 271 N.C. 276, 156 S.E.2d 265 (1967); Rhyne v. O'Brien, 54 N.C. App. 621, 284 S.E.2d 122 (1981).

AND MAY INVOLVE MANSLAUGHTER. --A violation of this section may subject the offender to both civil and criminal liability. There may be a violation of this section as a result of which the offender is subjected, in addition to civil liability, only to the penalty prescribed by statute, but when the negligent acts are reckless to the point of culpability and are sufficient to evince a complete and thoughtless disregard for the rights and safety of other persons using the highways, they then become criminally negligent and the driver of a motor vehicle so offending may be called upon to answer for manslaughter. State v. McLean, 234 N.C. 283, 67 S.E.2d 75 (1951).

Death caused by a violation of either subsection (b) of this section or G.S. 20-138 (now G.S. 20-138.1) may constitute manslaughter. State v. Griffith, 24 N.C. App. 250, 210 S.E.2d 431 (1974), cert. denied, 286 N.C. 546, 212 S.E.2d 168 (1975).

WHERE VIOLATION CAUSED ACCIDENT AND DEATH. --A condition precedent to a conviction of manslaughter for the violation of either subsection (b) of this section or G.S. 20-138 (now G.S. 20-138.1) or both is that the violation of either one or both must have caused the accident and the death of decedent. State v.

Griffith, 24 N.C. App. 250, 210 S.E.2d 431 (1974), cert. denied, 286 N.C. 546, 212 S.E.2d 168 (1975).

PROOF OF VIOLATION IN PROSECUTION FOR MURDER, MANSLAUGHTER OR ASSAULT. --North Carolina statutes on the subject of regulating the care to be used by those driving motor vehicles upon the State's highways are designed to secure the reasonable safety of persons in and upon the highways of the State, and where death or great bodily harm results, evidence that the accused was, at the time charged, violating these provisions may be properly received upon a trial for murder or for manslaughter in appropriate instances, or as evidence of an assault where no serious injury has resulted. State v. Sudderth, 184 N.C. 753, 114 S.E. 828 (1922).

PUNITIVE DAMAGES JUSTIFIED. --Evidence that defendant's tractor trailer was willfully and wantonly operated on the wrong side of the highway in the face of plaintiff's approaching vehicle in violation of several safety statutes, including this section, was sufficient to support an award of punitive damages. Marsh ex rel. Marsh v. Trotman, 96 N.C. App. 578, 386 S.E.2d 447 (1989).

III. EVIDENCE.

EVIDENCE OF RECKLESS DRIVING HELD SUFFICIENT TO GO TO JURY. --State's evidence tending to show that defendant, driving 60 miles an hour, crashed into the rear of a car driven in the same direction on its right-hand side of the highway at 20 or 25 miles an hour, and that the driver of the other car saw defendant approaching at an excessive speed but that defendant struck the car before its driver could get on the shoulders of the road, together with evidence showing that defendant's car struck the other car with terrific force, was sufficient to be submitted to the jury upon a warrant charging defendant with reckless driving under this section. State v. Wilson, 218 N.C. 769, 12 S.E.2d 654 (1941).

Evidence tending to show that defendant was driving some 80 to 90 miles per hour over a highway on which several other vehicles were moving at the time was sufficient to overrule defendant's motion to nonsuit and to sustain a conviction of reckless driving. State v. Vanhoy, 230 N.C. 162, 52 S.E.2d 278 (1949).

Where from the evidence it was inferable that defendant in rounding a curve failed to exercise due care to maintain a proper lookout and to keep his car under control, and that he was driving recklessly in violation of this section, the evidence was sufficient to carry the case to the jury on the issue of actionable negligence. Tatem v. Tatem, 245 N.C. 587, 96 S.E.2d 725 (1957).

Evidence tending to show that defendant driver saw a truck approaching with a red flashing light on its front and a fogging machine in the truck emitting chemical fog which completely obscured the entire highway, and that defendant driver slowed his vehicle but drove into the fog at a rather good rate of speed and so continued on his right side of the highway until he was hit head-on by a truck traveling in the opposite direction, was sufficient to require submission to the jury of the question whether defendant was operating his vehicle in violation of this section. Moore v. Plymouth, 249 N.C. 423, 106 S.E.2d 695 (1959).

Evidence that defendant was driving on the public highways of the State while under the influence of intoxicating liquor in violation of G.S. 20-138 (now G.S. 20-138.1), and was driving recklessly in violation of this section, which proximately caused the death of a passenger in his car, was sufficient to be submitted to the jury in a prosecution for manslaughter. State v. Blankenship, 229 N.C. 589, 50 S.E.2d 724 (1948).

For additional cases holding that the evidence was properly submitted to the jury on the question of reckless driving, see Puckett v. Dyer, 203 N.C. 684, 167 S.E. 43 (1932); State v. Holbrook, 228 N.C. 620, 46 S.E.2d 843 (1948); State v. Steelman, 228 N.C. 634, 46 S.E.2d 845 (1948); State v. Blankenship, 229 N.C. 589, 50 S.E.2d 724 (1948); State v. Sawyer, 230 N.C. 713, 55 S.E.2d 464 (1949); State v. Call, 236 N.C. 333, 72 S.E.2d 752 (1952); State v. Roberson, 240 N.C. 745, 83 S.E.2d 798 (1954); Stockwell v. Brown, 254 N.C. 662, 119 S.E.2d 795 (1961).

Where an officer stated defendant sped at a rate "very much" in excess of 15 miles per hour over the speed limit and driving into oncoming traffic prior to slamming on the brakes and sliding to a halt in front of an occupied mobile home, that was sufficient evidence for the jury to find defendant guilty of eluding an officer while speeding in excess of 15 miles over the speed limit and driving recklessly. State v. Davis, 163 N.C. App. 587, 594 S.E.2d 57 (2004), cert. denied, 358 N.C. 547, 599 S.E.2d 564 (2004).

State presented sufficient evidence of the aggravating factors necessary to support defendant's conviction for felony fleeing to elude arrest under G.S. 20-141.5(b); during a high-speed chase, defendant was driving more than 15 mph over the speed limit and he was driving recklessly under G.S. 20-140. State v. Smith, 178 N.C. App. 134, 631 S.E.2d 34 (2006).

EVIDENCE OF RECKLESS DRIVING HELD SUFFICIENT TO SURVIVE MOTION TO DISMISS. --Evidence that defendant drove his motorcycle at a speed and in a manner so as to endanger or be likely to endanger person or property was sufficient to survive a motion to dismiss the charge of reckless driving. State v. Teel, 180 N.C. App. 446, 637 S.E.2d 288 (2006).

Substantial evidence existed to support the trial court's denial of defendant's request that the charge against defendant of reckless driving pursuant to G.S. 20-140(b) be dismissed. The State presented evidence that: (1) defendant drove defendant's vehicle while impaired; and (2) defendant was driving the vehicle well above the speed limit. State v. Coffey, 189 N.C. App. 382, 658 S.E.2d 73 (2008).

Evidence that defendant was intoxicated, all four tires went off the road, distinctive marks were left on the road indicating that defendant lost control of the vehicle, and the vehicle traveled 131 feet from the point it went off the road and 108 feet after it flipped was sufficient to support defendant's conviction for reckless driving. State v. Geisslercrain, 233 N.C. App. 186, 756 S.E.2d 92 (April. 1, 2014).

There was substantial evidence to support the elements of reckless driving, plus there was more than a mere failure to keep a reasonable lookout, such that the trial court did not err in denying defendant's motion to dismiss; she was driving impaired, all four tires of the vehicle went off the road, and the vehicle traveled 131 feet from when it left the road until it flipped, and then another 108 feet after. State v. Geisslercrain, 233 N.C. App. 186, 756 S.E.2d 92 (2014).

Defendant's reckless driving charge was not dismissed because sufficient independent evidence corroborated defendant's statement that defendant ran a stop sign going 60 miles per hour. State v. Hines, 259 N.C. App. 358, 816 S.E.2d 182 (2018).

EVIDENCE HELD INSUFFICIENT TO SHOW VIOLATION OF SECTION. --Allegation that defendant violated the provisions of this section in that he operated his truck carelessly and heedlessly in willful and wanton disregard of rights and safety of others, at a speed and in a manner to endanger or be likely to endanger person and property, and by operating same to the left when he could have turned to the right and passed without striking plaintiff's testator, was not supported by evidence. Tysinger v. Coble Dairy Prods., 225 N.C. 717, 36 S.E.2d 246 (1945).

Evidence that an ambulance on emergency duty, with its siren sounding at "peak," was traveling north along a four-lane street and entered an intersection with another, more heavily traveled, four-lane street against a red light, that a car traveling east and a cab traveling west along the intersecting street stopped, but that defendant's bus, traveling west in the northern lane of the intersecting street with its view obstructed by the stationary cab, etc., proceeded into the intersection with the green light and struck the right side of the ambulance in the northeastern part of the intersection, failed to show negligence on the part of the operator of the bus under this section or G.S. 20-156. McEwen Funeral Serv. v. Charlotte City Coach Lines, 248 N.C. 146, 102 S.E.2d 816 (1958).

Evidence, while sufficient to present the question of negligence, did not disclose careless and reckless driving within the purview of this section. Williams v. Boulerice, 269 N.C. 499, 153 S.E.2d 95 (1967).

Denial of defendant juvenile's motion to dismiss a reckless driving under G.S. 20-140(b) charge was not supported by sufficient evidence as although the record contained evidence that defendant was driving a vehicle registered to his mother at the time of the wreck and that the vehicle that he was driving had collided with a utility pole, there was no evidence that the collision resulted from any careless or reckless driving by defendant; the mere fact that an unlicensed driver ran off the road and collided with a utility pole did not establish a violation of G.S. 20-140(b). In re A.N.C., 225 N.C. App. 315, 750 S.E.2d 835 (2013), review denied 367 N.C. 269, 752 S.E.2d 151, 2013 N.C. LEXIS 1386 (2013).

CIRCUMSTANTIAL EVIDENCE TENDING TO IDENTIFY DEFENDANT AS THE DRIVER OF CAR DRIVEN IN A RECKLESS MANNER WAS HELD SUFFICIENT to be submitted to the jury. State v. Dooley, 232 N.C. 311, 59 S.E.2d 808 (1950).

FOR CASE HOLDING EVIDENCE SUFFICIENT TO SUSTAIN NEGLIGENCE AND PROXIMATE CAUSE AS A MATTER OF LAW, see Smith v. Miller, 209 N.C. 170, 183 S.E. 370 (1936).

IV. INDICTMENTS, WARRANTS AND ALLEGATIONS.

AN INDICTMENT UNDER THIS SECTION MAY BE CONSOLIDATED FOR TRIAL WITH AN INDICTMENT UNDER G.S. 20-217, which prohibits the driver of a motor vehicle from passing a standing school bus on the highway without first bringing said motor vehicle to a complete stop. State v. Webb, 210 N.C. 350, 186 S.E. 241 (1936).

WARRANTS UNDER THIS SECTION WHICH CHARGE THE OFFENSE ALMOST LITERALLY IN THE WORDS OF THE STATUTE ARE SUFFICIENT. State v. Wallace, 251 N.C. 378, 111 S.E.2d 714 (1959).

PARTICULARITY REQUIRED IN PLEADING RECKLESS DRIVING. --To plead reckless driving effectively, the pleader must particularize with reference to the specific rules of the road which the motorist was violating and his manner of doing so. Ingle v. Roy Stone Transf. Corp., 271 N.C. 276, 156 S.E.2d 265 (1967).

To plead reckless driving effectively, a party must allege facts which show that the other was violating specific rules of the road in a criminally negligent manner. Roberts v. Pilot Freight Carriers, 273 N.C. 600, 160 S.E.2d 712 (1968); Nance v. Williams, 2 N.C. App. 345, 163 S.E.2d 47 (1968).

ALLEGATIONS OF RECKLESS DRIVING IN THE WORDS OF THIS SECTION, WITHOUT MORE, DO NOT JUSTIFY A CHARGE OF RECKLESS DRIVING. Roberts v. Pilot Freight Carriers, 273 N.C. 600, 160 S.E.2d 712 (1968); Nance v. Williams, 2 N.C. App. 345, 163 S.E.2d 47 (1968).

Allegations as to reckless driving in the words of this section, without specifying wherein the party was reckless, amount to no more than an allegation that the party charged was negligent. They are but conclusions of law which are not admitted by demurrer. They do not justify a charge on reckless driving. Ingle v. Roy Stone Transf. Corp., 271 N.C. 276, 156 S.E.2d 265 (1967).

WHERE A COMPLAINT ALLEGED RECKLESS DRIVING ON A UNIVERSITY CAMPUS as a violation of this section, the fact that the complaint alleged a violation of this section instead of a violation of former G.S. 20-140.1 was not fatal in the light of former G.S. 1-151, providing that pleadings shall be liberally construed, and in light of the theory of the trial court that campus roads were highways within the purview of this section. Rhyne v. Bailey, 254 N.C. 467, 119 S.E.2d 385 (1961).

WARRANTS HELD SUFFICIENT. --Warrant charging that defendant "did unlawfully and willfully operate a motor vehicle on a State highway in a careless and reckless manner and without due regard for the rights and safety of others and their property in violation" of municipal ordinances and contrary to the form of the statute was held sufficient to charge defendant with reckless driving under this section, since,

663

although the warrant failed to follow the language of the statute in accordance with the better practice, it did charge facts sufficient to enable the court to proceed to judgment, and the charge of violating the municipal ordinances could be treated as surplusage. State v. Wilson, 218 N.C. 769, 12 S.E.2d 654 (1941).

Warrant charging defendant with driving under the influence and reckless driving, which were treated as separate counts, was sufficient, since each count charged all the essential elements constituting the violation of law charged. State v. Fuller, 24 N.C. App. 38, 209 S.E.2d 805 (1974).

INDICTMENT HELD SUFFICIENT. --As the original language of the indictment tracked the language of G.S. 20-140(b), the indictment was sufficient to charge reckless driving. State v. Wade, 161 N.C. App. 686, 589 S.E.2d 379 (2003), cert. denied, 358 N.C. 241, 594 S.E.2d 33 (2004).

INDICTMENT SUFFICIENT TO CHARGE OF-FENSE OF FELONY SPEEDING TO ELUDE AR-REST WITH RECKLESS DRIVING AS AN AGGRA-VATING FACTOR. --Defendant's indictment was not facially invalid because it tracked the relevant language of the felony speeding to elude arrest statute, G.S. 20-141.5, and listed the essential elements of the offense; the body of the indictment provided defendant with enough information to prepare a defense for the offense of felony speeding to elude arrest with reckless driving as an aggravating factor. State v. Leonard, 213 N.C. App. 526, 711 S.E.2d 867 (2011).

V. INSTRUCTIONS.

IT IS NOT SUFFICIENT FOR THE JUDGE TO READ THIS SECTION AND THEN LEAVE IT TO THE JURY TO APPLY THE LAW TO THE FACTS and to decide for themselves what plaintiff did, if anything, which constituted reckless driving. Ingle v. Roy Stone Transf. Corp., 271 N.C. 276, 156 S.E.2d 265 (1967); Roberts v. Pilot Freight Carriers, Inc., 273 N.C. 600, 160 S.E.2d 712 (1968); Nance v. Williams, 2 N.C. App. 345, 163 S.E.2d 47 (1968); Ford v. Jones, 6 N.C. App. 722, 171 S.E.2d 103 (1969).

AS TO REQUIREMENTS IN CHARGING ON RECKLESS DRIVING UNDER FORMER G.S. 1-180, see State v. Vanhoy, 230 N.C. 162, 52 S.E.2d 278 (1949); Ingle v. Roy Stone Transf. Corp., 271 N.C. 276, 156 S.E.2d 265 (1967); Roberts v. Pilot Freight Carriers, Inc., 273 N.C. 600, 160 S.E.2d 712 (1968); Nance v. Williams, 2 N.C. App. 345, 163 S.E.2d 47 (1968); Ford v. Jones, 6 N.C. App. 722, 171 S.E.2d 103 (1969).

INSTRUCTION ERRONEOUS WHEN NOT SUP-PORTED BY EVIDENCE. --Where there is no evidence that the person charged with negligence drive his vehicle in such a manner as to constitute reckless driving, it is error for the court to charge that reckless driving is an element of negligence to be considered by the jury. Ford v. Jones, 6 N.C. App. 722, 171 S.E.2d 103 (1969).

FOR CASE HOLDING INSTRUCTION ON RECK-LESS DRIVING REVERSIBLE ERROR, see State v. Folger, 211 N.C. 695, 191 S.E. 747 (1937).

IN A MANSLAUGHTER CASE BASED ON RECK-LESS DRIVING OF DEFENDANT, an instruction on

reckless driving which did not charge the jury to find that such reckless driving was the proximate cause of the wreck and resultant death of the deceased was erroneous. State v. Mundy, 243 N.C. 149, 90 S.E.2d 312 (1955).

LEGAL PERIODICALS. --
For article on proof of negligence in North Carolina, see 48 N.C.L. Rev. 731 (1970).

N.C. Gen. Stat. § 20-140.1

Repealed by Session Laws 1973, c. 1330, s. 39.

§ 20-140.2. Overloaded or overcrowded vehicle

No person shall operate upon a highway or public vehicular area a motor vehicle which is so loaded or crowded with passengers or property, or both, as to obstruct the operator's view of the highway or public vehicular area, including intersections, or so as to impair or restrict otherwise the proper operation of the vehicle.

History.
1953, c. 1233; 1967, c. 674, s. 1; 1973, c. 1143, s. 2; c. 1330, s. 4

APPLIED in Snellings v. Roberts, 12 N.C. App. 476, 183 S.E.2d 872 (1971).

CITED in State v. Veazey, 191 N.C. App. 181, 662 S.E.2d 683 (2008).

§ 20-140.3. Unlawful use of National System of Interstate and Defense Highways and other controlled-access highways

On those sections of highways which are or become a part of the National System of Interstate and Defense Highways and other controlled-access highways, it shall be unlawful for any person:

(1) To drive a vehicle over, upon, or across any curb, central dividing section or other separation or dividing line on said highways.

(2) To make a left turn or a semicircular or U-turn except through an opening provided for that purpose in the dividing curb, separation section, or line on said highways.

(3) To drive any vehicle except in the proper lane provided for that purpose and in the proper direction and to the right of the central dividing curb, separation section, or line on said highways.

(4) To drive a vehicle onto or from any controlled-access highway except at such entrances and exits as are established by public authority.

(5) To stop, park, or leave standing any vehicle, whether attended or unattended, on any part or portion of the right-of-way of said highways, except in the case of an

emergency or as directed by a peace officer, or at designated parking areas.

(6) To fail to yield the right-of-way when entering the highway to any vehicle already travelling on the highway.

(7) Notwithstanding any other subdivision of this section, a law enforcement officer may cross the median of a divided highway when the officer has reasonable grounds to believe that a felony is being or has been committed, has personal knowledge that a vehicle is being operated at a speed or in a manner which is likely to endanger persons or property, or the officer has reasonable grounds to believe that the officer's presence is immediately required at a location which would necessitate crossing a median of a divided highway for this purpose. Fire department vehicles and public or private ambulances and rescue squad emergency service vehicles traveling in response to a fire alarm or other emergency call may cross the median of a divided highway when assistance is immediately required at a location which would necessitate the vehicle crossing a median of a divided highway for this purpose.

History.
1973, c. 1330, s. 5; 1977, c. 731, s. 1; 1999-330, s. 5

APPLIED in Oakes v. James, 68 N.C. App. 765, 315 S.E.2d 802 (1984).

CITED in State v. Dixon, 77 N.C. App. 27, 334 S.E.2d 433 (1985).

CROSS REFERENCES. --
For similar section, see G.S. 136-89.58.

§ 20-140.4. Special provisions for motorcycles and mopeds

(a) No person shall operate a motorcycle or moped upon a highway or public vehicular area:

(1) When the number of persons upon or within such motorcycle or moped, including the operator, shall exceed the number of persons which it was designed to carry.

(2) Unless the operator and all passengers thereon wear on their heads, with a retention strap properly secured, safety helmets of a type that complies with Federal Motor Vehicle Safety Standard (FMVSS) 218. This subdivision shall not apply to an operator of, or any passengers within, an autocycle that has completely enclosed seating or is equipped with a roll bar or roll cage.

(b) Violation of any provision of this section shall not be considered negligence per se or contributory negligence per se in any civil action.

(c) Any person convicted of violating this section shall have committed an infraction and shall pay a penalty of twenty-five dollars and fifty cents ($ 25.50) plus the following court costs: the General Court of Justice fee provided for in G.S. 7A-304(a)(4), the telephone facilities fee provided for in G.S. 7A-304(a)(2a), and the law enforcement training and certification fee provided for in G.S. 7A-304(a)(3b). Conviction of an infraction under this section has no other consequence.

(d) No drivers license points or insurance surcharge shall be assessed on account of violation of this section.

History.
1973, c. 1330, s. 6; 1989, c. 711, s. 1;2007-360, s. 7;2009-451, s. 15.20(k);2015-163, s. 11;2016-90, s. 12.5(b);2019-227, s. 6(a)

EDITOR'S NOTE. --
Session Laws 2015-163, s. 14, provides, in part: "Prosecutions for offenses committed before the effective date of this act are not abated or affected by this act, and the statutes that would be applicable but for this act remain applicable to those prosecutions."

Session Laws 2019-227, s. 6(b), provides: "This section is effective October 1, 2019. Prosecutions for offenses committed before the effective date of this section are not abated or affected by this section, and the statutes that would be applicable but for this section remain applicable to those prosecutions."

EFFECT OF AMENDMENTS. --
Session Laws 2007-360, s. 7, effective January 1, 2008, rewrote subdivision (a)(2).

Session Laws 2015-163, s. 11, effective October 1, 2015, inserted "or within" preceding "such motorcycle" in subdivision (a)(1); and added last sentence of subdivision (a)(2).

Session Laws 2016-90, s. 12.5(b), effective July 11, 2016, at the end of the last sentence in subdivision (a)(2), substituted "operator of, or any passengers within, an autocycle that has completely enclosed seating" for "operator of an autocycle or any passengers within an autocycle."

Session Laws 2019-227, s. 6(a), effective October 1, 2019, substituted "seating or is equipped with a roll bar or roll cage" for "seating" in subsection (a)(2). For effective date and applicability, see editor's note.

AS TO CONSTITUTIONALITY OF FORMER SUBSECTION (B) OF G.S. 20-140.2, see State v. Anderson, 275 N.C. 168, 166 S.E.2d 49 (1969).

STANDING TO CHALLENGE THIS STATUTE. --Respondents, who were not wearing safety helmets of any kind when they were cited, did not fall in the class of persons who might be adversely affected by this statute's alleged vagueness as to the type of helmet motorcyclists ought to wear and, therefore, lacked standing to challenge the statute on constitutional grounds. State v. Barker, 138 N.C. App. 304, 531 S.E.2d 228 (2000).

CITED in Fortson v. McClellan, 131 N.C. App. 635, 508 S.E.2d 549 (1998); State v. Shepley, 237 N.C. App. 174, 764 S.E.2d 658 (2014).

CROSS REFERENCES. --

For requirements for helmet use by persons below the age of 16 who are operating a bicycle or are a passenger on a bicycle, see G.S. 20-171.9.

LEGAL PERIODICALS. --

For note on statutory requirement of safety helmets for motorcyclists, see 6 Wake Forest Intra. L. Rev. 349 (1970).

§ 20-140.5. Special mobile equipment may tow certain vehicles

Special mobile equipment may not tow any vehicle other than the following:

(1) A single passenger vehicle that can carry no more than nine passengers and is carrying no passengers.

(2) A single property-hauling vehicle that has a registered weight of 5,000 pounds or less, is carrying no passengers, and does not exceed its registered weight.

History.

1991 (Reg. Sess., 1992), c. 1015, s. 3; 1999-438, s. 29

§ 20-141. Speed restrictions

(a) No person shall drive a vehicle on a highway or in a public vehicular area at a speed greater than is reasonable and prudent under the conditions then existing.

(b) Except as otherwise provided in this Chapter, it shall be unlawful to operate a vehicle in excess of the following speeds:

(1) Thirty-five miles per hour inside municipal corporate limits for all vehicles.

(2) Fifty-five miles per hour outside municipal corporate limits for all vehicles except for school buses and school activity buses.

(c) Except while towing another vehicle, or when an advisory safe-speed sign indicates a slower speed, or as otherwise provided by law, it shall be unlawful to operate a passenger vehicle upon the interstate and primary highway system at less than the following speeds:

(1) Forty miles per hour in a speed zone of 55 miles per hour.

(2) Forty-five miles per hour in a speed zone of 60 miles per hour or greater.

These minimum speeds shall be effective only when appropriate signs are posted indicating the minimum speed.

(d) (1) Whenever the Department of Transportation determines on the basis of an engineering and traffic investigation that any speed allowed by subsection (b) is greater than is reasonable and safe under the conditions found to exist upon any part of a highway outside the corporate limits of a municipality or upon any part of a highway designated as part of the Interstate Highway System or any part of a controlled-access highway (either inside or outside the corporate limits of a municipality), the Department of Transportation shall determine and declare a reasonable and safe speed limit.

(2) Whenever the Department of Transportation determines on the basis of an engineering and traffic investigation that a higher maximum speed than those set forth in subsection (b) is reasonable and safe under the conditions found to exist upon any part of a highway designated as part of the Interstate Highway System or any part of a controlled-access highway (either inside or outside the corporate limits of a municipality) the Department of Transportation shall determine and declare a reasonable and safe speed limit. A speed limit set pursuant to this subsection may not exceed 70 miles per hour.

Speed limits set pursuant to this subsection are not effective until appropriate signs giving notice thereof are erected upon the parts of the highway affected.

(e) Local authorities, in their respective jurisdictions, may authorize by ordinance higher speeds or lower speeds than those set out in subsection (b) upon all streets which are not part of the State highway system; but no speed so fixed shall authorize a speed in excess of 55 miles per hour. Speed limits set pursuant to this subsection shall be effective when appropriate signs giving notice thereof are erected upon the part of the streets affected.

(e1) Local authorities within their respective jurisdictions may authorize, by ordinance, lower speed limits than those set in subsection (b) of this section on school property. If the lower speed limit is being set on the grounds of a public school, the local school administrative unit must request or consent to the lower speed limit. If the lower speed limit is being set on the grounds of a private school, the governing body of the school must request or consent to the lower speed limit. Speed limits established pursuant to this subsection shall become effective when appropriate signs giving notice of the speed limit are erected upon affected property. A person who drives a motor vehicle on school property at a speed greater than the speed limit set and posted under this subsection is responsible for an infraction and is required to pay a penalty of two hundred fifty dollars ($ 250.00).

(f) Whenever local authorities within their respective jurisdictions determine upon the basis of an engineering and traffic investigation that a higher maximum speed than those set forth in subsection (b) is reasonable and safe, or that any speed hereinbefore set forth is greater than is reasonable and safe, under the conditions found to exist upon any part of a street within the corporate limits of a municipality and which street is a part of the State highway system (except those highways designated as part of the interstate highway system or other controlled-access highway) said local authorities shall determine and declare a safe and reasonable speed limit. A speed limit set pursuant to this subsection may not exceed 55 miles per hour. Limits set pursuant to this subsection shall become effective when the Department of Transportation has passed a concurring ordinance and signs are erected giving notice of the authorized speed limit.

When local authorities annex a road on the State highway system, the speed limit posted on the road at the time the road was annexed shall remain in effect until both the Department and municipality pass concurrent ordinances to change the speed limit.

The Department of Transportation is authorized to raise or lower the statutory speed limit on all highways on the State highway system within municipalities which do not have a governing body to enact municipal ordinances as provided by law. The Department of Transportation shall determine a reasonable and safe speed limit in the same manner as is provided in G.S. 20-141(d)(1) and G.S. 20-141(d)(2) for changing the speed limits outside of municipalities, without action of the municipality.

(g) Whenever the Department of Transportation or local authorities within their respective jurisdictions determine on the basis of an engineering and traffic investigation that slow speeds on any part of a highway considerably impede the normal and reasonable movement of traffic, the Department of Transportation or such local authority may determine and declare a minimum speed below which no person shall operate a motor vehicle except when necessary for safe operation in compliance with law. Such minimum speed limit shall be effective when appropriate signs giving notice thereof are erected on said part of the highway. Provided, such minimum speed limit shall be effective as to those highways and streets within the corporate limits of a municipality which are on the State highway system only when ordinances adopting the minimum speed limit are passed and concurred in by both the Department of Transportation and the local authorities. The provisions of this subsection shall not apply to farm tractors and other motor vehicles operating at reasonable speeds for the type and nature of such vehicles.

(h) No person shall operate a motor vehicle on the highway at such a slow speed as to impede the normal and reasonable movement of traffic except when reduced speed is necessary for safe operation or in compliance with law; provided, this provision shall not apply to farm tractors and other motor vehicles operating at reasonable speeds for the type and nature of such vehicles.

(i) The Department of Transportation shall have authority to designate and appropriately mark certain highways of the State as truck routes.

(j) Repealed by Session Laws 1997, c. 443, s. 19.26(b).

(j1) A person who drives a vehicle on a highway at a speed that is either more than 15 miles per hour more than the speed limit established by law for the highway where the offense occurred or over 80 miles per hour is guilty of a Class 3 misdemeanor.

(j2) A person who drives a motor vehicle in a highway work zone at a speed greater than the speed limit set and posted under this section shall be required to pay a penalty of two hundred fifty dollars ($ 250.00). This penalty shall be imposed in addition to those penalties established in this Chapter. A "highway work zone" is the area between the first sign that informs motorists of the existence of a work zone on a highway and the last sign that informs motorists of the end of the work zone. The additional penalty imposed by this subsection applies only if signs are posted at the beginning and end of any segment of the highway work zone stating the penalty for speeding in that segment of the work zone. The Secretary shall ensure that work zones shall only be posted with penalty signs if the Secretary determines, after engineering review, that the posting is necessary to ensure the safety of the traveling public due to a hazardous condition.

A law enforcement officer issuing a citation for a violation of this section while in a highway work zone shall indicate the vehicle speed and speed limit posted in the segment of the work zone, and determine whether the individual committed a violation of G.S. 20-141(j1). Upon an individual's conviction of a violation of this section while in a highway work zone, the clerk of court shall report that the vehicle was in a work zone at the time of the violation, the vehicle speed, and the speed limit of the work zone to the Division of Motor Vehicles.

(j3) A person is guilty of a Class 2 misdemeanor if the person drives a commercial motor vehicle carrying a load that is subject to the permit requirements of G.S. 20-119 upon a highway or any public vehicular area at a speed of 15 miles per hour or more above either:

(1) The posted speed; or

(2) The restricted speed, if any, of the permit, or if no permit was obtained, the speed that would be applicable to the load if a permit had been obtained.

(k) Repealed by Session Laws 1995 (Regular Session, 1996), c. 652, s. 1.

(l) Notwithstanding any other provision contained in G.S. 20-141 or any other statute or law of this State, including municipal charters, any speed limit on any portion of the public highways within the jurisdiction of this State shall be uniformly applicable to all types of motor vehicles using such portion of the highway, if on November 1, 1973, such portion of the highway had a speed limit which was uniformly applicable to all types of motor vehicles using it. Provided, however, that a lower speed limit may be established for any vehicle operating under a special permit because of any weight or dimension of such vehicle, including any load thereon. The requirement for a uniform speed limit hereunder shall not apply to any portion of the highway during such time as the condition of the highway, weather, an accident, or other condition creates a temporary hazard to the safety of traffic on such portion of the highway.

(m) The fact that the speed of a vehicle is lower than the foregoing limits shall not relieve the operator of a vehicle from the duty to decrease speed as may be necessary to avoid colliding with any person, vehicle or other conveyance on or entering the highway, and to avoid injury to any person or property.

(n) Notwithstanding any other provision contained in G.S. 20-141 or any other statute or law of this State, the failure of a motorist to stop his vehicle within the radius of its headlights or the range of his vision shall not be held negligence per se or contributory negligence per se.

(o) A violation of G.S. 20-123.2 shall be a lesser included offense in any violation of this section, and shall be subject to the following limitations and conditions:

(1) A violation of G.S. 20-123.2 shall be recorded in the driver's official record as "Improper equipment -- Speedometer."

(2) The lesser included offense under this subsection shall not apply to charges of speeding in excess of 25 miles per hour or more over the posted speed limit.

No drivers license points or insurance surcharge shall be assessed on account of a violation of this subsection.

(p) A driver charged with speeding in excess of 25 miles per hour over the posted speed limit shall be ineligible for a disposition of prayer for judgment continued.

History.
1937, c. 297, s. 2; c. 407, s. 103; 1939, c. 275; 1941, c. 347; 1947, c. 1067, s. 17; 1949, c. 947, s. 1; 1953, c. 1145; 1955, c. 398; c. 555, ss. 1, 2; c. 1042; 1957, c. 65, s. 11; c. 214; 1959, c. 640; c. 1264, s. 10; 1961, cc. 99, 1147; 1963, cc. 134, 456, 949; 1967, c. 106; 1971, c. 79, ss. 1-3; 1973, c. 507, s. 5; c. 1330, s. 7; 1975, c. 225; 1977, c. 367; c. 464, s. 34; c. 470; 1983, c. 131; 1985, c. 764, ss. 29, 30; 1985 (Reg. Sess., 1986), c. 852, s. 17; 1987, c. 164; 1991 (Reg. Sess., 1992), c. 818, s. 1; c. 1034, s. 1; 1993, c. 539, ss. 366, 367; 1994, Ex. Sess., c. 24, s. 14(c);1995 (Reg. Sess., 1996), c. 652, s. 1; 1997-341, s. 1;1997-443, s. 19.26(b);1997-488, s. 1;1999-330, s. 3;2000-109, s. 7(c);2003-110, s. 1;2004-203, s.

70(a);2005-349, s. 11;2007-380, ss. 1, 2; 2009-234, ss. 1, 2; 2011-64, s. 2;2012-194, s. 9;2013-360, s. 18B.14(k)

LOCAL MODIFICATION. --Burke: 1975, c. 533; Mecklenburg: 1983, c. 153; Richmond: 1975, c. 17; town of Bermuda Run: 2019-100, ss. 1 -4.

EDITOR'S NOTE. --
This section was amended by Session Laws 2009-234, s. 2, in the coded bill drafting format provided by G.S. 120-20.1. In subsection (j2), the word "signs" was substituted for "sign" but the substitution was not indicated by struck through and underlined text. Subsection (j2) has been set out in the form above at the direction of the Revisor of Statutes.

Subsection (j2) as amended by Session Laws 2009-234, s. 2, effective December 1, 2009, is applicable to offenses committed on or after that date.

EFFECT OF AMENDMENTS. --
Session Laws 2004-203, s. 70(a), effective December 1, 2004, added the last sentence of subsection (o).

Session Laws 2007-380, ss. 1 and 2, effective December 1, 2007, and applicable to offenses committed on or after that date, rewrote subsection (o), and added subsection (p).

Session Laws 2009-234, s. 1, effective June 30, 2009, added the second paragraph of subsection (f).

Session Laws 2011-64, s. 2, effective August 25, 2011, and applicable to offenses committed on or after that date, substituted "two hundred fifty dollars ($250.00)" for "not less than twenty-five dollars ($25.00)" in the last sentence of subsection (e1).

Session Laws 2012-194, s. 9, effective July 17, 2012, substituted "signs" for "sign" in the fourth sentence in subsection (j2).

Session Laws 2013-360, s. 18B.14(k), effective December 1, 2013, substituted "Class 3 misdemeanor" for "Class 2 misdemeanor" in subsection (j1). For applicability, see Editor's note.

I. IN GENERAL.
EDITOR'S NOTE. --Many of the cases cited below were decided under corresponding provisions of earlier laws or under this section as it stood before its revision by the second 1973 amendment.

CONSTITUTIONALITY OF FORMER PROVISIONS. --Former provisions of this section setting different speed limits for different types of vehicles were constitutional, since a difference in speed based upon weight and size of motor vehicles bears a real and substantial relationship to the public health, safety, morals or some other phase of the public welfare. State v. Bennor, 6 N.C. App. 188, 169 S.E.2d 393 (1969).

CONSTITUTIONALITY. --Subsection (m) of this section is not unconstitutionally vague. State v. Worthington, 89 N.C. App. 88, 365 S.E.2d 317 (1988).

PURPOSE OF SECTION. --This section was enacted for the protection of persons and property and in the interest of public safety and the preservation of human life. State v. Norris, 242 N.C. 47, 86 S.E.2d 916 (1955); State v. Bennor, 6 N.C. App. 188, 169 S.E.2d 393 (1969).

This section was enacted to promote safe operation of motor vehicles on the highways. Stephens v. Southern Oil Co., 259 N.C. 456, 131 S.E.2d 39 (1963).

Reckless driving and speed statutes are designed for the protection of life, limb and property. State v. Ward, 258 N.C. 330, 128 S.E.2d 673 (1962).

The obvious purpose of this section is to authorize specific speed limits and to establish a duty for all motorists to use due care in maintaining the speed of their vehicle. State v. Worthington, 89 N.C. App. 88, 365 S.E.2d 317 (1988).

THIS SECTION HAS BEEN SCRUTINIZED AND STUDIED BY THE LEGISLATURE AT EVERY SESSION of that body and has been amended, changed and altered constantly in keeping with changes in highway construction and public safety. State v. Bennor, 6 N.C. App. 188, 169 S.E.2d 393 (1969).

SCOPE OF PROTECTION. --This section does not limit its protection to motorists who are within the law; it enjoins all motorists to avoid causing injury to any person or property either on or off the highway, in compliance with legal requirements and the duty of all persons to use due care. McNair v. Goodwin, 264 N.C. 146, 141 S.E.2d 22 (1965).

THIS SECTION STATES SEVERAL OFFENSES, each of which is a separate crime independently of the others. State v. Mills, 181 N.C. 530, 106 S.E. 677 (1921). See also, State v. Rountree, 181 N.C. 535, 106 S.E. 669 (1921).

SUBSECTION (M) OF THIS SECTION MUST BE CONSTRUED CONSISTENT WITH THE REQUIREMENT OF SUBSECTION (A) that no person shall drive at a speed greater than is reasonable and prudent under the circumstances. State v. Worthington, 89 N.C. App. 88, 365 S.E.2d 317 (1988).

EFFECT OF SUBSECTION (M). --Subsection (m) of this section imposes liability on a motorist only when his failure to reduce speed to avoid a collision is not in keeping with the duty to use due care under the circumstances. State v. Worthington, 89 N.C. App. 88, 365 S.E.2d 317 (1988).

Subsection (m) of this section does not impose liability except in cases where a reasonable and ordinarily prudent person could and would have decreased his speed to avoid a collision. State v. Worthington, 89 N.C. App. 88, 365 S.E.2d 317 (1988).

RIGHTS OF MOTORIST ARE RELATIVE. --A motorist operates his vehicle on the public highways where others are apt to be. His rights are relative. Wagoner v. Butcher, 6 N.C. App. 221, 170 S.E.2d 151 (1969).

SECTION PRESCRIBES LAWFUL SPEEDS. --This section prescribes speeds at which motor vehicles may be lawfully operated on the highways of the State. Short v. Chapman, 261 N.C. 674, 136 S.E.2d 40 (1964).

This section establishes the maximum speed at which motor vehicles are permitted to travel lawfully on the highways of the State and in other places. Clark v. Jackson, 4 N.C. App. 277, 166 S.E.2d 501 (1969).

UNDER THIS SECTION 55 MILES PER HOUR IS THE GENERAL MAXIMUM SPEED LIMIT IN THE STATE, and the provisions of former subdivision (b)(5) [now subsection (d)] are in the nature of an exception. A defendant must bring himself within the provisions of the exception in order to receive its benefits. State v. Brown, 250 N.C. 209, 108 S.E.2d 233 (1959); Shue v. Scheidt, 252 N.C. 561, 114 S.E.2d 237 (1960).

EXEMPTION OF POLICE OFFICERS UNDER G.S. 20-145. --Section 20-145 exempts a police officer from observing the speed limit set out in this section when such officer is operating an automobile in the chase or apprehension of a violator of the law, or a person charged or suspected of such violation, as long as the officer drives with due regard to the safety of others. Goddard v. Williams, 251 N.C. 128, 110 S.E.2d 820 (1959), overruled in part, Young v. Woodall, 343 N.C. 459, 471 S.E.2d 357 (1996).

THE AUTHORITY OF THE STATE HIGHWAY COMMISSION (NOW DEPARTMENT OF TRANSPORTATION) UNDER SUBDIVISION (D)(1) of this section does not stop at city limits, but extends to all State highways maintained by it, regardless of whether such highways are within the corporate limits of a city or town. Davis v. Jessup, 257 N.C. 215, 125 S.E.2d 440 (1962).

AS TO UNENFORCEABILITY OF AN ORDINANCE IN CONFLICT WITH THIS SECTION, see State v. Stallings, 189 N.C. 104, 126 S.E. 187 (1925).

AS TO APPLICATION OF SECTION TO CRIMINAL ACTIONS, see James v. City of Charlotte, 183 N.C. 630, 112 S.E. 423 (1922); Piner v. Richter, 202 N.C. 573, 163 S.E. 561 (1932).

CRIMINAL LIABILITY FOR INJURY WHERE SPEED LIMIT EXCEEDED. --Where one recklessly drives an automobile without signal or warning in excess of the speed limit fixed by ordinance and the general statute, and thereby injures or kills another at a street intersection of the town, his violation of the law in this manner makes him criminally liable for the injury, without regard to the exercise of his judgment at the time in endeavoring to avoid the injury or contributory negligence on the part of the one injured or killed. State v. McIver, 175 N.C. 761, 94 S.E. 682 (1917).

A RECKLESS APPROACH AND TRAVERSE OF AN INTERSECTION MAY RENDER ONE CRIMINALLY LIABLE for the consequences of his acts, in addition to liability under this section. State v. Gash, 177 N.C. 595, 99 S.E. 337 (1919).

WHEN VIOLATION AMOUNTS TO MANSLAUGHTER. --Where one drives his automobile in violation of the statutory requirements, and thus directly, or without an independent intervening sole proximate cause, the death of another results, he is guilty of manslaughter, though the death was unintentionally caused by his act. But the violation also is insufficient unless it was the proximate cause of the death, and a charge disregarding the element of proximate cause is error. State v. Whaley, 191 N.C. 387, 132 S.E. 6 (1926).

WARRANT HELD SUFFICIENT TO CHARGE VI-
OLATION OF THIS SECTION by speeding 80 miles
per hour. State v. Daughtry, 236 N.C. 316, 72 S.E.2d
658 (1952).

CONVICTION FOR ASSAULT HELD NOT SUS-
TAINABLE. --Under an indictment of three counts
(assault with a deadly weapon, namely an automobile, operating a motor vehicle on a public highway
while under the influence of intoxicating liquor, and
operating a motor vehicle recklessly and in breach of
this section), wherein it was admitted by the State
that there was no evidence of intentional assault, and
where the jury returned for their verdict that defendant "was guilty of an assault, but not with reckless
driving," the State's admission and the verdict on the
last two counts dispelled the element of criminal negligence and criminal intent, and a conviction on the
first count would not be sustained. State v. Rawlings,
191 N.C. 265, 131 S.E. 632 (1926). See also, State v.
Rountree, 181 N.C. 535, 106 S.E. 669 (1921).

WHERE PLAINTIFF ALLEGED THAT DEFEN-
DANT WAS OPERATING HIS AUTOMOBILE AT A
SPEED WHICH WAS EXCESSIVE under the existing
conditions in violation of subsection (a), but made no
other allegation with reference to defendant's speed,
and did not allege that the approach to the scene of
the collision was either a business or a residential
district or that the proper authorities had posted any
signs giving notice of any determined speed limit for
the area, subsection (a) and former subdivision (b)(4)
[now subdivision (b)(2)] were pertinent in judging the
conduct of the defendant. Hensley v. Wallen, 257 N.C.
675, 127 S.E.2d 277 (1962).

DOUBLE JEOPARDY. --Defendant's convictions for
speeding, reckless driving, and speeding to elude arrest, aggravated to a felony for speeding and reckless
driving, violated double jeopardy because (1) speeding
and reckless driving were elements of the third crime,
since speeding and reckless driving increased the
maximum penalty, and (2) the legislature intended to
impose alternate, not separate, punishments, since all
the statutes sought to deter the same conduct. State v.
Mulder, 233 N.C. App. 82, 755 S.E.2d 98 (2014).

APPLIED in Gaffney v. Phelps, 207 N.C. 553, 178 S.E.
231 (1935) (speed in entering intersection); Hancock v.
Wilson, 211 N.C. 129, 189 S.E. 631 (1937); Sparks v.
Willis, 228 N.C. 25, 44 S.E.2d 343 (1947); State v. Blankenship, 229 N.C. 589, 50 S.E.2d 724 (1948); Bobbitt v.
Haynes, 231 N.C. 373, 57 S.E.2d 361 (1950); Whiteman
v. Seashore Transp. Co., 231 N.C. 701, 58 S.E.2d 752
(1950); Bumgardner v. Allison, 238 N.C. 621, 78 S.E.2d
752 (1953); McClamrock v. White Packing Co., 238 N.C.
648, 78 S.E.2d 749 (1953) (as to subsection (e)); Gantt v.
Hobson, 240 N.C. 426, 82 S.E.2d 384 (1954) (as to subsection (h)); Combs v. United States, 122 F. Supp. 280
(E.D.N.C. 1954) (as to subsection (a)); Wilson v. Web-
ster, 247 N.C. 393, 100 S.E.2d 829 (1957); Bass v. Lee,
255 N.C. 73, 120 S.E.2d 570 (1961); Powell v. Clark,
255 N.C. 707, 122 S.E.2d 706 (1961); Scarborough v.
Ingram, 256 N.C. 87, 122 S.E.2d 798 (1961); Bulluck
v. Long, 256 N.C. 577, 124 S.E.2d 716 (1962); Phillips
v. Alston, 257 N.C. 255, 125 S.E.2d 580 (1962); Benson

v. Sawyer, 257 N.C. 765, 127 S.E.2d 549 (1962); Parker
v. Bruce, 258 N.C. 341, 128 S.E.2d 561 (1962); Queen
v. Jarrett, 258 N.C. 405, 128 S.E.2d 894 (1963); State
v. Wells, 259 N.C. 173, 130 S.E.2d 299 (1963); Scott v.
Clark, 261 N.C. 102, 134 S.E.2d 181 (1964); Taney v.
Brown, 262 N.C. 438, 137 S.E.2d 827 (1964); Hall v.
Little, 262 N.C. 618, 138 S.E.2d 282 (1964); Carolina
Coach Co. v. Cox, 337 F.2d 101 (4th Cir. 1964); Knight v.
Seymour, 263 N.C. 790, 140 S.E.2d 410 (1965); Reeves v.
Campbell, 264 N.C. 224, 141 S.E.2d 296 (1965); Drum-
wright v. Wood, 266 N.C. 198, 146 S.E.2d 1 (1966); Wells
v. Bissette, 266 N.C. 774, 147 S.E.2d 210 (1966); Atwood
v. Holland, 267 N.C. 722, 148 S.E.2d 851 (1966); White
v. Mote, 270 N.C. 544, 155 S.E.2d 75 (1967); State v.
Massey, 271 N.C. 555, 157 S.E.2d 150 (1967); State v.
Moses, 272 N.C. 509, 158 S.E.2d 617 (1968); Pelkey v.
Bynum, 2 N.C. App. 183, 162 S.E.2d 586 (1968); Kin-
ney v. Goley, 6 N.C. App. 182, 169 S.E.2d 525 (1969);
Racine v. Boege, 6 N.C. App. 341, 169 S.E.2d 913 (1969);
State v. Zimmerman, 7 N.C. App. 522, 173 S.E.2d 35
(1970); Meeks v. Atkeson, 7 N.C. App. 631, 173 S.E.2d
509 (1970); Doggett v. Welborn, 18 N.C. App. 105, 196
S.E.2d 36 (1973); State v. Crabtree, 286 N.C. 541, 212
S.E.2d 103 (1975); McDougald v. Doughty, 27 N.C. App.
237, 218 S.E.2d 482 (1975); Farmer v. Chaney, 29 N.C.
App. 544, 225 S.E.2d 159 (1976); State v. Gainey, 292
N.C. 627, 234 S.E.2d 610 (1977); State v. Spellman, 40
N.C. App. 591, 253 S.E.2d 320 (1979); Harris v. Bridges,
59 N.C. App. 195, 296 S.E.2d 299 (1982); Murdock v.
Ratliff, 310 N.C. 652, 314 S.E.2d 518 (1984); State v.
Moore, 107 N.C. App. 388, 420 S.E.2d 691 (1992).

CITED in State v. Mickle, 194 N.C. 808, 140 S.E.
150 (1927); State v. Palmer, 197 N.C. 135, 147 S.E. 817
(1929); Burke v. Carolina Coach Co., 198 N.C. 8, 150
S.E. 636 (1929); Lancaster v. B. & H. Coast Line, 198
N.C. 107, 150 S.E. 716 (1929); Rudd v. Holmes, 198
N.C. 640, 152 S.E. 894 (1930); Pittman v. Downing,
209 N.C. 219, 183 S.E. 362 (1936); Taft v. Maryland
Cas. Co., 211 N.C. 507, 191 S.E. 10 (1937); Pearson v.
Luther, 212 N.C. 412, 193 S.E. 739 (1937); Reeves v.
Staley, 220 N.C. 573, 18 S.E.2d 239 (1942); Brown v.
Southern Paper Prods. Co., 222 N.C. 626, 24 S.E.2d
334 (1943); Crone v. Fisher, 223 N.C. 635, 27 S.E.2d
642 (1943); Hobbs v. Queen City Coach Co., 225 N.C.
323, 34 S.E.2d 211 (1945); State v. Sumner, 232 N.C.
386, 61 S.E.2d 84 (1950); Butler v. Allen, 233 N.C.
484, 64 S.E.2d 561 (1951); Matheny v. Central Motor
Lines, 233 N.C. 673, 65 S.E.2d 361 (1951); Hansley v.
Tilton, 234 N.C. 3, 65 S.E.2d 300 (1951); Adcox v. Austin, 235 N.C. 591, 70 S.E.2d 837 (1952); Pemberton v.
Lewis, 235 N.C. 188, 69 S.E.2d 512 (1952); Childress
v. Johnson Motor Lines, 235 N.C. 522, 70 S.E.2d 558
(1952); Jernigan v. Jernigan, 236 N.C. 430, 72 S.E.2d
912 (1952); Powell v. Daniel, 236 N.C. 489, 73 S.E.2d
143 (1952); Freshman v. Stallings, 128 F. Supp. 179
(E.D.N.C. 1955); Lowe v. Department of Motor Vehicles, 244 N.C. 353, 93 S.E.2d 448 (1956); Weaver v.
C.W. Myers Trading Post, Inc., 245 N.C. 106, 95 S.E.2d
533 (1956); as to subsection (e), in Keener v. Beal, 246
N.C. 247, 98 S.E.2d 19 (1957); Hennis Freight Lines v.
Burlington Mills Corp., 246 N.C. 143, 97 S.E.2d 850
(1957); Lookabill v. Regan, 247 N.C. 199, 100 S.E.2d

521 (1957); Durham v. McLean Trucking Co., 247 N.C. 204, 100 S.E.2d 348 (1957); Hollowell v. Archbell, 250 N.C. 716, 110 S.E.2d 262 (1959); Beaver v. Scheidt, 251 N.C. 671, 111 S.E.2d 881 (1960); Kennedy v. James, 252 N.C. 434, 113 S.E.2d 889 (1960); Pridgen v. Uzzell, 254 N.C. 292, 118 S.E.2d 755 (1961); Peeden v. Tait, 254 N.C. 489, 119 S.E.2d 450 (1961); Clifton v. Turner, 257 N.C. 92, 125 S.E.2d 339 (1962); Brewer v. Powers Trucking Co., 256 N.C. 175, 123 S.E.2d 608 (1962); Gilliam v. Propst Constr. Co., 256 N.C. 197, 123 S.E.2d 504 (1962); Dunlap v. Lee, 257 N.C. 447, 126 S.E.2d 62 (1962); Jewell Ridge Coal Corp. v. City of Charlotte, 204 F. Supp. 256 (W.D.N.C. 1962); Parlier v. Barnes, 260 N.C. 341, 132 S.E.2d 684 (1963); Upchurch v. Hudson Funeral Home, 263 N.C. 560, 140 S.E.2d 17 (1965); State Hwy. Comm'n v. Raleigh Farmers Mkt., Inc., 263 N.C. 622, 139 S.E.2d 904 (1965); Cogdell v. Taylor, 264 N.C. 424, 142 S.E.2d 36 (1965); Wilkins v. Turlington, 266 N.C. 328, 145 S.E.2d 892 (1966); Webb v. Felton, 266 N.C. 707, 147 S.E.2d 219 (1966); Barefoot v. Joyner, 270 N.C. 388, 154 S.E.2d 543 (1967); Kanoy v. Hinshaw, 273 N.C. 418, 160 S.E.2d 296 (1968); Reeves v. Hill, 272 N.C. 352, 158 S.E.2d 529 (1968); Anderson v. Carter, 272 N.C. 426, 158 S.E.2d 607 (1968); Swain v. Williamson, 4 N.C. App. 622, 167 S.E.2d 491 (1969); Brewer v. Harris, 279 N.C. 288, 182 S.E.2d 345 (1971); Southwire Co. v. Long Mfg. Co., 12 N.C. App. 335, 183 S.E.2d 253 (1971); McNair v. Boyette, 282 N.C. 230, 192 S.E.2d 457 (1972); Winters v. Burch, 284 N.C. 205, 200 S.E.2d 55 (1973); Wyatt v. Haywood, 22 N.C. App. 267, 206 S.E.2d 260 (1974); Caldwell v. Deese, 288 N.C. 375, 218 S.E.2d 379 (1975); State v. Hill, 31 N.C. App. 733, 230 S.E.2d 579 (1976); Smith v. Garrett, 32 N.C. App. 108, 230 S.E.2d 775 (1977); Cockrell v. Cromartie Transp. Co., 295 N.C. 444, 245 S.E.2d 497 (1978); Holt v. City of Statesville, 35 N.C. App. 381, 241 S.E.2d 362 (1978); Woods v. Smith, 297 N.C. 363, 255 S.E.2d 174 (1979); Sink v. Sumrell, 41 N.C. App. 242, 254 S.E.2d 665 (1979); State v. Clements, 51 N.C. App. 113, 275 S.E.2d 222 (1981); State v. Flaherty, 55 N.C. App. 14, 284 S.E.2d 565 (1981); White v. Greer, 55 N.C. App. 450, 285 S.E.2d 848 (1982); State v. Hefler, 60 N.C. App. 466, 299 S.E.2d 456 (1983); State v. Jones, 63 N.C. App. 411, 305 S.E.2d 221 (1983); State v. Hefler, 310 N.C. 135, 310 S.E.2d 310 (1984); State v. Scott, 71 N.C. App. 570, 322 S.E.2d 613 (1984); State v. McGill, 73 N.C. App. 206, 326 S.E.2d 345 (1985); State v. Braxton, 90 N.C. App. 204, 368 S.E.2d 56 (1988); Burgess v. Vestal, 99 N.C. App. 545, 393 S.E.2d 324 (1990); State v. Beasley, 104 N.C. App. 529, 410 S.E.2d 236 (1991); Body ex rel. Body v. Varner, 107 N.C. App. 219, 419 S.E.2d 208 (1992); Moreau v. Hill, 111 N.C. App. 679, 433 S.E.2d 10 (1993); Sparks v. Gilley Trucking Co., 992 F.2d 50 (4th Cir. 1993); Peal ex rel. Peal v. Smith, 115 N.C. App. 225, 444 S.E.2d 673 (1994); Jones v. Rochelle, 125 N.C. App. 82, 479 S.E.2d 231 (1996); State v. Phillips, 127 N.C. App. 391, 489 S.E.2d 890 (1997); State v. McClendon, 130 N.C. App. 368, 502 S.E.2d 902 (1998); State v. McClendon, 350 N.C. 630, 517 S.E.2d 128 (1999); State v. Jones, 353 N.C. 159, 538 S.E.2d 917 (2000); Hawley v. Cash, 155 N.C. App. 580,

574 S.E.2d 684 (2002); Williams v. Davis, 157 N.C. App. 696, 580 S.E.2d 85 (2003); State v. Mumford, 201 N.C. App. 594, 688 S.E.2d 458 (2010); Rabon v. Hopkins, 208 N.C. App. 351, 703 S.E.2d 181 (2010), review denied 365 N.C. 195, 710 S.E.2d 22, 2011 N.C. LEXIS 470 (N.C. 2011); State v. Leonard, 213 N.C. App. 526, 711 S.E.2d 867 (2011); State v. Castillo, 247 N.C. App. 327, 787 S.E.2d 48 (2016), review denied, 792 S.E.2d 784, 2016 N.C. LEXIS 765 (2016); State v. Evans, 251 N.C. App. 610, 795 S.E.2d 444 (2017).

II. STANDARD OF CARE AND NEGLIGENCE.

THIS SECTION PRESCRIBES A STANDARD OF CARE, and the standard fixed by the legislature is absolute. Aldridge v. Hasty, 240 N.C. 353, 82 S.E.2d 331 (1954); Kellogg v. Thomas, 244 N.C. 722, 94 S.E.2d 903 (1956); Lamm v. Gardner, 250 N.C. 540, 108 S.E.2d 847 (1959); Bondurant v. Mastin, 252 N.C. 190, 113 S.E.2d 292 (1960); Hutchens v. Southard, 254 N.C. 428, 119 S.E.2d 205 (1961); Pittman v. Swanson, 255 N.C. 681, 122 S.E.2d 814 (1961).

A DRIVER MUST OPERATE HIS VEHICLE AT A REASONABLE RATE OF SPEED AND KEEP A PROPER LOOKOUT for persons on or near the highway. Basden v. Sutton, 7 N.C. App. 6, 171 S.E.2d 77 (1969).

DUTY OF MOTORIST GENERALLY. --A motorist must operate his vehicle at a reasonable rate of speed, keep a lookout for persons on or near the highway, decrease his speed when any special hazard exists with respect to pedestrians, and, if circumstances warrant, he must give warning of his approach by sounding his horn. Morris v. Minix, 4 N.C. App. 634, 167 S.E.2d 494 (1969).

THE DUTY OF A DRIVER TO DECREASE HIS SPEED IS GOVERNED BY THE DUTY OF ALL PERSONS TO USE "DUE CARE," and is tested by the usual legal requirements and standards such as proximate cause. Day v. Davis, 268 N.C. 643, 151 S.E.2d 556 (1966).

THE SPEED LIMIT PRESCRIBED BY STATUTE DOES NOT ALONE EXCUSE THOSE WHO DRIVE WITHIN THE LIMIT SPECIFIED by the statute, and it is likewise required that they use proper care where other conditions require it within the limitations given. State v. Whaley, 191 N.C. 387, 132 S.E. 6 (1926).

The fact that a vehicle is being driven within the statutory speed limit does not render the speed lawful when by reason of special hazards the speed is greater than is reasonable and prudent under the existing conditions. Rollison v. Hicks, 233 N.C. 99, 63 S.E.2d 190 (1951).

The fact that the speed of a vehicle is lower than that fixed by statute does not relieve the driver from the duty to decrease speed when approaching and crossing an intersection, or when a hazard exists with respect to weather or highway conditions, and his speed shall be reduced as may be necessary to avoid colliding with any vehicle on the highway. Keller v. Security Mills of Greensboro, Inc., 260 N.C. 571, 133 S.E.2d 222 (1963).

AND A MOTORIST MAY NOT LAWFULLY DRIVE AT A SPEED WHICH IS NOT REASONABLE AND PRUDENT under the circumstances, notwithstanding that such speed is less than the limit set by this section. Kolman v. Silbert, 219 N.C. 134, 12 S.E.2d 915 (1941).

By provision of this section, speed in excess of that which is reasonable and prudent under the circumstances, when special hazards exist by reason of traffic, weather or highway conditions, is unlawful, notwithstanding that the speed may be less than the prima facie limits prescribed. Hoke v. Atlantic Greyhound Corp., 226 N.C. 692, 40 S.E.2d 345 (1946).

Speed in excess of that which is reasonable and prudent under the existing conditions is unlawful, notwithstanding that the speed may be less than the limits proscribed by statute. State v. Grissom, 17 N.C. App. 374, 194 S.E.2d 227, cert. denied, 283 N.C. 258, 195 S.E.2d 691 (1973).

The speed of a motor vehicle may be unlawful under the circumstances of a particular case, even though such speed is less than the definite statutory limit prescribed for the vehicle in the place where it is being driven. Sowers v. Marley, 235 N.C. 607, 70 S.E.2d 670 (1952); Wise v. Lodge, 247 N.C. 250, 100 S.E.2d 677 (1957); Lamm v. Gardner, 250 N.C. 540, 108 S.E.2d 847 (1959).

It is unlawful to drive at any time on a State highway at a speed greater than is reasonable and prudent under the conditions then existing. State v. Norris, 242 N.C. 47, 86 S.E.2d 916 (1955).

Violation of the standard of care required by subsection (h) of this section is negligence per se. Murdock v. Ratliff, 63 N.C. App. 306, 305 S.E.2d 48 (1983), rev'd on other grounds, 310 N.C. 652, 314 S.E.2d 518 (1984).

Subsections (g) and (m) of this section, construed together, establish a duty to drive with caution and circumspection and to reduce speed if necessary to avoid a collision, irrespective of the lawful speed limit or the speed actually driven. State v. Stroud, 78 N.C. App. 599, 337 S.E.2d 873 (1985).

THIS SECTION REQUIRES THE MOTORIST TO DECREASE HIS SPEED WHEN SPECIAL HAZARDS EXIST by reason of weather and highway conditions, to the end that others using the highway may not be injured. Williams v. Tucker, 259 N.C. 214, 130 S.E.2d 306 (1963); Sessoms v. Roberson, 47 N.C. App. 573, 268 S.E.2d 24 (1980).

A speed greater than is reasonable and prudent under the conditions then existing is prohibited by this section, and the duty is imposed upon the driver to decrease the speed of his automobile when special hazard exists with respect to pedestrians or other traffic. Baker v. Perrott, 228 N.C. 558, 46 S.E.2d 461 (1948). See Williams v. Henderson, 230 N.C. 707, 55 S.E.2d 462 (1949); Riggs v. Akers Motor Lines, 233 N.C. 160, 63 S.E.2d 197 (1951); Price v. Miller, 271 N.C. 690, 157 S.E.2d 347 (1967).

The driver of an automobile is required at all times to operate his vehicle with due regard to traffic and conditions of the highway and to keep his car under control and decrease his speed when special hazards exist by reason of weather or highway conditions or when necessary to avoid colliding with any other vehicle. This requirement, as expressed in this section and G.S. 20-140, constitutes the hub of the motor vehicle law around which other provisions regulating the operation of motor vehicles revolve. Cox v. Lee, 230 N.C. 155, 52 S.E.2d 355 (1949); Singletary v. Nixon, 239 N.C. 634, 80 S.E.2d 676 (1954); Lamm v. Gardner, 250 N.C. 540, 108 S.E.2d 847 (1959).

DUTY TO REFRAIN FROM ENTERING HIGHWAY OR TO STOP IN EXTREME CASES. --In extreme cases where by reason of fog or other conditions visibility is practically nonexistent, motorists are under a duty to refrain from entering the highway or to stop if already on the highway. Williams v. Tucker, 259 N.C. 214, 130 S.E.2d 306 (1963).

WHETHER A GIVEN SPEED IS LAWFUL DEPENDS ON CIRCUMSTANCES. --In light of the provisions of G.S. 20-140 and this section, it is clear that whether or not a speed of 55 miles an hour is lawful depends upon the circumstances at the time. These sections provide that a motorist must at all times drive with due caution and circumspection and at a speed and in a manner so as not to endanger or be likely to endanger any person or property. At no time may a motorist lawfully drive at a speed greater than is reasonable and prudent under the conditions then existing. Primm v. King, 249 N.C. 228, 106 S.E.2d 223 (1958).

DRIVING BELOW THE SPEED LIMIT IS NOT A DEFENSE to a charge of driving at a speed greater than is reasonable and prudent under existing conditions; regardless of the posted speed limit, motorists have a duty to decrease speed if necessary to avoid a collision. State v. Stroud, 78 N.C. App. 599, 337 S.E.2d 873 (1985).

SPEED LESS THAN 20 MILES PER HOUR MAY BE UNLAWFUL. --Speed less than 20 miles per hour in a business district, residential district or elsewhere, if greater than is reasonable and prudent under the conditions then existing, is unlawful and negligence per se. Hinson v. Dawson, 241 N.C. 714, 86 S.E.2d 585 (1955).

AS MAY SPEED OF 35 OR 40 MPH ON SNOWY HIGHWAY. --Speed of 40 miles per hour on a highway on which snow is beginning to stick may be excessive. Fox v. Hollar, 257 N.C. 65, 125 S.E.2d 334 (1962).

Speed of 35 to 40 miles per hour on a highway covered with ice and snow may be excessive; the driver of the vehicle under such conditions must exercise care commensurate with the danger so as to keep his vehicle under control. Redden v. Bynum, 256 N.C. 351, 123 S.E.2d 734 (1962).

CHARACTER OF DISTRICT MUST BE PROVED BEFORE SPEED LIMIT CAN BE DETERMINED. -- In the absence of a stipulation, it is necessary to prove the character of the district before the maximum speed permitted by law can be determined. Hensley v. Wallen, 257 N.C. 675, 127 S.E.2d 277 (1962).

WHAT IS THE SPEED LIMIT IS A MIXED QUESTION OF FACT AND LAW, except where the State

Chapter 20

Highway Commission (now the Board of Transportation) or local authorities, pursuant to the statute, have determined a reasonable and safe speed for a particular area and have declared it by erecting appropriate signs. Hensley v. Wallen, 257 N.C. 675, 127 S.E.2d 277 (1962).

REASONABLENESS OF SPEED IS QUESTION FOR JURY. --It is ultimately for the jury, not for a witness, to determine what speed under subsection (a) of this section would have been "reasonable and prudent under the conditions" which existed at the time and place of a collision. Peterson v. Taylor, 10 N.C. App. 297, 178 S.E.2d 227 (1971).

In a suit arising out of an accident between two tractor trailers, plaintiffs' negligence claims against defendant driver and defendant operator survived summary judgment because, inter alia, whether defendant driver's speed was unreasonably slow and whether traffic was impeded were questions of fact to be resolved by a jury. Pracht v. Saga Freight Logistics, LLC, 2015 U.S. Dist. LEXIS 138230 (W.D.N.C. Oct. 9, 2015).

WHETHER PLAINTIFF'S SPEED WAS UNREASONABLY SLOW AND WHETHER TRAFFIC WAS IMPEDED ARE QUESTIONS OF FACT FOR JURY. Page v. Tao, 56 N.C. App. 488, 289 S.E.2d 910, aff'd, 306 N.C. 739, 295 S.E.2d 470 (1982).

Where the evidence tended to show that plaintiff or defendant was traveling at a slow speed, a jury question was presented as to whether under the circumstances the speed was so slow as to impede reasonable movement of traffic, and whether there was justification for the slow speed. Fonville v. Dixon, 16 N.C. App. 664, 193 S.E.2d 406 (1972), cert. denied, 282 N.C. 672, 194 S.E.2d 152 (1973).

WHEN ROAD'S CONDITION IS SUCH THAT SKIDDING MAY BE REASONABLY ANTICIPATED, DRIVER MUST EXERCISE CARE COMMENSURATE WITH THE DANGER to keep his vehicle under control so as to avoid injury to occupants of the vehicle and others on or off the highway. Webb v. Clark, 264 N.C. 474, 141 S.E.2d 880 (1965); Clark v. Jackson, 4 N.C. App. 277, 166 S.E.2d 501 (1969).

BUT THE SKIDDING OF AN AUTOMOBILE IS NOT IN ITSELF, AND WITHOUT MORE, EVIDENCE OF NEGLIGENCE. Bass v. McLamb, 268 N.C. 395, 150 S.E.2d 856 (1966).

The mere skidding of a motor vehicle is not evidence of, and does not imply, negligence. Clark v. Jackson, 4 N.C. App. 277, 166 S.E.2d 501 (1969).

SKIDDING MAY BE EVIDENCE OF NEGLIGENCE, IF IT WAS CAUSED BY FAILURE TO EXERCISE REASONABLE PRECAUTION to avoid it, when the conditions at the time made such a result probable in the absence of such precaution. Clark v. Jackson, 4 N.C. App. 277, 166 S.E.2d 501 (1969).

THE MOTORIST UPON A PUBLIC HIGHWAY ON A DARK, MISTY AND FOGGY NIGHT IS REQUIRED TO REGULATE THE SPEED OF HIS CAR with a view to his own safety according to the distance the light from his headlights is thrown in front of him upon the highway, and to observe the rule of the ordinary prudent man. Weston v. Southern Ry., 194 N.C. 210, 139 S.E. 237 (1927). See also, Stewart v. Stewart, 221 N.C. 147, 19 S.E.2d 242 (1942).

CURVES AND DARKNESS ARE CONDITIONS A MOTORIST IS REQUIRED TO TAKE INTO CONSIDERATION in regulating his speed as may be necessary to avoid colliding with any person, vehicle, or other conveyance. Allen v. Dr. Pepper Bottling Co., 223 N.C. 118, 25 S.E.2d 388 (1943). See also, Tyson v. Ford, 228 N.C. 778, 47 S.E.2d 251 (1948).

BUT THE DUTY OF THE NOCTURNAL MOTORIST DOES NOT EXTEND SO FAR AS TO REQUIRE THAT HE MUST BE ABLE TO BRING HIS AUTOMOBILE TO AN IMMEDIATE STOP on the sudden arising of a dangerous situation which he could not reasonably have anticipated. Rouse v. Peterson, 261 N.C. 600, 135 S.E.2d 549 (1964).

INABILITY TO STOP WITHIN RADIUS OF LIGHTS IS NOT NEGLIGENCE OR CONTRIBUTORY NEGLIGENCE PER SE. --When a motorist is traveling within the maximum speed limit, his inability to stop his vehicle within the radius of his headlights will not be held negligence or contributory negligence per se. Short v. Chapman, 261 N.C. 674, 136 S.E.2d 40 (1964).

If the driver of a motor vehicle who is operating it within the maximum speed limits prescribed by this section fails to stop such vehicle within the radius of the lights of the vehicle or within the range of his vision, the courts may no longer hold such failure to be negligence per se, or contributory negligence per se, as the case may be, that is, negligence or contributory negligence, in and of itself; but the facts relating thereto may be considered by the jury, with other facts in such action, in determining whether the operator be guilty of negligence, or contributory negligence, as the case may be. Beasley v. Williams, 260 N.C. 561, 133 S.E.2d 227 (1963); Coleman v. Burris, 265 N.C. 404, 144 S.E.2d 241 (1965); Bass v. McLamb, 268 N.C. 395, 150 S.E.2d 856 (1966); Duke v. Tankard, 3 N.C. App. 563, 165 S.E.2d 524 (1969).

If a motorist is traveling within the legal speed limit, his inability to stop within the range of his headlights is not negligence per se, but is only evidence of negligence to be considered with the other evidence in the case. May v. Southern Ry., 259 N.C. 43, 129 S.E.2d 624 (1963).

NOR IS INABILITY TO STOP WITHIN RANGE OF VISION. --Plaintiff's inability to stop within the range of his vision was held not to be contributory negligence per se, but the facts relating thereto were held for consideration by the jury in determining the issue of contributory negligence. Brown v. Hale, 263 N.C. 176, 139 S.E.2d 210 (1964).

No universal absolute rule may be applied to the question of whether a motorist is contributorily negligent as a matter of law by proceeding when his or her vision becomes obscured by conditions on the highway; the conduct of each motorist must be evaluated in the light of the unique factors and circumstances with which he or she is confronted. Only in the clearest cases should a failure to stop completely be held to be negligence as a matter of law. Allen v. Pullen, 82 N.C. App. 61, 345 S.E.2d 469 (1986), cert. denied, 318 N.C. 691, 351 S.E.2d 738 (1987).

Defendant's failure to stop her vehicle within the range of her vision when confronted by a cloud of dust was not contributory negligence per se, and under the circumstances, where her vision was suddenly obscured, the question of her speed was properly one for the jury. Allen v. Pullen, 82 N.C. App. 61, 345 S.E.2d 469 (1986), cert. denied, 318 N.C. 691, 351 S.E.2d 738 (1987).

AND AN INSTRUCTION TO THE CONTRARY CONSTITUTES PREJUDICIAL ERROR. --The court committed prejudicial error in instructing the jury to the effect that failure or inability of defendant, who was driving the automobile within the maximum speed limit on the highway, to stop the automobile within the radius of his lights would constitute a breach of legal duty and would be negligence per se. Salter v. Lovick, 257 N.C. 619, 127 S.E.2d 273 (1962).

COLLISION WITH VEHICLE PARKED ON HIGHWAY AT NIGHT WITHOUT LIGHTS. --Plaintiff would not be held contributorily negligent as a matter of law in striking the rear of a vehicle left unattended on a highway at nighttime without lights, when plaintiff at the time was traveling within the statutory maximum speed limit. Beasley v. Williams, 260 N.C. 561, 133 S.E.2d 227 (1953).

Allegations held not to show contributory negligence as a matter of law in colliding with truck stopped on highway after dark without rear lights. Weavil v. Myers, 243 N.C. 386, 90 S.E.2d 733 (1956).

Where a motorist is traveling within the maximum legal speed, he will not be held contributorily negligent as a matter of law in colliding with the rear of a vehicle left in his lane of traffic at nighttime without lights. Dezern v. Asheboro City Bd. of Educ., 260 N.C. 535, 133 S.E.2d 204 (1963).

Motorist who is driving his automobile within the maximum speed limit cannot be held contributorily negligent as a matter of law in outrunning his headlights and striking the rear end of a pickup truck stopped on the highway without lights. Rouse v. Peterson, 261 N.C. 600, 135 S.E.2d 549 (1964); Sharpe v. Hanline, 265 N.C. 502, 144 S.E.2d 574 (1965).

A motorist is not required to anticipate that an automobile will be stopped on the highway ahead of him at night, without lights or warning signals required by statute, but this does not relieve him of the duty of exercising reasonable care for his own safety, of keeping a proper lookout, and proceeding as a reasonably prudent person would under the circumstances to avoid a collision with the rear of a vehicle stopped or standing on the road. Bass v. McLamb, 268 N.C. 395, 150 S.E.2d 856 (1966).

SPEED WHEN PERSON OR VEHICLE IS IN DRIVER'S LINE OF TRAVEL. --Any speed may be unlawful and excessive if the operator of a motor vehicle knows or by the exercise of due care should reasonably anticipate that a person or vehicle is standing in his line of travel. Murray v. Wyatt, 245 N.C. 123, 95 S.E.2d 541 (1956).

Any speed may be unlawful if the driver of a motor vehicle sees, or in the exercise of due care could and should have seen, a person or vehicle in his line of travel. Cassetta v. Compton, 256 N.C. 71, 123 S.E.2d 222 (1961).

THE LAW REQUIRES MORE THAN ORDINARY CARE IN REGARD TO CHILDREN. Moore v. Powell, 205 N.C. 636, 172 S.E. 327 (1934).

AS TO PASSING ANIMALS, see Tudor v. Bowen, 152 N.C. 441, 67 S.E. 1015 (1910); Gaskins v. Hancock, 156 N.C. 56, 72 S.E. 80 (1911); Curry v. Fleer, 157 N.C. 16, 72 S.E. 626 (1911).

AS TO CARE REQUIRED OF MOTORISTS AT INTERSECTIONS UNDER FORMER SUBSECTION (C) of this section, which expressly required drivers to decrease speed on approaching and crossing an intersection as necessary to avoid collisions, etc., see Hutchens v. Southard, 254 N.C. 428, 119 S.E.2d 205 (1961); Rogers v. Rogers, 2 N.C. App. 668, 163 S.E.2d 645 (1968); Murrell v. Jennings, 15 N.C. App. 658, 190 S.E.2d 686 (1972).

DRIVER HAS NO DUTY TO ANTICIPATE VIOLATION OF LAW BY ANOTHER. --The operator of an automobile traveling upon an intersecting highway traversing a designated main-traveled or through highway is under no duty to anticipate that the operator of an automobile upon such designated highway, approaching the intersection of the two highways, will fail to observe the speed regulations and the rules of the road. Hawes v. Atlantic Ref. Co., 236 N.C. 643, 74 S.E.2d 17 (1953).

BUT MUST EXERCISE DUE CARE TO AVOID CONSEQUENCES OF ANOTHER'S NEGLIGENCE. --The driver of an automobile upon a through highway did not have the right to assume absolutely that a driver approaching the intersection along a servient highway would obey the stop sign before entering or crossing the through highway, but was required to keep a proper lookout and to keep his car at a reasonable speed under the circumstances in order to avoid injury to life or limb, and the driver of the car along the through highway forfeited his right to rely upon the assumption that the other driver would stop before entering or crossing the intersection when he approached and attempted traverse it himself at an unlawful or excessive speed. Even when his speed was lawful he remained under duty to exercise due care to ascertain if the driver of the other car was going to violate the statutory requirement in order to avoid the consequences of such negligence. Groome v. Davis, 215 N.C. 510, 2 S.E.2d 771 (1939).

VIOLATION OF SECTION IS NEGLIGENCE PER SE -- IN GENERAL. --Operation of a motor vehicle in excess of the applicable limits set forth in this section is negligence per se. Edwards v. Mayes, 385 F.2d 369 (4th Cir. 1967).

It is negligence per se to drive an automobile upon a public highway at a speed greater than that permitted by statute. Albritton v. Hill, 190 N.C. 429, 130 S.E. 5 (1925). See also Norfleet v. Hall, 204 N.C. 573, 169 S.E. 143 (1933); James v. Carolina Coach Co., 207 N.C. 742, 178 S.E. 607 (1935); Exum v. Baumrind, 210 N.C.

650, 188 S.E. 200 (1936); Jones v. Horton, 264 N.C. 549, 142 S.E.2d 351 (1965); Raper v. Byrum, 265 N.C. 269, 144 S.E.2d 38 (1965).

One who fails to comply with the provisions of this section is negligent. Stephens v. Southern Oil Co., 259 N.C. 456, 131 S.E.2d 39 (1963).

Violation of this section constitutes negligence, because according to the uniform decisions of the Supreme Court, the violation of a statute imposing a rule of conduct in the operation of a motor vehicle and enacted in the interest of safety has been held to constitute negligence per se, unless otherwise provided in the statute. Bridges v. Jackson, 255 N.C. 333, 121 S.E.2d 542 (1961).

SAME -- SUBSECTION (A). -- Tarrant v. Pepsi-Cola Bottling Co., 221 N.C. 390, 20 S.E.2d 565 (1942); Black v. Gurley Milling Co., 257 N.C. 730, 127 S.E.2d 515 (1962); Rundle v. Grubb Motor Lines, 300 F.2d 333 (4th Cir. 1962); Page v. Tao, 56 N.C. App. 488, 289 S.E.2d 910, aff'd, 306 N.C. 739, 295 S.E.2d 470 (1982).

SAME -- FORMER SUBDIVISION (B)(3). -- Smart v. Fox, 268 N.C. 284, 150 S.E.2d 403 (1966).

SAME -- FORMER SUBDIVISION (B)(4). -- Stegall v. Sledge, 247 N.C. 718, 102 S.E.2d 115 (1958); Rudd v. Stewart, 255 N.C. 90, 120 S.E.2d 601 (1961); Price v. Miller, 271 N.C. 690, 157 S.E.2d 347 (1967); Basden v. Sutton, 7 N.C. App. 6, 171 S.E.2d 77 (1969).

SAME -- FORMER SUBSECTION (C). -- Hutchens v. Southard, 254 N.C. 428, 119 S.E.2d 205 (1961); Pittman v. Swanson, 255 N.C. 681, 122 S.E.2d 814 (1961); Redden v. Bynum, 256 N.C. 351, 123 S.E.2d 734 (1962); Rundle v. Grubb Motor Lines, 300 F.2d 333 (4th Cir. 1962).

DRIVING AT A SPEED GREATER THAN IS REASONABLE AND PRUDENT IS NEGLIGENCE. --If a person drives a vehicle on a highway at a speed greater than is reasonable and prudent under conditions then existing, such person is guilty of negligence per se, that is, as a matter of law, notwithstanding the fact that the speed does not exceed the applicable maximum limits set forth in subsection (b) of this section. Cassetta v. Compton, 256 N.C. 71, 123 S.E.2d 222 (1961); Edwards v. Mayes, 385 F.2d 369 (4th Cir. 1967).

It is unlawful for a person to operate a vehicle upon a public highway at a speed that is greater than is reasonable and prudent under existing circumstances. One who violates this statute is guilty of negligence. Rouse v. Jones, 254 N.C. 575, 119 S.E.2d 628 (1961).

If one drives an automobile at a speed greater than 55 miles per hour, or faster than is reasonable and prudent under existing conditions, he is negligent. Rector v. Roberts, 264 N.C. 324, 141 S.E.2d 482 (1965).

Operation at a speed in excess of that lawfully prescribed is a negligent act. Krider v. Martello, 252 N.C. 474, 113 S.E.2d 924 (1960).

A motorist is required to act as a reasonably prudent man and to drive with due caution and circumspection and at a speed or in a manner so as not to endanger or be likely to endanger any person or property, and his failure to do so is negligence. Crotts

v. Overnite Transp. Co., 246 N.C. 420, 98 S.E.2d 502 (1957).

TO BE ACTIONABLE NEGLIGENCE MUST BE PROXIMATE CAUSE OF INJURY. --A violation of this section constitutes negligence, although such negligence is not actionable unless it is the proximate cause of the injuries complained of. Davis v. Imes, 13 N.C. App. 521, 186 S.E.2d 641 (1972).

While violation of former subsection (c) constituted negligence per se, in order for there to be actionable negligence, such violation had to have been a proximate cause of the injury in suit, including the essential element of foreseeability. Day v. Davis, 268 N.C. 643, 151 S.E.2d 556 (1966).

If the negligence resulting from failure to comply with the provisions of this section proximately causes injury, liability results. Stephens v. Southern Oil Co., 259 N.C. 456, 131 S.E.2d 39 (1963).

AND VIOLATION OF THIS SECTION HAS LEGAL SIGNIFICANCE IN A CIVIL ACTION ONLY IF IT PROXIMATELY CAUSES INJURY. Cassetta v. Compton, 256 N.C. 71, 123 S.E.2d 222 (1961).

BURDEN OF SHOWING PROXIMATE CAUSE. --Plaintiff in a civil action has the burden of showing that excessive speed, when relied upon by him, was a proximate cause of injury. Hoke v. Atlantic Greyhound Corp., 226 N.C. 692, 40 S.E.2d 345 (1946).

EVIDENCE OF EXCESSIVE SPEED IS NOT PRIMA FACIE EVIDENCE OF PROXIMATE CAUSE. --Speed in excess of 21 miles per hour in a business district is prima facie evidence that the speed is excessive and unlawful, but such evidence is not prima facie proof of proximate cause; it is merely evidence to be considered with other evidence in determining actionable negligence. Templeton v. Kelley, 215 N.C. 577, 2 S.E.2d 696 (1939).

The mere fact that it can be reasonably inferred from the evidence that an automobile was traveling at a very rapid speed when it wrecked is not sufficient to permit a jury to find that such speed caused its wreck, and that its driver was guilty of actionable negligence. Crisp v. Medlin, 264 N.C. 314, 141 S.E.2d 609 (1965).

QUESTION OF PROXIMATE CAUSE FOR THE JURY. --Whether a violation of the provisions of this section was the proximate cause of an injury is for the jury to determine. Stephens v. Southern Oil Co., 259 N.C. 456, 131 S.E.2d 39 (1963).

EVIDENCE HELD SUFFICIENT TO SHOW ACTIONABLE NEGLIGENCE. --Evidence of greatly excessive speed in violation of the speed restrictions of this section, and of reckless driving in violation of G.S. 20-140, was sufficient to make out a case of actionable negligence. Bell v. Maxwell, 246 N.C. 257, 98 S.E.2d 33 (1957); Hutchens v. Southard, 254 N.C. 428, 119 S.E.2d 205 (1961).

All the evidence tended to show that plaintiff's decedent was killed by the actionable negligence of the driver of the automobile in which he was a passenger when the automobile was driven at an excessive speed in violation of this section and in a reckless manner in violation of G.S. 20-140. Bridges v. Graham, 246 N.C. 371, 98 S.E.2d 492 (1957).

Where there was evidence that defendant was driving his automobile on the highway at a speed of 65 miles per hour and that the injury in suit was proximately caused by such excessive speed, it was sufficient to be submitted to the jury on the issue of actionable negligence. Norfleet v. Hall, 204 N.C. 573, 169 S.E. 143 (1933).

AS TO EVIDENCE ESTABLISHING NEGLIGENCE PER SE BUT NOT WANTON NEGLIGENCE, see Turner v. Lipe, 210 N.C. 627, 188 S.E. 108 (1936). See also, Smart v. Rodgers, 217 N.C. 560, 8 S.E.2d 833 (1940).

EFFECT OF VIOLATION BY PLAINTIFF UPON RECOVERY FROM RAILROAD. --The mere fact that the speed of an automobile exceeded that allowed by law at the time of its collision with a railroad train at a public crossing does not of itself prevent a recovery by the owner where there is evidence of negligence on the part of the railroad, because it would, among other things, withdraw the question of proximate cause from the jury. Shepard v. Norfolk S.R.R., 169 N.C. 239, 84 S.E. 277 (1915).

DEPARTMENT OF TRANSPORTATION NOT NEGLIGENT FOR FAILURE TO LOWER SPEED LIMIT. --North Carolina Department of Transportation (DOT) was not liable for the deaths of two persons whose vehicle went into a lake, due to a failure to lower the speed limit on the road where the accident occurred, because DOT owed the persons no duty, under G.S. 143B-346, as no events triggering an engineering and traffic investigation on which a lowering of the speed limit could be based occurred prior to the accident in question. Turner v. N.C. DOT, 223 N.C. App. 90, 733 S.E.2d 871 (2012).

III. EVIDENCE.

MERE FACT OF A COLLISION WITH A VEHICLE AHEAD FURNISHES SOME EVIDENCE that the following motorist was negligent as to speed or was following too closely. Huggins v. Kye, 10 N.C. App. 221, 178 S.E.2d 127 (1970).

The principle that the mere fact of a collision with a vehicle ahead furnishes some evidence that the following motorist was negligent as to speed, was following too closely, or failed to keep a proper lookout is not absolute; the negligence, if any, depends upon the circumstances. Powell v. Cross, 263 N.C. 764, 140 S.E.2d 393 (1965).

THE PHYSICAL FACTS AT THE SCENE OF AN ACCIDENT may disclose that the operator of the vehicle was travelling at excessive speed. Keller v. Security Mills of Greensboro, Inc., 260 N.C. 571, 133 S.E.2d 222 (1963).

REASONABLE SUSPICION TO STOP DEFENDANT'S VEHICLE. --Officer had reasonable suspicion for stopping defendant for driving too quickly given the road conditions after the officer observed defendant abruptly accelerate his truck and turn left, causing the truck to fishtail in the snow before defendant regained control. State v. Johnson, 370 N.C. 32, 803 S.E.2d 137 (2017).

TESTIMONY OF WITNESS AS TO SPEED LIMIT IN PARTICULAR AREA VIOLATES OPINION RULE. --To permit a witness to say what a speed limit was for a particular area at a given time is to allow him to give his inferences from facts which he has observed. Such testimony violates the opinion rule and invades the province of the jury. Hensley v. Wallen, 257 N.C. 675, 127 S.E.2d 277 (1962).

BUT WITNESS MAY TESTIFY AS TO PRESENCE OF HIGHWAY SIGN. --If a highway sign declaring the speed limit to be a given speed has been posted, it would be competent for a witness to say so, describe the sign, and testify as to its location. Hensley v. Wallen, 257 N.C. 675, 127 S.E.2d 277 (1962).

INFERENCE IS THAT HIGHWAY SIGN WAS ERECTED BY PROPER AUTHORITIES. --When a sign is present, nothing else appearing, there is a logical inference that it was erected by the proper authorities pursuant to this section. Hensley v. Wallen, 257 N.C. 675, 127 S.E.2d 277 (1962).

COMPETENCY OF OPINION TESTIMONY AS TO SPEED OF VEHICLE. --It is the rule in this State that any person of ordinary intelligence who has had a reasonable opportunity to observe is competent to testify as to the rate of speed of an automobile. Jones v. Horton, 264 N.C. 549, 142 S.E.2d 351 (1965).

JUDGING SPEED BY MOVEMENT OF LIGHTS. --At night, a witness may judge the speed of an automobile by the movement of its lights, if his observation is for such a distance as to enable him to form an intelligent opinion. Jones v. Horton, 264 N.C. 549, 142 S.E.2d 351 (1965).

SUBMISSION OF CIRCUMSTANTIAL EVIDENCE. --Though the evidence on the part of plaintiff is not direct, but circumstantial, yet it may be sufficient evidence to be submitted to the jury that defendant was exceeding the speed limit contrary to this section. Jones v. Bagwell, 207 N.C. 378, 177 S.E. 170 (1934).

EVIDENCE WAS INSUFFICIENT TO BE SUBMITTED TO JURY ON THE QUESTION OF MAXIMUM SPEED LIMIT FOR BUSINESS DISTRICT where it did not bring the locale of the collision within the statutory definition of such district. Tillman v. Bellamy, 242 N.C. 201, 87 S.E.2d 253 (1955).

AS TO EVIDENCE SHOWING EXCESSIVE SPEED, see State v. Goins, 233 N.C. 460, 64 S.E.2d 289 (1951).

EVIDENCE TENDING TO SHOW SPEED GREATER THAN WAS REASONABLE AND PRUDENT. --Evidence tending to show that the driver of a truck was traveling 35 to 40 miles per hour in an early morning fog which limited visibility to 100 or 125 feet, that he had overtaken a vehicle traveling in the same direction and was attempting to pass such vehicle 250 or 300 feet before reaching a curve, and that he collided with plaintiff's car which approached from the opposite direction, was held sufficient to be submitted to the jury on the issue of the negligence of the driver of the truck. Winfield v. Smith, 230 N.C. 392, 53 S.E.2d 251 (1949).

EVIDENCE NEGATIVING EXCESSIVE SPEED.
--In the light of admitted facts as to the length of
marks on the shoulder of highway and the point at
which truck came to rest, suggestion of a speed of 45
miles per hour as the truck was leaving the highway
and going on the shoulder was contrary to human experience. Tysinger v. Coble Dairy Prods., 225 N.C. 717,
36 S.E.2d 246 (1945).

SUFFICIENT EVIDENCE TO OVERRULE DE-
FENDANT'S MOTION HELD FOR NONSUIT.
--Evidence that defendant was driving his car at a
speed of 50 to 55 miles per hour, on or near the center of the highway, when he collided with another car,
resulting in the death of the driver thereof, was held
sufficient to overrule defendant's motion for nonsuit
in a prosecution for manslaughter, although defendant introduced evidence in sharp conflict. State v.
Webber, 210 N.C. 137, 185 S.E. 659 (1936).

The State's evidence tending to show that defendant was driving some 80 to 90 miles per hour over a
highway whereon several other vehicles were moving
at the time was sufficient to overrule defendant's motion for nonsuit and to sustain a conviction of reckless
driving under G.S. 20-140 and of driving at a speed in
excess of 55 miles per hour in violation of this section.
State v. Vanhoy, 230 N.C. 162, 52 S.E.2d 278 (1949).

Evidence that defendant failed to yield the right-
of-way to plaintiff, who was on the right, and that defendant was driving at 50 miles per hour through intersection, raised the issue of defendant's negligence,
and motion for nonsuit at the close of all the evidence
was properly denied. Price v. Gray, 246 N.C. 162, 97
S.E.2d 844 (1957).

EVIDENCE HELD SUFFICIENT FOR SUBMIS-
SION TO JURY. --Evidence was sufficient to show
violation of this section, and to warrant submission
to the jury of the issue of defendants' negligence.
Winfield v. Smith, 230 N.C. 392, 53 S.E.2d 251 (1949);
Brafford v. Cook, 232 N.C. 699, 62 S.E.2d 327 (1950).

Evidence was sufficient to be submitted to the
jury on the question of the negligence of a driver in
traveling at excessive speed and in failing to maintain a proper lookout and in failing to keep his car
under proper control. Blalock v. Hart, 239 N.C. 475, 80
S.E.2d 373 (1954).

Mute evidence of extensive damage to front end of
defendant's car, of blood spots on car and of car coming to rest 365 feet from where other blood spots began, tended to show that defendant had not slackened
his speed of 75 to 80 miles per hour up to the moment
of striking deceased, and that he was violating this
section. State v. Phelps, 242 N.C. 540, 89 S.E.2d 132
(1955).

Evidence that a child less than five years old was
on the hard surface of a highway, unattended and
clearly visible to defendant while he traveled a distance of one-half mile, that the child ran across the
highway toward her companion, another small child,
when defendant was only some 40 feet away, and that
defendant could not then avoid striking the child, notwithstanding he had reduced his speed from some 45
miles per hour to 25 miles per hour, was sufficient to

be submitted to the jury. Henderson v. Locklear, 260
N.C. 582, 133 S.E.2d 164 (1963).

For case holding evidence sufficient to show a violation of subsection (a), see Register v. Gibbs, 233 N.C.
456, 64 S.E.2d 280 (1951).

For case holding evidence sufficient to show that
defendant was guilty of negligence in not decreasing
speed when approaching and entering an intersection
at a speed of 60 to 70 miles an hour in violation of
former subsection (c) of this section, see Stockwell v.
Brown, 254 N.C. 662, 119 S.E.2d 795 (1961).

For case holding that driver was driving at a speed
greater than was reasonable and prudent under the
conditions existing, see Cronenberg v. United States,
123 F. Supp. 693 (E.D.N.C. 1954).

Evidence that defendant, while operating an automobile under hazardous conditions, perceived an
automobile in her lane of travel, but that despite
"slamming on" her brakes she was unable to maintain
control of her automobile and slid into the rear end of
the automobile in front of her was sufficient to submit
the issue for determination by the jury. Masciulli v.
Tucker, 82 N.C. App. 200, 346 S.E.2d 305 (1986).

IV. INSTRUCTIONS.

NECESSITY OF INSTRUCTING ON CONDUCT
CONSTITUTING NEGLIGENCE PER SE. --Where
there is evidence from which the jury could draw a
reasonable inference that the defendant was driving
at a speed in excess of the statutory limit, the court
must instruct the jury, without special request therefor, that if it finds from the evidence that defendant
was operating his motor vehicle in excess of the speed
limit such conduct would constitute negligence per se.
A failure to so instruct the jury is prejudicial error
which requires reversal and a new trial. Edwards v.
Mayes, 385 F.2d 369 (4th Cir. 1967).

FAILURE TO INSTRUCT ON NEGLIGENCE PER
SE HELD NOT PREJUDICIAL ERROR. --Although
it is technically true that violation of this section's
"reasonable and prudent" standard is negligence per
se, the trial judge did not commit prejudicial error
in instructing the jury that violation of the statute
was negligence; the practical effect of an instruction
on negligence and negligence per se in regard to this
section would have been identical, and in either case,
the jury would be required to determine what was
"reasonable and prudent" under the circumstances.
Hinnant v. Holland, 92 N.C. App. 142, 374 S.E.2d 152
(1988), cert. denied, 324 N.C. 335, 378 S.E.2d 792
(1989).

FOR CASE HOLDING THAT INSTRUCTION
FAILING TO CHARGE PROVISIONS OF THIS SEC-
TION IN A CIVIL ACTION WAS ERROR, see Barnes
v. Teer, 219 N.C. 823, 15 S.E.2d 379 (1941).

INSTRUCTION ON DUTY NOT TO DRIVE AT
SPEED GREATER THAN REASONABLE. --Trial
judge did not err in refusing to instruct the jury on decedent's duty not to drive at a speed greater than was
reasonable and prudent under the conditions existing
at the time of the accident; configuration of stop lights,
fast-food mart, and police vehicles in bank parking lot
did not "heighten" decedent's duty under subsection

Chapter 20

(a) of this section and did not require judge to submit defendant's requested instruction notwithstanding the absence of any evidence about decedent's rate of speed, where, further, none of the evidence indicated that decedent saw, or should have seen, defendant turn in front of her in time for her to slow down or to sound her horn. Stutts v. Adair, 94 N.C. App. 227, 380 S.E.2d 411 (1989).

Trial court's refusal to instruct jury on decedent's duty not to drive at a speed greater than was reasonable and prudent under the conditions existing at the time of accident was not error; excessive speed is not inferred from vehicular damage. Stutts v. Adair, 94 N.C. App. 227, 380 S.E.2d 411 (1989).

Although a trial judge instructed the jury that every person was under a duty to follow standards of conduct established by a safety statute and that a person's failure to do so was negligence in and of itself, the only specific safety statute on which he then charged the jury was G.S. 20-141(a), to the effect that no person should drive a vehicle at a speed greater than was reasonable under the conditions then existing; this instruction was insufficient to act as substitute for a charge that defendant violated G.S. 20-146 because the jury was limited to finding negligence on the basis of defendant's violation of a safety statute if it found that he was driving his vehicle at a speed greater than was reasonable and prudent at the time instead of permitting the jury to consider, alternatively, that defendant was negligent because of actions that caused his vehicle to cross the center line and collide with plaintiff's car in plaintiff's lane of travel. Sobczak v. Vorholt, 181 N.C. App. 629, 640 S.E.2d 805 (2007).

INSTRUCTION OF DOCTRINE OF SUDDEN EMERGENCY HELD ERROR under the evidence. Masciulli v. Tucker, 82 N.C. App. 200, 346 S.E.2d 305 (1986).

INSTRUCTION AS TO SPECIAL HAZARDS HELD WITHOUT ERROR. --The trial court's instruction correctly defining "residential district" and charging that the lawful speed therein was 25 miles an hour, but that this limitation did not relieve the driver from further reducing his speed if made necessary by special hazards in order to avoid colliding with any person or vehicle, was without error. Reid v. City Coach Co., 215 N.C. 469, 2 S.E.2d 578, 123 A.L.R. 140 (1939).

INSTRUCTION ON DUTY TO DECREASE SPEED. --The trial judge committed reversible error in refusing to instruct the jury regarding the duty to decrease speed under subsection (m). Hinnant v. Holland, 92 N.C. App. 142, 374 S.E.2d 152 (1988), cert. denied, 324 N.C. 335, 378 S.E.2d 792 (1989).

Judge was not required to instruct the jury about decedent's duty to decrease her speed to the extent necessary to avoid a collision, where nothing in the record indicated that decedent had the opportunity to slow down when defendant entered her path of travel, and where there was no evidence that decedent saw, or should have seen, defendant in time to react to his

presence. Stutts v. Adair, 94 N.C. App. 227, 380 S.E.2d 411 (1989).

The trial court erred by refusing to instruct the jury that defendant had a duty to decrease her speed. Welling v. Walker, 117 N.C. App. 445, 451 S.E.2d 329 (1994), cert. dismissed as improvidently granted, 342 N.C. 411, 464 S.E.2d 43 (1995).

BAIL BONDSMAN CANNOT VIOLATE DRIVING LAW INSTRUCTION. --Defendant, a bail bondsman, was properly convicted of involuntary manslaughter, following a motor vehicle accident in which the defendant was pursuing in a high speed chase a person who had failed to appear in court, because the trial court did not err in instructing the jury that bail bondsmen could not violate North Carolina motor vehicle laws to make an arrest. State v. McGee, 234 N.C. App. 285, 758 S.E.2d 661 (2014).

AS TO INSTRUCTION REGARDING DUTY OF MOTORIST OPERATING A VEHICLE WITH WORN, SLICK TIRES ON A WET AND SLIPPERY HIGHWAY, see First Union Nat'l Bank v. Hackney, 270 N.C. 437, 154 S.E.2d 512 (1967).

AS TO INSTRUCTIONS UNDER FORMER SUBSECTION (C), see Kolman v. Silbert, 219 N.C. 134, 12 S.E.2d 915 (1941); Garvey v. Atlantic Greyhound Corp., 228 N.C. 166, 45 S.E.2d 58 (1947); Medlin v. Spurrier & Co., 239 N.C. 48, 79 S.E.2d 209 (1953); Pittman v. Swanson, 255 N.C. 681, 122 S.E.2d 814 (1961).

AS TO REQUIREMENTS OF CHARGE UNDER FORMER G.S. 1-180, see Lewis v. Watson, 229 N.C. 20, 47 S.E.2d 484 (1948); State v. Vanhoy, 230 N.C. 162, 52 S.E.2d 278 (1949).

CROSS REFERENCES. --
As to minimum speed on inside lanes of certain dual-lane highways, see G.S. 20-146(e).

LEGAL PERIODICALS. --
For comment on the 1941 amendment, see 19 N.C.L. Rev. 455 (1941).

For comment on the 1949 amendment, see 27 N.C.L. Rev. 473 (1949).

For comment on the 1953 amendment, see 31 N.C.L. Rev. 415 (1953).

For article on proof of negligence in North Carolina, see 48 N.C.L. Rev. 731 (1970).

OPINIONS OF THE ATTORNEY GENERAL

SUBSECTION (E) OF THIS SECTION SPECIFICALLY AUTHORIZES THE MUNICIPAL CORPORATION TO SET A SPEED LIMIT OF LESS THAN 35 miles per hour on streets within the municipality which are not part of the State highway system. See opinion of Attorney General to Mr. Robert M. Bennett, City Engineer, City of Fayetteville, 54 N.C.A.G. 65 (1985).

EFFECT OF SUBSECTION (M). --Subsection (m) of this section creates a criminal offense of failure to decrease speed as necessary to avoid a collision as well as a "standard of care" in establishing civil negligence. See opinion of Attorney General to Ms. Mary Claire McNaught, Public Safety Attorney, Winston-Salem, N.C., 48 N.C.A.G. 138 (1979).

A MUNICIPAL ORDINANCE LIMITING SPEED ON NONSYSTEM STREETS IS INEFFECTIVE

WITHOUT SIGNS. --See opinion of Attorney General to Mr. James B. Garland, Assistant Gastonia City Attorney, 41 N.C.A.G. 167 (1970).

REDUCTION OF SPEED LIMITS ON STATE HIGHWAYS IN SCHOOL ZONES WITHIN MUNICIPALITIES. --Section 20-141.1 must be construed together with this section, G.S. 20-169, and other statutes, and when so construed, the provision for concurring ordinances in this section when reducing speed limits on State highways in school zones within municipalities must be given effect and must be complied with. See opinion of the Attorney General to Mr. Ralph D. Karpinos, Town Attorney, Chapel Hill, N.C., 58 N.C.A.G. 17 (Feb. 26, 1988).

A municipal ordinance adopted pursuant to G.S. 20-141.1 reducing the speed in a school zone on a State Highway System street is not effective without a concurring ordinance by the Department of Transportation as provided for by subsection (f) of this section. See opinion of the Attorney General to Mr. Ralph D. Karpinos, Town Attorney, Chapel Hill, N.C., 58 N.C.A.G. 17 (Feb. 26, 1988).

OPERATING MILITARY TACTICAL VEHICLES AT SLOW SPEEDS DOES NOT VIOLATE THE NORTH CAROLINA MOTOR VEHICLE CODE. See opinion of Attorney General to Colonel Kenneth C. Sallenger, Command Logistics Officer, North Carolina National Guard, 1999 N.C.A.G. 4 (1/21/99).

§ 20-141.1. Speed limits in school zones

The Board of Transportation or local authorities within their respective jurisdictions may, by ordinance, set speed limits lower than those designated in G.S. 20-141 for areas adjacent to or near a public, private or parochial school. Limits set pursuant to this section shall become effective when signs are erected giving notice of the school zone, the authorized speed limit, and the days and hours when the lower limit is effective, or by erecting signs giving notice of the school zone, the authorized speed limit and which indicate the days and hours the lower limit is effective by an electronic flasher operated with a time clock. Limits set pursuant to this section may be enforced only on days when school is in session, and no speed limit below 20 miles per hour may be set under the authority of this section. A person who drives a motor vehicle in a school zone at a speed greater than the speed limit set and posted under this section is responsible for an infraction and is required to pay a penalty of two hundred fifty dollars ($ 250.00).

History.
1977, c. 902, s. 2; 1979, c. 613; 1997-341, s. 1.1;2011-64, s. 1

EFFECT OF AMENDMENTS. --
Session Laws 2011-64, s. 1, effective August 25, 2011, and applicable to offenses committed on or after that date, substituted "two hundred fifty dollars ($250.00)" for "not less than twenty-five dollars ($25.00)" in the last sentence.

CITED in State v. Leonard, 213 N.C. App. 526, 711 S.E.2d 867 (2011); State v. Hawk, 236 N.C. App. 177, 762 S.E.2d 883 (2014).

OPINIONS OF THE ATTORNEY GENERAL

PURPOSE OF SECTION. --The purpose of the act adopting this section was "to increase the drivers license points for speed violations in school zones" from two to three points. See opinion of the Attorney General to Mr. Ralph D. Karpinos, Town Attorney, Chapel Hill, N.C., 58 N.C.A.G. 17 (Feb. 26, 1988).

Without the adoption of this section there would have been no formal charge to correspond to the increased points provided for in G.S. 20-16(c). See opinion of the Attorney General to Mr. Ralph D. Karpinos, Town Attorney, Chapel Hill, N.C., 58 N.C.A.G. 17 (Feb. 26, 1988).

This section, when passed, was only incidental to increase the drivers license points for speed violations in school zones. Authorization to reduce speed in school zones was already provided for by other statutes and the "Manual on Uniform Traffic Control Devices", which the Department is required to comply with by federal-aid provisions and G.S. 20-169. See opinion of the Attorney General to Mr. Ralph D. Karpinos, Town Attorney, Chapel Hill, N.C., 58 N.C.A.G. 17 (Feb. 26, 1988).

REDUCTION OF SPEED LIMITS ON STATE HIGHWAYS IN SCHOOL ZONES WITHIN MUNICIPALITIES. --This section must be construed together with G.S. 20-141, G.S. 20-169, and other statutes, and when so construed, the provision for concurring ordinances in G.S. 20-141 when reducing speed limits on State highways in school zones within municipalities must be given effect and must be complied with. See opinion of the Attorney General to Mr. Ralph D. Karpinos, Town Attorney, Chapel Hill, N.C., 58 N.C.A.G. 17 (Feb. 26, 1988).

A municipal ordinance adopted pursuant to this section reducing the speed in a school zone on a State Highway System street is not effective without a concurring ordinance by the Department of Transportation as provided for by G.S. 20-141(f). See opinion of the Attorney General to Mr. Ralph D. Karpinos, Town Attorney, Chapel Hill, N.C., 58 N.C.A.G. 17 (Feb. 26, 1988).

§ 20-141.2. Prima facie rule of evidence as to operation of motor vehicle altered so as to increase potential speed

Proof of the operation upon any street or highway of North Carolina at a speed in excess of the limits provided by law of any motor vehicle when the motor, or any mechanical part or feature, or the design of the motor vehicle has been changed or altered so that there is a variation between such motor vehicle as changed or altered and the motor vehicle as constructed according to specification of the original motor vehicle manufacturer, with the result that the potential speed of such vehicle has been increased beyond that which existed prior to such change or alteration, or the proof of operation upon any street or highway of North Carolina at a speed in excess of the limits provided by law of any motor vehicle assembled from parts of two or more different makes of motor vehicles, whether or not any specially made or specially designed parts or appliances are included in the manufacture and assembly thereof, shall be prima facie evidence that such motor vehicle was operated at such time by the registered owner thereof.

History.
1953, c. 1220

LEGAL PERIODICALS. --
For brief comment on this section, see 31 N.C.L. Rev. 418 (1953).

§ 20-141.3. Unlawful racing on streets and highways

(a) It shall be unlawful for any person to operate a motor vehicle on a street or highway willfully in prearranged speed competition with another motor vehicle. Any person violating the provisions of this subsection shall be guilty of a Class 1 misdemeanor.

(b) It shall be unlawful for any person to operate a motor vehicle on a street or highway willfully in speed competition with another motor vehicle. Any person willfully violating the provisions of this subsection shall be guilty of a Class 2 misdemeanor.

(c) It shall be unlawful for any person to authorize or knowingly permit a motor vehicle owned by him or under his control to be operated on a public street, highway, or thoroughfare in prearranged speed competition with another motor vehicle, or to place or receive any bet, wager, or other thing of value from the outcome of any prearranged speed competition on any public street, highway, or thoroughfare. Any person violating the provisions of this subsection shall be guilty of a Class 1 misdemeanor.

(d) The Commissioner of Motor Vehicles shall revoke the driver's license or privilege to drive of every person convicted of violating the provisions of subsection (a) or subsection (c) of this section, said revocation to be for three years; provided any person whose license has been revoked under this section may apply for a new license after 18 months from revocation. Upon filing of such application the Division may issue a new license upon satisfactory proof that the former licensee has been of good behavior for the past 18 months and that his conduct and attitude are such as to entitle him to favorable consideration and upon such terms and conditions which the Division may see fit to impose for the balance of the three-year revocation period, which period shall be computed from the date of the original revocation.

(e) The Commissioner may suspend the driver's license or privilege to drive of every person convicted of violating the provisions of subsection (b) of this section. Such suspension shall be for a period of time within the discretion of the Commissioner, but not to exceed one year.

(f) All suspensions and revocations made pursuant to the provisions of this section shall be in the same form and manner and shall be subject to all procedures as now provided for suspensions and revocations made under the provisions of Article 2 of Chapter 20 of the General Statutes.

(g) When any officer of the law discovers that any person has operated or is operating a motor vehicle willfully in prearranged speed competition with another motor vehicle on a street or highway, he shall seize the motor vehicle and deliver the same to the sheriff of the county in which such offense is committed, or the same shall be placed under said sheriff's constructive possession if delivery of actual possession is impractical, and the vehicle shall be held by the sheriff pending the trial of the person or persons arrested for operating such motor vehicle in violation of subsection (a) of this section. The sheriff shall restore the seized motor vehicle to the owner upon execution by the owner of a good and valid bond, with sufficient sureties, in an amount double the value of the property, which bond shall be approved by said sheriff and shall be conditioned on the return of the motor vehicle to the custody of the sheriff on the day of trial of the person or persons accused. Upon the acquittal of the person charged with operating said motor vehicle willfully in prearranged speed competition with another motor vehicle, the sheriff shall return the motor vehicle to the owner thereof.

Notwithstanding the provisions for sale set out above, on petition by a lienholder, the court, in its discretion and upon such terms and conditions as it may prescribe, may allow reclamation of the vehicle by the lienholder. The lienholder shall file with the court an accounting of the proceeds of any subsequent sale of the vehicle and pay into the court any proceeds received in excess of the amount of the lien.

Upon conviction of the operator of said motor vehicle of a violation of subsection (a) of this section, the court shall order a sale at public auction of said motor vehicle and the officer making the sale, after deducting the expenses of keeping the motor vehicle, the fee for the seizure, and the costs of the sale, shall pay all liens, according to their priorities, which are established, by intervention or otherwise, at said hearing or in other proceeding brought for said purpose, as being bona fide, and shall pay the balance of the proceeds to the proper officer of the county who receives fines and forfeitures to be used for the school fund of the county. All liens against a motor vehicle sold under the provisions of this section shall be transferred from the motor vehicle to the proceeds of its sale. If, at the time of hearing, or other proceeding in which the matter is considered, the owner of the vehicle can establish to the satisfaction of the court that said motor vehicle was used in prearranged speed competition with another motor vehicle on a street or highway without the knowledge or consent of the owner, and that the owner had no reasonable grounds to believe that the motor vehicle would be used for such purpose, the court shall not order a sale of the vehicle but shall restore it to the owner, and the said owner shall, at his request, be entitled to a trial by jury upon such issues.

If the owner of said motor vehicle cannot be found, the taking of the same, with a description thereof, shall be advertised in some newspaper published in the city or county where taken, or, if there be no newspaper published in such city or county, in a newspaper having circulation in the county, once a week for two weeks and by handbills posted in three public places near the place of seizure, and if said owner shall not appear within 10 days after the last publication of the advertisement, the property shall be sold, or otherwise disposed of in the manner set forth in this section.

When any vehicle confiscated under the provisions of this section is found to be specially equipped or modified from its original manufactured condition so as to increase its speed, the court shall, prior to sale, order that the special equipment or modification be removed and destroyed and the vehicle restored to its original manufactured condition. However, if the court should find that such equipment and modifications are so extensive that it would be impractical to restore said vehicle to its original manufactured condition, then the court may order that the vehicle be turned over to such governmental agency or public official within the territorial jurisdiction of the court as the court shall see fit, to be used in the performance of official duties only, and not for resale, transfer, or disposition other than as junk: Provided, that nothing herein contained shall affect the rights of lienholders and other claimants to said vehicles as set out in this section.

History.

1955, c. 1156; 1957, c. 1358; 1961, c. 354; 1963, c. 318; 1967, c. 446; 1969, c. 186, s. 3; 1973, c. 1330, s. 8; 1975, c. 716, s. 5; 1979, c. 667, s. 31; 1993, c. 539, ss. 368-370; 1994, Ex. Sess., c. 24, s. 14(c);1995, c. 163, ss. 8, 9

THE WORD "RACE," when used in conjunction with the operation of a motor vehicle on the highway, describes "speed competition with another motor vehicle" and is sufficient to charge a violation of this section. State v. Turner, 13 N.C. App. 603, 186 S.E.2d 681, cert. denied, 281 N.C. 157, 187 S.E.2d 587 (1972).

VIOLATION OF THE RACING STATUTE IS NEGLIGENT PER SE. Harrington v. Collins, 40 N.C. App. 530, 253 S.E.2d 288, aff'd, 298 N.C. 535, 259 S.E.2d 275 (1979).

Violation of subsections (a) and (b) of this section is negligence per se. Those who participate are on a joint venture and are encouraging and inciting each other. The primary negligence involved is the race itself. Boykin v. Bennett, 253 N.C. 725, 118 S.E.2d 12 (1961).

A violation of subsection (b) of this section is negligence per se. Lewis v. Brunston, 78 N.C. App. 678, 338 S.E.2d 595 (1986).

VIOLATION AS WILFUL OR WANTON NEGLIGENCE. --A violation of subsection (b) of this section constitutes wilful or wanton negligence. Lewis v. Brunston, 78 N.C. App. 678, 338 S.E.2d 595 (1986).

ALL ENGAGED IN RACE ARE LIABLE. --Racing on the public highways is a plain and serious danger to every other person using the way. When persons are making such unlawful use of the highways and another is injured thereby, the former are liable in damages for the injuries sustained by the latter. And where a person is injured by such racing, all engaged in the race are liable even though only one, or even none, of the vehicles came in contact with the injured person. Boykin v. Bennett, 253 N.C. 725, 118 S.E.2d 12 (1961).

All who willfully participate in speed competition between motor vehicles on a public highway are jointly and concurrently negligent and if damage to one not involved in the race proximately results from it, all participants are liable, regardless of which of the racing cars actually inflicts the injury, and regardless of the fact that the injured person was a passenger in one of the racing vehicles. Boykin v. Bennett, 253 N.C. 725, 118 S.E.2d 12 (1961).

BUT PASSENGER MUST ACTIVELY PARTICIPATE TO BE NEGLIGENT. --In order for a passenger to be a party to the offense under subsection (a) of this section and to be jointly and concurrently negligent, he must do more than fail to speak, remonstrate or leave the car. The evidence must show that the passenger in some way participated or was involved in the race in order to constitute acquiescence. Harrington v. Collins, 40 N.C. App. 530, 253 S.E.2d 288, aff'd, 298 N.C. 535, 259 S.E.2d 275 (1979).

Where defendant driver's participation in a prearranged speed competition in violation of this section constituted willful or wanton conduct and was a proximate cause of plaintiff's injuries, and plaintiff had no notice of an agreement to race when he entered the car, plaintiff's failure to remonstrate or to leave the car at a rural crossroads minutes past midnight on a cold Christmas Eve did not constitute willful or wanton conduct as a matter of law which would bar his action against the driver of the second car involved in the race for injuries caused by defendant's willful or wanton conduct. Harrington v. Collins, 298 N.C. 535, 259 S.E.2d 275 (1979).

DEFENDANT'S PARTICIPATION IN A PREARRANGED AUTOMOBILE RACE CONSTITUTED WILLFUL OR WANTON CONDUCT and was, as a matter of law, a proximate cause of injuries received

Chapter 20

by plaintiff passenger in a collision during the race. Harrington v. Collins, 40 N.C. App. 530, 253 S.E.2d 288, aff'd, 298 N.C. 535, 259 S.E.2d 275 (1979).

PROXIMATE CAUSE OF COLLISION. --Evidence showing that about one-half mile before and immediately prior to the accident defendants were driving their cars at night "bumper to bumper" at speeds of 75 to 80 m.p.h. on road where the speed limit was 45 m.p.h., if believed by the jury, was sufficient to support a finding by the jury that defendants operated their cars wilfully in speed competition in violation of subsection (b) of this section and that their negligence in this respect proximately caused collision. Lewis v. Brunston, 78 N.C. App. 678, 338 S.E.2d 595 (1986).

ACQUITTAL OF RECKLESS DRIVING IN A COURT HAVING JURISDICTION TO TRY DEFENDANT FOR THAT OFFENSE WOULD NOT BAR DEFENDANT'S PROSECUTION IN SUPERIOR COURT FOR INVOLUNTARY MANSLAUGHTER arising out of the same occurrence. Reckless driving and speed competition are not lesser included offenses of the charge of involuntary manslaughter. State v. Sawyer, 11 N.C. App. 81, 180 S.E.2d 387 (1971).

INSTRUCTION IN PROSECUTION FOR INVOLUNTARY MANSLAUGHTER. --In a prosecution for involuntary manslaughter arising out of a violation of this section, an instruction which would permit the jury to find defendant guilty of involuntary manslaughter without first finding beyond a reasonable doubt that the speed competition was a proximate cause of the collision was erroneous. State v. Sawyer, 11 N.C. App. 81, 180 S.E.2d 387 (1971).

THE TRIAL COURT DID NOT ERR IN FAILING TO CHARGE the jury on the issue of whether or not the defendant engaged in a willful speed competition, where there was no evidence that the defendant purposely and deliberately engaged in a race. Hord v. Atkinson, 68 N.C. App. 346, 315 S.E.2d 339 (1984).

APPLIED in State v. Daniel, 255 N.C. 717, 122 S.E.2d 704 (1961); Mason v. Gillikin, 256 N.C. 527, 124 S.E.2d 537 (1962).

CITED in Orange Speedway, Inc. v. Clayton, 247 N.C. 528, 101 S.E.2d 406 (1958); State v. Triplett, 70 N.C. App. 341, 318 S.E.2d 913 (1984); Hinson v. Jarvis, 190 N.C. App. 607, 660 S.E.2d 604 (2008), review dismissed, as moot, 363 N.C. 126, 675 S.E.2d 365 (2009), review denied, 363 N.C. 126, 675 S.E.2d 366 (2009).

§ 20-141.4. Felony and misdemeanor death by vehicle; felony serious injury by vehicle; aggravated offenses; repeat felony death by vehicle

(a) Repealed by Session Laws 1983, c. 435, s. 27.

(a1) **Felony Death by Vehicle.** -- A person commits the offense of felony death by vehicle if:

　　(1) The person unintentionally causes the death of another person,

　　(2) The person was engaged in the offense of impaired driving under G.S. 20-138.1 or G.S. 20-138.2, and

　　(3) The commission of the offense in subdivision (2) of this subsection is the proximate cause of the death.

(a2) **Misdemeanor Death by Vehicle.** -- A person commits the offense of misdemeanor death by vehicle if:

　　(1) The person unintentionally causes the death of another person,

　　(2) The person was engaged in the violation of any State law or local ordinance applying to the operation or use of a vehicle or to the regulation of traffic, other than impaired driving under G.S. 20-138.1, and

　　(3) The commission of the offense in subdivision (2) of this subsection is the proximate cause of the death.

(a3) **Felony Serious Injury by Vehicle.** -- A person commits the offense of felony serious injury by vehicle if:

　　(1) The person unintentionally causes serious injury to another person,

　　(2) The person was engaged in the offense of impaired driving under G.S. 20-138.1 or G.S. 20-138.2, and

　　(3) The commission of the offense in subdivision (2) of this subsection is the proximate cause of the serious injury.

(a4) **Aggravated Felony Serious Injury by Vehicle.** -- A person commits the offense of aggravated felony serious injury by vehicle if:

　　(1) The person unintentionally causes serious injury to another person,

　　(2) The person was engaged in the offense of impaired driving under G.S. 20-138.1 or G.S. 20-138.2,

　　(3) The commission of the offense in subdivision (2) of this subsection is the proximate cause of the serious injury, and

　　(4) The person has a previous conviction involving impaired driving, as defined in G.S. 20-4.01(24a), within seven years of the date of the offense.

(a5) **Aggravated Felony Death by Vehicle.** -- A person commits the offense of aggravated felony death by vehicle if:

　　(1) The person unintentionally causes the death of another person,

　　(2) The person was engaged in the offense of impaired driving under G.S. 20-138.1 or G.S. 20-138.2,

　　(3) The commission of the offense in subdivision (2) of this subsection is the proximate cause of the death, and

　　(4) The person has a previous conviction involving impaired driving, as defined in G.S. 20-4.01(24a), within seven years of the date of the offense.

(a6) **Repeat Felony Death by Vehicle Offender.** -- A person commits the offense of repeat felony death by vehicle if:

(1) The person commits an offense under subsection (a1) or subsection (a5) of this section; and

(2) The person has a previous conviction under:

    a. Subsection (a1) of this section;

    b. Subsection (a5) of this section; or

    c. G.S. 14-17 or G.S. 14-18, and the basis of the conviction was the unintentional death of another person while engaged in the offense of impaired driving under G.S. 20-138.1 or G.S. 20-138.2.

The pleading and proof of previous convictions shall be in accordance with the provisions of G.S. 15A-928.

(b) **Punishments.** -- Unless the conduct is covered under some other provision of law providing greater punishment, the following classifications apply to the offenses set forth in this section:

(1) Repeat felony death by vehicle is a Class B2 felony.

(1a) Aggravated felony death by vehicle is a Class D felony. Notwithstanding the provisions of G.S. 15A-1340.17, the court shall sentence the defendant in the aggravated range of the appropriate Prior Record Level.

(2) Felony death by vehicle is a Class D felony. Notwithstanding the provisions of G.S. 15A-1340.17, intermediate punishment is authorized for a defendant who is a Prior Record Level I offender.

(3) Aggravated felony serious injury by vehicle is a Class E felony.

(4) Felony serious injury by vehicle is a Class F felony.

(5) Misdemeanor death by vehicle is a Class A1 misdemeanor.

(c) **No Double Prosecutions.** -- No person who has been placed in jeopardy upon a charge of death by vehicle may be prosecuted for the offense of manslaughter arising out of the same death; and no person who has been placed in jeopardy upon a charge of manslaughter may be prosecuted for death by vehicle arising out of the same death.

History.
1973, c. 1330, s. 9; 1983, c. 435, s. 27; 1993, c. 285, s. 10;c. 539, ss. 371, 1259; 1994, Ex. Sess., c. 24, s. 14(c);2006-253, s. 14;2007-493, s. 15;2009-528, s. 1;2012-165, s. 2, 3

EDITOR'S NOTE. --
Subdivision (b)(5) as amended by Session Laws 2009-528, s. 1, effective December 1, 2009, is applicable to offenses committed on or after that date.

Session Laws 2012-165, in its preamble provides: "Whereas, the State must prove that the defendant acted with malice to obtain a conviction of second degree murder; and

"Whereas, North Carolina case law holds that malice may be shown in three different ways: by hatred, ill will, or spite; a condition of the mind which prompts a person to take the life of another intentionally or to intentionally inflict serious bodily injury which proximately results in another's death, without just cause, excuse or justification; or the commission of an inherently dangerous act or omission, in such a reckless and wanton manner as to manifest a mind utterly without regard for human life and social duty and deliberately bent on mischief; Now, therefore;"

Session Laws 2012-165, s. 4, made the amendments to this section by Session Laws 2012-165, ss. 2 and 3, applicable to offenses committed on or after December 1, 2012.

EFFECT OF AMENDMENTS. --
Session Laws 2006-253, s. 14, effective December 1, 2006, and applicable to offenses committed on or after that date, rewrote the section.

Session Laws 2007-493, s. 15, effective August 30, 2007, rewrote subsection (a6). For applicability provision, see Editor's note.

Session Laws 2012-165, ss. 2 and 3, effective December 1, 2012, deleted the last paragraph of subsection (a)(6), which formerly read: "A person convicted under this subsection shall be subject to the same sentence as if the person had been convicted of second degree murder"; added present subdivision (b)(1) and redesignated former subdivision (b)(1) as present subdivision (b)(1a); added the last sentence in subdivision (b)(1a); and, in subdivision (b)(2), substituted "Class D felony" for "Class E felony" and added the last sentence. For applicability, see Editor's note.

EDITOR'S NOTE. --Some of the cases cited below were decided under corresponding provisions of former law and under this section as it read prior to the 1983 amendment and the 1993 amendment, which reduced the blood alcohol content for driving while impaired and related offenses from 0.10 to 0.08.

THIS SECTION HELD NOT UNCONSTITUTIONAL AS APPLIED TO DEFENDANT who was found to have caused victim's death in violating G.S. 20-150(a), which violation constituted ordinary negligence. State v. Smith, 90 N.C. App. 161, 368 S.E.2d 33 (1988) aff'd, 323 N.C. 703, 374 S.E.2d 866, cert. denied, 490 U.S. 1100, 109 S. Ct. 2453, 104 L. Ed. 2d 1007 (1989).

LEGISLATIVE INTENT. --The intention of the legislature in enacting this section was to define a crime of lesser degree of manslaughter wherein criminal responsibility for death by vehicle is not dependent upon the presence of culpable or criminal negligence. State v. Freeman, 31 N.C. App. 93, 228 S.E.2d 516, cert. denied, 291 N.C. 449, 230 S.E.2d 766 (1976).

FELONY MURDER RULE MAY BE USED IN AUTOMOBILE CASES where an underlying felony is committed, even though the General Assembly has enacted the more specific statutes of felony death by vehicle and misdemeanor death by vehicle. State v. Jones, 133 N.C. App. 448, 516 S.E.2d 405 (1999), aff'd in part, rev'd in part on other grounds, and remanded, 353 N.C. 159, 538 S.E.2d 917 (2000).

THE PURPOSE OF SUBSECTION (C) of this section is not to prevent the courts from treating one offense as a lesser included offense of the other, but rather to prevent the State from bringing a new prosecution against a defendant for death by vehicle after he has already been convicted or acquitted of manslaughter. State v. Freeman, 31 N.C. App. 93, 228 S.E.2d 516, cert. denied, 291 N.C. 449, 230 S.E.2d 766 (1976).

EVERY ELEMENT OF THIS SECTION IS EMBRACED IN THE COMMON-LAW DEFINITION OF INVOLUNTARY MANSLAUGHTER. State v. Freeman, 31 N.C. App. 93, 228 S.E.2d 516, cert. denied, 291 N.C. 449, 230 S.E.2d 766 (1976).

ELEMENTS OF FELONY DEATH BY VEHICLE. --The offense of felony death by vehicle requires the identical essential elements to those required for a conviction of involuntary manslaughter predicated on a violation of G.S. 20-138.1, to wit: a willful violation of G.S. 20-138.1 and a causal link between that violation and the death. State v. Williams, 90 N.C. App. 615, 369 S.E.2d 832, cert. denied, 323 N.C. 369, 373 S.E.2d 555 (1988).

STATUTE DID NOT PREVENT PROSECUTION UNDER BOTH DEATH BY VEHICLE AND MANSLAUGHTER THEORIES. --Trial court properly denied defendant's pretrial motion to dismiss and/or have the State elect between death by vehicle and manslaughter charges because, under G.S. 20-141.4(c), while defendant may not have been sentenced for both crimes, the statute did not prevent prosecution under both theories. State v. Elmore, 224 N.C. App. 331, 736 S.E.2d 568 (2012).

FELONY DEATH BY VEHICLE IS NOT A LESSER INCLUDED OFFENSE of involuntary manslaughter while driving under the influence of alcohol. State v. Williams, 90 N.C. App. 615, 369 S.E.2d 832, cert. denied, 323 N.C. 369, 373 S.E.2d 555 (1988).

DRIVING WHILE IMPAIRED IS A LESSER INCLUDED OFFENSE OF FELONY DEATH BY VEHICLE, and upon conviction of felony death by vehicle the lesser offense merges into the greater; thus, it was error to sentence defendant both for felony death by vehicle and the lesser included offense of driving while impaired. State v. Richardson, 96 N.C. App. 270, 385 S.E.2d 194 (1989).

ELEMENTS OF FELONY SERIOUS INJURY BY VEHICLE REQUIRE CONVICTION OF LESSER CRIME OF DRIVING WHILE IMPAIRED. --Trial court erred in accepting inconsistent verdict of not guilty of driving while impaired, under G.S. 20-138.1, yet guilty of felony serious injury by vehicle, under G.S. 20-141.4(a3), because the elements of the greater crime statutorily required conviction of the lesser crime. State v. Mumford, 201 N.C. App. 594, 688 S.E.2d 458 (2010).

SPECIFIC INTENT TO CAUSE DEATH NOT REQUIRED. --The phrase "intentionally causes the death of another person" as used within this section refers not to the presence of a specific intent to cause death, but rather to the fact that the act which resulted in death is intentionally committed and is an act of impaired driving under G.S. 20-138.1. State v.

Williams, 90 N.C. App. 615, 369 S.E.2d 832, cert. denied, 323 N.C. 369, 373 S.E.2d 555 (1988).

INTENTIONAL ACT OF IMPAIRED DRIVING REQUIRED FOR VIOLATION OF G.S. 20-141.4. --Trial court properly denied defendant's motion to dismiss the charge of felonious serious injury by motor vehicle, G.S. 20-141.4(a3), because there was evidence upon which the jury could find that defendant's intoxication was a proximate cause of the victim's injuries, and a man of ordinary prudence could have foreseen an accident resulting from drinking and driving; two officers testified that defendant appeared impaired, and at trial, defendant stipulated to a blood alcohol concentration of .10, which was over the legal driving limit. State v. Leonard, 213 N.C. App. 526, 711 S.E.2d 867 (2011).

DEFENDANT MAY ASSERT INTERVENING NEGLIGENCE OF ANOTHER. --A defendant charged with death by vehicle under this section may assert the intervening negligence of another as a defense. State v. Tioran, 65 N.C. App. 122, 308 S.E.2d 659 (1983).

EVIDENCE THAT DEFENDANT'S INTOXICATION PROXIMATE CAUSE OF INJURY. --Even if defendant's willful attempt to elude arrest in violation of G.S. 20-141.5 was a cause of the victim's injury, his driving under the influence in violation of G.S. 20-138.1 could also be a proximate cause of the injury under G.S. 20-141.4(a3) because defendant's violation of G.S. 20-138.1 did not have to be the only proximate cause of the victim's injury in order for defendant to be found criminally liable; a showing that defendant's action of driving while under the influence was one of the proximate causes was sufficient. State v. Leonard, 213 N.C. App. 526, 711 S.E.2d 867 (2011).

Trial court properly denied defendant's motion to dismiss the charge of felonious serious injury by motor vehicle, G.S. 20-141.4(a3), because there was evidence upon which the jury could find that defendant's intoxication was a proximate cause of the victim's injuries, and a man of ordinary prudence could have foreseen an accident resulting from drinking and driving; two officers testified that defendant appeared impaired, and at trial, defendant stipulated to a blood alcohol concentration of .10, which was over the legal driving limit. State v. Leonard, 213 N.C. App. 526, 711 S.E.2d 867 (2011).

PROSECUTION AFTER CONVICTION UNDER G.S. 20-158 AS DOUBLE JEOPARDY. --Where defendant entered a plea of guilty to a charge of failing to yield the right-of-way in violation of G.S. 20-158 and a passenger thereafter died from injuries received in the resultant accident, the trial of defendant on a charge of death by vehicle under this section "in that he did unlawfully and willfully fail to yield the right-of-way . . . in violation of General Statute 20-158" would place defendant in jeopardy for a second time on the charge of failure to yield the right-of-way in violation U.S. Const., Amend. V. State v. Griffin, 51 N.C. App. 564, 277 S.E.2d 77 (1981).

CHARGE BASED ON VIOLATION OF G.S. 20-174(E). --Where the evidence was sufficient to permit conviction for a violation of G.S. 20-174(e), submission of the charge of death by vehicle based on a violation of that section was proper. State v. Fearing, 48 N.C. App. 329, 269 S.E.2d 245 (1980), aff'd in part and rev'd in part on other grounds, 304 N.C. 471, 284 S.E.2d 448 (1981).

CHARGE PROPERLY REFUSED. --Trial court did not err in failing to submit to the jury a possible verdict of misdemeanor death by motor vehicle, as since the jury rejected involuntary manslaughter in favor of second degree murder, it would also have rejected the lesser offense of misdemeanor death by a vehicle. State v. Goodman, 149 N.C. App. 57, 560 S.E.2d 196 (2002), cert. granted, 356 N.C. 170, 568 S.E.2d 852 (2002).

A PLEA OF "RESPONSIBLE" TO THE INFRACTION OF DRIVING LEFT OF CENTER did not bar later prosecution, on double jeopardy grounds, of the defendant for misdemeanor death by vehicle, when the only basis for the misdemeanor death charge was the driving left of center infraction. State v. Hamrick, 110 N.C. App. 60, 428 S.E.2d 830, appeal dismissed, cert. denied, 334 N.C. 436, 433 S.E.2d 181 (1993).

FAILURE OF TRIAL JUDGE TO ALLOW JURY TO CONSIDER LESSER DEGREE OF HOMICIDE OF DEATH BY VEHICLE CONSTITUTED PREJUDICIAL ERROR that was not cured by a verdict of guilty of the more serious crime of involuntary manslaughter, where the evidence would have permitted the jury to find defendant guilty of death by vehicle. State v. Baum, 33 N.C. App. 633, 236 S.E.2d 31, cert. denied, 293 N.C. 253, 237 S.E.2d 536 (1977).

INSTRUCTION ON INTENTIONAL OR RECKLESS CONDUCT UPHELD. --A jury instruction which, in distinguishing death by vehicle from involuntary manslaughter, merely pointed out that with respect to the offense of death by vehicle the State is not required to prove any intentional or reckless conduct on the part of the defendant, comported with the definition in this section. State v. Thompson, 37 N.C. App. 444, 246 S.E.2d 81, cert. denied, 295 N.C. 652, 248 S.E.2d 257 (1978).

FAILURE TO INSTRUCT ON CONTRIBUTORY NEGLIGENCE. --Trial court's refusal to instruct the jury on contributory negligence when it submitted the charge of felony death by vehicle under G.S. 20-141.4(a1)to the jury did not amount to reversible error because defendant did not seek such an instruction, the requested instruction was counter to jurisprudence of North Carolina, and the jury was properly instructed. State v. Bailey, 184 N.C. App. 746, 646 S.E.2d 837 (2007).

AMENDMENT OF WARRANT'S ALLEGATIONS OF MOTOR VEHICLE VIOLATION. --Although the death by vehicle statute contemplates that some violation of a motor vehicle statute or ordinance be specified in a warrant charging death by vehicle, it is not essential that the motor vehicle violation alleged in the warrant as originally issued be the same as the motor vehicle violation alleged in the warrant as considered by the jury, where the substituted motor vehicle violation is substantially similar to that originally alleged. State v. Clements, 51 N.C. App. 113, 275 S.E.2d 222 (1981).

In a trial de novo in the superior court upon a warrant alleging death by vehicle, the trial court did not err in allowing the State to amend the warrant at the close of the State's evidence by striking an allegation of "following too closely" and adding an allegation of "failure to reduce speed to avoid an accident, a violation of G.S. 20-141(m)," since the nature of the offense with which the defendant was charged, death by vehicle, was not changed by the amendment. State v. Clements, 51 N.C. App. 113, 275 S.E.2d 222 (1981).

IT IS NOT ALWAYS NECESSARY TO HAVE AN EXPERT TESTIFY AS TO THE CAUSE OF DEATH where all of the facts disclose a set of circumstances from which any person of average intelligence could be satisfied beyond a reasonable doubt that the fatality occurred in the collision. State v. Smith, 37 N.C. App. 64, 245 S.E.2d 227 (1978).

JURISDICTION. --In a prosecution on separate bills of indictment for failing to stop an automobile at the scene of an accident in which an individual was killed under G.S. 20-166(a) and death by vehicle, where the two offenses were based on the same act or transaction, the superior court had jurisdiction of the misdemeanor offense of death by vehicle. State v. Fearing, 304 N.C. 471, 284 S.E.2d 487 (1981).

TRIAL COURT ERRED IN SENTENCING DEFENDANT FOR BOTH INVOLUNTARY MANSLAUGHTER AND FELONY DEATH BY VEHICLE ARISING OUT OF THE SAME DEATH UNDER G.S. 20-141.4(C), although the elements of both offenses were not the same, and also erred by sentencing him for both felony death by vehicle under G.S. 20-141.4(a1) and DWI under G.S. 20-138.1, because DWI was an element of felony death by vehicle. State v. Davis, 198 N.C. App. 443, 680 S.E.2d 239 (2009).

TRIAL COURT ERRED IN IMPOSING CONDITION ON DEFENDANT'S PROBATION for conviction of misdemeanor death by vehicle on payment of $500,000 restitution, with which she clearly could not comply. State v. Smith, 90 N.C. App. 161, 368 S.E.2d 33 (1988), aff'd, 323 N.C. 703, 374 S.E.2d 866 (1989), cert. denied, 490 U.S. 1100, 109 S. Ct. 2453, 104 L. Ed. 2d 1007 (1989).

Although the trial court properly used the wrongful death statute G.S. 28A-18-2 to compute the amount of restitution which defendant found guilty of misdemeanor death by vehicle should pay, it erred in its application of G.S. 28A-18-2. State v. Smith, 90 N.C. App. 161, 368 S.E.2d 33 (1988), aff'd, 323 N.C. 703, 374 S.E.2d 866 (1989), cert. denied, 490 U.S. 1100, 109 S. Ct. 2453, 104 L. Ed. 2d 1007 (1989).

MOTION TO DISMISS IMPROPERLY DENIED. --In a case in which defendant passed a tow truck on the shoulder and struck and killed the victim, the trial court erred in denying defendant's motion to dismiss the felony death by motor vehicle charge because driving while impaired (DWI) was a necessary element of that offense, and the DWI charge was dismissed on appeal. State v. Nazzal, -- N.C. App. --, 840 S.E.2d 881 (2020).

APPLIED in State v. Moore, 107 N.C. App. 388, 420 S.E.2d 691 (1992); State v. Jones, 353 N.C. 159, 538 S.E.2d 917 (2000).

CITED in State v. Hice, 34 N.C. App. 468, 238 S.E.2d 619 (1977); State v. Howard, 70 N.C. App. 487, 320 S.E.2d 17 (1984); State v. Stroud, 78 N.C. App. 599, 337 S.E.2d 873 (1985); State v. Worthington, 89 N.C. App. 88, 365 S.E.2d 317 (1988); State v. Ealy, 94 N.C. App. 707, 381 S.E.2d 185 (1989); State v. Beale, 324 N.C. 87, 376 S.E.2d 1 (1989); North Carolina v. Ivory, 906 F.2d 999 (4th Cir. 1990); State v. Byers, 105 N.C. App. 377, 413 S.E.2d 586 (1992); State v. Hudson, 123 N.C. App. 336, 473 S.E.2d 415 (1996), rev'd on other grounds, 345 N.C. 729, 483 S.E.2d 436 (1997); State v. Blackmon, 208 N.C. App. 397, 702 S.E.2d 833 (2010); State v. Ziglar, 209 N.C. App. 461, 705 S.E.2d 417 (2011), review denied 365 N.C. 200, 710 S.E.2d 30, 2011 N.C. LEXIS 438 (N.C. 2011); State v. Young, 368 N.C. 188, 775 S.E.2d 291 (2015); State v. Cox, 253 N.C. App. 306, 800 S.E.2d 692 (2017), review denied, 803 S.E.2d 153, 2017 N.C. LEXIS 579 (N.C. 2017).

LEGAL PERIODICALS. --

For survey of 1976 case law on criminal law, see 55 N.C.L. Rev. 976 (1977).

For 1997 legislative survey, see 20 Campbell L. Rev. 417.

§ 20-141.5. Speeding to elude arrest; seizure and sale of vehicles

(a) It shall be unlawful for any person to operate a motor vehicle on a street, highway, or public vehicular area while fleeing or attempting to elude a law enforcement officer who is in the lawful performance of his duties. Except as provided in subsection (b) of this section, violation of this section shall be a Class 1 misdemeanor.

(b) If two or more of the following aggravating factors are present at the time the violation occurs, violation of this section shall be a Class H felony.

(1) Speeding in excess of 15 miles per hour over the legal speed limit.

(2) Gross impairment of the person's faculties while driving due to:

    a. Consumption of an impairing substance; or

    b. A blood alcohol concentration of 0.14 or more within a relevant time after the driving.

(3) Reckless driving as proscribed by G.S. 20-140.

(4) Negligent driving leading to an accident causing:

    a. Property damage in excess of one thousand dollars ($ 1,000); or

    b. Personal injury.

(5) Driving when the person's drivers license is revoked.

(6) Driving in excess of the posted speed limit, during the days and hours when the posted limit is in effect, on school property or in an area designated as a school zone pursuant to G.S. 20-141.1, or in a highway work zone as defined in G.S. 20-141(j2).

(7) Passing a stopped school bus as proscribed by G.S. 20-217.

(8) Driving with a child under 12 years of age in the vehicle.

(b1) When a violation of subsection (a) of this section is the proximate cause of the death of any person, the person violating subsection (a) of this section shall be guilty of a Class H felony. When a violation of subsection (b) of this section is the proximate cause of the death of any person, the person violating subsection (b) of this section shall be guilty of a Class E felony.

(c) Whenever evidence is presented in any court or administrative hearing of the fact that a vehicle was operated in violation of this section, it shall be prima facie evidence that the vehicle was operated by the person in whose name the vehicle was registered at the time of the violation, according to the Division's records. If the vehicle is rented, then proof of that rental shall be prima facie evidence that the vehicle was operated by the renter of the vehicle at the time of the violation.

(d) The Division shall suspend, for up to one year, the drivers license of any person convicted of a misdemeanor under this section. The Division shall revoke, for two years, the drivers license of any person convicted of a felony under this section if the person was convicted on the basis of the presence of two of the aggravating factors listed in subsection (b) of this section. The Division shall revoke, for three years, the drivers license of any person convicted of a felony under this section if the person was convicted on the basis of the presence of three or more aggravating factors listed in subsection (b) of this section. In the case of a first felony conviction under this section where only two aggravating factors were present, the licensee may apply to the sentencing court for a limited driving privilege after a period of 12 months of revocation, provided the operator's license has not also been revoked or suspended under any other provision of law. A limited driving privilege issued under this subsection shall be valid for the period of revocation remaining in the same manner and under the terms and conditions prescribed in G.S. 20-16.1(b). If the person's license is revoked under any other statute, the limited driving privilege issued pursuant to this subsection is invalid.

(e) When the probable cause of the law enforcement officer is based on the prima facie evidence rule set forth in subsection (c) above, the officer shall make a reasonable effort to contact the registered owner of the vehicle prior to initiating criminal process.

(f) Each law enforcement agency shall adopt a policy applicable to the pursuit of fleeing or eluding motorists. Each policy adopted pursuant to this subsection shall specifically include factors to be considered by an officer in determining when to initiate or terminate a pursuit. The Attorney General shall develop a model policy or policies to be considered for use by law enforcement agencies.

(g) through (j) Repealed by Session Laws 2013-243, s. 6, effective December 1, 2013, and applicable to offenses committed on or after that date.

(k) If a person is convicted of a violation of subsection (b) or (b1) of this section, the motor vehicle that was driven by the defendant at the time the defendant committed the offense of felony speeding to elude arrest becomes property subject to forfeiture in accordance with the procedure set out in G.S. 20-28.2, 20-28.3, 20-28.4, and 20-28.5.

History.
1997-443, s. 19.26(a);2005-341, s. 1;2011-271, s. 1;2013-243, ss. 6, 7

EDITOR'S NOTE. --
Session Laws 2005-341, s. 1, effective December 1, 2005, and applicable to offenses committed on or after that date, added present subsection (c) and redesignated former subsections (c) through (f) as present subsections (d) through (g). At the direction of the Revisor of Statutes, the new subsection (c) has been redesignated as (b1) and subsections (c) through (f) have not been redesignated.

EFFECT OF AMENDMENTS. --
Session Laws 2011-271, s. 1, effective December 1, 2011, and applicable to offenses committed on or after that date, substituted "determining when to initiate or terminate a pursuit" for "determining when it is advisable to break off a chase to stop and apprehend a suspect" in the second sentence of subsection (f); and added subsections (g) through (j).

Session Laws 2013-243, ss. 6 and 7, effective December 1, 2013, repealed subsections (g) through (j) which pertained to procedures for seizure and sale at public auction of motor vehicles in cases where a felony violation has occurred and added subsection (k). For applicability, see Editor's note.

JURY'S DUTY AS TO FINDING TWO OR MORE VIOLATIONS. --The eight aggravating factors set out by this section are not separately chargeable, discrete criminal activities requiring a jury to unanimously agree on the same two factors for purposes of aggravation; rather, the statutory factors are merely alternative ways of proving the crime of felonious speeding to elude arrest and a defendant may be convicted pursuant to this section if the jury merely agrees that he committed two of those violations although they do not agree on which two. State v. Funchess, 141 N.C. App. 302, 540 S.E.2d 435 (2000).

BECAUSE THIS STATUTE ONLY REQUIRES PROOF OF TWO OR MORE FACTORS, the State was not required to prove all three factors pertinent to defendant's case although these were stated conjunctively in the indictment. State v. Funchess, 141 N.C. App. 302, 540 S.E.2d 435 (2000).

THE FAILURE OF THE TRIAL COURT TO CHARGE ON KNOWLEDGE OF REVOCATION pursuant to G.S. 20-28 in support of an aggravated sentence under this section was not erroneous where the State's evidence tended to show that it complied with the provisions for giving notice of revocation or suspension of a driver's license found in G.S. 20-48 and the defendant neither contested that evidence nor offered contrary evidence. State v. Funchess, 141 N.C. App. 302, 540 S.E.2d 435 (2000).

FLEEING TO ELUDE ARREST NOT ESSENTIAL ELEMENT FOR INDICTMENT. --Offense of fleeing to elude arrest was not dependent on the specific duty that the officer was performing at the time of the offense, and therefore it was not an essential element required to be set out in indictment. State v. Teel, 180 N.C. App. 446, 637 S.E.2d 288 (2006).

SHOWING THAT DEFENDANT WAS DRIVING ON HIGHWAY OR STREET NOT REQUIRED. --Driving while license revoked aggravating factor of felony speeding to elude arrest under G.S. 20-141.5(b)(5) did not require a showing that defendant was on a highway or street, as G.S. 20-141.5(a) specified that a defendant had to be operating a car in a public vehicular area while fleeing police. State v. Dewalt, 209 N.C. App. 187, 703 S.E.2d 872 (2011).

INTENT TO ELUDE. --Fact that defendant preferred to be arrested by a female officer was irrelevant to determining whether defendant did in fact intend to elude; the evidence demonstrated that defendant actually intended to operate a motor vehicle in order to elude law enforcement officers. State v. Cameron, 223 N.C. App. 72, 732 S.E.2d 386 (2012).

PROPERTY VALUE. --Statute does not specifically define how to determine the value of the property damage, and the value could be either the cost to repair the property damage or the decrease in value of the damaged property as a whole, but the evidence was sufficient to support either interpretation of the amount of property damage caused by defendant; besides hitting the guardrail, defendant drove through a house and damaged a nearby shed, and the jury could use common sense to determine the damages from driving through a house alone would be in excess of $ 1,000.00. State v. Gorham, 262 N.C. App. 483, 822 S.E.2d 313 (2018).

DEFENDANT'S PRIOR CONVICTION under G.S. 20-141.5(a) obviously presented a serious risk of injury to another in the abstract; it had not been necessary to consider evidence concerning the statutory definition, and thus, in sentencing the defendant, the federal district court correctly proceeded under the "otherwise" clause of 18 U.S.C.S. § 924(e)(2)(B). United States v. Green, 2002 U.S. App. LEXIS 9656 (4th Cir. May 22, 2002), cert. denied, 537 U.S. 940, 123 S. Ct. 42, 154 L. Ed. 2d 246 (2002).

REASONABLE SUSPICION FOR POLICE TO STOP. --Defendant's conduct in failing to stop at a road checkpoint, but instead, driving through it and nearly striking an officer, gave the officer reasonable suspicion that defendant had committed several crimes, including violations of G.S. 20-141.5(a) and G.S. 20-140(a); the officer's stop and arrest of defendant were valid. State v. Mitchell, 358 N.C. 63, 592 S.E.2d 543 (2004).

Trial court did not err by denying defendant's motion to dismiss for insufficient evidence because a police officer had reasonable suspicion that criminal activity was underway and thus, was lawfully performing his duties at the time of the stop; defendant was seized once the officers placed him in handcuffs and not at the time the officer activated his blue lights as he did not heed the order and pull over and thus, did not submit to the officer's show of authority. State v. Mahatha, -- N.C. App. --, 832 S.E.2d 914 (2019).

Trial court did not err by denying defendant's motion to dismiss for insufficient evidence because a police officer had reasonable suspicion that criminal activity was underway and thus, was lawfully performing his duties at the time of the stop; the officer's subsequent observations of defendant's traffic crimes enabled the officer to buttress an anonymous tip through sufficient police corroboration and to form the basis for suspicion of criminal activity. State v. Mahatha, -- N.C. App. --, 832 S.E.2d 914 (2019).

JURY INSTRUCTIONS. --Defendant's G.S. 20-141.5 conviction was not set aside as under G.S. 15A-1232, in instructing the jury, the judge was not required to state, summarize or recapitulate the evidence, or to explain the application of the law to the evidence. State v. Pierce, 216 N.C. App. 377, 718 S.E.2d 648 (2011), dismissed and review denied 365 N.C. 560, 723 S.E.2d 769, 2012 N.C. LEXIS 209 (N.C. 2012).

INDICTMENT SUFFICIENT. --Defendant's indictment was not facially invalid because it tracked the relevant language of the felony speeding to elude arrest statute, G.S. 20-141.5, and listed the essential elements of the offense; the body of the indictment provided defendant with enough information to prepare a defense for the offense of felony speeding to elude arrest with reckless driving as an aggravating factor. State v. Leonard, 213 N.C. App. 526, 711 S.E.2d 867 (2011).

JURY INSTRUCTION PROPER. --Trial court's disjunctive instruction on the charge of felony operation of a motor vehicle to elude arrest was not improper; while many of the enumerated aggravating factors are in fact separate crimes under various provisions of the general statutes, they are not separate offenses, but are merely alternate ways of enhancing the punishment for speeding to elude arrest from a misdemeanor to a class H felony. State v. Hazelwood, 187 N.C. App. 94, 652 S.E.2d 63 (2007), cert. denied, 363 N.C. 133, 673 S.E.2d 867 (2009), cert. denied, 558 U.S. 1013, 130 S. Ct. 553, 175 L. Ed. 2d 385 (2009).

In a case of felony speeding to elude a police officer, a jury instruction that allowed the jury to find either actual knowledge or implied knowledge that the person from whom the defendant was fleeing was a law-enforcement officer was not error. State v. Graves, 203 N.C. App. 123, 690 S.E.2d 545 (2010), cert. denied

365 N.C. 188, 707 S.E.2d 233, 2011 N.C. LEXIS 248 (2011).

JURY UNANIMOUS ON TWO FACTORS. --While the jury may not have been unanimous as to which aggravating factors were present, it was unanimous in finding defendant guilty of the felonious operation of a motor vehicle to elude arrest and thus, the disjunctive jury instruction given by the trial court did not constitute error. State v. Banks, 213 N.C. App. 599, 713 S.E.2d 754 (2011).

EVIDENCE HELD SUFFICIENT TO SUPPORT CONVICTION. --Where an officer stated defendant sped at a rate "very much" in excess of 15 miles per hour over the speed limit and driving into oncoming traffic prior to slamming on the brakes and sliding to a halt in front of an occupied mobile home, that was sufficient evidence for the jury to find defendant guilty of eluding an officer while speeding in excess of 15 miles over the speed limit and driving recklessly. State v. Davis, 163 N.C. App. 587, 594 S.E.2d 57 (2004), cert. denied, 358 N.C. 547, 599 S.E.2d 564 (2004).

Proof that defendant was grossly impaired while driving due the consumption of alcohol and was driving recklessly was sufficient to support a conviction for felonious fleeing to elude arrest; the State was not required to prove that defendant drove in excess of 15 miles per hour over the legal speed limit as well since G.S. 20-141.5 only requires proof of two of the three listed factors. State v. Stokes, 174 N.C. App. 447, 621 S.E.2d 311 (2005).

State presented sufficient evidence of the aggravating factors necessary to support defendant's conviction for felony fleeing to elude arrest under G.S. 20-141.5(b); during a high-speed chase, defendant was driving more than 15 mph over the speed limit and he was driving recklessly under G.S. 20-140. State v. Smith, 178 N.C. App. 134, 631 S.E.2d 34 (2006).

State's failure to present sufficient evidence in support of one of four alleged aggravating factors, driving while license revoked, did not require vacation of defendant's charge of felony speeding to elude under G.S. 20-141.5 because the State presented sufficient evidence in support of the other three aggravating factors. State v. Graves, 203 N.C. App. 123, 690 S.E.2d 545 (2010), cert. denied 365 N.C. 188, 707 S.E.2d 233, 2011 N.C. LEXIS 248 (2011).

In a prosecution for felonious operation of a motor vehicle to elude arrest under G.S. 20-141.5(a), the evidence was sufficient to show defendant drove recklessly, as a trooper testified to clocking defendant at 82 miles per hour in a 55 zone, and testimony allowed the jury to infer that defendant crossed a solid double yellow line while being pursued. State v. Jackson, 212 N.C. App. 167, 710 S.E.2d 414 (2011).

Any error which could or could not have resulted from the State's introduction of a North Carolina Department of Motor Vehicles employee's affidavit clearly did not result in prejudice to defendant because the evidence was sufficient to support a finding that at least two aggravating factors listed in G.S. 20-141.5(b) were present; even assuming that the employee's affidavit violated defendant's right to confrontation, no miscarriage of justice occurred, and the exclusion of the affidavit would not have altered the jury's verdict because the jury had ample evidence before it to find two aggravating factors were present so as to enhance his driving to elude arrest conviction to a Class H felony. State v. Leonard, 213 N.C. App. 526, 711 S.E.2d 867 (2011).

Defendant's G.S. 20-141.5(b1) conviction was supported by sufficient evidence as: (1) defendant fled from a corporal's attempted lawful stop and, in doing so, created a police exigency; (2) an officer nearby was informed of the exigency and sped to provide assistance and apprehend defendant; (2) on his way, the officer encountered an obstruction in the road, was unable to safely avoid the obstruction due to his speed, and perished after unsuccessfully attempting to avoid the obstruction; and (3) the decision to exclude some evidence of the officer's alleged negligence did not violate defendant's right to a full and fair defense. State v. Pierce, 216 N.C. App. 377, 718 S.E.2d 648 (2011), dismissed and review denied 365 N.C. 560, 723 S.E.2d 769, 2012 N.C. LEXIS 209 (N.C. 2012).

DEFENDANT PROXIMATELY CAUSED VICTIM'S INJURY. --Even if defendant's willful attempt to elude arrest in violation of G.S. 20-141.5 was a cause of the victim's injury, his driving under the influence in violation of G.S. 20-138.1 could also be a proximate cause of the injury under G.S. 20-141.4(a3) because defendant's violation of G.S. 20-138.1 did not have to be the only proximate cause of the victim's injury in order for defendant to be found criminally liable; a showing that defendant's action of driving while under the influence was one of the proximate causes was sufficient. State v. Leonard, 213 N.C. App. 526, 711 S.E.2d 867 (2011).

SENTENCING ISSUES. --Where defendant pled guilty to assault with a deadly weapon on a government officer and felony fleeing to elude arrest, as assault with a deadly weapon on a government officer was the more serious of the two underlying felonies, and all of the elements of assault with a deadly weapon on a government officer were not included in any of defendant's prior offenses, the trial court misapplied G.S. 15A-1340.14(b)(6) by including an additional point in calculating her sentence. State v. Gardner, 225 N.C. App. 161, 736 S.E.2d 826 (2013).

Defendant's two North Carolina convictions for felony speeding to elude arrest did not constitute violent felonies under Armed Career Criminal Act (ACCA) because they did not have an element of use, attempted use, or threatened use of physical force against the person of another, nor were they among listed violent felonies in ACCA. United States v. Barlow, 811 F.3d 133 (4th Cir. 2015).

DOUBLE JEOPARDY. --Defendant's convictions for speeding, reckless driving, and speeding to elude arrest, aggravated to a felony for speeding and reckless driving, violated double jeopardy because (1) speeding and reckless driving were elements of the third crime, since speeding and reckless driving increased the maximum penalty, and (2) the legislature intended to impose alternate, not separate,

punishments, since all the statutes sought to deter the same conduct. State v. Mulder, 233 N.C. App. 82, 755 S.E.2d 98 (2014).

APPLIED in State v. Jones, 157 N.C. App. 472, 579 S.E.2d 408 (2003); State v. Scott, 167 N.C. App. 783, 607 S.E.2d 10 (2005); State v. Spencer, 218 N.C. App. 267, 720 S.E.2d 901 (2012).

CITED in Parish v. Hill, 350 N.C. 231, 513 S.E.2d 547 (1999); State v. Bagley, 183 N.C. App. 514, 644 S.E.2d 615 (2007); State v. Maready, 205 N.C. App. 1, 695 S.E.2d 771 (2010).

§ 20-141.6. Aggressive Driving

(a) Any person who operates a motor vehicle on a street, highway, or public vehicular area is guilty of aggressive driving if the person:

(1) Violates either G.S. 20-141 or G.S. 20-141.1, and

(2) Drives carelessly and heedlessly in willful or wanton disregard of the rights or safety of others.

(b) For the purposes of this section only, in order to prove a violation of subsection (a)(2), the State must show that the person committed two or more of the below specified offenses while in violation of subsection (a)(1):

(1) Running through a red light in violation of G.S. 20-158(b)(2) or (b)(3), or G.S. 20-158(c)(2) or (c)(3).

(2) Running through a stop sign in violation of G.S. 20-158(b)(1) or (c)(1).

(3) Illegal passing in violation of G.S. 20-149 or G.S. 20-150.

(4) Failing to yield right-of-way in violation of G.S. 20-155, 20-156, 20-158(b)(4) or (c)(4) or 20-158.1.

(5) Following too closely in violation of G.S. 20-152.

(c) A person convicted of aggressive driving is guilty of a Class 1 misdemeanor.

(d) The offense of reckless driving under G.S. 20-140 is a lesser-included offense of the offense set forth in this section.

History.
2004-193, s. 1
EDITOR'S NOTE. --
Session Laws 2004-193, s. 6, made this section effective December 1, 2004, and applicable to offenses committed on or after that date.

N.C. Gen. Stat. § 20-142

Repealed by Session Laws 1991, c. 368, s. 2.
CROSS REFERENCES. --
For current law, see G.S. 20-142.1 to 20-142.5.

§ 20-142.1. Obedience to railroad signal

(a) Whenever any person driving a vehicle approaches a railroad grade crossing under any of the circumstances stated in this section, the driver of the vehicle shall stop within 50 feet, but not less than 15 feet from the nearest rail of the railroad and shall not proceed until he can do so safely. These requirements apply when:

(1) A clearly visible electrical or mechanical signal device gives warning of the immediate approach of a railroad train or on-track equipment;

(2) A crossing gate is lowered or when a human flagman gives or continues to give a signal of the approach or passage of a railroad train or on-track equipment;

(3) A railroad train or on-track equipment approaching within approximately 1500 feet of the highway crossing emits a signal audible from that distance, and the railroad train or on-track equipment is an immediate hazard because of its speed or nearness to the crossing; or

(4) An approaching railroad train or on-track equipment is plainly visible and is in hazardous proximity to the crossing.

(b) No person shall drive any vehicle through, around, or under any crossing gate or barrier at a railroad crossing while the gate or barrier is closed or is being opened or closed, nor shall any pedestrian pass through, around, over, or under any crossing gate or barrier at a railroad crossing while the gate or barrier is closed or is being opened or closed.

(c) When stopping as required at a railroad crossing, the driver shall keep as far to the right of the highway as possible and shall not form two lanes of traffic unless the roadway is marked for four or more lanes of traffic.

(d) Any person who violates any provisions of this section shall be guilty of an infraction and punished in accordance with G.S. 20-176. Violation of this section shall not constitute negligence per se.

(e) An employer who knowingly allows, requires, permits, or otherwise authorizes a driver of a commercial motor vehicle to violate this section shall be guilty of an infraction. Such employer will also be subject to a civil penalty under G.S. 20-37.21.

History.
1991, c. 368, s. 1;2005-349, s. 12;2019-36, s. 2
  EDITOR'S NOTE. --
  Session Laws 2019-36, s. 6, made the amendment to subsection (a) by Session Laws 2019-36, s. 2, effective December 1, 2019, and applicable to offenses committed on or after that date.
  EFFECT OF AMENDMENTS. --
  Session Laws 2005-349, s. 12, effective September 30, 2005, and applicable to offenses committed on or after that date, added subsection (e).
  Session Laws 2019-36, s. 2, effective December 1, 2019, inserted "or on-track equipment" following

"train" throughout the section. For effective date and applicability, see editor's note.
  CONTRIBUTORY NEGLIGENCE. --Decedent's own negligence contributed to his injuries and barred recovery on plaintiff's negligence claim where the evidence showed that engineer signaled train's approach, that plaintiff failed to explain what prevented decedent from hearing warning bell and horn, and that decedent also failed to stop within 50 feet of the crossing to determine whether it was safe to proceed. Parchment v. Garner, 135 N.C. App. 312, 520 S.E.2d 100 (1999).
  Trial court erred in granting defendants' motion to dismiss the personal representative's negligence action because the allegations of the complaint did not necessarily dictate a finding of contributory negligence by the decedent; the fact that the decedent bypassed the crossing gate, in violation of G.S. 20-142.1, was evidence that could be considered in deciding whether the decedent breached the duty of exercising ordinary care. Sharp v. CSX Transp., Inc., 160 N.C. App. 241, 584 S.E.2d 888 (2003).
  North Carolina Industrial Commission did not err in holding that an injured person was not contributorily negligent in that: (1) the injured party's attention was focused on the stop sign to the right side of the tracks and that she was slowing to obey that stop sign when she was struck by a train; (2) the evidence conflicted as to whether the train issued a signal audible from 1,500 feet of the highway crossing and whether the approaching train was plainly visible to invoke G.S. 20-142.1(a) (3), (3) a passenger in another driver's car's testimony was sufficient to support the Commission's finding that the injured party had slowed down in an attempt to obey the stop sign, and (4) a field support engineer with the Department of Transportation testified that the stop sign was confusing. Norman v. N.C. DOT, 161 N.C. App. 211, 588 S.E.2d 42 (2003), review dismissed, review denied, 358 N.C. 235, 595 S.E.2d 153 (2004), cert. denied, 358 N.C. 545, 599 S.E.2d 404 (2004).
  APPLIED in Gilliam v. McKnight, (M.D.N.C. Dec. 4, 2002).

§ 20-142.2. Vehicles stop at certain grade crossing

The Department of Transportation may designate particularly dangerous highway crossings of railroads and erect stop signs at those crossings. When a stop sign is erected at a highway crossing of a railroad, the driver of any vehicle shall stop within 50 feet but not less than 15 feet from the nearest rail of such grade crossing and shall proceed only upon exercising due care. Any person who violates this section shall be guilty of an infraction and punished in accordance with G.S. 20-176. Violation of this section shall not constitute negligence per se. An employer who knowingly allows, requires, permits, or otherwise authorizes a driver of a commercial motor vehicle to violate this section shall be guilty of an infraction. Such employer will also be subject to a civil penalty under G.S. 20-37.21.

History.

1991, c. 368, s. 1;2005-349, s. 13

EFFECT OF AMENDMENTS. --

Session Laws 2005-349, s. 13, effective September 30, 2005, and applicable to offenses committed on or after that date, added the last two sentences.

EDITOR'S NOTE. --The cases cited below were decided under corresponding provisions of earlier law.

NECESSITY FOR SECTION. --Although under Hinton v. Southern Ry., 172 N.C. 587, 90 S.E. 756 (1916), a railroad is a highway, an amendment of the statute was necessary in order to compel the operator of a motor vehicle to bring it to a full stop before crossing or attempting to cross a railroad track. State v. Stallings, 189 N.C. 104, 126 S.E. 187 (1925).

DUTY TO STOP AS MIXED QUESTION OF LAW AND FACT. --A driver of an automobile is not required under all circumstances to stop before driving upon a railroad grade crossing, and whether he is required to do so under the particular circumstances disclosed by the evidence is ordinarily a mixed question of law and fact to be submitted to the jury upon proper instruction from the court. Keller v. Southern Ry., 205 N.C. 269, 171 S.E. 73 (1933).

REASONABLY PRUDENT MAN TEST. --The test is whether a reasonably prudent man, knowing the custom of the crossing signals by bell and whistle and also the automatic signals, would approach the track in the reasonable belief that no train was approaching. Earnhardt v. Southern Ry., 281 F. Supp. 585 (M.D.N.C. 1968), aff'd, 405 F.2d 877 (4th Cir. 1969).

EXTENUATING CIRCUMSTANCES MAY RELAX DILIGENCE REQUIRED OF TRAVELLER. --While ordinarily a driver would be guilty of contributory negligence as a matter of law when he did not stop when he was 25 feet from the track where he could have seen the train if he had looked, extenuating circumstances may relax the diligence required of the traveller. Hence from the evidence the jury could reasonably have concluded that the driver was listening for crossing signals, but that they were not given, and looking for the automatic signals which normally would warn him if a train was approaching, and that at the time he got within 25 feet of the track, he was misled by the failure of the automatic signals and the failure of defendant to give any warning of any kind of the train which was approaching at 60 miles per hour or 88 feet per second. Earnhardt v. Southern Ry., 281 F. Supp. 585 (M.D.N.C. 1968), aff'd, 405 F.2d 877 (4th Cir. 1969).

FAILURE TO COME TO A FULL STOP BEFORE ENTERING RAILROAD CROSSING AS REQUIRED BY STATUTE IS NOT CONTRIBUTORY NEGLIGENCE PER SE, but such failure is a circumstance to be considered by the jury with the other evidence in the case upon the question. White v. North Carolina R.R., 216 N.C. 79, 3 S.E.2d 310 (1939).

Failure of a motorist to stop his automobile before crossing a railroad at a grade crossing on a public highway, as directed by this section, at a distance not exceeding 50 feet from the nearest rail, did not constitute contributory negligence per se in his action against railroad company to recover damages to his car caused by a collision with a train standing upon the tracks; but where the evidence tended only to show that the proximate cause of the plaintiff's injury was his own negligence in exceeding the speed he should have used under the circumstances, a judgment as of nonsuit thereon should have been entered on defendant's motion therefor properly entered. Weston v. Southern Ry., 194 N.C. 210, 139 S.E. 237 (1927).

§ 20-142.3. Certain vehicles must stop at railroad grade crossing

(a) Before crossing at grade any track or tracks of a railroad, the driver of any school bus, any activity bus, any motor vehicle carrying passengers for compensation, any commercial motor vehicle listed in 49 C.F.R. § 392.10, and any motor vehicle with a capacity of 16 or more persons shall stop the vehicle within 50 feet but not less than 15 feet from the nearest rail of the railroad. While stopped, the driver shall listen and look in both directions along the track for any approaching train or on-track equipment and shall not proceed until the driver can do so safely. Upon proceeding, the driver of the vehicle shall cross the track in a gear that allows the driver to cross the track without changing gears and the driver shall not change gears while crossing the track or tracks.

(b) Except for school buses and activity buses, the provisions of this section shall not require the driver of a vehicle to stop:

(1) At railroad tracks used exclusively for industrial switching purposes within a business district.

(2) At a railroad grade crossing which a police officer or crossing flagman directs traffic to proceed.

(3) At a railroad grade crossing protected by a gate or flashing signal designed to stop traffic upon the approach of a train or on-track equipment, when the gate or flashing signal does not indicate the approach of a train or on-track equipment.

(4) At an abandoned railroad grade crossing which is marked with a sign indicating that the rail line is abandoned.

(5) At an industrial or spur line railroad grade crossing marked with a sign reading "Exempt" erected by or with the consent of the appropriate State or local authority.

(c) A person violating the provisions of this section shall be guilty of an infraction and punished in accordance with G.S. 20-176. Violation of this section shall not constitute negligence per se.

(d), (e) Repealed by Session Laws 2001-487, s. 50(g).

(f) An employer who knowingly allows, requires, permits, or otherwise authorizes a driver of a commercial motor vehicle to violate this section shall be guilty of an infraction. Such employer will also be subject to a civil penalty under G.S. 20-37.21.

History.

1991, c. 368, s. 1;1999-274, ss. 1, 2; 2001-487, s. 50(g);2005-349, s. 14;2019-36, s. 3

LOCAL MODIFICATION. --Craven: 2010-20.

EDITOR'S NOTE. --

Subsection (f) was originally enacted by Session Laws 2005-349, s. 14, as subsection (e). The subsection has been redesignated at the direction of the Revisor of Statutes.

Session Laws 2019-36, s. 6, made the amendment to subsection (a) and subdivision (b)(3) by Session Laws 2019-36, s. 3, effective December 1, 2019, and applicable to offenses committed on or after that date.

EFFECT OF AMENDMENTS. --

Session Laws 2005-349, s. 14, effective September 30, 2005, and applicable to offenses committed on or after that date, added subsection (f).

Session Laws 2019-36, s. 3, effective December 1, 2019, inserted "or on-track equipment" in subsection (a); inserted "or on-track equipment" twice in subdivisions (b)(3). For effective date and applicability, see editor's note.

§ 20-142.4. Moving heavy equipment at railroad grade crossing

(a) No person shall operate or move any crawler-type tractor, crane, or roller or any equipment or structure having a normal operating speed of five or less miles per hour upon or across any tracks at a railroad crossing without first complying with this section.

(b) Notice of any intended crossing described in subsection (a) of this section shall be given to a superintendent of the railroad and a reasonable time be given to the railroad to provide protection at the crossing.

(c) Before making any crossing described in subsection (a) of this section, the person operating or moving the vehicle or equipment shall:

(1) Stop the vehicle or equipment not less than 15 feet nor more than 50 feet from the nearest rail of the railroad;

(2) While stopped, shall listen and look both directions along the track for any approaching train or on-track equipment and for signals indicating the approach of a train or on-track equipment; and

(3) Shall not proceed until the crossing can be made safely.

(d) No crossing described in subsection (a) of this section shall be made when warning is given by automatic signal or crossing gates or a flagman or otherwise of the immediate approach of a railroad train or on-track equipment.

(e) Subsection (c) of this section shall not apply at any railroad crossing where State or local authorities have determined that trains are not operating during certain periods or seasons of the year and have erected an official sign carrying the legend "Exempt".

(f) Any person who violates any provision of this section shall be guilty of an infraction and punished in accordance with G.S. 20-176. Violation of this section shall not constitute negligence per se.

(g) An employer who knowingly allows, requires, permits, or otherwise authorizes a driver of a commercial motor vehicle to violate this section shall be guilty of an infraction. Such employer will also be subject to a civil penalty under G.S. 20-37.21.

History.

1991, c. 368, s. 1;2005-349, s. 15;2019-36, s. 4

EDITOR'S NOTE. --

Session Laws 2019-36, s. 6, made the amendment to subsections (c) and (d) by Session Laws 2019-36, s. 4, effective December 1, 2019, and applicable to offenses committed on or after that date.

EFFECT OF AMENDMENTS. --

Session Laws 2005-349, s. 15, effective September 30, 2005, and applicable to offenses committed on or after that date, added subsection (g).

Session Laws 2019-36, s. 4, effective December 1, 2019, in subdivision (c)(2), inserted "or on-track equipment" following "approaching train", and substituted "train or on-track equipment" for "train"; and substituted "on-track equipment" for "car" at the end of subsection (d). For effective date and applicability, see editor's note.

§ 20-142.5. Stop when traffic obstructed

No driver shall enter an intersection or a marked crosswalk or drive onto any railroad grade crossing unless there is sufficient space on the other side of the intersection, crosswalk, or railroad grade crossing to accommodate the vehicle he is operating without obstructing the passage of other vehicles, pedestrians, or railroad trains or on-track equipment, notwithstanding the indication of any traffic control signal to proceed. Any person who violates any provision of this section shall be guilty of an infraction and punished in accordance with G.S. 20-176. Violation of this section shall not constitute negligence per se.

An employer who knowingly allows, requires, permits, or otherwise authorizes a driver of a commercial motor vehicle to violate this section shall be guilty of an infraction. Such employer will also be subject to a civil penalty under G.S. 20-37.21.

History.

1991, c. 368, s. 1;2005-349, s. 16;2019-36, s. 5

EDITOR'S NOTE. --

Session Laws 2019-36, s. 6, made the amendment to this section by Session Laws 2019-36, s. 5, effective

December 1, 2019, and applicable to offenses committed on or after that date.

EFFECT OF AMENDMENTS. --

Session Laws 2005-349, s. 16, effective September 30, 2005, and applicable to offenses committed on or after that date, added the last paragraph.

Session Laws 2019-36, s. 5, effective December 1, 2019, substituted "trains or on-track equipment" for "trains" in the first sentence. For effective date and applicability, see editor's note.

§§ 20-143, 20-143.1

Repealed by Session Laws 1991, c. 368, ss. 2, 3.

CROSS REFERENCES. --

For current law, see G.S. 20-142.1 to 20-142.5.

§ 20-144. Special speed limitation on bridges

It shall be unlawful to drive any vehicle upon any public bridge, causeway or viaduct at a speed which is greater than the maximum speed which can with safety to such structure be maintained thereon, when such structure is signposted as provided in this section.

The Department of Transportation, upon request from any local authorities, shall, or upon its own initiative may, conduct an investigation of any public bridge, causeway or viaduct, and if it shall thereupon find that such structure cannot with safety to itself withstand vehicles traveling at the speed otherwise permissible under this Article, the Division shall determine and declare the maximum speed of vehicles which such structure can withstand, and shall cause or permit suitable signs stating such maximum speed to be erected and maintained at a distance of 100 feet beyond each end of such structure. The findings and determination of the Department of Transportation shall be conclusive evidence of the maximum speed which can with safety to any such structure be maintained thereon.

History.

1937, c. 407, s. 106; 1957, c. 65, s. 11; 1973, c. 507, ss. 5, 21; 1975, c. 716, s. 5; 1977, c. 464, s. 34

INSTRUCTION IN PROSECUTION FOR INVOLUNTARY MANSLAUGHTER HELD ERRONEOUS. --In a prosecution for involuntary manslaughter arising out of a violation of this section, instruction which failed to require the jury to find beyond a reasonable doubt that the deliberate and intentional violation of the speed statute upon the part of defendant was a proximate cause of the collision which inflicted the injuries resulting in death was erroneous. State v. Sawyer, 11 N.C. App. 81, 180 S.E.2d 387 (1971).

CROSS REFERENCES. --

As to the power of the Department of Transportation to fix maximum load limits on bridges, see G.S. 136-72.

§ 20-145. When speed limit not applicable

The speed limitations set forth in this Article shall not apply to vehicles when operated with due regard for safety under the direction of the police in the chase or apprehension of violators of the law or of persons charged with or suspected of any such violation, nor to fire department or fire patrol vehicles when traveling in response to a fire alarm, nor to public or private ambulances and rescue squad emergency service vehicles when traveling in emergencies, nor to vehicles operated by county fire marshals and civil preparedness coordinators when traveling in the performances of their duties, nor to any of the following when either operated by a law enforcement officer in the chase or apprehension of violators of the law or of persons charged with or suspected of any such violation, when traveling in response to a fire alarm, or for other emergency response purposes: (i) a vehicle operated by the Division of Marine Fisheries of the Department of Environmental Quality or the Division of Parks and Recreation of the Department of Natural and Cultural Resources or (ii) a vehicle operated by the North Carolina Forest Service of the Department of Agriculture and Consumer Services. This exemption shall not, however, protect the driver of any such vehicle from the consequence of a reckless disregard of the safety of others.

History.

1937, c. 407, s. 107; 1947, c. 987; 1971, c. 5; 1977, c. 52, s. 3; 1985, c. 454, s. 5; 2013-415, s. 1(c);2015-241, s. 14.30(gg)

EFFECT OF AMENDMENTS. --

Session Laws 2013-415, s. 1(c), effective October 1, 2013, inserted "nor to any of the following when either operated by a law enforcement officer in the chase or apprehension of violators of the law or of persons charged with or suspected of any such violation, when traveling in response to a fire alarm, or for other emergency response purposes: (i) a vehicle operated by the Division of Marine Fisheries or the Division of Parks and Recreation of the Department of Environment and Natural Resources or (ii) a vehicle operated by the North Carolina Forest Service of the Department of Agriculture and Consumer Services."

Session Laws 2015-241, s. 14.30(gg), effective July 1, 2015, substituted "Fisheries of the Department of Environmental Quality" for "Fisheries" and substituted "Department of Natural and Cultural Resources" for "Department of Environment and Natural Resources."

OTHER EXEMPTIONS FOR POLICE VEHICLES NOT PRECLUDED. --The legislature, by including the express exemption for police vehicles when operated with due regard for safety in this section, did not thereby evidence an intent that there be no exemption under any circumstances from other sections of the Motor Vehicle Act for police vehicles while being

Chapter 20

similarly operated. Collins v. Christenberry, 6 N.C. App. 504, 170 S.E.2d 515 (1969).

POLICE RESPONDING TO NOTICE OF PURSUIT. --The language of this section is broad enough to include not only police in direct or immediate pursuit of law violators or suspected violators, but also police who receive notice of the pursuit and respond by proceeding to the scene for the purpose of assisting in the chase or apprehension. State v. Flaherty, 55 N.C. App. 14, 284 S.E.2d 565 (1981).

BALANCING TEST APPLIED BY POLICE OFFICERS. --In pursuing a fleeing suspect, a law enforcement officer must conduct a balancing test, weighing the interests of justice in apprehending the fleeing suspect with the interests of the public in not being subject to unreasonable risks of injury. Parish v. Hill, 350 N.C. 231, 513 S.E.2d 547 (1999).

STANDARD OF CARE APPLICABLE TO POLICE OFFICERS. --The fact that a police vehicle is exempt from the operation of traffic regulations or enjoys certain prior rights over other vehicles does not permit the operator of such vehicle to drive in reckless disregard of the safety of others, nor does it relieve him from the general duty of exercising due care. Goddard v. Williams, 251 N.C. 128, 110 S.E.2d 820 (1959), overruled in part, Young v. Woodall, 343 N.C. 459, 471 S.E.2d 357 (1996).

An officer, when in pursuit of a lawbreaker, is not to be deemed negligent merely because he fails to observe the requirements of the Motor Vehicle Act. His conduct is to be examined and tested by another standard. He is required to observe the care which a reasonably prudent man would exercise in the discharge of official duties of a like nature under like circumstances. Goddard v. Williams, 251 N.C. 128, 110 S.E.2d 820 (1959), overruled in part, Young v. Woodall, 343 N.C. 459, 471 S.E.2d 357 (1996).

For discussion of the action a reasonable man, who is serving as a member of the North Carolina state highway patrol should take when he tries to stop a motor vehicle for following too closely and the driver of the vehicle does not stop. McMillan v. Newton, 63 N.C. App. 751, 306 S.E.2d 470, cert. denied, 309 N.C. 821, 310 S.E.2d 350 (1983).

The standard of care under this section is the reckless disregard of the safety of others, i.e. gross negligence, and this standard applies whether or not the pursuing officer's vehicle was in the collision. Young v. Woodall, 343 N.C. 459, 471 S.E.2d 357 (1996).

Standard of care a police officer must use when acting within the contours of G.S. 20-145 is that of gross negligence. Jones v. City of Durham, 168 N.C. App. 433, 608 S.E.2d 387 (2005), aff'd, 360 N.C. 81, 622 S.E.2d 596 (2005).

City and one of its officers were granted summary judgment with regard to a pedestrian's gross negligence claim related to being struck by a police cruiser, because the pedestrian failed to show any triable issues of fact as to gross negligence on the part of the police officer responding to a backup call; the pedestrian's own deposition testimony showed that she had heard sirens and nevertheless had proceeded into the street, against a traffic light, and outside of any crosswalk. Jones v. City of Durham, 168 N.C. App. 433, 608 S.E.2d 387 (2005), aff'd, 360 N.C. 81, 622 S.E.2d 596 (2005).

GROSS OR WANTON NEGLIGENCE. --Gross negligence in the pursuit context is wanton conduct done with conscious or reckless disregard for the rights and safety of others. D'Alessandro v. Westall, 972 F. Supp. 965 (W.D.N.C. 1997).

Law enforcement officers were not entitled to summary judgment in claim brought against them under this section where a reasonable jury could conclude that the officers' pursuit of motorist constituted gross negligence. D'Alessandro v. Westall, 972 F. Supp. 965 (W.D.N.C. 1997).

Summary judgment was proper where plaintiff failed to demonstrate the existence of a genuine issue of material fact as to gross negligence on the part of the officers who attempted to apprehend a motorist suspected of driving while intoxicated and where the actions of the officers were otherwise exempt under this section. Norris v. Zambito, 135 N.C. App. 288, 520 S.E.2d 113 (1999).

Officer's speed of 10 to 25 miles per hour in excess of the 35 mile-per-hour speed limit in responding to an emergency call from another officer in peril did not support a finding of gross negligence under G.S. 20-145 in a claim for injuries sustained when the officer struck plaintiff; the officer's compliance with the authoritative training standard in this emergency situation fully supported the appropriateness of his decision to perform an evasive maneuver upon viewing the injured person in the road and negated the contention of gross negligence. Jones v. City of Durham, 360 N.C. 81, 622 S.E.2d 596 (2005).

G.

S. 20-145 provided an exception to the speed limit rules for emergency vehicles. Inclusion of the word "wanton" in police pursuit cases was a shorthand reference to the "reckless disregard" limitation of G.S. 20-145 and did not refer to the definition of the word from a wholly unrelated statute -- G.S. 1D-5(7), the punitive damages statute. Villepigue v. City of Danville, 190 N.C. App. 359, 661 S.E.2d 12 (2008), review denied, 362 N.C. 688, 671 S.E.2d 532 (2008).

CITY POLICY. --There was insufficient evidence that city and its police chief failed to develop a substantive policy on high speed chases, where the policy gave officers wide discretion in conducting high speed chases, but did delineate factors officers were to consider, and balanced the danger of pursuit against allowing the suspect to escape. Parish v. Hill, 130 N.C. App. 195, 502 S.E.2d 637 (1998), rev'd on other grounds, 350 N.C. 231, 513 S.E.2d 547 (1999).

Police officers did not act with "gross negligence" in pursuing a suspected traffic violator, where the officers were well behind the suspect when he crashed his car into a residence, killing his passenger, and the officers did not try to force the suspect's car off the road or to overtake it. Parish v. Hill, 350 N.C. 231, 513 S.E.2d 547 (1999).

Evidence of a violation of a city's pursuit policy does not show gross negligence; although it may provide evidence of some negligence, it does not conclusively establish negligence. Jones v. City of Durham, 168 N.C. App. 433, 608 S.E.2d 387 (2005), aff'd, 360 N.C. 81, 622 S.E.2d 596 (2005).

NO LIABILITY OF OFFICER FOR DEATH OF INNOCENT MOTORIST. --Where a police officer initiated the pursuit of a motorist who imposed an imminent threat to public safety, traveled at a high rate of speed, and passed multiple cars while using his blue lights and siren on a narrow two-lane road, the officer's conduct did not rise to the elevated standard of gross negligence that would impose liability on the officer for a citizen's death. The weather was clear; the road relatively straight, with only a slight bend and grade; it was approximately 2:30-3:00 p.m. on a Sunday afternoon; and the officer was unaware of the upcoming intersection's activity, the victim's car, or the stopped line of traffic directly in front of his vehicle. Villepigue v. City of Danville, 190 N.C. App. 359, 661 S.E.2d 12 (2008), review denied, 362 N.C. 688, 671 S.E.2d 532 (2008).

In a wrongful death suit arising from a collision between a police cruiser and decedent's vehicle, the trial court erred by denying defendants' motion for summary judgment because the officer's conduct during a high speed pursuit did not rise to the level of gross negligence per G.S. 20-145. The officer followed common procedure and exercised his discretion by waiting to activate the siren and lights; although he exceeded the speed limit and violated policy by failing to notify the police communications center of the pursuit, this did not constitute gross negligence. Greene v. City of Greenville, 225 N.C. App. 24, 736 S.E.2d 833 (2013), review denied, 747 S.E.2d 249, 2013 N.C. LEXIS 753 (2013).

APPLICATION TO BAIL BONDSMEN. --Defendant, a bail bondsman, was properly convicted of involuntary manslaughter following a motor vehicle accident in which defendant was pursuing in a high speed chase a person who had failed to appear in court, because the trial court did not err in instructing the jury that bail bondsmen could not violate North Carolina motor vehicle laws to make an arrest. State v. McGee, 234 N.C. App. 285, 758 S.E.2d 661 (2014).

BURDEN OF PROOF. --It would be a fair allocation of the burden of proof to require a defendant to prove that he comes within the exceptions recognized by this section. State v. Flaherty, 55 N.C. App. 14, 284 S.E.2d 565 (1981).

APPLIED in Campbell v. O'Sullivan, 4 N.C. App. 581, 167 S.E.2d 450 (1969); N.C. Dep't of Env't & Natural Res. v. Carroll, 358 N.C. 649, 599 S.E.2d 888 (2004).

CITED in Fowler v. North Carolina Dep't of Crime Control & Pub. Safety, 92 N.C. App. 733, 376 S.E.2d 11 (1989); Shaw v. Stroud, 13 F.3d 791 (4th Cir. 1994); Clayton v. Branson, 170 N.C. App. 438, 613 S.E.2d 259 (2005), cert. denied, 360 N.C. 174, 625 S.E.2d 785 (2005); Lunsford v. Lori Renn, 207 N.C. App. 298, 700 S.E.2d 94 (2010), review denied 365 N.C. 193, 707 S.E.2d 244, 2011 N.C. LEXIS 260 (2011).

LEGAL PERIODICALS. --

For note on municipal liability for accident involving fire truck responding to emergency call for inhalator, see 30 N.C.L. Rev. 89 (1951).

For note discussing the effect of this section on the standard of care required of police officers in the performance of official duties, see 39 N.C.L. Rev. 460 (1961).

For a survey of 1996 developments in tort law, see 75 N.C.L. Rev. 2468 (1997).

§ 20-146. Drive on right side of highway; exceptions

(a) Upon all highways of sufficient width a vehicle shall be driven upon the right half of the highway except as follows:

(1) When overtaking and passing another vehicle proceeding in the same direction under the rules governing such movement;

(2) When an obstruction exists making it necessary to drive to the left of the center of the highway; provided, any person so doing shall yield the right-of-way to all vehicles traveling in the proper direction upon the unobstructed portion of the highway within such distance as to constitute an immediate hazard;

(3) Upon a highway divided into three marked lanes for traffic under the rules applicable thereon; or

(4) Upon a highway designated and signposted for one-way traffic.

(a1) Self-propelled grain combines or other self-propelled farm equipment shall be operated to the right of the centerline except as provided in G.S. 20-116(j)(4).

(b) Upon all highways any vehicle proceeding at less than the legal maximum speed limit shall be driven in the right-hand lane then available for thru traffic, or as close as practicable to the right-hand curb or edge of the highway, except when overtaking and passing another vehicle proceeding in the same direction or when preparing for a left turn.

(c) Upon any highway having four or more lanes for moving traffic and providing for two-way movement of traffic, no vehicle shall be driven to the left of the centerline of the highway, except when authorized by official traffic-control devices designating certain lanes to the left side of the center of the highway for use by traffic not otherwise permitted to use such lanes or except as permitted under subsection (a)(2) hereof.

(d) Whenever any street has been divided into two or more clearly marked lanes for traffic, the following rules in addition to all others consistent herewith shall apply.

(1) A vehicle shall be driven as nearly as practicable entirely within a single lane and shall not be moved from such lane

until the driver has first ascertained that such movement can be made with safety.

(2) Upon a street which is divided into three or more lanes and provides for the two-way movement of traffic, a vehicle shall not be driven in the center lane except when overtaking and passing another vehicle traveling in the same direction when such center lane is clear of traffic within a safe distance, or in the preparation for making a left turn or where such center lane is at the time allocated exclusively to traffic moving in the same direction that the vehicle is proceeding and such allocation is designated by official traffic-control device.

(3) Official traffic-control devices may be erected directing specified traffic to use a designated lane or designating those lanes to be used by traffic moving in a particular direction regardless of the center of the street and drivers of vehicles shall obey the direction of every such device.

(4) Official traffic-control devices may be installed prohibiting the changing of lanes on sections of streets, and drivers of vehicles shall obey the directions of every such device.

(e) Notwithstanding any other provisions of this section, when appropriate signs have been posted, it shall be unlawful for any person to operate a motor vehicle over and upon the inside lane, next to the median of any dual-lane highway at a speed less than the posted speed limit when the operation of said motor vehicle over and upon said inside lane shall impede the steady flow of traffic except when preparing for a left turn. "Appropriate signs" as used herein shall be construed as including "Slower Traffic Keep Right" or designations of similar import.

History.

1937, c. 407, s. 108; 1965, c. 678, s. 2; 1973, c. 1330, s. 3; 1975, c. 593; 1985, c. 764, s. 25; 1985 (Reg. Sess., 1986), c. 852, s. 17; 2001-487, s. 11;2015-263, s. 6(b)

EFFECT OF AMENDMENTS. --
Session Laws 2015-263, s. 6.(b), effective September 30, 2015, added subsection (a1).

EDITOR'S NOTE. --Some of the cases cited below were decided under corresponding provisions of former law.

APPLICABILITY. --This statute does not apply only to situations where it is practicable for a motorist to stay within his current lane of traffic. Rather, it contains two disjunctive mandates: (1) a motorist must drive his vehicle as nearly as practicable entirely within a single lane; (2) a motorist must also refrain from changing lanes unless he has first ascertained that such movement can be made with safety. State v. Nazzal, -- N.C. App. --, 840 S.E.2d 881 (2020).

DOUBLE JEOPARDY. --A violation of this section constitutes an "offense" within the double jeopardy clause of the Fifth Amendment. State v. Hamrick, 110

N.C. App. 60, 428 S.E.2d 830, appeal dismissed, cert. denied, 334 N.C. 436, 433 S.E.2d 181 (1993).

THE PURPOSE OF THIS SECTION is the protection of occupants of other vehicles using the public highway and pedestrians and property thereon. Powell v. Clark, 255 N.C. 707; 122 S.E.2d 706 (1961); Sessoms v. Roberson, 47 N.C. App. 573, 268 S.E.2d 24 (1980).

THIS SECTION PRESCRIBES A STANDARD OF CARE for a motorist, and the standard fixed by the legislature is absolute. Bondurant v. Mastin, 252 N.C. 190, 113 S.E.2d 292 (1960).

A PERSON WALKING ALONG A PUBLIC HIGHWAY PUSHING A HANDCART IS A PEDESTRIAN within the purview of G.S. 20-174(d), and is not a driver of a vehicle within the meaning of this section and G.S. 20-149. Lewis v. Watson, 229 N.C. 20, 47 S.E.2d 484 (1948).

RIGHT TO ASSUME THAT APPROACHING VEHICLE WILL REMAIN ON OWN SIDE OF ROAD. --A motorist proceeding on his right side of the highway is not required to anticipate that an automobile which is coming from the opposite direction on its own side of the road will suddenly leave its side of the road and turn into his path. He has the right to assume under such circumstances that the approaching automobile will remain on its own side of the road until the vehicles meet and pass in safety. Johnson v. Douglas, 6 N.C. App. 109, 169 S.E.2d 505 (1969).

VIOLATION OF THIS SECTION IS NEGLIGENCE PER SE. Boyd v. Harper, 250 N.C. 334, 108 S.E.2d 598 (1959); Anderson v. Webb, 267 N.C. 745, 148 S.E.2d 846 (1966).

One who fails to comply with the provisions of this section is negligent. Stephens v. Southern Oil Co., 259 N.C. 456, 131 S.E.2d 39 (1963).

BUT NEGLIGENCE PER SE RULE IS INAPPLICABLE TO POLICE. --The principle that violation of this section constitutes negligence per se is not applicable to law-enforcement officers, who are not to be deemed negligent merely for failure to observe the rules of the road while engaged in the pursuit of lawbreakers. Wade v. Grooms, 37 N.C. App. 428, 246 S.E.2d 17 (1978).

WHEN VIOLATION CONSTITUTES CULPABLE NEGLIGENCE. --Violation of a safety statute which results in injury or death will constitute culpable negligence if the violation is willful, wanton or intentional. But where there is an unintentional or inadvertent violation of the statute, such violation standing alone does not constitute culpable negligence. The inadvertent or unintentional violation of the statute must be accompanied by recklessness of probable consequences of a dangerous nature, when tested by the rule of reasonable prevision, amounting altogether to a thoughtless disregard of consequences or of a heedless indifference to the safety of others. State v. Hancock, 248 N.C. 432, 103 S.E.2d 491 (1958).

VIOLATION CONSTITUTES ACTIONABLE NEGLIGENCE WHEN IT IS PROXIMATE CAUSE OF INJURY. --Violation of this section is negligence per se, which, when it is the proximate cause of injury, constitutes actionable negligence. Anderson v. Webb, 267 N.C. 745, 148 S.E.2d 846 (1966); Smith v. Kilburn, 13 N.C. App. 449, 186 S.E.2d 214, cert. denied, 281 N.C. 155, 187 S.E.2d 586 (1972).

A violation of this section is negligence per se, and when proximate cause of injury or damage is shown, such violation constitutes actionable negligence. Reeves v. Hill, 272 N.C. 352, 158 S.E.2d 529 (1968); Lassiter v. Williams, 272 N.C. 473, 158 S.E.2d 593 (1968); Sessoms v. Roberson, 47 N.C. App. 573, 268 S.E.2d 24 (1980).

A violation of this section is negligence per se, but to be actionable, such negligence must be the proximate cause of injury. Tysinger v. Coble Dairy Prods., 225 N.C. 717, 36 S.E.2d 246 (1945). See also, Hoke v. Atlantic Greyhound Corp., 226 N.C. 692, 40 S.E.2d 345 (1946); Watters v. Parrish, 252 N.C. 787, 115 S.E.2d 1 (1960); Davis v. Imes, 13 N.C. App. 521, 186 S.E.2d 641 (1972).

A violation of this section is negligence per se, but such negligence is not actionable unless there is a causal relation between the breach and the injury. Grimes v. Carolina Coach Co., 203 N.C. 605, 166 S.E. 599 (1932). See also, Stovall v. Ragland, 211 N.C. 536, 190 S.E. 899 (1937); McCombs v. McLean Trucking Co., 252 N.C. 699, 114 S.E.2d 683 (1960).

If the negligence resulting from the failure to comply with the provisions of this section proximately causes injury, liability results. Stephens v. Southern Oil Co., 259 N.C. 456, 131 S.E.2d 39 (1963).

A safety statute, such as this section, is pertinent when, and only when, there is evidence tending to show a violation thereof proximately caused the alleged injuries. Powell v. Clark, 255 N.C. 707, 122 S.E.2d 706 (1961).

PROXIMATE CAUSE AS A JURY QUESTION. --Whether a violation of the provisions of this section is the proximate cause of an injury is for the jury to determine. Stephens v. Southern Oil Co., 259 N.C. 456, 131 S.E.2d 39 (1963); Sessoms v. Roberson, 47 N.C. App. 573, 268 S.E.2d 24 (1980).

PRIMA FACIE CASE OF ACTIONABLE NEGLIGENCE IS MADE OUT BY EVIDENCE THAT DEFENDANT WAS DRIVING LEFT OF CENTER. --Evidence in action for injuries or damages caused by an automobile collision showing that defendant was driving left of the center of the highway when the collision occurred made out a prima facie case of actionable negligence. Reeves v. Hill, 272 N.C. 352, 158 S.E.2d 529 (1968); Lassiter v. Williams, 272 N.C. 473, 158 S.E.2d 593 (1968).

BUT DEFENDANT MAY SHOW CAUSE OF VIOLATION WAS NOT NEGLIGENCE. --A violation of this section, requiring a vehicle operator to drive on the right side of the highway, with certain exceptions, is negligence per se. However, a defendant may escape liability by showing that he was on the wrong side of the road from a cause other than his own negligence. Nationwide Mut. Ins. Co. v. Chantos, 298 N.C. 246, 258 S.E.2d 334 (1979).

When a plaintiff suing to recover damages for injuries sustained in a collision offers evidence tending to show that the collision occurred when the defendant was driving to the left of the center of the highway, such evidence made out a prima facie case of actionable negligence. The defendant, of course, could rebut the inference arising from such evidence by showing that he was on the wrong side of the road from a cause other than his own negligence. Anderson v. Webb, 267 N.C. 745, 148 S.E.2d 846 (1966); Smith v. Kilburn, 13 N.C. App. 449, 186 S.E.2d 214, cert. denied, 281 N.C. 155, 187 S.E.2d 586 (1972); Sessoms v. Roberson, 47 N.C. App. 573, 268 S.E.2d 24 (1980).

Decedent's initial act of negligence (being partially parked on the highway) justified the shift of defendant's vehicle to the left of the center line in the no passing zone; therefore, there was no negligence per se. Hurley v. Miller, 113 N.C. App. 658, 440 S.E.2d 286 (1994), rev'd on other grounds, 339 N.C. 601, 453 S.E.2d 861 (1995).

THE DOCTRINE OF SUDDEN EMERGENCY overrides the mandatory standards of subdivision (a) (2) of this section. Harris v. Guyton, 54 N.C. App. 434, 283 S.E.2d 538 (1981), cert. denied, 305 N.C. 152, 289 S.E.2d 380 (1982).

Where defendant failed to show that there was a "sudden emergencies" exception to G.S. 20-146 that allowed for a jury instruction on sudden emergency, and where defendant also failed to establish that the emergency which necessitated her sudden action of swerving into another lane of traffic in order to avoid a car that stopped short in front of her was not created by negligence on her part, there was no entitlement to such an instruction under G.S. 15A-1231. State v. Glover, 156 N.C. App. 139, 575 S.E.2d 835 (2003).

DRIVING TO LEFT TO AVOID COLLISION. --Where bus driver cut his bus to the left and crossed the centerline in an effort to avoid collision, such act was not negligence. Ingram v. Smoky Mt. Stages, Inc., 225 N.C. 444, 35 S.E.2d 337 (1945).

BURDEN ON PLAINTIFF TO ESTABLISH NEGLIGENCE. --Where plaintiff's evidence left in speculation and conjecture the determinative fact of whether defendant's car was being driven on the wrong side of the highway at the time of the collision, defendant's motion to nonsuit was properly granted, the burden being on plaintiff to establish defendant's negligence. Cheek v. Barnwell Whse. & Brokerage Co., 209 N.C. 569, 183 S.E. 729 (1936).

COMPETENCY OF CIRCUMSTANTIAL EVIDENCE. --Where evidence that defendant was driving to his left of the center of the highway when a collision occurred is circumstantial, i.e., based on testimony as to the physical facts at the scene, such evidence may be sufficiently strong to infer negligence and take the cause to the jury. Lassiter v. Williams, 272 N.C. 473, 158 S.E.2d 593 (1968).

COLLISION WITH GARBAGE TRUCK. --In negligence action in which plaintiff's van collided with defendant's garbage truck, despite the fact truck had stopped, trial judge properly submitted the issue of whether defendant violated this section, since there was evidence that while the garbage truck was stopped, the engine was left running. Smith v. Pass, 95 N.C. App. 243, 382 S.E.2d 781 (1989).

REASONABLE SUSPICION FOR TRAFFIC STOP. --Officer was allowed to pull defendant over based on reasonable suspicion because the officer reasonably suspected multiple traffic violations; defendant was driving ten miles per hour over the speed limit, following a truck too closely, and weaving over the white line marking the edge of the road, which was forbidden. State v. Bullock, 370 N.C. 256, 805 S.E.2d 671 (2017).

Deputy sheriff had reasonable suspicion to stop defendant's vehicle because the deputy saw defendant's vehicle barely cross the double yellow lines in the center of a road, which was a traffic violation. State v. Sutton, 259 N.C. App. 891, 817 S.E.2d 211 (2018), review denied, 818 S.E.2d 275, 2018 N.C. LEXIS 799 (N.C. 2018).

PROBABLE CAUSE TO STOP VEHICLE. --Where a police investigator saw defendant's vehicle commit a violation of G.S. 20-146(a), the traffic stop was proper under U.S. Const., Amend. IV, as it was based on a readily observed traffic violation and it was supported by probable cause. State v. Baublitz, 172 N.C. App. 801, 616 S.E.2d 615 (2005).

Superior court erred in affirming a district court's pretrial indication granting defendant's motion to suppress a traffic stop because defendant violated G.S. 20-146(d); when defendant crossed the double yellow line on a street he failed to stay in his lane in violation of G.S. 20-146(d)(1), and defendant failed to obey the double yellow line marker in violation of G.S. 20-146(d)(3)-(4). State v. Osterhoudt, 222 N.C. App. 620, 731 S.E.2d 454 (2012).

Superior court erred in affirming a district court's pretrial indication granting defendant's motion to suppress a traffic stop because a trooper had a reasonable articulable suspicion to stop defendant based on the observed traffic violations, and the stop was reasonable under the Fourth Amendment; the trooper's testimony that he initiated the stop of defendant after observing defendant drive over the double yellow line was sufficient to establish a violation of G.S. 20-146(d) and G.S. 20-153. State v. Osterhoudt, 222 N.C. App. 620, 731 S.E.2d 454 (2012).

Where the driver's conduct was in violation of statute, probable cause existed to stop the vehicle. United States v. Winstead, 2016 U.S. Dist. LEXIS 13860 (E.D.N.C. Feb. 4, 2016).

MOTION TO DISMISS PROPERLY DENIED. --Defendant's motion to dismiss the failure to maintain lane control charge was properly denied as there was substantial evidence from which the jury could infer that defendant did not ascertain that veering onto the shoulder and passing the tow truck on its right side could be done with safety because defendant was driving late at night at a speed unreasonably fast for the icy conditions; upon seeing a tow truck partially obstructing his current lane of traffic, defendant decided to pass the vehicle on the shoulder without first determining what, if any, further perils lay in his redirected course; and a reasonable motorist would not have attempted to pass the tow truck to its right along the shoulder. State v. Nazzal, -- N.C. App. --, 840 S.E.2d 881 (2020).

EVIDENCE HELD SUFFICIENT. --Testimony of witnesses who were at the scene of the collision almost immediately after it occurred to the effect that they saw glass, flour and mud on the south side of the highway, intestate's right side and defendant's left side of the highway, and nothing of the kind on the opposite side of the highway, the north side, was evidence that defendant's truck was being operated in violation of this section and §§ 20-147 and 20-148, which required defendant to drive his truck on his right side of the highway and to give plaintiff's coupe half of the main-traveled portion of the roadway as nearly as possible, and that this violation proximately caused the collision which resulted in the death of plaintiff's intestate. Wyrick v. Ballard & Ballard Co., 224 N.C. 301, 29 S.E.2d 900 (1944).

Testimony of passenger in truck driven by intestate to the effect that intestate was driving on his right side of the road in an ordinary manner, that defendant's tractor with trailer-tanker was traveling in the opposite direction, and that the truck hit the trailer-tanker which was sticking out to its left as the tractor was being driven to its right of the road, resulting in intestate's death, was sufficient to support an inference that defendant violated this section in failing to drive his tractor-trailer on his right half of the highway, proximately causing the death of plaintiff's intestate, and compulsory nonsuit was error. Gladden v. Setzer, 230 N.C. 269, 52 S.E.2d 804 (1949).

For case holding that blood spots indicated that when defendant's car struck deceased its left wheels were on or over the center of the highway in violation of this section, see State v. Phelps, 242 N.C. 540, 89 S.E.2d 132 (1955).

Where plaintiff passenger was injured in a head-on collision of two automobiles on a dirt road in the dust raised by a third car, testimony of witnesses that at least a part of each driver's vehicle was to the left of his center of the highway would take the issue as to the negligence of each driver to the jury. Forte v. Goodwin, 261 N.C. 608, 135 S.E.2d 552 (1964).

Plaintiff in a wrongful death action offered sufficient evidence, including physical evidence of tire marks at the scene and the defendant's statements to the investigating officer, to support a jury finding that defendant was driving on the left-hand side of the street when he struck plaintiff's intestate. Smith v. Kilburn, 13 N.C. App. 449, 186 S.E.2d 214, cert. denied, 281 N.C. 155, 187 S.E.2d 586 (1972).

For additional case holding evidence sufficient to show violation of section, see State v. Goins, 233 N.C. 460, 64 S.E.2d 289 (1951).

Trial court erred in refusing to instruct the jury that defendant violated G.S. 20-146(d) by failing to keep his vehicle in his lane of travel because plaintiff's evidence showed that defendant crossed the center line and struck plaintiff in the opposing lane of traffic; it was irrelevant that defendant did not intentionally drive his car across the center line, but rather the crucial inquiry was whether defendant's action culminating in the accident were negligent, and plaintiff's evidence that defendant was traveling at an unsafe speed for the icy road conditions at the time allowed a jury to find that defendant's negligence caused him to lose control of his vehicle. Sobczak v. Vorholt, 181 N.C. App. 629, 640 S.E.2d 805 (2007).

NO VIOLATION. --Defendant did not violate G.S. 20-146(a) because its requirement that drivers stay on the right half of the road would not apply since the street defendant was driving upon was a three-lane road. State v. Osterhoudt, 222 N.C. App. 620, 731 S.E.2d 454 (2012).

FOR CASE HOLDING EVIDENCE INSUFFICIENT TO SHOW AN INTENTIONAL, WILLFUL OR WANTON VIOLATION, see State v. Hancock, 248 N.C. 432, 103 S.E.2d 491 (1958); State v. Eller, 256 N.C. 706, 124 S.E.2d 806 (1962).

INSTRUCTION HELD WITHOUT ERROR. --An instruction that the violation of statutes regulating the operation of motor vehicles and the conduct of pedestrians on the highway would constitute negligence per se, and would be actionable if it was the proximate cause of injury, was without error when the instruction was applied solely to this section and G.S. 20-174, prescribing that vehicles should be operated on the right-hand side of the highway and that warning should be given pedestrians. Williams v. Woodward, 218 N.C. 305, 10 S.E.2d 913 (1940).

SUFFICIENCY OF INSTRUCTION. --Although a trial judge instructed the jury that every person was under a duty to follow standards of conduct established by a safety statute and that a person's failure to do so was negligence in and of itself, the only specific safety statute on which he then charged the jury was G.S. 20-141(a), to the effect that no person should drive a vehicle at a speed greater than was reasonable under the conditions then existing; this instruction was insufficient to act as substitute for a charge that defendant violated G.S. 20-146 because the jury was limited to finding negligence on the basis of defendant's violation of a safety statute if it found that he was driving his vehicle at a speed greater than was reasonable and prudent at the time instead of permitting the jury to consider, alternatively, that defendant was negligent because of actions that caused his vehicle to cross the center line and collide with plaintiff's car in plaintiff's lane of travel. Sobczak v. Vorholt, 181 N.C. App. 629, 640 S.E.2d 805 (2007).

APPLIED in Hancock v. Wilson, 211 N.C. 129, 189 S.E. 631 (1937); Newbern v. Leary, 215 N.C. 134, 1 S.E.2d 384 (1939). See also State v. Toler, 195 N.C. 481, 142 S.E. 715 (1928); State v. Durham, 201 N.C. 724, 161 S.E. 398 (1931); Queen City Coach Co. v. Lee, 218 N.C. 320, 11 S.E.2d 341 (1940); Horton v. Peterson, 238 N.C. 446, 78 S.E.2d 181 (1953); State v. Turberville, 239 N.C. 25, 79 S.E.2d 359 (1953); Combs v. United States, 122 F. Supp. 280 (E.D.N.C. 1954); Hennis Freight Lines v. Burlington Mills Corp., 246 N.C. 143, 97 S.E.2d 850 (1957); Kirkman v. Baucom, 246 N.C. 510, 98 S.E.2d 922 (1957); Parker v. Flythe, 256 N.C. 548, 124 S.E.2d 530 (1962); Hardin v. American Mut. Fire Ins. Co., 261 N.C. 67, 134 S.E.2d 142 (1964); Bass v. Roberson, 261 N.C. 125, 134 S.E.2d 157 (1964); Threadgill v. Kendall, 262 N.C. 751, 138 S.E.2d

625 (1964); Stewart v. Gallimore, 265 N.C. 696, 144 S.E.2d 862 (1965); Atwood v. Holland, 267 N.C. 722, 148 S.E.2d 851 (1966); State v. Massey, 271 N.C. 555, 157 S.E.2d 150 (1967); State v. Moses, 272 N.C. 509, 158 S.E.2d 617 (1968); Broadnax v. Deloatch, 8 N.C. App. 620, 175 S.E.2d 314 (1970); Asbury v. City of Raleigh, 48 N.C. App. 56, 268 S.E.2d 562 (1980); Belk v. Peters, 63 N.C. App. 196, 303 S.E.2d 641 (1983); Tate v. Christy, 114 N.C. App. 45, 440 S.E.2d 858 (1994).

CITED in Maddox v. Brown, 232 N.C. 542, 61 S.E.2d 613 (1950); White v. Cason, 251 N.C. 646, 111 S.E.2d 887 (1960); Brewer v. Powers Trucking Co., 256 N.C. 175, 123 S.E.2d 608 (1962); Wagner v. Eudy, 257 N.C. 199, 125 S.E.2d 598 (1962); McPherson v. Haire, 262 N.C. 71, 136 S.E.2d 224 (1964); State Hwy. Comm'n v. Raleigh Farmers Mkt., Inc., 263 N.C. 622, 139 S.E.2d 904 (1965); Hunt v. Carolina Truck Supplies, Inc., 266 N.C. 314, 146 S.E.2d 84 (1966); Champion v. Waller, 268 N.C. 426, 150 S.E.2d 783 (1966); Brewer v. Harris, 279 N.C. 288, 182 S.E.2d 345 (1971); State v. Boone, 16 N.C. App. 368, 192 S.E.2d 13 (1972); State v. Hefler, 60 N.C. App. 466, 299 S.E.2d 456 (1983); State v. Ealy, 94 N.C. App. 707, 381 S.E.2d 185 (1989); Body ex rel. Body v. Varner, 107 N.C. App. 219, 419 S.E.2d 208 (1992); Reynolds v. United States, 805 F. Supp. 336 (W.D.N.C. 1992); Peal ex rel. Peal v. Smith, 115 N.C. App. 225, 444 S.E.2d 673 (1994); Chaney v. Young, 122 N.C. App. 260, 468 S.E.2d 837 (1996); State v. Jones, 353 N.C. 159, 538 S.E.2d 917 (2000); State v. Hudson, 206 N.C. App. 482, 696 S.E.2d 577, review denied, 705 S.E.2d 360, 2010 N.C. LEXIS 1020 (2010); State v. McKenzie, 225 N.C. App. 208, 736 S.E.2d 591 (2013), rev'd 367 N.C. 112, 750 S.E.2d 521, 2013 N.C. LEXIS 1019 (2013), rev'd 748 S.E.2d 145, 2013 N.C. LEXIS 1019 (2013).

LEGAL PERIODICALS. --

For discussion of the subject matter of statutes similar to this and succeeding sections, see 2 N.C.L. Rev. 178 (1924) and 5 N.C.L. Rev. 248 (1927).

§ 20-146.1. Operation of motorcycles

(a) All motorcycles are entitled to full use of a lane and no motor vehicle shall be driven in such a manner as to deprive any motorcycle of the full use of a lane. This subsection shall not apply to motorcycles operated two abreast in a single lane.

(b) Motorcycles shall not be operated more than two abreast in a single lane. For purposes of this subsection, the term "motorcycle" shall not include autocycles. Autocycles shall not be operated more than one abreast in a single lane.

History.

1965, c. 909; 1973, c. 1330, s. 14; 1975, c. 786; 2015-163, s. 12

EDITOR'S NOTE. --

Session Laws 2015-163, s. 14, provides, in part: "Prosecutions for offenses committed before the effective date of this act are not abated or affected by this act, and the statutes that would be applicable but for this act remain applicable to those prosecutions."

Chapter 20

EFFECT OF AMENDMENTS. --
Session Laws 2015-163, s. 12, effective October 1, 2015, added the last two sentences of subsection (b).
APPLIED in Burrow v. Jones, 51 N.C. App. 549, 277 S.E.2d 97 (1981).

§ 20-146.2. Rush hour traffic lanes authorized

(a) **HOV Lanes. --** The Department of Transportation may designate one or more travel lanes as high occupancy vehicle (HOV) lanes on streets and highways on the State Highway System and cities may designate one or more travel lanes as high occupancy vehicle (HOV) lanes on streets on the Municipal Street System. HOV lanes shall be reserved for vehicles with a specified number of passengers as determined by the Department of Transportation or the city having jurisdiction over the street or highway. When HOV lanes have been designated, and have been appropriately marked with signs or other markers, they shall be reserved for privately or publicly operated buses, and automobiles or other vehicles containing the specified number of persons. Where access restrictions are applied on HOV lanes through designated signing and pavement markings, vehicles shall only cross into or out of an HOV lane at designated openings. A motor vehicle shall not travel in a designated HOV lane if the motor vehicle has more than three axles, regardless of the number of occupants. HOV lane restrictions shall not apply to any of the following:

(1) Motorcycles.

(2) Vehicles designed to transport 15 or more passengers, regardless of the actual number of occupants.

(3) Emergency vehicles. As used in this subdivision, the term "emergency vehicle" means any law enforcement, fire, police, or other government vehicle, and any public and privately owned ambulance or emergency service vehicle, when responding to an emergency.

(4) Plug-in electric vehicles as defined in G.S. 20-4.01(28b), regardless of the number of passengers in the vehicle. These vehicles must be able to travel at the posted speed limit while operating in the HOV lane.

(5) Dedicated natural gas vehicles as defined in G.S. 20-4.01(5a), regardless of the number of passengers in the vehicle. These vehicles must be able to travel at the posted speed limit while operating in the HOV lane.

(6) Fuel cell electric vehicles as defined in G.S. 20-4.01(12a), regardless of the number of passengers in the vehicle. These vehicles must be able to travel at the posted speed limit while operating in the HOV lane.

(a1) **Transitway Lanes. --** The Department of Transportation may designate one or more travel lanes as a transitway on streets and highways on the State Highway System and cities may designate one or more travel lanes as a transitway on streets on the Municipal Street System. Transitways shall be reserved for public transportation vehicles as determined by the Department of Transportation or the city having jurisdiction over the street or highway. When transitways have been designated, and they have been appropriately marked with signs or other markers, they shall be reserved for privately or publicly operated transportation vehicles as determined by the Department or the city having jurisdiction.

(b) **Temporary Peak Traffic Shoulder Lanes. --** The Department of Transportation may modify, upgrade, and designate shoulders of controlled access facilities and partially controlled access facilities as temporary travel lanes during peak traffic periods. When these shoulders have been appropriately marked, it shall be unlawful to use these shoulders for stopping or emergency parking. Emergency parking areas shall be designated at other appropriate areas, off these shoulders, when available.

(c) **Directional Flow Peak Traffic Lanes. --** The Department of Transportation may designate travel lanes for the directional flow of peak traffic on streets and highways on the State Highway System and cities may designate travel lanes for the directional flow of peak traffic on streets on the Municipal Street System. These travel lanes may be designated for time periods by the agency controlling the streets and highways.

History.
1987, c. 547, s. 1; 1999-350, s. 1;2003-184, s. 5;2011-95, s. 2;2011-206, s. 2;2012-194, s. 10;2020-73, s. 4

EDITOR'S NOTE. --
The reference to "G.S. 29-4.01(12a)" in subdivision (a)(6) appears to be incorrect and probably should be "G.S. 20-4.01(12a)."

Session Laws 2020-73, s. 7, made the amendment of subdivision (a)(4) by Session Laws 2020-73, s. 4, effective December 1, 2020, and applicable to offenses committed on or after that date.

EFFECT OF AMENDMENTS. --
Session Laws 2003-184, s. 5, effective December 1, 2003, and applicable to violations that occur on or after that date, added subsection catchlines in subsections (a) through (c); and added the fourth through last sentences in subsection (a).

Session Laws 2011-95, s. 2, effective May 26, 2011, subdivided former subsection (a), creating the introductory paragraph and the subdivision (1) through (3) designations; added "any of the following" at the end of the introductory paragraph of subsection (a); in subdivision (a)(3), substituted "Emergency vehicles" for "HOV lane restrictions shall not apply to emergency vehicles" and "subdivision" for "subsection"; and added subdivision (a)(4).

Session Laws 2011-206, s. 2, effective June 23, 2011, added subdivisions (a)(5) and (a)(6).

Session Laws 2012-194, s. 10, effective July 17, 2012, substituted "G.S. 20-4.01(12a)" for "G.S. 29-4.01(12a)" in subdivision (a)(6).

Session Laws 2020-73, s. 4, substituted "G.S. 20-4.01(28b)" for "G.S. 20-4.01(28a)" in the first sentence of subdivision (a)(4). For effective date and applicability, see editor's note.

§ 20-147. Keep to the right in crossing intersections or railroads

In crossing an intersection of highways or the intersection of a highway by a railroad right-of-way, the driver of a vehicle shall at all times cause such vehicle to travel on the right half of the highway unless such right side is obstructed or impassable.

History.
1937, c. 407, s. 109

EXERCISE OF ORDINARY CARE REQUIRED AT INTERSECTIONS. --The duties of motorists, both those on dominant and those on servient highways, when approaching, entering or traversing intersections, require that each driver exercise ordinary care under the particular circumstances in which he finds himself, and that the failure to do so can constitute actionable negligence where injury results. Murrell v. Jennings, 15 N.C. App. 658, 190 S.E.2d 686 (1972).

VIOLATION OF SECTION AS NEGLIGENCE. --A motorist is required by statute to remain on the right side of the highway at a crossing or intersection, and violation of this statute is negligence. Crotts v. Overnite Transp. Co., 246 N.C. 420, 98 S.E.2d 502 (1957).

APPLIED in Stutts v. Burcham, 271 N.C. 176, 155 S.E.2d 742 (1967).

CITED in Hardy v. Tesh, 5 N.C. App. 107, 167 S.E.2d 848 (1969); Rector v. James, 41 N.C. App. 267, 254 S.E.2d 633 (1979).

§ 20-147.1. Passenger vehicle towing other vehicles to keep right

Whenever a noncommercial passenger vehicle as defined in G.S. 20-4.01(27)*l*. is towing another vehicle as defined in G.S. 20-4.01(49), the driver of the towing vehicle shall at all times cause that vehicle to travel on the right half of the highway, and upon any highway having four or more lanes for moving traffic and providing for two-way movement of traffic, the vehicle shall not be driven in the left-most lane of the right half of the highway except when overtaking and passing another vehicle proceeding in the same direction, when preparing for a left

turn, or the right lanes are obstructed or impassable. These towing vehicles shall also comply with all signage for vehicles of three or more axles erected pursuant to G.S. 20-146(d)(3).

History.
2004-124, s. 30.6(a);2004-199, s. 56;2017-102, s. 5.2(b)

EDITOR'S NOTE. --
Session Laws 2004-124, s. 30.6(b), made this section effective December 1, 2004, and applicable to offenses committed on or after that date.

Session Laws 2017-102, s. 5.2(b) provides: "The Revisor of Statutes is authorized to reletter the definitions in G.S. 20-4.01(27) and G.S. 20-4.01(32b) to place them in alphabetical order. The Revisor of Statutes may conform any citations that change as a result of the relettering." Pursuant to that authority, the reference to G.S. 20-4.01(27)g. in this section was changed to G.S. 20-4.01(27)*l*.

EFFECT OF AMENDMENTS. --
Session Laws 2004-199, s. 56, effective August 17, 2004, substituted "and upon any highway having four or more lanes for moving traffic and providing for two-way movement of traffic, the vehicle shall not be driven in the left-most lane of the right half of the highway except when overtaking and passing another vehicle proceeding in the same direction, when preparing for a left turn, or the right lanes are" for "or if the highway is divided into two or more lanes in the right most lane of travel, unless that lane is" at the end of the first sentence.

§ 20-148. Meeting of vehicles

Drivers of vehicles proceeding in opposite directions shall pass each other to the right, each giving to the other at least one half of the main-traveled portion of the roadway as nearly as possible.

History.
1937, c. 407, s. 110

EDITOR'S NOTE. --Some of the cases cited below were decided under corresponding provisions of former law.

THIS SECTION PRESCRIBES A STANDARD OF CARE for a motorist and the standard fixed by the legislature is absolute. Bondurant v. Mastin, 252 N.C. 190, 113 S.E.2d 292 (1960); McGinnis v. Robinson, 258 N.C. 264, 128 S.E.2d 608 (1962).

FOR CASE HOLDING THIS SECTION IRRELEVANT WHERE COLLISION OCCURRED ON A THREE-LANE HIGHWAY, see State v. Duncan, 264 N.C. 123, 141 S.E.2d 23 (1965).

DRIVER HAS RIGHT TO ASSUME THAT OTHERS WILL OBSERVE THE LAW. --The driver of an automobile who is himself observing the law as set out in this section in meeting and passing an automobile proceeding in the opposite direction has the right ordinarily to assume that the driver of the approaching automobile will also observe the rule and avoid a collision. Lucas v. White, 248 N.C. 38, 102 S.E.2d 387 (1958).

When the driver of one of two automobiles is not observing the rule of this section, as the automobiles approach each other the other driver may assume that before the automobiles meet the driver of the approaching automobile will turn to his right, so that the two automobiles may pass each other in safety. Shirley v. Ayers, 201 N.C. 51, 158 S.E. 840 (1931). See also, James v. Carolina Coach Co., 207 N.C. 742, 178 S.E. 607 (1935); Hancock v. Wilson, 211 N.C. 129, 189 S.E. 631 (1937); Hoke v. Atlantic Greyhound Corp., 227 N.C. 412, 42 S.E.2d 593 (1947); Morgan v. Saunders, 236 N.C. 162, 72 S.E.2d 411 (1952).

BUT SUCH RIGHT IS NOT ABSOLUTE. --Ordinarily, a motorist has the right to assume that the driver of a vehicle approaching on the same side or on his left-hand side will yield half of the highway or turn out in time to avoid a collision, but this right is not absolute. It may be qualified by the particular circumstances existing at the time. Brown v. Southern Paper Prods. Co., 222 N.C. 626, 24 S.E.2d 334 (1943); Hoke v. Atlantic Greyhound Corp., 227 N.C. 412, 42 S.E.2d 593 (1947); Lamm v. Gardner, 250 N.C. 540, 108 S.E.2d 847 (1959).

The right of a motorist to assume that the driver of a negligently operated automobile will observe the law in time to avoid collision is not absolute, but may be qualified by the particular circumstances at the time, such as the proximity and movement of the other vehicle and the condition and width of the road. Morgan v. Saunders, 236 N.C. 162, 72 S.E.2d 411 (1952); Lamm v. Gardner, 250 N.C. 540, 108 S.E.2d 847 (1959).

The right of a motorist to assume that vehicles approaching from the opposite direction will remain on their right side of the highway is not absolute, and when a motorist approached a machine emitting a chemical fog obscuring the entire highway, he could not rely on such assumption when a reasonably prudent man might reasonably anticipate that a motorist might be on the highway meeting him and might be unable to keep safely on his side of the highway on account of the fog. Moore v. Town of Plymouth, 249 N.C. 423, 106 S.E.2d 695 (1959).

The rule that a motorist traveling on his right or seasonably turning thereto has the right to assume that a car approaching from the opposite direction will comply with this section and turn to its right in time to avoid a collision not applicable to a motorist who ran completely off the road to his right, lost control, and hit a car standing still completely off the hard surface on its left side of the highway with its lights on, since the rule merely absolves a motorist from blame if he continues at a reasonable rate of speed in his line of travel in reliance on the assumption, but does not relieve him from the duty of knowing the position of his car on the highway from his own observation. Webb v. Hutchins, 228 N.C. 1, 44 S.E.2d 350 (1947).

AND DRIVER MUST EXERCISE DUE CARE. --Notwithstanding the right of a motorist to so

assume, still this does not lessen his duty to conform to the requirement of exercising due care under the existing circumstances, that is, to conform to the rule of the reasonably prudent man. Sebastian v. Horton Motor Lines, 213 N.C. 770, 197 S.E. 539 (1938); Hoke v. Atlantic Greyhound Corp., 227 N.C. 412, 42 S.E.2d 593 (1947).

A motorist, although in his proper lane of traffic, must exercise ordinary care to avoid injuring persons or vehicles in his lane if he discovers their peril or in the exercise of ordinary care could discover it. It is his duty to slow down and have his vehicle under control and to pull over on the shoulder, if by doing so, he can avoid injury. Rundle v. Wyrick, 194 F. Supp. 630 (M.D.N.C. 1961), aff'd sub nom Rundle v. Grubb Motor Lines, 300 F.2d 333 (4th Cir. 1962).

VIOLATION OF THIS SECTION IS NEGLIGENCE PER SE. Hobbs v. Queen City Coach Co., 225 N.C. 323, 34 S.E.2d 211 (1945); Boyd v. Harper, 250 N.C. 334, 108 S.E.2d 598 (1959); McCombs v. McLean Trucking Co., 252 N.C. 699, 114 S.E.2d 683 (1960); Watters v. Parrish, 252 N.C. 787, 115 S.E.2d 1 (1960); Carswell v. Lackey, 253 N.C. 387, 117 S.E.2d 51 (1960); Anderson v. Webb, 267 N.C. 745, 148 S.E.2d 846 (1966).

AND CONSTITUTES ACTIONABLE NEGLIGENCE WHEN IT PROXIMATELY CAUSES INJURY. --A violation of this section would be negligence per se, and if such violation were the proximate cause of the injury it would be actionable. Wallace v. Longest, 226 N.C. 161, 37 S.E.2d 112 (1946); Hoke v. Atlantic Greyhound Corp., 226 N.C. 692, 40 S.E.2d 345 (1946); McGinnis v. Robinson, 258 N.C. 264, 128 S.E.2d 608 (1962); Anderson v. Webb, 267 N.C. 745, 148 S.E.2d 846 (1966).

A violation of this section is negligence per se, and, when proximate cause of injury or damage is shown, such violation constitutes actionable negligence. Reeves v. Hill, 272 N.C. 352, 158 S.E.2d 529 (1968); Lassiter v. Williams, 272 N.C. 473, 158 S.E.2d 593 (1968).

A violation of this section constitutes negligence, although such negligence is not actionable unless it is the proximate cause of the injuries complained of. Davis v. Imes, 13 N.C. App. 521, 186 S.E.2d 641 (1972).

A safety statute, such as this section, is pertinent when, and only when, there is evidence tending to show a violation thereof proximately caused the alleged injuries or death. State v. Duncan, 264 N.C. 123, 141 S.E.2d 23 (1965).

PROXIMATE CAUSE IS A MATTER FOR CONSIDERATION OF THE JURY under the law as declared by the court. Wallace v. Longest, 226 N.C. 161, 37 S.E.2d 112 (1946); McCombs v. McLean Trucking Co., 252 N.C. 699, 114 S.E.2d 683 (1960).

Where evidence tended to show that driver of defendant's truck, in meeting pickup truck in which plaintiffs were riding, was not passing on his right side of highway, and was not giving oncoming truck at least one half of the main-traveled portion of the roadway as nearly as possible, in violation of the provisions of this section, the question of whether defendant's truck was on left side of highway and, if so, whether this was the proximate cause of the collision would be for jury. Wallace v. Longest, 226 N.C. 161, 37 S.E.2d 112 (1946).

PRIMA FACIE CASE OF ACTIONABLE NEGLIGENCE IS MADE OUT BY EVIDENCE THAT DEFENDANT WAS DRIVING LEFT OF CENTER. --Where plaintiff sues for injuries or damages caused by an automobile collision and offers evidence showing that defendant was driving left of the center of the highway when the collision occurred, such evidence makes out a prima facie case of actionable negligence. Reeves v. Hill, 272 N.C. 352, 158 S.E.2d 529 (1968); Lassiter v. Williams, 272 N.C. 473, 158 S.E.2d 593 (1968).

BUT DEFENDANT MAY REBUT SUCH INFERENCE. --Evidence in an action for damages for injuries sustained in a collision, tending to show that the collision occurred when defendant was driving to his left of the center of the highway makes out a prima facie case of actionable negligence. The defendant, of course, may rebut the inference arising from such evidence by showing that he was on the wrong side of the road from a cause other than his own negligence. Anderson v. Webb, 267 N.C. 745, 148 S.E.2d 846 (1966).

WHEN VIOLATION CONSTITUTES CULPABLE NEGLIGENCE. --The violation of a safety statute which results in injury or death will constitute culpable negligence if the violation is willful, wanton, or intentional. But, where there is an unintentional or inadvertent violation of the statute, such violation standing alone does not constitute culpable negligence. The inadvertent or unintentional violation of the statute must be accompanied by recklessness of probable consequences of a dangerous nature when tested by the rule of reasonable prevision, amounting altogether to a thoughtless disregard of consequences or of a heedless indifference to the safety of others. State v. Roop, 255 N.C. 607, 122 S.E.2d 363 (1961).

COMPETENCY OF CIRCUMSTANTIAL EVIDENCE. --Where evidence that defendant was driving to the left of the center of the highway when a collision occurred is circumstantial, i.e., based on testimony as to the physical facts at the scene, such evidence may be sufficiently strong to infer negligence and take the case to the jury. Lassiter v. Williams, 272 N.C. 473, 158 S.E.2d 593 (1968).

EVIDENCE HELD SUFFICIENT. --Evidence tending to show that the driver of a truck was traveling 35 to 40 miles per hour in an early morning fog which limited visibility to 100 or 125 feet, that he had overtaken a vehicle traveling in the same direction and was attempting to pass such vehicle 250 or 300 feet before reaching a curve, and that he collided with plaintiff's car which approached from the opposite direction was held sufficient to be submitted to the jury on the issue of the negligence of the driver of the truck. Winfield v. Smith, 230 N.C. 392, 53 S.E.2d 251 (1949).

For additional cases holding evidence sufficient to show violation of this section, see State v. Wooten, 228 N.C. 628, 46 S.E.2d 868 (1948); Winfield v. Smith, 230 N.C. 392, 53 S.E.2d 251 (1949).

AS TO EVIDENCE SHOWING FAILURE TO YIELD ONE HALF OF ROADWAY, see State v. Goins, 233 N.C. 460, 64 S.E.2d 289 (1951).

INSTRUCTIONS UPHELD. --In an action for damages caused by the collision of two motor vehicles, a charge that "If plaintiff has satisfied you from the evidence and by the greater weight that on this occasion the driver of the defendant's truck at the time of the collision failed to drive the defendant's truck upon the right half of the highway, then that would constitute negligence on the part of defendant's driver" was in accord with this section. Hopkins v. Colonial Stores, Inc., 224 N.C. 137, 29 S.E.2d 455 (1944), overruled on other grounds in Jones v. Bailey, 246 N.C. 599, 99 S.E.2d 768 (1957).

An instruction on the right of a motorist to assume that an approaching vehicle would yield one half the highway in passing was held not objectionable in limiting such right to a motorist himself observing the requirements of the statute, when such instruction, considered in context, was to the effect that a motorist was not entitled to rely on such assumption if such motorist was himself then driving on his left side of the highway and was thereby contributing to the hazard and emergency that existed immediately prior to the collision. Blackwell v. Lee, 248 N.C. 354, 103 S.E.2d 703 (1958).

INSTRUCTION HELD ERRONEOUS. --An instruction confusing the provisions of G.S. 20-149, pertaining to the duty of the driver of any vehicle overtaking another vehicle proceeding in the same direction, with the provisions of this section, prescribing the respective duties of drivers of vehicles proceeding in opposite directions when meeting, was prejudicial error. Lookabill v. Regan, 245 N.C. 500, 96 S.E.2d 421 (1957).

APPLIED in Asbury v. City of Raleigh, 48 N.C. App. 56, 268 S.E.2d 562 (1980).

CITED in Harris v. Bridges, 46 N.C. App. 207, 264 S.E.2d 804 (1980); Williams v. Hall, 100 N.C. App. 655, 397 S.E.2d 767 (1990); Reynolds v. United States, 805 F. Supp. 336 (W.D.N.C. 1992); Peal ex rel. Peal v. Smith, 115 N.C. App. 225, 444 S.E.2d 673 (1994).

§ 20-149. Overtaking a vehicle

(a) The driver of any such vehicle overtaking another vehicle proceeding in the same direction shall pass at least two feet to the left thereof, and shall not again drive to the right side of the highway until safely clear of such overtaken vehicle. This subsection shall not apply when the overtaking and passing is done pursuant to the provisions of G.S. 20-150(e) or G.S. 20-150.1.

(b) Except when overtaking and passing on the right is permitted, the driver of an overtaken vehicle shall give way to the right in favor of the overtaking vehicle while being lawfully overtaken on audible signal and shall not increase the speed of his vehicle until completely passed by the overtaking vehicle.

Failure to comply with this subsection:

(1) Is a Class 1 misdemeanor when the failure is the proximate cause of a collision resulting in serious bodily injury.

(2) Is a Class 2 misdemeanor when the failure is the proximate cause of a collision resulting in bodily injury or property damage.

(3) Is, in all other cases, an infraction.

History.

1937, c. 407, s. 111; 1955, c. 913, s. 3; 1959, c. 247; 1973, c. 1330, s. 15; 1995, c. 283, s. 1;2016-90, s. 5.5(b) LOCAL MODIFICATION. --Durham, Mecklenburg (except as to City of Charlotte), Vance and Wake, as to subsection (a): 1953, c. 772; City of Charlotte: 2001-79.

EDITOR'S NOTE. --

Session Laws 2016-90, s. 5.5(d), made the substitution of "G.S. 20-150(e) or G.S. 20-150.1" for "G.S. 20-150.1" at the end of the last sentence in subsection (a) of this section by Session Laws 2016-90, s. 5.5(b), applicable to offenses committed on or after October 1, 2016.

EFFECT OF AMENDMENTS. --

Session Laws 2016-90, s. 5.5(b), effective October 1, 2016, in subsection (a), substituted "G.S. 20-150(e) or G.S. 20-150.1" for "G.S. 20-150.1." See editor's note for applicability.

I. IN GENERAL.

EDITOR'S NOTE. --Some of the cases cited below were decided under corresponding provisions of former law.

PURPOSE OF SECTION. --This section was enacted for the protection of the public upon the roads and highways of the State. Wolfe v. Independent Coach Line, 198 N.C. 140, 150 S.E. 876 (1929).

The principal purpose of this section is the protection of the "overtaken vehicle" and its occupants. McGinnis v. Robinson, 252 N.C. 574, 114 S.E.2d 365 (1960).

The object of this section is not only the protection of the overtaken vehicle and its occupants, but also the protection of the passing vehicle and its occupants. Boykin v. Bissette, 260 N.C. 295, 132 S.E.2d 616 (1963).

SECTION INAPPLICABLE WHERE FORWARD VEHICLE IS IN LEFT-TURN LANE. --The rule of the road contained in this section does not apply where there are three lanes available to the motorist and the forward vehicle is in the left-turn lane while the overtaking vehicle is in the through-traffic lane. Anderson v. Talman Office Supplies, Inc., 234 N.C. 142, 66 S.E.2d 677 (1951). See also, Anderson v. Talman Office Supplies, Inc., 236 N.C. 519, 73 S.E.2d 141 (1952).

OR WHERE VEHICLES ARE PROCEEDING IN OPPOSITE DIRECTIONS. --Absent unusual circumstances, this section has no bearing where collision is between vehicles proceeding in opposite directions. McGinnis v. Robinson, 252 N.C. 574, 114 S.E.2d 365 (1960).

A PERSON WALKING ALONG A PUBLIC HIGHWAY PUSHING A HANDCART IS A PEDESTRIAN within the purview of G.S. 20-174(d) and is not a driver of a vehicle within the meaning of G.S. 20-146 and this section. Lewis v. Watson, 229 N.C. 20, 47 S.E.2d 484 (1948).

COMMON-LAW RULE OF ORDINARY CARE APPLIES. Cowan v. Murrows Transf., Inc., 262 N.C. 550, 138 S.E.2d 228 (1964).

TWO-FOOT CLEARANCE REQUIREMENT IS A MINIMUM REQUIREMENT by the express terms of the statute. Murchison v. Powell, 269 N.C. 656, 153 S.E.2d 352 (1967).

WHICH APPLIES TO OVERTAKING AND PASSING ANOTHER VEHICLE. --The two-foot clearance required by this section applies to the overtaking and passing of another vehicle, not a horse subject to fright by a sudden noise. Murchison v. Powell, 269 N.C. 656, 153 S.E.2d 352 (1967).

SUBSECTION (A) OF THIS SECTION DOES NOT REQUIRE THAT A VEHICLE MUST PASS AT LEAST TWO FEET TO THE LEFT OF THE CENTERLINE of the highway in passing another vehicle traveling in the same direction, but only that it pass at least two feet to the left of the other vehicle. Eason v. Grimsley, 255 N.C. 494, 121 S.E.2d 885 (1961).

RULE OF THE ROAD SET OUT IN G.S. 20-152 DOES NOT APPLY WHERE ONE MOTORIST IS OVERTAKING AND PASSING ANOTHER, AS AUTHORIZED BY THIS SECTION, or where there are two lanes available to the motorist and the forward vehicle is in the outer lane and the overtaking vehicle is in the passing lane. Maddox v. Brown, 232 N.C. 542, 61 S.E.2d 613 (1950).

AS TO DUTY OF DRIVER OF OVERTAKING VEHICLE TO GIVE AUDIBLE WARNING and effect of his failure to do so under subsection (b) of this section as it stood before the 1973 amendment, see Ervin v. Cannon Mills Co., 233 N.C. 415, 64 S.E.2d 431 (1951); Ward v. Cruse, 236 N.C. 400, 72 S.E.2d 835 (1952); Lyerly v. Griffin, 237 N.C. 686, 75 S.E.2d 730 (1953); Sheldon v. Childers, 240 N.C. 449, 82 S.E.2d 396 (1954); Tallent v. Talbert, 249 N.C. 149, 105 S.E.2d 426 (1958); Schloss v. Hallman, 255 N.C. 686, 122 S.E.2d 513 (1961); Boykin v. Bissette, 260 N.C. 295, 132 S.E.2d 616 (1963); McPherson v. Haire, 262 N.C. 71, 136 S.E.2d 224 (1964); Cowan v. Murrows Transf., Inc., 262 N.C. 550, 138 S.E.2d 228 (1964); Webb v. Felton, 266 N.C. 707, 147 S.E.2d 219 (1966); Lowe v. Futrell, 271 N.C. 550, 157 S.E.2d 92 (1967); Kinney v. Goley, 4 N.C. App. 325, 167 S.E.2d 97, reaffirmed on rehearing, 6 N.C. App. 182, 169 S.E.2d 525 (1969).

There is no statutory requirement that a driver sound his horn when he begins to pass; thus, a driver's failure to sound his horn does not constitute negligence per se; rather, he is subject to the common-law duty to use reasonable care. Perry v. Aycock, 68 N.C. App. 705, 315 S.E.2d 791 (1984).

ABSENT A STATUTORY REQUIREMENT, A MOTORIST IS ONLY REQUIRED TO SOUND HIS HORN WHEN REASONABLY NECESSARY TO

GIVE WARNING. Perry v. Aycock, 68 N.C. App. 705, 315 S.E.2d 791 (1984).

DUTY ON APPROACHING STOPPED TRUCK. --Where driver of stopped truck standing on the right of the highway has given no clear signal of his intention to make a left turn, but merely has on the left rear and left fender a red light flashing on and off, the driver of an automobile approaching at night from the rear, in the exercise of ordinary care, is bound to approach with his automobile under control, so as to reduce his speed or stop, if necessary, to avoid injury. Weavil v. C.W. Myers Trading Post, Inc., 245 N.C. 106, 95 S.E.2d 533 (1956).

CONTRIBUTORY NEGLIGENCE IN OVERTAKING FORWARD VEHICLE FAILING TO SIGNAL INTENTION TO TURN LEFT. --Even though forward driver fails to signal before making a left turn, the driver overtaking and passing the forward driver may be guilty of contributory negligence for not complying with this section. Lyerly v. Griffin, 237 N.C. 686, 75 S.E.2d 730 (1953).

RIGHT TO PASS TO RIGHT OF FORWARD VEHICLE WHICH HAS SIGNALED INTENTION TO TURN LEFT. --Where the driver of a preceding vehicle traveling in the same direction gives a clear signal of his intention to turn left into an intersecting road and leaves sufficient space to his right to permit the overtaking vehicle to pass in safety, the provisions of subsection (a) of this section do not apply, and the overtaking vehicle may pass to the right of the overtaken vehicle, but this rule does not relieve the driver of the overtaking vehicle of the duty of observing other pertinent statutes. Ward v. Cruse, 236 N.C. 400, 72 S.E.2d 835 (1952).

Notwithstanding the provisions of this statute, a motorist may, in the exercise of ordinary care, pass another vehicle, going in the same direction, on the right of the overtaken vehicle when the driver of that vehicle has given a clear signal of his intention to make a left turn and has left sufficient space to the right to permit the overtaking vehicle to pass in safety. This rule, however, does not mean that the act of passing on the right of a left-turning vehicle at an intersection may not be accomplished in such a manner as to constitute negligence. Ford v. Smith, 6 N.C. App. 539, 170 S.E.2d 548 (1969).

Generally, the overtaking driver is justified in proceeding along the right side of the highway in attempting to pass the forward vehicle where the driver of the latter gives a left-turn signal or pulls over to the left as though intending to make a left turn. Ford v. Smith, 6 N.C. App. 539, 170 S.E.2d 548 (1969).

VIOLATION OF SECTION AS NEGLIGENCE PER SE. --Violation of this section is negligence per se, entitling the person injured to his damages when there is a causal connection between the negligent act and the injury complained of. Wolfe v. Independent Coach Line, 198 N.C. 140, 150 S.E. 876 (1929).

A violation of subsection (a) of this section is negligence per se. Kleibor v. Colonial Stores, Inc., 159 F.2d 894 (4th Cir. 1947).

Violation of subsection (a) of this section is negligence and if such negligence was the proximate cause of plaintiff's injuries, defendant, nothing else appearing, is liable to plaintiff. Stovall v. Ragland, 211 N.C. 536, 190 S.E. 899 (1937).

A violation of subsection (a) of this section would be negligence per se and if injury proximately result therefrom, it would be actionable. Tarrant v. Pepsi-Cola Bottling Co., 221 N.C. 390, 20 S.E.2d 565 (1942); Clark v. Emerson, 245 N.C. 387, 95 S.E.2d 880 (1957).

CONTRIBUTORY NEGLIGENCE HELD QUESTION FOR JURY. --Where the evidence tended to show that plaintiff's vehicle was following that of defendant, that defendant's truck slowed down and pulled to its left of the highway, that a person in the rear of the truck motioned plaintiff's driver to go ahead, and that as plaintiff's vehicle started to pass defendant's vehicle on its right, the driver of defendant's truck turned right to enter a private driveway and the two vehicles collided, nonsuit on the ground of contributory negligence was erroneously entered, since whether plaintiff's driver was guilty of contributory negligence in attempting to pass defendant's vehicle on the right was a question for the determination of the jury under the circumstances. Levy v. Carolina Aluminum Co., 232 N.C. 158, 59 S.E.2d 632 (1950).

EVIDENCE HELD SUFFICIENT TO RAISE ISSUE OF LAST CLEAR CHANCE. --Where the evidence tended to show that plaintiff, in order to avoid striking a chicken standing on the hard surface of the highway, drove his automobile gradually to the left, so that his car was traveling in about the center of the highway at the time of the accident in question, and that a bus belonging to defendant was traveling in the same direction and hit plaintiff's car when the bus attempted to pass, it was held that, conceding plaintiff was negligent in driving to the left without giving any signal or ascertaining if the car could be driven to the left in safety, defendant's motion to nonsuit was erroneously granted, since the pleadings and evidence were sufficient to raise the issue of last clear chance in tending to establish defendant's negligence in failing to keep a safe distance between the vehicles and in failing to take the precautions and give the signals required by this section for passing cars on the highway. Morris v. Seashore Transp. Co., 208 N.C. 807, 182 S.E. 487 (1935).

INSTRUCTIONS HELD ERRONEOUS. --In an action involving alleged negligence of defendant in failing to yield to plaintiff's intestate one half of highway as respective vehicles, traveling in opposite directions, passed each other, an instruction embracing the statutory duty of a driver of a vehicle overtaking and passing another vehicle traveling in the same direction was prejudicial error. Lookabill v. Regan, 245 N.C. 500, 96 S.E.2d 421 (1957).

Where the uncontroverted evidence supported a finding that the driver of defendant's car violated subsection (a) of this section as to the duty of the driver of an overtaking vehicle, but there was neither allegation nor evidence that such violation was a proximate cause of the collision, an instruction based on that subsection was erroneous and prejudicial. McGinnis v. Robinson, 252 N.C. 574, 114 S.E.2d 365 (1960).

APPLIED in State v. Holbrook, 228 N.C. 620, 46 S.E.2d 843 (1948); Clifton v. Turner, 257 N.C. 92, 125 S.E.2d 339 (1962); Pate v. Hair, 208 F. Supp. 455 (W.D.N.C. 1962); Bass v. Roberson, 261 N.C. 125, 134 S.E.2d 157 (1964); Farmers Oil Co. v. Miller, 264 N.C. 101, 141 S.E.2d 41 (1965); Simpson v. Lyerly, 265 N.C. 700, 144 S.E.2d 870 (1965); Welch v. Jenkins, 271 N.C. 138, 155 S.E.2d 763 (1967); Almond v. Bolton, 272 N.C. 78, 157 S.E.2d 709 (1967).

CITED in Citizens Nat'l Bank v. Phillips, 236 N.C. 470, 73 S.E.2d 323 (1952); Harris v. Davis, 244 N.C. 579, 94 S.E.2d 649 (1956); Rudd v. Stewart, 255 N.C. 90, 120 S.E.2d 601 (1961); Porter v. Philyaw, 204 F. Supp. 285 (W.D.N.C. 1962); Caudill v. Nationwide Mut. Ins. Co., 264 N.C. 674, 142 S.E.2d 616 (1965); Inman v. Harper, 2 N.C. App. 103, 162 S.E.2d 629 (1968); Bateman v. Elizabeth City State College, 5 N.C. App. 168, 167 S.E.2d 838 (1969); Bell v. Wallace, 32 N.C. App. 370, 232 S.E.2d 305 (1977); Davis v. Gamble, 55 N.C. App. 617, 286 S.E.2d 629 (1982); Whitley v. Owens, 86 N.C. App. 180, 356 S.E.2d 815 (1987).

II. DUTY OF DRIVER OF OVERTAKEN VEHICLE.

EDITOR'S NOTE. --Some of the cases treated below were decided under corresponding provisions of former law.

EXEMPTION OF POLICE VEHICLES IN CASE OF "RUNNING ROADBLOCK." --The provision of former G.S. 20-151 requiring the driver of a vehicle about to be overtaken to yield the right-of-way did not apply to a highway patrolman who set up a "running roadblock" in an attempt to stop a stolen car being pursued by another patrolman, since an exemption for police vehicles from that section in case of a running roadblock could be reasonably implied. Collins v. Christenberry, 6 N.C. App. 504, 170 S.E.2d 515 (1969).

DUTY TO TURN TO RIGHT. --The driver of an automobile, upon the signal of a faster car approaching from the rear, must turn to the right so that the other may pass to his left, when the conditions existing there at the time are reasonably safe to permit the other to pass. Dreher v. Divine, 192 N.C. 325, 135 S.E. 29 (1926).

DUTY NOT TO ACCELERATE. --Where driver was driving in the proper lane at approximately the maximum lawful speed, but when an overtaking car drew abreast of his car it was apparent that the overtaking vehicle was in a position of peril by reason of the near approach of a meeting vehicle, and the driver of car being overtaken did not reduce speed but accelerated and raced the passing car, under the circumstances thus presented, it was the duty of the driver of the car being overtaken not to increase the speed of his car until the overtaken car had completely passed. Rouse v. Jones, 254 N.C. 575, 119 S.E.2d 628 (1961).

DRIVER OF AN AUTOTRUCK IS NOT HELD TO THE SAME DEGREE OF CARE IN OBSERVING THOSE WHO MAY WISH TO PASS HIM COMING FROM THE REAR, as in front, and is not required to turn to the right for such purpose, unless he is appraised by the one who wishes to pass, by proper signal, of his intention to do so. Dreher v. Divine, 192 N.C. 325, 135 S.E. 29 (1926).

DUTY OF DRIVER PASSING FROM REAR. --The driver of an automobile who wishes to pass another ahead of him must keep his automobile under control, so as to avoid a collision if the driver ahead of him does not hear his signals or is not aware of his intention to pass, or if the condition of the road makes it unsafe not only to himself, but to those who are driving from the opposite direction. Dreher v. Divine, 192 N.C. 325, 135 S.E. 29 (1926).

CULPABLE NEGLIGENCE. --One who violated the provisions of former statute requiring driver to give way to overtaking vehicles, not intentionally or recklessly, but merely through a failure to exercise due care, and thereby proximately caused a death, would not be culpably negligent unless in the light of the attendant circumstances his negligent act was likely to result in death or bodily harm. State v. Stansell, 203 N.C. 69, 164 S.E. 580 (1932).

AS TO PROOF OF VIOLATION IN TRIAL FOR RESULTING CRIME, see State v. Rountree, 181 N.C. 535, 106 S.E. 669 (1921); State v. Jessup, 183 N.C. 771, 111 S.E. 523 (1922).

VIOLATION NOT EVIDENCE OF SPECIFIC INTENT TO ASSAULT. --Since the intentional driving of a motor vehicle on the wrong side of the road in disregard of former statutory provisions was malum prohibitum, not malum in se, the performance of this unlawful act was not evidence of a specific intent to commit an assault. State v. Rawlings, 191 N.C. 265, 131 S.E. 632 (1926).

SUBMISSION TO JURY REQUIRED. --Where there was evidence that plaintiff, desiring to pass a truck on the highway going in the same direction, blew his horn, and that the driver of the truck heard the signal, but instead of driving to the right of the center of the road to allow plaintiff to pass on the left, drove to the left and stopped or came almost to a stop, and that plaintiff, thinking that the truck was going to stop, and having his car under control, attempted to pass on the right, when the truck suddenly turned to the right, forcing plaintiff to turn to the right to avoid hitting the truck and causing plaintiff's car to run off embankment on the right of the road, resulting in injury, the evidence should have been submitted to the jury upon issues of negligence, contributory negligence and damages. Stevens v. Rostan, 196 N.C. 314, 145 S.E. 555 (1928).

WHERE THE DRIVER OF AN AUTOMOBILE VIOLATED THE STATUTES by turning to the right to avoid a motorcycle traveling in the same direction upon a public road, and collided therewith, and an action was brought to recover damages therefor, and the evidence was conflicting as to whether the motorcycle was unexpectedly turned out in the wrong direction, resulting in the injury, the question of proximate cause depended upon whether the driver of the automobile acted with reasonable prudence under the circumstances to avoid the injury, or whether the collision was caused by the wrongful and unexpected act of the one on the motorcycle. Cooke v. Jerome, 172 N.C. 626, 90 S.E. 767 (1916).

THE TRIAL JUDGE DID NOT ERR IN FAILING TO CHARGE THE JURY on the defendant's failure to yield to an overtaking vehicle, where there was no evidence presented that indicated that the other driver ever attempted to pass or to overtake the defendant once car chase had begun. Hord v. Atkinson, 68 N.C. App. 346, 315 S.E.2d 339 (1984).

§ 20-150. Limitations on privilege of overtaking and passing

(a) The driver of a vehicle shall not drive to the left side of the center of a highway, in overtaking and passing another vehicle proceeding in the same direction, unless such left side is clearly visible and is free of oncoming traffic for a sufficient distance ahead to permit such overtaking and passing to be made in safety.

(b) The driver of a vehicle shall not overtake and pass another vehicle proceeding in the same direction upon the crest of a grade or upon a curve in the highway where the driver's view along the highway is obstructed within a distance of 500 feet.

(c) The driver of a vehicle shall not overtake and pass any other vehicle proceeding in the same direction at any railway grade crossing nor at any intersection of highway unless permitted so to do by a traffic or police officer. For the purposes of this section the words "intersection of highway" shall be defined and limited to intersections designated and marked by the Department of Transportation by appropriate signs, and street intersections in cities and towns.

(d) The driver of a vehicle shall not drive to the left side of the centerline of a highway upon the crest of a grade or upon a curve in the highway where such centerline has been placed upon such highway by the Department of Transportation, and is visible.

(e) The driver of a vehicle shall not overtake and pass another on any portion of the highway which is marked by signs, markers or markings placed by the Department of Transportation stating or clearly indicating that passing should not be attempted. The prohibition in this section shall not apply when the overtaking and passing is done in accordance with all of the following:

(1) The slower moving vehicle to be passed is a bicycle or a moped.

(2) The slower moving vehicle is proceeding in the same direction as the faster moving vehicle.

(3) The driver of the faster moving vehicle either (i) provides a minimum of four feet between the faster moving vehicle and the slower moving vehicle or (ii) completely enters the left lane of the highway.

(4) The operator of the slower moving vehicle is not (i) making a left turn or (ii)

signaling in accordance with G.S. 20-154 that he or she intends to make a left turn.

(5) The driver of the faster moving vehicle complies with all other applicable requirements set forth in this section.

(e1) *(Effective December 1, 2020)* The driver of a vehicle shall not overtake and pass self-propelled farm equipment proceeding in the same direction when the farm equipment is (i) making a left turn or (ii) signaling that it intends to make a left turn.

(f) The foregoing limitations shall not apply upon a one-way street nor to the driver of a vehicle turning left in or from an alley, private road, or driveway.

History.
1937, c. 407, s. 112; 1955, c. 862; c. 913, s. 2; 1957, c. 65, s. 11; 1969, c. 13; 1973, c. 507, s. 5; c. 1330, s. 16; 1977, c. 464, s. 34; 1979, c. 472; 2016-90, s. 5.5(a);2020-18, s. 2(a)

EDITOR'S NOTE. --
Session Laws 2016-90, s. 5.5(d), made the last sentence and subdivisions (1) through (5) of subsection (e) of this section, as added by Session Laws 2016-90, s. 5.5(a), applicable to offenses committed on or after October 1, 2016.

Session Laws 2020-18, s. 2(b), made subsection (e1), as added by Session Laws 2020-18, s. 2(a), effective December 1, 2020, and applicable to offenses committed on or after that date.

Session Laws 2020-18, s. 16(a), is a severability clause.

EFFECT OF AMENDMENTS. --
Session Laws 2016-90, s. 5.5(a), effective October 1, 2016, in subsection (e), added "The prohibition in this section shall not apply when the overtaking and passing is done in accordance with all of the following" at the end of the introductory paragraph, and added subdivisions (e)(1), (e)(2), (e)(3), (e)(4), and (e)(5). See editor's note for applicability.

Session Laws 2020-18, s. 2(a), added subsection (e1). For effective date and applicability, see editor's note.

I. IN GENERAL.
EDITOR'S NOTE. --Some of the cases cited below were decided under corresponding provisions of former law.

PURPOSE OF SECTION. --The manifest purpose of this section is to promote safety in the operation of automobiles on the highways and not to obstruct vehicular traffic. Lawson v. Benton, 272 N.C. 627, 158 S.E.2d 805 (1968).

THIS SAFETY STATUTE MUST BE GIVEN A REASONABLE AND REALISTIC INTERPRETATION to effect the legislative purpose. Lawson v. Benton, 272 N.C. 627, 158 S.E.2d 805 (1968).

THIS SECTION APPLIES ONLY TO VEHICLES OVERTAKING AND PASSING ANOTHER VEHICLE TRAVELING IN THE SAME DIRECTION. State v. Boone, 16 N.C. App. 368, 192 S.E.2d 13 (1972).

APPLICABILITY OF SECTION TO LITIGATION BETWEEN OVERTAKING MOTORIST AND DRIVER OF OVERTAKEN VEHICLE. --Although this section is designed primarily to prevent collision between an overtaking automobile and a vehicle coming from the opposite direction, its provisions are germane to litigation between an overtaking motorist and the driver of an overtaken vehicle if there is evidence to the effect that the underlying accident was occasioned by an unsuccessful effort on the part of the former to pass the latter upon a marked curve. The driver of the overtaken vehicle is certainly not required in such case to anticipate that the latter will attempt to pass in violation of the section. Walker v. American Bakeries Co., 234 N.C. 440, 67 S.E.2d 459 (1951).

STATUTES OF THIS KIND HAVE NO APPLICATION TO MULTIPLE-LANE HIGHWAYS. Byerly v. Shell, 312 F.2d 141 (4th Cir. 1962).

The provisions of subsections (d) and (e) of this section were plainly not intended to apply to multiple highways which furnish parallel lanes on which vehicles moving in the same direction may pass without encountering traffic coming from the opposite direction. Byerly v. Shell, 312 F.2d 141 (4th Cir. 1962).

SUBSECTIONS (B) AND (D) HARMONIZED. --Subsections (b) and (d) of this section are harmonious rather than conflictive. They are not designed to regulate the behavior of the operator of an overtaking automobile in any event unless he is traveling upon a curve in the highway. Whether the one statutory regulation or the other applies to the driver of an overtaking vehicle proceeding upon a curve in the highway depends on whether the curve is marked by a visible centerline placed upon the highway by the State Highway Commission (now Department of Transportation). Where the curve is so marked, the action of the operator of the overtaking automobile is governed by subsection (d), which forbids him to drive to the left side of the centerline in order to pass the overtaken vehicle; and where the curve is not so marked, the conduct of the driver of the overtaking automobile is controlled by subsection (b), which permits him to pass the overtaken vehicle unless his view along the highway is obstructed within a distance of 500 feet. Walker v. American Bakeries Co., 234 N.C. 440, 67 S.E.2d 459 (1951).

NO RULE OF LAW COMPELS ONE VEHICLE TO TRAVEL INDEFINITELY BEHIND THE OTHER. Farmers Oil Co. v. Miller, 264 N.C. 101, 141 S.E.2d 41 (1965).

AND NO RULE GIVES ONE VEHICLE THE UNQUALIFIED RIGHT TO OVERTAKE AND PASS THE OTHER. Farmers Oil Co. v. Miller, 264 N.C. 101, 141 S.E.2d 41 (1965).

PURPOSE OF YELLOW LINES. --Yellow lines are designed primarily to prevent collision between an overtaking and passing automobile and a vehicle coming from the opposite direction, and to protect occupants of other cars, pedestrians and property on the highway. Rushing v. Polk, 258 N.C. 256, 128 S.E.2d

675 (1962); Farmers Oil Co. v. Miller, 264 N.C. 101, 141 S.E.2d 41 (1965).

PRESENCE AND CROSSING OF YELLOW LINE ARE EVIDENTIAL DETAILS in the totality of circumstances in a case. Farmers Oil Co. v. Miller, 264 N.C. 101, 141 S.E.2d 41 (1965).

TROOPER'S DIRECT OBSERVATIONS OF DRIVER'S ACTIONS PROVIDED REASONABLE SUSPICION FOR A VEHICLE STOP. Under North Carolina law, defendant's act of crossing the double yellow centerline clearly constituted a traffic violation. State v. Jones, 258 N.C. App. 643, 813 S.E.2d 668 (2018).

VIOLATION OF SECTION AS NEGLIGENCE PER SE. --A violation of this section, relating to the limitations on privilege of overtaking and passing another vehicle, is negligence per se, and, if injury proximately results therefrom, the injured party is entitled to recover. Johnson v. Harris, 166 F. Supp. 417 (M.D.N.C. 1958); Rouse v. Jones, 254 N.C. 575, 119 S.E.2d 628 (1961).

A violation of this section is negligence per se if injury proximately results therefrom. Duncan v. Ayers, 55 N.C. App. 40, 284 S.E.2d 561 (1981).

VIOLATION OF SUBSECTION (A) NEGLIGENCE PER SE. State v. Smith, 90 N.C. App. 161, 368 S.E.2d 33 (1988), aff'd, 323 N.C. 703, 374 S.E.2d 866, cert. denied, 490 U.S. 1100, 109 S. Ct. 2453, 104 L. Ed. 2d 1007 (1989).

VIOLATION NOT NEGLIGENCE PER SE --Decedent's initial act of negligence (being partially parked on the highway) justified the shift of defendant's vehicle to the left of the center line in the no passing zone; therefore, there was no negligence per se. Hurley v. Miller, 113 N.C. App. 658, 440 S.E.2d 286 (1994), rev'd on other grounds, 339 N.C. 601, 453 S.E.2d 861 (1995).

NOTICE OF SPECIAL HAZARD. --Signs in construction area marked "One-Way Road," "Slow" and "Men Working," the presence of dirt piled along the highway and a ditch-digging machine at work on side of the highway constituted notice to driver of oil transport truck that he was approaching a zone of special hazard. Sloan v. Glenn, 245 N.C. 55, 95 S.E.2d 81 (1956).

NEGLIGENCE AND CONTRIBUTORY NEGLIGENCE IN AREA OF SPECIAL HAZARD HELD JURY QUESTIONS. --Attempt of truck driver to pass a backfiller tractor traveling in the same direction in an area of special hazard was not negligence as a matter of law under the circumstances, but truck driver's negligence and contributory negligence of tractor driver were questions for the jury. Sloan v. Glenn, 245 N.C. 55, 95 S.E.2d 81 (1956).

FOR CASE HOLDING INSTRUCTION ERRONEOUS AS NULLIFYING PROVISIONS OF THIS SECTION, see Walker v. American Bakeries Co., 234 N.C. 440, 67 S.E.2d 459 (1951).

EVIDENCE HELD SUFFICIENT. --Evidence tending to show that defendant truck driver was traveling 35 to 40 miles per hour in an early morning fog which limited visibility to 100 or 126 feet, that he had overtaken a vehicle traveling in the same direction and was attempting to pass such vehicle 250 or 300 feet before reaching a curve, and that he collided with plaintiff's car which approached from the opposite direction was held sufficient to be submitted to the jury on the issue of the negligence of the truck driver. Winfield v. Smith, 230 N.C. 392, 53 S.E.2d 251 (1949).

Evidence that the driver of a truck, in attempting to pass cars going in the same direction, pulled out in the center of the road and hit car which plaintiff was driving in the opposite direction, causing damage to the car and injury to plaintiff, was sufficient to be submitted to the jury on the question of the actionable negligence of the driver of the truck. Joyner v. Dail, 210 N.C. 663, 188 S.E. 209 (1936).

For additional cases holding evidence sufficient to show violation of this section, see Winfield v. Smith, 230 N.C. 392, 53 S.E.2d 251 (1949); State v. Goins, 233 N.C. 460, 64 S.E.2d 289 (1951).

EVIDENCE HELD INSUFFICIENT. --Where plaintiff testified he passed in a passing zone and the evidence showed the collision occurred almost exactly where the passing zone ended, this evidence failed to establish plaintiff's negligence so clearly that no other reasonable inference could have been drawn. Therefore, the trial court did not err in denying defendant's motion for a directed verdict. Sass v. Thomas, 90 N.C. App. 719, 370 S.E.2d 73 (1988).

CONTRIBUTORY NEGLIGENCE HELD TO BAR RECOVERY. --Even though the driver of a truck which collided with plaintiff's automobile failed to observe certain statutory requirements, where the evidence was clear in showing that the collision occurred when plaintiff was attempting to overtake and pass the truck proceeding in the same direction at a highway intersection, without permission so to do by a traffic or police officer, in violation of this section, contributory negligence on the part of plaintiff barred recovery. Cole v. Fletcher Lumber Co., 230 N.C. 616, 55 S.E.2d 86 (1949).

NONSUIT ON THE GROUND OF CONTRIBUTORY NEGLIGENCE WAS ERRONEOUSLY ENTERED where plaintiff's evidence did not compel the inference that his negligence contributed as a proximate cause to his injury and damage. Pruett v. Inman, 252 N.C. 520, 114 S.E.2d 360 (1960).

APPLIED in Bass v. Roberson, 261 N.C. 125, 134 S.E.2d 157 (1964); Taney v. Brown, 262 N.C. 438, 137 S.E.2d 827 (1964); Knight v. Seymour, 263 N.C. 790, 140 S.E.2d 410 (1965); Duckworth v. Metcalf, 268 N.C. 340, 150 S.E.2d 485 (1966); Wands v. Cauble, 270 N.C. 311, 154 S.E.2d 425 (1967); Stutts v. Burcham, 271 N.C. 176, 155 S.E.2d 742 (1967); Watson Seafood & Poultry Co. v. George W. Thomas, Inc., 26 N.C. App. 6, 214 S.E.2d 605 (1975); Belk v. Peters, 63 N.C. App. 196, 303 S.E.2d 641 (1983).

CITED in State v. Palmer, 197 N.C. 135, 147 S.E. 817 (1929); Cook v. Horne, 198 N.C. 739, 153 S.E. 315 (1930); Queen City Coach Co. v. Lee, 218 N.C. 320, 11 S.E.2d 341 (1940); Tysinger v. Coble Dairy Prods., 225 N.C. 717, 36 S.E.2d 246 (1945); Citizens Nat'l Bank v. Phillips, 236 N.C. 470, 73 S.E.2d 323 (1952); Sheldon v. Childers, 240 N.C. 449, 82 S.E.2d 396 (1954) (as

to subsection (c)); Kirkman v. Baucom, 246 N.C. 510, 98 S.E.2d 922 (1957); McGinnis v. Robinson, 252 N.C. 574, 114 S.E.2d 365 (1960); Bundy v. Belue, 253 N.C. 31, 116 S.E.2d 200 (1960); McPherson v. Haire, 262 N.C. 71, 136 S.E.2d 224 (1964); Wyatt v. Haywood, 22 N.C. App. 267, 206 S.E.2d 260 (1974); Bell v. Brueggemyer, 35 N.C. App. 658, 242 S.E.2d 392 (1978); Rector v. James, 41 N.C. App. 267, 254 S.E.2d 633 (1979); Body ex rel. Body v. Varner, 107 N.C. App. 219, 419 S.E.2d 208 (1992).

II. PASSING AT RAILWAY GRADE CROSSINGS OR INTERSECTIONS.

SUBSECTION (C) OF THIS SECTION IS A SAFETY STATUTE enacted for the public's common safety and welfare. Watson Seafood & Poultry Co. v. George W. Thomas, Inc., 289 N.C. 7, 220 S.E.2d 536 (1975).

A PRIVATE DRIVEWAY IS NOT AN INTERSECTING HIGHWAY WITHIN THE MEANING OF SUBSECTION (C) of this section. Levy v. Carolina Aluminum Co., 232 N.C. 158, 59 S.E.2d 632 (1950); Farmers Oil Co. v. Miller, 264 N.C. 101, 141 S.E.2d 41 (1965).

ABSENT A STATUTORY REQUIREMENT, A MOTORIST IS ONLY REQUIRED TO SOUND HIS HORN WHEN REASONABLY NECESSARY TO GIVE WARNING. Perry v. Aycock, 68 N.C. App. 705, 315 S.E.2d 791 (1984).

NEED TO PROHIBIT PASSING AT INTERSECTIONS. --In the case of a two-lane roadway in which traffic moves in both directions, the need to prohibit passing at intersections is obvious, since the driver in the rear may reasonably anticipate that the car in the lead may desire to turn to the left. To such a situation the statute clearly applies. Byerly v. Shell, 312 F.2d 141 (4th Cir. 1962).

THE MEANING OF SUBSECTION (C) of this section is that one motorist may not pass another going in the same direction under either of two conditions: (1) At any place designated and marked by the State Highway Commission (now Department of Transportation) as an intersection; (2) At any street intersection in any city or town. Adams v. Godwin, 252 N.C. 471, 114 S.E.2d 76 (1960).

SUBSECTION (C) OF THIS SECTION REQUIRES ONE TO OBSERVE STREET INTERSECTIONS WITHIN CORPORATE LIMITS whether marked or unmarked. Watson Seafood & Poultry Co. v. George W. Thomas, Inc., 289 N.C. 7, 220 S.E.2d 536 (1975).

SINCE SUBSECTION (C) OF THIS SECTION DOES NOT CONTAIN THE WORDS "KNOWINGLY," "WILLFULLY" OR OTHER WORDS OF LIKE IMPORT, it was the obvious intent of the legislature to make the performance of a specific act a criminal violation and to thereby place upon the individual the burden to know whether his conduct is within the statutory prohibition. Watson Seafood & Poultry Co. v. George W. Thomas, Inc., 289 N.C. 7, 220 S.E.2d 536 (1975).

PASSING AT INTERSECTION ON DUAL HIGHWAY IS NOT NEGLIGENCE PER SE. --Under the proper interpretation of the North Carolina statutes, it is not unlawful and negligent per se for one vehicle to pass another at an intersection on a dual highway. Byerly v. Shell, 312 F.2d 141 (4th Cir. 1962).

BUT THE EXERCISE OF CAREFUL LOOKOUT IS ESPECIALLY INDICATED ON A HIGHWAY HAVING A PASSING LANE. State v. Fuller, 259 N.C. 111, 130 S.E.2d 61 (1963).

PASSING AT CROSSOVER NOT A VIOLATION OF SUBSECTION (C). --An intersection under subsection (c) of this section must be designated and marked by the Highway Commission (now Department of Transportation) by appropriate signs, and overtaking and passing another vehicle at "a crossover" is not a violation of this section and is therefore not negligence per se. Bennet v. Livingston, 250 N.C. 586, 108 S.E.2d 843 (1959).

PASSING AT RAILROAD GRADE CROSSING IS NEGLIGENCE PER SE. --It is negligence per se for the operator of a motor vehicle to overtake and pass another vehicle traveling in the same direction at a railroad grade crossing. Murray v. Atlantic C.L.R.R., 218 N.C. 392, 11 S.E.2d 326 (1940).

AS IS UNAUTHORIZED PASSING AT INTERSECTION. --It is negligence per se for a motorist to overtake and pass another vehicle proceeding in the same direction at an intersection of a highway, unless permitted to do so by a traffic officer. Donivant v. Swain, 229 N.C. 114, 47 S.E.2d 707 (1948); Cole v. Fletcher Lumber Co., 230 N.C. 616, 55 S.E.2d 86 (1949); Ferris v. Whitaker, 123 F. Supp. 356 (E.D.N.C. 1954); Adams v. Godwin, 252 N.C. 471, 114 S.E.2d 76 (1960).

This section prohibits a motorist from overtaking and passing at highway intersections, and the violation of this section is negligence. Crotts v. Overnite Transp. Co., 246 N.C. 420, 98 S.E.2d 502 (1957).

Where plaintiff's driver overtook and attempted to pass defendant's truck at an intersection within a municipality, he was guilty of negligence per se under subsection (c) of this section, and without regard to his knowledge of whether he was within the city limits of the municipality. Watson Seafood & Poultry Co. v. George W. Thomas, Inc., 289 N.C. 7, 220 S.E.2d 536 (1975).

WHERE INJURY PROXIMATELY RESULTS THEREFROM. --Violation of subsection (c) of this section constitutes negligence per se if injury proximately results therefrom. Carter v. Scheidt, 261 N.C. 702, 136 S.E.2d 105 (1964); Teachey v. Woolard, 16 N.C. App. 249, 191 S.E.2d 903, cert. denied, 288 N.C. 430, 192 S.E.2d 840 (1972).

FOR CASE HOLDING THAT ACT OF MOTORIST IN VIOLATING SUBSECTION (C) OF THIS SECTION WAS THE SOLE PROXIMATE CAUSE OF COLLISION which occurred when an overtaking motorist attempted to pass a truck while the latter was making a left turn at an intersection, without passing beyond the center of the intersection as was then required by G.S. 20-153, see Ferris v. Whitaker, 123 F. Supp. 356 (E.D.N.C. 1954).

FOR CASE HOLDING THAT EVIDENCE DID NOT COMPEL THE CONCLUSION THAT PLAINTIFF'S DRIVER ATTEMPTED TO PASS

DEFENDANT'S VEHICLE at an intersection in violation of this section, see Carolina Cas. Ins. Co. v. Cline, 238 N.C. 133, 76 S.E.2d 374 (1953).

FAILURE TO INSTRUCT ON SUBSECTION (C) HELD ERROR. --Where the evidence tended to show that the driver of an automobile overtook and attempted to pass a truck proceeding in the same direction at an intersection of streets in a municipality at which no traffic officer was stationed, and that the vehicle collided when the driver of the truck made a left turn at the intersection, it was error for the court to instruct the jury that the provisions of subsection (c) of this section did not apply. Donivant v. Swain, 229 N.C. 114, 47 S.E.2d 707 (1948).

DENIAL OF NONSUIT ON GROUNDS OF CONTRIBUTORY NEGLIGENCE UPHELD. --Where plaintiff's evidence tended to show that he started passing a truck 275 feet from an intersection, nonsuit on the ground that plaintiff was contributorily negligent in attempting to pass at an intersection was properly denied, since the evidence was susceptible to the inference that plaintiff could have passed the truck before it reached the intersection had not the driver of the truck turned suddenly to the left 75 feet from the intersection in "cutting the corner." Howard v. Bingham, 231 N.C. 420, 57 S.E.2d 401 (1950).

OPINIONS OF THE ATTORNEY GENERAL

SOLID CENTERLINES ARE CONSIDERED TO BE "MARKINGS" UNDER SUBSECTION (E) OF THIS SECTION. --See opinion of Attorney General to Ms. Clair McNaught, Public Safety Attorney, 49 N.C.A.G. 1 (1979).

§ 20-150.1. When passing on the right is permitted

The driver of a vehicle may overtake and pass upon the right of another vehicle only under the following conditions:

(1) When the vehicle overtaken is in a lane designated for left turns;

(2) Upon a street or highway with unobstructed pavement of sufficient width which have been marked for two or more lanes of moving vehicles in each direction and are not occupied by parked vehicles;

(3) Upon a one-way street, or upon a highway on which traffic is restricted to one direction of movement when such street or highway is free from obstructions and is of sufficient width and is marked for two or more lanes of moving vehicles which are not occupied by parked vehicles;

(4) When driving in a lane designating a right turn on a red traffic signal light.

History.
1953, c. 679

PASSING ON THE RIGHT, WHEN NOT SANCTIONED BY THIS SECTION, CONSTITUTES NEGLIGENCE PER SE if found to be the proximate cause of a collision. Teachey v. Woolard, 16 N.C. App. 249, 191 S.E.2d 903, cert. denied, 282 N.C. 430, 192 S.E.2d 840 (1972).

APPLIED in Schloss v. Hallman, 255 N.C. 686, 122 S.E.2d 513 (1961).

CITED in Oliver v. Royall, 36 N.C. App. 239, 243 S.E.2d 436 (1978); Duncan v. Ayers, 55 N.C. App. 40, 284 S.E.2d 561 (1981).

LEGAL PERIODICALS. --

For brief comment on this section, see 31 N.C.L. Rev. 418 (1953).

N.C. Gen. Stat. § 20-151

Repealed by Session Laws 1995, c. 283, s. 2.

§ 20-152. Following too closely

(a) The driver of a motor vehicle shall not follow another vehicle more closely than is reasonable and prudent, having due regard for the speed of such vehicles and the traffic upon and the condition of the highway.

(b) The driver of any motor vehicle traveling upon a highway outside of a business or residential district and following another motor vehicle shall, whenever conditions permit, leave sufficient space so that an overtaking vehicle may enter and occupy such space without danger, except that this shall not prevent a motor vehicle from overtaking and passing another motor vehicle. This provision shall not apply to funeral processions.

(c) Subsections (a) and (b) of this section shall not apply to the driver of any non-leading commercial motor vehicle traveling in a platoon on any roadway where the Department of Transportation has by traffic ordinance authorized travel by platoon. For purposes of this subsection, the term "platoon" means a group of individual commercial motor vehicles traveling at close following distances in a unified manner through the use of an electronically interconnected braking system.

History.

1937, c. 407, s. 114; 1949, c. 1207, s. 4; 1973, c. 1330, s. 17; 2017-169, s. 1

EDITOR'S NOTE. --

Session Laws 2017-169, s. 2, provides: "The Department shall submit a report on the implementation of this act to the Joint Legislative Transportation Oversight Committee on or before April 1, 2018."

Session Laws 2017-169, s. 3 made subsection (c) of this section as added by Session Laws 2017-169, s. 1, effective August 1, 2017, and further provides: "Prosecutions for offenses committed before the effective date of this act are not abated or affected by this act, and the statutes that would be applicable but for this act remain applicable to those prosecutions."

EFFECT OF AMENDMENTS. --

Session Laws 2017-169, s. 1, added subsection (c). For effective date and applicability, see editor's note.

SUBSECTION (A) OF THIS SECTION IS A STATUTORY DECLARATION OF THE COMMON LAW that the driver of a motor vehicle shall not follow another vehicle more closely than is reasonable and prudent, with regard for the safety of others and due regard to the speed of such vehicles and the traffic upon and condition of the highway. Black v. Gurley Milling Co., 257 N.C. 730, 127 S.E.2d 515 (1962).

THE RULE OF THE ROAD SET OUT IN THIS SECTION DOES NOT APPLY WHERE ONE MOTORIST IS OVERTAKING AND PASSING ANOTHER, as authorized by G.S. 20-149, or where there are two lanes available to the motorist and the forward vehicle is in the outer lane and the overtaking vehicle is in the passing lane. Maddox v. Brown, 232 N.C. 542, 61 S.E.2d 613 (1950).

If the defendant was in the act of passing, then this section would have no application and provide no standard by which the court might judge. Gowens v. Morgan & Sons Poultry Co., 238 F. Supp. 399 (M.D.N.C. 1964).

NOR TO VEHICLES STOPPING ONE BEHIND THE OTHER. --The statutory prohibition against following too closely a vehicle traveling in the same direction has no application to the distance between vehicles stopping one behind another on the highway. There is no prescribed distance within which one car must stop behind another stopped car. Royal v. McClure, 244 N.C. 186, 92 S.E.2d 762 (1956).

THIS SECTION FIXES NO SPECIFIC DISTANCE at which one automobile may lawfully follow another. Beanblossom v. Thomas, 266 N.C. 181, 146 S.E.2d 36 (1966).

DETERMINING PROPER SPACE TO BE MAINTAINED BETWEEN VEHICLES. --A motorist, in determining the proper space to be maintained between his vehicle and the one preceding him, must take into consideration such variables as the locality, road and weather conditions, other traffic on the highway, and the characteristics of the vehicle he is driving, as well as that of the one ahead, the relative speeds of the two, and his ability to control and stop his vehicle should an emergency require it. Thus, the space is determined according to the standard of reasonable care and should be sufficient to enable the operator of the car behind to avoid danger in case of a sudden stop or a decrease in speed by the vehicle ahead under circumstances which should reasonably be anticipated by the following driver. Beanblossom v. Thomas, 266 N.C. 181, 146 S.E.2d 36 (1966).

REASONABLE SUSPICION FOR TRAFFIC STOP. --Officer was allowed to pull defendant over based on reasonable suspicion because the officer reasonably suspected multiple traffic violations; defendant was driving ten miles per hour over the speed limit, following a truck too closely, and weaving over the white line marking the edge of the road, which was forbidden. State v. Bullock, 370 N.C. 256, 805 S.E.2d 671 (2017).

DRIVERS CHARGED WITH NOTICE THAT OPERATION OF EACH CAR IN LINE IS AFFECTED BY CAR IN FRONT. --Where plaintiff and defendant had been driving their cars behind a line of cars for a substantial distance, the drivers, in the exercise of reasonable care, were charged with notice that the operation of each car was affected by the one in front of it. They had to maintain such distance, keep such a lookout, and operate at such speed, under these conditions, that they could control their cars under ordinarily foreseeable developments. Griffin v. Ward, 267 N.C. 296, 148 S.E.2d 133 (1966).

CONDITION AND EFFECTIVENESS OF BRAKES MUST BE TAKEN INTO CONSIDERATION BY A MOTORIST in determining what is a safe distance and a safe speed at which he may follow another vehicle. Crotts v. Overnite Transp. Co., 246 N.C. 420, 98 S.E.2d 502 (1957).

EXERCISE OF CARE AFTER DISCOVERY OF SUDDEN PERIL WOULD NOT EXERCISE NEGLIGENT CONDUCT where the sudden peril was due to failure to keep a safe distance behind another vehicle and maintain a proper lookout. Gowens v. Morgan & Sons Poultry Co., 238 F. Supp. 399 (M.D.N.C. 1964).

CERTAIN INFERENCES ARE PERMITTED FROM FACT OF COLLISION. --Ordinarily the mere fact of a collision with the vehicle ahead furnishes some evidence that the motorist to the rear was not keeping a proper lookout or that he was following too closely. Burnett v. Corbett, 264 N.C. 341, 141 S.E.2d 468 (1965).

Unless the driver of the leading vehicle is himself guilty of negligence, or unless an emergency is created by some third person or other highway hazard, the mere fact of a collision with the vehicle ahead furnishes some evidence that the motorist in the rear was not keeping a proper lookout or that he was following too closely. Beanblossom v. Thomas, 266 N.C. 181, 146 S.E.2d 36 (1966).

The mere fact of a collision with a vehicle ahead furnishes some evidence that the following motorist was negligent as to speed or was following too closely. Griffin v. Ward, 267 N.C. 296, 148 S.E.2d 133 (1966); Huggins v. Kye, 10 N.C. App. 221, 178 S.E.2d 127 (1970).

Admission of defendant that his car collided with the rear of plaintiff's car permitted a legitimate inference by a jury that defendant was following plaintiff's automobile more closely than was reasonable and prudent, in violation of this section. Scher v. Antonucci, 77 N.C. App. 810, 336 S.E.2d 434 (1985).

BUT MERE PROOF OF COLLISION DOES NOT COMPEL CONCLUSIONS. --Though the mere fact of a collision with a vehicle furnishes some evidence of a violation of this section, or of failure to keep a proper lookout, the mere proof of a collision with a preceding vehicle does not compel either of these conclusions. It merely raises a question for the jury to determine. Ratliff v. Duke Power Co., 268 N.C. 605, 151 S.E.2d 641 (1966); Scher v. Antonucci, 77 N.C. App. 810, 336 S.E.2d 434 (1985).

THE FOLLOWING DRIVER IS NOT AN INSURER AGAINST REAR-END COLLISIONS, for, even when he follows at a distance reasonable under the existing conditions, the space may be too short to permit a stop under any and all eventualities. White v. Mote, 270 N.C. 544, 155 S.E.2d 75 (1967).

A VIOLATION OF THIS SECTION IS NEGLIGENCE PER SE. Burnett v. Corbett, 264 N.C. 341, 141 S.E.2d 468 (1965); Ratliff v. Duke Power Co., 268 N.C. 605, 151 S.E.2d 641 (1966); Scher v. Antonucci, 77 N.C. App. 810, 336 S.E.2d 434 (1985).

A motorist is prohibited by this section from following another vehicle more closely than is reasonable and prudent under the circumstances with regard to the traffic and the condition of the highway, and the violation of this section is negligence. Crotts v. Overnite Transp. Co., 246 N.C. 420, 98 S.E.2d 502 (1957).

A violation of subsection (a) of this section is negligence per se, and, if injury proximately results therefrom, it is actionable. Murray v. Atlantic C.L.R.R., 218 N.C. 392, 11 S.E.2d 326 (1940); Cozart v. Hudson, 239 N.C. 279, 78 S.E.2d 881 (1954); Smith v. Rawlins, 253 N.C. 67, 116 S.E.2d 184 (1960); Fox v. Hollar, 257 N.C. 65, 125 S.E.2d 334 (1962); Hamilton v. McCash, 257 N.C. 611, 127 S.E.2d 214 (1962); Gowens v. Morgan & Sons Poultry Co., 238 F. Supp. 399 (M.D.N.C. 1964); Beanblossom v. Thomas, 266 N.C. 181, 146 S.E.2d 36 (1966).

FOR CASE HOLDING THAT PLAINTIFF WAS NOT GUILTY OF CONTRIBUTORY NEGLIGENCE in following too closely a truck with which he collided, see Killough v. Williams, 224 N.C. 254, 29 S.E.2d 697 (1944).

INSTRUCTION REQUIRED. --Where violation of this section bore directly on the issue of defendant's negligence, which was a substantial feature of the case, the court should have declared and explained the section in its charge to the jury, and should also have explained that violation of this section was negligence per se. The court had this duty irrespective of plaintiff's request for special instructions. Scher v. Antonucci, 77 N.C. App. 810, 336 S.E.2d 434 (1985).

WHERE COURT, IN ITS CHARGE ON CONTRIBUTORY NEGLIGENCE, DID NOT CALL ATTENTION TO CORRESPONDING FORMER SECTION, an exception to the charge would not be sustained in the absence of a special request for such instruction. Alexander v. Southern Pub. Utils. Co., 207 N.C. 438, 177 S.E. 427 (1934).

JUDGMENT NOTWITHSTANDING VERDICT. --In a case in plaintiff brought an action seeking damages sustained when she collided with a utility line owned by defendant that was lying at ground level in a public roadway, the trial court did not err in denying defendant's motion for judgment notwithstanding the verdict with respect to defendant's contention that plaintiff was contributorily negligent as a matter of law for cycling too closely to the cyclist in front of her before she was injured, as the evidence presented to the jury was not such that the only reasonable conclusion to be drawn was in favor of defendant on the question of plaintiff's contributory negligence. Goins

v. Time Warner Cable Se., LLC, 258 N.C. App. 234, 812 S.E.2d 723 (2018), review denied, 371 N.C. 569, 819 S.E.2d 388, 2018 N.C. LEXIS 963 (2018).

APPLIED in State v. Holbrook, 228 N.C. 620, 46 S.E.2d 843 (1948); Pacific Fire Ins. Co. v. Sistrunk Motors, Inc., 241 N.C. 67, 84 S.E.2d 301 (1954); Hall v. Little, 262 N.C. 618, 138 S.E.2d 282 (1964); Brown v. Hale, 263 N.C. 176, 139 S.E.2d 210 (1964).

CITED in Hobbs v. Mann, 199 N.C. 532, 155 S.E. 163 (1930); Smith v. Carolina Coach Co., 214 N.C. 314, 199 S.E. 90 (1938); State v. Steelman, 228 N.C. 634, 46 S.E.2d 845 (1948); Clifton v. Turner, 257 N.C. 92, 125 S.E.2d 339 (1962); Dunlap v. Lee, 257 N.C. 447, 126 S.E.2d 62 (1962); Jones v. C.B. Atkins Co., 259 N.C. 655, 131 S.E.2d 371 (1963); Southwire Co. v. Long Mfg. Co., 12 N.C. App. 335, 183 S.E.2d 253 (1971); Shay v. Nixon, 45 N.C. App. 108, 262 S.E.2d 294 (1980); State v. Clements, 51 N.C. App. 113, 275 S.E.2d 222 (1981); State v. McGill, 73 N.C. App. 206, 326 S.E.2d 345 (1985); State v. McClendon, 130 N.C. App. 368, 502 S.E.2d 902 (1998); State v. McClendon, 350 N.C. 630, 517 S.E.2d 128 (1999); State v. Wilson, 155 N.C. App. 89, 574 S.E.2d 93 (2002), appeal dismissed, cert. denied, 356 N.C. 693, 579 S.E.2d 98, cert. denied, 540 U.S. 843, 124 S. Ct. 113, 157 L. Ed. 2d 78 (2003); Williams v. Davis, 157 N.C. App. 696, 580 S.E.2d 85 (2003); State v. Hernandez, 170 N.C. App. 299, 612 S.E.2d 420 (2005).

LEGAL PERIODICALS. --

For article on proof of negligence in North Carolina, see 48 N.C.L. Rev. 731 (1970).

§ 20-153. Turning at intersections

(a) **Right Turns.** -- Both the approach for a right turn and a right turn shall be made as close as practicable to the right-hand curb or edge of the roadway.

(b) **Left Turns.** -- The driver of a vehicle intending to turn left at any intersection shall approach the intersection in the extreme left-hand lane lawfully available to traffic moving in the direction of travel of that vehicle, and, after entering the intersection, the left turn shall be made so as to leave the intersection in a lane lawfully available to traffic moving in the direction upon the roadway being entered.

(c) Local authorities and the Department of Transportation, in their respective jurisdictions, may modify the foregoing method of turning at intersections by clearly indicating by buttons, markers, or other direction signs within an intersection the course to be followed by vehicles turning thereat, and it shall be unlawful for any driver to fail to turn in a manner as so directed.

History.

1937, c. 407, s. 115; 1955, c. 913, s. 5; 1973, c. 1330, s. 18; 1977, c. 464, s. 34; 1997-405, s. 1

SUBSECTION (B) DOES NOT DISTINGUISH TWO-LANE ROADS FROM ROADS WITH MORE THAN TWO LANES. --While subsection (a) of this section speaks in terms describing a portion of a roadway: "right-hand curb or edge," subsection (b) of this section speaks in terms of the "left-hand lane." The logical driver might expect another driver preparing to turn left at an intersection on a two-lane street to approach the intersection in the portion of the roadway nearest the center line on the left, but this is not what subsection (b) of this section says. Subsection (b) of this section makes no distinction between two-lane or more than two-lane roadways. Gay v. Walter, 58 N.C. App. 813, 294 S.E.2d 769 (1982).

INSTRUCTION ON SUBSECTION (B) HELD ERRONEOUS. --Where the evidence shows that a collision occurred between an automobile, which intended to turn left at the approaching intersection, traveling in the right-hand lane of a two-lane street with one lane of traffic in each direction and another automobile, which pulled out of a parking space in front of the first automobile, an instruction on the requirements of subsection (b) of this section is erroneous. Gay v. Walter, 58 N.C. App. 813, 294 S.E.2d 769 (1982).

AS TO PURPOSE OF PROVISION FORMERLY REQUIRING THAT DRIVER INTENDING TO TURN TO THE LEFT SHOULD PASS BEYOND CENTER OF INTERSECTION, see Ferris v. Whitaker, 123 F. Supp. 356 (E.D.N.C. 1954).

RIGHT TO PASS VEHICLE IN LEFT-TURN LANE ON THE RIGHT. --When a motorist approaches from the rear a vehicle standing in the left-turn lane, he has the right to assume that the driver of that vehicle will turn to the left upon the change of the traffic signal. He has the right, and it is his duty, to pass the vehicle on its right. Anderson v. Talman Office Supplies, Inc., 234 N.C. 142, 66 S.E.2d 677 (1951). See Anderson v. Talman Office Supplies, Inc., 236 N.C. 519, 73 S.E.2d 141 (1952).

INFERENCES FROM FACT OF COLLISION. --The principle that the mere fact of a collision with a vehicle ahead furnishes some evidence that the following motorist was negligent as to speed, was following too closely, or failed to keep a proper lookout is not absolute; negligence, if any, depends upon the circumstances. Powell v. Cross, 263 N.C. 764, 140 S.E.2d 393 (1965).

REASONABLE ARTICULABLE SUSPICION FOR STOP. --Superior court erred in affirming a district court's pretrial indication granting defendant's motion to suppress a traffic stop because a trooper had a reasonable articulable suspicion to stop defendant based on the observed traffic violations, and the stop was reasonable under the Fourth Amendment; the trooper's testimony that he initiated the stop of defendant after observing defendant drive over the double yellow line was sufficient to establish a violation of G.S. 20-146(d) and G.S. 20-153. State v. Osterhoudt, 222 N.C. App. 620, 731 S.E.2d 454 (2012).

A VIOLATION OF SUBSECTION (A) IS NEGLIGENCE PER SE, and if injury proximately results therefrom, such violation is actionable. Tarrant v. Pepsi-Cola Bottling Co., 221 N.C. 390, 20 S.E.2d 565 (1942); Simmons v. Rogers, 247 N.C. 340, 100 S.E.2d 849 (1957); Pearsall v. Duke Power Co., 258 N.C. 639, 129 S.E.2d 217 (1963).

PROXIMATE CAUSE FOR JURY. --If plaintiff violated this section and was guilty of contributory negligence per se, it was for the jury to say whether such negligence proximately caused or contributed to plaintiff's injuries and damage, bearing in mind that reasonable foreseeability is an essential element of proximate cause. White v. Lacey, 245 N.C. 364, 96 S.E.2d 1 (1957).

CHARGE TO JURY AS TO MAKING OF LEFT TURN. --When the failure to explain the law so the jury could apply it to the facts is specifically called to the court's attention by a juror's request for information, the court should tell the jury how to find the intersection of the streets and how, when the motorist reaches the intersection, he is required to drive in making a left turn. Pearsall v. Duke Power Co., 258 N.C. 639, 129 S.E.2d 217 (1963).

CIRCUMSTANCES HELD TO WARRANT INFERENCE OF NEGLIGENCE AND SUBMISSION TO JURY. --Where plaintiff was lawfully in an intersection, standing in a position where he was clearly visible to the driver of defendant's taxicab as the latter approached the intersection, and the taxi driver, had he been keeping a proper lookout, could have seen plaintiff in ample time to avoid a collision, but instead "cut the corner," in violation of subsection (a) of this section, without giving any signal or warning of his approach, resulting in a collision, these circumstances, unrebutted, warranted an inference of negligence and were sufficient to require the submission of appropriate issues to the jury. Ward v. Bowles, 228 N.C. 273, 45 S.E.2d 354 (1947).

VIOLATION ESTABLISHED. --Superior court erred in affirming a district court's pretrial indication granting defendant's motion to suppress a traffic stop because defendant violated G.S. 20-153; defendant violated G.S. 20-153 by failing to stay close to the right-hand curb when making the turn onto the street, and there was no practical reason why defendant would need to veer over the double yellow line. State v. Osterhoudt, 222 N.C. App. 620, 731 S.E.2d 454 (2012).

FOR CASE HOLDING EVIDENCE INSUFFICIENT TO SHOW A VIOLATION OF THIS SECTION, see Kidd v. Burton, 269 N.C. 267, 152 S.E.2d 162 (1967).

APPLIED in Cole v. Fletcher Lumber Co., 230 N.C. 616, 55 S.E.2d 86 (1949); Stewart v. Gallimore, 265 N.C. 696, 144 S.E.2d 862 (1965); Wands v. Cauble, 270 N.C. 311, 154 S.E.2d 425 (1967).

CITED in Ervin v. Cannon Mills Co., 233 N.C. 415, 64 S.E.2d 431 (1951); Smith v. United States, 94 F. Supp. 681 (W.D.N.C. 1951); Hudson v. Petroleum Transit Co., 250 N.C. 435, 108 S.E.2d 900 (1959); Ray v. French Broad Elec. Membership Corp., 252 N.C. 380, 113 S.E.2d 806 (1960); McPherson v. Haire, 262 N.C. 71, 136 S.E.2d 224 (1964); Almond v. Bolton, 272 N.C. 78, 157 S.E.2d 709 (1967); Hardy v. Tesh, 5 N.C. App. 107, 167 S.E.2d 848 (1969).

§ 20-154. Signals on starting, stopping or turning

(a) The driver of any vehicle upon a highway or public vehicular area before starting, stopping or turning from a direct line shall first see that such movement can be made in safety, and if any pedestrian may be affected by such movement shall give a clearly audible signal by sounding the horn, and whenever the operation of any other vehicle may be affected by such movement, shall give a signal as required in this section, plainly visible to the driver of such other vehicle, of the intention to make such movement. The driver of a vehicle shall not back the same unless such movement can be made with safety and without interfering with other traffic.

(a1) A person who violates subsection (a) of this section and causes a motorcycle or bicycle operator to change travel lanes or leave that portion of any public street or highway designated as travel lanes shall be responsible for an infraction and shall be assessed a fine of not less than two hundred dollars ($ 200.00). A person who violates subsection (a) of this section that results in a crash causing property damage or personal injury to a motorcycle or bicycle operator or passenger shall be responsible for an infraction and shall be assessed a fine of not less than five hundred dollars ($ 500.00) unless subsection (a2) of this section applies.

(a2) A person who violates subsection (a) of this section and the violation results in a crash causing property damage in excess of five thousand dollars ($ 5,000) or a serious bodily injury as defined in G.S. 20-160.1(b) to a motorcycle or bicycle operator or passenger shall be responsible for an infraction and shall be assessed a fine of not less than seven hundred fifty dollars ($ 750.00). A violation of this subsection shall be treated as a failure to yield right-of-way to a motorcycle or bicycle, as applicable, for purposes of assessment of points under G.S. 20-16(c). In addition, the trial judge shall have the authority to order the license of any driver violating this subsection suspended for a period not to exceed 30 days. If a judge orders suspension of a person's drivers license pursuant to this subsection, the judge may allow the licensee a limited driving privilege for a period not to exceed the period of suspension. The limited driving privilege shall be issued in the same manner and under the terms and conditions prescribed in G.S. 20-16.1(b)(1), (2), (3), (4), (5), and G.S. 20-16.1(g).

(b) The signal herein required shall be given by means of the hand and arm in the manner herein specified, or by any mechanical or electrical signal device approved by the Division, except that when a vehicle is so constructed or loaded as to prevent the hand and arm signal from being visible, both to the front and rear, the signal shall be given by a device of a type which has been approved by the Division.

Except as otherwise provided in subsection (b1) of this section, whenever the signal is given the driver shall indicate his intention to start, stop, or turn by extending the hand and arm from and beyond the left side of the vehicle as hereinafter set forth.

Left turn -- hand and arm horizontal, forefinger pointing.

Right turn -- upper arm horizontal, forearm and hand pointed upward.

Stop -- upper arm horizontal, forearm and hand pointed downward.

All hand and arm signals shall be given from the left side of the vehicle and all signals shall be maintained or given continuously for the last 100 feet traveled prior to stopping or making a turn. Provided, that in all areas where the speed limit is 45 miles per hour or higher and the operator intends to turn from a direct line of travel, a signal of intention to turn from a direct line of travel shall be given continuously during the last 200 feet traveled before turning.

Any motor vehicle in use on a highway shall be equipped with, and required signal shall be given by, a signal lamp or lamps or mechanical signal device when the distance from the center of the top of the steering post to the left outside limit of the body, cab or load of such motor vehicle exceeds 24 inches, or when the distance from the center of the top of the steering post to the rear limit of the body or load thereof exceeds 14 feet. The latter measurement shall apply to any single vehicle, also to any combination of vehicles except combinations operated by farmers in hauling farm products.

(b1) Notwithstanding the requirement set forth in subsection (b) of this section that a driver signal a right turn by extending his or her hand and arm from beyond the left side of the vehicle, an operator of a bicycle may signal his or her intention to make a right turn by extending his or her hand and arm horizontally, with the forefinger pointing, from beyond the right side of the bicycle.

(c) No person shall operate over the highways of this State a right-hand-drive motor vehicle or a motor vehicle equipped with the steering mechanism on the right-hand side thereof unless said motor vehicle is equipped with mechanical or electrical signal devices by which the signals for left turns and right turns may be given. Such mechanical or electrical devices shall be approved by the Division.

(d) A violation of this section shall not constitute negligence per se.

History.
1937, c. 407, s. 116; 1949, c. 1016, s. 1; 1951, cc. 293, 360; 1955, c. 1157, s. 9; 1957, c. 488, s. 2; 1965, c. 768; 1973, c. 1330, s. 19; 1975, c. 716, s. 5; 1981, c. 599, s. 4; 1985, c. 96; 2011-361, s. 1;2013-366, s. 5(a);2016-90, s. 5.5(c)

EDITOR'S NOTE. --
Session Laws 2016-90, s. 5.5(d), made the amendments to subsections (a1), (a2), (b), and (b1) of this section by Session Laws 2016-90, s. 5.5(c), applicable to offenses committed on or after October 1, 2016.

EFFECT OF AMENDMENTS. --
Session Laws 2011-361, s. 1, effective December 1, 2011, and applicable to offenses committed on or after that date, added subsection (a1).

Session Laws 2013-366, s. 5(a), effective October 1, 2013, added "unless subsection (a2) of this section applies" in subsection (a1); and added subsection (a2). For applicability, see Editor's note.

Session Laws 2016-90, s. 5.5(c), effective October 1, 2016, inserted "or bicycle" and "or bicycle, as applicable" throughout subsections (a1) and (a2); in subsection (b), substituted "Except as otherwise provided in subsection (b1) of this section, whenever" for "Whenever" and twice substituted "upper arm horizontal, forearm, and hand" for "hand and arm"; and added subsection (b1). See editor's note for applicability.

I. IN GENERAL.
EDITOR'S NOTE. --A number of the cases cited below were decided prior to the 1965 amendment to subsection (b) of this section, which added a former proviso as to violations not constituting negligence per se, and the 1973 amendment, which added subsection (d), to the same effect.

PURPOSE OF SECTION. --The manifest purpose of this section is to promote safety in the operation of automobiles on the highways, and not to obstruct vehicular traffic. Farmers Oil Co. v. Miller, 264 N.C. 101, 141 S.E.2d 41 (1965).

The manifest object of this section is to promote vehicular travel. Cooley v. Baker, 231 N.C. 533, 58 S.E.2d 115 (1950).

THIS SECTION MUST BE GIVEN A REASONABLE AND REALISTIC INTERPRETATION to effect the legislative purpose. Cooley v. Baker, 231 N.C. 533, 58 S.E.2d 115 (1950); Farmers Oil Co. v. Miller, 264 N.C. 101, 141 S.E.2d 41 (1965).

EVIDENCE SEIZED AFTER VALID STOP UNDER THIS SECTION HELD ADMISSIBLE. --Officer had probable cause to stop defendant because the officer, who was traveling behind defendant, saw defendant change lanes without signaling, which was a violation G.S. 20-154(a); the trial court's denial of defendant's motion to suppress evidence seized after the stop was proper. State v. Styles, 185 N.C. App. 271, 648 S.E.2d 214 (2007), aff'd, 362 N.C. 412, 665 S.E.2d 438 (2008).

Defendant's failure to use a turn signal provided an officer with reasonable suspicion justifying an investigative stop of defendant because defendant was traveling in a through lane in medium traffic, a short distance ahead of the officer's vehicle; the failure to use a signal could have affected another motor vehicle, violating G.S. 20-154(a). State v. McRae, 203 N.C. App. 319, 691 S.E.2d 56 (2010).

SECTION INAPPLICABLE WHERE DRIVER HAS NO CHOICE. --This section, which provides that the driver of a motor vehicle shall not stop without first seeing that he can do so in safety, and that he must give a signal of his intention where the operation of other cars might be affected, is not applicable where the driver has no choice but to stop, such as where he is confronted with a situation which demands that he stop because the line of cars in front of him has done so, he cannot turn left because of oncoming traffic, and it has been raining and the windows of his car are up so that he can give no hand signal. Griffin v. Ward, 267 N.C. 296, 148 S.E.2d 133 (1966).

Where plaintiff, whose vehicle was struck from the rear by defendant, had failed to give any signal indicating that he was going to stop, but defendant's own evidence established that plaintiff had no time in which to give a signal, plaintiff was not guilty of contributory negligence, because he was under no statutory duty to give a signal where he had no choice but to stop because of the situation. Harris v. Freeman, 18 N.C. App. 85, 196 S.E.2d 48 (1973).

THE APPROACH OF A POLICE VEHICLE GIVING A SIGNAL BY SIREN DOES NOT NULLIFY OR SUSPEND THE PROVISIONS OF THIS SECTION, or relieve a motorist of the duty to ascertain, before turning to his right, that such movement can be made in safety, or to signal any vehicle approaching from the rear. Anderson v. Talman Office Supplies Inc., 234 N.C. 142, 66 S.E.2d 677 (1951). See also, Anderson v. Talman Office Supplies, 236 N.C. 519, 73 S.E.2d 141 (1952).

TWO DUTIES IMPOSED ON MOTORIST ON STARTING, STOPPING OR TURNING. --This section requires of one operating a motor vehicle before starting, stopping or turning from the direct line that he is traveling to first see that such movement can be made in safety, and when the operation of another vehicle by such movement may be affected, to give a signal plainly visible to the driver of the other vehicle of his intent to make such movement. Porter v. Philyaw, 204 F. Supp. 285 (W.D.N.C. 1962).

This section imposes two duties upon a motorist intending to turn: (1) To see that the movement can be made in safety; and (2) To give the required signal when the operation of any other vehicle may be affected. Tart v. Register, 257 N.C. 161, 125 S.E.2d 754 (1962); Farmers Oil Co. v. Miller, 264 N.C. 101, 141 S.E.2d 41 (1965); Clarke v. Holman, 274 N.C. 425, 163 S.E.2d 783 (1968); Johnson v. Douglas, 6 N.C. App. 109, 169 S.E.2d 505 (1969); Taylor v. Hudson, 49 N.C. App. 296, 271 S.E.2d 70 (1980).

This section imposes two duties upon a motorist intending to turn from a direct line upon a highway: (1) To exercise reasonable care to see that such movement can be made in safety; and (2) To give the required signal whenever the operation of any other vehicle may be affected by such movement, plainly visible to the driver of such other vehicle, of the intention to make such movement. McNamara v. Outlaw, 262 N.C. 612, 138 S.E.2d 287 (1964).

The duties imposed upon the driver intending to turn from a direct line are twofold: (1) He must first ascertain whether the move can be made in safety; and (2) Upon ascertaining that another vehicle might be affected, he must give a signal, plainly visible, of his intention so to move. Sharpe v. Grindstaff, 329 F.

Supp. 405 (M.D.N.C. 1970), rev'd on other grounds, 446 F.2d 152 (4th Cir. 1971).

DRIVER MUST FIRST SEE THAT TURN CAN BE MADE IN SAFETY. --Every driver who intends to turn, or partly turn, from a direct line shall first see that such movement can be made in safety. Wagoner v. Butcher, 6 N.C. App. 221, 170 S.E.2d 151 (1969).

While it is true that subsection (a) of this section does not mean that a motorist may not make a left turn on a highway unless the circumstances are absolutely free from danger, he is required to exercise reasonable care in determining that his intended movement can be made in safety. Petree v. Johnson, 2 N.C. App. 336, 163 S.E.2d 87 (1968).

THE GIVING OF A SIGNAL FOR A LEFT TURN DOES NOT GIVE THE SIGNALER AN ABSOLUTE RIGHT TO MAKE THE TURN immediately, regardless of circumstances; the signaler must first ascertain that the movement may be made safely. Eason v. Grimsley, 255 N.C. 494, 121 S.E.2d 885 (1961); McNamara v. Outlaw, 262 N.C. 612, 138 S.E.2d 287 (1964).

A signal would be futile if a turn could not be made in safety; and, therefore, there is a complete failure of duty upon the part of the driver of the turning car if he does not first use reasonable care to see that the turn may be made in safety. Ervin v. Cannon Mills Co., 233 N.C. 415, 64 S.E.2d 431 (1951). *Under circumstances making subsection (a) of this section applicable,* the statute imposes both the duty of giving the required turn signal and the duty to see prior to turning that such movement can be made in safety. Brown v. Brown, 38 N.C. App. 607, 248 S.E.2d 397 (1978).

A person who drives a motor vehicle upon this State's highways must exercise reasonable care to ascertain that he can turn safely from a straight course of travel. Horne v. Trivette, 58 N.C. App. 77, 293 S.E.2d 290, cert. denied, 306 N.C. 741, 295 S.E.2d 759 (1982).

DRIVER MAKING A LEFT TURN MUST ALWAYS USE THE CARE WHICH A REASONABLE MAN WOULD USE under like circumstances. Ratliff v. Duke Power Co., 268 N.C. 605, 151 S.E.2d 641 (1966).

A CHANGE OF LANES BY A PASSING MOTORIST MAY REQUIRE THE SAME PRECAUTIONS AS AN ACTUAL TURN and such an interpretation promotes safe vehicular travel. This reading is a reasonable and realistic interpretation of the statute. Sass v. Thomas, 90 N.C. App. 719, 370 S.E.2d 73 (1988).

BUT CIRCUMSTANCES NEED NOT BE ABSOLUTELY FREE FROM DANGER. --The requirement that a motorist shall not turn from a straight line until he has first seen that the movement can be made in safety does not mean that he may not make a left turn on the highway unless the circumstances are absolutely free from danger, but only that he exercise reasonable care under the circumstances to ascertain that such movement can be made with safety. Cooley v. Baker, 231 N.C. 533, 58 S.E.2d 115 (1950); White v. Lacey, 245 N.C. 364, 96 S.E.2d 1 (1957); Tart v. Register, 257 N.C. 161, 125 S.E.2d 754 (1962); Williams v. Tucker, 259 N.C. 214, 130 S.E.2d 306 (1963); Farmers Oil Co. v. Miller, 264 N.C. 101, 141 S.E.2d 41

(1965); Clarke v. Holman, 274 N.C. 425, 163 S.E.2d 783 (1968); Johnson v. Douglas, 6 N.C. App. 109, 169 S.E.2d 505 (1969); Taylor v. Hudson, 49 N.C. App. 296, 271 S.E.2d 70 (1980).

A motorist is not required to ascertain that a turning motion is absolutely free from danger. Cowan v. Murrows Transf., Inc., 262 N.C. 550, 138 S.E.2d 228 (1964); Hales v. Flowers, 7 N.C. App. 46, 171 S.E.2d 113 (1969); Hudgens v. Goins, 15 N.C. App. 203, 189 S.E.2d 633 (1972).

The provisions of subsection (a) of this section do not require infallibility of a motorist, and do not mean that he cannot make a left turn upon a highway unless the circumstances are absolutely free from danger. McNamara v. Outlaw, 262 N.C. 612, 138 S.E.2d 287 (1964); Almond v. Bolton, 272 N.C. 78, 157 S.E.2d 709 (1967).

The statutory provision that "the driver of any vehicle upon a highway before.. turning from a direct line shall first see that such movement can be made in safety" does not mean that a motorist may not make a left turn on a highway unless the circumstances render such turning absolutely free from danger. It is simply designed to impose upon the driver of a motor vehicle who is about to make a left turn upon a highway the legal duty to exercise reasonable care under the circumstances in ascertaining that such movement can be made with safety to himself and others before he actually undertakes it. Hales v. Flowers, 7 N.C. App. 46, 171 S.E.2d 113 (1969).

This provision is designed to impose upon a driver the legal duty to exercise reasonable care under the circumstances in ascertaining that his movement can be made with safety to himself and others before he actually undertakes the movement. It does not mean that a motorist may not make a turn on a highway unless the circumstances render such turning absolutely free from danger. Sass v. Thomas, 90 N.C. App. 719, 370 S.E.2d 73 (1988).

TURNING DRIVER MAY ASSUME THAT APPROACHING MOTORIST WILL EXERCISE DUE CARE. --In considering whether he can turn with safety and whether he should give a statutory signal of his purpose, the driver of a motor vehicle who undertakes to make a left turn in front of an approaching motorist has the right to take it for granted, in the absence of notice to the contrary, that the oncoming motorist will maintain a proper lookout, drive at a lawful speed, and otherwise exercise due care to avoid collision with his turning vehicle. McNamara v. Outlaw, 262 N.C. 612, 138 S.E.2d 287 (1964); Johnson v. Douglas, 6 N.C. App. 109, 169 S.E.2d 505 (1969); Taylor v. Hudson, 49 N.C. App. 296, 271 S.E.2d 70 (1980); Sass v. Thomas, 90 N.C. App. 719, 370 S.E.2d 73 (1988).

GIVING OF BOTH HAND AND MECHANICAL SIGNALS IS NOT REQUIRED. --There is nothing in this section or in the case law that requires under any conditions that a hand signal and a mechanical or electrical signal shall both be given before making a left turn. Rudd v. Stewart, 255 N.C. 90, 120 S.E.2d 601 (1961).

THE DUTY TO GIVE A SIGNAL DOES NOT ARISE UNLESS THE OPERATION OF SOME OTHER VEHICLE MAY BE AFFECTED by such movement. When the surrounding circumstances afford a driver reasonable grounds to conclude that a left turn might affect the operation of another vehicle, then the duty to give the statutory signal is imposed upon him. Clarke v. Holman, 274 N.C. 425, 163 S.E.2d 783 (1968).

This section does not require that a motorist give a proper signal before making a left turn on the highway unless the surrounding circumstances afford him reasonable grounds for apprehending that such movement may affect the operation of another vehicle, and in exercising such prevision he may, in the absence of notice to the contrary, assume that other motorists will maintain a proper lookout, drive at a lawful speed, and otherwise exercise due care. Cooley v. Baker, 231 N.C. 533, 58 S.E.2d 115 (1950).

This section does not require the driver of a motor vehicle intending to make a left turn upon a highway to signal his purpose to turn in every case. The duty to give a statutory signal of an intended left turn does not arise in any event unless the operation of some other vehicle may be affected by such movement. And even then the law does not require infallibility of the motorist. It imposes upon him the duty of giving a statutory signal of his intended left turn only in case the surrounding circumstances afford him reasonable grounds for apprehending that his making the left turn upon the highway might affect the operation of another vehicle. Blanton v. Carolina Dairy, Inc., 238 N.C. 382, 77 S.E.2d 922 (1953).

The duty to signal is imposed only where the surrounding circumstances afford the driver reasonable grounds for apprehending his turn might affect the operation of another vehicle. Sass v. Thomas, 90 N.C. App. 719, 370 S.E.2d 73 (1988).

NO SIGNAL IS REQUIRED BY SUBSECTION (A) OF THIS SECTION WHEN THE OPERATION OF ANOTHER VEHICLE WILL NOT BE AFFECTED by starting, stopping, or turning. Clarke v. Holman, 1 N.C. App. 176, 160 S.E.2d 552, aff'd, 274 N.C. 425, 163 S.E.2d 783 (1968).

Subsection (a) of this section does not require that a motorist give a signal before turning unless the surrounding circumstances afford reasonable grounds for apprehending that the turn may affect the operation of another vehicle. Brown v. Brown, 38 N.C. App. 607, 248 S.E.2d 397 (1978).

PERSON OBSERVING NO VEHICLES IN EITHER DIRECTION IS UNDER NO OBLIGATION TO GIVE SIGNAL. --Where plaintiff first looked in both directions, and observed no automobile or other vehicle approaching from either direction, he was under no obligation under this section to give any signal of his purpose to turn to his left and enter the driveway to his home. Stovall v. Ragland, 211 N.C. 536, 190 S.E. 899 (1937).

One is not required to give a signal to a motorist who has yet appeared on the horizon. Clarke v. Holman, 274 N.C. 425, 163 S.E.2d 783 (1968).

BUT DRIVER MUST KEEP OUTLOOK IN DIRECTION OF TRAVEL. --It is the duty of the driver of a motor vehicle not merely to look, but to keep an outlook in the direction of travel. Clarke v. Holman, 274 N.C. 425, 163 S.E.2d 783 (1968).

DRIVER IS HELD TO THE DUTY OF SEEING WHAT HE OUGHT TO HAVE SEEN. Clarke v. Holman, 274 N.C. 425, 163 S.E.2d 783 (1968).

WHERE CARS ARE MEETING AT AN INTERSECTION AND ONE INTENDS TO TURN across the lane of travel of the other, subsection (b) of G.S. 20-155 and subsection (a) of this section apply, and the driver making the turn is under duty to give a plainly visible signal of his intention to turn, and to ascertain that such movement can be made in safety, without regard to which vehicle entered the intersection first. Fleming v. Drye, 253 N.C. 545, 117 S.E.2d 416 (1960); King v. Sloan, 261 N.C. 562, 135 S.E.2d 556 (1964).

GIVING SIGNAL DOES NOT RELIEVE DRIVER OF OTHER DUTIES. --The requirement in this section that a prescribed hand signal be given of intention to make a left turn in traffic does not constitute full compliance with the mandate also expressed that before turning from a direct line the driver shall first see that such movement can be made in safety, nor does the performance of this mechanical act alone relieve the driver of the common-law duty to exercise due care in other respects. Ervin v. Cannon Mills Co., 233 N.C. 415, 64 S.E.2d 431 (1951); Simmons v. Rogers, 247 N.C. 340, 100 S.E.2d 849 (1957).

THE DRIVER OF AN AUTOMOBILE MAY BE REQUIRED TO GIVE NOT ONLY THE STATUTORY SIGNALS, BUT ALSO OTHER SIGNALS, or to slacken speed or take other steps to avoid a collision, if the surrounding circumstances and conditions require it. The giving of the statutory signals is the least the law requires. Ervin v. Cannon Mills Co., 233 N.C. 415, 64 S.E.2d 431 (1951).

IT IS NOT NECESSARILY ENOUGH TO LOOK AND GIVE SIGNAL. --In making a left turn, it is not necessarily enough to absolve a driver from negligence that he looked and gave the statutory signal. When a turning vehicle is drawing behind it a 40-foot pole, it is obvious that a left turn at a right angle will involve some swinging of the end of the pole in an arc through part of the intersection. Evidence of such a turn with such a load is sufficient to permit, though not to require, the jury to find that reasonable care for the safety of other users of the highway demands the stationing of some person at the intersection to stop traffic which may otherwise be imperiled by the turn. Ratliff v. Duke Power Co., 268 N.C. 605, 151 S.E.2d 641 (1966).

An allegation that the proper turn signal was given does not support the conclusion that the signaler thereby acquired the right to make an uninterrupted turn, or that the turn made pursuant thereto was lawful. Tart v. Register, 257 N.C. 161, 125 S.E.2d 754 (1962).

RIGHT TO ASSUME THAT DRIVER WILL GIVE SIGNAL. --A person has the right to assume, and to act on the assumption, that the driver of a vehicle approaching from the opposite direction will comply with subsection (a) of this section before making a left turn across his path. Petree v. Johnson, 2 N.C. App. 336, 163 S.E.2d 87 (1968).

ASSUMPTION THAT DRIVER WILL DELAY TURN UNTIL SAFE. --Without regard to whether the turning driver gives the appropriate signal, other motorists affected have the right to assume that he will delay his movement until it may be made in safety. Brown v. Brown, 38 N.C. App. 607, 248 S.E.2d 397 (1978).

When the circumstances do not allow the signaler a reasonable margin of safety, other affected motorists have the right to assume that he will delay his movement until it may be made in safety. Eason v. Grimsley, 255 N.C. 494, 121 S.E.2d 885 (1961).

UNTIL ONE SEES OR OUGHT TO SEE TURN BEING MADE. --While ordinarily a motorist may assume and act on the assumption that the driver of vehicle approaching from the opposite direction will comply with statutory requirements as to signaling before making a left turn across his path, he is not entitled to indulge in this assumption after he sees or by exercise of due care ought to see that the approaching driver is turning to his left across the highway to enter an intersecting road. Jernigan v. Jernigan, 236 N.C. 430, 72 S.E.2d 912 (1952).

A SIGNAL MUST BE MAINTAINED FOR A SUFFICIENT DISTANCE AND LENGTH OF TIME to enable the driver of the following vehicle to observe it and to understand therefrom what movement is intended. Farmers Oil Co. v. Miller, 264 N.C. 101, 141 S.E.2d 41 (1965).

THE PRESCRIBED HAND SIGNAL SHOULD BE MAINTAINED FOR A SUFFICIENT LENGTH OF TIME to enable the driver of the following vehicle to observe it and to understand therefrom what movement is intended. Ervin v. Cannon Mills Co., 233 N.C. 415, 64 S.E.2d 431 (1951); McNamara v. Outlaw, 262 N.C. 612, 138 S.E.2d 287 (1964).

EFFECT OF TRAFFIC SIGNALS AT INTERSECTION. --Where street intersection had electrically operated traffic signals, with the usual red, yellow, and green lights, the rights of a motorist at such intersection were controlled by the traffic signals and not by the section. White v. Cothran, 260 N.C. 510, 133 S.E.2d 132 (1963).

Where the intersection of streets in a municipality has authorized electric traffic signals, requirements in regard to stopping are controlled by the traffic lights and not by subsection (b) of this section. Jones v. Holt, 268 N.C. 381, 150 S.E.2d 759 (1966).

When a motorist approaches an electrically controlled signal at an intersection of streets or highways, he is under the legal duty to maintain a proper lookout and to keep his motor vehicle under reasonable control in order that he may stop before entering the intersection if the green light changes to yellow or red before he actually enters the intersection. Likewise, another motorist, following immediately behind the first motorist, is not relieved of the legal duty to keep his motor vehicle under reasonable control in order that he might not collide with the motor vehicle in front of him in the event the driver of the first car is required to stop before entering the intersection by reason of the signal light changing from green to yellow or red. Jones v. Holt, 268 N.C. 381, 150 S.E.2d 759 (1966).

In subsection (a) of this section there is no hint of a legislative intent to create a clear dichotomy between those intersections with and those without traffic lights. A pedestrian following the lights and continuing his straight course has the right to rely on the presumption that the driver will obey the law as set forth in this section. Wagoner v. Butcher, 6 N.C. App. 221, 170 S.E.2d 151 (1969).

DUTY ON STARTING AFTER HAVING STOPPED FOR RED LIGHT. --After stopping for a red light at an intersection, before starting again a driver should not only have the green light or the go sign facing him, but he should also see and determine in the exercise of due care that such movement can be made in safety. Troxler v. Central Motor Lines, 240 N.C. 420, 82 S.E.2d 342 (1954).

VIOLATION OF SECTION AS QUESTION FOR JURY. --Whether defendant observed the rule of the road first, by ascertaining if a turn would affect the operation of any other vehicle, and second, by giving the required signal, under this section, raised an issue of fact for the jury. Mason v. Johnson, 215 N.C. 95, 1 S.E.2d 379 (1939).

Whether, according to the evidence, red signal lights on a stopped truck flashing on and off were sufficient to indicate a left turn of the truck was for the jury to decide. Weavil v. C.W. Myers Trading Post, Inc., 245 N.C. 106, 95 S.E.2d 533 (1956).

Whether signal lights would blink, and whether, if they would blink, they were "plainly visible," as required by this section, were questions for the jury. Eason v. Grimsley, 255 N.C. 494, 121 S.E.2d 885 (1961).

It was for the jury to determine whether plaintiff should have reasonably anticipated that the operation of any other vehicle might be affected by his making a right-hand turn. Kidd v. Burton, 269 N.C. 267, 152 S.E.2d 162 (1967).

FOR CASE HOLDING THAT EVIDENCE SHOWED VIOLATION OF SECTION, see Powell v. Lloyd, 234 N.C. 481, 67 S.E.2d 664 (1951).

VIOLATION OF SECTION NOT SHOWN. --Where a motorist made a left turn across a street, without signaling, to enter a filling station, when a vehicle approaching from the opposite direction was 900 feet away, and was struck by such other vehicle which was traveling at a speed of approximately 70 miles per hour, such motorist did not violate this section, since the motorist had every reason to believe that he could complete his turn with safety to himself and others without affecting in any way the operation of the approaching vehicle. Cooley v. Baker, 231 N.C. 533, 58 S.E.2d 115 (1950).

VIOLATION SHOWN. --Trial court's finding that at the time defendant's vehicle changed lanes without a signal, it was being operated by defendant immediately in front of an arresting officer's vehicle

indicated that defendant's failure to signal violated G.S. 20-154(a) because it was clear that changing lanes immediately in front of another vehicle might affect the operation of the trailing vehicle. State v. Styles, 362 N.C. 412, 665 S.E.2d 438 (2008).

DUTY OF BICYCLIST. --Under ordinary circumstances, it is the duty of a bicyclist, before turning from a direct line of travel, to ascertain that the movement can be made in safety, and to signal his intention to make the movement if the operation of any other vehicle will be thereby affected. Webb v. Felton, 266 N.C. 707, 147 S.E.2d 219 (1966).

VIOLATION OF THIS SECTION AND FORMER § 20-138 (NOW G.S. 20-138.1) IS NOT SUFFICIENT TO SUSTAIN A PROSECUTION FOR INVOLUNTARY MANSLAUGHTER unless a causal relation is shown between the breach of the statute and the death. State v. Lowery, 223 N.C. 598, 27 S.E.2d 638 (1943). See also, Templeton v. Kelley, 216 N.C. 487, 5 S.E.2d 555 (1939), modified in part on rehearing, 217 N.C. 164, 7 S.E.2d 380 (1940).

APPLIED in Badders v. Lassiter, 240 N.C. 413, 82 S.E.2d 357 (1954); Shoe v. Hood, 251 N.C. 719, 112 S.E.2d 543 (1960); Scarborough v. Ingram, 256 N.C. 87, 122 S.E.2d 798 (1961); Parker v. Bruce, 258 N.C. 341, 128 S.E.2d 561 (1962); Queen v. Jarrett, 258 N.C. 405, 128 S.E.2d 894 (1963); Faulk v. Althouse Chem. Co., 259 N.C. 395, 130 S.E.2d 684 (1963); Carolina Coach Co. v. Cox, 337 F.2d 101 (4th Cir. 1964); Mayberry v. Allred, 263 N.C. 780, 140 S.E.2d 406 (1965); Stewart v. Gallimore, 265 N.C. 696, 144 S.E.2d 862 (1965); Simpson v. Lyerly, 265 N.C. 700, 144 S.E.2d 870 (1965); Webb v. Felton, 266 N.C. 707, 147 S.E.2d 219 (1966); Stutts v. Burcham, 271 N.C. 176, 155 S.E.2d 742 (1967); Roberts v. Pilot Freight Carriers, 273 N.C. 600, 160 S.E.2d 712 (1968); Key v. Merritt-Holland Welding Supplies, 273 N.C. 609, 160 S.E.2d 687 (1968); Smith v. Perdue, 7 N.C. App. 314, 172 S.E.2d 246 (1970); Perry v. Aycock, 68 N.C. App. 705, 315 S.E.2d 791 (1984).

CITED in Smith v. Carolina Coach Co., 214 N.C. 314, 199 S.E. 90 (1938); Newbern v. Leary, 215 N.C. 134, 1 S.E.2d 384 (1939); Matheny v. Central Motor Lines, 233 N.C. 673, 65 S.E.2d 361 (1951); Morrisette v. A.G. Boone Co., 235 N.C. 162, 69 S.E.2d 239 (1952); Aldridge v. Hasty, 240 N.C. 353, 82 S.E.2d 331 (1954); Emerson v. Munford, 242 N.C. 241, 87 S.E.2d 306 (1955); Hollowell v. Archbell, 250 N.C. 716, 110 S.E.2d 262 (1959); McPherson v. Haire, 262 N.C. 71, 136 S.E.2d 224 (1964); Correll v. Gaskins, 263 N.C. 212, 139 S.E.2d 202 (1964); Vann v. Hayes, 266 N.C. 713, 147 S.E.2d 186 (1966); Underwood v. Gay, 268 N.C. 715, 151 S.E.2d 596 (1966); Kanoy v. Hinshaw, 273 N.C. 418, 160 S.E.2d 296 (1968); Hall v. Kimber, 6 N.C. App. 669, 171 S.E.2d 99 (1969); Bateman v. Elizabeth City State College, 5 N.C. App. 168, 167 S.E.2d 838 (1969); Brown v. Boren Clay Prods. Co., 5 N.C. App. 418, 168 S.E.2d 452 (1969); Kinney v. Goley, 6 N.C. App. 182, 169 S.E.2d 525 (1969); Strickland v. Powell, 279 N.C. 183, 181 S.E.2d 464 (1971); Odell v. Lipscomb, 12 N.C. App. 318, 183 S.E.2d 299 (1971); Southwire Co. v. Long Mfg. Co., 12 N.C. App. 335, 183

Chapter 20

S.E.2d 253 (1971); Teachey v. Woolard, 16 N.C. App. 249, 191 S.E.2d 903 (1972); Cardwell v. Ware, 36 N.C. App. 366, 243 S.E.2d 915 (1978); Jones v. Morris, 42 N.C. App. 10, 255 S.E.2d 619 (1979); Harris v. Bridges, 46 N.C. App. 207, 264 S.E.2d 804 (1980); Davis v. Gamble, 55 N.C. App. 617, 286 S.E.2d 629 (1982); Cunningham v. Brown, 62 N.C. App. 239, 302 S.E.2d 822 (1983); Williams v. Hall, 100 N.C. App. 655, 397 S.E.2d 767 (1990); Body ex rel. Body v. Varner, 107 N.C. App. 219, 419 S.E.2d 208 (1992); Williams v. Davis, 157 N.C. App. 696, 580 S.E.2d 85 (2003); State v. Barnard, 362 N.C. 244, 658 S.E.2d 643 (2008); State v. Watkins, 220 N.C. App. 384, 725 S.E.2d 400 (2012); Ward v. Carmona, 368 N.C. 35, 770 S.E.2d 70 (2015).

II. NEGLIGENCE AND PROXIMATE CAUSE.

VIOLATION AS FACTOR TO BE CONSIDERED IN DETERMINING BREACH OF DUTY TO EXERCISE DUE CARE. --Since a violation of this section is no longer to be considered negligence per se, the jury, if they find as a fact that this section was violated, must consider the violation along with all other facts and circumstances, and decide whether, when so considered, the violator has breached his common-law duty of exercising ordinary care. Kinney v. Goley, 4 N.C. App. 325, 167 S.E.2d 97, reaffirmed on rehearing, 6 N.C. App. 182, 169 S.E.2d 525 (1969); Harris v. Freeman, 18 N.C. App. 85, 196 S.E.2d 48 (1973); Mintz v. Foster, 35 N.C. App. 638, 242 S.E.2d 181 (1978); Spruill v. Summerlin, 51 N.C. App. 452, 276 S.E.2d 736 (1981).

Since a violation of this safety statute is not negligence per se, triers of the facts must consider all relevant facts and attendant circumstances in deciding whether the violator has breached his common-law duty to exercise due care. Sharpe v. Grindstaff, 329 F. Supp. 405 (M.D.N.C. 1970), rev'd on other grounds, 446 F.2d 152 (4th Cir. 1971).

Although subsection (d) of this section provides that the violation of this section is not negligence per se, a violation of subsection (a) of this section may be considered along with all other facts and circumstances in determining whether defendant driver breached duty of exercising ordinary, reasonable care. Phillips v. United States, 650 F. Supp. 114 (W.D.N.C. 1986).

While a driver's failure to meet the statutory requirements is not negligence per se, it must be considered along with all the other facts and circumstances as evidence of the driver's alleged contributory negligence. Blankley v. Martin, 101 N.C. App. 175, 398 S.E.2d 606 (1990).

FOR CASES HOLDING VIOLATION OF THIS SECTION TO BE NEGLIGENCE PER SE, DECIDED PRIOR TO THE 1965 AMENDMENT to this section, see Murphy v. Asheville-Knoxville Coach Co., 200 N.C. 92, 156 S.E. 550 (1931); Holland v. Strader, 216 N.C. 436, 5 S.E.2d 311 (1939); Bechtler v. Bracken, 218 N.C. 515, 11 S.E.2d 721 (1940); Conley v. Pearce-Young-Angel Co., 224 N.C. 211, 29 S.E.2d 740 (1944); Banks v. Shepard, 230 N.C. 86, 52 S.E.2d 215 (1949); Cooley v. Baker, 231 N.C. 533, 58 S.E.2d 115 (1950); Grimm v. Watson, 233 N.C. 65, 62 S.E.2d 538 (1950); Ervin v. Cannon Mills Co., 233 N.C. 415, 64

S.E.2d 431 (1951); Bradham v. McLean Trucking Co., 243 N.C. 708, 91 S.E.2d 891 (1956); Queen City Coach Co. v. Fultz, 246 N.C. 523, 98 S.E.2d 860 (1957); Hall v. Carroll, 255 N.C. 326, 121 S.E.2d 547 (1961); Tart v. Register, 257 N.C. 161, 125 S.E.2d 754 (1962); Wiggins v. Ponder, 259 N.C. 277, 130 S.E.2d 402 (1963); Cowan v. Murrows Transf., Inc., 262 N.C. 550, 138 S.E.2d 228 (1964); Farmers Oil Co. v. Miller, 264 N.C. 101, 141 S.E.2d 41 (1965); Lowe v. Futrell, 271 N.C. 550, 157 S.E.2d 92 (1967).

FOR CASES HOLDING THAT WHETHER THE VIOLATION OF THIS SECTION WAS A PROXIMATE CAUSE OF INJURY FOR THE JURY, see Holland v. Strader, 216 N.C. 436, 5 S.E.2d 311 (1939); White v. Lacey, 245 N.C. 364, 96 S.E.2d 1 (1957).

STOPPING ON TRAVELED PORTION OF HIGHWAY DOES NOT NECESSARILY CONSTITUTE NEGLIGENCE. --The mere fact that a driver stops his vehicle on the traveled portion of a highway for the purpose of receiving or discharging a passenger, nothing else appearing, does not constitute negligence. Strickland v. Powell, 10 N.C. App. 225, 178 S.E.2d 136 (1970), aff'd, 279 N.C. 183, 181 S.E.2d 464 (1971).

BUT MUST BE DONE WITH REGARD TO REQUIREMENTS OF SECTION. --The stopping on a bus on the traveled portion of the highway to receive or discharge a passenger must be done with due regard to the provisions of this section. Banks v. Shepard, 230 N.C. 86, 52 S.E.2d 215 (1949).

EVIDENCE THAT DEFENDANT DRIVER GAVE SIGNAL OF INTENTION TO TURN LEFT BY AN ELECTRICAL SIGNAL DEVICE operated by a lever on the steering column was competent to be considered by the jury on the issue of the contributory negligence of such operator, notwithstanding the absence of evidence that such signal device had been approved by the Department (now Division) of Motor Vehicles, since, apart from this section, it is for the jury to decide whether the signal was in fact given, whether it indicated a left turn by the operator of the car, and whether the driver of the other car was negligent in failing to observe and heed such signal. Queen City Coach Co. v. Fultz, 246 N.C. 523, 98 S.E.2d 860 (1957).

EVIDENCE HELD INSUFFICIENT TO SHOW THAT MECHANICAL OR ELECTRICAL SIGNAL WAS GIVEN. --Where plaintiff, a passenger in a bus, was injured when a truck following the bus collided with the rear thereof when the bus had stopped on the highway to permit a passenger to alight, and defendant bus company admitted that its driver gave no hand signal, but introduced evidence of a rule of the Utilities Commission as to the required lighting equipment on motor vehicles, along with evidence that the bus had been inspected and approved by an inspector of the Utilities Commission, and a certificate of title issued by the Department (now Division) of Motor Vehicles, together with testimony of the driver that the stoplights were on only when the brakes were on and then only if one stopped the bus suddenly, and that the driver slowed down gradually before stopping the bus, it was held that the evidence was insufficient to show that a mechanical or electrical signal as required by this section was given, and motion to nonsuit was properly denied. Banks v. Shepard, 230 N.C. 86, 52 S.E.2d 215 (1949).

EVIDENCE HELD SUFFICIENT TO SHOW NEGLIGENCE. --Evidence to the effect that defendant, traveling in the opposite direction, turned left to enter a private driveway and stopped with her vehicle partially blocking plaintiff's lane of travel, causing plaintiff to swerve off the hard surface to avoid a collision, was sufficient to show negligence by defendant under subsection (a) of this section. Black v. Wilkinson, 269 N.C. 689, 153 S.E.2d 333 (1967).

EVIDENCE OF NEGLIGENCE HELD SUFFICIENT FOR JURY. --Evidence that defendant driver attempted to turn left into a dirt road without giving a plain and visible signal of his intention to do so, did not keep a proper lookout, and did not heed plaintiff's warning horn, resulting in a collision with plaintiff's vehicle as plaintiff, traveling in the same direction, was attempting to pass, was sufficient to be submitted to the jury on the issue of negligence. Eason v. Grimsley, 255 N.C. 494, 121 S.E.2d 885 (1961).

INTERVENING NEGLIGENCE HELD TO INSULATE PRIMARY NEGLIGENCE. --Where plaintiff's evidence tended to show that plaintiff was standing at the rear of a car parked completely off the hard surface on the right, that a car traveling at a speed of 45 to 50 miles per hour slowed down rapidly as it came near the parked car, that the driver of a truck following 250 feet behind the car, when he saw the brake light on the car, immediately applied his brakes without effect and then applied his hand brake and skidded off the highway, striking the rear of the car and the plaintiff, oncoming traffic preventing the truck driver from turning to the left, and the driver of the truck testified that had his brakes been working properly he did not think he would have had any trouble stopping the truck, it was held that even conceding negligence on the part of the driver of the car in violating this section, the intervening negligence of the driver of the truck, in driving at excessive speed or in operating the truck with defective brakes, insulated any negligence of the driver of the car as a matter of law, since neither the intervening negligence nor the resulting injury could have been reasonably anticipated by the driver of the car from his act in rapidly decreasing his speed. Warner v. Lazarus, 229 N.C. 27, 47 S.E.2d 496 (1948).

CONTRIBUTORY NEGLIGENCE HELD TO BAR RECOVERY. --Where plaintiff's tractor-trailer, following defendants' tractor-trailer on the highway at night, rammed the rear of defendants' vehicle when it suddenly stopped on the highway, and plaintiff's allegations and evidence were to the effect that defendants' vehicle suddenly stopped without signal by hand or electrical device, while plaintiff's driver testified that he was familiar with the highway and knew he was approaching an intersection where traffic was congested, that he was traveling between 110 and 115 feet behind defendants' vehicle, that he did not see that it had stopped until he was within 75 feet of it, and that he immediately put on his brakes but was too close to stop before hitting its rear, it was held

that plaintiff's evidence disclosed contributory negligence as a matter of law, barring recovery. Fawley v. Bobo, 231 N.C. 203, 56 S.E.2d 419 (1949).

Even though the driver of a truck which collided with plaintiff's automobile failed to observe the requirements of this and other sections, where collision occurred when plaintiff was attempting to overtake and pass the truck proceeding in the same direction at the intersection of highways, without permission to do so by a traffic or police officer, in violation of provisions of G.S. 20-150(c), contributory negligence on the part of the plaintiff barred his recovery. Cole v. Fletcher Lumber Co., 230 N.C. 616, 55 S.E.2d 86 (1949).

Plaintiff truck driver was held guilty of contributory negligence in turning left without seeing that the movement could be made in safety, and he could not recover damages from colliding with a tractor-trailer. Gasperson v. Rice, 240 N.C. 660, 83 S.E.2d 665 (1954).

Plaintiff's admitted violation of this section in making a "U" turn to his left without ascertaining that he could do so in safety and without giving required signal was a proximate cause of the collision, justifying a nonsuit against him. Tallent v. Talbert, 249 N.C. 149, 105 S.E.2d 426 (1958).

FOR CASE HOLDING THAT THE EVIDENCE DID NOT COMPEL CONCLUSION THAT SOLE PROXIMATE CAUSE OF COLLISION WAS ILLEGAL LEFT TURN made by driver of other car, see Jernigan v. Jernigan, 236 N.C. 430, 72 S.E.2d 912 (1952).

FOR CASE HOLDING THAT FAILURE TO GIVE HAND SIGNAL WAS NOT THE PROXIMATE CAUSE OF COLLISION, see Cozart v. Hudson, 239 N.C. 279, 78 S.E.2d 881 (1954).

FOR CASES HOLDING THAT ALLEGATIONS OF COMPLAINT SHOWED THAT SOLE PROXIMATE CAUSE OF COLLISION WAS NEGLIGENT LEFT TURN made by first defendant across path of second defendant, despite allegations that second defendant was concurrently negligent, see Hout v. Harvell, 270 N.C. 274, 154 S.E.2d 41 (1967); Mabe v. Green, 270 N.C. 276, 154 S.E.2d 91 (1967).

PLAINTIFF'S FAILURE TO AGAIN LOOK FOR FOLLOWING OR PASSING VEHICLES BEFORE BEGINNING THE LEFT TURN was evidence that she violated this statute and was contributorily negligent. Since the evidence does not indicate how far following vehicles could be seen, ascertaining when 115 feet away that no vehicle was behind her and signaling for a left turn did not necessarily meet the statute's requirements. Church v. Greene, 100 N.C. App. 675, 397 S.E.2d 649 (1990).

INSTRUCTIONS HELD ERRONEOUS. --An instruction stating in substance that defendants had to prove first that plaintiff failed to ascertain safe turning conditions and, having proved this, had to prove that plaintiff failed to signal his intention to turn, and that the failure to signal was the proximate cause of the collision, placed an unwarranted burden on defendants. Mitchell v. White, 256 N.C. 437, 124 S.E.2d 137 (1962).

Where there was no evidence that defendant driver failed to give the signal for a left turn, as required by this section, and no evidence that defendant was traveling at excessive speed at the time, it was error for the court to instruct the jury upon the issue of the driver's negligence in regard to turn signals and excessive speed. Textile Motor Freight, Inc. v. DuBose, 260 N.C. 497, 133 S.E.2d 129 (1963).

LEGAL PERIODICALS. --

For note, "Turning and Stopping -- Signals by Drivers," see 29 N.C.L. Rev. 439 (1951).

For article on proof of negligence in North Carolina, see 48 N.C.L. Rev. 731 (1970).

§ 20-155. Right-of-way

(a) When two vehicles approach or enter an intersection from different highways at approximately the same time, the driver of the vehicle on the left shall yield the right-of-way to the vehicle on the right.

(b) The driver of a vehicle intending to turn to the left within an intersection or into an alley, private road, or driveway shall yield the right-of-way to any vehicle approaching from the opposite direction which is within the intersection or so close as to constitute an immediate hazard.

(c) The driver of any vehicle upon a highway within a business or residence district shall yield the right-of-way to a pedestrian crossing such highway within any clearly marked crosswalk, or any regular pedestrian crossing included in the prolongation of the lateral boundary lines of the adjacent sidewalk at the end of a block, except at intersections where the movement of traffic is being regulated by traffic officers or traffic direction devices.

(d) The driver of any vehicle approaching but not having entered a traffic circle shall yield the right-of-way to a vehicle already within such traffic circle.

History.

1937, c. 407, s. 117; 1949, c. 1016, s. 2; 1955, c. 913, ss. 6, 7; 1967, c. 1053; 1973, c. 1330, s. 20

I. IN GENERAL.

APPLIED in Wooten v. Smith, 215 N.C. 48, 200 S.E. 921 (1939); Primm v. King, 249 N.C. 228, 106 S.E.2d 223 (1958); Greene v. Meredith, 264 N.C. 178, 141 S.E.2d 287 (1965); Mims v. Dixon, 272 N.C. 256, 158 S.E.2d 91 (1967); White v. Hester, 1 N.C. App. 410, 161 S.E.2d 611 (1968); Douglas v. Booth, 6 N.C. App. 156, 169 S.E.2d 492 (1969); U.S. Indus., Inc. v. Tharpe, 47 N.C. App. 754, 268 S.E.2d 824 (1980); Cucina v. City of Jacksonville, (N.C. App. Apr. 4, 2000); Cucina v. City of Jacksonville, 138 N.C. App. 99, 530 S.E.2d 353 (2000), review denied, 352 N.C. 588, 544 S.E.2d 778 (2000).

CITED in Leary v. Norfolk S. Bus Corp., 220 N.C. 745, 18 S.E.2d 426 (1942); Bobbitt v. Haynes, 231 N.C. 373, 57 S.E.2d 361 (1950); Smith v. Buie, 243 N.C. 209, 90 S.E.2d 514 (1955); Jordan v. Blackwelder, 250 N.C.

189, 108 S.E.2d 429 (1959); Kelly v. Ashburn, 256 N.C. 338, 123 S.E.2d 775 (1962); Farrow v. Baugham, 266 N.C. 739, 147 S.E.2d 167 (1966); Anderson v. Carter, 272 N.C. 426, 158 S.E.2d 607 (1968); Hall v. Kimber, 6 N.C. App. 669, 171 S.E.2d 99 (1969); Hathcock v. Lowder, 16 N.C. App. 255, 192 S.E.2d 124 (1972); North Carolina v. Ivory, 906 F.2d 999 (4th Cir. 1990); Lonon v. Talbert, 103 N.C. App. 686, 407 S.E.2d 276 (1991).

II. INTERSECTIONS GENERALLY.

"RIGHT-OF-WAY" DEFINED. --The expression "right-of-way" has been interpreted to mean the right of a vehicle to proceed uninterruptedly in a lawful manner in the direction in which it is moving, in preference to another vehicle approaching from a different direction into its path. Bennett v. Stephenson, 237 N.C. 377, 75 S.E.2d 147 (1953).

RIGHT-OF-WAY IS NOT ABSOLUTE. --One who has the right-of-way at an intersection does not have the absolute right-of-way in the sense that he is not bound to use ordinary care in the exercise of his right. When he sees, or by the exercise of due care should see, that an approaching driver cannot or will not observe the traffic laws, he must use such care as an ordinarily prudent person would use under the same or similar circumstances to avoid collision and injury. His duty under such circumstances consists in keeping a reasonable lookout, keeping his vehicle under control, and taking reasonable precautions to avoid injury to persons and property. Carr v. Lee, 249 N.C. 712, 107 S.E.2d 544 (1959).

Even though a driver has the right-of-way at an intersection, it is incumbent upon him, in approaching and traversing the intersection, to drive at a speed no greater than is reasonable under the conditions then existing, to keep his vehicle under control, to keep a reasonably careful lookout and to take such action as a reasonably prudent person would take to avoid collision when the danger of one is discovered or should have been discovered. Dawson v. Jennette, 278 N.C. 438, 180 S.E.2d 121 (1971).

SECTION APPLIES TO INTERSECTIONS NOT COVERED BY OTHER RULES. --This section announces the rule with respect to use of intersections not covered by other rules. McEwen Funeral Serv. v. Charlotte City Coach Lines, 248 N.C. 146, 102 S.E.2d 816 (1958).

SECTION INAPPLICABLE WHERE ONE STREET IS FAVORED BY LIGHTS, SIGNS, ETC. --Where by reason of automatic traffic lights, stop or caution signs, or other devices, one street at an intersection is favored over the other, and one street is thereby made permanently or intermittently dominant and the other servient, this section has no application. White v. Phelps, 260 N.C. 445, 132 S.E.2d 902 (1963).

Ordinarily, when traffic lights are installed at an intersection, the relative rights of motorists approaching on intersecting streets are determinable with reference thereto rather than by the provisions of this section. Cogdell v. Taylor, 264 N.C. 424, 142 S.E.2d 36 (1965).

WHERE THERE ARE NO STOP SIGNS OR TRAFFIC CONTROL DEVICES AT AN INTERSECTION, NEITHER STREET IS FAVORED over the other, notwithstanding that one is paved and the other is not, and the right-of-way at such intersection is governed by subsections (a) and (b) of this section. Mallette v. Ideal Laundry & Dry Cleaners, Inc., 245 N.C. 652, 97 S.E.2d 245 (1957); Rhyne v. Bailey, 254 N.C. 467, 119 S.E.2d 385 (1961).

AND THIS SECTION APPLIES. --Absent traffic lights, the relative rights of motorists are determinable with reference to this section. Cogdell v. Taylor, 264 N.C. 424, 142 S.E.2d 36 (1965).

EFFECT OF DISAPPEARANCE OR REMOVAL OF STOP SIGN. --Where driver on a highway which a stop sign had designated as the dominant highway knew that the stop sign had been so erected, but did not know of its disappearance or removal, and driver of vehicle on the other highway, which the stop sign had designated as the servient highway, did not know there had ever been such a stop sign erected at the intersection, and approached the intersection from the right of the other driver, the removal of the stop sign would not take away the right of the driver of the vehicle on the highway designated by the sign as the dominant highway to treat the highway as such and to proceed into the intersection on the assumption that the other vehicle approaching from the right would yield the right-of-way to him. The responsibility of the driver of the vehicle on the highway designated by the sign as the servient highway, who did not know the highway had ever been so designated, would be judged in the light of conditions confronting him, namely, an unmarked intersection at which the other vehicle was approaching from his left. Dawson v. Jennette, 278 N.C. 438, 180 S.E.2d 121 (1971).

EFFECT OF PRIOR KNOWLEDGE OF MALFUNCTIONING TRAFFIC SIGNAL. --Where a traffic signal was malfunctioning, and each party knew how the traffic signal malfunctioned on his street, the rights and duties of the drivers would be determined on the basis of their prior knowledge and not on the objective condition of the intersection; hence, defendant was not entitled to a peremptory instruction that the vehicle approaching from the right had the right-of-way under this section. Bledsoe v. Gaddy, 10 N.C. App. 470, 179 S.E.2d 167 (1971).

NO DISTINCTION BETWEEN "T" INTERSECTION AND ONE AT WHICH HIGHWAYS CROSS. --With reference to the right-of-way as between two vehicles approaching and entering an intersection, the law of this State makes no distinction between a "T" intersection and one at which two highways cross each other completely. Dawson v. Jennette, 278 N.C. 438, 180 S.E.2d 121 (1971).

SUBSECTION (A) INAPPLICABLE TO VEHICLES PROCEEDING IN OPPOSITE DIRECTIONS. --Where motorists are proceeding in opposite directions and meeting at an intersection, subsection (a) of this section has no application. Fleming v. Drye, 253 N.C. 545, 117 S.E.2d 416 (1960).

Where motorists are proceeding in opposite directions and meeting at an intersection controlled by automatic traffic lights, subsection (a) of this section has no application. Shoe v. Hood, 251 N.C. 719, 112 S.E.2d 543 (1960); Wiggins v. Ponder, 259 N.C. 277, 130 S.E.2d 402 (1963); Rathburn v. Sorrells, 5 N.C. App. 212, 167 S.E.2d 800 (1969).

APPLICABILITY OF SUBSECTION (A) TO VEHICLES ENTERING INTERSECTION AT "APPROXIMATELY SAME TIME." --Subsection (a) of this section does not apply unless two vehicles approach or enter intersection at approximately the same time. When that condition does not exist, the vehicle first reaching and entering the intersection has the right-of-way over a vehicle subsequently reaching it, irrespective of their directions of travel; and it is the duty of the driver of the latter vehicle to delay his progress so as to allow the first arrival to pass in safety. State v. Hill, 233 N.C. 61, 62 S.E.2d 532 (1950); Brady v. Nehi Beverage Co., 242 N.C. 32, 86 S.E.2d 901 (1955); Downs v. Odom, 250 N.C. 81, 108 S.E.2d 65 (1959).

The test of the applicability of subsection (a) of this section is whether both vehicles approach or reach the intersection at "approximately the same time," and the right-of-way is not determined by a fraction of a second. Hathcock v. Lowder, 16 N.C. App. 255, 192 S.E.2d 124, cert. denied, 282 N.C. 426, 192 S.E.2d 836 (1972).

WHEN VEHICLES APPROACH OR ENTER INTERSECTION AT APPROXIMATELY SAME TIME. --Two motor vehicles approach or enter an intersection at approximately the same time within the purview of these rules whenever their respective distances from the intersection, their relative speeds, and the other attendant circumstances show that the driver of the vehicle on the left should reasonably apprehend that there is danger of collision unless he delays his progress until the vehicle on the right has passed. State v. Hill, 233 N.C. 61, 62 S.E.2d 532 (1950); Bennett v. Stephenson, 237 N.C. 377, 75 S.E.2d 147 (1953); Brady v. Nehi Beverage Co., 242 N.C. 32, 86 S.E.2d 901 (1955); Taylor v. Brake, 245 N.C. 553, 96 S.E.2d 686 (1957); Moore v. Butler, 10 N.C. App. 120, 178 S.E.2d 35 (1970); Dawson v. Jennette, 278 N.C. 438, 180 S.E.2d 121 (1971).

APPROACH OR ENTRY AT SAME TIME NOT SHOWN. --It could not be held as a matter of law that plaintiff's automobile and defendants' truck approached or entered intersection "at approximately the same time" when the latter was 125 feet away from the intersection when the former was entering it, and when plaintiff's automobile had crossed within four feet of the opposite curb when defendants' truck collided therewith. Crone v. Fisher, 223 N.C. 635, 27 S.E.2d 642 (1943).

Where defendant's automobile came to a stop at an intersection 23 feet wide while the automobile in which decedent was traveling was more than 125 feet away, and a collision occurred when defendant attempted to cross the intersection, the two vehicles did not approach or enter the intersection at approximately the same time, and therefore the automobile of the decedent did not have the right-of-way. State v. Hill, 233 N.C. 61, 62 S.E.2d 532 (1950).

DUTY OF DRIVER APPROACHING FROM LEFT. --If the driver of the automobile on the left approaching an intersection sees, or in the exercise of reasonable prudence should see, an automobile approaching from his right in such a manner that apparently the two automobiles will reach the intersection at approximately the same time, it is his duty to decrease his speed, bring his automobile under control, and if necessary stop, and to yield the right-of-way to the driver of the automobile on his right in order to enable him to proceed and thus avoid a collision. The law imposes this duty on the driver of an automobile approaching an intersecting highway unless the automobile coming from his right on the intersecting highway is a sufficient distance away to warrant the assumption that he can proceed before the other automobile, operated at a reasonable speed, reaches the crossing. Bennett v. Stephenson, 237 N.C. 377, 75 S.E.2d 147 (1953).

Where two drivers approach an uncontrolled intersection at the same time, it is the duty of the driver on the left to yield the right-of-way to the vehicle on his right. Wilder v. Harris, 266 N.C. 82, 145 S.E.2d 393 (1965).

WHEN THE DRIVER OF A MOTOR VEHICLE ON THE LEFT COMES TO AN INTERSECTION AND FINDS NO ONE APPROACHING IT on the other street within such distance as reasonably to indicate danger of collision, he is under no obligation to stop or wait, but may proceed to use such intersection as a matter of right. Carr v. Stewart, 252 N.C. 118, 113 S.E.2d 18 (1960).

RIGHT TO ASSUME THAT DRIVER APPROACHING FROM LEFT WILL YIELD RIGHT-OF-WAY. --If two automobiles approach an intersection at approximately the same time, the driver of the automobile on the right, in approaching the intersection, has the right to assume that the driver of the automobile coming from the left will yield the right-of-way and stop or slow down sufficiently to permit the other to pass in safety. Bennett v. Stephenson, 237 N.C. 377, 75 S.E.2d 147 (1953). See also, Finch v. Ward, 238 N.C. 290, 77 S.E.2d 661 (1953); Brady v. Nehi Beverage Co., 242 N.C. 32, 86 S.E.2d 901 (1955); Neal v. Stevens, 266 N.C. 96, 145 S.E.2d 325 (1965).

A driver with the right-of-way at an intersection is under no duty to anticipate disobedience of law or negligence on the part of others; rather, in the absence of anything which puts him on notice, or should put him on notice, to the contrary, he is entitled to assume, and to act on the assumption, that others will obey the law, exercise reasonable care and yield the right-of-way. Carr v. Lee, 249 N.C. 712, 107 S.E.2d 544 (1959).

A driver having the right-of-way may act upon the assumption, in the absence of notice to the contrary, that the other motorist will recognize his right-of-way and grant him a free passage over the intersection. Carr v. Stewart, 252 N.C. 118, 113 S.E.2d 18 (1960).

When two drivers approach an uncontrolled intersection at the same time, the driver on the right has the right to assume, and to act on the assumption, until given notice to the contrary, that the operator of any vehicle approaching the intersection to the left would obey the law and yield the right-of-way. Wilder v. Harris, 266 N.C. 82, 145 S.E.2d 393 (1965).

Nothing else appearing, the driver of a vehicle having the right-of-way at an intersection is entitled to assume and to act, until the last moment, on the assumption that the driver of another vehicle, approaching the intersection, will recognize his right-of-way and will stop or reduce his speed sufficiently to permit him to pass through the intersection in safety. Dawson v. Jennette, 278 N.C. 438, 180 S.E.2d 121 (1971).

RIGHT TO ASSUME ANOTHER DRIVER'S COMPLIANCE WITH LAW. --While plaintiff had a duty to drive no faster than was safe, to keep his vehicle under control, to maintain a careful lookout, and to take reasonably prudent steps to avoid a collision, he was entitled to assume, even to the last moment, that defendant would comply with the law before entering plaintiff's lane of travel, and nothing indicated that plaintiff failed to act reasonably. Daisy v. Yost, 250 N.C. App. 530, 794 S.E.2d 364 (2016).

EFFECT OF SPEED OF DRIVER ON RIGHT ON APPLICATION OF RULE. --Fact that defendant's automobile, which was approaching from plaintiff's right, was being driven at a speed of 35 to 40 miles per hour in a residential district with no other vehicle in view would not prevent the application of the rule as to right-of-way for automobiles entering an intersection at the same time, in the absence of evidence that the speed of defendant's automobile proximately caused the collision. Bennett v. Stephenson, 237 N.C. 377, 75 S.E.2d 147 (1953).

RIGHT-OF-WAY ON ENTERING INTERSECTION AHEAD OF OTHER CAR. --If plaintiff's automobile enters intersection of two streets at a time when defendant's approaching car is far enough away to justify a person in believing that, in the exercise of reasonable care and prudence, he may safely pass over the intersection ahead of the oncoming car, plaintiff has the right-of-way and it is the duty of defendant to reduce his speed and bring his car under control and yield. Yellow Cab Co. v. Sanders, 223 N.C. 626, 27 S.E.2d 631 (1943).

Where defendant's truck entered intersection before the automobile in which plaintiff was riding reached the intersection, and the truck approached the intersection from the automobile's right side of the road, the truck had the right-of-way. Brady v. Nehi Beverage Co., 242 N.C. 32, 86 S.E.2d 901 (1955).

RIGHT-OF-WAY WHERE VEHICLE ON LEFT HAS ALREADY ENTERED INTERSECTION. --This section does not apply if the driver on the right, at the time he approaches intersection and before reaching it, in the exercise of reasonable prudence ascertains that the vehicle on his left has already entered the intersection. Kennedy v. Smith, 226 N.C. 514, 39 S.E.2d 380 (1946); Taylor v. Brake, 245 N.C. 553, 96 S.E.2d 686 (1957).

If the automobile approaching from the left reaches intersection first and has already entered the intersection the driver of the automobile on the right is under the duty to permit the other automobile to pass in safety. Bennett v. Stephenson, 237 N.C. 377, 75 S.E.2d 147 (1953).

RULE WHERE DRIVER HAS BROUGHT AUTOMOBILE TO COMPLETE STOP. --The rule as to right-of-way prescribed by this section applies to moving vehicles approaching an intersection at approximately the same time. Where the driver has already brought his automobile to a complete stop, thereafter the duty would devolve upon him to exercise due care to observe approaching vehicles and to govern his conduct accordingly. One who is required to stop before entering a highway should not proceed, with oncoming vehicles in view, until in the exercise of due care he can determine that he can do so with reasonable assurance of safety. Matheny v. Central Motor Lines, 233 N.C. 673, 65 S.E.2d 361 (1951); Badders v. Lassiter, 240 N.C. 413, 82 S.E.2d 357 (1954).

A MOTORIST WHO DOES NOT KEEP A LOOKOUT IS NEVERTHELESS CHARGED WITH HAVING SEEN WHAT HE COULD HAVE SEEN had he looked, and his liability to one injured in a collision with his vehicle is determined as it would have been had he looked, observed the prevailing conditions and continued to drive as he did. Dawson v. Jennette, 278 N.C. 438, 180 S.E.2d 121 (1971).

RECOVERY HELD BARRED BY FAILURE TO MAINTAIN PROPER LOOKOUT. --Where plaintiff's testimony indicated that he did not slow down and yield the right-of-way to defendant for the reason that plaintiff was not maintaining a proper lookout and did not see defendant's vehicle, and where plaintiff's testimony further revealed that, while he looked before entering the intersection, he did so at a point where he could not see vehicles approaching the intersection from his right, his admitted conduct prohibited any recovery. Moore v. Butler, 10 N.C. App. 120, 178 S.E.2d 35 (1970).

EVIDENCE HELD SUFFICIENT TO GO TO JURY. --In an action to recover damages resulting from a collision at a street intersection, plaintiff's evidence that she entered intersection first and that defendants entered the intersection from her left was sufficient to take the case to the jury over defendants' motion to nonsuit. Harrison v. Kapp, 241 N.C. 408, 85 S.E.2d 337 (1955).

FOR CASE HOLDING FAILURE TO YIELD RIGHT-OF-WAY PROXIMATE CAUSE OF COLLISION, see Freeman v. Preddy, 237 N.C. 734, 76 S.E.2d 159 (1953).

AS TO EVIDENCE SUPPORTING INFERENCE THAT DEFENDANT NEGLIGENTLY FAILED TO YIELD RIGHT-OF-WAY, see Donlop v. Snyder, 234 N.C. 627, 68 S.E.2d 316 (1951); Tripp v. Harris, 260 N.C. 200, 132 S.E.2d 322 (1963).

ISSUE OF NEGLIGENCE RAISED BY EVIDENCE. --Evidence that defendant failed to yield the right-of-way to plaintiff, who was on the right, and that defendant was driving at 50 miles per hour through the intersection, raised the issue of defendant's negligence, and motion for nonsuit at the close of all the evidence was properly denied. Price v. Gray, 246 N.C. 162, 97 S.E.2d 844 (1957).

INSTRUCTION UPHELD. --Under this section, where damages were sought for defendant's negligent driving at a street intersection, and there was evidence tending to show that defendant was approaching the intersection at an unlawful rate of speed and did not slow up before collision with another car, an instruction correctly charging the rule of the right-of-way if both cars approached the intersection simultaneously and the rule that if one car was already in the intersection it was the duty of the driver of the other car to slow down and permit it to pass would not be held for error. Piner v. Richter, 202 N.C. 573, 163 S.E. 561 (1932).

COURT NOT REQUIRED TO READ APPLICABLE STATUTES TO JURY. --Where the trial court charges the law in regard to the statutory provisions in regard to the right-of-way at an intersection, and applies the law to the evidence in the case, an objection on the ground that the court failed to charge on the statutes is without merit, if not being required that the court read the applicable statutes to the jury. Kennedy v. James, 252 N.C. 434, 113 S.E.2d 889 (1960).

AS TO EXCEPTION OF EMERGENCY AMBULANCES FROM REQUIREMENTS OF THIS SECTION, see Upchurch v. Hudson Funeral Home, 263 N.C. 560, 140 S.E.2d 17 (1965).

III. LEFT TURNS.

DUTY OF DRIVER TURNING LEFT. --The driver desiring to turn left at an intersection may move into the intersection when the signal facing him is green, but before turning left is charged with the duty to yield the right-of-way under this section. Hudson v. Petroleum Transit Co., 250 N.C. 435, 108 S.E.2d 900 (1959).

It is incumbent upon a motorist, before making a left turn at an intersection, to give a plainly visible signal of his intention to turn and to ascertain that the movement can be made in safety, without regard to which vehicle enters the intersection first. Wiggins v. Ponder, 259 N.C. 277, 130 S.E.2d 402 (1963).

WHERE CARS ARE MEETING AT AN INTERSECTION AND ONE INTENDS TO TURN ACROSS THE LANE OF TRAVEL OF THE OTHER, subsection (b) of this section and subsection (a) of G.S. 20-154 apply, and the driver making the turn is under duty to give a plainly visible signal of his intention to turn, and to ascertain that such movement can be made in safety, without regard to which vehicle entered the intersection first. Fleming v. Drye, 253 N.C. 545, 117 S.E.2d 416 (1960); King v. Sloan, 261 N.C. 562, 135 S.E.2d 556 (1964). See also, Fowler v. Atlantic Co., 234 N.C. 542, 67 S.E.2d 496 (1951).

DUTY WHERE TURNING VEHICLE HAS ALREADY ENTERED INTERSECTION. --Under subsection (b) of this section, the vehicle first reaching an intersection which has no stop sign or traffic signal has the right-of-way over a vehicle subsequently reaching it, whether the vehicle in the intersection is proceeding straight ahead or turning in either direction; and it is the duty of the driver of the vehicle not having entered the intersection to delay his progress and allow the vehicle which first entered the intersection to pass in safety. Carr v. Stewart, 252 N.C. 118, 113 S.E.2d 18 (1960).

If plaintiff was already in the intersection, giving the statutory left-turn signal, at a time when defendant was 150-feet away, it was defendant's duty to delay her entrance into the intersection until plaintiff had cleared it entirely. Mayberry v. Allred, 263 N.C. 780, 140 S.E.2d 406 (1965).

RIGHT TO ASSUME THAT OTHER DRIVERS WILL NOT BLOCK LANE BY LEFT TURN. --A driver intending to go straight through an intersection has the right to assume, and to act on the assumption, that all other travelers will observe the law and will not block his lane of travel by a left turn without first ascertaining that such move can be made in safety. Harris v. Parris, 260 N.C. 524, 133 S.E.2d 195 (1963).

A through driver is required to give notice of any intended change in direction through an intersection, and in the absence of such notice, other travelers are required to assume that he intends to continue through in his proper lane of traffic. Harris v. Parris, 260 N.C. 524, 133 S.E.2d 195 (1963).

SUBSECTION (B) HELD APPLICABLE. --Where, at the time they were struck, defendants had fully complied with G.S. 20-158(a), subsection (b) of this section was then applicable. Todd v. Shipman, 12 N.C. App. 650, 184 S.E.2d 403 (1971).

FOR CASE HOLDING PLEADINGS AND EVIDENCE INSUFFICIENT to support plaintiff's theory that plaintiff had the right-of-way by virtue of subsection (b) of this section, see Taylor v. Brake, 245 N.C. 553, 96 S.E.2d 686 (1957).

PRIMA FACIE CASE OF NEGLIGENCE. --Where it may be inferred from plaintiff's evidence that defendant failed to observe either of the statutory requirements of G.S. 20-154(a) or subsection (b) of this section and that injury was suffered by plaintiff because of such failure, plaintiff has made out a prima facie case of actionable negligence. Wiggins v. Ponder, 259 N.C. 277, 130 S.E.2d 402 (1963).

IV. RIGHT-OF-WAY OF PEDESTRIANS.

PEDESTRIAN'S RIGHT-OF-WAY LIMITED BY GREEN LIGHT IN PRESENCE OF TRAFFIC SIGNALS. --The right-of-way given a pedestrian by subsection (c) of this section at an intersection where there is no traffic-control signal is limited at an intersection where there is a traffic-control signal to the pedestrian having the right-of-way only when he is moving with the green light. Wagoner v. Butcher, 6 N.C. App. 221, 170 S.E.2d 151 (1969), decided under this section and § 20-173(a) as it read prior to its amendment in 1973.

BUT RIGHT TO PROCEED IS SUPERIOR TO RIGHT TO TURN. --The pedestrian crossing with a favorable light is assisted by the principle that the right to proceed is superior to the right to turn. Wagoner v. Butcher, 6 N.C. App. 221, 170 S.E.2d 151 (1969).

SO THAT PEDESTRIAN'S RIGHTS ARE SUPERIOR TO TURNING MOTORIST'S WHERE LIGHTS ARE FAVORABLE. --Under subsection (c) of this section, where a pedestrian and a turning motorist are both proceeding at an intersection under favorable signal lights, the right of the pedestrian to proceed is superior to that of the turning motorist. Duke v. Meisky, 12 N.C. App. 329, 183 S.E.2d 292 (1971).

AND PEDESTRIAN'S RIGHT-OF-WAY IS NOT IMPAIRED WHEN HE CROSSES WITH LIGHTS. --Subsection (c) of this section may be construed to mean that a pedestrian's crosswalk right-of-way is not impaired when the movement of the pedestrian is in accord with the traffic lights. Wagoner v. Butcher, 6 N.C. App. 221, 170 S.E.2d 151 (1969).

NOR IS PEDESTRIAN'S RIGHT-OF-WAY ON GREEN LIGHT SUBORDINATED TO THAT OF TURNING MOTORIST. --The effect of the exception in subsection (c) of this section as to intersections where traffic is regulated by traffic officers or traffic direction devices is not to subordinate the right-of-way of a pedestrian moving on a green light to that of a turning motorist. Wagoner v. Butcher, 6 N.C. App. 221, 170 S.E.2d 151 (1969).

LEGAL PERIODICALS. --

For brief comment on right-of-way as between vehicles on a paved road and those entering from unpaved roads, see 34 N.C.L. Rev. 81 (1955).

§ 20-156. Exceptions to the right-of-way rule

(a) The driver of a vehicle about to enter or cross a highway from an alley, building entrance, private road, or driveway shall yield the right-of-way to all vehicles approaching on the highway to be entered.

(b) The driver of a vehicle upon the highway shall yield the right-of-way to police and fire department vehicles and public and private ambulances, vehicles used by an organ procurement organization or agency for the recovery or transportation of human tissues and organs for transplantation or a vehicle operated by a transplant coordinator who is an employee of an organ procurement organization or agency when the transplant coordinator is responding to a call to recover or transport human tissues or organs for transplantation, and to rescue squad emergency service vehicles and vehicles operated by county fire marshals and civil preparedness coordinators, and to a vehicle operated by the Division of Marine Fisheries of the Department of Environmental Quality or the Division of Parks and Recreation of the Department of Natural and Cultural Resources when used for law enforcement, firefighting, or other emergency response purpose, and to a vehicle operated by the North Carolina Forest Service of the Department of Agriculture and Consumer Services when used for a law enforcement, firefighting, or other emergency response purpose, when the operators of said vehicles are giving a warning signal by appropriate light and by bell, siren or exhaust whistle audible under normal conditions from a distance not less than 1,000 feet. When appropriate warning signals are being given, as provided in this subsection, an emergency vehicle may proceed through an intersection or other place when the emergency vehicle is facing a stop sign, a yield sign, or a traffic light which is emitting a flashing strobe signal or a beam of steady or flashing red light. This provision shall not operate to relieve the driver of a police or fire department vehicle, or a vehicle owned or operated by the Department of Environmental Quality, or the Department of Agriculture and Consumer Services, or public or private ambulance or vehicles used by an organ procurement organization or agency for the recovery or transportation of human tissues and organs for transplantation or a vehicle operated by a transplant coordinator who is an employee of an organ procurement organization or agency when the transplant coordinator is responding to a call to recover or transport human tissues or organs for transplantation, or rescue squad emergency service vehicle or county fire marshals or civil preparedness coordinators from the duty to drive with due regard for the safety of all persons using the highway, nor shall it protect the driver of any such vehicle or county fire marshal or civil preparedness coordinator from the consequence of any arbitrary exercise of such right-of-way.

History.
1937, c. 407, s. 118; 1971, cc. 78, 106; 1973, c. 1330, s. 21; 1977, c. 52, s. 4; c. 438, s. 3; 1985, c. 427; 1989, c. 537, s. 3;2013-415, s. 1(d);2015-241, s. 14.30(u), (hh)

EFFECT OF AMENDMENTS. --
Session Laws 2013-415, s. 1(d), effective October 1, 2013, in subsection (b), inserted "and to a vehicle operated by the Division of Marine Fisheries or the Division of Parks and Recreation of the Department of Environment and Natural Resources when used for law enforcement, firefighting, or other emergency response purpose, and to a vehicle operated by the North Carolina Forest Service of the Department of Agriculture and Consumer Services when used for a law enforcement, firefighting, or other emergency response purpose" in the first sentence and "or a vehicle owned or operated by the Department of Environment and Natural Resources, or the Department of Agriculture and Consumer Services" in the third sentence.

Session Laws 2015-241, s. 14.30(hh), effective July 1, 2015, in the first sentence in subsection (b), substituted "Fisheries of the Department of Environmental Quality" for "Fisheries" and substituted "Department of Natural and Cultural Resources" for "Department of Environment and Natural Resources."

Session Laws 2015-241, s. 14.30(u), effective July 1, 2015, in the third sentence in subsection (b), substituted "Department of Environmental Quality" for "Department of Environment and Natural Resources."

I. IN GENERAL.
APPLIED in Nantz v. Nantz, 255 N.C. 357, 121 S.E.2d 561 (1961); State v. Gurley, 257 N.C. 270, 125 S.E.2d 445 (1962); O'Berry v. Perry, 266 N.C. 77, 145 S.E.2d 321 (1965); Williams v. Bethany Volunteer Fire Dep't, 307 N.C. 430, 298 S.E.2d 352 (1983).

CITED in Bobbitt v. Haynes, 231 N.C. 373, 57 S.E.2d 361 (1950); Brady v. Nehi Beverage Co., 242 N.C. 32, 86 S.E.2d 901 (1955); Fleming v. Drye, 253 N.C. 545, 117 S.E.2d 416 (1960); Payne v. Lowe, 2 N.C. App. 369, 163 S.E.2d 74 (1968); Campbell v. O'Sullivan, 4 N.C. App. 581, 167 S.E.2d 450 (1969); White v. Reilly, 15 N.C. App. 331, 190 S.E.2d 303 (1972); Hathcock v. Lowder, 16 N.C. App. 255, 192 S.E.2d 124 (1972); Williams v. Bethany Volunteer Fire Dep't, 57 N.C. App. 114, 290 S.E.2d 794 (1982); Lopez v. Snowden, 96 N.C. App. 480, 386 S.E.2d 65 (1989).

II. ENTRY OR CROSSING OF HIGHWAY FROM PRIVATE ROAD, ETC.
REGULATORY POWER OF STATE. --Subsection (a) of this section and G.S. 20-165.1 illustrate the power of the State to regulate the time and manner of entering a public highway. Moses v. State Hwy. Comm'n, 261 N.C. 316, 134 S.E.2d 664, cert. denied, 379 U.S. 930, 85 S. Ct. 327, 13 L. Ed. 2d 342 (1964).

ABUTTING OWNER'S RIGHT OF ACCESS MUST BE EXERCISED WITH DUE REGARD TO THE SAFETY OF OTHERS who have an equal right to use the highway. State Hwy. Comm'n v. Raleigh Farmers Mkt., Inc., 263 N.C. 622, 139 S.E.2d 904, aff'd, 264 N.C. 139, 141 S.E.2d 10 (1965).

DUTY OF DRIVER ENTERING HIGHWAY TO LOOK FOR APPROACHING VEHICLES. --In order to comply with subsection (a) of this section, the driver of a vehicle entering a public highway from a private road or drive is required to look for vehicles approaching on such highway, at a time when this precaution may be effective. Gantt v. Hobson, 240 N.C. 426, 82 S.E.2d 384 (1954). See also, Clark v. Emerson, 245 N.C. 387, 95 S.E.2d 880 (1957).

AND TO DEFER ENTRY UNTIL IT IS SAFE. --In order to comply with this section, a driver entering a public highway from a private drive is required to look for vehicles approaching on such highway, at a time when the precaution may be effective, to yield the right-of-way to vehicles traveling on the highway, and to defer entry until the movement may be made in safety. C.C.T. Equip. Co. v. Hertz Corp., 256 N.C. 277, 123 S.E.2d 802 (1962); Davis v. Imes, 13 N.C. App. 521, 186 S.E.2d 641 (1972); Bigelow v. Johnson, 303 N.C. 126, 277 S.E.2d 347 (1981).

In order to comply with subsection (a) of this section, the driver of a vehicle about to enter or cross a highway from an alley, building entrance, private road or driveway is only required to look for vehicles approaching on the highway at a time when his lookout may be effective, to see what he should see, and to yield the right-of-way to vehicles on the highway which, in the exercise of reasonable care, he sees or should see are being operated at such a speed or distance as to make his entry onto the highway unsafe, by delaying his entry onto the highway until a reasonable and prudent man would conclude that the entry could be made in safety. Penland v. Greene, 289 N.C. 281, 221 S.E.2d 365 (1976); Bigelow v. Johnson, 303 N.C. 126, 277 S.E.2d 347 (1981).

Before entering a public highway from a private driveway, the operator of a motor vehicle is required to exercise due care to see that the intended movement can be made in safety. Smith v. Nunn, 257 N.C. 108, 125 S.E.2d 351 (1962).

SUBSECTION (A) OF THIS SECTION DOES NOT REQUIRE OMNISCIENCE on the part of a motorist entering a public highway from a private drive. Penland v. Greene, 289 N.C. 281, 221 S.E.2d 365 (1976).

APPLICABILITY OF SUBSECTION (A) TO PERSON RIDING ANIMAL. --The requirement that a person entering a public highway from a private road or drive must yield the right-of-way to vehicles on the public highway applies to a person riding an animal as well as to a person driving a motor vehicle. Watson v. Stallings, 270 N.C. 187, 154 S.E.2d 308 (1967).

RIGHT TO ASSUME THAT DRIVER ENTERING HIGHWAY WILL COMPLY WITH SECTION. --The operator of an automobile traveling upon a public highway in this State is under no duty to anticipate that the driver of an automobile entering a public highway from a private road or drive will fail to yield the right-of-way to all vehicles on such public highway, as required by subsection (a) of this section, and in the absence of anything which gives or should give notice to the contrary, he is entitled to assume and to act upon the assumption, even to the last moment, that the driver of the automobile so entering the public highway from a private road or drive will, in obedience to the section, yield the right-of-way. Garner v. Pittman, 237 N.C. 328, 75 S.E.2d 111 (1953).

One operating his motorcycle upon the highway was under no duty to assume that a motorist would fail to yield to him the right-of-way which was rightfully his, and he was entitled to this assumption even to the last moment. Whiteside v. Rooks, 197 F. Supp. 313 (W.D.N.C. 1961).

RIGHT-OF-WAY ON DIRT RAMP ACROSS HIGHWAY. --This section is applicable at such times as a dirt ramp across a highway is open for public travel, but it does not apply at such times as the ramp is closed by the flagmen. At the times when the ramp is closed, public travelers have no right to use it, but must stop and yield the right-of-way to contractor's machinery. The flagman's signal to stop is at least equivalent to a legally established stop sign or stoplight at an intersection. C.C.T. Equip. Co. v. Hertz Corp., 256 N.C. 277, 123 S.E.2d 802 (1962).

Irrespective of subsection (a) of this section, a contractor for the improvement of an airport who was granted permission to maintain a dirt ramp across a highway was under a duty, before operating its earth-moving equipment onto and across the ramp, to exercise due care to see that such movement could be made with safety and without injury to users of the highway. C.C. Mangum, Inc. v. Gasperson, 262 N.C. 32, 136 S.E.2d 234 (1964).

FAILURE TO YIELD RIGHT-OF-WAY TO TRAFFIC ON A PUBLIC HIGHWAY DID NOT COMPEL A FINDING OF CONTRIBUTORY NEGLIGENCE as a matter of law when there was evidence that traffic on the highway was faced with a red traffic light and there was no evidence of anything to give notice that a motorist on the highway would not obey the traffic control signal. Galloway v. Hartman, 271 N.C. 372, 156 S.E.2d 727 (1967).

USE OF TERMS "DOMINANT" AND "SERVIENT" IN CHARGE TO JURY. --While use of the words "dominant" and "servient" may not be precisely correct in referring to the roads in question under subsection (a) of this section in instructions to the jury, where the judge instructed upon the proper principles of law applicable to each motorist, defendant was not prejudiced thereby. Penland v. Greene, 289 N.C. 281, 221 S.E.2d 365 (1976).

There is no error prejudicial to defendant in the occasional use of the term "servient highway or street" instead of "private road or drive" in the charge to the jury. Penland v. Greene, 24 N.C. App. 240, 210 S.E.2d 505 (1974), aff'd, 289 N.C. 281, 221 S.E.2d 365 (1976).

There is no error prejudicial to defendant in the occasional use of the term "servient highway or street" instead of "private road or drive" in the charge to the jury. Penland v. Greene, 24 N.C. App. 240, 210 S.E.2d 505 (1974), aff'd, 289 N.C. 281, 221 S.E.2d 365 (1976).

III. RIGHT-OF-WAY OF EMERGENCY VEHICLES.

WHEN EMERGENCY VEHICLE HAS RIGHT-OF-WAY PRIVILEGE. --If the operator of an authorized emergency vehicle bona fide believes that an emergency exists which requires expeditious movement and meets the statutory test by giving warning, he is accorded the necessary privilege of the right-of-way. Williams v. Sossoman's Funeral Home, 248 N.C. 524, 103 S.E.2d 714 (1958).

WHEN RIGHT-OF-WAY MUST BE YIELDED TO EMERGENCY VEHICLE. --No duty rests on the operator of a motor vehicle making normal use of a highway to yield the right-of-way to another vehicle on an emergency mission until an appropriate warning has been directed to him, and he has reasonable opportunity to yield his prior right. McEwen Funeral Serv. v. Charlotte City Coach Lines, 248 N.C. 146, 102 S.E.2d 816 (1958).

RIGHT-OF-WAY PRIVILEGES OF EMERGENCY VEHICLES INAPPLICABLE TO INTERSECTIONS CONTROLLED BY TRAFFIC LIGHTS. --The General Assembly did not intend the right-of-way privileges accorded emergency ambulances by this section to be extended to apply to intersections controlled by automatic traffic lights. Upchurch v. Hudson Funeral Home, 263 N.C. 560, 140 S.E.2d 17 (1965); State v. Flaherty, 55 N.C. App. 14, 284 S.E.2d 565 (1981).

RIGHT OF OPERATOR OF EMERGENCY VEHICLE TO ASSUME THAT OTHER DRIVERS WILL

YIELD. --The operator of an authorized emergency vehicle, while on an emergency call, has the right to proceed upon the assumption that when the required signal by siren is given, other users of the highway will yield the right-of-way. Williams v. Sossoman's Funeral Home, 248 N.C. 524, 103 S.E.2d 714 (1958).

THE AUDIBLE SOUND WHICH THIS SECTION REQUIRES is such a sound as was in fact heard and comprehended, or which should have been heard and its meaning understood, by a reasonably prudent operator called upon to yield the right-of-way. McEwen Funeral Serv. v. Charlotte City Coach Lines, 248 N.C. 146, 102 S.E.2d 816 (1958); Williams v. Sossoman's Funeral Home, 248 N.C. 524, 103 S.E.2d 714 (1958).

LEGAL PERIODICALS. --

For note on liability of municipality for accident involving fire truck responding to an emergency call for an inhalator, see 30 N.C.L. Rev. 89 (1951).

§ 20-157. Approach of law enforcement, fire department or rescue squad vehicles or ambulances; driving over fire hose or blocking fire fighting equipment; parking, etc., near law enforcement, fire department, or rescue squad vehicle or ambulance

(a) Upon the approach of any law enforcement or fire department vehicle or public or private ambulance or rescue squad emergency service vehicle, or a vehicle operated by the Division of Marine Fisheries of the Department of Environmental Quality, or the Division of Parks and Recreation of the Department of Natural and Cultural Resources, or the North Carolina Forest Service of the Department of Agriculture and Consumer Services when traveling in response to a fire alarm or other emergency response purpose, giving warning signal by appropriate light and by audible bell, siren or exhaust whistle, audible under normal conditions from a distance not less than 1000 feet, the driver of every other vehicle shall immediately drive the same to a position as near as possible and parallel to the right-hand edge or curb, clear of any intersection of streets or highways, and shall stop and remain in such position unless otherwise directed by a law enforcement or traffic officer until the law enforcement or fire department vehicle, or the vehicle operated by the Division of Marine Fisheries of the Department of Environmental Quality, or the Division of Parks and Recreation of the Department of Natural and Cultural Resources, or the North Carolina Forest Service of the Department of Agriculture and Consumer Services, or the public or private ambulance or rescue squad emergency service vehicle shall have passed. Provided, however, this subsection shall not apply to vehicles traveling in the opposite direction of the vehicles herein enumerated when traveling on a four-lane limited access highway with a median divider dividing the highway for vehicles traveling in opposite directions, and provided further that the violation of this subsection shall be negligence per se. Violation of this subsection is a Class 2 misdemeanor.

(b) It shall be unlawful for the driver of any vehicle other than one on official business to follow any fire apparatus traveling in response to a fire alarm closer than one block or to drive into or park such vehicle within one block where fire apparatus has stopped in answer to a fire alarm.

(c) Outside of the corporate limits of any city or town it shall be unlawful for the driver of any vehicle other than one on official business to follow any fire apparatus traveling in response to a fire alarm closer than 400 feet or to drive into or park such vehicle within a space of 400 feet from where fire apparatus has stopped in answer to a fire alarm.

(d) It shall be unlawful to drive a motor vehicle over a fire hose or any other equipment that is being used at a fire at any time, or to block a fire-fighting apparatus or any other equipment from its source of supply regardless of its distance from the fire.

(e) It shall be unlawful for the driver of a vehicle, other than one on official business, to park and leave standing such vehicle within 100 feet of law enforcement or fire department vehicles, public or private ambulances, or rescue squad emergency vehicles which are engaged in the investigation of an accident or engaged in rendering assistance to victims of such accident.

(f) When an authorized emergency vehicle as described in subsection (a) of this section or any public service vehicle is parked or standing within 12 feet of a roadway and is giving a warning signal by appropriate light, the driver of every other approaching vehicle shall, as soon as it is safe and when not otherwise directed by an individual lawfully directing traffic, do one of the following:

(1) Move the vehicle into a lane that is not the lane nearest the parked or standing authorized emergency vehicle or public service vehicle and continue traveling in that lane until safely clear of the authorized emergency vehicle. This paragraph applies only if the roadway has at least two lanes for traffic proceeding in the direction of the approaching vehicle and if the approaching vehicle may change lanes safely and without interfering with any vehicular traffic.

(2) Slow the vehicle, maintaining a safe speed for traffic conditions, and operate the vehicle at a reduced speed and be prepared to stop until completely past the authorized emergency vehicle or public service vehicle. This paragraph applies only if the roadway has only one lane for traffic proceeding in

the direction of the approaching vehicle or if the approaching vehicle may not change lanes safely and without interfering with any vehicular traffic.

For purposes of this section, "public service vehicle" means a vehicle that (i) is being used to assist motorists or law enforcement officers with wrecked or disabled vehicles, (ii) is being used to install, maintain, or restore utility service, including electric, cable, telephone, communications, and gas, (iii) is being used in the collection of refuse, solid waste, or recycling, or (iv) is a highway maintenance vehicle owned and operated by or contracted by the State or a local government and is operating an amber-colored flashing light authorized by G.S. 20-130.2. Violation of this subsection shall be negligence per se.

(g) Except as provided in subsections (a), (h), and (i) of this section, violation of this section shall be an infraction punishable by a fine of two hundred fifty dollars ($ 250.00).

(h) A person who violates this section and causes damage to property in the immediate area of the authorized emergency vehicle or public service vehicle in excess of five hundred dollars ($ 500.00), or causes injury to a law enforcement officer, a firefighter, an emergency vehicle operator, an Incident Management Assistance Patrol member, a public service vehicle operator, or any other emergency response person in the immediate area of the authorized emergency vehicle or public service vehicle is guilty of a Class 1 misdemeanor.

(i) A person who violates this section and causes serious injury or death to a law enforcement officer, a firefighter, an emergency vehicle operator, an Incident Management Assistance Patrol member, a public service vehicle operator, or any other emergency response person in the immediate area of the authorized emergency vehicle or public service vehicle is guilty of a Class F felony. The Division may suspend, for up to six months, the drivers license of any person convicted under this subsection. If the Division suspends a person's license under this subsection, a judge may allow the licensee a limited driving privilege for a period not to exceed the period of suspension, provided the person's license has not also been revoked or suspended under any other provision of law. The limited driving privilege shall be issued in the same manner and under the terms and conditions prescribed in G.S. 20-16.1(b).

History.
1937, c. 407, s. 119; 1955, cc. 173, 744; 1971, c. 366, ss. 1, 2; 1985, c. 764, s. 31; 1985 (Reg. Sess., 1986), c. 852, s. 17; 1993, c. 539, s. 372;1994, Ex. Sess., c. 24, s. 14(c);2001-331, s. 1;2005-189, s. 1;2006-259, s. 9;2007-360, s. 1;2010-132, s. 12;2012-14, s. 1;2013-415, s. 1(e);2015-26, s. 3;2015-241, s. 14.30(ii);2019-157, s. 2

EDITOR'S NOTE. --
Session Laws 2015-26, s. 4, made the amendment to subsection (f) of this section by Session Laws 2015-26, s. 3, applicable to offenses committed on or after October 1, 2015.

Session Laws 2019-157, s. 1, provides: "This act shall be known and may be cited as the 'Officer Jason Quick Act.'"

Session Laws 2019-157, s. 4, makes the amendments to subsection (i) of this section by Session Laws 2019-157, s. 2, effective December 1, 2019, and applicable to offenses committed on or after that date.

EFFECT OF AMENDMENTS. --
Session Laws 2005-189, s. 1, effective July 1, 2006, and applicable to offenses committed on or after that date, substituted "law enforcement" for "police" in the section heading, and in subsections (a) and (e); in subsection (a), in the next-to-last sentence, substituted "shall be" for "shall not be"; in subsection (f), inserted "or any public service vehicle" in the introductory paragraph; in subdivision (f)(2), inserted "and be prepared to stop" in the first sentence; in the undesignated paragraph, added the first sentence, and in the second sentence, substituted "shall be" for "shall not be"; and added subsections (g) through (i).

Session Laws 2006-259, s. 9, effective August 23, 2006, added "or public service vehicle" in subdivisions (f)(1) and (f)(2).

Session Laws 2007-360, s. 1, effective August 17, 2007, deleted "has been called to the scene by a motorist or a law enforcement officer" following "means a vehicle that" in the last paragraph of subsection (f).

Session Laws 2010-132, s. 12, effective December 1, 2010, and applicable to offenses committed on or after that date, inserted "or is a vehicle being used to restore electric utility service due to an unplanned event" in the last paragraph in subsection (f).

Session Laws 2012-14, s. 1, effective October 1, 2012, substituted "install, maintain, or restore utility service, including electric, cable, telephone, communications, and gas, or is a highway maintenance vehicle owned and operated by or contracted by the State or a local government" for "restore electric utility service due to an unplanned event" in the last paragraph of subsection (f). For applicability, see Editor's note.

Session Laws 2013-415, s. 1(e), effective October 1, 2013, in subsection (a), inserted "or a vehicle operated by the Division of Marine Fisheries, or the Division of Parks and Recreation of the Department of Environment and Natural Resources, or the North Carolina Forest Service of the Department of Agriculture and Consumer Services when traveling in response to a fire alarm or other emergency response purpose" in the first sentence and "or the vehicle operated by the Division of Marine Fisheries, or the Division of Parks and Recreation of the Department of Environment and Natural Resources, or the North Carolina Forest Service of the Department of Agriculture and Consumer Services."

Session Laws 2015-26, s. 3, effective October 1, 2015, in the undesignated paragraph at the end of subsection (f), inserted designations (i), (ii), and (iv), inserted subdivision (iii), and made related changes. For applicability, see editor's note.

Session Laws 2015-241, s. 14.30(ii), effective July 1, 2015, in subsection (a), substituted "Fisheries of the Department of Environmental Quality" for "Fisheries" and substituted "Department of Natural and Cultural Resources" for "Department of Environment and Natural Resources" twice.

Session Laws 2019-157, s. 2, effective December 1, 2019, substituted "Class F" for "Class I" in subsection (i). For effective date and applicability, see editor's note.

§ 20-157.1. Funeral processions

(a) As used in this section, a "funeral procession" means two or more vehicles accompanying the remains of a deceased person, or traveling to the church, chapel, or other location at which the funeral services are to be held, in which the lead vehicle is either a State or local law enforcement vehicle, other vehicle designated by a law enforcement officer or the funeral director, or the lead vehicle displays a flashing amber or purple light, sign, pennant, flag, or other insignia furnished by a funeral home indicating a funeral procession.

(b) Each vehicle in the funeral procession shall be operated with its headlights illuminated, if so equipped, and its hazard warning signal lamps illuminated, if so equipped.

(c) The operator of the lead vehicle in a funeral procession shall comply with all traffic-control signals, but when the lead vehicle in a funeral procession has progressed across an intersection in accordance with the traffic-control sign or signal, or when directed to do so by a law enforcement officer or a designee of a law enforcement officer or the funeral director, or when the lead vehicle is a law enforcement vehicle which progresses across the intersection while giving appropriate warning by light or siren, all vehicles in the funeral procession may proceed through the intersection without stopping, except that the operator of each vehicle shall exercise reasonable care towards any other vehicle or pedestrian on the highway. An operator of a vehicle that is not part of the funeral procession shall not join the funeral procession for the purpose of securing the right-of-way granted by this subsection.

(d) Operators of vehicles in a funeral procession shall drive on the right-hand side of the roadway and shall follow the vehicle ahead as closely as reasonable and prudent having due regard for speed and existing conditions.

(e) Operators of vehicles in a funeral procession shall yield the right-of-way to law enforcement vehicles, fire protection vehicles, rescue vehicles, ambulances, and other emergency vehicles giving appropriate warning signals by light or siren and shall yield the right-of-way when directed to do so by a law enforcement officer.

(f) Operators of vehicles in a funeral procession shall proceed at the posted minimum speed, except that the operator of such vehicle shall exercise reasonable care having due regard for speed and existing conditions.

(g) The operator of a vehicle proceeding in the opposite direction as a funeral procession may yield to the funeral procession. If the operator chooses to yield to the procession, the operator must do so by reducing speed, or by stopping completely off the roadway when meeting the procession or while the procession passes, so that operators of other vehicles proceeding in the opposite direction of the procession can continue to travel without leaving their lane of traffic.

(h) The operator of a vehicle proceeding in the same direction as a funeral procession shall not pass or attempt to pass the funeral procession, except that the operator of such a vehicle may pass a funeral procession when the highway has been marked for two or more lanes of moving traffic in the same direction of the funeral procession.

(i) An operator of a vehicle shall not knowingly drive between vehicles in a funeral procession by crossing their path unless directed to do so by a person authorized to direct traffic. When a funeral procession is proceeding through a steady or strobe-beam stoplight emitting a red light as permitted by subsection (c), an operator of a vehicle that is not in the funeral procession shall not enter the intersection knowing a funeral procession is in progress, even if facing a steady or strobe-beam stoplight emitting a green light, unless the operator can do so safely without crossing the path of the funeral procession.

(j) Nothing in this section shall be construed to prevent State or local law enforcement officers from escorting funeral processions in law enforcement vehicles.

(k) A violation of this section shall not constitute negligence per se.

(l) To the extent that a local government unit's ordinance is in direct conflict with any part of this statute, the ordinance shall control and prevail over the conflicting part.

(m) A violation of this section shall not be considered a moving violation for purposes of G.S. 58-36-65 or G.S. 58-36-75.

History.
1999-441, s. 1

§ 20-158. Vehicle control signs and signals

(a) The Department of Transportation, with reference to State highways, and local authorities, with reference to highways under their jurisdiction, are hereby authorized to control vehicles:

(1) At intersections, by erecting or installing stop signs requiring vehicles to come to a complete stop at the entrance to that portion of the intersection designated as the main traveled or through highway. Stop signs may also be erected at three or more entrances to an intersection.

(2) At appropriate places other than intersections, by erecting or installing stop signs requiring vehicles to come to a complete stop.

(3) At intersections and other appropriate places, by erecting or installing steady-beam traffic signals and other traffic control devices, signs, or signals. All steady-beam traffic signals emitting alternate red and green lights shall be arranged so that the red light in vertical-arranged signal faces shall appear above, and in horizontal-arranged signal faces shall appear to the left of all yellow and green lights.

(4) At intersections and other appropriate places, by erecting or installing flashing red or yellow lights.

(b) **Control of Vehicles at Intersections. --**

(1) When a stop sign has been erected or installed at an intersection, it shall be unlawful for the driver of any vehicle to fail to stop in obedience thereto and yield the right-of-way to vehicles operating on the designated main-traveled or through highway. When stop signs have been erected at three or more entrances to an intersection, the driver, after stopping in obedience thereto, may proceed with caution.

(2) a. When a traffic signal is emitting a steady red circular light controlling traffic approaching an intersection, an approaching vehicle facing the red light shall come to a stop and shall not enter the intersection. After coming to a complete stop and unless prohibited by an appropriate sign, that approaching vehicle may make a right turn.

b. Any vehicle that turns right under this subdivision shall yield the right-of-way to:

1. Other traffic and pedestrians using the intersection; and

2. Pedestrians who are moving towards the intersection, who are in reasonably close proximity to the intersection, and who are preparing to cross in front of the traffic that is required to stop at the red light.

c. Failure to yield to a pedestrian under this subdivision shall be an infraction, and the court may assess a penalty of not more than five hundred dollars ($ 500.00) and not less than one hundred dollars ($ 100.00).

d. Repealed by Session Laws 2014-58, s. 4, effective July 7, 2014.

(2a) When a traffic signal is emitting a steady yellow circular light on a traffic signal controlling traffic approaching an intersection or a steady yellow arrow light on a traffic signal controlling traffic turning at an intersection, vehicles facing the yellow light are warned that the related green light is being terminated or a red light will be immediately forthcoming. When the traffic signal is emitting a steady green light, vehicles may proceed with due care through the intersection subject to the rights of pedestrians and other vehicles as may otherwise be provided by law.

(3) When a flashing red light has been erected or installed at an intersection, approaching vehicles facing the red light shall stop and yield the right-of-way to vehicles in or approaching the intersection. The right to proceed shall be subject to the rules applicable to making a stop at a stop sign.

(4) When a flashing yellow light has been erected or installed at an intersection, approaching vehicles facing the yellow flashing light may proceed through the intersection with caution, yielding the right-of-way to vehicles in or approaching the intersection.

(5) When a stop sign, traffic signal, flashing light, or other traffic-control device authorized by subsection (a) of this section requires a vehicle to stop at an intersection, the driver shall stop (i) at an appropriately marked stop line, or if none, (ii) before entering a marked crosswalk, or if none, (iii) before entering the intersection at the point nearest the intersecting street where the driver has a view of approaching traffic on the intersecting street.

(6) When a traffic signal is not illuminated due to a power outage or other malfunction, vehicles shall approach the intersection and proceed through the intersection as though such intersection is controlled by a stop sign on all approaches to the intersection. This subdivision shall not apply if the movement of traffic at the intersection is being directed by a law enforcement officer, another authorized person, or another type of traffic control device.

(c) **Control of Vehicles at Places other than Intersections. --**

(1) When a stop sign has been erected or installed at a place other than an intersection, it shall be unlawful for the driver of any vehicle to fail to stop in obedience thereto and yield the right-of-way to pedestrians and other vehicles.

(2) When a traffic signal has been erected or installed at a place other than an intersection, and is emitting a steady red light, vehicles facing the red light shall come to a complete stop. When the traffic signal is emitting a steady yellow light, vehicles facing the light shall be warned that a red light will be immediately forthcoming and that vehicles may not proceed through such a red light. When the traffic signal is emitting a steady green light, vehicles may proceed subject to the rights of pedestrians and other vehicles as may otherwise be provided by law.

(3) When a flashing red light has been erected or installed at a place other than an intersection, approaching vehicles facing the light shall stop and yield the right-of-way to pedestrians or other vehicles.

(4) When a flashing yellow light has been erected or installed at a place other than an intersection, approaching vehicles facing the light may proceed with caution, yielding the right-of-way to pedestrians and other vehicles.

(5) When a traffic signal, stop sign, or other traffic control device authorized by subsection (a) requires a vehicle to stop at a place other than an intersection, the driver shall stop at an appropriately marked stop line, or if none, before entering a marked crosswalk, or if none, before proceeding past the traffic control device.

(6) When a ramp meter is displaying a circular red display, vehicles facing the red light must stop. When a ramp meter is displaying a circular green display, a vehicle may proceed for each lane of traffic facing the meter. When the display is dark or not emitting a red or green display, a vehicle may proceed without stopping. A violation of this subdivision is an infraction. No drivers license points or insurance surcharge shall be assessed as a result of a violation of this subdivision.

(d) No failure to stop as required by the provisions of this section shall be considered negligence or contributory negligence per se in any action at law for injury to person or property, but the facts relating to such failure to stop may be considered with the other facts in the case in determining whether a party was guilty of negligence or contributory negligence.

(e) **Defense.** -- It shall be a defense to a violation of sub-subdivision (b)(2)a. of this section if the operator of a motorcycle, as defined in G.S. 20-4.01(27)h., shows all of the following:

(1) The operator brought the motorcycle to a complete stop at the intersection or stop bar where a steady red light was being emitted in the direction of the operator.

(2) The intersection is controlled by a vehicle actuated traffic signal using an inductive loop to activate the traffic signal.

(3) No other vehicle that was entitled to have the right-of-way under applicable law was sitting at, traveling through, or approaching the intersection.

(4) No pedestrians were attempting to cross at or near the intersection.

(5) The motorcycle operator who received the citation waited a minimum of three minutes at the intersection or stop bar where the steady red light was being emitted in the direction of the operator before entering the intersection.

History.
1937, c. 407, s. 120; 1941, c. 83; 1949, c. 583, s. 2; 1955, c. 384, s. 1; c. 913, s. 7; 1957, c. 65, s. 11; 1973, c. 507, s. 5; c. 1191; c. 1330, s. 22; 1975, c. 1; 1977, c. 464, s. 34; 1979, c. 298, s. 1; 1989, c. 285; 2004-141, ss. 1, 2; 2004-172, ss. 2, 5; 2006-264, s. 6;2007-260, s. 1;2007-360, ss. 2, 3; 2014-58, ss. 4, 10(b); 2017-102, s. 5.2(b)

LOCAL MODIFICATION. --Currituck: 1985, c. 288.

EDITOR'S NOTE. --
Session Laws 2004-172, s. 4, which was codified as G.S. 58-36-75(h) at the direction of the Revisor of Statutes, provides that the North Carolina Rate Bureau shall assign one insurance point under the Safe Driver Incentive Plan for persons who fail to yield to a pedestrian under G.S. 20-158(b)(2)b.

Session Laws 2004-172, s. 5, effective December 1, 2004, has been codified as sub-subdivision (b)(2)d. at the direction of the Revisor of Statutes.

Session Laws 2014-58, s. 14, made subdivision (c)(6), as added by Session Laws 2014-58, s. 10(b), effective December 1, 2014, and applicable to offenses committed on or after that date.

Session Laws 2017-102, s. 5.2(b) provides: "The Revisor of Statutes is authorized to reletter the definitions in G.S. 20-4.01(27) and G.S. 20-4.01(32b) to place them in alphabetical order. The Revisor of Statutes may conform any citations that change as a result of the relettering." Pursuant to that authority, the reference to G.S. 20-4.01(27)d. in subsection (e) was changed to G.S. 20-4.01(27)h.

EFFECT OF AMENDMENTS. --
Session Laws 2004-141, ss. 1 and 2, effective July 1, 2004, in subdivision (a)(3), substituted "traffic signals" for "stoplights" throughout, inserted "in vertical-arranged signal faces," preceding "shall appear above," and substituted "above, and in horizontal-arranged signal faces shall appear to the left of all yellow and green lights" for "at the top of the signaling unit and the green light shall appear at the bottom of the signaling unit"; in subdivision (b)(2), substituted "approaching" for "passing straight through" three times, substituted "with a steady-beam traffic signal" for "from a steady or strobe beam stoplight," substituted "traffic signal" for "steady or strobe beam stoplight," substituted "the" for "a"

preceding "red light," and deleted "controlling traffic passing straight through an intersection" preceding "provided that."

Session Laws 2004-172, s. 2, effective December 1, 2004, and applicable to violations committed on or after that date, rewrote former subdivision (b)(2) as present subdivisions (b)(2) and (b)(2a).

Session Laws 2006-264, s. 6, effective August 27, 2006, rewrote subdivision (b)(2) and (b)(2)a.

Session Laws 2007-260, s. 1, effective December 1, 2007, and applicable to offenses committed on or after that date, added subsection (e).

Session Laws 2007-360, ss. 2 and 3, effective August 17, 2007, in subsection (b), substituted "traffic signal is emitting a steady red circular light" for "steady beam traffic signal is emitting a red light" in subdivision (b)(2)a. and "traffic signal" for "stopligh" in subdivision (b)(5), and added subdivision (b)(6); and in subsection (c), substituted "traffic signal" for "stoplight" and "traffic control device" for "signaling device" throughout.

Session Laws 2014-58, s. 4, effective July 7, 2014, repealed subdivision (b)(2)d, which read "The Department of Transportation shall collect data regarding the number of individuals who are found responsible for violations of sub-subdivision b. of this subdivision and the number of pedestrians who are involved in accidents at intersections because of a driver's failure to yield the right-of-way while turning right at a red light. The data shall include information regarding the number of disabled pedestrians, including individuals with visual or mobility-related disabilities, who are involved in right turn on red accidents. The Department shall report the data annually to the Joint Legislative Transportation Oversight Committee beginning January 1, 2006."

Session Laws 2014-58, s. 10(b), effective December 1, 2014, added subdivision (c)(6). See Editor's note for applicability.

I. IN GENERAL.

APPLICABILITY TO U.S. HIGHWAYS. --Highways which are built and maintained in part out of funds contributed by the federal government and which form links in an interstate system and are designated as U.S. highways are State highways under the supervision and control of the State Highway Commission (now Board of Transportation) and this section is applicable to these just as it is to other State highways. Yost v. Hall, 233 N.C. 463, 64 S.E.2d 554 (1951).

UNNAMED DIRT ROAD AND NAMED PAVED ROAD WHICH INTERSECTED WERE PUBLIC ROADS OF EQUAL DIGNITY where neither was designated "main traveled or through highway" by the State Highway Commission (now Board of Transportation). Brady v. Nehi Beverage Co., 242 N.C. 32, 86 S.E.2d 901 (1955).

DESIGNATION OF STREETS BY MUNICIPAL AUTHORITIES. --Where two streets of a municipality intersect, testimony identifying one as the through street and the other as the cross street on which there is a stop sign to the right of a driver thereon approaching the intersection connotes that the streets

have been so designated and the sign erected by action of the municipal authorities. Smith v. Buie, 243 N.C. 209, 90 S.E.2d 514 (1955).

THIS SECTION REGULATES THE CONDUCT OF ONE ENTERING THE MAIN HIGHWAY from a private road. Penland v. Greene, 24 N.C. App. 240, 210 S.E.2d 505 (1974), aff'd, 289 N.C. 281, 221 S.E.2d 365 (1976).

THIS SECTION APPLIES TO A "T" INTERSECTION, as with reference to the right-of-way as between two vehicles approaching and entering an intersection, the law of this State makes no distinction between a "T" intersection and one at which the two highways cross each other completely. Dawson v. Jennette, 278 N.C. 438, 180 S.E.2d 121 (1971).

THE LEGISLATURE TOOK RECOGNITION OF THE FACT THAT ALL HIGHWAY INTERSECTIONS ARE NOT OF EQUAL IMPORTANCE because of the density of traffic on one highway as compared to the flow on an intersecting highway. Hence, a rule was prescribed for this situation by this section, requiring operators of motor vehicles on a servient highway to stop in accordance with signs commanding them to do so. This was supplemented in 1955 by the provisions of G.S. 20-158.1. McEwen Funeral Serv., Inc. v. Charlotte City Coach Lines, 248 N.C. 146, 102 S.E.2d 816 (1958).

THE AUTOMOBILE DRIVER ON A DOMINANT HIGHWAY APPROACHING AN INTERSECTING SERVIENT HIGHWAY is not under a duty to anticipate that the automobile driver on the servient highway will fail to stop as required by statute, and in the absence of anything which gives or should give notice to the contrary, he will be entitled to assume and to act upon the assumption, even to the last moment, that the automobile driver on the servient highway will obey the law and stop before entering the dominant highway. Lewis v. Brunston, 78 N.C. App. 68, 338 S.E.2d 595 (1986).

IT IS THE DUTY OF THE DRIVER OF A MOTOR VEHICLE ON A SERVIENT HIGHWAY TO STOP at such time and place as the physical conditions may require in order for him to observe traffic conditions on the highways and to determine when, in the exercise of due care, he may enter or cross the intersecting highway with reasonable safety. Derrick v. Ray, 61 N.C. App. 218, 300 S.E.2d 721 (1983).

THE DRIVER ON THE SERVIENT INTERSECTING HIGHWAY IS NOT UNDER A DUTY TO ANTICIPATE that the automobile driver on the dominant highway, approaching the intersection of the two highways, will fail to observe the speed regulations and the rules of the road, and in the absence of anything which gives or should give notice to the contrary, he is entitled to assume and to act upon the assumption that the automobile driver on the dominant highway will obey such regulations and the rules of the road. Lewis v. Brunston, 78 N.C. App. 68, 338 S.E.2d 595 (1986).

WHERE AT THE TIME THEY WERE STRUCK DEFENDANTS HAD FULLY COMPLIED WITH SUBSECTION (A) OF THIS SECTION, G.S.

20-155(B)WAS APPLICABLE. Todd v. Shipman, 12 N.C. App. 650, 184 S.E.2d 403 (1971).

THIS SECTION DOES NOT REQUIRE A SPECIFIC INTENT. State v. Wright, 52 N.C. App. 166, 278 S.E.2d 579 (1981).

INADVERTENT VIOLATION OF SECTION. --Where there is an unintentional or inadvertent violation of this section, such violation, standing alone, does not constitute culpable negligence in the law of crimes as distinguished from actionable negligence in the law of torts. The inadvertent or unintentional violation of the statute must be accompanied by recklessness of probable consequences of a dangerous nature, when tested by the rule of reasonable prevision, amounting altogether to a thoughtless disregard of consequences or of a heedless indifference to the safety of others. State v. Sealy, 253 N.C. 802, 117 S.E.2d 793 (1961).

PROXIMATE CAUSE IN PROSECUTION FOR INVOLUNTARY MANSLAUGHTER. --Where a conviction of involuntary manslaughter is sought for the failure to observe a positive duty imposed by statute with reference to the driving of automobiles upon the State highways, the question of proximate cause must be shown beyond a mere chance or casualty. State v. Satterfield, 198 N.C. 682, 153 S.E. 155 (1930).

The manifest object of this section is to protect the public by requiring the driver of an automobile upon the public highways of the State to stop and ascertain the circumstances and conditions at highway intersections, particularly with reference to traffic, with a view of determining whether in the exercise of due care he may go upon the intersecting highway with reasonable safety to himself and others. Hence, where the defendant in a prosecution for manslaughter failed to stop, but had knowledge of the conditions and an unobstructed view of the highway for a long distance, and there was no evidence tending to show that he had violated any other statute or that he was negligent in any other respect, the evidence alone that he had violated the statute in the respect stated was insufficient to take the case to the jury, as there was no evidence that the violation of the statute was a proximate cause of the death or in causal relation thereto, and defendant's motion as of nonsuit, made in apt time, should have been granted. State v. Satterfield, 198 N.C. 682, 153 S.E. 155 (1930).

EVIDENCE OF WANTON CONDUCT HELD SUFFICIENT TO GO TO JURY. --In a negligence action, the evidence of the defendant's wanton conduct was sufficient to go to the jury, where defendant admitted: Awareness of her own substantial intoxication, indifference to her duty under G.S. 20-138.1 to avoid operating a motor vehicle while impaired, and obliviousness to the duty under this section to stop at the five stoplights between the cocktail lounge and the accident. It was for the jury to determine whether defendant's negligence evinced a wilful or reckless indifference to the rights of others, and then, whether her wilful or wanton conduct was the proximate cause of the accident. King v. Allred, 76 N.C. App. 427, 333 S.E.2d 758, cert. denied, 315 N.C. 184, 337 S.E.2d 857

(1985); Field v. Sheriff of Wake County, 831 F.2d 530 (4th Cir. 1987).

SUBSEQUENT PROSECUTION UNDER G.S. 20-141.4 HELD DOUBLE JEOPARDY. --Where defendant entered a plea of guilty to a charge of failing to yield the right-of-way in violation of this section, which failure resulted in an automobile accident, and a passenger thereafter died from injuries received in the accident, the trial of defendant on a charge of death by vehicle under G.S. 20-141.4 "in that he did unlawfully and willfully fail to yield the right-of-way.. in violation of General Statute 20-158" would place defendant in jeopardy for a second time on the charge of failure to yield the right-of-way, in violation of U.S. Const., Amend. V. State v. Griffin, 51 N.C. App. 564, 277 S.E.2d 77 (1981).

CITY'S RED LIGHT CAMERA ORDINANCE. --County board of education was entitled to funds derived from a city's red light camera program, which program was implemented by an ordinance pursuant to G.S. 160A-300.1(c), as N.C. Const., Art. IX, § 7 applied to the civil penalties assessed by the city for violations of the ordinance regarding the failure to stop for a red stoplight. Further, pursuant to G.S. 115C-437, the city was to pay 90 percent of the amount collected by its red light camera program to the board. Shavitz v. City of High Point, 177 N.C. App. 465, 630 S.E.2d 4 (2006), cert. denied, appeal dismissed, 361 N.C. 430, 648 S.E.2d 845 (2007).

DRIVER'S DUTIES AT RED LIGHT. --Third-party defendant was attempting to make a left turn on a red circular light, and if he entered the intersection while the light was green and the light turned red, he was permitted to complete his turn as long as he maintained a lookout and exercised reasonable care, and if he had not yet entered the intersection when the light turned red, he had a duty to stop; the appellate court's decision did not create a new theory of motor vehicle negligence inconsistent with North Carolina statutes and case law. Ward v. Carmona, 368 N.C. 35, 770 S.E.2d 70 (2015).

Statute permits vehicles approaching an intersection with a red circular light to make a right turn; however, this statutory provision allows a driver to make a right turn on red only if the intersection is clear. Ward v. Carmona, 368 N.C. 35, 770 S.E.2d 70 (2015).

APPLIED in Jones v. Bagwell, 207 N.C. 378, 177 S.E. 170 (1934); Powell v. Daniel, 236 N.C. 489, 73 S.E.2d 143 (1952); Edens v. Carolina Freight Carriers Corp., 247 N.C. 391, 100 S.E.2d 878 (1957); State v. Wells, 259 N.C. 173, 130 S.E.2d 299 (1963); Keith v. King, 263 N.C. 118, 139 S.E.2d 21 (1964); Douglas v. Booth, 6 N.C. App. 156, 169 S.E.2d 492 (1969); Gregor v. Willis, 8 N.C. App. 538, 174 S.E.2d 702 (1970); State v. Gainey, 292 N.C. 627, 234 S.E.2d 610 (1977); Shavitz v. City of High Point, 270 F. Supp. 2d 702 (M.D.N.C. 2003); Fisk v. Murphy, 212 N.C. App. 667, 713 S.E.2d 100 (2011).

CITED in Camalier v. Jeffries, 340 N.C. 699, 460 S.E.2d 133; Leary v. Norfolk S. Bus Corp., 220 N.C. 745, 18 S.E.2d 426 (1942); Smith v. United States, 94

Chapter 20

F. Supp. 681 (W.D.N.C. 1951); State v. Bournais, 240 N.C. 311, 82 S.E.2d 115 (1954); Currin v. Williams, 248 N.C. 32, 102 S.E.2d 455 (1958); Tucker v. Moorefield, 250 N.C. 340, 108 S.E.2d 637 (1959); Hunt v. Cranford, 253 N.C. 381, 117 S.E.2d 18 (1960); Watson Seafood & Poultry Co. v. George W. Thomas, Inc., 289 N.C. 7, 220 S.E.2d 536 (1975); Penland v. Greene, 289 N.C. 281, 221 S.E.2d 365 (1976); Young v. Denning, 54 N.C. App. 361, 283 S.E.2d 164 (1981); Smith v. Stocks, 54 N.C. App. 393, 283 S.E.2d 819 (1981); State v. Jones, 63 N.C. App. 411, 305 S.E.2d 221 (1983); State v. Field, 75 N.C. App. 647, 331 S.E.2d 221 (1985); Field v. Sheriff of Wake County, 831 F.2d 530 (4th Cir. 1987); State v. Hamrick, 110 N.C. App. 60, 428 S.E.2d 830 (1993); State v. Barnard, 362 N.C. 244, 658 S.E.2d 643 (2008).

II. RIGHTS AND DUTIES EFFECTED BY STOP SIGNS.

THE PURPOSE OF HIGHWAY STOP SIGNS is to enable the driver of a motor vehicle to have the opportunity to observe the traffic conditions on highways and to determine when in the exercise of due care he might enter upon an intersecting highway with reasonable assurance of safety to himself and others. Morrisette v. A.G. Boone Co., 235 N.C. 162, 69 S.E.2d 239 (1952); Edwards v. Vaughn, 238 N.C. 89, 76 S.E.2d 359 (1953); Badders v. Lassiter, 240 N.C. 413, 82 S.E.2d 357 (1954).

THE PURPOSE TO BE SERVED BY PLACING A STOP SIGN SOME DISTANCE FROM INTERSECTION of a servient highway and a dominant highway is to give the motorist ample time to slow down and stop before entering the zone of danger. And when the driver of a motor vehicle stops at a stop sign on a servient highway and then proceeds into the intersection without keeping a lookout and ascertaining whether he can enter or cross the intersecting highway with reasonable safety, he ignores the intent and purpose of this section. Edwards v. Vaughn, 238 N.C. 89, 76 S.E.2d 359 (1953).

THE ERECTION OF STOP SIGNS ON AN INTERSECTING HIGHWAY OR STREET IS A METHOD OF GIVING THE PUBLIC NOTICE that traffic on one is favored over the other and that a motorist facing a stop sign must yield. Kelly v. Ashburn, 256 N.C. 338, 123 S.E.2d 775 (1962); Payne v. Lowe, 2 N.C. App. 369, 163 S.E.2d 74 (1968).

SECTION CREATES NO DUTY ON PART OF DEPARTMENT OF TRANSPORTATION. --G.S. 20-158(a)(1) only authorizes the North Carolina Department of Transportation to erect or install stop signs, and while the Department of Transportation has authority to install a stop sign at an intersection, the statute does not mandate that it do so; the statute does not, therefore, establish that the Department of Transportation has a duty to erect or necessarily had responsibility for a stop sign and the Department of Transportation cannot be held liable for negligence based solely on the failure to erect a properly located sign at the intersection unless it breached a duty independent of G.S. 20-158(a). Norman v. N.C. DOT, 161 N.C. App. 211, 588 S.E.2d 42 (2003), review dismissed, review denied, 358 N.C. 235, 595 S.E.2d 153

(2004), cert. denied, 358 N.C. 545, 599 S.E.2d 404 (2004).

SIGN 600 FEET FROM INTERSECTION NOT "AT THE ENTRANCE." --The stop signs referred to in this statute are signs erected "at the entrance" to the main traveled or through highway. A sign 600 feet away from an intersection cannot reasonably be said to be at the entrance thereto. Gilliland v. Ruke, 280 F.2d 544 (4th Cir. 1960).

PRESUMPTION THAT SIGNS WERE ERECTED BY LAWFUL AUTHORITY. --Stop signs at intersections are in such general use and their function is so well known that a motorist, in the absence of notice to the contrary, may presume that they were erected by lawful authority. The presumption is one of fact and, like other presumptions of fact, is rebuttable. Kelly v. Ashburn, 256 N.C. 338, 123 S.E.2d 775 (1962).

DUTY TO STOP DEPENDS UPON PRESENCE OF STOP SIGN. --The language of this section indicates that the duty to stop depends upon the presence of a stop sign at the time the driver approaches the intersection. He is commanded to stop "in obedience" to the stop sign. If no such sign is in sight and the driver is not aware that there should be one, there is nothing to obey and hence no statutory duty to stop. Gilliland v. Ruke, 280 F.2d 544 (4th Cir. 1960).

EFFECT OF REMOVAL OF STOP SIGN. --Where driver on a highway which a stop sign had designated as the dominant highway knew that the stop sign had been so erected but did not know of its disappearance or removal, and driver on the highway which the stop sign had designated as the servient highway did not know that there had ever been a stop sign erected at the intersection, and he approached the intersection from the right of the other driver, removal of the stop sign would not take away the right of the driver of the vehicle on the highway designated by the sign as the dominant highway to treat the highway as such and to proceed into the intersection on the assumption that the other vehicle approaching from the right would yield the right-of-way to him. The responsibility of the driver of the vehicle on the highway designated by the sign as the servient highway, who did not know that such highway had ever been so designated, would be judged in the light of conditions confronting him, namely, an unmarked intersection at which the other vehicle was approaching from his left. Dawson v. Jennette, 278 N.C. 438, 180 S.E.2d 121 (1971).

THIS SECTION DOES NOT REQUIRE THAT A MOTORIST STOP WHERE A STOP SIGN IS LOCATED. It requires that, in obedience to the notice provided by the stop sign, he bring his car to a full stop before entering the highway and yield the right-of-way to vehicles approaching the intersection on the highway. Clifton v. Turner, 257 N.C. 92, 125 S.E.2d 339 (1962); Howard v. Melvin, 262 N.C. 569, 138 S.E.2d 238 (1964).

DUTY OF DRIVER WHEN PRESENTED WITH STOP SIGN. --A driver along a servient street is required, in compliance with this section, to bring his vehicle to a stop in obedience to a stop sign lawfully erected, and not to proceed into an intersection with the dominant highway until, in the exercise of due care, he can determine that he can do so with reasonable assurance of safety. Todd v. Shipman, 12 N.C. App. 650, 184 S.E.2d 403 (1971).

Stop signs erected by the State Highway Commission (now Board of Transportation) and local authorities on an intersecting highway or street pursuant to subsection (a) of this section are a method of giving the public notice that traffic on one is favored over traffic on the other, and a motorist facing a stop sign must yield. Kelly v. Ashburn, 256 N.C. 338, 123 S.E.2d 775 (1962); Galloway v. Hartman, 271 N.C. 372, 156 S.E.2d 727 (1967).

A motorist traveling on a servient highway on which a stop sign has been erected at an intersection with a dominant highway may not lawfully enter such intersection until he has stopped and observed the traffic on the dominant highway and determined in the exercise of due care that he may enter such intersection with reasonable assurance of safety to himself and others. Primm v. King, 249 N.C. 228, 106 S.E.2d 223 (1958).

A driver of a motor vehicle about to enter a highway protected by stop signs must stop as directed, look in both directions and permit all vehicles to pass which are at such a distance and traveling at such a speed that it would be imprudent for him to proceed into the intersection. Matheny v. Central Motor Lines, 233 N.C. 673, 65 S.E.2d 361 (1951).

DRIVER TO EXERCISE DUE CARE BEFORE STARTING FROM POSITION ON SUBSERVIENT HIGHWAY. --It is the duty of a motorist before starting from his position on a subservient highway into a dominant highway to exercise due care to see that such movement can be made in safety. Morrisette v. A.G. Boone Co., 235 N.C. 162, 69 S.E.2d 239 (1952).

The driver on the subservient highway is not only required to stop, but, further, is required thereafter to exercise due care to see that he may enter the dominant highway in safety. Satterwhite v. Bocelato, 130 F. Supp. 825 (E.D.N.C. 1955).

This section not only requires the driver on the servient highway or street to stop, but such driver is further required, after stopping, to exercise due care to see that he may enter or cross the dominant highway or street in safety before entering thereon. Jordan v. Blackwelder, 250 N.C. 189, 108 S.E.2d 429 (1959); Wooten v. Russell, 255 N.C. 699, 122 S.E.2d 603 (1961); Howard v. Melvin, 262 N.C. 569, 138 S.E.2d 238 (1964).

This section not only requires the driver on a servient highway to stop, but such driver is further required to exercise due care to see that he may enter or cross the dominant highway or street in safety before entering thereon. This interpretation incorporates the requirements obtained in G.S. 20-154, that the motorist must see that such movement can be made in safety. Kanoy v. Hinshaw, 273 N.C. 418, 160 S.E.2d 296 (1968).

DELAY UNTIL APPROACHING VEHICLES HAVE PASSED. --When the driver of an automobile is required to stop at an intersection, he must yield the right-of-way to an automobile approaching on the intersecting highway, and unless the approaching automobile is far enough away to afford reasonable ground for the belief that he can cross in safety he must delay his progress until the other vehicle has passed. Matheny v. Central Motor Lines, 233 N.C. 673, 65 S.E.2d 361 (1951); Badders v. Lassiter, 240 N.C. 413, 82 S.E.2d 357 (1954).

This section requires the driver to remain in a private road until he ascertains, by proper lookout, that he can enter the main highway in safety to himself and to others on the highway. Warren v. Lewis, 273 N.C. 457, 160 S.E.2d 305 (1968).

The right of one starting from a stopped position to undertake to cross an intersection would depend largely upon the distance from the intersection of approaching vehicles and their speed, and unless under the circumstances he would reasonably apprehend no danger of collision from an approaching vehicle it would be his duty to delay his progress until the vehicle has passed. Badders v. Lassiter, 240 N.C. 413, 82 S.E.2d 357 (1954); Raper v. Byrum, 265 N.C. 269, 144 S.E.2d 38 (1965).

WHEN DRIVER SHOULD PROCEED. --The driver who is required to stop should not proceed, with oncoming vehicles in view, until in the exercise of due care he has determined that he can proceed safely. U.S. Indus., Inc. v. Tharpe, 47 N.C. App. 754, 268 S.E.2d 824, cert. denied, 301 N.C. 90, 273 S.E.2d 311 (1980).

DUTY TO DETERMINE SAFETY OF ENTRY OR CROSSING NOT RELIEVED BY LOCATION OF STOP SIGNS AT POINTS FROM WHICH DRIVER CANNOT GET UNOBSTRUCTED VIEW. --Fact that stop signs, due to surrounding physical conditions, are located at points from which the driver of a motor vehicle cannot get an unobscured vision of the intersecting highway for a sufficient distance to ascertain whether it can be entered or crossed with reasonable safety does not relieve a driver on a servient highway from the duty to look and observe traffic conditions on the dominant highway, and to make such observation, before entering or crossing the same, as may be necessary to determine whether or not it would be reasonably safe to enter or cross such highway. Edwards v. Vaughn, 238 N.C. 89, 76 S.E.2d 359 (1953).

RIGHT TO ASSUME THAT DRIVER ON DOMINANT HIGHWAY WILL OBEY LAW. --The driver along the servient highway is not required to anticipate that a driver on the dominant highway will travel at excessive speed or fail to observe the rules of the road applicable to him. Farmer v. Reynolds, 4 N.C. App. 554, 167 S.E.2d 480 (1969).

RIGHT TO ASSUME THAT AUTOMOBILE ON SERVIENT HIGHWAY WILL STOP AS REQUIRED BY STATUTE. --The operator of an automobile traveling upon a designated main-traveled or through highway and approaching an intersecting highway is under no duty to anticipate that the operator of an automobile approaching on such intersecting highway will fail to stop as required by the statute, and in the absence of anything which gives or should

Chapter 20

give notice to the contrary, he will be entitled to assume and to act upon the assumption, even to the last moment, that the operator of the automobile on the intersecting highway will act in obedience to the statute, and stop before entering such designated highway. Hawes v. Atlantic Ref. Co., 236 N.C. 643, 74 S.E.2d 17 (1953); Caughron v. Walker, 243 N.C. 153, 90 S.E.2d 305 (1955); Smith v. Buie, 243 N.C. 209, 90 S.E.2d 514 (1955); Jackson v. McCoury, 247 N.C. 502, 101 S.E.2d 377 (1958); King v. Powell, 252 N.C. 506, 114 S.E.2d 265 (1960); Wooten v. Russell, 255 N.C. 699, 122 S.E.2d 603 (1961); Raper v. Byrum, 265 N.C. 269, 144 S.E.2d 38 (1965); Moore v. Hales, 266 N.C. 482, 146 S.E.2d 385 (1966).

A motorist proceeding along a favored highway is entitled to assume that traffic on an intersecting secondary highway will yield him the right-of-way, and the effect of his right to rely on this assumption is not lost because warning signs have been misplaced or removed. Kelly v. Ashburn, 256 N.C. 338, 123 S.E.2d 775 (1962).

It is reasonable for the operator of an automobile, traveling upon a designated main-traveled or through highway and approaching an intersecting highway, to assume until the last moment that a motorist on the servient highway who has actually stopped in obedience to the stop sign will yield the right-of-way to him and will not enter the intersection until he has passed through it. Raper v. Byrum, 265 N.C. 269, 144 S.E.2d 38 (1965).

Nothing else appearing, the driver of a vehicle having the right-of-way at an intersection is entitled to assume and to act, until the last moment, on the assumption that the driver of another vehicle, approaching the intersection, will recognize his right-of-way and will stop or reduce his speed sufficiently to permit him to pass through the intersection in safety. Dawson v. Jennette, 278 N.C. 438, 180 S.E.2d 121 (1971); U.S. Indus., Inc. v. Tharpe, 47 N.C. App. 754, 268 S.E.2d 824, cert. denied, 301 N.C. 90, 273 S.E.2d 311 (1980).

DRIVER ON A FAVORED HIGHWAY PROTECTED BY A STATUTORY STOP SIGN DOES NOT HAVE AN ABSOLUTE RIGHT-OF-WAY in the sense that he is not bound to exercise care toward traffic approaching on an intersecting unfavored highway. It is his duty, notwithstanding his favored position, to observe ordinary care. Williamson v. Randall, 248 N.C. 20, 102 S.E.2d 381 (1958). See also, Scott v. Darden, 259 N.C. 167, 130 S.E.2d 42 (1963).

DRIVER ON DOMINANT HIGHWAY MUST EXERCISE DUE CARE. --While the driver of a car along the dominant highway is entitled to assume that the operator of a car along the intersecting servient highway will stop before entering the intersection, the driver along the dominant highway is nevertheless required to exercise the care of an ordinarily prudent person under similar circumstances to keep a reasonably careful lookout, not to exceed a speed which is reasonable and prudent under the circumstances, and to take such care as a reasonably prudent man would exercise to avoid collision when danger of a collision is

discovered or should have been discovered. Blalock v. Hart, 239 N.C. 475, 80 S.E.2d 373 (1954); Caughron v. Walker, 243 N.C. 153, 90 S.E.2d 305 (1955); Jackson v. McCoury, 247 N.C. 502, 101 S.E.2d 377 (1958).

The driver on a favored highway protected by a statutory stop sign does not have an absolute right-of-way in the sense that he is not bound to exercise care toward traffic approaching on an intersecting unfavored highway. It is his duty, notwithstanding his favored position, to observe ordinary care, that is, that degree of care which an ordinarily prudent person would exercise under similar circumstances. In the exercise of such duty it is incumbent upon him in approaching and traversing such an intersection (1) to drive at a speed no greater than is reasonable and prudent under the conditions then existing, (2) to keep his motor vehicle under control, (3) to keep a reasonably careful lookout, and (4) to take such action as an ordinarily prudent person would take in avoiding a collision with persons or vehicles upon the highway when, in the exercise of due care, the danger of such a collision is discovered or should have been discovered. Primm v. King, 249 N.C. 228, 106 S.E.2d 223 (1958); King v. Powell, 252 N.C. 506, 114 S.E.2d 265 (1960); Stockwell v. Brown, 254 N.C. 662, 119 S.E.2d 795 (1961); Raper v. Byrum, 265 N.C. 269, 144 S.E.2d 38 (1965); Murrell v. Jennings, 15 N.C. App. 658, 190 S.E.2d 686 (1972).

Even though a driver has the right-of-way at an intersection, it is incumbent upon him, in approaching and traversing the intersection, to drive at a speed no greater than is reasonable under the conditions then existing, to keep his vehicle under control, to keep a reasonably careful lookout and to take such action as a reasonably prudent person would take to avoid collision when the danger of one is discovered or should have been discovered. Dawson v. Jennette, 278 N.C. 438, 180 S.E.2d 121 (1971).

The driver of an automobile upon a through highway did not have the right to assume absolutely that a driver approaching the intersection along a servient highway would obey the stop sign before entering or crossing the through highway, but was required to keep a proper lookout and to keep his car at a reasonable speed under the circumstances in order to avoid injury to life or limb, and he forfeited his right to rely upon the assumption that the other driver would stop before entering or crossing the intersection when he approached and attempted to traverse it himself at an unlawful or excessive speed; moreover, even when his speed was lawful he remained under the duty of exercising due care to ascertain if the driver of the other car was going to violate the statutory requirement, in order to avoid the consequences of such negligence, it being necessary to construe the pertinent statutes in pari materia and this result being consonant with such construction. Groome v. Davis, 215 N.C. 510, 2 S.E.2d 771 (1939).

LIABILITY OF DRIVER REQUIRED TO STOP IS BASED ON WHAT HE SHOULD HAVE SEEN. --The motorist who is required to stop and ascertain whether he can proceed safely is deemed to have seen what he would have been able to see had he looked, and his liability to one injured in a collision with his vehicle is determined as it would have been had he looked, observed the prevailing conditions and continued to drive as he did. U.S. Indus., Inc. v. Tharpe, 47 N.C. App. 754, 268 S.E.2d 824, cert. denied, 301 N.C. 90, 273 S.E.2d 311 (1980).

RIGHT-OF-WAY WHERE DRIVER ON SERVIENT STREET IS IN INTERSECTION. --Where the driver on the servient street is already in the intersection before the vehicle approaching on the dominant street is near enough to the intersection to constitute an immediate hazard, the driver on the servient street has the right-of-way. Farmer v. Reynolds, 4 N.C. App. 554, 167 S.E.2d 480 (1969); Todd v. Shipman, 12 N.C. App. 650, 184 S.E.2d 403 (1971).

A vehicle traveling along a through street does not have the right-of-way at an intersection if a vehicle from the cross street is already in the intersection before the vehicle traveling along the through street is near enough to the intersection to constitute an immediate hazard. Pearson v. Luther, 212 N.C. 412, 193 S.E. 739 (1937).

FACT THAT A MOTORIST ON A SERVIENT ROAD REACHES INTERSECTION A HAIRS-BREADTH AHEAD of one on the dominant highway does not give him the right to proceed. It is his duty to stop and yield the right-of-way unless the motorist on the dominant highway is a sufficient distance from the intersection to warrant the assumption that he can cross in safety before the other vehicle, operated at a reasonable speed, reaches the crossing. Farmer v. Reynolds, 4 N.C. App. 554, 167 S.E.2d 480 (1969).

INSTRUCTION ON DEFENDANT'S DUTY UPHELD. --A charge of the court with reference to this section, which stated, "The test is whether or not a reasonable and careful and prudent person would have stopped and yielded the right-of-way under the circumstances as they existed," clearly told the jury that defendant's duty was reasonable care under the circumstances. Wright v. Holt, 18 N.C. App. 661, 197 S.E.2d 811, cert. denied, 283 N.C. 759, 198 S.E.2d 729 (1973).

III. NEGLIGENCE AND PROXIMATE CAUSE.

VIOLATION OF THIS SECTION IS NOT NEGLIGENT PER SE. State v. Williams, 3 N.C. App. 463, 165 S.E.2d 52 (1969).

BUT MAY BE EVIDENCE OF NEGLIGENCE OR CONTRIBUTORY NEGLIGENCE TO BE CONSIDERED. --Failure of a motorist traveling upon a servient highway to stop in obedience to a stop sign before entering an intersection with a dominant highway is not negligence per se and is insufficient, standing alone, to make out a prima facie case of negligence, but is only evidence of negligence to be considered along with other facts and circumstances adduced by the evidence, and an instruction that failure to stop in obedience to the sign is negligence must be held reversible error. Hill v. Lopez, 228 N.C. 433, 45 S.E.2d 539 (1947). See Nichols v. Goldston, 228 N.C. 514, 46 S.E.2d 320 (1948); Lee v. Robertson Chem. Corp., 229 N.C. 447, 50 S.E.2d 181 (1948); Bobbitt v. Haynes, 231

N.C. 373, 57 S.E.2d 361 (1950); Bailey v. Michael, 231 N.C. 404, 57 S.E.2d 372 (1950); Johnson v. Bell, 234 N.C. 522, 67 S.E.2d 658 (1951). See also, Satterwhite v. Bocelato, 130 F. Supp. 825 (E.D.N.C. 1955).

Failure to come to a complete stop before entering a through street intersection is not negligence per se, but only evidence of negligence to be considered with other facts in the case, such holding being a necessary corollary to the provision of this section that failure to stop before entering a through street intersection should not be considered contributory negligence per se, but only evidence to be considered with the other facts in the case upon the issue of contributory negligence. Sebastian v. Horton Motor Lines, 213 N.C. 770, 197 S.E. 539 (1938); Reeves v. Staley, 220 N.C. 573, 18 S.E.2d 239 (1942).

Failure of a driver along a servient highway to stop before entering an intersection with a dominant highway is not contributory negligence per se, but is to be considered with other facts in evidence in determining the issue. Hawes v. Atlantic Ref. Co., 236 N.C. 643, 74 S.E.2d 17 (1953); Primm v. King, 249 N.C. 228, 106 S.E.2d 223 (1958); State v. Sealy, 253 N.C. 802, 117 S.E.2d 793 (1961).

Failure to stop at a stop sign and yield the right-of-way is not negligence per se, but it is evidence of negligence that may be considered with other facts in the case in determining whether a party thereto was guilty of negligence or contributory negligence. Johnson v. Bass, 256 N.C. 716, 125 S.E.2d 19 (1962).

Directed verdict was properly granted as to an injured party's complaint for damages received in an automobile accident because the evidence, viewed most favorably to the injured party, showed his contributory negligence and violation of G.S. 20-158(b)(1) when he stopped at a stop sign before entering the intersection where the accident occurred, looked left and right, but did not look at an exit ramp from which a motorist who struck him entered the intersection, before proceeding into the intersection. Williams v. Davis, 157 N.C. App. 696, 580 S.E.2d 85 (2003).

While an injured party was not contributorily negligent per se under G.S. 20-158(d) when he entered an intersection after stopping at a stop sign, without looking at an exit ramp from which the vehicle that struck him entered the intersection, he was contributorily negligent, and his complaint was dismissed on a motion for directed verdict. Williams v. Davis, 157 N.C. App. 696, 580 S.E.2d 85 (2003).

AND WHEN IT IS THE PROXIMATE CAUSE OF INJURY MAY BE SUFFICIENT TO SUPPORT VERDICT. --While a failure to stop and yield the right-of-way to traffic on the dominant highway is not negligence per se, it is evidence of negligence, and, when the proximate cause of injury, is sufficient to support a verdict for plaintiff. Wooten v. Russell, 255 N.C. 699, 122 S.E.2d 603 (1961).

FAILURE TO EXERCISE ORDINARY CARE AS ACTIONABLE NEGLIGENCE. --The duties of motorists, both those on dominant and those on servient highways, when approaching, entering or traversing intersections, require that each driver exercise ordinary care under the particular circumstances in which he finds himself; the failure to do so can constitute actionable negligence where injury results. Murrell v. Jennings, 15 N.C. App. 658, 190 S.E.2d 686 (1972).

PEREMPTORY INSTRUCTION AS TO NEGLIGENCE WAS PROPER. --As the evidence was undisputed as to the driver's violation of G.S. 20-158(b)(1), the trial court did not err in giving a peremptory instruction to the jury as to her negligence. Oakes v. Wooten, 173 N.C. App. 506, 620 S.E.2d 39 (2005).

BURDEN OF PROVING PROXIMATE CAUSE. --It is not enough for plaintiff to show that defendant was negligent in driving at an excessive speed, in failing to reduce his speed as he approached an entered intersection, or in failing to maintain a reasonable and proper lookout. The burden is also upon the plaintiff to prove that such negligence by defendant was one of the proximate causes of the collision and of his intestate's death. Raper v. Byrum, 265 N.C. 269, 144 S.E.2d 38 (1965).

EVIDENCE HELD SUFFICIENT TO ESTABLISH NEGLIGENCE AND PROXIMATE CAUSE. --Where plaintiff's intestate brought automobile to a stop at a point where he had an unobstructed view of defendants' automobile approaching on the dominant highway, and resumed his progress into the intersection at a very slow rate of speed when defendants' automobile was so near to the intersection and moving at such a speed that in the exercise of reasonable prudence he should have seen that he could not cross in safety, his entry into the intersection in this manner and under these conditions was negligence and was one of the proximate causes of the collision and of his death, if not the sole proximate cause thereof. Raper v. Byrum, 265 N.C. 269, 144 S.E.2d 38 (1965).

COLLISION AT AN INTERSECTION WHERE A STOP SIGN HAS BEEN REMOVED OR DEFACED MAY RESULT FROM NEGLIGENCE of one party, or both, or neither. Kelly v. Ashburn, 256 N.C. 338, 123 S.E.2d 775 (1962).

INSTRUCTION AS TO NEGLIGENCE HELD ERROR since it was counter to the provisions of this section. Stephens v. Johnson, 215 N.C. 133, 1 S.E.2d 367 (1939).

AS TO CONTROLLING EFFECT OF THIS SECTION OVER A MUNICIPAL ORDINANCE making failure to stop unlawful, see Swinson v. Nance, 219 N.C. 772, 15 S.E.2d 284 (1941).

LEGAL PERIODICALS. --

For comment on the 1941 amendment, see 19 N.C.L. Rev. 455 (1941).

§ 20-158.1. Erection of "yield right-of-way" signs

The Department of Transportation, with reference to State highways, and cities and towns with reference to highways and streets under their jurisdiction, are authorized to designate main-traveled or through highways and streets by erecting at the entrance thereto from intersecting highways or streets, signs notifying

drivers of vehicles to yield the right-of-way to drivers of vehicles approaching the intersection on the main-traveled or through highway. Notwithstanding any other provisions of this Chapter, except G.S. 20-156, whenever any such yield right-of-way signs have been so erected, it shall be unlawful for the driver of any vehicle to enter or cross such main-traveled or through highway or street unless he shall first slow down and yield right-of-way to any vehicle in movement on the main-traveled or through highway or street which is approaching so as to arrive at the intersection at approximately the same time as the vehicle entering the main-traveled or through highway or street. No failure to so yield the right-of-way shall be considered negligence or contributory negligence per se in any action at law for injury to person or property, but the facts relating to such failure to yield the right-of-way may be considered with the other facts in the case in determining whether either party in such action was guilty of negligence or contributory negligence.

History.

1955, c. 295; 1957, c. 65, s. 11; 1973, c. 507, s. 5; c. 1330, s. 23; 1977, c. 464, s. 34

THIS SECTION SUPPLEMENTS G.S. 20-158. McEwen Funeral Serv., Inc. v. Charlotte City Coach Lines, 248 N.C. 146, 102 S.E.2d 816 (1958).

AS TO EXEMPTION OF EMERGENCY AMBULANCES FROM THE REQUIREMENTS OF THIS SECTION, see Upchurch v. Hudson Funeral Home, 263 N.C. 560, 140 S.E.2d 17 (1965).

WHERE THE DRIVER ON THE SERVIENT STREET IS ALREADY IN THE INTERSECTION before the vehicle approaching on the dominant street is near enough to the intersection to constitute an immediate hazard, the driver on the servient street has the right-of-way. Farmer v. Reynolds, 4 N.C. App. 554, 167 S.E.2d 480 (1969).

FACT THAT A MOTORIST ON A SERVIENT ROAD REACHES INTERSECTION A HAIRBREADTH AHEAD of one on the dominant highway does not give him the right to proceed. It is his duty to stop and yield the right-of-way unless the motorist on the dominant highway is a sufficient distance from the intersection to warrant the assumption that he can cross in safety before the other vehicle, operated at a reasonable speed, reaches the crossing. Farmer v. Reynolds, 4 N.C. App. 554, 167 S.E.2d 480 (1969).

DRIVER ON SERVIENT HIGHWAY NOT REQUIRED TO ANTICIPATE VIOLATION OF LAW BY DRIVER ON DOMINANT HIGHWAY. --Driver along servient highway is not required to anticipate that a driver on the dominant highway will travel at excessive speed or fail to observe the rules of the road applicable to him. Farmer v. Reynolds, 4 N.C. App. 554, 167 S.E.2d 480 (1969).

CITED in Johnson v. Bass, 256 N.C. 716, 125 S.E.2d 19 (1962); Hathcock v. Lowder, 16 N.C. App. 255, 192 S.E.2d 124 (1972).

§ 20-158.2. Control of vehicles on Turnpike System

The North Carolina Turnpike Authority may control vehicles at appropriate places by erecting traffic control devices to collect tolls.

History.
2002-133, s. 2
CROSS REFERENCES. --
As to public toll roads and bridges, generally, see G.S. 136-89.180 et seq. As to the North Carolina Turnpike Authority, see G.S. 136-89.182.

§ 20-158.3. Emergency entry to controlled access roads

Any person, association, or other legal entity having responsibility for a controlled access system on a road that is a public vehicular area shall provide a means of immediate access to all emergency service vehicles, which shall include law enforcement, fire, rescue, ambulance, and first responder vehicles. This section shall not apply to any entity where federal regulations and requirements on its activities preempt application of State regulations or requirements.

History.
2007-455, s. 2

N.C. Gen. Stat. § 20-159

Repealed by Session Laws 1973, c. 1330, s. 39.

§ 20-160. Driving through safety zone or on sidewalks prohibited

(a) The driver of a vehicle shall not at any time drive through or over a safety zone.

(b) No person shall drive any motor vehicle upon a sidewalk or sidewalk area except upon a permanent or temporary driveway.

History.
1937, c. 407, s. 122; 1973, c. 1330, s. 24
CITED in Kennedy v. Polumbo, 209 N.C. App. 394, 704 S.E.2d 916 (2011).
CROSS REFERENCES. --
For definition of safety zone, see G.S. 20-4.01(39).

§ 20-160.1. Failure to yield causing serious bodily injury; penalties

(a) Unless the conduct is covered under some other law providing greater punishment, a person who commits the offense of failure to yield while approaching or entering an intersection, turning at a stop or yield sign, entering a roadway, upon the approach of an emergency vehicle, or at highway construction or maintenance shall be punished under this section. When there is serious bodily injury but no death resulting from the violation, the violator shall be fined five hundred dollars ($ 500.00) and the violator's drivers license or commercial drivers license shall be suspended for 90 days.

(b) As used in this section, "serious bodily injury" means bodily injury that involves a substantial risk of death, extreme physical pain, protracted and obvious disfigurement, or protracted loss or impairment of the function of a bodily member, organ, or mental faculty.

History.
2004-172, s. 1

§ 20-161. Stopping on highway prohibited; warning signals; removal of vehicles from public highway

(a) No person shall park or leave standing any vehicle, whether attended or unattended, upon the main-traveled portion of any highway or highway bridge with the speed limit posted less than 45 miles per hour unless the vehicle is disabled to such an extent that it is impossible to avoid stopping and temporarily leaving the vehicle upon the paved or main traveled portion of the highway or highway bridge. This subsection shall not apply to a solid waste vehicle stopped on a highway while engaged in collecting garbage as defined in G.S. 20-118(c)(5)g. or recyclable material as defined in G.S. 130A-290(a)(26).

(a1) No person shall park or leave standing any vehicle, whether attended or unattended, upon the paved or main-traveled portion of any highway or highway bridge with the speed limit posted 45 miles per hour or greater unless the vehicle is disabled to such an extent that it is impossible to avoid stopping and temporarily leaving the vehicle upon the paved or main-traveled portion of the highway or highway bridge. This subsection shall not apply to a solid waste vehicle stopped on a highway while engaged in collecting garbage as defined in G.S. 20-118(c)(5)g. or recyclable material as defined in G.S. 130A-290(a)(26).

(b) No person shall park or leave standing any vehicle upon the shoulder of a public highway unless the vehicle can be clearly seen by approaching drivers from a distance of 200 feet in both directions and does not obstruct the normal movement of traffic.

(c) The operator of any truck, truck tractor, trailer or semitrailer which is disabled upon any portion of the highway shall display warning devices of a type and in a manner as required under the rules and regulations of the United States Department of Transportation as adopted by the Division of Motor Vehicles. Such warning devices shall be displayed as long as the vehicle is disabled.

Chapter 20

(d) The owner of any vehicle parked or left standing in violation of law shall be deemed to have appointed any investigating law-enforcement officer his agent:

    (1) For the purpose of removing the vehicle to the shoulder of the highway or to some other suitable place; and

    (2) For the purpose of arranging for the transportation and safe storage of any vehicle which is interfering with the regular flow of traffic or which otherwise constitutes a hazard, in which case the officer shall be deemed a legal possessor of the vehicle within the meaning of G.S. 44A-2(d).

(e) When any vehicle is parked or left standing upon the right-of-way of a public highway, including rest areas, for a period of 24 hours or more, the owner shall be deemed to have appointed any investigating law-enforcement officer his agent for the purpose of arranging for the transportation and safe storage of such vehicle and such investigating law-enforcement officer shall be deemed a legal possessor of the motor vehicle within the meaning of that term as it appears in G.S. 44A-2(d).

(f) An investigating law enforcement officer, with the concurrence of the Department of Transportation, or the Department of Transportation, with the concurrence of an investigating law enforcement officer, may immediately remove or cause to be removed from the State highway system any wrecked, abandoned, disabled, unattended, burned, or partially dismantled vehicle, cargo, or other personal property interfering with the regular flow of traffic or which otherwise constitutes a hazard. In the event of a motor vehicle crash involving serious personal injury or death, no removal shall occur until the investigating law enforcement officer determines that adequate information has been obtained for preparation of a crash report. No state or local law enforcement officer, Department of Transportation employee, or person or firm contracting or assisting in the removal or disposition of any such vehicle, cargo, or other personal property shall be held criminally or civilly liable for any damage or economic injury related to carrying out or enforcing the provisions of this section.

(g) The owner shall be liable for any costs incurred in the removal, storage, and subsequent disposition of a vehicle, cargo, or other personal property under the authority of this section.

History.

1937, c. 407, s. 123; 1951, c. 1165, s. 1; 1971, c. 294, s. 1; 1973, c. 1330, s. 25; 1985, c. 454, s. 6; 2003-310, s. 1;2007-360, ss. 4, 5; 2009-104, s. 1;2010-132, ss. 13, 14, 15; 2015-231, s. 1

LOCAL MODIFICATION. --Brunswick: 2005-266, s. 1.

EDITOR'S NOTE. --

Session Laws 2015-231, s. 4, made the amendment to subsection (f) of this section by Session Laws 2015-231, s. 1, applicable to any obstructions to traffic arising on or after 12:01 A.M. of August 26, 2015.

EFFECT OF AMENDMENTS. --

Session Laws 2007-360, ss. 4 and 5, effective August 17, 2007, in subsection (e), inserted "including rest areas" following "public highway" and substituted "24 hours" for "48 hours"; and in subsection (f), substituted "the State highway system" for "a controlled access highway" in the first sentence.

Session Laws 2009-104, s. 1, effective October 1, 2009, and applicable to offenses occurring on or after that date, added the last sentence in subsection (a).

Session Laws 2010-132, ss. 13 through 15, effective December 1, 2010, and applicable to offenses committed on or after that date, in the first sentence in subsection (a), substituted "upon the main-traveled portion of any highway or highway bridge with the speed limit posted less than 45 miles per hour" for "upon the paved or main-traveled portion of any highway or highway bridge outside municipal corporate limits"; added subsection (a1); and in subsection (b), deleted "outside municipal corporate limits" following "public highway."

Session Laws 2015-231, s. 1, effective August 25, 2015, substituted "An" for "Any" preceding "investigating law enforcement officer" at the beginning of subsection (f); inserted "or the Department of Transportation, with the concurrence of an investigating law enforcement officer" following "Department of Transportation" near the beginning of the first sentence. For applicability, see editor's note.

I. IN GENERAL.

MEANING OF "PARK" ON "LEAVE STANDING". --The word "park" means the permitting of a vehicle to remain standing on a public highway or street, while not in use. State v. Carter, 205 N.C. 761, 172 S.E. 415 (1934).

TO "PARK" MEANS SOMETHING MORE THAN A MERE TEMPORARY OR MOMENTARY STOPPAGE on the road for a necessary purpose. Stallings v. Buchan Transp. Co., 210 N.C. 201, 185 S.E. 643 (1936); Morris v. Jenrette Transp. Co., 235 N.C. 568, 70 S.E.2d 845 (1952); Meece v. Dickson, 252 N.C. 300, 113 S.E.2d 578 (1960), overruled on other grounds, Melton v. Crotts, 257 N.C. 121, 125 S.E.2d 396 (1962); Saunders v. Warren, 264 N.C. 200, 141 S.E.2d 308 (1965). See also, Williams v. Jones, 53 N.C. App. 171, 280 S.E.2d 474 (1981); Adams v. Mills, 68 N.C. App. 256, 314 S.E.2d 589, rev'd on other grounds, 312 N.C. 181, 322 S.E.2d 164 (1984).

The words "park" and "leave standing," as used in this section, are modified by the words "whether attended or unattended," so that they are synonymous, and neither term includes a mere temporary stop for a necessary purpose when there is no intent to break the continuity of the travel as starting and stopping on a highway in accordance with the exigencies of the occasion is an incident to the right of travel. Peoples v. Fulk, 220 N.C. 635, 18 S.E.2d 147 (1942); Morris

v. Jenrette Transp. Co., 235 N.C. 568, 70 S.E.2d 845 (1952); Royal v. McClure, 244 N.C. 186, 92 S.E.2d 762 (1956); Meece v. Dickson, 252 N.C. 300, 113 S.E.2d 578 (1960), overruled on other grounds, Melton v. Crotts, 257 N.C. 121, 125 S.E.2d 396 (1962); Wilson v. Miller, 20 N.C. App. 156, 201 S.E.2d 55 (1973).

"Park" and "leave standing," as used in subsection (a) of this section, are synonymous, and neither term includes a mere temporary or momentary stoppage on the highway for a necessary purpose when there is no intent to break the continuity of the travel. Faison v. T & S Trucking Co., 266 N.C. 383, 146 S.E.2d 450 (1966).

A mere temporary or momentary stoppage on the highway when there is no intent to break the continuity of the travel is not what is meant by the terms "parking" or "leave standing" as used in this section. Wilson v. Lee, 1 N.C. App. 119, 160 S.E.2d 107 (1968).

THIS SECTION HAS NO REFERENCE TO A MERE TEMPORARY STOP FOR A NECESSARY PURPOSE when there is no intent to break the continuity of "travel." Royal v. McClure, 244 N.C. 186, 92 S.E.2d 762 (1956).

BUT A TEMPORARY STOPPING MUST BE FOR A NECESSARY PURPOSE, and under such conditions that it is impossible to avoid leaving such vehicle in such position, that is, occupying the traveled portion of the highway. Melton v. Crotts, 257 N.C. 121, 125 S.E.2d 396 (1962).

WHETHER STOP, THOUGH TEMPORARY, WAS FOR A NECESSARY PURPOSE IS A FACTOR TO BE CONSIDERED IN DETERMINING A VIOLATION of this section. Williams v. Jones, 53 N.C. App. 171, 280 S.E.2d 474 (1981).

DEPUTY SHERIFF DID NOT VIOLATE THIS SECTION WHEN HE TEMPORARILY STOPPED HIS CAR on the right side of the highway in order to speak to an intoxicated pedestrian. Skinner v. Evans, 243 N.C. 760, 92 S.E.2d 209 (1956).

STOPPING OF A POLICE CAR TO DETERMINE WHETHER DRIVER OF ANOTHER CAR HAD A DRIVER'S LICENSE DID NOT CONSTITUTE A PARKING of the police car in violation of subsection (a) of this section. Kinsey v. Town of Kenly, 263 N.C. 376, 139 S.E.2d 686 (1965).

TRUCK STOPPED TO AVOID WRECK HELD NOT "PARKED." --Where the driver of a truck with a trailer stopped on the highway at night on the right-hand side, with lights burning, because two automobiles in front of him were interlocked in a wreck, and at the time of the collision the truck and trailer had been standing still only a fraction of a minute, and the truck remained parked for about five minutes thereafter, it was held that at the time of the collision the truck was not "parked" on the highway within the meaning of this section. Stallings v. Buchan Transp. Co., 210 N.C. 201, 185 S.E. 643 (1936).

FOR CASE HOLDING THAT DEFENDANT'S TRACTOR-TRAILER WAS NOT "PARKED" at place of collision, within the meaning of subsection (a) of this section, see Harris Express, Inc. v. Jones, 236 N.C. 542, 73 S.E.2d 301 (1952).

STOPPING OF BUS TO PICK UP PASSENGERS NOT "PARKING." --The stopping of a bus on the hard surface of a highway outside of a business or residential district to take on a passenger is not parking or leaving the vehicle standing within the meaning of the terms as used in this section. Peoples v. Fulk, 220 N.C. 635, 18 S.E.2d 147 (1942); Leary v. Norfolk S. Bus Corp., 220 N.C. 745, 18 S.E.2d 426 (1942); Morgan v. Carolina Coach Co., 225 N.C. 668, 36 S.E.2d 263 (1945). See also, Conley v. Pearce-Young-Angel Co., 224 N.C. 211, 29 S.E.2d 740 (1944); Banks v. Shepard, 230 N.C. 86, 52 S.E.2d 215 (1949).

EXEMPTION FOR POLICE ROADBLOCK. --Erection of some type of roadblock, whether stationary or running, may be the only practical method of stopping a determined and reckless lawbreaker. Under such circumstances, exemption for police vehicles from this section (in case of a stationary roadblock) or from former G.S. 20-151 (in case of a running roadblock) may be reasonably implied. Collins v. Christenberry, 6 N.C. App. 504, 170 S.E.2d 515 (1969).

THIS SECTION REQUIRES THAT NO PART OF A PARKED VEHICLE BE LEFT PROTRUDING into the traveled portion of the highway when there is ample room and it is practicable to park the entire vehicle off the traveled portion of the highway. Sharpe v. Hanline, 265 N.C. 502, 144 S.E.2d 574 (1965).

FACT THAT TAILLIGHT OF DEFENDANT'S TRUCK WAS STILL BURNING AFTER COLLISION DID NOT EXCUSE HIM from leaving it on the paved portion of a highway. Freshman v. Stallings, 128 F. Supp. 179 (E.D.N.C. 1955).

ONE STOPPING AN AUTOMOBILE ON THE HIGHWAY SHOULD USE ORDINARY CARE to prevent a collision with other vehicles operating thereon. Saunders v. Warren, 267 N.C. 735, 149 S.E.2d 19 (1966).

IRRESPECTIVE OF REASON FOR STOPPING. -- The operator of a standing or parked vehicle which constitutes a source of danger to other users of the highway is generally bound to exercise ordinary or reasonable care to give adequate warning or notice to approaching traffic of the presence of the standing vehicle, and such duty exists irrespective of the reason for stopping the vehicle on the highway. The driver of the stopped vehicle must take such precautions as would reasonably be calculated to prevent injury, whether by the use of lights, flags, guards, or other practical means, and failing to give such warning may constitute negligence. Saunders v. Warren, 267 N.C. 735, 149 S.E.2d 19 (1966).

A MOTORIST STOPPING ON A PRONOUNCED CURVE SHOULD ANTICIPATE THAT A FOLLOWING MOTORIST WILL HAVE AN OBSTRUCTED VIEW of the highway ahead. Saunders v. Warren, 267 N.C. 735, 149 S.E.2d 19 (1966).

APPLIED in Parkway Bus Co. v. Coble Dairy Prods. Co., 229 N.C. 352, 49 S.E.2d 623 (1948); Parrish v. Bryant, 237 N.C. 256, 74 S.E.2d 726 (1953); Chandler v. Forsyth Royal Crown Bottling Co., 257 N.C. 245, 125 S.E.2d 584 (1962); Carolina Coach Co. v. Cox, 337 F.2d 101 (4th Cir. 1964); Coleman v. Burris, 265 N.C. 404,

Chapter 20

144 S.E.2d 241 (1965); Williams v. Hall, 1 N.C. App. 508, 162 S.E.2d 84 (1968); Staples v. Carter, 5 N.C. App. 264, 168 S.E.2d 240 (1969); Grimes v. Gibert, 6 N.C. App. 304, 170 S.E.2d 65 (1969); Northwestern Distribs., Inc. v. North Carolina Dep't of Transp., 41 N.C. App. 548, 255 S.E.2d 203 (1979); King v. Allred, 309 N.C. 113, 305 S.E.2d 554 (1983); State v. Gooden, 65 N.C. App. 669, 309 S.E.2d 707 (1983); Sizemore v. Raxter, 73 N.C. App. 531, 327 S.E.2d 258 (1985); Meadows v. Cigar Supply Co., 91 N.C. App. 404, 371 S.E.2d 765 (1988); Reed v. Abrahamson, 108 N.C. App. 301, 423 S.E.2d 491 (1992).

CITED in Riggs v. Gulf Oil Corp., 228 N.C. 774, 47 S.E.2d 254 (1948); Thomas v. Thurston Motor Lines, 230 N.C. 122, 52 S.E.2d 377 (1949); Cronenberg v. United States, 123 F. Supp. 693 (E.D.N.C. 1954); Keener v. Beal, 246 N.C. 247, 98 S.E.2d 19 (1957); McDonald v. Patton, 240 F.2d 424 (4th Cir. 1957); Correll v. Gaskins, 263 N.C. 212, 139 S.E.2d 202 (1964); Lienthall v. Glass, 2 N.C. App. 65, 162 S.E.2d 596 (1968); Puryear v. Cooper, 2 N.C. App. 517, 163 S.E.2d 299 (1968); Choate Motor Co. v. Gray, 5 N.C. App. 643, 169 S.E.2d 77 (1969); Atkins v. Moye, 277 N.C. 179, 176 S.E.2d 789 (1970); Williamson v. Basinger, 30 N.C. App. 50, 226 S.E.2d 213 (1976); Digsby v. Gregory, 35 N.C. App. 59, 240 S.E.2d 491 (1978); Bowles Auto., Inc. v. N.C. DMV, 203 N.C. App. 19, 690 S.E.2d 728 (2010), review denied, 364 N.C. 324, 700 S.E.2d 746, 2010 N.C. LEXIS 590 (2010).

II. DISABLED VEHICLES.

MEANING OF "IMPOSSIBLE". --The word "impossible" in subsection (a) of this section does not mean physical, absolute impossibility, but means not reasonably practical under the circumstances. Williams v. Jones, 53 N.C. App. 171, 280 S.E.2d 474 (1981).

The word "impossible" must be construed as meaning that the car must be disabled to the extent that it is not reasonably practical to move it so as to leave room for the free passage of other cars. Melton v. Crotts, 257 N.C. 121, 125 S.E.2d 396 (1962).

"IMPOSSIBLE" IS TO BE CONSTRUED IN A REASONABLE, PRACTICAL SENSE. Melton v. Crotts, 257 N.C. 121, 125 S.E.2d 396 (1962).

EMERGENCY PARKING ON SHOULDER. --Prohibiting the parking or leaving of a vehicle on "the paved or main traveled portion of any highway" does not prohibit the emergency parking of a vehicle on the shoulder of a highway, paved or otherwise, which is outside the main traveled part. Thomas v. Deloatch, 45 N.C. App. 322, 263 S.E.2d 615, cert. denied, 300 N.C. 379, 267 S.E.2d 685 (1980).

This section does not prohibit the emergency parking of a vehicle on the shoulder of a highway where no part of the vehicle extends into the main traveled portion of the highway. Adams v. Miller, 312 N.C. 181, 322 S.E.2d 164 (1984).

CLAIM OF EXCEPTION TO BE TESTED BY FACTS. --Claim of protection by virtue exception of disabled vehicles from the prohibition in subsection (a) of this section where it is "impossible" to avoid leaving such vehicle on the paved or main traveled part of the highway must be tested by the facts of

each case. Melton v. Crotts, 257 N.C. 121, 125 S.E.2d 396 (1962).

APPLICABILITY OF EXCEPTION IS A JURY QUESTION. --Where there was evidence tending to show that defendant had parked his truck upon the hard surface of a highway in violation of this section, resulting in injury to plaintiff, but defendant claimed applicability of the exception as to disabled vehicles, under the statute and the facts disclosed by the record the matter should have been submitted to the jury under proper instructions, and the granting of defendant's motion as of nonsuit was error. Smithwick v. Colonial Pine Co., 200 N.C. 519, 157 S.E. 612 (1931).

AS IS QUESTION OF DISABLEMENT. --Whether a puncture or blowout is such disablement of a motor vehicle as to justify the driver in stopping partially on the paved portion of the highway is ordinarily a question for the jury, unless the facts are admitted. Melton v. Crotts, 257 N.C. 121, 125 S.E.2d 396 (1962); Adams v. Mills, 312 N.C. 181, 322 S.E.2d 164 (1984).

AS TO BURDEN OF ESTABLISHING EXCEPTION FOR DISABLED VEHICLE, see Melton v. Crotts, 257 N.C. 121, 125 S.E.2d 396 (1962).

EVIDENCE HELD INSUFFICIENT TO ESTABLISH EXCEPTION. --Where defendant's only evidence in excuse of parking on the paved portion of the highway was that he had a flat tire, such evidence was insufficient to bring defendant within the exception. Lambert v. Caronna, 206 N.C. 616, 175 S.E. 303 (1934).

SECTION HELD NOT VIOLATED. --The parking of a disabled vehicle as far as possible on the right shoulder, leaving more than 15 feet of the main traveled portion of the highway open for the free passage of traffic, at a place where the drivers of other cars had a clear view of the parked automobile for a distance of more than 200 feet in both directions, was not a violation of this section. Rowe v. Murphy, 250 N.C. 627, 109 S.E.2d 474 (1959).

For case holding that statute was not violated where disabled truck was parked on shoulder of highway, see State v. McDonald, 211 N.C. 672, 191 S.E. 733 (1937).

III. WARNING SIGNALS AND LIGHTS.

"TRUCK" DOES NOT INCLUDE THREE-QUARTER TON TRUCK. --The part of this section requiring the driver of a truck, trailer or semitrailer to display red flares or lanterns (now reflectors) when disabled upon the highway is not applicable to a three-quarter ton truck. Freshman v. Stallings, 128 F. Supp. 179 (E.D.N.C. 1955).

THE WORD "TRUCK," AS USED IN THIS SECTION, INCLUDES A MOBILE HIGHWAY POST-OFFICE VEHICLE. Cronenberg v. United States, 123 F. Supp. 693 (E.D.N.C. 1954).

FLARE OR REFLECTOR REQUIREMENT ONLY APPLICABLE TO TRUCKS, TRAILERS AND SEMI-TRAILERS. --The requirement of this section with respect to placing red flares or lanterns (now reflectors) on the highway applies to trucks, trailers or semitrailers disabled on the highway, and not to automobiles.

Rowe v. Murphy, 250 N.C. 627, 109 S.E.2d 474 (1959). See also, Exum v. Boyles, 272 N.C. 567, 158 S.E.2d 845 (1968).

BUT OBLIGATION TO LIGHT VEHICLES AT NIGHT IS NOT AFFECTED. --This section does not conflict with nor reduce the obligation imposed on the operator of a vehicle stopped or parked on the highway at night to light his vehicle as required by G.S. 20-129 and G.S. 20-134. Melton v. Crotts, 257 N.C. 121, 125 S.E.2d 396 (1962), overruling Meece v. Dickson, 252 N.C. 300, 113 S.E.2d 578 (1960), to the extent that it may be construed as conflicting.

AND WHETHER DEFENDANTS VIOLATED THIS SECTION WOULD HAVE NO BEARING UPON THEIR OBLIGATIONS IN RESPECT OF LIGHTING EQUIPMENT and lights imposed by G.S. 20-129 and G.S. 20-134. Faison v. T & S Trucking Co., 266 N.C. 383, 146 S.E.2d 450 (1966).

DRIVER OF A DISABLED TRUCK IS GIVEN A REASONABLE TIME TO DISPLAY WARNING SIGNALS, and the law will not hold him to be negligent in failing to do that which he has not had time to do. Morris v. Jenrette Transp. Co., 235 N.C. 568, 70 S.E.2d 845 (1952).

RIGHT TO ASSUME THAT DRIVER OF DISABLED TRUCK WILL DISPLAY WARNING SIGNALS. --A motorist has the right to assume that the driver of any truck becoming disabled on the highway after sundown will display red flares on lanterns (now reflectors) are required by this section. Chaffin v. Brame, 233 N.C. 377, 64 S.E.2d 276 (1951); United States v. First-Citizens Bank & Trust Co., 208 F.2d 280 (4th Cir. 1953); Towe v. Stokes, 117 F. Supp. 880 (M.D.N.C.), aff'd, 214 F.2d 563 (1954).

IV. NEGLIGENCE AND PROXIMATE CAUSE.

VIOLATION OF THIS SECTION IS NEGLIGENCE PER SE. Hughes v. Vestal, 264 N.C. 500, 142 S.E.2d 361 (1965); Wilson v. Miller, 20 N.C. App. 156, 201 S.E.2d 55 (1973); Furr v. Pinoca Volunteer Fire Dep't, 53 N.C. App. 458, 281 S.E.2d 174, cert. denied, 304 N.C. 587, 289 S.E.2d 377 (1981); King v. Allred, 60 N.C. App. 380, 299 S.E.2d 248 (1983); Clark v. Moore, 65 N.C. App. 609, 309 S.E.2d 579 (1983); Adams v. Mills, 312 N.C. 181, 322 S.E.2d 164 (1984).

The requirement of setting out proper warning flares is absolute, and a violation of it is negligence per se. Barrier v. Thomas & Howard Co., 205 N.C. 425, 171 S.E. 626 (1933); Caulder v. Cresham, 224 N.C. 402, 30 S.E.2d 312 (1944).

TO BE ACTIONABLE NEGLIGENCE MUST BE PROXIMATE CAUSE OF INJURY. --Negligence in parking an automobile on a public highway in violation of this section, to be actionable, must be a proximate cause of the injury in suit. Burke v. Carolina Coach Co., 198 N.C. 8, 150 S.E. 636 (1929); Adams v. Mills, 312 N.C. 181, 322 S.E.2d 164 (1984).

Failure to meet the requirements of this section relating to the display of warning signals when a truck, etc., is disabled on the highway convicts of negligence, which is actionable if such failure was one of the proximate causes of the collision. Taylor v. United States, 156 F. Supp. 763 (E.D.N.C. 1957).

PROXIMATE CAUSE IS JURY QUESTION. --Whether a violation of this section is the proximate cause of injury in a particular case is ordinarily a question for the jury. Hughes v. Vestal, 264 N.C. 500, 142 S.E.2d 361 (1965); Wilson v. Miller, 20 N.C. App. 156, 201 S.E.2d 55 (1973); Clark v. Moore, 65 N.C. App. 609, 309 S.E.2d 579 (1983).

Where violation of this section, which is negligence per se, is admitted or established by the evidence, it is ordinarily a question for the jury to determine whether such negligence is a proximate cause of injury which resulted in damages. Furr v. Pinoca Volunteer Fire Dep't, 53 N.C. App. 458, 281 S.E.2d 174, cert. denied, 304 N.C. 587, 289 S.E.2d 377 (1981).

STOPPING TO RECEIVE OR DISCHARGE PASSENGER DOES NOT NECESSARILY CONSTITUTE NEGLIGENCE. --The mere fact that a driver stops his vehicle on the traveled portion of a highway for the purpose of receiving or discharging a passenger, nothing else appearing, does not constitute negligence. Strickland v. Powell, 10 N.C. App. 225, 178 S.E.2d 136 (1970), aff'd, 279 N.C. 183, 181 S.E.2d 464 (1971).

PARKING A TRUCK ON A PAVED HIGHWAY AT NIGHT, WITHOUT FLARES OR OTHER WARNING, IS NEGLIGENCE. Allen v. Dr. Pepper Bottling Co., 223 N.C. 118, 25 S.E.2d 388 (1943).

THE PARKING OF A CAR ON THE HARD SURFACE OF A HIGHWAY AT NIGHT WITHOUT A TAILLIGHT in violation of statute is sufficient to sustain the jury's affirmative answer upon the issue of actionable negligence, and the question of contributory negligence in failing to see the parked car under the circumstances in time to have avoided the collision is also properly submitted to the jury. Lambert v. Caronna, 206 N.C. 616, 175 S.E. 303 (1934); Sharpe v. Hanline, 265 N.C. 502, 144 S.E.2d 574 (1965).

LEAVING A DISABLED MARINE CORPS WRECKER STANDING ON THE HIGHWAY IN THE NIGHTTIME WITHOUT LIGHTS and warning signals required by G.S. 20-134 and this section constituted negligence. United States v. First-Citizens Bank & Trust Co., 208 F.2d 280 (4th Cir. 1953).

FAILURE TO MOVE DISABLED TRUCK TO SHOULDER OF HIGHWAY. --Where one of truck's tires was flat and its motor was out of commission, but with the manpower present the truck could have been removed onto the shoulder, failure to do so constituted negligence. Freshman v. Stallings, 128 F. Supp. 179 (E.D.N.C. 1955).

NEGLIGENT PARKING NEED NOT BE ANTICIPATED. --Where defendant left his truck unattended, partly on a paved or improved portion of a State highway, between sunset and sunup, without displaying flares on lanterns (now reflectors) not less than 200 feet to the front and rear of the vehicle, he committed an act of negligence, and the driver of the car in which plaintiff was riding, traveling at about 30 to 35 miles per hour on the right side of the road under conditions which made it impossible for him to see more than a few feet ahead, although apparently guilty of negligence, was not under the duty of anticipating defendant's negligent parking, so that the concurrent negligence of the two made the resulting collision inevitable and an exception to the denial of a motion of nonsuit could not be sustained. Caulder v. Gresham, 224 N.C. 402, 30 S.E.2d 312 (1944).

COLLISION WITH GARBAGE TRUCK STOPPED TO COLLECT GARBAGE. --In a negligence action in which defendant employee parked garbage truck on the shoulder of the road facing oncoming traffic and van collided with the truck, evidence of alternative method for collecting customer's garbage prior to the accident, as well as testimony revealing defendant employee's rationale for stopping as he did, was relevant not only on the issue of whether defendant employer and defendant employee violated subsections (a) and (b) of this section, but also to the issue of defendant employee's alleged negligent conduct. Smith v. Pass, 95 N.C. App. 243, 382 S.E.2d 781 (1989).

In negligence action in which plaintiff's van collided with defendant's garbage truck, where there was conflicting evidence about the necessity of stopping the garbage truck on the shoulder and travelled portion of the road facing oncoming traffic and where there was conflicting evidence as to whether alternative means were available for defendant and his assistant to collect garbage at customer's residence, the court properly submitted this issue to the jury. Smith v. Pass, 95 N.C. App. 243, 382 S.E.2d 781 (1989).

EVIDENCE HELD TO MAKE OUT PRIMA FACIE CASE OF ACTIONABLE NEGLIGENCE. --Evidence that defendants left a wrecker standing on the highway in such manner that the wrecker and the cable attached blocked the entire highway, that the existing circumstances affected visibility of the cable, that no meaningful warning was given that the highway was completely obstructed, and that traffic, to avoid collision, would have had to come to a complete stop, made out a prima facie case of actionable negligence on the part of defendants. Montford v. Gilbhaar, 265 N.C. 389, 144 S.E.2d 31 (1965).

NEGLIGENCE HELD PROXIMATE CAUSE OF COLLISION. --Negligence of government's servants in failing to provide proper and statutory warning when a mobile highway post-office vehicle became disabled on the highway was one of the proximate causes of collision and resulting death and injuries. Cronenberg v. United States, 123 F. Supp. 693 (E.D.N.C. 1954).

FOR CASE HOLDING EVIDENCE INSUFFICIENT TO SHOW VIOLATION OF SECTION AS PROXIMATE CAUSE OF INJURY, see Saunders v. Warren, 264 N.C. 200, 141 S.E.2d 308 (1965).

EVIDENCE OF NEGLIGENCE HELD SUFFICIENT TO GO TO JURY. --Evidence that a disabled truck was left standing on the hard surface of a highway at night without warning flares or lanterns (now reflectors) as required by this section, and that a car, approaching from the rear, collided with the back of the truck, resulting in injuries to the driver and passengers in the car, was sufficient to be submitted to the jury on the issue of negligence in the actions instituted by the driver and occupants of the car against the driver and owner of the truck. Wilson v. Central Motor Lines, 230 N.C. 551, 54 S.E.2d 53 (1949).

Where defendant's truck, which was not disabled, was parked on the shoulder of a much-traveled, two-lane highway, and though the shoulder was wide enough with room to spare to accommodate the truck, part of it extended into the main-traveled portion of the highway far enough so that cars could not pass the truck without going into the other traffic lane, this was evidence enough of defendant's negligence and the issue was for the jury to determine, rather than the court. Wilkins v. Taylor, 76 N.C. App. 536, 333 S.E.2d 503 (1985).

EVIDENCE HELD TO DISCLOSE CONTRIBUTORY NEGLIGENCE. --Conceding that defendant was negligent in parking his car on the hard surface in violation of this section, the evidence disclosed contributory negligence of plaintiff as a matter of law in attempting to pass the parked car without first ascertaining that he could do so in safety. McNair v. Kilmer & Co., 210 N.C. 65, 185 S.E. 481 (1936).

Guest's contributory negligence barred recovery from driver for negligence in parking vehicle in violation of this section. Basnight v. Wilson, 245 N.C. 548, 96 S.E.2d 699 (1957).

Where plaintiff may have raised a question of fact for the jury as to whether her stop at an accident site to offer assistance was a "necessary" one, it was uncontested that plaintiff had no disabling condition which caused her to stop the vehicle; thus, she violated G.S. 20- 161(a), and it was proper for the trial court to direct a verdict in favor of defendant. Hutton v. Logan, 152 N.C. App. 94, 566 S.E.2d 782 (2002).

NONSUIT ON GROUND OF CONTRIBUTORY NEGLIGENCE HELD NOT WARRANTED. --Evidence disclosing that plaintiff's automobile was parked on a bridge 40 feet wide, leaving a space of 30 feet for the passage of traffic, that the driver of defendants' bus was blinded by the lights of an approaching car and hit the rear of plaintiff's car, and that the bridge constituted part of a city street and the parking of cars on the bridge was customary, was held not to warrant nonsuit on the ground of contributory negligence, since even though the parking of the car on the bridge was negligence per se, whether such negligence under the circumstances was a proximate cause of the injury was a question for the jury. Boles v. Hegler, 232 N.C. 327, 59 S.E.2d 796 (1950).

Where evidence tended to show that defendant's mud-spattered truck was parked on a dark, foggy morning, with all four wheels on the pavement without lights, flares, or any other mode of signal, and had been so parked for some time, and that plaintiff was compelled to dim his lights when about 20 feet south of defendant's truck, in response to the dimmed lights of an oncoming car, the lights of this car partly blinding plaintiff, who collided with the rear of defendant's truck, a motion for nonsuit on the ground of contributory negligence was properly refused. Cummins v. Southern Fruit Co., 225 N.C. 625, 36 S.E.2d 11 (1945).

AS TO NEGLIGENCE OF ONE DEFENDANT INSULATING NEGLIGENCE OF ANOTHER, see

McLaney v. Anchor Motor Freight, Inc., 236 N.C. 714, 74 S.E.2d 36 (1953).

NEGLIGENCE INSTRUCTION. --Where defendant offered no evidence that plaintiff's actions constituted negligence in violation of subsection (a) of this section or with regard to any other standard of care, the trial judge was not obligated to charge the jury on contributory negligence or to submit it as an issue to them. Adams v. Mills, 68 N.C. App. 256, 314 S.E.2d 589, rev'd on other grounds, 312 N.C. 181, 322 S.E.2d 164 (1984).

BURDEN OF PROOF. --The burden is on plaintiff to prove that defendant violated this section, while if defendant is to escape the consequences of this violation, defendant has the burden of bringing himself within the provision that "it is impossible to avoid stopping." Williams v. Jones, 53 N.C. App. 171, 280 S.E.2d 474 (1981).

INSTRUCTIONS ON BURDEN OF PROOF. --In an action to recover damages suffered by plaintiff when his vehicle collided with that of defendant, trial court should have instructed the jury that plaintiff had the burden of proving that defendant violated subsection (a) of this section by parking or leaving his vehicle standing on the paved portion of the highway when he had the opportunity to park the vehicle on the shoulder of the highway, and that the burden was on defendant to prove that he was excused from such parking because it was not reasonably practical under the circumstances to avoid stopping on the paved portion of the highway; failure to so charge was error prejudicial to plaintiff. Williams v. Jones, 53 N.C. App. 171, 280 S.E.2d 474 (1981).

SUDDEN EMERGENCY INSTRUCTION REQUIRED. --In an action to recover damages sustained in an automobile accident, the trial court erred in failing to charge on the doctrine of sudden emergency, as requested by plaintiff, where the evidence tended to show that plaintiff saw defendant's vehicle in his traffic lane when he was four car lengths away, that plaintiff did not pull onto the left lane because he was afraid that he would be hit by a tractor trailer behind him in that lane, that plaintiff probably could have pulled to the right but he would have been on a narrow grassy area and a guardrail was there, that the entire shoulder was only 10 feet wide, and that there was fog in the area at the time of the collision. Williams v. Jones, 53 N.C. App. 171, 280 S.E.2d 474 (1981).

§ 20-161.1. Regulation of night parking on highways

No person parking or leaving standing a vehicle at night on a highway or on a side road entering into a highway shall permit the bright lights of said vehicle to continue burning when such lights face oncoming traffic.

History.
1953, c. 1052

HAZARD AGAINST WHICH SECTION DIRECTED. --This section is directed against the hazard of bright lights on standing vehicles facing oncoming traffic at night. Lienthall v. Glass, 2 N.C. App. 65, 162 S.E.2d 596 (1968).

APPLICABILITY OF SECTION. --Section 20-168(b) makes this section, which prohibits bright lights on standing vehicles at night, inapplicable to street maintenance workers actually performing their duties. Pinkston v. Connor, 63 N.C. App. 628, 306 S.E.2d 132 (1983), aff'd, 310 N.C. 148, 310 S.E.2d 347 (1984).

FOR CASE HOLDING THAT GUEST'S CONTRIBUTORY NEGLIGENCE BARRED RECOVERY FROM DRIVER FOR NEGLIGENCE IN PARKING VEHICLE IN VIOLATION OF THIS SECTION, see Basnight v. Wilson, 245 N.C. 548, 96 S.E.2d 699 (1957).

APPLIED in Staples v. Carter, 5 N.C. App. 264, 168 S.E.2d 240 (1969); Tharpe v. Brewer, 7 N.C. App. 432, 172 S.E.2d 919 (1970).

N.C. Gen. Stat. § 20-161.2

Repealed by Session Laws 1983, c. 420, s. 1.
CROSS REFERENCES. --
As to post-towing procedures, see now G.S. 20-219.9 et seq.

§ 20-162. Parking in front of private driveway, fire hydrant, fire station, intersection of curb lines or fire lane

(a) No person shall park a vehicle or permit it to stand, whether attended or unattended, upon a highway in front of a private driveway or within 15 feet in either direction of a fire hydrant or the entrance to a fire station, nor within 25 feet from the intersection of curb lines or if none, then within 15 feet of the intersection of property lines at an intersection of highways; provided, that local authorities may by ordinance decrease the distance within which a vehicle may park in either direction of a fire hydrant.

(b) No person shall park a vehicle or permit it to stand, whether attended or unattended, upon any public vehicular area, street, highway or roadway in any area designated as a fire lane. This prohibition includes designated fire lanes in shopping center or mall parking lots and all other public vehicular areas. Provided, however, persons loading or unloading supplies or merchandise may park temporarily in a fire lane located in a shopping center or mall parking lot as long as the vehicle is not left unattended. The prima facie rule of evidence created by G.S. 20-162.1 is applicable to prosecutions for violation of this section. The owner of a vehicle parked in violation of this subsection shall be deemed to have appointed any State, county or municipal law-enforcement officer as his agent for the purpose of arranging for the transportation and safe storage of such vehicle. No law-enforcement officer removing such a vehicle shall be held criminally or civilly liable in any way for any acts or omissions arising out of or caused by carrying out or enforcing any provisions of this subsection, unless the conduct of the officer amounts to wanton misconduct or intentional wrongdoing.

History.

1937, c. 407, s. 124; 1939, c. 111; 1979, c. 552; 1981, c. 574, s. 1

LOCAL MODIFICATION. --City of Wilson: 1985, c. 137; Town of Manteo: 2002-141, s. 7.

APPLICABILITY OF RULE OF EVIDENCE IN G.S. 20-162.1. --The prima facie rule of evidence created by G.S. 20-162.1 is applicable to prosecutions for violation of this section. State v. Rumfelt, 241 N.C. 375, 85 S.E.2d 398 (1955).

VIOLATION OF SECTION AS MISDEMEANOR. --Violation of this section by parking within 25 feet from the intersection of curb lines at an intersection of highways within a municipality is a misdemeanor, notwithstanding that the prima facie rule of evidence created by G.S. 20-162.1 is invoked. State v. Rumfelt, 241 N.C. 375, 85 S.E.2d 398 (1955).

APPLIED in Sizemore v. Raxter, 73 N.C. App. 531, 327 S.E.2d 258 (1985); Richardson v. Hiatt, 95 N.C. App. 196, 381 S.E.2d 866 (1989).

CITED in Basnight v. Wilson, 245 N.C. 548, 96 S.E.2d 699 (1957).

§ 20-162.1. Prima facie rule of evidence for enforcement of parking regulations

(a) Whenever evidence shall be presented in any court of the fact that any automobile, truck, or other vehicle was found upon any street, alley or other public place contrary to and in violation of the provisions of any statute or of any municipal or Department of Transportation ordinance limiting the time during which any such vehicle may be parked or prohibiting or otherwise regulating the parking of any such vehicle, it shall be prima facie evidence in any court in the State of North Carolina that such vehicle was parked and left upon such street, alley or public way or place by the person, firm or corporation in whose name such vehicle is then registered and licensed according to the records of the department or agency of the State of North Carolina, by whatever name designated, which is empowered to register such vehicles and to issue licenses for their operation upon the streets and highways of this State; provided, that no evidence tendered or presented under the authorization contained in this section shall be admissible or competent in any respect in any court or tribunal, except in cases concerned solely with violation of statutes or ordinances limiting, prohibiting or otherwise regulating the parking of automobiles or other vehicles upon public streets, highways, or other public places.

Any person found responsible for an infraction pursuant to this section shall be subject to a penalty of not more than five dollars ($ 5.00).

(b) The prima facie rule of evidence established by subsection (a) shall not apply to the registered owner of a leased or rented vehicle parked in violation of law when the owner can furnish sworn evidence that the vehicle was, at the time of the parking violation, leased or rented, to another person or company. In those instances, the owner of the vehicle shall furnish sworn evidence to the courts within 30 days after notification of the violation in accordance with this subsection.

If the notification is given to the owner of the vehicle within 90 days after the date of the violation, the owner shall include in the sworn evidence the name and address of the person or company that leased or rented the vehicle. If notification is given to the owner of the vehicle after 90 days have elapsed from the date of the violation, the owner is not required to include the name or address of the lessee or renter of the vehicle in the sworn evidence.

History.

1953, c. 879, ss. 1, 1 1/2; c. 978; 1955, c. 566, s. 1; 1983, c. 753; 1985, c. 764, s. 32; 1985 (Reg. Sess., 1986), c. 852, s. 17; 1987, c. 736, s. 1; 1989, c. 243, s. 2;2001-259, s. 1

LOCAL MODIFICATION. --Mecklenburg: 1981, c. 239; city of Clinton: 1979, c. 326; city of Goldsboro: 1981, c. 314; city of Greenville: 1985 (Reg. Sess., 1986), c. 813; city of Jacksonville: 1985, c. 152; city of Sandford: 2006-28, s. 2;city of Winston-Salem: 1983, c. 160; town of Kernersville: 1987, c. 54; town of Pittsboro: 1987, c. 460, s. 27.

EDITOR'S NOTE. --

The act inserting this section exempted Madison and Sampson Counties. Session Laws 1953, c. 978, made the section applicable to Sampson County. Session Laws 1955, c. 566, s. 1, made the section applicable to Madison County.

ORIGIN OF SECTION. --It seems apparent that as a result of the decision in State v. Scoggin, 236 N.C. 19, 72 S.E.2d 54 (1952), holding that the court, in the absence of a legislative rule of evidence to the contrary, would not consider mere ownership of a motor vehicle parked in violation of a city ordinance sufficient to sustain a criminal conviction, the General Assembly at its 1953 Session enacted the statute which is now this section. State v. Rumfelt, 241 N.C. 375, 85 S.E.2d 398 (1955).

EFFECT OF SECTION. --This section creates no criminal offense, but prescribes that when the prima facie rule of evidence therein set forth is relied upon by the State in a criminal prosecution, the punishment shall be a penalty of $1.00. State v. Rumfelt, 241 N.C. 375, 85 S.E.2d 398 (1955).

THE WORD "PENALTY" IS USED IN THIS SECTION IN THE BROAD SENSE OF PUNISHMENT and not in the sense of a penalty recoverable in a civil action. State v. Rumfelt, 241 N.C. 375, 85 S.E.2d 398 (1955).

APPLICABILITY TO PROSECUTIONS UNDER G.S. 20-162. --Prima facie rule of evidence created by this section is applicable to prosecutions for violation of G.S. 20-162. State v. Rumfelt, 241 N.C. 375, 85 S.E.2d 398 (1955).

LEGAL PERIODICALS. --

For brief comment on this section, see 31 N.C.L. Rev. 410 (1953).

§§ 20-162.2, 20-162.3

Transferred to §§ 20-219.2, 20-219.3 by Session Laws 1973, c. 1330, s. 36.

§ 20-163. Unattended motor vehicles

No person driving or in charge of a motor vehicle shall permit it to stand unattended on a public highway or public vehicular area without first stopping the engine, effectively setting the brake thereon and, when standing upon any grade, turning the front wheels to the curb or side of the highway.

History.
1937, c. 407, s. 125; 1973, c. 1330, s. 26

VIOLATION OF SECTION IS NEGLIGENCE PER SE. --The violation of this section and other safety statutes is negligence per se, unless the statute expressly provides otherwise. McCall v. Dixie Cartage & Warehousing, Inc., 272 N.C. 190, 158 S.E.2d 72 (1967).

When a vehicle is parked, this section requires a setting of the brakes, and a violation of this statute is negligence. Bundy v. Belue, 253 N.C. 31, 116 S.E.2d 200 (1960).

BUT VIOLATION MUST BE PROXIMATE CAUSE OF INJURY TO BE ACTIONABLE. --Violation of this section is negligence per se, but it must be a proximate cause of the injury to be actionable. Arnett v. Yeago, 247 N.C. 356, 100 S.E.2d 855 (1957); Watts v. Watts, 252 N.C. 352, 113 S.E.2d 720 (1960).

VIOLATION INFERRED FROM RUNAWAY AUTOMOBILE. --The fact that an automobile ran down the street for a considerable distance immediately after it was parked permitted the inference that plaintiff's intestate did not turn the vehicle's front wheels to the curb of the street as required by G.S. 20-124 and this section. Watts v. Watts, 252 N.C. 352, 113 S.E.2d 720 (1960).

EXERCISE OF CARE OTHER THAN ON PUBLIC HIGHWAYS. --For case citing this statute for the purpose of indicating that due care in the operation of motor vehicles must be exercised in places other than upon public highways, see Wiggins v. Paramount Motor Sales, Inc., 89 N.C. App. 119, 365 S.E.2d 192 (1988).

EVIDENCE THAT DEFENDANT LEFT LOANER CAR, WHICH HE KNEW TO BE WITHOUT AN EMERGENCY BRAKE, PARKED WITH THE ENGINE RUNNING at a relatively high speed near the place where he was conversing with plaintiff was sufficient to take the case to the jury on the issue of whether defendant was negligent in the operation of his loaner car. Wiggins v. Paramount Motor Sales, Inc., 119 N.C. App. 89, 365 S.E.2d 192 (1988).

N.C. Gen. Stat. § 20-164

Repealed by Session Laws 1973, c. 1330, s. 39.

N.C. Gen. Stat. § 20-165

Repealed by Session Laws 1995, c. 379, s. 6.

§ 20-165.1. One-way traffic

In all cases where the Department of Transportation has heretofore, or may hereafter lawfully designate any highway or other separate roadway, under its jurisdiction for one-way traffic and shall erect appropriate signs giving notice thereof, it shall be unlawful for any person to willfully drive or operate any vehicle on said highway or roadway except in the direction so indicated by said signs.

History.
1957, c. 1177; 1973, c. 507, s. 5; c. 1330, s. 28; 1977, c. 464, s. 34

REGULATORY POWER OF STATE. --This section and G.S. 20-156(a) illustrate the power of the State to regulate the time and manner of entering a public highway. Moses v. State Hwy. Comm'n, 261 N.C. 316, 134 S.E.2d 664, cert. denied, 379 U.S. 930, 85 S. Ct. 327, 13 L. Ed. 2d 342 (1964).

WILLFUL VIOLATION OF THIS SECTION WOULD CONSTITUTE CULPABLE NEGLIGENCE IF IT WAS THE PROXIMATE CAUSE OF DEATH. State v. Atkins, 58 N.C. App. 146, 292 S.E.2d 744, cert. denied and appeal dismissed, 306 N.C. 744, 295 S.E.2d 480 (1982).

CITED in State Hwy. Comm'n v. Raleigh Farmers Mkt., Inc., 263 N.C. 622, 139 S.E.2d 904 (1965).

§ 20-166. Duty to stop in event of a crash; furnishing information or assistance to injured person, etc.; persons assisting exempt from civil liability

(a) The driver of any vehicle who knows or reasonably should know:

(1) That the vehicle which he or she is operating is involved in a crash; and

(2) That the crash has resulted in serious bodily injury, as defined in G.S. 14-32.4, or death to any person;

shall immediately stop his or her vehicle at the scene of the crash. The driver shall remain with the vehicle at the scene of the crash until a law-enforcement officer completes the investigation of the crash or authorizes the driver to leave and the vehicle to be removed, unless remaining at the scene places the driver or others at significant risk of injury.

Prior to the completion of the investigation of the crash by a law enforcement officer, or the consent of the officer to leave, the driver may not facilitate, allow, or agree to the removal of the vehicle from the scene for any purpose other than to call for a law enforcement officer, to call for medical assistance or medical treatment as set forth in subsection (b) of this section, or to remove oneself or others from significant risk of injury. If the driver does leave for a reason permitted by this subsection, then the driver must return with the vehicle to the accident scene within a reasonable period of time, unless otherwise instructed by a law enforcement officer. A willful violation of this subsection shall be punished as a Class F felony.

(a1) The driver of any vehicle who knows or reasonably should know:

(1) That the vehicle which he or she is operating is involved in a crash; and

(2) That the crash has resulted in injury;

shall immediately stop his or her vehicle at the scene of the crash. The driver shall remain with the vehicle at the scene of the crash until a law enforcement officer completes the investigation of the crash or authorizes the driver to leave and the vehicle to be removed, unless remaining at the scene places the driver or others at significant risk of injury.

Prior to the completion of the investigation of the crash by a law enforcement officer, or the consent of the officer to leave, the driver may not facilitate, allow, or agree to the removal of the vehicle from the scene for any purpose other than to call for a law enforcement officer, to call for medical assistance or medical treatment as set forth in subsection (b) of this section, or to remove oneself or others from significant risk of injury. If the driver does leave for a reason permitted by this subsection, then the driver must return with the vehicle to the crash scene within a reasonable period of time, unless otherwise instructed by a law enforcement officer. A willful violation of this subsection shall be punished as a Class H felony.

(b) In addition to complying with the requirements of subsections (a) and (a1) of this section, the driver as set forth in subsections (a) and

(a1) shall give his or her name, address, driver's license number and the license plate number of the vehicle to the person struck or the driver or occupants of any vehicle collided with, provided that the person or persons are physically and mentally capable of receiving such information, and shall render to any person injured in such crash reasonable assistance, including the calling for medical assistance if it is apparent that such assistance is necessary or is requested by the injured person. A violation of this subsection is a Class 1 misdemeanor.

(c) The driver of any vehicle, when the driver knows or reasonably should know that the vehicle which the driver is operating is involved in a crash which results:

(1) Only in damage to property; or

(2) In injury or death to any person, but only if the operator of the vehicle did not know and did not have reason to know of the death or injury;

shall immediately stop the vehicle at the scene of the crash. If the crash is a reportable crash, the driver shall remain with the vehicle at the scene of the crash until a law enforcement officer completes the investigation of the crash or authorizes the driver to leave and the vehicle to be removed, unless remaining at the scene places the driver or others at significant risk of injury.

Prior to the completion of the investigation of the crash by a law enforcement officer, or the consent of the officer to leave, the driver may not facilitate, allow, or agree to the removal of the vehicle from the scene, for any purpose other than to call for a law enforcement officer, to call for medical assistance or medical treatment, or to remove oneself or others from significant risk of injury. If the driver does leave for a reason permitted by this subsection, then the driver must return with the vehicle to the accident scene within a reasonable period of time, unless otherwise instructed by a law enforcement officer. A willful violation of this subsection is a Class 1 misdemeanor.

(c1) In addition to complying with the requirement of subsection (c) of this section, the driver as set forth in subsection (c) shall give his or her name, address, driver's license number and the license plate number of his vehicle to the driver or occupants of any other vehicle involved in the crash or to any person whose property is damaged in the crash. If the damaged property is a parked and unattended vehicle and the name and location of the owner is not known to or readily ascertainable by the driver of the responsible vehicle, the driver shall furnish the information required by this subsection to the nearest available peace officer, or, in the alternative, and provided the driver thereafter within 48 hours fully complies with

G.S. 20-166.1(c), shall immediately place a paper-writing containing the information in a conspicuous place upon or in the damaged vehicle. If the damaged property is a guardrail, utility pole, or other fixed object owned by the Department of Transportation, a public utility, or other public service corporation to which report cannot readily be made at the scene, it shall be sufficient if the responsible driver shall furnish the information required to the nearest peace officer or make written report thereof containing the information by U.S. certified mail, return receipt requested, to the North Carolina Division of Motor Vehicles within five days following the collision. A violation of this subsection is a Class 1 misdemeanor.

(c2) Notwithstanding subsections (a), (a1), and (c) of this section, if a crash occurs on a main lane, ramp, shoulder, median, or adjacent area of a highway, each vehicle shall be moved as soon as possible out of the travel lane and onto the shoulder or to a designated accident investigation site to complete the requirements of this section and minimize interference with traffic if all of the following apply:

(1) The crash has not resulted in injury or death to any person or the drivers did not know or have reason to know of any injury or death.

(2) Each vehicle can be normally and safely driven. For purposes of this subsection, a vehicle can be normally and safely driven if it does not require towing and can be operated under its own power and in its usual manner, without additional damage or hazard to the vehicle, other traffic, or the roadway.

(d) Any person who renders first aid or emergency assistance at the scene of a motor vehicle crash on any street or highway to any person injured as a result of the accident, shall not be liable in civil damages for any acts or omissions relating to the services rendered, unless the acts or omissions amount to wanton conduct or intentional wrongdoing.

(e) The Division of Motor Vehicles shall revoke the drivers license of a person convicted of violating subsection (a) or (a1) of this section for a period of one year, unless the court makes a finding that a longer period of revocation is appropriate under the circumstances of the case. If the court makes this finding, the Division of Motor Vehicles shall revoke that person's drivers license for two years. Upon a first conviction only for a violation of subsection (a1) of this section, a trial judge may allow limited driving privileges in the manner set forth in G.S. 20-179.3(b)(2) during any period of time during which the drivers license is revoked.

History.
1937, c. 407, s. 128; 1939, c. 10, ss. 1, 1 1/2; 1943, c. 439; 1951, cc. 309, 794, 823; 1953, cc. 394, 793; c. 1340, s. 1; 1955, c. 913, s. 8; 1965, c. 176; 1967, c. 445; 1971, c. 958, s. 1; 1973, c. 507, s. 5; 1975, c. 716, s. 5; 1977, c. 464, s. 34; 1979, c. 667, s. 32; 1983, c. 912, s. 1; 1985, c. 324, ss. 1-4; 1993, c. 539, ss. 373 -375, 1260; 1994, Ex. Sess., c. 24, s. 14(c);2003-310, s. 2;2003-394, s. 1;2005-460, s. 1;2008-128, s. 1

EFFECT OF AMENDMENTS. --
Session Laws 2003-394, s. 1, effective December 1, 2003, added subsection (e). See Editor's note for applicability.

Session Laws 2005-460, s. 1, effective December 1, 2005, and applicable to offenses committed on or after that date, rewrote subsections (a) and (c); added "Notwithstanding subsections (a) and (c) of this section" to the beginning of subsection (c2); and made minor stylistic and gender neutral changes.

Session Laws 2008-128, s. 1, effective December 1, 2008, and applicable to offenses committed on or after that date, substituted "crash" for "accident or collision" or "accident," and made related changes throughout the section; in subdivision (a)(2), substituted "serious bodily injury, as defined in G.S. 14-32.4" for "injury"; in the last paragraph of subsection (a), substituted "Class F" for "Class H"; added subsection (a1), and added references to subsection (a1) throughout the section; and made stylistic changes.

I. IN GENERAL.
EDITOR'S NOTE. --Many of the cases cited below were decided under this section as it read prior to the 1983 amendment.

PURPOSE OF SECTION. --The general purpose of this section is to facilitate investigation of automobile accidents and to assure immediate aid to anyone injured by such collision. State v. Fearing, 48 N.C. App. 329, 269 S.E.2d 245, aff'd in part and rev'd in part on other grounds, 304 N.C. 471, 284 S.E.2d 487 (1981).

The purpose of the requirement that a motorist stop and identify himself is to facilitate investigation. State v. Smith, 264 N.C. 575, 142 S.E.2d 149 (1965).

A plain reading of this section indicates it exists for safety purposes and imposes a duty of care upon a person whose vehicle collides with another person. Powell v. Doe, 123 N.C. App. 392, 473 S.E.2d 407 (1996).

AN OFFENSE UNDER THIS SECTION IS NOT RESTRICTED TO PUBLIC HIGHWAYS. -- State v. Smith, 264 N.C. 575, 142 S.E.2d 149 (1965).

ELEMENTS OF OFFENSE. --In prosecutions under subsection (a) of this section as it read prior to the 1983 amendment, the State had to prove that the defendant knew (1) that he had been involved in an accident or collision, and (2) that a person was killed or physically injured in the collision. The knowledge required could be actual or implied. State v. Fearing, 304 N.C. 471, 284 S.E.2d 487 (1981). *To support a verdict of guilty under subsection (a)* of this section as it read prior to the 1983 amendment, the State had to prove that defendant was driving the automobile involved in the accident at the time it occurred; that the vehicle defendant was driving came into contact with another person resulting in injury or death; and that defendant, knowing he had struck the victim, failed to stop immediately at the scene. State v. Fearing, 48 N.C. App. 329, 269 S.E.2d 245 (1980), aff'd in part and rev'd in part on other grounds, 304 N.C. 471, 284 S.E.2d 487 (1981).

In order to convict defendant on a count which charged a violation of subsection (a) of this section as it read prior to the 1983 amendment, it was necessary for the State to prove that on the occasion in question, defendant was the operator of a named automobile which the State contended drove down a given street; that this vehicle was involved in an accident or collision with the alleged victim; and that knowing he had struck the victim, defendant failed to stop his vehicle immediately at the scene. State v. Overman, 257 N.C. 464, 125 S.E.2d 920 (1962).

As to elements of offense under subsection (c) as it read prior to the 1983 amendment, see State v. Overman, 257 N.C. 464, 125 S.E.2d 920 (1962).

The essential elements of the offense of hit and run with personal injury are: (1) That the defendant was involved in an accident; (2) that someone was physically injured in this accident; (3) that at the time of the accident the defendant was driving the vehicle; (4) that the defendant knew that he had struck a pedestrian and that the pedestrian suffered physical injury; (5) that the defendant did not stop his vehicle immediately at the scene of the accident; and (6) that the defendant's failure to stop was wilful, that is, intentional and without justification or excuse. State v. Acklin, 71 N.C. App. 261, 321 S.E.2d 532 (1984).

Defendant was properly convicted of giving false information for a motor vehicle crash report in violation of G.S. 20-279.31(b) when defendant falsely stated that defendant drove a vehicle involved in a crash, because, inter alia, while G.S. 20-166.1(h) did not list "driver's identity" with the information that "shall be included," the remaining portions of the statute preceding and following that section imposed an explicit duty on drivers to provide the drivers' name, address, and other information in the event of a reportable accident, G.S. 20-166(b), (c1), G.S. 20-166.1(a) -- (c), so it could be inferred that the term "persons and vehicles involved" necessarily included the identity of the driver. State v. Hernandez, 188 N.C. App. 193, 655 S.E.2d 426 (2008).

Trial court plainly erred by failing to instruct the jury on willfulness because it was an essential element of the offense of hit and run and defendant's sole defense was that his departure from the accident site was authorized and required by statute as he left in an effort to get the victim medical assistance. State v. Scaturro, 253 N.C. App. 828, 802 S.E.2d 500 (2017), review denied, 804 S.E.2d 528, 2017 N.C. LEXIS 718 (N.C. 2017), dismissed, 804 S.E.2d 530, 2017 N.C. LEXIS 710 (N.C. 2017).

Trial court did not err by submitting to the jury and entering judgment upon conviction for felonious hit and run resulting in injury, an offense for which defendant was not indicted, because the essential elements of hit and run resulting in injury, the offense for which defendant was indicted, necessarily included the essential elements of hit and run resulting

in injury: the victim was injured as a result of the crash and his injury resulted in death. State v. Malloy, 257 N.C. App. 191, 809 S.E.2d 14 (2017).

NEGLIGENCE PER SE. --Violation of this type of statute is negligence per se if new injuries, or an aggravation of original injuries, occur after the hit and run driver leaves the scene without rendering aid. Powell v. Doe, 123 N.C. App. 392, 473 S.E.2d 407 (1996).

Any negligence in failing to stop after an accident cannot be the proximate cause of the occurrence of the accident itself, or of any immediate injury or death resulting therefrom; thus, use of this section as the standard for negligence per se will only be appropriate when the evidence shows that the hit and run driver's failure to stop and render aid either exacerbated the injury, resulted in unnecessary pain and suffering, or resulted in an avoidable death. Powell v. Doe, 123 N.C. App. 392, 473 S.E.2d 407 (1996).

EFFECT OF PROVISO REGARDING PARKED OR UNATTENDED VEHICLES. --Proviso in subsection (b) as it read prior to the 1983 amendment merely withdrew the case of a parked or unattended vehicle whose owner's identity was not readily ascertainable from the general language of the statute. It did not describe a separate offense, and therefore it did not need to be negatived in the warrant. State v. Norris, 26 N.C. App. 259, 215 S.E.2d 875, appeal dismissed, 288 N.C. 249, 217 S.E.2d 673 (1975), cert. denied, 423 U.S. 1073, 96 S. Ct. 856, 47 L. Ed. 2d 83 (1976).

LESSER INCLUDED OFFENSE. --The misdemeanor described in subsection (b) as it read prior to the 1983 amendment was not a lesser included offense of the crime described in subsection (c) as it read prior to the 1983 amendment. State v. Chavis, 9 N.C. App. 430, 176 S.E.2d 388 (1970).

MEANING OF "PERSON STRUCK" AND "DRIVER OR OCCUPANTS". --Under this section, "the person struck" means a pedestrian, and "the driver or occupants of any vehicle collided with" means the driver or passengers in a vehicle. State v. Gatewood, 46 N.C. App. 28, 264 S.E.2d 375, cert. denied, 300 N.C. 559, 270 S.E.2d 112 (1980).

NO VIOLATION IN FAILING TO GIVE INFORMATION TO DRIVER WHERE ONLY PEDESTRIAN INJURED. --Where defendant's car struck and killed a pedestrian and then sideswiped an approaching vehicle, but the collision did not result in injury or death to the driver or any passengers in the sideswiped vehicle collided with, defendant did not violate this section in failing to give the required information to the driver. State v. Gatewood, 46 N.C. App. 28, 264 S.E.2d 375, cert. denied, 300 N.C. 559, 270 S.E.2d 112 (1980).

PERSONAL INJURY OR DEATH IS A NECESSARY ELEMENT OF THE OFFENSE envisioned by this section. State v. Crutchfield, 5 N.C. App. 586, 169 S.E.2d 43 (1969).

AS IS KNOWLEDGE THAT ACCIDENT RESULTED IN INJURY OR DEATH. --Knowledge of the driver that his vehicle had been involved in an accident resulting in injury to a person is an essential element of the offense of "hit-and-run driving."

State v. Ray, 229 N.C. 40, 47 S.E.2d 494 (1948); State v. Fearing, 48 N.C. App. 329, 269 S.E.2d 245, cert. denied, 301 N.C. 99, 273 S.E.2d 303, 301 N.C. 403, 273 S.E.2d 448 (1980), aff'd in part and rev'd in part on other grounds, 304 N.C. 471, 284 S.E.2d 487 (1981).

Knowledge by a motorist that he had struck a pedestrian is an essential element of the offense of failing to stop and give such pedestrian aid. State v. Glover, 270 N.C. 319, 154 S.E.2d 305 (1967).

In order to lay the basis for punishment under former G.S. 20-182 for willful violation of this section, the State must show that defendant willfully violated subsection (a) of this section by failing to stop at the scene of an accident, knowing that there was an accident and knowing that a person had been injured or killed in the accident; therefore, in a prosecution of defendant for being an accessory after the fact to hit-and-run driving, trial court's instruction was erroneous where it gave the impression that, if the accident involved injury or death to a person, knowledge that an accident had occurred was sufficient to provide the element of willful failure to stop, and that a showing of the driver's knowledge of injury or death to a person was not required. State v. Fearing, 50 N.C. App. 475, 279 S.E.2d 356, aff'd in part and rev'd in part on other grounds, 304 N.C. 499, 284 S.E.2d 479 (1981). See also, State v. Fearing, 304 N.C. 471, 284 S.E.2d 487 (1981).

DUTY OF DRIVER INVOLVED IN ACCIDENT RESULTING IN PERSONAL INJURY OR DEATH. -- This section requires the driver of a vehicle, involved in an accident or collision resulting in injury or death to any person, to stop, render reasonable assistance and give certain specified information to the occupant or driver of the vehicle collided with. Branch v. Dempsey, 265 N.C. 733, 145 S.E.2d 395 (1965).

This section requires the driver of a vehicle involved in an accident to stop at the scene, and in the event the accident involves the injury of any person, it requires him to give his name, address, operator's license and the registration number of his vehicle, and to render reasonable assistance to the injured person. State v. Brown, 226 N.C. 681, 40 S.E.2d 34 (1946).

A DRIVER VIOLATES THIS SECTION IF HE DOES NOT IMMEDIATELY STOP AT THE SCENE. State v. Norris, 26 N.C. App. 259, 215 S.E.2d 875, appeal dismissed, 288 N.C. 249, 217 S.E.2d 673 (1975), cert. denied, 423 U.S. 1073, 96 S. Ct. 856, 47 L. Ed. 2d 83 (1976); State v. Fearing, 48 N.C. App. 329, 269 S.E.2d 245, cert. denied, 301 N.C. 99, 273 S.E.2d 303, 301 N.C. 403, 273 S.E.2d 448 (1980), aff'd in part and rev'd in part on other grounds, 304 N.C. 471, 284 S.E.2d 487 (1981); State v. Lucas, 58 N.C. App. 141, 292 S.E.2d 747, cert. denied, 306 N.C. 390, 293 S.E.2d 593 (1982).

FAILURE TO STOP IS THE GIST OF THE OFFENSE. State v. Smith, 264 N.C. 575, 142 S.E.2d 149 (1965).

GOOD FAITH IN OBTAINING AID FOR INJURED PARTY IMMATERIAL TO CHARGE OF FAILURE TO STOP. --Where defendant admitted that he knew he had hit a man and that he did not stop or return to the scene, his own testimony disclosed a violation of this section, and his good faith in stopping 200 yards away from the accident and obtaining aid for the injured man before proceeding on his way to his home was immaterial on the issue of guilt or innocence; hence, the exclusion of testimony to this effect was without error. State v. Brown, 226 N.C. 681, 40 S.E.2d 34 (1946).

AS IS ABSENCE OF FAULT. --Absence of fault on the part of the driver is not a defense to the charge of failure to stop. State v. Smith, 264 N.C. 575, 142 S.E.2d 149 (1965); State v. Fearing, 48 N.C. App. 329, 269 S.E.2d 245, cert. denied, 301 N.C. 99, 273 S.E.2d 303, 301 N.C. 403, 273 S.E.2d 448 (1980), aff'd in part and rev'd in part on other grounds, 304 N.C. 471, 284 S.E.2d 487 (1981).

FAILURE TO STOP OR FLIGHT FROM SCENE AS EVIDENCE OF CONSCIOUS WRONG. --A defendant's failure to stop, as required by this section, or his immediate flight from the scene of the injury, affords sufficient evidence of conscious wrong or dereliction on his part to warrant the jury in so concluding. Edwards v. Cross, 233 N.C. 354, 64 S.E.2d 6 (1951).

THIS SECTION DOES NOT REQUIRE A STATEMENT BY THE DRIVER AS TO HOW HE WAS DRIVING OR WHAT CAUSED THE COLLISION. Branch v. Dempsey, 265 N.C. 733, 145 S.E.2d 395 (1965).

GIVING OF NAME, ETC., NOT REQUIRED WHERE OTHER PARTIES TOO INJURED TO RECEIVE REPORT. --Defendant could not be convicted of the charge that he failed to give his name, address, etc., where the evidence showed that all others involved in the accident were either killed or so seriously injured that there was no one to whom defendant could give a report. State v. Wall, 243 N.C. 238, 90 S.E.2d 383 (1955).

Where evidence by the State was to the effect that the injured party was unconscious after the accident, no useful purpose could have been served by undertaking to give the unconscious man the information required by this section. The law does not require a party to do a vain and useless thing. State v. Coggin, 263 N.C. 457, 139 S.E.2d 701 (1965).

REQUIREMENT THAT DRIVER REMAIN ON SCENE DID NOT EQUAL FORMAL ARREST. --Admission of an officer's statement that defendant juvenile acknowledged being the driver of a wrecked vehicle did not violate G.S. 7B-2101 since although G.S. 20-166(c) required defendant to stay at the accident scene, the requirement that an individual involved in a motor vehicle accident remain on the scene of the accident did not equate with a restraint on that individual's freedom equivalent to a formal arrest for custodial interrogation purposes. In re A.N.C., 225 N.C. App. 315, 750 S.E.2d 835 (2013), review denied 367 N.C. 269, 752 S.E.2d 151, 2013 N.C. LEXIS 1386 (2013).

STATEMENT VOLUNTARY. --Defendant juvenile's statement to a police officer was voluntary for Fifth Amendment, U.S. Const. amend. V, purposes, even though G.S. 20-166(c1) required defendant

Chapter 20

to respond to the officer's questions, since the Fifth Amendment privilege could not be invoked to resist compliance with a regulatory regime constructed to effect the State's public purposes unrelated to the enforcement of its criminal laws, the mere requirement that an individual disclosed his name to an investigating officer on the scene of a motor vehicle accident did not necessarily have incriminating effect, and the record contained no additional information tending to suggest that defendant's admission that he had been driving the wrecked vehicle resulted from any coercive conduct on the part of the officer. In re A.N.C., 225 N.C. App. 315, 750 S.E.2d 835 (2013), review denied 367 N.C. 269, 752 S.E.2d 151, 2013 N.C. LEXIS 1386 (2013).

A DEFENDANT MAY NOT BE CONVICTED OF FAILING TO GIVE ASSISTANCE TO A PERSON INSTANTLY KILLED in collision. State v. Wall, 243 N.C. 238, 90 S.E.2d 383 (1955).

WHETHER INJURY WAS SUSTAINED IS JURY QUESTION. --Whether a person received personal injuries in an accident within the meaning of this section is a matter for determination by the jury. State v. Chavis, 9 N.C. App. 430, 176 S.E.2d 388 (1970).

BURDEN OF PROOF ON STATE. --The burden is on the State to satisfy beyond a reasonable doubt that defendant violated every element of a crime charged under this section. State v. Chavis, 9 N.C. App. 430, 176 S.E.2d 388 (1970).

The State has the burden of presenting sufficient evidence on each and every element of the offense of hit and run with personal injury to warrant submitting its case to the jury. State v. Acklin, 71 N.C. App. 261, 321 S.E.2d 532 (1984).

EVIDENCE HELD ADMISSIBLE. --No plain error existed in a trial court admitting evidence of defendant's empty prescription pill bottle, testimony by an officer identifying the pills from the label, and testimony by a pharmacist about the interaction between the pills and alcohol, as the evidence was relevant to show that defendant, who had been drinking, was driving while impaired at the time of an auto accident. State v. Edwards, 170 N.C. App. 381, 612 S.E.2d 394 (2005).

DEFENDANT WAS ENTITLED TO HAVE JUDGE INSTRUCT THE JURY THAT THE BURDEN WAS ON THE STATE to establish beyond a reasonable doubt that defendant knowingly or intentionally failed to render reasonable assistance to his injured passenger, including carrying him to a physician or surgeon for medical or surgical treatment if it was apparent that such treatment was necessary. State v. Coggin, 263 N.C. 457, 139 S.E.2d 701 (1965).

INSTRUCTION UPHELD. --In a prosecution for "hit-and-run driving," an instruction that defendant was charged with violation of one of the motor vehicle statutes designed for the protection of life and property could not be held error, as the statement was not related to any fact in issue or any evidence introduced in the case and contained no inference as to the guilt or innocence of defendant, where it further appeared that the court correctly charged upon the

presumption of innocence and the burden of proof. State v. King, 219 N.C. 667, 14 S.E.2d 803 (1941).

FOR CASE HOLDING THAT PROOF OF FAILURE TO STOP AUTOMOBILE AT SCENE OF ACCIDENT WAS WHOLLY LACKING, see State v. Wall, 243 N.C. 238, 90 S.E.2d 383 (1955).

EVIDENCE HELD SUFFICIENT FOR JURY. --Evidence which tended to show that the car of the prosecuting witness was struck by a car which was traveling at the time of the accident with its left wheels over the centerline of the highway, that an occupant in the car of the prosecuting witness was injured, and that the car which collided with her car failed to stop after the collision, in violation of this section, along with circumstantial evidence, including marks on the highway leading uninterruptedly from the point of collision to a car parked at defendant's place of business which defendant admitted to be his, the condition of defendant's car, a hub cap and other automobile parts found at the scene of the collision which were missing from defendant's car, and other circumstances tending to show efforts on the part of defendant to conceal the identity of his car as the one involved in the collision, together with testimony by defendant that no one else had driven his car on the evening in question, was held sufficient to have been submitted to the jury on the question of defendant's guilt, and his motions for judgment as of nonsuit were held properly refused. State v. King, 219 N.C. 667, 14 S.E.2d 803 (1941).

For case holding evidence sufficient to take case to jury as to whether defendant failed to render reasonable assistance to injured persons as required by this section, see State v. Wall, 243 N.C. 238, 90 S.E.2d 383 (1955). *For case holding evidence sufficient to support charge* of failing to stop an automobile after an accident resulting in the death of a person, see State v. Massey, 271 N.C. 555, 157 S.E.2d 150 (1967).

HIT-AND-RUN PROSECUTION NOT BARRED BY ACQUITTAL OF INVOLUNTARY MANSLAUGHTER. --In a prosecution for hit-and-run driving, the trial court properly refused to submit an issue of former acquittal based upon a prior prosecution for involuntary manslaughter arising out of the same collision, since the offenses are different, both in law and in fact, and therefore the plea of former jeopardy was inapposite as a matter of law. State v. Williams, 229 N.C. 415, 50 S.E.2d 4 (1948).

GUEST PASSENGER NOT NECESSARILY GUILTY AS AIDER AND ABETTOR. --Where the owner and driver of an automobile fails to stop and give his name, address and license number after an accident resulting in injury to a person, in violation of this section, an occupant of the car, merely because he is a guest passenger in the car driven by the owner, is not guilty as an aider and abettor. State v. Dutch, 246 N.C. 438, 98 S.E.2d 475 (1957).

EVIDENCE OF AIDING DRIVER IN AVOIDING ARREST HELD TO SUPPORT CHARGE AS ACCESSORY AFTER THE FACT. --In a prosecution of defendant for being an accessory after the fact to the willful failure immediately to stop a motor vehicle at the scene of an accident and collision resulting in injury or death, evidence was sufficient to be submitted to the jury where it tended to show that a third person, while driving an automobile owned by defendant, struck, injured and killed a named person; that the driver knew he had struck a person but did not stop at the scene of the accident; and that upon learning that the driver had struck a person and had not stopped, defendant, who was not in the car nor present at the scene of the accident, assisted the driver in avoiding apprehension, arrest and punishment for such offense. State v. Fearing, 50 N.C. App. 475, 274 S.E.2d 356, aff'd in part and rev'd in part on other grounds, 304 N.C. 499, 284 S.E.2d 479 (1981). See also, State v. Fearing, 304 N.C. 471, 284 S.E.2d 487 (1981).

EVIDENCE OF PRIOR CONVICTIONS FOR DRIVING UNDER THE INFLUENCE CAN PROPERLY BE CONSIDERED AS AN AGGRAVATING FACTOR in sentencing a defendant for hit and run personal injury, impairment not being an element of the offense. State v. Ragland, 80 N.C. App. 496, 342 S.E.2d 532 (1986).

EVIDENCE HELD SUFFICIENT FOR CONVICTION. --Evidence that defendant's truck had front end damage and defendant stated that he did not stop because he did not think he damaged the other vehicle supported defendant's conviction for failure to stop immediately after an accident involving property damage. State v. Braswell, 222 N.C. App. 176, 729 S.E.2d 697 (2012).

APPLIED in State v. Smith, 238 N.C. 82, 76 S.E.2d 363 (1953); State v. Nall, 239 N.C. 60, 79 S.E.2d 354 (1953); State v. Hollingsworth, 263 N.C. 158, 139 S.E.2d 235 (1964); State v. Harrelson, 265 N.C. 589, 144 S.E.2d 650 (1965); State v. Mohrmann, 265 N.C. 594, 144 S.E.2d 645 (1965); State v. Moses, 272 N.C. 509, 158 S.E.2d 617 (1968); State v. Markham, 5 N.C. App. 391, 168 S.E.2d 49 (1969); State v. Alston, 6 N.C. App. 200, 169 S.E.2d 520 (1969); State v. Moore, 19 N.C. App. 742, 200 S.E.2d 200 (1973); State v. Rimmer, 25 N.C. App. 637, 214 S.E.2d 225 (1975); State v. Cobbins, 66 N.C. App. 616, 311 S.E.2d 653 (1984); State v. Carrington, 74 N.C. App. 40, 327 S.E.2d 594 (1985); State v. Mobley, 86 N.C. App. 528, 358 S.E.2d 689 (1987); Hutton v. Logan, 152 N.C. App. 94, 566 S.E.2d 782 (2002).

CITED in State v. Newton, 207 N.C. 323, 177 S.E. 184 (1934); State v. Midgett, 214 N.C. 107, 198 S.E. 613 (1938); Leary v. Norfolk S. Bus Corp., 220 N.C. 745, 18 S.E.2d 426 (1942); State v. Collins, 247 N.C. 248, 100 S.E.2d 492 (1957); Punch v. Landis, 258 N.C. 114, 128 S.E.2d 224 (1962); State v. Tise, 39 N.C. App. 495, 250 S.E.2d 674 (1979); State v. Fearing, 304 N.C. 471, 284 S.E.2d 479 (1981); State v. Duvall, 304 N.C. 557, 284 S.E.2d 495 (1981); State v. Duvall, 50 N.C. App. 684, 275 S.E.2d 842 (1981); State v. Crabb, 55 N.C. App. 172, 284 S.E.2d 690 (1981); State v. Simpson, 61 N.C. App. 151, 300 S.E.2d 412 (1983); State v. Green, 77 N.C. App. 429, 335 S.E.2d 176 (1985); State v. Brown, 87 N.C. App. 13, 359 S.E.2d 265 (1987); State v. Brunson, 96 N.C. App. 347, 385 S.E.2d 542 (1989); State v. Brunson, 327 N.C. 244, 393 S.E.2d 860

(1990); State v. Davis, 208 N.C. App. 26, 702 S.E.2d 507 (2010); State v. Braswell, 222 N.C. App. 176, 729 S.E.2d 697 (2012); Prouse v. Bituminous Cas. Corp., 222 N.C. App. 111, 730 S.E.2d 239 (2012).

II. WARRANTS AND INDICTMENTS.

ALLEGATIONS OF FAILURE TO GIVE INFORMATION ONLY RELEVANT WHERE DEFENDANT STOPPED AT SCENE. --Allegations in warrant that defendant failed to give his name, address, operator's license number and the registration number of his vehicle would become relevant only if there was some evidence that he immediately stopped at the scene. State v. Lucas, 58 N.C. App. 141, 292 S.E.2d 747, cert. denied, 306 N.C. 390, 293 S.E.2d 593 (1982). *WARRANT HELD INSUFFICIENT. --Warrant was insufficient to charge the offense* of leaving the scene of an accident where it did not charge defendant with operating the motor vehicle involved in the accident and did not charge that he failed to give his name, address and driver's license number before leaving the scene of the accident. State v. Wiley, 20 N.C. App. 732, 203 S.E.2d 95 (1974).

For additional case holding warrant insufficient, see State v. Morris, 235 N.C. 393, 70 S.E.2d 23 (1952).

FAILURE OF INDICTMENT TO DESIGNATE STREET OR HIGHWAY ON WHICH COLLISION OCCURRED IS NOT FATAL. State v. Smith, 264 N.C. 575, 142 S.E.2d 149 (1965).

NOR IS FAILURE OF WARRANT TO SET OUT DESCRIPTION OR NAME OF OWNER OF PROPERTY DAMAGED. --In a prosecution under this section, charging defendant with failing to stop his automobile after an accident resulting in property damage, the fact that the warrant failed to set out any description of the property damaged other than the word "automobile" and failed to state the name of the owner was not fatal. State v. Crutchfield, 5 N.C. App. 586, 169 S.E.2d 43 (1969).

PROOF THAT ALL VICTIMS WERE KILLED AS ALLEGED HELD UNNECESSARY. --If the State satisfied the jury beyond a reasonable doubt that defendant was the driver of an automobile involved in an accident resulting in injuries to the six named persons in the indictment, and did unlawfully, willfully and feloniously fail to stop such automobile at the scene of the accident, it would be sufficient to justify conviction of the defendant on the first count in the indictment; it would not be necessary for the State to prove that all of the six named persons were killed, as alleged in the indictment. State v. Wilson, 264 N.C. 373, 141 S.E.2d 801 (1965).

WARRANT AS CURE FOR DEFECTIVE INDICTMENT IN CASE TRANSFERRED FOR JURY TRIAL. --Where a prosecution for violating this section, a misdemeanor in the exclusive jurisdiction of a municipal-county court, was transferred to the superior court upon defendant's demand for a jury trial, the jurisdiction of the superior court was limited to the charge in the warrant; therefore, the warrant constituted an essential part of the record, so that any failure of the indictment to identify the property damaged and the owner thereof was cured when the

Chapter 20

warrant supplied this information, thus affording defendant protection against another prosecution for the same offense. State v. Smith, 264 N.C. 575, 142 S.E.2d 149 (1965).

CROSS REFERENCES. --

As to immunity from liability of any person rendering first aid or emergency health care treatment to an unconscious, ill or injured person in certain circumstances, see G.S. 90-21.14.

LEGAL PERIODICALS. --

As to the effect of the 1939 amendment, see 17 N.C.L. Rev. 349 (1939).

For brief comment on the 1953 amendments, see 31 N.C.L. Rev. 419 (1953).

For note on North Carolina's "Good Samaritan" statute, see 44 N.C.L. Rev. 508 (1966).

For note on duty of tort-feasor and of innocent participant to render aid to accident victim, see 6 Wake Forest Intra. L. Rev. 537 (1970).

For survey of 1980 criminal law, see 59 N.C.L. Rev. 1123 (1981).

For survey of 1981 criminal law, see 60 N.C.L. Rev. 1289 (1982).

For article, "Senate Bill 33 Grants Protection to Emergency Room Providers.. and Just About Everyone Else, Too," see 91 N.C.L. Rev. 720 (2013).

For article, "When Cars Crash: The Automobile's Tort Law Legacy," see 53 Wake Forest L. Rev. 293 (2018).

§ 20-166.1. Reports and investigations required in event of accident

(a) **Notice of Accident.** -- The driver of a vehicle involved in a reportable accident must immediately, by the quickest means of communication, notify the appropriate law enforcement agency of the accident. If the accident occurred in a city or town, the appropriate agency is the police department of the city or town. If the accident occurred outside a city or town, the appropriate agency is the State Highway Patrol or the sheriff's office or other qualified rural police of the county where the accident occurred.

(b) **Insurance Verification.** -- When requested to do so by the Division, the driver of a vehicle involved in a reportable accident must furnish proof of financial responsibility.

(c) **Parked Vehicle.** -- The driver of a motor vehicle that collides with another motor vehicle left parked or unattended on a highway of this State must report the collision to the owner of the parked or unattended motor vehicle. This requirement applies to an accident that is not a reportable accident as well as to one that is a reportable accident. The report may be made orally or in writing, must be made within 48 hours of the accident, and must include the following:

    (1) The time, date, and place of the accident.

    (2) The driver's name, address, and drivers license number.

    (3) The registration plate number of the vehicle being operated by the driver at the time of the accident.

If the driver makes a written report to the owner of the parked or unattended vehicle and the report is not given to the owner at the scene of the accident, the report must be sent to the owner by certified mail, return receipt requested, and a copy of the report must be sent to the Division.

(d) Repealed by Session Laws 1995, c. 191, s. 2.

(e) **Investigation by Officer.** -- The appropriate law enforcement agency must investigate a reportable accident. A law-enforcement officer who investigates a reportable accident, whether at the scene of the accident or by subsequent investigations and interviews, must make a written report of the accident within 24 hours of the accident and must forward it as required by this subsection. The report must contain information on financial responsibility for the vehicle driven by the person whom the officer identified as at fault for the accident.

If the officer writing the report is a member of the State Highway Patrol, the officer must forward the report to the Division. If the officer is not a member of the State Highway Patrol, the officer must forward the report to the local law enforcement agency for the area where the accident occurred. A local law enforcement agency that receives an accident report must forward it to the Division within 10 days after receiving the report. Upon request of the driver of the motor vehicle involved in the accident or the insurance agent or company identified by the driver under subsection (b) of this section, and notwithstanding any provision of Chapter 132 of the General Statutes to the contrary, the officer writing the report may forward an uncertified copy of the report to the insurance agent or company identified by the driver under subsection (b) of this section if evidence satisfactory to the officer is provided showing a certified copy of the report has been requested from the Division and the applicable fee set in G.S. 20-42 has been paid. Nothing in this section shall prohibit a law enforcement agency from providing to the public accident reports or portions of accident reports that are public records.

When a person injured in a reportable accident dies as a result of the accident within 12 months after the accident and the death was not reported in the original report, the law enforcement officer investigating the accident must file a supplemental report that includes the death.

(f) **Medical Personnel.** -- A county medical examiner must report to the Division the death of any person in a reportable accident and the circumstances of the accident. The medical examiner must file the report within five days after the death. A hospital must notify the medical examiner of the county in which the accident occurred of the death within the hospital of any person who dies as a result of injuries apparently sustained in a reportable accident.

(g) Repealed by Session Laws 1987, c. 49.

(h) **Forms.** -- The Division shall provide forms or procedures for submitting crash data to persons required to make reports under this section and the reports shall be made in a format approved by the Commissioner. The following information shall be included about a reportable crash:

(1) The cause of the crash.

(2) The conditions existing at the time of the crash.

(3) The persons and vehicles involved, except that the name and address of a minor child involved in a school bus crash who is a passenger on a school bus may only be disclosed to (i) the local board of education, (ii) the State Board of Education, (iii) the parent or guardian of the child, (iv) an insurance company investigating a claim arising out of the crash, (v) an attorney representing a person involved in the crash, and (vi) law enforcement officials investigating the crash. As used in this subdivision, school bus also includes a school activity bus as defined by G.S. 20-4.01(27).

(4) Whether the vehicle has been seized and is subject to forfeiture under G.S. 20-28.2.

(i) **Effect of Report.** -- A report of an accident made under this section by a person who is not a law enforcement officer is without prejudice, is for the use of the Division, and shall not be used in any manner as evidence, or for any other purpose in any trial, civil or criminal, arising out of the accident. Any other report of an accident made under this section may be used in any manner as evidence, or for any other purpose, in any trial, civil or criminal, as permitted under the rules of evidence. At the demand of a court, the Division must give the court a properly executed certificate stating that a particular accident report has or has not been filed with the Division solely to prove a compliance with this section.

The reports made by persons who are not law enforcement officers or medical examiners are not public records. The reports made by law enforcement officers and medical examiners are public records and are open to inspection by the general public at all reasonable times. The Division must give a certified copy of one of these reports to a member of the general public who requests a copy and pays the fee set in G.S. 20-42.

(j) **Statistics.** -- The Division may periodically publish statistical information on motor vehicle accidents based on information in accident reports. The Division may conduct detailed research to determine more fully the cause and control of accidents and may conduct experimental field tests within areas of the State from time to time to prove the practicability of various ideas advanced in traffic control and accident prevention.

(k) **Punishment.** -- A violation of any provision of this section is a misdemeanor of the Class set in G.S. 20-176.

History.

1953, c. 1340, s. 2; 1955, c. 913, s. 9; 1963, c. 1249; 1965, c. 577; 1971, c. 55; c. 763, s. 1; c. 958, ss. 2, 3; 1973, c. 1133, ss. 1, 2; c. 1330, s. 29; 1975, c. 307; c. 716, s. 5; 1979, c. 667, s. 33; 1981, c. 690, s. 14; 1983, c. 229, ss. 1, 2; 1985, c. 764, s. 33; 1985 (Reg. Sess., 1986), c. 852, s. 17; 1987, c. 49; 1993, c. 539, ss. 376, 377; 1994, Ex. Sess., c. 24, s. 14(c);1995, c. 191, s. 2;1998-182, s. 12.1;1999-452, s. 19;2012-147, s. 1;2016-90, s. 13.8

EDITOR'S NOTE. --
Session Laws 2016-94, s. 35.25(a) -(d), provides: "(a) Establishment. -- The Division of Motor Vehicles shall, through an open request for proposal (RFP) process, seek to procure a contract with a private vendor for the statewide maintenance of the Crash Reporting Program. The Crash Reporting Program shall include at least all of the following components:

"(1) A comprehensive data repository for collision data.

"(2) A document repository for all collision reports in the State.

"(3) The capability to process paper reports, including scanning, data entry, validation of data against business edits, quality control application for reviewing reports, the ability to return or reject reports, and the ability to reprocess corrected reports.

"(4) The creation of an electronic submission application that incorporates all State validation rules to ensure that submitted reports are complete, accurate, and error-free.

"(5) A database capable of sharing statewide collision data with State and federal traffic safety partners, State law enforcement agencies, and the public.

"(6) A Web portal capability allowing authorized users to perform search functions and data extraction, obtain statistical traffic safety reports, map collision result sets, review configurable collision data dashboards, and perform data analysis against statewide collision data.

"(7) Compatibility with all data file formats and submission requirements for State and federal entities that require access to State collision data.

"(8) Capability to leverage predictive analytics to optimize resource allocation in order to improve traffic safety.

"(b) Vendor and Contract Requirements. -- By October 31, 2016, the Division shall issue an RFP in accordance with subsection (a) of this section. After review of the submitted proposals, the Department shall enter into a contract with the lowest responsible vendor

Chapter 20

who provides evidence satisfactory to the Division of a demonstrated history of providing similar statewide services.

"(c) Reports. -- The Division shall provide the following reports:

"(1) By April 30, 2017, a report to the Office of State Budget and Management and chairs of the House of Representatives Committee on Transportation Appropriations and the Senate Appropriations Committee on Department of Transportation on (i) the completion of the RFP process, including the name and qualifications of the firm awarded the contract; (ii) progress on the transition of the maintenance of the Program; and (iii) any other findings of interest determined by the Division.

"(2) By April 30, 2018, a report to the Office of State Budget and Management and chairs of the House of Representatives Committee on Transportation Appropriations and the Senate Appropriations Committee on Department of Transportation on (i) the number of accident reports purchased through the e-commerce site; (ii) the revenue generated to the Division through the contract with the vendor; and (iii) any savings realized by the Division from private vendor maintenance of the Program.

"(d) Use of Funds. -- Notwithstanding any provision of Section 7.14 of S.L. 2014-100 to the contrary, the Department of Transportation may use funds allocated in Section 7.14 of S.L. 2014-100 to the project titled 'Division of Motor Vehicles Channel Strategy' to cover costs associated with other Division of Motor Vehicles' modernization projects, including planning and design activities associated with (i) the Crash Reporting Program established under this section and (ii) the Division of Motor Vehicles' legacy systems."

Session Laws 2016-94, s. 1.2, provides: "This act shall be known as the 'Current Operations and Capital Improvements Appropriations Act of 2016.'"

Session Laws 2016-94, s. 39.4, provides: "Except for statutory changes or other provisions that clearly indicate an intention to have effects beyond the 2016-2017 fiscal year, the textual provisions of this act apply only to funds appropriated for, and activities occurring during, the 2016-2017 fiscal year."

Session Laws 2016-94, s. 39.7, is a severability clause.

EFFECT OF AMENDMENTS. --
Session Laws 2012-147, s. 1, effective October 1, 2012, rewrote subdivision (h)(3).

Session Laws 2016-90, s. 13.8, effective July 11, 2016, in subsection (e), added the fourth and fifth sentences in the second paragraph.

DUTIES IMPOSED ON DRIVER AND NOT OWNER. --The duties imposed by this section are duties which the law imposes upon the driver, not upon the owner. Branch v. Dempsey, 265 N.C. 733, 145 S.E.2d 395 (1965).

WHAT IS REQUIRED OF DRIVER BY THIS SECTION. --This section requires the driver of any vehicle involved in a collision resulting in the injury or death of any person to give notice of the collision to police officers and within 24 hours to make a written report to the Department (now Division) of Motor Vehicles upon a form supplied by it. Branch v. Dempsey, 265 N.C. 733, 145 S.E.2d 395 (1965).

INFORMATION REQUIRED FROM OPERATOR. --The operator of a motor vehicle was required by former G.S. 20-279.4 to inform the Department (now Division), when he notified it of the accident, whether he carried liability insurance or was exempt from the statutory provision. Robinson v. United States Cas. Co., 260 N.C. 284, 132 S.E.2d 629 (1963).

Defendant was properly convicted of giving false information for a motor vehicle crash report in violation of G.S. 20-279.31(b) when defendant falsely stated that defendant drove a vehicle involved in a crash, because, inter alia, while G.S. 20-166.1(h) did not list "driver's identity" with the information that "shall be included," the remaining portions of the statute preceding and following that section imposed an explicit duty on drivers to provide the drivers' name, address, and other information in the event of a reportable accident, G.S. 20-166(b), (c1), G.S. 20-166.1(a) -- (c), so it could be inferred that the term "persons and vehicles involved" necessarily included the identity of the driver. State v. Hernandez, 188 N.C. App. 193, 655 S.E.2d 426 (2008).

NO STATEMENT TO OFFICER REQUIRED. --This section contains no provision requiring a driver involved in a collision which must be reported to make any statement to the officer. Branch v. Dempsey, 265 N.C. 733, 145 S.E.2d 395 (1965).

DUTIES IMPOSED BY SUBSECTION (E). --Subsection (e) of this section makes it the duty of the State Highway Patrol to investigate all collisions required under this section to be reported to it, and requires the investigating officer to make his report in writing to the Department (now Division) of Motor Vehicles, which report is open to inspection by the public. Branch v. Dempsey, 265 N.C. 733, 145 S.E.2d 395 (1965).

RIGHT OF INJURED PARTY NOT IMPAIRED BY INSURED'S FAILURE TO NOTIFY INSURER OR REPORT ACCIDENT. --The right of an injured party, after recovery of unsatisfied judgment against insured, to recover against insurer in an assigned risk liability policy could not be defeated by the failure of insured to notify insurer of the accident or failure of insured to file an accident report with the Department (now Division) of Motor Vehicles. Lane v. Iowa Mut. Ins. Co., 258 N.C. 318, 128 S.E.2d 398 (1962).

APPLIED in Lane v. Iowa Mut. Ins. Co., 258 N.C. 318, 128 S.E.2d 398 (1962); Marks v. Thompson, 282 N.C. 174, 192 S.E.2d 311 (1972); Stalls v. Penny, 62 N.C. App. 511, 302 S.E.2d 912 (1983); State v. Carrington, 74 N.C. App. 40, 327 S.E.2d 594 (1985).

CITED in Robinson v. United States Cas. Co., 260 N.C. 284, 132 S.E.2d 629 (1963); Carter v. Scheidt, 261 N.C. 702, 136 S.E.2d 105 (1964); Forrester v. Garrett, 280 N.C. 117, 184 S.E.2d 858 (1971); State v. Francum, 39 N.C. App. 429, 250 S.E.2d 705 (1979); State v. Duvall, 50 N.C. App. 684, 275 S.E.2d 842 (1981); State v.

Adams, 88 N.C. App. 139, 362 S.E.2d 789 (1987); State v. Smathers, 232 N.C. App. 120, 753 S.E.2d 380 (2014), review denied, 755 S.E.2d 616, 2014 N.C. LEXIS 193 (2014).

LEGAL PERIODICALS. --

For brief comment on this section, see 31 N.C.L. Rev. 419 (1953).

For note on the State's inability to suspend the driver's license of a bankrupt who fails to satisfy an accident judgment debt, see 50 N.C.L. Rev. 350 (1972).

For comment on release of medical records by North Carolina hospitals, see 7 N.C. Cent. L.J. 299 (1976).

OPINIONS OF THE ATTORNEY GENERAL

CONFIDENTIALITY PROVISIONS OF G.S. 7A-675 [SEE NOW G.S. 7B-2901] DO NOT PROHIBIT IDENTIFICATION IN COLLISION REPORT filed pursuant to subsection (e) of person under 18 years involved in collision. See opinion of Attorney General to Mr. Maurice A. Cawn, Police Attorney, City of Greensboro, 58 N.C.A.G. 33 (May 17, 1988).

RELEASE OF DEPARTMENT OF MOTOR VEHICLE RECORDS. --The Department of Motor Vehicles is required by the Drivers Privacy Protection Act, 18 U.S.C. § 2721 et seq., to redact "personal information" and "highly restricted personal information" from documents, such as accident reports, provided to the public. Otherwise, the requirements of the Public Records Act, G.S. 132-1 et seq., should be complied with by DMV and local law enforcement agencies. Motor vehicle registration information provided by DMV to local taxing authorities should also be provided upon request in accordance with the Public Records Act. See opinion of Attorney General to Mr. George Tatum, Commissioner, North Carolina Division of Motor Vehicles, 2005 N.C.A.G. 1 (02/09/05).

§ 20-166.2. Duty of passenger to remain at the scene of an accident

(a) The passenger of any vehicle who knows or reasonably should know that the vehicle in which he or she is a passenger is involved in an accident or collision shall not willfully leave the scene of the accident by acting as the driver of a vehicle involved in the accident until a law enforcement officer completes the investigation of the accident or collision or authorizes the passenger to leave, unless remaining at the scene places the passenger or others at significant risk of injury.

Prior to the completion of the investigation of the accident by a law enforcement officer, or the consent of the officer to leave, the passenger may not facilitate, allow, or agree to the removal of the vehicle from the scene, for any purpose other than to call for a law enforcement officer, to call for medical assistance or medical treatment as set forth in subsection (b) of this section, or to remove oneself or others from a significant risk of injury. If the passenger does leave the scene of an accident by driving a vehicle involved in

the accident for a reason permitted by this subsection, the passenger must return with the vehicle to the accident scene within a reasonable period of time, unless otherwise instructed by a law enforcement officer. A willful violation of this subsection is a Class H felony if the accident or collision is described in G.S. 20-166(a). A willful violation of this subsection is a Class 1 misdemeanor if the accident or collision is a reportable accident described in G.S. 20-166(c).

(b) In addition to complying with the requirement of subsection (a) of this section, the passenger shall give the passenger's name, address, drivers license number, and the license plate number of the vehicle in which the passenger was riding, if possible, to the person struck or the driver or occupants of any vehicle collided with, provided that the person or persons are physically and mentally capable of receiving the information, and shall render to any person injured in the accident or collision reasonable assistance, including the calling for medical assistance if it is apparent that such assistance is necessary or is requested by the injured person. A violation of this subsection is a Class 1 misdemeanor.

History.

2005-460, s. 2

EDITOR'S NOTE. --

Session Laws 2005-460, s. 3, made this section effective December 1, 2005, and applicable to offenses committed on or after that date.

§ 20-166.3. Limit storage duration for vehicle damaged as a result of a collision

(a) **Limited Duration of Storage. --** A motor vehicle that is towed and stored at the direction of a law enforcement agency following a collision may be held for evidence for not more than 20 days without a court order. Absent a court order, the vehicle must be released to the vehicle owner, insurer, or lien holder upon payment of the towing and storage fees.

(b) **Application. --** This section shall not apply to a motor vehicle (i) seized as a result of a violation of law or (ii) abandoned by the owner.

History.

2015-188, s. 1

EDITOR'S NOTE. --

Session Laws 2015-188, s. 2 provides: "This act becomes effective August 1, 2015, and applies to motor vehicles impounded on or after that date."

§ 20-167. Vehicles transporting explosives

Any person operating any vehicle transporting any explosive as a cargo or part of a cargo upon a highway shall at all times comply with the rules and regulations of the United States

Department of Transportation as adopted by the Division of Motor Vehicles.

History.

1937, c. 407, s. 129; 1985, c. 454, s. 7

CITED in Latham v. Elizabeth City Orange Crush Bottling Co., 213 N.C. 158, 195 S.E. 372 (1938).

§ 20-167.1. Transportation of spent nuclear fuel

(a) No person, firm or corporation shall transport upon the highways of this State any spent nuclear fuel unless such person, firm, or corporation notifies the State Highway Patrol in advance of transporting the spent nuclear fuel.

(b) The provisions of this section shall apply whether or not the fuel is for delivery in North Carolina and whether or not the shipment originated in North Carolina.

(c) The Radiation Protection Commission is authorized to adopt, promulgate, amend, and repeal rules and regulations necessary to implement the provisions of this section.

(d) Any person, firm or corporation violating any provision of this section is guilty of a Class 3 misdemeanor and shall be punished only by a fine of not less than five hundred dollars ($ 500.00), and each unauthorized shipment shall constitute a separate offense.

History.

1977, c. 839, s. 1; 1985, c. 764, s. 33.1; 1985 (Reg. Sess., 1986), c. 852, s. 17; 1993, c. 539, s. 378;1994, Ex. Sess., c. 24, s. 14(c)

§ 20-168. Drivers of State, county, and city vehicles subject to the provisions of this Article

(a) Subject to the exceptions in subsection (b), the provisions of this Article applicable to the drivers of vehicles upon the highways shall apply to the drivers of all vehicles owned or operated by the State or any political subdivision thereof.

(b) While actually engaged in maintenance or construction work on the highways, but not while traveling to or from such work, drivers of vehicles owned or operated by the State or any political subdivision thereof are exempt from all provisions of this Article except:

(1) G.S. 20-138.1. Impaired driving.

(2) Repealed by Session Laws 1983, c. 435, s. 28.

(3) G.S. 20-139.1. Procedures governing chemical analyses; admissibility; evidentiary provisions; controlled-drinking programs.

(4) G.S. 20-140. Reckless driving.

(5) Repealed by Session Laws 1983, c. 435, s. 38.

(6) G.S. 20-141. Speed restrictions.

(7) G.S. 20-141.3. Unlawful racing on streets and highways.

(8) G.S. 20-141.4. Felony and misdemeanor death by vehicle.

History.

1937, c. 407, s. 130; 1973, c. 1330, s. 30; 1981, c. 412, s. 4; c. 747, s. 66; 1983, c. 435, s. 28

APPLIED in Northwestern Distribs., Inc. v. North Carolina Dep't of Transp., 41 N.C. App. 548, 255 S.E.2d 203 (1979); Pinkston v. Connor, 63 N.C. App. 628, 306 S.E.2d 132 (1983).

CITED in Babbs v. Eury, 206 N.C. 679, 175 S.E. 100 (1934).

§ 20-169. Powers of local authorities

Local authorities, except as expressly authorized by G.S. 20-141 and 20-158, shall have no power or authority to alter any speed limitations declared in this Article or to enact or enforce any rules or regulations contrary to the provisions of this Article, except that local authorities shall have power to provide by ordinances for any of the following:

(1) Regulating traffic by means of traffic or semaphores or other signaling devices on any portion of the highway where traffic is heavy or continuous.

(2) Prohibiting other than one-way traffic upon certain highways.

(3) Regulating the use of the highways by processions or assemblages.

(4) Regulating the speed of vehicles on highways in public parks.

(5) Authorizing law enforcement or fire department vehicles, ambulances, and rescue squad emergency service vehicles, equipped with a siren to preempt any traffic signals upon city streets within local authority boundaries or, with the approval of the Department of Transportation, on State highways within the boundaries of local authorities. The Department of Transportation shall respond to requests for approval within 60 days of receipt of a request.

Signs shall be erected giving notices of the special limits and regulations under subdivisions (1) through (4) of this section.

History.

1937, c. 407, s. 131; 1949, c. 947, s. 2; 1955, c. 384, s. 2; 1963, c. 559; 1973, c. 507, s. 5; 1979, c. 298, s. 2; 1991, c. 530, s. 5;1999-310, s. 1

LOCAL MODIFICATION. --City of Greensboro: 1953, c. 1075.

MUNICIPALITY CONFORMANCE WITH MUTCD. --Under the North Carolina General Statutes, municipalities are required to conform to the traffic control device standards promulgated in the Manual on Uniform Traffic Control Devices (MUTCD) only with respect to State highways. Talian v. City of Charlotte, 98 N.C. App. 281, 390 S.E.2d 737, aff'd, 327 N.C. 629, 398 S.E.2d 330 (1990).

THIS SECTION AUTHORIZES MUNICIPAL CORPORATIONS TO INSTALL AUTOMATIC TRAFFIC-CONTROL SIGNALS AND COMPEL THEIR OBSERVANCE by ordinance. Upchurch v. Hudson Funeral Home, 263 N.C. 560, 140 S.E.2d 17 (1965).

In consequence of this section, a town acted within the limits of its authority as a municipal corporation in installing automatic traffic-control signals and enacting an ordinance to compel their observance. Cox v. Hennis Freight Lines, 236 N.C. 72, 72 S.E.2d 25 (1952).

AMBULANCES MAY BE REQUIRED TO OBSERVE LIGHTS. --The provisions of this section are sufficiently broad to authorize the adoption of an ordinance requiring ambulances to observe traffic lights. Upchurch v. Hudson Funeral Home, 263 N.C. 560, 140 S.E.2d 17 (1965).

LEGAL RIGHTS DEPENDENT ON ORDINANCE. --When automatic traffic-control signals are installed pursuant to a municipal ordinance authorized by this section, the respective rights of motorists depend upon the provisions of the particular ordinance authorizing such installations. Cogdell v. Taylor, 264 N.C. 424, 142 S.E.2d 36 (1965).

ALLEGATION AND PROOF OF ORDINANCE. --Before legal rights may be predicated on an ordinance regulating traffic by means of automatic signal-control devices, such an ordinance must be alleged and established by proper evidence. Smith v. Buie, 243 N.C. 209, 90 S.E.2d 514 (1955).

VIOLATION OF ORDINANCE AS NEGLIGENCE PER SE. --Violation of a valid ordinance adopted pursuant to this section, requiring a motorist to stop in obedience to a red traffic-control signal, is negligence per se. Currin v. Williams, 248 N.C. 32, 102 S.E.2d 455 (1958).

FOR APPLICATION OF FORMER STATUTE PROHIBITING CONFLICTING ORDINANCES, see State v. Freshwater, 183 N.C. 762, 111 S.E. 161 (1922).

CITED in Stewart v. Yellow Cab Co., 225 N.C. 654, 36 S.E.2d 256 (1945); Rogers v. Rogers, 2 N.C. App. 668, 163 S.E.2d 645 (1968); Lonon v. Talbert, 103 N.C. App. 686, 407 S.E.2d 276 (1991); King v. Town of Chapel Hill, 367 N.C. 400, 758 S.E.2d 364 (2014).

OPINIONS OF THE ATTORNEY GENERAL

REDUCTION OF SPEED LIMITS ON STATE HIGHWAYS IN SCHOOL ZONES WITHIN MUNICIPALITIES. --G.S. 20-141.1 must be construed together with this section, G.S. 20-141, and other statutes, and when so construed, the provision for concurring ordinances in G.S. 20-141 when reducing speed limits on State highways in school zones within municipalities must be given effect and must be complied with. See opinion of the Attorney General to Mr. Ralph D. Karpinos, Town Attorney, Chapel Hill, N.C., 58 N.C.A.G. 17 (Feb. 26, 1988).

A municipal ordinance adopted pursuant to G.S. 20-141.1 reducing the speed in a school zone on a State Highway System street is not effective without a concurring ordinance by the Department of Transportation as provided for by G.S. 20-141(f). See opinion of the Attorney General to Mr. Ralph D. Karpinos, Town Attorney, Chapel Hill, N.C., 58 N.C.A.G. 17 (Feb. 26, 1988).

§ 20-170. This Article not to interfere with rights of owners of real property with reference thereto

Nothing in this Article shall be construed to prevent the owner of real property used by the public for purposes of vehicular travel by permission of the owner, and not as matter of right from prohibiting such use nor from requiring other or different or additional conditions than those specified in this Article or otherwise regulating such use as may seem best to such owner.

History.

1937, c. 407, s. 132

§ 20-171. Traffic laws apply to persons riding animals or driving animal-drawn vehicles

Every person riding an animal or driving any animal drawing a vehicle upon a highway shall be subject to the provisions of this Article applicable to the driver of a vehicle, except those provisions of the Article which by their nature can have no application.

History.

1939, c. 275

THE LEGISLATURE INTENDED the provisions of the traffic laws of North Carolina applicable to the drivers of "vehicles" to apply to horseback riders irrespective of whether a horse is a vehicle. State v. Dellinger, 73 N.C. App. 685, 327 S.E.2d 609 (1985).

REQUIREMENT THAT A PERSON ENTERING A PUBLIC HIGHWAY FROM A PRIVATE ROAD OR DRIVE MUST YIELD THE RIGHT-OF-WAY to vehicles on the public highway applies to a person riding an animal as well as to a person driving a motor vehicle. Watson v. Stallings, 270 N.C. 187, 154 S.E.2d 308 (1967).

PART 10A.
OPERATION OF BICYCLES

§ 20-171.1. Definitions

As used in this Part, except where the context clearly requires otherwise, the words and expressions defined in this section shall be held to have the meanings here given to them:

Bicycle. -- A nonmotorized vehicle with two or three wheels tandem, a steering handle, one or two saddle seats, and pedals by which the vehicle is propelled, or an electric assisted bicycle, as defined in G.S. 20-4.01(7a).

History.
1977, c. 1123, s. 1; 2016-90, s. 13(c)
  EDITOR'S NOTE. --
  Session Laws 2015-45, ss. 1 -4, provides: "Section 1. Study. -- The Department of Transportation shall study the bicycle safety laws in this State. The study shall focus on what statutory revisions, if any, are needed to better ensure the safety of bicyclists and motorists. In doing so, the Department shall consider at least all of the following:

  "(1) How faster-moving vehicles may safely overtake bicycles on roadways where sight distance may be inhibited.

  "(2) Whether bicyclists on a roadway should be required to ride single file or allowed to ride two or more abreast.

  "(3) Whether bicyclists should be required to carry a form of identification.

  (4) Any other issues determined relevant by the Department.

  "Section 2. Working Group. --

  In conducting the study required by this act, the Department shall convene a working group of interested parties knowledgeable and interested in the bicycle safety laws of this State. The working group shall include all of the following:

  "(1) A law enforcement officer.

  "(2) A representative from the bicycling industry.

  "(3) A representative from the agricultural industry.

  "(4) A representative from the trucking industry.

  "(5) A representative from county government, who may be a county law enforcement officer.

  "(6) A representative from municipal government, who may be a municipal law enforcement officer.

  "(7) A representative from the University of North Carolina Highway Safety Research Center.

  "(8) A minimum of two staff representatives from the Department.

  "(9) Any other expert or stakeholder the Department or working group determines may assist the Department in completing the study required by this act.

  "The Department shall designate the members listed in subdivisions (1) through (8) of this section, and the working group shall subsequently select a chair and designate the remaining members of the working group authorized under subdivision (9) of this section. In designating additional members, the working group shall ensure that membership composition includes representation of different operator and geographical perspectives.

  "Section 3. Maximum Number of Working Group Members. --

  The total number of members of the working group convened under Section 2 of this act shall not exceed 12 members.

  "Section 4. Report and Recommendations. --

  The Department shall report its findings and recommendations, including any legislative proposals, to the Joint Legislative Transportation Oversight Committee on or before December 31, 2015."
Session Laws 2016-90, s. 13(j), made the amendment to this section by Session Laws 2016-90, s. 13(c), applicable to offenses committed on or after December 1, 2016.

  EFFECT OF AMENDMENTS. --
  Session Laws 2016-90, s. 13(c), effective December 1, 2016, added "propelled, or an electric assisted bicycle, as defined in G.S. 20-4.01(7a)" at the end of the second paragraph. See editor's note for applicability.

§ 20-171.2. Bicycle racing

  (a) Bicycle racing on the highways is prohibited except as authorized in this section.

  (b) Bicycle racing on a highway shall not be unlawful when a racing event has been approved by State or local authorities on any highway under their respective jurisdictions. Approval of bicycle highway racing events shall be granted only under conditions which assure reasonable safety for all race participants, spectators and other highway users, and which prevent unreasonable interference with traffic flow which would seriously inconvenience other highway users.

  (c) By agreement with the approving authority, participants in an approved bicycle highway racing event may be exempted from compliance with any traffic laws otherwise applicable thereto, provided that traffic control is adequate to assure the safety of all highway users.

History.
1977, c. 1123, s. 1

§§ 20-171.3 through 20-171.5

  Reserved for future codification purposes.

PART 10B.
CHILD BICYCLE SAFETY ACT

§ 20-171.6. Short title

  This Article shall be known and may be cited as the "Child Bicycle Safety Act."

History.
2001-268, s. 1

§ 20-171.7. Legislative findings and purpose

  (a) The General Assembly finds and declares that:

(1) Disability and death of children resulting from injuries sustained in bicycling accidents are a serious threat to the public health, welfare, and safety of the people of this State, and the prevention of that disability and death is a goal of all North Carolinians.

(2) Head injuries are the leading cause of disability and death from bicycling accidents.

(3) The risk of head injury from bicycling accidents is significantly reduced for bicyclists who wear proper protective bicycle helmets; yet helmets are worn by fewer than five percent (5%) of child bicyclists nationwide.

(4) The risk of head injury or of any other injury to a small child who is a passenger on a bicycle operated by another person would be significantly reduced if any child passenger sat in a separate restraining seat.

(b) The purpose of this Article is to reduce the incidence of disability and death resulting from injuries incurred in bicycling accidents by requiring that while riding on a bicycle on the public roads, public bicycle paths, and other public rights-of-way of this State, all bicycle operators and passengers under the age of 16 years wear approved protective bicycle helmets; that all bicycle passengers who weigh less than 40 pounds or are less than 40 inches in height be seated in separate restraining seats; and that no person who is unable to maintain an erect, seated position shall be a passenger in a bicycle restraining seat, and all other bicycle passengers shall be seated on saddle seats.

History.
2001-268, s. 1

§ 20-171.8. Definitions

As used in this Article, the following terms have the following meanings:

(1) "Bicycle" means a human-powered vehicle with two wheels in tandem designed to transport, by the action of pedaling, one or more persons seated on one or more saddle seats on its frame. This term also includes a human-powered vehicle, designed to transport by the action of pedaling which has more than two wheels where the vehicle is used on a public roadway, public bicycle path, or other public right-of-way, but does not include a tricycle.

(2) "Operator" means a person who travels on a bicycle seated on a saddle seat from which that person is intended to and can pedal the bicycle.

(3) "Other public right-of-way" means any right-of-way other than a public roadway or public bicycle path that is under the jurisdiction and control of this State or a local political subdivision of the State and is designed for use and used by vehicular and/or pedestrian traffic.

(4) "Passenger" means a person who travels on a bicycle in any manner except as an operator.

(5) "Protective bicycle helmet" means a piece of headgear that meets or exceeds the impact standards for protective bicycle helmets set by the American National Standards Institute (ANSI) or the Snell Memorial Foundation.

(6) "Public bicycle path" means a right-of-way under the jurisdiction and control of this State or a local political subdivision of the State for use primarily by bicycles and pedestrians.

(7) "Public roadway" means a right-of-way under the jurisdiction and control of this State or a local political subdivision of the State for use primarily by motor vehicles.

(8) "Restraining seat" means a seat separate from the saddle seat of the operator of the bicycle that is fastened securely to the frame of the bicycle and is adequately equipped to restrain the passenger in such seat and protect such passenger from the moving parts of the bicycle.

(9) "Tricycle" means a three-wheeled, human-powered vehicle designed for use as a toy by a single child under the age of six years, the seat of which is no more than two feet from ground level.

History.
2001-268, s. 1

§ 20-171.9. Requirements for helmet and restraining seat use

With regard to any bicycle used on a public roadway, public bicycle path, or other public right-of-way:

(a) It shall be unlawful for any parent or legal guardian of a person below the age of 16 to knowingly permit that person to operate or be a passenger on a bicycle unless at all times when the person is so engaged he or she wears a protective bicycle helmet of good fit fastened securely upon the head with the straps of the helmet.

(b) It shall be unlawful for any parent or legal guardian of a person below the age of 16 to knowingly permit that person to be a passenger on a bicycle unless all of the following conditions are met:

(1) The person is able to maintain an erect, seated position on the bicycle.

(2) Except as provided in subdivision (3) of this subsection, the person is

properly seated alone on a saddle seat (as on a tandem bicycle).

(3) With respect to any person who weighs less than 40 pounds, or is less than 40 inches in height, the person can be and is properly seated in and adequately secured to a restraining seat.

(c) No negligence or liability shall be assessed on or imputed to any party on account of a violation of subsection (a) or (b) of this section.

(d) Violation of this section shall be an infraction. Except as provided in subsection (e) of this section, any parent or guardian found responsible for violation of this section may be ordered to pay a civil fine of up to ten dollars ($ 10.00), inclusive of all penalty assessments and court costs.

(e) In the case of a first conviction of this section, the court may waive the fine upon receipt of satisfactory proof that the person responsible for the infraction has purchased or otherwise obtained, as appropriate, a protective bicycle helmet or a restraining seat, and uses and intends to use it whenever required under this section.

History.
2001-268, s. 1
    CROSS REFERENCES. --
For requirements that operators and passengers on motorcycles and mopeds wear safety helmets, see G.S. 20-140.4.

§§ 20-171.10 through 20-171.14

Reserved for future codification purposes.

PART 10C.
OPERATION OF ALL-TERRAIN VEHICLES

§ 20-171.15. Age restrictions

(a) It is unlawful for any parent or legal guardian of a person less than eight years of age to knowingly permit that person to operate an all-terrain vehicle.

(b) Repealed by Session Laws 2015-286, s. 3.13(a), effective October 22, 2015.

(c) It is unlawful for any parent or legal guardian of a person less than 16 years of age to knowingly permit that person to operate an all-terrain vehicle in violation of the Age Restriction Warning Label affixed by the manufacturer as required by the applicable American National Standards Institute/Specialty Vehicle Institute of America (ANSI/SVIA) design standard.

(d) It is unlawful for any parent or legal guardian of a person less than 16 years of age to knowingly permit that person to operate an all-terrain

vehicle unless the person is under the continuous visual supervision of a person 18 years of age or older while operating the all-terrain vehicle.

(e) Subsection (c) of this section does not apply to any parent or legal guardian of a person born on or before August 15, 1997, who permits that person to operate an all-terrain vehicle and who establishes proof that the parent or legal guardian owned the all-terrain vehicle prior to August 15, 2005.

History.
2005-282, s. 2;2015-286, s. 3.13(a)
    EDITOR'S NOTE. --
Session Laws 2005-282, s. 3, made this section effective December 1, 2005, and applicable to offenses committed on or after that date.
    EFFECT OF AMENDMENTS. --
Session Laws 2015-286, s. 3.13(a), effective October 22, 2015, deleted former subsection (b); rewrote subsection (c); and substituted "Subsection (c) of this section does not apply" for "Subsections (b) and (c) of this section do not apply" in subsection (e).

§ 20-171.16. Passengers

No operator of an all-terrain vehicle shall carry a passenger, except on those vehicles specifically designed by the manufacturer to carry passengers in addition to the operator.

History.
2005-282, s. 2

§ 20-171.17. Prohibited acts by sellers

No person shall knowingly sell or offer to sell an all-terrain vehicle:

(1) For use by a person under the age of eight years.

(2) In violation of the Age Restriction Warning Label affixed by the manufacturer as required by the applicable American National Standards Institute/Specialty Vehicle Institute of America (ANSI/SVIA) design standard for use by a person less than 16 years of age.

(3) Repealed by Session Laws 2015-286, s. 3.13(b), effective October 22, 2015.

History.
2005-282, s. 2;2015-286, s. 3.13(b)
    EFFECT OF AMENDMENTS. --
Session Laws 2015-286, s. 3.13(b), effective October 22, 2015, rewrote subdivision (2); and deleted former subdivision (3).

§ 20-171.18. Equipment requirements

Every all-terrain vehicle sold, offered for sale, or operated in this State shall meet the following equipment standards:

Chapter 20

(1) It shall be equipped with a brake system maintained in good operating condition.

(2) It shall be equipped with an effective muffler system maintained in good working condition.

(3) It shall be equipped with a United States Forest Service qualified spark arrester maintained in good working condition.

History.
2005-282, s. 2

§ 20-171.19. Prohibited acts by owners and operators

(a) No person shall operate an all-terrain vehicle on a public street or highway or public vehicular area when such operation is otherwise permitted by law, unless the person wears eye protection and a safety helmet meeting United States Department of Transportation standards for motorcycle helmets.

(a1) No person under 18 years of age shall operate an all-terrain vehicle off a public street or highway or public vehicular area unless the person wears eye protection and a safety helmet meeting United States Department of Transportation standards for motorcycle helmets.

(a2) Notwithstanding subsection (a1) of this section, a person who is under 18 years of age and employed by a supplier of retail electric service, while engaged in power line inspection, may operate an all-terrain vehicle while wearing both of the following:

(1) Head protection equipped with a chin strap that conforms to the standards applicable to suppliers of retail electric service adopted by the Occupational Safety and Health Division of the North Carolina Department of Labor.

(2) Eye protection that conforms to the standards applicable to suppliers of retail electric service adopted by the Occupational Safety and Health Division of the North Carolina Department of Labor.

(b) No owner shall authorize an all-terrain vehicle to be operated contrary to this Part.

(c) No person shall operate an all-terrain vehicle while under the influence of alcohol, any controlled substance, or a prescription or nonprescription drug that impairs vision or motor coordination.

(d) No person shall operate an all-terrain vehicle in a careless or reckless manner so as to endanger or cause injury or damage to any person or property.

(e) Except as otherwise permitted by law, no person shall operate an all-terrain vehicle on any public street, road, or highway except for purposes of crossing that street, road, or highway.

(f) Except as otherwise permitted by law, no person shall operate an all-terrain vehicle at anytime on an interstate or limited-access highway.

(g) No person shall operate an all-terrain vehicle during the hours of darkness, from one-half hour after sunset to one-half hour before sunrise and at anytime when visibility is reduced due to insufficient light or atmospheric conditions, without displaying a lighted headlamp and taillamp, unless the use of lights is prohibited by other applicable laws.

History.
2005-282, s. 2;2006-259, s. 10(a);2011-68, s. 1;2013-410, s. 4.2
EFFECT OF AMENDMENTS. --
Session Laws 2006-259, s. 10(a), effective December 1, 2006, and applicable to acts committed on or after that date, added subsection (a1).
Session Laws 2011-68, s. 1, effective October 1, 2011, and applicable to offenses committed on or after that date, inserted "on a public street or highway or public vehicular area" in subsection (a); added present subsection (a1); and redesignated former subsection (a1) as present subsection (a2), and therein, in the introductory paragraph, substituted "Notwithstanding subsection (a1) of this section, a person who is under 18 years of age and employed" for "Notwithstanding subsection (a) of this section, any person employed."
Session Laws 2013-410, s. 4.2, effective August 23, 2013, inserted "when such operation is otherwise permitted by law" in subsection (a).

§ 20-171.20. Safety training and certificate

Effective October 1, 2006, every all-terrain vehicle operator born on or after January 1, 1990, shall possess a safety certificate indicating successful completion of an all-terrain vehicle safety course sponsored or approved by the All-Terrain Vehicle Safety Institute or by another all-terrain vehicle safety course approved by the Commissioner of Insurance. The North Carolina Community College System is authorized to provide all-terrain vehicle safety training, approved by the Commissioner, to persons less than 18 years of age.

History.
2005-282, s. 2;2007-433, s. 4
EFFECT OF AMENDMENTS. --
Session Laws 2007-433, s. 4, effective October 1, 2007, inserted inserted "or by another all-terrain vehicle.. 18 years of age" at the end of the section.

§ 20-171.21. Penalties

Any person violating any of the provisions of this Part shall be responsible for an infraction and may be subject to a penalty of not more than two hundred dollars ($ 200.00).

History.

2005-282, s. 2;2008-187, s. 11

EFFECT OF AMENDMENTS. --

Session Laws 2008-187, s. 11, effective August 7, 2008, substituted "penalty" for "fine."

§ 20-171.22. Exceptions

(a) The provisions of this Part do not apply to any owner, operator, lessor, or renter of a farm or ranch, or that person's employees or immediate family or household members, when operating an all-terrain vehicle while engaged in farming operations.

(a1) Any person may operate an all-terrain vehicle or utility vehicle on a public street or highway while engaged in farming operations.

(b) The provisions of this Part do not apply to any person using an all-terrain vehicle for hunting or trapping purposes if the person is otherwise lawfully engaged in those activities.

(c) The provisions of G.S. 20-171.19(a1) do not apply to any person 16 years of age or older if the person is otherwise lawfully using the all-terrain vehicle on any ocean beach area where such vehicles are allowed by law. As used in this subsection, "ocean beach area" means the area adjacent to the ocean and ocean inlets that is subject to public trust rights. Natural indicators of the landward extent of the ocean beaches include, but are not limited to, the first line of stable, natural vegetation; the toe of the frontal dune; and the storm trash line.

History.

2005-282, s. 2;2008-91, s. 1;2011-68, s. 2;2015-263, s. 8

EFFECT OF AMENDMENTS. --

Session Laws 2008-91, s. 1, effective July 11, 2008, added subsection (c).

Session Laws 2011-68, s. 2, effective October 1, 2011, and applicable to offenses committed on or after that date, corrected the section reference in the first sentence of subsection (c).

Session Laws 2015-263, s. 8, effective September 30, 2015, added subsection (a1).

§ 20-171.23. Motorized all-terrain vehicles of law enforcement officers and fire, rescue, and emergency medical services permitted on certain highways

(a) Law enforcement officers acting in the course and scope of their duties may operate motorized all-terrain vehicles owned or leased by the agency, or under the direct control of the incident commander, on: (i) public highways where the speed limit is 35 miles per hour or less; and (ii) nonfully controlled access highways with higher speeds for the purpose of traveling from a speed zone to an adjacent speed zone where the speed limit is 35 miles per hour or less.

(b) Fire, rescue, and emergency medical services personnel acting in the course and scope of their duties may operate motorized all-terrain vehicles and owned or leased by fire, rescue, or emergency medical services departments, or under the direct control of the incident commander, on: (i) public highways where the speed limit is 35 miles per hour or less; and (ii) nonfully controlled access highways with higher speeds for the purpose of traveling from a speed zone to an adjacent speed zone where the speed limit is 35 miles per hour or less.

(c) This Part and all other State laws governing the operation of all-terrain vehicles apply to the operation of all-terrain vehicles authorized by this section.

(d) An all-terrain vehicle operated pursuant to this section shall be equipped with operable front and rear lights and a horn.

(e) A person operating an all-terrain vehicle pursuant to this section shall observe posted speed limits and shall not exceed the manufacturer's recommended speed for the vehicle.

(f) A person operating an all-terrain vehicle pursuant to this section shall carry an official identification card or badge.

(g) For purposes of this section, the term "motorized all-terrain vehicle" has the same meaning as in G.S. 14-159.3, except that the term also includes utility vehicles, as defined in this Chapter.

History.

2007-433, s. 1;2015-26, ss. 1, 2.1

EFFECT OF AMENDMENTS. --

Session Laws 2015-26, s. 1, effective May 21, 2015, deleted "as defined in G.S. 14-159.3(b)" following "vehicles" in the introductory language in subsections (a) and (b); and added subsection (g).

Session Laws 2015-26, s. 2.1, effective May 21, 2015, substituted "all-terrain" for "all terrain" throughout.

§ 20-171.24. Motorized all-terrain vehicle use by municipal and county employees permitted on certain highways

(a) Municipal and county employees may operate motorized all-terrain vehicles owned or leased by the agency on: (i) public highways where the speed limit is 35 miles per hour or less; and (ii) nonfully controlled access highways with higher speeds for the purpose of traveling from a speed zone to an adjacent speed zone where the speed limit is 35 miles per hour or less.

(b) This Part and all other State laws governing the operation of all-terrain vehicles apply to the operation of all-terrain vehicles authorized by this section.

(c) An all-terrain vehicle operated pursuant to this section shall be equipped with operable front and rear lights and a horn.

(d) A person operating an all-terrain vehicle pursuant to this section shall observe posted speed limits and shall not exceed the manufacturer's recommended speed for the vehicle.

(e) A person operating an all-terrain vehicle pursuant to this section shall carry an official identification card or badge.

(e1) For purposes of this section, the term "motorized all-terrain vehicle" has the same meaning as in G.S. 14-159.3, except that the term also includes utility vehicles, as defined in this Chapter.

(f) Repealed by Session Laws 2015-26, s. 2, effective May 21, 2015.

History.
2007-433, s. 2;2008-99, s. 1;2010-19, s. 1;2010-46, s. 1;2014-32, s. 1;2015-26, ss. 2, 2.1; 2017-102, s. 7

EFFECT OF AMENDMENTS. --
Session Laws 2008-99, s. 1, effective July 15, 2008, inserted "Lowell, Manteo" in subsection (f).

Session Laws 2010-19, s. 1, effective June 24, 2010, added "Hamlet" in subsection (f).

Session Laws 2010-46, s. 1, effective July 1, 2010, added "Williamston" in subsection (f).

Session Laws 2014-32, s. 1, effective June 26, 2014, substituted "Wrightsville Beach, and Yanceyville" for "and Wrightsville Beach" in subsection (f).

Session Laws 2015-26, s. 2, effective May 21, 2015, in subsection (a), deleted "as defined in G.S. 14-159.3(b)" following "vehicles" and made a punctuation change; added subsection (e1); and deleted former subsection (f), which named the towns to which the section was applicable.

Session Laws 2015-26, s. 2.1, effective May 21, 2015, Session Laws 2015-26, s. 2.1, effective May 21, 2015, substituted "all-terrain" for "all terrain" throughout.

Session Laws 2017-102, s. 7, effective July 12, 2017, rewrote the section heading which formerly read: "Motorized all-terrain vehicle use by employees of listed municipalities and counties permitted on certain highways."

§ 20-171.25. Motorized all-terrain vehicle use by certain employees of natural gas utilities permitted on public highways and rights-of-way

(a) Natural gas utility employees and contractors engaged in pipeline safety, leak survey, and patrolling activities, acting in the course and scope of their employment, may operate motorized all-terrain vehicles owned or leased by the utility on public highways and rights-of-way only to the extent necessary to perform those activities.

(b) This Part and all other State laws governing the operation of all-terrain vehicles apply to the operation of all-terrain vehicles authorized by this section.

(c) An all-terrain vehicle operated pursuant to this section shall be equipped with operable front and rear lights and a horn.

(d) A person operating an all-terrain vehicle pursuant to this section shall observe posted speed limits and shall not exceed the manufacturer's recommended speed for the vehicle.

(e) A person operating an all-terrain vehicle pursuant to this section shall carry an official company identification card or badge.

History.
2008-156, s. 2

§ 20-171.26. Motorized all-terrain vehicle use by disabled sportsmen

(a) Persons qualified under the Disabled Sportsmen Program, pursuant to G.S. 113-296, are authorized to transverse public roadways using an all-terrain vehicle while engaging in licensed hunting or fishing activities. Use of the all-terrain vehicle shall be limited to driving across the roadway, in a perpendicular fashion, without travel in either direction along the roadway.

(b) This Part and all other State laws governing the operation of all-terrain vehicles apply to the operation of all-terrain vehicles authorized by this section.

(c) An all-terrain vehicle operated pursuant to this section shall be equipped with operable front and rear lights and a horn.

(d) A person operating an all-terrain vehicle pursuant to this section shall observe posted speed limits and shall not exceed the manufacturer's recommended speed for the vehicle.

(e) A person operating an all-terrain vehicle pursuant to this section shall carry evidence of membership in the Disabled Sportsmen Program and the appropriate license to engage in the hunting or fishing activity.

History.
2010-146, s. 1

PART 11.
PEDESTRIANS' RIGHTS AND DUTIES

§ 20-172. Pedestrians subject to traffic-control signals

(a) The Board of Transportation, with reference to State highways, and local authorities, with reference to highways under their jurisdiction, are hereby authorized to erect or install, at intersections or other appropriate places,

Chapter 20

special pedestrian control signals exhibiting the words or symbols "WALK" or "DON'T WALK" as a part of a system of traffic-control signals or devices.

(b) Whenever special pedestrian-control signals are in place, such signals shall indicate as follows:

(1) **WALK.** -- Pedestrians facing such signal may proceed across the highway in the direction of the signal and shall be given the right-of-way by the drivers of all vehicles.

(2) **DON'T WALK.** -- No pedestrian shall start to cross the highway in the direction of such signal, but any pedestrian who has partially completed his crossing on the "WALK" signal shall proceed to a sidewalk or safety island while the "DON'T WALK" signal is showing.

(c) Where a system of traffic-control signals or devices does not include special pedestrian-control signals, pedestrians shall be subject to the vehicular traffic-control signals or devices as they apply to pedestrian traffic.

(d) At places without traffic-control signals or devices, pedestrians shall be accorded the privileges and shall be subject to the restrictions stated in Part 11 of this Article.

History.

1937, c. 407, s. 133; 1973, c. 507, s. 5; c. 1330, s. 31; 1987, c. 125

A PEDESTRIAN AT A CROSSWALK ACQUIRES NO ADDITIONAL RIGHTS AGAINST A RED TRAFFIC LIGHT. Wagoner v. Butcher, 6 N.C. App. 221, 170 S.E.2d 151 (1969).

RIGHTS OF PEDESTRIANS PROCEEDING IN ACCORD WITH LIGHTS NOT IMPAIRED. --The legislature did not intend that the provisions subjecting pedestrians to traffic lights would impair their rights as pedestrians proceeding in accord with such lights. Wagoner v. Butcher, 6 N.C. App. 221, 170 S.E.2d 151 (1969).

PARTY HAVING GREEN LIGHT HAS SUPERIOR RIGHT. --Although one party may be a motorist and the other a pedestrian, whoever has the green light has the superior right to traverse the intersection and to assume that the other will recognize it and conduct himself accordingly. Wagoner v. Butcher, 6 N.C. App. 221, 170 S.E.2d 151 (1969).

CHARGE IN CIVIL ACTIONS. --It is the duty of the court to charge the statutory duty of drivers to pedestrians in an action for damages for their violation; this error is not cured by a general charge as to the use of necessary prudence and is reversible even in the absence of a prayer for more specific instructions. Bowen v. Schnibben, 184 N.C. 248, 114 S.E. 170 (1922).

CITED in Metcalf v. Foister, 232 N.C. 355, 61 S.E.2d 77 (1950); Spencer v. McDowell Motor Co., 236 N.C. 239, 72 S.E.2d 598 (1952).

§ 20-173. Pedestrians' right-of-way at crosswalks

(a) Where traffic-control signals are not in place or in operation the driver of a vehicle shall yield the right-of-way, slowing down or stopping if need be to so yield, to a pedestrian crossing the roadway within any marked crosswalk or within any unmarked crosswalk at or near an intersection, except as otherwise provided in Part 11 of this Article.

(b) Whenever any vehicle is stopped at a marked crosswalk or at any unmarked crosswalk at an intersection to permit a pedestrian to cross the roadway, the driver of any other vehicle approaching from the rear shall not overtake and pass such stopped vehicle.

(c) The driver of a vehicle emerging from or entering an alley, building entrance, private road, or driveway shall yield the right-of-way to any pedestrian, or person riding a bicycle, approaching on any sidewalk or walkway extending across such alley, building entrance, road, or driveway.

History.

1937, c. 407, s. 134; 1973, c. 1330, s. 32

RELATIVE RIGHTS OF PEDESTRIANS AND MOTORISTS IN ABSENCE OF SIGNALS. --In the absence of signals controlling traffic, the relative rights of pedestrians and motorists are prescribed by this section and G.S. 20-174. Griffin v. Pancoast, 257 N.C. 52, 125 S.E.2d 310 (1962).

ABSENCE OF SIDEWALKS AND TRAFFIC SIGNALS. --Where plaintiff-pedestrian crossed at an intersection where there were no traffic signals and no sidewalks on either side of the street, he was not entitled to an instruction based upon statute imposing duty of care on motorist toward a pedestrian. Tucker v. Bruton, 102 N.C. App. 117, 401 S.E.2d 130 (1991).

The North Carolina Supreme Court has defined an "unmarked crosswalk" as "that area within an intersection which also lies within the lateral boundaries of a sidewalk projected across the intersection." Under this definition, the plaintiff must show that he was crossing at an area which was the projected extension of the sidewalk from one side of the street to the other. Tucker v. Bruton, 102 N.C. App. 117, 401 S.E.2d 130 (1991).

THE TERM "UNMARKED CROSSWALK AT AN INTERSECTION," as used in subsection (a) of this section and G.S. 20-174(a), means that area within an intersection which also lies within the lateral boundaries of a sidewalk projected across the intersection. Anderson v. Carter, 272 N.C. 426, 158 S.E.2d 607 (1968); Bowen v. Gardner, 3 N.C. App. 529, 165 S.E.2d 545, rev'd on other grounds, 275 N.C. 363, 168 S.E.2d 47 (1969); Wagoner v. Butcher, 6 N.C. App. 221, 170 S.E.2d 151 (1969); Downs v. Watson, 8 N.C. App. 13, 173 S.E.2d 556 (1970).

This section extends the right-of-way to a pedestrian within "an unmarked crosswalk at an intersection." The focus is not on the lines, but on the proximity to an intersection, which is a place where a motorist should expect pedestrians will have to cross. Wagoner v. Butcher, 6 N.C. App. 221, 170 S.E.2d 151 (1969).

PEDESTRIAN'S RIGHT-OF-WAY NOT AFFECTED BY FAILURE TO MARK CROSSWALK. --If a pedestrian was crossing at an intersection, as defined in G.S. 20-38(12) (now G.S. 20-4.01(16)), he would have the right-of-way, regardless of the failure to mark a place at the intersection for pedestrians to use in crossing. Griffin v. Pancoast, 257 N.C. 52, 125 S.E.2d 310 (1962).

WHERE GUTTER REPAIR WORK AND BARRICADES PREVENTED EXIT FROM THE STREET WITHIN THE CROSSWALK LINES, it would be unreasonable and unjust to say that plaintiff forfeited her intersection crossing right-of-way by stepping a few feet outside the painted lines to skirt a barricade. Wagoner v. Butcher, 6 N.C. App. 221, 170 S.E.2d 151 (1969). *CROSSING AT PLACES OTHER THAN CROSSWALKS. --Subsection (a) of this section and G.S. 20-174(a) do not prohibit pedestrians from crossing streets or highways at places other than marked crosswalks or unmarked crosswalks at intersections.* Anderson v. Carter, 272 N.C. 426, 158 S.E.2d 607 (1968). But see § 20-174(c).

DUTY OF MOTORIST TO YIELD RIGHT-OF-WAY. --It is the duty of a motorist to yield the right-of-way to a pedestrian in an unmarked crosswalk at an intersection. Bowen v. Gardner, 3 N.C. App. 529, 165 S.E.2d 545, rev'd on other grounds, 275 N.C. 363, 168 S.E.2d 47 (1969).

DUTY OF PEDESTRIAN TO YIELD RIGHT-OF-WAY. --If a pedestrian elects to cross a street or a highway at a place which is neither a marked crosswalk nor an unmarked crosswalk at an intersection, subsection (a) of this section and G.S. 20-174(a) require that he yield the right-of-way to vehicles. Anderson v. Carter, 272 N.C. 426, 158 S.E.2d 607 (1968).

BOTH PEDESTRIAN AND MOTORIST HAVE THE RIGHT TO ASSUME THE OTHER WILL OBEY THE RULES of the road and accord the right-of-way to the one having that privilege. Griffin v. Pancoast, 257 N.C. 52, 125 S.E.2d 310 (1962).

A RIGHT-OF-WAY IS NOT ABSOLUTE, and even a pedestrian with the right-of-way must exercise ordinary care for her own safety. Wagoner v. Butcher, 6 N.C. App. 221, 170 S.E.2d 151 (1969).

BUT WHERE THE PEDESTRIAN HAS THE RIGHT-OF-WAY, HE IS NOT REQUIRED TO ANTICIPATE NEGLIGENCE on the part of others. Wagoner v. Butcher, 6 N.C. App. 221, 170 S.E.2d 151 (1969).

To a pedestrian the right-of-way means that he has the right to continue in his direction of travel without anticipating negligence on the part of motorists. Unless the circumstances are sufficient to give him notice to the contrary, he may act upon the assumption, even to the last moment, that motorists will recognize such a preferential right. Wagoner v. Butcher, 6 N.C. App. 221, 170 S.E.2d 151 (1969).

If a person is crossing in an unmarked crosswalk at an intersection, he is not required to anticipate negligence on the part of others. In the absence of anything which gives or should give notice to the contrary, he is entitled to assume, and to act upon the assumption, even to the last moment, that others will observe and obey the statute which requires them to yield the right-of-way. Bowen v. Gardner, 275 N.C. 363, 168 S.E.2d 47 (1969).

PEDESTRIAN WHO HAS THE RIGHT-OF-WAY AT A CROSSWALK MAY NOT BE HELD CONTRIBUTORILY NEGLIGENT AS A MATTER OF LAW for failure to see an approaching vehicle or for failure to use ordinary care for his or her own safety. The pedestrian is not required to anticipate negligence on the part of others. McCoy v. Dowdy, 16 N.C. App. 242, 192 S.E.2d 81 (1972).

Where a pedestrian had the right-of-way afforded her by an intersection crosswalk, it was erroneous to find contributory negligence as a matter of law simply because she failed to see defendant motorist approaching the intersection. Wagoner v. Butcher, 6 N.C. App. 221, 170 S.E.2d 151 (1969).

WHETHER A PEDESTRIAN, SIMPLY BY FAILING TO SEE A VEHICLE, FAILED TO EXERCISE DUE CARE IS A JURY QUESTION. The jury must determine whether the vehicle's speed, proximity or manner of operation would have put the pedestrian, had she seen the vehicle, on notice that the motorist did not intend to yield the right-of-way. Wagoner v. Butcher, 6 N.C. App. 221, 170 S.E.2d 151 (1969).

EFFECT OF TRAFFIC CONTROL SIGNAL ON PEDESTRIAN'S RIGHT-OF-WAY. --The right-of-way given a pedestrian by G.S. 20-155(c) at an intersection where there is no traffic-control signal is limited at an intersection where there is a traffic-control signal by subsection (a) of this section to the pedestrian having the right-of-way only when he is moving with the green light. Wagoner v. Butcher, 6 N.C. App. 221, 170 S.E.2d 151 (1969).

Section 20-155(c) may be construed to mean that a pedestrian's crosswalk right-of-way is not impaired when the movement of the pedestrian is in accord with the traffic lights. Wagoner v. Butcher, 6 N.C. App. 221, 170 S.E.2d 151 (1969).

The effect of the exception in G.S. 20-155(c) as to intersections where traffic is regulated by traffic officers or traffic direction devices is not to subordinate the right-of-way of a pedestrian moving on a green light to that of a turning motorist. Wagoner v. Butcher, 6 N.C. App. 221, 170 S.E.2d 151 (1969).

APPLIED in Keaton v. Blue Bird Taxi Co., 241 N.C. 589, 86 S.E.2d 93 (1955); Falls v. Williams, 261 N.C. 413, 134 S.E.2d 670 (1964); Blake v. Mallard, 262 N.C. 62, 136 S.E.2d 214 (1964); Nix v. Earley, 263 N.C. 795, 140 S.E.2d 402 (1965); Carter v. Murray, 7 N.C. App. 171, 171 S.E.2d 810 (1970).

CITED in Leary v. Norfolk S. Bus Corp., 220 N.C. 745, 18 S.E.2d 426 (1942); Spencer v. McDowell Motor Co., 236 N.C. 239, 72 S.E.2d 598 (1952); Reeves v. Campbell, 264 N.C. 224, 141 S.E.2d 296 (1965).

Chapter 20

§ 20-174. Crossing at other than crosswalks; walking along highway

(a) Every pedestrian crossing a roadway at any point other than within a marked crosswalk or within an unmarked crosswalk at an intersection shall yield the right-of-way to all vehicles upon the roadway.

(b) Any pedestrian crossing a roadway at a point where a pedestrian tunnel or overhead pedestrian crossing has been provided shall yield the right-of-way to all vehicles upon the roadway.

(c) Between adjacent intersections at which traffic-control signals are in operation pedestrians shall not cross at any place except in a marked crosswalk.

(d) Where sidewalks are provided, it shall be unlawful for any pedestrian to walk along and upon an adjacent roadway. Where sidewalks are not provided, any pedestrian walking along and upon a highway shall, when practicable, walk only on the extreme left of the roadway or its shoulder facing traffic which may approach from the opposite direction. Such pedestrian shall yield the right-of-way to approaching traffic.

(e) Notwithstanding the provisions of this section, every driver of a vehicle shall exercise due care to avoid colliding with any pedestrian upon any roadway, and shall give warning by sounding the horn when necessary, and shall exercise proper precaution upon observing any child or any confused or incapacitated person upon a roadway.

History.

1937, c. 407, s. 135; 1973, c. 1330, s. 33

I. IN GENERAL.

A PEDESTRIAN'S RIGHT-OF-WAY IS LIMITED BY THIS SECTION. Wagoner v. Butcher, 6 N.C. App. 221, 170 S.E.2d 151 (1969).

A PERSON WALKING ALONG A PUBLIC HIGHWAY PUSHING A HANDCART IS A "PEDESTRIAN" within the purview of subsection (d) of this section, and is not a driver of a vehicle within the meaning of G.S. 20-146 and 20-149. Lewis v. Watson, 229 N.C. 20, 47 S.E.2d 484 (1948).

THE TERM "UNMARKED CROSSWALK AT AN INTERSECTION," as used in G.S. 20-173(a) and subsection (a) of this section, means that area within an intersection which also lies within the lateral boundaries of a sidewalk projected across the intersection. Anderson v. Carter, 272 N.C. 426, 158 S.E.2d 607 (1968); Bowen v. Gardner, 3 N.C. App. 529, 165 S.E.2d 545, rev'd on other grounds, 275 N.C. 363, 168 S.E.2d 47 (1969); Wagoner v. Butcher, 6 N.C. App. 221, 170 S.E.2d 151 (1969); Downs v. Watson, 8 N.C. App. 13, 173 S.E.2d 556 (1970).

RIGHT-OF-WAY OF PEDESTRIAN CROSSING INTERSECTION. --A pedestrian crossing an intersection, as defined by G.S. 20-38(12) (now G.S. 20-4.01(16)), even though there is no marked crosswalk at that point, has the right-of-way over a motorist

traversing the intersection. Jenkins v. Thomas, 260 N.C. 768, 133 S.E.2d 694 (1963).

PEDESTRIAN NEED NOT YIELD RIGHT-OF-WAY AT UNMARKED INTERSECTIONS. --An instruction placing the duty upon a pedestrian to yield the right-of-way to vehicles in traversing a highway at an unmarked intersection of highways must be held for error. Gaskins v. Kelly, 228 N.C. 697, 47 S.E.2d 34 (1948).

SUBSECTION (A) AND G.S. 20-173(A) DO NOT PROHIBIT PEDESTRIANS FROM CROSSING STREETS OR HIGHWAYS AT PLACES OTHER THAN MARKED CROSSWALKS or unmarked crosswalks at intersections. Anderson v. Carter, 272 N.C. 426, 158 S.E.2d 607 (1968). But see subsection (c).

BUT PEDESTRIAN SO CROSSING MUST YIELD RIGHT-OF-WAY. --A pedestrian crossing the highway at a place which is not within a marked crosswalk or within an unmarked crosswalk at an intersection is under a duty to yield the right-of-way to vehicles along the highway, subject to the duty of a motorist to exercise due care to avoid colliding with any pedestrian and to give warning by sounding his horn whenever necessary. Garmon v. Thomas, 241 N.C. 412, 85 S.E.2d 589 (1955).

It is the duty of a pedestrian, in crossing a highway at a point other than within a marked crosswalk or within an unmarked crosswalk at an intersection, to yield the right-of-way to a truck approaching upon the roadway. Tysinger v. Coble Dairy Prods., 225 N.C. 717, 36 S.E.2d 246 (1945); Grisanti v. United States, 284 F. Supp. 308 (E.D.N.C. 1968).

If the pedestrian elects to cross a street or a highway at a place which is not a marked crosswalk and not an unmarked crosswalk at an intersection, G.S. 20-173(a) and subsection (a) of this section require that he yield the right-of-way to vehicles. Anderson v. Carter, 272 N.C. 426, 158 S.E.2d 607 (1968).

Where intestate was crossing the street diagonally within the block, at a point which was neither at an intersection nor within a marked crosswalk, and the evidence disclosed no traffic control signals at the adjacent intersections, under the provisions of subsection (a) it was intestate's duty to "yield the right-of-way to all vehicles upon the roadway." Wanner v. Alsup, 265 N.C. 308, 144 S.E.2d 18 (1965).

AND KEEP A TIMELY LOOKOUT. --It is the duty of pedestrians to look before starting across a highway, and in the exercise of reasonable care for their own safety, to keep a timely lookout for approaching motor traffic on the highway to see what should have been seen and could have been seen if they had looked before starting across the highway. Rosser v. Smith, 260 N.C. 647, 133 S.E.2d 499 (1963); Charles v. Dougal, 685 F. Supp. 508 (E.D.N.C. 1988), aff'd, 869 F.2d 593 (4th Cir. 1989).

A pedestrian who crosses the street at a point where he does not have the right-of-way must constantly watch for oncoming traffic before he steps into the street and while he is crossing. Brooks v. Boucher, 22 N.C. App. 676, 207 S.E.2d 282, cert. denied, 286

N.C. 211, 209 S.E.2d 319 (1974); Dendy v. Watkins, 288 N.C. 447, 219 S.E.2d 214 (1975).

A pedestrian crossing the road at any point other than a marked crosswalk, or walking along or upon a highway, has a statutory duty to yield the right of way to all vehicles on the roadway. Such a pedestrian also has a common law duty to exercise reasonable care for his own safety by keeping a proper lookout for approaching traffic before entering the road and while on the roadway. Whitley v. Owens, 86 N.C. App. 180, 356 S.E.2d 815 (1987).

While a pedestrian (or motorist) has a right to assume that other motorists will use due care and obey the rules of the road, that right does not relieve him of the legal duty to maintain a proper lookout and otherwise exercise a reasonable degree of care for his own safety. Whitley v. Owens, 86 N.C. App. 180, 356 S.E.2d 815 (1987).

SUBSECTION (A) WAS INAPPLICABLE to a case involving plaintiff who was struck by defendant's truck as she crossed in front of supermarket parking lot because plaintiff was crossing a public vehicular area rather than a roadway. The trial court therefore erred by imposing on plaintiff a duty to yield the right-of-way and by allowing the jury to evaluate plaintiff's conduct using an improper standard of care. Corns v. Hall, 112 N.C. App. 232, 435 S.E.2d 88 (1993).

IT IS UNLAWFUL TO WALK ON THE RIGHT-HAND SHOULDER OF A HIGHWAY along the traveled portion thereof. Simpson v. Wood, 260 N.C. 157, 132 S.E.2d 369 (1963).

APPLIED in Sparks v. Willis, 228 N.C. 25, 44 S.E.2d 343 (1947); Combs v. United States, 122 F. Supp. 280 (E.D.N.C. 1954); Holland v. Malpass, 255 N.C. 395, 121 S.E.2d 576 (1961); Nix v. Earley, 263 N.C. 795, 140 S.E.2d 402 (1965); Jones v. Smith, 3 N.C. App. 396, 165 S.E.2d 56 (1969); Swain v. Williamson, 4 N.C. App. 622, 167 S.E.2d 491 (1969); Anderson v. Mann, 9 N.C. App. 397, 176 S.E.2d 365 (1970); Clark v. Bodycombe, 27 N.C. App. 146, 218 S.E.2d 216 (1975); Brooks v. Smith, 27 N.C. App. 223, 218 S.E.2d 489 (1975); Sessoms v. Roberson, 47 N.C. App. 573, 268 S.E.2d 24 (1980); McNeil v. Gardner, 104 N.C. App. 692, 411 S.E.2d 174 (1991); State v. Moore, 107 N.C. App. 388, 420 S.E.2d 691 (1992); Phillips ex rel. Schultz v. Holland, 107 N.C. App. 688, 421 S.E.2d 608 (1992).

CITED in Pack v. Auman, 220 N.C. 704, 18 S.E.2d 247 (1942); Metcalf v. Foister, 232 N.C. 355, 61 S.E.2d 77 (1950); Keaton v. Blue Bird Taxi Co., 241 N.C. 589, 86 S.E.2d 93 (1955); Jenks v. Morrison, 258 N.C. 96, 127 S.E.2d 895 (1962); Webb v. Felton, 266 N.C. 707, 147 S.E.2d 219 (1966); Bowen v. Gardner, 275 N.C. 363, 168 S.E.2d 47 (1969); Duke v. Meisky, 12 N.C. App. 329, 183 S.E.2d 292 (1971); Tucker v. Bruton, 102 N.C. App. 117, 401 S.E.2d 130 (1991); Womack v. Stephens, 144 N.C. App. 57, 550 S.E.2d 18 (2001).

II. MOTORIST'S DUTY UNDER SUBSECTION (E).

SUBSECTION (E) STATES THE COMMON LAW. --Both the common law and subsection (e) of this section provide that notwithstanding the provisions of subsection (d) "every driver of a vehicle shall exercise due care to avoid colliding with any pedestrian upon any roadway." Lewis v. Watson, 229 N.C. 20, 47 S.E.2d 484 (1948); State v. Fearing, 48 N.C. App. 329, 269 S.E.2d 245, cert. denied, 301 N.C. 99, 273 S.E.2d 303, 301 N.C. 403, 273 S.E.2d 448 (1980), aff'd in part and rev'd in part, 304 N.C. 471, 284 S.E.2d 487 (1981).

Subsection (e) of this section states the common-law rule of negligence. Gathings v. Sehorn, 255 N.C. 503, 121 S.E.2d 873 (1961).

Independent of statute, it is the duty of the motorist at common law to exercise due care to avoid colliding with a pedestrian. Gamble v. Sears, 252 N.C. 706, 114 S.E.2d 677 (1960).

MOTORIST'S RIGHT-OF-WAY SUBJECT TO SUBSECTION (E). --If a pedestrian was not injured at an intersection, but was struck when he stepped into a street at some point between one intersection and the next, the motorist would have the right-of-way. This right-of-way would, of course, be subject to the provisions of subsection (e). Griffin v. Pancoast, 257 N.C. 52, 125 S.E.2d 310 (1962).

DUTY UNDER SUBSECTION (E) GENERALLY. --Under subsection (e) of this section, a motorist has the duty, which is applicable to all motorists generally, to operate his vehicle at a reasonable rate of speed, keep a lookout for persons on or near the highway, decrease his speed when special hazards exist with respect to pedestrians, and give warning of his approach by sounding his horn if the circumstances warrant. State v. Fearing, 48 N.C. App. 329, 269 S.E.2d 245, cert. denied, 301 N.C. 99, 273 S.E.2d 303, 301 N.C. 403, 273 S.E.2d 448 (1980), aff'd in part and rev'd in part on other grounds, 304 N.C. 471, 284 S.E.2d 487 (1981). See also, Morris v. Minix, 4 N.C. App. 634, 167 S.E.2d 494 (1969).

MOTORIST MUST EXERCISE DUE CARE. --It is the duty of a motor vehicle operator both at common law and under the express provisions of this section to "exercise due care to avoid colliding" with pedestrians on the highway. Rosser v. Smith, 260 N.C. 647, 133 S.E.2d 499 (1963); Wanner v. Alsup, 265 N.C. 308, 144 S.E.2d 18 (1965).

RIGHT OF MOTORIST TO ASSUME THAT PEDESTRIAN WILL OBEY LAW. --Where a pedestrian elects not to cross an intersection at a point where he has the right-of-way, but at a point where the motorist has the right-of-way, the motorist has the right to assume, until put on notice to the contrary, that the pedestrian will obey the law and yield the right-of-way. Jenkins v. Thomas, 260 N.C. 768, 133 S.E.2d 694 (1963).

DUTY OF MOTORIST WHERE PEDESTRIAN FAILS TO YIELD RIGHT-OF-WAY. --Even though a pedestrian failed to yield the right-of-way as required by this section, it was the duty of the driver of an approaching vehicle, both at common law and under the express provisions of subsection (e), to "exercise due care to avoid colliding with" the pedestrian. Simpson v. Curry, 237 N.C. 260, 74 S.E.2d 649 (1953); Landini v. Steelman, 243 N.C. 146, 90 S.E.2d 377 (1955); Gamble v. Sears, 252 N.C. 706, 114 S.E.2d 677 (1960).

OR WHERE PEDESTRIAN CROSSES UNLAWFULLY. --It is unlawful for a pedestrian to cross between intersections at which traffic-control signals are in operation except in a marked crosswalk, but where a pedestrian violates this provision a motorist is nonetheless required to exercise due care to avoid colliding with him. State v. Call, 236 N.C. 333, 72 S.E.2d 752 (1952).

A DRIVER MUST MAKE CERTAIN THAT PEDESTRIANS IN FRONT OF HIM ARE AWARE OF HIS APPROACH. Wanner v. Alsup, 265 N.C. 308, 144 S.E.2d 18 (1965).

DUTY TO GIVE WARNING TO PEDESTRIANS. --While ordinarily a motorist is not required to anticipate that a pedestrian will leave a place of safety and get in a line of travel, when the circumstances are such that it should appear to the motorist that a pedestrian is oblivious of his approach, or when he may reasonably anticipate that the pedestrian will come into his way, it is his duty to give warning by sounding his horn. Williams v. Henderson, 230 N.C. 707, 55 S.E.2d 462 (1949).

A workman crossing a highway in an area marked by signs reading "Men Working" is in a lawful place where he has a right to be, and when apparently oblivious of danger, he is entitled to a signal of approach as much as, if not more than, an ordinary pedestrian in the highway. Kellogg v. Thomas, 244 N.C. 722, 94 S.E.2d 903 (1956).

While a driver of a motor vehicle is not required to anticipate that a pedestrian seen in a place of safety will leave it and get in the danger zone until some demonstration or movement on his part reasonably indicates that fact, he must give warning to one who is on the highway or in close proximity to it and is not on a sidewalk, who is apparently oblivious of the approach of the car, or to one whom the driver in the exercise of ordinary care may reasonably anticipate will come into his way. Wanner v. Alsup, 265 N.C. 308, 144 S.E.2d 18 (1965).

It is a driver's duty to sound his horn in order that a pedestrian unaware of his approach may have timely warning. Wanner v. Alsup, 265 N.C. 308, 144 S.E.2d 18 (1965).

MOTORIST'S DUTY WHERE PEDESTRIAN IS OBLIVIOUS TO DANGER. --Where a pedestrian elects not to cross an intersection at a point where he has the right-of-way, but at a point where the motorist has the right-of-way, the mere fact that the pedestrian is oblivious to danger does not impose a duty on the motorist to yield the right-of-way; that duty arises when, and only when, the motorist sees, or in the exercise of reasonable care should see, that the pedestrian is not aware of the approaching danger and for that reason will continue to expose himself to peril. Jenkins v. Thomas, 260 N.C. 768, 133 S.E.2d 694 (1963).

If it appears that a pedestrian is oblivious for the moment to the nearness of a car and the speed at which it is approaching, ordinary care requires the driver to blow his horn, slow down and, if necessary, stop, to avoid inflicting injury. Wanner v. Alsup, 265 N.C. 308, 144 S.E.2d 18 (1965).

DUTY OF MOTORIST TO CHILD. --This section imposes upon a driver the legal duty to exercise proper precaution to avoid injury to a child, if by the exercise of reasonable care he can and should observe the child upon the street. Washington v. Davis, 249 N.C. 65, 105 S.E.2d 202 (1958).

The presence of children on or near the traveled portion of a highway, whom a driver sees or should see, places him under the duty to use due care to control the speed and movement of his vehicle and to keep a vigilant lookout to avoid injury. Anderson v. Smith, 29 N.C. App. 72, 223 S.E.2d 402 (1976).

The presence of children on or near a highway is a warning signal to a motorist, who must bear in mind that they have less capacity to shun danger than adults and are prone to act on impulse. Anderson v. Smith, 29 N.C. App. 72, 223 S.E.2d 402 (1976).

A motorist who sees, or by the exercise of reasonable care should see, children on or near the highway must recognize that children have less discretion than adults and may run out into the street in front of his approaching automobile unmindful of the danger. Therefore, proper care requires a motorist to maintain a vigilant lookout, to give a timely warning of his approach, and to drive at such speed and in such a manner that he can control his vehicle if a child, in obedience to a childish impulse, attempts to cross the street in front of his approaching automobile. Gupton v. McCombs, 74 N.C. App. 547, 328 S.E.2d 886, cert. denied, 314 N.C. 329, 333 S.E.2d 486 (1985).

FOR CASE HOLDING EVIDENCE SUFFICIENT TO SHOW NONCOMPLIANCE WITH SUBSECTION (E), see Register v. Gibbs, 233 N.C. 456, 64 S.E.2d 280 (1951).

MOTORIST HELD NOT ENTITLED TO SUDDEN EMERGENCY INSTRUCTION. --Motorist who observed a child standing at the side of the road but never sounded her horn to warn the child of her approach, failed to keep a vigilant lookout for the child and testified that she assumed that the child would wait for oncoming cars and her vehicle to pass before crossing the street was not entitled to sudden emergency instruction. Gupton v. McCombs, 74 N.C. App. 547, 328 S.E.2d 886, cert. denied, 314 N.C. 329, 333 S.E.2d 486 (1985).

III. NEGLIGENCE AND CONTRIBUTORY NEGLIGENCE.

CROSSING A STREET WITHOUT A RIGHT-OF-WAY IS NOT NEGLIGENCE PER SE. Wagoner v. Butcher, 6 N.C. App. 221, 170 S.E.2d 151 (1969).

AND VIOLATIONS OF THIS SECTION DO NOT CONSTITUTE NEGLIGENCE PER SE. Clark v. Bodycombe, 289 N.C. 246, 221 S.E.2d 506 (1976).

It is unlawful for a pedestrian to cross a street between intersections at which traffic lights are maintained unless there is a marked crosswalk between the intersections at which he may cross and on which he has the right-of-way over vehicles, and his failure to observe the statutory requirements is evidence of negligence, but not negligence per se. Templeton v. Kelley, 216 N.C. 487, 5 S.E.2d 555 (1939). See also Templeton v. Kelley, 215 N.C. 577, 2 S.E.2d 696 (1939), modified on other grounds, 217 N.C. 164, 7 S.E.2d 380 (1940); Bass v. Roberson, 261 N.C. 125, 134 S.E.2d 157 (1964).

Evidence of a violation of this section does not constitute negligence or contributory negligence per se, but rather is some proof of negligence, to be considered with the rest of the evidence in the case. Troy v. Todd, 68 N.C. App. 63, 313 S.E.2d 896 (1984).

BUT MUST BE CONSIDERED ALONG WITH OTHER EVIDENCE. --Violation by a pedestrian of subsections (a), (b) and (e) of this section is not negligence per se, but is evidence to be considered along with other evidence upon the question of a pedestrian's negligence. Moore v. Bezalla, 241 N.C. 190, 84 S.E.2d 817 (1954); Simpson v. Curry, 237 N.C. 260, 74 S.E.2d 649 (1953).

A violation of subsection (e) of this section may not be considered negligence per se; the jury, if they find as a fact that subsection (e) of this section was violated, must consider the violation along with all other facts and circumstances and decide whether, when so considered, the person found guilty of such violation breached his common law and statutory duty of exercising ordinary care. Pope v. Deal, 39 N.C. App. 196, 249 S.E.2d 866 (1978), cert. denied, 296 N.C. 737, 254 S.E.2d 178 (1979).

FAILURE TO YIELD THE RIGHT-OF-WAY AS REQUIRED UNDER THIS SECTION IS NOT CONTRIBUTORY NEGLIGENCE PER SE, but rather it is evidence of negligence to be considered with other evidence in the case in determining whether the actor is chargeable with negligence which proximately caused or contributed to his injury. Wanner v. Alsup, 265 N.C. 308, 144 S.E.2d 18 (1965); Wagoner v. Butcher, 6 N.C. App. 221, 170 S.E.2d 151 (1969); Pompey v. Hyder, 9 N.C. App. 30, 175 S.E.2d 319 (1970); Dendy v. Watkins, 288 N.C. 447, 219 S.E.2d 214 (1975).

Failure of a pedestrian to yield the right-of-way as required by subsection (a) is not contributory negligence per se, but is evidence to be considered with other evidence in the case upon the issue. Citizens Nat'l Bank v. Phillips, 236 N.C. 470, 73 S.E.2d 323 (1952); Simpson v. Curry, 237 N.C. 260, 74 S.E.2d 649 (1953); Goodson v. Williams, 237 N.C. 291, 74 S.E.2d 762 (1953); Landini v. Steelman, 243 N.C. 146, 90 S.E.2d 377 (1955); Gamble v. Sears, 252 N.C. 706, 114 S.E.2d 677 (1960); Brooks v. Boucher, 22 N.C. App. 676, 207 S.E.2d 282, cert. denied, 286 N.C. 211, 209 S.E.2d 319 (1974).

The failure of a pedestrian crossing a roadway at a point other than a crosswalk to yield the right-of-way to a motor vehicle is not contributory negligence per se; it is only evidence of negligence. Blake v. Mallard, 262 N.C. 62, 136 S.E.2d 214 (1964); Holloway v. Holloway, 262 N.C. 258, 136 S.E.2d 559 (1964); Price v. Miller, 271 N.C. 690, 157 S.E.2d 347 (1967); Oliver v. Powell, 47 N.C. App. 59, 266 S.E.2d 830 (1980).

The mere fact that a pedestrian attempts to cross a street at a point other than a crosswalk is not sufficient, standing alone, to support a finding of contributory negligence as a matter of law. Wanner v. Alsup, 265 N.C. 308, 144 S.E.2d 18 (1965); Lewis v. Dove, 39 N.C. App. 599, 251 S.E.2d 669, cert. denied, 297 N.C. 300, 254 S.E.2d 920 (1979).

Where the evidence disclosed that intestate was pushing his handcart on the right-hand side of the highway in violation of subsection (d) of this section and was struck from the rear by a vehicle traveling in the same direction, and plaintiff's evidence was to the effect that the operator of the vehicle was traveling at excessive speed and failed to keep a proper lookout, the fact that intestate was traveling on the wrong side of the road did not render him guilty of contributory negligence as a matter of law upon the evidence, since the operator of a vehicle is under the duty notwithstanding the provisions of subsection (d) to exercise due care to avoid colliding with any pedestrian upon the highway. Lewis v. Watson, 229 N.C. 20, 47 S.E.2d 484 (1948), commented on in 27 N.C.L. Rev. 274 (1949).

Although a violation of subsection (a) is not contributory negligence per se, a failure to yield the right-of-way to a motor vehicle may constitute contributory negligence as a matter of law. Meadows v. Lawrence, 75 N.C. App. 86, 330 S.E.2d 47 (1985), aff'd, 315 N.C. 383, 337 S.E.2d 851 (1986).

Failure to yield the right of way to traffic pursuant to this section does not constitute negligence per se, but is some evidence of negligence. Whitley v. Owens, 86 N.C. App. 180, 356 S.E.2d 815 (1987).

SUMMARY JUDGMENT PROPERLY GRANTED AS TO CONTRIBUTORY NEGLIGENCE OF INJURED PARTY. --Trial court properly granted summary judgment pursuant to G.S. 1A-1, N.C. R. Civ. P. 56, to defendants as to an injured party's contributory negligence in an automobile accident; the injured party was clearly in violation of G.S. 20-174 at the time of the accident, as he was walking on or crossing a highway outside of a marked cross-walk, was not wearing reflective clothing, and was under the influence of alcohol and drugs. Hofecker v. Casperson, 168 N.C. App. 341, 607 S.E.2d 664 (2005).

In a case dealing with an accident between defendant's vehicle and the pedestrian, the trial court properly granted summary judgment in favor of defendant as no duty was imposed on defendant requiring her to yield her right-of-way merely because the pedestrian was oblivious to her danger; defendant was driving 35 miles per hour and only saw the pedestrian immediately before the collision, and without enough time to slow down; and the last clear chance doctrine was inapplicable because defendant could not see the pedestrian or predict her movement as the pedestrian was standing out of view in front of another vehicle just before she darted into the street. Patterson v. Worley, -- N.C. App. --, 828 S.E.2d 744 (2019).

JURY TO DETERMINE ISSUE OF CONTRIBUTORY NEGLIGENCE. --It is to be left to the jury to consider a violation of this section as evidence of negligence along with the other evidence in determining whether or not a pedestrian contributed to his own injury and was, therefore, guilty of contributory negligence. Simpson v. Wood, 260 N.C. 157, 132 S.E.2d 369 (1963).

It is to be left to the jury to consider a violation of subsection (d) of this section as evidence of negligence

Chapter 20

along with other evidence in determining whether or not the plaintiff contributed to his own injury and was, therefore, guilty of contributory negligence. Clark v. Bodycombe, 289 N.C. 246, 221 S.E.2d 506 (1976).

CONTRIBUTORY NEGLIGENCE HELD PROPER ISSUE FOR JURY. --The issue of contributory negligence was properly submitted to the jury in an action by a pedestrian for personal injuries sustained when he was struck by defendant's car where the evidence showed that plaintiff was crossing the roadway at an unmarked crossing in the path of an oncoming car which had the right-of-way. Maness v. Ingram, 29 N.C. App. 26, 222 S.E.2d 737 (1976).

Upon consideration of a motion for a directed verdict, where it appeared that plaintiff was proceeding along a dirt pathway beyond the curb on the north side of a street and that when she was confronted with an automobile blocking a driveway which traversed the path plaintiff left the dirt path and walked along a gutter between the driveway and the portion of the street upon which vehicles ordinarily traveled, but that plaintiff was never more than 12 inches from the north curb of the street, and that just before she reached the curb on the western side of the driveway she was struck by defendant's automobile, the evidence permitted diverse inferences as to whether plaintiff acted in a reasonable manner and whether her acts proximately caused her injuries; thus, the issue of contributory negligence should have been submitted to the jury. Clark v. Bodycombe, 289 N.C. 246, 221 S.E.2d 506 (1976).

Garbage truck driver who was not engaged in carrying or dumping garbage or any other duties of employment which would divert his attention and thus confer upon him different status from an ordinary pedestrian on the roadway, but was merely walking alongside the truck in order to reenter the cab and was free to keep a proper lookout and otherwise take precautions for his own safety, was under a duty not only to look, but to keep a lookout, to see traffic that could be seen, and to yield the right-of-way, and the question of his contributory negligence in being struck by a passing car was properly presented to the jury. Whitley v. Owens, 86 N.C. App. 180, 356 S.E.2d 815 (1987).

CONTRIBUTORY NEGLIGENCE AS MATTER OF LAW ESTABLISHED. --In light of the safety risks associated with standing on a fallen tree that was largely obscured by branches and obstructing both lanes of traffic on a curvy road, along with the fact that plaintiff knew family members had died in similar circumstances but still made no immediate effort to leave the roadway, plaintiff's failure to yield the right of way amounted to contributory negligence as a matter of law. Proffitt v. Gosnell, 257 N.C. App. 148, 809 S.E.2d 200 (2017).

FOR CASES FINDING PEDESTRIANS GUILTY OF CONTRIBUTORY NEGLIGENCE, see Miller v. Lewis & Holmes Motor Freight Corp., 218 N.C. 464, 11 S.E.2d 300 (1940); Garmon v. Thomas, 241 N.C. 412, 85 S.E.2d 589 (1955); Barbee v. Perry, 246 N.C. 538, 98 S.E.2d 794 (1957).

PEDESTRIAN CROSSING AT NIGHT OUTSIDE CROSSWALK. --If the road is straight, visibility unobstructed, the weather clear, and the headlights of the vehicle in use, the failure of a pedestrian crossing a road at night outside a crosswalk to see and avoid a vehicle will consistently be deemed contributory negligence as a matter of law. Meadows v. Lawrence, 75 N.C. App. 86, 330 S.E.2d 47 (1985), aff'd, 315 N.C. 383, 337 S.E.2d 851 (1986).

NONSUIT WHERE CONTRIBUTORY NEGLIGENCE IS PROXIMATE CAUSE OF INJURY. --The court will nonsuit a plaintiff pedestrian on the ground of contributory negligence when all the evidence so clearly establishes his failure to yield the right-of-way as one of the proximate causes of his injuries that no other reasonable conclusion is possible. Blake v. Mallard, 262 N.C. 62, 136 S.E.2d 214 (1964); Price v. Miller, 271 N.C. 690, 157 S.E.2d 347 (1967); Foster v. Shearin, 28 N.C. App. 51, 220 S.E.2d 179 (1975); Oliver v. Powell, 47 N.C. App. 59, 266 S.E.2d 830 (1980).

EVIDENCE HELD TO WARRANT NONSUIT. --Evidence disclosing that plaintiff pedestrian, instead of crossing at an intersection where he had the right-of-way, elected to cross some 100 feet south of the intersection, and that he was struck by defendant motorist, who was traveling with his lights on some 25 miles per hour in a 35 mile per hour zone, warranted nonsuit, in the absence of evidence that plaintiff was oblivious to the danger or that defendant saw or in the exercise of reasonable care should have seen that plaintiff was not aware of the approaching danger. Jenkins v. Thomas, 260 N.C. 768, 133 S.E.2d 694 (1963).

TEST ON DEFENDANTS' MOTION FOR SUMMARY JUDGMENT IN PERSONAL INJURY ACTION. --In passing a defendants' motion for summary judgment in an action to recover damages incurred by plaintiff pedestrian when she was struck by defendants' car while crossing the highway at a point where there was neither a crosswalk nor an intersection, the evidence must be tested by the rule of the reasonably prudent man, in the light of the duties imposed upon both plaintiff and defendant by subsections (a) and (e) of this section. Ragland v. Moore, 299 N.C. 360, 261 S.E.2d 666 (1980).

SUMMARY JUDGMENT NOT WARRANTED. --In an action to recover for personal injuries sustained by plaintiff jogger when he was struck by defendant's automobile, the trial court erred in entering summary judgment for defendants where there were issues of fact as to (1) whether one defendant was negligent in driving the automobile into plaintiff on the highway while visibility was clear, thereby failing to keep a proper lookout or to keep the vehicle under control; (2) whether plaintiff's negligence in violating subsection (d) of this section by not jogging on the left-hand side of the road was a proximate cause of his injury; and (3) whether plaintiff failed to keep a proper lookout when he saw the vehicle, took three or four more steps, and then started to cross the road in front of the vehicle. Parker v. Windborne, 50 N.C. App. 410, 273 S.E.2d 750, cert. denied, 302 N.C. 398, 279 S.E.2d 352 (1981).

INSTRUCTION UPHELD. --An instruction that the violation of statutes regulating the operation of motor vehicles and the conduct of pedestrians on the highway would constitute negligence per se and would be actionable if it was the proximate cause of injury was without error when the instruction was applied solely to G.S. 20-146 and this section, prescribing that vehicles should be operated on the right-hand side of the highway and that warning should be given pedestrians. Williams v. Woodward, 218 N.C. 305, 10 S.E.2d 913 (1940).

INSTRUCTIONS HELD ERRONEOUS. --Where all the evidence tended to show that injured pedestrian had crossed the street in the middle of a block between intersections at which traffic-control signals were in operation, and there was no evidence that there was a marked crosswalk at the place, an instruction to the effect that the pedestrian had a right to cross in the middle of the block and that motorists were under a duty to do what was necessary for her protection constituted prejudicial error. State v. Call, 236 N.C. 333, 72 S.E.2d 752 (1952).

Where the evidence was conflicting as to whether plaintiff pedestrian was walking on left-hand or right-hand side of the highway, the court should have charged the jury on the various aspects of the evidence to the effect that if she was walking on her left-hand side of the highway it was her duty to yield the right-of-way to vehicles upon the roadway, and that if she was walking on her right-hand side she was in violation of subsections (a) and (d) of this section, and an instruction that the duty of a pedestrian to yield the right-of-way applies only to traffic approaching from the front when he is walking on his left side of the highway was in error. Spencer v. McDowell Motor Co., 236 N.C. 239, 72 S.E.2d 598 (1952).

Where the evidence disclosed that plaintiff's intestate was pushing a handcart on the right side of the highway and was struck from the rear by defendant's vehicle traveling in the same direction, and plaintiff contended that the handcart was a vehicle and that G.S. 20-146 and 20-149 applied, while defendant contended that intestate was a pedestrian and was required by subsection (d) of this section to push the handcart along the extreme left-hand side of the highway, an instruction failing to define intestate's status and failing to explain the law arising upon the evidence failed to meet the requirements of former G.S. 1-180. Lewis v. Watson, 229 N.C. 20, 47 S.E.2d 484 (1948).

INSTRUCTION HELD NECESSARY. --In prosecution of defendant motorist for manslaughter for the deaths of two small boys who were struck by defendant's car as he was attempting to pass another vehicle traveling in the same direction, evidence that the children were walking on the hard surface when they were struck and that the preceding car speeded up as defendant attempted to pass it required the court to instruct the jury upon the conduct of the children in walking on the hard surface and the conduct of the other driver in increasing his speed, as bearing upon the question of whether defendant's negligence was a proximate cause of the deaths. State v. Harrington, 260 N.C. 663, 133 S.E.2d 452 (1963).

FOR CASE HOLDING THAT FAILURE TO CHARGE THIS SECTION WAS NOT PREJUDICIAL TO PLAINTIFF where jury found that defendant was negligent, see Gathings v. Sehorn, 255 N.C. 503, 121 S.E.2d 873 (1961).

LEGAL PERIODICALS. --
For article on proof of negligence in North Carolina, see 48 N.C.L. Rev. 731 (1970).

§ 20-174.1. Standing, sitting or lying upon highways or streets prohibited

(a) No person shall willfully stand, sit, or lie upon the highway or street in such a manner as to impede the regular flow of traffic.

(b) Violation of this section is a Class 2 misdemeanor.

History.
1965, c. 137; 1969, c. 1012; 1993 (Reg. Sess., 1994), c. 761, s. 17

LOCAL MODIFICATION. --Ashe: 2008-78, s. 2.

LEGISLATIVE INTENT. --The legislative intent is to prohibit and punish those who willfully place themselves upon the streets and highways of the State in such manner as to impede the regular flow of traffic. State v. Spencer, 276 N.C. 535, 173 S.E.2d 765 (1970); State v. Frinks, 22 N.C. App. 584, 207 S.E.2d 380, appeal dismissed, 285 N.C. 761, 209 S.E.2d 285 (1974).

The legislature intended to make it unlawful for any person to impede the regular flow of traffic upon the streets and highways of the State by willfully placing his body thereon in either a standing, lying or sitting position. State v. Spencer, 276 N.C. 535, 173 S.E.2d 765 (1970); Self v. Dixon, 39 N.C. App. 679, 251 S.E.2d 661 (1979).

THE PUNISHMENT CEILING IMPOSED BY G.S. 20-176(B)DOES NOT APPLY TO THIS SECTION. State v. Spencer, 276 N.C. 535, 173 S.E.2d 765 (1970).

ACTS CONDEMNED BY SECTION. --A person may stand and walk, stand and strut, stand and run or stand still. All these acts are condemned by this section when done willfully in such a manner as to impede the regular flow of traffic upon a public street or highway. State v. Spencer, 276 N.C. 535, 173 S.E.2d 765 (1970); State v. Frinks, 22 N.C. App. 584, 207 S.E.2d 380, appeal dismissed, 285 N.C. 761, 209 S.E.2d 285 (1974).

CONDUCT HELD VIOLATIVE OF SECTION. --Conduct of defendants in walking slowly back and forth across a public highway in such a manner as to cause traffic to be blocked in both directions was within the purview of this section, and the trial court correctly charged that "if the defendants were on the highway and standing, whether they were standing still or walking is of no consequence," since standing is an integral and necessary part of the act of walking. State v. Spencer, 7 N.C. App. 282, 172 S.E.2d 280, modified and aff'd, 276 N.C. 535, 173 S.E.2d 765 (1970).

EVIDENCE HELD INSUFFICIENT TO SHOW VIOLATION OF SECTION. --Where the evidence showed that plaintiff in a personal injury action stood "half on and half off" the pavement for the purpose of picking up a rag dropped by her niece, and that she saw defendant's approaching automobile but was unable to get off the pavement before being struck, there was not sufficient evidence tending to show that the plaintiff willfully placed her body on the street to impede or block traffic in violation of this section. Self v. Dixon, 39 N.C. App. 679, 251 S.E.2d 661 (1979).

INSTRUCTION HELD NOT PREJUDICIAL. --Where trial court read the warrant, which charged defendants with "feloniously" sitting, in defining a violation of this section to the jury, such charge was not prejudicial when the charge was considered in its entirety. State v. Frinks, 22 N.C. App. 584, 207 S.E.2d 380, appeal dismissed, 285 N.C. 761, 209 S.E.2d 285 (1974).

INSTRUCTION IMPROPER. --Plaintiff who placed himself in the road while helping a stranded motorist to push his car off the highway did not intentionally impede traffic; thus, giving a jury instruction based on this section on the issue of plaintiff's contributory negligence was error. Haas v. Clayton, 125 N.C. App. 200, 479 S.E.2d 805 (1997).

APPLIED in In re Burruss, 275 N.C. 517, 169 S.E.2d 879 (1969); In re Burruss, 4 N.C. App. 523, 167 S.E.2d 454 (1969); In re Shelton, 5 N.C. App. 487, 168 S.E.2d 695 (1969); Sizemore v. Raxter, 73 N.C. App. 531, 327 S.E.2d 258 (1985).

CITED in State v. Gibbs, 8 N.C. App. 339, 174 S.E.2d 119 (1970); State v. Evans, 8 N.C. App. 469, 174 S.E.2d 680 (1970); McKeiver v. Pennsylvania, 403 U.S. 528, 91 S. Ct. 1976, 29 L. Ed. 2d 647 (1971); State v. Godwin, 13 N.C. App. 700, 187 S.E.2d 400 (1972); State v. Murrell, 18 N.C. App. 327, 196 S.E.2d 606 (1973); State v. Phifer, 226 N.C. App. 359, 741 S.E.2d 446 (2013).

LEGAL PERIODICALS. --

For article dealing with legal problems in southern desegregation, see 43 N.C.L. Rev. 689 (1965).

§ 20-174.2. Local ordinances; pedestrians gathering, picketing, or protesting on roads or highways

(a) A municipality or a county may adopt an ordinance regulating the time, place, and manner of gatherings, picket lines, or protests by pedestrians that occur on State roadways and State highways.

(b) Nothing in this section shall permit a municipality or a county to impose restrictions or prohibitions on the activities of any of the following persons who are engaged in construction or maintenance, or in making traffic or engineering surveys:

    (1) Licensees, employees, or contractors of the Department of Transportation.

    (2) Licensees, employees, or contractors of a municipality.

History.
2007-360, s. 6

§ 20-175. Pedestrians soliciting rides, employment, business or funds upon highways or streets

(a) No person shall stand in any portion of the State highways, except upon the shoulders thereof, for the purpose of soliciting a ride from the driver of any motor vehicle.

(b) No person shall stand or loiter in the main traveled portion, including the shoulders and median, of any State highway or street, excluding sidewalks, or stop any motor vehicle for the purpose of soliciting employment, business or contributions from the driver or occupant of any motor vehicle that impedes the normal movement of traffic on the public highways or streets: Provided that the provisions of this subsection shall not apply to licensees, employees or contractors of the Department of Transportation or of any municipality engaged in construction or maintenance or in making traffic or engineering surveys.

(c) Repealed by Session Laws 1973, c. 1330, s. 39.

(d) Local governments may enact ordinances restricting or prohibiting a person from standing on any street, highway, or right-of-way excluding sidewalks while soliciting, or attempting to solicit, any employment, business, or contributions from the driver or occupants of any vehicle. No local government may enact or enforce any ordinance that prohibits engaging in the distribution of newspapers on the non-traveled portion of any street or highway except when those distribution activities impede the normal movement of traffic on the street or highway. This subsection does not permit additional restrictions or prohibitions on the activities of licensees, employees, or contractors of the Department of Transportation or of any municipality engaged in construction or maintenance or in making traffic or engineering surveys except as provided in subsection (e) of this section.

(e) A local government shall have the authority to grant authorization for a person to stand in, on, or near a street or State roadway, within the local government's municipal corporate limits, to solicit a charitable contribution if the requirements of this subsection are met.

A person seeking authorization under this subsection to solicit charitable contributions shall file a written application with the local government. This application shall be filed not later than seven days before the date the solicitation event is to occur. If there are multiple events or one event occurring on more than one day, each event shall be subject to the application and permit requirements of this subsection for each day the event is to be held, to include the application fee.

The application must include:

(1) The date and time when the solicitation is to occur;

(2) Each location at which the solicitation is to occur; and

(3) The number of solicitors to be involved in the solicitation at each location.

This subsection does not prohibit a local government from charging a fee for a permit, but in no case shall the fee be greater than twenty-five dollars ($ 25.00) per day per event.

The applicant shall also furnish to the local government advance proof of liability insurance in the amount of at least two million dollars ($ 2,000,000) to cover damages that may arise from the solicitation. The insurance coverage must provide coverage for claims against any solicitor and agree to hold the local government harmless.

A local government, by acting under this section, does not waive, or limit, any immunity or create any new liability for the local government. The issuance of an authorization under this section and the conducting of the solicitation authorized are not considered governmental functions of the local government.

In the event the solicitation event or the solicitors shall create a nuisance, delay traffic, create threatening or hostile situations, any law enforcement officer with proper jurisdiction may order the solicitations to cease. Any individual failing to follow a law enforcement officer's lawful order to cease solicitation shall be guilty of a Class 2 misdemeanor.

History.
1937, c. 407, s. 136; 1965, c. 673; 1973, c. 507, s. 5; c. 1330, s. 39; 1977, c. 464, s. 34; 2005-310, s. 1;2006-250, ss. 7(a), 7(b); 2008-223, s. 1
LOCAL MODIFICATION. --City of Burlington: 2005-30, s. 1;city of Durham: 2007-113, ss. 1, 2.
  EFFECT OF AMENDMENTS. --
  Session Laws 2005-310, s. 1, effective August 25, 2005, added subsection (d).
  Session Laws 2006-250, s. 7(a) and (b), effective December 1, 2006, and applicable to offenses committed on or after that date, inserted "except as provide in subsection (e) of this section" at the end of subsection (d) and added subsection (e).
  Session Laws 2008-223, s. 1, effective August 17, 2008, added the second sentence in subsection (d).
  MUNICIPAL ORDINANCE NOT IN CONFLICT WITH SECTION. --City produced evidence that soliciting in the roadways and on the rights-of-way amongst traffic was a dangerous activity; the city's expert opinion evidence was uncontradicted. That Burlington, N.C., Ordinance 08-19 was designed to

protect the public interest was also evidenced by the fact the ordinance tracked G.S. 20-175(d) which authorized local governments to pass such ordinances to restrict solicitations on public roadways. Times-News Publ'g Co. v. City of Burlington, 2008 U.S. Dist. LEXIS 56451 (M.D.N.C. June 30, 2008).
  APPLIED in Pinkston v. Connor, 63 N.C. App. 628, 306 S.E.2d 132 (1983).
  OPINIONS OF THE ATTORNEY GENERAL
  MUNICIPAL ORDINANCE IN CONFLICT WITH SECTION. --A municipal ordinance which authorized the sale of newspapers and merchandise at intersectional traffic islands was in conflict with this section, to the extent that the ordinance purported to authorize acts resulting in the impeding of the normal flow of traffic on the public highways. See opinion of Attorney General to Mr. J.M. Lynch, P.E., State Traffic Engineer, North Carolina Department of Transportation, 59 N.C.A.G. 45 (1989).
  ACTS NOT CONSTITUTING VIOLATION OF SECTION. --Standing or loitering on the main traveled portion of the highway and soliciting employment, business or contributions from the driver or occupant of a motor vehicle does not constitute a violation of this section if the acts do not result in impeding the normal movement of traffic. See opinion of Attorney General to Mr. Carl V. Venters, 41 N.C.A.G. 528 (1971).

PART 11A.
BLIND PEDESTRIANS -- WHITE CANES OR GUIDE DOGS

§ 20-175.1. Public use of white canes by other than blind persons prohibited

It shall be unlawful for any person, except one who is wholly or partially blind, to carry or use on any street or highway, or in any other public place, a cane or walking stick which is white in color or white tipped with red.

History.
1949, c. 324, s. 1

§ 20-175.2. Right-of-way at crossings, intersections and traffic-control signal points; white cane or guide dog to serve as signal for the blind

At any street, road or highway crossing or intersection, where the movement of traffic is not regulated by a traffic officer or by traffic-control signals, any blind or partially blind pedestrian shall be entitled to the right-of-way at such crossing or intersection, if such blind or partially blind pedestrian shall extend before him at arm's length a cane white in color or white tipped with red, or if such person is accompanied by a guide dog. Upon receiving such a signal, all vehicles at or approaching such intersection or crossing shall come to a full stop, leaving a clear lane through which such pedestrian may pass, and such vehicle shall remain stationary until such blind or partially blind pedestrian has completed the passage of such crossing or intersection. At any street, road or highway crossing or intersection, where the movement of traffic is regulated by traffic-control signals, blind or partially blind pedestrians shall be entitled to the right-of-way if such person having such cane or accompanied by a guide dog shall be partly across such crossing or intersection at the time the traffic-control signals change, and all vehicles shall stop and remain stationary until such pedestrian has completed passage across the intersection or crossing.

History.
1949, c. 324, s. 2

§ 20-175.3. Rights and privileges of blind persons without white cane or guide dog

Nothing contained in this Part shall be construed to deprive any blind or partially blind person not carrying a cane white in color or white tipped with red, or being accompanied by a guide dog, of any of the rights and privileges conferred by law upon pedestrians crossing streets and highways, nor shall the failure of such blind or partially blind person to carry a cane white in color or white tipped with red, or to be accompanied by a guide dog, upon the streets, roads, highways or sidewalks of this State, be held to constitute or be evidence of contributory negligence by virtue of this Part.

History.
1949, c. 324, s. 3

N.C. Gen. Stat. § 20-175.4

Repealed by Session Laws 1973, c. 1330, s. 39.

PART 11B.
PEDESTRIAN RIGHTS AND DUTIES OF PERSONS WITH A MOBILITY IMPAIRMENT

§ 20-175.5. Use of motorized wheelchairs or similar vehicles not exceeding 1000 pounds gross weight

While a person with a mobility impairment as defined in G.S. 20-37.5 operates a motorized wheelchair or similar vehicle not exceeding 1000 pounds gross weight in order to provide that person with the mobility of a pedestrian,

that person is subject to all the laws, ordinances, regulations, rights and responsibilities which would otherwise apply to a pedestrian, but is not subject to Part 10 of this Article or any other law, ordinance or regulation otherwise applicable to motor vehicles.

History.
1991, c. 206, s. 1

PART 11C.
ELECTRIC PERSONAL ASSISTIVE MOBILITY DEVICES

§ 20-175.6. Electric personal assistive mobility devices

(a) **Electric Personal Assistive Mobility Device.** -- As defined in G.S. 20-4.01(7b).

(b) **Exempt From Registration.** -- As provided in G.S. 20-51.

(c) **Use of Device.** -- An electric personal assistive mobility device may be operated on public highways with posted speeds of 25 miles per hour or less, sidewalks, and bicycle paths. A person operating an electric personal assistive mobility device on a sidewalk, roadway, or bicycle path shall yield the right-of-way to pedestrians and other human-powered devices. A person operating an electric personal assistive mobility device shall have all rights and duties of a pedestrian, including the rights and duties set forth in Part 11 of this Article.

(d) **Municipal Regulation.** -- For the purpose of assuring the safety of persons using highways and sidewalks, municipalities having jurisdiction over public streets, sidewalks, alleys, bridges, and other ways of public passage may by ordinance regulate the time, place, and manner of the operation of electric personal assistive mobility devices, but shall not prohibit their use.

History.
2002-98, s. 5;2016-90, s. 13(d)

EDITOR'S NOTE. --

Session Laws 2016-90, s. 13(j), made the amendment to subsection (a) of this section by Session Laws 2016-90, s. 13(d), applicable to offenses committed on or after December 1, 2016.

EFFECT OF AMENDMENTS. --

Session Laws 2016-90, s. 13(d), effective December 1, 2016, in subsection (a), substituted "G.S. 20-4.01(7b)" for "G.S. 20-4.01(7a)." See editor's note for applicability.

CROSS REFERENCES. --

As to definition of electric personal assistive mobility device, see G.S. 20-4.01. As to exemption of electric personal assistive mobility device from registration and title under the motor vehicle laws, see G.S. 20-51.

PART 11D.
PERSONAL DELIVERY DEVICES

§ 20-175.15. Definitions

The following definitions apply to this Part:

(1) **Agent.** -- A director, officer, employee, or other person authorized to act on behalf of a business entity.

(2) **Business entity.** -- A corporation, limited liability company, partnership, sole proprietorship, or other legal entity authorized to conduct business under the laws of this State.

(3) **Operator.** -- An agent who is 16 years of age or older and is charged with the responsibility of monitoring and operating a personal delivery device.

(4) **Pedestrian area.** -- A sidewalk, crosswalk, school crosswalk, school crossing zone, or safety zone.

(5) **Personal delivery device.** -- As defined in G.S. 20-4.01.

History.
2020-73, s. 2

EDITOR'S NOTE. --
Session Law 2020-73, s. 7 made this Part, as added by Session Laws 2020-73, s. 2, effective December 1, 2020, and applicable to offenses committed on or after that date.

Session Laws 2020-73, s. 2, enacted G.S. 20-175.7. It was renumbered as this section at the direction of the Revisor of Statutes.

§ 20-175.16. Personal delivery devices authorized; operation; equipment

(a) A business entity may operate a personal delivery device in a pedestrian area or on a highway, with the rights and duties applicable to a pedestrian under this Chapter, subject to the requirements and restrictions of this Part. Except as authorized in this Part, no person may operate a personal delivery device in a pedestrian area or on a highway in this State.

(b) Operation of a personal delivery device shall comply with all of the following:

(1) The personal delivery device shall be monitored by an operator who is able to exercise remote control over the navigation and operation of the personal delivery device.

(2) The personal delivery device may not be operated in a pedestrian area at a speed greater than 10 miles per hour.

(3) The personal delivery device may not be operated on a highway except as necessary to cross a highway or along a highway if a sidewalk is not provided or accessible. When operating along a highway under this subdivision, the following additional restrictions apply:

    a. The personal delivery device shall be operated on the shoulder or as close as practicable to the extreme right of the highway in the direction of authorized traffic movement and shall yield the right-of-way to all vehicles.

    b. The personal delivery device may not be operated on a highway at a speed greater than 20 miles per hour.

    c. The personal delivery device may not be operated on a highway with a speed limit greater than 35 miles per hour.

(4) The personal delivery device shall obey all traffic and pedestrian control devices and signs.

(5) The personal delivery device shall yield the right-of-way to all human pedestrians.

(6) The personal delivery device shall not unreasonably interfere with any vehicle or pedestrian.

(7) The personal delivery device shall not transport materials regulated under the Hazardous Materials Transportation Act (49 U.S.C. §§ 5101 -- 5128) that require placarding pursuant to Subpart F of 49 C.F.R. Part 172 (49 C.F.R. §§ 172.500 -- 172.560).

(c) A personal delivery device shall be equipped with all of the following:

(1) A marker that clearly states the name and contact information of the owner and a unique identification number.

(2) A braking system that enables the device to come to a controlled stop.

(3) When operated at night, lights on the front and rear of the personal delivery device that are visible and recognizable under normal atmospheric conditions from at least 500 feet on all sides of the personal delivery device.

(d) A violation of this section is an infraction.

History.
2020-73, s. 2

EDITOR'S NOTE. --
Session Laws 2020-73, s. 2, enacted G.S. 20-175.8. It was renumbered as this section at the direction of the Revisor of Statutes.

This section has more than one version with varying effective dates. To view a complete list of the versions of this section see Table of Contents.

§ 20-175.17. (Effective until December 1, 2022) Local regulation

For the purpose of assuring the safety of persons using highways and sidewalks, a local government having jurisdiction over public streets, sidewalks, alleys, bridges, and other ways of public passage may by ordinance regulate time and place of the operation of personal delivery devices, but shall not prohibit their use.

History.

2020-73, s. 2

SECTION SET OUT TWICE. --The section above is effective until December 1, 2022. For the section as amended December 1, 2022, see the following section, also numbered G.S. 20-175.17.

EDITOR'S NOTE. --

Session Laws 2020-73, s. 2, enacted G.S. 20-175.9. It was renumbered as this section at the direction of the Revisor of Statutes.

This section has more than one version with varying effective dates. To view a complete list of the versions of this section see Table of Contents.

§ 20-175.17. (Effective December 1, 2022) Local regulation

For the purpose of assuring the safety of persons using highways and sidewalks, a local government having jurisdiction over public streets, sidewalks, alleys, bridges, and other ways of public passage may by ordinance prohibit operation of personal delivery devices within its jurisdiction if the local government determines that the prohibition is necessary.

History.

2020-73, ss. 2, 3(a)

SECTION SET OUT TWICE. --The section above is effective December 1, 2022. For the section as in effect until December 1, 2022, see the preceding section, also numbered G.S. 20-175.17.

EDITOR'S NOTE. --

Session Laws 2020-73, s. 3(b), provides: "This section becomes effective December 1, 2022. Any ordinance regulating time and place of operation of personal delivery devices adopted by a local government in accordance with G.S. 20-175.9 [G.S. 20-175.17] before the effective date of this section shall remain in effect until repealed by that local government."

EFFECT OF AMENDMENTS. --

Session Laws 2020-73, s. 3(a), substituted "prohibit operation of personal delivery devices within its jurisdiction if the local government determines that the prohibition is necessary" for "regulate time and place of the operation of personal delivery devices, but shall not prohibit their use" at the end of the section. For effective date and applicability, see editor's note.

§ 20-175.18. Insurance

A business entity that operates a personal delivery device under this Part shall maintain an insurance policy that includes general liability coverage of not less than one hundred thousand dollars (\$ 100,000) per claim for damages arising from the operation of the personal delivery device.

History.

2020-73, s. 2

EDITOR'S NOTE. --

Session Laws 2020-73, s. 2, enacted G.S. 20-175.10. It was renumbered as this section at the direction of the Revisor of Statutes.

PART 12.
SENTENCING; PENALTIES

§ 20-176. Penalty for misdemeanor or infraction

(a) Violation of a provision of Part 9, 10, 10A, or 11 of this Article is an infraction unless the violation is specifically declared by law to be a misdemeanor or felony. Except as otherwise provided in subsection (a1) of this section, violation of the remaining Parts of this Article is a misdemeanor unless the violation is specifically declared by law to be an infraction or a felony.

(a1) A person who does any of the following is responsible for an infraction:

(1) Fails to carry the registration card in the vehicle, in violation of G.S. 20-57(c).

(2) Repealed by Session Laws 2016-90, s. 12(b), effective December 1, 2016, and applicable to registration cards issued on or after that date.

(3) Fails to notify the Division of an address change for a vehicle registration card within 60 days after the change occurs, in violation of G.S. 20-67.

(b) Unless a specific penalty is otherwise provided by law, a person found responsible for an infraction contained in this Article may be ordered to pay a penalty of not more than one hundred dollars (\$ 100.00).

(c) Unless a specific penalty is otherwise provided by law, a person convicted of a misdemeanor contained in this Article is guilty of a Class 2 misdemeanor. A punishment is specific for purposes of this subsection if it contains a quantitative limit on the term of imprisonment or the amount of fine a judge can impose.

(c1) Repealed by Session Laws 2014-100, s. 16C.1(c), effective October 1, 2014.

(c2) Repealed by Session Laws 2013-385, s. 5, effective December 1, 2013.

(d) For purposes of determining whether a violation of an offense contained in this Chapter constitutes negligence per se, crimes and infractions shall be treated identically.

History.

1937, c. 407, s. 137; 1951, c. 1013, s. 7; 1957, c. 1255; 1967, c. 674, s. 3; 1969, c. 378, s. 3; 1973, c. 1330, s. 34; 1975, c. 644; 1985, c. 764, s. 20; 1985 (Reg. Sess., 1986), c. 852, ss. 7, 17; c. 1014, s. 202; 1993, c. 539, s. 379;1994, Ex. Sess., c. 24, s. 14(c);2013-360, s. 18B.14(h);2013-385, s. 5;2014-100, s. 16C.1(c);2016-90, s. 12(b)

LOCAL MODIFICATION. --City of Charlotte: 2001-88.

EDITOR'S NOTE. --

Session Laws 2014-100, s. 16C.1(g), made the repeal of subsection (c1) by Session Laws 2014-100, s. 16C.1(c), applicable to (i) persons placed on probation or sentenced to imprisonment for impaired driving under G.S. 20-138.1 on or after January 1, 2015, and (ii) persons placed on probation or sentenced to imprisonment for all other misdemeanors other than impaired driving under G.S. 20-138.1 on or after October 1, 2014.

Session Laws 2016-90, s. 12(c), made the repeal of former subdivision (a1)(2) of this section, which pertained to failure of owner to sign a registration card, by Session Laws 2016-90, s. 12(b), applicable to registration cards issued on or after December 1, 2016.

EFFECT OF AMENDMENTS. --

Session Laws 2013-360, s. 18B.14(h), effective December 1, 2013, added "Except as otherwise provided in subsection (c2) of this section, and" in subsection (c); and added subsection (c2). For applicability, see Editor's note.

Session Laws 2013-385, s. 5, effective December 1, 2013, added "Except as otherwise provided in subsection (a1) of this section" in subsection (a); added subsection (a1); deleted "Except as otherwise provided in subsection (c2) of this section, and" preceding "Unless" in subsection (c); and deleted subsection (c2). For applicability, see Editor's note.

Session Laws 2014-100, s. 16C.1(c), effective October 1, 2014, repealed subsection (c1), which read "Notwithstanding any other provision of law, no person convicted of a misdemeanor for the violation of any provision of this Chapter except G.S. 20-28(a) and (b), G.S. 20-141(j), G.S. 20-141.3(b) and (c), G.S. 20-141.4, or a second or subsequent conviction of G.S. 20-138.1 shall be imprisoned in the State prison system unless the person previously has been imprisoned in a local confinement facility, as defined by G.S. 153A-217(5), for a violation of this Chapter." For applicability, see Editor's note.

Session Laws 2016-90, s. 12(b), effective December 1, 2016, repealed subsection (a1)(2). See editor's note for applicability.

EDITOR'S NOTE. --Some of the cases cited below were decided under corresponding provisions of former law.

AS TO STRICT CONSTRUCTION OF PENAL PROVISIONS, see Security Fin. Co. v. Hendry, 189 N.C. 549, 127 S.E. 629 (1925); Carolina Disct. Corp. v. Landis Motor Co., 190 N.C. 157, 129 S.E. 414 (1925).

THIS SECTION DOES NOT APPLY TO THE VARIOUS SECTIONS WHERE PUNISHMENT IS SPECIFIED AS FINE OR IMPRISONMENT OR BOTH in the discretion of the court with no maximum limitation being specified. State v. Spencer, 7 N.C. App. 282, 172 S.E.2d 280, modified and aff'd, 276 N.C. 535, 173 S.E.2d 765 (1970).

THE PUNISHMENT CEILING IMPOSED BY SUBSECTION (B) OF THIS SECTION DOES NOT APPLY TO G.S. 20-174.1. State v. Spencer, 276 N.C. 535, 173 S.E.2d 765 (1970).

THE MAXIMUM PUNISHMENT FOR A VIOLATION OF §§ 20-63 OR 20-111 would be that prescribed by subsection (b) of this section, namely, a fine of not more than $100.00 or imprisonment in the county or municipal jail for not more than 60 days or both such fine and imprisonment. State v. Tolley, 271 N.C. 459, 156 S.E.2d 858 (1967).

VIOLATION OF G.S. 20-162 by parking within 25 feet from the intersection of curb lines at an intersection of highways within a municipality is a misdemeanor, notwithstanding invocation of the prima facie rule of evidence created by G.S. 20-162.1. State v. Rumfelt, 241 N.C. 375, 85 S.E.2d 398 (1955).

EVERY PERSON CONVICTED OF SPEEDING IN VIOLATION OF G.S. 20-141, where the speed is not in excess of 80 miles an hour, shall be punished by a fine of not more than $100.00 or by imprisonment in the county or municipal jail for not more than 60 days or by both such fine and imprisonment. State v. Tolley, 271 N.C. 459, 156 S.E.2d 858 (1967).

DRIVING WITHOUT LIGHTS. --Subsection (b) of this section prescribes the punishment for driving a motor vehicle without lights during the period from half hour after sunset to a half hour before sunrise in violation of G.S. 20-129. State v. Eason, 242 N.C. 59, 86 S.E.2d 774 (1955).

Operating a motor vehicle on a public highway at night without lights is a violation of G.S. 20-129. Such violation is a misdemeanor under this section, and is negligence per se. Williamson v. Varner, 252 N.C. 446, 114 S.E.2d 92 (1960).

AS TO VIOLATIONS OF THE MOTOR VEHICLE LAW AS EVIDENCE OF GUILT OF OTHER CRIMES, see State v. McIver, 175 N.C. 761, 94 S.E. 682 (1917); State v. Gash, 177 N.C. 595, 99 S.E. 337 (1919); State v. Sudderth, 184 N.C. 753, 114 S.E. 828 (1922).

WHERE DEFENDANT HAD BEEN CHARGED IN THE DISTRICT COURT WITH DRUNKEN DRIVING UNDER FORMER G.S. 20-138, BUT WAS CONVICTED OF THE LESSER INCLUDED OFFENSE under former G.S. 20-140(c), the trial judge, on trial de novo in the superior court, erred in instructing the jury on reckless driving under G.S. 20-140(a) and should have instructed on former G.S. 20-140(c), since the superior court has no jurisdiction to try an accused for a specific misdemeanor on the warrant of an inferior court unless he is first tried and convicted and then appeals to the superior court from the sentence pronounced. State v. Robinson, 40 N.C. App. 514, 253 S.E.2d 311 (1979).

Chapter 20

ALLOCATION OF FUNDS FROM A CITY'S RED LIGHT CAMERA ORDINANCE. --County board of education was entitled to funds derived from a city's red light camera program, which program was implemented by an ordinance pursuant to G.S. 160A-300.1(c), as N.C. Const., Art. IX, § 7 applied to the civil penalties assessed by the city for violations of the ordinance regarding the failure to stop for a red stoplight. Further, pursuant to G.S. 115C-437, the city was to pay 90 percent of the amount collected by its red light camera program to the board. Shavitz v. City of High Point, 177 N.C. App. 465, 630 S.E.2d 4 (2006), cert. denied, appeal dismissed, 361 N.C. 430, 648 S.E.2d 845 (2007).

APPLIED in State v. Daughtry, 236 N.C. 316, 72 S.E.2d 658 (1952); State v. Massey, 265 N.C. 579, 144 S.E.2d 649 (1965); State v. Craig, 21 N.C. App. 51, 203 S.E.2d 401 (1974); Kraemer v. Moore, 67 N.C. App. 505, 313 S.E.2d 610 (1984); Richmond Cnty. Bd. of Educ. v. Cowell, 243 N.C. App. 116, 776 S.E.2d 244 (2015).

CITED in State v. Mickle, 194 N.C. 808, 140 S.E. 150 (1927); Lancaster v. B. & H. Coach Line, 198 N.C. 107, 150 S.E. 716 (1929); State v. Wooten, 228 N.C. 628, 46 S.E.2d 868 (1948); Hinson v. Dawson, 241 N.C. 714, 86 S.E.2d 585 (1955); State v. Baucom, 244 N.C. 61, 92 S.E.2d 426 (1956); McEwen Funeral Serv., Inc. v. Charlotte City Coach Lines, 248 N.C. 146, 102 S.E.2d 816 (1958); State v. Zimmerman, 7 N.C. App. 522, 173 S.E.2d 35 (1970); State v. Speights, 280 N.C. 137, 185 S.E.2d 152 (1971); State v. Murrell, 18 N.C. App. 327, 196 S.E.2d 606 (1973); State v. Hudson, 103 N.C. App. 708, 407 S.E.2d 583 (1991); Glenn-Robinson v. Acker, 140 N.C. App. 606, 538 S.E.2d 601 (2000); State v. Smith, 192 N.C. App. 690, 666 S.E.2d 191 (2008), cert. denied 130 S. Ct. 3325, 2010 U.S. LEXIS 4297, 176 L. Ed. 2d 1221 (U.S. 2010).

§ 20-177. Penalty for felony

Any person who shall be convicted of a violation of any of the provisions of this Article herein or by the laws of this State declared to constitute a felony shall, unless a different penalty is prescribed herein or by the laws of this State, be punished as a Class I felon.

History.
1937, c. 407, s. 138; 1979, c. 760, s. 5; 1979, 2nd Sess., c. 1316, s. 47; 1981, c. 63, s. 1; c. 179, s. 14

§ 20-178. Penalty for bad check

When any person, firm, or corporation shall tender to the Division any uncertified check for payment of any tax, fee or other obligation due by him under the provisions of this Article, and the bank upon which such check shall be drawn shall refuse to pay it on account of insufficient funds of the drawer on deposit in such bank, and such check shall be returned to the Division, an additional tax shall be imposed by the Division upon such person, firm or corporation, which additional tax shall be equal to ten percent (10%) of the tax or fee in payment of which such check was tendered: Provided, that in no case shall the additional tax be less than ten dollars ($ 10.00); provided, further, that no additional tax shall be imposed if, at the time such check was presented for payment, the drawer had on deposit in any bank of this State funds sufficient to pay such check and by inadvertence failed to draw the check upon such bank, or upon the proper account therein. The additional tax imposed by this section shall not be waived or diminished by the Division.

History.
1937, c. 407, s. 139; 1953, c. 1144; 1975, c. 716, s. 5; 1981, c. 690, s. 24

§ 20-178.1. Payment and review of civil penalty imposed by Department of Public Safety

(a) **Procedure.** -- A person who is assessed a civil penalty under this Article by the Department of Public Safety must pay the penalty within 30 calendar days after the date the penalty was assessed or make a written request within this time limit to the Department for a Departmental review of the penalty. A person who does not submit a request for review within the required time waives the right to a review and hearing on the penalty.

(b) **Department Review.** -- Any person who denies liability for a penalty imposed by the Department may request an informal review by the Secretary of the Department or the Secretary's designee. The request must be made in writing and must contain sufficient information for the Secretary, or the Secretary's designee, to determine the specific basis upon which liability is being challenged. Upon receiving a request for informal review, the Secretary, or the Secretary's designee, shall review the record and determine whether the penalty was assessed in error. If, after reviewing the record, the Secretary, or the Secretary's designee, determines that the assessment or a portion thereof was not issued in error, the penalty must be paid within 30 days of the notice of decision.

(c) **Judicial Review.** -- Any person who is dissatisfied with the decision of the Secretary and who has paid the penalty in full within 30 days of the notice of decision, as required by subsection (b) of this section, may, within 60 days of the decision, bring an action for refund of the penalty against the Department in the Superior Court of Wake County or in the superior court of the county in which the civil penalty was assessed. The court shall review the Secretary's decision and shall make findings of fact and conclusions of law. The hearing shall be conducted by the court without a jury. In reviewing the case, the court shall not give deference to the prior decision of the Secretary. A superior court may award attorneys' fees to a prevailing plaintiff only upon a showing of bad faith on the part of the Department, and any order for attorneys' fees must be supported by findings of fact and conclusions of law.

(d) **Interest.** -- Interest accrues on a penalty that is overdue. A penalty is overdue if it is not paid within the time required by this section. Interest is payable on a penalty assessed in error from the date the penalty was paid. The interest rate set in G.S. 105-241.21 applies to interest payable under this section.

(e) The clear proceeds of all civil penalties assessed by the Department pursuant to this Article, minus any fees paid as interest, filing fees, attorneys' fees, or other necessary costs of court associated with the defense of penalties imposed by the Department pursuant to this Article shall be remitted to the Civil Penalty and Forfeiture Fund in accordance with G.S. 115C-457.2.

History.
2009-376, s. 2(a);2011-145, s. 19.1(g)
  EFFECT OF AMENDMENTS. --
  Session Laws 2011-145, s. 19.1(g), effective January 1, 2012, substituted "Public Safety" for "Crime Control and Public Safety" in subsection (a) and in the section heading.

§ 20-179. Sentencing hearing after conviction for impaired driving; determination of grossly aggravating and aggravating and mitigating factors; punishments

(a) **Sentencing Hearing Required.** -- After a conviction under G.S. 20-138.1, G.S. 20-138.2, a second or subsequent conviction under G.S. 20-138.2A, or a second or subsequent conviction under G.S. 20-138.2B, or when any of those offenses are remanded back to district court after an appeal to superior court, the judge shall hold a sentencing hearing to determine whether there are aggravating or mitigating factors that affect the sentence to be imposed. The following apply:

(1) The court shall consider evidence of aggravating or mitigating factors present in the offense that make an aggravated or mitigated sentence appropriate. The State bears the burden of proving beyond a reasonable doubt that an aggravating factor exists, and the offender bears the burden of proving by a preponderance of the evidence that a mitigating factor exists.

(2) Before the hearing the prosecutor shall make all feasible efforts to secure the defendant's full record of traffic convictions, and shall present to the judge that record for consideration in the hearing. Upon request of the defendant, the prosecutor shall furnish the defendant or the defendant's attorney a copy of the defendant's record of traffic convictions at a reasonable time prior to the introduction of the record into evidence. In addition, the prosecutor shall present all other appropriate grossly aggravating and aggravating factors of which the prosecutor is aware, and the defendant or the defendant's attorney may present all appropriate mitigating factors. In every instance in which a valid chemical analysis is made of the defendant, the prosecutor shall present evidence of the resulting alcohol concentration.

(a1) **Jury Trial in Superior Court; Jury Procedure if Trial Bifurcated. --**

(1) **Notice.** -- If the defendant appeals to superior court, and the State intends to use one or more aggravating factors under subsections (c) or (d) of this section, the State must provide the defendant with notice of its intent. The notice shall be provided no later than 10 days prior to trial and shall contain a plain and concise factual statement indicating the factor or factors it intends to use under the authority of subsections (c) and (d) of this section. The notice must list all the aggravating factors that the State seeks to establish.

(2) **Aggravating factors.** -- The defendant may admit to the existence of an aggravating factor, and the factor so admitted shall be treated as though it were found by a jury pursuant to the procedures in this section. If the defendant does not so admit, only a jury may determine if an aggravating factor is present. The jury impaneled for the trial may, in the same trial, also determine if one or more aggravating factors is present, unless the court determines that the interests of justice require that a separate sentencing proceeding be used to make that determination. If the court determines that a separate proceeding is required, the proceeding shall be conducted by the trial judge before the trial jury as soon as practicable after the guilty verdict is returned. The State bears the burden of proving beyond a reasonable doubt that an aggravating factor exists, and the offender bears the burden of proving by a preponderance of the evidence that a mitigating factor exists.

(3) **Convening the jury.** -- If prior to the time that the trial jury begins its deliberations on the issue of whether one or more aggravating factors exist, any juror dies, becomes incapacitated or disqualified, or is discharged for any reason, an alternate juror shall become a part of the jury and

serve in all respects as those selected on the regular trial panel. An alternate juror shall become a part of the jury in the order in which the juror was selected. If the trial jury is unable to reconvene for a hearing on the issue of whether one or more aggravating factors exist after having determined the guilt of the accused, the trial judge shall impanel a new jury to determine the issue.

(4) **Jury selection.** -- A jury selected to determine whether one or more aggravating factors exist shall be selected in the same manner as juries are selected for the trial of criminal cases.

(a2) **Jury Trial on Aggravating Factors in Superior Court.** --

(1) **Defendant admits aggravating factor only.** -- If the defendant admits that an aggravating factor exists, but pleads not guilty to the underlying charge, a jury shall be impaneled to dispose of the charge only. In that case, evidence that relates solely to the establishment of an aggravating factor shall not be admitted in the trial.

(2) **Defendant pleads guilty to the charge only.** -- If the defendant pleads guilty to the charge, but contests the existence of one or more aggravating factors, a jury shall be impaneled to determine if the aggravating factor or factors exist.

(a3) **Procedure When Jury Trial Waived.** -- If a defendant waives the right to a jury trial under G.S. 15A-1201, the trial judge shall make all findings that are conferred upon the jury under the provisions of this section.

(b) Repealed by Session Laws 1983, c. 435, s. 29.

(c) **Determining Existence of Grossly Aggravating Factors.** -- At the sentencing hearing, based upon the evidence presented at trial and in the hearing, the judge, or the jury in superior court, must first determine whether there are any grossly aggravating factors in the case. Whether a prior conviction exists under subdivision (1) of this subsection, or whether a conviction exists under subdivision (d)(5) of this section, shall be matters to be determined by the judge, and not the jury, in district or superior court. If the sentencing hearing is for a case remanded back to district court from superior court, the judge shall determine whether the defendant has been convicted of any offense that was not considered at the initial sentencing hearing and impose the appropriate sentence under this section. The judge must impose the Aggravated Level One punishment under subsection (f3) of this section if it is determined that three or more grossly aggravating factors apply. The judge must impose the Level One punishment under subsection (g) of this section if it is determined that the grossly aggravating

factor in subdivision (4) of this subsection applies or two of the other grossly aggravating factors apply. If the judge does not find that the aggravating factor at subdivision (4) of this subsection applies, then the judge must impose the Level Two punishment under subsection (h) of this section if it is determined that only one of the other grossly aggravating factors applies. The grossly aggravating factors are:

(1) A prior conviction for an offense involving impaired driving if:

a. The conviction occurred within seven years before the date of the offense for which the defendant is being sentenced; or

b. The conviction occurs after the date of the offense for which the defendant is presently being sentenced, but prior to or contemporaneously with the present sentencing; or

c. The conviction occurred in district court; the case was appealed to superior court; the appeal has been withdrawn, or the case has been remanded back to district court; and a new sentencing hearing has not been held pursuant to G.S. 20-38.7.

Each prior conviction is a separate grossly aggravating factor.

(2) Driving by the defendant at the time of the offense while the defendant's driver's license was revoked pursuant to G.S. 20-28(a1).

(3) Serious injury to another person caused by the defendant's impaired driving at the time of the offense.

(4) Driving by the defendant while (i) a child under the age of 18 years, (ii) a person with the mental development of a child under the age of 18 years, or (iii) a person with a physical disability preventing unaided exit from the vehicle was in the vehicle at the time of the offense.

In imposing an Aggravated Level One, a Level One, or a Level Two punishment, the judge may consider the aggravating and mitigating factors in subsections (d) and (e) of this section in determining the appropriate sentence. If there are no grossly aggravating factors in the case, the judge must weigh all aggravating and mitigating factors and impose punishment as required by subsection (f) of this section.

(c1) **Written Findings.** -- The court shall make findings of the aggravating and mitigating factors present in the offense. If the jury finds factors in aggravation, the court shall ensure that those findings are entered in the court's determination of sentencing factors form or any comparable document used to record the findings of sentencing factors. Findings shall be in writing.

(d) **Aggravating Factors to Be Weighed.** -- The judge, or the jury in superior court, shall determine before sentencing under subsection (f) of this section whether any of the aggravating factors listed below apply to the defendant. The judge shall weigh the seriousness of each aggravating factor in the light of the particular circumstances of the case. The factors are:

(1) Gross impairment of the defendant's faculties while driving or an alcohol concentration of 0.15 or more within a relevant time after the driving. For purposes of this subdivision, the results of a chemical analysis presented at trial or sentencing shall be sufficient to prove the person's alcohol concentration, shall be conclusive, and shall not be subject to modification by any party, with or without approval by the court.

(2) Especially reckless or dangerous driving.

(3) Negligent driving that led to a reportable accident.

(4) Driving by the defendant while the defendant's driver's license was revoked.

(5) Two or more prior convictions of a motor vehicle offense not involving impaired driving for which at least three points are assigned under G.S. 20-16 or for which the convicted person's license is subject to revocation, if the convictions occurred within five years of the date of the offense for which the defendant is being sentenced, or one or more prior convictions of an offense involving impaired driving that occurred more than seven years before the date of the offense for which the defendant is being sentenced.

(6) Conviction under G.S. 20-141.5 of speeding by the defendant while fleeing or attempting to elude apprehension.

(7) Conviction under G.S. 20-141 of speeding by the defendant by at least 30 miles per hour over the legal limit.

(8) Passing a stopped school bus in violation of G.S. 20-217.

(9) Any other factor that aggravates the seriousness of the offense.

Except for the factor in subdivision (5) of this subsection the conduct constituting the aggravating factor shall occur during the same transaction or occurrence as the impaired driving offense.

(e) **Mitigating Factors to Be Weighed.** -- The judge shall also determine before sentencing under subsection (f) of this section whether any of the mitigating factors listed below apply to the defendant. The judge shall weigh the degree of mitigation of each factor in light of the particular circumstances of the case. The factors are:

(1) Slight impairment of the defendant's faculties resulting solely from alcohol, and an alcohol concentration that did not exceed 0.09 at any relevant time after the driving.

(2) Slight impairment of the defendant's faculties, resulting solely from alcohol, with no chemical analysis having been available to the defendant.

(3) Driving at the time of the offense that was safe and lawful except for the impairment of the defendant's faculties.

(4) A safe driving record, with the defendant's having no conviction for any motor vehicle offense for which at least four points are assigned under G.S. 20-16 or for which the person's license is subject to revocation within five years of the date of the offense for which the defendant is being sentenced.

(5) Impairment of the defendant's faculties caused primarily by a lawfully prescribed drug for an existing medical condition, and the amount of the drug taken was within the prescribed dosage.

(6) The defendant's voluntary submission to a mental health facility for assessment after being charged with the impaired driving offense for which the defendant is being sentenced, and, if recommended by the facility, voluntary participation in the recommended treatment.

(6a) Completion of a substance abuse assessment, compliance with its recommendations, and simultaneously maintaining 60 days of continuous abstinence from alcohol consumption, as proven by a continuous alcohol monitoring system. The continuous alcohol monitoring system shall be of a type approved by the Division of Adult Correction and Juvenile Justice of the Department of Public Safety.

(7) Any other factor that mitigates the seriousness of the offense.

Except for the factors in subdivisions (4), (6), (6a), and (7) of this subsection, the conduct constituting the mitigating factor shall occur during the same transaction or occurrence as the impaired driving offense.

(f) **Weighing the Aggravating and Mitigating Factors.** -- If the judge or the jury in the sentencing hearing determines that there are no grossly aggravating factors, the judge shall weigh all aggravating and mitigating factors listed in subsections (d) and (e) of this section. If the judge determines that:

(1) The aggravating factors substantially outweigh any mitigating factors, the judge shall note in the judgment the factors found and the judge's finding that the defendant is subject to the Level Three punishment and impose a punishment within the limits defined in subsection (i) of this section.

(2) There are no aggravating and mitigating factors, or that aggravating factors

are substantially counterbalanced by mitigating factors, the judge shall note in the judgment any factors found and the finding that the defendant is subject to the Level Four punishment and impose a punishment within the limits defined in subsection (j) of this section.

(3) The mitigating factors substantially outweigh any aggravating factors, the judge shall note in the judgment the factors found and the judge's finding that the defendant is subject to the Level Five punishment and impose a punishment within the limits defined in subsection (k) of this section.

It is not a mitigating factor that the driver of the vehicle was suffering from alcoholism, drug addiction, diminished capacity, or mental disease or defect. Evidence of these matters may be received in the sentencing hearing, however, for use by the judge in formulating terms and conditions of sentence after determining which punishment level shall be imposed.

(f1) **Aider and Abettor Punishment.** -- Notwithstanding any other provisions of this section, a person convicted of impaired driving under G.S. 20-138.1 under the common law concept of aiding and abetting is subject to Level Five punishment. The judge need not make any findings of grossly aggravating, aggravating, or mitigating factors in such cases.

(f2) **Limit on Consolidation of Judgments.** -- Except as provided in subsection (f1) of this section, in each charge of impaired driving for which there is a conviction the judge shall determine if the sentencing factors described in subsections (c), (d) and (e) of this section are applicable unless the impaired driving charge is consolidated with a charge carrying a greater punishment. Two or more impaired driving charges may not be consolidated for judgment.

(f3) **Aggravated Level One Punishment.** -- A defendant subject to Aggravated Level One punishment may be fined up to ten thousand dollars ($ 10,000) and shall be sentenced to a term of imprisonment that includes a minimum term of not less than 12 months and a maximum term of not more than 36 months. Notwithstanding G.S. 15A-1371, a defendant sentenced to a term of imprisonment pursuant to this subsection shall not be eligible for parole. However, the defendant shall be released from the Statewide Misdemeanant Confinement Program on the date equivalent to the defendant's maximum imposed term of imprisonment less four months and shall be supervised by the Section of Community Supervision of the Division of Adult Correction and Juvenile Justice under and subject to the provisions of Article 84A of Chapter 15A of the General Statutes

and shall also be required to abstain from alcohol consumption for the four-month period of supervision as verified by a continuous alcohol monitoring system. For purposes of revocation, violation of the requirement to abstain from alcohol or comply with the use of a continuous alcohol monitoring system shall be deemed a controlling condition under G.S. 15A-1368.4.

The term of imprisonment may be suspended only if a condition of special probation is imposed to require the defendant to serve a term of imprisonment of at least 120 days. If the defendant is placed on probation, the judge shall impose as requirements that the defendant (i) abstain from alcohol consumption for a minimum of 120 days to a maximum of the term of probation, as verified by a continuous alcohol monitoring system pursuant to subsection (h1) of this section, and (ii) obtain a substance abuse assessment and the education or treatment required by G.S. 20-17.6 for the restoration of a drivers license and as a condition of probation. The judge may impose any other lawful condition of probation.

(g) **Level One Punishment.** -- A defendant subject to Level One punishment may be fined up to four thousand dollars ($ 4,000) and shall be sentenced to a term of imprisonment that includes a minimum term of not less than 30 days and a maximum term of not more than 24 months. The term of imprisonment may be suspended only if a condition of special probation is imposed to require the defendant to serve a term of imprisonment of at least 30 days. A judge may reduce the minimum term of imprisonment required to a term of not less than 10 days if a condition of special probation is imposed to require that a defendant abstain from alcohol consumption and be monitored by a continuous alcohol monitoring system, of a type approved by the Division of Adult Correction and Juvenile Justice of the Department of Public Safety, for a period of not less than 120 days. If the defendant is monitored on an approved continuous alcohol monitoring system during the pretrial period, up to 60 days of pretrial monitoring may be credited against the 120-day monitoring requirement for probation. If the defendant is placed on probation, the judge shall impose a requirement that the defendant obtain a substance abuse assessment and the education or treatment required by G.S. 20-17.6 for the restoration of a drivers license and as a condition of probation. The judge may impose any other lawful condition of probation.

(h) **Level Two Punishment.** -- A defendant subject to Level Two punishment may be fined up to two thousand dollars ($ 2,000) and shall be sentenced to a term of imprisonment that includes a minimum term of not less than seven days and a maximum term of not more than 12 months. The term of imprisonment may be suspended only if a condition of special probation is imposed to require the defendant to serve a term of imprisonment of at least seven days or to abstain from consuming alcohol for at least 90 consecutive days, as verified by a continuous alcohol monitoring system, of a type approved by the Division of Adult Correction and Juvenile Justice of the Department of Public Safety. If the defendant is subject to Level Two punishment based on a finding that the grossly aggravating factor in subdivision (1) or (2) of subsection (c) of this section applies, the conviction for a prior offense involving impaired driving occurred within five years before the date of the offense for which the defendant is being sentenced and the judge suspends all active terms of imprisonment and imposes abstention from alcohol as verified by a continuous alcohol monitory system, then the judge must also impose as an additional condition of special probation that the defendant must complete 240 hours of community service. If the defendant is monitored on an approved continuous alcohol monitoring system during the pretrial period, up to 60 days of pretrial monitoring may be credited against the 90-day monitoring requirement for probation. If the defendant is placed on probation, the judge shall impose a requirement that the defendant obtain a substance abuse assessment and the education or treatment required by G.S. 20-17.6 for the restoration of a drivers license and as a condition of probation. The judge may impose any other lawful condition of probation.

(h1) **Alcohol Abstinence as Condition of Probation for Level One and Level Two Punishments.** -- The judge may impose, as a condition of probation for defendants subject to Level One or Level Two punishments, that the defendant abstain from alcohol consumption for a minimum of 30 days, to a maximum of the term of probation, as verified by a continuous alcohol monitoring system. The defendant's abstinence from alcohol shall be verified by a continuous alcohol monitoring system of a type approved by the Division of Adult Correction and Juvenile Justice of the Department of Public Safety.

(h2) Repealed by Session Laws 2011-191, s. 1, effective December 1, 2011, and applicable to offenses committed on or after that date.

(h3) Repealed by Session Laws 2012-146, s. 9, effective December 1, 2012.

(i) **Level Three Punishment.** -- A defendant subject to Level Three punishment may be fined up to one thousand dollars ($ 1,000) and shall be sentenced to a term of imprisonment that includes a minimum term of not less than 72 hours and a maximum term of not more than six months. The term of imprisonment may be suspended. However, the suspended sentence shall include the condition that the defendant:

(1) Be imprisoned for a term of at least 72 hours as a condition of special probation; or

(2) Perform community service for a term of at least 72 hours; or

(3) Repealed by Session Laws 2006-253, s. 23, effective December 1, 2006, and applicable to offenses committed on or after that date.

(4) Any combination of these conditions.

If the defendant is placed on probation, the judge shall impose a requirement that the defendant obtain a substance abuse assessment and the education or treatment required by G.S. 20-17.6 for the restoration of a drivers license and as a condition of probation. The judge may impose any other lawful condition of probation.

(j) **Level Four Punishment.** -- A defendant subject to Level Four punishment may be fined up to five hundred dollars ($ 500.00) and shall be sentenced to a term of imprisonment that includes a minimum term of not less than 48 hours and a maximum term of not more than 120 days. The term of imprisonment may be suspended. However, the suspended sentence shall include the condition that the defendant:

(1) Be imprisoned for a term of 48 hours as a condition of special probation; or

(2) Perform community service for a term of 48 hours; or

(3) Repealed by Session Laws 2006-253, s. 23, effective December 1, 2006, and applicable to offenses committed on or after that date.

(4) Any combination of these conditions.

If the defendant is placed on probation, the judge shall impose a requirement that the defendant obtain a substance abuse assessment and the education or treatment required by G.S. 20-17.6 for the restoration of a drivers license and as a condition of probation. The judge may impose any other lawful condition of probation.

(k) **Level Five Punishment.** -- A defendant subject to Level Five punishment may be fined up to two hundred dollars ($ 200.00) and shall be sentenced to a term of imprisonment that includes a minimum term of not less than 24 hours and a maximum term of not more than 60 days. The term of imprisonment may be suspended. However, the suspended sentence shall include the condition that the defendant:

(1) Be imprisoned for a term of 24 hours as a condition of special probation; or

(2) Perform community service for a term of 24 hours; or

(3) Repealed by Session Laws 2006-253, s. 23, effective December 1, 2006, and applicable to offenses committed on or after that date.

(4) Any combination of these conditions.

If the defendant is placed on probation, the judge shall impose a requirement that the defendant obtain a substance abuse assessment and the education or treatment required by G.S. 20-17.6 for the restoration of a drivers license and as a condition of probation. The judge may impose any other lawful condition of probation.

(k1) **Credit for Inpatient Treatment.** -- Pursuant to G.S. 15A-1351(a), the judge may order that a term of imprisonment imposed as a condition of special probation under any level of punishment be served as an inpatient in a facility operated or licensed by the State for the treatment of alcoholism or substance abuse where the defendant has been accepted for admission or commitment as an inpatient. The defendant shall bear the expense of any treatment unless the trial judge orders that the costs be absorbed by the State. The judge may impose restrictions on the defendant's ability to leave the premises of the treatment facility and require that the defendant follow the rules of the treatment facility. The judge may credit against the active sentence imposed on a defendant the time the defendant was an inpatient at the treatment facility, provided such treatment occurred after the commission of the offense for which the defendant is being sentenced. This section shall not be construed to limit the authority of the judge in sentencing under any other provisions of law.

(k2) **Probationary Requirement for Abstinence and Use of Continuous Alcohol Monitoring.** -- The judge may order that as a condition of special probation for any level of offense under G.S. 20-179 the defendant abstain from alcohol consumption, as verified by a continuous alcohol monitoring system, of a type approved by the Division of Adult Correction and Juvenile Justice of the Department of Public Safety.

(k3) **Continuous Alcohol Monitoring During Probation.** -- The court, in the sentencing order, may authorize probation officers to require defendants to submit to continuous alcohol monitoring for assessment purposes if the defendant has been required to abstain from alcohol consumption during the term of probation and the probation officer believes the defendant is consuming alcohol. The defendant shall bear the costs of the continuous alcohol monitoring system if the use of the system has been authorized by a judge in accordance with this subsection.

(k4) **Continuous Alcohol Monitoring Exception.** -- Notwithstanding the provisions of subsections (g), (h), (k2), and (k3) of this section, if the court finds, upon good cause shown, that the defendant should not be required to pay the costs of the continuous alcohol monitoring system, the court shall not impose the use of a continuous alcohol monitoring system unless the local governmental entity responsible for the incarceration of the defendant in the local confinement facility agrees to pay the costs of the system.

(*l*) Repealed by Session Laws 1989, c. 691.

(m) Repealed by Session Laws 1995, c. 496, s. 2.

(n) **Time Limits for Performance of Community Service.** -- If the judgment requires the defendant to perform a specified number of hours of community service, a minimum of 24 hours must be ordered.

(o) **Evidentiary Standards; Proof of Prior Convictions.** -- In the sentencing hearing, the State shall prove any grossly aggravating or aggravating factor beyond a reasonable doubt, and the defendant shall prove any mitigating factor by the greater weight of the evidence. Evidence adduced by either party at trial may be utilized in the sentencing hearing. Except as modified by this section, the procedure in G.S. 15A-1334(b) governs. The judge may accept any evidence as to the presence or absence of previous convictions that the judge finds reliable but shall give prima facie effect to convictions recorded by the Division or any other agency of the State of North Carolina. A copy of such conviction records transmitted by the police information network in general accordance with the procedure authorized by G.S. 20-26(b) is admissible in evidence without further authentication. If the judge decides to impose an active sentence of imprisonment that would not have been imposed but for a prior conviction of an offense, the judge shall afford the defendant an opportunity to introduce evidence that the prior conviction had been obtained in a case in which the defendant was indigent, had no counsel, and had not waived the right to counsel. If the defendant proves by the preponderance of the evidence all three above facts concerning the prior case, the conviction may not be used as a grossly aggravating or aggravating factor.

(p) **Limit on Amelioration of Punishment.** -- For active terms of imprisonment imposed under this section:

(1) The judge may not give credit to the defendant for the first 24 hours of time spent in incarceration pending trial.

(2) The defendant shall serve the mandatory minimum period of imprisonment and good or gain time credit may not be used to reduce that mandatory minimum period.

(3) The defendant may not be released on parole unless the defendant is otherwise eligible, has served the mandatory minimum period of imprisonment, and has obtained a substance abuse assessment and completed any recommended treatment or training program or is paroled into a residential treatment program.

With respect to the minimum or specific term of imprisonment imposed as a condition of special probation under this section, the judge may not give credit to the defendant for the first 24 hours of time spent in incarceration pending trial.

(q) Repealed by Session Laws 1991, c. 726, s. 20.

(r) **Supervised Probation Terminated.** -- Unless a judge in the judge's discretion determines that supervised probation is necessary, and includes in the record that the judge has received evidence and finds as a fact that supervised probation is necessary, and states in the judgment that supervised probation is necessary, a defendant convicted of an offense of impaired driving shall be placed on unsupervised probation if the defendant meets three conditions. These conditions are that the defendant (i) has not been convicted of an offense of impaired driving within the seven years preceding the date of this offense for which the defendant is sentenced, (ii) is being sentenced under subsections (i), (j), and (k) of this section, and (iii) has obtained any necessary substance abuse assessment and completed any recommended treatment or training program.

When a judge determines in accordance with the above procedures that a defendant should be placed on supervised probation, the judge shall authorize the probation officer to modify the defendant's probation by placing the defendant on unsupervised probation upon the completion by the defendant of the following conditions of the suspended sentence:

(1) Community service; or

(2) Repealed by Session Laws 1995 c. 496, s. 2.

(3) Payment of any fines, court costs, and fees; or

(4) Any combination of these conditions.

(s) **Method of Serving Sentence.** -- The judge in the judge's discretion may order a term of imprisonment to be served on weekends, even if the sentence cannot be served in consecutive sequence. However, if the defendant is ordered to a term of 48 hours or more, or has 48 hours or more remaining on a term of imprisonment, the defendant shall be required to serve 48 continuous hours of imprisonment to be given credit for time served. All of the following apply to a sentence served under this subsection:

(1) Credit for any jail time shall only be given hour for hour for time actually served. The jail shall maintain a log showing number of hours served.

(2) The defendant shall be refused entrance and shall be reported back to court if the defendant appears at the jail and has remaining in the defendant's body any alcohol as shown by an alcohol screening device or controlled substance previously consumed, unless lawfully obtained and taken in therapeutically appropriate amounts.

(3) If a defendant has been reported back to court under subdivision (2) of this subsection, the court shall hold a hearing. The defendant shall be ordered to serve the defendant's jail time immediately and shall not be eligible to serve jail time on weekends if the court determines that, at the time of entrance to the jail, at least one of the following apply:

a. The defendant had previously consumed alcohol in the defendant's body as shown by an alcohol screening device.

b. The defendant had a previously consumed controlled substance in the defendant's body.

It shall be a defense to an immediate service of sentence of jail time and ineligibility for weekend service of jail time if the court determines that alcohol or controlled substance was lawfully obtained and was taken in therapeutically appropriate amounts.

(t) Repealed by Session Laws 1995, c. 496, s. 2.

History.
1937, c. 407, s. 140; 1947, c. 1067, s. 18; 1967, c. 510; 1969, c. 50; c. 1283, ss. 1-5; 1971, c. 619, s. 16; c. 1133, s. 1; 1975, c. 716, s. 5; 1977, c. 125; 1977, 2nd Sess., c. 1222, s. 1; 1979, c. 453, ss. 1, 2; c. 903, ss. 1, 2; 1981, c. 466, ss. 4-6; 1983, c. 435, s. 29; 1983 (Reg. Sess., 1984), c. 1101, ss. 21-29, 36; 1985, c. 706, s. 1; 1985 (Reg. Sess., 1986), c. 1014, s. 201(d); 1987, c. 139; c. 352, s. 1; c. 797, ss. 1, 2; 1989, c. 548, ss. 1, 2; c. 691, ss. 1-3, 4.1; 1989 (Reg. Sess., 1990), c. 1031, ss. 1, 2; c. 1039, s. 6; 1991, c. 636, s. 19(b), (c); c. 726, ss. 20, 21; 1993, c. 285, s. 9;1995, c. 191, s. 3;c. 496, ss. 2 -7; c. 506, ss. 11-13; 1997-379, ss. 2.1 -2.8; 1997-443, s. 19.26(c);1998-182, ss. 25, 31-35; 2006-253, s. 23;2007-165, ss. 2, 3; 2007-493, ss. 6, 20, 26; 2009-372, s. 14;2010-97, s. 2;2011-145, s. 19.1(h), (k); 2011-191, s. 1;2011-329, s. 1;2012-146, s. 9;2012-194, s. 51.5;2013-348, s. 2;2014-100, s. 16C.1(d);2015-186, s. 6;2015-264, ss. 38(b), 86; 2015-289, s. 2;2017-102, s. 7.1;2017-186, s. 2 (nnnn)

EDITOR'S NOTE. --
Session Laws 2006-253, s. 29, provides: "The North Carolina General Assembly requests that the Chief Justice of the North Carolina Supreme Court encourage the judges of this State to obtain continuing legal education on the laws of this State relating to driving while impaired offenses and related issues, and to promulgate any rules necessary to ensure that the judiciary receives necessary training and education on these laws."

Session Laws 2012-146, s. 11, made the amendments to this section by Session Laws 2012-146, s. 9, applicable to offenses committed or any custody and visitation orders issued on or after that date.

Session Laws 2014-100, s. 16C.1(g), made the amendments to subsection (f3) by Session Laws

2014-100, s. 16C.1(d), applicable to (i) persons placed on probation or sentenced to imprisonment for impaired driving under G.S. 20-138.1 on or after January 1, 2015, and (ii) persons placed on probation or sentenced to imprisonment for all other misdemeanors other than impaired driving under G.S. 20-138.1 on or after October 1, 2014.

Session Laws 2014-100, s. 1.1, provides: "This act shall be known as 'The Current Operations and Capital Improvements Appropriations Act of 2014.'"

Session Laws 2014-100, s. 38.7, is a severability clause.

Session Laws 2015-186, s. 1, provides: "This act shall be known as the 'North Carolina Drivers License Restoration Act.'"

Session Laws 2015-186, s. 7, as amended by Session Laws 2015-264, s. 86, provides: "This act becomes effective December 1, 2015, and applies to offenses committed on or after that date. Prosecutions for offenses committed before the effective date of this act are not abated or affected by this act, and the statutes that would be applicable but for this act remain applicable to those prosecutions." Session Laws 2015-186, s. 6, had substituted "G.S. 20-28(a1)" for "G.S. 20-28" in subdivision (c)(2).

Session Laws 2015-264, s. 38(c), provides: "This section becomes effective December 1, 2015, and applies to convictions on or after that date. Prosecutions for offenses committed before the effective date of this section are not abated or affected by this section, and the statutes that would be applicable but for this section remain applicable to those prosecutions." Session Laws 2015-264, s. 38(b), had substituted "pursuant to G.S. 20-28(a1)" for "under G.S. 20-28(a1)," and deleted "and the revocation was an impaired driving revocation under G.S. 20-28.2(a)" at the end of subdivision (c)(2).

Session Laws 2015-264, s. 91.7, is a severability clause.

Session Laws 2015-289, s. 4, made subsection (a3), as added by Session Laws 2015-289, s. 2, applicable to defendants waiving their right to trial by jury on or after October 1, 2015.

EFFECT OF AMENDMENTS. --

Session Laws 2006-253, s. 23, effective December 1, 2006, and applicable to offenses committed on or after that date, rewrote the section.

Session Laws 2007-493, ss. 6 and 20, effective August 30, 2007, substituted "G.S. 20-138.2B" for "G.S. 20-138.3" in subsection (a), deleted "G.S. 20-138.3" following "G.S. 20-138.2B"; in subsection (c), in the second sentence, inserted "or whether a conviction exists under subdivision (d)(5) of this section," and made a related change; added subdivision (c)(1)c, and made a minor stylistic change; in subdivision (p)(3), deleted "or is paroled into a residential treatment program" at the end; and, in subdivision (s)(3), deleted "if" at the end of the introductory language.

Session Laws 2007-493, s. 26, effective December 1, 2007, and applicable to offenses committed on or after that date, in subdivision (d)(1), substituted "0.15" for "0.16" in the first sentence and added the last sentence.

Session Laws 2009-372, s. 14, effective December 1, 2009, and applicable to offenses committed on or after that date, rewrote subsection (n).

Session Laws 2010-97, s. 2, effective July 20, 2010, added "or is paroled into a residential treatment program" in subdivision (p)(3).

Session Laws 2011-145, s. 19.1(h), (k), effective January 1, 2012, substituted "Division of Adult Correction of the Department of Public Safety" for "Department of Correction" in subdivision (e)(6a) and subsections (f3) and (h1); and substituted "Section of Prisons of the Division of Adult Correction" for "Division of Community Corrections" in subsection (f3).

Session Laws 2011-191, s. 1, effective December 1, 2011, and applicable to offenses committed on or after that date, in subsection (c), in the introductory paragraph, added the fourth sentence, and deleted "or more" following "two" in the fifth sentence, and in the last paragraph, substituted "imposing an Aggravated Level One, a Level One, or a Level Two punishment" for "imposing a Level One or Two punishment"; added subsection (f3); in subsection (h1), substituted "the term of probation" for "60 days" in the first sentence, and deleted the former second sentence, which read: "The total cost to the defendant for the continuous alcohol monitoring system may not exceed one thousand dollars ($1,000)"; deleted subsection (h2), which read: "Notwithstanding the provisions of subsection (h1), if the court finds, upon good cause shown, that the defendant should not be required to pay the costs of the continuous alcohol monitoring system, the court shall not impose the use of a continuous alcohol monitoring system unless the local governmental entity responsible for the incarceration of the defendant in the local confinement facility agrees to pay the costs of the system"; and in subsection (h3), substituted "subsection (h1)" for "subsections (h1) or (h2)."

Session Laws 2011-329, s. 1, effective December 1, 2011, and applicable to offenses committed on or after that date, in the introductory paragraph of subsection (c), in the fifth sentence, inserted "the grossly aggravating factor in subdivision (4) of this subsection applies or" and substituted "two of the other grossly aggravating factors" for "two or more grossly aggravating factors," and in the sixth sentence, added "If the judge does not find that the aggravating factor at subdivision (4) of this subsection applies then" and "other"; and in subdivision (c)(4), inserted "(i)," substituted "18 years" for "16 years," and inserted "(ii) a person with the mental development of a child under the age of 18 years, or (iii) a person with a physical disability preventing unaided exit from the vehicle."

Session Laws 2012-146, s. 9, effective December 1, 2012, added the third and fourth sentences in subsection (g); in subsection (h), added the language beginning "or to abstain from consuming" to the end of the second sentence, and added the third sentence; deleted subsection (h3), which read "Any fees or costs paid pursuant to subsection (h1) of this section shall be paid to the clerk of court for the county in which the judgment was entered or the deferred prosecution agreement was filed. Fees or costs collected under this subsection shall be transmitted to the entity providing the continuous alcohol monitoring system"; and added subsections (k2), (k3), and (k4). For applicability, see Editor's note.

Session Laws 2012-194, s. 51.5, effective upon enactment of Session Laws 2012-146, substituted "G.S. 20-179" for "G.S. 20-170" in subsection (k2).

Session Laws 2013-348, s. 2, effective October 1, 2013, added the third sentence in subsection (h). For applicability, see Editor's note.

Session Laws 2014-100, s. 16C.1(d), effective October 1, 2014, in the first paragraph of subsection (f3), substituted "Statewide Misdemeanant Confinement Program" for "Division of Adult Correction of the Department of Public Safety" and "Section of Community Supervision" for "Section of Prisons" in the third sentence. See Editor's note for applicability.

Session Laws 2015-186, s. 6, effective December 1, 2015, and applicable to convictions on or after that date, substituted "G.S. 20-28(a1)" for "G.S. 20-28" in subdivision (c)(2). For effective date and applicability, see Editor's note.

Session Laws 2015-264, s. 38(b), effective December 1, 2015, substituted "pursuant to G.S. 20-28(a1)" for "under G.S. 20-28(a1)", and deleted "and the revocation was an impaired driving revocation under G.S. 20-28.2(a)" at the end of subdivision (c)(2). For effective date and applicability, see Editor's note.

Session Laws 2015-289, s. 2, effective October 1, 2015, added subsection (a3). For applicability, see Editor's note.

Session Laws 2017-102, s. 7.1, effective July 12, 2017, rewrote the section.

Session Laws 2017-186, s. 2 (nnnn), effective December 1, 2017, inserted "and Juvenile Justice" following "Division of Adult Correction" throughout the section.

EDITOR'S NOTE. --Many of the cases cited below were decided under this section as it read prior to the 1983 amendment and the 1993 amendment, which reduced the blood alcohol content for driving while impaired and related offenses from 0.10 to 0.08.

CONSTITUTIONALITY. --Defendant lacked standing to challenge the constitutionality of this section. State v. Roberts, 237 N.C. App. 551, 767 S.E.2d 543 (2014).

BIFURCATED PROCEDURE CONSTITUTIONAL. --The bifurcated procedure that the legislature has established for impaired driving cases, with the jury determining whether G.S. 20-138.1 has been violated and the judge determining the length of punishment required under this section, is constitutional. State v. Field, 75 N.C. App. 647, 331 S.E.2d 221, cert. denied and appeal dismissed, 315 N.C. 186, 337 S.E.2d 582 (1985).

Because the factors before the trial judge in determining sentencing are not elements of the offense, their consideration for purposes of sentencing is a function of the judge and is therefore not susceptible to constitutional challenge based upon either the right to a jury trial under U.S. Const., Amend. VI or N.C. Const., Art. I, § 24. State v. Denning, 316 N.C.

523, 342 S.E.2d 855 (1986), involving sentencing under this section for impaired driving.

The North Carolina legislature did not overstep the bounds of the Constitution in the sentencing scheme of this section. Field v. Sheriff of Wake County, 831 F.2d 530 (4th Cir. 1987).

In a sentencing hearing conducted after defendant pled guilty to driving while impaired the trial court did not violate the Constitution by finding that defendant had caused serious injury as a result of his impaired driving, one of the aggravating factors in this section. Field v. Sheriff of Wake County, 831 F.2d 530 (4th Cir. 1987).

THIS SECTION RELATES ONLY TO PUNISHMENT. State v. White, 246 N.C. 587, 99 S.E.2d 772 (1957).

AS TO APPLICABILITY OF FORMER SUBDIVISION (B)(1) OF THIS SECTION TO OUT-OF-STATE CONVICTIONS, see In re Sparks, 25 N.C. App. 65, 212 S.E.2d 220 (1975).

UNDER G.S. 20-24(C), A BOND FORFEITURE IS EQUIVALENT TO A CONVICTION. In re Sparks, 25 N.C. App. 65, 212 S.E.2d 220 (1975).

SERIOUS INJURY TO ANOTHER NOT ELEMENT OF OFFENSE. --Whether the defendant seriously injured another person was not an element of the crime of driving while impaired; it was a sentencing factor that the General Assembly deemed to be important in punishing those convicted of driving while impaired. State v. Field, 75 N.C. App. 627, 331 S.E.2d 221, cert. denied and appeal dismissed, 315 N.C. 186, 337 S.E.2d 582 (1985).

IMPOSITION OF MINIMUM AND MAXIMUM SENTENCES WAS NOT ERROR. --Trial judge did not err in stating both a minimum and maximum sentence for driving while impaired as G.S. 20-179(i) on its face, provided for a sentencing range. State v. McQueen, 181 N.C. App. 417, 639 S.E.2d 131 (2007), cert. denied, appeal dismissed, 361 N.C. 365, 646 S.E.2d 535 (2007).

MEANING OF "GROSS IMPAIRMENT". --"Gross impairment" is a high level of impairment, higher than that impairment which must be shown to prove the offense of DUI. State v. Harrington, 78 N.C. App. 39, 336 S.E.2d 852 (1985).

EFFECT OF BAC ON DETERMINATION OF "GROSS IMPAIRMENT". --While the statutory blood alcohol concentration (BAC) of 0.20 (now 0.08) may provide a "bright line" for determining "gross impairment," the finding of a BAC of 0.20 clearly is not required for the court to make the finding of gross impairment. State v. Harrington, 78 N.C. App. 39, 336 S.E.2d 852 (1985).

EVIDENCE WAS SUFFICIENT TO ALLOW THE COURT TO CONSIDER WHETHER DEFENDANT WAS GROSSLY IMPAIRED, where police officer testified that defendant drove erratically and did not keep his car in its lane of travel, was obviously unsteady on his feet, slurred his speech, had difficulty answering routine questions, and could not perform any of the four field sobriety tests satisfactorily; that defendant's blood alcohol concentration (BAC) was .14;

and that he admitted to the officer that he was under the influence of alcohol. State v. Harrington, 78 N.C. App. 39, 336 S.E.2d 852 (1985).

ESPECIALLY RECKLESS OR DANGEROUS DRIVING. --The legislature wrote the aggravating factor "especially reckless or dangerous driving" in the disjunctive, intending that evidence of either especially reckless or especially dangerous driving was enough to support one aggravating factor. However, there would need to be at least one item of evidence not used to prove either an element of the offense or any other factor in aggravation to support each additional aggravating factor. State v. Mack, 81 N.C. App. 578, 345 S.E.2d 223 (1986).

Impaired driving is in and of itself "reckless" and "dangerous." Therefore, to determine whether there was enough evidence to prove that defendant's driving was both "especially reckless" and "especially dangerous," the facts of a case must disclose excessive aspects of recklessness and dangerousness not normally present in the offense of impaired driving. State v. Mack, 81 N.C. App. 578, 345 S.E.2d 223 (1986).

GROSSLY AGGRAVATING FACTOR. --Trial court erred in sentencing defendant on his conviction for driving while impaired by finding that a grossly aggravating factor applied and permitted enhancement of his sentence for that offense; the law required that a grossly aggravating factor that was used to increase defendant's sentence beyond the presumptive range had to be submitted to a jury and found by the jury to exist beyond a reasonable doubt. State v. Cruz, 173 N.C. App. 689, 620 S.E.2d 251 (2005).

Trial court did not err in allowing the State of North Carolina to present evidence of grossly aggravating factors regarding defendant's sentence for driving while impaired without having complied with the 10-day notice provisions of the amended G.S. 20-179(a1) (1) because the notice provision was not applicable at the time of defendant's offense. State v. Dalton, 197 N.C. App. 392, 677 S.E.2d 208 (2009).

Context of finding the existence of a grossly aggravating factor based upon a prior driving while impaired conviction in superior court requires an interpretation that a "prior conviction" not be limited to only those not pending on direct appeal in the appellate courts; because there is no language limiting that definition to a "final" conviction or only those not challenged on appeal, the courts have no authority to interpret the statute as imposing such a limitation. State v. Cole, 262 N.C. App. 466, 822 S.E.2d 456 (2018).

Superior court properly concluded that defendant's prior driving while impaired (DWI) conviction, despite it being pending on appeal, constituted a "prior conviction"; accordingly, the superior court properly found the existence of a grossly aggravating factor based on the prior DWI conviction. State v. Cole, 262 N.C. App. 466, 822 S.E.2d 456 (2018).

WHEN NO GROSSLY AGGRAVATING FACTOR FOUND. --No grossly aggravating factors were found to exist, so the trial court was required to determine whether a Level Three, Level Four, or Level Five

punishment was appropriate by weighing those factors pursuant to the factors. State v. Geisslercrain, 233 N.C. App. 186, 756 S.E.2d 92 (2014).

FALLING ASLEEP WHILE DRIVING IS ESPECIALLY DANGEROUS. --While evidence that defendant fell asleep and ran off the road was not enough evidence to support both the especially dangerous and the especially reckless aggravating factors, falling asleep while driving is at least especially dangerous. State v. Mack, 81 N.C. App. 578, 345 S.E.2d 223 (1986).

"ESPECIALLY RECKLESS" DRIVING NOT SHOWN. --Where although the assistant district attorney stated that defendant had been charged with passing through a red light without stopping, there was no evidence before the court to support this assertion, the court erred in finding as an aggravating factor that defendant's driving had been especially reckless. State v. Lockwood, 78 N.C. App. 205, 336 S.E.2d 678 (1985).

THE BURDEN TO PROVE A FACTOR UNDER THIS SECTION IS BY THE GREATER WEIGHT OF THE EVIDENCE, similar to the preponderance standard used in the Fair Sentencing Act, G.S. 15A-1340.4. State v. Harrington, 78 N.C. App. 39, 336 S.E.2d 852 (1985).

Provision of this section specifically requiring the State "to prove any grossly aggravating or aggravating factor by the greater weight of the evidence" is synonymous with the "preponderance of the evidence" standard which has passed constitutional muster with the courts. State v. Denning, 316 N.C. 523, 342 S.E.2d 855 (1986).

THE PLAIN MEANING OF THE TERM "SUBSTANTIALLY" USED IN SUBDIVISION (F)(1) of this section, may be found in Black's Law Dictionary 1281 (5th ed. 1979), which defines it as, "[e]ssentially; without material qualification; in the main; in substance; materially; in a substantial manner. About, actually, competently, and essentially." State v. Weaver, 91 N.C. App. 413, 371 S.E.2d 759 (1988).

ALCOHOLICS ANONYMOUS IS NOT A "TREATMENT PROGRAM," it is, in fact, a support group for recovering alcoholics. State v. McGill, 114 N.C. App. 479, 442 S.E.2d 166 (1994).

LEVEL THREE PUNISHMENT HELD NOT AN ABUSE OF DISCRETION. --Where the trial judge found as factors to be considered in sentencing: (a) that no grossly aggravating factors were present; (b) that as an aggravating factor, defendant had at least one prior conviction of an impaired driving offense which occurred over seven years before the date of the present offense charged; and (c) as a factor in mitigation, that defendant had a safe driving record, having no convictions of any serious motor vehicle offense for which at least four points are assessed, or for which defendant's license was subject to revocation, within five years of the date of the present offense, and the judge then imposed a level three punishment as provided in subsection (i) of this section, the judge did not abuse his discretion. State v. Weaver, 91 N.C. App. 413, 371 S.E.2d 759 (1988).

LEVEL FOUR PUNISHMENT IMPOSED IF MITIGATING AND AGGRAVATING FACTORS ARE EQUAL. --Only if mitigating factors are found to apply and to substantially outweigh aggravating factors will a defendant receive Level Five Punishment. If mitigating factors and aggravating factors are in equipoise, Level Four Punishment, which permits a maximum term of 120 days, is to be imposed. State v. Santon, 101 N.C. App. 710, 401 S.E.2d 117 (1991).

SENTENCE OF 30 DAYS AS CONDITION OF SUSPENSION IN IMPOSING LEVEL FOUR PUNISHMENT WAS ERROR. --If the court had correctly found that a level four punishment should have been imposed, it erred in requiring the defendant to serve 30 days as part of the conditions of a suspended sentence, as subdivision (j)(1) limits the term of imprisonment to 48 hours. State v. MaGee, 75 N.C. App. 357, 330 S.E.2d 825 (1985).

THE NORTH CAROLINA LEGISLATURE HAS ACCORDED THE TRIAL COURT BROAD DISCRETION IN SUBSECTION (K) in sentencing a person convicted of driving under the influence, subject to one important restriction regarding punishment: initially the State trial court cannot imprison the defendant more than 24 hours. This mandatory restriction in a very real sense is the maximum sentence a State trial judge can impose under subsection (k), unless the defendant later violates a condition of probation. United States v. Harris, 27 F.3d 111 (4th Cir. 1994).

THE "LIKE PUNISHMENT" CLAUSE OF 18 U.S.C. § 13, THE FEDERAL ASSIMILATIVE CRIMES ACT, PLACES THE SAME RESTRICTION ON A FEDERAL COURT that is implementing the Assimilative Crimes Act. Thus, the federal court, like its State counterpart, cannot imprison a defendant more than 24 hours, unless he violates probation, nor can the federal court impose a fine in excess of $100. United States v. Harris, 27 F.3d 111 (4th Cir. 1994).

PRIOR CONVICTIONS ARE NOT AN ELEMENT OF THE OFFENSE OF DRIVING WHILE IMPAIRED, but are now merely one of several factors relating to punishment. State v. Denning, 316 N.C. 523, 342 S.E.2d 855 (1986).

WHEN PRIOR CONVICTION MAY NOT BE USED. --Under this section, once the State has proven by the greater weight of the evidence a prior driving under the influence conviction, defendant has the burden of proving by the preponderance of the evidence that in the case of the prior conviction (1) he was indigent; (2) he had no counsel; and (3) he had not waived counsel. If defendant meets his burden on all three facts, then the prior conviction may not be used as a basis for imposing an active sentence. State v. Haislip, 79 N.C. App. 656, 339 S.E.2d 832 (1986).

ALLEGATION OF PRIOR CONVICTION. --As to necessity for allegation of prior conviction under this section as it read prior to the 1983 amendment, see Harrell v. Scheidt, 243 N.C. 735, 92 S.E.2d 182 (1956); State v. Owenby, 10 N.C. App. 170, 177 S.E.2d 749 (1970); State v. Williams, 21 N.C. App. 70, 203 S.E.2d 399 (1974).

ADMISSIBILITY OF EVIDENCE OF PRIOR CONVICTION. --Evidence that a defendant has been previously convicted of drunken driving (now impaired driving) is admissible in a prosecution charging defendant with a second offense, even though the defendant neither testifies as a witness nor offers evidence of good character. State v. Owenby, 10 N.C. App. 170, 177 S.E.2d 749 (1970).

CONVICTION OF A SIMILAR OFFENSE IN ANOTHER JURISDICTION. --Although the definitions of "impairment" under North Carolina and New York laws are not identical and the statutes do not "mirror" one another, they are "substantially equivalent"; consequently, the trial court did not err in determining that defendant's prior conviction under New York law was a grossly aggravating factor in sentencing him under North Carolina law. State v. Parisi, 135 N.C. App. 222, 519 S.E.2d 531 (1999).

FAILURE TO PROVIDE DEFENDANT WITH NOTICE. --State failed to provide defendant with the statutorily required notice of its intention to use an aggravating factor under G.S. 20-179(d). State v. Reeves, 218 N.C. App. 570, 721 S.E.2d 317 (2012).

State's failure to provide notice under the statute was error, and because the court already found that the punishment was inappropriate, the error was not harmless and the court remanded for resentencing. State v. Geisslercrain, 233 N.C. App. 186, 756 S.E.2d 92 (2014).

State's failure to comply with the notice requirements did not violate the defendant's Sixth Amendment rights because the defendant's sentence was enhanced based only on the defendant's prior convictions. State v. Williams, 248 N.C. App. 112, 786 S.E.2d 419 (2016).

Trial court did not err by denying defendant's motion to strike grossly aggravating and aggravating factors under G.S. 20-179 based on the fact that the defendant had only seven-days' notice of the factors because the charge was not on appeal to the superior court. State v. Williams, 248 N.C. App. 112, 786 S.E.2d 419 (2016).

When the State fails to give notice of its intent to use aggravating sentencing factors as required by G.S. 20-179(a1)(1), the trial court's use of those factors in determining a defendant's sentencing level is reversible error. State v. Hughes, 265 N.C. App. 80, 827 S.E.2d 318 (2019), review denied, 372 N.C. 705, 830 S.E.2d 827, 2019 N.C. LEXIS 720 (2019).

State's failure to provide notice of its intent to use aggravating factors defined in G.S. 20-179 prevents the trial court from considering those factors at sentencing for impaired driving. State v. Hughes, 265 N.C. App. 80, 827 S.E.2d 318 (2019), review denied, 372 N.C. 705, 830 S.E.2d 827, 2019 N.C. LEXIS 720 (2019).

Language of G.S. 20-179(a1)(1) requires notice of the State's intent to use aggravating sentencing factors in impaired driving cases appealed to superior court, even if evidence supporting those factors was presented in district court. It is not enough that the defendant simply be made aware of the existence of

Chapter 20

such evidence. State v. Hughes, 265 N.C. App. 80, 827 S.E.2d 318 (2019), review denied, 372 N.C. 705, 830 S.E.2d 827, 2019 N.C. LEXIS 720 (2019).

Trial court committed prejudicial error by applying the G.S. 20-179(a1)(1) aggravating factors where the State had not provided defendant with sufficient notice of its intent to use those factors at sentencing, use of the factors raised the level of punishment imposed, and defendant had not waived his right to receive such notice. State v. Hughes, 265 N.C. App. 80, 827 S.E.2d 318 (2019), review denied, 372 N.C. 705, 830 S.E.2d 827, 2019 N.C. LEXIS 720 (2019).

FORMAL RULES OF EVIDENCE NOT APPLICABLE TO SENTENCING HEARING UNDER SUBSECTION (O). --Evidence adduced by either party at trial may be used at the sentencing hearing, under subsection (o) of this section, and the formal rules of evidence do not apply. State v. Haislip, 79 N.C. App. 656, 339 S.E.2d 832 (1986).

BUT STATEMENT BY COUNSEL IS NOT EVIDENCE. --While the formal rules of evidence do not apply at a sentencing hearing under subsection (o) of this section, the statement by defendant's counsel that defendant was indigent at the time of his 1981 driving under the influence conviction was not evidence. State v. Haislip, 79 N.C. App. 656, 339 S.E.2d 832 (1986).

JUDGE'S DISCRETION. --Even where only one aggravating factor, rather than two, is found along with two mitigating factors, the trial court still has the discretion to sentence the defendant to a Level Four punishment since it could have determined, within its discretion, that the one aggravating factor substantially counterbalanced the two mitigating factors; however, in this case, without any aggravating factors properly found, the trial court had no discretion but to sentence defendant to a level five punishment. State v. Geisslercrain, 233 N.C. App. 186, 756 S.E.2d 92 (2014).

JUDGMENT UPON EX PARTE REQUEST HELD ABUSE OF DISCRETION. --Judge's execution judgments allowing limited driving privileges upon a mere ex parte request, where he made no effort nor conducted any inquiry to ascertain whether the facts recited in the judgments were true and whether he was lawfully entitled to enter the judgments, and did not give the State an opportunity to be heard, when in truth the judgments were supported neither in fact nor in law and were beyond the judge's jurisdiction to enter, constituted a gross abuse of important provisions of the motor vehicle statutes and amounted to conduct prejudicial to the administration of justice that brings the judicial office into disrepute. In re Crutchfield, 289 N.C. 597, 223 S.E.2d 822 (1975).

If there are only mitigating factors present, and no aggravating factors present, the trial court must impose a Level Five punishment, and if there are no aggravating or mitigating factors present or, alternatively, if the aggravating and mitigating factors are substantially counterbalanced, then the trial court must impose a Level Four punishment. State v. Geisslercrain, 233 N.C. App. 186, 756 S.E.2d 92 (2014).

WHAT LEVEL OF PUNISHMENT TO BE IMPOSED. --If there are only aggravating factors present, and no mitigating factors present, then the aggravating factors substantially outweigh the mitigating factors (as there are none) as a matter of law, and the trial court must impose a Level Three punishment, and if the trial court determines that the mitigating factors substantially outweigh any aggravating factors, the trial court must impose a Level Five punishment. State v. Geisslercrain, 233 N.C. App. 186, 756 S.E.2d 92 (2014).

LICENSE SUSPENSIONS HELD SEPARATE AND DISTINCT REVOCATIONS. --Suspension of a license for refusal to submit to a chemical test at the time of an arrest for drunken driving (now impaired driving) and a suspension which results from a plea of guilty or a conviction of that charge are separate and distinct revocations. Vuncannon v. Garrett, 17 N.C. App. 440, 194 S.E.2d 364 (1973).

SENTENCING FORMS NEED NOT BE SIGNED AT TIME OF SENTENCING. --There is no requirement in the sentencing provisions of the Safe Roads Act requiring sentencing forms to be signed at the time of sentencing. State v. Sigmon, 74 N.C. App. 479, 328 S.E.2d 843 (1985).

SENTENCE FOUND WITHIN PRESUMPTIVE RANGE. --Court acted within the sentencing authority conferred to it under G.S. 20-179 when, following defendant's conviction for impaired driving, it sentenced defendant to 120 days of imprisonment, suspended, and placed defendant on unsupervised probation for 12 months as the punishment was tantamount to a sentence within the presumptive range, even though the trial court found two aggravating factors. State v. Green, 209 N.C. App. 669, 707 S.E.2d 715 (2011).

IMPOSITION OF CONDITIONS HELD PROPER. --Each of the conditions imposed on defendant was a non-discretionary byproduct of the sentence that was imposed in open court, so there was no error in imposing those conditions without defendant's presence. State v. Arrington, 215 N.C. App. 161, 714 S.E.2d 777 (2011), decided under former G.S. 143B-262.4.

AGGRAVATING FACTOR IMPROPERLY FOUND BY JUDGE. --If the aggravating factor had not been considered by the trial court, then there would have been only the single mitigating factor present, and the trial court would have been required to sentence Defendant to a Level Five punishment; the aggravating factor, which was improperly found by the judge, increased the penalty beyond the prescribed maximum, and defendant's Level Four punishment had to be vacated. State v. Geisslercrain, 233 N.C. App. 186, 756 S.E.2d 92 (2014).

HARMLESS ERROR. --Error under *Blakely v. Washington*, 542 U.S. 296 (2004), of not submitting aggravating factors to the jury so that they could be found beyond a reasonable doubt, which occurred in sentencing defendant under G.S. 20-179, was harmless since the overwhelming and uncontroverted testimony was that defendant totaled the victim's car and that a passenger was bleeding from the face and was

Chapter 20

treated at the emergency room. State v. McQueen, 181 N.C. App. 417, 639 S.E.2d 131 (2007), cert. denied, appeal dismissed, 361 N.C. 365, 646 S.E.2d 535 (2007).

Although the trial court should have submitted the aggravating factor in G.S. 20-179(c)(2), providing that at the time of the offense, defendant was driving while defendant's license was revoked, as defined by G.S. 20-28, and the revocation was an impaired driving revocation under G.S. 20-28.2(a), the error was harmless beyond a reasonable doubt. Defendant's driving record, admitted by the State, showed that defendant's driver's license was indefinitely revoked due to an impaired driving conviction and that the license had not been reinstated, which meant that evidence of the aggravating factor was overwhelming and uncontroverted such that a sentence beyond the statutory maximum could be imposed. State v. Coffey, 189 N.C. App. 382, 658 S.E.2d 73 (2008).

APPLIED in State v. Blankenship, 229 N.C. 589, 50 S.E.2d 724 (1948); State v. Nall, 239 N.C. 60, 79 S.E.2d 354 (1953); State v. Broadway, 256 N.C. 608, 124 S.E.2d 568 (1962); State v. Morgan, 263 N.C. 400, 139 S.E.2d 708 (1965); State v. Gallamore, 6 N.C. App. 608, 170 S.E.2d 573 (1969); State v. Spencer, 276 N.C. 535, 173 S.E.2d 765 (1970); State v. Tuggle, 17 N.C. App. 329, 194 S.E.2d 50 (1973); In re Greene, 297 N.C. 305, 255 S.E.2d 142 (1979); State v. Daughtry, 61 N.C. App. 320, 300 S.E.2d 719 (1983); State v. Cooney, 72 N.C. App. 649, 325 S.E.2d 15 (1985); State v. Gunter, 111 N.C. App. 621, 433 S.E.2d 191 (1993); State v. Gregory, 154 N.C. App. 718, 572 S.E.2d 838 (2002); State v. Armstrong, 203 N.C. App. 399, 691 S.E.2d 433 (2010).

CITED in State v. Parker, 220 N.C. 416, 17 S.E.2d 475 (1941); Fox v. Scheidt, 241 N.C. 31, 84 S.E.2d 259 (1954); State v. Cole, 241 N.C. 576, 86 S.E.2d 203 (1955); State v. Stone, 245 N.C. 42, 95 S.E.2d 77 (1956); State v. White, 246 N.C. 587, 99 S.E.2d 772 (1957); State v. Lee, 247 N.C. 230, 100 S.E.2d 372 (1957); State v. Green, 251 N.C. 141, 110 S.E.2d 805 (1959); State v. Ball, 255 N.C. 351, 121 S.E.2d 604 (1961); State v. Thompson, 257 N.C. 452, 126 S.E.2d 58 (1962); Brewer v. Garner, 264 N.C. 384, 141 S.E.2d 806 (1965); State v. Broome, 269 N.C. 661, 153 S.E.2d 384 (1967); State v. Morris, 275 N.C. 50, 165 S.E.2d 245 (1969); State v. Grant, 3 N.C. App. 586, 165 S.E.2d 505 (1969); State v. Owenby, 10 N.C. App. 170, 177 S.E.2d 749 (1970); Joyner v. Garrett, 279 N.C. 226, 182 S.E.2d 553 (1971); State v. Michaels, 11 N.C. App. 110, 180 S.E.2d 442 (1971); State v. Brown, 13 N.C. App. 327, 185 S.E.2d 453 (1971); State v. Medlin, 15 N.C. App. 434, 190 S.E.2d 425 (1972); State v. Burris, 17 N.C. App. 710, 195 S.E.2d 345 (1973); State v. Hurley, 18 N.C. App. 285, 196 S.E.2d 542 (1973); Helms v. Powell, 32 N.C. App. 266, 231 S.E.2d 912 (1977); In re Gardner, 39 N.C. App. 567, 251 S.E.2d 723 (1979); State v. McLawhorn, 43 N.C. App. 695, 260 S.E.2d 138 (1979); State v. Woodson, 49 N.C. App. 696, 272 S.E.2d 167 (1980); State v. Gooden, 65 N.C. App. 669, 309 S.E.2d 707 (1983); State v. Midgett, 78 N.C. App. 387, 337 S.E.2d 117 (1985); United States v. Kendrick, 636 F. Supp. 189 (E.D.N.C. 1986); State v. Barber, 93 N.C. App. 42, 376 S.E.2d 497 (1989); In re Inquiry

Concerning Judge Tucker, 348 N.C. 677, 501 S.E.2d 67 (1998); State v. Jarman, 140 N.C. App. 198, 535 S.E.2d 875 (2000); State v. Alexander, 359 N.C. 824, 616 S.E.2d 914 (2005); State v. Hurt, 361 N.C. 325, 643 S.E.2d 915 (2007); State v. Green, 211 N.C. App. 599, 710 S.E.2d 292 (2011); State v. Petty, 212 N.C. App. 368, 711 S.E.2d 509 (2011); State v. Norman, 213 N.C. App. 114, 711 S.E.2d 849 (2011), review denied, 718 S.E.2d 401, 2011 N.C. LEXIS 940 (2011); State v. Clowers, 217 N.C. App. 520, 720 S.E.2d 430 (2011); State v. Powell, 223 N.C. App. 77, 732 S.E.2d 491 (2012).

CROSS REFERENCES. --
As to Division of Adult Correction and Juvenile Justice of the Department of Public Safety establishing regulations for continuous alcohol monitoring systems, see G.S. 15A-1343.3. For current provisions regarding limited driving privileges, see G.S. 20-179.3.

LEGAL PERIODICALS. --
For survey of 1979 law on criminal procedure, see 58 N.C.L. Rev. 1404 (1980).

For 1997 legislative survey, see 20 Campbell L. Rev. 417.

OPINIONS OF THE ATTORNEY GENERAL
EDITOR'S NOTE. --The opinions of the Attorney General cited below were issued prior to the 1983 amendment and the 1993 amendment to this section. The 1993 amendment reduced the blood alcohol content for driving while impaired and related offenses from 0.10 to 0.08.

AS TO THE 7 YEAR LIMITATION IN FORMER SUBDIVISION (B)(1), see opinion of Attorney General to Solicitor F. Ogden Parker, 41 N.C.A.G. 535 (1971); opinion of Attorney General to Mr. James W. Copeland, Jr., Assistant District Attorney, Eighth Judicial District, 50 N.C.A.G. 89 (1981).

TEN-YEAR LIMITATION IN G.S. 20-36 APPLIES ONLY TO DEPARTMENT (NOW DIVISION) OF MOTOR VEHICLE ACTION. --See opinion of Attorney General to Honorable Robert A. Collier, Jr., 41 N.C.A.G. 322 (1971).

AS TO THE GRANTING, SCOPE, MODIFICATION AND REVOCATION OF LIMITED DRIVING PRIVILEGES UNDER FORMER SUBSECTION (B), see opinion of Attorney General to Mr. Robert C. Powell, Attorney at Law, 40 N.C.A.G. 401 (1969); opinion of Attorney General to Mr. John B. Whitley, District Prosecutor, Twenty-sixth Judicial District, 40 N.C.A.G. 409 (1969); the Honorable Walter W. Cohoon, Resident Judge, First Judicial District, 40 N.C.A.G. 410 (1969); opinion of Attorney General to Commissioner Joe W. Garrett, Department of Motor Vehicles, 40 N.C.A.G. 415 (1969); opinion of Attorney General to the Honorable John S. Gardner, District Court Judge, Sixteenth Judicial District, 40 N.C.A.G. 420 (1969); opinion of Attorney General to the Honorable Wm. Pope Barfield, Magistrate, Harnett County, 40 N.C.A.G. 407 (1970); opinion of Attorney General to Commissioner Joe W. Garrett, N.C. Department of Motor Vehicles, 40 N.C.A.G. 414 (1970); opinion of Attorney General to the Honorable Charles M. Johnson, Clerk of Superior Court, Montgomery County, 40

N.C.A.G. 418 (1970); opinion of Attorney General to Lt. O.H. Page, 41 N.C.A.G. 596 (1971); opinion of Attorney General to Mr. J. E. Holshouser, Sr., 41 N.C.A.G. 659 (1971); opinion of Attorney General to the Honorable J. Ray Braswell, 41 N.C.A.G. 706 (1971); opinion of Attorney General to Mr. James W. Hardison, Assistant District Attorney, 49 N.C.A.G. 119 (1980).

AS TO APPLICABILITY OF LIMITED DRIVING PRIVILEGE PROVISIONS TO OFFENSES COMMITTED BEFORE JULY 2, 1969, see opinion of Attorney General to Representative G. Hunter Warlick, Hickory, 40 N.C.A.G. 412 (1969).

ELECTRONIC HOUSE ARREST PROBATION. -- The mandatory minimum 14 day sentence for Level 1 and 7 days for Level 2 DWI defendants under subsections (g) and (h) may not be served through electronic house arrest probation. See opinion of Attorney General to Mr. Steve A. Balog, District Attorney, Prosecutorial District 15-A, 59 N.C.A.G. 62 (1989).

FEE FOR REHABILITATION COURSE. --Under this section prior to its amendment in 1983, the fee charged for an alcohol rehabilitation course could not be imposed by the court as part of the cost and collected by the clerk and distributed to the provider of the rehabilitation course. Opinion of Attorney General to Honorable George M. Britt, Chief District Judge, Seventh Judicial District, 48 N.C.A.G. 2 (1979).

§ 20-179.1. Presentence investigation of persons convicted of offense involving impaired driving

When a person has been convicted of an offense involving impaired driving, the trial judge may request a presentence investigation to determine whether the person convicted would benefit from treatment for habitual use of alcohol or drugs. If the person convicted objects, no presentence investigation may be ordered, but the judge retains his power to order suitable treatment as a condition of probation, and must do so when required by statute.

History.
1973, c. 612; 1981, c. 412, s. 4; c. 747, s. 66; 1983, c. 435, s. 29

N.C. Gen. Stat. § 20-179.2

Repealed by Session Laws 1995, c. 496, s. 8.

§ 20-179.3. Limited driving privilege

(a) **Definition of Limited Driving Privilege.** -- A limited driving privilege is a judgment issued in the discretion of a court for good cause shown authorizing a person with a revoked driver's license to drive for essential purposes related to any of the following:
(1) The person's employment.
(2) The maintenance of the person's household.

(3) The person's education.
(4) The person's court-ordered treatment or assessment.
(5) Community service ordered as a condition of the person's probation.
(6) Emergency medical care.
(7) Religious worship.

(b) **Eligibility. --**
(1) A person convicted of the offense of impaired driving under G.S. 20-138.1 is eligible for a limited driving privilege if:
a. At the time of the offense the person held either a valid driver's license or a license that had been expired for less than one year;
b. At the time of the offense the person had not within the preceding seven years been convicted of an offense involving impaired driving;
c. Punishment Level Three, Four, or Five was imposed for the offense of impaired driving;
d. Subsequent to the offense the person has not been convicted of, or had an unresolved charge lodged against the person for, an offense involving impaired driving; and
e. The person has obtained and filed with the court a substance abuse assessment of the type required by G.S. 20-17.6 for the restoration of a drivers license.

A person whose North Carolina driver's license is revoked because of a conviction in another jurisdiction substantially similar to impaired driving under G.S. 20-138.1 is eligible for a limited driving privilege if the person would be eligible for it had the conviction occurred in North Carolina. Eligibility for a limited driving privilege following a revocation under G.S. 20-16.2(d) is governed by G.S. 20-16.2(e1).

(2) Any person whose licensing privileges are forfeited pursuant to G.S. 15A-1331.1 is eligible for a limited driving privilege if the court finds that at the time of the forfeiture, the person held either a valid drivers license or a drivers license that had been expired for less than one year and
a. The person is supporting existing dependents or must have a drivers license to be gainfully employed; or
b. The person has an existing dependent who requires serious medical treatment and the defendant is the only person able to provide transportation to the dependent to the health care facility where the dependent can receive the needed medical treatment.

The limited driving privilege granted under this subdivision must restrict the person to essential driving related to the purposes listed above, and any driving that is not related to those purposes is unlawful even though done at times and upon routes that may be authorized by the privilege.

(c) **Privilege Not Effective until after Compliance with Court-Ordered Revocation.** -- A person convicted of an impaired driving offense may apply for a limited driving privilege at the time the judgment is entered. A person whose license is revoked because of a conviction in another jurisdiction substantially similar to impaired driving under G.S. 20-138.1 may apply for a limited driving privilege only after having completed at least 60 days of a court-imposed term of nonoperation of a motor vehicle, if the court in the other jurisdiction imposed such a term of nonoperation.

(c1) **Privilege Restrictions for High-Risk Drivers.** -- Notwithstanding any other provision of this section, any limited driving privilege issued to a person convicted of an impaired driving offense with an alcohol concentration of 0.15 or more at the time of the offense shall:

(1) Not become effective until at least 45 days after the final conviction under G.S. 20-138.1;

(2) Require the applicant to comply with the ignition interlock requirements of subsection (g5) of this section; and

(3) Restrict the applicant to driving only to and from the applicant's place of employment, the place the applicant is enrolled in school, the applicant's place of religious worship, any court ordered treatment or substance abuse education, and any ignition interlock service facility.

For purposes of this subsection, the results of a chemical analysis presented at trial or sentencing shall be sufficient to prove a person's alcohol concentration, shall be conclusive, and shall not be subject to modification by any party, with or without approval by the court.

(d) **Application for and Scheduling of Subsequent Hearing.** -- The application for a limited driving privilege made at any time after the day of sentencing must be filed with the clerk in duplicate, and no hearing scheduled may be held until a reasonable time after the clerk files a copy of the application with the district attorney's office. The hearing must be scheduled before:

(1) The presiding judge at the applicant's trial if that judge is assigned to a court in the district court district as defined in G.S. 7A-133 or superior court district or set of districts as defined in G.S. 7A-41.1, as the case may be, in which the conviction for impaired driving was imposed.

(2) The senior regular resident superior court judge of the superior court district or set of districts as defined in G.S. 7A-41.1 in which the conviction for impaired driving was imposed, if the presiding judge is not available within the district and the conviction was imposed in superior court.

(3) The chief district court judge of the district court district as defined in G.S. 7A-133 in which the conviction for impaired driving was imposed, if the presiding judge is not available within the district and the conviction was imposed in district court.

If the applicant was convicted of an offense in another jurisdiction, the hearing must be scheduled before the chief district court judge of the district court district as defined in G.S. 7A-133 in which he resides. G.S. 20-16.2(e1) governs the judge before whom a hearing is scheduled if the revocation was under G.S. 20-16.2(d). The hearing may be scheduled in any county within the district court district as defined in G.S. 7A-133 or superior court district or set of districts as defined in G.S. 7A-41.1, as the case may be.

(e) **Limited Basis for and Effect of Privilege.** -- A limited driving privilege issued under this section authorizes a person to drive if the person's license is revoked solely under G.S. 20-17(a)(2) or as a result of a conviction in another jurisdiction substantially similar to impaired driving under G.S. 20-138.1; if the person's license is revoked under any other statute, the limited driving privilege is invalid.

(f) **Overall Provisions on Use of Privilege.** -- Every limited driving privilege must restrict the applicant to essential driving related to the purposes listed in subsection (a), and any driving that is not related to those purposes is unlawful even though done at times and upon routes that may be authorized by the privilege. If the privilege is granted, driving related to emergency medical care is authorized at any time and without restriction as to routes, but all other driving must be for a purpose and done within the restrictions specified in the privilege.

(f1) **Definition of "Standard Working Hours".** -- Under this section, "standard working hours" are 6:00 A.M. to 8:00 P.M. on Monday through Friday.

(g) **Driving for Work-Related Purposes in Standard Working Hours.** -- In a limited driving privilege, the court may authorize driving for work-related purposes during standard working hours without specifying the times and routes in which the driving must occur. If the applicant is not required to drive for essential work-related purposes except during standard working hours, the limited driving privilege must prohibit driving during nonstandard working hours unless the driving is for emergency medical care or is authorized by subsection (g2). The limited driving privilege must state the name and address of the applicant's place of work or employer, and may include other information and restrictions applicable to work-related driving in the discretion of the court.

(g1) **Driving for Work-Related Purposes in Nonstandard Hours.** -- If the applicant is required to drive during nonstandard working hours for an essential work-related purpose, the applicant must present documentation of that fact before the judge may authorize the applicant to drive for this purpose during those hours. If the applicant is self-employed, the documentation must be attached to or made a part of the limited driving privilege. If the judge determines that it is necessary for the applicant to drive during nonstandard hours for a work-related purpose, the judge may authorize the applicant to drive subject to these limitations:

(1) If the applicant is required to drive to and from a specific place of work at regular times, the limited driving privilege must specify the general times and routes in which the applicant will be driving to and from work, and restrict driving to those times and routes.

(2) If the applicant is required to drive to and from work at a specific place, but is unable to specify the times at which that driving will occur, the limited driving privilege must specify the general routes in which the applicant will be driving to and from work, and restrict the driving to those general routes.

(3) If the applicant is required to drive to and from work at regular times but is unable to specify the places at which work is to be performed, the limited driving privilege must specify the general times and geographic boundaries in which the applicant will be driving, and restrict driving to those times and within those boundaries.

(4) If the applicant can specify neither the times nor places in which the applicant will be driving to and from work, or if the applicant is required to drive during these nonstandard working hours as a condition of employment, the limited driving privilege must specify the geographic boundaries in which the applicant will drive and restrict driving to that within those boundaries.

The limited driving privilege must state the name and address of the applicant's place of work or employer, and may include other information and restrictions applicable to work-related driving, in the discretion of the court.

(g2) A limited driving privilege may not allow driving for maintenance of the household except during standard working hours, and the limited driving privilege may contain any additional restrictions on that driving, in the discretion of the court. The limited driving privilege must authorize driving essential to the completion of any community work assignments, course of instruction at an Alcohol and Drug Education Traffic School, or substance abuse assessment or treatment, to which the applicant is ordered by the court as a condition of probation for the impaired driving conviction. If this driving will occur during nonstandard working hours, the limited driving privilege must specify the same limitations required by subsection (g1) for work-related driving during those hours, and it must include or have attached to it the name and address of the Alcohol and Drug Education Traffic School, the community service coordinator, or mental health treatment facility to which the applicant is assigned. Driving for educational purposes other than the course of instruction at an Alcohol and Drug Education Traffic School is subject to the same limitations applicable to work related driving under subsections (g) and (g1). Driving to and from the applicant's place of religious worship is subject to the same limitations applicable to work-related driving under subsections (g) and (g1) of this section.

(g3) **Ignition Interlock Allowed.** -- A judge may include all of the following in a limited driving privilege order:

(1) A restriction that the applicant may operate only a designated motor vehicle.

(2) A requirement that the designated motor vehicle be equipped with a functioning ignition interlock system of a type approved by the Commissioner. The Commissioner shall not unreasonably withhold approval of an ignition interlock system and shall consult with the Division of Purchase and Contract in the Department of Administration to ensure that potential vendors are not discriminated against.

(3) A requirement that the applicant personally activate the ignition interlock system before driving the motor vehicle.

(g4) The restrictions set forth in subsection (g3) and (g5) of this section do not apply to a motor vehicle that meets all of the following requirements:

(1) Is owned by the applicant's employer.

(2) Is operated by the applicant solely for work-related purposes.

(3) Its owner has filed with the court a written document authorizing the applicant to drive the vehicle, for work-related purposes, under the authority of a limited driving privilege.

(g5) **Ignition Interlock Required.** -- If a person's drivers license is revoked for a conviction of G.S. 20-138.1, and the person had an alcohol concentration of 0.15 or more, a judge shall include all of the following in a limited driving privilege order:

(1) A restriction that the applicant may operate only a designated motor vehicle.

(2) A requirement that the designated motor vehicle be equipped with a functioning ignition interlock system of a type approved by the Commissioner, which is set to prohibit driving with an alcohol concentration of greater than 0.00. The Commissioner shall not unreasonably withhold approval of an ignition interlock system and shall consult with the Division of Purchase and Contract in the Department of Administration to ensure that potential vendors are not discriminated against.

(3) A requirement that the applicant personally activate the ignition interlock system before driving the motor vehicle.

For purposes of this subsection, the results of a chemical analysis presented at trial or sentencing shall be sufficient to prove a person's alcohol concentration, shall be conclusive, and shall not be subject to modification by any party, with or without approval by the court.

(h) **Other Mandatory and Permissive Conditions or Restrictions.** -- In all limited driving privileges the judge shall also include a restriction that the applicant not consume alcohol while driving or drive at any time while the applicant has remaining in the applicant's body any alcohol or controlled substance previously consumed, unless the controlled substance was lawfully obtained and taken in therapeutically appropriate amounts. The judge may impose any other reasonable restrictions or conditions necessary to achieve the purposes of this section.

(i) **Modification or Revocation of Privilege.** -- A judge who issues a limited driving privilege is authorized to modify or revoke the limited driving privilege upon a showing that the circumstances have changed sufficiently to justify modification or revocation. If the judge who issued the privilege is not presiding in the court in which the privilege was issued, a presiding judge in that court may modify or revoke a privilege in accordance with this subsection. The judge must indicate in the order of modification or revocation the reasons for the order, or the judge must make specific findings indicating the reason for the order and those findings must be entered in the record of the case.

(j) **Effect of Violation of Restriction.** -- A person holding a limited driving privilege who violates any of its restrictions commits the offense of driving while license is revoked for impaired driving under G.S. 20-28(a1) and is subject to punishment and license revocation as provided in that section. If a law-enforcement officer has reasonable grounds to believe that the person holding a limited driving privilege has consumed alcohol while driving or has driven while the person has remaining in the person's body any alcohol previously consumed, the suspected offense of driving while license is revoked is an alcohol-related offense subject to the implied-consent provisions of G.S. 20-16.2. If a person holding a limited driving privilege is charged with driving while license revoked by violating a restriction contained in the limited driving privilege, and a judicial official determines that there is probable cause for the charge, the limited driving privilege is suspended pending the resolution of the case, and the judicial official must require the person to surrender the limited driving privilege. The judicial official must also notify the person that the person is not entitled to drive until the case is resolved.

Notwithstanding any other provision of law, an alcohol screening test may be administered to a driver suspected of violating this section, and the results of an alcohol screening test or the driver's refusal to submit may be used by a law enforcement officer, a court, or an administrative agency in determining if alcohol was present in the driver's body. No alcohol screening tests are valid under this section unless the device used is one approved by the Department of Health and Human Services, and the screening test is conducted in accordance with the applicable regulations of the Department as to the manner of its use.

(j1) **Effect of Violation of Community Service Requirement.** -- Section of Community Corrections of the Division of Adult Correction and Juvenile Justice staff shall report significant violations of the terms of a probation judgment related to community service to the court that ordered the community service. The court shall then conduct a hearing to determine if there was a willful failure to comply. The hearing may be held in the district where the requirement was imposed, where the alleged violation occurred, or where the probationer resides. If the court determines that there was a willful failure to pay the prescribed fee or to complete the work as ordered within the applicable time limits, the court shall revoke any limited driving privilege issued in the impaired driving case until community service requirements have been met. In addition, the court may take any further action authorized by Article 82 of Chapter 15A of the General Statutes for violation of a condition of probation.

(k) **Copy of Limited Driving Privilege to Division; Action Taken if Privilege Invalid.** -- The clerk of court or the child support enforcement agency must send a copy of any limited driving privilege issued in the county to the Division. A limited driving privilege that is not authorized by this section, G.S. 20-16.2(e1),

20-16.1, 50-13.12, or 110-142.2, or that does not contain the limitations required by law, is invalid. If the limited driving privilege is invalid on its face, the Division must immediately notify the court and the person holding the privilege that it considers the privilege void and that the Division records will not indicate that the person has a limited driving privilege.

(*l*) Any judge granting limited driving privileges under this section shall, prior to granting such privileges, be furnished proof and be satisfied that the person being granted such privileges is financially responsible. Proof of financial responsibility shall be in one of the following forms:

(1) A written certificate or electronically-transmitted facsimile thereof from any insurance carrier duly authorized to do business in this State certifying that there is in effect a nonfleet private passenger motor vehicle liability policy for the benefit of the person required to furnish proof of financial responsibility. The certificate or facsimile shall state the effective date and expiration date of the nonfleet private passenger motor vehicle liability policy and shall state the date that the certificate or facsimile is issued. The certificate or facsimile shall remain effective proof of financial responsibility for a period of 30 consecutive days following the date the certificate or facsimile is issued but shall not in and of itself constitute a binder or policy of insurance or

(2) A binder for or policy of nonfleet private passenger motor vehicle liability insurance under which the applicant is insured, provided that the binder or policy states the effective date and expiration date of the nonfleet private passenger motor vehicle liability policy.

The preceding provisions of this subsection do not apply to applicants who do not own currently registered motor vehicles and who do not operate nonfleet private passenger motor vehicles that are owned by other persons and that are not insured under commercial motor vehicle liability insurance policies. In such cases, the applicant shall sign a written certificate to that effect. Such certificate shall be furnished by the Division. Any material misrepresentation made by such person on such certificate shall be grounds for suspension of that person's license for a period of 90 days.

For the purpose of this subsection "nonfleet private passenger motor vehicle" has the definition ascribed to it in Article 40 of General Statute Chapter 58.

The Commissioner may require that certificates required by this subsection be on a form approved by the Commissioner. Such granting of limited driving privileges shall

be conditioned upon the maintenance of such financial responsibility during the period of the limited driving privilege. Nothing in this subsection precludes any person from showing proof of financial responsibility in any other manner authorized by Articles 9A and 13 of this Chapter.

History.
1983, c. 435, s. 31; 1983 (Reg. Sess., 1984), c. 1101, ss. 30-33; 1985, c. 706, s. 2; 1987, c. 869, s. 13; 1987 (Reg. Sess., 1988), c. 1037, s. 78; 1989, c. 436, s. 6;1994, Ex. Sess., c. 20, s. 3;1995, c. 506, ss. 1, 2; c. 538, s. 2(h); 1995 (Reg. Sess., 1996), c. 756, s. 31; 1997-379, s. 5.6;1999-406, ss. 4 -6; 2000-155, ss. 7, 11-13; 2001-487, s. 55;2007-182, s. 2;2007-493, ss. 24, 29, 30; 2008-187, s. 36(c);2009-372, s. 15;2011-145, s. 19.1(k);2012-194, s. 45(c);2015-185, s. 2(a);2015-186, s. 5;2015-264, s. 86;2017-186, s. 2 (oooo)

EDITOR'S NOTE. --
Session Laws 1999-406, s. 18, states that this act does not obligate the General Assembly to appropriate additional funds, and that this act shall be implemented with funds available or appropriated to the Department of Transportation and the Administrative Office of the Courts.

Session Laws 2015-186, s. 1, provides: "This act shall be known as the 'North Carolina Drivers License Restoration Act.'"

Session Laws 2015-186, s. 7, as amended by Session Laws 2015-264, s. 86, provides: "This act becomes effective December 1, 2015, and applies to offenses committed on or after that date. Prosecutions for offenses committed before the effective date of this act are not abated or affected by this act, and the statutes that would be applicable but for this act remain applicable to those prosecutions." Session Laws 2015-186, s. 5, had rewritten the first sentence of the first designated paragraph of subsection (j).

EFFECT OF AMENDMENTS. --
Session Laws 2007-182, s. 2, effective July 5, 2007, substituted "Commission for Public Health" for "Commission for Health Services" in the second sentence of the second paragraph of subsection (j).

Session Laws 2007-493, s. 24, effective August 30, 2007, deleted the former second and third sentences of subsection (c), which read: "If the judgment does not require the person to complete a period of nonoperation pursuant to G.S. 20-179, the privilege may be issued at the time the judgment is issued. If the judgment requires the person to complete a period of nonoperation pursuant to G.S. 20-179, the limited driving privilege may not be effective until the person successfully completes that period of nonoperation." For applicability provision, see Editor's note.

Session Laws 2007-493, ss. 29 and 30, effective December 1, 2007, and applicable to offenses committed on or after that date, added subsection (c1); and in subsection (g5), substituted "0.15" for "0.16," and added the second paragraph. For effective applicability provision, see Editor's note.

Chapter 20

Session Laws 2008-187, s. 36(c), effective August 7, 2008, in the second paragraph of subsection (j), substituted "Department of Health and Human Services" for "Commission for Public Health" and substituted "Department" for "Commission."

Session Laws 2009-372, s. 15, effective December 1, 2009, and applicable to offenses committed on or after that date, added subsection (j1).

Session Laws 2011-145, s. 19.1(k), effective January 1, 2012, substituted "Section of Community Corrections of the Division of Adult Correction" for "Division of Community Corrections" in subsection (j1).

Session Laws 2012-194, s. 45(c), effective July 17, 2012, substituted "G.S. 15A-1331.1" for "G.S. 15A-1331A" in subdivision (b)(2).

Session Laws 2015-185, s. 2(a), effective October 1, 2015, and applicable to limited driving privileges issued on or after that date, added subdivision (a)(7), inserted "the applicant's place of religious worship" in subdivision (c1)(3), added the last sentence in subsection (g2), and made gender neutral changes throughout the section.

Session Laws 2015-186, s. 5, rewrote the first sentence of the first designated paragraph of subsection (j). For effective date and applicability, see Editor's note.

Session Laws 2017-186, s. 2 (oooo), effective December 1, 2017, inserted "and Juvenile Justice" in the first sentence of subsection (j1).

VIOLATION OF SEPARATION OF POWERS. --North Carolina Division of Motor Vehicles violated the separation of powers clause in the North Carolina Constitution and violated a driver's right to due process when it unilaterally voided a district court's order limiting a driver's driving privilege; furthermore, by allowing the North Carolina Division of Motor Vehicles to, in essence, invalidate a properly entered court order, G.S. 20-179.3(k) violated the provisions requiring separation of powers contained in N.C. Const., Art. I, § 6; N.C. Const., Art. IV, § 1; and N.C. Const., Art. IV, § 3. State v. Bowes, 159 N.C. App. 18, 583 S.E.2d 294 (2003), cert. denied, 358 N.C. 156, 592 S.E.2d 698 (2004).

DISCRETION OF COURT IN GRANTING PRIVILEGE. --The granting or denying of a limited driving privilege pursuant to subsection (a) of this section is for good cause shown, the decision resting in the sound discretion of the trial court. State v. Sigmon, 74 N.C. App. 479, 328 S.E.2d 843 (1985).

MODIFICATION OF LIMITED DRIVING PRIVILEGE DUE TO INABILITY CAUSED BY MEDICAL CONDITION. --Trial court did not have jurisdiction to exempt under G.S. 20-179.3(i) a driver who was seeking reinstatement of her driver's license after having it revoked for driving while impaired from complying with the ignition interlock device upon a showing that the driver could not use the ignition interlock device due to medical conditions substantiated by a doctor's note; the ignition interlock device provisions of G.S. 20-17.8 are mandatory and not subject to review. State v. Benbow, 169 N.C. App. 613, 610 S.E.2d 297 (2005).

DEFENDANT HAS NO ENTITLEMENT TO A LIMITED DRIVING PRIVILEGE. State v. Sigmon, 74 N.C. App. 479, 328 S.E.2d 843 (1985).

PROBABLE CAUSE TO APPROACH DEFENDANT. --Officer who had specific knowledge that defendant's license had been revoked, that defendant held a limited driving privilege, and that he might have been violating his privilege by driving for a social purpose had a reasonable or founded suspicion base on articulable facts sufficient to justify his approach of defendant in a public place and ask to see a valid license and North Carolina permit. State v. Badgett, 82 N.C. App. 270, 346 S.E.2d 281 (1986).

REFUSAL TO ALLOW SHOWING OF GOOD CAUSE AS ABUSE OF DISCRETION. --Trial court's refusal to allow defendant to show good cause for authorization of a limited driving privilege was an abuse of discretion, where defendant's official record of convictions for violations of motor vehicle laws and his driver's license record showed that he had no prior convictions for violations of this type, the court found no aggravating or grossly aggravating factors, and there was no showing of any subsequent violations of this nature. State v. Bailey, 93 N.C. App. 721, 379 S.E.2d 266 (1989).

EVIDENCE HELD INSUFFICIENT TO SUPPORT CONVICTION UNDER SUBSECTION (J). -- State v. Cooney, 313 N.C. 594, 330 S.E.2d 206 (1985).

CITED in State v. Bartlett, 130 N.C. App. 79, 502 S.E.2d 53 (1998).

N.C. Gen. Stat. § 20-179.4

Repealed by Session Laws 2009-372, s. 16, effective December 1, 2009, and applicable to offenses committed on or after that date.

EDITOR'S NOTE. --

The former section, community service alternative punishment, responsibilities of the Department of Correction and fees, was enacted by Session Laws 1983, c. 761, s. 154, and amended by Session Laws 1983 (Reg. Sess., 1984), c. 1101, ss. 34, 35; 1987 (Reg. Sess., 1988), c. 1037, s. 82; 1989, c. 752, s. 109;1995, c. 496, s. 9;1997-234, s. 1;2002-126, s. 29A.1(b);and 2004-199, s. 14.

Subsection (c) of the former section was further amended by Session Laws 2009-451, s. 19.26(b), as amended by Session Laws 2009-575, s. 16A, effective September 1, 2009, and applicable to persons ordered to perform community service on or after that date. The amendment increased the fee in subsection (c) to $225.00.

N.C. Gen. Stat. § 20-180

Repealed by Session Laws 1973, c. 1330, s. 39.

§ 20-181. Penalty for failure to dim, etc., beams of headlamps

Any person operating a motor vehicle on the highways of this State, who shall fail to shift, depress, deflect, tilt or dim the beams of the headlamps thereon whenever another vehicle is met on such highways or when following another vehicle at a distance of less than 200 feet, except when engaged in the act of overtaking and passing may, upon a determination of responsibility for the offense, be required to pay a penalty of not more than ten dollars ($ 10.00).

History.

1939, c. 351, s. 3; 1955, c. 913, s. 1; 1987, c. 581, s. 5

CARS ARE REQUIRED TO DIM OR SLANT THEIR HEADLIGHTS IN PASSING. Cummins v. Southern Fruit Co., 225 N.C. 625, 36 S.E.2d 11 (1945).

RIGHT TO ASSUME THAT APPROACHING DRIVER WILL DIM LIGHTS. --A motorist may assume that whenever he meets another motor vehicle traveling in the opposite direction, its driver will seasonably dim its headlights and not persist in projecting glaring light into his eyes. Chaffin v. Brame, 233 N.C. 377, 64 S.E.2d 276 (1951); United States v. First-Citizens Bank & Trust Co., 208 F.2d 280 (4th Cir. 1953).

APPLIED in Keener v. Beal, 246 N.C. 247, 98 S.E.2d 19 (1957); Beasley v. Williams, 260 N.C. 561, 133 S.E.2d 227 (1963).

CITED in State v. Roberts, 82 N.C. App. 733, 348 S.E.2d 151 (1986).

CROSS REFERENCES. --

As to conviction under this section not being a ground for revocation of a driver's license, see G.S. 20-18.

N.C. Gen. Stat. § 20-182

Repealed by Session Laws 1983, c. 912, s. 2.

§ 20-183. Duties and powers of law-enforcement officers; warning by local officers before stopping another vehicle on highway; warning tickets

(a) It shall be the duty of the law-enforcement officers of the State and of each county, city, or other municipality to see that the provisions of this Article are enforced within their respective jurisdictions, and any such officer shall have the power to arrest on sight or upon warrant any person found violating the provisions of this Article. Such officers within their respective jurisdictions shall have the power to stop any motor vehicle upon the highways of the State for the purpose of determining whether the same is being operated in violation of any of the provisions of this Article. Provided, that when any county, city, or other municipal law-enforcement officer operating a motor vehicle overtakes another vehicle on the highways of the State, outside of the corporate limits of cities and towns, for the purpose of stopping the same or apprehending the driver thereof, for a violation of any of the provisions of this Article, he shall, before

stopping such other vehicle, sound a siren or activate a special light, bell, horn, or exhaust whistle approved for law-enforcement vehicles under the provisions of G.S. 20-125(b).

(b) In addition to other duties and powers heretofore existing, all law-enforcement officers charged with the duty of enforcing the motor vehicle laws are authorized to issue warning tickets to motorists for conduct constituting a potential hazard to the motoring public which does not amount to a definite, clear-cut, substantial violation of the motor vehicle laws. Each warning ticket issued shall contain information necessary to identify the offender, and shall be signed by the issuing officer. A copy of each warning ticket issued shall be delivered to the offender. Information from issued warning tickets shall be made available to the Drivers License Section of the Division of Motor Vehicles in a manner approved by the Commissioner but shall not be filed with or in any manner become a part of the offender's driving record. Warning tickets issued as well as the fact of issuance shall be privileged information and available only to authorized personnel of the Division for statistical and analytical purposes.

History.

1937, c. 407, s. 143; 1961, c. 793; 1965, cc. 537, 999; 1975, c. 716, s. 5; 1998-149, s. 9.2

CONSTITUTIONALITY. --The provisions of subsection (a) of this section, when balanced with the State's obligation to preserve order and enforce safety on its streets and highways, do not constitute such an encroachment on the individual's constitutional rights as to render the statute invalid. State v. Allen, 282 N.C. 503, 194 S.E.2d 9 (1973), but see in Keziah v. Bostic, 452 F. Supp. 912 (W.D.N.C. 1978).

POWERS OF HIGHWAY PATROL OFFICERS. --Members of the highway patrol have the power of peace officers for the purpose of enforcing the provisions of Article 3 of this Chapter. Patrol members may (i) arrest on sight any person found violating the provisions of Article 3 and (ii) stop any motor vehicle on a North Carolina highway to determine whether the vehicle is being operated in violation of any provision of Article 3. State v. Green, 103 N.C. App. 38, 404 S.E.2d 363 (1991).

UNRESTRAINED DISCRETION TO STOP VEHICLE VIOLATES STANDARDS OF TERRY V. OHIO. --To permit vehicle stops in the unrestrained discretion of police officers is to allow such stops to be used as pretexts for investigations and to sanction stops which could not be justified under the standards set out in Terry v. Ohio, 392 U.S. 1, 88 S. Ct. 1868, 20 L. Ed. 2d 889 (1968); Keziah v. Bostic, 452 F. Supp. 912 (W.D.N.C. 1978).

STATE'S INTERESTS DO NOT JUSTIFY UNREASONABLE INTERFERENCE WITH INDIVIDUAL'S RIGHTS. --The decision in State v. Allen, 282 N.C. 503, 194 S.E.2d 9 (1973), is not sufficiently sensitive to the need to accommodate the State's interest in enforcing its vehicle laws to the individual's right to be free from unreasonable interference with his travel on the highways. Keziah v. Bostic, 452 F. Supp. 912 (W.D.N.C. 1978).

The State has the power to enforce its vehicle safety and registration laws through some system of vehicle stops, but U.S. Const., Amend. IV also requires some accommodation of the individual interest in being left alone. Keziah v. Bostic, 452 F. Supp. 912 (W.D.N.C. 1978).

STOPPING OF INDIVIDUAL IN PRIVATE DRIVEWAY CONSTITUTED FOURTH AMENDMENT "SEIZURE". --Where a patrolman, while not engaged in any patrol of the highway for purposes of observing traffic or making random license checks, spontaneously decided to stop petitioner while petitioner was in a private driveway, it would have been perfectly natural for the petitioner to assume that he was about to be subjected to a search or inquiry for some purpose other than a routine license check and that the officer meant to accost him for some purpose. There is no doubt that the officer's stop and demand was a "seizure" within the meaning of U.S. Const., Amend. IV. Keziah v. Bostic, 452 F. Supp. 912 (W.D.N.C. 1978).

VEHICLE LICENSE CHECKS MUST NOT BE USED AS PRETEXTS FOR HARASSMENT OR FOR BASELESS INVESTIGATIONS. Keziah v. Bostic, 452 F. Supp. 912 (W.D.N.C. 1978).

POWER TO STOP VEHICLE DOES NOT INCLUDE POWER TO SEARCH. --The power to stop a vehicle under this section does not include the power to search. The power to search incident to a warrantless arrest is clearly limited to situations where the officer, after stopping the vehicle, has found a person "violating the provisions of this Article." State v. Blackwelder, 34 N.C. App. 352, 238 S.E.2d 190 (1977).

POWER TO ARREST DOES NOT NECESSARILY INCLUDE AUTHORITY TO SEARCH MOTOR VEHICLE in absence of probable cause. State v. Braxton, 90 N.C. App. 204, 368 S.E.2d 56 (1988).

PERSONS STOPPED PURSUANT TO THIS SECTION MAY NOT BE INDISCRIMINATELY SEARCHED OR ARRESTED WITHOUT PROBABLE CAUSE in contravention of recognized constitutional principles. State v. Allen, 282 N.C. 503, 194 S.E.2d 9 (1973).

NO POWER TO STOP VEHICLE TO DETERMINE IF DRIVER POSSESSED CONTRABAND DRUGS. --Where there was no evidence that the officer stopped the vehicle operated by the defendant for the purpose of determining if he had violated a motor vehicle statute, but rather, the obvious purpose in stopping the vehicle was to determine if the defendant possessed contraband drugs, the officer had no right to remove the defendant from and search the vehicle. State v. Blackwelder, 34 N.C. App. 352, 238 S.E.2d 190 (1977).

SEIZURE OF CONTRABAND IN PLAIN VIEW UPHELD. --Seizure of marijuana from defendants' car and arrest for its possession did not amount to an unconstitutional invasion of defendants' rights where officers discovered the marijuana in plain view after lawfully stopping defendants' vehicle to check driver's license and vehicle registration. State v. Garcia, 16 N.C. App. 344, 192 S.E.2d 2, cert. denied, 282 N.C. 427, 192 S.E.2d 837 (1972).

CONVICTION FOR ASSAULTING PATROLMAN MAKING ILLEGAL STOP UPHELD. --Where a patrolman, while not engaged in any patrol of the highway for purposes of observing traffic or making random license checks, spontaneously decided to stop petitioner while petitioner was in a private driveway, although petitioner would have had a meritorious defense to any prosecution based on failure to display his license, he was not entitled to invoke self-help against what was, at the time, an arguable lawful arrest, and his conviction for assaulting the highway patrolman would survive despite the finding that the officer's initial stop and demand were illegal as an unreasonable search and seizure under the U.S. Const., Amend. IV. Keziah v. Bostic, 452 F. Supp. 912 (W.D.N.C. 1978).

AUTHORITY GRANTED LAW-ENFORCEMENT OFFICERS UNDER SECTION. --This section authorizes State law-enforcement officers to stop any motor vehicle upon the highways of the State for the purpose of determining whether the same is being operated in violation of any of the provisions of the Motor Vehicles Code, including the provisions requiring registration of the vehicle, operation by a properly licensed driver, etc. United States v. Kelley, 462 F.2d 372 (4th Cir. 1972).

THE POWER TO STOP A VEHICLE UNDER THIS SECTION IS NOT DEPENDENT ON PROBABLE CAUSE to believe a violation has occurred. State v. Blackwelder, 34 N.C. App. 352, 238 S.E.2d 190 (1977).

Although when a police officer first stopped and approached truck he had no probable cause to believe that defendant had committed any offense, nevertheless the officer had authority to stop the truck under this section, and the existence of probable cause at the time the truck was stopped was not essential to the validity of subsequent arrest. State v. Dark, 22 N.C. App. 566, 207 S.E.2d 290, cert. denied, 285 N.C. 760, 209 S.E.2d 284 (1974).

In view of their authority under this section, the police were acting properly when they turned on their siren and light and requested a truck to stop even though they had no probable cause to believe that a crime had been committed. United States v. Kelley, 462 F.2d 372 (4th Cir. 1972).

SUBDIVISIONS (2) AND (4) OF G.S. 20-49 ARE NOT IRRECONCILABLE WITH THIS SECTION. State v. Allen, 15 N.C. App. 670, 190 S.E.2d 714 (1972), rev'd on other grounds, 282 N.C. 503, 194 S.E.2d 9 (1973).

VERDICT OF NOT GUILTY NOT TANTAMOUNT TO A FINDING OF NO REASONABLE GROUNDS FOR ARREST. --Verdict of not guilty of the misdemeanor for which defendant was arrested (drunken driving) was not tantamount to a finding that the arresting officer did not have reasonable grounds to believe that defendant had committed such offense

Chapter 20

in his presence and that defendant therefore could lawfully have resisted the arrest. State v. Jefferies, 17 N.C. App. 195, 193 S.E.2d 388 (1972), cert. denied, 282 N.C. 673, 194 S.E.2d 153 (1973).

APPLIED in State v. Eason, 242 N.C. 59, 86 S.E.2d 774 (1955); State v. White, 18 N.C. App. 31, 195 S.E.2d 576 (1973); State v. Keziah, 24 N.C. App. 298, 210 S.E.2d 436 (1974); State v. Davis, 66 N.C. App. 98, 311 S.E.2d 19 (1984).

CITED in State v. Mobley, 240 N.C. 476, 83 S.E.2d 100 (1954); State v. Cole, 241 N.C. 576, 86 S.E.2d 203 (1955); Lowe v. Department of Motor Vehicles, 244 N.C. 353, 93 S.E.2d 448 (1956); State v. Borland, 21 N.C. App. 559, 205 S.E.2d 340 (1974); State v. Bridges, 35 N.C. App. 81, 239 S.E.2d 856 (1978); State v. Mc-Clendon, 350 N.C. 630, 517 S.E.2d 128 (1999); State v. Washington, 193 N.C. App. 670, 668 S.E.2d 622 (2008).

LEGAL PERIODICALS. --
For survey of 1977 law on criminal procedure, see 56 N.C.L. Rev. 983 (1978).

For survey of 1978 law on criminal procedure, see 57 N.C.L. Rev. 1007 (1979).

For comment on the warrantless "search within a search" of containers in motor vehicles, see 17 Wake Forest L. Rev. 425 (1981).

ARTICLE 3A.
SAFETY AND EMISSIONS INSPECTION PROGRAM

PART 1.
SAFE USE OF STREETS AND HIGHWAYS

N.C. Gen. Stat. § 20-183.1

Repealed by Session Laws 1993 (Reg. Sess., 1994), c. 754, s. 3.

EDITOR'S NOTE. --
Session Laws 1993 (Reg. Sess., 1994), c. 754, s. 2, effective October 1, 1994, substituted "Safety and Emissions Inspection Program" for "Motor Vehicle Law of 1947" as the heading for Article 3A.

PART 2.
SAFETY AND EMISSIONS INSPECTIONS OF CERTAIN VEHICLES

§ 20-183.2. Description of vehicles subject to safety or emissions inspection; definitions

(a) Safety. — A motor vehicle is subject to a safety inspection in accordance with this Part if it meets all of the following requirements:

(1) It is subject to registration with the Division under Article 3 of this Chapter.

(2) It is not subject to inspection under 49 C.F.R. Part 396, the federal Motor Carrier Safety Regulations.

(3) It is not a trailer whose gross weight is less than 4,000 pounds or a house trailer.

(a1) Safety Inspection Exceptions. — The following vehicles shall not be subject to a safety inspection pursuant to this Article:

(1) Historic vehicles, as described in G.S. 20-79.4(b)(90).

(2) Buses titled to a local board of education and subject to the school bus inspection requirements specified by the State Board of Education and G.S. 115C-248.

(b) Emissions. — A motor vehicle is subject to an emissions inspection in accordance with this Part if it meets all of the following requirements:

(1) It is subject to registration with the Division under Article 3 of this Chapter, except for motor vehicles operated on a federal installation as provided in sub-subdivision e. of subdivision (5) of this subsection.

(2) It is not a trailer whose gross weight is less than 4,000 pounds, a house trailer, or a motorcycle.

(3) *(Effective until contingency met — see note)* It is (i) a 1996 or later model and older than the three most recent model years or (ii) a 1996 or later model and has 70,000 miles or more on its odometer.

(3) *(Contingent effective date — see note)* It is (i) a vehicle with a model year within 20 years of the current year and older than the three most recent model years or (ii) a vehicle with a model year within 20 years of the current year and has 70,000 miles or more on its odometer.

(4) Repealed by Session Laws 1999-328, s. 3.11, effective July 21, 1999.

(5) It meets any of the following descriptions:

  a. It is required to be registered in an emissions county.

  b. It is part of a fleet that is operated primarily in an emissions county.

  c. It is offered for rent in an emissions county.

  d. It is a used vehicle offered for sale by a dealer in an emissions county.

  e. It is operated on a federal installation located in an emissions county and it is not a tactical military vehicle. Vehicles operated on a federal installation include those that are owned or leased by employees of the installation and are used to commute to the installation and those owned or operated by the federal agency that conducts business at the installation.

Chapter 20

f. It is otherwise required by 40 C.F.R. Part 51 to be subject to an emissions inspection.

(6) It is not licensed at the farmer rate under G.S. 20-88(b).

(7) It is not a new motor vehicle, as defined in G.S. 20-286(10)a. and has been a used motor vehicle, as defined in G.S. 20-286(10)b., for 12 months or more. However, a motor vehicle that has been leased or rented, or offered for lease or rent, is subject to an emissions inspection when it either:

a. Has been leased or rented, or offered for lease or rent, for 12 months or more.

b. Is sold to a consumer-purchaser.

(8) It is not a privately owned, nonfleet motor home or house car, as defined in G.S. 20-4.01(27)k., that is built on a single chassis, has a gross vehicle weight of more than 10,000 pounds, and is designed primarily for recreational use.

(9) It is not a plug-in electric vehicle as defined in G.S. 20-4.01(28b).

(10) It is not a fuel cell electric vehicle as defined in G.S. 20-4.01(12a).

(c) Definitions. — The following definitions apply in this Part:

(1) Electronic inspection authorization. — An inspection authorization that is generated electronically through the electronic accounting system that creates a unique nonduplicating authorization number assigned to the vehicle's inspection receipt upon successful passage of an inspection. The term "electronic inspection authorization" shall include the term "inspection sticker" during the transition period to use of electronic inspection authorizations.

(2) Emissions county. — A county listed in G.S. 143-215.107A(c) and certified to the Commissioner of Motor Vehicles as a county in which the implementation of a motor vehicle emissions inspection program will improve ambient air quality.

(3) Federal installation. — An installation that is owned by, leased to, or otherwise regularly used as the place of business of a federal agency.

History.
1965, c. 734, s. 1; 1967, c. 692, s. 1; 1969, c. 179, s. 2; cc. 219, 386; 1973, c. 679, s. 2; 1975, c. 683; c. 716, s. 5; 1979, c. 77; 1989, c. 467; 1991, c. 394, s. 1;c. 761, s. 7;1993 (Reg. Sess., 1994), c. 754, s. 1; 1995, c. 163, s. 10;1997-29, s. 12;1999-328, s. 3.11;2000-134, ss. 7, 7.1, 9, 11; 2001-504, ss. 4, 5, 6, 10; 2004-167, s. 10;2004-199, s. 59;2006-255, s. 1;2007-503, s. 2;2008-172, s. 1;2009-570, s. 33;2011-95, s. 3;2011-206, s. 3;2012-199, s. 1;2012-200, s. 12(b);2013-410, s. 5;2015-264, s. 9;2017-10, s. 3.5(b);2017-102, s. 5.2(b);2020-73, s. 5

SUBDIVISION (B)(3) SET OUT TWICE. —The first version of subdivision (b)(3) set out above is effective until the first day of month that is 60 days after the Secretary of the Department of Environmental Quality certifies to the Revisor of Statutes that the EPA has approved an amendment to the North Carolina State Implementation Plan. The second version of subdivision (b)(3) is effective on that date pursuant to Session Laws 2017-10, s. 3.5(d). See Editor's note.

EDITOR'S NOTE. —
This section has been set out in the Interim Supplement to correct a publishing error in the main volume.

EDITOR'S NOTE. —
Session Laws 1999-328, s. 5.1 provides that the act shall not be construed to obligate the General Assembly to appropriate any funds to implement the provisions of this act. Every State agency to which this act applies shall implement the provisions of this act from funds otherwise appropriated or available to that agency.

Session Laws, 2012-199, s. 2, provides: "The Department of Environment and Natural Resources shall submit for approval the emissions inspection program changes provided in Section 1 of this act to the United States Environmental Protection Agency as an amendment to the North Carolina State Implementation Plan under the federal Clean Air Act. If the United States Environmental Protection Agency approves the amendment, the Secretary of the Department of Environment and Natural Resources shall certify this approval to the Revisor of Statutes. In the certification, the Secretary of the Department of Environment and Natural Resources shall include the session law number of this act."

Session Laws 2012-199, s. 3, provides: "After the Motor Vehicle Inspection and Law Enforcement System (MILES) is retired and the replacement system for MILES is operational, the Commissioner of Motor Vehicles shall certify to the Revisor of Statutes that MILES has been replaced. In the certification, the Commissioner of Motor Vehicles shall include the session law number of this act."

Session Laws 2012-199, s. 4, provides: "Section 1 of this act [which amended subdivision (b)(3)] becomes effective on the later of the following dates and applies to motor vehicles inspected, or due to be inspected, on or after the effective date of Section 1 of this act:

"**(1)** January 1, 2014.

"**(2)** The first day of a month that is 30 days after both of the following have occurred:

"**a.** The Department of Environment and Natural Resources certifies to the Revisor of Statutes that the United States Environmental Protection Agency has approved the amendment to the North Carolina State Implementation Plan based on the change to the emissions inspection program provided in Section 1 of this act.

"**b.** The Commissioner of Motor Vehicles certifies to the Revisor of Statutes that the Motor Vehicle Inspection and Law Enforcement System (MILES) has been replaced."

The Department of Environment and Natural Resources provided the certification required under 2012-199, s. 4 by letter dated February 13, 2015. The Commissioner of Motor Vehicles provided the certification required under 2012-199, s. 4 by letter dated February 24, 2015. Therefore, the amendment of subsection (b)(3) of this section by 2012-199, s. 1 became effective on April 1, 2015.

Session Laws 2017-10, s. 3.5(c), provides: "No later than September 30, 2017, the Department of Environmental Quality shall prepare and submit to the United States Environmental Protection Agency for approval by that agency a proposed North Carolina State Implementation Plan amendment based on the change to the motor vehicle emissions testing program provided in this section."

Session Laws 2017-10, s. 3.5(d), provides: "Subsections (a) and (b) of this section become effective on the later of the following dates and apply to motor vehicles inspected, or due to be inspected, on or after that effective date:

"(1) October 1, 2017.

"(2) The first day of a month that is 60 days after the Secretary of the Department of Environmental Quality certifies to the Revisor of Statutes that the United States Environmental Protection Agency has approved an amendment to the North Carolina State Implementation Plan submitted as required by subsection (c) of this section. The Secretary shall provide this notice along with the effective date of this act on its Web site and by written or electronic notice to emissions inspection mechanic license holders, emissions inspection station licensees, and self-inspector licensees in the counties where motor vehicle emissions inspection requirements are removed by this section."

Session Laws 2017-10, s. 5.1, is a severability clause.

Session Laws 2017-102, s. 5.2(b), provides: "The Revisor of Statutes is authorized to reletter the definitions in G.S. 20-4.01(27) and G.S. 20-4.01(32b) to place them in alphabetical order. The Revisor of Statutes may conform any citations that change as a result of the relettering." Pursuant to that authority, the reference to G.S. 20-4.01(27)d2. in subdivision (b)(8) was changed to G.S. 20-4.01(27)k.

Session Laws 2017-211, s. 12(b), provides: "The Department of Transportation and the Department of Environmental Quality shall jointly study whether the frequency of vehicle safety inspections and vehicle emissions inspections should be decreased. The Departments shall consider public safety, air quality, savings to vehicle owners, impacts on State revenues, and any other factors the Departments deem necessary. No later than March 1, 2018, the Departments shall jointly report their findings and recommendations to the Joint Legislative Transportation Oversight Committee."

Session Laws 2020-73, s. 7, made the amendment of subdivision (b)(9) by Session Laws 2020-73, s. 5, effective December 1, 2020, and applicable to offenses committed on or after that date.

EFFECT OF AMENDMENTS. —

Session Laws 2000-134, s. 11, effective January 1, 2006, in subdivision (b)(3), substituted "It is a 1996 or later model" for "Except as provided in G.S. **20-183**.3(b), it is a 1996 or later model."

Session Laws 2004-167, s. 10, as amended by Session Laws 2004-199, s. 59, effective October 1, 2004, added subsection (a1).

Session Laws 2006-255, s. 1, effective August 23, 2006, added the exception in subdivision (b)(1).

Session Laws 2007-503, s. **2**, effective October 1, 2008, and applicable to offenses committed on or after that date, added subdivision (c)(1) and redesignated former subdivisions (c)(1) and (c)(2) as present subdivisions (c)(**2**) and (c)(3).

Session Laws 2008-172, s. 1, effective August 4, 2008, rewrote subsection (a1).

Session Laws 2009-570, s. 33, effective August 28, 2009, substituted "G.S. 115C-248" for "115C-248(a)" at the end of subdivision (a1)(**2**).

Session Laws 2011-95, s. 3, effective May 26, 2011, added subdivision (b)(9).

Session Laws 2011-206, s. 3, effective June 23, 2011, added subdivision (b)(10).

Session Laws 2012-199, s. 1, added "and older than the three most recent model years or (ii) a 1996 or later model and has 70,000 miles or more on its odometer" to the end of subdivision (b)(3). For effective date, see Editor's notes.

Session Laws 2012-200, s. 12(b), effective August 1, 2012, deleted "or designated by the Environmental Management Commission pursuant to G.S. 143-215.107A(d)" following "G.S. 143-215.107A(c)" in subdivision (c)(**2**).

Session Laws 2013-410, s. 5, effective August 23, 2013, substituted "described in G.S. 20-79.4(b)(88)" for "defined in G.S. 20-79.4(b)(63)" in subdivision (a1)(1).

Session Laws 2015-264, s. 9, effective October 1, 2015, substituted "G.S. 20-79.4(b)(90)" for "G.S. 20-79.4(b)(88)" in subdivision (a1)(1).

Session Laws 2017-10, s. 3.5(b), substituted "vehicle with a model year within 20 years of the current year" for "a 1996 or later model" twice in subdivision (b)(3). For effective date, see editor's note.

Session Laws 2020-73, s. 5, substituted "G.S. 20-4.01(28b)" for "G.S. 20-4.01(28a)" in subdivision (b)(9). For effective date and applicability, see editor's note.

Case Notes

SALE OF UNINSPECTED VEHICLE BY DEALER IS NEGLIGENCE PER SE. —The retail sale of an automobile by a dealer, without first having the official inspection required by this statute, is negligence per se. This is the general rule as to statutes enacted for the safety and protection of the public. In such cases, the only remaining question is whether such negligence was a proximate cause of the injury for which recovery is sought. Anderson v. Robinson, 8 N.C. App. 224, 174 S.E.2d 45 (1970).

CITED in State v. White, 3 N.C. App. 31, 164 S.E.2d 36 (1968).

§ 20-183.3. Scope of safety inspection and emissions inspection

(a) **Safety.** -- A safety inspection of a motor vehicle consists of an inspection of the following equipment to determine if the vehicle has the equipment required by Part 9 of Article 3 of this Chapter and if the equipment is in a safe operating condition:

(1) Brakes, as required by G.S. 20-124.

(2) Lights, as required by G.S. 20-129 or G.S. 20-129.1.

(3) Horn, as required by G.S. 20-125(a).

(4) Steering mechanism, as required by G.S. 20-123.1.

(5) Windows and windshield wipers, as required by G.S. 20-127. To determine if a vehicle window meets the window tinting restrictions, a safety inspection mechanic must first determine, based on use of an automotive film check card or knowledge of window tinting techniques, if after-factory tint has been applied to the window. If after-factory tint has been applied, the mechanic must use a light meter approved by the Commissioner to determine if the window meets the window tinting restrictions.

(6) Directional signals, as required by G.S. 20-125.1.

(7) Tires, as required by G.S. 20-122.1.

(8) Mirrors, as required by G.S. 20-126.

(9) Exhaust system and emissions control devices, as required by G.S. 20-128. For a vehicle that is subject to an emissions inspection in addition to a safety inspection, a visual inspection of the vehicle's emissions control devices is included in the emissions inspection rather than the safety inspection.

(b) Repealed by Laws 2000-134, s. 12, effective January 1, 2006.

(b1) **Emissions.** -- An emissions inspection of a motor vehicle consists of a visual inspection of the vehicle's emissions control devices to determine if the devices are present, are properly connected, and are the correct type for the vehicle and an analysis of data provided by the on-board diagnostic (OBD) equipment installed by the vehicle manufacturer to identify any deterioration or malfunction in the operation of the vehicle that violates standards for the model year of the vehicle set by the Environmental Management Commission. To pass an emissions inspection a vehicle must pass both the visual inspection and the OBD analysis. When an emissions inspection is performed on a vehicle, a safety inspection must be performed on the vehicle as well.

(c) **Reinspection After Failure.** -- The scope of a reinspection of a vehicle that has been repaired after failing an inspection is the same as the original inspection unless the vehicle is presented for reinspection within 60 days of failing the original inspection. If the vehicle is presented for reinspection within this time limit and the inspection the vehicle failed was a safety inspection, the reinspection is limited to an inspection of the equipment that failed the original inspection. If the vehicle is presented for reinspection within this time limit and the inspection the vehicle failed was an emissions inspection, the reinspection is limited to the portion of the inspection the vehicle failed and any other portion of the inspection that would be affected by repairs made to correct the failure.

History.
1965, c. 734, s. 1; 1969, c. 378, s. 2; 1971, c. 455, s. 2; c. 478, ss. 1, 2; 1979, 2nd Sess., c. 1180, s. 3; 1981 (Reg. Sess., 1982), c. 1261, s. 1; 1989, c. 391, s. 2;1991, c. 654, s. 2;1993 (Reg. Sess., 1994), c. 754, s. 1; 1995, c. 473, s. 2;2000-134, ss. 8, 10, 12; 2001-504, s. 7;2007-364, s. 1

EFFECT OF AMENDMENTS. --
Session Laws 2000-134, s. 12, effective January 1, 2006, repealed subsection (b), pertaining to emissions inspections.

Session Laws 2007-364, s. 1, effective January 1, 2009, substituted "60 days" for "30 days" in the first sentence of subsection (c).

VISUAL INSPECTION REQUIRED. --Suspension of a vehicle inspection facility's equipment inspection license was warranted where the facility failed to visually inspect a truck's exhaust emission system and determine that it did not have a catalytic converter, although the truck passed minimum exhaust emission requirements. Darryl Burke Chevrolet, Inc. v. Aikens, 131 N.C. App. 31, 505 S.E.2d 581 (1998), aff'd, 350 N.C. 83, 511 S.E.2d 639 (1999).

STATUTE DID NOT AUTHORIZE STOP OF DEFENDANT'S VEHICLE. --Defendant's Fourth Amendment rights were violated when defendant's vehicle was stopped due to a malfunctioning brake light because (1) G.S. 20-129(g) only required defendant to have one working brake light, which defendant did, (2) that statute did not require the vehicle's originally equipped stop lamps to be in good working order, as did G.S. 20-129(d), and (3) the malfunctioning brake light did not violate the safety inspection requirements of G.S. 20-183.3 or the requirements of NG.S. 20-129.1. State v. Heien, 214 N.C. App. 515, 714 S.E.2d 827 (2011).

APPLIED in State v. Heien, 366 N.C. 271, 737 S.E.2d 351 (2012).

CITED in Anderson v. Robinson, 8 N.C. App. 224, 174 S.E.2d 45 (1970).

§ 20-183.4. License required to perform safety inspection; qualifications for license

(a) **License Required.** -- A safety inspection must be performed by one of the following methods:

(1) At a station that has a safety inspection station license issued by the Division and by a mechanic who is employed by the station and has a safety inspection mechanic license issued by the Division.

(2) At a place of business of a person who has a safety self-inspector license issued by the Division and by an individual who has a safety inspection mechanic license issued by the Division.

(b) **Station Qualifications.** -- An applicant for a license as a safety inspection station must meet all of the following requirements:

(1) Have a place of business that has adequate facilities, space, and equipment to conduct a safety inspection. A place of business designated in a station license that has been suspended or revoked cannot be the designated place for any other license applicant during the period of the suspension or revocation, unless the Division finds that operation of the place of business as an inspection station during this period by the license applicant would not defeat the purpose of the suspension or revocation because the license applicant has no connection with the person whose license was suspended or revoked or because of another reason. A finding made by the Division under this subdivision must be set out in a written statement that includes the finding and the reason for the finding.

(2) Regularly employ at least one mechanic who has a safety inspection mechanic license.

(3) Designate the individual who will be responsible for the day-to-day operation of the station. The individual designated must be of good character and have a reputation for honesty.

(4) Have equipment and software approved by the Division to transfer information on safety inspections to the Division by electronic means. During the initial implementation of the electronic inspection process, the vendor selected by the Division shall provide the equipment and software at no cost to a station that holds a license on October 1, 2008.

(c) **Mechanic Qualifications.** -- An applicant for a license as a safety inspection mechanic must meet all of the following requirements:

(1) Have successfully completed an eight-hour course approved by the Division that teaches students about the safety equipment a motor vehicle is required to have to pass a safety inspection and how to conduct a safety inspection using equipment to electronically transmit the vehicle information and inspection results.

(2) Have a drivers license.

(3) Be of good character and have a reputation for honesty.

(d) **Self-Inspector Qualifications.** -- An applicant for a license as a safety self-inspector must meet all of the following requirements:

(1) Operate a fleet of at least 10 vehicles that are subject to a safety inspection.

(2) Regularly employ or contract with an individual who has a safety inspection mechanic license and who will perform a safety inspection on the vehicles that are part of the self-inspector's fleet.

History.
1965, c. 734, s. 1; 1967, c. 692, s. 2; 1975, c. 716, s. 5; 1993 (Reg. Sess., 1994), c. 754, s. 1; 1997-29, s. 1;2007-503, s. 3;2008-190, s. 2
LOCAL MODIFICATION. --City of Shelby: 2010-47.
EFFECT OF AMENDMENTS. --
Session Laws 2007-503, s. 3, effective October 1, 2008, and applicable to offenses committed on or after that date, added subdivision (b)(4); and added "using equipment to electronically transmit the vehicle information and inspection results" at the end of subdivision (c)(1).
Session Laws 2008-190, s. 2, effective October 1, 2008, inserted "approved by the Division" in the first sentence of subdivision (b)(4).

§ 20-183.4A. License required to perform emissions inspection; qualifications for license

(a) **License Required.** -- An emissions inspection must be performed by one of the following methods:

(1) At a station that has an emissions inspection station license issued by the Division and by a mechanic who is employed by the station and has an emissions inspection mechanic license issued by the Division.

(2) At a place of business of a person who has an emissions self-inspector license issued by the Division and by an individual who has an emissions inspection mechanic license.

(b) **Station Qualifications.** -- An applicant for a license as an emissions inspection station must meet all of the following requirements:

(1) Have a license as a safety inspection station.

(2) Repealed by Laws 2000-134, s. 15, effective January 1, 2006.

(2a) Have equipment to analyze data provided by the on-board diagnostic (OBD) equipment approved by the Environmental Management Commission.

(3) Have equipment and software to transfer information on emissions inspections to the Division by electronic means. During the initial implementation of the electronic inspection process, the vendor

selected by the Division shall provide the software at no cost to a station that holds a license on October 1, 2008.

(4) Regularly employ at least one mechanic who has an emissions inspection mechanic license.

(c) **Mechanic Qualifications.** -- An applicant for a license as an emissions inspection mechanic must meet all of the following requirements:

(1) Have a license as a safety inspection mechanic.

(2) Repealed by Laws 2000-134, s. 15, effective January 1, 2006.

(2a) Have successfully completed an eight-hour course approved by the Division that teaches students about the causes and effects of the air pollution problem, the purpose of the emissions inspection program, the vehicle emission standards established by the United States Environmental Protection Agency, the emission control devices on vehicles, how to conduct an emissions inspection using equipment to analyze data provided by the on-board diagnostic (OBD) equipment approved by the Environmental Management Commission, and any other topic required by 40 C.F.R. § 51.367 to be included in the course. Successful completion requires a passing score on a written test and on a hands-on test in which the student is required to conduct an emissions inspection of a motor vehicle.

(d) **Self-Inspector Qualifications.** -- An applicant for a license as an emissions self-inspector must meet all of the following requirements:

(1) Have a license as a safety self-inspector.

(2) Operate a fleet of at least 10 vehicles that are subject to an emissions inspection.

(3) Repealed by Laws 2000-134, s. 15, effective January 1, 2006.

(3a) Have, or have a contract with a person who has, equipment to analyze data provided by the on-board diagnostic (OBD) equipment approved by the Environmental Management Commission.

(4) Regularly employ or contract with an individual who has an emissions inspection mechanic license and who will perform an emissions inspection on the vehicles that are part of the self-inspector's fleet.

History.
1993 (Reg. Sess., 1994), c. 754, s. 1; 2000-134, ss. 13, 14, 15; 2007-503, s. 4
LOCAL MODIFICATION. --City of Shelby: 2010-47.

EFFECT OF AMENDMENTS. --
Session Laws 2000-134, s. 15, effective January 1, 2006, repealed subdivision (b)(2), requiring each station to have an emissions analyzer; repealed

subdivision (c)(2), requiring a mechanic to have successfully completed an approved course in air pollution and emissions control; and repealed subdivision (d)(3), requiring self-inspectors to have an emissions analyzer.

Session Laws 2007-503, s. 4, effective October 1, 2008, and applicable to offenses committed on or after that date, in subdivision (b)(3), inserted "and software" in the first sentence, and added the second sentence.

§ 20-183.4B. Application for license; duration of license; renewal of mechanic license

(a) **Application.** -- An applicant for a license issued under this Part must complete an application form provided by the Division. The application must contain the applicant's name and address and any other information needed by the Division to determine whether the applicant is qualified for the license. The Division must review an application for a license to determine if the applicant qualifies for the license. If the applicant meets the qualifications, the Division must issue the license. If the applicant does not meet the qualifications, the Division must deny the application and notify the applicant in writing of the reason for the denial.

(b) **Duration of License.** -- A safety inspection mechanic license expires four years after the date it is issued. An emissions mechanic inspection license expires two years after the date it is issued. A safety inspection station license, an emissions inspection station license, and a self-inspector license are effective until surrendered by the license holder or suspended or revoked by the Division.

(c) **Renewal of Mechanic License.** -- A safety or an emissions inspection mechanic may apply to renew a license by filing an application with the Division on a form provided by the Division. To renew an emissions inspection mechanic license, an applicant must have successfully completed a four-hour emissions refresher course approved by the Division within nine months of applying for renewal. Successful completion requires a passing score on a written test and on a hands-on test in which the student is required to conduct an emissions inspection of a motor vehicle.

History.
1993 (Reg. Sess., 1994), c. 754, s. 1

EDITOR'S NOTE. --
Session Laws 2020-3, s. 4.7(a) -(h), as amended by Session Laws 2020-97, ss. 3.15(a), 3.16(a), provides: "(a) Definition. -- For purposes of this section, 'credential' means any of the following issued by the Division of Motor Vehicles:
"(1) Drivers license.
"(2) Learner's permit.

"(3) Limited learner's permit.

"(4) Limited provisional license.

"(5) Full provisional license.

"(6) Commercial drivers license.

"(7) Commercial learner's permit.

"(8) Temporary driving certificate.

"(9) Special identification card.

"(10) Handicapped placard.

"(11) Vehicle registration.

"(12) Temporary vehicle registration.

"(13) Dealer license plate.

"(14) Transporter plate.

"(15) Loaner/Dealer 'LD' plate.

"(16) Vehicle inspection authorization.

"(17) Inspection station license.

"(18) Inspection mechanic license.

"(19) Transportation network company permit.

"(20) Motor vehicle dealer license.

"(21) Sales representative license.

"(22) Manufacturer license.

"(23) Distributor license.

"(24) Wholesaler license.

"(25) Driver training school license.

"(26) Driver training school instructor license.

"(27) Professional housemoving license.

"(b) Extend Validity of Credentials. -- Notwithstanding renewal, duration, or expiration provisions of G.S. 20-7, 20-11, 20-37.6, 20-37.7, 20-37.13, 20-50, 20-66, 20-79, 20-79.02, 20-79.2, 20-183.4B, 20-183.4D, 20-280.3, 20-288, 20-324, and 20-359, or any other provision of law to the contrary, the Division of Motor Vehicles shall extend for a period of five months the validity of any credential that expires on or after March 1, 2020, and before August 1, 2020. The Division shall extend for a period of five months the validity of any credential listed in subdivisions (6), (7), (9), (10), and (18) of subsection (a) of this section that expires on or after March 1, 2020, and before the date 30 days after the date the Governor (i) rescinds Executive Order No. 116 or (ii) issues another executive order lifting restrictions on Division of Motor Vehicles functions. Notwithstanding G.S. 20-37.13(h) and G.S. 20-37.13A(a), the Division of Motor Vehicles is authorized to waive the requirement that commercial drivers license and commercial learner's permit holders have a medical examination and certification, as required by federal law, consistent with any waiver of medical qualifications standards issued by the Federal Motor Carrier Safety Administration. A credential extended under this section shall expire five months from the date it otherwise expires as prescribed by law prior to this section. However, the subsequent expiration of a credential extended under this section shall occur on the date prescribed by law prior to this section without regard to the extension. The Division shall notify individuals affected by an extension granted under this section, including information on new expiration dates and how the extension affects subsequent renewal and expiration dates.

"(b1) Extension of Intrastate Medical Waivers. -- Notwithstanding the limitation on duration of waivers in G.S. 20-37.13A(b), the Division of Motor

Vehicles may extend for up to five months the validity of a medical waiver issued by the Division under G.S. 20-37.13A if the waiver expires on or after March 1, 2020, and before the date 30 days after the date the Governor (i) rescinds Executive Order No. 116 or (ii) issues another executive order lifting restrictions on Division of Motor Vehicles functions, and the Division's Medical Review Unit determines the extension is appropriate.

"(c) Driving Eligibility Certificates. -- Notwithstanding G.S. 20-11(n)(3), a driving eligibility certificate dated on or after February 9, 2020, and before March 10, 2020, remains valid and may be accepted by the Division of Motor Vehicles to meet the requirements for a license or permit issued under G.S. 20-11 until 30 days after the date the Governor rescinds Executive Order No. 116 or the date the Division reopens all drivers license offices, whichever is earlier.

"(d) Waive Penalties. -- Notwithstanding any provision of law to the contrary, the Division shall waive any fines, fees, or penalties associated with failing to renew a credential during the period of time the credential is valid by extension under subsection (b) of this section.

"(e) Motor Vehicle Taxes. -- Notwithstanding any provision of law to the contrary, due dates for motor vehicle taxes that are tied to registration expiration under Article 22A of Chapter 105 of the General Statutes shall be extended to correspond with extended expiration dates under subsection (b) of this section.

"(f) Validity by Extension a Defense. -- A person may not be convicted or found responsible for any offense resulting from failure to renew a credential issued by the Division if, when tried for that offense, the person shows that the offense occurred during the period of time the credential is valid by extension under subsection (b) of this section.

"(g) Report. -- Within 30 days of the extensions made under subsection (b) of this section, the Division shall submit a report to the Joint Legislative Transportation Oversight Committee and the Fiscal Research Division detailing implementation of this section.

"(h) Effective Date. -- This section is effective retroactively to March 1, 2020, and applies to expirations occurring on or after that date."

Session Laws 2020-3, s. 5, is a severability clause.
Session Laws 2020-97, s. 4.5, is a severability clause.

§ 20-183.4C. When a vehicle must be inspected; 10-day temporary license plate

(a) **Inspection.** -- A vehicle that is subject to a safety inspection, an emissions inspection, or both must be inspected as follows:

(1) A new vehicle must be inspected before it is delivered to a purchaser at retail in this State. Upon purchase, a receipt approved by the Division must be provided to the new owner certifying compliance.

(1a) A new motor vehicle dealer who is also licensed pursuant to this Article may, notwithstanding subdivision (1) of this section, examine the safety and emissions control devices on a new motor vehicle and perform such services necessary to ensure the motor vehicle conforms to the required specifications established by the manufacturer and contained in its predelivery check list. The completion of the predelivery inspection procedure required or recommended by the manufacturer on a new motor vehicle shall constitute the inspection required by subdivision (1) of this section. For the purposes of this subdivision, the date of inspection shall be deemed to be the date of the sale of the motor vehicle to a purchaser.

(2) A used vehicle must be inspected before it is offered for sale at retail in this State by a dealer. Upon purchase, a receipt approved by the Division must be provided to the new owner certifying compliance.

(3) Repealed by Session Law 2007-503, s. 5, effective October 1, 2008.

(4) Except as authorized by the Commissioner for a single period of time not to exceed 12 months from the initial date of registration, a new or used vehicle acquired by a resident of this State from outside the State must be inspected before the vehicle is registered with the Division.

(5) Except as authorized by the Commissioner for a single period of time not to exceed 12 months from the initial date of registration, a vehicle owned by a new resident of this State who transfers the registration of the vehicle from the resident's former home state to this State must be inspected before the vehicle is registered with the Division.

(5a) Repealed by Session Law 2007-503, s. 5, effective October 1, 2008.

(6) A vehicle that has been inspected in accordance with this Part must be inspected by the last day of the month in which the registration on the vehicle expires.

(7) A vehicle that is required to be inspected in accordance with this Part may be inspected 90 days prior to midnight of the last day of the month as designated by the vehicle registration sticker.

(8) A new or used vehicle acquired from a retailer or a private sale in this State and registered with the Division with a new registration or a transferred registration must be inspected in accordance with this Part when the current registration expires unless it has received a passing inspection within the previous 12 months.

(9) Repealed by Session Laws 2010-97, s. 3, effective July 20, 2010.

(10) An unregistered vehicle may be registered with the Division in accordance with G.S. 20-50(b) for a period not to exceed 10 days prior to the vehicle receiving a passing inspection in accordance with this Part.

(11) A person who owns a vehicle located outside of this State when its emissions inspection becomes due may obtain an emissions inspection in the jurisdiction where the vehicle is located, in lieu of a North Carolina emissions inspection, as long as the inspection meets the requirements of 40 C.F.R. § 51.

(b) **Temporary License Plate.** -- The Division may issue a temporary license plate under and in accordance with G.S. 20-50(b) that is valid for 10 days to a person that authorizes the person to drive a vehicle whose inspection authorization or registration has expired.

(c) **Exemption.** -- The Division may issue a temporary exemption from the inspection requirements of this Article for any vehicle that has been determined by the Division to be principally garaged, as defined under G.S. 58-37-1(11), in this State and is primarily operated outside a county subject to emissions inspection requirements or outside of this State.

History.
1993 (Reg. Sess., 1994), c. 754, s. 1; 1997-29, s. 2;2001-504, s. 11;2007-481, s. 2;2007-503, s. 5;2008-190, s. 3;2009-319, s. 2;2010-97, s. 3;2015-241, s. 29.35(a);2018-42, s. 5

EDITOR'S NOTE. --
Session Laws 2015-241, s. 29.35(c), provides: "Ten-day trip permits issued under G.S. 20-183.4C(b) prior to the effective date of this section shall remain valid for the duration of the issuance."

Session Laws 2015-241, s. 29.35(d), provides: "This section becomes effective January 1, 2016, and applies to temporary license plates issued on or after that date."

Session Laws 2015-241, s. 1.1, provides: "This act shall be known as 'The Current Operations and Capital Improvements Appropriations Act of 2015.'"

Session Laws 2015-241, s. 33.4, provides: "Except for statutory changes or other provisions that clearly indicate an intention to have effects beyond the 2015-2017 fiscal biennium, the textual provisions of this act apply only to funds appropriated for, and activities occurring during, the 2015-2017 fiscal biennium."

Session Laws 2015-241, s. 33.6, is a severability clause.

EFFECT OF AMENDMENTS. --
Session Laws 2007-481, s. 2, effective August 30, 2007, added subdivision (a)(1a).

Session Laws 2007-503, s. 5, effective October 1, 2008, and applicable to offenses committed on or after that date, added the second sentence in subdivision (a)(1); in subdivision (a)(2), deleted "a location other than a public auction" at the end of the first sentence, and added the second sentence; deleted subdivision (a)(3); in subdivision (a)(4), inserted "new or" and deleted "a person" preceding "outside the State"; deleted subdivision (a)(5a); in subdivision (a)(6), substituted "registration" for "inspection sticker" and deleted "unless another subdivision of this section requires it to be inspected sooner" from the end; and added subdivisions (a)(7) through (a)(11).

Session Laws 2008-190, s. 3, effective October 1, 2008, substituted "three-day" for "one-way" in the section heading; substituted "before" for "within 10 days after" in subdivisions (a)(4) and (a)(5); and rewrote subdivisions (a)(9), (a)(10), and subsection (b).

Session Laws 2009-319, s. 2, effective July 17, 2009, added the exceptions at the beginning of subdivisions (a)(4) and (a)(5); in subsection (b), substituted "a vehicle" for "an insured vehicle" in the first sentence, and added the second sentence; and added subsection (c).

Session Laws 2010-97, s. 3, effective July 20, 2010, in the section catchline and in the first sentence in subsection (b), substituted "10-day trip permit" for "three-day trip permit"; in subdivision (a)(8), inserted "or a private sale" and "unless it has received a passing inspection within the previous 12 months"; deleted subdivision (a)(9), which read: "A used vehicle acquired from a private sale in this State must be inspected in accordance with this Part before the vehicle is registered with the Division unless it has received a passing inspection within the previous 12 months"; in subdivision (a)(10), substituted the language "may be registered with the Division in accordance with G.S. 20-50(b)" for "must be inspected before the vehicle is registered with the Division unless it has received a passing inspection within the previous 12 months"; and in subsection (b), substituted "drive the described vehicle for a period not to exceed 10 days from the date of issuance" for "drive the described vehicle only from the place the vehicle is parked to an inspection station, repair shop, or Division or contract agent registration office" in the last sentence, and deleted the last paragraph, which pertained to the Division's authority to issue a 10-day temporary permit, which must describe the vehicle that failed to pass the inspection and the date that it failed to pass inspection.

Session Laws 2015-241, s. 29.35(a), effective January 1, 2016, substituted "temporary license plate" for "trip permit" in the section heading; and rewrote subsection (b). For applicability, see editor's note.

Session Laws 2018-42, s. 5, effective June 22, 2018, substituted "delivered to a purchaser at" for "sold at" in subdivision (a)(1).

§ 20-183.4D. Procedure when a vehicle is inspected

(a) **Receipt.** -- When a safety inspection mechanic or an emissions inspection mechanic inspects a vehicle, the mechanic must give the person who brought the vehicle in for inspection an inspection receipt. The inspection receipt must state the date of the inspection, identify the mechanic performing the inspection, identify the station or self-inspector where the inspection was performed, and list the components of the inspection performed and indicate for each component whether the vehicle passed or failed. A vehicle that fails a component of an inspection may be repaired at any repair facility chosen by the owner or operator of the vehicle.

(b) **Electronic Inspection Authorization.** -- When a vehicle that is subject to a safety inspection only passes the safety inspection, the safety inspection mechanic who performed the inspection must issue an electronic inspection authorization to the vehicle at the place designated by the Division. When a vehicle that is subject to both a safety inspection and an emissions inspection passes both inspections or passes the safety inspection and has a waiver for the emissions inspection, the emissions mechanic performing the inspection must issue an electronic inspection authorization to the vehicle at the place designated by the Division.

(c), (d) Repealed by Session Laws 2007-503, s. 6, effective October 1, 2008.

(e) **When Electronic Inspection Authorization Expires.** -- An electronic inspection authorization issued under this Part expires at midnight of the last day of the month designated by the vehicle registration sticker of the following year.

History.
1993 (Reg. Sess., 1994), c. 754, s. 1; 2007-503, s. 6
EDITOR'S NOTE. --
Session Laws 2020-3, s. 4.7(a) -(h), as amended by Session Laws 2020-97, ss. 3.15(a), 3.16(a), provides: "(a) Definition. -- For purposes of this section, 'credential' means any of the following issued by the Division of Motor Vehicles:

"(1) Drivers license.
"(2) Learner's permit.
"(3) Limited learner's permit.
"(4) Limited provisional license.
"(5) Full provisional license.
"(6) Commercial drivers license.
"(7) Commercial learner's permit.
"(8) Temporary driving certificate.
"(9) Special identification card.
"(10) Handicapped placard.
"(11) Vehicle registration.
"(12) Temporary vehicle registration.
"(13) Dealer license plate.
"(14) Transporter plate.
"(15) Loaner/Dealer 'LD' plate.
"(16) Vehicle inspection authorization.
"(17) Inspection station license.
"(18) Inspection mechanic license.
"(19) Transportation network company permit.
"(20) Motor vehicle dealer license.
"(21) Sales representative license.
"(22) Manufacturer license.
"(23) Distributor license.
"(24) Wholesaler license.
"(25) Driver training school license.
"(26) Driver training school instructor license.

"(27) Professional housemoving license.

"(b) Extend Validity of Credentials. -- Notwithstanding renewal, duration, or expiration provisions of G.S. 20-7, 20-11, 20-37.6, 20-37.7, 20-37.13, 20-50, 20-66, 20-79, 20-79.02, 20-79.2, 20-183.4B, 20-183.4D, 20-280.3, 20-288, 20-324, and 20-359, or any other provision of law to the contrary, the Division of Motor Vehicles shall extend for a period of five months the validity of any credential that expires on or after March 1, 2020, and before August 1, 2020. The Division shall extend for a period of five months the validity of any credential listed in subdivisions (6), (7), (9), (10), and (18) of subsection (a) of this section that expires on or after March 1, 2020, and before the date 30 days after the date the Governor (i) rescinds Executive Order No. 116 or (ii) issues another executive order lifting restrictions on Division of Motor Vehicles functions. Notwithstanding G.S. 20-37.13(h) and G.S. 20-37.13A(a), the Division of Motor Vehicles is authorized to waive the requirement that commercial drivers license and commercial learner's permit holders have a medical examination and certification, as required by federal law, consistent with any waiver of medical qualifications standards issued by the Federal Motor Carrier Safety Administration. A credential extended under this section shall expire five months from the date it otherwise expires as prescribed by law prior to this section. However, the subsequent expiration of a credential extended under this section shall occur on the date prescribed by law prior to this section without regard to the extension. The Division shall notify individuals affected by an extension granted under this section, including information on new expiration dates and how the extension affects subsequent renewal and expiration dates.

"(b1) Extension of Intrastate Medical Waivers. -- Notwithstanding the limitation on duration of waivers in G.S. 20-37.13A(b), the Division of Motor Vehicles may extend for up to five months the validity of a medical waiver issued by the Division under G.S. 20-37.13A if the waiver expires on or after March 1, 2020, and before the date 30 days after the date the Governor (i) rescinds Executive Order No. 116 or (ii) issues another executive order lifting restrictions on Division of Motor Vehicles functions, and the Division's Medical Review Unit determines the extension is appropriate.

"(c) Driving Eligibility Certificates. -- Notwithstanding G.S. 20-11(n)(3), a driving eligibility certificate dated on or after February 9, 2020, and before March 10, 2020, remains valid and may be accepted by the Division of Motor Vehicles to meet the requirements for a license or permit issued under G.S. 20-11 until 30 days after the date the Governor rescinds Executive Order No. 116 or the date the Division reopens all drivers license offices, whichever is earlier.

"(d) Waive Penalties. -- Notwithstanding any provision of law to the contrary, the Division shall waive any fines, fees, or penalties associated with failing to renew a credential during the period of time the credential is valid by extension under subsection (b) of this section.

"(e) Motor Vehicle Taxes. -- Notwithstanding any provision of law to the contrary, due dates for motor vehicle taxes that are tied to registration expiration under Article 22A of Chapter 105 of the General Statutes shall be extended to correspond with extended expiration dates under subsection (b) of this section.

"(f) Validity by Extension a Defense. -- A person may not be convicted or found responsible for any offense resulting from failure to renew a credential issued by the Division if, when tried for that offense, the person shows that the offense occurred during the period of time the credential is valid by extension under subsection (b) of this section.

"(g) Report. -- Within 30 days of the extensions made under subsection (b) of this section, the Division shall submit a report to the Joint Legislative Transportation Oversight Committee and the Fiscal Research Division detailing implementation of this section.

"(h) Effective Date. -- This section is effective retroactively to March 1, 2020, and applies to expirations occurring on or after that date."

Session Laws 2020-3, s. 5, is a severability clause.

Session Laws 2020-97, s. 4.5, is a severability clause.

EFFECT OF AMENDMENTS. --

Session Laws 2007-503, s. 6, effective October 1, 2008, and applicable to offenses committed on or after that date, in subsection (b), substituted "Electronic Inspection Authorization" for "Sticker" in the subsection heading, and substituted "issue an electronic inspection authorization to" for "put an inspection sticker on the windshield of" twice; deleted subsections (c) and (d) which defined content of sticker and when a sticker expires; and added subsection (e).

§ 20-183.5. When a vehicle that fails an emissions inspection may obtain a waiver from the inspection requirement

(a) **Requirements.** -- The Division may issue a waiver for a vehicle, excluding a vehicle owned or being held for retail sale by a motor vehicle dealer, that meets all of the following requirements:

(1) Fails an emissions inspection because it passes the visual inspection but fails the analysis of data provided by the on-board diagnostic (OBD) equipment.

(2) Has documented repairs costing at least the waiver amount made to the vehicle to correct the cause of the failure. The waiver amount is two hundred dollars ($ 200.00).

(3) Is reinspected and again fails the inspection because it passes the visual inspection but fails the analysis of data provided by the on-board diagnostic (OBD) equipment.

(4) Meets any other waiver criteria required by 40 C.F.R. § 51.360, or as designated by the Division.

(b) **Procedure.** -- To obtain a waiver, a person must contact a local enforcement office of the Division. Before issuing a waiver, an employee of the

Division must review the inspection receipts issued for the inspections of the vehicle, review the documents establishing what repairs were made to the vehicle and at what cost, review any statement denying warranty coverage of the repairs made, and do a visual inspection of the vehicle, if appropriate, to determine if the documented repairs were made. The Division must issue a waiver if it determines that the vehicle qualifies for a waiver. A person to whom a waiver is issued must present the waiver to the self-inspector or inspection station performing the inspection to obtain an electronic inspection authorization.

(c) **Repairs.** -- The following repairs and their costs cannot be considered in determining whether the cost of repairs made to a vehicle equals or exceeds the waiver amount:

(1) Repairs covered by a warranty that applies to the vehicle.

(2) Repairs needed as a result of tampering with an emission control device of the vehicle.

(3) Repairs made by an individual who is not professionally engaged in the business of repairing vehicles.

(4) OBD diagnostics without corresponding repairs.

(d) **Electronic Inspection Authorization.** -- An electronic inspection authorization issued to a vehicle after the vehicle receives a waiver from the requirement of passing the emissions inspection expires at the same time it would if the vehicle had passed the emissions inspection.

History.
1965, c. 734, s. 1; 1993 (Reg. Sess., 1994), c. 754, s. 1; 2000-134, ss. 16, 17; 2007-503, s. 7

EFFECT OF AMENDMENTS. --
Session Laws 2007-503, s. 7, effective October 1, 2008, and applicable to offenses committed on or after that date, inserted "excluding a vehicle owned or being held for retail sale by a motor vehicle dealer" in the introductory paragraph of subsection (a); rewrote subdivision (a)(2); inserted "or as designated by the Division" in subdivision (a)(4); substituted "electronic inspection authorization" for "inspection sticker" at the end of subsection (b); in subdivision (c)(3), deleted "If the vehicle is a 1981 or newer model" at the beginning, and inserted "professionally"; added subdivision (c)(4); and in subsection (d), substituted "Electronic Inspection Authorization" for "Sticker Expiration," and substituted "electronic inspection authorization issued to" for "inspection sticker put on."

§ 20-183.5A. When a vehicle that fails a safety inspection because of missing emissions control devices may obtain a waiver

(a) **Requirements.** -- The Division may issue a waiver for a vehicle that meets all of the following requirements:

(1) Fails a safety inspection because it does not have one or more emissions control devices.

(2) Has documented repairs within the previous calendar year to replace missing emissions control devices costing at least the waiver amount made to the vehicle to correct the cause of the failure. The waiver amount is two hundred dollars ($ 200.00) if the vehicle is a 1996 or newer model.

(b) **Procedure.** -- To obtain a waiver, a person must contact a local enforcement office of the Division. Before issuing a waiver, an employee of the Division must review the inspection receipts issued for the inspections of the vehicle, review the documents establishing what repairs were made to the vehicle and at what cost, review any statement denying warranty coverage of the repairs made, and do a visual inspection of the vehicle, if appropriate, to determine if the documented repairs were made. The Division must issue a waiver if it determines that the vehicle qualifies for a waiver. A person to whom a waiver is issued must present the waiver to the self-inspector or inspection station performing the inspection to obtain an electronic inspection authorization.

(c) **Repairs.** -- The following repairs and their costs cannot be considered in determining whether the cost of repairs made to a vehicle equals or exceeds the waiver amount:

(1) Repairs covered by a warranty that applies to the vehicle.

(2) Repairs needed as a result of tampering with an emission control device of the vehicle.

(3) Repairs made by an individual who is not professionally engaged in the business of repairing vehicles.

(d) **Electronic Inspection Authorization Expiration.** -- An electronic inspection authorization issued to a vehicle after the vehicle receives a waiver from the requirement of passing the safety inspection expires at the same time it would if the vehicle had passed the safety inspection.

History.
2007-503, ss. 8, 9

EFFECT OF AMENDMENTS. --
Session Laws 2007-503, ss. 8 and 9, effective October 1, 2008, and applicable to offenses committed on or after that date, in subdivision (a)(2), deleted "seventy-five dollars ($75.00) if the vehicle is a pre-1981 model and is" following "amount is" and substituted "1996" for "1981"; substituted "electronic inspection authorization" for "inspection sticker" at the end of subsection (b); in subdivision (c)(3), deleted "If the vehicle is a 1981 or newer model" from the beginning, and inserted "professionally"; and in subsection (d), substituted "Electronic Inspection Authorization" for "Sticker" and "electronic inspection authorization issued to" for "inspection sticker put on."

N.C. Gen. Stat. § 20-183.6

Repealed by Session Laws 2007-503, s. 10, effective October 1, 2008, and applicable to offenses committed on or after that date.

§ 20-183.6A. Administration of program; duties of license holders

(a) **Division.** -- The Division is responsible for administering the safety inspection and the emissions inspection programs. In exercising this responsibility, the Division must:

(1) Conduct performance audits, record audits, and equipment audits of those licensed to perform inspections to ensure that inspections are performed properly.

(2) Ensure that Division personnel who audit license holders are knowledgeable about audit procedures and about the requirements of both the safety inspection and the emissions inspection programs.

(3) Perform an emissions inspection on a vehicle when requested to do so by a vehicle owner so the owner can compare the result of the inspection performed by the Division with the result of an inspection performed at an emissions inspection station.

(4) Investigate complaints about a person licensed to perform inspections and reports of irregularities in performing inspections.

(5) Establish written procedures for the issuance of electronic inspection authorizations to persons licensed to perform electronic inspection authorizations.

(6) Submit information and reports to the federal Environmental Protection Agency as required by 40 C.F.R. Part 51.

(b) **License Holders.** -- A person who is licensed by the Division under this Part must post the license at the place required by the Division and must keep a record of inspections performed. The inspection record must identify the vehicle that was inspected, indicate the type of inspection performed and the date of inspection, and contain any other information required by the Division. A self-inspector or an inspection station must send its records of inspections to the Division in the form and at the time required by the Division. An auditor of the Division may review the inspection records of a person licensed by the Division under this Part during normal business hours.

History.

1993 (Reg. Sess., 1994), c. 754, s. 1; 2007-503, s. 11

EFFECT OF AMENDMENTS. --

Session Laws 2007-503, s. 11, effective October 1, 2008, and applicable to offenses committed on or after that date, substituted "electronic inspection authorizations" for "inspection stickers" and for "inspections" in subdivision (a)(5).

§ 20-183.7. Fees for performing an inspection and issuing an electronic inspection authorization to a vehicle; use of civil penalties

(a) **Fee Amount.** -- When a fee applies to an inspection of a vehicle or the issuance of an electronic inspection authorization, the fee must be collected. The following fees apply to an inspection of a vehicle and the issuance of an electronic inspection authorization:

Type	Inspection	Authorization
Safety Only	$ 12.75	$.85
Emissions and Safety	23.75	6.25.

The fee for performing an inspection of a vehicle applies when an inspection is performed, regardless of whether the vehicle passes the inspection. The fee for an electronic inspection authorization applies when an electronic inspection authorization is issued to a vehicle. The fee for inspecting after-factory tinted windows shall be ten dollars ($ 10.00), and the fee applies only to an inspection performed with a light meter after a safety inspection mechanic determined that the window had after-factory tint. A safety inspection mechanic shall not inspect an after-factory tinted window of a vehicle for which the Division has issued a medical exception permit pursuant to G.S. 20-127(f).

A vehicle that is inspected at an inspection station and fails the inspection is entitled to be reinspected at the same station at any time within 60 days of the failed inspection without paying another inspection fee.

The inspection fee for an emissions and safety inspection set out in this subsection is the maximum amount that an inspection station or an inspection mechanic may charge for an emissions and safety inspection of a vehicle. An inspection station or an inspection mechanic may charge the maximum amount or any lesser amount for an emissions and safety inspection of a vehicle. The inspection fee for a safety only inspection set out in this subsection may not be increased or decreased. The authorization fees set out in this subsection may not be increased or decreased.

(b) **Self-Inspector.** -- The fee for an inspection does not apply to an inspection performed by a self-inspector. The fee for issuing an electronic inspection authorization to a vehicle applies to an inspection performed by a self-inspector.

(c) **Fee Distribution.** -- Fees collected for electronic inspection authorizations are payable to the Division of Motor Vehicles. The amount of each fee listed in the table below shall be credited to the Highway Fund, the Volunteer Rescue/EMS Fund established in G.S. 58-87-5, the Rescue Squad Workers' Relief Fund established

Chapter 20

in G.S. 58-88-5, and the Division of Air Quality of the Department of Environmental Quality:

Recipient	Safety Only Electronic Authorization	Emissions and Safety Electronic Authorization
Highway Fund	.55	5.30
Volunteer Rescue/ EMS Fund	.18	.18
Rescue Squad Workers' Relief Fund	.12	.12
Division of Air Quality	.00	.65.

(d) Repealed by Session Laws 2013-360, s. 34.15(c), effective July 1, 2013.

(d1) Repealed by Session Laws 2013-360, s. 34.15(b), effective June 30, 2014.

(d2) Repealed by Session Laws 2001-504, s. 3, effective July 1, 2007.

(e) **Civil Penalties.** -- Civil penalties collected under this Part shall be credited to the Highway Fund as nontax revenue.

(f) **Inspection Stations Required to Post Fee Information.** -- The Division shall approve the form and style of one or more standard signs to be used to display the information required by this subsection. The Division shall require that one or more of the standard signs be conspicuously posted at each inspection station in a manner reasonably calculated to make the information on the sign readily available to each person who presents a motor vehicle to the station for inspection. The sign shall include the following information:

(1) The maximum and minimum amounts of the inspection fee authorized by this section.

(2) The amount of the inspection fee charged by the inspection station and a statement that clearly indicates that the amount of the inspection fee is determined by the inspection station, that the inspection fee is retained by the inspection station to compensate the station for performing the inspection, and that the inspection fee is not paid to the State.

(3) The amount of the electronic inspection authorization fee, if the motor vehicle passes the inspection, a statement that the electronic inspection authorization fee is paid to the State, and a brief summary of the purposes for which the electronic inspection authorization fee is collected.

(4) The total fee to be charged if the motor vehicle passes the inspection.

(5) A statement that a vehicle that fails an inspection may be reinspected at the same station within 60 days of the inspection without payment of another inspection fee.

(g) **Information on Receipt.** -- The information set out in subdivisions (1) through (5) of subsection (f) of this section shall be set out in not smaller than 12 point type and shall be shown graphically in the form of a pie chart on the inspection receipt.

(h) Subsections (f) and (g) of this section apply only to inspection stations that perform both emissions and safety inspections.

History.
1965, c. 734, s. 1; 1969, c. 1242; 1973, c. 1480; 1975, c. 547; c. 716, s. 5; c. 875, s. 4; 1979, c. 688; 1979, 2nd Sess., c. 1180, ss. 5, 6; 1981, c. 690, s. 17; 1981 (Reg. Sess., 1982), c. 1261, s. 2; 1985, c. 415, ss. 1-6; 1985 (Reg. Sess., 1986), c. 1018, s. 8; 1987, c. 584, ss. 1-3; 1987 (Reg. Sess., 1988), c. 1062, ss. 3-5; 1989, c. 391, s. 3;c. 534, s. 3;1989 (Reg. Sess., 1990), c. 1066, s. 33(b); 1991 (Reg. Sess., 1992), c. 943, s. 1; 1993, c. 385, s. 1;1993 (Reg. Sess., 1994), c. 754, s. 1; 1995, c. 473, s. 3;1995 (Reg. Sess., 1996), c. 743, s. 1; 1997-29, s. 4;1997-443, s. 11A.123;2000-75, s. 3;2001-504, ss. 1-3; 2006-230, s. 2;2007-364, s. 2;2007-503, s. 12;2009-319, s. 3;2010-96, s. 7;2011-145, s. 6A.15;2013-302, s. 1;2013-360, s. 34.15(b), (c); 2015-241, s. 14.30(u)

EDITOR'S NOTE. --
Session Laws 2014-100, s. 2.2(e), provides: "Notwithstanding G.S. 20-183.7(c), fees collected for electronic inspection authorizations during the 2014-2015 fiscal year that would have been credited to the I & M Air Pollution Control Account established under G.S. 143-215.3A(b1) shall be credited to the State's General Fund."

Session Laws 2014-100, s. 1.1, provides: "This act shall be known as 'The Current Operations and Capital Improvements Appropriations Act of 2014.'"

Session Laws 2014-100, s. 38.4, provides: "Except for statutory changes or other provisions that clearly indicate an intention to have effects beyond the 2014-2015 fiscal year, the textual provisions of this act apply only to funds appropriated for, and activities occurring during, the 2014-2015 fiscal year."

Session Laws 2014-100, s. 38.7, is a severability clause.

EFFECT OF AMENDMENTS. --
Session Laws 2001-504, s. 3, effective July 1, 2007, amends this section as amended by ss. 1 and 2 of the act, by doing the following: in subsection (a), in the entry labelled "Emissions and Safety", substitutes "23.75" for "23.50" and substitutes "6.25" for "6.50"; in subsection (c), deletes "the Highway Trust Fund Repayment Fee established in subsection (d2) of this section" following "subsection (d1) of this section" and in the table, deletes the entry labelled "Highway Trust Fund Repayment Fee"; and deletes subsection (d2), relating to the Highway Trust Fund Repayment Fee.

Session Laws 2006-230, s. 2, effective July 1, 2007, added the third sentence in the second paragraph of subsection (a).

Chapter 20

Session Laws 2007-364, s. 2, effective January 1, 2009, substituted "60 days" for "30 days" in the third paragraph of subsection (a).

Session Laws 2007-503, s. 12, effective October 1, 2008, and applicable to offenses committed on or after that date, substituted "issuing an electronic inspection authorization to" for "putting an inspection sticker on" in the section heading; in subsection (a), substituted "electronic inspection authorization" for "inspection sticker" twice in the first paragraph, in the table, substituted "Authorization" for "Sticker" in the column heading, and "$12.75" for "$8.25" in the entry for "Safety Only," in the third paragraph, substituted "electronic inspection authorization" for "inspection sticker" and "electronic inspection authorization is issued to" for "inspection sticker is put on" in the second sentence, and deleted the third sentence, which read: "The fee for an inspection sticker does not apply to a replacement inspection sticker for use on a windshield replaced by a business registered with the Division pursuant to G.S. 20-183.6," and in the last paragraph, substituted "authorization fees" for "sticker fees" near the end; substituted "issuing an electronic inspection authorization to" for "putting an inspection sticker on" in subsection (b); in subsection (c), substituted "electronic inspection authorizations" for "inspection stickers" in the introductory paragraph, and in the table, substituted "Electronic Authorization" for "Sticker" in both column headings; inserted "safety and" in subsection (d1); and substituted "electronic inspection authorization" for "sticker" three times in subdivision (f)(3).

Session Laws 2009-319, s. 3, effective July 17, 2009, substituted "Inspection Program Account" for "Emissions Program Account" throughout subsections (c) and (d), and in subsection (d), deleted "emissions" preceding "inspection" in the last sentence.

Session Laws 2010-96, s. 7, effective July 20, 2010, substituted "60 days" for "30 days" in subdivision (f)(5).

Session Laws 2011-145, s. 6A.15, effective July 1, 2011, added "and to fund replacement of the State Titling and Registration System and the State Automated Driver License System" in the last sentence of subsection (d).

Session Laws 2013-302, s. 1, effective October 1, 2013, deleted the former third sentence in the second paragraph of subsection (a), which read "The fee for an inspection sticker does not apply to a replacement inspection sticker for use on a windshield replaced by a business registered with the Division pursuant to G.S. 20-183.6." For applicability, see Editor's note.

Session Laws 2013-360, s. 34.15(b), effective June 30, 2014, repealed subsection (d1), pertaining to the Telecommunications Account. For applicability, see Editor's note.

Session Laws 2013-360, s. 34.15(c), effective July 1, 2013, in subsection (c), deleted "the Inspection Program Account established in subsection (d) of this section, the Telecommunications Account established in subsection (d1) of this section" following "Highway Fund" in the second sentence, and rewrote the table;

and deleted subsection (d), pertaining to the Inspection Program Account. For applicability, see Editor's note.

Session Laws 2015-241, s. 14.30(u), effective July 1, 2015, substituted "Department of Environmental Quality" for "Department of Environment and Natural Resources" in subsection (c).

§ 20-183.7A. Penalties applicable to license holders and suspension or revocation of license for safety violations

(a) **Kinds of Violations.** -- The civil penalty schedule established in this section applies to safety self-inspectors, safety inspection stations, and safety inspection mechanics. The schedule categorizes safety violations into serious (Type I), minor (Type II), and technical (Type III) violations. A serious violation is a violation of this Part or a rule adopted to implement this Part that directly affects the safety or emissions reduction benefits of the safety inspection program. A minor violation is a violation of this Part or a rule adopted to implement this Part that reflects negligence or carelessness in conducting a safety inspection or complying with the safety inspection requirements but does not directly affect the safety benefits or emission reduction benefits of the safety inspection program. A technical violation is a violation that is not a serious violation, a minor violation, or another type of offense under this Part.

(b) **Penalty Schedule.** -- The Division must take the following action for a violation:

(1) **Type I.** -- For a first or second Type I violation within three years by a safety self-inspector or a safety inspection station, assess a civil penalty of two hundred fifty dollars ($ 250.00) and suspend the license of the business for 180 days. For a third or subsequent Type I violation within three years by a safety self-inspector or a safety inspection station, assess a civil penalty of one thousand dollars ($ 1,000) and revoke the license of the business for two years. For a first or second Type I violation within seven years by a safety inspection mechanic, assess a civil penalty of one hundred dollars ($ 100.00) and suspend the mechanic's license for six months. For a third or subsequent Type I violation within seven years by a safety inspection mechanic, assess a civil penalty of two hundred fifty dollars ($ 250.00) and revoke the mechanic's license for two years.

(2) **Type II.** -- For a first or second Type II violation within three years by a safety self-inspector or a safety inspection station, assess a civil penalty of one hundred dollars ($ 100.00). For a third or subsequent Type II violation within three years by a safety self-inspector or a safety inspection

station, assess a civil penalty of two hundred fifty dollars ($ 250.00) and suspend the license of the business for 90 days. For a first or second Type II violation within seven years by a safety inspection mechanic, assess a civil penalty of fifty dollars ($ 50.00). For a third or subsequent Type II violation within seven years by a safety inspection mechanic, assess a civil penalty of one hundred dollars ($ 100.00) and suspend the mechanic's license for 90 days.

(3) **Type III.** -- For a first or second Type III violation within seven years by a safety self-inspector, a safety inspection station, or a safety inspection mechanic, send a warning letter. For a third or subsequent Type III violation within seven years by the same safety license holder, assess a civil penalty of twenty-five dollars ($ 25.00).

(c) **Station or Self-Inspector Responsibility.** -- It is the responsibility of a safety inspection station and a safety self-inspector to supervise the safety inspection mechanics it employs. A violation by a safety inspection mechanic is considered a violation by the station or self-inspector for whom the mechanic is employed. The Division may stay a term of suspension for a first occurrence of a Type I violation for a station if the station agrees to follow the reasonable terms and conditions of the stay as determined by the Division. In determining whether to suspend a first occurrence violation for a station, the Division may consider the supervision provided by the station over the individual or individuals who committed the violation, action that has been taken to remedy future violations, or prior knowledge of the station as to the acts committed by the individual or individuals who committed the violation, or a combination of these factors. The monetary penalty shall not be stayed or reduced.

(d) **Multiple Violations in a Single Safety Inspection.** -- If a safety self-inspector, a safety inspection station, or a safety inspection mechanic commits two or more violations in the course of a single safety inspection, the Division shall take only the action specified for the most significant violation.

(d1) **Multiple Violations in Separate Safety Inspections.** -- In the case of two or more violations committed in separate safety inspections, considered at one time, the Division shall consider each violation as a separate occurrence and shall impose a separate penalty for each violation as a first, second, or third or subsequent violation as found in the applicable penalty schedule. The Division may in its discretion direct that any suspensions for the first, second, or third or subsequent violations run concurrently. If the Division does not direct that the suspensions run concurrently, they shall run consecutively. Nothing in this section shall

prohibit or limit a reviewing court's ability to affirm, reverse, remand, or modify the Division's decisions, whether discretionary or otherwise, pursuant to Article 4 of Chapter 150B of the General Statutes.

(e) **Mechanic Training.** -- A safety inspection mechanic whose license has been suspended or revoked must retake the course required under G.S. 20-183.4 and successfully complete the course before the mechanic's license can be reinstated. Failure to successfully complete this course continues the period of suspension or revocation until the course is completed successfully.

History.
2001-504, s. 12;2013-302, s. 2
  EFFECT OF AMENDMENTS. --
  Session Laws 2013-302, s. 2, effective October 1, 2013, substituted "180 days" for "six months" in subdivision (b)(1); added the third through fifth sentences in subsection (c); added "in a Single Safety Inspection" in subsection (d) heading; and added subsection (d1). For applicability, see Editor's note.
CITED in Inspection Station No. 31327 v. N.C. DMV, 244 N.C. App. 416, 781 S.E.2d 79 (2015).

§ 20-183.7B. Acts that are Type I, II, or III safety violations

(a) **Type I.** -- It is a Type I violation for a safety self-inspector, a safety inspection station, or a safety inspection mechanic to do any of the following:

(1) Issue a safety electronic inspection authorization to a vehicle without performing a safety inspection of vehicle.

(2) Issue a safety electronic inspection authorization to a vehicle after performing a safety inspection of the vehicle and determining that the vehicle did not pass the inspection.

(3) Allow a person who is not licensed as a safety inspection mechanic to perform a safety inspection for a self-inspector or at a safety station.

(4) Sell, issue, or otherwise give an electronic inspection authorization to another, other than as the result of a vehicle inspection in which the vehicle passed the inspection.

(5) Repealed by Session Laws 2013-302, s. 3, effective October 1, 2013, and applicable to violations occurring on or after that date.

(6) Perform a safety-only inspection on a vehicle that is subject to both a safety and an emissions inspection.

(7) Repealed by Session Laws 2013-302, s. 3, effective October 1, 2013, and applicable to violations occurring on or after that date.

(8) Conduct a safety inspection of a vehicle without driving the vehicle and without raising the vehicle and without opening the hood of the vehicle to check equipment located therein.

(9) Solicit or accept anything of value to pass a vehicle other than as provided in this Part.

(b) **Type II.** -- It is a Type II violation for a safety self-inspector, a safety inspection station, or a safety inspection mechanic to do any of the following:

(1) Issue a safety electronic inspection authorization to a vehicle without driving the vehicle and checking the vehicle's braking reaction, foot brake pedal reserve, and steering free play.

(2) Issue a safety electronic inspection authorization to a vehicle without raising the vehicle to free each wheel and checking the vehicle's tires, brake lines, parking brake cables, wheel drums, exhaust system, and the emissions equipment.

(3) Issue a safety electronic inspection authorization to a vehicle without raising the hood and checking the master cylinder, horn mounting, power steering, and emissions equipment.

(4) Conduct a safety inspection of a vehicle outside the designated inspection area.

(5) Issue a safety electronic inspection authorization to a vehicle with inoperative equipment, or with equipment that does not conform to the vehicle's original equipment or design specifications, or with equipment that is prohibited by any provision of law.

(6) Issue a safety electronic inspection authorization to a vehicle without performing a visual inspection of the vehicle's exhaust system.

(7) Issue a safety electronic inspection authorization to a vehicle without checking the exhaust system for leaks.

(8) Issue a safety electronic inspection authorization to a vehicle that is required to have any of the following emissions control devices but does not have the device:

    a. Catalytic converter.
    b. PCV valve.
    c. Thermostatic air control.
    d. Oxygen sensor.
    e. Unleaded gas restrictor.
    f. Gasoline tank cap or capless fuel system.
    g. Air injection system.
    h. Evaporative emissions system.
    i. Exhaust gas recirculation (EGR) valve.

(9) Issue a safety electronic inspection authorization to a vehicle after failing to inspect four or more of following:

    a. Emergency brake.
    b. Horn.
    c. Headlight high beam indicator.
    d. Inside rearview mirror.
    e. Outside rearview mirror.
    f. Turn signals.
    g. Parking lights.
    h. Headlights -- operation and lens.
    i. Headlights -- aim.
    j. Stoplights.
    k. Taillights.
    l. License plate lights.
    m. Windshield wiper.
    n. Windshield wiper blades.
    o. Window tint.

(10) Impose no fee for a safety inspection of a vehicle or the issuance of a safety electronic inspection authorization or impose a fee for one of these actions in an amount that differs from the amount set in G.S. 20-183.7.

(c) **Type III.** -- It is a Type III violation for a safety self-inspector, a safety inspection station, or a safety inspection mechanic to do any of the following:

(1) Fail to post a safety inspection station license issued by the Division.

(2) Fail to send information on safety inspections to the Division at the time or in the form required by the Division.

(3) Fail to post all safety information required by federal law and by the Division.

(4) Fail to put the required information on an inspection receipt in a legible manner using ink.

(5) Issue a receipt that is signed by a person other than the safety inspection mechanic.

(6) Repealed by Session Laws 2013-302, s. 3, effective October 1, 2013, and applicable to violations occurring on or after that date.

(7) Issue a safety electronic inspection authorization to a vehicle after having failed to inspect three or fewer of the following:

    a. Emergency brake.
    b. Horn.
    c. Headlight high beam indicator.
    d. Inside rearview mirror.
    e. Outside rearview mirror.
    f. Turn signals.
    g. Parking lights.
    h. Headlights -- operation and lens.
    i. Headlights -- aim.
    j. Stoplights.
    k. Taillights.
    l. License plate lights.
    m. Windshield wiper.
    n. Windshield wiper blades.
    o. Window tint.

(d) **Other Acts.** -- The lists in this section of the acts that are Type I, Type II, or Type III

Chapter 20

violations are not the only acts that are one of these types of violations. The Division may designate other acts that are a Type I, Type II, or Type III violation.

History.
2001-504, s. 12;2007-503, s. 13;2013-302, s. 3

EFFECT OF AMENDMENTS. --

Session Laws 2007-503, s. 13, effective October 1, 2008, and applicable to offenses committed on or after that date, substituted "electronic inspection authorization to" for "inspection sticker on," "electronic inspection authorization" for "inspection sticker," "electronic inspection authorizations" for "inspection stickers," and "Issue a safety" for "Put a safety" everywhere they appear throughout the section; and inserted "issue" following "Sell" in subdivision (a)(4).

Session Laws 2013-302, s. 3, effective October 1, 2013, deleted subdivisions (a)(5), (a)(7), and (c)(6), which formerly read "Be unable to account for five or more electronic inspection authorizations at any one time upon the request of an officer of the Division," "Transfer an electronic inspection authorization from one vehicle to another," and "Place an incorrect expiration date on an electronic inspection authorization" respectively; and added "or capless fuel system" at the end of subdivision (b)(8)f. For applicability, see Editor's note.

CORPORATION REQUIRED TO BE REPRESENTED BY ATTORNEY IN HEARING BEFORE THE DMV. --Although corporations were not required to be represented by attorneys in hearings before the Office of Administrative Hearings (OAH), pursuant to G.S. 150B-23 (referring to "attorney or representative" of a party), the DMV was exempted from the provisions of the Administrative Procedure Act authorizing contested cases to be brought in the OAH, G.S. 150B-1(e)(8), and therefore, in a hearing before the DMV, a corporation was required to be represented by an attorney. In re Twin County Motorsports, Inc., 230 N.C. App. 259, 749 S.E.2d 474 (2013).

CITED in In re Twin County Motorsports, Inc., 367 N.C. 613, 766 S.E.2d 832 (2014); Inspection Station No. 31327 v. N.C. DMV, 244 N.C. App. 416, 781 S.E.2d 79 (2015).

§ 20-183.8. Infractions and criminal offenses for violations of inspection requirements

(a) **Infractions.** -- A person who does any of the following commits an infraction and, if found responsible, is liable for a penalty of up to fifty dollars ($ 50.00):

(1) Operates a motor vehicle that is subject to inspection under this Part on a highway or public vehicular area in the State when the vehicle has not been inspected in accordance with this Part, as evidenced by the vehicle's lack of a current electronic inspection authorization or otherwise.

(2) Allows an electronic inspection authorization to be issued to a vehicle owned or operated by that person, knowing that the vehicle was not inspected before the electronic inspection authorization was issued or was not inspected properly.

(3) Issues an electronic inspection authorization on a vehicle, knowing or having reasonable grounds to know that an inspection of the vehicle was not performed or was performed improperly. A person who is cited for a civil penalty under G.S. 20-183.8B for an emissions violation involving the inspection of a vehicle may not be charged with an infraction under this subdivision based on that same vehicle.

(4) Alters the original certified configuration or data link connectors of a vehicle in such a way as to make an emissions inspection by analysis of data provided by onboard diagnostic (OBD) equipment inaccurate or impossible.

(b) **Defenses to Infractions.** -- Any of the following is a defense to a violation under subsection (a) of this section:

(1) The vehicle was continuously out of State for at least the 30 days preceding the date the electronic inspection authorization expired and a current electronic inspection authorization was obtained within 10 days after the vehicle came back to the State.

(2) The vehicle displays a dealer license plate or a transporter plate, the dealer repossessed the vehicle or otherwise acquired the vehicle within the last 10 days, and the vehicle is being driven from its place of acquisition to the dealer's place of business or to an inspection station.

(3) Repealed by Session Laws 1997-29, s. 5.

(4) The charged infraction is described in subdivision (a)(1) of this section, the vehicle is subject to a safety inspection or an emissions inspection and the vehicle owner establishes in court that the vehicle was inspected after the citation was issued and within 30 days of the expiration date of the inspection sticker that was on the vehicle or the electronic inspection authorization was issued to the vehicle when the citation was issued.

(b1) A person who performs a safety inspection without a license, as required under G.S. 20-183.4, or an emissions inspection without a license, as required under G.S. 20-183.4A, is guilty of a Class 3 misdemeanor.

(c) **Felony.** -- A person who does any of the following commits a Class I felony:

(1) Forges an inspection sticker or inspection receipt.

(2) Buys, sells, issues, or possesses a forged inspection sticker or electronic inspection authorization.

(3) Buys, sells, issues, or possesses an electronic inspection authorization other than as the result of either of the following:

a. Having a license as an inspection station, a self-inspector, or an inspection mechanic and obtaining the electronic inspection authorization from the Division through an electronic authorization vendor in the course of business.

b. A vehicle inspection in which the vehicle passed the inspection or for which the vehicle received a waiver.

(4) Solicits or accepts anything of value in order to pass a vehicle that fails a safety or emissions inspection.

(5) Fails a vehicle for any reason not authorized by law.

History.
1965, c. 734, s. 1; 1967, c. 692, s. 3; 1969, c. 179, s. 1; c. 620; 1973, cc. 909, 1322; 1975, c. 716, s. 5; 1979, 2nd Sess., c. 1180, s. 4; 1985, c. 764, s. 23; 1985 (Reg. Sess., 1986), c. 852, s. 17; 1993 (Reg. Sess., 1994), c. 754, s. 1; 1997-29, s. 5;1999-452, s. 25;2001-504, s. 13;2007-503, s. 14;2009-319, s. 5

EFFECT OF AMENDMENTS. --
Session Laws 2009-319, s. 5, effective December 1, 2009, and applicable to offenses committed on or after that date, added subsection (b1).

§ 20-183.8A. Civil penalties against motorists for emissions violations; waiver

(a) **Civil Penalties. --** The Division must assess a civil penalty against a person who owns or leases a vehicle that is subject to an inspection and who engages in any of the emissions violations set out in this subsection. As provided in G.S. 20-54, the registration of a vehicle may not be renewed until a penalty imposed under this subsection has been paid. The civil penalties and violations are as follows:

(1) Fifty dollars ($ 50.00) for failure to have the vehicle inspected within four months after it is required to be inspected under this Part.

(2) Two hundred fifty dollars ($ 250.00) for instructing or allowing a person to tamper with an emission control device of the vehicle so as to make the device inoperative or fail to work properly.

(3) Two hundred fifty dollars ($ 250.00) for incorrectly stating the vehicle's county of registration to avoid having an emissions inspection of the vehicle.

(b) **Waiver. --** The Division must waive the civil penalty assessed under subdivision (a)(1) of this section against a person who establishes the following:

(1) The person was continuously out of the State on active military duty from the date the electronic authorization expired to the date the four-month grace period expired.

(2) No person operated the vehicle from the date the electronic authorization expired to the date the four-month grace period expired.

(3) The person obtained a current electronic authorization within 30 days after returning to the State.

History.
1993 (Reg. Sess., 1994), c. 754, ss. 1, 8; 1998-212, s. 27.6(b);2007-364, ss. 3, 4; 2007-503, s. 15;2009-319, s. 4

EFFECT OF AMENDMENTS. --
Session Laws 2007-364, s. 3, effective August 17, 2007, and applicable to civil penalties assessed for violations committed on or after that date, added "waiver" in the section heading; added subsection (b) and designated the former provisions of the section as subsection (a); and in subsection (a), added the subsection heading "Civil Penalties."

Session Laws 2007-364, s. 4, effective July 1, 2008, and applicable to civil penalties assessed for violations committed on or after that date, in the introductory paragraph of subsection (a), substituted "must assess" for "shall assess" near the beginning, substituted "in any of the emissions violations set out in this subsection" for "does any of the following," and added the last two sentences; rewrote subdivisions (a)(1) through (3); and deleted the former last paragraph of the subsection, which provided penalty amounts for certain vehicles.

Session Laws 2009-319, s. 4, effective July 17, 2009, in subsection (a), in the introductory language, deleted "emissions" preceding "inspection"; and in subsection (b), substituted "electronic authorization" for "inspection sticker" three times.

§ 20-183.8B. Civil penalties against license holders and suspension or revocation of license for emissions violations

(a) **Kinds of Violations. --** The civil penalty schedule established in this section applies to emissions self-inspectors, emissions inspection stations, and emissions inspection mechanics. The schedule categorizes emissions violations into serious (Type I), minor (Type II), and technical (Type III) violations.

A serious violation is a violation of this Part or a rule adopted to implement this Part that directly affects the emission reduction benefits of the emissions inspection program. A minor violation is a violation of this Part or a rule adopted to implement this Part that reflects negligence or carelessness in conducting an emissions inspection or complying with the emissions inspection requirements but does not directly affect the emission reduction benefits of the emissions inspection program. A technical violation is a violation that is not a serious violation, a minor violation, or another type of offense under this Part.

(b) Penalty Schedule. -- The Division must take the following action for a violation:

(1) **Type I. --** For a first or second Type I violation by an emissions self-inspector or an emissions inspection station, assess a civil penalty of two hundred fifty dollars ($ 250.00) and suspend the license of the business for 180 days. For a third or subsequent Type I violation within three years by an emissions self-inspector or an emissions inspection station, assess a civil penalty of one thousand dollars ($ 1,000) and revoke the license of the business for two years.

For a first or second Type I violation by an emissions inspection mechanic, assess a civil penalty of one hundred dollars ($ 100.00) and suspend the mechanic's license for 180 days. For a third or subsequent Type I violation within seven years by an emissions inspection mechanic, assess a civil penalty of two hundred fifty dollars ($ 250.00) and revoke the mechanic's license for two years.

(2) **Type II. --** For a first or second Type II violation by an emissions self-inspector or an emissions inspection station, assess a civil penalty of one hundred dollars ($ 100.00). For a third or subsequent Type II violation within three years by an emissions self-inspector or an emissions inspection station, assess a civil penalty of two hundred fifty dollars ($ 250.00) and suspend the license of the business for 90 days.

For a first or second Type II violation by an emissions inspection mechanic, assess a civil penalty of fifty dollars ($ 50.00). For a third or subsequent Type II violation within seven years by an emissions inspection mechanic, assess a civil penalty of one hundred dollars ($ 100.00) and suspend the mechanic's license for 90 days.

(3) **Type III. --** For a first or second Type III violation by an emissions self-inspector, an emissions inspection station, or an emissions inspection mechanic, send a warning letter. For a third or subsequent Type III violation within three years by the same emissions license holder, assess a civil penalty of twenty-five dollars ($ 25.00).

(c) Station or Self-Inspector Responsibility. -- It is the responsibility of an emissions inspection station and an emissions self-inspector to supervise the emissions mechanics it employs. A violation by an emissions inspector mechanic is considered a violation by the station or self-inspector for whom the mechanic is employed. The Division may stay a term of suspension for a first occurrence of a Type I violation for a station if the station agrees to follow the reasonable terms and conditions of the stay as determined by the Division. In determining whether to suspend a first occurrence violation

for a station, the Division may consider the supervision provided by the station over the individual or individuals who committed the violation, action that has been taken to remedy future violations, or prior knowledge of the station as to the acts committed by the individual or individuals who committed the violation, or a combination of these factors. The monetary penalty shall not be stayed or reduced.

(c1) Multiple Violations in a Single Emissions Inspection. -- If an emissions self-inspector, an emissions inspection station, or an emissions inspection mechanic commits two or more violations in the course of a single emissions inspection, the Division shall take only the action specified for the most significant violation.

(c2) Multiple Violations in Separate Emissions Inspections. -- In the case of two or more violations committed in separate emissions inspections, considered at one time, the Division shall consider each violation as a separate occurrence and shall impose a separate penalty for each violation as a first, second, or third or subsequent violation as found in the applicable penalty schedule. The Division may in its discretion direct that any suspensions for the first, second, or third or subsequent violations run concurrently. If the Division does not direct that the suspensions run concurrently, they shall run consecutively. Nothing in this section shall prohibit or limit a reviewing court's ability to affirm, reverse, remand, or modify the Division's decisions, whether discretionary or otherwise, pursuant to Article 4 of Chapter 150B of the General Statutes.

(d), (d1) Repealed by Session Laws 2013-302, s. 4, effective October 1, 2013, and applicable to violations occurring on or after that date.

(e) Mechanic Training. -- An emissions inspection mechanic whose license has been suspended or revoked must retake the course required under G.S. 20-183.4A and successfully complete the course before the mechanic's license can be reinstated. Failure to successfully complete this course continues the period of suspension or revocation until the course is completed successfully.

History.
1993 (Reg. Sess., 1994), c. 754, s. 1; 1997-29, s. 6;2001-504, s. 14;2013-302, s. 4

EFFECT OF AMENDMENTS. --
Session Laws 2013-302, s. 4, effective October 1, 2013, substituted "180 days" for "six months" twice in subdivision (b)(1); added the third through fifth sentences in subsection (c); added subsections (c1) and (c2); and deleted subsections (d) and (d1), pertaining to Missing Stickers and Penalty for Missing Stickers. For applicability, see Editor's note.

SUSPENSION WARRANTED. --Suspension of a vehicle inspection facility's equipment inspection license was warranted where the facility failed to visually inspect a truck's exhaust emission system and determine that it did not have a catalytic converter as the facility's violation had an effect on the emission reduction benefits of the testing program and thus was a Type I violation. Darryl Burke Chevrolet, Inc. v. Aikens, 131 N.C. App. 31, 505 S.E.2d 581 (1998), aff'd, 350 N.C. 83, 511 S.E.2d 639 (1999).

§ 20-183.8C. Acts that are Type I, II, or III emissions violations

(a) **Type I.** -- It is a Type I violation for an emissions self-inspector, an emissions inspection station, or an emissions inspection mechanic to do any of the following:

(1) Issue an emissions electronic inspection authorization on a vehicle without performing an emissions inspection of the vehicle.

(1a) Issue an emissions electronic inspection authorization to a vehicle after performing an emissions inspection of the vehicle and determining that the vehicle did not pass the inspection.

(2) Use a test-defeating strategy when conducting an emissions inspection by changing the emission standards for a vehicle by incorrectly entering the vehicle type or model year, or using data provided by the on-board diagnostic (OBD) equipment of another vehicle to achieve a passing result.

(3) Allow a person who is not licensed as an emissions inspection mechanic to perform an emissions inspection for a self-inspector or at an emissions station.

(4) Sell, issue, or otherwise give an electronic inspection authorization to another other than as the result of a vehicle inspection in which the vehicle passed the inspection or for which the vehicle received a waiver.

(5) Repealed by Session Laws 2013-302, s. 5, effective October 1, 2013, and applicable to violations occurring on or after that date.

(6) Perform a safety-only inspection on a vehicle that is subject to both a safety and an emissions inspection.

(7) Repealed by Session Laws 2013-302, s. 5, effective October 1, 2013, and applicable to violations occurring on or after that date.

(b) **Type II.** -- It is a Type II violation for an emissions self-inspector, an emissions inspection station, or an emissions inspection mechanic to do any of the following:

(1) Use the identification code of another to gain access to an emissions analyzer or to equipment to analyze data provided by on-board diagnostic (OBD) equipment.

(2) Keep compliance documents in a manner that makes them easily accessible to individuals who are not inspection mechanics.

(3) Issue a safety electronic inspection authorization or an emissions electronic inspection authorization on a vehicle that is required to have one of the following emissions control devices but does not have it:

    a. Catalytic converter.

    b. PCV valve.

    c. Thermostatic air control.

    d. Oxygen sensor.

    e. Unleaded gas restrictor.

    f. Gasoline tank cap or capless fuel system.

    g. Air injection system.

    h. Evaporative emissions system.

    i. Exhaust gas recirculation (EGR) valve.

(4) Issue a safety electronic inspection authorization or an emissions electronic inspection authorization on a vehicle without performing a visual inspection of the vehicle's exhaust system and checking the exhaust system for leaks.

(5) Impose no fee for an emissions inspection of a vehicle or the issuance of an emissions electronic inspection authorization or impose a fee for one of these actions in an amount that differs from the amount set in G.S. 20-183.7.

(6) Issue an emissions electronic inspection authorization to a vehicle with a faulty Malfunction Indicator Lamp (MIL) or to a vehicle that has been made inoperable.

(c) **Type III.** -- It is a Type III violation for an emissions self-inspector, an emissions inspection station, or an emissions inspection mechanic to do any of the following:

(1) Fail to post an emissions license issued by the Division.

(2) Fail to send information on emissions inspections to the Division at the time or in the form required by the Division.

(3) Fail to post emissions information required by federal law to be posted.

(4) Repealed by Session Laws 2007-503, s. 16, effective October 1, 2008.

(5) Fail to put the required information on an inspection receipt in a legible manner.

(6) Repealed by Session Laws 2007-503, s. 16, effective October 1, 2008.

(d) **Other Acts.** -- The lists in this section of the acts that are Type I, Type II, or Type III violations are not the only acts that are one of these types of violations. The Division may designate other acts that are a Type I, Type II, or Type III violation.

History.

1993 (Reg. Sess., 1994), c. 754, s. 1; 1995, c. 163, s. 11;1997-29, s. 7;1997-456, s. 35;2000-134, ss. 18, 19; 2001-504, ss. 15, 16, 19; 2007-503, s. 16;2013-302, s. 5

EFFECT OF AMENDMENTS. --

Session Laws 2013-302, s. 5, effective October 1, 2013, deleted subdivisions (a)(5) and (a)(7), which formerly read "Be unable to account for five or more electronic inspection authorizations at any one time upon the request of an auditor of the Division" and "Transfer an electronic inspection authorization from one vehicle to another" respectively; added "or capless fuel system" at the end of subdivision (b)(3)f.; and added subdivision (b)(6). For applicability, see Editor's note.

§ 20-183.8D. Suspension or revocation of license

(a) **Safety.** -- The Division may suspend or revoke a safety self-inspector license, a safety inspection station license, and a safety inspection mechanic license issued under this Part if the license holder fails to comply with this Part or a rule adopted by the Commissioner to implement this Part.

(b) **Emissions.** -- The Division may suspend or revoke an emissions self-inspector license, an emissions inspection station license, and an emissions inspection mechanic license issued under this Part for any of the following reasons:

    (1) The suspension or revocation is imposed under G.S. 20-183.8B.

    (2) Failure to pay a civil penalty imposed under G.S. 20-183.8B within 30 days after it is imposed.

History.

1993 (Reg. Sess., 1994), c. 754, s. 1; 1997-29, s. 8

FAILURE TO VISUALLY INSPECT. --Suspension of a vehicle inspection facility's equipment inspection license was warranted where the facility failed to visually inspect a truck's exhaust emission system and determine that it did not have a catalytic converter as the facility's violation had an effect on the emission reduction benefits of the testing program and thus was a Type I violation. Darryl Burke Chevrolet, Inc. v. Aikens, 131 N.C. App. 31, 505 S.E.2d 581 (1998), aff'd, 350 N.C. 83, 511 S.E.2d 639 (1999).

N.C. Gen. Stat. § 20-183.8E

Recodified as § 20-183.8G at the direction of the Revisor of Statutes.

EDITOR'S NOTE. --

This section was recodified as G.S. 20-183.8G at the direction of the Revisor of Statutes in order to place G.S. 20-183.8F between G.S. 20-183.8D and this section, as specified in Session Laws 1997-29, s.9.

§ 20-183.8F. Requirements for giving license holders notice of violations and for taking summary action

(a) Repealed by Session Laws 2011-145, s. 28.23B(a), effective July 1, 2011.

(b) **Notice of Charges.** -- When the Division decides to charge an inspection station, a self-inspector, or a mechanic with a violation that could result in the suspension or revocation of the person's license, the Division must deliver a written statement of the charges to the affected license holder. The statement of charges must inform the license holder of the right to request a hearing, instruct the person on how to obtain a hearing, and inform the license holder of the effect of not requesting a hearing. The license holder has the right to a hearing before the license is suspended or revoked. G.S. 20-183.8G sets out the procedure for obtaining a hearing.

(c) **Exception for Summary Action.** -- The right granted by subsection (b) of this section to have a hearing before a license is suspended or revoked does not apply if the Division summarily suspends or revokes the license after a judge has reviewed and authorized the proposed action. A license issued to an inspection station, a self-inspector, or a mechanic is a substantial property interest that cannot be summarily suspended or revoked without judicial review.

(d) A notice or statement prepared pursuant to this section or an order of the Division that is directed to a mechanic may be served on the mechanic by delivering a copy of the notice, statement, or order to the station or to the place of business of the self-inspector where the mechanic is employed. Delivery under this section to any person may be made via certified mail or by hand delivery.

History.

1997-29, s. 9;1999-328, s. 3.13;2001-504, s. 17;2011-145, s. 28.23B(a)

EDITOR'S NOTE. --

This section was originally enacted as G.S. 20-183.8D.1 and was renumbered as this section at the direction of the Revisor of Statutes.

Session Laws 1999-328, s. 5.1 provides that the act shall not be construed to obligate the General Assembly to appropriate any funds to implement the provisions of this act. Every State agency to which this act applies shall implement the provisions of this act from funds otherwise appropriated or available to that agency.

Session Laws 2011-145, s. 1.1, provides: "This act shall be known as the 'Current Operations and Capital Improvements Appropriations Act of 2011.'"

Session Laws 2011-145, s. 32.5 is a severability clause.

EFFECT OF AMENDMENTS. --

Session Laws 2011-145, s. 28.23B(a), effective July 1, 2011, deleted subsection (a), which pertained to the finding of a violation; in subsection (b), in the first sentence, substituted "or a mechanic" for "a mechanic, or a person who is engaged in the business of replacing windshields" and deleted "an auditor of" preceding "the Division," in the second sentence, substituted "inform the license holder of the right to request a hearing" for "inform the license holder of this right," and in the last sentence, updated the section reference; and added the last sentence in subsection (d).

CITED in Inspection Station No. 31327 v. N.C. DMV, 244 N.C. App. 416, 781 S.E.2d 79 (2015).

§ 20-183.8G. Administrative and judicial review

(a) **Right to Hearing.** -- A person who applies for a license or registration under this Part or who has a license or registration issued under this Part has the right to a hearing when any of the following occurs:

(1) The Division denies the person's application for a license or registration.

(2) The Division delivers to the person a written statement of charges of a violation that could result in the suspension or revocation of the person's license.

(3) The Division summarily suspends or revokes the person's license following review and authorization of the proposed adverse action by a judge.

(4) The Division assesses a civil penalty against the person.

(5) The Division issues a warning letter to the person.

(6) The Division cancels the person's registration.

(b) **Hearing After Statement of Charges.** -- When a license holder receives a statement of charges of a violation that could result in the suspension or revocation of the person's license, the person can obtain a hearing by making a request for a hearing. The person must make the request to the Division within 10 days after receiving the statement of the charges. A person who does not request a hearing within this time limit waives the right to a hearing.

The Division must hold a hearing requested under this subsection within 30 days after receiving the request, unless the matter is continued for good cause. The hearing must be held at the location designated by the Division. Suspension or revocation of the license is stayed until a decision is made following the hearing.

If a person does not request a hearing within the time allowed for making the request, the proposed suspension or revocation becomes effective the day after the time for making the request ends. If a person requests a hearing but does not attend the hearing, the proposed suspension or revocation becomes effective the day after the date set for the hearing.

(c) **Hearing After Summary Action.** -- When the Division summarily suspends a license issued under this Part after judicial review and authorization of the proposed action, the person whose license was suspended or revoked may obtain a hearing by filing with the Division a written request for a hearing. The request must be filed within 10 days after the person was notified of the summary action. The Division must hold a hearing requested under this subsection within 14 days after receiving the request.

(d) **All Other Hearings.** -- When this section gives a person the right to a hearing and subsection (b) or (c) of this section does not apply to the hearing, the person may obtain a hearing by filing with the Division a written request for a hearing. The request must be filed within 10 days after the person receives written notice of the action for which a hearing is requested. The Division must hold a hearing within 90 days after the Division receives the request, unless the matter is continued for good cause.

(e) **Review by Commissioner.** -- The Commissioner may conduct a hearing required under this section or may designate a person to conduct the hearing. When a person designated by the Commissioner holds a hearing and makes a decision, the person who requested the hearing has the right to request the Commissioner to review the decision. The procedure set by the Division governs the review by the Commissioner of a decision made by a person designated by the Commissioner.

(f) **Decision.** -- Upon the Commissioner's review of a decision made after a hearing on the imposition of a monetary penalty against a motorist for an emissions violation or on a Type I, II, or III violation by a license holder, the Commissioner must uphold any monetary penalty, license suspension, license revocation, or warning required by G.S. 20-183.7A, G.S. 20-183.8A or G.S. 20-183.8B, respectively, if the decision is based on evidence presented at the hearing that supports the hearing officer's determination that the motorist or license holder committed the act for which the monetary penalty, license suspension, license revocation, or warning was imposed. Pursuant to the authority under G.S. 20-183.7A(c) and G.S. 20-183.8B(c), the Commissioner may order a suspension for a first occurrence Type I violation of a station to be stayed upon reasonable compliance terms to be determined by the Commissioner. Pursuant to the authority under G.S. 20-183.7A(d1) and G.S. 183.8B(c2), the Commissioner may order the suspensions against a license holder to run consecutively or concurrently. The Commissioner may uphold, dismiss, or modify a decision made after a hearing on any other action.

(g) **Judicial Review.** -- Article 4 of Chapter 150B of the General Statutes governs judicial review of an administrative decision made under this section.

Chapter 20

History.

1993 (Reg. Sess., 1994), c. 754, s. 1; 1997-29, s. 10;1999-328, s. 3.14;1999-456, s. 69;2009-550, s. 3.1;2011-145, s. 28.23B(b);2013-302, s. 6;2014-58, s. 1

EDITOR'S NOTE. --

This section was formerly G.S. 20-183.8E. It has been renumbered as this section at the direction of the Revisor of Statutes.

Session Laws 1999-456, s. 69, provided that in Session Laws 1999-328, original s. 13.14 was redesignated as s. 3.14.

Session Laws 1999-328, s. 5.1 provides that this act shall not be construed to obligate the General Assembly to appropriate any funds to implement the provisions of this act. Every State agency to which this act applies shall implement the provisions of this act from funds otherwise appropriated or available to that agency.

Session Laws 2011-145, s. 1.1, provides: "This act shall be known as the 'Current Operations and Capital Improvements Appropriations Act of 2011.'"

Session Laws 2011-145, s. 32.5 is a severability clause.

EFFECT OF AMENDMENTS. --

Session Laws 2009-550, s. 3.1, effective August 28, 2009, rewrote the second paragraph of subsection (b).

Session Laws 2011-145, s. 28.23B(b), effective July 1, 2011, substituted "30 days" for "10 business days" in the second paragraph of subsection (b).

Session Laws 2013-302, s. 6, effective October 1, 2013, in subsection (f), inserted "Upon the Commissioner's review of," substituted "violation by a license holder, the Commissioner," for "emissions violation by an emissions license holder," inserted "G.S. 20-183.7A," and substituted "is based on evidence presented at the hearing that supports the hearing officer's determination" for "contains a finding" in the first sentence, added the second sentence, and in the third sentence, inserted "The Commissioner may uphold, dismiss, or modify" at the beginning and deleted "may uphold, or modify the action" at the end. For applicability, see Editor's note.

Session Laws 2014-58, s. 1, effective October 1, 2014, substituted "request, unless the matter is continued for good cause" for "request" at the end of the first sentence in the second paragraph of subsection (b), and at the end of subsection (d).

CORPORATION REQUIRED TO BE REPRE-SENTED BY ATTORNEY IN HEARING BEFORE THE DMV. --Although corporations were not required to be represented by attorneys in hearings before the Office of Administrative Hearings (OAH), pursuant to G.S. 150B-23 (referring to "attorney or representative" of a party), the DMV was exempted from the provisions of the Administrative Procedure Act authorizing contested cases to be brought in the OAH, G.S. 150B-1(e)(8), and therefore, in a hearing before the DMV, a corporation was required to be represented by an attorney. In re Twin County Motorsports, Inc., 230 N.C. App. 259, 749 S.E.2d 474 (2013).

CITED in Inspection Station No. 31327 v. N.C. DMV, 244 N.C. App. 416, 781 S.E.2d 79 (2015).

ARTICLE 3B.
PERMANENT WEIGH STATIONS AND PORTABLE SCALES

§ 20-183.9. Establishment and maintenance of permanent weigh stations

The Department of Public Safety is hereby authorized, empowered and directed to equip and operate permanent weigh stations equipped to weigh vehicles using the streets and highways of this State to determine whether such vehicles are being operated in accordance with legislative enactments relating to weights of vehicles and their loads. The permanent weigh stations shall be established at such locations on the streets and highways in this State as will enable them to be used most advantageously in determining the weight of vehicles and their loads. The Department of Transportation shall be responsible for the maintenance and upkeep of all permanent weigh stations established pursuant to this section.

History.

1951, c. 988, s. 1; 1957, c. 65, s. 11; 1973, c. 507, s. 5; 1977, c. 464, ss. 34, 37; 1979, c. 76; 2002-159, s. 31.5(b);2002-190, s. 7;2004-124, s. 18.3(b);2006-66, s. 21.8;2011-145, s. 19.1(g)

EDITOR'S NOTE. --

Session Laws 2002-190, s. 17, provides: "The Governor shall resolve any dispute between the Department of Transportation and the Department of Crime Control and Public Safety concerning the implementation of this act [Session Laws 2002-190]."

EFFECT OF AMENDMENTS. --

Session Laws 2004-124, s. 18.3(b), effective July 1, 2004, substituted "permanent weigh stations" for "permanent weighing stations" twice in the text of the section, and once in the section heading.

Session Laws 2006-66, s. 21.8, effective July 1, 2006, substituted "equip and operate" for "equip, operate, and maintain" in the first sentence and added the last sentence of the paragraph.

Session Laws 2011-145, s. 19.1(g), effective January 1, 2012, substituted "Public Safety" for "Crime Control and Public Safety."

§ 20-183.10. Operation of the permanent weigh stations by the Department of Public Safety, State Highway Patrol, uniformed personnel

The permanent weigh stations to be established pursuant to the provisions of this Article shall be operated by the Department of Public Safety, State Highway Patrol, who shall assign a sufficient number of sworn and nonsworn personnel to the various weigh stations. Sworn personnel of the State Highway Patrol shall supervise all nonsworn personnel assigned to weigh stations. The sworn and nonsworn personnel shall have authority to weigh vehicles and to assess civil penalties pursuant to Article 3, Part 9 of this Chapter and shall wear uniforms to be selected and furnished by the Department of Public Safety, State Highway Patrol. The uniformed sworn and nonsworn personnel assigned to the various permanent weigh stations shall weigh vehicles and complete various reports as may be necessary for recording violations relating to the weight of vehicles and their loads. The uniformed officers assigned to the various permanent weigh stations shall have the powers of peace officers for the purpose of enforcing the provisions of this Chapter and in making arrests, serving process, and appearing in court in all matters and things relating to the weight of vehicles and their loads.

History.

1951, c. 988, s. 2; 1975, c. 716, s. 5; 1977, c. 319; 2002-159, s. 31.5(b);2002-190, s. 8;2004-124, s. 18.3(c);2011-145, s. 19.1(g), (p); 2015-241, s. 16A.7(j)

EDITOR'S NOTE. --

Session Laws 2002-190, s. 17, provides: "The Governor shall resolve any dispute between the Department of Transportation and the Department of Crime Control and Public Safety concerning the implementation of this act [Session Laws 2002-190]."

EFFECT OF AMENDMENTS. --

Session Laws 2004-124, s. 18.3(c), effective July 1, 2004, rewrote the section; and rewrote the section heading, which formerly read "Operation by Department of Crime Control and Public Safety uniformed personnel with powers of peace officers."

Session Laws 2011-145, s. 19.1(g), (p), effective January 1, 2012, substituted "Public Safety" for "Crime Control and Public Safety" and substituted "State Highway Patrol Section" for "Division of State Highway Patrol" throughout the section.

Session Laws 2015-241, s. 16A.7(j), effective July 1, 2015, substituted "State Highway Patrol" for "State Highway Patrol Section" in the section heading and three times in the section text.

N.C. Gen. Stat. § 20-183.11

Repealed by Session Laws 1995, c. 109, s. 5.

N.C. Gen. Stat. § 20-183.12

Repealed by Session Laws 1995, c. 163, s. 12.

ARTICLE 3C.
VEHICLE EQUIPMENT SAFETY COMPACT

§ 20-183.13. Compact enacted into law; form of Compact

The Vehicle Equipment Safety Compact is hereby enacted into law and entered into with all other jurisdictions legally joining therein in the form substantially as follows:

VEHICLE EQUIPMENT SAFETY COMPACT

ARTICLE I.
Findings and Purposes.

(a) The party states find that:

(1) Accidents and deaths on their streets and highways present a very serious human and economic problem with a major deleterious effect on the public welfare.

(2) There is a vital need for the development of greater interjurisdictional cooperation to achieve the necessary uniformity in the laws, rules, regulations and codes relating to vehicle equipment, and to accomplish this by such means as will minimize the time between the development of demonstrably and scientifically sound safety features and their incorporation into vehicles.

(b) The purposes of this Compact are to:

(1) Promote uniformity in regulation of and standards for equipment.

(2) Secure uniformity of law and administrative practice in vehicular regulation and related safety standards to permit incorporation of desirable equipment changes in vehicles in the interest of greater traffic safety.

(3) To provide means for the encouragement and utilization of research which will facilitate the achievement of the foregoing purposes, with due regard for the findings set forth in subdivision (a) of this article.

(c) It is the intent of this Compact to emphasize performance requirements and not to determine the specific detail of engineering in the manufacture of vehicles or equipment except to the extent necessary for the meeting of such performance requirements.

ARTICLE II.
Definitions.

As used in this Compact:

(a) "Vehicle" means every device in, upon or by which any person or property is or may be transported or drawn upon a highway, excepting devices moved by human power or used exclusively upon stationary rails or tracks.

(b) "State" means a state, territory or possession of the United States, the District of Columbia, or the Commonwealth of Puerto Rico.

(c) "Equipment" means any part of a vehicle or any accessory for use thereon which affects the safety of operation of such vehicle or the safety of the occupants.

ARTICLE III.
The Commission.

(a) There is hereby created an agency of the party states to be known as the "Vehicle Equipment Safety Commission" hereinafter called the Commission. The Commission shall be composed of one commissioner from each party state who shall be appointed, serve and be subject to removal in accordance with the laws of the state which he represents. If authorized by the laws of his party state, a commissioner may provide for the discharge of his duties and the performance of his functions on the Commission, either for the duration of his membership or for any lesser period of time, by an alternate. No such alternate shall be entitled to serve unless notification of his identity and appointment shall have been given to the Commission in such form as the Commission may require. Each commissioner, and each alternate, when serving in the place and stead of a commissioner, shall be entitled to be reimbursed by the Commission for expenses actually incurred in attending Commission meetings or while engaged in the business of the Commission.

(b) The commissioners shall be entitled to one vote each on the Commission. No action of the Commission shall be binding unless taken at a meeting at which a majority of the total number of votes on the Commission are cast in favor thereof. Action of the Commission shall be only at a meeting at which a majority of the commissioners, or their alternates, are present.

(c) The Commission shall have a seal.

(d) The Commission shall elect annually, from among its members, a chairman, a vice-chairman and a treasurer. The Commission may appoint an Executive Director and fix his duties and compensation. Such Executive Director shall serve at the pleasure of the Commission, and together with the treasurer shall be bonded in such amount as the Commission shall determine. The Executive Director also shall serve as secretary. If there be no Executive Director, the Commission shall elect a secretary in addition to the other officers provided by this subdivision.

(e) Irrespective of the civil service, personnel or other merit system laws of any of the party states, the Executive Director with approval of the Commission, or the Commission if there be no Executive Director, shall appoint, remove or discharge such personnel as may be necessary for the performance of the Commission's functions, and shall fix the duties and compensation of such personnel.

(f) The Commission may establish and maintain independently or in conjunction with any one or more of the party states, a suitable retirement system for its full-time employees. Employees of the Commission shall be eligible for Social Security coverage in respect of old age and survivor's insurance provided that the Commission takes such steps as may be necessary pursuant to the laws of the United States, to participate in such program of insurance as a government agency or unit. The Commission may establish and maintain or participate in such additional programs of employee benefits as may be appropriate.

(g) The Commission may borrow, accept or contract for the services of personnel from any party state, the United States, or any subdivision or agency of the aforementioned governments, or from any agency of two or more of the party states or their subdivisions.

(h) The Commission may accept for any of its purposes and functions under this Compact any and all donations, and grants of money, equipment, supplies, materials, and services, conditional or otherwise, from any state, the United States, or any other governmental agency and may receive, utilize and dispose of the same.

(i) The Commission may establish and maintain such facilities as may be necessary for the transacting of its business. The Commission may acquire, hold, and convey real and personal property and any interest therein.

(j) The Commission shall adopt bylaws for the conduct of its business and shall have the power to amend and rescind these bylaws. The Commission shall publish its bylaws in convenient form and shall file a copy thereof and a copy of any amendment thereto, with the appropriate agency or officer in each of the party states. The bylaws shall provide for appropriate notice to the commissioners of all Commission meetings and hearings and the business to be transacted at such meetings or hearings. Such notice shall also be given to such agencies or officers of each party state as the laws of such party state may provide.

(k) The Commission annually shall make to the governor and legislature of each party state a report covering the activities of the Commission for the preceding year, and embodying such recommendations as may have been issued by the Commission. The Commission may make such additional reports as it may deem desirable.

ARTICLE IV.
Research and Testing.

The Commission shall have power to:

(a) Collect, correlate, analyze and evaluate information resulting or derivable from research and testing activities in equipment and related fields.

(b) Recommend and encourage the undertaking of research and testing in any aspect of equipment or related matters when, in its judgment, appropriate or sufficient research or testing has not been undertaken.

(c) Contract for such equipment research and testing as one or more governmental agencies may agree to have contracted for by the Commission, provided that such governmental agency or agencies shall make available the funds necessary for such research and testing.

(d) Recommend to the party states changes in law or policy with emphasis on uniformity of laws and administrative rules, regulations or codes which would promote effective governmental action or coordination in the prevention of equipment-related highway accidents or the mitigation of equipment-related highway safety problems.

ARTICLE V.
Vehicular Equipment.

(a) In the interest of vehicular and public safety, the Commission may study the need for or desirability of the establishment of or changes in performance requirements or restrictions for any item of equipment. As a result of such study, the Commission may publish a report relating to any item or items of equipment, and the issuance of such a report shall be a condition precedent to any proceedings or other action provided or authorized by this article. No less than 60 days after the publication of a report containing the results of such study, the Commission upon due notice shall hold a hearing or hearings at such place or places as it may determine.

(b) Following the hearing or hearings provided for in subdivision (a) of this article, and with due regard for standards recommended by appropriate professional and technical associations and agencies, the Commission may issue rules, regulations or codes embodying performance requirements or restrictions for any item or items of equipment covered in the report, which in the opinion of the Commission will be fair and equitable and effectuate the purposes of this Compact.

(c) Each party state obligates itself to give due consideration to any and all rules, regulations and codes issued by the Commission and hereby declares its policy and intent to be the promotion of uniformity in the laws of the several party states relating to equipment.

(d) The Commission shall send prompt notice of its action in issuing any rule, regulation or code pursuant to this article to the appropriate motor vehicle agency of each party state and such notice shall contain the complete text of the rule, regulation or code.

(e) If the constitution of a party state requires, or if its statutes provide, the approval of the legislature by appropriate resolution or act may be made a condition precedent to the taking effect in such party state of any rule, regulation or code. In such event, the commissioner of such party state shall submit any Commission rule, regulation or code to the legislature as promptly as may be in lieu of administrative acceptance or rejection thereof by the party state.

(f) Except as otherwise specifically provided in or pursuant to subdivisions (e) and (g) of this article, the appropriate motor vehicle agency of a party state shall in accordance with its constitution or procedural laws adopt the rule, regulation or code within six months of the sending of the notice, and, upon such adoption, the rule, regulation or code shall have the force and effect of law therein.

(g) The appropriate motor vehicle agency of a party state may decline to adopt a rule, regulation or code issued by the Commission pursuant to this article if such agency specifically finds, after public hearing on due notice, that a variation from the Commission's rule, regulation or code is necessary to the public safety, and incorporates in such finding the reasons upon which it is based. Any such finding shall be subject to review by such procedure for review of administrative determinations as may be applicable pursuant to the laws of the party state. Upon request, the Commission shall be furnished with a copy of the transcript of any hearings held pursuant to this subdivision.

ARTICLE VI.
Finance.

(a) The Commission shall submit to the executive head or designated officer or officers of each party state a budget of its estimated expenditures for such period as may be required by the laws of that party state for presentation to the legislature thereof.

(b) Each of the Commission's budgets of estimated expenditures shall contain specific recommendations of the amount or amounts to be appropriated by each of the party states. The total amount of appropriations under any such budget shall be apportioned among the party states as follows: one third in equal shares; and the remainder in proportion to the number of motor vehicles registered in each party state. In determining the number of such registrations, the Commission may employ such source or sources of information as, in its judgment present the most equitable and accurate comparisons among the party states. Each of the Commission's budgets of estimated expenditures and requests for appropriations shall indicate the source or sources used in obtaining information concerning vehicular registrations.

(c) The Commission shall not pledge the credit of any party state. The Commission may meet any of its obligations in whole or in part with funds available to it under Article III(h) of this Compact, provided that the Commission takes specific action setting aside such funds prior to incurring any obligation to be met in whole or in part in such manner. Except where the Commission makes use of funds available to it under Article III(h) hereof, the Commission shall not incur any obligation prior to the allotment of funds by the party states adequate to meet the same.

(d) The Commission shall keep accurate accounts of all receipts and disbursements. The receipts and disbursements of the Commission shall be subject to the audit and accounting procedures established under its rules. However, all receipts and disbursements of funds handled by the Commission shall be audited yearly by a qualified public accountant and the report of the audit shall be included in and become part of the annual reports of the Commission.

(e) The accounts of the Commission shall be open at any reasonable time for inspection by duly constituted officers of the party states and by any persons authorized by the Commission.

(f) Nothing contained herein shall be construed to prevent Commission compliance with laws relating to audit or inspection of accounts by or on behalf of any government contributing to the support of the Commission.

ARTICLE VII.
Conflict of Interest.

(a) The Commission shall adopt rules and regulations with respect to conflict of interest for the commissioners of the party states, and their alternates, if any, and for the staff of the Commission and contractors with the Commission to the end that no member or employee or contractor shall have a pecuniary or other incompatible interest in the manufacture, sale or distribution of motor vehicles or vehicular equipment or in any facility or enterprise employed by the Commission or on its behalf for testing, conduct of investigations or research. In addition to any penalty for violation of such rules and regulations as may be applicable under the laws of the violator's jurisdiction of residence, employment or business, any violation of a Commission rule or regulation adopted pursuant to this article shall require the immediate discharge of any violating employee and the immediate vacating of membership, or relinquishing of status as a member on the Commission by any commissioner or alternate. In the case of a contractor, any violation of any such rule or regulation shall make any contract of the violator with the Commission subject to cancellation by the Commission.

(b) Nothing contained in this article shall be deemed to prevent a contractor for the Commission from using any facilities subject to his control in the performance of the contract even though such facilities are not devoted solely to work of or done on behalf of the Commission; nor to prevent such a contractor from receiving remuneration or profit from the use of such facilities.

ARTICLE VIII.
Advisory and Technical Committees.

The Commission may establish such advisory and technical committees as it may deem necessary, membership on which may include private citizens and public officials, and may cooperate with and use the services of any such committees and the organizations which the members represent in furthering any of its activities.

ARTICLE IX.
Entry into Force and Withdrawal.

(a) This Compact shall enter into force when enacted into law by any six or more states. Thereafter, this Compact shall become effective as to any other state upon its enactment thereof.

(b) Any party state may withdraw from this Compact by enacting a statute repealing the same, but no such withdrawal shall take effect until one year after the executive head of the withdrawing state has given notice in writing of the withdrawal to the executive heads of all other party states. No withdrawal shall affect any liability already incurred by or chargeable to a party state prior to the time of such withdrawal.

ARTICLE X.
Construction and Severability.

This Compact shall be liberally construed so as to effectuate the purposes thereof. The provisions of this Compact shall be severable and if any phrase, clause, sentence or provision of this Compact is declared to be contrary to the Constitution of any state or of the United States or the applicability thereof to any government, agency, person or circumstance is held invalid, the validity of the remainder of this Compact and the applicability thereof to any government, agency, person or circumstance shall not be affected thereby. If this Compact shall be held contrary to the constitution of any state participating herein, the Compact shall remain in full force and effect as to the remaining party states and in full force and effect as to the state affected as to all severable matters.

History.
1963, c. 1167, s. 1

§ 20-183.14. Legislative findings

The General Assembly finds that:

(1) The public safety necessitates the continuous development, modernization and implementation of standards and requirements of law relating to vehicle equipment, in accordance with expert knowledge and opinion.

(2) The public safety further requires that such standards and requirements be uniform from jurisdiction to jurisdiction,

except to the extent that specific and compelling evidence supports variation.

(3) The Division of Motor Vehicles, acting upon recommendations of the Vehicle Equipment Safety Commission and pursuant to the Vehicle Equipment Safety Compact provides a just, equitable and orderly means of promoting the public safety in the manner and within the scope contemplated by this Article.

History.
1963, c. 1167, s. 2; 1975, c. 716, s. 5

§ 20-183.15. Approval of rules and regulations by General Assembly required

Pursuant to Article V(e) of the Vehicle Equipment Safety Compact, it is the intention of this State and it is hereby provided that no rule, regulation or code issued by the Vehicle Equipment Safety Commission in accordance with Article V of the Compact shall take effect until approved by act of the General Assembly.

History.
1963, c. 1167, s. 3

§ 20-183.16. Compact Commissioner

The Commissioner of this State on the Vehicle Equipment Safety Commission shall be the Secretary of Transportation or such other officer of the Department of Transportation as the Secretary may designate.

History.
1963, c. 1167, s. 4; 1975, c. 716, s. 5
STATE GOVERMENT REORGANIZATION. --The administration of the Vehicle Equipment Safety Compact was transferred to the Department of Transportation and Highway Safety by former G.S. 143A-108, enacted by Session Laws 1971, c. 864. For present provisions as to the Department of Transportation, see G.S. 143B-345 et seq.

§ 20-183.17. Cooperation of State agencies authorized

Within appropriations available therefor, the departments, agencies and officers of the government of this State may cooperate with and assist the Vehicle Equipment Safety Commission within the scope contemplated by Article III(h) of the Compact. The departments, agencies and officers of the government of this State are authorized generally to cooperate with said Commission.

History.
1963, c. 1167, s. 5

§ 20-183.18. Filing of documents

Filing of documents as required by Article III(j) of the Compact shall be with the Secretary of State.

History.
1963, c. 1167, s. 6

§ 20-183.19. Budget procedure

Pursuant to Article VI(a) of the Compact, the Vehicle Equipment Safety Commission shall submit its budgets to the Director of the Budget.

History.
1963, c. 1167, s. 7

§ 20-183.20. Inspection of financial records of Commission

Pursuant to Article VI(e) of the Compact, the operations of the Vehicle Equipment Safety Commission shall be subject to the oversight of the State Auditor pursuant to Article 5A of Chapter 147 of the General Statutes.

History.
1963, c. 1167, s. 8; 1983, c. 913, s. 6

§ 20-183.21. "Executive head" defined

The term "executive head" as used in Article IX(b) of the Compact shall, with reference to this State, mean the Governor.

History.
1963, c. 1167, s. 9

§§ 20-183.22 through 20-183.29

Reserved for future codification purposes.

ARTICLE 3D.
AUTOMATIC LICENSE PLATE READER SYSTEMS.

§ 20-183.30. Definitions

The following definitions apply in this Article:

(1) **Automatic license plate reader system.** -- A system of one or more mobile or fixed automated high-speed cameras used in combination with computer algorithms to convert images of license plates into computer-readable data. This term shall not include a traffic control photographic system, as that term is defined in G.S. 160A-300.1(a), or an open road tolling system, as that term is defined in G.S. 136-89.210(3).

(2) **Law enforcement agency.** -- Any agency or officer of the State of North Carolina or any political subdivision thereof who

is empowered by the laws of this State to conduct investigations or to make arrests and any attorney, including the Attorney General of North Carolina, authorized by the laws of this State to prosecute or participate in the prosecution of those persons arrested or persons who may be subject to civil actions related to or concerning an arrest.

History.
2015-190, s. 1

EDITOR'S NOTE. --
Session Laws 2015-190, s. 1, enacted this Article, effective December 1, 2015, as G.S. 20-183.22 through 20-183.24. The sections in this Article have been renumbered as G.S. 20-183.30 through 20-183.32 at the direction of the Revisor of Statutes.

§ 20-183.31. Regulation of use

(a) Any State or local law enforcement agency using an automatic license plate reader system must adopt a written policy governing its use before the automatic license plate reader system is operational. The policy shall address all of the following:

(1) Databases used to compare data obtained by the automatic license plate reader system.

(2) Data retention.

(3) Sharing of data with other law enforcement agencies.

(4) Training of automatic license plate reader system operators.

(5) Supervisory oversight of automatic license plate reader system use.

(6) Internal data security and access.

(7) Annual or more frequent auditing and reporting of automatic license plate reader system use and effectiveness to the head of the agency responsible for operating the system.

(8) Accessing data obtained by automatic license plate reader systems not operated by the law enforcement agency.

(9) Any other subjects related to automatic license plate reader system use by the agency.

(b) Data obtained by a law enforcement agency in accordance with this section or G.S. 20-183.32 shall be obtained, accessed, preserved, or disclosed only for law enforcement or criminal justice purposes.

(c) Any law enforcement agency using an automatic license plate reader system must keep maintenance and calibration schedules and records for the system on file.

History.
2015-190, s. 1

§ 20-183.32. Preservation and disclosure of records

(a) Captured plate data obtained by an automatic license plate reader system, operated by or on behalf of a law enforcement agency for law enforcement purposes, shall not be preserved for more than 90 days after the date the data is captured.

(b) Notwithstanding subsection (a) of this section, data obtained by an automatic license plate reader may be preserved for more than 90 days pursuant to any of the following:

(1) A preservation request under subsection (c) of this section.

(2) A search warrant issued pursuant to Article 11 of Chapter 15A of the General Statutes.

(3) A federal search warrant issued in compliance with the Federal Rules of Criminal Procedure.

(c) Upon the request of a law enforcement agency, the custodian of the captured plate data shall take all necessary steps to immediately preserve captured plate data in its possession. A requesting agency must specify in a written, sworn statement all of the following:

(1) The location of the particular camera or cameras for which captured plate data must be preserved and the particular license plate for which captured plate data must be preserved.

(2) The date or dates and time frames for which captured plate data must be preserved.

(3) Specific and articulable facts showing that there are reasonable grounds to believe that the captured plate data is relevant and material to an ongoing criminal or missing persons investigation or is needed to prove a violation of a motor carrier safety regulation.

(4) The case and identity of the parties involved in that case.

After one year from the date of the initial preservation request, the captured plate data obtained by an automatic license plate reader system shall be destroyed according to the custodian's own record or data retention policy, unless the custodian receives within that period another preservation request under this subsection, in which case the retention period established under this subsection shall reset.

(d) A law enforcement agency that uses an automatic license plate reader system in accordance with G.S. 20-183.31 shall update the system from the databases specified therein every 24 hours if such updates are available or as soon as practicable after such updates become available.

(e) Captured plate data obtained in accordance with this Article is confidential and not a public record as that term is defined in G.S. 132-1. Data shall not be disclosed except to a federal, State, or local law enforcement agency for a legitimate law enforcement or public safety purpose pursuant to a written request from the requesting agency. Written requests may be in electronic format. Nothing in this subsection shall be construed as requiring the disclosure of captured plate data if a law enforcement agency determines that disclosure will compromise an ongoing investigation. Captured plate data shall not be sold for any purpose.

History.
2015-190, s. 1
 EDITOR'S NOTE. --
 Session Laws 2015-190, s. 1, enacted this section, effective December 1, 2015, as G.S. 20-183.24. The section has been renumbered as G.S. 20-183.32 at the direction of the Revisor of Statutes.

ARTICLE 4.
STATE HIGHWAY PATROL

§ 20-184. Patrol under supervision of Department of Public Safety

The Secretary of Public Safety, under the direction of the Governor, shall have supervision, direction and control of the State Highway Patrol. The Secretary shall establish in the Department of Public Safety a State Highway Patrol Division, prescribe regulations governing the Division, and assign to the Division such duties as the Secretary may deem proper.

History.
1935, c. 324, s. 2; 1939, c. 387, s. 1; 1941, c. 36; 1975, c. 716, s. 5; 1977, c. 70, ss. 13, 14, 15; 2011-145, s. 19.1(g), (hh); 2015-241, s. 16A.7(i)
 EDITOR'S NOTE. --
 Session Laws 2009-461, ss. 1 and 2, provide: "SECTION 1. Notwithstanding the authority of the Secretary of Crime Control and Public Safety to adopt rules for the maintenance and operation of a Highway Patrol rotation wrecker system, the amendments to 14A NCAC 09H.0321(10), which became effective on July 18, 2008, are void and unenforceable to the extent such amendments:
 "(1) Limit submission of initial applications and re-applications for inclusion in the Highway Patrol rotation wrecker list to an annual open enrollment period.
 "(2) Limit vehicle storage fees to the maximum allowed by G.S. 20-28.3.

"(3) Require that towing and recovery fees be within fifteen percent (15%) of the median price charged within the applicable Highway Patrol Troop.
 "Notwithstanding the limitations set out in this section, the Highway Patrol may require that wrecker services, when responding to rotation wrecker calls, charge reasonable fees for services rendered and that any fee charged for rotation services not exceed the wrecker service's charges for nonrotation service calls that provide the same service, labor, and conditions.
 "SECTION 2.
 The Secretary of Crime Control and Public Safety shall adopt amendments to 14A NCAC 09H.0321(10) to conform to the requirements of this act."
 EFFECT OF AMENDMENTS. --
 Session Laws 2011-145, s. 19.1(g), (hh), effective January 1, 2012, substituted "Public Safety" for "Crime Control and Public Safety" and "Section" for "Division" throughout the section; and made minor stylistic changes.
 Session Laws 2015-241, s. 16A.7(i), effective July 1, 2015, substituted "Division" for "Section" in three places.
 POWER TO PRESCRIBE REGULATIONS. --Trial court did not err in granting summary judgment to the governor, state public safety agency, state highway patrol, and certain unidentified persons, and denying the wrecker service owner's motion for summary judgment on the wrecker service owner's declaratory judgment action seeking a determination that regulations used to remove his wrecker service business from the state's Wrecker Rotation Services List were illegal and that the regulations were preempted by federal law; the trial court had the authority to declare that the regulations were not illegal because the General Assembly granted to the state public safety agency the power to direct the state highway patrol to establish regulations for private wrecker services. Ramey v. Easley, 178 N.C. App. 197, 632 S.E.2d 178 (2006).
 WRECKER SERVICES. --Injunction order requiring wrecker services to have a land-based telephone line and to own in fee simple the property upon which its business or storage facilities were located was vacated because plaintiffs did not argue in their complaint, affidavits, or at the hearing that they were being subjected to such requirements; wrecker service rotation rules requiring a timely response to calls and imposing reasonable fees fall into the public safety regulatory exception set forth in 49 U.S.C.S. 14501(c)(2)(A). Danny's Towing 2, Inc. v. N.C. Dep't of Crime Control & Pub. Safety, 213 N.C. App. 375, 715 S.E.2d 176 (2011).
 Order declaring the parties' rights under the State's Wrecker Service Regulations, 14A N.C. Admin. Code 09H.0321(a), was vacated because the trial court failed to clearly declare the rights of the parties and effectively dispose of the dispute by making a full and complete declaration; the order enjoined specific portions of the regulations and then declared the remainder reasonable and enforceable as written,

and while the construction could permit a logical inference that the enjoined portions were unreasonable and unenforceable as written, that was not the issue before the trial court. Danny's Towing 2, Inc. v. N.C. Dep't of Crime Control & Pub. Safety, 213 N.C. App. 375, 715 S.E.2d 176 (2011).

Injunction prohibiting a driver holding a valid Commercial Drivers License from operating a wrecker while waiting on a certified driving record from the Division of Motor Vehicles was vacated because ensuring proper licensure was a matter genuinely responsive to safety concerns. Danny's Towing 2, Inc. v. N.C. Dep't of Crime Control & Pub. Safety, 213 N.C. App. 375, 715 S.E.2d 176 (2011).

CROSS REFERENCES. --
As to transfer of the State Highway Patrol to the Department of Public Safety, see G.S. 143A-242.

§ 20-185. Personnel; appointment; salaries

(a) The State Highway Patrol shall consist of a commanding officer, who shall be appointed by the Governor and whose rank shall be designated by the Governor, and such additional subordinate officers and members as the Secretary of Public Safety, with the approval of the Governor, shall direct. Members of the State Highway Patrol shall be appointed by the Secretary, with the approval of the Governor, and shall serve at the pleasure of the Governor and Secretary. The commanding officer, other officers and members of the State Highway Patrol shall be paid such salaries as may be established by the Division of Personnel of the Department of Administration. Notwithstanding any other provision of this Article, the number of supervisory personnel of the State Highway Patrol shall not exceed a number equal to twenty-one percent (21%) of the personnel actually serving as uniformed highway patrolmen. Nothing in the previous sentence is intended to require the demotion, reassignment or change in status of any member of the State Highway Patrol presently assigned in a supervisory capacity. If a reduction in the number of Highway Patrol personnel assigned in supervisory capacity is required in order for the State Highway Patrol to meet the mandatory maximum percentage of supervisory personnel as set out in the fourth sentence of this subsection, that reduction shall be achieved through normal attrition resulting from supervisory personnel resigning, retiring or voluntarily transferring from supervisory positions.

(a1) Applicants for employment as a State Trooper shall be at least 21 years of age and not more than 39 years of age as of the first day of patrol school. Highway Patrol enforcement personnel hired on or after July 1, 2013, shall retire not later than the end of the month in which their 62nd birthday falls.

(b) to (f) Repealed by Session Laws 1979, 2nd Session, c. 1272, s. 2.

(g), (h) Struck out by Session Laws 1961, c. 833, s. 6.2.

(i) Positions in the State Highway Patrol approved by the General Assembly in the first fiscal year of a biennium to be added in the second fiscal year of a biennium may not be filled before adjustments to the budget for the second fiscal year of the budget are enacted by the General Assembly. If a position to be added in the State Highway Patrol for the second fiscal year of the biennium requires training, no applicant may be trained to fill the position until the budget adjustments for the second fiscal year are enacted by the General Assembly.

History.
1929, c. 218, s. 1; 1931, c. 381; 1935, c. 324, s. 1; 1937, c. 313, s. 1; 1941, c. 36; 1947, c. 461, s. 1; 1953, c. 1195, s. 1; 1955, c. 372; 1957, c. 1394; 1959, cc. 370, 1320; 1961, c. 833, s. 6.2; 1973, c. 59; 1975, c. 61, ss. 1, 2; c. 716, s. 5; 1977, c. 70, ss. 6-8, 13; c. 329, ss. 1-3; cc. 749, 889; 1979, 2nd Sess., c. 1272, s. 2; 1989 (Reg. Sess., 1990), c. 1066, s. 133; 2011-145, s. 19.1(g), (p); 2013-289, s. 9;2015-241, s. 16A.7(j)

EFFECT OF AMENDMENTS. --
Session Laws 2011-145, s. 19.1(g), (p), effective January 1, 2012, substituted "Public Safety" for "Crime Control and Public Safety" in subsection (a); and substituted "Highway Patrol Section" for "Highway Patrol Division" twice in subsection (i).

Session Laws 2013-289, s. 9, effective July 18, 2013, added subsection (a1).

Session Laws 2015-241, s. 16A.7(j), effective July 1, 2015, substituted "State Highway Patrol" for "Highway Patrol Section" twice in subsection (i).

CROSS REFERENCES. --
As to payment of salaries of certain State law-enforcement officers incapacitated as the result of injury by accident or occupational disease arising out of and in the course of performance of their duties, see G.S. 143-166.13 et seq.

§ 20-185.1. Trooper training; reimbursement

(a) **Trooper Training Reimbursement.** -- The training of State Troopers is a substantial investment of State resources that provides individuals with skills that are transferable to other law enforcement opportunities. The State may require an individual to agree in writing to reimburse a portion of the training costs incurred if the individual completes the training and becomes a State Trooper but does not remain a State Trooper for 36 months. The portion of the State's cost to be reimbursed is thirty-six thousand dollars ($ 36,000), less one thousand dollars ($ 1,000) for each month an individual served as a State Trooper and member of the State Highway Patrol.

(b) **Administration.** -- The Secretary of Public Safety shall perform all of the administrative functions necessary to implement the reimbursement agreements required by this section, including rule making, disseminating information, implementing contracts, and taking other necessary actions.

(c) **Hardships.** -- No contract shall be enforced under this section if the Secretary finds that it is impossible for the individual to serve as a member of the State Highway Patrol due to death, health-related reasons, or other hardship.

(d) **Law Enforcement Agency Requirements.** -- If a State Trooper separates from the State Highway Patrol before 36 months of service following completion of the training program and the State Trooper is hired within six months of separation from the State Highway Patrol by a municipal law enforcement agency, a Sheriff's office, or a company police agency certified under Chapter 74E of the General Statutes, then that hiring entity is liable to the State in the amount of thirty-six thousand dollars (\$ 36,000), to be paid in full within 90 days of the date the State Trooper is employed by the hiring entity. No hiring entity shall make any arrangement to circumvent any portion of this subsection.

History.
2018-5, s. 35.25(c);2018-97, s. 8.1(a)

EDITOR'S NOTE. --
Session Laws 2018-5, s. 1.1, provides: "This act shall be known as the 'Current Operations Appropriations Act of 2018.'"

Session Laws 2018-5, s. 39.7, is a severability clause.

Session Laws 2018-5, s. 39.8, made this section effective July 1, 2018.

EFFECT OF AMENDMENTS. --
Session Laws 2018-97, s. 8.1(a), effective July 1, 2018, rewrote the section.

CROSS REFERENCES. --
As to annual report on trooper training reimbursement agreements, see G.S. 143B-602.1.

§ 20-186. Oath of office

Each member of the State Highway Patrol shall subscribe and file with the Secretary of Public Safety an oath of office for the faithful performance of his duties.

History.
1929, c. 218, s. 2; 1937, c. 339, s. 1; 1941, c. 36; 1977, c. 70, s. 9; 2011-145, s. 19.1(g)

EFFECT OF AMENDMENTS. --
Session Laws 2011-145, s. 19.1(g), effective January 1, 2012, substituted "Public Safety" for "Crime Control and Public Safety."

§ 20-187. Orders and rules for organization and conduct

The Secretary of Public Safety is authorized and empowered to make all necessary orders, rules and regulations for the organization, assignment, and conduct of the members of the State Highway Patrol. Such orders, rules and regulations shall be subject to the approval of the Governor.

History.
1929, c. 218, ss. 1, 3; 1931, c. 381; 1933, c. 214, ss. 1, 2; 1939, c. 387, s. 2; 1941, c. 36; 1977, c. 70, s. 13; 2011-145, s. 19.1(g)

EFFECT OF AMENDMENTS. --
Session Laws 2011-145, s. 19.1(g), effective January 1, 2012, substituted "Public Safety" for "Crime Control and Public Safety."

CITED in Darnell v. North Carolina Dep't of Transp. & Hwy. Safety, 30 N.C. App. 328, 226 S.E.2d 879 (1976).

§ 20-187.1. Awards

(a) The patrol commander shall appoint an awards committee consisting of one troop commander, one troop executive officer, one district sergeant, one corporal, two troopers and one member of patrol headquarters staff. All committee members shall serve for a term of one year. The member from patrol headquarters staff shall serve as secretary to the committee and shall vote only in case of ties. The committee shall meet at such times and places designated by the patrol commander.

(b) The award to be granted under the provisions of this section shall be the North Carolina State Highway Patrol award of honor. The North Carolina State Highway Patrol award of honor is awarded in the name of the people of North Carolina and by the Governor to a person who, while a member of the North Carolina State Highway Patrol, distinguishes himself conspicuously by gallantry and intrepidity at the risk of personal safety and beyond the call of duty while engaged in the preservation of life and property. The deed performed must have been one of personal bravery and self-sacrifice so conspicuous as to clearly distinguish the individual above his colleagues and must have involved risk of life. Proof of the performance of the service will be required and each recommendation for the award of this decoration will be considered on the standard of extraordinary merit.

(c) Recipients of the awards hereinabove provided for will be entitled to receive a framed certificate of the award and an insignia designed to be worn as a part of the State Highway Patrol uniform.

(d) The awards committee shall review and investigate all reports of outstanding service and shall make recommendations to the patrol commander with respect thereto. The committee shall consider members of the Patrol for the awards created by this section when properly recommended by any individual having personal knowledge of an act, achievement or service believed to warrant the award of a decoration. No recommendation shall be made except by majority vote of all members of the committee. All recommendations of the committee shall be in writing and shall be forwarded to the patrol commander.

(e) Upon receipt of a recommendation of the committee, the patrol commander shall inquire into the facts of the matter and shall reduce his recommendation to writing. The patrol commander shall forward his recommendation, together with the recommendation of the committee, to the Secretary of Public Safety. The Secretary shall have final authority to approve or disapprove recommendations affecting the issuance of all awards except the award of honor. All recommendations for the award of honor shall be forwarded to the Governor for final approval or disapproval.

(f) The patrol commander shall, with the approval of the Secretary, establish all necessary rules and regulations to fully implement the provisions of this section and such rules and regulations shall include, but shall not be limited to, the following:

(1) Announcement of awards

(2) Presentation of awards

(3) Recording of awards

(4) Replacement of awards

(5) Authority to wear award insignias.

History.
1967, c. 1179; 1971, c. 848; 1977, c. 70, s. 13; 2011-145, s. 19.1(g).

EFFECT OF AMENDMENTS. --
Session Laws 2011-145, s. 19.1(g), effective January 1, 2012, substituted "Public Safety" for "Crime Control and Public Safety" in subsection (e).

§ 20-187.2. Badges and service side arms of deceased or retiring members of State, city and county law-enforcement agencies; weapons of active members

(a) Surviving spouses, or in the event such members die unsurvived by a spouse, surviving children of members of North Carolina State, city and county law-enforcement agencies killed in the line of duty or who are members of such agencies at the time of their deaths, and retiring members of such agencies shall receive upon request and at no cost to them, the badge worn or carried by such deceased or retiring member. The governing body of a law-enforcement agency may, in its discretion, also award to a retiring member or surviving relatives as provided herein, upon request, the service side arm of such deceased or

retiring members, at a price determined by such governing body, upon determining that the person receiving the weapon is not ineligible to own, possess, or receive a firearm under the provisions of State or federal law, or if the weapon has been rendered incapable of being fired. Governing body shall mean for county and local alcohol beverage control officers, the county or local board of alcoholic control; for all other law-enforcement officers with jurisdiction limited to a municipality or town, the city or town council; for all other law-enforcement officers with countywide jurisdiction, the board of county commissioners; for all State law-enforcement officers, the head of the department.

(b) Active members of North Carolina State law-enforcement agencies, upon change of type of weapons, may purchase the weapon worn or carried by such member at a price which shall be the average yield to the State from the sale of similar weapons during the preceding year.

(c) For purposes of this section, certified probation and parole officers shall be considered members of a North Carolina State law enforcement agency.

History.
1971, c. 669; 1973, c. 1424; 1975, c. 44; 1977, c. 548; 1979, c. 882; 1987, c. 122; 2013-369, s. 19;2016-77, s. 9(b)

EFFECT OF AMENDMENTS. --
Session Laws 2013-369, s. 19, effective October 1, 2013, substituted "determining that the person receiving the weapon is not ineligible to own, posses, or receive a firearm under the provisions of State or federal law, or if the weapon has" for "securing a permit as required by G.S. 14-402 et seq. or 14-409.1 et seq., or without such permit provided the weapon shall have" in subsection (a).

Session Laws 2016-77, s. 9(b), effective July 1, 2016, added subsection (c).

OPINIONS OF THE ATTORNEY GENERAL
BADGE TO BE GIVEN TO OFFICERS RETIRING ON DISABILITY. --Subsection (a) of this section requires law enforcement agencies to give an officer retiring upon disability retirement, with less than 20 years creditable service or only with five years creditable service, the badge worn by the officer. See opinion of Attorney General to Mr. Robert F. Thomas, Jr., Police Attorney, City of Charlotte, 50 N.C.A.G. 77 (1981).

§ 20-187.3. Quotas prohibited

(a) The Secretary of Public Safety shall not make or permit to be made any order, rule, or regulation requiring the issuance of any minimum number of traffic citations, or ticket quotas, by any member or members of the State Highway Patrol. Pay and promotions of members of the Highway Patrol shall be based on their overall job performance and not on the basis of the volume of citations issued or arrests made. Members of the Highway Patrol shall be subject to the salary schedule established by the Secretary of Public Safety and shall receive longevity pay for service as applicable to other State employees generally.

(b) Repealed by Session Laws 2018-5, s. 35.25(b), effective July 1, 2018.

History.

1981, c. 429; 1983 (Reg. Sess., 1984), c. 1034, ss. 106, 107; c. 1116, s. 89; 2011-145, s. 19.1(g);2012-142, s. 25.2C(d);2013-382, s. 9.1(c);2018-5, s. 35.25(b)

EDITOR'S NOTE. --

Session Laws 2013-360, s. 35.8(d), as amended by Session Laws 2014-100, s. 35.7, provides: "The salary increase provisions of G.S. 20-187.3 are suspended for the 2013-2014 fiscal year."

Session Laws 2013-360, s. 1.1, provides: "This act shall be known as the 'Current Operations and Capital Improvements Appropriations Act of 2013.'"

Session Laws 2013-360, s. 38.2, provides: "Except for statutory changes or other provisions that clearly indicate an intention to have effects beyond the 2013-2015 fiscal biennium, the textual provisions of this act apply only to funds appropriated for, and activities occurring during, the 2013-2015 fiscal biennium."

Session Laws 2013-360, s. 38.5, is a severability clause.

Session Laws 2013-382, s. 9.1(b), provides: "The following entities and positions created by Chapter 126 of the General Statutes are hereby renamed by this act:

"(1) The State Personnel Commission is renamed the 'North Carolina Human Resources Commission.'

"(2) The Office of State Personnel is renamed the 'North Carolina Office of State Human Resources.'

"(3) The State Personnel Director is renamed the 'Director of the North Carolina Office of State Human Resources.'"

Session Laws 2013-382, s. 9.1(c), provides: "Modification of References. -- The Revisor of Statutes shall delete any references in the General Statutes to the State Personnel Act, State Personnel Commission, the State Personnel Director, and the Office of State Personnel (or any derivatives thereof) and substitute references to the North Carolina Human Resources Act, the State Human Resources Commission, the Director of the Office of State Human Resources, and the Office of Human Resources (or the appropriate derivative thereof) to effectuate the renaming set forth in this section wherever conforming changes are necessary."

Session Laws 2013-382, s. 9.2, provides: "No action or proceeding pending on the effective date of this section, brought by or against the State Personnel Commission, the Director of the Office of State Personnel, or the Office of State Personnel, shall be affected by any provision of this section, but the same may be prosecuted or defended in the new name of the Commission, Director, and Office. In these actions and proceedings, the renamed Commission, Director, or Office shall be substituted as a party upon proper application to the courts or other public bodies."

Session Laws 2013-382, s. 9.3, provides: "Any business or other matter undertaken or commanded by the former State Personnel Commission, State Personnel Director, or Office of State Personnel regarding any State program, office, or contract or pertaining to or connected with their respective functions, powers, obligations, and duties that are pending on the date this act becomes effective may be conducted and completed by the Commission, Director, or Office in the same manner and under the same terms and conditions and with the same effect as if conducted and completed by the formerly named commission, director, or office."

Session Laws 2014-100, s. 35.6B, provides: "Notwithstanding G.S. 20-187.3 for the 2014-2015 fiscal year, the annual salary of a member of the State Highway Patrol whose salary does not exceed the maximum of the applicable salary range shall be increased on a percentage basis according to the date the member received sworn law enforcement officer status with the Patrol, as follows, in the amount of:

"(1) Six percent (6%) for a member sworn between 2012 and June 30, 2014.

"(2) Five and five-tenths percent (5.5%) for a member sworn between 2008 and 2011.

"(3) Five percent (5%) for a member sworn between 2005 and 2007."

Session Laws 2014-100, s. 1.1, provides: "This act shall be known as 'The Current Operations and Capital Improvements Appropriations Act of 2014.' "

Session Laws 2014-100, s. 38.4, provides: "Except for statutory changes or other provisions that clearly indicate an intention to have effects beyond the 2014-2015 fiscal year, the textual provisions of this act apply only to funds appropriated for, and activities occurring during, the 2014-2015 fiscal year."

Session Laws 2014-100, s. 38.7, is a severability clause.

Session Laws 2015-241, s. 16A.11, as added by Session Laws 2015-268, s. 6.2, provides: "The relocation of the State Capitol Police as a Section within the Highway Patrol pursuant to Section 16A.7 of this act shall not affect the subject matter or territorial jurisdiction of such officers and shall not entitle such officers to the statutory increases provided by G.S. 20-187.3 or Section 30.15 of this act."

Session Laws 2018-5, s. 1.1, provides: "This act shall be known as the 'Current Operations Appropriations Act of 2018.'"

Session Laws 2018-5, s. 39.7, is a severability clause.

EFFECT OF AMENDMENTS. --

Session Laws 2011-145, s. 19.1(g), effective January 1, 2012, substituted "Public Safety" for "Crime Control and Public Safety" twice.

Session Laws 2012-142, s. 25.2C(d), effective July 1, 2012, in subsection (a), deleted the third sentence which read: "The provisions of G.S. 126-7 shall not apply to members of the State Highway Patrol.", and substituted "shall" for "shall, however," in the fourth sentence.

Session Laws 2013-382, s. 9.1(c), effective August 21, 2013, substituted "State Human Resources

Commission" for "State Personnel Commission" in the last sentence of subsection (a).

Session Laws 2018-5, s. 35.25(b), effective July 1, 2018, in the second sentence of subsection (a), substituted "the salary schedule established by the Secretary of Public Safety and shall receive longevity pay for service as applicable" for "salary classes, ranges and longevity pay for service as are applicable" and deleted the former last sentence, relating to annual salary increases for each member of the Highway Patrol; and deleted subsection (b), which read: "The Secretary of Public Safety, subject to the availability of funds as authorized by the Director of the Budget, may place a member of the State Highway Patrol in any step in the salary range for the class to which the member is assigned based on the member's rank so that no member is in a step lower than others of the same rank who have held that rank for less time than that member."

§ 20-187.4. Disposition of retired service animals

(a) Upon determination that any service animal is no longer fit or needed for public service, the State or unit of local government may transfer ownership of the animal at a price determined by the State or unit of local government and upon any other terms and conditions as the State or unit of local government deems appropriate, to any of the following individuals, if that individual agrees to accept ownership, care, and custody of the service animal:

(1) The officer or employee who had normal custody and control of the service animal during the service animal's public service to the State or unit of local government.

(2) A surviving spouse, or in the event such officer or employee dies unsurvived by a spouse, surviving children of the officer or employee killed in the line of duty who had normal custody and control of the service animal during the service animal's public service to the State or unit of local government.

(3) An organization or program dedicated to the assistance or support of service animals retired from public service.

(b) For purposes of this section, the following definitions apply:

(1) "Service animal." -- Any horse, dog, or other animal owned by the State or a unit of local government that performs law enforcement, public safety, or emergency service functions.

(2) "Unit of local government." -- As defined in G.S. 159-7(b)(15).

History.
2016-101, s. 1
EDITOR'S NOTE. --
Session Laws 2016-101, s. 2, made this section effective October 1, 2016.

Also in the 2015-2016 biennium, the General Assembly enacted similar local legislation for the City of Raleigh, the County of Mecklenburg, and the Counties of Cleveland, Gaston, and Yancey and the municipalities in those three counties in Session Laws 2015-174 and in Session Laws 2016-20, s. 2.
CROSS REFERENCES. --
As to disposition of county property, generally, see G.S. 153A-176 et seq. As to training and development programs for law enforcement, see G.S. 153A-211 et seq. As to use and disposal of municipal property, generally, see G.S. 160A-265 et seq.

§ 20-187.5. Trademark authorization

The North Carolina Troopers Association is authorized to use all trademarks identifying the North Carolina State Highway Patrol held by the North Carolina Department of Public Safety or its Divisions. The use authorized under this section shall be limited to purposes that support the State Highway Patrol, employees of the State Highway Patrol, and the family members of the employees of the State Highway Patrol.

History.
2017-57, s. 16B.8(a)
EDITOR'S NOTE. --
Session Laws 2017-57, s. 16B.8(b), made this section effective June 28, 2017.
Session Laws 2017-57, s. 1.1, provides: "This act shall be known as the 'Current Operations Appropriations Act of 2017.'"
Session Laws 2017-57, s. 39.6, is a severability clause.

§ 20-188. Duties of Highway Patrol

The State Highway Patrol shall be subject to such orders, rules and regulations as may be adopted by the Secretary of Public Safety, with the approval of the Governor, and shall regularly patrol the highways of the State and enforce all laws and regulations respecting travel and the use of vehicles upon the highways of the State and all laws for the protection of the highways of the State. To this end, the members of the Patrol are given the power and authority of peace officers for the service of any warrant or other process issuing from any of the courts of the State having criminal jurisdiction, and are likewise authorized to arrest without warrant any person who, in the presence of said officers, is engaged in the violation of any of the laws of the State regulating travel and the use of vehicles upon the highways, or of laws with respect to the protection of the highways, and they shall have jurisdiction anywhere within the State, irrespective of county lines. The State Highway Patrol shall enforce the provisions of G.S. 14-399.

The State Highway Patrol shall have full power and authority to perform such additional duties as peace officers as may from time to time be directed by the Governor, and such officers may at any time and without special authority, either upon their own motion or at the request of any sheriff or local police authority, arrest persons accused of highway robbery, bank robbery, murder, or other crimes of violence.

The Secretary of Public Safety shall direct the officers and members of the State Highway Patrol in the performance of such other duties as may be required for the enforcement of the motor vehicle laws of the State.

Members of the State Highway Patrol, in addition to the duties, power and authority hereinbefore given, shall have the authority throughout the State of North Carolina of any police officer in respect to making arrests for any crimes committed in their presence and shall have authority to make arrests for any crime committed on any highway.

Regardless of territorial jurisdiction, any member of the State Highway Patrol who initiates an investigation of an accident or collision may not relinquish responsibility for completing the investigation, or for filing criminal charges as appropriate, without clear assurance that another law-enforcement officer or agency has fully undertaken responsibility, and in such cases he shall render reasonable assistance to the succeeding officer or agency if requested.

The State Highway Patrol recognizes the need to utilize private wrecker services to remove vehicles from public roadways as part of its public safety responsibility. In order to assure that this public safety responsibility is accomplished, the Troop Commander shall include on the Highway Patrol's rotation wrecker list only those wrecker services which agree in writing to impose reasonable charges for work performed and present one bill to the owner or operator of any towed vehicle. Towing, storage, and related fees charged may not be greater than fees charged for the same service for nonrotation calls that provide the same service, labor, and conditions.

History.
1929, c. 218, s. 4; 1933, c. 214, ss. 1, 2; 1935, c. 324, s. 3; 1939, c. 387, s. 2; 1941, c. 36; 1945, c. 1048; 1947, c. 1067, s. 20; 1973, c. 689; 1975, c. 716, s. 5; 1977, c. 70, ss. 10, 13; c. 887, s. 3; 2009-461, s. 3;2011-145, s. 19.1(g)

EDITOR'S NOTE. --
Session Laws 2009-461, ss. 1 and 2, provide: "SECTION 1. Notwithstanding the authority of the Secretary of Crime Control and Public Safety to adopt rules for the maintenance and operation of a Highway Patrol rotation wrecker system, the amendments to 14A NCAC 09H.0321(10), which became effective on July 18, 2008, are void and unenforceable to the extent such amendments:

"(1) Limit submission of initial applications and re-applications for inclusion in the Highway Patrol rotation wrecker list to an annual open enrollment period.

"(2) Limit vehicle storage fees to the maximum allowed by G.S. 20-28.3.

"(3) Require that towing and recovery fees be within fifteen percent (15%) of the median price charged within the applicable Highway Patrol Troop.

"Notwithstanding the limitations set out in this section, the Highway Patrol may require that wrecker services, when responding to rotation wrecker calls, charge reasonable fees for services rendered and that any fee charged for rotation services not exceed the wrecker service's charges for nonrotation service calls that provide the same service, labor, and conditions.

"SECTION 2.
The Secretary of Crime Control and Public Safety shall adopt amendments to 14A NCAC 09H.0321(10) to conform to the requirements of this act."

EFFECT OF AMENDMENTS. --
Session Laws 2009-461, s. 3, effective August 7, 2009, added the last paragraph.

Session Laws 2011-145, s. 19.1(g), effective January 1, 2012, substituted "Public Safety" for "Crime Control and Public Safety" twice.

WHEN ACTING AS SUCH, A STATE HIGHWAY PATROLMAN IS A PUBLIC OFFICER within the purview of G.S. 14-223, relating to resisting officers. State v. Powell, 10 N.C. App. 443, 179 S.E.2d 153 (1971).

RIGHT TO EMPLOY REASONABLE MEANS IN FULFILLING DUTIES. --By this section the Patrol is directed to "enforce all laws and regulations respecting travel and use of vehicles upon the highways of the State." Imposition of this duty implies the right to employ reasonable means in a reasonable manner in fulfilling it. Collins v. Christenberry, 6 N.C. App. 504, 170 S.E.2d 515 (1969).

Trial court did not err in granting summary judgment to the governor, state public safety agency, state highway patrol, and certain unidentified persons, and denying the wrecker service owner's motion for summary judgment on the wrecker service owner's declaratory judgment action seeking a determination that regulations used to remove his wrecker service business from the state's Wrecker Rotation Services List were illegal and that the regulations were preempted by federal law; the trial court had the authority to declare that the regulations were not illegal because the General Assembly granted to the state public safety agency the power to direct the state highway patrol to establish regulations for private wrecker services. Ramey v. Easley, 178 N.C. App. 197, 632 S.E.2d 178 (2006).

THE USE OF AN AIRPLANE BY HIGHWAY PATROLMEN TO LOCATE A PERSON SOUGHT TO BE ARRESTED by them is not a departure from the terms of their employment. Galloway v. Department of Motor Vehicles, 231 N.C. 447, 57 S.E.2d 799 (1950).

CARE REQUIRED OF OFFICER IN PURSUIT OF LAWBREAKER. --It is not held that an officer, when in pursuit of a lawbreaker, is under no obligation to exercise a reasonable degree of care to avoid injury to others who may be on the public roads and streets. It is held that, when so engaged, he is not to be deemed negligent merely because he fails to observe the requirements of the Motor Vehicle Act. His conduct is to be examined and tested by another standard. He is required to observe the care which a reasonably prudent man would exercise in the discharge of official duties of a like nature under like circumstances. Collins v. Christenberry, 6 N.C. App. 504, 170 S.E.2d 515 (1969).

ARREST WITHOUT WARRANT. --A highway patrolman apprehending a person driving a motor vehicle on the public highway while under the influence of intoxicating liquor is authorized, by virtue of the provisions of this section and subdivision (1) of former G.S. 15-41 [now G.S. 15A-401(b)] to arrest such person without a warrant, and such arrest is legal. State v. Broome, 269 N.C. 661, 153 S.E.2d 384 (1967).

THE WORD "ACCUSED" IN THIS SECTION IS USED IN THE GENERIC SENSE and does not import that the person to be arrested must have been accused of crime by judicial procedure. Galloway v. Department of Motor Vehicles, 231 N.C. 447, 57 S.E.2d 799 (1950).

ARMED ROBBERY IS A CRIME OF VIOLENCE within the meaning of this section. Galloway v. Department of Motor Vehicles, 231 N.C. 447, 57 S.E.2d 799 (1950).

ARREST OF INTRUDER IN HOME. --Where a highway patrolman is advised by a person that an armed convict had come to her home, made threats, and demanded food, such patrolman is given authority under this section to arrest such convict. Galloway v. Department of Motor Vehicles, 231 N.C. 447, 57 S.E.2d 799 (1950).

WRECKER SERVICES. --Injunction order requiring wrecker services to have a land-based telephone line and to own in fee simple the property upon which its business or storage facilities were located was vacated because plaintiffs did not argue in their complaint, affidavits, or at the hearing that they were being subjected to such requirements; wrecker service rotation rules requiring a timely response to calls and imposing reasonable fees fall into the public safety regulatory exception set forth in 49 U.S.C.S. 14501(c)(2)(A). Danny's Towing 2, Inc. v. N.C. Dep't of Crime Control & Pub. Safety, 213 N.C. App. 375, 715 S.E.2d 176 (2011).

Order declaring the parties' rights under the State's Wrecker Service Regulations, 14A N.C. Admin. Code 09H.0321(a), was vacated because the trial court failed to clearly declare the rights of the parties and effectively dispose of the dispute by making a full and complete declaration; the order enjoined specific portions of the regulations and then declared the remainder reasonable and enforceable as written, and while the construction could permit a logical inference that the enjoined portions were unreasonable and unenforceable as written, that was not the issue before the trial court. Danny's Towing 2, Inc. v. N.C. Dep't of Crime Control & Pub. Safety, 213 N.C. App. 375, 715 S.E.2d 176 (2011).

CITED in State v. Green, 103 N.C. App. 38, 404 S.E.2d 363 (1991).

LEGAL PERIODICALS. --

As to power of highway patrolman to make arrests, see 23 N.C.L. Rev. 338 (1945).

§ 20-189. Patrolmen assigned to Governor's office

The Secretary of Public Safety, at the request of the Governor, shall assign and attach two members of the State Highway Patrol to the office of the Governor, there to be assigned such duties and perform such services as the Governor may direct. The salary of the State Highway Patrol members so assigned to the office of the Governor shall be paid from appropriations made to the office of the Governor and shall be fixed in an amount to be determined by the Governor.

History.

1941, cc. 23, 36; 1965, c. 1159; 1977, c. 70, s. 13; 1983, c. 717, s. 6; 1985 (Reg. Sess., 1986), c. 955, ss. 2, 3; 2006-203, s. 15;2011-145, s. 19.1(g);2012-83, s. 30

EFFECT OF AMENDMENTS. --

Session Laws 2006-203, s. 15, effective July 1, 2007, deleted the former last sentence which read: "Prior to taking any action under the previous sentence, the Governor may consult with the Advisory Budget Commission."

Session Laws 2011-145, s. 19.1(g), effective January 1, 2012, substituted "Public Safety" for "Crime Control and Public Safety."

Session Laws 2012-83, s. 30, effective June 26, 2012, substituted "Highway Patrol members" for "highway patrolmen" in the second sentence.

§ 20-189.1. Lieutenant Governor Executive Protection Detail

(a) **Creation. --** There is created within the Highway Patrol a Lieutenant Governor's Executive Protection Detail. The Lieutenant Governor shall submit the names of three sworn members in good standing of the North Carolina Highway Patrol to the Commander, and the Commander shall assign those officers to serve in the Lieutenant Governor's Executive Protection Detail. The Lieutenant Governor is authorized to remove any members of the detail, with or without cause. If the Lieutenant Governor removes a member of the detail, the Lieutenant Governor shall submit to the Commander the name of an officer to replace the member who has been removed and the Commander shall assign the replacement. Members of the Lieutenant Governor's Executive Protection Detail shall continue to be employed by the North Carolina Highway Patrol subject to the laws, rules, and regulations of the Highway Patrol. The North Carolina Highway Patrol shall

Chapter 20

provide vehicles necessary for the carrying out of the Detail's duties under this Article.

(b) **Duties.** -- The members of the Lieutenant Governor's Executive Protection Detail shall protect the Lieutenant Governor and the Lieutenant Governor's immediate family and perform duties as assigned by the Lieutenant Governor relating to the protection of the Lieutenant Governor.

History.
2017-57, s. 16B.4(a)

EDITOR'S NOTE. --

Session Laws 2017-57, s. 16B.4(b), made this section effective June 28, 2017.

Session Laws 2017-57, s. 1.1, provides: "This act shall be known as the 'Current Operations Appropriations Act of 2017.'"

Session Laws 2017-57, s. 39.6, is a severability clause.

§ 20-189.2. State Highway Patrol Security Detail

The Speaker of the House of Representatives and the President Pro Tempore of the Senate, while traveling within the State on State business, may request a security detail. The request shall be made to the commander of the State Highway Patrol. If the request is made at least 48 hours in advance, the commander shall provide the detail. If the request is made less than 48 hours in advance, the commander shall provide the detail unless doing so would otherwise impair the ability of the State Highway patrol to perform its lawful duties.

History.
2017-57, s. 16B.9

EDITOR'S NOTE. --

Session Laws 2017-57, s. 39.7, made this section effective July 1, 2017.

Session Laws 2017-57, s. 1.1, provides: "This act shall be known as the 'Current Operations Appropriations Act of 2017.'"

Session Laws 2017-57, s. 39.6, is a severability clause.

§ 20-190. Uniforms; motor vehicles and arms; expense incurred; color of vehicle

The Department of Public Safety shall adopt some distinguishing uniform for the members of said State Highway Patrol, and furnish each member of the Patrol with an adequate number of said uniforms and each member of said Patrol force when on duty shall be dressed in said uniform. The Department of Public Safety shall likewise furnish each member of the Patrol with a suitable motor vehicle, and necessary arms, and provide for all reasonable expense incurred by said Patrol while on duty, provided,

that not less than eighty-three percent (83%) of the number of motor vehicles operated on the highways of the State by members of the State Highway Patrol shall be painted a uniform color of black and silver.

History.
1929, c. 218, s. 5; 1941, c. 36; 1955, c. 1132, ss. 1, 1 1/4, 1 3/4; 1957, c. 478, s. 1; c. 673, s. 1; 1961, c. 342; 1975, c. 716, s. 5; 1977, c. 70, s. 15; 1979, c. 229; 2011-145, s. 19.1(g)

EFFECT OF AMENDMENTS. --

Session Laws 2011-145, s. 19.1(g), effective January 1, 2012, substituted "Public Safety" for "Crime Control and Public Safety" twice.

§ 20-190.1. Patrol vehicles to have sirens; sounding siren

Every motor vehicle operated on the highways of the State by officers and members of the State Highway Patrol shall be equipped with a siren. Whenever any such officer or member operating any unmarked car shall overtake another vehicle on the highway after sunset of any day and before sunrise for the purpose of stopping the same or apprehending the driver thereof, he shall sound said siren before stopping such other vehicle.

History.
1957, c. 478, s. 1 1/2

N.C. Gen. Stat. § 20-190.2

Repealed by Session Laws 2018-74, s. 16, effective July 1, 2018.

§ 20-190.3. Assignment of new highway patrol cars

All new highway patrol cars, whether marked or unmarked, placed in service after July 1, 1985, shall be assigned to all members of the Highway Patrol.

History.
1985, c. 757, s. 165; 1987, c. 738, s. 122; 1989, c. 752, s. 114

§ 20-191. Use of facilities

Office space and other equipment and facilities of the Division of Motor Vehicles, Department of Transportation, presently being used by the State Highway Patrol shall continue to be used by the Patrol, and joint use of space, equipment and facilities between any division of the Department of Transportation and the State Highway Patrol may continue, unless such arrangements are changed by agreements between the Secretary of Public Safety and the Secretary of Transportation.

History.

1929, c. 218, s. 6; 1937, c. 313, s. 1; 1941, c. 36; 1947, c. 461, s. 2; 1975, c. 716, s. 5; 1977, c. 70, s. 11; 2011-145, s. 19.1(g)

EFFECT OF AMENDMENTS. --

Session Laws 2011-145, s. 19.1(g), effective January 1, 2012, substituted "Public Safety" for "Crime Control and Public Safety."

§ 20-192. Shifting of personnel from one district to another

The commanding officer of the State Highway Patrol under such rules and regulations as the Department of Public Safety may prescribe shall have authority from time to time to shift the forces from one district to another, or to consolidate more than one district force at any point for special purposes. Whenever a member of the State Highway Patrol is transferred from one point to another for the convenience of the State or otherwise than upon the request of the Highway Patrol member, the Department shall be responsible for transporting the household goods, furniture and personal apparel of the Highway Patrol member and members of the Highway Patrol member's household.

History.

1929, c. 218, s. 7; 1937, c. 313, s. 1; 1941, c. 36; 1947, c. 461, s. 3; 1951, c. 285; 1975, c. 716, s. 5; 1977, c. 70, s. 15; 2011-145, s. 19.1(g);2012-83, s. 31

EFFECT OF AMENDMENTS. --

Session Laws 2011-145, s. 19.1(g), effective January 1, 2012, substituted "Public Safety" for "Crime Control and Public Safety."

Session Laws 2012-83, s. 31, effective June 26, 2012, substituted "personnel" for "patrolmen" in the section heading; and in the last sentence, substituted "Highway Patrol member" for "patrolman" twice, and substituted "the Highway Patrol member's household" for "his household."

N.C. Gen. Stat. § 20-193

Repealed by Session Laws 1993 (Reg. Sess., 1994), c. 761, s. 18.

§ 20-194. Defense of members and other State law-enforcement officers in civil actions; payment of judgments

(a) Repealed by Session Laws 2011-145, s. 28.27(d), effective July 1, 2011.

(b) In the event that a member of the Highway Patrol or any other State law-enforcement officer is sued in a civil action as an individual for acts occurring while such member was alleged to be acting within the course and scope of his office, employment, service, agency or authority, which was alleged to be a proximate cause of the injury or damage complained of, the Attorney General is hereby authorized to defend such employee through the use of a member of his staff or, in his discretion, employ private counsel, subject to the provisions of Article 31A of Chapter 143 of the General Statutes and G.S. 147-17(a) through (c) and (d). Any judgment rendered as a result of said civil action against such member of the Highway Patrol or other State law-enforcement officer, for acts alleged to be committed within the course and scope of his office, employment, service, agency or authority shall be paid as an expense of administration up to the limit provided in the Tort Claims Act.

(c) The coverage afforded under this Article shall be excess coverage over any commercial liability insurance up to the limit of the Tort Claims Act.

History.

1929, c. 218, s. 9; 1941, c. 36; 1957, c. 65, s. 11; 1973, c. 507, s. 5; c. 1323; 1975, c. 210; 1977, c. 70, s. 12; 2011-145, s. 28.27(d);2017-57, s. 6.7(d)

EDITOR'S NOTE. --

Session Laws 2011-145, s. 1.1, provides: "This act shall be known as the 'Current Operations and Capital Improvements Appropriations Act of 2011.'"

Session Laws 2011-145, s. 32.5 is a severability clause.

EFFECT OF AMENDMENTS. --

Session Laws 2011-145, s. 28.27(d), effective July 1, 2011, deleted "Expense of administration" from the beginning of the section heading; and deleted subsection (a), which read: "All expenses incurred in carrying out the provisions of this Article shall be paid out of the highway fund."

Session Laws 2017-57, s. 6.7(d), effective July 1, 2017, in subsection (b) added "of the General Statutes" following "Article 31A of Chapter 143" and substituted "G.S. 147-17(a) through (c) and (d)" for "G.S. 147-17."

§ 20-195. Cooperation between Patrol and local officers

The Secretary of Public Safety with the approval of the Governor, through the State Highway Patrol, shall encourage the cooperation between the Highway Patrol and the several municipal and county peace officers of the State for the enforcement of all traffic laws and the proper administration of the Uniform Drivers' License Law, and arrangements for compensation of special services rendered by such local officers out of the funds allotted to the State Highway Patrol may be made, subject to the approval of the Director of the Budget.

History.

1935, c. 324, s. 5; 1939, c. 387, s. 3; 1941, c. 36; 1977, c. 70, ss. 13, 14; 2011-145, s. 19.1(g), (p); 2015-241, s. 16A.7(j)

EFFECT OF AMENDMENTS. --

Session Laws 2011-145, s. 19.1(g), (p), effective January 1, 2012, substituted "Public Safety" for "Crime Control and Public Safety"; and substituted "State Highway Patrol Section" for "State Highway Patrol Division" twice.

Session Laws 2015-241, s. 16A.7(j), effective July 1, 2015, substituted "State Highway Patrol" for "State Highway Patrol Section" in two places.

§ 20-196. Statewide radio system authorized; use of telephone lines in emergencies

The Secretary of Public Safety, through the State Highway Patrol is hereby authorized and directed to set up and maintain a statewide radio system, with adequate broadcasting stations so situate as to make the service available to all parts of the State for the purpose of maintaining radio contact with the members of the State Highway Patrol and other officers of the State, to the end that the traffic laws upon the highways may be more adequately enforced and that the criminal use of the highways may be prevented. The Secretary of Public Safety, through the State Highway Patrol, is hereby authorized to establish a plan of operation in accordance with Federal Communication Commission rules so that all certified law-enforcement officers within the State may use the law enforcement emergency frequency of 155.475MHz.

The Secretary of Public Safety is likewise authorized and empowered to arrange with the various telephone companies of the State for the use of their lines for emergency calls by the members of the State Highway Patrol, if it shall be found practicable to arrange apparatus for temporary contact with said telephone circuits along the highways of the State.

In order to make this service more generally useful, the various boards of county commissioners and the governing boards of the various cities and towns are hereby authorized and empowered to provide radio receiving sets in the offices and vehicles of their various officers, and such expenditures are declared to be a legal expenditure of any funds that may be available for police protection.

History.

1935, c. 324, s. 6; 1941, c. 36; 1957, c. 65, s. 11; 1973, c. 507, s. 5; 1975, c. 716, s. 5; 1977, c. 70, ss. 13, 14; c. 464, s. 34; 1983, c. 717, s. 7; 1987, c. 525; 2011-145, s. 19.1(g), (p); 2015-241, s. 16A.7(j)

EFFECT OF AMENDMENTS. --

Session Laws 2011-145, s. 19.1(g), (p), effective January 1, 2012, substituted "Public Safety" for "Crime Control and Public Safety" and "State Highway Patrol Section" for "State Highway Patrol Division" throughout the section.

Session Laws 2015-241, s. 16A.7(j), effective July 1, 2015, substituted "State Highway Patrol" for "State Highway Patrol Section" twice in the first paragraph.

N.C. Gen. Stat. § 20-196.1

Repealed by Session Laws 1998-212, s. 19.6(a), effective December 1, 1998.

§ 20-196.2. Use of aircraft to discover certain motor vehicle violations; declaration of policy.

The State Highway Patrol is hereby permitted the use of aircraft to discover violations of Part 10 of Article 3 of Chapter 20 of the General Statutes relating to operation of motor vehicles and rules of the road. It is hereby declared the public policy of North Carolina that the aircraft should be used primarily for accident prevention and should also be used incident to the issuance of warning citations in accordance with the provisions of G.S. 20-183.

History.

1967, c. 513; 1998-212, s. 19.6(b)

§ 20-196.3. Who may hold supervisory positions over sworn members of the Patrol

Notwithstanding any other provision of the General Statutes, only the following individuals may hold a supervisory position over sworn members of the Patrol:

(1) The Governor.

(2) The Secretary of Public Safety.

(3) A uniformed member of the North Carolina State Highway Patrol who has met all requirements for employment within the Patrol, including completion of the basic Patrol school.

History.

1975, c. 47; 1977, c. 70, s. 14.1; 2002-159, ss. 31.5(a), (b); 2002-190, s. 9;2011-145, s. 19.1(g);2013-289, s. 10;2015-241, s. 16A.7(h)

EDITOR'S NOTE. --

Session Laws 2002-190, s. 17, provides: "The Governor shall resolve any dispute between the Department of Transportation and the Department of Crime Control and Public Safety concerning the implementation of this act [Session Laws 2002-190]."

EFFECT OF AMENDMENTS. --

Session Laws 2013-289, s. 10, effective July 18, 2013, rewrote the section, which formerly read: "Notwithstanding any other provision of the General Statutes of North Carolina, it shall be unlawful for any person other than the Governor and the Secretary of Public Safety and other than a uniformed member of the North Carolina State Highway Patrol who has met all requirements for employment within the Patrol, including but not limited to completion of the basic Patrol school, to hold any supervisory position over sworn members of the Patrol."

Session Laws 2015-241, s. 16A.7(h), effective July 1, 2015, deleted "or the Commissioner of the Law Enforcement Division" from the end of subdivision (2).

§ 20-196.4. Oversized and hazardous shipment escort fee

(a) Every person, firm, corporation, or entity required by the North Carolina Department of Transportation or any federal agency or commission to have a law enforcement escort provided by the State Highway Patrol for the transport of any oversized load or hazardous shipment by road or rail shall pay to the Department of Public Safety a fee covering the full cost to administer, plan, and carry out the escort within this State.

(b) If the State Highway Patrol provides an escort to accompany the transport of oversized loads or hazardous shipments by road or rail at the request of any person, firm, corporation, or entity that is not required to have a law enforcement escort pursuant to subsection (a) of this section, then the requester shall pay to the Department of Public Safety a fee covering the full cost to administer, plan, and carry out the escort within this State.

(c) A fee established under this section is subject to G.S. 12-3.1. The full cost of an escort includes costs for vehicle or equipment maintenance required before or after an escort to ensure the visibility and safety of the law enforcement escort and the motoring public.

(d) All fees collected pursuant to this section shall be placed in a special Escort Fee Account. Revenue in the account is annually appropriated to the Department to reimburse the Department for its expenses in providing escorts under this section.

(e) Repealed by Session Laws 2010-129, s. 4, effective July 21, 2010.

History.
2002-126, s. 26.17(a);2010-129, s. 4;2011-145, s. 19.1(g)

EFFECT OF AMENDMENTS. --
Session Laws 2010-129, s. 4, effective July 21, 2010, rewrote subsection (c), which formerly read: "The Department of Crime Control and Public Safety shall comply with the provisions of G.S. 12-3.1(a)(2) when establishing fees to implement this section"; in subsection (d), deleted "and shall remain unencumbered and unexpended until appropriated by the General Assembly" from the end of the first sentence, and added the last sentence; and deleted subsection (e),

which related to duty of the Department to report quarterly on the funds in the special account to various committee Chairs.

Session Laws 2011-145, s. 19.1(g), effective July 1, 2012, substituted "Public Safety" for "Crime Control and Public Safety" twice.

§ 20-196.5. Report on gang prevention recommendations

The State Highway Patrol, in conjunction with the State Bureau of Investigation and the Governor's Crime Commission, shall develop recommendations concerning the establishment of priorities and needed improvements with respect to gang prevention and shall report those recommendations to the chairs of the House of Representatives and Senate Appropriations Committees on Justice and Public Safety and to the chairs of the Joint Legislative Oversight Committee on Justice and Public Safety on or before March 1 of each year.

History.
2015-241, s. 16B.3(a)

ARTICLE 5.
ENFORCEMENT OF COLLECTION OF JUDGMENTS AGAINST IRRESPONSIBLE DRIVERS OF MOTOR VEHICLES

§§ 20-197 through 20-211

Repealed by Session Laws 1947, c. 1006, s. 58.

ARTICLE 6.
GIVING PUBLICITY TO HIGHWAY TRAFFIC LAWS THROUGH THE PUBLIC SCHOOLS

§§ 20-212 through 20-215

Repealed by Session Laws 1993 (Reg. Sess., 1994), c. 761, s. 19.

ARTICLE 6A.
MOTOR CARRIERS OF MIGRATORY FARM WORKERS

§ 20-215.1. Definitions

The following definitions apply in this Article:

(1) **Migratory farm worker. --** An individual who is employed in agriculture.

(2) **Motor carrier of migratory farm workers. --** A person who for compensation transports at any one time in North Carolina five or more migratory farm workers to or from their employment by any motor vehicle, other than a passenger automobile or station wagon. The term does not include any of the following:

a. A migratory farm worker who is transporting his or her immediate family.

b. A carrier of passengers regulated by the North Carolina Utilities Commission or the United States Department of Transportation.

c. The transportation of migratory farm workers on a vehicle owned by a farmer when the migratory farm workers are employed or to be employed by the farmer to work on a farm owned or controlled by the farmer.

(3) Repealed by Session Laws 1973, c. 1330, s. 39.

History.
1961, c. 505, s. 1; 1973, c. 1330, s. 39; 1995 (Reg. Sess., 1996), c. 756, s. 17

CROSS REFERENCES. --
For definitions applicable throughout this Chapter, see G.S. 20-4.01.

§ 20-215.2. Power to regulate; rules and regulations establishing minimum standards

Notwithstanding any other provisions of this Chapter the North Carolina Division of Motor Vehicles, hereinafter referred to as "Division," is hereby vested with the power and duty to make and enforce reasonable rules and regulations applicable to motor carriers of migratory farm workers to and from their places of employment. The rules promulgated shall establish minimum standards:

(1) For the construction and equipment of such vehicles, including coupling devices, lighting equipment, exhaust systems, rear vision mirrors, brakes, steering mechanisms, tires, windshield wipers and warning devices.

(2) For the operation of such vehicles, including driving rules, distribution of passengers and load, maximum hours of service for drivers, minimum requirements of age and skill of drivers, physical conditions of drivers and permits, licenses or other credentials required of drivers.

(3) For the safety and comfort of passengers in such vehicles, including emergency kits, fire extinguishers, first-aid equipment, sidewalls, seating accommodations, tail gates or doors, rest and meal stops, maximum number of passengers, and safe means of ingress and egress.

History.
1961, c. 505, s. 2; 1975, c. 716, s. 5

N.C. Gen. Stat. § 20-215.3

Repealed by Session Laws 1985, c. 454, s. 8.

§ 20-215.4. Violation of regulations a misdemeanor

The violation of any rule or regulation promulgated by the Division hereunder by any person, firm or corporation shall be a Class 3 misdemeanor.

History.
1961, c. 505, s. 4; 1975, c. 716, s. 5; 1993, c. 539, s. 381;1994, Ex. Sess., c. 24, s. 14(c)

§ 20-215.5. Duties and powers of law-enforcement officers

It shall be the duty of the law-enforcement officers of the State, and of each county, city or town, to enforce the rules promulgated hereunder in their respective jurisdictions; and such officers shall have the power to stop any motor vehicle upon the highways of this State for the purpose of determining whether or not such motor vehicle is being operated in violation of such rules.

History.
1961, c. 505, s. 5

ARTICLE 7.
MISCELLANEOUS PROVISIONS RELATING TO MOTOR VEHICLES

§ 20-216. Passing horses or other draft animals

Any person operating a motor vehicle shall use reasonable care when approaching or passing a horse or other draft animal whether ridden or otherwise under control.

History.
1917, c. 140, s. 15; C.S., s. 2616; 1969, c. 401
THE LAWS WITH RESPECT TO PASSING ANIMALS, with the exception of establishing a speed limit, are to a great extent an embodiment of general principles of law applicable to motor vehicles when operated on the highway and in places where their

use is likely to be a source of danger to others. Tudor v. Bowen, 152 N.C. 441, 67 S.E. 1015 (1910); Gaskins v. Hancock, 156 N.C. 56, 72 S.E. 80 (1911); Curry v. Fleer, 157 N.C. 16, 72 S.E. 626 (1911).

CITED in Goss v. Williams, 196 N.C. 213, 145 S.E. 169 (1928); York v. York, 212 N.C. 695, 194 S.E. 486 (1938).

§ 20-217. Motor vehicles to stop for properly marked and designated school buses in certain instances; evidence of identity of driver

(a) When a school bus is displaying its mechanical stop signal or flashing red lights and the bus is stopped for the purpose of receiving or discharging passengers, the driver of any other vehicle that approaches the school bus from any direction on the same street, highway, or public vehicular area shall bring that other vehicle to a full stop and shall remain stopped. The driver of the other vehicle shall not proceed to move, pass, or attempt to pass the school bus until after the mechanical stop signal has been withdrawn, the flashing red stoplights have been turned off, and the bus has started to move.

(b) For the purpose of this section, a school bus includes a public school bus transporting children or school personnel, a public school bus transporting senior citizens under G.S. 115C-243, or a privately owned bus transporting children. This section applies only in the event the school bus bears upon the front and rear a plainly visible sign containing the words "school bus."

(c) Notwithstanding subsection (a) of this section, the driver of a vehicle traveling in the opposite direction from the school bus, upon any road, highway or city street that has been divided into two roadways, so constructed as to separate vehicular traffic between the two roadways by an intervening space (including a center lane for left turns if the roadway consists of at least four more lanes) or by a physical barrier, need not stop upon meeting and passing any school bus that has stopped in the roadway across the dividing space or physical barrier.

(d) It shall be unlawful for any school bus driver to stop and receive or discharge passengers or for any principal or superintendent of any school, routing a school bus, to authorize the driver of any school bus to stop and receive or discharge passengers upon any roadway described by subsection (c) of this section where passengers would be required to cross the roadway to reach their destination or to board the bus; provided, that passengers may be discharged or received at points where pedestrians and vehicular traffic are controlled by adequate stop-and-go traffic signals.

(e) Except as provided in subsection (g) of this section, any person violating this section shall be guilty of a Class 1 misdemeanor and shall pay a minimum fine of five hundred dollars ($ 500.00). A person who violates subsection (a) of this section shall not receive a prayer for judgment continued under any circumstances.

(f) Expired.

(g) Any person who willfully violates subsection (a) of this section and strikes any person shall be guilty of a Class I felony and shall pay a minimum fine of one thousand two hundred fifty dollars ($ 1,250). Any person who willfully violates subsection (a) of this section and strikes any person, resulting in the death of that person, shall be guilty of a Class H felony and shall pay a minimum fine of two thousand five hundred dollars ($ 2,500).

(g1) The Division shall revoke, for a period of one year, the drivers license of a person convicted of a second misdemeanor violation under this section within a three-year period. The Division shall revoke, for a period of two years, the drivers license of a person convicted of a Class I felony violation under this section. The Division shall revoke, for a period of three years, the drivers license of a person convicted of a Class H felony violation under this section. The Division shall permanently revoke the drivers license of (i) a person convicted of a second felony violation under this section within any period of time and (ii) a person convicted of a third misdemeanor violation under this section within any period of time.

In the case of a first felony conviction under this section, the licensee may apply to the sentencing court for a limited driving privilege after a period of six months of revocation, provided the person's drivers license has not also been revoked or suspended under any other provision of law. A limited driving privilege issued under this subsection shall be valid for the period of revocation remaining in the same manner and under the terms and conditions prescribed in G.S. 20-16.1(b). If the person's drivers license is revoked or suspended under any other statute, the limited driving privilege issued pursuant to this subsection is invalid.

In the case of a permanent revocation of a person's drivers license for committing a third misdemeanor violation under this section within any period of time, the person may apply for a drivers license after two years. The Division may, with or without a hearing, issue a new drivers license upon satisfactory proof that the former licensee has not been convicted of a moving violation under this Chapter or the laws of another state. The Division may impose any restrictions or conditions on the new drivers license that the Division considers appropriate. Any conditions or restrictions imposed by the Division shall not exceed two years.

In the case of a permanent revocation of a person's drivers license for committing a second Class I felony violation under this section within any period of time, the person may apply for a drivers license after three years. The Division may, with or without a hearing, issue a new drivers license upon satisfactory proof that the former licensee has not been convicted of a moving violation under this Chapter or the laws of another state. The Division may impose any restrictions or conditions on the new drivers license that the Division considers appropriate. Any conditions or restrictions imposed by the Division shall not exceed three years.

Any person whose drivers license is revoked under this section is disqualified pursuant to G.S. 20-17.4 from driving a commercial motor vehicle for the period of time in which the person's drivers license remains revoked under this section.

(g2) Pursuant to G.S. 20-54, failure of a person to pay any fine or costs imposed pursuant to this section shall result in the Division withholding the registration renewal of a motor vehicle registered in that person's name. The clerk of superior court in the county in which the case was disposed shall notify the Division of any person who fails to pay a fine or costs imposed pursuant to this section within 40 days of the date specified in the court's judgment, as required by G.S. 20-24.2(a)(2). The Division shall continue to withhold the registration renewal of a motor vehicle until the clerk of superior court notifies the Division that the person has satisfied the conditions of G.S. 20-24.1(b) applicable to the person's case. The provisions of this subsection shall be in addition to any other actions the Division may take to enforce the payment of any fine imposed pursuant to this section.

(h) Automated school bus safety cameras, as defined in G.S. 115C-242.1, may be used to detect and prosecute violations of this section. Any photograph or video recorded by an automated school bus safety camera shall, if consistent with the North Carolina Rules of Evidence, be admissible as evidence in any proceeding alleging a violation of subsection (a) of this section. Failure to produce a photograph or video recorded by an automated school bus safety camera shall not preclude prosecution under this section.

History.
1925, c. 265; 1943, c. 767; 1947, c. 527; 1955, c. 1365; 1959, c. 909; 1965, c. 370; 1969, c. 952; 1971, c. 245, s. 1; 1973, c. 1330, s. 35; 1977, 2nd Sess., c. 1280, s. 4; 1979, 2nd Sess., c. 1323; 1983, c. 779, s. 1; 1985, c. 700, s. 1; 1991, c. 290, s. 1;1993, c. 539, s. 382;1994, Ex. Sess., c. 24, s. 14(c);1998-149, s. 10;2005-204, s. 1;2006-160, s. 1;2006-259, s. 11(a);2007-382, s. 1;2009-147, ss. 1, 2; 2013-293, s. 2;2017-188, s. 4;2019-243, s. 8

EFFECT OF AMENDMENTS. --
Session Laws 2005-204, s. 1, effective September 1, 2005, and applicable to offenses committed on or after that date, rewrote subsections (a) and (b); in

subsection (c), deleted "the provisions of" following "Notwithstanding", substituted "that" for "which" in two places, and substituted "the" for "such" preceding "dividing space"; rewrote subsection (e); and added subsection (g).

Session Laws 2006-160, s. 1, effective September 1, 2006, and applicable to offenses committed on or after that date, added the second sentence in subsection (e).

Session Laws 2006-259, s. 11(a), effective December 1, 2006, and applicable to acts committed on or after that date, in subsection (g), added "willfully" following "Any person who" and deleted "willfully" preceding "strikes any person."

Session Laws 2007-382, s. 1, effective December 1, 2007, and applicable to offenses committed on or after that date, substituted "person" for "person causing serious bodily injury to that person" in subsection (g).

Session Laws 2013-293, s. 2, effective December 1, 2013, inserted "and shall pay a minimum fine of five hundred dollars ($500.00)" in subsection (e); in subsection (g), inserted "and shall pay a minimum fine of one thousand two hundred fifty dollars ($1,250)" and "and shall pay a minimum fine of two thousand five hundred dollars ($2,500)"; and added subsections (g1) and (g2). For applicability, see Editor's note.

Session Laws 2017-188, s. 4, effective July 25, 2017, in subsection (h), substituted "Automated school bus safety cameras, as defined in G.S. 115C-242.1" for "Automated camera and video recording systems" in the first sentence, substituted "an automated school bus safety camera" for "a camera or video recording system" in the second sentence, and added the third sentence.

Session Laws 2019-243, s. 8, effective November 6, 2019, substituted "40 days" for "20 days" in the second sentence of (g)(2).

THIS SECTION IS A SAFETY STATUTE, designed for the protection of life, limb and property. State v. Weston, 273 N.C. 275, 159 S.E.2d 883 (1968).

This section is designed for the protection of life, limb and property. Slade v. New Hanover County Bd. of Educ., 10 N.C. App. 287, 178 S.E.2d 316, cert. denied, 278 N.C. 104, 179 S.E.2d 453 (1971).

THIS SECTION APPLIES TO PASSING A SCHOOL BUS FROM EITHER DIRECTION, from the rear or from the front. State v. Webb, 210 N.C. 350, 186 S.E. 241 (1936).

NO DUTY TO STOP WHEN BUS IS ACROSS MEDIAN. --This section imposes no duty on a motorist to stop for a stopped school bus across the median from him on a divided highway. Holder v. Moore, 22 N.C. App. 134, 205 S.E.2d 732 (1974).

A VIOLATION OF THIS SECTION IS NEGLIGENCE PER SE, but such violation must be proximate cause contributing to injury and death of intestate to warrant recovery on that ground. Morgan v. Carolina Coach Co., 225 N.C. 668, 36 S.E.2d 263 (1945).

CULPABLE NEGLIGENCE. --The violation of a safety statute which results in injury or death will constitute culpable negligence if the violation is willful, wanton, or intentional. But where there is an

Chapter 20

unintentional or inadvertent violation of the statute, such violation standing alone does not constitute culpable negligence. The inadvertent or unintentional violation of the statute must be accompanied by recklessness of probable consequences of a dangerous nature, when tested by the rule of reasonable prevision, amounting altogether to a thoughtless disregard of consequences or a heedless indifference to the safety of others. State v. Weston, 273 N.C. 275, 159 S.E.2d 883 (1968).

EVIDENCE HELD SUFFICIENT. --The state's evidence regarding the identity of driver of blue car which passed a stopped school bus in violation of this section held sufficient. State v. Williams, 90 N.C. App. 120, 367 S.E.2d 345 (1988).

EVIDENCE FAILING TO SHOW VIOLATION OF THIS SECTION. --The evidence tended to show that a school bus and two following cars stopped on the right side of the highway, that two children alighted, one of whom ran immediately in front of the bus across the highway, and the other, a boy eight years old waited until the three vehicles were in motion and crossed the highway after the third vehicle had passed, and was struck by defendant's truck operated by defendant's agent which was traveling in the opposite direction about 30 miles per hour, and which failed to give any warning of its approach and failed to reduce speed prior to the collision. It was held that, although the evidence failed to show a violation of the letter of this section, since the school bus was in motion and its stop signal had been withdrawn prior to the impact, the evidence was sufficient to be submitted to the jury upon the issues of the negligence of the driver of the truck and the contributory negligence of defendant's intestate. Hughes v. Thayer, 229 N.C. 773, 51 S.E.2d 488 (1949).

APPLIED in Reeves v. Campbell, 264 N.C. 224, 141 S.E.2d 296 (1965).

CITED in In re Fuller, 345 N.C. 157, 478 S.E.2d 641 (1996); State v. Dewalt, 209 N.C. App. 187, 703 S.E.2d 872 (2011); State v. Leonard, 213 N.C. App. 526, 711 S.E.2d 867 (2011).

OPINIONS OF THE ATTORNEY GENERAL
PUBLIC VEHICULAR AREA. --This section has no application to a "public vehicular area" as defined by G.S. 20-4.01(32). See opinion of Attorney General to Mr. Alan Leonard, District Attorney, Twenty-Ninth Judicial District, 57 N.C.A.G. 10 (Mar. 9, 1987).

PASSING A STOPPED SCHOOL BUS DISPLAYING A MECHANICAL STOP SIGNAL while receiving or discharging passengers on a driveway on school property, which is not a street or highway, does not violate this section. See opinion of Attorney General to Mr. Alan Leonard, District Attorney, Twenty-Ninth Judicial District, 57 N.C.A.G. 10 (Mar. 9, 1987).

N.C. Gen. Stat. § 20-217.1

Repealed by Session Laws 1983, c. 779, s. 2.

§ 20-218. Standard qualifications for school bus drivers; speed limit for school buses and school activity buses

(a) **Qualifications.** -- No person shall drive a school bus over the highways or public vehicular areas of North Carolina while it is occupied by one or more child passengers unless the person furnishes to the superintendent of the schools of the county in which the bus shall be operated a certificate from any representative duly designated by the Commissioner and from the Director of Transportation or a designee of the Director in charge of school buses in the county showing that the person has been examined by them and is fit and competent to drive a school bus over the highways and public vehicular areas of the State. The driver of a school bus must be at least 18 years of age and hold a Class A, B, or C commercial drivers license and a school bus driver's certificate. The driver of a school activity bus must meet the same qualifications as a school bus driver or must have a license appropriate for the class of vehicle being driven.

(b) **Speed Limits.** -- It is unlawful to drive a school bus occupied by one or more child passengers over the highways or public vehicular areas of the State at a greater rate of speed than 45 miles per hour. It is unlawful to drive a school activity bus occupied by one or more child passengers over the highways or public vehicular areas of North Carolina at a greater rate of speed than 55 miles per hour.

(c) **Punishment.** -- A person who violates this section commits a Class 3 misdemeanor.

History.
1937, c. 397, ss. 1-3; 1941, c. 21; 1943, c. 440; 1945, c. 216; 1957, cc. 139, 595; 1971, c. 293; 1977, c. 791, ss. 1, 2; c. 1102; 1979, c. 31, ss. 1, 2; c. 667, s. 36; 1981, c. 30; 1987, c. 337, s. 1; 1989, c. 558, s. 1;c. 771, s. 6;1991, c. 726, s. 22;1993, c. 217, s. 1;1993 (Reg. Sess., 1994), c. 761, s. 20; 2009-550, s. 3.2

EFFECT OF AMENDMENTS. --
Session Laws 2009-550, s. 3.2, effective August 28, 2009, in subsection (a), substituted "one or more child passengers" for "children"; and in subsection (b), substituted "occupied by one or more child passengers" for "loaded with children" twice.

CITED in Shue v. Scheidt, 252 N.C. 561, 114 S.E.2d 237 (1960); Irving v. Charlotte-Mecklenburg Bd. of Educ., 368 N.C. 609, 781 S.E.2d 282 (2016).

CROSS REFERENCES. --
As to selection and employment of school bus drivers, see G.S. 115C-245.

OPINIONS OF THE ATTORNEY GENERAL
THIS SECTION AS REWRITTEN BY SESSION LAWS 1977, C. 791, CONTAINED THE CORRECT VERSION OF THE STATUTE. Opinion of Attorney General to Major D.R. Emory, N.C. State Highway

Patrol, 47 N.C.A.G. 75 (1977), prior to the 1979 and 1981 amendments.

N.C. Gen. Stat. § 20-218.1

Repealed by Session Laws 1993 (Reg. Sess., 1994), c. 761, s. 21.

§ 20-218.2. Speed limit for nonprofit activity buses

It is unlawful to drive an activity bus that is owned by a nonprofit organization and is transporting persons in connection with nonprofit activities over the highways or public vehicular areas of North Carolina at a greater rate of speed than 55 miles per hour. A person who violates this section commits a Class 3 misdemeanor.

History.

1969, c. 1000, s. 2; 1987, c. 337, s. 2; 1993 (Reg. Sess., 1994), c. 761, s. 23

N.C. Gen. Stat. § 20-219

Repealed by Session Laws 1993 (Reg. Sess., 1994), c. 761, s. 24.

N.C. Gen. Stat. § 20-219.1

Repealed by Session Laws 1971, c. 294, s. 2.
CROSS REFERENCES. --
For present provision as to removal of vehicles parked or left standing on highways, see G.S. 20-161.

§ 20-219.2. Removal of unauthorized vehicles from private lots

(a) It shall be unlawful for any person other than the owner or lessee of a privately owned or leased parking space to park a motor or other vehicle in such private parking space without the express permission of the owner or lessee of such space if the private parking lot is clearly designated as such by legible signs no smaller than 24 inches by 24 inches prominently displayed at all entrances thereto, displaying the current name and current phone number of the towing and storage company, and, if individually owned or leased, the parking lot or spaces within the lot are clearly marked by signs setting forth the name of each individual lessee or owner. A vehicle parked in a privately owned parking space in violation of this section may be removed from such space upon the written request of the parking space owner or lessee to a place of storage and the registered owner of such motor vehicle shall become liable for removal and storage charges. Any person who removes a vehicle pursuant to this section shall not be held liable for damages for the removal of the vehicle to the owner, lienholder or other person legally entitled to the possession of the vehicle removed; however, any person who intentionally or negligently damages a vehicle in the removal of such vehicle, or intentionally or negligently inflicts injury upon any person in the removal of such vehicle, may be held liable for damages. The provisions of this section shall not apply until 72 hours after the required signs are posted.

(a1) If any vehicle is removed pursuant to this section and there is a place of storage within 15 miles, the vehicle shall not be transported for storage more than 15 miles from the place of removal. For all other vehicles, the vehicle shall not be transported for storage more than 25 miles from the place of removal.

(a2) Any person who tows or stores a vehicle subject to this section shall inform the owner in writing at the time of retrieval of the vehicle that the owner has the right to pay the amount of the lien asserted, request immediate possession, and contest the lien for towing charges pursuant to the provisions of G.S. 44A-4.

(a3) Any person who tows or stores a vehicle subject to this section shall not require any person retrieving a vehicle to sign any waiver of rights or other similar document as a condition of the release of the person's vehicle, other than a form acknowledging the release and receipt of the vehicle.

(b) Any person violating any of the provisions of this section shall be guilty of an infraction and upon conviction shall be only penalized not less than one hundred fifty dollars ($ 150.00) in the discretion of the court.

(c) This section shall apply only to the Counties of Craven, Cumberland, Dare, Forsyth, Gaston, Guilford, Mecklenburg, New Hanover, Orange, Richmond, Robeson, Wake, Wilson and municipalities in those counties, and to the Cities of Durham, Jacksonville, Charlotte and Fayetteville.

(d) The provisions of this section shall not be interpreted to preempt the authority of any county or municipality to enact ordinances regulating towing from private lots, as authorized by general law.

History.

1969, cc. 173, 288; 1971, c. 986; 1973, c. 183; c. 981, s. 1; c. 1330, s. 36; 1975, c. 575; 1979, c. 380; 1979, 2nd Sess., c. 1119; 1981 (Reg. Sess., 1982), c. 1251, s. 3; 1989, c. 417; c. 644, s. 1; 1993, c. 539, s. 383;1994, Ex. Sess., c. 24, s. 14(c);2008-68, s. 1;2010-134, s. 1;2013-190, s. 1;2013-241, s. 2

LOCAL MODIFICATION. --Forsyth: 1983, c. 459.
EDITOR'S NOTE. --
This section was originally codified as G.S. 20-162.2. It was transferred to its present position by Session Laws 1973, c. 1330, s. 36.

EFFECT OF AMENDMENTS. --

Session Laws 2008-68, s. 1, effective December 1, 2008, and applicable to offenses committed on or after that date, inserted "Richmond" in subsection (c).

Session Laws 2013-190, s. 1, effective December 1, 2013, substituted "less than one hundred fifty dollars ($150.00)" for "more than one hundred dollars ($100.00)" in subsection (b). For applicability, see Editor's note.

Session Laws 2013-241, s. 2, effective December 1, 2013, in subsection (a), substituted "legible signs" for "a sign," "all entrances" for "the entrance," and inserted "current" twice in the first sentence, and added the last sentence. For applicability, see Editor's note.

TOWING VEHICLES. --In a case involving the scope of a municipality's power to regulate both the business of towing vehicles parked in private lots and the use of mobile telephones while driving, the Supreme Court held that the Town of Chapel Hill is generally permitted to regulate vehicle towing and that it acted within its authority by enacting signage, notice, and payment requirements for towing from private lots; however, Chapel Hill exceeded those powers by imposing a fee schedule and prohibiting towing companies from charging credit card fees. King v. Town of Chapel Hill, 367 N.C. 400, 758 S.E.2d 364 (2014).

CITED in Kirschbaum v. McLaurin Parking Co., 188 N.C. App. 782, 656 S.E.2d 683 (2008).

§ 20-219.3. Removal of unauthorized vehicles from gasoline service station premises

(a) No motor vehicle shall be left for more than 48 hours upon the premises of any gasoline service station without the consent of the owner or operator of the service station.

(b) The registered owner of any motor vehicle left unattended upon the premises of a service station in violation of subsection (a) shall be given notice by the owner or operator of said station of said violation. The notice given shall be by certified mail return receipt requested addressed to the registered owner of the motor vehicle.

(c) Upon the expiration of 10 days from the return of the receipt showing that the notice was received by the addressee, such vehicle left on the premises of a service station in violation of this section may be removed from the station premises to a place of storage and the registered owner of such vehicle shall become liable for the reasonable removal and storage charges and the vehicle subject to the storage lien created by G.S. 44A-1 et seq. Any person who removes a vehicle pursuant to this section shall not be held liable for damages for the removal of the vehicle to the owner, lienholder or other person legally entitled to the possession of the vehicle removed; however, any person who intentionally or negligently damages a vehicle in the removal of such vehicle, or intentionally or negligently inflicts injury upon any person in the removal of such vehicle, may be held liable for damages.

(d) In the alternative, the station owner or operator may charge for storage, assert a lien, and dispose of the vehicle under the terms of G.S. 44A-4(b) through (g). The proceeds from the sale of the vehicle shall be disbursed as provided in G.S. 44A-5.

History.

1971, c. 1220; 1973, c. 1330, s. 36; 1989, c. 644, s. 2

EDITOR'S NOTE. --

This section was originally codified as G.S. 20-162.3. It was transferred to its present position by Session Laws 1973, c. 1330, s. 36.

Session Laws 1973, c. 720, s. 2, which enacted G.S. 20-137.6 to 20-137.14, relating to abandoned and derelict vehicles, provided that the act would not repeal or modify G.S. 20-162.3 (now G.S. 20-219.3).

CITED in Bowles Auto., Inc. v. N.C. DMV, 203 N.C. App. 19, 690 S.E.2d 728 (2010), review denied, 364 N.C. 324, 700 S.E.2d 746, 2010 N.C. LEXIS 590 (2010).

§ 20-219.4. Public vehicular area designated

(a) Any area of private property used for vehicular traffic may be designated by the property owner as a public vehicular area by registering the area with the Department of Transportation and by erecting signs identifying the area as a public vehicular area in conformity with rules adopted by the Department of Transportation.

(b) The Department of Transportation shall serve as a registry for registrations of public vehicular areas permitted under this section. The Department shall adopt rules for registration requirements and procedures. The Department shall also adopt rules governing the size and locations of signs designating public vehicular areas by private property owners in accordance with this section. These rules shall ensure that signs erected pursuant to this provision shall be placed so as to provide reasonable notice to motorists.

(c) The Department shall charge a fee not to exceed five hundred dollars ($ 500.00) per registration request authorized by this section. The Department may also charge the reasonable cost for furnishing a certified copy of a registration when requested. Funds collected under this subsection shall be used to cover the cost of maintaining the registry.

History.

2001-441, s. 2

§ 20-219.5. Dealer liability for third-party motor vehicle history reports

A motor vehicle dealer, as defined in G.S. 20-286(11), and the dealer's owners, shareholders, officers, employees, and agents who, in conjunction with the actual or potential sale or lease of a motor vehicle, arrange to provide, provide, or otherwise make available to a vehicle purchaser, lessee, or other person any third-party motor vehicle history report, shall not be liable to the vehicle purchaser, lessee, or other person for any errors, omissions, or other inaccuracies contained in the third-party motor vehicle history report that are not based on information provided directly to the preparer of the third-party motor vehicle history report by that dealer. For purposes of this section, a "third-party motor vehicle history report" means any information prepared by a party other than the dealer, relating to any one or more of the following: vehicle ownership or titling history; liens on the vehicle; vehicle service, maintenance, or repair history; vehicle condition; or vehicle accident or collision history.

History.
2019-181, s. 2
    EDITOR'S NOTE. --
    Session Laws 2019-181, s. 6, made this section effective July 26, 2019.

§§ 20-219.5 through 20-219.8

Reserved for future codification purposes.

ARTICLE 7A.
POST-TOWING PROCEDURES

§ 20-219.9. Definitions

As used in this Article, unless the context clearly requires otherwise:
    (1) "Tow" in any of its forms includes to remove a vehicle by any means including towing and to store the vehicle;
    (2) "Tower" means the person who towed the vehicle;
    (3) "Towing fee" means the fee charged for towing and storing.

History.
1983, c. 420, s. 2
    CROSS REFERENCES. --
    For provision authorizing certain private colleges or universities to provide alternative post-towing procedures, see G.S. 116-229.

§ 20-219.10. Coverage of Article

(a) This Article applies to each towing of a vehicle that is carried out pursuant to G.S. 115C-46(d) or G.S. 143-340(19), or pursuant to the direction of a law-enforcement officer except:
    (1) This Article applies to towings pursuant to G.S. 115D-21, 116-44.4, 116-229, 153A-132, 153A-132.2, 160A-303, and 160A-303.2 only insofar as specifically provided;
    (2) This Article does not apply to a seizure of a vehicle under G.S. 14-86.1, 18B-504,

90-112, 113-137, 20-28.2, 20-28.3, or to any other seizure of a vehicle for evidence in a criminal proceeding or pursuant to any other statute providing for the forfeiture of a vehicle;
    (3) This Article does not apply to a seizure of a vehicle pursuant to a levy under execution.
(b) A person who authorizes the towing of a vehicle covered by this Article, G.S. 115D-21, 116-44.4, 116-229, 153A-132, 153A-132.2, 160A-303 or 160A-303.2 is a legal possessor of the vehicle within the meaning of G.S. 44A-1(1).

History.
1983, c. 420, s. 2; 1989, c. 743, s. 3;1997-379, s. 1.7
    EDITOR'S NOTE. --
    Session Laws 1989, c. 743, which amended this section, provided in s. 4 that the act would not affect the validity of any ordinance passed prior to October 1, 1989.
    CITED in Bowles Auto., Inc. v. N.C. DMV, 203 N.C. App. 19, 690 S.E.2d 728 (2010), review denied, 364 N.C. 324, 700 S.E.2d 746, 2010 N.C. LEXIS 590 (2010).

§ 20-219.11. Notice and probable cause hearing

(a) Whenever a vehicle with a valid registration plate or registration is towed as provided in G.S. 20-219.10, the authorizing person shall immediately notify the last known registered owner of the vehicle of the following:
    (1) A description of the vehicle;
    (2) The place where the vehicle is stored;
    (3) The violation with which the owner is charged, if any;
    (4) The procedure the owner must follow to have the vehicle returned to him; and
    (5) The procedure the owner must follow to request a probable cause hearing on the towing.
    If the vehicle has a North Carolina registration plate or registration, notice shall be given to the owner within 24 hours; if the vehicle is not registered in this State, notice shall be given to the owner within 72 hours. This notice shall, if feasible, be given by telephone. Whether or not the owner is reached by telephone, notice shall be mailed to his last known address unless he or his agent waives this notice in writing.
(b) Whenever a vehicle with neither a valid registration plate nor registration is towed as provided in G.S. 20-219.10, the authorizing person shall make reasonable efforts, including checking the vehicle identification number, to determine the last known registered owner of the vehicle and to notify him of the information listed in subsection (a). Unless the owner has otherwise been given notice, it is presumed that the authorizing person has not made reasonable efforts, as required under this subsection,

unless notice that the vehicle would be towed was posted on the windshield or some other conspicuous place at least seven days before the towing actually occurred; except, no pretowing notice need be given if the vehicle impeded the flow of traffic or otherwise jeopardized the public welfare so that immediate towing was necessary.

(c) The owner or any other person entitled to claim possession of the vehicle may request in writing a hearing to determine if probable cause existed for the towing. The request shall be filed with the magistrate in the county where the vehicle was towed. If there is more than one magistrate's office in that county, the request may be filed with the magistrate in the warrant-issuing office in the county seat or in any other office designated to receive requests by the chief district court judge. The magistrate shall set the hearing within 72 hours of his receiving the request. The owner, the person who requested the hearing if someone other than the owner, the tower, and the person who authorized the towing shall be notified of the time and place of the hearing.

(d) The owner, the tower, the person who authorized the towing, and any other interested parties may present evidence at the hearing. The person authorizing the towing and the tower may submit an affidavit in lieu of appearing personally, but the affidavit does not preclude that person from also testifying.

(e) The only issue at this hearing is whether or not probable cause existed for the towing. If the magistrate finds that probable cause did exist, the tower's lien continues. If the magistrate finds that probable cause did not exist, the tower's lien is extinguished.

(f) Any aggrieved party may appeal the magistrate's decision to district court.

History.
1983, c. 420, s. 2

§ 20-219.12. Option to pay or post bond

At any stage in the proceedings, including before the probable cause hearing, the owner may obtain possession of his vehicle by:
(1) Paying the towing fee, or
(2) Posting a bond for double the amount of the towing fee.

History.
1983, c. 420, s. 2

§ 20-219.13. Hearing on lien

The tower may seek to enforce his lien or the owner may seek to contest the lien pursuant to Chapter 44A.

History.
1983, c. 420, s. 2

§ 20-219.14. Payment to tower guaranteed

Every agency whose law-enforcement officers act pursuant to this Article, G.S. 115D-21, 116-44.4, 116-229, 153A-132, or 160A-303 shall by contract or rules provide compensation to the tower if a court finds no probable cause existed for the towing.

History.
1983, c. 420, s. 2

§§ 20-219.15 through 20-219.19

Reserved for future codification purposes.

ARTICLE 7B.
NOTIFICATION OF TOWING

§ 20-219.20. Requirement to give notice of vehicle towing

(a) Whenever a vehicle is towed at the request of a person other than the owner or operator of the vehicle, the tower shall provide the following information to the local law enforcement agency having jurisdiction through calling the 10-digit telephone number designated by the local law enforcement agency having jurisdiction prior to moving the vehicle:
(1) A description of the vehicle.
(2) The place from which the vehicle was towed.
(3) The place where the vehicle will be stored.
(4) The contact information for the person from whom the vehicle owner may retrieve the vehicle.

If the vehicle is impeding the flow of traffic or otherwise jeopardizing the public welfare so that immediate towing is necessary, the notice to the local law enforcement agency having jurisdiction may be provided by a tower within 30 minutes of moving the vehicle rather than prior to moving the vehicle. If a caller to a local law enforcement agency having jurisdiction can provide the information required under subdivisions (1) and (2) of this subsection, then a local law enforcement agency having jurisdiction shall provide to the caller the information provided under subdivisions (3) and (4) of this subsection. The local law enforcement agency having jurisdiction shall preserve the information required under this subsection for a period of not less than 30 days from the date on which the tower provided the information to the local law enforcement agency having jurisdiction.

(b) This section shall not apply to vehicles that are towed at the direction of a law enforcement officer or to vehicles removed from a private lot where signs are posted in accordance with G.S. 20-219.2(a).

(c) Violation of this section shall constitute an infraction subject to a penalty of not more than one hundred dollars ($ 100.00).

History.
2013-241, s. 1
EDITOR'S NOTE. --
Session Laws 2013-241, s. 1, enacted Article 7A. It was redesignated Article 7B at the direction of the Revisor of Statutes.

ARTICLE 8.
HABITUAL OFFENDERS

§§ 20-220 through 20-231

Repealed by Session Laws 1977, c. 243, s. 1.

ARTICLE 8A.
ISSUANCE OF NEW LICENSES TO PERSONS ADJUDGED HABITUAL OFFENDERS

N.C. Gen. Stat. § 20-231.1

Repealed by Session Laws 1993 (Reg. Sess., 1994), c. 761, s. 25.

ARTICLE 9.
MOTOR VEHICLE SAFETY AND FINANCIAL RESPONSIBILITY ACT

§§ 20-232 through 20-279

Repealed by Session Laws 1953, c. 1300, s. 35.
EDITOR'S NOTE. --
The repealing act is codified as G.S. 20-279.35. For law now effective, see G.S. 20-279.1 to 20-279.39. And see G.S. 20-309 to 20-319.
Former G.S. 20-232 has been reenacted and renumbered as G.S. 20-17.1.

ARTICLE 9A.
MOTOR VEHICLE SAFETY AND FINANCIAL RESPONSIBILITY ACT OF 1953

§ 20-279.1. Definitions

The following words and phrases, when used in this Article, shall, for the purposes of this Article, have the meanings respectively ascribed to them in this section, except in those instances where the context clearly indicates a different meaning:

(1) Repealed by Session Laws 1973, c. 1330, s. 39.

(2) Repealed by Session Laws 1991, c. 726, s. 20.

(3) "Judgment": Any judgment which shall have become final by expiration without appeal of the time within which an appeal might have been perfected, or by final affirmation on appeal, rendered by a court of competent jurisdiction of any state or of the United States, upon a cause of action arising out of the ownership, maintenance or use of any motor vehicle, for damages, including damages for care and loss of services, because of bodily injury to or death of any person, or for damages because of injury to or destruction of property, including the loss of use thereof, or upon a cause of action on an agreement of settlement for such damages.

(4) to (6) Repealed by Session Laws 1973, c. 1330, s. 39.

(6a) **Motor vehicle.** -- This term includes mopeds, as that term is defined in G.S. 20-4.01.

(7) "Nonresident's operating privilege": The privilege conferred upon a nonresident by the laws of this State pertaining to the operation by him of a motor vehicle in this State.

(8) to (10) Repealed by Session Laws 1973, c. 1330, s. 39.

(11) "Proof of financial responsibility": Proof of ability to respond in damages for liability, on account of accidents occurring subsequent to the effective date of said proof, arising out of the ownership, maintenance or use of a motor vehicle, in the amount of thirty thousand dollars ($ 30,000) because of bodily injury to or death of one person in any one accident, and, subject to said limit for one person, in the amount of sixty thousand dollars ($ 60,000) because of bodily injury to or death of two or more persons in any one accident, and in the amount of twenty-five thousand dollars ($ 25,000) because of injury to or destruction of property of others in any one accident. Nothing contained herein shall prevent an insurer and an insured from entering into a contract, not affecting third parties, providing for a deductible as to property damage at a rate approved by the Commissioner of Insurance.

(12) Repealed by Session Laws 1973, c. 1330, s. 39.

History.

1953, c. 1300, s. 1; 1955, c. 1152, s. 3; c. 1355; 1967, c. 277, s. 1; 1971, c. 1205, s. 1; 1973, c. 745, s. 1; c. 1330, s. 39; 1979, c. 832, s. 1; 1991, c. 469, s. 1; c. 726, s. 20; 1999-228, s. 1; 2015-125, s. 2

EDITOR'S NOTE. --

Session Laws 2015-125, s. 10, made subdivision (6a) of this section, as added by Session Laws 2015-125, s. 2, applicable to offenses committed on or after July 1, 2016.

EFFECT OF AMENDMENTS. --

Session Laws 2015-125, s. 2, effective July 1, 2016, added subdivision (6a). For applicability, see Editor's note.

THIS CHAPTER SUPERSEDES G.S. 58-3-10. --- G.S. 58-3-10, adopted in 1901, falls within Chapter 58, Insurance, Article 3, General Regulations for Insurance. As an earlier and more general statement of insurance law, it is superseded with respect to automobile liability insurance by Chapter 20, Motor Vehicles, specifically by Article 9A, the Motor Vehicle Safety and Financial Responsibility Act of 1953, and Article 13, the Vehicle Financial Responsibility Act of 1957. Chapter 20 represents a complete and comprehensive legislative scheme for the regulation of motor vehicles, and as such, its insurance provisions regarding automobiles prevail over the more general insurance regulations of Chapter 58. Odum v. Nationwide Mut. Ins. Co., 101 N.C. App. 627, 401 S.E.2d 87, cert. denied, 329 N.C. 499, 407 S.E.2d 539 (1991).

THE OBJECT OF THE MOTOR VEHICLE SAFETY AND FINANCIAL RESPONSIBILITY ACT was to provide protection to the public. Indiana Lumbermens Mut. Ins. Co. v. Parton, 147 F. Supp. 887 (M.D.N.C. 1957).

It is the purpose of the Financial Responsibility Act to provide protection for persons injured or damaged by the negligent operation of automobiles. Hawley v. Indemnity Ins. Co. of N. Am., 257 N.C. 381, 126 S.E.2d 161 (1962); Fidelity & Cas. Co. v. North Carolina Farm Bureau Mut. Ins. Co., 16 N.C. App. 194, 192 S.E.2d 113, cert. denied, 282 N.C. 425, 192 S.E.2d 840 (1972).

The purpose of the Financial Responsibility Law is to protect victims of automobile accidents. Allstate Ins. Co. v. Shelby Mut. Ins. Co., 269 N.C. 341, 152 S.E.2d 436 (1967).

The purpose of the Financial Responsibility Act is to provide protection from damages or injuries resulting from the negligent operation of automobiles. Nationwide Mut. Ins. Co. v. Hayes, 276 N.C. 620, 174 S.E.2d 511 (1970).

The purpose of the Financial Responsibility Act is to provide protection to the public from damages resulting from the negligent operation of automobiles by irresponsible persons. Nationwide Mut. Ins. Co. v. Fireman's Fund Ins. Co., 279 N.C. 240, 182 S.E.2d 571 (1971); Haight v. Travelers/Aetna Property Cas. Corp., 132 N.C. App. 673, 514 S.E.2d 102 (1999).

OPERATORS MUST BE FINANCIALLY RESPONSIBLE. --The legislatures of 1953 and 1955 required operators of motor vehicles in this State to be "financially responsible," and proof of financial responsibility is defined in this section. Iowa Mut. Ins. Co. v. Fred M. Simmons, Inc., 262 N.C. 691, 138 S.E.2d 512 (1964).

THIS ARTICLE AND ARTICLE 13 TO BE CONSTRUED IN PARI MATERIA. --The Motor Vehicle Safety and Financial Responsibility Act of 1953 applies to drivers whose licenses have been suspended and relates to the restoration of drivers' licenses, while the Vehicle Financial Responsibility Act of 1957 applies to all motor vehicle owners and relates to the registration of motor vehicles. The two acts are complementary, and the latter does not repeal or modify the former but incorporates portions of the former by reference, and the two acts are to be construed in pari materia so as to harmonize them and give effect to both. Faizan v. Grain Dealers Mut. Ins. Co., 254 N.C. 47, 118 S.E.2d 303 (1961).

This Article and Article 13 of this Chapter are to be construed together so as to harmonize their provisions and to effectuate the purpose of the legislature. Harrelson v. State Farm Mut. Auto. Ins. Co., 272 N.C. 603, 158 S.E.2d 812 (1968).

The 1953 Act, found at G.S. 20-279.1 to 20-279.39, applies to drivers whose licenses have been suspended and relates to the restoration of driver's licenses, while the 1957 Act, found at G.S. 20-309 to 20-319, applies to all motor vehicles' owners and relates to vehicle registration. The two Acts are complementary and are to be construed in pari materia so as to harmonize them and give effect to both. Odum v. Nationwide Mut. Ins. Co., 101 N.C. App. 627, 401 S.E.2d 87, cert. denied, 329 N.C. 499, 407 S.E.2d 539 (1991).

ARTICLE 13 REQUIRES PROOF OF FINANCIAL RESPONSIBILITY TO BE GIVEN IN MANNER PRESCRIBED BY THIS ARTICLE. --The Vehicle Financial Responsibility Act of 1957, Article 13 of this Chapter, requires every owner of a motor vehicle, as a prerequisite to the registration thereof, to show "proof of financial responsibility" in the manner prescribed by this Article. Jones v. State Farm Mut. Auto. Ins. Co., 270 N.C. 454, 155 S.E.2d 118 (1967).

CONSTRUCTION OF ARTICLE. --Ambiguous provisions of the Financial Responsibility Law must be construed to accomplish the purpose of such law. Allstate Ins. Co. v. Shelby Mut. Ins. Co., 269 N.C. 341, 152 S.E.2d 436 (1967).

The Act is to be liberally construed so that its intended purpose may be accomplished. Wilmoth v. State Farm Mut. Auto. Ins. Co., 127 N.C. App. 260, 488 S.E.2d 628 (1997), cert. denied, 347 N.C. 410, 494 S.E.2d 601 (1997).

Although insureds argued that reversing a trial court's finding that one insurer's policy was primary while a second insurer's policy was excess coverage was inconsistent with the purpose of the Motor Vehicle Safety and Financial Responsibility Act (FRA), the policies did not conflict with the FRA; the "excess" clauses of the two policies were mutually repugnant and neither clause was given effect. Integon Nat'l Ins. Co. v. Phillips, 212 N.C. App. 623, 712 S.E.2d 381 (2011).

THE PROVISIONS OF THE FINANCIAL RE-
SPONSIBILITY ACT ARE WRITTEN INTO EVERY
AUTOMOBILE LIABILITY POLICY as a matter of
law. Wilmoth v. State Farm Mut. Auto. Ins. Co., 127
N.C. App. 260, 488 S.E.2d 628 (1997), cert. denied, 347
N.C. 410, 494 S.E.2d 601 (1997).

Superior court properly reformed an insurance
policy to include the amount of minimum coverage required by G.S. 20-309(a1); construing G.S. 20-279.21
and G.S. 20-309 in pari materia, just as provisions of
G.S. 20-279.21 were read into every insurance policy
as a matter of law, provisions of G.S. 20-309(a1) were
also read into every insurance policy as a matter of
law. N.C. Farm Bureau Mut. Ins. Co. v. Armwood, 181
N.C. App. 407, 638 S.E.2d 922 (2007), rev'd, 361 N.C.
576, 653 S.E.2d 392 (2007).

CONTRAVENING POLICY PROVISION IS VOID.
--A provision in a policy of liability insurance which
contravenes the Financial Responsibility Law is void.
Allstate Ins. Co. v. Shelby Mut. Ins. Co., 269 N.C. 341,
152 S.E.2d 436 (1967).

If there is a conflict between the Financial Responsibility Act and the language of the policy, the Act prevails. Wilmoth v. State Farm Mut. Auto. Ins. Co., 127
N.C. App. 260, 488 S.E.2d 628 (1997), cert. denied, 347
N.C. 410, 494 S.E.2d 601 (1997).

SECTION REDUCES IMPORTANCE OF FAMILY
PURPOSE DOCTRINE. --The importance of the family purpose doctrine in this State has been greatly reduced by this section. Smith v. Simpson, 260 N.C. 601,
133 S.E.2d 474 (1963).

DEFINITION OF "OWNER" IN G.S. 20-4.01
APPLIES TO THIS ARTICLE. --The definition of
"owner" in G.S. 20-4.01(26) applies throughout this
Chapter, and thus to this Article unless the context
otherwise requires. It thus must be read into every
liability insurance policy within the purview of this
Article, unless the context otherwise requires. Ohio
Cas. Ins. Co. v. Anderson, 59 N.C. App. 621, 298 S.E.2d
56 (1982); Indiana Lumbermens Mut. Ins. Co. v. Unigard Indem. Co., 76 N.C. App. 88, 331 S.E.2d 741, cert.
denied, 314 N.C. 666, 335 S.E.2d 494 (1985).

AND "OWNER" WAS DELETED FROM THIS SEC-
TION MERELY TO AVOID REPETITION. --Prior to
1973 the G.S. 20-4.01(26) definition of "owner" appeared in subdivision (9) of this section, which subdivision was repealed in 1973. The General Assembly
placed it in G.S. 20-4.01. The apparent purpose was to
eliminate unnecessary repetition of this definition in
separate articles of this Chapter, not to make the definition inapplicable to this Article. Ohio Cas. Ins. Co.
v. Anderson, 59 N.C. App. 621, 298 S.E.2d 56 (1982).

FOR PURPOSES OF TORT LAW AND LIABIL-
ITY INSURANCE COVERAGE, NO OWNERSHIP
PASSES to the purchaser of a motor vehicle which
requires registration until: (1) The owner executes,
in the presence of a person authorized to administer
oaths, an assignment and warranty of title on the
reverse of the certificate of title, including the name
and address of the transferee; (2) there is an actual
or constructive delivery of the motor vehicle; and (3)
the duly assigned certificate of title is delivered to

the transferee (or lienholder in secured transactions).
Jenkins v. Aetna Cas. & Sur. Co., 324 N.C. 394, 378
S.E.2d 773 (1989).

OWNERSHIP DOES NOT PASS UNTIL TRANS-
FER OF TITLE PURSUANT TO G.S. 20-72 (B). --For
purposes of liability insurance coverage, ownership of
a motor vehicle which requires registration under the
Motor Vehicle Act of 1937 does not pass until transfer
of legal title is effected as provided in G.S. 20-72(b).
Indiana Lumbermens Mut. Ins. Co. v. Unigard Indem.
Co., 76 N.C. App. 88, 331 S.E.2d 741, cert. denied, 314
N.C. 666, 335 S.E.2d 494 (1985).

WHERE AN INSURED DRIVER HAS THE UNRE-
STRICTED USE AND POSSESSION OF AN AUTO-
MOBILE, the certificate of title for which is retained
by another, the car is "furnished for the regular use
of" the "non-owned" clause of the policy. Indiana Lumbermens Mut. Ins. Co. v. Unigard Indem. Co., 76 N.C.
App. 88, 331 S.E.2d 741, cert. denied, 314 N.C. 666,
335 S.E.2d 494 (1985).

NO STATUTORY PRIORITY OF PAYMENT FOR
INSURANCE POLICIES. --There is no provision of
the act which expressly establishes a statutory priority of payment among different insurance policies.
However, G.S. 20-279.21(i) does allow an insurance
liability policy to "provide for the pro-rating of the
insurance thereunder with other valid and collectible insurance." North Carolina Farm Bureau Mut.
Ins. Co. v. Hilliard, 90 N.C. App. 507, 369 S.E.2d 386
(1988), decided under 1983 version of § 20-279.1.

COVERAGE WHEN OTHER POLICIES ARE
PRESENT. --Umbrella policy covering the car's owner
did not limit its exclusion of coverage to when the
driver of the vehicle was covered under some other
policy for the statutory minimum amount, however, it
did not provide excess coverage as to the car accident
and it had no duty to defend. Harleysville Mut. Ins.
Co. v. Zurich-American Ins. Co., 157 N.C. App. 317,
578 S.E.2d 701 (2003), cert. denied, 357 N.C. 250, 582
S.E.2d 269 (2003).

Trial court erred in holding that the owner's insurance policy terminated when the son's policy was issued on the same car because the automatic termination clause in the owner's policy's only applied if
the owner obtained other insurance, and since the
owner's policy and the son's policy were procured by
different persons, the owner's policy did not automatically terminate; both policies provided liability coverage, but the son's policy only provided coverage under
its liability provisions when the limit of the owner's
policy's coverage was met. Progressive Am. Ins. Co. v.
State Farm Mut. Auto. Ins. Co., 184 N.C. App. 688, 647
S.E.2d 111 (2007).

COVERAGE AVAILABLE TO SHERIFF'S DEP-
UTY. --County's policy controlled the underinsured
motorist coverage available to a deputy sheriff as the
North Carolina Motor Vehicle Safety and Financial
Responsibility Act, G.S. 20-279.1 et seq., did not ap-
ply due to G.S. 20-279.32. N.C. Counties Liab. & Prop.
Joint Risk Mgmt. Agency v. Curry, 191 N.C. App. 217,
662 S.E.2d 678 (2008).

Chapter 20

APPLIED in Manning v. State Farm Mut. Auto. Ins. Co., 243 F. Supp. 619 (W.D.N.C. 1965); Forrester v. Garrett, 280 N.C. 117, 184 S.E.2d 858 (1971); Wilfong v. Wilkins, 70 N.C. App. 127, 318 S.E.2d 540 (1984); Dutch v. Harleysville Mut. Ins. Co., 139 N.C. App. 602, 534 S.E.2d 262 (2000); Hlasnick v. Federated Mut. Ins. Co., 353 N.C. 240, 539 S.E.2d 274 (2000).

CITED in State v. Anderson, 3 N.C. App. 124, 164 S.E.2d 48 (1968); Marks v. Thompson, 282 N.C. 174, 192 S.E.2d 311 (1972); Reliance Ins. Co. v. Morrison, 59 N.C. App. 524, 297 S.E.2d 187 (1982); American Tours, Inc. v. Liberty Mut. Ins. Co., 315 N.C. 341, 338 S.E.2d 92 (1986); North Carolina Farm Bureau Mut. Ins. Co. v. Warren, 326 N.C. 444, 390 S.E.2d 138 (1990); Metropolitan Property & Cas. Ins. Co. v. Lindquist, 120 N.C. App. 847, 463 S.E.2d 574 (1995); Liberty Mut. Ins. Co. v. Pennington, 141 N.C. App. 495, 541 S.E.2d 503 (2000), aff'd, 356 N.C. 571, 573 S.E.2d 118 (2002); Tart v. Martin, 137 N.C. App. 371, 527 S.E.2d 708 (2000); Naddeo v. Allstate Ins. Co., 139 N.C. App. 311, 533 S.E.2d 501 (2000); North Carolina Farm Bureau Mut. Ins. Co. v. Perkinson, 140 N.C. App. 140, 535 S.E.2d 405 (2000); Moore v. Cincinnati Ins. Co., 147 N.C. App. 761, 556 S.E.2d 682 (2001); Farm Bureau Ins. Co. of N.C., Inc. v. Blong, 159 N.C. App. 365, 583 S.E.2d 307 (2003), cert. denied, 357 N.C. 578, 589 S.E.2d 125 (2003); Espino v. Allstate Indem. Co., 159 N.C. App. 686, 583 S.E.2d 376 (2003); Great American Ins. Co. v. Freeman, 192 N.C. App. 497, 665 S.E.2d 536 (2008); N.C. Farm Bureau Mut. Ins. Co. v. Simpson, 198 N.C. App. 190, 678 S.E.2d 753 (2009), review denied, 363 N.C. 806, 691 S.E.2d 13, N.C. LEXIS 56 (2010); Integon Nat'l Ins. Co. v. Villafranco, 228 N.C. App. 390, 745 S.E.2d 922 (2013); Lunsford v. Mills, 367 N.C. 618, 766 S.E.2d 297 (2014).

CROSS REFERENCES. --

For definitions applicable throughout this Chapter, see G.S. 20-4.01. As to Vehicle Financial Responsibility Act of 1957, see G.S. 20-309 to 20-319. As to liability insurance covering negligent operation of municipal vehicles, see G.S. 160A-485.

LEGAL PERIODICALS. --

For comment on this Article, see 31 N.C.L. Rev. 420 (1953).

For comment on insurer's liability for intentionally inflicted injuries, see 43 N.C.L. Rev. 436 (1965).

For case law survey as to automobile liability insurance, see 44 N.C.L. Rev. 1023 (1966).

For case law survey as to insurance, see 45 N.C.L. Rev. 955 (1967).

For comment on Allstate Ins. Co. v. Shelby Mut. Ins. Co., 269 N.C. 341, 152 S.E.2d 436 (1967), cited in the note below, see 46 N.C.L. Rev. 433 (1968).

For comment, "Compulsory Motor Vehicle Liability Insurance: Joinder of Insurers as Defendants in Actions Arising out of Automobile Accidents," see 14 Wake Forest L. Rev. 200 (1978).

For note on use of the family purpose doctrine when no outsiders are involved, in light of Carver v. Carver, 310 N.C. 669, 314 S.E.2d 739 (1984) see 21 Wake Forest L. Rev. 243 (1985).

For note, "Sutton v. Aetna Casualty & Surety Co.: The North Carolina Supreme Court Approves Stacking of Underinsured Motorist Coverage--Will Uninsured Coverage Follow?," see 68 N.C. L. Rev. 1281 (1990).

For note, "Underinsured Motorist Coverage: North Carolina's Multiple Claimant Wrinkle -- Ray v. Atlantic Casualty Insurance Co.," see 17 Campbell L. Rev. 147 (1995).

§ 20-279.2. Commissioners to administer Article; appeal to court

(a) Except for G.S. 20-279.21(d1), the Commissioner shall administer and enforce the provisions of this Article and may make rules and regulations necessary for its administration and shall provide for hearings upon request of persons aggrieved by orders or acts of the Commissioner under the provisions of this Article. The Commissioner of Insurance shall administer and enforce the provisions of G.S. 20-279.21(d1) and may make rules and regulations necessary for its administration.

(b) Any person aggrieved by an order or act of the Commissioner of Motor Vehicles requiring a suspension or revocation of the person's license under the provisions of this Article, or requiring the posting of security as provided in this Article, or requiring the furnishing of proof of financial responsibility, may file a petition in the superior court of the county in which the petitioner resides for a review, and the commencement of the proceeding shall suspend the order or act of the Commissioner pending the final determination of the review. A copy of the petition shall be served upon the Commissioner, and the Commissioner shall have 20 days after service in which to file answer. The appeal shall be heard in said county by the judge holding court in said county or by the resident judge. At the hearing upon the petition the judge shall sit without the intervention of a jury and shall receive any evidence deemed by the judge to be relevant and proper. Except as otherwise provided in this section, upon the filing of the petition herein provided for, the procedure shall be the same as in civil actions.

The matter shall be heard de novo and the judge shall enter an order affirming the act or order of the Commissioner, or modifying same, including the amount of bond or security to be given by the petitioner. If the court is of the opinion that the petitioner was probably not guilty of negligence or that the negligence of the other party was probably the sole proximate cause of the collision, the judge shall reverse the act or order of the Commissioner. Either party may appeal from the order to the Supreme Court in the same manner as in other appeals from the superior court and the appeal shall have the effect of further staying the act or order of the

Commissioner requiring a suspension or revocation of the petitioner's license.

No act, or order given or rendered in any proceeding hereunder shall be admitted or used in any other civil or criminal action.

History.
1953, c. 1300, s. 2; 2018-5, s. 34.26(a)
   EDITOR'S NOTE. --
   Session Laws 2018-5, s. 1.1, provides: "This act shall be known as the 'Current Operations Appropriations Act of 2018.'"
   Session Laws 2018-5, s. 39.7, is a severability clause.
   EFFECT OF AMENDMENTS. --
   Session Laws 2018-5, s. 34.26(a), effective July 1, 2018, in the heading, substituted "Commissioners" for "Commissioner"; in subsection (a), in the first sentence, substituted "Except for G.S.20-279.21(d1), the Commissioner" for "The Commissioner" and added the second sentence; in subsection (b), in the first sentence, inserted "of Motor Vehicles" and in the next-to-last sentence, substituted "any evidence deemed" for "such evidence as shall be deemed"; and made stylistic changes throughout.
   CONSTITUTIONALITY. --The provisions for suspension of an automobile driver's license fully comply with constitutional requirements. State v. Martin, 13 N.C. App. 613, 186 S.E.2d 647, cert. denied, 281 N.C. 156, 188 S.E.2d 364, appeal dismissed, 281 N.C. 156, 188 S.E.2d 365 (1972).
   AMPLE REVIEW IS PROVIDED before a driver's license suspension becomes effective. State v. Martin, 13 N.C. App. 613, 186 S.E.2d 647, cert. denied, 281 N.C. 156, 188 S.E.2d 364, appeal dismissed, 281 N.C. 156, 188 S.E.2d 365 (1972).
   THIS SECTION MAKES NO PROVISION FOR INTERVENTION BY PERSONS WHO MIGHT RECOVER DAMAGES from petitioner based on his actionable negligence in connection with an accident. Carter v. Scheidt, 261 N.C. 702, 136 S.E.2d 105 (1964).
   BUT COMMISSIONER MAY NOTIFY THEM OF HEARING. --Persons who might recover damages from petitioner based on petitioner's actionable negligence in connection with an accident have no standing in a proceeding under subsection (b) as a matter of right. Even so, it is appropriate that the Commissioner notify such persons of the petition and of the hearing to the end that all competent and relevant evidence may be brought forward. Carter v. Scheidt, 261 N.C. 702, 136 S.E.2d 105 (1964).
   AND COURT MAY PERMIT SUCH PERSONS TO FILE STATEMENTS AND PARTICIPATE IN HEARING. --While persons who might recover damages from petitioner based on petitioner's actionable negligence in connection with an accident may not be considered proper parties to the proceeding in a technical sense, the court, in its discretion, may permit such persons to file a statement relevant to the facts alleged in the petition and may permit them to participate in the hearing. Carter v. Scheidt, 261 N.C. 702, 136 S.E.2d 105 (1964).

HOWEVER, SUCH STATEMENTS ARE NOT EVIDENCE. --Statements by persons not considered proper parties to the proceeding in the technical sense, whether denominated an answer, affidavit, or otherwise, may not be considered competent evidence in the hearing. Carter v. Scheidt, 261 N.C. 702, 136 S.E.2d 105 (1964).
   COMMISSIONER MUST ANSWER PETITION. --Subsection (b) imposes upon the Commissioner (or his representative) the duty to answer all essential allegations of the petition and to be present and participate in the hearing before the judge. Carter v. Scheidt, 261 N.C. 702, 136 S.E.2d 105 (1964).
   AND PRODUCE ALL PERTINENT EVIDENCE. --While the statute provides that the court shall make the crucial determinations, the statute contemplates that the Commissioner shall bring forward for the court's consideration all evidence in his possession pertinent to decision. Carter v. Scheidt, 261 N.C. 702, 136 S.E.2d 105 (1964).
   FILING PETITION IS EQUIVALENT TO SUPERSEDEAS. --The filing of a petition under subsection (b) of this section to review the Commissioner's order is the equivalent of a supersedeas suspending the order until the question at issue has been determined by the superior court. Robinson v. United States Cas. Co., 260 N.C. 284, 132 S.E.2d 629 (1963).
   THE BURDEN OF PROOF is on petitioner to show he "was probably not guilty of negligence" or "that the negligence of the other party was probably the sole proximate cause of the collision." Carter v. Scheidt, 261 N.C. 702, 136 S.E.2d 105 (1964).
   APPEAL TO SUPREME COURT. --Where, upon petition for review of order of the Commissioner of Motor Vehicles suspending petitioners' operator's licenses, the owner of the other car involved in the collision is made a party by consent order and files answer, such owner must be served with statement of case on appeal to the Supreme Court. Johnson v. Scheidt, 246 N.C. 452, 98 S.E.2d 451 (1957).
   COMMISSIONER AND COURT HELD WITHOUT AUTHORITY TO GRANT RELIEF. --Where petitioner did not allege that he was probably not guilty of negligence or that the negligence of the other party was probably the sole proximate cause of the collision, nor did he allege that the amount of the security required was excessive or that such security was not required by the terms of the statute and there were no allegations which if proved would entitle the petitioner to any relief, and the only relief requested by the petitioner was that the court postpone the posting of the security required by the Commissioner under G.S. 20-279.5, neither the Commissioner nor the court had the authority to grant this relief and a motion to dismiss was properly granted. Forrester v. Garrett, 280 N.C. 117, 184 S.E.2d 858 (1971).
   INSURER REQUIRED TO DEFEND UNTIL SETTLEMENT OR JUDGMENT WAS REACHED. --Insurance company was required to continue defending the insured until a settlement or judgment was reached despite having paid its policy limits under G.S. 1-540.3. Brown v. Lumbermens Mut. Cas. Co.,

90 N.C. App. 464, 369 S.E.2d 367, cert. denied, 323 N.C. 363, 373 S.E.2d 542, cert. denied, 323 N.C. 363, 373 S.E.2d 541 (1988).

A CAUSE OF ACTION ALLEGING BREACH OF GOOD FAITH WILL NOT LIE when the insurer settles a claim within the monetary limits of the insured's policy; the insurer has the duty to consider the insured's interest but may act in its own interest in settlement of the claim. Cash v. State Farm Mut. Auto. Ins. Co., 137 N.C. App. 192, 528 S.E.2d 372 (2000).

STATUTE PREVAILS IN CONFLICT WITH POLICY. --The provisions of the Motor Vehicle Safety and Financial Responsibility Act are written into every automobile liability policy as a matter of law and where the provisions of the policy conflict with the provisions of the statute, the statute prevails. Brown v. Truck Ins. Exch., 103 N.C. App. 59, 404 S.E.2d 172, cert. denied, 329 N.C. 786, 408 S.E.2d 515 (1991).

COVERAGE WHICH IS IN ADDITION TO THE MANDATORY REQUIREMENTS OF THE STATUTE ARE VOLUNTARY and are not subject to the requirements of the act. Voluntary coverage must be measured by the terms of the policy as written. Brown v. Truck Ins. Exch., 103 N.C. App. 59, 404 S.E.2d 172, cert. denied, 329 N.C. 786, 408 S.E.2d 515 (1991).

LEGAL PERIODICALS. --

For article, "Toward a Codification of the Law of Evidence in North Carolina," see 16 Wake Forest L. Rev. 669 (1980).

OPINIONS OF THE ATTORNEY GENERAL

HEARING AND JUDICIAL REVIEW PROVISIONS COMPLY WITH DUE PROCESS REQUIREMENTS. --See opinion of Attorney General to Senator Clyde Norton, 41 N.C.A.G. 420 (1971).

§ 20-279.3. Commissioner to furnish operating record

The Commissioner shall upon request furnish any person a certified abstract of the operating record of any person required to comply with the provisions of this Article, which abstract shall also fully designate the motor vehicle, if any, registered in the name of such person, and if there shall be no record of any conviction of such person of violating any law relating to the operation of a motor vehicle or of any injury or damage caused by such person, the Commissioner shall so certify.

History.

1953, c. 1300, s. 3

N.C. Gen. Stat. § 20-279.4

Repealed by Session Laws 1995, c. 191, s. 4.

§ 20-279.5. Security required unless evidence of insurance; when security determined; suspension; exceptions

(a) When the Division receives a report of a reportable accident under G.S. 20-166.1, the Commissioner must determine whether the owner or driver of a vehicle involved in the accident must file security under this Article and, if so, the amount of security the owner or driver must file. The Commissioner must make this determination at the end of 20 days after receiving the report.

(b) The Commissioner shall, within 60 days after the receipt of such report of a motor vehicle accident, suspend the license of each operator and each owner of a motor vehicle in any manner involved in such accident, and if such operator or owner is a nonresident the privilege of operating a motor vehicle within this State, unless such operator or owner, or both, shall deposit security in the sum so determined by the Commissioner; provided, notice of such suspension shall be sent by the Commissioner to such operator and owner not less than 10 days prior to the effective date of such suspension and shall state the amount required as security; provided further, the provisions of this Article requiring the deposit of security and the suspension of license for failure to deposit security shall not apply to an operator or owner who would otherwise be required to deposit security in an amount not in excess of one hundred dollars ($ 100.00). Where erroneous information is given the Commissioner with respect to the matters set forth in subdivisions (1), (2) or (3) of subsection (c) of this section or with respect to the ownership or operation of the vehicle, the extent of damage and injuries, or any other matters which would have affected the Commissioner's action had the information been previously submitted, he shall take appropriate action as hereinbefore provided, within 60 days after receipt by him of correct information with respect to said matters. The Commissioner, upon request and in his discretion, may postpone the effective date of the suspension provided in this section by 15 days if, in his opinion, such extension would aid in accomplishing settlements of claims by persons involved in accidents.

(c) This section shall not apply under the conditions stated in G.S. 20-279.6 nor:

(1) To such operator or owner if such owner had in effect at the time of such accident an automobile liability policy with respect to the motor vehicle involved in such accident;

(2) To such operator, if not the owner of such motor vehicle, if there was in effect at the time of such accident a motor vehicle liability policy or bond with respect to his operation of motor vehicles not owned by him;

(3) To such operator or owner if the liability of such operator or owner for damages resulting from such accident is, in the judgment of the Commissioner, covered by any other form of liability insurance policy or

bond or sinking fund or group assumption of liability;

(4) To any person qualifying as a self-insurer, nor to any operator for a self-insurer if, in the opinion of the Commissioner from the information furnished him, the operator at the time of the accident was probably operating the vehicle in the course of the operator's employment as an employee or officer of the self-insurer; nor

(5) To any employee of the United States government while operating a vehicle in its service and while acting within the scope of his employment, such operations being fully protected by the Federal Tort Claims Act of 1946, which affords ample security to all persons sustaining personal injuries or property damage through the negligence of such federal employee.

No such policy or bond shall be effective under this section unless issued by an insurance company or surety company authorized to do business in this State, except that if such motor vehicle was not registered in this State, or was a motor vehicle which was registered elsewhere than in this State at the effective date of the policy or bond, or the most recent renewal thereof, or if such operator not an owner was a nonresident of this State, such policy or bond shall not be effective under this section unless the insurance company or surety company if not authorized to do business in this State shall execute a power of attorney authorizing the Commissioner to accept service on its behalf of notice or process in any action upon such policy, or bond arising out of such accident, and unless said insurance company or surety company, if not authorized to do business in this State, is authorized to do business in the state or other jurisdiction where the motor vehicle is registered or, if such policy or bond is filed on behalf of an operator not an owner who was a nonresident of this State, unless said insurance company or surety company, if not authorized to do business in this State, is authorized to do business in the state or other jurisdiction of residence of such operator; provided, however, every such policy or bond is subject, if the accident has resulted in bodily injury or death, to a limit, exclusive of interest and cost, of not less than thirty thousand dollars ($ 30,000) because of bodily injury to or death of one person in any one accident and, subject to said limit for one person, to a limit of not less than sixty thousand dollars ($ 60,000) because of bodily injury to or death of two or more persons in any one accident, and, if the accident has resulted in injury to or destruction of property, to a limit of not less than twenty-five thousand dollars ($ 25,000) because of injury to or destruction of property of others in any one accident.

History.

1953, c. 1300, s. 5; 1955, cc. 138, 854; c. 855, s. 1; c. 1152, ss. 4-8; c. 1355; 1967, c. 277, s. 2; 1971, c. 763, s. 3; 1973, c. 745, s. 2; 1979, c. 832, s. 2; 1983, c. 691, s. 2; 1991, c. 469, s. 2;1991 (Reg. Sess., 1992), c. 837, s. 10; 1995, c. 191, s. 5;1999-228, s. 2

THE LEGISLATIVE POLICY BEHIND UNINSURED MOTORIST INSURANCE LAWS is not to divide liability among insurers or limit insurers' liability, but to protect the motorist to the extent the statute requires protection against a specific class of tortfeasors. Hamilton v. Travelers Indem. Co., 77 N.C. App. 318, 335 S.E.2d 228 (1985), cert. denied, 315 N.C. 587, 341 S.E.2d 25 (1986).

There is nothing in the legislative scheme suggesting that insured persons should have to concern themselves with the liability insurance limits of tortfeasors; in fact, the very purpose of uninsured motorist coverage is to ameliorate that concern. Hamilton v. Travelers Indem. Co., 77 N.C. App. 318, 335 S.E.2d 228 (1985), cert. denied, 315 N.C. 587, 341 S.E.2d 25 (1986).

EFFECT OF CHANGE IN UNINSURED MOTORIST COVERAGE BY 1979 AMENDMENT. --Motorists who contracted and paid premiums for uninsured motorist coverage after the effective date of the new limits provided in subsection (c) of this section by its 1979 amendment should receive coverage up to those higher limits. Hamilton v. Travelers Indem. Co., 77 N.C. App. 318, 335 S.E.2d 228 (1985), cert. denied, 315 N.C. 587, 341 S.E.2d 25 (1986).

Motorists with existing policies, including uninsured motorist coverage, at the level specified in subsection (c) of this section prior to its 1979 amendment could not claim up to the new limits if they were struck by an uninsured motorist; if those insureds, before their routinely scheduled policy renewal, desired more uninsured motorist coverage at the higher level, they could renew their policies early. In the interim, they would not be in violation of the Motor Vehicle Safety and Financial Responsibility Act because they retained their existing, lower-limit policies, nor would their insurers be forced to assume additional, uncontracted for liability. Hamilton v. Travelers Indem. Co., 77 N.C. App. 318, 335 S.E.2d 228 (1985), cert. denied, 315 N.C. 587, 341 S.E.2d 25 (1986).

"STACKING" OR AGGREGATING COVERAGES UNDER THE COMPULSORY UNINSURED MOTORIST COVERAGE REQUIREMENT may occur where coverage is provided by two or more policies, each providing the mandatory minimum coverage. However, to the extent that the coverage provided by motor vehicle liability insurance policies exceeds the mandatory minimum coverage required by the statute, the additional coverage is voluntary, and is governed by the terms of the insurance contract. GEICO v. Herndon, 79 N.C. App. 365, 339 S.E.2d 472 (1986).

THERE IS NO REQUIREMENT THAT ALL THOSE COVERED UNDER A POLICY BE INSURED AT IDENTICAL LEVELS OF COVERAGE; thus, as long as the minimum coverage requirements are met, no reason exists to prevent an insured from obtaining multi-tiered coverage for its employees. Hlasnick v. Federated Mut. Ins. Co., 136 N.C. App. 320, 524 S.E.2d 386 (2000), aff'd, in part, and cert. dismissed, in part, 353 N.C. 240, 539 S.E.2d 274 (2000).

THIS SECTION MAKES IT THE DUTY OF THE COMMISSIONER TO SUSPEND THE DRIVER'S LICENSE if the owner-operator fails to discharge his liability for the damage resulting from the collision. Robinson v. United States Cas. Co., 260 N.C. 284, 132 S.E.2d 629 (1963).

MULTI-TIER UIM COVERAGE WAS UPHELD where the policy provided UIM coverage meeting the minimum statutory requirements of this section but the purchaser of the fleet policy paid additional premiums to provide higher limits of UIM coverage to certain persons insured in excess of the statutory floor. Hlasnick v. Federated Mut. Ins. Co., 353 N.C. 240, 539 S.E.2d 274 (2000).

ACT OF COMMISSIONER IN SUSPENDING A LICENSE IS QUASI-JUDICIAL. Robinson v. United States Cas. Co., 260 N.C. 284, 132 S.E.2d 629 (1963).

AND IT CANNOT BE COLLATERALLY ATTACKED. Robinson v. United States Cas. Co., 260 N.C. 284, 132 S.E.2d 629 (1963).

The driver of an automobile may not sue his insurer for damages resulting from the revocation of his driver's license resulting from the false representation of his insurer that the driver did not have insurance in force at the time he was involved in an accident, since such action amounts to a collateral attack upon the order of the Commissioner suspending the license and is based on subornation of perjury. Robinson v. United States Cas. Co., 260 N.C. 284, 132 S.E.2d 629 (1963).

PLAINTIFF IS ENTITLED TO HEARING ON FACTUAL QUESTION OF WHETHER HE WAS INSURED. Robinson v. United States Cas. Co., 260 N.C. 284, 132 S.E.2d 629 (1963).

The second sentence in subsection (b) of this section gives the owner-operator of the motor vehicle full opportunity to present his evidence to the Commissioner to establish the fact that he did carry insurance as required. Robinson v. United States Cas. Co., 260 N.C. 284, 132 S.E.2d 629 (1963).

ALLEGATIONS INSUFFICIENT TO AUTHORIZE POSTPONEMENT OF POSTING. --Where petitioner did not allege that he was probably not guilty of negligence or that the negligence of the other party was probably the sole proximate cause of the collision, nor did he allege that the amount of the security required was excessive or that such security was not required by the terms of the statute and there were no allegations which if proved would entitle the petitioner to any relief, and the only relief requested by the petitioner was that the court postpone the posting of the security required by the Commissioner under this section, neither the Commissioner nor the court had

the authority to grant this relief and a motion to dismiss was properly granted. Forrester v. Garrett, 280 N.C. 117, 184 S.E.2d 858 (1971).

APPLIED in Carter v. Scheidt, 261 N.C. 702, 136 S.E.2d 105 (1964); Carson v. Godwin, 269 N.C. 744, 153 S.E.2d 473 (1967); Moore v. Hartford Fire Ins. Co., 270 N.C. 532, 155 S.E.2d 128 (1967); Wilfong v. Wilkins, 70 N.C. App. 127, 318 S.E.2d 540 (1984).

CITED in Lichtenberger v. American Motorists Ins. Co., 7 N.C. App. 269, 172 S.E.2d 284 (1970); State v. Herald, 10 N.C. App. 263, 178 S.E.2d 120 (1970); Dildy v. Southeastern Fire Ins. Co., 13 N.C. App. 66, 185 S.E.2d 272 (1971); Cochran v. North Carolina Farm Bureau Mut. Ins. Co., 113 N.C. App. 260, 437 S.E.2d 910 (1994); Maryland Cas. Co. v. Smith, 117 N.C. App. 593, 452 S.E.2d 318 (1995); Progressive Am. Ins. Co. v. Vasquez, 129 N.C. App. 742, 502 S.E.2d 10 (1998), aff'd in part and rev'd in part and remanded on other grounds, 350 N.C. 386, 515 S.E.2d 8 (1999); Corbett v. Smith, 131 N.C. App. 327, 507 S.E.2d 303 (1998); Nationwide Prop. & Cas. Ins. Co. v. Martinson, 208 N.C. App. 104, 701 S.E.2d 390 (2010), review denied, 365 N.C. 84, 706 S.E.2d 256, 2011 N.C. LEXIS 190 (2011); Grimsley v. Gov't Emples. Ins. Co., 217 N.C. App. 530, 721 S.E.2d 706 (2011), review denied 365 N.C. 552, 724 S.E.2d 505, 2012 N.C. LEXIS 189 (N.C. 2012); Unitrin Auto & Home Ins. Co. v. Rikard, 217 N.C. App. 393, 722 S.E.2d 510 (2011).

CROSS REFERENCES. --
For provision requiring forms to carry statement concerning perjury, see G.S. 20-279.7A.

LEGAL PERIODICALS. --
For 1984 survey, "Employee Exclusion Clauses in Automobile Liability Insurance Policies," see 63 N.C.L. Rev. 1228 (1985).
For note, "Underinsured Motorist Coverage: North Carolina's Multiple Claimant Wrinkle -- Ray v. Atlantic Casualty Insurance Co.," see 17 Campbell L. Rev. 147 (1995).

§ 20-279.6. Further exceptions to requirement of security

The requirements as to security and suspension in G.S. 20-279.5 shall not apply:

(1) To the operator or the owner of a motor vehicle involved in an accident wherein no injury or damage was caused to the person or property of anyone other than such operator or owner;

(2) To the operator or the owner of a motor vehicle legally parked at the time of the accident;

(3) To the owner of a motor vehicle if at the time of the accident the vehicle was being operated without his permission, express or implied, or was parked by a person who had been operating such motor vehicle without such permission;

(4) If, prior to the date that the Commissioner would otherwise suspend the license or the nonresident's operating privilege under G.S. 20-279.5, there shall be filed with the

Commissioner evidence satisfactory to him that the person who would otherwise have to file security has been released from liability or been finally adjudicated not to be liable or has executed a duly acknowledged written agreement providing for the payment of an agreed amount, in installments or otherwise, with respect to all claims for injuries or damages resulting from the accident;

(5) If, prior to the date that the Commissioner would otherwise suspend the license or the nonresident's operating privilege under G.S. 20-279.5, there shall be filed with the Commissioner evidence satisfactory to him that the person who would otherwise be required to file security has in any manner settled the claims of the other persons involved in the accident and if the Commissioner determines that, considering the circumstances of the accident and the settlement, the purposes of this Article and of protection of operators and owners of other motor vehicles are best accomplished by not requiring the posting of security or the suspension of the license. For the purpose of administering this subdivision, the Commissioner may consider a settlement made by an insurance company as the equivalent of a settlement made directly by the insured; nor

(6) If, prior to the date that the Commissioner would otherwise suspend the license or the nonresident's operating privilege under G.S. 20-279.5, there shall be filed with the Commissioner evidence satisfactory to him that another person involved in the accident has been convicted by a court of competent jurisdiction of a crime involving the operation of a motor vehicle at the time of the accident, and if the Commissioner in his discretion determines, after considering the circumstances of the accident or the nature and the circumstances of the crime, that the purpose of this Article and of protection of operators and owners of other motor vehicles are best accomplished by not requiring the posting of security or the suspension of the license.

History.
1953, c. 1300, s. 6; 1955, c. 1152, ss. 9, 10

CROSS REFERENCES. --
For provision requiring forms to carry statement concerning perjury, see G.S. 20-279.7A.

LEGAL PERIODICALS. --
For 1984 survey, "Employee Exclusion Clauses in Automobile Liability Insurance Policies," see 63 N.C.L. Rev. 1228 (1985).

§ 20-279.6A. Minors

In determining whether or not any of the exceptions set forth in G.S. 20-279.6 have been satisfied, in the case of accidents involving minors, the Commissioner may accept, for the purpose of this Article only, as valid releases on account of claims for injuries to minors or damage to the property of minors releases which have been executed by the parent of the minor having custody of the minor or by the guardian of the minor if there be one. In the case of an emancipated minor, the Commissioner may accept a release signed by or a settlement agreed upon by the minor without the approval of the parents of the minor. If in the opinion of the Commissioner the circumstances of the accident, the nature and extent of the injuries or damage, or any other circumstances make it advisable for the best protection of the interest of the minor, the Commissioner may decline to accept such releases or settlements and may require the approval of the superior court.

History.
1955, c. 1152, s. 11

§ 20-279.7. Duration of suspension

The license and nonresident's operating privilege suspended as provided in G.S. 20-279.5 shall remain so suspended and shall not be renewed nor shall any such license be issued to such person until:

(1) Such person shall deposit or there shall be deposited on his behalf the security required under G.S. 20-279.5;

(2) One year shall have elapsed following the date of such suspension and evidence satisfactory to the Commissioner has been filed with him that during such period no action for damages arising out of the accident has been instituted; or

(3) Evidence satisfactory to the Commissioner has been filed with him of a release from liability, or a final adjudication of nonliability, or a duly acknowledged written agreement, in accordance with subdivision (4) of G.S. 20-279.6 or a settlement accepted by the Commissioner as provided in subdivision (5) of G.S. 20-279.6, or a conviction accepted by the Commissioner as provided in subdivision (6) of G.S. 20-279.6; provided, if there is a default in the payment of any installment or sum under a duly acknowledged written agreement, the Commissioner shall, upon notice of the default, immediately suspend the license or nonresident's operating privilege of the defaulting person and may not restore it until:

a. That person deposits and thereafter maintains security as required under G.S. 20-279.5 in an amount determined by the Commissioner; or

b. That person files evidence satisfactory to the Commissioner of a new duly acknowledged written agreement or a settlement.

History.

1953, c. 1300, s. 7; 1955, c. 1152, s. 12; 1983, c. 610, s. 1 APPLIED in Forrester v. Garrett, 280 N.C. 117, 184 S.E.2d 858 (1971).

CROSS REFERENCES. --

For provision requiring forms to carry statement concerning perjury, see G.S. 20-279.7A.

§ 20-279.7A. Forms to carry statement concerning perjury

A person who makes a false affidavit or falsely sworn or affirmed statement concerning information required to be submitted under this Article commits a Class I felony. The Division shall include a statement of this offense on a form that it provides under this Article and that must be completed under oath.

History.

1983, c. 610, s. 3; 1993 (Reg. Sess., 1994), c. 761, s. 26

§ 20-279.8. Application to nonresidents, unlicensed drivers, unregistered motor vehicles and accidents in other states

(a) In case the operator or the owner of a motor vehicle involved in an accident within this State has no license, or is a nonresident, he shall not be allowed a license until he has complied with the requirements of this Article to the same extent that it would be necessary if, at the time of the accident, he had held a license.

(b) When a nonresident's operating privilege is suspended pursuant to G.S. 20-279.5 or 20-279.7, the Commissioner shall transmit a certified copy of the record of such action to the official in charge of the issuance of licenses in the state in which such nonresident resides, if the law of such other state provides for action in relation thereto similar to that provided for in subsection (c) of this section.

(c) Upon receipt of such certification that the operating privilege of a resident of this State has been suspended or revoked in any such other state pursuant to a law providing for its suspension or revocation for failure to deposit security for the payment of judgments arising out of a motor vehicle accident, under circumstances which would require the Commissioner to suspend a nonresident's operating privilege had the accident occurred in this State the Commissioner shall suspend the license of such resident. Such suspension shall continue until such resident furnishes evidence of his compliance with the law of such other state relating to the deposit of such security.

History.

1953, c. 1300, s. 8

§ 20-279.9. Form and amount of security

The security required under this Article shall be in such form and in such amount as the Commissioner may require but in no case in excess of the limits specified in G.S. 20-279.5 in reference to the acceptable limits of a policy or bond. The person depositing security shall specify in writing the person or persons on whose behalf the deposit is made and, at any time while such deposit is in the custody of the Commissioner or State Treasurer, the person depositing it may, in writing, amend the specification of the person or persons on whose behalf the deposit is made to include an additional person or persons; provided, however, that a single deposit of security shall be applicable only on behalf of persons required to furnish security because of the same accident.

The Commissioner may reduce the amount of security ordered in any case if, in his judgment, the amount ordered is excessive. In case the security originally ordered has been deposited the excess deposited over the reduced amount ordered shall be returned to the depositor or his personal representative forthwith, notwithstanding the provisions of G.S. 20-279.10.

History.

1953, c. 1300, s. 9

§ 20-279.10. Custody, disposition and return of security; escheat

(a) Security deposited in compliance with the requirements of this Article shall be placed by the Commissioner in the custody of the State Treasurer and shall be applicable only to the payment of a judgment or judgments rendered against the person or persons on whose behalf the deposit was made, for damages arising out of the accident in question in an action at law, begun not later than one year after the date of such accident, or within one year after the date of deposit of any security under subdivision (3) of G.S. 20-279.7, or to the payment in settlement, agreed to by the depositor, of a claim or claims arising out of such accident. Such deposit or any balance thereof shall be returned to the depositor or his personal representative when evidence satisfactory to the Commissioner has been filed with him that there has been a release from liability, or a final adjudication of nonliability, or a duly acknowledged agreement, in accordance with subdivision (4) of G.S. 20-279.6, or a settlement accepted by the Commissioner as provided in subdivision (5) of G.S. 20-279.6, or a conviction accepted by the Commissioner as provided in subdivision (6) of G.S. 20-279.6, or whenever, after the expiration of one year from the date of the accident, or from the date of deposit of any security under subdivision (3) of G.S. 20-279.7, whichever is later, the Commissioner shall be given reasonable evidence that there is no such action pending and no judgment rendered in such action left unpaid.

(b) One year from the deposit of any security under the terms of this Article, the Commissioner shall notify the depositor thereof by registered mail addressed to his last known address that the depositor is entitled to a refund of the security upon giving reasonable evidence that no action at law for damages arising out of the accident in question is pending or that no judgment rendered in any such action remains unpaid. If, at the end of three years from the date of deposit, no claim therefor has been received, the Division shall notify the depositor thereof by registered mail and shall cause a notice to be posted at the courthouse door of the county in which is located the last known address of the depositor for a period of 60 days. Such notice shall contain the name of the depositor, his last known address, the date, amount and nature of the deposit, and shall state the conditions under which the deposit will be refunded. If, at the end of two years from the date of posting of such notice, no claim for the deposit has been received, the Commissioner shall certify such fact together with the facts of notice to the State Treasurer. These deposits shall be turned over to the Escheat Fund of the Department of State Treasurer.

History.
1953, c. 1300, s. 10; 1955, c. 1152, s. 13; 1967, c. 1227; 1975, c. 716, s. 5; 1981, c. 531, s. 16

§ 20-279.11. Matters not to be evidence in civil suits

Neither the information on financial responsibility contained in an accident report, the action taken by the Commissioner pursuant to this Article, the findings, if any, of the Commissioner upon which the action is based, or the security filed as provided in this Article shall be referred to in any way, nor be any evidence of the negligence or due care of either party, at the trial of any action at law to recover damages.

History.
1953, c. 1300, s. 11; 1995, c. 191, s. 6

§ 20-279.12. Courts to report nonpayment of judgments

Whenever any person fails within 60 days to satisfy any judgment, upon the written request of the judgment creditor or his attorney it shall be the duty of the clerk of the court, or of the judge of a court which has no clerk, in which any such judgment is rendered within this State, to forward to the Commissioner immediately after the expiration of said 60 days, a certified copy of such judgment.

If the defendant named in any certified copy of a judgment reported to the Commissioner is a nonresident, the Commissioner shall transmit a certified copy of the judgment to the official in charge of the issuance of licenses and registration certificates of the state of which the defendant is a resident.

History.
1953, c. 1300, s. 12

§ 20-279.13. Suspension for nonpayment of judgment; exceptions

(a) The Commissioner, upon the receipt of a certified copy of a judgment, which has remained unsatisfied for a period of 60 days, shall forthwith suspend the license and any nonresident's operating privilege of any person against whom such judgment was rendered, except as hereinafter otherwise provided in this section and in G.S. 20-279.16.

(b) The Commissioner shall not, however, revoke or suspend the license of an owner or driver if the insurance carried by him was in a company which was authorized to transact business in this State and which subsequent to an accident involving the owner or operator and prior to settlement of the claim therefor went into liquidation, so that the owner or driver is thereby unable to satisfy the judgment arising out of the accident.

(c) If the judgment creditor consents in writing, in such form as the Commissioner may prescribe, that the judgment debtor be allowed license or nonresident's operating privilege, the same may be allowed by the Commissioner, in his discretion, for six months from the date of such consent and thereafter until such consent is revoked in writing notwithstanding default in the payment of such judgment, or of any installments thereof prescribed in G.S. 20-279.16.

History.
1953, c. 1300, s. 13; 1965, c. 926, s. 1; 1969, c. 186, s. 4; 1979, c. 667, s. 37

A STATUTE AS FREE FROM AMBIGUITY AS THIS SECTION REQUIRES NO CONSTRUCTION, only adherence. Wilfong v. Wilkins, 70 N.C. App. 127, 318 S.E.2d 540, cert. denied, 312 N.C. 498, 322 S.E.2d 566 (1984).

CITED in Hunnicutt v. Shelby Mut. Ins. Co., 255 N.C. 515, 122 S.E.2d 74 (1961); Lupo v. Powell, 44 N.C. App. 35, 259 S.E.2d 777 (1979).

OPINIONS OF THE ATTORNEY GENERAL

APPLICABILITY OF SUBSECTION (A). --The mandatory provisions of subsection (a) are not applicable to unsatisfied judgments based on debt and/or conversion of a motor vehicle and damages resulting therefrom. Opinion of Attorney General to Mr. Charles Hensley, 44 N.C.A.G. 250 (1975).

Chapter 20

SATISFACTION OF JUDGMENT BY JOINT TORT-FEASOR MAY NOT SATISFY JUDGMENT FOR OTHER TORT-FEASOR FOR DRIVER LICENSE SUSPENSION PURPOSES. --See opinion of Attorney General to Mr. Donald N. Freeman, Supervisor, Department of Motor Vehicles, 41 N.C.A.G. 99 (1970).

SECOND JUDGMENT UPON EXPIRATION OF TEN YEARS AFTER FIRST JUDGMENT NOT GROUNDS FOR CONTINUED SUSPENSION OF LICENSE. --See opinion of Attorney General to Mr. Donald N. Freeman, Supervisor, Department of Motor Vehicles, 40 N.C.A.G. 99 (1970).

§ 20-279.14. Suspension to continue until judgments satisfied

Such license and nonresident's operating privilege shall remain so suspended and shall not be renewed, nor shall any such license be thereafter issued in the name of such person, including any such person not previously licensed, unless and until every such judgment:

(1) Is stayed, or

(2) Is satisfied in full, or

(3) Is subject to the exemptions stated in G.S. 20-279.13 or G.S. 20-279.16, or

(4) Is barred from enforcement by the statute of limitations pursuant to G.S. 1-47,

(5) Is discharged in bankruptcy.

History.
1953, c. 1300, s. 14; 1969, c. 186, s. 5; 1975, c. 301
EFFECT OF G.S. 20-279.36. --This section shall not apply with respect to any accident or judgment arising therefrom, or violation of the motor vehicle laws of this State, occurring prior to the effective date of this section, under the provisions of G.S. 20-279.36. Justice v. Scheidt, 252 N.C. 361, 113 S.E.2d 709 (1960).
OPINIONS OF THE ATTORNEY GENERAL
SATISFACTION OF JUDGMENT BY JOINT TORT-FEASOR MAY NOT SATISFY JUDGMENT FOR OTHER TORT-FEASOR FOR DRIVER LICENSE SUSPENSION PURPOSES. --See opinion of Attorney General to Mr. Freeman, Department of Motor Vehicles, 40 N.C.A.G. 99 (1970).

§ 20-279.15. Payment sufficient to satisfy requirements

In addition to other methods of satisfaction provided by law, judgments herein referred to shall, for the purpose of this Article, be deemed satisfied:

(1) When thirty thousand dollars ($ 30,000) has been credited upon any judgment or judgments rendered in excess of that amount because of bodily injury to or death of one person as the result of any one accident; or

(2) When, subject to such limit of thirty thousand dollars ($ 30,000) because of bodily injury to or death of one person, the sum of sixty thousand dollars ($ 60,000) has been credited upon any judgment or judgments rendered in excess of that amount because of bodily injury to or death of two or more persons as the result of any one accident; or

(3) When twenty-five thousand dollars ($ 25,000) has been credited upon any judgment or judgments rendered in excess of that amount because of injury to or destruction of property of others as a result of any one accident;

Provided, however, payments made in settlement of any claims because of bodily injury, death or property damage arising from a motor vehicle accident shall be credited in reduction of the amounts provided for in this section.

History.
1953, c. 1300, s. 15; 1963, c. 1238; 1967, c. 277, s. 3; 1973, c. 745, s. 3; c. 889; 1979, c. 832, ss. 3-5; 1991, c. 469, s. 3;1991 (Reg. Sess., 1992), c. 837, s. 10; 1999-228, s. 3

COVERAGE EXTENDS TO PROPERTY DAMAGE AS WELL AS PERSONAL INJURIES. --Under subdivision (3) of this section, coverage within this Article extends to property damage as well as to personal damages occurring to the victim of an accident. Nationwide Mut. Ins. Co. v. Knight, 34 N.C. App. 96, 237 S.E.2d 341, cert. denied, 293 N.C. 589, 239 S.E.2d 263 (1977).

PROPERTY DAMAGE FROM INTENTIONAL RAMMING OF DEFENDANT'S CAR. --An automobile insurer was required to compensate defendant for any property damage arising out of the intentional ramming of defendant's automobile by the insured. Nationwide Mut. Ins. Co. v. Knight, 34 N.C. App. 96, 237 S.E.2d 341, cert. denied, 293 N.C. 589, 239 S.E.2d 263 (1977).

APPLIED in Wilfong v. Wilkins, 70 N.C. App. 127, 318 S.E.2d 540 (1984).

§ 20-279.16. Installment payment of judgments; default

(a) A judgment debtor upon due notice to the judgment creditor may apply to the court in which such judgment was rendered for the privilege of paying such judgment in installments and the court, in its discretion and without prejudice to any other legal remedies which the judgment creditor may have, may so order and fix the amounts and times of payment of the installments.

(b) The Commissioner shall not suspend a license or a nonresident's operating privilege, and shall restore any license or nonresident's operating privilege suspended following nonpayment of a judgment, when the judgment debtor obtains such an order permitting the payment of such judgment in installments, and while the payment of any said installment is not in default.

(c) In the event the judgment debtor fails to pay any installment as specified by such order, then upon notice of such default, the

Commissioner shall forthwith suspend the license or nonresident's operating privilege of the judgment debtor until such judgment is satisfied, as provided in this Article.

History.

1953, c. 1300, s. 16; 1969, c. 186, s. 6

APPLIED in Wilfong v. Wilkins, 70 N.C. App. 127, 318 S.E.2d 540 (1984).

N.C. Gen. Stat. § 20-279.17

Repealed by Session Laws 1967, c. 866.

§ 20-279.18. Alternate methods of giving proof

Proof of financial responsibility when required under this Article with respect to a motor vehicle or with respect to a person who is not the owner of a motor vehicle may be given by filing:

(1) A certificate of insurance as provided in G.S. 20-279.19 or 20-279.20; or

(2) A bond as provided in G.S. 20-279.24; or

(3) A certificate of deposit of money or securities as provided in G.S. 20-279.25; or

(4) A certificate of self-insurance, as provided in G.S. 20-279.33, supplemented by an agreement by the self-insurer that, with respect to accidents occurring while the certificate is in force, he will pay the same judgments and in the same amounts that an insurer would have been obligated to pay under an owner's motor vehicle liability policy if it had issued such a policy to said self-insurer.

History.

1953, c. 1300, s. 18

CITED in Marks v. Thompson, 282 N.C. 174, 192 S.E.2d 311 (1972).

§ 20-279.19. Certificate of insurance as proof

Proof of financial responsibility may be furnished by filing with the Commissioner the written certificate of any insurance carrier duly authorized to do business in this State certifying that there is in effect a motor vehicle liability policy for the benefit of the person required to furnish proof of financial responsibility. Such certificate shall give the effective date of such motor vehicle liability policy, which date shall be the same as the effective date of the certificate, and shall designate by explicit description or by appropriate reference all motor vehicles covered thereby, unless the policy is issued to a person who is not the owner of a motor vehicle. The Commissioner may require that certificates filed pursuant to this section be on a form approved by the Commissioner.

History.

1953, c. 1300, s. 19; 1955, c. 1152, s. 16

FILING DOES NOT ESTOP INSURER FROM DENYING COVERAGE. --The filing, as required by this section, does not estop an insurance carrier from thereafter denying coverage under the policy. Seaford v. Nationwide Mut. Ins. Co., 253 N.C. 719, 117 S.E.2d 733 (1961).

CITED in Faizan v. Grain Dealers Mut. Ins. Co., 254 N.C. 47, 118 S.E.2d 303 (1961); Harrelson v. State Farm Mut. Auto. Ins. Co., 272 N.C. 603, 158 S.E.2d 812 (1968); Nationwide Mut. Ins. Co. v. Aetna Life & Cas. Co., 283 N.C. 87, 194 S.E.2d 834 (1973); Bailey v. Nationwide Mut. Ins. Co., 19 N.C. App. 168, 198 S.E.2d 246 (1973).

§ 20-279.20. Certificate furnished by nonresident as proof

(a) The nonresident owner of a motor vehicle not registered in this State may give proof of financial responsibility by filing with the Commissioner a written certificate or certificates of an insurance carrier authorized to transact business in the state in which the motor vehicle or motor vehicles described in such certificate is registered, or if such nonresident does not own a motor vehicle, then in the state in which the insured resides, provided such certificate otherwise conforms to the provisions of this Article, and the Commissioner shall accept the same upon condition that said insurance carrier complies with the following provisions with respect to the policies so certified:

(1) Said insurance carrier shall execute a power of attorney authorizing the Commissioner to accept service on its behalf of notice or process in any action arising out of a motor vehicle accident in this State; and

(2) Said insurance carrier shall agree in writing that such policies shall be deemed to conform with the laws of this State relating to the terms of motor vehicle liability policies issued herein.

(b) If any insurance carrier not authorized to transact business in this State, which has qualified to furnish proof of financial responsibility, defaults in any said undertakings or agreements, the Commissioner shall not thereafter accept as proof any certificate of said carrier whether theretofore filed or thereafter tendered as proof, so long as such default continues.

(c) The Commissioner may require that certificates and powers filed pursuant to this section be on forms approved by the Commissioner.

History.

1953, c. 1300, s. 20; 1955, c. 1152, s. 17

Chapter 20

CITED in Faizan v. Grain Dealers Mut. Ins. Co., 254 N.C. 47, 118 S.E.2d 303 (1961); Bailey v. Nationwide Mut. Ins. Co., 19 N.C. App. 168, 198 S.E.2d 246 (1973); Fortune Ins. Co. v. Owens, 351 N.C. 424, 526 S.E.2d 463 (2000).

§ 20-279.21. "Motor vehicle liability policy" defined

(a) A "motor vehicle liability policy" as said term is used in this Article shall mean an owner's or an operator's policy of liability insurance, certified as provided in G.S. 20-279.19 or 20-279.20 as proof of financial responsibility, and issued, except as otherwise provided in G.S. 20-279.20, by an insurance carrier duly authorized to transact business in this State, to or for the benefit of the person named therein as insured.

(b) Except as provided in G.S. 20-309(a2), such owner's policy of liability insurance:

(1) Shall designate by explicit description or by appropriate reference all motor vehicles with respect to which coverage is thereby to be granted;

(2) Shall insure the person named therein and any other person, as insured, using any such motor vehicle or motor vehicles with the express or implied permission of such named insured, or any other persons in lawful possession, against loss from the liability imposed by law for damages arising out of the ownership, maintenance or use of such motor vehicle or motor vehicles within the United States of America or the Dominion of Canada subject to limits exclusive of interest and costs, with respect to each such motor vehicle, as follows: thirty thousand dollars ($ 30,000) because of bodily injury to or death of one person in any one accident and, subject to said limit for one person, sixty thousand dollars ($ 60,000) because of bodily injury to or death of two or more persons in any one accident, and twenty-five thousand dollars ($ 25,000) because of injury to or destruction of property of others in any one accident; and

(3) No policy of bodily injury liability insurance, covering liability arising out of the ownership, maintenance, or use of any motor vehicle, shall be delivered or issued for delivery in this State with respect to any motor vehicle registered or principally garaged in this State unless coverage is provided therein or supplemental thereto, under provisions filed with and approved by the Commissioner of Insurance, for the protection of persons insured thereunder who are legally entitled to recover damages from owners or operators of uninsured motor vehicles and hit-and-run motor vehicles because of bodily injury, sickness or disease, including death, resulting therefrom.

The limits of such uninsured motorist bodily injury coverage shall be equal to the highest limits of bodily injury liability coverage for any one vehicle insured under the policy; provided, however, that (i) the limits shall not exceed one million dollars ($ 1,000,000) per person and one million dollars ($ 1,000,000) per accident regardless of whether the highest limits of bodily injury liability coverage for any one vehicle insured under the policy exceed those limits and (ii) a named insured may purchase greater or lesser limits, except that the limits shall not be less than the bodily injury liability limits required pursuant to subdivision (2) of this subsection, and in no event shall an insurer be required by this subdivision to sell uninsured motorist bodily injury coverage at limits that exceed one million dollars ($ 1,000,000) per person and one million dollars ($ 1,000,000) per accident. When the policy is issued and renewed, the insurer shall notify the named insured as provided in subsection (m) of this section. The provisions shall include coverage for the protection of persons insured under the policy who are legally entitled to recover damages from owners or operators of uninsured motor vehicles because of injury to or destruction of the property of such insured. The limits of such uninsured motorist property damage coverage shall be equal to the highest limits of property damage liability coverage for any one vehicle insured under the policy; provided, however, that (i) the limits shall not exceed one million dollars ($ 1,000,000) per accident regardless of whether the highest limits of property damage liability coverage for any one vehicle insured under the policy exceed those limits and (ii) a named insured may purchase lesser limits, except that the limits shall not be less than the property damage liability limits required pursuant to subdivision (2) of this subsection. When the policy is issued and renewed, the insurer shall notify the named insured as provided in subsection (m) of this section. For uninsured motorist property damage coverage, the limits purchased by the named insured shall be subject, for each insured, to an exclusion of the first one hundred dollars ($ 100.00) of such damages. The provision shall further provide that a written statement by the liability insurer, whose name appears on the certification of financial responsibility made by the owner of any vehicle involved in an accident with the insured, that the other motor vehicle was not covered by insurance at the time of the accident with the insured shall operate as a prima facie presumption that the operator of the other motor vehicle was uninsured at the time of the accident with the insured for the purposes of recovery under this provision of the insured's liability insurance policy.

If a person who is legally entitled to recover damages from the owner or operator of an uninsured motor vehicle is an insured under the uninsured motorist coverage of a policy that insures more than one motor vehicle, that person shall not be permitted to combine the uninsured motorist limit applicable to any one motor vehicle with the uninsured motorist limit applicable to any other motor vehicle to determine the total amount of uninsured motorist coverage available to that person. If a person who is legally entitled to recover damages from the owner or operator of an uninsured motor vehicle is an insured under the uninsured motorist coverage of more than one policy, that person may combine the highest applicable uninsured motorist limit available under each policy to determine the total amount of uninsured motorist coverage available to that person. The previous sentence shall apply only to insurance on nonfleet private passenger motor vehicles as described in G.S. 58-40-10(1) and (2).

In addition to the above requirements relating to uninsured motorist insurance, every policy of bodily injury liability insurance covering liability arising out of the ownership, maintenance or use of any motor vehicle, which policy is delivered or issued for delivery in this State, shall be subject to the following provisions which need not be contained therein.

a. A provision that the insurer shall be bound by a final judgment taken by the insured against an uninsured motorist if the insurer has been served with copy of summons, complaint or other process in the action against the uninsured motorist by registered or certified mail, return receipt requested, or in any manner provided by law; provided however, that the determination of whether a motorist is uninsured may be decided only by an action against the insurer alone. The insurer, upon being served as herein provided, shall be a party to the action between the insured and the uninsured motorist though not named in the caption of the pleadings and may defend the suit in the name of the uninsured motorist or in its own name. The insurer, upon being served with copy of summons, complaint or other pleading, shall have the time allowed by statute in which to answer, demur

or otherwise plead (whether the pleading is verified or not) to the summons, complaint or other process served upon it. The consent of the insurer shall not be required for the initiation of suit by the insured against the uninsured motorist: Provided, however, no action shall be initiated by the insured until 60 days following the posting of notice to the insurer at the address shown on the policy or after personal delivery of the notice to the insurer or its agent setting forth the belief of the insured that the prospective defendant or defendants are uninsured motorists. No default judgment shall be entered when the insurer has timely filed an answer or other pleading as required by law. The failure to post notice to the insurer 60 days in advance of the initiation of suit shall not be grounds for dismissal of the action, but shall automatically extend the time for the filing of an answer or other pleadings to 60 days after the time of service of the summons, complaint, or other process on the insurer.

b. Where the insured, under the uninsured motorist coverage, claims that he has sustained bodily injury as the result of collision between motor vehicles and asserts that the identity of the operator or owner of a vehicle (other than a vehicle in which the insured is a passenger) cannot be ascertained, the insured may institute an action directly against the insurer: Provided, in that event, the insured, or someone in his behalf, shall report the accident within 24 hours or as soon thereafter as may be practicable, to a police officer, peace officer, other judicial officer, or to the Commissioner of Motor Vehicles. The insured shall also within a reasonable time give notice to the insurer of his injury, the extent thereof, and shall set forth in the notice the time, date and place of the injury. Thereafter, on forms to be mailed by the insurer within 15 days following receipt of the notice of the accident to the insurer, the insured shall furnish to insurer any further reasonable information concerning the accident and the injury that the insurer requests. If the forms are not furnished within 15 days, the insured is deemed to have complied with the requirements for furnishing information to the insurer. Suit may not be instituted against the insurer in less than 60 days from the posting of the first notice of the injury or accident to the insurer at the address shown on the policy or after personal delivery of the notice to the insurer or its agent. The failure to post notice to the insurer 60 days before the initiation of the suit shall not be grounds for dismissal of the action, but shall automatically extend the time for filing of an answer or other pleadings to 60 days after the time of service of the summons, complaint, or other process on the insurer.

Provided under this section the term "uninsured motor vehicle" shall include, but not be limited to, an insured motor vehicle where the liability insurer thereof is unable to make payment with respect to the legal liability within the limits specified therein because of insolvency.

An insurer's insolvency protection shall be applicable only to accidents occurring during a policy period in which its insured's uninsured motorist coverage is in effect where the liability insurer of the tort-feasor becomes insolvent within three years after such an accident. Nothing herein shall be construed to prevent any insurer from affording insolvency protection under terms and conditions more favorable to the insured than is provided herein.

In the event of payment to any person under the coverage required by this section and subject to the terms and conditions of coverage, the insurer making payment shall, to the extent thereof, be entitled to the proceeds of any settlement for judgment resulting from the exercise of any limits of recovery of that person against any person or organization legally responsible for the bodily injury for which the payment is made, including the proceeds recoverable from the assets of the insolvent insurer.

For the purpose of this section, an "uninsured motor vehicle" shall be a motor vehicle as to which there is no bodily injury liability insurance and property damage liability insurance in at least the amounts specified in subsection (c) of G.S. 20-279.5, or there is that insurance but the insurance company writing the insurance denies coverage thereunder, or has become bankrupt, or there is no bond or deposit of money or securities as provided in G.S. 20-279.24 or 20-279.25 in lieu of the bodily injury and property damage liability insurance, or the owner of the motor vehicle has not qualified as a self-insurer under the provisions of G.S. 20-279.33, or a vehicle that is not subject to the provisions of the Motor Vehicle Safety and Financial Responsibility Act; but the term "uninsured motor vehicle" shall not include:

a. A motor vehicle owned by the named insured;

b. A motor vehicle that is owned or operated by a self-insurer within the meaning of any motor vehicle financial responsibility law, motor carrier law or any similar law;

c. A motor vehicle that is owned by the United States of America, Canada, a state, or any agency of any of the foregoing (excluding, however, political subdivisions thereof);

d. A land motor vehicle or trailer, if operated on rails or crawler-treads or while located for use as a residence or premises and not as a vehicle; or

e. A farm-type tractor or equipment designed for use principally off public roads, except while actually upon public roads.

For purposes of this section "persons insured" means the named insured and, while resident of the same household, the spouse of any named insured and relatives of either, while in a motor vehicle or otherwise, and any person who uses with the consent, expressed or implied, of the named insured, the motor vehicle to which the policy applies and a guest in the motor vehicle to which the policy applies or the personal representative of any of the above or any other person or persons in lawful possession of the motor vehicle.

Notwithstanding the provisions of this subsection, no policy of motor vehicle liability insurance applicable solely to commercial motor vehicles as defined in G.S. 20-4.01(3d) or applicable solely to fleet vehicles shall be required to provide uninsured motorist coverage. When determining whether a policy is applicable solely to fleet vehicles, the insurer may rely upon the number of vehicles reported by the insured at the time of the issuance of the policy for the policy term in question. In the event of a renewal of the policy, when determining whether a policy is applicable solely to fleet vehicles, the insurer may rely upon the number of vehicles reported by the insured at the time of the renewal of the policy for the policy term in question. Any motor vehicle liability policy that insures both commercial motor vehicles as defined in G.S. 20-4.01(3d) and noncommercial motor vehicles shall provide uninsured motorist coverage in accordance with the provisions of this subsection in amounts equal to the highest limits of bodily injury and property damage liability coverage for any one noncommercial motor vehicle insured under the policy, subject to the right of the insured to purchase greater or lesser uninsured motorist bodily injury coverage limits and lesser uninsured motorist property damage coverage limits as set forth in this subsection. For the purpose of the immediately preceding sentence, noncommercial motor vehicle shall mean any motor vehicle that is not a commercial motor vehicle as defined in G.S. 20-4.01(3d), but that is otherwise subject to the requirements of this subsection.

(4) Shall, in addition to the coverages set forth in subdivisions (2) and (3) of this subsection, provide underinsured motorist coverage, to be used only with a policy that is written at limits that exceed those prescribed by subdivision (2) of this subsection. The limits of such underinsured motorist bodily injury coverage shall be equal to the highest limits of bodily injury liability coverage for any one vehicle insured under the policy; provided, however, that (i) the limits shall not exceed one million dollars ($ 1,000,000) per person and one million dollars ($ 1,000,000) per accident regardless of whether the highest limits of bodily injury liability coverage for any one vehicle insured under the policy exceed those limits, (ii) a named insured may purchase greater or lesser limits, except that the limits shall exceed the bodily injury liability limits required pursuant to subdivision (2) of this subsection, and in no event shall an insurer be required by this subdivision to sell underinsured motorist bodily injury coverage at limits that exceed one million dollars ($ 1,000,000) per person and one million dollars ($ 1,000,000) per accident, and (iii) the limits shall be equal to the limits of uninsured motorist bodily injury coverage purchased pursuant to subdivision (3) of

this subsection. When the policy is issued and renewed, the insurer shall notify the named insured as provided in subsection (m) of this section. An "uninsured motor vehicle," as described in subdivision (3) of this subsection, includes an "underinsured highway vehicle," which means a highway vehicle with respect to the ownership, maintenance, or use of which, the sum of the limits of liability under all bodily injury liability bonds and insurance policies applicable at the time of the accident is less than the applicable limits of underinsured motorist coverage for the vehicle involved in the accident and insured under the owner's policy. For purposes of an underinsured motorist claim asserted by a person injured in an accident where more than one person is injured, a highway vehicle will also be an "underinsured highway vehicle" if the total amount actually paid to that person under all bodily injury liability bonds and insurance policies applicable at the time of the accident is less than the applicable limits of underinsured motorist coverage for the vehicle involved in the accident and insured under the owner's policy. Notwithstanding the immediately preceding sentence, a highway vehicle shall not be an "underinsured motor vehicle" for purposes of an underinsured motorist claim under an owner's policy insuring that vehicle unless the owner's policy insuring that vehicle provides underinsured motorist coverage with limits that are greater than that policy's bodily injury liability limits. For the purposes of this subdivision, the term "highway vehicle" means a land motor vehicle or trailer other than (i) a farm-type tractor or other vehicle designed for use principally off public roads and while not upon public roads, (ii) a vehicle operated on rails or crawler-treads, or (iii) a vehicle while located for use as a residence or premises. The provisions of subdivision (3) of this subsection shall apply to the coverage required by this subdivision. Underinsured motorist coverage is deemed to apply when, by reason of payment of judgment or settlement, all liability bonds or insurance policies providing coverage for bodily injury caused by the ownership, maintenance, or use of the underinsured highway vehicle have been exhausted. Exhaustion of that liability coverage for the purpose of any single liability claim presented for underinsured motorist coverage is deemed to occur when either (a) the limits of liability per claim have been paid upon the claim, or (b) by reason of multiple claims, the aggregate per occurrence limit of liability has been paid. Underinsured motorist coverage

Chapter 20

is deemed to apply to the first dollar of an underinsured motorist coverage claim beyond amounts paid to the claimant under the exhausted liability policy.

In any event, the limit of underinsured motorist coverage applicable to any claim is determined to be the difference between the amount paid to the claimant under the exhausted liability policy or policies and the limit of underinsured motorist coverage applicable to the motor vehicle involved in the accident. Furthermore, if a claimant is an insured under the underinsured motorist coverage on separate or additional policies, the limit of underinsured motorist coverage applicable to the claimant is the difference between the amount paid to the claimant under the exhausted liability policy or policies and the total limits of the claimant's underinsured motorist coverages as determined by combining the highest limit available under each policy; provided that this sentence shall apply only to insurance on nonfleet private passenger motor vehicles as described in G.S. 58-40-15(9) and (10). The underinsured motorist limits applicable to any one motor vehicle under a policy shall not be combined with or added to the limits applicable to any other motor vehicle under that policy.

An underinsured motorist insurer may at its option, upon a claim pursuant to underinsured motorist coverage, pay moneys without there having first been an exhaustion of the liability insurance policy covering the ownership, use, and maintenance of the underinsured highway vehicle. In the event of payment, the underinsured motorist insurer shall be either: (a) entitled to receive by assignment from the claimant any right or (b) subrogated to the claimant's right regarding any claim the claimant has or had against the owner, operator, or maintainer of the underinsured highway vehicle, provided that the amount of the insurer's right by subrogation or assignment shall not exceed payments made to the claimant by the insurer. No insurer shall exercise any right of subrogation or any right to approve settlement with the original owner, operator, or maintainer of the underinsured highway vehicle under a policy providing coverage against an underinsured motorist where the insurer has been provided with written notice before a settlement between its insured and the underinsured motorist and the insurer fails to advance a payment to the insured in an amount equal to the tentative settlement within 30 days following receipt of that notice. Further, the insurer shall have the right, at its election, to pursue its claim by assignment or

subrogation in the name of the claimant, and the insurer shall not be denominated as a party in its own name except upon its own election. Assignment or subrogation as provided in this subdivision shall not, absent contrary agreement, operate to defeat the claimant's right to pursue recovery against the owner, operator, or maintainer of the underinsured highway vehicle for damages beyond those paid by the underinsured motorist insurer. The claimant and the underinsured motorist insurer may join their claims in a single suit without requiring that the insurer be named as a party. Any claimant who intends to pursue recovery against the owner, operator, or maintainer of the underinsured highway vehicle for moneys beyond those paid by the underinsured motorist insurer shall before doing so give notice to the insurer and give the insurer, at its expense, the opportunity to participate in the prosecution of the claim. Upon the entry of judgment in a suit upon any such claim in which the underinsured motorist insurer and claimant are joined, payment upon the judgment, unless otherwise agreed to, shall be applied pro rata to the claimant's claim beyond payment by the insurer of the owner, operator or maintainer of the underinsured highway vehicle and the claim of the underinsured motorist insurer.

A party injured by the operation of an underinsured highway vehicle who institutes a suit for the recovery of moneys for those injuries and in such an amount that, if recovered, would support a claim under underinsured motorist coverage shall give notice of the initiation of the suit to the underinsured motorist insurer as well as to the insurer providing primary liability coverage upon the underinsured highway vehicle. Upon receipt of notice, the underinsured motorist insurer shall have the right to appear in defense of the claim without being named as a party therein, and without being named as a party may participate in the suit as fully as if it were a party. The underinsured motorist insurer may elect, but may not be compelled, to appear in the action in its own name and present therein a claim against other parties; provided that application is made to and approved by a presiding superior court judge, in any such suit, any insurer providing primary liability insurance on the underinsured highway vehicle may upon payment of all of its applicable limits of liability be released from further liability or obligation to participate in the defense of such proceeding. However, before approving any such application, the court shall be persuaded that the owner, operator, or maintainer of the underinsured highway vehicle against whom a claim has been made has been apprised of the nature of the proceeding and given his right to select counsel of his own choice to appear in the action on his separate behalf. If an underinsured motorist insurer, following the approval of the application, pays in settlement or partial or total satisfaction of judgment moneys to the claimant, the insurer shall be subrogated to or entitled to an assignment of the claimant's rights against the owner, operator, or maintainer of the underinsured highway vehicle and, provided that adequate notice of right of independent representation was given to the owner, operator, or maintainer, a finding of liability or the award of damages shall be res judicata between the underinsured motorist insurer and the owner, operator, or maintainer of underinsured highway vehicle.

As consideration for payment of policy limits by a liability insurer on behalf of the owner, operator, or maintainer of an underinsured motor vehicle, a party injured by an underinsured motor vehicle may execute a contractual covenant not to enforce against the owner, operator, or maintainer of the vehicle any judgment that exceeds the policy limits. A covenant not to enforce judgment shall not preclude the injured party from pursuing available underinsured motorist benefits, unless the terms of the covenant expressly provide otherwise, and shall not preclude an insurer providing underinsured motorist coverage from pursuing any right of subrogation.

Notwithstanding the provisions of this subsection, no policy of motor vehicle liability insurance applicable solely to commercial motor vehicles as defined in G.S. 20-4.01(3d) or applicable solely to fleet vehicles shall be required to provide underinsured motorist coverage. When determining whether a policy is applicable solely to fleet vehicles, the insurer may rely upon the number of vehicles reported by the insured at the time of the issuance of the policy for the policy term in question. In the event of a renewal of the policy, when determining whether a policy is applicable solely to fleet vehicles, the insurer may rely upon the number of vehicles reported by the insured at the time of the renewal of the policy for the policy term in question. Any motor vehicle liability policy that insures both commercial motor vehicles as defined in G.S. 20-4.01(3d) and noncommercial motor vehicles shall provide underinsured motorist coverage in accordance with the provisions of this subsection in an amount equal to

the highest limits of bodily injury liability coverage for any one noncommercial motor vehicle insured under the policy, subject to the right of the insured to purchase greater or lesser underinsured motorist bodily injury liability coverage limits as set forth in this subsection. For the purpose of the immediately preceding sentence, noncommercial motor vehicle shall mean any motor vehicle that is not a commercial motor vehicle as defined in G.S. 20-4.01(3d), but that is otherwise subject to the requirements of this subsection.

(c) Such operator's policy of liability insurance shall insure the person named as insured therein against loss from the liability imposed upon him by law for damages arising out of the use by him of any motor vehicle not owned by him, and within 30 days following the date of its delivery to him of any motor vehicle owned by him, within the same territorial limits and subject to the same limits of liability as are set forth above with respect to an owner's policy of liability insurance.

(d) Such motor vehicle liability policy shall state the name and address of the named insured, the coverage afforded by the policy, the premium charged therefor, the policy period and the limits of liability, and shall contain an agreement or be endorsed that insurance is provided thereunder in accordance with the coverage defined in this Article as respects bodily injury and death or property damage, or both, and is subject to all the provisions of this Article.

(d1) Such motor vehicle liability policy shall provide an alternative method of determining the amount of property damage to a motor vehicle when liability for coverage for the claim is not in dispute. For a claim for property damage to a motor vehicle against an insurer, the policy shall provide that if:

(1) The claimant and the insurer fail to agree as to the difference in fair market value of the vehicle immediately before the accident and immediately after the accident; and

(2) The difference in the claimant's and the insurer's estimate of the diminution in fair market value is greater than two thousand dollars ($ 2,000) or twenty-five percent (25%) of the fair market retail value of the vehicle prior to the accident as determined by the latest edition of the National Automobile Dealers Association Pricing Guide Book or other publications approved by the Commissioner of Insurance, whichever is less, then on the written demand of either the claimant or the insurer, each shall select a competent and disinterested appraiser and notify the other of the appraiser selected within 20 days after the demand. The appraisers shall then appraise

the loss. Should the appraisers fail to agree, they shall then select a competent and disinterested appraiser to serve as an umpire. If the appraisers cannot agree upon an umpire within 15 days, either the claimant or the insurer may request that a magistrate resident in the county where the insured motor vehicle is registered or the county where the accident occurred select the umpire. The appraisers shall then submit their differences to the umpire. The umpire then shall prepare a report determining the amount of the loss and shall file the report with the insurer and the claimant. The agreement of the two appraisers or the report of the umpire, when filed with the insurer and the claimant, shall determine the amount of the damages. In preparing the report, the umpire shall not award damages that are higher or lower than the determinations of the appraisers. In no event shall appraisers or the umpire make any determination as to liability for damages or as to whether the policy provides coverage for claims asserted. The claimant or the insurer shall have 15 days from the filing of the report to reject the report and notify the other party of such rejection. If the report is not rejected within 15 days from the filing of the report, the report shall be binding upon both the claimant and the insurer. Each appraiser shall be paid by the party selecting the appraiser, and the expenses of appraisal and umpire shall be paid by the parties equally. For purposes of this section, "appraiser" and "umpire" shall mean a person licensed as a motor vehicle damage appraiser under G.S. 58-33-26 and G.S. 58-33-30 and who as a part of his or her regular employment is in the business of advising relative to the nature and amount of motor vehicle damage and the fair market value of damaged and undamaged motor vehicles.

(e) Uninsured or underinsured motorist coverage that is provided as part of a motor vehicle liability policy shall insure that portion of a loss uncompensated by any workers' compensation law and the amount of an employer's lien determined pursuant to G.S. 97-10.2(h) or (j). In no event shall this subsection be construed to require that coverage exceed the applicable uninsured or underinsured coverage limits of the motor vehicle policy or allow a recovery for damages already paid by workers' compensation. The policy need not insure a loss from any liability for damage to property owned by, rented to, in charge of or transported by the insured.

(f) Every motor vehicle liability policy shall be subject to the following provisions which need not be contained therein:

(1) Except as hereinafter provided, the liability of the insurance carrier with respect to the insurance required by this Article shall become absolute whenever injury or damage covered by said motor vehicle liability policy occurs; said policy may not be canceled or annulled as to such liability by any agreement between the insurance carrier and the insured after the occurrence of the injury or damage; no statement made by the insured or on his behalf and no violation of said policy shall defeat or void said policy. As to policies issued to insureds in this State under the assigned risk plan or through the North Carolina Motor Vehicle Reinsurance Facility, a default judgment taken against such an insured shall not be used as a basis for obtaining judgment against the insurer unless counsel for the plaintiff has forwarded to the insurer, or to one of its agents, by registered or certified mail with return receipt requested, or served by any other method of service provided by law, a copy of summons, complaint, or other pleadings, filed in the action. The return receipt shall, upon its return to plaintiff's counsel, be filed with the clerk of court wherein the action is pending against the insured and shall be admissible in evidence as proof of notice to the insurer. The refusal of insurer or its agent to accept delivery of the registered mail, as provided in this section, shall not affect the validity of such notice and any insurer or agent of an insurer refusing to accept such registered mail shall be charged with the knowledge of the contents of such notice. When notice has been sent to an agent of the insurer such notice shall be notice to the insurer. The word "agent" as used in this subsection shall include, but shall not be limited to, any person designated by the insurer as its agent for the service of process, any person duly licensed by the insurer in the State as insurance agent, any general agent of the company in the State of North Carolina, and any employee of the company in a managerial or other responsible position, or the North Carolina Commissioner of Insurance; provided, where the return receipt is signed by an employee of the insurer or an employee of an agent for the insurer, shall be deemed for the purposes of this subsection to have been received. The term "agent" as used in this subsection shall not include a producer of record or broker, who forwards an application for insurance to the North Carolina Motor Vehicle Reinsurance Facility.

The insurer, upon receipt of summons, complaint or other process, shall be entitled, upon its motion, to intervene in the suit against its insured as a party defendant and to defend the same in the name of its insured. In the event of such intervention by an insurer it shall become a named party defendant. The insurer shall have 30 days from the signing of the return receipt acknowledging receipt of the summons, complaint or other pleading in which to file a motion to intervene, along with any responsive pleading, whether verified or not, which it may deem necessary to protect its interest: Provided, the court having jurisdiction over the matter may, upon motion duly made, extend the time for the filing of responsive pleading or continue the trial of the matter for the purpose of affording the insurer a reasonable time in which to file responsive pleading or defend the action. If, after receiving copy of the summons, complaint or other pleading, the insurer elects not to defend the action, if coverage is in fact provided by the policy, the insurer shall be bound to the extent of its policy limits to the judgment taken by default against the insured, and noncooperation of the insured shall not be a defense.

If the plaintiff initiating an action against the insured has complied with the provisions of this subsection, then, in such event, the insurer may not cancel or annul the policy as to such liability and the defense of noncooperation shall not be available to the insurer: Provided, however, nothing in this section shall be construed as depriving an insurer of its defenses that the policy was not in force at the time in question, that the operator was not an "insured" under policy provisions, or that the policy had been lawfully canceled at the time of the accident giving rise to the cause of action.

Provided further that the provisions of this subdivision shall not apply when the insured has delivered a copy of the summons, complaint or other pleadings served on him to his insurance carrier within the time provided by law for filing answer, demurrer or other pleadings.

(2) The satisfaction by the insured of a judgment for such injury or damage shall not be a condition precedent to the right or duty of the insurance carrier to make payment on account of such injury or damage;

(3) The insurance carrier shall have the right to settle any claim covered by the policy, and if such settlement is made in good faith, the amount thereof shall be deductible from the limits of liability specified in subdivision (2) of subsection (b) of this section;

(4) The policy, the written application therefor, if any, and any rider or endorsement which does not conflict with the provisions of the Article shall constitute the entire contract between the parties.

(g) Any policy which grants the coverage required for a motor vehicle liability policy may also grant any lawful coverage in excess of or in addition to the coverage specified for a motor vehicle liability policy and such excess or additional coverage shall not be subject to the provisions of this Article. With respect to a policy which grants such excess or additional coverage the term "motor vehicle liability policy" shall apply only to that part of the coverage which is required by this section.

(h) Any motor vehicle liability policy may provide that the insured shall reimburse the insurance carrier for any payment the insurance carrier would not have been obligated to make under the terms of the policy except for the provisions of this Article.

(i) Any motor vehicle liability policy may provide for the prorating of the insurance thereunder with other valid and collectible insurance.

(j) The requirements for a motor vehicle liability policy may be fulfilled by the policies of one or more insurance carriers which policies together meet such requirements.

(k) Any binder issued pending the issuance of a motor vehicle liability policy shall be deemed to fulfill the requirements for such a policy.

(l) A party injured by an uninsured motor vehicle covered under a policy in amounts less than those set forth in G.S. 20-279.5, may execute a contractual covenant not to enforce against the owner, operator, or maintainer of the uninsured vehicle any judgment that exceeds the liability policy limits, as consideration for payment of any applicable policy limits by the insurer where judgment exceeds the policy limits. A covenant not to enforce judgment shall not preclude the injured party from pursuing available uninsured motorist benefits, unless the terms of the covenant expressly provide otherwise, and shall not preclude an insurer providing uninsured motorist coverage from pursuing any right of subrogation.

(m) Every insurer that sells motor vehicle liability policies subject to the requirements of subdivisions (b)(3) and (b)(4) of this section shall, when issuing and renewing a policy, give reasonable notice to the named insured of all of the following:

(1) The named insured is required to purchase uninsured motorist bodily injury coverage, uninsured motorist property damage coverage, and, if applicable, underinsured motorist bodily injury coverage.

(2) The named insured's uninsured motorist bodily injury coverage limits shall be equal to the highest limits of bodily injury liability coverage for any one vehicle insured under the policy unless the insured elects to purchase greater or lesser limits for uninsured motorist bodily injury coverage.

(3) The named insured's uninsured motorist property damage coverage limits shall be equal to the highest limits of property damage liability coverage for any one vehicle insured under the policy unless the insured elects to purchase lesser limits for uninsured motorist property damage coverage.

(4) The named insured's underinsured motorist bodily injury coverage limits, if applicable, shall be equal to the highest limits of bodily injury liability coverage for any one vehicle insured under the policy unless the insured elects to purchase greater or lesser limits for underinsured motorist bodily injury coverage.

(5) The named insured may purchase uninsured motorist bodily injury coverage and, if applicable, underinsured motorist coverage with limits up to one million dollars ($ 1,000,000) per person and one million dollars ($ 1,000,000) per accident.

An insurer shall be deemed to have given reasonable notice if it includes the following or substantially similar language on the policy's original and renewal declarations pages or in a separate notice accompanying the original and renewal declarations pages in at least 12 point type:

NOTICE: YOU ARE REQUIRED TO PURCHASE UNINSURED MOTORIST BODILY INJURY COVERAGE, UNINSURED MOTORIST PROPERTY DAMAGE COVERAGE AND, IN SOME CASES, UNDERINSURED MOTORIST BODILY INJURY COVERAGE. THIS INSURANCE PROTECTS YOU AND YOUR FAMILY AGAINST INJURIES AND PROPERTY DAMAGE CAUSED BY THE NEGLIGENCE OF OTHER DRIVERS WHO MAY HAVE LIMITED OR ONLY MINIMUM COVERAGE OR EVEN NO LIABILITY INSURANCE. YOU MAY PURCHASE UNINSURED MOTORIST BODILY INJURY COVERAGE AND, IF APPLICABLE, UNDERINSURED MOTORIST COVERAGE WITH LIMITS UP TO ONE MILLION DOLLARS ($ 1,000,000) PER PERSON AND ONE MILLION DOLLARS ($ 1,000,000) PER ACCIDENT OR AT SUCH LESSER LIMITS YOU CHOOSE. YOU CANNOT PURCHASE COVERAGE FOR LESS THAN THE MINIMUM LIMITS FOR THE BODILY INJURY AND PROPERTY DAMAGE COVERAGE THAT ARE REQUIRED FOR YOUR OWN VEHICLE. IF YOU DO NOT CHOOSE A GREATER OR LESSER LIMIT FOR UNINSURED MOTORIST BODILY INJURY COVERAGE, A LESSER LIMIT FOR UNINSURED MOTORIST PROPERTY DAMAGE COVERAGE, AND/OR A GREATER OR LESSER LIMIT FOR UNDERINSURED MOTORIST BODILY INJURY COVERAGE, THEN THE LIMITS FOR THE UNINSURED MOTORIST BODILY INJURY COVERAGE AND, IF APPLICABLE, THE UNDERINSURED MOTORIST BODILY INJURY COVERAGE WILL BE THE SAME AS THE HIGHEST LIMITS FOR BODILY INJURY LIABILITY COVERAGE FOR ANY ONE OF YOUR OWN VEHICLES INSURED UNDER THE POLICY AND THE LIMITS FOR THE UNINSURED MOTORIST PROPERTY DAMAGE COVERAGE WILL BE THE SAME AS THE HIGHEST LIMITS FOR PROPERTY DAMAGE LIABILITY COVERAGE FOR ANY ONE OF YOUR OWN VEHICLES INSURED UNDER THE POLICY. IF YOU WISH TO PURCHASE UNINSURED MOTORIST AND, IF APPLICABLE, UNDERINSURED MOTORIST COVERAGE AT DIFFERENT LIMITS THAN THE LIMITS FOR YOUR OWN VEHICLE INSURED UNDER THE POLICY, THEN YOU SHOULD CONTACT YOUR INSURANCE COMPANY OR AGENT TO DISCUSS YOUR OPTIONS FOR OBTAINING DIFFERENT COVERAGE LIMITS. YOU SHOULD ALSO READ YOUR ENTIRE POLICY TO UNDERSTAND WHAT IS COVERED UNDER UNINSURED AND UNDERINSURED MOTORIST COVERAGES.

(n) Nothing in this section shall be construed to provide greater amounts of uninsured or underinsured motorist coverage in a liability policy than the insured has purchased from the insurer under this section.

(o) An insurer that fails to comply with subsection (d1) or (m) of this section is subject to a civil penalty under G.S. 58-2-70.

History.

1953, c. 1300, s. 21; 1955, c. 1355; 1961, c. 640; 1965, c. 156; c. 674, s. 1; c. 898; 1967, c. 277, s. 4; c. 854; c. 1159, s. 1; c. 1162, s. 1; c. 1186, s. 1; c. 1246, s. 1; 1971, c. 1205, s. 2; 1973, c. 745, s. 4; 1975, c. 326, ss. 1, 2; c. 716, s. 5; c. 866, ss. 1-4; 1979, cc. 190, 675; c. 832, ss. 6, 7; 1983, c. 777, ss. 1, 2; 1985, c. 666, s. 74; 1985 (Reg. Sess., 1986), c. 1027, ss. 41, 42; 1987, c. 529; 1987 (Reg. Sess., 1988), c. 975, s. 33; 1991, c. 469, s. 4;c. 636, s. 3;c. 646, ss. 1, 2; c. 761, s. 12.3; 1991 (Reg. Sess., 1992), c. 837, s. 9; 1997-396, ss. 2, 3; 1999-195, s. 1;1999-228, s. 4;2003-311, ss. 1, 2; 2008-124, ss. 1.1, 1.2; 2009-440, s. 1;2009-561, s. 1;2009-566, s. 28;2015-135, s. 4.4;2018-5, s. 34.26(b)

EDITOR'S NOTE. --

The 1991 amendment to subdivisions (b)(3) and (b)(4) of this section by Session Laws 1991, c. 646, ss. 1 and 2 became effective November 5, 1991, 60 days after approval by the Commissioner of Insurance of filings made by the Bureau under section 3 of the 1991 act.

Chapter 20

Session Laws 2009-566, s. 28, amended Session Laws 2009-440, s. 3, contingent on Senate Bill 660 [S.L. 2009-440] becoming law, which it did. The section made subsection (d1) effective January 1, 2010, and applicable to motor vehicle liability insurance policies issued or renewed on or after that date.

Session Laws 2015-135, s. 1.1, provides: "This act shall be known and may be cited as the 'Foster Care Family Act.'"

Session Laws 2018-5, s. 1.1, provides: "This act shall be known as the 'Current Operations Appropriations Act of 2018.'"

Session Laws 2018-5, s. 39.7, is a severability clause.

EFFECT OF AMENDMENTS. --
Session Laws 2003-311, ss. 1 and 2, effective January 1, 2004, and applicable to accidents occurring on or after that date, rewrote the second paragraph of subdivision (b)(3); and inserted the third and fourth sentences in the first paragraph of subdivision (b)(4).

Session Laws 2015-135, s. 4.4, effective October 1, 2015, added "Except as provided in G.S. 20-309(a2)" in the introductory language of subsection (b).

Session Laws 2018-5, s. 34.26(b), effective July 1, 2018, in subdivision (d1)(2), inserted "licensed as a motor vehicle damage appraiser under G.S. 58-33-26 and G.S. 58-33-30 and" in the last sentence; and in subsection (o), substituted "subsection (d1) or (m)" for "subsection (m)."

I. GENERAL CONSIDERATION.

THE MANIFEST PURPOSE OF THIS ARTICLE was to provide protection, within the required limits, to persons injured or damaged by the negligent operation of a motor vehicle; and, in respect of a "motor vehicle liability policy," to provide such protection notwithstanding violations of policy provisions by the owner subsequent to accidents on which such injured parties base their claims. Nixon v. Liberty Mut. Ins. Co., 255 N.C. 106, 120 S.E.2d 430 (1961), quoting Swain v. Nationwide Mut. Ins. Co., 253 N.C. 120, 116 S.E.2d 482 (1960); Lane v. Iowa Mut. Ins. Co., 258 N.C. 318, 128 S.E.2d 398 (1962); Jones v. State Farm Mut. Auto. Ins. Co., 270 N.C. 454, 155 S.E.2d 118 (1967).

The primary purpose of this Article is to compensate the innocent victims of financially irresponsible motorists. Nationwide Mut. Ins. Co. v. Aetna Life & Cas. Co., 283 N.C. 87, 194 S.E.2d 834 (1973).

The purpose of the Financial Responsibility Act has always been to protect innocent motorists from financially irresponsible motorists. Nationwide Mut. Ins. Co. v. Baer, 113 N.C. App. 517, 439 S.E.2d 202 (1994).

The primary purpose of compulsory motor vehicle liability insurance is to compensate innocent victims who have been injured by financially irresponsible motorists. Nationwide Mut. Ins. Co. v. Roberts, 261 N.C. 285, 134 S.E.2d 654 (1964); Jones v. State Farm Mut. Auto. Ins. Co., 270 N.C. 454, 155 S.E.2d 118 (1967); Strickland v. Hughes, 273 N.C. 481, 160 S.E.2d 313 (1968); Ohio Cas. Ins. Co. v. Anderson, 59 N.C. App. 621, 298 S.E.2d 56 (1982).

The mandatory coverage required by this Article is solely for the protection of innocent victims who may be injured by financially irresponsible motorists. Nationwide Mut. Ins. Co. v. Chantos, 293 N.C. 431, 238 S.E.2d 597 (1977); Engle v. State Farm Mut. Auto. Ins. Co., 37 N.C. App. 126, 245 S.E.2d 532, cert. denied, 295 N.C. 645, 248 S.E.2d 250 (1978).

The primary purpose of the compulsory motor vehicle liability insurance required by North Carolina's Financial Responsibility Act is to compensate innocent victims who have been injured by financially irresponsible motorists. Furthermore, the act is to be liberally construed so that the beneficial purpose intended by its enactment may be accomplished. South Carolina Ins. Co. v. Smith, 67 N.C. App. 632, 313 S.E.2d 856, cert. denied, 311 N.C. 306, 317 S.E.2d 682 (1984).

The purpose of this State's compulsory motor vehicle insurance laws, of which the underinsured motorist provisions are a part, was and is the protection of innocent victims who may be injured by financially irresponsible motorists. Proctor v. North Carolina Farm Bureau Mut. Ins. Co., 324 N.C. 221, 376 S.E.2d 761 (1989).

Protection of innocent victims who may be injured by financially irresponsible motorists has repeatedly been held to be the fundamental purpose of the Financial Responsibility Act. Hartford Underwriters Ins. Co. v. Becks, 123 N.C. App. 489, 473 S.E.2d 427 (1996).

THE PURPOSE OF UNINSURED MOTORIST (UM) AND UNDERINSURED MOTORIST (UIM) COVERAGE is to compensate the innocent victims of financially irresponsible motorists. Bray v. North Carolina Farm Bureau Mut. Ins. Co., 115 N.C. App. 438, 445 S.E.2d 79 (1994), cert. improvidently granted in part, aff'd in part and rev'd in part on other grounds, 341 N.C. 678, 462 S.E.2d 650 (1995).

The purpose of this statute is to provide some financial recompense to innocent persons who receive bodily injury or property damage due to the negligence of uninsured motorists or those unidentified drivers who leave the scene of an accident. Williams v. Holsclaw, 128 N.C. App. 205, 495 S.E.2d 166 (1998).

THE LEGISLATIVE PURPOSE IN PERMITTING STACKING is to provide the innocent victim of an inadequately insured driver with an additional source of recovery so that she may receive full compensation for her injuries. Smith v. Nationwide Mut. Ins. Co., 97 N.C. App. 363, 388 S.E.2d 624 (1990), rev'd on other grounds, 328 N.C. 139, 400 S.E.2d 44, rehearing denied, 328 N.C. 577, 403 S.E.2d 514 (1991).

THE ACT IS TO BE LIBERALLY CONSTRUED so that its intended purpose may be accomplished. Wilmoth v. State Farm Mut. Auto. Ins. Co., 127 N.C. App. 260, 488 S.E.2d 628 (1997), cert. denied, 347 N.C. 410, 494 S.E.2d 601 (1997).

SUPPLEMENTAL EFFECT OF G.S. 20-281. --Section 20-281, which applies specifically to automobile owners who lease their cars for profit, is a companion section to and supplements this section, which applies to automobile owners generally. American Tours, Inc. v. Liberty Mut. Ins. Co., 315 N.C. 341, 338 S.E.2d 92 (1986).

G.

S. 20-281 is a source of mandatory terms for automobile liability insurance policies in addition to and independent of this section. American Tours, Inc. v. Liberty Mut. Ins. Co., 315 N.C. 341, 338 S.E.2d 92 (1986).

G.

S. 20-281, which applies to entities in the business of leasing vehicles, supplements this section and is intended to protect innocent drivers from financially irresponsible drivers. Hertz Corp. v. New S. Ins. Co., 129 N.C. App. 227, 497 S.E.2d 448 (1998).

A COMPULSORY MOTOR VEHICLE INSURANCE ACT IS A REMEDIAL STATUTE and will be liberally construed so that the beneficial purpose intended by its enactment by the General Assembly may be accomplished. Moore v. Hartford Fire Ins. Co., 270 N.C. 532, 155 S.E.2d 128 (1967); State Capital Ins. Co. v. Nationwide Mut. Ins. Co., 78 N.C. App. 542, 337 S.E.2d 866 (1985), aff'd, 318 N.C. 534, 350 S.E.2d 66 (1986); Harris ex rel. Freedman v. Nationwide Mut. Ins. Co., 332 N.C. 184, 420 S.E.2d 124 (1992).

This statute was enacted as remedial legislation and is to be liberally construed to effectuate its purpose. Lichtenberger v. American Motorists Ins. Co., 7 N.C. App. 269, 172 S.E.2d 284 (1970).

This section was enacted as remedial legislation and is to be liberally construed to effectuate its purpose, that being to provide, within fixed limits, some financial recompense to innocent persons who receive bodily injury or property damage, and to the dependents of those who lose their lives through the wrongful conduct of an uninsured motorist who cannot be made to respond in damages. Hendricks v. United States Fid. & Guar. Co., 5 N.C. App. 181, 167 S.E.2d 876 (1969).

OBLIGATIONS IMPOSED BY ARTICLE. --The Motor Vehicle Financial Responsibility Act obliges a motorist either to post security or to carry liability insurance, not accident insurance, to indemnify all persons who might be injured by the insured's car. Moore v. Young, 263 N.C. 483, 139 S.E.2d 704 (1965); McKinney v. Morrow, 18 N.C. App. 282, 196 S.E.2d 585, cert. denied, 283 N.C. 665, 197 S.E.2d 874 (1973).

POLICIES ARE MANDATORY. --In this State, all insurance policies covering loss from liability arising out of the ownership, maintenance, or use of a motor vehicle are, to the extent required by this section, mandatory. Nationwide Mut. Ins. Co. v. Roberts, 261 N.C. 285, 134 S.E.2d 654 (1964); Moore v. Hartford Fire Ins. Co., 270 N.C. 532, 155 S.E.2d 128 (1967).

STATUTE APPLIES TO ALL FINANCIALLY IRRESPONSIBLE PERSONS, INCLUDING MINORS. --The language of the Financial Responsibility Act leaves no doubt that the legislature intended to make all financially irresponsible persons, including minors, subject to its provisions. Nationwide Mut. Ins. Co. v. Chantos, 293 N.C. 431, 238 S.E.2d 597 (1977).

THE PROVISIONS OF THIS SECTION ARE WRITTEN INTO EVERY POLICY AS A MATTER OF LAW. In case a provision of the policy conflicts with a provision of the statute favorable to the insured, the provision of the statute controls. As a consequence, an insurance company cannot avoid liability on a policy of insurance issued pursuant to a statute by omitting from the policy provisions favorable to the insured, which are required by the statute. Lichtenberger v. American Motorists Ins. Co., 7 N.C. App. 269, 172 S.E.2d 284 (1970).

The provisions of the Financial Responsibility Act are "written" into every automobile liability policy as a matter of law, and, when the terms of the policy conflict with the statute, the provisions of the statute will prevail. Nationwide Mut. Ins. Co. v. Chantos, 293 N.C. 431, 238 S.E.2d 597 (1977); Engle v. State Farm Mut. Auto. Ins. Co., 37 N.C. App. 126, 245 S.E.2d 532, cert. denied, 295 N.C. 645, 248 S.E.2d 250 (1978); Ohio Cas. Ins. Co. v. Anderson, 59 N.C. App. 621, 298 S.E.2d 56 (1982).

The provisions of a statute applicable to insurance policies are a part of the policy to the same extent as if therein written, and when the terms of the policy conflict with statutory provisions favorable to the insured, the provisions of the statute will prevail. Nationwide Mut. Ins. Co. v. Aetna Life & Cas. Co., 283 N.C. 87, 194 S.E.2d 834 (1973); American Tours, Inc. v. Liberty Mut. Ins. Co., 68 N.C. App. 668, 316 S.E.2d 105, modified on other grounds and aff'd, 315 N.C. 341, 338 S.E.2d 92 (1986).

When the insuring language of the policy conflicts with the coverage mandated by this section, the provisions of the statute will control. State Capital Ins. Co. v. Nationwide Mut. Ins. Co., 78 N.C. App. 542, 337 S.E.2d 866 (1985), aff'd, 318 N.C. 534, 350 S.E.2d 66 (1986), reading into insurance policy coverage for damages arising out of the use of an automobile.

This section and G.S. 20-281 prescribe mandatory terms which become part of every liability policy insuring automobile lessors. Insurance Co. of N. Am. v. Aetna Life & Cas. Co., 88 N.C. App. 236, 362 S.E.2d 836 (1987).

When a statute is applicable to the terms of an insurance policy, the provisions of the statute become the terms of the policy, as if written into it. If the terms of the statute and the policy conflict, the statute prevails. Bray v. North Carolina Farm Bureau Mut. Ins. Co., 115 N.C. App. 438, 445 S.E.2d 79 (1994), cert. improvidently granted in part, aff'd in part and rev'd in part on other grounds, 341 N.C. 678, 462 S.E.2d 650 (1995).

When a statute applies to the terms of an insurance policy, the provisions of the statute become terms of the policy to the same extent as if they were written in the policy, and if the terms of the policy conflict with the statute, the provisions of the statute control. Baxley v. Nationwide Mut. Ins. Co., 115 N.C. App. 718, 446 S.E.2d 597 (1994).

The provisions of the Financial Responsibility Act are written into every automobile liability policy as a matter of law. Wilmoth v. State Farm Mut. Auto. Ins. Co., 127 N.C. App. 260, 488 S.E.2d 628 (1997), cert. denied, 347 N.C. 410, 494 S.E.2d 601 (1997).

CONSTRUCTION OF STATUTE WITH TERMS OF POLICY. --When a statute is applicable to the terms of an insurance policy, the provisions of the statute become a part of the policy as if written into it. If the terms of the statute and the policy conflict, the statute prevails. Bray v. North Carolina Farm Bureau Mut. Ins. Co., 341 N.C. 678, 462 S.E.2d 650 (1995).

CONSTRUCTION IN PARI MATERIA WITH G.S. 20-309. --Superior court properly reformed an insurance policy to include the amount of minimum coverage required by G.S. 20-309(a1); construing G.S. 20-279.21 and G.S. 20-309 in pari materia, just as provisions of G.S. 20-279.21 were read into every insurance policy as a matter of law, provisions of G.S. 20-309(a1) were also read into every insurance policy as a matter of law. N.C. Farm Bureau Mut. Ins. Co. v. Armwood, 181 N.C. App. 407, 638 S.E.2d 922 (2007), rev'd, 361 N.C. 576, 653 S.E.2d 392 (2007).

ACT PREVAILS OVER CONFLICTING POLICY. --If there is a conflict between the Financial Responsibility Act and the language of the policy, the Act prevails. Wilmoth v. State Farm Mut. Auto. Ins. Co., 127 N.C. App. 260, 488 S.E.2d 628 (1997), cert. denied, 347 N.C. 410, 494 S.E.2d 601 (1997).

EXCLUSIONARY PROVISIONS CONTRAVENING ARTICLE ARE VOID. --If an exclusionary provision of an assigned risk policy contravenes this Article, it is void. Nationwide Mut. Ins. Co. v. Roberts, 261 N.C. 285, 134 S.E.2d 654 (1964).

The public policy embodied by the Financial Responsibility Act controls over an exclusionary provision in a policy issued pursuant to the Act. Allstate Ins. Co. v. Webb, 10 N.C. App. 672, 179 S.E.2d 803 (1971); Nationwide Mut. Ins. Co. v. Aetna Life & Cas. Co., 283 N.C. 87, 194 S.E.2d 834 (1973).

The public policy goals of the Financial Responsibility Act apply only when the Act itself is being construed or when determinations are being made regarding the extent to which the Act, as to its mandatory minimum coverages, may override conflicting insurance policy provisions. Newell v. Nationwide Mut. Ins. Co., 334 N.C. 391, 432 S.E.2d 284 (1993).

There is nothing in this Article which authorizes the insurance company to exclude by the terms of its policy liability of the operator of an automobile if it is an automobile owned by a member of his household, and such a clause in the policy being repugnant to and in conflict with the provisions of this Article is void and of no effect. Indiana Lumbermens Mut. Ins. Co. v. Parton, 147 F. Supp. 887 (M.D.N.C. 1957).

Provision of an owner's automobile liability policy excluding from coverage an owned automobile while used "in the automobile business" by any person other than the named insured and certain other persons is repugnant to the mandatory requirements of the Motor Vehicle and Financial Responsibility Act and is, therefore, invalid. Nationwide Mut. Ins. Co. v. Aetna Life & Cas. Co., 283 N.C. 87, 194 S.E.2d 834 (1973).

An exclusion which attempts to limit the protection available to those designated as insureds to only the insured vehicle would be contrary to subdivision (b)(3) of this section and void. Crowder v. North Carolina Farm Bureau Mut. Ins. Co., 79 N.C. App. 551, 340

S.E.2d 127, cert. denied, 316 N.C. 731, 345 S.E.2d 387 (1986).

RATE BUREAU FORM NOT REQUIRED. --This section did not require the defendant's fleet policy to use a form promulgated by the Rate Bureau. Hlasnick v. Federated Mut. Ins. Co., 136 N.C. App. 320, 524 S.E.2d 386 (2000), aff'd, in part, and cert. dismissed, in part, 353 N.C. 240, 539 S.E.2d 274 (2000).

THE DEFINITION OF "PERSONS INSURED" CONTAINED IN subsection (b)(3) does not apply to liability coverage. Haight v. Travelers/Aetna Property Cas. Corp., 132 N.C. App. 673, 514 S.E.2d 102 (1999).

IN ESSENCE, SUBDIVISION (B)(3) OF THIS SECTION ESTABLISHES TWO "CLASSES" OF "PERSONS INSURED": (1) The named insured and, while resident of the same household, the spouse of the named insured and relatives of either and (2) any person who uses with the consent, express or implied, of the named insured, the insured vehicle, and a guest in such vehicle. The latter class are "persons insured" under this section only when the insured vehicle is involved, while the former class are "persons insured" even where the insured vehicle is not involved in the insured's injuries. Crowder v. North Carolina Farm Bureau Mut. Ins. Co., 79 N.C. App. 551, 340 S.E.2d 127, cert. denied, 316 N.C. 731, 345 S.E.2d 387 (1986).

Under subdivision (b)(3) of this section there are two classes of "persons insured": (1) the named insured and, while resident of the same household, the spouse of the named insured and relatives of either and (2) any person who uses with the consent, express or implied, of the named insured, the insured vehicle, and a guest of such vehicle. In the first class, a person is insured whether or not the insured vehicle is involved in the injuries; a person is insured in the second class only when the insured vehicle is involved in the injuries. Busby v. Simmons, 103 N.C. App. 592, 406 S.E.2d 628 (1991).

POLICY PROVIDING COVERAGE IN EXCESS OF STATUTORY REQUIREMENT. --An assigned risk policy providing no coverage in excess of the statutory requirement must be construed in connection with the public policy which the Motor Vehicle Safety and Financial Responsibility Act embodies. Nationwide Mut. Ins. Co. v. Roberts, 261 N.C. 285, 134 S.E.2d 654 (1964).

Insurer was liable for injuries to passengers in a vehicle driven by an insured's fourteen-year-old son because the policy's plain language extended coverage to family members using the covered vehicle even when they did not have a reasonable belief they were entitled to use the covered motor vehicle; the son was in fact an insured under the terms of the policy. Integon Nat'l Ins. Co. v. Villafranco, 228 N.C. App. 390, 745 S.E.2d 922 (2013).

IS DEEMED VOLUNTARY POLICY TO EXTENT OF EXCESS. --All insurance policies which insure in excess of the compulsory coverage of this section are voluntary policies to the extent of the excess. Nationwide Mut. Ins. Co. v. Roberts, 261 N.C. 285, 134 S.E.2d 654 (1964).

Chapter 20

As automobile liability coverage in excess of the statutorily required minimum was not subject to the Financial Responsibility Act of 1953, the defense of material misrepresentation was an acceptable defense that was asserted by an insurer in defense of its denial of coverage for a driver who was involved in an accident in an insured vehicle. James v. Integon Nat'l Ins. Co., 228 N.C. App. 171, 744 S.E.2d 491 (2013).

AND IS NOT SUBJECT TO REQUIREMENTS OF SECTION. --Coverage furnished an insured which is in addition to the mandatory statutory requirements, and is therefore voluntary, is not subject to the requirements of this section. Nationwide Mut. Ins. Co. v. Aetna Life & Cas. Co., 283 N.C. 87, 194 S.E.2d 834 (1973).

To the extent that coverage provided by motor vehicle liability insurance policies exceeds the mandatory minimum coverage required by statute, the additional coverage is voluntary, and is governed by the terms of the insurance contract. Nationwide Mut. Ins. Co. v. Massey, 82 N.C. App. 448, 346 S.E.2d 268 (1986).

In general, liability insurance coverage in excess of the amounts required under subdivision (b)(2) of this section is voluntary and not controlled by the provisions of the act. Subsection (g) of this section specifically excludes such coverage in addition to and in excess of that required by subdivision (b)(2) of this section. Aetna Cas. & Sur. Co. v. Younts, 84 N.C. App. 399, 352 S.E.2d 850 (1987).

IN ABSENCE OF STATUTORY PROVISION, LIABILITY MEASURED BY TERMS OF POLICY. --In the absence of any provision in the Financial Responsibility Act broadening the liability of the insurer, such liability must be measured by the terms of its policy as written. Underwood v. National Grange Mut. Liab. Co., 258 N.C. 211, 128 S.E.2d 577 (1962); Younts v. State Farm Mut. Auto. Ins. Co., 281 N.C. 582, 189 S.E.2d 137 (1972).

LIABILITY ON VOLUNTARY POLICY MUST ACCRUE UNDER PROVISIONS IN CONTRACT. --The insurer under a voluntary policy is liable only if its liability accrues under the provisions set out in the contract of insurance between defendant and its insured. Younts v. State Farm Mut. Auto. Ins. Co., 281 N.C. 582, 189 S.E.2d 137 (1972).

AND INJURED PARTY HAS NO GREATER RIGHTS AGAINST INSURER THAN HAS INSURED. --With reference to an owner's policy of insurance, unless the action be based on policy provisions required by this section, an injured party who obtains a judgment against the insured has no greater rights against the insurer than those of the insured. Clemmons v. Nationwide Mut. Ins. Co., 267 N.C. 495, 148 S.E.2d 640 (1966).

COMPLIANCE WITH VOLUNTARY POLICY PROVISIONS IS CONDITION PRECEDENT TO RECOVERY. --Where coverage in a policy is in addition to the coverage required by the Motor Vehicle Safety and Financial Responsibility Act, provisions requiring that an insured give notice of an accident, and requiring the insured's cooperation in defense of any action against him are binding and enforceable.

Moreover, compliance with such policy provisions is a condition precedent to recovery, with the burden of proof on the insured to show compliance, where the policy provides, "No action shall lie against the Company unless, as a condition precedent thereto, the Insured shall have fully complied with all the terms of this policy," or words of like import. Clemmons v. Nationwide Mut. Ins. Co., 267 N.C. 495, 148 S.E.2d 640 (1966).

The failure of insured under an assigned risk policy to give notice of an accident occurring while he was driving an automobile other than the one named in the policy precludes recovery by the insured or by the injured third person against insurer, even though the policy contains additional coverage, if insured is driving another vehicle, since such additional coverage is not required by this Article, and therefore the provisions of this Article are not applicable thereto. Woodruff v. State Farm Mut. Auto. Ins. Co., 260 N.C. 723, 133 S.E.2d 704 (1963).

FAMILY MEMBER EXCLUSION. --Insurance policy's "family member" exclusion for UM coverage is repugnant to the purpose of UM and UIM coverage and is therefore invalid. Bray v. North Carolina Farm Bureau Mut. Ins. Co., 115 N.C. App. 438, 445 S.E.2d 79 (1994), cert. improvidently granted in part, aff'd in part and rev'd in part on other grounds, 341 N.C. 678, 462 S.E.2d 650 (1995).

Where a person is injured through the negligence of an insured family member while riding with that family member in an insured vehicle, the Financial Responsibility Act prevents the operation of a family member exclusion in the policy's liability section to bar coverage. Cartner v. Nationwide Mut. Fire Ins. Co., 123 N.C. App. 251, 472 S.E.2d 389 (1996).

TWO PUBLIC POLICIES ARE INHERENT IN SUBSECTION (E); first, the subsection relieves the employer of the burden of paying double premiums (one to its workers' compensation carrier and one to its automobile liability policy carrier), and second, the section denies the windfall of a double recovery to the employee. Manning v. Fletcher, 324 N.C. 513, 379 S.E.2d 854, rehearing denied, 325 N.C. 277, 384 S.E.2d 517 (1989).

SCOPE OF EXCLUSION UNDER SUBSECTION (E). --The revision of subsection (e) of this section indicates a legislative intent to broaden the scope of exclusion to include not only the situation in which the injured party might otherwise receive both workers' compensation payments and liability payments on behalf of the insured, but also the situation in which the injured party, as an insured under the uninsured coverage of a liability policy, might otherwise receive workers' compensation benefits as well as uninsured coverage payments for the same injury. Manning v. Fletcher, 324 N.C. 513, 379 S.E.2d 854, rehearing denied, 325 N.C. 277, 384 S.E.2d 517 (1989).

APPLICABILITY OF EXCLUSIONS OF SUBSECTION (E) TO UNINSURED AND UNDERINSURED COVERAGES. --The location of subsection (e) in this section and its reference to a "motor vehicle liability policy" shows a legislative intent that the exclusion permitted by subsection (e) be applicable to all subdivisions of subsection (b), including the uninsured and underinsured coverages defined therein. Manning v. Fletcher, 324 N.C. 513, 379 S.E.2d 854, rehearing denied, 325 N.C. 277, 384 S.E.2d 517 (1989).

SUBSECTION (E) PERMITS AN INSURANCE CARRIER TO REDUCE UNDERINSURED MOTORIST COVERAGE LIABILITY in a business auto insurance policy by amounts paid to the insured as workers' compensation benefits. Manning v. Fletcher, 324 N.C. 513, 379 S.E.2d 854, rehearing denied, 325 N.C. 277, 384 S.E.2d 517 (1989).

ADVANCEMENT OF FUNDS --Insurer could elect to advance to its insured the liability limits of a tortfeasor's policy and thereby preserve its subrogation rights against the tortfeasor. N.C. Farm Bureau Mut. Ins. Co. v. Edwards, 154 N.C. App. 616, 572 S.E.2d 805 (2002).

INSURABLE INTEREST IS ESSENTIAL TO VALIDITY OF CONTRACT. --It is a fixed rule of insurance law that an insurable interest on the part of the person taking out the policy is essential to the validity and enforceability of the insurance contract. Rea v. Hardware Mut. Cas. Co., 15 N.C. App. 620, 190 S.E.2d 708, cert. denied, 282 N.C. 153, 191 S.E.2d 759 (1972).

WHO HAS INSURABLE INTEREST. --A person has an insurable interest in the subject matter insured where he has such a relation or connection with, or concern in, such subject matter that he will derive pecuniary benefit or advantage from its preservation, or will suffer pecuniary loss or damage from its destruction, termination, or injury by the happening of the event insured against. Rea v. Hardware Mut. Cas. Co., 15 N.C. App. 620, 190 S.E.2d 708, cert. denied, 282 N.C. 153, 191 S.E.2d 759 (1972).

Where the general superintendent of the company used an automobile in the business of the insured as its employee and the decedent, an officer, director and owner of 98% of the stock of the insured, used the automobile in the business of the insured, applying the general principles of law to the facts, the company had an insurable interest in the automobile. Rea v. Hardware Mut. Cas. Co., 15 N.C. App. 620, 190 S.E.2d 708, cert. denied, 282 N.C. 153, 191 S.E.2d 759 (1972).

DEFINITION OF OWNER'S POLICY --An "owner's policy" is a motor vehicle liability policy that insures the holder against legal liability for injuries to others arising out of the ownership, use or operation of a motor vehicle owned by him or her. Progressive Am. Ins. Co. v. Vasquez, 350 N.C. 386, 515 S.E.2d 8 (1999).

ARTICLE PROVIDES FOR ISSUANCE OF OWNER'S POLICY AND OPERATOR'S POLICY. --This Article provides for motor vehicle insurance carriers to issue two types of motor vehicle liability policies. One is an owner's policy, which insures the holder against legal liability for injuries to others arising out of the ownership, use or operation of a motor vehicle owned by him; and the other is an operator's policy, which insures the holder against legal liability for injuries to others arising out of the use by him of a motor vehicle not owned by him. Woodruff v. State Farm Mut. Auto. Ins. Co., 260 N.C. 723, 133 S.E.2d 704 (1963).

AND WHETHER POLICY INSURES OWNER AS AN OWNER OR AS AN OPERATOR DEPENDS ON INTENT of parties. That intent must be ascertained from the language used in the written contract. Lofquist v. Allstate Ins. Co., 263 N.C. 615, 140 S.E.2d 12 (1965).

Whether one is insured as owner or as operator depends on intent of parties. Ohio Cas. Ins. Co. v. Anderson, 59 N.C. App. 621, 298 S.E.2d 56 (1982).

DISTINCTION BETWEEN OWNER'S POLICY AND OPERATOR'S POLICY. --The distinction between an owner's policy of liability insurance and an operator's policy of liability insurance, the required provisions of each being set forth in this section, is pointed out in Howell v. Travelers Indem. Co., 237 N.C. 227, 74 S.E.2d 610 (1953), and Lofquist v. Allstate Ins. Co., 263 N.C. 615, 140 S.E.2d 12 (1965). Clemmons v. Nationwide Mut. Ins. Co., 267 N.C. 495, 148 S.E.2d 640 (1966).

COVERAGE UNDER OWNER'S POLICY. --An owner's policy protects the owner, as the named insured; it also protects any other person using the insured vehicle, with the owner's permission. Issuance of an owner's policy thus is generally to a "named insured" who is the "owner" of the described vehicle. Ohio Cas. Ins. Co. v. Anderson, 59 N.C. App. 621, 298 S.E.2d 56 (1982).

COVERAGE OF OWNER'S POLICY LIMITED TO VEHICLE DESCRIBED. --An owner's policy does not protect against liability resulting from the use of a motor vehicle not described in the policy. Lofquist v. Allstate Ins. Co., 263 N.C. 615, 140 S.E.2d 12 (1965).

Where an assigned risk policy of automobile liability insurance provided for the payment of additional premium for application of the policy to a newly acquired vehicle, and insurer, upon notification that insured had traded in the vehicle covered for another, advised insured that it would issue endorsement covering the second vehicle upon payment of additional premium in a stipulated amount, and there was no evidence that the additional premium was ever paid or the endorsement issued under the Motor Vehicle Safety and Financial Responsibility Act of 1947, the policy did not cover loss inflicted in the operation of the second vehicle, nor was insurer estopped from denying liability by reason of its failure to return the unearned premium on the original policy or its failure to cancel it. Miller v. New Amsterdam Cas. Co., 245 N.C. 526, 96 S.E.2d 860 (1957).

As an insurance policy held by the parents of the alleged tortfeasor limited liability coverage to damages arising out of ownership or use of covered autos, and did not deal with uninsured/underinsured motorist coverage, exclusion denying liability coverage for ownership, maintenance, or use of any vehicles, other than the covered autos, was valid and not contrary to public policy. Griswold v. Integon Gen. Ins. Corp., 149 N.C. App. 301, 560 S.E.2d 861 (2002).

"FAMILY OWNED" VS. "HOUSEHOLD OWNED". --Although a "family-owned vehicle" or "household-owned vehicle" exclusion may be clear and unambiguous, it will not be upheld by our courts in the context of uninsured motorist/ underinsured motorist coverage. Nationwide Mut. Ins. Co. v. Lankford, 118 N.C. App. 368, 455 S.E.2d 484 (1995).

CLASSES OF INSUREDS. --There is nothing in this section which indicates that if a person is otherwise covered as a first class insured he loses this coverage if he is covered as a second class insured on another policy. Mitchell v. Nationwide Mut. Ins. Co., 335 N.C. 433, 439 S.E.2d 110 (1994).

THE INJURED PARTY IN AN AUTOMOBILE ACCIDENT IS AN INTENDED THIRD-PARTY BENEFICIARY to the insurance contract between insurer and the tortfeasor/insured party. Murray v. Nationwide Mut. Ins. Co., 123 N.C. App. 1, 472 S.E.2d 358 (1996).

AS IS COVERAGE OF OWNER'S ASSIGNED RISK POLICY. --This Article does not require an owner's assigned risk policy to cover any liability except that growing out of the operation of the motor vehicle described in the policy. Woodruff v. State Farm Mut. Auto. Ins. Co., 260 N.C. 723, 133 S.E.2d 704 (1963); Clemmons v. Nationwide Mut. Ins. Co., 267 N.C. 495, 148 S.E.2d 640 (1966).

An owner's policy issued pursuant to the assigned risk statute of this State obligates the insurer to pay any liability the insured becomes liable to pay by reason of the operation of the automobile described in the policy up to the limit of $5,000. Woodruff v. State Farm Mut. Auto. Ins. Co., 260 N.C. 723, 133 S.E.2d 704 (1963).

THERE IS NO INSURANCE SEPARATE AND DISTINCT FROM THE OWNERSHIP OF THE CAR because an owner's motor vehicle liability policy is a contract between the insurance company and the owner. Younts v. State Farm Mut. Auto. Ins. Co., 281 N.C. 582, 189 S.E.2d 137 (1972).

COVERAGE IN A POLICY WITH RESPECT TO THE USE OF OTHER AUTOMOBILES is in addition to the coverage required by this Article. Woodruff v. State Farm Mut. Auto. Ins. Co., 260 N.C. 723, 133 S.E.2d 704 (1963).

An assigned risk policy of automobile insurance specifying the vehicle covered by the policy does not cover another vehicle owned by insured in the absence of a provision in the policy for extension of coverage or approval by insurer of a change in the vehicle covered. Miller v. New Amsterdam Cas. Co., 245 N.C. 526, 96 S.E.2d 860 (1957), decided under repealed § 20-227, which covered the same subject matter as this section.

POLICY COVERING ONLY ONE OF TWO VEHICLES OWNED BY INSURED. --For a case applying the Motor Vehicle Safety and Financial Responsibility Act of 1947, where an insurance company issued an owner's policy of liability insurance upon an assigned risk covering only one of the two vehicles owned by insured, and the insurer was held not liable for damages caused during insured's operation of the other vehicle owned by him, see Graham v. Iowa Nat'l Mut. Ins. Co., 240 N.C. 458, 82 S.E.2d 381 (1954).

ADMISSIBILITY OF INSURER'S STATEMENTS REGARDING COVERAGE. --A written statement by the liability insurer creates a prima facie presumption of an operator's underinsurance as well as uninsurance. By establishing a prima facie presumption of underinsurance for such written statements, subdivisions (b)(3) and (b)(4) of this section implicitly make such statements admissible into evidence in order to trigger the operation of the presumption. Crowder v. North Carolina Farm Bureau Mut. Ins. Co., 79 N.C. App. 551, 340 S.E.2d 127, cert. denied, 316 N.C. 731, 345 S.E.2d 387 (1986).

ADDITIONAL COVERAGE IS VOLUNTARY and the liability of the carrier for such coverage must be determined according to the terms and conditions of the binder. Roseboro Ford, Inc. v. Bass, 77 N.C. App. 263, 335 S.E.2d 214 (1985).

STACKING OF COVERAGE. --Policy provisions which require that the terms of the policy should "apply separately" to separate automobiles insured under a single policy would allow stacking of medical payments coverages, except where there was unambiguous language establishing that the per accident limitations applied regardless of the number of automobiles insured under the policy or other unambiguous language tying the coverages to specific automobiles. Hamilton v. Travelers Indem. Co., 77 N.C. App. 318, 335 S.E.2d 228 (1985), cert. denied, 315 N.C. 587, 341 S.E.2d 25 (1986).

STACKING FLEET AND NON-FLEET POLICIES. --The interpolicy stacking of fleet and non-fleet policies is permissible. Isenhour v. Universal Underwriters Ins. Co., 341 N.C. 597, 461 S.E.2d 317 (1995).

INTERPOLICY AND INTRAPOLICY STACKING. --A person living in the household with relatives should be allowed to aggregate or stack, both interpolicy and intrapolicy, the underinsured motorist coverages of the relatives and to collect on those stacked coverages. Mitchell v. Nationwide Mut. Ins. Co., 335 N.C. 433, 439 S.E.2d 110 (1994).

ASSIGNED RISK POLICY DOES NOT COVER REPLACEMENT VEHICLE OWNED BY PERSON OTHER THAN NAMED INSURED. --Nothing in the statute requires any carrier to extend the coverage of an assigned risk policy to a replacement vehicle owned by and registered to a person other than the original named insured owner of the vehicle originally described and insured. Beasley v. Hartford Accident & Indem. Co., 11 N.C. App. 34, 180 S.E.2d 381, aff'd, 280 N.C. 177, 184 S.E.2d 841 (1971).

RETENTION OF EQUITABLE TITLE BY PURCHASER WHERE LEGAL TITLE IN ANOTHER. --To allow defeat of coverage by the technicality of placement of legal title in the purchaser's son, at the purchaser's direction and without the son's knowledge, while the purchaser retained all equitable interest in the vehicle, would defy the legislative intent to close all avenues of escape from the provisions of this Article. Ohio Cas. Ins. Co. v. Anderson, 59 N.C. App. 621, 298 S.E.2d 56 (1982).

Where the vendee paid the entire purchase price, had exclusive possession and use of the vehicle, obtained the insurance coverage for it, and paid the premiums therefor, this sufficed to give him a clear equitable interest in the vehicle, and that equitable interest sufficed, under the particular facts and circumstances, to make him the "owner" of the vehicle within the coverage intent of the policy, interpreted in light of the purpose and intent of this Article. Ohio Cas. Ins. Co. v. Anderson, 59 N.C. App. 621, 298 S.E.2d 56 (1982).

TRANSFER OF TITLE TO VEHICLE. --The Responsibility Act makes no requirement that insurance, in case of transfer of title, follow the vehicle. Underwood v. National Grange Mut. Liab. Co., 258 N.C. 211, 128 S.E.2d 577 (1962).

NONOWNED VEHICLE. --Since actual title had not passed, an insurer had to provide coverage to its insured while driving a non-owned vehicle, even though the insured was in the process of buying the vehicle, as North Carolina required actual title to pass for ownership under G.S. 20-4.01(26); the insurer was responsible to a passenger who was injured in a collision with a non-owned vehicle being driven by the insured. Hernandez v. Nationwide Mut. Ins. Co., 171 N.C. App. 510, 615 S.E.2d 425 (2005), cert. denied, 360 N.C. 63, 621 S.E.2d 624 (2005).

NEWLY ACQUIRED VEHICLE. --If the policy was an owner's policy, defendant was not required to provide automatic insurance for a newly acquired motor vehicle. Lofquist v. Allstate Ins. Co., 263 N.C. 615, 140 S.E.2d 12 (1965).

PHANTOM VEHICLE. --This section does not provide for uninsured motorist coverage where a phantom vehicle allegedly caused a collision between two other automobiles, but made no physical contact with either of the other automobiles. Andersen v. Baccus, 109 N.C. App. 16, 426 S.E.2d 105 (1993), modified on other grounds, 335 N.C. 526, 439 S.E.2d 136 (1994).

The legislature never intended for subdivisions (b)(3) and (b)(4) of this section to provide coverage where plaintiff was injured by an unknown/uninsured motorist without making contact with the unknown motorist's vehicle. Johnson v. North Carolina Farm Bureau Ins. Co., 112 N.C. App. 623, 436 S.E.2d 265 (1993).

An unidentified motor vehicle is statutorily treated as an uninsured motor vehicle. Johnson v. North Carolina Farm Bureau Ins. Co., 112 N.C. App. 623, 436 S.E.2d 265 (1993).

THE STATUTORY REQUIREMENT FOR AUTOMATIC INSURANCE FOR 30 DAYS for a motor vehicle acquired by an "operator" is as much a part of the policy as if expressly written therein. Lofquist v. Allstate Ins. Co., 263 N.C. 615, 140 S.E.2d 12 (1965).

"ACCIDENT". --The word "accident" as used in this section with reference to compulsory insurance is used in the popular sense and means any unfortunate occurrence causing injury for which the insured is liable. Nationwide Mut. Ins. Co. v. Roberts, 261 N.C. 285, 134 S.E.2d 654 (1964).

"ARISING OUT OF" OWNERSHIP, MAINTENANCE OR USE OF AUTOMOBILE. --Where a policy provision speaks of liability "arising out of the ownership, maintenance or use" of a motor vehicle, the words "arising out of" are not words of narrow and specific limitation but are broad, general, and comprehensive terms affecting broad coverage. They are intended to, and do, afford protection to the insured against liability imposed upon him for all damages caused by acts done in connection with or arising out of such use. Fidelity & Cas. Co. v. North Carolina Farm Bureau Mut. Ins. Co., 16 N.C. App. 194, 192 S.E.2d 113, cert. denied, 282 N.C. 425, 192 S.E.2d 840 (1972).

THE WORDS "ARISING OUT OF" are words of much broader significance than "caused by." They are ordinarily understood to mean "originating from," "having its origin in," "growing out of," or "flowing from," or in short, "incident to," or "having connection with" the use of the automobile. Fidelity & Cas. Co. v. North Carolina Farm Bureau Mut. Ins. Co., 16 N.C. App. 194, 192 S.E.2d 113, cert. denied, 282 N.C. 425, 192 S.E.2d 840 (1972).

For purposes of determining whether an injury is covered by policy or statutory language extending coverage to loss "arising out of the use" of a motor vehicle, the use need not be the proximate cause of the injury in the narrow legal sense. Coverage will be extended if there is a reasonable causal connection between the use and the injury. State Capital Ins. Co. v. Nationwide Mut. Ins. Co., 78 N.C. App. 542, 337 S.E.2d 866 (1985), aff'd, 318 N.C. 534, 350 S.E.2d 66 (1986).

THE TEST FOR DETERMINING WHETHER AN AUTOMOBILE LIABILITY POLICY PROVIDES COVERAGE FOR AN ACCIDENT is not whether the automobile was a proximate cause of the accident. Instead, the test is whether there is a causal connection between the use of the automobile and the accident. State Capital Ins. Co. v. Nationwide Mut. Ins. Co., 318 N.C. 534, 350 S.E.2d 66 (1986).

Personal automobile liability insurance policy provided compulsory liability coverage to a child who was injured when he was struck by a non-insured car while at a repair shop to have the insured car repaired, because a sufficient causal connection between the use and the injuries existed for purposes of G.S. 20-279.21(b)(2); a showing of proximate causation was not required. Integon Nat'l Ins. Co. v. Ward, 184 N.C. App. 532, 646 S.E.2d 395 (2007).

WHERE THE CAUSE OF INJURY IS DISTINCTLY INDEPENDENT OF THE USE OF THE VEHICLE, no causal connection can be said to exist, and coverage will not be afforded. State Capital Ins. Co. v. Nationwide Mut. Ins. Co., 78 N.C. App. 542, 337 S.E.2d 866 (1985), aff'd, 318 N.C. 534, 350 S.E.2d 66 (1986).

THE TERMS "OWNERSHIP, MAINTENANCE AND USE" should not be treated as mere surplusage. They were placed in the policy in order to cover situations distinct and separate from any other term. Williams v. Nationwide Mut. Ins. Co., 269 N.C. 235, 152 S.E.2d 102 (1967); Fidelity & Cas. Co. v. North Carolina Farm Bureau Mut. Ins. Co., 16 N.C. App. 194, 192 S.E.2d 113, cert. denied, 282 N.C. 425, 192 S.E.2d 840 (1972).

When a policy is silent on the point, loading and unloading is using an insured motor vehicle within the terms of the omnibus insurance clause, which insures against loss arising out of the ownership, maintenance and use of a motor vehicle. Fidelity & Cas. Co. v. North Carolina Farm Bureau Mut. Ins. Co., 16 N.C. App. 194, 192 S.E.2d 113, cert. denied, 282 N.C. 425, 192 S.E.2d 840 (1972).

OWNERSHIP, MAINTENANCE, OR USE REQUIREMENT WRITTEN INTO EVERY POLICY. -- An automobile liability policy providing that it would "pay damages for bodily injury or property damage for which any insured becomes responsible" meant damages arising out of the ownership, maintenance, or use of such motor vehicle, since the provisions of the Financial Responsibility Act were written into the policy. Nationwide Mut. Ins. Co. v. Webb, 132 N.C. App. 524, 512 S.E.2d 764 (1999).

THE "USE" OF A VEHICLE INCLUDES ITS LOADING AND UNLOADING and all persons actively engaged in the loading and unloading with the permission of the named insured are additional insureds under policy omnibus clauses. Fidelity & Cas. Co. v. North Carolina Farm Bureau Mut. Ins. Co., 16 N.C. App. 194, 192 S.E.2d 113, cert. denied, 282 N.C. 425, 192 S.E.2d 840 (1972).

"USING" A VEHICLE. --Where plaintiff was struck while walking on the shoulder of the road in search of mechanical assistance after the vehicle he was driving broke down, plaintiff was "using" the vehicle at the time of the accident. As such, plaintiff was an insured of the insurance company at the time of the accident. Falls v. North Carolina Farm Bureau Mut. Ins. Co., 114 N.C. App. 203, 441 S.E.2d 583, cert. denied, 337 N.C. 691, 448 S.E.2d 521 (1994).

Van which child had just left when she was hit by a truck was in "use" at the time of the accident where there was a casual connection between the use of the van and the accident, in that it was because van was parked where it was, child had to cross the roadway, therefore auto policy provided coverage. Nationwide Mut. Ins. Co. v. Davis, 118 N.C. App. 494, 455 S.E.2d 892 (1995).

Where an insured was towing his disabled truck with his car, the insured was using the truck when an accident occurred, thereby giving rise to liability coverage under an insurance policy for both the truck and the car. Floyd v. Integon Gen. Ins. Corp., 152 N.C. App. 445, 567 S.E.2d 823 (2002).

REGULAR AND NORMAL USE OF A VEHICLE. --In order for an injury to be compensable there must be a causal connection between the use of the vehicle and the injury; this connection is shown if the injury is the natural and reasonable consequence of the vehicle's use; however, an injury is not a "natural and reasonable consequence of the use" of the vehicle if the injury is the result of something wholly disassociated from, independent of, and remote from the vehicle's normal use. Clearly, an automobile chase with guns blazing is not a regular and normal use of a vehicle. Scales v. State Farm Mut. Auto. Ins. Co., 119 N.C. App. 787, 460 S.E.2d 201 (1995).

Injuries to a bicyclist caused by a soda bottle intentionally thrown from an insured vehicle by a passenger did not arise out of the use of a vehicle; therefore, the insured's automobile liability policy did not cover the incident. Nationwide Mut. Ins. Co. v. Webb, 132 N.C. App. 524, 512 S.E.2d 764 (1999).

PHRASE "APPLICABLE LIMITS OF LIABILITY UNDER THE OWNER'S POLICY," found in subdivision (b)(4), which deals exclusively with underinsured motorist (UIM) coverage, refers to the limits of liability under plaintiff's UIM coverage. Following an automobile accident, a tortfeasor's liability coverage is called upon to compensate the injured plaintiff, who then turns to his own UIM coverage when the tortfeasor's liability coverage is exhausted. In this situation, the injured plaintiff's liability coverages are not applicable to the accident and a comparison to the plaintiff's liability coverage is inappropriate. Taken in context, the "liability limits" referred to are clearly those under the UIM coverage portion of the owners' policy. Harris ex rel. Freedman v. Nationwide Mut. Ins. Co., 332 N.C. 184, 420 S.E.2d 124 (1992).

The "applicable limits" are the sum of all underinsured motorist (UIM) coverages provided in the policy which are applicable to the plaintiff's claim. Given the natural and ordinary meaning of the plural form of the word limit, with reference to a single policy, "applicable limits" refers to all available UIM limits under the policy. Harris ex rel. Freedman v. Nationwide Mut. Ins. Co., 332 N.C. 184, 420 S.E.2d 124 (1992).

"NONFLEET" VEHICLES. --Fire vehicles listed in policy were private passenger vehicles not used in insured's business and hence "nonfleet" vehicles to which the exception to intrapolicy stacking of subdivision (b)(4) as it read prior to 1991 did not apply. McCaskill v. Pennsylvania Nat'l Mut. Cas. Ins. Co., 118 N.C. App. 320, 454 S.E.2d 842 (1995).

MAKING REPAIRS. --In an action on the uninsured motorists clause of an automobile insurance policy, where the allegations were to the effect that plaintiff, while underneath the uninsured vehicle, raised on blocks, making repairs, was injured when the owner removed a front wheel and the car fell or rolled upon plaintiff, it was held that repairs are a necessary incident to maintenance, and the allegations brought plaintiff within the coverage of the policy. Williams v. Nationwide Mut. Ins. Co., 269 N.C. 235, 152 S.E.2d 102 (1967).

INJURIES TO THIRD PARTY FROM RIFLE WHICH DISCHARGED WHILE BEING REMOVED. --Automobile liability policy which, when properly construed, provided coverage for damages arising out of the ownership, maintenance, or use of the insured's automobile provided coverage from injuries to third party resulting when rifle accidentally discharged while being removed from the motor vehicle by the insured. State Capital Ins. Co. v. Nationwide Mut. Ins. Co., 318 N.C. 534, 350 S.E.2d 66 (1986).

WHERE VICTIM WAS ACCIDENTALLY SHOT BY PASSENGER WHILE DRIVING A TRUCK owned by the passenger's employer, the company's insurance policy covered victim's injuries. Harford Fire Ins. Co.

v. Pierce, 127 N.C. App. 123, 489 S.E.2d 179 (1997), appeal dismissed, 347 N.C. 576, 502 S.E.2d 592 (1998).

INJURY IN REACHING INTO TRUCK FOR RIFLE. --Where the insured frequently used his insured truck for hunting, the transportation of firearms being an integral part of that activity, and at the time of the accident, the insured was reaching into the cab for his rifle in order to shoot a deer, the requisite causal connection between victim's injury and the use of the truck was present, and thus the injury arose out of the use of the truck so as to be within the coverage provided by the automobile liability insurance policy. State Capital Ins. Co. v. Nationwide Mut. Ins. Co., 78 N.C. App. 542, 337 S.E.2d 866 (1985), aff'd, 318 N.C. 534, 350 S.E.2d 66 (1986).

INJURIES INTENTIONALLY INFLICTED ARE COVERED. --Injuries intentionally inflicted by the use of an automobile are within the coverage of a motor vehicle liability policy as defined by this section. Nationwide Mut. Ins. Co. v. Roberts, 261 N.C. 285, 134 S.E.2d 654 (1964).

The provisions of this section extend coverage to include liability for injuries intentionally inflicted by the use of an automobile. Allstate Ins. Co. v. Webb, 10 N.C. App. 672, 179 S.E.2d 803 (1971).

AS VICTIM'S RIGHTS ARE NOT DERIVED THROUGH INSURED. --The victim's rights against the insurer are not derived through the insured as in the case of voluntary insurance, but are statutory and become absolute, under subdivision (f)(1), of this section on the occurrence of an injury covered by the policy. Nationwide Mut. Ins. Co. v. Roberts, 261 N.C. 285, 134 S.E.2d 654 (1964).

The purpose of compulsory liability insurance is not, like that of ordinary insurance, to save harmless the tort-feasor himself; therefore, there is no reason why the victim's right to recover from the insurance carrier should depend upon whether the conduct of its insured was intentional or negligent. Nationwide Mut. Ins. Co. v. Roberts, 261 N.C. 285, 134 S.E.2d 654 (1964).

The victim's rights against the insurer are not derived through the insured. Such rights are statutory and become absolute upon the occurrence of injury or damage inflicted by the named insured, by one driving with his permission, or by one driving while in lawful possession of the named insured's car, regardless of whether or not the nature and circumstances of the injury are covered by the contractual terms of the policy. Ohio Cas. Ins. Co. v. Anderson, 59 N.C. App. 621, 298 S.E.2d 56 (1982).

BUT INSURER MAY RECOVER FROM INSURED AMOUNT PAID FOR INTENTIONAL INJURIES. --Where, but for the provisions of this section, the insurer would not have been liable under its policy for injury intentionally inflicted by the use of an automobile, it could recover from the insured the amount paid to a claimant for such injury, and also the amount of its expenses. Allstate Ins. Co. v. Webb, 10 N.C. App. 672, 179 S.E.2d 803 (1971).

INSURER IS LIABLE FOR PROPERTY DAMAGE INTENTIONALLY INFLICTED BY INSURED. --An automobile insurer in this State is liable, within the maximum coverage required by this Article, for property damage caused by an insured who intentionally drives an automobile into plaintiff's property. Nationwide Mut. Ins. Co. v. Knight, 34 N.C. App. 96, 237 S.E.2d 341, cert. denied, 293 N.C. 589, 239 S.E.2d 263 (1977).

An automobile insurer was required to compensate defendant for any property damage arising out of the intentional ramming of defendant's automobile by the insured. Nationwide Mut. Ins. Co. v. Knight, 34 N.C. App. 96, 237 S.E.2d 341, cert. denied, 293 N.C. 589, 239 S.E.2d 263 (1977).

A WOUND CAUSED BY GUNSHOTS FIRED FROM THE INSURED'S MOVING AUTOMOBILE did not constitute an accident arising out of the ownership, maintenance or use of such automobile. Nationwide Mut. Ins. Co. v. Knight, 34 N.C. App. 96, 237 S.E.2d 341, cert. denied, 293 N.C. 589, 239 S.E.2d 263 (1977).

There was no casual relationship between the ownership, maintenance and use of the insured's moving vehicle, and the injury sustained by the minor defendant as a result of gunshots fired from that moving vehicle. Nationwide Mut. Ins. Co. v. Knight, 34 N.C. App. 96, 237 S.E.2d 341, cert. denied, 293 N.C. 589, 239 S.E.2d 263 (1977).

THROWING AN OBJECT FROM A CAR at someone on the side of the road was an independent act disassociated from the use of an automobile, for which the insurance policy did not provide coverage through it's "arising from the ownership maintenance or use of" language. Providence Wash. Ins. Co. v. Locklear ex rel. Smith, 115 N.C. App. 490, 445 S.E.2d 418 (1994).

NEGLIGENTLY SELF-INFLICTED INJURY NOT COMPENSABLE. --This section was not intended to compensate an insured for injury and damage negligently inflicted upon himself. Strickland v. Hughes, 273 N.C. 481, 160 S.E.2d 313 (1968).

MEDICAL PAYMENT COVERAGE. --The mandatory coverage required by this Article does not require the insurer to extend medical payment coverage beyond the terms of the policy to one who receives liability coverage solely by virtue of this Article. Nationwide Mut. Ins. Co. v. Chantos, 293 N.C. 431, 238 S.E.2d 597 (1977).

THAT EACH DRIVER IN A TWO-CAR COLLISION WOULD RECOVER from the other's insurance carrier was not in the legislative contemplation when the legislature passed this Article. Moore v. Young, 263 N.C. 483, 139 S.E.2d 704 (1965); McKinney v. Morrow, 18 N.C. App. 282, 196 S.E.2d 585, cert. denied, 283 N.C. 665, 197 S.E.2d 874 (1973).

"OTHER INSURANCE" PROVISION HELD VALID. --A provision in a liability policy excluding coverage if the accident in question is covered by other insurance does not contravene the North Carolina Financial Responsibility Law. Allstate Ins. Co. v. Shelby Mut. Ins. Co., 269 N.C. 341, 152 S.E.2d 436 (1968), commented on in 46 N.C.L. Rev. 433; Government Employees Ins. Co. v. Lumbermens Mut. Cas. Co., 269 N.C. 354, 152 S.E.2d 445 (1967).

VICTIM'S RIGHT TO RECOVER IS STATUTORY. --Under the Motor Vehicle and Financial Responsibility Act the victim's right to recover against the insurer is not derived through the insured, as in cases of voluntary insurance; his right to recover is statutory. Nationwide Mut. Ins. Co. v. Aetna Life & Cas. Co., 283 N.C. 87, 194 S.E.2d 834 (1973).

AND BECOMES ABSOLUTE UPON OCCURRENCE OF AN INJURY COVERED BY THE POLICY. Nationwide Mut. Ins. Co. v. Aetna Life & Cas. Co., 283 N.C. 87, 194 S.E.2d 834 (1973).

Under subdivision (f)(1) of this section, if insured becomes legally obligated for the payment of damages on account of a collision, insurer's liability becomes absolute as of the date of the collision if the policy is then valid and in force, and subsequent violations of policy provisions by the insured cannot affect the liability of insurer to a person injured in such collision as the result of insured's negligence, although insured may be liable to insurer for damages resulting to insurer as the result of breach of the policy provision. Swain v. Nationwide Mut. Ins. Co., 253 N.C. 120, 116 S.E.2d 482 (1960).

Under this section insurer's liability (within the limits of the compulsory coverage) for the payment of the damages for which insured was "legally obligated" became absolute when the injured party's car was damaged, at which time the policy issued by insurer to insured was in full force and effect. Lane v. Iowa Mut. Ins. Co., 258 N.C. 318, 128 S.E.2d 398 (1962).

THE VICTIM'S RIGHTS UNDER THE ACT AGAINST THE INSURER ARE NOT DERIVED THROUGH THE INSURED, as in the case of voluntary insurance. Such rights are statutory and become absolute upon the occurrence of injury or damage inflicted by the named insured, by one driving with his permission, or by one driving while in lawful possession of the named insured's car, regardless of whether or not the nature or circumstances of the injury are covered by the contractual terms of the policy. Engle v. State Farm Mut. Auto. Ins. Co., 37 N.C. App. 126, 245 S.E.2d 532, cert. denied, 295 N.C. 645, 248 S.E.2d 250 (1978).

EFFECT OF ISSUANCE OF FORM FS-1. --By the issuance of an FS-1 an insurer represents that it has issued and there is in effect an owner's motor vehicle liability policy. Harris v. Nationwide Mut. Ins. Co., 261 N.C. 499, 135 S.E.2d 209 (1964).

By the issuance of an FS-1, the insurer represents that everything requisite for a binding insurance policy has been performed, including payment, or satisfactory arrangement for payment, of premium. Once the FS-1 has been issued, nonpayment of premium, nothing else appearing, is no defense in a suit by a third party beneficiary against insurer. Harris v. Nationwide Mut. Ins. Co., 261 N.C. 499, 135 S.E.2d 209 (1964).

As between insurer and insured, the issuance by insurer of Form FS-1 stating thereon that insurance was effective, does not estop insurer from denying that the policy was in force or that notice of the accident was given as required by the policy. Harris v. Nationwide Mut. Ins. Co., 261 N.C. 499, 135 S.E.2d 209 (1964).

CAUSE OF ACTION ARISES AT TIME OF COLLISION. --The provisions of subdivision (f)(1) of this section support the statement of law that any cause of action which a plaintiff may acquire against defendant as a result of a collision arises at the time of the collision, and any right which he may claim against defendant under the laws of this State and under the uninsured motorists insurance coverage of the policy must be determined by the facts existing at the time of the collision. Hardin v. American Mut. Fire Ins. Co., 261 N.C. 67, 134 S.E.2d 142 (1964).

EFFECT OF POLICY VIOLATIONS. --Under subdivision (f)(1) of this section, policy violations do not defeat or avoid the policy in respect of a plaintiff's right to recover from defendant insurer the amount of the judgment establishing insured's legal liability to plaintiff. Swain v. Nationwide Mut. Ins. Co., 253 N.C. 120, 116 S.E.2d 482 (1960).

As to the compulsory coverage provided by a motor vehicle liability policy as defined in this section, issued as proof of financial responsibility as defined in G.S. 20-279.1, subdivision (f)(1) of this section provides explicitly that "no violation of said policy shall defeat or void said policy." Swain v. Nationwide Mut. Ins. Co., 253 N.C. 120, 116 S.E.2d 482 (1960); Jones v. State Farm Mut. Auto. Ins. Co., 270 N.C. 454, 155 S.E.2d 118 (1967).

Under subdivision (f)(1) of this section, insured's failure to comply with policy provisions as to notice of accident and of suit did not defeat the injured party's right to recover from the insurer the amount of a judgment by which insured's legal obligation to the insured party was finally determined. Lane v. Iowa Mut. Ins. Co., 258 N.C. 318, 128 S.E.2d 398 (1962).

No violation of the provisions of an owner's policy as an assigned risk will void the policy where the liability thereunder has been incurred by reason of the insured's operation of the automobile described in the policy. Woodruff v. State Farm Mut. Auto. Ins. Co., 260 N.C. 723, 133 S.E.2d 704 (1963).

Subsection (f) provides that except with respect to liability insurance written under the assigned risk plan, the liability of the insurance carrier shall be the extent of coverage required by this Article become absolute when the injury or damage covered by motor vehicle liability occurs, and no violation of said policy shall defeat or void said policy. Beasley v. Hartford Accident & Indem. Co., 11 N.C. App. 34, 180 S.E.2d 381, aff'd, 280 N.C. 177, 184 S.E.2d 841 (1971).

Driver's admitted failure to forward copies of notices and legal papers to insurance company did not constitute a violation of its contract and did not void any coverage on behalf of the insured above the compulsory amount; this section provides that violation of an insurance policy on the part of an insured cannot be used by the insurer to void the compulsory coverage required by the State. Aetna Cas. & Sur. Co. v. Welch, 92 N.C. App. 211, 373 S.E.2d 887 (1988).

FRAUD IN APPLICATION. --As to coverage required by the Financial Responsibility Act, fraud in an application for motor vehicle liability insurance is not a defense to the insurer's liability once injury has occurred. Hartford Underwriters Ins. Co. v. Becks, 123 N.C. App. 489, 473 S.E.2d 427 (1996).

INSURER NOT LIABLE ON RETROACTIVE POLICY FRAUDULENTLY PROCURED AFTER ACCIDENT OCCURRED. --Judgment declaring that an insurer was obligated to provide liability coverage for accident was error under circumstances in which, on the day of the accident, after the accident had occurred, the driver went to the insurer's office and tendered the past due premium to the local agent, but did not tell the insurer about the accident; G.S. 20-279.21(f)(1) presupposed the existence of a policy at the time of injury or damage. An insurance company was not liable under an automobile insurance policy when a person fraudulently procured retroactive liability insurance after an accident occurred. N.C. Farm Bureau Mut. Ins. Co. v. Simpson, 198 N.C. App. 190, 678 S.E.2d 753 (2009), review denied, 363 N.C. 806, 691 S.E.2d 13, N.C. LEXIS 56 (2010).

LIABILITY UNDER ASSIGNED RISK POLICY BECOMES ABSOLUTE WHEN INJURY OR DAMAGE OCCURS. --As provided in subdivision (f)(1) of this section liability becomes absolute when a plaintiff's injury and damage occur, notwithstanding subsequent violations by the insured under an assigned risk policy of his obligations to the insurance company under the policy provisions. Jones v. State Farm Mut. Auto. Ins. Co., 270 N.C. 454, 155 S.E.2d 118 (1967), decided under this section as it stood before the 1967 amendments thereto.

AND INSURER IS DEPRIVED OF DEFENSES OTHERWISE AVAILABLE UNDER STANDARD POLICY PROVISIONS. --Subdivision (f)(1) of this section, as interpreted and applied by the Supreme Court, deprives the insurer under an assigned risk policy of the defenses otherwise available under its standard policy provisions. Jones v. State Farm Mut. Auto. Ins. Co., 270 N.C. 454, 155 S.E.2d 118 (1967), decided under this section as it stood before the 1967 amendments thereto.

AND THIS PROVISION DOES NOT VIOLATE STATE OR FEDERAL CONSTITUTION. --Subdivision (f)(1) of this section, when applied to an assigned risk policy issued in compliance with the plan set forth in former G.S. 20-279.34 and regulations pursuant thereto, does not deprive an insurance company of its property without due process of law and otherwise than by the law of the land in contravention of U.S. Const., Amend. XIV and N.C. Const., Art. I, § 1 and 19. Jones v. State Farm Mut. Auto. Ins. Co., 270 N.C. 454, 155 S.E.2d 118 (1967), decided under this section as it stood before the 1967 amendments thereto.

POLICY PROVISION REQUIRING FORWARDING OF SUIT PAPERS IS VALID. --Policy provisions in an insurance contract requiring prompt forwarding of legal process as a condition precedent to recovery on the policy are valid so long as they do not conflict with this Article. Rose Hill Poultry Corp. v. American Mut. Ins. Co., 34 N.C. App. 224, 237 S.E.2d 564 (1977).

HENCE, FAILURE TO FORWARD SUIT PAPERS RELIEVES INSURER OF LIABILITY. --While no decision of the Supreme Court involving a policy provision, "If claim is made or suit is brought against the Insured, he shall immediately forward to the Company every demand, notice, summons or other process received by him or his representative," has come to the court's attention, decisions in other jurisdictions hold this is an unambiguous, reasonable and valid stipulation, and that, unless the insured or his judgment creditor can show compliance by the insured with this policy requirement, the insurer is relieved of liability. Clemmons v. Nationwide Mut. Ins. Co., 267 N.C. 495, 148 S.E.2d 640 (1966).

UNLESS INSURER LOSES RIGHT TO DEFEAT RECOVERY BY WAIVER OR ESTOPPEL. --An automobile liability insurer may, by waiver or estoppel, lose its right to defeat a recovery under a liability policy because of the insured's failure to comply with the policy provision as to the forwarding of suit papers. Clemmons v. Nationwide Mut. Ins. Co., 267 N.C. 495, 148 S.E.2d 640 (1966).

THE ESSENTIAL ELEMENTS OF A WAIVER are: (1) The existence, at the time of the alleged waiver, of a right, advantage or benefit; (2) the knowledge, actual or constructive, of the existence thereof; and (3) an intention to relinquish such right, advantage or benefit. Clemmons v. Nationwide Mut. Ins. Co., 267 N.C. 495, 148 S.E.2d 640 (1966).

FAILURE TO FORWARD SUIT PAPERS DID NOT DEFEAT INSURER'S LIABILITY TO THIRD PARTY. --The insured's failure under the terms of a policy to forward suit papers or otherwise notify the insurer of an action instituted in another state by an injured third party did not defeat or void the insurer's liability under the policy with respect to the third party. Rose Hill Poultry Corp. v. American Mut. Ins. Co., 34 N.C. App. 224, 237 S.E.2d 564 (1977).

BUT RELIEVED INSURER OF LIABILITY TO INSURED. --The insured's failure under the terms of a policy to forward suit papers or otherwise notify the insurer of an action instituted in another state by an injured third party relieved the insurer of its obligations under the policy to afford protection for the insured. The insured was not the innocent victim this Article was designed to protect, and thus the provision requiring forwarding of legal process was not in conflict with the purpose of this Article. Rose Hill Poultry Corp. v. American Mut. Ins. Co., 34 N.C. App. 224, 237 S.E.2d 564 (1977).

PURPOSE OF REQUIREMENT THAT PLAINTIFF GIVE NOTICE TO ASSIGNED RISK INSURER. --A manifest purpose of subdivision (f)(1) of this section is to require the plaintiff to give the insurer of assigned risk or Reinsurance Facility individuals notice of actions brought against such persons so that the insurer may protect its interests. Love v. Nationwide Mut. Ins. Co., 45 N.C. App. 444, 263 S.E.2d 337, cert. denied, 300 N.C. 198, 269 S.E.2d 617 (1980).

NOTICE TO INSURER NOT REQUIRED UNDER SUBDIVISION (F)(1) WHEN INSURED NOT ASSIGNED RISK INSURER. --Plaintiff was not required to give the insurer the registered notice required by subdivision (f)(1) because the insured was not an "assigned risk insured" under the statute. To hold otherwise would require every plaintiff to send copy of summons and complaint by registered mail to the carrier of the liability insurance of the owner of the vehicle involved in every accident resulting in litigation to avoid the pitfall of the possibility of the vehicle involved being a replacement vehicle registered in a different name than the applicant for assignment of risk. This was obviously not intended by the General Assembly. Beasley v. Hartford Accident & Indem. Co., 11 N.C. App. 34, 180 S.E.2d 381, aff'd, 280 N.C. 177, 184 S.E.2d 841 (1971).

PLAINTIFF'S FAILURE TO SERVE INSURER DID NOT RENDER JUDGMENT AGAINST INSURED VOID --Where a default judgment was entered against an insured in an individual's negligence action, the trial court did not abuse its discretion in denying the intervening insurer's motion to set aside the judgment as void under G.S. 1A-1, Rule 60(b)(4) on the ground that the individual who sued the insured had not given the insurer proper notification of the suit under G.S. 20-279.21(b)(3), as the insurer failed to show that the lack of notice to the insurer deprived the trial court of jurisdiction or authority to enter the default judgment against the insured, or otherwise rendered the judgment void. Barton v. Sutton, 152 N.C. App. 706, 568 S.E.2d 264 (2002).

DEFAULT JUDGMENT. --"Default judgment," as this term is used in subdivision (f)(1) of this section, must be construed so as to include all judgments obtained where an insured person falling within the provisions of this subdivision has not timely filed a responsive pleading or has otherwise made himself subject to a G.S. 1A-1, Rule 55 default. Love v. Nationwide Mut. Ins. Co., 45 N.C. App. 444, 263 S.E.2d 337, cert. denied, 300 N.C. 198, 269 S.E.2d 617 (1980).

The giving of notice of a default judgment is a condition precedent to maintaining a subsequent action against the insurer on the judgment, and the failure to provide that notice operates as a bar to the action. Love v. Nationwide Mut. Ins. Co., 45 N.C. App. 444, 263 S.E.2d 337, cert. denied, 300 N.C. 198, 269 S.E.2d 617 (1980).

A trial which results in findings or a verdict against a nonappearing defendant does not take the resulting judgment for the appearing party out of the "default" category within the meaning of subdivision (f)(1) of this section. Love v. Nationwide Mut. Ins. Co., 45 N.C. App. 444, 263 S.E.2d 337, cert. denied, 300 N.C. 198, 269 S.E.2d 617 (1980).

SUBDIVISION (F)(1) WAS NOT INTENDED TO PROTECT BREACH OF CONTRACT. --Although a manifest purpose of subdivision (f)(1) of this section is to require the plaintiff to give the insurer of assigned risk or reinsurance facility individuals notice of actions brought against such persons so that the insurer may protect its interests, it was not within the contemplation of the legislature that subdivision (f)(1) would protect brokers or agents in breach of contract for failure to perform a contract to perform insurance. Johnson v. Smith, 58 N.C. App. 390, 293 S.E.2d 644 (1982).

ABSOLUTE OBLIGATION TO DEFEND. --The obligation of a liability insurer to defend an action brought by an injured third party against the insured is absolute when the allegations of the complaint bring the claim within the coverage of the policy. Indiana Lumbermen's Mut. Ins. Co. v. Champion, 80 N.C. App. 370, 343 S.E.2d 15 (1986).

NO STATUTORY OBLIGATION TO DEFEND INSURED. --An insurer's duty to defend its insured in a motor vehicle liability action arises from the language of the insurance contract since there exists no statutory obligation in North Carolina to provide a defense for the insured. Brown v. Lumbermens Mut. Cas. Co., 90 N.C. 464, 369 S.E.2d 367, aff'd, 326 N.C. 387, 390 S.E.2d 150 (1990), cert. denied, 323 N.C. 363, 373 S.E.2d 541 (1988).

There is no statutory requirement that an insurance company provide its insured with a defense. Brown v. Lumbermens Mut. Cas. Co., 326 N.C. 387, 390 S.E.2d 150 (1990).

BUT DUTY CAN BE ASSUMED VOLUNTARILY. --Where an insurance company utilized subdivision (b)(3)a to provide a defense to the insured party, it was a party in the tort actions, although unnamed; therefore, although it was not required to defend the lawsuit, but chose to do so, by so doing it became a defendant, liable for attorney's fees and costs. Turnage ex rel. Turnage v. Nationwide Mut. Ins. Co., 109 N.C. App. 300, 426 S.E.2d 433, aff'd per curium, 335 N.C. 168, 435 S.E.2d 772 (1993).

DUTY TO DEFEND SEPARATE FROM DUTY TO INDEMNIFY. --It is a well recognized legal principle that an insurer's duty to defend its insured is separate from and broader than the insurer's duty to indemnify the insured. Brown v. Lumbermens Mut. Cas. Co., 90 N.C. 464, 369 S.E.2d 367, cert. denied, 323 N.C. 363, 373 S.E.2d 542, cert. denied, 323 N.C. 363, 373 S.E.2d 541 (1988).

REFUSAL OF INSURER TO DEFEND. --Where a liability insurer denies liability for a claim asserted against the insured and unjustifiably refuses to defend an action therefor, the insured is released from a provision of the policy against settlement of claims without the insurer's consent, and from a provision making the liability of the insurer dependent on the obtaining of a judgment against the insured; and that under such circumstances, the insured may make a reasonable compromise or settlement in good faith without losing his right to recover on the policy. Nixon v. Liberty Mut. Ins. Co., 255 N.C. 106, 120 S.E.2d 430 (1961).

If insured in a liability policy gives timely notice of a suit against him within the coverage of the liability policy, and insurer refuses to defend such suit, insured is entitled to recover of insurer the amount he is reasonably required to spend by virtue of the failure of insurer to defend the suit. Harris v. Nationwide Mut. Ins. Co., 261 N.C. 499, 135 S.E.2d 209 (1964).

AN INSURER'S REFUSAL TO DEFEND IS UNJUSTIFIED IF IT IS DETERMINED THAT THE ACTION IS IN FACT WITHIN THE COVERAGE OF THE POLICY. This is so even if the refusal to defend is based on the insurer's honest but mistaken belief that the claim is outside the policy coverage. Indiana Lumbermen's Mut. Ins. Co. v. Champion, 80 N.C. App. 370, 343 S.E.2d 15 (1986).

Where the jury's verdict determined the action was within the coverage of the policy, defendant insurer's refusal to defend was unjustified; therefore, insurer could not, if it had the opportunity, assert that is was an honest mistake since that was irrelevant. Wilson v. State Farm Mut. Auto. Ins. Co., 92 N.C. App. 320, 374 S.E.2d 446 (1988), rev'd on other grounds, 327 N.C. 419, 394 S.E.2d 807 (1990), modified on reh'g, 329 N.C. 262, 404 S.E.2d 852 (1991).

INSURER UNJUSTIFIEDLY REFUSING TO DEFEND NOT ENTITLED TO INVOKE "NO ACTION" PROVISION. --Where claim against insured was within the coverage of insurer's policy, insurer's refusal to defend the action was unjustified, and therefore insurer was not entitled to successfully invoke the "no action" provision in its policy as a defense. Indiana Lumbermen's Mut. Ins. Co. v. Champion, 80 N.C. App. 370, 343 S.E.2d 15 (1986).

DEFENDANT-INSURER WAS PROPERLY PERMITTED TO PARTICIPATE IN THE TRIAL where there was no evidence that the insurer failed to participate in the pre-trial conference. Warren v. GMC, 142 N.C. App. 316, 542 S.E.2d 317 (2001).

SETTLEMENT OF CLAIMS BY INSURER. --This section, which contains a provision expressly authorizing insurance companies to make settlement with claimants, is not any indication that prior to its effective date liability insurers were prohibited from settling with some of several claimants for the protection of their insured. Alford v. Textile Ins. Co., 248 N.C. 224, 103 S.E.2d 8 (1958); Braddy v. Nationwide Mut. Liab. Ins. Co., 122 N.C. App. 402, 470 S.E.2d 820 (1996).

When exercised in good faith, subdivision (f)(3) of this section, authorizing the insurer to negotiate and settle claims, is valid and binding on the insured. Nationwide Mut. Ins. Co. v. Chantos, 293 N.C. 431, 238 S.E.2d 597 (1977).

A provision in a liability policy that insurer might negotiate and settle any claim or suit was not proscribed or rendered void under repealed G.S. 20-227 as it stood in 1947. Alford v. Textile Ins. Co., 248 N.C. 224, 103 S.E.2d 8 (1958).

A liability insurance carrier may settle part of multiple claims arising from the negligence of its insured, even though such settlements result in preference by exhausting the fund to which an injured party whose claim has not been settled might otherwise look for payment, provided the insurer acts in good faith and not arbitrarily, and the burden is upon a claimant whose claim is not paid in full because of prior payment made by insurer in

settlements of other claims, to allege and prove bad faith on the part of the insurer. Alford v. Textile Ins. Co., 248 N.C. 224, 103 S.E.2d 8 (1958), decided under repealed § 20-227.

Where an insurance carrier makes a settlement in good faith, such settlement is binding on the insured as between him and the insurer, but such settlement is not binding as between the insured and a third party where the settlement was made without the knowledge or consent of the insured or over his protest, unless the insured in the meantime has ratified such settlement. Bradford v. Kelly, 260 N.C. 382, 132 S.E.2d 886 (1963).

A payment by insurer in settlement of the claim of one motorist against insured motorist, solely for the purpose of terminating the liability of insurer and reserving the insured motorist's rights, does not preclude the insured motorist from thereafter maintaining an action against the other. Gamble v. Stutts, 262 N.C. 276, 136 S.E.2d 688 (1964).

The duty of the insurer in the exercise of its contract right to settle a pending liability claim or suit is to act diligently and in good faith in effecting settlements within policy limits and, if necessary to accomplish that purpose, to pay the full amount of the policy. Coca-Cola Bottling Co. v. Maryland Cas. Co., 325 F. Supp. 204 (W.D.N.C. 1971).

Every claim has some settlement value, but the existence of issues for the jury rather than the certainty of nonsuit does not demonstrate bad faith or even lack of due care if the insurer fails to settle. Coca-Cola Bottling Co. v. Maryland Cas. Co., 325 F. Supp. 204 (W.D.N.C. 1971).

Although the insurer may be unreasonable in not settling as seen in retrospect, it is liable for recovery beyond its policy limits only if it acts with wrongful or fraudulent purpose or with lack of good faith; an honest mistake of judgment is not actionable. Coca-Cola Bottling Co. v. Maryland Cas. Co., 325 F. Supp. 204 (W.D.N.C. 1971).

Insurance counsel do not have to be omniscient, and their opinions, whether they support or cast doubt on the action of the insurer in not settling, do not determine the issue of liability above policy limits. Coca-Cola Bottling Co. v. Maryland Cas. Co., 325 F. Supp. 204 (W.D.N.C. 1971).

A release or settlement of an action against the tortfeasor does not vitiate the express statutory terms of subdivision (b)(4) of this section, such that the action can continue with the insurance carrier remaining as an unnamed defendant. Sellers v. North Carolina Farm Bureau Mut. Ins. Co., 108 N.C. App. 697, 424 S.E.2d 669 (1993).

Because plaintiff was afforded the opportunity to be heard on his claim for damages against the tortfeasor, and his derivative claim for UIM coverage against his insurer sounded in tort, plaintiff's due process rights were not violated by allowing his insurer to proceed as an unnamed party after it settled with tortfeasor. Braddy v. Nationwide Mut. Liab. Ins. Co., 122 N.C. App. 402, 470 S.E.2d 820 (1996).

Chapter 20

PLAINTIFF INSURER WAS PRECLUDED FROM ASSERTING ITS POLICY DEFENSES BY ITS REFUSAL TO DEFEND where, due to the "possibility" that the claim would be covered by the policy, the insurer's refusal to defend was unjustified. Naddeo v. Allstate Ins. Co., 139 N.C. App. 311, 533 S.E.2d 501 (2000).

ACTION BY INSURED AGAINST OTHER MOTORIST AFTER SETTLEMENT. --See Bradford v. Kelly, 260 N.C. 382, 132 S.E.2d 886 (1963).

ACTION BY INSURED AGAINST INSURER. --A cause of action alleging breach of good faith will not lie when the insurer settles a claim, in spite of insured's protestations that the claimants acted fraudulently, within the monetary limits of the insured's policy; the insurer has the duty to consider the insured's interest but may act in its own interest in settlement of the claim. Cash v. State Farm Mut. Auto. Ins. Co., 137 N.C. App. 192, 528 S.E.2d 372 (2000).

PROVISION FOR COMPULSORY ARBITRATION CONFLICTS WITH STATUTE. --A provision in an insurance policy, in effect, ousting the jurisdiction of the court to judicially determine liability and damages and providing for compulsory arbitration between the insured and the company, if they do not agree, conflicts with the beneficent purposes of the uninsured motorist statute favorable to the insured, and the provision of the statute controls. Wright v. Fid. & Cas. Co., 270 N.C. 577, 155 S.E.2d 100 (1967).

AN INSURER MAY HAVE REIMBURSEMENT FROM A STRANGER to the insurance contract whose negligence caused the injuries and damages for which the insurer had paid as a result of liability imposed by statute. Nationwide Mut. Ins. Co. v. Chantos, 293 N.C. 431, 238 S.E.2d 597 (1977).

POLICY PROVISION FOR REIMBURSEMENT BY INSURED. --Subsection (h) of this section does not compel reimbursement by the insured, it merely allows the insurer and the insured to enter into such an agreement. Nationwide Mut. Ins. Co. v. Chantos, 293 N.C. 431, 238 S.E.2d 597 (1977).

A policy provision providing for reimbursement by the insured is merely a contractual agreement between the parties to the policy and does not have the effect or force of a statute. Nationwide Mut. Ins. Co. v. Chantos, 293 N.C. 431, 238 S.E.2d 597 (1977).

COUNTERCLAIM AGAINST INSURED UNDER SUBSECTION (H). --In insured's action against insurer to recover for sums expended in defending a suit against insured within the coverage of the policy, insured's allegations of the payment of a sum to insurer's agent under agreement for the issuance of a binder do not relate to liability imposed by the Financial Responsibility Act, and therefore furnish no basis for a counterclaim against insured under subsection (h) of this section. Harris v. Nationwide Mut. Ins. Co., 261 N.C. 499, 135 S.E.2d 209 (1964).

BURDEN ON PLAINTIFF TO PROVE DEFENDANT WAS INSURED. --In order for the plaintiff to recover on the policy, the burden is on plaintiff to allege and prove that the defendant was insured under the policy on the date of the accident in which plaintiff was injured. Younts v. State Farm Mut. Auto. Ins. Co., 281 N.C. 582, 189 S.E.2d 137 (1972).

LIABILITY COVERAGE DISTINGUISHED FROM UNINSURED AND UNDERINSURED COVERAGE. --The statutory schemes operate on the realization that the very nature of liability's insurance coverage is different from uninsured/underinsured motorist coverage. The former protects covered persons from the consequences of their own negligence; the latter protects covered persons from the consequences of the negligence of others. Smith v. Nationwide Mut. Ins. Co., 328 N.C. 139, 400 S.E.2d 44 (1991), rehearing denied, 328 N.C. 577, 403 S.E.2d 514 (1991).

The statutory scheme for liability insurance is primarily vehicle-oriented while uninsured/underinsured motorist insurance is essentially person-oriented. Liability coverage is third-party insurance while uninsured/underinsured motorist coverage is first-party insurance. Smith v. Nationwide Mut. Ins. Co., 328 N.C. 139, 400 S.E.2d 44 (1991), rehearing denied, 328 N.C. 577, 403 S.E.2d 514 (1991).

DUTY OF INSURER WHERE POLICY HOLDER HAS MINIMUM LIMITS LIABILITY INSURANCE. --An insurance agent does not negligently breach a fiduciary duty to a policy holder who has a minimum limits automobile liability insurance policy if she does not explain to the policy holder that he would be eligible for UIM coverage if he increased his automobile liability insurance coverage above the statutory minimum limits. Phillips ex rel. Phillips v. State Farm Mut. Auto. Ins. Co., 129 N.C. App. 111, 497 S.E.2d 325 (1998), cert. denied, 348 N.C. 500, 510 S.E.2d 653 (1998).

UNINSURED/UNDERINSURED MOTORIST COVERAGES NOT REQUIRED TO EQUAL LIABILITY OR MEDICAL COVERAGES. --The purpose of uninsured/underinsured motorist insurance differs from the purposes of medical payments insurance or liability insurance. Likewise, while the statutory scheme requires the insurance company to offer uninsured/underinsured motorist coverages only if liability coverages exceed the minimum statutory requirement and in an amount equal to the limits of bodily injury liability insurance, nothing in the statute requires that the scope of the coverage be the same. Smith v. Nationwide Mut. Ins. Co., 328 N.C. 139, 400 S.E.2d 44 (1991), rehearing denied, 328 N.C. 577, 403 S.E.2d 514 (1991).

REDUCING DEFENDANT'S LIABILITY TO INJURED PLAINTIFF BY AMOUNT OF WORKERS' COMPENSATION PAID TO PLAINTIFF WAS IMPROPER. --Where plaintiff's damages were established at amount far in excess of any kind of insurance that was available to her, reducing defendant's liability to her by worker's compensation she received would disserve dominant public policy behind Financial Responsibility Act (that of making insurance available for compensation of innocently injured accident victims) and leave unfulfilled plaintiff's purpose in buying her own coverage in first place; nothing in subsection (e) of this section suggests that General Assembly intended to authorize

Chapter 20

any such absurdity. Sproles v. Greene, 100 N.C. App. 96, 394 S.E.2d 691 (1990), rev'd on other grounds, Sproles v. Integon Insurance Co., 329 N.C. 603, 407 S.E.2d 497 (1991).

SUBROGATION OF WORKERS' COMPENSATION INSURANCE CARRIER TO EMPLOYER'S RIGHT TO PAYMENT OF PROCEEDS FROM UNINSURED/UNDERINSURED MOTORIST INSURANCE. --Section 97-10.2 provides for subrogation of workers' compensation insurance carrier to employer's right, upon reimbursement of the employee, to any payment, including uninsured/underinsured motorist insurance proceeds, made to employee by or on behalf of a third party as a result of employee's injury. Ohio Cas. Group v. Owens, 99 N.C. App. 131, 392 S.E.2d 647 (1990), review denied, 327 N.C. 483, 396 S.E.2d 614 (1990), overruled by McMillian v. North Carolina Farm Bureau Mut. Ins. Co., 347 N.C. 560, 495 S.E.2d 352 (1998).

POLICY EXCLUSIONS WHICH CONFLICT WITH MOTOR VEHICLES SAFETY AND FINANCIAL RESPONSIBILITY ACT ARE UNENFORCEABLE. --Where policy terms purporting to exclude certain risks from uninsured/underinsured coverage are in conflict with provisions of Motor Vehicle Safety and Financial Responsibility Act, such exclusions are unenforceable. Ohio Cas. Group v. Owens, 99 N.C. App. 131, 392 S.E.2d 647 (1990), review denied, 327 N.C. 483, 396 S.E.2d 614 (1990), overruled by McMillian v. North Carolina Farm Bureau Mut. Ins. Co., 347 N.C. 560, 495 S.E.2d 352 (1998).

MINIMUM COVERAGE REQUIREMENTS NOT VIOLATED BY "OTHER INSURANCE" CLAUSE. --The court rejected the contention that the plaintiff/insurance company's "other insurance" clause violated North Carolina law and public policy by allowing the defendant/insurer to defeat the statutory requirement of providing minimum limits of coverage under this section and paying only a pro rata share of an insurance claim. USAA Cas. Ins. Co. v. Universal Underwriters Ins. Co., 138 N.C. App. 684, 532 S.E.2d 250 (2000).

FRAUD IN APPLICATION NOT A DEFENSE AS TO MINIMUM COVERAGE AMOUNTS. --As to the mandatory amount of motor vehicle liability insurance coverage required by this section, fraud in an application for insurance is not a defense to the insurer's liability once injury has occurred, but as to any amount of coverage in excess of the statutory minimum, fraud is a defense under common law or contract law principles. Odum v. Nationwide Mut. Ins. Co., 101 N.C. App. 627, 401 S.E.2d 87, cert. denied, 329 N.C. 499, 407 S.E.2d 539 (1991).

BUT AS TO ANY COVERAGE IN EXCESS OF THE STATUTORY MINIMUM, THE INSURER IS NOT PRECLUDED BY STATUTE OR PUBLIC POLICY FROM ASSERTING THE DEFENSE of fraud. Such a defense, if successful, would insulate the insurer against liability as to both the insured, and the injured third party. Odum v. Nationwide Mut. Ins. Co., 101 N.C. App. 627, 401 S.E.2d 87, cert. denied, 329 N.C. 499, 407 S.E.2d 539 (1991).

TWO CLASSES OF "PERSONS INSURED." --Subdivision (b)(3) establishes two "classes" of "persons insured": (1) the named insured and, while resident of the same household, the spouse of the named insured and relatives of either, and (2) any person who uses with the consent, express or implied, of the named insured, the insured vehicle, and a guest in such vehicle. Members of the second class are "persons insured" for the purposes of uninsured motorist (UM) and underinsured motorist (UIM) coverage only when the insured vehicle is involved in the insured's injuries. Members of the first class are "persons insured" even where the insured vehicle is not involved in the insured's injuries. Smith v. Nationwide Mut. Ins. Co., 328 N.C. 139, 400 S.E.2d 44 (1991), rehearing denied, 328 N.C. 577, 403 S.E.2d 514 (1991).

"NAMED INSURED" DISTINGUISHED FROM OTHER COVERED PERSONS. --The term, "named insured," appears frequently in this section in such a way as to distinguish the "named insured" from other covered persons. Brown v. Truck Ins. Exch., 103 N.C. App. 59, 404 S.E.2d 172, cert. denied, 329 N.C. 786, 408 S.E.2d 515 (1991).

OPERATOR WITHIN SCOPE OF PERMISSION. --As an operator of one of garage automobiles within the scope of its permission, daughter of persons to whom car was loaned to was an insured under garage's insurance policy and insurer was responsible for providing liability coverage for her. Integon Indem. Corp. v. Universal Underwriters Ins. Co., 342 N.C. 166, 463 S.E.2d 389 (1995).

COVERAGE WHICH IS IN ADDITION TO THE MANDATORY REQUIREMENTS OF THE STATE ARE VOLUNTARY and are not subject to the requirements of the act. Voluntary coverage must be measured by the terms of the policy as written. Brown v. Truck Ins. Exch., 103 N.C. App. 59, 404 S.E.2d 172, cert. denied, 329 N.C. 786, 408 S.E.2d 515 (1991).

APPLICATION OF VOLUNTARY ADDITIONAL COVERAGE. --A policy insuring the owner of the vehicle hired by the named insured only if the actual use of the automobile is in the business of the named insured is beyond the requirements of the Motor Vehicle Safety and Financial Responsibility Act and is voluntary additional coverage. As such, it is to be applied according to its terms and limitations. Brown v. Truck Ins. Exch., 103 N.C. App. 59, 404 S.E.2d 172, cert. denied, 329 N.C. 786, 408 S.E.2d 515 (1991).

USE BY PROHIBITED PARTY. --This section did not impose coverage when owner's permittee gave possession to a third party who knew that he was prohibited from using the vehicle. Nationwide Mut. Ins. Co. v. Baer, 113 N.C. App. 517, 439 S.E.2d 202 (1994).

WHERE THE FORECAST OF EVIDENCE BEFORE THE TRIAL COURT SHOWED THERE WAS NO COLLISION OR CONTACT BETWEEN THE AUTOMOBILE DRIVEN BY THE UNKNOWN MOTORIST, which allegedly caused accident, and any other automobile, including that driven by plaintiff's intestate, defendant insurance company was entitled to judgment as a matter of law. Andersen v. Baccus, 335 N.C. 526, 439 S.E.2d 136 (1994).

APPLICABILITY OF ACT WHERE FOREIGN IN-SURER IS INVOLVED. --The Act was not triggered by a contract's conformity clause which stated that "if any provision of this policy is contrary to any law to which it is subject, such provision is hereby amended to conform thereto" where the defendant/insurance company was never authorized to transact business and issue insurance policies in North Carolina. The mere fact that the accident happened in North Carolina did not make the Florida policy subject to North Carolina law. Fortune Ins. Co. v. Owens, 351 N.C. 424, 526 S.E.2d 463 (2000).

OUT OF STATE LAW APPLIED. --Although North Carolina's legislature, in subsection (b), has determined that family members are not to be excluded from primary or uninsured motorist/ underinsured motorist coverage, where Tennessee law governed because significant connection existed with Tennessee and the connection with North Carolina was casual, family member exclusion in policy would be applied. Johns v. Automobile Club Ins. Co., 118 N.C. App. 424, 455 S.E.2d 466 (1995).

PAYMENTS MADE TO THE VICTIM PURSUANT TO UNDER-INSURED OR UNINSURED COVER-AGE ARE FROM A COLLATERAL SOURCE AS DE-FINED IN G.S. 15B-2; an award under the Crime Victims Compensation Act, Chapter 15B, will be reduced to the extent that the economic loss will be recouped from under-insured or uninsured coverage. Onley v. Nationwide Mut. Ins. Co., 118 N.C. App. 686, 456 S.E.2d 882 (1995).

LIABILITY NOT OWED BY RENTAL COMPANY. --Where driver had an operative liability insurance policy meeting the requirements of the Financial Responsibility Act, and where car rental company specifically excluded liability insurance in the lease agreement, car rental company owed driver no liability coverage. Jeffreys v. Snappy Car Rental, Inc., 128 N.C. App. 171, 493 S.E.2d 767 (1997).

FOR OTHER DECISIONS UNDER FORMER STATUTE, see Russell v. Lumbermen's Mut. Cas. Co., 237 N.C. 220, 74 S.E.2d 615 (1953); Howell v. Travelers Indem. Co., 237 N.C. 227, 74 S.E.2d 610 (1953); Sanders v. Chavis, 243 N.C. 380, 90 S.E.2d 749 (1956); Sanders v. Travelers Indem. Co., 144 F. Supp. 742 (M.D.N.C. 1956); Lynn v. Farm Bureau Mut. Auto. Ins. Co., 264 F.2d 921 (4th Cir. 1959).

APPLIED in Daniels v. Nationwide Mut. Ins. Co., 258 N.C. 660, 129 S.E.2d 314 (1963); Manning v. State Farm Mut. Auto. Ins. Co., 243 F. Supp. 619 (W.D.N.C. 1965); Abernethy v. Utica Mut. Ins. Co., 373 F.2d 565 (4th Cir. 1967); Beasley v. Hartford Accident & Indem. Co., 280 N.C. 177, 184 S.E.2d 841 (1971); McKinney v. Morrow, 18 N.C. App. 282, 196 S.E.2d 585 (1973); Nationwide Mut. Ins. Co. v. Chantos, 21 N.C. App. 129, 203 S.E.2d 421 (1974); Ford Marketing Corp. v. National Grange Mut. Ins. Co., 33 N.C. App. 297, 235 S.E.2d 82 (1977); Nationwide Mut. Ins. Co. v. Chantos, 298 N.C. 246, 258 S.E.2d 334 (1979); Tucker v. Peerless Ins. Co., 41 N.C. App. 302, 254 S.E.2d 656 (1979); Jones v. Nationwide Mut. Ins. Co., 42 N.C. App. 43, 255 S.E.2d 617 (1979); Caison v. Nationwide Ins.

Co., 45 N.C. App. 30, 262 S.E.2d 296 (1980); Love v. Moore, 305 N.C. 575, 291 S.E.2d 141 (1982); Wilfong v. Wilkins, 70 N.C. App. 127, 318 S.E.2d 540 (1984); State Farm Mut. Auto. Ins. Co. v. Blackwelder, 103 N.C. App. 656, 406 S.E.2d 301 (1991); Gurganious v. Integon Gen. Ins. Corp., 108 N.C. App. 163, 423 S.E.2d 317 (1992); North Carolina Farm Bureau Mut. Ins. Co. v. Knudsen, 109 N.C. App. 114, 426 S.E.2d 88 (1993); Wiggins v. Nationwide Mut. Ins. Co., 112 N.C. App. 26, 434 S.E.2d 642 (1993); Nationwide Mut. Ins. Co. v. Williams, 123 N.C. App. 103, 472 S.E.2d 220 (1996); Toole ex rel. Welch v. State Farm Mut. Auto. Ins. Co., 127 N.C. App. 291, 488 S.E.2d 833 (1997); Corbett v. Smith, 131 N.C. App. 327, 507 S.E.2d 303 (1998); Robinson v. Leach, 133 N.C. App. 436, 514 S.E.2d 567 (1999); Cash v. State Farm Mut. Auto. Ins. Co., 137 N.C. App. 192, 528 S.E.2d 372 (2000); State Farm Mut. Auto. Ins. Co. v. Gaylor, 190 N.C. App. 448, 660 S.E.2d 104 (2008), review denied, 363 N.C. 130, 676 S.E.2d 310 (2009).

CITED in Eaves v. Universal Underwriters Group, 107 N.C. App. 595, 421 S.E.2d 191; Taylor v. Green, 242 N.C. 156, 87 S.E.2d 11 (1955); Muncie v. Travelers Ins. Co., 253 N.C. 74, 116 S.E.2d 474 (1960); Fidelity & Cas. Co. v. Jackson, 297 F.2d 230 (4th Cir. 1961); Faizan v. Grain Dealers Mut. Ins. Co., 254 N.C. 47, 118 S.E.2d 303 (1961); Aldridge v. State, 4 N.C. App. 297, 166 S.E.2d 485 (1969); In re North Carolina Auto. Rate Admin. Office, 278 N.C. 302, 180 S.E.2d 155 (1971); Marks v. Thompson, 282 N.C. 174, 192 S.E.2d 311 (1972); Love v. Moore, 54 N.C. App. 406, 283 S.E.2d 801 (1981); Shew v. Southern Fire & Cas. Co., 58 N.C. App. 637, 294 S.E.2d 233 (1982); Wall v. Nationwide Mut. Ins. Co., 62 N.C. App. 127, 302 S.E.2d 302 (1983); Gardner v. North Carolina State Bar, 316 N.C. 285, 341 S.E.2d 517 (1986); Nationwide Mut. Ins. Co. v. Land, 318 N.C. 551, 350 S.E.2d 500 (1986); Davidson v. Knauff Ins. Agency, Inc., 93 N.C. App. 20, 376 S.E.2d 488 (1989); Lockwood v. Porter, 98 N.C. App. 410, 390 S.E.2d 742 (1990); Bass v. North Carolina Farm Bureau Mut. Ins. Co., 100 N.C. App. 728, 398 S.E.2d 47 (1990); Nationwide Mut. Ins. Co. v. Silverman ex rel. Radja, 104 N.C. App. 783, 411 S.E.2d 152 (1991); Patrick v. Ronald Williams, Professional Ass'n, 102 N.C. App. 355, 402 S.E.2d 452 (1991); Wilson v. State Farm Mut. Auto. Ins. Co., 329 N.C. 262, 404 S.E.2d 852 (1991); United Servs. Auto. Ass'n v. Universal Underwriters Ins. Co., 104 N.C. App. 206, 408 S.E.2d 750 (1991); Leonard v. North Carolina Farm Bureau Mut. Ins. Co., 104 N.C. App. 665, 411 S.E.2d 178 (1991); Eury v. Nationwide Mut. Ins. Co., 109 N.C. App. 303, 426 S.E.2d 442 (1993); Watson v. American Nat'l Fire Ins. Co., 333 N.C. 338, 425 S.E.2d 696 (1993); Cagle v. Teachy, 111 N.C. App. 244, 431 S.E.2d 801 (1993); Hackett v. Bonta, 113 N.C. App. 89, 437 S.E.2d 687 (1993); Ragan v. Hill, 337 N.C. 667, 447 S.E.2d 371 (1994); Metropolitan Property & Cas. Ins. Co. v. Lindquist, 120 N.C. App. 847, 463 S.E.2d 574 (1995); Vasseur v. St. Paul Mut. Ins. Co., 123 N.C. App. 418, 473 S.E.2d 15 (1996); Grimsley v. Nelson, 342 N.C. 542, 467 S.E.2d 92 (1996); Martin v. Continental Ins. Co., 123 N.C. App. 650, 474 S.E.2d 146

(1996); Morgan v. State Farm Mut. Auto. Ins. Co., 129 N.C. App. 200, 497 S.E.2d 834 (1998); Reese v. Barbee, 134 N.C. App. 728, 518 S.E.2d 571 (1999), cert. denied, 351 N.C. 188, 541 S.E.2d 716 (1999); Anderson v. Atlantic Cas. Ins. Co., 134 N.C. App. 724, 518 S.E.2d 786 (1999); Levasseur v. Lowery, 139 N.C. App. 235, 533 S.E.2d 511 (2000), cert. denied, in part, 352 N.C. 675, 545 S.E.2d 426 (2000), aff'd, 353 N.C. 358, 543 S.E.2d 476 (2001); Moore v. Cincinnati Ins. Co., 147 N.C. App. 761, 556 S.E.2d 682 (2001); N.C. Farm Bureau Mut. Ins. Co. v. Holt, 154 N.C. App. 156, 574 S.E.2d 6 (2002), cert. denied, appeal dismissed, 357 N.C. 63, 579 S.E.2d 391 (2003); Erwin v. Tweed, 159 N.C. App. 579, 583 S.E.2d 717 (2003), cert. denied, 358 N.C. 234, 593 S.E.2d 780 (2004), aff'd, 359 N.C. 64, 602 S.E.2d 359 (2004); State Farm Fire & Cas. Co. v. Darsie, 161 N.C. App. 542, 589 S.E.2d 391 (2003), cert. denied, 358 N.C. 241, 594 S.E.2d 194 (2004), cert. dismissed, 358 N.C. 241, 594 S.E.2d 193 (2004); Richardson v. Bank of Am., N.A., 182 N.C. App. 531, 643 S.E.2d 410 (2007); Piles v. Allstate Ins. Co., 187 N.C. App. 399, 653 S.E.2d 181 (2007), review denied, 362 N.C. 361, 663 S.E.2d 316 (2008); Herbert v. Marcaccio, 213 N.C. App. 563, 713 S.E.2d 531 (2011); James v. Integon Nat'l Ins. Co., 228 N.C. App. 171, 744 S.E.2d 491 (2013); Dion v. Batten, 248 N.C. App. 476, 790 S.E.2d 844 (2016).

II. THE OMNIBUS CLAUSE.

EDITOR'S NOTE. --Many of the cases under this analysis line were decided under this section as it stood before the enactment of Session Laws 1967, c. 1162, which inserted "or any other persons in lawful possession" in subdivision (b)(2) of this section.

LEGISLATIVE INTENT. --The preamble to chapter 1162 of the 1967 Session Laws, which reinstated the words "or any other persons in lawful possession" in subdivision (b)(2) of this section, suggests very strongly that the reason for adding the quoted words was to alleviate the necessity of proving that the operator of a vehicle belonging to another had the express or implied permission of the owner to drive (the vehicle) on the very trip and occasion of the collision. Engle v. State Farm Mut. Auto. Ins. Co., 37 N.C. App. 126, 245 S.E.2d 532, cert. denied, 295 N.C. 645, 248 S.E.2d 250 (1978).

CONSTRUCTION OF PROVISION REQUIRING "OMNIBUS CLAUSE". --Statutes requiring the insertion in automobile liability policies of the "omnibus clause," extending the provisions of the policy to persons using the automobile with the express or implied permission of the named insured, reflect a clear-cut policy to protect the public. They should be construed and applied so as to carry out this policy. Chatfield v. Farm Bureau Mut. Auto. Ins. Co., 208 F.2d 250 (4th Cir. 1953), decided under repealed § 20-227, which covered the same subject matter as this section.

In subdivision (b)(2) the legislature intended no more radical coverage than is expressed in the moderate rule of construction, i.e., coverage shall include use with permission, express or implied. Hawley v. Indemnity Ins. Co. of N. Am., 257 N.C. 381, 126 S.E.2d 161 (1962).

The omnibus clause has been interpreted by the Supreme Court of North Carolina according to the "moderate" rule rather than the "hell and high-water" rule, as recommended in 41 N.C.L. Rev. 232 (1963). Bailey v. General Ins. Co. of Am., 265 N.C. 675, 144 S.E.2d 898 (1965).

An omnibus clause should be construed liberally in favor of the insured and in accordance with the policy of the clause to protect the public. Fidelity & Cas. Co. v. North Carolina Farm Bureau Mut. Ins. Co., 16 N.C. App. 194, 192 S.E.2d 113, cert. denied, 282 N.C. 425, 192 S.E.2d 840 (1972).

Ambiguity in a policy which requires interpretation as to whether the policy provisions impose liability requires construction in favor of coverage and against the company. Fidelity & Cas. Co. v. North Carolina Farm Bureau Mut. Ins. Co., 16 N.C. App. 194, 192 S.E.2d 113 (1972).

In construing an omnibus clause, an injury cannot be said to arise out of the use of an automobile if it was directly caused by some independent act or intervening cause wholly disassociated from, independent of, and remote from the use of the automobile. Fidelity & Cas. Co. v. North Carolina Farm Bureau Mut. Ins. Co., 16 N.C. App. 194, 192 S.E.2d 113 (1972).

Lessor's fleet insurance policy did not exclude liability coverage for lessee, even though the lessee was insured under his own liability policy at the minimum limits, where the lessee was a person 'required by law to be an insured" within the meaning of the fleet policy. Integon Indem. Corp. v. Universal Underwriters Ins. Co., 131 N.C. App. 267, 507 S.E.2d 66 (1998).

THIS SECTION AND G.S. 20-281 COMPARED. --- G.S. 20-281 requires those engaged in the business of renting automobiles to the public to maintain liability insurance "insuring the owner and rentee . . . and their agents" against liability for damages for personal injury or death in the minimum amount of $25,000 per person and $50,000 per accident and for property damage in the amount of $10,000.00, while this section, which applies more generally to every policy insuring any automobile owner, whether or not that owner leases vehicles, requires that the coverage be extended to "any other persons in lawful possession" of the vehicle. Insurance Co. of N. Am. v. Aetna Life & Cas. Co., 88 N.C. App. 236, 362 S.E.2d 836 (1987).

COMPULSORY AUTOMOBILE INSURANCE COVERAGE IS PROVIDED TO A DRIVER IF HE IS IN LAWFUL POSSESSION OF THE AUTOMOBILE. Wilson v. State Farm Mut. Auto. Ins. Co., 92 N.C. App. 320, 374 S.E.2d 446 (1988), rev'd on other grounds, 327 N.C. 419, 394 S.E.2d 807, modified on reh'g, 329 N.C. 262, 404 S.E.2d 852 (1991).

AT LEAST THREE CLASSES OF PERSONS USING AN INSURED AUTOMOBILE MUST BE COVERED by the omnibus clause: (1) persons named in the insurance policy ("the person named therein"), (2) "original permittees," that is, persons using a vehicle with the express or implied permission of the named insured, and (3) other persons in lawful possession, including "second permittees," that is, third parties

Chapter 20

using a vehicle with the permission of an "original permittee." Pemberton v. Reliance Ins. Co., 83 N.C. App. 289, 350 S.E.2d 103 (1986).

LAWFUL POSSESSION BY THIRD PARTY. --Summary judgment in favor of the insurer on plaintiffs' claim of liability under the Motor Vehicle Safety and Financial Responsibility Act was not warranted because a genuine dispute of material fact existed as to whether the driver of the van, who was the wife of the insured's employee, was in "lawful possession" of the van at the time of the accident, given that, the insured had not given express or implied permission to an employee's wife to drive the van. Brown v. Penn Nat'l Sec. Ins. Co., 2014 U.S. Dist. LEXIS 34164 (M.D.N.C. Mar. 17, 2014).

NO RECOVERY WHERE DRIVER HAD NEITHER PERMISSION NOR LAWFUL POSSESSION. --Subdivision (b)(2) of this section does not permit victims of accidents to recover from the owner of a motor vehicle, or his insurer, where the offending driver of the vehicle had neither permission to drive it nor lawful possession of it. Nationwide Mut. Ins. Co. v. Land, 78 N.C. App. 342, 337 S.E.2d 180 (1985), aff'd, 318 N.C. 551, 350 S.E.2d 500 (1986).

LIBERAL CONSTRUCTION IN INTERPRETING SCOPE OF PERMISSION. --The 1967 amendment, adding the words "any other person in lawful possession," signifies that the legislature favors adoption of a liberal rule of construction in applying and interpreting the scope of permission under the omnibus clause. Jernigan v. State Farm Mut. Auto. Ins. Co., 16 N.C. App. 46, 190 S.E.2d 866 (1972); Pemberton v. Reliance Ins. Co., 83 N.C. App. 289, 350 S.E.2d 103 (1986).

The legislature favors adoption of a liberal rule of construction in applying the coverage under the omnibus clause. Packer v. Travelers Ins. Co., 28 N.C. App. 365, 221 S.E.2d 707 (1976).

It was the necessity of proof of permission that the 1967 amendment to subdivision (b)(2) was designed to obviate. Although lawful possession by the operator may be shown by evidence of permission granted to the operator to take the vehicle in the first instance, the plaintiff is not required to show more than lawful possession at the time of the accident. Packer v. Travelers Ins. Co., 28 N.C. App. 365, 221 S.E.2d 707 (1976).

When lawful possession is shown, further proof is not required that the operator had the owner's permission to drive on the very trip and occasion of a collision. Packer v. Travelers Ins. Co., 28 N.C. App. 365, 221 S.E.2d 707 (1976); Caison v. Nationwide Ins. Co., 36 N.C. App. 173, 243 S.E.2d 429 (1978).

THE TERMS "PERMISSION" AND "LAWFUL POSSESSION" ARE NOT SYNONYMOUS, and parties seeking recovery under a theory of permission must meet a higher standard than those seeking recovery under a theory of mere lawful possession. Caison v. Nationwide Ins. Co., 36 N.C. App. 173, 243 S.E.2d 429 (1978), overruling Jernigan v. State Farm Mut. Auto. Ins. Co., 16 N.C. App. 46, 190 S.E.2d 866 (1972).

PERMISSION NOT ESSENTIAL TO "LAWFUL POSSESSION". --The clear intent of the legislature as expressed in the preamble to the 1967 amendment was that permission, express or implied, is not an essential element of lawful possession. Packer v. Travelers Ins. Co., 28 N.C. App. 365, 221 S.E.2d 707 (1976), overruling Jernigan v. State Farm Mut. Auto. Ins. Co., 16 N.C. App. 46, 190 S.E.2d 866 (1972).

The clear intent of the legislature was that permission, express or implied, is not an essential element of lawful possession. Caison v. Nationwide Ins. Co., 36 N.C. App. 173, 243 S.E.2d 429 (1978).

IT IS NOT NECESSARY TO SHOW THAT ONE HAS THE OWNER'S "PERMISSION" to drive an automobile in order to show that he is in "lawful possession" of it within the meaning of subdivision (b)(2) of this section. Insurance Co. of N. Am. v. Aetna Life & Cas. Co., 88 N.C. App. 236, 362 S.E.2d 836 (1987).

PERMISSION MAY BE EXPRESSED OR INFERRED. --The owner's permission for the use of the insured vehicle may be expressed or, under certain circumstances, it may be inferred. Bailey v. General Ins. Co. of Am., 265 N.C. 675, 144 S.E.2d 898 (1965).

Permission may be either express or implied. Nationwide Mut. Ins. Co. v. Fireman's Fund Ins. Co., 279 N.C. 240, 182 S.E.2d 571 (1971); Nationwide Mut. Ins. Co. v. Land, 78 N.C. App. 342, 337 S.E.2d 180 (1985), aff'd, 318 N.C. 551, 350 S.E.2d 500 (1986).

EXPRESS PERMISSION. --Where express permission to use the insured vehicle is relied upon it must be on an affirmative character, directly and distinctly stated, clear and outspoken, and not merely implied or left to inference. Hawley v. Indemnity Ins. Co. of N. Am., 257 N.C. 381, 126 S.E.2d 161 (1962); Bailey v. General Ins. Co. of Am., 265 N.C. 675, 144 S.E.2d 898 (1965).

IMPLIED PERMISSION to use the insured vehicle involves an inference arising from a course of conduct or relationship between the parties, in which there is mutual acquiescence or lack of objection under circumstances signifying assent. Hawley v. Indemnity Ins. Co. of N. Am., 257 N.C. 381, 126 S.E.2d 161 (1962); Bailey v. General Ins. Co. of Am., 265 N.C. 675, 144 S.E.2d 898 (1965).

Implied permission may be a product of the present or past conduct of the insured. It is not confined alone to affirmative action, and is usually shown by usage and practice of the parties over a sufficient period of time prior to the day on which the insured car was being used. Nationwide Mut. Ins. Co. v. Fireman's Fund Ins. Co., 279 N.C. 240, 182 S.E.2d 571 (1971).

Implied permission may be established by a showing of a course of conduct or relationship between parties, including lack of objection to the use by the permittee which signifies acquiescence or consent of the injured. Nationwide Mut. Ins. Co. v. Fireman's Fund Ins. Co., 279 N.C. 240, 182 S.E.2d 571 (1971).

The relationship between the owner and the user, such as kinship, social ties, and the purpose of the use, all have bearing on the critical question of the owner's implied permission for the actual use. Bailey

Chapter 20

v. General Ins. Co. of Am., 265 N.C. 675, 144 S.E.2d 898 (1965).

A permission to use an automobile may be implied, and strong social relationships and ties between the owner and the bailee are relevant upon the question of the extent of such implied permission. Wilson v. Hartford Accident & Indem. Co., 272 N.C. 183, 158 S.E.2d 1 (1967).

"PERMISSION" IS SOMETHING APART FROM A GENERAL STATE OF MIND. Underwood v. National Grange Mut. Liab. Co., 258 N.C. 211, 128 S.E.2d 577 (1962).

A GENERAL OR COMPREHENSIVE PERMIS-SION is much more readily to be assumed where the use of the insured motor vehicle is for social or nonbusiness purposes than where the relationship of master and servant exists and the usage of the vehicle is for business purposes. Hawley v. Indemnity Ins. Co. of N. Am., 257 N.C. 381, 126 S.E.2d 161 (1962).

It does not seem reasonable to assume that parties to an insurance contract covering a vehicle used in business contemplate an indiscriminate use for the social and separate business purpose of employees of named insured unless permission, express or implied, is given for such additional uses. Hawley v. Indemnity Ins. Co. of N. Am., 257 N.C. 381, 126 S.E.2d 161 (1962).

"PERMISSION" CONNOTES POWER TO GRANT OR WITHHOLD IT. --Permission to drive a car, within the meaning of the omnibus coverage clause, connotes the power to grant or withhold it. Rea v. Hardware Mut. Cas. Co., 15 N.C. App. 620, 190 S.E.2d 708, cert. denied, 282 N.C. 153, 191 S.E.2d 759 (1972).

In order for one's use and operation of an automobile to be within the meaning of the omnibus coverage clause requiring the permission of the named insured, the latter must, as a general rule, own the insured vehicle or have such an interest in it that he is entitled to the possession and control of the vehicle and in a position to give permission. Rea v. Hardware Mut. Cas. Co., 15 N.C. App. 620, 190 S.E.2d 708, cert. denied, 282 N.C. 153, 191 S.E.2d 759 (1972).

WHO MAY GRANT PERMISSION. --In order to grant permission, as the word "permission" is used in the omnibus clause of a policy, there must be such ownership or control of the automobile as to confer the legal right to give or withhold assent. Underwood v. National Grange Mut. Liab. Co., 258 N.C. 211, 128 S.E.2d 577 (1962).

Ordinarily, one permittee within the coverage of a liability policy does not have authority to select another permittee without specific authority from the named insured. Bailey v. General Ins. Co. of Am., 265 N.C. 675, 144 S.E.2d 898 (1965).

Compliance with the requirements of this section necessitates coverage of all who use the insured vehicle with the permission, express or implied, of the named insured. Whether the permission be expressly granted or impliedly conferred, it must originate in the language or the conduct of the named insured or of someone having authority to bind him or it in that respect. Hawley v. Indemnity Ins. Co. of N. Am., 257 N.C. 381, 126 S.E.2d 161 (1962).

A person, driving only with the permission of a permittee, is not considered as using the automobile with either the express or implied permission of the owner so as to create omnibus clause coverage. Nationwide Mut. Ins. Co. v. Chantos, 25 N.C. App. 482, 214 S.E.2d 438, cert. denied, 287 N.C. 465, 215 S.E.2d 624 (1975).

Where the original permittee gives the defendant express permission, this makes him a person in "lawful possession" under subdivision (b)(2). Nationwide Mut. Ins. Co. v. Chantos, 25 N.C. App. 482, 214 S.E.2d 438, cert. denied, 287 N.C. 465, 215 S.E.2d 624 (1975).

Permission expressly granted by the original permittee is sufficient for purposes of the statute to place the second permittee in lawful possession. Nationwide Mut. Ins. Co. v. Chantos, 25 N.C. App. 482, 214 S.E.2d 438, cert. denied, 287 N.C. 465, 215 S.E.2d 624 (1975); Engle v. State Farm Mut. Auto. Ins. Co., 37 N.C. App. 126, 245 S.E.2d 532, cert. denied, 295 N.C. 645, 248 S.E.2d 250 (1978).

A person is in lawful possession of a vehicle under an omnibus clause if he is given possession of the automobile by the automobile's owner or owner's permittee under a good faith belief that giving possession of the vehicle to the third party would not be in violation of any law or contractual obligation. Belasco v. Nationwide Mut. Ins. Co., 73 N.C. App. 413, 326 S.E.2d 109, cert. denied, 313 N.C. 596, 332 S.E.2d 177 (1985).

A person may be in lawful possession of an automobile if he is given possession by someone using the automobile with the express permission of the owner, even though the permission granted by the owner did not include the authority to permit others to operate the automobile. Insurance Co. of N. Am. v. Aetna Life & Cas. Co., 88 N.C. App. 236, 362 S.E.2d 836 (1987).

CASUAL CONNECTION BETWEEN INJURY AND USE OF VEHICLE. --Insured's use of a van included moving the decedent into her residence as a part of the insured's transport service; there was a sufficient causal connection between the van's use and the decedent's injury requiring the insurance policy to provide coverage. Integon Nat'l Ins. Co. v. Helping Hands Specialized Transp., Inc., 233 N.C. App. 652, 758 S.E.2d 27 (2014).

THIRD PARTY HELD IN LAWFUL POSSESSION OF RENTAL CAR. --Although lessee violated his contract by permitting third parties to drive rental car, their possession of it was not unlawful. Thus, driver was in "lawful possession" of the car at the time of the accident, although he had neither express nor implied permission from the lessor to drive it, and therefore insurer was required, pursuant to subdivision (b)(2) of this section, and G.S. 20-281, to provide coverage for driver's negligent operation of the automobile, limited to the amounts of coverage required by subsection (g) of this section and G.S. 20-281. Insurance Co. of N. Am. v. Aetna Life & Cas. Co., 88 N.C. App. 236, 362 S.E.2d 836 (1987).

USE HELD WITH PERMISSION. --Evidence was sufficient to show that driver's brother was an "original permittee" of the car's owner, another brother, and that he gave lawful possession of the car to driver within the meaning of subdivision (b)(2) of this

Chapter 20

section. Pemberton v. Reliance Ins. Co., 83 N.C. App. 289, 350 S.E.2d 103 (1986).

EXTENDING COVERAGE TO SECOND PERMITTEE. --Regardless of the liberality of the rule of construction applied, permission of the named insured or of the original permittee is essential to extend coverage to a second permittee. Jernigan v. State Farm Mut. Auto. Ins. Co., 16 N.C. App. 46, 190 S.E.2d 866 (1972).

GARAGE OWNER'S POLICY. --A garage owner's policy complies with the Motor Vehicle Safety and Financial Responsibility Act although it does not provide liability coverage for an occurrence if the operator of the vehicle involved in the occurrence is covered by another policy. United Servs. Auto. Ass'n v. Universal Underwriters Ins. Co., 332 N.C. 333, 420 S.E.2d 155 (1992).

BAILEE'S USE MUST BE WITHIN SCOPE OF PERMISSION. --Under the omnibus clause, the coverage of a policy extends to the liability of a bailee of the automobile for an accident only where the bailee's use of the vehicle at the time of the accident is within the scope of the permission granted to him, the burden being upon the plaintiff to show that such use was within the scope of the permission. Wilson v. Hartford Accident & Indem. Co., 272 N.C. 183, 158 S.E.2d 1 (1967).

When the bailee deviates in a material respect from the grant of permission, his use of the vehicle, while such deviation continues, is not a permitted use within the meaning of the omnibus clause of a policy. Wilson v. Hartford Accident & Indem. Co., 272 N.C. 183, 158 S.E.2d 1 (1967).

EXPRESS LIMITATIONS NOT OVERCOME BY PROOF OF FRIENDLY RELATIONS. --Proof of friendly relations, which might otherwise imply permission, cannot overcome the effect of a limitation as to time, purpose or locality expressly imposed by the owner upon the bailee at the time of the delivery of the automobile to the bailee by the owner on the occasion in question. Wilson v. Hartford Accident & Indem. Co., 272 N.C. 183, 158 S.E.2d 1 (1967).

VIOLATION OF PERMISSION BY CARRYING GUESTS IN VEHICLE. --Where the violation of permission consists merely of carrying guests in the vehicle, and the employee's use of the vehicle is otherwise permitted, the fact alone that the employee permitted riders on the vehicle will not serve to annul the permission of the employer so as to take the employee out of the protection of the omnibus clause. Hawley v. Indemnity Ins. Co. of N. Am., 257 N.C. 381, 126 S.E.2d 161 (1962).

PLAINTIFF HAS BURDEN OF SHOWING PERMISSION. --Plaintiff has the burden of showing that there was permission to use the vehicle. Hawley v. Indemnity Ins. Co. of N. Am., 257 N.C. 381, 126 S.E.2d 161 (1962).

USE HELD WITHOUT PERMISSION. --Where a prospective purchaser was permitted to drive a dealer's vehicle seven miles to the purchaser's home to show it to his wife and was to return the vehicle within two and one-half hours, but he actually drove

70 miles to another municipality and had an accident resulting in plaintiff's injury more than 20 hours after he should have returned the vehicle, the court held the purchaser's use at time of accident was without permission of owner. Fehl v. Aetna Cas. & Sur. Co., 260 N.C. 440, 133 S.E.2d 68 (1963).

While an individual's initial use of an automobile was permitted under the terms of a written lease and was subject to the terms thereof, once he defaulted and failed to return the car as demanded by bank-lessor, his continued use was a material deviation from the permission granted in the lease. As such, it was not a permissive use within the meaning of bank's insurance policy or subdivision (b)(2) of this section. Nationwide Mut. Ins. Co. v. Land, 78 N.C. App. 342, 337 S.E.2d 180 (1985), aff'd, 318 N.C. 551, 350 S.E.2d 500 (1986).

Trial court properly granted summary judgment pursuant to G.S. 1A-1, N.C. R. Civ. P. 56 to defendant in a declaratory judgment action concerning the obligations of insurers in a wrongful death action; a passenger in the vehicle insured by defendant was not in possession of the vehicle pursuant to G.S. 20-279.21(b)(2) when she grabbed the steering wheel from the driver and took control of the car. N.C. Farm Bureau Ins. Co. v. Nationwide Mut. Ins. Co., 168 N.C. App. 585, 608 S.E.2d 112 (2005).

IF THE NAMED INSURED HAS SOLD THE VEHICLE, its subsequent use by the buyer is by virtue of the latter's ownership and his right to control it and not by virtue of the permission of the named insured seller. Underwood v. National Grange Mut. Liab. Co., 258 N.C. 211, 128 S.E.2d 577 (1962).

WHERE THE NAMED INSURED DID NOT HOLD LEGAL TITLE to the automobile involved in the collision and dealer plates affixed thereto constituted the sole relationship between the car and the dealership, standing alone this connection was simply too weak to impose mandatory liability coverage on the basis of the owner's policy provisions of subsection (b). McLeod v. Nationwide Mut. Ins. Co., 115 N.C. App. 283, 444 S.E.2d 487, cert. denied, 337 N.C. 694, 448 S.E.2d 528 (1994).

LAWFUL POSSESSION SUBMITTED TO JURY. --Plaintiff, once having offered evidence tending to show lawful possession of the truck by a driver, was entitled to have the issue of lawful possession submitted to the jury. Packer v. Travelers Ins. Co., 28 N.C. App. 365, 221 S.E.2d 707 (1976).

Where there was evidence that defendant had driven the car before the accident, and his wife, the insured, did not report the car as stolen or tell the investigating officer that defendant did not have permission to drive the car, this alone was some evidence of implied permission, and created an issue for the jury's resolution. Wilson v. State Farm Mut. Auto. Ins. Co., 92 N.C. App. 320, 374 S.E.2d 446 (1988), rev'd on other grounds, 327 N.C. 419, 394 S.E.2d 807, modified on reh'g, 329 N.C. 262, 404 S.E.2d 852 (1991).

SUMMARY JUDGMENT ON ISSUE OF PERMISSION HELD IMPROPER. --Where although driver of truck involved in accident did not have owner's permission to drive truck and did not have a valid driver's license, and owner's insurance policy excluded coverage for persons using insured vehicle without reasonable belief that he or she was entitled to do so, insurance company was not entitled to summary judgment on their claim denying coverage, as there was a question as to the driver's subjective belief of being entitled to drive the vehicle. Aetna Cas. & Sur. Co. v. Nationwide Mut. Ins. Co., 95 N.C. App. 178, 381 S.E.2d 874 (1989), aff'd, 326 N.C. 771, 392 S.E.2d 377 (1990).

A PASSENGER WHO GRABS THE STEERING WHEEL IS ACTUALLY INTERFERING WITH THE VEHICLE'S OPERATION, AND IS NOT ""IN POSSESSION" pursuant to G.S. 20-279.21(b)(2). N.C. Farm Bureau Ins. Co. v. Nationwide Mut. Ins. Co., 168 N.C. App. 585, 608 S.E.2d 112 (2005).

PERSON KNOWINGLY OPERATING MOTOR VEHICLE WITHOUT DRIVER'S LICENSE MAY NEVERTHELESS HAVE REASONABLE BELIEF THAT HE WAS ENTITLED TO OPERATE VEHICLE on given date and time. Aetna Cas. & Sur. Co. v. Nationwide Mut. Ins. Co., 326 N.C. 771, 392 S.E.2d 377 (1990).

III. UNINSURED MOTORIST COVERAGE.

PURPOSE OF UNINSURED MOTORIST PROVISIONS. --Subdivision (3) of subsection (b) of this section was enacted so as to include protection against uninsured motorists. Moore v. Hartford Fire Ins. Co., 270 N.C. 532, 155 S.E.2d 128 (1967); Wright v. Fidelity & Cas. Co., 270 N.C. 577, 155 S.E.2d 100 (1967); Hamilton v. Travelers Indem. Co., 77 N.C. App. 318, 335 S.E.2d 228 (1985), cert. denied, 315 N.C. 587, 341 S.E.2d 25 (1986).

The purpose of the uninsured motorist statute was to provide, within fixed limits, some financial recompense to innocent persons who receive bodily injury or property damage, and to the dependents of those who lose their lives through the wrongful conduct of an uninsured motorist who cannot be made to respond in damages. Moore v. Hartford Fire Ins. Co., 270 N.C. 532, 155 S.E.2d 128 (1967); Lichtenberger v. American Motorists Ins. Co., 7 N.C. App. 269, 172 S.E.2d 284 (1970).

Uninsured motorist coverage is intended, within fixed limits, to provide financial recompense to innocent persons who receive injuries and the dependents of those who are killed, through the wrongful conduct of motorists who, because they are uninsured and not financially responsible, cannot be made to respond in damages. Wright v. Fidelity & Cas. Co., 270 N.C. 577, 155 S.E.2d 100 (1967).

Uninsured motorist coverage is designed to close the gaps inherent in motor vehicle financial responsibility and compulsory insurance legislation. Wright v. Fidelity & Cas. Co., 270 N.C. 577, 155 S.E.2d 100 (1967).

The uninsured motorist statute was enacted by the General Assembly as a result of public concern over the increasingly important problem arising from property damage, personal injury, and death inflicted by motorists who are uninsured and financially irresponsible. Moore v. Hartford Fire Ins. Co., 270 N.C.

532, 155 S.E.2d 128 (1967); Lichtenberger v. American Motorists Ins. Co., 7 N.C. App. 269, 172 S.E.2d 284 (1970).

The uninsured motorist provision of this section was enacted in order to close "gaps" in the motor vehicle financial responsibility legislation and thus, to provide financial recompense to innocent persons who receive injuries through the wrongful conduct of motorists who are uninsured and financially irresponsible. Autry v. Aetna Life & Cas. Ins. Co., 35 N.C. App. 628, 242 S.E.2d 172, cert. denied, 295 N.C. 89, 244 S.E.2d 257 (1978).

Subdivision (3) of subsection (b) of this section provides for a limited type of compulsory automobile liability coverage against uninsured motorists. Moore v. Hartford Fire Ins. Co., 270 N.C. 532, 155 S.E.2d 128 (1967).

The nature of the uninsured motorist statute is remedial and therefore should be liberally construed to accomplish the beneficial purpose intended by the General Assembly. Williams v. Holsclaw, 128 N.C. App. 205, 495 S.E.2d 166 (1998).

THE LEGISLATIVE POLICY BEHIND UNINSURED MOTORIST INSURANCE LAWS is not to divide liability among insurers or limit insurers' liability, but to protect the motorist to the extent the statute requires protection against a specific class of tortfeasors. Hamilton v. Travelers Indem. Co., 77 N.C. App. 318, 335 S.E.2d 228 (1985), cert. denied, 315 N.C. 587, 341 S.E.2d 25 (1986).

There is nothing in the legislative scheme suggesting that insured persons should have to concern themselves with the liability insurance limits of tortfeasors; in fact, the very purpose of uninsured motorist coverage is to ameliorate that concern. Hamilton v. Travelers Indem. Co., 77 N.C. App. 318, 335 S.E.2d 228 (1985), cert. denied, 315 N.C. 587, 341 S.E.2d 25 (1986).

CONSTRUCTION OF UNINSURED MOTORIST COVERAGE PROVISIONS. --G.S. 20-279.21(b)(3)(b), is remedial in nature and is to be liberally construed so that the beneficial purpose intended by its enactment may be accomplished; the purpose of the uninsured motorist provisions is best served when every provision is interpreted to provide the innocent victim with the fullest possible protection. Hoffman v. Great Am. Alliance Ins. Co., 166 N.C. App. 422, 601 S.E.2d 908 (2004).

THE STATUTORY PHRASE "COLLISION BETWEEN MOTOR VEHICLES" does not require that the collision be with the unidentified vehicle; the clear indication is that the legislature intended to make the provisions available to all insureds who are injured in motor vehicular collisions caused by unidentified motorists. Petteway v. South Carolina Ins. Co., 93 N.C. App. 776, 379 S.E.2d 80, cert. denied, 325 N.C. 273, 384 S.E.2d 518 (1989).

SUBDIVISION (B)(3)B OF THIS SECTION REQUIRES PHYSICAL CONTACT between the vehicle operated by the insured motorist and the vehicle operated by the hit-and-run driver for the uninsured motorist provisions of the statute to apply. McNeil v.

Chapter 20

Hartford Accident & Indem. Co., 84 N.C. App. 438, 352 S.E.2d 915 (1987).

If plaintiff can show at trial that a collision occurred between the hit-and-run vehicle and another vehicle and that this collision propelled that vehicle into a third vehicle, and that this second collision propelled the third vehicle into plaintiff's vehicle, then under these circumstances, the physical contact requirement has been satisfied, albeit intermediately and indirectly. McNeil v. Hartford Accident & Indem. Co., 84 N.C. App. 438, 352 S.E.2d 915 (1987).

Where plaintiff was seriously injured when an automobile he was driving overturned after being forced off the highway by an unidentified motorist and where the incident was witnessed by another motorist, plaintiff's claim to the benefit of defendants' uninsured motorist coverages was not legally enforceable under this section; the record showed without contradiction that plaintiff's injuries did not result from a collision between motor vehicles. Petteway v. South Carolina Ins. Co., 93 N.C. App. 776, 379 S.E.2d 80, cert. denied, 325 N.C. 273, 384 S.E.2d 518 (1989).

Insured's breach of contract and related claims against his automobile insurer were properly dismissed under G.S. 20-278.21(b)(3)(b) when his complaint alleged that he had struck a pine tree log which had fallen off of a truck and was lying in the middle on the interstate, but no evidence showed from what vehicle, if any, the pine tree log fell from, when it fell, or how long it had been lying on the interstate prior to impact, and thus, the complaint did not satisfy the physical contact requirement. Moore v. Nationwide Mut. Ins. Co., 191 N.C. App. 106, 664 S.E.2d 326 (2008), aff'd, 362 N.C. 673, 669 S.E.2d 321 (2008).

As an insured was injured while a passenger in his employer's truck when something fell from an unidentified vehicle in front of the truck, the incident did not satisfy the physical contact requirement for a "hit and run accident," as defined in G.S. 20-279.21(b)(3); his action against insurers was properly dismissed. Prouse v. Bituminous Cas. Corp., 222 N.C. App. 111, 730 S.E.2d 239 (2012).

VEHICLES OWNED BY POLITICAL SUBDIVISIONS are expressly excepted from the statutory exception. Williams v. Holsclaw, 128 N.C. App. 205, 495 S.E.2d 166 (1998).

Plaintiffs, who were injured in a traffic accident with a police officer, were not barred from recovering UM benefits from insurer due to the immunity granted to police officer. Williams v. Holsclaw, 128 N.C. App. 205, 495 S.E.2d 166 (1998).

SELECTION PROVISION NOT APPLICABLE TO COUNTY-OWNED VEHICLES. --In an accident involving a county employee in a county vehicle acting in the scope of her employment, G.S. 20-279.32 provided that the county was not subject to the Motor Vehicle Safety and Responsibility Act. The county was not required to specifically select Uninsured Motorist coverage of less than $2,000,000 under G.S. 20-279.21(b)(4), and the county's policy capping Uninsured Motorist coverage at $100,000 was therefore

enforceable. Nolan v. Cooke, 198 N.C. App. 667, 679 S.E.2d 892 (2009).

COVERAGE FOR PERSON WALKING DOWN THE STREET. --As a person insured of the first class, plaintiff was entitled to UM benefits under the policy regardless of whether she was riding in the insured vehicle or walking down the street. Bray v. North Carolina Farm Bureau Mut. Ins. Co., 115 N.C. App. 438, 445 S.E.2d 79 (1994), cert. improvidently granted in part, aff'd in part and rev'd in part on other grounds, 341 N.C. 678, 462 S.E.2d 650 (1995).

EFFECT OF INCREASE IN COVERAGE UNDER 1979 AMENDMENT. --Motorists with existing policies including uninsured motorist coverage at the level specified in G.S. 20-279.5(c) prior to its 1979 amendment could not claim up to the new limits if they were struck by an uninsured motorist; if those insureds, before their routinely scheduled policy renewal, desired more uninsured motorist coverage at the higher level, they could renew their policies early. In the interim, they would not be in violation of the Motor Vehicle Safety and Financial Responsibility Act because they retained their existing, lower-limit policies, nor would their insurers be forced to assume additional, uncontracted for liability. Hamilton v. Travelers Indem. Co., 77 N.C. App. 318, 335 S.E.2d 228 (1985), cert. denied, 315 N.C. 587, 341 S.E.2d 25 (1986).

Motorists who contracted and paid premiums for uninsured motorist coverage after the effective date of the new limits provided in G.S. 20-279.5(c) following its 1979 amendment should receive coverage up to those higher limits. Hamilton v. Travelers Indem. Co., 77 N.C. App. 318, 335 S.E.2d 228 (1985), cert. denied, 315 N.C. 587, 341 S.E.2d 25 (1986).

THE TERM "UNINSURED MOTOR VEHICLE" in subdivision (b)(3) of this section is intended to include motor vehicles which should be insured under this Article but are not, and motor vehicles which, though not subject to compulsory insurance under this Article, are at some time operated on the public highways. Autry v. Aetna Life & Cas. Ins. Co., 35 N.C. App. 628, 242 S.E.2d 172, cert. denied, 295 N.C. 89, 244 S.E.2d 257 (1978).

VEHICLE "UNINSURED" UNLESS POLICY COVERS LIABILITY OF PERSON USING IT. --An automobile on which an automobile liability insurance policy has been issued is uninsured within the meaning of an uninsured motorists endorsement, unless such policy covers the liability of the person using it and inflicting injury on the occasion of the collision or mishap. Buck v. United States Fid. & Guar. Co., 265 N.C. 285, 144 S.E.2d 34 (1965).

NO COVERAGE OF INJURY ON PRIVATE PROPERTY BY VEHICLE NOT SUBJECT TO FINANCIAL RESPONSIBILITY LAW. --The uninsured motorist provision was not intended to provide financial recompense to one injured on private property by a vehicle not subject to the registration and compulsory insurance provisions of the motor vehicle financial responsibility legislation. Autry v. Aetna Life & Cas. Ins. Co., 35 N.C. App. 628, 242 S.E.2d 172, cert. denied, 295 N.C. 89, 244 S.E.2d 257 (1978).

"LEGALLY ENTITLED TO RECOVER" should be construed to mean that insurer's Underinsured Motorist (UIM) liability derives from the tortfeasor's liability. Silvers v. Horace Mann Ins. Co., 324 N.C. 289, 378 S.E.2d 21 (1989).

AND THE UIM CARRIER CAN RECOVER FROM THE TORTFEASOR. --An uninsured motorist coverage carrier may bind a tortfeasor for the amount the uninsured carrier paid the victim pursuant to an arbitration proceeding. Burger v. Doe, 143 N.C. App. 328, 546 S.E.2d 141 (2001), cert. denied, 354 N.C. 67, 553 S.E.2d 36 (2001).

POLICY TO INCLUDE CERTAIN PROVISIONS. --A close reading of subdivisions (b)(3)a and (b)(3)b indicates that they provide for the inclusion of certain provisions in the policy, namely, that the insurer shall be bound by a final judgment against the uninsured motorist, under certain conditions, and that suit may be against the insurer directly in case of injury from collision with an unidentifiable motorist. Hendricks v. United States Fid. & Guar. Co., 5 N.C. App. 181, 167 S.E.2d 876 (1969).

CONSTRUCTION OF UNINSURED MOTORISTS COVERAGE. --In determining whether the injury arose out of the "ownership, maintenance, or use" of the motor vehicle, the same rules of construction apply in construing uninsured motorists coverage as apply in construing a standard liability insurance policy. Williams v. Nationwide Mut. Ins. Co., 269 N.C. 235, 152 S.E.2d 102 (1967).

The term "uninsured vehicle," when used in an uninsured motorist's endorsement, must be interpreted in the light of the fact that such endorsement is designed to protect the insured, and any operator of the insured's car with the insured's consent, against injury caused by the negligence of uninsured or unknown motorists. Buck v. United States Fid. & Guar. Co., 265 N.C. 285, 144 S.E.2d 34 (1965).

Subdivision (b)(3) of this section is to be considered in conjunction with the principle that the provisions of this section enter into and form a part of the policy. Lichtenberger v. American Motorists Ins. Co., 7 N.C. App. 269, 172 S.E.2d 284 (1970).

Employees injured in an accident caused by an uninsured motorist (UM) did not qualify as "persons insured" who were required to be offered UM coverage by the insurer under G.S. 20-279.21(b)(3) because their employer was the named insured under the commercial automobile policy and they were not using an insured vehicle at the time of the collision. Reel v. Selective Ins. Co., 407 F. Supp. 2d 737 (E.D.N.C. 2005).

Plaintiff insurer was not obligated to provide $1,000,000 in uninsured motorist coverage. Applying the Williams doctrine so as to require the insurer to afford UM coverage subject to a limit of $1,000,000 under the policy would have conflicted with the plain language of G.S. 20-279(b)(3) and existing precedent of North Carolina Supreme Court. Progressive Southeastern Ins. Co. v. McLeod, 2011 U.S. Dist. LEXIS 139378 (E.D.N.C. Dec. 5, 2011).

IN THE ABSENCE OF REJECTION, THIS SECTION WRITES UNINSURED MOTORISTS COVERAGE INTO EVERY POLICY of automobile liability insurance although the policy may not indicate the coverage on its face. Lichtenberger v. American Motorists Ins. Co., 7 N.C. App. 269, 172 S.E.2d 284 (1970).

COVERAGE IS PROVIDED ALTHOUGH NOT REQUESTED BY INSURED. --A policy issued under subdivision (b)(3) of this section is substantially different from a "voluntary" policy. Where the provisions of the statute enter into and form a part of the policy, the coverage is provided although the insured has never requested that coverage. Lichtenberger v. American Motorists Ins. Co., 7 N.C. App. 269, 172 S.E.2d 284 (1970).

BUT COVERAGE DOES NOT APPLY IF NAMED INSURED REJECTS IT. --Compulsory uninsured motorist coverage as required by subdivision (b)(3) of this section does not apply where the insured named in the policy rejects the coverage. Lichtenberger v. American Motorists Ins. Co., 7 N.C. App. 269, 172 S.E.2d 284 (1970).

REJECTION OF COVERAGE. --Trial court erred in granting an insurer summary judgment and in ordering that an insured's wife was entitled to only $100,000 in uninsured motorist (UIM) coverage, as opposed to the $1,000,000 upper limit of G.S. 20-279.21(b)(4), because the evidence, coupled with the insured's deposition testimony that he did not remember the selection/rejection form being explained to him, presented a genuine issue of material fact as to whether he had been offered the opportunity to accept or reject UIM coverage; there was no direct contradiction in the testimony of the insured, and he was not barred from using his own affidavit to raise an issue of material fact as to the central question in the analysis of whether the UIM limits applied. Unitrin Auto & Home Ins. Co. v. McNeill, 215 N.C. App. 465, 716 S.E.2d 48 (2011).

AMENDMENT OF POLICY DOES NOT AFFECT REJECTION. --Where the husband refused uninsured motorist coverage and then added his wife to the insurance policy as a named insured party, this amendment did not require another offer of uninsured motorist coverage under G.S. 20-279.21(b)(3), because a new policy was not being issued. Weaver v. O'Neal, 151 N.C. App. 556, 566 S.E.2d 146 (2002).

BURDEN OF PROVING REJECTION OF COVERAGE. --The delivery or issuance of a motor vehicle liability policy carries with it as a matter of law the requisite uninsured motorist liability, unless it is shown that the statutory coverage is rendered inapplicable by a rejection. As is true with cancellation or termination, the burden of proving the defense of rejection shifts to the defendant. Lichtenberger v. American Motorists Ins. Co., 7 N.C. App. 269, 172 S.E.2d 284 (1970).

ACCEPTANCE OF POLICY WITHOUT UNINSURED MOTORIST PROVISIONS DOES NOT OPERATE AS REJECTION. --If the insurer cannot avoid liability on a policy of insurance issued pursuant to this statute by omitting from the policy provisions favorable to the insured, then neither can the insured's acceptance of the policy alone operate as a rejection of the coverage written into it by statute. Lichtenberger v. American Motorists Ins. Co., 7 N.C. App. 269, 172 S.E.2d 284 (1970).

COVERAGE NOT RESTRICTED TO INJURY OR DAMAGE OCCURRING IN THIS STATE. --It appears from subdivision (3) of subsection (b) of this section that the General Assembly clearly intended that automobile liability insurance policies delivered or issued for delivery in this State and covering motor vehicles registered or principally garaged in this State will provide protection, within certain limits, to insureds who are legally entitled to recover damages for bodily injury from owners or operators of uninsured motor vehicles. The section does not restrict the coverage to injury or damage occurring in this State. Dildy v. Southeastern Fire Ins. Co., 13 N.C. App. 66, 185 S.E.2d 272 (1971).

VEHICLE INSURED IN ANOTHER STATE. --In an action on the uninsured motorist clause in a collision policy, evidence that the vehicle causing the loss was injured in another state, where it was registered and licensed, by a company authorized to do business in that state but not in North Carolina, was insufficient to carry the burden of proving the allegation that the vehicle was an uninsured automobile. Rice v. Aetna Cas. & Sur. Co., 267 N.C. 421, 148 S.E.2d 223 (1966).

INSOLVENCY OF INSURER OF VEHICLE CAUSING LOSS. --Prior to the first 1965 amendment, which added the present third paragraph of subdivision (b) (3), in an action on the uninsured vehicle clause in a collision policy, evidence that the vehicle causing the loss was insured in another state, where it was registered and licensed, and that subsequent to the collision the insurer was placed in receivership because of its insolvency, and that a claim was filed with the insurer's receiver, was insufficient to carry the burden of proving that the vehicle causing the injury was an uninsured motor vehicle. Rice v. Aetna Cas. & Sur. Co., 267 N.C. 421, 148 S.E.2d 223 (1966).

Under an insurance policy providing that a vehicle is uninsured if the liability insurer "is or becomes insolvent" without specifying any period of time, an uninsured motorist claim may not be barred even though the minimum period specified in subsection (b)(3)(b) has elapsed. North Carolina Ins. Guar. Ass'n v. State Farm Mut. Auto. Ins. Co., 115 N.C. App. 666, 446 S.E.2d 364 (1994).

While the General Assembly has prescribed the minimum time period within which insolvency protection must be provided, it also has expressly permitted an insurer to include, within a policy, coverage which extends beyond the mandated minimum term. North Carolina Ins. Guar. Ass'n v. State Farm Mut. Auto. Ins. Co., 115 N.C. App. 666, 446 S.E.2d 364 (1994).

Trial court properly granted summary judgment to an administratrix on her claims against two uninsured motorist insurers because, on the date of the insolvency of the third insurer with whom the administratrix settled following the work related death of her husband, the two uninsured motorist insurers

became liable to the administratrix for the unfunded amount of the settlement with the insolvent insurer. Jones v. N.C. Ins. Guaranty Ass'n, 163 N.C. App. 105, 592 S.E.2d 600 (2004), cert. denied, 358 N.C. 544, 598 S.E.2d 382 (2004), cert. denied, -- N.C. --, 598 S.E.2d 381 (2004).

WHAT MUST BE SHOWN UNDER UNINSURED MOTORIST ENDORSEMENT. --The insured, in order to be entitled to the benefits of the uninsured motorist endorsement, must show (1) he is legally entitled to recover damages, (2) from the owner or operator of an uninsured automobile, (3) because of bodily injury, (4) caused by accident, and (5) arising out of the ownership, maintenance, or use of the uninsured automobile. Williams v. Nationwide Mut. Ins. Co., 269 N.C. 235, 152 S.E.2d 102 (1967).

ACTION UNDER UNINSURED MOTORIST POLICY IS ONE FOR TORT. --Despite the contractual relation between plaintiff insured and defendant insurer, an action under an uninsured vehicle policy is actually one for the tort allegedly committed by the uninsured motorist. Brown v. Lumbermens Mut. Cas. Co., 285 N.C. 313, 204 S.E.2d 829 (1974).

The three-year tort statute of limitations, which begins running on the date of an accident, also applies to the uninsured motorist carrier. Thomas v. Washington, 136 N.C. App. 750, 525 S.E.2d 839 (2000).

TWO-YEAR STATUTE OF LIMITATIONS APPLIES. --In an action for wrongful death under an uninsured motor vehicle policy the court held that plaintiff should not have three years to sue the insurance company under G.S. 1-52, the statute of limitations on actions on contracts when he had only two years in which to sue the individual primarily liable, by reason of G.S. 1-53, the statute of limitations applicable to tort claims. Brown v. Lumbermens Mut. Cas. Co., 285 N.C. 313, 204 S.E.2d 829 (1974).

Where the estate administrator filed a wrongful death action against the uninsured driver and later served the uninsured motorist insurer in the same action, the applicable statute of limitations was the two-year wrongful death statute of limitations under G.S. 1-53(4) and not the three-year contract statute of limitations under G.S. 1-52(1); this finding was consistent with the requirement under G.S. 20-279.21(b) (3)(a) that the uninsured motorist insurer be made a party to the underlying tort action. Sturdivant v. Andrews, 161 N.C. App. 177, 587 S.E.2d 510 (2003), cert. denied, cert. dismissed, 358 N.C. 242, 594 S.E.2d 34 (2004).

Trial court properly granted uninsured motorist insurer summary judgment in an executrix's wrongful death action where the two-year statutes of limitations applied to the case and the executrix failed to filed the complaint against the defendants within that time period. Eckard v. Smith, 166 N.C. App. 312, 603 S.E.2d 134 (2004), cert. denied, 359 N.C. 321, 611 S.E.2d 410 (2005), aff'd, 360 N.C. 51, 619 S.E.2d 503 (2005).

Where valid service of process was not made upon an uninsured motorist carrier pursuant to N.C. Civ. R. P. 4(j)(6) within the applicable statute of limitations period set forth in G.S. 20-279.21(b)(3)(a) (2013), the trial court did not err in granting the motion of the uninsured motorist carrier to dismiss a personal injury claim for insufficient process or insufficient service of process. Davis v. Urquiza, 233 N.C. App. 462, 757 S.E.2d 327 (2014).

RIGHT TO RECOVER IS DERIVATIVE AND CONDITIONAL. --Plaintiff's right to recover against his intestate's insurer under the uninsured motorist endorsement is derivative and conditional. Brown v. Lumbermens Mut. Cas. Co., 285 N.C. 313, 204 S.E.2d 829 (1974).

Unless a plaintiff is "legally entitled to recover damages" for the wrongful death of his intestate from the uninsured motorist, the contract upon which he sues precludes him from recovering against the insurance company. Brown v. Lumbermens Mut. Cas. Co., 285 N.C. 313, 204 S.E.2d 829 (1974); Brace v. Strother, 90 N.C. App. 357, 368 S.E.2d 447, cert. denied, 323 N.C. 171, 373 S.E.2d 104 (1988), modified on other grounds, 329 N.C. 262, 404 S.E.2d 852 (1991).

CARRIER MAY NOT SEEK CONTRIBUTION AND/OR INDEMNIFICATION. --An uninsured motorist carrier, in defending an uninsured motorist pursuant to subdivision (b)(3)(a), may not file a third party complaint seeking contribution and/or indemnification. Hunter v. Kennedy, 128 N.C. App. 84, 493 S.E.2d 327 (1997).

Plain language of G.S. 20-279.21(b)(3)(b) requires an insured, or someone on his behalf, to report an accident within 24 hours or as soon thereafter as may be practicable, to a police officer, and this statutory language is unequivocable. Hoffman v. Great Am. Alliance Ins. Co., 166 N.C. App. 422, 601 S.E.2d 908 (2004).

Good faith inquiry is a subjective inquiry that examines a plaintiff's actual knowledge at the time of an accident. Hoffman v. Great Am. Alliance Ins. Co., 166 N.C. App. 422, 601 S.E.2d 908 (2004).

Trier of fact determines whether good faith was exercised by an insured in providing notice as soon as practicable. Hoffman v. Great Am. Alliance Ins. Co., 166 N.C. App. 422, 601 S.E.2d 908 (2004).

NOTICE REQUIREMENT. --Insured's failure to give prompt notice of an alleged hit and run accident, in which he was struck by a car while riding his bicycle and incurred personal injuries, barred his claim against the insurers from uninsured motorist vehicle coverage; the insured was aware that he was injured later during the day of the alleged accident, but failed to make even a police report regarding the incident. Hoffman v. Great Am. Alliance Ins. Co., 166 N.C. App. 422, 601 S.E.2d 908 (2004).

THREE-PART TEST APPLIES TO DETERMINE WHETHER AN INSURED'S DELAY IN GIVING PROMPT NOTICE TO AN INSURER WAS AS SOON AS PRACTICABLE; when faced with a claim that notice was not timely given, (1) the trier of fact must first decide whether the notice was given as soon as practicable and, (2) if not, whether the insured has shown that he acted in good faith, and (3) then the burden shifts to the insurer to show that its ability to

investigate and defend was materially prejudiced by the delay. Hoffman v. Great Am. Alliance Ins. Co., 166 N.C. App. 422, 601 S.E.2d 908 (2004).

ANY DEFENSE AVAILABLE TO THE UNINSURED TORT-FEASOR SHOULD BE AVAILABLE TO THE INSURER. Brown v. Lumbermens Mut. Cas. Co., 285 N.C. 313, 204 S.E.2d 829 (1974); Brace v. Strother, 90 N.C. App. 357, 368 S.E.2d 447 (1988).

EXTENT OF INSURER'S LIABILITY LIMITED TO AMOUNT OF DAMAGES RECOVERABLE IN COURT OF LAW. --When defendant to an action under an uninsured vehicle policy undertook "to pay all sums which the insured or his legal representatives shall be legally entitled to recover as damages from the owner or operator of an uninsured automobile because of bodily injury, sickness or disease, including death resulting therefrom.." it assumed liability only for damages for which plaintiff could recover judgment in a court of law in an action against the uninsured motorist. Brown v. Lumbermens Mut. Cas. Co., 285 N.C. 313, 204 S.E.2d 829 (1974).

LIMITATION OF LIABILITY AND EXCLUSIONARY PROVISIONS DEEMED VALID. --Limitation of liability and exclusionary provisions in policies which reduced the amount of uninsured motorist coverage by the amount paid to the insured as workers' compensation benefits did not conflict with the Financial Responsibility Act and were enforceable, Liberty Mut. Ins. Co. v. Ditillo, 125 N.C. App. 701, 482 S.E.2d 743 (1997), rev'd in part, 348 N.C. 247, 499 S.E.2d 764 (1998).

SUBROGATION LIEN. --The workers' compensation carrier for plaintiffs had a subrogation lien on the uninsured motorist policy proceeds paid to plaintiff employee who was injured in an automobile accident occurring while within the scope of employment. Bailey v. Nationwide Mut. Ins. Co., 112 N.C. App. 47, 434 S.E.2d 625 (1993), overruled on other grounds, McMillian v. North Carolina Farm Bureau Mut. Ins. Co., 347 N.C. 560, 495 S.E.2d 352 (1998).

SUBDIVISION (B)(3) OF THIS SECTION IS DESIGNED TO PROTECT THE INSURED AS TO HIS ACTUAL LOSS WITHIN THE STATUTORY LIMIT for one person, but it was not intended by the General Assembly that an insured shall receive more from such coverage than his actual loss, although he is the beneficiary under multiple policies issued pursuant to the statute. Moore v. Hartford Fire Ins. Co., 270 N.C. 532, 155 S.E.2d 128 (1967).

"OTHER INSURANCE" CLAUSES CONTRARY TO STATUTORY AMOUNT OF COVERAGE NOT PERMITTED. --Subdivision (3) of subsection (b) of this section does not permit "other insurance" clauses in the policy which are contrary to the statutory limited amount of coverage. Moore v. Hartford Fire Ins. Co., 270 N.C. 532, 155 S.E.2d 128 (1967).

"OTHER INSURANCE" CLAUSES UNENFORCEABLE WHERE INSURED'S ACTUAL DAMAGES EXCEED STATUTORY MINIMUM. --"Other insurance" clauses in policies providing uninsured motorist coverage may not be enforced if such enforcement results in limiting an insured to recovery of an amount equal only to the coverage compelled by the act, when the actual damages suffered by the insured are greater than that amount. Turner v. Masias, 36 N.C. App. 213, 243 S.E.2d 401 (1978).

BUT WHERE ACTUAL DAMAGES ARE LESS, SUCH CLAUSES ARE VALID. --While an "other insurance" clause in uninsured motorist coverage would be invalid to prevent the insured from being made whole, the use of such clauses to establish the rights of insurers in cases in which the damages were less than the coverage required by the act is not offensive to either the terms or intent of the act. The fact that two policies of insurance of different types are combined to provide the uninsured motorist coverage required by the act does not contravene its terms and, in fact, is specifically provided for in subsection (j). Turner v. Masias, 36 N.C. App. 213, 243 S.E.2d 401 (1978).

NEITHER THE LANGUAGE OF THE ACT NOR THE PUBLIC POLICY SERVED BY IT IS CONCERNED WITH WHICH INSURANCE COMPANY MAKES THE INSURED WHOLE, so long as the "other insurance" clause is not used to defeat recovery of actual damages by an insured who has not rejected uninsured motorist coverage. Turner v. Masias, 36 N.C. App. 213, 243 S.E.2d 401 (1978).

PROVISION THAT UNINSURED MOTORIST CLAUSE SHALL CONSTITUTE ONLY EXCESS COVERAGE VIOLATES STATUTE. --A policy provision that its uninsured motorist clause should constitute only excess insurance over any other similar insurance available to the injured person, is contrary to the statutory provisions of subdivision (3) of subsection (b) of this section. Moore v. Hartford Fire Ins. Co., 270 N.C. 532, 155 S.E.2d 128 (1967).

INSURED IS NOT LIMITED TO ONE RECOVERY WHERE HE IS BENEFICIARY OF MORE THAN ONE POLICY. --This section does not limit an insured to only one recovery under uninsured motorist coverage where his loss for bodily injury or death is greater than the statutory limit and he is the beneficiary of more than one policy issued under subdivision (3) of subsection (b). Moore v. Hartford Fire Ins. Co., 270 N.C. 532, 155 S.E.2d 128 (1967); Turner v. Masias, 36 N.C. App. 213, 243 S.E.2d 401 (1978); Hamilton v. Travelers Indem. Co., 77 N.C. App. 318, 335 S.E.2d 228 (1985), cert. denied, 315 N.C. 587, 341 S.E.2d 25 (1986).

"STACKING" OR AGGREGATING COVERAGES UNDER THE COMPULSORY UNINSURED MOTORIST'S COVERAGE REQUIREMENT may occur where coverage is provided by two or more policies, each providing the mandatory minimum coverage. However, to the extent that the coverage provided by motor vehicle liability insurance policies exceeds the mandatory minimum coverage required by the statute, the additional coverage is voluntary, and is governed by the terms of the insurance contract. GEICO v. Herndon, 79 N.C. App. 365, 339 S.E.2d 472 (1986).

Trial court properly determined that G.S. 20-279.21(b)(3) prohibited an insured who was a co-owner of a vehicle with the insured's employer from stacking the full amount of uninsured motorist (UM) coverage provided under an insurance policy the insured purchased with the full amount of UM coverage provided by a second policy the insured's employer purchased; appellate court upheld the trial court's judgment awarding the insured the maximum amount of UM coverage provided under the policy that the insured's employer purchased, and apportioning that amount between the insured and the employer's insurance companies. Hoover v. State Farm Mut. Ins. Co., 156 N.C. App. 418, 576 S.E.2d 396 (2003).

STACKING NOT REQUIRED. --This section does not require that the uninsured motorist coverage limits on each vehicle insured in the policy be aggregated or "stacked;" nor did the nature of the policy itself and the language it employed require such stacking. Lanning ex rel. Estate of Lanning v. Allstate Ins. Co., 332 N.C. 309, 420 S.E.2d 180 (1992).

The language in insurance company's policy was unambiguous and straightforward and it did not permit the intrapolicy stacking of its uninsured motorist (UM) coverage; therefore, the UM policy coverages on the three separate vehicles covered by plaintiffs' auto liability insurance policy with defendant insurance company would not be stacked intrapolicy to satisfy husband and wife's damages. Bailey v. Nationwide Mut. Ins. Co., 112 N.C. App. 47, 434 S.E.2d 625 (1993), overruled on other grounds, McMillian v. North Carolina Farm Bureau Mut. Ins. Co., 347 N.C. 560, 495 S.E.2d 352 (1998).

Because an insured had more than one policy with coverage, and the plain language of the policies clearly limited the total uninsured motorist coverage to the highest applicable limit of liability under any one policy, the insurer was entitled to a setoff for the amount already received by the insured, the insured was not entitled to stack the UM coverage limits under the policies pursuant to G.S. 20-279.21(b)(3), and summary judgment was properly granted to the insurer. Trivette v. State Farm Mut. Auto. Ins. Co., 164 N.C. App. 680, 596 S.E.2d 448 (2004), cert. denied, 359 N.C. 75, 605 S.E.2d 149 (2004).

CLAIMANTS WERE NOT ENTITLED TO STACK UNINSURED MOTORIST (UM) COVERAGE LIMITS under an insurance policy since this section does not mandate UM stacking and the language of the policy under which claimants were only entitled to UM coverage in the amount of $50,000 per person with a limit of $100,000 per accident, these amounts representing the amount of coverage on the vehicle involved in the accident, did not allow stacking. Dungee v. Nationwide Mut. Ins. Co., 108 N.C. App. 599, 424 S.E.2d 234 (1993).

INSTITUTION OF ACTION AGAINST HIT-AND-RUN DRIVER MAY NOT BE MADE CONDITION PRECEDENT TO RECOVERY UNDER POLICY. --In many cases it is impossible to determine the identity of a hit-and-run driver. To hold that the institution of an action by the insured against a hit-and-run driver, and to recover damages from him for his tort, is a condition precedent to the insurer's liability under uninsured motorist coverage, would in most such cases defeat insurer's liability against uninsured motorist coverage. Wright v. Fidelity & Cas. Co., 270 N.C. 577, 155 S.E.2d 100 (1967).

PROVISION REQUIRING JOINDER AS PARTY DEFENDANT OF PERSON ALLEGEDLY RESPONSIBLE FOR DAMAGE TO INSURED HELD VOID. --The provision of an automobile liability policy which required the insured, in an action against the insurer, to join as a party defendant the person or organization allegedly responsible for the damage to the insured, was held void as a violation of G.S. 58-31 (now G.S. 58-3-35) where the party defendant was a nonresident uninsured motorist and not amendable to the jurisdiction of this State. Dildy v. Southeastern Fire Ins. Co., 13 N.C. App. 66, 185 S.E.2d 272 (1971).

SERVICE OF PROCESS ON UNINSURED MOTORIST CARRIER. --Although this section does not expressly require that separate process be issued for an uninsured motorist carrier, it does specifically require that a "copy" of the summons and complaint be served on the insurer, and the appellate courts have required strict compliance with the statutes which provide for service of process on insurance companies. Thomas v. Washington, 136 N.C. App. 750, 525 S.E.2d 839 (2000).

Although an attorney's affidavit complied with the statutory requirements, which created a rebuttable presumption of valid service, an affidavit of a registered agent's employee rebutted the presumption of valid service by showing that an insurer never received a copy of a summons on February 17, 2012. In order for the insurer to be bound by a judgment against an uninsured motorist, service of process had to be obtained upon the insurer; the uninsured motorist and the insurer providing uninsured motorist coverage were separate parties with independent interests. Kahihu v. Brunson, 234 N.C. App. 142, 758 S.E.2d 648 (2014).

Uninsured motorist claims by an insured against the insured's insurer were time-barred because the three-year statute of limitations applicable to automobile negligence actions expired. Although the accident victim instituted an action within the limitations period and properly served the motorists involved, the insurer was not served with the summons and complaint until outside of the three-year statute of limitations period. Powell v. Kent, 257 N.C. App. 488, 810 S.E.2d 241 (2018), review denied, 813 S.E.2d 857, 2018 N.C. LEXIS 479 (2018).

DEFAULT JUDGMENT AGAINST UNINSURED MOTORIST PROHIBITED. --The purpose of that portion of this section prohibiting entry of default judgments is to provide the insurer, who has filed a timely answer, an opportunity to defend the complaint without being prejudiced by the conduct of the uninsured motorist who may, and usually does, have absolutely no interest in the law suit; otherwise, the insurer's liability being derivative, the entry of a default or default judgment, against the uninsured motorist also establishes the liability of the insurer. Abrams v. Surrette, 119 N.C. App. 239, 457 S.E.2d 770 (1995).

FAILURE TO OBTAIN JUDGMENT AGAINST DEFENDANTS PRECLUDED DECLARATORY JUDGMENT AGAINST INSURERS. --Under the uninsured motorist coverages of defendant insurers, liability did not attach until a valid judgment was obtained against the uninsured motorist; therefore, where plaintiffs had not obtained any such judgment and there was no assurance that they ever would, there was no case in controversy to meet the jurisdictional requirements for declaratory judgment under G.S. 1-253. McLaughlin v. Martin, 92 N.C. App. 368, 374 S.E.2d 455 (1988).

NO CONFLICT BETWEEN STATUTE AND POLICY REQUIREMENT. --There is no conflict between the term "hit-and-run motor vehicle," as used in the statute relating to uninsured or hit-and-run motor vehicle coverage, and a policy requirement of "physical contact of such automobile" with the insured or with an automobile occupied by the insured. Hendricks v. United States Fid. & Guar. Co., 5 N.C. App. 181, 167 S.E.2d 876 (1969).

THE AUTHORITY OF THE COURT TO TAX COSTS in an action to recover under uninsured motorist provisions of an insurance policy is not dependent on either the insurance policy or subdivision (b)(3) of this section. Ensley v. Nationwide Mut. Ins. Co., 80 N.C. App. 512, 342 S.E.2d 567, cert. denied, 318 N.C. 414, 349 S.E.2d 594 (1986).

UNINSURED MOTORIST PROVISION OF INSURANCE POLICY HELD TO PROVIDE COVERAGE FOR PARENT'S CLAIM FOR MINOR CHILD'S MEDICAL EXPENSES; child's distinct claims and coverage, raised under his separate contract of insurance, were irrelevant. Nationwide Mut. Ins. Co. v. Lankford, 118 N.C. App. 368, 455 S.E.2d 484 (1995).

SUBDIVISION (B)(3)B OF THIS SECTION DOES NOT REQUIRE THAT INSURER BE A NAMED PARTY; therefore, failure by petitioner to name insurer as a party was not fatal. Since a major purpose of accurately identifying defendant is to provide notice, and insurer had actual notice of action, respondent insurer's argument that there is no statutory scheme for default judgment against fictitious person was without merit. Sparks v. Nationwide Mut. Ins. Co., 99 N.C. App. 148, 392 S.E.2d 415 (1990).

USE OF VEHICLE. --Where plaintiff policeman was directing traffic at the time of accident, as the plaintiff was using his vehicle to assist him in the performance of his duties as a police officer, the vehicle was being put to service for a purpose intended by city; therefore, the plaintiff was among those persons insured under the statute and was entitled to uninsured motorist coverage. Maring v. Hartford Cas. Ins. Co., 126 N.C. App. 201, 484 S.E.2d 417 (1997).

SETOFF FOR PAYMENTS UNDER MEDICAL PAYMENTS COVERAGE --In an arbitration concerning uninsured motorist coverage, an insurer was entitled to a setoff for amounts paid under medical payments coverage, as the setoff did not violate G.S. 20-279.21; the statute did not contain any language controlling the issue presented in the instant case as to duplication of compensation under uninsured motorist coverage and medical payments coverage, and did not violate the collateral source rule. Espino

v. Allstate Indem. Co., 159 N.C. App. 686, 583 S.E.2d 376 (2003).

REDUCTION BY AMOUNT OF WORKERS COMPENSATION PERMITTED. --Where plaintiff was covered by both a workers' compensation policy paid for by his employer and by UM policies not paid for by his employer, under subsection (e) the limit of liability provision in defendant's policies at issue in the action was authorized and defendant UM carriers were entitled to reduce coverage to plaintiff by the amount of workers compensation already received. McMillian v. North Carolina Farm Bureau Mut. Ins. Co., 347 N.C. 560, 495 S.E.2d 352 (1998).

THE COURT UPHELD UIM PROVISIONS WHICH EXCLUDED RELATIVES WHO DID NOT RESIDE IN THE SAME HOUSEHOLD as the named insured and who were occupying a vehicle other than the one covered by the policy when they were injured. North Carolina Farm Bureau Mut. Ins. Co. v. Perkinson, 140 N.C. App. 140, 535 S.E.2d 405 (2000).

STATUTE OF LIMITATIONS DEFENSE. --Although an insurer's liability under an uninsured motorist liability policy is derivative of the uninsured motorist's liability, the insurer is not precluded from asserting the statute of limitations as a defense, where the plaintiff has not timely commenced an action against the insurer, even though the defense might not be available to the tortfeasor. Reese v. Barbee, 129 N.C. App. 823, 501 S.E.2d 698 (1998), aff'd, 350 N.C. 60, 510 S.E.2d 374 (1999).

INSURER BOUND BY JUDGMENT OF FLORIDA COURT. --Insurer who was served by registered or certified mail, return receipt requested, or another manner provided by law, with a copy of the summons, complaint, or other process in an underlying Florida action against an uninsured motorist, was, under G.S. 20-279.51(b)(3), bound by the final judgment the injured party took against the uninsured motorist. Sawyers v. Farm Bureau Ins. Co. of N.C., Inc., 170 N.C. App. 17, 612 S.E.2d 184 (2005).

APPELLATE JURISDICTION. --Appellate court lacked jurisdiction to hear an appeal by an underinsured motorist insurer because the trial court's order on cross-motions for summary judgment was an interlocutory order, as pending issues remained in the case, and the order did not contain a certification for appeal. Moreover, although the insurer was permitted, but was not required, to participate in the proceedings as an unnamed underinsured motorist carrier, the insurer failed to show a substantial right, which would have been lost absent immediate appellate review. Peterson v. Dillman, 245 N.C. App. 239, 782 S.E.2d 362 (2016).

ILLUSTRATIVE CASE. --Where the liability limits of business automobile policy were $300,000 and there was no written rejection of uninsured motorist (UM) coverage by the plaintiff, they were entitled to $300,000 of UM coverage, an amount equal to the liability limits of the policy. Bray v. North Carolina Farm Bureau Mut. Ins. Co., 341 N.C. 678, 462 S.E.2d 650 (1995).

Insured was not precluded as a matter of law from recovering under the uninsured motorist policy because it was possible that a reasonable interpretation of the uninsured motorist policy at issue was that a rock, which flew off a dump truck carting a load of rocks (which was unquestionably an expected use of the truck) and hit a vehicle, was a sufficiently direct collision between the truck and the vehicle. Geico Ins. Co. v. Larson, 542 F. Supp. 2d 441 (E.D.N.C. 2008).

IV. UNDERINSURED MOTORIST COVERAGE.

LEGISLATIVE INTENT. --The amendments to this section do not indicate the General Assembly intended to change the focus of underinsured motorist (UIM) coverage from persons to vehicles; the anti-intrapolicy stacking provisions in the 1991 amendments simply prevent an insured from receiving multiple UIM recoveries under a single policy. They do not prevent an insured from being covered while operating an owned vehicle not listed in the policy. Honeycutt v. Walker, 119 N.C. App. 220, 458 S.E.2d 23 (1995).

Although the better practice would be for the insured to notify the UIM carrier when the insured has received an acceptable offer from the liability carrier, there is nothing in the statute which requires written notice to the UIM insurer be made directly by the insured. Daughtry v. Castleberry, 123 N.C. App. 671, 474 S.E.2d 137 (1996), cert. granted, 345 N.C. 341, 483 S.E.2d 165 (1997), aff'd, 346 N.C. 272, 485 S.E.2d 45 (1997).

There is no requirement that all those covered under a policy be insured at identical levels of coverage; thus, as long as the minimum coverage requirements are met, no reason exists to prevent an insured from obtaining multi-tiered coverage for its employees. Hlasnick v. Federated Mut. Ins. Co., 136 N.C. App. 320, 524 S.E.2d 386 (2000), aff'd, in part, and cert. dismissed, in part, 353 N.C. 240, 539 S.E.2d 274 (2000).

SUBSECTION (B)(4) DOES NOT REQUIRE THAT AN UNDERINSURED MOTORIST CARRIER BE NOTIFIED OF A CLAIM WITHIN THE STATUTE OF LIMITATIONS GOVERNING THE TORTFEASOR, although an insured would be barred from seeking coverage if she failed to bring an action against a tortfeasor within the statute of limitations governing tort actions. Liberty Mut. Ins. Co. v. Pennington, 141 N.C. App. 495, 541 S.E.2d 503 (2000), aff'd, 356 N.C. 571, 573 S.E.2d 118 (2002).

In injured party's negligence claim against the driver, in which the injured party sought to recover underinsured motorist coverage from her insurer, the insurer was not entitled to formal service of process under G.S. 20-279.21(b)(4). Darroch v. Lea, 150 N.C. App. 156, 563 S.E.2d 219 (2002).

Injured insureds, who learned that the insurance coverage for the tortfeasor who injured them was insufficient to cover their damages, were not required to give their underinsured motorist insurer notice of a possible underinsured motorist claim within the statute of limitations applicable to the underlying tort, in G.S. 1-52(16), because the plain language of G.S. 20-279.21(b)(4), requiring notice of such a claim to the insurer, did not impose this requirement. Liberty

Mut. Ins. Co. v. Pennington, 356 N.C. 571, 573 S.E.2d 118 (2002).

CONTRIBUTION. --Insurer's contribution claim against providers for allegedly serving alcohol to a driver and allowing the driver to drive and injure the insurer's insureds was properly dismissed because (1) the insurer had no right to assert such a claim, under G.S. 1B-1(b), which governed over the more general G.S. 20-279.21, and only allowed joint tort-feasors to assert the claim, and (2) neither the insurer nor the insurer's insureds were joint tort-feasors. Nationwide Prop. & Cas. Ins. Co. v. Smith, 256 N.C. App. 492, 808 S.E.2d 172 (2017).

PER CLAIMANT OR PER ACCIDENT COVERAGE. --This section does not mandate that underinsured coverage limits be provided per claimant, as opposed to per accident, and thus, a per accident limit in a business liability policy is valid. Progressive Am. Ins. Co. v. Vasquez, 350 N.C. 386, 515 S.E.2d 8 (1999).

The applicable UIM limit under this section will depend on two factors: (1) the number of claimants seeking coverage under the UIM policy; and (2) whether the negligent driver's liability policy was exhausted pursuant to a per-person or per-accident cap. When only one UIM claimant exists, the per-person limit under the policy will be the applicable UIM limit, but when more than one claimant is seeking UIM coverage, how the liability policy was exhausted will determine the applicable UIM limit. In particular, when the negligent driver's liability policy was exhausted pursuant to the per-person cap, the UIM policy's per-person cap will be the applicable limit. However, when the liability policy was exhausted pursuant to the per-accident cap, the applicable UIM limit will be the UIM policy's per-accident limit. North Carolina Farm Bureau Mut. Ins. Co. v. Gurley, 139 N.C. App. 178, 532 S.E.2d 846 (2000).

Where the injured parties' insurer provided $500,000 of underinsured motorist coverage in any single accident, and the injured parties were each paid $100,000 by the tortfeasor's insurer, in determining the amount due to the injured parties, the total amount paid by the tortfeasor's insurer to the injured parties, $200,000, was to be subtracted from the $500,000 policy limits of the injured parties' insurer. Nationwide Mut. Ins. Co. v. Haight, 152 N.C. App. 137, 566 S.E.2d 835 (2002), cert. denied sub nom. Nationwide Mut. Ins. Co. v. Mills, 356 N.C. 675, 577 S.E.2d 627 (2003).

REJECTION OF COVERAGE PRIOR TO AMENDMENT. --Insured's rejection of underinsured motorists coverage, prior to the 1991 statutory amendment and prior to the approval of new form reflecting the substance of the statutory amendment, was not still valid and effective with respect to an accident that occurred after the rejection form had been substantially revised and after the policy had been renewed. Maryland Cas. Co. v. Smith, 117 N.C. App. 593, 452 S.E.2d 318 (1995).

REJECTION OF UNDERINSURED MOTORIST COVERAGE BY CO-POLICY HOLDER. --Trial court did not err in granting an insurer's motion for summary judgment in its action seeking a declaratory judgment that an insured was not entitled to any UIM coverage regarding an automobile accident because a co-policy holder was given the opportunity to reject or select differing coverage amounts of UIM coverage pursuant to G.S. 20-279.21(b)(4), and she chose not to purchase UIM coverage; co-policy holder's affidavit showed that she was aware of her options as to UIM coverage and that she made a conscious decision not to purchase it. N.C. Farm Bureau Mut. Ins. Co. v. Jenkins, 207 N.C. App. 506, 700 S.E.2d 434 (2010).

PROVISION OF UNDERINSURANCE. --"Underinsurance" provides a type of insurance coverage that allows an insured to be indemnified by his own insurer, in whole or in part, for damages caused by a negligent motorist who is insured inadequately. North Carolina Farm Bureau Mut. Ins. Co. v. Hilliard, 90 N.C. App. 507, 369 S.E.2d 386 (1988), decided under 1983 version of § 20-279.21.

DEFINITION OF UNDERINSURED DOES NOT INCORPORATE DEFINITION OF UNINSURED. --The legislature did not intend to fully incorporate the definition of an uninsured motor vehicle into the definition of an underinsured highway vehicle. Cochran v. North Carolina Farm Bureau Mut. Ins. Co., 113 N.C. App. 260, 437 S.E.2d 910 (1994).

STRICT COMPLIANCE NEEDED FOR UIM REJECTION TO BE EFFECTIVE. --An automobile insurance policy issued by defendant provided underinsured motorist (UIM) coverage to plaintiff for injuries sustained as a passenger where insured had rejected UIM coverage on company's own form rather than on one promulgated by the Rate Bureau; "substantial compliance" was irrelevant. Sanders v. American Spirit Ins. Co., 135 N.C. App. 178, 519 S.E.2d 323 (1999).

Because the tortfeasor's insurance policy's limit for liability was less than the minimum limit specified by G.S. 20-279.21(b), and because the insurer failed to demonstrate that the underinsured coverage was rejected by the insured, the trial court erred in granting its N.Y. C.P.L.R. art. 75 petition to stay arbitration. Matter of State Farm Mut. Auto. Ins. Co. v. Gray, 891 N.Y.S.2d 151 (Dec. 15, 2009).

INSURER'S FAILURE TO PROVIDE OPPORTUNITY TO REJECT UNDERINSURED MOTORIST LIMITS. --G.S. 20-279.21 established that an insured must be given the initial opportunity to reject or select different underinsured motorist (UIM) limits; insurer's total failure to provide an opportunity to reject UIM coverage or select different limits violated this requirement, and thus entitled the insured to the highest available limit of UIM coverage of $1,000,000. Williams v. Nationwide Mut. Ins. Co., 174 N.C. App. 601, 621 S.E.2d 644 (2005).

INSURER WAS REQUIRED TO STRICTLY ADHERE TO THE REQUIRED FORMAT FOR REJECTION OF UNDERINSURED MOTORIST (UIM) COVERAGE; written rejection of UIM coverage was invalid where, although the written rejection had virtually identical language to the UIM rejection form promulgated by the North Carolina Rate Bureau, the insurance company had shrunk the rejection form and included it in its application. Erie Ins. Exch. v. Miller, 160 N.C. App. 217, 584 S.E.2d 857 (2003).

BUT CERTAIN ADDITIONAL LANGUAGE IS ALLOWED. --Additional, explanatory language, designed to aid the insured in making an informed decision on whether to select or reject UM and UIM coverage, did not render a selection/rejection form invalid. Blackburn v. State Farm Mut. Auto. Ins. Co., 353 N.C. 369, 141 N.C. App. 655, 540 S.E.2d 63, 540 S.E.2d 63 (2000).

Accident victim's insurer was properly granted summary judgment on its claim that it did not have to provide the victim with underinsured motorist coverage (UIM) because the victim rejected UIM when she completed her insurance application, and the insurer's UIM selection/rejection form complied with a form promulgated by the North Carolina Rate Bureau and approved by the Commissioner of the North Carolina Department of Insurance pursuant to G.S. 20-279.21(b)(4); the only deviations from the promulgated form were the insurer's inclusion of additional language which explained uninsured and underinsured motorist coverage, and the insurer's use of 10-point type rather than 12-point type. Stegenga v. Burney, 174 N.C. App. 196, 620 S.E.2d 302 (2005).

REJECTION OF COVERAGE AFTER AMENDMENT. --An automobile liability insurer is required to offer insureds the opportunity to select underinsured motorist coverage limits in an amount between the statutory minimum and $1,000,000 and to obtain a valid rejection or selection of different underinsured motorist coverage limits under this option, notwithstanding that the policy is a renewal policy. State Farm Mut. Auto. Ins. Co. v. Fortin, 350 N.C. 264, 513 S.E.2d 782 (1999).

REJECTION OF COVERAGE HELD INVALID. --Plaintiff's rejection of underinsured motorist coverage was not effective where she was not eligible for UIM coverage at the time the rejection was signed because her policy limits did not exceed the minimum referred to in subdivision (b)(4) of this section. McNally v. Allstate Ins. Co., 142 N.C. App. 680, 544 S.E.2d 807 (2001).

Insurance company could not produce any writing executed by the wife insured that showed she validly rejected underinsured motorist (UIM) coverage; therefore, the insurance company's failure to produce the requisite form compelled the conclusion that it was not in strict compliance with G.S. 20-279.21(b)(4), and the husband insured was entitled to UIM coverage based on injuries sustained in the accident. Since there was no evidence that the wife insured was given the opportunity to reject UIM coverage or to select different coverage limits, at the time of the accident, the insureds had UIM coverage in the amount of one million dollars. Progressive Southeastern Ins. Co. v. Greene, 2008 U.S. Dist. LEXIS 111775 (M.D.N.C. Oct. 27, 2008).

WHERE TERMS OF POLICY EXPRESSLY EXCLUDED UNDERINSURED MOTORIST (UIM) COVERAGE, this section did not require an excess personal liability policy to provide UIM coverage. Piazza v. Little, 350 N.C. 585, 515 S.E.2d 219 (1999).

STATE-OWNED VEHICLES CAN BE UNDERINSURED VEHICLES. --An underinsured highway vehicle as defined in subsection (b)(4) of this section can include a state-owned vehicle. Cochran v. North Carolina Farm Bureau Mut. Ins. Co., 113 N.C. App. 260, 437 S.E.2d 910 (1994).

DEFINITION OF "PERSON INSURED." --Underinsured motorist coverage (UIM), is governed by subdivision (b)(4) of this section which incorporates by reference the definition of "persons insured" that is found in subdivision (b)(3) of this section, dealing with uninsured motorists (UM) coverage. Thus, for both UM and UIM coverage, "persons insured" is defined by subdivision (b)(3) of this section. Brown v. Truck Ins. Exch., 103 N.C. App. 59, 404 S.E.2d 172, cert. denied, 329 N.C. 786, 408 S.E.2d 515 (1991).

When one member of a household purchases first-party underinsured motorist (UIM) coverage, it may fairly be said that he or she intends to protect all members of the family unit within the household. The legislature recognized this family unit for purposes of UIM coverage when it defined "persons insured" of the first class as "the named insured and, while resident of the same household, the spouse of any named insured and relatives of either." These persons insured of the first class are protected, based on their relationship, whether they are injured while riding in one of the covered vehicles or otherwise. Harris ex rel. Freedman v. Nationwide Mut. Ins. Co., 332 N.C. 184, 420 S.E.2d 124 (1992).

Where plaintiff lived in the same household as his father, the owner of an automobile insurance policy providing underinsured motorist (UIM) coverage for two vehicles, plaintiff was a "person insured" under the policy and was entitled to the same rights to stack coverages intrapolicy as the owner. Miller v. Nationwide Mut. Ins. Co., 112 N.C. App. 295, 435 S.E.2d 537 (1993), cert. denied, 335 N.C. 770, 442 S.E.2d 519 (1994).

A PERSON WHO WAS NOT A "NAMED INSURED" UNDER THIS STATUTE or as defined in the policy was not a "person insured" under subdivision (b)(4) of this section. Brown v. Truck Ins. Exch., 103 N.C. App. 59, 404 S.E.2d 172, cert. denied, 329 N.C. 786, 408 S.E.2d 515 (1991).

RECOVERY WHERE NO LEGAL ENTITY IS "NAMED INSURED". --Summary judgment for plaintiff was appropriate and the estate of plaintiff's son could recover under his parents' automobile insurance policy, although policy had been placed in the name of a piece of property parents owned which was incapable of being legally classified as an individual or as an entity, commercial or otherwise, as the insured; the court resolved the ambiguity created by designating a place as the insured in favor of the plaintiff who paid the premiums and obtained the family coverage. Stockton v. North Carolina Farm Bureau Mut. Ins. Co., 139 N.C. App. 196, 532 S.E.2d 566 (2000).

WHEN NAMED INSURED IS A CORPORATION. --The term "named insured" does not include officers, directors, or stockholders of a corporation when the named insured is the corporation. Busby v. Simmons, 103 N.C. App. 592, 406 S.E.2d 628 (1991).

EMPLOYEES OF A CORPORATION were not named insureds by the terms of the corporation's automobile liability policy and therefore were not class one insureds under this section for the purpose of underinsured motorist coverage. Sproles v. Greene, 329 N.C. 603, 407 S.E.2d 497 (1991).

ELIGIBILITY FOR UNDERINSURANCE WHEN COVERED UNDER (B)(3) AND (B)(4). --Where tortfeasor qualified as both an uninsured motorist pursuant to subdivision (b)(3) of this section, and as an underinsured motorist under subdivision (b)(4), plaintiff's claim seeking recovery for underinsured motorist insurance stated a claim upon which relief could be granted. Monti ex rel. United States v. United Servs. Auto. Ass'n, 108 N.C. App. 342, 423 S.E.2d 530 (1992), cert. denied, 334 N.C. 164, 432 S.E.2d 363 (1993).

THE DISTINCTION BETWEEN AN UNDERINSURED MOTORIST POLICY PURCHASED BY THE EMPLOYEE AND ONE COVERING THE EMPLOYEE BUT PURCHASED BY HIS SPOUSE while a resident of the same household is unimportant. Creed v. R.G. Swaim & Son, 123 N.C. App. 124, 472 S.E.2d 213 (1996).

INTENTIONAL AND FRAUDULENT MISREPRESENTATIONS. --An insurer may deny UIM coverage in excess of the statutory minimum based upon intentional and fraudulent misrepresentations or concealment by an insured in procurement of an automobile liability insurance policy. Hartford Underwriters Ins. Co. v. Becks, 123 N.C. App. 489, 473 S.E.2d 427 (1996).

CLAIM ESTIMATES PROPERLY EXCLUDED AS EVIDENCE. --In personal injury action against plaintiff's UIM insurer, admitting claim estimates prepared by the insurer as admissions of a party opponent would unduly prejudice the defense and circumvent the policy of having the jury focus on the facts and not the existence of liability insurance. Braddy v. Nationwide Mut. Liab. Ins. Co., 122 N.C. App. 402, 470 S.E.2d 820 (1996).

VEHICLE NOT INCLUDED. --An underinsured vehicle, as that term is used in subdivision (b)(4), does not include a tort-feasor's vehicle whose available liability insurance is less than the relevant underinsured motorist (UIM) coverage. Ray v. Atlantic Cas. Ins. Co., 112 N.C. App. 259, 435 S.E.2d 80, cert. denied, 335 N.C. 559, 439 S.E.2d 151 (1993).

An owned vehicle exclusion is contrary to the terms of subdivision (b)(4), whether it is judicially imposed or whether it is contained in the underinsured motorist (UIM) portion of the policy. Nationwide Mut. Ins. Co. v. Mabe, 115 N.C. App. 193, 444 S.E.2d 664 (1994), aff'd, 342 N.C. 482, 467 S.E.2d 34 (1996).

Because the limits of an insured's underinsured motorist coverage and her sister's personal injury coverage were equal, the sum of the limits of liability under the bodily injury liability policies was not less than the applicable limits of underinsured motorist coverage; the sister's vehicle, therefore, was not underinsured, and the insured was not entitled to underinsured motorist coverage under her policy. N.C. Farm Bureau Mut. Ins. Co. v. Lunsford, -- N.C. App. --, 843 S.E.2d 677 (2020).

POLICY PROVISIONS WHICH EXCLUDED "OWNED VEHICLES" FROM UNDERINSURED MOTORIST (UIM) COVERAGE WERE INVALID. -- An underinsured highway vehicle as defined in subdivision (b)(4) can include a motor vehicle owned by the named insured, and the provisions in policies issued by an insurer attempting to exclude such coverage are invalid and unenforceable. State Farm Mut. Auto. Ins. Co. v. Young, 122 N.C. App. 505, 470 S.E.2d 361 (1996).

FAMILY OWNED EXCLUSION CLAUSE. --The existence of a family-owned exclusion clause in insured's insurance policy did not affect whether plaintiffs were entitled to underinsured motorist (UIM) benefits; insured could collect UIM benefits under his automobile policy for injuries suffered while riding his motorcycle, notwithstanding the family-owned exclusion clause. Honeycutt v. Walker, 119 N.C. App. 220, 458 S.E.2d 23 (1995).

Policy, which under the underinsured clause excluded all other owned vehicles not listed in the policy, was in violation of subdivision (b)(4) of this section. Nationwide Mut. Ins. Co. v. Mabe, 342 N.C. 482, 467 S.E.2d 34 (1996).

An underinsured highway vehicle as defined in subdivision (b)(4) can include a motor vehicle owned by the named insured, and the provisions in policies issued by an insurer attempting to exclude such coverage are invalid and unenforceable. State Farm Mut. Auto. Ins. Co. v. Young, 122 N.C. App. 505, 470 S.E.2d 361 (1996).

TERMS OF COVERAGE ARE WITHIN CONTROL OF PARTIES. --Underinsured motorists coverage is not required by law, since the insured may reject the coverage, and therefore the terms of the coverage are within the control of the parties. Aills v. Nationwide Mut. Ins. Co., 88 N.C. App. 595, 363 S.E.2d 880 (1988).

WHERE THERE ARE SEPARATE AND DISTINCT EXCESS LIABILITY AND UNDERLYING POLICIES, underinsured coverage is not written into the excess liability policy by operation of law and exists only if it is provided by the contractual terms of the excess policy. Progressive Am. Ins. Co. v. Vasquez, 350 N.C. 386, 515 S.E.2d 8 (1999).

COVERAGE TIED TO VEHICLE OCCUPIED. --Prior to the 1991 amendment to this section by Session Laws 1991, c. 646, ss. 1 to 4, where an injured party was not a named insured or spouse, and was not a family member residing in the household of the named insured at the time of the accident, she was a "Class II" insured, and the underinsured motorist coverage available to her was tied to the vehicle occupied by her at the time of the accident. Nationwide Mut. Ins. Co. v. Silverman ex rel. Radja, 332 N.C. 633, 423 S.E.2d 68 (1992).

SCOPE OF PERMISSIVE USES. --Where a drunken rental car driver was using the rental car with the rental company's permission, the driver was insured under a liability policy; though the driver violated her rental agreement by driving drunk, she did not exceed the scope of permissive use. United Servs. Auto. Ass'n v. Rhodes, 156 N.C. App. 665, 577 S.E.2d 171 (2003).

EXHAUSTION CLAUSE OF INSURANCE POLICY and the similar wording of subdivision (b)(4) obligate the insurer to pay only after the applicable liability bonds or policies have been exhausted by payment of a judgment or settlement. Silvers v. Horace Mann Ins. Co., 90 N.C. App. 1, 367 S.E.2d 372 (1988) (decided prior to 1985 amendments).

Given the fact that plaintiff settled for the maximum amount available under the tortfeasor's liability policy, it would contravene the purposes behind underinsured motorists (UIM) coverage to read the "legally entitled to recover damages" provision as a bar to plaintiff's recovery. In addition, given the language of the exhaustion clause which urges settlement or judgment before obligating the UIM carrier, it was reasonable for plaintiff to believe that she was required to settle or obtain a judgment against the tortfeasors and their liability insurer before seeking payment from her insurer. Silvers v. Horace Mann Ins. Co., 90 N.C. App. 1, 367 S.E.2d 372 (1988) (decided prior to 1985 amendments).

Subdivision (b)(4) requires a uninsured motorist (UIM) plaintiff to exhaust all remedies by seeking payment of judgments or settlements from the tortfeasor and liability insurer before seeking payment form the UIM insurer. Spivey v. Lowery, 116 N.C. App. 124, 446 S.E.2d 835, cert. denied, 338 N.C. 312, 452 S.E.2d 312 (1994).

ONCE AN ADVANCEMENT IS MADE AND THE UNDERINSURED CLAIM IS SETTLED PRIOR TO EXHAUSTION OF PRIMARY POLICY LIMITS, the underinsured motorist carrier is pursuing "its claim" and not that of the insured. The underinsured motorist carrier is not required to be designated as a party plaintiff "except upon its own election." State Farm Mut. Auto. Ins. Co. v. Blackwelder, 332 N.C. 135, 418 S.E.2d 229 (1992).

EXHAUSTION REQUIREMENT SATISFIED. --Insured's employee was not compelled by the insurer to file a lawsuit because, in light of the employee's timely settlement with the tortfeasor, the employee satisfied the exhaustion requirement and did not have to sue the tortfeasor in order to preserve his rights to underinsured motorist coverage. Guessford v. Pa. Nat'l Mut. Cas. Ins. Co., 2013 U.S. Dist. LEXIS 155968 (M.D.N.C. Oct. 30, 2013).

DETERMINATION AS TO PRIMARY AND EXCESS COVERAGE. --Trial court erred in finding that insurance company which insured plaintiffs' two vehicles, neither of which was involved in the subject accident, was primary and that the underinsured motorist coverage for the vehicle involved in the accident was excess; the plaintiffs were second-class insureds on the defendant's UIM policy and first-class on their own policy, but there was no need to pro-rate or consider classes where the "other insurance" clauses were not mutually repugnant, but could be read together harmoniously. Hlasnick v. Federated Mut. Ins.

Co., 136 N.C. App. 320, 524 S.E.2d 386 (2000), aff'd, in part, and cert. dismissed, in part, 353 N.C. 240, 539 S.E.2d 274 (2000).

UNDERINSURED MOTORIST COVERAGE CAN NEVER BE "EXCESS OR ADDITIONAL COVERAGE" within the meaning of subsection (g) for the purpose of avoiding the requirement of subdivision (b)(4) of intrapolicy and interpolicy stacking; since underinsured motorist (UIM) coverage in any given policy must always equal the policy's basic liability coverage and that coverage must always exceed the minimum mandatory amount, there can never be any excess or additional UIM coverage. Sutton v. Aetna Cas. & Sur. Co., 325 N.C. 259, 382 S.E.2d 759, rehearing denied, 325 N.C. 437, 384 S.E.2d 546 (1989).

UIM COVERAGE IN SEPARATE POLICIES. --Underinsured motorist (UIM) coverage is available under a policy issued to a named insured; true when the vehicle owned by the named insured and involved in his injuries is insured under a separate policy not containing UIM coverage. Bass v. North Carolina Farm Bureau Mut. Ins. Co., 332 N.C. 109, 418 S.E.2d 221 (1992).

Insured was properly awarded the limits of a secondary policy's underinsured motorist (UIM) of $1,000,000 since a primary policy had a $250,000 limit and the $30,000 the insured had received from an operator's exhausted liability policy was credited against the UIM coverage under the primary policy; stacking was permitted under G.S. 20-279.21(b)(4). Martini v. Companion Prop. & Cas. Ins. Co., 198 N.C. App. 39, 679 S.E.2d 156 (2009), review denied, 363 N.C. 805, 690 S.E.2d 704, N.C. LEXIS 39 (2010), aff'd in part and rev'd in part 2010 N.C. LEXIS 412 (2010).

INSURED MAY COLLECT UNDER MULTIPLE UNDERINSURED MOTORIST POLICIES UP TO, BUT NOT MORE THAN, HIS ACTUAL LOSS and a carrier having accepted premium for underinsured motorist coverage may not deny coverage on ground that other such insurance is available to insured. Sproles v. Greene, 100 N.C. App. 96, 394 S.E.2d 691 (1990), rev'd on other grounds, Sproles v. Integon Insurance Co., 329 N.C. 603, 407 S.E.2d 497 (1991).

INSURED WAS HELD TO HAVE RECEIVED TWO SEPARATE POLICIES OF UNDERINSURED COVERAGE, although the insurance company contended that only one policy was issued and that it included the later-added fourth vehicle, where the insured was told she could not add her fourth vehicle to the existing policy, was billed separately, and where the billings showed different renewal dates for the two policies. Iodice v. Jones, 135 N.C. App. 740, 522 S.E.2d 593 (1999).

AVAILABILITY OF COVERAGE NOT DEPENDENT UPON TORTFEASOR'S LIABILITY LIMITS. --The availability of underinsured motorist coverage to an injured victim does not depend upon the tortfeasor's liability limits being less than those on the vehicle with the underinsured motorist coverage. Amos v. North Carolina Farm Bureau Mut. Ins. Co., 103 N.C. App. 629, 406 S.E.2d 652, aff'd, 332 N.C. 340, 420 S.E.2d 123 (1992).

STACKING. --The Underinsured Motorist (UIM) coverages provided in two separate automobile insurance policies issued to the individual plaintiff may be aggregated or "stacked" to compensate for the death of plaintiff's daughter, who was killed while driving a vehicle owned by the individual plaintiff and the daughter, even though the daughter and the vehicle were listed in only one of the policies. Smith v. Nationwide Mut. Ins. Co., 328 N.C. 139, 400 S.E.2d 44 (1991), rehearing denied, 328 N.C. 577, 403 S.E.2d 514 (1991).

CONTROLLING EFFECT OF ARTICLE ON TERMS OF STACKING. --Despite the fact that underinsured motorist coverage may ultimately be rejected by the insured, the provisions of the Motor Vehicle Safety and Financial Responsibility Act (this Article) relating to intrapolicy stacking of uninsured motorist coverage control; therefore, the terms of stacking are controlled not by the parties and the insurance contract, but by the Act. Sutton v. Aetna Cas. & Sur. Co., 325 N.C. 259, 382 S.E.2d 759, rehearing denied, 325 N.C. 437, 384 S.E.2d 546 (1989).

STACKING NOT REQUIRED PRIOR TO AMENDMENT. --The 1983 version of subdivision (b)(4), which was prior to 1985 amendment, did not require that the underinsured motorist coverages in the same policy be aggregated or stacked. Proctor v. North Carolina Farm Bureau Mut. Ins. Co., 335 N.C. 533, 439 S.E.2d 112 (1994).

SUMMARY JUDGMENT IMPROPER WHERE STACKING ISSUE UNRESOLVED. --Summary judgment was inappropriate where a genuine issue of material fact existed as to whether the policy covering a dump truck met any of the statutory definitions of a "private passenger motor vehicle" under G.S. 58-40-10(b) and could be stacked with the other policies under this section. Erwin v. Tweed, 142 N.C. App. 643, 544 S.E.2d 803 (2001), review denied, 353 N.C. 724, 551 S.E.2d 437 (2001).

INTERPOLICY AND INTRAPOLICY STACKING. --The legislature intended subdivision (b)(4) of this section to require both interpolicy and intrapolicy stacking of underinsured coverages. Sutton v. Aetna Cas. & Sur. Co., 325 N.C. 259, 382 S.E.2d 759, rehearing denied, 325 N.C. 437, 384 S.E.2d 546 (1989).

Interpreting subdivision (b)(4) to allow both interpolicy and intrapolicy stacking is consistent with the nature and purpose of the Act, which is to compensate innocent victims of financially irresponsible motorists. Sutton v. Aetna Cas. & Sur. Co., 325 N.C. 259, 382 S.E.2d 759, rehearing denied, 325 N.C. 437, 384 S.E.2d 546 (1989).

The language of Motor Vehicle Safety and Financial Responsibility Act is intended to permit both interpolicy and intrapolicy stacking of multiple vehicles for underinsured motorist (UIM) coverage by the policy owner and prevails over any inconsistent language found in a policy. No distinction exists for UIM coverage purposes between the policy owner and a nonowner family member covered by the policy. Harris v. Nationwide Mut. Ins. Co., 103 N.C. App. 101, 404 S.E.2d 499, aff'd, 332 N.C. 184, 420 S.E.2d 124 (1992).

PUBLIC POLICY REASONS FOR ALLOWING INTRAPOLICY STACKING of Underinsured Motorist (UIM) coverage are that stacking: (1) enhances the injured party's potential for full recovery of all damages; (2) prevents the anomalous situation that an insured is better off -- for purposes of the underinsured motorist coverage -- if separate policies were purchased for each vehicle; (3) gives the insured due consideration for the separate premiums paid for each UIM coverage within a policy; and (4) is consistent with preexisting common law by which automobile insurance policies have been construed to require intrapolicy stacking of medical payments coverage. Proctor v. North Carolina Farm Bureau Mut. Ins. Co., 107 N.C. App. 26, 418 S.E.2d 680 (1992), petition denied as to additional issues, 333 N.C. 346, 426 S.E.2d 709 (1993), modified on other grounds, 335 N.C. 533, 439 S.E.2d 112 (1994).

STACKING OF UIM COVERAGES WHERE INSURED HOLDS MORE THAN ONE POLICY COVERING SEVERAL VEHICLES. --Where insurer sold insured two policies which provided four vehicles with uninsured motorist coverage and where the policies limited the liability for underinsured (UIM) coverage, subdivision (b)(4) of this section controlled, and permitted the insured to stack or aggregate the UIM coverages for each vehicle in both policies. Sutton v. Aetna Cas. & Sur. Co., 325 N.C. 259, 382 S.E.2d 759, rehearing denied, 325 N.C. 437, 384 S.E.2d 546 (1989).

TO DETERMINE WHETHER PLAINTIFF COULD STACK THE UNDERINSURED MOTORIST COVERAGES UNDER TWO POLICIES, the court would examine the policy language found in the "Other Insurance" provision of the policy issued by defendant in which the Uninsured Motorist (UM)/UIM endorsement modified the "Other Insurance" provision of the UM coverage agreement with respect to the damages the plaintiff was entitled to recover from an uninsured or underinsured motorist. Bass v. North Carolina Farm Bureau Mut. Ins. Co., 103 N.C. App. 272, 405 S.E.2d 370, aff'd, 332 N.C. 109, 418 S.E.2d 221 (1992).

TRIAL COURT ERRED IN DENYING AN INSURANCE COMPANY'S SUMMARY JUDGMENT MOTION AND IN GRANTING INJURED PERSONS' SUMMARY JUDGMENT MOTION IN A CASE SEEKING A DECLARATION THAT THE INJURED PERSONS WERE ALLOWED TO STACK THE UIM COVERAGE OF THEIR TWO POLICIES; stacking of underinsured motorist (UIM) coverages is permitted where each of the multiple policies providing stackable UIM coverages were written at limits that exceeded the statutorily-required minimum liability amount, but where one of two policies at issue provided liability coverage with limits equal to the statutorily-required minimum amount of $25,000/$50,000, under G.S. 20-279.21(b)(4), no UIM coverage was available with that policy -- thus, there was no additional UIM coverage available to be stacked with the $100,000 UIM coverage provided by the first policy, which was equal to the amount already paid under the tortfeasor's exhausted liability policy. Purcell v. Downey, 162 N.C. App. 529, 591 S.E.2d 556 (2004).

FOR PURPOSES OF STACKING, COVERAGE FOLLOWED INSURED RATHER THAN VEHICLE. Where plaintiff was a named insured in two policies, but the vehicle involved in the accident was not listed in the policy issued by defendant, plaintiff could recover under the underinsured motorist (UIM) provision of the policy issued by defendant as well as the other policy. The definition of "persons insured" for UM/UIM coverage strongly suggested that the UM/UIM coverage for family members follows the person rather than the vehicle. Bass v. North Carolina Farm Bureau Mut. Ins. Co., 103 N.C. App. 272, 405 S.E.2d 370, aff'd, 332 N.C. 109, 418 S.E.2d 221 (1992).

STACKING PERMITTED FOR PRIVATE PASSENGER VEHICLES. --Insurance company's owned vehicle exclusion was unenforceable and the insureds were entitled to stack their underinsured motorist (UIM) coverage if the vehicles listed in the policy were private passenger motor vehicles. Nationwide Mut. Ins. Co. v. Mabe, 115 N.C. App. 193, 444 S.E.2d 664 (1994), aff'd, 342 N.C. 482, 467 S.E.2d 34 (1996).

STACKING NOT PERMITTED. --No underinsured motorist benefits were provided through decedent's business auto policy because the covered vehicle was not a "private passenger motor vehicle" as required for interpolicy stacking under subsection (b)(4). North Carolina Farm Bureau Mut. Ins. Co. v. Stamper, 122 N.C. App. 254, 468 S.E.2d 584 (1996).

STACKING ALLOWED IN DETERMINING WHETHER TORTFEASOR'S CAR IS AN "UNDERINSURED HIGHWAY VEHICLE" --The language of subdivision (b)(4) allows the stacking of an insured's coverages in determining whether a tortfeasor's vehicle is an "underinsured highway vehicle." The statute compares the aggregate liability coverage of the tortfeasor's vehicle to the applicable limits of liability under the owner's policy, meaning the aggregate or stacked "limits" under the policy. Harris ex rel. Freedman v. Nationwide Mut. Ins. Co., 332 N.C. 184, 420 S.E.2d 124 (1992).

Underinsured motorist (UIM) coverage for a nonowner Class I insured under one policy could be stacked with the UIM coverage under another policy in which the party was also a nonowner insured. Mitchell v. Nationwide Ins. Co., 110 N.C. App. 16, 429 S.E.2d 351 (1993), pet. disc. rev. granted, 334 N.C. 164, 432 S.E.2d 363 (1993), aff'd, 335 N.C. 433, 439 S.E.2d 110 (1994).

Vehicle passenger and the passenger's mother were entitled to stack the driver's and the mother's insurance policies in determining that the vehicle involved in a one vehicle accident was an underinsured highway vehicle under G.S. 20-279.21(b)(4) for purposes of underinsured motorist insurance coverage. Furthermore, the driver's insurer was entitled to the entire credit for its liability payment as the primary insurer. Benton v. Hanford, 195 N.C. App. 88, 671 S.E.2d 31 (2009), review denied, 363 N.C. 744, 688 S.E.2d 452, (2009).

When two passengers were hurt in a one-car accident, the multiple claimant underinsured motorist (UIM) exception did not bar the vehicle's classification as underinsured because the statute's amendment meant two injuries did not trigger the exception, which applied only if the sum paid to one claimant were less than the claimant's UIM limits after liability payments to multiple claimants, so (1) one claimant's liability payment did not reduce the other claimant's coverage, (2) the general definition of "underinsured highway vehicle" was used to find UIM coverage, and (3) two policies' UIM coverage were stacked to calculate UIM limits and find if the vehicle were an "underinsured highway vehicle," which the vehicle was since the total UIM coverage from the two policies was greater than the liability limits of a policy under which payment was made. Integon Nat'l Ins. Co. v. Maurizzio, 240 N.C. App. 38, 769 S.E.2d 415 (2015).

AN INDIVIDUAL NAMED IN -- BUT NOT THE "OWNER" OF -- A MOTOR VEHICLE INSURANCE POLICY IS PERMITTED TO "STACK" UNDERINSURED COVERAGE when the single policy insures two vehicles. Davis v. Nationwide Mut. Ins. Co., 106 N.C. App. 221, 415 S.E.2d 767, cert. denied, 332 N.C. 343, 421 S.E.2d 146 (1992).

FAMILY UNIT ENTITLED TO INTRAPOLICY STACKING. --The principles which allow intrapolicy stacking when the owner is injured also allow intrapolicy stacking when the injured party is a person insured of the first class. Harris ex rel. Freedman v. Nationwide Mut. Ins. Co., 332 N.C. 184, 420 S.E.2d 124 (1992).

THIS SECTION'S DEFINITION OF "UNDERINSURED HIGHWAY VEHICLE" DID NOT PROHIBIT THE ISSUANCE OF MULTI-TIER UIM COVERAGE where the policy provided UIM coverage meeting the minimum statutory requirements but the purchaser of the fleet policy paid additional premiums to provide higher limits of UIM coverage to certain persons insured in excess of the statutory floor. Hlasnick v. Federated Mut. Ins. Co., 353 N.C. 240, 539 S.E.2d 274 (2000).

Automobile accident victim was entitled to stack with his own policy providing underinsured motorist benefits the policies of his father and brother, both interpolicy and intrapolicy. Any amount he received under those policies would be reduced by the amount he received from the tortfeasor's exhausted liability policy. Harrington v. Stevens, 334 N.C. 586, 434 S.E.2d 212 (1993).

FAILURE TO OBTAIN INSURER'S CONSENT. Plaintiff's failure to obtain insurer's consent before entering into consent judgment does not bar its recovery against insurer for underinsured motorist coverage, unless insurer establishes material prejudice that was caused by plaintiff's failure to notify it and obtain consent to settlement as required by the policy. Silvers v. Horace Mann Ins. Co., 324 N.C. 289, 378 S.E.2d 21 (1989).

Where defendant insurer waived its rights to subrogation for the payment of uninsured and underinsured motorist claims, it suffered no prejudice by plaintiff's noncompliance with the notice provisions of the policy. Rinehart v. Hartford Cas. Ins. Co., 91 N.C. App. 368, 371 S.E.2d 788 (1988).

GENERAL RELEASE NOT ALTERED BY CONSENT. --Uninsured motorist (UIM) carrier's consent to settlement did not alter the legal effect of a general release signed by plaintiff. Spivey v. Lowery, 116 N.C. App. 124, 446 S.E.2d 835, cert. denied, 338 N.C. 312, 452 S.E.2d 312 (1994).

PRIMARY INSURER NOT ENTITLED TO CREDIT FOR SETTLEMENT WITH SECONDARY INSURER. --Since secondary insurer was not required to pay any of its UIM coverage until the policy limit of primary insurer's underinsured motorist coverage (UIM) had been exceeded, the primary insurer was not entitled to a credit for $25,000 settlement between plaintiff and the secondary insurance carrier. Isenhour v. Universal Underwriters Ins. Co., 345 N.C. 151, 478 S.E.2d 197 (1996).

to all three underinsured motorist insurance (UIM) policy providers, given that the respective excess clauses were mutually repugnant, and because the claimant was a Class I insured under all three UIM policies. Nationwide Mut. Ins. Co. v. Integon Nat'l Ins. Co., 232 N.C. App. 44, 753 S.E.2d 388 (2014).

LIMITS OF COVERAGE. --Subdivision (b)(4) of this section provides that the limit of payment for underinsured motorist coverage is only the difference between the liability insurance that is applicable (the limit on the tortfeasor's liability coverage) and the limits of the undersigned motorist coverage as specified in the owner's policy (the limit on the undersigned motorist coverage in the plaintiff's policy with the defendant). Davidson v. United States Fid. & Guar. Co., 78 N.C. App. 140, 336 S.E.2d 709 (1985), aff'd, 316 N.C. 551, 342 S.E.2d 523 (1986).

Where the unambiguous terms of plaintiff's underinsured motorist coverage provided that any amount payable by the defendant would be reduced by all sums paid because of bodily injury by those legally responsible, the $25,000.00 limit on the plaintiff's underinsured motorist coverage would be reduced by the $25,000.00 which the plaintiff received in settlement from tortfeasor, leaving nothing due to plaintiff from defendant. Davidson v. United States Fid. & Guar. Co., 78 N.C. App. 140, 336 S.E.2d 709 (1985), aff'd, 316 N.C. 551, 342 S.E.2d 523 (1986).

NO STATUTORY PRIORITY OF PAYMENTS FOR INSURANCE POLICIES. --There is no provision of the Act which expressly establishes a statutory priority of payment among different insurance policies. However, this section does allow an insurance liability policy to "provide for the pro-rating of the insurance thereunder with other valid and collectible insurance." North Carolina Farm Bureau Mut. Ins. Co. v. Hilliard, 90 N.C. App. 507, 369 S.E.2d 386 (1988) (decided under 1983 version of § 20-279.1).

COURT OF APPEALS DID NOT ERR in holding that the wife of the owner-insured was entitled as a Class I insured to underinsured motorist (UIM) coverage, when the wife was injured while riding in another car owned by her and insured by a different carrier under a separate policy not containing UIM coverage. Grain Dealers Mut. Ins. Co. v. Long, 332 N.C. 477, 421 S.E.2d 142 (1992).

UNDERINSURED CARRIER AS UNNAMED DEFENDANT. --An underinsured motorist carrier defendant, at its election, must be permitted to appear as an unnamed defendant in the liability phase of a trial, and this is a substantial right. Church v. Allstate Ins. Co., 143 N.C. App. 527, 547 S.E.2d 458 (2001).

In a mail carrier's negligence suit regarding a car accident, where the mail carrier argued it was error to deny the mail carrier's motion in limine seeking to allow the attorney for the mail carrier's underinsured motorist carrier to be referred to as representing the "unnamed defendant," the mail carrier's argument failed because the carrier did not claim any specific prejudice and the underinsured motorist insurer had the right to appear in defense of the claim without being named as a party. Seay v. Snyder, 181 N.C. App. 248, 638 S.E.2d 584 (2007).

UNINSURED MOTORIST CARRIER'S RIGHT OF SUBROGATION. --This section allows the primary liability insurer to apply for court approval for release from further liability or obligation to defend upon payment of its primary liability limits and establishes a right of subrogation for the uninsured motorist carrier against the underinsured motorist if, upon notice of a tentative settlement with the underinsured motorist, the underinsured motorist carrier advances to the claimant the amount of the tentative settlement. Gunn v. Whichard, 707 F. Supp. 196 (E.D.N.C. 1988).

In the absence of an underinsured motorist carrier, the settlement funds from the primary liability carrier would be paid to the claimant. However, in the underinsured motorist context, the operation of subdivision (b)(4) requires the underinsured motorist carrier to advance an amount equal to the primary carrier's tentative settlement in order to preserve its subrogation rights. Gunn v. Whichard, 707 F. Supp. 196 (E.D.N.C. 1988).

A provider of underinsured motorist coverage who advances the policy limits of the liability carrier does not obtain an independent and separate right of reimbursement and is therefore limited to the rights of the claimant to which it is subrogated. Nationwide Mut. Ins. Co. v. State Farm Mut. Auto. Ins. Co., 109 N.C. App. 281, 426 S.E.2d 298, cert. denied, 333 N.C. 792, 431 S.E.2d 26 (1993).

Where a drunk driver's carrier tendered policy limits ($50,000) to defendants -- an accident victim and the estates of four persons killed in a collision -- and plaintiff, the insurer of one the decedent's parents, paid $250,000 in underinsured motorist (UIM) benefits, pursuant to the policy, which tracked the language of G.S. 20-279.21(b)(3), plaintiff insurer was subrogated to the rights of defendants as to their dram shop claims against the bars that served the drunk driver; however, it was obliged to its pay proportionate share of the attorneys' fees defendants incurred in the dram shop litigation. Farm Bureau Ins. Co. of N.C., Inc. v.

Chapter 20

Blong, 159 N.C. App. 365, 583 S.E.2d 307 (2003), cert. denied, 357 N.C. 578, 589 S.E.2d 125 (2003).

Trial court properly denied plaintiff's motion to compel production of an underinsured motorist (UIM) carrier's insurance policy and to compel disclosure of whether the UIM carrier agreed to waive its subrogation rights was subrogated to the extent of its payments to plaintiff to a portion of plaintiff's judgment against defendant; G.S. 20-279.21(b)(4) controlled over the policy provisions. Whether the UIM carrier agreed to waive its subrogation rights as to defendant was a matter for resolution between the UIM carrier and defendant and was of no concern to plaintiff. Wood v. Nunnery, 222 N.C. App. 303, 730 S.E.2d 222 (2012).

BECAUSE OF INSURER'S SUBROGATION RIGHT, DEFENDANT NOT ENTITLED TO CREDIT FOR PAYMENTS MADE BY UNDERINSURED MOTORIST CARRIER. --Trial court erred in declaring that a judgment entered in favor of plaintiff and against defendant had been satisfied because the judgment was awarded against only defendant, and, under G.S. 20-279.21(b), an underinsured motorist (UIM) carrier would have been subrogated to plaintiff's right against defendant to the extent of its payment; because of this subrogation right, defendant was not entitled to a credit against the judgment for payments made by the UIM carrier. Wood v. Nunnery, 222 N.C. App. 303, 730 S.E.2d 222 (2012).

UNDERINSURED INSURANCE CARRIER CANNOT ASSERT A CLAIM OF CONTRIBUTION because the carrier is not a tortfeasor; however, the carrier can bring a direct action against one of the defendants even though that defendant executed a release in favor of the other defendants. Johnson v. Hudson, 122 N.C. App. 188, 468 S.E.2d 64 (1996).

BY REQUIRING POLICYHOLDER TO SPECIFICALLY REQUEST UNDERINSURED MOTORIST COVERAGE, insurer failed to comply with subdivision (b)(4) of this section. The statutory coverage was thus written into the policy by operation of law, and would be in an amount equal to her liability coverage. Proctor v. North Carolina Farm Bureau Mut. Ins. Co., 90 N.C. App. 746, 370 S.E.2d 258 (1988), aff'd, 324 N.C. 221, 376 S.E.2d 761 (1989).

UNDERINSURED MOTORIST ENDORSEMENT HELD APPLICABLE TO INSURED RIDING IN NONOWNED VEHICLE. --Plaintiff, who was injured while riding as a passenger in a Jeep owned and operated by another individual, was covered by his father's policy, which contained an underinsured motorist endorsement, even though his injuries were unrelated to the use or operation of his father's van, which was the insured vehicle under the policy. Crowder v. North Carolina Farm Bureau Mut. Ins. Co., 79 N.C. App. 551, 340 S.E.2d 127, cert. denied, 316 N.C. 731, 345 S.E.2d 387 (1986), expressly limiting its holding to allowing underinsured motorist coverage for insureds operating, or riding in, a nonowned vehicle.

USE OF PREVIOUS JUDGMENT AGAINST UNDERINSURED MOTORIST IN LATER ACTION AGAINST UNDERINSURANCE CARRIER. --When the insured fails to comply with subdivision (b)(3) as to service of summons, complaint or other process, he may not use the previous judgment against the underinsured motorist as res judicata on the issue of liability or damages in a later action against its underinsurance carrier. Silvers v. Horace Mann Ins. Co., 90 N.C. App. 1, 367 S.E.2d 372 (1988), modified on other grounds, 324 N.C. 289, 378 S.E.2d 21 (1989) (decided prior to 1985 amendments).

PROVISIONS OF STATUTE CONTROL OVER EXPRESSED INTENTIONS OF PARTIES. --Whatever the expressed intentions of the insurer and the insured, the rejection form executed by insured, because it failed to comply with the provisions of subsection (b)(4), did not constitute a proper and effective rejection of UIM coverage equal to the policy's liability limits. Hendrickson v. Lee, 119 N.C. App. 444, 459 S.E.2d 275 (1995).

CONFLICT OF STATUTE PROVISIONS RESOLVED IN FAVOR OF INSURED. --Plaintiff's entry of a consent judgment with tortfeasors and their carrier did not bar her as a matter of law from recovering under the Underinsured Motorist (UIM) coverage of her policy with insurer; where the statute provided that a release of the tortfeasor acts to release the UIM insurance carrier of its derivative liability and the statute and the policy terms regarding UIM coverage appeared to require the insured to exhaust all liability policies by judgment or settlement before the insurer was obligated to pay under the UIM coverage, the conflict was resolved in favor of the insured because of the ambiguity and because of the intent behind the statute. Silvers v. Horace Mann Ins. Co., 324 N.C. 289, 378 S.E.2d 21 (1989) (decided under law prior to 1985 amendments).

WHERE VEHICLE DRIVEN BY DECEDENT WAS A HOUSEHOLD-OWNED VEHICLE NOT INSURED UNDER ONE OF TWO POLICIES held by plaintiff, decedent's father, the underinsured motorist (UIM) coverage provided by that policy was not available to compensate plaintiff for decedent's death. Smith v. Nationwide Mut. Ins. Co., 97 N.C. App. 363, 388 S.E.2d 624 (1990).

BASIS FOR DECLARATORY JUDGMENT. --Exhaustion of the limits of the tortfeasor's liability policy by payment of the limits of the policy by tortfeasor's insurer into deceased's estate triggered the applicability of plaintiff's underinsured motorist (UIM) coverage. Refusal of decedent's insurer to state the extent of the UIM coverage under two policies at issue sparked the actual controversy between plaintiff and insurer which provided the basis for a declaratory judgment suit. Smith v. Nationwide Mut. Ins. Co., 97 N.C. App. 363, 388 S.E.2d 624 (1990), rev'd on other grounds, 328 N.C. 139, 400 S.E.2d 44, rehearing denied, 328 N.C. 577, 403 S.E.2d 514 (1991).

SET-OFF FROM UIM COVERAGE TO EXTENT WORKERS' COMPENSATION BENEFITS PAID. --Insurance companies that provided underinsured motorist (UIM) coverage to a person who was killed while working for the North Carolina Department of Transportation (DOT) were required to pay the amount of loss sustained by the decedent's estate that was not compensated by a person who caused the employee's death, up to the limits of the UIM coverage, but were given a credit for the amount of workers' compensation benefits the estate received from the DOT, less the amount of a lien which the DOT asserted. Austin v. Midgett, 159 N.C. App. 416, 583 S.E.2d 405 (2003).

Since G.S. 97-25 required the state industrial commission to find as fact that services were rehabilitative in nature and were reasonably required to effect a cure or give relief in order to find that a workers' compensation carrier was entitled to a lien against payments made for rehabilitative services, those services were not a benefit to an injured motorist who received worker's compensation benefits as a matter of law; since a specific determination was required as to whether the services conferred a benefit to the motorist, and since an underinsured motorist carrier did not provide any proof of such a benefit, a credit to the carrier for payments made through workers' compensation to a rehabilitative center were properly excluded from the calculation of how much credit the carrier was entitled to against the payments it had to make to the motorist. Walker v. Penn Nat'l Sec. Ins. Co., 168 N.C. App. 555, 608 S.E.2d 107 (2005).

UNDERINSURED BENEFITS REDUCED BY WORKERS' COMPENSATION BENEFITS AND LIABILITY PAYMENTS. --The liability of an automobile insurer, who was also the workers' compensation carrier, for underinsured motorist benefits had to be reduced by the amount of workers' compensation benefits after reduction of the amount received from the tort-feasor's liability insurer. Manning v. Fletcher, 102 N.C. App. 392, 402 S.E.2d 648 (1991), aff'd, 331 N.C. 114, 413 S.E.2d 798 (1992).

An underinsured motorist coverage carrier under a business automobile policy is entitled to reduce its coverage by the amount of workers' compensation benefits which the same insurer paid to an injured worker. Brantley v. Starling, 336 N.C. 567, 444 S.E.2d 170 (1994).

In order to have amounts payable under underinsured motorist coverage reduced by amounts paid under workers' compensation coverage, subsection (e) does not require that the same entity provide both coverages. Brantley v. Starling, 336 N.C. 567, 444 S.E.2d 170 (1994).

This section does not mandate that underinsured motorist coverage be reduced by the amount of worker's compensation benefits, but instead allows for the insurer to limit liability by appropriate language in the contract of insurance. Progressive Am. Ins. Co. v. Vasquez, 129 N.C. App. 742, 502 S.E.2d 10 (1998), aff'd in part and rev'd in part and remanded on other grounds, 350 N.C. 386, 515 S.E.2d 8 (1999).

Underinsured motorist carrier was improperly denied a credit for payments that a negligent driver's liability insurance carrier made to the motorist who was driving the insured's vehicle; however, a credit for payments made to the motorist through worker's compensation to a rehabilitative center was properly not incorporated into the calculation of the credit it

was entitled to for worker's compensation payment because the carrier failed to show any evidence existed in the appellate record that indicated the motorist received a benefit from that center -- the availability of a credit for rehabilitative services was not available as a matter of law, but had to be established by the facts. Walker v. Penn Nat'l Sec. Ins. Co., 168 N.C. App. 555, 608 S.E.2d 107 (2005).

WHERE INSURER PROVIDED BOTH UNDERINSURED MOTORIST COVERAGE AND WORKERS' COMPENSATION COVERAGE to employee injured in an automobile accident, in a business auto insurance policy insurer could reduce its underinsured motorist coverage obligation by the total amount of workers' compensation paid to employee. Manning v. Fletcher, 324 N.C. 513, 379 S.E.2d 854 (1989).

THE MANDATORY NATURE OF WORKERS' COMPENSATION INSURANCE CARRIER'S LIEN ON A RECOVERY FROM THE THIRD-PARTY TORT-FEASOR IS NOT ALTERED BY THE DISCRETIONARY AUTHORITY OF THE TRIAL JUDGE to apportion the recovery between the employee and the insurance carrier, if that recovery is inadequate to satisfy the insurance carrier's lien. Manning v. Fletcher, 102 N.C. App. 392, 402 S.E.2d 648 (1991), aff'd, 331 N.C. 114, 413 S.E.2d 798 (1992).

NO SET OFF FROM UIM COVERAGE TO EXTENT WORKERS' COMPENSATION BENEFITS PAID. --Insurance company was not entitled to a set off from its underinsured motorist (UIM) coverage to the extent that workers' compensation benefits were paid or payable to truck driver's estate. Bowser v. Williams, 108 N.C. App. 8, 422 S.E.2d 355 (1992), cert. granted, 333 N.C. 343, 426 S.E.2d 703 (1993).

Where truck, in which plaintiff was riding at the time of the accident, was a business vehicle covered by the terms of the business auto policy with respect to underinsured motorist coverage, the trial court erred in finding that defendant insurance company, the underinsured motorist coverage carrier, was entitled to reduce its coverage by the amount of workers' compensation benefits which the same company paid to plaintiff. Brantley v. Starling, 111 N.C. App. 669, 433 S.E.2d 1, aff'd, 336 N.C. 567, 444 S.E.2d 170 (1994).

AMOUNT OF UNDERINSURED MOTORIST COVERAGE. --Subdivision (b)(4) of this section explicitly requires, in substance, that unless rejected by policyholder, each automobile insurance policy issued in this State must have underinsured motorist coverage in same amount as personal injury liability coverage. Sproles v. Greene, 100 N.C. App. 96, 394 S.E.2d 691 (1990), rev'd on other grounds, Sproles v. Integon Insurance Co., 329 N.C. 603, 407 S.E.2d 497 (1991).

Trial court did not err by concluding that insurance company's policy provided plaintiff $750,000 underinsured motorist (UIM) coverage although insurance company argued that their uninsured motorist (UM) coverage was not issued under subsection (3), but was instead issued pursuant to the Reinsurance Facility's rules. The provisions of the Financial Responsibility Act, including this section, are written into every automobile liability policy as a matter of law. Although the policy purported to provide UIM coverage of only $25,000 per person and $50,000 per accident, subdivision (b)(4) of this section mandates that where UIM coverage is issued, it must be issued in an amount equal to the liability policy limits for bodily injury. Bowser v. Williams, 108 N.C. App. 8, 422 S.E.2d 355 (1992), cert. granted, 333 N.C. 343, 426 S.E.2d 703 (1993), overruled on other grounds, McMillan v. North Carolina Farm Bureau Mut. Ins. Co., 347 N.C. 560, 495 S.E.2d 352 (1998).

The requirement of this section that underinsured motorist coverage be available when an automobile liability insurance policy has coverage exceeding the minimum limits refers to bodily injury coverage only, and does not apply if only the property damage limits exceed the minimum. Trosch v. State Farm Auto. Ins. Co., 132 N.C. App. 227, 510 S.E.2d 409 (1999).

Although insureds claimed an insurer failed to properly notify them of their option to select a higher underinsured motorist (UIM) amount, a trial court properly concluded the statutory default amount of UIM coverage under the Financial Responsibility Act, G.S. 20-279.21(b)(4), applied because the insurer included an uninsured motorist/UIM selection/rejection form in each renewal packet mailed to the insureds. Unitrin Auto & Home Ins. Co. v. Rikard, 217 N.C. App. 393, 722 S.E.2d 510 (2011).

POLICYHOLDER MUST HAVE LIABILITY COVERAGE IN EXCESS OF MINIMUM. --Under subdivision (b)(4), underinsured motorist coverage may be obtained only if the policyholder has liability insurance in excess of the minimum statutory requirement and, in any event, the underinsured motorist coverage must be in an amount equal to the policy limits for bodily injury liability specified in the policy. Smith v. Nationwide Mut. Ins. Co., 328 N.C. 139, 400 S.E.2d 44 (1991), rehearing denied, 328 N.C. 577, 403 S.E.2d 514 (1991).

ADMISSION OF NO ENTITLEMENT TO COVERAGE. --Trial court did not err in granting an insurance company's motion to dismiss when insured, who had only maintained minimum coverage, admitted in his complaint that he was not entitled to underinsured motorist coverage. Pinney v. State Farm Mut. Ins. Co., 146 N.C. App. 248, 552 S.E.2d 186 (2001), cert. denied, 356 N.C. 438, 572 S.E.2d 788 (2002).

ENTITLEMENT TO UIM COVERAGE. --Insureds qualified under an endorsement of their insurance policy as "named insureds" for underinsured motorist (UIM) coverage because UIM coverage followed the person, not the vehicle; further, the appellate court could see no reason to make an exception to G.S. 20-279.21(b)(4) and allow an "owned vehicle" exclusion to apply simply because the insurer believed that the insureds purchased insurance for a different reason than what the policy expressly protected them against and for which they paid additional premiums. Beddard v. McDaniel, 183 N.C. App. 476, 645 S.E.2d 153 (2007).

While under G.S. 20-279.21(b)(4) an insurer was not subject to the jurisdiction of the North Carolina Rate Bureau and, therefore, was not required to use the Rate Bureau approved form, the insurer nonetheless was required to prove that an insured with a fleet

of covered vehicles had validly rejected underinsured motorist (UIM) coverage or selected alternative UIM coverage limits. Because the record was devoid of any evidence that the insured made such a rejection or selection, the policy's liability limit for any auto applied with respect to UIM coverage. Great American Ins. Co. v. Freeman, 192 N.C. App. 497, 665 S.E.2d 536 (2008).

Insured was not entitled to $1,000,000 in underinsured motorist (UIM) coverage at the time of his injury, pursuant to the former G.S. 20-279.21(b)(4), because the insured was given an opportunity to reject UIM coverage or to select different coverage limits, and, thus, there was no total failure on the part of the insurer to inform the insured of available coverage. The insurer's evidence of the general practice at its computerized mailing facility, along with the copies of the documents mailed to the insured and the affidavits asserting that the selection/rejection form was included, was sufficient to establish that the insurer mailed a selection/rejection form to the insured. Grimsley v. Gov't Emples. Ins. Co., 217 N.C. App. 530, 721 S.E.2d 706 (2011), review denied 365 N.C. 552, 724 S.E.2d 505, 2012 N.C. LEXIS 189 (N.C. 2012).

Where a decedent had bought a truck from a company insured by plaintiff, G.S. 20-279.21(b) did not require plaintiff to provide underinsured motorist (UIM) coverage equal to its bodily injury liability coverage for the decedent's truck because plaintiff's policy was applicable solely to the company's fleet vehicles and plaintiff thus was exempt under G.S. 20-279.21(b)(4) from the mandatory UIM coverage requirement. West Am. Ins. Co. v. Terra Designs, Inc., 2014 U.S. Dist. LEXIS 43395 (W.D.N.C. Mar. 30, 2014).

Unambiguous "hired autos" endorsement in plaintiff's policy with a company from which a decedent bought a pickup truck did not render the decedent's truck an "owned" vehicle under that policy; therefore, underinsured motorist coverage ceased when title to the truck was transferred to the decedent. West Am. Ins. Co. v. Terra Designs, Inc., 2014 U.S. Dist. LEXIS 43395 (W.D.N.C. Mar. 30, 2014).

Trial court properly granted two administrators' motions for summary judgment and denied an insurer's motion for summary judgment in the administrators' action to recover underinsured motorist coverage (UIM) from the insurer because the multiple claimant exception of the Financial Responsibility Act did not apply and the administrators could recover UIM coverage under their own policies and under the tortfeasor's policy with the insurer. Nationwide Affinity Ins. Co. of Am. v. Le Bei, 259 N.C. App. 626, 816 S.E.2d 251 (2018), review denied, 371 N.C. 571, 819 S.E.2d 382, 2018 N.C. LEXIS 938 (2018).

STANDARD OF NOTICE MET BY MAILING SELECTION/REJECTION FORM. --Mailing of an uninsured motorist/underinsured motorist (UIM) coverage selection/rejection form by an insurer to an insured was sufficient to satisfy the standard of notice established by G.S. 20-279.21(b)(3), even if the insured did not receive the form prior to an accident in which UIM coverage was claimed; thus, there was not a total failure on the part of the insurer to provide an opportunity for the insured to reject UIM coverage or select different UIM policy limits. Nationwide Prop. & Cas. Ins. Co. v. Martinson, 208 N.C. App. 104, 701 S.E.2d 390 (2010), review denied, 365 N.C. 84, 706 S.E.2d 256, 2011 N.C. LEXIS 190 (2011).

INSURER'S NOTICE OF CHANGE IN LAW REGARDING UIM COVERAGE DEEMED SUFFICIENT. --Insurer's notice sufficiently summarized the impact of the amendments to the North Carolina Motor Vehicle Safety and Financial Responsibility Act so as to give reasonable notice to the insured of the changes in the law regarding mandatory underinsured motorist coverage. West Am. Ins. Co. v. Terra Designs, Inc., 2014 U.S. Dist. LEXIS 43395 (W.D.N.C. Mar. 30, 2014).

CLAUSE IN POLICY LIMITING LIABILITY UNDER MULTIPLE POLICIES HELD VOID AS CONFLICTING WITH THIS SECTION. --Policy provision which states, "If this policy and any other auto insurance policy issued to you apply to the same accident, the maximum limit of liability for your injuries under all the policies shall not exceed the highest applicable limit of liability under any one policy," conflicts with subdivision (b)(4) of this section and is therefore unenforceable. Sproles v. Greene, 100 N.C. App. 96, 394 S.E.2d 691 (1990), rev'd on other grounds, Sproles v. Integon Insurance Co., 329 N.C. 603, 407 S.E.2d 497 (1991), overruled on other grounds, McMillian v. North Carolina Farm Bureau Mut. Ins. Co., 347 N.C. 560, 495 S.E.2d 352 (1998).

EXCLUSIONS FOR "HOUSEHOLD-OWNED" VEHICLE FOUND ONLY IN THE MEDICAL PAYMENTS AND LIABILITY PORTIONS OF THE POLICY DID NOT CREATE THE "FAMILY MEMBER" EXCLUSION under the underinsured motorist portion of the policy. Smith v. Nationwide Mut. Ins. Co., 328 N.C. 139, 400 S.E.2d 44 (1991), rehearing denied, 328 N.C. 577, 403 S.E.2d 514 (1991).

VAN WAS NOT A "PRIVATE PASSENGER MOTOR VEHICLE". --Van used to transport employees to and from their homes and place of employment was not a "private passenger motor vehicle" for purposes of allowing stacking of underinsured motorist coverage for various vehicles. Aetna Cas. & Sur. Co. v. Fields, 105 N.C. App. 563, 414 S.E.2d 69 (1992).

COVERAGE IN PERSON ORIENTED. --Plaintiff, as the named insured under defendant's policy, was a first class insured and entitled to benefits under the underinsured motorist (UIM) coverage contained in the policy covering his automobiles, even though he was injured while riding his motorcycle which was not covered by the policy; UIM insurance is essentially person oriented, unlike liability insurance which is vehicle oriented. Honeycutt v. Walker, 119 N.C. App. 220, 458 S.E.2d 23 (1995).

UMBRELLA COVERAGE. --A multiple-coverage fleet insurance policy which includes umbrella coverage must offer underinsured motorist coverage equal to the liability limits under its umbrella coverage section. Isenhour v. Universal Underwriters Ins. Co., 341 N.C. 597, 461 S.E.2d 317 (1995).

Where there was no evidence in the record that insured either rejected in writing uninsured motorist or underinsured motorist coverage for the umbrella section of policy or selected a different limit, the umbrella section of the policy provided underinsured motorist coverage in an amount equal to the policy limits for automobile bodily injury liability as specified in the owner's umbrella coverage section of the policy. Isenhour v. Universal Underwriters Ins. Co., 341 N.C. 597, 461 S.E.2d 317 (1995).

USE OF RATE BUREAU FORM DOES NOT CONFLICT WITH G.S. 58-36-1. --By requiring rejection of UIM coverage to be accomplished by use of a specific Rate Bureau form, subsection (b)(4) does not effectively confer additional jurisdictional authority to the Rate Bureau, but is merely concerned with avoiding confusion and ambiguity through the use of a single standard and approved form, and mandating use of a Rate Bureau form for rejection of UIM coverage within a fleet policy does not necessarily conflict with G.S. 58-36-1. Hendrickson v. Lee, 119 N.C. App. 444, 459 S.E.2d 275 (1995).

POLICY ENDORSEMENT NOT CONSIDERED SEPARATE POLICY. --An endorsement to an automobile insurance policy that provided additional liability coverage under certain circumstances was not a separate "owner's policy of liability insurance," but rather, was merely a part of the insured's larger comprehensive policy; thus, insurer was not required to have the insured execute another Selection/Rejection Form. American Mfrs. Mut. Ins. Co. v. Hagler, 132 N.C. App. 204, 511 S.E.2d 28 (1999).

FORM FOR THE REJECTION OF UNDERINSURED MOTORIST COVERAGE WAS AMBIGUOUS and was construed in favor of coverage, where it differed from the Rate Bureau directive for the rejection of underinsured motorist coverage in that the sole option available to an insured by the rejection form was to reject uninsured motorist coverage limits, and the rejection form limited an insured who rejected liability limits UM coverage to selection of UM coverage only at a state's statutory limits. Hendrickson v. Lee, 119 N.C. App. 444, 459 S.E.2d 275 (1995).

The form provided by an automobile liability insurer to its insured for selection of underinsured motorist benefits was invalid, where it was not the form promulgated by the appropriate State agency, and the insurer's form did not require that rejection of UIM coverage be made in writing, as required by this section, but by contacting the insured's agent. State Farm Mut. Auto. Ins. Co. v. Fortin, 350 N.C. 264, 513 S.E.2d 782 (1999).

ABSENT COMPLETION OF AN APPROVED SELECTION OR REJECTION FORM, the insured was, as a matter of law, entitled to $1,000,000 in underinsured motorist coverage. Metropolitan Property & Cas. Ins. Co. v. Caviness, 124 N.C. App. 760, 478 S.E.2d 665 (1996).

COVERAGE NOT REQUIRED. --Automobile insurance policy which provided only the minimum statutorily required coverage of $25,000 per person/$50,000 per accident, was not required to provide UIM coverage. Hollar v. Hawkins, 119 N.C. App. 795, 460 S.E.2d 337 (1995).

Chapter 20

Under this section, a commercial excess liability insurance policy is not a "policy of bodily injury liability insurance," and thus, an excess insurer is not required to offer uninsured motorist and underinsured motorist coverage, since a "policy of bodily injury liability insurance" is a motor vehicle liability policy. Progressive Am. Ins. Co. v. Vasquez, 350 N.C. 386, 515 S.E.2d 8 (1999).

UNDERINSURED MOTORIST COVERAGE IN ABSENCE OF SELECTION. --Where the insured failed to make a valid selection of underinsured motorist coverage limits, such coverage was equal to the insured's liability limits of $100,000 per person and $300,000 per accident. State Farm Mut. Auto. Ins. Co. v. Fortin, 350 N.C. 264, 513 S.E.2d 782 (1999).

WHEN COVERAGE TRIGGERED IN MULTI-ACCIDENT SITUATION. --Summary judgment to an insured on his claim of underinsured motorist (UIM) coverage against his insurer, arising from injuries he sustained while acting as a first responder to a motor vehicle accident, whereupon he was struck by a second motorist, was proper because the UIM coverage was triggered the moment that all policies applicable to the first driver's vehicle had been exhausted; the insurer could not wait until all tortfeasors' insurers had paid or settled their matters. Lunsford v. Mills, 229 N.C. App. 24, 747 S.E.2d 390 (2013).

Structure and plain language this section, the purpose behind the underinsured motorist (UIM) statute, and the North Carolina Legislature's inclusion of subrogation rights for insurers compel the conclusion that UIM coverage is triggered upon the exhaustion of the policy limits of a single at-fault motorist. Therefore, in a case where there were several alleged tortfeasors, upon a first insurer's tender of its policy limit of $50,000 on behalf of a first insured, UIM coverage was triggered, and a second insured was entitled to recover UIM benefits according to the terms of his policy with the second insurer. Lunsford v. Mills, 367 N.C. 618, 766 S.E.2d 297 (2014).

Underinsured motorist insurer did not have discretion to withhold coverage to the insured until he reached settlement agreements with insurers for a second motorist where more than one motor vehicle accident was involved because it could have pursued the second insurers thereafter through subrogation or reimbursement. Lunsford v. Mills, 229 N.C. App. 24, 747 S.E.2d 390 (2013).

SETTLEMENT AGREEMENT DID NOT BAR RECOVERY. --Injured claimant's entry into a settlement agreement with negligent driver and his carrier did not bar claimant, as a matter of law, from recovering under both son and daughter's UIM coverage as a first class insured. North Carolina Farm Bureau Mut. Ins. Co. v. Bost, 126 N.C. App. 42, 483 S.E.2d 452 (1997).

RECOVERY BY NON-OCCUPANT. --Decedent who was attempting to get a vehicle covered by the defendant insurance company out of a ditch by hooking it up to another car when a third vehicle hit and killed him was covered by the defendant's UIM policy although he did not own and was not actually occupying the vehicle. Dutch v. Harleysville Mut. Ins. Co., 139 N.C. App. 602, 534 S.E.2d 262 (2000).

COVENANT NOT TO ENFORCE JUDGMENT --G.S. 20-279.21(b)(4), providing that individuals injured in car accidents could execute contractual covenants not to enforce judgment in favor of the tortfeasor as consideration for the payment of the liability policy limits without precluding them from seeking any available underinsured motorist benefits, did not apply to the interpretation of a release which could not be characterized as a covenant not to enforce judgment. N.C. Farm Bureau Mut. Ins. Co. v. Edwards, 154 N.C. App. 616, 572 S.E.2d 805 (2002).

Given G.S. 20-279.21(b)(4)'s reference only to covenants not to enforce judgments and not limited releases, the statute does not require that a settlement must contain a covenant to preserve an injured party's underinsured motorist claims, in order to preserve such claims. N.C. Farm Bureau Mut. Ins. Co. v. Edwards, 154 N.C. App. 616, 572 S.E.2d 805 (2002).

DETERMINATION OF AMOUNT DUE PLAINTIFF ON UIM CLAIM. --During a N.C. R. App. P. 31 motion for rehearing, the appellate court determined that a remand to the trial court was necessary to determine the amount due to plaintiff from an insurance company on an underinsured motorist claim pursuant to G.S. 20-279.21, as the stipulation of the parties was not sufficient to determine the amount due since the stipulation did not specify the total loss incurred by plaintiff. Austin v. Midgett, 166 N.C. App. 740, 603 S.E.2d 855 (2004).

MOTION TO COMPEL ARBITRATION OF UIM CLAIM IMPROPERLY DENIED --Trial court erred in denying an insured's motion to compel arbitration pursuant to G.S. 1-567.3 of an underinsured motorist claim pursuant to G.S. 20-279.21; the contractual period to request arbitration did not begin to run until the insured settled a liability claim with another company, and therefore the arbitration request was timely pursuant to the terms of the contract and G.S. 1-52(16). Register v. White, 160 N.C. App. 657, 587 S.E.2d 95 (2003), cert. granted, 358 N.C. 155, 590 S.E.2d 862 (2003), aff'd, 358 N.C. 691, 599 S.E.2d 549 (2004).

Since a passenger's contractual right to underinsured motorist coverage was expressly conditioned on the exhaustion of the liability carrier's policy limits, which did not occur until the liability carrier tendered the limits of its policy in the passenger's action for bodily injuries following an automobile accident, accrual of the three-year time limit in the UIM policy for the passenger to demand arbitration did not run until the date the liability carrier tendered its policy limits; because the passenger's demand for arbitration was filed within three years of that date, the demand was timely and the trial court erred in holding the demand had to be filed within three years of the date of the accident, which was when the passenger's bodily injuries were apparent. Register v. White, 358 N.C. 691, 599 S.E.2d 549 (2004).

Trial court erred in denying an insured's motion to compel arbitration of his underinsured motorist (UIM) claim against insurers because, for purposes of G.S. 20-279.21(b)(4), exhaustion occurred on tender, rather than on payment, of a liability insurer's policy limit; the limits of the liability insurer's policy were exhausted when that insurer tendered payment of $50,000 to the insured. Thus, the insured's written request for binding arbitration occurred at a time when his right to UIM arbitration was available under both G.S. 20-279.21 and under the terms of the UIM policies. Creed v. Smith, 222 N.C. App. 330, 732 S.E.2d 162 (2012).

DECISIONS UNDER PRIOR LAW. --The legislature made the level of underinsured motorist coverage a function of liability coverage, not a function of uninsured coverage. Proctor v. North Carolina Farm Bureau Mut. Ins. Co., 324 N.C. 221, 376 S.E.2d 761 (1989) (decided under prior law).

The amount of underinsured motorist coverage required by law when an insurer has not complied with subdivision (b)(4) of this section and the liability insurance policy in which the underinsured motorist coverage is required does not state the existence or the amount of such coverage is equal to the maximum liability coverage provided by the policy. Proctor v. North Carolina Farm Bureau Mut. Ins. Co., 324 N.C. 221, 376 S.E.2d 761 (1989) (decided under prior law).

LEGAL PERIODICALS. --

For note on automobile liability policies, see 35 N.C.L. Rev. 313 (1957).

For note on permissive user under the omnibus clause, see 41 N.C.L. Rev. 232 (1963).

For note on liability of insurer without notice, see 41 N.C.L. Rev. 853 (1963).

For note on insurer's liability for injuries intentionally inflicted by insured by use of automobile, see 43 N.C.L. Rev. 436 (1965).

For note on the statutory definition of an "uninsured motor vehicle" when the liability insurer is insolvent or denies coverage, see 45 N.C.L. Rev. 551 (1967).

For note on liability of insurer beyond policy limits, see 47 N.C.L. Rev. 453 (1969).

For note, "Liability of Insurers under the Omnibus Clause to Protect Emergency Drivers -- The North Carolina Situation," see 48 N.C.L. Rev. 984 (1970).

For survey of 1973 case law with regard to the construction of the omnibus clause, see 52 N.C.L. Rev. 809 (1974).

For survey of 1977 law on insurance, see 56 N.C.L. Rev. 1084 (1978).

For survey of 1978 administrative law, see 57 N.C.L. Rev. 831 (1979).

For survey of 1980 law on civil procedure, see 59 N.C.L. Rev. 1060 (1981).

For note discussing interpretation of notice provisions in insurance contracts, in light of Great Am. Ins. Co. v. C.G. Tate Constr. Co., 303 N.C. 387, 279 S.E.2d 769 (1981), see 61 N.C.L. Rev. 167 (1982).

For comment on insurer's liability for injury to alighting passengers, see 18 Wake Forest L. Rev. 537 (1982).

For 1984 survey, "Employee Exclusion Clauses in Automobile Liability Insurance Policies," see 63 N.C.L. Rev. 1228 (1985).

For note on use of the family purpose doctrine when no outsiders are involved, in light of Carver v. Carver,

310 N.C. 669, 314 S.E.2d 739 (1984), see 21 Wake Forest L. Rev. 243 (1985).

For note, "Underinsured Motorist Coverage: Legislative Solutions to Settlement Difficulties," see 64 N.C.L. Rev. 1408 (1986).

For comment, "A Gap in the North Carolina Motor Vehicle Liability Policy Statute: Joint Tortfeasors -- When and How Does Underinsured Motorist Coverage Apply?," see 12 Campbell L. Rev. 99 (1989).

For note, "Sutton v. Aetna Casualty & Surety Co.: The North Carolina Supreme Court Approves Stacking of Underinsured Motorist Coverage--Will Uninsured Coverage Follow?," see 68 N.C.L. Rev. 1281 (1990).

For note, "The Duty to Defend -- Brown v. Lumbermens Mut. Cas. Co.," 13 Campbell L. Rev. 141 (1990).

For note, "Baxley v. Nationwide Mutual Insurance Company: A Key Loophole in the Financial Responsibility Act of 1953 Comes to Light," see 72 N.C.L. Rev. 1809 (1994).

For note, "Underinsured Motorist Coverage: North Carolina's Multiple Claimant Wrinkle -- Ray v. Atlantic Casualty Insurance Co.," see 17 Campbell L. Rev. 147 (1995).

For survey, "Reconciling North Carolina's Interpretation of 'Legally Entitled to Recover' with the Spirit of the Uninsured Motorist Statute: The Lessons of Grimsley v. Nelson," see 73 N.C.L. Rev. 2474 (1995).

For a note on the effect on underinsured motorist benefits of covenants not to enforce judgment, see 76 N.C.L. Rev. 2482 (1998).

§ 20-279.22. Notice of cancellation or termination of certified policy

When an insurance carrier has certified a motor vehicle liability policy under G.S. 20-279.19 or a policy under G.S. 20-279.20, the insurance so certified shall not be canceled or terminated until at least 20 days after a notice of cancellation or termination of the insurance so certified shall be filed in the office of the Commissioner, except that such a policy subsequently procured and certified shall, on the effective date of its certification, terminate the insurance previously certified with respect to any motor vehicle designated in both certificates.

History.

1953, c. 1300, s. 22

THIS SECTION APPLIES ONLY TO CERTIFIED ASSIGNED RISK POLICIES ISSUED UNDER THE MOTOR VEHICLE SAFETY AND RESPONSIBILITY ACT OF 1953. Nationwide Mut. Ins. Co. v. Davis, 7 N.C. App. 152, 171 S.E.2d 601 (1970); Bailey v. Nationwide Mut. Ins. Co., 19 N.C. App. 168, 198 S.E.2d 246 (1973).

IT HAS NO APPLICATION TO POLICIES ISSUED UNDER THE VEHICLE FINANCIAL RESPONSIBILITY ACT OF 1957. Faizan v. Grain Dealers Mut. Ins. Co., 254 N.C. 47, 118 S.E.2d 303 (1961); Harrelson v. State Farm Mut. Auto. Ins. Co., 272 N.C. 603, 158 S.E.2d 812 (1968); Bailey v. Nationwide Mut. Ins. Co., 19 N.C. App. 168, 198 S.E.2d 246 (1973).

STATUTES CONTROL POLICY PROVISIONS AS TO CANCELLATION. --The provisions of this Article and Article 13 of this Chapter, liberally construed to effectuate the legislative policy, control any provision written into a policy which otherwise would give an insurance company a greater right to cancel than is provided by the statute. Harrelson v. State Farm Mut. Auto. Ins. Co., 272 N.C. 603, 158 S.E.2d 812 (1968).

RIGHT OF CARRIER TO CANCEL POLICY ISSUED UNDER ASSIGNED RISK PLAN is subject to the provisions of Article 13 of this Chapter as so implemented by the provisions of this Article incorporated by reference therein. Harrelson v. State Farm Mut. Auto. Ins. Co., 272 N.C. 603, 158 S.E.2d 812 (1968).

NOTICE IS REQUIRED WHETHER COVERAGE IS TERMINATED BY INSURED OR BY INSURER. --Under the provisions of the Motor Vehicle Safety and Responsibility Act of 1953 it is incumbent upon the insurer to give the statutory notice of cancellation irrespective of whether the insurance coverage is terminated through acts of the insured or the insurer. Nationwide Mut. Ins. Co. v. Davis, 7 N.C. App. 152, 171 S.E.2d 601 (1970).

§ 20-279.23. Article not to affect other policies

(a) This Article shall not be held to apply to or affect policies of automobile insurance against liability which may now or hereafter be required by any other law of this State, and such policies, if they contain an agreement or are endorsed to conform to the requirements of this Article, may be certified as proof of financial responsibility under this Article.

(b) This Article shall not be held to apply to or affect policies insuring solely the insured named in the policy against liability resulting from the maintenance or use by persons in the insured's employ or on his behalf of motor vehicles not owned by the insured.

History.

1953, c. 1300, s. 23

§ 20-279.24. Bond as proof

(a) Proof of financial responsibility may be furnished by filing with the Commissioner the bond of a surety company duly authorized to transact business in the State or a bond with at least two individual sureties each owning real estate within this State, and together having equities in such real estate over and above any encumbrances thereon equal in value to at least twice the amount of such bond, which real estate shall be scheduled in the bond which shall be approved by the clerk of the superior court of the county wherein the real estate is situated. Such bond shall be conditioned for payments in amounts and under the same circumstances as would be required in a motor vehicle liability

policy, and shall not be cancellable except after 20 days' written notice to the Commissioner. A certificate of the county tax supervisor or person performing the duties of the tax supervisor, showing the assessed valuation of each tract or parcel of real estate for tax purposes shall accompany a bond with individual sureties and, upon acceptance and approval by the Commissioner, the execution of such bond shall be proved before the clerk of the superior court of the county or counties wherein the land or any part thereof lies, and such bond shall be recorded in the office of the register of deeds of such county or counties. Such bond shall constitute a lien upon the real estate therein described from and after filing for recordation to the same extent as in the case of ordinary mortgages and shall be regarded as the equivalent of a mortgage or deed of trust. In the event of default in the terms of the bond the Commissioner may foreclose the lien thereof by making public sale upon publishing notice thereof as provided by G.S. 45-21.17; provided, that any such sale shall be subject to the provisions for upset or increased bids and resales and the procedure therefor as set out in Part 2 of Article 2A of Chapter 45 of the General Statutes. The proceeds of such sale shall be applied by the Commissioner toward the discharge of liability upon the bond, any excess to be paid over to the surety whose property was sold. The Commissioner shall have power to so sell as much of the property of either or both sureties described in the bond as shall be deemed necessary to discharge the liability under the bond, and shall not be required to apportion or prorate the liability as between sureties.

If any surety is a married person, his or her spouse shall be required to execute the bond, but only for the purpose of releasing any dower or curtesy interest in the property described in the bond, and the signing of such bond shall constitute a conveyance of dower or curtesy interest, as well as the homestead exemption of the surety, for the purpose of the bond, and the execution of the bond shall be duly acknowledged as in the case of deeds of conveyance. The Commissioner may require a certificate of title of a duly licensed attorney which shall show all liens and encumbrances with respect to each parcel of real estate described in the bond and, if any parcel of such real estate has buildings or other improvements thereon, the Commissioner may, in his discretion, require the filing with him of a policy or policies of fire and other hazard insurance, with loss clauses payable to the Commissioner as his interest may appear. All costs and expenses in connection with furnishing such bond and the registration thereof, and the certificate of title, insurance and other necessary items of expense shall be borne by the principal obligor under the bond, except that the costs of foreclosure may be paid from the proceeds of sale.

(b) If such a judgment, rendered against the principal on such bond shall not be satisfied within 60 days after it has become final, the judgment creditor may, for his own use and benefit and at his sole expense, bring an action or actions in the name of the State against the company or persons executing such bond, including an action or proceeding to foreclose any lien that may exist upon the real estate of a person who has executed such bond.

History.
1953, c. 1300, s. 24; 1993, c. 553, s. 10

§ 20-279.25. Money or securities as proof

(a) Proof of financial responsibility may be evidenced by the certificate of the State Treasurer that the person named therein has deposited with him eighty-five thousand dollars ($ 85,000) in cash, or securities such as may legally be purchased by savings banks or for trust funds of a market value of eighty-five thousand dollars ($ 85,000). The State Treasurer shall not accept any such deposit and issue a certificate therefor and the Commissioner shall not accept such certificate unless accompanied by evidence that there are no unsatisfied judgments of any character against the depositor in the county where the depositor resides.

(b) Such deposit shall be held by the State Treasurer to satisfy, in accordance with the provisions of this Article, any execution on a judgment issued against such person making the deposit for damages, including damages for care and loss of services because of bodily injury to or death of any person, or for damages because of injury to or destruction of property, including the loss of use thereof, resulting from the ownership, maintenance, use or operation of a motor vehicle after such deposit was made. Money or securities so deposited shall not be subject to attachment, garnishment, or execution unless such attachment, garnishment, or execution shall arise out of a suit for damages as aforesaid.

History.
1953, c. 1300, s. 25; 1965, c. 358, s. 1; 1967, c. 277, s. 5; 1973, c. 745, s. 5; 1979, c. 832, s. 8; 1991, c. 469, s. 8;1999-228, s. 5

§ 20-279.26. Owner may give proof for others

Whenever any person required to give proof of financial responsibility hereunder is or later becomes an operator in the employ of any owner, or is or later becomes a member of the immediate family or household of the owner, the Commissioner shall accept proof given by such owner in lieu of proof by such other person to permit such other person to operate a motor vehicle for which the owner has given proof as herein provided. The Commissioner shall designate the restrictions imposed by this section on the face of such person's license.

History.
1953, c. 1300, s. 26

§ 20-279.27. Substitution of proof

The Commissioner shall consent to the cancellation of any bond or certificate of insurance or the Commissioner shall direct and the State Treasurer shall return any money or securities to the person entitled thereto upon the substitution and acceptance of other adequate proof of financial responsibility pursuant to this Article.

History.
1953, c. 1300, s. 27

§ 20-279.28. Other proof may be required

Whenever any proof of financial responsibility filed under the provisions of this Article no longer fulfills the purposes for which required, the Commissioner shall for the purpose of this Article, require other proof as required by this Article, or whenever it appears that proof filed to cover any motor vehicle owned by a person does not cover all motor vehicles registered in the name of such person, the Commissioner shall require proof covering all such motor vehicles. The Commissioner shall suspend the license or the nonresident's operating privilege pending the filing of such other proof.

History.
1953, c. 1300, s. 28

§ 20-279.29. Duration of proof; when proof may be canceled or returned

The Commissioner shall upon request consent to the immediate cancellation of any bond or certificate of insurance, or the Commissioner shall direct and the State Treasurer shall return to the person entitled thereto any money or securities deposited pursuant to this Article as proof of financial responsibility, or the Commissioner shall waive the requirement of filing proof, in any of the following events:

(1) At any time after two years from the date such proof was required when, during the two-year period preceding the request, the Commissioner has not received record of a conviction or a forfeiture of bail which would require or permit the suspension or revocation of the license, registration or

nonresident's operating privilege of the person by or for whom such proof was furnished; or

(2) In the event of the death of the person on whose behalf such proof was filed or the permanent incapacity of such person to operate a motor vehicle; or

(3) In the event the person who has given proof surrenders his license to the Commissioner.

Provided, however, that the Commissioner shall not consent to the cancellation of any bond or the return of any money or securities in the event any action for damages upon a liability covered by such proof is then pending or any judgment upon any such liability is then unsatisfied or in the event the person who has filed such bond or deposited such money or securities, has, within one year immediately preceding such request, been involved as an operator or owner in any motor vehicle accident resulting in injury or damage to the person or property of others. An affidavit of the applicant as to the nonexistence of such facts, or that he has been released from all of his liability, or has been finally adjudicated not to be liable, for such injury or damage, shall be sufficient evidence thereof in the absence of evidence to the contrary in the records of the Commissioner.

Whenever any person whose proof has been canceled or returned under subdivision (3) of this section applies for a license within a period of two years from the date proof was originally required, any such application shall be refused unless the applicant shall reestablish such proof for the remainder of such two-year period.

History.
1953, c. 1300, s. 29

§ 20-279.30. Surrender of license

Any person whose license shall have been suspended as herein provided, or whose policy of insurance or bond, when required under this Article, shall have been canceled or terminated, or who shall neglect to furnish other proof upon request of the Commissioner shall immediately return his license to the Commissioner. If any person shall fail to return to the Commissioner the license as provided herein, the Commissioner shall forthwith direct any peace officer to secure possession thereof and to return the same to the Commissioner.

History.
1953, c. 1300, s. 30

§ 20-279.31. Other violations; penalties

(a) The Commissioner shall suspend the license of a person who fails to report a reportable accident, as required by G.S. 20-166.1, until the Division receives a report and for an additional period set by the Commissioner. The additional period may not exceed 30 days.

(b) Any person who does any of the following commits a Class 1 misdemeanor:

(1) Gives information required in a report of a reportable accident, knowing or having reason to believe the information is false.

(2) Forges or without authority signs any evidence of proof of financial responsibility.

(3) Files or offers for filing any evidence of proof of financial responsibility, knowing or having reason to believe that it is forged or signed without authority.

(c) Any person willfully failing to return a license as required in G.S. 20-279.30 is guilty of a Class 3 misdemeanor.

(c1) Any person who makes a false affidavit or knowingly swears or affirms falsely to any matter under G.S. 20-279.5, 20-279.6, or 20-279.7 is guilty of a Class I felony.

(d) Any person who shall violate any provision of this Article for which no penalty is otherwise provided is guilty of a Class 2 misdemeanor.

History.
1953, c. 1300, s. 31; 1983, c. 610, s. 2; 1993, c. 539, ss. 384, 1261; 1994, Ex. Sess., c. 24, s. 14(c);1995, c. 191, s. 7

GIVING FALSE INFORMATION FOR A MOTOR VEHICLE CRASH REPORT. --Trial court committed error by vacating a jury's verdict convicting a female defendant of giving false information for a motor vehicle crash report in violation of G.S. 20-279.31(b) because: (1) the female defendant "gave information" by telling an officer she was the driver of a vehicle involved in an accident; (2) it could be inferred that a male defendant was the driver of the vehicle, so it could be inferred that the female defendant knowingly gave false information; and (3) the driver's identity was a required part of a reportable accident report. State v. Hernandez, 188 N.C. App. 193, 655 S.E.2d 426 (2008).

CITED in Lane v. Iowa Mut. Ins. Co., 258 N.C. 318, 128 S.E.2d 398 (1962).

§ 20-279.32. Exceptions

This Article does not apply to a motor vehicle registered under G.S. 20-382 by a for-hire motor carrier. This Article does not apply to any motor vehicle owned by the State of North Carolina, nor does it apply to the operator of a vehicle owned by the State of North Carolina who becomes involved in an accident while operating the state-owned vehicle if the Commissioner determines that the vehicle at the time of the accident was probably being operated in the course of the operator's employment as an employee or officer of the State. This Article does not apply to any motor vehicle owned by a county or municipality of the State of North

Carolina, nor does it apply to the operator of a vehicle owned by a county or municipality of the State of North Carolina who becomes involved in an accident while operating such vehicle in the course of the operator's employment as an employee or officer of the county or municipality. This Article does not apply to the operator of a vehicle owned by a political subdivision, other than a county or municipality, of the State of North Carolina who becomes involved in an accident while operating such vehicle if the Commissioner determines that the vehicle at the time of the accident was probably being operated in the course of the operator's employment as an employee or officer of the subdivision providing that the Commissioner finds that the political subdivision has waived any immunity it has with respect to such accidents and has in force an insurance policy or other method of satisfying claims which may arise out of the accident. This Article does not apply to any motor vehicle owned by the federal government, nor does it apply to the operator of a motor vehicle owned by the federal government who becomes involved in an accident while operating the government-owned vehicle if the Commissioner determines that the vehicle at the time of the accident was probably being operated in the course of the operator's employment as an employee or officer of the federal government.

History.
1953, c. 1300, s. 32; 1955, c. 1152, s. 19; 1979, c. 667, s. 38; 1989, c. 485, s. 54;1995 (Reg. Sess., 1996), c. 756, s. 18; 1999-330, s. 4.1

COVERAGE AVAILABLE TO SHERIFF'S DEPUTY. --County's policy controlled the underinsured motorist coverage available to a deputy sheriff as the North Carolina Motor Vehicle Safety and Financial Responsibility Act, G.S. 20-279.1, did not apply due to G.S. 20-279.32. N.C. Counties Liab. & Prop. Joint Risk Mgmt. Agency v. Curry, 191 N.C. App. 217, 662 S.E.2d 678 (2008).

COUNTY NOT REQUIRED TO SELECT UNINSURED MOTORIST COVERAGE FOR COUNTY-OWNED VEHICLES. --In an accident involving a county employee in a county vehicle acting in the scope of her employment, G.S. 20-279.32 provided that the county was not subject to the Motor Vehicle Safety and Responsibility Act. The county was not required to specifically select Uninsured Motorist coverage of less than $2,000,000 under G.S. 20-279.21(b)(4), and the county's policy capping Uninsured Motorist coverage at $100,000 was therefore enforceable. Nolan v. Cooke, 198 N.C. App. 667, 679 S.E.2d 892 (2009).

APPLIED in Watson v. American Nat'l Fire Ins. Co., 333 N.C. 338, 425 S.E.2d 696 (1993); Great American Ins. Co. v. Freeman, 192 N.C. App. 497, 665 S.E.2d 536 (2008).

CITED in Hand v. Connecticut Indemnity Co., 124 N.C. App. 774, 478 S.E.2d 661 (1996).

§ 20-279.32A. Exception of school bus drivers

The provisions of this Article shall not apply to school bus drivers with respect to accidents or collisions in which they are involved while operating school buses in the course of their employment.

History.
1955, c. 1282

§ 20-279.33. Self-insurers

(a) Any person in whose name more than 25 motor vehicles are registered may qualify as a self-insurer by obtaining a certificate of self-insurance issued by the Commissioner as provided in subsection (b) of this section. For the purpose of this Article, the State of North Carolina shall be considered a self-insurer.

(b) The Commissioner may, in his discretion, upon the application of such a person, issue a certificate of self-insurance when he is satisfied that such person is possessed and will continue to be possessed of ability to pay judgments obtained against such person.

(c) Upon not less than five days' notice and a hearing pursuant to such notice, the Commissioner may upon reasonable grounds cancel a certificate of self-insurance. Failure to pay any judgment within 30 days after such judgment shall have become final shall constitute a reasonable ground for the cancellation of a certificate of self-insurance.

History.
1953, c. 1300, s. 33

APPLIED in North Carolina Farm Bureau Mut. Ins. Co. v. Knudsen, 109 N.C. App. 114, 426 S.E.2d 88 (1993).

CITED in Cochran v. North Carolina Farm Bureau Mut. Ins. Co., 113 N.C. App. 260, 437 S.E.2d 910 (1994).

§ 20-279.33A. Religious organizations; self-insurance

(a) Notwithstanding any other provision of this Article or Article 13 of this Chapter, any recognized religious organization having established tenets or teachings and that has been in existence at all times since December 31, 1950, may qualify as a self-insurer by obtaining a certificate of self-insurance from the Commissioner as provided in subsection (c) of this section if the Commissioner determines that all of the following conditions are met:

(1) Members of the religious organization operate five or more vehicles that are registered in this State and are either owned or leased by them.

(2) Members of the religious organization hold a common belief in mutual financial assistance in time of need to the extent that they share in financial obligations of other members who would otherwise be unable to meet their obligations.

(3) The religious organization has met all of its insurance obligations for the five years preceding its application.

(4) The religious organization is financially solvent and not subject to any actions in bankruptcy, trusteeship, receivership, or any other court proceeding in which the financial solvency of the religious organization is in question.

(5) Neither the religious organization nor any of its participating members has any judgments arising out of the operation, maintenance, or use of a motor vehicle taken against them that have remained unsatisfied for more than 30 days after becoming final.

(6) There are no other factors that cause the Commissioner to believe that the religious organization and its participating members are not of sufficient financial ability to pay judgments against them.

(7) The religious organization and its participating members meet other requirements that the Commissioner by administrative rule prescribes.

(b) The Commissioner may, in the Commissioner's discretion, upon the application of a religious organization, issue a certificate of self-insurance when the Commissioner is satisfied that the religious organization is possessed and will continue to be possessed of an ability to pay any judgments that might be rendered against the religious organization. The certificate shall serve as evidence of insurance for the purposes of G.S. 20-7(c1), 20-13.2(e), 20-16.1, 20-19(k), and 20-179.3(*l*).

(c) A group issued a certificate of self-insurance under this section shall notify the Commissioner in writing if any person ceases to be a member of the group. The group shall notify the Commissioner within 10 days of the person's removal or departure from the group.

(d) The Commissioner may, at any time after the issuance of a certificate of self-insurance under this subsection, cancel the certificate by giving 30 days' written notice of cancellation to the religious organization whenever there is reason to believe that the religious organization to whom the certificate was issued is no longer qualified as a self-insurer under this section.

History.
2006-145, s. 5
EDITOR'S NOTE. --
Session Laws 2006-145, s. 7, makes this section effective January 1, 2007.

N.C. Gen. Stat. § 20-279.34

Repealed by Session Laws 1993 (Reg. Sess., 1994), c. 761, s. 27.

§ 20-279.35. Supplemental to motor vehicle laws; repeal of laws in conflict

This Article shall in no respect be considered as a repeal of any of the motor vehicle laws of this State but shall be construed as supplemental thereto.

The "Motor Vehicle Safety and Responsibility Act" enacted by the 1947 Session of the General Assembly, being Chapter 1006 of the Session Laws of 1947 (G.S. 20-224 to 20-279), is hereby repealed except with respect to any accident or violation of the motor vehicle laws of this State occurring prior to January 1, 1954, or with respect to any judgment arising from such accident or violation, and as to such accidents, violations or judgments Chapter 1006 of the Session Laws of 1947 shall remain in full force and effect. Except as herein stated, all laws and clauses of laws in conflict with this Article are hereby repealed.

History.
1953, c. 1300, s. 35
APPLIED in Miller v. New Amsterdam Cas. Co., 245 N.C. 526, 96 S.E.2d 860 (1957).
CITED in Graham v. Iowa Nat'l Mut. Ins. Co., 240 N.C. 458, 82 S.E.2d 381 (1954); Swain v. Nationwide Mut. Ins. Co., 253 N.C. 120, 116 S.E.2d 482 (1960).

§ 20-279.36. Past application of Article

This Article shall not apply with respect to any accident, or judgment arising therefrom, or violation of the motor vehicle laws of this State, occurring prior to January 1, 1954.

History.
1953, c. 1300, s. 37
APPLIED in Justice v. Scheidt, 252 N.C. 361, 113 S.E.2d 709 (1960).
CITED in Swain v. Nationwide Mut. Ins. Co., 253 N.C. 120, 116 S.E.2d 482 (1960).

§ 20-279.37. Article not to prevent other process

Nothing in this Article shall be construed as preventing the plaintiff in any action at law from relying for relief upon the other processes provided by law.

History.
1953, c. 1300, s. 38

§ 20-279.38. Uniformity of interpretation

This Article shall be so interpreted and construed as to effectuate its general purpose to make uniform the laws of those states which enact it.

History.
1953, c. 1300, s. 39

§ 20-279.39. Title of Article

This Article may be cited as the "Motor Vehicle Safety-Responsibility Act of 1953."

History.
1953, c. 1300, s. 41
APPLIED in Integon Nat'l Ins. Co. v. Phillips, 212 N.C. App. 623, 712 S.E.2d 381 (2011).
CITED in North Carolina Farm Bureau Mut. Ins. Co. v. Warren, 326 N.C. 444, 390 S.E.2d 138 (1990); Great American Ins. Co. v. Freeman, 192 N.C. App. 497, 665 S.E.2d 536 (2008); Integon Nat'l Ins. Co. v. Villafranco, 228 N.C. App. 390, 745 S.E.2d 922 (2013); Lunsford v. Mills, 367 N.C. 618, 766 S.E.2d 297 (2014).

ARTICLE 10.
FINANCIAL RESPONSIBILITY OF TAXICAB OPERATORS

§ 20-280. Filing proof of financial responsibility with governing board of municipality or county

(a) Within 30 days after March 27, 1951, every person, firm or corporation engaging in the business of operating a taxicab or taxicabs within a municipality shall file with the governing board of the municipality in which such business is operated proof of financial responsibility as hereinafter defined.

No governing board of a municipality shall hereafter issue any certificate of convenience and necessity, franchise, license, permit or other privilege or authority to any person, firm or corporation authorizing such person, firm or corporation to engage in the business of operating a taxicab or taxicabs within the municipality unless such person, firm or corporation first files with said governing board proof of financial responsibility as hereinafter defined.

Within 30 days after the ratification of this section, every person, firm or corporation engaging in the business of operating a taxicab or taxicabs without the corporate limits of a municipality or municipalities, shall file with the board of county commissioners of the county in which such business is operated proof of financial responsibility as hereinafter defined.

No person, firm or corporation shall hereafter engage in the business of operating a taxicab or taxicabs without the corporate limits of a municipality or municipalities in any county unless such person, firm or corporation first files with the board of county commissioners of the county in which such business is operated proof of financial responsibility as hereinafter defined.

(b) As used in this section "proof of financial responsibility" shall mean a certificate of any insurance carrier duly authorized to do business in the State of North Carolina certifying that there is in effect a policy of liability insurance insuring the owner and operator of the taxicab business, his agents and employees while in the performance of their duties against loss from any liability imposed by law for damages including damages for care and loss of services because of bodily injury to or death of any person and injury to or destruction of property caused by accident and arising out of the ownership, use or operation of such taxicab or taxicabs, subject to limits (exclusive of interests and costs) with respect to each such motor vehicle as follows: one hundred thousand dollars ($ 100,000) because of bodily injury to or death of one person in any one accident and, subject to said limit for one person, three hundred thousand dollars ($ 300,000) because of bodily injury to or death of two or more persons in any one accident, and fifty thousand dollars ($ 50,000) because of injury to or destruction of property of others in any one accident.

(c) Repealed by Session Laws 2017-137, s. 2.5, effective January 1, 2018.

History.
1951, c. 406; 1965, c. 350, s. 1; 1967, c. 277, s. 7; 1973, c. 745, s. 6; 1979, c. 832, ss. 9, 10; 1991, c. 469, s. 5;1999-228, s. 6;2017-137, s. 2.5;2017-212, s. 1.3
LOCAL MODIFICATION. --Durham: 1953, c. 597.
EDITOR'S NOTE. --
Session Laws 2017-137, s. 3, as amended by Session Laws 2017-212, s. 1.3, made amendments by Session Laws 2017-137, s. 2.5, effective January 1, 2018.
EFFECT OF AMENDMENTS. --
Session Laws 2017-137, s. 2.5, in subsection (b) substituted "one hundred thousand dollars ($100,000)" for "thirty thousand dollars ($30,000)," substituted "three hundred thousand dollars ($300,000)" for "sixty thousand dollars ($60,000)," substituted "fifty thousand dollars ($50,000)" for "twenty five thousand dollars ($25,000)"; and deleted subsection (c) which pertained to the taxicab business being in compliance with the financial responsibilities of this section. For effective date, see editor's note.
CITED in Perrell v. Beaty Serv. Co., 248 N.C. 153, 102 S.E.2d 785 (1958).
LEGAL PERIODICALS. --
For brief comment on this section, see 29 N.C.L. Rev. 402 (1951).

ARTICLE 10A.
TRANSPORTATION NETWORK COMPANIES

§ 20-280.1. Definitions

The following definitions apply in this Article:

(1) **Airport operator.** -- Any person with police powers that owns or operates an airport.

(2) **Brokering transportation network company.** -- A transportation network company, as defined by this section, that exclusively dispatches TNC drivers that operate either of the following:

    a. For-hire passenger vehicles regulated under G.S. 160A-304.

    b. For-hire passenger vehicles regulated under G.S. 62-260(f) and subject to the requirements for security for protection of the public and safety of operation established for regulated motor common carriers.

(3) **Prearranged transportation services.** -- Transportation services available by advance request excluding for-hire passenger vehicles soliciting passengers for immediate transportation. No minimum waiting period is required between the advance request and the provision of the transportation services.

(4) **TNC driver.** -- An individual that uses a passenger vehicle in connection with a transportation network company's online-enabled application or platform to connect with passengers in exchange for payment of a fee to the transportation network company.

(5) **TNC service.** -- Prearranged transportation service provided by a TNC driver in connection with a transportation network company. The TNC service begins when the TNC driver accepts a ride request on the transportation network company's online-enabled application or platform and ends at the later of the following:

    a. The time that the driver completes the transaction on the online-enabled application or platform.

    b. The time that all passengers exit the vehicle and complete unloading of the vehicle.

(6) **Transportation network company (TNC).** -- Any person that uses an online-enabled application or platform to connect passengers with TNC drivers who provide prearranged transportation services.

History.
2015-237, s. 1
EDITOR'S NOTE. --
Section Laws 2015-237, s. 7 made this Article 10A, effective October 1, 2015.

§ 20-280.2. Permissible services and limitations

(a) A transportation network company holding a valid permit issued under this Article and continuously meeting the requirements of this Article may operate in the State. The transportation network company may charge a fee for the TNC service. The fee must meet the following requirements:

(1) The transportation network company's online-enabled application or platform must disclose the fee calculation method before a passenger makes a ride request.

(2) The transportation network company's online-enabled application or platform must provide the option for a passenger to receive an estimated fee before the passenger makes a ride request.

(3) The transportation network company must send an electronic receipt to the customer that includes the following:

    a. The locations where the TNC service started and ended.

    b. The total time and distance of the TNC service.

    c. An itemization and calculation of the total fee paid.

(4) The fee must be paid electronically through the transportation network company's online-enabled application or platform. No cash may be exchanged for the TNC service.

(b) A TNC driver may provide TNC service for compensation in the State.

History.
2015-237, s. 1
EDITOR'S NOTE. --
Section Laws 2015-237, s. 7 made this section effective October 1, 2015.

§ 20-280.3. Permits

(a) Every transportation network company must obtain a permit from the Division before operating in the State. Every transportation network company must pay to the Division a nonrefundable application fee of five thousand dollars ($ 5,000).

(b) Every transportation network company must renew the permit annually and pay to the Division a nonrefundable renewal fee of five thousand dollars ($ 5,000).

(c) The Division must prescribe the form of the application for a permit and renewal of a permit.

(d) The initial application and renewal application must require information sufficient to confirm compliance with this Article and include the following:

(1) Proof of insurance meeting the requirements of G.S. 20-280.4. This subdivision does not apply to brokering transportation network companies.

(2) Resident agent for service of process.

(3) Proof the transportation network company is registered with the Secretary of State to do business in the State if the transportation network company is a foreign corporation.

(4) Policy of nondiscrimination based on customers' geographic departure point or destination.

(5) Policy of nondiscrimination based on customers' race, color, national origin, religious belief or affiliation, sex, disability, or age.

(e) The Division may retain the fees collected under this section and use the funds for its operations.

History.

2015-237, s. 1

EDITOR'S NOTE. --

Section Laws 2015-237, s. 7 made this section effective October 1, 2015.

Session Laws 2020-3, s. 4.7(a) -(h), as amended by Session Laws 2020-97, ss. 3.15(a), 3.16(a), provides: "(a) Definition. -- For purposes of this section, 'credential' means any of the following issued by the Division of Motor Vehicles:

"(1) Drivers license.

"(2) Learner's permit.

"(3) Limited learner's permit.

"(4) Limited provisional license.

"(5) Full provisional license.

"(6) Commercial drivers license.

"(7) Commercial learner's permit.

"(8) Temporary driving certificate.

"(9) Special identification card.

"(10) Handicapped placard.

"(11) Vehicle registration.

"(12) Temporary vehicle registration.

"(13) Dealer license plate.

"(14) Transporter plate.

"(15) Loaner/Dealer 'LD' plate.

"(16) Vehicle inspection authorization.

"(17) Inspection station license.

"(18) Inspection mechanic license.

"(19) Transportation network company permit.

"(20) Motor vehicle dealer license.

"(21) Sales representative license.

"(22) Manufacturer license.

"(23) Distributor license.

"(24) Wholesaler license.

"(25) Driver training school license.

"(26) Driver training school instructor license.

"(27) Professional housemoving license.

"(b) Extend Validity of Credentials. -- Notwithstanding renewal, duration, or expiration provisions of G.S. 20-7, 20-11, 20-37.6, 20-37.7, 20-37.13, 20-50, 20-66, 20-79, 20-79.02, 20-79.2, 20-183.4B, 20-183.4D, 20-280.3, 20-288, 20-324, and 20-359, or any other provision of law to the contrary, the Division of Motor Vehicles shall extend for a period of five months the validity of any credential that expires on or after March 1, 2020, and before August 1, 2020. The Division shall extend for a period of five months the validity of any credential listed in subdivisions (6), (7), (9), (10), and (18) of subsection (a) of this section that expires on or after March 1, 2020, and before the date 30 days after the date the Governor (i) rescinds Executive Order No. 116 or (ii) issues another executive order lifting restrictions on Division of Motor Vehicles functions. Notwithstanding G.S. 20-37.13(h) and G.S. 20-37.13A(a), the Division of Motor Vehicles is authorized to waive the requirement that commercial drivers license and commercial learner's permit holders have a medical examination and certification, as required by federal law, consistent with any waiver of medical qualifications standards issued by the Federal Motor Carrier Safety Administration. A credential extended under this section shall expire five months from the date it otherwise expires as prescribed by law prior to this section. However, the subsequent expiration of a credential extended under this section shall occur on the date prescribed by law prior to this section without regard to the extension. The Division shall notify individuals affected by an extension granted under this section, including information on new expiration dates and how the extension affects subsequent renewal and expiration dates.

"(b1) Extension of Intrastate Medical Waivers. -- Notwithstanding the limitation on duration of waivers in G.S. 20-37.13A(b), the Division of Motor Vehicles may extend for up to five months the validity of a medical waiver issued by the Division under G.S. 20-37.13A if the waiver expires on or after March 1, 2020, and before the date 30 days after the date the Governor (i) rescinds Executive Order No. 116 or (ii) issues another executive order lifting restrictions on Division of Motor Vehicles functions, and the Division's Medical Review Unit determines the extension is appropriate.

"(c) Driving Eligibility Certificates. -- Notwithstanding G.S. 20-11(n)(3), a driving eligibility certificate dated on or after February 9, 2020, and before March 10, 2020, remains valid and may be accepted by the Division of Motor Vehicles to meet the requirements for a license or permit issued under G.S. 20-11 until 30 days after the date the Governor rescinds Executive Order No. 116 or the date the Division reopens all drivers license offices, whichever is earlier.

"(d) Waive Penalties. -- Notwithstanding any provision of law to the contrary, the Division shall waive any fines, fees, or penalties associated with failing to renew a credential during the period of time the credential is valid by extension under subsection (b) of this section.

"(e) Motor Vehicle Taxes. -- Notwithstanding any provision of law to the contrary, due dates for motor vehicle taxes that are tied to registration expiration under Article 22A of Chapter 105 of the General Statutes shall be extended to correspond with extended expiration dates under subsection (b) of this section.

"(f) Validity by Extension a Defense. -- A person may not be convicted or found responsible for any offense resulting from failure to renew a credential

Chapter 20

issued by the Division if, when tried for that offense, the person shows that the offense occurred during the period of time the credential is valid by extension under subsection (b) of this section.

"(g) Report. -- Within 30 days of the extensions made under subsection (b) of this section, the Division shall submit a report to the Joint Legislative Transportation Oversight Committee and the Fiscal Research Division detailing implementation of this section.

"(h) Effective Date. -- This section is effective retroactively to March 1, 2020, and applies to expirations occurring on or after that date."

Session Laws 2020-3, s. 5, is a severability clause.

Session Laws 2020-97, s. 4.5, is a severability clause.

§ 20-280.4. Financial responsibility

(a) Except as provided in subsection (n) of this section, TNC drivers or transportation network companies must maintain primary automobile insurance that meets all of the following requirements:

(1) Recognizes that the driver is a TNC driver or uses a vehicle to transport passengers for compensation.

(2) The following automobile insurance requirements apply while a TNC driver is logged on to the transportation network company's online-enabled application or platform but is not providing TNC service:

    a. Primary automobile liability insurance in the amount of at least fifty thousand dollars ($ 50,000) because of death of or bodily injury to one person in any one accident and, subject to said limit for one person, one hundred thousand dollars ($ 100,000) because of death of or bodily injury to two or more persons in any one accident, and at least twenty-five thousand dollars ($ 25,000) because of injury to or destruction of property of others in any one accident.

    b. Combined uninsured and underinsured motorist coverage, with limits for combined uninsured and underinsured motorist bodily injury coverage which at least equals the bodily injury liability limits of the policy, and which otherwise complies with the requirements of G.S. 20-279.21(b)(3) and (b)(4).

(3) The following automobile insurance requirements apply while a TNC driver is engaged in TNC service:

    a. Primary automobile liability insurance in the amount of at least one million five hundred thousand dollars ($ 1,500,000) because of death of one or more persons, bodily injury to one or more persons, injury to or destruction of property of others, or any

combination thereof, in any one accident.

    b. Combined uninsured and underinsured motorist coverage, with limits for combined uninsured and underinsured motorist bodily injury coverage of at least one million dollars ($ 1,000,000), and which otherwise complies with the requirements of G.S. 20-279.21(b)(3) and (b)(4).

(4) The coverage requirements of subdivisions (2) and (3) of this subsection may be satisfied by any of the following:

    a. Automobile insurance maintained by the TNC driver.

    b. Automobile insurance maintained by the transportation network company.

    c. Any combination of subsubdivisions a. and b. of this subdivision.

(b) If insurance maintained by the TNC driver under subsection (a) of this section has lapsed or does not provide the required coverage, insurance maintained by the transportation network company must provide the coverage required under subsection (a) of this section beginning with the first dollar of a claim and must provide the defense of the claim.

(c) Insurance coverage under an automobile insurance policy maintained by the transportation network company must not be dependent on a personal automobile insurer denying a claim.

(d) Insurance required by this section may be placed with an insurer licensed in the State or with a surplus lines insurer eligible to write policies in the State.

(e) Insurance satisfying the requirements of this section satisfies the financial responsibility requirement for a motor vehicle.

(f) A TNC driver must carry proof of coverage satisfying the requirements of this section at all times during use of a vehicle in connection with a transportation network company's online-enabled application or platform. In the event of an accident, a TNC driver must provide insurance coverage information directly to interested parties, automobile insurers, and investigating police officers, upon request. Upon such request, a TNC driver must also disclose to directly interested parties, automobile insurers, and investigating police officers whether the TNC driver was logged on or off of the transportation network company's online-enabled application or platform at the time of the accident.

(g) Before any vehicle is used in connection with a transportation network company's online-enabled application or platform, a TNC driver must notify both the insurer of the vehicle and any lienholder with an interest in the vehicle of the TNC driver's intent to use the vehicle in connection with a transportation network company's online-enabled application or platform.

(h) Transportation network companies must disclose in writing to potential TNC drivers the following before the TNC driver provides TNC service:

(1) The insurance coverage, including the types of coverage and the limits for each coverage, that the transportation network company provides while the TNC driver uses a private passenger vehicle in connection with a transportation network company's online-enabled application or platform.

(2) The TNC driver may not have any coverage under a personal automobile insurance policy while using the transportation network company's online-enabled application or platform.

(3) The following notice in a distinctive clause: "If the vehicle with which you provide transportation network company services has a lien against it, you must notify the lienholder prior to providing transportation network company services of your intent to provide transportation services with the vehicle. You may disclose to the lienholder all insurance coverage information provided to you by the transportation network company. If you fail to provide the required insurance coverage under the terms of your contract with the lienholder or show evidence to the lienholder of the coverage provided by the transportation network company, you may violate the terms of your contract."

(i) Insurers that write automobile insurance in the State may exclude coverage under the policy issued to an owner or operator of a personal vehicle for any loss that occurs while the driver is logged on to a transportation network company's online-enabled application or platform or while the driver provides TNC service. This right to exclude all coverage applies to any coverage included in an automobile insurance policy, including all of the following:

(1) Liability coverage for bodily injury and property damage.

(2) Personal injury protection coverage.

(3) Uninsured and underinsured motorist coverage.

(4) Medical payments coverage.

(5) Comprehensive physical damage coverage.

(6) Collision physical damage coverage.

(j) Automobile insurers that exclude the coverage described in subsection (i) of this section have no duty to defend or indemnify any claim expressly excluded. An automobile insurer that defends or indemnifies a claim against a driver that is excluded under the terms of its policy has a right of contribution against other insurers that provide automobile insurance to the same driver in satisfaction of the coverage requirements of this section.

(k) No insurer is required to sell a policy of insurance providing the coverage required by this section.

(l) Notwithstanding G.S. 58-37-35(b)(1)e., no insurance policy providing coverage required by this section is cedable to the North Carolina Reinsurance Facility due solely to the requirements of this section.

(m) In a claims coverage investigation or accident, a TNC driver, transportation network companies, any insurer potentially providing coverage under this section, and other directly involved parties must exchange the following information:

(1) Description of the coverage, exclusions, and limits provided under any insurance policy.

(2) Precise times that a TNC driver logged on and off of the transportation network company's online-enabled application or platform in the 12-hour period immediately preceding and in the 12-hour period immediately following the accident.

(3) Precise times that a TNC driver provided TNC service in the 12-hour period immediately preceding and in the 12-hour period immediately following the accident.

(n) This section does not apply to brokering transportation network companies.

History.
2015-237, s. 1
EDITOR'S NOTE. --
Section Laws 2015-237, s. 7 made this section effective October 1, 2015.

§ 20-280.5. Safety requirements

(a) The transportation network company must require TNC drivers have their vehicles inspected annually to meet State safety requirements. The Division may, by regulation, specify alternative inspections that are acceptable as equivalent inspections, such as an inspection performed in another state. This subsection does not apply to brokering transportation network companies.

(b) The transportation network company's online-enabled application or platform must provide the following information to customers after a ride request is accepted by a TNC driver:

(1) Photograph of the TNC driver.

(2) License plate number of the TNC driver's vehicle.

(3) Description of the TNC driver's vehicle.

(4) Approximate location of the TNC driver's vehicle displayed on a map.

(c) The transportation network company must maintain the following records:

(1) The record of each TNC service provided in this State for one year from the date the TNC service occurred.

(2) The record of each TNC driver, which includes a driver's name and current address of the driver the TNC has on record at the time the driver's relationship with the TNC ended, in this State for one year from the date the TNC driver terminated their relationship with the transportation network company.

(d) The transportation network company must require a TNC driver to display the license plate number of the TNC driver's vehicle in a location that is visible from the front of the vehicle at the time a TNC service begins and at all times during a TNC service. The vehicle's license plate number displayed pursuant to this subsection must be printed in a legible and contrasting font no smaller than three inches in height but is not required to be permanently mounted on the vehicle. A TNC driver is not required to obtain approval from the transportation network company or the Division for a license plate number display required by this subsection.

(e) Except as provided in subsection (f) of this section, a transportation network company must require a TNC driver to display consistent and distinctive signage or emblems, known as a trade dress, trademark, branding, or logo of the TNC, on the TNC driver's vehicle at all times when the TNC driver is active on the TNC digital platform or when providing any TNC service that reasonably assists customers to identify or verify a TNC driver responding to a ride request. TNC signage or emblems required by this subsection may include magnetic or removable signage or emblems, must be approved by the Division before use, and must meet all of the following requirements:

(1) Be readable during daylight hours at a distance of 50 feet.

(2) Include an illuminated TNC-provided sign displaying the TNC's proprietary trademark or logo that is clearly visible so as to be seen in darkness.

(f) A transportation network company may seek approval from the Division for technological identifiers as an alternative to the distinctive signage or emblems required by subsection (e) of this section. The Division may approve an alternative technological identifier if it reasonably assists customers to identify or verify a TNC driver responding to a ride request. If approved by the Division, the approved technological identifier must be used by a TNC driver at all times when the TNC driver is active on the TNC digital platform or when providing any TNC service.

History.
2015-237, s. 1;2019-194, s. 2(a);2020-3, s. 4.36(a)

EDITOR'S NOTE. --
Section Laws 2015-237, s. 7 made this section effective October 1, 2015.

Session Laws 2019-194, s. 1, provides: "This act shall be known as the 'Passenger Protection Act' and may be cited by that name."

Session Laws 2019-194, s. 2(b), as amended by Session Laws 2020-3, s. 4.36(a), provides: "G.S. 20-280.5(e) and (f), as enacted by this section, become effective September 1, 2020. The remainder of this section becomes effective October 1, 2019."

Session Laws 2020-3, s. 5, is a severability clause.

EFFECT OF AMENDMENTS. --
Session Laws 2019-194, s. 2(a), inserted "which includes a driver's name and current address of the driver the TNC has on record at the time the driver's relationship with the TNC ended" in subdivision (c) (2); added subsections (d), (e) and (f). For effective date, see Editor's note.

§ 20-280.6. Background checks

(a) Prior to permitting an individual to act as a TNC driver, the transportation network company must do all of the following:

(1) Require the individual to submit an application to the transportation network company, including, at a minimum, the following:

    a. Address.

    b. Age.

    c. Drivers license number.

    d. Driving history.

    e. Motor vehicle registration.

    f. Automobile liability insurance information.

(2) Conduct, or have a third party conduct, a local and national criminal background check for each applicant, including, at a minimum, the following:

    a. Multi-State/Multi-Jurisdiction Criminal Records Locator or other similar commercial nationwide database with validation (primary source search).

    b. National Sex Offender Registry.

(3) Review, or have a third party review, a driving history research report for such individual.

(b) The transportation network company must confirm that every TNC driver continues to meet all the requirements of this section every five years starting from the date the TNC driver met all the requirements of this section.

(c) The transportation network company must not permit an individual to act as a TNC driver if any of the following apply:

(1) Has had more than three moving violations in the prior three-year period or one major violation in the prior three-year period, including attempting to evade the police, reckless driving, or driving on a suspended or revoked license.

(2) Has been convicted within the past seven years of driving under the influence of drugs or alcohol, fraud, sexual offenses, use of a motor vehicle to commit a felony, or a crime involving property damage, theft, acts of violence, or acts of terror.

(3) Is a match in the National Sex Offender Registry.

(4) Does not possess a valid drivers license.

(5) Does not possess proof of registration for the motor vehicle to be used to provide TNC services.

(6) Does not possess proof of automobile liability insurance for the motor vehicle to be used to provide TNC services.

(7) Is not at least 19 years of age.

(d) This section does not apply to brokering transportation network companies.

History.
2015-237, s. 1
EDITOR'S NOTE. --
Section Laws 2015-237, s. 7 made this section effective October 1, 2015.

§ 20-280.7. Authority of Division

The Division may issue regulations to implement this Article.

History.
2015-237, s. 1
EDITOR'S NOTE. --
Section Laws 2015-237, s. 7 made this section effective October 1, 2015.

§ 20-280.8. Presumption that TNC drivers are independent contractors

A rebuttable presumption exists that a TNC driver is an independent contractor and not an employee. The presumption may be rebutted by application of the common law test for determining employment status.

History.
2015-237, s. 1
EDITOR'S NOTE. --
Section Laws 2015-237, s. 7 made this section effective October 1, 2015.
LEGAL PERIODICALS. --
For article, "That's Not My Name: An Analysis of North Carolina Laws Used to Classify Employees and Independent Contractors of Sharing Economy Businesses," see 38 N.C. Cent. L. Rev. 161 (2016).

§ 20-280.9. Airport operators

(a) An airport operator is authorized to charge transportation network companies and TNC drivers a reasonable fee for their use of the airport's facility.

(b) An airport operator is authorized to require an identifying decal be displayed by TNC drivers.

(c) An airport operator is authorized to require the purchase and use of equipment or establish other appropriate mechanisms for monitoring and auditing compliance, including having a transportation network company provide data for purposes of monitoring and auditing compliance.

(d) An airport operator is authorized to designate a location where TNC drivers may stage on the airport operator's facility, drop off passengers, and pick up passengers.

History.
2015-237, s. 1
EDITOR'S NOTE. --
Section Laws 2015-237, s. 7 made this section effective October 1, 2015.

§ 20-280.10. Statewide regulation

(a) Notwithstanding any other provision of law and except as authorized by this Chapter, no county, city, airport operator, or other governmental agency is authorized to impose fees, require licenses, limit the operation of TNC services, or otherwise regulate TNC services. TNC services remain subject to all ordinances and local laws outside the scope of this Chapter, including parking and traffic regulation.

(b) Any contract provision or term of service in a transportation network company's contract with a State resident or person present in the State contrary to this Article is void as against public policy.

History.
2015-237, s. 1
EDITOR'S NOTE. --
Section Laws 2015-237, s. 7 made this section effective October 1, 2015.

ARTICLE 10B.
PEER-TO-PEER VEHICLE SHARING

§ 20-280.15. Definitions

The following definitions apply in this Article:

(1) **Airport operator.** -- As defined in G.S. 20-280.1.

(2) **Peer-to-peer vehicle sharing.** -- The authorized use of a shared vehicle by an individual other than the shared vehicle owner through a peer-to-peer vehicle sharing program.

(3) **Peer-to-peer vehicle sharing program.** -- A business platform that connects shared vehicle owners with drivers to enable the sharing of vehicles for financial consideration.

(4) **Shared vehicle.** -- A vehicle that is available for sharing through a peer-to-peer vehicle sharing program.

(5) **Shared vehicle owner.** -- The registered owner of a shared vehicle that is made available for sharing through a peer-to-peer vehicle sharing program.

(6) **Vehicle sharing provider.** -- The person or entity that operates, facilitates, or administers the provision of personal vehicle sharing through a peer-to-peer vehicle sharing program.

History.
2019-199, s. 9(a)

EDITOR'S NOTE. --
Session Laws 2019-199, s. 9(b), made the Article effective October 1, 2019.

§ 20-280.17. Airport operators

An airport operator may (i) charge peer-to-peer vehicle sharing programs a reasonable fee for the use of the airport's facility, (ii) require an identifying decal be displayed on all shared vehicles that operate on airport property, (iii) require the purchase and use of equipment or establish other appropriate mechanisms for monitoring and auditing compliance, including having a peer-to-peer vehicle sharing program provide data for purposes of monitoring and auditing compliance, and (iv) designate a location where shared vehicles may stage on the airport operator's facility.

History.
2019-199, s. 9(a)

ARTICLE 11.
LIABILITY INSURANCE REQUIRED OF PERSONS ENGAGED IN RENTING MOTOR VEHICLES

§ 20-281. Liability insurance prerequisite to engaging in business; coverage of policy

From and after July 1, 1953, it shall be unlawful for any person, firm or corporation to engage in the business of renting or leasing motor vehicles to the public for operation by the rentee or lessee unless such person, firm or corporation has secured insurance for his own liability and that of his rentee or lessee, in such an amount as is hereinafter provided,

from an insurance company duly licensed to sell motor vehicle liability insurance in this State. Each such motor vehicle leased or rented must be covered by a policy of liability insurance insuring the owner and rentee or lessee and their agents and employees while in the performance of their duties against loss from any liability imposed by law for damages including damages for care and loss of services because of bodily injury to or death of any person and injury to or destruction of property caused by accident arising out of the operation of such motor vehicle, subject to the following minimum limits: thirty thousand dollars ($ 30,000) because of bodily injury to or death of one person in any one accident, and sixty thousand dollars ($ 60,000) because of bodily injury to or death of two or more persons in any one accident, and twenty-five thousand dollars ($ 25,000) because of injury to or destruction of property of others in any one accident. Provided, however, that nothing in this Article shall prevent such operators from qualifying as self-insurers under terms and conditions to be prepared and prescribed by the Commissioner of Motor Vehicles or by giving bond with personal or corporate surety, as now provided by G.S. 20-279.24, in lieu of securing the insurance policy hereinbefore provided for.

History.
1953, c. 1017, s. 1; 1955, c. 1296; 1965, c. 349, s. 1; 1967, c. 277, s. 8; 1973, c. 745, s. 7; 1979, c. 832, s. 11; 1991, c. 469, s. 6;1999-228, s. 7

COVERAGE REQUIREMENT IS REASONABLE. --The requirement of this section that policies which insure automobile lessors provide coverage for lessees and their agents is reasonable in light of the statute's purpose. A lessor's insurance should cover lessees because lessees are unlikely to purchase insurance on account of what may be the temporary nature of a rental arrangement. A lessor's insurance also should cover lessees' agents because, being mere agents, they are also unlikely to obtain their own insurance. American Tours, Inc. v. Liberty Mut. Ins. Co., 315 N.C. 341, 338 S.E.2d 92 (1986).

THE PUBLIC POLICY EXPRESSED IN THIS SECTION is that even where automobile rental agreements are violated it is preferable to provide coverage for innocent motorists rather than to deny such coverage because of the violation. American Tours, Inc. v. Liberty Mut. Ins. Co., 315 N.C. 341, 338 S.E.2d 92 (1986).

THIS SECTION AND G.S. 20-279.21 PRESCRIBE MANDATORY TERMS which become part of every liability policy insuring automobile lessors. Insurance Co. of N. Am. v. Aetna Life & Cas. Co., 88 N.C. App. 236, 362 S.E.2d 836 (1987).

SECTION IS IN ADDITION TO G.S. 20-279.21. -- This section is a source of mandatory terms for automobile liability insurance policies in addition to and independent of G.S. 20-279.21. American Tours, Inc. v. Liberty Mut. Ins. Co., 315 N.C. 341, 338 S.E.2d 92 (1986).

This section, which applies specifically to automobile owners who lease their cars for profit, is a companion section to and supplements G.S. 20-279.21, which applies to automobile owners generally. American Tours, Inc. v. Liberty Mut. Ins. Co., 315 N.C. 341, 338 S.E.2d 92 (1986).

This section supplements G.S. 20-279.21 and is intended to protect innocent drivers from financially irresponsible drivers. Hertz Corp. v. New S. Ins. Co., 129 N.C. App. 227, 497 S.E.2d 448 (1998).

THIS SECTION AND G.S. 20-279.21 COMPARED. --This section requires those engaged in the business of renting automobiles to the public to maintain liability insurance "insuring the owner and rentee . . . and their agents" against liability for damages for personal injury or death in the minimum amount of $25,000 per person and $50,000 per accident and for property damage in the amount of $10,000.00, while G.S. 20-279.21, which applies more generally to every policy insuring any automobile owner whether or not that owner leases vehicles, requires that the coverage be extended to "any other persons in lawful possession" of the vehicle. Insurance Co. of N. Am. v. Aetna Life & Cas. Co., 88 N.C. App. 236, 362 S.E.2d 836 (1987).

A LIABILITY POLICY ISSUED TO ONE IN THE BUSINESS OF RENTING CARS MUST COMPLY WITH BOTH G.S. 20-279.21 AND THIS SECTION and provide all coverages required by both sections. American Tours, Inc. v. Liberty Mut. Ins. Co., 315 N.C. 341, 338 S.E.2d 92 (1986).

SECTION PROVIDES COVERAGE TO LESSEES AND THEIR AGENTS. --In every automobile liability policy insuring automobile lessors, this section provides coverage to lessees and lessees' agents. American Tours, Inc. v. Liberty Mut. Ins. Co., 315 N.C. 341, 338 S.E.2d 92 (1986), holding that if 19 year old was an agent of her father, the lessee, this section required that she be covered, even though she did not have lessors' permission to use the car.

AMOUNT OF COVERAGE. --When an automobile insurance policy providing coverage in amounts in excess of that statutorily required contains substantive coverages less than those statutorily required, the insurer's liability for an accident for which the statute requires but the policy does not provide coverage is limited to the minimum amount of coverage required by statutes. American Tours, Inc. v. Liberty Mut. Ins. Co., 315 N.C. 341, 338 S.E.2d 92 (1986).

Coverage, to the extent that it exceeded that required by this section, was "voluntary." Insurance Co. of N. Am. v. Aetna Life & Cas. Co., 88 N.C. App. 236, 362 S.E.2d 836 (1987).

EXTENSION OF COVERAGE UNTIL RELATIONSHIP IS TERMINATED. --The legislature intended that coverage under this section should be extended until such times as there has been a clear termination of the relationship of lessor-lessee. Nationwide Mut. Ins. Co. v. Land, 78 N.C. App. 342, 337 S.E.2d 180 (1985), aff'd, 318 N.C. 551, 350 S.E.2d 500 (1986).

BREACH OR DEFAULT BY LESSEE. --An insurer who issues a policy to satisfy the requirements of this section is not relieved from its duty to provide coverage for a lessee upon a mere breach of an automobile lease agreement, or even upon a default in its terms. Nationwide Mut. Ins. Co. v. Land, 78 N.C. App. 342, 337 S.E.2d 180 (1985), aff'd, 318 N.C. 551, 350 S.E.2d 500 (1986).

CONVERSION BY LESSEE. --Where individual's continued possession of automobile, after bank had given him notice that he was in default and demanded possession of the automobile, was adverse to the rights of bank as owner and lessor and amounted to a conversion of the automobile, the relationship of lessor-lessee ceased to exist. Therefore such individual was not operating the automobile as banks lessee at the time of collision some 12 months thereafter, and bank's insurer was not required by this section to extend coverage for personal injuries caused by defendant's operation of the automobile. Nationwide Mut. Ins. Co. v. Land, 78 N.C. App. 342, 337 S.E.2d 180 (1985), aff'd, 318 N.C. 551, 350 S.E.2d 500 (1986).

THIS SECTION DID NOT EXTEND INSURANCE COVERAGE TO THE DRIVER OF A RENTED VEHICLE WHERE there was neither evidence nor a finding that the driver at any time was a rentee or a lessee or an agent or employee of the owner of the vehicle. Iowa Nat'l Mut. Ins. Co. v. Broughton, 283 N.C. 309, 196 S.E.2d 243 (1973).

In view of lessee's default and the efforts of the lessor to repossess the automobile, no lessor-lessee relationship existed at the time of collision involving the lessee, nor did the lessee have express or implied permission to operate the vehicle, and the policy insuring the lessor afforded no coverage under this section. Nationwide Mut. Ins. Co. v. Land, 318 N.C. 551, 350 S.E.2d 500 (1986).

THIRD PARTY HELD IN LAWFUL POSSESSION OF RENTAL CAR. --Although lessee violated his contract by permitting third parties to drive rental car, their possession of it was not unlawful. Thus, driver was in "lawful possession" of the car at the time of the accident, although he had neither express nor implied permission from the lessor to drive it, and therefore insurer was required, pursuant to G.S. 20-279.21(b)(2) and this section, to provide coverage for driver's negligent operation of the automobile, limited to the amounts of coverage required by G.S. 20-279.21(g) and this section. Insurance Co. of N. Am. v. Aetna Life & Cas. Co., 88 N.C. App. 236, 362 S.E.2d 836 (1987).

RENTAL COMPANY WITHOUT LIABILITY. --Where driver had an operative liability insurance policy meeting the requirements of the Financial Responsibility Act, and where car rental company specifically excluded liability insurance in the lease agreement, car rental company owed driver no liability coverage. Jeffreys v. Snappy Car Rental, Inc., 128 N.C. App. 171, 493 S.E.2d 767 (1997).

LIABILITY COVERAGE FOR VEHICLE LESSEE NOT EXCLUDED. --Lessor's fleet insurance policy did not exclude liability coverage for lessee, even though the lessee was insured under his own liability policy at the minimum limits, where the lessee was a person "required by law to be an insured" within the meaning of the fleet policy. Integon Indem. Corp. v. Universal Underwriters Ins. Co., 131 N.C. App. 267, 507 S.E.2d 66 (1998).

APPLIED in American Tours, Inc. v. Liberty Mut. Ins. Co., 68 N.C. App. 668, 316 S.E.2d 105 (1984).

CITED in Travelers Ins. Co. v. Ryder Truck Rental, Inc., 34 N.C. App. 379, 238 S.E.2d 193 (1977); Engle v. State Farm Mut. Auto. Ins. Co., 37 N.C. App. 126, 245 S.E.2d 532 (1978); Belasco v. Nationwide Mut. Ins. Co., 73 N.C. App. 413, 326 S.E.2d 109 (1985).

CROSS REFERENCES. --
As to registration fees for U-Drive-It passenger vehicles, see G.S. 20-87(2).

§ 20-282. Cooperation in enforcement of Article

The provisions of this Article shall be enforced by the Commissioner of Motor Vehicles in cooperation with the Commissioner of Insurance, the North Carolina Automobile Rate Administrative Office and with all law-enforcement officers and agents and other agencies of the State and the political subdivisions thereof.

History.
1953, c. 1017, s. 2

§ 20-283. Compliance with Article prerequisite to issuance of license plates

No license plates shall be issued by the Division of Motor Vehicles to operate a motor vehicle, for lease or rent for operation by the rentee or lessee, until the applicant for such license plates demonstrates to the Commissioner of Motor Vehicles that he has complied with the provisions of this Article.

History.
1953, c. 1017, s. 3; 1975, c. 716, s. 5

§ 20-284. Violation a misdemeanor

Any person, firm or corporation violating the provisions of this Article shall be guilty of a Class 1 misdemeanor.

History.
1953, c. 1017, s. 4; 1993, c. 539, s. 385;1994, Ex. Sess., c. 24, s. 14(c)

ARTICLE 12.
MOTOR VEHICLE DEALERS AND MANUFACTURERS LICENSING LAW

§ 20-285. Regulation of motor vehicle distribution in public interest

The General Assembly finds and declares that the distribution of motor vehicles in the State of North Carolina vitally affects the general economy of the State and the public interest and public welfare, and in the exercise of its police power, it is necessary to regulate and license motor vehicle manufacturers, distributors, dealers, salesmen, and their representatives doing business in North Carolina, in order to prevent frauds, impositions and other abuses upon its citizens and to protect and preserve the investments and properties of the citizens of this State.

History.
1955, c. 1243, s. 1; 1983, c. 704, s. 1
CITED in Mazda Motors of Am., Inc. v. Southwestern Motors, Inc., 36 N.C. App. 1, 243 S.E.2d 793 (1978).
LEGAL PERIODICALS. --
For 1984 survey on commercial law, "Green Light to Territorial Security for Automobile Dealers," see 63 N.C.L. Rev. 1080 (1985).

§ 20-286. Definitions

The following definitions apply in this Article:
(1), (2) Repealed by Session Laws 1973, c. 1330, s. 39.
(2a) **Dealership facilities. --** The real estate, buildings, fixtures and improvements devoted to the conduct of business under a franchise.
(2b) **Designated family member. --** The spouse, child, grandchild, parent, brother, or sister of a dealer, who, in the case of a deceased dealer, is entitled to inherit the dealer's ownership interest in the dealership under the terms of the dealer's will; or who has otherwise been designated in writing by a deceased dealer to succeed him in the motor vehicle dealership; or who under the laws of intestate succession of this State is entitled to inherit the interest; or who, in the case of an incapacitated dealer, has been appointed by a court as the legal representative of the dealer's property. The term includes the appointed and qualified personal representative and testamentary trustee of a deceased dealer.
(3) **Distributor. --** A person, resident or nonresident of this State, who sells or distributes new motor vehicles to new motor

vehicle dealers in this State, maintains a distributor representative in this State, controls any person, resident or nonresident, who in whole or in part offers for sale, sells or distributes any new motor vehicle to any motor vehicle dealer in this State.

(4) **Distributor branch.** -- A branch office maintained by a distributor for the sale of new motor vehicles to new motor vehicle dealers, or for directing or supervising the distributor's representatives in this State.

(5) **Distributor representative.** -- A person employed by a distributor or a distributor branch for the purpose of selling or promoting the sale of new motor vehicles or otherwise conducting the business of the distributor or distributor branch.

(5a) **Established office.** -- An office that meets the following requirements:

    a. Contains at least 96 square feet of floor space in a permanent enclosed building.

    b. Is a place where the books, records, and files required by the Division under this Article are kept.

(6) **Established salesroom.** -- A salesroom that meets the following requirements:

    a. Contains at least 96 square feet of floor space in a permanent enclosed building.

    b. Displays, or is located immediately adjacent to, a sign having block letters not less than three inches in height on contrasting background, clearly and distinctly designating the trade name of the business.

    c. Is a place at which a permanent business of bartering, trading, and selling motor vehicles will be carried on in good faith on an ongoing basis whereby the dealer can be contacted by the public at reasonable times.

    d. Is a place where the books, records, and files required by the Division under this Article are kept.

The term includes the area contiguous to or located within 500 feet of the premises on which the salesroom is located. The term does not include a tent, a temporary stand, or other temporary quarters. The minimum area requirement does not apply to any place of business lawfully in existence and duly licensed on or before January 1, 1978.

(7) **Factory branch.** -- A branch office, maintained for the sale of new motor vehicles to new motor vehicle dealers, or for directing or supervising the factory branch's representatives in this State.

(8) **Factory representative.** -- A person employed by a manufacturer or a factory branch for the purpose of selling or promoting the sale of the manufacturer's motor vehicles or otherwise conducting the business of the manufacturer or factory branch.

(8a) **Franchise.** -- A written agreement or contract between any new motor vehicle manufacturer, and any new motor vehicle dealer which purports to fix the legal rights and liabilities of the parties to such agreement or contract, and pursuant to which the dealer purchases and resells the franchised product or leases or rents the dealership premises.

(8b) **Franchised motor vehicle dealer.** -- A dealer who holds a currently valid franchise as defined in G.S. 20-286(8a) with a manufacturer or distributor of new motor vehicles, trailers, or semitrailers.

(8c) **Good faith.** -- Honesty in fact and the observation of reasonable commercial standards of fair dealing as defined and interpreted in G.S. 25-1-201(b)(20).

(8d) **Independent motor vehicle dealer.** -- A dealer in used motor vehicles.

(8e) **Manufacturer.** -- A person, resident or nonresident, who manufactures or assembles new motor vehicles, or who imports new motor vehicles for distribution through a distributor, including any person who acts for and is under the control of the manufacturer or assembler in connection with the distribution of the motor vehicles. Additionally, the term "manufacturer" shall include the terms "distributor" and "factory branch."

(9) Repealed by Session Laws 1973, c. 1330, s. 39.

(10) **Motor vehicle.** -- Any motor propelled vehicle, trailer or semitrailer, required to be registered under the laws of this State. This term does not include mopeds, as that term is defined in G.S. 20-4.01.

    a. "New motor vehicle" means a motor vehicle that has never been the subject of a completed, successful, or conditional sale that was subsequently approved other than between new motor vehicle dealers, or between a manufacturer and a new motor vehicle dealer of the same franchise. For purposes of this subdivision, the use of a new motor vehicle by a new motor vehicle dealer for demonstration or service loaner purposes does not render the new motor vehicle a used motor vehicle, notwithstanding (i) the commencement of the manufacturer's original warranty as a result of the franchised dealer's use of the vehicle for demonstration or loaner purposes, or (ii) the dealer's receipt of incentive or warranty compensation or other

Chapter 20

reimbursement or consideration from a manufacturer, factory branch, distributor, distributor branch or from a third-party warranty, maintenance, or service contract company relating to the use of a vehicle as a demonstrator or service loaner.

b. "Used motor vehicle" means a motor vehicle other than a motor vehicle described in sub-subdivision a. of this subdivision.

c. The term "motor vehicle" does not include an electrically powered device that is equipped with automated driving technology that enables device operation with or without remote support and supervision of a human, and to which all of the following apply: (i) the device does not exceed a weight of 750 pounds, excluding cargo, (ii) the device does not exceed a length of 40 inches when not linked with other devices, and (iii) the device does not exceed a width of 36 inches. An electrically powered device that is equipped with automated driving technology that enables device operation with or without remote support and supervision of a human and that exceeds any of the dimensions set out in this sub-subdivision is included in the term "motor vehicle" under this Article, and the device is subject to the provisions of Article 18 of this Chapter if it falls within the definition of "fully autonomous vehicle" under G.S. 20-400(3).

(11) **Motor vehicle dealer or dealer. --**

a. A person who does any of the following:

1. For commission, money, or other thing of value, buys, sells, or exchanges, whether outright or on conditional sale, bailment lease, chattel mortgage, or otherwise, five or more motor vehicles within any 12 consecutive months, regardless of who owns the motor vehicles.

2. On behalf of another and for commission, money, or other thing of value, arranges, offers, attempts to solicit, or attempts to negotiate the sale, purchase, or exchange of an interest in five or more motor vehicles within any 12 consecutive months, regardless of who owns the motor vehicles.

3. Engages, wholly or in part, in the business of selling new motor vehicles or new or used motor vehicles, or used motor vehicles only, whether or not the motor vehicles

are owned by that person, and sells five or more motor vehicles within any 12 consecutive months.

4. Offers to sell, displays, or permits the display for sale for any form of compensation five or more motor vehicles within any 12 consecutive months.

5. Primarily engages in the leasing or renting of motor vehicles to others and sells or offers to sell those vehicles at retail.

b. The term "motor vehicle dealer" or "dealer" does not include any of the following:

1. Receivers, trustees, administrators, executors, guardians, or other persons appointed by or acting under the judgment or order of any court.

2. Public officers while performing their official duties.

3. Persons disposing of motor vehicles acquired for their own use or the use of a family member, and actually so used, when the vehicles have been acquired and used in good faith and not for the purpose of avoiding the provisions of this Article.

4. Persons who sell motor vehicles as an incident to their principal business but who are not engaged primarily in the selling of motor vehicles. This category includes financial institutions who sell repossessed motor vehicles and insurance companies who sell motor vehicles to which they have taken title as an incident of payments made under policies of insurance, and auctioneers who sell motor vehicles for the owners or the heirs of the owners of those vehicles as part of an auction of other personal or real property or for the purpose of settling an estate or closing a business or who sell motor vehicles on behalf of a governmental entity, and who do not maintain a used car lot or building with one or more employed motor vehicle sales representatives.

5. Persons manufacturing, distributing or selling trailers and semitrailers weighing not more than 2,500 pounds unloaded weight.

6. A licensed real estate broker or salesman who sells a mobile home for the owner as an incident to the sale of land upon which the mobile home is located.

7. An employee of an organization arranging for the purchase or lease by the organization of vehicles for use in the organization's business.

8. Any publication, broadcast, or other communications media when engaged in the business of advertising, but not otherwise arranging for the sale of motor vehicles owned by others.

9. Any person dealing solely in the sale or lease of vehicles designed exclusively for off-road use.

10. Any real property owner who leases any interest in property for use by a dealer.

11. Any person acquiring any interest in a motor vehicle for a family member.

12. Any auctioneer licensed pursuant to Chapter 85B of the General Statutes employed to be an auctioneer of motor vehicles for a licensed motor vehicle dealer, while conducting an auction for that dealer.

13. Any charitable organization operating under section 501(c)(3) of the Internal Revenue Code (26 U.S.C. § 501(c)(3)) where the vehicle was donated to the charitable organization solely for purposes of resale by the charitable organization.

(12) **Motor vehicle sales representative or salesman.** -- A person who is employed as a sales representative by, or has an agreement with, a motor vehicle dealer or a wholesaler to sell or exchange motor vehicles.

(13) **New motor vehicle dealer.** -- A motor vehicle dealer who buys, sells or exchanges, or offers or attempts to negotiate a sale or exchange of an interest in, or who is engaged, wholly or in part, in the business of selling, new or new and used motor vehicles.

(13a) **Person.** -- Defined in G.S. 20-4.01.

(13b) **Relevant market area or trade area.** -- The area within a radius of 20 miles around an existing dealer or the area of responsibility defined in the franchise, whichever is greater; except that, where a manufacturer is seeking to establish an additional new motor vehicle dealer the relevant market area shall be as follows:

a. If the population in an area within a radius of 10 miles around the proposed site is 250,000 or more, the relevant market area shall be that area within the 10 mile radius; or

b. If the population in an area within a radius of 10 miles around the proposed site is less than 250,000, but the population in an area within a radius of 15 miles around the proposed site is 150,000 or more, the relevant market area shall be that area within the 15 mile radius; or

c. Except as defined in subparts a. and b., the relevant market area shall be the area within a radius of 20 miles around an existing dealer.

In determining population for this definition the most recent census by the U.S. Bureau of the Census or the most recent population update either from Claritas Inc. or other similar recognized source shall be accumulated for all census tracts either wholly or partially within the relevant market area. In accumulating population for this definition, block group and block level data shall be used to apportion the population of census tracts which are only partially within the relevant market area so that population outside of the applicable radius is not included in the count.

(14) Repealed by Session Laws 1973, c. 1330, s. 39.

(15) **Retail installment sale.** -- A sale of one or more motor vehicles to a buyer for the buyer's use and not for resale, in which the price thereof is payable in one or more installments over a period of time and in which the seller has either retained title to the goods or has taken or retained a security interest in the goods under a form of contract designated as a conditional sale, bailment lease, chattel mortgage or otherwise.

(15a) **Special tool or essential tool.** -- A tool designed and required by the manufacturer or distributor and not readily available from another source that is utilized for the purpose of performing service repairs on a motor vehicle sold by a manufacturer or distributor to its franchised new motor vehicle dealers in this State.

(16) **Used motor vehicle dealer.** -- A motor vehicle dealer who buys, sells or exchanges, or offers or attempts to negotiate a sale or exchange of an interest in, or who is engaged, wholly or in part, in the business of selling, used motor vehicles only.

(17) **Wholesaler.** -- A person who sells or distributes used motor vehicles to motor vehicle dealers in this State, has a sales representative in this State, or controls any person who in whole or in part offers for sale, sells, or distributes any used motor vehicle to a motor vehicle dealer in this State. The provisions of G.S. 20-302, 20-305.1, and

20-305.2 that apply to distributors also apply to wholesalers.

History.

1955, c. 1243, s. 2; 1967, c. 1126, s. 1; c. 1173; 1973, c. 1330, s. 39; 1977, c. 560, s. 1; 1983, c. 312; c. 704, ss. 2, 3, 21; 1987, c. 381; 1991, c. 527, s. 1;c. 662, s. 1;1991 (Reg. Sess., 1992), c. 819, s. 23; 1993, c. 331, s. 1;1995, c. 234, s. 1;1997-456. s. 27; 2003-254, s. 1;2003-265, s. 1;2005-409, s. 7;2007-484, s. 6;2015-125, s. 8;2015-209, s. 1;2015-232, s. 1.2;2015-264, s. 42(a);2018-43, s. 3;2019-125, s. 1;2020-73, s. 6

EDITOR'S NOTE. --

The subdivisions of subsection (11) were renumbered pursuant to Session Laws 1997-456, s. 27 which authorized the Revisor of Statutes to renumber or reletter sections and parts of sections having a number or letter designation that is incompatible with the General Assembly's computer database.

Session Laws 2015-209, s. 11 provides: "This act is effective when it becomes law [August 11, 2015] and applies to all current and future franchises and other agreements in existence between any new motor vehicle dealer located in this State and a manufacturer or distributor as of the effective date of this act." Session Laws 2015-209, s. 1, had substituted "a motor vehicle described in sub-subdivision a. of this subdivision" for "described in paragraph (10)a above" at the end of the sentence in subdivision (10)(b).

Session Laws 2019-125, s. 12, is a severability clause.

Session Laws 2019-125, s. 13, made subdivision (15a), as added by Session Laws 2019-125, s. 1, effective July 19, 2019, and applicable to all current and future franchises and other agreements in existence between any new motor vehicle dealer located in this State and a manufacturer or distributor as of that date.

Session Laws 2020-73, s. 7, made sub-subdivision (10)c., as added by Session Laws 2020-73, s. 6, effective December 1, 2020, and applicable to offenses committed on or after that date.

EFFECT OF AMENDMENTS. --

Session Laws 2003-254, s. 1, effective July 1, 2003, and applicable to licenses issued or renewed on or after that date, substituted "2,500 pounds unloaded weight" for "750 pounds and carrying not more than a 1,500 pound load" in subdivision (11)b.5.

Session Laws 2005-409, s. 7, effective September 20, 2005, substituted "that has never been the subject of a completed, successful, or conditional sale that was subsequently approved" for "which has never been the subject of a sale" in subdivision (10)a.

Session Laws 2007-484, s. 6, effective August 30, 2007, in subdivision (8c), substituted "Honesty" for "Honest", deleted "in the trade" following "fair dealing," and substituted "G.S. 25-1-201(b)(20)" for "G.S. 25-2-103(1)(b)".

Session Laws 2015-125, s. 8, effective July 1, 2015, added the last sentence in the introductory language of subdivision (10).

Session Laws 2015-209, s. 1, effective August 11, 2015, substituted "a motor vehicle described in sub-subdivision a. of this subdivision" for "described in paragraph (10)a above" at the end of the sentence in subdivision (10)(b). For applicability, see Editor's note.

Session Laws 2015-232, s. 1.2, effective August 25, 2015, inserted "a new motor vehicle" near the end of the first sentence and added the second sentence in subdivision (10)(a).

Session Laws 2015-264, s. 42.(a), effective October 1, 2015, reconfigured the parsing of the second sentence in subdivision (10)(a).

Session Laws 2018-43, s. 3, effective June 22, 2018, added subdivision (11)b.13.

Session Laws 2019-125, s. 1, added subdivision (15a). For effective date and applicability, see editor's note.

Session Laws 2020-73, s. 6, added sub-subdivision (10)c. For effective date and applicability, see editor's note.

NEGATIVE EQUITY AND GAP INSURANCE DO NOT COME WITHIN THE DEFINITION OF "PURCHASE MONEY OBLIGATION," and thus cannot give rise to a purchase money security interest. Wells Fargo Fin. N.C. 1, Inc. v. Price, 2007 U.S. Dist. LEXIS 97420 (E.D.N.C. Nov. 14, 2007).

"GOOD FAITH" REQUIRED BY § 20-305(6) DEFINED BY THIS SECTION. --Manufacturer's withdrawal from the heavy duty truck market was in good faith as required by G.S. 20-305(6). Carolina Truck & Body Co. v. GMC, 102 N.C. App. 262, 402 S.E.2d 135, cert. denied, 329 N.C. 266, 407 S.E.2d 831 (1991).

EVIDENCE OF GOOD FAITH HELD SUFFICIENT. --Where manufacturer gave dealer at least a year's notice concerning the likelihood of cancellation, manufacturer treated dealer no differently than it did any of its other heavy-duty truck franchisees, and, more importantly, where there was no evidence of dishonesty by manufacturer, the record was replete with evidence of manufacturer's good faith in cancelling its heavy-duty truck franchises with dealer. Carolina Truck & Body Co. v. GMC, 102 N.C. App. 262, 402 S.E.2d 135, cert. denied, 329 N.C. 266, 407 S.E.2d 831 (1991).

RELEVANT MARKET AREA OR TRADE AREA. --The intent of the legislature was to exclude population outside the designated radius, and the Commissioner of the Division of Motor Vehicles erred by including population lying outside the designated radius when determining "relevant market area," though that population was within a census tract partially within that area. Al Smith Buick Co. v. Mazda Motor of Am., Inc., 122 N.C. App. 429, 470 S.E.2d 552 (1996), cert. denied, 473 S.E.2d 609 (1996).

CITED in Star Auto. Co. v. Jaguar Cars, Inc., 95 N.C. App. 103, 382 S.E.2d 226 (1989); Ferris v. Haymore, 967 F.2d 946 (4th Cir. 1992).

CROSS REFERENCES. --

For definitions applicable throughout this Chapter, see G.S. 20-4.01.

LEGAL PERIODICALS. --

For 1984 survey on commercial law, "Green Light to Territorial Security for Automobile Dealers," see 63 N.C.L. Rev. 1080 (1985).

§ 20-287. Licenses required; penalties

(a) **License Required. --** It shall be unlawful for any new motor vehicle dealer, used motor vehicle dealer, motor vehicle sales representative, manufacturer, factory branch, factory representative, distributor, distributor branch, distributor representative, or wholesaler to engage in business in this State without first obtaining a license as provided in this Article. If any motor vehicle dealer acts as a motor vehicle sales representative, the dealer shall obtain a motor vehicle sales representative's license in addition to a motor vehicle dealer's license. A sales representative may have only one license. The license shall show the name of the dealer or wholesaler employing the sales representative. An individual who has submitted an application to the Division for a sales representative license pursuant to G.S. 20-288(a) shall be permitted to engage in activities as a sales representative while the application is pending provided that the sales representative applicant is actively and directly supervised by a licensed motor vehicle dealer or a licensed sales representative designated by the dealer, provided further that the applicant certifies in the application that the applicant has not been previously denied a sales representative license for any dealer by the Division and that the applicant has not been previously convicted of a felony. Any license issued by the Division to a motor vehicle dealer, manufacturer, factory branch, factory representative, distributor, distributor branch, distributor representative, or wholesaler under this Article may not be assigned, sold, or otherwise transferred to any other person or entity.

(b) **Civil Penalty for Violations by Licensee. --** In addition to any other punishment or remedy under the law for any violation of this section, the Division may levy and collect a civil penalty, in an amount not to exceed one thousand dollars ($ 1,000) for each violation, against any person who has obtained a license pursuant to this section, if it finds that the licensee has violated any of the provisions of G.S. 20-285 through G.S. 20-303, Article 15 of this Chapter, or any statute or rule adopted by the Division relating to the sale of vehicles, vehicle titling, or vehicle registration.

(c) **Civil Penalty for Violations by Person Without a License. --** In addition to any other punishment or remedy under the law for any violation of this section, the Division may levy and collect a civil penalty, in an amount not to exceed five thousand dollars ($ 5,000) for each violation, against any person who is required to obtain a license under this section and has not obtained the license, if it finds that the person has violated any of the provisions of G.S. 20-285 through G.S. 20-303, Article 15 of this Chapter, or any statute or rule adopted by the Division relating to the sale of vehicles, vehicle titling, or vehicle registration.

History.
1955, c. 1243, s. 3; 1991, c. 662, s. 2;2001-345, s. 1;2005-99, s. 1;2019-181, s. 1

EDITOR'S NOTE. --

The preamble to Session Laws 2001-345 reads as follows: "Whereas, not only the setting of standards to protect purchasers of motor vehicles but also the enforcement of substantial penalties applicable when those standards are not met is one of the most effective means to obtain this protection; and

"Whereas, more complex laws governing regulation of the sale and distribution of motor vehicles such as the titling of a vehicle, warranties, collection of consumer debt pursuant to Federal Trade Commission regulations, and applicable tax provisions impose a greater number of duties upon independent automobile dealers; and

"Whereas, the most effective and consistent means of informing both applicants for licensure and experienced, licensed motor vehicle dealers of major changes and increasing complexities in the law is to develop a program insuring the development and requirement of appropriate continuing education; Now, therefore."

EFFECT OF AMENDMENTS. --

Session Laws 2001-345, s. 1, effective July 1, 2002, and applicable to violations and offenses committed on or after that date and licenses issued to used motor vehicle dealers on or after that date, added "penalties" to the section catchline; redesignated the text of the former section as present subsection (a) and added the subsection catchline; and added subsections (b) and (c).

Session Laws 2005-99, s. 1, effective January 1, 2006, substituted "name of the dealer" for "name of each dealer" in the fourth sentence of subsection (a).

Session Laws 2019-181, s. 1, effective July 26, 2019, rewrote the last two sentences in subsection (a), which formerly read: "The following license holders may operate as a motor vehicle dealer without obtaining a motor vehicle dealer's license or paying an additional fee: a manufacturer, a factory branch, a distributor, and a distributor branch. Any of these license holders who operates as a motor vehicle dealer may sell motor vehicles at retail only at an established salesroom."

§ 20-288. Application for license; license requirements; expiration of license; bond

(a) A new motor vehicle dealer, motor vehicle sales representative, manufacturer, factory branch, factory representative, distributor,

distributor branch, distributor representative, or wholesaler may obtain a license by filing an application with the Division. An application must be on a form provided by the Division and contain the information required by the Division. An application for a license must be accompanied by the required fee. The following requirements also apply to applicants under this section:

(1) An application for a new motor vehicle dealer license must be accompanied by an application for a dealer license plate. In addition, the Division shall require each applicant for a new motor vehicle dealer license to certify on the application whether the applicant or any parent, subsidiary, affiliate, or any other entity related to the applicant is a manufacturer, factory branch, factory representative, distributor, distributor branch, or distributor representative. In the event the applicant indicates on the application that the applicant or any parent, subsidiary, affiliate, or any other entity related to the applicant is a manufacturer, factory branch, factory representative, distributor, distributor branch, or distributor representative, the Division shall not issue a motor vehicle dealer license to the applicant until both of the following conditions are satisfied:

a. The applicant states on the application the specific exception or exceptions to the prohibition on the issuance of a motor vehicle dealer license to any manufacturer, factory branch, factory representative, distributor, distributor branch, or distributor representative for which the applicant contends it qualifies under G.S. 20-305.2(a).

b. If the applicant does not currently hold a motor vehicle dealer license issued by the Division, the Commissioner determines, after an evidentiary hearing, that the applicant qualifies under one or more of the exceptions to the prohibition against the issuance of a motor vehicle dealer license to any manufacturer, factory branch, factory representative, distributor, distributor branch, or distributor representative provided in G.S. 20-305.2(a). The applicant shall bear the burden of proving the applicant's qualification for the exception or exceptions claimed.

(2) Upon submission of a license application by a manufacturer, factory branch, factory representative, distributor, distributor branch, or distributor representative that has not previously been issued a license by the Division, the Division shall promptly publish notice of the license application in the North Carolina Register.

The notice shall include the applicant's name, address, application date, and the names and titles of any individual listed on the application as an owner, partner, member, or officer of the applicant. The Division shall not approve or issue any license for a manufacturer, factory branch, factory representative, distributor, distributor branch, or distributor representative earlier than 15 days from the date the notice of the license or license renewal application was published in the North Carolina Register.

(a1) A used motor vehicle dealer may obtain a license by filing an application, as prescribed in subsection (a) of this section, and providing the following:

(1) The required fee.

(2) Proof that the applicant, within the last 12 months, has completed a 12-hour licensing course approved by the Division if the applicant is seeking an initial license and a six-hour course approved by the Division if the applicant is seeking a renewal license. The requirements of this subdivision do not apply to a used motor vehicle dealer the primary business of which is the sale of salvage vehicles on behalf of insurers or to a manufactured home dealer licensed under G.S. 143-143.11 who complies with the continuing education requirements of G.S. 143-143.11B. The requirement of this subdivision does not apply to persons age 62 or older as of July 1, 2002, who are seeking a renewal license. This subdivision also does not apply to an applicant who holds a license as a new motor vehicle dealer as defined in G.S. 20-286(13) and operates from an established showroom located in an area within a radius of 30 miles around the location of the established showroom for which the applicant seeks a used motor vehicle dealer license. An applicant who also holds a license as a new motor vehicle dealer may designate a representative to complete the licensing course required by this subdivision.

(3) If the applicant is an individual, proof that the applicant is at least 18 years of age and proof that all salespersons employed by the dealer are at least 18 years of age.

(4) The application for a dealer license plate.

(5) A certification as to whether the applicant or any entity having any common ownership or affiliation with the applicant is a motor vehicle manufacturer, factory branch, factory representative, distributor, distributor branch, or distributor representative. In the event the applicant indicates on the application that the applicant or any parent, subsidiary, affiliate, or any other entity related to the applicant is a

manufacturer, factory branch, factory representative, distributor, distributor branch, or distributor representative, the applicant shall be required to state whether the applicant contends it qualifies for a motor vehicle dealer's license in accordance with any of the exceptions to the prohibition on the issuance of a motor vehicle dealer's license to any manufacturer, factory branch, factory representative, distributor, distributor branch, or distributor representative, as provided in G.S. 20-305.2(a).

(b) The Division shall require in such application, or otherwise, information relating to matters set forth in G.S. 20-294 as grounds for the refusing of licenses, and to other pertinent matters commensurate with the safeguarding of the public interest, all of which shall be considered by the Division in determining the fitness of the applicant to engage in the business for which he seeks a license. The Division shall not require submission of an applicant's fingerprints to be used in performing a criminal history record check of an applicant for a license or license renewal.

(b1) The Division shall require in such license application and each application for renewal of license a certification that the applicant is familiar with the North Carolina Motor Vehicle Dealers and Manufacturers Licensing Law and with other North Carolina laws governing the conduct and operation of the business for which the license or license renewal is sought and that the applicant shall comply with the provisions of these laws, with the provisions of Article 12 of Chapter 20 of the General Statutes, and with other lawful regulations of the Division.

(c) All licenses that are granted shall be for a period of one year unless sooner revoked or suspended. The Division shall vary the expiration dates of all licenses that are granted so that an equal number of licenses expire at the end of each month, quarter, or other period consisting of one or more months to coincide with G.S. 20-79(c).

(d) To obtain a license as a wholesaler, an applicant who intends to sell or distribute self-propelled vehicles must have an established office in this State, and an applicant who intends to sell or distribute only trailers or semitrailers of more than 2,500 pounds unloaded weight must have a place of business in this State where the records required under this Article are kept.

To obtain a license as a motor vehicle dealer, an applicant who intends to deal in self-propelled vehicles must have an established salesroom in this State, and an applicant who intends to deal in only trailers or semitrailers of more than 2,500 pounds unloaded weight must have a place of business in this State where the records required under this Article are kept.

An applicant for a license as a manufacturer, a factory branch, a distributor, a distributor branch, a wholesaler, or a motor vehicle dealer must have a separate license for each established office, established salesroom, or other place of business in this State. An application for any of these licenses shall include a list of the applicant's places of business in this State.

(e) Each applicant approved by the Division for license as a motor vehicle dealer, manufacturer, factory branch, distributor, distributor branch, or wholesaler shall furnish a corporate surety bond or cash bond or fixed value equivalent of the bond. The amount of the bond for an applicant for a motor vehicle dealer's license is fifty thousand dollars ($ 50,000) for one established salesroom of the applicant and twenty-five thousand dollars ($ 25,000) for each of the applicant's additional established salesrooms. The amount of the bond for other applicants required to furnish a bond is fifty thousand dollars ($ 50,000) for one place of business of the applicant and twenty-five thousand dollars ($ 25,000) for each of the applicant's additional places of business.

A corporate surety bond shall be approved by the Commissioner as to form and shall be conditioned that the obligor will faithfully conform to and abide by the provisions of this Article and Article 15. A cash bond or fixed value equivalent thereof shall be approved by the Commissioner as to form and terms of deposits as will secure the ultimate beneficiaries of the bond; and such bond shall not be available for delivery to any person contrary to the rules of the Commissioner. Any purchaser of a motor vehicle, including a motor vehicle dealer, who shall have suffered any loss or damage by the failure of any license holder subject to this subsection to deliver free and clear title to any vehicle purchased from a license holder or any other act of a license holder subject to this subsection that constitutes a violation of this Article or Article 15 of this Chapter shall have the right to institute an action to recover against the license holder and the surety. Every license holder against whom an action is instituted shall notify the Commissioner of the action within 10 days after served with process. Except as provided by G.S. 20-288(f) and (g), a corporate surety bond shall remain in force and effect and may not be canceled by the surety unless the bonded person stops engaging in business or the person's license is denied, suspended, or revoked under G.S. 20-294. That cancellation may be had only upon 30 days' written notice to the Commissioner and shall not affect any liability incurred or accrued prior to the termination of such 30-day period. This subsection does not apply to a license holder who deals only in trailers having an empty weight of 4,000 pounds or less. This subsection does not apply to manufacturers of, or dealers in, mobile or manufactured homes who furnish a corporate surety bond, cash bond, or fixed value equivalent thereof, pursuant to G.S. 143-143.12.

(f) A corporate surety bond furnished pursuant to this section or renewal thereof may also be canceled by the surety prior to the next premium anniversary date without the prior written consent of the license holder for the following reasons:

(1) Nonpayment of premium in accordance with the terms for issuance of the surety bond; or

(2) An act or omission by the license holder or his representative that constitutes substantial and material misrepresentation or nondisclosure of a material fact in obtaining the surety bond or renewing the bond.

Any cancellation permitted by this subsection is not effective unless written notice of cancellation has been delivered or mailed to the license holder and to the Commissioner not less than 30 days before the proposed effective date of cancellation. The notice must be given or mailed by certified mail to the license holder at its last known address. The notice must state the reason for cancellation. Cancellation for nonpayment of premium is not effective if the amount due is paid before the effective date set forth in the notice of cancellation. Cancellation of the surety shall not affect any liability incurred or accrued prior to the termination of the 30-day notice period.

(g) A corporate surety may refuse to renew a surety bond furnished pursuant to this section by giving or mailing written notice of nonrenewal to the license holder and to the Commissioner not less than 30 days prior to the premium anniversary date of the surety bond. The notice must be given or mailed by certified mail to the license holder at its last known address. Nonrenewal of the surety bond shall not affect any liability incurred or accrued prior to the premium anniversary date of the surety bond.

History.
1955, c. 1243, s. 4; 1975, c. 716, s. 5; 1977, c. 560, s. 2; 1979, c. 254; 1981, c. 952, s. 3; 1985, c. 262; 1991, c. 495, s. 1;c. 662, s. 3;1993, c. 440, s. 3;1997-429, s. 1;2001-345, s. 2;2001-492, s. 4;2003-254, s. 2;2004-167, s. 9;2004-199, s. 59;2005-99, s. 2;2006-105, s. 2.3;2006-191, s. 1;2006-259, s. 12;2011-290, ss. 1, 2; 2017-148, s. 1;2019-125, s. 11;2020-77, s. 5(a)

EDITOR'S NOTE. --
The preamble to Session Laws 2001-345 reads: "Whereas, not only the setting of standards to protect purchasers of motor vehicles but also the enforcement of substantial penalties applicable when those standards are not met is one of the most effective means to obtain this protection; and

"Whereas, more complex laws governing regulation of the sale and distribution of motor vehicles such as the titling of a vehicle, warranties, collection of consumer debt pursuant to Federal Trade Commission regulations, and applicable tax provisions impose a greater number of duties upon independent automobile dealers; and

"Whereas, the most effective and consistent means of informing both applicants for licensure and experienced, licensed motor vehicle dealers of major changes and increasing complexities in the law is to develop a program insuring the development and requirement of appropriate continuing education; Now, therefore."

Session Laws 2011-290, which, in ss. 1 and 2, substituted "20 miles" for "one mile" in the next-to-last sentence of subdivision (a1)(2), and added subsection (b1), in s. 12, provided: "The terms and provisions of this act shall be applicable to all current and future franchises and other agreements in existence between any new motor vehicle dealer located in this State and a manufacturer or distributor as of the effective date of this act [June 24, 2011]."

Session Laws 2011-290, s. 13 is a severability clause.

Session Laws 2017-148, s. 6, is a severability clause.

Session Laws 2019-125, s. 12, is a severability clause.

Session Laws 2020-3, s. 4.7(a) -(h), as amended by Session Laws 2020-97, ss. 3.15(a), 3.16(a), provides: "(a) Definition. -- For purposes of this section, 'credential' means any of the following issued by the Division of Motor Vehicles:

"(1) Drivers license.

"(2) Learner's permit.

"(3) Limited learner's permit.

"(4) Limited provisional license.

"(5) Full provisional license.

"(6) Commercial drivers license.

"(7) Commercial learner's permit.

"(8) Temporary driving certificate.

"(9) Special identification card.

"(10) Handicapped placard.

"(11) Vehicle registration.

"(12) Temporary vehicle registration.

"(13) Dealer license plate.

"(14) Transporter plate.

"(15) Loaner/Dealer 'LD' plate.

"(16) Vehicle inspection authorization.

"(17) Inspection station license.

"(18) Inspection mechanic license.

"(19) Transportation network company permit.

"(20) Motor vehicle dealer license.

"(21) Sales representative license.

"(22) Manufacturer license.

"(23) Distributor license.

"(24) Wholesaler license.

"(25) Driver training school license.

"(26) Driver training school instructor license.

"(27) Professional housemoving license.

"(b) Extend Validity of Credentials. -- Notwithstanding renewal, duration, or expiration provisions of G.S. 20-7, 20-11, 20-37.6, 20-37.7, 20-37.13, 20-50,

20-66, 20-79, 20-79.02, 20-79.2, 20-183.4B, 20-183.4D, 20-280.3, 20-288, 20-324, and 20-359, or any other provision of law to the contrary, the Division of Motor Vehicles shall extend for a period of five months the validity of any credential that expires on or after March 1, 2020, and before August 1, 2020. The Division shall extend for a period of five months the validity of any credential listed in subdivisions (6), (7), (9), (10), and (18) of subsection (a) of this section that expires on or after March 1, 2020, and before the date 30 days after the date the Governor (i) rescinds Executive Order No. 116 or (ii) issues another executive order lifting restrictions on Division of Motor Vehicles functions. Notwithstanding G.S. 20-37.13(h) and G.S. 20-37.13A(a), the Division of Motor Vehicles is authorized to waive the requirement that commercial drivers license and commercial learner's permit holders have a medical examination and certification, as required by federal law, consistent with any waiver of medical qualifications standards issued by the Federal Motor Carrier Safety Administration. A credential extended under this section shall expire five months from the date it otherwise expires as prescribed by law prior to this section. However, the subsequent expiration of a credential extended under this section shall occur on the date prescribed by law prior to this section without regard to the extension. The Division shall notify individuals affected by an extension granted under this section, including information on new expiration dates and how the extension affects subsequent renewal and expiration dates.

"(b1) Extension of Intrastate Medical Waivers. -- Notwithstanding the limitation on duration of waivers in G.S. 20-37.13A(b), the Division of Motor Vehicles may extend for up to five months the validity of a medical waiver issued by the Division under G.S. 20-37.13A if the waiver expires on or after March 1, 2020, and before the date 30 days after the date the Governor (i) rescinds Executive Order No. 116 or (ii) issues another executive order lifting restrictions on Division of Motor Vehicles functions, and the Division's Medical Review Unit determines the extension is appropriate.

"(c) Driving Eligibility Certificates. -- Notwithstanding G.S. 20-11(n)(3), a driving eligibility certificate dated on or after February 9, 2020, and before March 10, 2020, remains valid and may be accepted by the Division of Motor Vehicles to meet the requirements for a license or permit issued under G.S. 20-11 until 30 days after the date the Governor rescinds Executive Order No. 116 or the date the Division reopens all drivers license offices, whichever is earlier.

"(d) Waive Penalties. -- Notwithstanding any provision of law to the contrary, the Division shall waive any fines, fees, or penalties associated with failing to renew a credential during the period of time the credential is valid by extension under subsection (b) of this section.

"(e) Motor Vehicle Taxes. -- Notwithstanding any provision of law to the contrary, due dates for motor vehicle taxes that are tied to registration expiration under Article 22A of Chapter 105 of the General Statutes shall be extended to correspond with extended expiration dates under subsection (b) of this section.

"(f) Validity by Extension a Defense. -- A person may not be convicted or found responsible for any offense resulting from failure to renew a credential issued by the Division if, when tried for that offense, the person shows that the offense occurred during the period of time the credential is valid by extension under subsection (b) of this section.

"(g) Report. -- Within 30 days of the extensions made under subsection (b) of this section, the Division shall submit a report to the Joint Legislative Transportation Oversight Committee and the Fiscal Research Division detailing implementation of this section.

"(h) Effective Date. -- This section is effective retroactively to March 1, 2020, and applies to expirations occurring on or after that date."

Session Laws 2020-3, s. 5, is a severability clause.

Session Laws 2020-77, s. 5(c), made the last sentence in subsection (b) of this section, as added by Session Laws 2020-77, s. 5(a), effective July 1, 2020, and applicable to applications for licensure or renewal received on or after that date.

Session Laws 2020-97, s. 4.5, is a severability clause.

EFFECT OF AMENDMENTS. --

Session Laws 2001-345, s. 2, effective July 1, 2002, and applicable to violations and offenses committed on or after that date and licenses issued to used motor vehicle dealers on or after that date, substituted "A new motor vehicle dealer . . . or wholesaler" for "A person" at the beginning of the first sentence of subsection (a); and added subsection (a1).

Session Laws 2003-254, s. 2, effective July 1, 2003, and applicable to licenses issued or renewed on or after that date, in the first and second paragraphs of subsection (d), substituted "more than 2,500 punds" for "less than 2500 pounds."

Session Laws 2004-167, s. 9, as amended by Session Laws 2004-199, s. 59, effective January 1, 2006, in subsection (c), inserted "one year from the date issued" following "shall expire," deleted "sooner" following "unless," and deleted ", on June 30 of the year following the date of issue" following "suspended."

Session Laws 2005-99, s. 2, effective January 1, 2006, rewrote subsection (c).

Session Laws 2006-105, s. 2.3, effective October 1, 2006, substituted "Except as provided by G.S. 20-288(f) and (g), a" for "A" at the beginning of the fifth sentence in the second paragraph of subsection (e); and added subsections (f) and (g).

Session Laws 2006-191, s. 1, effective January 1, 2007, and applicable to applications for used motor vehicle dealer license filed on or after that date, added the fourth and fifth sentences to subdivision (a1)(2).

Session Laws 2006-259, s. 12, effective August 23, 2006, substituted "Nonrenewal" for "cancellation" in subsection (g).

Session Laws 2017-148, s. 1, effective July 20, 2017, substituted "located in an area within a radius of 30 miles around the location of" for "20 miles or less from" in the second to last sentence in subdivision (a1)(2).

Session Laws 2019-125, s. 11, effective July 19, 2019, substituted "fee. The following requirements also apply to applicants under this section:" for "fee and by an application for a dealer license plate" at the end of subsection (a); added subdivisions (a)(1) and (a)(2); and added subdivision (a1)(5).

Session Laws 2020-77, s. 5(a), added the last sentence in subsection (b). For effective date and applicability, see editor's note.

CONSTITUTIONALITY. --Subsection (e) is not unconstitutional in that it unreasonably restricts plaintiff's right to engage in his occupation of manufacturing trailers, since the complexities surrounding the sale, dealer servicing, warranties, financing, titling and registration of motor vehicles makes their distribution a business which easily could be conducted so as to become a medium of fraud and dishonesty; the State's power to regulate such a business includes the right to require a bond or security for the faithful performance of the obligations incident to the business. Hence, the regulation complained of in this case is based upon reasonable grounds, it is not arbitrary, and is therefore a proper exercise of the State's police power. Butler v. Peters, 52 N.C. App. 357, 278 S.E.2d 283, appeal dismissed, 303 N.C. 543, 281 S.E.2d 391 (1981).

The exemption of manufacturers and dealers of trailers of less than 4,000 pounds empty weight from the bonding requirement of this section does not deny equal protection of the law, since, under North Carolina law, trailers weighing less than 4,000 pounds are exempt from brake requirements, directional signals, lighting requirements, and clearance lamps; smaller trailers cost less, are of simpler construction, and involve warranty problems of less magnitude; and the difference in treatment between trailers over 4,000 pounds and trailers less than 4,000 pounds therefore has a reasonable basis in relation to the purpose of statute in question. Butler v. Peters, 52 N.C. App. 357, 278 S.E.2d 283, appeal dismissed, 303 N.C. 543, 281 S.E.2d 391 (1981).

THE TWO HURDLES TO RECOVERY THAT NEED TO BE OVERCOME WITHIN SUBSECTION (E) are 1) the dealer's violation of either Article 12 or Article 15 of this Chapter, and 2) the suffering of damages and losses by the consumer. Tomlinson v. Camel City Motors, Inc., 330 N.C. 76, 408 S.E.2d 853 (1991).

G. S. 20-294(4) DOES NOT ENLARGE COVERAGE OF SUBSECTION (E). --G.S. 20-294(4) only sets out grounds for which the State may suspend or revoke a license. It does not enlarge the coverage of subsection (e) of this section to any parties other than a purchaser. Triplett v. James, 45 N.C. App. 96, 262 S.E.2d 374, cert. denied, 300 N.C. 202, 269 S.E.2d 621 (1980).

Subsection (e) of this section grants only to purchasers the right to recover on the bond, and the fact that, under G.S. 20-294(4), a dealer may lose his license for defrauding any person in the conduct of his business does not mean that the bond specifically required by subsection (e) and specifically limited by that section

as a source of indemnity to purchasers only is available as a remedy to any defrauded party. Triplett v. James, 45 N.C. App. 96, 262 S.E.2d 374, cert. denied, 300 N.C. 202, 269 S.E.2d 621 (1980).

THE PRACTICE OF FRAUD BY AN AUTOMOBILE DEALER UPON A PURCHASER is a violation of Article 12 of this Chapter for purposes of subsection (e). Tomlinson v. Camel City Motors, Inc., 330 N.C. 76, 408 S.E.2d 853 (1991).

ONLY PURCHASERS OF MOTOR VEHICLES MAY RECOVER UNDER A MOTOR VEHICLE SURETY BOND. Fink v. Stallings 601 Sales, Inc., 64 N.C. App. 604, 307 S.E.2d 829 (1983).

SELLER AS PURCHASER. --Although plaintiff had already contracted to resell vehicle that turned out to be stolen prior to its purchase, he qualified as an aggrieved purchaser and was entitled to recover under surety bond. Perkins v. Helms, 133 N.C. App. 620, 515 S.E.2d 906 (1999).

JOINT VENTURER NOT ELIGIBLE TO RECOVER ON BOND. --Although plaintiff's testimony indicated that he tendered money to defendant and received title to a cadillac in return, the relationship of the parties was primarily that of joint venturers rather than seller-purchaser; whereby the two engaged in a short-term business deal for joint profit, with contributions of effort from each and risk taken by each, and as a joint venturer, plaintiff was not a purchaser under the ordinary meaning of the word and therefore could not recover on the bond secured to comply with this section. Taylor v. Johnson, 84 N.C. App. 116, 351 S.E.2d 831 (1987).

SCOPE OF CAUSE OF ACTION AGAINST SURETY. --North Carolina's motor vehicle dealer suretyship statute provides a cause of action against both the dealer and surety to "[a]ny purchaser" of a motor vehicle who suffers loss or damage as a result of a dealer's violation of the state's odometer law. Consistent with the plain language of the statute, North Carolina courts have refused relief to injured parties who did not "purchase" an illegally altered vehicle. Ferris v. Haymore, 967 F.2d 946 (4th Cir. 1992).

The statute creates a cause of action in favor of "any purchaser," which includes in-state and out-of-state purchasers. Ferris v. Haymore, 967 F.2d 946 (4th Cir. 1992).

ACCRUAL OF CAUSE OF ACTION AGAINST SURETY. --Causes of action of truck purchaser against dealer and against dealer's surety under a motor vehicle dealer surety bond both arose when purchaser discovered dealer's breach of contract or fraud, and could be no later than the date on which purchaser filed a complaint against the dealer in the superior court. And as nothing prevented purchaser from joining both defendants in one action or from instituting a separate action against surety while the case against dealer was pending, the three-year statute of limitations of G.S. 1-52(1) was not tolled. Bernard v. Ohio Cas. Ins. Co., 79 N.C. App. 306, 339 S.E.2d 20 (1986).

A plaintiff's cause of action against a surety begins to run when the fraud is discovered. Ferris v. Haymore, 967 F.2d 946 (4th Cir. 1992).

The cause of action against a surety under a motor vehicle dealer surety bond arises at the time that the cause of action arises against the surety's principal. Ferris v. Haymore, 967 F.2d 946 (4th Cir. 1992).

FACT THAT SURETY DID NOT APPEAL FROM UNDERLYING JUDGMENT AGAINST CAR DEALER did not mean that the surety should pay the entire award. At the time that the default judgment was entered against dealer, its principal, the surety could raise only defenses concerning the substance of the claims. The surety was entitled thereafter to assert this section in its own defense to buyer's claim. Tomlinson v. Camel City Motors, Inc., 330 N.C. 76, 408 S.E.2d 853 (1991).

SURETY NOT LIABLE FOR TREBLE DAMAGES. --Where dealer did not pay buyer's monthly car payments as required by agreement, the total of the unpaid payments was the amount "suffered" by the plaintiff; she did not "suffer" further compensatory damages. Thus under this section the surety was not liable for the trebled portion of damages imposed under G.S. 75-16. Tomlinson v. Camel City Motors, Inc., 330 N.C. 76, 408 S.E.2d 853 (1991).

The purchaser of an automobile is entitled to recover against a surety only to the extent of "loss or damage" actually "suffered" as a result of the fraudulent conduct by the surety's principal. The purchaser is not entitled to recover punitive treble damages. Ferris v. Haymore, 967 F.2d 946 (4th Cir. 1992).

BANK SUBROGATED TO RIGHTS OF PURCHASERS. --Bank, which after dealer sold used vehicles with unpaid first liens in which it had a security interest to eight customers, entered into agreements with each of the customers providing that it would pay off the prior liens and that in return the customers would assign their claims against dealer and surety to it, pursuant to which agreements it extinguished all prior liens on the encumbered vehicles so that the customers received title to their vehicles reflecting bank as first lienholder, was subrogated to all the claims of the customers against defendant surety, and thus had a right to sue the dealer on the bonds issued by defendant surety. NCNB Nat'l Bank v. Western Sur. Co., 88 N.C. App. 705, 364 S.E.2d 675 (1988).

Where a subrogee obtained a default judgment that subrogated the subrogee to the rights of a purchaser, the subrogee could sue on a surety bond issued pursuant to G.S. 20-288(e) and a surety could not collaterally attack the judgment; summary judgment in favor of the subrogee was proper. Reg'l Acceptance Corp. v. Old Republic Sur. Co., 156 N.C. App. 680, 577 S.E.2d 391 (2003).

SURETY HELD LIABLE ON BONDS. --Under the facts, defendant's act of selling used automobiles with outstanding liens was in violation of this Article, thereby invoking the liability of the surety to pay on the bonds issued to plaintiff bank as assignee of the rights, claims and title of car purchasers. NCNB Nat'l Bank v. Western Sur. Co., 88 N.C. App. 705, 364 S.E.2d 675 (1988).

TOTAL AMOUNT OF BOND RECOVERY. --Bond purchased in the middle of the first year entitled recovery of $25,000 for each of the three license years during which it was effective, not an aggregate total

of $25,000 for the three years. Perkins v. Helms, 133 N.C. App. 620, 515 S.E.2d 906 (1999).

APPLIED in Tomlinson v. Camel City Motors, Inc., 101 N.C. App. 419, 399 S.E.2d 147 (1991); Nixon v. Alan Vester Auto Group, Inc., 2009 U.S. Dist. LEXIS 10870 (M.D.N.C. Feb. 12, 2009).

CITED in Randolph County v. Coen, 99 N.C. App. 746, 394 S.E.2d 256 (1990); George v. Hartford Accident & Indem. Co., 330 N.C. 755, 412 S.E.2d 43 (1992); Krause v. Rk Motors, 252 N.C. App. 135, 797 S.E.2d 335 (2017).

LEGAL PERIODICALS. --

For survey on consumer law, see 70 N.C.L. Rev. 1959 (1992).

§ 20-289. License fees

(a) The license fee for each fiscal year, or part thereof, shall be as follows:

(1) For motor vehicle dealers, distributors, distributor branches, and wholesalers, ninety dollars ($ 90.00) for each place of business.

(2) For manufacturers, one hundred ninety-five dollars ($ 195.00) and for each factory branch in this State, one hundred thirty dollars ($ 130.00).

(3) For motor vehicle sales representatives, twenty dollars ($ 20.00).

(4) For factory representatives, or distributor representatives, twenty dollars ($ 20.00).

(5) Repealed by Session Laws 1991, c. 662, s. 4.

(b) The fees collected under this section shall be credited to the Highway Fund. These fees are in addition to all other taxes and fees.

History.

1955, c. 1243, s. 5; 1969, c. 593; 1977, c. 802, s. 8; 1981, c. 690, s. 16; 1991, c. 662, s. 4;c. 689, s. 335;2005-276, s. 44.1(o);2015-241, s. 29.30(p)

EDITOR'S NOTE. --

Session Laws 2015-241, s. 1.1, provides: "This act shall be known as 'The Current Operations and Capital Improvements Appropriations Act of 2015.'"

Session Laws 2015-241, s. 29.30(u), made the amendment to subsection (a) of this section by Session Laws 2015-241, s. 29.30(p), applicable to issuances, renewals, restorations, and requests on or after January 1, 2016.

Session Laws 2015-241, s. 33.6, is a severability clause.

EFFECT OF AMENDMENTS. --

Session Laws 2005-276, s. 44.1(o), effective October 1, 2005, and applicable to fees collected on or after that date, in subdivision (a)(1), substituted "seventy dollars ($70.00)" for "fifty dollars ($50.00)"; in subdivision (a)(2), substituted "one hundred fifty dollars ($150.00)" for "one hundred dollars ($100.00)" and "one hundred dollars ($100.00)" for "seventy dollars ($70.00)"; and in subdivisions (a)(3) and (a)(4), substituted "fifteen dollars ($15.00)" for "ten dollars ($10.00)."

Session Laws 2015-241, s. 29.30(p), effective January 1, 2016, rewrote the dollar amounts throughout subsection (a). For applicability, see editor's note.

§ 20-290. Licenses to specify places of business; display of license and list of salesmen; advertising

(a) The license of a motor vehicle dealer shall list each of the dealer's established salesrooms in this State. A license of a manufacturer, factory branch, distributor, distributor branch, or wholesaler shall list each of the license holder's places of business in this State. A license shall be conspicuously displayed at each place of business. In the event the location of a business changes, the Division shall endorse the change of location on the license, without charge.

(b) Each dealer shall keep a current list of his licensed salesmen, showing the name of each licensed salesman, posted in a conspicuous place in each place of business.

(c) Whenever any licensee places an advertisement in any newspaper or publication, the licensee's name shall appear in the advertisement.

History.

1955, c. 1243, s. 6; 1975, c. 716, s. 5; 1991, c. 662, s. 5;2005-99, s. 3

EFFECT OF AMENDMENTS. --

Session Laws 2005-99, s. 3, effective January 1, 2006, in subsection (b), substituted "the name of each licensed salesman" for "names, addresses, and serial numbers of their licenses"; and in subsection (c), substituted "licensee's name shall appear in the advertisement" for "type and serial number of license shall appear therein."

§ 20-291. Representatives to carry license and display it on request; license to name employer

Every person to whom a sales representative, factory representative, or distributor representative license is issued shall carry the license when engaged in business, and shall display it upon request. The license shall state the name of the representative's employer. If the representative changes employers, the representative shall immediately apply to the Division for a license that states the name of the representative's new employer. The fee for issuing a license stating the name of a new employer is ten dollars ($ 10.00).

History.

1955, c. 1243, s. 7; 1975, c. 716, s. 5; 1991, c. 662, s. 6;c. 689, s. 336;2005-99, s. 4;2005-276, s. 44.1(r)

EFFECT OF AMENDMENTS. --

Session Laws 2005-99, s. 4, effective January 1, 2006, deleted "one-half" following "a new employer is" in the last sentence.

Session Laws 2005-276, s. 44.1(r), effective October 1, 2005, and applicable to fees collected on or after that date, substituted "ten dollars ($10.00)" for "one-half the fee set in G.S. 20-289 for an annual license."

§ 20-292. Dealers may display motor vehicles for sale at retail only at established salesrooms

A new or used motor vehicle dealer may display a motor vehicle for sale at retail only at the dealer's established salesroom, unless the display is of a motor vehicle that meets any of the following descriptions:

(1) Contains the dealer's name or other sales information and is used by the dealer as a "demonstrator" for transportation purposes.

(2) Is displayed at a trade show or exhibit at which no selling activities relating to the vehicle take place.

(3) Is displayed at the home or place of business of a customer at the request of the customer.

This section does not apply to recreational vehicles, house trailers, or boat, animal, camping, or other utility trailers.

History.

1955, c. 1243, s. 8; 1991, c. 662, s. 7

§ 20-292.1. Supplemental temporary license for sale of antique and specialty vehicles

Any dealer licensed as a motor vehicle dealer under this Article may apply to the Commissioner and receive, at no additional charge, a supplemental temporary license authorizing the off-premises sales of antique motor vehicles and specialty motor vehicles for a period not to exceed 10 consecutive calendar days. To obtain a temporary supplemental license for the off-premises sale of antique motor vehicles and specialty motor vehicles, the applicant shall:

(1) Be licensed as a motor vehicle dealer under this Article.

(2) Notify the applicable local office of the Division of the specific dates and location for which the license is requested.

(3) Display a sign at the licensed location clearly identifying the dealer.

(4) Keep and maintain the records required for the sale of motor vehicles under this Article.

(5) Provide staff to work at the temporary location for the duration of the off-premises sale.

(6) Meet any local government permitting requirements.

(7) Have written permission from the property owner to sell at the location.

For purposes of this section, the term "antique motor vehicle" shall mean any motor vehicle for private use manufactured at least 25 years prior to the current model year, and the term "specialty motor vehicle" shall mean any model or series of motor vehicle for private use manufactured at least three years prior to the current model year of which no more than 5,000 vehicles were sold within the United States during the model year the vehicle was manufactured.

This section does not apply to a nonselling motor vehicle show or public display of new motor vehicles.

History.
2003-113, s. 1

EDITOR'S NOTE. --
This section was originally enacted by Session Laws 2003-113, s. 1, as G.S. 20-293. It was renumbered as G.S. 20-292.1 at the direction of the Revisor of Statutes.

N.C. Gen. Stat. § 20-293

Repealed by Session Laws 1993, c. 440, s. 10.

§ 20-294. Grounds for denying, suspending, placing on probation, or revoking licenses

The Division may deny, suspend, place on probation, or revoke a license issued under this Article for any one or more of the following grounds:

(1) Making a material misstatement in an application for a license.

(2) Willfully and intentionally failing to comply with this Article, Article 15 of this Chapter, or G.S. 20-52.1, 20-75, 20-79.1, 20-79.2, 20-108, 20-109, 20-109.3, or a rule adopted by the Division under this Article.

(3) Failing to have an established salesroom, if the license holder is a motor vehicle dealer, or failing to have an established office, if the license holder is a wholesaler.

(4) Willfully defrauding any retail buyer, to the buyer's damage, or any other person in the conduct of the licensee's business.

(5) Employing fraudulent devices, methods or practices in connection with compliance with the requirements under the laws of this State with respect to the retaking of motor vehicles under retail installment contracts and the redemption and resale of such motor vehicles.

(6) Using unfair methods of competition or unfair deceptive acts or practices.

(7) Knowingly advertising by any means, any assertion, representation or statement of fact which is untrue, misleading or deceptive in any particular relating to the conduct of the business licensed or for which a license is sought.

(8) Knowingly advertising a used motor vehicle for sale as a new motor vehicle.

(9) Being convicted of an offense set forth under G.S. 20-106, 20-106.1, 20-107, or 20-112 while holding such a license or within five years next preceding the date of filing the application; or being convicted of a felony involving moral turpitude under the laws of this State, another state, or the United States.

(10) Submitting a bad check to the Division of Motor Vehicles in payment of highway use taxes collected by the licensee.

(11) Knowingly giving an incorrect certificate of title, or failing to give a certificate of title to a purchaser, a lienholder, or the Division, as appropriate, after a vehicle is sold.

(12) Making a material misstatement in an application for a dealer license plate.

(13) Failure to pay a civil penalty imposed under G.S. 20-287.

History.
1955, c. 1243, s. 10; 1963, c. 1102; 1967, c. 1126, s. 2; 1975, c. 716, s. 5; 1977, c. 560, s. 3; 1983, c. 704, s. 4; 1985, c. 687; ss. 1, 2; 1991, c. 193, s. 2;1993, c. 440, s. 11;2001-345, ss. 3, 4; 2010-132, s. 16;2014-108, s. 5(a);2018-43, s. 4

EDITOR'S NOTE. --
The preamble of Session Laws 2001-345, reads: "Whereas, not only the setting of standards to protect purchasers of motor vehicles but also the enforcement of substantial penalties applicable when those standards are not met is one of the most effective means to obtain this protection; and

"Whereas, more complex laws governing regulation of the sale and distribution of motor vehicles such as the titling of a vehicle, warranties, collection of consumer debt pursuant to Federal Trade Commission regulations, and applicable tax provisions impose a greater number of duties upon independent automobile dealers; and

"Whereas, the most effective and consistent means of informing both applicants for licensure and experienced, licensed motor vehicle dealers of major changes and increasing complexities in the law is to develop a program insuring the development and requirement of appropriate continuing education; Now, therefore."

EFFECT OF AMENDMENTS. --
Session Laws 2001-345, ss. 3 and 4, effective July 1, 2002, and applicable to violations and offenses committed on or after that date and licenses issued to used motor vehicle dealers on or after that date, substituted "20-79.1" for "20-82" in subdivision (2); and added subdivision (13).

Chapter 20

Session Laws 2010-132, s. 16, effective December 1, 2010, and applicable to offenses committed on or after that date, inserted "20-79.2" in subdivision (2).

Session Laws 2014-108, s. 5(a), effective October 1, 2014, inserted "placing on probation" in the section heading and inserted "place on probation" in the introductory paragraph.

Session Laws 2018-43, s. 4, effective June 22, 2018, inserted "20-109.3" in subdivision (2).

SUBDIVISION (4) DOES NOT ENLARGE COVERAGE OF G.S. 20-288(E). --Subsection (4) of this section only sets out grounds for which the State may suspend or revoke a license. It does not enlarge the coverage of G.S. 20-288(e) to any parties other than a purchaser. Triplett v. James, 45 N.C. App. 96, 262 S.E.2d 374, cert. denied, 300 N.C. 202, 269 S.E.2d 621 (1980).

G.

S. 20-288(e) grants only to purchasers the right to recover on the bond, and the fact that, under subdivision (4) of this section, a dealer may lose his license for defrauding any person in the conduct of his business does not mean that the bond specifically required by G.S. 20-288(e) and specifically limited by that section as a source of indemnity to purchasers only is available as a remedy to any defrauded party. Triplett v. James, 45 N.C. App. 96, 262 S.E.2d 374, cert. denied, 300 N.C. 202, 269 S.E.2d 621 (1980).

DEALER'S FRAUDULENT INDUCEMENT. --Where dealer induced plaintiff to purchase a car by telling her that the dealer would make the remaining installment payments on the old car if the purchaser would trade it in with the dealer for another car, and these promised payments were not made, this fraudulent inducement by the dealer violated this section. Tomlinson v. Camel City Motors, Inc., 330 N.C. 76, 408 S.E.2d 853 (1991).

MORAL TURPITUDE. --Contrary to plaintiff's contention, the term "moral turpitude" is deeply rooted in American Law. The Supreme Court has defined crimes involving moral turpitude as acts of baseness, vileness, or depravity in the private and social duties that man owes to his fellowman or to society in general. Dew v. State ex rel. N.C. DMV, 127 N.C. App. 309, 488 S.E.2d 836 (1997).

MORAL TURPITUDE SHOWN. --The Court of Appeals held that as a matter of law the felony of conspiracy to possess with intent to distribute marijuana is a crime involving moral turpitude. Dew v. State ex rel. N.C. DMV, 127 N.C. App. 309, 488 S.E.2d 836 (1997).

APPLIED in Nixon v. Alan Vester Auto Group, Inc., 2009 U.S. Dist. LEXIS 10870 (M.D.N.C. Feb. 12, 2009).

CITED in NCNB Nat'l Bank v. Western Sur. Co., 88 N.C. App. 705, 364 S.E.2d 675 (1988).

OPINIONS OF THE ATTORNEY GENERAL

PRICE PROHIBITED BY SUBDIVISION (6). --Subdivision (6) of the section prohibits a licensed motor vehicle dealer from advertising, publishing, or representing a price which does not include all charges which constitute the total price to the retail customer, except the North Carolina sales tax. Opinion of Attorney General to Mr. Gonzalie Rivers, License and Theft Division, Department of Motor Vehicles, 43 N.C.A.G. 135 (1973).

§ 20-295. Action on application; grace period while application for license renewal is pending

(a) **Division Action. --** The Division shall either grant or deny an application for a license or license renewal within 30 days after receiving it. Any applicant denied a license shall, upon filing a written request within 30 days, be given a hearing at the time and place determined by the Commissioner or a person designated by the Commissioner. A hearing shall be public and shall be held with reasonable promptness.

(b) **Pending License Renewal Grace Period. --** When an application for license renewal has been timely submitted prior to expiration of the license, the license shall remain valid for up to 30 days after the expiration date until the Division grants or denies the application. The Division shall ensure that any database maintained by the Division that indicates the status of a license issued under this Article reflects that the license continues to be valid during this period.

History.
1955, c. 1243, s. 11; 1975, c. 716, s. 5; 1993, c. 440, s. 1; 2020-77, s. 6(a)

EDITOR'S NOTE. --

Session Laws 2020-77, s. 6(b), made the rewriting of this section by Session Laws 2020-77, s. 6(a), effective July 1, 2020, and applicable to licenses that expire on or after that date.

EFFECT OF AMENDMENTS. --

Session Laws 2020-77, s. 6(a), rewrote the section. For effective date and applicability, see editor's note.

§ 20-296. Notice and hearing upon denial, suspension, revocation, placing on probation, or refusal to renew license

No license shall be suspended, revoked, denied, placed on probation, or renewal thereof refused, until a written notice of the complaint made has been furnished to the licensee against whom the same is directed, and a hearing thereon has been had before the Commissioner, or a person designated by him. At least 10 days' written notice of the time and place of such hearing shall be given to the licensee by certified mail with return receipt requested to his last known address as shown on his license or other record of information in possession of the Division. At any such hearing, the licensee shall have the right to be heard personally or by counsel. After hearing, the Division shall have power to suspend, revoke, place on probation, or refuse to renew the license in question. Immediate notice of any such action shall be given to the licensee in accordance with G.S. 1A-1, Rule 4(j) of the Rules of Civil Procedure.

History.

1955, c. 1243, s. 12; 1975, c. 716, s. 5; 1981, c. 108; 2014-108, s. 6(a)

EDITOR'S NOTE. --

Session Laws 2014-108, s. 6(b) made amendments to this section by Session Laws 2014-108, s. 6(a), effective October 1, 2014, and applicable to notices given on or after that date.

EFFECT OF AMENDMENTS. --

Session Laws 2014-108, s. 6(a), inserted "placing on probation" in the section heading and in the section text, substituted "suspended, revoked, denied, placed on probation" for "suspended or revoked or denied" in the first sentence and in the last sentence inserted "place on probation" and substituted "accordance with G.S. 1A-1, Rule 4(j) of the Rules of Civil Procedure" for "the manner herein provided in the case of notices of hearing." See Editor's note for effective date and applicability.

§ 20-297. Retention and inspection of certain records

(a) **Vehicles.** -- A dealer must keep a record of all vehicles received by the dealer and all vehicles sold by the dealer. The records must contain the information that the Division requires and be made available for inspection by the Division within a reasonable period of time after being requested by the Division. A dealer may satisfy the record-keeping requirements contained in this subsection either by (i) keeping and maintaining written or paper records at the dealership facility where the vehicles were sold or at another site within this State provided that the location and the name of a designated contact agent are provided to the Division or (ii) maintaining electronic copies of the records required by this subsection, provided that the Division shall have access to these electronic records from a location within this State. For purposes of this section, the location where dealership written or electronic records are kept and maintained may be owned and operated by a party other than the dealer.

(b) **Inspection.** -- The Division may inspect the pertinent books, records, letters, and contracts of a licensee relating to any written complaint made to the Division against the licensee.

(c) **Records Format.** -- Any record required to be kept and maintained under this section may be converted to electronic form and retained by a dealer in electronic form without retention of the original or any copies of the record in paper or other nonelectronic form.

History.

1955, c. 1243, s. 13; 1975, c. 716, s. 5; 1995, c. 163, s. 5;2007-481, s. 3;2016-74, s. 1

EDITOR'S NOTE. --

Session Laws 2016-74, s. 2, provides: "The Department of Transportation, Division of Motor Vehicles, shall adopt rules consistent with the provisions of this act. Rules adopted pursuant to this section shall not be subject to G.S. 150B-19.1(e), 150B-19.1(f), and 150B-21.4."

EFFECT OF AMENDMENTS. --

Session Laws 2007-481, s. 3, effective August 30, 2007, added the last sentence in subsection (a).

Session Laws 2016-74, s. 1, effective June 30, 2016, rewrote subsection (a); and added subsection (c).

§ 20-297.1. Franchise-related form agreements

(a) All franchise-related form agreements, as defined in this subsection, offered to a motor vehicle dealer in this State shall provide that all terms and conditions in the agreement inconsistent with any of the laws or rules of this State are of no force and effect. For purposes of this section, the term "franchise-related form agreements" means one or more contracts between a franchised motor vehicle dealer and a manufacturer, factory branch, distributor, or distributor branch, including a written communication from a manufacturer or distributor in which a duty is imposed on the franchised motor vehicle dealer under which:

    (1) The franchised motor vehicle dealer is granted the right to sell and service new motor vehicles manufactured or distributed by the manufacturer or distributor or only to service motor vehicles under the contract and a manufacturer's warranty;

    (2) The franchised motor vehicle dealer is a component of the manufacturer or distributor's distribution system as an independent business;

    (3) The franchised motor vehicle dealer is substantially associated with the manufacturer or distributor's trademark, trade name, and commercial symbol;

    (4) The franchised motor vehicle dealer's business substantially relies on the manufacturer or distributor for a continued supply of motor vehicles, parts, and accessories; or

    (5) Any right, duty, or obligation granted or imposed by this Chapter is affected.

(b) Notwithstanding the terms of any franchise or agreement, it shall be unlawful for any manufacturer, factory branch, distributor, or distributor branch to offer to a dealer, revise, modify, or replace a franchise-related form agreement, as defined above in this section, which agreement, modification, or replacement may adversely affect or alter the rights, obligations, or liability of a motor vehicle dealer or may adversely impair the sales, service obligations, investment, or profitability of any motor vehicle dealer located in this State, unless:

    (1) The manufacturer, factory branch, distributor, or distributor branch provides prior

Chapter 20

written notice by registered or certified mail to each affected dealer, the Commissioner, and the North Carolina Automobile Dealers Association, Inc., of the modification or replacement in the form and within the time frame set forth within this section and in subsection (c) of this section; and

(2) If a protest is filed under this section, the Commissioner approves the modification or replacement.

(c) The notice required by subdivision (b)(1) of this section shall:

(1) Be given not later than the 60th day before the effective date of the modification or replacement;

(2) Contain on its first page a conspicuous statement that reads: "NOTICE TO DEALER: YOU MAY BE ENTITLED TO FILE A PROTEST WITH THE COMMISSIONER OF THE NORTH CAROLINA DIVISION OF MOTOR VEHICLES AND HAVE A HEARING IN WHICH YOU MAY PROTEST THE PROPOSED INITIAL OFFERING, MODIFICATION, OR REPLACEMENT OF CERTAIN FRANCHISE-RELATED FORM AGREEMENTS UNDER THE TERMS OF THE MOTOR VEHICLE DEALERS AND MANUFACTURERS LICENSING LAW, IF YOU OPPOSE THIS ACTION"; and

(3) Contain a separate letter or statement that identifies all substantive modifications or revisions and the principal reasons for each such modification or revision.

(d) A franchised dealer may file a protest with the Commissioner of the offering, modification, or replacement pursuant to this section not later than the latter of:

(1) The 60th day after the date of the receipt of the notice; or

(2) The time specified in the notice.

(e) After a protest is filed, the Commissioner shall determine whether the manufacturer, factory branch, distributor, or distributor branch has established by a preponderance of the evidence that there is good cause for the proposed offering, modification, or replacement. The prior franchise-related form agreement, if any, continues in effect until the Commissioner resolves the protest.

(f) The Commissioner is authorized and directed to investigate and prevent violations of this section, including inconsistencies of any franchise-related form agreement with the provisions of this Article.

(g) Nothing contained in this section shall in any way limit a dealer's rights under any other provision of this Article or other applicable law.

History.
1997-319, s. 1; 2005-409, s. 1

EFFECT OF AMENDMENTS. --
Session Laws 2005-409, s. 1, effective September 20, 2005, rewrote this section.

§ 20-298. Insurance

It shall be unlawful for any dealer or salesman or any employee of any dealer, to coerce or offer anything of value to any purchaser of a motor vehicle to provide any type of insurance coverage on said motor vehicle. No dealer, salesman or representative of either shall accept any policy as collateral on any vehicle sold by him to secure an interest in such vehicle in any company not qualified under the insurance laws of this State: Provided, nothing in this Article shall prevent a dealer or his representative from requiring adequate insurance coverage on a motor vehicle which is the subject of an installment sale.

History.
1955, c. 1243, s. 14

§ 20-298.1. Provision of certain products and services to those covered under the Military Lending Act

A motor vehicle dealer that does not market or extend to a covered borrower a loan or credit transaction covered by Section 987 of Title 10 of the United States Code, or any subsequent amendments thereto, and Part 232 (commencing with Section 232.1) of Subchapter M of Chapter I of Subtitle A of Title 32 of the Code of Federal Regulations, or any subsequent amendments thereto, shall not be in violation of G.S. 127B-11 or otherwise under the law with respect to all transactions entered into on or after October 3, 2016, regardless of whether the motor vehicle dealer markets or extends the loan or credit transaction to other persons who are not covered borrowers. For purposes of this section, "covered borrower" has the same meaning as provided in Part 232 (commencing with Section 232.1) of Subchapter M of Chapter I of Subtitle A of Title 32 of the Code of Federal Regulations and any subsequent amendments thereto.

History.
2019-181, s. 4
EDITOR'S NOTE. --
Session Laws 2019-181, s. 6, made this section effective July 26, 2019.

§ 20-299. Acts of officers, directors, partners, salesmen and other representatives

(a) If a licensee is a copartnership or a corporation, it shall be sufficient cause for the denial, suspension or revocation of a license that any officer, director or partner of the copartnership or corporation has committed any act or omitted any duty which would be cause for refusing, suspending or revoking a license to such party as an individual. Each licensee shall be responsible for the acts of any or all of his salesmen while acting as his agent.

(b) Every licensee who is a manufacturer or a factory branch shall be responsible for the acts of any or all of its agents and representatives while acting in the conduct of said licensee's business whether or not such licensee approved, authorized, or had knowledge of such acts.

History.
1955, c. 1243, s. 15; 1973, c. 559

§ 20-300. Appeals from actions of Commissioner

Appeals from actions of the Commissioner shall be governed by the provisions of Chapter 150B of the General Statutes.

History.
1955, c. 1243, s. 16; 1973, c. 1331, s. 3; 1987, c. 827, s. 1
REVIEW OF A DECISION BY THE COMMISSIONER OF MOTOR VEHICLES is governed by G.S. 150A-51 (see now G.S. 150B-51). GMC v. Kinlaw, 78 N.C. App. 521, 338 S.E.2d 114 (1985).

THE STANDARD OF REVIEW for the court of appeals of a decision by the Commissioner of Motor Vehicles is governed by G.S. 150A-51 (recodified as G.S. 150B-51). Carolina Truck & Body Co. v. GMC, 102 N.C. App. 262, 402 S.E.2d 135, cert. denied, 329 N.C. 266, 407 S.E.2d 831 (1991).

APPLIED in Smith's Cycles, Inc. v. Alexander, 27 N.C. App. 382, 219 S.E.2d 282 (1975).

CITED in State ex rel. N.C. Utils. Comm'n v. Old Fort Finishing Plant, 264 N.C. 416, 142 S.E.2d 8 (1965); Star Auto. Co. v. Jaguar Cars, Inc., 95 N.C. App. 103, 382 S.E.2d 226 (1989).

§ 20-301. Powers of Commissioner

(a) The Commissioner shall promote the interests of the retail buyer of motor vehicles.

(b) The Commissioner shall have power to prevent unfair methods of competition and unfair or deceptive acts or practices and other violations of this Article. Any franchised new motor vehicle dealer who believes that a manufacturer, factory branch, distributor, or distributor branch with whom the dealer holds a currently valid franchise has violated or is currently violating any provision of this Article may file a petition before the Commissioner setting forth the factual and legal basis for such violations. The Commissioner shall promptly forward a copy of the petition to the named manufacturer, factory branch, distributor, or distributor branch

requesting a reply to the petition within 30 days. Allowing for sufficient time for the parties to conduct discovery, the Commissioner or his designee shall then hold an evidentiary hearing and render findings of fact and conclusions of law based on the evidence presented. Any parties to a hearing by the Commissioner concerning the establishment or relocating of a new motor vehicle dealer shall have a right of review of the decision in a court of competent jurisdiction pursuant to Chapter 150B of the General Statutes.

(c) The Commissioner shall have the power in hearings arising under this Article to enter scheduling orders and limit the time and scope of discovery; to determine the date, time, and place where hearings are to be held; to subpoena witnesses; to take depositions of witnesses; and to administer oaths.

(d) The Commissioner may, whenever he shall believe from evidence submitted to him that any person has been or is violating any provision of this Article, in addition to any other remedy, bring an action in the name of the State against that person and any other persons concerned or in any way participating in, or about to participate in practices or acts so in violation, to enjoin any persons from continuing the violations.

(e) The Commissioner may issue rules and regulations to implement the provisions of this section and to establish procedures related to administrative proceedings commenced under this section.

(f) In the event that a dealer, who is permitted or required to file a notice, protest, or petition before the Commissioner within a certain period of time in order to adjudicate, enforce, or protect rights afforded the dealer under this Article, voluntarily elects to appeal a policy, determination, or decision of the manufacturer through an appeals board or internal grievance procedure of the manufacturer, or to participate in or refer the matter to mediation, arbitration, or other alternative dispute resolution procedure or process established or endorsed by the manufacturer, the applicable period of time for the dealer to file the notice, protest, or petition before the Commissioner under this Article shall not commence until the manufacturer's appeal board or internal grievance procedure, mediation, arbitration, or appeals process of the manufacturer has been completed and the dealer has received notice in writing of the final decision or result of the procedure or process. Nothing, however, contained in this subsection shall be deemed to require that any dealer exhaust any internal grievance or other alternative dispute process required or established by the manufacturer before seeking redress from the Commissioner as provided in this Article.

(g) Notwithstanding any other statute, regulation, or rule or the existence of a pending legal or administrative proceeding in any other forum any franchised new motor vehicle dealer or any manufacturer, factory branch, distributor, or distributor branch may elect to file a petition before the Commissioner for resolution of any dispute that may arise with respect to any of the rights or obligations of the dealer or of the manufacturer, factory branch, distributor, or distributor branch related to a franchise or franchise-related form agreement. The Commissioner shall have the authority to apply principles of law, equity, and good faith in determining such matters. The filing of a petition by a dealer or a manufacturer, factory branch, distributor, or distributor branch pursuant to this section shall not preclude the party filing the petition from pursuing any other form of recourse it may have, either before the Commissioner or in another form, including any damages and injunctive relief. The Commissioner shall have the authority to receive and evaluate the facts in the matter of controversy and render a decision by entering an order which shall thereafter become binding and enforceable with respect to the parties, subject to the right of review of the decision in a court of competent jurisdiction pursuant to Chapter 150B of the General Statutes.

History.

1955, c. 1243, s. 17; 1983, c. 704, s. 23; 1991, c. 510, s. 1;1997-319, s. 2;1999-335, s. 1;2011-290, s. 3

GRANTING FRANCHISE IN VIOLATION OF G.S. 20-305(5) WOULD BE AN UNFAIR ACT OR PRACTICE, which the Commissioner is empowered to prevent under this section. American Motors Sales Corp. v. Peters, 58 N.C. App. 684, 294 S.E.2d 764 (1982).

POWER TO FORESTALL FRANCHISE TERMINATION. --Neither this section nor G.S. 20-305(6) expressly vests the Commissioner with the power to order parties to enter into a contract. However, the statutory prohibition on franchise termination except for cause remains intact. Thus it is not necessary that the Commissioner have the power to order parties to enter into contracts to enable the agency to function properly. GMC v. Kinlaw, 78 N.C. App. 521, 338 S.E.2d 114 (1985).

Commissioner's order finding that GMC failed to renew dealer's franchise agreements without cause and directing that the agreements not be terminated was proper. However, the Commissioner exceeded his authority in ordering GMC to enter "a regular five (5) year motor vehicle dealer sales agreement" with dealer. GMC v. Kinlaw, 78 N.C. App. 521, 338 S.E.2d 114 (1985).

APPLIED in American Motors Sales Corp. v. Peters, 311 N.C. 311, 317 S.E.2d 351 (1984).

CITED in Sandhill Motors, Inc. v. American Motors Sales Corp., 667 F.2d 1112 (4th Cir. 1981).

§ 20-301.1. Notice of additional charges against dealer's account; informal appeals procedure

(a) Notwithstanding the terms of any contract, franchise, novation, or agreement, it shall be unlawful for any manufacturer, factory branch, distributor, or distributor branch to charge or assess one of its franchised motor vehicle dealers located in this State, or to charge or debit the account of the franchised motor vehicle dealer for merchandise, tools, or equipment, or other charges or amounts which total more [than] five thousand dollars ($ 5,000), other than the published cost of new motor vehicles, and merchandise, tools, or equipment specifically ordered by the franchised motor vehicle dealer, unless the franchised motor vehicle dealer receives a detailed itemized description of the nature and amount of each charge in writing at least 10 days prior to the date the charge or account debit is to become effective or due. For purposes of this subsection, the prior written notice required pursuant to this subsection includes, but is not limited to, all charges or debits to a dealer's account for advertising or advertising materials; advertising or showroom displays; customer informational materials; computer or communications hardware or software; special tools; equipment; dealership operation guides; Internet programs; and any additional charges or surcharges made or proposed for merchandise, tools, or equipment previously charged to the dealer; and any other charges or amounts which total more than five thousand dollars ($ 5,000). If the franchised new motor vehicle dealer disputes all or any portion of an actual or proposed charge or debit to the dealer's account, the dealer may proceed as provided in G.S. 20-301(b) and G.S. 20-308.1. Upon the filing of a petition pursuant to G.S. 20-301(b) or a civil action pursuant to G.S. 20-308.1, the affected manufacturer, factory branch, distributor, or distributor branch shall not require payment from the dealer, or debit or charge the dealer's account, unless and until a final judgment supporting the payment or charge has been rendered by the Commissioner or court.

(b) Any franchised new motor vehicle dealer who seeks to challenge an actual or proposed charge, debit, payment, reimbursement, or credit to the franchised new motor vehicle dealer or to the franchised new motor vehicle dealer's account in an amount less than or equal to ten thousand dollars ($ 10,000) and that is in violation of this Article or contrary to the terms of the franchise may, prior to filing a formal petition before the Commissioner as provided in G.S. 20-301(b) or a civil action in any court of competent jurisdiction under G.S. 20-308.1, request and obtain a mediated settlement conference as provided in this subsection. Unless objection to the timeliness of the franchised new motor vehicle dealer's request for mediation under this subsection is waived in writing by the affected manufacturer, factory branch, distributor, or distributor branch, a franchised new motor vehicle dealer's request to mediate must be sent to the Commissioner within 75 days after the franchised new motor vehicle dealer's receipt of written notice from a manufacturer, factory branch, distributor, or distributor branch of the charges, debits, payments, reimbursements, or credits challenged by the franchised new motor vehicle dealer. If the franchised new motor vehicle dealer has requested in writing that the manufacturer, factory branch, distributor, or distributor branch review the questioned charges, debits, payments, reimbursements, or credits, a franchised new motor vehicle dealer's request to mediate must be sent to the Commissioner within 30 days after the franchised new motor vehicle dealer's receipt of the final written determination on the issue from the manufacturer, factory branch, distributor, or distributor branch.

(1) It is the policy and purpose of this subsection to implement a system of settlement events that are designed to reduce the cost of litigation under this Article to the general public and the parties, to focus the parties' attention on settlement rather than on trial preparation, and to provide a structured opportunity for settlement negotiations to take place.

(2) The franchised new motor vehicle dealer shall send a letter to the Commissioner by certified or registered mail, return receipt requested, identifying the actual or proposed charges the franchised new motor vehicle dealer seeks to challenge and the reason or basis for the challenge. The charges, debits, payments, reimbursements, or credits challenged by the franchised new motor vehicle dealer need not be related, and multiple issues may be resolved in a single proceeding. The franchised new motor vehicle dealer shall send a copy of the letter to the affected manufacturer, factory branch, distributor, or distributor branch, addressed to the current district, zone, or regional manager in charge of overseeing the dealer's operations, or the registered agent for acceptance of legal process in this State. Upon the mailing of a letter to the Commissioner and the manufacturer, factory branch, distributor, or distributor branch pursuant to this subsection, any chargeback to or any payment required of a franchised new motor vehicle dealer by a manufacturer, factory branch, distributor, or distributor branch shall be stayed during the pendency of the mediation. Upon

the mailing of a letter to the Commissioner and manufacturer, factory branch, distributor, or distributor branch pursuant to this subsection, any statute of limitation or other time limitation for filing a petition before the Commissioner or civil action shall be tolled during the pendency of the mediation.

(3) Upon receipt of the written request of the franchised new motor vehicle dealer, the Commissioner shall appoint a mediator and send notice of that appointment to the parties. A person is qualified to serve as mediator as provided by this subdivision if the person is certified to serve as a mediator under Rule 8 of the North Carolina Rules Implementing Statewide Mediated Settlement Conferences in Superior Court Civil Actions and does not represent motor vehicle dealers or manufacturers, factory branches, distributors, or distributor branches. A mediator acting pursuant to this subdivision shall have judicial immunity in the same manner and to the same extent as a judge of the General Court of Justice.

(4) The parties shall by written agreement select a venue and schedule for the mediated settlement conference conducted under this subsection. If the parties are unable to agree on a venue and schedule, the mediator shall select a venue and schedule. Except by written agreement of all parties, a mediation proceeding and mediated settlement conference under this subsection shall be held in North Carolina.

(5) In this subsection, "mediation" means a nonbinding forum in which an impartial person, the mediator, facilitates communication between parties to promote reconciliation, settlement, or understanding among them. A mediator may not impose his or her own judgment on the issues for that of the parties.

(6) At least 10 days prior to the mediated settlement conference, the affected manufacturer, factory branch, distributor, or distributor branch shall, by certified or registered mail, return receipt requested, send the mediator and the franchised new motor vehicle dealer a detailed response to the allegations raised in the franchised new motor vehicle dealer's written request. The mediation may be conducted by officers or employees of the parties themselves without the appearance of legal counsel. However, at least 10 days prior to the mediated settlement conference, either party may give notice to the other and to the mediator of its intention to appear at the mediation with legal counsel, in which event either party may appear at the mediation with legal counsel.

Chapter 20

(7) A mediation proceeding conducted pursuant to this subsection shall be complete not later than the sixtieth day after the date of the Commissioner's notice of the appointment of the mediator; this deadline may be extended by written agreement of the parties. The parties shall be solely responsible for the compensation and expenses of the mediator on a 50/50 basis. The Commissioner is not liable for the compensation paid or to be paid a mediator employed pursuant to this subsection.

(8) A party may attend a mediated settlement conference telephonically in lieu of personal appearance. If a party or other person required to attend a mediated settlement conference fails to attend without good cause, the Commissioner may impose upon the party or person any appropriate monetary sanction, including the payment of fines, attorneys' fees, mediator fees, expenses, and loss of earnings incurred by persons attending the conference.

(9) If the mediation fails to result in a resolution of the dispute, the franchised new motor vehicle dealer may proceed as provided in G.S. 20-301(b) and G.S. 20-308.1. Upon the filing of a petition pursuant to G.S. 20-301(b) or a civil action pursuant to G.S. 20-308.1, the affected manufacturer, factory branch, distributor, or distributor branch shall not require payment from the dealer, or debit or charge the dealer's account, unless and until a final judgment supporting the payment or charge has been rendered by the Commissioner or court. All communications made during a mediation proceeding, including, but not limited to, those communications made during a mediated settlement conference are presumed to be made in compromise negotiation and shall be governed by Rule 408 of the North Carolina Rules of Evidence.

History.
2001-510, s. 1;2011-290, s. 4
EDITOR'S NOTE. --
This section was amended by Session Laws 2011-290, s. 4, in the coded bill drafting format provided by G.S. 120-20.1. In subdivision (a), the word "than" in the phrase "or other charges or amounts which total more than five thousand dollars ($5,000)," was not underscored. Subsection (a) has been set out in the form above at the direction of the Revisor of Statutes.

§ 20-302. Rules and regulations

The Commissioner may make such rules and regulations, not inconsistent with the provisions of this Article, as he shall deem necessary or proper for the effective administration and enforcement of this Article, provided that the Commissioner shall make a copy of such rules and regulations available on a Web site maintained by the Division or the Department of Transportation 30 days prior to the effective date of such rules and regulations.

History.
1955, c. 1243, s. 18; 2018-74, s. 8
EFFECT OF AMENDMENTS. --
Session Laws 2018-74, s. 8, effective July 1, 2018, substituted "the Commissioner shall make a copy of such rules and regulations available on a Web site maintained by the Division or the Department of Transportation" for "a copy of such rules and regulations shall be mailed to each motor vehicle dealer licensee."
CITED in Murray v. Justice, 96 N.C. App. 169, 385 S.E.2d 195 (1989).

§ 20-303. Installment sales to be evidenced by written instrument; statement to be delivered to buyer

(a) Every retail installment sale shall be evidenced by one or more instruments in writing, which shall contain all the agreements of the parties and shall be signed by the buyer.

(b) For every retail installment sale, prior to or about the time of the delivery of the motor vehicle, the seller shall deliver to the buyer a written statement describing clearly the motor vehicle sold to the buyer, the cash sale price thereof, the cash paid down by the buyer, the amount credited the buyer for any trade-in and a description of the motor vehicle traded, the amount of the finance charge, the amount of any other charge specifying its purpose, the net balance due from the buyer, the terms of the payment of such net balance and a summary of any insurance protection to be effected. The written statement shall be signed by the buyer.

History.
1955, c. 1243, s. 19; 2007-513, s. 1
DESCRIPTION OF AMOUNT OWED. --Automobile dealership was granted summary judgment on a truck purchaser's G.S. 20-303 claim where there was no evidence that the description of the amount the purchaser owed was inaccurate. Comer v. Pers. Auto Sales, Inc., 368 F. Supp. 2d 478 (M.D.N.C. 2005).

§ 20-304. Coercion of retail dealer by manufacturer or distributor in connection with installment sales contract prohibited

(a) It shall be unlawful for any manufacturer, wholesaler or distributor, or any officer, agent or representative of either, to coerce, or attempt to coerce, any retail motor vehicle dealer or prospective retail motor vehicle dealer in this State to sell, assign or transfer any retail installment sales contract, obtained by such dealer in connection with the sale by him in this State of motor vehicles manufactured or sold by such manufacturer, wholesaler, or distributor, to a specified finance company or class of such companies, or to any other specified persons, by any of the acts or means hereinafter set forth, namely:

(1) By any statement, suggestion, promise or threat that such manufacturer, wholesaler, or distributor will in any manner benefit or injure such dealer, whether such statement, suggestion, threat or promise is expressed or implied, or made directly or indirectly,

(2) By any act that will benefit or injure such dealer,

(3) By any contract, or any expressed or implied offer of contract, made directly or indirectly to such dealer, for handling motor vehicles, on the condition that such dealer sell, assign or transfer his retail installment sales contract thereon, in this State, to a specified finance company or class of such companies, or to any other specified person,

(4) By any expressed or implied statement or representation, made directly or indirectly, that such dealer is under any obligation whatsoever to sell, assign or transfer any of his retail sales contracts, in this State, on motor vehicles manufactured or sold by such manufacturer, wholesaler, or distributor to such finance company, or class of companies, or other specified person, because of any relationship or affiliation between such manufacturer, wholesaler, or distributor and such finance company or companies or such other specified person or persons.

(b) Any such statements, threats, promises, acts, contracts, or offers of contracts, when the effect thereof may be to lessen or eliminate competition, or tend to create a monopoly, are declared unfair trade practices and unfair methods of competition and against the public policy of this State, are unlawful and are hereby prohibited.

History.
1955, c. 1243, s. 20

§ 20-305. Coercing dealer to accept commodities not ordered; threatening to cancel franchise; preventing transfer of ownership; granting additional franchises; terminating franchises without good cause; preventing family succession

It shall be unlawful for any manufacturer, factory branch, distributor, or distributor branch, or any field representative, officer, agent, or any representative whatsoever of any of them:

(1) To require, coerce, or attempt to coerce any dealer to accept delivery of any motor vehicle or vehicles, parts or accessories therefor, or any other commodities, which shall not have been ordered by that dealer, or to accept delivery of any motor vehicle or vehicles which have been equipped in a manner other than as specified by the dealer.

(2) To require, coerce, or attempt to coerce any dealer to enter into any agreement with such manufacturer, factory branch, distributor, or distributor branch, or representative thereof, or do any other act unfair to such dealer, by threatening to cancel any franchise existing between such manufacturer, factory branch, distributor, distributor branch, or representative thereof, and such dealer;

(3) *(See Editor's note for applicability)* Unfairly without due regard to the equities of the dealer, and without just provocation, to cancel the franchise of such dealer;

(4) Notwithstanding the terms of any franchise agreement, to prevent or refuse to approve the sale or transfer of the ownership of a dealership by the sale of the business, stock transfer, or otherwise, or the transfer, sale or assignment of a dealer franchise, or a change in the executive management or principal operator of the dealership, change in use of an existing facility to provide for the sales or service of one or more additional line-makes of new motor vehicles, or relocation of the dealership to another site within the dealership's relevant market area, if the Commissioner has determined, if requested in writing by the dealer within 30 days after receipt of an objection to the proposed transfer, sale, assignment, relocation, or change, and after a hearing on the matter, that the failure to permit or honor the transfer, sale, assignment, relocation, or change is unreasonable under the circumstances. No franchise may be transferred, sold, assigned, relocated, or the executive management or principal operators changed, or the use of an existing facility changed, unless the franchisor has been given at least 30 days' prior written notice as to the proposed transferee's name and address, financial ability, and qualifications of the proposed transferee, a copy of the purchase agreement between the dealership and the proposed transferee, the identity and qualifications of the persons proposed to be involved in executive management or as principal operators, and the location and site plans of any proposed

Chapter 20

relocation or change in use of a dealership facility. The franchisor shall send the dealership and the proposed transferee notice of objection, by registered or certified mail, return receipt requested, to the proposed transfer, sale, assignment, relocation, or change within 30 days after receipt of notice from the dealer, as provided in this section. The notice of objection shall state in detail all factual and legal bases for the objection on the part of the franchisor to the proposed transfer, sale, assignment, relocation, or change that is specifically referenced in this subdivision. An objection to a proposed transfer, sale, assignment, relocation, or change in the executive management or principal operator of the dealership or change in the use of the facility may only be premised upon the factual and legal bases specifically referenced in this subdivision or G.S. 20-305(11), as it relates to change in the use of a facility. A manufacturer's notice of objection which is based upon factual or legal issues that are not specifically referenced in this subdivision or G.S. 20-305(11) with respect to a change in the use of an existing facility as being issues upon which the Commissioner shall base his determination shall not be effective to preserve the franchisor's right to object to the proposed transfer sale, assignment, relocation, or change, provided the dealership or proposed transferee has submitted written notice, as required above, as to the proposed transferee's name and address, financial ability, and qualifications of the proposed transferee, a copy of the purchase agreement between the dealership and the proposed transferee, the identity and qualifications of the persons proposed to be involved in the executive management or as principal operators, and the location and site plans of any proposed relocation or change in the use of an existing facility. Failure by the franchisor to send notice of objection within 30 days shall constitute waiver by the franchisor of any right to object to the proposed transfer, sale, assignment, relocation, or change. If the franchisor requires additional information to complete its review, the franchisor shall notify the dealership within 15 days after receipt of the proposed transferee's name and address, financial ability, and qualifications, a copy of the purchase agreement between the dealership and the proposed transferee, the identity and qualifications of the persons proposed to be involved in executive management or as principal operators, and the location and site plans of any proposed relocation or change in use of the dealership facility. If the franchisor fails to request additional information from the dealer or proposed transferee within 15 days of receipt of this initial information, the 30-day time period within which the franchisor may provide notice of objection shall be deemed to run from the initial receipt date. Otherwise, the 30-day time period within which the franchisor may provide notice of objection shall run from the date the franchisor has received the supplemental information requested from the dealer or proposed transferee; provided, however, that failure by the franchisor to send notice of objection within 60 days of the franchisor's receipt of the initial information from the dealer shall constitute waiver by the franchisor of any right to object to the proposed transfer, sale, assignment, relocation, or change. With respect to a proposed transfer of ownership, sale, or assignment, the sole issue for determination by the Commissioner and the sole issue upon which the Commissioner shall hear or consider evidence is whether, by reason of lack of good moral character, lack of general business experience, or lack of financial ability, the proposed transferee is unfit to own the dealership. For purposes of this subdivision, the refusal by the manufacturer to accept a proposed transferee who is of good moral character and who otherwise meets the written, reasonable, and uniformly applied business experience and financial requirements, if any, required by the manufacturer of owners of its franchised automobile dealerships is presumed to demonstrate the manufacturer's failure to prove that the proposed transferee is unfit to own the dealership. With respect to a proposed change in the executive management or principal operator of the dealership, the sole issue for determination by the Commissioner and the sole issue on which the Commissioner shall hear or consider evidence shall be whether, by reason of lack of training, lack of prior experience, poor past performance, or poor character, the proposed candidate for a position within the executive management or as principal operator of the dealership is unfit for the position. For purposes of this subdivision, the refusal by the manufacturer to accept a proposed candidate for executive management or as principal operator who is of good moral character and who otherwise meets the written, reasonable, and uniformly applied standards or qualifications, if any, of the manufacturer relating to the business experience and prior performance of executive management required by the manufacturers of its dealers is presumed to demonstrate the manufacturer's failure to prove the proposed candidate for executive management or as principal operator is unfit to serve the capacity. With respect to a proposed change in use of a dealership facility to provide for the sales or service of one or more additional line-makes of new motor vehicles, the sole issue for determination by the Commissioner is whether the new motor vehicle dealer has a reasonable line of credit for each make or line of motor vehicle and remains in compliance with any reasonable capital standards and facilities requirements of the manufacturer or distributor. The reasonable facilities requirements of the manufacturer or distributor shall not include any requirement that a new motor vehicle dealer establish or maintain exclusive facilities, personnel, or display space. With respect to a proposed relocation or other proposed change, the issue for determination by the Commissioner is whether the proposed relocation or other change is unreasonable under the circumstances. For purposes of this subdivision, the refusal by the manufacturer to agree to a proposed relocation which meets the written, reasonable, and uniformly applied standards or criteria, if any, of the manufacturer relating to dealer relocations is presumed to demonstrate that the manufacturer's failure to prove the proposed relocation is unreasonable under the circumstances. The manufacturer shall have the burden of proof before the Commissioner under this subdivision. It is unlawful for a manufacturer to, in any way, condition its approval of a proposed transfer, sale, assignment, change in the dealer's executive management, principal operator, or appointment of a designated successor, on the existing or proposed dealer's willingness to construct a new facility, renovate the existing facility, acquire or refrain from acquiring one or more line-makes of vehicles, separate or divest one or more line-makes of vehicle, or establish or maintain exclusive facilities, personnel, or display space. It is unlawful for a manufacturer to, in any way, condition its approval of a proposed relocation on the existing or proposed dealer's willingness to acquire or refrain from acquiring one or more line-makes of vehicles, separate or divest one or more line-makes of vehicle, or establish or maintain exclusive facilities, personnel, or display space. The opinion or determination of a franchisor that the continued existence of one of its franchised dealers situated in this State is not viable, or that the dealer holds or fails to hold licensing rights for the sale of other line-makes of vehicles in a manner consistent with the franchisor's existing or future distribution or marketing plans, shall not constitute a lawful basis for the franchisor to fail or refuse to approve a dealer's proposed change in use of a dealership facility or relocation: provided, however, that nothing contained in this subdivision shall be deemed to prevent or prohibit a franchisor from failing to approve a dealer's proposed relocation on grounds that the specific site or facility proposed by the dealer is otherwise unreasonable under the circumstances. Approval of a relocation pursuant to this subdivision shall not in itself constitute the franchisor's representation or assurance of the dealer's viability at that location.

(5) To enter into a franchise establishing an additional new motor vehicle dealer or relocating an existing new motor vehicle dealer into a relevant market area where the same line make is then represented without first notifying in writing the Commissioner and each new motor vehicle dealer in that line make in the relevant market area of the intention to establish an additional dealer or to relocate an existing dealer within or into that market area. Within 30 days of receiving such notice or within 30 days after the end of any appeal procedure provided by the manufacturer, any new motor vehicle dealer may file with the Commissioner a protest to the establishing or relocating of the new motor vehicle dealer. When a protest is filed, the Commissioner shall promptly inform the manufacturer that a timely protest has been filed, and that the manufacturer shall not establish or relocate the proposed new motor vehicle dealer until the Commissioner has held a hearing and has determined that there is good cause for permitting the addition or relocation of such new motor vehicle dealer.

a. This section does not apply:

1. To the relocation of an existing new motor vehicle dealer within that dealer's relevant market area, provided that the relocation not be at a site within 10 miles of a licensed new motor vehicle dealer for the same line make of motor vehicle. If this sub-subdivision is applicable, only dealers trading in the same line-make of vehicle that are located within the 10-mile radius shall be entitled to notice from the manufacturer and have the protest rights afforded under this section.

2. If the proposed additional new motor vehicle dealer is to be established at or within two miles of a location at which a former licensed new motor vehicle dealer for the same line make of new motor vehicle had ceased operating within the previous two years.

3. To the relocation of an existing new motor vehicle dealer within two miles of the existing site of the new motor vehicle dealership if the franchise has been operating on a regular basis from the existing site for a minimum of three years immediately preceding the relocation.

4. To the relocation of an existing new motor vehicle dealer if the proposed site of the relocated new motor vehicle dealership is further away from all other new motor vehicle dealers of the same line make in that relevant market area.

5. Repealed by Session Laws 2008-156, s. 3, effective August 3, 2008.

b. In determining whether good cause has been established for not entering into or relocating an additional new motor vehicle dealer for the same line make, the Commissioner shall take into consideration the existing circumstances, including, but not limited to:

1. The permanency of the investment of both the existing and proposed additional new motor vehicle dealers;

2. Growth or decline in population, density of population, and new car registrations in the relevant market area;

3. Effect on the consuming public in the relevant market area;

4. Whether it is injurious or beneficial to the public welfare for an additional new motor vehicle dealer to be established;

5. Whether the new motor vehicle dealers of the same line make in that relevant market area are providing adequate competition and convenient customer care for the motor vehicles of the same line make in the market area which shall include the adequacy of motor vehicle sales and service facilities, equipment, supply of motor vehicle parts, and qualified service personnel;

6. Whether the establishment of an additional new motor vehicle dealer or relocation of an existing new motor vehicle dealer in the relevant market area would increase competition in a manner such as to be in the long-term public interest; and

7. The effect on the relocating dealer of a denial of its relocation into the relevant market area.

c. The Commissioner shall try to conduct the hearing and render his final determination if possible, within 180 days after a protest is filed.

d. Any parties to a hearing by the Commissioner concerning the establishment or relocating of a new motor vehicle dealer shall have a right of review of the decision in a court of competent jurisdiction pursuant to Chapter 150B of the General Statutes.

e. In a hearing involving a proposed additional dealership, the manufacturer or distributor has the burden of proof under this section. In a proceeding involving the relocation of an existing dealership, the dealer seeking to relocate has the burden of proof under this section.

f. If the Commissioner determines, following a hearing, that good cause exists for permitting the proposed additional or relocated motor vehicle dealership, the dealer seeking the proposed additional or relocated motor vehicle dealership must, within two years, obtain a license from the Commissioner for the sale of vehicles at the relevant site, and actually commence operations at the site selling new motor vehicles of all line makes, as permitted by the Commissioner. Failure to obtain a permit and commence sales within two years shall constitute waiver by the dealer of the dealer's right to the additional or relocated dealership, requiring renotification, a new hearing, and a new determination as provided in this section. If the Commissioner fails to determine that good cause exists for permitting the proposed additional or relocated motor vehicle dealership, the manufacturer seeking the proposed additional dealership or dealer seeking to relocate may not again provide notice of its intention or otherwise attempt to establish an additional dealership or relocate to any location within 10 miles of the site of the original proposed additional dealership or relocation site for a minimum of three years from the date of the Commissioner's determination.

g. *(See Editor's note for applicability)* For purposes of this subdivision, the addition, creation, or operation of a "satellite" or other facility, not physically part of or contiguous to an existing licensed new motor vehicle dealer, whether or not owned or operated by a person or other entity holding a franchise as defined by G.S.

20-286(8a), at which warranty service work authorized or reimbursed by a manufacturer is performed or at which new motor vehicles are offered for sale to the public, shall be considered an additional new motor vehicle dealer requiring a showing of good cause, prior notification to existing new motor vehicle dealers of the same line make of vehicle within the relevant market area by the manufacturer and the opportunity for a hearing before the Commissioner as provided in this subdivision.

(6) Notwithstanding the terms, provisions or conditions of any franchise or notwithstanding the terms or provisions of any waiver, to terminate, cancel or fail to renew any franchise with a licensed new motor vehicle dealer unless the manufacturer has satisfied the notice requirements of sub-subdivision c. of this subdivision and the Commissioner has determined, if requested in writing by the dealer within (i) the time period specified in G.S. 20-305(6) c.1.II., III., or IV., as applicable, or (ii) the effective date of the franchise termination specified or proposed by the manufacturer in the notice of termination, whichever period of time is longer, and after a hearing on the matter, that there is good cause for the termination, cancellation, or nonrenewal of the franchise and that the manufacturer has acted in good faith as defined in this act regarding the termination, cancellation or nonrenewal. When such a petition is made to the Commissioner by a dealer for determination as to the existence of good cause and good faith for the termination, cancellation or nonrenewal of a franchise, the Commissioner shall promptly inform the manufacturer that a timely petition has been filed, and the franchise in question shall continue in effect pending the Commissioner's decision. The Commissioner shall try to conduct the hearing and render a final determination within 180 days after a petition has been filed. If the termination, cancellation or nonrenewal is pursuant to G.S. 20-305(6)c.1.III. then the Commissioner shall give the proceeding priority consideration and shall try to render his final determination no later than 90 days after the petition has been filed. Any parties to a hearing by the Commissioner under this section shall have a right of review of the decision in a court of competent jurisdiction pursuant to Chapter 150B of the General Statutes. Any determination of the Commissioner under this section finding that good cause exists for the nonrenewal, cancellation, or termination of any franchise shall automatically be stayed during any period that the affected dealer shall have the right to judicial review or appeal of the determination before the superior court or any other appellate court and during the pendency of any appeal; provided, however, that within 30 days of entry of the Commissioner's order, the affected dealer provide such security as the reviewing court, in its discretion, may deem appropriate for payment of such costs and damages as may be incurred or sustained by the manufacturer by reason of and during the pendency of the stay. Although the right of the affected dealer to such stay is automatic, the procedure for providing such security and for the award of damages, if any, to the manufacturer upon dissolution of the stay shall be in accordance with G.S. 1A-1, Rule 65(d) and (e). No such security provided by or on behalf of any affected dealer shall be forfeited or damages awarded against a dealer who obtains a stay under this subdivision in the event the ownership of the affected dealership is subsequently transferred, sold, or assigned to a third party in accordance with this subdivision or subdivision (4) of this section and the closing on such transfer, sale, or assignment occurs no later than 180 days after the date of entry of the Commissioner's order. Furthermore, unless and until the termination, cancellation, or nonrenewal of a dealer's franchise shall finally become effective, in light of any stay or any order of the Commissioner determining that good cause exists for the termination, cancellation, or nonrenewal of a dealer's franchise as provided in this subdivision, a dealer who receives a notice of termination, cancellation, or nonrenewal from a manufacturer as provided in this subdivision shall continue to have the same rights to assign, sell, or transfer the franchise to a third party under the franchise and as permitted under G.S. 20-305(4) as if notice of the termination had not been given by the manufacturer. Any franchise under notice or threat of termination, cancellation, or nonrenewal by the manufacturer which is duly transferred in accordance with G.S. 20-305(4) shall not be subject to termination by reason of failure of performance or breaches of the franchise on the part of the transferor.

a. Notwithstanding the terms, provisions or conditions of any franchise or the terms or provisions of any waiver, good cause shall exist for the purposes of a termination, cancellation or nonrenewal when:

1. There is a failure by the new motor vehicle dealer to comply with a provision of the franchise

Chapter 20

which provision is both reasonable and of material significance to the franchise relationship provided that the dealer has been notified in writing of the failure within 180 days after the manufacturer first acquired knowledge of such failure;

2. If the failure by the new motor vehicle dealer relates to the performance of the new motor vehicle dealer in sales or service, then good cause shall be defined as the failure of the new motor vehicle dealer to comply with reasonable performance criteria established by the manufacturer if the new motor vehicle dealer was apprised by the manufacturer in writing of the failure; and

I. The notification stated that notice was provided of failure of performance pursuant to this section;

II. The new motor vehicle dealer was afforded a reasonable opportunity, for a period of not less than 180 days, to comply with the criteria; and

III. The new motor vehicle dealer failed to demonstrate substantial progress towards compliance with the manufacturer's performance criteria during such period and the new motor vehicle dealer's failure was not primarily due to economic or market factors within the dealer's relevant market area which were beyond the dealer's control.

b. The manufacturer shall have the burden of proof under this section.

c. **Notification of Termination, Cancellation and Nonrenewal. --**

1. Notwithstanding the terms, provisions or conditions of any franchise prior to the termination, cancellation or nonrenewal of any franchise, the manufacturer shall furnish notification of termination, cancellation or nonrenewal to the new motor vehicle dealer as follows:

I. In the manner described in G.S. 20-305(6)c2 below; and

II. Not less than 90 days prior to the effective date of such termination, cancellation or nonrenewal; or

III. Not less than 15 days prior to the effective date of such termination, cancellation or nonrenewal with respect to any of the following:

A. Insolvency of the new motor vehicle dealer, or filing of any petition by or against the new motor vehicle dealer under any bankruptcy or receivership law;

B. Failure of the new motor vehicle dealer to conduct its customary sales and service operations during its customary business hours for seven consecutive business days, except for acts of God or circumstances beyond the direct control of the new motor vehicle dealer;

C. Revocation of any license which the new motor vehicle dealer is required to have to operate a dealership;

D. Conviction of a felony involving moral turpitude, under the laws of this State or any other state, or territory, or the District of Columbia.

IV. Not less than 180 days prior to the effective date of such termination, cancellation, or nonrenewal which occurs as a result of any change in ownership, operation, or control of all or any part of the business of the manufacturer, factory branch, distributor, or distributor branch whether by sale or transfer of assets, corporate stock or other equity interest, assignment, merger, consolidation, combination, joint venture, redemption, operation of law or otherwise; or the termination, suspension, or cessation of a part or all of the business operations of the manufacturers, factory branch, distributor, or distributor branch; or discontinuance of the sale of the line-make or brand, or a change in distribution system by the manufacturer whether through a change in distributors or the manufacturer's decision to cease conducting business through a distributor altogether.

V. Unless the failure by the new motor vehicle dealer relates to the performance of the new motor vehicle dealer in sales or service, not more than one year after the manufacturer first acquired knowledge of the basic facts comprising the failure.

2. Notification under this section shall be in writing; shall be by certified mail or personally delivered to the new motor vehicle dealer; and shall contain:

I. A statement of intention to terminate, cancel or not to renew the franchise;

II. A detailed statement of all of the material reasons for the termination, cancellation or nonrenewal; and

III. The date on which the termination, cancellation or nonrenewal takes effect.

3. Notification provided in G.S. 20-305(6)c1II of 90 days prior to the effective date of such termination, cancellation or renewal may run concurrent with the 180 days designated in G.S. 20-305(6)a2II provided the notification is clearly designated by a separate written document mailed by certified mail or personally delivered to the new motor vehicle dealer.

d. Payments.

1. Notwithstanding the terms of any franchise, agreement, or waiver, upon the termination, nonrenewal or cancellation of any franchise by the manufacturer or distributor, the cessation of business or the termination, nonrenewal, or cancellation of any franchise by any new motor vehicle dealer located in this State, or upon any of the occurrences set forth in G.S. 20-305(6).c.1.IV., the manufacturer or distributor shall purchase from and compensate the new motor vehicle dealer for all of the following:

I. Each new and unsold motor vehicle within the new motor vehicle dealer's inventory that has been acquired within 24 months of the effective date of the termination from the manufacturer or distributor or another same line-make dealer in the ordinary course of business, and which has not been substantially altered or damaged to the prejudice of the manufacturer or

distributor while in the new motor vehicle dealer's possession, and which has been driven less than 1,000 miles or, for purposes of a recreational vehicle motor home as defined in G.S. 20-4.01(32b) c., less than 1,500 miles following the original date of delivery to the dealer, and for which no certificate of title has been issued. For purposes of this sub-subdivision, the term "ordinary course of business" shall include inventory transfers of all new, same line-make vehicles between affiliated dealerships, or otherwise between dealerships having common or interrelated ownership, provided that the transfer is not intended solely for the purpose of benefiting from the termination assistance described in this sub-subdivision.

II. Unused, undamaged and unsold supplies and parts purchased from the manufacturer or distributor or sources approved by the manufacturer or distributor, at a price not to exceed the original manufacturer's price to the dealer, provided such supplies and parts are currently offered for sale by the manufacturer or distributor in its current parts catalogs and are in salable condition.

III. Equipment, signs, and furnishings that have not been substantially altered or damaged and that have been required by the manufacturer or distributor to be purchased by the new motor vehicle dealer from the manufacturer or distributor, or their approved sources.

IV. Special tools that have not been altered or damaged, normal wear and tear excepted, and that have been required by the manufacturer or distributor to be purchased by the new motor vehicle dealer from the manufacturer or distributor, or their approved sources within five years immediately preceding the termination, nonrenewal or

Chapter 20

cancellation of the franchise. The amount of compensation which shall be paid to the new motor vehicle dealer by the manufacturer or distributor shall be the net acquisition price if the item was acquired in the 12 months preceding the date of receipt of the dealer's request for compensation; seventy-five percent (75%) of the net acquisition price if the item was acquired between 13 and 24 months preceding the dealer's request for compensation; fifty percent (50%) of the net acquisition price if the item was acquired between 25 and 36 months preceding the dealer's request for compensation; twenty-five percent (25%) of the net acquisition price if the item was acquired between 37 and 60 months preceding the dealer's request for compensation.

2. The compensation provided above shall be paid by the manufacturer or distributor not later than 90 days after the manufacturer or distributor has received notice in writing from or on behalf of the new motor vehicle dealer specifying the elements of compensation requested by the dealer; provided the new motor vehicle dealer has, or can obtain, clear title to the inventory and has conveyed, or can convey, title and possession of the same to the manufacturer or distributor. Within 15 days after receipt of the dealer's written request for compensation, the manufacturer or distributor shall send the dealer detailed written instructions and forms required by the manufacturer or distributor to effectuate the receipt of the compensation requested by the dealer. The manufacturer or distributor shall be obligated to pay or reimburse the dealer for any transportation charges associated with the repurchase obligations of the manufacturer or distributor under this sub-subdivision. The manufacturer or distributor shall also compensate the dealer for any handling, packing, or similar payments contemplated in the franchise. In no event may the manufacturer or distributor charge the dealer any handling, restocking, or other similar costs or fees associated with items repurchased by the manufacturer under this sub-subdivision.

3. In addition to the other payments set forth in this section, if a termination, cancellation, or nonrenewal is premised upon any of the occurrences set forth in G.S. 20-305(6)c.1.IV., then the manufacturer or distributor shall be liable to the dealer for an amount at least equivalent to the fair market value of the franchise on (i) the date the franchisor announces the action which results in termination, cancellation, or nonrenewal; or (ii) the date the action which results in termination, cancellation, or nonrenewal first became general knowledge; or (iii) the day 18 months prior to the date on which the notice of termination, cancellation, or nonrenewal is issued, whichever amount is higher. Payment is due not later than 90 days after the manufacturer or distributor has received notice in writing from, or on behalf of, the new motor vehicle dealer specifying the elements of compensation requested by the dealer. Any contract, agreement, or release entered into between any manufacturer and any dealer in which the dealer waives the dealer's right to receive monetary compensation in any sum or amount not less than the fair market value of the franchise as provided in this subdivision, including any contract, agreement, or release in which the dealer would accept the right to continue to offer and be compensated for service, parts, or both service and parts provided by the dealer in lieu of receiving all or a portion of the fair market value of the franchise, shall be voidable at the election of the dealer within 90 days of the effective date of the agreement. If the termination, cancellation, or nonrenewal is due to a manufacturer's change in distributors, but the line-make or brand in this State would continue to be sold through the new distributor, the manufacturer may avoid paying fair market value to the dealer if the new distributor or the manufacturer offers the dealer

a franchise agreement with terms acceptable to the dealer.

e. Dealership Facilities Assistance upon Termination, Cancellation or Nonrenewal.

In the event of the occurrence of any of the events specified in G.S. 20-305(6)d.1. above, except termination, cancellation or nonrenewal for license revocation, conviction of a crime involving moral turpitude, or fraud by a dealer-owner:

1. Subject to sub-sub-subdivision 3. of this sub-subdivision, if the new motor vehicle dealer is leasing the dealership facilities from a lessor other than the manufacturer or distributor, the manufacturer or distributor shall pay the new motor vehicle dealer a sum equivalent to the rent for the unexpired term of the lease or three year's rent, whichever is less, or such longer term as is provided in the franchise agreement between the dealer and manufacturer; except that, in the case of motorcycle dealerships, the manufacturer shall pay the new motor vehicle dealer the sum equivalent to the rent for the unexpired term of the lease or one year's rent, whichever is less, or such longer term as provided in the franchise agreement between the dealer and manufacturer; or

2. Subject to sub-sub-subdivision 3. of this sub-subdivision, if the new motor vehicle dealer owns the dealership facilities, the manufacturer or distributor shall pay the new motor vehicle dealer a sum equivalent to the reasonable rental value of the dealership facilities for three years, or for one year in the case of motorcycle dealerships.

3. In order to be entitled to facilities assistance from the manufacturer or distributor, as provided in this sub-subdivision, the dealer, owner, or lessee, as the case may be, shall have the obligation to mitigate damages by listing the demised premises for lease or sublease with a licensed real estate agent within 30 days after the effective date of the termination of the franchise and thereafter by reasonably cooperating with said real estate agent in the performance of the agent's duties and responsibilities. In the event that the dealer, owner, or lessee is able to lease or sublease the demised premises, the dealer shall be obligated to pay the manufacturer the net revenue received from such mitigation up to the total amount of facilities assistance which the dealer has received from the manufacturer pursuant to sub-subdivisions 1. and 2. To the extent and for such uses and purposes as may be consistent with the terms of the lease, a manufacturer who pays facilities assistance to a dealer under this sub-subdivision shall be entitled to occupy and use the dealership facilities during the years for which the manufacturer shall have paid rent under sub-subdivisions 1. and 2.

4. In the event the termination relates to fewer than all of the franchises operated by the dealer at a single location, the amount of facilities assistance which the manufacturer or distributor is required to pay the dealer under this sub-subdivision shall be based on the proportion of gross revenue received from the sale and lease of new vehicles by the dealer and from the dealer's parts and service operations during the three years immediately preceding the effective date of the termination (or any shorter period that the dealer may have held these franchises) of the line-makes being terminated, in relation to the gross revenue received from the sale and lease of all line-makes of new vehicles by the dealer and from the total of the dealer's and parts and service operations from this location during the same three-year period.

5. The compensation required for facilities assistance under this sub-subdivision shall be paid by the manufacturer or distributor within 90 days after the manufacturer or distributor has received notice in writing from, or on behalf of, a new motor vehicle dealer specifying the elements of compensation requested by the dealer.

f. The provisions of sub-subdivision e. above shall not be applicable when the termination, nonrenewal, or cancellation of the franchise agreement by a new motor vehicle dealer is the result of the sale of assets or stock of the motor vehicle dealership. The provisions of sub-subdivisions d. and e. above shall not be applicable when the termination, nonrenewal, or cancellation of the franchise agreement is at the initiation of a new motor vehicle dealer of recreational vehicle motor homes, as defined in G.S. 20-4.01(32b) c., provided that at the time of the termination, nonrenewal, or cancellation, the recreational vehicle manufacturer or distributor has paid to the dealer all claims for warranty or recall work, including payments for labor, parts, and other expenses, which were submitted by the dealer 30 days or more prior to the date of termination, nonrenewal, or cancellation.

g. A franchise shall continue in full force and operation notwithstanding a change, in whole or in part, of an established plan or system of distribution of the motor vehicles offered for sale under the franchise. The appointment of a new manufacturer, factory branch, distributor, or distributor branch for motor vehicles offered for sale under the franchise agreement shall be deemed to be a change of an established plan or system of distribution.

Upon the occurrence of the change, the Division shall deny an application of a manufacturer, factory branch, distributor, or distributor branch for a license or license renewal unless the applicant for a license as a manufacturer, factory branch, distributor, or distributor branch offers to each motor vehicle dealer who is a party to a franchise for that line-make a new franchise agreement containing substantially the same provisions which were contained in the previous franchise agreement or files an affidavit with the Division acknowledging its undertaking to assume and fulfill the rights, duties, and obligations of its predecessor under the previous franchise agreement.

(7) Notwithstanding the terms of any contract or agreement, to prevent or refuse to honor the succession to a dealership, including the franchise, by a motor vehicle dealer's designated successor as provided for under this subsection.

a. Any owner of a new motor vehicle dealership may appoint by will, or any other written instrument, a designated successor to succeed in the respective ownership interest or interest as principal operator of the owner in the new motor vehicle dealership, including the franchise, upon the death or incapacity of the owner or principal operator. In order for succession to the position of principal operator to occur by operation of law in accordance with sub-subdivision c. below, the owner's choice of a successor must be approved by the dealer, in accordance with the dealer's bylaws, if applicable, either prior or subsequent to the death or incapacity of the existing principal operator.

b. Any objections by a manufacturer or distributor to an owner's appointment of a designated successor shall be asserted in accordance with the following procedure:

1. Within 30 days after receiving written notice of the identity of the owner's designated successor and general information as to the financial ability and qualifications of the designated successor, the franchisor shall send the owner and designated successor notice of objection, by registered or certified mail, return receipt requested, to the appointment of the designated successor. The notice of objection shall state in detail all facts which constitute the basis for the contention on the part of the manufacturer or distributor that good cause, as defined in this sub-subdivision below, exists for rejection of the designated successor. Failure by the franchisor to send notice of objection within 30 days and otherwise as provided in this sub-subdivision shall constitute waiver by the franchisor of any right to object to the appointment of the designated successor.

2. Any time within 30 days of receipt of the manufacturer's notice of objection the owner or the designated successor may file a request in writing with the Commissioner that the Commissioner hold an evidentiary hearing and determine whether good cause exists for rejection of the designated successor. When such a request is filed, the Commissioner shall promptly inform the affected manufacturer or distributor that a timely request has been filed.

3. The Commissioner shall endeavor to hold the evidentiary hearing required under this sub-subdivision and render a determination within 180 days after receipt of the written request from the owner or designated successor. In determining whether good cause exists for rejection of the owner's appointed designated successor, the manufacturer or distributor has the burden of proving that the designated successor is

a person who is not of good moral character or does not meet the franchisor's existing written and reasonable standards and, considering the volume of sales and service of the new motor vehicle dealer, uniformly applied minimum business experience standards in the market area.

4. Any parties to a hearing by the Commissioner concerning whether good cause exists for the rejection of the dealer's designated successor shall have a right of review of the decision in a court of competent jurisdiction pursuant to Chapter 150B of the General Statutes.

5. Nothing in this subsubdivision shall preclude a manufacturer or distributor from, upon its receipt of written notice from an owner of the identity of the owner's designated successor, requiring that the designated successor promptly provide personal and financial data that is reasonably necessary to determine the financial ability and qualifications of the designated successor; provided, however, that such a request for additional information shall not delay any of the time periods or constraints contained herein.

6. In the event death or incapacity of the owner or principal operator occurs prior to the time a manufacturer or distributor receives notice of the owner's appointment of a designated successor or before the Commissioner has rendered a determination as provided above, the existing franchise shall remain in effect and the designated successor shall be deemed to have succeeded to all of the owner's or principal operator's rights and obligations in the dealership and under the franchise until a determination is made by the Commissioner or the rights of the parties have otherwise become fixed in accordance with this subsubdivision.

c. Except as otherwise provided in sub-subdivision d. of this subdivision, any designated successor of a deceased or incapacitated owner or principal operator of a new motor vehicle dealership appointed by such owner in substantial compliance with this section shall, by operation of law, succeed at the time of such death or incapacity to all of the rights and obligations of the owner or principal operator in the new motor vehicle dealership and under either the existing franchise or any other successor, renewal, or replacement franchise.

d. Within 60 days after the death or incapacity of the owner or principal operator, a designated successor appointed in substantial compliance with this section shall give the affected manufacturer or distributor written notice of his or her succession to the position of owner or principal operator of the new motor vehicle dealership; provided, however, that the failure of the designated successor to give the manufacturer or distributor written notice as provided above within 60 days of the death or incapacity of the owner or principal operator shall not result in the waiver or termination of the designated successor's right to succeed to the ownership of the new motor vehicle dealership unless the manufacturer or distributor gives written notice of this provision to either the designated successor or the deceased or incapacitated owner's executor, administrator, guardian or other fiduciary by certified or registered mail, return receipt requested, and said written notice grants not less than 30 days time within which the designated successor may give the notice required hereunder, provided the designated successor or the deceased or incapacitated owner's executor, administrator, guardian or other fiduciary has given the manufacturer reasonable notice of death or incapacity. Within 30 days of receipt of the notice by the manufacturer or distributor from the designated successor provided in this sub-subdivision, the manufacturer or distributor may request that the designated successor complete the application forms generally utilized by the manufacturer or distributor to review the designated successor's qualifications to establish a successor dealership. Within 30 days of receipt of the completed forms, the manufacturer or distributor shall send a letter by certified or registered mail, return receipt requested, advising the designated successor of facts and circumstances which have changed since the manufacturer's or distributor's original approval of the designated successor, and which have caused the manufacturer or distributor to object to the designated successor. Upon receipt of such notice, the designated successor may either designate an alternative successor or may file a request for evidentiary hearing in accordance with the procedures provided in sub-subdivisions b.2.-5. of this subdivision. In any such hearing, the manufacturer or distributor shall be limited to facts and circumstances which did not exist at the time the designated successor was originally approved or evidence which was originally requested to be produced by the designated successor at the time of the original request and was fraudulent.

e. The designated successor shall agree to be bound by all terms and conditions of the franchise in effect between the manufacturer or distributor and the owner at the time of the owner's or principal operator's death or incapacity, if so requested in writing by the manufacturer or distributor subsequent to the owner's or principal operator's death or incapacity.

f. This section does not preclude an owner of a new motor vehicle dealership from designating any person as his or her successor by written instrument filed with the manufacturer or distributor, and, in the event there is an inconsistency between the successor named in such written instrument and the designated successor otherwise appointed by the owner consistent with the provisions of this section, and that written instrument has not been revoked by the owner of the new motor vehicle dealership in writing to the manufacturer or distributor, then the written instrument filed with the manufacturer or distributor shall govern as to the appointment of the successor.

(8) To require, coerce, or attempt to coerce any new motor vehicle dealer in this State to order or accept delivery of any new motor vehicle with special features, accessories or equipment not included in the list price of those motor vehicles as publicly advertised by the manufacturer or distributor.

(9) To require, coerce, or attempt to coerce any new motor vehicle dealer in this State to purchase or lease a specific dealer management computer system for communication with the manufacturer, factory branch, distributor, or distributor branch or any computer hardware or software used for any purpose other than the maintenance or repair of motor vehicles, to participate monetarily in an advertising campaign or contest, or to purchase unnecessary or unreasonable quantities of any promotional materials, training materials, training programs, showroom or other display decorations, materials, computer equipment or programs, or special tools at the expense of the new motor vehicle dealer, provided that nothing in this subsection shall preclude a manufacturer or distributor from including an unitemized uniform charge in the base price of the new motor vehicle charged to the dealer where such charge is

attributable to advertising costs incurred or to be incurred by the manufacturer or distributor in the ordinary courses of its business. Notwithstanding the terms or conditions of any franchise or other agreement, a franchised dealer that sells fewer than 250 new motor vehicles per year may request approval from the manufacturer to enter into a tool loaner agreement with another dealer, in lieu of purchasing or leasing any special tools required by any manufacturer, factory branch, distributor, or distributor branch, provided, however, that all of the following conditions are satisfied:

a. The manufacturer does not offer its dealers a special tool loaner/sharing program in which the dealer would be eligible to participate.

b. Eligible special tools exceed a cost of two thousand dollars ($ 2,000) per special tool, are easily and readily transportable, and would be utilized for service on less than 10 vehicles per month at the requesting dealer's dealership.

c. The dealers participating in a special tools loaner agreement do so pursuant to a written agreement, including designation of the dealer responsible for purchasing the specified tools.

d. All participating dealers are of the same line-make franchise with the manufacturer.

e. All participating dealers are located within a 40-mile radius of the dealer responsible for purchasing the specified special tools.

f. No more than five dealers participate in a special tool loaner agreement.

g. The manufacturer has approved the special tool loaner agreement, including the list of participating dealers and the list of eligible special tools to be included, which approval shall not be unreasonably withheld, conditioned, or delayed.

h. The manufacturer, factory branch, distributor, or distributor branch shall have the right to disapprove or terminate, upon 30 days written notice to all of the affected dealers, any special tool loaner agreement, if it determines that the agreement has resulted or is likely to result in a warranty repair delay of more than 48 hours, excessive warranty expense, or significant customer dissatisfaction.

(10) To require, coerce, or attempt to coerce any new motor vehicle dealer in this State to change the capital structure of the new motor vehicle dealer or the means by or through which the new motor vehicle dealer finances the operation of the dealership provided that the new motor vehicle dealer at all times meets any reasonable capital standards determined by the manufacturer in accordance with uniformly applied criteria; and also provided that no change in the capital structure shall cause a change in the principal management or have the effect of a sale of the franchise without the consent of the manufacturer or distributor, provided that said consent shall not be unreasonably withheld.

(11) To require, coerce, or attempt to coerce any new motor vehicle dealer in this State to refrain from participation in the management of, investment in, or the acquisition of any other line of new motor vehicle or related products; Provided, however, that this subsection does not apply unless the new motor vehicle dealer maintains a reasonable line of credit for each make or line of new motor vehicle, and the new motor vehicle dealer remains in compliance with any reasonable capital standards and facilities requirements of the manufacturer. The reasonable facilities requirements shall not include any requirement that a new motor vehicle dealer establish or maintain exclusive facilities, personnel, or display space.

(12) To require, coerce, or attempt to coerce any new motor vehicle dealer in this State to change location of the dealership, or to make any substantial alterations to the dealership premises or facilities, when to do so would be

unreasonable, or without written assurance of a sufficient supply of new motor vehicles so as to justify such an expansion, in light of the current market and economic conditions.

(13) To require, coerce, or attempt to coerce any new motor vehicle dealer in this State to prospectively assent to a release, assignment, novation, waiver or estoppel which would relieve any person from liability to be imposed by this law or to require any controversy between a new motor vehicle dealer and a manufacturer, distributor, or representative, to be referred to any person other than the duly constituted courts of the State or the United States of America, or to the Commissioner, if such referral would be binding upon the new motor vehicle dealer.

(14) To delay, refuse, or fail to deliver motor vehicles or motor vehicle parts or accessories in reasonable quantities relative to the new motor vehicle dealer's facilities and sales potential in the new motor vehicle dealer's market area as determined in accordance with reasonably applied economic principles, or within a reasonable time, after receipt of an order from a dealer having a franchise for the retail sale of any new motor vehicle sold or distributed by the manufacturer or distributor, any new vehicle, parts or accessories to new vehicles as are covered by such franchise, and such vehicles, parts or accessories as are publicly advertised as being available or actually being delivered. The delivery to another dealer of a motor vehicle of the same model and similarly equipped as the vehicle ordered by a motor vehicle dealer who has not received delivery thereof, but who has placed his written order for the vehicle prior to the order of the dealer receiving the vehicle, shall be evidence of a delayed delivery of, or refusal to deliver, a new motor vehicle to a motor vehicle dealer within a reasonable time, without cause. Additionally, except as may be required by any consent decree of the Commissioner or other order of the Commissioner or court of competent jurisdiction, any sales

objectives which a manufacturer, factory branch, distributor, or distributor branch establishes for any of its franchised dealers in this State must be reasonable, and every manufacturer, factory branch, distributor, or distributor branch must allocate its products within this State in a manner that does all of the following:

a. Provides each of its franchised dealers in this State an adequate supply of vehicles by series, product line, and model in a fair, reasonable, and equitable manner based on each dealer's historical selling pattern and reasonable sales standards as compared to other same line-make dealers in the State.

b. Allocates an adequate supply of vehicles to each of its dealers by series, product line, and model so as to allow the dealer to achieve any performance standards established by the manufacturer and distributor.

c. Is fair and equitable to all of its franchised dealers in this State.

d. Makes available to each of its franchised dealers in this State a minimum of one of each vehicle series, model, or product line that the manufacturer makes available to any dealer in this State and advertises in the State as being available for purchase.

e. Does not unfairly discriminate among its franchised dealers in its allocation process.

This subsection is not violated, however, if such failure is caused solely by the occurrence of temporary international, national, or regional product shortages resulting from natural disasters, unavailability of parts, labor strikes, product recalls, and other factors and events beyond the control of the manufacturer that temporarily reduce a manufacturer's product supply. The willful or malicious maintenance, creation, or alteration of a vehicle allocation process or formula by a manufacturer, factory branch, distributor, or distributor branch that is in any part designed or intended to force or coerce a dealer in this State to close or sell the dealer's franchise, cause the dealer financial distress, or to relocate, update, or renovate the dealer's existing dealership facility shall constitute an unfair and deceptive trade practice under G.S. 75-1.1.

(15) To refuse to disclose to any new motor vehicle dealer, handling the same line make, the manner and mode of distribution of that line make within the State.

(16) To award money, goods, services, or any other benefit to any new motor vehicle dealership employee, either directly or indirectly, unless such benefit is promptly accounted for, and transmitted to, or approved by, the new motor vehicle dealer.

(17) To increase prices of new motor vehicles which the new motor vehicle dealer had ordered and which the manufacturer or distributor has accepted for immediate delivery for private retail consumers prior to the new motor vehicle dealer's receipt of the written official price increase notification. A sales contract signed by a private retail consumer shall constitute evidence of each such order provided that the vehicle is in fact delivered to that customer. Price differences applicable to new model or series shall not be considered a price increase or price decrease. Price changes caused by either: (i) the addition to a new motor vehicle of required or optional equipment; or (ii) revaluation of the United States dollar, in the case of foreign-make vehicles or components; or (iii) an increase in transportation charges due to increased rates imposed by carriers; or (iv) new tariffs or duties imposed by the United States of America or any other governmental authority, shall not be subject to the provisions of this subsection.

(18) To prevent or attempt to prevent a dealer from receiving fair and reasonable compensation for the value of the franchised business transferred in accordance with G.S. 20-305(4) above, or to prevent or attempt to prevent, through the exercise of any contractual right of first refusal or otherwise, a dealer located in this State from transferring the franchised business to such persons or other entities as the dealer shall designate in accordance with G.S. 20-305(4). The opinion or determination of a manufacturer that the existence or location of one of its franchised dealers situated in this State is not viable or is not consistent with the manufacturer's distribution or marketing forecast or plans shall not constitute a lawful basis for the manufacturer to fail or refuse to approve a dealer's proposed transfer of ownership submitted in accordance with G.S. 20-305(4), or "good cause" for the termination, cancellation, or nonrenewal of the franchise under G.S. 20-305(6) or grounds for the objection to an owner's designated successor appointed pursuant to G.S. 20-305(7).

(19) To offer any refunds or other types of inducements to any person for the purchase of new motor vehicles of a certain line make to be sold to the State or any political subdivision thereof without making the same offer available upon request to all other new motor vehicle dealers in the same line make within the State.

(20) To release to any outside party, except under subpoena or as otherwise required by law or in an administrative, judicial or arbitration proceeding involving the manufacturer or new motor vehicle dealer, any confidential business, financial, or personal information which may be from time to time provided by the new motor vehicle dealer to the manufacturer, without the express written consent of the new motor vehicle dealer.

(21) To deny any new motor vehicle dealer the right of free association with any other new motor vehicle dealer for any lawful purpose.

(22) To unfairly discriminate among its new motor vehicle dealers with respect to warranty reimbursements or authority granted its new motor vehicle dealers to make warranty adjustments with retail customers.

(23) To engage in any predatory practice against or unfairly compete with a new motor vehicle dealer located in this State.

(24) To terminate any franchise solely because of the death or incapacity of an owner who is not listed in the franchise as one on whose expertise and abilities the manufacturer relied in the granting of the franchise.

(25) To require, coerce, or attempt to coerce a new motor vehicle dealer in this State to either establish or maintain exclusive facilities, personnel, or display space.

(26) To resort to or to use any false or misleading advertisement in the conducting of its business as a manufacturer or distributor in this State.

(27) To knowingly make, either directly or through any agent or employee, any material statement which is false or misleading or conceal any material facts which induce any new motor vehicle dealer to enter into any agreement or franchise or to take any action which is materially prejudicial to that new motor vehicle dealer or his business.

(28) To require, coerce, or attempt to coerce any new motor vehicle dealer to purchase or order any new motor vehicle as a precondition to purchasing, ordering, or receiving any other new motor vehicle or vehicles. Nothing herein shall prevent a manufacturer from requiring that a new motor vehicle dealer fairly represent and inventory the full line of current model year new motor vehicles which are covered by the franchise agreement, provided that such inventory representation requirements are not unreasonable under the circumstances.

(29) To require, coerce, or attempt to coerce any new motor vehicle dealer to sell, transfer, or otherwise issue stock or other ownership interest in the dealership corporation to a general manager or any other person involved in the management of the dealership other than the dealer principal or dealer operator named in the franchise, unless the dealer principal or dealer operator is an absentee owner who is not involved in the operation of the dealership on a regular basis.

(30) To vary the price charged to any of its franchised new motor vehicle dealers located in this State for new motor vehicles based on the dealer's purchase of new facilities, supplies, tools, equipment, or other merchandise from the manufacturer, the dealer's relocation, remodeling, repair, or renovation of existing dealerships or construction of a new facility, the dealer's participation in training programs sponsored, endorsed, or recommended by the manufacturer, whether or not the dealer is dualed with one or more other line makes of new motor vehicles, or the dealer's sales penetration. Except as provided in this subdivision, it shall be unlawful for any manufacturer, factory branch, distributor, or distributor branch, or any field representative, officer, agent, or any representative whatsoever of any of them to vary the price charged to any of its franchised new motor vehicle dealers located in this State for new motor vehicles based on the dealer's sales volume, the dealer's level of sales or customer service satisfaction, the dealer's purchase of advertising materials, signage, nondiagnostic computer hardware or software, communications devices, or furnishings, or the dealer's participation in used motor vehicle inspection or certification programs sponsored or endorsed by the manufacturer.

The price of the vehicle, for purposes of this subdivision shall include the manufacturer's use of rebates, credits, or other consideration that has the effect of causing a variance in the price of new motor vehicles offered to its franchised dealers located in the State.

Notwithstanding the foregoing, nothing in this subdivision shall be deemed to preclude a manufacturer from establishing sales contests or promotions that provide or award dealers or consumers rebates or incentives; provided, however, that the manufacturer complies with all of the following conditions:

a. With respect to manufacturer to consumer rebates and incentives, the manufacturer's criteria for determining eligibility shall:

1. Permit all of the manufacturer's franchised new motor vehicle dealers

in this State to offer the rebate or incentive; and

2. Be uniformly applied and administered to all eligible consumers.

b. With respect to manufacturer to dealer rebates and incentives, the rebate or incentive program shall:

1. Be based solely on the dealer's actual or reasonably anticipated sales volume or on a uniform per vehicle sold or leased basis;

2. Be uniformly available, applied, and administered to all of the manufacturer's franchised new motor vehicle dealers in this State; and

3. Provide that any of the manufacturer's franchised new motor vehicle dealers in this State may, upon written request, obtain the method or formula used by the manufacturer in establishing the sales volumes for receiving the rebates or incentives and the specific calculations for determining the required sales volumes of the inquiring dealer and any of the manufacturer's other franchised new motor vehicle dealers located within 75 miles of the inquiring dealer.

Nothing contained in this subdivision shall prohibit a manufacturer from providing assistance or encouragement to a franchised dealer to remodel, renovate, recondition, or relocate the dealer's existing facilities, provided that this assistance, encouragement, or rewards are not determined on a per vehicle basis.

It is unlawful for any manufacturer to charge or include the cost of any program or policy prohibited under this subdivision in the price of new motor vehicles that the manufacturer sells to its franchised dealers or purchasers located in this State.

In the event that as of October 1, 1999, a manufacturer was operating a program that varied the price charged to its franchised dealers in this State in a manner that would violate this subdivision, or had in effect a documented policy that had been conveyed to its franchised dealers in this State and that varied the price charged to its franchised dealers in this State in a manner that would violate this subdivision, it shall be lawful for that program or policy, including amendments to that program or policy that are consistent with the purpose and provisions of the existing program or policy, or a program or policy similar thereto implemented after October 1, 1999, to continue in effect as to the manufacturer's franchised dealers located in this State until June 30, 2022.

In the event that as of June 30, 2001, a manufacturer was operating a program that varied the price charged to its franchised dealers in this State in a manner that would violate this subdivision, or had in effect a documented policy that had been conveyed to its franchised dealers in this State and that varied the price charged to its franchised dealers in this State in a manner that would violate this subdivision, and the program or policy was implemented in this State subsequent to October 1, 1999, and prior to June 30, 2001, and provided that the program or policy is in compliance with this subdivision as it existed as of June 30, 2001, it shall be lawful for that program or policy, including amendments to that program or policy that comply with this subdivision as it existed as of June 30, 2001, to continue in effect as to the manufacturer's franchised dealers located in this State until June 30, 2022.

Any manufacturer shall be required to pay or otherwise compensate any franchise dealer who has earned the right to receive payment or other compensation under a program in accordance with the manufacturer's program or policy.

The provisions of this subdivision shall not be applicable to multiple or repeated sales of new motor vehicles made by a new motor vehicle dealer to a single purchaser under a bona fide fleet sales policy of a manufacturer, factory branch, distributor, or distributor branch.

(31) Notwithstanding the terms of any contract, franchise, agreement, release, or waiver, to require that in any civil or administrative proceeding in which a new motor vehicle dealer asserts any claims, rights, or defenses arising under this Article or under the franchise, that the dealer or any nonprevailing party compensate the manufacturer or prevailing party for any court costs, attorneys' fees, or other expenses incurred in the litigation.

(32) To require that any of its franchised new motor vehicle dealers located in this State pay any extra fee, purchase unreasonable or unnecessary quantities of

advertising displays or other materials, or remodel, renovate, or recondition the dealers' existing facilities in order to receive any particular model or series of vehicles manufactured or distributed by the manufacturer for which the dealers have a valid franchise. Notwithstanding the foregoing, nothing contained in this subdivision shall be deemed to prohibit or prevent a manufacturer from requiring that its franchised dealers located in this State purchase special tools or equipment, stock reasonable quantities of certain parts, or participate in training programs which are reasonably necessary for those dealers to sell or service any model or series of vehicles.

(33) To fail to reimburse a dealer located in this State in full for the actual cost of providing a loaner vehicle to any customer who is having a vehicle serviced at the dealership if the provision of such a loaner vehicle is required by the manufacturer.

(34) To require, coerce, or attempt to coerce any new motor vehicle dealer in this State to participate monetarily in any training program whose subject matter is not expressly limited to specific information necessary to sell or service the models of vehicles the dealer is authorized to sell or service under the dealer's franchise with that manufacturer. Examples of training programs with respect to which a manufacturer is prohibited from requiring the dealer's monetary participation include, but are not limited to, those which purport to teach morale-boosting employee motivation, teamwork, or general principles of customer relations. A manufacturer is further prohibited from requiring the personal attendance of an owner or dealer principal of any dealership located in this State at any meeting or training program at which it is reasonably possible for another member of the dealer's management to attend and later relate the subject matter of the meeting or training program to the dealership's owners or principal operator.

(35) Notwithstanding the terms of any franchise, agreement,

waiver or novation, to limit the number of franchises of the same line make of vehicle that any franchised motor vehicle dealer, including its parent(s), subsidiaries, and affiliates, if any, may own or operate or attach any restrictions or conditions on the ownership or operation of multiple franchises of the same line make of motor vehicle without making the same limitations, conditions, and restrictions applicable to all of its other franchisees.

(36) With regard to any manufacturer, factory branch, distributor, distributor branch, or subsidiary thereof that owns and operates a new motor vehicle dealership, directly or indirectly through any subsidiary or affiliated entity as provided in G.S. 20-305.2, to unreasonably discriminate against any other new motor vehicle dealer in the same line make in any matter governed by the motor vehicle franchise, including the sale or allocation of vehicles or other manufacturer or distributor products, or the execution of dealer programs for benefits.

(37) Subdivisions (11) and (25) of this section shall not apply to any manufacturer, manufacturer branch, distributor, distributor branch, or any affiliate or subsidiary thereof of new motor vehicles which manufactures or distributes exclusively new motor vehicles with a gross weight rating of 8,500 pounds or more, provided that the following conditions are met: (i) the manufacturer has, as of November 1, 1996, an agreement in effect with at least three of its franchised dealers within the State, and which agreement was, in fact, being enforced by the manufacturer, requiring the dealers to maintain separate and exclusive facilities for the vehicles it manufactures or distributes; and (ii) there existed at least seven dealerships (locations) of that manufacturer within the State as of January 1, 1999.

(38) Notwithstanding the terms, provisions, or conditions of any agreement, franchise, novation, waiver, or other written instrument, to assign or change a franchised new motor vehicle dealer's

area of responsibility under the franchise arbitrarily or without due regard to the present or projected future pattern of motor vehicle sales and registrations within the dealer's market and without having provided the affected dealer with written notice of the change in the dealer's area of responsibility and a detailed description of the change in writing by registered or certified mail, return receipt requested. A franchised new motor vehicle dealer who believes that a manufacturer, factory branch, distributor, or distributor branch with whom the dealer has entered into a franchise has assigned or changed the dealer's area of responsibility, is proposing to assign or change the dealer's area of responsibility arbitrarily or without due regard to the present or projected future pattern of motor vehicle sales and registrations within the dealer's market, or failed to provide the dealer with the notice required under this subdivision may file a petition within 60 days of receiving notice of a manufacturer, factory branch, distributor, or distributor branch's proposed assignment or change to the dealer's area of responsibility and have an evidentiary hearing before the Commissioner as provided in G.S. 20-301(b) contesting the franchised new motor vehicle dealer's assigned area of responsibility. Provided that the dealer has not previously filed a petition pursuant to this subdivision within the preceding 48 months regarding the dealer's currently assigned area of responsibility, a franchised new motor vehicle dealer who believes that it is unreasonable for a manufacturer, factory branch, distributor, or distributor branch with whom that dealer has entered into a franchise to include one or more portions of the dealer's existing area of responsibility previously assigned to that dealer by the manufacturer, factory branch, distributor, or distributor branch may request the elimination of the contested territory from the dealer's area of responsibility by submitting the request in writing via U.S. registered or certified mail, return receipt requested, to

the manufacturer, factory branch, distributor, or distributor branch. The dealer shall state in its request that the request is being made pursuant to this subdivision, describe the territory the dealer seeks to remove from its area of responsibility, and provide a general statement as to the factual basis for the dealer's contention of the changed factors warranting modification of the dealer's area of responsibility. The dealer's request shall be deemed accepted by the manufacturer, factory branch, distributor, or distributor branch if the manufacturer, factory branch, distributor, or distributor branch has not sent the dealer notice of objection to the dealer's request via U.S. registered or certified mail, return receipt requested, within 90 days after receipt of the dealer's request. Within 30 days of the dealer's receipt of notice from the manufacturer, factory branch, distributor, or distributor branch of the manufacturer's rejection, in whole or in part, of the dealer's request for the elimination of the contested territory from the dealer's area of responsibility, either party may request mediation under the manufacturer's internal mediation program, if any. Any such mediation shall commence within 60 days after the request for mediation is made and be concluded within 120 days after the date the manufacturer, factory branch, distributor, or distributor branch objected to the dealer's proposed change in its area of responsibility. Within 60 days of the conclusion of a requested mediation process, or, if a mediation process has not been timely requested under this subdivision, within 60 days of receiving notice from the manufacturer, factory branch, distributor, or distributor branch of the manufacturer's rejection, in whole or in part, of the dealer's request for the elimination of the contested territory from the dealer's area of responsibility, a dealer may file a petition and have an evidentiary hearing before the Commissioner as provided in G.S. 20-301(b) contesting the manufacturer's rejection, in whole or in part, of the dealer's request for the elimination of the contested territory from the franchised new motor vehicle dealer's assigned area of responsibility. In determining at an evidentiary hearing requested under this subdivision whether all or any portion of the existing or proposed area of responsibility assigned to the dealer is unreasonable or has been assigned arbitrarily or without due regard to the present or projected future pattern of motor vehicle sales and registrations within the dealer's market, the Commissioner may take into consideration the relevant circumstances, including, but not limited to:

a. The investment of time, money, or other resources made for the purpose of developing the market for the vehicles of the same line-make in the existing or proposed area of responsibility by the petitioning dealer, other same line-make dealers who would be affected by the change in the area of responsibility, or by the manufacturer, factory branch, distributor, distributor branch, or any dealer or regional advertising association.

b. The present and future projected traffic patterns and drive times between consumers and the same line-make franchised dealers of the affected manufacturer, factory branch, distributor, or distributor branch who are located within the market.

c. The historical and projected future pattern of new vehicle sales and registrations of the affected manufacturer, factory branch, distributor, or distributor branch within various portions of the area of responsibility and within the market as a whole.

d. The growth or decline in population, density of population, and new car registrations in the market.

e. If the affected manufacturer, factory branch, distributor, or distributor branch has removed territory from a dealer's area of responsibility or is proposing to remove

territory from a dealer's area of responsibility, the projected economic effects, if any, that these changes in the dealer's area of responsibility will have on the petitioning dealer, other same line-make dealers, the public, and the manufacturer, factory branch, distributor, or distributor branch.

f. The projected effects that the changes in the petitioning dealer's area of responsibility that have been made or proposed by the affected manufacturer, manufacturer branch, distributor, or distributor branch will have on the consuming public within the market.

g. The presence or absence of natural geographical obstacles or boundaries, such as mountains and rivers.

h. The proximity of census tracts or other geographic units used by the affected manufacturer, factory branch, distributor, or distributor branch in determining same line-make dealers' respective areas of responsibility.

i. The public interest, consumer welfare, and customer convenience.

j. The reasonableness of the change or proposed change to the dealer's area of responsibility considering the benefits and harm to the petitioning dealer, other same line-make dealers, and the manufacturer, factory branch, distributor, or distributor branch.

At the evidentiary hearing before the Commissioner, following the filing of a petition by a dealer contesting the proposed assignment or change to the dealer's area of responsibility by a manufacturer, factory branch, distributor, or distributor branch, the affected manufacturer, factory branch, distributor, or distributor branch shall have the burden of proving that all portions of its current or proposed area of responsibility for the petitioning franchised new motor vehicle dealer are reasonable in light of the present or projected future pattern of motor vehicle sales and registrations within the franchised new motor vehicle dealer's market. At an evidentiary hearing before the Commissioner held pursuant to a franchised new motor vehicle dealer's petition to eliminate contested territory from the dealer's existing area of responsibility previously assigned to the dealer by the manufacturer, factory branch, distributor, or distributor branch, the franchised new motor vehicle dealer shall have the burden of proving that it would be unreasonable to continue to include the contested territory in the dealer's area of responsibility due to changes in circumstances under sub-subdivisions a. through j. of this subdivision that are beyond the control of the dealer. A policy or protocol of a manufacturer, factory branch, distributor, or distributor branch that determines a dealer's area of responsibility based solely on the proximity of census tracts or other geographic units to its franchised dealers and the existence of natural boundaries fails to satisfy the burden of proof on the affected manufacturer, factory branch, distributor, or distributor branch under this subdivision. Upon the filing of a petition before the Commissioner under this subdivision, any changes in the petitioning franchised new motor vehicle dealer's area of responsibility that have been proposed by the affected manufacturer, factory branch, distributor, or distributor branch shall be stayed during the pendency of the determination by the Commissioner. If a protest is or has been filed under G.S. 20-305(5) and the franchised new motor vehicle dealer's area of responsibility is included in the relevant market area under the protest, any protest filed under this subdivision shall be consolidated with that protest for

hearing and joint disposition of all of the protests. Nothing in this subdivision shall apply to the determination of whether good cause exists for the establishment by a manufacturer, factory branch, distributor, or distributor branch of an additional new motor vehicle dealer or relocation of an existing new motor vehicle dealer, which shall be governed in accordance with the requirements and criteria contained in G.S. 20-305(5) and not this subdivision.

(39) Notwithstanding the terms, provisions, or conditions of any agreement, franchise, novation, waiver, or other written instrument, to require, coerce, or attempt to coerce any of its franchised motor vehicle dealers in this State to purchase, lease, erect, or relocate one or more signs displaying the name of the manufacturer or franchised motor vehicle dealer upon unreasonable or onerous terms or conditions or if installation of the additional signage would violate local signage or zoning laws to which the franchised motor vehicle dealer is subject. Any term, provision, or condition of any agreement, franchise, waiver, novation, or any other written instrument which is in violation of this subdivision shall be deemed null and void and without force and effect.

(40) Notwithstanding the terms, provisions, or conditions of any agreement or franchise, to require any dealer to floor plan any of the dealer's inventory or finance the acquisition, construction, or renovation of any of the dealer's property or facilities by or through any financial source or sources designated by the manufacturer, factory branch, distributor, or distributor branch, including any financial source or sources that is or are directly or indirectly owned, operated, or controlled by the manufacturer, factory branch, distributor, or distributor branch.

(41) Notwithstanding the terms, provisions, or conditions of any agreement or franchise, to use or consider the performance of any of its franchised new motor vehicle dealers located in this State

relating to the sale of the manufacturer's new motor vehicles or ability to satisfy any minimum sales or market share quota or responsibility relating to the sale of the manufacturer's new motor vehicles in determining:

a. The dealer's eligibility to purchase program, certified, or other used motor vehicles from the manufacturer;

b. The volume, type, or model of program, certified, or other used motor vehicles the dealer shall be eligible to purchase from the manufacturer;

c. The price or prices of any program, certified, or other used motor vehicles that the dealer shall be eligible to purchase from the manufacturer; or

d. The availability or amount of any discount, credit, rebate, or sales incentive the dealer shall be eligible to receive from the manufacturer for the purchase of any program, certified, or other used motor vehicles offered for sale by the manufacturer.

(42) Notwithstanding the terms, provisions, or conditions of any agreement or waiver, to directly or indirectly condition the awarding of a franchise to a prospective new motor vehicle dealer, the addition of a line make or franchise to an existing dealer, the renewal of a franchise of an existing dealer, the approval of the relocation of an existing dealer's facility, or the approval of the sale or transfer of the ownership of a franchise on the willingness of a dealer, proposed new dealer, or owner of an interest in the dealership facility to enter into a site control agreement or exclusive use agreement. For purposes of this subdivision, the terms "site control agreement" and "exclusive use agreement" include any agreement that has the effect of either: (i) requiring that the dealer establish or maintain exclusive dealership facilities; or (ii) restricting the ability of the dealer, or the ability of the dealer's lessor in the event the dealership facility is being leased, to transfer, sell, lease, or change the use of the dealership premises, whether by sublease, lease, collateral pledge of lease, right of first refusal to purchase or lease, option to purchase, option to lease, or other similar agreement, regardless of the parties to such agreement. Any provision contained in any agreement entered into on or after August 26, 2009, that is inconsistent with the provisions of this subdivision shall be voidable at the election of the affected dealer, prospective dealer, or owner of an interest in the dealership facility.

(43) Notwithstanding the terms, provisions, or conditions of any agreement, franchise, novation, waiver, or other written instrument, to require, coerce, or attempt to coerce any of its franchised motor vehicle dealers in this State to change the principal operator, general manager, or any other manager or supervisor employed by the dealer. Any term, provision, or condition of any agreement, franchise, waiver, novation, or any other written instrument that is inconsistent with this subdivision shall be deemed null and void and without force and effect.

(44) Notwithstanding the terms, provisions, or conditions of any agreement or franchise, to require, coerce, or attempt to coerce any new motor vehicle dealer located in this State to refrain from displaying in the dealer's showroom or elsewhere within the dealership facility any sports-related honors, awards, photographs, displays, or other artifacts or memorabilia; provided, however, that such sports-related honors, awards, photographs, displays, or other artifacts or memorabilia (i) pertain to an owner, investor, or executive manager of the dealership; (ii) relate to professional sports; (iii) do not reference or advertise a competing brand of motor vehicles; and (iv) do not conceal or disparage any of the required branding elements that are part of the dealership facility.

(45) Notwithstanding the terms, provisions, or conditions of any agreement or franchise, to discriminate against a new motor vehicle dealer located in this State for selling or offering for sale a service contract, debt cancellation

agreement, maintenance agreement, or similar product not approved, endorsed, sponsored, or offered by the manufacturer, distributor, affiliate, or captive finance source. For purposes of this subdivision, discrimination includes any of the following:

a. Requiring or coercing a dealer to exclusively sell or offer for sale service contracts, debt cancellation agreements, or similar products approved, endorsed, sponsored, or offered by the manufacturer, distributor, affiliate, or captive finance source.

b. Taking or threatening to take any adverse action against a dealer (i) because the dealer sells or offers for sale any service contracts, debt cancellation agreements, maintenance agreements, or similar products that have not been approved, endorsed, sponsored, or offered by the manufacturer, distributor, affiliate, or captive finance source or (ii) because the dealer fails to sell or offer for sale service contracts, debt cancellation agreements, maintenance agreements, or similar products approved, endorsed, sponsored, or offered by the manufacturer, distributor, their affiliate, or captive finance source.

c. Measuring a dealer's performance under a franchise in any part based upon the dealer's sale of service contracts, debt cancellation agreements, or similar products approved, endorsed, sponsored, or offered by the manufacturer, distributor, affiliate, or captive finance source.

d. Requiring a dealer to exclusively promote the sale of service contracts, debt cancellation agreements, or similar products approved, endorsed, sponsored, or offered by the manufacturer, distributor, affiliate, or captive finance source.

e. Considering the dealer's sale of service contracts, debt cancellation agreements, or similar products approved,

endorsed, sponsored, or offered by the manufacturer, distributor, affiliate, or captive finance source in determining any of the following:

1. The dealer's eligibility to purchase any vehicles, parts, or other products or services from the manufacturer or distributor.

2. The volume of vehicles or other parts or services the dealer shall be eligible to purchase from the manufacturer or distributor.

3. The price or prices of any vehicles, parts, or other products or services that the dealer shall be eligible to purchase from the manufacturer or distributor.

4. The availability or amount of any vehicle discount, credit, special pricing, rebate, or sales or service incentive the dealer shall be eligible to receive from the manufacturer, distributor, affiliate, or captive finance source in which the incentives are calculated or paid on a per-vehicle basis or any vehicle discount, credit, special pricing, or rebate that are calculated or paid on a per-vehicle basis.

For purposes of this subdivision, discrimination does not include, and nothing shall prohibit a manufacturer, distributor, affiliate, or captive finance source from, offering discounts, rebates, or other incentives to dealers who voluntarily sell or offer for sale service contracts, debt cancellation agreements, or similar products approved, endorsed, sponsored, or offered by the manufacturer, distributor, affiliate, or captive finance source; provided, however, that such discounts, rebates, or other incentives are based solely on the sales volume of the service contracts, debt cancellation agreements, or similar products sold by the dealer and do not provide vehicle sales or service incentives.

For purposes of this subdivision, a service contract

provider or its representative shall not complete any sale or transaction of an extended service contract, extended maintenance plan, or similar product using contract forms that do not disclose the identity of the service contract provider.

(46) To require, coerce, or attempt to coerce a dealer located in this State to purchase goods or services of any nature from a vendor selected, identified, or designated by a manufacturer, distributor, affiliate, or captive finance source when the dealer may obtain goods or services of substantially similar quality and design from a vendor selected by the dealer, provided the dealer obtains prior approval from the manufacturer, distributor, affiliate, or captive finance source, for the use of the dealer's selected vendor. Such approval by the manufacturer, distributor, affiliate, or captive finance source may not be unreasonably withheld. For purposes of this subdivision, the term "goods" does not include moveable displays, brochures, and promotional materials containing material subject to the intellectual property rights of a manufacturer or distributor, or special tools or parts as reasonably required by the manufacturer to be used in repairs under warranty obligations of a manufacturer or distributor. If the manufacturer, distributor, affiliate, or captive finance source claims that a vendor chosen by the dealer cannot supply goods and services of substantially similar quality and design, the dealer may file a protest with the Commissioner. When a protest is filed, the Commissioner shall promptly inform the manufacturer, distributor, affiliate, or captive finance source that a protest has been filed. The Commissioner shall conduct a hearing on the merits of the protest within 90 days following the filing of a response to the protest. The manufacturer, distributor, affiliate, or captive finance source shall bear the burden of proving that the goods or services chosen by the dealer are not of substantially similar quality and design to those required by the

manufacturer, distributor, affiliate, or captive finance source.

(47) To fail to provide to a dealer, if the goods or services to be supplied to the dealer by a vendor selected, identified, or designated by the manufacturer or distributor are signs or other franchisor image elements to be purchased or leased to the dealer, the right to purchase or lease the signs or other franchisor image elements of similar quality and design from a vendor selected by the dealer. This subdivision and subdivision (46) of this section shall not be construed to allow a dealer or vendor to violate directly or indirectly the intellectual property rights of the manufacturer or distributor, including, but not limited to, the manufacturer's or distributor's intellectual property rights in any trademarks or trade dress, or other intellectual property interests owned or controlled by the manufacturer or distributor, or to permit a dealer to erect or maintain signs that do not conform to the reasonable intellectual property right or trademark and trade dress usage guidelines of the manufacturer or distributor.

(48) To unreasonably interfere with a dealer's independence in staffing the dealership by engaging in any of the following conduct: (i) requiring, coercing, or attempting to coerce a dealer located in this State to employ, appoint, or designate an individual to serve full-time or exclusively in any specific capacity, role, or job function at the dealership, other than the employment or appointment of a full-time general manager; (ii) requiring a dealer to employ, appoint, or designate an individual to serve full-time or exclusively in any specific capacity, role, or job function at the dealership, other than the employment or appointment of a full-time general manager, in order to participate in or qualify for any incentive program offered or sponsored by the manufacturer or distributor or to otherwise receive any discounts, credits, rebates, or incentives of any kind that are calculated or paid on a per-vehicle basis; or (iii) requiring that the dealer obtain the approval of the manufacturer or

distributor prior to employing or appointing any individual in any capacity, role, or job function at the dealership, other than the employment or appointment of a full-time general manager. Except as expressly provided above, nothing contained in this subdivision shall be deemed to prevent or prohibit a manufacturer or distributor from requiring that a dealer employ a reasonable number of trained employees to sell and service the factory's vehicles.

(49) A manufacturer or distributor may not charge a dealer more than a reasonable cost for any tool that the manufacturer or distributor sells to a dealer and designates as a special or essential tool. A manufacturer or distributor that collects tool fees as a convenience for the dealer and passes the payment through to a tool manufacturer or supplier which is not owned, operated, or controlled by the manufacturer, distributor, or affiliate shall not be considered to be selling the tool provided that the manufacturer or distributor's involvement does not increase the cost of the special tool or essential tool. Nothing in this subdivision shall prohibit a manufacturer or distributor from charging a reasonable nominal fee in addition to the cost of the special or essential tool that includes manufacturer or distributor handling costs. For any special or essential tool that the manufacturer or distributor sells to the dealer at a price exceeding two hundred fifty dollars ($ 250.00), the manufacturer or distributor shall disclose on an invoice or similar billing statement submitted to the dealer for the tool, the actual cost of the special or essential tool paid by the manufacturer or distributor.

(50) To require, coerce, or attempt to coerce any new motor vehicle dealer located in this State to change location of its dealership, or to make any substantial alterations to its dealership premises or facilities, if the dealer (i) has changed the location of its dealership or made substantial alterations to its dealership premises or facilities within the preceding 10 years at a cost of more than

two hundred fifty thousand dollars ($ 250,000), indexed to the Consumer Price Index, over this 10-year period, and (ii) the change in location or alteration was made toward compliance with a facility initiative or facility program that was sponsored or supported by the manufacturer, factory branch, distributor, or distributor branch, with the approval of the manufacturer, factory branch, distributor, or distributor branch. For any dealer that did not change the location of its dealership or make substantial alterations to its dealership premises or facilities within the preceding 10 years at a cost of more than two hundred fifty thousand dollars ($ 250,000), indexed to the Consumer Price Index, the dealer's obligation to change location of its dealership, or to make any substantial alteration to its dealership premises or facilities, at the request of a manufacturer, factory branch, distributor, or distributor branch, or to satisfy a requirement or condition of an incentive program sponsored by a manufacturer, factory branch, distributor, or distributor branch, shall be governed by the applicable provisions of subdivisions (4), (11), (12), (25), (30), (32), and (42) of this section. This section shall not apply to any facility or premises improvement or alteration that is voluntarily agreed to by the new motor vehicle dealer and for which the dealer receives facilities-related compensation from the manufacturer or distributor for the facility improvement or alteration equivalent to at least a majority of the cost incurred by the dealer for the facility improvement or alteration.

(51) To establish, implement, or enforce criteria for measuring the sales or service performance of any of its franchised new motor vehicle dealers in this State for any of the purposes in sub-subdivisions a. through c. of this subdivision that (i) are unfair, unreasonable, arbitrary, or inequitable; (ii) do not consider available relevant and material State and regional criteria, data, and facts. Relevant and material criteria, data, or facts include those of motor vehicle dealerships

Chapter 20

of comparable size in comparable markets; and (iii) if such performance measurement criteria are based, in whole or in part, on a survey, such survey must be based on a statistically significant and valid random sample. In any proceeding under this subdivision, the applicable manufacturer or distributor shall bear the burden of proof (i) with regard to all issues raised in the proceeding and (ii) that the dealer performance measurements comply with all of the provisions hereof and are, and have been, implemented and enforced uniformly by the manufacturer or distributor among its franchised dealers in this State. Prior to taking a final action on an event described in sub-subdivisions a. through c. of this subdivision, if the dealer's current or past sales or service performance constitute any part of the basis for the final action, a manufacturer or distributor shall allow a dealer to present relevant local criteria, data, and facts beyond the control of the dealer, which the manufacturer or distributor shall consider. In the event it is determined that the performance criteria employed by a manufacturer or distributor for measuring the sales, service, or customer satisfaction performance of any of its franchised motor vehicle dealers in this State are unfair, unreasonable, arbitrary, or inequitable, or that the performance criteria does not consider available State and regional criteria, data, and facts required in this subsection, or that the performance criteria have not been implemented and enforced uniformly by the manufacturer or distributor among its franchised dealers in this State, or that the performance criteria do not consider relevant local criteria, data, and facts presented by the dealer in accordance with this subdivision, the performance criteria of the manufacturer or distributor may not constitute any part of the basis for a determination in any franchise-related decision pertaining to any of the following:

a. Whether to allow a dealer's proposed transfer of ownership pursuant to subdivision (4) of this section.

b. Whether good cause exists for the termination of a dealer's franchise pursuant to subdivision (6) of this section.

c. Whether to allow appointment of a designated successor to a franchise pursuant to subdivision (7) of this section.

If a dealer's current or past performance in sales or service constitutes any part of the basis for the decision of the manufacturer, factory branch, distributor, or distributor branch pertaining to sub-subdivisions a. through c. of this subdivision, the dealer and the applicable manufacturer, factory branch, distributor, or distributor branch shall have the right to present local criteria, data, and facts in any petition or hearing before the Commissioner requested by the dealer pursuant to subdivision (4), (6), or (7) of this section.

(52) To prohibit or to in any way unreasonably limit or restrict a dealer from offering for sale over the Internet, including online e-commerce marketplaces, parts and accessories obtained by the dealer from the manufacturer, factory branch, distributor, or distributor branch, or from any source recommended or approved by the manufacturer, factory branch, distributor, or distributor branch. Nothing in this subdivision shall eliminate or impair the intellectual property rights of a manufacturer, factory branch, distributor, or distributor branch.

History.
1955, c. 1243, s. 21; 1973, c. 88, ss. 1, 2; 1983, c. 704, ss. 5-10; 1987, c. 827, s. 1; 1991, c. 510, ss. 2 -4; 1993, c. 123, s. 1;c. 331, s. 2;1995, c. 163, s. 13;c. 480, s. 3;1997-319, s. 3;1999-335, s. 2;1999-336, s. 1;2001-510, ss. 2, 6; 2003-113, ss. 2, 3, 4; 2005-409, s. 2;2005-463, s. 2;2007-513, ss. 2 -4, 9, 12; 2008-156, s. 3;2008-187, s. 50;2009-338, ss. 1, 2, 5; 2009-496, s. 1;2011-290, ss. 5 -9; 2013-302, s. 7;2014-58, s. 10(e), (f); 2015-209, ss. 2, 3, 4, 5; 2017-102, s. 5.2(b);2017-148, s. 2;2018-27, ss. 1, 4; 2019-125, ss. 2 -5

EDITOR'S NOTE. --
Subdivision (3) of this section was repealed by Session Laws 1973, c. 88. However, s. 4 of the 1973 act provides: "The provisions of this act shall not apply to manufacturers of, or dealers in, mobile or manufactured type housing or recreational trailers." In view

of s. 4, subdivision (3) has not been deleted from the section as set out above.

Session Laws 1997-319, s. 5, provides that the amendment adding subdivision (5)g. of this section shall not apply to satellite facilities licensed before July 1, 1997.

Session Laws 2013-302, s. 11, provides: "The terms and provisions of Sections 7 through 12 of this act shall be applicable to all current and future franchises and other agreements in existence between any new motor vehicle dealer located in this State and a manufacturer or distributor as of the effective date of this act."

Session Laws 2013-302, s. 12, is a severability clause.

Session Laws 2015-209, s. 10, is a severability clause.

Session Laws 2015-209, which, in ss. 2-5, amended this section, in s. 11 provides: "This act is effective when it becomes law [August 11, 2015] and applies to all current and future franchises and other agreements in existence between any new motor vehicle dealer located in this State and a manufacturer or distributor as of the effective date of this act."

Session Laws 2017-102, s. 5.2(b), provides: "The Revisor of Statutes is authorized to reletter the definitions in G.S. 20-4.01(27) and G.S. 20-4.01(32b) to place them in alphabetical order. The Revisor of Statutes may conform any citations that change as a result of the relettering." Pursuant to that authority, G.S. 20-4.01(32b)a. was redesignated as G.S. 20-4.01(32b)c. Conforming changes were made in subdivisions (6)d. and f. of this section.

Session Laws 2017-148, s. 6, is a severability clause.

Session Laws 2018-27, s. 5, is a severability clause.

Session Laws 2019-125, s. 13, made the amendments to this section by Session Laws 2019-125, ss. 2-5, effective July 19, 2019, and applicable to all current and future franchises and other agreements in existence between any new motor vehicle dealer located in this State and a manufacturer or distributor as of that date.

Session laws 2019-125, s. 12, is a severability clause.

EFFECT OF AMENDMENTS. --

Session Laws 2005-409, s. 2, effective September 20, 2005, in subdivision (30), substituted "that has" for "which has" in the second paragraph, substituted "that provide" for "which provide" in the third paragraph and substituted "2010" for "2006" in the sixth and seventh paragraphs.

Session Laws 2005-463, s. 2, effective October 3, 2005, added sub-subdivision (5)a.5.; and made a minor stylistic change.

Session Laws 2011-290, s. 6, effective January 1, 2014, substituted "18 months" for "12 months" in clause (iii) of the first sentence in subdivision (6)d.3.

Session Laws 2013-302, s. 7, effective July 18, 2013, substituted "2018" for "2014" at the end of the sixth and seventh paragraphs in subdivision (30); and added subdivisions (44) through (48).

Session Laws 2014-58, s. 10(e) and (f), effective December 1, 2014, updated internal references in subdivisions (6)d.1.I. and (6)f. See Editor's note for applicability.

Session Laws 2015-209, ss. 2-5, effective August 11, 2015, substituted "subdivision" for "paragraph" and "sub-subdivision" for "subparagraph" throughout subdivisions (6) and (7); substituted "line-make or brand" for "product line" in (6)c.1.IV; in (6)d.3., added the next-to-last sentence and inserted "but the line-make or brand in this State would continue to be sold through the new distributor" in the last sentence; substituted "sub-subdivision" for "paragraph" near the middle of the of the second sentence of subdivision (7)(d); rewrote subdivision (38); and added subdivision (49). For applicability, see editor's note.

Session Laws 2017-148, s. 2, effective July 20, 2017, substituted "June 30, 2022" for "June 30, 2018" at the end of the sixth and seventh full paragraphs in subdivision (30).

Session Laws 2018-27, ss. 1 and 4, effective June 22, 2018, added subdivisions (50) and (51).

Session Laws 2019-125, ss. 2-5, effective July 19, 2019, rewrote subdivisions (9), (38), and (51), added subdivision (52); and substituted "or parts as reasonably required by the manufacturer" for "as reasonably required by the manufacturer, or parts" in the third sentence of subdivision (46). For effective date and applicability, see editor's note.

THE NOTICE PROVISION CONTEMPLATES AN ANALYSIS OF RELEVANT MARKET CONDITIONS within the trade area at or about the time that the notice of the new dealership is made, not the distant past or future. Smith's Cycles, Inc. v. Alexander, 27 N.C. App. 382, 219 S.E.2d 282 (1975).

SUBDIVISION (5) IS NOT UNCONSTITUTIONAL ON ITS FACE AS ALLOWING MONOPOLIES. American Motors Sales Corp. v. Peters, 58 N.C. App. 684, 294 S.E.2d 764 (1982).

While subdivision (5) of this section prohibiting additional franchises amounts to a restraint of trade, the restraint of intra-band trade contemplated by the statute is not such as to amount to the creation of a monopoly. More than a mere adverse effect on competition must arise before a restraint of trade becomes monopolistic. American Motors Sales Corp. v. Peters, 311 N.C. 311, 317 S.E.2d 351 (1984).

AMENDMENT NOT IMPAIRMENT OF RIGHT TO CONTRACT. --The amendment to this section, which provided a procedure by which an automobile dealer could seek administrative review of its franchisor's refusal to approve a relocation, was a patently reasonable exercise of the State's police power and was not an unconstitutional impairment of the parties' right to contract. Nissan Div. of Nissan Motor Corp. in United States v. Nissan, 111 N.C. App. 748, 434 S.E.2d 224 (1993).

LEGISLATIVE INTENT. --The legislature did not intend that a franchise agreement could be cancelled for "good cause" only when the dealer did some affirmative act which would give the manufacturer "good cause" to cancel the franchise. Carolina Truck & Body

Co. v. GMC, 102 N.C. App. 262, 402 S.E.2d 135, cert. denied, 329 N.C. 266, 407 S.E.2d 831 (1991).

The legislature would not enact a statute prohibiting a manufacturer from cancelling a franchise agreement if it decided to stop manufacturing that product because it was unprofitable. Carolina Truck & Body Co. v. GMC, 102 N.C. App. 262, 402 S.E.2d 135, cert. denied, 329 N.C. 266, 407 S.E.2d 831 (1991).

The legislature does not require a manufacturer to continue on a road to certain bankruptcy by requiring the manufacturer to continue to make and sell unprofitable models of cars or trucks. Carolina Truck & Body Co. v. GMC, 102 N.C. App. 262, 402 S.E.2d 135, cert. denied, 329 N.C. 266, 407 S.E.2d 831 (1991).

EXCLUSIVE DEALERSHIP IN TRADE AREA IS PERMISSIBLE. --Under subdivision (5) of this section, an automobile manufacturer may give a dealer the exclusive right to sell its automobiles in a trade area without violating N.C. Const., Art. I, § 34. For the General Assembly to require the manufacturer to do what it could bargain to do if it desired to execute a contract is not the granting of a monopoly. American Motors Sales Corp. v. Peters, 58 N.C. App. 684, 294 S.E.2d 764 (1982).

FRANCHISE IS NOT AGREEMENT NOT TO COMPETE. --The grant of a franchise to an automobile dealer is not an agreement between competitors not to compete, but a contract between a manufacturer and a dealer. The State has enacted legislation which gives automobile dealers some protection after they have made investments and taken other action, relying on contracts they have made. The State has the power to do this. American Motors Sales Corp. v. Peters, 58 N.C. App. 684, 294 S.E.2d 764 (1982).

STATE CAN REQUIRE THAT FRANCHISE BE EXCLUSIVE IF DEALER ABIDES BY TERMS. --The State can require that if an automobile manufacturer gives a franchise to a dealer to sell automobiles, that the manufacturer include in the terms of the franchise agreement the right that the dealer have an exclusive franchise in a certain trade area so long as the dealer abides by the terms of the franchise agreement. American Motors Sales Corp. v. Peters, 58 N.C. App. 684, 294 S.E.2d 764 (1982).

GRANTING FRANCHISE IN VIOLATION OF SUBDIVISION (5) WOULD BE AN UNFAIR ACT OR PRACTICE, which the Commissioner is empowered to prevent under G.S. 20-301. American Motors Sales Corp. v. Peters, 58 N.C. App. 684, 294 S.E.2d 764 (1982).

NOTIFICATION BY REGISTERED OR CERTIFIED MAIL. --The General Assembly intended for the phrase registered or certified mail, return receipt requested to refer exclusively to the delivery service offered by the U.S. Mail and not to notice delivered by any private delivery service. Nissan Div. of Nissan Motor Corp. in United States v. Fred Anderson Nissan, 337 N.C. 424, 445 S.E.2d 600 (1994).

DELIVERY BY FEDERAL EXPRESS, with return receipt, was held to be registered mail within the meaning of this section. Nissan Div. of Nissan Motor

Corp. in United States v. Nissan, 111 N.C. App. 748, 434 S.E.2d 224 (1993).

Since the language of this section requires that notice be sent through registered or certified mail, return receipt requested and provides that failure to do so shall constitute waiver, car manufacturer waived any objection to dealer's proposed relocation by sending its notice by Federal Express. Nissan Div. of Nissan Motor Corp. in United States v. Fred Anderson Nissan, 337 N.C. 424, 445 S.E.2d 600 (1994).

VERBAL NOTICE DOES NOT COMPLY WITH SUBDIVISION (5). --Subdivision (5) of this section requires that written notice be given to a franchisee before a new franchise may be granted. Verbal notice does not comply with the statute. American Motors Sales Corp. v. Peters, 58 N.C. App. 684, 294 S.E.2d 764 (1982).

FURTHER NOTICE UNDER SUBDIVISION (5) REQUIRED. --Where a motorcycle manufacturer gave plaintiff dealer notice under subdivision (5) of this section of its intention to grant a new motorcycle franchise in plaintiff's trade area on or before Sept. 1, 1973, but the manufacturer did not grant such a franchise by that date, the failure of plaintiff to request a hearing by the Commissioner of Motor Vehicles within 30 days after receipt of such notice did not give the manufacturer the right to grant a new franchise at any time in the future without giving plaintiff further notice under subdivision (5); and where the manufacturer granted a new franchise on Oct. 14, 1974, without giving additional notice to plaintiff, the 30-day time limitation never began to run, and plaintiff properly filed its petition for a hearing on Oct. 19, 1974. Smith's Cycles, Inc. v. Alexander, 27 N.C. App. 382, 219 S.E.2d 282 (1975).

DEALER'S PERFORMANCE DOES NOT AFFECT RIGHT TO SEEK TO PROHIBIT OTHER FRANCHISES. --The fact that an automobile dealer may not have been as competent in business as it could have been does not show he had engaged in any sharp practice or inequitable conduct which would give rise to a holding that he had unclean hands in a proceeding to prohibit establishment of additional franchises. American Motors Sales Corp. v. Peters, 58 N.C. App. 684, 294 S.E.2d 764 (1982).

APPEAL FROM INJUNCTION AGAINST NEW FRANCHISE. --Where the Commissioner has enjoined the granting of additional franchises in a certain area, a court's refusal to stay this order is appealable, where it affects substantial rights and will work an injury to the petitioners if not corrected before an appeal from the final judgment. American Motors Sales Corp. v. Peters, 58 N.C. App. 684, 294 S.E.2d 764 (1982).

CANCELLATION OF FRANCHISE WHEN PRODUCT DISCONTINUED. --Subdivision (6)c.1.IV of this section implies that a manufacturer may cancel a franchise if discontinuing the sale of the product line. Carolina Truck & Body Co. v. GMC, 102 N.C. App. 262, 402 S.E.2d 135, cert. denied, 329 N.C. 266, 407 S.E.2d 831 (1991).

Cancellation of a franchise if discontinuing a product line is a "good cause" under the statute. Carolina Truck & Body Co. v. GMC, 102 N.C. App. 262, 402 S.E.2d 135, cert. denied, 329 N.C. 266, 407 S.E.2d 831 (1991).

"GOOD FAITH" DEFINED. --Manufacturer's withdrawal from the heavy duty truck market was in good faith as required by subdivision (6) of this section. Good faith is defined in G.S. 20-286(8b) as "honest in fact and the observation of reasonable commercial standards of fair dealing in the trade as defined and interpreted in G.S. 25-2-103(1)(b)(subdivision (1)(b) was deleted in 2006)." Carolina Truck & Body Co. v. GMC, 102 N.C. App. 262, 402 S.E.2d 135, cert. denied, 329 N.C. 266, 407 S.E.2d 831 (1991).

EVIDENCE OF GOOD FAITH HELD SUFFICIENT. --Where manufacturer gave dealer at least a year's notice concerning the likelihood of cancellation, manufacturer treated dealer no differently than it did any of its other heavy-duty truck franchisees, and more importantly, where, there was no evidence of dishonesty by manufacturer, the record was replete with evidence of manufacturer's good faith in cancelling its heavy-duty truck franchises with dealer. Carolina Truck & Body Co. v. GMC, 102 N.C. App. 262, 402 S.E.2d 135, cert. denied, 329 N.C. 266, 407 S.E.2d 831 (1991).

SUBDIVISION (6) IS CONSTITUTIONAL. --The General Assembly reasonably concluded that subdivision (6) of this section promotes the public welfare in an area vitally affecting the general economy of the State, and it is constitutional. Mazda Motors of Am., Inc. v. Southwestern Motors, Inc., 36 N.C. App. 1, 243 S.E.2d 793 (1978), aff'd in part, rev'd in part, 296 N.C. 357, 250 S.E.2d 250 (1979).

SUBDIVISION (6) DOES NOT UNCONSTITUTIONALLY "IMPAIR THE OBLIGATIONS OF CONTRACTS". --Subdivision (6) of this section is not a state "law impairing the obligations of contracts" in the constitutional sense. Mazda Motors of Am., Inc. v. Southwestern Motors, Inc., 36 N.C. App. 1, 243 S.E.2d 793 (1978), aff'd in part, rev'd in part, 296 N.C. 357, 250 S.E.2d 250 (1979).

SUBDIVISION (6) DOES NOT UNCONSTITUTIONALLY TAKE PROPERTY WITHOUT COMPENSATION. --Subdivision (6) of this section does not involve any disturbance of essential or core expectations arising from contract or amount to a taking without compensation. Rather, it constitutes a reasonable exercise of the police power by the State in furtherance of the public welfare. Mazda Motors of Am., Inc. v. Southwestern Motors, Inc., 36 N.C. App. 1, 243 S.E.2d 793 (1978), aff'd in part, rev'd in part, 296 N.C. 357, 250 S.E.2d 250 (1979).

SUBDIVISION (6) IS NOT UNCONSTITUTIONALLY RETROACTIVE. --Subdivision (6) of this section, which requires a filing of notice prior to termination of automobile franchise contracts, is not made unconstitutional by retroactive application to existing contracts. Mazda Motors of Am., Inc. v. Southwestern Motors, Inc., 36 N.C. App. 1, 243 S.E.2d 793 (1978), aff'd in part, rev'd in part, 296 N.C. 357, 250 S.E.2d 250 (1979).

SUBDIVISION (6) IS NOT AN EX POST FACTO LAW. --Although this Article provides criminal sanctions for violations of subdivision (6) of this section, its retroactive application to an existing contract does not constitute it an ex post facto law prohibited by U.S. Const., Art. I, § 10, cl. 1. That clause applies only in cases in which a crime is created or punishment for a criminal act is increased after the fact and does not speak to the effect of statutes passed after the fact when employed in civil cases. Mazda Motors of Am., Inc. v. Southwestern Motors, Inc., 36 N.C. App. 1, 243 S.E.2d 793 (1978), aff'd in part, rev'd in part, 296 N.C. 357, 250 S.E.2d 250 (1979).

THE PROVISIONS OF SUBDIVISION (6) OF THIS SECTION ARE FREE FROM AMBIGUITY, apply solely to unilateral franchise terminations by the manufacturer, and do not extend to mutual agreements between manufacturer and dealer to terminate a franchise. Mazda Motors of Am., Inc. v. Southwestern Motors, Inc., 296 N.C. 357, 250 S.E.2d 250 (1979).

SUBDIVISION (6) APPLIES TO UNILATERAL ACTION BY MANUFACTURERS, NOT MUTUAL AGREEMENTS BETWEEN MANUFACTURER AND DEALER. --In effect, the express language of subdivision (6) of this section imposes substantial curbs on the unilateral actions of a manufacturer with respect to franchise termination. The express language does not cover voluntary mutual termination agreements between manufacturer and dealer. Mazda Motors of Am., Inc. v. Southwestern Motors, Inc., 296 N.C. 357, 250 S.E.2d 250 (1979).

VOLUNTARINESS OF TERMINATION IRRELEVANT TO QUESTION OF NOTICE TO COMMISSIONER. --Subdivision (6) of this section specifically commands that the Commissioner of Motor Vehicles be given the required notice prior to termination or expiration of an automobile dealership franchise. Failure to give the required notice prior to termination or expiration is specifically declared to be unlawful. The voluntariness of such agreements is irrelevant. Mazda Motors of Am., Inc. v. Southwestern Motors, Inc., 36 N.C. App. 1, 243 S.E.2d 793 (1978), aff'd in part, rev'd in part, 296 N.C. 357, 250 S.E.2d 250 (1979).

GOOD CAUSE FOR FAILURE TO RENEW FRANCHISE. --To prove that poor sales performance constitutes good cause for its failure to renew respondent's franchise agreements, petitioner must demonstrate that: (1) respondent failed to comply with a provision of the franchise agreements which required satisfactory sales performance; (2) petitioner's performance standards are reasonable; and (3) respondent's failure was not due primarily to economic or market factors beyond his control. GMC v. Kinlaw, 78 N.C. App. 521, 338 S.E.2d 114 (1985).

POWER TO FORESTALL FRANCHISE TERMINATION. --Neither G.S. 20-301 nor subdivision (6) of this section expressly vest the Commissioner with the power to order parties to enter into a contract. However, the statutory prohibition on franchise termination except for cause remains intact. Thus it is not necessary that the Commissioner have the power to order parties to enter into contracts to enable the

Chapter 20

agency to function properly. GMC v. Kinlaw, 78 N.C. App. 521, 338 S.E.2d 114 (1985).

Commissioner's order finding that GMC failed to renew dealer's franchise agreements without cause and directing that the agreements not be terminated was proper. However, the Commissioner exceeded his authority in ordering GMC to enter "a regular five (5) year motor vehicle dealer sales agreement" with dealer. GMC v. Kinlaw, 78 N.C. App. 521, 338 S.E.2d 114 (1985).

JUDICIAL REVIEW OF COMMISSIONER'S DECISION. --The decision of the Motor Vehicles Commissioner on the termination of a franchise is reviewable pursuant to Chapter 150B of the General Statutes. GMC v. Carolina Truck & Body Co., 102 N.C. App. 349, 402 S.E.2d 139 (1991).

FILING OF PETITION WITH DMV. --The actual stamping of a petition mailed by dealer on Oct. 26, 1982, on Nov. 2, 1982 by the party responsible for processing petitions for the DMV did not constitute the required filing, but instead, the receipt of the petition by the DMV constituted its filing. Star Auto. Co. v. Saab-Scania of Am., Inc., 84 N.C. App. 531, 353 S.E.2d 260 (1987).

WRITTEN NOTICE TO FRANCHISEE MUST STATE REASONS FOR NONRENEWAL WITH SUFFICIENT SPECIFICITY to inform the dealer of the legal grounds for nonrenewal. Star Auto. Co. v. Jaguar Cars, Inc., 95 N.C. App. 103, 382 S.E.2d 226, cert. denied, 325 N.C. 710, 388 S.E.2d 463 (1989).

EVALUATION OF WRITTEN NOTICE. --Information which the franchisee has received, other than that included in the written notice, may not be taken into account in evaluating the legal sufficiency of the written notice to the franchise. Star Auto. Co. v. Jaguar Cars, Inc., 95 N.C. App. 103, 382 S.E.2d 226, cert. denied, 325 N.C. 710, 388 S.E.2d 463 (1989).

RELEVANT MARKET AREA WHERE SAME LINE MAKE REPRESENTED. --The intent of the legislature was to exclude population outside the designated radius, and the Commissioner of the Division of Motor Vehicles erred by including population lying outside the designated radius when determining "relevant market area," though that population was within a census tract partially within that area. Al Smith Buick Co. v. Mazda Motor of Am., Inc., 122 N.C. App. 429, 470 S.E.2d 552 (1996), cert. denied, 473 S.E.2d 609 (1996).

COMMISSIONER'S RULING BECAME LAW OF THE CASE. --Commissioner of the Division of Motor Vehicles erred when he found dealer was precluded from pursuing further legal challenges to the establishment of an additional dealership based upon prior consent order, because the commissioner had ruled the consent order ceased to be effective after the lapse of a reasonable time and the manufacturer failed to appeal that ruling, which became the law of the case. Al Smith Buick Co. v. Mazda Motor of Am., Inc., 122 N.C. App. 429, 470 S.E.2d 552 (1996), cert. denied, 473 S.E.2d 609 (1996).

WRITTEN NOTICE HELD SUFFICIENT. --Letter from car distributor to car dealer was sufficiently specific to inform dealer of distributor's basis for nonrenewal and to inform dealer of its statutory rights, where the notice stated that distributor had made the decision not to renew dealer's franchise as part of an "overall effort" to "upgrade and reorganize," and where distributor's letter also recited the factors that it used to make its nonrenewal determination, namely, facilities, location, after-sales service, financial resources and managerial skills and commitment, and that dealer's alleged deficiencies in these areas were distributor's reasons for nonrenewal. Star Auto. Co. v. Jaguar Cars, Inc., 95 N.C. App. 103, 382 S.E.2d 226, cert. denied, 325 N.C. 710, 388 S.E.2d 463 (1989). APPLIED in Smith's Cycles, Inc. v. American Honda Motor Co., 26 N.C. App. 76, 214 S.E.2d 785 (1975); Sandhill Motors, Inc. v. American Motors Sales Corp., 667 F.2d 1112 (4th Cir. 1981).

CROSS REFERENCES. --

As to application of subdivisions (4) through (28) of this section, see G.S. 20-305.5.

LEGAL PERIODICALS. --

For survey of 1978 constitutional law, see 57 N.C.L. Rev. 958 (1979).

For comment on the Business Opportunity Sales Act of 1977, see 17 Wake Forest L. Rev. 623 (1981).

For article discussing unfair methods of competition, deceptive trade practices, and unfair trade practices, see 5 Campbell L. Rev. 119 (1982).

For survey of 1982 law on commercial law, see 61 N.C.L. Rev. 1018 (1983).

For 1984 survey on commercial law, "Green Light to Territorial Security for Automobile Dealers," see 63 N.C.L. Rev. 1080 (1985).

§ 20-305.1. Automobile dealer warranty and recall obligations

(a) Each motor vehicle manufacturer, factory branch, distributor or distributor branch, shall specify in writing to each of its motor vehicle dealers licensed in this State the dealer's obligations for preparation, delivery, warranty, and recall service on its products. The disclosure required under this subsection shall include the schedule of compensation to be paid the dealers for parts, work, and service in connection with preparation, delivery, warranty, and recall service, and the time allowances for the performance of the work and service. In no event shall the schedule of compensation fail to include reasonable compensation for diagnostic work and associated administrative requirements as well as repair service and labor. Time allowances for the performance of preparation, delivery, warranty, and recall work and service shall be reasonable and adequate for the work to be performed. The compensation paid under this section shall be reasonable, provided, however, that under no circumstances shall the reasonable compensation under this section for warranty and recall service be in an amount less than the dealer's current retail labor rate and the amount charged to retail customers for the manufacturer's or distributor's original parts for nonwarranty work of like kind, provided the amount is competitive with the retail rates charged for parts and labor by other franchised dealers of the same line-make located within the dealer's market. If there is no other same line-make dealer located in the dealer's market or if all other same line-make dealers in the dealer's market are owned or operated by the same entities or individuals as the dealership being compared, the retail rates charged for parts and labor by other franchised dealers located in the dealer's market that sell competing line-make motor vehicles as the dealer may be considered when determining whether the dealer's rates are competitive.

(a1) The retail rate customarily charged by the dealer for parts and labor may be established at the election of the dealer by the dealer submitting to the manufacturer or distributor 100 sequential nonwarranty customer-paid service repair orders which contain warranty-like parts, or 60 consecutive days of nonwarranty customer-paid service repair orders which contain warranty-like parts, whichever is less, covering repairs made no more than 180 days before the submission and declaring the average percentage markup. The average of the parts markup rate and the average labor rate shall both be presumed to be reasonable, however, a manufacturer or distributor may, not later than 30 days after submission, rebut that presumption by reasonably substantiating that the rate is unfair and unreasonable in light of the retail rates charged for parts and labor by all other franchised motor vehicle dealers in the dealer's market offering the same line-make vehicles. In the event there are no other franchised dealers offering the same line-make of vehicle in the dealer's market, the manufacturer or distributor may compare the dealer's retail rate for parts and labor with the retail rates charged for parts and labor by other franchised dealers who are selling competing line-makes of vehicles within the dealer's market. The retail rate and the average labor rate shall go into effect 30 days following the manufacturer's approval, but in no event later than 60 days following the declaration, subject to audit of the submitted repair orders by the manufacturer or distributor and a rebuttal of the declared rate as described above. If the declared rate is rebutted, the manufacturer or distributor shall propose an adjustment of the average percentage markup based on that rebuttal not later than 30 days after such audit, but in no event later than 60 days after submission. If the dealer does not agree with the proposed average percentage markup, the dealer may file a protest with the Commissioner not later than 30 days after receipt of that proposal by the manufacturer or

distributor. If such a protest is filed, the Commissioner shall inform the manufacturer or distributor that a timely protest has been filed and that a hearing will be held on such protest. In any hearing held pursuant to this subsection, the manufacturer or distributor shall have the burden of proving by a preponderance of the evidence that the rate declared by the dealer was unreasonable as described in this subsection and that the proposed adjustment of the average percentage markup is reasonable pursuant to the provisions of this subsection. If the dealer prevails at a protest hearing, the dealer's proposed rate, affirmed at the hearing, shall be effective as of 60 days after the date of the dealer's initial submission of the customer-paid service orders to the manufacturer or distributor. If the manufacturer or distributor prevails at a protest hearing, the rate proposed by the manufacturer or distributor, that was affirmed at the hearing, shall be effective beginning 30 days following issuance of the final order.

(a2) In calculating the retail rate customarily charged by the dealer for parts and labor, the following work shall not be included in the calculation:

(1) Repairs for manufacturer or distributor special events, specials, coupons, or other promotional discounts for retail customer repairs.

(2) Parts sold at wholesale or at reduced or specially negotiated rates for insurance repairs.

(3) Engine assemblies.

(4) Routine maintenance, including fluids, filters, alignments, flushes, oil changes, belts, and brake drums/rotors and shoes/pads not provided in the course of repairs.

(5) Nuts, bolts, fasteners, and similar items that do not have an individual part number.

(6) Tires and vehicle alignments.

(7) Vehicle reconditioning.

(8) Batteries and light bulbs.

(a3) If a manufacturer or distributor furnishes a part or component to a dealer, at reduced or no cost, to use in performing repairs under a recall, campaign service action, or warranty repair, the manufacturer or distributor shall compensate the dealer for the part or component in the same manner as warranty parts compensation under this section by compensating the dealer on the basis of the dealer's average markup on the cost for the part or component as listed in the manufacturer's or distributor's price schedule less the cost for the part or component.

(a4) A manufacturer or distributor may not require a dealer to establish the retail rate customarily charged by the dealer for parts and labor by an unduly burdensome or time-consuming method or by requiring information that is unduly burdensome or time consuming to provide, including, but not limited to, part-by-part or transaction-by-transaction calculations.

(b) Notwithstanding the terms of any franchise agreement, it is unlawful for any motor vehicle manufacturer, factory branch, distributor, or distributor branch to fail to perform any of its warranty or recall obligations with respect to a motor vehicle, to fail to fully compensate its motor vehicle dealers licensed in this State for a qualifying used motor vehicle pursuant to subsections (i) and (j) of this section or warranty and recall parts other than parts used to repair the living facilities of recreational vehicles, including motor homes, travel trailers, fifth-wheel trailers, camping trailers, and truck campers as defined in G.S. 20-4.01(32b), at the prevailing retail rate according to the factors in subsection (a) of this section, or, in service in accordance with the schedule of compensation provided the dealer pursuant to subsection (a) of this section, or to otherwise recover all or any portion of its costs for compensating its motor vehicle dealers licensed in this State for warranty or recall parts and service or for payments for a qualifying used motor vehicle pursuant to subsections (i) and (j) of this section either by reduction in the amount due to the dealer, or by separate charge, surcharge, or other imposition, and to fail to indemnify and hold harmless its franchised dealers licensed in this State against any judgment for damages or settlements agreed to by the manufacturer, including, but not limited to, court costs and reasonable attorneys' fees of the motor vehicle dealer, arising out of complaints, claims or lawsuits including, but not limited to, strict liability, negligence, misrepresentation, express or implied warranty, or recision or revocation of acceptance of the sale of a motor vehicle as defined in G.S. 25-2-608, to the extent that the judgment or settlement relates to the alleged defective negligent manufacture, assembly or design of new motor vehicles, parts or accessories or other functions by the manufacturer, factory branch, distributor or distributor branch, beyond the control of the dealer. Any audit, other than an audit conducted for cause, for warranty or recall parts or service compensation, or compensation for a qualifying used motor vehicle in accordance with subsections (i) and (j) of this section may only be conducted one time within any 12-month period and shall only be for the 12-month period immediately following the date of the payment of the claim by the manufacturer, factory branch, distributor, or distributor branch. Any audit, other than an audit conducted for cause, for sales incentives, service incentives, rebates, or other forms of incentive compensation may only be conducted one time within any 12-month period and shall only be for the 12-month period immediately following the date of the payment of the claim by the manufacturer, factory branch, distributor, or distributor branch pursuant to a sales incentives program, service incentives program, rebate program, or other form of incentive compensation program. Provided, however, these limitations shall not be effective in the case of fraudulent claims. For purposes of this subsection, the term "audit conducted for cause" is defined as an audit based on any of the following: (i) statistical evidence that the dealer's claims are unreasonably high in comparison to other dealers similarly situated or the dealer's claim history, (ii) that the dealer's claims submissions violate reasonable claims documentation or other requirements of the applicable manufacturer, factory branch, distributor, or distributor branch, (iii) a follow up to an earlier audit in which the dealer was notified of a claim documentation procedure violation that occurred within the prior 12-month period, provided the audit and any chargeback are in compliance with subdivision (b1) of this section and are limited in scope to just the specific violation determined previously, or (iv) reasonable evidence of malfeasance or fraud. In the event a manufacturer, factory branch, distributor, or distributor branch elects to perform an audit conducted for cause, the manufacturer, factory branch, distributor, or distributor branch, simultaneously with providing the affected dealer with written notice of the audit, shall further be required to explain in detail in the notice the data or other foundation upon which the cause is based.

(b1) All claims made by motor vehicle dealers pursuant to this section for compensation for delivery, preparation, warranty, and recall work, including compensation for a qualifying used motor vehicle in accordance with subsection (i) of this section, labor, parts, and other expenses, shall be paid by the manufacturer within 30 days after receipt of claim from the dealer. When any claim is disapproved, the dealer shall be notified in writing of the grounds for disapproval. Any claim not specifically disapproved in writing within 30 days after receipt shall be considered approved and payment is due immediately. No claim which has been approved and paid may be charged back to the dealer unless it can be shown that the claim was false or fraudulent, that the repairs were not properly made or were unnecessary to correct the defective condition, or the dealer failed to reasonably substantiate the claim either in accordance with the manufacturer's reasonable written procedures or by other reasonable means. A manufacturer or distributor shall not deny a claim or reduce the amount to be reimbursed to the dealer as long as the dealer has provided reasonably sufficient documentation that the dealer:

(1) Made a good faith attempt to perform the work in compliance with the written policies and procedures of the manufacturer; and

(2) Actually performed the work.

Notwithstanding the foregoing, a manufacturer shall not fail to fully compensate a dealer for warranty or recall work or make any chargeback to the dealer's account based on the dealer's failure to comply with the manufacturer's claim documentation procedure or procedures unless both of the following requirements have been met:

(1) The dealer has, within the previous 12 months, failed to comply with the same specific claim documentation procedure or procedures; and

(2) The manufacturer has, within the previous 12 months, provided a written warning to the dealer by certified United States mail, return receipt requested, identifying the specific claim documentation procedure or procedures violated by the dealer.

Nothing contained in this subdivision shall be deemed to prevent or prohibit a manufacturer from adopting or implementing a policy or procedure which provides or allows for the self-audit of dealers, provided, however, that if any such self-audit procedure contains provisions relating to claim documentation, such claim documentation policies or procedures shall be subject to the prohibitions and requirements contained in this subdivision. Notices sent by a manufacturer under a bona fide self-audit procedure shall be deemed sufficient notice to meet the requirements of this subsection provided that the dealer is given reasonable opportunity through self-audit to identify and correct any out-of-line procedures for a period of at least 60 days before the manufacturer conducts its own audit of the dealer warranty operations and procedures. A manufacturer may further not charge a dealer back subsequent to the payment of the claim unless a representative of the manufacturer has met in person at the dealership, or by telephone, with an officer or employee of the dealer designated by the dealer and explained in detail the basis for each of the proposed charge-backs and thereafter given the dealer's representative a reasonable opportunity at the meeting, or during the telephone call, to explain the dealer's position relating to each of the proposed charge-backs. In the event the dealer was selected for audit or review on the basis that some or all of the dealer's claims were viewed as excessive in comparison to average, mean, or aggregate data accumulated by the manufacturer, or in relation to claims submitted by a group of other franchisees of the manufacturer, the manufacturer shall, at or prior to the meeting or telephone call with the dealer's representative, provide the dealer with a written statement containing the basis or methodology upon which the dealer was selected for audit or review.

(b2) A manufacturer may not deny a motor vehicle dealer's claim for sales incentives, service incentives, rebates, or other forms of incentive compensation, reduce the amount to be paid to the dealer, or charge a dealer back subsequent to the payment of the claim unless it can be shown that the claim was false or fraudulent or that the dealer failed to reasonably substantiate the claim either in accordance with the manufacturer's reasonable written procedures or by other reasonable means.

(b3) (1) For purposes of this subsection, the term "manufacturer" shall include the terms "manufacturer," "manufacturer branch," "distributor," and "distributor branch," as those terms are defined in G.S. 20-286.

(2) Notwithstanding the terms of any franchise or other agreement, or the terms of any program, policy, or procedure of any manufacturer, it shall be unlawful for any manufacturer to take or threaten to take any adverse action against a dealer located in this State, or to otherwise discriminate against any dealer located in this State when:

a. The dealer failed to ensure that the purchaser or lessee paid personal property tax on the vehicle purchased or leased from the dealer;

b. The dealer failed to ensure that the vehicle being purchased or leased had been permanently registered in this State or in any other state in which the dealer was not required to ensure that the vehicle's permanent registration was processed or submitted at the time of the vehicle's purchase or lease;

c. The manufacturer extrapolated the imposition of any adverse action based on a certain number or percentage of the vehicles sold or leased by a dealer over a specified period of time having been exported or brokered; or

d. The dealer sold or leased a motor vehicle to a customer who either exported the vehicle to a foreign country or who resold the vehicle to a third party, unless:

1. The dealer reasonably should have known that the customer intended to export or resell the motor vehicle prior to the customer's purchase or lease of the vehicle from the dealer;

2. The vehicle sold or leased by the dealer was exported to a foreign country within 180 days after the date of sale or lease by the dealer; and

3. The affected manufacturer provided written notification to the affected motor vehicle dealer of the resale or export within 12 months from the date of sale or lease.

Notwithstanding the provisions of sub-subdivision d. of this subdivision, a manufacturer may take adverse action against a dealer located in this State if the dealer sold or leased a motor vehicle to a customer who either exported the vehicle to a foreign country or who resold the vehicle to a third party and the dealer, prior to the customer's purchase or lease of the vehicle from the dealer, had actual knowledge that the customer intended to export or resell the motor vehicle.

(3) The adverse action and discrimination prohibited under this subsection includes, but is not limited to, a manufacturer's actual or threatened:

a. Failure or refusal to allocate, sell, or deliver motor vehicles to the dealer;

b. Discrimination against any dealer in the allocation of vehicles;

c. Charging back or withholding payments or other compensation or consideration that a dealer is otherwise entitled to receive and that is not otherwise the subject of a dispute for warranty reimbursement or under a sales promotion, incentive program, contest, or other program or policy that would provide any compensation or support for the dealer;

d. Disqualification of a dealer from participating in, or discrimination against any dealer relating to, any sales promotion, incentive program, contest, or other program or policy that would provide any compensation or support for the dealer;

e. Termination of a franchise; or

f. The imposition of any fine, penalty, chargeback, or other disciplinary or punitive measure.

(4) In any proceeding brought pursuant to this subsection, the affected manufacturer shall have the burden of proving that the dealer knew or reasonably should have known that the customer intended to export or resell the motor vehicle prior to the customer's purchase or lease of the vehicle

from the dealer, subject to the following provisions:

a. There shall be a rebuttable presumption that the dealer, prior to the customer's purchase or lease of the vehicle, did not know nor should have reasonably known that the customer intended to export or resell the motor vehicle, if:

1. Following the sale or lease, the dealer submitted the requisite documentation to the appropriate governmental entity to enable the vehicle to be titled, registered and, where applicable, sales or highway use tax paid in any state or territory within the United States in the name of a customer who was physically present at the dealership at or prior to the time of sale or lease; and

2. The customer's identifying information was not included on a list of known or suspected exporters or resellers identified and made readily accessible to the dealer by the applicable manufacturer at the time of the sale or lease.

b. There shall be a rebuttable presumption that the dealer, prior to the customer's purchase or lease of the vehicle, knew or reasonably should have known that the customer intended to export or resell the motor vehicle if the customer's identifying information was included on a list of known or suspected exporters or resellers identified and made readily accessible to the dealer by the applicable manufacturer at the time of the sale or lease.

c. Nothing contained in subdivision (2) of this subsection shall be deemed to prevent or prohibit the Commissioner or the affected manufacturer from considering one or more of the factors delineated in sub-subdivisions a. through c. of subdivision (2) of this subsection in determining whether the dealer knew or reasonably should have known that the customer intended to export or resell the motor vehicle prior to the customer's purchase or lease of the vehicle from the dealer.

(5) Any audit of a dealer by a manufacturer for sales or leases made to known exporters or brokers may only be conducted one time within any 12-month period and shall only be for the 12-month period immediately preceding the audit, provided, however, that nothing in this subsection shall prohibit or limit the ability of

a manufacturer, factory branch, distributor, or distributor branch to conduct any audit of sales or leases made by one of its franchised dealers to known exporters or brokers for cause at any time during the permitted time period. For purposes of this subdivision, the term "for cause" means the dealer's sale or lease of motor vehicles to individuals identified on a list of known motor vehicle exporters or brokers previously provided by or posted on a Web site made accessible to the dealer by the manufacturer, factory branch, distributor, or distributor branch or reasonable evidence that the dealer knew or reasonably should have known that the customer intended to export or resell the motor vehicle.

(b4) Any person or other entity employed or contracted by a manufacturer, factory branch, distributor, or distributor branch to conduct an audit of a motor vehicle dealer regulated by this section shall comply with all the requirements of this section. It shall be unlawful for any manufacturer, factory branch, distributor, or distributor branch to contract with or employ any person or other entity to conduct an audit of any motor vehicle dealer located in this State regulated under this section for which the person or other entity conducting the audit of the dealer would be in any part compensated on the basis of the dollar amount, volume, or number of chargebacks that would result to the dealer from the audit.

(c) In the event there is a dispute between the manufacturer, factory branch, distributor, or distributor branch, and the dealer with respect to any matter referred to in subsection (a), (b), (b1), (b2), (b3), (d), or (i) of this section, either party may petition the Commissioner in writing, within 30 days after either party has given written notice of the dispute to the other, for a hearing on the subject and the decision of the Commissioner shall be binding on the parties, subject to rights of judicial review and appeal as provided in Chapter 150B of the General Statutes; provided, however, that nothing contained herein shall give the Commissioner any authority as to the content of any manufacturer's or distributor's warranty. Upon the filing of a petition before the Commissioner under this subsection, any chargeback to or any payment required of a dealer by a manufacturer relating to warranty or recall parts or service compensation, or to sales incentives, service incentives, rebates, other forms of incentive compensation, or the withholding or chargeback of other compensation or support that a dealer would otherwise be eligible to receive, shall be stayed during the pendency of the determination by the Commissioner.

(d) **Transportation damages. --**
    (1) Notwithstanding the terms, provisions or conditions of any agreement or franchise, the manufacturer is liable for all damages to motor vehicles before delivery to a carrier or transporter.

    (2) If a new motor vehicle dealer determines the method of transportation, the risk of loss passes to the dealer upon delivery of the vehicle to the carrier.

    (3) In every other instance, the risk of loss remains with the manufacturer until such time as the new motor vehicle dealer or his designee accepts the vehicle from the carrier.

    (4) Whenever a motor vehicle is damaged while in transit when the carrier or the means of transportation is designated by the manufacturer or distributor, or whenever a motor vehicle is otherwise damaged prior to delivery to the dealer, the dealer must:

        a. Notify the manufacturer or distributor of such damage within three working days or within such additional time as authorized by the franchise agreement of the occurrence of the delivery of the motor vehicle as defined in subsection (1) of this section; and

        b. Must request from the manufacturer or distributor authorization to repair the damages sustained or to replace the parts or accessories damaged.

    (5) In the event the manufacturer or distributor refuses or fails to authorize repair or replacement of any such damage within ten working days after receipt of notification of damage by the dealer, ownership of the motor vehicle shall revert to the manufacturer or distributor, and the dealer shall incur no obligation, financial or otherwise, for such damage to the motor vehicle.

    (5a) No manufacturer shall fail to disclose in writing to a new motor vehicle dealer, at the time of delivery of a new motor vehicle, the nature and extent of any and all damage and post-manufacturing repairs made to such motor vehicle while in the possession or under the control of the manufacturer if the cost of such post-manufacturing repairs exceeds three percent (3%) of the manufacturer's suggested retail price. A manufacturer is not required to disclose to a new motor vehicle dealer that any glass, tires or bumper of a new motor vehicle was damaged at any time if the damaged item has been replaced with original or comparable equipment.

    (6) Nothing in this subsection (d) shall relieve the dealer of the obligation to cooperate with the manufacturer as necessary in filing any transportation damage claim with the carrier.

(e) **Damage/Repair Disclosure. --** Notwithstanding the provisions of subdivision (d)(4) of this section and in supplementation thereof, a new motor vehicle dealer shall disclose in writing to a purchaser of the new motor vehicle prior to entering into a sales contract any damage and repair to the new motor vehicle if the damage exceeds five percent (5%) of the manufacturer's suggested retail price as calculated at the rate of the dealer's authorized warranty rate for labor and parts.

(1) A new motor vehicle dealer is not required to disclose to a purchaser that any damage of any nature occurred to a new motor vehicle at any time if the total cost of all repairs fails to exceed five percent (5%) of the manufacturer's suggested retail price as calculated at the time the repairs were made based upon the dealer's authorized warranty rate for labor and parts and the damaged item has been replaced with original or comparable equipment.

(2) If disclosure is not required under this section, a purchaser may not revoke or rescind a sales contract or have or file any cause of action or claim against the dealer or manufacturer for breach of contract, breach of warranty, fraud, concealment, unfair and deceptive acts or practices, or otherwise due solely to the fact that the new motor vehicle was damaged and repaired prior to completion of the sale.

(3) For purposes of this section, "manufacturer's suggested retail price" means the retail price of the new motor vehicle suggested by the manufacturer including the retail delivered price suggested by the manufacturer for each accessory or item of optional equipment physically attached to the new motor vehicle at the time of delivery to the new motor vehicle dealer which is not included within the retail price suggested by the manufacturer for the new motor vehicle.

(f) The provisions of subsections (a), (b), (b1), (d) and (e) shall not apply to manufacturers and dealers of "motorcycles" as defined in G.S. 20-4.01(27).

(f1) The provisions of subsections (a), (b), (b1), (b2), and (c) of this section applicable to a motor vehicle manufacturer shall also apply to a component parts manufacturer. For purposes of this section, a component parts manufacturer means a person, resident, or nonresident of this State who manufactures or assembles new motor vehicle "component parts" and directly warrants the component parts to the consumer. For purposes of this section, component parts means an engine, power train, rear axle, or other part of a motor vehicle that is not warranted by the final manufacturer of the motor vehicle.

(f2) The provisions of subsections (d) and (e) of this section shall not apply to a State agency that assists the United States Department of Defense with purchasing, transferring, or titling a vehicle to another State agency, a unit of local government, a volunteer fire department, or a volunteer rescue squad.

(g) **Truck Dealer Cost Reimbursement.** -- Every manufacturer, manufacturer branch, distributor, or distributor branch of new motor vehicles, or any affiliate or subsidiary thereof, which manufactures or distributes new motor vehicles with a gross vehicle weight rating of 16,000 pounds or more shall compensate its new motor vehicle dealers located in this State for the cost of special tools, equipment, and training for which its dealers are liable when the applicable manufacturer, manufacturer branch, distributor, or distributor branch sells a portion of its vehicle inventory to converters and other nondealer retailers. The purpose of this reimbursement is to compensate truck dealers for special additional costs these dealers are required to pay for servicing these vehicles when the dealers are excluded from compensation for these expenses at the point of sale. The compensation which shall be paid pursuant to this subsection shall be applicable only with respect to new motor vehicles with a gross vehicle weight rating of 16,000 pounds or more which are registered to end users within this State and that are sold by a manufacturer, manufacturer branch, distributor, or distributor branch to either of the following:

(1) Persons or entities other than new motor vehicle dealers with whom the manufacturer, manufacturer branch, distributor, or distributor branch has entered into franchises.

(2) Persons or entities that install custom bodies on truck chassis, including, but not limited to, mounted equipment or specialized bodies for concrete distribution, firefighting equipment, waste disposal, recycling, garbage disposal, buses, utility service, street sweepers, wreckers, and rollback bodies for vehicle recovery; provided, however, that no compensation shall be required to be paid pursuant to this subdivision with respect to vehicles sold for purposes of manufacturing or assembling school buses. Additionally, no compensation shall be required to be paid pursuant to this subdivision with respect to any vehicles that were sold to the end user by a franchised new motor vehicle dealer.

The amount of compensation that shall be payable by the applicable manufacturer, manufacturer branch, distributor, or distributor branch shall be one thousand five hundred dollars ($ 1,500) per new motor vehicle registered in this State whose chassis has a gross vehicle weight rating of 16,000 pounds or more. The compensation required pursuant to this subsection shall be paid by the applicable manufacturer, manufacturer branch, distributor, or distributor branch to its franchised new motor vehicle dealer in closest proximity to the registered address of the end user to whom the motor vehicle has been registered within 30 days after registration of the vehicle. Upon receiving a request in writing from one of its franchised dealers located in this State, a manufacturer, manufacturer branch, distributor, or distributor branch shall promptly make available to the dealer its records relating to the registered addresses of its new motor vehicles registered in this State for the previous 12 months and its payment of compensation to dealers as provided in this subsection.

(h) **Right to Return Unnecessary Parts or Accessories.** -- Notwithstanding the terms of any franchise agreement, it is unlawful for any motor vehicle manufacturer, factory branch, distributor, or distributor branch to deny a franchised new motor vehicle dealer the right to return any part or accessory that the dealer has not sold after 15 months where the part or accessory was not obtained through a specific order initiated by the franchised new motor vehicle dealer, but instead was specified for, sold to, and shipped to the dealer pursuant to an automated ordering system, provided that the part or accessory is in the condition required for return to the manufacturer, factory branch, distributor, or distributor branch and the dealer returns the part within 60 days of it becoming eligible under this subsection. For purposes of this subsection, an "automated ordering system" shall be a computerized system required by the manufacturer that automatically specifies parts and accessories for sale and shipment to the dealer without specific order thereof initiated by the dealer. The manufacturer, factory branch, distributor, or distributor branch shall not charge a restocking or handling fee for any part or accessory being returned under this subsection.

(i) **Compensation for Used Motor Vehicle Recall.** -- Notwithstanding the terms of any franchise or other agreement other than an agreement permitted by this subsection (i) of this section, it is unlawful for any motor vehicle manufacturer, factory branch, distributor, or distributor branch to fail to compensate a franchised motor vehicle dealer for any qualifying used motor vehicle in the inventory of a dealer authorized to sell new motor vehicles of the same line-make or by a dealer authorized to perform recall repairs on vehicles of the same line-make in the manner specified in this subsection. The manufacturer, factory branch, distributor, or distributor branch shall compensate the dealer for any qualifying used motor vehicle in the inventory of the dealer at the prorated rate of at least one and one-half percent (1.5%)

per month of the average trade-in value of the qualifying used motor vehicle beginning on the date the vehicle becomes a qualifying used motor vehicle and ending on and including the date the vehicle ceases to be a qualifying used motor vehicle pursuant to subsection (j) of this section. Any claim by a dealer for compensation owed under this subsection may be submitted by the dealer on a monthly basis, and the manufacturer, factory branch, distributor, or distributor branch shall approve or disapprove the claim within 30 days of receipt of the claim and shall process and pay the claim within 60 days after the approval of the claim. Every manufacturer, manufacturer branch, distributor, and distributor branch licensed by the Commissioner under this Article shall establish a simple, convenient, and efficient process for its franchised dealers to submit claims for compensation under this subsection on a monthly basis. Such process shall provide for a manner and method for a dealer to demonstrate the inventory status of a qualifying used motor vehicle, provided the manner and method is reasonable and does not require information that is unduly burdensome. Nothing in this subsection shall prohibit a manufacturer, factory branch, distributor, or distributor branch from compensating a dealer for a qualifying used motor vehicle under a national recall compensation program instead of the basis established in this section, provided that the compensation paid to dealers under the program is equal to or exceeds the level of compensation required by this subsection on a monthly basis and the compensation payments are made within the time periods required by this section. Nothing in this subsection shall prohibit a dealer and a manufacturer, factory branch, distributor, or distributor branch from voluntarily entering an agreement the sole subject matter of which is compensation for a dealer for a used motor vehicle subject to a recall and which provides a compensation amount or other related terms that differ from the compensation amount and other requirements specified in subsection (j) of this section provided that the dealer's ability to participate in or qualify for any incentive program offered or sponsored by the manufacturer or distributor or to otherwise receive any discounts, credits, rebates, or incentives of any kind is not conditioned upon the dealer's willingness to enter such an agreement. Nothing in this subsection shall require a manufacturer, factory branch, distributor, or distributor branch to provide total compensation in excess of the total average trade-in value of the qualifying used motor vehicle.

(j) Definitions -- The following definitions apply in this section:

(1) "Average trade-in value" means the value of a used motor vehicle as determined by reference to a generally accepted,

nationally published, third-party used vehicle valuation guide book.

(2) "Qualifying used motor vehicle" means a motor vehicle that meets all of the following: (i) a used motor vehicle of a line-make for which the dealer holds an active franchise with the manufacturer to sell and service new motor vehicles; (ii) a used motor vehicle of a model subject to a recall notice and subject to or covered under a stop-sale or do-not-drive order issued by the manufacturer of the motor vehicle or issued by the National Highway Traffic Safety Administration; (iii) parts or other remedy sufficient to fully repair the underlying defect that resulted in the recall of the motor vehicle to the extent that the motor vehicle is no longer subject to or covered by a stop-sale or do-not-drive order issued by the manufacturer of the motor vehicle were not made available to the dealer within 30 days of the date of the notice of recall by the manufacturer; (iv) a motor vehicle in the dealer's inventory or otherwise owned by the dealer at the time a stop-sale or do-not-drive order is issued or taken into the used motor vehicle inventory of the dealer as a consumer trade-in incident to the purchase of a motor vehicle from the dealer after the stop-sale or do-not-drive order is issued. A motor vehicle meeting the definition of a "qualifying used motor vehicle" pursuant to this subdivision shall cease to be a "qualifying used motor vehicle" on the earlier of the following: (i) the date the remedy or parts to fully repair the underlying defect that resulted in the recall of the motor vehicle to an extent that the motor vehicle is no longer subject to or covered by a stop-sale or do-not-drive order issued by the manufacturer of the motor vehicle are made available to the dealer; (ii) the date the dealer sells, trades, or otherwise disposes of the qualifying used motor vehicle; or (iii) the date the manufacturer provides notice to the dealer that the stop-sale or do-not-drive order is no longer in effect.

(3) "Stop-sale or do-not-drive order" means a notification, directive, or order issued by a manufacturer, factory branch, distributor, or distributor branch to its franchised dealers or issued by the National Highway Traffic Safety Administration stating that motor vehicle models of certain used vehicles in inventory shall not be sold or leased, at either retail or wholesale, due to a federal safety recall for a defect or a noncompliance recall, or a federal emissions recall.

Nothing in this subsection shall be construed as excluding from the definition of a qualifying used motor vehicle a motor vehicle on which a previously issued notice of recall or a stop-sale or do-not-drive order remains in effect as of the effective date of this subsection, or a motor vehicle that becomes subject to a notice of recall or a stop-sale or do-not drive order on or after the effective date of this subsection, provided that the motor vehicle otherwise meets the criteria for a qualifying used motor vehicle. Subsections (i) and (j) of this section shall not be applicable to any manufacturer, factory branch, distributor, or distributor branch that manufactures or distributes recreational vehicles.

(k) Any compensation provided to the dealer that meets the minimum requirements of subsection (i) of this section is exclusive and may not be combined with any other state or federal recall compensation civil remedy for used motor vehicles subject to recall.

History.

1973, c. 88, s. 3; c. 1331, s. 3; 1983, c. 704, ss. 11-13; 1987, c. 827, s. 1; 1989, c. 614, ss. 1, 2; 1991, c. 561, ss. 1 -4; 1993, c. 116, ss. 1, 2; 1995, c. 156, s. 1;1997-319, s. 4;1999-335, ss. 3, 3.1, 4; 2003-113, s. 5;2003-258, s. 4;2007-513, ss. 5 -7, 11; 2009-338, ss. 3, 4; 2009-550, s. 2(c);2011-290, s. 10;2013-302, s. 10;2015-209, ss. 6, 7, 8, 9; 2017-148, s. 3;2018-27, s. 2;2019-125, ss. 6, 9

EDITOR'S NOTE. --

Subsection (b1), amended by Session Laws 2007-513, s. 6, as set out above, has two subdivisions designated (b1)(1) and two subdivisions designated (b1)(2).

Session Laws 2015-209, s. 10, is a severability clause.

Session Laws 2015-209, which, in ss. 6-9, amended this section, in s. 11 provides: "This act is effective when it becomes law [August 11, 2015] and applies to all current and future franchises and other agreements in existence between any new motor vehicle dealer located in this State and a manufacturer or distributor as of the effective date of this act."

Session Laws 2017-148, s. 6, is a severability clause.

Session Laws 2018-27, s. 5, is a severability clause.

Session laws 2019-125, s. 12, is a severability clause.

Session Laws 2019-125, s. 13, made the amendments to subsections (b), (b3), (b4), and (g) by Session Laws 2019-125, ss. 6, 9, effective July 19, 2019, and applicable to all current and future franchises and other agreements in existence between any new motor vehicle dealer located in this State and a manufacturer or distributor as of that date.

EFFECT OF AMENDMENTS. --

Session Laws 2009-550, s. 2(c), effective August 28, 2009, added subsection (f2).

Session Laws 2013-302, s. 10, effective July 18, 2013, inserted "the retail rates charged for parts and labor by" in the last sentence of subsection (a); in subsection (a1), deleted "fair and" preceding "reasonable" in the second and eighth sentences, and "unfair and" preceding "unreasonable" in the eighth sentence, substituted "retail rates charged for parts and labor by" for "practices of" in the second and third sentences, added "retail" following "dealer's" in the third sentence, and added the last two sentences; deleted "and transmission assemblies" following "assemblies" in subdivision (a2)(3); added subdivision (a2)(8); and made minor stylistic changes.

Session Laws 2015-209, ss. 6 -9, effective August 11, 2015, substituted "specials, coupons, or other promotional discounts" for "specials, or promotional discounts" in subdivision (a2)(1); rewrote subdivision (a2)(4); inserted "and vehicle alignments" following "Tires" in subdivision (a2)(6); rewrote subsection (b3); inserted "(b3)" following "(b1), (b2)," in the first sentence of subsection (c); and rewrote the last sentence of subsection (c); and added the last sentence in subdivision (g)(2) and substituted "nine hundred dollars ($900.00)" for "six hundred dollars ($600.00)" in the first sentence in the last paragraph in subsection (g). For effective date, see editor's note.

Session Laws 2017-148, s. 3, effective July 20, 2017, substituted "other than parts used to repair the living facilities of recreational vehicles, including motor homes, travel trailers, fifth-wheel trailers, camping trailers, and truck campers as defined in G.S. 20-4.01(32b)" for "other than parts used to repair the living facilities of recreational vehicles" in the first sentence of subsection (b).

Session Laws 2018-27, s. 2, effective June 22, 2018, in the section heading, inserted "and recall"; rewrote subsection (a); in subsection (a3), inserted "reduced or" near the beginning and substituted "dealer on the basis of the dealer's average" for "dealer the average" near the end; in subsection (b), in the first sentence, inserted "or recall" twice, inserted "a qualifying used motor vehicle pursuant to subsections (i) and (j) of this section or," inserted "and recall," and inserted "or for payments for a qualifying used motor vehicle pursuant to subsections (i) and (j) of this section," and in the second sentence, substituted "or recall parts or service compensation, or compensation for a qualifying used motor vehicle in accordance with subsections (i) and (j) of this section" for "parts or service compensation"; in subsection (b1), substituted "warranty, and recall work, including compensation for a qualifying used motor vehicle in accordance with subsection (i) of this section, labor," for "warranty and recall work including labor" in the first sentence of the introductory paragraph; in subsection (c), in the first sentence, substituted "(b3), (d), or (i)" for "(b3), or (d)" and in the last sentence, inserted "or recall"; in subsection (h), added the subsection heading; and added subsections (i) through (k); and made minor stylistic changes.

Session Laws 2019-125, ss. 6 and 9, effective July 19, 2019, in subsection (b), inserted "other than an audit conducted for cause" and "may only be conducted one time within any 12-month period and" in the second and third sentences, and added the fifth and sixth sentences; rewrote subdivision (b3)(5), added subsection (b4), and in subsection (g), substituted "one thousand five hundred dollars ($1,500)" for "nine hundred dollars ($900.00)" in the second

paragraph. For effective date and applicability, see editor's note.

CROSS REFERENCES. --
As to inapplicability of this section to certain manufacturers and dealers, see G.S. 20-305.5.

§ 20-305.2. Unfair methods of competition; protection of car-buying public

(a) It is unlawful for any motor vehicle manufacturer, factory branch, distributor, distributor branch, or subsidiary thereof, to directly or indirectly through any parent, subsidiary, or affiliated entity, whether or not such motor vehicle manufacturer, factory branch, distributor, distributor branch, or subsidiary thereof has entered into a franchise, within the meaning of G.S. 20-286(8a), with any person or entity in this State, own any ownership interest in, operate, or control any motor vehicle dealer in this State or any entity in this State that provides warranty service or repairs at retail, to file a motor vehicle dealer application with the Division pursuant to G.S. 20-288, or to be licensed by the Division as a motor vehicle dealer, provided that this section shall not be construed to prohibit any of the following:

(1) The operation by a manufacturer, factory branch, distributor, distributor branch, or subsidiary thereof, of a dealership for a temporary period (not to exceed one year) during the transition from one owner or operator to another.

(2) The ownership or control of a dealership by a manufacturer, factory branch, distributor, distributor branch, or subsidiary thereof, while in a bona fide relationship with an economically disadvantaged or other independent person, other than a manufacturer, factory branch, distributor, distributor branch, or an agent or affiliate thereof, who has made a bona fide, unencumbered initial investment of at least six percent (6%) of the total sales price that is subject to loss in the dealership and who can reasonably expect to acquire full ownership of the dealership within a reasonable period of time, not to exceed 12 years, and on reasonable terms and conditions.

(3) The ownership, operation or control of a dealership by a manufacturer, factory branch, distributor, distributor branch, or subsidiary thereof, if such manufacturer, factory branch, distributor, distributor branch, or subsidiary has been engaged in the retail sale of motor vehicles through such dealership for a continuous period of three years prior to March 16, 1973, and if the Commissioner determines, after a hearing on the matter at the request of any party, that there is no independent dealer available in the relevant market area to

own and operate the franchise in a manner consistent with the public interest.

(4) Repealed by Session Laws 2019-125, s. 10, effective July 19, 2019.

(4a) The ownership, operation, or control of a maximum total number of five motor vehicle dealership locations within this State prior to December 31, 2020, or a maximum total number of six motor vehicle dealership locations within this State on or after January 1, 2021, by a manufacturer that manufactures and sells only motor vehicles that are plug-in electric vehicles that do not rely on any nonelectric source of power in all modes of operation; provided, however, that this subdivision shall be applicable only to a manufacturer that had at least one motor vehicle dealership licensed in this State by the Division as of March 1, 2019. The Division shall deny any motor vehicle dealer application that, if granted by the Division, would allow said manufacturer, or any parent, subsidiary, or other person or entity affiliated with the manufacturer, to own, operate, or control any more than the maximum total number of motor vehicle dealership locations in this State permitted by this subdivision. Provided further, that the Commissioner shall promptly revoke any motor vehicle dealer license granted under this section upon discovery of the occurrence of any of the following events:

a. The manufacturer ceases to manufacturer or distribute only motor vehicles that are electric vehicles that do not rely on any nonelectric source of power in all modes of operation.

b. The manufacturer enters into a franchise with any dealer located in this State.

c. The manufacturer acquires a substantial affiliation with any motor vehicle manufacturer or distributor that currently has or at any point in the past has ever entered into a franchise with a dealer located in this State. For purposes of this sub-subdivision, the term "substantial affiliation" means either of the following:

1. The ownership by the manufacturer of a direct or indirect interest of greater than thirty percent (30%) of the shareholder voting control of an entity that is a motor vehicle manufacturer, factory branch, distributor, or distributor branch, as these terms are defined in G.S. 20-286.

2. The combined direct or indirect ownership by one or more motor vehicle manufacturers, factory branches, distributors, or distributor branches, as these terms are defined in G.S. 20-286, or one of their affiliates, of greater than thirty percent (30%) of the shareholder voting control of the manufacturer.

d. The manufacturer sells or offers for sale any new motor vehicles identified as, or bearing the logo or brand of, a motor vehicle manufacturer or distributor which has any franchised dealers within this State, provided, however, that this provision shall not be deemed to be violated if any component parts of a motor vehicle are branded with the name of or logo of another motor vehicle manufacturer as long as the vehicle as a whole is clearly identified as, and branded exclusively with the brand of the electric vehicle manufacturer that holds the motor vehicle dealer license.

(5) The ownership, operation, or control of any facility (location) of a new motor vehicle dealer in this State at which the dealer sells only new and used motor vehicles with a gross weight rating of 8,500 pounds or more, provided that both of the following conditions have been met:

a. The facility is located within 35 miles of manufacturing or assembling facilities existing as of January 1, 1999, and is owned or operated by the manufacturer, manufacturing branch, distributor, distributor branch, or any affiliate or subsidiary thereof which assembles, manufactures, or distributes new motor vehicles with a gross weight rating of 8,500 pounds or more by such dealer at said location; and

b. The facility is located in the largest Standard Metropolitan Statistical Area (SMSA) in the State.

(6) As to any line make of motor vehicle for which there is in aggregate no more than 13 franchised new motor vehicle dealers (locations) licensed and in operation within the State as of January 1, 1999, the ownership, operation, or control of one or more new motor vehicle dealership trading solely in such line make of vehicle by the manufacturer, factory branch, distributor, distributor branch, or subsidiary or affiliate thereof, provided however, that all of the following conditions are met:

a. The manufacturer, factory branch, distributor, distributor branch, or subsidiary or affiliate thereof does not own directly or indirectly, in aggregate, in excess of forty-five percent (45%) interest in the dealership;

Chapter 20

b. At the time the manufacturer, factory branch, distributor, distributor branch, or subsidiary or affiliate thereof first acquires ownership or assumes operation or control with respect to any such dealership, the distance between the dealership thus owned, operated, or controlled and the nearest other new motor vehicle dealership trading in the same line make of vehicle, is no less than 35 miles;

c. All the manufacturer's franchise agreements confer rights on the dealer of the line make to develop and operate within a defined geographic territory or area, as many dealership facilities as the dealer and manufacturer shall agree are appropriate; and

d. That as of July 1, 1999, not fewer than half of the dealers of the line make within the State own and operate two or more dealership facilities in the geographic territory or area covered by the franchise agreement with the manufacturer.

(7) The ownership, operation, or control of a dealership that sells primarily recreational vehicles as defined in G.S. 20-4.01 by a manufacturer, factory branch, distributor, or distributor branch, or subsidiary thereof, if the manufacturer, factory branch, distributor, or distributor branch, or subsidiary thereof, owned, operated, or controlled the dealership as of October 1, 2001.

(8) A manufacturer that manufactures and distributes only low-speed vehicles that meet the applicable NHTSA standards for low-speed vehicles; provided, however, that this subdivision is applicable only to a manufacturer that had at least one motor vehicle dealership licensed in this State by the Division as of March 1, 2019.

(b) Subsection (a) of this section does not apply to manufacturers or distributors of trailers or semitrailers that are not recreational vehicles as defined in G.S. 20-4.01.

(c) For purposes of subsection (d) of this section, the following definitions apply:

(1) **Former Franchisee.** -- A new motor vehicle dealer, as defined in G.S. 20-286(13), that has entered into a franchise, as defined in G.S. 20-286(8a) with a predecessor manufacturer and that has either:

a. Entered into a termination agreement or deferred termination agreement with a predecessor or successor manufacturer related to such franchise; or

b. Has had such franchise canceled, terminated, nonrenewed, noncontinued, rejected, nonassumed, or otherwise ended.

(2) **Relevant market area.** -- The area within a 10-, 15-, or 20-mile radius around the site of the previous franchisee's dealership facility, as determined in the same manner that the relevant market area is determined under G.S. 20-286(13b) when a manufacturer is seeking to establish an additional new motor vehicle dealer.

(3) **Successor manufacturer.** -- Any motor vehicle manufacturer, as defined in G.S. 20-286(8e), that, on or after January 1, 2009, acquires, succeeds to, or assumes any part of the business of another manufacturer, referred to as the "predecessor manufacturer," as the result of any of the following:

a. A change in ownership, operation, or control of the predecessor manufacturer by sale or transfer of assets, corporate stock or other equity interest, assignment, merger, consolidation, combination, joint venture, redemption, court-approved sale, operation of law or otherwise.

b. The termination, suspension, or cessation of a part or all of the business operations of the predecessor manufacturer.

c. The discontinuance of the sale of the product line.

d. A change in distribution system by the predecessor manufacturer, whether through a change in distributor or the predecessor manufacturer's decision to cease conducting business through a distributor altogether.

(d) For a period of four years from the date that a successor manufacturer acquires, succeeds to, or assumes any part of the business of a predecessor manufacturer, it shall be unlawful for such successor manufacturer to enter into a same line make franchise with any person, as defined in G.S. 20-4.01(28), or to permit the relocation of any existing same line make franchise, for a line make of the predecessor manufacturer that would be located or relocated within the relevant market area of a former franchisee who owned or leased a dealership facility in that relevant market area without first offering the additional or relocated franchise to the former franchisee, or the designated successor of such former franchisee in the event the former franchisee is deceased or disabled, at no cost and without any requirements or restrictions other than those imposed generally on the manufacturer's other franchisees at that time, unless one of the following applies:

(1) As a result of the former franchisee's cancellation, termination, noncontinuance, or nonrenewal of the franchise, the predecessor manufacturer had consolidated the line make with another of its line makes for

which the predecessor manufacturer had a franchisee with a then-existing dealership facility located within that relevant market area.

(2) The successor manufacturer has paid the former franchisee, or the designated successor of such former franchisee in the event the former franchisee is deceased or disabled, the fair market value of the former franchisee's franchise calculated as prescribed in G.S. 20-305(6)d.3.

(3) The successor manufacturer proves that the former franchisee, or the designated successor of such former franchisee in the event the former franchisee is deceased or disabled, by reason of lack of training, lack of prior experience, poor past performance, lack of financial ability, or poor character, is unfit to own or manage the dealership. A successor manufacturer who seeks to assert that a former franchisee is unfit to own or manage the dealership must file a petition seeking a hearing on this issue before the Commissioner and shall have the burden of proving lack of fitness at such hearing. The Commissioner shall try to conduct the hearing and render a final determination within 120 days after the manufacturer's petition has been filed. No successor dealer, other than the former franchisee, may be appointed or franchised by the successor manufacturer within the relevant market area until the Commissioner has held a hearing and rendered a determination on the issue of the fitness of the previous franchisee to own or manage the dealership.

(e) For purposes of this section, an unfair method of competition includes any physical or mechanical warranty repair made or provided directly by a manufacturer or distributor to any motor vehicle located within this State requiring the direct participation of a dealer franchised by the manufacturer or distributor and without such dealer receiving reasonable compensation, equal to an amount no less than the amount provided in G.S. 20-305.1.

(f) No claim or cause of action may be brought against a dealer in this State arising out of any warranty repair, fix, repair, or update that was provided by the manufacturer or distributor without the direct involvement and participation of the dealer. Any manufacturer or distributor that provides or attempts to provide a warranty repair, fix, repair, update, or adjustment directly to any motor vehicle located within this State without the direct participation of a dealer franchised by the manufacturer or distributor shall fully indemnify and hold harmless any dealer located in this State for all claims, demands, judgments, damages, attorneys' fees, litigation expenses, and all other costs and expenses incurred by the dealer arising out of the actual or attempted warranty repair, fix, repair, update, or adjustment.

History.
1973, c. 88, s. 3; 1983, c. 704, ss. 14, 15; 1999-335, s. 5;2001-510, s. 3;2002-72, ss. 19(d), 19(e); 2003-416, s. 11;2009-496, s. 2;2013-302, s. 8;2019-125, s. 10

EDITOR'S NOTE. --
Subdivisions (c)(1) and (c)(3) were renumbered as subdivisions (c)(3) and (c)(1), respectively, at the direction of the Revisor of Statutes to maintain alphabetical order.

Session Laws 2009-496, s. 3, provides: "The terms and provisions of this act [s. 2 of which amended subsection (b) and added subsections (c) and (d) of this section] shall be applicable to all franchises and other agreements entered into on or after the effective date of this act [August 26, 2009] between any new motor vehicle dealer located in this State and a manufacturer or distributor."

Session Laws 2009-496, s. 4, is a severability clause.

Session Laws 2013-302, s. 11, provides: "The terms and provisions of Sections 7 through 12 of this act shall be applicable to all current and future franchises and other agreements in existence between any new motor vehicle dealer located in this State and a manufacturer or distributor as of the effective date of this act."

Session laws 2019-125, s. 12, is a severability clause.

EFFECT OF AMENDMENTS. --
Session Laws 2003-416, s. 11, effective August 14, 2003, made minor stylistic changes in subdivision (a)(7).

Session Laws 2013-302, s. 8, effective July 18, 2013, added subsections (e) and (f).

Session Laws 2019-125, s. 10, effective July 19, 2019, inserted "protection of car-buying public" in the catchline; in subsection (a), rewrote the introductory paragraph, deleted subdivision (4), added subdivisions (4a) and (8), and made stylistic changes.

CITED in American Motors Sales Corp. v. Peters, 311 N.C. 311, 317 S.E.2d 351 (1984).

CROSS REFERENCES. --
As to inapplicability of this section to certain manufacturers and dealers, see G.S. 20-305.5.

§ 20-305.3. Hearing notice

In every case of a hearing before the Commissioner authorized under this Article, the Commissioner shall give reasonable notice of each such hearing to all interested parties, and the Commissioner's decision shall be binding on the parties, subject to the rights of judicial review and appeal as provided in Chapter 150B of the General Statutes. The costs of such hearings shall be assessed by the Commissioner.

History.
1973, c. 88, s. 3; c. 1331, s. 3; 1987, c. 827, s. 1

CITED in Sandhill Motors, Inc. v. American Motors Sales Corp., 667 F.2d 1112 (4th Cir. 1981); American Motors Sales Corp. v. Peters, 58 N.C. App. 684, 294 S.E.2d 764 (1982).

CROSS REFERENCES. --

As to inapplicability of this section to certain manufacturers and dealers, see G.S. 20-305.5.

§ 20-305.4. Motor Vehicle Dealers' Advisory Board

(a) The Motor Vehicle Dealers' Advisory Board shall consist of six members; three of which shall be appointed by the Speaker of the House of Representatives, and three of which shall be appointed by the President Pro Tempore of the Senate to consult with and advise the Commissioner with respect to matters brought before the Commissioner under the provisions of G.S. 20-304 through 20-305.4.

(b) Each member of the Motor Vehicle Dealers' Advisory Board shall be a resident of North Carolina. Three members of the Board shall be franchised dealers in new automobiles or trucks, duly licensed and engaged in business as such in North Carolina, provided that no two of such dealers may be franchised to sell automobiles or trucks manufactured or distributed by the same person or a subsidiary or affiliate of the same person. Three members of the Board shall not be motor vehicle dealers or employees of a motor vehicle dealer.

(c) The Speaker shall appoint two of the dealer members and one of the public members and shall fill any vacancy in said positions and the President Pro Tempore of the Senate shall appoint one of the dealer members and two of the public members and shall fill any vacancy in said positions. In making the initial appointments the Speaker shall designate that the two dealer members shall serve for one and three years respectively and the public member shall serve for two years, and in making the initial appointments the Lieutenant Governor shall designate that the dealer member shall serve for two years and the two public members shall serve for one and three years respectively.

(d) Two members of the first Board appointed shall serve for a period of three years, two members of the first Board shall serve for a period of two years, and two members of the first Board shall serve for a period of one year. Subsequent appointments shall be for terms of three years, except appointments to fill vacancies which shall be for the unexpired terms. Members of the Board shall meet at the call of the Commissioner and shall receive as compensation for their services seven dollars ($ 7.00) for each day actually engaged in the exercise of the duties of the Board and such travel expenses and subsistence allowances as are generally allowed other State commissions and boards.

History.

1973, c. 88, s. 3; 1995, c. 490, s. 36

CROSS REFERENCES. --

As to inapplicability of this section to certain manufacturers and dealers, see G.S. 20-305.5.

§ 20-305.5. Recreational vehicle manufacturer warranty recall obligations

(a) It is unlawful for any manufacturer, factory branch, distributor, or distributor branch that manufactures or distributes recreational vehicles to fail to fully compensate its dealers located in this State in accordance with this section for warranty or recall work performed by the dealers related to the living facilities of the vehicle, including all labor and parts used to repair such living facilities and any equipment, plumbing, appliances, and other options included by the manufacturer, factory branch, distributor, or distributor branch in the purchase price paid by the dealer for the vehicle. For purposes of this section, the term "recreational vehicle" includes motor homes, travel trailers, fifth-wheel trailers, camping trailers, and truck campers as defined by G.S. 20-4.01(32b). With respect to those portions of the living facilities of recreational vehicles and any equipment, plumbing, appliances, and other options that are part of such living facilities and that are included by the recreational vehicle manufacturer, factory branch, distributor, or distributor branch in the purchase price paid by the dealer for the vehicle, the term "warrantor" shall mean any manufacturer or distributor of such living facilities or any equipment, plumbing, appliances, and other options that are part of such living facilities that offers a warranty in writing to either the recreational vehicle dealer or to the ultimate purchaser of the recreational vehicle. The term "warrantor" does not include a person that provides a service contract, mechanical or other insurance, or an extended warranty sold for separate consideration by a dealer or other person not controlled by a warrantor. Notwithstanding the terms or conditions of any contract or agreement, it is unlawful for any recreational vehicle manufacturer, factory branch, distributor, or distributor branch to fail to fully and timely compensate any of its franchised recreational vehicle dealers located in this State in accordance with this section for all parts and labor used by such franchised dealers in making warranty or recall repairs to such living facilities of recreational vehicles, including any equipment, plumbing, appliances, and other options included by the recreational vehicle manufacturer, factory branch, distributor, or distributor branch in the purchase price paid by the dealer for the vehicle, to the extent that the individual components of such living facilities are not separately warranted by the manufacturers or distributors of such components. Notwithstanding the terms or conditions of any warranty, contract, or agreement, it is unlawful for any warrantor, as defined in this subdivision, to fail to fully and timely compensate any franchised recreational vehicle dealer located in this State in accordance with this section for all parts and labor used by such franchised recreational vehicle dealer in making warranty or recall repairs to any component parts of the living facilities of recreational vehicles manufactured or distributed by such warrantor, including any equipment, plumbing, appliances, and other options included by a recreational vehicle manufacturer, factory branch, distributor, or distributor branch in the purchase price paid by the dealer for the vehicle.

(b) Each warrantor as defined in this subdivision and each recreational vehicle manufacturer, factory branch, distributor, and distributor branch that sells or distributes recreational vehicles in this State shall specify in writing to each recreational vehicle dealer licensed in this State who sells products manufactured or distributed by such warrantor or such recreational vehicle manufacturer, factory branch, distributor, or distributor branch, the recreational vehicle dealer's obligations for preparation, delivery, and warranty and recall service on its products, the schedule of compensation to be paid such dealers for parts, work, and service in connection with warranty or recall service, and the time allowances for the performance of such work and service. In no event shall such schedule of compensation fail to include reasonable compensation for diagnostic work and associated administrative requirements as well as repair service, labor, and transportation provided by the dealer to transport a recreational vehicle to and from a location at which the repairs can be made. Provided, however, that with respect to reimbursement for a recreational vehicle dealer's transportation expenses, the dealer is required to obtain the prior written authorization of the affected warrantor before incurring any transportation expenses, which authorization shall not be unreasonably denied by the warrantor, and provided further that any such request for transportation reimbursement must be denied by the warrantor within 5 business days of the warrantor's receipt of the dealer's request for reimbursement or the request shall be deemed authorized and allowed. Time allowances for the performance of warranty work and service shall be reasonable and adequate for the work to be performed. The compensation which must be paid under this section must be reasonable; provided, however, that under no circumstances may the reasonable compensation

under this section be in an amount less than the recreational vehicle dealer's current retail labor rate for nonwarranty work of like kind, provided such amount is competitive with the retail rates charged for parts and labor by other franchised recreational dealers within the dealer's market.

(c) A warrantor may not require a dealer to establish the rate customarily charged by the recreational vehicle dealer for labor by an unduly burdensome or time-consuming method or by requiring information that is unduly burdensome or time-consuming to provide, including, but not limited to, part-by-part or transaction-by-transaction calculations.

(d) For any part, equipment, plumbing system or device, or appliance or option, a warrantor shall reimburse the dealer the cost of the part, equipment, plumbing system or device, appliance or option, plus a minimum of a thirty percent (30%) handling charge and pay the cost, if any, of freight to return the part, equipment, appliance, or option to the warrantor.

(e) If a warrantor furnishes a part or component to a dealer, at reduced or no cost, to use in performing repairs under a warranty or recall repair, the warrantor shall compensate the dealer for the part or component in the same manner as warranty parts compensation under this section, by compensating the dealer on the basis of a thirty percent (30%) handling charge for the part or component as listed in the warrantor's price schedule less the cost for the part or component.

(f) Notwithstanding the terms of any warranty, contract, or agreement, all claims made by recreational dealers pursuant to this section for compensation for delivery, preparation, warranty and recall work, and transportation costs, including labor, parts, and other expenses, shall be paid by the affected warrantor within 30 days after receipt of claim from the dealer. When any claim is disapproved, the dealer shall be notified in writing of the grounds for disapproval. Any claim not specifically disapproved in writing within 30 days after receipt shall be considered approved and payment is due immediately. No claim which has been approved and paid may be charged back to the dealer unless it can be shown that the claim was false or fraudulent, that the repairs were not properly made or were unnecessary to correct the defective condition, or the dealer failed to reasonably substantiate the claim either in accordance with the manufacturer's reasonable written procedures or by other reasonable means. A warrantor shall not deny a claim or reduce the amount to be reimbursed to the dealer as long as the dealer has provided reasonably sufficient documentation that the dealer (i) made a good-faith attempt to perform the work in compliance with the written policies and procedures of the warrantor and (ii) actually performed the work.

Notwithstanding the foregoing, a warrantor shall not fail to fully compensate a dealer for warranty or recall work or make any charge-back to the dealer's account based on the dealer's failure to comply with the warrantor's claim documentation procedure or procedures unless both of the following requirements have been met:

(1) The dealer has, within the previous 12 months, failed to comply with the same specific claim documentation procedure or procedures.

(2) The warrantor has, within the previous 12 months, provided a written warning to the dealer by certified United States mail, return receipt requested, identifying the specific claim documentation procedure or procedures violated by the dealer.

(g) Every recreational vehicle manufacturer, factory branch, distributor, or distributor branch that manufactures or distributes recreational vehicles for sale in this State shall designate at least one of its employees knowledgeable in warranty administration who shall be the designated warranty contact person with whom its franchised dealers licensed in this State can communicate to assist them in filing and getting paid on warranty claims related to all component parts of all recreational vehicles such recreational vehicle manufacturer, factory branch, distributor, or distributor branch sells or distributes in this State. Each recreational vehicle manufacturer, factory branch, distributor, or distributor branch shall promptly notify, in writing, all of its franchised recreational vehicle dealers licensed in this State, the Commissioner, and the North Carolina Automobile Dealers Association, Incorporated, of the identity and contact information of the designated warranty contact person and any changes in this information. A recreational vehicle manufacturer or distributor that represents multiple suppliers or multiple line-makes of vehicles shall be permitted to designate a single individual as the designated warranty contact person for all such suppliers and line-makes of vehicles represented by such recreational vehicle manufacturer or distributor.

(h) It shall be unlawful for any warrantor or for any recreational vehicle manufacturer, factory branch, distributor, or distributor branch to recover or attempt to recover all or any portion of its costs for compensating recreational vehicle dealers licensed in this State for warranty or recall parts and service either by reduction in the amount due to the dealer or by separate charge, surcharge, or other imposition.

(i) It shall be unlawful for any recreational vehicle manufacturer, factory branch, distributor, or distributor branch to fail to indemnify and hold harmless its franchised dealers licensed in this State against any judgment

for damages or settlements agreed to by the manufacturer, including, but not limited to, court costs and reasonable attorneys' fees of the recreational vehicle dealer, arising out of complaints, claims, or lawsuits, including, but not limited to, strict liability, negligence, misrepresentation, express or implied warranty, or rescission or revocation of acceptance of the sale of a vehicle as defined in G.S. 25-2-608, to the extent that the judgment or settlement relates to the alleged defective or negligent manufacture, assembly, or design of new recreational vehicles, parts, or accessories or other functions by the manufacturer, factory branch, distributor, or distributor branch beyond the control of the dealer. It shall be unlawful for any warrantor to fail to indemnify and hold harmless any recreational vehicle dealer located in this State who sold one or more products warranted by such warrantor against any judgment for damages or settlements agreed to by the warrantor, including, but not limited to, court costs and reasonable attorneys' fees of the recreational vehicle dealer, arising out of complaints, claims, or lawsuits, including, but not limited to, strict liability, negligence, misrepresentation, express or implied warranty, or rescission or revocation of acceptance of the sale of a vehicle or vehicle part, component, or accessory, as defined in G.S. 25-2-608, to the extent that the judgment or settlement relates to the alleged defective or negligent manufacture, assembly, or design of a product warranted by the warrantor or other functions of the warrantor beyond the control of the dealer. Any audit for warranty or recall parts or service compensation shall only be for the 12-month period immediately following the date of the payment of the claim by the manufacturer, factory branch, distributor, distributor branch, or warrantor. Any audit for sales incentives, service incentives, rebates, or other forms of incentive compensation shall only be for the 12-month period immediately following the date of the payment of the claim by the manufacturer, factory branch, distributor, distributor branch, or warrantor. Provided, however, these limitations shall not be effective in the case of fraudulent claims.

(j) It shall be unlawful for any warrantor or for any recreational vehicle manufacturer, factory branch, distributor, or distributor branch to direct or encourage any owner or purchaser of a recreational vehicle to have warranty or recall service work or other repairs on a recreational vehicle made by a repair facility other than either the franchised dealer that sold the vehicle owner the recreational vehicle or the franchised dealer closest in proximity to such recreational vehicle owner or purchaser, provided that the recreational vehicle dealer who sold the vehicle to the owner or purchaser or who is located in closest proximity to such recreational vehicle owner or purchaser has sufficiently trained personnel and the necessary tools and equipment to make the required repairs to the vehicle, has not expressly stated in writing its desire to have the repairs made elsewhere, and is willing to make the repairs within a reasonable period of time after the necessary parts have been supplied to the dealer.

(k) In the event there is a dispute between a recreational vehicle dealer and a warrantor or a recreational vehicle manufacturer, factory branch, distributor, or distributor branch, with relating to any matter referred to in this section, either party may petition the Commissioner in writing, within 30 days after either party has given written notice of the dispute to the other, for a hearing on the subject and the decision of the Commissioner shall be binding on the parties, subject to rights of judicial review and appeal as provided in Chapter 150B of the General Statutes; provided, however, that nothing contained herein shall give the Commissioner any authority as to the content of any warrantor's warranty. Upon the filing of a petition before the Commissioner under this subsection, any chargeback to or any payment required of a recreational vehicle dealer by a warrantor or by a recreational vehicle manufacturer, factory branch, distributor, or distributor branch relating to warranty or recall parts or service compensation, or to sales incentives, service incentives, rebates, other forms of incentive compensation, or the withholding or chargeback of other compensation or support that a dealer would otherwise be eligible to receive, shall be stayed during the pendency of the determination by the Commissioner.

(*l*) The provisions of G.S. 20-305(4) through G.S. 20-305(28) and G.S. 20-305.2 to G.S. 20-305.4 shall not apply to manufacturers of or dealers in mobile or manufactured type housing or who sell or distribute only nonmotorized recreational trailers; provided, however, that unless specifically exempted, each of these provisions shall be applicable to all recreational vehicle manufacturers, factory branches, distributors, and distributor branches who sell or distribute any motorized recreational vehicles in this State. The provisions of G.S. 20-305.1 shall not apply to manufacturers of or dealers in mobile or manufactured type housing.

(m) To the extent not expressly inconsistent with the provisions of this section, all of the terms and provisions of G.S. 20-305.1 shall be applicable to recreational vehicle dealers and to recreational vehicle manufacturers, factory branches, distributors, and distributor branches under this section. For purposes of this section and Article 12 of Chapter 20 of the General Statutes of North Carolina, the relationship between a recreational vehicle manufacturer or recreational vehicle distributor, on

the one part, and a recreational vehicle dealer that is located within this State, on the other part, pursuant to which the recreational vehicle dealer purchases and resells new recreational vehicles from the recreational vehicle manufacturer or recreational vehicle distributor, shall be considered a "franchise", as this term is defined in G.S. 20-286(8a), whether or not the rights and responsibilities of the parties have been delineated in a written agreement or contract.

History.
1973, c. 88, s. 4; 1983, c. 704, s. 18; 2017-148, s. 4
   EDITOR'S NOTE. --
Session Laws 2017-148, s. 6, is a severability clause.
   EFFECT OF AMENDMENTS. --
Session Laws 2017-148, s. 4, effective July 20, 2017, rewrote the section, which formerly read: "Recreational vehicle manufacturer warranty recall obligations. The provisions of G.S. 20-305(4) through G.S. 20-305(28) and 20-305.1 to 20-305.4 shall not apply to manufacturers of, or dealers in, mobile or manufactured type housing or recreational trailers."
   CROSS REFERENCES. --
See the Editor's note under G.S. 20-305, regarding the applicability of subdivision (3) of that section.

§ 20-305.6. Unlawful for manufacturers to unfairly discriminate among dealers

Notwithstanding the terms of any contract, franchise, novation, or agreement, it shall be unlawful for any manufacturer, factory branch, distributor, or distributor branch to do any of the following:

(1) Discriminate against any similarly situated franchised new motor vehicle dealers in this State.

(2) Unfairly discriminate against franchised new motor vehicle dealers located in this State who have dualed facilities at which the vehicles distributed by the manufacturer, factory branch, distributor, or distributor branch are sold or serviced with one or more other line makes of vehicles.

(3) Unfairly discriminate against one of its franchised new motor vehicle dealers in this State with respect to any aspect of the franchise agreement.

(4) Use any financial services company or leasing company owned or controlled by the manufacturer or distributor to accomplish what would otherwise be illegal conduct on the part of the manufacturer or distributor pursuant to this section. This section shall not limit the right of the financial services or leasing company to engage in business practices in accordance with the trade.

History.
2001-510, s. 4

§ 20-305.7. (Effective until May 1, 2021) Protecting dealership data and consent to access dealership information

(a) Except as expressly authorized in this section, no manufacturer, factory branch, distributor, or distributor branch shall require a new motor vehicle dealer to provide its customer lists, customer information, consumer contact information, transaction data, or service files. Any requirement by a manufacturer, factory branch, distributor, or distributor branch that a new motor vehicle dealer provide its customer lists, customer information, consumer contact information, transaction data, or service files as a condition to the dealer's participation in any incentive program or contest for a customer or dealer to receive any incentive payments otherwise earned under an incentive program or contest, for the dealer to obtain consumer or customer leads, or for the dealer to receive any other benefits, rights, merchandise, or services for which the dealer would otherwise be entitled to obtain under the franchise or any other contract or agreement, or which shall customarily be provided to dealers, shall be voidable at the option of the dealer, unless all of the following conditions are satisfied: (i) the customer information requested relates solely to the specific program requirements or goals associated with such manufacturer's or distributor's own vehicle makes and does not require that the dealer provide general customer information or other information related to the dealer; (ii) such requirement is lawful and would also not require the dealer to allow any customer the right to opt out under the federal Gramm-Leach-Bliley Act, 15 U.S.C., Subchapter I, § 1608, et seq.; and (iii) the dealer is not required to allow the manufacturer or distributor or any third party to have direct access to the dealer's computer system, but the dealer is instead permitted to provide the same dealer, consumer, or customer data or information specified by the manufacturer or distributor by timely obtaining and pushing or otherwise furnishing the required data in a widely accepted file format such as comma delimited in accordance with subsection (g1) of this section. Nothing contained in this section shall limit the ability of the manufacturer, factory branch, distributor, or distributor branch to require that the dealer provide, or use in accordance with the law, such customer information related solely to such manufacturer's or distributor's own vehicle makes to the extent necessary to do any of the following:

(1) Satisfy any safety or recall notice obligations.

(2) Complete the sale and delivery of a new motor vehicle to a customer.

(3) Validate and pay customer or dealer incentives.

(4) Submit to the manufacturer, factory branch, distributor, or distributor branch claims for any services supplied by the dealer for any claim for warranty parts or repairs.

At the request of a manufacturer or distributor or of a third party acting on behalf of a manufacturer or distributor, a dealer may only be required to provide customer information related solely to such manufacturer's or distributor's own vehicle makes for reasonable marketing purposes, market research, consumer surveys, market analysis, and dealership performance analysis, but the dealer is only required to provide such customer information to the extent lawfully permissible; to the extent the requested information relates solely to specific program requirements or goals associated with such manufacturer's or distributor's own vehicle makes and does not require the dealer to provide general customer information or other information related to the dealer; and to the extent the requested information can be provided without requiring that the dealer allow any customer the right to opt out under the federal Gramm-Leach-Bliley Act, 15 U.S.C., Subchapter I, § 6801, et seq.

No manufacturer, factory branch, distributor, or distributor branch shall access or obtain dealer or customer data from or write dealer or customer data to a dealer management computer system utilized by a motor vehicle dealer located in this State, or require or coerce a motor vehicle dealer located in this State to utilize a particular dealer management computer system, unless the dealer management computer system allows the dealer to reasonably maintain the security, integrity, and confidentiality of the data maintained in the system. No manufacturer, factory branch, distributor, distributor branch, dealer management computer system vendor, or any third party acting on behalf of any manufacturer, factory branch, distributor, distributor branch, or dealer management computer system vendor shall prohibit a dealer from providing a means to regularly and continually monitor the specific data accessed from or written to the dealer's computer system and from complying with applicable State and federal laws and any rules or regulations promulgated thereunder. These provisions shall not be deemed to impose an obligation on a manufacturer, factory branch, distributor, distributor branch, dealer management computer system vendor, or any third party acting on behalf of any manufacturer, factory branch, distributor, distributor branch, or dealer management computer system vendor to provide such capability.

(b) No manufacturer, factory branch, distributor, distributor branch, dealer management computer system vendor, or any third party acting on behalf of any manufacturer, factory branch, distributor, distributor branch, or dealer management computer system vendor may access or utilize customer or prospect information maintained in a dealer management computer system utilized by a motor vehicle dealer located in this State for purposes of soliciting any such customer or prospect on behalf of, or directing the customer or prospect to, any other dealer. The limitations in this subsection do not apply to any of the following:

(1) A customer that requests a reference to another dealership.

(2) A customer that moves more than 60 miles away from the dealer whose data was accessed.

(3) Customer or prospect information that was provided to the dealer by the manufacturer, factory branch, distributor, or distributor branch.

(4) Customer or prospect information obtained by the manufacturer, factory branch, distributor, or distributor branch where the dealer agrees to allow the manufacturer, factory branch, distributor, distributor branch, dealer management computer system vendor, or any third party acting on behalf of any manufacturer, factory branch, distributor, distributor branch, or dealer management computer system vendor the right to access and utilize the customer or prospect information maintained in the dealer's dealer management computer system for purposes of soliciting any customer or prospect of the dealer on behalf of, or directing the customer or prospect to, any other dealer in a separate, stand-alone written instrument dedicated solely to the authorization.

No manufacturer, factory branch, distributor, distributor branch, dealer management computer system vendor, or any third party acting on behalf of any manufacturer, factory branch, distributor, distributor branch, or dealer management computer system vendor may provide access to customer or dealership information maintained in a dealer management computer system utilized by a motor vehicle dealer located in this State, without first obtaining the dealer's prior express written consent, revocable by the dealer upon five business days written notice, to provide the access. Prior to obtaining this consent and prior to entering into an initial contract or renewal of a contract with a dealer located in this State, the manufacturer, factory branch,

distributor, distributor branch, dealer management computer system vendor, or any third party acting on behalf of, or through any manufacturer, factory branch, distributor, distributor branch, or dealer management computer system vendor shall provide to the dealer a written list of all specific third parties to whom any data obtained from the dealer has actually been provided within the 12-month period ending November 1 of the prior year. The list shall further describe the scope and specific fields of the data provided. In addition to the initial list, a dealer management computer system vendor or any third party acting on behalf of or through a dealer management computer system vendor shall provide to the dealer an annual list of each and every third party to whom the data is actually being provided on November 1 of each year and each and every third party to whom the data was actually provided in the preceding 12 months and for each and every third party identified, the scope and specific fields of the data provided to the third party during the 12-month period. This list shall be provided to the dealer by January 1 of each year. The lists required in this subsection of the third parties to whom any data obtained from the dealer has actually been provided shall be specific to each affected dealer. It is insufficient and unlawful for the provider of this information to furnish any dealer a list of third parties who could or may have received any of the affected dealer's data, as the information required to be provided in this subsection requires the provider of this information to state the identity and other specified information of each and every third party to whom the data was actually provided during the relevant period of time. Any dealer management computer system vendor's contract that directly relates to the transfer or accessing of dealer or dealer customer information must conspicuously state, "NOTICE TO DEALER: THIS AGREEMENT RELATES TO THE TRANSFER AND ACCESSING OF CONFIDENTIAL INFORMATION AND CONSUMER RELATED DATA". This consent does not change any such person's obligations to comply with the terms of this section and any additional State or federal laws (and any rules or regulations adopted under these laws) applicable to the person with respect to the access. In addition, no dealer management computer system vendor shall refuse to provide a dealer management computer system to a motor vehicle dealer located in this State if the dealer refuses to provide any consent under this subsection.

(c) No dealer management computer system vendor, or third party acting on behalf of or through any dealer management computer system vendor, may access or obtain data from or write data to a dealer management computer system utilized by a motor vehicle dealer located in this State, unless the dealer management computer system allows the dealer to reasonably maintain the security, integrity, and confidentiality of the customer and dealership information maintained in the system. No dealer management computer system vendor, or third party acting on behalf of or through any dealer management computer system vendor, shall prohibit a dealer from providing a means to regularly and continually monitor the specific data accessed from or written to the dealer's computer system and from complying with applicable State and federal laws and any rules or regulations adopted under these laws. This section does not impose an obligation on a manufacturer, factory branch, distributor, distributor branch, dealer management computer system vendor, or any third party acting on behalf of any manufacturer, factory branch, distributor, distributor branch, or dealer management computer system vendor to provide this capability.

(d) Any manufacturer, factory branch, distributor, distributor branch, dealer management computer system vendor, or any third party acting on behalf of or through any dealer management computer system vendor, having electronic access to customer or motor vehicle dealership data in a dealership management computer system utilized by a motor vehicle dealer located in this State shall provide notice to the dealer of any security breach of dealership or customer data obtained through the access, which at the time of the breach was in the possession or custody of the manufacturer, factory branch, distributor, distributor branch, dealer management computer system vendor, or third party. The disclosure notification shall be made without unreasonable delay by the manufacturer, factory branch, distributor, distributor branch, dealer management computer system vendor, or third party following discovery by the person, or notification to the person, of the breach. The disclosure notification shall describe measures reasonably necessary to determine the scope of the breach and corrective actions that may be taken in an effort to restore the integrity, security, and confidentiality of the data. These measures and corrective actions shall be implemented as soon as practicable by all persons responsible for the breach.

(e) Nothing in this section precludes, prohibits, or denies the right of the manufacturer, factory branch, distributor, or distributor branch to receive customer or dealership information from a motor vehicle dealer located in this State for the purposes of complying with federal or State safety requirements or implementing steps related to manufacturer recalls at such times as necessary in order to comply with federal and State requirements or manufacturer recalls so long as receiving this information from the dealer does not impair, alter, or reduce the security, integrity, and confidentiality of the customer and dealership information collected or generated by the dealer.

(f) The following definitions apply to this section:

(1) **Dealer management computer system. --** A computer hardware and software system that is owned or leased by the dealer, including a dealer's use of Web applications, software, or hardware, whether located at the dealership or provided at a remote location and that provides access to customer records and transactions by a motor vehicle dealer located in this State and that allows the motor vehicle dealer timely information in order to sell vehicles, parts, or services through the motor vehicle dealership.

(2) **Dealer management computer system vendor. --** A seller or reseller of dealer management computer systems, a person that sells computer software for use on dealer management computer systems, or a person that services or maintains dealer management computer systems, but only to the extent that each of the sellers, resellers, or other persons listed in this subdivision are engaged in these activities.

(3) **Security breach. --** An incident of unauthorized access to and acquisition of records or data containing dealership or dealership customer information where unauthorized use of the dealership or dealership customer information has occurred or is reasonably likely to occur or that creates a material risk of harm to a dealership or a dealership's customer. Any incident of unauthorized access to and acquisition of records or data containing dealership or dealership customer information or any incident of disclosure of dealership customer information to one or more third parties that has not been specifically authorized by the dealer or customer constitutes a security breach.

(g) G.S. 20-308.1(d) does not apply to an action brought under this section against a dealer management computer system vendor.

(g1) Notwithstanding any of the terms or provisions contained in this section or in any consent, authorization, release, novation, franchise, or other contract or agreement, whenever any manufacturer, factory branch, distributor,

distributor branch, dealer management computer system vendor, or any third party acting on behalf of or through, or approved, referred, endorsed, authorized, certified, granted preferred status, or recommended by, any manufacturer, factory branch, distributor, distributor branch, or dealer management computer system vendor requires that a new motor vehicle dealer provide any dealer, consumer, or customer data or information through direct access to a dealer's computer system, the dealer is not required to provide, and shall not be required to consent to provide in any written agreement, such direct access to its computer system. The dealer may instead provide the same dealer, consumer, or customer data or information specified by the requesting party by timely obtaining and pushing or otherwise furnishing the requested data to the requesting party in a widely accepted file format such as comma delimited. When a dealer would otherwise be required to provide direct access to its computer system under the terms of a consent, authorization, release, novation, franchise, or other contract or agreement, a dealer that elects to provide data or information through other means may be charged a reasonable initial set-up fee and a reasonable processing fee based on the actual incremental costs incurred by the party requesting the data for establishing and implementing the process for the dealer. Any term or provision contained in any consent, authorization, release, novation, franchise, or other contract or agreement that is inconsistent with any term or provision contained in this subsection is voidable at the option of the dealer.

(g2) Notwithstanding the terms or conditions of any consent, authorization, release, novation, franchise, or other contract or agreement, every manufacturer, factory branch, distributor, distributor branch, dealer management computer system vendor, or any third party acting on behalf of or through any manufacturer, factory branch, distributor, distributor branch, or dealer management computer system vendor, having electronic access to consumer or customer data or other information in a computer system utilized by a new motor vehicle dealer, or who has otherwise been provided consumer or customer data or information by the dealer, shall fully indemnify and hold harmless any dealer from whom it has acquired the consumer or customer data or other information from all damages, costs, and expenses incurred by the dealer. This indemnification by the manufacturer, factory branch, distributor, distributor branch, dealer management computer system vendor, or third party acting on behalf of these entities includes, but is not limited to, judgments, settlements, fines, penalties, litigation costs, defense costs, court costs, costs related to the disclosure of security

breaches, and attorneys' fees arising out of complaints, claims, civil or administrative actions, and, to the fullest extent allowable under the law, governmental investigations and prosecutions to the extent caused by a security breach; the access, storage, maintenance, use, sharing, disclosure, or retention of the dealer's consumer or customer data or other information; or maintenance or services provided to any computer system utilized by a new motor vehicle dealer.

(h) This section applies to contracts entered into on or after November 1, 2005.

History.
2005-409, s. 4;2007-513, s. 10;2011-290, s. 11;2013-302, s. 9;2018-27, s. 3;2019-177, s. 4.2
SECTION SET OUT TWICE. --The section above is effective until May 1, 2021. For the section as amended May 1, 2021, see the following section, also numbered G.S. 20-305.7.

EDITOR'S NOTE. --
Subsections (h) and (i) were added to this section by Session Laws 2011-290, s. 11. Since subsection (h) already existed, subsections (h) and (i), as added by this act, have been renumbered as subsections (g1) and (g2), respectively, at the direction of the Revisor of Statutes. The reference to "subsection (h) of this section" in subsection (a), has been changed to "subsection (g1) of this section" to conform to the renumbering.

Session Laws 2011-290, which, in ss. 5 and 7 through 9, amended this section by adding the first paragraph, subdivisions (a)(1) through (a)(4), and the next-to-last paragraph in subsection (a), in the last paragraph of subsection (b), inserting "specific" and substituting "any data obtained from the dealer has actually been provided" for "any North Carolina dealer management computer system data has been provided" in the second sentence, inserting "and specific fields" in the third sentence, twice inserting "actually" and inserting "and specific fields" in the fourth sentence, and deleting "except to the extent that consent is deemed by the parties to be reasonably necessary in order for the vendor to provide the system to the dealer" from the end of the last sentence, in subdivision (f)(1), substituting "software system that is owned or leased by the dealer, including a dealer's use of Web applications, software, or hardware, whether located at the dealership or provided at a remote location and that provides access" for "software system having dealer business process management modules that provide real time access" and making a minor stylistic change, in the last sentence of subdivision (f)(3), inserting "or any incident of disclosure of dealership customer information to one or more third parties which shall not have been specifically authorized by the dealer or customer," and adding subsections (g1) and (g2), in s. 12, provided: "The terms and provisions of this act shall be applicable to all current and future franchises and other agreements in existence between any new motor vehicle dealer located in this State and a manufacturer or distributor as of the effective date of this act [June 24, 2011]."

Session Laws 2011-290, s. 13 is a severability clause.

Session Laws 2013-302, s. 11, provides: "The terms and provisions of Sections 7 through 12 of this act shall be applicable to all current and future franchises and other agreements in existence between any new motor vehicle dealer located in this State and a manufacturer or distributor as of the effective date of this act."

Session Laws 2013-302, s. 12, is a severability clause.

This section was amended by Session Laws 2018-27, s. 3, in the coded bill drafting format provided by G.S. 120-20.1. The act amended subsection (b), in part by adding the sentence "The lists required in this paragraph of the third parties to whom any data obtained from the dealer has actually been provided shall be specific to each affected dealer and it shall be insufficient and unlawful for the provider of this information to furnish any dealer a list of third parties who could or may have received any of the affected dealer's data, as the information required to be provided in this paragraph requires the provider of this information to state the identity and other specified information of each and every third party to whom such data was actually provided during the relevant period of time." The words "the third parties to whom any data obtained from the dealer has actually been provided" were not underlined, however. The sentence was later amended by Session Laws 2019-177, s. 4.2, to remove that language.

This section was amended by Session Laws 2018-27, s. 3, in the coded bill drafting format provided by G.S. 120-20.1. The act amended subsection (b), in part by adding the sentence "The lists required in this paragraph of the third parties to whom any data obtained from the dealer has actually been provided shall be specific to each affected dealer and it shall be insufficient and unlawful for the provider of this information to furnish any dealer a list of third parties who could or may have received any of the affected dealer's data, as the information required to be provided in this paragraph requires the provider of this information to state the identity and other specified information of each and every third party to whom such data was actually provided during the relevant period of time." The words "the third parties to whom any data obtained from the dealer has actually been provided" were not underlined, however. The sentence is set out in the form above, with the non-coded added language in brackets, at the direction of the Revisor of Statutes.

Session Laws 2018-27, s. 5, is a severability clause.

EFFECT OF AMENDMENTS. --
Session Laws 2007-513, s. 10, effective August 30, 2007, in subsection (b), added the introductory paragraph and subdivisions (b)(1) through (b)(4). For applicability, see Editor's notes.

Session Laws 2013-302, s. 9, effective July 18, 2013, in subdivision (f)(2), substituted "a person that sells computer software for use on dealer management computer systems, or a person who services or maintains dealer management computer systems, but only to the extent that each of the sellers, resellers, or other persons listed in this subdivision are engaged in such activities" for "(but only to the extent that such person is engaged in such activities"; added "or approved, referred, endorsed, authorized, certified, granted preferred status, or recommended by" in subsection (g1); in subsections (g2), substituted "dealer. Such indemnification by the manufacturer, factory branch, distributor, distributor branch, dealer management computer system vendor, or third party acting on behalf of these entities includes" for "dealer, including" and "or maintenance or services provided to any computer system utilized by a new motor vehicle dealer" for "by the manufacturer, factory branch, distributor, distributor branch, dealer management computer system vendor, or third party acting on behalf of or through such manufacturer, factory branch, distributor, distributor branch, or dealer management computer system vendor" and inserted "costs related to the disclosure of security breaches" and "a security breach or"; and made minor stylistic changes.

Session Laws 2018-27, s. 3, effective June 22, 2018, in the last paragraph of subsection (b), rewrote the fourth sentence and added the sixth sentence.

Session Laws 2019-177, s. 4.2, effective July 26, 2019, inserted "the third parties to whom any data obtained from the dealer has actually been provided" in subsection (b) to correct an error; and made numerous stylistic changes in subsections (b)-(h).

This section has more than one version with varying effective dates. To view a complete list of the versions of this section see Table of Contents.

§ 20-305.7. (Effective May 1, 2021) Protecting dealership data and consent to access dealership information

(a) Except as expressly authorized in this section, no manufacturer, factory branch, distributor, or distributor branch shall require a new motor vehicle dealer to provide its customer lists, customer information, consumer contact information, transaction data, or service files. Any requirement by a manufacturer, factory branch, distributor, or distributor branch that a new motor vehicle dealer provide its customer lists, customer information, consumer contact information, transaction data, or service files to the manufacturer, factory branch, distributor, or distributor branch, or to any third party as a condition to the dealer's participation in any incentive program or contest, for a customer or dealer to receive any incentive payments otherwise earned under an incentive program or contest, for the dealer to obtain consumer or customer leads, or for the dealer to receive any other benefits, rights, merchandise, or services for which the dealer would otherwise be entitled to obtain under the franchise or any other contract or agreement, or which shall customarily be provided to dealers, shall be voidable at the option of the dealer, and the dealer shall automatically be entitled to all benefits earned under the applicable incentive program or contest or any other contract or agreement, unless all of the following conditions are satisfied: (i) the customer information requested relates solely to the specific program requirements or goals associated with such manufacturer's or distributor's own vehicle makes and does not require that the dealer provide general customer information or other information related to the dealer; (ii) such requirement is lawful and would also not require the dealer to allow any customer the right to opt out under the federal Gramm-Leach-Bliley Act, 15 U.S.C., Subchapter I, § 1608, et seq.; and (iii) the dealer is either permitted to restrict the data fields that may be accessed in the dealer's dealer management computer system, or the dealer is permitted to provide the same dealer, consumer, or customer data or information specified by the manufacturer or distributor by timely obtaining and pushing or otherwise furnishing the required data in a widely accepted file format such as comma delimited in accordance with subsection (g1) of this section. Nothing contained in this section shall limit the ability of the manufacturer, factory branch, distributor, or distributor branch to require that the dealer provide, or use in accordance with the law, such customer information related solely to such manufacturer's or distributor's own vehicle makes to the extent necessary to do any of the following:

(1) Satisfy any safety or recall notice obligations.

(2) Complete the sale and delivery of a new motor vehicle to a customer.

(3) Validate and pay customer or dealer incentives.

(4) Submit to the manufacturer, factory branch, distributor, or distributor branch claims for any services supplied by the dealer for any claim for warranty parts or repairs.

At the request of a manufacturer or distributor or of a third party acting on behalf of a manufacturer or distributor, a dealer may only be required to provide customer information related solely to such manufacturer's or distributor's own vehicle makes for reasonable marketing purposes, market research, consumer surveys, market analysis, and dealership performance analysis, but the dealer is only required to provide such customer information to the extent lawfully permissible; to the extent the requested information relates solely to specific program requirements or goals associated with such manufacturer's or distributor's own vehicle makes and does not require the dealer to provide general customer information or other information related to the dealer; and to the extent the requested information can be provided without requiring that the dealer allow any customer the right to opt out under the federal Gramm-Leach-Bliley Act, 15 U.S.C., Subchapter I, § 6801, et seq.

No manufacturer, factory branch, distributor, or distributor branch shall access or obtain dealer or customer data from or write dealer or customer data to a dealer management computer system utilized by a motor vehicle dealer located in this State, or require or coerce a motor vehicle dealer located in this State to utilize a particular dealer management computer system, unless the dealer management computer system allows the dealer to reasonably maintain the security, integrity, and confidentiality of the data maintained in the system. No manufacturer, factory branch, distributor, distributor branch, dealer management computer system vendor, or any third party acting on behalf of any manufacturer, factory branch, distributor, distributor branch, or dealer management computer system vendor shall prohibit a dealer from providing a means to regularly and continually monitor the specific data accessed from or written to the dealer's computer system and from complying with applicable State and federal laws and any rules or regulations promulgated thereunder. These provisions shall not be deemed to impose an obligation on a manufacturer, factory branch, distributor, distributor branch, dealer management computer system vendor, or any third party acting on behalf of any manufacturer, factory branch, distributor, distributor branch, or dealer management computer system vendor to provide such capability. Notwithstanding the terms or conditions of any incentive program or contest that is either required or voluntary on the part of the dealer, or the terms or conditions of any other contract or agreement, it shall be unlawful for any manufacturer, factory branch, distributor, or distributor branch to fail or refuse to provide dealer notice, in a standalone written document, at least 30 days prior to making any changes in any of the dealer or customer data the dealer is requested or required to share with a manufacturer, factory branch, distributor, or distributor branch, or any third party. The changes in any of the dealer or customer data the dealer is required or requested to provide shall be void unless the applicable manufacturer, factory branch, distributor, or distributor branch complies with the notice requirements contained in this paragraph.

(b) No manufacturer, factory branch, distributor, distributor branch, dealer management computer system vendor, or any third party acting on behalf of any manufacturer, factory branch, distributor, distributor branch, or dealer management computer system vendor may access or utilize customer or prospect information maintained in a dealer management computer system utilized by a motor vehicle dealer located in this State for purposes of soliciting any such customer or prospect on behalf of, or directing the customer or prospect to, any other dealer. The limitations in this subsection do not apply to any of the following:

(1) A customer that requests a reference to another dealership.

(2) A customer that moves more than 60 miles away from the dealer whose data was accessed.

(3) Customer or prospect information that was provided to the dealer by the manufacturer, factory branch, distributor, or distributor branch.

(4) Customer or prospect information obtained by the manufacturer, factory branch, distributor, or distributor branch where the dealer agrees to allow the manufacturer, factory branch, distributor, distributor branch, dealer management computer system vendor, or any third party acting on behalf of any manufacturer, factory branch, distributor, distributor branch, or dealer management computer system vendor the right to access and utilize the customer or prospect information maintained in the dealer's dealer management computer system for purposes of soliciting any customer or prospect of the dealer on behalf of, or directing the customer or prospect to, any other dealer in a separate, stand-alone written instrument dedicated solely to the authorization.

No manufacturer, factory branch, distributor, distributor branch, dealer management computer system vendor, or any third party acting on behalf of any manufacturer, factory branch, distributor, distributor branch, or dealer management computer system vendor may provide access to customer or dealership information maintained in a dealer management computer system utilized by a motor vehicle dealer located in this State, without first obtaining the dealer's prior express written consent, revocable by the dealer upon five business days written notice, to provide the access. Prior to obtaining this consent and prior to entering into an initial contract or renewal of a contract with a dealer located in this State, the manufacturer, factory branch, distributor, distributor branch, dealer management computer system vendor, or any third party acting on behalf of, or through any manufacturer, factory branch, distributor, distributor branch, or dealer management computer system vendor shall provide to the dealer a written list of all specific third parties to whom any data obtained from the dealer has actually been provided within the 12-month period ending November 1 of the prior year. The list shall further describe the scope and specific fields of the data provided. In addition to the initial list, a dealer management computer system vendor or any third party acting on behalf of or through a dealer management computer system vendor shall provide to the dealer an annual list of each and every third party to whom the data is actually being provided on November 1 of each year and each and every third party to whom the data was actually provided in the preceding 12 months and for each and every third party identified, the scope and specific fields of the data provided to the third party during the 12-month period. This list shall be provided to the dealer by January 1 of each year. The lists required in this subsection of the third parties to whom any data obtained from the dealer has actually been provided shall be specific to each affected dealer. It is insufficient and unlawful for the provider of this information to furnish any dealer a list of third parties who could or may have received any of the affected dealer's data, as the information required to be provided in this subsection requires the provider of this information to state the identity and other specified information of each and every third party to whom the data was actually provided during the relevant period of time. Any dealer management computer system vendor's contract that directly relates to the transfer or accessing of dealer or dealer customer information must conspicuously state, "NOTICE TO DEALER: THIS AGREEMENT RELATES TO THE TRANSFER AND ACCESSING OF CONFIDENTIAL INFORMATION AND CONSUMER RELATED DATA". This consent does not change any such person's obligations to comply with the terms of this section and any additional State or federal laws (and any rules or regulations adopted under these laws) applicable to the person with respect to the access. In addition, no dealer management computer system vendor shall refuse to provide a dealer management computer system to a motor vehicle dealer located in this State if the dealer refuses to provide any consent under this subsection.

(b1) Notwithstanding the terms of any contract or agreement with a dealer management computer system vendor or third party, for purposes of this subsection, the dealer's data contained in or on a dealer management computer system owned, leased, or licensed by a dealer located in this State is the property of the dealer. For purposes of this section, the terms "dealer data" and "dealer's data" shall be defined as any information or other data that has been entered, by direct entry or otherwise, or stored on the dealer's dealer management computer system by an officer or employee of the dealer or third party contracted by the dealer, whether stored or hosted on-site at a dealer location or on the cloud or at any other remote location, that contains data or other information about any of the following: (i) the dealer's sales, service, or parts customers or the dealer's customer transactions, (ii) customer leads generated by or provided to the dealer, (iii) the tracking, history, or performance of the dealer's internal processing of customer orders and work, (iv) customer deal files, (v) customer recommendations or complaints communicated by any means to the dealer, (vi) the tracking of dealer or customer incentive payments sought or received from any manufacturer or distributor, (vii) business plans, goals, objectives, or strategies created by any officer, employer, or contractee of the dealer; (viii) the dealer's internal bank, financial, or business records, (ix) email, voice, and other communications between or among the dealer's officers or employees, (x) email, voice, and other communications between the dealer's officers or employees and third parties, (xi) contracts and agreements with third parties and all records related to the performance of such contracts and agreements, (xii) employee performance, (xiii) dealer personnel records, and (xiv) dealer inventory data. The terms "dealer data" and "dealer's data" specifically exclude the proprietary software, intellectual property, data, or information of a dealer management computer system vendor, manufacturer, factory branch, distributor, or distributor branch, data specifically licensed from a third party by a dealer management computer system vendor, manufacturer, factory branch, distributor, or distributor branch, and data provided to a dealer by a manufacturer, factory branch, distributor, distributor branch, subsidiary, or affiliate.

Notwithstanding the terms of any contract or agreement, it shall be unlawful for any dealer management computer system vendor, or any third party having access to any dealer management computer system, to:

(1) Unreasonably interfere with a dealer's ability to protect, store, copy, share, or use any dealer data downloaded from a dealer management computer system utilized by a new motor vehicle dealer located in this State. Unlawful conduct prohibited by this section includes, but is not limited to:

a. Imposing any unreasonable fees or other restrictions on the dealer or any third party for access to or sharing of dealer data. For purposes of this section, the term "unreasonable fees" means charges for access to customer or dealer data beyond any direct costs incurred by any dealer management computer system vendor in providing access to the dealer's customer or dealer data to a third party that the dealer has authorized to access its dealer management computer system or allowing any third party that the dealer has authorized to access its dealer management computer system to write data to its dealer management computer system. Nothing contained in this subdivision shall be deemed to prohibit the charging of a fee, which includes the ability of the service provider to recoup development costs incurred to provide the services involved and to make a reasonable profit on the services provided. Any charges must be both (i) reasonable in amount and (ii) disclosed to the dealer in reasonably sufficient detail prior to the fees being charged to the dealer, or they will be deemed prohibited, unreasonable fees.

b. Imposing unreasonable restrictions on secure integration by any third party that the dealer has explicitly authorized to access its dealer management computer system for the purpose of accessing dealer data. Examples of unreasonable restrictions include, but are not limited to, any of the following:

1. Unreasonable restrictions on the scope or nature of the dealer's data shared with a third party authorized by the dealer to access the dealer's dealer management computer system.

2. Unreasonable restrictions on the ability of a third party authorized by the dealer to securely access the dealer's dealer management computer system to share dealer data or securely write dealer data to a dealer management computer system.

3. Requiring unreasonable access to sensitive, competitive, or other confidential business

information of a third party as a condition for access dealer data.

4. It shall not be an unreasonable restriction to condition a third party's access to the dealer management computer system on that third party's compliance with reasonable security standards or operational protocols that the dealer management computer system vendor specifies.

c. Sharing dealer data with any third party, if sharing the data is not authorized by the dealer.

d. Prohibiting or unreasonably limiting a dealer's ability to store, copy, securely share, or use dealer data outside the dealer's dealer management computer system in any manner and for any reason once it has been downloaded from the dealer management computer system.

e. Permitting access to or accessing dealer data without first obtaining the dealer's express written consent in a standalone document or contractual provision that is conspicuous in appearance, contained in a separate page or screen from any other written material, and requires an independent mark or affirmation from a dealer principal, general manager, or other management level employee of the dealership expressly authorized in writing by the dealer principal or general manager.

f. Upon receipt of a written request from a dealer, failing or refusing to block specific data fields containing dealer data from being shared with one or more third parties. Where blocking hinders, blocks, diminishes, or otherwise interferes with the functionality of a third party's service or product or the dealer's ability to participate in an incentive or other program of a manufacturer, factory branch, distributor, or distributor branch, or other third party authorized by the dealer, the dealer management computer system vendor shall be held harmless from the dealer's decision to block specified data fields, so long as the dealer management computer system vendor was acting at the direction of the dealer.

(2) Access, use, store, or share any dealer data from a dealer management computer system in any manner other than as expressly permitted in its written agreement with the dealer.

(3) Fail to provide the dealer with the option and ability to securely obtain and push or otherwise distribute specified dealer data within the dealer's dealer management computer system to any third party instead of the third party receiving the dealer data directly from the dealer's dealer management computer system vendor or providing the third party direct access to the dealer's dealer management computer system. A dealer management computer system vendor shall be held harmless for any errors, breach, misuse, or any harms directly or indirectly caused by a dealer sharing data with any third party beyond the control of the dealer management computer system vendor. In the event a dealer sharing data with a third party outside of the control of the dealer computer management system vendor causes damage to the dealer management computer system or any third party, the party or parties that caused the damage shall be liable for the damage.

(4) Fail to provide the dealer, within seven days of receiving a dealer's written request, access to any SOC 2 audit conducted on behalf of the dealer management computer system vendor and related to the services licensed by the dealer.

(5) Fail to promptly provide a dealer, upon the dealer's written request, a written listing of all entities with whom it is currently sharing any data from the dealer's dealer management computer system and with whom it has, within the immediately 12 preceding months, shared any data from the dealer's dealer management computer system, the specific data fields shared with each entity identified, and the dates any data was shared, to the extent that information can reasonably be stored by the dealership management computer system vendor.

(6) Upon receipt of a dealer's written request to terminate any contract or agreement for the provision of hardware or software related to the dealer's dealer management computer system, to fail to promptly provide a copy of the dealer's data maintained on its dealership management computer system to the dealer in a secure, usable format.

Nothing in this section prevents the charging of a fee, which includes the ability of the dealer management computer system vendor to recoup costs incurred to provide the services involved and to make a reasonable profit on the services provided. Charges must be disclosed to and approved by the dealer prior to the time the dealer incurs the charges.

Nothing in this section prevents any dealer or third party from discharging its obligations as a service provider under

Chapter 20

federal, State, or local law to protect and secure protected dealer data.

Nothing in this section shall be deemed to prohibit a dealer management computer system vendor from conditioning a party's access to, or integration with, a dealer's dealer management computer system on that party's compliance with reasonable security standards or other operational protocols that the dealer's computer management system vendor specifies.

For purposes of this subsection, the term "third party" shall not be applicable to any manufacturer, factory branch, distributor, distributor branch, or subsidiary or affiliate thereof.

(b2) The rights conferred on dealers in this section are not waivable and may not be reduced or otherwise modified by any contract or agreement.

(c) No dealer management computer system vendor, or third party acting on behalf of or through any dealer management computer system vendor, may access or obtain data from or write data to a dealer management computer system utilized by a motor vehicle dealer located in this State, unless the dealer management computer system allows the dealer to reasonably maintain the security, integrity, and confidentiality of the customer and dealership information maintained in the system. No dealer management computer system vendor, or third party acting on behalf of or through any dealer management computer system vendor, shall prohibit a dealer from providing a means to regularly and continually monitor the specific data accessed from or written to the dealer's computer system and from complying with applicable State and federal laws and any rules or regulations adopted under these laws. This section does not impose an obligation on a manufacturer, factory branch, distributor, distributor branch, dealer management computer system vendor, or any third party acting on behalf of any manufacturer, factory branch, distributor, distributor branch, or dealer management computer system vendor to provide this capability.

(d) Any manufacturer, factory branch, distributor, distributor branch, dealer management computer system vendor, or any third party acting on behalf of or through any dealer management computer system vendor, having electronic access to customer or motor vehicle dealership data in a dealership management computer system utilized by a motor vehicle dealer located in this State shall provide notice to the dealer of any security breach of dealership or customer data obtained through the access, which at the time of the breach was in the possession or custody of the manufacturer, factory branch, distributor, distributor branch,

dealer management computer system vendor, or third party. The disclosure notification shall be made without unreasonable delay by the manufacturer, factory branch, distributor, distributor branch, dealer management computer system vendor, or third party following discovery by the person, or notification to the person, of the breach. The disclosure notification shall describe measures reasonably necessary to determine the scope of the breach and corrective actions that may be taken in an effort to restore the integrity, security, and confidentiality of the data. These measures and corrective actions shall be implemented as soon as practicable by all persons responsible for the breach.

(e) Nothing in this section precludes, prohibits, or denies the right of the manufacturer, factory branch, distributor, or distributor branch to receive customer or dealership information from a motor vehicle dealer located in this State for the purposes of complying with federal or State safety requirements or implementing steps related to manufacturer recalls at such times as necessary in order to comply with federal and State requirements or manufacturer recalls so long as receiving this information from the dealer does not impair, alter, or reduce the security, integrity, and confidentiality of the customer and dealership information collected or generated by the dealer.

(f) The following definitions apply to this section:

(1) **Dealer management computer system. --** A computer hardware and software system that is owned or leased by the dealer, including a dealer's use of Web applications, software, or hardware, whether located at the dealership or provided at a remote location and that provides access to customer records and transactions by a motor vehicle dealer located in this State and that allows the motor vehicle dealer timely information in order to sell vehicles, parts, or services through the motor vehicle dealership.

(2) **Dealer management computer system vendor. --** A seller or reseller of dealer management computer systems, a person that sells computer software for use on dealer management computer systems, or a person that services or maintains dealer management computer systems, but only to the extent that each of the sellers, resellers, or other persons listed in this subdivision are engaged in these activities.

(3) **Security breach. --** An incident of unauthorized access to and acquisition of records or data containing dealership or dealership customer information where unauthorized use of the dealership or dealership customer information has occurred or is reasonably likely to occur or that creates

a material risk of harm to a dealership or a dealership's customer. Any incident of unauthorized access to and acquisition of records or data containing dealership or dealership customer information or any incident of disclosure of dealership customer information to one or more third parties that has not been specifically authorized by the dealer or customer constitutes a security breach.

(g) G.S. 20-308.1(d) does not apply to an action brought under this section against a dealer management computer system vendor.

(g1) Notwithstanding any of the terms or provisions contained in this section or in any consent, authorization, release, novation, franchise, or other contract or agreement, whenever any manufacturer, factory branch, distributor, distributor branch, dealer management computer system vendor, or any third party acting on behalf of or through, or approved, referred, endorsed, authorized, certified, granted preferred status, or recommended by, any manufacturer, factory branch, distributor, distributor branch, or dealer management computer system vendor requires that a new motor vehicle dealer provide any dealer, consumer, or customer data or information through direct access to a dealer's computer system, the dealer is not required to provide, and shall not be required to consent to provide in any written agreement, such direct access to its computer system. The dealer may instead provide the same dealer, consumer, or customer data or information specified by the requesting party by timely obtaining and pushing or otherwise furnishing the requested data to the requesting party in a widely accepted file format such as comma delimited. When a dealer would otherwise be required to provide direct access to its computer system under the terms of a consent, authorization, release, novation, franchise, or other contract or agreement, a dealer that elects to provide data or information through other means may be charged a reasonable initial set-up fee and a reasonable processing fee based on the actual incremental costs incurred by the party requesting the data for establishing and implementing the process for the dealer. Any term or provision contained in any consent, authorization, release, novation, franchise, or other contract or agreement that is inconsistent with any term or provision contained in this subsection is voidable at the option of the dealer.

(g2) Notwithstanding the terms or conditions of any consent, authorization, release, novation, franchise, or other contract or agreement, every manufacturer, factory branch, distributor, distributor branch, dealer management computer system vendor, or any third party acting on behalf of or through any manufacturer, factory branch, distributor, distributor branch, or dealer management computer system vendor, having electronic access to consumer or customer data or other information in a computer system utilized by a new motor vehicle dealer, or who has otherwise been provided consumer or customer data or information by the dealer, shall fully indemnify and hold harmless any dealer from whom it has acquired the consumer or customer data or other information from all damages, costs, and expenses incurred by the dealer. This indemnification by the manufacturer, factory branch, distributor, distributor branch, dealer management computer system vendor, or third party acting on behalf of these entities includes, but is not limited to, judgments, settlements, fines, penalties, litigation costs, defense costs, court costs, costs related to the disclosure of security breaches, and attorneys' fees arising out of complaints, claims, civil or administrative actions, and, to the fullest extent allowable under the law, governmental investigations and prosecutions to the extent caused by a security breach; the access, storage, maintenance, use, sharing, disclosure, or retention of the dealer's consumer or customer data or other information; or maintenance or services provided to any computer system utilized by a new motor vehicle dealer.

(h) This section applies to contracts entered into on or after November 1, 2005.

History.

2005-409, s. 4;2007-513, s. 10;2011-290, s. 11;2013-302, s. 9;2018-27, s. 3;2019-125, s. 7;2019-177, s. 4.2;2020-51, s. 2

SECTION SET OUT TWICE. --The section above is effective May 1, 2021. For the section as in effect until May 1, 2021, see the preceding section, also numbered G.S. 20-305.7.

EDITOR'S NOTE. --

Subsections (h) and (i) were added to this section by Session Laws 2011-290, s. 11. Since subsection (h) already existed, subsections (h) and (i), as added by this act, have been renumbered as subsections (g1) and (g2), respectively, at the direction of the Revisor of Statutes. The reference to "subsection (h) of this section" in subsection (a), has been changed to "subsection (g1) of this section" to conform to the renumbering.

Session Laws 2011-290, which, in ss. 5 and 7 through 9, amended this section by adding the first paragraph, subdivisions (a)(1) through (a)(4), and the next-to-last paragraph in subsection (a), in the last paragraph of subsection (b), inserting "specific" and substituting "any data obtained from the dealer has actually been provided" for "any North Carolina dealer management computer system data has been provided" in the second sentence, inserting "and specific fields" in the third sentence, twice inserting "actually" and inserting "and specific fields" in the fourth sentence, and deleting "except to the extent that consent is deemed by the parties to be reasonably necessary in order for the vendor to provide the system to the dealer" from the end of the last sentence, in sub-division (f)(1), substituting "software system that is owned or leased by the dealer, including a dealer's use of Web applications, software, or hardware, whether located at the dealership or provided at a remote location and that provides access" for "software system having dealer business process management modules that provide real time access" and making a minor stylistic change, in the last sentence of subdivision (f)(3), inserting "or any incident of disclosure of dealership customer information to one or more third parties which shall not have been specifically authorized by the dealer or customer," and adding subsections (g1) and (g2), in s. 12, provided: "The terms and provisions of this act shall be applicable to all current and future franchises and other agreements in existence between any new motor vehicle dealer located in this State and a manufacturer or distributor as of the effective date of this act [June 24, 2011]."

Session Laws 2011-290, s. 13 is a severability clause.

Session Laws 2013-302, s. 11, provides: "The terms and provisions of Sections 7 through 12 of this act shall be applicable to all current and future franchises and other agreements in existence between any new motor vehicle dealer located in this State and a manufacturer or distributor as of the effective date of this act."

Session Laws 2013-302, s. 12, is a severability clause.

This section was amended by Session Laws 2018-27, s. 3, in the coded bill drafting format provided by G.S. 120-20.1. The act amended subsection (b), in part by adding the sentence "The lists required in this paragraph of the third parties to whom any data obtained from the dealer has actually been provided shall be specific to each affected dealer and it shall be insufficient and unlawful for the provider of this information to furnish any dealer a list of third parties who could or may have received any of the affected dealer's data, as the information required to be provided in this paragraph requires the provider of this information to state the identity and other specified information of each and every third party to whom such data was actually provided during the relevant period of time." The words "the third parties to whom any data obtained from the dealer has actually been provided" were not underlined, however. The sentence is set out in the form above at the direction of the Revisor of Statutes.

This section was amended by Session Laws 2018-27, s. 3, in the coded bill drafting format provided by G.S. 120-20.1. The act amended subsection (b), in part by adding the sentence "The lists required in this paragraph of the third parties to whom any data obtained from the dealer has actually been provided shall be specific to each affected dealer and it shall be insufficient and unlawful for the provider of this information to furnish any dealer a list of third parties who could or may have received any of the affected dealer's data, as the information required to be provided in this paragraph requires the provider of this

information to state the identity and other specified information of each and every third party to whom such data was actually provided during the relevant period of time." The words "the third parties to whom any data obtained from the dealer has actually been provided" were not underlined, however. The sentence was later amended by Session Laws 2019-177, s. 4.2, to remove that language.

Session Laws 2018-27, s. 5, is a severability clause.

Session Laws 2019-125, s. 12, is a severability clause.

Session Laws 2019-125, s. 13, as amended by Session Laws 2020-51, s. 2, made subsections (b1) and (b2) and the amendment of subsection (a) by Session Laws 2019-125, s. 7, effective May 1, 2021, and applicable to all current and future franchises and other agreements in existence between any new motor vehicle dealer located in this State and a manufacturer, distributor, dealer management computer system vendor, or third party as of that date.

EFFECT OF AMENDMENTS. --

Session Laws 2007-513, s. 10, effective August 30, 2007, in subsection (b), added the introductory paragraph and subdivisions (b)(1) through (b)(4). For applicability, see Editor's notes.

Session Laws 2013-302, s. 9, effective July 18, 2013, in subdivision (f)(2), substituted "a person that sells computer software for use on dealer management computer systems, or a person who services or maintains dealer management computer systems, but only to the extent that each of the sellers, resellers, or other persons listed in this subdivision are engaged in such activities" for "(but only to the extent that such person is engaged in such activities"; added "or approved, referred, endorsed, authorized, certified, granted preferred status, or recommended by" in subsection (g1); in subsections (g2), substituted "dealer. Such indemnification by the manufacturer, factory branch, distributor, distributor branch, dealer management computer system vendor, or third party acting on behalf of these entities includes" for "dealer, including" and "or maintenance or services provided to any computer system utilized by a new motor vehicle dealer" for "by the manufacturer, factory branch, distributor, distributor branch, dealer management computer system vendor, or third party acting on behalf of or through such manufacturer, factory branch, distributor, distributor branch, or dealer management computer system vendor" and inserted "costs related to the disclosure of security breaches" and "a security breach or"; and made minor stylistic changes.

Session Laws 2018-27, s. 3, effective June 22, 2018, in the last paragraph of subsection (b), rewrote the fourth sentence and added the sixth sentence.

Session Laws 2019-125, s. 7, as amended by Session Laws 2020-51, s. 2, rewrote subsection (a); and added subsections (b1) and (b2). For effective date and applicability, see editor's note.

Session Laws 2019-177, s. 4.2, effective July 26, 2019, inserted "the third parties to whom any data obtained from the dealer has actually been provided" in subsection (b) to correct an error; and made numerous stylistic changes in subsections (b)-(h).

§ 20-306. Unlawful for salesman to sell except for his employer; multiple employment; persons who arrange transactions involving the sale of new motor vehicles

It shall be unlawful for any motor vehicle salesman licensed under this Article or an individual who has submitted an application for a license as required in G.S. 20-288 and who is engaging in activities as a supervised sales representative applicant while the application is pending pursuant to G.S. 20-287(a) to sell or exchange or offer or attempt to sell or exchange any motor vehicle other than his own except for the licensed motor vehicle dealer or dealers by whom he is employed, or to offer, transfer or assign, any sale or exchange, that he may have negotiated, to any other dealer or salesman. A salesman may be employed by more than one dealer provided such multiple employment is clearly indicated on his license. It shall be unlawful for any person to, for a fee, commission, or other valuable consideration, arrange or offer to arrange a transaction involving the sale of a new motor vehicle; provided, however, this prohibition shall not be applicable to:

    (1) A franchised motor vehicle dealer as defined in G.S. 20-286(8b) who is licensed under this Article or a sales representative who is licensed under this Article when acting on behalf of the dealer;

    (2) A manufacturer who is licensed under this Article or bona fide employee of such manufacturer when acting on behalf of the manufacturer;

    (3) A distributor who is licensed under this Article or a bona fide employee of such distributor when acting on behalf of the distributor; or

    (4) At any point in the transaction the bona fide owner of the vehicle involved in the transaction.

    (5) A motor vehicle dealer, as defined in G.S. 20-286(11), who offers valuable consideration to a person not licensed under this Article, or a person who is offered or receives valuable consideration from a motor vehicle dealer for the referral of a customer to the dealer, provided that the consideration paid by the motor vehicle dealer does not exceed two hundred fifty dollars ($ 250.00) in value per referral and the person receiving the consideration has received no more than five referral payments from that motor vehicle dealer in the same calendar year.

History.
1955, c. 1243, s. 22; 1993, c. 331, s. 3;2019-181, s. 3
EDITOR'S NOTE. --
Session Laws 1993, c. 331, which amended this section, by adding at the end of the section catchline "persons who arrange transactions involving the sale of new motor vehicles"; in the second sentence substituting "A salesman" for "Salesmen"; and adding the third sentence with subdivisions (1) through (4), in s. 4 provides: "Sections 2 and 3 of this act shall not apply to manufacturers of or dealers in mobile or manufactured type housing or recreational trailers."
EFFECT OF AMENDMENTS. --
Session Laws 2019-181, s. 3, effective July 26, 2019, inserted "or an individual who has submitted an application for a license as required in G.S. 20-288 and who is engaging in activities as a supervised sales representative applicant while the application is pending pursuant to G.S. 20-287(a)" in the first sentence of the introductory paragraph; and added subdivision (5).

§ 20-307. Article applicable to existing and future franchises and contracts

The provisions of this Article shall be applicable to all franchises and contracts existing between dealers and manufacturers, factory branches, and distributors at the time of its ratification, and to all such future franchises and contracts.

History.
1955, c. 1243, s. 23

§ 20-307.1. Jurisdiction

A franchisee who is substantially and primarily engaged in the sale of motor vehicles or parts, materials, or components of motor vehicles, including batteries, tires, transmissions, mufflers, painting, lubrication or tune-ups may bring suit against any franchisor, engaged in commerce, in the General Court of Justice in the State of North Carolina that has proper venue.

History.
1983, c. 704, s. 24

§ 20-308. Penalties

Any person violating any of the provisions of this Article, except for G.S. 20-305.7, shall be guilty of a Class 1 misdemeanor.

History.
1955, c. 1243, s. 24; 1993, c. 539, s. 386;1994, Ex. Sess., c. 24, s. 14(c);2005-409, s. 5
EFFECT OF AMENDMENTS. --
Session Laws 2005-409, s. 5, effective September 20, 2005, inserted "except for G.S. 20-305.7" preceding "shall be guilty"; and made minor punctuation changes.

§ 20-308.1. Civil actions for violations

(a) Notwithstanding the terms, provisions or conditions of any agreement or franchise or other terms or provisions of any novation, waiver or other written instrument, any motor vehicle dealer who is or may be injured by a violation of a provision of this Article, or any party to a franchise who is so injured in his business or property by a violation of a provision of this Article relating to that franchise, or an arrangement which, if consummated, would be in violation of this Article may, notwithstanding the initiation or pendency of, or failure to initiate an administrative proceeding before the Commissioner concerning the same parties or subject matter, bring an action for damages and equitable relief, including injunctive relief, in any court of competent jurisdiction with regard to any matter not within the jurisdiction of the Commissioner or that seeks relief wholly outside the authority or jurisdiction of the Commissioner to award.

(b) Where the violation of a provision of this Article can be shown to be willful, malicious, or wanton, or if continued multiple violations of a provision or provisions of this Article occur, the court may award punitive damages, attorneys' fees and costs in addition to any other damages under this Article.

(c) A new motor vehicle dealer, if he has not suffered any loss of money or property, may obtain final equitable relief if it can be shown that the violation of a provision of this Article by a manufacturer or distributor may have the effect of causing a loss of money or property.

(d) In order to prevent injury or harm to all or a substantial number of its members or to prevent injury or harm to the franchise distribution system of new motor vehicles within this State, any association that is comprised of a minimum of 400 new motor vehicle dealers, or a minimum of 10 motorcycle dealers or recreational vehicle dealers, substantially all of whom are new motor vehicle dealers located within North Carolina, and which represents the collective interests of its members, shall have standing to intervene as a party in any civil or administrative proceeding in any of the courts or administrative agencies of this State, or to file a petition before the Commissioner or a civil action or cause of action in any court of competent jurisdiction for itself, or on behalf of any or all of its members, seeking declaratory and injunctive relief. An action brought pursuant to this subsection may seek a determination whether one or more manufacturers, factory branches, distributors, or distributor branches doing business in this State have violated any of the provisions of this Article, or for the determination of any rights created or defined by this Article, so long as the association alleges an injury to the collective interest of its members cognizable under this section. A cognizable injury to the collective interest of the members of the association shall be deemed to occur if a manufacturer, factory branch, distributor, or distributor branch doing business in this State, or seeking to be licensed by the Division in any capacity or to otherwise engage in business in this State, applies for licensure to own, operate, or control a motor vehicle dealership in this State in violation of this Article or engages in any conduct or takes any action that either: (i) has harmed or would harm or which has adversely affected or would adversely affect a majority of its franchised new motor vehicle dealers in this State or a majority of all franchised new motor vehicle dealers in this State, or (ii) would erode or cause any other damage or injury to the franchise system of distribution of new motor vehicles within this State, whether or not the manufacturer, factory branch, distributor, or distributor branch currently has or proposes to have any franchised dealer in this State. Notwithstanding the foregoing, nothing in this subsection shall be construed to convey standing for an association to intervene in the denial of a renewal license or revocation of existing licenses issued by the Division pursuant to this Chapter or other enforcement actions taken against individual dealers or other individual licensees that may be initiated by the Division pursuant to G.S. 20-294 or other statute. Intervention by the association shall be limited to seeking declaratory relief, injunctive relief, or both declaratory and injunctive relief. With respect to any administrative or civil action filed by an association pursuant to this subsection, the relief granted shall be limited to declaratory and injunctive relief and in no event shall the Commissioner or court enter an award of monetary damages. In the event that, in any civil action before a court of this State in which an association has exercised standing in accordance with this subsection and becomes a party to the action, the court enters a declaratory ruling as to the facial applicability of any of the provisions contained in this Article, or interpreting the rights and obligations of one or more manufacturers or distributors or the rights and obligations of one or more dealers, the court's determination shall be collateral estoppel in any subsequent civil action or administrative proceeding involving the same manufacturer or manufacturers, or the same distributor or distributors, or the same dealer or dealers on all issues of fact and law decided in the original civil action in which the association was a party, provided the same decision or specific portion of the decision qualifies for application of collateral estoppel under North Carolina law. Notwithstanding anything contained herein, this subsection shall not be applicable to motor vehicle dealer licenses issued by the Division to a manufacturer pursuant to G.S. 20-305.2(a)(4a), provided that this exclusion from association standing shall not be applicable in the event the manufacturer applies for or is issued more than the maximum total number of motor vehicle dealer licenses permitted in G.S. 20-305.2(a)(4a) or upon the occurrence of any of the events listed in sub-subdivisions a. through d. of G.S. 20-305.2(a)(4a).

History.
1983, c. 704, s. 16; 1991, c. 510, s. 5;2001-510, s. 5;2007-513, s. 8;2019-125, s. 8

EDITOR'S NOTE. --
Session Laws 2019-125, s. 12, is a severability clause.

Session Laws 2019-125, s. 13, made the rewriting of subsection (d) by Session Laws 2019-125, s. 8, effective July 19, 2019, and applicable to all current and future franchises and other agreements in existence between any new motor vehicle dealer located in this State and a manufacturer or distributor as of that date.

EFFECT OF AMENDMENTS. --
Session Laws 2019-125, s. 8, rewrote subsection (d). For effective date and applicability, see editor's note.

CITED in Huberth v. Holly, 120 N.C. App. 348, 462 S.E.2d 239 (1995).

§ 20-308.2. Applicability of this Article

(a) Any person who engages directly or indirectly in purposeful contacts within this State in connection with the offering or advertising for sale, or has business dealings, with respect to a new motor vehicle sale within this State, shall be subject to the provisions of this Article and shall be subject to the jurisdiction of the courts of this State.

(b) The applicability of this Article shall not be affected by a choice of law clause in any franchise, agreement, waiver, novation, or any other written instrument.

(c) Any provision of any agreement, franchise, waiver, novation or any other written instrument which is in violation of any section of this Article shall be deemed null and void and without force and effect.

(d) It shall be unlawful for a manufacturer or distributor to use any subsidiary corporation, affiliated corporation, or any other controlled corporation, partnership, association or person to accomplish what would otherwise be illegal conduct under this Article on the part of the manufacturer or distributor.

(e) The provisions of this Article shall apply to all written agreements between a manufacturer, wholesaler, or distributor with a motor vehicle dealer including, but not limited to, the franchise offering, the franchise agreement, sales of goods, services or advertising, leases or deeds of trust of real or personal property, promises to pay, security interests, pledges, insurance contracts, advertising contracts, construction or installation contracts, servicing contracts, and all other such agreements between a motor vehicle dealer and a manufacturer, wholesaler, or distributor.

History.
1983, c. 704, s. 17; 2005-409, s. 6

EFFECT OF AMENDMENTS. --
Session Laws 2005-409, s. 6, effective September 20, 2005, added subsection (e).

§§ 20-308.3 through 20-308.12

Reserved for future codification purposes.

ARTICLE 12A.
MOTOR VEHICLE CAPTIVE FINANCE SOURCE LAW

§ 20-308.13. Regulation of motor vehicle captive finance sources

The General Assembly finds and declares that the distribution of motor vehicles in the State of North Carolina vitally affects the general economy of the State and the public interest and public welfare, and in the exercise of its police power, it is necessary to regulate motor vehicle captive finance sources doing business in North Carolina to protect and preserve the investments and properties of the citizens of this State.

History.
2005-409, s. 3

EDITOR'S NOTE. --
Session Laws 2005-409, s. 3, originally enacted this Article as G.S. 20-308.3 through 20-308.12. It has been renumbered as G.S. 20-308.13 through 20-308.22 at the direction of the Revisor of Statutes.

§ 20-308.14. Definitions

The definitions contained in G.S. 20-286 shall be applicable to the provisions of this Article.

History.
2005-409, s. 3

§ 20-308.15. Prohibited contractual requirements imposed by manufacturer, distributor, or captive finance source

It shall be unlawful for any manufacturer, factory branch, captive finance source, distributor, or distributor branch, or any field representative, officer, agent, or any representative of them, notwithstanding the terms, provisions, or conditions of any agreement or franchise, to require any of its franchised dealers located in this State to agree to any terms, conditions, or requirements that are set forth in subdivisions (1) through (8) below in order for any such dealer to sell to any captive finance source (defined below) any retail installment contract, loan, or lease of any motor vehicles purchased or leased by any of the dealer's customers ("contract for sale or lease"), or to be able to participate in, or otherwise, directly or indirectly, obtain the benefits of any consumer transaction incentive program payable to the consumer or the dealer and offered by or through any financial source that provides automotive-related loans or purchases retail installment contracts or lease contracts for motor vehicles in North Carolina and is, directly or indirectly, owned, operated, or controlled by such manufacturer, factory branch, distributor, or distributor branch ("captive finance source"):

(1) Require a dealer to grant such captive finance source a power of attorney to do anything on behalf of the dealer other than sign the dealer's name on any check, draft, or other instrument received in payment or proceeds under any contract for the sale or lease of a motor vehicle that is made payable to the dealer but which is properly payable to the captive finance source, is for the purpose of correcting an error in a customer's finance application or title processing document, or is for the purpose of processing regular titling of the vehicle.

(2) Require a dealer to warrant or guarantee the accuracy and completeness of any personal, financial, or credit information provided by the customer on the credit application and/or in the course of applying for credit other than to require that the dealer make reasonable inquiry regarding the accuracy and completeness of such information and represent that such information is true and correct to the best of the dealer's knowledge.

(3) Require a dealer to repurchase, pay off, or guaranty any contract for the sale or lease of a motor vehicle or to require a dealer to indemnify, defend, or hold harmless the captive finance source for settlements, judgments, damages, litigation expenses, or other costs or expenses incurred by such captive finance source unless the obligation to repurchase, pay off, guaranty, indemnify, or hold harmless resulted directly from (i) the subject dealer's material breach of the terms of a written agreement with the captive finance source or the terms for the purchase of an individual contract for sale or lease that the captive finance

source communicates to the dealer before each such purchase, except to the extent the breached terms are otherwise prohibited under subdivisions (1) through (8) of this section, or (ii) the subject dealer's violation of applicable law. For purposes of this section, the dealer may, however, contractually obligate itself to warrant the accuracy of the information provided on the finance contact, but such warranty can only be enforced if the captive finance source gives the dealer a reasonable opportunity to cure or correct any errors on the finance contract where cure or correction is possible. For purposes of this section, any allegation by a third party that would constitute a breach of the terms of a written agreement between the dealer and a captive finance source shall be considered a material breach.

(4) Notwithstanding the terms of any contract or agreement, treat a dealer's breach of an agreement between the dealer and a captive finance source with respect to the captive finance source's purchase of individual contracts for the sale or lease of a motor vehicle as a breach of such agreement with respect to purchase of other such contracts, nor shall such a breach, in and of itself, constitute a breach of any other agreement between the dealer and the captive finance source, or between the dealer and any affiliate of such captive finance source.

(5) Require a dealer to waive any defenses that may be available to it under its agreements with the captive finance source or under any applicable laws.

(6) Require a dealer to settle or contribute any of its own funds or financial resources toward the settlement of any multiparty or class action litigation without obtaining the dealer's voluntary and written consent subsequent to the filing of such litigation.

(7) Require a dealer to contribute to any reserve or contingency account established or maintained by the captive finance source, for the financing of the sale or lease of any motor vehicles purchased or leased by any of the dealer's customers, in any amount or on any basis other than the reasonable expected amount of future finance reserve chargebacks to the dealer's account. This section shall not apply to or limit (i) reasonable amounts reserved and maintained related to the sale or financing of any products ancillary to the sale, lease, or financing of the motor vehicle itself; (ii) a delay or reduction in the payment of dealer's portion of the finance income pursuant to an agreement between the dealer and a captive finance source under which the dealer agrees to such delay or reduction in exchange for the limitation, reduction, or elimination of

the dealer's responsibility for finance reserve chargebacks; or (iii) a chargeback to a dealer (or offset of any amounts otherwise payable to a dealer by the captive finance source) for any indebtedness properly owing from a dealer to the captive finance source as part of a specific program covered by this section, the terms of which have been agreed to by the dealer in advance, except to the extent such chargeback would otherwise be prohibited under subdivisions (1) through (8) of this section.

(8) Require a dealer to repossess or otherwise gain possession of a motor vehicle at the request of or on behalf of the captive finance source. This section shall not apply to any requirements contained in any agreement between the dealer and the captive finance source wherein the dealer agrees to receive and process vehicles that are voluntarily returned by the customer or returned to the lessor at the end of the lease term.

Any clause or provision in any franchise or agreement between a dealer and a manufacturer, factory branch, distributor, or distributor branch, or between a dealer and any captive finance source, that is in violation of or that is inconsistent with any of the provisions of this section shall be voidable, to the extent that it violates this section, at any time at the election of the dealer.

History.
2005-409, s. 3

§ 20-308.16. Powers of Commissioner

(a) The Commissioner shall promote the interests of the retail buyer of motor vehicles.

(b) The Commissioner shall have power to prevent unfair or deceptive acts or practices and other violations of this Article. Any franchised new motor vehicle dealer who believes that a captive finance source with whom the dealer does business in North Carolina has violated or is currently violating any provision of this Article may file a petition before the Commissioner setting forth the factual and legal basis for such violations. The Commissioner shall promptly forward a copy of the petition to the named captive finance source requesting a reply to the petition within 30 days. Allowing for sufficient time for the parties to conduct discovery, the Commissioner or his designee shall then hold an evidentiary hearing and render findings of fact and conclusions of law based on the evidence presented.

(c) The Commissioner shall have the power in hearings arising under this Article to enter scheduling orders and limit the time and scope of discovery; to determine the date, time, and place where hearings are to be held; to subpoena witnesses; to take depositions of witnesses; and to administer oaths.

(d) The Commissioner may, whenever he shall believe from evidence submitted to him that any person has been or is violating any provision of this Article, in addition to any other remedy, bring an action in the name of the State against that person and any other persons concerned or in any way participating in, or about to participate in, practices or acts so in violation, to enjoin any persons from continuing the violations.

(e) The Commissioner may issue rules and regulations to implement the provisions of this section and to establish procedures related to administrative proceedings commenced under this section.

(f) In the event that a dealer, who is permitted or required to file a notice, protest, or petition before the Commissioner within a certain period of time in order to adjudicate, enforce, or protect rights afforded the dealer under this Article, voluntarily elects to appeal a policy, determination, or decision of the captive finance source through an appeals board or internal grievance procedure of the captive finance source, or to participate in or refer the matter to mediation, arbitration, or other alternative dispute resolution procedure or process established or endorsed by the captive finance source, the applicable period of time for the dealer to file the notice, protest, or petition before the Commissioner under this Article shall not commence until the captive finance source's appeal board or internal grievance procedure, mediation, arbitration, or appeals process of the captive finance source has been completed and the dealer has received notice in writing of the final decision or result of the procedure or process. Nothing, however, contained in this subsection shall be deemed to require that any dealer exhaust any internal grievance or other alternative dispute process required or established by the captive finance source before seeking redress from the Commissioner as provided in this Article.

History.
2005-409, s. 3

§ 20-308.17. Rules and regulations

The Commissioner may make such rules and regulations, not inconsistent with the provisions of this Article, as he shall deem necessary or proper for the effective administration and enforcement of this Article, provided that a copy of such rules and regulations shall be mailed to each motor vehicle dealer licensee and captive finance source 30 days prior to the effective date of such rules and regulations.

History.
2005-409, s. 3

§ 20-308.18. Hearing notice

In every case of a hearing before the Commissioner authorized under this Article, the Commissioner shall give reasonable notice of each such hearing to all interested parties, and the Commissioner's decision shall be binding on the parties, subject to the rights of judicial review and appeal as provided in Chapter 150B of the General Statutes. The costs of such hearings shall be assessed by the Commissioner.

History.
2005-409, s. 3

§ 20-308.19. Article applicable to existing and future agreements

The provisions of this Article shall be applicable to all contracts and agreements existing between dealers and captive finance sources at the time of its ratification and to all such future contracts and agreements.

History.
2005-409, s. 3

§ 20-308.20. Jurisdiction

A new motor vehicle dealer located in this State may bring suit against any captive finance source engaged in commerce in this State in the General Court of Justice in the State of North Carolina that has proper venue.

History.
2005-409, s. 3

§ 20-308.21. Civil actions for violations

(a) Notwithstanding the terms, provisions, or conditions of any agreement or other terms or provisions of any novation, waiver, arbitration agreement, or other written instrument, any person who is or may be injured by a violation of a provision of this Article, or any party to an agreement who is so injured in his business or property by a violation of a provision of this Article relating to that agreement, or an arrangement which, if consummated, would be in violation of this Article may, notwithstanding the initiation or pendency of, or failure to initiate an administrative proceeding before the Commissioner concerning the same parties or subject matter, bring an action for damages and equitable relief, including injunctive relief, in any court of competent jurisdiction with regard to any matter not within the jurisdiction of the Commissioner or that seeks relief wholly outside the authority or jurisdiction of the Commissioner to award.

(b) Where the violation of a provision of this Article can be shown to be willful, malicious, or wanton, or if continued multiple violations of a provision or provisions of this Article occur, the court may award punitive damages, attorneys' fees and costs in addition to any other damages under this Article.

(c) A new motor vehicle dealer, if he has not suffered any loss of money or property, may obtain final equitable relief if it can be shown that the violation of a provision of this Article by a captive finance source may have the effect of causing a loss of money or property.

(d) Any association that is comprised of a minimum of 400 new motor vehicle dealers, or a minimum of 10 motorcycle dealers, substantially all of whom are new motor vehicle dealers located within North Carolina, and which represents the collective interests of its members, shall have standing to file a petition before the Commissioner or a cause of action in any court of competent jurisdiction for itself, or on behalf of any or all of its members, seeking declaratory and injunctive relief. Prior to bringing an action, the association and captive finance source shall initiate mediation as set forth in G.S. 20-301.1(b). An action brought pursuant to this subsection may seek a determination whether one or more captive finance sources doing business in this State have violated any of the provisions of this Article, or for the determination of any rights created or defined by this Article, so long as the association alleges an injury to the collective interest of its members cognizable under this section. A cognizable injury to the collective interest of the members of the association shall be deemed to occur if a captive finance source doing business in this State has engaged in any conduct or taken any action which actually harms or affects all of the franchised new motor vehicle dealers holding agreements with that captive finance source in this State. With respect to any administrative or civil action filed by an association pursuant to this subsection, the relief granted shall be limited to declaratory and injunctive relief and in no event shall the Commissioner or court enter an award of monetary damages.

History.
2005-409, s. 3

§ 20-308.22. Applicability of this Article

(a) Any captive finance source who engages directly or indirectly in purposeful contacts within this State in connection with the offering or advertising the availability of financing for the sale or lease of motor vehicles within this State, or who has business dealings within this State, shall be subject to the provisions of this

Article and shall be subject to the jurisdiction of the courts of this State.

(b) The applicability of this Article shall not be affected by a choice of law clause in any agreement, waiver, novation, or any other written instrument.

(c) Any provision of any agreement, waiver, novation, or any other written instrument which is in violation of any section of this Article shall be deemed null and void and without force and effect to the extent it violates this section.

(d) It shall be unlawful for a captive finance source to use any subsidiary corporation, affiliated corporation, or any other controlled corporation, partnership, association, or person to accomplish what would otherwise be illegal conduct under this Article on the part of the captive finance source.

History.
2005-409, s. 3

ARTICLE 13.
THE VEHICLE FINANCIAL RESPONSIBILITY ACT OF 1957

§ 20-309. Financial responsibility prerequisite to registration; must be maintained throughout registration period

(a) No motor vehicle shall be registered in this State unless the owner at the time of registration provides proof of financial responsibility for the operation of such motor vehicle, as provided in this Article. The owner of each motor vehicle registered in this State shall maintain financial responsibility continuously throughout the period of registration. For purposes of this Article, the term "motor vehicle" includes mopeds, as that term is defined in G.S. 20-4.01.

(a1) An owner of a commercial motor vehicle, as defined in G.S. 20-4.01(3d), shall have financial responsibility for the operation of the motor vehicle in an amount equal to that required for for-hire carriers transporting nonhazardous property in interstate or foreign commerce in 49 C.F.R. § 387.9.

(a2) Notwithstanding any other provision of this Chapter, an owner's policy of liability insurance issued to a foster parent or parents, which policy includes an endorsement excluding coverage for one or more foster children residing in the foster parent's or parents' household, may be certified as proof of financial responsibility, provided that each foster child for whom coverage is excluded is insured in an amount equal to or greater than the minimum limits required by G.S. 20-279.21 under some other owner's policy of liability insurance or a named nonowner's policy of liability insurance. The North Carolina Rate Bureau shall establish, with the approval of the Commissioner of Insurance, a named driver exclusion endorsement or endorsements for foster children as described herein.

(b) Financial responsibility shall be a liability insurance policy or a financial security bond or a financial security deposit or by qualification as a self-insurer, as these terms are defined and described in Article 9A, Chapter 20 of the General Statutes of North Carolina, as amended.

(c) When it is certified that financial responsibility is a liability insurance policy, the Commissioner of Motor Vehicles may require that the owner produce records to prove the fact of such insurance, and failure to produce such records shall be prima facie evidence that no financial responsibility exists with regard to the vehicle concerned. It shall be the duty of insurance companies, upon request of the Division, to verify the accuracy of any owner's certification.

(c1) The proof of insurance required to demonstrate financial responsibility under subsection (c) of this section may be satisfied by producing records of insurance in either physical or electronic format. Acceptable electronic formats include display of electronic images on a mobile phone or other portable electronic device produced through an application or Web site of the insurer.

(d) When liability insurance with regard to any motor vehicle is terminated by cancellation or failure to renew, or the owner's financial responsibility for the operation of any motor vehicle is otherwise terminated, the owner shall forthwith surrender the registration certificate and plates of the vehicle to the Division of Motor Vehicles unless financial responsibility is maintained in some other manner in compliance with this Article.

(e) Repealed by Session Laws 2006-213, s. 5, effective July 1, 2008, and applicable to lapses occurring on or after that date.

(f) The Commissioner shall administer and enforce the provisions of this Article and may make rules and regulations necessary for its administration and shall provide for hearings upon request of persons aggrieved by orders or acts of the Commissioner under the provisions of this Article.

(g) Repealed by Session Laws 2007-484, s. 7(a), effective July 1, 2008, and applicable to lapses occurring on or after that date.

(h) Recodified as G.S. 20-311(g) by Session Laws 2007-484, s. 7(d), effective July 1, 2008, and applicable to lapses occurring on or after that date.

History.

1957, c. 1393, s. 1; 1959, c. 1277, s. 1; 1963, c. 964, s. 1; 1965, c. 272; c. 1136, ss. 1, 2; 1967, c. 822, ss. 1, 2; c. 857, ss. 1, 2; 1971, c. 477, ss. 1, 2; c. 924; 1975, c. 302; c. 348, ss. 1-3; c. 716, s. 5; 1979, 2nd Sess., c. 1279, s. 1; 1981, c. 690, s. 25; 1983, c. 761, s. 146; 1983 (Reg. Sess., 1984), c. 1069, ss. 1, 2; 1985, c. 666, s. 84; 1991, c. 402, s. 1;1999-330, s. 4;1999-452, s. 20;2000-140, s. 100(a);2000-155, s. 20;2005-276, s. 6.37(p);2006-213, s. 5;2006-264, s. 38;2007-484, ss. 7(a), (d); 2009-550, s. 4;2015-125, s. 3;2015-135, s. 4.3;2015-146, s. 4

EDITOR'S NOTE. --

Session Laws 2005-276, s. 6.37(w), provides: "The Office of State Budget and Management shall develop a methodology for computing the actual costs of collection of civil penalties by State departments and agencies. This methodology shall apply to all State departments and agencies, effective July 1, 2006."

Session Laws 2005-276, s. 1.2, provides: "This act shall be known as the 'Current Operations and Capital Improvements Appropriations Act of 2005.'"

Session Laws 2005-276, s. 46.3, provides: "Except for statutory changes or other provisions that clearly indicate an intention to have effects beyond the 2005-2007 fiscal biennium, the textual provisions of this act apply only to funds appropriated for, and activities occurring during, the 2005-2007 fiscal biennium."

Session Laws 2005-276, s. 46.5, is a severability clause.

Session Laws 2015-125, s. 10, made the amendment to subsection (a) of this section by Session Laws 2015-125, s. 3, applicable to offenses committed on or after July 1, 2016.

Session Laws 2015-135, s. 1.1, provides: "This act shall be known and may be cited as the 'Foster Care Family Act.'"

EFFECT OF AMENDMENTS. --

Session Laws 2005-276, s. 6.37(p), effective July 1, 2005, added subsection (g).

Session Laws 2006-213, s. 5, effective July 1, 2008, and applicable to lapses occurring on or after that date, repealed subsection (e).

Session Laws 2006-264, s. 38, effective August 27, 2006, added subsection (h).

Session Laws 2009-550, s. 4, effective August 28, 2009, substituted "provide proof of financial" for "has financial" in subsection (a).

Session Laws 2015-125, s. 3, effective July 1, 2016, added the present last sentence in subsection (a).

Session Laws 2015-135, s. 4.3, effective October 1, 2015, added subsection (a2).

Session Laws 2015-146, s. 4, effective July 13, 2015, added subsection (c1).

THIS ARTICLE IS A REMEDIAL STATUTE AND WILL BE LIBERALLY CONSTRUED to carry out its beneficent purpose of providing compensation to those who have been injured by automobiles. Jones v. State Farm Mut. Auto. Ins. Co., 270 N.C. 454, 155 S.E.2d 118 (1967).

THE MANIFEST PURPOSE OF THIS ARTICLE is to provide protection, within the required limits, to persons injured or damaged by the negligent

operation of a motor vehicle; and in respect of a motor vehicle liability policy to provide such protection notwithstanding violations of policy provisions by the owner subsequent to accidents on which such injured parties base their claims. To bar recovery from the insurer on account of such policy violations would practically nullify the statute by making the enforcement of the rights of the person intended to be protected dependent upon the acts of the very person who caused the injury. Swain v. Nationwide Mut. Ins. Co., 253 N.C. 120, 116 S.E.2d 482 (1960).

The manifest purpose of this Article was to provide protection, within the required limits, to persons injured or damaged by the negligent operation of a motor vehicle. Perkins v. American Mut. Fire Ins. Co., 274 N.C. 134, 161 S.E.2d 536 (1968).

The purpose of this Article is to assure the protection of liability insurance, or other type of established financial responsibility, up to the minimum amount specified in this Article, to persons injured by the negligent operation of a motor vehicle upon the highways of this State. To that end, the act makes it mandatory that the owner of a registered motor vehicle maintain proof of financial responsibility throughout such registration of the vehicle. This may be done by the owner's obtaining, and maintaining in effect, a policy of automobile liability insurance (G.S. 20-279.19, 20-314). To enable an owner so to comply with this requirement of the act, even though he is unable to procure such insurance in the usual way, the act provides that the provisions of the Financial Responsibility Act of 1953, with reference to the assigned risk plan, "shall apply to filing and maintaining proof of financial responsibility required by" the Act of 1957 (G.S. 20-314). Harrelson v. State Farm Mut. Auto. Ins. Co., 272 N.C. 603, 158 S.E.2d 812 (1968).

The manifest purpose of this Article was to provide protection, within the required limits, to persons injured or damaged by the negligent operation of a motor vehicle, and, in respect of a "motor vehicle liability policy," to provide such protection notwithstanding violations of policy provisions by the owner subsequent to accidents on which such injured parties base their claims. Jones v. State Farm Mut. Auto. Ins. Co., 270 N.C. 454, 155 S.E.2d 118 (1967).

The primary purpose of the law requiring compulsory insurance is to furnish at least partial compensation to innocent victims who have suffered injury and damage as a result of the negligent operation of a motor vehicle upon the public highway. Allstate Ins. Co. v. Hale, 270 N.C. 195, 154 S.E.2d 79 (1967).

It is manifest that the purpose of this Article is to provide protection, within the required limits, to persons injured or damaged by the negligent operation of a motor vehicle. Nationwide Mut. Ins. Co. v. Cotten, 12 N.C. App. 212, 182 S.E.2d 801, rev'd on other grounds, 280 N.C. 20, 185 S.E.2d 182 (1971).

THE DEFINITION OF "OWNER" given in G.S. 20-4.01(26) applies to all Chapter 20 and to the Financial Responsibility Act unless the context requires otherwise. Jenkins v. Aetna Cas. & Sur. Co., 91 N.C. App.

388, 371 S.E.2d 761 (1988), rev'd on other grounds, 324 N.C. 394, 378 S.E.2d 773 (1989).

PASSAGE OF TITLE FOR PURPOSES OF TORT LAW AND INSURANCE COVERAGE. --For purposes of tort law and liability insurance coverage, no ownership passes to the purchaser of a motor vehicle which requires registration until transfer of legal title is effected as provided in G.S. 20-72(b). The general rule then, as between vendor and vendee, is that the vendee does not acquire valid owner's liability insurance until legal title has been transferred or assigned to the vendee by the vendor. Jenkins v. Aetna Cas. & Sur. Co., 91 N.C. App. 388, 371 S.E.2d 761 (1988), rev'd on other grounds, 324 N.C. 394, 378 S.E.2d 773 (1989).

THIS ARTICLE OBLIGES A MOTORIST EITHER TO POST SECURITY OR TO CARRY LIABILITY INSURANCE, NOT ACCIDENT INSURANCE to indemnify all persons who might be injured by the insured's car. When the legislature passed the act it was not in the legislative contemplation that each driver in a two-car collision would recover from the other's insurance carrier. Moore v. Young, 263 N.C. 483, 139 S.E.2d 704 (1965); McKinney v. Morrow, 18 N.C. App. 282, 196 S.E.2d 585, cert. denied, 283 N.C. 665, 197 S.E.2d 874 (1973).

THIS ARTICLE AND ARTICLE 9A ARE TO BE CONSTRUED IN PARI MATERIA. --The Motor Vehicle Safety and Financial Responsibility Act of 1953 applies to drivers whose licenses have been suspended and relates to the restoration of drivers' licenses, while the Vehicle Financial Responsibility Act of 1957 applies to all motor vehicle owners and relates to the registration of motor vehicles. The two acts are complementary and the latter does not repeal or modify the former, but incorporates portions of the former by reference, and the two acts are to be construed in pari materia so as to harmonize them and give effect to both. Faizan v. Grain Dealers Mut. Ins. Co., 254 N.C. 47, 118 S.E.2d 303 (1961).

This Article requires every owner of a motor vehicle, as a prerequisite to the registration thereof to show proof of financial responsibility in the manner prescribed by Article 9A of this Chapter. Swain v. Nationwide Mut. Ins. Co., 253 N.C. 120, 116 S.E.2d 482 (1960); First Union Nat'l Bank v. Hackney, 266 N.C. 17, 145 S.E.2d 352 (1965); Jones v. State Farm Mut. Auto. Ins. Co., 270 N.C. 454, 155 S.E.2d 118 (1967).

This Article and Article 9A are to be construed together so as to harmonize their provisions and to effectuate the purpose of the legislature. Harrelson v. State Farm Mut. Auto. Ins. Co., 272 N.C. 603, 158 S.E.2d 812 (1968).

The 1953 Act, found at G.S. 20-279.1 to 20-279.39, applies to drivers whose licenses have been suspended and relates to the restoration of driver's licenses while this article, the 1957 Act, found at G.S. 20-309 to 20-319, applies to all motor vehicles' owners and relates to vehicle registration. The two Acts are complementary and are to be construed in pari materia so as to harmonize them and give effect to both. Odum v. Nationwide Mut. Ins. Co., 101 N.C. App. 627,

401 S.E.2d 87, cert. denied, 329 N.C. 499, 407 S.E.2d 539 (1991).

THIS ARTICLE AND ARTICLE 9 OF CHAPTER 20 SUPERSEDE G.S. 58-3-10. --G.S. 58-3-10, adopted in 1901, falls within Chapter 58, Insurance, Article 3, General Regulations for Insurance. As an earlier and more general statement of insurance law, it is superseded with respect to automobile liability insurance by Chapter 20, Motor Vehicles, specifically by Article 9A, the Motor Vehicle Safety and Financial Responsibility Act of 1953, and Article 13, the Vehicle Financial Responsibility Act of 1957. Chapter 20 represents a complete and comprehensive legislative scheme for the regulation of motor vehicles and, as such, its insurance provisions regarding automobiles prevail over the more general insurance regulations of Chapter 58. Odum v. Nationwide Mut. Ins. Co., 101 N.C. App. 627, 401 S.E.2d 87, cert. denied, 329 N.C. 499, 407 S.E.2d 539 (1991).

FINANCIAL RESPONSIBILITY MUST BE MAINTAINED ON ALL MOTOR VEHICLES. --Under this section financial responsibility as provided in Article 9A of Chapter 20 of the General Statutes--i.e., the Financial Responsibility Act--must be maintained upon all motor vehicles registered in this State. Hendrickson v. Lee, 119 N.C. App. 444, 459 S.E.2d 275 (1995).

EFFECT OF ISSUANCE OF CERTIFICATE BY INSURER. --By the issuance of the certificate an insurer represents that it has issued and there is in effect an owner's motor vehicle liability policy. Crisp v. State Farm Mut. Auto. Ins. Co., 256 N.C. 408, 124 S.E.2d 149 (1962).

By the issuance of the certificate the insurer represents that everything requisite for a binding insurance policy has been performed, including payment, or satisfactory arrangement for payment, of premium. Once the certificate has been issued, nonpayment of premium, nothing else appearing, is no defense in a suit by a third party beneficiary against insurer. To avoid liability insurer must allege and prove cancellation and termination of the insurance policy in accordance with the applicable statute, unless it is established by plaintiff's evidence or admissions. Crisp v. State Farm Mut. Auto. Ins. Co., 256 N.C. 408, 124 S.E.2d 149 (1962).

REFORMATION OF INSURANCE POLICY TO COMPLY WITH STATUTE. --Superior court properly reformed an insurance policy to include the amount of minimum coverage required by G.S. 20-309(a1); construing G.S. 20-279.21 and G.S. 20-309 in pari materia, just as provisions of G.S. 20-279.21 were read into every insurance policy as a matter of law, provisions of G.S. 20-309(a1) were also read into every insurance policy as a matter of law. N.C. Farm Bureau Mut. Ins. Co. v. Armwood, 181 N.C. App. 407, 638 S.E.2d 922 (2007), rev'd, 361 N.C. 576, 653 S.E.2d 392 (2007).

TIME GAPS IN COVERAGE PERMITTED. --The Vehicle Financial Responsibility Act of 1957 permits the possibility of time gaps in insurance coverage; that is, short periods in which vehicles are uninsured. Fincher v. Rhyne, 266 N.C. 64, 145 S.E.2d 316 (1965).

THE REQUIREMENTS OF THIS SECTION WITH RESPECT TO CANCELLATION MUST BE OBSERVED or the attempt at cancellation fails. Allstate Ins. Co. v. Hale, 270 N.C. 195, 154 S.E.2d 79 (1967).

Subsection (e) of this section prescribe the procedure pursuant to which a policy issued for the purpose of complying with the requirements of this Article may be cancelled by the insurance carrier having the right to cancel. In order to cancel such policy, the carrier must comply with these procedural requirements of the statute or the attempt at cancellation fails. Harrelson v. State Farm Mut. Auto. Ins. Co., 272 N.C. 603, 158 S.E.2d 812 (1968).

IN ORDER TO BE EFFECTIVE, A PURPORTED CANCELLATION MUST COMPLY WITH THE PROVISIONS OF SUBSECTION (E) OF THIS SECTION AND G.S. 20-310. Redmon v. United States Fid. & Guar. Co., 21 N.C. App. 704, 206 S.E.2d 298, cert. denied, 285 N.C. 661, 207 S.E.2d 755 (1974).

An insurer may not cancel for nonpayment of premiums without following the provisions of subsection (e) of this section and G.S. 20-310. Nationwide Mut. Ins. Co. v. Davis, 7 N.C. App. 152, 171 S.E.2d 601 (1970).

Before an insurer may cancel or refuse to renew a policy of automobile liability insurance for failure to pay a premium due, the insurer must follow the provisions of G.S. 20-310 and subsection (e) of this section. Smith v. Nationwide Mut. Ins. Co., 72 N.C. App. 400, 324 S.E.2d 868, rev'd on other grounds, 315 N.C. 262, 337 S.E.2d 569 (1985).

PURPOSE OF NOTICE REQUIREMENT. --The purpose of the notice to the Department (now Division) is to enable it to recall the registration and license plate issued for the vehicle unless the owner makes other provision for compliance with the Vehicle Financial Responsibility Act. Nationwide Mut. Ins. Co. v. Cotten, 280 N.C. 20, 185 S.E.2d 182 (1971).

NOTICE BY INSURER TO INSURED IS NOT REQUIRED WHERE INSURED HAS TERMINATED POLICY. --Where a policy is terminated or cancelled by an insured, the insurer is not required to give notice of cancellation to the insured. Nationwide Mut. Ins. Co. v. Davis, 7 N.C. App. 152, 171 S.E.2d 601 (1970).

AND FAILURE TO GIVE NOTICE TO DEPARTMENT OF TERMINATION BY INSURED DID NOT AFFECT VALIDITY OF CANCELLATION. --Where the insured terminated a policy issued pursuant to the Vehicle Responsibility Act of 1957, the insurer was required to notify the Department (now Division) of Motor Vehicles, but failure to give such notice did not affect the validity or binding effect of the cancellation. Nationwide Mut. Ins. Co. v. Davis, 7 N.C. App. 152, 171 S.E.2d 601 (1970), decided under this section as it stood before the 1979 (2nd Sess.) amendment.

DISTINCTION BETWEEN TERMINATION BY INSURER AND BY INSURED UNDER FORMER LAW. --See Nationwide Mut. Ins. Co. v. Cotten, 280 N.C. 20, 185 S.E.2d 182 (1971); Bailey v. Nationwide Mut. Ins. Co., 19 N.C. App. 168, 198 S.E.2d 246 (1973).

THE MANDATORY LANGUAGE OF SUBSECTION (E) of this section did not invest the Commissioner of the Division of Motor Vehicles with authority to override the notification requirement contained therein. Allstate Ins. Co. v. McCrae, 325 N.C. 411, 384 S.E.2d 1 (1989), decided under law in effect prior to 1984 amendment.

EFFECT OF DEFECTIVE NOTICE OF CANCELLATION TO DIVISION OF MOTOR VEHICLES. --Defective notice of cancellation to the insured can result in ineffective termination of the policy and thus in continued coverage by the insurer; however, this is not true when the defective notice is directed to the Division of Motor Vehicles. Allstate Ins. Co. v. McCrae, 325 N.C. 411, 384 S.E.2d 1 (1989), decided under law in effect prior to 1984 amendment.

PAYMENTS AUTHORIZED BY G.S. 20-309(E) ARE IN THE NATURE OF SANCTIONS and are thus subject to N.C. Const., Art. IX, § 7. N.C. Sch. Bds. Ass'n v. Moore, 160 N.C. App. 253, 585 S.E.2d 418 (2003).

CIVIL PENALTY AS EXCLUSIVE SANCTION FOR DEFECTIVE NOTICE OF CANCELLATION TO DIVISION OF MOTOR VEHICLES. --The General Assembly appears to have intended that the civil penalty be the exclusive sanction for failure to give the Division of Motor Vehicles the required notice of termination. Allstate Ins. Co. v. McCrae, 325 N.C. 411, 384 S.E.2d 1 (1989), decided under law in effect prior to 1984 amendment.

POLICY VIOLATIONS A DEFENSE PRIOR TO JANUARY 1, 1958. --As to accidents occurring prior to the effective date (January 1, 1958) of this Article, policy violations constitute a valid and complete defense as to the insurer. Swain v. Nationwide Mut. Ins. Co., 253 N.C. 120, 116 S.E.2d 482 (1960).

APPLIED in Underwood v. National Grange Mut. Liab. Co., 258 N.C. 211, 128 S.E.2d 577 (1962); Lofquist v. Allstate Ins. Co., 263 N.C. 615, 140 S.E.2d 12 (1965); Harris v. Scotland Neck Rescue Squad, Inc., 75 N.C. App. 444, 331 S.E.2d 695 (1985).

CITED in High Point Sav. & Trust Co. v. King, 253 N.C. 571, 117 S.E.2d 421 (1960); Fidelity & Cas. Co. v. Jackson, 297 F.2d 230 (4th Cir. 1961); Smart Fin. Co. v. Dick, 256 N.C. 669, 124 S.E.2d 862 (1962); Griffin v. Hartford Accident & Indem. Co., 264 N.C. 212, 141 S.E.2d 300 (1965); Hayes v. Hartford Accident & Indem. Co., 274 N.C. 73, 161 S.E.2d 552 (1968); Grant v. State Farm Mut. Auto. Ins. Co., 1 N.C. App. 76, 159 S.E.2d 368 (1968); Nationwide Mut. Ins. Co. v. Hayes, 276 N.C. 620, 174 S.E.2d 511 (1970); In re North Carolina Auto. Rate Admin. Office, 278 N.C. 302, 180 S.E.2d 155 (1971); State ex rel. Hunt v. North Carolina Reinsurance Facility, 49 N.C. App. 206, 271 S.E.2d 302 (1980); Shew v. Southern Fire & Cas. Co., 58 N.C. App. 637, 294 S.E.2d 233 (1982); Ohio Cas. Ins. Co. v. Anderson, 59 N.C. App. 621, 298 S.E.2d 56 (1982); Lowe v. Tarble, 312 N.C. 467, 323 S.E.2d 19 (1984); Smith v. Nationwide Mut. Ins. Co., 315 N.C. 262, 337 S.E.2d 569 (1985); N.C. Farm Bureau Mut. Ins. Co. v. Simpson, 198 N.C. App. 190, 678 S.E.2d 753 (2009), review denied, 363 N.C. 806, 691 S.E.2d 13, N.C. LEXIS 56 (2010); State v. Sullivan, 201 N.C. App. 540, 687 S.E.2d 504 (2009), appeal denied, 364 N.C. 247, 699 S.E.2d 921 (2010), cert. denied, 562

U.S. 1138, 131 S. Ct. 937, 178 L. Ed. 2d 754, 2011 U.S. LEXIS 574 (U.S. 2011).

CROSS REFERENCES. --

As to Motor Vehicle Safety and Financial Responsibility Act of 1953, see G.S. 20-279.1 to 20-279.39.

LEGAL PERIODICALS. --

For case law survey on insurance, see 41 N.C.L. Rev. 484 (1963).

For note on the State's inability to suspend the driver's license of a bankrupt who fails to satisfy an accident judgment debt, see 50 N.C.L. Rev. 350 (1972).

For 1984 survey, "Employee Exclusion Clauses in Automobile Liability Insurance Policies," see 63 N.C.L. Rev. 1228 (1985).

For note as to terminating an insurance policy according to North Carolina's financial responsibility legislation, in light of Peerless Ins. Co. v. Freeman, 78 N.C. App. 774, 338 S.E.2d 570, aff'd per curiam, 317 N.C. 145, 343 S.E.2d 539 (1986), see 65 N.C.L. Rev. 1409 (1987).

For note, "Sutton v. Aetna Casualty & Surety Co.: The North Carolina Supreme Court Approves Stacking of Underinsured Motorist Coverage--Will Uninsured Coverage Follow?," see 68 N.C. L. Rev. 1281 (1990).

N.C. Gen. Stat. § 20-309.1

Repealed by Session Laws 1993 (Reg. Sess., 1994), c. 761, s. 28.

§ 20-309.2. Insurer shall notify Division of actions on insurance policies

(a) **Notice Required.** -- An insurer shall notify the Division upon any of the following with regard to a motor vehicle liability policy:

(1) Issues a new or replacement policy.

(2) Terminates a policy, either by cancellation or failure to renew, unless the same insurer issues a replacement policy complying with this Article at the same time the insurer terminates the old policy and no lapse in coverage results.

(3) Reinstates a policy after the insurer has notified the Division of a cancellation or termination.

(b) **Time Period.** -- An insurer shall notify the Division as required by subsection (a) of this section within 20 business days.

(c) **Form of Notice.** -- Any insurer with twenty-five million dollars ($ 25,000,000) or more in annual vehicle insurance premium volume shall submit the notices required under this section by electronic means. All other insurers may submit the notices required under this section by either paper or electronic means.

(d) **Trade Secret Protection.** -- The names of insureds and the beginning date and termination date of insurance coverage provided to the Division by an insurer under this section constitutes a designated trade secret under G.S. 132-1.2.

(e) **Civil Penalty.** -- The Commissioner of Insurance may assess a civil penalty of two hundred dollars ($ 200.00) against an insurer that fails to notify the Division as required by this section. The Commissioner may waive the penalty if the insurer establishes good cause for the failure.

(f) **Clear Proceeds of Penalties.** -- The clear proceeds of all civil penalties, civil forfeitures, and civil fines that are collected by the Department of Transportation pursuant to this section shall be remitted to the Civil Penalty and Forfeiture Fund in accordance with G.S. 115C-457.2.

History.

2006-213, s. 1;2007-484, s. 7(b)

EDITOR'S NOTE. --

Session Laws 2006-213, s. 6, made this section effective July 1, 2008, and applicable to lapses occurring on or after that date.

N.C. Gen. Stat. § 20-310

Repealed by Session Laws 1993 (Reg. Sess., 1994), c. 761, s. 29.

CROSS REFERENCES. --

This section was repealed by Session Laws 1993 (Reg. Sess., 1994), c. 761, s. 29, effective February 1, 1995. For provisions concerning termination of a nonfleet private passenger motor vehicle insurance policy effective February 1, 1995, see G.S. 58-36-85.

N.C. Gen. Stat. § 20-310.1

Repealed by Session Laws 1963, c. 964, s. 3.

N.C. Gen. Stat. § 20-310.2

Repealed by Session Laws 1993 (Reg. Sess., 1994), c. 761, s. 31.

CROSS REFERENCES. --

This section was repealed by Session Laws 1993 (Reg. Sess., 1994), c. 761, s. 31, effective February 1, 1995. For provisions concerning termination of a nonfleet private passenger motor vehicle insurance policy effective February 1, 1995, see G.S. 58-36-85.

§ 20-311. Action by the Division when notified of a lapse in financial responsibility

(a) **Action.** -- When the Division receives evidence, by a notice of termination of a motor vehicle liability policy or otherwise, that the owner of a motor vehicle registered or required to be registered in this State does not have financial responsibility for the operation of the vehicle, the Division shall send the owner a letter. The letter shall notify the owner of the evidence and inform the owner that the owner shall respond to the letter within 10 days of the date on the letter and explain how the owner has met the duty to have

Chapter 20

continuous financial responsibility for the vehicle. Based on the owner's response, the Division shall take the appropriate action listed:

(1) **Division correction.** -- If the owner responds within the required time and the response establishes that the owner has not had a lapse in financial responsibility, the Division shall correct its records.

(2) **Penalty only.** -- If the owner responds within the required time and the response establishes all of the following, the Division shall assess the owner a penalty in the amount set in subsection (b) of this section:

a. The owner had a lapse in financial responsibility, but the owner now has financial responsibility.

b. The vehicle was not involved in an accident during the lapse in financial responsibility.

c. The owner did not operate the vehicle or allow the vehicle to be operated during the lapse with knowledge that the owner had no financial responsibility for the vehicle.

(3) **Penalty and revocation.** -- If the owner responds within the required time and the response establishes either of the following, the Division shall assess the owner a penalty in the amount set in subsection (b) of this section and revoke the registration of the owner's vehicle for the period set in subsection (c) of this section:

a. The owner had a lapse in financial responsibility and still does not have financial responsibility.

b. The owner now has financial responsibility even though the owner had a lapse, but the response also establishes any of the following:

1. The vehicle was involved in an accident during the lapse.

2. The owner operated the vehicle during the lapse with knowledge that the owner had no financial responsibility for the vehicle.

3. The owner allowed the vehicle to be operated during the lapse with knowledge that the owner had no financial responsibility for the vehicle.

(4) **Penalty and revocation for failure to respond.** -- Except as otherwise provided in this subdivision, if the owner does not respond within the required time, the Division shall assess a penalty in the applicable amount set forth in subsection (b) of this section and shall revoke the registration of the owner's vehicle for the period set in subsection (c) of this section. If the owner does not respond within the required time, but later responds and establishes

that the owner has not had a lapse in financial responsibility, the Division shall correct its records, rescind any revocation under this subdivision of the registration of the owner's vehicle, and the owner shall not be responsible for any fee or penalty arising under this section from the owner's failure to timely respond.

(b) **Penalty Amount.** -- The following table determines the amount of a penalty payable under this section by an owner who has had a lapse in financial responsibility; the amount is based on the number of times the owner has been assessed a penalty under this section during the three-year period before the date the owner's current lapse began:

Number of Lapses in Previous Three Years	Penalty Amount
None	$ 50.00
One	$ 100.00
Two or More	$ 150.00

(c) **Revocation Period.** -- The revocation period for a revocation based on a response that establishes that a vehicle owner does not have financial responsibility is indefinite and ends when the owner obtains financial responsibility or transfers the vehicle to an owner who has financial responsibility. The revocation period for a revocation based on a response that establishes the occurrence of an accident during a lapse in financial responsibility or the knowing operation of a vehicle without financial responsibility is 30 days. The revocation period for a revocation based on failure of a vehicle owner to respond is indefinite and ends when the owner (i) establishes that the owner has not had a lapse in financial responsibility, (ii) obtains financial responsibility, or (iii) transfers the vehicle to an owner who has financial responsibility, whichever occurs first.

(d) **Revocation Notice.** -- When the Division revokes the registration of an owner's vehicle, it shall notify the owner of the revocation. The notice shall inform the owner of the following:

(1) That the owner shall return the vehicle's registration plate and registration card to the Division, if the owner has not done so already, and that failure to do so is a Class 2 misdemeanor under G.S. 20-45.

(2) That the vehicle's registration plate and registration card are subject to seizure by a law enforcement officer.

(3) That the registration of the vehicle cannot be renewed while the registration is revoked.

(4) That the owner shall pay any penalties assessed within 30 days of the date of the notice, a restoration fee, and the fee for a registration plate when the owner applies

to the Division to register a vehicle whose registration was revoked.

(5) That failure of an owner to pay any penalty or fee assessed pursuant to this section shall result in the Division withholding the registration renewal of any motor vehicle registered in that owner's name.

(e) **Registration After Revocation.** -- A vehicle whose registration has been revoked may not be registered during the revocation period in the name of the owner, a child of the owner, the owner's spouse, or a child of the owner's spouse. This restriction does not apply to a spouse who is living separate and apart from the owner. At the end of a revocation period, a vehicle owner who has financial responsibility may apply to register a vehicle whose registration was revoked. The owner shall provide proof of current financial responsibility and pay any penalty assessed, a restoration fee of fifty dollars ($ 50.00), and the fee for a registration plate. Pursuant to G.S. 20-54, failure of an owner to pay any penalty or fee assessed pursuant to this section shall result in the Division withholding the registration renewal of any motor vehicle registered in that owner's name.

(f) **Clear Proceeds of Penalties.** -- The clear proceeds of all civil penalties, civil forfeitures, and civil fines that are collected by the Department of Transportation pursuant to this section shall be remitted to the Civil Penalty and Forfeiture Fund in accordance with G.S. 115C-457.2.

(g) **Military Waiver.** -- Notwithstanding the penalty and restoration fee provisions of this section, any monetary penalty or restoration fee shall be waived for any person who, at the time of notification of a lapse in financial responsibility, was deployed as a member of the Armed Forces of the United States outside of the continental United States for a total of 45 or more days. In addition, no insurance points under the Safe Driver Incentive Plan shall be assessed for any violation for which a monetary penalty or restoration fee is waived pursuant to this subsection. All of the following apply to a person qualifying under this subsection:

(1) The person shall have an affirmative defense to any criminal charge based upon the failure to return any registration card or registration plate to the Division.

(2) Upon reregistration, the person shall receive without cost from the Division all necessary registration cards or plates.

(3) Upon notice of revocation, the person shall be permitted to transfer the vehicle's registration immediately to his or her spouse, child, or spouse's child, notwithstanding the provisions of subsection (e) of this section.

(g1) **Out-of-State Waiver.** -- Notwithstanding the penalty and restoration fee provisions of this section, any monetary penalty or restoration fee shall be waived for any person who meets all of the following requirements:

(1) The owner has become a resident of another state and has registered the owner's vehicle in that state within 30 days of the cancellation or expiration of the owner's North Carolina motor vehicle liability policy.

(2) The owner has submitted a copy of their current out-of-state registration card to the Division.

(3) The owner has returned the North Carolina registration plate or has submitted an affidavit indicating that the North Carolina registration plate has been lost, stolen, or destroyed.

(h) **Applicability.** -- The penalty and revocation imposed under this section do not apply when the sole owner of a vehicle dies and that owner had financial responsibility for the vehicle as of the date of the owner's death.

History.
1957, c. 1393, s. 3; 1959, c. 1277, s. 2; 1963, c. 964, s. 4; 1965, c. 205; c. 1136, s. 3; 1967, c. 822, s. 3; c. 857, s. 4; 1971, c. 477, s. 3; 1975, c. 348, s. 4; c. 716, s. 5; 1979, 2nd Sess., c. 1279, s. 2; 1983, c. 761, s. 147; 1983 (Reg. Sess., 1984), c. 1069, s. 2; 2006-213, s. 2;2006-264, s. 38;2007-484, ss. 7(c), (d); 2011-183, s. 24;2015-241, s. 29.31(a);2019-227, s. 4

EDITOR'S NOTE. --
Subsection (g) was formerly codified as G.S. 20-309(h). It was recodified as G.S. 20-311(g) by Session Laws 2007-484, s. 7(d), which was effective on the effective date of Session Laws 2006-213 (July 1, 2008), and applicable to lapses occurring on or after that date.

Session Laws 2015-241, s. 29.31(c), made subsection (h), as added by Session Laws 2015-241, s. 29.31(a), effective September 18, 2015, and made the remainder of the amendments to this section by Session Laws 2015-241, s. 29.31(a), effective January 1, 2016, and applicable to lapses in financial responsibility occurring on or after that date.

Session Laws 2015-241, s. 1.1, provides: "This act shall be known as 'The Current Operations and Capital Improvements Appropriations Act of 2015.'"

Session Laws 2015-241, s. 33.6, is a severability clause.

EFFECT OF AMENDMENTS. --
Session Laws 2011-183, s. 24, effective June 20, 2011, substituted "Armed Forces of the United States" for "United States Armed Forces" in the first sentence of subsection (g).

Session Laws 2015-241, s. 29.31(a), rewrote the section. For effective date and applicability, see editor's note.

Session Laws 2019-227, s. 4, effective September 27, 2019, added subsection (g1).

CITED in Griffin v. Hartford Accident & Indem. Co., 264 N.C. 212, 141 S.E.2d 300 (1965).

N.C. Gen. Stat. § 20-312

Repealed by Session Laws 2006-213, s. 5, effective July 1, 2008, and applicable to lapses occurring on or after that date.

§ 20-313. Operation of motor vehicle without financial responsibility a misdemeanor

(a) On or after July 1, 1963, any owner of a motor vehicle registered or required to be registered in this State who shall operate or permit such motor vehicle to be operated in this State without having in full force and effect the financial responsibility required by this Article shall be guilty of a Class 3 misdemeanor.

(b) Evidence that the owner of a motor vehicle registered or required to be registered in this State has operated or permitted such motor vehicle to be operated in this State, coupled with proof of records of the Division of Motor Vehicles indicating that the owner did not have financial responsibility applicable to the operation of the motor vehicle in the manner certified by him for purposes of G.S. 20-309, shall be prima facie evidence that such owner did at the time and place alleged operate or permit such motor vehicle to be operated without having in full force and effect the financial responsibility required by the provisions of this Article.

History.
1957, c. 1393, s. 5; 1959, c. 1277, s. 3; 1963, c. 964, s. 5; 1975, c. 716, s. 5; 1993, c. 539, s. 388;1994, Ex. Sess., c. 24, s. 14(c);2013-360, s. 18B.14 (*l*)

EDITOR'S NOTE. --
Session Laws 2013-360, s. 18B.14(n), provides: "This section becomes effective December 1, 2013. Prosecutions for offenses committed before the effective date of this section are not abated or affected by this section, and the statutes that would be applicable but for this section remain applicable to those prosecutions."

Session Laws 2013-360, s. 1.1, provides: "This act shall be known as the 'Current Operations and Capital Improvements Appropriations Act of 2013.'"

Session Laws 2013-360, s. 38.5 is a severability clause.

EFFECT OF AMENDMENTS. --
Session Laws 2013-360, s. 18B.14 (*l*), effective December 1, 2013, substituted "Class 3 misdemeanor" for "Class 1 misdemeanor" in subsection (a). For applicability, see Editor's note.

CONSTITUTIONALITY. --G.S. 20-111(1) and G.S. 20-313 bear a real and substantial relationship to public safety, and, therefore, he General Assembly had ample authority, under its police power, to enact the sections of the statute and to make their violation a criminal offense because there are ample public

safety justifications for the vehicle registration and financial responsibility requirements; if a defendant does not wish to follow these statutory requirements, he may exercise his right to travel in a variety of other ways, and if he wishes, he may walk, ride a bicycle or horse, or travel as a passenger in an automobile, bus, airplane or helicopter, but he cannot operate a motor vehicle on the public highways. State v. Sullivan, 201 N.C. App. 540, 687 S.E.2d 504 (2009), appeal denied, 364 N.C. 247, 699 S.E.2d 921 (2010), cert. denied, 562 U.S. 1138, 131 S. Ct. 937, 178 L. Ed. 2d 754, 2011 U.S. LEXIS 574 (U.S. 2011).

G.
S. 20-111 and G.S. 20-313 are not void for vagueness because the purpose of the statutes is very clear, and there is nothing in these statutes that forbids or requires doing an act in terms so vague that men of common intelligence must necessarily guess at its meaning and differ as to its application; defendant failed to demonstrate how the statutes failed to give him the type of fair notice that was necessary to enable him or anyone else operating a motor vehicle to conform their conduct to the law. State v. Sullivan, 201 N.C. App. 540, 687 S.E.2d 504 (2009), appeal denied, 364 N.C. 247, 699 S.E.2d 921 (2010), cert. denied, 562 U.S. 1138, 131 S. Ct. 937, 178 L. Ed. 2d 754, 2011 U.S. LEXIS 574 (U.S. 2011).

FAILURE TO PROVE OWNERSHIP. --State failed to adequately prove that defendant owned vehicle in question where the only evidence tending to prove his ownership was defendant's statement to a wrecker crew demanding that they not remove "his" car; such an "admission" was insufficient to prove ownership absent substantial independent evidence tending to establish its trustworthiness. State v. Harrell, 96 N.C. App. 426, 386 S.E.2d 103 (1989).

APPLIED in Underwood v. National Grange Mut. Liab. Co., 258 N.C. 211, 128 S.E.2d 577 (1962); State v. Green, 266 N.C. 785, 147 S.E.2d 377 (1966).

CITED in Griffin v. Hartford Accident & Indem. Co., 264 N.C. 212, 141 S.E.2d 300 (1965); State v. Scott, 71 N.C. App. 570, 322 S.E.2d 613 (1984); State v. Golden, 96 N.C. App. 249, 385 S.E.2d 346 (1989); State v. Washington, 193 N.C. App. 670, 668 S.E.2d 622 (2008).

§ 20-313.1. Making false certification or giving false information a misdemeanor

(a) Any owner of a motor vehicle registered or required to be registered in this State who shall make a false certification concerning his financial responsibility for the operation of such motor vehicle shall be guilty of a Class 1 misdemeanor.

(b) Any person, firm, or corporation giving false information to the Division concerning another's financial responsibility for the operation of a motor vehicle registered or required to be registered in this State, knowing or having reason to believe that such information is false, shall be guilty of a Class 1 misdemeanor.

History.

1963, c. 964, s. 6; 1975, c. 716, s. 5; 1993, c. 539, s. 389;1994, Ex. Sess., c. 24, s. 14(c)

§ 20-314. Applicability of Article 9A; its provisions continued

The provisions of Article 9A, Chapter 20 of the General Statutes, as amended, which pertain to the method of giving and maintaining proof of financial responsibility and which govern and define "motor vehicle liability policy" and assigned risk plans shall apply to filing and maintaining proof of financial responsibility required by this Article. It is intended that the provisions of Article 9A, Chapter 20 of the General Statutes, as amended, relating to proof of financial responsibility required of each operator and each owner of a motor vehicle involved in an accident, and relating to nonpayment of a judgment as defined in G.S. 20-279.1, shall continue in full force and effect.

History.

1957, c. 1393, s. 6; 1963, c. 964, s. 7

OWNER MUST SHOW PROOF OF FINANCIAL RESPONSIBILITY AS PREREQUISITE TO REGISTRATION. --This Article requires every owner of a motor vehicle, as a prerequisite to the registration thereof, to show "proof of financial responsibility" in the manner prescribed by the Motor Vehicle Safety and Financial Responsibility Act of 1953, Chapter 20, Article 9A. Jones v. State Farm Mut. Auto. Ins. Co., 270 N.C. 454, 155 S.E.2d 118 (1967).

INSURANCE POLICIES AND INSURERS' CERTIFICATES required by both Article 9A of this Chapter and this Article, are defined by Article 9A. Faizan v. Grain Dealers Mut. Ins. Co., 254 N.C. 47, 118 S.E.2d 303 (1961).

G.

S. 20-279.34 IS INCORPORATED BY REFERENCE into the Financial Responsibility Act of 1957 by this section. Harrelson v. State Farm Mut. Auto. Ins. Co., 272 N.C. 603, 158 S.E.2d 812 (1968).

THIS SECTION DOES NOT INCORPORATE G.S. 20-279.22 in this Article. Faizan v. Grain Dealers Mut. Ins. Co., 254 N.C. 47, 118 S.E.2d 303 (1961).

CITED in Swain v. Nationwide Mut. Ins. Co., 253 N.C. 120, 116 S.E.2d 482 (1960); Nixon v. Liberty Mut. Ins. Co., 258 N.C. 41, 127 S.E.2d 892 (1962); Daniels v. Nationwide Mut. Ins. Co., 258 N.C. 660, 129 S.E.2d 314 (1963).

§ 20-315. Commissioner to administer Article; rules and regulations

The Commissioner of Motor Vehicles shall administer and enforce the provisions of this Article relating to registration of motor vehicles and may make necessary rules and regulations for its administration.

History.

1957, c. 1393, s. 7

CITED in Levinson v. Travelers Indem. Co., 258 N.C. 672, 129 S.E.2d 297 (1963); GEICO v. Lumbermens Mut. Cas. Co., 269 N.C. 354, 152 S.E.2d 445 (1967).

§ 20-316. Divisional hearings upon lapse of liability insurance coverage

Any person whose registration plate has been revoked under G.S. 20-311 may request a hearing. Upon receipt of such request, the Division shall, as early as practical, afford an opportunity for hearing. At the hearing the duly authorized agents of the Division may administer oaths and issue subpoenas for the attendance of witnesses and the production of relevant books and documents. If it appears that continuous financial responsibility existed for the vehicle involved, or if it appears the lapse of financial responsibility is not reasonably attributable to the neglect or fault of the person whose registration plate was revoked, the Division shall withdraw its order of revocation and such person may retain the registration plate. Otherwise, the order of revocation shall be affirmed and the registration plate surrendered.

History.

1971, c. 1218, s. 1; 1973, c. 1144, ss. 1, 2; 1975, c. 716, s. 5; 2006-213, s. 3

N.C. Gen. Stat. § 20-316.1

Repealed by Session Laws 2006-213, s. 5, effective July 1, 2008, and applicable to lapses occurring on or after that date.

§ 20-317. Insurance required by any other law; certain operators not affected

This Article shall not be held to apply to or affect policies of automobile insurance against liability which may now or hereafter be required by any other law of this State, and such policies, if they contain an agreement or are endorsed to conform to the requirements of this Article, may be certified as proof of financial responsibility under this Article. This Article applies to vehicles of motor carriers required to register with the Division under G.S. 20-382 or G.S. 20-382.1 only to the extent that the amount of financial responsibility required by this Article exceeds the amount required by the United States Department of Transportation.

History.

1957, c. 1393, s. 9; 1959, c. 1252, s. 1; 1975, c. 716, s. 5; 1995 (Reg. Sess., 1996), c. 756, s. 19

Chapter 20

§ 20-318. Federal, State and political subdivision vehicles excepted

This Article does not apply to any motor vehicle owned by the State of North Carolina or by a political subdivision of the State, nor to any motor vehicle owned by the federal government.

History.
1957, c. 1393, s. 10

§ 20-319. Effective date

This Article shall be effective from and after January 1, 1958.

History.
1957, c. 1393, s. 12; 1961, c. 276
CITED in Faizan v. Grain Dealers Mut. Ins. Co., 254 N.C. 47, 118 S.E.2d 303 (1961); Grant v. State Farm Mut. Auto. Ins. Co., 1 N.C. App. 76, 159 S.E.2d 368 (1968).

LEGAL PERIODICALS. --
For note on the State's inability to suspend the driver's license of a bankrupt who fails to satisfy an accident judgment debt, see 50 N.C.L. Rev. 350 (1972).

ARTICLE 13A.
CERTIFICATION OF AUTOMOBILE INSURANCE COVERAGE BY INSURANCE COMPANIES

§ 20-319.1. Company to forward certification within seven days after receipt of request

Upon the receipt by an insurance company at its home office of a registered letter from an insured requesting that it certify to the North Carolina Division of Motor Vehicles whether or not a previously issued policy of automobile liability insurance was in full force and effect on a designated day, it shall be the duty of such insurance company to forward such certification within seven days.

History.
1967, c. 908, s. 1; 1975, c. 716, s. 5

§ 20-319.2. Penalty for failure to forward certification

If any insurance company shall without good cause fail to forward said certification within seven days after its receipt of such registered letter, the North Carolina Commissioner of Insurance shall be authorized in his discretion to impose a civil penalty upon said company in the amount of two hundred dollars ($ 200.00) for such violation.

History.
1967, c. 908, s. 2

ARTICLE 14.
DRIVER TRAINING SCHOOL LICENSING LAW

§ 20-320. Definitions

As used in this Article:

(1) "Commercial driver training school" or "school" means a business enterprise conducted by an individual, association, partnership or corporation which educates or trains persons to operate or drive motor vehicles or which furnishes educational materials to prepare an applicant for an examination given by the State for a driver's license or learner's permit, and charges a consideration or tuition for such service or materials.

(2) "Commissioner" means the Commissioner of Motor Vehicles.

(3) "Instructor" means any person who operates a commercial driver training school or who teaches, conducts classes, gives demonstrations, or supervises practical training of persons learning to operate or drive motor vehicles in connection with operation of a commercial driver training school.

History.
1965, c. 873; 1979, c. 667, s. 39
CITED in Charlotte Truck Driver Training School, Inc. v. North Carolina DMV, 95 N.C. App. 209, 381 S.E.2d 861 (1989).

§ 20-321. Enforcement of Article by Commissioner

(a) The Commissioner shall adopt and prescribe such regulations concerning the administration and enforcement of this Article as are necessary to protect the public. The Commissioner or his authorized representative shall have the duty of examining applicants for commercial driver training schools and instructor's licenses, licensing successful applicants, and inspecting school facilities, records, and equipment.

(b) The Commissioner shall administer and enforce the provisions of this Article, and may call upon the State Superintendent of Public Instruction for assistance in developing and formulating appropriate regulations.

History.
1965, c. 873; 1973, c. 1331, s. 3; 1987, c. 69; c. 827, § 3

§ 20-322. Licenses for schools necessary; regulations as to requirements

(a) No commercial driver training school shall be established nor any such existing school be continued on or after July 1, 1965, unless such school applies for and obtains from the Commissioner a license in the manner and form prescribed by the Commissioner.

(b) Regulations adopted by the Commissioner shall state the requirements for a school license, including requirements concerning location, equipment, courses of instruction, instructors, financial statements, schedule of fees and charges, character and reputation of the operators, insurance, bond or other security in such sum and with such provisions as the Commissioner deems necessary to protect adequately the interests of the public, and such other matters as the Commissioner may prescribe. A driver education course offered to prepare an individual for a limited learner's permit or another provisional license must meet the requirements set in G.S. 115C-215 for the program of driver education offered in the public schools.

History.
1965, c. 873; 1997-16, s. 4;1997-443, s. 32.20;2011-145, s. 28.37(e)

EDITOR'S NOTE. --
Session Laws 1997-16, s. 10 provides that this act does not appropriate funds to the Division to implement this act nor does it obligate the General Assembly to appropriate funds to implement this act.

EFFECT OF AMENDMENTS. --
Session Laws 2011-145, s. 28.37(e), effective July 1, 2011, updated the section reference in the last sentence of subsection (b).

§ 20-323. Licenses for instructors necessary; regulations as to requirements

(a) No person shall act as an instructor on or after July 1, 1965, unless such person applies for and obtains from the Commissioner a license in the manner and form prescribed by the Commissioner.

(b) Regulations adopted by the Commissioner shall state the requirements for an instructor's license, including requirements concerning moral character, physical condition, knowledge of the courses of instruction, knowledge of the motor vehicle laws and safety principles, previous personal and employment records, and such other matters as the Commissioner may prescribe, for the protection of the public.

History.
1965, c. 873

§ 20-324. Expiration and renewal of licenses; fees

(a) **Renewal.** -- A license issued under this Article expires two years after the date the license is issued. To renew a license, the license holder must file an application for renewal with the Division.

(b) **Fees.** -- An application for an initial license or the renewal of a license must be accompanied by the application fee for the license. The application fee for a school license is eighty dollars ($ 80.00). The application fee for an instructor license is sixteen dollars ($ 16.00). The application fee for a license is not refundable. Fees collected under this section must be credited to the Highway Fund.

History.
1965, c. 873; 1977, c. 802, s. 9; 1981, c. 690, s. 15; 1997-33, s. 1

EDITOR'S NOTE. --
Session Laws 2020-3, s. 4.7(a) -(h), as amended by Session Laws 2020-97, ss. 3.15(a), 3.16(a), provides: "(a) Definition. -- For purposes of this section, 'credential' means any of the following issued by the Division of Motor Vehicles:

"(1) Drivers license.

"(2) Learner's permit.

"(3) Limited learner's permit.

"(4) Limited provisional license.

"(5) Full provisional license.

"(6) Commercial drivers license.

"(7) Commercial learner's permit.

"(8) Temporary driving certificate.

"(9) Special identification card.

"(10) Handicapped placard.

"(11) Vehicle registration.

"(12) Temporary vehicle registration.

"(13) Dealer license plate.

"(14) Transporter plate.

"(15) Loaner/Dealer 'LD' plate.

"(16) Vehicle inspection authorization.

"(17) Inspection station license.

"(18) Inspection mechanic license.

"(19) Transportation network company permit.

"(20) Motor vehicle dealer license.

"(21) Sales representative license.

"(22) Manufacturer license.

"(23) Distributor license.

"(24) Wholesaler license.

"(25) Driver training school license.

"(26) Driver training school instructor license.

"(27) Professional housemoving license.

"(b) Extend Validity of Credentials. -- Notwithstanding renewal, duration, or expiration provisions of G.S. 20-7, 20-11, 20-37.6, 20-37.7, 20-37.13, 20-50, 20-66, 20-79, 20-79.02, 20-79.2, 20-183.4B, 20-183.4D, 20-280.3, 20-288, 20-324, and 20-359, or any other provision of law to the contrary, the Division of Motor Vehicles shall extend for a period of five months the validity of any credential that expires on or after

March 1, 2020, and before August 1, 2020. The Division shall extend for a period of five months the validity of any credential listed in subdivisions (6), (7), (9), (10), and (18) of subsection (a) of this section that expires on or after March 1, 2020, and before the date 30 days after the date the Governor (i) rescinds Executive Order No. 116 or (ii) issues another executive order lifting restrictions on Division of Motor Vehicles functions. Notwithstanding G.S. 20-37.13(h) and G.S. 20-37.13A(a), the Division of Motor Vehicles is authorized to waive the requirement that commercial drivers license and commercial learner's permit holders have a medical examination and certification, as required by federal law, consistent with any waiver of medical qualifications standards issued by the Federal Motor Carrier Safety Administration. A credential extended under this section shall expire five months from the date it otherwise expires as prescribed by law prior to this section. However, the subsequent expiration of a credential extended under this section shall occur on the date prescribed by law prior to this section without regard to the extension. The Division shall notify individuals affected by an extension granted under this section, including information on new expiration dates and how the extension affects subsequent renewal and expiration dates.

"(b1) Extension of Intrastate Medical Waivers. -- Notwithstanding the limitation on duration of waivers in G.S. 20-37.13A(b), the Division of Motor Vehicles may extend for up to five months the validity of a medical waiver issued by the Division under G.S. 20-37.13A if the waiver expires on or after March 1, 2020, and before the date 30 days after the date the Governor (i) rescinds Executive Order No. 116 or (ii) issues another executive order lifting restrictions on Division of Motor Vehicles functions, and the Division's Medical Review Unit determines the extension is appropriate.

"(c) Driving Eligibility Certificates. -- Notwithstanding G.S. 20-11(n)(3), a driving eligibility certificate dated on or after February 9, 2020, and before March 10, 2020, remains valid and may be accepted by the Division of Motor Vehicles to meet the requirements for a license or permit issued under G.S. 20-11 until 30 days after the date the Governor rescinds Executive Order No. 116 or the date the Division reopens all drivers license offices, whichever is earlier.

"(d) Waive Penalties. -- Notwithstanding any provision of law to the contrary, the Division shall waive any fines, fees, or penalties associated with failing to renew a credential during the period of time the credential is valid by extension under subsection (b) of this section.

"(e) Motor Vehicle Taxes. -- Notwithstanding any provision of law to the contrary, due dates for motor vehicle taxes that are tied to registration expiration under Article 22A of Chapter 105 of the General Statutes shall be extended to correspond with extended expiration dates under subsection (b) of this section.

"(f) Validity by Extension a Defense. -- A person may not be convicted or found responsible for any offense resulting from failure to renew a credential issued by the Division if, when tried for that offense, the person shows that the offense occurred during the period of time the credential is valid by extension under subsection (b) of this section.

"(g) Report. -- Within 30 days of the extensions made under subsection (b) of this section, the Division shall submit a report to the Joint Legislative Transportation Oversight Committee and the Fiscal Research Division detailing implementation of this section.

"(h) Effective Date. -- This section is effective retroactively to March 1, 2020, and applies to expirations occurring on or after that date."

Session Laws 2020-3, s. 5, is a severability clause.

Session Laws 2020-97, s. 4.5, is a severability clause.

§ 20-325. Cancellation, suspension, revocation, and refusal to issue or renew licenses

The Commissioner may cancel, suspend, revoke, or refuse to issue or renew a school or instructor's license in any case where he finds the licensee or applicant has not complied with, or has violated any of the provisions of this Article or any regulation adopted by the Commissioner hereunder. A suspended or revoked license shall be returned to the Commissioner by the licensee, and its holder shall not be eligible to apply for a license under this Article until 12 months have elapsed since the date of such suspension or revocation.

History.

1965, c. 873

§ 20-326. Exemptions from Article

The provisions of this Article shall not apply to any person giving driver training lessons without charge, to employers maintaining driver training schools without charge for their employees only, or to schools or classes conducted by colleges, universities and high schools.

History.

1965, c. 873

§ 20-327. Penalties for violating Article or regulations

Violation of any provision of this Article or any regulation promulgated pursuant hereto, shall constitute a Class 3 misdemeanor.

History.

1965, c. 873; 1993, c. 539, s. 390; 1994, Ex. Sess., c. 24, s. 14(c)

§ 20-328. Administration of Article

This Article shall be administered by the Division of Motor Vehicles with no additional appropriations.

History.

1965, c. 873; 1973, c. 440; 1975, c. 716, s. 5

§§ 20-329 through 20-339

Reserved for future codification purposes.

ARTICLE 15.
VEHICLE MILEAGE ACT

§ 20-340. Purpose

This Article shall provide State remedies for persons injured by motor vehicle odometer alteration, and to provide purchasers of motor vehicles with information to assist them in determining the condition and value of such vehicles. Such remedies shall be in addition to remedies provided by the federal odometer law (Motor Vehicle Information and Cost Savings Act, Public Law 92-513, 86 Stat. 947, enacted October 20, 1972).

History.

1973, c. 679, s. 1
CITED in Miller v. Triangle Volkswagen, Inc., 55 N.C. App. 593, 286 S.E.2d 608 (1982); Washburn v. Vandiver, 93 N.C. App. 657, 379 S.E.2d 65 (1989).

§ 20-341. Definitions

As used in this Article:

(1) The term "odometer" means an instrument for measuring and recording the actual distance a motor vehicle travels while in operation; but shall not include any auxiliary odometer designed to be reset by the operator of the motor vehicle for the purpose of recording mileage on trips.

(2) The term "repair and replacement" means to restore to a sound working condition by replacing the odometer or any part thereof or by correcting what is inoperative.

(3) The term "transfer" means to change ownership by purchase, gift, or any other means.

(4) The term "transferee" means any person to whom the ownership in a motor vehicle is transferred or any person who, as agent, accepts transfer of ownership in a motor vehicle for another by purchase, gift, or any means other than by creation of a security interest.

(5) The term "transferor" means any person who or any person who, as agent, transfers his ownership in a motor vehicle by sale, gift or any means other than by creation of a security interest.

(6) The term "lessee" means any person, or the agent for any person, to whom a motor vehicle has been leased for a term of at least four months.

(7) The term "lessor" means any person, or the agent for any person, who has leased five or more vehicles in the past 12 months.

(8) The term "mileage" means the actual distance that a vehicle has traveled.

History.

1973, c. 679, s. 1; 1989, c. 482, s. 1

§ 20-342. Unlawful devices

It is unlawful for any person knowingly to advertise for sale, to sell, to use, or to install or to have installed, any device which causes an odometer to register any mileage other than the true mileage driven. For the purposes of this section, the true mileage driven is that mileage driven by the vehicle as registered by the odometer within the manufacturer's designed tolerance.

History.

1973, c. 679, s. 1

§ 20-343. Unlawful change of mileage

It is unlawful for any person or his agent to disconnect, reset, or alter the odometer of any motor vehicle with the intent to change the number of miles indicated thereon. Whenever evidence shall be presented in any court of the fact that an odometer has been reset or altered to change the number of miles indicated thereon, it shall be prima facie evidence in any court in the State of North Carolina that the resetting or alteration was made by the person, firm or corporation who held title or by law was required to hold title to the vehicle in which the reset or altered odometer was installed at the time of such resetting or alteration or if such person has more than 20 employees and has specifically and in writing delegated responsibility for the motor vehicle to an agent, that the resetting or alteration was made by the agent.

History.

1973, c. 679, s. 1; 1979, c. 696
EFFECT OF 1979 AMENDMENT. --The 1979 amendment, which added the second sentence to this section, is a procedural statute establishing a prima facie case upon the presentation of the required evidence; it does not alter the substantive law but is solely procedural, not affecting any vested rights of defendant. Duffer v. Royal Dodge, Inc., 51 N.C. App. 129, 275 S.E.2d 206 (1981).

ODOMETER ALTERATION PROHIBITED BY THIS SECTION IS A VIOLATION OF MOTOR VEHICLE LAWS OF NORTH CAROLINA as that term is used in G.S. 20-28.1(c). Evans v. Roberson, 314 N.C. 315, 333 S.E.2d 228 (1985).

§ 20-344. Operation of vehicle with intent to defraud

It is unlawful for any person with the intent to defraud to operate a motor vehicle on any street or highway knowing that the odometer of such vehicle is disconnected or nonfunctional.

History.

1973, c. 679, s. 1

§ 20-345. Conspiracy

No person shall conspire with any other person to violate G.S. 20-342, 20-343, 20-344, 20-346, 20-347, or 20-347.1.

History.

1973, c. 679, s. 1; 1989, c. 482, s. 7

§ 20-346. Lawful service, repair, or replacement of odometer

Nothing in this Article shall prevent the service, repair, or replacement of an odometer, provided the mileage indicated thereon remains the same as before the service, repair, or replacement. Where the odometer is incapable of registering the same mileage as before such service, repair, or replacement, the odometer shall be adjusted to read zero and a notice in writing shall be attached to the left door frame of the vehicle by the owner or his agent specifying the mileage prior to repair or replacement of the odometer and the date on which it was repaired or replaced. Any removal or alteration of such notice so affixed shall be unlawful.

History.

1973, c. 679, s. 1

APPLIED in Roberts v. Buffaloe, 43 N.C. App. 368, 258 S.E.2d 861 (1979).

CITED in Miller v. Triangle Volkswagen, Inc, 55 N.C. App. 593, 286 S.E.2d 608 (1982); McCracken v. Anderson Chevrolet-Olds, Inc., 82 N.C. App. 521, 346 S.E.2d 683 (1986).

§ 20-347. Disclosure requirements

(a) In connection with the transfer of a motor vehicle, the transferor shall disclose the mileage to the transferee in writing on the title or on the document used to reassign the title. This written disclosure must be signed by the transferor,

including the printed name, and shall contain the following information:

(1) The odometer reading at the time of the transfer (not to include tenths of miles);

(2) The date of the transfer;

(3) The transferor's name and current address;

(3a) The transferee's printed name, signature and current address;

(4) The identity of the vehicle, including its make, model, body type, and vehicle identification number, and the license plate number most recently used on the vehicle; and

(5) Certification by the transferor that to the best of his knowledge the odometer reading

a. Reflects the actual mileage; or

b. Reflects the amount of mileage in excess of the designed mechanical odometer limit; or

c. Does not reflect the actual mileage and should not be relied on.

(6), (7) Repealed by Session Laws 1989, c. 482, s. 2.

(a1) Before executing any transfer of ownership document, each lessor of a leased motor vehicle shall notify the lessee in writing that the lessee is required to provide written disclosure to the lessor regarding mileage. In connection with the transfer of ownership of the leased motor vehicle, the lessee shall furnish to the lessor a written statement signed by the lessee containing the following information:

(1) The printed name of the person making the disclosure;

(2) The current odometer reading (not to include tenths of miles);

(3) The date of the statement;

(4) The lessee's printed name and current address;

(5) The lessor's printed name, signature, and current address;

(6) The identity of the vehicle, including its make, model, year, body type, and vehicle identification number;

(7) The date that the lessor notified the lessee of the disclosure requirements and the date the lessor received the completed disclosure statement; and

(8) Certification by the lessee that to the best of his knowledge the odometer reading:

a. Reflects the actual mileage;

b. Reflects the amount of mileage in excess of the designed mechanical odometer limit; or

c. Does not reflect the actual mileage and should not be relied on.

If the lessor transfers the leased vehicle without obtaining possession of it, the lessor may indicate on the title the mileage disclosed by the lessee under this subsection, unless the lessor has reason to believe that the disclosure by the lessee does not reflect the actual mileage of the vehicle.

(b) Repealed by Session Laws 1973, c. 1088.

(c) It shall be unlawful for any transferor to violate any rules under this section or to knowingly give a false statement to a transferee in making any disclosure required by such rules.

(d) The provisions of this disclosure statement section shall not apply to the following transfers:

(1) A vehicle having a gross vehicle weight rating of more than 16,000 pounds.

(2) A vehicle that is not self-propelled.

(2a) A vehicle sold directly by the manufacturer to any agency of the United States in conformity with contractual specifications.

(3) A vehicle that is 10 years old or older.

(4) A new vehicle prior to its first transfer for purposes other than resale.

(5) A vehicle that is transferred by a State agency that assists the United States Department of Defense with purchasing, transferring, or titling a vehicle to another State agency, a unit of local government, a volunteer fire department, or a volunteer rescue squad.

History.

1973, c. 679, s. 1; c. 1088; 1983, c. 387; 1989, c. 482, ss. 2 -5; 1993, c. 553, s. 11;2009-550, s. 2(d)

EFFECT OF AMENDMENTS. --

Session Laws 2009-550, s. 2(d), effective August 28, 2009, added subdivision (d)(5) and made related changes.

IN ORDER TO ESTABLISH LIABILITY UNDER THIS SECTION AND G.S. 20-348, THE PLAINTIFF MUST SHOW (1) that the seller had either actual or constructive knowledge that the odometer was materially incorrect, and (2) that the seller acted with gross negligence or recklessness. McCraken v. Anderson Chevrolet-Olds, Inc., 82 N.C. App. 521, 346 S.E.2d 683 (1986).

Recovery pursuant to this section and G.S. 20-348 imposes no requirement to allege each element of fraud. However, plaintiff must show that defendant's failure to comply with the disclosure requirements was more than a technical failure; the noncompliance must have been induced by an intent to defraud. Schon v. Beeker, 94 N.C. App. 738, 381 S.E.2d 464 (1989).

INTENT TO DEFRAUD FOUND WHERE DEALER HAD REASON TO QUESTION ODOMETER MILEAGE. --The dealer acted with the intent to defraud, where the evidence showed that the dealer had some question as to the verity of the odometer mileage, yet all it did to confirm the mileage was to drive the vehicle, examine the interior and compare the mileage on the inspection sticker with the mileage on the odometer, and the evidence also showed that any mechanic could ascertain from the grease buildup on the chassis that the vehicle had been driven more

than the number of miles shown on the odometer, that several pieces of equipment, most noticeably the tires, were not of the original brand, and that the truck showed other signs of wear. To allow a dealer with expertise to ignore such indicators of wear would be to eviscerate the purpose of the statute. Levine v. Parks Chevrolet, Inc., 76 N.C. App. 44, 331 S.E.2d 747, cert. denied, 315 N.C. 184, 337 S.E.2d 858 (1985).

FOR EXAMPLE OF A COMPLAINT sufficient to allege a cause of action based upon this section and G.S. 20-348, see Schon v. Beeker, 94 N.C. App. 738, 381 S.E.2d 464 (1989).

APPLIED in Roberts v. Buffaloe, 43 N.C. App. 368, 258 S.E.2d 861 (1979); Duffer v. Royal Dodge, Inc., 51 N.C. App. 129, 275 S.E.2d 206 (1981).

CITED in United States v. Cotoia, 785 F.2d 497 (4th Cir. 1986).

§ 20-347.1. Odometer disclosure record retention

(a) Dealers and distributors of motor vehicles who are required by this Part to execute an odometer disclosure statement shall retain, for five years, a photostat, carbon, or other facsimile copy of each odometer mileage statement which they issue or receive. They shall retain all odometer disclosure statements at their primary place of business in an order that is appropriate to business requirements and that permits systematic retrieval.

(b) Lessors shall retain, for five years following the date they transfer ownership of the leased vehicle, each odometer disclosure statement which they receive from a lessee. They shall retain all odometer disclosure statements at their primary place of business in an order that is appropriate to business requirements and that permits systematic retrieval.

(c) Each auction company shall establish and retain at its primary place of business in an order that is appropriate to business requirements and that permits systematic retrieval, for five years following the date of sale of each motor vehicle, the following records:

(1) The name of the most recent owner (other than the auction company);

(2) The name of the buyer;

(3) The vehicle identification number; and

(4) The odometer reading on the date which the auction company took possession of the motor vehicle.

(d) Records required to be kept under this section shall be open to inspection and copying by law enforcement officers of the Division in order to determine compliance with this Article.

History.

1989, c. 482, s. 6

§ 20-348. Private civil action

(a) Any person who, with intent to defraud, violates any requirement imposed under this Article shall be liable in an amount equal to the sum of:

(1) Three times the amount of actual damages sustained or one thousand five hundred dollars ($ 1,500), whichever is the greater; and

(2) In the case of any successful action to enforce the foregoing liability, the costs of the action together with reasonable attorney fees as determined by the court.

(b) An action to enforce any liability created under subsection (a) of this section may be brought in any court of the trial division of the General Court of Justice of the State of North Carolina within four years from the date on which the liability arises.

History.

1973, c. 679, s. 1; 1981 (Reg. Sess., 1982), c. 1280, s. 1

IN ORDER TO ESTABLISH LIABILITY UNDER G.S. 20-347 AND THIS SECTION, THE PLAINTIFF MUST SHOW (1) that the seller had either actual or constructive knowledge that the odometer was materially incorrect, and (2) that the seller acted with gross negligence or recklessness. McCraken v. Anderson Chevrolet-Olds, Inc., 82 N.C. App. 521, 346 S.E.2d 683 (1986).

TO MAKE OUT A PRIMA FACIE CASE UNDER SUBSECTION (A) OF THIS SECTION, a plaintiff must establish (1) a violation of a requirement imposed under this Article, (2) that was made with the intent to defraud. McCracken v. Anderson Chevrolet-Olds, Inc., 82 N.C. App. 521, 346 S.E.2d 683 (1986).

CONSTRUCTIVE KNOWLEDGE THAT THE ODOMETER IS INCORRECT is established upon proof that the transferor either (a) recklessly disregarded indications that it was incorrect, or (b) in the exercise of reasonable care, should have known the odometer was incorrect. McCracken v. Anderson Chevrolet-Olds, Inc., 82 N.C. App. 521, 346 S.E.2d 683 (1986).

INTENT TO DEFRAUD ESSENTIAL TO ACTION FOR DAMAGES. --There must be more than a technical failure to comply in order to give rise to an action for damages under the Vehicle Mileage Act. The noncompliance must be accompanied by an intent to defraud. American Imports, Inc. v. G.E. Employees W. Region Fed. Credit Union, 37 N.C. App. 121, 245 S.E.2d 798 (1978).

Although knowledge of an incorrect odometer reading may, in some cases, be evidence of gross negligence or recklessness, a mere negligent violation of a disclosure requirement or even a knowing violation cannot support a private cause of action under subsection (a) of this section, absent evidence sufficient to demonstrate an intent to defraud. McCracken v. Anderson Chevrolet-Olds, Inc., 82 N.C. App. 521, 346 S.E.2d 683 (1986).

It was not error for the trial court to award plaintiffs $1,500 on each of the odometer statute violations since the issues submitted included a question of defendant's intent and the court properly explained the meaning of an intent to defraud to the jury. Washburn v. Vandiver, 93 N.C. App. 657, 379 S.E.2d 65 (1989).

Recovery pursuant to this section and G.S. 20-347 imposes no requirement to allege each element of fraud. However, plaintiff must show that defendant's failure to comply with the disclosure requirements was more than a technical failure; the noncompliance must have been induced by an intent to defraud. Schon v. Beeker, 94 N.C. App. 738, 381 S.E.2d 464 (1989).

In order to properly plead a cause of action under G.S. 20-71.4(a), and G.S. 20-348(a), a plaintiff must allege fraudulent intent in addition to a violation of the disclosure provisions of G.S. 20-71.4(a). Bowman v. Alan Vester Ford Lincoln Mercury, 151 N.C. App. 603, 566 S.E.2d 818 (2002).

WHERE PLAINTIFF SEEKS TREBLE DAMAGES AND PUNITIVE DAMAGES in an action against defendant car dealer in which he alleges that defendant sold him a car and alleged that the odometer reading was accurate when he knew that the true mileage was far in excess of that shown on the odometer, plaintiff's prayer for punitive damages cannot be sustained, even if the jury answers the liability issue in favor of plaintiff. Plaintiff's recovery, if any, will be the greater of three times his actual damages or $1,500, costs and reasonable attorneys' fees as determined by the court. Roberts v. Buffaloe, 43 N.C. App. 368, 258 S.E.2d 861 (1979).

PLAINTIFF MUST ELECT REMEDIES. --Pursuant to the doctrine of election of remedies, a party may not recover twice based on the same conduct; trial court erred in awarding the buyers in a used car purchase transaction treble damages under both G.S. 20-348(a) and G.S. ch. 75. Blankenship v. Town & Country Ford, Inc., 174 N.C. App. 764, 622 S.E.2d 638 (2005).

ASSESSMENT OF DAMAGES ON BOTH AN UNFAIR TRADE PRACTICES CLAIM AND ODOMETER STATUTE VIOLATIONS DID NOT AMOUNT TO A DOUBLE RECOVERY since an action for unfair or deceptive acts or practices is a distinct action apart from fraud, breach of contract, or violation of State and federal odometer statutes; where jury concluded that plaintiffs had been damaged in the amount of $1,300 pursuant to the unfair trade practices claim and the trial court then trebled this amount and where the trial court then assessed $1,500 on each of the odometer statute violations as required by statute plaintiffs were not awarded double recovery. Washburn v. Vandiver, 93 N.C. App. 657, 379 S.E.2d 65 (1989).

FOR EXAMPLE OF A COMPLAINT sufficient to allege a cause of action based upon G.S. 20-347 and this section, see Schon v. Beeker, 94 N.C. App. 738, 381 S.E.2d 464 (1989).

DEFENDANTS COMMITTED UNFAIR AND DECEPTIVE TRADE PRACTICES where car sold by

Chapter 20

defendants was severely structurally damaged, was not safe to operate, and plaintiff was misled by defendants into believing otherwise. Huff v. Autos Unlimited, Inc., 124 N.C. App. 410, 477 S.E.2d 86 (1996), cert. denied, 346 N.C. 279, 486 S.E.2d 546 (1997).

EVIDENCE HELD INSUFFICIENT. --Under the evidence, there was no more than a suspicion that defendant was grossly negligent or recklessly disregarded any indications that truck had been driven more than 19,000 miles in 14 months, and judgment under subsection (a) of this section would be reversed. McCracken v. Anderson Chevrolet-Olds, Inc., 82 N.C. App. 521, 346 S.E.2d 683 (1986).

APPLIED in Levine v. Parks Chevrolet, Inc., 76 N.C. App. 44, 331 S.E.2d 747 (1985); Payne v. Parks Chevrolet, Inc., 119 N.C. App. 383, 458 S.E.2d 716 (1995).

CITED in Wilson v. Sutton, 124 N.C. App. 170, 476 S.E.2d 467 (1996); Blankenship v. Town & Country Ford, Inc., 155 N.C. App. 161, 574 S.E.2d 132 (2002), cert. denied, appeal dismissed, 357 N.C. 61, 579 S.E.2d 384 (2003).

§ 20-349. Injunctive enforcement

Upon petition by the Attorney General of North Carolina, a violation of this Article may be enjoined as an unfair and deceptive trade practice, as prohibited by G.S. 75-1.1.

History.
1973, c. 679, s. 1
INTENT TO DEFRAUD NOT REQUIRED. --Intent to defraud the plaintiff is not required in an action for injunctive relief against a violator under this section, or to impose misdemeanor criminal penalties under G.S. 20-350, although both of these statutes require proof of knowledge by the transferor. McCracken v. Anderson Chevrolet-Olds, Inc., 82 N.C. App. 521, 346 S.E.2d 683 (1986).

§ 20-350. Criminal offense

Any person, firm or corporation violating G.S. 20-343 shall be guilty of a Class I felony. A violation of any remaining provision of this Article shall be a Class 1 misdemeanor.

History.
1973, c. 679, s. 1; 1989, c. 482, s. 7.1;1993, c. 539, ss. 391, 1262; 1994, Ex. Sess., c. 24, s. 14(c)
INTENT TO DEFRAUD NOT REQUIRED. --Intent to defraud the plaintiff is not required in an action for injunctive relief against a violator under G.S. 20-349, or to impose misdemeanor criminal penalties under this section, although both of these statutes require proof of knowledge by the transferor. McCracken v. Anderson Chevrolet-Olds, Inc., 82 N.C. App. 521, 346 S.E.2d 683 (1986) (decided prior to 1993 amendment).
CITED in Evans v. Roberson, 69 N.C. App. 644, 317 S.E.2d 715 (1984).

ARTICLE 15A.
NEW MOTOR VEHICLES WARRANTIES ACT

§ 20-351. Purpose

This Article shall provide State and private remedies against motor vehicle manufacturers for persons injured by new motor vehicles failing to conform to express warranties.

History.
1987, c. 385, s. 1
LEGISLATIVE INTENT -- EFFECTIVE DATE. --The legislature did not express the intent that G.S. 20-351 to 351.10 be applied retroactively; nor is there any clear implication from the statute that the legislature intended to apply the statute retroactively. Instead, the legislature passed the statute in June of 1987 and made its intention clear that the statute become effective in October of 1987. Estridge v. Ford Motor Co., 101 N.C. App. 716, 401 S.E.2d 85 (1991), cert. denied, 329 N.C. 267, 404 S.E.2d 867 (1991).

ACT IS INAPPLICABLE TO LEASES EXECUTED PRIOR TO EFFECTIVE DATE. --Plaintiff's claim based on the New Motor Vehicles Warranties Act was properly dismissed even though no defects existed prior to the enactment of statute. Application of "Lemon Law" to lease executed prior to effective date of statute is retroactive and improper, without legislative intent for retroactive application. Estridge v. Ford Motor Co., 101 N.C. App. 716, 401 S.E.2d 85 (1991), cert. denied, 329 N.C. 267, 404 S.E.2d 867 (1991).

MANUFACTURER'S DEFICIENT DISCLOSURE regarding the necessity of a written notification of nonconformity relieved plaintiff from the written notice requirement as well as the requirement that the manufacturer be allowed a reasonable time to make repairs; therefore, defendant manufacturer was not entitled to summary judgment on plaintiff's claim under the New Vehicles Act. Anders v. Hyundai Motor Am. Corp., 104 N.C. App. 61, 407 S.E.2d 618, cert. denied, 330 N.C. 440, 412 S.E.2d 69 (1991).

THE LEMON LAW HAS SEVERAL PURPOSES; it protects consumers who purchase defective new vehicles, it encourages private settlement between consumers and manufacturers, and it seeks a fair result that neither unduly benefits nor unduly burdens either party to a dispute. Buford v. GMC, 339 N.C. 396, 451 S.E.2d 293 (1994).

ORDER TO REPURCHASE VEHICLE PROPER. --Trial court properly ordered a manufacturer to repurchase a vehicle in a claim under the Lemon Law, G.S. 20-351, because there was no fact issue as to the sufficiency of the buyers' notice of nonconformity, the 15-day period to cure an alleged defect under G.S. 20-351.5(a) began when manufacturer received written notice of the nonconformity, the buyers afforded a reasonable period, not to exceed 15 days, to correct the nonconformity, and the manufacturer failed to timely repair the vehicle; however, the attorney's fees award was error because there was no evidence that the manufacturer acted unreasonably, and the record was devoid of evidence that the manufacturer did anything but act altogether reasonably from the time it learned of the buyers' complaints about their vehicle. Further, the buyers were not entitled to treble damages where, after receiving the buyers' letter alleging violations on July 27, 2010, the manufacturer successfully contacted the buyers' attorney via faxed letter on August 6, 2010, the manufacturer made several settlement offers and ultimately set up an inspection and repair, although outside of the 15-day cure period, and when the manufacturer's representative performed an inspection, he was able to identify and resolve the problem within a few days. Hardison v. Kia Motors Am., Inc., 226 N.C. App. 22, 738 S.E.2d 814 (2013).

APPLIED in Adventure Travel World, Ltd. v. GMC, 107 N.C. App. 573, 421 S.E.2d 173 (1992).

CITED in Dallaire v. Bank of Am., N.A., 224 N.C. App. 248, 738 S.E.2d 731 (2012), rev'd 760 S.E.2d 263, 2014 N.C. LEXIS 408 (2014). Stunzi v. Medlin Motors, Inc., 214 N.C. App. 332, 714 S.E.2d 770 (2011).

LEGAL PERIODICALS. --
For note on North Carolina's automobile warranty legislation, see 66 N.C.L. Rev. 1080 (1988).

§ 20-351.1. Definitions

As used in this Article:

(1) "Consumer" means the purchaser, other than for purposes of resale, or lessee from a commercial lender, lessor, or from a manufacturer or dealer, of a motor vehicle, and any other person entitled by the terms of an express warranty to enforce the obligations of that warranty.

(2) "Manufacturer" means any person or corporation, resident or nonresident, who manufactures or assembles or imports or distributes new motor vehicles which are sold in the State of North Carolina.

(3) "Motor vehicle" includes a motor vehicle as defined in G.S. 20-4.01 that is sold or leased in this State, but does not include "house trailer" as defined in G.S. 20-4.01 or any motor vehicle that weighs more than 10,000 pounds.

(4) "New motor vehicle" means a motor vehicle for which a certificate of origin, as required by G.S. 20-52.1 or a similar requirement in another state, has never been supplied to a consumer, or which a manufacturer, its agent, or its authorized dealer states in writing is being sold as a new motor vehicle.

History.
1987, c. 385, s. 1; 1989, c. 43, s. 2;c. 519, s. 2;2005-436, s. 1

EFFECT OF AMENDMENTS. --
Session Laws 2005-436, s. 1, effective October 1, 2005, and applicable to contracts entered into on or after that date, rewrote subdivision (3).

CITED in Anders v. Hyundai Motor Am. Corp., 104 N.C. App. 61, 407 S.E.2d 618 (1991); Taylor v. Volvo N. Am. Corp., 107 N.C. App. 678, 421 S.E.2d 617 (1992); Buford v. GMC, 339 N.C. 396, 451 S.E.2d 293 (1994).

§ 20-351.2. Require repairs; when mileage warranty begins to accrue

(a) Express warranties for a new motor vehicle shall remain in effect at least one year or 12,000 miles. If a new motor vehicle does not conform to all applicable express warranties for a period of one year, or the term of the express warranties, whichever is greater, following the date of original delivery of the motor vehicle to the consumer, and the consumer reports the nonconformity to the manufacturer, its agent, or its authorized dealer during such period, the manufacturer shall make, or arrange to have made, repairs necessary to conform the vehicle to the express warranties, whether or not these repairs are made after the expiration of the applicable warranty period.

(b) Any express warranty for a new motor vehicle expressed in terms of a certain number of miles shall begin to accrue from the mileage on the odometer at the date of original delivery to the consumer.

History.
1987, c. 385, s. 1; 1989, c. 14

A MANUFACTURER'S EXPRESS WARRANTIES DO NOT NECESSARILY INCLUDE that the vehicle will meet its owner's, or lessor's, expectations. Taylor v. Volvo N. Am. Corp., 339 N.C. 238, 451 S.E.2d 618 (1994).

CAUSE OF NONCONFORMITY. --There is no statutory requirement that the buyer in all cases prove the cause of the nonconformity or identify any specific mechanical defect related to the nonconformity. Taylor v. Volvo N. Am. Corp., 339 N.C. 238, 451 S.E.2d 618 (1994).

ALTHOUGH PLAINTIFF DID NOT SHOW THE PRECISE MECHANICAL DEFECT WITHIN HIS BRAKING SYSTEM, he produced enough evidence to establish that shimmy and clicking were caused by a "defect" in the braking system; since, the warranty covered shimmying and clicking caused by a "defect," plaintiff's evidence was sufficient to support the trial court's finding that the shimmy and clicking constituted a nonconformity to, or breach of, the warranty. Taylor v. Volvo N. Am. Corp., 339 N.C. 238, 451 S.E.2d 618 (1994).

APPLIED in Taylor v. Volvo N. Am. Corp., 107 N.C. App. 678, 421 S.E.2d 617 (1992).

CITED in Anders v. Hyundai Motor Am. Corp., 104 N.C. App. 61, 407 S.E.2d 618 (1991); Estridge v. Ford Motor Co., 101 N.C. App. 716, 401 S.E.2d 85 (1991).

§ 20-351.3. Replacement or refund; disclosure requirement

(a) When the consumer is the purchaser or a person entitled by the terms of the express warranty to enforce the obligations of the warranty, if the manufacturer is unable, after a reasonable number of attempts, to conform the motor vehicle to any express warranty by repairing or correcting, or arranging for the repair or correction of, any defect or condition or series of defects or conditions which substantially impair the value of the motor vehicle to the consumer, and which occurred no later than 24 months or 24,000 miles following original delivery of the vehicle, the manufacturer shall, at the option of the consumer, replace the vehicle with a comparable new motor vehicle or accept return of the vehicle from the consumer and refund to the consumer the following:

(1) The full contract price including, but not limited to, charges for undercoating, dealer preparation and transportation, and installed options, plus the non-refundable portions of extended warranties and service contracts;

(2) All collateral charges, including but not limited to, sales tax, license and registration fees, and similar government charges;

(3) All finance charges incurred by the consumer after he first reports the nonconformity to the manufacturer, its agent, or its authorized dealer; and

(4) Any incidental damages and monetary consequential damages.

(b) When consumer is a lessee, if the manufacturer is unable, after a reasonable number of attempts, to conform the motor vehicle to any express warranty by repairing or correcting, or arranging for the repair or correction of, any defect or condition or series of defects or conditions which substantially impair the value of the motor vehicle to the consumer, and which occurred no later than 24 months or 24,000 miles following original delivery of the vehicle, the manufacturer shall, at the option of the consumer, replace the vehicle with a comparable new motor vehicle or accept return of the vehicle from the consumer and refund the following:

(1) To the consumer:

a. All sums previously paid by the consumer under the terms of the lease;

b. All sums previously paid by the consumer in connection with entering into the lease agreement, including, but not limited to, any capitalized cost reduction, sales tax, license and registration fees, and similar government charges; and

c. Any incidental and monetary consequential damages.

(2) To the lessor, a full refund of the lease price, plus an additional amount equal to five percent (5%) of the lease price, less eighty-five percent (85%) of the amount actually paid by the consumer to the lessor pursuant to the lease. The lease price means the actual purchase cost of the vehicle to the lessor.

In the case of a refund, the leased vehicle shall be returned to the manufacturer and the consumer's written lease shall be terminated by the lessor without any penalty to the consumer. The lessor shall transfer title of the motor vehicle to the manufacturer as necessary to effectuate the consumer's rights pursuant to this Article, whether the consumer chooses vehicle replacement or refund.

(c) Refunds shall be made to the consumer, lessor, and any lienholders as their interests may appear. The refund to the consumer shall be reduced by a reasonable allowance for the consumer's use of the vehicle. A reasonable allowance for use is calculated from the number of miles used by the consumer up to the date of the third attempt to repair the same nonconformity which is the subject of the claim, or the twentieth cumulative business day when the vehicle is out of service by reason of repair of one or more nonconformities, whichever occurs first. The number of miles used by the consumer is multiplied by the purchase price of the vehicle or the lessor's actual lease price, and divided by 120,000.

(d) If a manufacturer, its agent, or its authorized dealer resells a motor vehicle that was returned pursuant to this Article or any other State's applicable law, regardless of whether there was any judicial determination that the motor vehicle had any defect or that it failed to conform to all express warranties, the manufacturer, its agent, or its authorized dealer shall disclose to the subsequent purchaser prior to the sale:

(1) That the motor vehicle was returned pursuant to this Article or pursuant to the applicable law of any other State; and

(2) The defect or condition or series of defects or conditions which substantially impaired the value of the motor vehicle to the consumer.

Any subsequent purchaser who purchases the motor vehicle for resale with notice of the return, shall make the required disclosures to any person to whom he resells the motor vehicle.

History.
1987, c. 385, s. 1; 1989, c. 43, s. 1;c. 519, s. 1;2005-436, s. 2

Chapter 20

EFFECT OF AMENDMENTS. --
Session Laws 2005-436, s. 2, effective October 1, 2005, and applicable to contracts entered into on or after that date, rewrote subsection (c).

A MANUFACTURER'S EXPRESS WARRANTIES DO NOT NECESSARILY INCLUDE that the vehicle will meet its owner's, or lessor's, expectations. Taylor v. Volvo N. Am. Corp., 339 N.C. 238, 451 S.E.2d 618 (1994).

CONSTRUCTION WITH OTHER PROVISIONS. --The remedies provision, G.S. 20-351.8, by referring directly to this section, fully incorporates the amount and type of relief available at the consumer's option into a jury's calculation of monetary damages. Buford v. GMC, 339 N.C. 396, 451 S.E.2d 293 (1994).

A CONSUMER MAY NOT RETAIN A VEHICLE FOR WHICH HE HAS RECEIVED A REFUND under the Lemon Law whether the refund arises out of a request by the consumer pursuant to subsection (a) or out of a judgment for monetary damages. Buford v. GMC, 339 N.C. 396, 451 S.E.2d 293 (1994).

DAMAGE CAUSED BY NON-MANUFACTURER PARTS WERE EXCLUDED FROM THE MANUFACTURER'S EXPRESS WARRANTY COVERAGE. --Under the express warranty related to a vehicle lease, damage caused by non-manufacturer parts were excluded from the manufacturer's express warranty coverage and thus could not have been the basis of relief under the New Motor Vehicles Warranties Act, G.S. 20-351.3; an affidavit submitted by the lessee did not create a fact issue as to whether the maker of the device at issue was authorized by the manufacturer, as it did not indicate how affiant had personal knowledge, but, in contrast, affidavits submitted by the manufacturer stated that their information was based on the affiants' personal knowledge. Eugene Tucker Builders, Inc. v. Ford Motor Co., 175 N.C. App. 151, 622 S.E.2d 698 (2005), cert. denied, 360 N.C. 479, 630 S.E.2d 926 (2006).

APPLIED in Taylor v. Volvo N. Am. Corp., 107 N.C. App. 678, 421 S.E.2d 617 (1992).

CITED in Anders v. Hyundai Motor Am. Corp., 104 N.C. App. 61, 407 S.E.2d 618 (1991); Estridge v. Ford Motor Co., 101 N.C. App. 716, 401 S.E.2d 85 (1991); Stunzi v. Medlin Motors, Inc., 214 N.C. App. 332, 714 S.E.2d 770 (2011).

§ 20-351.4. Affirmative defenses

It is an affirmative defense to any claim under this Article that an alleged nonconformity or series of nonconformities are the result of abuse, neglect, odometer tampering by the consumer or unauthorized modifications or alterations of a motor vehicle.

History.
1987, c. 385, s. 1
CITED in Taylor v. Volvo N. Am. Corp., 107 N.C. App. 678, 421 S.E.2d 617 (1992).

§ 20-351.5. Presumption

(a) It is presumed that a reasonable number of attempts have been undertaken to conform a motor vehicle to the applicable express warranties if:

(1) The same nonconformity has been presented for repair to the manufacturer, its agent, or its authorized dealer four or more times but the same nonconformity continues to exist; or

(2) The vehicle was out of service to the consumer during or while awaiting repair of the nonconformity or a series of nonconformities for a cumulative total of 20 or more business days during any 12-month period of the warranty,

provided that the consumer has notified the manufacturer directly in writing of the existence of the nonconformity or series of nonconformities and allowed the manufacturer a reasonable period, not to exceed 15 calendar days, in which to correct the nonconformity or series of nonconformities. The manufacturer must clearly and conspicuously disclose to the consumer in the warranty or owners manual that written notification of a nonconformity is required before a consumer may be eligible for a refund or replacement of the vehicle and the manufacturer shall include in the warranty or owners manual the name and address where the written notification may be sent. Provided, further, that notice to the manufacturer shall not be required if the manufacturer fails to make the disclosures provided herein.

(b) The consumer may prove that a defect or condition substantially impairs the value of the motor vehicle to the consumer in a manner other than that set forth in subsection (a) of this section.

(c) The term of an express warranty, the one-year period, and the 20-day period shall be extended by any period of time during which repair services are not available to the consumer because of war, strike, or natural disaster.

History.
1987, c. 385, s. 1
MANUFACTURER'S DEFICIENT DISCLOSURE regarding the necessity of a written notification of nonconformity relieved plaintiff from the written notice requirement as well as the requirement that the manufacturer be allowed a reasonable time to make repairs; therefore, defendant manufacturer was not entitled to summary judgment on plaintiff's claim under the New Vehicles Act. Anders v. Hyundai Motor Am. Corp., 104 N.C. App. 61, 407 S.E.2d 618, cert. denied, 330 N.C. 440, 412 S.E.2d 69 (1991).

ORDER TO REPURCHASE VEHICLE PROPER. --Trial court properly ordered a manufacturer to repurchase a vehicle in a claim under the Lemon Law, G.S. 20-351, because there was no fact issue as to the sufficiency of the buyers' notice of nonconformity, the 15-day period to cure an alleged defect under G.S. 20-351.5(a) began when manufacturer received written notice of the nonconformity, the buyers afforded a reasonable period, not to exceed 15 days, to correct the nonconformity, and the manufacturer failed to timely repair the vehicle; however, the attorney's fees award was error because there was no evidence that the manufacturer acted unreasonably, and the record was devoid of evidence that the manufacturer did anything but act altogether reasonably from the time it learned of the buyers' complaints about their vehicle. Further, the buyers were not entitled to treble damages where, after receiving the buyers' letter alleging violations on July 27, 2010, the manufacturer successfully contacted the buyers' attorney via faxed letter on August 6, 2010, the manufacturer made several settlement offers and ultimately set up an inspection and repair, although outside of the 15-day cure period, and when the manufacturer's representative performed an inspection, he was able to identify and resolve the problem within a few days. Hardison v. Kia Motors Am., Inc., 226 N.C. App. 22, 738 S.E.2d 814 (2013).

CITED in Taylor v. Volvo N. Am. Corp., 107 N.C. App. 678, 421 S.E.2d 617 (1992).

§ 20-351.6. Civil action by the Attorney General

Whenever, in his opinion, the interests of the public require it, it shall be the duty of the Attorney General upon his ascertaining that any of the provisions of this Article have been violated by the manufacturer to bring a civil action in the name of the State, or any officer or department thereof as provided by law, or in the name of the State on relation of the Attorney General.

History.
1987, c. 385, s. 1

§ 20-351.7. Civil action by the consumer

A consumer injured by reason of any violation of the provisions of this Article may bring a civil action against the manufacturer; provided, however, the consumer has given the manufacturer written notice of his intent to bring an action against the manufacturer at least 10 days prior to filing such suit. Nothing in this section shall prevent a manufacturer from requiring a consumer to utilize an informal settlement procedure prior to litigation if that procedure substantially complies in design and operation with the Magnuson-Moss Warranty Act, 15 USC § 2301 et seq., and regulations promulgated thereunder, and that requirement is written clearly and conspicuously, in the written warranty and any warranty instructions provided to the consumer.

History.
1987, c. 385, s. 1

§ 20-351.8. Remedies

In any action brought under this Article, the court may grant as relief:

(1) A permanent or temporary injunction or other equitable relief as the court deems just;

(2) Monetary damages to the injured consumer in the amount fixed by the verdict. Such damages shall be trebled upon a finding that the manufacturer unreasonably refused to comply with G.S. 20-351.2 or G.S. 20-351.3. The jury may consider as damages all items listed for refund under G.S. 20-351.3;

(3) A reasonable attorney's fee for the attorney of the prevailing party, payable by the losing party, upon a finding by the court that:

a. The manufacturer unreasonably failed or refused to fully resolve the matter which constitutes the basis of such action; or

b. The party instituting the action knew, or should have known, the action was frivolous and malicious.

History.
1987, c. 385, s. 1

CONSTRUCTION WITH OTHER PROVISIONS. --This section, by referring directly to G.S. 20-351.3, fully incorporates the amount and type of relief available at the consumer's option into a jury's calculation of monetary damages. Buford v. GMC, 339 N.C. 396, 451 S.E.2d 293 (1994).

ONLY THE NET LOSS TO THE CONSUMER SHOULD BE TREBLED. Taylor v. Volvo N. Am. Corp., 339 N.C. 238, 451 S.E.2d 618 (1994).

REDUCTION OF DAMAGES BY REASONABLE ALLOWANCE FOR USE. --Trial court improperly calculated plaintiff's recovery by failing to reduce plaintiff's damages by the reasonable allowance for use before trebling damages; since the allowance for plaintiff's use of vehicle exceeded his damages, plaintiff recovered no damages on his claim under the act. Taylor v. Volvo N. Am. Corp., 339 N.C. 238, 451 S.E.2d 618 (1994).

ATTORNEY'S FEES. --The term "court" as used in subdivision (3) of this section was interpreted to mean the trial judge. Therefore, for purposes of awarding attorney's fees, it is the trial judge, not the jury, that is to make the finding required by subdivision (3). After making such a finding, the court may, in its discretion, award attorney's fees. Buford v. GMC, 112 N.C. App. 437, 435 S.E.2d 782 (1993), reversed on other ground, 339 N.C. 396, 451 S.E.2d 293 (1994).

BUYERS NOT ENTITLED TO ATTORNEY'S FEES OR TREBLE DAMAGES. --Trial court properly ordered a manufacturer to repurchase a vehicle in a claim under the Lemon Law, G.S. 20-351, because there was no fact issue as to the sufficiency of the buyers' notice of nonconformity, the 15-day period to cure an alleged defect under G.S. 20-351.5(a) began when manufacturer received written notice of the nonconformity, the buyers afforded a reasonable period, not to exceed 15 days, to correct the nonconformity, and the manufacturer failed to timely repair the vehicle; however, the attorney's fees award was error because there was no evidence that the manufacturer acted unreasonably, and the record was devoid of evidence that the manufacturer did anything but act altogether reasonably from the time it learned of the buyers' complaints about their vehicle. Further, the buyers were not entitled to treble damages where, after receiving the buyers' letter alleging violations on July 27, 2010, the manufacturer successfully contacted the buyers' attorney via faxed letter on August 6, 2010, the manufacturer made several settlement offers and ultimately set up an inspection and repair, although outside of the 15-day cure period, and when the manufacturer's representative performed an inspection, he was able to identify and resolve the problem within a few days. Hardison v. Kia Motors Am., Inc., 226 N.C. App. 22, 738 S.E.2d 814 (2013).

LEGAL PERIODICALS. --

For note, "A Public Goods Approach to Calculating Reasonable Fees under Attorney Fee Shifting Statutes," see 1989 Duke L.J. 438.

§ 20-351.9. Dealership liability

No authorized dealer shall be held liable by the manufacturer for any refunds or vehicle replacements in the absence of evidence indicating that dealership repairs have been carried out in a manner substantially inconsistent with the manufacturers' instructions. This Article does not create any cause of action by a consumer against an authorized dealer.

History.
1987, c. 385, s. 1

§ 20-351.10. Preservation of other remedies

This Article does not limit the rights or remedies which are otherwise available to a consumer under any other law.

History.
1987, c. 385, s. 1

§ 20-351.11. Manufacturer's warranty for State motor vehicles that operate on diesel fuel

Every new motor vehicle purchased by the State that is designed to operate on diesel fuel shall be covered by an express manufacturer's warranty that allows the use of B-20 fuel, as defined in G.S. 143-58.4. This section does not apply if the intended use, as determined by the agency, of the new motor vehicle requires a type of vehicle for which an express manufacturer's warranty allows the use of B-20 fuel is not available.

History.
2007-420, s. 1

EDITOR'S NOTE. --

Session Laws 2007-420, s. 4, made this section effective January 1, 2008, and applicable to motor vehicles transferred to or purchased by the State on or after that date.

CITED in Stunzi v. Medlin Motors, Inc., 214 N.C. App. 332, 714 S.E.2d 770 (2011).

§§ 20-352, 20-353

Reserved for future codification purposes.

ARTICLE 15B.
NORTH CAROLINA MOTOR VEHICLE REPAIR ACT

§ 20-354. Short title

This act shall be known and may be cited as the "North Carolina Motor Vehicle Repair Act."

History.
1999-437, s. 1

EDITOR'S NOTE. --

The numbers §§ 20-354.1 to 20-354.9 were assigned by the Revisor of Statutes, the sections having been numbered §§ 20-354A to 20-354I by Session Laws 1999-437, s.1.

§ 20-354.1. Scope and application

This act shall apply to all motor vehicle repair shops in North Carolina, except:

(1) Any motor vehicle repair shop of a municipal, county, State, or federal government when carrying out the functions of the government.

(2) Any person who engages solely in the repair of any of the following:

    a. Motor vehicles that are owned, maintained, and operated exclusively by that person for that person's own use.

    b. For-hire vehicles which are rented for periods of 30 days or less.

(3) Any person who repairs only motor vehicles which are operated principally for

agricultural or horticultural pursuits on farms, groves, or orchards and which are operated on the highways of this State only incidentally en route to or from the farms, groves, or orchards.

(4) Motor vehicle auctions or persons in the performance of motor vehicle repairs solely for motor vehicle auctions.

(5) Any motor vehicle repair shop in the performance of a motor vehicle repair if the cost of the repair does not exceed three hundred fifty dollars ($ 350.00).

(6) Any person or motor vehicle repair shop in the performance of repairs on commercial construction equipment or motor vehicles that have a GVWR of at least 26,001 pounds.

(7) When a third party has waived in writing the right to receive written estimates from the motor vehicle repair shop; the third party indicates to the motor vehicle repair shop that the repairs will be paid for by the third party under an insurance policy, service contract, mechanical breakdown contract, or manufacturer's warranty; and the third party further indicates that the customer's share of the cost of repairs, if any, will not exceed three hundred fifty dollars ($ 350.00).

History.
1999-437, s. 1;2001-298, s. 1
EDITOR'S NOTE. --
This section was originally enacted by Session Laws 1999-437, s. 1, as G.S. 20-354A. It has been renumbered as this section at the direction of the Revisor of Statutes.

§ 20-354.2. Definitions

As used in this act:

(1) "Customer" means the person who signs the written repair estimate or any other person whom that person designates as a person who may authorize repair work.

(2) "Employee" means an individual who is employed full time or part time by a motor vehicle repair shop and performs motor vehicle repairs.

(3) "Motor vehicle" means any automobile, truck, bus, recreational vehicle, motorcycle, motor scooter, or other motor-powered vehicle, but does not include trailers, mobile homes, travel trailers, or trailer coaches without independent motive power, or watercraft or aircraft.

(4) "Motor vehicle repair" means all maintenance of and modification and repairs to motor vehicles and the diagnostic work incident to those repairs, including, but not limited to, the rebuilding or restoring of rebuilt vehicles, body work, painting, warranty work, shop supply fees, hazardous

material disposal fees incident to a repair, and other work customarily undertaken by motor vehicle repair shops. Motor vehicle repair does not include the sale or installation of tires when authorized by the customer.

(5) "Motor vehicle repair shop" means any person who, for compensation, engages or attempts to engage in the repair of motor vehicles owned by other persons and includes, but is not limited to:

    a. Mobile motor vehicle repair shops.

    b. Motor vehicle and recreational vehicle dealers.

    c. Garages.

    d. Service stations.

    e. Self-employed individuals.

    f. Truck stops.

    g. Paint and body shops.

    h. Brake, muffler, or transmission shops.

    i. Shops doing glasswork.

Any person who engages solely in the maintenance or repair of the coach portion of a recreational vehicle is not a motor vehicle repair shop.

History.
1999-437, s. 1;2005-463, s. 1
EDITOR'S NOTE. --
This section was originally enacted by Session Laws 1999-437, s. 1, as G.S. 20-354B. It has been renumbered as this section at the direction of the Revisor of Statutes.
EFFECT OF AMENDMENTS. --
Session Laws 2005-463, s. 1, effective October 3, 2005, inserted "shop supply fees, hazardous material disposal fees incident to a repair" in subdivision (4).
IN CONSTRUING A HOMEOWNERS ASSOCIATION'S DECLARATION OF COVENANTS, CONDITIONS AND RESTRICTIONS (CC&RS), PROPERTY OWNERS' RELIANCE ON G.S. 20-4.01(32A) AND (27)D2, AND G.S. 20-354.2 (defining travel trailer, camping trailer, motor vehicle, and motor home or house car) was misplaced; the statutes were enacted between six and sixteen years after the association's CC&Rs (referring to campers and all similar property) were drafted and recorded. The statutory provisions were not material to the issue of the drafters' intent in 1985 when the CC&Rs were drafted and recorded. Schwartz v. Banbury Woods Homeowners Ass'n, 196 N.C. App. 584, 675 S.E.2d 382 (2009), review denied, 363 N.C. 856, 694 S.E.2d 391, 2010 N.C. LEXIS 230 (2010).

§ 20-354.3. Written motor vehicle repair estimate and disclosure statement required

(a) When any customer requests a motor vehicle repair shop to perform repair work on a motor vehicle, the cost of which repair work will exceed three hundred fifty dollars ($ 350.00) to the customer, the shop shall prepare a written repair estimate, which is a form setting forth the estimated cost of repair work, including diagnostic work, before effecting any diagnostic work or repair. In determining under this section whether the cost of the repair work exceeds three hundred fifty dollars ($ 350.00), the cost of the repair work shall consist of the cost of parts and labor necessary for the repair work and any charges for necessary diagnostic work and teardown, if any, and shall include any taxes, any other repair shop supplies or overhead, and any other extra services that are incidental to the repair work. The written repair estimate shall also include a statement allowing the customer to indicate whether replaced parts should be saved for inspection or return and a statement indicating the daily charge for storing the customer's motor vehicle after the customer has been notified that the repair work has been completed.

(b) The information required by subsection (a) of this section need not be provided if the customer waives in writing his or her right to receive a written estimate. A customer may waive his or her right to receive any written estimates from a motor vehicle repair shop for a period of time specified by the customer in the waiver.

(c) Except as provided in subsection (e) of this section, a copy of the written repair estimate required by subsection (a) of this section shall be given to the customer before repair work is begun.

(d) If the customer leaves his or her motor vehicle at a motor vehicle repair shop during hours when the shop is not open, or if the motor vehicle repair shop reasonably believes that an accurate estimate of the cost of repairs cannot be made until after the diagnostic work has been completed, or if the customer permits the shop or another person to deliver the motor vehicle to the shop, there shall be an implied partial waiver of the written estimate; however, upon completion of the diagnostic work necessary to estimate the cost of repair, the shop shall notify the customer as required by G.S. 20-354.5(a).

(e) Nothing in this section shall be construed to require a motor vehicle repair shop to give a written estimate price if the motor vehicle repair shop does not agree to perform the requested repair.

History.
1999-437, s. 1;2001-298, s. 2;2005-304, s. 1
    EDITOR'S NOTE. --
    This section was originally enacted by Session Laws 1999-437, s. 1, as G.S. 20-354C. It has been renumbered as this section at the direction of the Revisor of Statutes.

EFFECT OF AMENDMENTS. --
Session Laws 2005-304, s. 1, effective October 1, 2005, and applicable to repair estimates that are made on or after that date, inserted the present second sentence of subsection (a).

§ 20-354.4. Charges for motor vehicle repair estimate; requirement of waiver of rights prohibited

(a) Before proceeding with preparing an estimate, the shop shall do both of the following:
    (1) Disclose to the customer the amount, if any, of the charge for preparing the estimate.
    (2) Obtain a written authorization to prepare an estimate if there is a charge for that estimate.

(b) It is a violation of this Article for any motor vehicle repair shop to require that any person waive his or her rights provided in this Article as a precondition to the repair of his or her vehicle by the shop or to impose or threaten to impose any charge which is clearly excessive in relation to the work involved in making the price estimate for the purpose of inducing the customer to waive his or her rights provided in this Article.

History.
1999-437, s. 1
    EDITOR'S NOTE. --
    This section was originally enacted by Session Laws 1999-437, s. 1, as G.S. 20-354D. It has been renumbered as this section at the direction of the Revisor of Statutes.

§ 20-354.5. Notification of charges in excess of repair estimate; prohibited charges; refusal to return vehicle prohibited; inspection of parts

(a) In the event that any of the following applies, the customer shall be promptly notified by telephone, telegraph, mail, or other means of the additional repair work and estimated cost of the additional repair work:
    (1) The written repair estimate contains only an estimate for diagnostic work necessary to estimate the cost of repair and such diagnostic work has been completed.
    (2) A determination is made by a motor vehicle repair shop that the actual charges for the repair work will exceed the written estimate by more than ten percent (10%).
    (3) An implied partial waiver exists for diagnostic work, and the diagnostic work has been completed.

When a customer is notified, he or she shall, orally or in writing, authorize, modify, or cancel the order for repair.

(b) If a customer cancels the order for repair or, after diagnostic work is performed, decides not to have the repairs performed, and if the customer authorizes the motor vehicle repair shop to reassemble the motor vehicle, the shop shall expeditiously reassemble the motor vehicle in a condition reasonably similar to the condition in which it was received.

After cancellation of the repair order or a decision by the customer not to have repairs made after diagnostic work has been performed, the shop may charge for and the customer is obligated to pay the cost of repairs actually completed that were authorized by the written repair estimate as well as the cost of diagnostic work and teardown, the cost of parts and labor to replace items that were destroyed by teardown, and the cost to reassemble the component or the vehicle, provided the customer was notified of these possible costs in the written repair estimate or at the time the customer authorized the motor vehicle repair shop to reassemble the motor vehicle.

(c) It is a violation of this Article for a motor vehicle repair shop to charge more than the written estimate and the amount by which the motor vehicle repair shop has obtained authorization to exceed the written estimate in accordance with subsections (a) or (b) of this section, plus ten percent (10%).

(d) It is a violation of this Article for any motor vehicle repair shop to refuse to return any customer's motor vehicle because the customer refused to pay for repair charges that exceed a written estimate and any amounts authorized by the customer in accordance with subsection (a) or (b) of this section by more than ten percent (10%), provided that the customer has paid the motor vehicle repair shop the amount of the estimate and the amounts authorized by the customer in accordance with subsections (a) and (b) of this section, plus ten percent (10%).

(e) Upon request made at the time the repair work is authorized by the customer, the customer is entitled to inspect parts removed from his or her vehicle or, if the shop has no warranty arrangement or exchange parts program with a manufacturer, supplier, or distributor, have them returned to him or her. A motor vehicle repair shop may discard parts removed from a customer's vehicle or sell them and retain the proceeds for the shop's own account if the customer fails to take possession of the parts at the shop within two business days after taking delivery of the repaired vehicle.

History.
1999-437, s. 1;2001-298, ss. 3, 4

EDITOR'S NOTE. --
This section was originally enacted by Session Laws 1999-437, s. 1, as G.S. 20-354E. It has been renumbered as this section at the direction of the Revisor of Statutes.

§ 20-354.6. Invoice required of motor vehicle repair shop

The motor vehicle repair shop shall provide each customer, upon completion of any repair, with a legible copy of an invoice for such repair. The invoice shall include the following information:

(1) A statement indicating what was done to correct the problem or a description of the service provided.

(2) An itemized description of all labor, parts, and merchandise supplied and the costs of all labor, parts, and merchandise supplied. No itemized description is required to be provided to the customer for labor, parts, and merchandise supplied when a third party has indicated to the motor vehicle repair shop that the repairs will be paid for under a service contract, under a mechanical breakdown contract, or under a manufacturer's warranty, without charge to the customer.

(3) A statement identifying any replacement part as being used, rebuilt, or reconditioned, as the case may be.

History.
1999-437, s. 1;2001-298, s. 5;2002-159, s. 32

EDITOR'S NOTE. --
This section was originally enacted by Session Laws 1999-437, s. 1, as G.S. 20-354F. It has been renumbered as this section at the direction of the Revisor of Statutes.

§ 20-354.7. Required disclosure; signs; notice to customers

A sign, at least 24 inches on each side, shall be posted in a manner conspicuous to the public. The sign shall contain:

(1) That the consumer has a right to receive a written estimate or to waive receipt of that estimate if the cost of repairs will exceed three hundred fifty dollars ($ 350.00).

(2) That the consumer may request, at the time the work order is taken, the return or inspection of all parts that have been replaced during the motor vehicle repair.

History.
1999-437, s. 1

EDITOR'S NOTE. --
This section was originally enacted by Session Laws 1999-437, s. 1, as G.S. 20-354G. It has been

Chapter 20

renumbered as this section at the direction of the Revisor of Statutes.

§ 20-354.8. Prohibited acts and practices

It shall be a violation of this Article for any motor vehicle repair shop or employee of a motor vehicle repair shop to do any of the following:

(1) Charge for repairs which have not been expressly or impliedly authorized by the customer.

(2) Misrepresent that repairs have been made to a motor vehicle.

(3) Misrepresent that certain parts and repairs are necessary to repair a vehicle.

(4) Misrepresent that the vehicle being inspected or diagnosed is in a dangerous condition or that the customer's continued use of the vehicle may be harmful or cause great damage to the vehicle.

(5) Fraudulently alter any customer contract, estimate, invoice, or other document.

(6) Fraudulently misuse any customer's credit card.

(7) Make or authorize in any manner or by any means whatever any written or oral statement which is untrue, deceptive, or misleading, and which is known, or which by the exercise of reasonable care should be known, to be untrue, deceptive, or misleading, related to this Article.

(8) Make fraudulent promises of a character likely to influence, persuade, or induce a customer to authorize the repair, service, or maintenance of a motor vehicle.

(9) Substitute used, rebuilt, salvaged, or straightened parts for new replacement parts without notice to the motor vehicle owner and to his or her insurer if the cost of repair is to be paid pursuant to an insurance policy and the identity of the insurer or its claims adjuster is disclosed to the motor vehicle repair shop.

(10) Cause or allow a customer to sign any work order that does not state the repairs requested by the customer.

(11) Refuse to give to a customer a copy of any document requiring the customer's signature upon completion or cancellation of the repair work.

(12) Rebuild or restore a rebuilt vehicle without the knowledge of the owner in a manner that does not conform to the original vehicle manufacturer's established repair procedures or specifications and allowable tolerances for the particular model and year.

(13) Perform any other act that is a violation of this Article or that constitutes fraud or misrepresentation under this Article.

History.
1999-437, s. 1

EDITOR'S NOTE. --
This section was originally enacted by Session Laws 1999-437, s. 1, as G.S. 20-354H. It has been renumbered as this section at the direction of the Revisor of Statutes.

§ 20-354.9. Remedies

Any customer injured by a violation of this Article may bring an action in the appropriate court for relief. The prevailing party in that action may be entitled to damages plus court costs and reasonable attorneys' fees. The customer may also bring an action for injunctive relief in the appropriate court. A violation of this Article is not punishable as a crime; however, this Article does not limit the rights or remedies which are otherwise available to a consumer under any other law.

History.
1999-437, s. 1

EDITOR'S NOTE. --
This section was originally enacted by Session Laws 1999-437, s. 1, as G.S. 20-354I. It has been renumbered as this section at the direction of the Revisor of Statutes.

ATTORNEYS' FEES AWARD IMPROPER. --Award of attorneys' fees pursuant to the statute was reversed because a driver's case against a collision repair shop was not tried under the North Carolina Motor Vehicle Repair Act, and the jury was neither given instructions on nor asked to render a verdict on any cause of action related to the Act; the driver brought his case without reference to, or reliance upon, the Act, and neither his pleadings nor his evidence gave any indication he was relying on the Act to remedy his loss. Ridley v. Wendel, 251 N.C. App. 452, 795 S.E.2d 807 (2016).

§§ 20-354.10 through 20-355

Reserved for future codification purposes.

ARTICLE 16.
PROFESSIONAL HOUSEMOVING

§ 20-356. Definitions

As used in this Article, the following terms mean:

(1) **Department. --** The Department of Transportation.

(2) **House. --** A dwelling, building, or other structure in excess of 15 feet in width. Mobile homes, manufactured homes, or modular homes, or portions thereof, are not within this definition when being

transported from the manufacturer or from a licensed retail dealer location to the first set-up site.

(3) **Housemover.** -- A person licensed under this Article.

(4) **Person.** -- An individual, corporation, partnership, association, or any other business entity.

(5) **Secretary.** -- The Secretary of the Department of Transportation.

(6) **Unsafe practices.** -- Any act that is determined by a final agency decision of an enforcing agency or by a court of competent jurisdiction to create a hazard to the motoring public, or any citations under the Occupational Safety and Health Act that have become a final order within the last three years for willful serious violations or for failing to abate serious violations, as defined in G.S. 95-127.

History.
1977, c. 720, s. 1; 1979, c. 475, s. 2; 2001-424, s. 27.17(a);2005-354, s. 1;2008-89, s. 1

EDITOR'S NOTE. --
This section, as rewritten by Session Laws 2008-89, s. 1, effective December 1, 2008, is applicable to licenses issued and offenses committed on or after that date, rewrote the section.

EFFECT OF AMENDMENTS. --
Session Laws 2005-354, s. 1, effective October 1, 2005, substituted "15" for "14" and inserted "or from a licensed retail dealer location" in the second sentence.

§ 20-357. Housemovers to be licensed

All persons who engage in the profession of housemoving on roads and highways on the State Highway System shall be licensed by the Department.

History.
1977, c. 720, s. 2

§ 20-358. Qualifications to become licensed

The Department shall issue annual printed licenses to applicants meeting the following conditions:

(1) The applicant must be at least 21 years of age; present acceptable evidence of good character and show sufficient housemoving experience on the application form furnished by the Department. Proof of creditable housemoving experience must be furnished at the time of application for those applicants not previously licensed by the Department. Creditable housemoving experience means extensive and responsible training gained by the applicant while engaged actively and directly on a full-time basis in the moving of houses and structures on public roads and highways with at least five years of experience. Examples of the capacity in which a person may work in gaining experience include the following in building moving operations:

    a. Moving superintendent,

    b. Moving foreman, and

    c. General mechanic and helper in the housemoving profession or trade.

To comply with the requirement of proof of creditable housemoving experience, each applicant not previously licensed under this Article shall submit to the Department an affidavit from a certified public accountant that the applicant has documented employment records for a period of five continuous years from a person or persons licensed by this State or another state for housemoving. Each applicant not previously licensed under this Article shall also submit to the Department affidavits from a person or persons licensed in this State or another state in housemoving, who have employed the applicant in housemoving, providing in detail the applicant's full-time experience, including any supervisory duties and experience, in housemoving.

(2) Repealed by Session Laws 1981, c. 818, s. 3.

(3) The applicant must furnish proof that all of the vehicles, excluding "beams and dollies" and "hauling units," to be used in the movement of buildings, structures, or other extraordinary objects wider than 15 feet have met the requirements of G.S. 20-183.2 pertaining to the equipment inspection of motor vehicles; provided that the "beams and dollies" and "hauling units" are excluded from inspection under G.S. 20-183.2 and, further, are not required to be equipped with brakes.

(4) The applicant must exhibit his federal employer's identification number.

(5) The applicant must pay an annual license fee of one hundred dollars ($ 100.00).

History.
1977, c. 720, s. 3; 1981, c. 818, s. 3; 1991 (Reg. Sess., 1992), c. 813, s. 2; 2005-354, s. 2;2008-89, s. 2

EDITOR'S NOTE. --
Session Laws 2008-89, s. 6, provides: "An applicant for a housemoving license under Article 16 of Chapter 20 of the General Statutes with at least 24 months' experience under G.S. 20-358(1) as of December 1, 2008, may be initially licensed without additional experience until December 1, 2011."

EFFECT OF AMENDMENTS. --
Session Laws 2005-354, s. 2, effective October 1, 2005, in subdivision (1), inserted the second sentence; and in subdivision (3), substituted "15" for "14."

Session Laws 2008-89, s. 2, effective December 1, 2008, and applicable to licenses issued and offenses committed on or after that date, in subdivision (1), substituted "21 years" for "18 years" in the first sentence, in the third sentence, substituted "Creditable housemoving" for "Housemoving" at the beginning, and substituted "five years of experience" for "24 months experience" at the end, and added the last paragraph.

CROSS REFERENCES. --
For present provisions similar to the subject matter of repealed subdivision (2), see G.S. 20-359.1.

§ 20-359. Effective period of license

A license issued hereunder shall be effective from date of issuance and expire on July 31 of each year and shall be renewable on an annual basis.

History.
1977, c. 720, s. 4; 2005-354, s. 3

EDITOR'S NOTE. --
Session Laws 2020-3, s. 4.7(a) -(h), as amended by Session Laws 2020-97, ss. 3.15(a), 3.16(a), provides:
"(a) Definition. -- For purposes of this section, 'credential' means any of the following issued by the Division of Motor Vehicles:
"(1) Drivers license.
"(2) Learner's permit.
"(3) Limited learner's permit.
"(4) Limited provisional license.
"(5) Full provisional license.
"(6) Commercial drivers license.
"(7) Commercial learner's permit.
"(8) Temporary driving certificate.
"(9) Special identification card.
"(10) Handicapped placard.
"(11) Vehicle registration.
"(12) Temporary vehicle registration.
"(13) Dealer license plate.
"(14) Transporter plate.
"(15) Loaner/Dealer 'LD' plate.
"(16) Vehicle inspection authorization.
"(17) Inspection station license.
"(18) Inspection mechanic license.
"(19) Transportation network company permit.
"(20) Motor vehicle dealer license.
"(21) Sales representative license.
"(22) Manufacturer license.
"(23) Distributor license.
"(24) Wholesaler license.
"(25) Driver training school license.
"(26) Driver training school instructor license.
"(27) Professional housemoving license.
"(b) Extend Validity of Credentials. -- Notwithstanding renewal, duration, or expiration provisions of G.S. 20-7, 20-11, 20-37.6, 20-37.7, 20-37.13, 20-50, 20-66, 20-79, 20-79.02, 20-79.2, 20-183.4B,

20-183.4D, 20-280.3, 20-288, 20-324, and 20-359, or any other provision of law to the contrary, the Division of Motor Vehicles shall extend for a period of five months the validity of any credential that expires on or after March 1, 2020, and before August 1, 2020. The Division shall extend for a period of five months the validity of any credential listed in subdivisions (6), (7), (9), (10), and (18) of subsection (a) of this section that expires on or after March 1, 2020, and before the date 30 days after the date the Governor (i) rescinds Executive Order No. 116 or (ii) issues another executive order lifting restrictions on Division of Motor Vehicles functions. Notwithstanding G.S. 20-37.13(h) and G.S. 20-37.13A(a), the Division of Motor Vehicles is authorized to waive the requirement that commercial drivers license and commercial learner's permit holders have a medical examination and certification, as required by federal law, consistent with any waiver of medical qualifications standards issued by the Federal Motor Carrier Safety Administration. A credential extended under this section shall expire five months from the date it otherwise expires as prescribed by law prior to this section. However, the subsequent expiration of a credential extended under this section shall occur on the date prescribed by law prior to this section without regard to the extension. The Division shall notify individuals affected by an extension granted under this section, including information on new expiration dates and how the extension affects subsequent renewal and expiration dates.

"(b1) Extension of Intrastate Medical Waivers. -- Notwithstanding the limitation on duration of waivers in G.S. 20-37.13A(b), the Division of Motor Vehicles may extend for up to five months the validity of a medical waiver issued by the Division under G.S. 20-37.13A if the waiver expires on or after March 1, 2020, and before the date 30 days after the date the Governor (i) rescinds Executive Order No. 116 or (ii) issues another executive order lifting restrictions on Division of Motor Vehicles functions, and the Division's Medical Review Unit determines the extension is appropriate.

"(c) Driving Eligibility Certificates. -- Notwithstanding G.S. 20-11(n)(3), a driving eligibility certificate dated on or after February 9, 2020, and before March 10, 2020, remains valid and may be accepted by the Division of Motor Vehicles to meet the requirements for a license or permit issued under G.S. 20-11 until 30 days after the date the Governor rescinds Executive Order No. 116 or the date the Division reopens all drivers license offices, whichever is earlier.

"(d) Waive Penalties. -- Notwithstanding any provision of law to the contrary, the Division shall waive any fines, fees, or penalties associated with failing to renew a credential during the period of time the credential is valid by extension under subsection (b) of this section.

"(e) Motor Vehicle Taxes. -- Notwithstanding any provision of law to the contrary, due dates for motor vehicle taxes that are tied to registration expiration under Article 22A of Chapter 105 of the General

Statutes shall be extended to correspond with extended expiration dates under subsection (b) of this section.

"(f) Validity by Extension a Defense. -- A person may not be convicted or found responsible for any offense resulting from failure to renew a credential issued by the Division if, when tried for that offense, the person shows that the offense occurred during the period of time the credential is valid by extension under subsection (b) of this section.

"(g) Report. -- Within 30 days of the extensions made under subsection (b) of this section, the Division shall submit a report to the Joint Legislative Transportation Oversight Committee and the Fiscal Research Division detailing implementation of this section.

"(h) Effective Date. -- This section is effective retroactively to March 1, 2020, and applies to expirations occurring on or after that date."

Session Laws 2020-3, s. 5, is a severability clause.

Session Laws 2020-97, s. 4.5, is a severability clause.

EFFECT OF AMENDMENTS. --

Session Laws 2005-354, s. 3, effective October 1, 2005, deleted "for a period of one year" following "shall be effective," and inserted "and expire on July 31 of each year."

§ 20-359.1. Insurance requirements

(a) No license shall be issued or renewed pursuant to this Article unless the applicant files with the Department a certificate or certificates of insurance, from an insurance company or companies authorized to do business in this State, providing:

    (1) Motor vehicle insurance for bodily injury to or death of one or more persons in any one accident and for injury to or destruction of property of others in any one accident with minimum coverage of three hundred fifty thousand dollars ($ 350,000) combined single limit of liability;

    (2) Comprehensive general liability insurance with a minimum coverage of three hundred fifty thousand dollars ($ 350,000) combined single limit of liability, including coverage of operations on North Carolina streets and highways that are not covered by motor vehicle insurance; and

    (3) Workers' compensation insurance that complies with Chapter 97 for all employees if the person is licensed as a professional housemover. The exemptions in G.S. 97-13 from the provisions of Chapter 97 shall not apply to licensed professional housemovers.

(b) The certificate or certificates shall provide for continuous coverage during the effective period of the license issued pursuant to this Article. At the time the certificate is filed, the applicant shall also file with the Department a current list of all motor vehicles covered by the certificate. The applicant shall file amendments to the list within 15 days of any changes.

(c) An insurance company issuing any insurance policy required by subsection (a) of this section shall notify the Department of any of the following events at least 30 days before its occurrence: (i) cancellation of the policy, (ii) non-renewal of the policy, or (iii) any change in the policy.

(d) In addition to all coverages required by this section, the applicant shall file with the Department a copy of either: (i) a bond or other acceptable surety providing coverage in the amount of twenty-five thousand dollars ($ 25,000) for the benefit of a person contracting with the housemover to move that person's structure for all claims for property damage arising from the movement of a structure pursuant to this Article, or (ii) a policy of cargo insurance in the amount of fifty thousand dollars ($ 50,000).

History.

1981, c. 818, s. 1; 1991 (Reg. Sess., 1992), c. 813, s. 1

OPINIONS OF THE ATTORNEY GENERAL

LIABILITY FOR THE MOVEMENT OF ANY BUILDING OR STRUCTURE by automobile or mobile equipment cannot be excluded from the insurance coverage required to be furnished for licensure by a professional house mover pursuant to this section. See opinion of Attorney General to Mr. W.F. Rosser, P.E., Head of Maintenance, North Carolina Department of Transportation, 52 N.C.A.G. 105 (1983).

§ 20-360. Requirements for permit

(a) Persons licensed as professional housemovers shall also be required to secure a permit from the Department for every move undertaken on the State Highway System of roads; that permit shall be issued by the Department after determining that the applicant is (i) properly licensed, (ii) furnished special surety bonds as required by the Department, and (iii) complying with such other regulations as required by the Department.

(b) It shall be the duty of the applicant to see that the "beams and dollies" and "hauling units" used shall be constructed with proper material in a suitable manner and utilized so as to provide for the safety of the general public and the structure being relocated. Any violation of this duty may result in suspension or revocation of his license by the Department.

(c) A license shall not be required for an individual owner of a towing vehicle moving their own buildings from or to property owned individually by those persons; however, a permit will be required for all moves.

(d) Licensed housemovers shall furnish front and rear certified escort vehicles on all moves, one or both of which may be a marked police, sheriff or State Highway Patrol vehicle as determined by the issuing agent, or one or two properly equipped certified escort vehicles depending on the number of law-enforcement vehicles escorting the move; escort vehicles shall operate where possible at a distance of 300 feet from the structure being moved; that this interval will be closed in cities and other congested areas to protect other traffic from the swing of the load at corners and turns, and the certified escort vehicles shall comply with all restrictions as provided on the permit secured for movement of the structure.

History.
1977, c. 720, s. 5; 1981, c. 818, s. 2; 2005-354, s. 4
   EFFECT OF AMENDMENTS. --
   Session Laws 2005-354, s. 4, effective October 1, 2005, substituted "an individual owner of a towing vehicle" for "individuals" in subsection (c) and rewrote subsection (d).

§ 20-361. Application for permit and permit fee

Application for a permit to move a structure must be made to the division or district engineer having jurisdiction at least two days prior to the date of the move. For good cause shown, this time may be waived by the district or division engineer. A travel plan and a permit application fee of twenty dollars ($ 20.00) shall accompany the application. Division or district engineers are authorized to issue permits for individual moves of a structure or building whose width does not exceed 36 feet. The travel plan will show the proposed route, the time estimated for each segment of the move, a plan to handle traffic so that no one delay to other highway users shall exceed 20 minutes. The division or district engineers shall review the travel plan and if the route cannot accommodate the move due to roadway weight limits, bridge size or weight limits, or will cause undue interruption of traffic flow, the permit shall not be issued. The applicant may submit alternate plans if desired until an acceptable route is determined. If the width of the building or structure to be relocated is more than 36 feet, or if no acceptable travel plan has been filed, and the denial of the permit would cause a hardship, the application and travel plan may be submitted to the Department on appeal. After reviewing the route and travel plan, the Department may in its discretion issue the permit after considering the practical physical limitations of the route, the nature and purpose of the move, the size and weight of the structure, the distance the structure is to be moved, and the safety and convenience of the traveling public. A surety

bond in an amount to cover the cost of any damage to the pavement, structures, bridges, roadway or other damages that may occur can be required if deemed necessary by the Department.

History.
1977, c. 720, s. 6; 1991 (Reg. Sess., 1992), c. 813, s. 3

§ 20-362. Liability of housemovers

The permittee assumes all responsibility for injury to persons or damage to property of any kind and agrees to hold the Department harmless for any claims arising out of his conduct or actions.

History.
1977, c. 720, s. 7

§ 20-363. Removal and replacement of obstructions

All obstructions, including mailboxes, traffic signals, signs, and utility lines will be removed immediately prior to and replaced immediately after the move at the expense of the mover. Any property, real or personal, to be removed, which is not located in the right-of-way, shall not be removed until the owner is notified and arrangements for and approval from the owner are obtained.

History.
1977, c. 720, s. 8; 2008-89, s. 3
   EDITOR'S NOTE. --
   This section, as amended by Session Laws 2008-89, s. 3, effective December 1, 2008, is applicable to licenses issued and offenses committed on or after that date.

§ 20-364. Route changes

Irrespective of the route shown on the permit, an alternate route will be followed:
   (1) If directed by a peace officer.
   (2) If directed by a uniformed officer assigned to a weigh station to follow a route to a weighing device.
   (3) If the specified route is officially detoured. Should a detour be encountered, the driver shall check with the office issuing permit on which he is traveling prior to proceeding.

History.
1977, c. 720, s. 9; 2004-124, s. 18.3(d)
   EFFECT OF AMENDMENTS. --
   Session Laws 2004-124, s. 18.3(d), effective July 1, 2004, substituted "weigh station" for "weighing station" in subdivision (2).

§ 20-365. Loading or parking on right-of-way

The object to be transported will not be loaded, unloaded, nor parked, day or night, on highway right-of-way without specific permission from the district or division engineer.

History.
1977, c. 720, s. 10

§ 20-366. Effect of weather

No move will be made when atmospheric conditions render visibility lower than safe for travel. Moves will not be made when highway is covered with snow or ice, or at any time travel conditions are considered unsafe by the Department or Highway Patrol or other law-enforcement officers having jurisdiction.

History.
1977, c. 720, s. 11

§ 20-367. Obtaining license or permit by fraud

The permit may be voided if any conditions of the permit are violated. Upon any violation, the permit must be surrendered and a new permit obtained before proceeding. Misrepresentation of information on application to obtain a license, fraudulently obtaining a permit, alteration of a permit, or unauthorized use of a permit will render the permit void.

History.
1977, c. 720, s. 12

§ 20-368. Municipal regulations

All moves on streets on the municipal system of streets shall comply with local regulations.

History.
1977, c. 720, s. 13
CITED in King v. Town of Chapel Hill, 367 N.C. 400, 758 S.E.2d 364 (2014).

§ 20-369. Out-of-state licenses and permits

An out-of-state person, partnership, or corporation engaging in the structural moving business may apply to the Department for a license to engage in the housemoving profession in North Carolina, and obtain permits for moves by complying with the provisions of this Article and the regulations of the Department in the same manner as is required of North Carolina residents and by showing that the state in which the housemover operates his business extends similar privileges to housemovers licensed in North Carolina.

History.
1977, c. 720, s. 14; 1979, c. 475, s. 1

§ 20-370. Speed limits

The speed of moves will be that which is reasonable and prudent for the load, considering weight and bulk, under conditions existing at the time.

History.
1977, c. 720, s. 15

§ 20-371. Penalties

(a) Any person violating the provisions of this Article or the regulations of the Department governing housemoving shall be guilty of a Class 1 misdemeanor.

(b) The Department is hereby authorized in the name of the State to apply for relief by injunction, in the established manner provided in cases of civil procedure, without bond, to enforce the provisions of this Article, or to restrain any violation thereof. In such proceedings, it shall not be necessary to allege or prove either that an adequate remedy at law does not exist, or that substantial or irreparable damage would result from the continued violation thereof.

History.
1977, c. 720, s. 16; 1993, c. 539, s. 392;1994, Ex. Sess., c. 24, s. 14(c);2008-89, s. 4

§ 20-372. Invalid section; severability

If any of the provisions of this Article, or if the application of such provisions to any person or circumstance shall be held invalid, the remainder of this Article and the application of such provision of this Article other than those as to which it is held valid, shall not be affected thereby.

History.
1977, c. 720, s. 17

N.C. Gen. Stat. § 20-373

Reserved for future codification purposes.

§ 20-374. Unsafe practices

(a) If the Department determines that a housemover has engaged in unsafe practices, all licenses, permits, and authorizations issued to the person pursuant to this Article shall be revoked for a period of six months.

(b) Any person whose license, permit, or authorization issued under this Article is revoked pursuant to this section may request a hearing to be held before the Secretary or a person designated by the Secretary. The licensee shall be notified in writing no less than 10 days prior to the hearing of the time and place of the hearing. At the hearing, the parties shall be given an opportunity to present evidence on issues of fact, examine and cross-examine witnesses, and present arguments on issues of law. The decision of the Secretary or of the person designated by the Secretary shall be final. Any person aggrieved by the final decision may seek judicial review of the decision in accordance with the provisions of Article 4 of Chapter 150B of the General Statutes.

History.

2008-89, s. 5

EDITOR'S NOTE. --

Session Laws 2008-89, s. 7, made this section effective December 1, 2008, and applicable to licenses issued and offenses committed on or after that date.

N.C. Gen. Stat. § 20-375

Reserved for future codification purposes.

ARTICLE 17.
MOTOR CARRIER SAFETY REGULATION UNIT

PART 1.
GENERAL PROVISIONS

§ 20-376. Definitions

The following definitions apply in this Article:

(1) **Federal safety and hazardous materials regulations.** -- The federal motor carrier safety regulations contained in 49 C.F.R. Parts 171 through 180, 382, and 390 through 398.

(2) **Foreign commerce.** -- Commerce between any of the following:

a. A place in the United States and a place in a foreign country.

b. Places in the United States through any foreign country.

(3) **Interstate commerce.** -- As defined in 49 C.F.R. Part 390.5.

(3a) **Interstate motor carrier.** -- Any person, firm, or corporation that operates or controls a commercial motor vehicle as defined in 49 C.F.R. § 390.5 in interstate commerce.

(4) **Intrastate commerce.** -- As defined in 49 C.F.R. Part 390.5.

(5) **Intrastate motor carrier.** -- Any person, firm, or corporation that operates or controls a motor vehicle in intrastate commerce when the vehicle:

a. Is a vehicle having a gross vehicle weight rating (GVWR) or gross combination weight rating (GCWR) or gross vehicle weight (GVW) or gross combination weight (GCW) of 26,001 pounds or more, whichever is greater.

b. Is designed or used to transport 16 or more passengers, including the driver.

c. Is used in transporting a hazardous material in a quantity requiring placarding pursuant to 49 C.F.R. Parts 170 through 185.

History.

1985, c. 454, s. 1; 1993 (Reg. Sess., 1994), c. 621, s. 5; 1995 (Reg. Sess., 1996), c. 756, s. 20; 1997-456, s. 36;1998-149, s. 11;1999-452, s. 21;2002-152, s. 3;2010-129, s. 5

EFFECT OF AMENDMENTS. --

Session Laws 2010-129, s. 5, effective October 1, 2010, and applicable to offenses committed on or after that date, in the introductory paragraph in subdivision (5), substituted "controls a motor vehicle in intrastate commerce when the vehicle:" for "controls a commercial motor vehicle as defined in G.S. 20-401(3d) in intrastate commerce"; and added subdivisions (5)a. through (5)c.

OPINIONS OF THE ATTORNEY GENERAL

PRIVATELY OWNED BUSES NOT ENGAGED IN FOR-HIRE TRANSPORTATION OF PASSENGERS. --The Division of Motor Vehicles has no regulatory authority under Article 17, Chapter 20 of the North Carolina General Statutes (Motor Carrier Safety Regulations), over privately owned buses not engaged in for-hire transportation of passengers. See opinion of Attorney General to Mr. William S. Hiatt, Commissioner of Motor Vehicles, 58 N.C.A.G. 1 (Jan. 5, 1988).

PART 2.
AUTHORITY AND POWERS OF DEPARTMENT OF PUBLIC SAFETY

§ 20-377. General powers of Department of Public Safety

The Department of Public Safety shall have and exercise such general power and authority to supervise and control the motor carriers of the State as may be necessary to carry out the laws providing for their regulation, and all such other powers and duties as may be necessary or incident to the proper discharge of its duties.

History.

1985, c. 454, s. 1; 2002-159, s. 31.5(b);2002-190, s. 2;2011-145, s. 19.1(g)

EDITOR'S NOTE. --

Session Laws 2002-190, s. 17, provides: "The Governor shall resolve any dispute between the Department of Transportation and the Department of Crime Control and Public Safety concerning the implementation of this act [Session Laws 2002-190]."

EFFECT OF AMENDMENTS. --

Session Laws 2011-145, s. 19.1(g), effective January 1, 2012, substituted "Public Safety" for "Crime Control and Public Safety."

N.C. Gen. Stat. § 20-378

Repealed by Session Laws 1995 (Regular Session, 1996), c. 756, s. 21.

§ 20-379. Department of Public Safety to audit motor carriers for compliance

The Department of Public Safety must periodically audit each motor carrier to determine if the carrier is complying with this Article and, if the motor carrier is subject to regulation by the North Carolina Utilities Commission, with Chapter 62 of the General Statutes. In conducting the audit, the Department of Public Safety may examine a person under oath, compel the production of papers and the attendance of witnesses, and copy a paper for use in the audit. An employee of the Department of Public Safety may enter the premises of a motor carrier during reasonable hours to enforce this Article. When on the premises of a motor carrier, an employee of the Department of Public Safety may set up and use equipment needed to make the tests required by this Article.

History.

1985, c. 454, s. 1; 1995 (Reg. Sess., 1996), c. 756, s. 22; 2002-159, s. 31.5(b);2002-190, s. 2;2011-145, s. 19.1(g)

EDITOR'S NOTE. --

Session Laws 2002-190, s. 17, provides: "The Governor shall resolve any dispute between the Department of Transportation and the Department of Crime Control and Public Safety concerning the implementation of this act [Session Laws 2002-190]."

EFFECT OF AMENDMENTS. --

Session Laws 2011-145, s. 19.1(g), effective January 1, 2012, substituted "Public Safety" for "Crime Control and Public Safety" throughout the section.

§ 20-380. Department of Public Safety may investigate accidents involving motor carriers and promote general safety program

The Department of Public Safety may conduct a program of accident prevention and public safety covering all motor carriers with special emphasis on highway safety and transport safety and may investigate the causes of any accident on a highway involving a motor carrier. Any information obtained in an investigation shall be reduced to writing and a report thereof filed in the office of the Department of Public Safety, which shall be subject to public inspection but such report shall not be admissible in evidence in any civil or criminal proceeding arising from such accident. The Department of Public Safety may adopt rules for the safety of the public as affected by motor carriers and the safety of motor carrier employees. The Department of Public Safety shall cooperate with and coordinate its activities for motor carriers with other agencies and organizations engaged in the promotion of highway safety and employee safety.

History.

1985, c. 454, s. 1; 1995 (Reg. Sess., 1996), c. 756, s. 23; 2002-159, s. 31.5(b);2002-190, s. 2;2011-145, s. 19.1(g)

EDITOR'S NOTE. --

Session Laws 2002-190, s. 17, provides: "The Governor shall resolve any dispute between the Department of Transportation and the Department of Crime Control and Public Safety concerning the implementation of this act [Session Laws 2002-190]."

EFFECT OF AMENDMENTS. --

Session Laws 2011-145, s. 19.1(g), effective January 1, 2012, substituted "Public Safety" for "Crime Control and Public Safety" throughout the section.

§ 20-381. Specific powers and duties of Department of Public Safety applicable to motor carriers; agricultural exemption

(a) The Department of Public Safety has the following powers and duties concerning motor carriers:

(1) To prescribe qualifications and maximum hours of service of drivers and their helpers.

(1a) To set safety standards for vehicles of motor carriers engaged in foreign, interstate, or intrastate commerce over the highways of this State and for the safe operation of these vehicles. The Department of Public Safety may stop, enter upon, and perform inspections of motor carriers' vehicles in operation to determine compliance with these standards and may conduct any investigations and tests it finds necessary to promote the safety of equipment and the safe operation on the highway of these vehicles.

(1b) To enforce this Article, rules adopted under this Article, and the federal safety and hazardous materials regulations.

Chapter 20

(2) To enter the premises of a motor carrier to inspect a motor vehicle or any equipment used by the motor carrier in transporting passengers or property.

(2a) To prohibit the use by a motor carrier of any motor vehicle or motor vehicle equipment the Department of Public Safety finds, by reason of its mechanical condition or loading, would be likely to cause a crash or breakdown in the transportation of passengers or property on a highway. If an agent of the Department of Public Safety finds a motor vehicle of a motor carrier in actual use upon the highways in the transportation of passengers or property that, by reason of its mechanical condition or loading, would be likely to cause a crash or breakdown, the agent shall declare the vehicle "Out of Service." The agent shall require the operator thereof to discontinue its use and to substitute therefor a safe vehicle, parts or equipment at the earliest possible time and place, having regard for both the convenience and the safety of the passengers or property. When an inspector or agent stops a motor vehicle on the highway, under authority of this section, and the motor vehicle is declared "Out of Service," no motor carrier operator shall require, or permit, any person to operate, nor shall any person operate, any motor vehicle equipment declared "Out of Service" until all repairs required by the "Out of Service" notice have been satisfactorily completed. Such agents or inspectors shall also have the right to stop any motor vehicle which is being used upon the public highways for the transportation of passengers or property by a motor carrier subject to the provisions of this Article and to eject therefrom any driver or operator who shall be operating or be in charge of such motor vehicle while under the influence of alcoholic beverages or impairing substances. It shall be the duty of all inspectors and agents of the Department of Public Safety to make a written report, upon a form prescribed by the Department of Public Safety, of inspections of all motor equipment and a copy of each such written report, disclosing defects in such equipment, shall be served promptly upon the motor carrier operating the same, either in person by the inspector or agent or by mail. Such agents and inspectors shall also make and serve a similar written report in cases where a motor vehicle is operated in violation of this Chapter or, if the motor vehicle is subject to regulation by the North Carolina Utilities Commission, of Chapter 62 of the General Statutes.

(3) To relieve the highways of all undue burdens and safeguard traffic thereon by adopting and enforcing rules and orders designed and calculated to minimize the dangers attending transportation on the highways of all hazardous materials and other commodities.

(4) To determine the safety fitness of intrastate motor carriers, to assign safety ratings to intrastate motor carriers as defined in 49 C.F.R. § 385.3, to direct intrastate motor carriers to take remedial action when required, to prohibit the operation of intrastate motor carriers when subject to an out-of-service order issued by the Federal Motor Carrier Safety Administration or the Department.

(5) To enforce any order issued by the Federal Motor Carrier Safety Administration including the authority to seize registration plates pursuant to the provisions of G.S. 20-45 from motor carriers whose registration was rescinded and cancelled pursuant to G.S. 20-110(m) or G.S. 20-110(n).

(b) The definitions set out in 49 Code of Federal Regulations § 171.8 apply to this subsection. The transportation of an agricultural product, other than a Class 2 material, over local roads between fields of the same farm by a farmer operating as an intrastate private motor carrier is exempt from the requirements of Parts 171 through 180 of 49 CFR as provided in 49 CFR § 173.5(a). The transportation of an agricultural product to or from a farm within 150 miles of the farm by a farmer operating as an intrastate private motor carrier is exempt from the requirements of Subparts G and H of Part 172 of 49 CFR as provided in 49 CFR § 173.5(b).

(c) For purposes of 49 C.F.R. § 395.1(k) and any other federal law or regulation relating to hours-of-service rules for drivers engaged in the transportation of agricultural commodities and farm supplies for agricultural purposes, the terms "planting and harvesting season" and "planting and harvesting period" refer to the period from January 1 through December 31 of each year.

(d) The definitions set out in 49 C.F.R. § 390.5 apply to this subsection. A covered farm vehicle engaged in intrastate commerce is exempt from the requirements of 49 C.F.R. § 390.21.

History.
1985, c. 454, s. 1; 1995 (Reg. Sess., 1996), c. 756, s. 24; 1997-456, ss. 37, 38; 1998-149, s. 12;1998-165, s. 1;1999-452, s. 22;2002-152, ss. 4, 5; 2002-159, s. 31.5(b);2002-190, s. 2;2009-376, s. 9;2011-145, s. 19.1(g);2014-103, s. 5;2017-108, s. 17;2019-196, s. 4

EDITOR'S NOTE. --
Session Laws 1981, c. 412, s. 4, and c. 747, s. 66, changed the term "intoxicating liquors" to "alcoholic beverages" throughout the General Statutes as then

in effect. However, Session Laws 1985, c. 454, s. 1, used "intoxicating liquors" in enacting this section.

Session Laws 2002-190, s. 17, provides: "The Governor shall resolve any dispute between the Department of Transportation and the Department of Crime Control and Public Safety concerning the implementation of this act [Session Laws 2002-190]."

Session Laws 2017-108, s. 17.1(a)-(d), provides: "(a) Rule. -- Until the effective date of the revised permanent rule that the State Highway Patrol is required to adopt pursuant to subsection (c) of this section, the State Highway Patrol shall implement 14B NCAC 07C.0101 (Safety of Operation and Equipment), as provided in subsection (b) of this section.

"(b) Implementation. -- Notwithstanding 14B NCAC 07C.0101, the State Highway Patrol shall exempt covered farm vehicles engaged in intrastate commerce from the requirements of 49 C.F.R. § 390.21.

"(c) Additional Rule-Making Authority. -- The State Highway Patrol shall adopt rules to amend 14B NCAC 07C.0101, consistent with subsection (b) of this section.

"(d) Effective Date. -- Subsection (b) of this section expires on the date that rules adopted pursuant to subsection (c) of this section become effective. The remainder of this section is effective when it becomes law."

Session Laws 2017-108, s. 21, is a severability clause.

EFFECT OF AMENDMENTS. --

Session Laws 2011-145, s. 19.1(g), effective January 1, 2012, substituted "Public Safety" for "Crime Control and Public Safety" throughout the section.

Session Laws 2014-103, s. 5, effective August 6, 2014, added subsection (c).

Session Laws 2017-108, s. 17, effective July 12, 2017, added subsection (d).

Session Laws 2019-196, s. 4, effective November 12, 2019, rewrote subdivisions (a)(4) and (a)(5).

§ 20-382. For-hire motor carrier registration, insurance verification, and temporary trip permit authority

(a) **UCRA.** -- The Commissioner may enter into the Unified Carrier Registration Agreement (UCRA), established pursuant to Section 4305 of Public Law 109-73, and into agreements with jurisdictions participating in the UCRA to exchange information for any audit or enforcement activity required by the UCRA. Upon entry into the UCRA, the requirements set under the UCRA apply to the Division. If a requirement set under the UCRA conflicts with this section, the UCRA controls. Rules adopted to implement this section must ensure compliance with mandates of the Federal Motor Carrier Safety Administration and the United States Department of Transportation.

(a1) **Carrier Registration.** -- A motor carrier may not operate a for-hire motor vehicle in interstate commerce in this State unless the motor carrier has complied with all of the following requirements:

(1) Registered its operations with its base state.

(1a) Done one of the following:

a. Filed a copy of the certificate of authority issued to it by the United States Department of Transportation allowing it to transport regulated items in this State and any amendments to that authority.

b. Certified to the Division that it carries only items that are not regulated by the United States Department of Transportation.

(2) Verified, in accordance with subsection (b) of this section, that it has insurance for each for-hire motor vehicle it operates.

(3) Paid the fees set in G.S. 20-385.

(b) **Insurance Verification.** -- A motor carrier that operates a for-hire motor vehicle in interstate commerce in this State and is regulated by the United States Department of Transportation must verify to the Division that each for-hire motor vehicle the motor carrier operates in this State is insured in accordance with the requirements set by the United States Department of Transportation. A motor carrier that operates a for-hire motor vehicle in interstate commerce in this State and is exempt from regulation by the United States Department of Transportation must verify to the Division that each for-hire motor vehicle the motor carrier operates in this State is insured in accordance with the requirements set by the North Carolina Utilities Commission.

(c) **Trip Permit.** -- A motor carrier that is not registered as required by this section may obtain an emergency trip permit. An emergency trip permit allows the motor carrier to operate a for-hire motor vehicle in this State for a period not to exceed 10 days.

History.
1985, c. 454, s. 1; 1993 (Reg. Sess., 1994), c. 621, s. 1; 1995 (Reg. Sess., 1996), c. 756, s. 25; 2007-492, s. 3; 2010-97, s. 4

EDITOR'S NOTE. --
Session Laws 2007-492, s. 6, provides: "If the Commissioner of Motor Vehicles enters into the Unified Carrier Registration Agreement, the Agreement must specify the date on which any fees required under the Agreement become effective in this State. The date must ensure adequate time to implement the fee provisions."

EFFECT OF AMENDMENTS. --
Session Laws 2007-492, s. 3, effective August 30, 2007, rewrote this section and the section heading.

Session Laws 2010-97, s. 4, effective July 20, 2010, deleted "by filing an application for it with the Division" from the end of the first sentence in subsection (c).

§ 20-382.1. Registration of for-hire intrastate motor carriers and verification that their vehicles are insured

(a) **Registration.** -- A for-hire motor carrier may not operate a for-hire motor vehicle in intrastate commerce in this State unless the motor carrier has complied with all of the following requirements:

    (1) For a motor carrier that hauls household goods, registered its operations with the State by doing one of the following:

        a. Obtaining a certificate of authority from the North Carolina Utilities Commission.

        b. Obtaining a certificate of exemption from the Division.

    (1a) For a motor carrier that does not haul household goods, registered its operations with the Division.

    (2) Verified, in accordance with subsection (b) of this section, that it has insurance for each for-hire motor vehicle it operates in this State.

    (3) Paid the fees set in G.S. 20-385.

(b) **Insurance Verification.** -- A for-hire motor carrier that operates a for-hire vehicle in intrastate commerce in this State must verify to the Division that each for-hire motor vehicle it operates in this State is insured. To do this, the motor carrier must submit an insurance verification form to the Division and must file annually with the Division a list of the for-hire vehicles it operates in this State.

History.
1993 (Reg. Sess., 1994), c. 621, s. 2; 1995 (Reg. Sess., 1996), c. 756, s. 26

§ 20-382.2. Penalty for failure to comply with registration or insurance verification requirements

(a) **Acts.** -- A motor carrier who does any of the following is subject to a civil penalty of one thousand dollars ($ 1,000):

    (1) Operates a for-hire motor vehicle in this State without registering its operations, as required by this Part.

    (2) Repealed by Session Laws 2007-492, s. 4, effective August 30, 2007.

    (3) Operates a for-hire motor vehicle in intrastate commerce in this State for which it has not verified it has insurance, as required by G.S. 20-382.1.

(b) **Payment and Review.** -- When the Department of Public Safety finds that a for-hire motor vehicle is operated in this State in violation of the registration and insurance verification requirements of this Part, the Department must place the motor vehicle out of service until the motor carrier is in compliance and the penalty imposed under this section is paid unless the officer that imposes the penalty determines that operation of the motor vehicle will not jeopardize collection of the penalty. A motor carrier that denies liability for a penalty imposed under this section may pay the penalty under protest and follow the procedure in G.S. 20-178.1 for a departmental review of the penalty.

(c) **Judicial Restriction.** -- A court of this State may not issue a restraining order or an injunction to restrain or enjoin the collection of a penalty imposed under this section or to permit the operation of a vehicle placed out of service under this section without payment of the penalty.

(d) **Proceeds.** -- A penalty imposed under this section is payable to the Department of Transportation, Fiscal Section. The clear proceeds of all civil penalties assessed by the Department pursuant to this section, minus any fees paid as interest, filing fees, attorneys' fees, or other necessary costs of court associated with the defense of penalties imposed pursuant to this section shall be remitted to the Civil Penalty and Forfeiture Fund in accordance with G.S. 115C-457.2.

History.
1993 (Reg. Sess., 1994), c. 621, s. 3; 1997-466, s. 3;2002-159, s. 31.5(b);2002-190, ss. 2, 3; 2005-64, s. 1;2007-492, s. 4;2009-376, ss. 2(b), 14; 2011-145, s. 19.1(g)

EDITOR'S NOTE. --
Session Laws 2002-190, s. 17, provides: "The Governor shall resolve any dispute between the Department of Transportation and the Department of Crime Control and Public Safety concerning the implementation of this act [Session Laws 2002-190]."

EFFECT OF AMENDMENTS. --
Session Laws 2005-64, s. 1, effective May 26, 2005, substituted "shall be placed out of service until the motor carrier is in compliance and" for "may not be driven for a purpose other than to park the motor vehicle until" in subsection (b).

Session Laws 2007-492, s. 4, effective August 30, 2007, deleted subdivision (a)(2), which read: "Operates a for-hire motor vehicle in interstate commerce in this State that does not carry a copy of either an insurance registration receipt issued to the motor carrier or a cab card with an identification stamp issued for the vehicle, as required by G.S. 20-382."

Session Laws 2009-376, s. 14, effective July 31, 2009, rewrote subsection (d).

Session Laws 2011-145, s. 19.1(g), effective January 1, 2012, substituted "Public Safety" for "Crime Control and Public Safety."

§ 20-383. Inspectors and officers given enforcement authority

Only designated inspectors, officers, and personnel of the Department of Public Safety shall have the authority to enforce the provisions of this Article and provisions of Chapter 62 applicable to motor transportation, and they are empowered to make complaint for the issue of appropriate warrants, information, presentments or other lawful process for the enforcement and prosecution of violations of the transportation laws against all offenders, whether they be regulated motor carriers or not, and to appear in court or before the North Carolina Utilities Commission and offer evidence at the trial pursuant to such processes.

History.

1985, c. 454, s. 1; 2002-159, s. 31.5(b);2002-190, s. 2;2011-145, s. 19.1(g);2012-78, s. 10

EDITOR'S NOTE. --

Session Laws 2002-190, s. 17, provides: "The Governor shall resolve any dispute between the Department of Transportation and the Department of Crime Control and Public Safety concerning the implementation of this act [Session Laws 2002-190]."

Session Laws 2012-78, s. 18, provides: "Prosecutions for offenses committed before the effective date of the section of this act [June 26, 2012] that modifies the offense are not abated or affected by this act, and the statutes that would be applicable but for this act remain applicable to those prosecutions."

EFFECT OF AMENDMENTS. --

Session Laws 2011-145, s. 19.1(g), effective January 1, 2012, substituted "Public Safety" for "Crime Control and Public Safety."

Session Laws 2012-78, s. 10, effective June 26, 2012, substituted "inspectors, officers, and personnel" for "inspectors and officers" and deleted "Crime Control and" preceding "Public Safety".

§ 20-384. Penalty for certain violations

A motor carrier who fails to conduct a safety inspection of a vehicle as required by Part 396 of the federal safety regulations or who fails to mark a vehicle that has been inspected as required by that Part commits an infraction and, if found responsible, is liable for a penalty of up to fifty dollars ($ 50.00).

History.

1985, c. 454, s. 1; c. 757, s. 164(b); 1985 (Reg. Sess., 1986), c. 1018, s. 13; 1993 (Reg. Sess., 1994), c. 754, s. 6; 1995 (Reg. Sess., 1996), c. 756, s. 27

EDITOR'S NOTE. --

Session Laws 1985 (Reg. Sess., 1986), c. 1018, s. 13, effective June 30, 1986, repealed the amendment to this section by Session Laws 1985, c. 757, s. 164(b). The 1985 amendment would have been effective July 1, 1986, and therefore never went into effect. The section is set out above as enacted by Session Laws 1985, c. 454, s. 1.

PUBLIC POLICY. --Where employer forced employee-at-will to drive truck in violation of federal law or lose his job, employer's conduct violated the public policy of this State regarding highway safety, as evidenced by this section, G.S. 20-397 and provisions in the North Carolina Administrative Code; therefore, employee's suit based upon wrongful termination of his at-will employment stated a cause of action. Coman v. Thomas Mfg. Co., 325 N.C. 172, 381 S.E.2d 445 (1989).

OPINIONS OF THE ATTORNEY GENERAL

PRIVATELY OWNED BUSES NOT ENGAGED IN FOR-HIRE TRANSPORTATION OF PASSENGERS. --The Division of Motor Vehicles has no regulatory authority under Article 17, Chapter 20 of the North Carolina General Statutes (Motor Carrier Safety Regulations), over privately owned buses not engaged in for-hire transportation of passengers. See opinion of Attorney General to Mr. William S. Hiatt, Commissioner of Motor Vehicles, 58 N.C.A.G. 1 (Jan. 5, 1988).

PART 3.
FEES AND CHARGES

§ 20-385. Fee schedule

(a) The fees listed in this section apply to a motor carrier. These fees are in addition to any fees required under the Unified Carrier Registration Agreement.

    (1) Repealed by Session Laws 2007-492, s. 5, effective August 30, 2007.

    (2) Application by an intrastate motor carrier for a certificate of exemption......$ 60.00

    (3) Certification by an interstate motor carrier that it is not regulated by the United States Department of Transportation......60.00

    (4) Application by an interstate motor carrier for an emergency trip permit........23.00

(b) Repealed by Session Laws 2007-492, s. 5, effective August 30, 2007.

History.

1985, c. 454, s. 1; 1993 (Reg. Sess., 1994), c. 621, s. 4; 1995 (Reg. Sess., 1996), c. 756, s. 28; 2005-276, s. 44.1(p);2007-492, s. 5;2015-241, s. 29.30(q)

EDITOR'S NOTE. --

Session Laws 2007-492, s. 6, provides: "If the Commissioner of Motor Vehicles enters into the Unified Carrier Registration Agreement, the Agreement must specify the date on which any fees required under the Agreement become effective in this State. The date must ensure adequate time to implement the fee provisions."

Session Laws 2015-241, s. 29.30(u), made the amendment to subsection (a) of this section by Session Laws 2015-241, s. 29.30(q), applicable to issuances, renewals, restorations, and requests on or after January 1, 2016.

Session Laws 2015-241, s. 1.1, provides: "This act shall be known as 'The Current Operations and Capital Improvements Appropriations Act of 2015.'"

Session Laws 2015-241, s. 33.6, is a severability clause.

EFFECT OF AMENDMENTS. --

Session Laws 2005-276, s. 44.1(p), effective October 1, 2005, and applicable to fees collected on or after that date, in subdivisions (a)(2) and (a)(3), substituted "45.00" for "25.00" and in subdivision (a)(4), substituted "18.00" for "10.00."

Session Laws 2007-492, s. 5, effective August 30, 2007, rewrote this section.

Session Laws 2015-241, s. 29.30(q), effective January 1, 2016, substituted "60.00" for "45.00" in subdivisions (a)(2) and (a)(3), and "23.00" for "18.00" in subdivision (a)(4). For applicability, see editor's note.

§ 20-386. Fees, charges and penalties; disposition

All fees and charges received by the Division under G.S. 20-385 shall be in addition to any other tax or fee provided by law and shall be placed in the Highway Fund.

History.

1985, c. 454, s. 1

PART 4.
PENALTIES AND ACTIONS

§ 20-387. Motor carrier violating any provision of Article, rules or orders; penalty

Any motor carrier which violates any of the provisions of this Article or refuses to conform to or obey any rule, order or regulation of the Division or Department of Public Safety shall, in addition to the other penalties prescribed in this Article forfeit and pay a sum up to one thousand dollars ($ 1,000) for each offense, to be recovered in an action to be instituted in the Superior Court of Wake County, in the name of the State of North Carolina on the relation of the Department of Public Safety; and each day such motor carrier continues to violate any provision of this Article or continues to refuse to obey or perform any rule, order or regulation prescribed by the Division or Department of Public Safety shall be a separate offense.

History.

1985, c. 454, s. 1; 2002-159, s. 31.5(b);2002-159, s. 31.5(b);2002-190, s. 10;2011-145, s. 19.1(g)

EDITOR'S NOTE. --

Session Laws 2002-190, s. 17, as amended by Session Laws 2002-159, s. 31.5, provides: "The Governor shall resolve any dispute between the Department of Transportation and the Department of Crime Control and Public Safety concerning the implementation of this act [Session Laws 2002-190]."

EFFECT OF AMENDMENTS. --

Session Laws 2011-145, s. 19.1(g), effective January 1, 2012, substituted "Public Safety" for "Crime Control and Public Safety" throughout the section.

§ 20-388. Willful acts of employees deemed those of motor carrier

The willful act of any officer, agent, or employee of a motor carrier, acting within the scope of his official duties of employment, shall, for the purpose of this Article, be deemed to be the willful act of the motor carrier.

History.

1985, c. 454, s. 1

§ 20-389. Actions to recover penalties

Except as otherwise provided in this Article, an action for the recovery of any penalty under this Article shall be instituted in Wake County, and shall be instituted in the name of the State of North Carolina on the relation of the Department of Public Safety against the person incurring such penalty; or whenever such action is upon the complaint of any injured person, it shall be instituted in the name of the State of North Carolina on the relation of the Department of Public Safety upon the complaint of such injured person against the person incurring such penalty. Such action may be instituted and prosecuted by the Attorney General, the District Attorney of the Wake County Superior Court, or the injured person. The procedure in such actions, the right of appeal and the rules regulating appeals shall be the same as provided by law in other civil actions.

History.

1985, c. 454, s. 1; 2002-159, s. 31.5(b);2002-190, s. 2;2011-145, s. 19.1(g)

EDITOR'S NOTE. --

Session Laws 2002-190, s. 17, provides: "The Governor shall resolve any dispute between the Department of Transportation and the Department of Crime Control and Public Safety concerning the implementation of this act [Session Laws 2002-190]."

EFFECT OF AMENDMENTS. --

Session Laws 2011-145, s. 19.1(g), effective January 1, 2012, substituted "Public Safety" for "Crime Control and Public Safety" twice.

§ 20-390. Refusal to permit Department of Public Safety to inspect records made misdemeanor

Any motor carrier, its officers or agents in charge thereof, that fails or refuses upon the written demand of the Department of Public Safety to permit its authorized representatives or employees to examine and inspect its books, records, accounts and documents, or its plant, property, or facilities, as provided for by law, shall be guilty of a Class 3 misdemeanor. Each day of such failure or refusal shall constitute a separate offense and each such offense shall be punishable only by a fine of not less than five hundred dollars ($ 500.00) and not more than five thousand dollars ($ 5,000).

History.

1985, c. 454, s. 1; 1993, c. 539, s. 393;1994, Ex. Sess., c. 24, s. 14(c);2002-159, s. 31.5(b);2002-190, s. 2;2011-145, s. 19.1(g)

EDITOR'S NOTE. --

Session Laws 2002-190, s. 17, provides: "The Governor shall resolve any dispute between the Department of Transportation and the Department of Crime Control and Public Safety concerning the implementation of this act [Session Laws 2002-190]."

EFFECT OF AMENDMENTS. --

Session Laws 2011-145, s. 19.1(g), effective January 1, 2012, substituted "Public Safety" for "Crime Control and Public Safety."

§ 20-391. Violating rules, with injury to others

If any motor carrier doing business in this State by its agents or employees shall be guilty of the violations of the rules and regulations provided and prescribed by the Division or the Department of Public Safety, and if after due notice of such violation given to the principal officer thereof, if residing in the State, or, if not, to the manager or superintendent or secretary or treasurer if residing in the State, or, if not, then to any local agent thereof, ample and full recompense for the wrong or injury done thereby to any person as may be directed by the Division or Department of Public Safety shall not be made within 30 days from the time of such notice, such motor carrier shall incur a penalty for each offense of five hundred dollars ($ 500.00).

History.

1985, c. 454, s. 1; 2002-159, s. 31.5(b);2002-190, s. 11;2011-145, s. 19.1(g)

EDITOR'S NOTE. --

Session Laws 2002-190, s. 17, provides: "The Governor shall resolve any dispute between the Department of Transportation and the Department of Crime Control and Public Safety concerning the implementation of this act [Session Laws 2002-190]."

EFFECT OF AMENDMENTS. --

Session Laws 2011-145, s. 19.1(g), effective January 1, 2012, substituted "Public Safety" for "Crime Control and Public Safety" twice.

§ 20-392. Failure to make report; obstructing Division or Department of Public Safety

Every officer, agent or employee of any motor carrier, who shall willfully neglect or refuse to make and furnish any report required by the Division or Department of Public Safety for the purposes of this Article, or who shall willfully or unlawfully hinder, delay or obstruct the Division or Department of Public Safety in the discharge of the duties hereby imposed upon it, shall forfeit and pay five hundred dollars ($ 500.00) for each offense, to be recovered in an action in the name of the State. A delay of 10 days to make and furnish such report shall raise the presumption that the same was willful.

History.

1985, c. 454, s. 1; 2002-159, s. 31.5(b);2002-190, s. 12;2011-145, s. 19.1(g)

EDITOR'S NOTE. --

Session Laws 2002-190, s. 17, provides: "The Governor shall resolve any dispute between the Department of Transportation and the Department of Crime Control and Public Safety concerning the implementation of this act [Session Laws 2002-190]."

EFFECT OF AMENDMENTS. --

Session Laws 2011-145, s. 19.1(g), effective January 1, 2012, substituted "Public Safety" for "Crime Control and Public Safety" throughout the section.

§ 20-393. Disclosure of information by employee of Department of Public Safety unlawful

It shall be unlawful for any agent or employee of the Department of Public Safety knowingly and willfully to divulge any fact or information which may come to his knowledge during the course of any examination or inspection made under authority of this Article, except to the Department of Public Safety or as may be directed by the Department of Public Safety or upon approval of a request to the Department of Public Safety by the Utilities Commission or by a court or judge thereof.

History.

1985, c. 454, s. 1; 2002-159, s. 31.5(b);2002-190, s. 2;2011-145, s. 19.1(g)

EDITOR'S NOTE. --

Session Laws 2002-190, s. 17, provides: "The Governor shall resolve any dispute between the Department of Transportation and the Department of Crime Control and Public Safety concerning the implementation of this act [Session Laws 2002-190]."

EFFECT OF AMENDMENTS. --

Session Laws 2011-145, s. 19.1(g), effective January 1, 2012, substituted "Public Safety" for "Crime Control and Public Safety" throughout the section.

§ 20-394. Remedies for injuries cumulative

The remedies given by this Article to persons injured shall be regarded as cumulative to the remedies otherwise provided by law against motor carriers.

History.
1985, c. 454, s. 1

§ 20-395. Willful injury to property of motor carrier a misdemeanor

If any person shall willfully do or cause to be done any act or acts whatever whereby any building, construction or work of any motor carrier, or any engine, machine or structure of any matter or thing appertaining to the same shall be stopped, obstructed, impaired, weakened, injured or destroyed, he shall be guilty of a Class 1 misdemeanor.

History.
1985, c. 454, s. 1; 1993, c. 539, s. 394;1994, Ex. Sess., c. 24, s. 14(c)

§ 20-396. Unlawful motor carrier operations

(a) Any person, whether carrier, shipper, consignee, or any officer, employee, agent, or representative thereof, who by means of any false statement or representation, or by the use of any false or fictitious bill, bill of lading, receipt, voucher, roll, account, claim, certificate, affidavit, deposition, lease, or bill of sale, or by any other means or device, shall knowingly and willfully seek to evade or defeat regulations as in this Article provided for motor carriers, shall be deemed guilty of a Class 3 misdemeanor and only punished by a fine of not more than five hundred dollars ($ 500.00) for the first offense and not more than two thousand dollars ($ 2,000) for any subsequent offense.

(b) Any motor carrier, or other person, or any officer, agent, employee, or representative thereof, who shall willfully fail or refuse to make a report to the Division or Department of Public Safety as required by this Article, or other applicable law, or to make specific and full, true, and correct answer to any question within 30 days from the time it is lawfully required by the Division or Department of Public Safety so to do, or to keep accounts, records, and memoranda in the form and manner prescribed by the Division or Department of Public Safety or shall knowingly and willfully falsify, destroy, mutilate, or alter any such report, account, record, or memorandum, or shall knowingly and willfully neglect or fail to make true and correct entries in such accounts, records, or memoranda of all facts and transactions appertaining to the business of the carrier, or person required under this Article to keep the same, or shall knowingly and willfully keep any accounts, records, or memoranda contrary to the rules, regulations, or orders of the Division or Department of Public Safety with respect thereto, shall be deemed guilty of a Class 3 misdemeanor and be punished for each offense only by a fine of not more than five thousand dollars ($ 5,000). As used in this subsection the words "kept" and "keep" shall be construed to mean made, prepared or compiled as well as retained.

History.
1985, c. 454, s. 1; 1993, c. 539, s. 395;1994, Ex. Sess., c. 24, s. 14(c);2002-159, s. 31.5(b);2002-190, s. 13;2011-145, s. 19.1(g)

EDITOR'S NOTE. --
Session Laws 2002-190, s. 17, provides: "The Governor shall resolve any dispute between the Department of Transportation and the Department of Crime Control and Public Safety concerning the implementation of this act [Session Laws 2002-190]."

EFFECT OF AMENDMENTS. --
Session Laws 2011-145, s. 19.1(g), effective January 1, 2012, substituted "Public Safety" for "Crime Control and Public Safety" throughout the section.

§ 20-397. Furnishing false information to the Department of Public Safety; withholding information from the Department of Public Safety

(a) Every person, firm or corporation operating under the jurisdiction of the Department of Public Safety or who is required by law to file reports with the Department of Public Safety who shall knowingly or willfully file or give false information to the Department of Public Safety in any report, reply, response, or other statement or document furnished to the Department of Public Safety shall be guilty of a Class 1 misdemeanor.

(b) Every person, firm, or corporation operating under the jurisdiction of the Department of Public Safety or who is required by law to file reports with the Department of Public Safety who shall willfully withhold clearly specified and reasonably obtainable information from the Department of Public Safety in any report, response, reply or statement filed with the Department of Public Safety in the performance of the duties of the Department of Public Safety or who shall fail or refuse to file any report, response, reply or statement required by the Department of Public Safety in the performance of the duties of the Department of Public Safety shall be guilty of a Class 1 misdemeanor.

History.

1985, c. 454, s. 1; 1993, c. 539, s. 396;1994, Ex. Sess., c. 24, s. 14(c);2002-159, s. 31.5(b);2002-190, s. 2;2011-145, s. 19.1(g)

EDITOR'S NOTE. --

Session Laws 2002-190, s. 17, provides: "The Governor shall resolve any dispute between the Department of Transportation and the Department of Crime Control and Public Safety concerning the implementation of this act [Session Laws 2002-190]."

EFFECT OF AMENDMENTS. --

Session Laws 2011-145, s. 19.1(g), effective January 1, 2012, substituted "Public Safety" for "Crime Control and Public Safety" throughout the section.

PUBLIC POLICY. --Where employer forced employee-at-will to drive truck in violation of federal law or lose his job, employer's conduct violated the public policy of this State regarding highway safety, evidenced by G.S. 20-384 and this section and provisions in the North Carolina Administrative Code; therefore, employee's suit based upon wrongful termination of his at-will employment stated a cause of action. Coman v. Thomas Mfg. Co., 325 N.C. 172, 381 S.E.2d 445 (1989). CITED in Harrison v. Edison Bros. Apparel Stores, 924 F.2d 530 (4th Cir. 1991).

§ 20-398. Household goods carrier; marking or identification of vehicles

(a) No carrier shall operate any motor vehicle upon a highway, public street, or public vehicular area within the State in the transportation of household goods for compensation unless the name or trade name and the North Carolina number assigned to the carrier by the North Carolina Utilities Commission appear on each side of the vehicle in letters and figures not less than three inches high. The North Carolina number assigned to the carrier shall also be placed on the rear left upper quadrant of the vehicle in letters and figures not less than three inches high. In case of a tractor-trailer unit, the side markings must be on the tractor and the rear markings must be on the trailer. The markings required may be printed on the vehicle or on durable placards securely fastened on the vehicle.

(b) Except as provided in subsection (b) of this section, the provisions of this section shall apply to every vehicle used by the carrier in his or her operation whether owned, rented, leased, or otherwise. However, if a vehicle is rented or leased, the words "Operated By" shall also appear above or preceding the name of the carrier, unless the vehicles are under permanent lease, in which case the name of the lessor and the words "Operated By" need not appear.

(c) The provisions of this section do not apply to carriers engaged only in interstate commerce. If the carrier is engaged in both interstate and intrastate commerce and is marked as required by the Federal Motor Carrier Safety Administration, then in that case, it will only be necessary for the carrier to print his or her North Carolina number in a conspicuous place near his or her name in letters and figures corresponding in size with Federal Motor Carrier Safety Administration regulations.

(d) Any person, whether carrier or any officer, employee, agent, or representative thereof, who violates this section shall be guilty of a Class 3 misdemeanor and punished only by a fine of not more than five hundred dollars ($ 500.00) for the first offense and not more than two thousand dollars ($ 2,000) for any subsequent offense.

History.

2011-244, s. 1

CROSS REFERENCES. --

As to civil penalty for violations of this section, see G.S. 62-280. As to penalty for false representation of household goods carrier certificate, see G.S. 62-280.1.

ARTICLE 18.
REGULATION OF FULLY AUTONOMOUS VEHICLES

§ 20-400. Definitions

The following definitions apply in this Article:

(1) **Automated driving system.** -- The hardware and software that are collectively capable of performing the entire dynamic driving task on a sustained basis, regardless of whether it is operating within a limited or unlimited operational design domain.

(2) **Dynamic driving task.** -- All of the real-time operational and tactical control functions required to operate a motor vehicle in motion or which has the engine running, such as:

a. Lateral vehicle motion control via steering.

b. Longitudinal motion control via acceleration and deceleration.

c. Monitoring the driving environment via object and event detection, recognition, classification, and response preparation.

d. Object and event response execution.

e. Maneuver planning.

f. Enhancing conspicuity via lighting, signaling, and gesturing.

(3) **Fully autonomous vehicle.** -- A motor vehicle equipped with an automated driving system that will not at any time require an occupant to perform any portion of the dynamic driving task when

the automated driving system is engaged. If equipment that allows an occupant to perform any portion of the dynamic driving task is installed, it must be stowed or made unusable in such a manner that an occupant cannot assume control of the vehicle when the automated driving system is engaged.

(4) **Minimal risk condition.** -- An operating mode in which a fully autonomous vehicle with the automated driving system engaged achieves a reasonably safe state, bringing the vehicle to a complete stop, upon experiencing a failure of the automatic driving system that renders the vehicle unable to perform any portion of the dynamic driving task.

(5) **Operator.** -- For the purposes of this Article, is a person as defined in G.S. 20-4.01. An operator does not include an occupant within a fully autonomous vehicle performing solely strategic driving functions.

(6) **Operational design domain.** -- Specific conditions under which an automated driving system is limited to effectively operate, such as geographical limitations, roadway types, speed range, and environmental conditions.

(7) **Strategic driving functions.** -- Control of navigational parameters such as trip scheduling or the selection of destinations and waypoints but does not include any portion of the dynamic driving task.

History.
2017-166, s. 1
EDITOR'S NOTE. --
Session Laws 2017-166, s. 2 provides: "This act [which enacted this Article] becomes effective December 1, 2017, and applies to offenses committed on or after that date. Prosecutions for offenses committed before the effective date of this act are not abated or affected by this act, and the statutes that would be applicable but for this act remain applicable to those prosecutions."
LEGAL PERIODICALS. --
For article, "The Regulatory Sweet Spot for Autonomous Vehicles," see 53 Wake Forest L. Rev. 337 (2018).

§ 20-401. Regulation of fully autonomous vehicles

(a) **Driver's License Not Required.** -- Notwithstanding the provisions of G.S. 20-7 and this Chapter, the operator of a fully autonomous vehicle with the automated driving system engaged is not required to be licensed to operate a motor vehicle.

(b) **Vehicle Registration Card in Vehicle.** -- For a fully autonomous vehicle, the provisions of G.S. 20-49(4) and G.S. 20-57(c) are satisfied if the vehicle registration card is in the vehicle, physically or electronically, and readily available to be inspected by an officer or inspector.

(c) **Parent or Legal Guardian Responsible for Certain Violations.** -- The parent or legal guardian of a minor is responsible for a violation of G.S. 20-135.2B, the prohibition on children in an open bed of a pickup, or G.S. 20-137.1, the child restraint law, if the violation occurs in a fully autonomous vehicle.

(d) **Minimum Age for Unsupervised Minors in Fully Autonomous Vehicles.** -- It is unlawful for any parent or legal guardian of a person less than 12 years of age to knowingly permit that person to occupy a fully autonomous vehicle in motion or which has the engine running unless the person is under the supervision of a person 18 years of age or older.

(e) **Registered Owner Responsible for Moving Violations.** -- The person in whose name the fully autonomous vehicle is registered is responsible for a violation of this Chapter that is considered a moving violation, if the violation involves a fully autonomous vehicle.

(f) **Unattended Vehicle.** -- A vehicle shall not be considered unattended pursuant to G.S. 20-163 or any other provision of Chapter 20 of the General Statutes merely because it is a fully autonomous vehicle with the automated driving system engaged.

(g) **Duty to Stop in the Event of a Crash.** -- If all of the following conditions are met when a fully autonomous vehicle is involved in a crash, then the provisions of subsections (a) through (c2) and subsection (e) of G.S. 20-166 and subsections (a) and (c) of G.S. 20-166.1 shall be considered satisfied, and no violation of those provisions shall be charged:

(1) The vehicle or the operator of the vehicle promptly contacts the appropriate law enforcement agency to report the crash.

(2) The vehicle or operator of the vehicle promptly calls for medical assistance, if appropriate.

(3) For a reportable crash, the vehicle remains at the scene of the crash until vehicle registration and insurance information is provided to the parties affected by the crash and a law enforcement officer authorizes the vehicle to be removed.

(4) For a nonreportable crash, the vehicle remains at the scene or in the immediate vicinity of the crash until vehicle registration and insurance information is provided to the parties affected by the crash.

(h) **Operation.** -- A person may operate a fully autonomous vehicle if the vehicle meets all of the following requirements:

(1) Unless an exception or exemption has been granted under applicable State or federal law, the vehicle:

    a. Is capable of being operated in compliance with Articles 3, 3A, 7, 11, and 13 of this Chapter;

    b. Complies with applicable federal law and regulations; and

    c. Has been certified in accordance with federal regulations in 49 C.F.R. Part 567 as being in compliance with applicable federal motor vehicle safety standards and bears the required certification label or labels.

(2) The vehicle has the capability to meet the requirements of subsection (g) of this section.

(3) The vehicle can achieve a minimal risk condition.

(4) The vehicle is covered by a motor vehicle liability policy meeting the applicable requirements of G.S. 20-279.21.

(5) The vehicle is registered in accordance with Part 3 of Article 3 of this Chapter, and, if registered in this State, the vehicle shall be identified on the registration and registration card as a fully autonomous vehicle.

(i) **Preemption.** -- No local government shall enact any local law or ordinance related to the regulation or operation of fully autonomous vehicles or vehicles equipped with an automated driving system, other than regulation specifically authorized in Chapter 153A and Chapter 160A of the General Statutes that is not specifically related to those types of motor vehicles.

History.
2017-166, s. 1
   EDITOR'S NOTE. --
   Session Laws 2017-166, s. 2 provides: "This act [which enacted this Article] becomes effective December 1, 2017, and applies to offenses committed on or after that date. Prosecutions for offenses committed before the effective date of this act are not abated or affected by this act, and the statutes that would be applicable but for this act remain applicable to those prosecutions."

§ 20-402. Applicability to vehicles other than fully autonomous vehicles

(a) **Definitions.** -- As used in this section, a "request to intervene" means notification by a vehicle to the human operator that the operator should promptly begin or resume performance of part or all of the dynamic driving task.

(b) **Applicability.** -- Operation of a motor vehicle equipped with an automated driving system capable of performing the entire dynamic driving task with the expectation that a human operator will respond appropriately to a request to intervene is lawful under this Chapter and subject to the provisions of this Chapter.

History.
2017-166, s. 1
   EDITOR'S NOTE. --
   Session Laws 2017-166, s. 2 provides: "This act [which enacted this Article] becomes effective December 1, 2017, and applies to offenses committed on or after that date. Prosecutions for offenses committed before the effective date of this act are not abated or affected by this act, and the statutes that would be applicable but for this act remain applicable to those prosecutions."

§ 20-403. Fully Autonomous Vehicle Committee

(a) **Committee Established.** -- There is hereby created a Fully Autonomous Vehicle Committee within the Department of Transportation.

(b) **Membership.** -- The following persons shall serve on the Committee:

(1) Secretary of Transportation, or the Secretary's designee.

(2) The Secretary of Commerce, or the Secretary's designee.

(3) The Commissioner of Insurance, or the Commissioner's designee.

(4) A representative of the Highway Patrol, designated by the Commander.

(5) A representative of the North Carolina Association of Chiefs of Police, designated by its Executive Director.

(6) A representative of the North Carolina Sheriffs' Association, designated by its President.

(7) A representative of the University of North Carolina Highway Safety Research Center, designated by the Director.

(8) At least two representatives from the autonomous vehicle industry, designated by the Secretary of Transportation.

(9) A representative of the Attorney General's Office, designated by the Attorney General, who is familiar with motor vehicle law.

(10) A representative of local law enforcement, designated by the Secretary of Transportation.

(11) A representative of the trucking industry, designated by the North Carolina Trucking Association.

(12) A planner from an urban area, designated by the North Carolina League of Municipalities.

(13) A planner from a rural area, designated by the North Carolina Association of County Commissioners.

Chapter 20

(14) Two members of the North Carolina Senate, designated by the President Pro Tempore of the Senate.

(15) Two members of the North Carolina House of Representatives, designated by the Speaker of the House.

(c) **Duties.** -- The Committee shall meet regularly, and at a minimum four times a year, to consider matters relevant to fully autonomous vehicle technology, review State motor vehicle law as they relate to the deployment of fully autonomous vehicles onto the State highway system and municipal streets, make recommendations concerning the testing of fully autonomous vehicles, identify and make recommendations for Department of Transportation traffic rules and ordinances, and make recommendations to the General Assembly on any needed changes to State law.

(d) **Staff.** -- The Department of Transportation shall provide staff and meeting space, from reasonably available resources, to the Committee.

History.

2017-166, s. 1

EDITOR'S NOTE. --

Session Laws 2017-166, s. 2 provides: "This act [which enacted this Article] becomes effective December 1, 2017, and applies to offenses committed on or after that date. Prosecutions for offenses committed before the effective date of this act are not abated or affected by this act, and the statutes that would be applicable but for this act remain applicable to those prosecutions."

Chapter 20

PART II.
RELATED LAWS

CHAPTER 1.
CIVIL PROCEDURE

SUBCHAPTER 05.
COMMENCEMENT OF ACTIONS

ARTICLE 8.
SUMMONS

§ 1-105. Service upon nonresident drivers of motor vehicles and upon the personal representatives of deceased nonresident drivers of motor vehicles

The acceptance by a nonresident of the rights and privileges conferred by the laws now or hereafter in force in this State permitting the operation of motor vehicles, as evidenced by the operation of a motor vehicle by such nonresident on the public highways of this State, or at any other place in this State, or the operation by such nonresident of a motor vehicle on the public highways of this State or at any other place in this State, other than as so permitted or regulated, shall be deemed equivalent to the appointment by such nonresident of the Commissioner of Motor Vehicles, or his successor in office, to be his true and lawful attorney and the attorney of his executor or administrator, upon whom may be served all summonses or other lawful process in any action or proceeding against him or his executor or administrator, growing out of any accident or collision in which said nonresident may be involved by reason of the operation by him, for him, or under his control or direction, express or implied, of a motor vehicle on such public highways of this State, or at any other place in this State, and said acceptance or operation shall be a signification of his agreement that any such process against him or his executor or administrator shall be of the same legal force and validity as if served on him personally, or on his executor or administrator. Service of such process shall be made in the following manner:

(1) By leaving a copy thereof, with a fee of ten dollars ($ 10.00), in the hands of the Commissioner of Motor Vehicles, or in his office. Such service, upon compliance with the other provisions of this section, shall be sufficient service upon the said nonresident.

(2) Notice of such service of process and copy thereof must be forthwith sent by certified or registered mail by plaintiff or the Commissioner of Motor Vehicles to the defendant, and the entries on the defendant's return receipt shall be sufficient evidence of the date on which notice of service upon the Commissioner of Motor Vehicles and copy of process were delivered to the defendant, on which date service on said defendant shall be deemed completed. If the defendant refuses to accept the certified or registered letter, service on the defendant shall be deemed completed on the date of such refusal to accept as determined by notations by the postal authorities on the original envelope, and if such date cannot be so determined, then service shall be deemed completed on the date that the certified or registered letter is returned to the plaintiff or Commissioner of Motor Vehicles, as determined by postal marks on the original envelope. If the certified or registered letter is not delivered to the defendant because it is unclaimed, or because he has removed himself from his last known address and has left no forwarding address or is unknown at his last known address, service on the defendant shall be deemed completed on the date that the certified or registered letter is returned to the plaintiff or Commissioner of Motor Vehicles.

(3) The defendant's return receipt, or the original envelope bearing a notation by the postal authorities that receipt was refused, and an affidavit by the plaintiff that notice of mailing the registered letter and refusal to accept was forthwith sent to the defendant by ordinary mail, together with the plaintiff's affidavit of compliance with the provisions of this section, must be appended to the summons or other process and filed with said summons, complaint and other papers in the cause.

Provided, that where the nonresident motorist has died prior to the commencement of an action brought pursuant to this section, service of process shall be made on the executor or administrator of such nonresident motorist in the same manner and on the same notice as is provided in the case of a nonresident motorist.

The court in which the action is pending shall order such continuance as may be necessary to afford the defendant reasonable opportunity to defend the action.

History.
1929, c. 75, s. 1; 1941, c. 36, s. 4; 1951, c. 646; 1953, c. 796; 1955, c. 1022; 1961, c. 1191; 1963, c. 491; 1967, c. 954, s. 4; 1971, c. 420, ss. 1, 2; 1975, c. 294;　1989, c. 645, s. 1

I. GENERAL CONSIDERATION.

THIS SECTION IS CONSTITUTIONAL and valid. Bigham v. Foor, 201 N.C. 14, 158 S.E. 548 (1931); Wynn v. Robinson, 216 N.C. 347, 4 S.E.2d 884 (1939); Davis v. Martini, 233 N.C. 351, 64 S.E.2d 1 (1951); Ewing v. Thompson, 233 N.C. 564, 65 S.E.2d 17 (1951).

The fundamental requisites of due process are notice and opportunity to be heard, both of which are adequately provided for by this section. Denton v. Ellis, 258 F. Supp. 223 (E.D.N.C. 1966).

This section has been considered against a constitutional background and upheld as giving adequate notice to the defendant and as a reasonable exercise of jurisdiction. Denton v. Ellis, 258 F. Supp. 223 (E.D.N.C. 1966).

A state may, in the exercise of its police power, provide that a nonresident motorist using its highways shall be deemed to have appointed a state official his agent to receive service of process in any action growing out of such use, if the statute provides a proper method for notifying the defendant of such service. Denton v. Ellis, 258 F. Supp. 223 (E.D.N.C. 1966).

The requirement of this section for mailing a copy of the process to a nonresident motorist's last known address provides sufficient assurance of actual notice so as to meet minimum due process requirements and to provide a constitutional basis for personal jurisdiction of a nonresident motorist who is served in conformity with this section. Humprey v. Sinnott, 84 N.C. App. 263, 352 S.E.2d 443 (1987).

IT AFFECTS A SUBSTANTIAL RIGHT. --This section is not remedial or curative, but affects a substantial right. Ashley v. Brown, 198 N.C. 369, 151 S.E. 725 (1930).

AND IS NOT RETROACTIVE. --Appointment of the Commissioner under this section is contractual, and the statute is not to be given retroactive effect; hence, service of process under this section in an action accruing before the effective force thereof is void. Ashley v. Brown, 198 N.C. 369, 151 S.E. 725 (1930).

PURPOSE OF SECTION. --The broad purpose of this section is to enable a resident motorist to bring a nonresident motorist, who would otherwise be beyond this jurisdiction by the time suit could be instituted, within the jurisdiction of our courts to answer for a negligent injury inflicted while the nonresident was using the highways of this State. Hart v. Queen City Coach Co., 241 N.C. 389, 85 S.E.2d 319 (1955).

The evident purpose of this section is to extend the State's judicial power broadly to permit North Carolina residents to acquire jurisdiction over nonresidents who may be held responsible for injuries or death caused by their automobiles. Davis v. St. Paul-Mercury Indem. Co., 294 F.2d 641 (4th Cir. 1961).

Although this section enables a North Carolina resident to obtain personal jurisdiction over any nonresident involved in an automobile accident in this state by virtue of the operation of a motor vehicle in North Carolina, the purpose of the statute is to provide jurisdiction over the driver who inflicted the injuries. Riddick v. Myers, 131 N.C. App. 871, 509 S.E.2d 469 (1998).

A NARROW INTERPRETATION OF THIS SECTION WOULD DEFEAT ITS PURPOSE. Davis v. St. Paul-Mercury Indem. Co., 294 F.2d 641 (4th Cir. 1961).

THIS SECTION MUST BE STRICTLY CONSTRUED. --Substituted or constructive service of process is a radical departure from the rule of the common law, and therefore statutes authorizing it must be strictly construed, both as to the proper grant of authority for such service and in determining whether effective service under the statute has been made. Coble v. Brown, 1 N.C. App. 1, 159 S.E.2d 259 (1968).

AND STRICTLY COMPLIED WITH. --The provisions of this section are in derogation of the common law and must be strictly complied with. Carolina Plywood Distribs., Inc. v. McAndrews, 270 N.C. 91, 153 S.E.2d 770 (1967).

The provisions of this section are in derogation of the common law and must be strictly complied with, to the extent that actual notice given in any manner other than that prescribed by the statute cannot supply constitutional validity to it or to service under it. Philpott v. Kerns, 285 N.C. 225, 203 S.E.2d 778 (1974).

While this section must be strictly construed because it is in derogation of the common law, where the possibility of confusion among people of ordinary intelligence is virtually impossible, a summons should not be found invalid simply because of technical mistakes or poor wording. Humprey v. Sinnott, 84 N.C. App. 263, 352 S.E.2d 443 (1987).

THIS SECTION DOES NOT IN ANY WAY CHANGE OR AMEND THE LAW GOVERNING THE COMMENCEMENT OF ACTIONS or the contents of a summons. Carolina Plywood Distribs., Inc. v. McAndrews, 270 N.C. 91, 153 S.E.2d 770 (1967).

BUT PROVIDES ARTIFICIAL METHOD OF SERVING PROCESS. --This section provides a statutory and artificial method by which duly issued process may be served on nonresident motorists. Carolina Plywood Distribs., Inc. v. McAndrews, 270 N.C. 91, 153 S.E.2d 770 (1967).

STATUTES IN PARI MATERIA. --G.S. 20-22, 20-37, 20-38 (now repealed) and 20-78, dealing with the privilege and responsibilities of persons operating motor vehicles on the public highways of the State, and this section relating to service of process on a nonresident who has committed a tort in the operation of a vehicle on the public highways of the State, deal with the same subject matter and must be considered in pari materia. Morrisey v. Crabtree, 143 F. Supp. 105 (M.D.N.C. 1956).

THIS SECTION AND FORMER G.S. 1-89, RELATING TO CONTENTS AND RETURN OF SUMMONS,

WERE TO BE CONSTRUED TOGETHER and strictly complied with. Carolina Plywood Distribs., Inc. v. McAndrews, 270 N.C. 91, 153 S.E.2d 770 (1967). As to summons, see now G.S. 1A-1, Rule 4.

SECTION NOT IN CONFLICT WITH G.S. 1-21. -- This section and G.S. 1-105.1 are not in conflict with and do not repeal G.S. 1-21, even though there is no need for a tolling statute when a nonresident defendant is amenable to process. Travis v. McLaughlin, 29 N.C. App. 389, 224 S.E.2d 243, cert. denied, 290 N.C. 555, 226 S.E.2d 513 (1976).

THIS SECTION DOES NOT WARRANT SERVICE UPON A NONRESIDENT OWNER IN AN ACTION FOR ABUSE OF PROCESS based upon such owner's arrest of plaintiff after a collision between their cars in this State, since the action for abuse of process does not arise out of a collision in which defendant was involved by reason of the operation of his automobile in this State. Lindsay v. Short, 210 N.C. 287, 186 S.E. 239 (1936).

SECTION APPLIES TO ACTION ON JUDGMENT ENTERED IN ANOTHER STATE. --This section applies to an action against an alleged joint tort-feasor based upon judgments entered in courts of other states, arising from an accident in this State. Carolina Coach Co. v. Cox, 337 F.2d 101 (4th Cir. 1964).

NONRESIDENT WIFE LIVING WITH HER HUSBAND IN ANOTHER STATE MAY SERVE SUMMONS ON HIM BY SERVICE ON COMMISSIONER in her action instituted in a county in this State, to recover for injuries sustained in an automobile accident which occurred in this State and which resulted from his alleged negligence. Alberts v. Alberts, 217 N.C. 443, 8 S.E.2d 523 (1940).

Where plaintiff is the wife of defendant, both are nonresidents, and the action was instituted to recover for injuries sustained by plaintiff in an automobile accident which occurred in this State, service of process on defendant by service on the Commissioner under the provisions of this section is valid. Bogen v. Bogen, 219 N.C. 51, 12 S.E.2d 649 (1941), rev'd on other grounds, 220 N.C. 648, 18 S.E.2d 162 (1942).

G. S. 1-105.1 MAKES THIS SECTION APPLICABLE TO RESIDENTS OF THE STATE WHO LEAVE and remain without the State subsequent to an accident. Denton v. Ellis, 258 F. Supp. 223 (E.D.N.C. 1966).

Before the enactment of G.S. 1-105.1, the method of serving process on a nonresident provided in this section and former G.S. 1-106 was ineffective to obtain service of process on a citizen and resident of this State while such citizen was residing temporarily outside the State, or was in the armed services of the United States and stationed in another state or foreign country. Foster v. Holt, 237 N.C. 495, 75 S.E.2d 319 (1953).

BEFORE THE 1953 AMENDMENT, THIS SECTION MADE NO PROVISION FOR SERVICE ON THE PERSONAL REPRESENTATIVE of a deceased automobile owner who died after an accident occurring in this State and before service of process, and service under the statute upon such personal representative conferred no jurisdiction on our courts, since an agency, unless coupled with an interest, is terminated by the death of the principal. Dowling v. Winters, 208 N.C. 521, 181 S.E. 751 (1935).

PURPOSE AND SCOPE OF 1953 AMENDMENT. --Except for changes in respect of the manner of service, it seems clear that the authorization of an action and service of process upon nonresident drivers of motor vehicles and upon the personal representatives of deceased nonresident drivers of motor vehicles was the only purpose and significant effect of the 1953 amendment. Franklin v. Standard Cellulose Prods., Inc., 261 N.C. 626, 135 S.E.2d 655 (1964).

1953 AMENDMENT AUTHORIZES SERVICE ON PERSONAL REPRESENTATIVE OF DECEASED NONRESIDENT. --The 1953 amendment to this section authorizes service of process on and the maintenance of an action against a foreign administrator of a nonresident driver fatally injured in a collision in this State to recover for the alleged negligent operation of the vehicle by the nonresident. Franklin v. Standard Cellulose Prods., Inc., 261 N.C. 626, 135 S.E.2d 655 (1964).

This section clearly permits nonresident administrators to be sued in the State, in actions "growing out of any accident or collision in which said nonresident may be involved by reason of the operation by him, for him, or under his control or direction, express or implied, of a motor vehicle [anywhere within the State]." Tolson v. Hodge, 411 F.2d 123 (4th Cir. 1969).

THE OVERWHELMING WEIGHT OF AUTHORITY SUSTAINS THE ASSERTION OF JURISDICTION OVER PERSONAL REPRESENTATIVES of nonresident motorists. Tolson v. Hodge, 411 F.2d 123 (4th Cir. 1969).

While North Carolina, by virtue of this section, permits a suit against the nonresident administrator of a motorist who became involved in an auto accident in North Carolina, nonresident administrators are otherwise held to lack the capacity to sue or be sued. However, the argument that the lack of capacity to initiate suit, while having capacity to be sued, renders a statute like this section "grossly unfair" has been specifically rejected. Tolson v. Hodge, 411 F.2d 123 (4th Cir. 1969).

THE LEGISLATURE, BY THE 1955 AMENDMENT, INTENDED ONLY TO BROADEN THE AREA OF VEHICULAR OPERATION to include private ways and places on land not within the confines of public highways. Byrd v. Piedmont Aviation, Inc., 256 N.C. 684, 124 S.E.2d 880 (1962).

AND DID NOT INTEND TO ENLARGE AND EXTEND THE MEANING OF THE WORDS "MOTOR VEHICLE." The 1955 amendment did not undertake to change the type of vehicle, but merely enlarged the sphere of its operation. Byrd v. Piedmont Aviation, Inc., 256 N.C. 684, 124 S.E.2d 880 (1962).

MEANING OF "MOTOR VEHICLE". --The ordinary, popular and common acceptance of the term "motor vehicle" has no relation to machines used in travel by air; it involves only motor-driven devices used in travel by land. Byrd v. Piedmont Aviation, Inc., 256 N.C. 684, 124 S.E.2d 880 (1962).

AN AIRPLANE IS NOT A "MOTOR VEHICLE" within the purview of this section. Byrd v. Piedmont Aviation, Inc., 256 N.C. 684, 124 S.E.2d 880 (1962).

TERM "PUBLIC HIGHWAYS" INCLUDES PUBLIC STREETS. --When the legislature authorized the service of process on a nonresident in an action for damages growing out of an accident occurring on the "public highways" of North Carolina, it covered accidents on public streets as well as public roads, for both are public highways. Morrisey v. Crabtree, 143 F. Supp. 105 (M.D.N.C. 1956).

APPLIED in MacClure v. Accident & Cas. Ins. Co., 229 N.C. 305, 49 S.E.2d 742 (1948); Todd v. Thomas, 202 F. Supp. 45 (E.D.N.C. 1962); Lamb v. McKibbon, 15 N.C. App. 229, 189 S.E.2d 547 (1972); Hargett v. Reed, 95 N.C. App. 292, 382 S.E.2d 791 (1989).

CITED in Howard v. Queen City Coach Co., 212 N.C. 201, 193 S.E. 138 (1937); Townsend v. Carolina Coach Co., 231 N.C. 81, 56 S.E.2d 39 (1949); Hodges v. Home Ins. Co., 232 N.C. 475, 61 S.E.2d 372 (1950); Ellington v. Milne, 14 F.R.D. 241 (E.D.N.C. 1953); Howard v. Sasso, 253 N.C. 185, 116 S.E.2d 341 (1960); Nationwide Mut. Ins. Co. v. Roberts, 261 N.C. 285, 134 S.E.2d 654 (1964); Franklin v. Standard Cellulose Prods., Inc., 261 N.C. 626, 135 S.E.2d 655 (1964); DeArmon v. B. Mears Corp., 312 N.C. 749, 325 S.E.2d 223 (1985); Seabrooke v. Hagin, 83 N.C. App. 60, 348 S.E.2d 614 (1986); Gibson v. Mena, 144 N.C. App. 125, 548 S.E.2d 745 (2001).

II. PROOF TO SUSTAIN SERVICE OF PROCESS.

TO SUSTAIN SERVICE OF PROCESS UPON DEFENDANT UNDER THIS SECTION PURSUANT TO § 1-105.1, THE PLAINTIFFS MUST SHOW EITHER: (1) That defendant had established a residence outside the State subsequent to the accident or collision, or (2) That he had left the State subsequent to the collision complained of and remained absent from the State for 60 days or more continuously. Coble v. Brown, 1 N.C. App. 1, 159 S.E.2d 259 (1968).

DEFENDANT HELD SUFFICIENTLY IDENTIFIED IN SUMMONS. --In an action for damages against a nonresident arising from his operation of a motor vehicle in this state, where summons was served to the Commissioner of Motor Vehicles pursuant to this statute, there was no possibility of misunderstanding as to who the true defendant was where defendant's name and address were listed directly under the Commissioner and defendant's name appeared both in the caption of the case and in the accompanying complaint. Smith v. Schraffenberger, 90 N.C. App. 589, 369 S.E.2d 90, cert. denied, 323 N.C. 366, 373 S.E.2d 549 (1988).

RESIDENCE OF DEFENDANT AT TIME OF ACCIDENT CONTROLLED the application of this section, G.S. 1-105.1 and former G.S. 1-107 under federal Rule 4(d)7. Denton v. Ellis, 258 F. Supp. 223 (E.D.N.C. 1966).

RESIDENT OF CANADA IS "NONRESIDENT". --A resident of Canada who operated an automobile involved in an accident on a public highway in this State was a "nonresident" within the purview of this section. Ewing v. Thompson, 233 N.C. 564, 65 S.E.2d 17 (1951).

MEMBER OF ARMED SERVICES AND WIFE STATIONED HERE UNDER MILITARY ORDERS. --Where the evidence tended to show that a member of the armed services, accompanied by his wife, was stationed in this State under military orders at the time of the accident in suit, that prior to his entry into service he was a resident of another state, and that at the time of the service of summons both had moved to another state incident to his orders, without evidence that they were in this State for any purpose other than that contemplated by his military service or that they ever formed any intention of making this State their place of residence, was sufficient to support the trial court's finding of fact that at the time of the accident they were nonresidents so as to subject them to service of summons under this section. Hart v. Queen City Coach Co., 241 N.C. 389, 85 S.E.2d 319 (1955).

CONCLUSIVE EFFECT OF FINDING OF NONRESIDENCE ON APPEAL. --The finding of the trial court that defendants were nonresidents on the date of the automobile collision in suit, and were, therefore, subject to service under this section, is conclusive on appeal if such finding is supported by evidence. Hart v. Queen City Coach Co., 241 N.C. 389, 85 S.E.2d 319 (1955).

Upon motion to dismiss an action on the ground that the defendant was a resident of this State and was served with summons under a statute authorizing service on nonresidents, the finding of fact by the superior court judge that the defendant was a nonresident, based upon competent evidence, was conclusive on appeal. Bigham v. Foor, 201 N.C. 14, 158 S.E. 548 (1931).

STATE MAY ASSERT JURISDICTION OVER OWNER AS WELL AS DRIVER. --The State has a strong interest in being able to provide a convenient forum where its citizens may be able to seek, from the owner as well as from the actual operator, compensation for injuries that will often be extremely serious. Jurisdiction over the driver who inflicted the injury does not exhaust the State's interest; it is not pushing the matter too far to recognize that the State may also assert the jurisdiction of its courts over the owner who placed the vehicle in the driver's hands to take it onto the State's highways. Davis v. St. Paul-Mercury Indem. Co., 294 F.2d 641 (4th Cir. 1961).

Ownership of property, particularly that which is capable of inflicting serious injury, may fairly be coupled with an obligation upon the owner to stand suit where the property is or has been taken with his consent. Davis v. St. Paul-Mercury Indem. Co., 294 F.2d 641 (4th Cir. 1961).

BUT NEITHER OWNERSHIP NOR PHYSICAL PRESENCE IS NECESSARY. --By the express language of this section, the operation of a motor vehicle by a nonresident on the highways is the equivalent of the appointment of the Commissioner of Motor Vehicles as process agent for the nonresident. Neither ownership nor physical presence in the motor vehicle is necessary for valid service. It is sufficient if the nonresident had the legal right to exercise control at the moment the asserted cause of action arose. Pressley v. Turner, 249 N.C. 102, 105 S.E.2d 289 (1958).

Under this section, the ownership or lack of ownership by the nonresident defendant of the motor vehicle involved in the accident is of no legal consequence insofar as his amenability to constructive service of process is concerned. Davis v. Martini, 233 N.C. 351, 64 S.E.2d 1 (1951).

CAR MUST BE OPERATED BY, FOR OR UNDER DIRECTION OR CONTROL OF NONRESIDENT DEFENDANT. --This section provides for constructive service of process upon a nonresident defendant in either of the following situations: (1) Where the nonresident was personally operating the vehicle; or (2) Where the vehicle was being operated for the nonresident, or under his control or direction, express or implied. Davis v. Martini, 233 N.C. 351, 64 S.E.2d 1 (1951).

To sustain service of process under this section there must be a finding to the effect that the owner's motor vehicle, on the occasion of the collision, was being operated "for him, or under his control or direction." Howard v. Sasso, 253 N.C. 185, 116 S.E.2d 341 (1960).

In order to hold an attempted service upon a nonresident valid under this section there must be sufficient evidence to support a finding that the automobile was operated under the "control or direction, express or implied" of the nonresident defendant. Smith v. Haughton, 206 N.C. 587, 174 S.E. 506 (1934); Howard v. Sasso, 253 N.C. 185, 116 S.E.2d 341 (1960).

OWNER MAY BE PRESUMED TO HAVE RIGHT OF CONTROL. --An automobile owner may not unreasonably be presumed to have a right to exercise control. Davis v. St. Paul-Mercury Indem. Co., 294 F.2d 641 (4th Cir. 1961).

AND UNLIKELIHOOD THAT HE WILL EXERCISE IT IS IMMATERIAL. --The unlikelihood that the owner will in fact exercise his legal right to control the operation of the automobile is immaterial. Davis v. St. Paul-Mercury Indem. Co., 294 F.2d 641 (4th Cir. 1961).

OWNER NEED NOT BE PHYSICALLY IN A POSITION TO DIRECT DRIVER. --This section does not require that the owner be physically in a position to direct the driver's every move. Davis v. St. Paul-Mercury Indem. Co., 294 F.2d 641 (4th Cir. 1961).

THE WORDS "EXPRESS OR IMPLIED" SUGGEST ONLY A MINIMAL CONNECTION BETWEEN THE DRIVER AND THE OWNER, which is satisfied if the owner has a legal right to control the operation of the automobile. Davis v. St. Paul-Mercury Indem. Co., 294 F.2d 641 (4th Cir. 1961).

DRIVER NEED NOT BE ACTING FOR PECUNIARY BENEFIT OF OWNER. --This section does not require that the driver be acting for the pecuniary benefit of the owner. Davis v. St. Paul-Mercury Indem. Co., 294 F.2d 641 (4th Cir. 1961).

THE "FAMILY PURPOSE" DOCTRINE IS NOT DETERMINATIVE in interpreting this section where "control or direction" are the standards. Davis v. St. Paul-Mercury Indem. Co., 294 F.2d 641 (4th Cir. 1961).

FAMILY-PURPOSE AUTOMOBILE OPERATED BY SON OF OWNER. --A family-purpose automobile, owned by a resident of Canada, and operated by her son on a public highway in this State, is operated for the owner, or under her control or direction, express or implied, within the purview of this section. Ewing v. Thompson, 233 N.C. 564, 65 S.E.2d 17 (1951).

EVIDENCE HELD SUFFICIENT TO SHOW CONTROL BY NONRESIDENT DEFENDANT. --An affidavit of a salesman that the details of his schedule and the control of his automobile were determined by him, subject to the approval of his corporate employer, supported the finding of the court that the automobile was being operated for the corporate employer and under its control and direction, express or implied, within the meaning of this section, and in an action to recover for alleged negligent operation of the car, service of process on the corporate employer through the Commissioner was valid. Wynn v. Robinson, 216 N.C. 347, 4 S.E.2d 884 (1939). See also, Queen City Coach Co. v. Chattanooga Medicine Co., 220 N.C. 442, 17 S.E.2d 478 (1941).

Averments in affidavits that the automobile causing the injury in suit, admittedly owned by the nonresident corporate defendant and driven in this State by its salesman, was being driven here with the corporation's permission for the purpose of effecting a sale, was sufficient evidence to support the court's finding that the automobile was being driven at the time of the injury for the corporation or was under its implied control and direction so as to support service of process on it by service on the Commissioner. Crabtree v. Burroughs-White Chevrolet Sales Co., 217 N.C. 587, 9 S.E.2d 23 (1940).

For additional case holding evidence sufficient to show control of motor vehicle by nonresident defendant, see Davis v. Martini, 233 N.C. 351, 64 S.E.2d 1 (1951).

EVIDENCE HELD INSUFFICIENT TO SHOW CONTROL. --Where a deputy sheriff of the state of South Carolina was traveling through this State to return a prisoner to that state in his own car, which was driven by another whom he engaged to drive the car and to assist in returning the prisoner, it was held that the deputy sheriff was without authority to designate another to act for the sheriff, and the driver of the car was not operating same for the sheriff and under the sheriff's direction and control within the purview of this section, and therefore service of process on the sheriff by service on the Commissioner was void. Blake v. Allen, 221 N.C. 445, 20 S.E.2d 552 (1942).

FOR CASE HOLDING FINDINGS OF FACT SUFFICIENT TO SUPPORT SERVICE UNDER THIS SECTION, see Winborne v. Stokes, 238 N.C. 414, 78 S.E.2d 171 (1953).

Chapter 1

III. PROCEDURE FOR SERVICE AND NOTICE.

EITHER SERVICE UNDER THIS SECTION OR UNDER FORMER PARAGRAPH (J)(9) OF G.S. 1A-1, RULE 4 IS AVAILABLE to serve a nonresident operator of a motor vehicle under appropriate circumstances, since validity of this section does not make it exclusive. House v. House, 22 N.C. App. 686, 207 S.E.2d 339 (1974).

THE ISSUANCE OF A VALID SUMMONS IS NECESSARY for there to be compliance with the provisions of this section. Carolina Plywood Distribs., Inc. v. McAndrews, 270 N.C. 91, 153 S.E.2d 770 (1967).

THE SUMMONS MUST COMMAND THE SHERIFF OR OTHER PROPER OFFICER TO SUMMON THE DEFENDANT OR DEFENDANTS. Carolina Plywood Distribs., Inc. v. McAndrews, 270 N.C. 91, 153 S.E.2d 770 (1967).

SUMMONS WHICH WAS DIRECTED TO THE COMMISSIONER OF MOTOR VEHICLES RATHER THAN TO DEFENDANT WAS NOT FATALLY DEFECTIVE where it was clearly directed to the Commissioner in his representative capacity as process agent for defendant. Humprey v. Sinnott, 84 N.C. App. 263, 352 S.E.2d 443 (1987).

SUMMONS HELD DEFECTIVE WHERE DIRECTED TO COMMISSIONER RATHER THAN DEFENDANTS. --A summons was held patently defective when it was directed not to the nonresident defendants as required by G.S. 1A-1, Rule 4(c), but instead was directed to the Commissioner of Motor Vehicles, who was summoned and notified to appear and answer the complaint. Philpott v. Kerns, 285 N.C. 225, 203 S.E.2d 778 (1974).

Where the summons commanded the sheriff to summons the Commissioner of Motor Vehicles only and did not command the sheriff to summons the defendants at all, and the Commissioner duly mailed a copy to the nonresident defendants, the nonresidents were not summoned and the court had no jurisdiction in the absence of a general appearance by them. Carolina Plywood Distribs., Inc. v. McAndrews, 270 N.C. 91, 153 S.E.2d 770 (1967).

MEANING OF SUBDIVISION (2). --The provision in subdivision (2) of this section making the defendant's return receipt "sufficient evidence of the date on which notice of service upon the Commissioner of Motor Vehicles and copy of process were delivered to the defendant" does not mean that all that is required to effect service upon a nonresident motorist is the return of a receipt for registered mail signed by the defendant. This provision did not replace the statutory scheme for substituted service; rather, it merely provided a conclusive means of determining when that service had been accomplished. Service is still to be made "by leaving" the process with the Commissioner of Motor Vehicles. Byrd v. Pawlick, 362 F.2d 390 (4th Cir. 1966).

"UNCLAIMED" REQUIREMENT NOT PREDICATED ON OPPORTUNITY TO CLAIM. --Because the plain language of subdivision (2) of this section does not expressly predicate the classification of a forwarded package as "unclaimed" on non-resident defendants' first being afforded an opportunity to claim it, constructive service on defendant was complete under this section. Coiner v. Cales, 135 N.C. App. 343, 520 S.E.2d 61 (1999).

UNLIKE SERVICE BY PUBLICATION, THERE APPEARS TO BE NO DUE DILIGENCE REQUIREMENT UNDER SUBDIVISION (2); all that is required is "sufficient compliance," and using the address on a three-year old accident report was deemed sufficient. Coiner v. Cales, 135 N.C. App. 343, 520 S.E.2d 61 (1999).

SERVICE HELD INSUFFICIENT DESPITE DEFENDANT'S RECEIPT OF NOTICE. --Where, apparently through inadvertence, the order for service of process upon a nonresident motorist under this section was directed to the sheriff of one county, but was forwarded by the plaintiff's attorneys to the sheriff of another county and by him served upon the Commissioner of Motor Vehicles, service was insufficient, notwithstanding that notice of service of process upon the Commissioner and a copy thereof did reach the defendant by registered mail as required by subdivision (2) of this section. Byrd v. Pawlick, 362 F.2d 390 (4th Cir. 1966).

WHAT SHERIFF'S RETURN MUST SHOW. -- When service of process on a nonresident through the Commissioner of Motor Vehicles, as provided in this section, is sought, it is essential that the sheriff's return show that such service was made as specifically required, and that a copy of the process be sent defendant by registered mail and return receipt therefor and plaintiff's affidavit of compliance be attached to summons and filed. Propst v. Hughes Trucking Co., 223 N.C. 490, 27 S.E.2d 152 (1943).

DEFAULT JUDGMENT NOT VACATED BY DEFENDANTS' REFUSAL TO ACCEPT REGISTERED MAIL. --A default judgment will not be vacated where nonresident defendants knew plaintiff was injured by a truck owned and operated by them, and was demanding damages, and they refused to accept registered mail in order to avoid service. Morrisey v. Crabtree, 143 F. Supp. 105 (M.D.N.C. 1956).

REQUIREMENT IN SUBDIVISION (3) THAT REFUSED REGISTERED LETTER BE SENT BY ORDINARY MAIL applies only to those letters which were in fact "refused," and does not apply to those which are unclaimed or marked "moved, not forwardable." Ridge v. Wright, 35 N.C. App. 643, 242 S.E.2d 389, cert. denied, 295 N.C. 467, 246 S.E.2d 10 (1978).

EFFECT OF FILING AFFIDAVIT OF COMPLIANCE AFTER HEARING ON MOTION TO DISMISS. --Failure of plaintiff to file an affidavit of compliance required under subdivision (3) of this section until after the hearing on the motion to dismiss, which was more than three years after the accident and 114 days after service of the summons on the Commissioner of Motor Vehicles, did not render service on the nonresident defendant invalid, since filing of the affidavit did not affect the completeness of the service but rather merely perfected the record and furnished proof of compliance with this section for the guidance of the courts. Quattrone v. Rochester, 46 N.C. App. 799, 266 S.E.2d 40, cert. denied, 301 N.C. 95, 273 S.E.2d 300 (1980).

AFFIDAVIT HELD SUFFICIENT TO SUPPORT SERVICE BY CERTIFIED MAIL. --Where the plaintiff filed an affidavit of compliance, as required by subdivision (3) of this section, showing that a copy of summons and complaint was mailed to the defendant at her last known address by certified mail, return receipt requested, and that it was returned undelivered because it was unclaimed, the plaintiff showed sufficient compliance with subdivision (2) of this section, to confer jurisdiction, notwithstanding his use of certified rather than registered mail. Humprey v. Sinnott, 84 N.C. App. 263, 352 S.E.2d 443 (1987).

AFFIDAVIT HELD INSUFFICIENT TO SUPPORT SERVICE UNDER THIS SECTION AND G.S. 1-105.1. --Where plaintiffs' affidavits, stripped of incompetent evidence, were left with the statement of deputy sheriff that he went to defendant's last-known address on two occasions and defendant was not there and that he made further investigations and could not locate the whereabouts of defendant, conceding, for the purpose of argument only, that this might be held sufficient to support an averment of due diligence under the requirements of former G.S. 1-98.2, it was insufficient to make out a prima facie case to support service of process under this section and G.S. 1-105.1. Coble v. Brown, 1 N.C. App. 1, 159 S.E.2d 259 (1968).

SERVICE UNDER FEDERAL RULE. --If the requirements of this section and G.S. 1-105.1 are met, service under Rule 4 of the federal Rules of Civil Procedure is valid. Denton v. Ellis, 258 F. Supp. 223 (E.D.N.C. 1966).

AMENDMENT OF PROCESS AND PLEADING. --When the procedural requirements of this section are strictly complied with, the process and pleading are subject to amendment in accordance with general rules. Bailey v. McPherson, 233 N.C. 231, 63 S.E.2d 559 (1951); Carolina Plywood Distribs., Inc. v. McAndrews, 270 N.C. 91, 153 S.E.2d 770 (1967).

PROCEDURAL ERROR CORRECTED WHEN ANOTHER SUMMONS SERVED AND RETURNED. --If the initial service failed to comply with this section, the procedural error is corrected when another summons, dated subsequently, is served and returned as having been served on defendant by leaving a copy with the Commissioner of Motor Vehicles as process agent for defendant. Tolson v. Hodge, 411 F.2d 123 (4th Cir. 1969).

SERVICE HELD SUFFICIENT. --Where the person sought to be sued personally received notice by registered mail of summons and complaint giving him unmistakable notice that it was he who was intended to be sued, although the process ran against a nonexistent corporation of the same name as the firm operated by him, it was held that the service in strict accord with this section was sufficient to meet the requirements of due process of law. Bailey v. McPherson, 233 N.C. 231, 63 S.E.2d 559 (1951).

Where defendant refused to accept a copy of the complaint and summons because the word "Jr." was not included after his name, the Supreme Court held that the suffix "Jr." is no part of a person's name; it is a mere descriptio personae; names are to designate persons, and where the identity is certain a variance in the name is immaterial. Sink v. Schafer, 266 N.C. 347, 145 S.E.2d 860 (1966).

MOTION TO QUASH SERVICE DENIED. --Where, in an action against a nonresident bus owner to recover for the negligent operation of a bus in this State, service on the nonresident was had by service on the Commissioner of Motor Vehicles, the nonresident's motion to quash the service would be denied when the nonresident offered no evidence in support of its allegations that it had leased the bus to be operated solely by and under the exclusive control of a resident corporation and under the resident corporation's franchise right. Israel v. Baltimore & A.R.R., 262 N.C. 83, 136 S.E.2d 248 (1964).

EXTENSION OF TIME TO PLEAD. --The statutes pertaining to service of process upon a nonresident motorist contemplate giving such a defendant an opportunity to defend even beyond the right of the judge in his discretion to extend the time. Mills v. McCuen, 1 N.C. App. 403, 161 S.E.2d 628 (1968).

LEGAL PERIODICALS. --

For comment on the 1953 amendment, see 31 N.C.L. Rev. 395 (1953).

For brief comment on the 1955 amendment, see 33 N.C.L. Rev. 530 (1955).

For case law survey on process, see 41 N.C.L. Rev. 524 (1963).

For case law survey on pleading and parties, see 43 N.C.L. Rev. 873 (1965).

For case law survey on trial practice, see 43 N.C.L. Rev. 938 (1965).

For article, "Modern Statutory Approaches to Service of Process outside the State -- Comparing the North Carolina Rules of Civil Procedure with the Uniform Interstate and International Procedure Act," see 49 N.C.L. Rev. 235 (1971).

For survey of 1980 law on civil procedure, see 59 N.C.L. Rev. 1049 (1981).

OPINIONS OF THE ATTORNEY GENERAL

SERVICE OF PROCESS. --Service upon the Commissioner of Motor Vehicles, in a manner consistent with G.S. 1A-1, Rule 4, meets the requirement of this section. See opinion of Attorney General to Mr. J.M. Penny, Deputy Commissioner of Motor Vehicles, 55 N.C.A.G. 26 (1985).

Service of process pursuant to this section and G.S. 1-105.1 upon the Commissioner of Motor Vehicles may be made by leaving a copy thereof with a fee of three dollars ($3.00) in the hands of the Commissioner of Motor Vehicles, or in his office. Service by Sheriff or Marshal is not required. See opinion of Attorney General to Mr. J.M. Penny, Deputy Commissioner of Motor Vehicles, 55 N.C.A.G. 26 (1985).

Chapter 1

§ 1-105.1. Service on residents who establish residence outside the State and on residents who depart from the State

The provisions of G.S. 1-105 of this Chapter shall also apply to a resident of the State at the time of the accident or collision who establishes residence outside the State subsequent to the accident or collision and to a resident of the State at the time of the accident or collision who departs from the State subsequent to the accident or collision and remains absent therefrom for 60 days or more, continuously whether such absence is intended to be temporary or permanent.

History.

1955, c. 232; 1967, c. 954, s. 4; 1971, c. 420, ss. 1, 2

STRICT CONSTRUCTION OF SECTION. --Substituted or constructive service of process is a radical departure from the rule of the common law, and therefore statutes authorizing it must be strictly construed, both as to the proper grant of authority for such service and in determining whether effective service under the statute has been made. Coble v. Brown, 1 N.C. App. 1, 159 S.E.2d 259 (1968).

SECTION NOT IN CONFLICT WITH G.S. 1-21. -- This section and G.S. 1-105, providing for substitute service of a nonresident motorist by service upon the Commissioner of Motor Vehicles, are not in conflict with and do not repeal G.S. 1-21, even though there is no need for a tolling statute when a nonresident defendant is amenable to process. Travis v. McLaughlin, 29 N.C. App. 389, 224 S.E.2d 243, cert. denied, 290 N.C. 555, 226 S.E.2d 513 (1976).

DOMICILE IN STATE BRINGS DEFENDANT WITHIN REACH OF STATE'S JURISDICTION. --Domicile in the State is alone sufficient to bring an absent defendant within the reach of the State's jurisdiction for purposes of a personal judgment by means of appropriate substituted service, provided proper notice and opportunity for hearing were given. Denton v. Ellis, 258 F. Supp. 223 (E.D.N.C. 1966).

WHEN PLAINTIFF MUST SHOW FACTS BRINGING DEFENDANT WITHIN PURVIEW OF SECTION. --This section does not require that plaintiffs must set forth in their complaint or by affidavit the facts giving rise to the conclusion that defendant comes within the purview of the statute; nevertheless, upon attack by special appearance and motion to quash, a showing is required of the facts essential to jurisdiction. Coble v. Brown, 1 N.C. App. 1, 159 S.E.2d 259 (1968).

MERE AVERMENT OF DUE DILIGENCE IS INSUFFICIENT. --A mere averment of due diligence such as is sufficient to support service by publication in an in rem action is not sufficient for a case which arises under this section. Coble v. Brown, 1 N.C. App. 1, 159 S.E.2d 259 (1968).

AFFIDAVITS HELD INSUFFICIENT TO SUPPORT SERVICE. --Where plaintiffs' affidavits, stripped of incompetent evidence, were left with the statement of the deputy sheriff that he went to defendant's last known address on two occasions and defendant was not there and that he made further investigations and could not locate the whereabouts of defendant, conceding, for the purpose of argument only, that this might be held sufficient to support an averment of due diligence under the requirements of former G.S. 1-98.2, it was insufficient to make out a prima facie case to support service of process under this section and G.S. 1-105. Coble v. Brown, 1 N.C. App. 1, 159 S.E.2d 259 (1968).

AVERMENT AND AFFIDAVIT BASED ON HEARSAY. --Where one plaintiff simply averred that he was informed and believed that defendant had removed himself from his last known address and had left the State and remained absent for more than 60 days continuously subsequent to the collision complained of and was residing somewhere in Florida, and the deputy sheriff's affidavit averred that he talked with a woman who he was informed and believed was defendant's sister, who told him that it was her information and belief that defendant was living in Florida and that he was informed and believed that the only information he was able to obtain concerning the whereabouts of defendant indicated that the said defendant was residing in the state of Florida, address unknown, this evidence was manifestly inadmissible hearsay evidence and defendant's objection thereto was entirely proper. Coble v. Brown, 1 N.C. App. 1, 159 S.E.2d 259 (1968).

CITED in Nationwide Mut. Ins. Co. v. Roberts, 261 N.C. 285, 134 S.E.2d 654 (1964); Harrison v. Hanvey, 265 N.C. 243, 143 S.E.2d 593 (1965); Byrd v. Pawlick, 362 F.2d 390 (4th Cir. 1966); Kennedy v. Starr, 62 N.C. App. 182, 302 S.E.2d 497 (1983).

OPINIONS OF THE ATTORNEY GENERAL

SERVICE OF PROCESS pursuant to G.S. 1-105 and this section upon the Commissioner of Motor Vehicles may be made by leaving a copy thereof with a fee of three dollars ($3.00) in the hands of the Commissioner of Motor Vehicles, or in his office. Service by Sheriff or Marshal is not required. See opinion of Attorney General to Mr. J.M. Penny, Deputy Commissioner of Motor Vehicles, 55 N.C.A.G. 26 (1985).

CHAPTER 8.
EVIDENCE

ARTICLE 7.
COMPETENCY OF WITNESSES

N.C. Gen. Stat. § 8-50.3

Expired effective September 30, 2007.

EDITOR'S NOTE. --

Session Laws 2003-280, s. 5 , as amended by Session Laws 2005-27, made this section effective July 1, 2003, and expiring September 30, 2007.

USER NOTE:

For more generally applicable notes, see notes under the first section of this subpart, part, article, or chapter.

Chapter 8

CHAPTER 14.
CRIMINAL LAW

SUBCHAPTER 01.
GENERAL PROVISIONS

ARTICLE 2F.
CRIMES BY UNMANNED AIRCRAFT SYSTEMS

§ 14-7.45. Crimes committed by use of unmanned aircraft systems

All crimes committed by use of an unmanned aircraft system, as defined in G.S. 15A-300.1, while in flight over this State shall be governed by the laws of this State, and the question of whether the conduct by an unmanned aircraft system while in flight over this State constitutes a crime by the owner of the unmanned aircraft system shall be determined by the laws of this State.

History.
2014-100, 34.30(b)
ISSUE SUBMITTED TO JURY. --Trial court erred in sentencing defendant as a habitual felon when the issue was not submitted to the jury. State v. Cannon, 254 N.C. App. 794, 804 S.E.2d 199 (2017), aff'd, 2018 N.C. LEXIS 51 (N.C. 2018) aff'd, 809 S.E.2d 567, 2018 N.C. LEXIS 51 (2018).
CROSS REFERENCES. --
As to operation of unmanned aircraft systems, see G.S. 63-95.

SUBCHAPTER 05.
OFFENSES AGAINST PROPERTY

ARTICLE 16.
LARCENY

§ 14-72.7. Chop shop activity

(a) A person is guilty of a Class G felony if that person engages in any of the following activities, without regard to the value of the property in question:

(1) Altering, destroying, disassembling, dismantling, reassembling, or storing any motor vehicle or motor vehicle part the person knows or has reasonable grounds to believe has been illegally obtained by theft, fraud, or other illegal means.

(2) Permitting a place to be used for any activity prohibited by this section, where the person either owns or has legal possession of the place, and knows or has reasonable grounds to believe that the place is being used for any activity prohibited by this section.

(3) Purchasing, disposing of, selling, transferring, receiving, or possessing a motor vehicle or motor vehicle part either knowing or having reasonable grounds to believe that the vehicle identification number of the motor vehicle, or vehicle part identification number of the vehicle part, has been altered, counterfeited, defaced, destroyed, disguised, falsified, forged, obliterated, or removed.

(4) Purchasing, disposing of, selling, transferring, receiving, or possessing a motor vehicle or motor vehicle part to or from a person engaged in any activity prohibited by this section, knowing or having reasonable grounds to believe that the person is engaging in that activity.

(b) **Innocent Activities. --** The provisions of this section shall not apply to either of the following:

(1) Purchasing, disposing of, selling, transferring, receiving, possessing, crushing, or compacting a motor vehicle or motor vehicle part in good faith and without knowledge of previous illegal activity in regard to that vehicle or part, as long as the person engaging in the activity does not remove a vehicle identification number or vehicle part identification number before or during the activity.

(2) Purchasing, disposing of, selling, transferring, receiving, possessing, crushing, or compacting a motor vehicle or motor vehicle part after law enforcement proceedings are completed or as a part of law enforcement proceedings, as long as the activity is not in conflict with law enforcement proceedings.

(c) **Civil Penalty. --** Any court with jurisdiction of a criminal prosecution under this section may also assess a civil penalty. The clear proceeds of the civil penalties shall be remitted to the Civil Penalty and Forfeiture Fund in accordance with G.S. 115C-457.2. The civil penalty shall not exceed three times the assets obtained by the defendant as a result of violations of this section.

(d) **Private Actions. --** Any person aggrieved by a violation of this section may, in a civil action in any court of competent jurisdiction, obtain appropriate relief, including preliminary and other equitable or declaratory relief, compensatory and punitive damages, reasonable investigation expenses, costs of suit, and any attorneys' fees as may be provided by law.

Chapter 14

(e) **Seizure and Forfeiture.** -- Any instrumentality possessed or used to engage in the activities prohibited by this section are subject to the seizure and forfeiture provisions of G.S. 14-86.1. The real property of a place used to engage in the activities prohibited by this section is subject to the abatement and forfeiture provisions of Chapter 19 of the General Statutes.

(f) **Definitions.** -- For the purposes of this section, the following definitions apply:

(1) **Instrumentality.** -- Motor vehicle, motor vehicle part, other conveyance, tool, implement, or equipment possessed or used in the activities prohibited under this section.

(2) **Vehicle identification number.** -- A number, a letter, a character, a datum, a derivative, or a combination thereof, used by the manufacturer or the Division of Motor Vehicles for the purpose of uniquely identifying a motor vehicle.

(3) **Vehicle part identification number.** -- A number, a letter, a character, a datum, a derivative, or a combination thereof, used by the manufacturer for the purpose of uniquely identifying a motor vehicle part.

History.

2007-178, s. 1 ; 2013-323, s. 1

EFFECT OF AMENDMENTS. --

Session Laws 2013-323, s. 1 , effective December 1, 2013, in subsection (a), in the introductory language, substituted "Class G" for "Class H" and deleted "knowingly" preceding "engages"; substituted "or has reasonable grounds to believe has been illegally" for "to be illegally" in subdivision (a)(1); inserted "or has reasonable grounds to believe" in subdivision (a)(2); substituted "either knowing or having reasonable grounds to believe" for "with the knowledge" in subdivision (a)(3); and inserted "or having reasonable grounds to believe" in subdivision (a)(4). For applicability, see Editor's note.

§ 14-72.8. Felony larceny of motor vehicle parts

Unless the conduct is covered under some other provision of law providing greater punishment, larceny of a motor vehicle part is a Class I felony if the cost of repairing the motor vehicle is one thousand dollars ($ 1,000) or more.

For purposes of this section, the cost of repairing a motor vehicle means the cost of any replacement part and any additional costs necessary to install the replacement part in the motor vehicle.

History.

2009-379, s. 1

VALUE. --Statute makes larceny of a motor vehicle part a Class I felony if the cost of repairing the motor vehicle is $ 1,000 or more, and it would appear that if a defendant removed a part worth $ 500.00 from a vehicle, but the cost to repair by replacing the part would be over $ 1,000.00 because of the labor, the larceny would be elevated to a Class I felony. The statute expressly does not depend upon the fair market value of the car itself in its damaged condition as compared to its original condition or even just the value of the stolen part. State v. Gorham, 262 N.C. App. 483, 822 S.E.2d 313 (2018).

INDICTMENT. --Trial court lacked jurisdiction to try defendant for larceny of motor vehicle parts because the indictment failed to allege the cost of repairing a single motor vehicle, and thus, the indictment was invalid on its face. State v. Stephenson, -- N.C. App. --, 833 S.E.2d 393 (2019).

SUBCHAPTER 07.
OFFENSES AGAINST PUBLIC MORALITY AND DECENCY

ARTICLE 27A.
SEX OFFENDER AND PUBLIC PROTECTION REGISTRATION PROGRAMS

PART 2.
SEX OFFENDER AND PUBLIC PROTECTION REGISTRATION PROGRAM

§ 14-208.19A. Commercial drivers license restrictions

(a) The Division of Motor Vehicles, in compliance with G.S. 20-37.14A, shall not issue or renew a commercial drivers license with a P or S endorsement to any person required to register under this Article.

(b) The Division of Motor Vehicles, in compliance with G.S. 20-37.13(f) shall not issue a commercial driver learner's permit with a P or S endorsement to any person required to register under this Article.

(c) A person who is convicted of a violation that requires registration under Article 27A of Chapter 14 of the General Statutes is disqualified under G.S. 20-17.4 from driving a commercial motor vehicle that requires a commercial drivers license with a P or S endorsement for the period of time during which the person is required to maintain registration under Article 27A of Chapter 14 of the General Statutes.

(d) A person who drives a commercial passenger vehicle or a school bus and who does not have a commercial drivers license with a P or S endorsement because the person was convicted of a violation that requires registration under Article

27A of Chapter 14 of the General Statutes shall be punished as provided by G.S. 20-27.1.

History.

2009-491, s. 1

EDITOR'S NOTE. --

Session Laws 2009-491, s. 1 , enacted this section as G.S. 14-208.19. It has been renumbered as this section at the direction of the Revisor of Statutes.

Session Laws 2009-491, s. 7 , provides: "This act becomes effective December 1, 2009. This act applies to persons whose initial registration under Article 27A of Chapter 14 of the General Statutes occurs on or after December 1, 2009, and to persons who are registered under Article 27A of Chapter 14 of the General Statutes prior to December 1, 2009, and continue to be registered on or after December 1, 2009. The criminal penalties enacted by this act apply to offenses occurring on or after December 1, 2009."

SUBCHAPTER 10.
OFFENSES AGAINST THE PUBLIC SAFETY

ARTICLE 36.
OFFENSES AGAINST THE PUBLIC SAFETY

§ 14-280.3. Interference with manned aircraft by unmanned aircraft systems

(a) Any person who willfully damages, disrupts the operation of, or otherwise interferes with a manned aircraft through use of an unmanned aircraft system, while the manned aircraft is taking off, landing, in flight, or otherwise in motion, is guilty of a Class H felony.

(b) The following definitions apply to this section:

(1) **Manned aircraft.** -- As defined in G.S. 15A-300.1.

(2) **Unmanned aircraft system.** -- As defined in G.S. 15A-300.1.

History.

2014-100, s. 34.30(c)

CROSS REFERENCES. --

As to operation of unmanned aircrafts, see 63-95.

SUBCHAPTER 11.
GENERAL POLICE REGULATIONS

ARTICLE 52.
MISCELLANEOUS POLICE REGULATIONS

§ 14-401.4. Identifying marks on machines and apparatus; application to Division of Motor Vehicles for numbers

(a) No person, firm or corporation shall willfully remove, deface, destroy, alter or cover over the manufacturer's serial or engine number or any other manufacturer's number or other distinguishing number or identification mark upon any machine or other apparatus, including but not limited to farm equipment, machinery and apparatus, but excluding electric storage batteries, nor shall any person, firm or corporation place or stamp any serial, engine, or other number or mark upon such machinery, apparatus or equipment except as provided for in this section, nor shall any person, firm or corporation purchase or take into possession or sell, trade, transfer, devise, give away or in any manner dispose of such machinery, apparatus, or equipment except by intestate succession or as junk or scrap after the manufacturer's serial or engine number or mark has been willfully removed, defaced, destroyed, altered or covered up unless a new number or mark has been added as provided in this section: Provided, however, that this section shall not prohibit or prevent the owner or holder of a mortgage, conditional sales contract, title retaining contract, or a trustee under a deed of trust from taking possession for the purpose of foreclosure under a power of sale or by court order, of such machinery, apparatus, or equipment, or from selling the same by foreclosure sale under a power contained in a mortgage, conditional sales contract, title retaining contract, deed of trust, or court order; or from taking possession thereof in satisfaction of the indebtedness secured by the mortgage, deed of trust, conditional sales contract, or title retaining contract pursuant to an agreement with the owner.

(b) Each seller of farm machinery, farm equipment or farm apparatus covered by this section shall give the purchaser a bill of sale for such machinery, equipment or apparatus and shall include in the bill of sale the manufacturer's serial number or distinguishing number or identification mark, which the seller warrants to be true and correct according to his invoice or bill of sale as received from his manufacturer, supplier, or distributor or dealer.

(c) Each user of farm machinery, farm equipment or farm apparatus whose manufacturer's serial number, distinguishing number or identification mark has been obliterated or is now unrecognizable, may obtain a valid identification number for any such machinery, equipment or apparatus upon application for such number to the Division of Motor Vehicles accompanied by satisfactory proof of ownership and a subsequent certification to the Division by a member of the North Carolina Highway Patrol that said applicant has placed the number on the proper machinery, equipment or apparatus. The Division of Motor Vehicles is hereby authorized and empowered to issue appropriate identification marks or distinguishing numbers for machinery, equipment or apparatus upon application as provided in this section and the Division is further authorized and empowered to designate the place or places on the machinery, equipment or apparatus at which the identification marks or distinguishing numbers shall be placed. The Division is also authorized to designate the method to be used in placing the identification marks or distinguishing numbers on the machinery, equipment or apparatus: Provided, however, that the owner or holder of the mortgage conditional sales contract, title retaining contract, or trustee under a deed of trust in possession of such encumbered machinery, equipment, or apparatus from which the manufacturer's serial or engine number or other manufacturer's number or distinguishing mark has been obliterated or has become unrecognizable or the purchaser at the foreclosure sale thereof, may at any time obtain a valid identification number for any such machinery, equipment or apparatus upon application therefor to the Division of Motor Vehicles.

(d) Any person, firm or corporation who shall violate any part of this section shall be guilty of a Class 1 misdemeanor.

History.
1949, c. 928; 1951, c. 1110 s. 1; 1953, c. 257; 1975, c. 716, s. 5; 1993, c. 539, s. 274 ; 1994, Ex. Sess., c. 24, s. 14(c)

§ 14-401.24. Unlawful possession and use of unmanned aircraft systems

(a) It shall be a Class E felony for any person to possess or use an unmanned aircraft or unmanned aircraft system that has a weapon attached.

(b) It shall be a Class 1 misdemeanor for any person to fish or to hunt using an unmanned aircraft system.

(c) The following definitions apply to this section:

    (1) **To fish.** -- As defined in G.S. 113-130.

    (2) **To hunt.** -- As defined in G.S. 113-130.

    (3) **Unmanned aircraft.** -- As defined in G.S. 15A-300.1.

    (4) **Unmanned aircraft system.** -- As defined in G.S. 15A-300.1.

    (5) **Weapon.** -- Those weapons specified in G.S. 14-269, 14-269.2, 14-284.1, or 14-288.8 and any other object capable of inflicting serious bodily injury or death when used as a weapon.

(d) This section shall not prohibit possession or usage of an unmanned aircraft or unmanned aircraft system that is authorized by federal law or regulation.

History.
2014-100, s. 34.30(d)
  LEGAL PERIODICALS. --
  For article, "Drone Zoning," see 95 N.C.L. Rev. 133 (2016).

§ 14-401.26. TNC driver failure to display license plate information

It shall be unlawful for a transportation network company (TNC) driver, as defined in G.S. 20-280.1, to fail to display the license plate number of the TNC driver's vehicle as required by G.S. 20-280.5(d). A violation of this section shall be an infraction and shall be punishable by a fine of two hundred fifty dollars ($ 250.00).

History.
2019-194, s. 3(a)
  EDITOR'S NOTE. --
  Session Laws 2019-194, s. 1 , provides: "This act shall be known as the 'Passenger Protection Act' and may be cited by that name."
  Session Laws 2019-194, s. 3(b) , made this section, as added by Session Laws 2019-194, s. 3(a) , effective December 1, 2019, and applicable to offenses committed on or after that date.

§ 14-401.27. Impersonation of a transportation network company driver

It shall be unlawful for any person to impersonate a transportation network company (TNC) driver, as defined in G.S. 20-280.1, by a false statement, false display of distinctive signage or emblems known as a trade dress, trademark, branding, or logo of the TNC, or any other act which falsely represents that the person has a current connection with a transportation network company or falsely represents that the person is responding to a passenger ride request for a transportation network company. A violation of this section is a Class H felony if the person impersonates a TNC driver during the commission of a separate felony offense. Any other violation of this section is a Class 2 misdemeanor.

History.
2019-194, s. 3.3(a)
  EDITOR'S NOTE. --
  Session Laws 2019-194, s. 1 , provides: "This act shall be known as the 'Passenger Protection Act' and may be cited by that name."
  Session Laws 2019-194, s. 3.3(b) , made this section, as added by Session Laws 2019-194, s. 3.3(a) , effective December 1, 2019, and applicable to offenses committed on or after that date.

Chapter 14

CHAPTER 15A.
CRIMINAL PROCEDURE ACT

SUBCHAPTER 02.
LAW-ENFORCEMENT AND INVESTIGATIVE PROCEDURES

ARTICLE 16B.
USE OF UNMANNED AIRCRAFT SYSTEMS

§ 15A-300.1. Restrictions on use of unmanned aircraft systems

(a) **Definitions.** -- The following definitions apply to this Article:

(1) **Manned aircraft.** -- An aircraft, as defined in G.S. 63-1, that is operated with a person in or on the aircraft.

(2) Repealed by Session Laws 2017-160, s. 1 , effective December 1, 2017, and applicable to offenses committed on or after that date and acts occurring and causes of action arising on or after that date.

(3) **Unmanned aircraft.** -- An aircraft, as defined in G.S. 63-1, that is operated without the possibility of human intervention from within or on the aircraft.

(4) **Unmanned aircraft system.** --- An unmanned aircraft and associated elements, including communication links and components that control the unmanned aircraft that are required for the pilot in command to operate safely and efficiently in the national airspace system.

(b) **General Prohibitions.** -- Except as otherwise provided in this section, no person, entity, or State agency shall use an unmanned aircraft system to do any of the following:

(1) Conduct surveillance of:

a. A person or a dwelling occupied by a person and that dwelling's curtilage without the person's consent.

b. Private real property without the consent of the owner, easement holder, or lessee of the property.

(2) Photograph an individual, without the individual's consent, for the purpose of publishing or otherwise publicly disseminating the photograph. This subdivision shall not apply to newsgathering, newsworthy events, or events or places to which the general public is invited.

(c) **Law Enforcement Exceptions.** -- Notwithstanding the provisions of subsection (b) of this section, the use of unmanned aircraft systems by law enforcement agencies of the State or a political subdivision of the State is not prohibited in the following instances:

(1) To counter a high risk of a terrorist attack by a specific individual or organization if the United States Secretary of Homeland Security or the Secretary of the North Carolina Department of Public Safety determines that credible intelligence indicates that such a risk exists.

(2) To conduct surveillance in an area that is within a law enforcement officer's plain view when the officer is in a location the officer has a legal right to be.

(3) If the law enforcement agency first obtains a search warrant authorizing the use of an unmanned aircraft system.

(4) If the law enforcement agency possesses reasonable suspicion that, under particular circumstances, swift action is needed to prevent imminent danger to life or serious damage to property, to forestall the imminent escape of a suspect or the destruction of evidence, to conduct pursuit of an escapee or suspect, or to facilitate the search for a missing person.

(5) To photograph gatherings to which the general public is invited on public or private land.

(c1) **Emergency Management Exception.** -- Notwithstanding the provisions of subsection (b) of this section, an emergency management agency, as defined in G.S. 166A-19.3, may use unmanned aircraft systems for all functions and activities related to emergency management, including incident command, area reconnaissance, search and rescue, preliminary damage assessment, hazard risk management, and floodplain mapping.

(d) Repealed by Session Laws 2017-160, s. 2 , effective July 21, 2017.

(e) Any person who is the subject of unwarranted surveillance, or whose photograph is taken in violation of the provisions of this section, shall have a civil cause of action against the person, entity, or State agency that conducts the surveillance or that uses an unmanned aircraft system to photograph for the purpose of publishing or otherwise disseminating the photograph. In lieu of actual damages, the person whose photograph is taken may elect to recover five thousand dollars ($ 5,000) for each photograph or video that is published or otherwise disseminated, as well as reasonable costs and attorneys' fees and injunctive or other relief as determined by the court.

(f) Evidence obtained or collected in violation of this section is not admissible as evidence in a criminal prosecution in any court of law in this

State except when obtained or collected under the objectively reasonable, good-faith belief that the actions were lawful.

History.
2014-100, s. 34.30(a) ; 2017-160, ss. 1 -3

EDITOR'S NOTE. --
Session Laws 2017-160, s. 6 made the amendment to this section by Session Laws 2017-160, s. 1 , which deleted subdivision (a)(2) which formerly read: "Model aircraft. -- An aircraft, as defined in G.S. 63 1, that is mechanically driven or launched into flight and that meets all of the following requirements: a. Is flown solely for hobby or recreational purposes. b. Is not used for payment, consideration, gratuity, or benefit, directly or indirectly charged, demanded, received, or collected, by any person for the use of the aircraft or any photographic or video image produced by the aircraft."; and deleted "and that does not meet the definition of model aircraft" at the end of subdivision (a)(3), effective December 1, 2017, and applicable to offenses committed on or after that date and acts occurring and causes of action arising on or after that date.

EFFECT OF AMENDMENTS. --
Session Laws 2017-160, s. 1 , deleted subdivision (a)(2) which formerly read: "Model aircraft. -- An aircraft, as defined in G.S. 63 1, that is mechanically driven or launched into flight and that meets all of the following requirements: a. Is flown solely for hobby or recreational purposes. b. Is not used for payment, consideration, gratuity, or benefit, directly or indirectly charged, demanded, received, or collected, by any person for the use of the aircraft or any photographic or video image produced by the aircraft."; and deleted "and that does not meet the definition of model aircraft" at the end of subdivision (a)(3). For effective date and applicability, see editor's note.

Session Laws 2017-160, ss. 2 and 3, effective July 21, 2017, added subsection (c1) and deleted subsection (d) which limited the use of certain special imaging technology such as infrared and thermal imaging to scientific investigation and research, mapping, and evaluating farming operations, forestry, and investigations of vegetation or wildlife.

LEGAL PERIODICALS. --
For note, "The Peering Predator: Drone Technology Leaves Children Unprotected from Registered Sex Offenders," see 39 Campbell L. Rev. 167 (2017).
For article, "Drone Zoning," see 95 N.C.L. Rev. 133 (2016).

NOTES APPLICABLE TO ENTIRE CHAPTER
OFFICIAL COMMENTARY

This commentary is based upon the commentary included in the January 1973 report of the Criminal Code Commission with its proposed code of pretrial procedure. The consultant-draftsmen of the Commission have revised the commentary to reflect changes that were made by the General Assembly in the course of passage.

The Commission's commentary was drafted by the consultant-draftsmen in an effort to explain the rationale behind policy decisions, to enlighten practitioners as to the aims and intent of the Commission, and in some cases to draw attention to pertinent cases or factual situations which either made the inclusion of a provision desirable or necessary.

The Commission's debates and debates in committees of the legislature and on the floor are the source of much of this commentary but neither the commission nor any legislative official has reviewed and approved this commentary on a line-by-line basis.

EDITOR'S NOTE. --Session Laws 1973, c. 1286, repealed many, but not all, of the sections of Chapter 15, Criminal Procedure, and a number of sections elsewhere in the General Statutes, and enacted in their place Chapter 15A, Criminal Procedure Act, effective July 1, 1975. Certain sections in Chapter 15 and in other chapters of the General Statutes were transferred and renumbered as sections in Chapter 15A. Where appropriate, the historical citations to the repealed sections have been added to corresponding sections in Chapter 15A.

The "Official Commentary" under Articles 1 to 34, 36 to 61 of this Chapter appears as originally drafted by the Criminal Code Commission and does not reflect amendments or changes in the law since the enactment of Session Laws 1973, c. 1286.

Where they appear in this Chapter, "Amended Comment" usually means that an error in the original comment has been corrected by a subsequent amendment, and "Supplemental Comment" pertains to a later development, such as an amendment to the statute text.

Many of the cases cited in the annotations under the various sections of this Chapter were decided under former similar provisions of Chapter 15 and earlier statutes.

Session Laws 1973, c. 1286, ss. 27, 28 and 31, provided:

"Sec. 27. All statutes which refer to sections repealed or amended by this act shall be deemed, insofar as possible, to refer to those provisions of this act which accomplish the same or an equivalent purpose.

"Sec. 28. None of the provisions of this act providing for the repeal of certain sections of the General Statutes shall constitute a reenactment of the common law.

"Sec. 31. This act becomes effective on July 1, 1975, and is applicable to all criminal proceedings begun on and after that date and each provision is applicable to criminal proceedings pending on that date to the extent practicable, except § 12 [§§ 15-176.3 through 15-176.5] of this act which becomes effective on July 1, 1974."

Session Laws 1975, c. 573, amended Session Laws 1973, c. 1286, s. 31, so as to make the 1973 act effective Sept. 1, 1975, rather than July 1, 1975.

Session Laws 1975, c. 166, ss. 27 and 28, provided:

"Sec. 27. Chapter 15A of the General Statutes is hereby amended by striking out the words 'district solicitor' wherever the words appear throughout Chapter 15A, and inserting in lieu thereof the words 'district attorney,' and by striking out the word 'solicitor,' wherever the word appears throughout Chapter 15A and inserting in lieu thereof the word 'prosecutor.' The Michie Company, publishers of the General Statutes of North Carolina, is authorized and directed to make the changes directed above wherever they might appear appropriate in the text of Chapter 15A of the General Statutes.

"Sec. 28. This act shall become effective on the date that Chapter 1286 of the 1973 Session Laws becomes effective."

§ 15A-300.2. Regulation of launch and recovery sites

(a) No unmanned aircraft system may be launched or recovered from any State or private property without consent.

(b) A unit of local government may adopt an ordinance to regulate the use of the local government's property for the launch or recovery of unmanned aircraft systems.

History.
2014-100, s. 34.30(a)
   USER NOTE:
   For more generally applicable notes, see notes under the first section of this subpart, part, article, or chapter.

§ 15A-300.3. Use of an unmanned aircraft system near a confinement or correctional facility prohibited

(a) **Prohibition. --** No person, entity, or State agency shall use an unmanned aircraft system within either a horizontal distance of 500 feet, or a vertical distance of 250 feet from any local confinement facility, as defined in G.S. 153A-217, or State or federal correctional facility. For the purpose of this section, horizontal distance shall extend outward from the furthest exterior building walls, perimeter fences, and permanent fixed perimeter, or from another boundary clearly marked with posted notices. Posted notices shall be conspicuously posted not more than 100 yards apart along a marked boundary and comply with Department of Transportation guidelines.

(b) **Exceptions. --** Unless the use of the unmanned aircraft system is otherwise prohibited under State or federal law, the distance restrictions of subsection (a) of this section do not apply to any of the following:

(1) A person operating an unmanned aircraft system with written consent from the official in responsible charge of the facility.

(2) A law enforcement officer using an unmanned aircraft system in accordance with G.S. 15A-300.1(c).

(3) A public utility, as defined in G.S. 62-3(23), a provider, as defined in G.S. 146-29.2(a)(6), or a commercial entity, provided that the public utility, provider, or commercial entity complies with all of the following:

a. The unmanned aircraft system must not be used within either a horizontal distance of 150 feet, or within a vertical distance of 150 feet from any local confinement facility or State or federal correctional facility.

b. Notifies the official in responsible charge of the facility at least 24 hours prior to operating the unmanned aircraft system. A commercial entity operating in compliance with G.S.15A-300.1 and pursuant to the provisions of this subdivision is exempt from the 24-hour notice requirement.

c. Uses the unmanned aircraft system for the purpose of inspecting public utility or provider transmission lines, equipment, or communication infrastructure or for another purpose directly related to the business of the public utility, provider, or commercial entity.

d. Uses the unmanned aircraft system for commercial purposes pursuant to and in compliance with (i) Federal Aviation Administration regulations, authorizations, or exemptions and (ii) Article 10 of Chapter 63 of the General Statutes.

e. The person operating the unmanned aircraft system does not physically enter the prohibited space without an escort from the facility.

(4) An emergency management agency, as defined in G.S. 166A-19.3, emergency medical services personnel, firefighters, and law enforcement officers, when using an unmanned aircraft system in response to an emergency.

(c) **Penalty. --** The following penalties apply for violations of this section:

(1) A person who uses an unmanned aircraft system (i) in violation of subsection (a) of this section or (ii) pursuant to an exception in subsection (b) of this section and who delivers, or attempts to deliver, a weapon to a local confinement facility or State or federal correctional facility is guilty of a Class H felony, which shall include a fine of one thousand five hundred dollars ($ 1,500). For purposes of this subdivision, the term "weapon" is as defined in G.S. 14-401.24(c).

(2) A person who uses an unmanned aircraft system (i) in violation of subsection (a) of this section or (ii) pursuant to an exception in subsection (b) of this section and who delivers, or attempts to deliver, contraband to a local confinement facility or State or federal correctional facility is guilty of

a Class I felony, which shall include a fine of one thousand dollars ($ 1,000). For purposes of this subdivision, the term "contraband" includes controlled substances, as defined in G.S. 90-87, cigarettes, alcohol, and communication devices, but does not include weapons.

(3) A person who uses an unmanned aircraft system in violation of subsection (a) of this section for any other purpose is guilty of a Class 1 misdemeanor, which shall include a fine of five hundred dollars ($ 500.00).

(d) **Seizure, Forfeiture, and Disposition of Seized Property.** -- A law enforcement agency may seize an unmanned aircraft system and any attached property, weapons, and contraband used in violation of this section. An unmanned aircraft system used in violation of this section and seized by a law enforcement agency is subject to forfeiture and disposition pursuant to G.S. 18B-504. An innocent owner or holder of a security interest applying to the court for release of the unmanned aircraft system, in accordance with G.S. 18B-504(h), shall also provide proof of ownership or security interest and written certification that the unmanned aircraft system will not be returned to the person who was charged with the violation of subsection (a) of this section. The court shall forfeit and dispose of any other property, weapons, or contraband seized by a law enforcement agency in connection with a violation of this section pursuant to G.S. 18B-504, 14-269.1, 90-112, or any combination thereof.

History.
2017-179, s. 1

EDITOR'S NOTE. --
Session Laws 2017-179, s. 2 , provides: "2. For the purpose of restricting the operation of an unmanned aircraft system in accordance with Section 1 of this act, the Division of Aviation of the Department of Transportation shall petition the Federal Aviation Administration (FAA) to designate any local confinement facility, as defined in G.S. 153A-217, or State or federal correctional facility in the State as a fixed site facility, pursuant to rules and regulations adopted pursuant to section 2209 of the FAA Extension, Safety, and Security Act of 2016, Public Law No. 114-190. The Division shall follow all guidance from the FAA in submitting and processing the petition. The Division shall publish designations by the FAA in accordance with this act on the Division Web site.

"At the request of the Division, the Social Services Commission of the Department of Health and Human Services shall provide to the Division a list of local confinement facilities, as defined in G.S. 153A-217, including facility location and a contact person for each facility. At the request of the Division, the Department of Public Safety shall provide to the Division a list of State correctional facilities, including facility location, a contact person for each facility, and each facility's operational status."

Session Laws 2017-179, s. 3 , provides: "3. The Division of Aviation of the Department of Transportation shall develop guidelines for the content and dimensions for posted notices to mark boundaries in accordance with Section 1 of this act."

Session Laws 2017-179, s. 4 made this section effective December 1, 2017, and applicable to offenses committed on or after that date.

USER NOTE:
For more generally applicable notes, see notes under the first section of this subpart, part, article, or chapter.

Chapter 15A

CHAPTER 25.
UNIFORM COMMERCIAL CODE

ARTICLE 1.
GENERAL PROVISIONS

PART 2.
GENERAL DEFINITIONS AND PRINCIPLES OF INTERPRETATION

§ 25-1-201. General definitions

(a) Unless the context otherwise requires, words or phrases defined in this section, or in the additional definitions contained in other Articles of this Chapter that apply to particular Articles or Parts thereof, have the meanings stated.

(b) Subject to definitions contained in other articles of this Chapter that apply to particular articles or parts thereof:

(1) "Action," in the sense of a judicial proceeding, includes recoupment, counterclaim, setoff, suit in equity, and any other proceeding in which rights are determined.

(2) "Aggrieved party" means a party entitled to pursue a remedy.

(3) "Agreement," as distinguished from "contract," means the bargain of the parties in fact, as found in their language or inferred from other circumstances, including course of performance, course of dealing, or usage of trade as provided in G.S. 25-1-303.

(4) "Bank" means a person engaged in the business of banking and includes a savings bank, savings and loan association, credit union, and trust company.

(5) "Bearer" means a person in control of a negotiable electronic document of title or a person in possession of a negotiable instrument, negotiable tangible document of title, or certificated security that is payable to bearer or indorsed in blank.

(6) "Bill of lading" means a document of title evidencing the receipt of goods for shipment issued by a person engaged in the business of directly or indirectly transporting or forwarding goods. The term does not include a warehouse receipt.

(7) "Branch" includes a separately incorporated foreign branch of a bank.

(8) "Burden of establishing" a fact means the burden of persuading the trier of fact that the existence of the fact is more probable than its nonexistence.

(9) "Buyer in ordinary course of business" means a person that buys goods in good faith, without knowledge that the sale violates the rights of another person in the goods, and in the ordinary course from a person, other than a pawnbroker, in the business of selling goods of that kind. A person buys goods in the ordinary course if the sale to the person comports with the usual or customary practices in the kind of business in which the seller is engaged or with the seller's own usual or customary practices. A person that sells oil, gas, or other minerals at the wellhead or minehead is a person in the business of selling goods of that kind. A buyer in ordinary course of business may buy for cash, by exchange of other property, or on secured or unsecured credit, and may acquire goods or documents of title under a preexisting contract for sale. Only a buyer that takes possession of the goods or has a right to recover the goods from the seller under Article 2 of this Chapter may be a buyer in ordinary course of business. "Buyer in ordinary course of business" does not include a person that acquires goods in a transfer in bulk or as security for or in total or partial satisfaction of a money debt.

(10) "Conspicuous," with reference to a term, means so written, displayed, or presented that a reasonable person against which it is to operate ought to have noticed it. Whether a term is "conspicuous" or not is a decision for the court. Conspicuous terms include the following:

a. A heading in capitals equal to or greater in size than the surrounding text, or in contrasting type, font, or color to the surrounding text of the same or lesser size; and

b. Language in the body of a record or display in larger type than the surrounding text, or in contrasting type, font, or color to the surrounding text of the same size, or set off from surrounding text of the same size by symbols or other marks that call attention to the language.

(11) "Consumer" means an individual who enters into a transaction primarily for personal, family, or household purposes.

(12) "Contract," as distinguished from "agreement," means the total legal obligation that results from the parties' agreement as determined by this Chapter as supplemented by any other applicable laws.

(13) "Creditor" includes a general creditor, a secured creditor, a lien creditor, and any representative of creditors, including

an assignee for the benefit of creditors, a trustee in bankruptcy, a receiver in equity, and an executor or administrator of an insolvent debtor's or assignor's estate.

(14) "Defendant" includes a person in the position of defendant in a counterclaim, cross-claim, or third-party claim.

(15) "Delivery," with respect to an electronic document of title means voluntary transfer of control and with respect to an instrument, a tangible document of title, or chattel paper, means voluntary transfer of possession.

(16) "Document of title" means a record (i) that in the regular course of business or financing is treated as adequately evidencing that the person in possession or control of the record is entitled to receive, control, hold, and dispose of the record and the goods the record covers and (ii) that purports to be issued by or addressed to a bailee and to cover goods in the bailee's possession which are either identified or are fungible portions of an identified mass. The term includes a bill of lading, transport document, dock warrant, dock receipt, warehouse receipt, and order for delivery of goods. An electronic document of title means a document of title evidenced by a record consisting of information stored in an electronic medium. A tangible document of title means a document of title evidenced by a record consisting of information that is inscribed on a tangible medium.

(17) "Fault" means a default, breach, or wrongful act or omission.

(18) "Fungible goods" means:
a. Goods of which any unit, by nature or usage of trade, are the equivalent of any other like unit; or
b. Goods that by agreement are treated as equivalent.

(19) "Genuine" means free of forgery or counterfeiting.

(20) "Good faith," except as otherwise provided in Article 5 of this Chapter, means honesty in fact and the observance of reasonable commercial standards of fair dealing.

(21) "Holder" means:
a. The person in possession of a negotiable instrument that is payable either to bearer or to an identified person that is the person in possession;
b. The person in possession of a negotiable tangible document of title if the goods are deliverable either to bearer or to the order of the person in possession; or
c. The person in control of a negotiable electronic document of title.

(22) "Insolvency proceeding" includes an assignment for the benefit of creditors or other proceeding intended to liquidate or rehabilitate the estate of the person involved.

(23) "Insolvent" means:
a. Having generally ceased to pay debts in the ordinary course of business other than as a result of bona fide dispute;
b. Being unable to pay debts as they become due; or
c. Being insolvent within the meaning of federal bankruptcy law.

(24) "Money" means a medium of exchange currently authorized or adopted by a domestic or foreign government. The term includes a monetary unit of account established by an intergovernmental organization or by agreement between two or more countries.

(25) "Organization" means a person other than an individual.

(26) "Party," as distinguished from "third party," means a person that has engaged in a transaction or made an agreement subject to this Chapter.

(27) "Person" means an individual, corporation, business trust, estate, trust, partnership, limited liability company, association, joint venture, government, governmental subdivision, agency, or instrumentality, public corporation, or any other legal or commercial entity.

(28) "Present value" means the amount as of a date certain of one or more sums payable in the future, discounted to the date certain by use of either an interest rate specified by the parties if that rate is not manifestly unreasonable at the time the transaction is entered into or, if an interest rate is not so specified, a commercially reasonable rate that takes into account the facts and circumstances at the time the transaction is entered into.

(29) "Purchase" means taking by sale, lease, discount, negotiation, mortgage, pledge, lien, security interest, issue or reissue, gift, or any other voluntary transaction creating an interest in property.

(30) "Purchaser" means a person that takes by purchase.

(31) "Record" means information that is inscribed on a tangible medium or that is stored in an electronic or other medium and is retrievable in perceivable form.

(32) "Remedy" means any remedial right to which an aggrieved party is entitled with or without resort to a tribunal.

(33) "Representative" means a person empowered to act for another, including an agent, an officer of a corporation or association, and a trustee, executor, or administrator of an estate.

(34) "Right" includes remedy.

(35) "Security interest" means an interest in personal property or fixtures which secures payment or performance of an obligation. "Security interest" includes any interest of a consignor and a buyer of accounts, chattel paper, a payment intangible, or a promissory note in a transaction that is subject to Article 9 of this Chapter. "Security interest" does not include the special property interest of a buyer of goods on identification of those goods to a contract for sale under G.S. 25-2-401, but a buyer may also acquire a "security interest" by complying with Article 9 of this Chapter. Except as otherwise provided in G.S. 25-2-505, the right of a seller or lessor of goods under Article 2 or 2A of this Chapter to retain or acquire possession of the goods is not a "security interest," but a seller or lessor may also acquire a "security interest" by complying with Article 9 of this Chapter. The retention or reservation of title by a seller of goods notwithstanding shipment or delivery to the buyer under G.S. 25-2-401 is limited in effect to a reservation of a "security interest." Whether a transaction in the form of a lease creates a "security interest" is determined pursuant to G.S. 25-1-203.

(36) "Send" in connection with a writing, record, or notice means:

    a. To deposit in the mail or deliver for transmission by any other usual means of communication with postage or cost of transmission provided for and properly addressed and, in the case of an instrument, to an address specified thereon or otherwise agreed, or if there be none to any address reasonable under the circumstances; or

    b. In any other way to cause to be received any record or notice within the time it would have arrived if properly sent.

(37) "Signed" includes using any symbol executed or adopted with present intention to adopt or accept a writing.

(38) "State" means a State of the United States, the District of Columbia, Puerto Rico, the United States Virgin Islands, or any territory or insular possession subject to the jurisdiction of the United States.

(39) "Surety" includes a guarantor or other secondary obligor.

(40) "Term" means a portion of an agreement that relates to a particular matter.

(41) "Unauthorized signature" means a signature made without actual, implied, or apparent authority. The term includes a forgery.

(42) "Warehouse receipt" means a document of title issued by a person engaged in the business of storing goods for hire.

(43) "Writing" includes printing, typewriting, or any other intentional reduction to tangible form. "Written" has a corresponding meaning.

History.
1899, c. 733, ss. 25, 56, 191; Rev., ss. 2173, 2205, 2340, 3032; 1917, c. 37, ss. 4, 5, 58; 1919, c. 65, ss. 1, 10, 32, 42; c. 290; C.S., ss. 280, 283, 292, 314, 2976, 3005, 3037, 4037, 4044, 4046; 1941, c. 353, s. 22; G.S., s. 55-102; 1955, c. 1371, s. 2; 1961, c. 574; 1965, c. 700, s. 1; 1967, c. 562, s. 1; 1975, c. 862, ss. 2, 3; 1989 (Reg. Sess., 1990), c. 1024, s. 8(a)-(c); 1993, c. 463, s. 2 ; 1995, c. 232, s. 3 ; 2000-169, ss. 5 -7; 2006-112, ss. 1 , 26

OFFICIAL COMMENTS

Source: Former Section 1-201.

Changes from former law: In order to make it clear that all definitions in the Uniform Commercial Code (not just those appearing in Article 1, as stated in former Section 1-201, but also those appearing in other Articles) do not apply if the context otherwise requires, a new subsection (a) to that effect has been added, and the definitions now appear in subsection (b). The reference in subsection (a) to the "context" is intended to refer to the context in which the defined term is used in the Uniform Commercial Code. In other words, the definition applies whenever the defined term is used unless the context in which the defined term is used in the statute indicates that the term was not used in its defined sense. Consider, for example, Sections 3-103(a)(9) (defining "promise," in relevant part, as "a written undertaking to pay money signed by the person undertaking to pay") and 3-303(a)(1) (indicating that an instrument is issued or transferred for value if "the instrument is issued or transferred for a promise of performance, to the extent that the promise has been performed." It is clear from the statutory context of the use of the word "promise" in Section 3-303(a)(1) that the term was not used in the sense of its definition in Section 3-103(a)(9). Thus, the Section 3-103(a)(9) definition should not be used to give meaning to the word "promise" in Section 3-303(a).

Some definitions in former Section 1-201 have been reformulated as substantive provisions and have been moved to other sections. See Sections 1-202 (explicating concepts of notice and knowledge formerly addressed in Sections 1-201(25)-(27)), 1-204 (determining when a person gives value for rights, replacing the definition of "value" in former Section 1-201(44)), and 1-206 (addressing the meaning of presumptions, replacing the definitions of "presumption" and "presumed" in former Section 1-201(31)). Similarly, the portion of the definition of "security interest" in former Section 1-201(37) which explained the difference between a security interest and a lease has been relocated to Section 1-203.

Two definitions in former Section 1-201 have been deleted. The definition of "honor" in former Section 1-201(21) has been moved to Section 2-103(1)(b), inasmuch as the definition only applies to the use of the word in Article 2. The definition of "telegram" in

Chapter 25

former Section 1-201(41) has been deleted because that word no longer appears in the definition of "conspicuous."

Other than minor stylistic changes and renumbering, the remaining definitions in this section are as in former Article 1 except as noted below.

1. "Action." Unchanged from former Section 1-201, which was derived from similar definitions in Section 191, Uniform Negotiable Instruments Law; Section 76, Uniform Sales Act; Section 58, Uniform Warehouse Receipts Act; Section 53, Uniform Bills of Lading Act.

2. "Aggrieved party." Unchanged from former Section 1-201.

3. "Agreement." Derived from former Section 1-201. As used in the Uniform Commercial Code the word is intended to include full recognition of usage of trade, course of dealing, course of performance and the surrounding circumstances as effective parts thereof, and of any agreement permitted under the provisions of the Uniform Commercial Code to displace a stated rule of law. Whether an agreement has legal consequences is determined by applicable provisions of the Uniform Commercial Code and, to the extent provided in Section 1-103, by the law of contracts.

4. "Bank." Derived from Section 4A-104.

5. "Bearer." Unchanged from former Section 1-201, which was derived from Section 191, Uniform Negotiable Instruments Law.

6. "Bill of Lading." Derived from former Section 1-201. The reference to, and definition of, an "airbill" has been deleted as no longer necessary.

7. "Branch." Unchanged from former Section 1-201.

8. "Burden of establishing a fact." Unchanged from former Section 1-201.

9. "Buyer in ordinary course of business." Except for minor stylistic changes, identical to former Section 1-201 (as amended in conjunction with the 1999 revisions to Article 9). The major significance of the phrase lies in Section 2-403 and in the Article on Secured Transactions (Article 9).

The first sentence of paragraph (9) makes clear that a buyer from a pawnbroker cannot be a buyer in ordinary course of business. The second sentence explains what it means to buy "in the ordinary course." The penultimate sentence prevents a buyer that does not have the right to possession as against the seller from being a buyer in ordinary course of business. Concerning when a buyer obtains possessory rights, see Sections 2-502 and 2-716. However, the penultimate sentence is not intended to affect a buyer's status as a buyer in ordinary course of business in cases (such as a "drop shipment") involving delivery by the seller to a person buying from the buyer or a donee from the buyer. The requirement relates to whether as against the seller the buyer or one taking through the buyer has possessory rights.

10. "Conspicuous." Derived from former Section 1-201(10). This definition states the general standard that to be conspicuous a term ought to be noticed by a reasonable person. Whether a term is conspicuous is an issue for the court. Subparagraphs (A) and (B) set out several methods for making a term conspicuous. Requiring that a term be conspicuous blends a notice function (the term ought to be noticed) and a planning function (giving guidance to the party relying on the term regarding how that result can be achieved). Although these paragraphs indicate some of the methods for making a term attention-calling, the test is whether attention can reasonably be expected to be called to it. The statutory language should not be construed to permit a result that is inconsistent with that test.

11. "Consumer." Derived from Section 9-102(a)(25).

12. "Contract." Except for minor stylistic changes, identical to former Section 1-201.

13. "Creditor." Unchanged from former Section 1-201.

14. "Defendant." Except for minor stylistic changes, identical to former Section 1-201, which was derived from Section 76, Uniform Sales Act.

15. "Delivery." Derived from former Section 1-201. The reference to certificated securities has been deleted in light of the more specific treatment of the matter in Section 8-301.

16. "Document of title." Unchanged from former Section 1-201, which was derived from Section 76, Uniform Sales Act. By making it explicit that the obligation or designation of a third party as "bailee" is essential to a document of title, this definition clearly rejects any such result as obtained in *Hixson v. Ward,* 254 Ill.App. 505 (1929), which treated a conditional sales contract as a document of title. Also the definition is left open so that new types of documents may be included. It is unforeseeable what documents may one day serve the essential purpose now filled by warehouse receipts and bills of lading. Truck transport has already opened up problems which do not fit the patterns of practice resting upon the assumption that a draft can move through banking channels faster than the goods themselves can reach their destination. There lie ahead air transport and such probabilities as teletype transmission of what may some day be regarded commercially as "Documents of Title." The definition is stated in terms of the function of the documents with the intention that any document which gains commercial recognition as accomplishing the desired result shall be included within its scope. Fungible goods are adequately identified within the language of the definition by identification of the mass of which they are a part.

Dock warrants were within the Sales Act definition of document of title apparently for the purpose of recognizing a valid tender by means of such paper. In current commercial practice a dock warrant or receipt is a kind of interim certificate issued by steamship companies upon delivery of the goods at the dock, entitling a designated person to have issued to him at the company's office a bill of lading. The receipt itself is invariably nonnegotiable in form although it may indicate that a negotiable bill is to be forthcoming. Such a document is not within the general compass of the definition, although trade usage may in some cases entitle such paper to be treated as a document

Chapter 25

of title. If the dock receipt actually represents a storage obligation undertaken by the shipping company, then it is a warehouse receipt within this section regardless of the name given to the instrument.

The goods must be "described," but the description may be by marks or labels and may be qualified in such a way as to disclaim personal knowledge of the issuer regarding contents or condition. However, baggage and parcel checks and similar "tokens" of storage which identify stored goods only as those received in exchange for the token are not covered by this Article.

The definition is broad enough to include an airway bill.

17. "Fault." Derived from former Section 1-201. "Default" has been added to the list of events constituting fault.

18. "Fungible goods." Derived from former Section 1-201. References to securities have been deleted because Article 8 no longer uses the term "fungible" to describe securities. Accordingly, this provision now defines the concept only in the context of goods.

19. "Genuine." Unchanged from former Section 1-201.

20. "Good faith." Former Section 1-201(19) defined "good faith" simply as honesty in fact; the definition contained no element of commercial reasonableness. Initially, that definition applied throughout the Code with only one exception. Former Section 2-103(1)(b) provided that "in this Article. . good faith in the case of a merchant means honesty in fact and the observance of reasonable commercial standards of fair dealing in the trade." This alternative definition was limited in applicability in three ways. First, it applied only to transactions within the scope of Article 2. Second, it applied only to merchants. Third, strictly construed it applied only to uses of the phrase "good faith" in Article 2; thus, so construed it would not define "good faith" for its most important use -- the obligation of good faith imposed by former Section 1-203.

Over time, however, amendments to the Uniform Commercial Code brought the Article 2 merchant concept of good faith (subjective honesty and objective commercial reasonableness) into other Articles. First, Article 2A explicitly incorporated the Article 2 standard. See Section 2A-103(7). Then, other Articles broadened the applicability of that standard by adopting it for all parties rather than just for merchants. See, e.g., Sections 3-103(a)(4), 4A-105(a)(6), 8-102(a)(10), and 9-102(a)(43). All of these definitions are comprised of two elements- honesty in fact and the observance of reasonable commercial standards of fair dealing. Only revised Article 5 defines "good faith" solely in terms of subjective honesty, and only Article 6 and Article 7 are without definitions of good faith. (It should be noted that, while revised Article 6 did not define good faith, Comment 2 to revised Section 6-102 states that "this Article adopts the definition of 'good faith' in Article 1 in all cases, even when the buyer is a merchant.") Given these developments, it is appropriate to move the broader definition of "good faith" to Article 1. Of course, this definition is subject to the applicability of the narrower definition in revised Article 5.

21. "Holder." Derived from former Section 1-201. The definition has been reorganized for clarity.

22. "Insolvency proceedings." Unchanged from former Section 1-201.

23. "Insolvent." Derived from former Section 1-201. The three tests of insolvency- "generally ceased to pay debts in the ordinary course of business other than as a result of a bona fide dispute as to them," "unable to pay debts as they become due," and "insolvent within the meaning of the federal bankruptcy law" -- are expressly set up as alternative tests and must be approached from a commercial standpoint.

24. "Money." Substantively identical to former Section 1-201. The test is that of sanction of government, whether by authorization before issue or adoption afterward, which recognizes the circulating medium as a part of the official currency of that government. The narrow view that money is limited to legal tender is rejected.

25. "Organization." The former definition of this word has been replaced with the standard definition used in acts prepared by the National Conference of Commissioners on Uniform State Laws.

26. "Party." Substantively identical to former Section 1-201. Mention of a party includes, of course, a person acting through an agent. However, where an agent comes into opposition or contrast to the principal, particular account is taken of that situation.

27. "Person." The former definition of this word has been replaced with the standard definition used in acts prepared by the National Conference of Commissioners on Uniform State Laws.

28. "Present value." This definition was formerly contained within the definition of "security interest" in former Section 1-201(37).

29. "Purchase." Derived from former Section 1-201. The form of definition has been changed from "includes" to "means."

30. "Purchaser." Unchanged from former Section 1-201.

31. "Record." Derived from Section 9-102(a)(69).

32. "Remedy." Unchanged from former Section 1-201. The purpose is to make it clear that both remedy and right (as defined) include those remedial rights of "self help" which are among the most important bodies of rights under the Uniform Commercial Code, remedial rights being those to which an aggrieved party may resort on its own.

33. "Representative." Derived from former Section 1-201. Reorganized, and form changed from "includes" to "means."

34. "Right." Except for minor stylistic changes, identical to former Section 1-201.

35. "Security Interest." The definition is the first paragraph of the definition of "security interest" in former Section 1-201, with minor stylistic changes. The remaining portion of that definition has been moved to Section 1-203. Note that, because of the scope of Article 9, the term includes the interest of certain outright buyers of certain kinds of property.

36. "Send." Derived from former Section 1-201. Compare "notifies".

37. "Signed." Derived from former Section 1-201. Former Section 1-201 referred to "intention to authenticate"; because other articles now use the term "authenticate," the language has been changed to "intention to adopt or accept." The latter formulation is derived from the definition of "authenticate" in Section 9-102(a)(7). This provision refers only to writings, because the term "signed," as used in some articles, refers only to writings. This provision also makes it clear that, as the term "signed" is used in the Uniform Commercial Code, a complete signature is not necessary. The symbol may be printed, stamped or written; it may be by initials or by thumbprint. It may be on any part of the document and in appropriate cases may be found in a billhead or letterhead. No catalog of possible situations can be complete and the court must use common sense and commercial experience in passing upon these matters. The question always is whether the symbol was executed or adopted by the party with present intention to adopt or accept the writing.

38. "State." This is the standard definition of the term used in acts prepared by the National Conference of Commissioners on Uniform State Laws.

39. "Surety." This definition makes it clear that "surety" includes all secondary obligors, not just those whose obligation refers to the person obligated as a surety. As to the nature of secondary obligations generally, see Restatement (Third), Suretyship and Guaranty Section 1 (1996).

40. "Term." Unchanged from former Section 1-201.

41. "Unauthorized signature." Unchanged from former Section 1-201.

42. "Warehouse receipt." Unchanged from former Section 1-201, which was derived from Section 76(1), Uniform Sales Act; Section 1, Uniform Warehouse Receipts Act. Receipts issued by a field warehouse are included, provided the warehouseman and the depositor of the goods are different persons.

43. "Written" or "writing." Unchanged from former Section 1-201.

EFFECT OF AMENDMENTS. --
Session Laws 2006-112, s. 26 , effective October 1, 2006, in subsection (b), inserted "a person in control of a negotiable electronic document of title or" and "negotiable tangible" in subdivision (5), inserted "of title" and "directly or indirectly" in the first sentence and added the second sentence of subdivision (6), inserted "to an electronic document of title means voluntary transfer of control and with respect" and "a tangible" in subdivision (15), rewrote subdivision (16), inserted "negotiable tangible" in subdivision (21)b., added subdivision (21)c., and made minor stylistic changes, and substituted "document of title" for "receipt" in subdivision (42).

EDITOR'S NOTE. --Some of the cases cited below were decided under former G.S. 25-1-201.

STANDING TO SEEK STAY RELIEF. --Bank had standing to seek stay relief under 11 U.S.C.S. § 362(d), as the bank had possession of the original note specially endorsed to it. It was not necessary for the bank to establish its ownership of the note and deed of trust in the real property records; nor was it required to prove that each transfer of the note and security agreement was by an authorized seller. In re Sears, 2013 Bankr. LEXIS 2010 (Bankr. W.D.N.C. May 16, 2013).

THE UCC PROTECTS BUYERS IN THE ORDINARY COURSE OF BUSINESS from the claims of predecessors in interest who place items into the stream of commerce without warning that they subsequently will claim ownership. North Carolina Nat'l Bank v. Robinson, 78 N.C. App. 1, 336 S.E.2d 666 (1985).

"CONSPICUOUSNESS". --Determination on conspicuousness is a question of law for the court. Billings v. Joseph Harris Co., 27 N.C. App. 689, 220 S.E.2d 361 (1975), aff'd, 290 N.C. 502, 226 S.E.2d 321 (1976); Angola Farm Supply & Equip. Co. v. FMC Corp., 59 N.C. App. 272, 296 S.E.2d 503 (1982).

Language on herbicide to the effect that seller made "no other express or implied warranty of fitness or merchantability or any other express or implied warranty," which was in darker and larger type than the other language on the label, was "conspicuous," as defined by subdivision (10) of this section, and served to effectively disclaim any implied warranties of merchantability or fitness. Tyson v. Ciba-Geigy Corp., 82 N.C. App. 626, 347 S.E.2d 473 (1986).

Forum selection clause was conspicuous where, although the font used in the forum selection clause could have been made larger, the forum selection language was found in two places on the front page of an agreement, both times in bold print and underlined. Price v. Leasecomm Corp., (M.D.N.C. Mar. 31, 2004).

"DELIVERY" --Delivery of a deed or instrument to the named payee, subject to the control of the person delivering it or subject to an agreed condition, does not constitute delivery in the eyes of the law. State v. First Resort Properties, 81 N.C. App. 499, 344 S.E.2d 354 (1986).

"PURCHASE." --"Hanging paragraph" of 11 U.S.C.S. § 1325 did not bar bifurcation of creditor's secured claim because original financing of the car was not within 910-day period prior to bankruptcy filing; a subsequent refinancing did not constitute a "purchase" under G.S. 25-1-201(b)(29) because refinancing did not create an interest in property. In re Cunningham, 2012 Bankr. LEXIS 2025 (Bankr. W.D.N.C. May 8, 2012).

"PURCHASER." --Bank was granted relief from automatic stay based on lack of equity because it had security interest in securities accounts, it was purchaser, and it was identified as person having a security entitlement in accounts. Security interest was perfected because bank, as purchaser, became entitlement holder over accounts, and it had control over all security entitlements held in accounts. In re Bressler, 2013 Bankr. LEXIS 4763 (Bankr. M.D.N.C. Nov. 6, 2013).

"SEND." --Creditor's effort to notify debtors of private sale by sending a first class letter to debtors' last known address was reasonable where there was no evidence that the letter was returned, or that the debtors did not receive such notice, or that the debtors had provided creditor with a new address. In re Marshall, 219 Bankr. 687 (Bankr. M.D.N.C. 1997).

GOOD FAITH ("HONESTY IN FACT") AND "NOTICE," although not synonymous, are inherently intertwined. Therefore, the relation between the two cannot be ignored. Branch Banking & Trust Co. v. Gill, 293 N.C. 164, 237 S.E.2d 21 (1977).

The same facts which call a party's "good faith" into question may also give him "notice of a defense." Branch Banking & Trust Co. v. Gill, 293 N.C. 164, 237 S.E.2d 21 (1977).

Albeit "good faith" is literally defined as "honesty in fact in the conduct or transaction concerned," the Uniform Commercial Code does not permit parties to intentionally keep themselves in ignorance of facts which, if known, would defeat their rights in a negotiable document of title. Branch Banking & Trust Co. v. Gill, 293 N.C. 164, 237 S.E.2d 21 (1977).

HONESTY IN FACT REQUIRED OF SUPPLIER. --A good faith duty requiring a supplier of products to disclose its internal strategies to distributors was inappropriate, as the breadth of good faith required was limited to the "honesty in fact" definition of this section, which governed distributor's claim under G.S. 25-1-203, rather than the more expansive "reasonable commercial standards of fair dealing in the trade" definition of G.S. 25-2-103. L.C. Williams Oil Co. v. Exxon Corp., 625 F. Supp. 477 (M.D.N.C. 1985).

"HOLDER." --The definition of "holder" in subdivision (20) of this section is applicable to G.S. 45-21.16. In re Cooke, 37 N.C. App. 575, 246 S.E.2d 801 (1978).

Ownership is not indispensable to holdership. In re Cooke, 37 N.C. App. 575, 246 S.E.2d 801 (1978).

There was ample evidence that the beneficiaries of a deed of trust were holders of a valid debt where the notes secured by the deed of trust were payable to the beneficiaries or order, the notes were not endorsed, and the notes were in the possession of the original beneficiary-payees. In re Cooke, 37 N.C. App. 575, 246 S.E.2d 801 (1978).

As evidence that a plaintiff is holder of a note is an essential element of a cause of action upon such note, the defendant was entitled to demand strict proof of this element. The incorporation by reference into the complaint of a copy of the note was not in itself sufficient evidence to establish for purposes of summary judgment that the plaintiff was the holder of the note. Liles v. Myers, 38 N.C. App. 525, 248 S.E.2d 385 (1978).

Where a negotiable instrument is made payable to order, one becomes a holder of the instrument when it is properly endorsed and delivered to him, and mere possession of a note payable to order does not suffice to prove ownership or holder status. Econo-Travel Motor Hotel Corp. v. Taylor, 301 N.C. 200, 271 S.E.2d 54 (1980).

Where a negotiable instrument is made payable to order, one becomes a holder of the instrument when it is properly endorsed and delivered to him, and mere possession of a note payable to order does not suffice to prove ownership or holder status. Econo-Travel Motor Hotel Corp. v. Taylor, 301 N.C. 200, 271 S.E.2d 54 (1980).

It is the fact of possession which is significant in determining whether a person is a holder, and the absence of possession defeats that status. Connolly v. Potts, 63 N.C. App. 547, 306 S.E.2d 123 (1983).

Bank which had cancelled and released a promissory note because of a clerical error, and therefore was not a "holder" in the traditional sense, could still meet the burden required by this section by showing that debtor never satisfied the underlying obligation. G.E. Capital Mtg. Servs. v. Neely, 135 N.C. App. 187, 519 S.E.2d 553 (1999).

Party seeking to foreclose did not show that it was the current holder of a note under G.S. 25-1-201(21) as although the photocopies of the note and deed of trust established the required elements under G.S. 45-21.16(d) since the debtors did not dispute that they were correct copies, the photocopies indicated that the original holder of both instruments was not the party seeking to foreclose; the photocopies did not indicate that the original holder negotiated, indorsed, or transferred the note to the party seeking to foreclose. In re Foreclosure of a Deed of Trust Executed by Hannia M. Adams & H. Clayton Adams, 204 N.C. App. 318, 693 S.E.2d 705 (2010).

Trial court erred in permitting a substitute trustee to proceed with foreclosure proceedings under G.S. 45-21.16(d) because there was no competent evidence that the trustee was the owner and holder of a mortgagor's adjustable rate note and deed of trust, and production of an original note at trial did not, in itself, establish that the note was transferred to the party presenting the note with the purpose of giving that party the right to enforce the instrument; the trial court's findings of fact did not address who had possession of the mortgagor's note at the time of the de novo hearing, and without a determination of who had physical possession of the note, the trial court could determine, under the Uniform Commercial Code, G.S. 25-1-201(b)(21), the entity that was the holder of the note. In re Foreclosure by David A. Simpson, P.C., 211 N.C. App. 483, 711 S.E.2d 165 (2011).

Assuming that production of a mortgagor's adjustable rate note was evidence of a transfer of the note pursuant to the Uniform Commercial Code and that a substitute trustee was in possession of the note, that was not sufficient evidence that the trustee was the "holder" of the note under the UCC, G.S. 25-1-201(b)(21); the note was not indorsed to the trustee or to bearer, a prerequisite to confer upon the trustee the status of holder under G.S. 25-1-201(b)(21). In re Foreclosure by David A. Simpson, P.C., 211 N.C. App. 483, 711 S.E.2d 165 (2011).

Substitute trustee did not offer sufficient evidence that a bank, as trustee, was the holder of a mortgagor's adjustable rate note and, thus, the party entitled to proceed with a foreclosure action under G.S. 45-21.16(d) because pursuant to the Uniform Commercial Code, G.S. 25-3-110(c), the note was payable to the

Chapter 25

bank as trustee; the note was clearly indorsed to the bank as trustee. In re Foreclosure by David A. Simpson, P.C., 211 N.C. App. 483, 711 S.E.2d 165 (2011).

Lender's successor's evidence, including a letter from the Comptroller of the Currency officially certifying a merger between the successor and the lender, was sufficient to establish the merger. The successor, as the surviving corporation after the merger, succeeded by operation of law to the lender's status as holder of a note, pursuant to G.S. 55-11-06(a)(2). In re Foreclosure of N.C. Deed of Trust by Carver Pond I L.P., 217 N.C. App. 352, 719 S.E.2d 207 (2011).

Trustee's summary foreclosure proceeding under G.S. 45.21.16 was properly dismissed because the trustee was not the legal holder of the promissory note executed by the borrower and, therefore, lacked authorization to foreclose on the borrower's property securing the note under a deed of trust. In re Foreclosure of a Deed of Trust of Bass, 217 N.C. App. 244, 720 S.E.2d 18 (2011).

Petitioner was the holder of a note as it had physical possession of the note at the hearing and submitted a copy of that note, and a Non-Home Loan Certificate that stated that petitioner was successor by merger to the mortgagee was not challenged; because of the merger, petitioner had all the rights and powers the mortgagee had before the merger under G.S. 53-17 [repealed]. As the mortgagee was the indorser of the note in blank, petitioner received those rights in the merger. In re Yopp, 217 N.C. App. 488, 720 S.E.2d 769 (2011).

Affiant's conclusion that petitioner was the holder of a note and a deed of trust petitioner sought to foreclose was a legal conclusion and was disregarded; whether an entity was a holder under G.S. 25-1-201(b) (21) was a legal conclusion that was to be determined by a court on the basis of factual allegations. In re Yopp, 217 N.C. App. 488, 720 S.E.2d 769 (2011).

Bank was a holder under G.S. 25-1-201(b)(21) of a note entitled to foreclose under G.S. 45-21.16(d) where: (1) a challenged stamp was a signature and an indorsement; (2) the presumption in favor of the validity of the signature prevailed; (3) the mortgagor was in default; and (4) the indorsements on the note unambiguously indicated an intent to transfer the note under G.S. 25-3-201(b) from each lender to the next, and finally to the bank. In re Foreclosure of a Deed of Trust Executed by Bass, 366 N.C. 464, 738 S.E.2d 173 (2013).

Although the Federal Deposit Insurance Corporation (FDIC) did not produce an original promissory note in response to a debtor's demand for strict proof, the FDIC was the holder of the note within the meaning of G.S. 25-1-201(b)(21) and G.S. 25-3-301 because the note was payable to a bank, the FDIC succeeded to all rights of the bank when it was appointed as the bank's receiver, a true and accurate copy of the note was in the record, and the debtor did not produce any evidence suggesting that the copy of the note in the record was somehow inaccurate or anything but a true and correct copy. FDIC v. Cashion, 720 F.3d 169 (4th Cir. 2013).

Transferee bank attained holder status of the borrowers' promissory note because the bank, which had physical possession of the note, presented the original note in open court, the note was unambiguously indorsed in blank by the vice president of the bank's predecessor in interest, and did not identify a person to whom it was payable. In re Dispute over the Sum of $375,757.47, 240 N.C. App. 505, 771 S.E.2d 800 (2015).

Trial court did not err in authorizing a substitute trustee to proceed with a foreclosure sale of property a buyer purchased at an execution sale because an assignee was the holder of the promissory note; the assignee produced the original note indorsed in blank, and that was sufficient to support the trial court's conclusion that it was the holder of the note. In re Foreclosure of a Deed of Trust Executed by Rawls, 243 N.C. App. 316, 777 S.E.2d 796 (2015).

"Holder" of a promissory note may be a bank or other lending institution that is in possession of a note that has been indorsed in blank; a petitioner's production of an original note indorsed in blank establishes that the petitioner is the holder of the note. In re Foreclosure of a Deed of Trust Executed by Rawls, 243 N.C. App. 316, 777 S.E.2d 796 (2015).

Superior court properly authorized a bank to proceed with foreclosure on property a purchaser bought at a foreclosure sale because the bank was the holder of the promissory note secured by the deed of trust encumbering the property; the note was indorsed in blank, and the bank had possession of the note. Greene v. Tr. Servs. of Carolina, LLC, 244 N.C. App. 583, 781 S.E.2d 664 (2016).

AN INDORSEMENT BY AN AUTHORIZED AGENT OF THE "HOLDER" IS SUFFICIENT TO VALIDATE THE TRANSACTION. Summerlin v. National Serv. Indus., Inc., 72 N.C. App. 476, 325 S.E.2d 12 (1985).

"MONEY." --Debtors' interest in unearned portion of a retainer paid to a law firm was a general intangible and as such, a creditor with a properly perfected security interest had a lien on the balance of the retainer fund; in reaching its determination that the retainer was a general intangible, the bankruptcy court reasoned that the debtors' interest in the retainer was neither a deposit account (because the law firm was not a bank or financial institution) or "money" (because the debtors had only the right to receive a refund on the unearned portion of the retainer fund). In re E-Z Serve Convenience Stores, Inc., 299 B.R. 126 (Bankr. M.D.N.C. 2003), aff'd, 318 Bankr. 637 (M.D.N.C. 2004).

"RIGHTS." --The term "all rights" in an assignment included the contractual right of assignor to receive C.O.D. payment from defendant. Gunby v. Pilot Freight Carriers, Inc., 82 N.C. App. 427, 346 S.E.2d 188 (1986).

"SECURITY INTEREST." --This section defines "security interest" without reference to whether title is in the vendor or the vendee under the security agreement. Szabo Food Serv., Inc. v. Balentine's, Inc., 285 N.C. 452, 206 S.E.2d 242 (1974).

Clause (b) of subsection (37) is not consistent with the fundamental proposition that to create a security interest the parties must have intended to create one. Szabo Food Serv., Inc. v. Balentine's, Inc., 285 N.C. 452, 206 S.E.2d 242 (1974).

The language of a promissory note considered together with the terms and language of a financing statement may be sufficient to create a security interest in collateral owned by the debtor on the note. Mitchell v. Rock Hill Nat'l Bank (In re Mid-Atlantic Piping Prods., Inc.), 24 Bankr. 314 (Bankr. W.D.N.C. 1982).

A financing statement can serve as a written security agreement to satisfy G.S. 25-9-203(1)(b). Mitchell v. Rock Hill Nat'l Bank (In re Mid-Atlantic Piping Prods., Inc.), 24 Bankr. 314 (Bankr. W.D.N.C. 1982).

Article 9 of this Chapter applies to a transaction intended to create a security interest, regardless of whom the certificate lists as the owner. Carter v. Holland (In re Carraway), 65 Bankr. 51 (Bankr. E.D.N.C. 1986).

Deed of trust executed in 1999 by a borrower, who guaranteed two promissory notes made by the borrower's family business in 2004 and 2005, did not provide a basis for the lender to foreclose on the deed of trust following non-payment of the 2004 and 2005 notes, which did not refer to a security interest or right to foreclose. The 1999 note signed in connection with the deed of trust had been paid, extinguishing the security interest pursuant to G.S. 25-1-201(a)(35). Tr. Servs. v. R.C. Koonts & Sons Masonry, Inc., 202 N.C. App. 317, 688 S.E.2d 737 (2010).

Anti-modification provision prevented debtors' proposed modification of creditor's claim because the creditor was secured only by real property that was the debtors' principal residence and no additional security interest was created by boilerplate language in the deed of trust form that granted creditor rights in an escrow account and miscellaneous proceeds. In re Adams, 2015 Bankr. LEXIS 4457 (Bankr. E.D.N.C. Nov. 30, 2015).

SECURITY INTEREST V. LEASE. --Where a debtor could terminate her rental agreement for a VCR and a washing machine at any time with no further obligation to continue paying rent, the agreement was a "true" lease, not a security interest, under subdivision (37) of this section. In re Frady, 141 Bankr. 600 (Bankr. W.D.N.C. 1991).

An agreement purporting to lease equipment actually was a secured loan, where the lessee could purchase the equipment for $1 upon termination of the lease, the total monthly lease payments approximated the purchase price, the lessor was a financing company, the lessee was not responsible for maintenance, insurance, taxes, and expenses, and the transaction was referred to as a loan in the parties' agreement. L.C. Williams Oil Co. v. NAFCO Capital Corp., 130 N.C. App. 286, 502 S.E.2d 415 (1998).

Although a bankruptcy debtor had a right to terminate an agreement to lease a storage barn at any time, the agreement was properly treated as a true lease rather than a disguised security agreement based on economic reality, since the lack of evidence concerning the value of the barn prevented any finding that the lessor retained a meaningful reversionary interest, a purchase option was for a nominal amount, or the debtor had a right to gain equity in the barn. In re Johnson, 571 B.R. 167 (Bankr. E.D.N.C. 2017).

NO ASSIGNMENT OF SECURITY INTEREST. --Where a bank loaned money to a debtor and filed a financing statement in 1999 and a partnership entered into a factoring agreement with the debtor but did not file a statement until 2003, the bank had a priority lien on the proceeds at issue because it perfected its security interest several years before the partnership; also, a purported financing statement amendment failed to include a security agreement showing an assignment of the security interest in certain accounts receivable. Rentenbach Constructors, Inc. v. CM P'ship, 181 N.C. App. 268, 639 S.E.2d 16 (2007).

"SIGNED." --Because of the importance placed upon financing statements, in cases dealing with the debtor's signature on financing statements the courts should apply the liberal definition of "signed" in subsection (39) of this section with caution. Provident Fin. Co. v. Beneficial Fin. Co., 36 N.C. App. 401, 245 S.E.2d 510, cert. denied, 295 N.C. 549, 248 S.E.2d 728 (1978).

Contested stamp from an original lender to a transferee was a signature under G.S. 25-1-201(b)(37) as: (1) it indicated an intent to transfer the debt to a transferee; (2) the original note was transferred in accordance with the stamp's intent; and (3) the stamp showed that it was executed or adopted by the party with the intention to adopt or accept the writing. In re Foreclosure of a Deed of Trust Executed by Bass, 366 N.C. 464, 738 S.E.2d 173 (2013).

"WAREHOUSE RECEIPT." --"Household Goods Descriptive Inventory" was sufficient to constitute a warehouse receipt for purposes of holding defendant moving company responsible under Art. 7 for its actions as a warehouseman where the document listed each item picked up, its condition, the owner's name, the origin loading address, and was signed and dated by defendant's authorized agent and driver. Tate v. Action Moving & Storage, Inc., 95 N.C. App. 541, 383 S.E.2d 229 (1989), cert. denied, 326 N.C. 54, 389 S.E.2d 104 (1990).

ARBITRATION IS NEITHER AN "ACTION" NOR A "JUDICIAL PROCEEDING." --By its terms the limitations period stated in G.S. 25-2-725 applies only to an "action," which, under subsection (1) is a "judicial proceeding," and an arbitration is neither an "action" nor a "judicial proceeding," but a nonjudicial, out-of-court proceeding which makes an action or judicial proceeding unnecessary. In re Cameron, 91 N.C. App. 164, 370 S.E.2d 704 (1988).

APPLIED in First Fed. Bank v. Aldridge, 230 N.C. App. 187, 749 S.E.2d 289 (2013).

CITED in Singletary v. P & A Invs., Inc., 212 N.C. App. 469, 712 S.E.2d 681 (2011); In re Foreclosure of the Deed of Trust from Manning, 228 N.C. App. 591, 747 S.E.2d 286 (2013).

LEGAL PERIODICALS. --

For article concerning liens on personal property not governed by the Uniform Commercial Code, see 44 N.C.L. Rev. 322 (1966).

For article on waiver of defense clauses in consumer contracts, see 48 N.C.L. Rev. 545 (1970).

For note on consignments and the consignor's duty to satisfy public notice requirements, see 13 Wake Forest L. Rev. 507 (1977).

For note on commercial reasonableness and the public sale in North Carolina, see 17 Wake Forest L. Rev. 153 (1981).

For comment, "Return to the Conservative View of Security Agreements in Commercial Transactions," see 8 Campbell L. Rev. 505 (1986).

For article, "Court Adjustment of Long-Term Contracts: An Analysis Under Modern Contract Law," see 1987 Duke L.J. 1 (1987).

For article, "Public Filing and Personal Property Leases: Questions of Definition and Doctrine," see 22 Wake Forest L. Rev. 425 (1987).

For comment, "Is it a Sale or a Lease?: The Implications of Article 2A and Revised U.C.C. Section 1-201(37) in North Carolina," see 18 N.C. Cent. L.J. 187 (1989).

NOTES APPLICABLE TO ENTIRE CHAPTER

EDITOR'S NOTE. --Former G.S. 25-1 to 25-199 (the N.I.L.) were repealed by Session Laws 1965, c. 700, which enacted the U.C.C.

To maintain uniformity with the commercial codes adopted by other states, the designation and indentation of subsections, subdivisions and further divisions of sections in Chapter 25 have not been changed to conform to the system and style employed elsewhere in the General Statutes. The numbering of sections corresponds to that used in the 1962 Official Text of the U.C.C., as amended, except that each number is preceded by the chapter number "25." Thus, "G.S. 1-101" of the Official Text is "G.S. 25-1-101" in this chapter.

Where sections of the U.C.C. are similar to sections repealed by Session Laws 1965, c. 700, the historical citations to the former sections have been added to the historical citations to the sections of the U.C.C.

Following each section of the U.C.C., Official Comments have been included. The Comments headed "North Carolina Comment" first appeared in "North Carolina Annotations -- The Uniform Commercial Code," a 1965 report of the former Legislative Council to the General Assembly of North Carolina. Appropriate comments were selected at the time of initial publication of Chapter 25 and edited under the supervision of the Division of Legislative Drafting and Codification of Statutes of the Department of Justice. The Comments headed "Official Comment" are the Comments of the National Conference of Commissioners on Uniform State Laws and The American Law Institute which appeared in the "1962 Official Text with Comments" of the U.C.C., with the exceptions noted hereafter.

Official Comments, copyright 1978, 1987, 1989, 1990, 1991, 1993, 1994, 1995, 1998-2000 are reprinted in Articles 1 to 11 with the permission of The American Law Institute and the National Conference of Commissioners on Uniform State Laws. It is believed that the Official Comments will prove of value to the practitioner in understanding and applying the text of this Chapter.

Where they appear in this Chapter, "Amended Comment" usually means that an error in the original comment has been corrected by a subsequent amendment, and "Supplemental Comment" pertains to a later development, such as an amendment to the statute text. North Carolina Comments explain where the General Assembly has enacted variations to the text of the Uniform Act.

Article 8 of Chapter 25 was amended in 1989 and again in 1997, and contains Amended Official Comments thereto.

Articles 2A and 4A of Chapter 25 were enacted by the General Assembly in 1993, and contain the Official Comments thereto.

Article 5 of Chapter 25 was revised in 1999 and contains revised Official Comments.

Article 9 was revised in 2000 and contains revised Official Comments thereto. This revised Article 9 supersedes the revision of Article 9 by Session Laws 1975, c. 862, s. 1.

Article 8 of Chapter 25 contains a North Carolina Comment to the 1989 revision. Articles 3 and 4 of Chapter 25 contain revised North Carolina Comments to the 1995 Revision. Article 5 of Chapter 25 contains two North Carolina Comments to the 1999 Revision.

The Official Comments and the North Carolina Comments printed in this Chapter have been printed by the publisher as received, without any significant editorial change.

The user should also note that Amended Official Comments have not been received in conjunction with all amendments to sections of the U.C.C., and therefore, subsequent amendments to the Official Comments and the North Carolina Comments may not be reflected in some instances.

The Comment under the title of the Act states in part: "Uniformity throughout American jurisdictions is one of the main objectives of this Code; and that objective cannot be obtained without substantial uniformity of construction. To aid in uniform construction these Comments set forth the purpose of various provisions of this Act to promote uniformity, to aid in viewing the Act as an integrated whole, and to safeguard against misconstruction."

NOTES APPLICABLE TO ENTIRE ARTICLE

EDITOR'S NOTE. --Official Comments in Article 1: Copyright 2001 by the American Law Institute and the National Conference of Commissioners on Uniform State Laws. Reprinted with permission of the Permanent Editorial Board of the Uniform Commercial Code.

The Official Comments appearing under individual sections in this Article have been printed by the publisher as received, without editorial change, and relate to the Article as originally enacted. However,

Chapter 25

not all sections in this Article may carry Official Comments. Furthermore, Official Comments may or may not have been received or updated in conjunction with subsequent amendments to this Article and, therefore, may not reflect all changes to the sections under which they appear.

Session Laws 2006-112, s. 1 , effective October 1, 2006, rewrote Article 1 of Chapter 25 of the General Statutes. At the end of Article 1 are tables showing comparable sections and their disposition in new Article 1. Where appropriate, historical citations to sections of former Article 1 have been placed under corresponding sections of revised Article 1.

Session Laws 2006-112, s. 61 , provides: "The Revisor of Statutes shall cause to be printed along with this act all relevant portions of the official comments to Uniform Commercial Code Revised Article 1 and Uniform Commercial Code Revised Article 7 and all explanatory comments of the drafters of this act as the Revisor deems appropriate."

ARTICLE 9.
SECURED TRANSACTIONS

PART 3.
PERFECTION AND PRIORITY

SUBPART 1.
LAW GOVERNING PERFECTION AND PRIORITY

§ 25-9-301. Law governing perfection and priority of security interests

Except as otherwise provided in G.S. 25-9-303 through G.S. 25-9-306, the following rules determine the law governing perfection, the effect of perfection or nonperfection, and the priority of a security interest in collateral:

(1) Except as otherwise provided in this section, while a debtor is located in a jurisdiction, the local law of that jurisdiction governs perfection, the effect of perfection or nonperfection, and the priority of a security interest in collateral.

(2) While collateral is located in a jurisdiction, the local law of that jurisdiction governs perfection, the effect of perfection or nonperfection, and the priority of a possessory security interest in that collateral.

(3) Except as otherwise provided in paragraph (4) of this section, while tangible negotiable documents, goods, instruments, money, or tangible chattel paper is located in a jurisdiction, the local law of that jurisdiction governs:

a. Perfection of a security interest in the goods by filing a fixture filing;

b. Perfection of a security interest in timber to be cut; and

c. The effect of perfection or nonperfection and the priority of a nonpossessory security interest in the collateral.

(4) The local law of the jurisdiction in which the wellhead or minehead is located governs perfection, the effect of perfection or nonperfection, and the priority of a security interest in as-extracted collateral.

History.

1945, c. 196, s. 2; 1957, c. 564; 1965, c. 700, s. 1; 1967, c. 562, s. 1; 1975, c. 862, s. 7; 1989 (Reg. Sess., 1990), c. 1024, s. 8(e), (f); 1997-181, s. 2 ; 1999-73, s. 4(a) , (b); 2000-169, s. 1 ; 2006-112, s. 48

AMENDED OFFICIAL COMMENT (2010 EDITION)

1. *Source.* Former sections 9-103(1)(a) and (b), 9-103(3)(a) and (b), and 9-103(5), substantially modified.

2. *Scope of this Subpart.* Part 3, subpart 1 (sections 9-301 through 9-307) contains choice of law rules similar to those of former section 9-103. Former section 9-103 generally addresses which state's law governs "perfection and the effect of perfection or nonperfection of" security interests. See, e.g., former section 9-103(1)(b). This article follows the broader and more precise formulation in former section 9-103(6)(b), which was revised in connection with the promulgation of revised article 8 in 1994: "Perfection, the effect of perfection or nonperfection, and the priority of" security interests. Priority, in this context, subsumes all of the rules in part 3, including "cut off" or "take free" rules such as sections 9-317(b), (c), and (d), 9-320(a), (b), and (d), and 9-332. This subpart does not address choice of law for other purposes. For example, the law applicable to issues such as attachment, validity, characterization (e.g., true lease or security interest), and enforcement is governed by the rules in section 1-301; that governing law typically is specified in the same agreement that contains the security agreement. And, another jurisdiction's law may govern other third-party matters addressed in this article. See section 9-401, comment 3.

3. *Scope of Referral.* In designating the jurisdiction whose law governs, this article directs the court to apply only the substantive ("local") law of a particular jurisdiction and not its choice of law rules.

Example 1: Litigation over the priority of a security interest in accounts arises in State X. State X has adopted the official text of this article, which provides that priority is determined by the local law of the jurisdiction in which the debtor is located. See section 9-301(1). The debtor is located in State Y. Even if State Y has retained former article 9 or enacted a nonuniform choice of law rule (e.g., one that provides that perfection is governed by the law of State Z), a State X court should look only to the substantive law of State Y and disregard State Y's choice of law rule. State Y's substantive law (e.g., its section 9-501) provides that financing statements should be filed in a filing office in State Y. Note, however, that if the identical perfection issue were to be litigated in State Y, the court would look to State Y's former section 9-103 or nonuniform section 9-301 and conclude that a filing in State Y is ineffective.

Example 2: In the preceding example, assume that State X has adopted the official text of this article, and State Y has adopted a nonuniform section 9-301(1) under which perfection is governed by the whole law of State X, including its choice of law rules. If litigation occurs in State X, the court should look to the substantive law of State Y, which provides that financing statements are to be filed in a filing office in State Y. If litigation occurs in State Y, the court should look to the law of State X, whose choice of law rule requires that the court apply the substantive law of State Y. Thus, regardless of the jurisdiction in which the litigation arises, the financing statement should be filed in State Y.

4. *Law Governing Perfection: General Rule.* Paragraph (1) contains the general rule: The law governing perfection of security interests in both tangible and intangible collateral, whether perfected by filing or automatically, is the law of the jurisdiction of the debtor's location, as determined under section 9-307.

Paragraph (1) substantially simplifies the choice of law rules. Former section 9-103 contained different choice of law rules for different types of collateral. Under section 9-301(1), the law of a single jurisdiction governs perfection with respect to most types of collateral, both tangible and intangible. Paragraph (1) eliminates the need for former section 9-103(1)(c), which concerned purchase-money security interests in tangible collateral that is intended to move from one jurisdiction to the other. It is likely to reduce the frequency of cases in which the governing law changes after a financing statement is properly filed. (Presumably, debtors change their own location less frequently than they change the location of their collateral.) The approach taken in paragraph (1) also eliminates some difficult priority issues and the need to distinguish between "mobile" and "ordinary" goods, and it reduces the number of filing offices in which secured parties must file or search when collateral is located in several jurisdictions.

5. *Law Governing Perfection: Exceptions.* The general rule is subject to several exceptions. It does not apply to goods covered by a certificate of title (see section 9-303), deposit accounts (see section 9-304), investment property (see section 9-305), or letter-of-credit rights (see section 9-306). Nor does it apply to possessory security interests, i.e., security interests that the secured party has perfected by taking possession of the collateral (see paragraph (2)), security interests perfected by filing a fixture filing (see subparagraph (3)(A)), security interests in timber to be cut (subparagraph (3)(B)), or security interests in as-extracted collateral (see paragraph (4)).

a. *Possessory Security Interests.* Paragraph (2) applies to possessory security interests and provides that perfection is governed by the local law of the jurisdiction in which the collateral is located. This is the rule of former section 9-103(1)(b), except paragraph (2) eliminates the troublesome "last event" test of former law.

The distinction between nonpossessory and possessory security interests creates the potential for the same jurisdiction to apply two different choice of law rules to determine perfection in the same collateral. For example, were a secured party in possession of an instrument or document to relinquish possession in reliance on temporary perfection, the applicable law immediately would change from that of the location of the collateral to that of the location of the debtor. The applicability of two different choice of law rules for perfection is unlikely to lead to any material practical problems. The perfection rules of one article 9 jurisdiction are likely to be identical to those of another. Moreover, under paragraph (3), the relative priority of competing security interests in tangible collateral is resolved by reference to the law of the jurisdiction in which the collateral is located, regardless of how the security interests are perfected.

b. *Fixture Filings.* Under the general rule in paragraph (1), a security interest in fixtures may be perfected by filing in the office specified by section 9-501(a) as enacted in the jurisdiction in which the debtor is located. However, application of this rule to perfection of a security interest by filing a fixture filing could yield strange results. For example, perfection of a security interest in fixtures located in Arizona and owned by a Delaware corporation would be governed by the law of Delaware. Although Delaware law would send one to a filing office in Arizona for the place to file a financing statement as a fixture filing, see section 9-501, Delaware law would not take account of local, nonuniform, real property filing and recording requirements that Arizona law might impose. For this reason, paragraph (3)(A) contains a special rule for security interests perfected by a fixture filing; the law of the jurisdiction in which the fixtures are located governs perfection, including the formal requisites of a fixture filing. Under paragraph (3)(C), the same law governs priority. Fixtures are "goods" as defined in section 9-102.

The filing of a financing statement to perfect a security interest in collateral of a transmitting utility constitutes a fixture filing with respect to goods that are or become fixtures. See section 9-501(b). Accordingly, to perfect a security interest in goods of this kind by a fixture filing, a financing statement must be filed in the office specified by section 9-501(b) as enacted in the jurisdiction in which the goods are located. If the fixtures collateral is located in more than one State, filing in all of those States will be necessary to perfect a security interest in all the fixtures collateral by a fixture filing. Of course, a security interest in nearly all types of collateral (including fixtures) of a transmitting utility may be perfected by filing in the office specified by section 9-501(b) as enacted in the jurisdiction in which the transmitting utility is located. However, such a filing will not be effective as a fixture filing except with respect to goods that are located in that jurisdiction.

c. *Timber to Be Cut.* Application of the general rule in paragraph (1) to perfection of a security interest in timber to be cut would yield undesirable results analogous to those described with respect to fixtures. Paragraph (3)(B) adopts a similar solution: Perfection is governed by the law of the jurisdiction in which the timber is located. As with fixtures, under paragraph (3)(C), the same law governs priority. Timber to be cut also is "goods" as defined in section 9-102.

Paragraph (3)(B) applies only to "timber to be cut," not to timber that has been cut. Consequently, once the timber is cut, the general choice of law rule in paragraph (1) becomes applicable. To ensure continued perfection, a secured party should file in both the jurisdiction in which the timber to be cut is located and in the state where the debtor is located. The former filing would be with the office in which a real property mortgage would be filed, and the latter would be a central filing. See section 9-501.

d. *As-Extracted Collateral.* Paragraph (4) adopts the rule of former section 9-103(5) with respect to certain security interests in minerals and related accounts. Like security interests in fixtures perfected by filing a fixture filing, security interests in minerals that are as-extracted collateral are perfected by filing in the office designated for the filing or recording of a mortgage on the real property. For the same reasons, the law governing perfection and priority is the law of the jurisdiction in which the wellhead or minehead is located.

6. *Change in Law Governing Perfection.* When the debtor changes its location to another jurisdiction, the jurisdiction whose law governs perfection under paragraph (1) changes, as well. Similarly, the law governing perfection of a possessory security interest in collateral under paragraph (2) changes when the collateral is removed to another jurisdiction. Nevertheless, these changes will not result in an immediate loss of perfection. See section 9-316(a) and (b).

7. *Law Governing Effect of Perfection and Priority: Goods, Documents, Instruments, Money, Negotiable Documents, and Tangible Chattel Paper.* Under former section 9-103, the law of a single jurisdiction governed both questions of perfection and those of priority. This article generally adopts that approach. See paragraph (1). But the approach may create problems if the debtor and collateral are located in different jurisdictions. For example, assume a security interest in equipment located in Pennsylvania is perfected by filing in Illinois, where the debtor is located. If the law of the jurisdiction in which the debtor is located were to govern priority, then the priority of an execution lien on goods located in Pennsylvania would be governed by rules enacted by the Illinois legislature.

To address this problem, paragraph (3)(C) divorces questions of perfection from questions of "the effect of perfection or nonperfection and the priority of a security interest." Under paragraph (3)(C), the rights of competing claimants to tangible collateral are resolved by reference to the law of the jurisdiction in which the collateral is located. A similar bifurcation applied to security interests in investment property under former section 9-103(6). See section 9-305.

Paragraph (3)(C) applies the law of the situs to determine priority only with respect to goods (including fixtures), instruments, money, negotiable documents, and tangible chattel paper. Compare former section 9-103(1), which applied the law of the location of the collateral to documents, instruments, and "ordinary" (as opposed to "mobile") goods. This article does not distinguish among types of goods. The ordinary/mobile goods distinction appears to address concerns about where to file and search, rather than concerns about priority. There is no reason to preserve this distinction under the bifurcated approach.

Particularly serious confusion may arise when the choice of law rules of a given jurisdiction result in each of two competing security interests in the same collateral being governed by a different priority rule. The potential for this confusion existed under former section 9-103(4) with respect to chattel paper: Perfection by possession was governed by the law of the location of the paper, whereas perfection by filing was governed by the law of the location of the debtor. Consider the mess that would have been created if the language or interpretation of former section 9-308 were to differ in the two relevant states, or if one of the relevant jurisdictions (e.g., a foreign country) had not adopted article 9. The potential for confusion could have been exacerbated when a secured party perfected both by taking possession in the state where the collateral is located (State A) and by filing in the state where the debtor is located (State B)--a common practice for some chattel paper financers. By providing that the law of the jurisdiction in which the collateral is located governs priority, paragraph (3) substantially diminishes this problem.

8. *Non-U.S. Debtors.* This article applies the same choice of law rules to all debtors, foreign and domestic. For example, it adopts the bifurcated approach for determining the law applicable to security interests in goods and other tangible collateral. See comment 5(a), above. The article contains a new rule specifying the location of non-U.S. debtors for purposes of this part. The rule appears in section 9-307 and is explained in the Comments to that section. Former section 9-103(3)(c), which contained a special choice of law rule governing security interests created by debtors located in a non-U.S. jurisdiction, proved unsatisfactory and was deleted.

EDITOR'S NOTE. --

Session Laws 2012-70, s. 27 , provides: "The Revisor of Statutes shall cause to be printed, as annotations to the published General Statutes, all relevant portions of the Official Comments to the 2010 Amendments to Article 9 of the Uniform Commercial Code and all explanatory comments of the drafters of this act as the Revisor may deem appropriate."

The Revision of Uniform Commercial Code Article 9 -- Secured Transactions was drafted by the National Conference of Commissioners on Uniform State Laws and The American Law Institute on April 27, 2011. The Official Commentary for the 2010 revision are copyrighted 2010 by The American Law Institute and National Conference of Commissioners on Uniform

State Laws. The affected portions of the Official Comment to this section have been set out at this section with the appropriate amendments.

EFFECT OF AMENDMENTS. --

Session Laws 2006-112, s. 48 , effective October 1, 2006, inserted "tangible" preceding "negotiable documents" in the introductory language of subdivision (3).

EDITOR'S NOTE. --Some of the cases below were decided under former Article 9 of the Uniform Commercial Code prior to its revision by Session Laws 2000-169.

IT IS THE EXCLUSION OF THIRD PARTIES WHICH IS THE ESSENCE OF PERFECTION OF A SECURITY INTEREST. Westchase I Assocs. v. Lincoln Nat'l Life Ins. Co., 126 Bankr. 692 (W.D.N.C. 1991).

SECURITY INTERESTS IN MOTOR VEHICLES. --With reference to vehicles subject to registration with the Division of Motor Vehicles, the provisions of G.S. 20-58 et seq. are the exclusive statutory authority governing the perfecting of security interests in motor vehicles. In re Holder, 94 Bankr. 395 (Bankr. M.D.N.C. 1988), aff'd, 892 F.2d 29 (4th Cir. 1989).

APPLIED in In re Augusta Tissue Mill, LLC, 2007 Bankr. LEXIS 3040 (Bankr. M.D.N.C. Sept. 5, 2007).

CITED in Rentenbach Constructors, Inc. v. CM P'ship, 181 N.C. App. 268, 639 S.E.2d 16 (2007).

LEGAL PERIODICALS. --

For comment, "Return to the Conservative View of Security Agreements in Commercial Transactions," see 8 Campbell L. Rev. 505 (1986).

For article, "Certainty, Efficiency, and Realism: Rights in Collateral Under Article 9 of the Uniform Commercial Code," see 73 N.C.L. Rev. 115 (1994).

NOTES APPLICABLE TO ENTIRE CHAPTER

EDITOR'S NOTE. --Former G.S. 25-1 to 25-199 (the N.I.L.) were repealed by Session Laws 1965, c. 700, which enacted the U.C.C.

To maintain uniformity with the commercial codes adopted by other states, the designation and indentation of subsections, subdivisions and further divisions of sections in Chapter 25 have not been changed to conform to the system and style employed elsewhere in the General Statutes. The numbering of sections corresponds to that used in the 1962 Official Text of the U.C.C., as amended, except that each number is preceded by the chapter number "25." Thus, "G.S. 1-101" of the Official Text is "G.S. 25-1-101" in this chapter.

Where sections of the U.C.C. are similar to sections repealed by Session Laws 1965, c. 700, the historical citations to the former sections have been added to the historical citations to the sections of the U.C.C.

Following each section of the U.C.C., Official Comments have been included. The Comments headed "North Carolina Comment" first appeared in "North Carolina Annotations -- The Uniform Commercial Code," a 1965 report of the former Legislative Council to the General Assembly of North Carolina. Appropriate comments were selected at the time of initial publication of Chapter 25 and edited under the supervision of the Division of Legislative Drafting and Codification of Statutes of the Department of Justice. The Comments headed "Official Comment" are the Comments of the National Conference of Commissioners on Uniform State Laws and The American Law Institute which appeared in the "1962 Official Text with Comments" of the U.C.C., with the exceptions noted hereafter.

Official Comments, copyright 1978, 1987, 1989, 1990, 1991, 1993, 1994, 1995, 1998-2000 are reprinted in Articles 1 to 11 with the permission of The American Law Institute and the National Conference of Commissioners on Uniform State Laws. It is believed that the Official Comments will prove of value to the practitioner in understanding and applying the text of this Chapter.

Where they appear in this Chapter, "Amended Comment" usually means that an error in the original comment has been corrected by a subsequent amendment, and "Supplemental Comment" pertains to a later development, such as an amendment to the statute text. North Carolina Comments explain where the General Assembly has enacted variations to the text of the Uniform Act.

Article 8 of Chapter 25 was amended in 1989 and again in 1997, and contains Amended Official Comments thereto.

Articles 2A and 4A of Chapter 25 were enacted by the General Assembly in 1993, and contain the Official Comments thereto.

Article 5 of Chapter 25 was revised in 1999 and contains revised Official Comments.

Article 9 was revised in 2000 and contains revised Official Comments thereto. This revised Article 9 supersedes the revision of Article 9 by Session Laws 1975, c. 862, s. 1.

Article 8 of Chapter 25 contains a North Carolina Comment to the 1989 revision. Articles 3 and 4 of Chapter 25 contain revised North Carolina Comments to the 1995 Revision. Article 5 of Chapter 25 contains two North Carolina Comments to the 1999 Revision.

The Official Comments and the North Carolina Comments printed in this Chapter have been printed by the publisher as received, without any significant editorial change.

The user should also note that Amended Official Comments have not been received in conjunction with all amendments to sections of the U.C.C., and therefore, subsequent amendments to the Official Comments and the North Carolina Comments may not be reflected in some instances.

The Comment under the title of the Act states in part: "Uniformity throughout American jurisdictions is one of the main objectives of this Code; and that objective cannot be obtained without substantial uniformity of construction. To aid in uniform construction these Comments set forth the purpose of various provisions of this Act to promote uniformity, to aid in viewing the Act as an integrated whole, and to safeguard against misconstruction."

Chapter 25

NOTES APPLICABLE TO ENTIRE ARTICLE

EDITOR'S NOTE. --Session Laws 2000-169, s. 1, effective July 1, 2001, rewrote Article 9 of Chapter 25 of the Uniform Commercial Code. At the end of Article 9 are tables showing comparable sections and their disposition in new Article 9. This revised Article 9 supersedes the revision of Article 9 by Session Laws 1975, c. 862, s. 1. Where appropriate, historical citations to sections of former Article 9 have been placed under corresponding sections of revised Article 9.

Session Laws 2000-169, s. 49, directs the Revisor of Statutes to cause to be printed along with the act all relevant portions of the official comments to the Uniform Commercial Code, Revised Article 9 and conforming amendments to Articles 1, 2, 2A, 4, 5, 6, 7, and 8 and all explanatory comments of the drafters of this act as the Revisor deems appropriate.

Session Laws 2001-218, s. 6, provides: "The Revisor of Statutes shall cause to be printed along with the portions of this act amending Article 9 of Chapter 25 of the General Statutes, such North Carolina official comments explaining the amendments made by this act as the Revisor deems appropriate."

Session Laws 2012-70, s. 27, provides: "The Revisor of Statutes shall cause to be printed, as annotations to the published General Statutes, all relevant portions of the Official Comments to the 2010 Amendments to Article 9 of the Uniform Commercial Code and all explanatory comments of the drafters of this act as the Revisor may deem appropriate."

The Revision of Uniform Commercial Code Article 9 -- Secured Transactions was drafted by the National Conference of Commissioners on Uniform State Laws and The American Law Institute on April 27, 2011. The Official Commentary for the 2010 revision are copyrighted 2010 by The American Law Institute and National Conference of Commissioners on Uniform State Laws. The affected portions of the Official Comment to this Article have been set out in this Article with the appropriate amendments.

Official Comments in Article 9: Copyright 1998-2000 by the American Law Institute and the National Conference of Commissioners on Uniform State Laws. Reprinted with permission of the Permanent Editorial Board of the Uniform Commercial Code.

The Official Comments appearing under individual sections in this Article have been printed by the publisher as received, without editorial change, and relate to the Article as originally enacted. However, not all sections in this Article may carry Official Comments. Furthermore, Official Comments may or may not have been received or updated in conjunction with subsequent amendments to this Article and, therefore, may not reflect all changes to the sections under which they appear.

§ 25-9-302. Law governing perfection and priority of agricultural liens

While farm products are located in a jurisdiction, the local law of that jurisdiction governs perfection, the effect of perfection or nonperfection, and the priority of an agricultural lien on the farm products.

History.

2000-169, s. 1

AMENDED OFFICIAL COMMENT (2010 EDITION)

1. *Source.* New.

2. *Agricultural Liens.* This section provides choice of law rules for agricultural liens on farm products. Perfection, the effect of perfection or nonperfection, and priority all are governed by the law of the jurisdiction in which the farm products are located. Other choice of law rules, including section 1-301, determine which jurisdiction's law governs other matters, such as the secured party's rights on default. See section 9-301, comment 2. Inasmuch as no agricultural lien on proceeds arises under this article, this section does not expressly apply to proceeds of agricultural liens. However, if another statute creates an agricultural lien on proceeds, it may be appropriate for courts to apply the choice of law rule in this section to determine priority in the proceeds.

EDITOR'S NOTE. --

Session Laws 2012-70, s. 27, provides: "The Revisor of Statutes shall cause to be printed, as annotations to the published General Statutes, all relevant portions of the Official Comments to the 2010 Amendments to Article 9 of the Uniform Commercial Code and all explanatory comments of the drafters of this act as the Revisor may deem appropriate."

The Revision of Uniform Commercial Code Article 9 -- Secured Transactions was drafted by the National Conference of Commissioners on Uniform State Laws and The American Law Institute on April 27, 2011. The Official Commentary for the 2010 revision are copyrighted 2010 by The American Law Institute and National Conference of Commissioners on Uniform State Laws. The affected portions of the Official Comment to this section have been set out at this section with the appropriate amendments.

PRIORITY BASED ON FIRST TO FILE. --Where a bank loaned money to a debtor and filed a financing statement in 1999 and a partnership entered into a factoring agreement with the debtor but did not file a statement until 2003, the bank had a priority lien on the proceeds at issue because it perfected its security interest several years before the partnership; also, a purported financing statement amendment failed to include a security agreement showing an assignment of the security interest in certain accounts receivable. Rentenbach Constructors, Inc. v. CM P'ship, 181 N.C. App. 268, 639 S.E.2d 16 (2007).

USER NOTE:

For more generally applicable notes, see notes under the first section of this subpart, part, article, or chapter.

§ 25-9-307. Location of debtor

(a) "Place of business." -- In this section, "place of business" means a place where a debtor conducts its affairs.

(b) Debtor's location: general rules. -- Except as otherwise provided in this section, the following rules determine a debtor's location:

(1) A debtor who is an individual is located at the individual's principal residence.

(2) A debtor that is an organization and has only one place of business is located at its place of business.

(3) A debtor that is an organization and has more than one place of business is located at its chief executive office.

(c) **Limitation of applicability of subsection (b).** -- Subsection (b) of this section applies only if a debtor's residence, place of business, or chief executive office, as applicable, is located in a jurisdiction whose law generally requires information concerning the existence of a nonpossessory security interest to be made generally available in a filing, recording, or registration system as a condition or result of the security interest's obtaining priority over the rights of a lien creditor with respect to the collateral. If subsection (b) of this section does not apply, the debtor is located in the District of Columbia.

(d) Continuation of location: cessation of existence, etc. -- A person that ceases to exist, have a residence, or have a place of business continues to be located in the jurisdiction specified by subsections (b) and (c) of this section.

(e) **Location of registered organization organized under state law.** -- A registered organization that is organized under the law of a state is located in that state.

(f) **Location of registered organization organized under federal law; bank branches and agencies.** -- Except as otherwise provided in subsection (i) of this section, a registered organization that is organized under the law of the United States and a branch or agency of a bank that is not organized under the law of the United States or a state are located:

(1) In the state that the law of the United States designates, if the law designates a state of location;

(2) In the state that the registered organization, branch, or agency designates, if the law of the United States authorizes the registered organization, branch, or agency to designate its state of location, including by designating its main office, home office, or other comparable office; or

(3) In the District of Columbia, if neither subdivision (1) nor subdivision (2) of this subsection applies.

(g) Continuation of location: change in status of registered organization. -- A registered organization continues to be located in the jurisdiction specified by subsection (e) or (f) of this section notwithstanding:

(1) The suspension, revocation, forfeiture, or lapse of the registered organization's status as such in its jurisdiction of organization; or

(2) The dissolution, winding up, or cancellation of the existence of the registered organization.

(h) **Location of United States.** -- The United States is located in the District of Columbia.

(i) **Location of foreign bank branch or agency if licensed in only one state.** -- A branch or agency of a bank that is not organized under the law of the United States or a state is located in the state in which the branch or agency is licensed, if all branches and agencies of the bank are licensed in only one state.

(j) **Location of foreign air carrier.** -- A foreign air carrier under the Federal Aviation Act of 1958, as amended, is located at the designated office of the agent upon which service of process may be made on behalf of the carrier.

(k) **Section applies only to this Part.** --- This section applies only for purposes of this Part.

History.
2000-169, s. 1 ; 2012-70, s. 3
AMENDED OFFICIAL COMMENT (2010 EDITION)

1.   *Source.* Former section 9-103(3)(d), substantially revised.

2.   *General Rules.* As a general matter, the location of the debtor determines the jurisdiction whose law governs perfection of a security interest. See sections 9-301(1) and 9-305(c). It also governs priority of a security interest in certain types of intangible collateral, such as accounts, electronic chattel paper, and general intangibles. This section determines the location of the debtor for choice of law purposes, but not for other purposes. See subsection (k).

Subsection (b) states the general rules: An individual debtor is deemed to be located at the individual's principal residence with respect to both personal and business assets. Any other debtor is deemed to be located at its place of business if it has only one, or at its chief executive office if it has more than one place of business.

As used in this section, a "place of business" means a place where the debtor conducts its affairs. See subsection (a). Thus, every organization, even eleemosynary institutions and other organizations that do not conduct "for profit" business activities, has a "place of business." Under subsection (d), a person who ceases to exist, have a residence, or have a place of business continues to be located in the jurisdiction determined by subsection (b).

The term "chief executive office" is not defined in this section or elsewhere in the Uniform Commercial

Chapter 25

Code. "Chief executive office" means the place from which the debtor manages the main part of its business operations or other affairs. This is the place where persons dealing with the debtor would normally look for credit information, and is the appropriate place for filing. With respect to most multistate debtors, it will be simple to determine which of the debtor's offices is the "chief executive office." Even when a doubt arises, it would be rare that there could be more than two possibilities. A secured party in such a case may protect itself by perfecting under the law of each possible jurisdiction.

Similarly, the term "principal residence" is not defined. If the security interest in question is a purchase-money security interest in consumer goods which is perfected upon attachment, see section 9-309(1), the choice of law may make no difference. In other cases, when a doubt arises, prudence may dictate perfecting under the law of each jurisdiction that might be the debtor's "principal residence."

Questions sometimes arise about the location of the debtor with respect to collateral held in a common-law trust. A typical common-law trust is not itself a juridical entity capable of owning property and so would not be a "debtor" as defined in section 9-102. Rather, the debtor with respect to property held in a common-law trust typically is the trustee of the trust acting in the capacity of trustee. (The beneficiary would be a "debtor" with respect to its beneficial interest in the trust, but not with respect to the property held in the trust.) If a common-law trust has multiple trustees located in different jurisdictions, a secured party who perfects by filing would be well advised to file a financing statement in each jurisdiction in which a trustee is located, as determined under section 9-307. Filing in all relevant jurisdictions would insure perfection and minimize any priority complications that otherwise might arise.

The general rules are subject to several exceptions, each of which is discussed below.

3. *Non-U.S. Debtors.* Under the general rules of this section, a non-U.S. debtor normally would be located in a foreign jurisdiction and, as a consequence, foreign law would govern perfection. When foreign law affords no public notice of security interests, the general rule yields unacceptable results.

Accordingly, subsection (c) provides that the normal rules for determining the location of a debtor (i.e., the rules in subsection (b)) apply only if they yield a location that is "a jurisdiction whose law generally requires information concerning the existence of a nonpossessory security interest to be made generally available in a filing, recording, or registration system as a condition or result of the security interest's obtaining priority over the rights of a lien creditor with respect to the collateral." The phrase "generally requires" is meant to include legal regimes that generally require notice in a filing or recording system as a condition of perfecting nonpossessory security interests, but which permit perfection by another method (e.g., control, automatic perfection, temporary perfection) in limited circumstances. A jurisdiction that has

adopted this article or an earlier version of this article is such a jurisdiction. If the rules in subsection (b) yield a jurisdiction whose law does not generally require notice in a filing or registration system and none of the special rules in subsections (e), (f), (i), and (j) applies, the debtor is located in the District of Columbia.

4. *Registered Organizations Organized Under Law of a State.* Under subsection (e), a "registered organization" (defined in section 9-102 so as to ordinarily include corporations, limited partnerships, limited liability companies, and statutory trusts) organized under the law of a "State" (defined in section 9-102) is located in its State of organization. The term "registered organization" includes a business trust described in the second sentence of the term's definition. See section 9-102. The trust's public organic record, typically the trust agreement, usually will indicate the jurisdiction under whose law the trust is organized.

Subsection (g) makes clear that events affecting the status of a registered organization, such as the dissolution of a corporation or revocation of its charter, do not affect its location for purposes of subsection (e). However, certain of these events may result in, or be accompanied by, a transfer of collateral from the registered organization to another debtor. This section does not determine whether a transfer occurs, nor does it determine the legal consequences of any transfer.

Determining the registered organization-debtor's location by reference to the jurisdiction of organization could provide some important side benefits for the filing systems. A jurisdiction could structure its filing system so that it would be impossible to make a mistake in a registered organization-debtor's name on a financing statement. For example, a filer would be informed if a filed record designated an incorrect corporate name for the debtor. Linking filing to the jurisdiction of organization also could reduce pressure on the system imposed by transactions in which registered organizations cease to exist-as a consequence of merger or consolidation, for example. The jurisdiction of organization might prohibit such transactions unless steps were taken to ensure that existing filings were refiled against a successor or terminated by the secured party.

5. *Registered Organizations Organized Under Law of United States; Branches and Agencies of Banks Not Organized Under Law of United States.* Subsection (f) specifies the location of a debtor that is a registered organization organized under the law of the United States. It defers to the law of the United States, to the extent that that law determines, or authorizes the debtor to determine, the debtor's location. Thus, if the law of the United States designates a particular state as the debtor's location, that state is the debtor's location for purposes of this article's choice of law rules. Similarly, if the law of the United States authorizes the registered organization to designate its state of location, the state that the registered organization designates is the state in which it is located for purposes

of this article's choice of law rules. In other cases, the debtor is located in the District of Columbia.

In some cases, the law of the United States authorizes the registered organi-zation to designate a main office, home office, or other comparable office. See, e.g., 12 U.S.C. §§ 22 and 1464(a); 12 C.F.R. § 552.3. Designation of such an office constitutes the designation of the State of location for purposes of section 9-307(f)(2).

Subsection (f) also specifies the location of a branch or agency in the United States of a foreign bank that has one or more branches or agencies in the United States. The law of the United States authorizes a foreign bank (or, on behalf of the bank, a federal regulatory agency) to designate a single home state for all of the foreign bank's branches and agencies in the United States. See 12 U.S.C. § 3103(c) and 12 C.F.R. § 211.22. The designated State constitutes the State of location for the branch or agency for purposes of section 9-307(f): however if all of the foreign bank's branches or agencies that are in the United States are licensed in only one State, the branches and agencies are located in that State. See subsection (i).

In cases not governed by subsection (f) or (i), the location of a foreign bank is determined by subsections (b) and (c).

6. *United States.* To the extent that article 9 governs (see sections 1-301 and 9-109(c)), the United States is located in the District of Columbia for purposes of this article's choice of law rules. See subsection (h).

7. *Foreign Air Carriers.* Subsection (j) follows former section 9-103(3)(d). To the extent that it is applicable, the Convention on the International Recognition of Rights in Aircraft (Geneva Convention) supersedes state legislation on this subject, as set forth in section 9-311(b), but some nations are not parties to that convention.

TRANSITION PROVISIONS. --For transition provisions related to the 2010 amendments to Article 9 by Session Laws 2012-70, see the Appendix following Part 7 at the end of this Article.

Session Laws 2012-70, s. 26(a) , (b), provides: "(a) Pre-Effective-Date Transactions or Liens. -- Except as otherwise provided in Part II of this act, this act applies to a transaction or lien within its scope, even if the transaction or lien was entered into or created before this act becomes effective [July 1, 2013].

"(b) Pre-Effective-Date Proceedings. -- This act does not affect an action, case, or proceeding commenced before this act becomes effective [July 1, 2013]."

EDITOR'S NOTE. --
Session Laws 2012-70, s. 27 , provides: "The Revisor of Statutes shall cause to be printed, as annotations to the published General Statutes, all relevant portions of the Official Comments to the 2010 Amendments to Article 9 of the Uniform Commercial Code and all explanatory comments of the drafters of this act as the Revisor may deem appropriate."

The Revision of Uniform Commercial Code Article 9 -- Secured Transactions was drafted by the National Conference of Commissioners on Uniform State Laws

and The American Law Institute on April 27, 2011. The Official Commentary for the 2010 revision are copyrighted 2010 by The American Law Institute and National Conference of Commissioners on Uniform State Laws. The affected portions of the Official Comment to this section have been set out at this section with the appropriate amendments.

EFFECT OF AMENDMENTS. --
Session Laws 2012-70, s. 3 , effective July 1, 2013, substituted "location, including by designating its main office, home office, or other comparable office" for "location" in subsection (f). See note for Transition Provisions governing these amendments.

APPLIED in In re Augusta Tissue Mill, LLC, 2007 Bankr. LEXIS 3040 (Bankr. M.D.N.C. Sept. 5, 2007).

CITED in Community Sav. Bank, Inc. v. Rountree (In re Rountree), 2002 Bankr. LEXIS 2132 (Bankr. M.D.N.C. Apr. 30, 2002).

USER NOTE:
For more generally applicable notes, see notes under the first section of this subpart, part, article, or chapter.

SUBPART 3.
PRIORITY

§ 25-9-318. No interest retained in right to payment that is sold; rights and title of seller of account or chattel paper with respect to creditors and purchasers

(a) **Seller retains no interest. --** A debtor that has sold an account, chattel paper, payment intangible, or promissory note does not retain a legal or equitable interest in the collateral sold.

(b) **Deemed rights of debtor if buyer's security interest unperfected. --** For purposes of determining the rights of creditors of, and purchasers for value of an account or chattel paper from, a debtor that has sold an account or chattel paper, while the buyer's security interest is unperfected, the debtor is deemed to have rights and title to the account or chattel paper identical to those the debtor sold.

History.
2000-169, s. 1

AMENDED OFFICIAL COMMENT (2010 EDITION)

1. *Source.* New.

2. *Sellers of Accounts, Chattel Paper, Payment Intangibles, and Promissory Notes.* Section 1-201(b)(35) defines "security interest" to include the interest of a buyer of accounts, chattel paper, payment intangibles, or promissory notes. See also section 9-109(a) and comment 5. Subsection (a) makes explicit what was implicit, but perfectly obvious, under former article 9: The fact that a sale of an account or chattel paper gives rise to a "security interest" does not imply that the seller retains an interest in the property that has

been sold. To the contrary, a seller of an account or chattel paper retains no interest whatsoever in the property to the extent that it has been sold. Subsection (a) also applies to sales of payment intangibles and promissory notes, transactions that were not covered by former article 9. Neither this article nor the definition of "security interest" in section 1-201 provides rules for distinguishing sales transactions from those that create a security interest securing an obligation.

3. *Buyers of Accounts and Chattel Paper.* Another aspect of sales of accounts and chattel paper also was implicit, and equally obvious, under former article 9: If the buyer's security interest is unperfected, then for purposes of determining the rights of certain third parties, the seller (debtor) is deemed to have all rights and title that the seller sold. The seller is deemed to have these rights even though, as between the parties, it has sold all its rights to the buyer. Subsection (b) makes this explicit. As a consequence of subsection (b), if the buyer's security interest is unperfected, the seller can transfer, and the creditors of the seller can reach, the account or chattel paper as if it had not been sold.

Example: Debtor sells accounts or chattel paper to Buyer-1 and retains no interest in them. Buyer-1 does not file a financing statement. Debtor then sells the same receivables to Buyer-2. Buyer-2 files a proper financing statement. Having sold the receivables to Buyer-1, Debtor would not have any rights in the collateral so as to permit Buyer-2's security (ownership) interest to attach. Nevertheless, under this section, for purposes of determining the rights of purchasers for value from Debtor, Debtor is deemed to have the rights that Debtor sold. Accordingly, Buyer-2's security interest attaches, is perfected by the filing, and, under section 9-322, is senior to Buyer-1's interest.

4. *Effect of Perfection.* If the security interest of a buyer of accounts or chattel paper is perfected the usual result would take effect: Transferees from and creditors of the seller could not acquire an interest in the sold accounts or chattel paper. The same result generally would occur if payment intangibles or promissory notes were sold, inasmuch as the buyer's security interest is automatically perfected under section 9-309. However, in certain circumstances a purchaser who takes possession of a promissory note will achieve priority, under sections 9-330 or 9-331, over the security interest of an earlier buyer of the promissory note. It necessarily follows that the seller in those circumstances retains the power to transfer the promissory note, as if it had not been sold, to a purchaser who obtains priority under either of those sections. See section 9-203(b)(3), comment 6.

EDITOR'S NOTE. --
Session Laws 2012-70, s. 27 , provides: "The Revisor of Statutes shall cause to be printed, as annotations to the published General Statutes, all relevant portions of the Official Comments to the 2010 Amendments to Article 9 of the Uniform Commercial Code and all explanatory comments of the drafters of this act as the Revisor may deem appropriate."

The Revision of Uniform Commercial Code Article 9 -- Secured Transactions was drafted by the National Conference of Commissioners on Uniform State Laws and The American Law Institute on April 27, 2011. The Official Commentary for the 2010 revision are copyrighted 2010 by The American Law Institute and National Conference of Commissioners on Uniform State Laws. The affected portions of the Official Comment to this section have been set out at this section with the appropriate amendments.

PRIORITY BASED ON FIRST TO FILE. --Where a bank loaned money to a debtor and filed a financing statement in 1999 and a partnership entered into a factoring agreement with the debtor but did not file a statement until 2003, the bank had a priority lien on the proceeds at issue because it perfected its security interest several years before the partnership; also, a purported financing statement amendment failed to include a security agreement showing an assignment of the security interest in certain accounts receivable. Rentenbach Constructors, Inc. v. CM P'ship, 181 N.C. App. 268, 639 S.E.2d 16 (2007).

USER NOTE:
For more generally applicable notes, see notes under the first section of this subpart, part, article, or chapter.

PART 4.
RIGHTS OF THIRD PARTIES

§ 25-9-406. Discharge of account debtor; notification of assignment; identification and proof of assignment; restrictions on assignment of accounts, chattel paper, payment intangibles, and promissory notes ineffective

(a) **Discharge of account debtor; effect of notification. --** Subject to subsections (b) through (i) of this section, an account debtor on an account, chattel paper, or a payment intangible may discharge its obligation by paying the assignor until, but not after, the account debtor receives a notification, authenticated by the assignor or the assignee, that the amount due or to become due has been assigned and that payment is to be made to the assignee. After receipt of the notification, the account debtor may discharge its obligation by paying the assignee and may not discharge the obligation by paying the assignor.

(b) **When notification ineffective. --** Subject to subsection (h) of this section, notification is ineffective under subsection (a) of this section:

(1) If it does not reasonably identify the rights assigned;

(2) To the extent that an agreement between an account debtor and a seller of a payment intangible limits the account debtor's duty to pay a person other than the

seller and the limitation is effective under law other than this Article; or

(3) At the option of an account debtor, if the notification notifies the account debtor to make less than the full amount of any installment or other periodic payment to the assignee, even if:

a. Only a portion of the account, chattel paper, or payment intangible has been assigned to that assignee;

b. A portion has been assigned to another assignee; or

c. The account debtor knows that the assignment to that assignee is limited.

(c) **Proof of assignment.** -- Subject to subsection (h) of this section, if requested by the account debtor, an assignee shall seasonably furnish reasonable proof that the assignment has been made. Unless the assignee complies, the account debtor may discharge its obligation by paying the assignor, even if the account debtor has received a notification under subsection (a) of this section.

(d) **Term restricting assignment generally ineffective.** -- Except as otherwise provided in subsection (e) of this section and G.S. 25-2A-303 and G.S. 25-9-407, and subject to subsection (h) of this section, a term in an agreement between an account debtor and an assignor or in a promissory note is ineffective to the extent that it:

(1) Prohibits, restricts, or requires the consent of the account debtor or person obligated on the promissory note to the assignment or transfer of, or the creation, attachment, perfection, or enforcement of a security interest in, the account, chattel paper, payment intangible, or promissory note; or

(2) Provides that the assignment or transfer or the creation, attachment, perfection, or enforcement of the security interest may give rise to a default, breach, right of recoupment, claim, defense, termination, right of termination, or remedy under the account, chattel paper, payment intangible, or promissory note.

(e) **Inapplicability of subsection (d) to certain sales.** -- Subsection (d) of this section does not apply to the sale of a payment intangible or promissory note, other than a sale pursuant to a disposition under G.S. 25-9-610 or an acceptance of collateral under G.S. 25-9-620.

(f) **Legal restrictions on assignment generally ineffective.** -- Except as otherwise provided in G.S. 25-2A-303 and G.S. 25-9-407 and subject to subsections (h) and (i) of this section, a rule of law, statute, or regulation that prohibits, restricts, or requires the consent of a government, governmental body or official, or account debtor to the assignment or transfer of, or creation of a security interest in, an account

or chattel paper is ineffective to the extent that the rule of law, statute, or regulation:

(1) Prohibits, restricts, or requires the consent of the government, governmental body or official, or account debtor to the assignment or transfer of, or the creation, attachment, perfection, or enforcement of a security interest in the account or chattel paper; or

(2) Provides that the assignment or transfer or the creation, attachment, perfection, or enforcement of the security interest may give rise to a default, breach, right of recoupment, claim, defense, termination, right of termination, or remedy under the account or chattel paper.

(g) **Subdivision (b)(3) not waivable.** --- Subject to subsection (h) of this section, an account debtor may not waive or vary its option under subdivision (b)(3) of this section.

(h) **Rule for individual under other law.** -- This section is subject to law other than this Article which establishes a different rule for an account debtor who is an individual and who incurred the obligation primarily for personal, family, or household purposes.

(i) **Inapplicability.** -- This section does not apply to an assignment of a health-care-insurance receivable or an interest in a partnership or limited liability company. Subsection (f) of this section does not apply to an assignment or transfer of, or the creation, attachment, perfection, or enforcement of a security interest in, a right the transfer of which is prohibited or restricted by any of the following statutes to the extent that the statute is inconsistent with subsection (f) of this section:

(1) North Carolina Structured Settlement Act (Article 44B of Chapter 1 of the General Statutes).

(2) North Carolina Crime Victims Compensation Act (Chapter 15B of the General Statutes).

(3) North Carolina Consumer Finance Act (Article 15 of Chapter 53 of the General Statutes).

(4) North Carolina Firefighters' and Rescue Squad Workers' Pension Fund (Article 86 of Chapter 58 of the General Statutes).

(5) Employment Security Law (Chapter 96 of the General Statutes).

(6) North Carolina Workers' Compensation Fund Act (Article 1 of Chapter 97 of the General Statutes).

(7) Programs of Public Assistance (Article 2 of Chapter 108A of the General Statutes).

(8) North Carolina State Lottery Act (Chapter 18C of the General Statutes).

(j) **Section prevails over inconsistent law.** -- Except to the extent otherwise provided in subsection (i) of this section, this section prevails over any inconsistent provision of an existing or future statute, rule, or regulation of this State unless the provision is contained in a statute of this State, refers expressly to this section, and states that the provision prevails over this section.

History.
1945, c. 196, s. 6; 1961, c. 574; 1965, c. 700, s. 1; 1975, c. 862, s. 7; 2000-169, s. 1 ; 2012-70, s. 8 ; 2013-157, s. 31 ; 2013-284, s. 1(b)

OFFICIAL COMMENT

1. *Source.* Former section 9-318(3), (4).

2. *Account Debtor's Right to Pay Assignor Until Notification.* Subsection (a) provides the general rule concerning an account debtor's right to pay the assignor until the account debtor receives appropriate notification. The revision makes clear that once the account debtor receives the notification, the account debtor cannot discharge its obligation by paying the assignor. It also makes explicit that payment to the assignor before notification, or payment to the assignee after notification, discharges the obligation. No change in meaning from former section 9-318 is intended. Nothing in this section conditions the effectiveness of a notification on the identity of the person who gives it. An account debtor that doubts whether the right to payment has been assigned may avail itself of the procedures in subsection (c). See comment 4.

An effective notification under subsection (a) must be authenticated. This requirement normally could be satisfied by sending notification on the notifying person's letterhead or on a form on which the notifying person's name appears. In each case the printed name would be a symbol adopted by the notifying person for the purpose of identifying the person and adopting the notification. See section 9-102 (defining "authenticate").

Subsection (a) applies only to account debtors on accounts, chattel paper, and payment intangibles. (Section 9-102 defines the term "account debtor" more broadly, to include those obligated on all general intangibles.) Although subsection (a) is more precise than its predecessor, it probably does not change the rule that applied under former article 9. Former section 9-318(3) referred to the account debtor's obligation to "pay," indicating that the subsection was limited to account debtors on accounts, chattel paper, and other payment obligations.

3. *Limitations on Effectiveness of Notification.* Subsection (b) contains some special rules concerning the effectiveness of a notification under subsection (a).

Subsection (b)(1) tracks former section 9-318(3) by making ineffective a notification that does not reasonably identify the rights assigned. A reasonable identification need not identify the right to payment with specificity, but what is reasonable also is not left to the arbitrary decision of the account debtor. If an account debtor has doubt as to the adequacy of a notification, it may not be safe in disregarding the notification unless it notifies the assignee with reasonable promptness as to the respects in which the account debtor considers the notification defective.

Subsection (b)(2), which is new, applies only to sales of payment intangibles. It makes a notification ineffective to the extent that other law gives effect to an agreement between an account debtor and a seller of a payment intangible that limits the account debtor's duty to pay a person other than the seller. Payment intangibles are substantially less fungible than accounts and chattel paper. In some (e.g., commercial bank loans), account debtors customarily and legitimately expect that they will not be required to pay any person other than the financial institution that has advanced funds.

It has become common in financing transactions to assign interests in a single obligation to more than one assignee. Requiring an account debtor that owes a single obligation to make multiple payments to multiple assignees would be unnecessarily burdensome. Thus, under subsection (b)(3), an account debtor that is notified to pay an assignee less than the full amount of any installment or other periodic payment has the option to treat the notification as ineffective, ignore the notice, and discharge the assigned obligation by paying the assignor. Some account debtors may not realize that the law affords them the right to ignore certain notices of assignment with impunity. By making the notification ineffective at the account debtor's option, subsection (b)(3) permits an account debtor to pay the assignee in accordance with the notice and thereby to satisfy its obligation pro tanto. Under subsection (g), the rights and duties created by subsection (b)(3) cannot be waived or varied.

4. *Proof of Assignment.* Subsection (c) links payment with discharge, as in subsection (a). It follows former section 9-318(3) in referring to the right of the account debtor to pay the assignor if the requested proof of assignment is not seasonably forthcoming. Even if the proof is not forthcoming, the notification of assignment would remain effective, so that, in the absence of reasonable proof of the assignment, the account debtor could discharge the obligation by paying either the assignee or the assignor. Of course, if the assignee did not in fact receive an assignment, the account debtor cannot discharge its obligation by paying a putative assignee who is a stranger. The observations in comment 3 concerning the reasonableness of an identification of a right to payment also apply here. An account debtor that questions the adequacy of proof submitted by an assignor would be well advised to promptly inform the assignor of the defects.

An account debtor may face another problem if its obligation becomes due while the account debtor is awaiting reasonable proof of the assignment that it has requested from the assignee. This section does not excuse the account debtor from timely compliance with its obligations. Consequently, an account debtor that has received a notification of assignment and who has requested reasonable proof of the assignment may discharge its obligation by paying the assignor at the time (or even earlier if reasonably necessary to avoid risk of default) when a payment is due, even if the account debtor has not yet received a response to its request for proof. On the other hand, after requesting reasonable proof of the assignment, an account debtor may not discharge its obligation by paying the assignor substantially in advance of the time that the payment is due unless the assignee has failed to provide the proof seasonably.

5. *Contractual Restrictions on Assignment.* Former section 9-318(4) rendered ineffective an agreement between an account debtor and an assignor which prohibited assignment of an account (whether outright or to secure an obligation) or prohibited a security assignment of a general intangible for the payment of money due or to become due. Subsection (d) essentially follows former section 9-318(4), but expands the rule of free assignability to chattel paper (subject to sections 2A-303 and 9-407) and promissory notes and explicitly overrides both restrictions and prohibitions of assignment. The policies underlying the ineffectiveness of contractual restrictions under this section build on common-law developments that essentially have eliminated legal restrictions on assignments of rights to payment as security and other assignments of rights to payment such as accounts and chattel paper. Any that might linger for accounts and chattel paper are addressed by new subsection (f). See comment 6.

Former section 9-318(4) did not apply to a sale of a payment intangible (as described in the former provision, "a general intangible for money due or to become due") but did apply to an assignment of a payment intangible for security. Subsection (e) continues this approach and also makes subsection (d) inapplicable to sales of promissory notes. Section 9-408 addresses anti-assignment clauses with respect to sales of payment intangibles and promissory notes.

Like former section 9-318(4), subsection (d) provides that anti-assignment clauses are "ineffective." The quoted term means that the clause is of no effect whatsoever; the clause does not prevent the assignment from taking effect between the parties and the prohibited assignment does not constitute a default under the agreement between the account debtor and assignor. However, subsection (d) does not override terms that do not directly prohibit, restrict, or require consent to an assignment but which might, nonetheless, present a practical impairment of the assignment. Properly read, however, subsection (d) reaches only covenants that prohibit, restrict, or require consents to assignments; it does not override all terms that might "impair" an assignment in fact.

Example: Buyer enters into an agreement with Seller to buy equipment that Seller is to manufacture according to Buyer's specifications. Buyer agrees to make a series of prepayments during the construction process. In return, Seller agrees to set aside the prepaid funds in a special account and to use the funds solely for the manufacture of the designated equipment. Seller also agrees that it will not assign any of its rights under the sale agreement with Buyer. Nevertheless, Seller grants to Secured Party a security interest in its accounts. Seller's anti-assignment agreement is ineffective under subsection (d); its agreement concerning the use of prepaid funds, which is not a restriction or prohibition on assignment, is not. However, if Secured Party notifies Buyer to make all future payments directly to Secured Party, Buyer will be obliged to do so under subsection (a) if it wishes the payments to discharge its obligation. Unless Secured Party releases the funds to Seller so that Seller can comply with its use-of-funds covenant, Seller will be in breach of that covenant.

In the example, there appears to be a plausible business purpose for the use-of-funds covenant. However, a court may conclude that a covenant with no business purpose other than imposing an impediment to an assignment actually is a direct restriction that is rendered ineffective by subsection (d).

6. *Legal Restrictions on Assignment.* Former section 9-318(4), like subsection (d) of this section, addressed only contractual restrictions on assignment. The former section was grounded on the reality that legal, as opposed to contractual, restrictions on assignments of rights to payment had largely disappeared. New subsection (f) codifies this principle of free assignability for accounts and chattel paper. For the most part the discussion of contractual restrictions in comment 5 applies as well to legal restrictions rendered ineffective under subsection (f).

7. *Multiple Assignments.* This section, like former section 9-318, is not a complete codification of the law of assignments of rights to payment. In particular, it is silent concerning many of the ramifications for an account debtor in cases of multiple assignments of the same right. For example, an assignor might assign the same receivable to multiple assignees (which assignments could be either inadvertent or wrongful). Or, the assignor could assign the receivable to assignee-1, which then might reassign it to assignee-2, and so forth. The rights and duties of an account debtor in the face of multiple assignments and in other circumstances not resolved in the statutory text are left to the common-law rules. See, e.g., Restatement (2d), Contracts sections 338(3) and 339. The failure of former article 9 to codify these rules does not appear to have caused problems.

8. *Consumer Account Debtors.* Subsection (h) is new. It makes clear that the rules of this section are subject to other law establishing special rules for consumer account debtors.

9. *Account Debtors on Health-Care-Insurance Receivables.* Subsection (i) also is new. The obligation of an insurer with respect to a health-care-insurance receivable is governed by other law. Section 9-408 addresses contractual and legal restrictions on the assignment of a health-care-insurance receivable.

NORTH CAROLINA COMMENT

Subsection (i) is modified by adding the last sentence. Subsection (j) is rewritten.

TRANSITION PROVISIONS. --For transition provisions related to the 2010 amendments to Article 9 by Session Laws 2012-70, see the Appendix following Part 7 at the end of this Article.

Session Laws 2012-70, s. 26(a) , (b), provides: "(a) Pre-Effective-Date Transactions or Liens. -- Except as otherwise provided in Part II of this act, this act applies to a transaction or lien within its scope, even if the transaction or lien was entered into or created before this act becomes effective [July 1, 2013].

"(b) Pre-Effective-Date Proceedings. -- This act does not affect an action, case, or proceeding commenced before this act becomes effective [July 1, 2013]."

EFFECT OF AMENDMENTS. --

Session Laws 2012-70, s. 8 , effective July 1, 2013, in subsection (e), substituted "note, other than a sale pursuant to a disposition under G.S. 25-9-610 or an acceptance of collateral under G.S. 25-9-620" for "note"; in subsection (i), deleted "North Carolina Structured Settlement Act (Article 44B of Chapter 1 of the General Statutes); North Carolina Crime Victims Compensation Act (Chapter 15B of the General Statutes); North Carolina Consumer Finance Act (Article 15 of Chapter 53 of the General Statutes); North Carolina Firemen's and Rescue Squad Workers' Pension Fund (Article 86 of Chapter 58 of the General Statutes); Employment

Security Law (Chapter 96 of the General Statutes); North Carolina Workers' Compensation Fund Act (Article 1 of Chapter 97 of the General Statutes); and Programs of Public Assistance (Article 2 of Chapter 108A of the General Statutes)" following "subsection (f) of this section," and added subdivisions (i)(1) through (i) (8); and made minor punctuation changes. See note for Transition Provisions governing these amendments.

Session Laws 2013-157, s. 31 , effective January 1, 2014, added "or an interest in a partnership or limited liability company" at the end of the first sentence of subsection (i).

Session Laws 2013-284, s. 1(b) , effective July 1, 2013, substituted "Firefighters'" for "Firemen's" in subdivision (i)(4).

USER NOTE:

For more generally applicable notes, see notes under the first section of this subpart, part, article, or chapter.

CHAPTER 44A.
STATUTORY LIENS
AND CHARGES

ARTICLE 1.
POSSESSORY LIENS ON
PERSONAL PROPERTY

§ 44A-1. Definitions

As used in this Article:

(1) "Legal possessor" means

a. Any person entrusted with possession of personal property by an owner thereof, or

b. Any person in possession of personal property and entitled thereto by operation of law.

(2) "Lienor" means any person entitled to a lien under this Article.

(2a) "Motor Vehicle" has the meaning provided in G.S. 20-4.01.

(3) "Owner" means

a. Any person having legal title to the property, or

b. A lessee of the person having legal title, or

c. A debtor entrusted with possession of the property by a secured party, or

d. A secured party entitled to possession, or

e. Any person entrusted with possession of the property by his employer or principal who is an owner under any of the above.

(4) "Secured party" means a person holding a security interest.

(5) "Security interest" means any interest in personal property which interest is subject to the provisions of Article 9 of the Uniform Commercial Code, or any other interest intended to create security in real or personal property.

(6) "Vessel" has the meaning provided in G.S. 75A-2.

History.
1967, c. 1029, s. 1; 1991, c. 731, s. 1

THIS CHAPTER DID NOT PURPORT TO ABROGATE LONG ESTABLISHED PRINCIPLES under which equitable liens have been enforced by our courts in a variety of situations. Embree Constr. Group, Inc. v. Rafcor, Inc., 97 N.C. App. 418, 388 S.E.2d 604 (1990), modified on other grounds, 330 N.C. 487, 411 S.E.2d 916 (1992).

PRIORITY OF LIENS. --For priority purposes, liens duly perfected under this Chapter relate back to the time of first furnishing labor or materials. As between a statutory lien and the lien created by a deed of trust, the general rule is that the lien which is first in time has priority. RDC, Inc. v. Brookleigh Bldrs., Inc., 60 N.C. App. 375, 299 S.E.2d 448, rev'd on other grounds, 309 N.C. 182, 305 S.E.2d 722 (1983).

Defendant properly met the requirements of this chapter, and judgment signed by trial judge properly referred to the site upon which defendant wanted a lien declared and related the lien back to the date when labor and materials were first furnished at the site; therefore, defendant's lien had priority over the deed of trust held by plaintiff. Metropolitan Life Ins. Co. v. Rowell, 115 N.C. App. 152, 444 S.E.2d 231, cert. denied, 338 N.C. 518, 452 S.E.2d 813 (1994).

Debtor's motion for summary judgment on the adversary proceeding of the Chapter 44A claimants to recover on liens for unpaid labor and materials was denied because the motion relied on G.S. 25-9-334, which was not applicable to priority questions involving nonpossessory statutory liens under Chapter 44A. All Points Capital Corp. v. Laurel Hill Paper Co. (In re Laurel Hill Paper Co.), 387 B.R. 677 (Bankr. M.D.N.C. 2008).

PRESERVATION FOR REVIEW. --In a case in which a bankruptcy court awarded a debtor damages and attorney's fees for conversion by a creditor and the creditor argued on appeal that even if the layaway plan became an installment sales contract, he nevertheless obtained a possessory lien on the sewing/embroidery machine for repairs pursuant to G.S. 44A-1 et seq., which, he contended, authorized his retention of the machine until the debtor paid for repairs, he had not raised that argument in the bankruptcy court, and the district court could not consider the argument because there was no showing of exceptional circumstances. Hancock v. Renshaw, 421 B.R. 738 (M.D.N.C. 2009).

APPLIED in MSR Enters., Inc. v. GMC, 27 N.C. App. 94, 218 S.E.2d 234 (1975); Drummond v. Cordell, 72 N.C. App. 262, 324 S.E.2d 301 (1985); Peace River Elec. Coop. v. Ward Transformer Co., 116 N.C. App. 493, 449 S.E.2d 202 (1994); Monteau v. Reis Trucking & Constr., Inc., 147 N.C. App. 121, 553 S.E.2d 709 (2001); Bowles Auto., Inc. v. N.C. DMV, 203 N.C. App. 19, 690 S.E.2d 728 (2010), review denied, 364 N.C. 324, 700 S.E.2d 746, 2010 N.C. LEXIS 590 (2010).

CITED in Floyd S. Pike Elec. Contractor v. Goodwill Missionary Baptist Church, 25 N.C. App. 563, 214 S.E.2d 276 (1975); Paccar Fin. Corp. v. Harnett Transf., Inc., 51 N.C. App. 1, 275 S.E.2d 243 (1981); State v. Davy, 100 N.C. App. 551, 397 S.E.2d 634 (1990); Vaseleniuck Engine Dev., LLC v. Sabertooth Motorcycles, LLC, 219 N.C. App. 540, 727 S.E.2d 308 (2012).

LEGAL PERIODICALS. --
For article concerning liens on personal property not governed by the Uniform Commercial Code, see 44 N.C.L. Rev. 322 (1966).

§ 44A-2. Persons entitled to lien on personal property

(a) Any person who tows, alters, repairs, stores, services, treats, or improves personal property other than a motor vehicle or an aircraft in the ordinary course of his business pursuant to an express or implied contract with an owner or legal possessor of the personal property has a lien upon the property. The amount of the lien shall be the lesser of

(1) The reasonable charges for the services and materials; or

(2) The contract price; or

(3) One hundred dollars ($ 100.00) if the lienor has dealt with a legal possessor who is not an owner.

This lien shall have priority over perfected and unperfected security interests.

(b) Any person engaged in the business of operating a hotel, motel, or boardinghouse has a lien upon all baggage, vehicles and other personal property brought upon his premises by a guest or boarder who is an owner thereof to the extent of reasonable charges for the room, accommodations and other items or services furnished at the request of the guest or boarder. This lien shall not have priority over any security interest in the property which is perfected at the time the guest or boarder brings the property to said hotel, motel or boardinghouse.

(c) Any person engaged in the business of boarding animals has a lien on the animals boarded for reasonable charges for such boarding which are contracted for with an owner or legal possessor of the animal. This lien shall have priority over perfected and unperfected security interests.

(d) Any person who repairs, services, tows, or stores motor vehicles in the ordinary course of the person's business pursuant to an express or implied contract with an owner or legal possessor of the motor vehicle, except for a motor vehicle seized pursuant to G.S. 20-28.3, has a lien upon the motor vehicle for reasonable charges for such repairs, servicing, towing, storing, or for the rental of one or more substitute vehicles provided during the repair, servicing, or storage. This lien shall have priority over perfected and unperfected security interests. Payment for towing and storing a motor vehicle seized pursuant to G.S. 20-28.3 shall be as provided for in G.S. 20-28.2 through G.S. 20-28.5.

(e) Any lessor of nonresidential demised premises has a lien on all furniture, furnishings, trade fixtures, equipment and other personal property to which the tenant has legal title and which remains on the demised premises if (i) the tenant has vacated the premises for 21 or more days after the paid rental period has expired, and (ii) the lessor has a lawful claim for damages against the tenant. If the tenant has vacated the premises for 21 or more days after the expiration of the paid rental period, or if the lessor has received a judgment for possession of the premises which is executable and the tenant has vacated the premises, then all property

remaining on the premises may be removed and placed in storage. If the total value of all property remaining on the premises is less than one hundred dollars ($ 100.00), then it shall be deemed abandoned five days after the tenant has vacated the premises, and the lessor may remove it and may donate it to any charitable institution or organization. Provided, the lessor shall not have a lien if there is an agreement between the lessor or his agent and the tenant that the lessor shall not have a lien. This lien shall be for the amount of any rents which were due the lessor at the time the tenant vacated the premises and for the time, up to 60 days, from the vacating of the premises to the date of sale; and for any sums necessary to repair damages to the premises caused by the tenant, normal wear and tear excepted; and for reasonable costs and expenses of sale. The lien created by this subsection shall be enforced by sale at public sale pursuant to the provisions of G.S. 44A-4(e). This lien shall not have priority over any security interest in the property which is perfected at the time the lessor acquires this lien.

(e1) This Article shall not apply to liens created by storage of personal property at a self-service storage facility.

(e2) Any lessor of a space for a manufactured home as defined in G.S. 143-143.9(6) has a lien on all furniture, furnishings, and other personal property including the manufactured home titled in the name of the tenant if (i) the manufactured home remains on the demised premises 21 days after the lessor is placed in lawful possession by writ of possession and (ii) the lessor has a lawful claim for damages against the tenant. If the lessor has received a judgment for possession of the premises which has been executed, then all property remaining on the premises may be removed and placed in storage. Prior to the expiration of the 21-day period, the landlord shall release possession of the personal property and manufactured home to the tenant during regular business hours or at a time mutually agreed upon. This lien shall be for the amount of any rents which were due the lessor at the time the tenant vacated the premises and for the time, up to 60 days, from the vacating of the premises to the date of sale; and for any sums necessary to repair damages to the premises caused by the tenant, normal wear and tear excepted; and for reasonable costs and expenses of the sale. The lien created by this subsection shall be enforced by public sale under G.S. 44A-4(e). The landlord may begin the advertisement for sale process immediately upon execution of the writ of possession by the sheriff, but may not conduct the sale until the lien has attached. This lien shall not have any priority over any security interest in the property that is perfected at the time the lessor acquires this lien. The lessor shall not have a lien under this subsection if there is an agreement between the lessor or the lessor's agent and the tenant that the lessor shall not have a lien.

(f) Any person who improves any textile goods in the ordinary course of his business pursuant to an express or implied contract with the owner or legal possessor of such goods shall have a lien upon all goods of such owner or possessor in his possession for improvement. The amount of such lien shall be for the entire unpaid contracted charges owed such person for improvement of said goods including any amount owed for improvement of goods, the possession of which may have been relinquished, and such lien shall have priority over perfected and unperfected security interests. "Goods" as used herein includes any textile goods, yarns or products of natural or man-made fibers or combination thereof. "Improve" as used herein shall be construed to include processing, fabricating or treating by throwing, spinning, knitting, dyeing, finishing, fabricating or otherwise.

(g) Any person who fabricates, casts, or otherwise makes a mold or who uses a mold to manufacture, assemble, or otherwise make a product pursuant to an express or implied contract with the owner of such mold shall have a lien upon the mold. For a lien to arise under this subsection, there must exist written evidence that the parties understood that a lien could be applied against the mold, with the evidence being in the form either of a written contract or a separate written statement provided by the potential holder of the lien under this subsection to the owner of the mold prior to the fabrication or use of the mold. The written contract or separate written statement must describe generally the amount of the potential lien as set forth in this subsection. The amount of the lien under this subsection shall equal the total of (i) any unpaid contracted charges due from the owner of the mold for making the mold, plus (ii) any unpaid contracted charges for all products made with the mold. The lien under this subsection shall not have priority over any security interest in the mold which is perfected at the time the person acquires this lien. As used in this subsection, the word "mold" shall include a mold, die, form, or pattern.

(h) Any landlord of nonresidential property, including any storage or self-storage space, in which potentially confidential materials, as that term is defined in G.S. 42-14.4(a), remain after the landlord has obtained possession of the property must provide notice to the North Carolina State Bar and comply with the provisions of G.S. 42-14.4, if the landlord has actual knowledge that the former tenant is an attorney. Potentially confidential materials shall not be the subject of a lien under the provisions of this Article.

History.
1967, c. 1029, s. 1; 1971, cc. 261, 403; c. 544, s. 1; c. 1197; 1973, c. 1298, s. 1; 1975, c. 461; 1981, c. 566, s. 2; c. 682, s. 9; 1981 (Reg. Sess., 1982), c. 1275, s. 2; 1995, c. 460, s. 9 ; c. 480, s. 1 ; 1995 (Reg. Sess., 1996), c. 744, s. 1; 1998-182, s. 14 ; 1999-278, s. 5 ; 2006-222, s. 1.2 ; 2012-76, s. 2

EFFECT OF AMENDMENTS. --
Session Laws 2006-222, s. 1.2 , effective October 1, 2006, and applicable to labor, skills, or materials furnished on an aircraft, or storage provided for an aircraft, on or after that date, inserted "or an aircraft" in the first sentence of the introductory language of subsection (a).

Session Laws 2012-76, s. 2 , effective October 1, 2012, added subsection (h).

PROVISIONS FOR RETENTION OF MOTOR VEHICLE ARE NOT UNCONSTITUTIONAL. --The provisions of the possessory lien statute which provide for the retention of the motor vehicle by any person who repairs, services, tows or stores such vehicle in his business, without prior notice or hearing, do not violate the due process clause of U.S. Const., Amend. XIV. Caesar v. Kiser, 387 F. Supp. 645 (M.D.N.C. 1975).

THIS SECTION AND G.S. 44A-3 ARE CODIFICATIONS OF THE COMMON-LAW PRINCIPLE that a garageman has a possessory interest in a vehicle left in his care by the owner or legal possessor and in which he has invested labor and materials. Caesar v. Kiser, 387 F. Supp. 645 (M.D.N.C. 1975).

THE LIENOR'S POSSESSOR INTEREST REPRESENTS A BALANCING OF THE INTERESTS between ownership rights and the right of a craftsman to have security for payment for his service. Caesar v. Kiser, 387 F. Supp. 645 (M.D.N.C. 1975).

BOARDING LIEN. --Parties who provided services under production agreements with a Chapter 11 debtor that was in business of finishing genetically specific pigs did not have valid "boarding liens" within the meaning of G.S. 44A-2(c) because the parties that were claiming liens were not engaged in business of boarding within the meaning of the statute, and because, in any event, any such liens were expressly waived in the agreement between the parties. Newkirk Farms, Inc. v. First Nat'l Bank, N.A. (In re Coastal Plains Pork, LLC), 2010 Bankr. LEXIS 1776 (Bankr. E.D.N.C. May 21, 2010).

WAREHOUSEMAN'S LIEN. --Any rights a warehouseman had to plaintiff's personal property stored in his warehouse were to be analyzed as a warehouseman's lien under chapter 25 rather than as a possessory lien under chapter 44A. Smithers v. Tru-Pak Moving Sys., 121 N.C. App. 542, 468 S.E.2d 410 (1996).

CONTINUED STORAGE OF PROPERTY SUSTAINED LIEN, BUT DID NOT AMOUNT TO VIOLATION OF AUTOMATIC STAY. --Default judgment was not entered against a towing company because a debtor's complaint alleging violation of the automatic stay, 11 U.S.C.S. § 362(a)(5), lacked merit, as the company's continued storage of the vehicle sustained its state law lien, G.S. 44A-2(d) and G.S. 44A-3, but did not amount to enforcement of the lien or a willful violation of the automatic stay. Green v. Univ. Auto Care (In re Green), 2010 Bankr. LEXIS 477 (Bankr. E.D.N.C. Feb. 16, 2010).

OWNER OF GARAGE AND WRECKER SERVICE WITH WHOM SHERIFF CONTRACTED to store certain cars levied on pursuant to court order was a legal possessor, and under subsection (d) of this section had a lien on the cars from the time he began towing them away; his lien was enforceable in the principal action under the explicit language of G.S. 1A-1, Rule 24, and G.S. 1-440.43 by intervention. Case v. Miller, 68 N.C. App. 729, 315 S.E.2d 737 (1984).

OWNER OF STORAGE OR TOWING COMPANY WAS ENTITLED TO RECOVERY under this section because the company had an implied contract with the sheriff. Green Tree Fin. Servicing v. Young, 133 N.C. App. 339, 515 S.E.2d 223 (1999).

MECHANIC'S LIEN SURVIVED CREDIT UNION'S REPOSSESSION OF A CAR --While a mechanic who performed a diagnostic analysis of an automobile had a valid lien against the credit union that financed the purchase of the automobile and repossessed the automobile from the mechanic's premises late at night without the mechanic's knowledge or consent, the trial court erred in awarding the mechanic actual and treble damages, as the mechanic's proper remedy was to be awarded possession of the automobile. Old Salem Foreign Car Serv., Inc. v. Webb, 159 N.C. App. 93, 582 S.E.2d 673 (2003).

COURT OF APPEALS WOULD DECLINE TO CREATE A JUDICIAL EXCEPTION TO THIS ARTICLE and hold that when property is seized by a law enforcement agency who thereafter directs the local storage facility to store and retain said property at their direction, the lawful owner is entitled to immediate possession of said property and the law enforcement agency is thereafter held accountable for all storage liens. State v. Davy, 100 N.C. App. 551, 397 S.E.2d 634 (1990).

A LAW ENFORCEMENT AGENCY IS NOT ACCOUNTABLE for storage liens attaching, pursuant to this section, to property seized by the agency and stored, at the agency's direction, by a local storage facility. To hold otherwise would be to create a judicial exception to this Article. State v. Davy, 100 N.C. App. 551, 397 S.E.2d 634 (1990).

AMOUNT OF LIEN ESTABLISHED. --Under the plain language of G.S. 44A-4, where the lien amount was designated as $100.00 in plaintiff's complaint and that allegation was not challenged in the statutorily specified manner, the amount of the lien was conclusively established as being $100.00. Thus, regardless of any labels attached to the various parties herein, the clerk of court did not err in ordering defendant to relinquish possession of transformer upon plaintiff's tender of $100.00. Peace River Elec. Coop. v. Ward Transformer Co., 116 N.C. App. 493, 449 S.E.2d 202 (1994), cert. denied, 339 N.C. 739, 454 S.E.2d 655 (1995).

LIEN NOT EXTINGUISHED WHERE CHECK BOUNCED. --Where, before an automobile was delivered to owner, defendant had a lien on the vehicle for the entire amount due to it for repairs and services pursuant to subsection (d) of this section, and in order to obtain the vehicle the owner gave defendant a check for the balance due, which was returned uncashed because of insufficient funds, defendant's lien was not extinguished and the property was subject to redelivery to defendant through the remedy of claim and delivery. Adder v. Holman & Moody, Inc., 288 N.C. 484, 219 S.E.2d 190 (1975).

WHERE PURCHASER OF PERSONAL PROPERTY SUBJECT TO A VALID, ENFORCEABLE, PERFECTED SECURITY INTEREST BUYS IN THE COLLATERAL at a foreclosure sale conducted pursuant to this Chapter to satisfy an account for repairs which the purchaser has failed to pay, for a purchase price which essentially represents payment of the account, the purchaser does not thereby extinguish the security interest; rather, the security property or collateral remains subject to the security interest, and if the indebtedness for payment of which the collateral was pledged remains in default, the right to possession continues to be with the holder of the security interest. Paccar Fin. Corp. v. Harnett Transf., Inc., 51 N.C. App. 1, 275 S.E.2d 243, cert. denied, 302 N.C. 629, 280 S.E.2d 441 (1981).

WHERE NO CONTRACT WITH AMOUNTS OWED. --Plaintiff had not shown that it had a lien on certain bottle cap molds because, among other reasons, it had not shown that it had a contract with the purchaser upon which there were amounts owed, as required by G.S. 44A-2(g). Weener Plastics, Inc. v. HNH Packaging, LLC, 590 F. Supp. 2d 760 (E.D.N.C. 2008).

SUMMARY JUDGMENT ON CONVERSION AND TRESPASS TO CHATTELS CLAIMS IMPROPER. --Partial summary judgment on conversion and trespass to chattels claims was error because, as it was uncontroverted that plaintiff had altered the condition of the engines in its possession and had not been paid in full, plaintiff was entitled to an G.S. 44A-2(a) possessory lien on the engines. Vaseleniuck Engine Dev., LLC v. Sabertooth Motorcycles, LLC, 219 N.C. App. 540, 727 S.E.2d 308 (2012).

LESSOR'S LIEN NOT ESTABLISHED. --Claim was not nondischargeable under 11 U.S.C.S. § 523(a)(2) and (a)(6) where a creditor/lessor failed to prove that it had a statutory lien on items removed from leased premises under G.S. 44A-2(e), as there was no evidence that the lessee had vacated the premises for at least 21 days on the day that the lessor changed the locks. Even if it did have a valid lien, the evidence showed that the items removed were the personal property of the debtor (who personally guaranteed the lease and who was the lessee's principal officer) and of the lessee's employees, not of the lessee. Walton Holding of NC, LLC v. Young (In re Young), 2012 Bankr. LEXIS 3802 (Bankr. M.D.N.C. Aug. 17, 2012).

APPLIED in Marlen C. Robb & Son Boatyard & Marina, Inc. v. Vessel Bristol, 893 F. Supp. 526 (E.D.N.C. 1994); Bowles Auto., Inc. v. N.C. DMV, 203 N.C. App. 19, 690 S.E.2d 728 (2010), review denied, 364 N.C. 324, 700 S.E.2d 746, 2010 N.C. LEXIS 590 (2010).

CITED in Griffin v. Holmes, 843 F. Supp. 81 (E.D.N.C. 1993); In re Aerospace Technologies, Inc., 199 Bankr. 331 (Bankr. M.D.N.C. 1996); North Carolina Farm Bureau Mut. Ins. Co. v. Weaver, 134 N.C. App. 359, 517 S.E.2d 381 (1999); Triad Int'l Maint. Corp. v. Guernsey Air Leasing, Ltd., 178 F. Supp. 2d 547 (M.D.N.C. 2001).

LEGAL PERIODICALS. --

For note on garagemen's liens and duress of goods, see 54 N.C.L. Rev. 1106 (1976).

For comment on landlords' eviction remedies in the light of Spinks v. Taylor, 303 N.C. 256, 278 S.E.2d 501 (1981), and the 1981 Act to clarify landlord eviction remedies in residential tenancies, see 60 N.C.L. Rev. 885 (1982).

For survey of 1981 commercial law, see 60 N.C.L. Rev. 1238 (1982).

For article discussing unfair methods of competition, deceptive trade practices, and unfair trade practices, see 5 Campbell L. Rev. 119 (1982).

For article discussing self help residential eviction by landlords in light of the Landlord Eviction Remedies Act, see 13 N.C. Cent. L.J. 195 (1982).

For comment on the Landlord Eviction Remedies Act in light of Spinks v. Taylor, 303 N.C. 256, 278 S.E.2d 501 (1981), see 18 Wake Forest L. Rev. 25 (1982).

§ 44A-3. When lien arises and terminates

Liens conferred under this Article arise only when the lienor acquires possession of the property and terminate and become unenforceable when the lienor voluntarily relinquishes the possession of the property upon which a lien might be claimed, or when an owner, his agent, a legal possessor or any other person having a security or other interest in the property tenders prior to sale the amount secured by the lien plus reasonable storage, boarding and other expenses incurred by the lienor. The reacquisition of possession of property voluntarily relinquished shall not reinstate the lien. Liens conferred under this Article do not terminate when the lienor involuntarily relinquishes the possession of the property.

History.

1967, c. 1029, s. 1; 1991, c. 344, s. 3 ; c. 731, s. 2

PROVISIONS FOR RETENTION OF MOTOR VEHICLE ARE NOT UNCONSTITUTIONAL. --The provisions of the possessory lien statute which provide for the retention of the motor vehicle by any person who repairs, services, tows or stores such vehicle in his business, without prior notice or hearing, do not violate the due process clause of U.S. Const., Amend. XIV. Caesar v. Kiser, 387 F. Supp. 645 (M.D.N.C. 1975).

THIS SECTION AND G.S. 44A-2 ARE CODIFICATIONS OF THE COMMON-LAW PRINCIPLE that a garageman has a possessory interest in a vehicle left in his care by the owner or legal possessor and in which he has invested labor and materials. Caesar v. Kiser, 387 F. Supp. 645 (M.D.N.C. 1975).

THE LIENOR'S POSSESSORY INTEREST REPRESENTS A BALANCING OF THE INTERESTS between ownership rights and the right of a craftsman to have security for payment for his service. Caesar v. Kiser, 387 F. Supp. 645 (M.D.N.C. 1975).

RELINQUISHMENT TERMINATES LIEN ONLY WHEN IT IS VOLUNTARY. --While it is true that possessory liens generally terminate when the lienor relinquishes possession, that rule only applies when possession is surrendered voluntarily. Case v. Miller, 68 N.C. App. 729, 315 S.E.2d 737 (1984).

While a mechanic who performed a diagnostic analysis of an automobile had a valid lien against the credit union that financed the purchase of the automobile and repossessed the automobile from the mechanic's premises late at night without the mechanic's knowledge or consent, the trial court erred in awarding the mechanic actual and treble damages, as the mechanic's proper remedy was to be awarded possession of the automobile. Old Salem Foreign Car Serv., Inc. v. Webb, 159 N.C. App. 93, 582 S.E.2d 673 (2003).

CONTINUED STORAGE OF PROPERTY SUSTAINED LIEN, BUT DID NOT AMOUNT TO VIOLATION OF AUTOMATIC STAY. --Default judgment was not entered against a towing company because a debtor's complaint alleging violation of the automatic stay, 11 U.S.C.S. § 362(a)(5), lacked merit, as the company's continued storage of the vehicle sustained its state law lien, G.S. 44A-2(d) and G.S. 44A-3, but did not amount to enforcement of the lien or a willful violation of the automatic stay. Green v. Univ. Auto Care (In re Green), 2010 Bankr. LEXIS 477 (Bankr. E.D.N.C. Feb. 16, 2010).

WHERE POSSESSION OF VEHICLES WAS SURRENDERED IN OBEDIENCE TO A COURT ORDER directing their sale, obedience to the court order did not work a forfeiture of the rights of the lienholder. Case v. Miller, 68 N.C. App. 729, 315 S.E.2d 737 (1984).

AMOUNT OF LIEN ESTABLISHED. --Under the plain language of G.S. 44A-4, where the lien amount was designated as $100.00 in plaintiff's complaint and that allegation was not challenged in the statutorily specified manner, the amount of the lien was conclusively established as being $100.00. Thus, regardless of any labels attached to the various parties herein, the clerk of court did not err in ordering defendant to relinquish possession of transformer upon plaintiff's tender of $100.00. Peace River Elec. Coop. v. Ward Transformer Co., 116 N.C. App. 493, 449 S.E.2d 202 (1994), cert. denied, 339 N.C. 739, 454 S.E.2d 655 (1995).

WHERE OWNER OBTAINED DELIVERY OF HIS PROPERTY BY GIVING THE LIENHOLDER A WORTHLESS CHECK, the property was not voluntarily relinquished by the lienholder. Adder v. Holman & Moody, Inc., 288 N.C. 484, 219 S.E.2d 190 (1975).

BECAUSE AN AIRCRAFT MAINTENANCE FACILITY NEVER ACQUIRED POSSESSION of the complete set of an aircraft's maintenance records, it never acquired a mechanic's lien on those items; when the maintenance facility returned the aircraft's engines to the owner, its interest in the engines terminated and it no longer held an enforceable interest in the engines. Triad Int'l Maint. Corp. v. Guernsey Air Leasing, Ltd., 178 F. Supp. 2d 547 (M.D.N.C. 2001).

AMENDMENT OF COMPLAINT HELD TIMELY. --When plaintiff filed motion to amend his complaint to add a cause of action to enforce a materialman's or laborer's lien on December 8, 1983, and the last day he had furnished material or labor to defendants' property was June 15, 1983, his motion was filed within the 180-day period set forth in subsection (a) of this section, the date of the filing of the motion, rather than the date the court rules on it, being the crucial date in measuring the period of limitations. Plaintiff's amendment was therefore not barred by the statute of limitations, and whether it would "relate back" to the filing of the original complaint was immaterial. Mauney v. Morris, 316 N.C. 67, 340 S.E.2d 397 (1986).

CITED in Paccar Fin. Corp. v. Harnett Transf., Inc., 51 N.C. App. 1, 275 S.E.2d 243 (1981); Griffin v. Holmes, 843 F. Supp. 81 (E.D.N.C. 1993); North Carolina Farm Bureau Mut. Ins. Co. v. Weaver, 134 N.C. App. 359, 517 S.E.2d 381 (1999).

LEGAL PERIODICALS. --

For note on garagemen's liens and duress of goods, see 54 N.C.L. Rev. 1106 (1976).

§ 44A-4. Enforcement of lien by sale

(a) **Enforcement by Sale. --** If the charges for which the lien is claimed under this Article remain unpaid or unsatisfied for 30 days or, in the case of towing and storage charges on a motor vehicle, 10 days following the maturity of the obligation to pay any such charges, the lienor may enforce the lien by public or private sale as provided in this section. The lienor may bring an action on the debt in any court of competent jurisdiction at any time following maturity of the obligation. Failure of the lienor to bring such action within a 180-day period following the commencement of storage shall constitute a waiver of any right to collect storage charges which accrue after such period. Provided that when property is placed in storage pursuant to an express contract of storage, the lien shall continue and the lienor may bring an action to collect storage charges and enforce his lien at any time within 120 days following default on the obligation to pay storage charges.

The owner or person with whom the lienor dealt may at any time following the maturity of the obligation bring an action in any court of competent jurisdiction as by law provided. If in any such action the owner or other party requests immediate possession of the property and pays the amount of the lien asserted into the clerk of the court in which such action is pending, the clerk shall issue an order to the lienor to relinquish possession of the property to the owner or other party. The request for immediate possession may be made in the complaint, which shall also set forth the amount of the asserted lien and the portion thereof which is not in dispute, if any. If within three days after service of the summons and complaint, as the number of days is computed in G.S. 1A-1, Rule 6, the lienor does not file a contrary statement of the amount of the lien at the time of the filing of the complaint, the amount set forth in the complaint shall be deemed to be the amount of the asserted lien. The clerk may at any time disburse to the lienor that portion of the cash bond, which the plaintiff says in his complaint is not in dispute, upon application of the lienor. The magistrate or judge shall direct appropriate disbursement of the disputed or undisbursed portion of the bond in the judgment of the court. In the event an action by the owner pursuant to this section is heard in district or superior court, the substantially prevailing party in such court may be awarded a reasonable attorney's fee in the discretion of the judge.

(b) **Notice and Hearings. --**

(1) If the property upon which the lien is claimed is a motor vehicle that is required to be registered, the lienor following the expiration of the relevant time period provided by subsection (a) shall give notice to the Division of Motor Vehicles that a lien is asserted and sale is proposed and shall remit to the Division a fee of thirteen dollars ($ 13.00). The Division of Motor Vehicles shall issue notice by certified mail, return receipt requested, to the person having legal title to the property, if reasonably ascertainable, to the person with whom the lienor dealt if different, and to each secured party and other person claiming an interest in the property who is actually known to the Division or who can be reasonably ascertained. The notice shall state that a lien has been asserted against specific property and shall identify the lienor, the date that the lien arose, the general nature of the services performed and materials used or sold for which the lien is asserted, the amount of the lien, and that the lienor intends to sell the property in satisfaction of the lien. The notice shall inform the recipient that the recipient has the right to a judicial hearing at which time a determination will be made as to the validity of the lien prior to a sale taking place. The notice shall further state that the recipient has a period of 10 days from the date of receipt in which to notify the Division by certified mail, return receipt requested, that a hearing is desired and that if the recipient wishes to contest the sale of his property pursuant to such lien, the recipient should notify the Division that a hearing is desired. The notice shall state the required information in simplified terms and shall contain a form

Chapter 44A

whereby the recipient may notify the Division that a hearing is desired by the return of such form to the Division. The Division shall notify the lienor whether such notice is timely received by the Division. In lieu of the notice by the lienor to the Division and the notices issued by the Division described above, the lienor may issue notice on a form approved by the Division pursuant to the notice requirements above. If notice is issued by the lienor, the recipient shall return the form requesting a hearing to the lienor, and not the Division, within 10 days from the date the recipient receives the notice if a judicial hearing is requested. If the certified mail notice has been returned as undeliverable and the notice of a right to a judicial hearing has been given to the owner of the motor vehicle in accordance with G.S. 20-28.4, no further notice is required. Failure of the recipient to notify the Division or lienor, as specified in the notice, within 10 days of the receipt of such notice that a hearing is desired shall be deemed a waiver of the right to a hearing prior to the sale of the property against which the lien is asserted, and the lienor may proceed to enforce the lien by public or private sale as provided in this section and the Division shall transfer title to the property pursuant to such sale. If the Division or lienor, as specified in the notice, is notified within the 10-day period provided above that a hearing is desired prior to sale, the lien may be enforced by sale as provided in this section and the Division will transfer title only pursuant to the order of a court of competent jurisdiction.

If the certified mail notice has been returned as undeliverable, or if the name of the person having legal title to the vehicle cannot reasonably be ascertained and the fair market value of the vehicle is less than eight hundred dollars ($ 800.00), the lienor may institute a special proceeding in the county where the vehicle is being held, for authorization to sell that vehicle. Market value shall be determined by the schedule of values adopted by the Commissioner under G.S. 105-187.3.

In such a proceeding a lienor may not include more than ten vehicles, but the proceeds of the sale of each shall be subject only to valid claims against that vehicle, and any excess proceeds of the sale shall be paid immediately to the Treasurer for disposition pursuant to Chapter 116B of the General Statutes.

The application to the clerk in such a special proceeding shall contain the notice of sale information set out in subsection (f) hereof. If the application is in proper form

the clerk shall enter an order authorizing the sale on a date not less than 14 days therefrom, and the lienor shall cause the application and order to be sent immediately by first-class mail pursuant to G.S. 1A-1, Rule 5, to each person to whom notice was mailed pursuant to this subsection. Following the authorized sale the lienor shall file with the clerk a report in the form of an affidavit, stating that the lienor has complied with the public or private sale provisions of G.S. 44A-4, the name, address, and bid of the high bidder or person buying at a private sale, and a statement of the disposition of the sale proceeds. The clerk then shall enter an order directing the Division to transfer title accordingly.

If prior to the sale the owner or legal possessor contests the sale or lien in a writing filed with the clerk, the proceeding shall be handled in accordance with G.S. 1-301.2.

(2) If the property upon which the lien is claimed is other than a motor vehicle required to be registered, the lienor following the expiration of the 30-day period provided by subsection (a) shall issue notice to the person having legal title to the property, if reasonably ascertainable, and to the person with whom the lienor dealt if different by certified mail, return receipt requested. Such notice shall state that a lien has been asserted against specific property and shall identify the lienor, the date that the lien arose, the general nature of the services performed and materials used or sold for which the lien is asserted, the amount of the lien, and that the lienor intends to sell the property in satisfaction of the lien. The notice shall inform the recipient that the recipient has the right to a judicial hearing at which time a determination will be made as to the validity of the lien prior to a sale taking place. The notice shall further state that the recipient has a period of 10 days from the date of receipt in which to notify the lienor by certified mail; return receipt requested, that a hearing is desired and that if the recipient wishes to contest the sale of his property pursuant to such lien, the recipient should notify the lienor that a hearing is desired. The notice shall state the required information in simplified terms and shall contain a form whereby the recipient may notify the lienor that a hearing is desired by the return of such form to the lienor. Failure of the recipient to notify the lienor within 10 days of the receipt of such notice that a hearing is desired shall be deemed a waiver of the right to a hearing prior to sale of the property against which the lien is asserted and the lienor may proceed to enforce the lien by public

or private sale as provided in this section. If the lienor is notified within the 10-day period provided above that a hearing is desired prior to sale, the lien may be enforced by sale as provided in this section only pursuant to the order of a court of competent jurisdiction.

(c) **Private Sale.** -- Sale by private sale may be made in any manner that is commercially reasonable. If the property upon which the lien is claimed is a motor vehicle, the sale may not be made until notice is given to the Commissioner of Motor Vehicles pursuant to G.S. 20-114(c). Not less than 30 days prior to the date of the proposed private sale, the lienor shall cause notice to be mailed, as provided in subsection (f) hereof, to the person having legal title to the property, if reasonably ascertainable, to the person with whom the lienor dealt if different, and to each secured party or other person claiming an interest in the property who is actually known to the lienor or can be reasonably ascertained. Notices provided pursuant to subsection (b) hereof shall be sufficient for these purposes if such notices contain the information required by subsection (f) hereof. The lienor shall not purchase, directly or indirectly, the property at private sale and such a sale to the lienor shall be voidable.

(d) **Request for Public Sale.** -- If an owner, the person with whom the lienor dealt, any secured party, or other person claiming an interest in the property notifies the lienor prior to the date upon or after which the sale by private sale is proposed to be made, that public sale is requested, sale by private sale shall not be made. After request for public sale is received, notice of public sale must be given as if no notice of sale by private sale had been given.

(e) **Public Sale.** --

(1) Not less than 20 days prior to sale by public sale the lienor:

a. Shall notify the Commissioner of Motor Vehicles as provided in G.S. 20-114(c) if the property upon which the lien is claimed is a motor vehicle; and

a1. Shall cause notice to be mailed to the person having legal title to the property if reasonably ascertainable, to the person with whom the lienor dealt if different, and to each secured party or other person claiming an interest in the property who is actually known to the lienor or can be reasonably ascertained, provided that notices provided pursuant to subsection (b) hereof shall be sufficient for these purposes if such notices contain the information required by subsection (f) hereof; and

b. Shall advertise the sale by posting a copy of the notice of sale at the courthouse door in the county where the sale is to be held;

and shall publish notice of sale once a week for two consecutive weeks in a newspaper of general circulation in the same county, the date of the last publication being not less than five days prior to the sale. The notice of sale need not be published if the vehicle has a market value of less than three thousand five hundred dollars ($ 3,500), as determined by the schedule of values adopted by the Commissioner under G.S. 105-187.3.

(2) A public sale must be held on a day other than Sunday and between the hours of 10:00 A.M. and 4:00 P.M.:

a. In any county where any part of the contract giving rise to the lien was performed, or

b. In the county where the obligation secured by the lien was contracted for.

(3) A lienor may purchase at public sale.

(f) **Notice of Sale.** -- The notice of sale shall include:

(1) The name and address of the lienor;

(2) The name of the person having legal title to the property if such person can be reasonably ascertained and the name of the person with whom the lienor dealt;

(3) A description of the property;

(4) The amount due for which the lien is claimed;

(5) The place of the sale;

(6) If a private sale the date upon or after which the sale is proposed to be made, or if a public sale the date and hour when the sale is to be held.

(g) **Damages for Noncompliance.** -- If the lienor fails to comply substantially with any of the provisions of this section, the lienor shall be liable to the person having legal title to the property or any other party injured by such noncompliance in the sum of one hundred dollars ($ 100.00), together with a reasonable attorney's fee as awarded by the court. Damages provided by this section shall be in addition to actual damages to which any party is otherwise entitled.

History.

1967, c. 1029, s. 1; 1975, c. 438, s. 1; c. 716, s. 5; 1977, c. 74, s. 4; c. 793, s. 1; 1981, c. 690, s. 26; 1983, c. 44, ss. 1, 2; 1985, c. 655, ss. 4, 5; 1989, c. 770, s. 10 ; 1991, c. 344, s. 1 ; c. 731, s. 3 ; 1995 (Reg. Sess., 1996), c. 635, ss. 2-4; 1998-182, s. 15 ; 1999-216, s. 10 ; 1999-460, s. 7 ; 2004-128, s. 5 ; 2012-175, s. 12(a) ; 2015-241, s. 29.30(r) ; 2019-243, s. 17(a)

EDITOR'S NOTE. --

Session Laws 2015-241, s. 29.30(u) , made the amendment to subdivision (b)(1) of this section by Session Laws 2015-241, s. 29.30(r) , applicable to issuances, renewals, restorations, and requests on or after January 1, 2016.

Session Laws 2015-241, s. 1.1 , provides: "This act shall be known as 'The Current Operations and Capital Improvements Appropriations Act of 2015.'"

Session Laws 2015-241, s. 33.6 , is a severability clause.

Session Laws 2019-243, s. 17(b) , made the amendment of subdivision (b)(1) by Session Laws 2019-243, s. 17(a) , effective December 1, 2019, and applicable to applications filed on or after that date.

EFFECT OF AMENDMENTS. --

Session Laws 2012-175, s. 12(a) , effective July 12, 2012, deleted "registered or" preceding "certified mail" throughout subsection (b).

Session Laws 2015-241, s. 29.30(r) , effective January 1, 2016, substituted "thirteen dollars ($13.00)" for "ten dollars ($10.00)" in the first sentence of subdivision (b)(1). For applicability, see editor's note.

Session Laws 2019-243, s. 17(a) , substituted "may not include more than ten vehicles" for "may include more than one vehicle" in the third paragraph of subdivision (b)(1). For effective date and applicability, see editor's note.

FORMER PROVISIONS AS TO SALE UNCONSTITUTIONAL. --The sale provision of this section as it stood before the 1975 amendment permitted the sale of motor vehicles by a lienor without affording the owner an opportunity for notice and a hearing to judicially determine the validity of the underlying debt, and in this respect the statute violated the due process clause of U.S. Const., Amend. XIV. Caesar v. Kiser, 387 F. Supp. 645 (M.D.N.C. 1975).

"STATE ACTION" INVOLVED. --The State is actively involved in the creation and enforcement of the lien on motor vehicles and such must be held to constitute "state action" as that term is used in 42 U.S.C. § 1983. Caesar v. Kiser, 387 F. Supp. 645 (M.D.N.C. 1975).

Under North Carolina law, the sale could not be accomplished without the affirmative acts of the Department (now Division) of Motor Vehicles in transferring the indicia of ownership. Caesar v. Kiser, 387 F. Supp. 645 (M.D.N.C. 1975).

LIENOR MUST COMPLY WITH SECTION WHEN MAIL NOTICE UNDELIVERABLE. --Subdivision (b)(1) of this section did not allow a lienor of an abandoned motor vehicle to dispose of it without complying with the requirements of this section as they pertain to other types of personal property when the registered or certified mail notice had been returned as undeliverable. Ernie's Tire Sales & Serv. v. Riggs, 106 N.C. App. 460, 417 S.E.2d 75 (1992).

LIENOR MAY NOT SELL VEHICLE WITHOUT PRIOR JUDICIAL DETERMINATION OR OWNER'S WAIVER. --The lienor may still retain his possessory lien on the motor vehicle if the owner or legal possessor fails to pay his charges, but the lienor may not, without a prior judicial determination or the owner's waiver, sell the motor vehicle to satisfy his claim. Caesar v. Kiser, 387 F. Supp. 645 (M.D.N.C. 1975).

AMOUNT DESIGNATED IN COMPLAINT ESTABLISHED AMOUNT OF LIEN. --Under the plain language of this section, where the lien amount was designated as $100.00 in plaintiff's complaint and that allegation was not challenged in the statutorily specified manner, the amount of the lien was conclusively established as being $100.00. Thus, regardless of any labels attached to the various parties herein, the clerk of court did not err in ordering defendant to relinquish possession of transformer upon plaintiff's tender of $100.00. Peace River Elec. Coop. v. Ward Transformer Co., 116 N.C. App. 493, 449 S.E.2d 202 (1994), cert. denied, 339 N.C. 739, 454 S.E.2d 655 (1995).

TIME FOR COLLECTION BY LIENHOLDER. --In view of the proviso of subsection (a) of this section, which states that when property is placed in storage pursuant to an express contract of storage, the lien shall continue and the lienor may bring an action to collect storage charges and enforce his lien at any time within 120 days following default on the obligation to pay storage charges, and in view of the fact that storage was under an express contract with the sheriff, subject to the control of court, lienholder's right to collect did not end 180 days after storage began, but 120 days after the default, if any, occurred. Case v. Miller, 68 N.C. App. 729, 315 S.E.2d 737 (1984).

APPLICABILITY OF BOND PROVISION. --The bond provision is located only in the second paragraph of subsection (a), the paragraph governing lien actions filed by the owner of property subject to a lien; accordingly, the bond provision applies only to lien actions filed by the owner of property subject to a lien, not to lien actions filed by the lienor. Griffin v. Holmes, 843 F. Supp. 81 (E.D.N.C. 1993).

G.

S. 44A-4(B)(2) PROVIDES THAT THE LIENOR HAS TO ISSUE NOTICE TO THE PERSON HAVING LEGAL TITLE TO PROPERTY and specifies what the notice should contain; where defendant failed to comply substantially with the provisions of that subdivision, defendant was liable for statutory and actual damages. Rowell v. N.C. Equip. Co., 146 N.C. App. 431, 552 S.E.2d 274 (2001).

SUMMARY JUDGMENT IMPROPER. --Summary judgment for defendant on its claim that plaintiff violated G.S. 44A-4 was error because, although the evidence raised an inference that plaintiff failed to comply with G.S. 44A-4, this was a factual issue to have been determined only by the jury. Vaseleniuck Engine Dev., LLC v. Sabertooth Motorcycles, LLC, 219 N.C. App. 540, 727 S.E.2d 308 (2012).

CALCULATION OF DAMAGES. --Determination of actual damages, if any, was reserved for the jury, and the measure of actual damages was the difference between the fair market value of the property at the time of the sale and the amount for which the property was actually sold. Rowell v. N.C. Equip. Co., 146 N.C. App. 431, 552 S.E.2d 274 (2001).

ATTORNEY FEES. --Where defendant neither prevailed nor defended under the theory that he had a chapter 44A lien, but it was a warehouseman's lien under chapter 25, the trial court erred by awarding attorney fees under this section. Smithers v. Tru-Pak Moving Sys., 121 N.C. App. 542, 468 S.E.2d 410 (1996).

APPLIED in Drummond v. Cordell, 72 N.C. App. 262, 324 S.E.2d 301 (1985); Drummond v. Cordell, 73 N.C. App. 438, 326 S.E.2d 292 (1985); AT & T Family Fed. Credit Union v. Beaty Wrecker Serv., Inc., 108 N.C. App. 611, 425 S.E.2d 427 (1993); Rowell v. N.C. Equip. Co., 146 N.C. App. 431, 552 S.E.2d 274 (2001); Triad Int'l Maint. Corp. v. Guernsey Air Leasing, Ltd., 178 F. Supp. 2d 547 (M.D.N.C. 2001); Bowles Auto., Inc. v. N.C. DMV, 203 N.C. App. 19, 690 S.E.2d 728 (2010), review denied, 364 N.C. 324, 700 S.E.2d 746, 2010 N.C. LEXIS 590 (2010).

CITED in Old Salem Foreign Car Serv., Inc. v. Webb, 159 N.C. App. 93, 582 S.E.2d 673 (2003).

LEGAL PERIODICALS. --

For note on garagemen's liens and duress of goods, see 54 N.C.L. Rev. 1106 (1976).

OPINIONS OF THE ATTORNEY GENERAL

ENFORCEMENT OF LIEN BY WAREHOUSE-MAN. --Warehouseman with liens pursuant to both Article 1 of Chapter 44A and Article 7 of the U.C.C. may enforce lien under G.S. 25-7-210 without allowing the owner a judicial hearing under G.S. 44A-4. See opinion of Attorney General to Resa L. Harris, Legal Officer, Office of the Clerk of Superior Court, Mecklenburg County, 48 N.C.A.G. 111 (1979).

§ 44A-5. Proceeds of sale

The proceeds of the sale shall be applied as follows:

(1) Payment of reasonable expenses incurred in connection with the sale. Expenses of sale include but are not limited to reasonable storage and boarding expenses after giving notice of sale.

(2) Payment of the obligation secured by the lien.

(3) Any surplus shall be paid to the person entitled thereto; but when such person cannot be found, the surplus shall be paid to the clerk of superior court of the county in which the sale took place, to be held by the clerk for the person entitled thereto.

History.

1967, c. 1029, s. 1; 1971, c. 544, s. 2

EFFECT OF SALE. --The sale of property encumbered by a statutory lien does not extinguish the lien; instead, its obligations are collectable from the proceeds of sale. Case v. Miller, 68 N.C. App. 729, 315 S.E.2d 737 (1984).

CITED in Drummond v. Cordell, 73 N.C. App. 438, 326 S.E.2d 292 (1985).

§ 44A-6. Title of purchaser

A purchaser for value at a properly conducted sale, and a purchaser for value without constructive notice of a defect in the sale, whether or not the purchaser is the lienor or an agent of the lienor, acquires title to the property free of any interests over which the lienor was entitled to priority.

History.

1967, c. 1029, s. 1; 1995, c. 480, s. 2

WHERE PURCHASER OF PERSONAL PROPERTY SUBJECT TO A VALID, ENFORCEABLE, PERFECTED SECURITY INTEREST BUYS IN THE COLLATERAL at a foreclosure sale conducted pursuant to this chapter to satisfy an account for repairs which the purchaser has failed to pay for a purchase price which essentially represents payment of the account, the purchaser does not thereby extinguish the security interest; rather, the security property or collateral remains subject to the security interest, and if the indebtedness for payment of which the collateral was pledged remains in default, the right to possession continues to be with the holder of the security interest. Paccar Fin. Corp. v. Harnett Transf., Inc., 51 N.C. App. 1, 275 S.E.2d 243, cert. denied, 302 N.C. 629, 280 S.E.2d 441 (1981).

APPLIED in Caesar v. Kiser, 387 F. Supp. 645 (M.D.N.C. 1975).

LEGAL PERIODICALS. --

For survey of 1981 commercial law, see 60 N.C.L. Rev. 1238 (1982).

§ 44A-6.1. Action to regain possession of a motor vehicle or vessel

(a) When the lienor involuntarily relinquishes possession of the property and the property upon which the lien is claimed is a motor vehicle or vessel, the lienor may institute an action to regain possession of the motor vehicle or vessel in small claims court any time following the lienor's involuntary loss of possession and following maturity of the obligation to pay charges. The lienor shall serve a copy of the summons and the complaint pursuant to G.S. 1A-1, Rule 4, on each secured party claiming an interest in the vehicle or vessel. For purposes of this section, involuntary relinquishment of possession includes only those situations where the owner or other party takes possession of the motor vehicle or vessel without the lienor's permission or without judicial process. If in the court action the owner or other party retains possession of the motor vehicle or vessel, the owner or other party shall pay the amount of the lien asserted as bond into the clerk of the court in which the action is pending.

If within three days after service of the summons and complaint, as the number of days is computed in G.S. 1A-1, Rule 6, neither the defendant nor a secured party claiming an interest in the vehicle or vessel files a contrary statement of the amount of the lien at the time of the filing of the complaint, the amount set forth in the complaint shall be deemed to be the amount of the asserted lien. The clerk may at any time disburse to the lienor that portion of the cash bond which is not in dispute, upon application of the lienor. The magistrate shall:

(1) Direct appropriate disbursement of the disputed or undisbursed portion of the bond; and

(2) Direct appropriate possession of the motor vehicle or vessel if, in the judgment of the court, the plaintiff has a valid right to a lien.

(b) Either party to an action pursuant to subsection (a) of this section may appeal to district court for a trial de novo.

History.

1991, c. 344, s. 2 ; c. 731, s. 4

MECHANIC'S LIEN SURVIVED CREDIT UNION'S REPOSSESSION OF A CAR --While a mechanic who performed a diagnostic analysis of an automobile had a valid lien against the credit union that financed the purchase of the automobile and repossessed the automobile from the mechanic's premises late at night without the mechanic's knowledge or consent, the trial court erred in awarding the mechanic actual and treble damages, as the mechanic's proper remedy was to be awarded possession of the automobile. Old Salem Foreign Car Serv., Inc. v. Webb, 159 N.C. App. 93, 582 S.E.2d 673 (2003).

FAILURE TO USE LEGAL REMEDIES MAY PRECLUDE INSURANCE COVERAGE. --The actions of defendant, who had available legal remedies under subsection (a) of this section but attempted to repossess car by means not authorized by law, were not "necessary or incidental" to "garage operations" and insurance contract did not provide coverage for conduct complained of in wrongful death action. North Carolina Farm Bureau Mut. Ins. Co. v. Weaver, 134 N.C. App. 359, 517 S.E.2d 381 (1999).

Chapter 44A

CHAPTER 62.
PUBLIC UTILITIES

ARTICLE 12.
MOTOR CARRIERS

§ 62-278. Revocation of license plates by Utilities Commission

(a) The license plates of any carrier of persons or household goods by motor vehicle for compensation may be revoked and removed from the vehicles of any such carrier for wilful violation of any provision of this Chapter, or for the wilful violation of any lawful rule or regulation made and promulgated by the Utilities Commission. To that end the Commission shall have power upon complaint or upon its own motion, after notice and hearing, to order the license plates of any such offending carrier revoked and removed from the vehicles of such carrier for a period not exceeding 30 days, and it shall be the duty of the Department of Motor Vehicles to execute such orders made by the Utilities Commission upon receipt of a certified copy of the same.

(b) This section shall be in addition to and independent of other provisions of law for the enforcement of the motor carrier laws of this State.

History.

1951, c. 1120; 1963, c. 1165, s. 1; 1995, c. 523, s. 27

CHAPTER 63.
AERONAUTICS

ARTICLE 10.
OPERATION OF UNMANNED AIRCRAFT SYSTEMS

§ 63-95. Training required for operation of unmanned aircraft systems

(a) As used in this Article, the term "Division" means the Division of Aviation of the Department of Transportation.

(b) The Division shall develop a knowledge test for operating an unmanned aircraft system that complies with all applicable State and federal regulations and shall provide for administration of the test. The test shall ensure that the operator of an unmanned aircraft system is knowledgeable of the State statutes and regulations regarding the operation of unmanned aircraft systems. The Division may permit a person, including an agency of this State, an agency of a political subdivision of this State, an employer, or a private training facility, to administer the test developed pursuant to this subsection, provided the test is the same as that administered by the Division and complies with all applicable State and federal regulations.

(c) No agent or agency of the State, or agent or agency of a political subdivision of the State, may operate an unmanned aircraft system within the State without completion of the test set forth in subsection (b) of this section.

History.
2014-100, s. 34.30(g) ; 2015-232, s. 2.3

EDITOR'S NOTE. --
Session Laws 2014-100, s. 34.30 (*l*), made this section effective August 7, 2014.

Session Laws 2014-100, s. 34.30(h) , provides: "The Division of Aviation of the Department of Transportation shall develop and implement the knowledge and skills test required by G.S. 63-95, as enacted in subsection (g) of this section, no later than May 31, 2015, and shall report to the Joint Legislative Transportation Oversight Committee on the status of implementation by June 15, 2015."

Session Laws 2014-100, s. 34.30(i) , provides: "The Division of Aviation of the Department of Transportation shall immediately begin developing the licensing system for commercial operation required by G.S. 63-96, as enacted in subsection (g) of this section, and shall ensure that the system complies with Federal Aviation Administration (FAA) guidelines on commercial operation, as those guidelines become available. Within 60 days of issuance of the FAA guidelines and authorization by the FAA for commercial

operations to begin, the Division shall implement the licensing system required by G.S. 63-96, as enacted in subsection (g) of this section."

Session Laws 2014-100, s. 34.30(j) , as amended by Session Laws 2015-232, s. 2.2 , provides: "Except as authorized under Section 7.16(e) of S.L. 2013-360, as amended by Section 7.11(a) of S.L. 2014-100, no operation of unmanned aircraft systems by agents or agencies of the State or a political subdivision of the State shall be authorized in this State until the knowlege test required by G.S. 63-95, as enacted in subsection (g) of this section, has been implemented."

Session Laws 2014-100, s. 34.30(k) , provides: "The Division of Aviation of the Department of Transportation shall use funds appropriated in this act to the Division to cover the administration costs incurred from developing and implementing the knowledge and skills test and licensing system for commercial operation required by this section."

Session Laws 2014-100, s. 1.1 , provides: "This act shall be known as 'The Current Operations and Capital Improvements Appropriations Act of 2014.'"

Session Laws 2014-100, s. 38.4 , provides: "Except for statutory changes or other provisions that clearly indicate an intention to have effects beyond the 2014-2015 fiscal year, the textual provisions of this act apply only to funds appropriated for, and activities occurring during, the 2014-2015 fiscal year."

Session Laws 2014-100, s. 38.7 , is a severability clause.

EFFECT OF AMENDMENTS. --
Session Laws 2015-232, s. 2.3 , effective August 25, 2015, in subsection (b), deleted "and skills" following "knowledge" in the first sentence, and added the second sentence.

§ 63-96. Permit required for commercial operation of unmanned aircraft systems

(a) No person shall operate an unmanned aircraft system, as defined in G.S. 15A-300.1, in this State for commercial purposes unless the person is in possession of a permit issued by the Division valid for the unmanned aircraft system being operated. Application for the permit shall be made in the manner provided by the Division. Unless suspended or revoked, the permit shall be effective for a period to be established by the Division not exceeding eight years.

(b) No person shall be issued a permit under this section unless all of the following apply:

(1) The person is at least the minimum age required by federal regulation for operation of an unmanned aircraft system.

(2) The person possesses a valid government-issued photographic identification acceptable to the Federal Aviation Administration for issuing authorization to operate an unmanned aircraft system.

(3) The person has passed the knowledge test for operating an unmanned aircraft system as prescribed in G.S. 63-95(b).

Chapter 63

(4) The person has satisfied all other applicable requirements of this Article or federal regulation.

(c) A permit to operate an unmanned aircraft system for commercial purposes shall not be issued to a person while the person's license or permit to operate an unmanned aircraft system is suspended, revoked, or cancelled in any state.

(d) The Division shall develop and administer a program that complies with all applicable federal regulations to issue permits to operators of unmanned aircraft systems for commercial purposes, including a fee structure for permits. Criteria and requirements established under the subdivisions set forth in this subsection shall be no more restrictive than the rules or regulations adopted by the Federal Aviation Administration setting forth the criteria and requirements under which a person may operate an unmanned aircraft system for commercial purposes. The program must include the following components:

(1) A system for classifying unmanned aircraft systems based on characteristics determined to be appropriate by the Division.

(2) Repealed by Session Laws 2017-160, s. 4 , effective July 21, 2017.

(3) A permit application process, which shall include a requirement that the Division provide notice to an applicant of the Division's decision on issuance of a permit no later than 10 days from the date the Division receives the applicant's application.

(4) Technical guidance for complying with program requirements.

(5) Criteria under which the Division may suspend or revoke a permit.

(6) Criteria under which the Division may waive permitting requirements for applicants currently holding a valid license or permit to operate unmanned aircraft systems issued by another state or territory of the United States, the District of Columbia, or the United States.

(7) A designation of the geographic area within which a permittee shall be authorized to operate an unmanned aircraft system.

(8) Requirements pertaining to the collection, use, and retention of data by permittees obtained through the operation of unmanned aircraft systems, to be established in consultation with the State Chief Information Officer.

(9) Requirements for the marking of each unmanned aircraft system operated pursuant to a permit issued under this section sufficient to allow identification of the owner of the system and the person issued a permit to operate it.

(10) A system for providing agencies that conduct other operations within regulated airspace with the identity and contact information of permittees and the geographic areas within which the permittee is authorized to operate an unmanned aircraft system.

(e) A person who operates an unmanned aircraft system for commercial purposes other than as authorized under this section shall be guilty of a Class 1 misdemeanor.

(f) Subject to the limitations set forth in subsection (d) of this section, the Division may issue rules and regulations to implement the provisions of this section.

History.
2014-100, s. 34.30(g) ; 2015-232, s. 2.4 ; 2016-90, s. 14.5 ; 2017-160, s. 4

EDITOR'S NOTE. --
Session Laws 2014-100, s. 34.30 (*l*), made this section effective August 7, 2014.

Session Laws 2014-100, s. 34.30(h) , provides: "The Division of Aviation of the Department of Transportation shall develop and implement the knowledge and skills test required by G.S. 63-95, as enacted in subsection (g) of this section, no later than May 31, 2015, and shall report to the Joint Legislative Transportation Oversight Committee on the status of implementation by June 15, 2015."

Session Laws 2014-100, s. 34.30(i) , provides: "The Division of Aviation of the Department of Transportation shall immediately begin developing the licensing system for commercial operation required by G.S. 63-96, as enacted in subsection (g) of this section, and shall ensure that the system complies with Federal Aviation Administration (FAA) guidelines on commercial operation, as those guidelines become available. Within 60 days of issuance of the FAA guidelines and authorization by the FAA for commercial operations to begin, the Division shall implement the licensing system required by G.S. 63-96, as enacted in subsection (g) of this section."

Session Laws 2014-100, s. 34.30(j) , as amended by Session Laws 2015-232, s. 2.2 , provides: "Except as authorized under Section 7.16(e) of S.L. 2013-360, as amended by Section 7.11(a) of S.L. 2014-100, no operation of unmanned aircraft systems by agents or agencies of the State or a political subdivision of the State shall be authorized in this State until the knowlege test required by G.S. 63-95, as enacted in subsection (g) of this section, has been implemented."

Session Laws 2014-100, s. 34.30(k) , provides: "The Division of Aviation of the Department of Transportation shall use funds appropriated in this act to the Division to cover the administration costs incurred from developing and implementing the knowledge and skills test and licensing system for commercial operation required by this section."

Session Laws 2014-100, s. 1.1 , provides: "This act shall be known as 'The Current Operations and Capital Improvements Appropriations Act of 2014.'"

Session Laws 2014-100, s. 38.4 , provides: "Except for statutory changes or other provisions that clearly indicate an intention to have effects beyond the 2014-2015 fiscal year, the textual provisions of this act apply only to funds appropriated for, and activities occurring during, the 2014-2015 fiscal year."

Session Laws 2014-100, s. 38.7 , is a severability clause.

Session Laws 2015-232, s. 2.5 , provides: "Prior to the implementation of the knowledge test and permitting process required by G.S. 63-96, any person authorized by the FAA for commercial operation of an unmanned aircraft system in this State shall not be in violation of that statute, provided that the person makes application for a State permit for commercial operation within 60 days of the full implementation of the permitting process and is issued a State commercial operation permit in due course."

EFFECT OF AMENDMENTS. --

Session Laws 2015-232, s. 2.4 , effective August 25, 2015, rewrote the section.

Session Laws 2016-90, s. 14.5 , effective July 11, 2016, in subdivision (b)(1), substituted "16" for "17."

Session Laws 2017-160, s. 4 , effective July 21, 2017, substituted "the minimum age required by federal regulation for operation of an unmanned aircraft system." for "16 years of age." in subdivision (b)(1); rewrote subdivision (b)(2), which read: "The person possesses a valid drivers license issued by any state or territory of the United States or the District of Columbia."; rewrote subsection (d), which read: "The Division shall develop and administer a program that complies with all applicable federal regulations to issue permits to operators of unmanned aircraft systems for commercial purposes. The program must include the following components:"; deleted subdivision (d)(2), which read: "A fee structure for permits."; deleted the former second sentence in subsection (d)(7), which read: "The rules adopted by the Division for designating a geographic area pursuant to this subdivision shall be no more restrictive than the rules or regulations adopted by the Federal Aviation Administration for designating a geographic area for the commercial operation of unmanned aircraft systems."; and added "Subject to the limitations set forth in subsection (d) of this section," to the beginning of subsection (f) and made a related stylistic change.

LEGAL PERIODICALS. --

For article, "Drone Zoning," see 95 N.C.L. Rev. 133 (2016).

CHAPTER 97.
WORKERS'
COMPENSATION ACT

ARTICLE 1.
WORKERS'
COMPENSATION ACT

§ 97-29. Rates and duration of compensation for total incapacity

(a) When an employee qualifies for total disability, the employer shall pay or cause to be paid, as hereinafter provided by subsections (b) through (d) of this section, to the injured employee a weekly compensation equal to sixty-six and two-thirds percent (662/3%) of his average weekly wages, but not more than the amount established annually to be effective January 1 as provided herein, nor less than thirty dollars ($ 30.00) per week.

(b) When a claim is compensable pursuant to G.S. 97-18(b), paid without prejudice pursuant to G.S. 97-18(d), agreed by the parties pursuant to G.S. 97-82, or when a claim has been deemed compensable following a hearing pursuant to G.S. 97-84, the employee qualifies for temporary total disability subject to the limitations noted herein. The employee shall not be entitled to compensation pursuant to this subsection greater than 500 weeks from the date of first disability unless the employee qualifies for extended compensation under subsection (c) of this section.

(c) An employee may qualify for extended compensation in excess of the 500-week limitation on temporary total disability as described in subsection (b) of this section only if (i) at the time the employee makes application to the Commission to exceed the 500-week limitation on temporary total disability as described in subsection (b) of this section, 425 weeks have passed since the date of first disability and (ii) pursuant to the provisions of G.S. 97-84, unless agreed to by the parties, the employee shall prove by a preponderance of the evidence that the employee has sustained a total loss of wage-earning capacity. If an employee makes application for extended compensation pursuant to this subsection and is awarded extended compensation by the Commission, the award shall not be stayed pursuant to G.S. 97-85 or G.S. 97-86 until the full Commission or an appellate court determines otherwise. Upon its own motion or upon the application of any party in interest, the Industrial Commission may review an award for extended compensation in excess of the 500-week limitation on temporary total

disability described in subsection (b) of this section, and, on such review, may make an award ending or continuing extended compensation. When reviewing a prior award to determine if the employee remains entitled to extended compensation, the Commission shall determine if the employer has proven by a preponderance of the evidence that the employee no longer has a total loss of wage-earning capacity. When an employee is receiving full retirement benefits under section 202(a) of the Social Security Act, after attainment of retirement age, as defined in section 216(*l*) of the Social Security Act, the employer may reduce the extended compensation by one hundred percent (100%) of the employee's retirement benefit. The reduction shall consist of the employee's primary benefit paid pursuant to section 202(a) of the Social Security Act but shall not include any dependent or auxiliary benefits paid pursuant to any other section of the Social Security Act, if any, or any cost-of-living increases in benefits made pursuant to section 215(i) of the Social Security Act.

(d) An injured employee may qualify for permanent total disability only if the employee has one or more of the following physical or mental limitations resulting from the injury:

(1) The loss of both hands, both arms, both feet, both legs, both eyes, or any two thereof, as provided by G.S. 97-31(17).

(2) Spinal injury involving severe paralysis of both arms, both legs, or the trunk.

(3) Severe brain or closed head injury as evidenced by severe and permanent:

    a. Sensory or motor disturbances;

    b. Communication disturbances;

    c. Complex integrated disturbances of cerebral function; or

    d. Neurological disorders.

(4) Second-degree or third-degree burns to thirty-three percent (33%) or more of the total body surface.

An employee who qualifies for permanent total disability pursuant to this subsection shall be entitled to compensation, including medical compensation, during the lifetime of the injured employee, unless the employer shows by a preponderance of the evidence that the employee is capable of returning to suitable employment as defined in G.S. 97-2(22). Provided, however, the termination or suspension of compensation because the employee is capable of returning to suitable employment as defined in G.S. 97-2(22) does not affect the employee's entitlement to medical compensation. An employee who qualifies for permanent total disability under subdivision (1) of this subsection is entitled to lifetime compensation, including medical compensation, regardless of whether or not the employee has returned to work in any capacity. In no other case shall an employee be eligible for lifetime compensation for permanent total disability.

(e) An employee shall not be entitled to benefits under this section or G.S. 97-30 and G.S. 97-31 at the same time.

(f) Where an employee can show entitlement to compensation pursuant to this section or G.S. 97-30 and a specific physical impairment pursuant to G.S. 97-31, the employee shall not collect benefits concurrently pursuant to both this section or G.S. 97-30 and G.S. 97-31, but rather is entitled to select the statutory compensation which provides the more favorable remedy.

(g) The weekly compensation payment for members of the North Carolina National Guard and the North Carolina State Defense Militia shall be the maximum amount established annually in accordance with subsection (i) of this section per week as fixed herein. The weekly compensation payment for deputy sheriffs, or those acting in the capacity of deputy sheriffs, who serve upon a fee basis, shall be thirty dollars ($ 30.00) a week as fixed herein.

(h) An officer or member of the State Highway Patrol shall not be awarded any weekly compensation under the provisions of this section for the first two years of any incapacity resulting from an injury by accident arising out of and in the course of the performance by him of his official duties if, during such incapacity, he continues to be an officer or member of the State Highway Patrol, but he shall be awarded any other benefits to which he may be entitled under the provisions of this Article.

(i) Notwithstanding any other provision of this Article, on July 1 of each year, a maximum weekly benefit amount shall be computed. The amount of this maximum weekly benefit shall be derived by obtaining the average weekly insured wage, as defined in G.S. 96-1, by multiplying such average weekly insured wage by 1.10, and by rounding such figure to its nearest multiple of two dollars ($ 2.00), and this said maximum weekly benefit shall be applicable to all injuries and claims arising on and after January 1 following such computation. Such maximum weekly benefit shall apply to all provisions of this Chapter and shall be adjusted July 1 and effective January 1 of each year as herein provided.

(j) If death results from the injury or occupational disease, then the employer shall pay compensation in accordance with the provisions of G.S. 97-38.

History.
1929, c. 120, s. 29; 1939, c. 277, s. 1; 1943, c. 502, s. 3; c. 543; c. 672, s. 2; 1945, c. 766; 1947, c. 823; 1949, c. 1017; 1951, c. 70, s. 1; 1953, c. 1135, s. 1; c. 1195, s. 2; 1955, c. 1026, s. 5; 1957, c. 1217; 1963, c. 604, s. 1; 1967, c. 84, s. 1; 1969, c. 143, s. 1; 1971, c. 281, s. 1; c. 321, s. 1; 1973, c. 515, s. 1; c. 759, s. 1; c. 1103, s. 1; c. 1308, ss. 1, 2; 1975, c. 284, s. 4; 1979, c. 244; 1981, c. 276, s. 2; c. 378, s. 1; c. 421, s. 3; c. 521, s. 2; c. 920, s. 1; 1987, c. 729, s. 6; 1991, c. 703, s. 4 ; 1999-456, s. 33(d) ; 2009-281, s. 1 ; 2011-287, s. 10 ; 2012-135, s. 6 ; 2013-2, s. 9(e) ; 2013-224, s. 19 ; 2013-410, s. 19

EFFECT OF AMENDMENTS. --
Session Laws 2009-281, s. 1 , effective July 10, 2009, substituted "National Guard" for "national guard" in the first sentence of the third paragraph.

Session Laws 2011-287, s. 10 , effective June 24, 2011, and applicable to claims arising on or after that date, substituted "Rates and duration of compensation" for "Compensation rates" in the section catchline; and rewrote the section.

Session Laws 2012-135, s. 6 , substituted "when a claim has been deemed compensable following a hearing pursuant to G.S. 97-84" for "when an employee proves by a preponderance of the evidence that the employee is unable to earn the same wages the employee had earned before the injury, either in the same or other employment" in the first sentence of subsection (b). For effective date and applicability, see editor's note.

Session Laws 2013-2, s. 9(e) , substituted "wage, as defined in G.S. 96-1" for "wage in accordance with G.S. 96-8(22)" in the second sentence of subsection (i). For effective date and applicability, see editor's note.

Session Laws 2013-410, s. 19 , effective August 23, 2013, substituted "subsection (i)" for "the last paragraph" in the first sentence of subsection (g).

I. IN GENERAL.
LEGISLATIVE INTENT. --The legislature's expansion of this section in 1973 reflects an obvious intent to address the plight of a worker who suffers an injury permanently abrogating his earning ability. Whitley v. Columbia Lumber Mfg. Co., 318 N.C. 89, 348 S.E.2d 336 (1986).

THIS SECTION IS NOT CONSTITUTIONALLY INFIRM; its application bears a rational relationship to a legitimate state interest. Clark v. Sanger Clinic, P.A., 142 N.C. App. 350, 542 S.E.2d 668, cert. denied, 353 N.C. 450, 548 S.E.2d 524 (2001).

THE NORTH CAROLINA INDUSTRIAL COMMISSION IS THE SOLE JUDGE OF THE WEIGHT AND CREDIBILITY OF THE EVIDENCE in an industrial injury matter. Hensley v. Indus. Maint. Overflow, 166 N.C. App. 413, 601 S.E.2d 893 (2004), cert. denied, 359 N.C. 631, 613 S.E.2d 690 (2005), cert. dismissed, 359 N.C. 631, -- S.E.2d -- (2005).

FINDINGS MUST SUPPORT AWARD AND COMMISSION, NOT COURT OF APPEALS, MUST MAKE FINDINGS. --While the Court of Appeals was correct that no finding of fact supported the Industrial Commission's conclusion that plaintiff was totally disabled under this section because his business was not "employment" and his earnings were not "wages," the Court of Appeals erred when it usurped the Commission's fact-finding role and determined that plaintiff's management skills were marketable in the labor market and that plaintiff was "actively involved in the personal management of [his] business." Lanning

Chapter 97

v. Fieldcrest-Cannon, Inc., 352 N.C. 98, 530 S.E.2d 54 (2000).

JUDICIAL REVIEW. --If there is competent evidence to support the North Carolina Industrial Commission's findings of fact, those findings must stand, even if there is evidence to the contrary and a reviewing court must affirm an opinion and award. Hensley v. Indus. Maint. Overflow, 166 N.C. App. 413, 601 S.E.2d 893 (2004), cert. denied, 359 N.C. 631, 613 S.E.2d 690 (2005), cert. dismissed, 359 N.C. 631, -- S.E.2d -- (2005).

COST-EFFECTIVENESS IS NOT THE SOLE GOAL OF THE WORKERS' COMPENSATION ACT. Grantham v. Cherry Hosp., 98 N.C. App. 34, 389 S.E.2d 822, cert. denied, 327 N.C. 138, 394 S.E.2d 454 (1990).

FOR DISCUSSION OF THE TWO LINES OF CASE LAW RELATING TO THE CONCEPT OF MAXIMUM MEDICAL IMPROVEMENT and its applicability to G.S. 97-29, 97-30 and 97-31, see Effingham v. Kroger Co., 149 N.C. App. 105, 561 S.E.2d 287 (2002).

CONCEPT OF MAXIMUM MEDICAL IMPROVEMENT IS NOT APPLICABLE TO G.S. 97-29 OR G.S. 97-30. --While G.S. 97-31 contemplates a "healing period" followed by a statutory period of time corresponding to the specific physical injury, and allows an employee to receive scheduled benefits for a specific physical impairment only once "the healing period" ends, neither G.S. 97-29 nor G.S. 97-30 contemplates a framework similar to that established by G.S. 97-31. Under G.S. 97-29 or G.S. 97-30, an employee may receive compensation once the employee has established a total or partial loss of wage-earning capacity, and the employee may receive such compensation for as long as the loss of wage-earning capacity continues, for a maximum of 300 weeks in cases of partial loss of wage-earning capacity. Hence, the primary significance of the concept of Maximum Medical Improvement (MMI) is to delineate a crucial point in time only within the context of a claim for scheduled benefits under G.S. 97-31; the concept of MMI does not have any direct bearing upon an employee's right to continue to receive temporary disability benefits once the employee has established a loss of wage-earning capacity pursuant to G.S. 97-29 or G.S. 97-30. Knight v. Wal-Mart Stores, Inc., 149 N.C. App. 1, 562 S.E.2d 434 (2002), cert. denied, 355 N.C. 749, 565 S.E.2d 667 (2002), aff'd, 357 N.C. 44, 577 S.E.2d 620 (2003).

MAXIMUM MEDICAL IMPROVEMENT AS PREREQUISITE TO PERMANENT DISABILITY. --An employee may seek a determination of her entitlement to permanent disability under G.S. 97-29, 97-30, or 97-31 only after reaching maximum medical improvement. Effingham v. Kroger Co., 149 N.C. App. 105, 561 S.E.2d 287 (2002).

THIS SECTION AND G.S. 97-30 ARE MUTUALLY EXCLUSIVE. A claimant cannot simultaneously be both totally and partially incapacitated. Carothers v. Ti-Caro, 83 N.C. App. 301, 350 S.E.2d 95 (1986).

When an employee suffers a diminution of the power or capacity to earn, he or she is entitled to benefits under G.S. 97-30; when the power or capacity to earn is totally obliterated, he or she is entitled to benefits under this section. Gupton v. Builders Transp., 320 N.C. 38, 357 S.E.2d 674 (1987).

Award of benefits by the North Carolina Industrial Commission was remanded to allow an employer and its insurer a credit for an award of permanent partial disability because an employee was unable to recover simultaneous benefits under G.S. 97-29 or G.S. 97-30 and G.S. 97-31. Guerrero v. Brodie Contrs., Inc., 158 N.C. App. 678, 582 S.E.2d 346 (2003).

CONSTRUCTION WITH G.S. 97-31. --This section should be construed in pari materia with G.S. 97-31, allowing compensation for the loss of members, and so construed it is held that where an employee has suffered an injury to his hand arising out of and in the course of his employment, and the injury causes him total temporary disability in the course of its healing, and renders it necessary to amputate certain parts of certain fingers of the hand, he is entitled to receive compensation under this section for total temporary disability, and in addition thereto compensation for the loss of the parts of his fingers under G.S. 97-31, there being no provision in the act that the latter should preclude the former, compensation for the latter to begin upon expiration of the compensation for the former. Rice v. Denny Roll & Panel Co., 199 N.C. 154, 154 S.E. 69 (1930); Whitley v. Columbia Lumber Mfg. Co., 78 N.C. App. 217, 336 S.E.2d 642 (1985).

Deceased employee's estate, which recovered death benefits, did not have a vested right in additional compensation resulting from the employee's loss of vision under G.S. 97-31 because the employee was not entitled to recover once under G.S. 97-29 and then again under G.S. 97-31. Kelly v. Duke Univ., 190 N.C. App. 733, 661 S.E.2d 745 (2008), review denied, stay denied, 363 N.C. 128, 675 S.E.2d 367 (2009).

SAME -- AWARD UNDER THIS SECTION MORE FAVORABLE. --In many instances, an award under this section better fulfills the policy of the Workers' Compensation Act than an award under G.S. 97-31, because it is a more favorable remedy and is more directly related to compensating inability to work. West v. Bladenboro Cotton Mills, Inc., 62 N.C. App. 267, 302 S.E.2d 645 (1983).

SAME -- AWARD WHEN ALL INJURIES NOT COVERED UNDER G.S. 97-31. --When all of a worker's injuries are not covered by the schedule contained in G.S. 97-31 and the worker's earning capacity has been totally and permanently impaired, he is entitled to an award for permanent and total disability under the provisions of this section. Jones v. Murdoch Center, 74 N.C. App. 128, 327 S.E.2d 294 (1985).

Where all of a worker's injuries are compensable under G.S. 97-31, the compensation provided for under that section is in lieu of all other compensation. When, however, an employee cannot be fully compensated under G.S. 97-31 and is permanently incapacitated, he or she is entitled to compensation under this section for total incapacity or under G.S. 97-30 for partial incapacity. Kendrick v. City of Greensboro, 80

N.C. App. 183, 341 S.E.2d 122, cert. denied, 317 N.C. 335, 346 S.E.2d 500 (1986).

An employee who suffers an injury scheduled in G.S. 97-31 may recover compensation under this section instead of G.S. 97-31 if he is totally and permanently disabled. Whitley v. Columbia Lumber Mfg. Co., 318 N.C. 89, 348 S.E.2d 336 (1986).

When all of an employee's injuries are included in the schedule set out in G.S. 97-31, the employee's entitlement to compensation is exclusively under that section. However, if an employee receives an injury which is compensable and the injury causes him to become so emotionally disturbed that he is unable to work, he is entitled to compensation for total incapacity under this section. Hill v. Hanes Corp., 79 N.C. App. 67, 339 S.E.2d 1 (1986), aff'd in part, rev'd in part, 319 N.C. 167, 353 S.E.2d 392 (1987).

An employee may be compensated for both a scheduled compensable injury under G.S. 97-31 and total incapacity for work under this section when the total incapacity is caused by a psychiatric disorder brought on by the scheduled injury. Hill v. Hanes Corp., 319 N.C. 167, 353 S.E.2d 392 (1987).

If a claimant is totally and permanently disabled within the meaning of this section, then he is not limited to a recovery under the schedule of compensation of G.S. 97-31. Mitchell v. Fieldcrest Mills, Inc., 84 N.C. App. 661, 353 S.E.2d 638 (1987).

Where claimant is totally disabled as a result of injuries not included in G.S. 97-31 schedule, claimant is entitled to an award for total disability under this section. Weaver v. Swedish Imports Maintenance, Inc., 319 N.C. 243, 354 S.E.2d 477 (1987).

SAME -- AWARD WHEN G.S. 97-31 COVERS ALL INJURIES. --When all of a worker's injuries are included in the schedule set out in G.S. 97-31 his compensation is limited to that provided for in the statutory schedule without regard to his ability or inability to earn wages. Jones v. Murdoch Center, 74 N.C. App. 128, 327 S.E.2d 294 (1985).

SAME -- DISABLEMENT PRESUMED UNDER G.S. 97-31. --In all cases in which compensation is sought under this section or G.S. 97-30, total or partial disablement must be shown; however, if compensation is sought in the alternative under G.S. 97-31, disablement is presumed from the injury and compensation is accordingly based on the schedule. Grant v. Burlington Indus., Inc., 77 N.C. App. 241, 335 S.E.2d 327 (1985).

SAME -- ILLUSTRATIVE CASES. --Plaintiff, who suffered a fall causing a permanent partial impairment to his back of 20% and whom the Commission found unable to work at his previous job as a nurse or at any other employment, was totally and permanently disabled and was entitled to recover under this section, and was not limited to recovery under G.S. 97-31. Taylor v. Margaret R. Pardee Mem. Hosp., 83 N.C. App. 385, 350 S.E.2d 148 (1986), cert. denied, 319 N.C. 410, 354 S.E.2d 729 (1987).

THE "IN LIEU OF" CLAUSE IN G.S. 97-31DOES NOT PREVENT A WORKER WHO QUALIFIES FROM RECOVERING LIFETIME BENEFITS UNDER THIS SECTION. Whitley v. Columbia Lumber Mfg. Co., 318 N.C. 89, 348 S.E.2d 336 (1986), overruling Perry v. Hibriten Furn. Co., 296 N.C. 88, 249 S.E.2d 397 (1978).

The interpretation of Perry v. Hibriten Furn. Co., 296 N.C. 88, 249 S.E.2d 397 (1978), that when all of a plaintiff's disability resulting from an injury is covered by G.S. 97-31, an employee is entitled to no compensation for permanent total disability, was overruled in Whitley v. Columbia Lumber Mfg. Co., 318 N.C. 89, 348 S.E.2d 336 (1986), which held that the "in lieu of" clause of G.S. 97-31 does not prevent a worker who qualifies from recovering lifetime benefits under this section. Harrington v. Pait Logging Company/ Georgia Pac., 86 N.C. App. 77, 356 S.E.2d 365 (1987).

This section is an alternate source of compensation for an employee who suffers an injury which is also included under the schedule under G.S. 97-31; the injured worker is allowed to select the more favorable remedy, but he or she cannot recover compensation under both sections, because G.S. 97-31 is "in lieu of all other compensation." Harrington v. Pait Logging Company/Georgia Pac., 86 N.C. App. 77, 356 S.E.2d 365 (1987); McKenzie v. McCarter Elec. Co., 86 N.C. App. 619, 359 S.E.2d 249 (1987).

Often an award under this section, and by implication G.S. 97-30, better fulfills the policy of the Workers' Compensation Act than an award under G.S. 97-31(24). Strickland v. Burlington Indus., Inc., 87 N.C. App. 507, 361 S.E.2d 394 (1987).

RIGHT TO ELECT COVERAGE UNDER THIS SECTION. --Even if all injuries are covered under G.S. 97-31, the scheduled injury section, an employee may nevertheless elect to claim under this section if this section is more favorable, but he may not recover under both sections. Hill v. Hanes Corp., 319 N.C. 167, 353 S.E.2d 392 (1987).

CONSTRUCTION WITH G.S. 97-47. --North Carolina Industrial Commission erred by awarding a workers' compensation claimant additional disability compensation as the claimant did not prove the claimant had sustained a change of condition under G.S. 97-47, and the only way an award could be modified under G.S. 97-29 was if the claimant showed a change in condition. Ward v. Floors Perfect, 183 N.C. App. 541, 645 S.E.2d 109 (2007), review denied, 361 N.C. 575, 651 S.E.2d 565, rev'd, remanded, 362 N.C. 280, 658 S.E.2d 656 (2008).

ADDITIONAL RECOVERY FOR CONCURRENT SYMPTOMS NOT AVAILABLE. --Where an employee has received compensation for a brain injury under the total disability provisions of this section, additional recovery is not available for concurrent symptoms caused by that injury. Dishmond v. International Paper Co., 132 N.C. App. 576, 512 S.E.2d 771 (1999).

THE INDUSTRIAL COMMISSION IS REQUIRED TO CONDUCT A FULL INVESTIGATION and a determination that a Form 26 compensation agreement is fair and just, in order to assure that the settlement is in accord with the intent and purpose of the Workers' Compensation Act that an injured employee receive the disability benefits to which he is entitled, and, particularly, that an employee qualifying for disability compensation under both this section and G.S. 97-31 have the benefit of the more favorable remedy. Vernon v. Steven L. Mabe Bldrs., 336 N.C. 425, 444 S.E.2d 191 (1994).

FAILURE OF COMMISSION TO DETERMINE FAIRNESS OF AGREEMENT. --Where plaintiff may have been entitled to permanent total disability benefits under this section, as well as permanent partial disability benefits under G.S. 97-31, but under this section plaintiff would receive such benefits for as long as he remained totally disabled rather than 45 weeks, and claims employee assumed, rather than determined, that plaintiff was knowledgeable about workers' compensation benefits and his rights, in approving the Form 26 compensation agreement between plaintiff and defendants, the Industrial Commission did not, as the statute requires, act in a judicial capacity to determine the fairness of the agreement. Vernon v. Steven L. Mabe Bldrs., 336 N.C. 425, 444 S.E.2d 191 (1994).

Where an employee suffered a back injury and entered into a compromise settlement agreement with an insurance carrier, the North Carolina Industrial Commission erred by not setting aside the agreement because, inter alia, the Commission failed to undertake a full investigation to determine if the agreement was fair and just since the employee may have been entitled to total disability benefits instead of a scheduled injury or partial disability benefits. Kyle v. Holston Group, 188 N.C. App. 686, 656 S.E.2d 667 (2008), review denied, 362 N.C. 359, 662 S.E.2d 905 (2008).

WORKER MAY SELECT MORE FAVORABLE REMEDY. --This section is an alternative source of compensation for an employee who suffers an injury which is also included in the schedule, and the worker may select the more favorable remedy. Wilder v. Barbour Boat Works, 84 N.C. App. 188, 352 S.E.2d 690 (1987).

This section and G.S. 97-31 are alternate sources of compensation for an employee who suffers a disabling injury which is also included as a scheduled injury. The injured worker is allowed to select the more favorable remedy, but he cannot recover compensation under both sections. Cockman v. PPG Indus., 84 N.C. App. 101, 351 S.E.2d 771 (1987); Dishmond v. International Paper Co., 132 N.C. App. 576, 512 S.E.2d 771 (1999).

COMMISSION ERRED BY NOT ASSESSING MOST MUNIFICENT REMEDY. --The Industrial Commission erred when it awarded permanent disability compensation solely for plaintiff's scheduled hand injury under G.S. 97-31 without assessing whether this section or G.S. 97-30 would provide him a more munificent remedy. McLean v. Eaton Corp., 125 N.C. App. 391, 481 S.E.2d 289 (1997).

VERSION OF STATUTE IN EFFECT FOR DETERMINING COMPENSATION. --Plaintiff, who became partially disabled in 1973 and was compensated pursuant to the laws in effect at that time, was

entitled to compensation for total disability (arising out of the same injury) under the laws in effect in 1981, when he became totally disabled. Peace v. J.P. Stevens Co., 95 N.C. App. 129, 381 S.E.2d 798 (1989).

CALCULATION OF AVERAGE WEEKLY WAGE AND COMPENSATION RATE. --North Carolina Industrial Commission's findings, under G.S. 97-29, as to an injured city employee's average weekly wage and compensation rate was supported by competent evidence based on the employee's total yearly earnings, longevity bonus, and overtime adjustment for longevity, which were then divided by the number of weeks the employee worked in the year. Cox v. City of Winston-Salem, 171 N.C. App. 112, 613 S.E.2d 746 (2005).

North Carolina Industrial Commission's finding that an employee retained only minimal earning capacity was supported by the medical and record evidence and accorded to the appellate court's mandate in an earlier remand; the commission properly took judicial notice of the federal minimum wage to conclude that the employee was entitled to $14,181 more under G.S. 97-30 than he was under the Form 26 agreement, and to set the agreement aside and award the employee $14,181. Lewis v. Craven Reg'l Med. Ctr., 174 N.C. App. 561, 621 S.E.2d 259 (2005), cert. denied, -- N.C. --, 629 S.E.2d 853 (2006).

North Carolina Industrial Commission correctly determined that decedent's average weekly wages for 1987 were $807 based on G.S. 97-2(5), but the Commission erred by failing to apply the average weekly wages in conjunction with G.S. 97-38 because the Commission failed to apply the 66 percent aspect of the statute to the average weekly wages of $807; upon applying the 66 percent, the compensation became $538, and because $538 was below the maximum compensation rate of $730 for 2006, the year a decedent was diagnosed, the decedent's dependent was entitled to the full amount of $538 for 400 weeks. Johnson v. Covil Corp., 212 N.C. App. 407, 711 S.E.2d 500 (2011).

North Carolina Industrial Commission erred in figuring that a decedent had average weekly wages of $807 based on his 1987 wages and in concluding that the maximum compensation rate of $308 for 1987 applied because although the proper year for determining his average weekly wages was 1987, G.S. 97-29 did not provide an unjust result but required that the maximum compensation rate for 2006 be used, as that was the year of the decedent's diagnosis; the North Carolina Industrial Commission made the correct determination that to have a just and fair result it had to resort to using a decedent's average weekly wages from his last year of employment with the employer, but the Commission erred in failing to explain why the first method of G.S. 97-2(5) would produce unjust results. Johnson v. Covil Corp., 212 N.C. App. 407, 711 S.E.2d 500 (2011).

Where the North Carolina Industrial Commission determined that plaintiff was disabled as the result of the effects of two separate compensable injuries and that plaintiff was entitled to temporary total disability benefits under G.S. 97-29(a), the Commission's findings regarding plaintiff's weekly compensation rate were insufficient to permit a proper application of the formula prescribed in G.S. 97-34 because the Commission did not determine whether plaintiff received an injury for which compensation was payable while being entitled to compensation for a previous injury in the same employment and, if so, which of the applicable compensation rates would cover the longest period and provide the largest amount payable. Thus, it was necessary to remand the case to the Commission for the entry of a new order containing adequate findings and conclusions. Helfrich v. Coca-Cola Bottling Co. Consol., 225 N.C. App. 701, 741 S.E.2d 408 (2013).

PAYMENT OF EMPLOYEE'S CONSUMER DEBTS AS REHABILITATIVE SERVICE NOT AUTHORIZED. --The Workers' Compensation Act does not authorize the Commission to order an employer to pay an employee's common consumer debts as a rehabilitative service. Grantham v. Cherry Hosp., 98 N.C. App. 34, 389 S.E.2d 822 (1990).

It is not a reasonable interpretation of the Workers' Compensation Act to classify the payment of consumer debt as a rehabilitative service. Grantham v. Cherry Hosp., 98 N.C. App. 34, 389 S.E.2d 822 (1990).

WHERE AN EMPLOYEE IS PROPERLY DETERMINED TO BE TOTALLY AND PERMANENTLY DISABLED UNDER THIS SECTION, § 97-32 HAS NO APPLICATION. Peoples v. Cone Mills Corp., 316 N.C. 426, 342 S.E.2d 798 (1986).

INABILITY TO OBTAIN FUTURE EMPLOYMENT. --Where an employee's effort to obtain employment would be futile because of age, inexperience, lack of education or other preexisting factors, the employee should not be precluded from compensation for failing to engage in the meaningless exercise of seeking a job which does not exist. Lackey v. R.L. Stowe Mills, Inc., 106 N.C. App. 658, 418 S.E.2d 517, cert. denied, 332 N.C. 345, 421 S.E.2d 150 (1992).

THIS SECTION IS NOT SUBJECT TO THE LIMITATION IMPOSED BY THE PROVISO OF G.S. 97-37. Inman v. Meares, 247 N.C. 661, 101 S.E.2d 692 (1958).

Where an employee filed a claim for total temporary disability under this section and thereafter recovered from his disabling injury and returned to his employment and was fatally injured in a compensable accident unconnected with the prior claim, the claim for disability did not come within the proviso of G.S. 97-37 and the right to payments accrued at the time of the employee's death had vested and survived to his personal representative. Inman v. Meares, 247 N.C. 661, 101 S.E.2d 692 (1958).

SELF-EMPLOYMENT. --Questions regarding whether a claimant's self-employment involves marketable skills and whether a claimant's active involvement in the day-to-day operation of a business are questions of fact. Hensley v. Indus. Maint. Overflow, 166 N.C. App. 413, 601 S.E.2d 893 (2004), cert. denied, 359 N.C. 631, 613 S.E.2d 690 (2005), cert. dismissed, 359 N.C. 631, -- S.E.2d -- (2005).

TERMINATION DATE OF TEMPORARY TOTAL DISABILITY BENEFITS NOT REQUIRED. --This section does not require a finding nor a conclusion regarding the termination date of temporary total disability benefits. Such a requirement would be illogical since a case of temporary total disability is one in which the duration of the disability is uncertain. Kennedy v. Duke Univ. Medical Center, 101 N.C. App. 24, 398 S.E.2d 677 (1990).

CLAIMANT UNABLE TO EARN WAGES IN ANY JOB FOR WHICH QUALIFIED WAS TOTALLY, NOT PARTIALLY, DISABLED. --The Commission erred as a matter of law by awarding claimant compensation for partial disability when it found as fact that plaintiff was incapable of earning wages in any employment for which plaintiff was qualified. Based on the Commission's findings, plaintiff was totally disabled within the meaning of this section. Carothers v. Ti-Caro, 83 N.C. App. 301, 350 S.E.2d 95 (1986).

ACCRUED UNPAID COMPENSATION IS ASSET OF DECEASED WORKER'S ESTATE. --Compensation which accrues under this section during the lifetime of an injured worker, but is unpaid at his death, becomes an asset of his estate. McCulloch v. Catawba College, 266 N.C. 513, 146 S.E.2d 467 (1966).

DISABILITY, as used in the act, means impairment of wage earning capacity rather than physical impairment. Priddy v. Blue Bird Cab Co., 9 N.C. App. 291, 176 S.E.2d 26 (1970).

A person may be wholly incapable of working and earning wages even though her ability to carry out normal life functions has not been wholly destroyed and even though she has not lost 100 percent use of her nervous system. Little v. Anson County Schools Food Serv., 295 N.C. 527, 246 S.E.2d 743 (1978).

In order to support a conclusion of disability, the Industrial Commission must find that after the injury, the plaintiff was incapable of earning the same wages he or she earned before the injury in the same or any other employment and that the plaintiff's incapacity to earn was caused or significantly contributed to by the injury. Harrington v. Pait Logging Company/Georgia Pac., 86 N.C. App. 77, 356 S.E.2d 365 (1987); Strickland v. Burlington Indus., Inc., 86 N.C. App. 598, 359 S.E.2d 19, modified and aff'd on rehearing, 87 N.C. App. 507, 361 S.E.2d 394 (1987).

IN ORDER TO PROVE DISABILITY THE BURDEN IS ON THE EMPLOYEE to show that he is unable to earn the same wages he had earned before the injury, either in the same employment or in other employment. The employee may meet this burden in one of four ways: (1) the production of medical evidence that he is physically or mentally, as a consequence of the work related injury, incapable of work in any employment; (2) the production of evidence that he is capable of some work, but that he has, after a reasonable effort on his part, been unsuccessful in his effort to obtain employment; (3) the production of evidence that he is capable of some work but that it would be futile because of preexisting conditions, i.e., age, inexperience, lack of education, to seek other employment; or (4) the production of evidence that he has obtained other employment at a wage less than that earned prior to the injury. Russell v. Lowes Prod. Distrib., 108 N.C. App. 762, 425 S.E.2d 454 (1993).

AGREEMENT AFFECTS CONSEQUENT BURDEN OF PROOF. --The Commission erred in concluding that as a matter of law because defendants had the burden of proof to present evidence sufficient to rebut a presumption of continued total disability raised by Form 21 agreement, and defendants had not met that burden, plaintiff was entitled to a continuing presumption of total disability; plaintiff employee's later Form 26 agreement with its specific duration superseded the earlier Form 21 agreement which covered her total disability for an indefinite period, and consequently, she had the burden of rebutting the existing presumption of partial disability through the presentation of evidence supporting total disability. Dancy v. Abbott Labs., 139 N.C. App. 553, 534 S.E.2d 601 (2000), review dismissed, 353 N.C. 370 (2001), aff'd, 353 N.C. 446, 545 S.E.2d 211 (2001).

THE RELEVANT INQUIRY UNDER THIS SECTION is not whether all or some persons with plaintiff's degree of injury are capable of working and earning wages, but whether plaintiff herself has such capacity. Little v. Anson County Schools Food Serv., 295 N.C. 527, 246 S.E.2d 743 (1978); Allen v. Standard Mineral Co., 71 N.C. App. 597, 322 S.E.2d 644 (1984), cert. denied, 313 N.C. 327, 329 S.E.2d 384 (1985).

If preexisting conditions such as the employee's age, education and work experience are such that an injury causes the employee a greater degree of incapacity for work than the same injury would cause some other person, the employee must be compensated for the actual incapacity he or she suffers, and not for the degree of disability which would be suffered by someone who is younger or who possesses superior education or work experience. Peoples v. Cone Mills Corp., 316 N.C. 426, 342 S.E.2d 798 (1986).

UNDER THE TRADITIONAL FOUR-WAY CLASSIFICATION OF DISABILITIES, a total disability under this section must be either permanent or temporary. Gamble v. Borden, Inc., 45 N.C. App. 506, 263 S.E.2d 280, cert. denied, 300 N.C. 372, 267 S.E.2d 675 (1980).

OCCUPATIONAL DISEASE IS NOT COMPENSABLE UNTIL IT CAUSES INCAPACITY TO WORK. --An occupational disease does not become compensable under this section (relating to total incapacity) or G.S. 97-30 (relating to partial incapacity) until it causes incapacity for work. This incapacity is the basic "loss" for which the worker receives compensation. Caulder v. Mills, 314 N.C. 70, 331 S.E.2d 646 (1985).

IN DETERMINING THE EXTENT OF A PARTICULAR EMPLOYEE'S CAPACITY FOR WORK, the Commission may consider such factors as the individual's degree of pain and the individual's age, education and work experience. Niple v. Seawell Realty & Indus. Co., 88 N.C. App. 136, 362 S.E.2d 572 (1987).

FACT THAT PLAINTIFF CAN PERFORM SEDENTARY WORK DOES NOT IN ITSELF PRECLUDE THE COMMISSION FROM MAKING AN AWARD for total disability if it finds upon supporting evidence that plaintiff, because of other preexisting limitations, is not qualified to perform the kind of sedentary jobs that might be available in the marketplace. Peoples v. Cone Mills Corp., 316 N.C. 426, 342 S.E.2d 798 (1986).

WHERE OCCUPATIONAL LUNG DISEASE INCAPACITATES AN EMPLOYEE FROM ALL BUT SEDENTARY EMPLOYMENT, and because of the employee's age, limited education or work experience no sedentary employment for which the employee is qualified exists, the employee is entitled to compensation for total disability. Peoples v. Cone Mills Corp., 316 N.C. 426, 342 S.E.2d 798 (1986).

DISABILITY RELATED TO ASBESTOSIS. --The claimant could not recover compensation for total or partial incapacity to earn wages, both of which require a showing of disablement, where his prior award of 104-weeks' compensation for asbestosis did not establish his disablement, but he was entitled to compensation for permanent injury to his lungs. Davis v. Weyerhaeuser Co., 132 N.C. App. 771, 514 S.E.2d 91 (1999).

WHEN AN INJURY TO THE BACK CAUSES REFERRED PAIN TO THE EXTREMITIES of the body and this pain impairs the use of the extremities, then the award of workers' compensation must take into account such impairment. Harmon v. Public Serv. of N.C., Inc., 81 N.C. App. 482, 344 S.E.2d 285, cert. denied, 318 N.C. 415, 349 S.E.2d 595 (1986).

When an injury to the back causes referred pain to the extremities of the body, and this pain impairs the use of the extremities, then the award of workers' compensation must take into account such impairment; furthermore, a disabled plaintiff suffering from "chronic back and leg pain" as a result of a work-related injury to the back cannot be fully compensated under G.S. 97-31(23) and is entitled to compensation under this section. Therefore, the Industrial Commission's failure to make findings as to disability to the plaintiff's legs caused by the arachnoiditis was error and required a remand to the Commission for appropriate findings. McKenzie v. McCarter Elec. Co., 86 N.C. App. 619, 359 S.E.2d 249 (1987).

REMAND FOR FINDINGS AS TO OTHER EMPLOYMENT FOR WHICH QUALIFIED. --Where the Commission found that plaintiff had chronic obstructive pulmonary disease caused in part by her exposure to respirable cotton dust during her employment, but that her impairment was not sufficient to render plaintiff incapable of performing types of employment which did not require very strenuous activity or exposure to cotton dust, but the Commission's findings did not address evidence that due to plaintiff's education, age and experience she was probably not capable of earning wages in any employment which did not require substantial physical exertion, the case was remanded for appropriate findings and conclusions of plaintiff's capacity to earn wages in employment for which she might be qualified. Webb v. Pauline Knitting Indus., 78 N.C. App. 184, 336 S.E.2d 645 (1985).

REMAND FOR FINDINGS AS TO WAGE EARNING CAPACITY. --Where plaintiff suffered a permanent disability to her lungs, the Industrial

Commission committed error in compensating her under G.S. 97-31, but failing to consider or make findings of fact as to whether her disability affected her wage earning capacity under either this section, or G.S. 97-30, as this prevented plaintiff from electing to recover under either this section or G.S. 97-30, if she was so entitled. Strickland v. Burlington Indus., Inc., 87 N.C. App. 507, 361 S.E.2d 394 (1987).

PRESUMPTION OF DURATION OF DISABILITY. --The Supreme Court has held that "if an award is made, payable during disability, and there is a presumption that disability lasts until the employee returns to work, there is likewise a presumption that disability ended when the employee returned to work." Tucker v. Lowdermilk, 233 N.C. 185, 63 S.E.2d 109 (1951).

WHEELCHAIR ACCESSIBLE RESIDENCE. -- The employer's obligation to furnish "other treatment or care" may include the duty to furnish alternate, wheelchair accessible housing. Derebery v. Pitt County Fire Marshall, 318 N.C. 192, 347 S.E.2d 814 (1986).

Evidence that plaintiff's present rented home had not been modified to accommodate his wheelchair, that the owners would not permit such modification, and that plaintiff could not enter the bathroom or kitchen and thus could not use the bath or toilet facilities or prepare meals for himself supported the Commission's finding of fact that plaintiff's present residence was not satisfactory and its award for wheelchair accessible housing. Derebery v. Pitt County Fire Marshall, 318 N.C. 192, 347 S.E.2d 814 (1986).

Employer could be ordered, under G.S. 97-29, to pay to rent handicapped accessible housing for a quadriplegic employee because: (1) the employee had no home that could be renovated; (2) the employer had paid to house the employee in a skilled nursing or long-term care facility; and (3) such facilities were not in the employee's medical best interest. Tinajero v. Balfour Beatty Infrastructure, Inc., 233 N.C. App. 748, 758 S.E.2d 169 (2014).

North Carolina Industrial Commission did not err in requiring a worker to contribute $400 per month toward the cost of renting his apartment. Hall v. United States Xpress, Inc., 256 N.C. App. 635, 808 S.E.2d 595 (2017), review dismissed, 813 S.E.2d 249, 2018 N.C. LEXIS 339 (2018) review denied, stay lifted, stay denied, 813 S.E.2d 235, 2018 N.C. LEXIS 344 (2018).

HANDICAPPED ACCESSIBLE HOUSING. --An employer's duty to provide other treatment or care is sufficiently broad to include the duty to provide handicapped accessible housing. Timmons v. North Carolina DOT, 123 N.C. App. 456, 473 S.E.2d 356 (1996), aff'd, 346 N.C. 173, 484 S.E.2d 551 (1997).

SPECIALLY EQUIPPED VAN. --Neither the phrase "other treatment or care" nor the term "rehabilitative services" in this section can reasonably be interpreted to include a specially equipped van. McDonald v. Brunswick Elec. Membership Corp., 77 N.C. App. 753, 336 S.E.2d 407 (1985), affirming the Commission's opinion and award, however, to the extent that it required defendants to reimburse plaintiff for the cost of special adaptive equipment in his specially equipped van.

It was not error to deny a quadriplegic employee's request to order an employer to provide an adaptable van because the record showed transportation services available to the employee were satisfactory. Tinajero v. Balfour Beatty Infrastructure, Inc., 233 N.C. App. 748, 758 S.E.2d 169 (2014).

PSYCHOLOGICAL INJURIES ARE COMPENSABLE, if at all, under this section or G.S. 97-31 and wage-earning capacity is critical to the assessment of a plaintiff's entitlement to benefits under these sections. McLean v. Eaton Corp., 125 N.C. App. 391, 481 S.E.2d 289 (1997).

EVIDENCE HELD SUFFICIENT TO SHOW THAT INJURIOUS EXPOSURE OCCURRED DURING COURSE OF EMPLOYMENT. --Where the record disclosed that plaintiff did not continue earning wages after 1969, her unsuccessful attempts to work during the years 1969 to 1980, when considered in conjunction with the medical evidence, merely demonstrated her total incapacity to earn wages; thus the commission's determination that plaintiff's last injurious exposure to the hazards of her occupational disease occurred while she was employed in 1968, and its order that employer and its carrier in 1968 pay her an award under the provisions of this section in effect on October 1, 1968, would be affirmed. Gregory v. Sadie Cotton Mills, Inc., 90 N.C. App. 433, 368 S.E.2d 650, cert. denied, 322 N.C. 835, 371 S.E.2d 277 (1988).

Testimony of two doctors and a vocational rehabilitation counselor was amply competent to support the Commission's finding that employee had no capacity to earn wages in either the same or any other employment up to the date of a hearing before a deputy commissioner. Kennedy v. Duke Univ. Medical Center, 101 N.C. App. 24, 398 S.E.2d 677 (1990).

Where an employee, who was a traveling nursing assistant, had traveled to a patient's home, left on a personal errand, and was injured in an automobile accident on her return to the patient's home, the full North Carolina Industrial Commission's award of temporary total disability benefits was upheld on appeal, because the personal errand had been completed and the employee had resumed her business travel route when the accident occurred; thus, the accident was properly determined to have occurred in the course of employment, making the injury compensable. Chavis v. TLC Home Health Care, 172 N.C. App. 366, 616 S.E.2d 403 (2005).

EMPLOYEE BORE BURDEN OF REBUTTING PRESUMPTION THAT SHE WAS TEMPORARILY PARTIALLY DISABLED. --The plaintiff bore the burden of proving total disability at the hearing before the Commission where--after entering into a Form 21 agreement which did not specifically note the type of disability for which plaintiff was being compensated but in which the weekly compensation rate was fixed at a level equivalent to the amount payable for total disability under this section--she entered a Form 26 agreement which created the presumption that plaintiff was temporarily partially disabled, and not totally disabled. Saunders v. Edenton Ob/Gyn Ctr., 352 N.C. 136, 530 S.E.2d 62 (2000).

BURDEN OF PROOF. --A claimant who asserts that he is entitled to compensation under this section has the burden of proving that he is, as a result of the injury arising out of and in the course of his employment, totally unable to earn wages which in the same or any other employment. Burwell v. Winn-Dixie Raleigh, Inc., 114 N.C. App. 69, 441 S.E.2d 145 (1994).

Industrial Commission's findings that an employee had not unjustifiably refused suitable employment, after having received temporary disability benefits due to a slip and fall during her employment, was supported by the evidence which indicated that she had called in sick daily, as directed by her supervisor; accordingly, her discharge a week later for her failure to report to work was not credible as a refusal to work and the Commission's award of continuing benefits was upheld due to the failure of the employer to meet its burden pursuant to G.S. 97-29 and 97-30. Whitfield v. Lab. Corp., 158 N.C. App. 341, 581 S.E.2d 778 (2003).

Employee's additional indemnity compensation claim for a work-related injury failed because, (1) after the employer met Seagraves by showing the employee's post-injury termination was not due to the employee's workers' compensation claim, the employee did not show the employee was disabled except for the time when benefits were paid, and (2) the employee did not show the employee suffered loss or permanent damage to an important organ or body part. Anders v. Universal Leaf North Am., 253 N.C. App. 241, 800 S.E.2d 99 (2017), superseded, 803 S.E.2d 463, 2017 N.C. App. LEXIS 642 (N.C. Ct. App. 2017).

DEFENDANTS HELD NOT ENTITLED TO CREDIT FOR SCHEDULED AWARD. --Where temporary total disability payments for stress-induced depression resulting from injury were to begin approximately six months after the final payment on the scheduled award for permanent partial disability, the defendants would not be given credit on the compensation awarded for temporary total disability for compensation previously awarded under G.S. 97-31(15). Hill v. Hanes Corp., 79 N.C. App. 67, 339 S.E.2d 1 (1986), aff'd in part, rev'd in part, 319 N.C. 167, 353 S.E.2d 392 (1987).

FINDINGS IMPLYING TEMPORARY TOTAL DISABILITY HELD SUFFICIENT. --Commission's findings implying that plaintiff's disability was a temporary total one were sufficiently definite to determine the rights of the parties, even though the Commission failed to make specific findings regarding both the extent and the permanency of the plaintiff's injury. Kennedy v. Duke Univ. Medical Center, 101 N.C. App. 24, 398 S.E.2d 677 (1990).

EVIDENCE SUFFICIENT TO SUPPORT TEMPORARY TOTAL DISABILITY RATING. --Evidence held sufficient to support the Commission's award of compensation for temporary total disability based on stress-induced depression resulting from injury. Hill v. Hanes Corp., 79 N.C. App. 67, 339 S.E.2d 1 (1986),

aff'd in part, rev'd in part, 319 N.C. 167, 353 S.E.2d 392 (1987).

Where plaintiff testified that his arm was "no good;" that he had worked as a roofer in the United States, although he had no green card and was not a citizen, since 1995; that he was in continuous pain and had been unable to work since he fell from a forklift; and that his doctor assigned him a 10% impairment rating for his left wrist, the Industrial Commission did not err in assigning plaintiff a rating of temporary total disability under this section. Rivera v. Trapp, 135 N.C. App. 296, 519 S.E.2d 777 (1999).

EVIDENCE INSUFFICIENT TO SUPPORT TEMPORARY TOTAL DISABILITY RATING. --Because there was no evidence a claimant had leg injuries or pain due to a work-related accident, and given a doctor's statement that any such pain was not causally related to the accident, the North Carolina Industrial Commission's finding that the claimant sustained injuries to her legs due to the accident, and thus was entitled to temporary total disability benefits, was without evidentiary support. Williams v. Law Cos. Group, Inc., 188 N.C. App. 235, 654 S.E.2d 725 (2008), rev'd, remanded, 362 N.C. 506, 666 S.E.2d 750 (2008).

EVIDENCE SUFFICIENT TO SHOW PERMANENT TOTAL INCAPACITY. --Where physician testified that plaintiff suffered continuous pain in his back, both hips, and legs and continuous numbness of the right foot, and that he was 100% disabled, and opined that plaintiff's pain was caused by the use of his back in coordination with his hips and legs, the Commission could determine that plaintiff would not be totally compensated for his injuries under G.S. 97-31 and that, as a result, he was entitled to compensation for permanent total incapacity under this section. Kendrick v. City of Greensboro, 80 N.C. App. 183, 341 S.E.2d 122, cert. denied, 317 N.C. 335, 346 S.E.2d 500 (1986).

EVIDENCE SUFFICIENT TO AWARD PERMANENT PARTIAL DISABILITY. --Plaintiff, who received temporary total disability benefits under this section for a compensable heart attack in April, 1979, was properly awarded permanent partial disability under G.S. 97-30 on his application under G.S. 97-47 for modification of the prior award following three additional heart attacks, where the Commission found that he had been permanently and totally disabled since June, 1981, partially as a result of his compensable heart attack in 1979. Weaver v. Swedish Imports Maintenance, Inc., 80 N.C. App. 432, 343 S.E.2d 205 (1986), modified, 319 N.C. 243, 354 S.E.2d 477 (1987).

NO CHANGE IN CONDITION FOUND. --North Carolina Industrial Commission properly found that a workers' compensation claimant was not entitled to benefits under G.S. 97-29 as the only method by which a change in the award could be made was that provided by G.S. 97-47; the claimant's award could not be modified as the claimant failed to prove a change of condition under G.S. 97-47. Ward v. Floors Perfect, 183 N.C. App. 541, 645 S.E.2d 109 (2007), review denied, 361 N.C. 575, 651 S.E.2d 565, rev'd, remanded, 362 N.C. 280, 658 S.E.2d 656 (2008).

EVIDENCE OF AN EMPLOYER'S REFUSAL TO ALLOW AN EMPLOYEE TO RETURN TO WORK BECAUSE THERE WAS NO "LIGHT" WORK AVAILABLE supports a finding that the employee is not capable of earning wages in the same employment. Moore v. Davis Auto Serv., 118 N.C. App. 624, 456 S.E.2d 847 (1995).

RETURN TO WORK ASSERTION DOES NOT NECESSARILY RAISE WAGE EARNING CAPACITY ISSUE. --Where defendants did not assert any other reason for termination of plaintiff's benefits besides "return to work" on the Form 28T, the record revealed that the plaintiff denied that she ever attempted a "trial return to work" and that she, therefore, was not required to file a Form 28U, and it was undisputed that defendants did not file a Form 24 seeking to terminate plaintiff's compensation on grounds other than plaintiff's "return to work", the only issue before the Full Commission was whether or not plaintiff had returned to work, warranting termination of benefits pursuant to N.C. Gen. Stat. G.S. 97-18.1(b); thus it did not consider the issue of whether or not plaintiff had wage earning capacity and neither would the Court of Appeals. Lewis v. Sonoco Prods. Co., 137 N.C. App. 61, 526 S.E.2d 671 (2000).

TRIAL RETURN TO WORK. --Employee may attempt a trial return to work for a period not to exceed nine months and, during a trial return to work period, the employee shall be paid any compensation that may be owed for partial disability pursuant to G.S. 97-30. If the trial return to work was unsuccessful, the employee's right to continuing compensation under G.S. 97-29 shall be unimpaired unless terminated or suspended thereafter for other reasons. Richardson v. Maxim Healthcare/Allegis Group, -- N.C. App. --, 2007 N.C. App. LEXIS 2112 (Oct. 2, 2007).

NO BENEFITS FOR UNJUSTIFIABLE REFUSAL OF EMPLOYMENT. --If an employer shows that an employee has unjustifiably refused employment procured for the employee that is suitable to the employee's capacity and the evidence is accepted by the Industrial Commission, the employee is not entitled to any benefits pursuant to this section or G.S. 97-30. Franklin v. Broyhill Furn. Indus., 123 N.C. App. 200, 472 S.E.2d 382 (1996).

When deciding whether an employee who sought salary continuation benefits refused suitable employment, it was error for the North Carolina Industrial Commission to apply a workers' compensation analysis under G.S. 97-29 and G.S. 97-30 because the distinct governing standard was whether the employee refused to perform duties to which the employee was properly assigned, under G.S. 143-166.19. Yerby v. N.C. Dep't of Pub. Safety/Div. of Juvenile Justice, 232 N.C. App. 515, 754 S.E.2d 209 (2014).

AS TO CONSTRUCTION OF SECTION PRIOR TO ITS EARLY AMENDMENT, see Smith v. Carolina Power & Light Co., 198 N.C. 614, 152 S.E. 805 (1930).

EFFECT OF LITIGATION OF EARNING CAPACITY ON REVIEW OF FORM 26 AGREEMENT. --Where plaintiff's earning capacity was actually litigated and necessary to the outcome of his G.S. 97-47 hearing, the Industrial Commission was bound by that finding in determining if a Form 26 agreement was fair and just; therefore, its finding that the agreement was "improvidently approved" on the grounds that plaintiff had no earning capacity, thus qualifying him for benefits under this section, had to be reversed. Lewis v. Craven Reg'l Med. Ctr., 134 N.C. App. 438, 518 S.E.2d 1 (1999).

CONCEPT OF MAXIMUM MEDICAL IMPROVEMENT IS NOT APPLICABLE TO TEMPORARY DISABILITY PAYMENTS. --Employee's reaching of maximum medical improvement (MMI) did not affect the employee's right to continue to receive temporary disability workers' compensation benefits and MMI did not represent the point in time at which a loss of wage-earning capacity automatically converted from temporary to permanent. Hooker v. Stokes-Reynolds Hospital/North Carolina Baptist Hosp. Inc., 161 N.C. App. 111, 587 S.E.2d 440 (2003).

NO DOUBLE RECOVERY. --There was no double recovery in a workers' compensation case because the amount paid to a claimant for temporary total disability was deducted from the balance of the permanent partial disability benefits awarded. Lewis v. N.C. Dep't of Corr., 234 N.C. App. 376, 760 S.E.2d 15 (2014).

APPLIED in Aldridge v. Foil Motor Co., 262 N.C. 248, 136 S.E.2d 591 (1964); Anderson v. Lincoln Constr. Co., 265 N.C. 431, 144 S.E.2d 272 (1965); Bryan v. First Free Will Baptist Church, 267 N.C. 111, 147 S.E.2d 633 (1966); Swaney v. George Newton Constr. Co., 5 N.C. App. 520, 169 S.E.2d 90 (1969); Starr v. Charlotte Paper Co., 8 N.C. App. 604, 175 S.E.2d 342 (1970); Blalock v. Roberts Co., 12 N.C. App. 499, 183 S.E.2d 827 (1971); Gaddy v. Kern, 17 N.C. App. 680, 195 S.E.2d 141 (1973); Lewallen v. National Upholstery Co., 27 N.C. App. 652, 219 S.E.2d 798 (1975); Morrison v. Burlington Indus., 304 N.C. 1, 282 S.E.2d 458 (1981); McKee v. Crescent Spinning Co., 54 N.C. App. 558, 284 S.E.2d 175 (1981); Roper v. J.P. Stevens & Co., 65 N.C. App. 69, 308 S.E.2d 485 (1983); Ballenger v. Burris Indus., Inc., 66 N.C. App. 556, 311 S.E.2d 881 (1984); Harrell v. Harriet & Henderson Yarns, 314 N.C. 566, 336 S.E.2d 47 (1985); Vandiford v. Stewart Equip. Co., 98 N.C. App. 458, 391 S.E.2d 193 (1990); Cratt v. Perdue Farms, Inc., 102 N.C. App. 336, 401 S.E.2d 771 (1991); Gilliam v. Perdue Farms, 112 N.C. App. 535, 435 S.E.2d 780 (1993); Brown v. Family Dollar Distribution Ctr., 129 N.C. App. 361, 499 S.E.2d 197 (1998); Trivette v. Mid-South Mgmt., Inc., 154 N.C. App. 140, 571 S.E.2d 692 (2002); Davis v. Harrah's Cherokee Casino, 362 N.C. 133, 655 S.E.2d 392 (2008); Thompson v. STS Holdings, Inc., 213 N.C. App. 26, 711 S.E.2d 827 (2011); Yerby v. N.C. Dep't of Pub. Safety/Division of Juvenile Justice, 246 N.C. App. 182, 782 S.E.2d 545 (2016).

CITED in Murray v. Nebel Knitting Co., 214 N.C. 437, 199 S.E. 609 (1938); Stanley v. Hyman-Michaels Co., 222 N.C. 257, 22 S.E.2d 570 (1942); Branham v. Denny Roll & Panel Co., 223 N.C. 233, 25 S.E.2d 865 (1943); Duncan v. Carpenter, 233 N.C. 422, 64 S.E.2d 410 (1951); Brinkley v. United Feldspar & Minerals Corp., 246 N.C. 17, 97 S.E.2d 419 (1957); McDowell

v. Town of Kure Beach, 251 N.C. 818, 112 S.E.2d 390 (1960); Brewer v. Powers Trucking Co., 256 N.C. 175, 123 S.E.2d 608 (1962); Morgan v. Thomasville Furn. Indus., Inc., 2 N.C. App. 126, 162 S.E.2d 619 (1968); Dudley v. Downtowner Motor Inn, 13 N.C. App. 474, 186 S.E.2d 188 (1972); Schofield v. Great Atl. & Pac. Tea Co., 32 N.C. App. 508, 232 S.E.2d 874 (1977); Baldwin v. North Carolina Mem. Hosp., 32 N.C. App. 779, 233 S.E.2d 600 (1977); Hogan v. Johnson Motor Lines, 38 N.C. App. 288, 248 S.E.2d 61 (1978); Sebastian v. Mona Watkins Hair Styling, 40 N.C. App. 30, 251 S.E.2d 872 (1979); In re Annexation Ordinance, 300 N.C. 337, 266 S.E.2d 661 (1980); Morrison v. Burlington Indus., 301 N.C. 226, 271 S.E.2d 364 (1980); Gasperson v. Buncombe County Pub. Schools, 52 N.C. App. 154, 277 S.E.2d 872 (1981); Peeler v. State Hwy. Comm., 302 N.C. 183, 273 S.E.2d 705 (1981); Rutledge v. Tultex Corp./Kings Yarn, 308 N.C. 85, 301 S.E.2d 359 (1983); Cook v. Bladenboro Cotton Mills, Inc., 61 N.C. App. 562, 300 S.E.2d 852 (1983); Hogan v. Cone Mills Corp., 63 N.C. App. 439, 305 S.E.2d 213 (1983); Dolbow v. Holland Indus., Inc., 64 N.C. App. 695, 308 S.E.2d 335 (1983); Fleming v. K-Mart Corp., 67 N.C. App. 669, 313 S.E.2d 890 (1984); Peoples v. Cone Mills Corp., 69 N.C. App. 263, 317 S.E.2d 120 (1984); Frady v. Groves Thread/General Accident Ins. Co., 312 N.C. 316, 321 S.E.2d 835 (1984); Lumley v. Dancy Constr. Co., 79 N.C. App. 114, 339 S.E.2d 9 (1986); Moretz v. Richards & Assocs., 316 N.C. 539, 342 S.E.2d 844 (1986); Costner v. A.A. Ramsey & Sons, 81 N.C. App. 121, 343 S.E.2d 607 (1986); Hendrix v. Linn-Corriher Corp., 317 N.C. 179, 345 S.E.2d 374 (1986); Gupton v. Builders Transp., 83 N.C. App. 1, 348 S.E.2d 601 (1986); Heffner v. Cone Mills Corp., 83 N.C. App. 84, 349 S.E.2d 70 (1986); Haponski v. Constructor's Inc., 87 N.C. App. 95, 360 S.E.2d 109 (1987); Estes v. North Carolina State Univ., 89 N.C. App. 55, 365 S.E.2d 160 (1988); Thomas v. Hanes Printables, 91 N.C. App. 45, 370 S.E.2d 419 (1988); Gaddy v. Anson Wood Prods., 92 N.C. App. 483, 374 S.E.2d 477 (1988); Hunt v. Scotsman Convenience Store No. 93, 95 N.C. App. 620, 383 S.E.2d 390 (1989); Wall v. North Carolina Dep't of Human Resources, 99 N.C. App. 330, 393 S.E.2d 109 (1990); Daughtry v. Metric Constr. Co., 115 N.C. App. 354, 446 S.E.2d 590, cert. denied, 338 N.C. 515, 452 S.E.2d 808 (1994); Gray v. Carolina Freight Carriers, Inc., 105 N.C. App. 480, 414 S.E.2d 102 (1992); Freeman v. Freeman, 107 N.C. App. 644, 421 S.E.2d 623 (1992); Bowden v. Boling Co., 110 N.C. App. 226, 429 S.E.2d 394 (1993); Conklin v. Carolina Narrow Fabrics Co., 113 N.C. App. 542, 439 S.E.2d 239 (1994); Baker v. City of Sanford, 120 N.C. App. 783, 463 S.E.2d 559 (1995); Brown v. S & N Communications, Inc., 124 N.C. App. 320, 477 S.E.2d 197 (1996); Neal v. Carolina Mgt., 130 N.C. App. 220, 502 S.E.2d 424 (1998), rev'd on other grounds, 350 N.C. 63, 510 S.E.2d 375 (1999); Timmons v. North Carolina DOT, 351 N.C. 177, 522 S.E.2d 62 (1999); Shah v. Howard Johnson, 140 N.C. App. 58, 535 S.E.2d 577 (2000); Clark v. ITT Grinnell Indus. Piping, Inc., 141 N.C. App. 417, 539 S.E.2d 369 (2000); Bond v. Foster Masonry, Inc., 139 N.C. App. 123, 532 S.E.2d 583 (2000); Royce v. Rushco

Food Stores, Inc., 139 N.C. App. 322, 533 S.E.2d 284 (2000); Devlin v. Apple Gold, Inc., 153 N.C. App. 442, 570 S.E.2d 257 (2002); Gordon v. City of Durham, 153 N.C. App. 782, 571 S.E.2d 48 (2002); Arnold v. Wal-Mart Stores, 154 N.C. App. 482, 571 S.E.2d 888 (2002); Dial v. Cozy Corner Rest., Inc., 161 N.C. App. 694, 589 S.E.2d 146 (2003); White v. Weyerhaeuser Co., 167 N.C. App. 658, 606 S.E.2d 389 (2005); Chambers v. Transit Mgmt., 360 N.C. 609, 636 S.E.2d 553 (2006); Outerbridge v. Perdue Farms, Inc., 181 N.C. App. 50, 638 S.E.2d 564 (2007); Richardson v. Maxim Healthcare/ Allegis Group, 188 N.C. App. 337, 657 S.E.2d 34 (2008), aff'd in part, rev'd in part, 362 N.C. 657, 669 S.E.2d 582 (2008); Cross v. Falk Integrated Techs., Inc., 190 N.C. App. 274, 661 S.E.2d 249 (2008); Cross v. Capital Transaction Group, Inc., 191 N.C. App. 115, 661 S.E.2d 778 (2008), review denied, 363 N.C. 124, 672 S.E.2d 687 (2009); Polk v. Nationwide Recyclers, Inc., 192 N.C. App. 211, 664 S.E.2d 619 (2008); Scarboro v. Emery Worldwide Freight Corp., 192 N.C. App. 488, 665 S.E.2d 781 (2008); Meares v. Dana Corp., 193 N.C. App. 86, 666 S.E.2d 819 (2008), review denied, stay denied, 363 N.C. 129, 673 S.E.2d 359 (2009); Jones v. Modern Chevrolet, 194 N.C. App. 86, 671 S.E.2d 333 (2008); Shackleton v. Southern Flooring & Acoustical Co., 211 N.C. App. 233, 712 S.E.2d 289 (2011); Lipscomb v. Mayflower Vehicle Sys., 213 N.C. App. 440, 716 S.E.2d 345 (2011); Wynn v. United Health Services/Two Rivers Health - Trent Campus, 214 N.C. App. 69, 716 S.E.2d 373 (2011); Mehaffey v. Burger King, 217 N.C. App. 318, 718 S.E.2d 720 (2011), rev'd in part 367 N.C. 120, 749 S.E.2d 252, 2013 N.C. LEXIS 1161 (2013); Keeton v. Circle K, 217 N.C. App. 332, 719 S.E.2d 244 (2011); Burnham v. McGee Bros. Co., 221 N.C. App. 341, 727 S.E.2d 724 (2012), cert. denied 366 N.C. 437, 737 S.E.2d 106, 2013 N.C. LEXIS 161 (2013); Espinosa v. Tradesource, Inc., 231 N.C. App. 174, 752 S.E.2d 153 (2013).

II. PERMANENT AND TOTAL DISABILITY.

TEMPORARY TOTAL DISABILITY BENEFITS ALLOWED IN LIGHT OF AGREEMENTS. --The Commission did not err in awarding employee temporary total disability (TTD) benefits, given that the parties had entered into a Form 21 agreement and a Form 26 supplemental agreement stipulating to TTD benefits. Foster v. U.S. Airways, Inc., 149 N.C. App. 913, 563 S.E.2d 235 (2002), cert. denied, 356 N.C. 299, 570 S.E.2d 505 (2002).

THIS SECTION CONTAINS A MANDATORY PROVISION that applies when the Commission finds a permanent and total disability. Robinson v. J.P. Stevens & Co., 57 N.C. App. 619, 292 S.E.2d 144 (1982).

ESTABLISHMENT OF PERMANENT INCAPACITY. --Once an employee has reached their maximum medical improvement, the employee may establish permanent incapacity pursuant to either this section, G.S. 97-30 or G.S. 97-31. Franklin v. Broyhill Furn. Indus., 123 N.C. App. 200, 472 S.E.2d 382 (1996).

OTHER TREATMENT PROVISION IS IN ADDITION TO NAMED ITEMS. --The provision for other treatment or care goes beyond and is in addition to the specific named essential items and services set out in this section. Godwin v. Swift & Co., 270 N.C. 690, 155 S.E.2d 157 (1967).

MEDICAL EXPENSES COMPENSATED ONLY WHERE DISABILITY IS TOTAL AND PERMANENT. --This section entitles a claimant to recover compensation for medical care only where disability is found to be total and permanent. Peeler v. State Hwy. Comm., 48 N.C. App. 1, 269 S.E.2d 153 (1980), aff'd, 302 N.C. 183, 273 S.E.2d 705 (1981).

AN EMPLOYEE'S PRESUMPTION OF DISABILITY may not be defeated merely by a return to work. Kisiah v. W.R. Kisiah Plumbing, Inc., 124 N.C. App. 72, 476 S.E.2d 434 (1996).

Once the Form 21 agreement was entered into by the parties and approved by the Commission, a concomitant presumption of disability attached in favor of employee, and the burden of proof was on the employer, not the employee, to demonstrate that plaintiff was no longer entitled to his disability award. Kisiah v. W.R. Kisiah Plumbing, Inc., 124 N.C. App. 72, 476 S.E.2d 434 (1996).

North Carolina Industrial Commission's conclusion that the claimant had not proven that the claimant was totally disabled or had diminished wage-earning capacity was erroneous, because the parties' final Form 26 gave the claimant the benefit of a continuing presumption of disability and the burden rested on defendants to prove the claimant's employability. Alphin v. Tart L.P. Gas Co., 192 N.C. App. 576, 666 S.E.2d 160 (2008), review denied, 363 N.C. 257, 676 S.E.2d 899 (2009).

COMBINATION OF COMPENSABLE AND NON-COMPENSABLE ILLNESSES. --Where a claimant is rendered totally unable to earn wages, partially as a result of a compensable injury and partially as a result of a non-work-related medical condition, the claimant is entitled to an award for total disability under this section. Counts v. Black & Decker Corp., 121 N.C. App. 387, 465 S.E.2d 343 (1996).

There was competent evidence before the Industrial Commission to support its finding that plaintiff's work-related shoulder injury combined with her non-work-related arthritic condition to render her totally disabled. Counts v. Black & Decker Corp., 121 N.C. App. 387, 465 S.E.2d 343 (1996).

TOTAL INCAPACITY FROM EMOTIONAL DISTURBANCE CAUSED BY INJURY. --Where employee receives a compensable injury which causes her to become so emotionally disturbed that she is unable to work, she is entitled to compensation for total incapacity under this section. Fayne v. Fieldcrest Mills, Inc., 54 N.C. App. 144, 282 S.E.2d 539 (1981), cert. denied, 304 N.C. 725, 288 S.E.2d 380 (1982).

If an employee suffers a compensable injury and the injury causes an emotional disturbance which renders him unable to work, he is entitled to compensation for total incapacity under this section. McLean v. Eaton Corp., 125 N.C. App. 391, 481 S.E.2d 289 (1997).

COMPENSATION FOR BYSSINOSIS. --It was not until 1975, when the General Assembly enacted the amendments to this section, that employees suffering from byssinosis were able to receive unlimited weekly benefits for their total and permanent disability. Prior to that time, this section only provided lifetime weekly benefits for persons disabled due to paralysis resulting from injury to the brain or spinal cord or from loss of mental capacity due to injury to the brain. In all other cases of total disability, compensation was restricted in the amount of money paid per week, in the amount of weeks paid and in the maximum amount which the claimant could receive. Taylor v. J.P. Stevens & Co., 57 N.C. App. 643, 292 S.E.2d 277 (1982), modified and aff'd, 307 N.C. 392, 298 S.E.2d 681 (1983).

An award for damage to the lungs may be made under subdivision (24) of G.S. 97-31. But such an award, by the express terms of the statute, would be in lieu of all other compensation. Such award may also be based on this section, as had been done in many other reported cases involving byssinosis disability. West v. Bladenboro Cotton Mills, Inc., 62 N.C. App. 267, 302 S.E.2d 645 (1983).

LOSS OF BOTH LEGS. --G.S. 97-31(17) provides that the loss of both legs constitutes total and permanent disability to be compensated according to this section, which provides for lifetime benefits. Timmons v. North Carolina DOT, 123 N.C. App. 456, 473 S.E.2d 356 (1996), aff'd, 346 N.C. 173, 484 S.E.2d 551 (1997).

Although plaintiff, who had lost both legs, returned to full-time employment, the employee was entitled to on-going benefits. Timmons v. North Carolina DOT, 123 N.C. App. 456, 473 S.E.2d 356 (1996), aff'd, 346 N.C. 173, 484 S.E.2d 551 (1997).

DEPRESSION CAUSED BY INJURY. --Evidence held sufficient to support the Commission's conclusion that employee was entitled to compensation under this section for total disability due to stress induced depression caused by on-the-job physical injuries which rendered him totally disabled. Hill v. Hanes Corp., 319 N.C. 167, 353 S.E.2d 392 (1987).

CHRONIC FATIGUE SYNDROME. --Evidence that an employee of a waste company whose job was to collect and dispose of raw sewage developed chronic fatigue syndrome and other ailments after being accidentally sprayed with raw sewage and that the employee's illnesses were most probably the result of the accident supported a ruling of the North Carolina Industrial Commission awarding the employee permanent workers' compensation disability benefits. Norton v. Waste Mgmt., 146 N.C. App. 409, 552 S.E.2d 702 (2001).

AGGRAVATION OF LATENT CONDITION. --When a pre-existing, nondisabling, non-job-related condition is aggravated or accelerated by an accidental injury arising out of and in the course of employment or by an occupational disease so that disability results, then the employer must compensate the employee for the entire resulting disability, even though it would not have disabled a normal person to that extent. In such a case, where an injury has aggravated an existing condition and thus proximately caused the incapacity, the relative contributions of the accident and the pre-existing condition will not be weighed. Wilder v. Barbour Boat Works, 84 N.C. App. 689, 352 S.E.2d 690 (1987).

Evidence held to clearly indicate that plaintiff's 1983 injury to his leg aggravated a latent condition due to an unrelated 1977 injury and therefore proximately contributed to his total disability. Although a normal person may not have been disabled to that extent, plaintiff's entire disability was compensable. Wilder v. Barbour Boat Works, 84 N.C. App. 689, 352 S.E.2d 690 (1987).

Where an injury has aggravated an existing condition and thus proximately caused the incapacity, the relative contributions of the accident and the pre-existing condition will not be weighed. McKenzie v. McCarter Elec. Co., 86 N.C. App. 619, 359 S.E.2d 249 (1987).

Although evidence in the record supported the North Carolina Industrial Commission's judgment that an employee's cancer was accelerated by injuries the employee sustained in a work-related accident, and the appellate court affirmed the Commission's decision to award temporary total disability benefits to the employee, the court remanded the case to the Commission for further proceedings because the record did not explain how the Commission had determined the employee's average weekly wage, a determination that was central to its award of benefits, and because there was conflicting evidence in the record which raised questions about the Commission's findings that a city which employed the employee was entitled to a credit for long-term disability benefits it paid the employee, and that the employee was not entitled to an award of attorney's fees. Cox v. City of Winston-Salem, 157 N.C. App. 228, 578 S.E.2d 669 (2003).

TOTAL INCAPACITY RESULTING FROM MORE THAN ONE INJURY. --If an injured employee is permanently and totally disabled, then he or she is entitled to receive compensation under this section, even if no single injury resulted in total and permanent disability, so long as the combined effect of all of the injuries caused permanent and total disability. McKenzie v. McCarter Elec. Co., 86 N.C. App. 619, 359 S.E.2d 249 (1987).

WHEN APPORTIONMENT NOT PERMITTED. --Apportionment is not permitted when an employee becomes totally and permanently disabled due to a compensable injury's aggravation or acceleration of the employee's nondisabling, pre-existing disease or infirmity. Errante v. Cumberland County Solid Waste Mgt., 106 N.C. App. 114, 415 S.E.2d 583 (1992).

An employee is also entitled to full compensation for total disability without apportionment when the nature of the employee's total disability makes any attempt at apportionment between work-related and non-work-related causes speculative. Errante v. Cumberland County Solid Waste Mgt., 106 N.C. App. 114, 415 S.E.2d 583 (1992).

In a workers' compensation case wherein the employee was awarded compensation after being found permanently and totally disabled, the North Carolina Industrial Commission properly determined that the employee's impairment could not be apportioned between occupational and non-occupational causes and that the employee was entitled to continued compensation as competent evidence in the record supported the Commission's finding that the employee's disability could not reasonably be apportioned between the work-related asbestosis and the other non-work-related lung disease and, in turn, the Commission's findings of fact supported its conclusion that the employer was liable to compensate the employee for the entire disability. Bolick v. ABF Freight Sys., 188 N.C. App. 294, 654 S.E.2d 793 (2008), cert. denied, 362 N.C. 233, 659 S.E.2d 436 (2008), review denied, 362 N.C. 355, 661 S.E.2d 242 (2008).

APPORTIONMENT HELD NECESSARY. --Where it is clear that claimant's permanent and total disability was only partially a result of the initial compensable heart attack, the award must be apportioned to reflect the extent to which claimant's permanent total disability was caused by the compensable heart attack. Weaver v. Swedish Imports Maintenance, Inc., 319 N.C. 243, 354 S.E.2d 477 (1987).

The apportionment rule established by Morrison v. Burlington Indus., 304 N.C. 1, 282 S.E.2d 458 (1981), was applicable to a silicosis case in which there was some evidence of the existence of a nonwork-related disease or condition which independently contributed to the employee's incapacity to earn wages. Pitman v. Feldspar Corp., 87 N.C. App. 208, 360 S.E.2d 696 (1987), cert. denied, 321 N.C. 474, 364 S.E.2d 924 (1988), remanding for specific findings as to what extent plaintiff's silicosis caused his incapacity for work.

PLAINTIFF COULD PROVE TOTAL LOSS OF WAGE-EARNING CAPACITY BY PRODUCING EVIDENCE that he was capable of some work but, after a reasonable effort on his part, was unsuccessful in his effort to obtain employment. Zimmerman v. Eagle Elec. Mfg. Co., 147 N.C. App. 748, 556 S.E.2d 678 (2001).

EVIDENCE OF TOTAL DISABILITY HELD SUFFICIENT. --Evidence provided by plaintiff's treating physician, occupational therapists, psychological associates, and vocational rehabilitation specialists supported the Commission's finding that plaintiff was unable, as a result of injury sustained in the course and scope of his employment, to earn wages in his former employment or in any other employment. Moore v. Davis Auto Serv., 118 N.C. App. 624, 456 S.E.2d 847 (1995).

Award of ongoing permanent and total disability compensation to plaintiff pursuant to G.S. 97-29 was upheld upon appellate court review where defendants, the former employer and its insurer, failed to meet their burden of showing that plaintiff was capable of returning to gainful employment and the greater weight of the evidence showed, by the testimony of an orthopedic specialist, that it was unlikely plaintiff would ever return to gainful employment due to her osteoporosis and compression fractures; defendants failed to present any evidence that employment opportunities existed for plaintiff that she had not explored given her age, education, physical

Chapter 97

limitations, vocational skills, and experience and the specialist's opinion that plaintiff would not be able to return to work and his reservation of plaintiff's ability to perform a sedentary job with no lifting requirements showed her incapacity to earn any wages on a permanent basis. Clark v. Wal-Mart, 163 N.C. App. 686, 594 S.E.2d 433 (2004).

Award finding a claimant totally disabled was upheld, despite the claimant receiving a tobacco allotment and owning a mobile home park, because the claimant did not perform any physical activity involved with either enterprise, and competent evidence showed that the claimant was unable to (1) walk or stand for any sustained period of time, (2) sleep for more than a few hours at a time because of continuous knee pain, and (3) remain balanced for any length of time. Hensley v. Indus. Maint. Overflow, 166 N.C. App. 413, 601 S.E.2d 893 (2004), cert. denied, 359 N.C. 631, 613 S.E.2d 690 (2005), cert. dismissed, 359 N.C. 631, -- S.E.2d -- (2005).

North Carolina Industrial Commission's denial of a workers' compensation claimant's application for temporary total disability benefits was affirmed as: (1) the Commission was entitled to give greater weight to the testimony of some doctors over others, (2) the Commission made findings sufficient to address the issues and evidence before it, and (3) a doctor's testimony did not justify overturning the Commission's findings that a lightning strike was the precipitating event for the claimant's somatization disorder, but did not establish causation. Perkins v. U.S. Airways, 177 N.C. App. 205, 628 S.E.2d 402 (2006), review denied, 361 N.C. 356, 644 S.E.2d 231 (2007).

Employee's estate was entitled to permanent and total disability benefits under G.S. 97-29 and G.S. 97-54 because: (1) testimony by a physician appointed by the industrial commission supported the commission's finding of fact that the employee suffered from asbestosis as a result of his employment with the employer as an asbestos tile installer; (2) the employee's medical course continued as the appointed physician had predicted that it would based on his diagnosis; and (3) the employee suffered from breathing problems as a result of asbestosis that severely impaired his daily activities and rendered him unable to perform gainful employment. Estate of Gainey v. S. Flooring & Acoustical Co., 184 N.C. App. 497, 646 S.E.2d 604 (2007).

Employee was properly awarded temporary total disability benefits for bilateral carpal tunnel syndrome (CTS) because, inter alia, (1) there was sufficient evidence that the employee's CTS was a compensable occupational disease, (2) the evidence tended to show that any current effort by the employee to obtain sedentary light-duty employment would have been futile based on the employee's medical problems, limited education, limited work experience, and limited training, and (3) there was insufficient evidence for apportionment. Johnson v. City of Winston-Salem, 188 N.C. App. 383, 656 S.E.2d 608 (2008), review denied, -- N.C. --, -- S.E.2d --, 2008 N.C. LEXIS 514 (N.C. 2008), aff'd, 362 N.C. 676, 669 S.E.2d 319 (2008).

EVIDENCE OF TOTAL DISABILITY HELD INSUFFICIENT. --There was no evidence in the medical records submitted to the Commission that supported an award of permanent total disability benefits under this section. Salaam v. North Carolina DOT, 122 N.C. App. 83, 468 S.E.2d 536 (1996), review denied, 345 N.C. 494, 480 S.E.2d 51 (1997).

No finding of fact supported the Commission's conclusion of law that an injured employee was entitled to permanent and total disability where because of an accident the employee may have aggravated her pre-existing condition, but all the evidence showed that she was not totally incapable of earning wages, and instead the competent evidence showed that her wage earning capacity was greater than or equal to that prior to her fall at work. Frazier v. McDonald's, 149 N.C. App. 745, 562 S.E.2d 295 (2002), cert. denied, 356 N.C. 670, 577 S.E.2d 117 (2003).

Although evidence in the record supported the North Carolina Industrial Commission's judgment that an employee's cancer was accelerated by injuries the employee sustained in a work-related accident, and the appellate court affirmed the Commission's decision to award temporary total disability benefits to the employee, the court remanded the case to the Commission for further proceedings because the record did not explain how the Commission had determined the employee's average weekly wage, a determination that was central to its award of benefits, and because there was conflicting evidence in the record which raised questions about the Commission's findings that a city which employed the employee was entitled to a credit for long-term disability benefits it paid the employee, and that the employee was not entitled to an award of attorney's fees. Cox v. City of Winston-Salem, 157 N.C. App. 228, 578 S.E.2d 669 (2003).

Workers' compensation claimant was not entitled to compensation under G.S. 97-29 or G.S. 97-30 after a Form 24 was approved as the evidence supported the North Carolina Industrial Commission's determinations that the claimant was capable of returning to full-duty work without restrictions and that she failed in her burden of proving that she remained disabled as a result of the compensable injury where, while there was medical evidence to support a determination that the claimant could not return to full-time work as a flight attendant, this alone was insufficient to establish that she was incapable of earning wages at any job; the claimant's one contact with her employer about a light duty position was insufficient to establish she had made a reasonable effort to obtain employment under the second Russell option. Perkins v. U.S. Airways, 177 N.C. App. 205, 628 S.E.2d 402 (2006), review denied, 361 N.C. 356, 644 S.E.2d 231 (2007).

North Carolina Industrial Commission erred in awarding employee temporary total disability compensation because the Commission's finding that the employee was unable to work at her job or any other job was not based on medical evidence, but only on employee's testimony. Everett v. N.C. Indus. Comm'n

Chapter 97

No. 102217 Well Care & Nursing Servs., 180 N.C. App. 314, 636 S.E.2d 824 (2006).

Industrial Commission's opinion and award concluding that plaintiff was entitled to temporary total disability benefits from May 15 through Nov. 29, 2000, under G.S. 97-29, and was limited to benefits thereafter under G.S. 97-31 based on a five percent impairment rating, was remanded for additional findings of fact, because the Commission determined the existence of plaintiff's disability, but did not determine the extent of plaintiff's disability because it failed to address whether plaintiff was capable of earning the same wages he was earning at the time of his injury. Outerbridge v. Perdue Farms, Inc., 181 N.C. App. 50, 638 S.E.2d 564 (2007).

RETIREMENT. --Plaintiff was not barred from seeking disability benefits if his retirement was for reasons unrelated to his occupational disease; the pertinent issue was whether plaintiff, subsequent to retirement, experienced a loss in wage-earning capacity. Stroud v. Caswell Ctr., 124 N.C. App. 653, 478 S.E.2d 234 (1996).

Claimant was not barred from receiving workers' compensation benefits for an occupational disease solely because he or she was retired; the commission's award of benefits based on a worker's asbestosis was not error based on the fact that the worker "retired voluntarily" and not due to pulmonary problems. Austin v. Cont'l Gen. Tire, 185 N.C. App. 488, 648 S.E.2d 570 (2007).

III. MAXIMUM WEEKLY BENEFIT.

LEGISLATIVE INTENT. --The legislature intended the maximums to be separate and independent provisions of this section. Taylor v. J.P. Stevens Co., 307 N.C. 392, 298 S.E.2d 681 (1983).

THE 1973 AMENDMENT TO THIS SECTION GOVERNING THE MAXIMUM WEEKLY WORKERS' COMPENSATION BENEFIT APPLIES TO G.S. 97-38, so that G.S. 97-38 no longer limited recovery for death claims to $80.00 per week. Andrews v. Nu-Woods, Inc., 43 N.C. App. 591, 259 S.E.2d 306 (1979), aff'd, 299 N.C. 723, 264 S.E.2d 99 (1980).

The 1973 amendment clearly establishes maximum weekly benefits for all sections of the Workers' Compensation Act, including benefits for total incapacity and death, and benefits under G.S. 97-38 are no longer limited to $80.00 per week. Andrews v. Nu-Woods, Inc., 299 N.C. 723, 264 S.E.2d 99 (1980).

APPLICATION OF SECTION AS AMENDED IN 1978 UPHELD. --Where all of the evidence disclosed that plaintiff did not become totally disabled until 1978, no right to recover for permanent total disability vested until after the enactment of the 1978 version of this section (Session Laws 1973, c. 1308, G.S. 1, 2) and no possible liability accrued to defendants as a result of plaintiff's permanent total disability until after the enactment and effective date of the 1973 revision of this section; hence, the application of the 1978 version of this section did not constitute an unconstitutional application of substantive law. Smith v. American & Efird Mills, 305 N.C. 507, 290 S.E.2d 634 (1982).

In a workers' compensation case, plaintiff was compensated for his permanent and total disability under this section as it read in 1978 when his disability became permanent and total, rather than as it read in 1970 when he first became disabled and was entitled to compensation for partial disability under G.S. 97-30, since plaintiff had no right to claim compensation, nor was the employer exposed to liability, under this section until 1978 when plaintiff appeared to have become totally disabled. Smith v. American & Efird Mills, 51 N.C. App. 480, 277 S.E.2d 83, cert. denied and appeal dismissed, 304 N.C. 197, 285 S.E.2d 101 (1981), aff'd, 305 N.C. 507, 290 S.E.2d 634 (1982).

G.

S. 97-29.1 PROVIDES PARITY WITH CERTAIN BENEFITS UNDER THIS SECTION. --The import of G.S. 97-29.1 was to effectuate some economic parity in benefits afforded persons who prior to G.S. 97-29.1 received lifetime weekly benefits with those who received lifetime weekly benefits by virtue of the 1975 amendment to this section. Taylor v. J.P. Stevens & Co., 57 N.C. App. 643, 292 S.E.2d 277 (1982), modified and aff'd, 307 N.C. 392, 298 S.E.2d 681 (1983).

STACKING OF BENEFITS UNDER G.S. 97-30 AND THIS SECTION NOT PERMITTED. --If the Industrial Commission in workers' compensation actions should find that a plaintiff is totally and permanently disabled, the plaintiff's compensation should be to the fullest extent allowed under this section and should be awarded without regard to compensation previously awarded the plaintiff under G.S. 97-30 for partial disability; however, a plaintiff should receive full compensation under this section only where an award under G.S. 97-30 was fully paid before the plaintiff became totally disabled, since, if the period for partial disability award overlapped the period for the total award, the stacking of total benefits on top of partial benefits for the same time period would allow the plaintiff a greater recovery than the legislature intended. Smith v. American & Efird Mills, 51 N.C. App. 480, 277 S.E.2d 83, cert. denied and appeal dismissed, 304 N.C. 197, 285 S.E.2d 101 (1981), aff'd, 305 N.C. 507, 290 S.E.2d 634 (1982).

At a given point in time, the provisions of this section and G.S. 97-30 must be mutually exclusive; that is, a claimant cannot simultaneously be both totally and partially incapacitated. Smith v. American & Efird Mills, 51 N.C. App. 480, 277 S.E.2d 83, cert. denied and appeal dismissed, 304 N.C. 197, 285 S.E.2d 101 (1981), aff'd, 305 N.C. 507, 290 S.E.2d 634 (1982).

THIS SECTION DID NOT ENTITLE THE PLAINTIFF-REGISTERED NURSE TO YEARLY INCREASES commensurate with the maximum rate calculated per annum. Clark v. Sanger Clinic, P.A., 142 N.C. App. 350, 542 S.E.2d 668, cert. denied, 353 N.C. 450, 548 S.E.2d 524 (2001).

WEEKLY WAGES IMPROPERLY CALCULATED. --Although an employee was entitled to temporary total disability benefits, pursuant to G.S. 97-29, the employee's average weekly wage was improperly calculated because the Industrial Commission erroneously found the employee worked less than 52 weeks for the employer, and the Commission's erroneous finding improperly triggered method three under G.S. § 97-2(5). James v. Carolina Power & Light, 212 N.C. App. 441, 713 S.E.2d 50 (2011).

North Carolina Industrial Commission erred in determining a workers' compensation claimant's average weekly wage for G.S. 97-29 purposes based solely on G.S. 97-2(5) as it did not specify which of the five methods it used in calculating the claimant's average weekly wage. Mauldin v. A.C. Corp., 217 N.C. App. 36, 719 S.E.2d 110 (2011), rev'd in part 366 N.C. 140, 727 S.E.2d 874, 2012 N.C. LEXIS 415 (N.C. 2012).

AWARD HELD PROPER. --Industrial commission did not err in awarding the claimant, as a temporary total disability benefit, his average weekly wage multiplied by the maximum percentage award he was entitled to under statutory law, for a two-month period rather than including the seven months that passed from his injury that occurred prior to the two-month period; the evidence did not show that claimant was disabled during that seven-month time period, and the claimant did not show that an alternate calculation should have been used to determine his average weekly wage used to determine the temporary total disability benefit award. France v. Murrow's Transfer, 163 N.C. App. 340, 593 S.E.2d 450 (2004).

CROSS REFERENCES. --
As to certain State law-enforcement officers, see G.S. 143-166.16.

LEGAL PERIODICALS. --
For a discussion of this section, see 8 N.C.L. Rev. 427 (1930).

For comment on the 1943 amendments, see 21 N.C.L. Rev. 384 (1943).

As to the 1949 amendment, see 27 N.C.L. Rev. 495 (1949).

For a discussion of the increase in allowable recovery by the 1951 amendment, see 29 N.C.L. Rev. 428 (1951).

For note on average weekly wage and combination of wages, see 44 N.C.L. Rev. 1177 (1966).

For survey of 1978 administrative law, see 57 N.C.L. Rev. 831 (1979).

For note discussing the use of age, education, and work experience in determining disability in workers' compensation cases, see 15 Wake Forest L. Rev. 570 (1979).

For survey of 1980 tort law, see 59 N.C.L. Rev. 1239 (1981).

For comment on Morrison v. Burlington Indus., 304 N.C. 1, 282 S.E.2d 458 (1981), see 4 Campbell L. Rev. 107 (1981).

For survey of 1981 administrative law, see 60 N.C.L. Rev. 1165 (1982).

For survey, "Vernon v. Stephen L. Mabe Builders: The Requirements of Fairness in Settlement Agreements Under the North Carolina Workers' Compensation Act," see 73 N.C.L. Rev. 2529 (1995).

For article, "Why Aren't You Working?: Medlin with Proof of Disability Under the North Carolina Workers' Compensation Act," see 38 Campbell L. Rev. 211 (2016).

§ 97-29.1. Increase in payments in cases for total and permanent disability occurring prior to July 1, 1973

In all cases of total and permanent disability occurring prior to July 1, 1973, weekly compensation payments shall be increased effective July 1, 1977, to an amount computed by multiplying the number of calendar years prior to July 1, 1973, that the case arose by five percent (5%). Payments made by the employer or its insurance carrier by reason of such increase in weekly benefits may be deducted by such employer or insurance carrier from the tax levied on such employer or carrier pursuant to G.S. 105-228.5 or G.S. 97-100. Every employer or insurance carrier claiming such deduction or credit shall verify such claim to the Secretary of Revenue or the Industrial Commission by affidavit or by such other method as may be prescribed by the Secretary of Revenue or the Industrial Commission.

History.
1977, c. 651

PURPOSE. --In enacting this section, the legislature did not intend to do anything other than increase the weekly benefits of claimants who were totally and permanently disabled. Taylor v. J.P. Stevens & Co., 57 N.C. App. 643, 292 S.E.2d 277 (1982), modified and aff'd, 307 N.C. 392, 298 S.E.2d 681 (1983).

The legislative history of this section reveals an intent to provide additional benefits for persons who were disabled prior to 1973. Taylor v. J.P. Stevens & Co., 57 N.C. App. 643, 292 S.E.2d 277 (1982), modified and aff'd, 307 N.C. 392, 298 S.E.2d 681 (1983).

By enacting this section, the legislature intended only to affect those cases in which the claimant received lifetime weekly benefits under G.S. 97-29 prior to 1975 amendment to that statute which provided lifetime weekly benefits for total and permanent disability regardless of the cause of disability. Taylor v. J.P. Stevens Co., 57 N.C. App. 643, 292 S.E.2d 277 (1982), modified and aff'd, 307 N.C. 392, 298 S.E.2d 681 (1983).

EFFECT OF SECTION. --This section increases only the weekly compensation benefits in all cases of total and permanent disability occurring prior to July 1, 1973; no provision has been made for an increase in total benefits. It is a well-settled principle of statutory construction that where a statute is intelligible without any additional words, no additional words may be supplied. Taylor v. J.P. Stevens & Co., 307 N.C. 392, 298 S.E.2d 681 (1983).

SECTION PROVIDES PARITY WITH CERTAIN BENEFITS UNDER G.S. 97-29. --The import of this section was to effectuate some economic parity in benefits afforded persons who prior to this section received lifetime weekly benefits with those who received lifetime weekly benefits by virtue of the 1975 amendment to G.S. 97-29. Taylor v. J.P. Stevens & Co., 57 N.C. App. 643, 292 S.E.2d 277 (1982), modified and aff'd, 307 N.C. 392, 298 S.E.2d 681 (1983).

Chapter 97

COMMISSION PROPERLY FOUND NO CAUSATION. --North Carolina Industrial Commission properly held that a workers' compensation claimant's arthritic condition in her knees was not compensable as, although a prior award included "problems caused by falls" as compensable conditions, the degenerative arthritis was not the very injury that the Commission had previously determined to be the result of a compensable accident. Clark v. Sanger Clinic, P.A., 175 N.C. App. 76, 623 S.E.2d 293 (2005).

North Carolina Industrial Commission properly found that a workers' compensation claimant's arthritic condition in her knees was not compensable where, although tears in the claimant's knees were related to falls, and therefore were compensable, the claimant failed to establish that she had a pre-existing arthritic condition in her knees and an expert testified that a long-standing tear could not cause arthritis of the knee; while there was evidence that the claimant's falls could have aggravated her degenerative knee condition, there was also testimony that the claimant's pre-existing obesity could have aggravated the degenerative changes in her knees. Clark v. Sanger Clinic, P.A., 175 N.C. App. 76, 623 S.E.2d 293 (2005).

North Carolina Industrial Commission did not err in holding that the causal relationship between a workers' compensation claimant's compensable injuries and the need for restorative dental treatment was tenuous as an expert testified that the claimant's dental condition could have been caused by poor hygiene, xerostomia ("dry mouth" syndrome), possibly brought on by plaintiff's medications, stones in her salivary glands, or the six weeks that the claimant was in a coma following her unrelated gastric bypass procedure; while another expert testified that "dry mouth" syndrome was a potential side effect of several of the claimant's medications, there was no testimony as to what actually caused the claimant's dental condition. Clark v. Sanger Clinic, P.A., 175 N.C. App. 76, 623 S.E.2d 293 (2005).

North Carolina Industrial Commission properly failed to specify treatment for a workers' compensation claimant's esophageal reflux, constipation, and nausea as compensable as there was no testimony as to what actually caused the conditions; while a treating physician testified that many of the claimant's medications had esophageal reflux, constipation, and nausea as side effects, there was no testimony that these conditions were causally related to the claimant's compensable injuries. Further, the physician testified that the claimant had ample reason to have nausea due to her gastric surgery, the complications from that, and her pain medication; further, if the claimant could establish that the conditions were related to her compensable injuries, her employer was obligated to provide the treatment for the ailments. Clark v. Sanger Clinic, P.A., 175 N.C. App. 76, 623 S.E.2d 293 (2005).

§ 97-30. Partial incapacity

Except as otherwise provided in G.S. 97-31, where the incapacity for work resulting from the injury is partial, the employer shall pay, or cause to be paid, as hereinafter provided, to the injured employee during such disability, a weekly compensation equal to sixty-six and two-thirds percent (66⅔%) of the difference between his average weekly wages before the injury and the average weekly wages which he is able to earn thereafter, but not more than the amount established annually to be effective January 1 as provided in G.S. 97-29 a week, and in no case shall the employee receive more than 500 weeks of payments under this section. Any weeks of payments made pursuant to G.S. 97-29 shall be deducted from the 500 weeks of payments available under this section. An officer or member of the State Highway Patrol shall not be awarded any weekly compensation under the provisions of this section for the first two years of any incapacity resulting from an injury by accident arising out of and in the course of the performance by him of his official duties if, during such incapacity, he continues to be an officer or member of the State Highway Patrol, but he shall be awarded any other benefits to which he may be entitled under the provisions of this Article.

History.
1929, c. 120, s. 30; 1943, c. 502, s. 4; 1947, c. 823; 1951, c. 70, s. 2; 1953, c. 1195, s. 3; 1955, c. 1026, s. 6; 1957, c. 1217; 1963, c. 604, s. 2; 1967, c. 84, s. 2; 1969, c. 143, s. 2; 1971, c. 281, s. 2; 1973, c. 515, s. 2; c. 759, s. 2; 1981, c. 276, s. 1; 2011-287, s. 11

EDITOR'S NOTE. --
Session Laws 2011-287, s. 1 , provides: "This act shall be known as the 'Protecting and Putting North Carolina Back to Work Act.'"

Session Laws 2011-287, s. 11 , which, in the first sentence, substituted "January 1" for "October 1" and substituted "in no case shall the employee receive more than 500 weeks of payments under this section" for "in no case shall the period covered by such compensation be greater than 300 weeks from the date of injury," added the present second sentence, and deleted the former second sentence, was applicable to claims arising on or after June 24, 2011.

EFFECT OF AMENDMENTS. --
Session Laws 2011-287, s. 11 , effective June 24, 2011, and applicable to claims arising on or after that date, in the first sentence, substituted "January 1" for "October 1" and "in no case shall the employee receive more than 500 weeks of payments under this section" for "in no case shall the period covered by such compensation be greater than 300 weeks from the date of injury," added the second sentence, and deleted the former second sentence, which read: "In case the partial disability begins after a period of total disability, the latter period shall be deducted from the maximum period herein allowed for partial disability."

APPLICATION OF SEAGRAVES TEST. --Issue of whether the Seagraves test was properly applied in a case in which an employer denied an injured

Chapter 97

employee's claim for workers' compensation benefits on the grounds that the employee had been terminated for reasons unrelated to his injury was not resolved by the appellate court; although the test was appropriate if circumstances surrounding termination warranted preclusion or discontinuation of injury related benefits under G.S. 97-32, the commission failed to make the necessary findings or conclusions to explain why it applied Seagraves. Jones v. Modern Chevrolet, 194 N.C. App. 86, 671 S.E.2d 333 (2008).

Employee's additional indemnity compensation claim for a work-related injury failed because, (1) after the employer met Seagraves by showing the employee's post-injury termination was not due to the employee's workers' compensation claim, the employee did not show the employee was disabled except for the time when benefits were paid, and (2) the employee did not show the employee suffered loss or permanent damage to an important organ or body part. Anders v. Universal Leaf North Am., 253 N.C. App. 241, 800 S.E.2d 99 (2017), superseded, 803 S.E.2d 463, 2017 N.C. App. LEXIS 642 (N.C. Ct. App. 2017).

THE WORKERS' COMPENSATION ACT IS ONLY INTENDED TO FURNISH COMPENSATION FOR LOSS OF EARNING CAPACITY. Without such loss, there is no provision for compensation in this section, even if permanent physical injury is suffered. Branham v. Denny Roll & Panel Co., 223 N.C. 233, 25 S.E.2d 865 (1943).

TEST OF EARNING CAPACITY. --Under the act, wages earned, or the capacity to earn wages, is the test of earning capacity, or to state it differently, the diminution of the power or capacity to earn is the measure of compensability. Branham v. Denny Roll & Panel Co., 223 N.C. 233, 25 S.E.2d 865 (1943), in which claimant, who was found to have suffered one-third "general partial disability" due to back injury, returned to lighter work but was paid the same wage as before the injury, and the Supreme Court rejected his contention that he was unable to work as he had before the injury and was thus entitled to compensation although still receiving the same wage, decided prior to the 1955 amendment to G.S. 97-31, which made back injuries compensable as specific disabilities under that section. Wilhite v. Liberty Veneer Co., 47 N.C. App. 434, 267 S.E.2d 566, rev'd on other grounds, 303 N.C. 281, 278 S.E.2d 234 (1981).

The disability of an employee is to be measured by his capacity or incapacity to earn the wages he was receiving at the time of the injury. Loss of earning capacity is the criterion. Dail v. Kellex Corp., 233 N.C. 446, 64 S.E.2d 438 (1951).

Compensation must be based upon loss of wage-earning power rather than the amount actually received. Hill v. DuBose, 234 N.C. 446, 67 S.E.2d 371 (1951). See also Evans v. Asheville Citizens Times Co., 246 N.C. 669, 100 S.E.2d 75 (1957).

VERSION OF STATUTE IN EFFECT FOR DETERMINING COMPENSATION. --Plaintiff, who became partially disabled in 1973 and was compensated pursuant to the laws in effect at that time, was entitled to compensation for total disability (arising out of the same injury) under the laws in effect in 1981, when he became totally disabled. Peace v. J.P. Stevens Co., 95 N.C. App. 129, 381 S.E.2d 798 (1989).

MEDICAL SERVICES TO EMPLOYEE WHO LOSES NO WAGES. --The rule that denies compensation to an injured employee who has lost no wages is necessarily applied in some cases growing out of this section in order to determine the amount of compensation due, but it is not applicable to medical, surgical, hospital, and nursing services under G.S. 97-25, as medical and hospital expenses are not a part of, and are not included in, determining recoverable compensation. Ashley v. Rent-A-Car Co., 271 N.C. 76, 155 S.E.2d 755 (1967).

RETURN TO WORK -- GENERALLY. --If there is a presumption that disability lasts until the employee returns to work, there is likewise a presumption that disability ended when the employee returned to work. Tucker v. Lowdermilk, 233 N.C. 185, 63 S.E.2d 109 (1951).

Employee may attempt a trial return to work for a period not to exceed nine months and, during a trial return to work period, the employee shall be paid any compensation that may be owed for partial disability pursuant to G.S. 97-30. If the trial return to work was unsuccessful, the employee's right to continuing compensation under G.S. 97-29 shall be unimpaired unless terminated or suspended thereafter for other reasons. Richardson v. Maxim Healthcare/Allegis Group, -- N.C. App. --, 2007 N.C. App. LEXIS 2112 (Oct. 2, 2007).

SAME -- AT HIGHER WAGES. --Employee was receiving compensation under this section for permanent partial disability resulting from injury to his back. He obtained a new job in which he earned more than he was earning at the time of injury. His physical condition remained unchanged. The Supreme Court held that he had undergone a change of condition within the meaning of G.S. 97-47 justifying a modification of the award and reduction of the compensation payable. Smith v. Swift & Co., 212 N.C. 608, 194 S.E. 106 (1937), decided prior to the 1955 amendment to G.S. 97-31 which made back injuries compensable as specific disabilities under that section.

ESTABLISHMENT OF PERMANENT INCAPACITY. --Once an employee has reached their maximum medical improvement, the employee may establish permanent incapacity pursuant to either this section, G.S. 97-29 or G.S. 97-31. Franklin v. Broyhill Furn. Indus., 123 N.C. App. 200, 472 S.E.2d 382 (1996).

FOR DISCUSSION OF THE TWO LINES OF CASE LAW RELATING TO THE CONCEPT OF MAXIMUM MEDICAL IMPROVEMENT and its applicability to G.S. 97-29, 97-30 and 97-31, see Effingham v. Kroger Co., 149 N.C. App. 105, 561 S.E.2d 287 (2002).

CONCEPT OF MAXIMUM MEDICAL IMPROVEMENT IS NOT APPLICABLE TO G.S. 97-29 OR G.S. 97-30. --While G.S. 97-31 contemplates a "healing period" followed by a statutory period of time corresponding to the specific physical injury, and allows an employee to receive scheduled benefits for a specific physical impairment only once "the healing period" ends, neither G.S. 97-29 nor G.S. 97-30 contemplates a framework similar to that established by G.S. 97-31. Under G.S. 97-29 or G.S. 97-30, an employee may receive compensation once the employee has established a total or partial loss of wage-earning capacity, and the employee may receive such compensation for as long as the loss of wage-earning capacity continues, for a maximum of 300 weeks in cases of partial loss of wage-earning capacity. Hence, the primary significance of the concept of Maximum Medical Improvement (MMI) is to delineate a crucial point in time only within the context of a claim for scheduled benefits under G.S. 97-31; the concept of MMI does not have any direct bearing upon an employee's right to continue to receive temporary disability benefits once the employee has established a loss of wage-earning capacity pursuant to G.S. 97-29 or G.S. 97-30. Knight v. Wal-Mart Stores, Inc., 149 N.C. App. 1, 562 S.E.2d 434 (2002), cert. denied, 355 N.C. 749, 565 S.E.2d 667 (2002), aff'd, 357 N.C. 44, 577 S.E.2d 620 (2003).

MAXIMUM MEDICAL IMPROVEMENTS PREREQUISITE TO PERMANENT DISABILITY. --An employee may seek a determination of her entitlement to permanent disability under G.S. 97-29, 97-30, or 97-31 only after reaching maximum medical improvement. Effingham v. Kroger Co., 149 N.C. App. 105, 561 S.E.2d 287 (2002).

EXTENT OF DISABILITY MUST BE KNOWN. -- The Commission is not in a position to make a proper award until the extent of disability or permanent injury, if any, is determined. Hall v. Thomason Chevrolet, Inc., 263 N.C. 569, 139 S.E.2d 857 (1965).

SINCE DEGREE OF DISABILITY IS MEASURE FOR COMPENSATION. --Under this section, compensation for permanent partial disability is measured by the degree of disability, except in case of loss of a member as specified in G.S. 97-31. Ashley v. Rent-A-Car Co., 271 N.C. 76, 155 S.E.2d 755 (1967).

VERSION OF STATUTE IN EFFECT FOR DETERMINING COMPENSATION. --Plaintiff, who became partially disabled in 1973 and was compensated pursuant to the laws in effect at that time, was entitled to compensation for total disability (arising out of the same injury) under the laws in effect in 1981, when he became totally disabled. Peace v. J.P. Stevens Co., 95 N.C. App. 129, 381 S.E.2d 798 (1989).

THIS SECTION AND G.S. 97-29 ARE MUTUALLY EXCLUSIVE. A claimant cannot simultaneously be both totally and partially incapacitated. Carothers v. Ti-Caro, 83 N.C. App. 301, 350 S.E.2d 95 (1986).

When an employee suffers a diminution of the power or capacity to earn, he or she is entitled to benefits under this section; when the power or capacity to earn is totally obliterated, he or she is entitled to benefits under G.S. 97-29. Gupton v. Builders Transp., 320 N.C. 38, 357 S.E.2d 674 (1987).

Award of benefits by the North Carolina Industrial Commission was remanded to allow an employer and its insurer a credit for an award of permanent partial disability because an employee was unable to recover

simultaneous benefits under G.S. 97-29 or G.S. 97-30 and G.S. 97-31. Guerrero v. Brodie Contrs., Inc., 158 N.C. App. 678, 582 S.E.2d 346 (2003).

STACKING OF BENEFITS UNDER G.S. 97-29 AND THIS SECTION NOT PERMITTED. --If the Industrial Commission in workers' compensation actions should find that a plaintiff became totally and permanently disabled, the plaintiff's compensation should be to the fullest extent allowed under G.S. 97-29 and should be awarded without regard to compensation previously awarded the plaintiff under this section for partial disability; however, a plaintiff should receive full compensation under G.S. 97-29 only where an award under this section was fully paid before the plaintiff became totally disabled, since if the period for the partial disability award overlapped the period for the total award, the stacking of total benefits on top of partial benefits, for the same time period, would allow the plaintiff a greater recovery than the legislature intended. Smith v. American & Efird Mills, 51 N.C. App. 480, 277 S.E.2d 83, cert. denied and appeal dismissed, 304 N.C. 197, 285 S.E.2d 101 (1981), aff'd, 305 N.C. 507, 290 S.E.2d 634 (1982).

At a given point in time, the provisions of G.S. 97-29 and this section must be mutually exclusive; that is, a claimant cannot simultaneously be both totally and partially incapacitated. Smith v. American & Efird Mills, 51 N.C. App. 480, 277 S.E.2d 83, cert. denied and appeal dismissed, 304 N.C. 197, 285 S.E.2d 101 (1981), aff'd, 305 N.C. 507, 290 S.E.2d 634 (1982).

THE PROPER FORMULA FOR COMPENSATION UNDER THIS SECTION would be the difference between wages before and after the disease multiplied by 662/3 percent multiplied by the percentage of disability for work on account of work-related causes rather than by the percentage of the physical impairment that is work-related. Parrish v. Burlington Indus., Inc., 71 N.C. App. 196, 321 S.E.2d 492 (1984).

Industrial Commission's (Commission) temporary partial disability compensation award was vacated because the Commission's factual findings of the employee's wage-earning capacity differed from the Commission's conclusions on that capacity, and it could not be determined how either figure was reached, nor did applying the formula in G.S. 97-30 to either figure yield the award that was ordered, so competent evidence did not support the award. Lipscomb v. Mayflower Vehicle Sys., 213 N.C. App. 440, 716 S.E.2d 345 (2011).

G.

S. 97-31 COMPARED. --In all cases in which compensation is sought under G.S. 97-29 or this section, total or partial disablement must be shown; however, if compensation is sought in the alternative under G.S. 97-31, disablement is presumed from the injury and compensation is accordingly based on the schedule. Grant v. Burlington Indus., Inc., 77 N.C. App. 241, 335 S.E.2d 327 (1985).

Often an award under G.S. 97-29, and by implication of this section, better fulfills the policy of the Workers' Compensation Act than an award under G.S.

97-31(24). Strickland v. Burlington Indus., Inc., 87 N.C. App. 507, 361 S.E.2d 394 (1987).

An employee who suffers injuries resulting in partial disability of a general nature is entitled to compensation under this section, while an employee who sustains injuries of a specific nature is entitled to recover pursuant to the schedule provided in G.S. 97-31. In fact, an employee who sustains both general and specific injuries may recover benefits under both this section and G.S. 97-31. Gray v. Carolina Freight Carriers, Inc., 105 N.C. App. 480, 414 S.E.2d 102 (1992).

WHERE ALL OF A WORKER'S INJURIES ARE INCLUDED IN THE SCHEDULE SET OUT IN G.S. 97-31 his compensation is limited to that provided for in the statutory schedule without regard to his ability or inability to earn wages. Jones v. Murdoch Center, 74 N.C. App. 128, 327 S.E.2d 294 (1985).

UNJUSTIFIABLE REFUSAL OF EMPLOYMENT. --If an employer shows that the employee has unjustifiably refused employment procured for him that is suitable to the employee's capacity and the evidence is accepted by the Industrial Commission, the employee is not entitled to any benefits pursuant to this section or G.S. 97-29. Franklin v. Broyhill Furn. Indus., 123 N.C. App. 200, 472 S.E.2d 382 (1996).

Industrial Commission's findings that an employee had not unjustifiably refused suitable employment, after having received temporary disability benefits due to a slip and fall during her employment, was supported by the evidence that indicated that she had called in sick daily, as directed by her supervisor; accordingly, her discharge a week later for her failure to report to work was not credible as a refusal to work and the Commission's award of continuing benefits was upheld due to the failure of the employer to meet its burden pursuant to G.S. 97-29 and 97-30. Whitfield v. Lab. Corp., 158 N.C. App. 341, 581 S.E.2d 778 (2003).

When deciding whether an employee who sought salary continuation benefits refused suitable employment, it was error for the North Carolina Industrial Commission to apply a workers' compensation analysis under G.S. 97-29 and G.S. 97-30 because the distinct governing standard was whether the employee refused to perform duties to which the employee was properly assigned, under G.S. 143-166.19. Yerby v. N.C. Dep't of Pub. Safety/Div. of Juvenile Justice, 232 N.C. App. 515, 754 S.E.2d 209 (2014).

SECTION CONSTRUED WITH G.S. 97-42. --Where the employer and insurer paid workers' compensation benefits to the employee while he was incarcerated to which the employee was not entitled, the employer and insurer were entitled to credit under G.S. 97-42; because the award was for an indefinite period, the employer and insurer were permitted to reduce the amount of the employee's payments, as shortening the period of benefits was not possible because the employee's benefits were to terminate pursuant to G.S. 97-30, G.S. 97-31 when the employee returned to work and there would be no opportunity to shorten the period of disability. Easton v. J.D. Denson Mowing, 173 N.C. App. 439, 620 S.E.2d 201 (2005).

WHERE ALL OF A WORKER'S INJURIES ARE NOT INCLUDED IN THE SCHEDULE CONTAINED IN G.S. 97-31 and the worker's earning capacity has been permanently, but only partially, impaired he is entitled to the scheduled compensation provided for in G.S. 97-31 and an award for permanent partial disability as provided for in this section. Jones v. Murdoch Ctr., 74 N.C. App. 128, 327 S.E.2d 294 (1985).

INJURIES ALSO ENTITLING EMPLOYEE TO COMPENSATION UNDER G.S. 97-31. --An employee sustained injuries resulting in disability of a general nature such as would entitle him to compensation under this section. In addition to such injuries, he had also sustained injuries of a specific nature such as to entitle him to compensation under G.S. 97-31. He is entitled to compensation for the specific injuries under G.S. 97-31, and then, if still disabled as a result of the other injuries, compensation will be paid under this section. Morgan v. Town of Norwood, 211 N.C. 600, 191 S.E. 345 (1937).

Where all of a worker's injuries are compensable under G.S. 97-31, the compensation provided for under that section is in lieu of all other compensation. When, however, an employee cannot be fully compensated under G.S. 97-31 and is permanently incapacitated, he or she is entitled to compensation under G.S. 97-29 for total incapacity or this section for partial incapacity. Kendrick v. City of Greensboro, 80 N.C. App. 183, 341 S.E.2d 122, cert. denied, 317 N.C. 335, 346 S.E.2d 500 (1986).

Because stacking of benefits covering the same injury for the same time period is prohibited, and because the prevention of double recovery, not exclusivity of remedy, is patently the intent of the "in lieu of all other compensation" clause in G.S. 97-31, a plaintiff entitled to select a remedy under either G.S. 97-31 or this section may receive benefits under the provisions offering the more generous benefits, less the amount he or she has already received. Gupton v. Builders Transp., 320 N.C. 38, 357 S.E.2d 674 (1987).

AWARD FOR BOTH PARTIAL INCAPACITY UNDER THIS SECTION AND FOR DISFIGUREMENT UNDER G.S. 97-31(22) is now permissible for injuries occurring since July 1, 1963. Hall v. Thomason Chevrolet, Inc., 263 N.C. 569, 139 S.E.2d 857 (1965).

WHEN AN EMPLOYEE'S POWER TO EARN IS DIMINISHED BUT NOT OBLITERATED, he is entitled to benefits under this section for a permanent partial disability. Brown v. S & N Communications, Inc., 124 N.C. App. 320, 477 S.E.2d 197 (1996).

AWARD FOR PARTIAL DISABILITY NOT INCREASED TO COMPENSATION FOR TOTAL DISABILITY. --Where an award was entered for total disability for a certain length of time, and for partial disability thereafter for a total of 300 weeks under this section, the Industrial Commission could not increase the award of compensation to that allowed for total disability, upon its finding that at the time of the review of the award claimant's condition was unchanged and that he was at the time only 50 percent disabled. Murray v. Nebel Knitting Co., 214 N.C. 437,

199 S.E. 609 (1938), distinguishing Smith v. Swift & Co., 212 N.C. 608, 194 S.E. 106 (1937).

OCCUPATIONAL DISEASE IS NOT COMPENSABLE UNTIL IT CAUSES INCAPACITY FOR WORK. --An occupational disease does not become compensable under G.S. 97-29 (relating to total incapacity) or this section (relating to partial incapacity) until it causes incapacity for work. This incapacity is the basic "loss" for which the worker receives compensation under those statutes. Caulder v. Mills, 314 N.C. 70, 331 S.E.2d 646 (1985).

AMOUNT OF BENEFIT. --Subject to the limitations and percentages stated in the statute in partial disability cases, the weekly benefit due is based on the difference between the employee's average weekly wage before the injury and average weekly wage which he is able to earn thereafter. Thomason v. Fiber Indus., 78 N.C. App. 159, 336 S.E.2d 632 (1985), cert. denied, 316 N.C. 202, 341 S.E.2d 573 (1986).

Where the evidence tended to show that plaintiff was permanently partially disabled by reason of occupational disease and that after failing to obtain employment in the cotton textile industry in which he had been employed for 29 years, the plaintiff made an earnest and highly commendable search for other employment, and was able to obtain a permanent job with a restaurant at the minimum wage but was released from that employment only because business conditions resulted in the restaurant going out of business, the Commission was required to enter an award setting the plaintiff's compensation at two-thirds of the difference between his average wage of $196.91 a week while working for the defendant and the minimum wage of $134.00 a week which he received thereafter, an award of $41.94 per week, not to exceed 300 weeks. Hendrix v. Linn-Corriher Corp., 317 N.C. 179, 345 S.E.2d 374 (1986).

Compensation under this section is to be computed upon the basis of the difference in the average weekly earnings before the injury and the average weekly wages the employee is able to earn thereafter. Gupton v. Builders Transp., 320 N.C. 38, 357 S.E.2d 674 (1987).

COMMISSION ERRED BY NOT ASSESSING MOST MUNIFICIENT REMEDY. --The Industrial Commission erred when it awarded permanent disability compensation solely for plaintiff's scheduled hand injury under G.S. 97-31 without assessing whether G.S. 97-29 or this section would provide him a more munificent remedy. McLean v. Eaton Corp., 125 N.C. App. 391, 481 S.E.2d 289 (1997).

THE COMMISSION DID NOT ERR IN ALLOWING DEFENDANTS A CREDIT ONLY FOR THE WAGES ACTUALLY EARNED by employee after he was found to be disabled, as implicit in the Commission's finding that employee was entitled to compensation at two-thirds the difference between his wages prior to disability and his average weekly wages immediately thereafter was a finding that the wages actually earned by the employee after he was found to be disabled were the wages he was capable of earning. Calloway v. Mills, 78 N.C. App. 702, 338 S.E.2d 548 (1986), remanding, however, for further findings

so that the exact amount of credit could be set and compensation could be properly calculated.

SHOWING NECESSARY TO SECURE AWARD UNDER SECTION. --In order to secure an award under this section, the claimant has the burden of proving (1) that the injury resulted from accident arising out of and in the course of his employment; (2) that there resulted from that injury a loss of earning capacity (disability); and (3) the extent of that disability. Without such proof, there is no authority upon which to make an award, even though permanent physical injury may have been suffered. Gaddy v. Kern, 17 N.C. App. 680, 195 S.E.2d 141, cert. denied, 283 N.C. 585, 197 S.E.2d 873 (1973).

In order to secure an award under this section, the plaintiff has the burden of showing not only permanent partial disability, but also its degree. Gupton v. Builders Transp., 320 N.C. 38, 357 S.E.2d 674 (1987).

AN EMPLOYEE'S PRESUMPTION OF DISABILITY may not be defeated merely by a return to work. Kisiah v. W.R. Kisiah Plumbing, Inc., 124 N.C. App. 72, 476 S.E.2d 434 (1996).

BURDEN IS ON CLAIMANT TO SHOW PERMANENT PARTIAL DISABILITY. Hall v. Thomason Chevrolet, Inc., 263 N.C. 569, 139 S.E.2d 857 (1965).

AND ALSO ITS DEGREE. See Hall v. Thomason Chevrolet, Inc., 263 N.C. 569, 139 S.E.2d 857 (1965).

PRESUMPTION OF DISABILITY NOT REBUTTED. --Where the parties executed a Form 21 Agreement relieving the employee of the burden of proving his disability, the fact that plaintiff held a job one year before the matter was initially heard was not sufficient to prove that suitable jobs were available to him and that he was capable of getting one. Flores v. Stacy Penny Masonry Co., 134 N.C. App. 452, 518 S.E.2d 200 (1999).

Determination that a plaintiff suffered a fractured wrist was supported by competent evidence and he was properly found entitled to 300 weeks of partial disability payments, as the employer failed to show that the plaintiff was capable of earning his pre-injury wages post-injury since the plaintiff was not in professional football player condition due to his injury; in the future, the defendant was entitled to file a motion with the Commission pursuant to G.S. 97-47 for a modification of the plaintiff's award. Renfro v. Richardson Sports, Ltd. Partners, 172 N.C. App. 176, 616 S.E.2d 317 (2005), cert. denied, 360 N.C. 535, 633 S.E.2d 821 (2006), cert. dismissed, 360 N.C. 535, 633 S.E.2d 821 (2006).

BECAUSE PLAINTIFF'S PRESUMPTION OF POST-INJURY DIMINISHED EARNING CAPACITY WAS ESTABLISHED by plaintiff and unrebutted by defendant, plaintiff was allowed to elect benefits pursuant to this section. Shaw v. UPS, 116 N.C. App. 598, 449 S.E.2d 50 (1994), aff'd per curiam, 342 N.C. 189, 463 S.E.2d 78 (1995).

ENTITLEMENT TO PARTIAL DISABILITY COMPENSATION SHOWN. --Plaintiff, who received temporary total disability benefits under G.S. 97-29 for a compensable heart attack in April, 1979, was properly awarded permanent partial disability under this section on his application under G.S. 97-47 for modification of the prior award following three additional heart attacks, where the Commission found that he had been permanently and totally disabled since June 1981, partially as a result of his compensable heart attack in 1979. Weaver v. Swedish Imports Maintenance, Inc., 80 N.C. App. 432, 343 S.E.2d 205 (1986), modified, 319 N.C. 243, 354 S.E.2d 477 (1987).

Individual who retired from job in which he had 47 years of experience at age 70, and subsequently attempted to return to work but could not obtain comparable employment, was entitled to partial disability compensation based on the difference between his present and former wages, in view of environmental restriction, caused by his occupational disease (COPD), which combined with other factors to limit the scope of his potential employment. Preslar v. Cannon Mills Co., 80 N.C. App. 610, 343 S.E.2d 209 (1986).

Truck driver, who suffered a 7% loss in the visual field of one eye in a job-related accident and was unable thereafter to find work at wages comparable to those he had been earning as a truck driver, was not precluded from receiving benefits under this section merely because he had received some compensation under G.S. 97-31 for a scheduled injury. Gupton v. Builders Transp., 320 N.C. 38, 357 S.E.2d 674 (1987).

The record contained competent evidence to support the plaintiff's temporary partial disability compensation: the Commission's determination that, but for his injury, plaintiff would have received the Panthers contract amount of $ 86,000; its finding that plaintiff was unable to obtain other professional football employment; plaintiff's failure to obtain employment with the Dallas Cowboys; and his three treating physicians' note that a symptomatic disc would contraindicate his playing professional football. Larramore v. Richardson Sports, Ltd., 141 N.C. App. 250, 540 S.E.2d 768 (2000), aff'd, 353 N.C. 520, 546 S.E.2d 87 (2001).

Employee met burden of proving employment at a diminished capacity after a work-related injury by showing employment at a wage lower than pre-injury employment wage and because employer did not prove that the employee was able to earn higher wages, the North Carolina Industrial Commission did not err by finding that the employee was eligible to receive partial disability compensation. Osmond v. Carolina Concrete Specialties, 151 N.C. App. 541, 568 S.E.2d 204 (2002), review denied, 356 N.C. 676, 577 S.E.2d 631 (2003).

Where an employee suffered a general partial disability, but continued to receive the same wages, which amounted to more than the assessable compensation for his injury, he could not receive additional compensation. But to protect the employee against the possibility that the employer might, after the expiration of the time limit specified in G.S. 97-24, discontinue the employment and thus defeat the rights of the employee, the Commission, after finding the existing of the disability, directed that an award issue subject to specified limitations. It directed compensation at the statutory rate "at any time it is shown that the claimant is earning less," etc., during the statutory period

of 300 weeks. By this order the Commission, in effect retained jurisdiction for future adjustments. In so doing it did not exceed its authority. Branham v. Denny Roll & Panel Co., 223 N.C. 233, 25 S.E.2d 865 (1943).

PARTIAL DISABILITY BENEFITS NOT WARRANTED. --An award also containing a provision by which the Commission sought to retain jurisdiction during 300 weeks so that claimant might be paid more compensation if he had a wage loss as a result of his injury within that time was held to be error by the Supreme Court, which said, "There is nothing in the statute . . . that contemplates or authorizes an anticipatory finding by the Commission that a physical impairment may develop into a compensable disability. Neither does the statute vest in the Commission the power to retain jurisdiction of a claim, after compensation has been awarded, merely because some physical impairment suffered by the claimant may, at some time in the future, cause a loss of wages. The Commission is concerned with conditions existing prior to and at the time of the hearing. If such conditions change in the future, to the detriment of the claimant, the statute affords the claimant a remedy and fixes the time within which he must seek it. G.S. 97-47." Dail v. Kellex Corp., 233 N.C. 446, 64 S.E.2d 438 (1951).

In Harris v. Asheville Contracting Co., 240 N.C. 715, 83 S.E.2d 802 (1954), the court again stated that the Commission was without jurisdiction to retain jurisdiction for 300 weeks. Branham v. Denny Roll & Panel Co., 223 N.C. 233, 25 S.E.2d 865 (1943), was distinguished. See also Hill v. DuBose, 234 N.C. 446, 67 S.E.2d 371 (1951); Hill v. DuBose, 237 N.C. 501, 75 S.E.2d 401 (1953).

Workers' compensation claimant was not entitled to compensation under G.S. 97-29 or G.S. 97-30 after a Form 24 was approved as the evidence supported the North Carolina Industrial Commission's determinations that the claimant was capable of returning to full-duty work without restrictions and that she failed in her burden of proving that she remained disabled as a result of the compensable injury where, while there was medical evidence to support a determination that the claimant could not return to full-time work as a flight attendant, this alone was insufficient to establish that she was incapable of earning wages at any job; the claimant's one contact with her employer about a light duty position was insufficient to establish she had made a reasonable effort to obtain employment under the second Russell option. Perkins v. U.S. Airways, 177 N.C. App. 205, 628 S.E.2d 402 (2006), review denied, 361 N.C. 356, 644 S.E.2d 231 (2007).

APPORTIONMENT HELD PROPER. --Where evidence supported the Industrial Commission's conclusion that claimant was totally disabled and that 55 percent of her disability was due to an occupational disease while 45 percent was due to other physical infirmities, it was not error for the Industrial Commission to award claimant compensation for a 55 percent partial disability rather than for total disability. Morrison v. Burlington Indus., 304 N.C. 1, 282 S.E.2d 458 (1981).

Chapter 97

Plaintiff cannot aggregate or combine his or her wages from more than one employment in calculating his or her compensation rate, and thus, for purposes of computing compensation rate where a plaintiff worked two separate jobs at the time of injury, his or her average weekly wages are determined only from the earnings of the employment in which he or she was injured. Tunell v. Res. MFG/Prologistix, 222 N.C. App. 271, 731 S.E.2d 844 (2012).

Since North Carolina statutes and case law do not allow aggregation of wages from concurrent employment in calculating a plaintiff's average weekly wages pursuant to G.S. 97-2(5), by extension, an employer cannot deduct wages earned from concurrent employment in calculating the employer's obligation to pay partial disability compensation pursuant to G.S. 97-30; however, that this holding may not apply in situations where the post-injury employment is found to have been enlarged or used as a substitute for the loss of earnings in the injury producing employment. Tunell v. Res. MFG/Prologistix, 222 N.C. App. 271, 731 S.E.2d 844 (2012).

AGGREGATION OF WAGES NOT ALLOWED. --North Carolina Industrial Commission erred by subtracting an employee's post-injury earnings from a second employer in calculating a first employer's obligation to pay temporary partial disability compensation because the employee's earnings from the second employer were not included in his average weekly wages before his injury; because North Carolina law does not allow aggregation of wages from concurrent employment in calculating a plaintiff's average weekly wages, by extension, an employer cannot deduct wages earned from a concurrent employer in calculating partial disability compensation. Tunell v. Res. MFG/Prologistix, 222 N.C. App. 271, 731 S.E.2d 844 (2012).

EMPLOYER'S FAILURE TO TELL EMPLOYEE ABOUT BENEFITS PROVIDED UNDER THIS SECTION was not sufficient reason to set aside the award where employee-plaintiff entered into an agreement, accepted all the benefits from it, and chose not to contest it until almost two years after entering the agreement. Crump v. Independence Nissan, 112 N.C. App. 587, 436 S.E.2d 589 (1993).

FAILURE OF COMMISSION TO DETERMINE FAIRNESS OF AGREEMENT. --Where an employee suffered a back injury and entered into a compromise settlement agreement with an insurance carrier, the North Carolina Industrial Commission erred by not setting aside the agreement because, inter alia, the Commission failed to undertake a full investigation to determine if the agreement was fair and just since the employee may have been entitled to total disability benefits instead of a scheduled injury or partial disability benefits. Kyle v. Holston Group, 188 N.C. App. 686, 656 S.E.2d 667 (2008), review denied, 362 N.C. 359, 662 S.E.2d 905 (2008).

EXAGGERATED POST-INJURY EARNINGS. --Where plaintiff's hourly wage after he terminated his employment due to lung impairment was less than he had earned; however, his weekly income was approximately the same as pre-injury due to his working more hours post-injury, plaintiff's actual post-injury earnings were exaggerated and were not a reliable indicator of his earning capacity. Harris v. North Am. Prods., 125 N.C. App. 349, 481 S.E.2d 321 (1997).

FACTORS OTHER THAN ACTUAL POST-INJURY EARNINGS may be considered in determining an injured employee's post-injury earning capacity. Harris v. North Am. Prods., 125 N.C. App. 349, 481 S.E.2d 321 (1997).

FAILURE TO MAKE REQUIRED FINDINGS AS TO EARNING CAPACITY. --Industrial commission erred in determining a worker's permanent partial disability rating pursuant to G.S. 97-31; disability was defined by a diminished capacity to earn wages, not by physical infirmity alone, G.S. 97-2(9), and the commission failed to make required findings pursuant to G.S. 97-30 on whether the job offered to the worker by her employer accurately reflected her ability to earn wages. Baker v. Sam's Club, 161 N.C. App. 712, 589 S.E.2d 387 (2003).

North Carolina Industrial Commission erred in awarding an employee temporary partial disability compensation at varying rates not to exceed $442 per week for up to 300 weeks from the date of his injury because the Commission made no findings about the employee's wages or earnings in the years following his injury; while the Commission made a finding of futility, it was related only to the employee's temporary total disability, which began two weeks before August 30, 2001, and its findings of fact did not address the employee's ability to earn wages in fields other than stunt work for the period between October 1993 and July 1999. Barrett v. All Payment Servs., Inc., 201 N.C. App. 522, 686 S.E.2d 920 (2009), review denied 363 N.C. 853, 693 S.E.2d 915, 2010 N.C. LEXIS 260 (2010).

REMAND FOR FINDINGS AS TO WAGE EARNING CAPACITY. --Where plaintiff suffered a permanent disability to her lungs, the Industrial Commission committed error in compensating her under G.S. 97-31, but failing to consider or make findings of fact as to whether her disability affected her wage earning capacity under either G.S. 97-29 or this section, as this prevented plaintiff from electing to recover under either this section or G.S. 97-29, if she was so entitled. Strickland v. Burlington Indus., Inc., 87 N.C. App. 507, 361 S.E.2d 394 (1987).

PSYCHOLOGICAL INJURIES ARE COMPENSABLE, if at all, under G.S. 97-29 or this section and wage-earning capacity is critical to the assessment of a plaintiff's entitlement to benefits under these sections. McLean v. Eaton Corp., 125 N.C. App. 391, 481 S.E.2d 289 (1997).

DISABILITY RELATED TO ASBESTOSIS. --The claimant could not recover compensation for total or partial incapacity to earn wages, both of which require a showing of disablement, where his prior award of 104-weeks compensation for asbestosis did not establish his disablement, but he was entitled to compensation for permanent injury to his lungs.

Davis v. Weyerhaeuser Co., 132 N.C. App. 771, 514 S.E.2d 91 (1999).

CONCEPT OF MAXIMUM MEDICAL IMPROVEMENT IS NOT APPLICABLE TO TEMPORARY DISABILITY PAYMENTS. --Employee's reaching of maximum medical improvement (MMI) did not affect the employee's right to continue to receive temporary disability workers' compensation benefits and MMI did not represent the point in time at which a loss of wage-earning capacity automatically converted from temporary to permanent. Hooker v. Stokes-Reynolds Hospital/North Carolina Baptist Hosp. Inc., 161 N.C. App. 111, 587 S.E.2d 440 (2003).

AWARD FINDING A CLAIMANT TOTALLY DISABLED WAS UPHELD, despite the claimant receiving a tobacco allotment and owning a mobile home park, because the claimant did not perform any physical activity involved with either enterprise, and competent evidence showed that the claimant was unable to (1) walk or stand for any sustained period of time, (2) sleep for more than a few hours at a time because of continuous knee pain, and (3) remain balanced for any length of time. Hensley v. Indus. Maint. Overflow, 166 N.C. App. 413, 601 S.E.2d 893 (2004), cert. denied, 359 N.C. 631, 613 S.E.2d 690 (2005), cert. dismissed, 359 N.C. 631, -- S.E.2d -- (2005).

AWARD SUPPORTED BY THE EVIDENCE. --North Carolina Industrial Commission's finding that an employee retained only minimal earning capacity was supported by the medical and record evidence and accorded to the appellate court's mandate in an earlier remand; the commission properly took judicial notice of the federal minimum wage to conclude that the employee was entitled to $14,181 more under G.S. 97-30 than he was under the Form 26 agreement, and to set the agreement aside and award the employee $14,181. Lewis v. Craven Reg'l Med. Ctr., 174 N.C. App. 561, 621 S.E.2d 259 (2005), cert. denied, -- N.C. --, 629 S.E.2d 853 (2006).

APPLIED in Dowdy v. Fieldcrest Mills, Inc., 308 N.C. 701, 304 S.E.2d 215 (1983); Roper v. J.P. Stevens & Co., 65 N.C. App. 69, 308 S.E.2d 485 (1983); Fleming v. K-Mart Corp., 312 N.C. 538, 324 S.E.2d 214 (1985); Weaver v. Swedish Imports Maintenance, Inc., 319 N.C. 243, 354 S.E.2d 477 (1987); King v. Yeargin Constr. Co., 124 N.C. App. 396, 476 S.E.2d 898 (1996); Trivette v. Mid-South Mgmt., Inc., 154 N.C. App. 140, 571 S.E.2d 692 (2002); Yerby v. N.C. Dep't of Pub. Safety/Division of Juvenile Justice, 246 N.C. App. 182, 782 S.E.2d 545 (2016).

CITED in Honeycutt v. Carolina Asbestos Co., 235 N.C. 471, 70 S.E.2d 426 (1952); Little v. Anson County Schools Food Serv., 295 N.C. 527, 246 S.E.2d 743 (1978); Morrison v. Burlington Indus., 301 N.C. 226, 271 S.E.2d 364 (1980); Gamble v. Borden, Inc., 45 N.C. App. 506, 263 S.E.2d 280 (1980); Smith v. American & Efird Mills, 305 N.C. 507, 290 S.E.2d 634 (1982); Cloutier v. State, 57 N.C. App. 239, 291 S.E.2d 362 (1982); West v. Bladenboro Cotton Mills, Inc., 62 N.C. App. 267, 302 S.E.2d 645 (1983); Dolbow v. Holland Indus., Inc., 64 N.C. App. 695, 308 S.E.2d 335 (1983); Hill v. Hanes Corp., 79 N.C. App. 67, 339 S.E.2d 1 (1986); Whitley v.

Columbia Lumber Mfg. Co., 318 N.C. 89, 348 S.E.2d 336 (1986); Gupton v. Builders Transp., 83 N.C. App. 1, 348 S.E.2d 601 (1986); Heffner v. Cone Mills Corp., 83 N.C. App. 84, 349 S.E.2d 70 (1986); Hill v. Hanes Corp., 319 N.C. 167, 353 S.E.2d 392 (1987); Thomas v. Hanes Printables, 91 N.C. App. 45, 370 S.E.2d 419 (1988); Freeman v. Freeman, 107 N.C. App. 644, 421 S.E.2d 623 (1992); Charlotte-Mecklenburg Hosp. Auth. v. North Carolina Indus. Comm'n, 336 N.C. 200, 443 S.E.2d 716 (1994); McGee v. Estes Express Lines, 125 N.C. App. 298, 480 S.E.2d 416 (1997); Daughtry v. Metric Constr. Co., 115 N.C. App. 354, 446 S.E.2d 590, cert. denied, 338 N.C. 515, 452 S.E.2d 808 (1994); Neal v. Carolina Mgt., 130 N.C. App. 220, 502 S.E.2d 424 (1998), rev'd on other grounds, 350 N.C. 63, 510 S.E.2d 375 (1999); Lanning v. Fieldcrest-Cannon, Inc., 352 N.C. 98, 530 S.E.2d 54 (2000); Lewis v. Sonoco Prods. Co., 137 N.C. App. 61, 526 S.E.2d 671 (2000); Bond v. Foster Masonry, Inc., 139 N.C. App. 123, 532 S.E.2d 583 (2000); Oliver v. Lane Co., 143 N.C. App. 167, 544 S.E.2d 606 (2001); Devlin v. Apple Gold, Inc., 153 N.C. App. 442, 570 S.E.2d 257 (2002); Arnold v. Wal-Mart Stores, 154 N.C. App. 482, 571 S.E.2d 888 (2002); White v. Weyerhaeuser Co., 167 N.C. App. 658, 606 S.E.2d 389 (2005); Smith v. Richardson Sports Ltd. Partners, 168 N.C. App. 410, 608 S.E.2d 342 (2005); Smith v. Richardson Sports Ltd. Partners, 172 N.C. App. 200, 616 S.E.2d 245 (2005), cert. denied, 360 N.C. 536, 633 S.E.2d 824 (2006), cert. dismissed, 360 N.C. 536, 633 S.E.2d 824 (2006); Swift v. Richardson Sports, Inc., -- N.C. App. --, 2005 N.C. App. LEXIS 725 (Apr. 5, 2005); Everett v. N.C. Indus. Comm'n No. 102217 Well Care & Nursing Servs., 180 N.C. App. 314, 636 S.E.2d 824 (2006); Outerbridge v. Perdue Farms, Inc., 181 N.C. App. 50, 638 S.E.2d 564 (2007); Richardson v. Maxim Healthcare/ Allegis Group, 188 N.C. App. 337, 657 S.E.2d 34 (2008), aff'd in part, rev'd in part, 362 N.C. 657, 669 S.E.2d 582 (2008); Kelly v. Duke Univ., 190 N.C. App. 733, 661 S.E.2d 745 (2008), review denied, stay denied, 363 N.C. 128, 675 S.E.2d 367 (2009); Cross v. Falk Integrated Techs., Inc., 190 N.C. App. 274, 661 S.E.2d 249 (2008); Alphin v. Tart L.P. Gas Co., 192 N.C. App. 576, 666 S.E.2d 160 (2008), review denied, 363 N.C. 257, 676 S.E.2d 899 (2009); Wynn v. United Health Services/ Two Rivers Health - Trent Campus, 214 N.C. App. 69, 716 S.E.2d 373 (2011); Keeton v. Circle K, 217 N.C. App. 332, 719 S.E.2d 244 (2011); Falin v. Roberts Co. Field Servs., 245 N.C. App. 144, 782 S.E.2d 75 (2016), review denied, 793 S.E.2d 226, 2016 N.C. LEXIS 837 (2016).

CROSS REFERENCES. --

As to credits, see G.S. 97-42. As to certain State law-enforcement officers, see G.S. 143-166.16.

LEGAL PERIODICALS. --

For comment on the 1943 amendment, which increased the maximum weekly compensation, see 21 N.C.L. Rev. 384 (1943).

For survey of 1978 administrative law, see 57 N.C.L. Rev. 831 (1979).

For comment on Morrison v. Burlington Indus., 304 N.C. 1, 282 S.E.2d 458 (1981), see 4 Campbell L. Rev. 107 (1981).

Chapter 97

For survey, "The North Carolina Workers' Compensation Act of 1994: A Step in the Direction of Restoring Balance," see 73 N.C.L. Rev. 2502 (1995).

For article, "Why Aren't You Working?: Medlin with Proof of Disability Under the North Carolina Workers' Compensation Act," see 38 Campbell L. Rev. 211 (2016).

CHAPTER 105. TAXATION

SUBCHAPTER 01. LEVY OF TAXES

ARTICLE 5A. NORTH CAROLINA HIGHWAY USE TAX

§ 105-187.1. Definitions

(a) The following definitions and the definitions in G.S. 105-164.3 apply to this Article:

(1) **Commissioner. --** The Commissioner of Motor Vehicles.

(2) **Division. --** The Division of Motor Vehicles, Department of Transportation.

(2a) **Limited possession commitment. --** Long-term lease or rental, short-term lease or rental, and vehicle subscriptions.

(3) **Long-term lease or rental. --** A lease or rental made under a written agreement to lease or rent one or more vehicles to the same person for a period of at least 365 continuous days and that is not a vehicle subscription.

(3a) **Park model RV. --** A vehicle that meets all of the following conditions:

a. Is designed and marketed as temporary living quarters for recreational, camping, travel, or seasonal use.

b. Is certified by the manufacturer as complying with ANSI A119.5.

c. Is built on a single chassis mounted on wheels with a gross trailer area not exceeding 400 square feet in the setup mode.

(4) **Recreational vehicle. --** Defined in G.S. 20-4.01. The term also includes a park model RV.

(5) **Rescue squad. --** An organization that provides rescue services, emergency medical services, or both.

(6) **Retailer. --** A retailer as defined in G.S. 105-164.3 who is engaged in the business of selling, leasing, renting, or offering vehicle subscriptions for motor vehicles.

(7) **Short-term lease or rental. --** A lease or rental of a motor vehicle or motor vehicles, including a vehicle sharing service, that is not a long-term lease or rental or a vehicle subscription.

(8) **Vehicle sharing service. --** A service for which a person pays a membership fee for the right to use a motor vehicle or motor vehicles upon payment of an additional time-based or mileage-based fee.

(9) **Vehicle subscription. --** A written agreement that grants a person the right to use and exchange motor vehicles owned, directly or indirectly, by the person offering the agreement upon payment of a subscription fee, but it does not include a vehicle sharing service. The subscription fee must provide a person exclusive use of an agreed-upon number of motor vehicles at any given time during the full term of the subscription.

(b) This section does not apply to Chapter 20 of the General Statutes, including the licensing requirements, restrictions, limitations, and prohibitions on unfair methods of competition contained in Article 12 of that Chapter.

History.

1989, c. 692, s. 4.1; 1991, c. 79, s. 4; 2000-173, s. 10(a); 2001-424, s. 34.24(e); 2001-497, s. 2(b); 2002-72, s. 19(a); 2016-5, s. 3.19(a); 2019-69, s. 1

EDITOR'S NOTE. --

Session Laws 2003-383, s. 4, provides: "The General Assembly reaffirms its intent that the proceeds of the issuance of any bonds pursuant to the Highway Bond Act of 1996, Chapter 590 of the 1995 Session Laws, shall be used only for the purposes stated in that act, and for no other purpose."

The section as amended by Session Laws 2016-5, s. 3.19(a), added the definition of "Park model RV" and designated it as subdivision (4), redesignating former subdivisions (4) through (7) as subdivisions (5) through (8), respectively. The definition of "Park model RV" has been redesignated as subdivision (3a), and the subsequent definitions have retained their former designations, at the direction of the Revisor of Statutes.

Subdivision (a)(2a) was added by Session Laws 2019-69, s. 1, as subdivision (a)(3c), and was redesignated at the direction of the Revisor of Statutes to maintain alphabetical order.

Session Laws 2019-69, s. 6, made the amendment to this section by Session Laws 2019-69, s. 1, effective October 1, 2019, and applicable to vehicle subscription agreements entered into on or after that date.

EFFECT OF AMENDMENTS. --

Session Laws 2016-5, s. 3.19(a), effective May 11, 2016, added the definition of "Park model RV"; and added the last sentence in subdivision (4).

Session Laws 2019-69, s. 1, designated the previously existing provisions as subsection (a); substituted "one or more vehicles" for "property" and "days and that is not a vehicle subscription" for "days" in subdivision (a)(3); and added subdivisions (a)(3c), (a)(6) through (a)(9), and subsection (b). For effective date and applicability, see editor's note.

§ 105-187.2. Highway use tax imposed

A tax is imposed on the privilege of using the highways of this State. This tax is in addition to all other taxes and fees imposed.

History.

1989, c. 692, s. 4.1

§ 105-187.3. Rate of tax

(a) **Tax Base.** -- The tax imposed by this Article is applied to the sum of the retail value of a motor vehicle for which a certificate of title is issued and any fee regulated by G.S. 20-101.1. The tax does not apply to the sales price of a service contract, provided the charge is separately stated on the bill of sale or other similar document given to the purchaser at the time of the sale.

(a1) **Tax Rate.** -- The tax rate is three percent (3%). The maximum tax is two thousand dollars ($ 2,000) for each certificate of title issued for a Class A or Class B motor vehicle that is a commercial motor vehicle, as defined in G.S. 20-4.01, and for each certificate of title issued for a recreational vehicle. The tax is payable as provided in G.S. 105-187.4.

(b) **Retail Value.** -- The retail value of a motor vehicle for which a certificate of title is issued because of a sale of the motor vehicle by a retailer is the sales price of the motor vehicle, including all accessories attached to the vehicle when it is delivered to the purchaser, less the amount of any allowance given by the retailer for a motor vehicle taken in trade as a full or partial payment for the purchased motor vehicle.

The retail value of a motor vehicle for which a certificate of title is issued because of a sale of the motor vehicle by a seller who is not a retailer is the market value of the vehicle, less the amount of any allowance given by the seller for a motor vehicle taken in trade as a full or partial payment for the purchased motor vehicle. A transaction in which two parties exchange motor vehicles is considered a sale regardless of whether either party gives additional consideration as part of the transaction.

The retail value of a motor vehicle for which a certificate of title is issued because of a reason other than the sale of the motor vehicle is the market value of the vehicle. The market value of a vehicle is presumed to be the value of the vehicle set in a schedule of values adopted by the Commissioner.

The retail value of a vehicle for which a certificate of title is issued because of a transfer by a State agency that assists the United States Department of Defense with purchasing, transferring, or titling a vehicle to another State agency, a unit of local government, a volunteer fire department, or a volunteer rescue squad is the sales price paid by the State agency, unit of local government, volunteer fire department, or volunteer rescue squad.

(c) **Schedules.** -- In adopting a schedule of values for motor vehicles, the Commissioner shall adopt a schedule whose values do not exceed the wholesale values of motor vehicles as published in a recognized automotive reference manual.

History.

1989, c. 692, ss. 4.1, 4.2; c. 770, s. 74.13; 1993, c. 467, s. 3; 1995, c. 349, s. 1; c. 390, s. 30; 2001-424, s. 34.24(a); 2001-497, s. 2(a); 2009-550, s. 2(e); 2010-95, s. 5; 2013-360, s. 34.29(a); 2013-363, s. 8.1; 2014-3, s. 6.1(g); 2014-39, s. 3; 2015-241, s. 29.34A(a); 2015-259, s. 5(d); 2015-268, s. 10.1(d)

EDITOR'S NOTE. --

Session Laws 2013-360, s. 1.1, provides: "This act shall be known as the 'Current Operations and Capital Improvements Appropriations Act of 2013.'"

Session Laws 2013-360, s. 38.5 is a severability clause.

Session Laws 2013-363, s. 8.1, amended Session Laws 2013-360, s. 34.29(b), by changing the effective date of the amendment to subsection (a) of this section by Session Laws 2013-360, s. 34.29(a), to July 1, 2014.

Session Laws 2014-3, s. 6.1(g), and Session Laws 2014-39, s. 3, both amended subsection (a) of this section in the coded bill drafting format provided by G.S. 120-20.1. However, the amendment by Session Laws 2014-3, s. 6.1(g) did not account for the changes made by Session Laws 2014-39, s. 3, and the section has been set out in the form above at the direction of the Revisor of Statutes.

Session Laws 2015-241, s. 29.34A(c), as amended by Session Laws 2015-268, s. 10.1(d), provides: "This section becomes effective January 1, 2016, and applies to sales made on or after that date, or, for purposes of G.S. 105-187.5, a lease or rental agreement entered into on or after that date."

Session Laws 2015-241, s. 1.1, provides: "This act shall be known as 'The Current Operations and Capital Improvements Appropriations Act of 2015.'"

Session Laws 2015-241, s. 33.6, is a severability clause.

Session Laws 2015-259, s. 5(f), provides: "This section becomes effective March 1, 2016, and applies to service contracts purchased on or after date, if House Bill 97 of the 2015 Regular Session of the General Assembly is enacted." House Bill 97 was enacted as Session Laws 2015-241.

Session Laws 2016-94, s. 38.5(a), provides: "A retailer is not liable for an undercollection of sales or use tax as a result of the changes made under Section 32.18 of S.L. 2015-241 and under Part V of S.L. 2015-259 if the retailer made a good-faith effort to comply with the law and collect the proper amount of tax. This applies only to the period beginning March 1, 2016, and ending December 31, 2016."

Session Laws 2016-94, s. 1.2, provides: "This act shall be known as the 'Current Operations and Capital Improvements Appropriations Act of 2016.'"

Session Laws 2016-94, s. 39.4, provides: "Except for statutory changes or other provisions that clearly indicate an intention to have effects beyond the 2016-2017 fiscal year, the textual provisions of this act apply only to funds appropriated for, and activities occurring during, the 2016-2017 fiscal year."

Session Laws 2016-94, s. 39.7, is a severability clause.

EFFECT OF AMENDMENTS. --

Session Laws 2009-550, s. 2(e), effective August 28, 2009, added subsection (b1).

Session Laws 2010-95, s. 5, effective July 17, 2010, subdivided former subsection (b) into three paragraphs; and redesignated former subsection (b1) as the present fourth paragraph of subsection (b) by deleting the subsection (b1) designation and the subsection head, which read: "Retail Value of Transferred Department of Defense Vehicles."

Session Laws 2013-360, s. 34.29(a), as amended by Session Laws 2013-363, s. 8.1, effective July 1, 2014, rewrote subsection (a).

Session Laws 2014-3, s. 6.1(g), effective October 1, 2014, rewrote former subsection (a) as present subsections (a) and (a1). See Editor's note for applicability.

Session Laws 2015-241, s. 29.34A(a), effective January 1, 2016, rewrote subsection (a1). For applicability, see editor's note.

Session Laws 2015-259, s. 5(d), in subsection (a), added "provided the charge is separately stated on the bill of sale or other similar document given to the purchaser at the time of the sale" at the end of the last sentence, and deleted the former last sentence, which read: "The sales price of a service contract is subject to the sales tax imposed under Article 5 of this Chapter." For effective date and applicability, see editor's note.

§ 105-187.4. Payment of tax

(a) **Method.** -- The tax imposed by this Article must be paid to the Commissioner when applying for a certificate of title for a motor vehicle. The Commissioner may not issue a certificate of title for a vehicle until the tax imposed by this Article has been paid. The tax may be paid in cash or by check.

(b) **Sale by Retailer.** -- When a certificate of title for a motor vehicle is issued because of a sale of the motor vehicle by a retailer, the applicant for the certificate of title must attach a copy of the bill of sale for the motor vehicle to the application. A retailer who sells a motor vehicle may collect from the purchaser of the vehicle the tax payable upon the issuance of a certificate of title for the vehicle, apply for a certificate of title on behalf of the purchaser, and remit the tax due on behalf of the purchaser. If a check submitted by a retailer in payment of taxes collected under this section is not honored by the financial institution upon which it is drawn because the retailer's account did not have sufficient funds to pay the check or the retailer did not have an account at the institution, the Division may suspend or revoke the license issued to the retailer under Article 12 of Chapter 20 of the General Statutes.

History.
1989, c. 692, s. 4.1; 1991, c. 193, s. 1

§ 105-187.5. Alternate tax for a limited possession commitment

(a) **Election.** -- A retailer may elect not to pay the tax imposed by this Article at the rate set in G.S. 105-187.3 when applying for a certificate of title for a motor vehicle purchased by the retailer for a limited possession commitment. A retailer who makes this election shall pay a tax on the gross receipts of the limited possession commitment of the vehicle. The portion of a limited possession commitment billing or payment that represents any amount applicable to the sales price of a service contract as defined in G.S. 105-164.3 should not be included in the gross receipts subject to the tax imposed by this Article. The charge must be separately stated on documentation given to the purchaser at the time the limited possession commitment goes into effect, or on the monthly billing statement or other documentation given to the purchaser. When a limited possession commitment is sold to another retailer, the seller of the limited possession commitment should provide to the purchaser of the limited possession commitment the documentation showing that the service contract and applicable sales taxes were separately stated at the time the limited possession commitment went into effect and the new retailer must retain the information to support an allocation for tax computed on the gross receipts subject to highway use tax. Like the tax imposed by G.S. 105-187.3, this alternate tax is a tax on the privilege of using the highways of this State. The tax is imposed on a retailer, but is to be added to the limited possession commitment of a motor vehicle and thereby be paid by the person who enters into a limited possession commitment with a retailer.

(b) **Rate.** -- The applicable tax rates on the gross receipts from a limited possession commitment are as listed in this subsection. Gross receipts does not include the amount of any allowance given for a motor vehicle taken in trade as a partial payment on the limited possession commitment. The maximum tax in G.S. 105-187.3(a1) on certain motor vehicles applies to a continuous limited possession commitment of such a motor vehicle to the same person. The applicable tax rates are as follows:

Type of Limited Possession Commitment	Tax Rate
Short-term lease or rental	8%
Vehicle subscription	5%
Long-term lease or rental	3%

(c) **Method.** -- A retailer who elects to pay tax on the gross receipts of the limited possession commitment of a motor vehicle shall make this election when applying for a certificate of title for the vehicle. To make the election, the retailer shall complete a form provided by the Division giving information needed to collect the alternate tax based on gross receipts. Once made, an election is irrevocable.

(d) **Administration.** -- The Division shall notify the Secretary of Revenue of a retailer who makes the election under this section. A retailer who makes this election shall report and remit to the Secretary the tax on the gross receipts of the limited possession commitment of the motor vehicle. The Secretary shall administer the tax imposed by this section on gross receipts in the same manner as the tax levied under G.S. 105-164.4(a)(2). The administrative provisions and powers of the Secretary that apply to the tax levied under G.S. 105-164.4(a)(2) apply to the tax imposed by this section. In addition, the Division may request the Secretary to audit a retailer who elects to pay tax on gross receipts under this section. When the Secretary conducts an audit at the request of the Division, the Division shall reimburse the Secretary for the cost of the audit, as determined by the Secretary. In conducting an audit of a retailer under this section, the Secretary may audit any sales of motor vehicles made by the retailer.

History.

1989, c. 692, s. 4.1; 1991, c. 79, s. 5; c. 193, s. 3; 1995, c. 410, s. 1; 2000-173, s. 10(b); 2001-424, s. 34.24(b); 2001-497, s. 2(c); 2014-3, s. 6.1(h); 2015-259, s. 5(e); 2016-92, s. 2.7; 2016-94, s. 38.5(k); 2019-69, s. 2

EDITOR'S NOTE. --

Session Laws 2015-259, s. 5(f), provides: "This section becomes effective March 1, 2016, and applies to service contracts purchased on or after date, if House Bill 97 of the 2015 Regular Session of the General Assembly is enacted." House Bill 97 was enacted as Session Laws 2015-241.

Session Laws 2016-94, s. 38.5(a), provides: "A retailer is not liable for an undercollection of sales or use tax as a result of the changes made under Section 32.18 of S.L. 2015-241 and under Part V of S.L. 2015-259 if the retailer made a good-faith effort to comply with the law and collect the proper amount of tax. This applies only to the period beginning March 1, 2016, and ending December 31, 2016."

Session Laws 2015-94, s. 38.5 (*l*), provides: "The Department of Revenue must issue written guidance on the implementation of the sales tax changes imposed by this act by November 15, 2016."

Session Laws 2016-94, s. 38.5(q) made the amendments to this section by Session Laws 2016-94, s. 38.5(k), applicable to sales made on or after January 1, 2017.

Session Laws 2016-94, s. 1.2, provides: "This act shall be known as the 'Current Operations and Capital Improvements Appropriations Act of 2016.'"

Session Laws 2016-94, s. 39.4, provides: "Except for statutory changes or other provisions that clearly indicate an intention to have effects beyond the 2016-2017 fiscal year, the textual provisions of this act apply only to funds appropriated for, and activities occurring during, the 2016-2017 fiscal year."

Session Laws 2016-94, s. 39.7, is a severability clause.

Session Laws 2019-69, s. 6, made the amendment to this section by Session Laws 2019-69, s. 2, effective October 1, 2019, and applicable to vehicle subscription agreements entered into on or after that date.

EFFECT OF AMENDMENTS. --

Session Laws 2014-3, s. 6.1(h), effective October 1, 2014, inserted the third and fourth sentences in subsection (a). See Editor's note for applicability.

Session Laws 2015-259, s. 5(e), rewrote subsection (a). For effective date and applicability, see Editor's note.

Session Laws 2016-92, s. 2.7, effective July 11, 2016, substituted "G.S. 105-187.3(a1)" for "G.S. 105-187.3(a)" in the last sentence of subsection (b).

Session Laws 2016-94, s. 38.5(k), effective January 1, 2017, in subsection (a), substituted "charge must" for "charge should" in the fourth sentence, deleted the former fifth sentence, which read: "Where a retailer fails to separately state any portion of a lease or rental billing or payment that represents an amount applicable to the sale price of a service contract, the amount is deemed to be part of the gross receipts of a lease or rental of a vehicle," and added the present fifth sentence; and substituted "G.S. 105-187.3(a1)" for "G.S. 105-187.3(a)" in the last sentence of subsection (b). See editor's note for applicability.

Session Laws 2019-69, s. 2, rewrote the section heading, which formerly read "Alternate tax for those who rent or lease motor vehicles"; substituted "limited possession commitment" for "lease or rental" throughout the section; substituted "enters into a limited possession commitment with a retailer" for "leases or rents the vehicle" in the last sentence of subsection (a); and, in subsection (b), rewrote the first sentence and added the last sentence. For effective date and applicablity, see editor's note.

§ 105-187.6. Exemptions from highway use tax

(a) **Full Exemptions.** -- The tax imposed by this Article does not apply when a certificate of title is issued as the result of a transfer of a motor vehicle:

(1) To (i) the insurer of the motor vehicle under G.S. 20-109.1 because the vehicle is a salvage vehicle or (ii) a used motor vehicle dealer under G.S. 20-109.1 because the vehicle is a salvage vehicle that was abandoned.

(2) To either a manufacturer, as defined in G.S. 20-286, or a motor vehicle retailer for the purpose of resale.

(3) To the same owner to reflect a change or correction in the owner's name.

(3a) To one or more of the same co-owners to reflect the removal of one or more other co-owners, when there is no consideration for the transfer.

(4) By will or intestacy.

(5) By a gift between a husband and wife, a parent and child, or a stepparent and a stepchild.

(6) By a distribution of marital or divisible property incident to a marital separation or divorce.

(7) Repealed by Session Laws 2009-445, s. 16, effective August 7, 2009.

(8) To a local board of education for use in the driver education program of a public school when the motor vehicle is transferred:

    a. By a retailer and is to be transferred back to the retailer within 300 days after the transfer to the local board.

    b. By a local board of education.

(9) To a volunteer fire department or volunteer rescue squad that is not part of a unit of local government, has no more than two paid employees, and is exempt from State income tax under G.S. 105-130.11, when the motor vehicle is one of the following:

    a. A fire truck, a pump truck, a tanker truck, or a ladder truck used to suppress fire.

    b. A four-wheel drive vehicle intended to be mounted with a water tank and hose and used for forest fire fighting.

    c. An emergency services vehicle.

(10) To a State agency from a unit of local government, volunteer fire department, or volunteer rescue squad to enable the State agency to transfer the vehicle to another unit of local government, volunteer fire department, or volunteer rescue squad.

(11) To a revocable trust from an owner who is the sole beneficiary of the trust.

(12) To a charitable organization operating under section 501(c)(3) of the Internal Revenue Code (26 U.S.C. § 501(c)(3)) where the vehicle was donated to the charitable organization solely for purposes of resale by the charitable organization.

(b) **Partial Exemptions.** -- A maximum tax of forty dollars ($ 40.00) applies when a certificate of title is issued as the result of a transfer of a motor vehicle:

(1) To a secured party who has a perfected security interest in the motor vehicle.

(2) To a partnership, limited liability company, corporation, trust, or other person where no gain or loss arises on the transfer of the motor vehicle under section 351 or section 721 of the Code, or because the transfer is treated under the Code as being to an entity that is not a separate entity from its owner or whose separate existence is otherwise disregarded, or to a partnership, limited liability company, or corporation by merger, conversion, or consolidation in accordance with applicable law.

(c) **Out-of-state Vehicles.** -- A maximum tax of two hundred fifty dollars ($ 250.00) applies when a certificate of title is issued for a motor vehicle that, at the time of applying for a certificate of title, is and has been titled in the name of the owner of the motor vehicle in another state for at least 90 days prior to the date of application for a certificate of title in this State.

(d) **Exemption Limitation.** -- The full exemptions set out in subsection (a) of this section, except for those set out in subdivisions (1), (2), (9), and (10) of subsection (a) of this section, do not apply to a certificate of title issued for a motor vehicle titled in another state at the time of the transfer. The partial exemptions set out in subsection (b) of this section do not apply to a certificate of title issued for a motor vehicle titled in another state at the time of the transfer.

History.

1989, c. 692, s. 4.1; c. 770, ss. 74.9, 74.10; 1991, c. 193, s. 4; c. 689, s. 323; 1993, c. 467, s. 1; 1995, c. 390, s. 31; 1997-443, s. 11A.118(a); 1998-98, s. 15.1; 1999-369, s. 5.9; 2000-140, s. 68; 2001-387, s. 151; 2001-424, s. 34.24(d); 2001-487, s. 68; 2009-81, s. 2; 2009-445, s. 16; 2010-95, s. 6; 2013-400, s. 6; 2015-241, ss. 29.34(a), 29.34A(b); 2015-268, s. 10.1(d); 2017-69, s. 1; 2018-43, s. 5

EDITOR'S NOTE. --

Session Laws 2015-241, s. 29.34A(c), as amended by Session Laws 2015-268, s. 10.1(d), provides: "This section becomes effective January 1, 2016, and applies to sales made on or after that date, or, for purposes of G.S. 105-187.5, a lease or rental agreement entered into on or after that date."

EFFECT OF AMENDMENTS. --

Session Laws 2009-81, s. 2, effective June 11, 2009, added subdivision (a)(10).

Session Laws 2009-445, s. 16, effective August 7, 2009, deleted subdivision (a)(7), which read: "To a handicapped person from the Department of Health and Human Services after the vehicle has been equipped by the Department for use by the handicapped."

Session Laws 2010-95, s. 6, effective July 17, 2010, added subdivision (a)(11).

Session Laws 2013-400, s. 6, effective October 1, 2013, in subdivision (a)(1), inserted "(i)" and added "or (ii) a used motor vehicle dealer under G.S. 20-109.1 because the vehicle is a salvage vehicle that was abandoned."

Session Laws 2015-241, s. 29.34(a), effective September 30, 2015, in subsection (c), inserted "in the name of the owner of the motor vehicle" and added

Chapter 105

"prior to the date of application for a certificate of title in this State."

Session Laws 2015-241, s. 29.34A(b), substituted "tax of two hundred fifty dollars ($250.00)" for "tax of one hundred fifty dollars ($150.00)." in subsection (c). For effective date and applicability, see Editor's note.

Session Laws 2017-69, s. 1, effective June 28, 2017, added subsection (d).

Session Laws 2018-43, s. 5, effective June 22, 2018, added subdivision (a)(12).

§ 105-187.7. Credits

(a) **Tax Paid in Another State.** -- A person who, within 90 days before applying for a certificate of title for a motor vehicle on which the tax imposed by this Article is due, has paid a sales tax, an excise tax, or a tax substantially equivalent to the tax imposed by this Article on the vehicle to a taxing jurisdiction outside this State is allowed a credit against the tax due under this Article for the amount of tax paid to the other jurisdiction.

(b) **Tax Paid Within One Year.** -- A person who applies for a certificate of title for a motor vehicle that is titled in another state but was formerly titled in this State is allowed a credit against the tax due under this Article for the amount of tax paid under this Article by that person on the same vehicle within one year before the application for a certificate of title.

History.
1989, c. 692, s. 4.1; 1995, c. 390, s. 32; c. 512, s. 1

§ 105-187.8. Refund for return of purchased motor vehicle

When a purchaser of a motor vehicle returns the motor vehicle to the seller of the motor vehicle within 90 days after the purchase and receives a vehicle replacement for the returned vehicle or a refund of the price paid the seller, whether from the seller or the manufacturer of the vehicle, the purchaser may obtain a refund of the privilege tax paid on the certificate of title issued for the returned motor vehicle.

To obtain a refund, the purchaser must apply to the Division for a refund within 30 days after receiving the replacement vehicle or refund of the purchase price. The application must be made on a form prescribed by the Commission and must be supported by documentation from the seller of the returned vehicle.

History.
1989, c. 692, s. 4.1; 1995, c. 390, s. 33

§ 105-187.9. Disposition of tax proceeds

(a) **Distribution.** -- Of the taxes collected under this Article at the rate of five percent (5%)

and eight percent (8%), the sum of ten million dollars ($ 10,000,000) shall be credited annually to the Highway Fund, and the remainder shall be credited to the General Fund. Taxes collected under this Article at the rate of three percent (3%) shall be credited to the North Carolina Highway Trust Fund.

(b) Repealed by Session Laws 2010-31, s. 28.7(i), and Session Laws 2013-183, s. 4.1, effective July 1, 2013.

(c) Repealed by Session Laws 2013-183, s. 4.1, effective July 1, 2013.

History.
1989, c. 692, s. 4.1; c. 799, s. 33; 1993, c. 321, s. 164(a); 2001-424, s. 34.24(c); 2001-513, s. 15; 2008-107, s. 25.5(a), (c), (e); 2010-31, s. 28.7(f), (h)-(j); 2011-145, ss. 28.33(c), (d); 2011-391, s. 57; 2012-142, s. 24.8(b); 2013-183, s. 4.1; 2017-57, s. 2.2(f); 2019-69, s. 3

EDITOR'S NOTE. --
Session Laws 2013-183, s. 7.1(b), provided: "This act is effective only if the General Assembly appropriates funds in the Current Operations and Capital Improvements Appropriations Act of 2013 to implement this act." Session Laws 2013-360, s. 34.30, effective July 1, 2013, repealed Session Laws 2013-183, s. 7.1(b).

Session Laws 2017-57, s. 2.2(g), made the amendment to subsection (a) of this section by Session Laws 2017-57, s. 2.2(f), effective June 28, 2017, and applicable to taxes collected on or after that date.

Session Laws 2017-57, s. 1.1, provides: "This act shall be known as the 'Current Operations Appropriations Act of 2017.'"

Session Laws 2017-57, s. 39.6, is a severability clause.

Session Laws 2019-69, s. 6, made the amendment to this section by Session Laws 2019-69, s. 3, effective October 1, 2019, and applicable to vehicle subscription agreements entered into on or after that date.

EFFECT OF AMENDMENTS. --
Session Laws 2008-107, s. 25.5(a), effective July 1, 2008, substituted "forty-five million dollars ($145,000,000)" for "seventy million dollars ($170,000,000)" in subdivision (b)(1).

Session Laws 2008-107, s. 25.5(c), effective July 1, 2009, substituted "one hundred six million dollars ($106,000,000)" for "one hundred forty-five million dollars ($145,000,000)" in subdivision (b)(1).

Session Laws 2008-107, s. 25.5(e), effective July 1, 2010, substituted "seventy-one million dollars ($71,000,000)" for "one hundred six million dollars ($106,000,000)" in subdivision (b)(1).

Session Laws 2010-31, s. 28.7(f), effective July 1, 2011, in the introductory paragraph of subsection (b), substituted "General Fund Transfer" for "Transfer" and made a minor punctuation change; in subdivision (b)(1), substituted "forty million dollars ($40,000,000)" for "seventy-one million dollars ($71,000,000)"; and added subsection (c).

Session Laws 2010-31, s. 28.7(h), effective July 1, 2012, in subdivision (b)(1), substituted "twenty-six million dollars ($26,000,000)" for "forty million dollars ($40,000,000)"; and in subsection (c), substituted "forty-five million dollars ($45,000,000)" for "thirty-one million dollars ($31,000,000)."

Session Laws 2010-31, s. 28.7(i), (j), effective July 1, 2013, deleted subsection (b), relating to "General Land Transfers"; and substituted "fifty-eight million dollars ($58,000,000)" for "forty-five million dollars ($45,000,000)" in the first sentence of subsection (c).

Session Laws 2013-183, s. 4.1, effective July 1, 2013, deleted subsections (b) and (c), which pertained to general fund transfer and mobility fund transfer, respectively.

Session Laws 2017-57, s. 2.2(f), in subsection (a), in the first sentence, substituted "Of the taxes collected" for "Taxes collected" at the beginning, and inserted ", the sum of ten million dollars ($10,000,000) shall be credited annually to the Highway Fund, and the remainder" near the middle. For effective date and applicability, see editor's note.

Session Laws 2019-69, s. 3, inserted "five percent (5%) and" in subsection (a). For effective date and applicability, see editor's note.

TRANSFER FROM TRUST FUND TO GENERAL FUND. --Because one of the objects of the North Carolina Highway Trust Fund is to supplement the State's General Fund, use of the Trust Fund monies for this purpose cannot be viewed as a "raid" of the Trust Fund for purposes not previously sanctioned by the General Assembly; the Trust Fund lacks the indicia of a trust, the language creating the Trust Fund is ambiguous concerning whether the Trust Fund was intended to be a "true" trust fund because G.S. 136-176 merely states that a special account is created within the State treasury, not a trust fund, the Trust Fund is not constitutionally protected, and G.S. 105-187.9 evinces the intention of the General Assembly to use part of the Trust Fund money to supplement the General Fund. Goldston v. State, 199 N.C. App. 618, 683 S.E.2d 237 (2009), review denied, 363 N.C. 802, 690 S.E.2d 536 (2010).

STATUTORY TRANSFER OF MONEY BY THE GENERAL ASSEMBLY FROM THE NORTH CAROLINA HIGHWAY TRUST FUND TO THE STATE'S GENERAL FUND WAS APPROPRIATE; an Executive Order was read to refer to the General Assembly and the Governor in proclamations as the appropriate bodies to make adjustments, and that action was consistent with the text of the Constitution with regard to the manner in which public money was spent; the Current Operations and Capital Improvements Appropriations Act of 2001, the historical practice that led up to the adoption of N.C. Const., Art. III, § 5, and the legislative history of the money involved. Goldston v. State, 199 N.C. App. 618, 683 S.E.2d 237 (2009), review denied, 363 N.C. 802, 690 S.E.2d 536 (2010).

§ 105-187.10. Penalties and remedies

(a) **Penalties.** -- The penalty for bad checks in G.S. 105-236(1) applies to a check offered in payment of the tax imposed by this Article.

In addition, if a check offered to the Division in payment of the tax imposed by this Article is returned unpaid and the tax for which the check was offered, plus the penalty imposed under G.S. 105-236(1), is not paid within 30 days after the Commissioner demands its payment, the Commissioner may revoke the registration plate of the vehicle for which a certificate of title was issued when the check was offered.

(b) **Unpaid Taxes.** -- The remedies for collection of taxes in Article 9 of this Chapter apply to the taxes levied by this Article and collected by the Commissioner. In applying these remedies, the Commissioner has the same authority as the Secretary.

(c) **Appeals.** -- A taxpayer who disagrees with the presumed value of a motor vehicle must pay the tax based on the presumed value, but may appeal the value to the Commissioner. A taxpayer who appeals the value must provide two estimates of the value of the vehicle to the Commissioner. If the Commissioner finds that the value of the vehicle is less than the presumed value of the vehicle, the Commissioner shall refund any overpayment of tax made by the taxpayer with interest at the rate specified in G.S. 105-241.21 from the date of the overpayment.

History.
1989, c. 692, s. 4.1; c. 770, s. 74.8; 2007-491, ss. 21, 44(1)b

EDITOR'S NOTE. --
Session Laws 2007-491, s. 47, provides: "G.S. 105-241.10, as enacted by Section 1 of this act, and Sections 6, 15, 16, 17, and 22 are effective for taxable years beginning on or after January 1, 2007. Section 14 is effective for taxable years beginning on or after January 1, 2008. Sections 45, 46, and 47 are effective when they become law. The remainder of this act becomes effective January 1, 2008. The procedures for review of disputed tax matters enacted by this act apply to assessments of tax that are not final as of the effective date of this act and to claims for refund pending on or filed on or after the effective date of this act. This act does not affect matters for which a petition for review was filed with the Tax Review Board under G.S. 105-241.2 [repealed] before the effective date of this act. The repeal of G.S. 105-122(c) and G.S. 105-130.4(t) and Sections 11 and 12 apply to requests for alternative apportionment formulas filed on or after the effective date of this act. A petition filed with the Tax Review Board for an apportionment formula before the effective date of this act is considered a request under G.S. 105-122(c1) or G.S. 105-130.4(t1), as appropriate."

EFFECT OF AMENDMENTS. --
Session Laws 2007-491, ss. 21, 44(1)b., effective January 1, 2008, in subsection (b), substituted "Article 9 of this Chapter" for "G.S. 20-99" in the first sentence, and added the last sentence; and in subsection (c), substituted "G.S. 105-241.21" for "G.S. 105-241.1"

in the last sentence. For applicability, see Editor's note.

N.C. Gen. Stat. § 105-187.11

Repealed by Session Laws 2007-527, s. 30, effective August 31, 2007.

ARTICLE 9.
GENERAL ADMINISTRATION; PENALTIES AND REMEDIES

§ 105-269.3. Enforcement of Subchapter V and fuel inspection tax

The State Highway Patrol and law enforcement officers and other appropriate personnel in the Department of Public Safety may assist the Department of Revenue in enforcing Subchapter V of this Chapter and Article 3 of Chapter 119 of the General Statutes. The State Highway Patrol and law enforcement officers of the Department of Public Safety have the power of peace officers in matters concerning the enforcement of Subchapter V of this Chapter and Article 3 of Chapter 119 of the General Statutes.

History.
1963, c. 1169, s. 6; 1991, c. 42, s. 16; 1991 (Reg. Sess., 1992), c. 1007, s. 17; 1993, c. 485, s. 15; 1993 (Reg. Sess., 1994), c. 745, s. 19; 2002-159, s. 31.5(b); 2002-190, s. 2; 2011-145, s. 19.1(g)

EDITOR'S NOTE. --
Session Laws 2002-190, s. 17, provides: "The Governor shall resolve any dispute between the Department of Transportation and the Department of Crime Control and Public Safety [now Department of Public Safety] concerning the implementation of this act."

EFFECT OF AMENDMENTS. --
Session Laws 2002-190, s. 2, as amended by Session Laws 2002-159, s. 31.5(b), effective January 1, 2003, substituted "Department of Crime Control and Public Safety" for "Division of Motor Vehicles of the Department of Transportation" in the first sentence and for "Division of Motor Vehicles" in the second sentence.
Session Laws 2011-145, s. 19.1(g), effective January 1, 2012, substituted "Public Safety" for "Crime Control and Public Safety" in the first and last sentences.

SUBCHAPTER 02.
LISTING, APPRAISAL, AND ASSESSMENT OF PROPERTY AND COLLECTION OF TAXES ON PROPERTY

ARTICLE 18.
REPORTS IN AID OF LISTING

N.C. Gen. Stat. § 105-314

Repealed by Session Laws 1993, c. 761, s. 37.4.

ARTICLE 22A.
MOTOR VEHICLES

§ 105-330. Definitions

The following definitions apply in this Article:
(1) **Classified motor vehicle.** -- A motor vehicle classified under this Article.
(1a) **Collecting authority.** -- The Division of Motor Vehicles or an agent contracting with the Division of Motor Vehicles.
(2) **Motor vehicle.** -- Defined in G.S. 20-4.01(23).
(2a) **Municipal corporation.** -- Defined in G.S. 105-273(11).
(3) **Public service company.** -- Defined in G.S. 105-333(14).
(4) **Registered classified motor vehicle.** -- Any of the following:
a. A classified motor vehicle that has a registration plate issued under Article 3 of Chapter 20 of the General Statutes and whose registration is current.
b. A classified motor vehicle transferred to an owner who has applied for a registration plate for the motor vehicle.
(5) **Registration fees.** -- Fees set out in G.S. 20-87 and G.S. 20-88.
(6) **Unregistered classified motor vehicle.** -- A classified motor vehicle that is not a registered classified motor vehicle.

History.
1991, c. 624, s. 1; 2005-294, s. 1; 2006-259, s. 31.5; 2007-527, s. 22(b); 2008-134, s. 65; 2009-445, s. 24(a); 2010-95, s. 22(c); 2011-330, s. 42(a); 2012-79, s. 3.6; 2013-414, s. 70(b), (d)

EDITOR'S NOTE. --
Subdivisions (3) and (4), as added by Session Laws 2005-294, s. 1, were redesignated as subdivisions (1a) and (2a) at the direction of the Revisor of Statutes to maintain alphabetical order.
Session Laws 2005-294, s. 13, as amended by Session Laws 2006-259, s. 31.5, as amended by Session Laws 2007-527, s. 22(b), as amended by Session Laws 2008-134, s. 65, as amended by Session Laws 2012-79, s. 3.6, and as amended by Session Laws 2013-414, s. 70(d), provides: "Sections 4 and 8 of this act become effective January 1, 2006. Sections 1, 2, 3, 5, 6, 7, 10 and 11 of this act become effective July 1, 2013, and apply to combined tax and registration notices issued on or after that date. Counties may continue to

collect property taxes on motor vehicles for taxable years beginning on or before September 1, 2013, under the provisions of Article 22A of Chapter 105 of the General Statutes as those statutes are in effect on June 30, 2013. Sections 12 and 13 of this act are effective when they become law. Nothing in this act shall require the General Assembly to appropriate funds to implement it for the biennium ending June 30, 2007."

Session Laws 2020-3, s. 4.7(a) -(h), as amended by Session Laws 2020-97, ss. 3.15(a), 3.16(a), provides: "(a) Definition. -- For purposes of this section, 'credential' means any of the following issued by the Division of Motor Vehicles:

"(1) Drivers license.

"(2) Learner's permit.

"(3) Limited learner's permit.

"(4) Limited provisional license.

"(5) Full provisional license.

"(6) Commercial drivers license.

"(7) Commercial learner's permit.

"(8) Temporary driving certificate.

"(9) Special identification card.

"(10) Handicapped placard.

"(11) Vehicle registration.

"(12) Temporary vehicle registration.

"(13) Dealer license plate.

"(14) Transporter plate.

"(15) Loaner/Dealer 'LD' plate.

"(16) Vehicle inspection authorization.

"(17) Inspection station license.

"(18) Inspection mechanic license.

"(19) Transportation network company permit.

"(20) Motor vehicle dealer license.

"(21) Sales representative license.

"(22) Manufacturer license.

"(23) Distributor license.

"(24) Wholesaler license.

"(25) Driver training school license.

"(26) Driver training school instructor license.

"(27) Professional housemoving license.

"(b) Extend Validity of Credentials. --

Notwithstanding renewal, duration, or expiration provisions of G.S. 20-7, 20-11, 20-37.6, 20-37.7, 20-37.13, 20-50, 20-66, 20-79, 20-79.02, 20-79.2, 20-183.4B, 20-183.4D, 20-280.3, 20-288, 20-324, and 20-359, or any other provision of law to the contrary, the Division of Motor Vehicles shall extend for a period of five months the validity of any credential that expires on or after March 1, 2020, and before August 1, 2020. The Division shall extend for a period of five months the validity of any credential listed in subdivisions (6), (7), (9), (10), and (18) of subsection (a) of this section that expires on or after March 1, 2020, and before the date 30 days after the date the Governor (i) rescinds Executive Order No. 116 or (ii) issues another executive order lifting restrictions on Division of Motor Vehicles functions. Notwithstanding G.S. 20-37.13(h) and G.S. 20-37.13A(a), the Division of Motor Vehicles is authorized to waive the requirement that commercial drivers license and commercial learner's permit holders have a medical examination and certification, as required by federal law, consistent with any waiver of medical qualifications standards issued by the Federal Motor Carrier Safety Administration. A credential extended under this section shall expire five months from the date it otherwise expires as prescribed by law prior to this section. However, the subsequent expiration of a credential extended under this section shall occur on the date prescribed by law prior to this section without regard to the extension. The Division shall notify individuals affected by an extension granted under this section, including information on new expiration dates and how the extension affects subsequent renewal and expiration dates.

"(b1) Extension of Intrastate Medical Waivers. --

Notwithstanding the limitation on duration of waivers in G.S. 20-37.13A(b), the Division of Motor Vehicles may extend for up to five months the validity of a medical waiver issued by the Division under G.S. 20-37.13A if the waiver expires on or after March 1, 2020, and before the date 30 days after the date the Governor (i) rescinds Executive Order No. 116 or (ii) issues another executive order lifting restrictions on Division of Motor Vehicles functions, and the Division's Medical Review Unit determines the extension is appropriate.

"(c) Driving Eligibility Certificates. --

Notwithstanding G.S. 20-11(n)(3), a driving eligibility certificate dated on or after February 9, 2020, and before March 10, 2020, remains valid and may be accepted by the Division of Motor Vehicles to meet the requirements for a license or permit issued under G.S. 20-11 until 30 days after the date the Governor rescinds Executive Order No. 116 or the date the Division reopens all drivers license offices, whichever is earlier.

"(d) Waive Penalties. --

Notwithstanding any provision of law to the contrary, the Division shall waive any fines, fees, or penalties associated with failing to renew a credential during the period of time the credential is valid by extension under subsection (b) of this section.

"(e) Motor Vehicle Taxes. --

Notwithstanding any provision of law to the contrary, due dates for motor vehicle taxes that are tied to registration expiration under Article 22A of Chapter 105 of the General Statutes shall be extended to correspond with extended expiration dates under subsection (b) of this section.

"(f) Validity by Extension a Defense. --

A person may not be convicted or found responsible for any offense resulting from failure to renew a credential issued by the Division if, when tried for that offense, the person shows that the offense occurred during the period of time the credential is valid by extension under subsection (b) of this section.

"(g) Report. --

Within 30 days of the extensions made under subsection (b) of this section, the Division shall submit a report to the Joint Legislative Transportation Oversight Committee and the Fiscal Research Division detailing implementation of this section.

"(h) Effective Date. --

This section is effective retroactively to March 1, 2020, and applies to expirations occurring on or after that date."

Session Laws 2020-3, s. 5, is a severability clause.

Session Laws 2020-97, s. 4.5, is a severability clause.

EFFECT OF AMENDMENTS. --

Session Laws 2005-294, s. 1, added subdivisions (1a) and (2a). For effective date, see editor's note.

Session Laws 2009-445, s. 24(a), added subdivisions (4) through (6). See Editor's note for effective date and applicability.

CROSS REFERENCES. --

As to the use and confidential nature of actual addresses of Address Confidentiality Program participants by boards of elections for election-related purposes, see G.S. 15C-8.

§ 105-330.1. Classification of motor vehicles

(a) **Classification. --** All motor vehicles other than the motor vehicles listed in subsection (b) of this section are designated a special class of property under Article V, Sec. 2(2) of the North Carolina Constitution and are considered classified motor vehicles. Classified motor vehicles must be listed and assessed as provided in this Article and taxes on classified motor vehicles must be collected as provided in this Article.

(b) **Exceptions. --** The following motor vehicles are not classified under subsection (a) of this section:

(1) Motor vehicles exempt from registration pursuant to G.S. 20-51.

(2) Manufactured homes, mobile classrooms, and mobile offices.

(3) Semitrailers or trailers registered on a multiyear basis.

(4) Motor vehicles owned or leased by a public service company and appraised under G.S. 105-335.

(5) Repealed by Session Laws 2000, c. 140, s. 75(a), effective July 1, 2000.

(6) Motor vehicles registered under the International Registration Plan.

(7) Motor vehicles issued permanent registration plates under G.S. 20-84.

(8) Self-propelled property-carrying vehicles issued three-month registration plates at the farmer rate under G.S. 20-88.

(9) Motor vehicles owned by participants in the Address Confidentiality Program authorized under Chapter 15C of the General Statutes.

History.

1991, c. 624, s. 1; 1991 (Reg. Sess., 1992), c. 961, s. 3; 1993, c. 485, s. 18; c. 543, s. 4; 1993 (Reg. Sess., 1994), c. 745, s. 1; 2000-140, s. 75(a); 2007-471, s. 6; 2009-445, ss. 24(a), 25(a); 2010-95, s. 22(c), (d); 2013-414, ss. 70(b), (c), 72

EFFECT OF AMENDMENTS. --

Session Laws 2007-471, s. 6, added subdivision (b)(6). For effective date, see Editor's note.

Session Laws 2009-445, s. 24(a), in subsection (a), in the first sentence, deleted "authority of" preceding "Article V" near the middle, and added "and are considered classified motor vehicles" at the end; in the second sentence, substituted "must" for "shall" twice; and added subdivisions (b)(7) and (b)(8). For effective date and applicability, see Editor's note.

Session Laws 2013-414, s. 72, effective July 1, 2013, added subdivision (b)(9).

§ 105-330.2. Appraisal, ownership, and situs

(a) **Determination Date for Registered Vehicle. --** The ownership, situs, and taxability of a registered classified motor vehicle is determined annually as of the date on which the vehicle's current registration is renewed, regardless of whether the registration is renewed after it has expired, or on the date an application for a new registration is submitted. The situs of a registered classified motor vehicle may not be changed until the next registration date. The value of a registered classified motor vehicle is determined as follows:

(1) For a registration expiring or an application for a new registration during the period January 1 through August 31, the value is determined as of January 1 of the current year.

(2) For a registration expiring or an application for a new registration during the period September 1 through December 31, the value is determined as of January 1 of the following year.

(3) For a new motor vehicle whose value cannot be determined as of January 1 of the year specified in subdivision (1) or (2) of this subsection, the value is determined as of the date that model of motor vehicle is first offered for sale at retail in this State.

(4) For a motor vehicle whose value cannot be determined as of the date set under any other subdivision in this subsection, the value is determined using the most currently available January 1 retail value of the vehicle.

(a1) **Determination Date for Unregistered Vehicle. --** The ownership, situs, and taxability of an unregistered classified motor vehicle is determined as of January 1 of the year in which the registration of the motor vehicle expires and is not renewed or the motor vehicle is acquired and the owner does not submit an application for registration. The value of an unregistered classified motor vehicle is determined as of January 1 of the year the vehicle is required to be listed.

(b) **Value. --** An assessor must appraise a classified motor vehicle at its true value in money as prescribed by G.S. 105-283. The sales price of a classified motor vehicle purchased from a dealer, including all accessories attached to the vehicle when it is delivered to the purchaser, is considered the true value of the vehicle, and the assessor must appraise the vehicle at this value. The sales price excludes the tax imposed under Article 5A of this Chapter. The Property Tax Division of the Department of Revenue must annually adopt a schedule of values, standards, and rules to be used in the valuation of all other classified motor vehicles to ensure equitable statewide valuations, taking into account local market conditions and allowing adjustments for mileage and the condition of the vehicles.

(b1) **Valuation Appeal.** -- The owner of a classified motor vehicle may appeal the appraised value of the vehicle by filing a request for appeal with the assessor within 30 days of the date taxes are due on the vehicle under G.S. 105-330.4. An owner who appeals the appraised value of a classified motor vehicle must pay the tax on the vehicle when due, subject to a full or partial refund if the appeal is decided in the owner's favor.

The combined tax and registration notice or tax receipt for a classified motor vehicle must explain the right to appeal the appraised value of the vehicle. A lessee of a vehicle that is required by the terms of the lease to pay the tax on the vehicle is considered the owner of the vehicle for purposes of filing an appeal under this subsection. Appeals filed under this subsection shall proceed in the manner provided in G.S. 105-312(d).

(b2) **Exemption or Exclusion Appeal.** -- The owner of a classified motor vehicle may appeal the vehicle's eligibility for an exemption or exclusion by filing a request for appeal with the assessor within 30 days of the assessor's initial decision on the exemption or exclusion application filed by the owner pursuant to G.S. 105-330.3(b). Appeals filed under this subsection shall proceed in the manner provided in G.S. 105-312(d).

(c) Repealed by Session Laws 2008-134, s. 61, effective July 28, 2008.

History.
1991, c. 624, s. 1; 1991 (Reg. Sess., 1992), c. 961, s. 4; 1995, c. 510, s. 1; 1995 (Reg. Sess., 1996), c. 646, s. 24; 1997-6, s. 10; 1999-353, s. 1; 2005-294, s. 2; 2005-303, s. 1; 2006-259, s. 31.5; 2007-527, s. 22(b); 2008-134, ss. 61, 65; 2009-445, s. 24(a); 2010-95, s. 22(c); 2011-330, s. 42(a); 2012-79, ss. 3.2, 3.6; 2013-414, ss. 70(b), (d), 71(a), (b)

EFFECT OF AMENDMENTS. --
Session Laws 2005-294, s. 2, rewrote subsection (b); and added the last sentence in subsection (c). For effective date, see Editor's note.

Session Laws 2005-303, s. 1, effective for taxes imposed for taxable years beginning on or after July 1, 2005, inserted the second sentence of subsection (b).

Session Laws 2008-134, s. 61, effective July 28, 2008, deleted subsection (c), regarding the administration of a memorandum of understanding for the administration of the listing, appraisal, and assessment of classified motor vehicles.

Session Laws 2009-445, s. 24(a), rewrote the section. For effective date and applicability, see Editor's note.

Session Laws 2013-414, s. 71(b), effective July 1, 2013, in subsection (b1), in the first paragraph, added "Valuation" at the beginning of the subsection heading, and deleted "or taxability" following "appraised value" in the first and second sentences; in the second paragraph, deleted "and taxability" following "appraised value" and added the last sentence; and added subsection (b2).

§ 105-330.3. Listing requirements for classified motor vehicles; application for exempt status

(a1) **Unregistered Vehicles.** -- The owner of an unregistered classified motor vehicle must list the vehicle for taxes by filing an abstract with the assessor of the county in which the vehicle is located on or before January 31 following the date the owner acquired the unregistered vehicle or, in the case of a registration that is not renewed, January 31 following the date the registration expires, and on or before January 31 of each succeeding year that the vehicle is unregistered. If a classified motor vehicle required to be listed pursuant to this subsection is registered before the end of the fiscal year for which it was required to be listed, the following applies:

(1) The vehicle is taxed as a registered vehicle, and the tax assessed pursuant to this subsection for the fiscal year in which the vehicle was required to be listed shall be released and/or refunded.

(2) *(Effective for taxes imposed for taxable years beginning before July 1, 2017)* For any months for which the vehicle was not taxed between the date the registration expired and the start of the current registered vehicle tax year, the vehicle is taxed as an unregistered vehicle as follows:

a. The value of the motor vehicle is determined as of January 1 of the year in which the registration of the motor vehicle expires.

b. In computing the taxes, the assessor must use the tax rates and any additional motor vehicle taxes of the various taxing units in effect on the date the taxes are computed.

c. The tax on the motor vehicle is the product of a fraction and the number of months for which the vehicle was not taxed between the date the registration expires and the start of the

Chapter 105

current registered vehicle tax year. The numerator of the fraction is the product of the appraised value of the motor vehicle and the tax rate of the various taxing units. The denominator of the fraction is 12.

d. The taxes are due on the first day of the second month following the month the notice was prepared.

e. Interest accrues on unpaid taxes for these unregistered classified motor vehicles at the rate of five percent (5%) for the remainder of the month following the month the taxes are due. Interest accrues at the rate of three-fourths percent (3/4%) for each following month until the taxes are paid, unless the notice is prepared after the date the taxes are due. In that circumstance, the interest accrues beginning the second month following the date of the notice until the taxes are paid.

(2) *(Effective for taxes imposed for taxable years beginning on or after July 1, 2017)* For any months for which the vehicle was not taxed between the date the registration expired and the start of the current registered vehicle tax year, the vehicle is taxed as an unregistered vehicle as follows:

a. The value of the motor vehicle is determined as of January 1 of the year in which the taxes are computed.

b. In computing the taxes, the assessor must use the tax rates and any additional motor vehicle taxes of the various taxing units in effect on the date the taxes are computed.

c. The tax on the motor vehicle is the product of a fraction and the number of months for which the vehicle was not taxed between the date the registration expires and the start of the current registered vehicle tax year. The numerator of the fraction is the product of the appraised value of the motor vehicle and the tax rate of the various taxing units. The denominator of the fraction is 12.

d. The taxes are due on September 1 following the date the notice was prepared. Taxes are payable at par or face amount if paid before January 6 following the due date. Taxes paid on or after January 6 following the due date are subject to interest charges. Interest accrues on taxes paid on or after January 6 pursuant to G.S. 105-360.

e. Repealed by Session Laws 2017-204, s. 5.1(a), effective for taxable years beginning on or after July 1, 2017.

(3) A vehicle required to be listed pursuant to this subsection that is not listed

by January 31 and is not registered before the end of the fiscal year for which it was required to be listed is subject to discovery pursuant to G.S. 105-312.

(b) **Exemption or Exclusion.** -- The owner of a classified motor vehicle who claims an exemption or exclusion from tax under this Subchapter has the burden of establishing that the vehicle is entitled to the exemption or exclusion. The owner may establish prima facie entitlement to exemption or exclusion of the classified motor vehicle by filing an application for exempt status with the assessor within 30 days of the date taxes on the vehicle are due. When an approved application is on file, the assessor must omit from the tax records the classified motor vehicles described in the application. An application is not required for vehicles qualifying for the exemptions or exclusions listed in G.S. 105-282.1(a)(1). The remaining provisions of G.S. 105-282.1 do not apply to classified motor vehicles.

(c) **Duty to report changes.** -- The owner of a classified motor vehicle that has been omitted from the tax records as provided in subsection (b) of this section must report to the assessor any classified motor vehicle registered in the owner's name or owned by that person but not registered in the person's name that does not qualify for exemption or exclusion for the current year. This report must be made within 30 days after the renewal of registration or initial registration of the vehicle or, for an unregistered vehicle, on or before January 31 of the year in which the vehicle is required to be listed by subsection (a1) of this section. A classified motor vehicle that does not qualify for exemption or exclusion but has been omitted from the tax records as provided in subsection (b) is subject to discovery under the provisions of G.S. 105-312, except that in lieu of the penalties prescribed by G.S. 105-312(h) a penalty of one hundred dollars ($ 100.00) is assessed for each registration period that elapsed before the disqualification was discovered.

(d) **Criminal Sanction.** -- A person who willfully attempts, or who willfully aids or abets another person to attempt, in any manner to evade or defeat the taxes subject to this Article, whether by removal or concealment of property or otherwise, is guilty of a Class 2 misdemeanor.

History.
1991, c. 624, s. 1; 2008-134, s. 62; 2009-445, s. 24(a); 2010-95, s. 22(c); 2012-79, s. 3.3; 2013-414, ss. 70(b), 71(a), (c); 2017-204, s. 5.1(a)

SUBDIVISION (A1)(2) SET OUT TWICE. --The first version of subdivision (a1)(2) set out above is effective for taxes imposed for taxable years before July 1, 2017. The second version of subdivision (a1)(2) set out above is effective for taxes imposed for taxable years beginning on or after July 1, 2017.

EDITOR'S NOTE. --
Session Laws 2017-204, s. 7.1, is a severability clause.

EFFECT OF AMENDMENTS. --
Session Laws 2008-134, s. 62, effective July 28, 2008, in subdivision (a)(2), added "unless the vehicle has been taxed as a registered vehicle for the current year" to the end; and in subsection (b), added the last sentence.

Session Laws 2009-445, s. 24(a), rewrote the section. For effective date and applicability, see Editor's note.

Session Laws 2013-414, s. 71(c), effective July 1, 2013, rewrote subsection (a1); and, in subsection (b), added "within 30 days of the date taxes on the vehicle are due" at the end of the second sentence.

Session Laws 2017-204, s. 5.1(a), effective for taxes imposed for taxable years beginning on or after July 1, 2017, substituted "the taxes are computed" for "the registration of the motor vehicle expires" in subsubdivision (a1)(2)a., rewrote sub-subdivision (a1)(2) d., and deleted sub-subdivision (a1)(2)e., related to interest due on unpaid taxes for unregistered classified motor vehicles.

§ 105-330.4. Due date, interest, and enforcement remedies

(a) **Due Date.** -- The registration of a classified motor vehicle may not be issued unless a temporary registration plate is issued for the motor vehicle under G.S. 20-79.1A or the taxes for the motor vehicle's tax year that begins after the issuance of the registration are paid upon registration. A registration of a classified motor vehicle may not be renewed unless the taxes for the motor vehicle's tax year that begins after the registration expires are paid upon registration. If the registration of a classified motor vehicle is renewed earlier than the date the taxes are due, the taxes must be paid as if they were due. Taxes on a classified motor vehicle are due as follows:

(1) For an unregistered classified motor vehicle, the taxes are due on September 1 following the date by which the vehicle was required to be listed.

(2) For a registered classified motor vehicle that is registered under the staggered system, the taxes are due each year on the date the owner applies for a new registration or the fifteenth day of the month following the month in which the registration renewal sticker expires pursuant to G.S. 20-66(g).

(3) For a registered classified motor vehicle that is registered under the annual system, taxes are due on the date the owner applies for a new registration or 45 days after the registration expires.

(4) For a registered classified motor vehicle that has a temporary registration plate issued under G.S. 20-79.1 or a limited registration plate issued under G.S. 20-79.1A, the taxes are due on the last day of the second month following the date the owner applied for the plate.

(a1) Repealed by Session Laws 2009-445, s. 24(a), effective July 1, 2013, and applicable to combined tax and registration notices issued on or after that date.

(b) **Interest.** -- Interest accrues on unpaid taxes and unpaid registration fees for registered classified motor vehicles at the rate of five percent (5%) for the remainder of the month the taxes are due under subsection (a) of this section. Interest does not accrue for the first month following the due date. Interest accrues at the rate of three-fourths percent (3/4%) beginning the second month following the due date and for each following month until the taxes and fees are paid. Subject to the provisions of G.S. 105-395.1, interest accrues on delinquent taxes on unregistered classified motor vehicles as provided in G.S. 105-360(a) and the discounts allowed in G.S. 105-360(a) apply to the payment of the taxes.

(c) **Remedies.** -- The enforcement remedies in this Subchapter apply to unpaid taxes on an unregistered classified motor vehicle and to unpaid taxes on a registered classified motor vehicle for which the tax year begins before October 1, 2013.

(d) **Payments.** -- Tax payments submitted by mail are deemed to be received as of the date shown on the postmark affixed by the United States Postal Service. If no date is shown on the postmark or if the postmark is not affixed by the United States Postal Service, the tax payment is deemed to be received when the payment is received by the collecting authority. In any dispute arising under this subsection, the burden of proof is on the taxpayer to show that the payment was timely made.

(e) **Waiver.** -- Notwithstanding G.S. 105-380, the governing board of a county may adopt a resolution to create a uniform policy to allow the reduction or waiver of interest or penalties on delinquent motor vehicle taxes for registered classified motor vehicles for tax years prior to July 1, 2013.

History.
1991, c. 624, s. 1; 1991 (Reg. Sess., 1992), c. 961, s. 5; 1995, c. 510, s. 2; 2001-139, s. 8; 2005-294, ss. 3, 4, 5; 2006-259, s. 31.5; 2007-471, s. 3; 2007-527, s. 22(b); 2008-134, s. 65; 2009-445, ss. 24(a), 25(a); 2010-95, s. 22(c), (d); 2011-330, ss. 40, 42(a); 2012-79, ss. 3.4, 3.6; 2013-414, ss. 70(b) -(d), 71(a), (d); 2015-204, s. 1

EFFECT OF AMENDMENTS. --
Session Laws 2005-294, ss. 3 and 5, rewrote subsection (a); and rewrote the first two sentences in subsection (b). For effective date, see editor's note.

Session Laws 2005-294, s. 4, effective January 1, 2006, in subsection (b), substituted "five percent (5%)" for "two percent (2%)" and deleted "tax" preceding "notice required by" in the introductory language.

Session Laws 2007-471, s. 3, added subsection (a1). For effective date, see Editor's note.

Session Laws 2009-445, s. 24(a), rewrote the section. For effective date and applicability, see Editor's note.

Session Laws 2011-330, s. 40, effective June 27, 2011, added subsection (d).

Session Laws 2013-414, s. 71(d), effective July 1, 2013, rewrote the introductory paragraph of subsection (a); rewrote subsections (b) and (c); and in subsection (d), added "Payments" as the subsection heading, and substituted "by the collecting authority" for "in the office of the tax collector" in the second sentence.

Session Laws 2015-204, s. 1, effective August 11, 2015, added subsection (e).

OPINIONS OF THE ATTORNEY GENERAL

COUNTY MAY NOT IMPOSE LATE PAYMENT PENALTY OR ADMINISTRATIVE FEE UPON DELINQUENT PROPERTY TAX ACCOUNTS. --Because the statutes authorizing property taxes provide for interest and/or penalties, a county may not, by ordinance, impose a late payment penalty or administrative fee upon delinquent property tax accounts. See opinion of Attorney General to Lloyd C. Smith, Jr., Pritchett & Burch, PLLC, 2001 N.C. AG LEXIS 6 (3/6/2001).

§ 105-330.5. Notice required; distribution and collection fees

(a) **Notice for Registered Vehicle.** -- The Property Tax Division of the Department of Revenue or a third-party contractor selected by the Property Tax Division must prepare a combined tax and registration notice for each registered classified motor vehicle. The combined tax and registration notice must contain all county and municipal corporation taxes and fees due on the motor vehicle as computed by the assessor in the county of registration. If the motor vehicle has a temporary or limited registration plate issued under G.S. 20-79.1 or G.S. 20-79.1A, the combined tax and registration notice must state that the vehicle registration fees for the plate have been paid and that the vehicle's registration becomes valid for the remainder of the year upon payment of the county and municipal corporation taxes and fees that are due. A combined tax and registration notice that sets out the required information on a vehicle issued a limited registration plate constitutes the registration certificate for that vehicle.

In computing the taxes, the assessor must appraise the motor vehicle in accordance with G.S. 105-330.2 and must use the tax rates and any additional motor vehicle taxes of the various taxing units in effect on the date the taxes are computed. The tax on the motor vehicle is the product of a fraction and the number of months in the motor vehicle tax year. The numerator of the fraction is the product of the appraised value of the motor vehicle and the tax rate of the various taxing units. The denominator of the fraction is 12. This procedure constitutes the listing and assessment of each classified motor vehicle for taxation.

The combined tax and registration notice must contain the following:

(1) The appraised value of the motor vehicle.

(2) The tax rate of each taxing unit.

(3) A statement that the appraised value and the taxability of the motor vehicle may be appealed to the assessor in writing within 30 days of the due date.

(4) The registration fee imposed by the Division of Motor Vehicles and any other information required by the Division of Motor Vehicles to comply with the provisions of Chapter 20 of the General Statutes.

(5) Instructions for payment.

(a1) **Proration.** -- When a new registration is obtained for a registered classified motor vehicle that is registered under the annual system, the taxes are prorated for the remainder of the calendar year. The amount of prorated taxes due is the product of the proration fraction and the taxes computed according to subsection (a) of this section. The numerator of the proration fraction is the number of full months remaining in the calendar year following the registration application date and the denominator of the fraction is 12.

(a2) Repealed by Session Laws 2009-445, s. 24(a), effective July 1, 2011, and applicable to combined tax and registration notices issued on or after that date, or when the Division of motor vehicles and the Department of Revenue certify that the integrated computer system or registration renewal and property tax collection for motor vehicles is in operation, whichever occurs first.

(b) **Distribution and Collection Fees.** -- The Property Tax Division of the Department of Revenue or a third-party contractor selected by the Property Tax Division must send a copy of the combined tax and registration notice for a registered classified motor vehicle to the motor vehicle owner, as defined in G.S. 20-4.01. Upon receiving written consent from the motor vehicle owner, the notice required under this subsection may be sent electronically to an e-mail address provided by the motor vehicle owner. The Department must establish a fee equal to the actual cost of preparing, printing, and sending the notice. The Department may receive a fee for each notice generated for a vehicle registered in a county or municipal corporation from the taxes and fees remitted to the county or municipal corporation in which the vehicle is registered. The collecting authority is responsible for collecting county and municipal taxes and fees assessed under this Article and may receive a fee for collecting these taxes and fees. The amount of this fee for an agent contracting with the Division of Motor Vehicles must equal at least the applicable amount set under G.S. 20-63(h). The amount of this fee for the Division of Motor Vehicles is the amount set by the memorandum of understanding entered into under G.S. 105-330.11 but shall not exceed the amount set under G.S. 20-63. The Property Tax Division must establish procedures to ensure that tax payments and fees received pursuant to this Article and Chapter 20 of the General Statutes are properly accounted for and taxes and fees due other taxing units and the Division of Motor Vehicles are remitted at least once each month.

(b1) Repealed by Session Laws 1995, c. 329, s. 2.

(c) **Notice for Unregistered Vehicle.** -- The assessor must prepare and send a tax notice for each unregistered classified motor vehicle before September 1 following the January 31 listing date. The notice must include all county and special district taxes due on the motor vehicle. In computing the taxes, the assessor must use the tax rates of the taxing units in effect for the fiscal year that begins on July 1 following the January 31 listing date. Municipalities must list, assess, and tax unregistered classified motor vehicles as provided in G.S. 105-326, 105-327, and 105-328.

(d) **Scope of Levy.** -- A county must include taxes on registered classified motor vehicles in the tax levy for the fiscal year in which the taxes are collected.

(e) Repealed by Session Laws 2012-79, s. 3.5, effective June 26, 2012.

History.
1991, c. 624, s. 1; 1991 (Reg. Sess., 1992), c. 961, s. 6; 1995, c. 24, s. 1; c. 329, s. 2; c. 510, s. 3; 2005-294, s. 6; 2005-313, s. 8; 2006-259, s. 31.5; 2007-471, ss. 4, 5; 2007-527, s. 22(b); 2008-134, s. 65; 2009-445, ss. 24(a), 25(a); 2010-95, s. 22(c), (d); 2011-330, s. 42(a); 2012-71, ss. 3.5, 3.6; 2013-372, s. 2(b); 2013-414, s. 70(b) -(d); 2014-3, s. 13.3; 2015-108, s. 1

EDITOR'S NOTE. --
Session Laws 2005-294, s. 13, as amended by Session Laws 2006-259, s. 31.5, as amended by Session Laws 2007-527, s. 22, as amended by Session Laws 2008-134, s. 65, as amended by Session Laws 2012-79, s. 3.6, and as amended by Session Laws 2013-414, s. 70(d), provides, in part, that s. 6 of the act becomes effective July 1, 2013, and apply to combined tax and registration notices issued on or after that date. Counties may continue to collect property taxes on motor vehicles for taxable years beginning on or before September 1, 2013, under the provisions of Article 22A of Chapter 105 of the General Statutes as

those statutes are in effect on June 30, 2013. Nothing in this act shall require the General Assembly to appropriate funds to implement it for the biennium ending June 30, 2007.

Session Laws 2012-142, s. 24.10(a) -(c), as amended by Session Laws 2015-241, s. 29.37, and as amended by Session Laws 2016-94, s. 35.15(a), provides: "(a) Upon request from the Department of Transportation and notwithstanding any other provision of law to the contrary, the Office of State Budget and Management may authorize the creation of permanent, full-time positions within the Department of Transportation and its Division of Motor Vehicles in excess of the positions authorized by this act for the purposes of implementing and administering the combined motor vehicle registration and property tax collection system and providing other support as determined necessary by the Commissioner of the Division of Motor Vehicles. Positions created under this authorization shall be funded with receipts from the fee assessed under G.S. 105-330.5(b). "(b) Beginning October 1, 2012, the Office of State Budget and Management shall report quarterly on all transfers of funds from the Combined Motor Vehicle and Registration Account (Combined Account) and positions supported by the Combined Account during the 2012-2013 fiscal year to the House Appropriations Subcommittee on Transportation, the Senate Appropriations Committee on Department of Transportation, the Joint Legislative Transportation Oversight Committee, and the Fiscal Research Division. The report shall include, at a minimum, the following:

"(1) A summary of activities funded by the Combined Account to date.

"(2) Amounts transferred from the Combined Account and expended per activity.

"(3) A detailed listing of positions funded by receipts to the Combined Account, identifying the position number, title, effective date and duration, cost, functions performed, and organizational unit to which the position is assigned.

"(c) No later than May 1, 2013, the Department of Revenue and the Department of Transportation shall jointly report on the status of the Memorandum of Understanding required by G.S. 105-330.11 to the following: the House Appropriations Subcommittee on Transportation, the Senate Appropriations Committee on Department of Transportation, the cochairs of the House Appropriations Committee, the cochairs of the Senate Appropriations/Base Budget Committee, and the Fiscal Research Division. The report shall identify the estimated recurring costs of system administration and proposed administrative fees to support the costs of combined notice generation and collection of registration fees and vehicle property taxes."

Session Laws 2012-142, s. 1.2, provides: "This act shall be known as 'The Current Operations and Capital Improvements Appropriations Act of 2012.'"

Session Laws 2012-142, s. 27.4, provides: "Except for statutory changes or other provisions that clearly indicate an intention to have effects beyond the

Chapter 105

2012-2013 fiscal year, the textual provisions of this act apply only to funds appropriated for, and activities occurring during, the 2012-2013 fiscal year."

Session Laws 2012-142, s. 27.7 is a severability clause.

Session Laws 2015-241, s. 1.1, provides: "This act shall be known as 'The Current Operations and Capital Improvements Appropriations Act of 2015.'"

Session Laws 2015-241, s. 33.4, provides: "Except for statutory changes or other provisions that clearly indicate an intention to have effects beyond the 2015-2017 fiscal biennium, the textual provisions of this act apply only to funds appropriated for, and activities occurring during, the 2015-2017 fiscal biennium."

Session Laws 2015-241, s. 33.6, is a severability clause.

Session Laws 2016-94, s. 35.15(b), effective June 30, 2016, provides: "Nothing in subsection (a) of this section shall be construed as authorizing the creation of any positions in addition to the 45 remaining positions authorized under Section 24.10(a) of S.L. 2012-142."

Session Laws 2016-94, s. 1.2, provides: "This act shall be known as the 'Current Operations and Capital Improvements Appropriations Act of 2016.'"

Session Laws 2016-94, s. 39.4, provides: "Except for statutory changes or other provisions that clearly indicate an intention to have effects beyond the 2016-2017 fiscal year, the textual provisions of this act apply only to funds appropriated for, and activities occurring during, the 2016-2017 fiscal year."

Session Laws 2016-94, s. 39.7, is a severability clause.

EFFECT OF AMENDMENTS. --

Session Laws 2005-294, s. 6, in subsection (a), rewrote the first two sentences, and inserted "combined" and "and registration" in the last sentence and in subdivision (a)(1); substituted "before the taxes and fees become delinquent" for "within 30 days after the date of the notice" in subdivision (a)(4); added subdivision (a)(5); in subsection (a1), substituted "taxes" for "assessor" and "be prorated" for "prorate the taxes due"; rewrote subsection (b) and made minor stylistic changes. For effective date, see editor's note.

Session Laws 2007-471, ss. 4 and 5, added subsection (a2); and inserted "or (a2) of this section" in the first sentence of subsection (b). For effective date, see Editor's note.

Session Laws 2009-445, s. 24(a), rewrote the section. For effective date and applicability, see Editor's note.

Session Laws 2012-79, s. 3.5, effective June 26, 2012, repealed subsection (e), which pertained to the collection of small underpayments and refunds of small overpayments of taxes and fees due on motor vehicles.

Session Laws 2013-372, s. 2(b), effective July 1, 2013, substituted "the applicable amount set" for "one-third of the compensation paid for registration renewals conducted by contract agents" in the next-to-last sentence of subsection (b).

Session Laws 2014-3, s. 13.3, effective July 1, 2014, in subsection (b), inserted "for an agent contracting with the Division of Motor Vehicles" in the fifth sentence, and added the present sixth sentence. See Editor's note for applicability.

Session Laws 2015-108, s. 1, effective January 1, 2015, added the second sentence of subsection (b).

§ 105-330.6. Motor vehicle tax year; transfer of plates; surrender of plates

(a) **Tax Year.** -- The tax year for a classified motor vehicle listed pursuant to G.S. 105-330.3(a)(1) and registered under the staggered system begins on the first day of the first month following the date on which the former registration expires or the new registration is applied for and ends on the last day of the month in which the current registration expires. The tax year for a classified motor vehicle listed pursuant to G.S. 105-330.3(a)(1) and registered under the annual system begins on the first day of the first month following the date on which the registration expires or the new registration is applied for and ends the following December 31. The tax year for a classified motor vehicle listed pursuant to G.S. 105-330.3(a)(2) is the fiscal year that opens in the calendar year in which the vehicle is required to be listed.

(a1) **Change in Tax Year.** -- If the tax year for a classified motor vehicle changes because of a change in its registration for a reason other than the transfer of its registration plates to another classified motor vehicle pursuant to G.S. 20-64, and the new tax year begins before the expiration of the vehicle's original tax year, the taxpayer may receive a credit, in the form of a release, against the taxes on the vehicle for the new tax year. The amount of the credit is equal to a proportion of the taxes paid on the vehicle for the original tax year. The proportion is the number of full calendar months remaining in the original tax year as of the first day of the new tax year, divided by the number of months in the original tax year. To obtain the credit allowed in this subsection, the taxpayer must apply within 30 days after the taxes for the new tax year are due and must provide the county tax collector information establishing the original tax year of the vehicle, the amount of taxes paid on the vehicle for that year, and the reason for the change in registration.

(b) **Transfer of Plates.** -- If the owner of a classified motor vehicle listed pursuant to G.S. 105-330.3(a)(1) transfers the registration plates from the listed vehicle to another classified motor vehicle pursuant to G.S. 20-64 during the listed vehicle's tax year, the vehicle to which the plates are transferred is not required to be listed or taxed until the current registration expires or is renewed.

(c) **Surrender of Plates.** -- If the owner of a classified motor vehicle, who pays the tax as required by G.S. 105-330.4(a), either transfers the motor vehicle to a new owner or moves out-of-state and registers the vehicle in another jurisdiction, and the owner surrenders the registration plates from the listed vehicle to the Division of Motor Vehicles, then the owner may apply for a release or refund of taxes on the vehicle for any full calendar months remaining in the vehicle's tax year after the date of surrender. To apply for a release or refund, the owner must present to the county tax collector within one year after surrendering the plates the receipt received from the Division of Motor Vehicles accepting surrender of the registration plates. The county tax collector shall then multiply the amount of the taxes for the tax year on the vehicle by a fraction, the denominator of which is the number of months in the tax year and the numerator of which is the number of full calendar months remaining in the vehicle's tax year after the date of surrender of the registration plates. The product of the multiplication is the amount of taxes to be released or refunded. If the taxes have not been paid at the date of application, the county tax collector shall make a release of the prorated taxes and credit the owner's tax notice with the amount of the release. If the taxes have been paid at the date of application, the county tax collector shall direct an order for a refund of the prorated taxes to the county finance officer, and the finance officer shall issue a refund to the vehicle owner.

History.
1991, c. 624, s. 1; 1991 (Reg. Sess., 1992), c. 961, s. 7; 1995, c. 510, s. 4; 1998-139, s. 3; 2001-406, s. 1; 2001-497, s. 1(a); 2005-313, s. 9; 2017-204, s. 5.2

EFFECT OF AMENDMENTS. --

Session Laws 2005-313, s. 9, effective January 1, 2006, in the first sentence of subsection (a), inserted "former" and substituted "the month in which the current registration expires" for "the twelfth month following the date on which the registration expires or the new registration is applied for"; in subsection (a1), substituted "divided by the number of months in the original tax year" for "divided by 12" at the end of the third sentence; and in subsection (c), substituted "the number of months in the tax year" for "12" near the middle of the third sentence.

Session Laws 2017-204, s. 5.2, effective August 11, 2017, substituted "motor vehicle, who pays the tax as required by G.S. 105-330.4(a)" for "motor vehicle listed pursuant to G.S. 105-330.3(a)(1)" in the first sentence of subsection (c).

LEGAL PERIODICALS. --

See legislative survey, 21 Campbell L. Rev. 323 (1999).

N.C. Gen. Stat. § 105-330.7

Repealed by Session Laws 2005-294, s. 7, effective July 1, 2013, and applicable to combined tax and registration notices issued on or after that date.

History.
1991, c. 624, s. 1; 1991 (Reg. Sess., 1992), c. 961, s. 8; 2005-294, s. 13; 2006-259, s. 31.5; 2007-527, s. 22; 2008-134, s. 65; 2005-294, s. 7; 2011-330, s. 42(a); 2012-79, s. 3.6; 2013-414, s. 70(d); repealed by 2005-294, s. 7, effective July 1, 2013

EDITOR'S NOTE. --

Former G.S. 105-330.7 pertained to list of delinquents sent to Division of Motor Vehicles.

Session Laws 2005-294, s. 13, as amended by Session Laws 2006-259, s. 31.5, as amended by Session Laws 2007-527, s. 22, as amended by Session Laws 2008-134, s. 65, as amended by Session Laws 2012-79, s. 3.6, and as amended by Session Laws 2013-414, s. 70(d), provides, in part, that this section is repealed effective July 1, 2013, and applicable to combined tax and registration notices issued on or after that date. Counties may continue to collect property taxes on motor vehichles for taxable years beginning on or before September 1, 2013, under the provisions of Article 22A of Chapter 105 of the General Statutes as those statutes are in effect on June 30, 2013. Nothing in this act shall require the General Assembly to appropriate funds to implement it for the biennium ending June 30, 2007.

Session Laws 2011-330, s. 42(a), effective June 27, 2011, corrected a citation in Session Laws 2008-134, s. 65, which amended the effective date of the repeal of this section by Session Laws 2005-294, s. 7.

§ 105-330.8. Deadlines not extended

Except as otherwise provided in this Article, the following sections of the General Statutes do not apply:

(1) G.S. 105-395.1 and G.S. 103-5.
(2) G.S. 105-321(f).
(3) G.S. 105-360.

History.
1991, c. 624, s. 1; 2009-445, s. 24(a); 2010-95, s. 22(c); 2013-414, s. 70(b)

EFFECT OF AMENDMENTS. --

Session Laws 2009-445, s. 24(a), effective July 1, 2013, substituted "following sections of the General Statutes do not apply" for "provisions of G.S. 105-395.1 and G.S. 103-5 do not apply to deadlines established in this Article" in the introductory language, and added subdivisions (1) through (3). For effective date and applicability, see Editor's note.

§ 105-330.10. Disposition of interest

The interest collected on unpaid registration fees pursuant to G.S. 105-330.4 shall be

transferred on a monthly basis to the North
Carolina Highway Fund.

History.

2005-294, ss. 8, 9; 2006-30, s. 3; 2006-259, s. 31.5;
2007-471, s. 7(a); 2007-527, s. 22(a) -(c); 2008-134, ss.
63, 65, 66, 79; 2009-445, s. 25(b); 2010-95, s. 22(a), (b),
(e); 2011-330, s. 42(a) -(c); 2013-414, s. 70(a), (c), (d);
2015-241, s. 29.30(n)

EDITOR'S NOTE. --

Session Laws 2005-294, s. 13, as amended by Session Laws 2006-259, s. 31.5, as amended by Session
Laws 2007-527, s. 22(b), as amended by Session Laws
2008-134, s. 65, as amended by Session Laws 2012-79,
s. 3.6, and as amended by Session Laws 2013-414, s.
70(d), provides: "Sections 4 and 8 of this act become
effective January 1, 2006. Sections 1, 2, 3, 5, 6, 7, 10
and 11 of this act become effective July 1, 2013, and
apply to combined tax and registration notices issued on or after that date. Counties may continue to
collect property taxes on motor vehicles for taxable
years beginning on or before September 1, 2013, under the provisions of Article 22A of Chapter 105 of the
General Statutes as those statutes are in effect on
June 30, 2013. Sections 12 and 13 of this act are effective when they become law. Nothing in this act shall
require the General Assembly to appropriate funds to
implement it for the biennium ending June 30, 2007."

This section was amended by Session Laws 2007-
527, s. 22(c), effective January 1, 2011, in the coded
bill drafting format prescribed by G.S. 120-20.1. The
section was subsequently completely rewritten by
Session Laws 2008-134, s. 63, effective July 28, 2008,
without taking into account the 2007 amendments.
Session Laws 2008-134, s. 79, as amended by Session
Laws 2009-445, s. 25(b), repealed Session Laws 2008-
134, s. 63, effective July 1, 2011, thus resolving the
conflict, as of that point.

Session Laws 2007-527, s. 22(d), as amended by
Session Laws 2008-134, s. 66, provided that the
amendments to this section by s. 22(c) of Session
Laws 2007-527 would become effective January 1,
2011, or when the Division of Motor Vehicles of the
Department of Transportation and the Department of
Revenue certify that the integrated computer system
for registration renewal and property tax collection
for motor vehicles is in operation, whichever occurs
first. Session Laws 2010-95, s. 22(a), amended Session Laws 2007-527, s. 22(d) to change the effective
date of the amendment by Session Laws 2007-527,
s. 22(c) to July 1, 2010; however, Session Laws 2010-
95, s. 22(b) also amended Session Laws 2007-527, s.
22(d), as amended by Session Laws 2008-134, s. 66,
(the exact same amendment) to change the effective
date of Session Laws 2007-527, s. 22(c) to July 1, 2013,
thus creating a conflict as to when that amendment
is effective. Session Laws 2011-330, s. 42(b) repealed
Session Laws 2010-95, s. 22(a) and, thus, eliminated
the conflict as to the effective date of the amendment,
which is July 1, 2013.

Furthermore, Session Laws 2010-95, s. 22(e),
amended Session Laws 2008-134, s. 79, "as amended
by Section 25(b) of S.L. 2009-445," to add the following sentence: "Section 63 of this act is repealed July 1,
2013." Although Session Laws 2010-95, s. 22(e) indicates that it is amending Session Laws 2008-134, s.
79, as amended by Session Laws 2009-445, s. 25(b),
the illustrative text set out in the act omits the following sentence added by the 2009 act: "Section 63 of
this act is repealed July 1, 2011." Therefore, pursuant to the coded bill drafting format provided by G.S.
120-20.1, the amendment by Session Laws 2010-95,
s. 22(e) did not eliminate that sentence, resulting in
a conflict in the date of repeal for Session Laws 2008-
134, s. 63. However, Session Laws 2011-330, s. 42(c)
amended Session Laws 2010-95, s. 22(e) to delete the
repeal date of July 1, 2011 for s. 63 of Session Laws
2008-134, and replace it with a repeal date of July 1,
2013," thus eliminating the conflict in the repeal date
for Session Laws 2008-134, s. 63.

Session Laws 2013-414, s. 70(a), amended Session
laws 2007-527, s. 22(d), as amended by Session Laws
2008-134, s. 66, and as amended by Session Laws
2010-95, s. 22(b), to read as follows: "Subsection (c)
of this section becomes effective July 1, 2013. The remainder of this section is effective when it becomes
law."

Session Laws 2011-330, s. 42(a), effective June 27,
2011, corrected a citation in Session Laws 2008-134,
s. 65, which amended the effective date of the enactment of this section by Session Laws 2005-294, s. 8.

Session Laws 2012-142, s. 24.10(a) -(c), as amended
by Session Laws 2015-241, s. 29.37, and as amended
by Session Laws 2016-94, s. 35.15(a), provides: "(a)
Upon request from the Department of Transportation
and notwithstanding any other provision of law to the
contrary, the Office of State Budget and Management
may authorize the creation of permanent, full-time
positions within the Department of Transportation
and its Division of Motor Vehicles in excess of the
positions authorized by this act for the purposes of
implementing and administering the combined motor
vehicle registration and property tax collection system and providing other support as determined necessary by the Commissioner of the Division of Motor
Vehicles. Positions created under this authorization
shall be funded with receipts from the fee assessed
under G.S. 105-330.5(b). "(b) Beginning October 1,
2012, the Office of State Budget and Management
shall report quarterly on all transfers of funds from
the Combined Motor Vehicle and Registration Account (Combined Account) and positions supported
by the Combined Account during the 2012-2013 fiscal
year to the House Appropriations Subcommittee on
Transportation, the Senate Appropriations Committee on Department of Transportation, the Joint Legislative Transportation Oversight Committee, and the
Fiscal Research Division. The report shall include, at
a minimum, the following:

"(1) A summary of activities funded by the Combined Account to date.

Chapter 105

"(2) Amounts transferred from the Combined Account and expended per activity.

"(3) A detailed listing of positions funded by receipts to the Combined Account, identifying the position number, title, effective date and duration, cost, functions performed, and organizational unit to which the position is assigned.

"(c) No later than May 1, 2013, the Department of Revenue and the Department of Transportation shall jointly report on the status of the Memorandum of Understanding required by G.S. 105-330.11 to the following: the House Appropriations Subcommittee on Transportation, the Senate Appropriations Committee on Department of Transportation, the cochairs of the House Appropriations Committee, the cochairs of the Senate Appropriations/Base Budget Committee, and the Fiscal Research Division. The report shall identify the estimated recurring costs of system administration and proposed administrative fees to support the costs of combined notice generation and collection of registration fees and vehicle property taxes."

Session Laws 2012-142, s. 1.2, provides: "This act shall be known as 'The Current Operations and Capital Improvements Appropriations Act of 2012.'"

Session Laws 2012-142, s. 27.4, provides: "Except for statutory changes or other provisions that clearly indicate an intention to have effects beyond the 2012-2013 fiscal year, the textual provisions of this act apply only to funds appropriated for, and activities occurring during, the 2012-2013 fiscal year."

Session Laws 2012-142, s. 27.7 is a severability clause.

Session Laws 2013-372, s. 3, provides: "Implementation by the Division of Motor Vehicles of the Department of Transportation of an integrated computer system that combines vehicle registration with the collection of property tax includes training commission contractors under G.S. 20-63(h) on the use of that integrated computer system. The cost of the system training required of the commission contractors on or after April 1, 2013, and before July 1, 2013, is a cost of the combined motor vehicle registration renewal and property tax collection system and is payable from the Combined Motor Vehicle and Registration Account, established under G.S. 105-330.10."

Session Laws 2015-241, s. 29.30(u), made the amendment to this section by Session Laws 2015-241, s. 29.30(n), applicable to issuances, renewals, restorations, and requests on or after January 1, 2016.

Session Laws 2015-241, s. 1.1, provides: "This act shall be known as 'The Current Operations and Capital Improvements Appropriations Act of 2015.'"

Session Laws 2015-241, s. 33.4, provides: "Except for statutory changes or other provisions that clearly indicate an intention to have effects beyond the 2015-2017 fiscal biennium, the textual provisions of this act apply only to funds appropriated for, and activities occurring during, the 2015-2017 fiscal biennium."

Session Laws 2015-241, s. 33.6, is a severability clause.

Session Laws 2016-94, s. 35.15(b), effective June 30, 2016, provides: "Nothing in subsection (a) of this section shall be construed as authorizing the creation of any positions in addition to the 45 remaining positions authorized under Section 24.10(a) of S.L. 2012-142."

Session Laws 2016-94, s. 1.2, provides: "This act shall be known as the 'Current Operations and Capital Improvements Appropriations Act of 2016.'"

Session Laws 2016-94, s. 39.4, provides: "Except for statutory changes or other provisions that clearly indicate an intention to have effects beyond the 2016-2017 fiscal year, the textual provisions of this act apply only to funds appropriated for, and activities occurring during, the 2016-2017 fiscal year."

Session Laws 2016-94, s. 39.7, is a severability clause.

EFFECT OF AMENDMENTS. --

Session Laws 2007-527, s. 22(c), as amended by Session Laws 2008-134, s. 66, effective January 1, 2011, rewrote the section.

Session Laws 2008-134, s. 63, effective July 28, 2008, rewrote the section.

Session Laws 2015-241, s. 29.30(n), effective January 1, 2016, substituted "Fund." for "Fund for technology improvements within the Division of Motor Vehicles." For applicability, see editor's note.

§ 105-330.11. Memorandum of understanding

The Department of Revenue, acting through the Property Tax Division, and the Department of Transportation, acting through the Division of Motor Vehicles are directed to enter into a memorandum of understanding concerning the administration of this Article. The memorandum of understanding must include the following:

(1) A procedure for the administration of the listing, appraisal, and assessment of classified motor vehicles.

(2) Information concerning vehicle identification, the name and address of a vehicle's owner, and other information that will be required on a motor vehicle registration form to implement the tax listing and collection provisions of this Article.

(3) A procedure for the business practices, accounting, and costs of carrying out the integrated computer system for registration renewal and property tax collection for motor vehicles once the system has been certified to be in operation by the Department of Revenue and the Department of Transportation. The Departments must consult with the North Carolina Association of County Commissioners, acting on behalf of the counties, and the North Carolina League of Municipalities, acting on behalf of the municipalities, in developing the procedures under this subdivision and obtain their signed endorsements before any part of this procedure is implemented.

Chapter 105

History.

2008-134, s. 64; 2009-445, s. 24(a); 2013-414, s. 70(b)

EDITOR'S NOTE. --

Session Laws 2012-142, s. 24.10(a) -(c), as amended by Session Laws 2015-241, s. 29.37, and as amended by Session Laws 2016-94, s. 35.15(a), provides: "(a) Upon request from the Department of Transportation and notwithstanding any other provision of law to the contrary, the Office of State Budget and Management may authorize the creation of permanent, full-time positions within the Department of Transportation and its Division of Motor Vehicles in excess of the positions authorized by this act for the purposes of implementing and administering the combined motor vehicle registration and property tax collection system and providing other support as determined necessary by the Commissioner of the Division of Motor Vehicles. Positions created under this authorization shall be funded with receipts from the fee assessed under G.S. 105-330.5(b). "(b) Beginning October 1, 2012, the Office of State Budget and Management shall report quarterly on all transfers of funds from the Combined Motor Vehicle and Registration Account (Combined Account) and positions supported by the Combined Account during the 2012-2013 fiscal year to the House Appropriations Subcommittee on Transportation, the Senate Appropriations Committee on Department of Transportation, the Joint Legislative Transportation Oversight Committee, and the Fiscal Research Division. The report shall include, at a minimum, the following:

"(1) A summary of activities funded by the Combined Account to date.

"(2) Amounts transferred from the Combined Account and expended per activity.

"(3) A detailed listing of positions funded by receipts to the Combined Account, identifying the position number, title, effective date and duration, cost, functions performed, and organizational unit to which the position is assigned.

"(c) No later than May 1, 2013, the Department of Revenue and the Department of Transportation shall jointly report on the status of the Memorandum of Understanding required by G.S. 105-330.11 to the following: the House Appropriations Subcommittee on Transportation, the Senate Appropriations Committee on Department of Transportation, the cochairs of the House Appropriations Committee, the cochairs of the Senate Appropriations/Base Budget Committee, and the Fiscal Research Division. The report shall identify the estimated recurring costs of system administration and proposed administrative fees to support the costs of combined notice generation and collection of registration fees and vehicle property taxes."

Session Laws 2012-142, s. 1.2, provides: "This act shall be known as 'The Current Operations and Capital Improvements Appropriations Act of 2012.'"

Session Laws 2012-142, s. 27.4, provides: "Except for statutory changes or other provisions that clearly indicate an intention to have effects beyond the 2012-2013 fiscal year, the textual provisions of this act apply only to funds appropriated for, and activities occurring during, the 2012-2013 fiscal year."

Session Laws 2012-142, s. 27.7 is a severability clause.

Session Laws 2015-241, s. 1.1, provides: "This act shall be known as 'The Current Operations and Capital Improvements Appropriations Act of 2015.'"

Session Laws 2015-241, s. 33.4, provides: "Except for statutory changes or other provisions that clearly indicate an intention to have effects beyond the 2015-2017 fiscal biennium, the textual provisions of this act apply only to funds appropriated for, and activities occurring during, the 2015-2017 fiscal biennium."

Session Laws 2015-241, s. 33.6, is a severability clause.

Session Laws 2016-94, s. 35.15(b), effective June 30, 2016, provides: "Nothing in subsection (a) of this section shall be construed as authorizing the creation of any positions in addition to the 45 remaining positions authorized under Section 24.10(a) of S.L. 2012-142."

Session Laws 2016-94, s. 1.2, provides: "This act shall be known as the 'Current Operations and Capital Improvements Appropriations Act of 2016.'"

Session Laws 2016-94, s. 39.4, provides: "Except for statutory changes or other provisions that clearly indicate an intention to have effects beyond the 2016-2017 fiscal year, the textual provisions of this act apply only to funds appropriated for, and activities occurring during, the 2016-2017 fiscal year."

Session Laws 2016-94, s. 39.7, is a severability clause.

EFFECT OF AMENDMENTS. --

Session Laws 2009-445, s. 24(a), effective August 7, 2009, substituted "the name and address of a vehicle's owner" for "identification of a vehicle owner by name and address" in subdivision (2).

SUBCHAPTER 05.
MOTOR FUEL TAXES

ARTICLE 36B.
TAX ON MOTOR CARRIERS

§ 105-449.37. Definitions; tax liability; application

(a) **Definitions. --** The following definitions apply in this Article:

(1) **International Fuel Tax Agreement. --** The Articles of Agreement adopted by the International Fuel Tax Association, Inc., as amended as of December 1, 2018.

(2) **Motor carrier. --** A person who operates or causes to be operated on any highway in this State a motor vehicle that is a qualified motor vehicle. The term does not include the United States, a state, or a political subdivision of a state.

(3) **Motor vehicle.** -- Defined in G.S. 20-4.01.

(4) **Operations.** -- The movement of a qualified motor vehicle by a motor carrier, whether loaded or empty and whether or not operated for compensation.

(5) **Person.** -- Defined in G.S. 105-228.90.

(6) **Qualified motor vehicle.** -- Defined in the International Fuel Tax Agreement.

(7) **Secretary.** -- Defined in G.S. 105-228.90.

(b) **Liability.** -- A motor carrier who operates on one or more days of a reporting period is liable for the tax imposed by this Article for that reporting period and is entitled to the credits allowed for that reporting period.

(c) **Application.** -- A motor carrier who operates a qualified motor vehicle in this State must submit an application, as provided in this Article, and obtain the appropriate license and decals for the vehicle. The Article applies to both an interstate motor carrier subject to the International Fuel Tax Agreement and to an intrastate motor carrier.

History.

1955, c. 823, s. 1; 1973, c. 476, s. 193; 1983, c. 713, s. 55; 1989, c. 7, s. 1; 1991, c. 182, s. 2; c. 487, s. 2; 1991 (Reg. Sess., 1992), c. 913, s. 8; 1993, c. 354, s. 28; 1999-337, s. 36; 2000-140, s. 74; 2008-134, s. 16; 2010-95, s. 27; 2014-3, s. 9.5(b); 2017-39, s. 11; 2020-58, s. 2.9

EDITOR'S NOTE. --

Session Laws 2014-3, s. 9.5(a), effective May 29, 2014, rewrote the Article 36B heading, which formerly read "Tax on Carriers Using Fuel Purchased Outside State."

EFFECT OF AMENDMENTS. --

Session Laws 2008-134, s. 16, effective January 1, 2009, rewrote subsection (a).

Session Laws 2010-95, s. 27, effective July 17, 2010, substituted "June 1, 2010" for "June 1, 2008" in subdivision (a)(1).

Session Laws 2014-3, s. 9.5(b), effective May 29, 2014, added "application" at the end of the section heading; substituted "July 1, 2013" for "June 1, 2010" in subdivision (a)(1); and added subsection (c).

Session Laws 2017-39, s. 11, effective June 21, 2017, substituted "January 1, 2017" for "July 1, 2013" in subdivision (a)(1); and, in subsection (c), substituted "submit an application," for "register the vehicle'" and made a stylistic change.

Session Laws 2020-58, s. 2.9, effective June 30, 2020, substituted "December 1, 2018" for "January 1, 2017" in subdivision (a)(1).

§ 105-449.38. Tax levied

A road tax for the privilege of using the streets and highways of this State is imposed upon every motor carrier on the amount of motor fuel or alternative fuel used by the carrier in its operations within this State. The tax shall be at the rate established by the Secretary pursuant to G.S. 105-449.80 or G.S. 105-449.136, as appropriate. This tax is in addition to any other taxes imposed on motor carriers.

History.

1955, c. 823, s. 2; 1969, c. 600, s. 22; 1981, c. 690, s. 3; 1985 (Reg. Sess., 1986), c. 982, s. 16; 1995, c. 390, s. 16; 2001-205, s. 2; 2008-134, s. 17

EFFECT OF AMENDMENTS. --

Session Laws 2008-134, s. 17, effective January 1, 2009, made a minor punctuation change.

§ 105-449.39. Credit for payment of motor fuel tax

Every motor carrier subject to the tax levied by this Article is entitled to a credit on its quarterly return for tax paid by the carrier on fuel purchased in the State. The amount of the credit is determined using the tax rate in effect under G.S. 105-449.80 for the time period covered by the return. To obtain a credit, the motor carrier must furnish evidence satisfactory to the Secretary that the tax for which the credit is claimed has been paid.

If the amount of a credit to which a motor carrier is entitled for a quarter exceeds the motor carrier's liability for that quarter, the excess is refundable in accordance with G.S. 105-241.7.

History.

1955, c. 823, s. 3; 1969, c. 600, s. 22; c. 1098; 1973, c. 476, s. 193; 1979, 2nd Sess., c. 1098; 1981, c. 690, s. 3; 1985 (Reg. Sess., 1986), c. 982, s. 17; 1987, c. 315; 1989, c. 692, s. 5.7; 1991, c. 182, s. 3; c. 487, s. 3; 1998-146, s. 1; 1999-337, s. 37; 2005-435, s. 3; 2007-491, s. 40; 2010-95, s. 26(a); 2016-5, s. 4.10(a)

EDITOR'S NOTE. --

Session Laws 2007-491, s. 47, provides: "G.S. 105-241.10, as enacted by Section 1 of this act, and Sections 6, 15, 16, 17, and 22 are effective for taxable years beginning on or after January 1, 2007. Section 14 is effective for taxable years beginning on or after January 1, 2008. Sections 45, 46, and 47 are effective when they become law. The remainder of this act becomes effective January 1, 2008. The procedures for review of disputed tax matters enacted by this act apply to assessments of tax that are not final as of the effective date of this act and to claims for refund pending on or filed on or after the effective date of this act. This act does not affect matters for which a petition for review was filed with the Tax Review Board under G.S. 105-241.2 [repealed] before the effective date of this act. The repeal of G.S. 105-122(c) and G.S. 105-130.4(t) and Sections 11 and 12 apply to requests for alternative apportionment formulas filed on or after the effective date of this act. A petition filed with the Tax Review Board for an apportionment formula before the effective date of this act is considered a request under G.S. 105-122(c1) or G.S. 105-130.4(t1), as appropriate."

EFFECT OF AMENDMENTS. --

Session Laws 2005-435, s. 3, effective September 27, 2005, substituted "carrier in accordance with G.S. 105-266(a)(3)" for "carrier" in the last paragraph.

Session Laws 2007-491, s. 40, effective January 1, 2008, substituted "excess is refundable in accordance with G.S. 105-241.7" for "Secretary must refund the excess to the motor carrier in accordance with G.S. 105-266(a)(3)" in the second paragraph. For applicability, see Editor's note.

Session Laws 2010-95, s. 26(a), effective July 17, 2010, twice substituted "return" for "report" in the first paragraph.

Session Laws 2016-5, s. 4.10(a), effective January 1, 2016, substituted "the tax rate in effect under G.S. 105-449.80 for the time period" for "the flat cents-per-gallon rate plus the variable cents-per-gallon rate of tax in effect during the quarter" in the second sentence of the first paragraph.

§ 105-449.40. Secretary may require bond

(a) **Authority.** -- The Secretary may require a motor carrier to furnish a bond when any of the following occurs:

(1) The motor carrier fails to file a return within the time required by this Article.

(2) The motor carrier fails to pay a tax when due under this Article.

(3) After auditing the motor carrier's records, the Secretary determines that a bond is needed to protect the State from loss in collecting the tax due under this Article.

(b) **Amount.** -- A bond required of a motor carrier under this section may not be more than the larger of the following amounts:

(1) Five hundred dollars ($ 500.00).

(2) Four times the motor carrier's average tax liability or refund for a reporting period.

A bond must be in the form required by the Secretary.

History.

1955, c. 823, s. 4; 1967, c. 1110, s. 15; 1973, c. 476, s. 193; 1991, c. 487, s. 4; 2010-95, s. 26(b).

EFFECT OF AMENDMENTS. --

Session Laws 2010-95, s. 26(b), effective July 17, 2010, substituted "return" for "report" in subdivision (a)(1).

N.C. Gen. Stat. § 105-449.41

Repealed by Session Laws 2002-108, s. 2, effective January 1, 2003.

§ 105-449.42. Payment of tax

The tax levied by this Article is due when a motor carrier files a quarterly return under G.S. 105-449.45. The amount of tax due is calculated on the amount of motor fuel or alternative fuel used by the motor carrier in its operations within this State during the quarter covered by the return.

History.

1955, c. 823, s. 6; 1973, c. 476, s. 193; 1979, 2nd Sess., c. 1086, s. 2; 1983, c. 29, s. 2; 1991, c. 182, s. 4; 1999-337, s. 38; 2010-95, s. 26(c)

EFFECT OF AMENDMENTS. --

Session Laws 2010-95, s. 26(c), effective July 17, 2010, twice substituted "return" for "report."

§ 105-449.42A. Leased motor vehicles

(a) **Lessor in Leasing Business.** -- A lessor who is regularly engaged in the business of leasing or renting motor vehicles without drivers for compensation is the motor carrier for a leased or rented motor vehicle unless the lessee of the leased or rented motor vehicle gives the Secretary written notice, by filing a return or otherwise, that the lessee is the motor carrier. In that circumstance, the lessee is the motor carrier for the leased or rented motor vehicle.

Before a lessee gives the Secretary written notice under this subsection that the lessee is the motor carrier, the lessee and lessor must make a written agreement for the lessee to be the motor carrier. Upon request of the Secretary, the lessee must give the Secretary a copy of the agreement.

(b) **Independent Contractor.** -- The lessee of a motor vehicle that is leased from an independent contractor is the motor carrier for the leased motor vehicle unless one of the circumstances listed in this subsection applies. If either of these circumstances applies, the lessor is the motor carrier for the leased motor vehicle.

(1) The motor vehicle is leased for fewer than 30 days.

(2) The motor vehicle is leased for at least 30 days and the lessor gives the Secretary written notice, by filing a return or otherwise, that the lessor is the motor carrier.

Before a lessor gives the Secretary written notice that the lessor is the motor carrier, the lessor and lessee must make a written agreement for the lessor to be the motor carrier. Upon request of the Secretary, the lessor must give the Secretary a copy of the agreement.

(c) **Liability.** -- An independent contractor who leases a motor vehicle to another for fewer than 30 days is liable for compliance with this Article and the person to whom the motor vehicle is leased is not liable. Otherwise, both the lessor and lessee of a motor vehicle are jointly and severally liable for compliance with this Article.

History.

1983, c. 29, s. 3; 1985 (Reg. Sess., 1986), c. 826, s. 11; 1991, c. 487, s. 5; 1991 (Reg. Sess., 1992), c. 913, s. 9; 2010-95, s. 26(d).

EFFECT OF AMENDMENTS. --

Session Laws 2010-95, s. 26(d), effective July 17, 2010, in the first paragraph of subsection (a) and the first sentence of subdivision (b)(2), substituted "return" for "report"; in the introductory paragraph of subsection (b), in the first sentence, substituted "unless one of the circumstances listed in this subsection applies" for "unless either of the following applies," and added the last sentence; added the last two sentences in subdivision (b)(2); and deleted the last three sentences in subsection (b), which read: "If either of these circumstances applies, the lessor is the motor carrier for the leased motor vehicle. Before a lessor gives the Secretary written notice under subdivision (2) that the lessor is the motor carrier, the lessor and lessee must make a written agreement for the lessor to be the motor carrier. Upon request of the Secretary, the lessor must give the Secretary a copy of the agreement."

§ 105-449.43. Application of tax proceeds

Tax revenue collected under this Article and tax refunds or credits allowed under this Article shall be allocated among and charged to the funds and accounts listed in G.S. 105-449.125 in accordance with that section.

History.

1955, c. 823, s. 7; 1981 (Reg. Sess., 1982), c. 1211, s. 3; 1989, c. 692, s. 1.16; 1995, c. 390, s. 17

§ 105-449.44. How to determine the amount of fuel used in the State; presumption of amount used

(a) **Calculation.** -- The amount of motor fuel or alternative fuel a motor carrier uses in its operations in this State for a reporting period is the number of miles the motor carrier travels in this State during that period divided by the calculated miles per gallon for the motor carrier for all qualified motor vehicles during that period.

(b) **Presumption.** -- The Secretary must check returns filed under this Article against the weigh station records and other records of the Division of Motor Vehicles of the Department of Transportation and the State Highway Patrol of the Department of Public Safety concerning motor carriers to determine if motor carriers that are operating in this State are filing the returns required by this Article. If the records indicate that a motor carrier operated in this State in a quarter and either did not file a return for that quarter or understated its mileage in this State on a return filed for that quarter by at least twenty-five percent

(25%), the Secretary may assess the motor carrier for an amount based on the motor carrier's presumed operations. The motor carrier is presumed to have mileage in this State equal to 10 trips of 450 miles each for each of the motor carrier's qualified motor vehicles and to have fuel usage of four miles per gallon.

(c) **Vehicles.** -- The number of qualified motor vehicles of a motor carrier that is licensed under this Article is the number of sets of decals issued to the carrier. The number of qualified motor vehicles of a carrier that is not licensed under this Article is the number of qualified motor vehicles licensed or registered by the motor carrier in the carrier's base state under the International Registration Plan.

History.

1955, c. 823, s. 8; 1995, c. 390, s. 35; 1999-337, s. 39; 2000-173, s. 12; 2005-435, s. 4; 2008-134, s. 18; 2010-95, s. 26(e); 2011-145, s. 19.1(g); 2017-204, s. 4.4(a).

EDITOR'S NOTE. --

Session Laws 2017-204, s. 4.9, provides in part: "The remainder of this part is effective when it becomes law [August 11, 2017] and applies to requests for review filed on or after that date and to requests for review pending on that date for which the Department reissues a request for additional information, allows the taxpayer time to respond by the requested response date, and provides notification to the taxpayer that failure to timely respond to the request will result in the request for review being subject to the provisions of G.S. 105-241.13A."

Session Laws 2017-204, s. 7.1, is a severability clause.

EFFECT OF AMENDMENTS. --

Session Laws 2005-435, s. 4, effective September 27, 2005, rewrote subsection (a).

Session Laws 2008-134, s. 18, effective January 1, 2009, in subsection (a), substituted "motor vehicles" for "vehicles" near the end; rewrote subsection (b); and in subsection (c), substituted "qualified motor vehicles" for "vehicles" all three times it appears, and substituted "sets of decals" for "identification markers" near the end of the first sentence.

Session Laws 2010-95, s. 26(e), effective July 17, 2010, in subsection (b), twice substituted "returns" for "reports" in the first sentence, and twice substituted "return" for "report" in the second sentence.

Session Laws 2011-145, s. 19.1(g), effective January 1, 2012, substituted "Public Safety" for "Crime Control and Public Safety" in the first sentence of subsection (b).

Session Laws 2017-204, s. 4.4(a), effective August 11, 2017, in subsection (c), substituted "licensed" for "registered" in the first and second sentences, and inserted "licensed or" in the second sentence. For applicability, see editor's note.

§ 105-449.45. Returns of carriers

(a) **Return.** -- A motor carrier must report its operations to the Secretary on a quarterly basis unless subsection (b) of this section exempts the motor carrier from this requirement. A quarterly return covers a calendar quarter and is due by the last day in April, July, October, and January. A return must be filed in the form required by the Secretary.

(b) **Exemptions. --** A motor carrier is not required to file a quarterly return if any of the following applies:

(1) All the motor carrier's operations during the quarter were made under a temporary permit issued under G.S. 105-449.49.

(2) The motor carrier is an intrastate motor carrier, as indicated on the motor carrier's application for licensure with the Secretary.

(c) **Informational Returns. --** A motor carrier must file with the Secretary any informational returns concerning its operations that the Secretary requires.

(d) **Penalties. --** A motor carrier that fails to file a return under this section by the required date is subject to a penalty of fifty dollars ($ 50.00).

(e) **Interest. --** Interest on overpayments and underpayments of tax imposed on motor carriers under this Article is subject to the interest rate adopted in the International Fuel Tax Agreement.

History.

1955, c. 823, s. 9; 1973, c. 476, s. 193; 1979, 2nd Sess., c. 1086, s. 2; 1981 (Reg. Sess., 1982), c. 1254, s. 2; 1989 (Reg. Sess., 1990), c. 1050, s. 1; 1991, c. 182, s. 5; 1995, c. 17, s. 13.1; 1998-212, s. 29A.14(q); 1999-337, s. 40; 2009-445, s. 31(a); 2010-95, s. 26(f); 2016-5, s. 4.8; 2017-204, s. 4.4(b)

EDITOR'S NOTE. --

Session Laws 2017-204, s. 4.9, provides in part: "The remainder of this part is effective when it becomes law [August 11, 2017] and applies to requests for review filed on or after that date and to requests for review pending on that date for which the Department reissues a request for additional information, allows the taxpayer time to respond by the requested response date, and provides notification to the taxpayer that failure to timely respond to the request will result in the request for review being subject to the provisions of G.S. 105-241.13A."

Session Laws 2017-204, s. 7.1, is a severability clause.

EFFECT OF AMENDMENTS. --

Session Laws 2009-445, s. 31(a), effective January 1, 2010, added the last sentence in subsection (a).

Session Laws 2010-95, s. 26(f), effective July 17, 2010, in the section catchline, substituted "Returns" for "Reports"; throughout the section, substituted "return" for "report," or similar language; and in subsection (c), substituted "Informational Returns" for "Other Reports" and "must file with the Secretary any informational returns" for "must file with the Secretary other reports."

Session Laws 2016-5, s. 4.8, effective May 11, 2016, added subsection (e).

Session Laws 2017-204, s. 4.4(b), effective August 11, 2017, substituted "licensure" for "registration" in subdivision (b)(2). For applicability, see editor's note.

§ 105-449.46. Inspection of books and records

The Secretary and his authorized agents and representatives shall have the right at any reasonable time to inspect the books and records of any motor carrier subject to the tax imposed by this Article or to the registration fee imposed by Article 3 of Chapter 20 of the General Statutes.

History.

1955, c. 823, s. 10; 1973, c. 476, s. 193; 2005-435, s. 5

EFFECT OF AMENDMENTS. --

Session Laws 2005-435, s. 5, effective September 27, 2005, substituted "Article or to the registration fee imposed by Article 3 of Chapter 20 of the General Statutes" for "Article" at the end of the paragraph.

§ 105-449.47. Licensure of vehicles

(a) **Requirement. --** A motor carrier may not operate or cause to be operated in this State a qualified motor vehicle unless both the motor carrier and at least one qualified motor vehicle are licensed as provided in this subsection. This subsection applies to a motor carrier that operates a recreational vehicle that is used in connection with any business endeavor. A motor carrier that is subject to the International Fuel Tax Agreement must be licensed with the motor carrier's base state jurisdiction. A motor carrier that is not subject to the International Fuel Tax Agreement must be licensed with the Secretary for purposes of the tax imposed by this Article.

(a1) **License and Decal. --** When the Secretary licenses a motor carrier, the Secretary must issue a license for the motor carrier and a set of decals for each qualified motor vehicle. A motor carrier must keep records of decals issued to it and must be able to account for all decals it receives from the Secretary. Licenses and decals issued by the Secretary are for a calendar year. All decals issued by the Secretary remain the property of the State. The Secretary may revoke a license or a decal when a motor carrier fails to comply with this Article or Article 36C or 36D of this Subchapter.

A motor carrier must carry a copy of its license in each motor vehicle operated by the motor carrier when the vehicle is in this State. Unless operating under a temporary permit under G.S. 105-449.49, a motor vehicle must clearly display one decal on each side of the vehicle at all times. A decal must be affixed to the qualified motor vehicle for which it was issued in the place and manner designated by the authority that issued it.

(b) **Exemption.** -- This section does not apply to the operation of a qualified motor vehicle that is licensed in another state and is operated temporarily in this State by a public utility, a governmental or cooperative provider of utility services, or a contractor for one of these entities for the purpose of restoring utility services in an emergency outage.

History.

1955, c. 823, s. 11; 1973, c. 746, s. 193; 1983, c. 713, s. 56; 1985 (Reg. Sess., 1986), c. 937, s. 20; 1989, c. 692, s. 6.2; 1991, c. 487, s. 6; 1995, c. 50, s. 5; c. 390, s. 18; 1999-337, s. 41; 2002-108, s. 3; 2004-170, s. 24; 2005-435, s. 6; 2008-134, s. 19; 2014-3, s. 9.5(c); 2017-204, s. 4.4(c); 2020-58, s. 2.10(a)

EDITOR'S NOTE. --

Session Laws 2017-204, s. 4.9, provides in part: "The remainder of this part is effective when it becomes law [August 11, 2017] and applies to requests for review filed on or after that date and to requests for review pending on that date for which the Department reissues a request for additional information, allows the taxpayer time to respond by the requested response date, and provides notification to the taxpayer that failure to timely respond to the request will result in the request for review being subject to the provisions of G.S. 105-241.13A."

Session Laws 2017-204, s. 7.1, is a severability clause.

EFFECT OF AMENDMENTS. --

Session Laws 2002-108, s. 3, effective January 1, 2003, redesignated the former second and third paragraphs of subsection (a) as present subsection (a1); and in subsection (a1), inserted "Registration and Identification Marker" at the beginning, and inserted the second sentence.

Session Laws 2004-170, s. 24, effective August 2, 2004, deleted the former fourth sentence which read: "The Secretary may renew a registration or an identification marker without issuing a new registration or identification marker."

Session Laws 2005-435, s. 6, effective September 27, 2005, in subsection (a1), deleted "withhold or" preceding "revoke a registration" and substituted "Article" for "Article, former Article 36 or 36A of this Subchapter" in the last sentence.

Session Laws 2008-134, s. 19, effective January 1, 2009, rewrote the section.

Session Laws 2014-3, s. 9.5(c), effective May 29, 2014, rewrote subsection (a).

Session Laws 2017-204, s. 4.4(c), effective August 11, 2017, substituted "Licensure" for "Registration" or similar language, in the section heading and throughout the section; substituted "used in connection with any business endeavor" for "considered a qualified motor vehicle" in the second sentence of subsection (a); and deleted "the motor carrier registers" following "motor vehicle" in the first sentence of subsection (a1). For applicability, see editor's note.

Session Laws 2020-58, s. 2.10(a), effective June 30, 2020, added "Unless operating under a temporary permit under G.S. 105-449.49" at the beginning of the second sentence in the second paragraph of subsection (a1).

§ 105-449.47A. Denial of license application and decal issuance

The Secretary may refuse to license and issue a decal to an applicant that does not meet the requirements set out in G.S. 105-449.69(b) or that has done any of the following:

(1) Had a license issued under Chapter 105 or Chapter 119 of the General Statutes revoked by the Secretary.

(2) Had a license issued by another jurisdiction, pursuant to the International Fuel Tax Agreement, revoked.

(3) Been convicted of fraud or misrepresentation.

(4) Been convicted of any other offense that indicates that the applicant may not comply with this Article if licensed and issued a decal.

(5) Failed to remit payment for a tax debt under Chapter 105 or Chapter 119 of the General Statutes. The term "tax debt" has the same meaning as defined in G.S. 105-243.1.

(6) Failed to file a return due under Chapter 105 or Chapter 119 of the General Statutes.

(7) Failed to maintain motor vehicle registration on the qualified motor vehicle.

History.

2005-435, s. 7; 2008-134, s. 20; 2009-445, s. 32; 2010-95, s. 28; 2017-204, s. 4.4(d); 2019-169, s. 4.10

EDITOR'S NOTE. --

Session Laws 2008-134, s. 20, amended this section in the coded bill drafting format provided by G.S. 120-20.1. The word "to" was inadvertently stricken from subdivision (2). The error was corrected by Session Laws 2009-445, s. 32.

Session Laws 2017-204, s. 4.9, provides in part: "The remainder of this part is effective when it becomes law [August 11, 2017] and applies to requests for review filed on or after that date and to requests for review pending on that date for which the Department reissues a request for additional information, allows the taxpayer time to respond by the requested response date, and provides notification to the taxpayer that failure to timely respond to the request will result in the request for review being subject to the provisions of G.S. 105-241.13A."

Session Laws 2017-204, s. 7.1, is a severability clause.

EFFECT OF AMENDMENTS. --

Session Laws 2008-134, s. 20, effective January 1, 2009, in the section heading, substituted "decals" for "identification markers"; in the introductory language, substituted "a decal" for "an identification marker"; in subdivision (2), substituted "the International Fuel Tax Agreement" for "to G.S. 105-449.57"; and in subdivision (4), substituted "a decal" for "an identification marker."

Session Laws 2009-445, s. 32, effective August 7, 2009, inserted "to" in subdivision (2).

Session Laws 2010-95, s. 28, effective July 17, 2010, inserted "does not meet the requirements set out in G.S. 105-449.69(b) or that" in the introductory language.

Session Laws 2017-204, s. 4.4(d), effective August 11, 2017, rewrote the section heading; substituted "license" for "registration" or similar language throughout the section; substituted "revoked by the Secretary" for "cancelled by the Secretary for cause" in subdivision (1); and substituted "revoked" for "cancelled for cause" in subdivision (2). For applicability, see editor's note.

Session Laws 2019-169, s. 4.10, effective July 26, 2019, added subdivision (7).

N.C. Gen. Stat. § 105-449.48

Repealed by Session Laws 2006-162, s. 12(c), effective July 24, 2006.

§ 105-449.49. Temporary permits

(a) **Permitting Service. --** Upon application to the Secretary and payment of a fee of fifty dollars ($ 50.00), a permitting service may obtain a temporary permit authorizing a motor carrier to operate a vehicle in the State for three days without licensing the vehicle in accordance with G.S. 105-449.47. The permitting service may sell the temporary permit to a motor carrier. A motor carrier to whom a temporary permit has been issued may elect not to report its operation of the vehicle during the three-day period. Fees collected under this subsection are credited to the Highway Fund.

(b) Repealed by Session Laws 2016-5, s. 4.6, effective May 11, 2016.

(c) **Licensed Motor Carrier. --** A licensed motor carrier in North Carolina, who is subject to the International Fuel Tax Agreement, may apply for a temporary permit authorizing the motor carrier to operate a qualified motor vehicle in the State for 30 days without a decal. The licensed motor carrier must be in compliance with this Article, and the application must be on a form prescribed by the Secretary and contain information required by the Secretary.

(d) **Permit. --** A motor carrier operating under a temporary permit issued pursuant to this section must keep a copy of the permit in the motor vehicle.

History.

1955, c. 823, s. 13; 1973, c. 476, s. 193; 1979, c. 11; 1981 (Reg. Sess., 1982), c. 1254, s. 1; 1983, c. 713, s. 58;

1991, c. 182, s. 6; c. 487, s. 7; 1991 (Reg. Sess., 1992), c. 913, s. 10; 2003-349, s. 10.1; 2006-162, s. 12(d); 2016-5, s. 4.6; 2017-204, s. 4.4(e); 2020-58, s. 2.10(b)

EDITOR'S NOTE. --

Session Laws 2017-204, s. 4.9, provides in part: "The remainder of this part is effective when it becomes law [August 11, 2017] and applies to requests for review filed on or after that date and to requests for review pending on that date for which the Department reissues a request for additional information, allows the taxpayer time to respond by the requested response date, and provides notification to the taxpayer that failure to timely respond to the request will result in the request for review being subject to the provisions of G.S. 105-241.13A."

Session Laws 2017-204, s. 7.1, is a severability clause.

EFFECT OF AMENDMENTS. --

Session Laws 2003-349, s. 10.1, effective January 1, 2004, in the first sentence of the introductory paragraph, substituted "three days" for "20 days" and in the second sentence, substituted "three-day period" for "20-day period."

Session Laws 2006-162, s. 12(d), effective July 24, 2006, added the subsection designations and subsection catchlines; and, in present subsection (a), inserted "for three days" following "State" and deleted "for not more than three days" at the end of the first sentence and added the last sentence.

Session Laws 2016-5, s. 4.6, effective May 11, 2016, in subsection (a), in the first sentence, substituted "a permitting service" for "a motor carrier" near the beginning and substituted "a motor carrier" for "the carrier" near the middle, and added the second sentence; and deleted former subsection (b) pertaining to refusal to issue a temporary permit.

Session Laws 2017-204, s. 4.4(e), effective August 11, 2017, substituted "licensing" for "registering" in the first sentence of subsection (a). For applicability, see editor's note.

Session Laws 2020-58, s. 2.10(b), effective June 30, 2020, substituted "Permitting Service" for "Issuance" in the heading of subsection (a); and added subsections (c) and (d).

N.C. Gen. Stat. § 105-449.50

Repealed by Session Laws 2008-134, s. 21, effective January 1, 2009.

§ 105-449.51. Violations declared to be misdemeanors

A person who operates or causes to be operated on a highway in this State a qualified motor vehicle that does not carry a license as required by this Article, does not properly display a decal as required by this Article, or is not licensed in accordance with this Article commits a Class 3 misdemeanor and is punishable by a fine of two hundred dollars ($ 200.00). Each day's operation in violation of this section constitutes a separate offense.

History.

1955, c. 823, s. 15; 1973, c. 476, s. 193; 1983, c. 713, s. 59; 1993, c. 539, s. 734; 1994, Ex. Sess., c. 24, s. 14(c); 2005-435, s. 8; 2008-134, s. 22; 2017-204, s. 4.4(f)

EDITOR'S NOTE. --

Session Laws 2017-204, s. 4.9, provides in part: "The remainder of this part is effective when it becomes law [August 11, 2017] and applies to requests for review filed on or after that date and to requests for review pending on that date for which the Department reissues a request for additional information, allows the taxpayer time to respond by the requested response date, and provides notification to the taxpayer that failure to timely respond to the request will result in the request for review being subject to the provisions of G.S. 105-241.13A."

Session Laws 2017-204, s. 7.1, is a severability clause.

EFFECT OF AMENDMENTS. --

Session Laws 2005-435, s. 8, effective January 1, 2006, deleted "only" preceding "be fined" and "no less than ten dollars ($10.00) nor more than" thereafter in the introductory language.

Session Laws 2008-134, s. 22, effective January 1, 2009, inserted "qualified" preceding "motor vehicle," substituted "a decal" for "an identification marker," "Article commits" for "Article is guilty of," and "and is punishable by a fine of" for "and, upon conviction thereof, shall be fined," deleted "of any provision" following "operation in violation," and substituted "constitutes a separate" for "shall constitute a separate."

Session Laws 2017-204, s. 4.4(f), effective August 11, 2017, in the first sentence, substituted "A person" for "Any person," "license" for "registration card" and "licensed" for "registered." For applicability, see editor's note.

§ 105-449.52. Civil penalties applicable to motor carriers

(a) **Penalty.** -- A motor carrier who does any of the following is subject to a civil penalty:

(1) Operates in this State or causes to be operated in this State a qualified motor vehicle that either fails to carry the license required by this Article or fails to display a decal in accordance with this Article. The amount of the penalty is one hundred dollars ($ 100.00).

(2) Is unable to account for a decal the Secretary issues the motor carrier, as required by G.S. 105-449.47. The amount of the penalty is one hundred dollars ($ 100.00) for each decal for which the carrier is unable to account.

(3) Displays a decal on a qualified motor vehicle operated by a motor carrier that was not issued to the carrier by the Secretary under G.S. 105-449.47. The amount of the penalty is one thousand dollars ($ 1,000) for each decal unlawfully obtained. Both the licensed motor carrier to whom the Secretary issued the decal and the motor carrier displaying the unlawfully obtained decal are jointly and severally liable for the penalty under this subdivision.

(a1) **Payment.** -- A penalty imposed under this section is payable to the agency that assessed the penalty. When a qualified motor vehicle is found to be operating without a license or a decal or with a decal the Secretary did not issue for the vehicle, the qualified motor vehicle may not be driven for a purpose other than to park it until the penalty imposed under this section is paid unless the officer that imposes the penalty determines that operating it will not jeopardize collection of the penalty.

(b) **Penalty Reduction.** -- The Secretary may reduce or waive the penalty as provided under G.S. 105-449.119.

History.

1955, c. 823, s. 16; 1957, c. 948; 1973, c. 476, s. 193; 1975, c. 716, s. 5; 1981, c. 690, s. 18; 1983, c. 713, s. 60; 1991, c. 42, s. 14; 1991 (Reg. Sess., 1992), c. 913, s. 11; 1998-146, s. 2; 1999-337, s. 43; 2002-108, s. 4; 2004-170, s. 25; 2007-527, s. 16(a); 2008-134, ss. 8, 23; 2014-3, s. 9.8(a); 2017-204, s. 4.4(g)

EDITOR'S NOTE. --

Session Laws 2017-204, s. 4.9, provides in part: "The remainder of this part is effective when it becomes law [August 11, 2017] and applies to requests for review filed on or after that date and to requests for review pending on that date for which the Department reissues a request for additional information, allows the taxpayer time to respond by the requested response date, and provides notification to the taxpayer that failure to timely respond to the request will result in the request for review being subject to the provisions of G.S. 105-241.13A."

Session Laws 2017-204, s. 7.1, is a severability clause.

EFFECT OF AMENDMENTS. --

Session Laws 2002-108, s. 4, effective January 1, 2003, rewrote the section heading and subsection (a).

Session Laws 2004-170, s. 25, effective August 2, 2004, in subdivision (a)(1), substituted "either fails" for "does not" and "fails" for "does not"; and inserted "the Department of Crime Control and Public Safety," following "Department of Revenue" in the first sentence of the paragraph following subdivision (a)(3).

Session Laws 2007-527, s. 16(a), effective August 31, 2007, redesignated the former second paragraph of subdivision (a)(3) as present subsection (a1); and in subsection (a1), added the subsection heading, and substituted "agency that assessed the penalty" for "Department of Revenue, the Department of Crime Control and Public Safety, or the Division of Motor Vehicles."

Session Laws 2008-134, s. 8, effective July 28, 2008, in subsection (b), substituted "Review." for "Hearing." at the beginning, and substituted "reviewing a penalty" for "protesting a penalty."

Session Laws 2008-134, s. 23, effective January 1, 2009, in subdivision (a)(1), substituted "a qualified motor vehicle" for "a motor vehicle" and "a decal" for "an identification marker"; in subdivision (a)(2), substituted "a decal" for "identification markers," "decal for which" for "identification marker," and "account" for "account for"; in subdivision (a)(3), substituted "a decal on a qualified" for "an identification marker on a," and substituted "decal" for "an identification marker" three times; and in subsection (a1), substituted "qualified motor vehicle" for "motor vehicle" twice, "a decal" for "an identification marker" twice, "park it until" for "park the motor vehicle until," and "operating it" for "operation of the motor vehicle."

Session Laws 2014-3, s. 9.8(a), effective May 29, 2014, rewrote subsection (b).

Session Laws 2017-204, s. 4.4(g), effective August 11, 2017, substituted "license" for "registration card" in subdivision (a)(1) and subsection (a1); and substituted "Penalty Reduction" for "Penalty" in the heading for subsection (b). For applicability, see editor's note.

N.C. Gen. Stat. § 105-449.53

Repealed by Session Laws 1963, c. 1169, s. 6.

§ 105-449.54. Commissioner of Motor Vehicles made process agent of nonresident motor carriers

By operating a motor vehicle on the highways of this State, a nonresident motor carrier consents to the appointment of the Commissioner of Motor Vehicles as its attorney in fact and process agent for all summonses or other lawful process or notice in any action, assessment, or other proceeding under this Chapter.

History.
1955, c. 823, s. 18; 2004-170, s. 26
EFFECT OF AMENDMENTS. --
Session Laws 2004-170, s. 26, effective August 2, 2004, rewrote the section.

§§ 105-449.55, 105-449.56

Repealed by Session Laws 1991, c. 42, s. 17.
CROSS REFERENCES. --
As to enforcement of Subchapter V, see now G.S. 105-269.3.

§ 105-449.57. Cooperative agreements between jurisdictions

(a) **Authority.** -- The Secretary may enter into cooperative agreements with other jurisdictions for exchange of information in administering the tax imposed by this Article. No agreement, arrangement, declaration, or amendment to an agreement is effective until stated in writing and approved by the Secretary or the Secretary's designee.

(b) **Content.** -- An agreement may provide for determining the base state for motor carriers, records requirements, audit procedures, exchange of information, persons eligible for tax licensing, defining qualified motor vehicles, determining if bonding is required, specifying reporting requirements and periods, including defining uniform penalty and interest rates for late reporting, determining methods for collecting and forwarding of motor carrier taxes and penalties to another jurisdiction, and any other provisions that will facilitate the administration of the agreement.

(c) **Disclosure.** -- In accordance with G.S. 105-259, the Secretary may, as required by the terms of an agreement, forward to officials of another jurisdiction any information in the Department's possession relative to the administration and collection of a tax imposed on the use of motor fuel or alternative fuel by any motor carrier. The Secretary may disclose to officials of another jurisdiction the location of offices, motor vehicles, and other real and personal property of motor carriers.

(d) **Audits.** -- An agreement may provide for each jurisdiction to audit the records of motor carriers based in the jurisdiction to determine if the taxes due each jurisdiction are properly reported and paid. Each jurisdiction must forward the findings of the audits performed on motor carriers based in the jurisdiction to each jurisdiction in which the carrier has taxable use of motor fuel or alternative fuel. For motor carriers not based in this State, the Secretary may utilize the audit findings received from another jurisdiction as the basis upon which to propose assessments of taxes against the carrier as though the audit had been conducted by the Secretary. Penalties and interest must be assessed at the rates provided in the agreement.

No agreement entered into pursuant to this section may preclude the Department from auditing the records of any motor carrier covered by this Chapter.

The provisions of Article 9 of this Chapter apply to any assessment or order made under this section.

(e) **Restriction.** -- The Secretary or the Secretary's designee may not enter into any agreement that would increase or decrease taxes and fees imposed under Subchapter V of Chapter 105 of the General Statutes. Any provision to the contrary is void.

History.
1989, c. 667, s. 1; 1993, c. 485, s. 36; 1995 (Reg. Sess., 1996), c. 647, s. 50; 1999-337, s. 42; 2016-5, ss. 4.5(b), 4.7(a), (b)
EFFECT OF AMENDMENTS. --
Session Laws 2016-5, ss. 4.5(b) and 4.7(a), (b), effective May 11, 2016, added "or the Secretary's designee" at the end of subsection (a); inserted "administration and collection of a tax imposed on the" in the first sentence of subsection (c); and inserted "or the Secretary's designee" near the beginning of subsection (e).

CHAPTER 115C.
ELEMENTARY AND SECONDARY EDUCATION

SUBCHAPTER 04.
EDUCATION PROGRAM

ARTICLE 14.
DRIVER EDUCATION

§ 115C-215. Administration of driver education program by the Department of Public Instruction

(a) In accordance with criteria and standards approved by the State Board of Education, the State Superintendent of Public Instruction shall organize and administer a standardized program of driver education to be offered at the public high schools of this State for all physically and mentally qualified persons who (i) are older than 14 years and six months, (ii) are approved by the principal of the school, pursuant to rules adopted by the State Board of Education, (iii) are enrolled in a public or private high school within the State or are receiving instruction through a home school as provided by Part 3 of Article 39 of Chapter 115C of the General Statutes, and (iv) have not previously enrolled in the program. The driver education program shall be for the purpose of making available public education to all students on driver safety and training. The State Board of Education shall use for this purpose all funds appropriated pursuant to subsection (f) of this section to the Department of Public Instruction and may use all other funds that become available for its use for this purpose.

(b) The driver education curriculum shall include the following:

(1) Instruction on the rights and privileges of the handicapped and the signs and symbols used to assist the handicapped relative to motor vehicles, including the "international symbol of accessibility" and other symbols and devices as provided in Article 2A of Chapter 20 of the General Statutes.

(2) At least six hours of instruction on the offense of driving while impaired and related subjects.

(3) At least six hours of actual driving experience. To the extent practicable, this experience may include at least one hour of instruction on the techniques of defensive driving.

(4) At least one hour of motorcycle safety awareness training.

(5) Instruction on law enforcement procedures for traffic stops that is developed in consultation with the State Highway Patrol, the North Carolina Sheriff's Association, and the North Carolina Association of Chiefs of Police. The instruction shall provide a description of the actions that a motorist should take during a traffic stop, including appropriate interactions with law enforcement officers.

(c) The State Board of Education shall establish and implement a strategic plan for the driver education program. At a minimum, the strategic plan shall consist of goals and performance indicators, including the number of program participants as compared to the number of persons projected to be eligible to participate in the program, the implementation of a standard curriculum for the program, expenditures for the program, and the success rate of program participants in receiving a drivers license as reported by the Division of Motor Vehicles. The strategic plan shall also outline specific roles and duties of an advisory committee consisting of employees of the Division of Motor Vehicles and the Department of Public Instruction and other stakeholders in driver education.

(c1) If a local school administrative unit does not comply with any reporting requirements imposed on the unit for the purposes of implementing the strategic plan established by the State Board of Education pursuant to subsection (c) of this section, the Department of Public Instruction may withhold up to five percent (5%) of the State funds allocated to a local school administrative unit for driver education until the unit reports the information required by the Department.

(d) The State Board of Education shall adopt a salary range for the delivery of driver education courses by driver education instructors who are public school employees. The salary range shall be based on the driver education instructor's qualifications, certification, and licensure specific to driver education.

(e) The State Board of Education shall adopt rules to permit local boards of education to enter contracts with public or private entities to provide a program of driver education at public high schools. All driver education instructors shall meet the requirements established by the State Board of Education; provided, however, driver education instructors shall not be required to hold teacher certificates.

(f) The clear proceeds of the newly established motor vehicle registration late fee charged pursuant to G.S. 20-88.03, as enacted by S.L. 2015-241, shall be used to provide a dedicated source of revenue for the drivers education program administered by the Department of Public

Instruction in accordance with this section and shall be appropriated by the General Assembly for this purpose for the 2016-2017 fiscal year and subsequent fiscal years thereafter.

(g) The Department of Public Instruction shall have a full-time director and other professional, administrative, technical, and clerical personnel as may be necessary for the statewide administration of the driver education program. Of the funds appropriated to the Department each fiscal year pursuant to subsection (f) of this section, the Department may use up to two percent (2%) of those funds for the direct costs for the statewide administration of the program, including any necessary positions.

History.

1953, c. 1196; 1955, c. 1372, art. 23, s. 4; 1959, c. 573, s. 16; 1981, c. 423, s. 1; 1991, c. 689, s. 32(b); 2011-145, s. 28.37(a); 2011-334, s. 1; 2015-241, ss. 5.3(c), 8.39(a); 2016-94, ss. 5.2, 8.5; 2017-95, s. 2; 2018-5, s. 7.11(b)

EDITOR'S NOTE. --

Session Laws 2011-145, s. 28.37(f) -(i), provides: "(f) The State Board of Education shall report to the Joint Legislative Program Evaluation Oversight Committee by July 15, 2011, on the status of the implementation of Section 7.12 of S.L. 2010-31, which mandates the creation of a standard curriculum to be used for the driver education program in the Department of Public Instruction.

"(g) For the 2011-2012 school year, no State funds shall be used for driver education programs that do not use the standard driver education curriculum created in accordance with Section 7.12 of S.L. 2010-31.

"(h) The State Board of Education shall establish a pilot program to deliver driver education by electronic means. At least five local school administrative units shall participate in the pilot program. Funds appropriated for driver education shall be used to implement the pilot program. The State Board shall report on the implementation of the pilot program to the Joint Legislative Education Oversight Committee and the Joint Legislative Program Evaluation Oversight Committee by June 15, 2012. The report shall include the cost per student of delivering the instruction and the success rate of program participants in receiving a drivers license.   "(i) The State Board of Education shall report to the Joint Legislative Education Oversight Committee and to the Joint Legislative Program Evaluation Oversight Committee by June 15, 2012, on the following:

"(1) The most cost-effective method of delivering driver education in the short- and long-term. In making this determination, the State Board of Education shall consider the results of the pilot program implemented pursuant to Section 5 of this act.

"(2) The strategic plan adopted by the State Board of Education in accordance with G.S. 115C-215."

Session Laws 2011-145, s. 1.1, provides: "This act shall be known as the 'Current Operations and Capital Improvements Appropriations Act of 2011.'"

Session Laws 2011-145, s. 32.2, provides: "Except for statutory changes or other provisions that clearly indicate an intention to have effects beyond the 2011-2013 fiscal biennium, the textual provisions of this act apply only to funds appropriated for, and activities occurring during, the 2011-2013 fiscal biennium."

Session Laws 2011-145, s. 32.5, is a severability clause.

Session Laws 2014-100, s. 8.15(b), provides: "It is the intent of the General Assembly that, beginning with the 2015-2016 fiscal year, the driver education program administered by the Department of Public Instruction in accordance with G.S. 115C-215 shall no longer be paid out of the Highway Fund based on an annual appropriation by the General Assembly. Local boards of education shall use funds available to them, including a fee for instruction charged to students pursuant to G.S. 115C-216(g), to offer noncredit driver education courses in high schools."

Session Laws 2014-100, s. 1.1, provides: "This act shall be known as 'The Current Operations and Capital Improvements Appropriations Act of 2014.'"

Session Laws 2014-100, s. 38.4, provides: "Except for statutory changes or other provisions that clearly indicate an intention to have effects beyond the 2014-2015 fiscal year, the textual provisions of this act apply only to funds appropriated for, and activities occurring during, the 2014-2015 fiscal year."

Session Laws 2014-100, s. 38.7, is a severability clause.

Session Laws 2015-241, s. 5.3(c), as amended by Session Laws 2016-94, s. 5.2, was codified as subsection (f) of this section at the direction of the Revisor of Statutes.

Session Laws 2015-241, s. 8.39(d), provides: "Local boards of education shall report to the State Board of Education no later than December 15, 2015, on the following related to driver education programs offered by and through the local school administrative unit for the 2012-2013, 2013-2014, 2014-2015, and 2015-2016 school years, by year:

"(1) How driver education is provided. The local board of education shall provide detailed information regarding whether the driver education program is offered by the local school administrative unit or whether it contracts with an outside provider. If the local school administrative unit contracts with an outside provider to provide any portion of the driver education program, such as instruction, materials, or the fleet used for driver training, the unit shall provide a detailed summary of information as to the terms of the contract, what the unit is responsible for providing, and what the outside provider has contracted to provide, and a copy of all contracts related to driver education.

"(2) Total cost for the driver education program and per student cost for the program. The local board shall include a detailed explanation of expenditures of all funds associated with the driver education program, written in plain English.

"(3) How the fleet used for driver training is provided and maintained. If the local school administrative unit maintains its own fleet, information regarding the number of vehicles in the fleet, procurement, maintenance, and fuel cost of those vehicles, replacement cycle for the vehicles, and source of funds for the fleet.

"(4) Numbers of students eligible to participate in the driver education program, number of students participating in the program, and numbers of students successfully completing the program.

"(5) Materials used for instruction of the standardized driver education curriculum.

"(6) Methodology for transfer to agencies of student information related to driver education.

"(7) Role of parents and legal guardians in driver education instruction.

"(8) Process for filing and resolving complaints related to the driver education program. If the local school administrative unit has a process, the unit shall provide information on the numbers, types, and resolutions of filed complaints.

"(9) Assessments and evaluations used to determine quality and success of the driver education program.

"(10) Average and maximum length of time between classroom instruction and behind-the-wheel instruction.

"(11) Average and maximum number of classroom hours taught per day on regular school days and on any other day.

"(12) Average and maximum number of behind-the-wheel hours taught per day on regular school days and on any other day.

"(13) Process, if any, for reviewing driving records for driver education instructors.

"(14) Tracking, if any, of student outcomes when seeking a graduated drivers license. If the local school administrative unit tracks this information, the unit shall provide data on student outcomes, including numbers of students who successfully completed or unsuccessfully completed the written and driving portions of the graduated drivers license examination, respectively.

"(15) If fees are charged for driver education, fee waivers or reductions, if any, provided to students. If fee waivers or reductions are provided, the local school administrative unit should provide data on the policy for fee waivers or reductions, how many students are eligible for and use the waiver or reduction, and the amounts waived or reduced."

Session Laws 2015-241, s. 8.39(e) , provides: "The State Board of Education shall report to the Joint Legislative Education Oversight Committee (Committee) on the information provided by local boards of education on driver education programs under subsection (d) of this section no later than February 15, 2016."

Session Laws 2015-241, s. 8.39(f) , provides: "The Committee shall study the provision of driver education by examining information, findings, and recommendations in the following reports and any additional information that it deems necessary and relevant:

"(1) The National Highway Traffic Safety Administration report issued in May 2015, entitled "State of

North Carolina: Technical Assessment of the Driver Education Program.

"(2) The North Carolina Driver Education Strategic Plan prepared in June 2012 by the Driver Education Advisory Committee of the State Board of Education.

"(3) The North Carolina's Driver Education Program Management Review prepared in November 2010 by the Office of State Budget and Management.

"(4) The Program Evaluation Division's report issued in March 2014, entitled "Performance Measurement and Monitoring Would Strengthen Accountability of North Carolina's Driver Education Program.

"(5) Information provided by local boards of education on driver education programs, as reported by the State Board of Education pursuant to subsection (e) of this section."

Session Laws 2015-241, s. 8.39(g) , provides: "The Committee shall make recommendations, which may include proposed legislation, on the study required under subsection (f) of this section to the 2015 General Assembly upon its convening of the 2016 Regular Session on the following issues:

"(1) Lowering the cost of delivery for driver education.

"(2) Adjusting or removing fees for driver education.

"(3) The appropriate level of involvement for parents and legal guardians.

"(4) Appropriate level of involvement of the Department of Transportation, Division of Motor Vehicles.

"(5) Recommendations on alternate providers, such as community colleges or private entities."

Session Laws 2015-241, s. 8.39(h) , as amended by Session Laws 2016-94, s. 8.5 , made the amendments by Session Laws 2015-241, s. 8.39(a) , effective July 1, 2016, and applicable beginning with the 2016-2017 school year.

Session Laws 2015-241, s. 1.1 , provides: "This act shall be known as 'The Current Operations and Capital Improvements Appropriations Act of 2015.'"

Session Laws 2015-241, s. 33.4 , provides: "Except for statutory changes or other provisions that clearly indicate an intention to have effects beyond the 2015-2017 fiscal biennium, the textual provisions of this act apply only to funds appropriated for, and activities occurring during, the 2015-2017 fiscal biennium."

Session Laws 2015-241, s. 33.6 , is a severability clause.

Session Laws 2016-23, s. 5(a) , made current North Carolina students who are eligible to attend North Carolina schools before boundary certification, and who lose eligibility as a result of certification, to attend North Carolina schools.

Session Laws 2016-23, s. 6(a) -(c), provides: "(a) Notwithstanding State Board of Education policy, GCS-R-004, or any other provision of law, if a student enrolled in a North Carolina public school or charter school under subsection (a) of Section 5 of this act obtains a beginner's permit in South Carolina, the student shall be eligible to participate in behind-the-wheel instruction as part of a driver education course offered by the local school administrative unit in which the student is enrolled "(b) Notwithstanding G.S. 20-11(b)(1), a student who (i) as a result of the boundary certification becomes a legal resident of North Carolina on the date of the certification and (ii) is enrolled in a South Carolina school district in which his or her residence was located prior to certification or in the South Carolina statewide public charter school district may meet the requirement in G.S. 20-11(b)(1) for obtaining a limited learner's permit if the student passes a course of driver education offered by the South Carolina high school in which the student is enrolled.

"(c) The Department of Transportation, Division of Motor Vehicles, in collaboration with the State Board of Education, shall develop a procedure for any North Carolina resident who is a student enrolled in a South Carolina school pursuant to the conditions described in subsection (b) of this section to satisfy the driver eligibility certificate requirements of G.S. 20-11 to obtain and continue to hold a limited or full provisional license under this section."

Session Laws 2016-23, s. 12(a) , is a severability clause.

Session Laws 2017-95, s. 3 , made subdivision (b) (5), as added by Session Laws 2017-95, s. 2 , effective July 12, 2017, and applicable beginning with the 2017-2018 school year.

Session Laws 2018-5, s. 1.1 , provides: "This act shall be known as the 'Current Operations Appropriations Act of 2018.'"

Session Laws 2018-5, s. 39.7 , is a severability clause.

Session Laws 2020-30, s. 2 , provides: "Notwithstanding G.S. 115C-215(b)(1), (2), (4), and (5) and G.S. 115C-216, and the requirements of State Board of Education Policy DRIV-0004, for students enrolled in classroom driver education between January 2020 and March 16, 2020, in a public school or a licensed commercial driver training school, students shall be deemed to have completed all classroom instruction requirements for driver education if the student completed at least 15 hours of classroom instruction prior to March 16, 2020. A student who has not completed at least 15 hours of classroom instruction may be offered the opportunity to take and pass the proficiency examination developed by the Department of Public Instruction, as provided in the State Board of Education Policy DRIV-0004, to waive the classroom instruction requirement. All students enrolled in driver education in the spring semester of 2020 shall be required to complete a minimum of six hours of behind-the-wheel instruction before being issued a North Carolina Driver Education Completion Certificate. Public schools are authorized to resume driver education programs in accordance with guidance issued by the Department of Public Instruction."

EFFECT OF AMENDMENTS. --
Session Laws 2011-145, s. 28.37(a) , effective July 1, 2011, rewrote the section catchline, which formerly read: "Instruction in driver training and safety education"; and rewrote the section, which formerly read: "There shall be organized and administered under the general supervision of the Superintendent of Public Instruction a program of driver training and safety education in the public schools of this State, said courses to be non-credit courses taught by instructors who meet the requirements established by the State Board of Education. Instructors shall not be required to hold teacher certificates."

Session Laws 2011-334, s. 1 , effective July 1, 2011, in subsection (d), in the first sentence, inserted "the delivery of" and "courses by driver education," and deleted "and who do not hold teacher certificates" from the end, and added the last sentence, and deleted the last paragraph, which pertained to driver education instructors being paid on the teacher salary schedule.

Session Laws 2015-241, s. 8.39(a) , as amended by Session Laws 2016-94, s. 8.5 , added the next-to-the-last sentence in subsection (a). For effective date and applicability, see editor's note.

Session Laws 2017-95, s. 2 , added subdivision (b) (5). For effective date and applicability, see editor's note.

Session Laws 2018-5, s. 7.11(b) , effective July 1, 2018, in subsection (a), substituted "pursuant to subsection (f) of this section to the Department of Public Instruction" for "to it for this purpose"; and added subsections (c1) and (g).

THE DRIVER-TRAINING VEHICLE IS A NECESSARY COMPONENT IN DRIVER EDUCATION COURSES and must, therefore, be considered as a component of school instructional service rather than school transportation service. Smith v. McDowell County Bd. of Educ., 68 N.C. App. 541, 316 S.E.2d 108 (1984).

CROSS REFERENCES. --
As to driver education, generally, see G.S. 20-88.1.

§ 115C-216. Boards of education required to provide courses in operation of motor vehicles

(a) **Course of Training and Instruction Required in Public High Schools. --** Local boards of education shall offer noncredit driver education courses in high schools using the standardized curriculum provided by the Department of Public Instruction.

(b) **Inclusion of Expense in Budget. --** The local boards of education shall include as an item of instructional service and as a part of the current expense fund of the budget of the high schools under their supervision, the expense necessary to offer the driver education course.

(c) through (f) Repealed by Session Laws 1991, c. 689, s. 32(c) .

(g) **Fee for Instruction. --** The local boards of education shall fund driver education courses from funds available to them and may charge each student participating in a driver education course a fee of up to sixty-five dollars ($ 65.00) to offset the costs of providing the training and instruction. If a local board of education charges a fee for participation in a driver education course, the local board shall provide a process for reduction or waiver of that fee for students unable to pay the fee due to economic hardship.

History.
1955, c. 817; 1965, c. 397; 1981, c. 423, s. 1; 1991, c. 689, s. 32(c) ; 2011-145, ss. 28.37(b) , 31.1; 2013-360, s. 34.20(a) ; 2014-100, s. 8.15(c) ; 2015-241, s. 8.39(b) ; 2016-94, s. 8.5

EDITOR'S NOTE. --
Session Laws 2011-145, s. 28.37(f) -(i), provides: "(f) The State Board of Education shall report to the Joint Legislative Program Evaluation Oversight Committee by July 15, 2011, on the status of the implementation of Section 7.12 of S.L. 2010-31, which mandates the creation of a standard curriculum to be used for the driver education program in the Department of Public Instruction.

"(g) For the 2011-2012 school year, no State funds shall be used for driver education programs that do not use the standard driver education curriculum created in accordance with Section 7.12 of S.L. 2010-31.

"(h) The State Board of Education shall establish a pilot program to deliver driver education by electronic means. At least five local school administrative units shall participate in the pilot program. Funds appropriated for driver education shall be used to implement the pilot program. The State Board shall report on the implementation of the pilot program to the Joint Legislative Education Oversight Committee and the Joint Legislative Program Evaluation Oversight Committee by June 15, 2012. The report shall include the cost per student of delivering the instruction and the success rate of program participants in receiving a drivers license. "(i) The State Board of Education shall report to the Joint Legislative Education Oversight Committee and to the Joint Legislative Program Evaluation Oversight Committee by June 15, 2012, on the following:

"(1) The most cost-effective method of delivering driver education in the short- and long-term. In making this determination, the State Board of Education shall consider the results of the pilot program implemented pursuant to Section 5 of this act.

"(2) The strategic plan adopted by the State Board of Education in accordance with G.S. 115C-215."
Session Laws 2011-145, s. 1.1 , provides: "This act shall be known as the 'Current Operations and Capital Improvements Appropriations Act of 2011.'"
Session Laws 2011-145, s. 32.2 , provides: "Except for statutory changes or other provisions that clearly indicate an intention to have effects beyond the 2011-2013 fiscal biennium, the textual provisions of this act apply only to funds appropriated for, and activities occurring during, the 2011-2013 fiscal biennium."
Session Laws 2011-145, s. 32.5 , is a severability clause.
Session Laws 2013-360, s. 34.20(b) , provides: "The Division of Motor Vehicles and the Department of Public Instruction shall collaborate to revise the driver knowledge test and to create a process for administration of the test and certification of passage by public schools administering driver education programs. The Division and the Department shall report to the Joint Legislative Transportation Oversight Committee, the Joint Legislative Program Evaluation Oversight Committee, the Joint Legislative Education Oversight Committee, and the Fiscal Research Division no later than March 1, 2014, on their progress in meeting the requirements of this subsection."

Session Laws 2013-360, s. 1.1 , provides: "This act shall be known as the 'Current Operations and Capital Improvements Appropriations Act of 2013.'"
Session Laws 2013-360, s. 38.2 , provides: "Except for statutory changes or other provisions that clearly indicate an intention to have effects beyond the 2013-2015 fiscal biennium, the textual provisions of this act apply only to funds appropriated for, and activities occurring during, the 2013-2015 fiscal biennium."
Session Laws 2013-360, s. 38.5 , is a severability clause.
Session Laws 2014-100, s. 8.15(b) , provides: "It is the intent of the General Assembly that, beginning with the 2015-2016 fiscal year, the driver education program administered by the Department of Public Instruction in accordance with G.S. 115C-215 shall no longer be paid out of the Highway Fund based on an annual appropriation by the General Assembly. Local boards of education shall use funds available to them, including a fee for instruction charged to students pursuant to G.S. 115C-216(g), to offer noncredit driver education courses in high schools."
Session Laws 2014-100, s. 1.1 , provides: "This act shall be known as 'The Current Operations and Capital Improvements Appropriations Act of 2014.'"
Session Laws 2014-100, s. 38.4 , provides: "Except for statutory changes or other provisions that clearly indicate an intention to have effects beyond the 2014-2015 fiscal year, the textual provisions of this act apply only to funds appropriated for, and activities occurring during, the 2014-2015 fiscal year."
Session Laws 2014-100, s. 38.7 , is a severability clause.
Session Laws 2015-241, s. 8.39(h) , as amended by Session Laws 2016-94, s. 8.5 , made the amendments by Session Laws 2015-241, s. 8.39(b) , effective July 1, 2016, applicable beginning with the 2016-2017 school year.
Session Laws 2015-241, s. 1.1 , provides: "This act shall be known as 'The Current Operations and Capital Improvements Appropriations Act of 2015.'"
Session Laws 2015-241, s. 33.4 , provides: "Except for statutory changes or other provisions that clearly indicate an intention to have effects beyond the 2015-2017 fiscal biennium, the textual provisions of this act apply only to funds appropriated for, and activities occurring during, the 2015-2017 fiscal biennium."
Session Laws 2015-241, s. 33.6 , is a severability clause.
Session Laws 2016-94, s. 1.2 , provides: "This act shall be known as the 'Current Operations and Capital Improvements Appropriations Act of 2016.'"
Session Laws 2016-94, s. 39.7 , is a severability clause.

Session Laws 2020-30, s. 2 , provides: "Notwithstanding G.S. 115C-215(b)(1), (2), (4), and (5) and G.S. 115C-216, and the requirements of State Board of Education Policy DRIV-0004, for students enrolled in classroom driver education between January 2020 and March 16, 2020, in a public school or a licensed commercial driver training school, students shall be deemed to have completed all classroom instruction requirements for driver education if the student completed at least 15 hours of classroom instruction prior to March 16, 2020. A student who has not completed at least 15 hours of classroom instruction may be offered the opportunity to take and pass the proficiency examination developed by the Department of Public Instruction, as provided in the State Board of Education Policy DRIV-0004, to waive the classroom instruction requirement. All students enrolled in driver education in the spring semester of 2020 shall be required to complete a minimum of six hours of behind-the-wheel instruction before being issued a North Carolina Driver Education Completion Certificate. Public schools are authorized to resume driver education programs in accordance with guidance issued by the Department of Public Instruction."

EFFECT OF AMENDMENTS. --

Session Laws 2011-145, ss. 28.37(b) , 31.1, effective July 1, 2011, rewrote subsections (a) and (b) and added subsection (g).

Session Laws 2013-360, s. 34.20(a) , effective July 26, 2013, substituted "fifty-five dollars ($55.00)" for "forty-five dollars ($45.00)" in subsection (g). For applicability, see Editor's note.

Session Laws 2014-100, s. 8.15(c) , effective July 1, 2014, in subsection (g), inserted "shall fund driver education courses from funds available to them and," and substituted "sixty-five dollars ($65.00)" for "fifty-five dollars ($55.00)."

Session Laws 2015-241, s. 8.39(b) , as amended by Session Laws 2016-94, s. 8.5 , added the last sentence in subsection (g). For effective date and applicability, see editor's note.

THE DRIVER-TRAINING VEHICLE IS A NECESSARY COMPONENT IN DRIVER EDUCATION COURSES and must, therefore, be considered as a component of school instructional service rather than school transportation service. Smith v. McDowell County Bd. of Educ., 68 N.C. App. 541, 316 S.E.2d 108 (1984).

CROSS REFERENCES. --

As to driver education, generally, see G.S. 20-88.1.

ARTICLE 17.
SUPPORTING SERVICES

PART 1.
TRANSPORTATION

§ 115C-240. Authority and duties of State Board of Education

(a) The State Board of Education shall promulgate rules and regulations for the operation of a public school transportation system.

(b) The State Board of Education shall be under no duty to supply transportation to any pupil or employee enrolled or employed in any school. Neither the State nor the State Board of Education shall in any manner be liable for the failure or refusal of any local board of education to furnish transportation, by school bus or otherwise, to any pupil or employee of any school, or for any neglect or action of any county or city board of education, or any employee of any such board, in the operation or maintenance of any school bus.

(c) The State Board of Education shall from time to time adopt such rules and regulations with reference to the construction, equipment, color, and maintenance of school buses, the number of pupils who may be permitted to ride at the same time upon any bus, and the age and qualifications of drivers of school buses as it shall deem to be desirable for the purpose of promoting safety in the operation of school buses. Every school bus that is capable of operating on diesel fuel shall be capable of operating on diesel fuel with a minimum biodiesel concentration of B-20, as defined in G.S. 143-58.4. No school bus shall be operated for the transportation of pupils unless such bus is constructed and maintained as prescribed in such regulations and is equipped with adequate heating facilities, a standard signaling device for giving due notice that the bus is about to make a turn, an alternating flashing stoplight on the front of the bus, an alternating flashing stoplight on the rear of the bus, and such other warning devices, fire protective equipment and first aid supplies as may be prescribed for installation upon such buses by the regulation of the State Board of Education.

(d) The State Board of Education shall assist local boards of education by establishing guidelines and a framework through which local boards may establish, review and amend school bus routes prepared pursuant to G.S. 115C-246. The State Board shall also require local boards to implement the Transportation Information Management System or an equivalent system approved by the State Board of Education, no later than September 1, 1992. The State Board of Education shall also assist local boards of education with reference to the acquisition and maintenance of school buses or any other question which may arise in connection with the organization and operation of school bus transportation systems of local boards.

(e) The State Board of Education shall allocate to the respective local boards of education funds appropriated from time to time by the General Assembly for the purpose of providing transportation to the pupils enrolled in the public schools within this State. Such funds shall be allocated by the State Board of Education in accordance with the number of pupils to be transported, the length of bus routes, road conditions and all other circumstances affecting the cost of the transportation of pupils by school bus to the end that the funds so appropriated may be allocated on a fair and equitable basis, according to the needs of the respective local school administrative units and so as to provide the most efficient use of such funds. Such allocation shall be made by the State Board of Education at the beginning of each fiscal year, except that the State Board may reserve for future allocation from time to time within such fiscal year as the need therefor shall be found to exist, a reasonable amount not to exceed ten percent (10%) of the total funds available for transportation in such fiscal year from such appropriation. If there is evidence of inequitable or inefficient use of funds, the State Board of Education shall be empowered to review school bus routes established by local boards pursuant to G.S. 115C-246 as well as other factors affecting the cost of the transportation of pupils by school bus.

(f) The respective local boards shall use such funds for the purposes of replacing, maintaining, insuring, and operating public school buses and service vehicles in accordance with the provisions of G.S. 115C-239 to 115C-246, 115C-248 to 115C-254 and 115C-256 to 115C-259 and for no other purpose, but in the making of expenditures for such purposes shall be subject to rules and regulations promulgated by the State Board of Education.

History.

1955, c. 1372, art. 21, p. 2; 1981, c. 423, s. 1; 1983, c. 630, ss. 3-6; 1989 (Reg. Sess., 1990), c. 1066, s. 96(a); 1991 (Reg. Sess., 1992), c. 900, s. 77(a); 2007-423, s. 1

EDITOR'S NOTE. --

Subsection (c), as amended by Session Laws 2007-423, s. 1 , effective June 1, 2008, to add the second and third sentences, is applicable to vehicles transferred or purchased on or after that date.

EFFECT OF AMENDMENTS. --

Session Laws 2007-423, s. 1 , effective June 1, 2008, and applicable to vehicles transferred or purchased on or after that date, added the second sentence in subsection (c).

EDITOR'S NOTE. --Some of the cases annotated below were decided under corresponding provisions of former Chapter 115.

AS TO LIMIT ON AUTHORITY AND CONTROL BY STATE BOARD, see Styers v. Phillips, 277 N.C. 460, 178 S.E.2d 583 (1971).

STATE BOARD NOT RESPONSIBLE FOR OPERATION OF SCHOOL BUSES. --The General Assembly has relieved the State Board of all responsibility for the operation of school buses. Styers v. Phillips, 277 N.C. 460, 178 S.E.2d 583 (1971).

THE STATE BOARD DOES NOT AUTHORIZE THE TRANSPORTATION OF ANY PUPILS. It allocates available funds to those boards which elect to operate transportation systems. Styers v. Phillips, 277 N.C. 460, 178 S.E.2d 583 (1971).

STATE BOARD TO ALLOCATE FUNDS. --The State Board is authorized and directed to allocate, without restriction, the funds appropriated for transportation during the school year to the boards of education which have elected to provide school bus transportation. Styers v. Phillips, 277 N.C. 460, 178 S.E.2d 583 (1971).

BURDEN OF PRODUCING EVIDENCE THAT BOARD FAILED TO MAKE ALLOCATIONS. --The burden is upon plaintiffs to produce evidence that the State Board has failed to make the allocations required. Styers v. Phillips, 277 N.C. 460, 178 S.E.2d 583 (1971).

CITED in Irving v. Charlotte-Mecklenburg Bd. of Educ., 230 N.C. App. 265, 750 S.E.2d 1 (2013), rev'd, 368 N.C. 609, 781 S.E.2d 282, 2016 N.C. LEXIS 30 (2016); Irving v. Charlotte-Mecklenburg Bd. of Educ., 368 N.C. 609, 781 S.E.2d 282 (2016).

§ 115C-242.1. Installation and operation of automated school bus safety camera

(a) **Definition.** -- An "automated school bus safety camera" is a device that is affixed to a school bus, as that term is used in G.S. 20-217, that is synchronized to automatically record photographs or video of a vehicle at the time the vehicle is detected for a violation of (i) G.S. 20-217 or (ii) an ordinance adopted under G.S. 153A-246.

(b) **Installation and Operation.** -- Automated school bus safety cameras may be installed and operated on any school bus operated by a local board of education within a county that has adopted an ordinance under G.S. 153A-246 as follows:

(1) A local board of education may install and operate automated school bus safety cameras without contracting with a private vendor.

(2) A local board of education may enter into a service contract to install and operate automated school bus safety cameras with a private vendor. Contracts shall be let in accordance with the provisions of G.S. 143-129 applicable to purchases of apparatus, supplies, materials, or equipment. The maximum length of any contract entered into under this subdivision shall be three years. A contract entered into under this subdivision may contain an option to renew or extend the contract for only one additional term not to exceed three years.

(3) Upon request by one or more local boards of education, the State Board of Education shall enter into a contract for a statewide service or contracts for regional

services to install and operate automated school bus safety cameras with a private vendor. These contracts shall be let in accordance with the provisions of Article 3 of Chapter 143 of the General Statutes.

(c) **Interlocal Agreements.** -- Any local board of education, board of county commissioners, and law enforcement agency may enter into an interlocal agreement pursuant to Part 1 of Article 20 of Chapter 160A of the General Statutes that is necessary and proper to effectuate the purpose and intent of this section and G.S. 153A-246. Any agreement entered into pursuant to this subsection may include provisions on cost-sharing and reimbursement to which the local board of education, board of county commissioners, or law enforcement agency freely and voluntarily agree for the purposes of effectuating this section and G.S. 153A-246.

(d) **Evidence in Criminal Proceeding.** --- Any photographs or videos recorded by an automated school bus safety camera that capture a violation of G.S. 20-217 shall also be provided to the investigating law enforcement agency for use as evidence in any proceeding alleging a violation of G.S. 20-217.

History.
2017-188, s. 2
    EDITOR'S NOTE. --
    Session Laws   2017-188, s. 7 , reads in part: "The requirements in G.S. 115C-242.1(b)(2), as enacted by Section 2 of this act, shall not apply to a local board of education that, prior to the effective date of this act [July 25, 2017], entered into a contract with a private vendor to install and operate automated school bus safety cameras."

CHAPTER 115D.
COMMUNITY COLLEGES

ARTICLE 2.
LOCAL ADMINISTRATION

§ 115D-21. Traffic regulations; fines and penalties

(a) All of the provisions of Chapter 20 of the General Statutes relating to the use of highways of the State of North Carolina and the operation of motor vehicles thereon shall apply to the streets, roads, alleys and driveways on the campuses of all institutions in the North Carolina Community College System. Any person violating any of the provisions of Chapter 20 of the General Statutes in or on the streets, roads, alleys and driveways on the campuses of institutions in the North Carolina Community College System shall, upon conviction thereof, be punished as prescribed in this section and as provided by Chapter 20 of the General Statutes relating to motor vehicles. Nothing contained in this section shall be construed as in any way interfering with the ownership and control of the streets, roads, alleys and driveways on the campuses of institutions in the system as is now vested by law in the trustees of each individual institution in the North Carolina Community College System.

(b) The trustees are authorized and empowered to make additional rules and regulations and to adopt additional ordinances with respect to the use of the streets, roads, alleys and driveways and to establish parking areas on or off the campuses not inconsistent with the provisions of Chapter 20 of the General Statutes of North Carolina. Upon investigation, the trustees may determine and fix speed limits on streets, roads, alleys, and driveways subject to such rules, regulations, and ordinances, lower than those provided in G.S. 20-141. The trustees may make reasonable provisions for the towing or removal of unattended vehicles found to be in violation of rules, regulations and ordinances. All rules, regulations and ordinances adopted pursuant to the authority of this section shall be recorded in the proceedings of the trustees; shall be printed; and copies of such rules, regulations and ordinances shall be filed in the office of the Secretary of State of North Carolina. Violation of any such rules, regulations, or ordinances, is an infraction punishable by a penalty of not more than one hundred dollars ($ 100.00).

Regardless of whether an institution does its own removal and disposal of motor vehicles or contracts with another person to do so, the institution shall provide a hearing procedure for the owner. For purposes of this subsection, the definitions in G.S. 20-219.9 apply:

(1) If the institution operates in such a way that the person who tows the vehicle is responsible for collecting towing fees, all provisions of Article 7A, Chapter 20, apply.

(2) If the institution operates in such a way that it is responsible for collecting towing fees, it shall:

a. Provide by contract or ordinance for a schedule of reasonable towing fees,

b. Provide a procedure for a prompt fair hearing to contest the towing,

c. Provide for an appeal to district court from that hearing,

d. Authorize release of the vehicle at any time after towing by the posting of a bond or paying of the fees due, and

e. If the institution chooses to enforce its authority by sale of the vehicle, provide a sale procedure similar to that provided in G.S. 44A-4, 44A-5, and 44A-6, except that no hearing in addition to the probable cause hearing is required. If no one purchases the vehicle at the sale and if the value of the vehicle is less than the amount of the lien, the institution may destroy it.

(c) The trustees may by rules, regulations, or ordinances provide for a system of registration of all motor vehicles where the owner or operator does park on the campus or keeps said vehicle on the campus. The trustees shall cause to be posted at appropriate places on campus notice to the public of applicable parking and traffic rules, regulations, and ordinances governing the campus over which it has jurisdiction. The trustees may by rules, regulations, or ordinances establish or cause to have established a system of citations that may be issued to owners or operators of motor vehicles who violate established rules, regulations, or ordinances. The trustees shall provide for the administration of said system of citations; establish or cause to be established a system of fines to be levied for the violation of established rules, regulations and ordinances; and enforce or cause to be enforced the collection of said fines. The fine for each offense shall not exceed twenty-five dollars ($ 25.00). The trustees shall be empowered to exercise the right to prohibit repeated violators of such rules, regulations, or ordinances from parking on the campus.

(d) The clear proceeds of all civil penalties collected pursuant to this section shall be remitted to the Civil Penalty and Forfeiture Fund in accordance with G.S. 115C-457.2.

History.
1971, c. 795, ss. 1-3; 1979, c. 462, s. 2; 1983, c. 420, s. 4; 1985, c. 764, s. 38; 2012-142, s. 8.9

Chapter 115D

EFFECT OF AMENDMENTS. --

Session Laws 2012-142, s. 8.9 , effective July 1, 2012, substituted "twenty-five dollars ($25.00)" for "five dollars ($5.00), which funds shall be retained in the institution and expended in the discretion of the trustees" in the fifth sentence of subsection (c), and added subsection (d).

CROSS REFERENCES. --

As to post-towing procedure for motor vehicles towed pursuant to the provisions of this section, see G.S. 20-219.9 et seq.

§ 115D-21.1. Campus law enforcement agencies

(a) The board of trustees of any community college may establish a campus law enforcement agency and employ campus police officers. These officers shall meet the requirements of Article 1 of Chapter 17C of the General Statutes, shall take the oath of office prescribed by Article VI, Section 7 of the Constitution, and shall have all the powers of law enforcement officers generally. The territorial jurisdiction of a campus police officer shall include all property owned or leased to the community college employing the officer and that portion of any public road or highway passing through the property and immediately adjoining it, wherever located.

(b) The board of trustees of any community college that establishes a campus law enforcement agency under subsection (a) of this section may enter into joint agreements with the governing board of any municipality to extend the law enforcement authority of campus police officers into the municipality's jurisdiction and to determine the circumstances under which this extension of authority may be granted.

(c) The board of trustees of any community college that establishes a campus law enforcement agency under subsection (a) of this section may enter into joint agreements with the governing board of any county, with the consent of the sheriff, to extend the law enforcement authority of campus police officers into the county's jurisdiction and to determine the circumstances under which this extension of authority may be granted.

History.

1999-68, s. 1

EDITOR'S NOTE. --

"Article 1 of Chapter 17C" has been substituted for "Chapter 17C" in this section at the direction of the Revisor of Statutes.

CHAPTER 116.
HIGHER EDUCATION

ARTICLE 1.
THE UNIVERSITY OF NORTH CAROLINA

PART 6.
TRAFFIC AND PARKING

§ 116-44.3. Definitions

Unless the context clearly requires another meaning, the following words and phrases have the meanings indicated when used in this Part:

(1) "Board of trustees" and "constituent institution" have the meanings assigned in G.S. 116-2.

(2) "Campus" means that University property, without regard to location, which is used wholly or partly for the purposes of a particular constituent institution of the University of North Carolina.

(3) "University" means a constituent institution as defined in G.S. 116-2.

(4) "University property" means property that is owned or leased in whole or in part by the State of North Carolina and which is subject to the general management and control of the Board of Governors of the University of North Carolina.

History.
1973, c. 495, s. 1

§ 116-44.4. Regulation of traffic and parking and registration of motor vehicles

(a) Except as otherwise provided in this Part, all of the provisions of Chapter 20 of the General Statutes relating to the use of highways of the State and the operation of motor vehicles thereon are applicable to all streets, alleys, driveways, parking lots, and parking structures on University property. Nothing in this section modifies any rights of ownership or control of University property, now or hereafter vested in the Board of Governors of the University of North Carolina or the State of North Carolina.

(b) Each board of trustees may by ordinance prohibit, regulate, divert, control, and limit pedestrian or vehicular traffic and the parking of motor vehicles and other modes of conveyance on the campus. In fixing speed limits, the board of trustees is not subject to G.S. 20-141(f1) or (g2), but may fix any speed limit reasonable and safe under the circumstances as conclusively determined by the board of trustees. The board of trustees may not regulate traffic on streets open to the public as of right, except as specifically provided in this Part.

(c) Each board of trustees may by ordinance provide for the registration of motor vehicles maintained or operated on the campus by any student, faculty member, or employee of the University, and may fix fees for such registration. The ordinance may make it unlawful for any person to operate an unregistered motor vehicle on the campus when the vehicle is required by the ordinance to be registered.

(d) Each board of trustees may by ordinance set aside parking lots and other parking facilities on the campus for use by students, faculty, and employees of the University and members of the general public attending schools, conferences, or meetings at the University, visiting or making use of any University facilities, or attending to official business with the University. The board of trustees may issue permits to park in these lots and garages and may charge a fee therefor. The board of trustees may also by ordinance make it unlawful for any person to park a motor vehicle in any lot or other parking facility without procuring the requisite permit and displaying it on the vehicle. No permit to park shall be issued until the student requesting the permit provides the name of the insurer, the policy number under which the student has financial responsibility, and the student certifies that the motor vehicle is insured at the levels set in G.S. 20-279.1(11) or higher. This subsection applies to motor vehicles that are registered in other states as well as motor vehicles that are registered in this State pursuant to Chapter 20 of the General Statutes.

(e) Each board of trustees may by ordinance set aside spaces in designated parking areas or facilities in which motor vehicles may be parked for specified periods of time. To regulate parking in such spaces, the board of trustees may install a system of parking meters and make it unlawful for any person to park a motor vehicle in a metered space without activating the meter for the entire time that the vehicle is parked, up to the maximum length of time allowed for that space. The meters may be activated by coins of the United States. The board of trustees may also install automatic gates, employ attendants, and use any other device or procedure to control access to and collect the fees for using its parking areas and facilities.

(f) The board of trustees may by ordinance provide for the issuance of stickers, decals, permits, or other indicia representing the registration status of vehicles or the eligibility of vehicles to park on the campus and may by ordinance prohibit the forgery, counterfeiting, unauthorized transfer, or unauthorized use of them.

Chapter 116

(g) Violation of an ordinance adopted under any portion of this Part is an infraction as defined in G.S. 14-3.1 and is punishable by a penalty of not more than fifty dollars ($ 50.00). An ordinance may provide that certain prohibited acts shall not be infractions and in such cases the provisions of subsection (h) may be used to enforce the ordinance.

(h) An ordinance adopted under any portion of this Part may provide that violation subjects the offender to a civil penalty. Penalties may be graduated according to the seriousness of the offense or the number of prior offenses by the person charged. Each board of trustees may establish procedures for the collection of these penalties and they may be enforced by civil action in the nature of debt. The board of trustees may also provide for appropriate administrative sanctions if an offender does not pay a validly due penalty or upon repeated offenses. Appropriate administrative sanctions include, but are not limited to, revocation of parking permits, termination of vehicle registration, and termination or suspension of enrollment in or employment by the University.

(i) An ordinance adopted under any portion of this Part may provide that any vehicle illegally parked may be removed to a storage area. Regardless of whether a constituent institution does its own removal and disposal of motor vehicles or contracts with another person to do so, the institution shall provide a hearing procedure for the owner. For purposes of this subsection, the definitions in G.S. 20-219.9 apply.

   (1) If the institution operates in such a way that the person who tows the vehicle is responsible for collecting towing fees, all provisions of Article 7A, Chapter 20, apply.

   (2) If the institution operates in such a way that it is responsible for collecting towing fees, it shall:

      a. Provide by contract or ordinance for a schedule of reasonable towing fees,

      b. Provide a procedure for a prompt fair hearing to contest the towing,

      c. Provide for an appeal to district court from that hearing,

      d. Authorize release of the vehicle at any time after towing by the posting of a bond or paying of the fees due, and

      e. If the institution chooses to enforce its authority by sale of the vehicle, provide a sale procedure similar to that provided in G.S. 44A-4, 44A-5, and 44A-6, except that no hearing in addition to the probable cause hearing is required. If no one purchases the vehicle at the sale and if the value of the vehicle is less than the amount of the lien, the institution may destroy it.

(j) Evidence that a motor vehicle was found parked or unattended in violation of an ordinance of the board of trustees is prima facie evidence that the vehicle was parked by:

   (1) The person holding a University parking permit for the vehicle, or

   (2) If no University parking permit has been issued for the vehicle, the person in whose name the vehicle is registered with the University pursuant to subsection (c), or

   (3) If no University parking permit has been issued for the vehicle and the vehicle is not registered with the University, the person in whose name it is registered with the North Carolina Division of Motor Vehicles or the corresponding agency of another state or nation.

The rule of evidence established by this subsection applies only in civil, criminal, or administrative actions or proceedings concerning violations of ordinances of the board of trustees. G.S. 20-162.1 does not apply to such actions or proceedings.

(k) Each board of trustees shall cause to be posted appropriate notice to the public of applicable traffic and parking restrictions.

(l) All ordinances adopted under this Part shall be recorded in the minutes of the board of trustees and copies thereof shall be filed in the offices of the President of the University of North Carolina and the Secretary of State. Each board of trustees shall provide for printing and distributing copies of its traffic and parking ordinances.

(m) All moneys received pursuant to this Part, except for the clear proceeds of all civil penalties collected pursuant to subsection (h) of this section, shall be placed in a trust account in each constituent institution, are appropriated, and may be used for any of the following purposes:

   (1) To defray the cost of administering and enforcing ordinances adopted under this Part;

   (2) To develop, maintain, and supervise parking areas and facilities;

   (3) To provide bus service or other transportation systems and facilities, including payments to any public or private transportation system serving University students, faculty, or employees;

   (4) As a pledge to secure revenue bonds for parking facilities issued under Article 21 of this Chapter;

   (5) Other purposes related to parking, traffic, and transportation on the campus.

The clear proceeds of all civil penalties collected pursuant to subsection (h) of this section shall be remitted to the Civil Penalty and Forfeiture Fund in accordance with G.S. 115C-457.2.

History.
1973, c. 495, s. 1; 1975, c. 716, s. 5; 1981 (Reg. Sess., 1982), c. 1239, s. 3; 1983, c. 420, s. 5; 1985, c. 764, s. 36; 2001-336, s. 1 ; 2005-276, s. 6.37(r) ; 2006-203, s. 51

The references to G.S. 20-141(f1) and (g2) in subsection (b) of this section are to subsections existing prior to the 1973 amendment of G.S. 20-141.

Session Laws 2005-276, s. 6.37(w) , provides: "The Office of State Budget and Management shall develop a methodology for computing the actual costs of collection of civil penalties by State departments and agencies. This methodology shall apply to all State departments and agencies, effective July 1, 2006."

Session Laws 2005-276, s. 1.2 , provides: "This act shall be known as the 'Current Operations and Capital Improvements Appropriations Act of 2005'."

Session Laws 2005-276, s. 46.3 , provides: "Except for statutory changes or other provisions that clearly indicate an intention to have effects beyond the 2005-2007 fiscal biennium, the textual provisions of this act apply only to funds appropriated for, and activities occurring during, the 2005-2007 fiscal biennium."

Session Laws 2005-276, s. 46.5 , is a severability clause.

EFFECT OF AMENDMENTS. --
Session Laws 2005-276, s. 6.37(r) , effective July 1, 2005, in subsection (m), in the introductory paragraph, inserted ", except for the clear proceeds of all civil penalties collected pursuant to subsection (h) of this section," and added the last sentence.

Session Laws 2006-203, s. 51 , effective July 1, 2007, and applicable to the budget for the 2007-2009 biennium and each subsequent biennium thereafter, substituted "institution, are appropriated" for "institution" in subsection (m).

BECAUSE THE NORTH CAROLINA GENERAL ASSEMBLY ENACTED G.S. 116-44.4 PURSUANT TO A CLEAR GRANT OF CONSTITUTIONAL AUTHORITY to establish a mechanism for administering the "maintenance and management" of traffic and parking on each University of North Carolina campus, G.S. 116-44.4 is constitutional under N.C. Const., Art. IX, § 8, which is a co-equal provision with N.C. Const., Art. IX, § 7. N.C. Sch. Bds. Ass'n v. Moore, 160 N.C. App. 253, 585 S.E.2d 418 (2003).

PROCEEDS OF PENALTIES THAT ARE COLLECTED FOR VIOLATION OF CAMPUS TRAFFIC AND PARKING ORDINANCES AS "INFRACTIONS" under G.S. 116-44.4(g) are subject to N.C. Const., Art. IX, § 7. N.C. Sch. Bds. Ass'n v. Moore, 160 N.C. App. 253, 585 S.E.2d 418 (2003).

"CIVIL PENALTIES" IMPOSED BY G.S. 116-44.4(H), which are intended to compensate campuses for the expense of establishing and maintaining parking-and transportation-related services, are remedial in nature and thus are not subject to N.C. Const., Art. IX, § 7. N.C. Sch. Bds. Ass'n v. Moore, 160 N.C. App. 253, 585 S.E.2d 418 (2003).

§ 116-44.5. Special provisions applicable to identified constituent institutions of the University of North Carolina

In addition to the powers granted by G.S. 116-44.4, the board of trustees of each of the constituent institutions enumerated hereinafter shall have the additional powers prescribed:

(1) The Board of Trustees of the University of North Carolina at Chapel Hill may by ordinance prohibit, regulate, and limit the parking of motor vehicles on those portions of the following public streets in the Town of Chapel Hill where parking is not prohibited by an ordinance of the Town of Chapel Hill:

    a. Battle Lane;

    b. Country Club Road, between Raleigh Street and South Road;

    c. Manning Drive;

    d. McCauley Street, between Columbia Street and Pittsboro Street;

    e. Pittsboro Street, between South Columbia Street and Cameron Avenue;

    f. Boundary Street, between Country Club Road and East Franklin Street;

    g. Park Place, between Boundary Street and East Franklin Street;

    h. South Columbia Street, between Franklin Street and Manning Drive;

    i. Cameron Avenue, between South Columbia Street and Raleigh Street;

    j. Raleigh Street;

    k. Ridge Road;

    l. South Road, between Columbia Street and Country Club Road.

In addition, the Board of Trustees of the University of North Carolina at Chapel Hill may regulate traffic on Cameron Avenue, between Raleigh Street and South Columbia Street, and on Raleigh Street, in any manner not inconsistent with ordinances of the Town of Chapel Hill.

(2) The Board of Trustees of Appalachian State University may by ordinance prohibit, regulate, and limit the parking of motor vehicles on those portions of the following public streets in the Town of Boone where parking is not prohibited by an ordinance of the Town of Boone:

    a. Rivers Street, between U.S. 221--U.S. 321 (Hardin Street) and Water Street;

    b. Stadium Drive, between Rivers Street and Hemlock Drive;

    c. College Street, to the extent that it is bounded on both sides by the university campus;

    d. Appalachian Street, between Locust Street and Howard Street;

    e. Brown Street, between Locust Street and Howard Street;

    f. Hill Street, only on the half of Hill Street bounded by the university campus;

    g. Stansberry Circle, from Holmes Drive to the end of Stansberry Circle;

h. Locust Street, from U.S. 221-U.S. 321 (Hardin Street) to the end of Locust Street; and

i. Dale Street, from State Farm Road to the end of Dale Street.

(3) The Board of Trustees of the University of North Carolina at Charlotte may by ordinance prohibit, regulate, and limit the parking of motor vehicles on those portions of the following public roads in the County of Mecklenburg where parking is not prohibited by ordinance or other source of legal regulation of the County of Mecklenburg or other governmental entity with jurisdiction to regulate parking on such public road:

a. Mary Alexander Boulevard (State Road No. 2834), between its intersection with N.C. Highway 49 and its intersection with Mallard Creek Church Road.

In addition, the Board of Trustees of the University of North Carolina at Charlotte may regulate traffic on Mary Alexander Boulevard (State Road No. 2834), between its intersection with N.C. Highway 49 and its intersection with Mallard Creek Church Road, in any manner not inconsistent with any ordinances or other sources of legal regulation of the County of Mecklenburg or other governmental entity with jurisdiction to regulate traffic on such public road.

(3a) The Board of Trustees of the University of North Carolina at Wilmington may by ordinance prohibit, regulate, and limit the parking of motor vehicles on those portions of the following public streets in the City of Wilmington where parking is not prohibited by an ordinance of the City of Wilmington:

a. "H" Street.

(3b) The Board of Trustees of the University of North Carolina at Greensboro may by ordinance prohibit, regulate, and limit the parking of motor vehicles for those portions of any of the following public streets in the City of Greensboro where parking is not prohibited by an ordinance of the City of Greensboro:

a. Forest Street between Oakland Avenue and Spring Garden Street.

b. Highland Avenue between Oakland Avenue and Spring Garden Street.

c. Jefferson Street between Spring Garden Street and the Walker/Aycock parking lot.

d. Kenilworth Street between Oakland Avenue and Walker Avenue.

e. McIver Street between Walker Avenue and West Market Street.

f. Stirling Street between Oakland Avenue and Walker Avenue.

g. Theta Street between Kenilworth Street and Stirling Street.

h. Walker Avenue between Aycock Street and Jackson Library and between Tate Street and McIver Street.

(3c) The Board of Trustees of North Carolina Agricultural and Technical State University may by ordinance prohibit, regulate, and limit the parking of motor vehicles on those portions of the following streets in the City of Greensboro where parking is not prohibited by an ordinance of the City of Greensboro:

a. Dudley Street between Market Street and Bluford Street.

b. Bluford Street between Regan Street and Luther Street.

c. Laurel Street between Lindsay Street and East Market Street.

d. Benbow Road between Sullivan Street and East Market Street.

e. Sullivan Street between O'Henry Boulevard overpass and Lindsay Street.

f. Beech Street between Bluford Street and Lindsay Street.

g. Obermeyer Street between Bluford Street and Market Street.

h. Daniel Street between Bluford Street and Market Street.

i. Nocho Street between Bluford Street and Market Street.

In addition, the Board of Trustees of North Carolina A&T State University may regulate traffic on the following streets for the portion of those streets that abut the university: Benbow Road, Dudley Street, Lindsay Street, and Market Street, provided that the regulation is not inconsistent with ordinances of the City of Greensboro.

(4) This section does not diminish the authority of any affected municipality, county or other governmental entity to prohibit parking on any public street or road listed herein. It is intended only to authorize the respective boards of trustees of the constituent institutions identified hereinabove to further prohibit, regulate, and limit parking on certain public streets and roads running through or adjacent to the campuses of the constituent institutions where parking is not prohibited by ordinance or other law of any affected municipality, county or other governmental entity. When an ordinance or other law of an affected municipality, county or other governmental entity is adopted to prohibit parking on any portion of any public street or road then regulated by an ordinance of a board of trustees, the ordinance of the board of trustees is superseded and the University, upon request

of the municipality, county or other governmental entity, shall immediately remove any signs, devices, or markings erected or placed by the University on that portion of the street or road pursuant to the superseded ordinance.

History.
1973, c. 495, s. 1; 1979, c. 238;   2001-170, s. 1 ;   2003-213, s. 1 ;   2005-165, s. 1
EFFECT OF AMENDMENTS. --
Session Laws 2005-165, s. 1 , effective July 7, 2005, added subdivision (3c).

CHAPTER 122C.
MENTAL HEALTH, DEVELOPMENTAL DISABILITIES, AND SUBSTANCE ABUSE ACT OF 1985

ARTICLE 6.
SPECIAL PROVISIONS

PART 1.
CAMP BUTNER AND COMMUNITY OF BUTNER

§ 122C-402. Application of State highway and motor vehicle laws at State institutions on Camp Butner reservation

The provisions of Chapter 20 of the General Statutes relating to the use of the highways of the State and the operation of motor vehicles thereon are made applicable to the streets, alleys, and driveways on the Camp Butner reservation that are on the grounds of any State facility or any State institution operated by the Department or by the Division of Adult Correction and Juvenile Justice of the Department of Public Safety. Any person violating any of the provisions of Chapter 20 of the General Statutes in or on these streets, alleys, or driveways shall upon conviction be punished as prescribed in that Chapter. This section does not interfere with the ownership and control of the streets, alleys, and driveways on the grounds as is now vested by law in the Department.

History.
1949, c. 71, s. 2; 1955, c. 887, s. 1; 1959, c. 1028, s. 4; 1963, c. 1166, s. 10; 1973, c. 476, s. 133; 1985, c. 589, s. 2; 2011-145, s. 19.1(h) ; 2017-186, s. 2 (qqqqq)
    EFFECT OF AMENDMENTS. --
    Session Laws 2017-186, s. 2 (qqqqq), effective December 1, 2017, inserted "and Juvenile Justice" in the first sentence of the section

CHAPTER 130A.
PUBLIC HEALTH

ARTICLE 4.
VITAL STATISTICS

§ 130A-121. List of deceased residents for county jury commission and Commissioner of Motor Vehicles

(a) Repealed by Session Laws 2012-180, s. 12, effective July 12, 2012.

(b) The State Registrar shall provide to the Commissioner of Motor Vehicles an alphabetical list of all residents of the State who have died in the two years prior to July 1 of each odd-numbered year, unless an annual jury list is being prepared under G.S. 9-2(a), in which case the list shall be of all residents of the State who have died in the year prior to July 1 of each year. The list shall include the name and address of each deceased resident and may be in either printed or computerized form, as requested by the Commissioner of Motor Vehicles.

History.
2007-512, s. 2 ; 2012-180, s. 12

EFFECT OF AMENDMENTS. --
Session Laws 2012-180, s. 12 , effective July 12, 2012, repealed subsection (a), which read: "The State Registrar shall provide to each county's jury commission an alphabetical list of all residents of that county who have died in the two years prior to July 1 of each odd-numbered year, unless an annual jury list is being prepared under G.S. 9-2(a), in which case the list shall be of all residents of the county who have died in the year prior to July 1 of each year. The list shall include the name and address of each deceased resident and may be in either printed or computerized form, as requested by the jury commission."

CHAPTER 136. TRANSPORTATION

ARTICLE 2.
POWERS AND DUTIES OF DEPARTMENT AND BOARD OF TRANSPORTATION

§ 136-26. Closing of State transportation infrastructure during construction or for dangerous conditions; driving through, removal, injury to barriers, warning signs, etc

(a) If it shall appear necessary to the Department of Transportation, its officers, or appropriate employees, to close any transportation infrastructure coming under its jurisdiction so as to permit proper completion of construction work which is being performed, or to prohibit traffic on transportation infrastructure due to damage posing a danger to public safety, the Department of Transportation, its officers or employees, may close, or cause to be closed, the whole or any portion of transportation infrastructure deemed necessary to be excluded from public travel. While any transportation infrastructure, or portion thereof, is so closed, or while any transportation infrastructure, or portion thereof, is in process of construction or maintenance, the Department of Transportation, its officers or appropriate employees, or its contractor, under authority from the Department of Transportation, may erect, or cause to be erected, suitable barriers or obstruction thereon; may post, or cause to be posted, conspicuous notices to the effect that the transportation infrastructure, or portion thereof, is closed; and may place warning signs, lights and lanterns on transportation infrastructure, or portions thereof.

(b) When infrastructure is closed to the public as provided herein, any person who willfully drives onto transportation infrastructure closed pursuant to this section or removes, injures or destroys any such barrier or barriers or obstructions on the road closed or being constructed, or tears down, removes or destroys any such notices, or extinguishes, removes, injures or destroys any such warning signs, lights, or lanterns so erected, posted, or placed pursuant to this section, shall be guilty of a Class 1 misdemeanor.

(c) This prohibition [in this section] does not apply to law enforcement, first responders, personnel of emergency management agencies, or Department of Transportation personnel acting in the course of, and within the scope of, their official duties; or personnel acting in the course of, and within the scope of, installation, restoration or maintenance of utility services in coordination with the Department of Transportation.

History.
1921, c. 2, s. 12; C.S., s. 3846(t); 1933, c. 172, s. 17; 1957, c. 65, s. 11; 1973, c. 507, s. 5; 1977, c. 464, s. 7.1; 1993, c. 539, s. 980 ; 2009-266, s. 10 ; 2019-84, s. 1

EDITOR'S NOTE. --
The previously undesignated provisions of this section were divided into subsections (a), (b), and (c) at the direction of the Revisor of Statutes.

Session Laws 2019-84, s. 2 , made the amendments to this section by Session Laws 2019-84, s. 1 , effective December 1, 2019, and applicable to offenses committed on or after that date.

EFFECT OF AMENDMENTS. --
Session Laws 2009-266, s. 10 , effective August 1, 2009, substituted "transportation infrastructure" for "highways" in the section catchline, and substituted "transportation infrastructure" for "road or highway" and "such road or highway" throughout the section; in the first sentence, deleted "of" preceding "proper", substituted "infrastructure" for "such road or highway" in the last sentence, and made stylistic changes throughout the section.

Session Laws 2019-84, s. 1 , rewrote the section heading; and rewrote the section. For division of existing provisions into subsections, see editor's note. For effective date and applicability, see editor's note.

POWERS OF DEPARTMENT IN CARRYING OUT GRADING WORK. --This section, together with the general powers of the State Highway Commission (now Department of Transportation), authorized the State Highway Commission (now Department of Transportation) directly or by implication, in the prosecution of the grading work, to direct and permit soil to be conveyed across a highway, the dirt ramp to be placed on the highway for its protection from injury by heavy equipment, the placing of warning signs along the highway, the stationing of flagmen at the ramp to stop traffic along the highway and close that portion of the road when in use by earthmovers, and its grade inspector to give supervision and instruction to the contractor and its employees in carrying out the grading work. C.C.T. Equip. Co. v. Hertz Corp., 256 N.C. 277, 123 S.E.2d 802 (1962).

PURPOSE OF CLOSING HIGHWAYS. --The closing or temporary closing of highways or portions thereof during construction and repair operations is designed to avoid interruptions and delays in the prosecution of the work. C.C. Mangum, Inc. v. Gasperson, 262 N.C. 32, 136 S.E.2d 234 (1964).

The exercise of authority to close a highway, which relates to a highway "in process of construction or maintenance," is for the public benefit. C.C. Mangum, Inc. v. Gasperson, 262 N.C. 32, 136 S.E.2d 234 (1964).

PUBLIC TRAVEL MAY BE TEMPORARILY SUSPENDED. --Public travel on a street or other highway may be temporarily suspended for a necessary or proper purpose, as for example to permit repairs or reconstruction. C.C.T. Equip. Co. v. Hertz Corp., 256 N.C. 277, 123 S.E.2d 802 (1962).

This section authorizes the State Highway Commission (now Department of Transportation) through "its officers or appropriate employees, or its contractor," to close a highway to public travel while a ramp is in use by its contractor's equipment. C.C. Mangum, Inc. v. Gasperson, 262 N.C. 32, 136 S.E.2d 234 (1964).

LIABILITY OF CONTRACTOR FOR INJURY. --A contractor constructing a highway was not relieved, by an order of the State Highway Commission (now Department of Transportation) closing the road to travel, of liability for injuries in an automobile collision with an unlighted disabled truck left by defendant on the side of the highway, where on the part of the road where the accident happened barriers had been removed and to defendant's knowledge many people habitually traversed it. Thompson Caldwell Constr. Co. v. Young, 294 F. 145 (4th Cir. 1923).

CONTRACTOR HAS DUTY TO EXERCISE ORDINARY CARE. --When a contractor undertakes to perform work under contract with the State Highway Commission (now Department of Transportation), the positive legal duty devolves on him to exercise ordinary care for the safety of the general public traveling over the road on which he is working. C.C.T. Equip. Co. v. Hertz Corp., 256 N.C. 277, 123 S.E.2d 802 (1962).

The contractor doing the work is there for a lawful purpose and is not obliged to stop the work every time a traveler drives along. But while the traveler assumes certain risks, he is still a traveler on a public way, and the contractor still owes him due care, and is liable for injuries suffered by him as a result of negligence in the performance of the work. C.C.T. Equip. Co. v. Hertz Corp., 256 N.C. 277, 123 S.E.2d 802 (1962).

IN PROVIDING AND MAINTAINING WARNINGS AND SAFEGUARDS. --Contractors must exercise ordinary care in providing and maintaining reasonable warnings and safeguards against conditions existent at the time and place. C.C.T. Equip. Co. v. Hertz Corp., 256 N.C. 277, 123 S.E.2d 802 (1962).

REQUIREMENTS AS TO SIGNS AND FLAGMEN DO NOT GIVE CONTRACTOR SPECIAL PRIVILEGES. --Where a contractor for the improvement of an airport is granted permission by the State Highway Commission (now Department of Transportation) to construct a dirt ramp over the highway to protect it from heavy equipment, the Commission's (now Department's) requirements with reference to signs and flagmen are primarily for the protection of the users of the highway and do not confer on the contractor special privileges in respect to right-of-way. C.C. Mangum, Inc. v. Gasperson, 262 N.C. 32, 136 S.E.2d 234 (1964).

DEPARTMENT CANNOT IMPOSE DIFFERENT STANDARD OF CARE. --The State Highway Commission (now Department of Transportation) cannot by contract or by supervisory instructions prescribe for contractors a different standard of care from that imposed by the common law in a given situation, as it affects third parties. But in its use of and authority over a highway, for purposes of construction, repair or maintenance, it may create circumstances which bring into play rules of conduct which would not apply if such purposes were not involved. C.C.T. Equip. Co. v. Hertz Corp., 256 N.C. 277, 123 S.E.2d 802 (1962).

SUFFICIENCY OF WARNING. --Actual notice of every special obstruction or defect in a highway is not required to be given to a traveler, nor need the way be so barricaded as to preclude all possibility of injury, but it is sufficient if a plain warning of danger is given, and the traveler has notice or knowledge of facts sufficient to put him on inquiry. The test of the sufficiency of the warning is whether the means employed, whatever they may be, are reasonably sufficient for the purpose. C.C.T. Equip. Co. v. Hertz Corp., 256 N.C. 277, 123 S.E.2d 802 (1962).

RED LIGHT OR RED FLAG. --A red light is recognized by common usage as a method of giving warning of danger during hours of darkness, and a driver seeing a red light ahead in the highway is required in the exercise of due care to heed its warning. The same is equally true of a red flag in daylight hours when properly displayed. C.C.T. Equip. Co. v. Hertz Corp., 256 N.C. 277, 123 S.E.2d 802 (1962).

CARE REQUIRED OF TRAVELER. --When extraordinary conditions exist on a highway by reason of construction or repair operations, the motorist is required by law to take notice of them. The traveler's care must be commensurate with the obvious danger. C.C.T. Equip. Co. v. Hertz Corp., 256 N.C. 277, 123 S.E.2d 802 (1962).

One who operates an automobile on a public highway which is under construction or repair, or in use for such purposes, cannot assume that there are no obstructions, defects or dangers ahead. In such instances it is the duty of the motorist, in the exercise of due care, to keep his vehicle under such control that it can be stopped within the distance within which a proper barrier or obstruction, or an obvious danger can be seen. C.C.T. Equip. Co. v. Hertz Corp., 256 N.C. 277, 123 S.E.2d 802 (1962).

Where travel on the highway was closed temporarily by means of warning signs and flagmen's signals it was the duty of the motorist to stop and yield the right-of-way to the contractor's earth movers. C.C. Mangum, Inc. v. Gasperson, 262 N.C. 32, 136 S.E.2d 234 (1964).

APPLIED in Luther v. Asheville Contracting Co., 268 N.C. 636, 151 S.E.2d 649 (1966).

CITED in Payne v. Lowe, 2 N.C. App. 369, 163 S.E.2d 74 (1968).

§ 136-30. Uniform signs and other traffic control devices on highways, streets, and public vehicular areas

(a) **State Highway System.** -- The Department of Transportation may number and mark highways in the State highway system. All traffic signs and other traffic control devices placed on a highway in the State highway system must conform to the Uniform Manual. The

Chapter 136

Department of Transportation shall have the power to control all signs within the right-of-way of highways in the State highway system. The Department of Transportation may erect signs directing persons to roads and places of importance.

(b) **Municipal Street System.** -- All traffic signs and other traffic control devices placed on a municipal street system street must conform to the appearance criteria of the Uniform Manual. All traffic control devices placed on a highway that is within the corporate limits of a municipality but is part of the State highway system must be approved by the Department of Transportation.

(c) **Public Vehicular Areas.** -- Except as provided in this subsection, all traffic signs and other traffic control devices placed on a public vehicular area, as defined in G.S. 20-4.01, must conform to the Uniform Manual. The owner of private property that contains a public vehicular area may place on the property a traffic control device, other than a sign designating a parking space for handicapped persons, as defined in G.S. 20-37.5, that differs in material from the uniform device but does not differ in shape, size, color, or any other way from the uniform device. The owner of private property that contains a public vehicular area may place on the property a sign designating a parking space for handicapped persons that differs in material and color from the uniform sign but does not differ in shape, size, or any other way from the uniform device.

(d) **Definition.** -- As used in this section, the term "Uniform Manual" means the Manual on Uniform Traffic Control Devices for Streets and Highways, published by the United States Department of Transportation, and any supplement to that Manual adopted by the North Carolina Department of Transportation.

(e) **Exception for Public Airport Traffic Signs.** -- Publicly owned airports, as defined in Chapter 63 of the General Statutes, shall be exempt from the requirements of subsections (b) and (c) of this section with respect to informational and directional signs, but not with respect to regulatory traffic signs.

History.
1921, c. 2, ss. 9(a), 9(b); C.S., ss. 3846(q), 3846(r); 1927, c. 148, s. 54; 1933, c. 172, s. 17; 1957, c. 65, s. 11; 1973, c. 507, s. 5; 1977, c. 464, s. 7.1; 1991, c. 530, s. 1 ; 1991 (Reg. Sess., 1992), c. 818, s. 2; 1993, c. 51, s. 1

EDITOR'S NOTE. --
Session Laws 1991 (Reg. Sess., 1992), c. 860, s. 1, effective July 7, 1992, inserted "appearance criteria of the" in the first sentence of subsection (b). Section 2 of c. 860 made the act applicable to the City of Charlotte only, and provided that the act would expire when Session Laws 1991 (Reg. Sess., 1992), c. 818, s. 2 became effective. Chapter 818, s. 2 made the same

amendment to this section in the form of general legislation, and became effective October 1, 1992, and applicable to offenses committed on or after that date.

Session Laws 1981-1194, s. 7.2, as added by Session Laws 2005-276, s. 28.14(a) , provides: "At the request of the Roanoke Voyages Corridor Commission, the Department of Transportation may manufacture and install, on Roanoke Island and up to 30 miles off the island, way-finding signs that, by color, design, and lettering, do not comply with normal transportation signage standards. These signs shall be used to identify and give directions to historic, educational, and cultural attractions on the island. The Department of Transportation shall not erect any signage that would be impracticable, unfeasible, or that would result in an unsafe or hazardous condition."

Session Laws 2005-276, s. 28.14(b) , provides: "At the request of the Blue Ridge National Heritage Area Partnership, as established by Public Law 108-108, Title I, Section 140(d)(3), the Department of Transportation may manufacture and install way-finding signs that, by color, design, and lettering, do not comply with normal transportation signage standards. Signage throughout the 25-county area, as defined in Public Law 108-108, Title I, Section 140(d)(2), of the Blue Ridge National Heritage Area shall be used to identify and give directions to historic, educational, and cultural attractions. The Department of Transportation shall not erect any signage that would be impracticable, unfeasible, or that would result in an unsafe or hazardous condition."

Session Laws 2005-276, s. 1.2 , provides: "This act shall be known as the 'Current Operations and Capital Improvements Appropriations Act of 2005.'"

Session Laws 2005-276, s. 46.3 , provides: "Except for statutory changes or other provisions that clearly indicate an intention to have effects beyond the 2005-2007 fiscal biennium, the textual provisions of this act apply only to funds appropriated for, and activities occurring during, the 2005-2007 fiscal biennium."

Session Laws 2005-276, s. 46.5 , is a severability clause.

RESPONSIBILITY FOR CITY STREETS WHICH BECOME PART OF STATE SYSTEM. --When a city street becomes a part of the State highway system, the Board (now the Department) of Transportation is responsible for its maintenance thereafter which includes the control of all signs and structures within the right-of-way. Therefore, in the absence of any control over a State highway within its border, a municipality has no liability for injuries resulting from a dangerous condition of such street unless it created or increased such condition. Shapiro v. Toyota Motor Co., 38 N.C. App. 658, 248 S.E.2d 868 (1978).

DEPARTMENT OF TRANSPORTATION CAN BE FOUND NEGLIGENT. --North Carolina Department of Transportation can, under G.S. 136-30(a), be found negligent based on a failure to comply with the United States Department of Transportation's Manuel on Uniform Control Devices for Streets and Highways when erecting a stop sign. Norman v. N.C. DOT, 161 N.C. App. 211, 588 S.E.2d 42 (2003), review dismissed, review denied, 358 N.C. 235, 595 S.E.2d 153 (2004), cert. denied, 358 N.C. 545, 599 S.E.2d 404 (2004).

DEPARTMENT OF TRANSPORTATION NOT NEGLIGENT. --North Carolina Department of Transportation (DOT) was not liable for the deaths of two persons whose vehicle went into a lake, due to a failure to place warning signs on the road where the accident occurred, because DOT owed the persons no duty, under G.S. 143B-346, as nothing showed DOT did not act pursuant to the Manual on Uniform Traffic Control Devices and the DOT's policies, since nothing showed DOT knew of an unsafe condition on the road where the accident occurred. Turner v. N.C. DOT, 223 N.C. App. 90, 733 S.E.2d 871 (2012).

APPLIED in Estate of Jiggetts v. City of Gastonia, 128 N.C. App. 410, 497 S.E.2d 287 (1998); State v. Osterhoudt, 222 N.C. App. 620, 731 S.E.2d 454 (2012).

CITED in Davis v. J.M.X., Inc., 137 N.C. App. 267, 528 S.E.2d 56 (2000), aff'd, 352 N.C. 662, 535 S.E.2d 356 (2000).

§ 136-32.1. Misleading signs prohibited

No person shall erect or maintain within 100 feet of any highway right-of-way any warning or direction sign or marker of the same shape, design, color and size of any official highway sign or marker erected under the provisions of G.S. 136-30, or otherwise so similar to an official sign or marker as to appear to be an official highway sign or marker. Any person who violates any of the provisions of this section is guilty of a Class 1 misdemeanor.

History.
1955, c. 231; 1991 (Reg. Sess., 1992), c. 1030, s. 40; 1993, c. 539, s. 982 ; 1994, Ex. Sess., c. 24, s. 14(c)

§ 136-32.2. Placing blinding, deceptive or distracting lights unlawful

(a) If any person, firm or corporation shall place or cause to be placed any lights, which are flashing, moving, rotating, intermittent or steady spotlights, in such a manner and place and of such intensity:

(1) Which, by the use of flashing or blinding lights, blinds, tends to blind and effectively hampers the vision of the operator of any motor vehicle passing on a public highway; or

(2) Which involves red, green or amber lights or reflectorized material and which resembles traffic signal lights or traffic control signs; or

(3) Which, by the use of lights, reasonably causes the operator of any motor vehicle passing upon a public highway to mistakenly believe that there is approaching or situated in his lane of travel some other motor vehicle or obstacle, device or barricade, which would impede his traveling in such lane;

[he or it] shall be guilty of a Class 3 misdemeanor.

(b) Each 10 days during which a violation of the provisions of this section is continued after conviction therefor shall be deemed a separate offense.

(c) The provisions of this section shall not apply to any lights or lighting devices erected or maintained by the Department of Transportation or other properly constituted State or local authorities and intended to effect or implement traffic control and safety. Nothing contained in this section shall be deemed to prohibit the otherwise reasonable use of lights or lighting devices for advertising or other lawful purpose when the same do not fall within the provisions of subdivisions (1) through (3) of subsection (a) of this section.

(d) The enforcement of this section shall be the specific responsibility and duty of the State Highway Patrol in addition to all other law-enforcement agencies and officers within this State; provided, however, no warrant shall issue charging a violation of this section unless the violation has continued for 10 days after notice of the same has been given to the person, firm or corporation maintaining or owning such device or devices alleged to be in violation of this section.

History.
1959, c. 560; 1973, c. 507, s. 5; 1975, c. 716, s. 5; 1977, c. 464, ss. 7.1, 17; 1993, c. 539, s. 983 ; 1994, Ex. Sess., c. 24, s. 14(c)

§ 136-32.3. Litter enforcement signs

The Department of Transportation shall place signs on the Interstate Highway System notifying motorists of the penalties for littering. The signs shall include the amount of the maximum penalty for littering. The Department of Transportation shall determine the locations of and distance between the signs.

History.
2001-512, s. 4
EDITOR'S NOTE. --
Session Laws 2001-512, s. 15 , provides: "This act shall not be construed to obligate the General Assembly to appropriate any funds to implement the provisions of this act. Every agency to which this act applies shall implement the provisions of this act from funds otherwise appropriated or available to the agency."

N.C. Gen. Stat. § 136-33.2

Repealed by Session Laws 2007-164, s. 2 , effective July 1, 2007.
CROSS REFERENCES. --
For current provisions as to signs marking beginning of speed zones, see G.S. 136-33.2A.

§ 136-33.2A. Signs marking beginning of reduced speed zones

If a need to reduce speed in a speed zone is determined to exist by an engineer of the Department, there shall be a sign erected, of adequate size, at least 600 feet in advance of the beginning of any speed zone established by any agency of the State authorized to establish the same, which shall indicate a change in the speed limit.

History.
2007-164, s. 3

ARTICLE 2A.
STATE TRANSPORTATION GENERALLY

§ 136-44.3A. Highway Maintenance Improvement Program

(a) **Definitions.** -- The following definitions apply in this Article:

(1) **Cape seal treatment.** -- A chip seal treatment followed by a slurry seal treatment.

(2) **Chip seal treatment.** -- A type of pavement preservation treatment applied to existing asphalt pavement. The treatment involves spraying an asphalt emulsion onto the roadway, applying a layer of aggregate chips, and rolling the chips into the emulsion. This term includes single, double, and triple chip seal treatments.

(3) **Highway Maintenance Improvement Program.** -- The schedule of State highway maintenance projects required under G.S. 143B-350(f)(4a).

(4) **Highway Maintenance Improvement Program Needs Assessment.** -- A report of the amount of funds needed, the number of affected lane miles, and the percentage of the primary and secondary system roads that are rated to need a resurfacing or pavement preservation treatment within the Highway Maintenance Improvement Program's five-year time period but are not programmed due to funding constraints.

(5) **Microsurfacing treatment.** -- A type of pavement preservation treatment that involves mixing fine aggregate, asphalt emulsion, minerals, water, and a polymer additive, and applying the mixture to the roadway.

(6) **Pavement preservation treatment.** -- Includes full-width surface treatments used to extend or renew the pavement life.

(7) **Rehabilitation.** -- A contract resurfacing maintenance program that involves applying multiple layers of pavement that exceed two inches.

(8) **Resurfacing.** -- A contract resurfacing program that involves applying one layer that does not exceed two inches of pavement.

(9) **Slurry seal treatment.** -- A type of pavement preservation treatment that involves mixing fine aggregate, asphalt emulsion, minerals, and water, and applying the mixture to the roadway.

(b) **Road Quality Improvement of Pavement Preservation Treatments.** -- It is the intent of the General Assembly that (i) the Department use asphalt pavement preservation treatments that are high-quality, long-lasting, and provide a smooth road surface and (ii) the Department increase its contractual use of pavement preservation treatments.

(c) **(Effective until January 1, 2020) Highway Maintenance Improvement Program.** -- After the annual inspection of roads within the State highway system, each highway division shall determine and report to the Chief Engineer on the need for rehabilitation, resurfacing, or pavement preservation treatments. The Chief Engineer shall establish a five-year priority list for each highway division based on the Chief Engineer's estimate of need. In addition, the Chief Engineer shall establish a five-year improvement schedule, sorted by county, for rehabilitation, resurfacing, and pavement preservation treatment activities. The schedule shall be based on the amount of funds appropriated to the contract resurfacing program and the pavement preservation program in the fiscal year preceding the issuance of the Highway Maintenance Improvement Program for all five years of the Highway Maintenance Improvement Program. State funding for the Highway Maintenance Improvement Program shall be limited to funds appropriated from the State Highway Fund.

(c) **(Effective January 1, 2020) Highway Maintenance Improvement Program.** -- After the annual inspection of roads within the State highway system, each highway division shall determine and report to the Chief Engineer on (i) the need for rehabilitation, resurfacing, or pavement preservation treatments, (ii) the need for bridge and general maintenance, and (iii) projected changes to the condition of pavement on primary and secondary roads for each year over a five-year period. The Chief Engineer shall establish a five-year priority list for each highway division based on the Chief Engineer's estimate of need. In addition, the Chief Engineer shall establish a five-year improvement schedule, sorted by county, for rehabilitation, resurfacing, and pavement preservation treatment activities. The schedule shall be based on the amount of funds appropriated to the contract resurfacing program and the pavement preservation program in the fiscal year preceding the issuance of the Highway Maintenance Improvement Program for all five years of the Highway Maintenance Improvement Program. State funding for the Highway Maintenance Improvement Program shall be limited to funds appropriated from the State Highway Fund.

(d) Repealed by Session Laws 2015-241, s. 29.17C(b), effective July 1, 2015.

(d1) **Restriction and Encumbrance Schedule.** -- Notwithstanding any other provision of law, funds appropriated for the contract maintenance resurfacing program may not be transferred to another account to be used for another purpose. Beginning in the 2015-2016 fiscal year, the Department of Transportation shall spend or encumber all funds appropriated for the contract maintenance resurfacing program by June 30 of the fiscal year in which the funds were appropriated.

(e) **Single Chip Seal Treatment Prohibited on Access Routes.** -- Except as authorized in subsection (f) of this section, and unless used in combination with a slurry seal, microsurfacing, or resurfacing treatment, the Department shall not use single chip seal treatment on access routes for Surface Transportation Assistance Act Dimensioned Vehicles.

(f) Authorized Use of Single Chip Seal Treatment on Secondary Roads. The Department may use single chip seal treatments on secondary roads only under any of the following conditions:

(1) The secondary road has a daily traffic volume of less than 15,000 vehicles. Single chip treatments used under this subdivision shall be capped with a final riding surface of sand or material of equivalent size to fill voids to create a smooth riding surface.

(2) The single chip seal treatment is used in combination with a slurry seal, microsurfacing, or resurfacing treatment.

(3) The condition of the secondary road requires a rough surface to improve traction, such as a secondary road in a mountainous community or another area with low skid resistance.

(f1) Chip Seal Treatment Prohibited on Subdivision Streets. Unless used in combination with a fog seal, the Department shall not use chip seal treatment on subdivision streets.

(g) **Report.** -- The Department shall submit the Highway Maintenance Improvement Program and Highway Maintenance Improvement Program Needs Assessment to the General Assembly by April 1 of each year. If the General Assembly is in session, the Department shall report to the House of Representatives Appropriations Subcommittee on Transportation, the Senate Appropriations Committee on Transportation, and the Fiscal Research Division. If the General Assembly is not in session, the Department shall report to the Joint Legislative Transportation Oversight Committee and the Fiscal Research Division.

History.
2014-100, s. 34.11(b); 2015-241, s. 29.17C(b); 2016-94, s. 35.23; 2017-57, s. 34.11(a), (b)
SUBSECTION (C) SET OUT TWICE. --The first version of subsection (c) set out above is effective until January 1, 2020. The second version of subsection (c) set out above is effective January 1, 2020.
EDITOR'S NOTE. --
Session Laws 2014-100, s. 38.8, made this section effective July 1, 2014.
Session Laws 2014-100, s. 1.1, provides: "This act shall be known as 'The Current Operations and Capital Improvements Appropriations Act of 2014.'"
Session Laws 2014-100, s. 38.7, is a severability clause.
Session Laws 2015-241, s. 1.1, provides: "This act shall be known as 'The Current Operations and Capital Improvements Appropriations Act of 2015.'"
Session Laws 2015-241, s. 33.6, is a severability clause.
Session Laws 2016-94, s. 1.2, provides: "This act shall be known as the 'Current Operations and Capital Improvements Appropriations Act of 2016.'"
Session Laws 2016-94, s. 39.7, is a severability clause.
Session Law 2017-57, s. 34.11(d), made the amendment to subdivision (a)(4) and to subsection (c) of the section by Session Laws 2017-57, s. 34.11(a), effective July 1, 2017, and applicable to priority lists and improvement schedules submitted on or after that date.
Session Law 2017-57, s. 34.11(d), made the amendment to subsection (c) of the section by Session Laws 2017-57, s. 34.11(b), effective January 1, 2020, and applicable beginning with the report due April 1, 2020.
Session Laws 2017-57, s. 34.11(c), provides: "(c) By January 1, 2020, and for the purpose of forming a consolidated report of all maintenance activities, the Department of Transportation shall merge the Bridge Maintenance Improvement Program and the General Maintenance Improvement Program into the Highway Maintenance Improvement Program established under G.S. 136-44.3A."
Session Laws 2017-57, s. 1.1, provides: "This act shall be known as the 'Current Operations Appropriations Act of 2017.'"
Session Laws 2017-57, s. 39.4, provides: "Except for statutory changes or other provisions that clearly indicate an intention to have effects beyond the 2017-2019 fiscal biennium, the textual provisions of this act apply only to funds appropriated for, and activities occurring during, the 2017-2019 fiscal biennium."
Session Laws 2017-57, s. 39.6, is a severability clause.

EFFECT OF AMENDMENTS. --
Session Laws 2015-241, s. 29.17C(b) , effective July 1, 2015, deleted former subsection (d), which related to contract maintenance resurfacing program letting schedule; and added subsection (d1).

Session Laws 2016-94, s. 35.23 , effective July 1, 2016, deleted "subdivision streets" preceding "access routes" twice and made related changes in subsection (e); and added subsection (f1).

Session Laws 2017-57, s. 34.11(a) , substituted "five-year" for "three year" in subdivision (a)(4); and, in subsection (c), substituted "five-year" or variants for "three-year" or variants wherever it appeared. For effective date and applicability, see editor's note.

Session Laws 2017-57, s. 34.11(b) , rewrote the first sentence in subsection (c), which read: "Highway Maintenance Improvement Program. -- After the annual inspection of roads within the State highway system, each highway division shall determine and report to the Chief Engineer on the need for rehabilitation, resurfacing, or pavement preservation treatments." For effective date and applicability, see editor's note.

§ 136-44.17. Pavement preservation program

(a) **Program Established. --** The Department of Transportation shall establish the pavement preservation program.

(b) **Eligible Activities or Treatments. ---** Applications eligible for funding under the pavement preservation program include the following preservation activities or treatments for asphalt pavement structures:

(1) Chip seals, slurry seals, fog seals, sand seals, scrub seals, and cape seals.

(2) Microsurfacing.

(3) Profile milling not covered by resurfacing.

(4) Asphalt rejuvenators.

(5) Open graded asphalt friction course.

(6) Overlays less than 1,000 feet in length.

(7) Diamond grinding.

(8) Joint sealing.

(9) Dowel bar retrofit.

(10) Partial-depth or full-depth repairs and reclamations.

(11) Ultra-thin whitetopping.

(12) Thin lift and sand asphalt overlays.

(13) Asphalt crack sealing.

(14) Pavement markers and markings.

(c) **Ineligible Activities or Treatments. ---** The pavement preservation program shall not include the following preservation activities or treatments:

(1) Contract resurfacing activities or major pavement rehabilitation treatments and pretreatments that are used in combination with a resurfacing treatment, such as profile milling or chip seals.

(2) Routine maintenance activities used to maintain and preserve the condition of roads. Treatments include, but are not limited to, pothole patching, rut filling, cleaning of roadside ditches and structures, shoulder maintenance, and retracing of pavement markings.

(3) Maintenance and preservation activities performed on bridges or culverts.

(4) Activities related to positive guidance or signal maintenance program functions.

(d) **Encumbrance Schedule. --** Beginning in the 2015-2016 fiscal year, the Department of Transportation shall spend or encumber all funds appropriated by the General Assembly to the Department for the pavement preservation program by June 30 of the fiscal year for which the funds were appropriated.

History.
2014-100, s. 34.11(f) ; 2015-241, s. 29.17(a) ; 2017-57, s. 34.9

EDITOR'S NOTE. --
Session Laws 2014-100, s. 34.11(g) , provides: "Establishment of Account. -- The Department of Transportation shall establish a new account within its maintenance account to receive funds allocated under this section for pavement preservation."

Session Laws 2014-100, s. 34.11(h) , provides: "2014-2015 Outsourcing Target. -- Of funds allocated in this act for pavement preservation, no more than eighty percent (80%) may be used for projects undertaken by the Department, with the remaining funds used for projects outsourced to private contractors."

Session Laws 2014-100, s. 34.11(i) , provides: "Future Outsourcing Targets. -- The Department shall increase its use of outsourcing of pavement preservation activities to reach the following targets for outsourcing of pavement preservation projects:

"(1) Thirty percent (30%) of pavement preservation program funds allocated by the 2015-2016 fiscal year.

"(2) Fifty-five percent (55%) of pavement preservation program funds allocated by the 2016-2017 fiscal year.

"(3) Eighty percent (80%) of pavement preservation program funds allocated by the 2017-2018 fiscal year and subsequent fiscal years thereafter."

Session Laws 2014-100, s. 34.11(j) , provides: "Increased Use of the Paving Industry. -- It is the intent of the General Assembly that the Department work cooperatively with the paving industry so that the industry grows in size, scope, and geographic reach and has the capability to fulfill contracts for pavement preservation work across the State. Therefore, the Department is directed to conduct workshops, trainings, or other meetings to encourage greater privatization of pavement preservation activities with the intent of reducing the amount of pavement preservation activities conducted by the Department."

Session Laws 2014-100, s. 34.11 (*l*), as amended by Session Laws 2015-241, s. 29.17(c) , provides: "Report. -- The Department shall report to the Joint Legislative

Transportation Oversight Committee and the Fiscal Research Division by no later than September 1, 2014, on its plan for increasing its use of outsourcing of pavement preservation activities in accordance with subsection (i) of this section. The Department shall report no later than December 1, 2014, and annually thereafter, to the Joint Legislative Transportation Oversight Committee and the Fiscal Research Division on the Department's progress toward achieving the goals set forth in subsection (i) of this section. The annual report shall include the following:

"(1) A monthly examination of expenditures, by treatment type, indicating the amount and percentage performed by contract.

"(2) The number of lane miles covered, by treatment type, along with an average cost per lane miles, by treatment type, indicating costs for each type for work performed by the Department and by contract.

"(3) The statewide cost per lane mile (hereafter 'unit cost') along with unit cost for each division and for each type of treatment. The Department shall provide an explanation for unit costs that vary by more than ten percent (10%) from the statewide unit cost."

Session Laws 2014-100, s. 34.11(m) provides: "Subsection (j) of this section expires June 30, 2017. Subsection (*l*) of this section expires December 31, 2018."

Session Laws 2014-100, s. 1.1 , provides: "This act shall be known as 'The Current Operations and Capital Improvements Appropriations Act of 2014.'"

Session Laws 2014-100, s. 38.4 , provides: "Except for statutory changes or other provisions that clearly indicate an intention to have effects beyond the 2014-2015 fiscal year, the textual provisions of this act apply only to funds appropriated for, and activities occurring during, the 2014-2015 fiscal year."

Session Laws 2014-100, s. 38.7 , is a severability clause.

Session Laws 2015-241, s. 1.1 , provides: "This act shall be known as 'The Current Operations and Capital Improvements Appropriations Act of 2015.'"

Session Laws 2015-241, s. 33.6 , is a severability clause.

EFFECT OF AMENDMENTS. --
Session Laws 2015-241, s. 29.17(a) , effective July 1, 2015, added subdivision (b)(13); deleted "asphalt crack sealing" preceding "pothole patching" in the second sentence of subdivision (c)(2); and added subsection (d).

Session Laws 2017-57, s. 34.9 , effective July 1, 2017, added subdivision (b)(14).

ARTICLE 6D.
CONTROLLED-ACCESS FACILITIES

§ 136-89.58. Unlawful use of National System of Interstate and Defense Highways and other controlled-access facilities

On those sections of highways which are or become a part of the National System of Interstate and Defense Highways and other controlled-access facilities it shall be unlawful for any person:

(1) To drive a vehicle over, upon or across any curb, central dividing section or other separation or dividing line on said highways.

(2) To make a left turn or a semicircular or U-turn except through an opening provided for that purpose in the dividing curb section, separation, or line on said highways.

(3) To drive any vehicle except in the proper lane provided for that purpose and in the proper direction and to the right of the central dividing curb, separation section, or line on said highways.

(4) To drive any vehicle into the main travel lanes or lanes of connecting ramps or interchanges except through an opening or connection provided for that purpose by the Department of Transportation.

(5) To stop, park, or leave standing any vehicle, whether attended or unattended, on any part or portion of the right-of-way of said highways, except in the case of an emergency or as directed by a peace officer, or as designated parking areas.

(6) To willfully damage, remove, climb, cross or breach any fence erected within the rights-of-way of said highways.

(7) Repealed by Session Laws 1999-330, s. 6 , effective December 1, 1999.

Any person who violates any of the provisions of this section shall be guilty of a Class 2 misdemeanor.

History.
1959, c. 647; 1965, c. 474, s. 2; 1973, c. 507, s. 5; 1977, c. 464, s. 7.1; c. 731, s. 2; 1993, c. 539, s. 988 ; 1994, Ex. Sess., c. 24, s. 14(c) ; 1999-330, s. 6

PERMIT TO ERECT AND MAINTAIN ADVERTISING SIGNS WAS NOT SUBJECT TO REVOCATION pursuant to a regulation providing for revocation for "unlawful violation of control of access on interstate . . . facilities," where employees of the permit holder had parked their truck on the shoulder of the interstate and were servicing a sign, but had not crossed any access control fence or other barrier in order to do so. Ace-Hi, Inc. v. Department of Transp., 70 N.C. App. 214, 319 S.E.2d 294 (1984).

OUTDOOR ADVERTISING --Outdoor advertising companies who were appealing the revocations of their permits for certain outdoor advertising signs did not show that they would be required to violate certain State statutes, such as G.S. 136-89.56, prohibiting commercial enterprises on certain highways, or G.S. 136.89.58, prohibiting standing vehicles on the right-of-way of certain highways, to measure the height of those signs, nor was this argument raised before the trial court, as required by Rule 10(b)(1). Capital Outdoor, Inc. v. Tolson, 159 N.C. App. 55, 582 S.E.2d 717 (2003).

CITED in North Carolina State Hwy. Comm'n v. Asheville School, Inc., 276 N.C. 556, 173 S.E.2d 909 (1970).

CROSS REFERENCES. --
For similar section, see G.S. 20-140.3.

ARTICLE 7.
MISCELLANEOUS PROVISIONS

§ 136-102. Billboard obstructing view at entrance to school, church or public institution on public highway

(a) It shall be unlawful for any person, firm, or corporation to construct or maintain outside the limits of any city or town in this State any billboard larger than six square feet at or nearer than 200 feet to the point where any walk or drive from any school, church, or public institution located along any highway enters such highway except under the following conditions:

(1) Such billboard is attached to the side of a building or buildings which are or may be erected within 200 feet of any such walk or drive and the attachment thereto causes no additional obstruction of view.

(2) A building or other structure is located so as to obstruct the view between such walk or drive and such billboard.

(3) Such billboard is located on the opposite side of the highway from the entrance to said walk or drive.

(b) Any person, firm, or corporation convicted of violating the provisions of this section shall be guilty of a Class 3 misdemeanor and punished only by a fine of ten dollars ($ 10.00), and each day that such violation continues shall be considered a separate offense.

History.
1947, c. 304, ss. 1, 2; 1993, c. 539, s. 994 ; 1994, Ex. Sess., c. 24, s. 14(c)

§ 136-102.8. Subdivision streets; traffic calming devices

The Department shall establish policies and procedures for the installation or utilization of traffic tables or traffic calming devices erected on State-maintained subdivision streets adopted by the Department, pursuant to G.S. 136-102.6, if all of the following requirements are met:

(1) A traffic engineering study has been approved by the Department detailing

types and locations of traffic calming devices.

(2) Installation and utilization of traffic tables or traffic calming devices is within one of the following areas:

a. A subdivision with a homeowners association.

b. A neighborhood in which the property owners have established a contractual agreement outlining responsibility for traffic calming devices installed in the neighborhood.

(3) The traffic tables or traffic calming devices are paid for and maintained by the subdivision homeowners association, or its successor, or pursuant to a neighborhood agreement.

(4) The homeowners association has the written support, for the installation of each traffic table or traffic calming device approved by the Department pursuant to this section, of at least sixty percent (60%) of the member property owners, or the neighborhood agreement is signed by at least sixty percent (60%) of the neighborhood property owners.

(5) The homeowners association, or neighborhood pursuant to its agreement, posts a performance bond with the Department sufficient to fund maintenance or removal of the traffic tables or calming devices, if the homeowners association, or neighborhood pursuant to its agreement, fails to maintain them, or is dissolved. The bond shall remain in place for a period of three years from the date of installation.

History.
2009-310, s. 1 ; 2015-217, s. 2
EDITOR'S NOTE. --
Session Laws 2009-310, s. 2 , made this section effective October 1, 2009, and applicable to traffic tables and traffic calming devices installed on or after that date.

Session Laws 2015-217, s. 1(a) , provides: "Study. -- The Department of Transportation shall study the process that must be followed, and the requirements that must be met, for the Department of Transportation to accept subdivision streets dedicated as public on the State highway system for maintenance, including (i) whether the process that must be followed is efficient and timely, (ii) whether the minimum right-of-way and construction standards established by the Board of Transportation for acceptance on the State highway system are reasonable, (iii) what the financial impact is on the State and homeowners when subdivision streets are or are not accepted on the State highway system for maintenance, and (iv) any other matters the Department of Transportation deems relevant to the study."

Session Laws 2015-217, s. 1(b) , provides: "Report. -- The Department shall report its findings and recommendations, including any legislative proposals, to the Joint Legislative Transportation Oversight Committee no later than February 1, 2016."

EFFECT OF AMENDMENTS. --
Session Laws 2015-217, s. 2 , effective August 18, 2015, substituted "sixty percent (60%)" for "seventy percent (70%)" two times in subdivision (4).

ARTICLE 11B.
TOURIST-ORIENTED DIRECTIONAL SIGN PROGRAM

§ 136-140.15. Scope of operations

(a) **Program.** -- The Department of Transportation shall administer a tourist-oriented directional signs (TODS) program.

(b) **Definitions.** -- The following definitions apply in this Article:

(1) **TODS.** -- Tourist-oriented directional signs (TODS) are guide signs that display the business identification of and directional information for tourist-oriented businesses and tourist-oriented facilities or for classes of businesses or facilities that are tourist-oriented.

(2) **Tourist-oriented business.** -- A business, the substantial portion of whose products or services is of significant interest to tourists. The term may include a business involved with seasonal agricultural products. When used in this Article, the term "business" means a tourist-oriented business.

(3) **Tourist-oriented facility.** -- A business, service, or activity facility that derives a major portion of income or visitors during the normal business season from road users not residing in the immediate area of the facility. When used in this Article, the term "facility" means a tourist-oriented facility.

(c) **Limitation.** -- The Department shall not install TODS for a business or facility if the signs would be required at intersections where, due to the number of conflicting locations of other highway signs or traffic control devices or other physical or topographical features of the roadside, their presence would be impractical or unfeasible or result in an unsafe or hazardous condition.

(d) **Duplication.** -- If a business or facility is currently shown on another official highway guide sign, such as a logo sign or supplemental guide sign, on the same approach to an intersection where a TODS panel for that business or facility would be located, the business or facility may elect to keep the existing highway guide sign or have it removed and participate in the TODS program. If the business or facility elects to retain the existing highway guide sign, the business or facility is ineligible for the TODS program at that intersection.

History.
2001-383, s. 1

EDITOR'S NOTE. --
Session Laws 2004-199, s. 61 , provides: "The Department of Transportation shall install highway directional guide signs at limited-access highway terminals for the nonresidential campuses of colleges or universities located in North Carolina, if the nonresidential campus is located within one mile from the limited-access highway terminal and if the college or university is licensed by the Board of Governors of The University of North Carolina, offers both undergraduate and graduate degree programs, and has a minimum of 350 students enrolled at the nonresidential campus. The college or university requesting the sign installment shall pay for all charges related to the construction of the sign."

§ 136-140.16. Eligibility criteria

A business or facility is eligible to participate in the TODS program if it meets all of the following conditions:

(1) It is open to the general public and is not restricted to "members only".

(2) It does not restrict access to its facilities by the general public.

(3) It complies with all applicable laws, ordinances, rules, and regulations concerning the provision of public accommodations without regard to race, religion, color, age, sex, national origin, disability, and any other category protected by federal or State constitutional or statutory law concerning the granting of licenses and approvals for public facilities.

(4) It meets the following standards:

a. It is in continuous operation at least eight hours a day, five days a week during its normal season or the normal operating season for the type of business or facility.

b. It is licensed and approved by the appropriate State and local agencies regulating the particular type of business or activity.

History.
2001-383, s. 1

§ 136-140.17. Terminating participation in program

A business or facility may terminate its participation in the TODS program at any time. The business or facility is not entitled to a refund of any part of any fees paid because of voluntary termination of participation by the business or facility, for any reason, before the end of its current contract period.

History.
2001-383, s. 1

§ 136-140.18. Temporary modification of TODS panels

(a) The Department shall allow a participating business or facility to close for remodeling or to repair damage from fire or other natural disaster if its TODS panels are covered or removed while the business or facility is closed. No refund of fees or extension of the time remaining in the contract for participation will be provided for the period of closure.

(b) The Department may, at its discretion, remove or cover TODS panels for roadway construction or maintenance, for routine maintenance of the TODS assembly, for traffic research study, or for any other reason it considers appropriate. Businesses or facilities are not entitled to any refunds of fee amounts for the period that the TODS panels are covered or removed under this subsection unless the period exceeds seven days.

(c) The TODS panels for seasonal businesses or facilities shall have an appropriate message added during the period in which the businesses or facilities are open to the public as part of their normal seasonal operation.

History.
2001-383, s. 1

§ 136-140.19. Board of Transportation to adopt rules to implement the TODS program

The Board of Transportation shall adopt rules to implement the TODS program created by this Article. The rules shall include all of the following:

(1) The Board shall set fees to cover the initial costs of signs, sign installation, and maintenance, and the costs of administering the program.

(2) The Board shall establish a standard for the size, color, and letter height of the TODS as specified in the National Manual of Uniform Traffic Control Devices for Streets and Highways.

(3) TODS shall not be placed more than five miles from the business or facility.

(4) TODS shall not be placed where prohibited by local ordinance.

(5) The number of TODS panels shall not exceed six per intersection with only one business or facility on each panel.

(6) If a business or facility is not directly on a State highway, it is eligible for TODS panels only if both of the following requirements are met:

　　a. It is located on a street that directly connects with a State road.

　　b. It is located so that only one directional sign, placed on a State road, will lead the tourist to the business or facility.

(7) A TODS shall not be placed immediately in advance of the business or facility if the business or facility and its on-premise advertising signs are readily visible from the roadway.

(8) The Board shall limit the placement of TODS to highways other than fully controlled access highways and to rural areas in and around towns or cities with a population of less than 40,000.

History.
2001-383, s. 1 ; 2014-100, s. 34.14(b)
EDITOR'S NOTE. --
Session Laws 2014-100, s. 1.1 , provides: "This act shall be known as 'The Current Operations and Capital Improvements Appropriations Act of 2014.'"
Session Laws 2014-100, s. 38.7 , is a severability clause.
EFFECT OF AMENDMENTS. --
Session Laws 2014-100, s. 34.14(b) , effective July 1, 2014, substituted "Board of Transportation" for "Department" in the section heading and the introductory language; substituted "Board" for "Department" in subdivisions (1), (2), (8); and, in subdivision (1), inserted "installation, and" and "the costs of."

ARTICLE 18A.
NORTH CAROLINA AND SOUTH CAROLINA RAIL COMPACT

§§ 136-225, 136-226

Repealed by Session Laws 2018-142, s. 18 , effective December 14, 2018.

History.
§ 136-225. 2014-121, s. 1 ; repealed by Session Laws 2018-142, s. 18 , effective December 14, 2018; § 136-225. 2014-121, s. 1 ; repealed by Session Laws 2018-142, s. 18 , effective December 14, 2018
EDITOR'S NOTE. --
Session Laws 2014-121, ss. 1 and 2, effective September 20, 2014, were codified as this Article at the direction of the Revisor of Statutes.
Pursuant to G.S. 136-226(j), the North Carolina and South Carolina Rail Compact is effective when approved by both the North Carolina General Assembly and South Carolina General Assembly, except that, if approval is required by the United States Congress, then the compact is also contingent on such approval.
Former G.S. 136-225 pertained to Short Title. Former G.S. 136-226 pertained to Compact provisions.

CHAPTER 153A.
COUNTIES

ARTICLE 12.
ROADS AND BRIDGES

§ 153A-246. Use of photographs or videos recorded by automated school bus safety cameras

(a) **Definitions.** -- The following definitions apply in this section:

(1) **Automated school bus safety camera.** -- As defined in G.S. 115C-242.1.

(2) **Officials or agents.** -- This term includes a local board of education located within the county or a private vendor contracted with under G.S. 115C-242.1.

(3) **School bus.** -- As used in G.S. 20-217.

(b) **Civil Enforcement.** -- A county may adopt an ordinance for the civil enforcement of G.S. 20-217 by means of an automated school bus safety camera installed and operated on any school bus located within that county. An ordinance adopted pursuant to this section shall not apply to any violation of G.S. 20-217 that results in injury or death. Notwithstanding the provisions of G.S. 14-4, in the event that a county adopts an ordinance pursuant to this section, a violation of the ordinance shall not be an infraction. An ordinance authorized by this subsection shall provide all of the following:

(1) The notice of the violation shall be given in the form of a citation and shall be received by the registered owner of the vehicle no more than 60 days after the date of the violation.

(2) The registered owner of a vehicle shall be responsible for a violation unless the vehicle was, at the time of the violation, in the care, custody, or control of another person or unless the citation was not received by the registered owner within 60 days after the date of the violation.

(3) A person wishing to contest a citation shall, within 30 days after receiving the citation, deliver to the officials or agents of the county that issued the citation a written request for a hearing accompanied by an affidavit stating the basis for contesting the citation, including, as applicable:

a. The name and address of the person other than the registered owner who had the care, custody, or control of the vehicle.

b. A statement that the vehicle involved was stolen at the time of the violation, with a copy of any insurance report or police report supporting this statement.

c. A statement that the citation was not received within 60 days after the date of the violation, and a statement of the date on which the citation was received.

d. A copy of a criminal pleading charging the person with a violation of G.S. 20-217 arising out of the same facts as those for which the citation was issued.

(4) The citation shall include all of the following:

a. The date and time of the violation, the location of the violation, the amount of the civil monetary penalty imposed, and the date by which the civil monetary penalty shall be paid or contested.

b. An image taken from the recorded image showing the vehicle involved in the violation.

c. A copy of a statement or electronically generated affirmation of a law enforcement officer employed by a law enforcement agency with whom an agreement has been reached pursuant to G.S. 115C-242.1(c) stating that, based upon inspection of the recorded images, the owner's motor vehicle was operated in violation of the ordinance adopted pursuant to this subsection.

d. Instructions explaining the manner in which, and the time within which, liability under the citation may be contested pursuant to subdivision (3) of this subsection.

e. A warning that failure to pay the civil monetary penalty or to contest liability in a timely manner shall waive any right to contest liability and shall result in a late penalty of one hundred dollars ($ 100.00), in addition to the civil monetary penalty.

f. In citations issued to the registered owner of the vehicle, a warning that failure to pay the civil monetary penalty or to contest liability in a timely manner shall result in refusal by the Division of Motor Vehicles to register the motor vehicle, in addition to imposition of the civil monetary penalty and late penalty.

(5) Violations of the ordinance shall be deemed a noncriminal violation for which a civil penalty shall be assessed and for which no points authorized by G.S. 20-16(c) and no insurance points authorized by G.S. 58-36-65 shall be assigned to the registered owner or driver of the vehicle. The amount of such penalty shall be four hundred

dollars ($ 400.00) for the first offense, seven hundred fifty dollars ($ 750.00) for the second violation, and one thousand dollars ($ 1,000) for each subsequent violation of the ordinance.

(6) If a registered owner provides an affidavit that the vehicle was, at the time of the violation, in the care, custody, or control of another person or company, the identified person or company may be issued a citation complying with the requirements of subdivision (4) of this subsection.

(7) The citation shall be processed by officials or agents of the county and shall be served by any method permitted for service of process pursuant to G.S. 1A-1, Rule 4 of the North Carolina Rules of Civil Procedure, or by first-class mail to the address of the registered owner of the vehicle provided on the motor vehicle registration or, as applicable, to the address of the person identified in an affidavit submitted by the registered owner of the vehicle.

(8) If the person to whom a citation is issued makes a timely request for a hearing pursuant to subdivision (3) of this subsection, a summons shall be issued by any method permitted for service of process pursuant to G.S. 1A-1, Rule 4 of the North Carolina Rules of Civil Procedure, directing the person to appear at the place and time specified in the summons in order to contest the citation at an administrative hearing.

(9) A citation recipient who, within 30 days after receiving the citation, fails either to pay the civil penalty or to request a hearing to contest the citation shall have waived the right to contest responsibility for the violation and shall be subject to a late penalty of one hundred dollars ($ 100.00) in addition to the civil penalty assessed under this subsection.

(10) The county shall institute a nonjudicial administrative hearing to hear contested citations or penalties issued or assessed under this section. The decision on a contested citation shall be rendered in writing within five days after the hearing and shall be served upon the person contesting the citation by any method permitted for service of process pursuant to G.S. 1A-1, Rule 4 of the North Carolina Rules of Civil Procedure. If the decision is adverse to the person contesting the citation, the decision shall contain instructions explaining the manner and the time within which the decision may be appealed pursuant to subdivision (11) of this subsection.

(11) A person may appeal to the district court division of the General Court of Justice from any adverse decision on a contested citation by filing notice of appeal in the office of the clerk of superior court. Enforcement of an adverse decision shall be stayed pending the outcome of a timely appeal. Except as otherwise provided in this subdivision, appeal shall be in accordance with the procedure set forth in Article 19 of Chapter 7A of the General Statutes applicable to appeals from the magistrate to the district court. For purposes of calculating the time within which any action must be taken to meet procedural requirements of the appeal, the date upon which the person contesting the citation is served with the adverse decision shall be deemed to be the date of entry of judgment.

(12) In the event a person is charged in a criminal pleading with a violation of G.S. 20-217, all of the following shall apply:

a. The charging law enforcement agency shall provide written notice to the county office responsible for processing civil citations pursuant to subdivision (7) of subsection (b) of this section containing the name and address of the person charged with violation of G.S. 20-217 and the date of the violation.

b. After receiving notice pursuant to this subdivision that a person has been charged in a criminal pleading with a violation of G.S. 20-217, the county shall not impose a civil penalty against that person arising out of the same facts as those for which the person was charged in the criminal pleading.

c. The county shall issue a full refund of any civil penalty payment received from a person who was charged in a criminal pleading with a violation of G.S. 20-217 if the civil penalty arose out of the same facts as those for which that person was charged in the criminal pleading, together with interest at the legal rate as provided by G.S. 24-1 from the date the penalty was paid until the date of refund.

(13) If a citation is not contested pursuant to subdivision (3) of this subsection, payment of the civil penalty is due within 30 days after receipt of the citation. If the citation is contested, and the result of the administrative hearing held pursuant to subdivision (10) of this subsection is a decision adverse to the citation recipient, then payment is due within 30 days after receipt of the adverse decision, unless the citation recipient appeals the adverse decision pursuant to subdivision (11) of this subsection. If the adverse decision is appealed, and if the final decision on appeal is adverse to the citation recipient, then payment of the civil penalty is due within 30 days after the

citation recipient receives notice of the final adverse decision on appeal.

(14) If the registered owner of a motor vehicle who receives a citation fails to pay the civil penalty when due, the Division of Motor Vehicles shall refuse to register the motor vehicle for the owner in accordance with G.S. 20-54(11). The county may establish procedures for providing notice to the Division of Motor Vehicles and for the collection of these penalties and may enforce the penalties by civil action in the nature of debt.

(15) The county shall provide each law enforcement agency within its jurisdiction with the name and address of the county official to whom written notice of persons charged with violation of G.S. 20-217 should be given pursuant to subdivision (12) of this subsection.

(c) **Notice.** -- An automated school bus safety camera installed on a school bus must be identified by appropriate warning signs conspicuously posted on the school bus. All warning signs shall be consistent with a statewide standard adopted by the State Board of Education in conjunction with local boards of education that install and operate automated school bus safety cameras on their school buses.

(d) **Application.** -- Nothing in this section shall be construed to do any of the following:

(1) Require the installation and operation of automated school bus safety cameras on a school bus.

(2) Prohibit the use and admissibility of any photograph or video recorded by an automated school bus safety camera in any criminal proceeding alleging a violation of G.S. 20-217.

(3) Prohibit the imposition of penalties, including the assignment of points authorized by G.S. 20-16(c) and insurance points authorized by G.S. 58-36-65, on any registered owner or driver of the vehicle convicted of a misdemeanor or felony violation of G.S. 20-217.

(e) **Criminal Prosecution Encouraged.** --- The General Assembly of North Carolina encourages criminal prosecution for violation of G.S. 20-217 whenever photographs or videos recorded by an automated school bus safety camera provide evidence sufficient to support such prosecution.

(f) A county that adopts an ordinance as provided in this section, shall maintain records of all violations of that ordinance for which a civil penalty is assessed. Upon request, the county shall provide at least five years of those records to the North Carolina Child Fatality Task Force and the North Carolina General Assembly.

History.
2017-188, ss. 1 , 5
EDITOR'S NOTE. --
Session Laws 2017-188, s. 5 , effective July 25, 2017, was codified as subsection (f) of this section and set out in the form above at the direction of the Revisor of Statutes.

Index